W9-BUT-152

THE SAGE HANDBOOK OF QUALITATIVE RESEARCH

THIRD EDITION

INTERNATIONAL ADVISORY BOARD

ABOUT THE COVER

Some readers will be curious about the cover photograph. Beginning with the 2nd edition of the *Handbook*, we have used the cover to symbolize some theme or themes of the *Handbook*. This is no less true in this edition's cover photograph. We deliberately chose a photograph that is both non-Western in its orientation and also clearly performance-driven. We have been fortunate enough, with the good offices of the Sage Publications art division, to locate a photograph with three critical elements: performers, a group that appears to be getting instruction, and an audience. For those familiar with the performance in the right-hand side of the photograph, the introduction of the whirling dervishes will come as as a familiar scene. The dervishes are Muslims, members of one of several sects, who take vows of poverty and austerity. The dance they perform is a sacred ritual, carried out to gradually reduce the body to focus on Allah and holy matters only. The performance itself—now shared with Westerners and non-Muslim audiences—is an intensely spiritual experience, as it is intended to be, even for non-Muslim audiences.

We have intended this photograph to do several things at once in the "reading": to indicate a broader reach for this *Handbook*, incorporating the perspectives of non-Western, indigenous, First Nations, and other non-U.S. and non-European sources; to signify the performance aspects of performance ethnography and performative, communitarian social justice; to indicate the "experience-near" quality of a new generation of ethnography, via showing the audience both near to the performers and, simultaneously, on the same level; and to signal the return of the spiritual and the sacred to the practices of sciences, foretold in the previous editions. It is our hope that other readers, from other standpoints, will locate and resonate to other extended meanings in the cover and find that its multiple levels sets them, too, to dreaming of a re-envisioned ethnography and a set of qualitative practices that summon a wider view of the purposes of a re-imagined social science.

—*Yvonna S. Lincoln*
—*Norman K. Denzin*

THE SAGE HANDBOOK OF QUALITATIVE RESEARCH

THIRD EDITION

EDITORS

NORMAN K. DENZIN

University of Illinois at Urbana-Champaign

YVONNA S. LINCOLN

Texas A&M University

For information:

Sage Publications, Inc.
2455 Teller Road
Thousand Oaks, California 91320
E-mail: order@sagepub.com

Sage Publications Ltd.
1 Oliver's Yard
55 City Road
London EC1Y 1SP
United Kingdom

Sage Publications India Pvt. Ltd.
B-42, Panchsheel Enclave
Post Box 4109
New Delhi 110 017 India

Printed in the United States of America.

This book is printed on acid-free paper.

Library of Congress Cataloging-in-Publication Data

The SAGE handbook of qualitative research / edited by Norman K. Denzin,
Yvonna S. Lincoln.—3rd ed.
p. cm.
Rev. ed. of: Handbook of qualitative research. 2nd ed. c2000.
Includes bibliographical references and index.
ISBN 978-0-7619-2757-0 (cloth)
1. Social sciences—Research. I. Denzin, Norman K. II. Lincoln, Yvonna S.
III. Handbook of qualitative research.
H62.H2455 2005
001.4′2—dc22

2004026085

07 08 09 10 9 8 7 6 5 4 3

Acquiring Editor: Lisa Cuevas Shaw
Associate Editor: Margo Crouppen
Project Editor: Claudia A. Hoffman
Copy Editors: D. J. Peck, Judy Selhorst, and A. J. Sobczak
Typesetter: C&M Digitals (P) Ltd.
Indexer: Kathleen Paparchontis
Cover Designer: Ravi Balasuriya

CONTENTS

PREFACE

This third edition of the *Handbook of Qualitative Research,* like the second edition, is virtually a new volume. Nearly two-thirds of the authors in this edition are new contributors. Indeed, this edition includes 42 new chapters, authors, and/or coauthors. Among the chapter topics in this edition, 16 are totally new, including contributions on indigenous inquiry, decolonizing methodologies, critical ethnography, critical humanism and queer theory, performance ethnography, narrative inquiry, arts-based inquiry, online ethnography, analytic methodologies, Foucault's methodologies, talk and text, focus groups and critical pedagogy, relativism, criteria and politics, the poetics of place, cultural and investigative poetics, qualitative evaluation and social policy, social science inquiry in the new millennium, and an anthropology of the contemporary. All returning authors have either substantially revised their original contributions or have produced chapters that are completely new.

This third edition of the *Handbook of Qualitative Research* continues where the second edition ended. Over the past quarter century, a quiet methodological revolution has been occurring in the social sciences; a blurring of disciplinary boundaries is taking place. The social and policy sciences and the humanities are drawing closer together in a mutual focus on an interpretive, qualitative approach to research and theory. These are not new trends, but the extent to which the "qualitative revolution" is taking over the social sciences and related professional fields is nothing short of amazing. The overwhelmingly positive reactions to the first and second editions of the *Handbook* affirm these observations. We continue to be astonished at the reception the previous editions have received. Researchers and teachers alike have found useful materials in them from which to teach and launch new inquiries.

Not surprisingly, however, this quiet revolution has been met by resistance, which we discuss in Chapter 1, our introduction to this edition. Needless to say, this resistance grows out of neoconservative discourses (e.g., the No Child Left Behind Act) and the recent report published by the National Research Council (see Feuer, Towne, & Shavelson, 2002), which have appropriated neopositivist, so-called evidence-based epistemologies. Leaders of this movement assert that qualitative research is nonscientific, should not receive federal funds, and is of little value in the social policy arena (see Lincoln & Cannella, 2004).

There continue to be multiple social science and humanities audiences for this *Handbook:* graduate students who want to do learn how to do qualitative research, interested faculty hoping to become better informed about the field, individuals working in policy settings who understand the value of qualitative research methodologies and want to learn about the latest developments in the field, and faculty who are experts in one or more areas covered by the *Handbook* but who also want to be informed about the most recent developments in the field. We never imagined these audiences would be so large. Nor did we imagine that the *Handbook* would become a text used in undergraduate and graduate research methods courses, but it did. In 2003, we created from the *Handbook*'s second edition three new paperback volumes for classroom use: *The Landscape of Qualitative Research, Strategies of Qualitative Inquiry,* and *Collecting and Interpreting Qualitative Materials.*

Qualitative inquiry, among other things, is the name for a "reformist movement that began in the early 1970s in the academy" (Schwandt, 2000, p. 189). The interpretive and critical paradigms, in their multiple forms, are central to this movement. Indeed, this movement encompasses multiple paradigmatic formulations. It also includes complex epistemological and ethical criticisms of traditional social science research. The movement now has its own journals, scientific associations, conferences, annual workshops, and faculty positions.

The transformations in the field of qualitative research that were taking place in the early 1990s continued to gain momentum as the decade unfolded. Many scholars began to judge the days of value-free inquiry based on a God's-eye view of reality to be over. Today many agree that all inquiry is moral and political. By century's end, few looked back with skepticism on the narrative turn. The turn had been taken, and that was all there was to say about it. Many have now told their tales from the field. Further, today we know that men and women write culture differently, and that writing itself is not an innocent practice.

Experimental, reflexive ways of writing first-person ethnographic texts are now commonplace. Critical personal narratives have become a central feature of counterhegemonic, decolonizing methodologies (Mutua & Swadener, 2004, p. 16). Sociologists, anthropologists, and educators continue to explore new ways of composing ethnography, writing fiction, drama, performance texts, and ethnographic poetry. Social science journals are holding fiction contests. Civic journalism is shaping calls for a civic, or public, ethnography, and cultural criticism is now accepted practice.

Today there is a pressing need to show how the practices of qualitative research can help change the world in positive ways. So at the beginning of the 21st century it is necessary to reengage the promise of qualitative research as a form of radical democratic practice (Peshkin, 1993). In our letter inviting authors to contribute to this volume, we stated:

> This will be the third generation of the handbook. The first edition established the fact that qualitative research had come of age as a field, and needed to be taken seriously. The second edition said we need to show how qualitative research can be used to address issues of social justice. Now, in the third edition, we want to be even more explicit politically. We agree with Ginnie Olesen (2000, p. 215), "Rage is not enough."[1] We want you to help lead the way. How do we move the current generation of critical, interpretive thought and inquiry beyond rage to progressive political action, to theory and method that connect politics, pedagogy, and ethics to action in the world? We want the third edition to carry qualitative inquiry well into the next century. We want the new edition to advance a democratic project committed to social justice in an age of uncertainty. At the same time, we want authors who can write chapters that will address practical, concrete issues of implementation while critiquing the field and mapping key current and emergent themes, debates, and developments.

This is the agenda of this third edition, to show how scholars can use the discourses of qualitative research to help create and imagine a free democratic society. Each of the chapters in this volume is defined by these commitments, in one way or another.

■ ■ ■

We ask of a handbook that it do many things. A handbook, ideally, should represent a distillation of the knowledge of a field; it should be a benchmark volume that synthesizes an existing literature, helping to define and shape the present and future of that discipline. A handbook charts the past, the present, and the future of the discourses at hand. It represents the very best thinking of the very best scholars in the world. It is reflexive, comprehensive, dialogical, accessible. It is authoritative and definitive. Its subject matter is clearly defined. Its authors work within a shared framework. Its authors and editors seek to impose order on a field and a discipline, yet they respect and attempt to honor diversity across disciplinary and paradigmatic perspectives.

A handbook is more than a review of the literature. It speaks to graduate students, to established scholars, and to scholars who wish to learn about the field. It includes information useful for hands-on research. It shows scholars how they can move from ideas to inquiry, from inquiry to interpretation, from interpretation to praxis, to action in the world. It locates its project within larger disciplinary and historical formations. It takes a stand on social justice issues—it is not just about pure scholarship. It is humble. It is indispensable.

These understandings organized the first and second editions of this *Handbook*. In metaphoric terms, if you were to take one book on qualitative research with you to a desert island (or choose one book to read before a comprehensive graduate examination), that book would be a handbook. In the spring and summer of 2002 we returned to this mandate, asking ourselves how best to map what had happened in the field since the first and second editions were published.

▣ The "Field" of Qualitative Research

Our choice of a photograph of the Brooklyn Bridge for the cover of the second edition was deliberate. Like that complex structure, in that edition as well as this, the *Handbook* bridges the new and the old. It joins multiple interpretive communities; it stretches across different landscapes. It offers a pathway back and forth between the public and the private, between science and the sacred, between disciplined inquiry and artistic expression.

Methodological Fundamentalism

It did not take us long to discover that the "field" of qualitative research had undergone quantum leaps since the spring of 1991, when we had planned the first edition. We once again learned that the field of qualitative research is defined primarily by a series of essential tensions, contradictions, and hesitations. These tensions—many of which emerged after 1991—work back and forth between competing definitions and conceptions of the field. These tensions are lodged within and outside the field. In recent years, the methodological conservatism embedded in the educational initiatives of George W. Bush's presidential administration have inscribed narrowly defined governmental regimes of truth. The new "gold standard" for producing knowledge that is worthwhile is based on quantitative, experimental design studies (Lincoln & Canella, 2004, p. 7).

This "methodological fundamentalism" (Lincoln & Cannella, 2004, p. 7) returns to a much discredited model of empirical inquiry. The experimental quantitative model is ill suited to "examining the complex and dynamic contexts of public education in its many forms, sites, and variations, especially considering the . . . subtle social differences produced by gender, race, ethnicity, linguistic status, or class. Indeed, multiple kinds of knowledge, produced by multiple epistemologies and methodologies, are not only worth having but also demanded if policy, legislation, and practice are to be sensitive to social needs" (Lincoln & Cannella, 2004, p. 7). Qualitative researchers twist and turn within this politicized space (Lather, 2004).

Clearly, the tensions and contradictions that characterize the field do not exist within a unified arena. The issues and concerns of qualitative researchers in nursing and health care, for example, are decidedly different from those of researchers in cultural anthropology, where statistical and evidence-based models of inquiry are of less importance. The questions that indigenous scholars deal with are often different from those of interest to critical theorists in educational research. Nor do the international disciplinary networks of qualitative researchers necessarily cross one another, speak to one another, read one another.

Our attempt in this volume, then, once again, is to solidify, interpret, and organize a "field" of qualitative research in the face of essential political, paradigmatic differences and inherent contradictions among styles and types of research, and over the barriers of disciplinary, national, racial, cultural, and gender differences. We present our discussion of how these tensions resolve themselves in our introductory and concluding chapters. We also address these tensions in the implicit dialogue we carry on with various contributors to this volume, many of whom view the field quite differently than we. For you, the reader, to understand why we have resolved these dilemmas as we have, we must first locate ourselves in these tensions and contradictions.

Norman Denzin is committed to a critical pedagogy, critical race, cultural studies, performance-based, poststructural position that stresses the importance of politics and social justice. Yvonna Lincoln is an avowed constructionist, postmodernist, and feminist, likewise committed to social justice, who also places great value on theory and paradigm formation. We share a belief in the limitations of positivism and its successor, postpositivism. Lincoln brings to the project the disciplines of education, psychology, and history, whereas Denzin's grounding is in sociology, communications, anthropology, and the humanities. Our respective biases have shaped the construction of this volume and have entered directly into our dialogues with each other. Although we do not always agree—for example, on the question of whether paradigms can be crossed or integrated—our two voices are heard often in the following pages. Other editors, working from different perspectives, would define the field and construct this book in different ways, choose different spokespersons for the various topics, focus on other concerns, emphasize different methods, or otherwise organize the contents differently.

▣ Organization of This Volume

The organization of the *Handbook* moves from the general to the specific, the past to the present. Part I locates the field, starting with applied qualitative research traditions in the academy, then takes up the topics of critical theorizing and analysis on social (in)justice, researching natives in the "age of uncertainty," resisting neocolonial domination in the Māori context, and the politics and ethics of field research. Part II isolates what we regard as the major historical and contemporary paradigms now structuring and influencing qualitative research in the human disciplines. The chapters move from competing paradigms (positivist, postpositivist, constructivist, critical theory) to specific interpretive perspectives (critical ethnography, feminist discourse, critical race theory, cultural studies, and critical humanism and queer theory).

Part III isolates the major strategies of inquiry—historically the research methods—that researchers can utilize in concrete studies. The contributors to this section embed their discussions of specific strategies of inquiry (performance ethnography, case study, public ethnography, interpretive practice, grounded theory, critical ethnography, *testimonio,* participatory action research, clinical research) in social justice topics. These chapters extensively explore the histories and uses of these strategies.

Still, the question of methods begins with the design of the qualitative research project. This always begins with a socially situated researcher who moves from a research question to a paradigm or perspective, to the empirical world. So located, the researcher then addresses the range of methods that can be employed in any study. In Chapter 15, Julianne Cheek wisely observes that questions surrounding the practice and politics of funding qualitative research are often paramount at this point in any study. Globally, funding for qualitative research becomes more difficult as methodological conservatism gains momentum in neoliberal political regimes.

Part IV examines methods of collecting and analyzing empirical materials. These include narrative inquiry; arts-based inquiry; interviewing; observation; the use of artifacts, documents, and records from the past; visual, auto-, and online ethnography; interpretive perspectives; Foucault's methodologies; analyses of talk and text; and focus groups. Part V takes up the art and practices of interpretation, evaluation, and presentation, including criteria for judging the adequacy of qualitative materials in an age of relativism, the interpretive process, writing as a method of inquiry, the poetics of place, cultural poeisis, investigative poetry and the politics of witnessing, and qualitative evaluation and changing social policy. The three chapters in Part VI speculate on the future and promise of the social sciences and qualitative research in an age of global uncertainty.

▣ Preparation of the Revised *Handbook*

The idea of a new edition of the *Handbook* was taken up seriously in an all-day meeting in New Orleans in April 2002. There the two of us met with our editors at Sage, Alison Muddитt and Margaret Seawell. Once again it became clear in our lengthy discussions that we needed input from individuals with perspectives different from our own. To accomplish this, we assembled an international and interdisciplinary editorial board made up of highly prestigious scholars who assisted us in the selection of chapters written by equally prestigious authors, the preparation of the table of contents, and the reading of (often multiple drafts of) each chapter (the names of all editorial board members are listed on the page facing this volume's title page). We used our editorial board members as windows into their respective disciplines. We sought information from them on key topics, perspectives, and controversies that needed to be addressed. In our selection of editorial board members and chapter authors, we attempted to crosscut disciplinary, gender, race, paradigm, and national boundaries. Our hope was that by seeking board members' views we would minimize our own disciplinary blinders.

We received extensive feedback from the board members, including suggestions for new chapters, different slants to take on each of the chapters, and suggestions of authors for different chapters. In addition to asking each *Handbook* author—internationally recognized in his or her subject matter—to consider social justice issues, we asked each to address such topics as history, epistemology, ontology, exemplary texts, key controversies, competing paradigms, and predictions about the future.

Responding to Critics

We have been gratified by the tremendous response from the field to the previous editions of the *Handbook;* it has been especially gratifying that hundreds of professors around the world have chosen the *Handbook* (in one form or another) to be part of their assigned readings for students. We have also been gratified by the critical responses to the work. The *Handbook* has helped open space for a dialogue that was long overdue. Many readers have found problems with our approach to the field, and these problems indicate places where more conversations need to take place. Among the criticisms of the first and second editions have been the following: The *Handbook*'s framework was unwieldy; the contributions did not give enough attention to the Chicago school; there was too much emphasis on the postmodern period; we employed an arbitrary historical model; the contents were too eclectic; we overemphasized the fifth and sixth moments and the crisis of representation; we gave too much attention to political correctness, and not enough to knowledge for its own sake; there was not enough on how to do qualitative research. Some felt that a revolution had not occurred, and they wondered, too, how we proposed to evaluate qualitative research now that the narrative turn has been taken.

We cannot speak for the more than 120 authors who have contributed chapters to the first, second, and third editions. Each person has taken a stance on these issues. As editors, we have attempted to represent a number of competing or at least contesting ideologies and frames of reference. This *Handbook* is not, nor is it intended to be, Denzin's or Lincoln's view from the bridge. We are not saying that there is only one way to do research, or that our way is best, or that the so-called old ways are bad. We are just saying this is one way to conceptualize this field, and it is a way that we find useful.

Of course the *Handbook* is not a single thing. It even transcends the sum of its parts, and there is enormous diversity both within and between these chapters. It is our hope that readers find spaces within these spaces that work for them. It is our desire that new dialogue take place within these spaces. This will be a gentle, probing, neighborly, and critical conversation, a conversation that bridges the many diverse interpretive communities that today make up this field called qualitative research. We value passion, we invite criticism, we seek to initiate a discourse of resistance. Internationally, qualitative researchers must struggle against neoliberal regimes of truth, science, and justice.

Defining the Field

The qualitative research community consists of groups of globally dispersed persons who are attempting to implement a critical interpretive approach that will help them (and others) make sense of the terrifying conditions that define daily life in the first decade of this new century. These individuals employ constructivist theory, critical theory, feminist theory, queer theory, critical race theory, and cultural studies models of interpretation. They locate themselves on the borders between postpositivism and poststructuralism. They use any and all of the research strategies (case study, ethnography, phenomenology, grounded theory, biographical, historical, participatory, and clinical) discussed in Part III of the *Handbook*. As interpretive *bricoleurs* (see Harper, 1987, pp. 9, 74), the members of this group are adept at using all of the methods of collecting and analyzing empirical materials discussed by the authors of the chapters in Part IV. And, as writers and interpreters, these individuals wrestle with positivist, postpositivist, poststructural, and postmodern criteria for evaluating their written work.[2]

These scholars constitute a loosely defined international interpretive community. They are slowly coming to agreement on what constitutes "good" and "bad," or banal, or emancipatory, troubling both analysis and interpretation. They are constantly challenging the distinction between the "real" and that which is constructed, understanding that all events and understandings are mediated and made real through interactional and material practices, through discourse, conversation, writing, and narrative; through scientific articles and realist, postrealist, and performance tales from the field.

This group works at both the centers and the margins of those emerging interdisciplinary, transnational formations that crisscross the borders that separate communications, race and ethnicity, religion, women's studies, sociology, history, anthropology, literary criticism, political science, economics, social work, health care, and education. This work is characterized by a quiet change in outlook, a transdisciplinary conversation, a pragmatic change in practices, politics, and habits.

It is at this juncture—the uneasy, troubled crossroads where neoliberalism, pragmatism, and postmodernism meet—that a quiet revolution is occurring. This revolution is defined by the politics of representation, which asks, What is represented in a text, and how should it be judged? We have left the world of naive realism, knowing now that a text does not mirror the world, it creates the world. Further, there is no external world or final arbiter—lived experience, for example—against which a text can be judged.

Pragmatism is central to this conversation, for it is itself a theoretical and philosophical concern, firmly rooted in the postrealist tradition. As such, it is a theoretical position that privileges practice and method over reflection and deliberative action. Indeed, postmodernism itself has no predisposition to privilege discourse or text over observation. Instead, postmodernism (and poststructuralism) would simply have us attend to discourse and performance as seriously as we attend to observation (or any other fieldwork methods) and recognize that our discourses are the vehicles for sharing our observations with those who were not in the field with us.

It is precisely the angst attending our recognition of the hidden powers of discourses that leaves us now at the threshold of postmodernism and that signals the advent of questions that will leave none of us untouched. It is true that contemporary qualitative, interpretive research exists within competing fields of discourse. Our present history of the field locates seven moments—and an eighth and ninth, the future. These moments all circulate in the present, competing with and defining one another. This discourse is moving in several directions at the same time. This has the effect of simultaneously creating new spaces, new possibilities, and new formations for qualitative research methods while closing down others.

There are those who would marginalize and politicize the postmodern, poststructural versions of qualitative research, equating it with political correctness, with radical relativism, narratives of the self, and armchair commentary. Some would chastise this *Handbook* for not paying adequate homage to the hands-on, nuts-and-bolts approach to fieldwork, to texts that tell us how to study the "real" world. Still others would seek a preferred, canonical, but flexible version of this project, returning to the Chicago school or more recent formal, analytic, realist versions. Some would criticize the formation from within, contending that the privileging of discourse over observation does not yield adequate criteria for evaluating interpretive work, wondering what to do when left only with voice and interpretation. Many ask for a normative framework for evaluating their own work. None of these desires is likely to be satisfied anytime soon, however. Contestation, contradiction, and philosophical tensions make the achievement of consensus on any of these issues less than imminent.

We are not collating history here, although every chapter describes the history of a subfield. Our intention, which our contributors share, is to point to the future, where the field of qualitative research methods will be 10 years from now. Of course, many scholars in the field still work within frameworks defined by earlier historical moments. This is how it should be. There is no one way to do interpretive, qualitative inquiry. We are all interpretive *bricoleurs* stuck in the present working against the past as we move into a politically charged and challenging future.

Competing Definitions of Qualitative Research Methods

The open-ended nature of the qualitative research project leads to a perpetual resistance against attempts to impose a single, umbrellalike paradigm over the entire project. There are multiple interpretive projects, including the decolonizing methodological project of indigenous scholars; theories of critical pedagogy; performance (auto) ethnographies; standpoint epistemologies; critical race theory; critical, public, poetic, queer, materialist, feminist, and reflexive ethnographies; projects connected to the British cultural studies and Frankfurt schools; grounded theories of several varieties; multiple strands of ethnomethodology; African American, prophetic, postmodern, and neopragmatic Marxism; a U.S.-based critical cultural studies model; and transnational cultural studies projects.

The generic focus of each of these versions of qualitative research moves in five directions at the same time: (a) the "detour through interpretive theory" and a politics of the local, linked (b) to the analysis of the politics of representation and the textual analyses of literary and cultural forms, including their production, distribution, and consumption; (c) the ethnographic, qualitative study and representation of these forms in everyday life; (d) the investigation of new pedagogical and interpretive practices that interactively engage critical cultural analysis in the classroom and the local community; and (e) a utopian politics of possibility (Madison, 1998) that redresses social injustices and imagines a radical democracy that is not yet a reality (Weems, 2002, p. 3).

Whose Revolution?

To summarize: A single, several-part thesis organizes our reading of where the field of qualitative research methodology is today. First, this project has changed because the world that qualitative research confronts, within and outside the academy, has changed. It has also changed because of the increasing sophistication—both theoretical and methodological—of interpretivist researchers everywhere. Disjuncture and difference, violence and terror, define the global political economy. This is a post- or neocolonial world. It is necessary to think beyond the nation, or the local group, as the focus of inquiry.

Second, this is a world where ethnographic texts circulate like other commodities in an electronic world economy. It may be that ethnography is one of the major discourses of the neomodern world. But if this is so, it is no longer possible to take for granted what anyone means by *ethnography,* even in traditional, realist qualitative research (see Snow, 1999, p. 97).[3] Global and local legal processes have erased the personal and institutional distance between the ethnographer and those he or she writes about. We do not "own" the field notes we make about those we study. We do not have an undisputed warrant to study anyone or anything. Subjects now challenge how they have been written about, and more than one ethnographer has been taken to court.

Third, this is a gendered project. Feminist, postcolonial, and queer theorists question the traditional logic of the heterosexual narrative ethnographic text that reflexively positions the ethnographer's gender-neutral (or masculine) self within a realist story. Today there is no solidified ethnographic identity. The ethnographer works within a "hybrid" reality. Experience, discourse, and self-understandings collide with larger cultural assumptions concerning race, ethnicity, nationality, gender, class, and age. A certain identity is never possible; the ethnographer must always ask not "*Who* am I?" but "*When, where, how* am I?" (Trinh, 1992, p. 157).

Fourth, qualitative research is an inquiry project, but it is also a moral, allegorical, and therapeutic project. Ethnography is more than the record of human experience. The ethnographer writes tiny moral tales, tales that do more than celebrate cultural difference or bring another culture alive. The researcher's story is written as a prop, a pillar that, to paraphrase William Faulkner (1967, p. 724), will help men and women endure and prevail in the opening years of the 21st century.

Fifth, although the field of qualitative research is defined by constant breaks and ruptures, there is a shifting center to the project: the avowed humanistic and social justice commitment to study the social world from the perspective of the interacting individual. From this principle flow the liberal and radical politics of action that are held by feminist, clinical, ethnic, critical, queer, critical race theory, and cultural studies researchers. Although multiple interpretive communities now circulate within the field of qualitative research, they are all united on this single point.

Sixth, qualitative research's seventh and eighth moments will be defined by the work that ethnographers do as they implement the above assumptions. These situations set the stage for qualitative research's transformations in the 21st century. Finally, we anticipate a continued performance turn in qualitative inquiry, with writers performing their texts for others.

▣ Tales of the *Handbook*

Many of the difficulties we have encountered in developing this volume are common to any project of substantial magnitude. Others arose from the essential tensions and contradictions that operate in this field at this historical moment. As was the case when we were working on the first and second editions, the "right" chapter authors were sometimes unavailable, too busy, or overcommitted. Consequently, we sought out others, who turned out to be more "right" than we had imagined possible. Few overlapping networks cut across the many disciplines we were attempting to cover. We were fortunate, in more than one instance, to have an editorial board member point us in a direction we had not previously been aware existed. We are grateful to Michelle Fine for connecting us with the community of indigenous scholars in New Zealand, in particular Linda Tuhiwai Smith and Russell Bishop.

Although we knew the territory somewhat better this time around, there were still spaces we blundered into with little knowledge about whom we should ask to do what. We confronted disciplinary and generational blinders—including our own—and discovered there are separate traditions surrounding each of our topics within distinct interpretive communities. It was often difficult to know how to bridge these differences, and our "bridges" were often makeshift constructions. We also had to cope with vastly different styles of thinking about a variety of topics based on disciplinary, epistemological, gender, racial, ethnic, cultural, and national beliefs, boundaries, and ideologies.

In many instances we unwittingly entered into political battles over who should write a given chapter, or over how a chapter should be written or evaluated. These disputes clearly pointed to the political nature of this project and to the fact that each chapter is a potential, if not real, site for multiple interpretations. Many times the politics of meaning came into play as we attempted to negotiate and navigate our way through areas fraught with emotion. On more than one occasion we disagreed with both an author and an editorial board member. We often found ourselves adjudicating between competing editorial reviews, working the hyphens between meaning making and diplomacy. Regrettably, in some cases we hurt feelings and perhaps even damaged long-standing friendships. In such moments we sought forgiveness. With the clarity of hindsight, we can see that there are many things we would do differently today, and we apologize for the damage we have done.

We, as well as our authors and advisers, struggled with the meanings we wanted to bring to such terms as *theory, paradigm, epistemology, interpretive framework, empirical materials* versus *data,* and *research strategies.* We discovered that the very term *qualitative research* means different things to many different people.

We abandoned the goal of being comprehensive, even with 2,000 manuscript pages. We fought with authors over deadlines and over the number of pages we would give them. We also fought with authors over how to conceptualize their chapter and found that what was clear to us was not necessarily clear to anyone else. We fought with authors too over when their chapters were done, constantly seeking their forbearance as we requested yet another revision.

Reading the *Handbook*

Were we to write our own critique of this book, we would point to the shortcomings we see in it, which in many senses are the same as those we saw in the 1994 and 2000 editions. These include an overreliance on the perspectives of our respective disciplines (sociology, communications, and education) as well as a failure to involve more scholars from international indigenous communities. This volume does not provide a detailed treatment of the intersection of critical and indigenous inquiry, nor does it include a comprehensive chapter on human subject research and institutional review boards. We worked hard to avoid these problems, yet they remain. On the other hand, in this edition we do address some of the problems that were present in the second edition. We have made a greater effort to cover more areas of applied qualitative work. We have helped to initiate dialogues between the authors of various chapters. We have created spaces for more voices from other disciplines, especially anthropology and communications, but we still have a shortfall of voices representing people of color and of the Third World. You, the reader, will certainly have your own responses to this book, responses that may highlight other issues that we have not yet seen.

This is all in the nature of the *Handbook,* and in the nature of doing qualitative research. This book is a social construction, a socially enacted, cocreated entity, and although it exists in a material form, will no doubt be re-created in subsequent iterations as generations of scholars and graduate students use it, adapt it, and launch from it additional methodological, paradigmatic, theoretical, and practical work. It is not a final statement. It is a starting point, a springboard for new thought and new work, work that is fresh and sensitive, that blurs the boundaries of our disciplines but always sharpens our understandings of the larger human project.

It is our hope that this third edition, with all its strengths and all its flaws, will contribute to the growing maturity and global influence of qualitative research in the human disciplines. And, as we were originally mandated, we hope this convinces you, the reader, that qualitative research now constitutes a field of study in its own right, allowing you to better anchor and locate your own work in the qualitative research tradition and its central place in a radical democratic project. If this happens, we will have succeeded in building a bridge that serves us all well.

Acknowledgments

This *Handbook* would not exist without its authors and the editorial board members who gave freely, often on very short notice, of their time, advice, and ever-courteous suggestions. We acknowledge en masse the support of the authors and the editorial board members, whose names are listed facing the title page. These individuals were able to offer both long-term, sustained commitments to the project and short-term emergency assistance.

There are other debts, intensely personal and closer to home. The *Handbook* would never have been possible without the ever-present help, support, wisdom, and encouragement of our editors and publishers at Sage: Alison Mudditt, Margaret Seawell, and Lisa Cuevas Shaw. Their grasp of this field, its history, and diversity is extraordinary. Their conceptions of what this project should look like have been extremely valuable. Their energy kept us moving forward. Furthermore, whenever we confronted a problem, Lisa was there with her assistance and good-natured humor. Judy Selhorst, Astrid Virding, and Claudia Hoffman moved the project through production with their usual grace and humor. Aisha Durham, Grant Kien, James Salvo, and Li Xiung provided outstanding proofreading skills. Ravi Balasuriya designed the cover.

We would also like to thank the following individuals and institutions for their assistance, support, insights, and patience: our respective universities and departments, especially, at Yvonna's university, Dean Jane Conoley, Associate Dean Ernest Goetz, and Department Head Bryan R. Cole, each of whom facilitated this work in some important way. In Urbana, David Monje was the sine qua non. His good humor and grace kept our ever-growing files in order and everyone on the same timetable. Without David, who inherited the mantle from Jack Bratich, this project would never have been completed.

Norman also gratefully acknowledges the moral, intellectual, and financial support given to this project by Dean Ron Yates of the College of Communication and by Paula Treichler and Bruce Williams, past and present directors, respectively, of the Institute of Communication. He also thanks Nina Richards and Tom Galer-Unti, who kept the financial accounts straight. Claudia Hoffman at Sage helped move this project through production; we are extremely grateful to her, as well as to D. J. Peck, A. J. Sobczak, Judy Selhorst, and Kathleen Paparchontis for their excellent work during the copyediting, proofreading, and indexing phases of production. Our spouses, Katherine Ryan and Egon Guba, helped keep us on track, listened to our complaints, and generally displayed extraordinary patience, forbearance, and support.

Finally, there are two groups of individuals who gave unstintingly of their time and energy to provide us with their expertise and thoughtful reviews when we needed additional guidance. The first group is our International Advisory Board—the names of all board members are listed opposite this volume's title page. The second group consists of invited guest readers, whose names are listed below. Without the help of all these individuals we would often have found ourselves with less than complete understandings of the various traditions, perspectives, and methods represented in this volume. We would like to acknowledge the important contributions of the following special readers to this project: Bryant Alexander, Tom Barone, Jack Z. Bratich, Susan Chase, Shing-Ling Sarina Chen, Nadine Dolby, Susan Finley, Andrea Fontana, Jaber Gubrium, Stephen Hartnett, Stacy Holman Jones, Steve Jones, Ruthellen Josselson, Luis Miron, Ronald J. Pelias, John Prosser, Johny Saldaña, Paula Saukko, Thomas Schwandt, Patrick Slattery, and Linda Tuhiwai Smith.

—Norman K. Denzin
University of Illinois at Urbana-Champaign

—Yvonna S. Lincoln
Texas A&M University

Notes

1. Focusing her remarks on feminist issues, Olesen (2000) calls for "incisive scholarship to frame, direct, and harness passion in the interests of redressing grievous problems in many areas of women's health" (p. 215).

2. These criteria range from those endorsed by postpositivists (variations on validity and reliability, including credibility and trustworthiness) to poststructural, feminist standpoint concerns emphasizing collaborative, evocative, performance texts that create ethically responsible relations between researchers and those they study.

3. The realist text, Jameson (1990) argues, constructed its version of the world by "programming . . . readers; by training them in new habits and practices. . . . such narratives must ultimately produce that very category of Reality . . . of the real, of the 'objective' or 'external' world, which is itself historical, may undergo decisive modification in other modes of production, if not in later stages of this one" (p. 166). The new ethnographic text is producing its versions of reality and teaching readers how to engage this view of the social world.

References

Faulkner, W. (1967). Address upon receiving the Nobel Prize for Literature. In M. Cowley (Ed.), *The portable Faulkner* (Rev. ed., pp. 723–724). New York: Viking.

Feuer, M. J., Towne, L., & Shavelson, R. J. (2002). Scientific culture and educational research. *Educational Researcher, 31*(8), 4–14.

Harper, D. (1987). *Working knowledge: Skill and community in a small shop.* Chicago: University of Chicago Press.

Jameson, F. (1990). *Signatures of the visible.* New York: Routledge.

Lather, P. (2004). This *is* your father's paradigm: Government intrusion and the case of qualitative research in education. *Qualitative Inquiry, 10,* 15–34.

Lincoln, Y. S., & Cannella, G. S. (2004). Dangerous discourses: Methodological conservatism and governmental regimes of truth. *Qualitative Inquiry, 10,* 5–14.

Madison, D. S. (1998). Performances, personal narratives, and the politics of possibility. In S. J. Dailey (Ed.), *The future of performance studies: Visions and revisions* (pp. 276–286). Washington, DC: National Communication Association.

Mutua, K., & Swadener, B. B. (2004). Introduction. In K. Mutua & B. B. Swadener (Eds.), *Decolonizing research in cross-cultural contexts: Critical personal narratives* (pp. 1–23). Albany: State University of New York Press.

Olesen, V. L. (2000). Feminisms and qualitative research at and into the millennium. In N. K. Denzin & Y. S. Lincoln (Eds.), *Handbook of qualitative research* (2nd ed., pp. 215–255). Thousand Oaks, CA: Sage.

Peshkin, A. (1993). The goodness of qualitative research. *Educational Researcher, 22*(2), 24–30.

Schwandt, T. A. (2000). Three epistemological stances for qualitative inquiry: Interpretivism, hermeneutics, and social constructionism. In N. K. Denzin & Y. S. Lincoln (Eds.), *Handbook of qualitative research* (2nd ed., pp. 189–213). Thousand Oaks, CA: Sage.

Snow, D. (1999). Assessing the ways in which qualitative/ethnographic research contributes to social psychology: Introduction to special issue. *Social Psychology Quarterly, 62,* 97–100.

Trinh T. M. (1992). *Framer framed.* New York: Routledge.

Weems, M. (2002). *I speak from the wound that is my mouth.* New York: Peter Lang.

1

INTRODUCTION

The Discipline and Practice of Qualitative Research

Norman K. Denzin and Yvonna S. Lincoln

Writing about scientific research, including qualitative research, from the vantage point of the colonized, a position that she chooses to privilege, Linda Tuhiwai Smith (1999) states that "the term 'research' is inextricably linked to European imperialism and colonialism." She continues, "The word itself is probably one of the dirtiest words in the indigenous world's vocabulary. . . . It is implicated in the worst excesses of colonialism," with the ways in which "knowledge about indigenous peoples was collected, classified, and then represented back to the West" (p. 1). This dirty word stirs up anger, silence, distrust. "It is so powerful that indigenous people even write poetry about research" (p. 1). It is one of colonialism's most sordid legacies.

Sadly, qualitative research, in many if not all of its forms (observation, participation, interviewing, ethnography), serves as a metaphor for colonial knowledge, for power, and for truth. The metaphor works this way. Research, quantitative and qualitative, is scientific. Research provides the foundation for reports about and representations of "the Other." In the colonial context, research becomes an objective way of representing the dark-skinned Other to the white world.

Colonizing nations relied on the human disciplines, especially sociology and anthropology, to produce knowledge about strange and foreign worlds. This close involvement with the colonial project contributed, in significant ways, to qualitative research's long and anguished history, to its becoming a dirty word (for reviews, see in this volume Foley & Valenzuela, Chapter 9; Tedlock, Chapter 18). In sociology, the work of the "Chicago school" in the 1920s and 1930s established the importance of qualitative inquiry for the study of human group life. In anthropology during the same period, the discipline-defining studies of Boas, Mead, Benedict, Bateson, Evans-Pritchard, Radcliffe-Brown, and Malinowski charted the outlines of the fieldwork method (see Gupta & Ferguson, 1997; Stocking, 1986, 1989).

Authors' Note. We are grateful to many who have helped with this chapter, including Egon Guba, Mitch Allen, David Monje, and Katherine E. Ryan.

The agenda was clear-cut: The observer went to a foreign setting to study the culture, customs, and habits of another human group. Often this was a group that stood in the way of white settlers. Ethnographic reports of these groups where incorporated into colonizing strategies, ways of controlling the foreign, deviant, or troublesome Other. Soon qualitative research would be employed in other social and behavioral science disciplines, including education (especially the work of Dewey), history, political science, business, medicine, nursing, social work, and communications (for criticisms of this tradition, see Smith, 1999; Vidich & Lyman, 2000; see also Rosaldo 1989, pp. 25–45; Tedlock, Chapter 18, this volume).

By the 1960s, battle lines were drawn within the quantitative and qualitative camps. Quantitative scholars relegated qualitative research to a subordinate status in the scientific arena. In response, qualitative researchers extolled the humanistic virtues of their subjective, interpretive approach to the study of human group life. In the meantime, indigenous peoples found themselves subjected to the indignities of both approaches, as each methodology was used in the name of colonizing powers (see Battiste, 2000; Semali & Kincheloe, 1999).

Vidich and Lyman (1994, 2000) have charted many key features of this painful history. In their now-classic analysis they note, with some irony, that qualitative research in sociology and anthropology was "born out of concern to understand the 'other'" (Vidich & Lyman, 2000, p. 38). Furthermore, this "other" was the exotic Other, a primitive, nonwhite person from a foreign culture judged to be less civilized than ours. Of course, there were colonialists long before there were anthropologists and ethnographers. Nonetheless, there would be no colonial, and now no neocolonial, history were it not for this investigative mentality that turned the dark-skinned Other into the object of the ethnographer's gaze. From the very beginning, qualitative research was implicated in a racist project.[1]

In this introductory chapter, we define the field of qualitative research, then navigate, chart, and review the history of qualitative research in the human disciplines. This will allow us to locate this volume and its contents within their historical moments. (These historical moments are somewhat artificial; they are socially constructed, quasi-historical, and overlapping conventions. Nevertheless, they permit a "performance" of developing ideas. They also facilitate an increasing sensitivity to and sophistication about the pitfalls and promises of ethnography and qualitative research.) We also present a conceptual framework for reading the qualitative research act as a multicultural, gendered process and then provide a brief introduction to the chapters that follow. Returning to the observations of Vidich and Lyman as well as those of hooks, we conclude with a brief discussion of qualitative research and critical race theory (see also Ladson-Billings & Donnor, Chapter 11, this volume). We also discuss the threats to qualitative, human subject research from the methodological conservatism movement mentioned briefly in our preface. As we note in the preface, we use the metaphor of the bridge to structure what follows. This volume is intended to serve as a bridge connecting historical moments, politics, the decolonization project, research methods, paradigms, and communities of interpretive scholars.

Definitional Issues

Qualitative research is a field of inquiry in its own right. It crosscuts disciplines, fields, and subject matters.[2] A complex, interconnected family of terms, concepts, and assumptions surround the term *qualitative research*. These include the traditions associated with foundationalism, positivism, postfoundationalism, postpositivism, poststructuralism, and the many qualitative research perspectives, and/or methods connected to cultural and interpretive studies (the chapters in Part II take up these paradigms).[3] There are separate and detailed literatures on the many methods and approaches that fall under the category of qualitative research, such as case study, politics and ethics, participatory inquiry, interviewing, participant observation, visual methods, and interpretive analysis.

In North America, qualitative research operates in a complex historical field that crosscuts at least eight historical moments. (We discuss these moments in detail below.) These moments overlap and simultaneously operate in the present.[4] We define them as the *traditional* (1900–1950); the *modernist*, or golden age (1950–1970); *blurred genres* (1970–1986); the *crisis of representation* (1986–1990); the *postmodern*, a period of experimental and new ethnographies (1990–1995); *postexperimental inquiry* (1995–2000); the *methodologically contested present* (2000–2004); and the *fractured future*, which is now (2005–). The future, the eighth moment, confronts the methodological backlash associated with the evidence-based social movement. It is concerned with moral discourse, with the development of sacred textualities. The eighth moment asks that the social sciences and the humanities become sites for critical conversations about democracy, race, gender, class, nation-states, globalization, freedom, and community.[5]

The postmodern and postexperimental moments were defined in part by a concern for literary and rhetorical tropes and the narrative turn, a concern for storytelling, for composing ethnographies in new ways (Bochner & Ellis, 2002; Ellis, 2004; Goodall, 2000; Pelias, 2004; Richardson & Lockridge, 2004; Trujillo, 2004). Laurel Richardson (1997) observes that this moment was shaped by a new sensibility, by doubt, by a refusal to privilege any method or theory (p. 173). But now at the dawn of this new century we struggle to connect qualitative research to the hopes, needs, goals, and promises of a free democratic society.

Successive waves of epistemological theorizing move across these eight moments. The traditional period is associated with the positivist, foundational paradigm. The modernist or golden age and blurred genres moments are connected to the appearance of postpositivist arguments. At the same time, a variety of new interpretive, qualitative perspectives were taken up, including hermeneutics, structuralism, semiotics, phenomenology, cultural studies, and feminism.[6] In the blurred genres phase, the humanities became central resources for critical, interpretive theory, and the qualitative research project broadly conceived. The researcher became a *bricoleur* (see below), learning how to borrow from many different disciplines.

The blurred genres phase produced the next stage, the crisis of representation. Here researchers struggled with how to locate themselves and their subjects in reflexive texts. A kind of methodological diaspora took place, a two-way exodus. Humanists migrated to the social sciences, searching for new social theory, new ways to study popular culture and its local, ethnographic contexts. Social scientists turned to the humanities, hoping to learn how to do complex structural and poststructural readings of social texts. From the humanities, social scientists also learned how to produce texts that refused to be read in simplistic, linear, incontrovertible terms. The line between text and context blurred. In the postmodern, experimental moment, researchers continued to move away from foundational and quasi-foundational criteria (see in this volume Smith & Hodkinson, Chapter 36; Richardson & St. Pierre, Chapter 38). Alternative evaluative criteria were sought, criteria that might prove evocative, moral, critical, and rooted in local understandings.

Any definition of qualitative research must work within this complex historical field. *Qualitative research* means different things in each of these moments. Nonetheless, an initial, generic definition can be offered: Qualitative research is a situated activity that locates the observer in the world. It consists of a set of interpretive, material practices that make the world visible. These practices transform the world. They turn the world into a series of representations, including field notes, interviews, conversations, photographs, recordings, and memos to the self. At this level, qualitative research involves an interpretive, naturalistic approach to the world. This means that qualitative researchers study things in their natural settings, attempting to make sense of, or interpret, phenomena in terms of the meanings people bring to them.[7]

Qualitative research involves the studied use and collection of a variety of empirical materials—case study; personal experience; introspection; life story; interview; artifacts; cultural texts and productions; observational, historical, interactional, and visual texts—that describe routine and problematic moments and meanings in individuals' lives. Accordingly, qualitative researchers deploy a wide range of interconnected interpretive practices, hoping always to get a better understanding of the subject matter at hand. It is understood, however, that each practice makes the world visible in a different way. Hence there is frequently a commitment to using more than one interpretive practice in any study.

The Qualitative Researcher as *Bricoleur* and Quilt Maker

The qualitative researcher may be described using multiple and gendered images: scientist, naturalist, field-worker, journalist, social critic, artist, performer, jazz musician, filmmaker, quilt maker, essayist. The many methodological practices of qualitative research may be viewed as soft science, journalism, ethnography, bricolage, quilt making, or montage. The researcher, in turn, may be seen as a *bricoleur,* as a maker of quilts, or, as in filmmaking, a person who assembles images into montages. (On montage, see Cook, 1981, pp. 171–177; Monaco, 1981, pp. 322–328; and the discussion below. On quilting, see hooks, 1990, pp. 115–122; Wolcott, 1995, pp. 31–33.)

Harper (1987, pp. 9, 74–75, 92), de Certeau (1984, p. xv), Nelson, Treichler, and Grossberg (1992, p. 2), Lévi-Strauss (1966, p. 17), Weinstein and Weinstein (1991, p. 161), and Kincheloe (2001) clarify the meanings of *bricolage* and *bricoleur.*[8] A *bricoleur* makes do by "adapting the *bricoles* of the world. *Bricolage* is 'the poetic making do'" (de Certeau, 1984, p. xv) with "such bricoles—the odds and ends, the bits left over" (Harper, 1987, p. 74). The *bricoleur* is a "Jack of all trades, a kind of professional do-it-yourself" (Lévi-Strauss, 1966, p. 17). In their work, *bricoleurs* define and extend themselves (Harper, 1987, p. 75). Indeed, the *bricoleur's* life story, or biography, "may be thought of as bricolage" (Harper, 1987, p. 92).

There are many kinds of *bricoleurs*—interpretive, narrative, theoretical, political, methodological (see below). The interpretive *bricoleur* produces a bricolage—that is, a pieced-together set of representations that is fitted to the specifics of a complex situation. "The solution (bricolage) which is the result of the *bricoleur's* method is an [emergent] construction" (Weinstein & Weinstein, 1991, p. 161) that changes and takes new forms as the *bricoleur* adds different tools, methods, and techniques of representation and interpretation to the puzzle. Nelson et al. (1992) describe the methodology of cultural studies as "a bricolage. Its choice of practice, that is, is pragmatic, strategic and self-reflexive" (p. 2). This understanding can be applied, with qualifications, to qualitative research.

The qualitative researcher as *bricoleur,* or maker of quilts, uses the aesthetic and material tools of his or her craft, deploying whatever strategies, methods, and empirical materials are at hand (Becker, 1998, p. 2). If the researcher needs to invent, or piece together, new tools or techniques, he or she will do so. Choices regarding which interpretive practices to employ are not necessarily made in advance. As Nelson et al. (1992) note, the "choice of research practices depends upon the questions that are asked, and the questions depend on their context" (p. 2), what is available in the context, and what the researcher can do in that setting.

These interpretive practices involve aesthetic issues, an aesthetics of representation that goes beyond the pragmatic or the practical. Here the concept of *montage* is useful (see Cook, 1981, p. 323; Monaco, 1981, pp. 171–172). Montage is a method of editing cinematic images. In the history of cinematography, montage is most closely associated with the work of Sergei Eisenstein, especially his film *The Battleship Potemkin* (1925). In montage, several different images are juxtaposed to or superimposed on one another to create a picture. In a sense, montage is like *pentimento,* in which something that has been painted out of a picture (an image the painter "repented," or denied) becomes visible again, creating something new. What is new is what had been obscured by a previous image.

Montage and pentimento, like jazz, which is improvisation, create the sense that images, sounds, and understandings are blending together, overlapping, forming a composite, a new creation. The images seem to shape and define one another, and an emotional, gestalt effect is produced. In film montage, images are often combined in a swiftly run sequence that produces a dizzily revolving collection of several images around a central or focused picture or sequence; directors often use such effects to signify the passage of time.

Perhaps the most famous instance of montage in film is the Odessa Steps sequence in *The Battleship Potemkin*. In the climax of the film, the citizens of Odessa are being massacred by czarist troops on the stone steps leading down to the harbor. Eisenstein cuts to a young mother as she pushes her baby in a carriage across the landing in front of the firing troops.[9] Citizens rush past her, jolting the carriage, which she is afraid to push down to the next flight of stairs. The troops are above her, firing at the citizens. She is trapped between the troops and the steps. She screams. A line of rifles points to the sky, the rifle barrels erupting in smoke. The mother's head sways back. The wheels of the carriage teeter on the edge of the steps. The mother's hand clutches the silver buckle of her belt. Below her, people are being beaten by soldiers. Blood drips over the mother's white gloves. The baby's hand reaches out of the carriage. The mother sways back and forth. The troops advance. The mother falls back against the carriage. A woman watches in horror as the rear wheels of the carriage roll off the edge of the landing. With accelerating speed, the carriage bounces down the steps, past dead citizens. The baby is jostled from side to side inside the carriage. The soldiers fire their rifles into a group of wounded citizens. A student screams as the carriage leaps across the steps, tilts, and overturns (Cook, 1981, p. 167).[10]

Montage uses brief images to create a clearly defined sense of urgency and complexity. It invites viewers to construct interpretations that build on one another as a scene unfolds. These interpretations are based on associations among the contrasting images that blend into one another. The underlying assumption of montage is that viewers perceive and interpret the shots in a "montage sequence not *sequentially*, or one at a time, but rather *simultaneously*" (Cook, 1981, p. 172). The viewer puts the sequences together into a meaningful emotional whole, as if at a glance, all at once.

The qualitative researcher who uses montage is like a quilt maker or a jazz improviser. The quilter stitches, edits, and puts slices of reality together. This process creates and brings psychological and emotional unity—a pattern—to an interpretive experience. There are many examples of montage in current qualitative research (see Diversi, 1998; Holman Jones, 1999; Lather & Smithies, 1997; Ronai, 1998; see also Holman Jones, Chapter 30, this volume). Using multiple voices, different textual formats, and various typefaces, Lather and Smithies (1997) weave a complex text about AIDS and women who are HIV-positive. Holman Jones (1999) creates a performance text using lyrics from the blues songs sung by Billie Holiday.

In texts based on the metaphors of montage, quilt making, and jazz improvisation, many different things are going on at the same time—different voices, different perspectives, points of views, angles of vision. Like autoethnographic performance texts, works that use montage simultaneously create and enact moral meaning. They move from the personal to the political, from the local to the historical and the cultural. These are dialogical texts. They presume an active audience. They create spaces for give-and-take between reader and writer. They do more than turn the Other into the object of the social science gaze (see in this volume Alexander, Chapter 16; Holman Jones, Chapter 30).

Qualitative research is inherently multimethod in focus (Flick, 2002, pp. 226–227). However, the use of multiple methods, or triangulation, reflects an attempt to secure an in-depth understanding of the phenomenon in question. Objective reality can never be captured. We know a thing only through its representations. Triangulation is not a tool or a strategy of validation, but an alternative to validation (Flick, 2002, p. 227). The combination of multiple methodological practices, empirical materials, perspectives, and observers in a single study is best understood, then, as a strategy that adds rigor, breadth, complexity, richness, and depth to any inquiry (see Flick, 2002, p. 229).

In Chapter 38 of this volume, Richardson and St. Pierre dispute the usefulness of the concept of triangulation, asserting that the central image for qualitative inquiry should be the crystal, not the triangle. Mixed-genre texts in the postexperimental moment have more than three sides. Like crystals, Eisenstein's montage, the jazz solo, or the pieces in a quilt, the mixed-genre text "combines symmetry and substance with an infinite variety of shapes, substances, transmutations.... Crystals grow, change, alter.... Crystals are prisms that reflect externalities and refract within themselves, creating different colors, patterns, arrays, casting off in different directions" (Richardson, 2000, p. 934).

In the crystallization process, the writer tells the same tale from different points of view. For example, in *A Thrice-Told Tale* (1992), Margery Wolf uses fiction, field notes, and a scientific article to give three different accounts of the same set of experiences in a native village. Similarly, in her play *Fires in the Mirror* (1993), Anna Deavere Smith presents a series of performance pieces based on interviews with people who were involved in a racial conflict in Crown Heights, Brooklyn, on August 19, 1991. The play has multiple speaking parts, including conversations with gang members, police officers, and anonymous young girls and boys. There is no one "correct" telling of this event. Each telling, like light hitting a crystal, reflects a different perspective on this incident.

Viewed as a crystalline form, as a montage, or as a creative performance around a central theme, triangulation as a form of, or alternative to, validity thus can be extended. Triangulation is the simultaneous display of multiple, refracted realities. Each of the metaphors "works" to create simultaneity rather than the sequential or linear. Readers and audiences are then invited to explore competing visions of the context, to become immersed in and merge with new realities to comprehend.

The methodological *bricoleur* is adept at performing a large number of diverse tasks, ranging from interviewing to intensive self-reflection and introspection. The theoretical *bricoleur* reads widely and is knowledgeable about the many interpretive paradigms (feminism, Marxism, cultural studies, constructivism, queer theory) that can be brought to any particular problem. He or she may not, however, feel that paradigms can be mingled or synthesized. That is, one cannot easily move between paradigms as overarching philosophical systems denoting particular ontologies, epistemologies, and methodologies. They represent belief systems that attach users to particular worldviews. Perspectives, in contrast, are less well developed systems, and one can move between them more easily. The researcher as *bricoleur*-theorist works between and within competing and overlapping perspectives and paradigms.

The interpretive *bricoleur* understands that research is an interactive process shaped by his or her own personal history, biography, gender, social class, race, and ethnicity, and by those of the people in the setting. The critical *bricoleur* stresses the dialectical and hermeneutic nature of interdisciplinary inquiry, knowing that the boundaries that previously separated traditional disciplines no longer hold (Kincheloe, 2001, p. 683). The political *bricoleur* knows that science is power, for all research findings have political implications. There is no value-free science. This researcher seeks a civic social science based on a politics of hope (Lincoln, 1999). The gendered, narrative *bricoleur* also knows that researchers all tell stories about the worlds they have studied. Thus the narratives, or stories, scientists tell are accounts couched and framed within specific storytelling traditions, often defined as paradigms (e.g., positivism, postpositivism, constructivism).

The product of the interpretive *bricoleur*'s labor is a complex, quiltlike bricolage, a reflexive collage or montage—a set of fluid, interconnected images and representations. This interpretive structure is like a quilt, a performance text, a sequence of representations connecting the parts to the whole.

Qualitative Research as a Site of Multiple Interpretive Practices

Qualitative research, as a set of interpretive activities, privileges no single methodological practice over another. As a site of discussion, or discourse, qualitative research is difficult to define clearly. It has no theory or paradigm that is distinctly its own. As the contributions to Part II of this volume reveal, multiple theoretical paradigms claim use of qualitative research methods and strategies, from constructivist to cultural studies, feminism, Marxism, and ethnic models of study. Qualitative research is used in many separate disciplines, as we will discuss below. It does not belong to a single discipline.

Nor does qualitative research have a distinct set of methods or practices that are entirely its own. Qualitative researchers use semiotics, narrative, content, discourse, archival and phonemic analysis, even statistics, tables, graphs, and numbers. They also draw on and utilize the approaches, methods, and techniques of ethnomethodology, phenomenology, hermeneutics, feminism, rhizomatics, deconstructionism, ethnography, interviewing, psychoanalysis, cultural studies, survey research, and participant observation, among others.[11] All of these research practices "can provide important insights and knowledge" (Nelson et al., 1992, p. 2). No specific method or practice can be privileged over any other.

Many of these methods, or research practices, are used in other contexts in the human disciplines. Each bears the traces of its own disciplinary history. Thus there is an extensive history of the uses and meanings of ethnography and ethnology in education (see in this volume Ladson-Billings & Donnor, Chapter 11; Kincheloe & McLaren, Chapter 12); of participant observation and ethnography in anthropology (see Foley & Valenzuela, Chapter 9; Tedlock, Chapter 18; Brady, Chapter 39), sociology (see Holstein & Gubrium, Chapter 19; Fontana & Frey, Chapter 27; Harper, Chapter 29), communications (see Alexander, Chapter 16; Holman Jones, Chapter 30), and cultural studies (see Saukko, Chapter 13); of textual, hermeneutic, feminist, psychoanalytic, arts-based, semiotic, and narrative analysis in cinema and literary studies (see Olesen, Chapter 10; Finley, Chapter 26; Brady, Chapter 39); and of narrative, discourse, and conversational analysis in sociology, medicine, communications, and education (see Miller & Crabtree, Chapter 24; Chase, Chapter 25; Perakyla, Chapter 34).

The many histories that surround each method or research strategy reveal how multiple uses and meanings are brought to each practice. Textual analyses in literary studies, for example, often treat texts as self-contained systems. On the other hand, a researcher working from a cultural studies or feminist perspective reads a text in terms of its location within a historical moment marked by a particular gender, race, or class ideology. A cultural studies use of ethnography would bring a set of understandings from feminism, postmodernism, and poststructuralism to the project. These understandings would not be shared by mainstream postpositivist sociologists. Similarly, postpositivist and poststructural historians bring different understandings and uses to the methods and findings of historical research (see Tierney, 2000). These tensions and contradictions are all evident in the chapters in this volume.

These separate and multiple uses and meanings of the methods of qualitative research make it difficult for scholars to agree on any essential definition of the field, for it is never just one thing.[12] Still, we must establish a definition for purposes of this discussion. We borrow from, and paraphrase, Nelson et al.'s (1992, p. 4) attempt to define cultural studies:

> Qualitative research is an interdisciplinary, transdisciplinary, and sometimes counterdisciplinary field. It crosscuts the humanities and the social and physical sciences. Qualitative research is many things at the same time. It is multiparadigmatic in focus. Its practitioners are sensitive to the value of the multimethod approach. They are committed to the naturalistic perspective and to the interpretive understanding of human experience. At the same time, the field is inherently political and shaped by multiple ethical and political positions.
>
> Qualitative research embraces two tensions at the same time. On the one hand, it is drawn to a broad, interpretive, postexperimental, postmodern, feminist, and critical sensibility. On the other hand, it is drawn to more narrowly defined positivist, postpositivist, humanistic, and naturalistic conceptions of human experience and its analysis. Further, these tensions can be combined in the same project, bringing both postmodern and naturalistic, or both critical and humanistic, perspectives to bear.

This rather awkward statement means that qualitative research, as a set of practices, embraces within its own multiple disciplinary histories constant tensions and contradictions over the project itself, including its methods and the forms its findings and interpretations take. The field sprawls between and cuts across all of the human disciplines, even including, in some cases, the physical sciences. Its practitioners are variously committed to modern, postmodern, and postexperimental sensibilities and the approaches to social research that these sensibilities imply.

Resistances to Qualitative Studies

The academic and disciplinary resistances to qualitative research illustrate the politics embedded in this field of discourse. The challenges to qualitative research are many. As Seale, Gobo, Gubrium, and Silverman (2004) observe, we can best understand these criticisms by "distinguish[ing] analytically the political (or external) role of [qualitative] methodology from the procedural (or internal) one" (p. 7). Politics situate methodology within and outside the academy. Procedural issues define how qualitative methodology is used to produce knowledge about the world.

Often, the political and the procedural intersect. Politicians and "hard" scientists sometimes call qualitative researchers journalists or soft scientists. The work of qualitative scholars is termed unscientific, or only exploratory, or subjective. It is called criticism rather than theory or science, or it is interpreted politically, as a disguised version of Marxism or secular humanism (see Huber, 1995; see also Denzin, 1997, pp. 258–261).

These political and procedural resistances reflect an uneasy awareness that the interpretive traditions of qualitative research commit the researcher to a critique of the positivist or postpositivist project. But the positivist resistance to qualitative research goes beyond the "ever-present desire to maintain a distinction between hard science and soft scholarship" (Carey, 1989, p. 99; see also Smith & Hodkinson, Chapter 36, this volume). The experimental (positivist) sciences (physics, chemistry, economics, and psychology, for example) are often seen as the crowning achievements of Western civilization, and in their practices it is assumed that "truth" can transcend opinion and personal bias (Carey, 1989, p. 99; Schwandt, 1997b, p. 309). Qualitative research is seen as an assault on this tradition, whose adherents often retreat into a "value-free objectivist science" (Carey, 1989, p. 104) model to defend their position. They seldom attempt to make explicit, or to critique, the "moral and political commitments in their own contingent work" (Carey, 1989, p. 104; see also Guba & Lincoln, Chapter 8, this volume).

Positivists further allege that the so-called new experimental qualitative researchers write fiction, not science, and that these researchers have no way of verifying their truth statements. Ethnographic poetry and fiction signal the death of empirical science, and there is little to be gained by attempting to engage in moral criticism. These critics presume a stable, unchanging reality that can be studied using the empirical methods of objective social science (see Huber, 1995). The province of qualitative research, accordingly, is the world of lived experience, for this is where individual belief and action intersect with culture. Under this model there is no preoccupation with discourse and method as material interpretive practices that constitute representation and description. Thus is the textual, narrative turn rejected by the positivists.

The opposition to positive science by the poststructuralists is seen, then, as an attack on reason and truth. At the same time, the positivist science attack on qualitative research is regarded as an attempt to legislate one version of truth over another.

Politics and Reemergent Scientism

The scientifically based research (SBR) movement initiated in recent years by the National Research Council (NRC) has created a hostile political environment for qualitative research. Connected to the federal legislation known as the No Child Left Behind Act of 2001, SBR embodies a reemergent scientism (Maxwell, 2004), a positivist, evidence-based epistemology. The movement encourages researchers to employ "rigorous, systematic, and objective methodology to obtain reliable and valid knowledge " (Ryan & Hood, 2004, p. 80). The preferred methodology employs well-defined causal models and independent and dependent variables. Researchers examine causal models in the context of randomized controlled experiments, which allow for replication and generalization of their results (Ryan & Hood, 2004, p. 81).

Under such a framework, qualitative research becomes suspect. Qualitative research does not require well-defined variables or causal models. The observations and measurements of qualitative scholars are not based on subjects' random assignment to experimental groups. Qualitative researchers do not generate "hard evidence" using such methods. At best, through case study, interview, and ethnographic methods, researchers can gather descriptive materials that can be tested with experimental methods. The epistemologies of critical race, queer, postcolonial, feminist, and postmodern theories are rendered useless by the SBR perspective, relegated at best to the category of scholarship, not science (Ryan & Hood, 2004, p. 81; St. Pierre, 2004, p. 132).

Critics of the SBR movement are united on the following points. "Bush science" (Lather, 2004, p. 19) and its experimental, evidence-based methodologies represent a racialized, masculinist backlash to the proliferation of qualitative inquiry methods over the past two decades. The movement endorses a narrow view of science (Maxwell, 2004) that celebrates a "neoclassical experimentalism that is a throwback to the Campbell-Stanley era and its dogmatic adherence to an exclusive reliance on quantitative methods" (Howe, 2004, p. 42). The movement represents "nostalgia for a simple and ordered universe of science that never was" (Popkewitz, 2004, p. 62). With its emphasis on only one form of scientific rigor, the NRC ignores the value of using complex historical, contextual, and political criteria to evaluate inquiry (Bloch, 2004).

As Howe (2004) observes, neoclassical experimentalists extol evidence-based "medical research as the model for educational research, particularly the random clinical trial" (p. 48). But dispensing a pill in a random clinical trial is quite unlike "dispensing a curriculum," and the "effects" of an educational experiment cannot be easily measured, unlike a "10-point reduction in diastolic blood pressure" (p. 48; see also Miller & Crabtree, Chapter 24, this volume).

Qualitative researchers must learn to think outside the box as they critique the NRC and its methodological guidelines (Atkinson, 2004). They must apply their imaginations and find new ways to define such terms as *randomized design, causal model, policy studies,* and *public science* (Cannella & Lincoln, 2004a, 2004b; Lincoln & Cannella, 2004a, 2004b; Lincoln & Tierney, 2004; Weinstein, 2004). More deeply, qualitative researchers must resist conservative attempts to discredit qualitative inquiry by placing it back inside the box of positivism.

Mixed-Methods Experimentalism

As Howe (2004) notes, the SBR movement finds a place for qualitative methods in mixed-methods experimental designs. In such designs, qualitative methods may be "employed either singly or in combination with quantitative methods, including the use of randomized experimental designs" (p. 49). Mixed-methods designs are direct descendants of classical experimentalism. They presume a methodological hierarchy in which quantitative methods are at the top and qualitative methods are relegated to "a largely auxiliary role in pursuit of the *technocratic* aim of accumulating knowledge of 'what works'" (pp. 53–54).

The mixed-methods movement takes qualitative methods out of their natural home, which is within the critical, interpretive framework (Howe, 2004, p. 54; but see Teddlie & Tashakkori, 2003, p. 15). It divides inquiry into dichotomous categories: exploration versus confirmation. Qualitative work is assigned to the first category, quantitative research to the second (Teddlie & Tashakkori, 2003, p. 15). Like the classic experimental model, it excludes stakeholders from dialogue and active participation in the research process. This weakens its democratic and dialogical dimensions and decreases the likelihood that previously silenced voices will be heard (Howe,

2004, pp. 56–57). As Howe (2004) cautions, it is not just the "'methodological fundamentalists' who have bought into [this] approach. A sizable number of rather influential . . . educational researchers . . . have also signed on. This might be a compromise to the current political climate; it might be a backlash against the perceived excesses of postmodernism; it might be both. It is an ominous development, whatever the explanation" (p. 57).

Pragmatic Criticisms of Antifoundationalism

Seale et al. (2004) contest what they regard as the excesses of an antimethodological, "anything goes," romantic postmodernism that is associated with our project. They assert that too often the approach we value produces "low quality qualitative research and research results that are quite stereotypical and close to common sense" (p. 2). In contrast, they propose a practice-based, pragmatic approach that places research practice at the center. They note that research involves an engagement "with a variety of things and people: research materials . . . social theories, philosophical debates, values, methods, tests . . . research participants" (p. 2). (Actually, this approach is quite close to our own, especially our view of the *bricoleur* and bricolage.) Seale et al.'s situated methodology rejects the antifoundational claim that there are only partial truths, that the dividing line between fact and fiction has broken down (p. 3). These scholars believe that this dividing line has not collapsed, and that qualitative researchers should not accept stories if they do not accord with the best available facts (p. 6).

Oddly, these pragmatic procedural arguments reproduce a variant of the evidence-based model and its criticisms of poststructural, performative sensibilities. They can be used to provide political support for the methodological marginalization of the positions advanced by many of the contributors to this volume.

The complex political terrain described above defines the many traditions and strands of qualitative research: the British tradition and its presence in other national contexts; the American pragmatic, naturalistic, and interpretive traditions in sociology, anthropology, communications, and education; the German and French phenomenological, hermeneutic, semiotic, Marxist, structural, and poststructural perspectives; feminist studies, African American studies, Latino studies, queer studies, studies of indigenous and aboriginal cultures. The politics of qualitative research creates a tension that informs each of these traditions. This tension itself is constantly being reexamined and interrogated as qualitative research confronts a changing historical world, new intellectual positions, and its own institutional and academic conditions.

To summarize: Qualitative research is many things to many people. Its essence is twofold: a commitment to some version of the naturalistic, interpretive approach to its subject matter and an ongoing critique of the politics and methods of postpositivism. We turn now to a brief discussion of the major differences between qualitative and quantitative approaches to research. We then discuss ongoing differences and tensions within qualitative inquiry.

Qualitative Versus Quantitative Research

The word *qualitative* implies an emphasis on the qualities of entities and on processes and meanings that are not experimentally examined or measured (if measured at all) in terms of quantity, amount, intensity, or frequency. Qualitative researchers stress the socially constructed nature of reality, the intimate relationship between the researcher and what is studied, and the situational constraints that shape inquiry. Such researchers emphasize the value-laden nature of inquiry. They seek answers to questions that stress *how* social experience is created and given meaning. In contrast, quantitative studies emphasize the measurement and analysis of causal relationships between variables, not processes. Proponents of such studies claim that their work is done from within a value-free framework.

Research Styles: Doing the Same Things Differently?

Of course, both qualitative and quantitative researchers "think they know something about society worth telling to others, and they use a variety of forms, media and means to communicate their ideas and findings" (Becker, 1986, p. 122). Qualitative research differs from quantitative research in five significant ways (Becker, 1996). These points of difference, discussed in turn below, all involve different ways of addressing the same set of issues. They return always to the politics of research and to who has the power to legislate correct solutions to social problems.

Uses of positivism and postpositivism. First, both perspectives are shaped by the positivist and postpositivist traditions in the physical and social sciences (see the discussion below). These two positivist science traditions hold to naïve and critical realist positions concerning reality and its perception. In the positivist version it is contended that there is a reality out there to be studied, captured, and understood, whereas the postpositivists argue that reality can never be fully apprehended, only approximated (Guba, 1990, p. 22). Postpositivism relies on multiple methods as a way of capturing as much of reality as possible. At the same time, it emphasizes the discovery and verification of theories. Traditional evaluation criteria, such as internal and external validity, are stressed, as is the use of qualitative procedures that lend themselves to structured (sometimes statistical) analysis. Computer-assisted methods of analysis that permit frequency counts, tabulations, and low-level statistical analyses may also be employed.

The positivist and postpositivist traditions linger like long shadows over the qualitative research project. Historically, qualitative research was defined within the positivist paradigm, where qualitative researchers attempted to do good positivist research with less rigorous methods and procedures. Some mid-20th-century qualitative researchers reported participant observation findings in terms of quasi-statistics (e.g., Becker, Geer, Hughes, & Strauss, 1961). As recently as 1998, Strauss and Corbin, two leading proponents of the grounded theory approach to qualitative research, attempted to modify the usual canons of good (positivist) science to fit their own postpositivist conception of rigorous research (but see Charmaz, Chapter 20, this volume; see also Glaser, 1992). Some applied researchers, while claiming to be atheoretical, often fit within the positivist or postpositivist framework by default.

Flick (2002) usefully summarizes the differences between these two approaches to inquiry, noting that the quantitative approach has been used for purposes of isolating "causes and effects . . . operationalizing theoretical relations . . . [and] measuring and . . . quantifying phenomena . . . allowing the generalization of findings" (p. 3). But today doubt is cast on such projects: "Rapid social change and the resulting diversification of life worlds are increasingly confronting social researchers with new social contexts and perspectives. . . . traditional deductive methodologies . . . are failing. . . . thus research is increasingly forced to make use of inductive strategies instead of starting from theories and testing them. . . . knowledge and practice are studied as *local* knowledge and practice" (p. 2).

Spindler and Spindler (1992) summarize their qualitative approach to quantitative materials: "Instrumentation and quantification are simply procedures employed to extend and reinforce certain kinds of data, interpretations and test hypotheses across samples. Both must be kept in their place. One must avoid their premature or overly extensive use as a security mechanism" (p. 69).

Although many qualitative researchers in the postpositivist tradition use statistical measures, methods, and documents as a way of locating a group of subjects within a larger population, they seldom report their findings in terms of the kinds of complex statistical measures or methods to which quantitative researchers are drawn (e.g., path, regression, and log-linear analyses).

Acceptance of postmodern sensibilities. The use of quantitative, positivist methods and assumptions has been rejected by a new generation of qualitative researchers who are attached to poststructural and/or postmodern sensibilities. These researchers argue that positivist methods are but one way of telling stories about societies or social worlds. These methods may be no better or no worse than any other methods; they just tell different kinds of stories.

This tolerant view is not shared by all qualitative researchers (Huber, 1995). Many members of the critical theory, constructivist, poststructural, and postmodern schools of thought reject positivist and postpositivist criteria when evaluating their own work. They see these criteria as irrelevant to their work and contend that such criteria reproduce only a certain kind of science, a science that silences too many voices. These researchers seek alternative methods for evaluating their work, including verisimilitude, emotionality, personal responsibility, an ethic of caring, political praxis, multivoiced texts, and dialogues with subjects. In response, positivists and postpositivists argue that what they do is good science, free of individual bias and subjectivity. As noted above, they see postmodernism and poststructuralism as attacks on reason and truth.

Capturing the individual's point of view. Both qualitative and quantitative researchers are concerned with the individual's point of view. However, qualitative investigators think they can get closer to the actor's perspective through detailed interviewing and observation. They argue that quantitative researchers are seldom able to capture their subjects' perspectives because they have to rely on more remote, inferential empirical methods and materials. Many quantitative researchers regard the empirical materials produced by interpretive methods as unreliable, impressionistic, and not objective.

Examining the constraints of everyday life. Qualitative researchers are more likely to confront and come up against the constraints of the everyday social world. They see this world in action and embed their findings in it. Quantitative researchers abstract from this world and seldom study it directly. They seek a nomothetic or etic science based on probabilities derived from the study of large numbers of randomly selected cases. These kinds of statements stand above and outside the constraints of everyday life. Qualitative researchers, on the other hand, are committed to an emic, idiographic, case-based position that directs attention to the specifics of particular cases.

Securing rich descriptions. Qualitative researchers believe that rich descriptions of the social world are valuable, whereas quantitative researchers, with their etic, nomothetic commitments, are less concerned with such detail. Quantitative researchers are deliberately unconcerned with rich descriptions because such detail interrupts the process of developing generalizations.

▣ ▣ ▣

The five points of difference described above reflect qualitative and quantitative scholars' commitments to different styles of research, different epistemologies, and different forms of representation. Each work tradition is governed by a different set of genres; each has its own classics, its own preferred forms of representation, interpretation, trustworthiness, and textual evaluation (see Becker, 1986, pp. 134–135). Qualitative researchers use ethnographic prose, historical narratives, first-person accounts, still photographs, life histories, fictionalized "facts," and biographical and autobiographical materials, among others. Quantitative researchers use mathematical models, statistical tables, and graphs, and they usually write about their research in impersonal, third-person prose.

▣ Tensions Within Qualitative Research

It is erroneous to presume that all qualitative researchers share the same assumptions about the five points of difference described above. As the following discussion reveals, positivist, postpositivist, and poststructural differences define and shape the discourses of qualitative research. Realists and postpositivists within the interpretive, qualitative research tradition criticize poststructuralists for taking the textual, narrative turn. These critics contend that such work is navel gazing. It produces the conditions "for a dialogue of the deaf between itself and the community" (Silverman, 1997, p. 240). Critics accuse those who attempt to capture the point of view of the interacting subject in the world of naïve humanism, of reproducing "a Romantic impulse which elevates the experiential to the level of the authentic" (Silverman, 1997, p. 248).

Still others assert that those who take the textual, performance turn ignore lived experience. Snow and Morrill (1995) argue that "this performance turn, like the preoccupation with discourse and storytelling, will take us further from the field of social action and the real dramas of everyday life and thus signal the death knell of ethnography as an empirically grounded enterprise" (p. 361). Of course, we disagree.

Critical Realism

For some, there is a third stream, between naïve positivism and poststructuralism. Critical realism is an antipositivist movement in the social sciences closely associated with the works of Roy Bhaskar and Rom Harré (Danermark, Ekström, Jakobsen, & Karlsson, 2002). Critical realists use the word *critical* in a particular way. This is not "Frankfurt school" critical theory, although there are traces of social criticism here and there (see Danermark et al., 2002, p. 201). Instead, *critical* in this context refers to a transcendental realism that rejects methodological individualism and universal claims to truth. Critical realists oppose logical positivist, relativist, and antifoundational epistemologies. Critical realists agree with the positivists that there is a world of events out there that is observable and independent of human consciousness. They hold that knowledge about this world is socially constructed. Society is made up of feeling, thinking human beings, and their interpretations of the world must be studied (Danermark et al., 2002, p. 200). Critical realists reject a correspondence theory of truth. They believe that reality is arranged in levels and that scientific work must go beyond statements of regularity to analysis of the mechanisms, processes, and structures that account for the patterns that are observed.

Still, as postempiricist, antifoundational, critical theorists, we reject much of what the critical realists advocate. Throughout the past century, social science and philosophy have been continually tangled up with one another. Various "isms" and philosophical movements have crisscrossed sociological and educational discourses, from positivism to postpositivism, to analytic and linguistic philosophy, to hermeneutics, structuralism, poststructuralism, Marxism, feminism, and current post-post versions of all of the above. Some have said that the logical positivists steered the social sciences on a rigorous course of self-destruction.

We do not think that critical realism will keep the social science ship afloat. The social sciences are normative disciplines, always already embedded in issues of value, ideology, power, desire, sexism, racism, domination, repression, and control. We want a social science that is committed up front to issues of social justice, equity, nonviolence, peace, and universal human rights. We do not want a social science that says it can address these issues if it wants to. For us, that is no longer an option.

With these differences within and between interpretive traditions in hand, we must now briefly discuss the history of qualitative research. We break this history into eight historical moments, mindful that any history is always somewhat arbitrary and always at least partially a social construction.

The History of Qualitative Research

The history of qualitative research reveals that the modern social science disciplines have taken as their mission "the analysis and understanding of the patterned conduct and social processes of society" (Vidich & Lyman, 2000, p. 37). The notion that social scientists could carry out this task presupposed that they had the ability to observe this world objectively. Qualitative methods were a major tool of such observations.[13]

Throughout the history of qualitative research, qualitative investigators have defined their work in terms of hopes and values, "religious faiths, occupational and professional ideologies" (Vidich & Lyman, 2000, p. 39). Qualitative research (like all research) has always been judged on the "standard of whether the work communicates or 'says' something to us" (Vidich & Lyman, 2000, p. 39), based on how we conceptualize our reality and our images of the world. *Epistemology* is the word that has historically defined these standards of evaluation. In the contemporary period, as we have argued above, many received discourses on epistemology are now being reevaluated.

Vidich and Lyman's (2000) work on the history of qualitative research covers the following (somewhat) overlapping stages: early ethnography (to the 17th century), colonial ethnography (17th-, 18th-, and 19th-century explorers), the ethnography of the American Indian as "Other" (late-19th- and early-20th-century anthropology), community studies and ethnographies of American immigrants (early 20th century through the 1960s), studies of ethnicity and assimilation (midcentury through the 1980s), and the present, which we call the *eighth moment.*

In each of these eras, researchers were and have been influenced by their political hopes and ideologies, discovering findings in their research that confirmed their prior theories or beliefs. Early ethnographers confirmed the racial and cultural diversity of peoples throughout the globe and attempted to fit this diversity into a theory about the origins of history, the races, and civilizations. Colonial ethnographers, before the professionalization of ethnography in the 20th century, fostered a colonial pluralism that left natives on their own as long as their leaders could be co-opted by the colonial administration.

European ethnographers studied Africans, Asians, and other Third World peoples of color. Early American ethnographers studied the American Indian from the perspective of the conqueror, who saw the lifeworld of the primitive as a window to the prehistoric past. The Calvinist mission to save the Indian was soon transferred to the mission of saving the "hordes" of immigrants who entered the United States with the beginnings of industrialization. Qualitative community studies of the ethnic Other proliferated from the early 1900s to the 1960s and included the work of E. Franklin Frazier, Robert Park, and Robert Redfield and their students, as well as William Foote Whyte, the Lynds, August Hollingshead, Herbert Gans, Stanford Lyman, Arthur Vidich, and Joseph Bensman. The post-1960 ethnicity studies challenged the "melting pot" hypotheses of Park and his followers and corresponded to the emergence of ethnic studies programs that saw Native Americans, Latinos, Asian Americans, and African Americans attempting to take control over the study of their own peoples.

The postmodern and poststructural challenge emerged in the mid-1980s. It questioned the assumptions that had organized this earlier history in each of its colonizing moments. Qualitative research that crosses the "postmodern divide" requires the scholar, Vidich and Lyman (2000) argue, to "abandon all established and preconceived values, theories, perspectives . . . and prejudices as resources for ethnographic study" (p. 60). In this new era the qualitative researcher does more than observe history; he or she plays a part in it. New tales from the field will now be written, and they will reflect the researchers' direct and personal engagement with this historical period.

Vidich and Lyman's analysis covers the full sweep of ethnographic history. Ours is confined to the 20th and 21st centuries and complements many of their divisions. We begin with the early foundational work of the British and French as well as the Chicago, Columbia, Harvard, Berkeley, and British schools of sociology and anthropology. This early foundational period established the norms of classical qualitative and ethnographic research (see Gupta & Ferguson, 1997; Rosaldo, 1989; Stocking, 1989).

▣ The Eight Moments of Qualitative Research

As we have noted above, we divide our history of qualitative research in North America in the 20th century and beyond into eight phases, which we describe in turn below.

The Traditional Period

We call the first moment the traditional period (this covers the second and third phases discussed by Vidich & Lyman, 2000). It begins in the early

1900s and continues until World War II. In this period, qualitative researchers wrote "objective," colonizing accounts of field experiences that were reflective of the positivist scientist paradigm. They were concerned with offering valid, reliable, and objective interpretations in their writings. The "Other" whom they studied was alien, foreign, and strange.

Here is Malinowski (1967) discussing his field experiences in New Guinea and the Trobriand Islands in the years 1914–15 and 1917–18. He is bartering his way into field data:

> Nothing whatever draws me to ethnographic studies.... On the whole the village struck me rather unfavorably. There is a certain disorganization ... the rowdiness and persistence of the people who laugh and stare and lie discouraged me somewhat.... Went to the village hoping to photograph a few stages of the *bara* dance. I handed out half-sticks of tobacco, then watched a few dances; then took pictures—but results were poor.... they would not pose long enough for time exposures. At moments I was furious at them, particularly because after I gave them their portions of tobacco they all went away. (quoted in Geertz, 1988, pp. 73–74)

In another work, this lonely, frustrated, isolated field-worker describes his methods in the following words:

> In the field one has to face a chaos of facts.... in this crude form they are not scientific facts at all; they are absolutely elusive, and can only be fixed by interpretation.... *Only laws and generalizations are scientific facts,* and field work consists only and exclusively in the interpretation of the chaotic social reality, in subordinating it to general rules. (Malinowski, 1916/1948, p. 328; quoted in Geertz, 1988, p. 81)

Malinowski's remarks are provocative. On the one hand they disparage fieldwork, but on the other they speak of it within the glorified language of science, with laws and generalizations fashioned out of this selfsame experience.

During this period the field-worker was lionized, made into a larger-than-life figure who went into the field and returned with stories about strange peoples. Rosaldo (1989) describes this as the period of the Lone Ethnographer, the story of the man-scientist who went off in search of his native in a distant land. There this figure "encountered the object of his quest ... [and] underwent his rite of passage by enduring the ultimate ordeal of 'fieldwork'" (p. 30). Returning home with his data, the Lone Ethnographer wrote up an objective account of the culture studied. This account was structured by the norms of classical ethnography. This sacred bundle of terms (Rosaldo, 1989, p. 31) organized ethnographic texts around four beliefs and commitments: a commitment to objectivism, a complicity with imperialism, a belief in monumentalism (the ethnography would create a museumlike picture of the culture studied), and a belief in timelessness (what was studied would never change). The Other was an "object" to be archived. This model of the researcher, who could also write complex, dense theories about what was studied, holds to the present day.

The myth of the Lone Ethnographer depicts the birth of classic ethnography. The texts of Malinowski, Radcliffe-Brown, Margaret Mead, and Gregory Bateson are still carefully studied for what they can tell the novice about fieldwork, taking field notes, and writing theory. But today the image of the Lone Ethnographer has been shattered. Many scholars see the works of the classic ethnographers as relics from the colonial past (Rosaldo, 1989, p. 44). Whereas some feel nostalgia for this past, others celebrate its passing. Rosaldo (1989) quotes Cora Du Bois, a retired Harvard anthropology professor, who lamented this passing at a conference in 1980, reflecting on the crisis in anthropology: "[I feel a distance] from the complexity and disarray of what I once found a justifiable and challenging discipline.... It has been like moving from a distinguished art museum into a garage sale" (p. 44).

Du Bois regards the classic ethnographies as pieces of timeless artwork contained in a museum. She feels uncomfortable in the chaos of the garage sale. In contrast, Rosaldo (1989) is drawn to this metaphor because "it provides a precise image of the postcolonial situation where cultural artifacts flow between unlikely places, and nothing is sacred, permanent, or sealed off. The image of anthropology as a garage sale depicts our present global situation" (p. 44). Indeed, many valuable treasures may be found in unexpected places, if one is willing to look long and hard. Old standards no longer hold. Ethnographies do not produce timeless truths. The commitment to objectivism is now in doubt. The complicity with imperialism is openly challenged today, and the belief in monumentalism is a thing of the past.

The legacies of this first period begin at the end of the 19th century, when the novel and the social sciences had become distinguished as separate systems of discourse (Clough, 1998, pp. 21–22). However, the Chicago school, with its emphasis on the life story and the "slice-of-life" approach to ethnographic materials, sought to develop an interpretive methodology that maintained the centrality of the narrated life history approach. This led to the production of texts that gave the researcher-as-author the power to represent the subject's story. Written under the mantle of straightforward, sentiment-free social realism, these texts used the language of ordinary people. They articulated a social science version of literary naturalism, which often produced the sympathetic illusion that a solution to a social problem had been found. Like the Depression-era juvenile delinquent and other "social problems" films (Roffman & Purdy, 1981), these accounts romanticized the subject. They turned the deviant into a sociological version of a screen hero. These sociological stories, like their film counterparts, usually had happy endings, as they followed individuals through the three stages of the classic morality tale: being in a state of grace, being seduced by evil and falling, and finally achieving redemption through suffering.

Modernist Phase

The modernist phase, or second moment, builds on the canonical works from the traditional period. Social realism, naturalism, and slice-of-life ethnographies are still valued. This phase extended through the postwar years to the 1970s and is still present in the work of many (for reviews, see Wolcott, 1990, 1992, 1995; see also Tedlock, Chapter 18, this volume). In this period many texts sought to formalize qualitative methods (see, e.g., Bogdan & Taylor, 1975; Cicourel, 1964; Filstead, 1970; Glaser & Strauss, 1967; Lofland, 1971, 1995; Lofland & Lofland, 1984, 1995; Taylor & Bogdan, 1998).[14] The modernist ethnographer and sociological participant observer attempted rigorous qualitative studies of important social processes, including deviance and social control in the classroom and society. This was a moment of creative ferment.

A new generation of graduate students across the human disciplines encountered new interpretive theories (ethnomethodology, phenomenology, critical theory, feminism). They were drawn to qualitative research practices that would let them give a voice to society's underclass. Postpositivism functioned as a powerful epistemological paradigm. Researchers attempted to fit Campbell and Stanley's (1963) model of internal and external validity to constructionist and interactionist conceptions of the research act. They returned to the texts of the Chicago school as sources of inspiration (see Denzin, 1970, 1978).

A canonical text from this moment remains *Boys in White* (Becker et al., 1961; see also Becker, 1998). Firmly entrenched in mid-20th-century methodological discourse, this work attempted to make qualitative research as rigorous as its quantitative counterpart. Causal narratives were central to this project. This multimethod work combined open-ended and quasi-structured interviewing with participant observation and the careful analysis of such materials in standardized, statistical form. In his classic article "Problems of Inference and Proof in Participant Observation," Howard S. Becker (1958/1970) describes the use of quasi-statistics:

> Participant observations have occasionally been gathered in standardized form capable of being transformed into legitimate statistical data. But the exigencies of the field usually prevent the collection of data in such a form to meet the assumptions of statistical tests, so that the observer deals in what have been called "quasi-statistics." His conclusions, while implicitly numerical, do not require precise quantification. (p. 31)

In the analysis of data, Becker notes, the qualitative researcher takes a cue from more quantitatively oriented colleagues. The researcher looks for probabilities or support for arguments concerning the likelihood that, or frequency with which, a conclusion in fact applies in a specific situation (see also Becker, 1998, pp. 166–170). Thus did work in the modernist period clothe itself in the language and rhetoric of positivist and postpositivist discourse.

This was the golden age of rigorous qualitative analysis, bracketed in sociology by *Boys in White* (Becker et al., 1961) at one end and *The Discovery of Grounded Theory* (Glaser & Strauss, 1967) at the other. In education, qualitative research in this period was defined by George and Louise Spindler, Jules Henry, Harry Wolcott, and John Singleton. This form of qualitative research is still present in the work of scholars such as Strauss and Corbin (1998) and Ryan and Bernard (2000).

The "golden age" reinforced the picture of qualitative researchers as cultural romantics. Imbued with Promethean human powers, they valorized villains and outsiders as heroes to mainstream society. They embodied a belief in the contingency of self and society, and held to emancipatory ideals for "which one lives and dies." They put in place a tragic and often ironic view of society and self, and joined a long line of leftist cultural romantics that included Emerson, Marx, James, Dewey, Gramsci, and Martin Luther King, Jr. (West, 1989, chap. 6).

As this moment came to an end, the Vietnam War was everywhere present in American society. In 1969, alongside these political currents, Herbert Blumer and Everett Hughes met with a group of young sociologists called the "Chicago Irregulars" at the American Sociological Association meetings held in San Francisco and shared their memories of the "Chicago years." Lyn Lofland (1980) describes this time as a

> moment of creative ferment—scholarly and political. The San Francisco meetings witnessed not simply the Blumer-Hughes event but a "counter-revolution." . . . a group first came to . . . talk about the problems of being a sociologist and a female. . . . the discipline seemed literally to be bursting with new . . . ideas: labelling theory, ethnomethodology, conflict theory, phenomenology, dramaturgical analysis. (p. 253)

Thus did the modernist phase come to an end.

Blurred Genres

By the beginning of the third phase (1970–1986), which we call the moment of blurred genres, qualitative researchers had a full complement of paradigms, methods, and strategies to employ in their research. Theories ranged from symbolic interactionism to constructivism, naturalistic inquiry, positivism and postpositivism, phenomenology, ethnomethodology, critical theory, neo-Marxist theory, semiotics, structuralism, feminism, and various racial/ethnic paradigms. Applied qualitative research was gaining in stature, and the politics and ethics of qualitative research—implicated as they were in various applications of this work—were topics of considerable concern. Research strategies and formats for reporting research ranged from grounded theory to the case study, to methods of historical, biographical, ethnographic, action, and clinical research. Diverse ways of collecting and analyzing empirical materials were also available, including qualitative interviewing (open-ended and quasi-structured) and observational, visual, personal experience, and documentary methods. Computers were entering the situation, to be fully developed as aids in the analysis of qualitative data in the next decade, along with narrative, content, and semiotic methods of reading interviews and cultural texts.

Two books by Clifford Geertz, *The Interpretation of Cultures* (1973) and *Local Knowledge* (1983), defined the beginning and the end of this moment. In these two works, Geertz argued that the old functional, positivist, behavioral, totalizing approaches to the human disciplines were giving way to a more pluralistic, interpretive, open-ended perspective. This new perspective took cultural representations and their meanings as its points of departure. Calling for "thick description" of particular events, rituals, and customs, Geertz suggested that all anthropological writings are interpretations of interpretations.[15] The observer has no privileged voice in the interpretations that are written. The central task of theory is to make sense out of a local situation.

Geertz went on to propose that the boundaries between the social sciences and the humanities had become blurred. Social scientists were now turning to the humanities for models, theories, and methods of analysis (semiotics, hermeneutics). A form of genre diaspora was occurring: documentaries that read like fiction (Mailer), parables posing as ethnographies (Castañeda), theoretical treatises that look like travelogues (Lévi-Strauss). At the same time, other new approaches were emerging: poststructuralism (Barthes), neopositivism (Philips), neo-Marxism (Althusser), micro-macro descriptivism (Geertz), ritual theories of drama and culture (V. Turner), deconstructionism (Derrida), ethnomethodology (Garfinkel). The golden age of the social sciences was over, and a new age of blurred, interpretive genres was upon us. The essay as an art form was replacing the scientific article. At issue now was the author's presence in the interpretive text (Geertz, 1988). How can the researcher speak with authority in an age when there are no longer any firm rules concerning the text, including the author's place in it, its standards of evaluation, and its subject matter?

The naturalistic, postpositivist, and constructionist paradigms gained power in this period, especially in education, in the works of Harry Wolcott, Frederick Erickson, Egon Guba, Yvonna Lincoln, Robert Stake, and Elliot Eisner. By the end of the 1970s, several qualitative journals were in place, including *Urban Life and Culture* (now *Journal of Contemporary Ethnography*), *Cultural Anthropology, Anthropology and Education Quarterly, Qualitative Sociology,* and *Symbolic Interaction,* as well as the book series *Studies in Symbolic Interaction.*

Crisis of Representation

A profound rupture occurred in the mid-1980s. What we call the fourth moment, or the crisis of representation, appeared with *Anthropology as Cultural Critique* (Marcus & Fischer, 1986), *The Anthropology of Experience* (Turner & Bruner, 1986), *Writing Culture* (Clifford & Marcus, 1986), *Works and Lives* (Geertz, 1988), and *The Predicament of Culture* (Clifford, 1988). These works made research and writing more reflexive and called into question the issues of gender, class, and race. They articulated the consequences of Geertz's "blurred genres" interpretation of the field in the early 1980s.[16]

Qualitative researchers sought new models of truth, method, and representation (Rosaldo, 1989). The erosion of classic norms in anthropology (objectivism, complicity with colonialism, social life structured by fixed rituals and customs, ethnographies as monuments to a culture) was complete (Rosaldo, 1989, pp. 44–45; see also Jackson, 1998, pp. 7–8). Critical theory, feminist theory, and epistemologies of color now competed for attention in this arena. Issues such as validity, reliability, and objectivity, previously believed settled, were once more problematic. Pattern and interpretive theories, as opposed to causal, linear theories, were now more common, as writers continued to challenge older models of truth and meaning (Rosaldo, 1989).

Stoller and Olkes (1987, pp. 227–229) describe how they felt the crisis of representation in their fieldwork among the Songhay of Niger. Stoller observes: "When I began to write anthropological texts, I followed the conventions of my training. I 'gathered data,' and once the 'data' were arranged in neat piles, I 'wrote them up.' In one case I reduced Songhay insults to a series of neat logical formulas" (p. 227). Stoller became dissatisfied with this form of writing, in part because he learned "everyone had lied to me and . . . the data I has so painstakingly collected were worthless. I learned a lesson: Informants routinely lie to their anthropologists" (Stoller & Olkes, 1987, p. 9). This discovery led to a second—that he had, in following the conventions of ethnographic realism, edited himself out of his text. This led Stoller to produce a different type of text, a memoir, in which he became a central character in the story he told. This story, an account of his experiences in the Songhay world, became an analysis of the clash between his world and the world of Songhay sorcery. Thus Stoller's journey represents an attempt to confront the crisis of representation in the fourth moment.

Clough (1998) elaborates this crisis and criticizes those who would argue that new forms of writing represent a way out of the crisis. She argues:

> While many sociologists now commenting on the criticism of ethnography view writing as "downright central to the ethnographic enterprise" [Van Maanen, 1988, p. xi], the problems of writing are still viewed as different from the problems of method or fieldwork itself. Thus the solution usually offered is experiments in writing, that is a self-consciousness about writing. (p. 136)

It is this insistence on the difference between writing and fieldwork that must be analyzed. (Richardson & St. Pierre are quite articulate about this issue in Chapter 38 of this volume).

In writing, the field-worker makes a claim to moral and scientific authority. This claim allows the realist and experimental ethnographic texts to function as sources of validation for an empirical science. They show that the world of real lived experience can still be captured, if only in the writer's memoirs, or fictional experimentations, or dramatic readings. But these works have the danger of directing attention away from the ways in which the text constructs sexually situated individuals in a field of social difference. They also perpetuate "empirical science's hegemony" (Clough, 1998, p. 8), for these new writing technologies of the subject become the site "for the production of knowledge/power . . . [aligned] with . . . the capital/state axis" (Aronowitz, 1988, p. 300; quoted in Clough, 1998, p. 8). Such experiments come up against, and then back away from, the difference between empirical science and social criticism. Too often they fail to engage fully a new politics of textuality that would "refuse the identity of empirical science" (Clough, 1998, p. 135). This new social criticism "would intervene in the relationship of information economics, nation-state politics, and technologies of mass communication, especially in terms of the empirical sciences" (Clough, 1998, p. 16). This, of course, is the terrain occupied by cultural studies.

In Chapter 38 of this volume, Richardson and St. Pierre develop the above arguments, viewing writing as a method of inquiry that moves through successive stages of self-reflection. As a series of written representations, the fieldworker's texts flow from the field experience, through intermediate works, to later work, and finally to the research text, which is the public presentation of the ethnographic and narrative experience. Thus fieldwork and writing blur into one another. There is, in the final analysis, no difference between writing and fieldwork. These two perspectives inform one another throughout every chapter in this volume. In these ways the crisis of representation moves qualitative research in new and critical directions.

A Triple Crisis

The ethnographer's authority remains under assault today (Behar, 1995, p. 3; Gupta & Ferguson, 1997, p. 16; Jackson, 1998; Ortner, 1997, p. 2). A triple crisis of representation, legitimation, and praxis confronts qualitative researchers in the human disciplines. Embedded in the discourses of poststructuralism and postmodernism (Vidich & Lyman, 2000; see also Richardson & St. Pierre, Chapter 38, this volume), these three crises are coded in multiple terms, variously called and associated with the *critical, interpretive, linguistic, feminist,* and *rhetorical* turns in social theory. These new turns make problematic two key assumptions of qualitative research. The first is that qualitative researchers can no longer directly capture lived experience. Such experience, it is argued, is created in the social text written by the researcher. This is the representational crisis. It confronts the inescapable problem of representation, but does so within a framework that makes the direct link between experience and text problematic.

The second assumption makes problematic the traditional criteria for evaluating and interpreting qualitative research. This is the legitimation crisis. It involves a serious rethinking of such terms as *validity, generalizability,* and *reliability,* terms already retheorized in postpositivist (Hammersley, 1992), constructionist-naturalistic (Guba & Lincoln, 1989, pp. 163–183), feminist (Olesen, Chapter 10, this volume), interpretive and performative (Denzin, 1997, 2003), poststructural (Lather, 1993; Lather & Smithies, 1997), and critical discourses (Kincheloe & McLaren, Chapter 12, this volume). This crisis asks, How are qualitative studies to be evaluated in the contemporary, poststructural moment? The first two crises shape the third, which asks, Is it possible to effect change in the world if society is only and always a text? Clearly these crises intersect and blur, as do the answers to the questions they generate (see Ladson-Billings, 2000; Schwandt, 2000; Smith & Deemer, 2000).

The fifth moment, the postmodern period of experimental ethnographic writing, struggled to make sense of these crises. New ways of composing ethnography were explored (Ellis & Bochner, 1996). Theories were read as tales from the field. Writers struggled with different ways to represent the "Other," although they were now joined by new representational concerns (Fine, Weis, Weseen, & Wong, 2000; see also Fine & Weis, Chapter 3, this volume). Epistemologies from previously silenced groups emerged to offer solutions to these problems. The concept of the aloof observer was abandoned. More action, participatory, and activist-oriented research was on the horizon. The search for grand narratives was being replaced by more local, small-scale theories fitted to specific problems and specific situations.

The sixth moment, postexperimental inquiry (1995–2000), was a period of great excitement, with AltaMira Press, under the direction of Mitch Allen, taking the lead. AltaMira's book series titled Ethnographic Alternatives, for which Carolyn Ellis and Arthur Bochner served as series editors, captured this new excitement and brought a host of new authors into the interpretive community. The following description of the series from the publisher reflects its experimental tone: "Ethnographic Alternatives publishes experimental forms of qualitative writing that blur the boundaries between social sciences and humanities. Some volumes in the series . . . experiment with novel forms of expressing lived experience, including literary, poetic, autobiographical, multivoiced, conversational, critical, visual, performative and co-constructed representations."

During this same period, two major new qualitative journals began publication: *Qualitative Inquiry* and *Qualitative Research*. The editors of these journals were committed to publishing the very best new work. The success of these ventures framed the seventh moment, what we are calling the methodologically contested present (2000–2004). As discussed above, this is a period of conflict, great tension, and, in some quarters, retrenchment.

The eighth moment is now, the future (2005–). In this moment scholars, as reviewed above, are confronting the methodological backlash associated with "Bush science" and the evidence-based social movement.

Reading History

We draw several conclusions from this brief history, noting that it is, like all histories, somewhat arbitrary. First, each of the earlier historical moments is still operating in the present, either as legacy or as a set of practices that researchers continue follow or argue against. The multiple and fractured histories of qualitative research now make it possible for any given researcher to attach a project to a canonical text from any of the above-described historical moments. Multiple criteria of evaluation compete for attention in this field. Second, an embarrassment of choices now characterizes the field of qualitative research. Researchers have never before had so many paradigms, strategies of inquiry, and methods of analysis to draw upon and utilize. Third, we are in a moment of discovery and rediscovery, as new ways of looking, interpreting, arguing, and writing are debated and discussed. Fourth, the qualitative research act can no longer be viewed from within a neutral or objective positivist perspective. Class, race, gender, and ethnicity shape inquiry, making research a multicultural process. Fifth, we are clearly not implying a progress narrative with our history. We are not saying that the cutting edge is located in the present. We are saying that the present is a politically charged space. Complex pressures both within and outside of the qualitative community are working to erase the positive developments of the past 30 years.

Qualitative Research as Process

Three interconnected, generic activities define the qualitative research process. They go by a variety of different labels, including *theory, analysis, ontology, epistemology,* and *methodology.* Behind these terms stands the personal biography of the researcher, who speaks from a particular class, gender, racial, cultural, and ethnic community perspective. The gendered, multiculturally situated researcher approaches the world with a set of ideas, a framework (theory, ontology) that specifies a set of questions (epistemology) that he or she then examines in specific ways (methodology, analysis). That is, the researcher collects empirical materials bearing on the question and then analyzes and writes about those materials. Every researcher speaks from within a distinct interpretive community that configures, in its special way, the multicultural, gendered components of the research act.

In this volume we treat these generic activities under five headings, or phases: the researcher and the researched as multicultural subjects, major paradigms and interpretive perspectives, research strategies, methods of collecting and analyzing empirical materials, and the art of interpretation. Behind and within each of these phases stands the biographically situated researcher. This individual enters the research process from inside an interpretive community. This community has its own historical research traditions, which constitute a distinct point of view. This perspective leads the researcher to adopt particular views of the "Other" who is studied. At the same time, the politics and the ethics of research must also be considered, for these concerns permeate every phase of the research process.

The Other as Research Subject

Since its early-20th-century birth in modern, interpretive form, qualitative research has been haunted by a double-faced ghost. On the one hand, qualitative researchers have assumed that qualified, competent observers can, with objectivity, clarity, and precision, report on their own observations of the social world, including the experiences of others. Second, researchers have held to the belief in a real subject, or real individual, who is present in the world and able, in some form, to report on his or her experiences. So armed, researchers could blend their own observations with the self-reports provided by subjects through interviews and life story, personal experience, and case study documents.

These two beliefs have led qualitative researchers across disciplines to seek a method that will allow them to record accurately their own observations while also uncovering the meanings their subjects bring to their life experiences. Such a method would rely on the subjective verbal and written expressions of meaning given by the individuals studied as windows into the inner lives of these persons. Since Dilthey (1900/1976), this search for a method has led to a perennial focus in the human disciplines on qualitative, interpretive methods.

Recently, as noted above, this position and its beliefs have come under assault. Poststructuralists and postmodernists have contributed to the understanding that there is no clear window into the inner life of an individual. Any gaze is always filtered through the lenses of language, gender, social class, race, and ethnicity. There are no objective observations, only observations socially situated in the worlds of—and between—the observer and the observed. Subjects, or individuals, are seldom able to give full explanations of their actions or intentions; all they can offer are accounts, or stories, about what they have done and why. No single method can grasp all the subtle variations in ongoing human experience. Consequently, qualitative researchers deploy a wide range of interconnected interpretive methods, always seeking better ways to make more understandable the worlds of experience they have studied.

Table 1.1 depicts the relationships we see among the five phases that define the research process. Behind all but one of these phases stands the biographically situated researcher. These five levels of activity, or practice, work their way through the biography of the researcher. We take them up briefly in order here; we discuss these phases more fully in our introductions to the individual parts of this volume.

Phase 1: The Researcher

Our remarks above indicate the depth and complexity of the traditional and applied qualitative research perspectives into which a socially situated researcher enters. These traditions locate the researcher in history, simultaneously guiding and constraining the work that is done in any specific study. This field has always been characterized by diversity and conflict, and these are its most enduring traditions (see Greenwood & Levin, Chapter 2, this volume). As a carrier of this complex and contradictory history, the researcher must also confront the ethics and politics of research (see in this volume Fine & Weis, Chapter 3; Smith, Chapter 4; Bishop, Chapter 5; Christians, Chapter 6). Researching the native, the indigenous Other, while claiming to engage in value-free inquiry for the human disciplines is over. Today researchers struggle to develop situational and transsituational ethics that apply to all forms of the research act and its human-to-human relationships. We no longer have the option of deferring the decolonization project.

Phase 2: Interpretive Paradigms

All qualitative researchers are philosophers in that "universal sense in which all human beings . . . are guided by highly abstract principles" (Bateson, 1972, p. 320). These principles combine beliefs about ontology (What kind of being is the human being? What is the nature of reality?), epistemology (What is the relationship between the inquirer and the known?), and methodology (How do we know the world, or gain knowledge of it?) (see Guba, 1990, p. 18; Lincoln & Guba, 1985, pp. 14–15; see also Guba & Lincoln, Chapter 8, this volume). These beliefs shape how the qualitative researcher sees the world and acts in it. The researcher is "bound within a net of epistemological and ontological premises which—regardless of ultimate truth or falsity—become partially self-validating" (Bateson, 1972, p. 314).

The net that contains the researcher's epistemological, ontological, and methodological premises may be termed a *paradigm*, or an interpretive framework, a "basic set of beliefs that guides action" (Guba, 1990, p. 17). All research is interpretive; it is guided by the researcher's set of beliefs and feelings about the world and how it should be understood and studied. Some beliefs may be taken for granted, invisible, only assumed, whereas others are highly problematic and controversial. Each interpretive paradigm makes particular demands on the researcher, including the questions the researcher asks and the interpretations he or she brings to them.

At the most general level, four major interpretive paradigms structure qualitative research: positivist and postpositivist, constructivist-interpretive, critical (Marxist, emancipatory), and feminist-poststructural. These four abstract paradigms become more complicated at the level of concrete specific interpretive communities. At this level it is possible to identify not only the constructivist, but also multiple versions of feminism (Afrocentric and poststructural),[17] as well as specific ethnic, Marxist, and cultural studies paradigms. These perspectives, or paradigms, are examined in Part II of this volume.

The paradigms examined in Part II work against and alongside (and some within) the positivist and postpositivist models. They all work within relativist ontologies (multiple constructed realities), interpretive epistemologies (the knower and known interact and shape one another), and interpretive, naturalistic methods.

Table 1.2 presents these paradigms and their assumptions, including their criteria for evaluating research, and the typical form that an interpretive or theoretical statement assumes in each paradigm.[18] These paradigms are explored in considerable detail in the chapters in Part II by Guba and Lincoln (Chapter 8), Olesen (Chapter 10), Ladson-Billings and Donnor (Chapter 11), Kincheloe and McLaren (Chapter 12), Saukko

Table 1.1. The Research Process

Phase 1: The Researcher as a Multicultural Subject

History and research traditions
Conceptions of self and the Other
The ethics and politics of research

Phase 2: Theoretical Paradigms and Perspectives

Positivism, postpositivism
Interpretivism, constructivism, hermeneutics
Feminism(s)
Racialized discourses
Critical theory and Marxist models
Cultural studies models
Queer theory

Phase 3: Research Strategies

Design
Case study
Ethnography, participant observation, performance ethnography
Phenomenology, ethnomethodology
Grounded theory
Life history, *testimonio*
Historical method
Action and applied research
Clinical research

Phase 4: Methods of Collection and Analysis

Interviewing
Observing
Artifacts, documents, and records
Visual methods
Autoethnography
Data management methods
Computer-assisted analysis
Textual analysis
Focus groups
Applied ethnography

Phase 5: The Art, Practices, and Politics of Interpretation and Evaluation

Criteria for judging adequacy
Practices and politics of interpretation
Writing as interpretation
Policy analysis
Evaluation traditions
Applied research

Table 1.2. Interpretive Paradigms

Paradigm/Theory	*Criteria*	*Form of Theory*	*Type of Narration*
Positivist/ postpositivist	Internal, external validity	Logical-deductive, grounded	Scientific report
Constructivist	Trustworthiness, credibility, transferability, confirmability	Substantive-formal	Interpretive case studies, ethnographic fiction
Feminist	Afrocentric, lived experience, dialogue, caring, accountability, race, class, gender, reflexivity, praxis, emotion, concrete grounding	Critical, standpoint	Essays, stories, experimental writing
Ethnic	Afrocentric, lived experience, dialogue, caring, accountability, race, class, gender	Standpoint, critical, historical	Essays, fables, dramas
Marxist	Emancipatory theory, falsifiability dialogical, race, class, gender	Critical, historical, economic	Historical, economic, sociocultural analyses
Cultural studies	Cultural practices, praxis, social texts, subjectivities	Social criticism	Cultural theory-as criticism
Queer theory	Reflexivity, deconstruction	Social criticism, historical analysis	Theory as criticism, autobiography

(Chapter 13), and Plummer (Chapter 14). We have discussed the positivist and postpositivist paradigms above. They work from within a realist and critical realist ontology and objective epistemologies, and they rely on experimental, quasi-experimental, survey, and rigorously defined qualitative methodologies. Ryan and Bernard (2000) have developed elements of this paradigm.

The constructivist paradigm assumes a relativist ontology (there are multiple realities), a subjectivist epistemology (knower and respondent cocreate understandings), and a naturalistic (in the natural world) set of methodological procedures. Findings are usually presented in terms of the criteria of grounded theory or pattern theories (see in this volume Guba & Lincoln, Chapter 8; Charmaz, Chapter 20; see also Ryan and Bernard, 2000). Terms such as *credibility, transferability, dependability,* and *confirmability* replace the usual positivist criteria of internal and external validity, reliability, and objectivity.

Feminist, ethnic, Marxist, cultural studies, and queer theory models privilege a materialist-realist ontology; that is, the real world makes a material difference in terms of race, class, and gender. Subjectivist epistemologies and naturalistic methodologies (usually ethnographies) are also employed. Empirical materials and theoretical arguments are evaluated in terms of their emancipatory implications. Criteria from gender and racial communities (e.g., African American) may be applied (emotionality and feeling, caring, personal accountability, dialogue).

Poststructural feminist theories emphasize problems with the social text, its logic, and its inability ever to represent the world of lived experience fully. Positivist and postpositivist criteria of evaluation are replaced by other criteria, including the reflexive, multivoiced text that is grounded in the experiences of oppressed peoples.

The cultural studies and queer theory paradigms are multifocused, with many different strands drawing from Marxism, feminism, and the postmodern sensibility (see in this volume Saukko, Chapter 13; Plummer, Chapter 14; Richardson and St. Pierre, Chapter 38). There is a tension between a humanistic cultural studies, which stresses lived experiences (meaning), and a more structural cultural studies project, which stresses the structural and material determinants (race, class, gender) and effects of experience. Of course, there are two sides to every coin, and both sides are needed—indeed, both are critical. The cultural studies and queer theory paradigms use methods strategically—that is, as resources for understanding and for producing resistances to local structures of domination. Scholars may do close textual readings and discourse analyses of cultural texts (see in this volume Olesen, Chapter 10; Saukko, Chapter 13; Chase, Chapter 25) as well as local, online, reflexive, and critical ethnographies, open-ended interviewing, and participant observation. The focus is on how race, class, and gender are produced and enacted in historically specific situations.

Paradigm and personal history in hand, focused on a concrete empirical problem to examine, the researcher now moves to the next stage of the research process—namely, working with a specific strategy of inquiry.

Phase 3: Strategies of Inquiry and Interpretive Paradigms

Table 1.1 presents some of the major strategies of inquiry a researcher may use. Phase 3 begins with research design, which, broadly conceived, involves a clear focus on the research question, the purposes of the study, and "what information most appropriately will answer specific research questions, and which strategies are most effective for obtaining it" (LeCompte & Preissle, 1993, p. 30; see also Cheek, Chapter 15, this volume). A research design describes a flexible set of guidelines that connect theoretical paradigms first to strategies of inquiry and second to methods for collecting empirical materials. A research design situates the researcher in the empirical world and connects him or her to specific sites, persons, groups, institutions, and bodies of relevant interpretive material, including documents and archives. A research design also specifies how the investigator will address the two critical issues of representation and legitimation.

A strategy of inquiry comprises a bundle of skills, assumptions, and practices that the researcher employs as he or she moves from paradigm to the empirical world. Strategies of inquiry put paradigms of interpretation into motion. At the same time, strategies of inquiry also connect the researcher to specific methods of collecting and analyzing empirical materials. For example, the case study strategy relies on interviewing, observing, and document analysis. Research strategies implement and anchor paradigms in specific empirical sites or in specific methodological practices, such as making a case an object of study. These strategies include the case study, phenomenological and ethnomethodological techniques, and the use of grounded theory, as well as biographical, autoethnographic, historical, action, and clinical methods. Each of these strategies is connected to a complex literature, and each has a separate history, exemplary works, and preferred ways of putting the strategy into motion.

Phase 4: Methods of Collecting and Analyzing Empirical Materials

Qualitative researchers employ several methods for collecting empirical materials.[19] These methods, which are taken up in Part IV of this volume, include interviewing; direct observation; the analysis of artifacts, documents, and cultural records; the use of visual materials; and the use of personal experience. The researcher may also read and analyze interviews or cultural texts in a variety of different ways, including content, narrative, and semiotic strategies. Faced with large amounts of qualitative materials, the investigator seeks ways of managing and interpreting these documents, and here data management methods and computer-assisted models of analysis may be of use.

Phase 5: The Art and Politics of Interpretation and Evaluation

Qualitative research is endlessly creative and interpretive. The researcher does not just leave the field with mountains of empirical materials and then easily write up his or her findings. Qualitative interpretations are constructed. The researcher first creates a field text consisting of field notes and documents from the field, what Roger Sanjek (1990, p. 386) calls "indexing" and David Plath (1990, p. 374) calls "filework." The writer-as-interpreter moves from this text to a research text: notes and interpretations based on the field text. This text is then re-created as a working interpretive document that contains the writer's initial attempts to make sense of what he or she has learned. Finally, the writer produces the public text that comes to the reader. This final tale from the field may assume several forms: confessional, realist, impressionistic, critical, formal, literary, analytic, grounded theory, and so on (see Van Maanen, 1988).

The interpretive practice of making sense of one's findings is both artistic and political. Multiple criteria for evaluating qualitative research now exist, and those that we emphasize stress the situated, relational, and textual structures of the ethnographic experience. There is no single interpretive truth. As we argued earlier, there are multiple interpretive communities, each with its own criteria for evaluating interpretations.

Program evaluation is a major site of qualitative research, and qualitative researchers can influence social policy in important ways. The chapters in this volume by Greenwood and Levin (Chapter 2), Kemmis and McTaggart (Chapter 23), Miller and Crabtree (Chapter 24), Tedlock (Chapter 18), Smith and Hodkinson (Chapter 36), and House (Chapter 42) trace and discuss the rich history of applied qualitative research in the social sciences. This is the critical site where theory, method, praxis, action, and policy all come together. Qualitative researchers can isolate target populations, show the immediate effects of certain programs on such groups, and isolate the constraints that operate against policy changes in such settings. Action-oriented and clinically oriented qualitative researchers can also create spaces where those who are studied (the Other) can speak. The evaluator becomes the conduit for making such voices heard.

▣ Bridging the Historical Moments: What Comes Next?

In Chapter 38 of this volume, Richardson and St. Pierre argue that we are already in the post-"post" period—post-poststructuralism, post-postmodernism, post-postexperimentalism. What this means for interpretive ethnographic practices is still not clear, but it is certain that things will never again be the same. We are in a new age where messy, uncertain, multivoiced texts, cultural criticism, and new experimental works will become more common, as will more reflexive forms of fieldwork, analysis, and intertextual representation. The subject of our final essay in this volume is these sixth, seventh, eighth, and ninth moments. It is true that, as the poet said, the center no longer holds. We can reflect on what should be at the new center.

Thus we come full circle. Returning to our bridge metaphor, the chapters that follow take the researcher back and forth through every phase of the research act. Like a good bridge, the chapters provide for two-way traffic, coming and going between moments, formations, and interpretive communities. Each chapter examines the relevant histories, controversies, and current practices that are associated with each paradigm, strategy, and method. Each chapter also offers projections for the future, where a specific paradigm, strategy, or method will be 10 years from now, deep into the formative years of the 21st century.

In reading the chapters that follow, it is important to remember that the field of qualitative research is defined by a series of tensions, contradictions, and hesitations. These tensions work back and forth between and among the broad, doubting postmodern sensibility; the more certain, more traditional positivist, postpositivist, and naturalistic conceptions of this project; and an increasingly conservative, neoliberal global environment. All of the chapters that follow are caught in and articulate these tensions.

Notes

1. Recall bell hooks's (1990, p. 127) reading of the famous photo of Stephen Tyler doing fieldwork in India that appears on the cover of *Writing Culture* (Clifford & Marcus, 1986). In the picture, Tyler is seated at some distance from three dark-skinned persons. One, a child, is poking his or her head out of a basket. A woman is hidden in the shadows of the hut. A man, a checkered white-and-black shawl across his shoulder, elbow propped on his knee, hand resting along the side of his face, is staring at Tyler. Tyler is writing in a field journal. A piece of white cloth is attached to his glasses, perhaps shielding him from the sun. This patch of whiteness marks Tyler as the white male writer studying these passive brown and black persons. Indeed, the brown male's gaze signals some desire, or some attachment to Tyler. In contrast, the female's gaze is completely hidden by the shadows and by the words of the book's title, which are printed across her face.

2. Qualitative research has separate and distinguished histories in education, social work, communications, psychology, history, organizational studies, medical science, anthropology, and sociology.

3. Some definitions are in order here. *Positivism* asserts that objective accounts of the real world can be given. *Postpositivism* holds that only partially objective accounts of the world can be produced, for all methods for examining such accounts are flawed. According to *foundationalism,* we can have an ultimate grounding for our knowledge claims about the world, and this involves the use of empiricist and positivist epistemologies (Schwandt, 1997a, p. 103). *Nonfoundationalism* holds that we can make statements about the world without "recourse to ultimate proof or foundations for that knowing" (Schwandt, 1997a, p. 102). *Quasi-foundationalism* holds that we can make certain knowledge claims about the world based on neorealist criteria, including the correspondence concept of truth; there is an independent reality that can be mapped (see Smith & Hodkinson, Chapter 36, this volume).

4. Jameson (1991, pp. 3–4) reminds us that any periodization hypothesis is always suspect, even one that rejects linear, stagelike models. It is never clear to what reality a stage refers, and what divides one stage from another is always debatable. Our eight moments are meant to mark discernible shifts in style, genre, epistemology, ethics, politics, and aesthetics.

5. Several scholars have termed this model a *progress narrative* (Alasuutari, 2004, pp. 599–600; Seale et al., 2004, p. 2). Critics assert that we believe that the most recent moment is the most up-to-date, the avant-garde, the cutting edge (Alasuutari, 2004, p. 601). Naturally, we dispute this reading. Teddlie and Tashakkori (2003, pp. 5–8) have modified our historical periods to fit their historical analysis of the major moments in the emergence of the use of mixed methods in social science research in the past century.

6. Some additional definitions are needed here. *Structuralism* holds that any system is made up of a set of oppositional categories embedded in language. *Semiotics* is the science of signs or sign systems—a structuralist project. According to *poststructuralism,* language is an unstable system of referents, thus it is impossible ever to capture completely the meaning of an action, text, or intention. *Postmodernism* is a contemporary sensibility, developing since World War II, that privileges no single authority, method, or paradigm. *Hermeneutics* is an approach to the analysis of texts that stresses how prior understandings and prejudices shape the interpretive process. *Phenomenology* is a complex system of ideas associated with the works of Husserl, Heidegger, Sartre, Merleau-Ponty, and Alfred Schutz. *Cultural studies* is a complex, interdisciplinary field that merges critical theory, feminism, and poststructuralism.

7. Of course, all settings are natural—that is, places where everyday experiences take place. Qualitative researchers study people doing things together in the places where these things are done (Becker, 1986). There is no field site or natural place where one goes to do this kind of work (see also Gupta & Ferguson, 1997, p. 8). The site is constituted through the researcher's interpretive practices. Historically, analysts have distinguished between experimental (laboratory) and field (natural) research settings, hence the argument that qualitative research is naturalistic. Activity theory erases this distinction (Keller & Keller, 1996, p. 20; Vygotsky, 1978).

8. According to Weinstein and Weinstein (1991), "The meaning of *bricoleur* in French popular speech is 'someone who works with his (or her) hands and uses devious means compared to those of the craftsman.' . . . the *bricoleur* is practical and gets the job done" (p. 161). These authors provide a history of the term, connecting it to the works of the German sociologist and social theorist Georg Simmel and, by implication, Baudelaire. Hammersley (1999) disputes our use of this term. Following Lévi-Strauss, he reads the *bricoleur* as a mythmaker. He suggests that the term be replaced with the notion of the boatbuilder. Hammersley also quarrels with our "moments" model of the history of qualitative research, contending that it implies some sense of progress.

9. Brian De Palma reproduced this baby carriage scene in his 1987 film *The Untouchables*.

10. In the harbor, the muzzles of the *Potemkin*'s two huge guns swing slowly toward the camera. Words on the screen inform us, "The brutal military power answered by guns of the battleship." A final famous three-shot montage sequence shows first a sculpture of a sleeping lion, then a lion rising from his sleep, and finally the lion roaring, symbolizing the rage of the Russian people (Cook, 1981, p. 167). In this sequence Eisenstein uses montage to expand time, creating a psychological duration for this horrible event. By drawing out this sequence, by showing the baby in the carriage, the soldiers firing on the citizens, the blood on the mother's glove, the descending carriage on the steps, he suggests a level of destruction of great magnitude.

11. Here it is relevant to make a distinction between techniques that are used across disciplines and methods that are used within disciplines. Ethnomethodologists, for example, employ their approach as a method, whereas others selectively borrow that method as a technique for their own applications. Harry Wolcott (personal communication, 1993) suggests this distinction. It is also relevant to make distinctions among topic, method, and resource. Methods can be studied as topics of inquiry; that is how a case study gets done. In this ironic, ethnomethodological sense, method is both a resource and a topic of inquiry.

12. Indeed, any attempt to give an essential definition of qualitative research requires a qualitative analysis of the circumstances that produce such a definition.

13. In this sense all research is qualitative, because "the observer is at the center of the research process" (Vidich & Lyman, 2000, p. 39).

14. See Lincoln and Guba (1985) for an extension and elaboration of this tradition in the mid-1980s, and for more recent extensions see Taylor and Bogdan (1998) and Creswell (1998).

15. Greenblatt (1997, pp. 15–18) offers a useful deconstructive reading of the many meanings and practices Geertz brings to the term *thick description*.

16. These works marginalized and minimized the contributions of standpoint feminist theory and research to this discourse (see Behar, 1995, p. 3; Gordon, 1995, p. 432).

17. Olesen (Chapter 10, this volume) identifies three strands of feminist research: mainstream empirical, standpoint and cultural studies, and poststructural, postmodern. She places Afrocentric and other models of color under the cultural studies and postmodern categories.

18. These, of course, are our interpretations of these paradigms and interpretive styles.

19. *Empirical materials* is the preferred term for what traditionally have been described as data.

References

Alasuutari, P. (2004). The globalization of qualitative research. In C. Seale, G. Gobo, J. F. Gubrium, & D. Silverman (Eds.), *Qualitative research practice* (pp. 595–608). London: Sage.

Aronowitz, S. (1988). *Science as power: Discourse and ideology in modern society.* Minneapolis: University of Minnesota Press.

Atkinson, E. (2004). Thinking outside the box: An exercise in heresy. *Qualitative Inquiry, 10,* 111–129.

Bateson, G. (1972). *Steps to an ecology of mind.* New York: Ballantine.

Battiste, M. (2000). Introduction: Unfolding lessons of colonization. In M. Battiste (Ed.), *Reclaiming indigenous voice and vision* (pp. xvi–xxx). Vancouver: University of British Columbia Press.

Becker, H. S. (1970). Problems of inference and proof in participant observation. In H. S. Becker, *Sociological work: Method and substance.* Chicago: Aldine. (Reprinted from *American Sociological Review,* 1958, *23,* 652–660)

Becker, H. S. (1986). *Doing things together.* Evanston, IL: Northwestern University Press.

Becker, H. S. (1996). The epistemology of qualitative research. In R. Jessor, A. Colby, & R. A. Shweder (Eds.), *Ethnography and human development: Context and meaning in social inquiry* (pp. 53–71). Chicago: University of Chicago Press.

Becker, H. S. (1998). *Tricks of the trade: How to think about your research while you're doing it.* Chicago: University of Chicago Press.

Becker, H. S., Geer, B., Hughes, E. C., & Strauss, A. L. (1961). *Boys in white: Student culture in medical school.* Chicago: University of Chicago Press.

Behar, R. (1995). Introduction: Out of exile. In R. Behar & D. A. Gordon (Eds.), *Women writing culture* (pp. 1–29). Berkeley: University of California Press.

Bloch, M. (2004). A discourse that disciplines, governs, and regulates: The National Research Council's report on scientific research in education. *Qualitative Inquiry, 10,* 96–110.

Bochner, A. P., & Ellis, C. (Eds.). (2002). *Ethnographically speaking: Autoethnography, literature, and aesthetics.* Walnut Creek, CA: AltaMira.

Bogdan, R., & Taylor, S. J. (1975). *Introduction to qualitative research methods: A phenomenological approach to the social sciences.* New York: John Wiley.

Campbell, D. T., & Stanley, J. C. (1963). *Experimental and quasi-experimental designs for research.* Chicago: Rand McNally.

Cannella, G. S., & Lincoln, Y. S. (2004a). Dangerous discourses II: Comprehending and countering the redeployment of discourses (and resources) in the generation of liberatory inquiry. *Qualitative Inquiry, 10,* 165–174.

Cannella, G. S., & Lincoln, Y. S. (2004b). Epilogue: Claiming a critical public social science—reconceptualizing and redeploying research. *Qualitative Inquiry, 10,* 298–309.

Carey, J. W. (1989). *Communication as culture: Essays on media and society.* Boston: Unwin Hyman.

Cicourel, A. V. (1964). *Method and measurement in sociology.* New York: Free Press.

Clifford, J. (1988). *The predicament of culture: Twentieth-century ethnography, literature, and art.* Cambridge, MA: Harvard University Press.

Clifford, J., & Marcus, G. E. (Eds.). (1986). *Writing culture: The poetics and politics of ethnography.* Berkeley: University of California Press.

Clough, P. T. (1998). *The end(s) of ethnography: From realism to social criticism* (2nd ed.). New York: Peter Lang.

Cook, D. A. (1981). *A history of narrative film.* New York: W. W. Norton.

Creswell, J. W. (1998). *Qualitative inquiry and research design: Choosing among five traditions.* Thousand Oaks, CA: Sage.

Danermark, B., Ekström, M., Jakobsen, L., & Karlsson, J. C. (2002). *Explaining society: Critical realism in the social sciences.* London: Routledge.

de Certeau, M. (1984). *The practice of everyday life.* Berkeley: University of California Press.

Denzin, N. K. (1970). *The research act.* Chicago: Aldine.

Denzin, N. K. (1978). *The research act: A theoretical introduction to sociological methods* (2nd ed.). New York: McGraw-Hill.

Denzin, N. K. (1997). *Interpretive ethnography: Ethnographic practices for the 21st century.* Thousand Oaks, CA: Sage.

Denzin, N. K. (2003). *Performance ethnography: Critical pedagogy and the politics of culture.* Thousand Oaks, CA: Sage.

Dilthey, W. L. (1976). *Selected writings.* Cambridge: Cambridge University Press. (Original work published 1900)

Diversi, M. (1998). Glimpses of street life: Representing lived experience through short stories. *Qualitative Inquiry, 4,* 131–137.

Ellis, C. (2004). *The ethnographic I: A methodological novel about autoethnography.* Walnut Creek, CA: AltaMira.

Ellis, C., & Bochner, A. P. (Eds.). (1996). *Composing ethnography: Alternative forms of qualitative writing.* Walnut Creek, CA: AltaMira.

Filstead, W. J. (Ed.). (1970). *Qualitative methodology.* Chicago: Markham.

Fine, M., Weis, L., Weseen, S., & Wong, L. (2000). For whom? Qualitative research, representations, and social responsibilities. In N. K. Denzin & Y. S. Lincoln (Eds.), *Handbook of qualitative research* (2nd ed., pp. 107–131). Thousand Oaks, CA: Sage.

Flick, U. (2002). *An introduction to qualitative research* (2nd ed.). London: Sage.

Geertz, C. (1973). *The interpretation of cultures: Selected essays.* New York: Basic Books.

Geertz, C. (1983). *Local knowledge: Further essays in interpretive anthropology.* New York: Basic Books.

Geertz, C. (1988). *Works and lives: The anthropologist as author.* Stanford, CA: Stanford University Press.

Glaser, B. G. (1992). *Emergence vs. forcing: Basics of grounded theory.* Mill Valley, CA: Sociology Press.

Glaser, B. G., & Strauss, A. L. (1967). *The discovery of grounded theory: Strategies for qualitative research.* Chicago: Aldine.

Goodall, H. L., Jr. (2000). *Writing the new ethnography.* Walnut Creek, CA: AltaMira.

Gordon, D. A. (1995). Culture writing women: Inscribing feminist anthropology. In R. Behar & D. A. Gordon (Eds.), *Women writing culture* (pp. 429–441). Berkeley: University of California Press.

Greenblatt, S. (1997). The touch of the real. In S. B. Ortner (Ed.), The fate of "culture": Geertz and beyond [Special issue]. *Representations, 59,* 14–29.

Guba, E. G. (1990). The alternative paradigm dialog. In E. G. Guba (Ed.), *The paradigm dialog* (pp. 17–30). Newbury Park, CA: Sage.

Guba, E. G., & Lincoln, Y. S. (1989). *Fourth generation evaluation.* Newbury Park, CA: Sage.

Gupta, A., & Ferguson, J. (Eds.). (1997). Discipline and practice: "The field" as site, method, and location in anthropology. In A. Gupta & J. Ferguson (Eds.), *Anthropological locations: Boundaries and grounds of a field science* (pp. 1–46). Berkeley: University of California Press.

Hammersley, M. (1992). *What's wrong with ethnography? Methodological explorations.* London: Routledge.

Hammersley, M. (1999). Not bricolage but boatbuilding: Exploring two metaphors for thinking about ethnography. *Journal of Contemporary Ethnography, 28,* 574–585.

Harper, D. (1987). *Working knowledge: Skill and community in a small shop.* Chicago: University of Chicago Press.

Holman Jones, S. (1999). Torch. *Qualitative Inquiry, 5,* 235–250.

hooks, b. (1990). *Yearning: Race, gender, and cultural politics.* Boston: South End.

Howe, K. R. (2004). A critique of experimentalism. *Qualitative Inquiry, 10,* 42–61.

Huber, J. (1995). Centennial essay: Institutional perspectives on sociology. *American Journal of Sociology, 101,* 194–216.

Jackson, M. (1998). *Minima ethnographica: Intersubjectivity and the anthropological project.* Chicago: University of Chicago Press.

Jameson, F. (1991). *Postmodernism; or, The cultural logic of late capitalism.* Durham, NC: Duke University Press.

Keller, C. M., & Keller, J. D. (1996). *Cognition and tool use: The blacksmith at work.* New York: Cambridge University Press.

Kincheloe, J. L. (2001). Describing the bricolage: Conceptualizing a new rigor in qualitative research. *Qualitative Inquiry, 7,* 679–692.

Ladson-Billings, G. (2000). Socialized discourses and ethnic epistemologies. In N. K. Denzin & Y. S. Lincoln (Eds.), *Handbook of qualitative research* (2nd ed., pp. 257–277). Thousand Oaks, CA: Sage.

Lather, P. (1993). Fertile obsession: Validity after poststructuralism. *Sociological Quarterly, 35,* 673–694.

Lather, P. (2004). This *is* your father's paradigm: Government intrusion and the case of qualitative research in education. *Qualitative Inquiry, 10,* 15–34.

Lather, P., & Smithies, C. (1997). *Troubling the angels: Women living with HIV/AIDS.* Boulder, CO: Westview.

LeCompte, M. D., & Preissle, J. (with Tesch, R.). (1993). *Ethnography and qualitative design in educational research* (2nd ed.). New York: Academic Press.

Lévi-Strauss, C. (1966). *The savage mind* (2nd ed.). Chicago: University of Chicago Press.

Lincoln, Y. S. (1999, June). *Courage, vulnerability and truth.* Keynote address delivered at the conference "Reclaiming Voice II: Ethnographic Inquiry and Qualitative Research in a Postmodern Age," University of California, Irvine.

Lincoln, Y. S., & Cannella, G. S. (2004a). Dangerous discourses: Methodological conservatism and governmental regimes of truth. *Qualitative Inquiry, 10,* 5–14.

Lincoln, Y. S., & Cannella, G. S. (2004b). Qualitative research, power, and the radical Right. *Qualitative Inquiry, 10,* 175–201.

Lincoln, Y. S., & Guba, E. G. (1985). *Naturalistic inquiry.* Beverly Hills, CA: Sage.

Lincoln, Y. S., & Tierney, W. G. (2004). Qualitative research and institutional review boards. *Qualitative Inquiry, 10,* 219–234.

Lofland, J. (1971). *Analyzing social settings.* Belmont, CA: Wadsworth.

Lofland, J. (1995). Analytic ethnography: Features, failings, and futures. *Journal of Contemporary Ethnography, 24,* 30–67.

Lofland, J., & Lofland, L. H. (1984). *Analyzing social settings: A guide to qualitative observation and analysis* (2nd ed.). Belmont, CA: Wadsworth.

Lofland, J., & Lofland, L. H. (1995). *Analyzing social settings: A guide to qualitative observation and analysis* (3rd ed.). Belmont, CA: Wadsworth.

Lofland, L. H. (1980). The 1969 Blumer-Hughes Talk. *Urban Life and Culture, 8,* 248–260.

Malinowski, B. (1948). *Magic, science and religion, and other essays.* New York: Natural History Press. (Original work published 1916)

Malinowski, B. (1967). *A diary in the strict sense of the term* (N. Guterman, Trans.). New York: Harcourt, Brace & World.

Marcus, G. E., & Fischer, M. M. J. (1986). *Anthropology as cultural critique: An experimental moment in the human sciences.* Chicago: University of Chicago Press.

Maxwell, J. A. (2004). Reemergent scientism, postmodernism, and dialogue across differences. *Qualitative Inquiry, 10,* 35–41.

Monaco, J. (1981). *How to read a film: The art, technology, language, history and theory of film* (Rev. ed.). New York: Oxford University Press.

Nelson, C., Treichler, P. A., & Grossberg, L. (1992). Cultural studies: An introduction. In L. Grossberg, C. Nelson, & P. A. Treichler (Eds.), *Cultural studies* (pp. 1–16). New York: Routledge.

Ortner, S. B. (1997). Introduction. In S. B. Ortner (Ed.), The fate of "culture": Geertz and beyond [Special issue]. *Representations, 59,* 1–13.

Pelias, R. J. (2004). *A methodology of the heart: Evoking academic and daily life.* Walnut Creek, CA: AltaMira.

Plath, D. W. (1990). Fieldnotes, filed notes, and the conferring of note. In R. Sanjek (Ed.), *Fieldnotes: The makings of anthropology* (pp. 371–384). Ithaca, NY: Cornell University Press.

Popkewitz, T. S. (2004). Is the National Research Council committee's report on scientific research in education scientific? On trusting the manifesto. *Qualitative Inquiry, 10,* 62–78.

Richardson, L. (1997). *Fields of play: Constructing an academic life.* New Brunswick, NJ: Rutgers University Press.

Richardson, L. (2000). Writing: A method of inquiry. In N. K. Denzin & Y. S. Lincoln (Eds.), *Handbook of qualitative research* (2nd ed., pp. 923–948). Thousand Oaks, CA: Sage.

Richardson, L., & Lockridge, E. (2004). *Travels with Ernest: Crossing the literary/sociological divide.* Walnut Creek, CA: AltaMira.

Roffman, P., & Purdy, J. (1981). *The Hollywood social problem film.* Bloomington: Indiana University Press.

Ronai, C. R. (1998). Sketching with Derrida: An ethnography of a researcher/erotic dancer. *Qualitative Inquiry, 4,* 405–420.

Rosaldo, R. (1989). *Culture and truth: The remaking of social analysis.* Boston: Beacon.

Ryan, G. W., & Bernard, H. R. (2000). Data management and analysis methods. In N. K. Denzin & Y. S. Lincoln (Eds.), *Handbook of qualitative research* (2nd ed., pp. 769–802). Thousand Oaks, CA: Sage.

Ryan, K. E., & Hood, L. K. (2004). Guarding the castle and opening the gates. *Qualitative Inquiry, 10,* 79–95.

St. Pierre, E. A. (2004). Refusing alternatives: A science of contestation. *Qualitative Inquiry, 10,* 130–139.

Sanjek, R. (1990). On ethnographic validity. In R. Sanjek (Ed.), *Fieldnotes: The makings of anthropology* (pp. 385–418). Ithaca, NY: Cornell University Press.

Schwandt, T. A. (1997a). *Qualitative inquiry: A dictionary of terms.* Thousand Oaks, CA: Sage.

Schwandt, T. A. (1997b). Textual gymnastics, ethics and angst. In W. G. Tierney & Y. S. Lincoln (Eds.), *Representation and the text: Re-framing the narrative voice* (pp. 305–311). Albany: State University of New York Press.

Schwandt, T. A. (2000). Three epistemological stances for qualitative inquiry: Interpretivism, hermeneutics, and social constructionism. In N. K. Denzin & Y. S. Lincoln (Eds.), *Handbook of qualitative research* (2nd ed., pp. 189–213). Thousand Oaks, CA: Sage.

Seale, C., Gobo, G., Gubrium, J. F., & Silverman, D. (2004). Introduction: Inside qualitative research. In C. Seale, G. Gobo, J. F. Gubrium, & D. Silverman (Eds.), *Qualitative research practice* (pp. 1–11). London: Sage.

Semali, L. M., & Kincheloe, J. L. (1999). Introduction: What is indigenous knowledge and why should we study it?" In L. M. Semali & J. L. Kincheloe (Eds.), *What is indigenous knowledge? Voices from the academy* (pp. 3–57). New York: Falmer.

Silverman, D. (1997). Towards an aesthetics of research. In D. Silverman (Ed.), *Qualitative research: Theory, method and practice* (pp. 239–253). London: Sage.

Smith, A. D. (1993). *Fires in the mirror: Crown Heights, Brooklyn, and other identities.* New York: Anchor.

Smith, J. K., & Deemer, D. K. (2000). The problem of criteria in the age of relativism. In N. K. Denzin & Y. S. Lincoln (Eds.), *Handbook of qualitative research* (2nd ed., pp. 877–896). Thousand Oaks, CA: Sage.

Smith, L. T. (1999). *Decolonizing methodologies: Research and indigenous peoples.* Dunedin, New Zealand: University of Otago Press.

Snow, D., & Morrill, C. (1995). Ironies, puzzles, and contradictions in Denzin and Lincoln's vision of qualitative research. *Journal of Contemporary Ethnography, 22,* 358–362.

Spindler, G., & Spindler, L. (1992). Cultural process and ethnography: An anthropological perspective. In M. D. LeCompte, W. L. Millroy, & J. Preissle (Eds.), *The handbook of qualitative research in education* (pp. 53–92). New York: Academic Press.

Stocking, G. W., Jr. (1986). Anthropology and the science of the irrational: Malinowski's encounter with Freudian psychoanalysis. In G. W. Stocking, Jr. (Ed.), *Malinowski, Rivers, Benedict and others: Essays on culture and personality* (pp. 13–49). Madison: University of Wisconsin Press.

Stocking, G. W., Jr. (1989). The ethnographic sensibility of the 1920s and the dualism of the anthropological tradition. In G. W. Stocking, Jr. (Ed.), *Romantic motives: Essays on anthropological sensibility* (pp. 208–276). Madison: University of Wisconsin Press.

Stoller, P., & Olkes, C. (1987). *In sorcery's shadow: A memoir of apprenticeship among the Songhay of Niger.* Chicago: University of Chicago Press.

Strauss, A. L., & Corbin, J. (1998). *Basics of qualitative research: Techniques and procedures for developing grounded theory* (2nd ed.). Thousand Oaks, CA: Sage.

Taylor, S. J., & Bogdan, R. (1998). *Introduction to qualitative research methods: A guidebook and resource* (3rd ed.). New York: John Wiley.

Teddlie, C., & Tashakkori, A. (2003). Major issues and controversies in the use of mixed methods in the social and behavioral sciences. In A. Tashakkori & C. Teddlie (Eds.), *Handbook of mixed methods in social and behavioral research* (pp. 3–50). Thousand Oaks, CA: Sage.

Tierney, W. G. (2000). Undaunted courage: Life history and the postmodern challenge. In N. K. Denzin & Y. S. Lincoln (Eds.), *Handbook of qualitative research* (2nd ed., pp. 537–553). Thousand Oaks, CA: Sage.

Trujillo, N. (2004). *In search of Naunny's grave: Age, class, gender, and ethnicity in an American family.* Walnut Creek, CA: AltaMira.

Turner, V., & Bruner, E. (Eds.). (1986). *The anthropology of experience.* Urbana: University of Illinois Press.

Van Maanen, J. (1988). *Tales of the field: On writing ethnography.* Chicago: University of Chicago Press.

Vidich, A. J., & Lyman, S. M. (1994). Qualitative methods: Their history in sociology and anthropology. In N. K. Denzin & Y. S. Lincoln (Eds.), *Handbook of qualitative research* (pp. 23–59). Thousand Oaks, CA: Sage.

Vidich, A. J., & Lyman, S. M. (2000). Qualitative methods: Their history in sociology and anthropology. In N. K. Denzin & Y. S. Lincoln (Eds.), *Handbook of qualitative research* (2nd ed., pp. 37–84). Thousand Oaks, CA: Sage.

Vygotsky, L. S. (1978). *Mind in society: The development of higher psychological processes* (M. Cole, V. John-Steiner, S. Scribner, & E. Souberman, Eds.). Cambridge, MA: Harvard University Press.

Weinstein, D., & Weinstein, M. A. (1991). Georg Simmel: Sociological flaneur bricoleur. *Theory, Culture & Society, 8,* 151–168.

Weinstein, M. (2004). Randomized design and the myth of certain knowledge: Guinea pig narratives and cultural critique. *Qualitative Inquiry, 10,* 246–260.

West, C. (1989). *The American evasion of philosophy: A genealogy of pragmatism.* Madison: University of Wisconsin Press.

Wolf, M. A. (1992). *A thrice-told tale: Feminism, postmodernism, and ethnographic responsibility.* Stanford, CA: Stanford University Press.

Wolcott, H. F. (1990). *Writing up qualitative research.* Newbury Park, CA: Sage.

Wolcott, H. F. (1992). Posturing in qualitative inquiry. In M. D. LeCompte, W. L. Millroy, & J. Preissle (Eds.), *The handbook of qualitative research in education* (pp. 3–52). New York: Academic Press.

Wolcott, H. F. (1995). *The art of fieldwork.* Walnut Creek, CA: AltaMira.

Part I

LOCATING THE FIELD

This part of the *Handbook* begins with the suggested reform of the social sciences and the academy through action research. It then moves to issues surrounding compositional studies and critical theorizing. Inquiry under neocolonial regimes is examined next. The discussion then turns to the social, political, and moral responsibilities of the researcher as well as the ethics and politics of qualitative inquiry.

History and the Participatory Action Tradition

The opening chapter, by Greenwood and Levin, reveals the depth and complexity of the traditional and applied qualitative research perspectives that are consciously and unconsciously inherited by the researcher-as-interpretive-bricoleur.[1] These traditions locate the investigator in a system of historical (and organizational) discourse. This system guides and constrains the interpretive work that is being done in any specific study.

In their monumental chapter ("Qualitative Methods: Their History in Sociology and Anthropology"), reprinted in the second edition of the *Handbook*, Vidich and Lyman (2000) show how the ethnographic tradition extends from the Greeks through the 15th- and 16th-century interests of Westerners in the origins of primitive cultures; to colonial ethnology connected to the empires of Spain, England, France, and Holland; to several 20th-century transformations in America and Europe. Throughout this history, the users of qualitative research have displayed commitments to a small set of beliefs, including objectivism, the desire to contextualize experience, and a willingness to interpret theoretically what has been observed.

These beliefs supplement the positivist tradition of complicity with colonialism, the commitments to monumentalism, and the production of timeless texts discussed in our introductory Chapter 1. The colonial model located qualitative inquiry in racial and sexual discourses that privileged white patriarchy. Of course, as indicated in our introductory chapter, recently these beliefs have come under considerable attack. Vidich and Lyman, as well as Smith (Chapter 4), Bishop (Chapter 5), and Ladson-Billings and Donnor (Chapter 11), document the extent to which early as well as contemporary qualitative researchers were (and remain) implicated in these systems of oppression.

Greenwood and Levin expand and extend this line of criticism. They are quite explicit that scholars have a responsibility to do work that is socially meaningful and socially responsible. The relationship between researchers, universities, and society must change. Politically informed action research, inquiry committed to praxis and social change, is the vehicle for accomplishing this transformation.

Action researchers are committed to a set of disciplined, material practices that produce radical, democratizing transformations in the civic sphere. These practices involve collaborative dialogue, participatory decision making, inclusive democratic deliberation, and the maximal participation and representation of all relevant parties (Ryan & Destefano, 2000, p. 1). Action researchers literally help transform inquiry into praxis, or action. Research subjects become coparticipants and stakeholders in the process of inquiry. Research becomes praxis—practical, reflective, pragmatic action—directed to solving problems in the world.

These problems originate in the lives of the research coparticipants—they do not come down from on high, by way of grand theory. Together, stakeholders and action researchers co-create knowledge that is pragmatically useful and is grounded in local knowledge. In the process, they jointly define research objectives and political goals, co-construct research questions, pool knowledge, hone shared research skills, fashion interpretations and performance texts that implement specific strategies for social change, and measure validity and credibility by the willingness of local stakeholders to act on the basis of the results of the action research.

Academic science has a history in the past century of not being able to accomplish consistently goals such as these. According to Greenwood and Levin, there several reasons for this failure, including the inability of a so-called positivistic, value-free social science to produce useful social research; the increasing tendency of outside corporations to define the needs and values of the university; the loss of research funds to entrepreneurial and private sector research organizations; and bloated, inefficient internal administrative infrastructures.

Greenwood and Levin are not renouncing the practices of science; rather, they are calling for a reformulation of what science and the academy are all about. Their model of pragmatically grounded action research is not a retreat from disciplined scientific inquiry.[2] This form of inquiry reconceptualizes science as a collaborative, communicative, communitarian, context-centered, moral project. They want to locate action research at the center of the contemporary university. Their chapter is a call for a civic social science, a pragmatic science that will lead to the radical reconstruction of the university's relationships with society, state, and community in this new century.

▣ Critical Theorizing, Social Responsibility, Decolonizing Research, and the Ethics of Inquiry

The contributions of Michelle Fine and Lois Weis (Chapter 3), Linda Tuhiwai Smith (Chapter 4), Russell Bishop (Chapter 5), Clifford Christians (Chapter 6), and Yvonna Lincoln (Chapter 7) extend this call for a committed, civic moral social science. Fine and Weis offer a theory of method, a new approach to ethnography, a new way of reading and writing this complex, fragmented, and fractured social puzzle we call America. Compositional studies are contextual, relational, and sensitive to the fluidity of social identities. Fine and Weis seek to create compositional works that place race, class, gender, and ethnicity in relation to one another, in ways that work back and forth among history, economy, and politics. Their chapter offers brief looks at two compositional designs: Weis's long-term study of white working-class men and women, and Fine's participatory action project involving youth as critical researchers of desegregation. Each of these ethnographic projects is designed to understand how "global and national formations, as well as relational interactions, seep through the lives, identities, relations, and communities of youth and adults, ultimately refracting back on the larger formations that give rise to them to begin with" (p. 69). They offer a series of stories that reveal a set of knotty, emergent ethical and rhetorical dilemmas that were encountered as they attempted to write for, with, and about poor and working-class stakeholders.

These are the problems of qualitative inquiry in the current historical moment. They turn on the issues of voice, reflexivity, "race," informed consent, good and bad stories, and "coming clean at the hyphen." Voice and reflexivity are primary. Fine and Weis struggled with how to locate themselves and their stakeholders in the text. They also struggled with how to write about "race," a floating, unstable fiction that is also an inerasable aspect of the self and its personal history. With them, we take heart in the observations of Nikoury, a youth researcher from the Lower East Side of Manhattan who stunned an audience with these words: "I used to see flat. No more . . . now I know things are much deeper than they appear. And it's my job to find out what's behind the so-called facts. I can't see flat anymore" (p. 80).

Fine and Weis are hopeful that compositional studies can "provide a scholarly mirror of urgency, refracting back on a nation . . . [asking] us to re-view the very structures of power upon which the country, the economy, our schools, and our fragile sense of selves . . . are premised, and to imagine, alternatively, what could be" (p. 80).

Linda Tuhiwai Smith, a Mâori scholar, discusses research in and on indigenous communities—those who have witnessed, have been excluded from, and have survived modernity and imperialism. She analyses how indigenous peoples, the native Other, historically have been vulnerable to neocolonial research. Recently, as part of the decolonization process, indigenous communities have begin to resist hegemonic research and to invent new research methodologies. Mâori scholars have developed a research approach known as Kaupapa Mâori. Smith (Chapter 4) and Bishop (Chapter 5) outline this approach, which makes research a highly political activity.

In indigenous communities, research ethics involves both establishing and maintaining nurturing reciprocal and respectful relationships. This ethical framework is very much at odds with the Western, Institutional Review Board type of apparatus, with its informed consent forms. Indigenous research activity offers genuine utopian hope for creating and living in a more just and humane social world.

Russell Bishop shows how a Kaupapa Mâori position can be used by the Mâori to get free of neocolonial domination. Kaupapa Mâori creates the conditions for self-determination. It emphasizes five issues of power that become criteria for evaluating research: initiation, benefits, representation, legitimation, and accountability. Indigenous researchers should initiate research, not be the subject of someone else's research agenda. The community should benefit from the research, which should represent the voices of indigenous peoples. The indigenous community should have the power to legitimate and produce the research texts that are written, as well as the power to hold researchers accountable for what is written. When these five criteria are addressed in the affirmative, empowering knowledge is created, allowing indigenous persons to free themselves from neocolonial domination.

A Feminist, Communitarian Ethical Framework

Clifford Christians (Chapter 6) locates the ethics and politics of qualitative inquiry within a broader historical and intellectual framework. He first examines the Enlightenment model of positivism, value-free inquiry, utilitarianism, and utilitarian ethics. In a value-free social science, codes of ethics for professional societies become the conventional format for moral principles. By the 1980s, each of the major social science associations (contemporaneous with passage of federal laws and promulgation of national guidelines) had developed its own ethical code, with an emphasis on several guidelines: informed consent, nondeception, the absence of psychological or physical harm, privacy and confidentiality, and a commitment to collecting and presenting reliable and valid empirical materials. Institutional Review Boards (IRBs) implemented these guidelines, including ensuring that informed consent is always obtained in human subject research. However, Christians notes, as do Smith and Bishop, that in reality IRBs protect institutions and not individuals.

Several events challenged the Enlightenment model, including the Nazi medical experiments, the Tuskegee Syphilis Study, Project Camelot in the 1960s, Milgram's deception of subjects in his psychology experiments, Humphrey's deceptive study of homosexuals, and the complicity of social scientists with military initiatives in Vietnam. In addition, charges of fraud, plagiarism, data tampering, and misrepresentation continue to the present day.

Christians details the poverty of this model. It creates the conditions for deception, for the invasion of private spaces, for duping subjects, and for challenges to the subjects' moral worth and dignity (see also Angrosino, Chapter 28, this volume; Guba & Lincoln, 1989, pp. 120–141). Christians calls for its replacement with an ethics based on the values of feminist communitarianism.

This is an evolving, emerging ethical framework that serves as a powerful antidote to the deception-based, utilitarian IRB system. It presumes a community that is ontologically and axiologically prior to the person. This community has common moral values, and research is rooted in a concept of care, of shared governance, of neighborliness, and of love, kindness, and the moral good. Accounts of social life should display these values and be based on interpretive sufficiency. They should have sufficient depth to allow the reader to form a critical understanding about the world studied. These texts should exhibit an absence of racial, class, and gender stereotyping. These texts should generate social criticism and should lead to resistance, empowerment, and social action—to positive change in the social world.

In the feminist communitarian model, as with the model of participatory action research advocated by Greenwood and Levin, Fine and Weis, Smith, Bishop, and Kemmis and McTaggart, participants have a co-equal say in how research should be conducted, what should be studied, which methods should be used, which findings are valid and acceptable, how the findings are to be implemented, and how the consequences of such action are to be assessed. Spaces for disagreement are recognized, and discourse aims for mutual understanding and for the honoring of moral commitments.

A sacred, existential epistemology places us in a noncompetitive, nonhierarchical relationship to the earth, to nature, and to the larger world (Bateson, 1972, p. 335). This sacred epistemology stresses the values of empowerment, shared governance, care, solidarity, love, community, covenant, morally involved observers, and civic transformation. As Christians observes, this ethical epistemology recovers the moral values that were excluded by the rational, Enlightenment science project. This sacred epistemology is based on a philosophical anthropology which declares that "all humans are worthy of dignity and sacred status without exception for class or ethnicity" (Christians, 1995, p. 129). A universal human ethic, stressing the sacredness of life, human dignity, truth-telling, and nonviolence derives from this position (Christians, 1997, pp. 12–15). This ethic is based on locally experienced, culturally prescribed protonorms (Christians, 1995, p. 129). These primal norms provide a defensible "conception of good rooted in universal human solidarity" (Christians, 1995, p. 129; see also Christians, 1997, 1998). This sacred epistemology recognizes and interrogates the ways in which race, class, and gender operate as important systems of oppression in the world today.

Thus does Christians outline a radical ethical path for the future. In so doing, he transcends the usual middle-of-the-road ethical models that focus on the problems associated with betrayal, deception, and harm in qualitative research. Christians's call for a collaborative social science research model makes the researcher responsible not to a removed discipline (or institution) but rather to those studied. This implements critical, action, and feminist traditions that forcefully align the ethics of research with a politics of the oppressed. Christians's framework reorganizes existing discourses on ethics and the social sciences.[3]

The Biomedical Model of Ethics[4]

Christians reviews the criticisms of the biomedical model of ethics, the apparatus of the Institutional Review Board, and Common Rule understandings. Criticisms center on four key terms and their definitions: human subjects, human subject research, harm, and ethical conduct.

A note on the relationship between science and ethics is in order. As Christians notes in Chapter 6, the Common Rule principles reiterate the basic themes of "value-neutral experimentalism—individual autonomy, maximum benefits with minimal risks, and ethical ends exterior to scientific means" (p. 146). These principles "dominate the codes of ethics: informed consent, protection of privacy, and nondeception" (p. 146). These rules do not conceptualize research in participatory or collaborative formats. Christians observes that in reality the guidelines do not stop other ethical violations, including plagiarism, falsification, fabrication, and violations of confidentiality.

Pritchard (2002, pp. 8–9) notes that there is room for ethical conflict as well. The three principles contained in the Common Rule rest on three different ethical traditions: respect, from Kant; beneficence, from Mill and the utilitarians; and justice as a distributive ideal, from Aristotle. These ethical traditions are not compatible: They rest on different moral, ontological, and political assumptions, as well as on different understandings of what is right, just, and respectful. The Kantian principle of respect may contradict the utilitarian principle of beneficence, for instance.

Respect, *beneficence*, and *justice* are problematic terms. Surely there is more to respect than informed consent—more, that is, than getting people to agree to be participants in a study. Respect involves caring for others, honoring them, and treating them with dignity. An informed consent form does not do this, and it does not confer respect on another person.

Beneficence, including risks and benefits, cannot be quantified, nor can a clear meaning be given to acceptable risk or to benefits that clearly serve a larger cause. Smith (Chapter 4) and Bishop (Chapter 5), for instance, both argue that the collectivity must determine collectively what are the costs and benefits for participating in research.

Furthermore, individuals may not have the individual right to allow particular forms of research to be done if the research has negative effects for the greater social whole. A cost-benefit model of society and inquiry does injustice to the empowering, participatory model of research that many peoples are now advocating.

Justice extends beyond implementing fair selection procedures or unfairly distributing the benefits of research across a population. Justice involves principles of care, love, kindness, and fairness, as well as commitments to shared responsibility and to honesty, truth, balance, and harmony. Taken out of their Western utilitarian framework, respect, beneficence, and justice must be seen as principles that are felt as they are performed; that is, they can serve as performative guidelines to a moral way of being in the world with others. As currently enforced by IRBs, however, they serve as coldly calculating devices that may position persons against one another.

Regarding research, Pritchard (2002) contends that the biomedical model's concept of research does not adequately deal with procedural changes in research projects and with unforeseen contingencies that lead to changes in purpose and intent. Often, anonymity cannot be maintained, nor is it always desirable; for example, participatory action inquiry presumes full community participation in a research project.

Staffing presents another level of difficulty. IRBs often are understaffed or have members who either reject or are uninformed about the newer, critical qualitative research tradition. Many IRBs lack proper appeal procedures or methods for expediting research that should be exempted.

Recent summaries by the American Association of University Professors (AAUP) (2001, 2002) raise additional reservations, which also center on the five issues discussed above. These reservations involve the following topics.

Research and Human Subjects

- A failure by IRBs to be aware of new interpretive and qualitative developments in the social sciences, including participant observation, ethnography, autoethnography, and oral history research
- The application of a concept of research and science that privileges the biomedical model of science and not the model of trust, negotiation, and respect that must be established in ethnographic or historical inquiry, where research is not *on*, but is rather *with*, other human beings
- An event-based and not a process-based conception of research and the consent process

Ethics

- A failure to see human beings as social creatures located in complex historical, political, and cultural spaces
- Infringements on academic freedom resulting from failure to allow certain types of inquiry to go forward
- Inappropriate applications of the "Common Rule" in assessing potential harm
- Overly restrictive applications of the informed consent rule

IRBs as Institutional Structures

- A failure to have an adequate appeal system in place
- The need to ensure that IRBs have members from the newer interpretive paradigms

Academic Freedom

- First Amendment and academic freedom infringements
- Policing of inquiry in the humanities, including oral history research
- Policing and obstruction of research seminars and dissertation projects
- Constraints on critical inquiry, including historical or journalistic work that contributes to the public knowledge of the past, while incriminating, or passing negative judgment on, persons and institutions
- A failure to consider or incorporate existing forms of regulation into the Common Rule, including laws and rules regarding libel, copyright, and intellectual property rights
- The general extension of IRB powers across disciplines, creating a negative effect on what will, or will not, be studied
- Vastly different applications of the Common Rule across campus communities

Important Topics Not Regulated

- The conduct of research with indigenous peoples (see below)
- The regulation of unorthodox or problematic conduct in the field (e.g., sexual relations)
- Relations between IRBs and ethical codes involving universal human rights
- Disciplinary codes of ethics and IRBs, and new codes of ethics and moral perspectives coming from the standpoints of feminist, queer, and racialized epistemologies
- Appeal mechanisms for any human subject who needs to grieve and who seeks some form of restorative justice as a result of harm experienced as a research subject
- Indigenous discourses and alternative views of research, science, and human beings

Disciplining and Constraining Ethical Conduct

The consequence of these restrictions is a disciplining of qualitative inquiry, with the discipline process extending from oversight by granting agencies to the policing of qualitative research seminars and even the conduct of qualitative dissertations (Lincoln & Cannella, 2004a, 2004b). In some cases, lines of critical inquiry have not been funded and have not gone forward because of criticisms from local IRBs. Pressures from the political right discredit critical interpretive inquiry. From the federal to the local levels, a trend seems to be emerging. In too many instances, there seems to be a move away from protecting human subjects and toward increased monitoring, censuring, and policing of projects that are critical of conservative politics.

Lincoln and Tierney (2004) observe that these policing activities have at least five important implications for critical, social justice inquiry. First, the widespread rejection of alternative forms of research means that qualitative inquiry will be heard less and less in federal and state policy forums. Second, it appears that qualitative researchers are being deliberately excluded from this national dialogue. Consequently, third, young researchers trained in the critical tradition are not being listened to. Fourth, the definition of research has not changed to fit newer models of inquiry. Fifth, in rejecting qualitative inquiry, traditional researchers are endorsing a more distanced form of research that is compatible with existing stereotypes concerning persons of color.

Lincoln extends this analysis in Chapter 7, underscoring the negative effects of these recent developments on academic freedom, graduate student training, and qualitative inquiry. These developments threaten academic freedom in four ways: (a) They lead to increased scrutiny of human subject research, as well as (b) new scrutiny of classroom research and training in qualitative research involving human subjects; (c) they connect to evidence-based discourses, which define qualitative research as being unscientific; and (d) by endorsing methodological conservatism, they reinforce the status quo on many campuses. This conservatism produces new constraints on graduate training, leads to the improper review of faculty research, and creates conditions for politicizing the IRB review process, while protecting institutions and not individuals from risk and harm.

These constraints must be resisted, and the local IRB is a good place to start.

Conclusions

As does Christians, we endorse a *feminist, communitarian ethic* that calls, after Smith and Bishop, for collaborative, trusting, nonoppressive relationships between researchers and those studied. Such an ethic presumes that investigators are committed to stressing personal accountability, caring, the value of individual expressiveness, the capacity for empathy, and the sharing of emotionality (Collins, 1990, p. 216).

Notes

1. Any distinction between applied and non-applied qualitative research traditions is somewhat arbitrary. Both traditions are scholarly. Each has a long history, and each carries basic implications for theory and social change. Good theoretical research should also have applied relevance and implications. On occasion, it is argued that applied and action research are non-theoretical, but even this conclusion can be disputed, as Kemmis and McTaggart (Chapter 23, this volume) demonstrate.

2. We will develop a notion of a sacred science below and in our concluding chapter (Epilogue).

3. Given Christians's framework, there are two primary ethical models: utilitarian and non-utilitarian. Historically and most recently, however, one of five ethical stances (absolutist, consequentialist, feminist, relativist, deceptive) has been followed, and often these stances merge with one another. The *absolutist* position argues that any method that contributes to a society's self-understanding is acceptable, but only conduct in the public sphere should be studied. The *deception* model says that any method, including the use of lies and misrepresentation, is justified in the name of truth. The *relativist* stance says that researchers have absolute freedom to study what they want and that ethical standards are a matter of individual conscience. Christians's feminist-communitarian framework elaborates a *contextual-consequential framework* that stresses mutual respect, noncoercion, nonmanipulation, and the support of democratic values (see Guba & Lincoln, 1989, pp. 120–141; Smith, 1990; also Collins, 1990, p. 216; Mitchell, 1993).

4. This section draws from Denzin (2003, pp. 248–257).

References

American Association of University Professors. (2001). Protecting human beings: Institutional Review Boards and social science research. *Academe, 87*(3), 55–67.

American Association of University Professors. (2002). Should all disciplines be subject to the Common Rule? Human subjects of social science research. *Academe, 88*(1), 1–15.

Bateson, G. (1972). *Steps to an ecology of mind.* New York: Ballantine.

Christians, G. C. (1995). The naturalistic fallacy in contemporary interactionist-interpretive research. *Studies in Symbolic Interaction, 19,* 125–130.

Christians, G. C. (1997). The ethics of being in a communications context. In C. Christians & M. Traber (Eds.), *Communication ethics and universal values* (pp. 3–23). Thousand Oaks, CA: Sage.

Christians, G. C. (1998). The sacredness of life. *Media Development, 2,* 3–7.

Collins, P. H. (1990). *Black feminist thought.* New York: Routledge.

Guba, E. G., & Lincoln, Y. S. (1989). *Fourth generation evaluation.* Newbury Park, CA: Sage.

Lincoln, Y. S., & Cannella, G. S. (2004a). Dangerous discourses: Methodological conservatism and governmental regimes of truth. *Qualitative Inquiry, 10*(1), 5–14.

Lincoln, Y. S., & Cannella, G. S. (2004b). Qualitative research, power, and the radical right. *Qualitative Inquiry, 10*(2), 175–201.

Lincoln, Y. S., & Tierney, W. G. (2004). Qualitative research and Institutional Review Boards. *Qualitative Inquiry, 10*(2), 219–234.

Mitchell, R. J., Jr. (1993). *Secrecy and fieldwork.* Newbury Park, CA: Sage.

Pritchard, I. A. (2002). Travelers and trolls: Practitioner research and Institutional Review Boards. *Educational Researcher, 31,* 3–13.

Ryan, K., & Destefano, L. (2000). Introduction. In K. Ryan & L. Destefano (Eds.), *Evaluation in a democratic society: Deliberation, dialogue and inclusion* (pp. 1–20). San Francisco: Jossey-Bass.

Smith, L. M. (1990). Ethics, field studies, and the paradigm crisis. In E. G. Guba (Ed.), *The paradigm dialog* (pp. 137–157). Newbury Park, CA: Sage.

Vidich, A. J., & Lyman, S. M. (2000). Qualitative methods: Their history in sociology and anthropology. In N. K. Denzin & Y. S. Lincoln (Eds.), *Handbook of qualitative research* (2nd ed., pp. 37-84). Thousand Oaks, CA: Sage.

2

REFORM OF THE SOCIAL SCIENCES AND OF UNIVERSITIES THROUGH ACTION RESEARCH

Davydd J. Greenwood and Morten Levin

When dissatisfied practitioners seek to explain why important, innovative, transdisciplinary developments such as feminism, grounded theory, cultural studies, social studies of science, naturalistic inquiry, and action research have difficulty gaining a foothold and then surviving in universities, the analysis focuses on the organizational structures created by the disciplines and their aggregations into centrifugal colleges (Messer-Davidow, 2002). Most critics account for the conservative behavior of which they do not approve by referring to academic "politics," to the maintenance of mini-cartels and disciplinary monopolies that control publication, promotion, research funding, and similar processes. The apparent cause is the political power of the owners of the various disciplinary bunkers on campuses.

As "political" as this behavior seems, it is obvious worldwide that the relationship between what is done in universities—especially what we do in the social sciences—and what the rest of society (on which we depend) wants is not being handled with much political skill. In our opinion, university relationships to key external constituencies (e.g., taxpayers, national and state government funders, private foundations, our surrounding communities, and public and private sector organizations) embody politically (and economically) self-destructive behavior.

A great number of university social scientists write about each other and for each other, purposely engaging as little as possible in public debates and in issues that are socially salient. Often, their research is written up in a language and with concepts that are incomprehensible to the people who are the "subjects" of research and to those outside the university who might want to use the findings. That philosophers, mathematicians, or musicologists do this fits their image as humanists conserving and enhancing ideas and productions of human value, regardless of their direct applicability. That social scientists do this as well, despite their claims to study and comprehend the workings of society, is more problematic.

Put more bluntly, most social science disciplines have excused themselves from social engagement by defining doing "social science" as separate from the application of their insights. The remaining gestures toward social engagement are left mainly to the social science associations' mission statements. The cost of this disengagement to the social sciences is visible in the small state and federal research allocations for academic social science research.[1]

These observations raise the following questions: How can social scientists be at once so "political" on campus and so impolitic in relation to society at large? Why is it that the knowledge created by social science research seldom leads to solutions to major societal problems? Why is it that social disengagement is more typical than atypical for social scientists? This chapter is our effort to sort out these issues. We seek to account for the disconnection between the internal politics of professional practice and the external constituencies of the conventional social sciences (e.g., sociology, anthropology, political science, and many branches of economics) in view of the fact that those external constituencies provide the financial and institutional support needed for the survival of the social sciences. We then present an alternative approach to social science and action research, because we believe that action research is key to the needed fundamental transformation of the behaviors engaged in by social scientists.

▣ Why Is There Such a Disconnection Between the Social Sciences and Society at Large?

There is no one right way to conceptualize and understand the relationship between social science work at universities and society at large, and different perspectives lead to different insights. What we offer is simply our view, based on the use of three elements: Marxism, the sociology of the professions, and historical/developmental perspectives.

Marxist or Neo-Marxist Views

These analytical frameworks stress the impact of the larger political economy on institutions and ideologies, including those of the academy (Silva & Slaughter, 1984; Slaughter & Leslie, 1997). From this perspective, the principal function of universities is the reproduction of social class differences through teaching, research, and the provision of new generations with access to key positions of power within the class system. From a Marxist perspective, universities contain a complex mix of elements that involve both promoting and demoting the claims of aspirants to social mobility.

Universities emphasize respect for the past and its structuring value schemes while simultaneously engaging in research designed to change the human condition. Much of this research is externally funded, placing universities in a service relationship to existing structures of power. Furthermore, most universities are both tax exempt and tax subsidized, placing them in a relationship of subordination to the state and to the public. Despite this, it is quite typical for many of those employed in universities to forget that they are beneficiaries of public subsidies.

As work organizations, universities are characterized by strong hierarchical structures and a number of superimposed networks. They are divided into colleges, with further division of the colleges into disciplinary departments and the departments into subdisciplines, with nationally and internationally networked sets of relationships linking individual researchers to each other. Teaching is strongly controlled bureaucratically, but the organization of research is more entrepreneurial and more determined by the researchers themselves. Despite the recruitment of some senior faculty into administrative roles, universities increasingly are run by managers who often have strongly Tayloristic visions of work organization and who operate at a great distance from the site of value production.

As in feudalism, administrative power is wielded by enforcing competitiveness among the units. Academic management philosophies and schemes generally mimic those of the private sector, but with a time delay measured in years. As a result, most of the recent efforts to become more "businesslike" in universities involve the application of management strategies already tried and discarded by the private sector (Birnbaum, 2000).

Ideologically, universities claim to serve the "public good" by educating the young for good jobs and conducting research that is in society's interest or that directly creates value for society. Internal management ideologies stress cost-effectiveness, encouragement of entrepreneurial activity in university operations, competitiveness in student admissions and support services, and entrepreneurialism in attracting research money and alumni gifts.

The Tayloristic and economistic ideologies of cost-effectiveness and market tests, increasingly used by university administrators and boards of trustees to discipline campus activities, have to deal with the crippling inconvenience that there are few true "market tests" for academic activity. As a result, administrative "impressions" and beliefs often substitute for market tests, and framing them in "market" language serves mainly to obscure the constant shifts of power within the system, including shifts in the structures of patron-client relationships, changes in favoritisms, and the ongoing consolidation of administrative power. This situation is basically the same in most industrial societies, even if the university forms part of the public administrative system, as it does in many European countries.

At the level of work organization, universities are characterized by intensely hierarchical relationships between senior and junior faculty; between faculty and staff; and among faculty, students, and staff. The same contradictions between public political expressions of prosocial values and privately competitive and entrepreneurial behaviors that characterize major corporations and political parties are visible within university structures at all levels. The notion of egalitarian collegiality, often used to describe relationships between "disciplinary" peers, rarely is visible and arises usually when a disciplinary peer group is under threat or is trying to wrest resources from other such groups. Most people involved in the workings of universities—faculty, students, administrators, and staff—experience them as profoundly authoritarian workplaces.

Sociology of the Professions Views

Perhaps the most abundant literature on the issues discussed in this chapter is found in the many variants of the sociology of the professions. These approaches range among Marxist, functionalist, and intepretivist strategies and resist easy summary (see Abbott, 1988; Brint, 1996; Freidson, 1986; Krause, 1996). What they share is a more "internalist" perspective than is commonly found in the more comprehensive Marxist/neo-Marxist framings of these issues. The sociology of the professions focuses on the multiple structurings of professional powers. These structurings involve centrally the development of boundary maintenance mechanisms that serve to include, exclude, certify, and decertify practitioners and groups of practitioners. This literature also emphasizes the development of internal professional power structures that set agendas for work, that define the "discipline" of which the profession is an embodiment, and that establish the genealogies of some of the most powerful subgroups of practitioners and turn these partisan genealogies into a "history" of the profession (Madoo Lengermann & Niebrugge-Brantley, 1998).

In these approaches, the self-interest of the established academic practitioners is central. Essential to professionalism is that a strong boundary exist between what is inside and what is outside the profession. This is key to the development of academic professional structures and also directly requires that groups of professional colleagues engage in numerous transactions with superordinate systems of power in order to be certified by them. To function, the academic professions must be accepted and accredited by those in power at universities, yet members of the profession owe principal allegiance to their professional peers, not to their universities.

Within the university structure, disciplinary department chairs—no matter how important their discipline might be—are subordinate to deans, provosts, and presidents. Thus, a department chair who might be a major player in the national and international disciplinary associations in his or her field is, on campus, a relatively low-level functionary. This situation often leads to a double strategy. Ambitious department chairs work on the ranking of their departments in various national schemes in order to acquire and control university resources. Deans, provosts, and vice-chancellors must pay attention to these rankings because declines in the rankings of the units in their charge are part of the pseudo-market test of their abilities as academic administrators.

Such professional strategies have some advantages for senior academic administrators or public higher education officials because they encourage the faculty and the departments to compete mainly with each other. In this way, the disciplines "discipline" each other and permit higher administrators to behave like referees in a contest. Clearly, organizations structured this way are generally passive in relation to central power and are relatively easy to control. These campus controls are backed up by national ranking schemes that encourage further competitiveness and by state and national funding schemes that set the terms of the competition within groups and that privilege and punish professional groups according to extradisciplinary criteria.

Students and junior colleagues are socialized into these structures through required curricula, examinations, ideological pressures, and threats to their ability to continue in the profession. Their attention is driven inward and away from the external relations or social roles/responsibilities of their professions, and certainly away from issuing any challenges to higher authorities.

These structures, of course, are highly sensitive to the larger management schemes into which they fit and to the larger political economy. As a result, there are quite dramatic national differences in the composition, mission, and ranking of different professions, as Elliott Krause has shown (1996), but pursuing this topic would take us beyond the scope of this chapter.

Historical/Developmental Views

Perhaps the best-developed literature on these topics comes from history. Scholars such as Mary Furner (1975), Ellen Messer-Davidow (2002), Dorothy Ross (1991), and George Stocking, Jr. (1968) have documented and analyzed the long-run transitions in the social sciences and the humanities. There are also scores of self-promoting and self-protective professional association histories (i.e., the "official stories"). We ignore this latter set here, finding them useful as ethnographic documents but not as explanations of the processes involved. There is an advantage in having a long time perspective because large-scale changes in the disciplines often become sharply visible only when viewed as they develop over several decades.

The literature on the history of the social sciences in the United States suggests something like the following narrative. It begins with the founding of the American Social Science Association in 1865 as an association of senior academics who would study and debate major issues of public policy and provide governments and corporate leaders with supposedly balanced advice. By the 1880s, this approach began to wane, and the various social science disciplinary associations emerged, beginning with economics. The link between the founding of these associations and the emergence of disciplinary departments in PhD-granting institutions was a sea change in the trajectory of the social sciences and resulted in many of the structures that exist today.

The works of Mary Furner (1975), Patricia Madoo Lengermann and Jill Niebrugge-Brantley (1998), Ellen Messer-Davidow (2002), and Edward Silva and Sheila Slaughter (1984) amplify this larger picture by showing how the institutionalization of the disciplines and their professional associations was achieved through homogenizing the intellectual and political agendas of each field, ejecting the reformers, and creating the self-regulating and self-regarding disciplinary structures that are so powerful in universities today.

These histories also show that these outcomes were human products, were context dependent, and were fought over for decades at a time. Despite differences in the disciplines and in timing, the overall trajectory from "advocacy to objectivity" (as Furner [1975] phrased it) seems to be overdetermined. One of the sobering apparent lessons of these histories is that the prospect of rebuilding a socially connected or, less likely, a socially reformist agenda in the conventional social sciences not only faces negative odds but also runs directly counter to the course of 120 years of disciplinary histories.

Just how this process of disciplinarization and domestication applies to the newer social sciences (e.g., policy studies, management studies, organizational behavior) is not clear, as there is little critical historical work available. Impressionistically, it seems to us that these newer social sciences are beginning to repeat the process undergone in conventional social sciences, a process that resulted in their current disciplinarization and separation from engagement in the everyday world of social practice.

The consistent divergence between theory and practice in all the social science fields is especially notable. How this develops in a group of disciplines explicitly founded to inform social practice should puzzle everyone. Even the great national differences that appear in these trajectories and their organizational contexts do not overcome the global dynamics of disciplinarization and the segregation of theory from practice in academic work. Whatever the causes of these consistent phenomena, they must be both powerful and global. There appear to be direct links among disciplinarization, the purging of reformers, and the splitting of theory and practice, with theory becoming the focus of the academic social sciences. Having better understandings of these dynamics obviously is crucial to the future of the social sciences.

The above, highly selective, survey suggests a few things about this subject. There is ample reason to agree with Pierre Bourdieu's (1994) observation that academics resist being self-reflective about their professional practice. As interesting as the materials we have cited are, they are a very small window into a largely unstudied world. We social scientists generally do not apply our own social science frameworks to the study of our professional behavior. Instead, we permit ourselves to inhabit positions and espouse ideologies often in direct conflict with the very theories and methods we claim to have created (Bourdieu, 1994). For example, Greenwood has pointed out repeatedly that when threatened, anthropologists—who for generations assiduously have deconstructed the notion of the homogeneity and stability of notions like "tradition"—often refer to the "traditions" of anthropology as an ideological prop to defend their professional interests.

It is also striking how little academics reflect upon and understand the idea that they are members of a larger work organization in which relationships both to colleagues and to management have important effects on their capacity to do academic work. "Social" scientists regularly conceptualize themselves as solo entrepreneurs, leaving aside their professional knowledge of social structures and power relations, as if these were only disguises they wear while making their way into the "discipline."

The Political Economy Within Institutions of Higher Education

Whatever else one concludes from the above, it should be clear that what happens on university campuses is not isolated from what happens in society at large. The notion of the "ivory tower" notwithstanding, universities are both "in" and "of" their societies, but it is important to understand that these external forces do not apply across a smooth, undifferentiated internal academic surface. Universities show a high degree of internal differentiation, and this differentiation matters a great deal to our topic of university reform.

The internal political economy of universities is heterogeneous. In the United States and in other industrialized societies, one of the strongly emergent features of university life is the highly entrepreneurial behavior in the sciences and in engineering. Driven by the governmental and private sector markets and by explicit higher education policy designs, these fields have become expert in and structurally organized to capture, manage, and recapture the governmental and private sector funds that keep their research operations going. A complex web of interpenetrated interests links governments, businesses, and university scientists and engineers in a collaborative activity in which senior scientists and engineers basically become entrepreneurs who manage large laboratories and research projects, with the assistance of large numbers of graduate assistants, lab technicians, and grants administrators.

Social scientists, except those in the relatively rare environments of major contract research shops (such as the University of Michigan's Survey Research Center), are not so organized. Groups of economists, some psychologists, and some sociologists occasionally manage to mount multi-person projects, found institutes, support some graduate students, and bring some resources into the university. In this regard, from a university budgetary point of view, they are scientist-like, with the virtue that their research does not require the large infrastructural investments typical of much scientific research. The activities of even the most successful economists, psychologists, and sociologists, however, appear minuscule financially when compared to the scale of what goes on in the natural sciences and engineering.

Generally speaking, in political science, anthropology, and the qualitative branches of sociology and psychology, the funding sources brought in for external research are derisory. As a consequence, from the point of view of a central financial officer at a university, large proportions of the budgets for the social sciences and the humanities in the U.S. context represent calls on the university's resources that are not matched by an external revenue source. Instead, the social sciences and humanities, focused as they are on issues of social critique, interdisciplinary research, gender, and positionality, provide a kind of prestige to universities. They are part of the university "offering" that makes an institution seem appropriately academic, but their activities are maintained by cross-subsidies, justified in ideological rather than economic terms, and always in danger of being cut off.

Because self-justification in terms of financial revenues in excess of costs is not possible, the social sciences generally focus on being highly ranked nationally among their competitor departments at other universities. That is, they substitute one kind of market test for another. These national rankings follow a variety of reputational and accountancy schemes and are the subject of both strong critique and constant attention in the United States, the United Kingdom, and, increasingly, elsewhere.

Explaining how these ranking systems were generated and are maintained would take us beyond the scope of this chapter, but such an explanation must be provided. Suffice it to say that the disciplinary departments need to do well in national rankings in order to carry clout on campus, to recruit bright faculty, and to attract good undergraduate and graduate students. A great deal of energy goes into assessing, managing, and debating these rankings.

These dynamics create a heterogeneous surface within universities. The sciences, engineering, parts of economics, psychology (mainly laboratory work) and sociology (mainly quantitative), the applied fields of management, and law all generate significant revenues. Most are either organized as profit centers or are understood to be self-financing and to be good investments. By contrast, the rest of the social sciences (including all those practicing qualitative methods) and the humanities depend for their survival on redistributions from these "profitable" units and on subsidies from tuition, the general fund, alumni giving, and earnings on university investments. That is to say, a competitive, market-based research economy—in which the deans, individual entrepreneurial academics, and others seek to minimize costs and maximize earnings—coexists with a redistributive economy in which those who generate expenses without revenues are the net beneficiaries of the profits of others.

Whatever else this means, it suggests that a university "economy" is a complex organization in which a variety of economic principles are at work and in which the relationships among the sciences, engineering, the social sciences, and the humanities are negotiated through the central administration. Counterintuitively, there currently exists no overall management model that explicitly conceptualizes these conditions or provides guidance about how to manage them effectively for the ongoing growth of the organization. Rather, given the hierarchical structure of decision making described above, senior administrators are faced with attempting to keep a complex system afloat while not being able to operate most of the units in an "economic" way. To put it more bluntly, the complexity of university "economies" is such that neither faculty nor senior administrators have relevant understandings to guide them in making choices. No one can turn to well-argued visions about the principles that should be used to operate a university, about how much entrepreneurial activity is compatible with university life, and about what happens when and if tuition revenues, research contracts, patent income, and alumni gifts start oscillating wildly. Neither social democratic nor neoliberal models are adequate to the task. In the absence of intelligently structured models, simplistic neoliberal fiscal fantasies take over, to the detriment of everyone (Rhind, 2003).

This is the internal "political economy" of the contemporary research university. Because its structures are neither widely understood nor carefully studied, most university administrators and public authorities apply less differentiated, monodimensional management models to universities, succumbing often to the temptation of attempting to view whole universities as for-profit businesses and thereby making both "irrational" and counterproductive decisions, engaging in anti-economic behavior, and supporting unjustified and highly politicized cross-subsidies while not guaranteeing the survival of their institutions.

What Counts as Knowledge in Contemporary Universities?

If, among other things, one of the key missions of universities is the production and transmission of knowledge, then what counts as knowledge is central to any definition and proposed reform of universities. Within this, what counts as social science knowledge is quite problematic.

Just because universities are, among other things, knowledge producing systems, it is not necessarily the case that universities have a very clear idea about what constitutes relevant knowledge. There are some conventional views of knowledge in the sciences and engineering that at least keep their enterprises funded, but the views of knowledge in current circulation are not much help when we try to think about the social sciences.

The conventional understanding of knowledge tends to be grounded in its explicit forms: what can be recorded in words, numbers, and figures and thus is explicitly accessible for humans. Based on this understanding, knowledge tends to be treated as an individualistic, cognitive phenomenon formed by the ability to capture insights (Fuller, 2002). This conception of knowledge is of very little use in the social sciences and the humanities, and challenging this view is necessary to our argument.

Social Science Knowledge

If we attempt to conceptualize social science knowledge, consistent with its origins, as the knowledge that is necessary to create a bridge between social research and the knowledge needs of society at large, then the disconnection between what currently counts as social science knowledge and what serves society's needs is nearly complete. In what follows, we intend to create a different picture by expanding the understanding of what counts as knowledge to include bridging concrete practical intelligence and reflective and value-based reflectivity.

Knowing

Very limited organizational and administrative meanings attach to knowledge concepts at universities. Contemporary debates about what constitutes knowledge can add three important dimensions to commonsense notions, dimensions that have the potential for shifting the way universities generate and apply knowledge.

Tacit Knowing

Much of our knowing is tacit; it expresses itself in our actions. We focus on the verb *knowing* instead of the noun *knowledge* because knowing emphasizes the point that knowledge is linked to people's actions. Tacit knowing is a term generally attributed to Michael Polanyi (1974), and Polanyi's argument is partially built on the arguments in *The Concept of Mind* written by Oxford philosopher Gilbert Ryle (1949). In Polanyi's view, tacit knowing connotes the "hidden" understandings that guide our actions without our ability to explicitly communicate what the knowledge is.

Knowing How

Although Polanyi's work is more recent, in our view, Ryle created a more fruitful concept than Polanyi's "tacit knowing" by introducing the notion of "knowing how." "Knowing how" grounds knowledge in actions and, because this is precisely how we are able to identify tacit knowing, knowing how seems a more direct anchor to use.

Collective Knowing

Knowledge is also inherently collective. Work by Berger and Luckmann (1967) and Schutz (1967/1972) on the social construction of social realities paved the road for a deeper understanding of knowing as a socially constructed and socially distributed phenomenon. People working together develop and share knowledge as a collective effort and collective product, the petty commodity view of knowledge production notwithstanding (Greenwood, 1991).

Bent Flyvbjerg (2001) follows a somewhat different path but ends up making some of the same distinctions. He refers to the work of Aristotle in making a taxonomy based on *episteme* (theoretical knowledge), *techne* (pragmatic and context-dependent practical rationality[2]), and *phronesis* (practical and context-dependent deliberation about values).

He seeks a solution to the current dilemmas of the social sciences by advocating a closer link to *phronesis.*[3] The argument is that *techne* and *phronesis* constitute the necessary "know-how" for organizational change, social reform, and regional economic development. Neither we nor Flyvbjerg assign any special priority to *episteme,* the conventional and favored form of explicit and theoretical knowledge and the form that currently dominates the academic social sciences.

The Aristotelian distinctions between *episteme*, *techne*, and *phronesis* center on distinguishing three kinds of knowledge. One is not superior to the other; all are equally valid forms of knowing in particular contexts. The key here is the equal validity of these forms of knowing when they are properly contextualized and deployed.

Episteme centers fundamentally on contemplative ways of knowing aimed at understanding the eternal and unchangeable operations of the world. The sources of *episteme* are multiple—speculative, analytical, logical, and experiential—but the focus is always on eternal truths beyond their materialization in concrete situations. Typically, the kinds of complexity found in *episteme* take the form of definitional statements, logical connections, and building of models and analogies. *Episteme* is highly self-contained because it is deployed mainly in theoretical discourses themselves. Although *episteme* obviously is not a self-contained activity, it aims to remove as many concrete empirical referents as possible in order to achieve the status of general truth.

If this meaning of *episteme* accords rather closely to everyday usage of the term *theory*, this is not the case with *techne* and *phronesis. Techne* is one of two other kinds of knowledge beyond *episteme. Techne* arises from Aristotle's poetical episteme. It is a form of knowledge that is inherently action oriented and inherently productive. *Techne* engages in the analysis of what should be done in the world in order to increase human happiness. The sources of *techne* are multiple. They necessarily involve sufficient experiential engagement in the world to permit the analysis of "what should be done." It is a mode of knowing and acting of its own. To quote Flyvbjerg, "*Techne* is thus craft and art, and as an activity it is concrete, variable, and context-dependent. The objective of *techne* is application of technical knowledge and skills according to a pragmatic instrumental rationality, what Foucault calls 'a practical rationality governed by a conscious goal'" (Flyvbjerg, 2001, p. 56).

The development of *techne* involves, first and foremost, the creation of that conscious goal, the generation of ideas of better designs for living that will increase human happiness. The types of complexity involved in *techne* arise around the debate among ideal ends, the complex contextualization of these ends, and the instrumental design of activities to enhance the human condition. *Techne* is not the application of *episteme* and, indeed, its link to *episteme* is tenuous in many situations. *Techne* arises from its own sources in moral/ethical debate and visions of an ideal society.

Techne is evaluated primarily by impact measures developed by the professional experts themselves who decide whether or not their projects have enhanced human happiness and, if not, why not. Practitioners of *techne* do engage with local stakeholders, power holders, and other experts, often being contracted by those in power to attempt to achieve positive social changes. Their relationship to the subjects of their work is often close and collaborative, but they are first and foremost professional experts who do things "for," not "with," the local stakeholders. They bring general designs and habits of work to the local case and privilege their own knowledge over that of the local stakeholders.

Phronesis is a less well-known idea. Formally defined by Aristotle as internally consistent reasoning that deals with all possible particulars, *phronesis* is best understood as the design of action through collaborative knowledge construction with the legitimate stakeholders in a problematic situation.

The sources of *phronesis* are collaborative arenas for knowledge development in which the professional researcher's knowledge is combined with the local knowledge of the stakeholders in defining the problem to be addressed. Together, they design and implement the research that needs to be done to understand the problem. They then design the actions to improve the situation together, and they evaluate the adequacy of what was done. If they are not satisfied, they cycle through the process again until the results are satisfactory to all the parties.

The types of complexity involved in *phronesis* are at once intellectual, contextual, and social, as *phronesis* involves the creation of a new space for collaborative reflection, the contrast and integration of many kinds of knowledge systems, the linking of the general and the particular through action and analysis, and the collaborative design of both the goals and the actions aimed at achieving them.

Phronesis is a practice that is deployed in groups in which all the stakeholders—both research experts and local collaborators—have legitimate knowledge claims and rights to determine the outcome. It is evaluated by the collaborators diversely according to their interests, but all share an interest in the adequacy of the outcomes achieved in relation to the goals they collaboratively developed. Thus, *phronesis* involves an egalitarian engagement across knowledge systems and diverse experiences.

This praxis-oriented knowing, which is collective, develops out of communities of practice, to use the wording of Brown and Duguid (1991) and Wenger (1998). This literature pinpoints how people, through working together, develop and cultivate knowledge that enables the participants to take the appropriate actions to achieve the goals they seek. The core perspective is a conceptualization of knowledge as inscribed in actions that are collectively developed and shared by people working together. Explicit knowledge is present and necessary but not dominant.

This kind of knowing linked to action inherently has physical and technological dimensions. Theoretical capability is necessary, but no results ever will be achieved unless local actors learn how to act in appropriate and effective ways and use suitable tools and methods. Thus technique, technology, and knowledge merge in an understanding of *knowing how to act* to reach certain desired goals. Knowledge is not a passive form of reflection but emerges through actively struggling to know how to act in real-world contexts with real-world materials.

When knowledge is understood as *knowing how to act*, skillful actions are always highly contextual. It is impossible to conceptualize action as taking place in a "generalized" environment. To act is to contextualize behavior, and being able to act skillfully implies that actions are appropriate to the given context. The actor needs to make sense of the context to enable appropriate actions. "Knowing how" thus implies knowing how in a given context in which appropriate actions emerge from contextual knowing. The conventional understanding of general knowledge that treats it as supracontextual and thus universally applicable is of very little interest to us because we do not believe that what constitutes knowledge in the social sciences can be addressed usefully from the hothouse of armchair intellectual debate.

Why Knowledge Matters to Universities

Universities increasingly view themselves as knowledge generation and knowledge management organizations, and they attempt to profit from knowledge generation efforts and gain or retain control over knowledge products that have a value in the marketplace (Fuller, 2002). In this regard, scientific and engineering knowledge has led the way, creating patentable discoveries and processes that, at least in the United States, make significant contributions to the financial well-being of research universities. There are pressures for the expansion of this commodity production notion of knowledge into broader spheres, pressures that go along with increasing emphasis on cost-benefit models in decision making by higher education managers.

Just how this struggle over the university generation, management, and sale of knowledge will turn out is not clear. On one hand, research universities increasingly act to commoditize knowledge production to create regular revenue flows (as well as academic prestige in the commodity production–based ranking systems). In the sciences, this has led to a spate of applied research and a de-emphasis on basic research. In the social sciences, the bulk of the external research money available to university social science is for positivistic research on economic issues, demographic trends, and public attitudes.

Whatever else it does, the current academic fiscal regime does not support unequivocally *episteme*-centered views of social science knowledge. However, it is also clear that few universities support "knowing how" work either, because such work focuses attention on fundamental needs for social and economic reform and thus often irritates public and private sector constituencies and wealthy donors. There is almost no indication that existing research funding patterns support more linked efforts between multiple academic partners and relevant non-university stakeholders.

The "Humpty Dumpty" Problem

Another difficulty in the way universities, most particularly in the social sciences, organize knowledge production activities has been called the "Humpty Dumpty" problem by Waddock and Spangler:

> Specialization in professions today resembles all the king's horses and all the king's men tackling the puzzle created by the fragments of Humpty Dumpty's broken body. Professionals . . . are tackling problems with only some of the knowledge needed to solve the problems. . . . Despite the fragmentation into professional specialties, professionals and managers are expected to somehow put their—and only their—pieces of Humpty Dumpty back together again. Further, they are to accomplish this task without really understanding what Humpty looked like in the first place, or what the other professions can do to make him whole again. Clearly, this model does not work. In addition to their traditional areas of expertise, professionals must be able to see society holistically, thorough lenses capable of integrating multiple perspectives simultaneously. (Waddock & Spangler, 2000, p. 211)

The Humpty Dumpty problem is relevant because the world does not issue problems in neat disciplinary packages. Problems come up as complex, multidimensional, and often confusing congeries of issues. To deal with them, their multiple dimensions must be understood, as well as what holds them together as problems. Only a university work organization that moves easily across boundaries between forms of expertise and between insider and outsider knowledges can deal with such problems.

Action Research as "Science"[4]

We reject arguments for separating praxis and theory in social research. Either social research is collaboratively applied or we do not believe that it deserves to be called research. It should simply be called what it is: speculation. The terms "pure" and "applied" research, current everywhere in university life, imply that a division of labor between the "pure" and the "applied" can exist. We believe that this division makes social research impossible. Thus, for us, the world divides into action research, which we support and practice, and conventional social research (subdivided into pure and applied social research and organized into professional subgroupings) that we reject on combined epistemological, methodological, and ethical/political grounds (Greenwood & Levin, 1998a, 1998b, 2000a, 2000b, 2001a, 2001b; Levin & Greenwood, 1998).

Because of the dominance of positivistic frameworks and *episteme* in the organization of the conventional social sciences, our view automatically is heard as a retreat from the scientific method into "activism." To hard-line interpretivists, we are seen as so epistemologically naïve as not to understand that it is impossible to commit ourselves to any course of action on the basis of any kind of social research, since all knowledge is contingent and positional—the ultimate form of self-justifying inaction. The operating assumptions in the conventional social sciences are that greater relevance and engagement automatically involves a loss of scientific validity or a loss of courage in the face of the yawning abyss of endless subjectivity.

Pragmatism

A different grounding for social research can be found in pragmatic philosophy. Dewey, James, Pierce, and others (Diggins, 1994) offer an interesting and fruitful foundation for ontological and epistemological questions inherent in social research that is action relevant. Pragmatism links theory and praxis. The core reflection process is connected to action outcomes that involve manipulating material and social factors in a given context. Experience emerges in a continual interaction between people and their environment; accordingly, this process constitutes both the subjects and objects of inquiry. The actions taken are purposeful and aim at creating desired outcomes. Hence, the knowledge creation process is based on the inquirers' norms, values, and interests.

Validity claims are identified as "warranted" assertions resulting from an inquiry process in which an indeterminate situation is made determinate through concrete actions in an actual context. The research logic is constituted in the inquiry process itself, and it guides the knowledge generation process.

Although it seems paradoxical to positivists, with their *episteme*-based views of knowledge, as action researchers we strongly advocate the use of scientific methods and emphasize the importance and possibility of the creation of valid knowledge in social research (see Greenwood & Levin, 1998b). Furthermore, we believe that this kind of inquiry is a foundational element in democratic processes in society and is the core mission of the "social" sciences.

These general characteristics of the pragmatist position ground the action research approach. Two central parameters stand out clearly: knowledge generation through action and experimentation in context, and participative democracy as both a method and a goal. Neither of these is routinely found in the current academic social sciences.

The Action Research Practice of Science

Everyone is supposed to know by now that social research is different from the study of atoms, molecules, rocks, tigers, slime molds, and other physical objects. Yet one can only be amazed by the emphasis that so many conventional social scientists still place on the claim that being "scientific" requires researchers to sever all relations with the observed. Though epistemologically and methodologically indefensible, this view is still largely dominant in social science practice, most particularly in the fields gaining the bulk of social science research money and dominating the world of social science publications: economics, sociology, and political science. This positivistic credo obviously is wrong, and it leads away from producing reliable information, meaningful interpretations, and social actions in social research. It has been subjected to generations of critique, even from within the conventional social sciences.[5] Yet it persists, suggesting that its social embeddedness itself deserves attention.

We believe that strong interventions in the organization of universities and the academic professions are required to root it out. Put more simply, the epistemological ideas underlying action research are not new ideas; they simply have been purged as conventional social researchers (and the social interests they serve—consciously or unconsciously) have rejected university engagement in social reform.

Cogenerative Inquiry

Action research aims to solve pertinent problems in a given context through democratic inquiry in which professional researchers collaborate with local stakeholders to seek and enact solutions to problems of major importance to the stakeholders. We refer to this as cogenerative inquiry because it is built on professional researcher–stakeholder collaboration and aims to solve real-life problems in context. Cogenerative inquiry processes involve trained professional researchers and knowledgeable local stakeholders who work together to define the problems to be addressed, to gather and organize relevant knowledge and data, to analyze the resulting information, and to design social change interventions. The relationship between the professional researcher and the local stakeholders is based on bringing the diverse bases of their knowledge and their distinctive social locations to bear on a problem collaboratively. The professional researcher often brings knowledge of other relevant cases and of relevant research methods, and he or she often has experience in organizing research processes. The insiders have extensive and long-term knowledge of the problems at hand and the contexts in which they occur, as well as knowledge about how and from whom to get additional information. They also contribute urgency and focus to the process, because it centers on problems they are eager to solve. Together, these partners create a powerful research team.

Local Knowledge and Professional Knowledge

For cogenerative inquiry to occur, the collaboration must be based on an interaction between local knowledge and professional knowledge. Whereas conventional social research and consulting privileges professional knowledge over local knowledge, action research does not. Given the complexity of the problems addressed, only local stakeholders, with their years of experience in a particular situation, have sufficient information and knowledge about the situation to design effective social change processes. We do not, however, romanticize local knowledge and denigrate professional knowledge. Both forms of knowledge are essential to cogenerative inquiry.

Validity, Credibility, and Reliability

Validity, credibility, and reliability in action research are measured by the willingness of local stakeholders to act on the results of the action research, thereby risking their welfare on the "validity" of their ideas and the degree to which the outcomes meet their expectations. Thus, cogenerated contextual knowledge is deemed valid if it generates warrants for action. The core validity claim centers on the workability of the actual social change activity engaged in, and the test is whether or not the actual solution to a problem arrived at solves the problem.

Dealing With Context-Centered Knowledge

Communicating context-centered knowledge effectively to academics and to other potential users is a complex process. The action research inquiry process is linked intimately to action in context. This means considerable challenges in communicating and abstracting results in a way that others who did not participate in a particular project, including other stakeholder groups facing comparable but not identical situations, will understand. Precisely because the knowledge is cogenerated, includes local knowledge and analyses, and is built deeply into the local context, comparison of results across cases and the creation of generalizations is a challenge.[6]

Comparison and Generalization

We do not think that these complexities justify having handed over the territory of comparative generalization and abstract theorization to conventional social researchers working in an *episteme* mode only. The approach of positivistic research to generalization has been to abstract from context, average out cases, lose sight of the world as lived in by human beings, and generally make the knowledge gained impossible to apply (which, for us, means that it is not "knowledge" at all). Despite the vast sums of money and huge numbers of person-hours put into this kind of research, we find the theoretical harvest scanty. On the other side, the rejection of the possibility of learning and generalizing at all, typical of much interpretivism, constructivism, and vulgar postmodernism, strikes us as an equally open invitation to intellectual posturing without any sense of social or moral responsibility.

Central to the action research view of generalization is that any single case that runs counter to a generalization invalidates it (Lewin, 1948) and requires the generalization to be reformulated. In contrast, positivist research often approaches exceptional cases by attempting to disqualify them, in order to preserve the existing generalization. Rather than welcoming the opportunity to revise the generalization, the reaction often is to find a way to ignore it.

Greenwood became particularly well aware of this during his period of action research in the labor-managed cooperatives of Mondragón, Spain, the most successful labor-managed industrial cooperatives anywhere (see Greenwood, González Santos, et al., 1992). Because the "official story" is that cooperatives cannot succeed, that Spaniards are religious fanatics, and that they are not good at working hard or at making money, the bulk of the literature on Mondragón in the 1960s and 1970s attempted to explain the case away as a mere oddity. Basque cultural predispositions, charismatic leadership, and solidarity were all tried as ways of making this exception one that could be ignored, letting the celebration of the supposed greater competitiveness of the standard capitalist firm go on unaffected by this, and other, glaring exceptions. Positivist theorists did not want to learn from the case, in direct contravention of the requirements of scientific thinking that view important exceptions as the most potentially valuable sources of new knowledge.

William Foote Whyte (1982) captured the idea of the productivity of exceptions in his concept of "social inventions." He proposed that all forms of business organizations could learn from this Basque case by trying to figure out how the unique social inventions they had made helped explain their success. Having identified these inventions, researchers could then begin the process of figuring out which of them could be generalized and diffused to other contexts where their utility could be tested, again in collaborative action. Of course, the key to this approach is that the validity of the comparison is also tested in action and not treated as a thought experiment.

If we readdress generalizations in light of what we have argued above, we reframe generalization in action research terms as necessitating a process of reflective action rather than as being based on structures of rule-based interpretation. Given our position that knowledge is context bound, the key to utilizing this knowledge in a different setting is to follow a two-step model. First, it is important to understand the contextual conditions under which the knowledge has been created. This recognizes the inherent contextualization of the knowledge itself. Second, the transfer of this knowledge to another setting implies understanding the contextual conditions of the new setting, how these differ from the setting in which the knowledge was produced, and it involves a reflection on what consequences this has for applying the actual knowledge in the new context. Hence, generalization becomes an active process of reflection in which involved actors must make up their minds whether the previous knowledge makes sense in the new context or not and begin working on ways of acting in the new context.

Although it would take much more space to make the full case (see Greenwood & Levin, 1998b), we have said enough to make it clear that action research is not some kind of a social science dead end. It is a disciplined way of developing valid knowledge and theory while promoting positive social change.

Reconstructing the Relationships Between Universities and Social Stakeholders

We believe that the proper response to the epistemological, methodological, political economic, and ethical issues we have been raising is to reconstruct the relationships between the universities and the multiple stakeholders in society. We believe that a significant part of the answer is to make action research *the* central strategy in social research and organizational development. This is because action research, as we have explained above, involves research efforts in which the users (such as governments, social service agencies, corporations large and small, communities, and nongovernmental organizations) have a definite stake in the problems under study and in which the research process integrates collaborative teaching/learning among multiple disciplines with groups of these non-university partners. We know that this kind of university-based action research is possible because a number of successful examples exist. We will end this chapter by providing an account of two such examples, drawn from a much larger set.

Social Science–Engineering Research Relationships and University-Industry Cooperation: The "Offshore Yard"[7]

This project began when the Norwegian Research Council awarded a major research and development contract to SINTEF, a Norwegian research organization located in Trondheim and closely linked to the Norwegian University of Science and Technology. This contract focused on what is called "enterprise modeling," an information systems–centered technique for developing models of complex organizational processes, both to improve efficiency and to restructure organizational behavior. SINTEF received the contract for this work as part of a major national initiative to support applied research and organizational development in manufacturing industries.

A key National Research Council requirement for this program was that engineering research on enterprise modeling had to be linked to social science research on organization and leadership. This required the collaboration of engineers and social scientists within SINTEF of a more intensive sort than usual. The National Research Council argued that enterprise modeling could not be reduced to a technical effort and that the enterprise models themselves had to deal with organizational issues as well, because their deployment would depend on the employees' ability to use the models as "tools" in everyday work.

The research focus of this activity was not clear at the outset. The instrumental goal for the national research organization was to create a useful enterprise model rather than one that would be only a nice puzzle for information technologists to solve. The research focus emerged in the form of an engineering focus on enterprise models as learning opportunities for all employees and a social science focus on participatory change processes.

The Offshore Yard agreed to be a partner in this effort, and the project was launched in early 1996. The Yard employs approximately 1,000 persons and is located a 90-minute drive north of Trondheim on the Trondheim fjord. The yard has a long history of specializing in the design and construction of the large and complex offshore installations used in North Sea oil exploration.

The project was to be comanaged by a joint group of engineers and social scientists. The key researchers were Ivar Blikø, Terje Skarlo, Johan Elvemo, and Ida Munkeby, two engineers and two social scientists, all employed at SINTEF. The expectation was that cooperation across professional boundaries would somehow arise as an automatic feature of their being engaged in the same project.

The process was by no means so simple. Throughout the initial phase of the project, the only cooperation seen meant merely that team members were present at the company site at the same time. In part, this was because the two engineers on the team had a long history with the company. They had many years of contact with the company as consulting researchers, and, before that, they worked as engineers on the staff in the Yard. As a result, the engineers took the lead in the early project activity.[8] They were running the project, and the social scientists seemed fairly passive. The engineers were working concretely on computer-based mockups of enterprise models and, because this was a strong focus of planning interest in the company, they accordingly received a great deal of attention from the senior management of the yard.

While this was going on, the social scientists were devoting their attention to a general survey of the company and making an ethnographic effort to learn about the organization and social realities of the company. This was considered important to give the social scientists a grasp of what the company was like. This research-based knowledge generation meant little to company people, as this work was neither understood nor valued by the company or by the engineering members of the team.

The first opening for social science knowledge came when the social researchers organized a search conference[9] to address the problems of the organization of work at the shop floor level. This search conference produced results that captured the attention of both the local union and management and made it clear locally that the social scientists had skills that offered significant opportunities for learning and collaborative planning in the company. This was also the first time the researchers managed to include a fairly large number of employees from different layers of the organization in the same knowledge production process.

As a consequence of this experience, cooperation between the university and Offshore Yard began to deepen. At the time, the company was developing a leadership training program. Through the social scientists, company officials learned about other experiences in running such programs, and this helped them plan locally. They were better able to plan their overall organizational development activity in their own training program because knowing about other programs helped them with their design. In addition, they felt it would be an advantage to them if company participants in the training also could get official university credits for their involvement. Thus, the resulting program was designed through a university-company dialogue and, in the end, one of the social scientists on the team ran it. The program also gave official university-based credits to those participants who decided to take a formal exam. The leadership program became an effort that enhanced the formal skill level of the participants, and the university credits gave them recognition outside the context of the yard.

The program was very successful, making evident how close collaboration between the company and the university could be mutually rewarding. The university people could experiment professionally and pedagogically in real-life contexts, while the company got access to cutting-edge knowledge both from the university and from other companies, through the university's contacts. As an interesting side effect, the Yard decided to invite managers from neighboring plants to participate. The Yard recognized that its own future depended on its having good relations with its neighbors and suppliers. Company officials decided that one way to improve this cooperation was to share their program, as a gesture symbolizing the interdependent relationships they have and the mutual stakes in each other's success.

Over the course of the project, the cooperation between engineers and social scientists began to grow and create new insights. A key first move in this direction was a redesign of the tube manufacturing facility in the Yard. The reorganization of work processes that was cogeneratively developed through workers' participation meant that shop floor workers gained direct access to the computer-based production planning and scheduling the company engineers used. Instead of having information from the system filtered through the foreman, workers at the shop floor level could utilize the information system and decide for themselves how to manage the production process. This form of organizational leveling probably would not have come about had it not been for the increased mutual understanding between the SINTEF engineers and social scientists and their company partners that emerged through their working together on the same concrete problems as a team.

Gradually, based on these experiences, a reconceptualization emerged of the whole way to develop enterprise models. The conventional engineering take on enterprise models was that the experts (the engineers) collected information, made an analysis, and then made expert decisions regarding what the model should look like. A new approach to enterprise modeling in the Yard was developed in which the involved employees actually have a direct say. Although this is a modest step in the direction of participation, it is potentially a very important one. It is fair to say that this changed focus toward participation would not have occurred unless the social scientists had presented substantive knowledge on issues of organization and leadership that were testable through participatory processes.

As more mutual trust developed between company people and researchers, the marginalized position of the social scientists gradually changed, and the company came to count on the social scientists as well. For example, one of the major challenges for the company in the future will be how to manage with a significant reduction in the number of employees humanely and without destroying company morale. These changes originate both from restructuring of the corporation the Yard is part of and from new engineering and production processes that led to a reduced need for laborers. The Yard has invited the researchers to take a serious role in this process by asking them to draw, from all over the world, knowledge and diverse perspectives on this difficult subject. The researchers have been able to support new and often critical knowledge that has changed or extended the company's understanding of its downsizing challenge.

The research team also has been asked to assist in working on the learning atmosphere in the Yard. This has involved extensive interviewing of a broad spectrum of employees to build a view about how to improve the Yard's capacity for ongoing learning. The results of these interviews were fed back to the involved employees, and the researchers shaped dialogues with them that aimed both at presenting the results and at examining the inferences made by the researchers through comparison with the local knowledge of the workers. Again, we can see how models of learning with an origin in social science circles can be applied to the local learning process, and the results are important factors in the researchers' assessments of the strength and value of their academic findings.

Perhaps the most interesting overall development in this project is how the company–university relationship developed. The senior executive officer is now a strong supporter of the fruitfulness of the company's relationship with the university. In public presentations, he credits the researchers with bringing relevant and important knowledge to the company and explains that he can see how this relationship can become increasingly important. It took him several years of cooperation to see these possibilities, but now he does, and the university is glad to respond. Although there is no reason to romanticize the relationship, because differences of opinion and interest do emerge, the relationship seems so robust that further developments are likely.

In the end, only through multidisciplinary action research over a sustained period of time were these results possible. The research values and the action values in the process have both been respected, and all the partners in the process have benefited.

Collaborative Research for Organizational Transformation Within the Walls of the University

Here we report on an example of an action research initiative that occurred at Cornell University, resulting in reform of a major, required university course: introductory physics. The protagonist of this effort was Michael Reynolds, who wrote this work up as a doctoral dissertation in science education at Cornell (Reynolds, 1994).[10] Because universities are redoubts of hierarchical and territorial behavior, changes initiated by students or by graduate assistants and lecturers are rare, making this case particularly interesting.

At the time the project began, Reynolds was employed as a teaching assistant in an introductory physics course that is one of the requirements for students wishing to go to medical school. This makes the course a key gatekeeping mechanism in the very competitive process of acquiring access to the medical profession and makes the stake the students have in doing well high and the power of the faculty and university over their lives considerable. It also means that the course has a guaranteed clientele, almost no matter how badly it is taught.

Although there is more than one physics course, this particular one is crucial in completing premedical requirements. Because of a comprehensive reform undertaken in the late 1960s, this course was and is delivered in what is called an "auto-tutorial" format. This means that students work through the course materials at their own pace (within limits), doing experiments and studying in a learning center, asking for advice there, and taking examinations on each unit (often many times) until they have achieved the mastery of the material and grade they seek. Despite the inviting and apparently flexible format, the course had become notoriously unpopular among students. Performance on standardized national exams was poor, morale among the students and staff was relatively low, and the Physics department was concerned.

The staff structure included a professor in charge, a senior lecturer who was the de facto principal course manager, and some graduate assistants. Among these, Reynolds was working as a teaching assistant in the course to support himself while he worked on his PhD in Education. Having heard about action research and finding it consistent with his view of the world, he proposed to the professor and lecturer in charge that they attempt an action research evaluation and reform of the course. With Greenwood's help, they got funding from the office of the Vice President for Academic Programs to support the reform effort.

There followed a long and complex process that was skillfully guided by Reynolds. It involved the undergraduate students, teaching assistants, lecturers, professor, and members of Reynolds's PhD committee in a long-term process. It began with an evaluation of the main difficulties students had with the course, then involved the selection of a new text and piloting the revised course. Reynolds guided this process patiently and consistently. Ultimately, the professor, the lecturer, instructors, teaching assistants, and students collaborated in redesigning the course through intensive meetings and debates.

One of the things they discovered was that the course had become unworkable in part because of its very nature. As new concepts and theories were developed in physics, they were added to the course, but there was no overall system for examining what materials should be eliminated or consolidated to make room for the new ones. The result was an increasingly overstuffed course that the students found increasingly difficult to deal with. In bringing the whole course before all the stakeholders and in examining the choice of a possible new textbook, it was possible for the group to confront these issues.

There were many conflicts on issues of substance and authority during the process, which was stressful for all involved, yet they stayed together and kept at the process until they had completely redesigned the course. It was then piloted, and the results were a dramatic improvement in student performance on national tests and a considerable increase in student satisfaction with the course.

Reynolds then wrote the process up from his detailed field notes and journals and drafted his dissertation. He submitted the draft to his collaborators for comment and revision, then explained to them the revisions he would make. He also offered them the option to add their own written comments in a late chapter of the dissertation, using either their real names or pseudonyms.

This iteration of the process produced some significant changes in the dissertation and solidified the group's own learning process. Eventually, many of the collaborators attended Reynolds's dissertation defense and were engaged in the discussion, the first time we know of that such a "collaborative" defense occurred at Cornell. Subsequently, that kind of defense, with collaborators present, has been repeated with other PhD candidates (Boser, 2001; Grudens-Schuck, 1998).

Interestingly, though the process was extremely stressful for the participants, the results were phenomenally good for the students. A proposal was made to extend this approach to curriculum reform to other courses at Cornell, but the university administration was unprepared to underwrite the process, despite its obvious great success in this case.

Perhaps the reform of a single course does not seem like much of a social change, but we think it has powerful implications. This case demonstrates the possibility of an action research–based reform being initiated from a position of little power within a profoundly bureaucratic and hierarchical organization, the university. The value of the knowledge of each category of stakeholder was patent throughout, and the shared interests of all in a good outcome for the students helped hold the process together. That such reform is possible and successful means that those who write off the possibility of significant university reforms are simply wrong. Of course, it also shows that an isolated success does not add up to ongoing institutional change without a broader strategy to back it up. Thus, it was a success, but an isolated one.

Although this is a very modest amount of case material to present in support of our contentions, we believe that the cases at least give the reader a general sense of the kind of vision of social research we advocate.

Institutionalizing AR in Academic Environments

One of the major challenges facing modern universities that are funded with private or public money lies in making visible their contribution to important social and technological challenges in the larger society. This cannot be done unless research and teaching are clearly aligned to extra-university needs.

Although such an argument is often heard in the current debates about the social obligations of universities, little progress has been made at mediating university–society relationships because of the profound differences between what is considered appropriate research and teaching by academics and what the public wants and expects. Few processes are in place to work toward creating a shared understanding of what a desired focus of collaboration should be. The parties operate in two different worlds, with very limited cross-boundary communication and learning, and they operate with the inconvenience that the public has the power to make decisions affecting future university budgets.

Action research meets the need for this kind of mediated communication and action. It deals with real-life problems in context, and it is built on participation by the non-university problem owners. It creates mutual learning opportunities for researchers and participants, it produces tangible results. Hence, action research, if managed skillfully, can respond in a positive way to the changing and increasingly interventionist public and private sector environments in which universities must operate.

How, then, do we envisage a university operating within the frame of reference of action research? Given what we have already said about how research would have to be organized, it is clear that problem definition must be accomplished cooperatively with the actors who experience the actual problem situations. Thus, research will have to be conducted in "natural" settings without trying to create a university-centered substitute experimental situation.

Conducting research this way guarantees that research foci will not emerge from reading about the latest fashionable theory within an academic profession, but rather as a negotiated joint understanding of what the problem in focus should be, an understanding in which both professionals and problem owners have a say in setting the issue the group will deal with. For academic researchers, this places a premium on the ability and willingness to frame researchable questions in concrete problem situations, a process that certainly forces the researchers to adopt perspectives that often are not central or even well known within their own disciplines.

One way to create this potential is to train researchers who are capable of embracing perspectives beyond those of single, constrained professional disciplinary territories. Another possibility is to create teams that contain enough varieties of expertise relevant to the problem at hand so that the internal capacity to mobilize the needed forms of knowledge exists. In both situations, the centerpiece is the requirement that academic researchers be able to operate in a transdisciplinary environment, where the challenges center on actively transforming their own perspectives in order to accommodate and help build the necessary knowledge platform needed for working through the problem. They also would also have to understand their accountability to the extra-university stakeholders' evaluation of the results through action. Thus, team-based research and breaking down boundaries between different professional positions are central features of the deployment of action research in universities.

Teaching would have to change in much the same way. In fact, it is possible to envisage a teaching process that mirrors the action research process we have articulated above. The obvious starting point would be use of concrete problem situations in classrooms, probably accomplished by use of real cases. Starting here, the development of learning foci (e.g., problem definitions) would have to emerge from the concrete problem situations, a position that is the centerpiece of John Dewey's pedagogy.

In this regard, this teaching situation is parallel to an action research project. The main difference is that there are three types of principal actors in the classroom: the problem owners, the students, and the teachers. As in action research, they will all be linked in a mutual learning process. Even though students might themselves be participants, without many of the necessary skills and insights, they will discover that, as students, they bring a different set of experiences and points of view into the collaborative learning arena and can make important contributions as they gain confidence in their own abilities. Thus, all three parties will be teachers and colearners.

The professional academics will have a special obligation to structure the learning situation effectively and to provide necessary substantive knowledge to the participants in the learning process. As is generally the case in teaching, the professors would start the course using their conception of what are key substantive issues in the situation under examination. Because this kind of teaching is problem driven, however, all predetermined plans will have to be adjusted to the concrete teaching situation as new, cogenerated understandings emerge from the learning group.

Focusing on real-life problems also forces the different disciplines to cooperate because relevant knowledge must be sought from any and all sources. No single discipline or strand of thinking can dominate action research because real-world problems are not tailored to match disciplinary structures and standards of academic popularity. The valuable academic professional thus is not the world's leading expert in discipline "X" or theory "Y" but instead is the person who can bring relevant knowledge for solving the problem to the table.

Through such pedagogical processes, whatever else they do, it is certain that students will learn how to apply what they know and how to learn from each other, from the professors, and from the problem owners. What they will not develop is a narrow allegiance to a particular discipline or to a university world separated from life in society at large. And together, the professors and students will be of service to the world outside the academy. Thus, universities that focus their teaching on action research will be able to supply practical results and insights to the surrounding society.

Is This Possible?

The question is not whether action research can be accommodated in contemporary universities, but how to create experimental situations to make it happen. We can find examples of this in undergraduate education, in professional degree courses, and in PhD programs. Programs in action research at both of the authors' institutions (Cornell and the Norwegian University of Science and Technology) have shown that such programs are possible, albeit on a very small scale at present.

The biggest obstacle is how to integrate this type of alternative educational process fully in the current structures of universities. Everything we have said above constitutes a challenge to the current division of labor and to the disciplinary and administrative structures of universities. Pursuing this would weaken the hegemony of separate professional and disciplinary structures, would force professional activity to move toward meeting social needs, and would limit the self-serving and self-regarding academic professionalism that is the hallmark of contemporary universities.

Despite how difficult it appears to be, there are reasons to think that progress can be made along these lines. The increasing public and fiscal pressure on universities to justify themselves and their activities creates a risky but promising situation in which experimenting with action research approaches may be the only possible solution for universities that wish to survive into the next generation.

There is a choice. One strategy some universities have adopted is that, as the public financial support for universities drops, they consider themselves even less accountable to the public. Another is to try to renegotiate this relationship and reverse the negative trend. We believe in using action research to try to repair the deeply compromised relationships universities have with their publics and governments.

Notes

1. The exceptions to this poverty are positivistic, policy-oriented economic research and bits of policy-relevant social science research anchored primarily in schools of business, planning, and public policy.

2. *Techne* can also be interpreted as the technical rationality that is in the heads and the hands of experts, but, in the context of this essay, it denotes the kind of knowing necessary for making skilled transformation processes and therefore is not connected to the experts' power position.

3. These arguments have been made in much more detail and with a much more comprehensive understanding of their Greek origins by Olav Eikeland (1997).

4. A version of this section was delivered by Greenwood as a paper titled *La antropología "inaplicable": El divorcio entre la teoría y la práctica y el declive de la antropología universitaria* (Inapplicable Anthropology: The Divorce Between Theory and Practice and the Decline of University Anthropology) at the conference of Sociedad Española de Antropología Aplicada in Granada, Spain, in November of 2002.

5. A critique of this kind of blind positivism was central to the ideas of the major social thinkers who gave rise to the social sciences in the first place (Adam Smith, Karl Marx, Max Weber, Emile Durkheim, and John Dewey, among others). A good source of current critiques is James Scheurich (1997).

6. For a full discussion of these issues, see Robert Stake (1995).

7. This is a pseudonym.

8. Levin observed much of this process because he served as a member of the local steering committee for the project. He recollects how little linkage there was at the outset between engineering and the social sciences.

9. A search conference is a democratically organized action research means for bringing a group of problem owners together for an intensive process of reflection, analysis, and action planning. For a more detailed description, see Greenwood and Levin (1998b).

10. Greenwood served as a member of Reynolds's PhD committee and worked with him throughout this research. However, the ideas, processes, and interpretations offered here are those Reynolds generated, not Greenwood's. Because Reynolds is now hard at work in secondary school reform, he has not made a further write-up of his work, so we encourage the interested reader to consult his dissertation directly.

References

Abbott, A. (1988). *The system of professions.* Chicago: University of Chicago Press.

Berger, P., & Luckmann, T. (1967). *The social construction of reality: A treatise in the sociology of knowledge.* New York: Anchor.

Birnbaum, R. (2000). *Management fads in higher education.* San Francisco: Jossey-Bass.

Boser, S. (2001). *An action research approach to reforming rural health and human services administration through Medicaid managed care: Implication for the policy sciences.* Unpublished doctoral dissertation, Cornell University.

Bourdieu, P. (1994). *Homo academicus* (Peter Collier, Trans.). Stanford, CA: Stanford University Press.

Brint, S. (1996). *In an age of experts: The changing roles of professionals in politics and public life.* Princeton, NJ: Princeton University Press.

Brown, J. S., & Duguid, P. (1991). Organizational learning and communities-of-practice: Toward a unified view of working, learning, and innovation. *Organization Science, 2,* 40–57.

Diggins, J. (1994). *The promise of pragmatism.* Chicago: University of Chicago Press.

Eikeland, O. (1997). *Erfaring, dialogikk og politickk.* Oslo: Acta Humaniora, Scandinavian University Press.

Flyvbjerg, B. (2001). *Making social science matter: Why social inquiry fails and how it can succeed again.* Cambridge, UK: Cambridge University Press.

Freidson, E. (1986). *Professional powers: A study of the institutionalization of formal knowledge.* Chicago: University of Chicago Press.

Fuller, S. (2002). *Knowledge management foundations.* Boston: Butterworth/Heinemann.

Furner, M. (1975). *From advocacy to objectivity.* Lexington: University of Kentucky Press.

Greenwood, D. J. (1991). Collective reflective practice through participatory action research: A case study from the Fagor cooperatives of Mondragón. In D. A. Schön (Ed.), *The reflective turn: Case studies in and on educational practice* (pp. 84–107). New York: Teachers College Press.

Greenwood, D. J., & González Santos, J. L., with Cantón Alonso, J., Galparsoro Markaide, I., Goiricelaya Arruza, A., Legarreta Ruin, I., & Salaberría Amesti, K. (1992). *Industrial democracy as process: Participatory action research in the Fagor cooperative group of Mondragón.* Assen-Maastricht, Netherlands: Van Gorcum.

Greenwood, D., & Levin, M. (1998a). Action research, science, and the co-optation of social research. *Studies in Cultures, Organizations and Societies, 4*(2), 237–261.

Greenwood, D. J., & Levin, M. (1998b). *Introduction to action research: Social research for social change.* Thousand Oaks, CA: Sage.

Greenwood, D. J., & Levin, M. (2000a). Reconstructing the relationships between universities and society through action research. In N. K. Denzin & Y. S. Lincoln (Eds.), *Handbook of qualitative research* (2nd ed., pp. 85–106). Thousand Oaks, CA: Sage.

Greenwood, D. J., & Levin, M. (2000b). Recreating university-society relationships: Action research versus academic Taylorism. In O. N. Babüroglu, M. Emery, and Associates (Eds.), *Educational futures: Shifting paradigms of universities and education* (pp. 19–30). Istanbul: Fred Emery Memorial Book, Sabanci University.

Greenwood, D. J., & Levin, M. (2001a). Pragmatic action research and the struggle to transform universities into learning communities. In P. Reason & H. Bradbury (Eds.), *Handbook of action research* (pp. 103–113). London: Sage.

Greenwood, D. J., & Levin, M. (2001b). Re-organizing universities and "knowing how": University restructuring and knowledge creation for the twenty-first century. *Organization, 8*(2), 433–440.

Grudens-Schuck, N. (1998). *When farmers design curriculum: Participatory education for sustainable agriculture in Ontario, Canada.* Unpublished doctoral dissertation, Cornell University.

Krause, E. (1996). *The death of the guilds.* New Haven, CT: Yale University Press.

Levin, M., & Greenwood, D. (1998). The reconstruction of universities: Seeking a different integration into knowledge development processes. *Concepts and Transformation, 2*(2), 145–163.

Lewin, K. (1948). The conflict between Aristotelian and Galilean modes of thought in contemporary psychology. In *A dynamic theory of personality* (pp. 1–42). New York: McGraw-Hill.

Madoo Lengermann, P., & Niebrugge-Brantley, J. (1998). *The women founders.* Boston: McGraw-Hill.

Messer-Davidow, E. (2002). *Disciplining feminism: From social activism to academic discourse.* Durham, NC: Duke University Press.

Polanyi, M. (1974). *Personal knowledge: Toward a post-critical philosophy.* Chicago: University of Chicago Press.

Reynolds, M. (1994). *Democracy in higher education: Participatory action research in the Physics 101–102 curriculum revision project at Cornell University.* Unpublished doctoral dissertation, Cornell University.

Rhind, D. (2003). *Great expectations: The social sciences in Britain.* London: Commission on the Social Sciences.

Ross, D. (1991). *The origin of American social science.* Cambridge, UK: Cambridge University Press.

Ryle, G. (1949). *The concept of mind.* Chicago: University of Chicago Press.

Scheurich, J. (1997). *Research method in the postmodern.* London: Falmer.

Schutz, A. (1972). *The phenomenology of the social world.* Chicago: Northwestern University Press. (Original work published 1967)

Silva, E., & Slaughter, S. (1984). *Serving power: The making of a modern social science expert.* Westport, CT: Greenwood.

Slaughter, S., & Leslie, L. (1997). *Academic capitalism: Politics, policies, and the entrepreneurial university.* Baltimore: Johns Hopkins University Press.

Stake, R. (1995). *The art of case study research.* Thousand Oaks, CA: Sage.

Stocking, G., Jr. (1968). *Race, culture, and evolution: Essays in the history of anthropology.* Chicago: University of Chicago Press.

Waddock, S. A., & Spangler, E. (2000). Action learning in leadership for change: Partnership, pedagogy, and projects for responsible management development. In F. Sherman & W. Torbert (Eds.), *Transforming social inquiry, transforming social action: New paradigms for crossing the theory/practice divide in universities and communities* (pp. 207–228). Boston: Kluwer.

Wenger, E. (1998). *Communities of practice: Learning, meaning, and identity.* Cambridge, UK: Cambridge University Press.

Whyte, W. F. (1982). Social inventions for solving human problems. *American Sociological Review, 47,* 1–13.

3

COMPOSITIONAL STUDIES, IN TWO PARTS

Critical Theorizing and Analysis on Social (In)Justice

Michelle Fine and Lois Weis

Like the artist, we explicitly explore the negative bridging spaces within the composition; we intentionally explore the relationship between "negative" and "positive" spaces and understand that no "positive" exists except in relation to the "negative."

—Fine and Weis, from this chapter

We offer here a detailed explanation of what we are putting forward as "compositional studies," in which analyses of public and private institutions, groups, and lives are lodged in relation to key social and economic structures. We draw on what some have described as oscillation (Alford, 1998; Deleuze, 1990; Farmer, 2001; Hitchcock, 1999), a deliberate movement between theory "in the clouds" and empirical materials "on the ground." In this chapter, we articulate our theory of method, offering a critical look at compositional studies as frame and a serious elaboration as to how we oscillate from local to structural, how we analyze in ways that reveal what photographers call the "varied depths of field," and how we try to position the work to "have legs," that is, to be useful to struggles for social justice. We write to name the assumptions of our compositional studies, reflect upon its possibilities for theory and activism, and consider the limits of this work.

We write as well-educated and influenced by ethnographers who have written powerful "oscillating" works (see Anzaldúa, 1999; Crenshaw,

Authors' Note. Our continued thanks to Craig Centrie, who offered great insight into our artistic metaphor. Craig, a visual artist in his own right, prompted us to think through the relationship between the visual arts and what we do as ethnographers.

1995; Fanon, 1967; hooks, 1984; Ladson-Billings, 2000; Matsuda, 1995). Paul Willis (1977) and Valerie Walkerdine (e.g., Walkerdine, Lacey, & Melody, 2001), for instance, have crafted analyses of white working-class youth situated explicitly in historical and class politics, with a keen eye toward development and identity. Patricia Hill Collins (1991), Mari Matsuda (1995), Gloria Ladson-Billings (2000), and Patricia Williams (1992) have crafted Critical Race Theory to speak explicitly back to the webbed relations of history, the political economy, and everyday lives of women and men of color. Barrie Thorne (1993) has boldly broadened our understandings of gender, arguing fervently against "sex difference" research, insisting instead that gender be analyzed as relational performance. Paul Farmer (2001) moves from biography of individuals living in Haiti who suffer tuberculosis to the international politics of epidemiology, illness, and health care, while Angela Valenzuela (1999) skillfully helps us come to know Mexican American youth across contexts in the school, home, and community. These scholars produce writings centered on the rich complexity within a given group, offering complex, detailed, and sophisticated analyses of a slice of the social matrix and theorizing its relation to the whole (see also Bourgois, 2002; Duneier, 1994; Foley, 1990; Rubin, 1976; Scheper-Hughes & Sargent, 1998; Stepick, Stepick, Eugene, & Teed 2001; Stack, 1997; Twine, 2000; Waters, 1999).

In compositional studies, we take up a companion project, writing through the perspectives of multiple groups of this social puzzle we call America, fractured by jagged lines of power, so as to theorize carefully this relationality and, at the same time, recompose the institution, community, and nation as series of fissures and connections. Although there is always a risk that the in-group depth may be compromised in the pursuit of cross-group analysis, we try, in this chapter, to articulate how this method responds to questions of social critique and imagination, social justice theory, and advocacy.

To be more specific, in *The Unknown City* (Fine & Weis, 1998) and in *Working Class Without Work* (Weis, 1990), analytically speaking, we have argued that white working-class men (at least in the urban Northeast of the United States) can be understood only in relation to a constructed African American "other," with the most powerful refraction occurring in relation to African American men. These white working-class men must be theorized about and their words analyzed, then, in relation to "bordering" groups—white women, African American men and women, gay men across racial/ethnic groups, and so forth. Although their narrations rarely reference history or the global economy explicitly, we have had to situate these men, as they move through their daily lives and narrate their social relations, in the shifting historic sands of social, economic, and political conditions.

The key point here is that social theory and analyses can no longer afford to isolate a "group," or to re-present their stories as "transparent," as though that group were coherent and bounded; instead, we must theorize explicitly—that is, "connect the dots"—to render visible relations to other "groups" and to larger sociopolitical formations. The emergent montage of groups must simultaneously be positioned within historically shifting social and economic relations in the United States and across the globe. Although the specific "bordering" groups are uncovered ethnographically and may vary by site, deep theorizing and deep analysis are required to join these seemingly separate and isolated groups and to link them institutionally and ideologically. More broadly speaking, our notion and practice of qualitative work suggests that *no* one group can be understood as if outside the relational and structural aspects of identity formation.

At the heart of compositional studies lie three analytic moves we seek to make explicit. The first is the deliberate placement of ethnographic and narrative material into a contextual and historic understanding of economic and racial formations (see Sartre, 1968). Without presuming a simple determinism of economics to identity, we nevertheless take as foundational the idea that individuals navigate lives in what Martín-Baró (1994) and Freire (1982) would call "limit situations," within historic moments, unequal power relations, and the everyday activities of life. As Jean-Paul Sartre articulated in 1968, weaving a method between Marxism and existentialism, "If one wants to grant to Marxist thought its full complexity, one would have to say that man [*sic*] in a period of exploitation is at once both the product of his own product and a historical agent who can under no circumstances be taken as a product. This contradiction is not fixed; it must be grasped in the very movement of *praxis*" (1968, p. 87).

Yet when we engage ethnographically, speak to people, collect survey data, or conduct a focus group, it is most unusual for individuals to connect the dots between their "personal lives" and the historic, economic, and racial relations within which they exist (Mills, 1959). History appears as a "foreign force"; people do not recognize the "meaning of their enterprise . . . in the total, objective result" (Sartre, 1968, p. 89). That is, indeed, the insidious victory of neoliberal ideology: People speak as if they are self-consciously immune and independent, disconnected and insulated from history, the state, the economic context, and "others." As social theorists, we know well that the webs that connect structures, relations, and lives are essential to understanding the rhythm of daily life, possibilities for social change, and the ways in which individuals take form in, and transform, social relations. Thus, we work hard to situate our analyses of communities, schools, and lives, positioning them historically, economically, and socially so that the material context within which individuals are "making sense" can be linked to their very efforts to reflect upon and transform these conditions.

Second, in our work we rely more on categories of social identity than do many of our poststructural scholar-friends. That is, while we refuse essentialism, resisting the mantra-like-categories of social life—race, ethnicity, class, gender—as coherent, in the body, "real," consistent, or homogeneous, we also take very seriously the notion that these categories become "real" inside institutional life, yielding dire political and economic consequences. Even if resisted, they come to be foundational to social identities. Even as performed, multiple, shifting, and fluid, the technologies of surveillance ensure partial penetration of the politics of social identities (Butler, 1999; Foucault, 1977; Scott, 1990). You simply can't hang out in poor and working-class communities, a suburban mall, a prison, or an elite suburban golf course and come away believing that race, ethnicity, and class are simply inventions. Thus, with theoretical ambivalence and political commitment, we analytically embrace these categories of identity as social, porous, flexible, and yet profoundly political ways of organizing the world. By so doing, we seek to understand how individuals make sense of, resist, embrace, and embody social categories, and, just as dramatically, how they situate "others," at times even essentializing and reifying "other" categories, in relation to themselves. This is, we argue, what demands a relational method.

Third, as a corollary to our interest in categories as fluid sites for meaning making, we seek to elaborate the textured variations of identities that can be found within any single category. Thus, as you will read, our method enables us to search explicitly for variety, dissent within, outliers who stand (by "choice" or otherwise) at the dejected or radical margins, those who deny category membership, and those who challenge the existence of categories at all. Analytically, it is crucial to resist searching for in-group coherence or consensus as anything other than a hegemonic construction, although, as we argue, the search for modal forms is exceedingly useful. Nevertheless, it is critical to theorize how variation and outliers in relation to such modality re-present the larger group (Bhavnani, 1994).

These three moves—contextual, relational, and potentially focusing on and through individual variation while seeking modal forms—are crucial to what we are calling our "theory of method." Indeed, we would argue that this "theory of method" is conceptually akin to what an artist does, and this leads us to call our articulated method "compositional studies." A visual artist can have no composition without paying explicit attention to both the positive and the negative spaces of a composition. Positive space (the main object) must have a negative referent, and the negative referent, visually speaking, is as important as the positive to the composition as a whole. It is these "blank" or "black" spaces in relation to "color" or "white" that we pay attention to in our work. Like the artist, we explicitly explore the negative bridging spaces within the composition; we intentionally explore the relationship between "negative" and "positive" spaces and understand that no "positive" exists except in relation to the "negative." Again, this is an artistic metaphor, but it is one that offers great power as we reflect upon and name our ethnographic practice. Under our theory and practice of method, then, relevant bordering groups (those groups that border the primary subject of interest in the ethnography) are as essential to the ethnographic composition as any primary group under consideration. Thus, our specific genre of ethnographic practice historically implies a particular analytic method, one that considers the in-between, the gauze that glues groups together, even as it is narrated to distinguish "them." The in-between, like DuBois's color line, grows to be as theoretically and politically critical as that group which initially captures our ethnographic attention. Like the Black arts movement in the 1960s and 1970s, then, we intentionally and self-consciously politicize our artistic/compositional metaphor, arguing that our ethnographic compositions sit at the nexus of structural forces and individual lives/agency.[1]

Extending our notion of "compositional studies," we also argue that no group, even as in relation to other bordering groups, can be understood without reference to the larger economic and racial formations within which interactions take place. Given kaleidoscopic changes in the world economy in the past several decades, for instance, Lois Weis's follow-up study of individuals who initially were the subjects in *Working Class Without Work* (Weis, 1990) drives home the point that none of this is static and that it is important to watch the ways in which this all plays out over time. Identities are constructed in relation to the constructed identities of others, as well as dialectically in relation to the broader economy and culture. But none of this remains unchanged. Long-term ethnographic investigations enable us to track this set of interactions and relationships over time. Here is the unique contribution of Weis's *Class Reunion* (2004); she uses data gathered in 1985 in a working-class high school and then re-interviews students from that school 15 years later. This form of ethnographic longitudinality enables us to shift our eye from pieces drawn at one point in time to those drawn at another, opening ever further the spectrum of compositional ethnography. We thus begin here—with a clear(ish) focus as to what the economic and racial formations look like over time, and as to what the field of relational interactions is within this broader, evolving context.

Importantly, our notion of compositional studies invites a rotating position for the writer/researcher; that is, compositional studies affords researchers the opportunity and obligation to be at once grounded and analytically oscillating between engagement and distance; explicitly committed to deep situatedness yet able to embrace shifting perspectives as to the full composition. Our theory of method, then, extends an invitation to the researcher as multiply positioned: grounded, engaged, reflective, well versed in scholarly discourse, knowledgeable as to external circumstances, and able to move between theory and life "on the ground." Whether in a school, a prison, a neighborhood, a cultural arts center, a community center, a religious institution, or wherever, we invite researchers/writers to travel between theory "in the clouds," so to speak, and the everyday practices of individuals living in communities as they (and we) negotiate, make sense of, and change their/our positionalities and circumstance. This method suggests, then, an articulate, intellectually and personally flexible, and engaged individual who really does enjoy and respect what others have to say. The responsibility of placing these interactions/narrations and all that we have come to refer to as "data," then, lies largely with us.

We offer, in this chapter, a brief look at two compositional designs, both of which will be elaborated elsewhere (Fine et al., 2004; Weis, 2004): a longitudinal analysis of white working-class men and women, followed by Lois Weis after 15 years as their lives, stories, and homes carry the seams of the economic and racial formations in contemporary white working-class America, and a participatory action research project that Michelle Fine has coordinated, in which youth across suburban and urban districts learn to be critical researchers of "desegregation" through an analysis of race, ethnicity, class, and opportunity in their own schools and in the New York metropolitan region. In putting these two pieces forward, we argue that both projects are fundamentally rooted in what we call compositional studies—ethnographic inquiry designed to understand how global and national formations, as well as relational interactions, seep through the lives, identities, relations, and communities of youth and adults, ultimately refracting back on the larger formations that give rise to them to begin with.

Class Reunion

Amid cries of "farewell to the working class" (Gorz, 1982) and the assertion of the complete eclipse of this class given the lack of "direct representations of the interaction among workers on American television" (Aronowitz, 1992), I (Lois) offer *Class Reunion* (2004)—a volume aimed at targeting and explicating the remaking of the American white working class in the latter quarter of the 20th century. Arguing that we cannot write off the white working class simply because white men no longer have access to well-paying laboring jobs in the primary labor market (Edwards, 1979), jobs that created a distinctive place for labor in the capital-labor accord (Apple, 2001; Hunter, 1987), and that we cannot assume that this class can be understood only as a tapestry that seamlessly integrates people across ethnicity, race, and gender (Bettie, 2003), I explore empirically and longitudinally the remaking of this class both discursively and behaviorally inside radical, globally based economic restructuring (Reich, 1991, 2002).

Beginning in 1985 with my ethnographic investigation of Freeway High (*Working Class Without Work: High School Students in a De-Industrializing Economy*; Weis, 1990) and culminating with intensive follow-up interviews with these same students in 2000–2001, I track a group of the sons and daughters of the workers of "Freeway Steel" over a 15-year time period. The original volume, *Working Class Without Work* (1990), explores identity formation among white working-class male and female students in relation to the school, economy, and family of origin, capturing the complex relations among secondary schooling, human agency, and the formation of collective consciousness within a radically changing economic and social context. I suggest in the volume that young women exhibit a "glimmer of critique" regarding traditional gender roles in the working-class family and that young men are ripe for New Right consciousness given their strident racism and male-dominant stance in an economy that, like the ones immortalized in the justly celebrated films *The Full Monty* and *The Missing Postman* (Walkerdine et al., 2001), offers them little.

Fifteen years later, I return to these same students as they (and we) meet in *Class Reunion*, a study lodged firmly in our theory of method as outlined earlier. Through a careful look at the high school and young adult years (ages 18–31) of the sons and daughters of the industrial proletariat in the northeastern "Rust Belt" of the United States, I capture and theorize the reshaping of this class under a wholly restructured global economy. Traversing the lives of these men and women in line with our larger working method of compositional ethnography, I argue that the remaking of this class can be understood only through careful and explicit attention to issues that swirl around theories of whiteness, masculinity, violence, representations, and the economy. Reflective of the triplet of theoretical and analytic moves that we put forward here as signature of our work—deep work within one group (over a 15-year time period in this case); serious relational analyses between and among relevant bordering groups; and broad structural connections to social, economic, and political arrangements—I argue that the remaking of the white working class can be understood only in relation to gendered constructions within that group and the construction of relevant "others" outside itself—in this case, African Americans and Yemenites, particularly men—as well as deep shifts in large social formations, particularly the global economy.

▣ Changing Economies, Changing Gender

In this chapter, I (Lois) probe varying ways in which white working-class men remake class and masculinity in the context of massive changes in the global economy, changes that most specifically target the former industrial proletariat. Stretching to situate themselves within the postindustrial world, young white working-class Freeway men take their selves as forged in relation to the three primary definitional axes that are defining characteristics of their youth identity: (a) an emerging contradictory code of respect toward school knowledge and culture not in evidence in key previous studies of this group conducted when the economy was kinder to the white working class, (b) a set of virulently patriarchal constructions of home/family life that position future wives in particular kinds of subordinate relationships, and (c) constructed notions of racial "others" (Weis, 1990). Through careful engagement with data collected in 2000–2001, I argue here that it is the ways in which individual white working-class men simultaneously position themselves and are positioned vis-à-vis these three major axes that determine, to some extent at least, both where they individually land 15 years later *and* the broader contours of white working-class culture. Specifically, in the case of the men, it is in the pulling away from what are defined within peer groups in high school as normative or perhaps hegemonic masculine cultural forms that we begin to see young people, in this case young men, move toward adulthood. Tracing the push and pull of hegemonic cultural forms as defined in high school, I suggest here that it is within this push and pull, as lived inside the new global economy and accompanying tighter sorting mechanisms, that we can begin to understand both the generalized shape of the new working class and the individual positions within this class as well as potentially outside it.

In this section, we meet, for illustrative purposes, Jerry and Bob, both of whom were in the honors bubble in high school (constituting 20 students out of a class of 300—the only students specifically pursuing college prep work in high school) and thus already were outside, to some extent at least, the dominant white working-class male culture as described in *Working Class Without Work* (Weis, 1990). Jerry, a star athlete, in high school lived mainly inside the honors group. Bob, on the other hand, did not. When I first met him, when he was 16 years old, Bob loved heavy metal bands and wore their T-shirts. He often got into fights, and he frequently got stoned and drunk. He exhibited a set of attitudes and behaviors that placed him squarely within the hegemonic working-class masculinity exhibited during the high school years of Freeway students. Most of his friends were in the non-honors classes, leaving him little time or interest for his peers in the honors bubble. Ultimately, however, both men distanced themselves from the normative male white working-class youth culture—Jerry is now a middle school math teacher, and Bob is completing his degree in veterinary medicine at what is arguably the most prestigious veterinary school in the country.

Jerry: I grew up in the second ward which is, so the first ward is definitely the lower class, lower than most of Freeway, but it's [where] I live now, it's similar to where I grew up, I'd say a little bit more, you know, where I may have grown up in a lower-middle class neighborhood, I'd say maybe where I live now it's middle class. And so it's a little step above. . . . My dad was definitely proud of me; he got to expect that of me and always congratulated me, and I think I made him very proud of me. All my siblings went to college. None of them were scored as well academically. I'm a little bit more serious than the rest of them. . . . Yeah, it is weird that our close immediate five to ten group of people [not including Bob] that were in that advanced group together all had a lot of similar beliefs and goals and we all wanted to go to college, wanted to succeed. And that's the minority. If you look overall at that class [Freeway High], you wouldn't find as much success, but in that group, I don't know. We were all competitive with each other, and yet still friends.

Lois: What do you think happened to some of the rest of the kids that were not in that [advanced] class?

Jerry: I don't know. Probably just went out to work wherever they found a job and maybe they'd have high goals for themselves, but a lot of them are still living in Freeway.

Lois: [Fifteen years ago] We talked about your parents, what kind of work they did. You said your mom is not educated past 8th Grade. How does she talk about her work? Does she work now?

Jerry: No. She's retired also [like his dad]. She actually made envelopes. She worked full-time and then there were times when she worked part-time when the kids were really young, and I remember once for a few years, when I was very young, she worked on the night shift and she stayed home with the kids during the day. Then my dad came home and she went to work at night. I remember going with my dad to go pick her up late at night. How did she talk about it? I never once heard her say, "I hate my job." I never heard her say she loved her job. She never really talked about it a whole lot. . . . Except when she was happy when she brought a box of envelopes home that she got at work.

Lois: You're describing [earlier he did so] your dad as a pretty traditional Italian man. Sometimes those men are not real happy when their wives work outside the home. How did that play out in your household?

Jerry: I never sensed that he might feel that. We needed . . . with all the kids [five kids] we needed two incomes in the family . . . I don't know, it was pretty, like I said, traditional, what I think of back to the 1950s, how when my mom cooked, my dad expected a meal when he came home. You look back now at how silly it was. But that's how they grew up and that's how it was.

Lois: Can you describe a typical weekday in your house [now]?

Jerry: Typical weekday, yeah. From morning, getting up and coming to school here, extra early, always having kids here before school. Giving, really giving of what I have as I teach. I kind of work very hard until the school day is over. Then I'm involved with extracurricular activities, whether it be running the fitness program after school, or when softball season comes, coaching the teams, which involves practice every day. But then, coming home and cooking dinner. I like to cook dinner . . . I do it more because I like to, and so she'll [his wife] do more of the cleanup work, which I hate to do. So, we share that responsibility. And then, whether it be working out or just relaxing watching TV or going to a sporting event or coming back to school to watch a sporting event, watch the kids play. . . . So, that's a typical day. . . . Weekend? Sundays are pretty typical of going to Mom's at one and having a big dinner and staying there for a couple of hours. And then coming home, doing the laundry, grocery shopping and planning for the next school week. But Saturdays are the ones that are changing. Usually we'll do more fun things. That would be going to a movie or something.

Jerry had several things going for him that enabled him to stake out a nonhegemonic form of white working-class masculinity as far back as middle school. Although solidly in the white manual-laboring working class, his parents worked to instill a strong work ethic in their children. This, though, is not enough to explain Jerry's class repositioning. Many, but certainly not all, of the Freeway parents had a strong work ethic tied to manual labor, and many in the 1980s desired that their children go on to school (Weis, 1990), feeling strongly that schooling was their only chance to secure an economic future. Jerry's break came when his measured intelligence (whatever "measured intelligence" is, it can have serious consequences) placed him in the honors classes in middle school, classes that he took seriously for the next 6 years. By his own admission, and that of most of the honors students whom I interviewed in the mid-1980s, he associated only with this group of students, the majority of them holding together as a group formed in relation to the non-honors students. For the men, this meant elaborating a form of masculinity forged centrally around academic achievement rather than physical prowess, sexism, and racism, as I suggested earlier were the valued norms in Freeway High. This does not mean that Jerry did not have in mind marrying a girl like his mother, who could take care of him. Indeed, evidence suggests that he did have such a girl in mind whom he dated throughout high school. But as he grew into his twenties, he changed that opinion and now participates in family life wherein he does a good portion of the domestic activity. He does all of the cooking, for example—something unheard of in his father's generation—while she "cleans up." The honors bubble encouraged the formation of a different kind of working-class masculinity, one exempt in many respects from that outlined above as hegemonic within this class faction. The majority of the 20 students in the honors bubble socialized and learned only with one another over a 6-year period. The young men thus could stand squarely on the space of a different kind of masculinity, and virtually every one of them (all but two) did so in the mid-1980s, when I engaged in the original work. The honors bubble, in fact, enabled and encouraged young working-class men to forge a masculinity different from that embedded in the broader class and gendered culture. Significantly, the honors bubble had no African American students or Puerto Rican students (unlike the broader school) and only two Yemenites, one male and one female, in spite of the much larger representation of students of color in the school as a whole. The just-mentioned woman is of mixed heritage (Yemenite and Vietnamese), and she grew up on the "white" side of town. Thus, core masculinist culture in the honors bubble was not formed in relation to people of color, women who were positioned as "less than" in precisely the same way as occurred in the larger class cultural configuration, or the contradictory code of respect outlined earlier. Rather, like the men from professional families whom Bob Connell talks about (1993, 1995), the men in this tiny segment of the working class have a dominant masculinity etched around academics, offering a distinct alternative to the blasting hegemonic masculinity that permeated the 1980s white youth in Freeway and the broader class cultural relations at the time. Jerry's hard work, parental support, connection to athletics, winning personality, and sheer smarts allowed him to move off the class space into which he was born. Jerry is now married to a young woman from an affluent suburban family, and his class background is now largely invisible.

Space does not permit an intensive analysis of Bob, who, in contrast to Jerry, lived a hegemonic form of white working-class masculinity in high school despite being placed in the honors bubble. Suffice it to say that Bob moved off that space as he embarked on a trajectory that ultimately led to the near completion of a highly valued veterinary school program. Working against and with the image of his father—a ne'er-do-well who had a distant relationship with his son—Bob never wants to "stagnate." Living in a church-owned house rented for a small sum of money to an obviously poor family, Bob's mother augmented family income, which could never be counted on, by taking in one foster child after another. As a youth and teenager, Bob walked between the cracks of the foster care system, listening to his music, frequently getting drunk and stoned, engaging in physical fights, and impregnating his 17-year-old girlfriend when he was 18. Working at Home

Depot, earning the minimum wage, and eventually entering the service, Bob appeared to have a clear life trajectory, in that he would play off of and live out deeply rooted and well-articulated hegemonic working-class masculinist forms in the early 21-century economy. Ironically, Bob's Army service interrupted this, offering space within which his marriage was brutally severed, he was mentored by his platoon sergeant, and ultimately he found God (Weis, 2004). Now desirous of a male-female relationship in which he takes seriously his role as protector, he claims that his wife, although highly educated and the daughter of a university faculty member, would like to bake pies, make quilts, and ultimately "open a Christian bookstore." Whether or not his wife would agree with this or not is open to debate, but I would argue that for many reasons, her agreement is irrelevant for the purpose of the current discussion. Bob has been catapulted, or has catapulted himself, across whatever class border may exist for a man from his social class background. Whatever fantasies Bob may or may not have about his wife's future pie-making activity, the fact is that his wife, born into a professional family, is highly educated, possessing a research-based master's degree and working toward a PhD in the sciences; she has a job and, by Bob's own admission, they share on a day-to-day basis all household tasks. He is, in fact, almost totally responsible for his two teenage sons when they come to visit, which is often (the entire summer and two weekends per month in spite of the fact that he lives 3 hours from them). Bob has moved far from his high school enactment of working-class core white male masculinity. He, like Jerry, is headed for a new space within the economy, one very different from that occupied by their parents and substantially different from the majority of their peers. Significantly, both men are physically distanced from Freeway, although Jerry lives, for the moment at least, in a bordering inner-ring white working-class suburb. Nevertheless, both men metaphorically and actually crossed the bridge that links working-class Freeway with the wider society. Jerry is a well-respected middle school teacher and, by the time of this writing, Bob will have become a veterinarian, having graduated from one of the top vet schools in the world.

In terms of our theory and method of compositional studies, *Class Reunion* allows us to interrogate the relation of large-scale economic and social relations on individual and group identities—to excavate the social psychological relations "between" genders and races, as narrated by white men, and to explore the nuanced variations among these men. We come to see identities carved in relation, in solidarity, and in opposition to other marked groups and, importantly, in relation to what the economy "offers up" over time. It is in the push and pull of these men, both within hegemonic high school masculinist forms *and* the currency of such forms in the restructured economy, that we can begin to understand the remaking of the white working class. Significantly, for white working-class males, struggles to ensure symbolic dominance in an ever-fragile economy sit perched on the unsteady fulcrum of racial and gender hierarchy (Weis, 2004).

For an alternative construction of compositional studies, designed with some of the same epistemological commitments, we turn now to a broad-based qualitative study of racial justice and public education, conducted by Michelle Fine and colleagues through a participatory design with youth. In this case, we witness compositional design in the critical study of race-, ethnicity-, and class-based academic opportunities within and across the New York City (NYC) metropolitan area, investigating in particular the ways in which white, African American, Latino, Afro-Caribbean, and Asian American youth conceptualize themselves and their opportunities, their "place" in the United States and in their schools, at the very revealing fractures of social hierarchies.

◼ Compositional Studies on the Fault Lines of Racial Justice and Public Education

Almost 50 years after *Brown v. Board of Education*, we continue to confront what is problematically coined an "achievement gap" between African Americans and Latinos, on one hand, and whites and Asian Americans, on the other; a similar gap appears between middle-class and poor children (Anyon, 1997; Bowles & Gintis, 1976; Ferguson, 1998; Fine, 1991; Fordham, 1996; Hochschild, 2003; New York Association of Community Organizations for Reform Now [ACORN], 2000; Orfield & Easton, 1996; Wilson, 1987; Woodson, 1972).[2] In 2001, a series of school districts within the New York metropolitan area, in suburban New York and New Jersey, joined to form a consortium to take up this question of the "gap" and invited Michelle and students from the Graduate Center, City University of New York, to collaborate on critical research into the production of, performance of, and resistance to the "gap." Drawing on Ron Hayduk's (1999) call for regional analyses (rather than urban or suburban analyses in isolation), we conceptualized an ethnographic analysis of the political economy of schooling as lived by youth in and around the NYC metropolitan area.

By crossing the lines separating suburbs and urban areas, we designed the work to reveal similarities across county lines and identify important contrasts. We sought to document the codependent growth of the suburbs and the defunding of urban America, as well as to reveal the fractures of inequity that echo within "desegregated" suburban communities and schools. We hoped, finally, to capture some of the magic of those spaces in which rich, engaging education flourishes for youth across lines of race, ethnicity, class, geography, and "track." With graduate students Maria Elena Torre, Janice Bloom, April Burns, Lori Chajet, Monique Guishard, Yasser Payne, and Kersha Smith, Michelle undertook this work committed to a textured, multimethod critical ethnographic analysis of urban and suburban schooling with youth, designed to speak back to questions of racial, ethnic, and class (in)justice in American education (see Torre & Fine, 2003, for design). To reach deep into the varied standpoints that constitute these schools, we created a participatory action research design with youth representing the full ensemble of standpoints within these urban and suburban desegregated settings (Anand, Fine, Perkins, Surrey, & the graduating class of 2000, Renaissance Middle School, 2001; Fals-Borda, 1979; Fine, Torre, et al., 2001, 2002; Freire, 1982; Hartsock, 1983).

The Design, in Brief

We have, over the past 18 months, been collaborating with more than 70 diverse youth from 11 racially integrated suburban school districts and 3 New York City high schools, crossing racial, ethnic, class, gender, academic, geographic, and sexuality lines. We designed a series of research camps in schools, on college campuses, and in communities ranging from wealthy Westchester suburbs to the South Bronx of New York City.

At the first research camp, a 2-day overnight at a New Jersey college, youth participated in "methods training," learning about qualitative design, critical race theory, and a series of methods including interview, focus group, observation, and survey design (e.g., we read with them Collins, 1991, and Harding, 1983). Urban and suburban students and those of us from the Graduate Center crafted a survey of questions to be distributed across districts, focusing on youth views of distributive (in)justice in the nation and their schools. The youth insisted that the survey *not* look like a test, so they creatively subverted the representations of "science" by including photos, cartoons for respondents to interpret, a chart of the achievement gap, and open-ended questions such as "What is the most powerful thing a teacher has ever said to you?" Available in English, French, Spanish, and Braille, as well as on tape, the survey was administered to nearly 5,000 9th and 12th graders in 13 urban and suburban districts. Within 6 weeks, we received 3,799 surveys—brimming with rich qualitative and quantitative data that could be disaggregated by race, ethnicity, gender, and "track." Beyond the surveys, over the past year we have engaged in participant observations within four suburban and two urban schools, arranged for four cross-school visitations, and conducted more than 20 focus group interviews. In addition, five school "teams" and one community-based activist group pursued their own inquiry crafted under the larger "opportunity gap" umbrella.

We offer here a slice into our material on racial, ethnic, and class justice in public education, to understand how differently positioned youth, like the men in *Class Reunion*, spin meaningful identities as students, researchers, and activists when they "discover" how deeply historic inequities are woven into the fabric of U.S. public education. The empirical material presented has been carved out of the larger project, at a key fracture point where youth confront structures, policies, practices, and relations that organize, naturalize, and ensure persistent inequity. We enter through this crack because we find it to be a compelling window into how privileged and marginalized youth negotiate political and intellectual identities, dreams, and imaginations in a (national and local) Grand Hall of mirrors in which privilege comes to be read as merit and in which being poor and/or of color gets read as worth-less.

Separate and Unequal? The Interior Life of "Desegregated" Schools

As we visited and worked with a number of desegregated suburban schools, 49 years after *Brown v. Board of Education*, we couldn't help but notice that diverse bodies indeed pass through the integrated school doors of historic victory but then funnel into classes largely segregated by race, ethnicity, and social class. Compared to urban schools, these schools are indeed well resourced. However, within these schools, we were struck by the persistence of "separate and unequal" access to educational rigor and quality. Unlike most students in U.S. schools, youth in desegregated schools must theorize their own identities relationally all the time and every day, because they are making selves in spaces where "difference" matters. That is, they are learning, claiming, and negotiating their places in a microcosmic racial/classed hierarchy on a daily basis.

To understand how youth make sense of their positions in these global/local race, ethnic, and class hierarchies, we enter a focus group composed of diverse youth from across schools, zip codes, and tracks who have come together to discuss academic tracking within their schools. These students attend desegregated schools in which almost 70% of whites and Asians are in advanced placement (AP) and/or honors classes, but only about 35% of African American and Latino students are. We listen now as students justify and challenge the America in which they are being educated, the space of the racial dream of integration, about which they know far too much.

Charles: My thoughts? When we just had [one group in a class] . . . you really don't get the full perspective of everything. You know what I mean? If they were in tracked classes, they wouldn't get to interact. And like . . . when you're in class with like all white people, because I know the same thing happens at [my school] like sometimes *I'm the only black male in class, and you do feel sort of inferior, or you do like sort of draw back a little bit* [authors' emphasis] because you have nobody else to relate with, you know. If it's more integrated, like, you know, you feel more comfortable and the learning environment is better . . . you just get more sides of it because, I don't know, it's hard to, even with math, everybody learns the same thing in math, but if it's all white people, you know what I mean? They're going to learn it somewhat different. *It's not that they don't get the same education, but they're going to miss that one little thing that a Latino person or a black person could add to the class. . . .* [authors' emphasis]

◘ ◘ ◘

Jack: [I don't think we should detrack entirely], maybe not in like all classes, but that really like what they, like maybe if they just had all freshman classes like that, you know, it would help out a lot . . . [to change it all] . . . you know the *kids that might not have achieved so much in the past could see* *like, you know, like "I do have a chance"* [authors' emphasis]. And you know, "I don't . . . I just don't have to stop. I can keep going and keep learning more stuff." So I don't know, maybe not like every class should be tracked, but *they* [authors' emphasis] should definitely be exposed.

▣ ▣ ▣

Tarik: It starts from when you graduate eighth grade. In eighth grade they ask you, "would you want to be in [top track]?" It depends on your grades. If your grades are good enough to be in top, then you can, but if not, you have to *choose* [authors' emphasis] the [regular] level.

▣ ▣ ▣

Jane: Because, like you know, some people even say that, you know, *the smart kids* [authors' emphasis] should be in a class by themselves because it's more conductive to their learning. But then the other people would say like well the special education kids . . . they need to be *with their kind so they'll learn better* [authors' emphasis].

Charles (African American, high- and medium-track classes) opens by revealing his discomfort with racial stratifications in his school. In one sweep, he poses a critique of the school, and he smuggles in the possibility that African American or Latino students may have "one little thing" to contribute. Jack (white, high-achieving boy) quickly navigates the "presenting problem" away from school structure or black/Latino contributions. Reverting to a discourse of pity, he detours the group's focus onto the students' presumed (lack of) motivation. Tarik, who sits at the top of an underresourced school composed entirely of students of color, lengthens Jack's line of analysis by foregrounding individual motivation and "choice." Jane, a white girl in top tracks, returns the conversation to school structure, but now—given that low motivation and bad grades are "in the room"—she justifies tracks as responsive to, indeed "needed" by, students at the top and at the bottom.

In less than 2 minutes, race has been evacuated from the conversation, replaced by the tropes of "smart" and "special education." Collectively performing a "color-blind" exchange, the group has evacuated the politics of race. Black and Latino students have degenerated from potential contributors to needy. Tracks have been resuscitated from racist to responsive. Melanie and Emily (both biracial, high-achieving young women) try to reassert questions of race and racism by introducing aspects of racializing by educators (Deleuze, 1990):

Melanie: Like tracking has been in the whole school system that I've been going to like from beginning, and if you grow up in a tracking system, that's all you can know. So if you grow up and the whole time I've been in honors classes, and a lot of the time, and I'm mixed so a lot of the time when, if you want to hang out with different people and you're forced, and the other students in your classes and you're kind of forced to hang out with some people that you don't normally, wouldn't normally like hang around with. And at the same time, it's like a lot of emphasis is put on by the parents and teacher, I remember a lot of the time, like "You're a good" . . . like teachers would tell me, "You're a good student, but you need to watch out who you hang out with, because they're going to have a bad influence on you." They didn't see me doing anything. I was just walking down the hallway talking to somebody. It wasn't like, you know, we were out doing whatever. But a lot of times it is the teachers and the parents' first impressions of their ideas that come off . . .

▣ ▣ ▣

Emily: But I want to say like . . . Melanie and I are a lot alike because we're both interracial and we were both in like honors classes. But with her, a lot of her friends are black and with me a lot of my friends are white. And *I get really tired of being the only . . . one of the very few people in my class to actually speak up* [authors' emphasis] if I see something that's like . . . or if I hear something that's not . . . that bothers me. And then I feel like *I'm all of a sudden the black voice* [authors' emphasis], you know. Like I'm all black people. And it's not true at all. I . . . lots of people have different kinds of opinions and I want to hear them. It's just that I think a lot of the time, like Charles was saying, when you're the only person in the class, you do get intimidated. And voices aren't heard any more then because of everyone else overpowering.

Across this focus group, we hear youth identities constructed in relation to state school practices that reify and stratify race, as well as in relation to "others" (whites, blacks, teachers, parents, "them," unmotivated students, students with bad grades). These youths sculpt themselves in a nation, in a community, and in local school buildings in which racial signifiers have come to be the organizational mortar with which intellectual hierarchies are built, sustained, and resisted. Although stratified schools, and perhaps focus groups, undoubtedly invite a set of essentialized performances (Butler, 1999; Phoenix, Frosh, & Pattman, 2003), these youth, like the men in *Class Reunion*, scaffold identities through the thick (and sometimes toxic) fog of national and local policies, and within local representations of themselves as value-ful or worth-less. Note that Jack, Tarik, and Jane frame the problem (and their worth) as one of lacks in "others." Charles, Melanie, and Emily try to insert critique of racial formations within the school building. All these youth are growing selves amid social and academic relations stinging with power, privilege, and inequity. All define themselves, and are defined, in relation and in hierarchy; fortunately, they are also defined in flux and in complexity. Although their personal selves may be fluid and performed wildly differently across sites, "others" are fixed, in ways that legitimate existing structures, buttress their own position within, and anesthetize themselves to their anxieties about inequity.

April Burns (2004) argues powerfully that privileged (primarily but not solely white) students are indeed discomforted with their advantage within the tight quarters of internal segregation. In a close discursive analysis of high achiever focus groups, she documents the reversals, critiques, and momentary interruptions that students offer as they reflect on the racialized hierarchies within their presumably integrated schools. More expressly, we hear African American, biracial, and Latino students—like Charles, Emily, and Melanie—struggling with the hall of mirrors in which they attend school—mirrors that typically represent them in ways discrepant from how they see themselves. Students of color traverse and negotiate social policies and practices of symbolic and material violence as they survive a torrent of everyday representations within their desegregated schools. Some do beautifully; others fall. To this task they all import DuBois's "double consciousness" by which the "seventh son" watches through a veil.

> The Negro is a sort of seventh son, born with a veil and gifted with second sight in this American world—a world which yields him no true self consciousness but only lets him see himself through the revelation of the other world. It is a peculiar sensation, this double-consciousness, this sense of always looking at one's self through the eyes of others, of measuring one's soul by the tape of a world that looks on in amused contempt and pity. One ever feels his two-ness—an American, a Negro; two souls, two thoughts, two unreconciled strivings; two warring ideals in one dark body, whose dogged strength alone keeps it from being torn asunder. (DuBois, 1990, p. 9)

The veil is critical to compositional studies because it is the lens that, at once, connects and separates. It is gauze, a way of seeing, shifty. It is not a tattoo, an inoculation, a stain on the soul. And yet the veil is, itself, work, both intellectual and psychological. We heard about the veil in various forms, from sons and daughters, beneficiaries of *Brown v. Board of Education*. With access to suburban schools of material wealth and opportunity, African American and Latino youth, compared to white and Asian American youth, offer vastly different responses to survey items related to alienation: Does your teacher know you? Understand you? Give you a second chance?

Black and Latino students score much higher on alienation, and lower on being known—even and especially those in high-track courses—than white and Asian American students. When asked "What was the most powerful thing a teacher has ever said to you—positively or negatively?," Black and Latino students, in sharp and biting contrast to their white and Asian American peers, were far more likely to write such words as "No effect" or "No teacher ever said anything to me that affected me."

The veil doubles. A prophylactic against engagement, it also facilitates other forms of connection. As a shield of protection, it is a way to view the world without assault. It also fills a moat of alienation. The veil, like the color line, constitutes a relational analysis; it recognizes the ironies of walls that at once separate and connect. Through the veil, youth of color witness all. Some narrate pain, some pleasure, and a significant group claims they do not allow the words to penetrate. This is not to say that youth internalize fully the blaring messages, nor that they are fully inoculated by the wisdom of their critical analysis. The veil is the social psychological texture through which the gap is produced, lived, witnessed, and embodied.

The "gap" is a trope for the most penetrating fissures that have formed America. Urban/suburban finance inequities guarantee the gap; academic tracks vivify and produce an embodiment of the gap. The "gap" is neither inevitable nor natural. Schools do not have to reproduce social formations; many of the small, detracked urban schools in our study were designed, indeed, to resist.[3] But broadly conceived, the structures and praxis of class and racial formations constitute public schooling (Noguera, 2003; Payne, 1995). Inequitable state financing, school organization, school size, and classed and racialized access to rigor, as well as deep-pocket private supports that privileged students enjoy—rather than the "bodies" or "cultures" of race/ethnicity—produce consistent differential outcomes within and across schools (Gramsci, 1971). The "gap" is overdetermined but not fully inhaled by all.

Although social analysis may reveal the effects of the long arm of the state, the economy, and racial formations on the lives of youth and young adults, it is interesting, for a moment, to consider who does, and who doesn't, acknowledge the presence (and stranglehold) of the arm. As in the focus group narrative and our survey material, we see that youth of privilege and success largely (for critical re-examination see Burns, 2004) re-present themselves "as if" untouched by these structural forces, "as if" they are gracefully moving forward simply on the basis of merit, hard work, good luck, and/or committed parenting. In contrast, youth of color and/or poverty—never immune to hegemonic discourse—season their words with critique, outrage, and the twinned relations of structural and personal responsibility. Like the men in *Class Reunion* (and maybe even more so), these young women and men speak through a relational, comparative sense of the "other." But in their formulations, they are saddened to realize that they have become the "other."

All lives are formed in history, power inequities, institutional arrangements, and relational negotiations. Compositional studies are well suited to reveal these relations. Youth of color and in poverty know these relations and consistently narrate them for us all.

This project, like *Class Reunion*, reveals the complexity and, we believe, the power of compositional studies. Across and within institutions of public education, we come to see how finance inequities tattoo shame and lack on the intellectually hungry souls of poor and working-class urban youth, as well as how, within racially desegregated high schools, the theater of tracking organizes and produces differences associated with race, ethnicity, and class within buildings, radically differentiating students' access to rigorous curriculum and teaching. The interior politics of these schools have been linked theoretically and systematically to the economic, racial, and policy environments in the states; the production of the "gap" has been empirically tied to the production of privilege-as-merit; and the identity formations of "high-track" and "low-track" youth are interrogated as they define themselves with and against one another. Then—better developed elsewhere—we enter the vast variation within groups: the struggles of low-achieving Asian American students confronting the "model minority myth" (Lee, 1996), the high-track African American students who report loyalty oaths and mixed messages from faculty, and the high-achieving white students who recognize and are discomforted by the structural props and private supports that enable segregation and assure their advantage (Burns, 2004). It is this compositional capacity to move, theoretically and empirically, between structures, groups, and lives and behind the scenes, that enables us to produce work that speaks back to larger struggles for social and educational justice.

A Note on Social Justice and Compositional Studies

Compositional studies responds to the question of social research for social justice in varied ways. In its largest sense, compositional studies makes explicit a mapping of economic, racial, and political formations inside the structures, relations, and identities of youth and young adults. Our invitation toward method asks researchers to render visible the long arms of the state, capital, and racial formations as they saturate communities, homes, schools, souls, identities, and dreams of poor and working-class, middle and upper middle-class America. As Lois's work reveals, the trajectory of young white working-class men and women can be understood only in relation to the economy, gendered constructions and relations, and the constructions and benefits of whiteness—all of which will be occluded in the typical narrative and, as such, must be instantiated through theory. The tracking of the remaking of the white working class in the last quarter of the 20th century speaks volumes about economic justice and injustice, the ways in which groups and individuals at one and the same time refuse to be "slotted" even as they are "slotted" into "appropriate" and predetermined positions. The white working-class men and women have, in fact, fought back in the past 15 years, demanding cultural and economic space within the new economy, but, as Lois suggests in the larger project, this is not without contradictory impulses and outcomes. Surely this "fighting back" is not simply around white male demands expressed through union activities, as was largely the case in the past. The desire to reposition and maintain relative privilege in relation to groups of color continues—a set of struggles that revolves around reconstituted notions of appropriate gender relations and roles. It is the pain and delight of these understandings through which we gain a deeper sense of social and economic injustice. We can also witness the contradictory impulses embedded within narrow identity movements. Here, "compositional studies" reveals the power of what could be a class-based movement across working people, as well as the political shortsightedness and divisiveness of organizing exclusively for white males.

So, too, in Michelle's work, youth across race/ethnic groups, rich and poor, yearn for schools and societies "not yet" (Greene, 1995). We hear discomfort from all with the current states of finance inequities and tracking; we hear the dire price, paid most dearly by urban youth of color, but also suburban youth, of inequitable state policies, tracking systems, and perverse local (mis)representations. Yet we see the power of youth standing together—across lines of race, ethnicity, class, geography, and "academic level"—to speak back to educators and to America.

We leave you with a scene of ambivalence from a recent "speak back." Youth researchers in a suburban school were presenting their "findings" to the faculty. Quite critical of racial and ethnic stratification in his school's academics and disciplinary policies, Derrick explained to the almost-all-white teacher group that he, as an African American male, spends "lots of time in the suspension room . . . and you notice it's mostly black, right?" Hesitant nods were erased rapidly by awkward discursive gymnastics, "Well, no, actually in June it gets whiter when the kids who haven't shown up for detention have to come in," followed by "Sometimes there are white students, maybe when you're not there." But Derrick persists, with the courage of speaking his mind to educators who may or may not listen; standing with peers across racial and ethnic groups and a few adults willing to bear witness as he speaks truth to power.

Derrick is no more optimistic than we that in his school, at this moment, his critique will transform local policy. In our research camps, we rehearse the presentation, expecting engagement and resistance. In the folded arms of disbelieving faculty, the institution declares, "We are coherent, we are integrated, we are fair, it's not about race." But now, skillfully able to slice the school-based analyses by race, ethnicity, and track, able to read the tables and the discursive analyses, Derrick knows he stands not alone. He insists, "I don't speak just for me. I'm speaking for 1,179 other Black and Latino students who completed the survey and report high rates of suspensions." Suddenly his dismissible, personal "anecdote" transforms into fact. He stands tall and represents the concerns of hundreds of African American and Latino students in his school, and from more than a dozen other schools, who report that suspensions, and access to rigor, are unevenly distributed, and opportunities are denied or discouraged. Flanked by white, African American, and biracial students—allies—together they have a job to do. He writes, after his presentation, that he will not "walk away, to swagger to the policies of life . . ." He will, instead, continue to deepen his analysis and outrage, surrounded by allies and representing hundreds, with the critical skills of participatory research directed toward social justice.

When asked, "Do you think it's fair to teach students of color about racism and critical consciousness and involve them in this work? Doesn't it depress you?" Jeneusse, a youth researcher from the South Bronx, assured an audience at Columbia University, "We've long known about racism; that's not news. What I know now, though, is that I can study it, speak about it, and we need to do something to change it." Nikoury, a youth researcher from the Lower East Side of Manhattan, stunned an audience with her astute reflection on participatory action research and its benefits: "I used to see flat. No more . . . now I know things are much deeper than they appear. And it's my job to find out what's behind the so-called facts. I can't see flat anymore." These young women and men have, indeed, come to appreciate the complexity of the composition, the shape of the fractures, and their own capacity to repaint the canvas of the future.

Compositional studies will require scholars willing to dip into the waters of history and political economy, while sharpening the skills of case study, ethnography, and autoethnography. We may witness a delicate, perhaps clumsy, choreography balancing over the waters of structural and cultural explanations, as Sartre wrote, through both Marxism and existentialism (1968; see O'Connor, 2001). The costs may be overtheorizing and underattending to the material before us, or losing the fine-grained analyses of what Geertz calls "thick description" inside a group, a space, a fraction of the nation. Yet we are hopeful that compositional studies can provide a scholarly mirror of urgency, refracting back on a nation, constructed and represented as if we were simply individuals flourishing or languishing in parallel lives, as we move toward conquering chunks of the globe in our own frightening image.

In both instances, *Class Reunion* and critical analysis of the "gap," compositional studies speaks back to our nation and ask us to re-view the very fractures of power upon which the country, the economy, our schools, and our fragile sense of selves/comfort/leisure are premised, and to imagine, alternatively, what could be.

Notes

1. We are indebted to Norman Denzin for stretching our thinking on this point. See Maulana Karenga (1982), a theorist of the Black arts movement, as a reaction to "high" European art.

2. Race-, ethnicity-, and class-based inequities in educational opportunities and outcomes persist despite struggles for finance equity (Hochschild, 2003; Kozol, 1991), teacher quality in poor urban districts (Darling-Hammond, 2000; Education Trust, 1998; Iatarola, 2001), school integration (see Cross, 1991; Fine, Anand, Jordan, & Sherman, 2000; Fullilove, 2000), affirmative action (Bok & Bowen, 1998), small schools (Wasley et al., 1999), special education and bilingual reform (Nieto, 1996; Rousso & Wehmeyer, 2001; Stanton-Salazar, 1997), and parent organizing (Fruchter, Galletta, & White, 1992), as well as struggles against high-stakes standardized testing (Haney, Russell, & Jackson, 1997) and tracking (Dauber, Alexander, & Entwisle, 1996; Hurtado, Haney, & Garcia, 1998; New York ACORN, 2000; Noguera, 2003; Oakes, Wells, Yonezawa, & Ray, 1997; Useem, 1990; Wheelock,1992).

3. The youth researchers attend East Side Community High School, a small, detracked urban school on the Lower East Side of New York City. Most of the students come from poor and working-class families, many are recent immigrants from Central and South America, and resources are low and academic expectations high. They are, indeed, neighborhood kids who were lucky enough to find an "alternative" school committed to rigorous education for all.

References

Alford, R. (1998). *The craft of inquiry: Theories, methods, evidence.* New York: Oxford University Press.

Anand, B., Fine, M., Perkins, T., Surrey, D., & the graduating class of 2000 Renaissance School. (2001). *The struggle never ends: An oral history of desegregation in a northern community.* New York: Teachers College Press.

Anyon, J. (1997). *Ghetto schooling.* New York: Teachers College Press.

Anzaldúa, G. (1999). *Borderlands/La Frontera.* San Francisco: Aunt Lute Publishers.

Apple, M. (2001). *Educating the "right" way: Markets, standards, God and inequality.* New York: Routledge.

Aronowitz, S. (1992). *False promises: The shaping of American working class consciousness* (2nd ed.). Durham, NC: Duke University Press.

Bettie, J. (2003). *Women without class.* Berkeley: University of California Press.

Bhavnani, K. (1994). Tracing the contours: Feminist research and objectivity. In H. Afshar & M. Maynard (Eds.), *The dynamics of "race" and gender: Some feminist interventions.* London: Taylor & Francis.

Bok, W., & Bowen, D. (1998). *The shape of the river: Long-term consequences of considering race in college and university admissions.* Princeton, NJ: Princeton University Press.

Bourgois, P. (2002). *In search of respect: Selling crack in El Barrio.* Cambridge, UK: Cambridge University Press.

Bowles, S., & Gintis, H. (1976). *Schooling in capitalist society.* New York: Basic Books.

Burns, A. (2004). The racing of capability and the culpability in desegregated schools: Discourses of merit and responsibility. In M. Fine, L. Weis, L. Pruitt, & A. Burns (Eds.), *Off white: Readings on power, privilege and resistance* (2nd ed.). New York: Routledge.

Butler, J. (1999).*Gender trouble: Tenth anniversary.* New York: Routledge.

Collins, P. H. (1991). *Black feminist thought: Knowledge, consciousness, and the politics of empowerment.* New York: Routledge.

Connell, R. W. (1993). Disruptions: Improper masculinities and schooling. In L. Weis & M. Fine (Eds.), *Beyond silenced voices.* Albany: SUNY Press.

Connell, R. W. (1995). *Masculinities.* Cambridge, UK: Polity.

Crenshaw, K. (1995). Mapping the margins: Intersectionality, identity politics, and violence against women of colour. In K. Crenshaw, N. Gotanda, G. Peller, & K. Thomas (Eds.), *Critical race theory: The key writings that formed the movement.* New York: New Press.

Cross, W. E., Jr. (1991). *Shades of black: Diversity in African-American identity.* Philadelphia: Temple University Press.

Darling-Hammond, L. (2000). Teaching quality and student achievement. *Education Policy Analysis Archives, 8*(1), 27–54.

Dauber, S., Alexander, K. L., & Entwisle, D. R. (1996). Tracking and transitions through the middle grades: Channeling educational trajectories. *Sociology of Education, 69*(3), 290–307.

Deleuze, G. (1990, May). Postscript on societies of control. *L'Autre Journal, 1.*

DuBois, W. E. B. (1990). *Souls of black folks.* New York: First Vintage Books.

Duneier, M. (1994). *Slim's table: Race, respectability, and masculinity.* Chicago: University of Chicago Press.

Education Trust. (1998). Good teaching matters: How well-qualified teachers can close the gap. *Thinking K-16, 3*(2), 1–14.

Edwards, R. (1979). *Contested terrain.* New York: Basic Books.

Fals-Borda, O. (1979). Investigating the reality in order to transform it: The Colombian experience. *Dialectical Anthropology, 4,* 33–55.

Fanon, F. (1967). *Black skin, white masks.* New York: Grove.

Farmer, P. (2001). *Infections and inequalities: The modern plagues.* Berkeley: University of California Press.

Ferguson, R. (1998). Can schools narrow the Black-White test score gap? In C. Jencks & M. Phillips (Eds.), *The Black-White test score gap.* Washington, DC: Brookings Institution.

Fine, M. (1991). *Framing dropouts: Notes on the politics of an urban high school.* Albany: SUNY Press.

Fine, M., Anand, B., Jordan, C., & Sherman, D. (2000). Before the bleach gets us all. In L. Weis & M. Fine (Eds.), *Construction sites: Spaces for urban youth to reimagine race, class, gender and sexuality.* New York: Teachers College Press.

Fine, M., Roberts, R., Torre, M., Bloom, J., Burns, A., Chajet, L., et al. (2004). *Echoes of Brown: Youth documenting and performing the legacy of Brown v. Board of Education.* New York: Teachers College Press.

Fine, M., Torre, M., Boudin, K., Bowen, I., Clark, J., Hylton, D., et al. (2001). *Changing minds: The impact of college in a maximum security prison.* New York: The Graduate Center, City University of New York.

Fine, M., Torre, M., Boudin, K., Bowen, I., Clark, J., Hylton, D., et al. (2002). Participatory action research: From within and beyond prison bars. In P. Camic, J. E. Rhodes, & L. Yardley (Eds.), *Qualitative research in psychology: Expanding perspectives in methodology and design.* Washington, DC: American Psychological Association.

Fine, M., & Weis, L. (1998). *The unknown city.* Boston: Beacon Press.

Foley, D. (1990). *Learning capitalist culture: Deep in the heart of Texas.* Philadelphia: University of Pennsylvania Press.

Fordham, S. (1996). *Black out: Dilemmas of race, identity and success at Capital High School.* Chicago: University of Chicago Press.

Foucault, M. (1977). *Discipline and punish: The birth of the prison.* New York: Pantheon.

Freire, P. (1982). Creating alternative research methods. Learning to do it by doing it. In B. Hall, A. Gillette, & R. Tandon (Eds.), *Creating knowledge: A monopoly.* New Delhi: Society for Participatory Research in Asia.

Fruchter, N., Galletta, A., & White, J. (1992). *New directions in parent involvement.* Washington, DC: Academy for Educational Development.

Fullilove, M. (2000). The house of Joshua. In L. Weis & M. Fine (Eds.), *Construction sites.* New York: Teachers College Press.

Gorz, A. (1982). *Farewell to the working class.* London: Pluto.

Gramsci, A. (1971). *Selections from prison notebooks.* New York: International.

Greene, M. (1995). *Releasing the imagination: Essays on education, the arts, and social change.* San Francisco: Jossey-Bass.

Haney, W., Russell, M., & Jackson, L. (1997). *Using drawings to study and change education.* Boston: Center for the Study of Testing, Evaluation and Educational Policy at Boston College.

Harding, S. (1983). *Discovering reality: Feminist perspectives on epistemology, metaphysics, methodology, and philosophy of science.* Dordrecht, Holland: D. Reidel.

Hartstock, N.C.M. (1983). *Money, sex, and power: Toward a feminist historical materialism.* New York: Longman.

Hayduk, R. (1999). *Regional analyses and structural racism.* Aspen, CO: Aspen Roundtable on Comprehensive Community Reform.

Hitchcock, P. (1999). *Oscillate wildly.* Minneapolis: University of Minnesota Press.

Hochschild, J. (2003). Social class meets the American dream in public schools. *Journal of Social Issues, 59*(4), 821–840.

hooks, b. (1984). *Feminist theory from margin to center.* Boston: South End.

Hunter, A. (1987). The role of liberal political culture in the construction of middle America. *University of Miami Law Review, 42*(1).

Hurtado, A., Haney, C., & Garcia, E. (1998). Becoming the mainstream: Merit, changing demographics and higher education in California. *La Raza Law Journal, 10*(2), 645–690.

Iatarola, P. (2001). *Distributing teacher quality equitably: The case of New York City* [Policy brief]. New York: Institute for Education and Social Policy.

Karenga, M. (1982). *Introduction to black studies.* Inglewood, CA: Kawaida.

Kozol, J. (1991). *Savage inequalities.* New York: Crown.

Ladson-Billings, G. (2000). Racialized discourses and ethnic epistemologies. In N. K. Denzin & Y. S. Lincoln (Eds.), *Handbook of qualitative research* (2nd ed.). Thousand Oaks, CA: Sage.

Lee, S. J. (1996). *Unraveling the "model minority" stereotype: Listening to Asian American youth.* New York: Teachers College Press.

Martín-Baró, I. (1994). *Writings for a liberation psychology.* Cambridge, MA: Harvard University Press.

Matsuda, M. (1995). Looking to the bottom: Critical legal studies and reparations. In K. Crenshaw, N. Gotanda, G. Peller, & K. Thomas (Eds.), *Critical race theory: The key writings that formed the movement.* New York: New Press.

Mills, C. W. (1959). *The sociological imagination.* London: Oxford University Press.

New York Association of Community Organizations for Reform Now. (2000). *The secret apartheid.* New York: ACORN Organizing Project.

Nieto, S. (1996). *Affirming diversity: The sociopolitical context of multicultural education* (2nd ed.). New York: Longman.

Noguera, P. (2003). *City schools and the American dream: Fulfilling the promise of public education.* New York: Teachers College Press.

Oakes, J., Wells, A., Yonezawa, S., & Ray, K. (1997). Equity lessons from detracking schools. In A. Hargreaves (Ed.), *Rethinking educational change with heart and mind.* Alexandria, VA: Association for Supervision and Curriculum Development.

O'Connor, C. (2001). Making sense of the complexity of social identity in relation to achievement: A sociological challenge in the new millennium. *Sociology of Education, 74,* 159–169.

Orfield, G., & Easton, S. (1996). *Dismantling desegregation.* New York: New Press.

Payne, C. (1995). *I've got the light of freedom: The organizing tradition and the Mississippi freedom struggle.* Berkeley: University of California Press.

Phoenix, A., Frosh, S., & Pattman, R. (2003). Producing contradictory masculine subject positions: Narrative of threat, homophobia and bulling in 11-14-year-old boys. *Journal of Social Issues, 59*(1), 179–196.

Reich, R. (1991). *The work of nations.* London: Simon and Schuster.

Reich, R. (2002). *The future of success.* New York: Alfred Knopf.

Rousso, H., & Wehmeyer, M. (2001). *Double jeopardy: Addressing gender equity in special education.* Albany: SUNY Press.

Rubin, L. (1976). *Worlds of pain: Life in the working-class family.* New York: Basic Books.

Sartre, J.-P. (1968). *Search for method.* New York: Vintage.

Scheper-Hughes, N., & Sargent, N. (1998). *Small wars: The cultural politics of childhood.* Berkeley: University of California Press.

Scott, J. (1990). *Domination and the art of resistance: Hidden transcripts.* New Haven, CT: Yale University Press.

Stack, C. B. (1997). *All our kin.* New York: Basic Books.

Stanton-Salazar, R. (1997). A social capital framework for understanding the socialization of racial minority children and youths. *Harvard Educational Review, 67,* 1–38.

Stepick, A., Stepick, C., Eugene, E., & Teed, D. (2001). Shifting identities. In A. Portes & R. Rumbaut (Eds.), *Ethnicities: Coming of age in immigrant America.* Berkeley: University of California Press.

Thorne, B. (1993). *Gender play: Girls and boys in school.* New Brunswick, NJ: Rutgers University Press.

Torre, M. E., & Fine, M. (2003). Critical perspectives on the "gap": Participatory action research with youth in "integrated" and segregated school settings. *Harvard Evaluation Exchange Newsletter.*

Twine, F. (2000). Racial ideologies and racial methodologies. In F. Twine & J. Warren (Eds.), *Racing research, researching race: Methodological dilemmas in the critical race studies.* New York: New York University Press.

Useem, E. (1990). Tracking students out of advanced mathematics. *American Educator, 14,* 24–46.

Valenzuela, A. (1999). *Subtractive schooling.* Albany: SUNY Press.

Walkerdine, V., Lacey, H., & Melody, J. (2001). *Growing up girl.* New York: New York University Press.

Wasley, P., Fine, M., King, S., Powell, L., Holland, N., & Gladden, M. (1999). *Small schools: Great strides.* New York: Bank Street College of Education.

Waters, M. (1999). *Black identities: West Indian immigrant dreams and American realities.* New York: Russell Sage Foundation.

Weis, L. (1990). *Working class without work: High school students in a de-industrializing economy.* New York: Routledge.

Weis, L. (2004). *Class reunion: The new working class.* New York: Routledge.

Wheelock, A. (1992). *Crossing the tracks.* New York: New Press.

Williams, P. (1992). *The alchemy of race and rights.* Cambridge, MA: Harvard University Press.

Willis, P. (1977). *Learning to labour.* Farnborough, UK: Saxon House.

Wilson, W. J. (1987). *The truly disadvantaged: The inner city, the underclass and public policy.* Chicago: University of Chicago Press.

Woodson, C. G. (1972). *The mis-education of the Negro.* New York: AMS Press. (Original work published 1933)

4

ON TRICKY GROUND

Researching the Native in the Age of Uncertainty

Linda Tuhiwai Smith

INTRODUCTION

In the spaces between research methodologies, ethical principles, institutional regulations, and human subjects as individuals and as socially organized actors and communities is tricky ground. The ground is tricky because it is complicated and changeable, and it is tricky also because it can play tricks on research and researchers. Qualitative researchers generally learn to recognize and negotiate this ground in a number of ways, such as through their graduate studies, their acquisition of deep theoretical and methodological understandings, apprenticeships, experiences and practices, conversations with colleagues, peer reviews, their teaching of others. The epistemological challenges to research—to its paradigms, practices, and impacts—play a significant role in making those spaces richly nuanced in terms of the diverse interests that occupy such spaces and at the same time much more dangerous for the unsuspecting qualitative traveler. For it is not just the noisy communities of difference "out there" in the margins of society who are moving into the research domain with new methodologies, epistemological approaches, and challenges to the way research is conducted. The neighbors are misbehaving as well. The pursuit of new scientific and technological knowledge, with biomedical research as a specific example, has presented new challenges to our understandings of what is scientifically possible and ethically acceptable. The turn back to the modernist and imperialist discourse of discovery, "hunting, racing, and gathering" across the globe to map the human genome or curing disease through the new science of genetic engineering, has an impact on the work of qualitative social science researchers. The discourse of discovery speaks through globalization and the marketplace of knowledge. "Hunting, racing, and gathering" is without doubt about winning. But wait—there is more. Also lurking around the corners are countervailing conservative forces that seek to disrupt any agenda of social justice that may form on such tricky ground. These forces have little tolerance for public debate, have little patience for alternative views, and have no interest in qualitative richness or complexity. Rather, they are nostalgic for a return to a research paradigm that, like life in general, should be simple.

It is often at the level of specific communities in the margins of a society that these complex currents intersect and are experienced. Some indigenous communities are examples of groups that have been historically vulnerable to research and remain vulnerable in many ways, but also have been able to resist as a group and to attempt to reshape and engage in research around their own interests. This chapter applies indigenous perspectives to examine the intersecting challenges of methodologies, ethics, institutions, and communities. It is a chapter about arriving at and often departing from commonly accepted understandings about the relationships between methodology, ethics, institutional demands, and the communities in which we live and with whom we research. Rather than a story of how complex the world is and how powerless we are to change it, this chapter is framed within a sense of the possible, of what indigenous communities have struggled for, have tried to assert and have achieved.

Indigenous Research and the Spaces From Which It Speaks

Indigenous peoples can be defined as the assembly of those who have witnessed, been excluded from, and have survived modernity and imperialism. They are peoples who have experienced the imperialism and colonialism of the modern historical period beginning with the Enlightenment. They remain culturally distinct, some with their native languages and belief systems still alive. They are minorities in territories and states over which they once held sovereignty. Some indigenous peoples do hold sovereignty, but of such small states that they wield little power over their own lives because they are subject to the whims and anxieties of large and powerful states. Some indigenous communities survive outside their traditional lands because they were forcibly removed from their lands and connections. They carry many names and labels, being referred to as natives, indigenous, autochthonous, tribal peoples, or ethnic minorities. Many indigenous peoples come together at regional and international levels to argue for rights and recognition. In some countries, such as China, there are many different indigenous groups and languages. In other places, such as New Zealand, there is one indigenous group, known as Māori, with one common language but multiple ways of defining themselves.

There are, of course, other definitions of indigenous or native peoples, stemming in part from international agreements and understandings, national laws and regulations, popular discourses, and the self-defining identities of the peoples who have been colonized and oppressed (Burger, 1987; Pritchard, 1998; Wilmer, 1993). The category of the native Other is one that Fanon (1961/1963) and Memmi (1957/1967) have argued is implicated in the same category as the settler and the colonizer. As opposing identities, they constitute each other as much as they constitute themselves. Rey Chow (1993) reminds us, however, that the native did exist before the "gaze" of the settler and before the image of "native" came to be constituted by imperialism, and that the native does have an existence outside and predating the settler/native identity. Chow (1993) refers to the "fascination" with the native as a "labor with endangered authenticities." The identity of "the native" is regarded as complicated, ambiguous, and therefore troubling even for those who live the realities and contradictions of being native and of being a member of a colonized and minority community that still remembers other ways of being, of knowing, and of relating to the world. What is troubling to the dominant cultural group about the definition of "native" is not what necessarily troubles the "native" community. The desire for "pure," uncontaminated, and simple definitions of the native by the settler is often a desire to continue to know and define the Other, whereas the desire by the native to be self-defining and self-naming can be read as a desire to be free, to escape definition, to be complicated, to develop and change, and to be regarded as fully human. In between such desires are multiple and shifting identities and hybridities with much more nuanced positions about what constitutes native identities, native communities, and native knowledge in anti/postcolonial times. There are also the not-insignificant matters of disproportionately high levels of poverty and underdevelopment, high levels of sickness and early death from preventable illnesses, disproportionate levels of incarceration, and other indices of social marginalization experienced by most indigenous communities.

There are some cautionary notes to these definitions, as native communities are not homogeneous, do not agree on the same issues, and do not live in splendid isolation from the world. There are internal relations of power, as in any society, that exclude, marginalize, and silence some while empowering others. Issues of gender, economic class, age, language, and religion are also struggled over in contemporary indigenous communities. There are native indigenous communities in the developed and in the developing world, and although material conditions even for those who live in rich countries are often horrendous, people in those countries are still better off than those in developing countries. There are, however, still many native and indigenous families and communities who possess the ancient memories of another way of knowing that informs many of their contemporary practices. When the foundations of those memories are disturbed, space sometimes is created for alternative imaginings to be voiced, to be sung, and to be heard (again).

The genealogy of indigenous approaches to research and the fact that they can be reviewed in this chapter is important because they have not simply appeared overnight, nor do they exist—as with other critical research approaches—without a politics of support around them or a history of ideas. This chapter speaks from particular historical, political, and moral spaces, along with a set of relationships and connections between indigenous aspirations, political activism, scholarship, and other social justice movements and scholarly work. Indigenous communities and researchers from different parts of the globe have long and often voiced concern about the "problem of research" and represented themselves to be among the "most researched" peoples of the world. The critique of research came to be voiced in the public domain in the 1970s, when indigenous political activism was also reasserting itself (Eidheim, 1997; Humphery, 2000; Langton, 1981; L. T. Smith, 1999). The history of research from many indigenous perspectives is so deeply embedded in colonization that it has been regarded as a tool only of colonization and not as a potential tool for self-determination and development. For indigenous peoples, research has a significance that is embedded in our history as natives under the gaze of Western science and colonialism. It is framed by indigenous attempts to escape the penetration and surveillance of that gaze while simultaneously reordering, reconstituting, and redefining ourselves as peoples and communities in a state of ongoing crisis. Research is a site of contestation not simply at the level of epistemology or methodology but also in its broadest sense as an organized scholarly activity that is deeply connected to power. That resistance to research, however, is changing ever so slightly as more indigenous and minority scholars have engaged in research methodologies and debates about research with communities (Bishop, 1998; Cram, Keefe, Ormsby, & Ormsby, 1998; Humphery, 2000; Pidgeon & Hardy, 2002; Smith, 1985; Worby & Rigney, 2002). It is also changing as indigenous communities and nations have mobilized internationally and have engaged with issues related to globalization, education systems, sovereignty, and the development of new technologies.

Indigenous peoples are used to being studied by outsiders; indeed, many of the basic disciplines of knowledge are implicated in studying the Other and creating expert knowledge of the Other (Helu Thaman, 2003; Said, 1978; Minh-ha, 1989; Vidich & Lyman, 2000). More recently, however, indigenous researchers have been active in seeking ways to disrupt the "history of exploitation, suspicion, misunderstanding, and prejudice" of indigenous peoples in order to develop methodologies and approaches to research that privilege indigenous knowledges, voices, experiences, reflections, and analyses of their social, material, and spiritual conditions (Rigney, 1999, p. 117). This shift in position, from seeing ourselves as passive victims of all research to seeing ourselves as activists engaging in a counterhegemonic struggle over research, is significant. The story of that progression has been told elsewhere in more depth and is not unique to indigenous peoples; women, gay and lesbian communities, ethnic minorities, and other marginalized communities have made similar journeys of critical discovery of the role of research in their lives (Hill Collins, 1991; Ladson-Billings, 2000; Mies, 1983; Moraga & Anzaldúa, 1983; Sedgwick, 1991). There have been multiple challenges to the epistemic basis of the dominant scientific paradigm of research, and these have led to the development of approaches that have offered a promise of counterhegemonic work. Some broad examples of these include oral history as stories of the working class, the range of feminist methodologies in both quantitative and qualitative research, the development of cultural and anti/postcolonial studies, critical race theory, and other critical approaches within disciplines (Beverley, 2000; Ladson-Billings, 2000; McLaren, 1993; Mohanty, 1984; Reinharz, 1992; Spivak, 1987; Stanley & Wise, 1983). Critical theorists have held out the hope that research could lead to emancipation and social justice for oppressed groups if research understood and addressed unequal relations of power. Feminism has challenged the deep patriarchy of Western knowledge and opened up new spaces for the examination of epistemological difference. Third World women, African American women, black women, Chicanas, and other minority group women have added immensely to our understandings of the intersections of gender, race, class, and imperialism and have attempted to describe what that means for themselves as researchers choosing to research in the margins (Aldama, 2001; Elabor-Idemudia, 2002; Hill Collins, 1991; Ladson-Billings, 2000; Mohanty, 1984; Moraga & Anzaldúa, 1983; Te Awekotuku, 1999). Indigenous women have played important roles in exploring the intersections of gender, race, class, and difference through the lens of native people and against the frame of colonization and oppression (K. Anderson, 2000; Maracle, 1996; Moreton-Robinson, 2000; L. T. Smith, 1992; Te Awekotuku, 1991; Trask, 1986).

The decolonization project in research engages in multiple layers of struggle across multiple sites. It involves the unmasking and deconstruction of imperialism, and its aspect of colonialism, in its old and new formations alongside a search for sovereignty; for reclamation of knowledge, language, and culture; and for the social transformation of the colonial relations between the native and the settler. It has been argued elsewhere that indigenous research needs an agenda that situates approaches and programs of research in the decolonization politics of the indigenous peoples movement (L. T. Smith, 1999). I would emphasize the importance of retaining the connections between the academy of researchers, the diverse indigenous communities, and the larger political struggle of decolonization because the disconnection of that relationship reinforces the colonial approach to education as divisive and destructive. This is not to suggest that such a relationship is, has been, or ever will be harmonious and idyllic; rather, it suggests that the connections, for all their turbulence, offer the best possibility for a transformative agenda that moves indigenous communities to someplace better than where they are now. Research is not just a highly moral and civilized search for knowledge; it is a set of very human activities that reproduce particular social relations of power. Decolonizing research, then, is not simply about challenging or making refinements to qualitative research. It is a much broader but still purposeful agenda for transforming the institution of research, the deep underlying structures and taken-for-granted ways of organizing, conducting, and disseminating research and knowledge. To borrow from Edward Said (1978), research can also be described as "a corporate institution" that has made statements about indigenous peoples, "authorising views" of us, "describing [us], teaching about [us], settling [us] and ruling over [us]." It is the corporate institution of research, as well as the epistemological foundations from which it springs, that needs to be decolonized.

> *I name this research methodology as Indigenist.*
>
> —Lester Rigney (1999, p. 118)

Becoming an indigenous researcher is somewhat like Maxine Green's (2000) description of

Table 4.1. Corporate Layers of Research

- Foundations, genealogies, and disciplines of knowledge that define its methodologies and its systems of classification and representation
- Historical embeddedness in imperialism, the production of knowledge, and the development of science
- Cultures and subcultures of its institutions and infrastructures
- Communities of like-minded or trained scholars, disciplinary bodies, and research associations
- Ways in which research is regulated and inscribed through notions of ethics, ethical review boards, and codes of conduct
- Practices of reporting and publishing
- National and international funding agencies and their links to particular agendas
- Ways in which some forms of research legitimate dominant forms of knowledge and maintain hegemony or dominant myths
- Chain and distribution of benefits from research
- Intersection of research with policy and the design and implementation of interventions

how artists from the margins come to re-imagine public spaces. "Through resistance in the course of their becoming—through naming what stood in their way, through coming together in efforts to overcome—people are likely to find out the kinds of selves they are creating" (p. 301). Indigenous researchers are "becoming" a research community. They have connected with each other across borders and have sought dialogue and conversations with each other. They write in ways that deeply resonate shared histories and struggles. They also write about what indigenous research ought to be. Australian Aborigine scholar Lester Rigney (1999), emphasizing Ward Churchill's (1993) earlier declarations of indigenist positioning, has argued for an indigenist approach to research that is formed around the three principles of *resistance*, *political integrity*, and *privileging* indigenous voices. He, like other indigenous researchers, connects research to liberation and to the history of oppression and racism. Rigney argues that research must serve and inform the political liberation struggle of indigenous peoples. It is also a struggle for development, for rebuilding leadership and governance structures, for strengthening social and cultural institutions, for protecting and restoring environments, and for revitalizing language and culture. Some indigenous writers would argue that indigenous research is research that is carried out by indigenous researchers with indigenous communities for indigenous communities (Cram, 2001; Rigney, 1999). Implicit in such a definition is that indigenous researchers are committed to a platform for changing the status quo and see the engagement by indigenous researchers as an important lever for transforming institutions, communities, and society. Other writers state that purpose more explicitly in that they define indigenous research as being a transformative project that is active in pursuit of social and institutional change, that makes space for indigenous knowledge, and that has a critical view of power relations and inequality (Bishop, 1998; Brady, 1999; Pihama, 2001; L. T. Smith, 1991). Others emphasize the critical role of research in enabling peoples and communities to reclaim and tell their stories in their own ways and to give *testimonio* to their collective herstories and struggles (Battiste, 2000; Beverley, 2000; The Latina Feminist Group, 2001). Embedded in these stories are the ways of knowing, deep metaphors, and motivational drivers that inspire the transformative praxis that many indigenous researchers identify as a powerful agent for resistance and change. These approaches connect and draw from indigenous knowledge and privilege indigenous pedagogies in their practices, relationships, and methodologies. Most indigenous researchers would claim that their research validates an ethical and culturally defined approach that enables indigenous communities to theorize their own lives and that connects their past histories with their future lives (Marker, 2003). Indigenous approaches are also mindful of and sensitive to the audiences of research and therefore of the accountabilities of researchers as storytellers, documenters of culture, and witnesses of the realities of indigenous lives, of their ceremonies, their aspirations, their incarcerations, their deaths. (Pihama, 1994; Steinhauer, 2003; Te Hennepe, 1993; Warrior, 1995).

In New Zealand, Māori scholars have coined their research approach as Kaupapa Māori or Māori research rather than employing the term "indigenist." There are strong reasons for such a naming, as the struggle has been seen as one over Māori language and the ability by Māori as Māori to name the world, to theorize the world, and to research back to power. The genealogy of indigenous research for Māori has one of its beginnings in the development of alternative Māori immersion-based schooling (Pihama, Cram, & Walker, 2002; G. H. Smith, 1990; L. T. Smith, 2000). Graham Smith (1990) has argued that the struggle to develop alternative schools known as Kura Kaupapa Māori helped produce a series of educational strategies that engaged with multiple levels of colonization and social inequality. These strategies included engagement with theory and research in new ways. Kaupapa Māori research has developed its own life, and as an approach or theory of research methodology, it has been applied across different disciplinary fields, including the sciences. It can be argued that researchers who employ a Kaupapa Māori approach are employing quite consciously a set of arguments, principles, and frameworks that relate to the purpose, ethics, analyses, and outcomes of research (Bishop & Glynn, 1999; Durie, 1992; Johnston, 2003; Pihama, 1993; L. T. Smith, 1991; Tomlins-Jahnke, 1997). It is a particular approach that sets out to make a positive difference for Māori, that incorporates a model of social change or transformation, that privileges Māori knowledge and ways of being, that sees the engagement in theory as well as empirical research as a significant task, and that sets out a framework for organizing, conducting, and evaluating Māori research (Jahnke & Taiapa, 1999; Pihama et al., 2002). It is also an approach that is active in building capacity and research infrastructure in order to sustain a sovereign research agenda that supports community aspirations and development (L. T. Smith, 1999). Those who work within this approach would argue that Kaupapa Māori research comes out of the practices, value systems, and social relations that are evident in the taken-for-granted ways that Māori people live their lives.

Indigenist research also includes a critique of the "rules of practice" regarding research, the way research projects are funded, and the development of strategies that address community concerns about the assumptions, ethics, purposes, procedures, and outcomes of research. These strategies often have led to innovative research questions, new methodologies, new research relationships, deep analyses of the researcher in context, and analyses, interpretations, and the making of meanings that have been enriched by indigenous concepts and language. To an extent, these strategies have encouraged nonindigenous researchers into a dialogue about research and, on occasion, to a reformulated and more constructive and collaborative research relationship with indigenous communities (Cram, 1997; Haig-Brown & Archibald, 1996; Simon & Smith, 2001; G. H. Smith, 1992). Critical and social justice approaches to qualitative research have provided academic space for much of the early work of indigenous research. Denzin and Lincoln (2000) describe a moment in the history of qualitative research (1970–1986) as the moment of "blurred genres" when local knowledge and lived realities became important, when a diversity of paradigms and methods developed, and when a theoretical and methodological blurring across boundaries occurred. Arguably, an indigenist research voice emerged in that blurred and liminal space as it paralleled the rise in indigenous political activism, especially in places like Australia, New Zealand,

Norway, and North America. For indigenous activists, this moment was also one of recognition that decolonization needed a positive and more inclusive social vision and needed more tools for development and self-determination (as an alternative to violent campaigns of resistance). Research, like schooling, once the tool of colonization and oppression, is very gradually coming to be seen as a potential means to reclaim languages, histories, and knowledge, to find solutions to the negative impacts of colonialism and to give voice to an alternative way of knowing and of being. Indigenous research focuses and situates the broader indigenous agenda in the research domain. This domain is dominated by a history, by institutional practices, and by particular paradigms and approaches to research held by academic communities and disciplines. The spaces within the research domain through which indigenous research can operate are small spaces on a shifting ground. Negotiating and transforming institutional practices and research frameworks is as significant as the carrying out of actual research programs. This makes indigenous research a highly political activity that can be perceived as threatening, destabilizing, and privileging of indigeneity over the interests and experiences of other diverse groups. Decolonization is political and disruptive even when the strategies employed are pacifist because anything that requires a major change of worldview, that forces a society to confront its past and address it at a structural and institutional level that challenges the systems of power, is indeed political. Indigenous research presents a challenge to the corporate institution of research to change its worldview, to confront its past and make changes.

Indigenous research approaches, like feminist methodologies, have not emerged into a neutral context, although their arrival has been predicted by those working with silenced and marginalized communities. As Lincoln (1993) forewarned, however, social sciences cannot simply develop grand narratives of the silenced without including the voices and understandings of marginalized and silenced communities. There continues to be vigorous critique of indigenous approaches and claims to knowledge, and, indeed, the indigenous presence in the academy. In some cases, this critique is framed by the discourses of anti–affirmative action, such as calls for "color- and race-free" policies. In other cases, the critique is a very focused attack on the possibility that indigenous people have a knowledge that can be differentiated from dogma and witchcraft or is a very focused and personal attack on an individual (Trask, 1993). In other examples, the critique does reflect attempts by nonindigenous scholars to engage seriously with indigenous scholarship and understand its implications for the practices of nonindigenous scholars and their disciplines. In a limited sense, there has been an attempt at dialogue between indigenous and nonindigenous scholars, usually occurring after indigenous scholars have provided a critique of the discipline—for example Vine Deloria's (1995) critique of anthropology and Ngugi wa Thiong'o's (1981/1987) critique of what counted as African literature. Kenyan writer Ngugi wa Thiong'o viewed the language of the settler/colonizer as being implicated in the "colonization of the mind" and came to the decision that he would not write in the language of the colonizer but instead would write in his own language of Gikuyu or Ki-Swahili. Ngugi's stance helped create further space for debate about "postcolonial" literature and the role of literature in colonial education systems (Ashcroft, Griffiths, & Tiffin, 1989). Vine Deloria's sustained political critique of the place of the American Indian in the American system has created space for the further development of American Indian Studies and a dialogue with other disciplines (Biolsi & Zimmerman, 1997). Unfortunately, dialogue is often the solution to fractures created through lack of dialogue between those with power and marginalized groups. Similar debates have occurred and continue to occur in other fields, including literature (Cook-Lynn, 1996; Harjo & Bird, 1997; Womack, 1999), feminist studies (Maracle, 1996; Moraga & Anzaldúa, 1983; Moreton-Robinson, 2000), and multicultural and ethnic studies (Mihesuah, 1998). Some debates are very public media campaigns that invoke the prejudices and attitudes toward indigenous peoples held by the dominant social group.[1] In some of these campaigns, the ethnicity of the dominant group is masked behind such social categories as "the public," "the taxpayers," or "the rest of society." The fears and attitudes of the dominant social group, and of other minority social groups, are employed quite purposefully in public debates about indigenous knowledge as the arbiters of what indigenous people are permitted to do, of what they are allowed to know, and indeed of who they are.

An important task of indigenous research in "becoming" a community of researchers is about capacity building, developing and mentoring researchers, and creating the space and support for new approaches to research and new examinations of indigenous knowledge. That activity can now be seen in a range of strategies that are being applied by diverse communities across the world to build research capability. Conversations about indigenous methodologies—albeit in different historical, disciplinary, and institutional spaces—are being discussed and applied by a diverse range of indigenous scholars across the globe. These include Sami scholars in northern Norway, Finland, Sweden, and Russia (Keskitalo, 1997) and native scholars in the Pacific Islands (Helu Thaman, 2003; Kaomea, 2003). Sami literary scholar Harald Gaski (1997), for example, argues that "Ever since the world's various indigenous peoples began turning their efforts to co-operative endeavours in the 1970s, the Sami have participated actively in the struggle to make these peoples' and their own voice heard. Art and literature have always played an important role in this endeavour. Therefore, the time for Sami literature to join world literature is past due" (p. 6). Jan Henri Keskitalo (1997) points to a research agenda for Sami people that is "based on the freedom to define, initiate and organize research, and the possibility to prioritise what kind of research should be defined as Sami research, at least when using public funding" (p. 169). All these discussions represent cross-border conversations and activism, as the territorial boundaries of many indigenous communities have been intersected and overlaid by the formation of modern states. Some discussions occur through specific indigenous forums, or through feminist or environmentalist networks, and others occur through the diaspora of the Third World, the "developing world," and regional gatherings (Alexander & Mohanty, 1997; Saunders, 2002; Shiva, 1993; Spivak, 1987).

Researching the Native in the Knowledge Economy

Knowledge is a key commodity in the 21st century. We understand this at a commonsense level simply as an effect of living in the era of globalization, although it is also expressed as the consequences of life in the postindustrial age, the age of information and postmodernity. Knowledge as a

Table 4.2. Strategies for Building Indigenous Research Capability

- The training of indigenous people as researchers
- The employment of indigenous people as researchers
- Participation by indigenous people in a wide range of research projects employing different kinds of approaches and methodologies
- The generating of research questions by communities
- Developing indigenous research methodologies
- Developing research protocols for working with communities
- The support by various individuals and communities of research-based decision making
- The establishment of indigenous research organizations
- Presentation of their research by indigenous researchers to other indigenous researchers
- Engagements and dialogue between indigenous and nonindigenous researchers and communities

commodity is a conception of knowledge (and curriculum) that is situated in the intersection of different visions of and alliances for globalization (Peters, 2003). Michael Apple (2001) refers to this alliance as one that brings together neoliberals, neoconservatives, authoritarian populists, and the new middle class. Apple defines neoliberals as those who are "deeply committed to markets and to freedom as 'individual choice,'" neoconservatives as ones who "want a return to discipline and traditional knowledge," authoritarian populists as ones who "want a return to (their) God in all of our institutions" (p. 11), and the new middle class as those who have created and stand to benefit most from this configuration of interests. The neoliberal economic vision of globalization is one in which the market shapes and determines most, if not all, human activities. Far from being simply an economic theory, neoliberal proponents have used their access to power to attempt to reform all aspects of society, including the relationships between the state and society. New Zealand is often used as a model, the "experiment" for how far this agenda can be pursued, because of the significant neoliberal reforms undertaken over the last 20 years (Kelsey, 1995). The reforms have included a "hollowing out" of the state; the reform and re-regulation of the welfare system—education, health, banking, and finance; and the removal of tariffs and other barriers to free trade (Moran, 1999). The reforms have been supported by a powerful ideological apparatus that has denied empirical evidence that groups were being marginalized further by policies and that the gaps between the rich and poor, the well and the sick, were widening under the reform regime. This ideological apparatus is most visible in its discursive strategies with rhetoric and slogans such as "user pays," privatization, increased competition, freedom of choice, and voucher education. It is also evident in the construction of new, idealized neoliberal subjects who are supposed to be "self-regulating selective choosers, highly competitive and autonomous individuals liberated from their locations in history, the economy, culture and community in order to become consumers in a global market" (L. T. Smith et al., 2002, p. 170).

The significance of the neoliberal agenda for social science research is that the "social," the "science," and the "research" have also been re-envisioned and re-regulated according to the neoliberal ideologies. One site where this re-envisioning and re-regulation of the social, the science, and the research intersects is in the economy of knowledge. As with other strategies of power, it is often the marginalized and silenced communities of society who experience the brunt and the cruelty of both the slogans and the material changes in their lives. The "knowledge economy" is a term used by businesspeople such as Thomas Stewart (1997) to define the ways in which changes in technology such as the Internet, the removal of barriers to travel and trade, and the shift to a postindustrial economy have created conditions in which the knowledge content of all goods and services will underpin wealth creation and determine competitive advantage. As a commodity, knowledge is produced under capitalist labor market conditions: it can be bought and sold, and it is private rather than public property. Researchers are knowledge workers who produce new knowledge. In this environment, new and unique knowledge products become highly prized objects of capitalist desire. Mapping the human genome and searching for cures to various diseases that will require the manufacturing of special products are just two examples of the "race" now on for "knowledge," the new El Dorado. Now, where can one discover new knowledge that is not already under private ownership? The laboratories? The rain forests? The human body? The knowledge and practices of those who have maintained their unique ways of living? The answer to all the above is "Yes," and there is more. Indigenous knowledge once denied by science as irrational and dogmatic is one of those new frontiers of knowledge. The efforts by indigenous peoples to reclaim and protect their traditional knowledge now coincides and converges with scientific interests in discovering how that knowledge can offer new possibilities for discovery (Stewart-Harawira, 1999).

One convergence of indigenous knowledge and science is in the field of ethnobotany, a field that has botanists and biologists working closely with indigenous communities in the collection and documentation of plants, medicinal remedies, and other practices. In doing science, ethnobotanists are also doing qualitative research, talking to community experts, observing practices, and developing word banks and other resources. The protocols that have been developed by the International Society of Ethnobotany will be discussed again later in this chapter. One use of the research that its members gather lies in the identification of medicinal properties that can be reproduced in the laboratory and developed for commercialization. The pharmaceutical industry has a keen hunger for such research, and there is real intensity in the hunt for new miracles to cure or alleviate both old and modern diseases. The search for new knowledge knows no borders. It is competitive and expensive, and only a few can participate. In the biomedical field, the rapid advances in knowledge and technology—for example, in reproductive birth technologies and in genetic engineering—present new challenges to what society thinks is ethically acceptable. Issues raised in relation to cloning a human being, new genetic therapies, and other remedies and practices stretch our understandings of what life is about. Although the science can develop the new knowledge, it is the *social* science that has an understanding of the nature of social change. Scientists, however, can also be powerful advocates of their own discoveries and fields of research, such that institutions and industries "buy into" the promise of new technologies and expect society to "catch up" to the ethical implications of the new knowledge. For qualitative research, new technologies present new vistas in a sense, new attitudes to examine and new dilemmas to resolve. For indigenous and other marginalized communities, the new vistas present new threats and risks in terms of their ability to protect their traditional knowledge and the likelihood of the benefits of research being distributed equitably to the poor rather than to the rich.

As Apple (2001) reminds, us, however, the neoliberal agenda also converges with the countervailing neoconservative and authoritarian tendencies that seek to protect and strengthen certain "traditional" forms of privilege. The "traditional" values and forms of knowledge being reified by these interest groups are not the same traditional values and ways of knowing that indigenous peoples speak of but are in fact the very antithesis of any form of non-Western, nonheterosexual, nonfeminist knowledge. Graham Hingangaroa Smith (1994) argues that there are new types of colonization in the neoliberal version of globalization that enable dominant interests in society to be maintained. Smith (1994) further contends that in the global marketplace, where everything can be commodified, local communities, cultures, practices, and values are put at accelerated risk, with little room to maneuver or develop resistance. One analogy of how the global marketplace works to put local communities and knowledge at risk is the impact of the large multinational or national company that sets up its store or its mall in a town that has small and struggling businesses. There are powerful driving forces that shape the ways in which individual interests come to be either aligned with or marginalized from the new development. For example, some people may need employment and others may need access to cheaper products; some people need to retain their businesses or see their community as being defined by the "Main Street," not the Mall. Young people may see the Mall as presenting new social possibilities that would cater more to their tastes by providing access to more global brands. In the end, the community becomes divided by economic interests, although all may ultimately wish for a united community. In the end, the Mall wins: The small businesses either collapse or struggle on; Main Street looks even more depressing, driving more people to the Mall; and everyone in town begins wearing the global brands, just like the people on television and the people who live in the next community, the next state, the next country. Local products, if they are made, find their way to a boot sale or a market day, basically consigned to the margins of the economy and community consciousness. Some local or native products are selected as marketable in the Mall, such as native medicine wheels and small hanging crystals. These products are not produced locally, because that would cost too much, so the *image* is reproduced at a cheaper price in countries with poor labor market conditions and then sold in every mall in the world. Imagine this as a global process having an impact in every little community of the world. It is a very seductive process, but something gets lost, in this process, for the community. For indigenous communities, the "something lost" has been defined as indigenous knowledge and culture. In biological terms, the "something lost" is our diversity; in sociolinguistics, it is the diversity of minority languages; culturally, it is our uniqueness of stories and experiences and how they are expressed. These are the "endangered authenticities" of which Rey Chow (1993) speaks, ones that are being erased through the homogenization of culture.

The knowledge economy, as one theme of globalization, constitutes the new identities of the self-regulating and selective chooser, the consumer of knowledge products, the knowledge worker and knowledge manager, and the clients of knowledge organizations. McLaren (1993, p. 215) calls these *market identities* that reflect the corporate model of market education and educational consumption. One might think that this makes for a very educated and knowledgeable society—not so. The knowledge economy is about creating and processing knowledge, trading and using knowledge for competitive advantage—it is not about knowing or knowledge for its own sake, it is not about the pursuit of knowledge but about "creating" knowledge by turning knowledge into a commodity or product. Research plays an important role in the creation of knowledge and, as argued by Steven Jordan (2003) in an article he entitled "Who stole my methodology?," even the most participatory research models are being subjected to the processes of commodification "for the purposes of supporting and reproducing the social relations of accumulation in their multifarious forms" (p. 195). Jordan further suggests that the methodology of participatory research is being appropriated and reconstituted by neoliberal discourses of participation "in ways that are antithetical to both its founding principles and traditions" (p. 195).

The neoliberal version of globalization is not, however, the only ideology at work across the globe. There are other interests at work, some repressive and others progressive. Trafficking in drugs and people, catering to pedophilia, and other organized criminal activities also have gone global. More recently, global terrorism (recognizing that some communities have been terrorized for hundreds of years by various forms of colonialism) has heightened the impulses and fears of neoconservatives and authoritarian populists and simultaneously has created threats to the free operations of the global marketplace. The powerful nostalgia of neoconservatives and authoritarian populists for a curriculum of the right (Apple, 2001), a curriculum of simple "facts," and a reification of what Denzin (1991) refers to as "ancient narratives" augurs dangers for education, for educational research, and for any social justice research. Neoconservative and authoritarian interest groups seek to disrupt any agenda for social justice and already have been effective in peeling back gains in social justice programs, although Roman and Eyre (1997) caution us to see the dangers of "applying 'backlash' exclusively to Right-wing political reactions [that] fail to draw attention to reactionary and defensive politics within and across left-wing/progressive groups—whether feminist, critical multicultural/anti-racist, or anti-heterosexist" (p. 3). The neoliberal agenda crosses the left and right of the political spectrum, and to some extent the fellow travelers of neoliberalism manage to infiltrate a wide spectrum of politics.

Other, more progressive groups also have managed to go global and make use of knowledge in the pursuit of a social justice agenda. Nongovernmental organizations and communities of interest have managed to put up resistance to the powerful interests of wealthy nations and corporations. Some of these coalitions have brought together diverse interests and unusual bedfellows to contest free trade; others have organized important consciousness-raising activities to keep information about injustice in the public eye. Small communities still cling to their own schools and identities as they attempt to build democratic community consensus. One of the perspectives that indigenous research brings to an understanding of this moment in the history of globalization is that it is simply another historical moment (one of many that indigenous communities have survived) that reinscribes imperialism with new versions of old colonialisms. This is not as cynical as it may sound; rather, it comes from the wisdom of survival on the margins. This moment can be analyzed, understood, and disrupted by holding onto and rearticulating an alternative vision of life and society. It is also not the only defining moment: Other changes have occurred that make communities somewhat more prepared to act or resist. For example, more indigenous researchers are choosing to research alongside their own communities. There are more allies. There also are other imperatives that have driven an agenda of transformation; among them is language regeneration. Language regeneration programs have created a momentum, especially in New Zealand, that neoliberal reforms have not been able or willing to subvert, as these programs have a strong hold on the community's aspirations. Indigenous development is optimistic despite what often appear to be huge barriers.

The new subjectivities of the free market and the knowledge economy also include the re-envisioning and re-regulation of new native subjects, a reworked Other, still raced and gendered, idealized and demonized, but now in possession of "market potential." Some of these new subjectivities resonate with the global market, where evoking of "the image" is a powerful mechanism for distancing the material conditions of the people from the image itself. Other subjectivities are "turning the gaze" back onto the dominant settler society, reflecting the momentum of political, educational, and economic change that already has occurred in many indigenous communities. These identities are formed "in translation," in the constant negotiation for meaning in a changing context. New identities form and re-form in response to or as a consequence of other changes and other identities. New voices are expressed, new leaders emerge, new organizations form, and new narratives of identity get told.

One newly worked native identity is that of the native intellectual as scientist. This is a small, emerging group of native scientists with strong connections to their native knowledge and practices. These scientists represent a new type of translator or interlocutor, one who bridges different knowledge traditions in ways that Western scientists find difficult to dismiss and indigenous communities find acceptable (Little Bear, 2000; Thomas, 2001). The native scientist not only is the native healer, herbalist, or spiritual expert but also is someone who understands the philosophies, knowledge, and histories that underpin cultural practices and beliefs and who generates his or her science from these foundations. As Basso (1996) and Marker (2003) have suggested, these people are not in the academy to "play word and idea games" but intend to contribute to change for the benefit of communities, to ensure that science listens to, acknowledges, and benefits indigenous communities. The role of these indigenous professionals is similar to the role played by the first generation of indigenous teachers and nurses and by the first generation of medical doctors and social workers in native communities, a difficult role of translating, mediating, and negotiating values, beliefs, and practices from different worldviews in difficult political contexts.

Ethics and Research

One area of research being vigorously contested by indigenous communities is that of research ethics and the definitions and practices that exemplify ethical and respectful research. Indigenous researchers often situate discussions about ethics in the context of indigenous knowledge and values and in the context of imperialism, colonialism, and racism (Cram, 1993; 2001; Menzies, 2001; Rigney, 1999). Indigenous understandings of research ethics have often been informed by indigenous scholars' broad experience of research and other interactions with the media, health system, museums, schools, and government agencies. Increasingly, however, research ethics has come to be a focus of indigenous efforts to transform research and institutions (Worby & Rigney, 2002). Research ethics is often much more about institutional and professional regulations and codes of conduct than it is about the needs, aspirations, or worldviews of "marginalized and vulnerable" communities.

Institutions are bound by ethical regulations designed to govern conduct within well-defined principles that have been embedded in international agreements and national laws. The Nuremberg Code (1949) was the first major international expression of principles that set out to protect the rights of people from research abuse, but there are other significant agreements, such as the World Medical Association Declaration of Helsinki Agreement of 1964 and the Belmont Report of 1979. National jurisdictions and professional societies have their own regulations that govern ethical conduct of research with human subjects. Increasingly, the challenges of new biotechnologies—for example, new birth technologies, genetic engineering, and issues related to cloning—also have given rise to ethical concerns, reviews, and revised guidelines.

For indigenous and other marginalized communities, research ethics is at a very basic level about establishing, maintaining, and nurturing reciprocal and respectful relationships, not just among people as individuals but also with people as individuals, as collectives, and as members of communities, and with humans who live in and with other entities in the environment. The abilities to enter preexisting relationships; to build, maintain, and nurture relationships; and to strengthen connectivity are important research skills in the indigenous arena. They require critical sensitivity and reciprocity of spirit by a researcher. Bishop (1998) refers to an example of relationship building in the Māori context as whakawhanaungatanga, "the process of establishing family (whânau) relationships, literally by means of identifying, through culturally appropriate means, your bodily linkage, your engagement, your connectedness, and therefore, an unspoken but implicit commitment to other people" (p. 203). Worby and Rigney (2002) refer to the "Five Rs: Resources, Reputations, Relationships, Reconciliation and Research" (pp. 27–28) as informing the process of gaining ethical consent. They argue that "The dynamic relationship between givers and receivers of knowledge is a reminder that dealing with indigenous issues is one of the most sensitive and complex tasks facing teachers, learners and researchers at all levels . . ." (p. 27). Bishop and Glynn (1992) also make the point that relationships are not simply about making friends. They argue that researchers must be self-aware of their position within the relationship and aware of their need for engagement in power-sharing processes.

In *Decolonizing Methodologies* (L. T. Smith, 1999), I also gave some examples of the ways in which my communities may describe respect, respectful conduct, trustworthiness, and integrity at a day-to-day level of practice and community assessment. My concern was to show that community people, like everyone else, make assessments of character at every interaction. They assess people from the first time they see them, hear them, and engage with them. They assess them by the tone of a letter that is sent, as well as by the way they eat, dress, and speak. These are applied to strangers as well as insiders. We all do it. Different cultures, societies, and groups have ways of masking, revealing, and managing how much of the assessment is actually conveyed to the other person and, when it is communicated, in what form and for what purpose. A colleague, Fiona Cram (2001), has translated how the selected value statements in *Decolonizing Methodologies* could be applied by researchers to reflect on their own codes of conduct. This could be described as an exercise of "bottom-up" or "community-up" defining of ethical behaviors that create opportunities to discuss and negotiate what is meant by the term "respect." Other colleagues have elaborated on the values, adding more and reframing some to incorporate other cultural expressions. One point to make is that most ethical codes are top down, in the sense of "moral" philosophy framing the meanings of ethics and in the sense that the powerful still make decisions for the powerless. The discussions, dialogues, and conversations about what ethical research conduct looks like are conducted in the meeting rooms of the powerful.

No one would dispute the principle of *respect*; indeed, it is embedded in all the major ethical protocols for researching with human subjects. However, what is *respect*, and how do we know when researchers are behaving respectfully? What does *respect* entail at a day-to-day level of interaction?

Table 4.3. "Community-Up" Approach to Defining Researcher Conduct

Cultural Values (Smith, 1999)	*Researcher Guideline (Cram, 2001)*
Aroha ki te tangata	A respect for people—allow people to define their own space and meet on their own terms.
He kanohi kitea	It is important to meet people face to face, especially when introducing the idea of the research, "fronting up" to the community before sending out long, complicated letters and materials.
Titiro, whakarongo . . . kôrero	Looking and listening (and then maybe speaking). This value emphasizes the importance of looking/observing and listening in order to develop understandings and find a place from which to speak.
Manaaki ki te tangata	Sharing, hosting, being generous. This is a value that underpins a collaborative approach to research, one that enables knowledge to flow both ways and that acknowledges the researcher as a learner and not just a data gatherer or observer. It is also facilitates the process of "giving back," of sharing results and of bringing closure if that is required for a project but not to a relationship.
Kia tupato	Be cautious. This suggests that researchers need to be politically astute, culturally safe, and reflective about their insider/outsider status. It is also a caution to insiders and outsiders that in community research, things can come undone without the researcher being aware or being told directly.
Kaua e takahia te mana o te tangata	Do not trample on the "mana" or dignity of a person. This is about informing people and guarding against being paternalistic or impatient because people do not know what the researcher may know. It is also about simple things like the way Westerners use wit, sarcasm, and irony as discursive strategies or where one sits down. For example, Māori people are offended when someone sits on a table designed and used for food.
Kaua e mahaki	Do not flaunt your knowledge. This is about finding ways to share knowledge, to be generous with knowledge without being a "show-off" or being arrogant. Sharing knowledge is about empowering a process, but the community has to empower itself.

To be respectful, what else does a researcher need to understand? It is when we ask questions about the apparently universal value of respect that things come undone, because the basic premise of that value is quintessentially Euro-American. What at first appears a simple matter of *respect* can end up as a complicated matter of cultural protocols, languages of respect, rituals of respect, dress codes: in short, the "p's and q's" of etiquette specific to cultural, gender, and class groups and subgroups. *Respect*, like other social values, embraces quite complex social norms, behaviors, and meanings, as one of many competing and active values in any given social situation. As an ethical principle, *respect* is constructed as universal partly through the process of defining what it means in philosophical and moral terms, partly through a process of distancing the social value and practice of *respect* from the messiness of any particular set of social interactions, and partly through a process of wrapping up the principle in a legal and procedural framework. The practice of *respect* in research is interpreted and expressed in very different ways on the basis of methodology, theoretical paradigms, institutional preparation, and individual idiosyncrasies and "manners."

Similarly, the principle and practice of *informed consent* presents real-world problems for researchers and for the researched. Fine, Weis, Weseen, and Wong (2000) already have discussed the ways in which "the consent form sits at the contradictory base of the institutionalisation of research" (p. 113). The form itself can be, as they argue, a "crude tool—a conscience—to remind us of our accountability and position" (p. 113). They argue that a consent form makes the power relations between researchers and researched concrete, and this can present challenges to researchers and researched alike, with some participants *wanting* to share their stories while others may feel *compelled* to share. The form itself can be the basis of dialogue and mediation, but the individual person who is participating in the research still must sign it. The principle of *informed consent* is based on the right of individuals to give consent to participation once they have been informed about the project and believe that they understand the project. In some jurisdictions, this right does not necessarily apply to children, prisoners, or people who have a mental illness. Nevertheless, the right is an individual one. However, what if participating in a research project, unwittingly or wittingly, reveals collective information to researchers—for example, providing DNA, sharing the making of a medicine, or revealing secret women's or men's business as may occur in societies like Aboriginal Australian communities, where men's knowledge and women's knowledge is strictly differentiated? Researching with children already has opened up the possibility that family secrets, especially stories of abuse, require actions to be taken beyond the simple gathering of data. One concern of indigenous communities about the *informed consent* principle is about the bleeding of knowledge away from collective protection through individual participation in research, with knowledge moving to scientists and organizations in the world at large. This process weakens indigenous collectively shared knowledge and is especially risky in an era of knowledge hunting and gathering. Another concern is about the nature of what it really means to be informed for people who may not be literate or well educated, who may not speak the language of the researcher, and who may not be able to differentiate the *invitation* to participate in research from the enforced compliance in signing official forms for welfare and social service agencies.

The claim to universal principles is one of the difficulties with ethical codes of conduct for research. It is not just that the concepts of respect, beneficence, and justice have been defined through Western eyes; there are other principles that inform ethical codes that can be problematic under certain conditions. In some indigenous contexts, the issue is framed more around the concept of *human rights* rather than principles or values. However, whether it is about principles, values, or rights, there is a common underpinning. Ethics codes are for the most part about protecting the individual, not the collective. Individuals can be "picked off" by researchers even when a community signals it does not approve of a project. Similarly, the claim to beneficence, the "save mankind" claim made even before research has been completed, is used to provide a moral imperative that certain forms of research must be supported at the expense of either individual or community consent. Research is often assumed to be beneficial simply because it is framed as research; its benefits are regarded as "self-evident" because the intentions of the researcher are "good." In a review of health research literature reporting on research involving indigenous Australians, I. Anderson, Griew, and McAullay (2003) suggest that very little attention is paid to the concept of benefit by researchers, and even less attention is paid to the assessment of research benefit. A consequence of the lack of guidelines in this area, they argue, is that "in the absence of any other guidelines the values that guide such a judgement will reflect those of the ethics committee as opposed to those of the Indigenous community in which research is proposed" (p. 26).

A more significant difficulty, already alluded to, can be expressed more in terms of "who" governs, regulates, interprets, sanctions, and monitors ethical codes of conduct" "Who" is responsible if things go terribly wrong? And "who" really governs and regulates the behaviors of scientists outside institutions and voluntary professional societies? For example, rogue scientists and quirky religious groups are already competing for the glory of cloning human beings with those whose research is at least held to a acceptable standards because of their employment in recognized institutions. From an indigenous perspective, the "who" on ethical review boards is representative of narrow class, religious, academic, and ethnic groups rather than reflecting the diversity of society. Because these boards are fundamentally supportive of research for advancing knowledge and other high-level aims, their main task is to advance research, not to limit it. In other words, their purpose is not neutral; it is to assist institutions to undertake research—within acceptable standards. These boards are not where larger questions about society's interests in research ought to be discussed; they generally are the place where already determined views about research are processed, primarily to protect institutions. Marginalized and vulnerable groups are not, by and large, represented on such boards. If a marginalized group is represented, its voice is muted as one of many voices of equal weight but not of equal power. Hence, even if a representative of a marginalized group is included on a review board, the individual may not have the support, the knowledge, or the language to debate the issue among those who accept the dominant Western view of ethics and society. These are difficult concerns to resolve but need to be discussed in an ongoing way, as ethical challenges will always exist in societies.

King, Henderson, and Stein (1999) suggest that there are two paradigms of ethics, the one we know as principalist and a potentially new one in process that is about relationships. King, Henderson, and Stein argue that the ethics regulations that researchers currently work under are based on three factors:

- Balancing principles: autonomy, beneficence, justice, informed consent, and confidentiality
- Ethical universalism (not moral relativism): truth (not stories)
- Atomistic focus: small frame, centered on individuals.

In the case of the International Society of Ethnobiology (ISE), a society of scientists whose work involves indigenous communities, the Code of Ethics that was developed with indigenous participation identifies 15 principles upon which ethical conduct rests. These principles include such things as the principles of self-determination, inalienability, traditional guardianship, and active participation. The ISE Code of Ethics suggests that research needs to be built on meaningful partnerships and collaboration with indigenous communities. Similarly, the Australian Institute of Aboriginal and Torres Strait Islander Studies published the *Guidelines for Ethical Research in Indigenous Studies* (2000) after conducting workshops with indigenous studies researchers. The *Guidelines* connect the notion of ethical principles with human rights and seek to "embody the best standards of ethical research and human rights" (p. 4). The *Guidelines* propose three major principles, inside of which are fuller explanations of the principles and practical applications. The three main principles are

- Consultation, negotiation, and mutual understanding
- Respect, recognition, and involvement
- Benefits, outcomes, and agreement.

Within the principles of the *Guidelines* are further subprinciples, such as respect for indigenous knowledge systems and processes, recognition of the diversity and uniqueness of peoples and individuals, and respect for intellectual and cultural property rights and involvement of indigenous individuals and communities as research collaborators.

Principles are balancing factors that still rest upon the assumption that the principles are understood as meaning the same thing to all people under all circumstances. As Denzin (2003) argues, this approach implies a singular approach to all forms of inquiry that oversimplifies and dehumanizes the human subject. Indigenous communities and other marginalized groups may not understand the history of the ethical code of conduct or its basis in Western moral philosophy, but they do understand breaches of respect and negative impacts from research such as the removal of their rights and lands. Qualitative researchers also know that emerging methodologies and emerging researchers have a difficult time making their way through the review process to gain approval. Kathleen M. Cumiskey (1998) narrates her experiences in dealing with her institutional review board as ones that came down to a reminder that graduate students would not be indemnified if she happened to be arrested or her work subpoenaed. The emphasis on procedural issues, including the balancing of risks and benefits, inhibits or limits the potential for institutions and society to examine ethics against a much broader social and epistemological framework.

What does an indigenous approach to research contribute to a discussion about ethical standards? Indigenous perspectives challenge researchers to reflect upon two significant contributions. In the first instance, indigenous communities share with other marginalized and vulnerable communities a collective and historically sustained experience of research as the Object. They also share the use of a "research as expert" representation of who they are. It is an experience indigenous communities associate with colonialism and racism, with inequality and injustice. More important, indigenous communities hold an alternative way of knowing about themselves and the environment that has managed to survive the assaults of colonization and its impacts. This alternative way of knowing may be different from what was known several hundred years ago by a community, but it is still a way of knowing that provides access to a different epistemology, an alternative vision of society, an alternative ethics for human conduct. It is not, therefore, a question of whether the knowledge is "pure" and authentic but whether it has been the means through which people have made sense of their lives and circumstances, that has sustained them and their cultural practices over time, that forms the basis for their understanding of human conduct, that enriches their creative spirit and fuels their determination to be free. The first contribution of an indigenous perspective to any discussion about research ethics is one that challenges those of us who teach about research ethics, who participate in approving and monitoring ethics proposals, to understand the historical development of research as a corporate, deeply colonial institution that is structurally embedded in society and its institutions. It is not just about training and then policing individual researchers, nor about ensuring that research with human subjects is an ethical activity. One thing we must have learned from the past is that when research subjects are not regarded as human to begin with, when they have been dehumanized, when they have been marginalized from "normal" human society, the human researcher does not see human subjects. To unravel the story of research ethics with human subjects, teachers and students must understand that research ethics is not just a body of historical "hiccups" and their legal solutions. It is a study of how societies, institutions, disciplines, and individuals *authorize, describe, settle, and rule.* It is a study of historical imperialism, racism, and patriarchy and the new formations of these systems in contemporary relations of power. It is a study of how humans fail and succeed at treating each other with respect.

Just as important, the second contribution indigenous research offers is a rich, deep, and diverse resource of alternative ways of knowing and thinking about ethics, research relationships, personal conduct, and researcher integrity. There are other ways to think about ethics that are unique to each culture. There are other ways to guide researcher conduct and ensure the integrity of research and the pursuit of knowledge. In New Zealand, as one example, Māori are discussing ethics in relation to *tikanga*, defined briefly by Mead (2003) as "A body of knowledge and customary practices carried out characteristically by communities" (p. 15). Mead (2003) argues that Tikanga has three main aspects, of knowledge, practices, and actors, and that among, other things, tikanga provides guidelines about moral and behavioral issues and informs ethical matters. He proposes five "tests" that can be applied to an ethical dilemma from a *tikanga Māori* perspective. These "tests" draw on Māori values to provide a framework for arriving at a Māori position on a specific ethical issue. The "tests" include the following:

- Applying cultural understandings of knowledge (for example applying *mauri*, the view that every living thing has a *mauri or life force*)
- Genealogical stories (such as those that explain how living things were created)
- Precedents in history
- Relationships
- Cultural values (such as the value of looking after people).

Mead suggests that examining an ethical issue against each of the five "tests" provides a framework that enables the dilemma created by new technologies to be thought through in a way that meets cultural and ethical scrutiny while remaining open to new possibilities. It is also a way to build a cultural and community body of knowledge about new discoveries, technologies, and research ethics.

It may be that these and other explorations connect with King, Henderson, and Stein's (1999) conception of a relationships paradigm that includes the following elements:

Layering of relevant relationships—individuals and groups

Context based—what are the relevant contexts? Culture, gender, race/ethnicity, community, place, others

Crosscutting issues, wider frame of reference

Narrative focus

Continuity—issues arise before and continue after projects

Change—in relationships over time

It may also be a way that connects with Denzin's (2003) call for a more inclusive and flexible model that would apply to all forms of inquiry. Also, as suggested by I. Anderson, Griew, and McAullay (2003), there is a tension between the regulations of practice and the development of ethical relationships. They argue that there is a need to develop at least two layers of responsiveness, one involving institutional collaborations with communities and the other involving researcher relationships with communities that are also mediated by reformed research structures. Indigenous research offers access to a range of epistemic alternatives. I would not want to suggest that such ways are simply out there waiting to be discovered, but certainly there are people and communities willing to engage in a meaningful dialogue, and there is much to talk about.

Qualitative Travelers on Tricky Ground

Qualitative research in an age of terrorism, in a time of uncertainty, and in an era when knowledge as power is reinscribed through its value as a commodity in the global market place presents tricky ground for researchers. It is often at the local level of marginalized communities that these complex currents intersect and are experienced as material conditions of poverty, injustice, and oppression. It is also at this level that responses to such currents are created on the ground, for seemingly pragmatic reasons. Sometimes this approach may indeed be a reasonable solution, but at other times it draws into question the taken-for-granted understandings that are being applied to decisions made under pressure. What maps should qualitative researchers study before venturing onto such terrain? This is not a trick question but rather one that suggests that we do have some maps. We can begin with all the maps of qualitative research we currently have, then draw some new maps that enrich and extend the boundaries of our understandings beyond the margins. We need to draw on all our maps of understanding. Even those tired and retired maps of qualitative research may hold important clues such as the origin stories or genealogical beginnings of certain trends and sticking points in qualitative research.

Qualitative researchers, however, must be more than either travelers or cultural tourists. Qualitative research is an important tool for indigenous communities because it is the tool that seems most able to *wage the battle of representation* (Fine et al., 2000); to weave and unravel competing *storylines* (Bishop, 1998); to situate, place, and contextualize; to create spaces for decolonizing (Aldama, 2001, Tierney, 2000); to provide frameworks for hearing silence and listening to the voices of the silenced (LeCompte, 1993, L. T. Smith, 2001); to create spaces for dialogue across difference; to analyze and make sense of complex and shifting experiences, identities, and realities; and to understand little and big changes that affect our lives. Qualitative research approaches have the potential to respond to epistemic challenges and crises, to unravel and weave, to fold in and unmask the layers of the social life and depth of human experience. This is not an argument for reducing qualitative research to social activism, nor is it an argument that suggests that quantitative research cannot also do some of the same things, but rather an argument for the tools, strategies, insights, and expert knowledge that can come with having a focused mind trained on the qualitative experience of people.

Qualitative research has an expanding set of tools that enable finer-grained interpretations of social life. Expanding the understandings and tools of qualitative researchers is important in an era when the diversity of human experience in social groups and communities, with languages and epistemologies, is undergoing profound cultural and political shifts. Although it could be argued that this has always been the case because societies always are dynamic, there is an argument to be made about the rapid loss of languages and cultures, the homogenization of cultures through globalization, and the significance for many communities of the impact of human beings on the environment. Indigenous communities live with the urgency that these challenges present to the world and have sought, through international mobilization, to call attention to these concerns. It is considered a sign of success when the Western world, through one of its institutions, pauses even momentarily to consider an alternative possibility. Indigenous research actively seeks to extend that momentary pause into genuine engagement with indigenous communities and alternative ways of seeking to live with and in the world.

Note

1. For example, in January, 2004, a series of speeches was made in New Zealand by a conservative political leader that attacked the role of the Treaty of Waitangi in legislation, that claimed Māori had extra holiday entitlements, that Māori with academic qualifications had lower standards because of affirmative action entry practices, and that purported to represent a "race free" vision for New Zealand. The speeches were quickly taken up as a populist message even though they were based on information later found to be incorrect and exaggerated and were clearly underpinned by an understanding of race and ethnicity that resonated with the racist messages of Australia's One Nation Leader Pauline Hanson.

References

Aldama, A. J. (2001). *Disrupting savagism: Intersecting Chicana/o, Mexican immigrant, and Native American struggles for self-representation.* Durham, NC: Duke University Press.

Alexander, M. J., & Mohanty, C. T. (1997). *Feminist genealogies, colonial legacies, democratic futures.* New York: Routledge.

Anderson, I., Griew, R., & McAullay, D. (2003). Ethics guidelines, health research and indigenous Australians. *New Zealand Bioethics Journal, 4*(1), 20–29.

Anderson, K. (2000). *A recognition of being: Reconstructing native womanhood.* Toronto: Sumach Press.

Apple, M. (2001). *Educating the "right" way: Markets, standards, God, and inequality.* New York: RoutledgeFalmer.

Ashcroft, B., Griffiths, G., & Tiffin, H. (1989). *The empire writes back: Theory and practice in post-colonial literatures.* London: Routledge.

Australian Institute of Aboriginal and Torres Strait Islander Studies. (2000). *Guidelines for ethical research in indigenous studies.* Canberra: Author.

Basso, K. H. (1996). *Wisdom sits in places: Landscape and language among the Western Apache.* Albuquerque: University of New Mexico Press.

Battiste, M. (Ed.). (2000). *Reclaiming indigenous voice and vision.* Vancouver: University of British Columbia Press.

Beverley, J. (2000). Testimonio, subalternity, and narrative authority. In N. Denzin & Y. S. Lincoln (Eds.), *Handbook of qualitative research* (2nd ed., pp. 555–566). Thousand Oaks: Sage.

Biolsi, T., & Zimmerman, L. J. (Eds.). (1997). *Indians and anthropologists: Vine Deloria and the critique of anthropology.* Tucson: University of Arizona Press.

Bishop, R. (1998). Freeing ourselves from neo-colonial domination in research: A Māori approach to creating knowledge. *Qualitative Studies in Education, 11*(2), 199–219.

Bishop, R., & Glynn, T. (1992). He kanohi kitea: Conducting and evaluating educational research. *New Zealand Journal of Educational Studies, 27*(2), 125–135.

Bishop, R., & Glynn, T. (1999). Researching in Māori contexts: An interpretation of participatory consciousness. *Journal of Intercultural Studies,* 20(2), 167–182.

Brady, W. (1999). Observing the Other. *Eureka Street,* 9(1), 28–30.

Burger, J. (1987). *Report from the frontier: The state of the world's indigenous peoples.* London: Zed Books.

Chow, R. (1993). *Writing diaspora: Tactics of intervention in contemporary cultural studies.* Bloomington: Indiana University Press.

Churchill, W. (1993). I am indigenist. In W. Churchill (Ed.), *Struggle for the land: Indigenous resistance to genocide, ecocide, and expropriation in contemporary North America* (pp. 403–451). Monroe, ME: Common Courage Press.

Cook-Lynn, E. (1996). *Why I can't read Wallace Stegner and other essays: A tribal voice.* Madison: University of Wisconsin Press.

Cram, F. (1993). Ethics in Māori research. In L. Nikora (Ed.), *Cultural justice and ethics.* [Proceedings of the Cultural Justice and Ethics Symposium held as part of the New Zealand Psychological Society's annual conference]. Wellington, New Zealand: Victoria University.

Cram, F. (1997). Developing partnerships in research: Pâkehâ researchers and Māori research. *Sites, 35,* 44–63.

Cram, F. (2001). Rangahau Māori: Tona tika, tona pono—The validity and integrity of Māori research. In M. Tolich (Ed.), *Research ethics in Aotearoa New Zealand* (pp. 35–52). Auckland, New Zealand: Pearson Education.

Cram, F., Keefe, V., Ormsby, C., & Ormsby, W. (1998). Memorywork and Māori health research: Discussion of a qualitative method. *He Pukenga Kôrero: A Journal of Māori Studies,* 37–45.

Cumiskey, K. M. (1998). (De)facing the Institutional Review Board: Wrangling the fear and fantasy of ethical dilemmas and research on "at-risk" youth. In J. Ayala et al. (Eds.), *Speed bumps: Reflections on the politics and methods of qualitative work* (pp. 28–31). New York: State University of New York, Graduate School of Education.

Deloria, V., Jr. (1995). *Red earth, white lies: Native Americans and the myth of scientific fact.* New York: Scribner.

Denzin, N. (1991). *Images of postmodern society: Social theory and contemporary cinema.* Newbury Park, CA: Sage.

Denzin, N., & Lincoln, Y. S. (2000). The discipline and practice of qualitative research. In N. Denzin & Y. S. Lincoln (Eds.), *Handbook of qualitative research* (2nd ed., pp. 128). Thousand Oaks, CA: Sage.

Durie, A. (1992). *Whaia te Ara Tika: Research methodologies and Māori.* Seminar on Māori research at Massey University, Palmerston North, New Zealand.

Eidheim, H. (1997). Ethno-political development among the Sami after World War II: The invention of self-hood. In H. Gaski (Ed.), *Sami culture in a new era: The Norwegian Sami experience* (pp. 29–61). Kárásjohka, Norway: Davvi Girji.

Elabor-Idemudia, P. (2002). Participatory research: A tool in the production of knowledge in development discourse. In K. Saunders (Ed.), *Feminist development and thought: Rethinking modernity, post-colonialism and representation* (pp. 227–242). London: Zed Books.

Fanon, F. (1963). *Wretched of the earth* (C. Farrington, Trans.). New York: Grove Press. (Original work published 1961)

Fine, M., Weis, L., Weseen, S., & Wong, L. (2000). For whom? Qualitative research, representations, and social responsibilities. In N. Denzin & Y. S. Lincoln (Eds.), *Handbook of qualitative research* (2nd ed., pp. 107–132). Thousand Oaks, CA: Sage.

Gaski, H. (Ed.). (1997). *In the shadow of the midnight sun: Contemporary Sami prose and literature.* Kárásjohka, Norway: Davvi Girji.

Green, M. (2000). Lived spaces, shared spaces, public spaces. In L. Weis & M. Fine (Eds.), *Construction sites: Excavating race, class, and gender among urban youth* (pp. 293–304). New York: Teachers College Press.

Haig-Brown, C., & Archibald, J. (1996). Transforming First Nations research with respect and power. *Qualitative Studies in Education, 9*(3), 245–267.

Harjo, J., & Bird, G. (1997). *Reinventing the enemy's language. Contemporary native women's writing of North America.* New York: W. W. Norton and Company.

Helu Thaman, K. (2003). *Re-presenting and re-searching Oceania: A suggestion for synthesis.* Keynote address to the Pacific Health Research Fono, Health Research Council of New Zealand, Auckland.

Hill Colllins, P. (1991). Learning from the outsider within. In M. Fonow & J. A. Cook (Eds.), *Beyond methodology: Feminist scholarship as lived research* (pp. 35–57). Bloomington: Indiana University Press.

Humphery, K. (2000). *Indigenous health and "Western research"* (Discussion paper for VicHealth Koori Health Research and Community Development Unit). Melbourne: Centre for the Study of Health and Society, University of Melbourne.

Humphery, K. (2002). Dirty questions: Indigenous health and "Western research." *Australian and New Zealand Journal of Public Health, 25*(3), 197–202.

Jahnke, H., & Taiapa, J. (1999). Māori research. In C. Davidson & M. Tolich (Eds.), *Social science research in New Zealand: Many paths to understanding* (pp. 39–50). Auckland, New Zealand: Longman Pearson Education.

Johnston, P. M. (2003). Research in a bicultural context: The case in Aotearoa/New Zealand. In J. Swann & J. Pratt (Eds.), *Educational research practice: Making sense of methodology* (pp. 98–110). London: Continuum.

Jordan, S. (2003). Who stole my methodology? Co-opting PAR. *Globalisation, Societies and Education, 1*(2), 185–200.

Kaomea, J. (2003). Reading erasures and making the familiar strange: Defamiliarizing methods for research in formerly colonized and historically oppressed communities. *Educational Researcher, 32*(2), 14–25.

Kelsey, J. (1995). *The New Zealand experiment.* Auckland, New Zealand: Auckland University Press.

Keskitalo, J. H. (1997). Sami post-secondary education—Ideals and realities. In H. Gaski (Ed.), *Sami culture in a new era: The Norwegian Sami experience* (pp. 155–171). Kárásjohka, Norway: Davvi Girji.

King, N., Henderson, G. E., & Stein, J. E. (1999). *Beyond regulations. Ethics in human subjects research.* Chapel Hill: University of North Carolina Press.

Ladson-Billings, G. (2000). Racialized discourses and ethnic epistemologies. In N. K. Denzin & Y. S. Lincoln (Eds.), *Handbook of qualitative research* (2nd ed., pp. 257–278). Thousand Oaks, CA: Sage.

Langton, M. (1981). Anthropologists must change. *Identity, 4*(4), 11.

The Latina Feminist Group. (2001). *Telling to live: Latina feminist testimonios.* Durham, NC: Duke University Press.

LeCompte, M. (1993). A framework for hearing silence: What does telling stories mean when we are supposed to be doing science? In D. McLaughlin & W. G. Tierney (Eds.), *Naming silenced lives* (pp. 9–28). New York: Routledge.

Lincoln, Y. S. (1993). I and thou: Method, voice, and roles in research with the silenced. In D. McLaughlin & W. G. Tierney (Eds.), *Naming silenced lives* (pp. 29–50). New York: Routledge.

Little Bear, L. (2000). Jagged worldviews colliding. In M. Battiste (Ed.), *Reclaiming indigenous voice and vision* (pp. 77–85). Vancouver: University of British Columbia Press.

Maracle, L. (1996). *I am woman: A native perspective on sociology and feminism.* Vancouver: Press Gang Publishers.

Marker, M. (2003). Indigenous voice, community, and epistemic violence: The ethnographer's "interests" and what "interests" the ethnographer. *Qualitative Studies in Education, 16*(3), 361–375.

McLaren, P. (1993). Border disputes: Multicultural narrative, identity formation, and critical pedagogy in postmodern America. In D. McLaughlin & W. G. Tierney (Eds.), *Naming silenced lives* (pp. 201–236). New York: Routledge.

Mead, H. M. (2003). *Tikanga Māori: Living by Māori values.* Wellington, New Zealand: Huia Publications and Te Whare Wananga o Awanuiarangi Press.

Memmi, A. (1967). *The colonizer and the colonized.* Boston: Beacon Press. (Original work published 1957)

Menzies, C. (2001). Researching with, for and among indigenous peoples. *Canadian Journal of Native Education, 25*(1), 19–36.

Mies, M. (1983). Towards a methodology for feminist research. In G. Bowles & R. D. Klein (Eds.), *Theories of women's studies* (pp. 117–139). New York: Routledge.

Minh-ha, T. T. (1989). *Woman, native, other: Writing, postcoloniality and feminism.* Bloomington: Indiana University Press.

Mohanty, C. (1984). Under Western eyes: Feminist scholarship and colonial discourses. *Boundary, 12*(3) and *13*(1), 338–358.

Moraga, C., & Anzaldúa, G. (Eds.). (1983). *This bridge called my back.* New York: Kitchen Table Press.

Moran, W. (1999). Democracy and geography in the reregulation of New Zealand. In D. B. Knight & A. E. Joseph (Eds.), *Restructuring societies: Insights from the social sciences* (pp. 33–58). Ottawa: Carleton University Press.

Moreton-Robinson, A. (2000). *Talkin' up to the white woman: Indigenous women and feminism.* St. Lucia: University of Queensland Press.

Ngugi Wa Thiong'o. (1997). *Writers in politics: A re-engagement with issues of literature and society.* Oxford, UK: James Currey. (Original work published 1981)

Peters, M. A. (2003). Classical political economy and the role of universities in the new knowledge economy. *Globalization, Societies and Education, 1*(2), 153–168.

Pidgeon, M., & Hardy, C. (2002). Researching with Aboriginal peoples: Practices and principles. *Canadian Journal of Native Education, 26*(2), 96–106.

Pihama, L. (1993). *Tungia te ururua kia tupu whakarirorito te tupu o te harakeke.* Unpublished master's thesis, University of Auckland.

Pihama, L. (1994). Are films dangerous?: A Māori woman's perspective on *The Piano*. *Hecate, 20*(2), 239–242.

Pihama, L. (2001). *Tihei Mauriora: Honouring our voices—mana wahine as a kaupapa Māori theoretical framework.* Unpublished doctoral thesis, University of Auckland.

Pihama, L., Cram, F., & Walker, S. (2002). Creating methodological space: A literature review of Kaupapa Māori research. *Canadian Journal of Native Education, 26*(1), 30–43.

Pritchard, S. (Ed.). (1998). *Indigenous peoples, the United Nations and human rights.* London: Zed Books.

Reinharz, S. (1992). *Feminist methods in social research.* New York: Oxford University Press.

Rigney, L. (1999). Internationalization of an indigenous anticolonial cultural critique of research methodologies. A guide to indigenist research methodology and its principles. *Wicazo SA Journal of Native American Studies Review, 14*(2), 109–121.

Roman, L. G., & Eyre, L. (1997). *Dangerous territories: Struggles for difference and equality in education.* New York: Routledge.

Said, E. (1978). *Orientalism.* London: Vintage Books.

Saunders, K. (Ed.). (2002). *Feminist development and thought: Rethinking modernity, post-colonialism and representation.* London. Zed Books.

Sedgwick, E. K. (1991). *Epistemology of the closet.* New York: Harvester Wheatsheaf.

Shiva, V. (1993). *Monocultures of the mind.* London: Zed Books.

Simon, J., & Smith, L. T. (Eds.). (2001). *A civilising mission? Perceptions and representations of the New Zealand Native Schools system.* Auckland, New Zealand: Auckland University Press.

Smith, G. H. (1990).The politics of reforming Māori education: The transforming potential of kura kaupapa Māori. In H. Lauder & C. Wylie (Eds.), *Towards successful schooling* (pp. 73–89). Basingstoke: Falmer.

Smith, G. H. (1992). *Research issues related to Māori education.* Auckland, New Zealand: Research Unit for Māori Education, The University of Auckland.

Smith, G. H. (1994). For sale: Indigenous language, knowledge and culture. *Polemic: A Journal of the University of Sydney Law School, 4*(3).

Smith, L. T. (1991). Te rapunga i te ao marama (the search for the world of light): Māori perspectives on research in education. In T. Linzey & J. Morss (Eds.), *Growing up: The politics of human learning* (pp. 46–55). Auckland, New Zealand: Longman Paul.

Smith, L. T. (1992). Māori women: Discourses, projects and mana wahine. In S. Middleton & A. Jones (Eds.), *Women and education in Aotearoa 2* (pp. 33–51). Wellington, New Zealand Bridget Williams Books.

Smith, L. T. (1999). *Decolonizing methodologies: Research and indigenous peoples.* London: Zed Books.

Smith, L. T. (2000). Kaupapa Māori research. In M. Battiste (Ed.), *Reclaiming indigenous voice and vision* (pp. 225–247). Vancouver: University of British Columbia Press.

Smith, L. T. (2001). Troubling spaces. *Journal of Critical Psychology, 4,* 175–182.

Smith, L. T., Smith, G. H., Boler, M., Kempton, M., Ormond, A., Chueh, H. C., et al. (2002). "Do you guys hate Aucklanders too?" Youth: Voicing difference from the rural heartland. *Journal of Rural Studies, 18,* 169–178.

Spivak, G. (1987). *In other worlds: Essays in cultural politics.* New York: Methuen.

Stanley, L., & Wise, S. (1983). *Breaking out: Feminist consciousness and feminist research.* London: Routledge & Kegan Paul.

Steinhauer, E. (2003). Thoughts on an indigenous research methodology. *Canadian Journal of Native Education, 26*(2), 69–81.

Stewart, T. A. (1997). *Intellectual capital: The new wealth of organizations.* New York. Doubleday/Currency.

Stewart-Harawira, M. (1999, October). Neo-imperialism and the (mis)appropriation of indigenousness. *Pacific World, 54,* pp. 10–15.

Te Awekotuku, N. (1991). *Mana wahine Māori.* Auckland, New Zealand: New Women's Press.

Te Awekotuku, N. (1999). Māori women and research: Researching ourselves. In *Māori psychology: Research and practice* (pp. 57–63) [Proceedings of a symposium sponsored by the Māori and Psychology Research Unit, University of Waikato]. Hamilton, New Zealand: University of Waikato.

Te Hennepe, S. (1993). Issues of respect: Reflections of First Nations students' experiences in post-secondary anthropology classrooms. *Canadian Journal of Native Education, 20,* 193–260.

Thomas, G. (2001). The value of scientific engineering training for Indian communities. In K. James (Ed.), *Science and Native American communities* (pp. 149–154). Lincoln: University of Nebraska Press.

Thompson, P. (1978). *The voices of the past.* London: Oxford University Press.

Tierney, W. G. (2000) Undaunted courage: Life history and the postmodern challenge. In N. K. Denzin & Y. S. Lincoln (Eds.), *Handbook of qualitative research* (2nd ed., pp. 537–554). Thousand Oaks, CA: Sage.

Tomlins-Jahnke, H. (1997). Towards a theory of mana wahine. *He Pukenga Kôrero: A Journal of Māori Studies, 3*(1), 27–36.

Trask, H.-K. (1986). *Eros and power: The promise of feminist theory.* Philadelphia: University of Pennsylvania Press.

Trask, H.-K. (1993). *From a native daughter: Colonialism and sovereignty in Hawai'i.* Monroe, ME: Common Courage Press.

Vidich, A. J., & Lyman, S. M. (2000). Qualitative methods: Their history in sociology and anthropology. In N. K. Denzin & Y. S. Lincoln (Eds.), *Handbook of qualitative research* (pp. 37–84). Thousand Oaks, CA: Sage.

Warrior, R. A. (1995). *Tribal secrets: Recovering American Indian intellectual traditions.* Minneapolis: University of Minnesota Press.

Wilmer, F. (1993). *The indigenous voice in world politics.* Newbury Park, CA: Sage.

Womack, C. S. (1999). *Red on red: Native American literary separatism.* Minneapolis: University of Minnesota Press.

Worby, G., & Rigney, D. (2002). Approaching ethical issues: Institutional management of indigenous research. *Australian Universities Review, 45*(1), 24–33.

5

FREEING OURSELVES FROM NEOCOLONIAL DOMINATION IN RESEARCH

A Kaupapa Māori Approach to Creating Knowledge[1]

Russell Bishop

> *One of the challenges for Māori researchers . . . has been to retrieve some space—first, some space to convince Māori people of the value of research for Māori; second, to convince the various, fragmented but powerful research communities of the need for greater Māori involvement in research; and third, to develop approaches and ways of carrying out research which take into account, without being limited by, the legacies of previous research, and the parameters of both previous and current approaches. What is now referred to as Kaupapa Māori approaches to research . . . is an attempt to retrieve that space and to achieve those general aims.*
>
> —L. T. Smith (1999, p. 183)

This chapter seeks to identify how issues of power, including initiation, benefits, representation, legitimation, and accountability, are addressed in practice within an indigenous Kaupapa Māori approach in such a way as to promote the self-determination of the research participants. In addition, this chapter questions how such considerations may affect Western-trained and -positioned researchers.

Author's Note. I am very grateful to Lous Heshusius, Norman Denzin, and Donna Deyhle for their careful consideration of earlier drafts of this chapter. I am also grateful to Susan Sandretto for her thoughtful assistance in preparing this chapter. To those of my family and friends who have worked on this and other research projects over the years, I want to express my gratitude. Ma te Runga Rawa koutou, e tiaki, e manaaki.

Māori people, along with many other minoritized peoples, are concerned that educational researchers have been slow to acknowledge the importance of culture and cultural differences as key components in successful research practice and understandings. As a result, key research issues of power relations, initiation, benefits, representation, legitimization, and accountability continue to be addressed in terms of the researchers' own cultural agendas, concerns, and interests. This chapter seeks to identify how such domination can be addressed by both Māori and non-Māori educational researchers through their conscious participation within the cultural aspirations, preferences, and practices of the research participants.

It is important to position this chapter within the growing body of literature that questions traditional approaches to researching on/for/with minoritized peoples by placing the culture of "an ethnic group at the center of the inquiry" (Tillman, 2002, p. 4). Notable among these authors are: Frances Rains, Jo-Ann Archibald, and Donna Deyhle (2000), who, in editing and introducing a special edition of the *International Journal of Qualitative Studies in Education* (*QSE*) titled *Through Our Eyes and in Our Own Words—The Voices of Indigenous Scholars*, featured examples of "American-Indian/Native American intellectualism, culture, culture-based curriculum, and indigenous epistemologies and paradigms" (Tillman, 2002, p. 5). K. Tsianina Lomawaima's (2000) analysis of the history of power struggles between academic researchers and those whom they study identified how the history of scholarly research (including education) in Native America "has been deeply implicated in the larger history of the domination and oppression of Native American communities" (p. 14). On a positive note, however, she identified how the development of new research protocols by various tribes shows the way toward more respectful and responsible scholarship. Similarly, Verna Kirkness, Carl Urion, and Jo-Anne Archibald in Canada and their work with the *Canadian Journal of Native Education* have brought issues of researching with respect to the fore. In addition, Donna Deyhle and Karen Swisher (1997) have examined the growth of self-determination approaches among indigenous peoples of North America. Others involved in such scholarship include African American scholars (Ladson-Billings, 1995, 2000; Stanfield, 1994; Tillman, 2002) and Chicana and Chicano scholars (González, 2001; Moll, 1992; Reyes, Scribner, & Scribner, 1999; Villegas & Lucas, 2002) who are calling for greater attention to power relations and the role of culture in the research process.

While drawing on the work of these scholars and others to illustrate some of the arguments in this chapter, however, this discussion of culturally responsive research will focus on Māori people's experiences of research as an example of the wider argument.

Māori People's Concerns About Research: Issues of Power

Despite the guarantees of the Treaty of Waitangi,[2] the colonization of Aotearoa/NewZealand and the subsequent neocolonial dominance of majority interests in social and educational research have continued. The result has been the development of a tradition of research[3] into Māori people's lives that addresses concerns and interests of the predominantly non-Māori researchers' own making, as defined and made accountable in terms of the researchers' own cultural worldview(s).

Researchers in Aotearoa/New Zealand have developed a tradition of research that has perpetuated colonial power imbalances, thereby undervaluing and belittling Māori knowledge and learning practices and processes in order to enhance those of the colonizers and adherents of colonial paradigms. A social pathology research approach has developed in Aotearoa/New Zealand that has become implied in all phases of the research process: the "inability" of Māori culture to cope with human problems and propositions that Māori culture was and is inferior to that of the colonizers in human terms. Furthermore, such practices have perpetuated an ideology of cultural superiority that precludes the development of power-sharing processes and the legitimization of diverse cultural epistemologies and cosmologies.

Furthermore, traditional research has misrepresented Māori understandings and ways of knowing by simplifying, conglomerating, and commodifying Māori knowledge for "consumption" by the colonizers. These processes have consequently misrepresented Māori experiences, thereby denying Māori authenticity and voice. Such research has displaced Māori lived experiences and the meanings that these experiences have with the "authoritative" voice of the methodological "expert," appropriating Māori lived experience in terms defined and determined by the "expert." Moreover, many misconstrued Māori cultural practices and meanings are now part of our everyday myths of Aotearoa/New Zealand, believed by Māori and non-Māori alike, and traditional social and educational research has contributed to this situation. As a result, Māori people are deeply concerned about the issue of to whom researchers are accountable. Who has control over the initiation, procedures, evaluations, construction, and distribution of newly defined knowledge? Analyses by myself (Bishop, 1996, 1998b) and Linda Tuhiwai Smith (1999) have concluded that control over legitimization and representation is maintained within the domain of the colonial and neocolonial paradigms and that locales of initiation and accountability are situated within Western cultural frameworks, thus precluding Māori cultural forms and processes of initiation and accountability.

Traditional research epistemologies have developed methods of initiating research and accessing research participants that are located within the cultural preferences and practices of the Western world, as opposed to the cultural preferences and practices of Māori people themselves. For example, the preoccupation with neutrality, objectivity, and distance by educational researchers has emphasized these concepts as criteria for authority, representation, and accountability and, thus, has distanced Māori people from participation in the construction, validation, and legitimization of knowledge. As a result, Māori people are increasingly becoming concerned about who will directly gain from the research. Traditionally, research has established an approach in which the research has served to advance the interests, concerns, and methods of the researcher and to locate the benefits of the research at least in part with the researcher, other benefits being of lesser concern.

Table 5.1 summarizes these concerns, noting that this analysis of Māori people's concerns about research reveals five crises that affect indigenous peoples.

▣ Insiders/Outsiders: Who Can Conduct Research in Indigenous Settings?

The concerns about initiation, benefits, representation, legitimacy, and accountability raise a number of questions about how research with Māori and indigenous peoples should be conducted, but perhaps initially it is important to consider by whom that research should be conducted.

One answer to this question might well be to take an essentializing position and suggest that cultural "insiders" might well undertake research in a more sensitive and responsive manner than "outsiders." As Merriam et al. (2001) suggest, it has "commonly been assumed that being an insider means easy access, the ability to ask more meaningful questions and read non-verbal cues, and most importantly be able to project a more truthful, authentic understanding of the culture under study" (p. 411). On the other hand, of course, there are concerns that insiders are inherently biased, or that they are too close to the culture to ask critical questions.

Whatever the case, such understandings assume a homogeneity that is far from the reality of the diversity and complexity that characterizes indigenous peoples' lives and that ignores the impacts that age, class, gender, education, and color, among other variables, might have upon the research relationship. Such understandings might arise even among researchers who might consider themselves to be "insiders." A number of studies by researchers who had initially considered themselves to be "insiders" (Brayboy & Deyhle, 2000;

Table 5.1. Māori People's Concerns About Research Focuses on the Locus of Power Over Issues of Initiation, Benefits, Representation, Legitimacy, and Accountability Being With the Researcher

Initiation	This concern focuses on how the research process begins and whose concerns, interests, and methods of approach determine/define the outcomes. Traditional research has developed methods of initiating research and accessing research participants that are located within the cultural concerns, preferences, and practices of the Western world.
Benefits	The question of benefits concerns who will directly gain from the research, and whether anyone actually will be disadvantaged. Māori people are increasingly becoming concerned about this important political aspect because traditional research has established an approach to research in which the benefits of the research serve to advance the interests, concerns, and methods of the researcher and that locates the benefits of the research at least in part with the researcher, others being of lesser concern.
Representation	Whose research constitutes an adequate depiction of social reality? Traditional research has misrepresented, that is, simplified/conglomerated and commodified, Māori knowledge for "consumption" by the colonizers and denied the authenticity of Māori experiences and voice. Such research has displaced Māori lived experiences with the "authoritative" voice of the "expert" voiced in terms defined/determined by the "expert." Furthermore, many misconstrued Māori cultural practices and meanings are now part of our everyday myths of Aotearoa/New Zealand, believed by Māori and non-Māori alike.
Legitimacy	This issue concerns what authority we claim for our texts. Traditional research has undervalued and belittled Māori knowledge and learning practices and processes in order to enhance those of the colonizers, and adherents of neocolonial paradigms. Such research has developed a social pathology research approach that has focused on the "inability" of Māori culture to cope with human problems, and it has proposed that Māori culture was inferior to that of the colonizers in human terms. Such practices have perpetuated an ideology of cultural superiority that precludes the development of power-sharing processes and the legitimation of diverse cultural epistemologies and cosmologies.
Accountability	This concern questions researchers' accountability. Who has control over the initiation, procedures, evaluations, text constructions, and distribution of newly defined knowledge? Traditional research has claimed that all people have an inalienable right to utilize all knowledge and has maintained that research findings be expressed in term of criteria located within the epistemological framework of traditional research, thus creating locales of accountability that are situated within Western cultural frameworks.

Johnson-Bailey, 1999; Merriam et al., 2001; L. T. Smith, 1999) attest to this problem. Further, as Linda Tuhiwai Smith (1999) argues, even Western-trained indigenous researchers who are intimately involved with community members typically will employ research techniques and methodologies that will likely marginalize the communities' contribution to the investigation. This suggests that indigenous researchers will not automatically conduct research in a culturally appropriate manner even when researching their own communities.

However, as Native American scholar Karen Swisher (1998) argues, the dilemma remains, for despite developments in research that attempt to listen to the voices and the stories of the people under study and present them in ways "to encourage readers to see through a different lens . . . much research still is presented from an outsider's perspective" (p. 191). Nevertheless, despite the problems that indigenous researchers might well face, she argues that American Indian scholars need to become involved in leading research rather than being the subjects or consumers of research. She suggests that this involvement will assist in keeping control over the research in the hands of those involved. She cites (among other sources) a 1989 report of regional dialogues, *Our Voices, Our Vision: American Indians Speak Out for Educational Excellence*, as an example of research that addressed the self-determination of the people involved because from the "conception of the dialogue format to formulation of data and publication, Indian people were in charge of and guided the project; and the voices and concerns of the people were clearly evident" (p. 192).

Swisher (1998) argues that what is missing from the plethora of books, journals, and articles produced by non-Indians about Indians is "the passion from within and the authority to ask new and different questions based on histories and experiences as indigenous people" (p. 193). Furthermore, she argues that the difference involves more than just diverse ways of knowing; it concerns "knowing that what we think is grounded in principles of sovereignty and self-determination; and that it has credibility" (p. 193). In this way, Swisher is clear that "Indian people also believe that they have the answers for improving Indian education and feel they must speak for themselves" (p. 192). If we were to extrapolate this argument to other indigenous settings, we could see this as a call for the power of definition over issues of research, with initiation, benefits, representation, legitimation, and accountability being with indigenous peoples. Swisher (1998) identifies an attitude of "we can and must do it ourselves," yet it is also clear that nonindigenous people must help, but not in the impositional ways of the past. Of course, this raises the question of just what are the new positions on offer to nonindigenous researchers—and to indigenous researchers, for that matter.

Tillman (2002), when considering who should conduct research in African American communities, suggests that it is not simply a matter of saying that the researcher must be African American, but "[r]ather it is important to consider whether the researcher has the cultural knowledge to accurately interpret and validate the experiences of African-Americans within the context of the phenomenon under study" (p. 4). Margie Maaka, at the 2003 joint conference of the New Zealand Association for Research in Education and Australian Association for Research in Education, extended this understanding of where nonindigenous peoples should be positioned by stating that Māori must be in control of the research agenda and must be the ones who set the parameters; however, others can participate at the invitation of the indigenous people. In other words, it is Māori research by Māori, for Māori with the help of invited others.

For native scholars, Jacobs-Huey (2002) and L. T. Smith (1999) emphasize the power of critical reflexivity. The former states that "critical reflexivity in both writing and identification as a native researcher may act to resist charges of having played the 'native card' via a non-critical privileging of one's insider status" (Jacobs-Huey, 2002, p. 799). Smith emphasizes that "at a general level insider researchers have to have ways of thinking critically about their processes, their relationships and the quality and richness of their data and analysis. So too do outsiders . . ." (Smith, 1999, p. 137).

Researchers such as Narayan (1993), Griffiths (1998), and Bridges (2001) explain that it is no longer useful to think of researchers as insiders or outsiders; instead, researchers might be positioned "in terms of shifting identifications amid a field of interpenetrating communities and power relations" (Narayan, 1993, p. 671). Narayan proposes that instead of trying to define insider or outsider status,

> what we must focus our attention on is the quality of relations with the people we seek to represent in our texts: are they viewed as mere fodder for professionally self-serving statements about a generalized Other, or are they accepted as subjects with voices, views, and dilemmas—people to whom we are bonded through ties of reciprocity . . . ? (1993, p. 672)

This chapter suggests how these concerns and aspirations might be met by invoking a discursive repositioning of all researchers into those positions that operationalize self-determination for indigenous peoples.

Kaupapa[4] Māori Research

Out of the discontent with traditional research and its disruption of Māori life, an indigenous approach to research has emerged in Aotearoa/New Zealand. This approach, termed Kaupapa Māori research, is challenging the dominance of the Pâkehâ worldview in research. Kaupapa Māori research emerged from within the wider ethnic revitalization movement that developed in New Zealand following the rapid Māori urbanization of the post–World War II period. This revitalization movement blossomed in the 1970s and 1980s with the intensifying of a political consciousness among Māori communities. More recently, in the late 1980s and the early 1990s, this consciousness has featured the revitalization of Māori cultural aspirations, preferences, and practices as a philosophical and productive educational stance, along with a resistance to the hegemony[5] of the dominant discourse.[6] In effect, therefore, Kaupapa Māori presupposes positions that are committed to a critical analysis of the existing unequal power relations within the wider New Zealand society that were created with the signing of the Treaty of Waitangi in 1840, those structures that work to oppress Māori people. These include rejection of hegemonic, belittling "Māori can't cope" discourses, together with a commitment to the power of conscientization and politicization through struggle for wider community and social freedoms (G. H. Smith, 1997).

A number of significant dimensions to Kaupapa Māori research serve to set it apart from traditional research. One main focus of a Kaupapa Māori approach to research is the operationalization of self-determination (*tino rangatiratanga*) by Māori people (Bishop, 1996; Durie, 1994, 1995,1998; Pihama, Cram, & Walker, 2002; G. H. Smith, 1997; L. T. Smith, 1999). Self-determination in Durie's (1995) terms "captures a sense of Māori ownership and active control over the future" (p. 16). Such a position is consistent with the Treaty of Waitangi, in which Māori people are able "to determine their own policies, to actively participate in the development and interpretation of the law, to assume responsibility for their own affairs and to plan for the needs of future generations" (Durie, 1995, p. 16). In addition, the promotion of self-determination has benefits beyond these aspects. A 10-year study of Māori households conducted by Durie (1998) shows that the development of a secure identity offers Māori people advantages that may

> afford some protection against poor health; it is more likely to be associated with active educational participation and with positive employment profiles. The corollary is that reduced access to the Māori resources, and the wider Māori world, may be associated with cultural, social and economic disadvantage. (pp. 58–59)

Such an approach challenges the locus of power and control over the research issues of initiation, benefits, representation, legitimation, and accountability as outlined above, being located in another cultural frame of reference/worldview. Kaupapa Māori is, therefore, challenging the dominance of traditional, individualistic research that primarily, at least in its present form, benefits the researchers and their agenda. In contrast, Kaupapa Māori research is collectivistic and is oriented toward benefiting all the research participants and their collectively determined agendas, defining and acknowledging Māori aspirations for research, while developing and implementing Māori theoretical and methodological preferences and practices for research.

Kaupapa Māori is a discourse that has emerged from and is legitimized from within the Māori community. Māori educationalist Graham Hingangaroa Smith (1992) describes Kaupapa Māori as "the philosophy and practice of being and acting Māori" (p. 1). It assumes the taken-for-granted social, political, historical, intellectual, and cultural legitimacy of Māori people, in that it is an orientation in which "Māori language, culture, knowledge and values are accepted in their own right" (p. 13). Linda Tuhiwai Smith (1999), another leading Māori exponent of this approach, argues that such naming provides a means whereby communities of the researched and the researchers can "engage in a dialogue about setting directions for the priorities, policies, and practices of research for, by, and with Māori" (p. 183).

One fundamental understanding of a Kaupapa Māori approach to research is that it is the discursive practice that is Kaupapa Māori that positions researchers in such a way as to operationalize self-determination in terms of agentic positioning and behavior for research participants. This understanding challenges the essentializing dichotomization of the insider/outsider debate by offering a discursive position for researchers, irrespective of ethnicity. This positioning occurs because the cultural aspirations, understandings, and practices of Māori people are used both literally and figuratively to implement and organize the research process. Furthermore, the associated research issues of initiation, benefits, representation, legitimization, and accountability are addressed and understood in practice by practitioners of Kaupapa Māori research within the cultural context of the research participants.

Such understandings challenge traditional ways of defining, accessing, and constructing knowledge about indigenous peoples and the process of self-critique, sometimes termed "paradigm shifting," that is used by Western scholars as a means of "cleansing" thought and attaining what becomes their version of the "truth." Indigenous peoples are challenging this process because it maintains control over the research agenda within the cultural domain of the researchers or their institutions.

A Kaupapa Māori position is predicated on the understanding that Māori means of accessing, defining, and protecting knowledge existed before European arrival in New Zealand. Such Māori cultural processes were protected by the Treaty of Waitangi then subsequently marginalized; however, they have always been legitimate within Māori cultural discourses. As with other Kaupapa Māori initiatives in education, health, and welfare, Kaupapa Māori research practice is, as Irwin (1994) explains, epistemologically based within Māori cultural specificities, preferences, and practices.[7] In Olssen' s (1993) terms, Māori initiatives are "epistemologically productive where in constructing a vision of the world and positioning people in relation to its classifications, it takes its shape from its interrelations with an infinitely proliferating series of other elements within a particular social field" (p. 4).

However, this is not to suggest that such an analysis promotes an essentialist view of Māori in which all Māori must act in prescribed ways, for Māori are just as diverse a people as any other. One of the main outcomes of Durie's (1998) longitudinal study of Māori families, Te Hoe Nuku Roa, is the identification of this very diversity within Māori peoples. To Pihama et al. (2002), this means that Kaupapa Māori analysis must take this diversity of Māori peoples into account. They argue that Kaupapa Māori analysis is for all Māori, "not for select groups or individuals. Kaupapa Māori is not owned by any group, nor can it be defined in ways that deny Māori people access to its articulation" (p. 8). In other words, Kaupapa Māori analysis must benefit Māori people in principle and in practice in such a way that the current realities of marginalization and the heritage of colonialism and neocolonialism are addressed.

Examples of Culturally Responsive Research Practices

This analysis is based on a number of studies conducted by the author using Kaupapa Māori research. The first study, *Collaborative Research Stories: Whakawhanaungatanga* (1996; also see Bishop, 1998b), was a collaborative meta-study of five projects that addressed Māori agendas in research in order to ascertain the ways in which a group of researchers were addressing Māori people's concerns about research and what the researchers' experiences of these projects meant to them individually. The experiences of the various researchers and their understandings of their experiences were investigated by co-constructing collaborative research stories. The objective was to engage in a process of critical reflection and build a discourse based on the formal and informal meetings that were part of each of the projects in order to connect epistemological questions to indigenous ways of knowing by way of descriptions of actual research projects. The meta-study examined how a group of researchers addressed the importance of devolving power and control in the research exercise in order to promote tino Rangatiratanga of Māori people—that is, to act as educational professionals in ways consistent with Article Two of the Treaty of Waitangi.[8] I talked with other researchers who had accepted the challenge of being repositioned by and within the discursive practice that is Kaupapa Māori.

The meta-study in effect sought to investigate my own position as a researcher within a conjoint reflection on shared experiences and conjoint construction of meanings about these experiences, a position where the stories of the other research participants merged with my own to create new stories. Such *collaborative stories* go beyond an approach that simply focuses on the cooperative sharing of experiences and focuses on connectedness, engagement, and involvement with the other research participants within the cultural worldview/discursive practice within which they function. This study sought to identify what constitutes this engagement and what implications this constitution has for promoting self-determination/agency/voice in the research participants by examining concepts of *participatory and cultural consciousness* and *connectedness* within Māori discursive practice.

The second study, *Te Toi Huarewa: Teaching and Learning in Total Immersion Māori Language Educational Settings* (Bishop, Berryman, & Richardson, 2002), sought to identify effective teaching and learning strategies, effective teaching and learning materials, and the ways in which teachers assess and monitor the effectiveness of their teaching in Māori-medium reading and writing programs for students aged 5 to 9 years. Following a period of establishing relationships and developing a joint agenda for the research to identify what effective teachers do in their classrooms and why they teach in a particular manner, the researchers sought to operationalize Kaupapa Māori concerns that the self-determination of the research participants over issues of representation and legitimation be paramount. The strategy consisted of conducting interviews and directed observations, followed by facilitated teacher reflections on what had been observed by using stimulated recall interviews (Calderhead, 1981). The stimulated recall interviews that followed the observation sessions focused on specific interactions observed in the classrooms. In the stimulated recall interviews, the teachers were encouraged to reflect upon what had been observed and to bring their own sense-making processes to the discussions in order to co-construct a "rich" descriptive picture of their classroom practices. In other words, they were encouraged to reflect upon and explain why they did what they did, in their own terms. Through the use of this process, they explained for us that they all placed the culture of the child at the center of learning relationships by developing in their classrooms what we later termed (after Gay, 2000; Villegas & Lucas, 2002) a *culturally appropriate and responsive context for learning.*

The third study, *Te Kotahitanga: The Experiences of Year 9 and 10 Māori Students in Mainstream Classrooms* (Bishop, Berryman, & Richardson, 2003), is a work-in-progress, a research/professional development project that is now entering its third phase of implementation in 12 schools with some 360 teachers. The project commenced in 2001, seeking to address the self-determination of Māori secondary school students by talking with them and other participants in their education about just what is involved in limiting and/or improving their educational achievement. The project commenced with the gathering of a number of narratives of students' classroom experience from a range of engaged and non-engaged Māori students (as defined by their schools), in five non–structurally modified mainstream secondary schools using the process of collaborative storying. This approach is very similar to that termed *testimonio,* in that it is the intention of the direct narrator (research participant) to use an interlocutor (the researcher) to bring their situation to the attention of an audience "to which he or she would normally not have access because of their very condition of subalternity to which the *testimonio* bears witness" (Beverley, 2000, p. 556). In this research project, the students were able to share their narratives about their experiences of schooling, so that teachers who otherwise might not have had access to the narratives could reflect upon them in terms of their own experiences and understandings.

It was from these amazing stories that the rest of this project developed. In their narratives, the students clearly identified the main influences on their educational achievement by articulating the impacts and consequences of their living in a marginalized space. That is, they explained how they were perceived in pathological terms by their teachers and how this perception has had negative effects on their lives. In addition, the students told the research team how teachers, in changing how they related to and interacted with Māori students in their classrooms, could create a context for learning wherein Māori students' educational achievement could improve, again by placing the self-determination of Māori students at the center of classroom relationships.

Such an approach is consistent with Ryan (1999), who suggests that a solution to the one-sidedness of representations that are promoted by the dominance of the powerful—in this case, pathologizing discourses—is to portray events as was done in the collaborative stories of the Māori students, in terms of "competing discourses rather than as simply the projection of inappropriate images" (p. 187). He suggests that this approach, rather than seeking the truth or "real pictures," allows for previously marginalized discourses "to emerge and compete on equal terms with previously dominant discourses" (p. 187).

On the basis of the suggestions from Year 9 and Year 10 (ages 14–16) Māori students, the research team developed an "Effective Teaching Profile." Together with other information from narratives of experiences from those parenting the students, from their principals and their teachers, and from the literature, this Effective Teaching Profile has formed the basis of a professional development program that, when implemented with a group of teachers in four schools, was associated with improved learning, behavior, and attendance outcomes for Māori students in the classrooms of those teachers who had been able to participate fully in the professional development program (Bishop, Berryman, et al., 2003).

Addressing Issues of Self-Determination

Western approaches to operationalizing self-determination (agentic positioning and behavior) in others are, according to Noddings (1986) and B. Davies (1990), best addressed by those who position themselves within empowering relationships. Authors such as Oakley (1981), Tripp (1983), Burgess (1984), Lather (1986, 1991), Patton (1990), Delamont (1992), Eisner (1991), Reinharz (1992), and Sprague and Hayes (2000) suggest that an "empowering" relationship could be attained by developing what could be termed an "enhanced research relationship," in which there occurs a long-term development of mutual purpose and intent between the researcher and the researched. To facilitate this development of mutuality, the research must recognize the need for personal investment in the form of self-disclosure and openness.[1] Sprague and Hayes (2000) explain that such relationships are mutual

> [to] the degree to which each party negotiates a balance between commitment to the other's and to one's own journey of self-determination. In mutual relationships each strives to recognize the other's unique and changing needs and abilities, [and] takes the other's perspectives and interests into account. (p. 684)

In the practice of Kaupapa Māori research, however, there develops a degree of involvement on the part of the researcher, constituted as a way of knowing, that is fundamentally different from the concepts of personal investment and collaboration suggested by the above authors. Although it appears that "personal investment" is essential, this personal investment is not on terms determined by the "investor." Instead, the investment is made on terms of mutual understanding and control by all participants, so that the investment is reciprocal and could not be otherwise. In other words, the "personal investment" by the researcher is not an act by an individual agent but instead emerges out of the context within which the research is constituted.

Traditional conceptualizations of knowing do not adequately explain this understanding. Elbow (1986, as cited in Connelly & Clandinin, 1990) identifies a different form of reciprocity, one he terms "connected knowing," in which the "knower is attached to the known" (p. 4). In other words, there is common understanding and a common basis for such an understanding, where the concerns, interests, and agendas of the researcher become the concerns, interests, and agendas of the researched and vice versa. Hogan (as cited in Connelly & Clandinin, 1990, p. 4) refers to this as a "feeling of connectedness." Heshusius (1994, 2002) transforms this notion by suggesting the need to move from an alienated mode of consciousness that sees the knower as separate from the known to a *participatory mode of consciousness.* Such a mode of consciousness addresses a fundamental reordering of understandings of the relationship "between self and other (and therefore of reality), and indeed between self and the world, in a manner where such a reordering not only includes connectedness but necessitates letting go of the focus on self" (Heshusius, 1994, p. 15).

Heshusius (1994) identifies this form of knowing as involving, that which Polanyi (1966) calls "tacit knowing," which Harman calls "compassionate consciousness" (as cited in Heshusius, 1994), and which Berman calls "somatic" or "bodily" knowing (as cited in Heshusius, 1994). Barbara Thayer-Bacon (1997) describes a relational epistemology that views "knowledge as something that is socially constructed by embedded, embodied people who are in relation with each other" (p. 245). Each of these authors is referring to an embodied way of being and of a knowing that is a nonaccountable, nondescribable way of knowing. Heshusius (1994) suggests that "the act of coming to know is not a subjectivity that one can explicitly account for," but rather it is of a "direct participatory nature one cannot account for" (p. 17). Heshusius (1996) also suggests that

> In a participatory mode of consciousness the *quality* of attentiveness is characterised by an absence of the need to separate, distance and to insert predetermined thought patterns, methods and formulas between self and other. It is characterised by an absence of the need to be in charge. (p. 627)

Heshusius (1994) identifies the ground from which a participatory mode of knowing emerges as "the recognition of the deeper kinship between ourselves and other" (p. 17). This form of knowing speaks in a very real sense to Māori ways of knowing, for the Māori term for connectedness and engagement by kinship is *whanaungatanga.* This concept is one of the most fundamental ideas within Māori culture, both as a value and as a social process.[9] Whanaungatanga literally consists of kin relationships between ourselves and others, and it is constituted in ways determined by the Māori cultural context.

▣ WHAKAWHANAUNGATANGA AS A KAUPAPA MĀORI RESEARCH APPROACH

Whakawhanaungatanga is the process of establishing *whânau* (extended family) relationships, literally by means of identifying, through culturally appropriate means, your bodily linkage, your engagement, your connectedness, and, therefore, an unspoken but implicit commitment to other people. For example, a *mihimihi* (formal ritualized introduction) at a *hui* (Māori ceremonial gathering) involves stating your own *whakapapa* in order to establish relationships with the hosts/others/visitors. A mihimihi does not identify you in terms of your work, in terms of your academic rank or title, for example. Rather, a mihimihi is a statement of where you are from and of how you can be related and connected to these other people and the land, in both the past and the present.

For Māori people, the process of whakawhanaungatanga identifies how our identity comes from our whakapapa and how our whakapapa and its associated *raranga kôrero* (those stories that explain the people and events of a whakapapa) link us to all other living and inanimate creatures and to the very earth we inhabit. Our mountain, our river, our island are us. We are part of them, and they are part of us. We know this in a bodily way, more than in a recitation of names. More than in the actual linking of names, we know it because we are related by blood and body. We are of the same bones (*iwi*) and of the same people (iwi). We are from the same pregnancies (*hapû*) and of the same subtribe (hapû). We are of the same family (*whânau*), the family into which we were born (whânau). We were nurtured by the same land (*whenua*), by the same placenta (whenua). In this way, the language reminds us that we are part of each other.

So when Māori people introduce ourselves as *whanaunga* (relatives), whether it be to engage in research or not, we are introducing part of one to another part of the same oneness. Knowing who we are is a somatic acknowledgment of our connectedness with and commitment to our surroundings, human and nonhuman. For example, from this positioning it would be very difficult to undertake research in a "nonsomatic," distanced manner. To invoke "distance" in a Māori research project would be to deny that it is a Māori project. It would have different goals, not Māori goals.

Establishing and maintaining whânau relationships, which can be either literal or metaphoric within the discursive practice that is Kaupapa Māori, is an integral and ongoing constitutive element of a Kaupapa Māori approach to research. Establishing a research group as if it were an extended family is one form of embodying the process of whakawhanaungatanga as a research strategy.

In a Kaupapa Māori approach to research, research groups constituted as whânau attempt to develop relationships and organizations based on similar principles to those that order a traditional or literal whânau. Metge (1990) explains that to use the term *whânau* is to identify a series of rights and responsibilities, commitments and obligations, and supports that are fundamental to the collectivity. These are the *tikanga* (customs) of the whânau: warm interpersonal interactions, group solidarity, shared responsibility for one another, cheerful cooperation for group ends, corporate responsibility for group property, and material or nonmaterial (e.g., knowledge) items and issues. These attributes can be summed up in the words *aroha* (love in the broadest sense, also mutuality), *awhi* (helpfulness), *manaaki* (hospitality), and *tiaki* (guidance).

The whânau is a location for communication, for sharing outcomes, and for constructing shared common understandings and meanings. Individuals have responsibilities to care for and to nurture other members of the group, while still adhering to the kaupapa of the group. The group will operate to avoid singling out particular individuals for comment and attention and to avoid embarrassing individuals who are not yet succeeding within the group. Group products and achievement frequently take the form of group performances, not individual performances.[10] The group typically will begin and end each session with prayer and also will typically share food together. The group will make major decisions as a group and then refer those decisions to kaumâtua (respected elders of either gender) for approval, and the group will seek to operate with the support and encouragement of kaumâtua. This feature acknowledges the multigenerational constitution of a whânau with associated hierarchically determined rights, responsibilities, and obligations.[11]

Determining Benefits: Identifying Lines of Accountability Using Māori Metaphor

Determining who benefits from the research and to whom the researchers are accountable also can be understood in terms of Māori discursive practices. What non-Māori people would refer to as management or control mechanisms are traditionally constituted in a whânau as *taonga tuku iho*—literally, those treasures passed down to us from the ancestors, those customs that guide our behavior. In this manner, the structure and function of a whânau describes and constitutes the relationship among research participants—in traditional research terminology, between the researcher and the researched—within Kaupapa Māori research practice. Research thus cannot proceed unless whânau support is obtained, unless kaumâtua provide guidance, and unless there is aroha between the participants, evidenced by an overriding feeling of tolerance, hospitality, and respect for others, their aspirations, and their preferences and practices. The research process is participatory as well as *participant driven* in the sense that the concerns, interests, and preferences of the whânau are what guide and drive the research processes. The research itself is driven by the participants in terms of setting the research questions, ascertaining the likely benefits, outlining the design of the work, undertaking the work that had to be done, distributing rewards, providing access to research findings, controlling the distribution of the knowledge, and deciding to whom the researcher is accountable.

This approach has much in common with that described by Kemmis and McTaggart (2000) as participatory and collaborative action research, which emerged "more or less deliberately as forms of resistance to conventional research practices that were perceived by particular kinds of participants as acts of colonization" (p. 572). To Esposito and Murphy (2000), participatory action research emphasizes the political nature of knowledge production and places a premium on self-emancipation (p. 180), where

> [s]uch research groups are typically comprised of both professionals and ordinary people, all of whom are regarded as authoritative sources of knowledge. By making minorities the authorized representatives of the knowledge produced, their experiences and concerns are brought to the forefront of the research. The resulting information is applied to resolving the problems they define collectively as significant. As a result, the integrity of distinct racial groups is not annihilated or subsumed within dominant narratives that portray them as peripheral members of society. (p. 181)

For researchers, this approach means that they are not information gatherers, data processors, and sense-makers of other people's lives; rather, they are expected to be able to communicate with individuals and groups, to participate in appropriate cultural processes and practices, and to interact in a dialogic manner with the research participants. Esposito and Murphy (2000) explain that research "methods are geared to offer opportunities for discussion. After all, information is not transmitted between researchers and individuals; instead, information is cocreated, . . . data are coproduced intersubjectively in a manner that preserves the existential nature of the information" (p. 182).

Esposito and Murphy (2000) also suggest that such an approach may facilitate the development of the kind of research that Lomawaima (2000) and Fine and Weis (1996) describe, a type in which investigators are more attuned to "locally meaningful expectations and concerns" (Lomawaima, 2000, p. 15). In addition, they suggest that researchers become actively involved in the solutions and promote the well-being of communities, instead of merely using locations as sites for data collection. As Lomawaima (2000) suggests, researchers should thus open up the "possibilities for directly meaningful research—research that is as informative and useful to tribes as it is to academic professionals and disciplinary theories" (p. 15).

What is crucial to an understanding of what it means to be a researcher in a Kaupapa Māori approach is that it is through the development of a participatory mode of consciousness that a researcher becomes part of this process. He or she does not start from a position outside the group and then choose to invest or reposition himself or herself. Rather, the (re)positioning is part of participation. The researcher cannot "position" himself or herself or "empower" the other. Instead, through entering a participatory mode of consciousness, the individual agent of the "I" of the researcher is released in order to enter a consciousness larger than the self.

One example of how whânau processes in action affect the position of the researcher is the way in which different individuals take on differing discursive positionings within the collective. These positionings fulfill different functions oriented toward the collaborative concerns, interests, and benefits of the whânau as a group, rather than toward the benefit of any one member—a member with a distanced research agenda, for example. Such positionings are constituted in ways that are generated by Māori cultural practices and preferences. For example, the leader of a research whânau, here termed a *whânau of interest* to identify it as a metaphoric whânau, will not necessarily be the researcher. Kaumâtua, which is a Māori-defined and -apportioned position (which can be singular or plural), will be the leader. Leadership in a whânau of interest, however, is not in the sense of making all the decisions, but instead in the sense of being a guide to *kawa* (culturally appropriate procedures) for decision making and a listener to the voices of all members of the whânau. The kaumâtua are the consensus seekers for the collective and are the producers of the collaborative voice of the members. By developing research within such existing culturally constituted practices, concerns about voice and agency can be addressed.

This emphasis on positionings within a group constituted as a whânau also addresses concerns about accountability, authority, and control. A Māori collective whânau contains a variety of discursively determined positions, some of which are open to the researcher and some of which are not. The extent to which researchers can be positioned within a whânau of interest is therefore tied very closely to *who* they are, often more so than to *what* they are. Therefore, positioning is not simply a matter of the researchers' choice, because this would further researcher imposition. That is, researchers are not free to assume any position that they think the whânau of interest needs in order for the whânau to function. The researchers' choice of positions is generated by the structure of the whânau and the customary ways of behaving constituted within the whânau. The clear implication is that researchers are required to locate themselves within new "story lines" that address the contradictory nature of the traditional researcher/researched relationship.

The language used by researchers working in Kaupapa Māori contexts in research reported by Bishop (1996, 1998b), for example, contains the key to the new story lines. The metaphors and imagery these researchers used to explain their participation in the research were those located within the research participants' domains, and the researchers either were moved or needed to move to become part of this domain. Researchers were positioned within the discursive practices of Kaupapa Māori by the use of contextually constituted metaphor within the domain where others constituted themselves as agentic. Furthermore, within this domain existed discursive practices that provided the researchers with positions that enabled them to carry through their negotiated lines of action whether they were insiders or outsiders. As a result of these negotiations, they had differing positions and expectations/tasks offered to them.

From this analysis, it can be seen that through developing a research group by using Māori customary sociopolitical processes, the research participants become members of a research whânau of interest, which, as a metaphoric whânau, is a group constituted in terms understandable and controllable by Māori cultural practices. These whânau of interest determine the research questions and the methods of research, and they use Māori cultural processes for addressing and acknowledging the construction and validation/legitimization of knowledge. Furthermore, the whânau of interest develops a collaborative approach to processing and constructing meaning/theorizing about the information, again by culturally constituted means. It is also important to recognize that whânau of interest are not isolated groups but rather are constituted and conduct their endeavors in terms of the wider cultural aspirations, preferences, and practices of Māori cultural revitalization within which their projects are composed.

Spiral Discourse

Whanâu of interest are developed by and use a Māori cultural process in both its literal and its metaphoric senses. This process is termed here *spiral discourse*, a culturally constituted discursive practice found in many Māori cultural practices associated, for example, with hui. A hui generally commences with a *pôwhiri* (formal welcome), a welcome rich in cultural meaning, imagery, and practices that fulfill the enormously important task of recognizing the relative *tapu* (specialness; being with potentiality for power) and *mana* (power) of the two sides, the hosts and the visitors (Salmond, 1975; Shirres, 1982). Once the formal welcome is complete and once the participants have been ritually joined together by the process of the welcoming ceremony, hui participants move on to the discussion of the matter under consideration (the kaupapa of the hui). This usually takes place within the meeting house, a place designated for this very purpose, free of distractions and interruptions. This house is symbolically the embodiment of an ancestor, which further emphasizes the normality of a somatic approach to knowing in such a setting and within these processes.

The participants address the matters under consideration, under the guidance of respected and authoritative elders (kaumâtua), whose primary function is to provide and monitor the correct spiritual and procedural framework within which the participants can discuss the issues before them. People get a chance to address the issue without fear of being interrupted. Generally, the procedure is for people to speak one after another, in sequence of left to right. People get a chance to state and restate their meanings, to revisit their meanings, and to modify, delete, and adapt their meanings according to tikanga (customary practices).

The discourse spirals, in that the flow of talk may seem circuitous and opinions may vary and waver, but the seeking of a collaboratively constructed story is central. The controls over proceedings are temporal and spiritual, as in all Māori cultural practices. The procedures are steeped in metaphoric meanings, richly abstract allusions being made constantly to cultural messages, stories, events of the past, and aspirations for the future. Such procedures are time proven and to the participants are highly effective in dealing with contemporary issues and concerns of all kinds.[12] The aim of a hui is to reach a consensus, to arrive at a jointly constructed meaning. This takes time, days if need be, or sometimes a series of hui will be held in order that the elders monitoring proceedings can tell when a constructed "voice" has been found.

▣ Initiating Research Using Māori Metaphor: Rejecting Empowerment

Addressing the self-determination of participants is embedded within many Māori cultural practices and understandings. For example, during the proceedings of a hui, one visible manifestation of this reality is seen in the ways that visitors make contributions toward the cost of the meeting. This contribution is termed a *koha.* In the past, this koha was often a gift of food to contribute to the running of the hui; nowadays, it is usually money that is laid down on the ground, by the last speaker of the visitors' side, between the two groups of people who are coming together at the welcoming ceremony. The koha remains an important ritualized part of a ceremony that generally proceeds without too much trouble. What must not be forgotten, however, is that the reception of the koha is up to the hosts. The koha, as a gift or an offering of assistance toward the cost of running the hui, goes with the full mana of the group so offering. It is placed in a position, such as laying it on the ground between the two groups coming together, so as to be able to be considered by the hosts. It is not often given into the hands of the hosts, but whatever the specific details of the protocol, the process of " laying down" is a very powerful recognition of the right of others to self-determination, that is, to choose whether to pick it up or not.

The koha generally precedes the final coming together of the two sides. The placing of the koha comes at a crucial stage in the ceremony, at which the hosts can refuse to accept the mana of the visitors, the hosts can display their ultimate control over events, and the hosts can choose whether they want to become one with the *manuhiri* (visitors) by the process of the *hôngi* and *haruru* (pressing noses and shaking hands). Symbolically, with the koha, the hosts are taking on the kaupapa of the guests by accepting that which the manuhiri are bringing for debate and mediation. Overall, however, it is important that the kaupapa the guests laid down at the hui is now the "property" of the whole whânau. It is now the task of the whole whânau to deliberate the issues and to own the problems, concerns, and ideas in a way that is real and meaningful, the way of *whakakotahitanga* (developing unity), where all will work for the betterment of the idea.

By invoking these processes in their metaphoric sense, Kaupapa Māori research is conducted within the discursive practices of Māori culture. Figuratively, laying down a koha as a means of initiating research, for example, or of offering solutions to a problem challenges notions of empowerment, which is a major concern within contemporary Western-defined research. It also challenges what constitutes "self" and "other" in Western thought. Rather than figuratively saying "I am giving you power" or "I intend to empower you," the laying down of a koha and stepping away for the others to consider your gift means that your mana is intact, as is theirs, and that you are acknowledging their power of self-determination. The three research projects referred to above all saw the researchers either laying out their potential contributions as researchers, or asking research participants to explain what has been observed in their classrooms or seeking the meaning that participants construct about their experiences as young people in secondary schools. In each of these cases, the researchers indicated that they did not have the power to make sense of the events or experiences alone and, indeed, did not want anything from the relationship that was not a product of the relationship. In this way, it is up to the others to exert agency, to decide if they wish to "pick it up," to explain the meanings of their own experiences on their own terms. Whatever they do, both sides have power throughout the process. Both sides have tapu that is being acknowledged.

In this sense, researchers in Kaupapa Māori contexts are repositioned in such a way that they no longer need to seek to *give voice to others*, to *empower* others, to *emancipate* others, or to refer to others as *subjugated voices*. Instead, they are able to listen to and participate with those traditionally "othered" as constructors of meanings of their own experiences and agents of knowledge. Not wanting anything from the experience for one's "self" is characteristic of what Schachtel (as cited in Heshusius, 1994) calls "allocentric knowing." It is only when nothing is desired for the self, not even the desire to empower someone, that complete attention and participation in "kinship" terms is possible.

In such ways, researchers can participate in a process that facilitates the development in people of a sense of themselves as agentic and of having an authoritative voice. This is not a result of the researcher "allowing" this to happen or "empowering" participants; it is the function of the cultural context within which the research participants are positioned, negotiate, and conduct the research.[13] In effect, the cultural context positions the participants by constructing the story lines, and with them the cultural metaphors and images, as well as the "thinking as usual," the talk/language through which research participants are constituted and researcher/researched relationships are organized. Thus, the joint development of new story lines is a collaborative effort. The researcher and the researched together rewrite the constitutive metaphors of the relationship. What makes it Māori is that it is done using Māori metaphor within a Māori cultural context.[14]

Such approaches are essential to move the power dynamics of research relationships because, as was mentioned earlier, differential power relations among participants, while construed and understood as collaborative by the researcher, may still enable researcher concerns and interests to dominate how understandings are constructed. This can happen even within relations constructed as reciprocal, if the research outcome remains one determined by the researcher as a data-gathering exercise (Goldstein, 2000; Tripp,

1983). When attempts at developing dialogue move beyond efforts to gather "data" and move toward mutual, symmetrical, dialogic construction of meaning within appropriate culturally constituted contexts, as is illustrated in the three examples introduced earlier, then the voice of the research participants is heard and their agency is facilitated.

Such understandings seeks to address the self/other relationship by examining how researchers shift themselves from a "speaking for" position to a situation that Michelle Fine (1994) describes as *taking place* "when we construct texts collaboratively, self-consciously examining our relations with/for/despite those who have been contained as Others, we move against, we enable resistance to, Othering" (p. 74). Fine (1994) attempts to

> unravel, critically, the blurred boundaries in our relation, and in our texts; to understand the political work of our narratives; to decipher how the traditions of social science serve to inscribe; and to imagine how our practice can be transformed to resist, self-consciously, acts of othering. (p. 57)

Fine and her colleagues Lois Weis, Susan Weseen, and Loonmun Wong (2000) stress "that questions of responsibility-for-whom will, and should, forever be paramount" (p. 125). Reciprocity in indigenous research, however, is not just a political understanding, an individual act, or a matter of refining and/or challenging the paradigms within which researchers work. Instead, every worldview within which the researcher becomes immersed holds the key to knowing. For example, establishing relationships and developing research whânau by invoking the processes of whakawhanaungatanga establishes interconnectedness, commitment, and engagement, within culturally constituted research practices, by means of constitutive metaphor from within the discursive practice of Kaupapa Māori. It is the use of such metaphor that reorders the relationship of the researcher/researched from within, from one focused on the researcher as "self" and on the researched as "other" to one of a common consciousness of all research participants.

Similarly, a Kaupapa Māori approach suggests that concepts of "distance," "detachment," and "separation," epistemological and methodological concerns on which researchers have spent much time in the recent past (Acker, Barry, & Esseveld, 1991; Stacey, 1991; Troyna, 1992, personal communication), do not characterize these research relationships in any way. Rather, Kaupapa Māori research experiences insist that the focus on "self" is blurred and that the focus turns to what Heshusius (1994) describes as a situation where "reality is no longer understood as truth to be interpreted but as mutually evolving" (p. 18). In an operational sense, it is suggested that researchers address the concerns and issues of the participants in ways that are understandable and able to be controlled by the research participants so that these concerns and issues also are, or become, those of the researchers. In other words, spiral discourse provides a means of effecting a qualitative shift in how participants relate to one another.

Sidorkin (2002) suggests that such understandings have major implications for how we understand the "self" and "invites us to think about the possibilities of a relational self" (p. 96), one in which "only analysis of specific relations in their interaction can provide a glimpse of the meaning of the self" (p. 97). To this end, Fitzsimons and Smith (2000) describe Kaupapa Māori philosophy as that which is "call[ing] for a relational identity through an interpretation of kinship and genealogy and current day events, but not a de-contextualised retreat to a romantic past" (p. 39).

This reordering of what constitutes the research relationship, with its implications and challenges to the essential enlightenment-generated self, is not on terms or within understandings constructed by the researcher, however well-intentioned contemporary impulses to "empower" the "other" might be. From an indigenous perspective, such impulses are misguided and perpetuate neocolonial sentiments. In other words, rather than using researcher-determined criteria for participation in a research process, whakawhanaungatanga uses Māori cultural practices, such as those found in hui, to set the pattern for research relationships, collaborative storying being but one example of this principle in practice. Whakawhanaungatanga as a research process uses methods and principles similar to those used to establish relationships among Māori people. These principles are invoked to address the means of research initiation, to establish the research questions, to facilitate participation in the work of the project, to address issues of representation and accountability, and to legitimate the ownership of knowledge that is defined and created.

Kincheloe and McLaren (2000) demonstrate how developments in critical ethnography, as one example, have benefited from such new understandings of culture and cultural practices and processes, used in both literal and figurative senses, to identify "possibilities for cultural critique, that have been opened up by the current blurring and mixing of disciplinary genres—those that emphasize experience, subjectivity, reflexivity and dialogical understanding" (p. 302). One major benefit from such analysis is that social life is "not viewed as preontologically available for the researcher to study" (p. 302). Kincheloe and McLaren suggest that this is a major breakthrough in the domain of critical theory, which previously remained rooted in the Western-based dialectic of binary analysis of oppositional pairings that viewed emancipation in terms of emancipating "others" (Kincheloe & McLaren, 2000) and, in many cases, conflated economic marginalization with ethnicity and gender and other axes of domination (see Bishop & Glynn, 1999, Chap. 2, for a detailed critique of this approach in New Zealand).

▣ Addressing Issues of Representation and Legitimation: A Narrative Approach

Interviewing as collaborative storying (Bishop, 1997), as used in the three studies identified earlier, addresses what Lincoln and Denzin (1994) identify as the twin crises of qualitative research—representation and legitimation. It does so by suggesting that rather than there being distinct stages in the research, from gaining access to data gathering to data processing, there is a process of continually revisiting the agenda and the sense-making processes of the research participants within the interview. In this way, meanings are negotiated and co-constructed between the research participants within the cultural frameworks of the discourses within which they are positioned. This process is captured by the image of a spiral. The concept of the spiral not only speaks in culturally preferred terms, the fern or koru,[15] but also indicates that the accumulation is always reflexive. This means that the discourse always returns to the original initiators, where control lies.

Mishler (1986) and Ryan (1999) explain these ideas further by suggesting that in order to construct meaning, it is necessary to appreciate how meaning is grounded in, and constructed through, discourse. Discursive practice is contextually, culturally, and individually related. Meanings in discourse are neither singular nor fixed. Terms take on "specific and contextually grounded meanings within and through the discourse as it develops and is shaped by speakers" (Mishler, 1986, p. 65). To put it another way, "meaning is constructed in the dialogue between individuals and the images and symbols they perceive" (Ryan, 1999, p. 11). A "community of interest" between researchers and participants (call them what you will) cannot be created unless the interview, as one example, is constructed so that interviewers and respondents strive to arrive together at meanings that both can understand. The relevance and appropriateness of questions and responses emerge through and are realized in the discourse itself. The standard process of analysis of interviews abstracts both questions and responses from this process. By suppressing the discourse and by assuming shared and standard meanings, this approach short-circuits the problem of obtaining meaning (Mishler, 1986).

This analysis suggests that when interviewing—one of the most commonly used qualitative methods—there needs to be a trade-off between two extremes. The first position claims "the words of an interview are the most accurate data and that the transcript of those words carries that accuracy with negligible loss" (Tripp, 1983, p. 40). In other words, what people say should be presented unaltered and not analyzed in any way beyond that which the respondent undertook. The second position maximizes researcher interpretation, editorial control, and ownership by introducing researcher coding and analysis in the form often referred to as "grounded theory" (after Glaser & Strauss, 1967). This chapter suggests there is a third position, in which the "coding" procedure is established and developed by the research participants as a process of storying and restorying, that is the co-joint construction of further meaning within a sequence of interviews. In other words, there is an attempt within the interview, or rather, within a series of in-depth, semistructured interviews as "conversations" (see Bishop, 1996, 1997), to actually co-construct a mutual understanding by means of sharing experiences and meanings.

The three examples of research outlined at the start of this chapter all used research approaches associated with the process of collaborative storying so that the research participants were able to recollect, to reflect on, and to make sense of their experiences within their own cultural context and, in particular, in their own language, hence being able to position themselves within those discourses wherein explanations/meanings lie. In such ways, their interpretations and analyses became "normal" and "accepted," as opposed to those of the researcher being what is legitimate.

Indeed, when indigenous cultural ways of knowing and aspirations—in this case, for self-determination—are central to the creation of the research context, then the situation goes beyond empowerment to one in which sense making, decision making, and theorizing take place in situations that are "normal" to the research participants rather than constructed by the researcher. Of course, the major implication for researchers is that they should be able to participate in these sense-making contexts rather than expecting the research participants to engage in theirs, emphasizing, as Tillman (2002, p. 3) suggests, the centrality of culture to the research process and "the multidimensional aspects of African-American cultures(s) and the possibilities for the resonance of the cultural knowledge of African-Americans in educational research" (p. 4).

This is not to suggest that only interviews as collaborative stories are able to address Māori concerns and aspirations for self-determination. Indeed, Sleeter (2001) has even argued that "quantitative research can be used for liberatory as well as oppressive ends" (p. 240). My own experiences when researching within secondary schools demonstrate that when spiral discourse occurs "with full regard for local complexities, power relations and previously ignored life experiences" (Sleeter, 2001, p. 241), then powerful outcomes are possible using a variety of research approaches. What is fundamental is not the approach per se, but rather establishing and maintaining relationships that address the power of the participants for self-determination.

The considerations above demonstrate the usefulness of the notion of collaborative storying as a generic approach, not just as a research method that speaks of a reordering of the relationships between researchers and research participants. Sidorkin (2002) suggests that this understanding addresses power imbalances because "[r]elations cannot belong to one thing: they are the joint property of at least two things" (p. 94). Scheurich and Young (1997) describe this as deconstructing research practices that arise out of the "social history and culture of the dominant race" and that "reflect and reinforce that social history and the controlling position of that racial group" (p. 13). Such practices are, as a result, epistemologically racist in that they deny the relational constructedness of the world in order to promote and maintain the hegemony of one of the supposed partners.

Approaches to Authority and Validity

Many of the problems identified above arise from researchers positioning themselves within modernist discourses. It is essential to challenge modernist discourses, with their concomitant concerns regarding validity that are addressed by such strategies as objectivity/subjectivity, replicability, and external measures for validity. These discourses are so pervasive that Māori/indigenous researchers may automatically revert to using such means of establishing validity for their texts, but problematically so because these measures of validity are all positioned/defined within another worldview. As bell hooks (1993) explains, the Black Power movement in the United States in the 1960s was influenced by the modernist discourses on race, gender, and class that were current at the time. As a result of not addressing these discourses and the ways they affected the condition of black people, issues such as patriarchy were left unaddressed within the Black Liberation movement. Unless black people address these issues themselves, hooks insists, others will do so for them, in ways determined by the concerns and interests of others rather than those that "women of color" would prefer.[16] Indeed, Linda Tillman (2002) promotes a culturally sensitive research approach for African Americans that focuses on "how African Americans understand and experience the world" (p. 4) and that advocates the use of an approach to qualitative research wherein "interpretative paradigms offer greater possibilities for the use of alternative frameworks, co-construction of multiple realities and experiences, and knowledge that can lead to improved educational opportunities for African Americans" (p. 5).

Yet historically, traditional forms of nonreflective research conducted within what Lincoln and Denzin (1994) term as positivist and post-positivist frames of reference perpetuate problems of outsiders determining what is valid for Māori. This occurs by the very process of employing non-Māori methodological frameworks and conventions for writing about such research processes and outcomes. For example, Lincoln and Denzin (1994) argue that terms such as "logical, construct, internal, ethnographic, and external validity, text-based data, triangulation, trustworthiness, credibility, grounding, naturalistic indicators, fit, coherence, comprehensiveness, plausibility, truth and relevance . . . [are] all attempts to reauthorize a text's authority in the post-positivist moment" (Lincoln & Denzin, 1994, p. 579).

These concepts, and the methodological frameworks within which they exist, represent attempts to contextualize the grounding of a text in the external, empirical world. "They represent efforts to develop a set of transcendent rules and procedures that lie outside any specific research project" (Lincoln & Denzin, 1994, p. 579). These externalized rules are the criteria by which the validity of a text is then judged. The author of the text is thus able to present the text to the reader as valid, replacing the sense making, meaning construction, and voice of the researched person with that of the researcher by representing the text as an authoritative re-presentation of the experiences of others by using a system of researcher-determined and -dominated coding and analytical tools.

Ballard (1994), referring to Donmoyer' s work, suggests that formulaic research procedures are rarely in fact useful as "prescriptions for practice" because people use their own knowledge, experience, feelings, and intuitions "when putting new ideas into practice or when working in new settings" (pp. 301–302). Furthermore, personal knowledge and personal experience can be seen as crucial in the application of new knowledge and/or working in new settings. This means that the application of research findings is filtered through the prior knowledge, feelings, and intuitions we already have. Donmoyer (as cited in Ballard, 1994) proposes that experience compounds, and this compounded knowledge/experience, when brought to a new task, provides for the occurrence of an even more complex process of understandings. Experience builds on and compounds experience, and, as Ballard suggests, this is why there is such value placed on colleagues with experience in the Pâkehâ world and on kaumâtua (elders) in the Māori world.

A related, and somewhat more complex, danger of referring to an existing methodology of participation is that there may be a tendency to construct a set of rules and procedures that lie outside any one research project. In doing so, researchers might take control over what constitutes legitimacy and validity, that is, what authority is claimed for the text will be removed from the participants. With such recipes comes the danger of outsiders controlling what constitutes reality for other people.

It is important to note, though, that the Kaupapa Māori approach does not suggest that all knowledge is completely relative. Instead, as Heshusius (1996) states:

> the self of the knower and the larger self of the community of inquiry are, from the very starting point, intimately woven into the very fabric of that which we claim as knowledge and of what we agree to be the proper ways by which we make knowledge claims. It is to say that the knower and the known are one movement. Moreover, any inquiry is an expression of a particular other-self relatedness. (p. 658)

Kaupapa Māori research, based in a different worldview from that of the dominant discourse, makes this political statement while at the same time rejecting a meaningless relativism by acknowledging the need to recognize and address the ongoing effects of racism and colonialism in the wider society.

Kaupapa Māori rejects outside control over what constitutes the text's call for authority and truth. A Kaupapa Māori position promotes what Lincoln and Denzin (1994) term an epistemological version of validity, one in which the authority of the text is "established through recourse to a set of rules concerning knowledge, its production and representation" (p. 578). Such an approach to validity locates the power within Māori cultural practices, where what are acceptable and what are not acceptable research, text, and/or processes is determined and defined by the research community itself in reference to the cultural context within which it operates.

As was explained above, Māori people have always had criteria for evaluating whether a process or a product is valid for them. *Taonga tuku iho* are literally the treasures from the ancestors. These treasures are the collected wisdom of ages, the means that have been established over a long period of time that guide and monitor people's very lives, today and in the future. Within these treasures are the messages of kawa,[17] those principles that, for example, guide the process of establishing relationships. Whakawhanaungatanga is not a haphazard process, decided on an ad hoc basis, but rather is based on time-honored and proven principles. How each of these principles is addressed in particular circumstances varies from tribe to tribe and hapu to hapu. Nevertheless, it is important that these principles are addressed.

For example, as described earlier, the meeting of two groups of people at a hui on a marae (ceremonial meeting place) involves acknowledgment of the tapu of each individual and of each group, by means of addressing and acknowledging the sacredness, specialness, genealogy, and connectedness of the guests with the hosts. Much time will be spent establishing this linkage, a connectedness between the people involved. How this actually is done is the subject of local customs, which are the correct ways to address these principles of kawa. *Tikanga* are an ongoing fertile ground for debate, but all participants know that if the kawa is not observed, then the event is "invalid": It does not have authority.

Just as Māori practices are epistemologically validated within Māori cultural contexts, so are Kaupapa Māori research practices and texts. Research conducted within a Kaupapa Māori framework has rules established as taonga tuku iho that are protected and maintained by the tapu of Māori cultural practices, such as the multiplicity of rituals within the hui and within the central cultural processes of whanaungatanga. Furthermore, the use of these concepts as constitutive research metaphors is subject to the same culturally determined processes of validation, and the same rules concerning knowledge, its production, and its representation, as are the literal phenomena. Therefore, the verification of a text, the authority of a text, and the quality of its representation of the experiences and its perspective of the participants are judged by criteria constructed and constituted within the culture.

By using such Māori concepts as *whânau*, *hui*, and *whakawhanaungatanga* as metaphors for the research process itself, Kaupapa Māori research invokes and claims authority for the processes and for the texts that are produced in terms of the principles, processes, and practices that govern such events in their literal sense. Metaphoric whânau are governed by the same principles and processes that govern a literal whânau and, as such, are understandable to and controllable by Māori people. Literal whânau have means of addressing contentious issues, resolving conflicts, constructing narratives, telling stories, raising children, and addressing economic and political issues, and, contrary to popular non-Māori opinion, such practices change over time to reflect changes going on in the wider world. Research whânau-of-interest also conduct their deliberations in a whânau style. Kaumâtua preside, others get their say according to who they are, and positions are defined in terms of how the definitions will benefit the whânau.

Subjectivities/Objectivities

As was discussed above, an indigenous Kaupapa Māori approach to research challenges colonial and neocolonial discourses that inscribe " otherness." Much quantitative research has dismissed, marginalized, or maintained control over the voice of others by insistence on the imposition of researcher-determined positivist and neopositivist evaluative criteria, internal and external validity, reliability, and objectivity. Nonetheless, a paradigm shift to qualitative research does not necessarily obviate this problem. Much qualitative research has also maintained a colonizing discourse of the "other" by seeking to hide the researcher/writer under a veil of neutrality or of objectivity or subjectivity, a situation in which the interests, concerns, and power of the researcher to determine the outcome of the research remain hidden in the text (B. Davies & Harré, 1990).

Objectivity, "that pathology of cognition that entails silence about the speaker, about [his or her] interests and [his or her] desires, and how these are socially situated and structurally maintained" (Gouldner, as cited in Tripp, 1983, p. 32), is a denial of identity. Just as identity to Māori people is tied up with being part of a whânau, a hapu, and an iwi, in the research relationship, membership in a metaphoric whânau of interest also provides its members with identity and hence the ability to participate. In Thayer-Bacon's (1997) view, "we develop a sense of 'self' through our relationships with others" (p. 241). For Māori researchers to stand aside from involvement in such a sociopolitical organization is to stand aside from their identity. This would signal the ultimate victory of colonization. For non-Māori researchers, denial of membership of the research whânau of interest is, similarly, to deny them a means of identification and hence participation within the projects. Furthermore, for non-Māori researchers to stand aside from participation in these terms is to promote colonization, albeit participation in ways defined by indigenous peoples may well pose difficulties for them. What is certain is that merely shifting one's position within the Western-dominated research domain need not address questions of interest to Māori people, because paradigm shifting is really a concern from another worldview. Non-Māori researchers need to seek inclusion on Māori terms, in terms of kin/metaphoric kin relationships and obligations—that is, within Māori-constituted practices and understandings—in order to establish their identity within research projects.

This does not mean, however, that researchers need to try to control their subjectivities. Heshusius (1994) suggests that managing subjectivity is just as problematic for qualitative researchers as managing objectivity is for the positivists. Esposito and Murphy (2000) similarly raise this problem of the preoccupation of many researchers who, while ostensibly locating themselves within critical race theory, for example, remain focused "strictly on subjectivity" and employ analytic tools "to interpret the discursive exchanges that, in the end, silence the study participants . . . [because] the investigator's subjectivity replaces the co-produced knowledge her research presumably represents" (p. 180).

This problem is epistemic in that the development of objectivity, through borrowing methodology from the natural sciences, introduced the concept of distance into the research relationship. Heshusius (1994) argues that the displacement of "objective positivism" by qualitative concerns about managing and controlling subjectivities perpetuates the fundamental notion that knowing is possible through constructing and regulating distance, a belief that presumes that the knower is separable from the known, a belief that is anathema to many indigenous people's ways of knowing. Heshusius (1994) suggests that the preoccupation with "managing subjectivity" is a "subtle form of empiricist thought" (p. 16) in that it assumes that if one can know subjectivity, then one can control it. Intellectualizing "the other's impact on self" perpetuates the notion of distance; validates the notions of "false consciousness" in others, emancipation as a project, and "othering" as a process; and reduces the self-other relationship to one that is mechanistic and methodological.

Operationally, Heshusius (1994) questions what we as researchers do after being confronted with "subjectivities": "Does one evaluate them and try to manage and to restrain them? And then believe one has the research process once again under control?" (p. 15). Both these positions address "meaningful" epistemological and methodological questions of the researcher's own choosing. Instead, Heshusius suggests that researchers need to address those questions that would address moral issues, such as "what kind of society do we have or are we constructing?" (p. 20). For example, how can racism be addressed unless those who perpetuate it become aware, through a participatory consciousness, of the lived reality of those who suffer? How can researchers become aware of the meaning of Māori schooling experiences if they perpetuate an artificial "distance" and objectify the "subject," dealing with issues in a manner that is of interest to the researchers rather than of concern to the subjects? The message is that you have to "live" the context in which schooling experiences occur. For example, the third study referred to before, *Te Kotahitanga* (Bishop, Berryman, et al., 2003), commenced by providing teachers with *testimonios* of students' experiences as a means of critically reflecting on the teachers' positioning in respect to deficit thinking and racism.

Preoccupations with managing and controlling one's subjectivities also stand in contrast with Berman's historical analysis, which suggests that "before the scientific revolution (and presumably the enlightenment) the act of knowing had always been understood as a form of participation and enchantment" (cited in Heshusius, 1994, p. 16). Berman states that "for most of human history, man [*sic*] saw himself as an integral part of it" (cited in Heshusius, 1994, p. 16). The very act of participation was knowing. Participation was direct, somatic (bodily), psychic, spiritual, and emotional involvement. "The belief that one can actually distance oneself, and then regulate that distance in order to come to know [has] left us alienated from each other, from nature and from ourselves" (Heshusius, 1994, p. 16).

Heshusius (1994) suggests that instead of addressing distance, researchers need to acknowledge their participation and attempt to develop a "participatory consciousness." This means becoming involved in a "somatic, non-verbal quality of attention that necessitates letting go of the focus of self" (p. 15). The three examples of Kaupapa Māori research projects identified earlier demonstrate that the researchers understand themselves to be involved somatically in a group process, a process whereby the researcher becomes part of a research whânau, limiting the development of insider/outsider dualisms. To be involved somatically means to be involved bodily—that is, physically, ethically, morally, and spiritually, not just in one's capacity as a "researcher" concerned with methodology. Such involvement is constituted as a way of knowing that is fundamentally different from the concepts of personal investment and collaboration that are suggested in traditional approaches to research. Although it appears that "personal investment" is essential, this personal investment is not on terms determined by the "investor." Instead, the investment is on terms mutually understandable and controllable by all participants, so that the investment is reciprocal and could not be otherwise. The "personal investment" by the researcher is not an act by an individual agent but instead emerges out of the context within which the research is constituted.

The process of colonization developed an alienated and alienating mode of consciousness and, thus, has tried to take a fundamental principle of life away from Māori people—that we do not objectify nature, nor do we subjectify nature. As we learn our whakapapa, we learn of our total integration, connectedness, and commitment to the world and the need to let go of the focus on self. We know that there is a way of knowing that is different from that which was taught to those colonized into the Western way of thought. We know about a way that is born of time, connectedness, kinship, commitment, and participation.

Epilogue: A Means of Evaluating Researcher Positioning

This chapter has concluded that researchers and research participants need a means whereby they can critically reflect upon the five issues of power that are identified in Figure 5.1. Figure 5.1 provides a series of critical questions that can be used by researchers and research participants to evaluate power relations prior to and during research activity. The outer circle shows some of the metaphors that might constitute a discursive position within which researchers can be positioned.

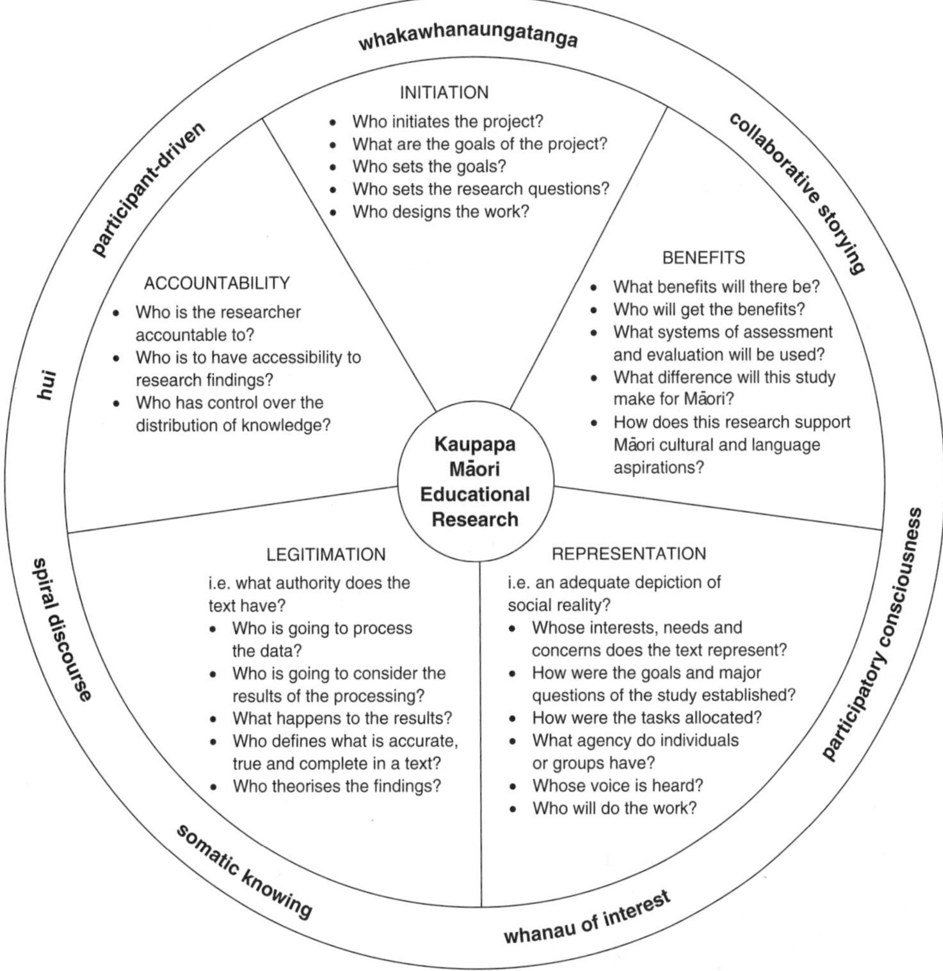

Figure 5.1. A Means of Evaluating Researcher Positioning

Source: Reproduced with permission from Bishop and Glynn (1999, p. 129).

Appendix: Glossary of Māori Terms

aroha	love in its broadest sense; mutuality
awhi	helpfulness
hapu	subtribe, usually linked to a common ancestor; pregnant
haruru	greeting others by shaking hands and performing a hôngi
hôngi	greeting another person by pressing noses together, to share the breath of life
hui	ceremonial, ritualized meeting
iwi	tribe; bones
kaumâtua	respected elder
kaupapa	agenda, philosophy
kawa	protocol
koha	gift
mana	power
manaaki	hospitality, caring
manuhiri	guest(s)
Māori	indigenous people of Aotearoa/New Zealand
marae	ceremonial meeting place
mihimihi	ritualized self-introduction
Pâkehâ	New Zealanders of European descent
pôwhiri	formal welcome
raranga kôrero	those stories that explain the people and events of a whakapapa
taonga	treasures, including physical, social, cultural, and intellectual
taonga tuku iho	treasures passed down to the present generation from the ancestors
tapu	sacred, to be treated with respect, a restriction, a being with potentiality for power, integrity, specialness
tiaki	to look after; guidance
tikanga	customs, values, beliefs, and attitudes
tino Rangatiratanga	self-determination
whakakotahitanga	developing unity
whakapapa	genealogy
whakawhanaungatanga	establishing relationships
whânau	extended family; to be born
whanaunga	relatives
whanaungatanga	kin relationships

Notes

1. This chapter is based on Bishop (1998a, 1998b).

2. Two peoples created Aotearoa/New Zealand when, in 1840, lieutenant-governor Hobson and the chiefs of New Zealand signed the Treaty of Waitangi on behalf of the British Crown and the Māori descendants of New Zealand. The treaty is seen as a charter for power sharing in the decision-making processes of this country and for Māori determination of their own destiny as the indigenous people of New Zealand (Walker, 1990). The history of Māori and Pâkehâ relations since the signing of the treaty has not been one of partnership, of two peoples developing a nation, but instead one of domination by Pâkehâ and marginalization of the Māori people (Bishop, 1991b; Simon, 1990; Walker, 1990). This has created the myth of our nation being "one people" with equal opportunities (Hohepa, 1975; Simon, 1990; Walker, 1990). Results of this domination are evident today in the lack of equitable participation by Māori in all positive and beneficial aspects of life in New Zealand and by their overrepresentation in the negative aspects (Pomare, 1988; Simon, 1990). In education, for example, the central government' s sequential policies of assimilation, integration, and multiculturalism (Irwin, 1989; Jones, McCulloch, Marshall, Smith, & Smith, 1990) and Taha Māori (Holmes, Bishop, & Glynn, 1993; G. H. Smith, 1990), while concerned for the welfare of Māori people, effectively stress the need for Māori people to subjugate their destiny to the needs of the nation-state, whose goals are determined by the Pâkehâ majority.

3. "Traditional" is used here to denote that "tradition" of research that has grown in New Zealand as a result of the dominance of the Western worldview in research institutions. Māori means of accessing, defining, and protecting knowledge, however, existed before European arrival. Such Māori cultural processes were protected by the Treaty of Waitangi, subsequently marginalized, but are today legitimized within Māori cultural discursive practice.

4. Please see the glossary of Māori terms for English translations.

5. The concept of hegemony is used here in the sense defined by Michel Foucault (Smart, 1986), who suggests that hegemony is an insidious process that is acquired most effectively through "practices, techniques, and methods which infiltrate minds and bodies, cultural practices which cultivate behaviors and beliefs, tastes, desires and needs as seemingly naturally occurring qualities and properties embodied in the psychic and physical reality of the human subject" (p. 159).

6. I am using the term "discourse" to mean language in social use or in action.

7. Irwin (1992a) argues that prior to the signing of the Treaty of Waitangi and the colonization of New Zealand, there existed a "complex, vibrant Māori education system" that had "Māori development [as] its vision, its educational processes and its measurable outcomes" (p. 9). Protection of this education system was guaranteed under Article Two of the Treaty of Waitangi, just as Article Three guaranteed Māori people, as citizens of New Zealand, the right to equitable educational outcomes. This promise had been negated by subsequent practice, and the outcome is the present educational crisis (L. Davies & Nicholl, 1993; Jones et al., 1990). The posttreaty education system that developed in New Zealand—the mission schools (Bishop, 1991a), the Native schools (Simon, 1990), and the present mainstream schools (Irwin, 1992a)—has been unable to "successfully validate matauranga Māori, leaving it marginalised and in a precarious state" (Irwin, 1992a, p. 10). Furthermore, while mainstream schooling does not serve Māori people well (L. Davies & Nicholl, 1993), the Māori schooling initiatives of Te Kohanga reo (Māori medium preschools), Kura Kaupapa Māori (Māori medium primary schools), Whare Kura (Māori medium secondary schools), and Whare Waananga (Māori tertiary institutions), "which have developed from within Māori communities to intervene in Māori language, cultural, educational, social and economic crises *are successful in the eyes of the Māori people*" (G. H. Smith, 1992, p. 1, emphasis added).

8. Article Two of an English translation of the Māori version of the Treaty of Waitangi states: "The Queen of England agrees to protect the Chiefs, the subtribes and all the people of New Zealand in the unqualified exercise of their chieftainship over their lands, villages and all their treasures. But on the other hand the Chiefs of the Confederation and all the Chiefs will sell land to the Queen at a price agreed to by the person owning it and by the person buying it (the latter being) appointed by the Queen as her purchase agent" (Kawharu, as cited in Consedine & Consedine, 2001, p. 236). It is the first part of this article that has relevance to this argument, that is, the promise that Māori people were guaranteed chiefly control over that which they treasured.

9. Whânau is a primary concept (a cultural preference) that underlies narratives of Kaupapa

Māori research practice. This concept contains both values (cultural aspirations) and social processes (cultural practices). The root word of "whânau" literally means "family" in its broad, "extended" sense. However, the word "whânau" is increasingly being used in a metaphoric sense (Metge, 1990). This generic concept of whânau subsumes other related concepts: whanaunga (relatives), whanaungatanga (relationships), whakawhanaungatanga (the process of establishing relationships), and whakapapa (literally, the means of establishing relationships). (The prefix "whaka" means "to make"; the suffix "tanga" has a naming function.)

10. This poses major challenges for assessment in education settings.

11. It is important to emphasize at this point that the use of Māori cultural practices (literally and/or metaphorically) in research might lead those not familiar with New Zealand to question how relevant such an analysis is to the lived realities of Māori people today. Because Māori people today are a Fourth World nation or nations—that is, within a larger entity—it is more a matter of degree as to who participates and when they participate. Therefore, rather than being able to quantify which portion of the Māori population still acts in this way, it is perhaps more realistic to say that most Māori do at some time. For some, it might be only at funerals or weddings; others, of course, (albeit a small proportion) live this way all the time, but increasingly more and more Māori people are participating in (for example) kaupapa Māori educational initiatives, and these are all run in a Māori manner. Thus, most people do sometimes, some all the time, and others not so often. What is perhaps more critical is that most Māori people are able to understand the processes and are able to participate. Much is said of the impact of urbanization on Māori people and the removal of young people from their tribal roots and the consequent decline in language abilities and cultural understandings. It is a measure of the strength of the whânau (the extended family) and the strength of genealogical linkages, however, that when Māori people gather, the hui (formal meetings) process is usually the one that is used, almost as a "default setting," despite more than a century of colonization. Indeed, it is a measure of the strength of these cultural practices and principles that they have survived the onslaught of the last 150 years. It is to these underlying strengths that I turn also as inspiration for developing an approach to Māori research. My argument, then, is not an attempt to identify "past practices" or reassemble a romantic past, but rather to examine what might constitute the emerging field of Kaupapa Māori research in reference to present Māori cultural practices that are guided by the messages from the past. Māori, along with many other indigenous people, are guided by the principle of guidance from the ancestors. It is not a matter of studying how people did things in the past but more an ongoing dynamic interactive relationship between those of us alive today as the embodiment of all those who have gone before. It seems to me that, in practice, Māori cultural practices are alive and well and that, when used either literally or metaphorically, they enable Māori people to understand and control what is happening.

12. Eminent Māori scholar Rose Pere (1991) describes the key qualities of a hui as

> respect, consideration, patience, and cooperation. People need to feel that they have the right and the time to express their point of view. You may not always agree with the speakers, but it is considered bad form to interrupt their flow of speech while they are standing on their feet; one has to wait to make a comment. People may be as frank as they like about others at the hui, but usually state their case in such a way that the person being criticized can stand up with some dignity in his/her right of reply. Once everything has been fully discussed and the members come to some form of consensus, the hui concludes with a prayer and the partaking of food. (p. 44)

13. This may appear to be somewhat patronizing; however, our experience when conducting Kaupapa Māori research is that research participants are often surprised by our insistence that we wish to enter into a dialogue with them about the meaning they construct from their experiences. Our experience is that the traditional "speaking for" type of research is so pervasive and dominant that participants are initially surprised that they might have an authoritative voice in the process rather than just being a source of data for an outside researcher. What are truly heartening are the positive responses we have had from participants of all ages, once they realized that they were able to engage in a dialogue.

14. For further details of the use of Māori metaphor, see Bishop (1996) and Bishop and Glynn (1999).

15. In New Zealand, the koru represents growth, new beginnings, renewal, and hope for the future.

16. Donna Awatere (1981) and Kathie Irwin (1992b) are two Māori feminist scholars who have taken up this challenge in Aotearoa/New Zealand, in a way that has clearly delineated their stance as different from white feminisms. In operationalizing Māori feminisms, they have critiqued modernist issues from a Māori worldview in Māori ways. Awatere critiqued white modernist feminists for hegemonically voicing Māori feminist concerns as identical to their own. Kathie Irwin's (1992b) critique addressed a question that is vexatious to non-Māori modernist feminists: "Why don't women speak on a marae?" She responded with other questions, such as "What do you mean by speaking? . . . Is a karanga not speaking?" and "Who is defining what speaking is?" She asserts that rather than taking an essentialist position, the validity of a text written about Māori women "speaking" on a marae is understandable only in terms of the rules established within Māori cultural practices associated with marae protocols. In this, she is not only addressing a Māori issue but also is addressing modernist feminists in poststructural terms of epistemological validity.

17. People often use the term *kawa* to refer to marae protocols. For example, at the time of whaikorero (ritualized speechmaking), some tribes conduct this part of the pôwhiri by a tikanga known as paeke, where all the male speakers of the hosts' side will speak at one time, then turn the marae over to the visitors' speaker, who then follows. Other tribes prefer to follow a tikanga termed utuutu, where hosts and visitors alternate. Some tribes welcome visitors into their meeting house following a hôngi; others keep the hôngi until the end of the welcoming time. It is clear that these various tikanga are practices that are correct in certain tribal or hapu contexts, but underneath is the practice of the kawa being handed down from those who have gone before, concerning the need to recognize the tapu of people, their mana, their wairua, and the mauri of the place and events. See Salmond (1975) for a detailed ethnographic study.

References

Acker, F., Barry, K., & Esseveld, J. (1991). Objectivity and truth problems in doing feminist research. In M. Fonow & J. Cook (Eds.), *Beyond methodology: Feminist scholarship as lived research* (pp. 133–154). Bloomington: Indiana University Press.

Awatere, D. (1981). *Māori sovereignty.* Auckland, New Zealand: Broadsheet.

Ballard, K. (Ed.). (1994). *Disability, family, whanau and society.* Palmerston North, New Zealand: Dunmore Press.

Beverley, J. (2000). Testimonio, subalternity, and narrative authority. In N. K. Denzin & Y. S. Lincoln (Eds.), *Handbook of qualitative research* (2nd ed., pp. 555–565). Thousand Oaks, CA: Sage.

Bishop, R. (1991a). *He whakawhanaungatanga tikanga rua. Establishing links: A bicultural experience.* Unpublished master's thesis, University of Otago, Dunedin, New Zealand.

Bishop, R. (1991b, December). *Te ropu rangahau tikanga rua: The need for emancipatory research under the control of the* Māori *people for the betterment of* Māori *people.* Paper presented at the 13th Annual New Zealand Association for Research in Education, Knox College, Dunedin, New Zealand.

Bishop, R. (1996). *Collaborative research stories: Whakawanaungatanga.* Palmerston North, New Zealand: Dunmore Press.

Bishop, R. (1997). Interviewing as collaborative storying. *Educational Research and Perspectives, 24*(1), 28–47.

Bishop, R. (1998a). Examples of culturally specific research practices: A response to Tillman and López. *Qualitative Studies in Education, 11*(3), 419–434.

Bishop, R. (1998b). Freeing ourselves from neocolonial domination in research: A Māori approach to creating knowledge. *Qualitative Studies in Education, 11*(2), 199–219.

Bishop, R., Berryman, M., & Richardson, C. (2002). Te toi huarewa: Effective teaching and learning in total immersion Māori language educational settings. *Canadian Journal of Native Education, 26*(1), 44–61.

Bishop, R., Berryman, M., & Richardson, C. (2003). *Te Kotahitanga: The experiences of year 9 and 10 Māori students in mainstream classrooms.* Wellington, New Zealand: Ministry of Education. Retrieved from www.minedu.govt.nz/goto/tekotahitanga

Bishop, R., & Glynn, T. (1999). *Culture counts: Changing power relations in education.* Palmerston North, New Zealand: Dunmore Press.

Brayboy, B. M., & Deyhle, D. (2000). Insider-outsider: Researchers in American Indian communities. *Theory Into Practice, 39*(3), 163–169.

Bridges, D. (2001). The ethics of outsider research. *Journal of Philosophy of Education, 35*(3), 371–386.

Burgess, R. G. (1984). *In the field: An introduction to field research.* New York: Falmer.

Calderhead, J. (1981). Stimulated recall: A method for research on teaching. *British Journal of Educational Psychology, 51,* 211–217.

Connelly, F. M., & Clandinin, D. J. (1990). Stories of experience and narrative inquiry. *Educational Researcher, 19*(5), 2–14.

Consedine, R., & Consedine, J. (2001). *Healing our history: The challenge of the Treaty of Waitangi.* Auckland, New Zealand: Penguin Books.

Davies, B. (1990). Agency as a form of discursive practice: A classroom observed. *British Journal of Sociology of Education, 11*(3), 341–361.

Davies, B., & Harré, R. (1990). Positioning: The discursive production of selves. *Journal of the Theory of Social Behaviour, 20*, 43–65.

Davies, L., & Nicholl, K. (1993). *Te Māori i roto i nga mahi whakaakoranga: Māori in education.* Wellington, New Zealand: Ministry of Education.

Delamont, S. (1992). *Fieldwork in educational settings: Methods, pitfalls and perspectives.* London: Falmer.

Deyhle, D., & Swisher, K. (1997). Research in American Indian and Alaska Native education: From assimilation to self-determination. In M. W. Apple (Ed.), *Review of Research in Education* (Vol. 22, pp. 113–194). Washington, DC: American Educational Research Association.

Durie, M. (1994). *Whaiora: Māori health development.* Auckland, New Zealand: Oxford University Press.

Durie, M. (1995). *Principles for the development of Māori policy.* Paper presented at the *Māori* Policy Development, Māori Policy Development Conference, Wellington, New Zealand.

Durie, M. (1998). *Te mana, te kawanatonga: The politics of Māori self-determination.* Auckland, New Zealand: Oxford University Press.

Eisner, E. W. (1991). *The enlightened eye: Qualitative inquiry and the enhancement of educational practice.* New York: Teachers College Press.

Esposito, L., & Murphy, J. W. (2000). Another step in the study of race relations. *The Sociological Quarterly, 41*(2), 171–187.

Fine, M. (1994). Working the hyphens: Reinventing the self and other in qualitative research. In N. K. Denzin & Y. S. Lincoln (Eds.), *Handbook of qualitative research* (1st ed., pp. 70–82). Thousand Oaks, CA: Sage.

Fine, M., & Weis, L. (1996). Writing the "wrongs" of fieldwork: Confronting our own research/writing dilemmas in urban ethnographies. *Qualitative Inquiry, 2*(3), 251–274.

Fine, M., Weis, L., Weseen, S., & Wong, L. (2000). For whom? Qualitative research, representations, and social responsibilities. In N. K. Denzin & Y. S. Lincoln (Eds.), *Handbook of qualitative research* (2nd ed., pp. 107–131). Thousand Oaks, CA: Sage.

Fitzsimons, P., & Smith, G. H. (2000). Philosophy and indigenous cultural transformation. *Educational Philosophy and Theory, 32*(1), 25–41.

Gay, G. (2000). *Culturally responsive teaching: Theory, research and practice.* New York: Teachers College Press.

Glaser, B. G., & Strauss, A. L. (1967). *The discovery of grounded theory: Strategies for qualitative research.* London: Weidenfeld and Nicolson.

Goldstein, L. S. (2000). Ethical dilemmas in designing collaborative research: Lessons learned the hard way. *Qualitative Studies in Education, 13*(5), 517–530.

González, F. E. (2001). *Haciendo que hacer*—cultivating a Mestiz worldview and academic achievement: Braiding cultural knowledge into educational research, policy, practice. *International Journal of Qualitative Studies in Education, 14*(5), 641–656.

Griffiths, M. (1998). *Educational research for social justice: Getting off the fence.* Buckingham, UK: Open University Press.

Heshusius, L. (1994). Freeing ourselves from objectivity: Managing subjectivity or turning toward a participatory mode of consciousness? *Educational Researcher, 23*(3), 15–22.

Heshusius, L. (1996). Modes of consciousness and the self in learning disabilities research: Considering past and future. In D. K. Reid, W. P. Hresko, & H. L. Swanson (Eds.), *Cognitive approaches to learning disabilities* (3rd ed., pp. 651–671). Austin, TX: PRO-ED.

Heshusius, L. (2002). More than the (merely) rational: Imagining inquiry for ability diversity. An essay response to Jim Paul. *Disability, Culture and Education, 1*(2), 95–118.

Hohepa, P. (1975). The one people myth. In M. King (Ed.), *Te ao hurihuri: The world moves on: Aspects of Māoritanga* (pp. 98–111). Auckland, New Zealand: Hicks Smith.

Holmes, H., Bishop, R., & Glynn, T. (1993). *Tu mai kia tu ake: Impact of taha Māori in Otago and Southland schools* (Te Ropu Rangahau Tikanga Rua Monograph No. 4). Dunedin, New Zealand: Department of Education, University of Otago.

hooks, b. (1993). Postmodern blackness. *Postmodern Culture, 1*(1). Retrieved from http://muse.jhu.edu/journals/pmc/index.html

Irwin, K. (1989). Multicultural education: the New Zealand response. *New Zealand Journal of Educational Studies, 24*(1), 3–18.

Irwin, K. (1992a). *Māori research methods and processes: An exploration and discussion.* Paper presented at the Joint New Zealand Association for Research in Education/Australian Association for Research in Education Conference, Geelong, Australia.

Irwin, K. (1992b). Towards theories of Māori feminisms. In R. Du Plessis (Ed.), *Feminist voices: Women's studies texts for Aotearoa/New Zealand* (pp. 1–21). Auckland, New Zealand: Oxford University Press.

Irwin, K. (1994). Māori research methods and processes: An exploration. *Sites: A Journal for Radical Perspectives on Culture, 28,* 25–43.

Jacobs-Huey, L. (2002). The natives are gazing and talking back: Review the problematics of positionality, voice and accountability among "Native" anthropologists. *American Anthropologist, 104*(3), 791–804.

Johnson-Bailey, J. (1999). The ties that bind and the shackles that separate: Race, gender, class, and color in a research process. *Qualitative Studies in Education, 12*(6), 659–670.

Jones, A., McCulloch, G., Marshall, J. D., Smith, G. H., & Smith, L. T. (1990). *Myths and realities: Schooling in New Zealand.* Palmerston North, New Zealand: Dunmore Press.

Kemmis, S., & McTaggart, R. (2000). Participatory action research. In N. K. Denzin & Y. S. Lincoln (Eds.), *Handbook of qualitative research* (2nd ed., pp. 567–605). Thousand Oaks, CA: Sage.

Kincheloe, J. L., & McLaren, P. (2000). Rethinking critical theory and qualitative research. In N. K. Denzin & Y. S. Lincoln (Eds.), *Handbook of qualitative research* (2nd ed., pp. 279–313). Thousand Oaks, CA: Sage.

Ladson-Billings, G. (1995). Toward a theory of culturally relevant pedagogy. *American Educational Research Journal, 32*(3), 465–491.

Ladson-Billings, G. (2000). Racialized discourses and ethnic epistemologies. In N. K. Denzin & Y. S. Lincoln (Eds.), *Handbook of qualitative research* (2nd ed., pp. 257–277). Thousand Oaks, CA: Sage.

Lather, P. (1986). Research as praxis. *Harvard Educational Review, 56*(3), 257–274.

Lather, P. (1991). *Getting smart: Feminist research and pedagogy with/in the postmodern.* New York: Routledge.

Lincoln, Y. S., & Denzin, N. K. (1994). The fifth moment. In N. K. Denzin & Y. S. Lincoln (Eds.), *Handbook of qualitative research* (1st ed., pp. 575–586). Thousand Oaks, CA: Sage.

Lomawaima, K. T. (2000). Tribal sovereigns: Reframing research in American Indian education. *Harvard Educational Review, 70*(1), 1–21.

Merriam, S. B., Johnson-Bailey, J., Lee, M.-Y., Kee, Y., Ntseane, G., & Muhamad, M. (2001). Power and positionality: Negotiating insider/outsider status within and across cultures. *International Journal of Lifelong Education, 20*(5), 405–416.

Metge, J. (1990). Te rito o te harakeke: Conceptions of the Whaanau. *Journal of the Polynesian Society, 99*(1), 55–91.

Mishler, E. G. (1986). *Research interviewing: Context and narrative.* Cambridge, MA: Harvard University Press.

Moll, L. C. (1992). Bilingual classroom studies and community analysis: Some recent trends. *Educational Researcher, 21,* 20–24.

Narayan, K. (1993). How native is a "native" anthropologist? *American Anthropologist, 95,* 671–686.

Noddings, N. (1986). Fidelity in teaching, teacher education, and research for teaching. *Harvard Educational Review, 56*(4), 496–510.

Oakley, A. (1981). Interviewing women: A contradiction in terms. In H. Roberts (Ed.), *Doing feminist research* (pp. 30–61). London: Routledge.

Olssen, M. (1993, April). *Habermas, post-modernism and the science question for education.* Paper presented at the Staff Seminar, University of Otago, Dunedin, New Zealand.

Patton, M. (1990). *Qualitative evaluation and research methods* (2nd ed.). Newbury Park, CA: Sage.

Pere, R. (1991). *Te wheke: A celebration of infinite wisdom.* Gisborne, New Zealand: Ao Ako.

Pihama, L., Cram, F., & Walker, S. (2002). Creating a methodological space: A literature review of Kaupapa Māori research. *Canadian Journal of Native Education, 26*(1), 30–43.

Polanyi, M. (1966). *The tacit dimension.* New York: Doubleday.

Pomare, E. (1988). *Hauora: Māori standards of health.* Wellington, New Zealand: Department of Health.

Rains, F. V., Archibald, J.-A., & Deyhle, D. (2000). Introduction: Through our eyes and in our own words. *International Journal of Qualitative Studies in Education, 13*(4), 337–342.

Reinharz, S. (1992). *Feminist methods in social research.* New York: Oxford University Press.

Reyes, P., Scribner, J., & Scribner, A. P. (Eds.). (1999). *Lessons from high-performing Hispanic schools: Greater learning communities.* New York: Teachers College Press.

Ryan, J. (1999). *Race and ethnicity in multi-ethnic schools: A critical case study.* Clevedon, UK: Multilingual Matters.

Salmond, A. (1975). *Hui: A study of Māori ceremonial greetings.* Auckland, New Zealand: Reed & Methuen.

Scheurich, J. J., & Young, M. D. (1997). Coloring epistemologies: Are our research epistemologies racially biased? *Educational Researcher, 26*(4), 4–16.

Shirres, M. (1982). Tapu. *Journal of the Polynesian Society, 91*(1), 29–52.

Sidorkin, A. M. (2002). *Learning relations: Impure education, deschooled schools, and dialogue with evil.* New York: Peter Lang.

Simon, J. A. (1990). *The role of schooling in Māori-Pâkehâ relations.* Unpublished doctoral dissertation, Auckland University, Auckland, New Zealand.

Sleeter, C. E. (2001). Epistemological diversity in research on preservice teacher preparation for historically underserved children. In W. G. Secada (Ed.), *Review of Research in Education* (Vol. 6, pp. 209–250). Washington, DC: American Educational Research Association.

Smart, B. (1986). The politics of truth and the problems of hegemony. In D. C. Hoy (Ed.), *Foucault: A critical reader* (pp. 157–173). Oxford, UK: Basil Blackwell.

Smith, G. H. (1990). Taha Māori: Pâkehâ capture. In J. Codd, R. Harker & R. Nash (Eds.), *Political issues in New Zealand education* (pp. 183–197). Palmerston North, New Zealand: Dunmore Press.

Smith, G. H. (1992, November). *Tane-nui-a-rangi's legacy: Propping up the sky: Kaupapa Māori as resistance and intervention.* Paper presented at the New Zealand Association for Research in Education/Australian Association for Research in Education Joint Conference, Deakin University, Australia. Retrieved from www.swin.edu/.au/aare/conf92/SMITG92.384

Smith, G. H. (1997). *Kaupapa Māori as transformative praxis.* Unpublished doctoral dissertation, University of Auckland, Auckland.

Smith, L. T. (1999). *Decolonizing methodologies: Research and indigenous peoples.* London: Zed Books.

Sprague, J., & Hayes, J. (2000). Self-determination and empowerment: A feminist standpoint analysis of talk about disability. *American Journal of Community Psychology, 28*(5), 671–695.

Stacey, J. (1991). Can there be a feminist ethnography? In S. B. Gluck & D. Patai (Eds.), *Women's words: The feminist practice of oral history* (pp. 111–119). New York: Routledge.

Stanfield, J. H. (1994). Ethnic modeling in qualitative research. In N. K. Denzin & Y. S. Lincoln (Eds.), *Handbook of qualitative research* (1st ed., pp. 175–188). Thousand Oaks, CA: Sage.

Swisher, K. G. (1998). Why Indian people should be the ones to write about Indian education. In D. A. Mihesuah (Ed.), *Natives and academics: Researching and writing about American Indians* (pp. 190–200). Lincoln: University of Nebraska Press.

Thayer-Bacon, B. (1997). The nurturing of a relational epistemology. *Educational Theory, 47*(2), 239–260.

Tillman, L. C. (2002). Culturally sensitive research approaches: An African-American perspective. *Educational Researcher, 31*(9), 3–12.

Tripp, D. H. (1983). Co-authorship and negotiation: The interview as act of creation. *Interchange, 14*(3), 32–45.

Villegas, A. M., & Lucas, T. (2002). *Educating culturally responsive teachers: A coherent approach.* New York: State University of New York Press.

Walker, R. (1990). *Ka whawhai tonu matou: Struggle without end.* Auckland, New Zealand: Penguin.

6

ETHICS AND POLITICS IN QUALITATIVE RESEARCH

Clifford G. Christians

The Enlightenment mind clustered around an extraordinary dichotomy. Intellectual historians usually summarize this split in terms of subject/object, fact/value, or material/spiritual dualisms. All three of these are legitimate interpretations of the cosmology inherited from Galileo, Descartes, and Newton. None of them, however, puts the Enlightenment into its sharpest focus. Its deepest root was a pervasive autonomy. The cult of human personality prevailed in all its freedom. Human beings were declared a law unto themselves, set loose from every faith that claimed their allegiance. Proudly self-conscious of human autonomy, the 18th-century mind saw nature as an arena of limitless possibilities in which the sovereignty of human personality was demonstrated by its mastery over the natural order. Release from nature spawned autonomous individuals who considered themselves independent of any authority. The freedom motif was the deepest driving force, first released by the Renaissance and achieving maturity during the Enlightenment.[1]

Obviously, one can reach autonomy by starting with the subject/object dualism. In constructing the Enlightenment worldview, the prestige of natural science played a key role in setting people free. Achievements in mathematics, physics, and astronomy allowed humans to dominate nature, which formerly had dominated them. Science provided unmistakable evidence that by applying reason to nature and to human beings in fairly obvious ways, people could live progressively happier lives. Crime and insanity, for example, no longer needed repressive theological explanations, but instead were deemed capable of mundane empirical solutions.

Likewise, one can get to the autonomous self by casting the question in terms of a radical discontinuity between hard facts and subjective values. The Enlightenment did push values to the fringe through its disjunction between knowledge of what is and what ought to be, and Enlightenment materialism in all its forms isolated reason from faith, and knowledge from belief. As Robert Hooke insisted in 1663, when he helped found London's Royal Society, "To improve the knowledge of natural things, this Society will not meddle with Divinity, Metaphysics, Morals, Politics and Rhetoric" (Lyons, 1944, p. 41). With factuality gaining a stranglehold on the Enlightenment mind, those regions of human interest that implied oughts, constraints, and imperatives simply ceased to appear. Certainly those who see the Enlightenment as separating facts and values have identified a cardinal difficulty. Likewise, the realm of the spirit can easily dissolve into mystery and intuition. If the spiritual world contains no binding force, it is surrendered to speculation by the divines, many of whom accepted the Enlightenment belief that their pursuit was ephemeral.

But the Enlightenment's autonomy doctrine created the greatest mischief. Individual self-determination stands as the centerpiece, bequeathing to us the universal problem of integrating human freedom with moral order. In struggling with the complexities and conundrums of this relationship, the Enlightenment, in effect, refused to sacrifice personal freedom. Even though the problem had a particular urgency in the 18th century, its response was not resolution but a categorical insistence on autonomy. Given the despotic political regimes and oppressive ecclesiastical systems of the period, such an uncompromising stance for freedom at this juncture is understandable. The Enlightenment began and ended with the assumption that human liberty ought to be cut away from the moral order, never integrated meaningfully with it.

Jean-Jacques Rousseau was the most outspoken advocate of this radical freedom. He gave intellectual substance to free self-determination of the human personality as the highest good. Rousseau is a complicated figure. He refused to be co-opted by Descartes's rationalism, Newton's mechanistic cosmology, or Locke's egoistic selves. He was not merely content to isolate and sacralize freedom, either, at least not in his *Discourse on Inequality* or in the *Social Contract*, where he answers Hobbes.

Rousseau represented the romantic wing of the Enlightenment, revolting against its rationalism. He won a wide following well into the 19th century for advocating immanent and emergent values rather than transcendent and given ones. While admitting that humans were finite and limited, he nonetheless promoted a freedom of breathtaking scope—not just disengagement from God or the Church, but freedom from culture and from any authority. Autonomy became the core of the human being and the center of the universe. Rousseau's understanding of equality, social systems, axiology, and language were anchored in it. He recognized the consequences more astutely than those comfortable with a shrunken negative freedom. The only solution that he found tolerable, however, was a noble human nature that enjoyed freedom beneficently and, therefore, one could presume, lived compatibly in some vague sense with a moral order.

Value-Free Experimentalism

Typically, debates over the character of the social sciences revolve around the theory and methodology of the natural sciences. However, the argument here is not how they resemble natural science, but rather their inscription into the dominant Enlightenment worldview. In political theory, the liberal state as it emerged in 17th- and 18th-century Europe left citizens free to lead their own lives without obeisance to the Church or the feudal order. Psychology, sociology, and economics—known as the human or moral sciences in the 18th and 19th centuries—were conceived as "liberal arts" that opened minds and freed the imagination. As the social sciences and liberal state emerged and overlapped historically, Enlightenment thinkers in Europe advocated the "facts, skills, and techniques" of experimental reasoning to support the state and citizenry (Root, 1993, pp. 14–15).

Consistent with the presumed priority of individual liberty over the moral order, the basic institutions of society were designed to ensure "neutrality between different conceptions of the good" (Root, 1993, p. 12). The state was prohibited "from requiring or even encouraging citizens to subscribe to one religious tradition, form of family life, or manner of personal or artistic expression over another" (Root, 1993, p. 12). Given the historical circumstances in which shared conceptions of the good were no longer broad and deeply entrenched, taking sides on moral issues and insisting on social ideals were considered counterproductive. Value neutrality appeared to be the logical alternative "for a society whose members practiced many religions, pursued many different occupations, and identified with many different customs and traditions" (Root, 1993, p. 11). The theory and practice of mainstream social science reflect liberal Enlightenment philosophy, as do education, science, and politics. Only a reintegration of autonomy and the moral order provides an alternative paradigm for the social sciences today.[2]

Mill's Philosophy of Social Science

For John Stuart Mill, "neutrality is necessary in order to promote autonomy. . . . A person cannot be forced to be good, and the state should not dictate the kind of life a citizen should lead; it would be better for citizens to choose badly than for them to be forced by the state to choose well" (Root, 1993, pp. 12–13). Planning our lives according to our own ideas and purposes is sine qua non for autonomous beings in Mill's *On Liberty* (1859/1978): "The free development of individuality is one of the principal ingredients of human happiness, and quite the chief ingredient of individual and social progress" (p. 50; see also Copleston, 1966, p. 303, n. 32). This neutrality, based on the supremacy of individual autonomy, is the foundational principle in his *Utilitarianism* (1861/1957) and in *A System of Logic, Ratiocinative and Inductive* (1843/1893) as well. For Mill, "the principle of utility demands that the individual should enjoy full liberty, except the liberty to harm others" (Copleston, 1966, p. 54). In addition to bringing classical utilitarianism to its maximum development and establishing with Locke the liberal state, Mill delineated the foundations of inductive inquiry as social scientific method. In terms of the principles of empiricism, he perfected the inductive techniques of Francis Bacon as a problem-solving methodology to replace Aristotelian deductive logic.

According to Mill, syllogisms contribute nothing new to human knowledge. If we conclude that because "all men are mortal" the Duke of Wellington is mortal by virtue of his manhood, then the conclusion does not advance the premise (see Mill, 1843/1893, II, 3, 2, p. 140). The crucial issue is not reordering the conceptual world but discriminating genuine knowledge from superstition. In the pursuit of truth, generalizing and synthesizing are necessary to advance inductively from the known to the unknown. Mill seeks to establish this function of logic as inference from the known, rather than certifying the rules for formal consistency in reasoning (Mill, 1843/1893, Bk. 3). Scientific certitude can be approximated when induction is followed rigorously, with propositions empirically derived and the material of all our knowledge provided by experience.[3] For the physical sciences, he establishes four modes of experimental inquiry: agreement, disagreement, residues, and the principle of concomitant variations (Mill, 1843/1893, III, 8, pp. 278–288). He considers them the only possible methods of proof for experimentation, as long as one presumes the realist position that nature is structured by uniformities.[4]

In Book 6 of *A System of Logic,* "On the Logic of the Moral Sciences," Mill (1843/1893) develops an inductive experimentalism as the scientific method for studying "the various phenomena which constitute social life" (VI, 6, 1, p. 606). Although he conceived of social science as explaining human behavior in terms of causal laws, he warned against the fatalism of full predictability. "Social laws are hypothetical, and statistically-based generalizations by their very nature admit of exceptions" (Copleston, 1966, p. 101; see also Mill, 1843/1893, VI, 5, 1, p. 596). Empirically confirmed instrumental knowledge about human behavior has greater predictive power when it deals with collective masses than when we are dealing with individual agents.

Mill's positivism is obvious throughout his work on experimental inquiry.[5] Based on the work of Auguste Comte, he defined matter as the "permanent possibility of sensation" (Mill, 1865, p. 198) and believed that nothing else can be said about metaphysical substances.[6] With Hume and Comte, Mill insisted that metaphysical substances are not real and that only the facts of sense phenomena exist. There are no essences or ultimate reality behind sensations; therefore, Mill (1865/1907, 1865) and Comte (1848/1910) argued that social scientists should limit themselves to particular data as a factual source out of which experimentally valid laws can be derived. For both, this is the only kind of knowledge that yields practical benefits (Mill, 1865, p. 242); in fact, society's salvation is contingent upon such scientific knowledge (p. 241).[7]

As with his consequentialist ethics, Mill's philosophy of social science is built on a dualism of means and ends. Citizens and politicians are responsible for articulating ends in a free society, and science is responsible for the know-how to achieve them. Science is amoral, speaking to questions of means but with no wherewithal or authority to dictate ends. Methods in the social sciences must be disinterested regarding substance and content, and rigorously limited to the risks and benefits of possible courses of action. Protocols for practicing liberal science "should be prescriptive, but not morally or politically prescriptive and should direct against bad science but not bad conduct" (Root, 1993, p. 129). Research cannot be judged right or wrong, only true or false. "Science is political only in its applications" (Root, 1993, p. 213). Given his democratic liberalism, Mill advocates neutrality "out of concern for the autonomy of the individuals or groups" social science seeks to serve. It should "treat them as thinking, willing, active beings who bear responsibility for their choices and are free to choose" their own conception of the good life by majority rule (Root, 1993, p. 19).

Value Neutrality in Max Weber

When 20th-century mainstream social scientists contended that ethics is not their business, they typically invoked Weber's essays written between 1904 and 1917. Given Weber's importance, methodologically and theoretically, for sociology and economics, his distinction between political judgments and scientific neutrality is given canonical status.

Weber distinguishes between value freedom and value relevance. He recognizes that in the discovery phase, "personal, cultural, moral, or political values cannot be eliminated; . . . what social scientists choose to investigate . . . they choose on the basis of the values" they expect their research to advance (Root, 1993, p. 33). But he insists that social science be value-free in the presentation phase. Findings ought not to express any judgments of a moral or political character. Professors should hang up their values along with their coats as they enter their lecture halls.

"An attitude of moral indifference," Weber (1904/1949b) writes, "has no connection with scientific objectivity" (p. 60). His meaning is clear from the value-freedom/value-relevance distinction. For the social sciences to be purposeful and rational, they must serve the "values of relevance."

> The problems of the social sciences are selected by the value relevance of the phenomena treated. . . . The expression "relevance to values" refers simply to the philosophical interpretation of that specifically scientific "interest" which determines the selection of a given subject matter and problems of empirical analysis. (Weber, 1917/1949a, pp. 21–22)

> In the social sciences the stimulus to the posing of scientific problems is in actuality always given by practical "questions." Hence, the very recognition of the existence of a scientific problem coincides personally with the possession of specifically oriented motives and values. . . . (Weber, 1904/1949b, p. 61)

> Without the investigator's evaluative ideas, there would be no principle of selection of subject matter and no meaningful knowledge of the concrete reality. Without the investigator's conviction regarding the significance of particular cultural facts, every attempt to analyze concrete reality is absolutely meaningless. (Weber, 1904/1949b, p. 82)

Whereas the natural sciences, in Weber's (1904/1949b, p. 72) view, seek general laws that govern all empirical phenomena, the social sciences study those realities that our values consider significant. Whereas the natural world itself indicates what reality to investigate, the infinite possibilities of the social world are ordered in terms of "the cultural values with which we approach reality" (1904/1949b, p. 78).[8] However, even though value relevance directs the social sciences, as with the natural sciences, Weber considers the former value-free. The subject matter in natural science makes value judgments unnecessary, and social scientists by a conscious decision can exclude judgments of "desirability or undesirability" from their publications and lectures (1904/1949b, p. 52). "What is really at issue is the intrinsically simple demand that the investigator and teacher should keep unconditionally separate the establishment of empirical facts . . . and his own political evaluations" (Weber, 1917/1949a, p. 11).

Weber's opposition to value judgments in the social sciences was driven by practical circumstances. Academic freedom for the universities of Prussia was more likely if professors limited their professional work to scientific know-how. With university hiring controlled by political officials, only if the faculty refrained from policy commitments and criticism would officials relinquish their control.

Few of the offices in government or industry in Germany were held by people who were well trained to solve questions of means. Weber thought that the best way to increase the power and economic prosperity of Germany was to train a new managerial class learned about means and silent about ends. The mission of the university, in Weber's view, should be to offer such training (Root, 1993, p. 41; see also Weber, 1973, pp. 4–8).[9]

Weber's practical argument for value freedom and his apparent limitation of it to the reporting phase have made his version of value neutrality attractive to 21st-century social science. He is not a positivist such as Comte or a thoroughgoing empiricist in the tradition of Mill. He disavowed the positivists' overwrought disjunction between discovery and justification, and he developed no systematic epistemology comparable to Mill's. His nationalism was partisan compared to Mill's liberal political philosophy. Nevertheless, Weber's value neutrality reflects Enlightenment autonomy in a fundamentally similar fashion. In the process of maintaining his distinction between value relevance and value freedom, he separates facts from values and means from ends. He appeals to empirical evidence and logical reasoning rooted in human rationality. "The validity of a practical imperative as a norm," he writes, "and the truth-value of an empirical proposition are absolutely heterogeneous in character" (Weber, 1904/1949b, p. 52). "A systematically correct scientific proof in the social sciences" may not be completely attainable, but that is most likely "due to faulty data," not because it is conceptually impossible (1904/1949b, p. 58).[10] For Weber, as with Mill, empirical science deals with questions of means, and his warning against inculcating political and moral values presumes a means-ends dichotomy (see Weber, 1917/1949a, pp. 18–19; 1904/1949b, p. 52).

As Michael Root (1993) concludes, "John Stuart Mill's call for neutrality in the social sciences is based on his belief" that the language of science "takes cognizance of a phenomenon and endeavors to discover its laws" (p. 205). Max Weber likewise "takes it for granted that there can be a language of science—a collection of truths—that excludes all value-judgments, rules, or directions for conduct" (Root, 1993, p. 205). In both cases, scientific knowledge exists for its own sake as morally neutral. For both, neutrality is desirable "because questions of value are not rationally resolvable" and neutrality in the social sciences is presumed to contribute "to political and personal autonomy" (Root, 1993, p. 229). In Weber's argument for value relevance in social science, he did not contradict the larger Enlightenment ideal of scientific neutrality between competing conceptions of the good.

Utilitarian Ethics

In addition to its this-worldly humanism, utilitarian ethics was attractive for its compatibility with scientific thought. It fit the canons of rational calculation as they were nourished by the Enlightenment's intellectual culture.

> In the utilitarian perspective, one validated an ethical position by hard evidence. You count the consequences for human happiness of one or another course, and you go with the one with the highest favorable total. What counts as human happiness was thought to be something conceptually unproblematic, a scientifically establishable domain of facts. One could abandon all the metaphysical or theological factors which made ethical questions scientifically undecidable. (Taylor, 1982, p. 129)

Utilitarian ethics replaces metaphysical distinctions with the calculation of empirical quantities. It follows the procedural demand that if "the happiness of each agent counts for one . . . the right course of action should be what satisfies all, or the largest number possible" (Taylor, 1982, p. 131). Autonomous reason is the arbiter of moral disputes.

With moral reasoning equivalent to calculating consequences for human happiness, utilitarianism presumes there is "a single consistent domain of the moral, that there is one set of considerations which determines what we ought morally to do." This "epistemologically-motivated reduction and homogenization of the moral" marginalizes the qualitative languages of admiration and contempt—integrity, healing, liberation, conviction, dishonesty, and self-indulgence, for example (Taylor, 1982, pp. 132–133). In utilitarian terms, these languages designate subjective factors that "correspond to nothing in reality. . . . They express the way we feel, not the way things are" (Taylor, 1982, p. 141). This single-consideration theory not only demands that we maximize general happiness but also considers irrelevant other moral imperatives that conflict with it, such as equal distribution. One-factor models appeal to the "epistemological squeamishness" of value-neutral social science, which "dislikes contrastive languages." Moreover, utilitarianism appealingly offers "the prospect of exact calculation of policy through . . . rational choice theory" (Taylor, 1982, p. 143). "It portrays all moral issues as discrete problems amenable to largely technical solutions" (Euben, 1981, p. 117). However, to its critics, this kind of exactness represents "a semblance of validity" by leaving out whatever cannot be calculated (Taylor, 1982, p. 143).[11]

Given the dualism of means and ends in utilitarian theory, the domain of the good in utilitarianism is extrinsic. All that is worth valuing is a function of its consequences. Prima facie duties are literally inconceivable. The degree to which one's actions and statements truly express what is important to someone does not count. Ethical and political thinking in consequentialist terms legislates intrinsic valuing out of existence (Taylor, 1982, p. 144). The exteriority of ethics is seen to guarantee the value neutrality of experimental procedures.[12]

▣ Codes of Ethics

In value-free social science, codes of ethics for professional and academic associations are the conventional format for moral principles. By the 1980s, each of the major scholarly associations had adopted its own code, with an overlapping emphasis on four guidelines for directing an inductive science of means toward majoritarian ends.

1. *Informed consent.* Consistent with its commitment to individual autonomy, social science in the Mill and Weber tradition insists that research subjects have the right to be informed about the nature and consequences of experiments in which they are involved. Proper respect for human freedom generally includes two necessary conditions. First, subjects must agree voluntarily to participate—that is, without physical or psychological coercion. Second, their agreement must be based on full and open information. "The Articles of the Nuremberg Tribunal and the Declaration of Helsinki both state that subjects must be told the duration, methods, possible risks, and the purpose or aim of the experiment" (Soble, 1978, p. 40; see also Veatch, 1996).

The self-evident character of this principle is not disputed in rationalist ethics. Meaningful application, however, generates ongoing disputes. As Punch (1994) observes, "In much fieldwork there seems to be no way around the predicament that informed consent—divulging one's identity and research purpose to all and sundry—will kill many a project stone dead" (p. 90). True to the privileging of means in a means-ends model, Punch reflects the general conclusion that codes of ethics should serve as a guideline prior to fieldwork but not intrude on full participation. "A strict application of codes" may "restrain and restrict" a great deal of "innocuous" and "unproblematic" research (p. 90).

2. *Deception.* In emphasizing informed consent, social science codes of ethics uniformly oppose deception. Even paternalistic arguments for possible deception of criminals, children in elementary schools, or the mentally incapacitated are no longer credible. The ongoing exposé of deceptive practices since Stanley Milgram's experiments have given this moral principle special status—deliberate misrepresentation is forbidden. Bulmer (1982) is typical of hard-liners who conclude with the codes that deception is "neither ethically justified nor practically necessary, nor in the best interest of sociology as an academic pursuit" (p. 217; see also Punch, 1994, p. 92).

The straightforward application of this principle suggests that researchers design different experiments free of active deception. But with ethical constructions exterior to the scientific enterprise, no unambiguous application is possible. Given that the search for knowledge is obligatory and deception is codified as morally unacceptable, in some situations both criteria cannot be satisfied. Within both psychology and medicine, some information cannot be obtained without at least deception by omission. The standard resolution for this dilemma is to permit a modicum of deception when there are explicit utilitarian reasons for doing so. Opposition to deception in the codes is de facto redefined in these terms: If "the knowledge to be gained from deceptive experiments" is clearly valuable to society, it is "only a minor defect that persons must be deceived in the process" (Soble, 1978, p. 40).

3. *Privacy and confidentiality.* Codes of ethics insist on safeguards to protect people's identities and those of the research locations. Confidentiality must be assured as the primary safeguard against unwanted exposure. All personal data ought to be secured or concealed and made public only behind a shield of anonymity. Professional etiquette uniformly concurs that no one deserves harm or embarrassment as a result of insensitive research practices. "The single most likely source of harm in social science inquiry" is the disclosure of private knowledge considered damaging by experimental subjects (Reiss, 1979, p. 73; see also Punch, 1994, p. 93).

As Enlightenment autonomy was developed in philosophical anthropology, a sacred innermost self became essential to the construction of unique personhood. Already in John Locke, this private domain received nonnegotiable status. Democratic life was articulated outside these atomistic units, a secondary domain of negotiated contracts and problematic communication. In the logic of social science inquiry revolving around the same autonomy inscribed in being, invading persons' fragile but distinctive privacy is intolerable.

Despite the signature status of privacy protection, watertight confidentiality has proved to be impossible. Pseudonyms and disguised locations often are recognized by insiders. What researchers consider innocent is perceived by participants as misleading or even betrayal. What appears neutral on paper is often conflictual in practice. When government agencies or educational institutions or health organizations are studied, what private parts ought not be exposed? And who is blameworthy if aggressive media carry the research further? Encoding privacy protection is meaningless when "there is no consensus or unanimity on what is public and private" (Punch, 1994, p. 94).

4. *Accuracy.* Ensuring that data are accurate is a cardinal principle in social science codes as well. Fabrications, fraudulent materials, omissions, and contrivances are both nonscientific and unethical. Data that are internally and externally valid are the coin of the realm, experimentally and morally. In an instrumentalist, value-neutral social science, the definitions entailed by the procedures themselves establish the ends by which they are evaluated as moral.

Institutional Review Boards

As a condition of funding, government agencies in various countries have insisted that review and monitoring bodies be established by institutions engaged in research involving human subjects. Institutional Review Boards (IRBs) embody the utilitarian agenda in terms of scope, assumptions, and procedural guidelines.

In 1978, the U.S. National Commission for the Protection of Human Subjects in Biomedical and Behavioral Research was established. As a result, three principles, published in what became known as the Belmont Report, were developed as the moral standards for research involving human subjects: respect for persons, beneficence, and justice.

1. The section on respect for persons reiterates the codes' demands that subjects enter the research voluntarily and with adequate information about the experiment's procedures and possible consequences. On a deeper level, respect for persons incorporates two basic ethical tenets: "First, that individuals should be treated as autonomous agents, and second, that persons with diminished autonomy [the immature and incapacitated] are entitled to protection" (University of Illinois at Urbana-Champaign, 2003).

2. Under the principle of beneficence, researchers are enjoined to secure the well-being of their subjects. Beneficent actions are understood in a double sense as avoiding harm altogether and, if risks are involved for achieving substantial benefits, minimizing as much harm as possible:

> In the case of particular projects, investigators and members of their institutions are obliged to give forethought to the maximization of benefits and the reduction of risks that might occur from the research investigation. In the case of scientific research in general, members of the larger society are obliged to recognize the longer term benefits and risks that may result from the improvement of knowledge and from the development of novel medical, psychotherapeutic, and social procedures. (University of Illinois at Urbana-Champaign, 2003)

3. The principle of justice insists on fair distribution of both the benefits and the burdens of research. An injustice occurs when some groups (e.g., welfare recipients, the institutionalized, or particular ethnic minorities) are overused as research subjects because of easy manipulation or their availability. And when research supported by public funds leads to "therapeutic devices and procedures, justice demands that these not provide advantages only to those who can afford them" (University of Illinois at Urbana-Champaign, 2003).

These principles reiterate the basic themes of value-neutral experimentalism—individual autonomy, maximum benefits with minimal risks, and ethical ends exterior to scientific means. The policy procedures based on them reflect the same guidelines as dominate the codes of ethics: informed consent, protection of privacy, and nondeception. The authority of IRBs was enhanced in 1989 when Congress passed the NIH Revitalization Act and formed the Commission on Research Integrity. The emphasis at that point was on the invention, fudging, and distortion of data. Falsification, fabrication, and plagiarism continue as federal categories of misconduct, with a new report in 1996 adding warnings against unauthorized use of confidential information, omission of important data, and interference (that is, physical damage to the materials of others).

With IRBs, the legacy of Mill, Comte, and Weber comes into its own. Value-neutral science is accountable to ethical standards through rational procedures controlled by value-neutral academic institutions in the service of an impartial government. Consistent with the way anonymous bureaucratic regimes become refined and streamlined toward greater efficiency, the regulations rooted in scientific and medical experiments now extend to humanistic inquiry. Protecting subjects from physical harm in laboratories has grown to encompass human behavior, history, and ethnography in natural settings. In Jonathon Church's metaphor, "a biomedical paradigm is used like some threshing machine with ethnographic research the resulting chaff" (2002, p. 2). Whereas Title 45/Part 46 of the Code of Federal Regulations (45 CFR 46) designed protocols for research funded by 17 federal agencies, at present most universities have multiple project agreements that consign all research to a campus IRB under the terms of 45 CFR 46 (Shopes, 2000, pp. 1–2).

While this bureaucratic expansion has gone on unremittingly, most IRBs have not changed the composition of their membership. Medical and behavioral scientists under the aegis of value-free neutrality continue to dominate, and the changes in procedures generally have stayed within the biomedical model. Expedited review under the Common Rule, for social research with no risk of physical or psychological harm, depends on enlightened IRB chairs and organizational flexibility. Informed consent, mandatory before medical experiments, is simply incongruent with interpretive research that interacts with human beings in their natural settings, rather than analyzing human subjects in a laboratory (Shopes, 2000, p. 5).[13] Despite technical improvements, "Intellectual curiosity remains actively discouraged by the IRB. Research projects must ask only surface questions and must not deviate from a path approved by a remote group of people. . . . Often the review process seems to be more about gamesmanship than anything else. A better formula for stultifying research could not be imagined" (Blanchard, 2002, p. 11).

In its conceptual structure, IRB policy is designed to produce the best ratio of benefits to costs. IRBs ostensibly protect the subjects who fall under the protocols they approve. However, given the interlocking utilitarian functions of social science, the academy, and the state that Mill identified and promoted, IRBs in reality protect their own institutions rather than subject populations in society at large (see Vanderpool, 1996, chaps. 2–6). Only if professional associations like the American Anthropological Association could create their own best practices for ethnographic research would IRBs take a significant step in the right direction. Such renovations are contrary to the centralizing homogeneity of closed systems such as the IRBs.[14]

The Current Crisis

Mill and Comte, each in his own way, presumed that experimental social science benefited society by uncovering facts about the human condition. Durkheim and Weber believed that a scientific study of society could help people come to grips with "the development of capitalism and the industrial revolution" (Jennings & Callahan, 1983, p. 3). The American Social Science Association was created in 1865 to link "real elements of the truth" with "the great social problems of the day" (Lazarsfeld & Reitz, 1975, p. 1). This myth of beneficence was destroyed with "the revelations at the Nuremberg trials (recounting the Nazis' 'medical experiments' on concentration camp inmates) and with the role of leading scientists in the Manhattan Project" (Punch, 1994, p. 88).

The crisis of confidence multiplied with the exposure to actual physical harm in the Tuskegee Syphilis Study and the Willowbrook Hepatitis Experiment. In the 1960s, Project Camelot, a U.S. Army attempt to use social science to measure and forecast revolutions and insurgency, was bitterly opposed around the world and had to be canceled. Stanley Milgram's (1974) deception of unwitting subjects and Laud Humphreys's (1970, 1972) deceptive research on homosexuals in a public toilet, and later in their homes, were considered scandalous for psychologically abusing research subjects. Noam Chomsky exposed the complicity of social scientists with military initiatives in Vietnam.

Vigorous concern for research ethics since the 1980s, support from foundations, and the development of ethics codes and the IRB apparatus are credited by their advocates with curbing outrageous abuses. However, the charges of fraud, plagiarism, and misrepresentation continue on a lesser scale, with dilemmas, conundrums, and controversies unabated over the meaning and application of ethical guidelines. Entrepreneurial faculty competing for scarce research dollars are generally compliant with institutional control, but the vastness of social science activity in universities and research entities makes full supervision impossible.

Underneath the pros and cons of administering a responsible social science, the structural deficiencies in its epistemology have become transparent (Jennings, 1983, pp. 4–7). A positivistic philosophy of social inquiry insists on neutrality regarding definitions of the good, and this worldview has been discredited. The Enlightenment model setting human freedom at odds with the moral order is bankrupt. Even Weber's weaker version of contrastive languages rather than oppositional entities is not up to the task. Reworking the ethics codes so that they are more explicit and less hortatory will make no fundamental difference. Requiring ethics workshops for graduate students and strengthening government policy are desirable but of marginal significance. Refining the IRB process and exhorting IRBs to account for the pluralistic nature of academic research are insufficient.

In utilitarianism, moral thinking and experimental procedures are homogenized into a unidimensional model of rational validation. Autonomous human beings are clairvoyant about aligning means and goals, presuming that they can objectify the mechanisms for understanding themselves and the social world surrounding them (see Taylor, 1982, p. 133). This restrictive definition of ethics accounts for some of the goods we seek, such as minimal harm, but those outside a utility calculus are excluded. "Emotionality and intuition" are relegated "to a secondary position" in the decision-making process, for example, and no attention is paid to an "ethics of caring" grounded in "concrete particularities" (Denzin, 1997, p. 273; see also Ryan, 1995, p. 147). The way power and ideology influence social and political institutions is largely ignored. Under a rhetorical patina of deliberate choice and the illusion of autonomous creativity, a means-ends system operates in fundamentally its own terms.

This constricted environment no longer addresses adequately the complicated issues we face in studying the social world. Celebrity social scientists generate status and prestige—McGeorge Bundy in the Kennedy years, political scientist Henry Kissinger, Daniel Moynihan while in the Senate. But failure in the War on Poverty, contradictions over welfare, and ill-fated studies of urban housing have dramatized the limitations of a utility calculus that occupies the entire moral domain.[15]

Certainly, levels of success and failure are open to dispute even within the social science disciplines themselves. More unsettling and threatening to the empirical mainstream than disappointing performance is the recognition that neutrality is not pluralistic but imperialistic. Reflecting on past experience, disinterested research under presumed conditions of value freedom is increasingly seen as de facto reinscribing the agenda in its own terms. Empiricism is procedurally committed to equal reckoning, regardless of how research subjects may constitute the substantive ends of life. But experimentalism is not a neutral meeting ground for all ideas; rather, it is a "fighting creed" that imposes its own ideas on others while uncritically assuming the very "superiority that powers this imposition."[16] In Foucault's (1979, pp. 170–195) more decisive terms, social science is a regime of power that helps maintain social order by normalizing subjects into categories designed by political authorities (see Root, 1993, chap. 7). A liberalism of equality is not neutral but represents only one range of ideals, and it is itself incompatible with other goods.

This noncontextual, nonsituational model that assumes that "a morally neutral, objective observer will get the facts right" ignores "the situatedness of power relations associated with gender, sexual orientation, class, ethnicity, race, and nationality." It is hierarchical (scientist-subject) and biased toward patriarchy. "It glosses the ways in which the observer-ethnographer is implicated and embedded in the 'ruling apparatus' of the society and the culture." Scientists "carry the mantle" of university-based authority as they venture out into "local community to do research" (Denzin, 1997, p. 272; see also Ryan, 1995, pp. 144–145).[17] There is no sustained questioning of expertise itself in democratic societies that belong in principle to citizens who do not share this specialized knowledge (see Euben, 1981, p. 120).

▣ Feminist Communitarianism

Social Ethics

Over the past decade, social and feminist ethics have made a radical break with the individual autonomy and rationalist presumption of canonical ethics (see Koehn, 1998). The social ethics of Agnes Heller (1988, 1990, 1996, 1999), Charles Taylor (1989, 1991, 1995; Taylor et al., 1994), Carole Pateman (1985, 1988, 1989), Edith Wyschogrod (1974, 1985, 1990, 1998), Kwasi Wiredu (1996), and Cornel West (1989, 1991, 1993) and the feminist ethics of Carol Gilligan (1982, 1983; Gilligan, Ward, & Taylor, 1988), Nel Noddings (1984, 1989, 1990), Virginia Held (1993), and Seyla Benhabib (1992) are fundamentally reconstructing ethical theory (see Code, 1991). Rather than searching for neutral principles to which all parties can appeal, social ethics rests on a complex view of moral judgments as integrating into an organic whole various perspectives—everyday experience, beliefs about the good, and feelings of approval and shame—in terms of human relations and social structures. This is a philosophical approach that situates the moral domain within the general purposes of human life that people share contextually and across cultural, racial, and historical boundaries. Ideally, it engenders a new occupational role and normative core for social science research (White, 1995).

Carol Gilligan (1982, 1983; Gilligan et al., 1988) characterizes the female moral voice as an ethic of care. This dimension of moral development is rooted in the primacy of human relationships. Compassion and nurturance resolve conflicting responsibilities among people, and as such these standards are totally the opposite of merely avoiding harm.[18] In *Caring,* Nel Noddings (1984) rejects outright the "ethics of principle as ambiguous and unstable" (p. 5), insisting that human care should play the central role in moral decision making. For Julia Wood (1994), "an interdependent sense of self" undergirds the ethic of care, wherein we are comfortable acting independently while "acting cooperatively . . . in relationship with others" (pp. 108, 110). Feminism in Linda Steiner's work critiques the conventions of impartiality and formality in ethics while giving precision to affection, intimacy, nurturing, egalitarian and collaborative processes, and empathy. Feminists' ethical self-consciousness also identifies subtle forms of oppression and imbalance, and it teaches us to "address questions about whose interests are regarded as worthy of debate" (Steiner, 1991, p. 158; see also Steiner, 1997).

While sharing in the turn away from an abstract ethics of calculation, Charlene Seigfried (1996) argues against the Gilligan-Noddings tradition. Linking feminism to pragmatism, in which gender is socially constructed, she contradicts "the simplistic equation of women with care and nurturance and men with justice and autonomy" (p. 206). Gender-based moralities de facto make one gender subservient to another. In her social ethics, gender is replaced with engendering: "To be female or male is not to instantiate an unchangeable nature but to participate in an ongoing process of negotiating cultural expectations of femininity and masculinity" (p. 206). Seigfried challenges us to a social morality in which caring values are central but contextualized in webs of relationships and constructed toward communities with "more autonomy for women and more connectedness for men" (p. 219). Agnes Heller and Edith Wyschogrod are two promising examples of proponents of social ethics that meet Seigfried's challenge while confronting forthrightly today's contingency, mass murder, conceptual upheavals in ethics, and hyperreality.

Heller, a former student of Georg Lukács and a dissident in Hungary, is the Hannah Arendt Professor of Philosophy at the New School for Social Research. Her trilogy developing a contemporary theory of social ethics (Heller, 1988, 1990, 1996) revolves around what she calls the one decisive question: "Good persons exist—how are they possible?" (1988, p. 7). She disavows an ethics of norms, rules, and ideals external to human beings. Only exceptional acts of responsibility under duress and predicaments, each in their own way, are "worthy of theoretical interest" (1996, p. 3). Accumulated wisdom, moral meaning from our own choices of decency, and the ongoing summons of the Other together reintroduce love, happiness, sympathy, and beauty into a modern, nonabsolutist, but principled theory of morals.

In *Saints and Postmodernism*, Edith Wyschogrod (1990) asserts that antiauthority struggles are possible without assuming that our choices are voluntary. She represents a social ethics of self and Other in the tradition of Emmanuel Levinas (see Wyschogrod, 1974).[19] "The other person opens the venue of ethics, the place where ethical existence occurs." The Other, "the touchstone of moral existence, is not a conceptual anchorage but a living force." Others function "as a critical solvent." Their existence carries "compelling moral weight" (Wyschogrod, 1990, p. xxi). As a professor of philosophy and religious thought at Rice University, with a commitment to moral narrative, Wyschogrod believes that one venue for Otherness is the saintly life, defined as one in "which compassion for the Other, irrespective of cost to the saint, is the primary trait." Saints put their own "bodies and material goods at the disposal of the Other.... Not only do saints contest the practices and beliefs of institutions, but in a more subtle way they contest the order of narrativity itself" (1990, pp. xxii–xxiii).

In addition to the Other-directed across a broad spectrum of belief systems who have "lived, suffered, and worked in actuality," Wyschogrod (1990, p. 7) examines historical narratives for illustrations of how the Other's self-manifestation is depicted. Her primary concern is the way communities shape shared experience in the face of cataclysms and calamities, arguing for historians who situate themselves "in dynamic relationship to them" (1998, p. 218). The overriding challenge for ethics, in Wyschogrod's view, is how historians enter into communities that create and sustain hope in terms of immediacy—"a presence here and now" but "a presence that must be deferred" to the future (1998, p. 248). Unless it is tangible and actionable, hope serves those in control. Hope that merely projects a future redemption obscures abuses of power and human need in the present.

Martin Buber (1958) calls the human relation a primal notion in his famous lines, "in the beginning is the relation" (p. 69) and "the relation is the cradle of life" (p. 60). Social relationships are preeminent. "The one primary word is the combination I-Thou" (p. 3). This irreducible phenomenon—the relational reality, the in-between, the reciprocal bond, the interpersonal—cannot be decomposed into simpler elements without destroying it. Given the primacy of relationships, unless we use our freedom to help others flourish, we deny our own well-being.

Rather than privileging an abstract rationalism, the moral order is positioned close to the bone, in the creaturely and corporeal rather than the conceptual. "In this way, ethics . . . is as old as creation. Being ethical is a primordial movement in the beckoning force of life itself" (Olthuis, 1997, p. 141). The ethics of Levinas is one example:

> The human face is the epiphany of the nakedness of the Other, a visitation, a meeting, a saying which comes in the passivity of the face, not threatening, but obligating. My world is ruptured, my contentment interrupted. I am already obligated. Here is an appeal from which there is no escape, a responsibility, a state of being hostage. It is looking into the face of the Other that reveals the call to a responsibility that is before any beginning, decision or initiative on my part. (Olthuis, 1997, p. 139)

Humans are defined as communicative beings within the fabric of everyday life. Through dialogic encounter, subjects create life together and nurture one another's moral obligation to it. Levinas's ethics presumes and articulates a radical ontology of social beings in relation (see, e.g., Levinas, 1985, 1991).

Moreover, in Levinasian terms, when I turn to the face of the Other, I not only see flesh and blood, but a third party also arrives—the whole of humanity. In responding to the Other's need, a baseline is established across the human race. For Benhabib (1992), this is interactive universalism.[20] Our universal solidarity is rooted in the principle that "we have inescapable claims on one another which cannot be renounced except at the cost of our humanity" (Peukert, 1981, p. 11).

A Feminist Communitarian Model

Feminist communitarianism is Denzin's (1997, pp. 274–287; 2003, pp. 242–258) label for the ethical theory to lead us forward at this juncture.[21] This is a normative model that serves as an antidote to individualist utilitarianism. It presumes that the community is ontologically and axiologically prior to persons. Human identity is constituted through the social realm. We are born into a sociocultural universe where values, moral commitments, and existential meanings are negotiated dialogically. Fulfillment is never achieved in isolation, but only through human bonding at the epicenter of social formation.

For communitarians, the liberalism of Locke and Mill confuses an aggregate of individual pursuits with the common good. Moral agents need a context of social commitments and community ties for assessing what is valuable. What is worth preserving as a good cannot be self-determined in isolation, but can be ascertained only within specific social situations where human identity is nurtured. The public sphere is conceived as a mosaic of particular communities, a pluralism of ethnic identities and worldviews intersecting to form a social bond but each seriously held and competitive as well. Rather than pay lip service to the social nature of the self while presuming a dualism of two orders, communitarianism interlocks personal autonomy with communal well-being. Morally appropriate action intends community. Common moral values are intrinsic to a community's ongoing existence and identity.

Therefore, the mission of social science research is enabling community life to prosper—equipping people to come to mutually held conclusions. The aim is not fulsome data per se, but community transformation. The received view assumes that research advances society's interests by feeding our individual capacity to reason and make calculated decisions. Research is intended to be collaborative in its design and participatory in its execution. Rather than ethics codes in the files of academic offices and research reports prepared for clients, the participants themselves are given a forum to activate the polis mutually. In contrast to utilitarian experimentalism, the substantive conceptions of the good that drive the problems reflect the conceptions of the community rather than the expertise of researchers or funding agencies.

In the feminist communitarian model, participants have a say in how the research should be conducted and a hand in actually conducting it, "including a voice or hand in deciding which problems should be studied, what methods should be used to study them, whether the findings are valid or acceptable, and how the findings are to be used or implemented" (Root, 1993, p. 245). This research is rooted in "community, shared governance . . . and neighborliness." Given its cooperative mutuality, it serves "the community in which it is carried out, rather than the community of knowledge producers and policymakers" (Lincoln, 1995, pp. 280, 287; see also Denzin, 1997, p. 275). It finds its genius in the maxim that "persons are arbitrators of their own presence in the world" (Denzin, 1989, p. 81).

For feminist communitarians, humans have the discursive power "to articulate situated moral rules that are grounded in local community and group understanding." Moral reasoning goes forward because people are "able to share one another's point of view in the social situation." Reciprocal care and understanding, rooted in emotional experience and not in formal consensus, are the basis on which moral discourse is possible (Denzin, 1997, p. 277; see also Denzin, 1984, p. 145; Reinharz, 1993).

Multiple moral and social spaces exist within the local community, and "every moral act is a contingent accomplishment" measured against the ideals of a universal respect for the dignity of every human being regardless of gender, age, race, or religion (Denzin, 1997, p. 274; see also Benhabib, 1992, p. 6). Through a moral order, we resist those social values that are divisive and exclusivist.

Interpretive Sufficiency

Within a feminist communitarian model, the mission of social science research is interpretive sufficiency. In contrast to an experimentalism of instrumental efficiency, this paradigm seeks to open up the social world in all its dynamic dimensions. The thick notion of sufficiency supplants the thinness of the technical, exterior, and statistically precise received view. Rather than reducing social issues to financial and administrative problems for politicians, social science research enables people to come to terms with their everyday experience themselves.

Interpretive sufficiency means taking seriously lives that are loaded with multiple interpretations and grounded in cultural complexity (Denzin, 1989, pp. 77, 81). Ethnographic accounts "should possess that amount of depth, detail, emotionality, nuance, and coherence that will permit a critical consciousness to be formed by the reader. Such texts should also exhibit representational adequacy, including the absence of racial, class, and gender stereotyping" (Denzin, 1997, p. 283; see also Christians et al., 1993, pp. 120–122).

From the perspective of a feminist communitarian ethics, interpretive discourse is authentically sufficient when it fulfills three conditions: it represents multiple voices, enhances moral discernment, and promotes social transformation. Consistent with the community-based norms advocated here, the focus is not on professional ethics per se but on the general morality.[22]

Multivocal and Cross-Cultural Representation

Within social and political entities are multiple spaces that exist as ongoing constructions of everyday life. The dialogical self is situated and articulated within these decisive contexts of gender, race, class, and religion. In contrast to contractarianism, where tacit consent or obligation is given to the state, people make and sustain the promises to one another. Research narratives reflect a community's multiple voices through which promise keeping takes place.

In Carole Pateman's communitarian philosophy, sociopolitical entities are not to be understood first of all in terms of contracts. Making promises is one of the basic ways in which consenting human beings "freely create their own social relationships" (Pateman, 1989, p. 61; see also Pateman, 1985, pp. 26–29). We assume an obligation by making a promise. When individuals promise, they are obliged to act accordingly. But promises are made not primarily to authorities through political contracts, but to fellow citizens. If obligations are rooted in promises, obligations are owed to other colleagues in institutions and to participants in community practices. Therefore, only under conditions of participatory democracy can there be self-assumed moral obligation.

Pateman understands the nature of moral agency. We know ourselves primarily in relation, and derivatively as thinkers withdrawn from action. Only by overcoming the traditional dualisms between thinker and agent, mind and body, reason and will, can we conceive of being as "the mutuality of personal relationships" (MacMurray, 1961a, p. 38). Moral commitments arise out of action and return to action for their incarnation and verification. From a dialogical perspective, promise keeping through action and everyday language is not a supercilious pursuit, because our way of being is not inwardly generated but socially derived.

> We become full human agents, capable of understanding ourselves, and hence of defining our identity, through . . . rich modes of expression we learn through exchange with others. . . .
>
> My discovering my own identity doesn't mean that I work it out in isolation, but that I negotiate it through dialogue, partly overt, partly internal, with others. My own identity crucially depends on my dialogical relations with others. . . .
>
> In the culture of authenticity, relationships are seen as the key loci of self discovery and self-affirmation. (Taylor et al., 1994, pp. 32, 34, 36)

If moral bondedness flows horizontally and obligation is reciprocal in character, the affirming and sustaining of promises occur cross-culturally. But the contemporary challenge of cultural diversity has raised the stakes and made easy solutions impossible. One of the most urgent and vexing issues on the democratic agenda at present is not just the moral obligation to treat ethnic differences with fairness, but how to recognize explicit cultural groups politically.

Communitarianism as the basis for ethnic plurality rejects melting pot homogeneity and replaces it with the politics of recognition. The basic issue is whether democracies are discriminating against their citizens in an unethical manner, when major institutions fail to account for the identities of their members (Taylor et al., 1994, p. 3). In what sense should the specific cultural and social features of African Americans, Asian Americans, Native Americans, Buddhists, Jews, the physically disabled, or children publicly matter? Should not public institutions insure only that democratic citizens share an equal right to political liberties and due process without regard to race, gender, or religion? Beneath the rhetoric is a fundamental philosophical dispute that Taylor calls the "politics of recognition." As he puts it, "Nonrecognition or miscrecognition can inflict harm, can be a form of oppression, imprisoning someone in a false, distorted, and reduced mode of being. Due recognition is not just a courtesy we owe people. It is a vital human need" (Taylor et al., 1994, p. 26). This foundational issue regarding the character of cultural identity needs to be resolved for cultural pluralism to come into its own. Feminist communitarianism is a non-assimilationist framework in which such resolution can occur.

However, liberal proceduralism cannot meet this vital human need. Emphasizing equal rights with no particular substantive view of the good life "gives only a very restricted acknowledgement of distinct cultural identities" (Taylor et al., 1994, p. 52). Insisting on neutrality, and without collective goals, produces at best personal freedom, safety, and economic security understood homogeneously. As Bunge (1996) puts it: "Contractualism is a code of behavior for the powerful and the hard—those who write contracts, not those who sign on the dotted line" (p. 230). However, in promise-based communal formation, the flourishing of particular cultures, religions, and ethnic groups is the substantive goal to which we are morally committed as human beings.

Norman Denzin (2002) demonstrates how multicultural representation ought to operate in the media's construction of the American racial order. An ethnic cinema that honors racial difference is not assimilationist, nor does it "celebrate exceptional blackness" supporting white values; and it refuses to pit "the ethnic other against a mainstream white America" as well as "dark skin against dark skin" (p. 6). Rather than "a didactic film aesthetic based on social problems realism"—one that is "trapped by the modernist agenda"—Denzin follows Hal Foster and bell hooks in arguing for an anti-aesthetic or postmodern aesthetic that is cross-disciplinary, oriented to the vernacular, and denies "the idea of a privileged aesthetic realm" (pp. 11, 180). A "feminist, Chicana/o and black performance-based aesthetic" creates "a critical counter-hegemonic race consciousness" and implements critical race theory (p. 180).

In feminist communitarian terms, this aesthetic is simultaneously political and ethical. Racial difference is imbricated in social theories and in conceptions of the human being, of justice, and of the common good. It requires an aesthetic that "in generating social criticism . . . also engenders resistance" (Denzin, 2002, p. 181). It is not a "protest or integrationist initiative" aimed at "informing a white audience of racial injustice," but instead "offers new forms of representation that create the space for new forms of critical race consciousness" (p. 182). The overarching standard made possible by this aesthetic is enhancing moral agency, that is, serving as a catalyst for moral discernment (Christians, 2002a, p. 409).

With the starting hypothesis that all human cultures have something important to say, social science research recognizes particular cultural values consistent with universal human dignity (Christians, 1997a, pp. 11–14). Interpretive sufficiency in its multicultural dimension "locates persons in a non-competitive, non-hierarchical relationship to the larger moral universe." It helps persons "imagine how things could be different in the everyday world. It imagines new forms of human transformation and emancipation. It enacts those transformations through dialogue" (Denzin, 2002, p. 181).

Moral Discernment

Societies are embodiments of institutions, practices, and structures recognized internally as legitimate. Without allegiance to a web of ordering relations, society becomes, as a matter of fact, inconceivable. Communities not only are linguistic entities but also require at least a minimal moral commitment to the common good. Because social entities are moral orders and not merely functional arrangements, moral commitment constitutes the self-in-relation. Our identity is defined by what we consider good or worth opposing. Only through the moral dimension can we make sense of human agency. As Mulhall and Swift (1996) write:

> Developing, maintaining and articulating [our moral intuitions and reactions] is not something humans could easily or even conceivably dispense with. . . . We can no more imagine a human life that fails to address the matter of its bearings in moral space than we can imagine one in which developing a sense of up and down, right and left is regarded as an optional human task. . . . A moral orientation is inescapable because the questions to which the framework provides answers are themselves inescapable. (pp. 106–108; see also Taylor, 1989, pp. 27–29)

A self exists only within "webs of interlocution," and all self-interpretation implicitly or explicitly "acknowledges the necessarily social origin of any and all their conceptions of the good and so of themselves" (Mulhall & Swift, 1996, pp. 112–113). Moral frameworks are as fundamental for orienting us in social space as the need to establish ourselves in physical space. The moral dimension must, therefore, be considered intrinsic to human beings, not a system of rules, norms, and ideals external to society. Moral duty is nurtured by the demands of social linkage and not produced by abstract theory.

The core of a society's common morality is pretheoretical agreement. However, "what counts as common morality is not only imprecise but variable . . . and a difficult practical problem" (Bok, 1995, p. 99). Moral obligation must be articulated within the fallible and irresolute voices of everyday life. Among disagreements and uncertainty, we look for criteria and wisdom in settling disputes and clarifying confusions; and normative theories of an interactive sort can invigorate our common moral discourse. But generally accepted theories are not necessary for the common good to prosper. The common good is not "the complete morality of every participant . . . but a set of agreements among people who typically hold other, less widely shared ethical beliefs" (Bok, 1995, p. 99). Instead of expecting more theoretical coherence than history warrants, Reinhold Niebuhr inspires us to work through inevitable social conflicts while maintaining "an untheoretical jumble of agreements" called here the common good (Barry, 1967, pp. 190–191). Through a common morality, we can approximate consensus on issues and settle disputes interactively. In Jürgen Habermas's (1993) terms, discourse in the public sphere must be oriented "toward mutual understanding" while allowing participants "the communicative freedom to take positions" on claims to final validity (p. 66; see also Habermas, 1990).

Communitarians challenge researchers to participate in a community's ongoing process of moral articulation. In fact, culture's continued existence depends on the identification and defense of its normative base. Therefore, ethnographic texts must enable us "to discover moral truths about ourselves"; narratives ought to "bring a moral compass into readers' lives" by accounting for things that matter to them (Denzin, 1997, p. 284). Feminist communitarianism seeks to engender moral reasoning internally. Communities are woven together by narratives that invigorate their common understanding of good and evil, happiness and reward, the meaning of life and death. Recovering and refashioning moral vocabulary help to amplify our deepest humanness. Researchers are not constituted as ethical selves antecedently, but moral discernment unfolds dialectically between researchers and the researched who collaborate with them.

Our widely shared moral convictions are developed through discourse within a community. These communities, where moral discourse is nurtured and shared, are a radical alternative to the utilitarian individualism of modernity. But in feminist communitarianism, communities are entered from the universal. The total opposite of an ethics of individual autonomy is universal human solidarity. Our obligation to sustain one another defines our existence. The primal sacredness of all without exception is the heart of the moral order and the new starting point for our theorizing (Christians, 1997b, 1998).

The rationale for human action is reverence for life on Earth. Living nature reproduces itself as its very character. Embedded in the animate world is the purposiveness of bringing forth life. Therefore, within the natural order is a moral claim on us for its own sake and in its own right. Nurturing life has a taken-for-granted character outside subjective preferences. Reverence for life on Earth is a pretheoretical given that makes the moral order possible. The sacredness of life is not an abstract imperative but the ground of human action.[23] It is a primordial generality that underlies reification into ethical principles, an organic bond that everyone shares inescapably. In our systematic reflection on this protonorm, we recognize that it entails such basic ethical principles as human dignity and nonviolence.

Reverence for life on Earth establishes a level playing floor for cross-cultural collaboration in ethics. It represents a universalism from the ground up. Various societies articulate this protonorm in different terms and illustrate it locally, but every culture can bring to the table this fundamental norm for ordering political relationships and social institutions. We live out our values in a community setting where the moral life is experienced and a moral vocabulary articulated. Such protonorms as reverence for life can be recovered only locally. Language situates them in history. The sacredness of life reflects our common condition as a species, but we act on it through the immediate reality of geography, ethnicity, and ideology. But according to feminist communitarianism, if we enter this communal arena not from individual decision making but from a universal commonness, we have the basis for believing that researchers and the researched can collaborate on the moral domain. Researchers do not bring a set of prescriptions into which they school their subjects. Instead, they find ways interactively to bring the sacredness of life into its own—each culture and all circumstances providing an abundance of meaning and application.

How the moral order works itself out in community formation is the issue, not first of all what researchers consider virtuous. The challenge for those writing culture is not to limit their moral perspectives to their own generic and neutral principles, but to engage the same moral space as the people they study. In this perspective, research strategies are not assessed first of all in terms of "experimental robustness," but for their "vitality and vigor in illuminating how we can create human flourishing" (Lincoln & Denzin, 2000, p. 1062).

Politics of Resistance

Ethics in the feminist communitarian mode generates social criticism, leads to resistance, and empowers to action those who are interacting (see Habermas, 1971, pp. 301–317). Thus, a basic norm for interpretive research is enabling the humane transformation of the multiple spheres of community life, such as religion, politics, ethnicity, and gender.

From his own dialogic perspective, Paulo Freire speaks of the need to reinvent the meaning of power:

> For me the principal, real transformation, the radical transformation of society in this part of the century demands not getting power from those who have it today, or merely to make some reforms, some changes in it. . . . The question, from my point of view, is not just to take power but to reinvent it. That is, to create a different kind of power, to deny the need power has as if it were metaphysics, bureaucratized, anti-democratic. (quoted in Evans, Evans, & Kennedy, 1987, p. 229)

Certainly oppressive power blocs and monopolies—economic, technological, and political—need the scrutiny of researchers and their collaborators. Given Freire's political-institutional bearing, power for him is a central notion in social analysis. But, in concert with him, feminist communitarian research refuses to deal with power in cognitive terms only. The issue is how people can empower themselves instead.

The dominant understanding of power is grounded in nonmutuality; it is interventionist power, exercised competitively and seeking control. In the communitarian alternative, power is relational, characterized by mutuality rather than sovereignty. Power from this perspective is reciprocity between two subjects, a relationship not of domination, but of intimacy and vulnerability—power akin to that of Alcoholics Anonymous, in which surrender to the community enables the individual to gain mastery. As understood so clearly in the indigenous Kaupapa Māori approach to research, "the researcher is led by the members of the community and does not presume to be a leader, or to have any power that he or she can relinquish" (Denzin, 2003, p. 243).

Dialogue is the key element in an emancipatory strategy that liberates rather than imprisons us in manipulation or antagonistic relationships. Although the control version of power considers mutuality weakness, the empowerment mode maximizes our humanity and thereby banishes powerlessness. In the research process, power is unmasked and engaged through solidarity as a researched-researcher team. There is certainly no monologic "assumption that the researcher is giving the group power" (Denzin, 2003, p. 243). Rather than play semantic games with power, researchers themselves are willing to march against the barricades. As Freire insists, only with everyone filling his or her own political space, to the point of civil disobedience as necessary, will empowerment mean anything revolutionary (see, e.g., Freire, 1970b, p. 129).

What is nonnegotiable in Freire's theory of power is participation of the oppressed in directing cultural formation. If an important social issue needs resolution, the most vulnerable will have to lead the way: "Revolutionary praxis cannot tolerate an absurd dichotomy in which the praxis of the people is merely that of following the [dominant elite's] decisions" (Freire, 1970a, p. 120; see also Freire, 1978, pp. 17ff.).[24] Arrogant politicians—supported by a bevy of accountants, lawyers, economists, and social science researchers—trivialize the nonexpert's voice as irrelevant to the problem or its solution. On the contrary, transformative action from the inside out is impossible unless the oppressed are active participants rather than being a leader's objects of action. "Only power that springs from the weakness of the oppressed will be sufficiently strong to free both" (Freire, 1970b, p. 28).[25]

In Freire's (1973) terms, the goal is conscientization, that is, a critical consciousness that directs the ongoing flow of praxis and reflection in everyday life. In a culture of silence, the oppressor's language and way of being are fatalistically accepted without contradiction. But a critical consciousness enables us to exercise the uniquely human capacity of "speaking a true word" (Freire, 1970b, p. 75). Under conditions of sociopolitical control, "the vanquished are dispossessed of their word, their expressiveness, their culture" (1970b, p. 134). Through conscientization, the oppressed gain their own voice and collaborate in transforming their culture (1970a, pp. 212–213). Therefore, research is not the transmission of specialized data but, in style and content, a catalyst for critical consciousness. Without what Freire (1970b, p. 47) calls "a critical comprehension of reality" (that is, the oppressed "grasping with their minds the truth of their reality"), there is only acquiescence in the status quo.

The resistance of the empowered is more productive at the interstices—at the fissures in social institutions where authentic action is possible. Effective resistance is nurtured in the backyards, the open spaces, and voluntary associations, and among neighborhoods, schools, and interactive settings of mutual struggle without elites. Because only nonviolence is morally acceptable for sociopolitical change, there is no other option except an educational one—having people movements gain their own voice, and nurturing a critical conscience through dialogic means. People-based development from below is not merely an end in itself but a fundamental condition of social transformation.

◼ Transforming the IRB

Interpretive sufficiency as a philosophy of social science fundamentally transforms the IRB system in form and content. As with IRBs, it emphasizes relentless accuracy but understands it as the researcher's authentic resonance with the context and the subject's self-reflection as a moral agent. In an indigenous Māori approach to knowledge, for example, "concrete experience is the criterion of meaning and truth" and researchers are "led by the members of the community to discover them" (Denzin, 2003, p. 243). However, because the research-subject relation is reciprocal, the IRB's invasion of privacy, informed consent, and deception are nonissues. In communitarianism, conceptions of the good are shared by the research subjects, and researchers collaborate in bringing these definitions into their own. "Participants have a co-equal say in how research should be conducted, what should be studied, which methods should be used, which findings are valid and acceptable, how the findings are to be implemented, and how the consequences of such actions are to be assessed" (Denzin, 2003, p. 257).

Interpretive sufficiency transcends the current regulatory system governing research on human subjects. Therefore, it recommends a policy of strict territorialism for the IRB regime. Given its historical roots in biomedicine, and with the explosion in both genetic research and privately funded biomedical research, 45 CFR 46 should be confined to medical, biological, and clinic studies, and the positivist and postpositivist social science that is epistemologically identical to them. Research methodologies that have broken down the walls between subjects and researchers ought to be excluded from IRB oversight. As Denzin observes:

> Performance autoethnography, for example, falls outside this [IRB] model, as do many forms of participatory action research, reflexive ethnography, and qualitative research involving testimonies, life stories, life-history inquiry, personal narrative inquiry, performance autobiography, conversation analysis, and ethnodrama. In all of these cases, subjects and researchers develop collaborative, public, pedagogical relationships. (2003, p. 249)

Because participation is voluntary, subjects do not need "to sign forms indicating that their consent is 'informed.'" . . . Confidentiality is not an issue, "for there is nothing to hide or protect." Participants are not subjected to preapproved procedures, but "acting together, researchers and subjects work to produce change in the world" (Denzin, 2003, pp. 249–250).

Given the different understandings of human inquiry, the review of research protocols ought to be given to peers in academic departments or units familiar with these methodologies. The Oral History Association, for example, has codified a set of principles and responsibilities for guiding work in oral history. These "Evaluation Guidelines," as they are commonly called, would serve as the framework for assessing research practice.[26] In her reference to oral history, Linda Shopes speaks for feminist communitarianism as a whole:

> The current regulatory system governing research on human subjects is simply incongruent with oral history interviewing. It has been used inappropriately to inhibit critical inquiry, and it is based on a definition of research far removed from historical practice. Moreover, historians are acutely aware of the ethical dimensions of our work and have well-developed professional standards governing oral history interviewing. I would like to see oral history recognized as lying outside the domain inscribed by the Common Rule. (Shopes, 2000, p. 8)

Denzin enriches feminist communitarian ethics by integrating it with an indigenous research ethic, particularly that of the Kaupapa Māori (2003, pp. 242–248, 257–258). The charters of various indigenous peoples are rooted in a participatory mode of knowing and presume collective, not individual, rights.

> These rights include control and ownership of the community's cultural property . . . and the rights of indigenous peoples to protect their culture's new knowledge and its dissemination. These charters embed codes of ethics within this larger perspective. They spell out specifically how researchers are to protect and respect the rights and interests of indigenous peoples, using the same protocols that regulate daily moral life in these cultures. (Denzin, 2003, p. 257)

This collaborative research model "makes the researcher responsible not to a removed discipline (or institution), but to those he or she studies."

It aligns the ethics of research "with a politics of resistance, hope, and freedom" (Denzin, 2003, p. 258).

▣ Conclusion

As Guba and Lincoln (1994) argue, the issues in social science ultimately must be engaged at the worldview level. "Questions of method are secondary to questions of paradigm, which we define as the basic belief system or worldview that guides the investigator, not only in choices of method but in ontologically and epistemologically fundamental ways" (p. 105). The conventional view, with its extrinsic ethics, gives us a truncated and unsophisticated paradigm that needs to be ontologically transformed. This historical overview of theory and practice points to the need for an entirely new model of research ethics in which human action and conceptions of the good are interactive.

"Since the relation of persons constitutes their existence as persons, . . . morally right action is [one] which intends community" (MacMurray, 1961b, p. 119). In feminist communitarianism, personal being is cut into the very heart of the social universe. The common good is accessible to us only in personal form; it has its ground and inspiration in a social ontology of the human.[27] "Ontology must be rescued from submersion in things by being thought out entirely from the viewpoint of person and thus of Being" (Lotz, 1963, p. 294). "Ontology is truly itself only when it is personal and persons are truly themselves only as ontological" (Lotz, 1963, p. 297).

When rooted in a positivist worldview, explanations of social life are considered incompatible with the renderings offered by the participants themselves. In problematics, lingual form, and content, research production presumes greater mastery and clearer illumination than the nonexperts who are the targeted beneficiaries. Protecting and promoting individual autonomy have been the philosophical rationale for value neutrality since its origins in Mill. But the incoherence in that view of social science is now transparent. By limiting the active involvement of rational beings or judging their self-understanding to be false, empiricist models contradict the ideal of rational beings who "choose between competing conceptions of the good" and make choices "deserving of respect." The verification standards of an instrumentalist system "take away what neutrality aims to protect: a community of free and equal rational beings legislating their own principles of conduct" (Root, 1993, p. 198). The social ontology of feminist communitarianism escapes this contradiction by reintegrating human life with the moral order.

▣ Notes

1. For greater detail regarding this argument than I can provide in the summary below, see Christians, Ferre, and Fackler (1993, pp. 18–32, 41–44).

2. Michael Root (1993) is unique among philosophers of the social sciences in linking social science to the ideals and practices of the liberal state on the grounds that both institutions "attempt to be neutral between competing conceptions of the good" (p. xv). As he elaborates:

> Though liberalism is primarily a theory of the state, its principles can be applied to any of the basic institutions of a society; for one can argue that the role of the clinic, the corporation, the scholarly associations, or professions is not to dictate or even recommend the kind of life a person should aim at. Neutrality can serve as an ideal for the operations of these institutions as much as it can for the state. Their role, one can argue, should be to facilitate whatever kind of life a student, patient, client, customer, or member is aiming at and not promote one kind of life over another. (p. 13)

Root's interpretations of Mill and Weber are crucial to my own formulation.

3. Although committed to what he called "the logic of the moral sciences" in delineating the canons or methods for induction, Mill shared with natural science a belief in the uniformity of nature and the presumption that all phenomena are subject to cause-and-effect relationships. His five principles of induction reflect a Newtonian cosmology.

4. Utilitarianism in John Stuart Mill's thought was essentially an amalgamation of Jeremy Bentham's greatest happiness principle, David Hume's empirical philosophy and concept of utility as a moral good, and Auguste Comte's positivist tenets that things-in-themselves cannot be known and knowledge is restricted to sensations. In his influential *A System of Logic,* Mill (1843/1893) typically is characterized as combining the principles of French positivism (as developed by Comte) and British empiricism into a single system.

5. For an elaboration of the complexities in positivism—including reference to its Millian connections—see Lincoln and Guba (1985, pp. 19–28).

6. Mill's realism is most explicitly developed in his *Examination of Sir William Hamilton's Philosophy* (1865). Our belief in a common external world, in his view, is rooted in the fact that our sensations of physical reality "belong as much to other human or sentient beings as to ourselves" (p. 196; see also Copleston, 1966, p. 306, n. 97).

7. Mill (1873/1969) specifically credits to Comte his use of the inverse deductive or historical method: "This was an idea entirely new to me when I found it in Comte; and but for him I might not soon (if ever) have arrived at it" (p. 126). Mill explicitly follows Comte in distinguishing social statics and social dynamics. He published two essays on Comte's influence in the *Westminster Review*, which were reprinted as *Auguste Comte and Positivism* (Mill, 1865/1907; see also Mill, 1873/1969, p. 165).

8. Emile Durkheim is more explicit and direct about causality in both the natural and the social worlds. Although he argued for sociological over psychological causes of behavior and did not believe intention could cause action, he unequivocally saw the task of social science as discovering the causal links between social facts and personal behavior (see, e.g., Durkheim, 1966, pp. 44, 297–306).

9. As one example of the abuse Weber resisted, Root (1993, pp. 41–42) refers to the appointment of Ludwig Bernhard to a professorship of economics at the University of Berlin. Though he had no academic credentials, the Ministry of Education gave Bernhard this position without a faculty vote (see Weber, 1973, pp. 4–30). In Shils's (1949) terms, "A mass of particular, concrete concerns underlies [his 1917] essay—his recurrent effort to penetrate to the postulates of economic theory, his ethical passion for academic freedom, his fervent nationalist political convictions and his own perpetual demand for intellectual integrity" (p. v).

10. The rationale for the creation of the Social Science Research Council in 1923 is multilayered, but in its attempt to link academic expertise with policy research, as well as in its preference for rigorous social scientific methodology, the SSRC reflects and implements Weber.

11. Often in professional ethics at present, we isolate consequentialism from a full-scale utilitarianism. We give up on the idea of maximizing happiness, but "still try to evaluate different courses of action purely in terms of their consequences, hoping to state everything worth considering in our consequence-descriptions." However, even this broad version of utilitarianism, in Taylor's terms, "still legislates certain goods out of existence" (Taylor, 1982, p. 144). It is likewise a restrictive definition of the good that favors the mode of reasoned calculation and prevents us from taking seriously all facets of moral and normative political thinking (Taylor, 1982). As Yvonna Lincoln observes, utilitarianism's inescapable problem is that "in advocating the greatest good for the greatest number, small groups of people (all minority groups, for example) experience the political regime of the 'tyranny of the majority.'" She refers correctly to "liberalism's tendency to reinscribe oppression by virtue of the utilitarian principle" (personal communication, February 16, 1999).

12. Given the nature of positivist inquiry, Jennings and Callahan (1983) conclude that only a short list of ethical questions is considered and, these questions "tend to merge with the canons of professional scientific methodology. . . . Intellectual honesty, the suppression of personal bias, careful collection and accurate reporting of data, and candid admission of the limits of the scientific reliability of empirical studies—these were essentially the only questions that could arise. And, since these ethical responsibilities are not particularly controversial (at least in principle), it is not surprising that during this period [the 1960s] neither those concerned with ethics nor social scientists devoted much time to analyzing or discussing them" (p. 6).

13. Most biomedical research occurs in a laboratory. Researchers are obliged to inform participants of potential risk and obtain consent before the research takes place. Ethnographic research occurs in settings where subjects live, and informed consent is a process of "ongoing interaction between the researcher and the members of the community being studied. . . . One must establish bonds of trust and negotiate consent . . . taking place over weeks or months—not prior to a structured interview" (Church, 2002, p. 3).

14. For a sociological and epistemological critique of IRBs, see Denzin (2003, pp. 248–257).

15. As Taylor (1982) puts it, "The modern dispute about utilitarianism is not about whether it occupies some of the space of moral reason, but whether it fills the whole space." "Comfort the dying" is a moral imperative in contemporary Calcutta, even though "the dying are in an extremity that makes [utilitarian] calculation irrelevant" (p. 134).

16. This restates the well-known objection to a democratic liberalism of individual rights:

> Liberalism is not a possible meeting ground for all cultures, but is the political expression of one range of cultures, and quite incompatible with other ranges. Liberalism can't and shouldn't claim complete cultural neutrality. Liberalism is also a fighting creed. Multiculturalism as it is often debated today has a lot to do with the imposition of some cultures on others, and with the assumed superiority that powers this imposition. Western liberal societies are thought to be supremely guilty in this regard, partly because of their colonial past, and partly because of their marginalization of segments of their populations that stem from other cultures. (Taylor et al., 1994, pp. 62–63).

17. Denzin in this passage credits Smith (1987, p. 107) with the concept of a "ruling apparatus."

18. Gilligan's research methods and conclusions have been debated by a diverse range of scholars. For this debate and related issues, see Brabeck (1990), Card (1991), Tong (1989, pp. 161–168; 1993, pp. 80–157), Wood (1994), and Seigfried (1996).

19. Levinas (b. 1905) was a professor of philosophy at the University of Paris (Nanterre) and head of the Israelite Normal School in Paris. In Wyschogrod's (1974) terms, "He continues the tradition of Martin Buber and Franz Rosenweig" and was "the first to introduce Husserl's work into . . . the French phenomenological school" (pp. vii-viii). Although Wyschogrod is a student of Heidegger, Hegel, and Husserl (see, e.g., Wyschogrod, 1985)—and engaged Derrida, Lyotard, Foucault, and Deleuze—her work on ethics appeals not to traditional philosophical discourse but to concrete expressions of self–Other transactions in the visual arts, literary narrative, historiography, and the normalization of death in the news.

20. Martha Nussbaum (1993) argues for a version of virtue ethics in these terms, contending for a model rooted in Aristotle that has cross-cultural application without being detached from particular forms of social life. In her model, various spheres of human experience that are found in all cultures represent questions to answer and choices to make—attitudes toward the ill or good fortune of others, how to treat strangers, management of property, control over bodily appetites, and so forth. Our experiences in these areas "fix a subject for further inquiry" (p. 247), and our reflection on each sphere will give us a "thin or nominal definition" of a virtue relevant to this sphere. On this basis, we can talk across cultures about behavior appropriate in each sphere (see Nussbaum, 1999).

21. Root (1993, chap. 10) also chooses a communitarian alternative to the dominant paradigm. In his version, critical theory, participatory research, and feminist social science are three examples of the communitarian approach. This chapter offers a more complex view of communitarianism developed in political philosophy and intellectual history, rather than limiting it to social theory and practical politics. Among the philosophical communitarians (Sandel, 1998; Taylor, 1989; Walzer, 1983, 1987), Carole Pateman (1985, 1989) is explicitly feminist, and her promise motif forms the axis for the principle of multivocal representation outlined below. In this chapter's feminist communitarian model, critical theory is integrated into the third ethical imperative—empowerment and resistance. In spite of that difference in emphasis, I agree with Root's (1993) conclusion: "Critical theories are always critical for a particular community, and the values they seek to advance are the values of that community. In that respect, critical theories are communitarian. . . . For critical theorists, the standard for choosing or accepting a social theory is the reflective acceptability of the theory by members of the community for whom the theory is critical" (pp. 233–234). For a review of communitarian motifs in terms of Foucault, see Olssen (2002).

22. For an elaboration of interpretive sufficiency in terms of news reporting, see Christians (2004, pp. 46–55).

23. The sacredness of life as a protonorm differs fundamentally from the Enlightenment's monocultural ethical rationalism, in which universal imperatives were considered obligatory for all nations and epochs. Cartesian foundationalism and Kant's formalism presumed noncontingent starting points. Universal human solidarity does not. Nor does it flow from Platonism, that is, the finite participating in the infinite and receiving its essence from it (see Christians, 1997b, pp. 3–6). In addition to the sacredness of life as a protonorm,

there are other appeals to universals that neither are Western nor presume a Newtonian cosmology; for a summary, see Christians (2002b).

24. Mutuality is a cardinal feature of the feminist communitarian model generally, and therefore is crucial to the principle of empowerment. For this reason, critical theory is inscribed into the third principle here, rather than following Root (see note 18, above), allowing it to stand by itself as an illustration of communitarianism. Root (1993, p. 238) himself observes that critical theorists often fail to transfer the "ideals of expertise" to their research subjects or give them little say in the research design and interpretation. Without a fundamental shift to communitarian interactivity, research in all modes is prone to the distributive fallacy.

25. Because of his fundamental commitment to dialogue, empowering for Freire avoids the weaknesses of monologic concepts of empowerment in which researchers are seen to free up the weak and unfortunate (summarized by Denzin [2003, pp. 242–245] citing Bishop, 1998). Although Freire represents a radical perspective, he does not claim, "as more radical theorists" do, that "only they and their theories can lead" the researched into freedom (Denzin, 2003, p. 246; citing Bishop, 1998).

26. Thomas Puglisi (2001) contends that the Oral History Association's (OHA) "Evaluation Guidelines" are not incompatible with federal regulations. However, actual experience with IRBs from oral historians indicates their disjuncture in theory and practice.

27. Michael Theunissen (1984) argues that Buber's relational self (and therefore its legacy in Levinas, Freire, Heller, Wyschogrod, and Taylor) is distinct from the subjectivity of Continental existentialism. The subjective sphere of Husserl and Sartre, for example, "stands in no relation to a Thou and is not a member of a We" (p. 20; see also p. 276). "According to Heidegger the self can only come to itself in a voluntary separation from other selves; according to Buber, it has its being solely in the relation" (p. 284).

References

Barry, B. (1967). Justice and the common good. In A. Quinton (Ed.), *Political philosophy* (pp. 190–191). Oxford, UK: Oxford University Press.

Benhabib, S. (1992). *Situating the self: Gender, community and postmodernism in contemporary ethics.* Cambridge, UK: Polity.

Bishop, R. (1998). Freeing ourselves from neo-colonial domination in research: A Māori approach to creating knowledge. *International Journal of Qualitative Studies in Education, 11,* 199–219.

Blanchard, M. A. (2002, January). *Should all disciplines be subject to the Common Rule? Human subjects of social science research.* Panel, U.S. Department of Health and Human Services. Retrieved from www.aaup.org/publications/Academe/2002/02m/02mjftr.htm

Bok, S. (1995). *Common values.* Columbia: University of Missouri Press.

Brabeck, M. M. (Ed.). (1990). *Who cares? Theory, research, and educational implications of the ethic of care.* New York: Praeger.

Buber, M. (1958). *I and thou* (2nd ed.; R. G. Smith, Trans.). New York: Scribner's.

Bulmer, M. (1982). The merits and demerits of covert participant observation. In M. Bulmer (Ed.), *Social research ethics* (pp. 217–251). London: Macmillan.

Bunge, M. (1996). *Finding philosophy in social science.* New Haven, CT: Yale University Press.

Card, C. (Ed.). (1991). *Feminist ethics.* Lawrence: University of Kansas Press.

Christians, C. G. (1997a). The ethics of being. In C. G. Christians & M. Traber (Eds.), *Communication ethics and universal values* (pp. 3–23). Thousand Oaks, CA: Sage.

Christians, C. G. (1997b). Social ethics and mass media practice. In J. M. Makau & R. C. Arnett (Eds.), *Communication ethics in an age of diversity* (pp. 187–205). Urbana: University of Illinois Press.

Christians, C. G. (1998). The sacredness of life. *Media Development, 45*(2), 3–7.

Christians, C. G. (2002a). Ethical theorists and qualitative research. *Qualitative Inquiry, 8*(1), 407–410.

Christians, C. G. (2002b). The latest developments in world ethics. *Proceedings: Media ethics preconference, cross-cultural ethics in a digitalized age* (pp. 3–11). Gwangju City, Korea: Chonnam National University.

Christians, C. G. (2004). The changing news paradigm: From objectivity to interpretive sufficiency. In S. H. Iorio (Ed.), *Qualitative research in journalism: Taking it to the streets* (pp. 41–56). Mahwah, NJ: Lawrence Erlbaum.

Christians, C. G., Ferre, J. P., & Fackler, P. M. (1993). *Good news: Social ethics and the press.* New York: Oxford University Press.

Church, J. T. (2002, January). *Should all disciplines be subject to the Common Rule? Human subjects of social science research.* Panel, U. S. Department of Health and Human Services. Retrieved from www.aaup.org/publications/Academe/2002/02m/02mjftr.htm

Code, L. (1991). *What can she know? Feminist theory and the construction of knowledge.* Ithaca, NY: Cornell University Press.

Comte, A. (1910). *A general view of positivism* (J. H. Bridges, Trans.). London: Routledge. (Original work published 1848)

Copleston, F. (1966). *A history of philosophy: Vol. 8. Modern philosophy: Bentham to Russell.* Garden City, NY: Doubleday.

Denzin, N. K. (1984).*On understanding emotion.* San Francisco: Jossey-Bass.

Denzin, N. K. (1989). *Interpretive biography.* Newbury Park, CA: Sage.

Denzin, N. K. (1997). *Interpretive ethnography: Ethnographic practices for the 21st century.* Thousand Oaks, CA: Sage.

Denzin, N. K. (2002). *Reading race: Hollywood and the cinema of racial violence.* Thousand Oaks, CA: Sage.

Denzin, N. K. (2003). *Performance ethnography: Critical pedagogy and the politics of culture.* Thousand Oaks, CA: Sage.

Durkheim, E. (1966). *Suicide: A study of sociology.* New York: Free Press.

Euben, J. P. (1981). Philosophy and the professions. *Democracy, 1*(2), 112–127.

Evans, A. F., Evans, R. A., & Kennedy, W. B. (1987). *Pedagogies for the non-poor.* Maryknoll, NY: Orbis.

Foucault, M. (1979). *Discipline and punish: The birth of the prison* (A. Sheridan, Trans.). New York: Random House.

Freire, P. (1970a). *Education as the practice of freedom: Cultural action for freedom.* Cambridge, MA: Harvard Educational Review/Center for the Study of Development.

Freire, P. (1970b). *Pedagogy of the oppressed.* New York: Seabury.

Freire, P. (1973). *Education for critical consciousness.* New York: Seabury.

Freire, P. (1978). *Pedagogy in process: The letters of Guinea-Bissau.* New York: Seabury.

Gilligan, C. (1982). *In a different voice: Psychological theory and women's development.* Cambridge, MA: Harvard University Press.

Gilligan, C. (1983). Do the social sciences have an adequate theory of moral development? In N. Haan, R. N. Bellah, P. Rabinow, & W. M. Sullivan (Eds.), *Social science as moral inquiry* (pp. 33–51). New York: Columbia University Press.

Gilligan, C., Ward, J. V., & Taylor, J. M. (1988). *Mapping the moral domain.* Cambridge, MA: Harvard University, Graduate School of Education.

Guba, E. G., & Lincoln, Y. S. (1994). Competing paradigms in qualitative research. In N. K. Denzin & Y. S. Lincoln (Eds.), *Handbook of qualitative research* (pp. 105–117). Thousand Oaks, CA: Sage.

Habermas, J. (1971). *Knowledge and human interests* (J. J. Shapiro, Trans.). Boston: Beacon.

Habermas, J. (1990). *Moral consciousness and communicative action* (C. Lenhardt & S. W. Nicholson, Trans.). Cambridge, MA: MIT Press.

Habermas, J. (1993). *Justification and application: Remarks on discourse ethics* (C. Cronin, Trans.). Cambridge, MA: MIT Press.

Held, V. (1993). *Feminist morality: Transforming culture, society, and politics.* Chicago: University of Chicago Press.

Heller, A. (1988). *General ethics.* Oxford, UK: Blackwell.

Heller, A. (1990). *A philosophy of morals.* Oxford, UK: Blackwell.

Heller, A. (1996). *An ethics of personality.* Oxford, UK: Blackwell.

Heller, A. (1999). *A theory of modernity.* Oxford, UK: Blackwell.

Humphreys, L. (1970). *Tearoom trade: Impersonal sex in public places.* Chicago: Aldine.

Humphreys, L. (1972). *Out of the closet.* Englewood Cliffs, NJ: Prentice Hall.

Jennings, B. (1983). Interpretive social science and policy analysis. In D. Callahan & B. Jennings (Eds.), *Ethics, the social sciences, and policy analysis* (pp. 3–35). New York: Plenum.

Jennings, B., & Callahan, D. (1983, February). Social sciences and the policy-making process. *Hastings Center Report,* pp. 3–8.

Koehn, D. (1998). *Rethinking feminist ethics: Care, trust and empathy.* New York: Routledge.

Lazarsfeld, P., & Reitz, J. G. (1975). *An introduction to applied sociology.* New York: Elsevier.

Levinas, E. (1985). *Ethics and infinity* (R. A. Cohen, Trans.). Pittsburgh, PA: Duquesne University Press.

Levinas, E. (1991). *Otherwise than being or beyond essence* (A. Lingis, Trans.). Dordrecht, Netherlands: Kluwer Academe.

Lincoln, Y. S. (1995). Emerging criteria for quality in qualitative and interpretive inquiry. *Qualitative Inquiry, 1*, 275–289.

Lincoln, Y. S., & Denzin, N. K. (2000). The seventh moment: Out of the past. *Handbook of Qualitative Research* (2nd ed. pp. 1047–1065). Thousand Oaks, CA: Sage.

Lincoln, Y. S., & Guba, E. G. (1985). *Naturalistic inquiry.* Beverly Hills, CA: Sage.

Lotz, J. B. (1963). Person and ontology. *Philosophy Today, 7*, 294–297.

Lyons, H. (1944). *The Royal Society 1660–1940.* Cambridge, UK: Cambridge University Press.

MacMurray, J. (1961a). *The form of the personal: Vol. 1. The self as agent.* London: Faber & Faber.

MacMurray, J. (1961b). *The form of the personal: Vol. 2. Persons in relation.* London: Faber & Faber.

Milgram, S. (1974). *Obedience to authority.* New York: Harper & Row.

Mill, J. S. (1865). *Examination of Sir William Hamilton's philosophy and of the principal philosophical questions discussed in his writings.* London: Longman, Green, Roberts & Green.

Mill, J. S. (1893). *A system of logic, ratiocinative and inductive: Being a connected view of the principles of evidence and the methods of scientific investigation* (8th ed.). New York: Harper & Brothers. (Original work published 1843)

Mill, J. S. (1907). *Auguste Comte and positivism.* London: Kegan Paul, Trench, Trubner & Co. (Original work published 1865)

Mill, J. S. (1957). *Utilitarianism.* Indianapolis: Bobbs-Merrill. (Original work published 1861)

Mill, J. S. (1969). *Autobiography.* Boston: Houghton Mifflin. (Original work published 1873)

Mill, J. S. (1978). *On liberty.* Indianapolis: Hackett. (Original work published 1859)

Mulhall, S., & Swift, A. (1996). *Liberals and communitarians* (2nd ed.). Oxford, UK: Blackwell.

Noddings, N. (1984). *Caring: A feminine approach to ethics and moral education.* Berkeley: University of California Press.

Noddings, N. (1989). *Women and evil.* Berkeley: University of California Press.

Noddings, N. (1990). Ethics from the standpoint of women. In D. L. Rhode (Ed.), *Theoretical perspectives on sexual difference* (pp. 160–173). New Haven, CT: Yale University Press.

Nussbaum, M. (1993). Non-relative virtues: An Aristotelian approach. In M. Nussbaum & A. Sen, *The quality of life* (pp. 242–269). Oxford, UK: Clarendon.

Nussbaum, M. (1999). *Sex and social justice.* New York: Oxford University Press.

Olssen, M. (2002). Michel Foucault as "thin" communitarian: Difference, community, democracy. *Cultural Studies—Critical Methodologies, 2*(4), 483–513.

Olthuis, J. (1997). Face-to-face: Ethical asymmetry or the symmetry of mutuality? In J. Olthuis (Ed.), *Knowing other-wise* (pp. 134–164). New York: Fordham University Press.

Pateman, C. (1985). *The problem of political obligation: A critique of liberal theory.* Cambridge, UK: Polity.

Pateman, C. (1988). *The sexual contract.* Stanford, CA: Stanford University Press.

Pateman, C. (1989). *The disorder of women: Democracy, feminism and political theory.* Stanford, CA: Stanford University Press.

Peukert, H. (1981). Universal solidarity as the goal of ethics. *Media Development, 28*(4), 10–12.

Puglisi, T. (2001). IRB review: It helps to know the regulatory framework. *American Psychological Society Observer, 1*(May/June), 34–35.

Punch, M. (1994). Politics and ethics in qualitative research. In N. K. Denzin & Y. S. Lincoln (Eds.), *Handbook of qualitative research* (pp. 83–97). Thousand Oaks, CA: Sage.

Reinharz, S. (1993). *Social research methods: Feminist perspectives.* New York: Elsevier.

Reiss, A. J., Jr. (1979). Governmental regulation of scientific inquiry: Some paradoxical consequences. In C. B. Klockars & F. W. O'Connor (Eds.), *Deviance and decency: The ethics of research with human subjects* (pp. 61–95). Beverly Hills, CA: Sage.

Root, M. (1993). *Philosophy of social science: The methods, ideals, and politics of social inquiry.* Oxford, UK: Blackwell.

Ryan, K. E. (1995). Evaluation ethics and issues of social justice: Contributions from female moral thinking. In N. K. Denzin (Ed.), *Studies in symbolic interaction: A research annual* (Vol. 19, pp. 143–151). Greenwich, CT: JAI.

Sandel, M. J. (1998). *Liberalism and the limits of justice* (2nd ed.). Cambridge, UK: Cambridge University Press.

Seigfried, C. H. (1996). *Pragmatism and feminism: Reweaving the social fabric.* Chicago: University of Chicago Press.

Shils, E. A. (1949). Foreword. In M. Weber, *The methodology of the social sciences* (pp. iii–x). New York: Free Press.

Shopes, L. (2000). Institutional Review Boards have a chilling effect on oral history. *Perspectives online.* Retrieved from www.theaha.org/perspectives/issues/2000/0009/0009vie1.cfm

Smith, D. E. (1987). *The everyday world as problematic: A feminist sociology.* Boston: Northeastern University Press.

Soble, A. (1978, October). Deception in social science research: Is informed consent possible? *Hastings Center Report,* pp. 40–46.

Steiner, L. (1991). Feminist theorizing and communication ethics. *Communication, 12*(3), 157–174.

Steiner, L. (1997). A feminist schema for analysis of ethical dilemmas. In F. L. Casmir (Ed.), *Ethics in intercultural and international communication* (pp. 59–88). Mahwah, NJ: Lawrence Erlbaum.

Taylor, C. (1982). The diversity of goods. In A. Sen & B. Williams (Eds.), *Utilitarianism and beyond* (pp. 129–144). Cambridge, UK: Cambridge University Press.

Taylor, C. (1989). *Sources of the self: The making of the modern identity.* Cambridge, MA: Harvard University Press.

Taylor, C. (1991). *The ethics of authenticity.* Cambridge, MA: Harvard University Press.

Taylor, C. (1995). *Philosophical arguments.* Cambridge, MA: Harvard University Press.

Taylor, C., Appiah, K. A., Habermas, J., Rockefeller, S. C., Walzer, M., & Wolf, S. (1994). *Multiculturalism: Examining the politics of recognition* (A. Gutmann, Ed.). Princeton, NJ: Princeton University Press.

Theunissen, M. (1984). *The other: Studies in the social ontology of Husserl, Heidegger, Sartre, and Buber* (C. Macann, Trans.). Cambridge, MA: MIT Press.

Tong, R. (1989). *Feminist thought.* Boulder, CO: Westview.

Tong, R. (1993). *Feminine and feminist ethics.* Belmont, CA: Wadsworth.

University of Illinois at Urbana-Champaign, Institutional Review Board. (2003, January). Part I: Fundamental principles for the use of human subjects in research. In *Handbook for investigators: For the protection of human subjects in research.* Urbana: Author. (Available from www.irb.uiuc.edu)

Vanderpool, H. Y. (Ed.). (1996). *The ethics of research involving human subjects: Facing the 21st century.* Frederick, MD: University Publishing Group.

Veatch, R. M. (1996). From Nuremberg through the 1990s: The priority of autonomy. In H. Y. Vanderpool (Ed.), *The ethics of research involving human subjects: Facing the 21st century* (pp. 45–58). Frederick, MD: University Publishing Group.

Walzer, M. (1983). *Spheres of justice: A defense of pluralism and equality.* New York: Basic Books.

Walzer, M. (1987). *Interpretation and social criticism.* Cambridge, MA: Harvard University Press.

Weber, M. (1949a). The meaning of ethical neutrality in sociology and economics. In M. Weber, *The methodology of the social sciences* (E. A. Shils & H. A. Finch, Eds. & Trans., pp. 1–47). New York: Free Press. (Original work published 1917)

Weber, M. (1949b). Objectivity in social science and social policy. In M. Weber, *The methodology of the social sciences* (E. A. Shils & H. A. Finch, Eds. & Trans., pp. 50–112). New York: Free Press. (Original work published 1904)

Weber, M. (1973). *Max Weber on universities* (E. A. Shils, Ed. & Trans.). Chicago: University of Chicago Press.

West, C. (1989). *The American evasion of philosophy: A genealogy of pragmatism.* Madison: University of Wisconsin Press.

West, C. (1991). *The ethical dimensions of Marxist thought.* New York: Monthly Review Books.

West, C. (1993). *Race matters.* Boston: Beacon Press.

White, R. (1995). From codes of ethics to public cultural truth. *European Journal of Communication, 10,* 441–460.

Wiredu, K. (1996). *Cultural universals: An African perspective.* Bloomington: Indiana University Press.

Wood, J. (1994). *Who cares? Women, care, and culture.* Carbondale: Southern Illinois University Press.

Wyschogrod, E. (1974). *Emmanuel Levinas: The problem of ethical metaphysics.* The Hague: Martinus Nijhoff.

Wyschogrod, E. (1985). *Spirit in ashes: Hegel, Heidegger, and man-made death.* Chicago: University of Chicago Press.

Wyschogrod, E. (1990). *Saints and postmodernism: Revisioning moral philosophy.* Chicago: University of Chicago Press.

Wyschogrod, E. (1998). *An ethics of remembering: History, heterology, and the nameless others.* Chicago: University of Chicago Press.

7

INSTITUTIONAL REVIEW BOARDS AND METHODOLOGICAL CONSERVATISM

The Challenge to and from Phenomenological Paradigms

Yvonna S. Lincoln

Qualitative research, as exemplified by this *Handbook*, hundreds of other books, and perhaps thousands of journal articles, has not only gained a foothold but has established a small stronghold in education and the social and clinical sciences. The number of national and international conferences, small and large, devoted to qualitative research and its practitioners has grown geometrically in recent years, and several annual conferences are now in their second decade.

As the variety of qualitative methods has expanded and been refined, paradigms, theoretical perspectives, and epistemological stances have been elaborated (e.g., feminist theory, race/ethnic studies theories, subaltern and postcolonial epistemologies, queer theory), and interpretive lenses have been developed (postmodernism, poststructuralism), increasing numbers of practitioners and would-be practitioners have been attracted to the promise and democratic and pluralistic ethics of qualitative practices. The inclusionary bent (Mertens, 1998) and social justice orientation (see Denzin, Chapter 37, this volume; Lincoln & Denzin, 2000) of the new social science has drawn a fresh cadre of methodologists committed to seeing social science used for democratic and liberalizing social purposes.

The resurgence of "high modernism" (Giddens, 1990), however, carries with it a return to some presumed "golden age" of methodological purity (and innocence) when broad consensus on the constituent elements of science supposedly reigned. Voices in the biomedical community (the Campbell and Cochrane Collaborations) and in the educational research community bespeak a turn toward "methodological conservatism" (Cannella & Lincoln, 2004a, 2004b; Lincoln & Cannella, 2004a, 2004b).

A recent series of legislative actions and committee policy changes, however, may directly and indirectly influence paradigmatic and methodological issues in ways unforeseen a scant decade ago. In turn, qualitative research may be compromised or even threatened by the new methodological conservatism being propagated in the name of evidence-based research and "scientifically based educational research."

Currently, there appear to be four ways in which the work of qualitative researchers and scholars who teach qualitative research philosophies and methods is constrained by the manner in which new paradigms encounter institutional review board (IRB) regulation on campuses: (a) increased scrutiny surrounding research with human subjects (a response to failures in biomedical research), (b) new scrutiny of classroom research and training in qualitative methods involving human subjects, (c) new discourses regarding what constitutes "evidence-based research," and (d) the long-term effects of the recent National Research Council (NRC, 2002) report on what should be considered to be scientific inquiry. After presenting a brief history of IRBs, I offer below a set of suggestions to help scholars cope with these constraints in both qualitative research and the teaching of qualitative methods.

▣ A Brief History of Institutional Review Boards

As I have noted elsewhere, the "original impulse to regulate U.S. scientific research federally followed World War II and the Nuremberg trials," where testimony regarding medical and psychological experiments performed on prisoners of war and inmates in the Nazi death camps left the civilized world reeling with anguish and horror (Denzin & Lincoln, in press). The Helsinki Agreement was formulated in response to the nightmares uncovered during those trials.

Following closely on the Nuremberg trials, however, were public revelations about a series of medical and psychological experiments conducted in the United States. The publicity surrounding the scandals of the Tuskegee Syphilis Study, the Willowbrook hepatitis experiments, Project Camelot in the 1960s (a series of military and CIA experiments with psychotropic drugs, including LSD, involving enlisted U.S. Army recruits), Stanley Milgram's psychological deception studies involving deliberately delivered electroshock torture, and the work of social scientists directed toward military purposes in Vietnam, particularly covert espionage activities, prompted the federal government to undertake reexamination of its own policies and procedures around ethics in human subjects research. In 1974, the Belmont Report, which embodied a code for human subjects protections, was adopted as the standard for overseeing U.S. Public Health Service grants and contracts. Originally limited to use in decisions regarding PHS grants, the federal regulations and ethics guidelines were soon extended to cover all federally funded research with human subjects. Eventually, they came to be applied to all human subjects research, whether funded or not, undertaken by federal grantees, foundation researchers, biomedical researchers, and social science and educational researchers as well.

Although the four broad areas covered by the Belmont Report (and subsequent federal legislation, including, for example, the Buckley Amendment)—informed consent, deception, privacy of records, and confidentiality and protection of research participants' identities—were a strong start for a research ethics code, the guidelines as they are now deployed have failed to keep pace with developments in research methodologies, particularly qualitative and action research methodologies, with their high emphasis on collaboration between researchers and those researched, high levels of interactivity, and new mandates for a reformulated communitarian and democratic ethics in the field. In light of emergent epistemologies deeply rooted in cultural practices but divorced from federal concerns, federal standards for research ethics (as well as newer legislation such as the No Child Left Behind Act of 2001) "collide with other understandings circulating in the field of qualitative research" (Denzin & Lincoln, in press). In the face of this collision, a reexamination of the role of IRBs vis-à-vis qualitative research appears to be critical at this juncture (Denzin & Lincoln, in press; see also in this volume Cheek, Chapter 15; Miller & Crabtree, Chapter 24).

The Challenges to Qualitative Research Posed by IRBs

Increased Scrutiny in Research With Human Subjects

New regulations regarding the protection of human subjects, created largely in response to tragic incidents involving biomedical and drug testing and informed consent, have acted to limit or severely constrain what teachers and students can do as part of classroom training as well as research (Gillespie, 1997). Two such incidents—one death resulting from an experimental procedure in a New York hospital and one from an experimental drug at Johns Hopkins—were sufficient to raise questions regarding whether participants in clinical and experimental trials of drugs and biomedical procedures receive enough information, and accurate information, on informed consent forms to understand fully the risks involved in their research participation. As a consequence, any and all research with human subjects, regardless of level of risk, has become the focus of increased regulation and oversight.

To be very clear: Classroom teachers have always gone to IRBs for approval of class activities and research training that involves human participants outside of class, including observation targets, potential interviewees, and survey respondents. But the arrangements between IRBs and researchers in the past were often much less formal than they are now, and they were assuredly not mandated by federal policies and procedures.

Today, the question of risk is rarely examined thoroughly (Gordon, Sugarman, & Kass, 1998) or taken into account in IRB deliberations. After conducting a series of nationwide hearings with social scientists, the American Association of University Professors (AAUP, 2001) recently concluded that IRBs are treating the level of risk in research with human subjects as though it were irrelevant, although information about risk level is clearly vital to considerations of what harm research is likely to do, if any. The AAUP report states that whereas biomedical and clinical trial research deserves maximum scrutiny for risk, many issues in social science and educational research may need only expedited review (p. 62). The recent federal policy decision, announced via the *Federal Register,* to remove oral history work from the list of the kinds of projects that must undergo IRB scrutiny is a tantalizing example of what may be a site-by-site battle around qualitative research methods.

An intriguing sidebar: Many of the individuals tapped for testimony because of their concerns about the new IRB regulations were oral historians who were worried that their inquiries might provoke levels of review not previously encountered in history departments or historical studies. In a somewhat stunning move, the federal government, on the recommendation of the National Research Council, has simply made oral history research permanently exempt from IRB review, imputing such little rigor to this work that it is not considered "social science" at all, but rather something else. I will have more to say about this later; for now, I simply want to note that this decision, in and of itself, although it frees historians who engage in oral history research from IRB review and therefore permits the broadest level of academic freedom in that research arena, can be seen as insulting and demeaning to those who do this kind of work.

The most prominent effects of increased IRB scrutiny cataloged so far have been the multiple rereviews of faculty proposals for qualitative research projects and in the rereviews and denials of proposed student research (particularly dissertation research) projects that utilize action research and participatory action research methods, research in the subjects' own settings (e.g., high schools), and/or research that is predominantly qualitative in nature (although not all researchers or their students have this problem; D. J. Greenwood, personal communication, 2003).[1] I have cited several examples of increased IRB scrutiny in my own previous work (Lincoln & Tierney, 2004), and scholars are collecting additional examples every month around the country. Qualitative researchers and doctoral students pursuing largely ethnographic and/or action research dissertations, however, are not the only researchers facing such additional scrutiny.

Increased Scrutiny in Qualitative Research Classroom Training and Course Work

The high-profile cases of failed medical protocols and ensuing deaths at two separate teaching hospitals mentioned earlier have led to renewed caution on the part of university IRBs and the researchers they serve. Increased attention to biomedical research has been accompanied by increased attention to regular course work and student training. One way in which this sharpened focus has been expressed has been in new requirements surrounding graduate teaching for qualitative research.

In the past, graduate course work in qualitative research required of a professor little more than an amicable visit with the IRB on some regular, but distant, basis—perhaps once every 5 to 10 years, unless a course was radically altered in substance or presentation. Formal procedures were rarely, if ever, followed, and IRB members were quite content to receive a complete course syllabus outlining the readings and assignments and describing the nature of the training students would undertake. In the past few years, however, the relationships between IRBs and professors have been seriously and profoundly restructured. Today, professors who teach qualitative methods, and whose assignments require students to move outside the classroom and begin practicing observational and interview skills on their own, are required to complete the entire IRB protocol, requesting permission even to teach courses in a manner that permits students to practice the skills they need to conduct research in a trained and ethical way.

The central point of much of graduate work is to prepare advanced students and college-trained scientists and intellectuals to undertake even more advanced intellectual and scientific exploration independent of their graduate advisers—as is the case in universities and laboratories around the world. The idea that graduate students may be trained in the use of nuclear reactors, the application of medical protocols, the techniques of electron microscopy, or any of the many other techniques they may need to continue scientific exploration on their own, largely without any IRB intervention at all, but students must seek IRB approval to interview professors on campus about their research in order to become familiar with interview techniques strikes many scholars as somewhat unreasonable. Although there has been some explication of the circumstances under which professors may use students, especially students in their own classrooms, as research subjects, particularly when the research concerns the classroom experience itself (DuBois, 2002; Hammack, 1997), little guidance is available about what experiences students themselves may have as part of their formal training.

I am not referring here to the kind of scrutiny that goes on as a result of the "political correctness" battles currently being waged between the political Right and much of academia based on the perception of members of the Right, or of the National Association of Scholars, that American colleges and universities are indoctrinating students with left-wing ideology (Burris & Diamond, 1991; Giroux, 1995). That form of scrutiny and reporting has far more to do with political agendas aimed at limiting academic freedom (Benjamin, Kurland, & Molotsky, 1985) than it does with research oversight. It is, furthermore, unofficial and intimidating in intent. As Giroux (1995) points out, "Many subordinate groups argue that the act of knowing is integrally related to the power of self-definition, which, in part, necessitates that more diverse histories and narratives be included in the curriculum. For many conservatives, however, such inclusiveness represents both a call to politicize the curriculum and a social practice that promotes national disunity and cultural decay" (p. 133).

Although academic freedom is deeply implicated in this set of arguments and, indeed, is being represented by political conservatives as a "casualty of this process" of politicization and the presumed lowering of academic standards, the reality is quite likely the reverse. Academic freedom is under assault from the Right's tactics of intimidation (e.g., public denunciation, Web sites that list the names of "ultraliberal" professors, Lynne Cheney's announced monitoring of specific professors who do not support the war in Iraq) and ongoing media assaults on "political correctness" (Devine, 1996; Diamond, 1991; Teller, 1988). In addition, students and other resident hecklers on campuses who shout down unpopular ideas represent a danger to academic freedom in the form of a "threat from within," as Trow (1985) aptly puts it.

Rather, I am referring in this chapter to scrutiny that represents increasing activism on the part of IRB structures. For example, when IRB review requirements were extended from public health research to all research involving human subjects under the National Research Act of 1974, "the original guidelines stated simply that informed consent must be obtained from subjects, [but] the present regulations contain a list of six specific topics which must be disclosed to subjects" (Gray, 1978, p. 35). The issue of research conducted within a classroom setting or, more specifically, as part of classroom assignments but *not* within the classroom or with class members themselves, is a critical one. Hecht (1995) labels this question "When is it teaching and when is it research?" (p. 9). He notes that his own institution arrived at a set of definitions and circumstances that many other institutions have now adopted:

> Within the confines of a class . . . there appears to be adequate provisions for protecting the rights of all individuals involved. Whether it happens within the physical classroom or outside, both faculty and students have an *academic* responsibility and obligation to behave in certain ways.
>
> Such protections, however, are not found when a faculty or student actively encounters individuals not enrolled in the class. An outsider is most likely unfamiliar with the requirements of the course, the particular assignment being accomplished, or the protections available through academic channels. Further, if the activity is a research activity—one where an [*sic*] systematic observation or interaction is made of human subjects in a naturally occurring or purposefully manipulated condition—those human subjects may be totally unaware of their participation. For these reasons, the . . . IRB has defined teaching as an activity that occurs between and among students and teachers. If the activity is to be a research activity (as defined above) but is to take place solely among the students and teachers as part of a recognized instructional process, where the students and teachers all know of the design and purpose (such as through a syllabus or handout), the activity is not considered research for IRB purposes. If, on the other hand, the activity is to involve individuals not students or faculty *in the course,* or is to involve activities where the students and/or teachers are unaware of their participation (such as a faculty systematically studying their students' responses to manipulated conditions) the activity would be considered research and subject to IRB review and approval. (pp. 9–10)

This set of principles—between teachers and students, where the syllabus serves as the learning contract, versus between students and those outside the classroom, where participants are unaware of the specific assignments, purposes, and so on—appears to be the one that guides most IRBs' reviews of even advanced graduate classes in qualitative research today. Although qualitative researchers across the United States have long engaged with IRBs in discussions of the kinds of exercises that students may carry out as part of their class assignments, until recent years such discussions have been rather informal. The paperwork associated with such discussions previously took the form of only class syllabi, which professors thoroughly discussed with IRB committee members in amicable and informal conversations prior to teaching their first classes.

One might argue that, at least on some campuses, the extended IRB review that is the norm today—often every time the same course is taught—has a chilling effect on qualitative methods teaching, especially given that no other courses in methods (e.g., statistics, practice teaching, medical internships) are subject to such rigorous oversight. Further, whereas the whole issue of inadequate protection of human subjects arose as a result of some profoundly questionable medical experiments (such as the Tuskegee Syphilis Study and the Willowbrook studies), it is difficult to find examples of such egregious research conduct in the human or social sciences. That is not to argue that such is not possible, only that it has thus far not happened, or is very rare.

Taking the opposite, and equally reasonable, side of this argument, Howe and Dougherty (1993) tactfully point out that "although moral abominations in social research are rare (but consider Milgram), other pressures—for instance, pressures to 'publish or perish'—are real and ubiquitous, and one need not be a bad person to be tempted to cut ethical corners in response to them, especially if cutting corners is the norm" (p. 16). Howe and Dougherty go on to argue that much of qualitative research should indeed be subject to review, for two reasons: the "open-ended and intimate" nature of qualitative research, especially as it puts researchers and research participants into face-to-face contact with each other; and the fact that its open-endedness requires that researchers and research participants negotiate meanings. These characteristics, they suggest, make qualitative research both more "ethically charged and unpredictable from the outset" (p. 19).

Although most qualitative researchers would strongly agree with Howe and Dougherty's description, many would also object that too often their research is subject to review by researchers who know nothing about qualitative research, who feel that it is not "good science," and/or who have no special sensitivity to social science research conducted using qualitative methods. Some IRBs go out of their way to ensure that proposals for qualitative research are reviewed by board members who have expertise in nonclinical, natural, and field settings; others make no such efforts. For qualitative researchers, the first type of review board rarely presents any problem for well-designed, strongly supervised student work. When the IRB is of the second kind, however, trying to secure approval is frequently a demoralizing endeavor.

New Discourses Around Evidence

IRBs are not always forces for methodological "purity" or conservatism on campuses, but they have been and they can be. When that is the case, qualitative researchers may find themselves subject to an additional set of pressures, as embodied in the NCR report *Scientific Research in Education* (2002) and new discourses emerging around the topic of what constitutes "scientific evidence."

As long ago as 1978, Gray recognized that it is "desirable for research to be considered from a variety of viewpoints" (p. 35). Gray was referring not only to research modes but also to research audiences, including individuals who themselves might be considered (at some point) research participants/subjects, and their participation in deliberations and debates regarding proposed research projects. Although the suggestion concerning increased participation on the part of "community members" (rather than simply other academic researchers) has not traveled very far in many institutions (but see Bauer, 2001), the discourse about modes of research has taken a decidedly alarming turn.

The rise of a neoconservative and neoliberal discourse (Baez & Slaughter, 2001; Messer-Davidow, 1993) regarding "political correctness" on campuses has been extended and reconfigured into a discourse around "standards" (Giroux, 1995), attaching to the criticisms of French political theories, feminist theories, critical theories, and gay, race/ethnic, border, postcolonial, and other emerging streams of thought that have been so prominent in the strident attacks on the "liberal campus" (Parenti, 1995). Although some have pointed out that it is a myth that campuses are liberal (Burris & Diamond, 1991), and Parenti (1995) has described "most college professors and students ... [as] drearily conventional in their ideological proclivities" (p. 20), an emphasis on *standards for research* has arisen from the broader accusation that multiculturalism has watered down standards. The No Child Left Behind Act of 2001 and the more recent report of the National Research Council (2002) on scientific research in education amount to a manifesto concerning the standards for "true" scientific research, especially what should be considered meaningful "evidence" and what (in the case of No Child Left Behind) will be funded for research and evaluation purposes.

The NRC (2002) report in particular has sent shock waves through the educational research community, supporting as it does "evidence-based research" and randomized controlled experiments based on clinical field trial models. Although the report does not disallow qualitative research as a strategy or set of methods that may produce evidence for research purposes, its clear focus on objectivity and causal connections, as well as generalizability, indicates a distinctly modernist and experimental bent that acts to freeze out inquiry models that take explicit account of alternative epistemologies or the emergent critiques of contemporary science that make alternative epistemologies so compelling and socially trenchant.

The questions that have been raised regarding the NRC (2002) report have less to do with the "principles for scientific inquiry" (p. 52) it lays out than with the report's underlying assumptions regarding what constitutes "evidence." The report asserts that two characteristics of scientific inquiry are replication and generalizability (p. 74). It then takes two examples—Elliot Eisner's notion of educational *connoisseurship* and Sara Lawrence-Lightfoot's qualitative methodology for *portraiture*—and demonstrates, using the NRC's own criteria, why neither of these well-recognized methods in educational research constitutes scientific inquiry (pp. 74–77). For the NRC, evidence is apparently not what is produced through the processes that Cronbach and Suppes (1969) describe in their groundbreaking work: "The report of a disciplined inquiry has a texture that displays the raw materials entering the argument and the logical processes by which they were compressed and rearranged to make the conclusion credible" (p. 16). Cronbach and Suppes themselves were sufficiently sophisticated to avoid the particular traps the NRC sets in limiting what constitutes evidence (primarily quantitative, generated by experimental method, replicable—never mind that few studies are ever replicated unless they are in high-stakes biomedical or technology-oriented arenas—empirically verifiable). Rather, the NRC's standards concerning what constitutes scientific research are based in the criteria for establishing the rigor of conventional experimental research: internal validity, external validity (generalizability), replicability, and objectivity. These criteria have been criticized as inappropriate for phenomenological inquiry (see Guba & Lincoln, 1994; Lincoln & Guba, 2000; see also Lincoln & Guba, 1985), and race and ethnic studies theorists, feminist theorists, and postcolonial and border studies theorists have proposed new formulations more appropriate to their own inquiry concerns as well as criteria more meaningful to the communities with which they work (Collins, 2000; Reinharz, 1992; Sandoval, 2000; Smith, 1999; Stanfield & Dennis, 1993).

The claims advanced in the NRC report concerning what constitutes scientific inquiry function on multiple levels. First, these claims act to narrow the range of what is to be considered "scientific," effectively shutting out of the scientific community a wide range of critical and alternate epistemology researchers. By defining nonexperimentalists as "the Other" and therefore outsiders to the community of scientific research, the NRC undermines serious and indeed lethal criticisms of the very practices it proclaims as "true" science. Philosophers, feminist theorists, race and ethnic theorists, and alternative paradigm practitioners have mounted pointed critiques around two issues regarding the kind of "scientific inquiry" the NRC supports: its claims to knowledge hegemony (Cowen, 1995) and, indeed, scientific supremacy; and its claims that other forms of inquiry, while they may be "scholarship" (NRC, 2002, pp. 73–74), are not "science" because of their inability to achieve science's principal aims of generalizability, disinterestedness, objectivity, and replicability. Scholars of all stripes and political leanings, including such experimentalists as Lee J. Cronbach himself, have recognized the inherent shortcomings of conventional scientific inquiry and have rejected the neomodernist formulation as unachievable and likely impractical in the social sphere.

On a second level, the NRC report lends support to IRBs in their attempts to limit the range of activities that researchers can undertake with human subjects. As I have reported elsewhere (Lincoln & Tierney, 2004), IRBs are rarely favorably disposed toward emergent research methods, paradigms, and methodologies (e.g., action research, participatory action research, constructivist inquiries, qualitative studies), especially when these boards are constituted primarily of hard scientists and experimentalists, as they have traditionally been (although D. J. Greenwood provides evidence of the opposite situation; personal communication, 2003). In all fairness, as much of this can be blamed on board members' lack of knowledge of such methods or their intended usages as on scientific "sacerdotalism" and a desire to maintain a kind of secular priesthood of science. Whatever the source, however, the effects are the same. Just as alternative epistemologies and qualitative methods are beginning to gain a foothold in the social sciences and educational research, the NRC report threatens an academic lockout of paradigmatic dissidents and alternative epistemology practitioners. Indeed, some members of the community strongly supported by the NRC are sufficiently threatened by alternative paradigm practitioners to declare: "Theorists of educational evaluation such as [here several names are listed, including my own] . . . have explicitly rejected this method [random assignment]. . . . By now, they have influenced the practice of many generations of young educational evaluators and *are probably a major cause of the impoverished current state of knowledge about what reform initiatives in American education have actually achieved*" (Cook & Payne, 2002, pp. 150–151; emphasis added). Although it is unnerving to be blamed for impoverishing the "current state of knowledge" about what works in American education, it is also refreshing to see an admission from the "gold standard" side of the debate that a handful of solid theorists have been responsible for such a profound alteration in the scholarly landscape.

This imputation that certain specific individuals are "probably a major cause of the impoverished current state of knowledge" does nothing, however, to open the academy to its promise as a marketplace of ideas. Quite the opposite: By defining some social scientists as practitioners of scientific inquiry, some as merely scholars, and others as perhaps responsible for outright ignorance (Cook & Payne, 2002), the NRC and others who are vocal in their support of randomized field trials (the clinical model for educational research) have attempted to re-create a class system that acts to define some knowledge as worthy of being utilized to address serious and weighty issues, such as policy formulation, or for serious purposes such as evaluation funding, and other knowledge as merely the purview of a nonscientific minority whose findings should not enter into the political fray of policy and/or legislative action. Thus practitioners of alternative paradigm inquiry are obliquely defined as dilettantes, scholars of no consequence, or, as one scholar has acerbically put it, "not good enough to play with the Big Boys."

On a third level, the aggrandizement of the power to define what should be considered scientific and what should not to a rather small group of individuals represents precisely the reification of a number of substantial criticisms of the practices of conventional inquiry, including maintenance of status, power, and privilege for a few; maintenance of the status quo, particularly with regard to the counterclaims of knowledges and ways of knowing that are outside of the Eurocentric and frequently patriarchal "Western canon"; and a limiting of the diversity and openness that a pluralistic society needs to flourish. A community of specialized elites is reinscribed by the public assertion of a single, true way—the "gold standard"—of conducting scientific inquiry. As Trow (1985) describes it, from another and more political context:

> Membership in such communities is very comfortable and rewarding; it often gives one a sense of personal worth and security. . . . But the good teacher and effective university environment do not make life more comfortable, but on the contrary, make it less comfortable by challenging positions that students already hold. And by challenging political and social pieties, higher education always threatens to disrupt the communities of partisans that live by rhetoric, slogans, symbols of

unity and *a claim to a monopoly on the truth.* (p. 64; emphasis added)

On a fourth level, such declarations must be taken seriously because of their ability, directly and indirectly, to *limit discussions on individual campuses* concerning what constitutes disciplined scientific inquiry and, therefore, what studies are approved by IRBs and which researchers find that their academic freedom to engage in significant research on social problems may be curtailed or abrogated altogether. The NRC report acts as a kind of political barometer, albeit one that masquerades as a disinterested and objective "scientific" barometer, that indicates the extent to which a given study may be classified as scientific or nonscientific and, therefore, even worthy of IRB review, federal funding (as in the No Child Left Behind Act), or federally supported research and evaluation activities.

Oral history is a case in point. As noted above, oral history is now classified as some other form of scholarly enterprise, so far removed from science that even though it deals exclusively with humans, it is automatically exempt from IRB review. Such classification—as sufficiently far removed from the scientific enterprise that scholars using this method needn't even bother with IRB review—is apt to make some important studies (e.g., the history of reform in a particular school as recounted by a former principal, a life history of practice in the teaching profession, the recounting of a scholar's experiences in entering and navigating the community of science or academia, an African American woman's experiences of growing up in the segregated South) fall outside the purview of meaningful or critical knowledge. Narrow definitions of scientific inquiry—and evidence—serve ultimately to circumscribe painfully and dangerously the range of what is considered useful knowledge and, consequently, to limit the kinds of studies supported by a range of administrative and managerial structures, including IRBs, funding agencies, foundations, and state governments and agencies. The long-term results are systemic constriction of academic freedom (for individual researchers) (Akker, 2002), a seeping loss of institutional autonomy (for institutions of higher education), and a loss of needed epistemological perspectives on persistent social justice issues.

Long-Term Effects of the NRC Report

The new discourse on "evidence-based research"—as well as "evidence-based teaching" (Pressley, Duke, & Boling, 2004), "evidence-based medicine," and other arenas where "evidence" is considered the "gold standard"—obscures the larger discourse of what evidence, which evidence, whose evidence, evidence gathered under what circumstances, evidence gathered for what uses, and for whom, shall be considered worthwhile, and thereby usable. No reasonable individual would argue that clinical field trials, or randomized experiments, do not have sound purposes under some conditions. Double-blind experiments have proven efficacy in testing pharmaceuticals, and some kinds of clinical trials of medical protocols have proven the effectiveness of revolutionary new therapies. But such randomized treatment procedures constitute a fairly narrow application of scientific method by themselves (see, e.g., Howe, 2004; Popkewitz, 2004; see also House, Chapter 42, this volume). Nevertheless, the NRC (2002) report comes rather closer to a "manifesto" on what constitutes scientific truth (Popkewitz, 2004) than it does to a reasoned argument that takes into account the many varieties of recognized epistemologies and methodologies abroad in the social sciences today. The many levels of unexamined assumptions in the NRC report itself—it is no misrepresentation to call it a manifesto—cast it clearly into the category of an ideological statement.

To take one example, consider the question of *knowledge for whom.* It is clear, on multiple readings of the report, that the NRC assumes that the major "consumers" of scientific research, particularly scientific research in education, are other scientists and the policy community. This assumption is true of others as well (Mosteller & Boruch, 2002). Although it is no doubt true that other scientists and academic researchers, as well as policy community members, are major consumers of educational and other social science research, it is not inappropriate to consider community members also as users and consumers of research. With an increasing amount of political and social action now emanating from local-level agencies and community organizations, it is not unreasonable to expect that communities themselves (broadly defined as neighborhoods, municipalities, organizations, and other coherent groups) will want to have access to information, data, knowledge, and interpretations regarding their own circumstances and possibilities for action. As communities acquire systematic information about themselves, they are empowered to participate in designing their own futures and to take action where it is meaningful: locally. If the assumption, however, is that scientific (or other systematic) social knowledge belongs to the knowledge-production community alone, then social action is curtailed in favor of official action. Democratic participation in social change, especially social change on behalf of social justice, is impaired or discouraged altogether. If methodological conservatism is not challenged, it can have the effect of undermining a democratic polity.

The NRC report's focus on "appropriate" inquiry methods (as opposed to those used by Eisner, Lawrence-Lightfoot, and many postmodern theorists, to name some of those whose work the NRC rejects from the panoply of acceptable "science"), especially when fortified with legislative intent to fund nothing but experimental and random assignment research and evaluation studies, creates a discourse that seeks to discipline, govern, and regulate (Bloch, 2004) the *practices* of research as well as the *practitioners* of research (Cannella & Lincoln, 2004a, 2004b; Lincoln & Cannella, 2004a, 2004b; Lincoln & Tierney, 2004). Such conservatism, especially when repeated and reinscribed in the practices of local institutional IRBs, disciplines scholars either by forcing them to use research designs that are inappropriate to the questions they raise (a matter of *fit;* see, for instance, Lincoln & Guba, 1985) or by subjecting them to multiple reviews in which they must define and redefine the nature of the "problems" proposed, often until the researchers simply give up and abandon those particular studies.

Methodological conservatism governs by prescribing a set of practices that are to be considered normative and standard, and relegating all others to subsidiary status, frequently with the threat of disapproval. Such conservatism also regulates by ensuring conformity to certain sets of practices and discouraging nonconformity by dismissing some forms of inquiry as "dangerous," "unscientific," or harmful to the institution. In one actual case of which I am personally aware, the chairman of the IRB made it quite clear, when challenged, that his first responsibility was to protect the institution from any untoward event. This is, of course, a complete perversion/inversion of what human subjects protection laws were created to do. Although the institution's reputation and integrity (as well as its standing with funding agencies) must be protected, the purposes of the IRB are to ensure freedom from harm for human subjects, to establish the likelihood of beneficence for a larger group (of similar research participants), and to ensure that subjects' consent to participate in the research is fully and authentically informed.

Meanwhile, some forms of dismissed or disapproved research might well be classified as "innovative . . . or novel nonvalidated practices" (Schaffner, 1997, p. 6) that have the potential to lead to new insights or theoretically advanced formulations, even by adherents of "gold standard" scientific method. The power of this methodologically conservative discourse to interrupt the pursuit of serious social insight cannot and should not be underestimated, for the discourse itself encodes a set of political assumptions regarding the nature of truth, the kinds of researchers who are able to deliver this "truth," and the kinds of findings that will be admitted into the policy arena. Conflicting, contradictory, and contested findings will not gain admission and will find few audiences. The emphasis on causal inference will short-circuit other forms of explanatory power and, consequently, lead to less, rather than more, deep understanding of social and educational microprocesses, especially the processes of oppression, injustice, economic and educational failure, and discrimination.

The "quick fix" focus on "what works," rather than on the patient and thorough work that leads to greater understanding of *what is at work,* will ultimately prove a chimera. "What works" is a mythical beast, and the search for this beast leads us farther and farther astray, away from research that addresses serious liberatory aims with a purpose-driven social science.

◙ Potential Constraints on Qualitative Research From Methodological Conservatism

That the rising chorus of opinions from experimentalists and methodological conservatives has led to serious constraints on counterdiscourses is not in doubt. The outcry from the research community has been strong and steady (Cannella & Lincoln, 2004a, 2004b; Lincoln & Cannella, 2004a, 2004b; see also two entire issues of *Qualitative Inquiry,* vol. 10, nos. 1 and 2, 2004, for commentary from many segments of the educational research community). The stakes are high, especially for qualitative researchers. Further, the amount of influence on IRBs of statements such as the NRC report is, at present, unknown. The largely conservative bent of many local IRBs, however, particularly in their mistrust of action research, participatory action research, and other "experience-near" projects, suggests that methodological conservatism will reestablish itself firmly on some campuses unless opponents undertake proactive educative intervention. Some of this reestablishment can already be seen in contextual constraints that are currently in operation, as I describe below.

Constraint 1: Oversight of graduate training. For example, whereas academics who teach statistical research methods are not constrained in how or what they teach, professors who teach qualitative research methods now must undergo full IRB review of their proposed courses, limit (probably correctly) the populations with which students may work, and submit extensive paperwork verifying the studies to be done, the studies completed, and the populations sought both before and after they teach the courses. The slightest error in protocol can now have the effect of preventing a required graduate-level research preparation course from being taught at all. This may have a somewhat chilling effect on the issues that students can raise in their research and on the kinds of discussions that normally take place in classrooms around problems that students face in the communities outside of academia. Two issues are at stake here. First is professors' ability to teach what they believe to be important and/or critical topic areas for students who will also join the academy. Second is the limitation placed on the nature of studies that students can do, for example, in schools, although a large number of students who go through education doctoral programs are likely to go back into schools, where they must conduct studies, assessments, testing, and other forms of research virtually on a daily basis. If they do not receive training in these arenas from teachers who are familiar with ethical and protocol issues, from whom will they receive appropriate socialization (Wolf, Croughan, & Lo, 2002)?

IRB approval processes now also act to limit the kinds of research, as well as the research methodologies, that students may employ in their doctoral dissertation work. The IRBs in some institutions often disapprove newer strategies such as action research, participatory action research, and research in, for example, a teacher's own district or school—even when such research is both desired and approved by the district-level IRB. In my own previous work, I have reported on a number of instances in which student work was turned down by campus-level IRBs even though the work was requested by school districts (Lincoln & Tierney, 2004).

Between federal imperatives for how research projects should be designed and IRB scrutiny and disapproval of nonconventional forms of inquiry, qualitative research is undergoing radical challenge. The stark politicization of research and its methods no doubt poses the gravest threat to qualitative researchers that has been seen in the past half century.

Concerned researchers can use several strategies to counter this problem. First, they must be active with their own institutional IRBs, whether by communicating with the boards on a regular basis or by agreeing to serve on them (Cannella, 2004), as some of my colleagues have done. Nothing appears to work so well as serving an educative function, not only to students but to colleagues as well. Those of us on campuses with large hard science, engineering, and agriculture complexes frequently find that IRBs are dominated by members from these units, most of whom know little about social scientific methods, processes, and questions, or about emerging paradigms in the social sciences. Efforts to enhance board members' awareness of competing paradigms for scientific inquiry are virtually always rewarded with increased sophistication. Active members who provide other members with opportunities to learn about alternative epistemologies, research methods, special problems in international research, and research with indigenous peoples (e.g., the American Anthropological Association has created a stunning database of thoughtful pieces on ethics in work with indigenous peoples) create IRBs that are educated about and responsive to multiple frameworks and multiple methods.

Constraint 2: Improper review of faculty research. Just as IRBs sometimes improperly review the proposals of students who wish to undertake research utilizing newer and more participatory methodologies—that is, the IRBs conduct their reviews with inappropriate criteria in mind—faculty research is likewise in jeopardy from IRB members who lack the training or sophistication to make appropriate scientific judgments. An underlying principle of academic freedom is that, in conducting research wherever they believe the critical questions lie, faculty will exercise care, thought, and due diligence in selecting the research models and methodologies they believe will best answer the critical questions. IRBs, however, sometimes dictate other research strategies that the researchers who are proposing the work believe to be inadequate or inappropriate. This happened prior to the publication of the NRC report, and there is some danger that it will happen with more frequency now that the NRC has created a discourse that serves to regulate and govern what is deemed "scientific" and what is not.

A critical principle of academic freedom is at stake in this discourse. If academics are no longer quite as free to utilize the models and methodologies they believe to be the most efficacious for answering critical social science questions, then a portion of the principle of academic freedom has been compromised. Vigilance on the part of concerned researchers, as well as some empirical studies examining which research projects are approved and which denied by IRBs from campus to campus, is necessary to determine whether this aspect of academic freedom is at risk and, if so, to what extent.

Constraint 3: Threats to institutional autonomy. The extent to which the NRC report will influence local IRBs is currently unknown and theoretically unknowable. Certainly, criticism of the report, which has issued from many quarters, is not likely to be dampened over time, especially as individual researchers see their options for conducting research and acquiring external funding limited by both the report and the No Child Left Behind legislation. It seems likely that on some campuses, IRBs will use the NRC report to support the kinds of decisions they have made all along—that is, to deny project approval for research that does not fit with experimental, quasi-experimental, or other conventional models.

The NRC report has the potential to politicize the IRB review process further if concerned researchers do nothing. The discourse around "standards" for research obscures the ideological persuasions of conventional inquiry, shrouding ideology as it does in the language of objectivity, disinterest, rationality, and random assignment (Lincoln & Cannella, 2004b; Weinstein, 2004). This discourse confronts liberatory social science with the *j'accuse* of "advocacy," a tactic that effectively disguises the particular and pernicious advocacies embedded in terms such as *rationality* and *objectivity* and the standpoints of those who evoke rationality and/or objectivity.

Although it has long been assumed that IRBs are strictly, or at least primarily, local oversight groups, and therefore a part of the local decision making that accrues to institutions as loci of knowledge creation, the NRC report jeopardizes that traditional institutional autonomy by "disciplining" (in a Foucauldian sense) what constitutes acceptable research and, therefore, who has the right to practice it. Consequently, whether they believe it is necessary now or not, institutions should give some thought to resisting the National Research Council's role in dictating research methodologies to those responsible for creating knowledge. At a minimum, institutions should be protesting as well as lobbying against the particularly narrow provisions of the No Child Left Behind Act, which prevents the use of federal funds for research that falls outside any but the most limiting criteria for inquiry.

To the extent that IRBs themselves resist the NRC's intellectually limited definition of scientific inquiry, institutions will have leverage in the fight to protect institutional autonomy. To the extent that IRBs are "captured" by this pinched and illiberal discursive strategy, institutions will have lost ground in the battle for autonomy and self-determination. Indeed, as Neave (1996) observes, there is "a growing chorus amongst political parties, anxious to rally a skeptical electorate to their flagging programmes, which holds academic freedom and institutional autonomy as examples of unjustified privilege wielded by the 'producers', i.e., by the academic estate" (p. 263). This description most assuredly fits with current neoconservative efforts to "tame liberal faculties" and rein in their presumed power. If institutions permit this to happen, they will surrender all pretense of intellectual freedom for faculty (Verbitskaya, 1996).

Constraint 4: Inappropriate decision making in the weighing of risks and benefits. One direct role of IRBs has always been, under current legislation, to weigh the risks and benefits of proposed research. Any risk to human research participants has to be outweighed, or at least counterbalanced, by potential benefits, not only to participants but also to a number of assumed and projected audiences (Amdur & Bankert, 1997; Howe & Dougherty, 1993; Oakes, 2002; Olivier, 2002; Pritchard, 2002; Wagner, 2003; Weijer, 1999). As noted above, in one case I have reported on previously, a professor who spoke with his institutional IRB on behalf of a student's dissertation research was told in no uncertain terms that the IRB sought to "protect" the institution before it protected the human participants who were supposedly at risk (Lincoln & Tierney, 2004). Nor were the board members ashamed or in any way embarrassed by this admission. Although it is surely the case that IRBs protect institutions (from lawsuits, from researchers who conduct haphazard or sloppy or unethical research)—and should do so—protection of the institution is assumed to be a *by-product* of the oversight and review process, not a primary goal. The weighing of risks and benefits is presumed to be directed toward research subjects and scientific findings. The intent of the law, one presumes, is to protect human subjects through this risk assessment process, not to ensure that the university's general counsel has a nice day.

Institutions can use several strategies to counter this kind of misguided decision making on the part of IRBs. Clear guidance for IRB members regarding the law and their roles in the review process from superordinate supervisors who are themselves well versed in the legal ramifications of research activities will help. Periodic training for board members—perhaps each time one group exits IRB service and another group enters—can counter the kind of groupthink that may lead them to believe their role is to act solely on behalf of the institution. Continuing education, perhaps in the form of workshops each semester, can help to keep IRB members informed of their proper roles. Institutions can also help to prevent IRBs from tilting in favor of institutional protectionism rather than human subject protection by assuring that IRB membership includes balanced numbers of representatives from the hard sciences, the social sciences, the humanities, and medical research units.

The Challenges of Qualitative Research to Ethics Regulations

At this moment in history, a concatenation of forces led by the "conservative cultural logics of neo-liberalism" (Denzin & Lincoln, in press) seeks to shape a definition of inquiry that precludes multiple paradigms, epistemologies, and theoretical perspectives from the policy arena. The constraints on qualitative scholars take several forms: constraints on what they may teach and on what classroom activities require IRB review, constraints on the kinds of research they may conduct, constraints on institutional autonomy, and constraints related to IRBs' weighing of risks and benefits, as concerns about protecting human subjects are subordinated to concerns about avoiding legal actions against the institution. These constraints on methodology are interactive, and all coalesce in a context in which federal initiatives aimed at regulating, governing, and/or disciplining the discourse around "what works" and definitions of "evidence" and "scientific inquiry" constitute genuine threats to academic freedom, to continued federal funding for research, to free and open inquiry, and to individual researcher integrity in determining best practices for pursuing research questions.

More important, these conservative discourses act to stamp out inquiry—particularly, but not exclusively, qualitative inquiry—aimed at democratic action and liberatory, antioppressive, social justice–oriented aims. They also act to silence voices that have only in the past quarter century begun to be heard in any great numbers—voices of the poor, of the members of underrepresented groups, of the disabled, the oppressed, and postcolonial peoples, among others. For conspiracy theorists, it is no large leap to see a connection between the rise of nonmajority scholarship and the current conservative backlash. Faludi (1991) has carefully explicated the backlash that women experienced when their gains in the job market and legal arenas threatened the status quo. The so-called culture wars, led by Lynne Cheney and members of the National Association of Scholars, among others, represents a backlash against challenges to the Eurocentric knowledge of the Western canon (D'Souza, 1991; Graff, 1992) and efforts to expand awareness of non-Western literatures and philosophies on campuses around the nation as a consequence of rapid globalization. Yet another backlash is currently taking place against the rights achieved by nonheterosexual individuals, as illustrated by the drive to "protect marriage" that has led to a proposal to amend the U.S. Constitution. In light of the startling gains in visibility and stature of alternative paradigm practices and practitioners in the past decade, it should neither surprise nor shock anyone that a backlash is taking place against qualitative and other alternative methodologies and epistemologies.

The current challenge for qualitative researchers is to work toward legal and policy changes that reflect the reconfigured relationships of qualitative research. These new relationships are cooperative, mutual, democratic, open-ended, communitarian. They are highly incompatible with the asymmetrical power, informed consent, risk-beneficence model of research ethics currently in force. Participatory, social justice–oriented social science demands a research ethics attuned to the postmodern, postfoundational, postcolonial, and globalized inquiry environment of alternative paradigms.

As the ground rules for trade, economics, diplomacy, and education shift, so should the ground rules for conducting research. As we move toward a postcolonial, globalized, "McDonaldized" (Ritzer, 1996), homogenized, corporatized world order, there is some danger that, for the purposes of rationalization and in the name of modernity, legislation regarding research ethics will become frozen where it now stands. The system that exists now in the United States, which is highly appropriate for the decade in which it was forged, was outgrown and inadequate once phenomenological philosophies began to permeate the inquiry environment and once qualitative researchers realized they were dealing with far more than a shift to a separate set of methods (Lincoln & Guba, 1989). Reformulated relationships between researcher and researched, the potential for trading and sharing roles between them, and the mandate to exercise moral discretion regarding the purposes and representations of social inquiry (Fine, Weis, Weseen, & Wong, 2000) re-created research in the image of democracy, care/caring, and social justice.

Clearly, the current system is not attuned to the needs, purposes, concerns, or relationships now being generated by postmodern and poststructural critical inquiry of a variety of paradigms, perspectives, and models. It seems unlikely, even with the reassertion of a modernist stance on the part of the National Research Council, that participatory, antihegemonic inquiry will quietly go away. Its practitioners and theoreticians deeply intuit the communitarian qualities of such inquiry, and, having switched epistemological communities from the academy to the communities they see themselves as serving, they will not readily readopt outmoded standards for research ethics.

The axiological challenge for this new epistemological community will be to find the means not only to influence their own IRBs (for instance, on how to present arguments to one's own IRB, see Cheek, Chapter 15, this volume) but also to effect a shift in legislation, policy, and legislative intent. That will be no easy task. It will require activism of a different sort: not in the field, but rather in the halls of power. In the current neoliberal pinched and conservative environment, it seems nearly impossible to begin such a conversation. Nevertheless, qualitative researchers must undertake it, because, as always—whether in technology, science, or social science—practice has far outstripped policy and civic dialogue. Concerned scholars are likely to find that thoughtful analysis of the issues, careful strategizing, and thinking globally while acting locally are the best strategies for countering these narrow, illiberal discourses. And local IRBs are good places to begin a mutually educative and liberalizing process.

Note

1. By *rereviews,* I mean multiple reviews that are conducted as the result of an IRB's denial of permission to conduct proposed research because of what the IRB believes to be inappropriate methodology. In such a case, the IRB tells the researcher to provide "additional clarification," which may range from primarily trivial changes to major revisions in the research plans.

References

Akker, J. (2002). Protecting academic freedom worldwide. *Academe, 88*(3), 44–45.

Amdur, R. J., & Bankert, E. (1997). Continuing IRB review when research activity is limited to routine follow-up evaluations. *IRB: Ethics and Human Research, 19*(1), 7–11.

American Association of University Professors. (2001). Protecting human beings: Institutional review boards and social science research. *Academe, 87*(3), 55–67.

Baez, B., & Slaughter, S. (2001). Academic freedom and the federal courts in the 1990s: The legitimation of the conservative entrepreneurial state. In J. C Smart (Ed.), *Higher education: Handbook of theory and research* (Vol. 16, pp. 73–118). New York: Agathon.

Bauer, P. E. (2001). A few simple truths about your community IRB members. *IRB: Ethics and Human Research, 23*(1), 7–8.

Benjamin, E., Kurland, J. E., & Molotsky, I. F. (1985). On "accuracy in academia" and academic freedom. *Academe, 71*(5), 4.

Bloch, M. (2004). A discourse that disciplines, governs, and regulates: The National Research Council's report on scientific research in education. *Qualitative Inquiry, 10*(1), 96–110.

Burris, V., & Diamond, S. (1991). Academic freedom, conspicuous benevolence and the National Association of Scholars. *Critical Sociology, 18*(3), 125–142.

Cannella, G. S. (2004). Regulatory power: Can a feminist poststructuralist engage in research oversight? *Qualitative Inquiry, 10,* 235–245.

Cannella, G. S., & Lincoln, Y. S. (2004a). Dangerous discourses II: Comprehending and countering the redeployment of discourses (and resources) in the generation of liberatory inquiry. *Qualitative Inquiry, 10,* 165–174.

Cannella, G. S., & Lincoln, Y. S. (2004b). Epilogue: Claiming a critical public social science—reconceptualizing and redeploying research. *Qualitative Inquiry, 10,* 298–309.

Collins, P. H. (2000). *Black feminist thought: Knowledge, consciousness, and the politics of empowerment* (2nd ed.). New York: Routledge.

Cook, T. D., & Payne, M. R. (2002). Objecting to the objections to using random assignment in educational research. In F. Mosteller & R. Boruch (Eds.), *Evidence matters: Randomized trials in education research* (pp. 150–178). Washington, DC: Brookings Institution Press.

Cowen, R. C. (1995, June 20). Scientists rally to quell anti-science political movements. *Christian Science Monitor,* p. 13.

Cronbach, L. J., & Suppes, P. (1969). *Research for tomorrow's schools: Disciplined inquiry in education.* New York: Macmillan.

Denzin, N. K., & Lincoln, Y. S. (in press). Preface. In Y. S. Lincoln & N. K. Denzin (Eds.), *IRBs and qualitative research.* Walnut Creek, CA: AltaMira.

Devine, P. E. (1996). Academic freedom in the postmodern world. *Public Affairs Quarterly, 10,* 185–201.

Diamond, S. (1991, February). Readin', writin', and repressin'. *Z Magazine, 4,* 44–48.

D'Souza, D. (1991). *Illiberal education: The politics of race and sex on campus.* New York: Free Press.

DuBois, J. M. (2002). When is informed consent appropriate in educational research? Regulatory and ethical issues. *IRB: Ethics and Human Research, 24*(1), 1–8.

Faludi, S. (1991). *Backlash: The undeclared war against American women.* New York: Crown.

Fine, M., Weis, L., Weseen, S., & Wong, L. (2000). For whom? Qualitative research, representations, and social responsibilities. In N. K. Denzin & Y. S. Lincoln (Eds.), *Handbook of qualitative research* (2nd ed., pp. 107–131). Thousand Oaks, CA: Sage.

Giddens, A. (1990). *The consequences of modernity.* Stanford, CA: Stanford University Press.

Gillespie, J. F. (1997, August). *Institutional review boards and university student research learning opportunities.* Paper presented at the 105th Annual Meeting of the American Psychological Association, Chicago.

Giroux, H. A. (1995). Teaching in the age of "political correctness." *Educational Forum, 50*(2), 130–139.

Gordon, V. M., Sugarman, J., & Kass, N. (1998). Toward a more comprehensive approach to protecting human subjects. *IRB: Ethics and Human Research, 20*(1), 1–5.

Graff, G. (1992). *Beyond the culture wars: How teaching the conflicts can revitalize American education.* New York: W. W. Norton.

Gray, B. H. (1978, May). *Institutional review boards as an instrument of assessment: Research involving human subjects.* Paper presented at the U.S. Conference on the Social Assessment of Science, University of Bielefeld, West Germany.

Guba, E. G., & Lincoln, Y. S. (1994). Competing paradigms in qualitative research. In N. K. Denzin & Y. S. Lincoln (Eds.), *Handbook of qualitative research* (pp. 105–117). Thousand Oaks, CA: Sage.

Hammack, F. M. (1997). Ethical issues in teacher research. *Teachers College Record, 99,* 247–265.

Hecht, J. B. (1995, October). *The institutional review board in social science research.* Paper presented at the annual meeting of the Mid-Western Educational Research Association, Chicago.

Howe, K. R. (2004). A critique of experimentalism. *Qualitative Inquiry, 10,* 42–61.

Howe, K. R., & Dougherty, K. C. (1993). Ethics, institutional review boards, and the changing face of educational research. *Educational Researcher, 22*(9), 16–21.

Lincoln, Y. S., & Cannella, G. S. (2004a). Dangerous discourses: Methodological conservatism and governmental regimes of truth. *Qualitative Inquiry, 10,* 5–14.

Lincoln, Y. S, & Cannella, G. S. (2004b). Qualitative research, power, and the radical Right. *Qualitative Inquiry, 10,* 175–201.

Lincoln, Y. S., & Denzin, N. K. (2000). The seventh moment: Out of the past. In N. K. Denzin & Y. S. Lincoln (Eds.), *Handbook of qualitative research* (2nd ed., pp. 1047–1065). Thousand Oaks, CA: Sage.

Lincoln, Y. S., & Guba, E. G. (1985). *Naturalistic inquiry.* Beverly Hills, CA: Sage.

Lincoln, Y. S., & Guba, E. G. (1989). Ethics: The failure of positivist science. *Review of Higher Education, 12,* 221–240.

Lincoln, Y. S., & Guba, E. G. (2000). Paradigmatic controversies, contradictions, and emerging confluences. In N. K. Denzin & Y. S. Lincoln (Eds.), *Handbook of qualitative research* (2nd ed., pp. 163–188). Thousand Oaks, CA: Sage.

Lincoln, Y. S., & Tierney, W. G. (2004). Qualitative research and institutional review boards. *Qualitative Inquiry, 10,* 219–234.

Mertens, D. M. (1998). *Research methods in education and psychology: Integrating diversity with quantitative and qualitative approaches.* Thousand Oaks, CA: Sage.

Messer-Davidow, E. (1993, Autumn). Manufacturing the attack on liberalized higher education. *Social Text, 36,* 40–80.

Mosteller, F., & Boruch, R. (Eds.). (2002). *Evidence matters: Randomized trials in education research.* Washington, DC: Brookings Institution Press.

National Research Council. (2002). *Scientific research in education.* Committee on Scientific Principles for Education Research (R. J. Shavelson & L. Towne, Eds.). Center for Education, Division of Behavioral and Social Sciences and Education. Washington, DC: National Academy Press.

Neave, G. (1996). Academic freedom and university autonomy: An abiding concern. *Higher Education Policy, 9,* 263–266.

Oakes, J. M. (2002). Risks and wrongs in social science research: An evaluator's guide to the IRB. *Evaluation Review, 26,* 443–479.

Olivier, S. (2002). Ethics review of research projects involving human subjects. *Quest, 54,* 196–204.

Parenti, M. (1995). The myth of the liberal campus. *Humanist, 55*(5), 20–24.

Popkewitz, T. S. (2004). Is the National Research Council committee's report on scientific research in education scientific? On trusting the manifesto. *Qualitative Inquiry, 10,* 62–78.

Pressley, M., Duke, N. K., & Boling, E. C. (2004). The educational science and scientifically based instruction we need: Lessons from reading research and policymaking. *Harvard Educational Review, 74,* 30–61.

Pritchard, I. A. (2002). Travelers and trolls: Practitioner research and institutional review boards. *Educational Researcher, 31*(3), 3–13.

Reinharz, S. (1992). *Feminist methods in social research.* New York: Oxford University Press.

Ritzer, G. (1996). *The McDonaldization of society* (Rev. ed.). Thousand Oaks, CA: Pine Forge.

Sandoval, C. (2000). *Methodology of the oppressed.* Minneapolis: University of Minnesota Press.

Schaffner, K. F. (1997). Ethical considerations in human investigation involving paradigm shifts: Organ transplantation in the 1990s. *IRB: Ethics and Human Research, 19*(6), 5–11.

Smith, L. T. (1999). *Decolonizing methodologies: Research and indigenous peoples.* Dunedin, New Zealand: University of Otago Press.

Stanfield, J. H., II, & Dennis, R. M. (Eds.). (1993). *Race and ethnicity in research methods.* Newbury Park, CA: Sage.

Teller, E. (1988). Freedom of speech and advocacy in academia: The debate on "Star Wars." In L. Csorba III (Ed.), *Academic license: The war on academic freedom* (pp. 123–129). Evanston, IL: UCA.

Trow, M. (1985, September-October). The threat from within: Academic freedom and negative evidence. *Change, 17,* 8–9, 61–64.

Verbitskaya, L. A. (1996). Academic freedom and university autonomy: A variety of concepts. *Higher Education Policy, 9,* 289–294.

Wagner, R. M. (2003). Ethical review of research involving human subjects: When and why is IRB review necessary? *Muscle & Nerve, 28,* 27–39.

Weijer, C. (1999). Thinking clearly about research risk: Implications of the work of Benjamin Freedman. *IRB: Ethics and Human Research, 21*(6), 1–5.

Weinstein, M. (2004). Randomized design and the myth of certain knowledge: Guinea pig narratives and cultural critique. *Qualitative Inquiry, 10,* 246–260.

Wolf, L. W., Croughan, M., & Lo, B. (2002). The challenges of IRB review and human subjects protections in practice-based research. *Medical Care, 40,* 521–529.

Additional Resources

Hammerschmidt, D. E. (1997). "There is no substantive due process right to conduct human-subjects research": The saga of the Minnesota gamma hydroxybutyrate study. *IRB: Ethics and Human Research, 19*(3–4), 13–15.

Huer, J. (1991). *Tenure for Socrates: A study in the betrayal of the American professor.* New York: Bergin & Garvey.

Pinsker, S. (1998, August 20). Politicized academia? *Christian Science Monitor,* p. 11.

Rabban, D. M. (2001). Academic freedom, individual or institutional? *Academe, 87*(6), 16–20.

Rajagopal, B. (2003). Academic freedom as a human right: An internationalist perspective. *Academe, 89*(3), 25–28.

Reilly, P. K. (2001). Been there; done that (we've been there; they've done that). *IRB: Ethics and Human Research, 23*(1), 8–9.

Russell, C. (1993). *Academic freedom.* London: Routledge.

University of Illinois at Chicago Research Ethics Study Group. (2002). "Doing it right—together": Study groups and research agendas. *IRB: Ethics and Human Research, 24*(1), 9–10.

Part II

PARADIGMS AND PERSPECTIVES IN CONTENTION

In our introductory chapter, following Guba (1990, p. 17), we defined a paradigm as a basic set of beliefs that guide action. Paradigms deal with first principles, or ultimates. They are human constructions. They define the worldview of the researcher-as-interpretive-bricoleur. These beliefs can never be established in terms of their ultimate truthfulness. Perspectives, in contrast, are not as solidified, nor as well unified, as paradigms, although a perspective may share many elements with a paradigm—for example, a common set of methodological assumptions or a particular epistemology.

A paradigm encompasses four terms: ethics (axiology), epistemology, ontology, and methodology. *Ethics* asks, "How will I be as a moral person in the world?" *Epistemology* asks "How do I know the world?" "What is the relationship between the inquirer and the known?" Every epistemology, as Christians (Chapter 6, this volume) indicates, implies an ethical-moral stance toward the world and the self of the researcher. *Ontology* raises basic questions about the nature of reality and the nature of the human being in the world. *Methodology* focuses on the best means for acquiring knowledge about the world.

Part II of the *Handbook* examines the major paradigms and perspectives that now structure and organize qualitative research. These paradigms and perspectives are positivism, postpositivism, constructivism, and participatory action frameworks. Alongside these paradigms are the perspectives of feminism (in its multiple forms), critical race theory, queer theory, and cultural studies. Each of these perspectives has developed its own criteria, assumptions, and methodological practices. These practices are then applied to disciplined inquiry within that framework. (Tables 6.1 and 6.2 in Lincoln and Guba [2000, pp. 165–166] outline the major differences between the positivist, postpositivist, critical theory, constructivist, and participatory paradigms.)

We have provided a brief discussion of each paradigm and perspective in Chapter 1; here we elaborate them in somewhat more detail. However, before turning to this discussion, it is important to note three interconnected events. Within the last decade, the borders and boundary lines between these paradigms and perspectives have begun to blur. As Lincoln and Guba observe, the "pedigrees" of various paradigms are themselves beginning to "interbreed." However, though the borders have blurred, perceptions of differences between perspectives have hardened. Even as this occurs, the discourses of methodological conservatism, discussed in our Preface and in Chapter 1, threaten to narrow the range and effectiveness of qualitative research practices. Hence, the title of this section, "Paradigms and Perspectives in Contention."

▣ Major Issues Confronting All Paradigms

Lincoln and Guba (2000) suggest that in the present moment, all paradigms must confront seven basic, critical issues. These issues involve axiology (ethics and values), accommodation and commensurability (can paradigms be fitted into one another?), action (what the researcher does in the world), control (who initiates inquiry, who asks questions), foundations of truth (foundationalism vs. anti- and nonfoundationalism), validity (traditional positivist models vs. poststructural-constructionist criteria), and voice, reflexivity, and postmodern representation (single- vs. multivoiced).

Each paradigm takes a different stance on these topics. Of course, the *positivist* and *postpositivist* paradigms provide the backdrop against which these other paradigms and perspectives operate. Lincoln and Guba analyze these two traditions in considerable detail, including their reliance on naïve realism; their dualistic epistemologies; their verificational approach to inquiry; and their emphasis on reliability, validity, prediction, control, and a building block approach to knowledge. Lincoln and Guba discuss the inability of these paradigms to address adequately issues surrounding voice, empowerment, and praxis. They also allude to the failure to satisfactorily address the theory- and value-laden nature of facts, the interactive nature of inquiry, and the fact that the same set of "facts" can support more than one theory.

Constructivism, Interpretivism, and Hermeneutics

According to Lincoln and Guba, *constructivism* adopts a relativist ontology (relativism), a transactional epistemology, and a hermeneutic, dialectical methodology. Users of this paradigm are oriented to the production of reconstructed understandings of the social world. The traditional positivist criteria of internal and external validity are replaced by such terms as *trustworthiness* and *authenticity*. Constructivists value transactional knowledge. Their work overlaps with the several different participatory action approaches discussed by Kemmis and McTaggart (Chapter 23, this volume). Constructivism connects action to praxis and builds on antifoundational arguments while encouraging experimental and multivoiced texts.

▣ Critical Ethnography

Douglas Foley and Angela Valenzuela (Chapter 9, this volume) offer a history and analysis of critical ethnography, giving special attention to critical ethnographers who do applied policy studies and also involve themselves in political movements. They observe that post-1960s critical ethnographers began advocating cultural critiques of modern society. These scholars revolted against positivism and sought to pursue a politically progressive agenda using multiple standpoint epistemologies. Various approaches were taken up in this time period, including action anthropology; global, neo-Marxist, Marxist feminist, and critical ethnography; and participatory action research.

Their chapter presents two case studies, Foley's career as doing activist anthropology, including his involvement in the Chicano civil rights movement, and Valenzuela's activities as an activist sociologist working on educational policy studies within the Latina/o activist community in Texas. Foley experimented with an evolving research methodology involving collaborative relationships, dialogic interviewing, community review of what was written, and the use of an engaging narrative style. Valenzuela was involved directly in everyday struggles of Chicana/o legislators to craft new legislation, including calling for more humanizing assessment measures. She was both researcher and advocate.

In reflexively exploring their own careers as critical ethnographers, Foley and Valenzuela illustrate different forms of collaboration and different forms of activism. Foley joined the ideological struggle against scientism. Valenzuela formed a passionate moral bond with her ethnic group. She collaborated with her subjects in a deep psychological and political way. Both authors conclude that critical ethnography will truly serve the public only when the academy has been transformed, which would involve, Smith (Chapter 4, this volume) and Bishop (Chapter 5, this volume) remind us, embracing the complex process of decolonization.

The Feminisms

Virginia Olesen (Chapter 10, this volume) observes that feminist qualitative research, at the dawn of this new century, is a highly diversified and contested site. Already we see multiple articulations of gender, as well as its enactment in post-9/11 spaces. Competing models, on a global scale, blur together. But beneath the fray and the debate, there is agreement that feminist inquiry in the new millennium is committed to action in the world. Feminists insist that a social justice agenda address the needs of men and women of color, because gender, class, and race are intimately interconnected. Olesen's is an impassioned feminism. "Rage is not enough," she exclaims. We need "incisive scholarship to frame, direct, and harness passion in the interests of redressing grievous problems in the many areas of women's health" (p. 236).

In 1994, Olesen identified three major strands of feminist inquiry (standpoint epistemology, empiricist, postmodernism-cultural studies). A decade later, these strands continue to multiply. There are today separate feminisms associated with specific disciplines; with the writings of women of color; women problematizing Whiteness; postcolonial discourse; decolonizing arguments of indigenous women; lesbian research and queer theory; disabled women; standpoint theory; and postmodern and deconstructive theory. This complexity has made the researcher-participant relationship more complicated. It has destabilized the insider-outsider model of inquiry. Within indigenous spaces, it has produced a call for the decolonization of the academy. This is linked to a deconstruction of such traditional terms as experience, difference, and gender.

A gendered decolonizing discourse focuses on the concepts of bias and objectivity, validity and trustworthiness, voice, and feminist ethics. On this last point, Olesen's masterful chapter elaborates the frameworks presented by Smith (Chapter 4), Bishop (Chapter 5), and Christians (Chapter 6) presented in Part I.

Moral Activism and Critical Race Theory Scholarship

Gloria Ladson-Billings and Jamel Donnor (Chapter 11, this volume) move critical race theory directly into the fields of politics and qualitative inquiry. They advocate an activist, moral, and ethical epistemology committed to social justice and a revolutionary habitus. They focus their analysis on the meaning of the "call," an epiphanic moment when persons of color are reminded that they are locked into a hierarchical racial structure. The "N word" can be invoked at any time to hail a person of color. Racialized others occupy the liminal space of alterity in white society; they are forced to play the role of alter ego to the ideal self prescribed by the dominant cultural model. Critical race theory (CRT) "seeks to decloak the seemingly race-neutral, and color-blind ways . . . of constructing and administering race-based appraisals . . . of the law, administrative policy, electoral politics . . . political discourse [and education] in the USA" (Parker, Deyhle, Villenas, & Nebeker, 1998, p. 5). Critical race theory uses multiple interpretive methodologies—stories, plays, performances. Critical race theory enacts an ethnic and ethical epistemology, arguing that ways of knowing and being are shaped by one's standpoint, or position in the world. This standpoint undoes the cultural, ethical, and epistemological logic (and racism) of the Eurocentric, Enlightenment paradigm. At the same time, it contests positivism's hegemonic control over what is and what is not acceptable research. Thus do they criticize the National Research Council's report on Scientific Research in Education (Shavelson & Towne, 2003).

Drawing on recent work by African American, Asian Pacific Islander, Asian American, Latina/o, and Native American scholars, Ladson-Billings and Donnor introduce the concepts of multiple or double consciousness, mestiza consciousness, and tribal secrets. The analysis of these terms allows them to show how the dominant cultural paradigms have produced fractured, racialized identities and experiences of exclusion for minority scholars. American society, they observe, has been constructed as a nation of white people whose politics and culture are designed to serve the interests of whites. Critical race theorists experiment with multiple interpretive strategies, ranging from storytelling to autoethnography, case studies, textual and narrative analyses, traditional fieldwork, and, most important, collaborative, action-based inquiries and studies of race, gender, law, education, and racial oppression in daily life.

Using the construct of "political race," they call for street-level cross-racial coalitions and alliances involving grassroots workers seeking to invigorate democracy. Connections with the hip-hop generation are central to this project. Political race enlarges the critical race project. It is not color-blind. It proposes multitextured political strategies that go beyond traditional legal or economic solutions to issues of racial justice. Ladson-Billings and Donnor show, drawing from Patricia Hill Collins, how "political" race embodies a nonviolent visionary pragmatism that is "actualized in the hearts and minds of ordinary people" (p. 292). For this to happen, the academy must change; it must embrace the principles of decolonization outlined by Smith and Bishop. A reconstructed university will become a home for racialized others, a place where indigenous, liberating, empowering pedagogies have become commonplace. In such a place, Ladson-Billings and Donnor argue, a new version of the call will be answered.

Critical Theory

Multiple *critical theories*, among them *Marxist* and *neo-Marxist models*, now circulate within the discourses of qualitative research (see Kincheloe and McLaren, Chapter 12, this volume). In Lincoln and Guba's framework, this paradigm, in its many formulations, articulates an ontology based on historical realism, an epistemology that is transactional, and a methodology that is both dialogic and dialectical. Kincheloe and McLaren trace the history of critical research (and Marxist theory), from the Frankfurt School through more recent transformations in poststructural, postmodern, feminist, critical pedagogy, and cultural studies theory.

They outline a critical theory, what they call critical humility, an evolving criticality for the new millennium, beginning with the assumption that the societies of the West are not unproblematically democratic and free. Their version of critical theory rejects economic determinism and focuses on the media, culture, language, power, desire, critical enlightenment, and critical emancipation. Their framework embraces a critical hermeneutics. They read instrumental rationality as one of the most repressive features of contemporary society. Building on Dewey and Gramsci, they present a critical, pragmatic approach to texts and their relationships to lived experience. This leads to a "resistance" version of critical theory, a version connected to critical ethnography, and partisan, critical inquiry committed to social criticism. Critical theorists, as bricoleurs, seek to produce practical, pragmatic knowledge, a bricolage that is cultural and structural, judged by its degree of historical situatedness and its ability to produce praxis, or action.

This chapter, like Olesen's and Ladson-Billings and Donnor's, is a call to arms. Getting mad no longer is enough. We must learn how to act in the world in ways that allow us to expose the workings of an invisible empire that has given us yet another Gulf War and another economic agenda that leaves even more children behind.

Cultural Studies

Cultural studies cannot be contained within a single framework. There are multiple cultural studies projects, including those connected to the Birmingham school and to the work of Stuart Hall and his associates (see Hall, 1996). Cultural studies research is historically self-reflective, critical, interdisciplinary, conversant with high theory, and focused on the global and the local; it takes into account historical, political, economic, cultural, and everyday discourses. It focuses on questions of community, identity, agency, and change (Grossberg & Pollock, 1998).

In its generic form, cultural studies involves an examination of how the history people live is produced by structures that have been handed down from the past. Each version of cultural studies is joined by a threefold concern with cultural texts, lived experience, and the articulated relationship between texts and everyday life. Within the cultural text tradition, some scholars examine the mass media and popular culture as sites where history, ideology, and subjective experiences come together. These scholars produce critical ethnographies of the audience in relation to particular historical moments. Other scholars read texts as sites where hegemonic meanings are produced, distributed, and consumed. Within the ethnographic tradition, there is a postmodern concern for the social text and its production.

The open-ended nature of the cultural studies project leads to a perpetual resistance against attempts to impose a single definition over the entire project. There are critical-Marxist, constructionist, and postpositivist paradigmatic strands within the formation, as well as emergent feminist and ethnic models. Scholars within the cultural studies project are drawn to historical realism and relativism as their ontology, to transactional epistemologies, and to dialogic methodologies, while remaining committed to a historical and structural framework that is action oriented.

Paula Saukko (Chapter 13, this volume) outlines a critical materialist, hermeneutic, poststructural, contextualist cultural studies project. Drawing on her own research on testing for genetic thrombophilia, she outlines a methodological program in cultural studies that is defined by its interest in lived, discursive, and contextual dimensions of reality. Weaving back and forth between culturalist and realist agendas, she identifies three key methodological currents or strands in cultural studies today: hermeneutics, poststructuralism, and contextualism. She translates these three dimensions into three validities (contextual, dialogic, self-reflexive), focused, respectively, on historical reality, authenticity, and deconstruction. These strands yield critical analyses of postindustrialism, globalization, neoliberalism, postcolonialism, and the recent trend toward the corporatization of universities, a trend that threatens to erase cultural studies.

Contextualism and contextual validity move back and forth in time, from the particular and the situational to the general and the historical. It shows how each instance of a phenomenon is embedded in its historical space, a space marked by politics, culture, and biography. In moving back and forth in time, the researcher situates a subject's projects in time and space. Dialogic validity grounds interpretation in lived reality. Self-reflexive validity analyzes how social discourses shape or mediate experience.

Saukko's contextualism confronts the hard, lived local facts of life in a global economy. Discursively, her project shows how the real is mediated by systems of discourse, which are themselves embedded in socially mediated realities. Thus does she move back and forth between the local and the global, the cultural and the real, the personal and the political.

The disciplinary boundaries that define cultural studies keep shifting, and there is no agreed upon standard genealogy of its emergence as a serious academic discipline. Nonetheless, there are certain prevailing tendencies, including feminist understandings of the politics of the everyday and the personal; disputes between proponents of textualism, ethnography, and autoethnography; and continued debates surrounding the dreams of modern citizenship.

Critical Humanism and Queer Theory

Critical race theory brought race and the concept of a complex racial subject squarely into qualitative inquiry. It remained for queer theory to do the same; namely, to question and deconstruct the concept of a unified sexual (and racialized) subject. Ken Plummer (Chapter 14, this volume) takes queer theory in a new direction. He writes from his own biography as a postgay humanist, a sort of feminist, a little queer, a critical humanist who wants to move on. He thinks that in the postmodern moment certain terms, like *family*, and much of our research methodology language are obsolete. He calls them zombie categories. They are no longer needed. They are dead.

With the arrival of queer theory, the social sciences are in a new space. This is the age of postmodern fragmentation, globalization, posthumanism. This is a time for new research styles, styles that take up the reflexive queer, polyphonic, narrative, ethical turn. Plummer's critical humanism, with its emphasis on symbolic interactionism, pragmatism, democratic thinking, storytelling, moral progress, and social justice, enters this space. It is committed to reducing human suffering, to an ethics of care and compassion, a politics of respect, and the importance of trust.

His queer theory is radical. It encourages the postmodernization of sexual and gender studies. It deconstructs all conventional categories of sexuality and gender. It is transgressive, gothic, and romantic. It challenges the heterosexual/homosexual binary; the deviance paradigm is abandoned. His queer methodology takes the textual turn seriously and endorses subversive ethnographies, scavenger methodologies, ethnographic performances, and queered case studies.

By troubling the place of the homo/heterosexual binary in everyday life, queer theory has created spaces for multiple discourses on transgendered, bisexual, lesbian, and gay subjects. This means that researchers must examine how any social arena is structured, in part by this homo/hetero dichotomy. They must ask how the epistemology of the closet is central to the sexual and material practices of everyday life. Queer theory challenges this epistemology, just as it deconstructs the notion of unified subjects. Queerness becomes a topic and a resource for investigating the way group boundaries are created, negotiated, and changed. Institutional and historical analyses are central to this project, for they shed light on how the self and its identities are embedded in institutional and cultural practices.

In Conclusion

The researcher-as-interpretive-bricoleur cannot afford to be a stranger to any of the paradigms and perspectives discussed in Part II of the *Handbook*. The researcher must understand the basic ethical, ontological, epistemological, and methodological assumptions of each, and be able to engage them in dialogue. The differences between paradigms and perspectives have significant and important implications at the practical, material, everyday level. The blurring of paradigm differences is likely to continue as long as proponents continue to come together to discuss their differences while seeking to build on those areas where they are in agreement.

It is also clear that there is no single "truth." All truths are partial and incomplete. There will be no single conventional paradigm, as Lincoln and Guba (2000) argue, to which all social scientists might ascribe. We occupy a historical moment marked by multivocality, contested meanings, paradigmatic controversies, and new textual forms. This is an age of emancipation, freedom from the confines of a single regime of truth, emancipation from seeing the world in one color.

References

Grossberg, L., & Pollock, D. (1998). Editorial statement. *Cultural Studies, 12*(2), 114.

Guba, E. (1990). The alternative paradigm dialog. In E. Guba (Ed.), *The paradigm dialog* (pp. 17–30). Newbury Park, CA: Sage.

Hall, S. (1996). Gramsci's relevance for the study of race and ethnicity. In D. Morley & K.-H. Chen (Eds.), *Stuart Hall: Critical dialogues in cultural studies* (pp. 411–444). London: Routledge.

Lincoln, Y. S., & Guba, E. (2000). Paradigmatic controversies, contradictions, and emerging confluences. In N. K. Denzin & Y. S. Lincoln (Eds.), *Handbook of qualitative research* (2nd ed., pp. 163–188). Thousand Oaks, CA: Sage.

Olesen, V. (1994). Feminisms and models of qualitative research. In N. K. Denzin & Y. S. Lincoln (Eds.), *Handbook of qualitative research* (pp. 158-174). Thousand Oaks, CA: Sage.

Parker, L., Deyhle, D., Villenas, S., & Nebeker, K. C. (1998). Guest editor's introduction: Critical race theory and qualitative studies in education. *Qualitative Studies in Education, 11,* 5–6.

Shavelson, R., & Towne, L. (Eds.). (2003). *Scientific research in education.* Washington, DC: National Academies Press.

8

PARADIGMATIC CONTROVERSIES, CONTRADICTIONS, AND EMERGING CONFLUENCES

Egon G. Guba and Yvonna S. Lincoln

In our chapter for the first edition of the *Handbook of Qualitative Research,* we focused on the contention among various research paradigms for legitimacy and intellectual and paradigmatic hegemony (Guba & Lincoln, 1994). The postmodern paradigms that we discussed (postmodernist critical theory and constructivism)[1] were in contention with the received positivist and postpositivist paradigms for legitimacy, and with one another for intellectual legitimacy. In the more than 10 years that have elapsed since that chapter was published, substantial changes have occurred in the landscape of social scientific inquiry.

On the matter of legitimacy, we observe that readers familiar with the literature on methods and paradigms reflect a high interest in ontologies and epistemologies that differ sharply from those undergirding conventional social science. Second, even those established professionals trained in quantitative social science (including the two of us) want to learn more about qualitative approaches, because new young professionals being mentored in graduate schools are asking serious questions about and looking for guidance in qualitatively oriented studies and dissertations. Third, the number of qualitative texts, research papers, workshops, and training materials has exploded. Indeed, it would be difficult to miss the distinct turn of the social sciences toward more interpretive, postmodern, and criticalist practices and theorizing (Bloland, 1989, 1995). This nonpositivist orientation has created a context (surround) in which virtually no study can go unchallenged by proponents of contending paradigms. Further, it is obvious that the number of practitioners of new-paradigm inquiry is growing daily. There can be no question that the legitimacy of postmodern paradigms is well established and at least equal to the legitimacy of received and conventional paradigms (Denzin & Lincoln, 1994).

On the matter of hegemony, or supremacy, among postmodern paradigms, it is clear that Geertz's (1988, 1993) prophecy about the "blurring of genres" is rapidly being fulfilled. Inquiry methodology can no longer be treated as a set of universally applicable rules or abstractions. Methodology is inevitably interwoven with and emerges from the nature of particular disciplines (such as sociology and psychology) and particular perspectives (such as Marxism, feminist theory, and queer theory). So, for instance, we can read feminist critical theorists such as Olesen (2000) or queer theorists such as Gamson (2000), or we can follow arguments about teachers as researchers (Kincheloe, 1991) while we understand the secondary text to be teacher empowerment and democratization of schooling practices. Indeed, the various paradigms are beginning to "interbreed" such that two theorists previously thought to be in irreconcilable conflict may now appear, under a different theoretical rubric, to be informing one another's arguments. A personal example is our own work, which has been heavily influenced by action research practitioners and postmodern critical theorists. Consequently, to argue that it is paradigms that are in contention is probably less useful than to probe where and how paradigms exhibit confluence and where and how they exhibit differences, controversies, and contradictions.

▣ Major Issues Confronting All Paradigms

In our chapter in the first edition of this *Handbook,* we presented two tables that summarized our positions, first, on the axiomatic nature of paradigms (the paradigms we considered at that time were positivism, postpositivism, critical theory, and constructivism; Guba & Lincoln, 1994, p. 109, Table 6.1); and second, on the issues we believed were most fundamental to differentiating the four paradigms (p. 112, Table 6.2). These tables are reproduced here as a way of reminding our readers of our previous statements. The axioms defined the ontological, epistemological, and methodological bases for both established and emergent paradigms; these are shown here in Table 8.1. The issues most often in contention that we examined were inquiry aim, nature of knowledge, the way knowledge is accumulated, goodness (rigor and validity) or quality criteria, values, ethics, voice, training, accommodation, and hegemony; these are shown in Table 8.2. An examination of these two tables will reacquaint the reader with our original *Handbook* treatment; more detailed information is, of course, available in our original chapter.

Since publication of that chapter, at least one set of authors, John Heron and Peter Reason, have elaborated on our tables to include the *participatory/cooperative* paradigm (Heron, 1996; Heron & Reason, 1997, pp. 289–290). Thus, in addition to the paradigms of positivism, postpositivism, critical theory, and constructivism, we add the participatory paradigm in the present chapter (this is an excellent example, we might add, of the hermeneutic elaboration so embedded in our own view, constructivism).

Our aim here is to extend the analysis further by building on Heron and Reason's additions and by rearranging the issues to reflect current thought. The issues we have chosen include our original formulations and the additions, revisions, and amplifications made by Heron and Reason (1997), and we have also chosen what we believe to be the issues most important today. We should note that *important* means several things to us. An important topic may be one that is widely debated (or even hotly contested)—validity is one such issue. An important issue may be one that bespeaks a new awareness (an issue such as recognition of the role of values). An important issue may be one that illustrates the influence of one paradigm on another (such as the influence of feminist, action research, critical theory, and participatory models on researcher conceptions of action within and with the community in which research is carried out). Or issues may be important because new or extended theoretical and/or field-oriented treatments for them are newly available—voice and reflexivity are two such issues.

Table 8.3 reprises the original Table 6.1 but adds the axioms of the participatory paradigm proposed by Heron and Reason (1997). Table 8.4 deals with seven issues and represents an update of selected issues first presented in the old Table 6.2. "Voice" in the 1994 version of Table 6.2 has been renamed "inquirer posture," and we have inserted a redefined "voice" in the current

(text continues, p. 197)

Table 8.1. Basic Beliefs (Metaphysics) of Alternative Inquiry Paradigms

Item	*Positivism*	*Postpositivism*	*Critical Theory et al.*	*Constructivism*
Ontology	Naïve realism—"real" reality but apprehendible	Critical realism—"real" reality but only imperfectly and probabilistically apprehendible	Historical realism—virtual reality shaped by social, political, cultural, economic, ethnic, and gender values; crystallized over time	Relativism—local and specific constructed and co-constructed realities
Epistemology	Dualist/objectivist; findings true	Modified dualist/objectivist; critical tradition/community; findings probably true	Transactional/subjectivist; value-mediated findings	Transactional/subjectivist; created findings
Methodology	Experimental/manipulative; verification of hypotheses; chiefly quantitative methods	Modified experimental/manipulative; critical multiplism; falsification of hypotheses; may include qualitative methods	Dialogic/dialectical	Hermeneutical/dialectical

Table 8.2. Paradigm Positions on Selected Practical Issues

Item	*Positivism*	*Postpositivism*	*Critical Theory et al.*	*Constructivism*
Inquiry aim	Explanation: prediction and control		Critique and transformation; restitution and emancipation	Understanding; reconstruction
Nature of knowledge	Verified hypotheses established as facts or laws	Nonfalsified hypotheses that are probable facts or laws	Structural/historical insights	Individual or collective reconstructions coalescing around consensus
Knowledge accumulation	Accretion—"building blocks" adding to "edifice of knowledge"; generalizations and cause-effect linkages		Historical revisionism; generalization by similarity	More informed and sophisticated reconstructions; vicarious experience
Goodness or quality criteria	Conventional benchmarks of "rigor": internal and external validity, reliability, and objectivity		Historical situatedness; erosion of ignorance and misapprehension; action stimulus	Trustworthiness and authenticity, including catalyst for action
Values	Excluded—influence denied		Included—formative	Included—formative
Ethics	Extrinsic: tilt toward deception		Intrinsic: moral tilt toward revelation	Intrinsic: process tilt toward revelation; special problems
Voice	"Disinterested scientist" as informer of decision makers, policy makers, and change agents		"Transformative intellectual" as advocate and activist	"Passionate participant" as facilitator of multivoice reconstruction
Training	Technical and quantitative; substantive theories	Technical; quantitative and qualitative; substantive theories	Resocialization; qualitative and quantitative; history; values of altruism, empowerment, and liberation	
Accommodation	Commensurable		Incommensurable with previous two	
Hegemony	In control of publication, funding, promotion, and tenure		Seeking recognition and input; offering challenges to predecessor paradigms, aligned with postcolonial aspirations	

Table 8.3. Basic Beliefs of Alternative Inquiry Paradigms—Updated

Issue	*Positivism*	*Postpositivism*	*Critical Theory et al.*	*Constructivism*	*Participatory*[a]
Ontology	Naïve realism—"real" reality but apprehendible	Critical realism—"real" reality but only imperfectly and probabilistically apprehendible	Historical realism—virtual reality shaped by social, political, cultural, economic, ethnic, and gender values; crystallized over time	Relativism—local and specific co-constructed realities	Participative reality—subjective-objective reality, cocreated by mind and given cosmos
Epistemology	Dualist/objectivist; findings true	Modified dualist/objectivist; critical tradition/community; findings probably true	Transactional/ subjectivist; value-mediated findings	Transactional/ subjectivist; co-created findings	Critical subjectivity in participatory transaction with cosmos; extended epistemology of experiential, propositional, and practical knowing; cocreated findings
Methodology	Experimental/ manipulative; verification of hypotheses; chiefly quantitative methods	Modified experimental/ manipulative; critical multiplism; falsification of hypotheses; may include qualitative methods	Dialogic/dialectical	Hermeneutical/ dialectical	Political participation in collaborative action inquiry; primacy of the practical; use of language grounded in shared experiential context

a. Entries in this column are based on Heron and Reason (1997).

Table 8.4. Paradigm Positions on Selected Issues—Updated

Issue	*Positivism*	*Postpositivism*	*Critical Theories*	*Constructivism*	*Participatory*[a]
Nature of knowledge	Verified hypotheses established as facts or laws	Nonfalsified hypotheses that are probable facts or laws	Structural/ historical insights	Individual and collective reconstructions sometimes coalescing around consensus	Extended epistemology: primacy of practical knowing; critical subjectivity; living knowledge
Knowledge accumulation	Accretion—"building blocks" adding to "edifice of knowledge"; generalizations and cause-effect linkages		Historical revisionism; generalization by similarity	More informed and sophisticated reconstructions; vicarious experience	In communities of inquiry embedded in communities of practice
Goodness or quality criteria	Conventional benchmarks of "rigor": internal and external validity, reliability, and objectivity		Historical situatedness; erosion of ignorance and misapprehensions; action stimulus	Trustworthiness and authenticity including catalyst for action	Congruence of experiential, presentational, propositional, and practical knowing; leads to action to transform the world in the service of human flourishing
Values	Excluded—influence denied		Included—formative		
Ethics	Extrinsic—tilt toward deception		Intrinsic—moral tilt toward revelation	Intrinsic—process tilt toward revelation	
Inquirer posture	"Disinterested scientist" as informer of decision makers, policy makers, and change agents		"Transformative intellectual" as advocate and activist	"Passionate participant" as facilitator of multivoice reconstruction	Primary voice manifest through aware self-reflective action; secondary voices in illuminating theory, narrative, movement, song, dance, and other presentational forms
Training	Technical and quantitative; substantive theories	Technical; quantitative and qualitative; substantive theories	Resocialization; qualitative and quantitative; history; values of altruism, empowerment and liberation		Coresearchers are initiated into the inquiry process by facilitator/researcher and learn through active engagement in the process; facilitator/researcher requires emotional competence, democratic personality and skills

a. Entries in this column are based on Heron and Reason (1997), except for "ethics" and "values."

Table 8.5. In all cases except "inquirer posture," the entries for the participatory paradigm are those proposed by Heron and Reason; in the one case not covered by them, we have added a notation that we believe captures their intention.

We make no attempt here to reprise the material well discussed in our earlier *Handbook* chapter. Instead, we focus solely on the issues in Table 8.5: axiology; accommodation and commensurability; action; control; foundations of truth and knowledge; validity; and voice, reflexivity, and postmodern textual representation. We believe these seven issues to be the most important at this time.

While we believe these issues to be the most contentious, we also believe they create the intellectual, theoretical, and practical space for dialogue, consensus, and confluence to occur. There is great potential for interweaving of viewpoints, for the incorporation of multiple perspectives, and for borrowing, or *bricolage,* where borrowing seems useful, richness enhancing, or theoretically heuristic. For instance, even though we are ourselves social constructivists/constructionists, our call to action embedded in the authenticity criteria we elaborated in *Fourth Generation Evaluation* (Guba & Lincoln, 1989) reflects strongly the bent to action embodied in critical theorists' perspectives. And although Heron and Reason have elaborated a model they call the *cooperative paradigm,* careful reading of their proposal reveals a form of inquiry that is post-postpositive, postmodern, and criticalist in orientation. As a result, the reader familiar with several theoretical and paradigmatic strands of research will find that echoes of many streams of thought come together in the extended table. What this means is that the categories, as Laurel Richardson (personal communication, September 12, 1998) has pointed out, "are fluid, indeed what should be a category keeps altering, enlarging." She notes that "even as [we] write, the boundaries between the paradigms are shifting." This is the paradigmatic equivalent of the Geertzian "blurring of genres" to which we referred earlier.

Our own position is that of the constructionist camp, loosely defined. We do not believe that criteria for judging either "reality" or validity are absolutist (Bradley & Schaefer, 1998); rather, they are derived from community consensus regarding what is "real," what is useful, and what has meaning (especially meaning for action and further steps). We believe that a goodly portion of social phenomena consists of the meaning-making activities of groups and individuals around those phenomena. The meaning-making activities themselves are of central interest to social constructionists/constructivists, simply because it is the meaning-making/sense-making/attributional activities that shape action (or inaction). The meaning-making activities themselves can be changed when they are found to be incomplete, faulty (e.g., discriminatory, oppressive, or nonliberatory), or malformed (created from data that can be shown to be false).

We have tried, however, to incorporate perspectives from other major nonpositivist paradigms. This is not a complete summation; space constraints prevent that. What we hope to do in this chapter is to acquaint readers with the larger currents, arguments, dialogues, and provocative writings and theorizing, the better to see perhaps what we ourselves do not even yet see: where and when confluence is possible, where constructive rapprochement might be negotiated, where voices are beginning to achieve some harmony.

Axiology

Earlier, we placed values on the table as an "issue" on which positivists or phenomenologists might have a "posture" (Guba & Lincoln, 1989, 1994; Lincoln & Guba, 1985). Fortunately, we reserved for ourselves the right to either get smarter or just change our minds. We did both. Now, we suspect (although Table 8.5 does not yet reflect it) that "axiology" should be grouped with "basic beliefs." In *Naturalistic Inquiry* (Lincoln & Guba, 1985), we covered some of the ways in which values feed into the inquiry process: choice of the problem, choice of paradigm to guide the problem, choice of theoretical framework, choice of major data-gathering and data-analytic methods, choice of context, treatment of values already resident

Table 8.5. Critical Issues of the Time

Issue	*Positivism*	*Postpositivism*	*Critical Theory et al.*	*Constructivism*	*Participatory*
Axiology	Propositional knowing about the world is an end in itself, is intrinsically valuable.		Propositional, transactional knowing is instrumentally valuable as a means to social emancipation, which is an end in itself, is intrinsically valuable.		Practical knowing about how to flourish with a balance of autonomy, cooperation, and hierarchy in a culture is an end in itself, is intrinsically valuable.
Accommodation and commensurability	Commensurable for all positivist forms		Incommensurable with positivist forms; some commensurability with constructivist, criticalist, and participatory approaches, especially as they merge in liberationist approaches outside the West		
Action	Not the responsibility of the researcher; viewed as "advocacy" or subjectivity, and therefore a threat to validity and objectivity		Found especially in the form of empowerment; emancipation anticipated and hoped for; social transformation, particularly toward more equity and justice, is end goal	Intertwined with validity; inquiry often incomplete without action on the part of participants; constructivist formulation mandates training in political action if participants do not understand political systems	
Control	Resides solely in researcher		Often resides in "transformative intellectual"; in new constructions, control returns to community	Shared between inquirer and participants	Shared to varying degrees
Relationship to foundations of truth and knowledge	Foundational	Foundational	Foundational within social critique	Antifoundational	Nonfoundational

Issue	*Positivism*	*Postpositivism*	*Critical Theory et al.*	*Constructivism*	*Participatory*
Extended considerations of validity (goodness criteria)	Traditional positivist constructions of validity; rigor, internal validity, external validity, reliability, objectivity		Action stimulus (see above); social transformation, equity, social justice	Extended constructions of validity: (a) crystalline validity (Richardson); (b) authenticity criteria (Guba & Lincoln); (c) catalytic, rhizomatic, voluptuous validities (Lather); (d) relational and ethics-centered criteria (Lincoln); (e) community-centered determinations of validity	See "action" above
Voice, reflexivity, postmodern textual representations	Voice of the researcher, principally; reflexivity may be considered a problem in objectivity; textual representation unproblematic and somewhat formulaic		Voices mixed between researcher and participants	Voices mixed, with participants' voices sometimes dominant; reflexivity serious and problematic; textual representation an extended issue	Voices mixed; textual representation rarely discussed but problematic; reflexivity relies on critical subjectivity and self-awareness
			Textual representation practices may be problematic—i.e., "fiction formulas" or unexamined "regimes of truth"		

within the context, and choice of format(s) for presenting findings. We believed those were strong enough reasons to argue for the inclusion of values as a major point of departure between positivist, conventional modes of inquiry and interpretive forms of inquiry.

A second "reading" of the burgeoning literature and subsequent rethinking of our own rationale have led us to conclude that the issue is much larger than we first conceived. If we had it to do all over again, we would make values or, more correctly, axiology (the branch of philosophy dealing with ethics, aesthetics, and religion) a part of the basic foundational philosophical dimensions of paradigm proposal. Doing so would, in our opinion, begin to help us see the embeddedness of ethics within, not external to, paradigms (see, for instance, Christians, 2000) and would contribute to the consideration of and dialogue about the role of spirituality in human inquiry. Arguably, axiology has been "defined out of" scientific inquiry for no larger a reason than that it also concerns "religion." But defining "religion" broadly to encompass spirituality would move constructivists closer to participative inquirers and would move critical theorists closer to both (owing to their concern with liberation from oppression and freeing of the human spirit, both profoundly spiritual concerns). The expansion of basic issues to include axiology, then, is one way of achieving greater confluence among the various interpretivist inquiry models. This is the place, for example, where Peter Reason's profound concerns with "sacred science" and human functioning find legitimacy; it is a place where Laurel Richardson's "sacred spaces" become authoritative sites for human inquiry; it is a place—or *the* place—where the spiritual meets social inquiry, as Reason (1993), and later Lincoln and Denzin (1994), proposed some years earlier.

▣ Accommodation and Commensurability

Positivists and postpositivists alike still occasionally argue that paradigms are, in some ways, commensurable; that is, they can be retrofitted to each other in ways that make the simultaneous practice of both possible. We have argued that at the paradigmatic, or philosophical, level, commensurability between positivist and postpositivist worldviews is not possible, but that within each paradigm, mixed methodologies (strategies) may make perfectly good sense (Guba & Lincoln, 1981, 1982, 1989, 1994; Lincoln & Guba, 1985). So, for instance, in *Effective Evaluation* we argued:

> The guiding inquiry paradigm most appropriate to responsive evaluation is . . . the naturalistic, phenomenological, or ethnographic paradigm. It will be seen that qualitative techniques are typically most appropriate to support this approach. There are times, however, when the issues and concerns voiced by audiences require information that is best generated by more conventional methods, especially quantitative methods. . . . In such cases, the responsive conventional evaluator will not shrink from the appropriate application. (Guba & Lincoln, 1981, p. 36)

As we tried to make clear, the "argument" arising in the social sciences was *not about method*, although many critics of the new naturalistic, ethnographic, phenomenological, and/or case study approaches assumed it was.[2] As late as 1998, Weiss could be found to claim that "some evaluation theorists, notably Guba and Lincoln (1989), hold that it is impossible to combine qualitative and quantitative approaches responsibly within an evaluation" (p. 268), even though we stated early on in *Fourth Generation Evaluation* (1989) that

> those claims, concerns, and issues that have *not* been resolved become the advance organizers for information collection by the evaluator. . . . *The information may be quantitative or qualitative.* Responsive evaluation does not rule out quantitative modes, as is mistakenly believed by many, but deals with whatever information is responsive to the unresolved claim, concern, or issue. (p. 43)

We had also strongly asserted earlier, in *Naturalistic Inquiry* (1985), that

> qualitative methods are stressed within the naturalistic paradigm not because the paradigm is antiquantitative but because qualitative methods

> come more easily to the human-as-instrument. *The reader should particularly note the absence of an antiquantitative stance,* precisely because the naturalistic and conventional paradigms are so often—mistakenly—equated with the qualitative and quantitative paradigms, respectively. Indeed, *there are many opportunities for the naturalistic investigator to utilize quantitative data—probably more than are appreciated.* (pp. 198–199; emphasis added)

Having demonstrated that we were not then (and are not now) talking about an antiquantitative posture or the exclusivity of *methods,* but rather about the philosophies of which paradigms are constructed, we can ask the question again regarding commensurability: Are paradigms commensurable? Is it possible to blend elements of one paradigm into another, so that one is engaging in research that represents the best of both worldviews? The answer, from our perspective, has to be a cautious *yes.* This is especially so if the models (paradigms) share axiomatic elements that are similar, or that resonate strongly between them. So, for instance, *positivism* and *postpositivism* are clearly commensurable. In the same vein, elements of *interpretivist/postmodern* critical theory, constructivist and participative inquiry, fit comfortably together. Commensurability is an issue only when researchers want to "pick and choose" among the axioms of positivist and interpretivist models, because the axioms are contradictory and mutually exclusive.

▣ The Call to Action

One of the clearest ways in which the paradigmatic controversies can be demonstrated is to compare the positivist and postpositivist adherents, who view action as a form of contamination of research results and processes, and the interpretivists, who see action on research results as a meaningful and important outcome of inquiry processes. Positivist adherents believe action to be either a form of advocacy or a form of subjectivity, either or both of which undermine the aim of objectivity. Critical theorists, on the other hand, have always advocated varying degrees of social action, from the overturning of specific unjust practices to radical transformation of entire societies. The call for action—whether in terms of internal transformation, such as ridding oneself of false consciousness, or of external social transformation—differentiates between positivist and postmodern criticalist theorists (including feminist and queer theorists). The sharpest shift, however, has been in the constructivist and participatory phenomenological models, where a step beyond interpretation and *Verstehen,* or understanding, toward social action is probably one of the most conceptually interesting of the shifts (Lincoln, 1997, 1998a, 1998b). For some theorists, the shift toward action came in response to widespread nonutilization of evaluation findings and the desire to create forms of evaluation that would attract champions who might follow through on recommendations with meaningful action plans (Guba & Lincoln, 1981, 1989). For others, embracing action came as both a political and an ethical commitment (see, for instance, Carr & Kemmis, 1986; Christians, 2000; Greenwood & Levin, 2000; Schratz & Walker, 1995; Tierney, 2000).

Whatever the source of the problem to which inquirers were responding, the shift toward connecting research, policy analysis, evaluation, and/or social deconstruction (e.g., deconstruction of the patriarchal forms of oppression in social structures, which is the project informing much feminist theorizing, or deconstruction of the homophobia embedded in public policies) with action has come to characterize much new-paradigm inquiry work, both at the theoretical and at the practice and *praxis*-oriented levels. Action has become a major controversy that limns the ongoing debates among practitioners of the various paradigms. The mandate for social action, especially action designed and created by and for research participants with the aid and cooperation of researchers, can be most sharply delineated between positivist/postpositivist and new-paradigm inquirers. Many positivist and postpositivist inquirers still consider "action" the domain of communities other than researchers and research participants: those of policy personnel, legislators, and civic and political officials. Hard-line foundationalists presume that the taint of action will interfere with, or even negate, the objectivity that is a (presumed) characteristic of rigorous scientific method inquiry.

▣ Control

Another controversy that has tended to become problematic centers on *control* of the study: Who initiates? Who determines salient questions? Who determines what constitutes findings? Who determines how data will be collected? Who determines in what forms the findings will be made public, if at all? Who determines what representations will be made of participants in the research? Let us be very clear: The issue of control is deeply embedded in the questions of voice, reflexivity, and issues of postmodern textual representation, which we shall take up later, *but only for new-paradigm inquirers.* For more conventional inquirers, the issue of control is effectively walled off from voice, reflexivity, and issues of textual representation, because each of those issues in some way threatens claims to rigor (particularly objectivity and validity). For new-paradigm inquirers who have seen the preeminent paradigm issues of ontology and epistemology effectively folded into one another, and who have watched as methodology and axiology logically folded into one another (Lincoln, 1995, 1997), control of an inquiry seems far less problematic, except insofar as inquirers seek to obtain participants' genuine participation (see, for instance, Guba & Lincoln, 1981, on contracting and attempts to get some stakeholding groups to do more than stand by while an evaluation is in progress).

Critical theorists, especially those who work in community organizing programs, are painfully aware of the necessity for members of the community, or research participants, to take control of their futures. Constructivists desire participants to take an increasingly active role in nominating questions of interest for any inquiry and in designing outlets for findings to be shared more widely within and outside the community. Participatory inquirers understand action controlled by the local context members to be the aim of inquiry within a community. For none of these paradigmatic adherents is control an issue of advocacy, a somewhat deceptive term usually used as a code within a larger metanarrative to attack an inquiry's rigor, objectivity, or fairness. Rather, for new-paradigm researchers control is a means of fostering emancipation, democracy, and community empowerment, and of redressing power imbalances such that those who were previously marginalized now achieve voice (Mertens, 1998) or "human flourishing" (Heron & Reason, 1997). Control as a controversy is an excellent place to observe the phenomenon that we have always termed "Catholic questions directed to a Methodist audience." We use this description—given to us by a workshop participant in the early 1980s—to refer to the ongoing problem of illegitimate questions: questions that have no meaning because the frames of reference are those for which they were never intended. (We could as well call these "Hindu questions to a Muslim," to give another sense of how paradigms, or overarching philosophies—or theologies—are incommensurable, and how questions in one framework make little, if any, sense in another.) Paradigmatic formulations interact such that control becomes inextricably intertwined with mandates for objectivity. Objectivity derives from the Enlightenment prescription for knowledge of the physical world, which is postulated to be separate and distinct from those who would know (Polkinghorne, 1989). But if knowledge of the social (as opposed to the physical) world resides in meaning-making mechanisms of the social, mental, and linguistic worlds that individuals inhabit, then knowledge cannot be separate from the knower, but rather is rooted in his or her mental or linguistic designations of that world (Polkinghorne, 1989; Salner, 1989).

▣ Foundations of Truth and Knowledge in Paradigms

Whether or not the world has a "real" existence outside of human experience of that world is an open question. For modernist (i.e., Enlightenment, scientific method, conventional, positivist) researchers, most assuredly there is a "real" reality "out there," apart from the flawed human apprehension of it. Further, that reality can be approached (approximated) only through the utilization of methods that prevent human contamination of its apprehension or comprehension. For foundationalists in the empiricist tradition, the foundations of scientific truth and knowledge about reality reside in rigorous application of testing phenomena against a template as much devoid of human bias, misperception, and other "idols" (Francis Bacon, cited in Polkinghorne, 1989) as instrumentally possible. As Polkinghorne (1989) makes clear:

> The idea that the objective realm is independent of the knower's subjective experiences of it can be found in Descartes's dual substance theory, with its distinction between the objective and subjective realms.... In the splitting of reality into subject and object realms, what can be known "objectively" is only the objective realm. True knowledge is limited to the objects and the relationships between them that exist in the realm of time and space. Human consciousness, which is subjective, is not accessible to science, and thus not truly knowable. (p. 23)

Now, templates of truth and knowledge can be defined in a variety of ways—as the end product of rational processes, as the result of experiential sensing, as the result of empirical observation, and others. In all cases, however, the referent is the physical or empirical world: rational engagement with it, experience of it, empirical observation of it. Realists, who work on the assumption that there is a "real" world "out there," may in individual cases also be foundationalists, taking the view that all of these ways of defining are rooted in phenomena existing outside the human mind. Although we can think about them, experience them, or observe them, they are nevertheless transcendent, referred to but beyond direct apprehension. Realism is an ontological question, whereas foundationalism is a criterial question. Some foundationalists argue that real phenomena necessarily imply certain final, ultimate criteria for testing them as truthful (although we may have great difficulty in determining what those criteria are); nonfoundationalists tend to argue that there are no such ultimate criteria, only those that we can agree upon at a certain time and under certain conditions. Foundational criteria are discovered; nonfoundational criteria are negotiated. It is the case, however, that most realists are also foundationalists, and many nonfoundationalists or antifoundationalists are relativists.

An ontological formulation that connects realism and foundationalism within the same "collapse" of categories that characterizes the ontological-epistemological collapse is one that exhibits good fit with the other assumptions of constructivism. That state of affairs suits new-paradigm inquirers well. Critical theorists, constructivists, and participatory/cooperative inquirers take their primary field of interest to be precisely that subjective and intersubjective social knowledge and the active construction and cocreation of such knowledge by human agents that is produced by human consciousness. Further, new-paradigm inquirers take to the social knowledge field with zest, informed by a variety of social, intellectual, and theoretical explorations. These theoretical excursions include Saussurian linguistic theory, which views all relationships between words and what those words signify as the function of an internal relationship within some linguistic system; literary theory's deconstructive contributions, which seek to disconnect texts from any *essentialist* or transcendental meaning and resituate them within both author and reader historical and social contexts (Hutcheon, 1989; Leitch, 1996); feminist (Addelson, 1993; Alpern, Antler, Perry, & Scobie, 1992; Babbitt, 1993; Harding, 1993), race and ethnic (Kondo, 1990, 1997; Trinh, 1991), and queer theorizing (Gamson, 2000), which seeks to uncover and explore varieties of oppression and historical colonizing between dominant and subaltern genders, identities, races, and social worlds; the postmodern historical moment (Michael, 1996), which problematizes truth as partial, identity as fluid, language as an unclear referent system, and method and criteria as potentially coercive (Ellis & Bochner, 1996); and criticalist theories of social change (Carspecken, 1996; Schratz & Walker, 1995). The realization of the richness of the mental, social, psychological, and linguistic worlds that individuals and social groups create and constantly re-create and cocreate gives rise, in the minds of new-paradigm postmodern and poststructural inquirers, to endlessly fertile fields of inquiry rigidly walled off from conventional inquirers. Unfettered from the pursuit of transcendental scientific truth, inquirers are now free to resituate themselves within texts, to reconstruct their relationships with research participants in less constricted fashions, and to create re-presentations (Tierney & Lincoln, 1997) that grapple openly with problems of inscription, reinscription, metanarratives, and other rhetorical devices that obscure the extent to which human action is locally and temporally shaped. The processes of uncovering forms of inscription and the rhetoric of metanarratives are *genealogical*—"expos[ing] the origins of the view that have become *sedimented and accepted as truths*" (Polkinghorne, 1989, p. 42; emphasis added)—or *archaeological* (Foucault, 1971; Scheurich, 1997).

New-paradigm inquirers engage the foundational controversy in quite different ways. Critical theorists, particularly critical theorists more positivist in orientation, who lean toward Marxian interpretations, tend toward foundational perspectives, with an important difference. Rather than locating foundational truth and knowledge in some external reality "out there," such critical theorists tend to locate the foundations of truth in specific historical, economic, racial, and social infrastructures of oppression, injustice, and marginalization. Knowers are not portrayed as *separate from* some objective reality, but may be cast as unaware actors in such historical realities ("false consciousness") or as aware of historical forms of oppression, but unable or unwilling, because of conflicts, to act on those historical forms to alter specific conditions in this historical moment ("divided consciousness"). Thus the "foundation" for critical theorists is a duality: social critique tied in turn to raised consciousness of the possibility of positive and liberating social change. Social critique may exist apart from social change, but both are necessary for criticalist perspectives.

Constructivists, on the other hand, tend toward the antifoundational (Lincoln, 1995, 1998b; Schwandt, 1996). *Antifoundational* is the term used to denote a refusal to adopt any permanent, unvarying (or "foundational") standards by which truth can be universally known. As one of us has argued, truth—and any agreement regarding what is valid knowledge—arises from the relationship between members of some stakeholding community (Lincoln, 1995). Agreements about truth may be the subject of community *negotiations* regarding what will be accepted as truth (although there are difficulties with that formulation as well; Guba & Lincoln, 1989). Or agreements may eventuate as the result of a *dialogue* that moves arguments about truth claims or validity past the warring camps of objectivity and relativity toward "a communal test of validity through the argumentation of the participants in a discourse" (Bernstein, 1983; Polkinghorne, 1989; Schwandt, 1996). This "communicative and pragmatic concept" of validity (Rorty, 1979) is never fixed or unvarying. Rather, it is created by means of a community narrative, itself subject to the temporal and historical conditions that gave rise to the community. Schwandt (1989) has also argued that these discourses, or community narratives, can and should be bounded by moral considerations, a premise grounded in the emancipatory narratives of the critical theorists, the philosophical pragmatism of Rorty, the democratic focus of constructivist inquiry, and the "human flourishing" goals of participatory and cooperative inquiry.

The controversies around foundationalism (and, to a lesser extent, essentialism) are not likely to be resolved through dialogue between paradigm adherents. The likelier event is that the "postmodern turn" (Best & Kellner, 1997), with its emphasis on the social construction of social reality, fluid as opposed to fixed identities of the self, and the partiality of all truths, will simply overtake modernist assumptions of an objective reality, as indeed, to some extent, it has already done in the physical sciences. We might predict that, if not in our lifetimes, at some later time the dualist idea of an objective reality suborned by limited human subjective realities will seem as quaint as flat-earth theories do to us today.

Validity: An Extended Agenda

Nowhere can the conversation about paradigm differences be more fertile than in the extended controversy about validity (Howe & Eisenhart, 1990; Kvale, 1989, 1994; Ryan, Greene, Lincoln, Mathison, & Mertens, 1998; Scheurich, 1994, 1996). Validity is not like objectivity. There are fairly strong theoretical, philosophical, and pragmatic rationales for examining the concept of objectivity and finding it wanting. Even within positivist frameworks it is viewed as conceptually flawed. But validity is a more irritating construct, one neither easily dismissed nor readily configured by new-paradigm practitioners (Enerstvedt, 1989; Tschudi, 1989). Validity cannot be dismissed simply because it points to a question that has to be answered in one way or another: Are these findings sufficiently authentic (isomorphic to some reality, trustworthy, related to the way others construct their social worlds) that I may trust myself in acting on their implications? More to the point, would I feel sufficiently secure about these findings to construct social policy or legislation based on them? At the same time, radical reconfigurations of validity leave researchers with multiple, sometimes conflicting, mandates for what constitutes rigorous research.

One of the issues around validity is the conflation between method and interpretation. The postmodern turn suggests that no method can deliver on ultimate truth, and in fact "suspects all methods," the more so the larger their claims to delivering on truth (Richardson, 1994). Thus, although one might argue that some methods are more suited than others for conducting research on human construction of social realities (Lincoln & Guba, 1985), no one would argue that a single method—or collection of methods—is the royal road to ultimate knowledge. In new-paradigm inquiry, however, it is not merely method that promises to deliver on some set of local or context-grounded truths, it is also the processes of interpretation. Thus we have two arguments proceeding simultaneously. The first, borrowed from positivism, argues for a kind of rigor in the application of method, whereas the second argues for both a community consent and a form of rigor—defensible reasoning, plausible alongside some other reality that is known to author and reader—in ascribing salience to one interpretation over another and for framing and bounding an interpretive study itself. Prior to our understanding that there were, indeed, two forms of rigor, we assembled a set of methodological criteria, largely borrowed from an earlier generation of thoughtful anthropological and sociological methodological theorists. Those methodological criteria are still useful for a variety of reasons, not the least of which is that they ensure that such issues as prolonged engagement and persistent observation are attended to with some seriousness.

It is the second kind of rigor, however, that has received the most attention in recent writings: Are we *interpretively* rigorous? Can our cocreated constructions be trusted to provide some purchase on some important human phenomenon?

Human phenomena are themselves the subject of controversy. Classical social scientists would like to see "human phenomena" limited to those social experiences from which (scientific) generalizations may be drawn. New-paradigm inquirers, however, are increasingly concerned with the single experience, the individual crisis, the epiphany or moment of discovery, with that most powerful of all threats to conventional objectivity, feeling and emotion. Social scientists concerned with the expansion of what count as social data rely increasingly on the experiential, the embodied, the emotive qualities of human experience that contribute the narrative quality to a life. Sociologists such as Ellis and Bochner (2000) and Richardson (2000) and psychologists such as Michelle Fine (see Fine, Weis, Weseen, & Wong, 2000) concern themselves with various forms of autoethnography and personal experience methods, both to overcome the abstractions of a social science far gone with quantitative descriptions of human life and to capture those elements that make life conflictual, moving, problematic.

For purposes of this discussion, we believe the adoption of the most radical definitions of social science is appropriate, because the paradigmatic controversies are often taking place at the edges of those conversations. Those edges are where the border work is occurring, and, accordingly, they are the places that show the most promise for projecting where qualitative methods will be in the near and far future.

Whither and Whether Criteria

At those edges, several conversations are occurring around validity. The first—and most radical—is a conversation opened by Schwandt (1996), who suggests that we say "farewell to criteriology," or the "regulative norms for removing doubt and settling disputes about what is correct or incorrect, true or false" (p. 59), which have created a virtual cult around criteria. Schwandt does not, however, himself say farewell to criteria forever; rather, he resituates social inquiry, with other contemporary philosophical pragmatists, within a framework that transforms professional social inquiry into a form of practical philosophy, characterized by "aesthetic, prudential and moral considerations as well as more conventionally scientific ones" (p. 68). When social inquiry becomes the practice of a form of practical philosophy—a deep questioning about how we shall get on in the world and what we conceive to be the potentials and limits of human knowledge and functioning—then we have some preliminary understanding of what entirely different criteria might be for judging social inquiry.

Schwandt (1996) proposes three such criteria. First, he argues, we should search for a social inquiry that "generate[s] knowledge that complements or supplements rather than displac[ing] lay probing of social problems," a form of knowledge for which we do not yet have the *content,* but from which we might seek to understand the aims of practice from a variety of perspectives, or with different lenses. Second, he proposes a "social inquiry as practical philosophy" that has as its aim "enhancing or cultivating *critical* intelligence in parties to the research encounter," critical intelligence being defined as "the capacity to engage in moral critique." And finally, he proposes a third way in which we might judge social inquiry as practical philosophy: We might make judgments about the social inquirer-as-practical-philosopher. He or she might be "evaluated on the success to which his or her reports of the inquiry enable the training or calibration of human judgment" (p. 69) or "the capacity for practical wisdom" (p. 70).

Schwandt is not alone, however, in wishing to say "farewell to criteriology," at least as it has been previously conceived. Scheurich (1997) makes a similar plea, and in the same vein, Smith (1993) also argues that validity, if it is to survive at all, must be radically reformulated if it is ever to serve phenomenological research well (see also Smith & Deemer, 2000).

At issue here is not whether we shall have criteria, or whose criteria we as a scientific community might adopt, but rather what the nature of social inquiry ought to be, whether it ought to undergo a transformation, and what might be the basis for criteria within a projected transformation. Schwandt (1989; also personal communication, August 21, 1998) is quite clear that both the transformation and the criteria are rooted in dialogic efforts. These dialogic efforts are quite clearly themselves forms of "moral discourse." Through the specific connections of the dialogic, the idea of practical wisdom, and moral discourses, much of Schwandt's work can be seen to be related to, and reflective of, critical theorist and participatory paradigms, as well as constructivism, although Schwandt specifically denies the relativity of truth. (For a more sophisticated explication and critique of forms of constructivism, hermeneutics, and interpretivism, see Schwandt, 2000. In that chapter, Schwandt spells out distinctions between realists and nonrealists, and between foundationalists and nonfoundationalists, far more clearly than it is possible for us to do in this chapter.)

To return to the central question embedded in validity: How do we know when we have specific social inquiries that are faithful enough to some human construction that we may feel safe in acting on them, or, more important, that members of the community in which the research is conducted may act on them? To that question, there is no final answer. There are, however, several discussions of what we might use to make both professional and lay judgments regarding any piece of work. It is to those versions of validity that we now turn.

Validity as Authenticity

Perhaps the first nonfoundational criteria were those we developed in response to a challenge by John K. Smith (see Smith & Deemer, 2000). In those criteria, we attempted to locate criteria for judging the *processes* and *outcomes* of naturalistic or constructivist inquiries (rather than the application of methods; see Guba & Lincoln, 1989). We described five potential outcomes of a social constructionist inquiry (evaluation is one form of disciplined inquiry; see Guba & Lincoln, 1981), each grounded in concerns specific to the paradigm we had tried to describe and construct, and apart from any concerns carried over from the positivist legacy. The criteria were instead rooted in the axioms and assumptions of the constructivist paradigm, insofar as we could extrapolate and infer them.

Those authenticity criteria—so called because we believed them to be hallmarks of authentic, trustworthy, rigorous, or "valid" constructivist or phenomenological inquiry—were fairness, ontological authenticity, educative authenticity, catalytic authenticity, and tactical authenticity (Guba & Lincoln, 1989, pp. 245–251). *Fairness* was thought to be a quality of balance; that is, all stakeholder views, perspectives, claims, concerns, and voices should be apparent in the text. Omission of stakeholder or participant voices reflects, we believe, a form of bias. This bias, however, was and is not related directly to the concerns of objectivity that flow from positivist inquiry and that are reflective of inquirer blindness or subjectivity. Rather, this fairness was defined by deliberate attempts to prevent marginalization, to act affirmatively with respect to inclusion, and to act with energy to ensure that all voices in the inquiry effort had a chance to be represented in any texts and to have their stories treated fairly and with balance.

Ontological and educative authenticity were designated as criteria for determining a raised level of awareness, in the first instance, by individual research participants and, in the second, by individuals about those who surround them or with whom they come into contact for some social or organizational purpose. Although we failed to see it at that particular historical moment (1989), there is no reason these criteria cannot be—at this point in time, with many miles under our theoretic and practice feet—reflective also of Schwandt's (1996) "critical intelligence," or capacity to engage in moral critique. In fact, the authenticity criteria we originally proposed had strong moral and ethical overtones, a point to which we later returned (see, for instance, Lincoln, 1995, 1998a, 1998b). It was a point to which our critics strongly objected before we were sufficiently self-aware to realize the implications of what we had proposed (see, for instance, Sechrest, 1993).

Catalytic and tactical authenticities refer to the ability of a given inquiry to prompt, first, action on the part of research participants and, second, the involvement of the researcher/evaluator in training participants in specific forms of social and political action if participants desire such training. It is here that constructivist inquiry practice begins to resemble forms of critical theorist action, action research, or participative or cooperative inquiry, each of which is predicated on creating the capacity in research participants for positive social change and forms of emancipatory community action. It is also at this specific point that practitioners of positivist and postpositivist social inquiry are the most critical, because any action on the part of the inquirer is thought to destabilize objectivity and introduce subjectivity, resulting in bias. The problem of subjectivity and bias has a long theoretical history, and this chapter is simply too brief for us to enter into the various formulations that either take account of subjectivity or posit it as a positive learning experience, practical, embodied, gendered, and emotive. For purposes of this discussion, it is enough to say that we are persuaded that objectivity is a chimera: a mythological creature that never existed, save in the imaginations of those who believe that knowing can be separated from the knower.

Validity as Resistance, Validity as Poststructural Transgression

Laurel Richardson (1994, 1997) has proposed another form of validity, a deliberately "transgressive" form, the *crystalline.* In writing experimental (i.e., nonauthoritative, nonpositivist) texts, particularly poems and plays, Richardson (1997) has sought to "problematize reliability, validity and truth" (p. 165) in an effort to create new relationships: to her research participants, to her work, to other women, to herself. She says that transgressive forms permit a social scientist to "conjure a different kind of social science . . . [which] means changing one's relationship to one's work, *how* one knows and tells about the sociological" (p. 166). In order to see "how transgression looks and how it feels," it is necessary to "find and deploy methods that allow us to uncover the hidden assumptions and life-denying repressions of sociology; resee/refeel sociology. Reseeing and retelling are inseparable" (p. 167).

The way to achieve such validity is by examining the properties of a crystal in a metaphoric sense. Here we present an extended quotation to give some flavor of how such validity might be described and deployed:

> I propose that the central imaginary for "validity" for postmodernist texts is not the triangle—a rigid, fixed, two-dimensional object. Rather the central imaginary is the crystal, which combines symmetry and substance with an infinite variety of shapes, substances, transmutations, multidimensionalities, and angles of approach. Crystals grow, change, alter, but are not amorphous. Crystals are prisms that reflect externalities *and* refract within themselves, creating different colors, patterns, arrays, casting off in different directions. What we see depends upon our angle of repose. Not triangulation, crystallization. In postmodernist mixed-genre texts, we have moved from plane geometry to light theory, where light can be *both* waves *and* particles. Crystallization, without losing structure, deconstructs the traditional idea of "validity" (we feel how there is no single truth, we see how texts validate themselves); and crystallization provides us with a deepened, complex, thoroughly partial understanding of the topic. Paradoxically, we know more and doubt what we know. (Richardson, 1997, p. 92)

The metaphoric "solid object" (crystal/text), which can be turned many ways, which reflects and refracts light (light/multiple layers of meaning), through which we can see both "wave" (light wave/human currents) and "particle" (light as "chunks" of energy/elements of truth, feeling, connection, processes of the research that "flow" together) is an attractive metaphor for validity. The properties of the crystal-as-metaphor help writers and readers alike see the interweaving of processes in the research: discovery, seeing, telling, storying, re-presentation.

Other "Transgressive" Validities

Laurel Richardson is not alone in calling for forms of validity that are "transgressive" and disruptive of the status quo. Patti Lather (1993) seeks "an incitement to discourse," the purpose of which is "to rupture validity as a regime of truth, to displace its historical inscription . . . via a dispersion, circulation and proliferation of counter-practices of authority that take the crisis of representation into account" (p. 674). In addition to catalytic validity (Lather, 1986), Lather (1993) poses *validity as simulacra/ironic validity; Lyotardian paralogy/neopragmatic validity,* a form of validity that "foster[s] heterogeneity, refusing disclosure" (p. 679); *Derridean rigor/rhizomatic validity,* a form of behaving "via relay, circuit, multiple openings" (p. 680); and *voluptuous/situated validity,* which "embodies a situated, partial tentativeness" and "brings ethics and epistemology together . . . via practices of engagement and self-reflexivity" (p. 686). Together, these form a way of interrupting, disrupting, and transforming "pure" presence into a disturbing, fluid, partial, and problematic presence—a poststructural and decidedly postmodern form of discourse theory, hence textual revelation.

Validity as an Ethical Relationship

As Lather (1993) points out, poststructural forms for validities "bring ethics and epistemology together" (p. 686); indeed, as Parker Palmer (1987) also notes, "every way of knowing contains its own moral trajectory" (p. 24). Peshkin reflects on Noddings's (1984) observation that "the search for justification often carries us farther and farther from the heart of morality" (p. 105; quoted in Peshkin, 1993, p. 24). The *way* in which we know is most assuredly tied up with both *what* we know and our *relationships with our research participants.* Accordingly, one of us worked on trying to understand the ways in which the ethical intersects both the interpersonal and the epistemological (as a form of authentic or valid knowing; Lincoln, 1995). The result was the first set of understandings about emerging criteria for quality that were also rooted in the epistemology/ethics nexus. Seven new standards were derived from that search: positionality, or standpoint, judgments; specific discourse communities and research sites as arbiters of quality; voice, or the extent to which a text has the quality of polyvocality; critical subjectivity (or what might be termed intense self-reflexivity); reciprocity, or the extent to which the research relationship becomes reciprocal rather than hierarchical; sacredness, or the profound regard for how science can (and does) contribute to human flourishing; and sharing the perquisites of privilege that accrue to our positions as academics with university positions. Each of these standards was extracted from a body of research, often from disciplines as disparate as management, philosophy, and women's studies (Lincoln, 1995).

Voice, Reflexivity, and Postmodern Textual Representation

Texts have to do a lot more work these days than they used to. Even as they are charged by poststructuralists and postmodernists to reflect upon their representational practices, representational practices themselves become more problematic. Three of the most engaging, but painful, issues are the problem of voice, the status of reflexivity, and the problematics of postmodern/poststructural textual representation, especially as those problematics are displayed in the shift toward narrative and literary forms that directly and openly deal with human emotion.

Voice

Voice is a multilayered problem, simply because it has come to mean many things to different researchers. In former eras, the only appropriate "voice" was the "voice from nowhere"—the "pure presence" of representation, as Lather terms it. As researchers became more conscious of the abstracted realities their texts created, they became simultaneously more conscious of having readers "hear" their informants—permitting readers to hear the exact words (and, occasionally, the paralinguistic cues, the lapses, pauses, stops, starts, reformulations) of the informants. Today voice can mean, especially in more participatory forms of research, not only having a real researcher—and a researcher's voice—in the text, but also letting research participants speak for themselves, either in text form or through plays, forums, "town meetings," or other oral and performance-oriented media or communication forms designed by research participants themselves. Performance texts, in particular, give an emotional immediacy to the voices of researchers and research participants far beyond their own sites and locales (see McCall, 2000). Rosanna Hertz (1997) describes voice as

> a struggle to figure out how to present the author's self while simultaneously writing the respondents' accounts and representing their selves. Voice has multiple dimensions: First, there is the voice of the author. Second, there is the presentation of the voices of one's respondents within the text. A third dimension appears when the self is the subject of the inquiry. . . . Voice is how authors express themselves within an ethnography. (pp. xi–xii)

But knowing how to express ourselves goes far beyond the commonsense understanding of "expressing ourselves." Generations of ethnographers trained in the "cooled-out, stripped-down rhetoric" of positivist inquiry (Firestone, 1987) find it difficult, if not nearly impossible, to "locate" themselves deliberately and squarely within their texts (even though, as Geertz [1988] has demonstrated finally and without doubt, the authorial voice is rarely genuinely absent, or even hidden).[3] Specific textual experimentation can help; that is, composing ethnographic work into various literary forms—the poetry and plays of Laurel Richardson are good examples—can help a researcher to overcome the tendency to write in the distanced and abstracted voice of the disembodied "I." But such writing exercises are hard work. This is also work that is embedded in the practices of reflexivity and narrativity, without which achieving a voice of (partial) truth is impossible.

Reflexivity

Reflexivity is the process of reflecting critically on the self as researcher, the "human as instrument" (Guba & Lincoln, 1981). It is, we would assert, the critical subjectivity discussed early on in Reason and Rowan's edited volume *Human Inquiry* (1981). It is a conscious experiencing of the self as both inquirer and respondent, as teacher and learner, as the one coming to know the self within the processes of research itself.

Reflexivity forces us to come to terms not only with our choice of research problem and with those with whom we engage in the research process, but with our selves and with the multiple identities that represent the fluid self in the research setting (Alcoff & Potter, 1993). Shulamit Reinharz (1997), for example, argues that we not only "*bring* the self to the field . . . [we also] *create* the self in the field" (p. 3). She suggests that although we all have many selves we bring with us, those selves fall into three categories: research-based selves, brought selves (the selves that historically, socially, and personally create our standpoints), and situationally created selves (p. 5). Each of those selves comes into play in the research setting and consequently has a distinctive voice. Reflexivity—as well as the poststructural and postmodern sensibilities concerning quality in qualitative research—demands that we interrogate each of our selves regarding the ways in which research efforts are shaped and staged around the binaries, contradictions, and paradoxes that form our own lives. We must question our selves, too, regarding how those binaries and paradoxes shape not only the identities called forth in the field and later in the discovery processes of writing, but also our interactions with respondents, in who we become to them in the process of *becoming* to ourselves. Someone once characterized qualitative research as the twin processes of "writing up" (field notes) and "writing down" (the narrative). But Clandinin and Connelly (1994) have made clear that this bitextual reading of the processes of qualitative research is far too simplistic. In fact, many texts are created in the process of engaging in fieldwork. As Richardson (1994, 1997, 2000; see also Richardson & St. Pierre, Chapter 38, this volume) makes clear, writing is not merely the transcribing of some reality. Rather, writing—of all the texts, notes, presentations, and possibilities—is also a process of discovery: discovery of the subject (and sometimes of the problem itself) and discovery of the self.

There is good news and bad news with the most contemporary of formulations. The good news is that the multiple selves—ourselves and our respondents—of postmodern inquiries may give rise to more dynamic, problematic, open-ended, and complex forms of writing and representation. The bad news is that the multiple selves we create and encounter give rise to more dynamic, problematic, open-ended, and complex forms of writing and representation.

Postmodern Textual Representations

There are two dangers inherent in the conventional texts of scientific method: that they may lead us to believe the world is rather simpler than it is, and that they may reinscribe enduring forms of historical oppression. Put another way, we are confronted with a crisis of authority (which tells us the world is "this way" when perhaps it is some other way, or many other ways) and a crisis of representation (which serves to silence those whose lives we appropriate for our social sciences, and which may also serve subtly to re-create *this* world, rather than some other, perhaps more complex, but just one). Catherine Stimpson (1988) has observed:

> Like every great word, "representation/s" is a stew. A scrambled menu, it serves up several meanings at once. For a representation can be an image—visual, verbal, or aural. . . . A representation can also be a narrative, a sequence of images and ideas. . . . Or, a representation can be the product of ideology, that vast scheme for showing forth the world and justifying its dealings. (p. 223)

One way to confront the dangerous illusions (and their underlying ideologies) that texts may foster is through the creation of new texts that break boundaries; that move from the center to the margins to comment on and decenter the center; that forgo closed, bounded worlds for those more open-ended and less conveniently encompassed; that transgress the boundaries of conventional social science; and that seek to create a social science about human life rather than *on* subjects.

Experiments with how to do this have produced "messy texts" (Marcus & Fischer, 1986). Messy texts are not typographic nightmares (although they may be typographically nonlinear); rather, they are texts that seek to break the binary between science and literature, to portray the contradiction and truth of human experience, to break the rules in the service of showing, even partially, how real human beings cope with both the eternal verities of human existence and the daily irritations and tragedies of living that existence. Postmodern representations search out and experiment with narratives that expand the range of understanding, voice, and storied variations in human experience. As much as they are social scientists, inquirers also become storytellers, poets, and playwrights, experimenting with personal narratives, first-person accounts, reflexive interrogations, and deconstruction of the forms of tyranny embedded in representational practices (see Richardson, 2000; Tierney & Lincoln, 1997).

Representation may be arguably the most open-ended of the controversies surrounding phenomenological research today, for no other reasons than that the ideas of what constitutes legitimate inquiry are expanding and, at the same time, the forms of narrative, dramatic, and rhetorical structure are far from being either explored or exploited fully. Because, too, each inquiry, each inquirer, brings a unique perspective to our understanding, the possibilities for variation and exploration are limited only by the number of those engaged in inquiry and the realms of social and intrapersonal life that become interesting to researchers. The only thing that can be said for certain about postmodern representational practices is that they will proliferate as forms and they will seek, and demand much of, audiences, many of whom may be outside the scholarly and academic world. In fact, some forms of inquiry may never show up in the academic world, because their purpose will be use in the immediate context, for the consumption, reflection, and use of indigenous audiences. Those that are produced for scholarly audiences will, however, continue to be untidy, experimental, and driven by the need to communicate social worlds that have remained private and "nonscientific" until now.

A Glimpse of the Future

The issues raised in this chapter are by no means the only ones under discussion for the near and far future. But they are some of the critical ones, and discussion, dialogue, and even controversies are bound to continue as practitioners of the various new and emergent paradigms continue either to look for common ground or to find ways in which to distinguish their forms of inquiry from others.

Some time ago, we expressed our hope that practitioners of both positivist and new-paradigm forms of inquiry might find some way of resolving their differences, such that all social scientists could work within a common discourse—and perhaps even several traditions—once again. In retrospect, such a resolution appears highly unlikely and would probably even be less than useful. This is not, however, because neither positivists nor phenomenologists will budge an inch (although that, too, is unlikely). Rather, it is because, in the postmodern moment, and in the wake of poststructuralism, the assumption that there is no single "truth"—that all truths are but partial truths; that the slippage between signifier and signified in linguistic and textual terms creates re-presentations that are only and always shadows of the actual people, events, and places; that identities are fluid rather than fixed—leads us ineluctably toward the insight that there will be no single "conventional" paradigm to which all social scientists might ascribe in some common terms and with mutual understanding. Rather, we stand at the threshold of a history marked by multivocality, contested meanings, paradigmatic controversies, and new textual forms. At some distance down this conjectural path, when its history is written, we will find that this has been the era of emancipation: emancipation from what Hannah Arendt calls "the coerciveness of Truth," emancipation from hearing only the voices of Western Europe, emancipation from generations of silence, and emancipation from seeing the world in one color.

We may also be entering an age of greater spirituality within research efforts. The emphasis on inquiry that reflects ecological values, on inquiry that respects communal forms of living that are not Western, on inquiry involving intense reflexivity regarding how our inquiries are shaped by our own historical and gendered locations, and on inquiry into "human flourishing," as Heron and Reason (1997) call it, may yet reintegrate the sacred with the secular in ways that promote freedom and self-determination. Egon Brunswik, the organizational theorist, wrote of "tied" and "untied" variables—variables that are linked, or clearly not linked, with other variables—when studying human forms of organization. We may be in a period of exploring the ways in which our inquiries are both tied and untied, as a means of finding where our interests cross and where we can both be and promote others' being, as whole human beings.

Notes

1. There are several versions of critical theory, including classical critical theory, which is most closely related to neo-Marxist theory; postpositivist formulations, which divorce themselves from Marxist theory but are positivist in their insistence on conventional rigor criteria; and postmodernist, poststructuralist, or constructivist-oriented varieties. See, for instance, Fay (1987), Carr and Kemmis (1986), and Lather (1991). See also Kemmis and McTaggart (2000) and Kincheloe and McLaren (2000).

2. For a clearer understanding of how methods came to stand in for paradigms, or how our initial (and, we thought, quite clear) positions came to be misconstrued, see Lancy (1993) or, even more currently, Weiss (1998, esp. p. 268).

3. For example, compare this chapter with, say, the work of Richardson (2000) and Ellis and Bochner (2000), where the authorial voices are clear, personal, vocal, and interior, interacting subjectivities. Although some colleagues have surprised us by correctly identifying which chapters each of us has written in given books, nevertheless, the style of this chapter more closely approximates the more distanced forms of "realist" writing than it does the intimate, personal "feeling tone" (to borrow a phrase from Studs Terkel) of other chapters. Voices also arise as a function of the material being covered. The material we chose as most important for this chapter seemed to demand a less personal tone, probably because there appears to be much more "contention" than calm dialogue concerning these issues. The "cool" tone likely stems from our psychological response to trying to create a quieter space for discussion around controversial issues. What can we say?

References

Addelson, K. P. (1993). Knowers/doers and their moral problems. In L. Alcoff & E. Potter (Eds.), *Feminist epistemologies* (pp. 265–294). New York: Routledge.

Alcoff, L., & Potter, E. (Eds.). (1993). *Feminist epistemologies.* New York: Routledge.

Alpern, S., Antler, J., Perry, E. I., & Scobie, I. W. (Eds.). (1992). *The challenge of feminist biography: Writing the lives of modern American women.* Urbana: University of Illinois Press.

Babbitt, S. (1993). Feminism and objective interests: The role of transformation experiences in rational deliberation. In L. Alcoff & E. Potter (Eds.), *Feminist epistemologies* (pp. 245–264). New York: Routledge.

Bernstein, R. J. (1983). *Beyond objectivism and relativism: Science, hermeneutics, and praxis.* Oxford: Blackwell.

Best, S., & Kellner, D. (1997). *The postmodern turn.* New York: Guilford.

Bloland, H. (1989). Higher education and high anxiety: Objectivism, relativism, and irony. *Journal of Higher Education, 60,* 519–543.

Bloland, H. (1995). Postmodernism and higher education. *Journal of Higher Education, 66,* 521–559.

Bradley, J., & Schaefer, K. (1998). *The uses and misuses of data and models.* Thousand Oaks, CA: Sage.

Carr, W. L., & Kemmis, S. (1986). *Becoming critical: Education, knowledge and action research.* London: Falmer.

Carspecken, P. F. (1996). *Critical ethnography in educational research: A theoretical and practical guide.* New York: Routledge.

Christians, C. G. (2000). Ethics and politics in qualitative research. In N. K. Denzin & Y. S. Lincoln (Eds.), *Handbook of qualitative research* (2nd ed., pp. 133–155). Thousand Oaks, CA: Sage.

Clandinin, D. J., & Connelly, F. M. (1994). Personal experience methods. In N. K. Denzin & Y. S. Lincoln (Eds.), *Handbook of qualitative research* (pp. 413–427). Thousand Oaks, CA: Sage.

Denzin, N. K., & Lincoln, Y. S. (Eds.). (1994). *Handbook of qualitative research.* Thousand Oaks, CA: Sage.

Ellis, C., & Bochner, A. P. (Eds.). (1996). *Composing ethnography: Alternative forms of qualitative writing.* Walnut Creek, CA: AltaMira.

Ellis, C., & Bochner, A. P. (2000). Autoethnography, personal narrative, reflexivity: Researcher as subject. In N. K. Denzin & Y. S. Lincoln (Eds.), *Handbook of qualitative research* (2nd ed., pp. 733–768). Thousand Oaks, CA: Sage.

Enerstvedt, R. (1989). The problem of validity in social science. In S. Kvale (Ed.), *Issues of validity in qualitative research* (pp. 135–173). Lund, Sweden: Studentlitteratur.

Fay, B. (1987). *Critical social science.* Ithaca, NY: Cornell University Press.

Fine, M., Weis, L., Weseen, S., & Wong, L. (2000). For whom? Qualitative research, representations, and social responsibilities. In N. K. Denzin & Y. S. Lincoln (Eds.), *Handbook of qualitative research* (2nd ed., pp. 107–131). Thousand Oaks, CA: Sage.

Firestone, W. (1987). Meaning in method: The rhetoric of quantitative and qualitative research. *Educational Researcher, 16*(7), 16–21.

Foucault, M. (1971). *The order of things: An archaeology of the human sciences.* New York: Pantheon.

Gamson, J. (2000). Sexualities, queer theory, and qualitative research. In N. K. Denzin & Y. S. Lincoln (Eds.), *Handbook of qualitative research* (2nd ed., pp. 347–365). Thousand Oaks, CA: Sage.

Geertz, C. (1988). *Works and lives: The anthropologist as author.* Cambridge: Polity.

Geertz, C. (1993). *Local knowledge: Further essays in interpretive anthropology.* London: Fontana.

Greenwood, D. J., & Levin, M. (2000). Reconstructing the relationships between universities and society through action research. In N. K. Denzin & Y. S. Lincoln (Eds.), *Handbook of qualitative research* (2nd ed., pp. 85–106). Thousand Oaks, CA: Sage.

Guba, E. G., & Lincoln, Y. S. (1981). *Effective evaluation: Improving the usefulness of evaluation results through responsive and naturalistic approaches.* San Francisco: Jossey-Bass.

Guba, E. G., & Lincoln, Y. S. (1982). Epistemological and methodological bases for naturalistic inquiry. *Educational Communications and Technology Journal, 31,* 233–252.

Guba, E. G., & Lincoln, Y. S. (1989). *Fourth generation evaluation.* Newbury Park, CA: Sage.

Guba, E. G., & Lincoln, Y. S. (1994). Competing paradigms in qualitative research. In N. K. Denzin & Y. S. Lincoln (Eds.), *Handbook of qualitative research* (pp. 105–117). Thousand Oaks, CA: Sage.

Harding, S. (1993). Rethinking standpoint epistemology: What is "strong objectivity"? In L. Alcoff & E. Potter (Eds.), *Feminist epistemologies* (pp. 49–82). New York: Routledge.

Heron, J. (1996). *Cooperative inquiry: Research into the human condition.* London: Sage.

Heron, J., & Reason, P. (1997). A participatory inquiry paradigm. *Qualitative Inquiry, 3,* 274–294.

Hertz, R. (1997). Introduction: Reflexivity and voice. In R. Hertz (Ed.), *Reflexivity and voice.* Thousand Oaks, CA: Sage.

Howe, K., & Eisenhart, M. (1990). Standards for qualitative (and quantitative) research: A prolegomenon. *Educational Researcher, 19*(4), 2–9.

Hutcheon, L. (1989). *The politics of postmodernism.* New York: Routledge.

Kemmis, S., & McTaggart, R. (2000). Participatory action research. In N. K. Denzin & Y. S. Lincoln (Eds.), *Handbook of qualitative research* (2nd ed., pp. 567–605). Thousand Oaks, CA: Sage.

Kincheloe, J. L. (1991). *Teachers as researchers: Qualitative inquiry as a path to empowerment.* London: Falmer.

Kincheloe, J. L., & McLaren, P. (2000). Rethinking critical theory and qualitative research. In N. K. Denzin & Y. S. Lincoln (Eds.), *Handbook of qualitative research* (2nd ed., pp. 279–313). Thousand Oaks, CA: Sage.

Kondo, D. K. (1990). *Crafting selves: Power, gender, and discourses of identity in a Japanese workplace.* Chicago: University of Chicago Press.

Kondo, D. K. (1997). *About face: Performing race in fashion and theater.* New York: Routledge.

Kvale, S. (Ed.). (1989). *Issues of validity in qualitative research.* Lund, Sweden: Studentlitteratur.

Kvale, S. (1994, April). *Validation as communication and action.* Paper presented at the annual meeting of the American Educational Research Association, New Orleans.

Lancy, D. F. (1993). *Qualitative research in education: An introduction to the major traditions.* New York: Longman.

Lather, P. (1986). Issues of validity in openly ideological research: Between a rock and a soft place. *Interchange, 17*(4), 63–84.

Lather, P. (1991). *Getting smart: Feminist research and pedagogy with/in the postmodern.* New York: Routledge.

Lather, P. (1993). Fertile obsession: Validity after poststructuralism. *Sociological Quarterly, 34,* 673–693.

Leitch, V. B. (1996). *Postmodern: Local effects, global flows.* Albany: State University of New York Press.

Lincoln, Y. S. (1995). Emerging criteria for quality in qualitative and interpretive research. *Qualitative Inquiry, 1,* 275–289.

Lincoln, Y. S. (1997). What constitutes quality in interpretive research? In C. K. Kinzer, K. A. Hinchman, & D. J. Leu (Eds.), *Inquiries in literacy: Theory and practice* (pp. 54–68). Chicago: National Reading Conference.

Lincoln, Y. S. (1998a). The ethics of teaching qualitative research. *Qualitative Inquiry, 4,* 305–317.

Lincoln, Y. S. (1998b). From understanding to action: New imperatives, new criteria, new methods for interpretive researchers. *Theory and Research in Social Education, 26*(1), 12–29.

Lincoln, Y. S., & Denzin, N. K. (1994). The fifth moment. In N. K. Denzin & Y. S. Lincoln (Eds.), *Handbook of qualitative research* (pp. 575–586). Thousand Oaks, CA: Sage.

Lincoln, Y. S., & Guba, E. G. (1985). *Naturalistic inquiry.* Beverly Hills, CA: Sage.

Marcus, G. E., & Fischer, M. M. J. (1986). *Anthropology as cultural critique: An experimental moment in the human sciences.* Chicago: University of Chicago Press.

McCall, M. M. (2000). Performance ethnography: A brief history and some advice. In N. K. Denzin & Y. S. Lincoln (Eds.), *Handbook of qualitative research* (2nd ed., pp. 421–433). Thousand Oaks, CA: Sage.

Mertens, D. (1998). *Research methods in education and psychology: Integrating diversity with quantitative and qualitative methods.* Thousand Oaks, CA: Sage.

Michael, M. C. (1996). *Feminism and the postmodern impulse: Post–World War II fiction.* Albany: State University of New York Press.

Noddings, N. (1984). *Caring: A feminine approach to ethics and moral education.* Berkeley: University of California Press.

Olesen, V. L. (2000). Feminisms and qualitative research at and into the millennium. In N. K. Denzin & Y. S. Lincoln (Eds.), *Handbook of qualitative research* (2nd ed., pp. 215–255). Thousand Oaks, CA: Sage.

Palmer, P. J. (1987, September-October). Community, conflict, and ways of knowing. *Change, 19,* 20–25.

Peshkin, A. (1993). The goodness of qualitative research. *Educational Researcher, 22*(2), 24–30.

Polkinghorne, D. E. (1989). Changing conversations about human science. In S. Kvale (Ed.), *Issues of validity in qualitative research* (pp. 13–46). Lund, Sweden: Studentlitteratur.

Reason, P. (1993). Sacred experience and sacred science. *Journal of Management Inquiry, 2,* 10–27.

Reason, P., & Rowan, J. (Eds.). (1981). *Human inquiry.* London: John Wiley.

Reinharz, S. (1997). Who am I? The need for a variety of selves in the field. In R. Hertz (Ed.), *Reflexivity and voice* (pp. 3–20). Thousand Oaks, CA: Sage.

Richardson, L. (1994). Writing: A method of inquiry. In N. K. Denzin & Y. S. Lincoln (Eds.), *Handbook of qualitative research* (pp. 516–529). Thousand Oaks, CA: Sage.

Richardson, L. (1997). *Fields of play: Constructing an academic life.* New Brunswick, NJ: Rutgers University Press.

Richardson, L. (2000). Writing: A method of inquiry. In N. K. Denzin & Y. S. Lincoln (Eds.), *Handbook of qualitative research* (2nd ed., pp. 923–948). Thousand Oaks, CA: Sage.

Rorty, R. (1979). *Philosophy and the mirror of nature.* Princeton, NJ: Princeton University Press.

Ryan, K. E., Greene, J. C., Lincoln, Y. S., Mathison, S., & Mertens, D. (1998). Advantages and challenges of using inclusive evaluation approaches in evaluation practice. *American Journal of Evaluation, 19,* 101–122.

Salner, M. (1989). Validity in human science research. In S. Kvale (Ed.), *Issues of validity in qualitative research* (pp. 47–72). Lund, Sweden: Studentlitteratur.

Scheurich, J. J. (1994). Policy archaeology. *Journal of Educational Policy, 9,* 297–316.

Scheurich, J. J. (1996). Validity. *International Journal of Qualitative Studies in Education, 9,* 49–60.

Scheurich, J. J. (1997). *Research method in the postmodern.* London: Falmer.

Schratz, M., & Walker, R. (1995). *Research as social change: New opportunities for qualitative research.* New York: Routledge.

Schwandt, T. A. (1989). Recapturing moral discourse in evaluation. *Educational Researcher, 18*(8), 11–16, 34.

Schwandt, T. A. (1996). Farewell to criteriology. *Qualitative Inquiry, 2,* 58–72.

Schwandt, T. A. (2000). Three epistemological stances for qualitative inquiry: Interpretivism, hermeneutics, and social constructionism. In N. K. Denzin & Y. S. Lincoln (Eds.), *Handbook of qualitative research* (2nd ed., pp. 189–213). Thousand Oaks, CA: Sage.

Sechrest, L. (1993). *Program evaluation: A pluralistic enterprise.* San Francisco: Jossey-Bass.

Smith, J. K. (1993). *After the demise of empiricism: The problem of judging social and educational inquiry.* Norwood, NJ: Ablex.

Smith, J. K., & Deemer, D. K. (2000). The problem of criteria in the age of relativism. In N. K. Denzin & Y. S. Lincoln (Eds.), *Handbook of qualitative research* (2nd ed., pp. 877–896). Thousand Oaks, CA: Sage.

Stimpson, C. R. (1988). Nancy Reagan wears a hat: Feminism and its cultural consensus. *Critical Inquiry, 14,* 223–243.

Tierney, W. G. (2000). Undaunted courage: Life history and the postmodern challenge. In N. K. Denzin & Y. S. Lincoln (Eds.), *Handbook of qualitative research* (2nd ed., pp. 537–553). Thousand Oaks, CA: Sage.

Tierney, W. G., & Lincoln, Y. S. (Eds.). (1997). *Representation and the text: Re-framing the narrative voice.* Albany: State University of New York Press.

Trinh, T. M. (1991). *When the moon waxes red: Representation, gender and cultural politics.* New York: Routledge.

Tschudi, F. (1989). Do qualitative and quantitative methods require different approaches to validity? In S. Kvale (Ed.), *Issues of validity in qualitative research* (pp. 109–134). Lund, Sweden: Studentlitteratur.

Weiss, C. H. (1998). *Evaluation* (2nd ed.). Upper Saddle River, NJ: Prentice Hall.

9

CRITICAL ETHNOGRAPHY

The Politics of Collaboration

Douglas Foley and Angela Valenzuela

INTRODUCTION

The purpose of this chapter is to highlight differences between "critical ethnographers" who do academic cultural critiques, who write applied policy studies, and who involve themselves directly in political movements. As we shall see, not all critical ethnographers are politically active. Nor do all produce knowledge that is both universalistic/theoretical and local/practical. Nor do all use reflexive, collaborative research methods. The rubric of critical ethnography glosses over many important differences between practitioners. After characterizing recent trends in contemporary critical ethnography, we portray our own ethnographic practice, which in some ways represents a continuum. On one end, Foley does academic "cultural critiques" and struggles to be more collaborative and politically involved. On the other end, Valenzuela does academic cultural critiques but is much more directly involved in public policy processes. We hope our reflections will encourage others to explore and publish more about their collaborative methodological and political practices.

Some Recent Trends in Critical Ethnography

In the 1960s, "critical ethnography" (Carspecken, 1996) often was based on classic Marxism or neo-Marxist critical theory. As new race, gender, sexual identity, and postcolonial social movements emerged, the philosophical basis for critical ethnography expanded greatly (Foley, Levinson, & Hurtig, 2001; Levinson & Holland, 1996; Villenas & Foley, 2002). These literature reviews underscore the growing disenchantment with the positivist notion of an objective social science that produces value-free ethnographies. Post-1960s critical ethnographers began advocating "cultural critiques" of modern society and its institutions (Marcus, 1998; Marcus & Fischer, 1986). Critical ethnographers not only rejected positivism but also worked the divide between the powerful and the powerless. Most ethnographic cultural critiques studied ruling groups and ruling ideologies and/or the sentiments and struggles of various oppressed peoples. Most were deeply committed to research that promotes an egalitarian society. Most hoped to produce both universalistic theoretical knowledge and local practical knowledge.

As the editors of this handbook have pointed out, qualitative research has become *the* site of philosophical and methodological revolt against positivism. This academic revolt is "political" in the sense that it seeks to transform the knowledge production of the academy. We have both participated in this revolt, which educational philosopher Thomas Schwandt (2000) aptly characterizes as having interpretive, hermeneutic, and constructivist alternatives. Were Schwandt to classify our ethnographic practice, he would note that we have greater affinities with hermeneutic and neo-Marxist critical theorists than with postmodern constructivists. In an earlier article, Foley (2002) advocated utilizing the following complementary reflexive practices: confessional, theoretical, intertextual, and deconstructive. Explicating these types of reflexivity is beyond this chapter, but it is important to note that he situated reflexive practices in a feminist perspective of science.

Donna Haraway (1988) and Sandra Harding (1998) share similar concepts of science that allow politically progressive critical ethnographers to make strong knowledge claims. Harding's discussion of "standpoint theory" and Haraway's notion of "situated knowledge" are so well known that there is little need to elaborate here. Suffice it to say that many critical ethnographers have replaced the grand positivist vision of speaking from a universalistic, objective standpoint with a more modest notion of speaking from a historically and culturally situated standpoint. Speaking from a historically specific standpoint acknowledges the impossibility of what Haraway aptly calls the "god trick" of speaking from an omnipotent standpoint. Critical ethnographers are mere culture-bound mortals speaking from very particular race, class, gender, and sexual identity locations. Because all standpoints represent particular interests and positions in a hierarchical society, they are "ideological" in the sense that they are partial.

Once an ethnographer abandons the positivist fallacy that research techniques can produce a detached, objective standpoint, it makes little sense to ignore more intuitive or subjective ways of knowing. Hence, contemporary critical ethnographers are beginning to use multiple epistemologies. They often value introspection, memory work, autobiography, and even dreams as important ways of knowing. The new, more reflexive critical ethnographer explores the intense self–other interaction that usually marks fieldwork and mediates the production of ethnographic narratives. In the current experimental moment (Denzin & Lincoln, 2000), the road to greater objectivity goes through the ethnographer's critical reflections on her subjectivity and intersubjective relationships. For most critical ethnographers, in a class society marked by class, racial, and sexual conflict, no producers of knowledge are innocent or politically neutral.

One of the early, forceful exponents of this perspective was existentialist sociologist Jack Douglas (1976). He urged social science researchers to abandon the ideal of grand theorizing and universalistic knowledge production. He preferred an "investigative" posture that aggressively studied social and political problems. Tapping into muckraking "new journalism" (T. Wolfe, 1974), Douglas also advocated operating covertly to expose corrupt bureaucrats or hate group leaders. He argued that in a politically corrupt, conflict-filled society, any means used to "get the story" was justifiable if it exposed harmful public practices.

Meanwhile, other anthropologists in the post-1960s era called for "reinventing" the field (Hymes, 1972), "studying up" (Nader, 1996), and studying "people without history" (E. Wolfe, 1982). For the first time, anthropologists began seriously studying imperialism, class and racial oppression, and social movements. They began to occupy the same methodological and ideological terrain occupied by the earlier community sociologists who studied social class inequality. Vidich and Lyman (2000) note that urban sociologists such as the Lynds (Lynd, 1956) and native Americanist anthropologists of the 1920s and 1930s were writing positive portraits of marginalized and stigmatized social, cultural, and occupational groups. Through the post–World War II years, C. Wright Mills (1959) led the way with a series of incisive studies of the national power elites. These early sociological studies of class inequalities and elites were even more critical than the Chicago school of urban sociology. Most of the pre–World War II "critical ethnographers" broke decisively with the positivist idea of value-free ethnographies.

One anthropologist who is often forgotten in histories of critical ethnography is Sol Tax. After doing a classic ethnography of Guatemalan markets (Tax, 1963), he became disenchanted with the academic, structural-functionalist ethnography of the 1940s and 1950s. In the late 1940s, he created a field school on the Mesquaki settlement in my hometown of Tama, Iowa (Foley, 1999). It was to be the testing ground for a new kind of anthropology. Tax advocated that "action anthropologists" be much more collaborative and produce research that the research subjects felt would resolve community problems. Bennett (1996) characterized Tax's orientation as rooted in American pragmatism's liberal, practical notion of science. Consequently, Tax distinguished his approach from academic anthropology and "applied anthropology" in several important ways.

First, action anthropologists were to operate without the sponsorship of government bureaucracies or private nongovernmental organizations (NGO's). They were to find independent funding and work more directly with and for the people they were studying. Second, Tax argued that because action anthropologists became accepted insiders, they were positioned to collect better data on social change and acculturation than were detached scientific ethnographers. Consequently, action anthropologists would help the community while they wrote trustworthy ethnographies. In effect, Tax envisioned a social science that created knowledge that was as practical and useful as it was theoretical and universal. For him, academic social scientists had produced a false notion of science and knowledge that privileged the theoretical over applied, practical knowledge.

Regrettably, Tax's action anthropology project on the Mesquaki settlement promised more than it delivered (Foley, 1999). It produced few lasting changes in the community and even less high-quality ethnography. Moreover, the field of academic anthropology never really embraced Tax's action anthropology. Nevertheless, a former student (Rubinstein, 1986) argues that Tax anticipated much of post-1960s anthropology. He contends that Tax's notion of "action anthropology" has become widely practiced in contemporary anthropology. After reviewing many contemporary studies of American culture, Foley and Moss (2001) would beg to differ. The continental philosophies of post-Marxism, postmodernism, and feminism have had a much greater impact on American anthropology than has philosophical pragmatism. Space does not permit a recapitulation of that review, but the work of Berkeley sociologist Michael Burawoy (1991, 2000) illustrates nicely the "new" critical ethnography, or what Marcus and Fischer (1986) call "the anthropology of cultural critiques." Burawoy and his students try to make the public aware of social inequalities and injustices as they revise the conventional wisdom of reigning academic theories. Because Burawoy explicitly advocates revising and generating social theory, his cultural critiques retain the basic goal of producing universal, scientific knowledge. That makes his studies publishable in the journals of various academic disciplines. The same holds true for many other neo-Marxist and Marxist feminist critical ethnographers (e.g., Brodkin, 2001; Fine & Weis, 1998; Susser, 2001; Zavella, 1987).

Most of these cultural critics break decisively with the positivist notion of value-free, scientific studies. On the other hand, most retain a strong notion of the author as expert and thus still operate in the field much like earlier scientific ethnographers. Their ethnographic practices are not particularly representative of the new postmodern experimental moment in ethnography (Denzin, 1997). The new critical ethnographers usually set the research agenda, collect the data, and write the account with relatively little input from subjects. They are not always inclined to work the self–other hyphen reflexively and to invite their research subjects to co-construct their ethnographic accounts. Characterizing the methodological and political practices of contemporary critical ethnographers is, however, risky business. For whatever reason, many do not report extensively on the extent of their political and methodological collaborations. Fine and Weis's (1998) study of the urban poor is, however, somewhat of an exception. Their formal ethnography and subsequent reflections on field methods (Fine & Weis, 2000; Fine, Weis, Weseen, & Wong, 2000) try to give some idea how collaborative they were politically and methodologically.

The current crop of critical ethnographers seems to be focusing more on dramatic public issues, and they are finding ways to reach wider audiences. Peggy Sanday (1976) was an early advocate of anthropological research that truly served the public interest. Her recent work (1990, 1996) on campus date rape, as well as her involvement and coverage of rape trials, is a case in point. Nancy Scheper-Hughes's (1992; Scheper-Hughes & Sargent, 1998) study of child welfare issues and Third World organ harvesting also is exemplary. Finally, our colleague at Rice University, Linda McNeil (2000), has forcefully critiqued many of the political right's educational accountability schemes in Texas. She also has worked tirelessly with local teachers and community educational leaders to reform these educational practices and has appeared on national TV shows such as *60 Minutes.* Increasingly, anthropologists interested in policy studies are advocating a more politicized type of policy studies (Kane & Mason, 2001; Levinson & Sutton, 2001; Okongwu & Mencher, 2000). These surveys of the field and a recent School of American Research conference on critical ethnography (Marcus, 1999) describe a host of new politically relevant cultural critiques in such areas as corporate agriculture, environmental pollution, pharmaceutical dumping, transnational labor migration, the publishing industry, cyberspace hackers, the AIDS crises, media and legal system demonization, and criminalization of urban street life and informal economies based on drugs, sex, and cultural rebellion.

Space does not permit an extensive review of the new, more political policy–oriented ethnographies, but the old labels of "critical ethnography" and "cultural critiques" may no longer capture the new diversity. The number of social scientists who are critiquing questionable legal, medical, educational, media, and corporate practices seems to be exploding. More important, these new critical ethnographers are beginning to write more accessible, less jargon-filled accounts. A few have also "crossed over" into the public sphere and have appeared as "experts" on talk and news shows. They have found new ways to bring their investigations to the public through opinion makers such as Oprah Winfrey, Larry King, and Ted Koppel. Meanwhile, they have quietly provided reporters with expert testimony for their journalistic exposés. Others have become policy advisers to politicians, and they directly influence legislation.

The final type of critical ethnographer is a distinct minority of activists who are deeply involved in progressive social movements and community-based reforms. In the field of educational research, Kemmis and McTaggart (2000) label such activities "participatory action research (PAR)." PAR researchers often base their approach on the philosophy of Latin American social activists Paulo Friere and Fals-Borda. PAR researchers have strong affinities with the more activist-oriented applied anthropologists (Eddy & Partridge, 1987). They often play the role of democratic facilitator and consciousness-raiser, or "cultural broker" between powerful institutions and the disenfranchised citizens. Anthropology has produced a few activists who are even more collaborative methodologically and politically than are most PAR action researchers. For example, in the early 1970s, anthropologist Carol Talbert, who joined the American Indian Movement (AIM) activists at Wounded Knee, gave an American Anthropological Association presentation about her role as a "pen for hire for AIM." In this particular case, she sought to document the FBI's dubious actions to prop up an anti-AIM faction and indict various AIM members for crimes they may not have committed. Talbert exemplifies a much more direct form of political collaboration. She joined the social movement and gave up much of her academic autonomy and authority to be an independent cultural critic. She researched and wrote what the movement needed.

Another anthropologist, Charles Valentine (1968), joined African American community action groups that conducted studies of landlords and police brutality, and that initiated rent strikes. At an American Anthropological Association meeting in the early 1970s, Valentine and several African American community members dramatized the difference between themselves and academic anthropologists. They flatly refused to present their findings to fellow anthropologists. Their intent was to convey contempt for the politically ineffectual nature of much academic anthropological research. In response, the discussant, Margaret Mead, expressed her anger that a fellow anthropologist would distrust a field that had labored to help the downtrodden. Her rather patronizing commentary set off a lively debate about the political utility/futility of anthropological research.

Although Valentine (1968) produced a classic published critique of the culture of poverty construct, we suspect that many "activist anthropologists" who became deeply involved in local political struggles have stopped writing academic books and articles. Contrary to right-wing propaganda that these "radicals" are taking over academia, our more politically active colleagues often either fail to get tenure or simply leave the academy altogether. For whatever reason, they apparently have been unable to find a way to combine their academic and political work. Unfortunately, we know precious little about where these "pushed out" activists go. To our knowledge, no one has bothered to tell their stories. Are they teaching in community colleges? Are they writing articles for local newspapers? Or have they succumbed to political disillusionment?

Despite such losses, as previously noted, the number of politically active anthropologists and sociologists appears to be growing. The Department of Anthropology at the University of Texas is an excellent case in point. The department now prides itself in ideological, cultural, and gender diversity, as well as a strong "activist anthropology" orientation. Several of our colleagues seem to have found the formula for balancing academic and political activities. For example, Charlie Hale has worked extensively in the land rights struggles of Nicaraguan indigenous groups. He recruits and trains indigenous Mayan anthropologists who actively work for these social movements and write highly critical accounts of Mayan ethnology. He and his students have done very specific research that aids their clients in legal cases, where he has been called upon to testify as an expert witness.

Another UT colleague, Ted Gordon, is a longtime activist among the African Creole populations of Nicaragua. Like Hale, Gordon works directly with ethnic political movements, and his highly successful African Diaspora program has trained many African American and Afro-Caribbean anthropologists. Yet other UT colleagues, Martha Menchaca, director of the borderlands program, and Richard Flores, director of the folklore program, have trained a number of activist Latina/o students. Menchaca has participated directly in legal research on racism and voter redistricting legislation as well. Flores (2002) has written a strong critique of Texas's most sacred cultural icon, the Alamo. Our politically active UT colleagues have all published scholarly, academic cultural critiques (Gordon, 1997; Hale, 1994; Menchaca, 2002). Nevertheless, Hale (n.d.) distances his own ethnographic practice from the Marcus and Fischer (1986) notion of cultural critiques. He contends that too many of the new cultural critics place greater emphasis on creating a "safe academic space" and publishing than on community service and political activism. In contrast, a genuinely "activist anthropologist" is more involved in local political struggles, and, like Sol Tax, Hale claims that such involvement produces better ethnographies.

It would seem that progressive social scientists have gained a foothold in the academy and have created a space for themselves. The browning, queering, and gendering of the academy and the social sciences surely is at work here. People of color, women, gays, and working-class academics are slowly replacing upper-middle-class, white, male gentleman scholars. Furthermore, the emergence of the interdisciplinary field of critical cultural studies has created many new journals and special series in university presses. A market for more critical, investigative ethnographies that expose relations of power and exploitation clearly has evolved. But these developments have their limits.

From a professional survival point of view, the idea of a safe space from which to publish makes considerable sense. It is no secret that Division I research institutions are "publish or perish" meat grinders. You either publish articles in the refereed journals of your field—and books if your department is a "book department"—or you get fired. The rub for many critical ethnographers is that their scholarship must be political in an academically acceptable manner. Consequently, many progressive academics spend most of their time writing and publishing cultural critiques that satisfy the demands of the academy and their peers. This observation is not intended to diminish the exceptional quality of many cultural critiques (Foley & Moss, 2001). Rather, it is meant to highlight the institutional pressures that many activist academics face. Unfortunately, there are few accounts of how the 21st-century knowledge production industry is changing. Most critical ethnographers, our UT colleagues included, rarely chronicle the psychological and monetary price that they pay for their political activism. As we shall see in the following case studies, we have both experienced enough pressures of political correctness to warn fledgling "critical ethnographers" what they too may face.

Case Study 1: A Cultural Critic in Search of Collaborative Methods

Being someone who has written several cultural critiques (Foley, 1990, 1995), I generally agree with Hale's assessment that such studies often are not particularly collaborative or directly political. When I left the anti–Vietnam War movement for academia, I found it a hostile environment for activist social scientists. I have written about my troubled adaptation to academia elsewhere (Foley, 2000). Put simply, in 1970 the University of Texas was a pretty conservative place. George I. Sanchez, a noted Chicano scholar, was the only colleague who encouraged me to do activist research. Like many young scholars with progressive political views, I had to make a number of agonizing compromises. It was the Vietnam war years, which made publishing my dissertation on American neocolonialism in the Philippines difficult. Consequently, I followed Sanchez's advice and began studying colonialism and racism in nearby South Texas. There I was, a former Student for Democratic Society (SDS) activist, wondering whether I was a sold-out academic. Political correctness pressures came from both sides of the American racial divide. Many white faculty saw little point to political activism, and many Chicana/o faculty distrusted *gringo* social scientists who wanted to join the *movimento.* Moreover, being the first ethnographer in a college of education filled with unrepentant positivists, it was difficult to garner high merit evaluations. It seemed as though I would have to produce twice as much as my apolitical colleagues to survive professionally. I felt compelled to cut down on time-consuming political activities so I could produce more publications, and that pattern of adaptation has dogged me throughout my career.

But old political habits die hard, and being a critical ethnographer involves much more than simply writing good cultural critiques. It also involves fighting for institutional reforms, for example, recruiting faculty and mentoring students who have experienced class, race, and gender discrimination. During that era, battling positivism was also a form of political struggle. More important, however, we found a few ways to be directly involved in the Chicano civil rights movement that we were studying (Foley, 1990; Foley with Mota, Post, & Lozano, 1989). Our research team, which included Brazilian Clarice Mota and local Chicano Ignacio Lozano, lived in the barrio, and we frequently voiced our opinions to local Raza Unida Party leaders regarding their political strategies and tactics (Foley, 1999). We also encouraged many local Chicano/a youth to go beyond their high school education. Finally, when La Raza Unida's director of the health care study quit, I went to work for the party and wrote up its research findings.

Nevertheless, our research team also tried to maintain a degree of detachment and neutrality. We wanted to produce a balanced ethnography that spanned the racial divide and included Anglo perspectives as well. We used all the classic methods of good ethnography, including participant observation, interviews, and informant work, in order to write a complex, rich portrait of race relations and the Chicano movement inside and outside schools. In the end, writing a critical ethnography that valorized the Chicano movement's efforts became more important than any direct local political work. As the project evolved, I rationalized my relative lack of political action with a cultural critique argument. We were giving voice to the voiceless Chicana and Chicano masses, thus raising the consciousness of the nation regarding inequality in South Texas. If what I wrote made a few Chicano/as be proud of their movement, or made a few Anglos question their racial attitudes, then my cultural critique was having—to use Patti Lather's (1991) apt phrase—a "catalytic [i.e., political] effect." In addition, the historical ethnography I wrote would have the "professional effect" of getting tenure for me and keeping bread on the family table.

Because we approached the research task in a rather traditional manner, there was very little effort to involve local people in the research process itself. We set the research agenda and wrote the ethnography that we deemed important. Being the lead author, I theorized the data and told the story I wanted to tell. Nevertheless, it is important to underscore some key ways that we tried to make our cultural critique more collaborative than are most "scientific" and/or critical ethnographies. First, like most good ethnographers, we developed a set of intimate, trusting relationships with several highly knowledgeable key community residents. These relationships helped us develop an "insider's" perspective on local life. At times, these relationships evolved into friendships, and some local residents became our "anthropological confidants" or "collaborators." They helped us focus and correct our understanding of local events and relationships. We often shared our interpretations with these locals, and as the relationships developed, we shared more of our mutual biographies. The point here is that good cultural critiques usually are based on a number of intimate, "collaborative" relations with research subjects.

Second, we used a conversational or dialogic style of interviewing, which encouraged the subjects to participate more. We interviewed in a very informal manner, and at times we shared more personal information about ourselves than do conventional interviewers. When these free-flowing conversations were transcribed, they often were shared with the respondents. That provided key informants with the opportunity to see how their own speech objectified and represented them. If they did not like their self-representations, they were free to edit their comments. This, of course, led some informants to censor their negative remarks, but sharing the interviews clearly enhanced local confidence in our intentions to be fair. In short, a more open-ended, conversational interviewing style generated more engaged personal narratives and more candid opinions. It also tended to humanize the interviewer and diminish her power and control of the interview process.

Third, we had a number of community members review our ethnographic manuscript before publication. Very few anthropologists were doing this sort of collaboration with their research subjects in the mid-1970s. I have elaborated elsewhere (Foley, with Mota et al., 1989) just how valuable and ethical this methodological procedure is. It allows us to correct a number of interpretations and representations.

Later, I used the same community review technique in a study of my hometown (Foley, 1995), and it added an important collaborative dimension to our cultural critique. Although this sort of collaboration does not relinquish authorial authority, it does add a great deal of reflexivity to the data collection and representational process. When local actors criticized our representations as slanted or partial, we made a serious effort to better corroborate our interpretations. We also changed the tone and tried to nuance the portrayals of several events and individuals. We took seriously what our local readers criticized, but we did not give them complete control over what we wrote. We created a dialogic, negotiated process that gave them some input into what we wrote, but in the end I wrote what I deemed important. In retrospect, we definitely amended the classic notion of the detached, all-knowing ethnographic scientist, but not entirely.

Finally, I sought to write our ethnography in a much more accessible, engaging ethnographic narrative style. Very early in my career, I came to see the cultural and linguistic gap between the anthropological observer and his subject as elitist and politically unprogressive. Over the years, it became clear that many of my undergraduates could not understand fully the ethnographies we assigned them to read. For political reasons, I came to embrace the ideal that ordinary people must be able to read and understand my ethnography. How can academics possibly serve the people they write about if their subjects cannot understand what they write?

It now seems obvious that academics have to liberate themselves from the pedantic, technical discourse of their disciplines if they hope to write useful stories. Methodologically, writing better is absolutely crucial for creating a kind of linguistic reciprocity between the research subjects and the researcher. This is an important, often unacknowledged form of "collaboration" that leads to more politically useful critical ethnographies.

Unfortunately, no young scholar who has been thoroughly socialized in an academic PhD program can accomplish this easily. At every turn, dissertation committee members, journal editors, and fellow students/colleagues will press a young scholar to retain a pedantic, technical, academic, storytelling style. One's personal identity and professional success seem to depend upon mastering this peculiar form of self-expression. Recent experimentation with mixed genres like autoethnographies has opened up some space in the academy, but the technical, theory-driven academic ethnography remains the standard toward which young scholars must aspire. The senior scholars who control the machinery of academic production and promotion maintain a tight grip on the conventions of social scientific writing. This surely will be the last bastion to fall, if ever it does. In the meantime, the social sciences remain a rather elitist, "high culture" form of social commentary.

To sum up, we opened up the process of producing ethnographies through the following means: a dialogic style of interviewing; intimate, highly personal informant relations; a community review of the manuscript; and writing in ordinary language. These practices, and many more being invented as we speak, make fieldwork—and telling stories about one's fieldwork—more open, more collaborative, and less hierarchical in character. We tried to break significantly with the attitudes and practices of positivistic scientific ethnography and scientific realism (Marcus & Cushman, 1982). Nevertheless, we fell far short of the ethical and political standard that Mâori scholar Linda Tuhiwai Smith (1999) advocates. She urges non-Mâori scholars to collaborate with the tribal elders, who help scholars define what they research and review what they write. In the Mesquaki study (Foley, 1995), I worked with tribal leaders and the tribal council, but the tribal elders neither set my research agenda nor monitored my fieldwork. I also acknowledged their way of knowing through dreams and vision quests, but I made no attempts to utilize those epistemologies. I retained more authorial authority than I would have under the Mâori community review process. Ultimately, I wrote the story I wanted to write—with, however, a good deal of input from key informants and from the community review. As we shall see, I was not as directly involved in community political processes as my coauthor has been.

The most politically active form of action anthropology emphasizes direct involvement in political movements, court cases, and aggressive organizing activities such as rent strikes. Other policy-oriented social scientists "work within the system" and write prizewinning cultural critiques as well as actively shape the public policy process. Accordingly, what follows is Angela Valenzuela's account of how she blends academic research and political commitment in a unique way.

Case Study 2: An "Activist Sociologist" and Her Legislative Involvement

I write to impart my craft—at least with respect to a certain kind of research in which I am currently involved. That is, I conduct "regular" ethnographic research—mostly in schools—using standard qualitative techniques in an attempt to generate better theoretical frameworks through which to both understand social problems and promote the development of just policies and practices in schools. The account that follows, however, reveals how my general interest in politics has evolved into a research approach that may be termed either "the ethnography of public policy" or the "public ethnography of policy."[1]

I am a third-generation Mexican American from West Texas reared in a community where the race and class lines between Anglos and Mexican Americans were sharply drawn for the greater part of the last century. I am also a product of the Texas public school system. I thus have a firsthand sense of its strengths and limitations with respect to the U.S.-Mexican community. I write primarily from my current vantage point as a member of the faculty at the University of Texas at Austin who is involved in the affairs of the Latino community at various levels. As an academic, I currently hold a tenured, joint appointment in two colleges, Education and Liberal Arts, at the University of Texas. In the College of Education, my appointment is in the Department of Curriculum and Instruction (C & I), and in Liberal Arts, it is in the Center for Mexican American Studies (CMAS). I see myself as situated within a tradition of activist-scholarship previously undertaken by Chicano faculty at the University of Texas at Austin that includes the work of Américo Paredes, George I. Sanchez, and Carlos Castañeda.

Like my colleague Doug Foley, I, too, have endured a prolonged and painful struggle to find my voice and write in a broadly accessible style. However, unlike my colleague, I have long felt a special sense of responsibility that comes precisely from my social and political location as a member of a community lacking in voice, status, and representation at all levels. Acquiring my voice thus has been inseparable from my community's broader agenda to also be heard, and in so doing, to acquire power and political representation. Moreover, my profound desire to write to, and for, my community is what has encouraged me to persist.

I sometimes contemplate how, unlike my Anglo academic colleagues, I have probably been "more liberated" to pursue other rhetorical avenues in both writing and speech. More pointedly, as a minority female scholar, I always suspected that no matter what or how I wrote, I would never quite reap the same privileges and status within the academic hierarchy. The experiences of other minority academics taught me that both acquiring tenure and the goal of institutional validation and legitimacy, generally, are risky pursuits that frequently are characterized by uncertainty and struggle regardless of one's chosen research approach. Consequently, and despite the risks involved, soon after graduating from a positivistic, quantitative Sociology Department at Stanford University, I decided to follow my heart and develop a more humanistic, qualitative research approach. I did so within the context of my first job, a tenure-track position in the Department of Sociology at Rice University in Houston, Texas. It is relevant to note that to date, I am the only Mexican American female professor ever to have been hired for a tenure-track faculty position at Rice.

To best explain my craft, I must first situate myself within my academic/scholarly community and within the broader Latina/o activist community in Texas. What my personal account reveals is the importance of my insider status within the Latino community, coupled with my desire to use research to address the inequities of political and policymaking processes. Although I am less reflexive than some experimental ethnographers (Denzin, 1997), I am collaborative in the first sense that we outline. That is, I have always developed intimate, trusting relationships with collaborators. With respect to the second sense of collaboration, wherein community members review my manuscripts before publication, this has proven somewhat problematic. The process of "studying up" and exposing how elites wield power in my community makes this kind of collaboration either impossible or limited (especially see Valenzuela, 2004a, 2004b). Although I do share my legislative work with select Latina/o leadership, legislators, and State Board of Education members, I nevertheless preserve a great deal of authorial authority. To best explain my current status and position in the legislature, my research background in Houston, Texas, must first be taken into account.

While working at Rice University, I conducted a case study of a local high school that culminated in my book *Subtractive Schooling: U.S.-Mexican Youth and the Politics of Caring* (Valenzuela, 1999). Spanning a 3-year time period, I generated a ground-level ethnography that examined the assimilation experiences of high school youth and how these, in turn, related to achievement and school orientations. Because I wanted the study to appeal directly to the Latino community in Houston, I incorporated an historical perspective and wrote in a language that made it accessible to them. I should add, however, that my desire to be tenured led me to invest a great deal in becoming a "real scholar" within the academy. Combined with my Stanford-based "programming" to develop theory, my academic past had proven to be a constraint of sorts. For example, my deductive-nomological interest in assimilation kept me from seeing, for an extended amount of time, how caring theory could fit into an argument about assimilation (see Valenzuela, 1999, Appendix). It also kept me from seeing—at least to the degree that I now see it—how the testing system itself subtracts resources from students (see Valenzuela, 2000).

My fieldwork on *Subtractive Schooling* nevertheless provided me with an in-depth perspective on local and district policies and politics. I attended various churches, frequented parks, purchased goods and services, exercised, and attended numerous functions in the community surrounding the school that I studied. This experience further provided me with firsthand experiences concerning the frequently challenging conditions of urban life for working-class, Mexican-origin people living in Houston at that time. In short, through my research, I became a trusted member of Houston's inner-city Latino community.

While in Houston, I also was a founding member and chair of the Latino Education Policy Committee (LEPC). The LEPC was composed of researchers, parents, clergy, and community activists. When the former U.S. Secretary of Education, Rodney Paige, was superintendent, the LEPC fought district battles pertaining to the representation of minorities in the district's magnet school programs, as well as another regarding certain Houston Independent School District (HISD) board members' decisions to curtail the bilingual education program in the district. These activities brought me into contact with a rather large array of individuals including League of United Latin American Citizens (LULAC) leadership and council members, city council members, school board members, and state senators and representatives, including State Representative Dora Olivo (D-Rosenberg), with whom I later worked.

Through my work as an associate with the Rice University Center for Education, my network also included large numbers of Houston-area researchers, teachers, administrators, school personnel, and board members. I myself was a board member of the following organizations: Annenberg Foundation, Teach for America, and the Inter-Ethnic Forum. Because of my personal relationship with Lee Brown, I even participated on his transition team when he became Houston's first African American mayor. Despite my multiple political commitments in Houston—which always were part of my larger goal of getting to know the city from multiple perspectives—my professional life continued, primarily through my involvement in professional associations like the American Sociological Association, the American Educational Research Association, and the National Association for Chicana and Chicano Studies.

My family situation also is an important part of my current role as a "participatory action researcher" in the Texas state legislature. My husband, Emilio Zamora, is a Texas historian, award-winning author, and community activist. With my return to Texas from California, I inherited his Houston and Texas network, permitting a smooth and quick transition into the Houston Latino community. Marriage to an academic in a related field also has meant a continuous flow of intellectual and political ideas. We have two children, ages 8 and 11, and in 1998, our family won "Family of the Year" for Houston's 16 of September celebration (marking Mexico's acquisition of independence from Spain in 1810). City officials held a banquet in our honor, and our story appeared as an insert in the city's only major newspaper, the *Houston Chronicle.* Our picture was posted on all of the Metro buses throughout the week of festivities. It is not an overstatement to suggest that at least for a time, the Zamora-Valenzuela family became a virtual household name in the Houston Latino community.

From my standpoint as an activist sociologist, this kind of activity and notoriety had both an upside and a downside. Unfortunately, matters soured for me at Rice University, and I ended up filing a claim against my employer with the Equal Employment Opportunity Commission, alleging gender and national origins discrimination. After a protracted struggle with my employer, we arrived at a mutually agreed upon and amicable settlement. Notwithstanding this moment of personal and familial strife, my research approach surely facilitated my deeper involvement in community political processes. The payoff for me was the community's generous support throughout my tenure review in the form of letters, meetings with university officials, and public recognition of our contributions to Houston's Latino community. In the end, these relationships with key political players helped me both to produce my critical ethnography and to expose the harmful aspects of current educational policies.

During my final year in Houston in 1999, Al Kauffman, lead counsel of the Mexican American Legal Defense and Educational Fund (MALDEF), called on me to testify in a federal suit against the Texas Education Agency and the State Board of Education. The plaintiff's case argued that the state's testing system discriminated against them. All were either Latino/a or African American. They all had obtained the necessary credits for graduation but were denied diplomas because of their inability to pass the high-stakes standardized test. Of all students who fail the state exam statewide, 87% are either Latina/o or African American. During the trial, I was able to bring my own data on immigrant achievement to bear on the questions at hand (see Valenzuela, 1999, 2000).

Unfortunately, MALDEF won the argument that minorities are disproportionately affected by the state's testing system but lost the case because the judge decided that the harm against the plaintiffs did not reach a "constitutional level" (*GI Forum et al. v. Texas Educational Agency et al.*, 2000). That is, due process allegedly was followed in the development of the test and also by allowing students multiple opportunities to take it (see Valenzuela, 2004b). The MALDEF case was transformative because it situated me in the center of crucial state- and national-level policy debates and political activities. I was handed the file for the state, which acquainted me with the policies, evidence, and justifications for the state's testing system. This information helped me to see new ways that the state reproduced educational inequalities while cleverly obscuring them (especially see McNeil & Valenzuela, 2001). My earlier research presented a bottom-up perspective, but participation in the trial helped me develop a more comprehensive, policy-based, top-down analysis as well (Valenzuela, 2002, 2004a, 2004b).

After a year of commuting from Houston to Austin in 1999, during which Emilio secured employment in the School of Information at UT, my family eventually relocated to Austin in the summer of 2000. My work in the legislature began almost immediately upon my arrival when State Representative Dora Olivo asked me to testify on the state's testing system. My Houston network thus followed me, providing me with relatively easy entrée into the Austin lawmaking community.

My interest in policy was further abetted by the CMAS position for which I was hired. That is, my duties included teaching lower- and upper-division courses in public policy, which many CMAS students must take in order to major in Mexican American Studies (the rest pursue a cultural studies concentration). This position forced me to retool and learn more about Texas government, statutes, history, and the policymaking process. Upon completing their policy studies courses, many of our CMAS students pursue internships at the state capitol for which they simultaneously earn college credit. My Mexican American Studies students, in turn, have taught me a great deal and provided me with information that I fold into my writings on educational policy.

At the graduate level, I also offer a course on policy titled Latino Education Policy in Texas. The course is cross-listed with the Lyndon B. Johnson (LBJ) School of Public Affairs. I offer it during every other year when the legislature is in session, and my students, some of whom are former CMAS undergraduates, typically are policy studies majors from either the LBJ school or the College of Education.

Today, I hold the following community-based posts: Education Committee Chair for the Texas League of United Latin American Citizens (LULAC), the nation's oldest Latino civil rights organization; member of an Austin LULAC council called Legislative LULAC; member of the Legislative Committee for the Texas Association for Bilingual Education (TABE); and member of the newly revived La Raza Unida working education group. All of these activities reflect my current position as an advocate for Latina/o youth in the legislature. My legislative activities include advising representatives and senators on different kinds of legislation in the areas of assessment, limited English proficient youth, bilingual education, school vouchers, and school finance. My most intense work has been with State Representative Olivo, with whom I have worked for two biennial legislative sessions to craft and promote legislation in the area of assessment (for a review of this work, see Valenzuela, 2004b, 2000).

Prior to Austin, my research and policy work—particularly through the Latino Education Policy Committee—were somewhat separate tasks. That is, my role was one of bringing my expertise to bear on certain issues. In time, my professional role has evolved from being an ethnographer in the classic sense to being a direct advocate for change. This redefinition of my role as a researcher grew primarily out of a process that began with a deeply felt identification with the political associations—such as LULAC, MALDEF, TABE, and the Intercultural Development Research Association (IDRA)—that advocate on behalf of the U.S.-Mexican community.

Whenever I testified in committee hearings at the state capitol, I found myself generating field notes from all of my experiences. Then I discovered a virtual gold mine of audio archives of committee hearings (at the legislature's Web site, www.capitol.state.tx.us), "data" that are used more by attorneys and legislative staff than researchers. These discoveries dovetailed neatly with my more general interest in informing my community of the politics and process of policy making.

My preference always was (and is) to be the person who merely chronicled and analyzed the unfolding of legislation. My experiences at the capitol, however, have taught me that a number of policy areas, such as assessment and accountability, are woefully underresearched. Upon losing the federal MALDEF trial, the Chicano caucus members anticipated that an appeal would not likely fare well in the conservative Fifth Circuit Court. Consequently, the struggle for a more just assessment system would shift back to the state legislature, where most educational policies originate.

In Fall, 2000, upon moving to Austin, I had hoped to chronicle just such an effort, but I soon realized that both majority and minority advocates were operationally defining equity as *equal access to mandated testing*. That is, the legislative concerns that predominated centered around which students were getting which tests rather than whether a numbers-based, single-number accountability system is a flawed design (McNeil & Valenzuela, 2001; Valenzuela, 2004b). This impoverished definition of equity meant that no one was initiating progressive legislation on the uses of assessment.

In light of this vacuum in leadership, I downloaded the accountability law and revised it from a single-indicator system based on test scores to a multiple-indicator system based on test scores, grades, and teacher recommendations. In this revised version, multiple indicators were to figure into all retention, promotion, and graduation decisions. Much like the admissions processes in most Texas colleges and universities, multiple indicators help compensate for poor test scores. Moreover, because assessment drives curriculum, use of multiple indicators would minimize the teaching to the test, the narrowing of curricula, and the further marginalizing of students that Linda McNeil and I observed to be the case in Houston's inner-city schools (for a more elaborate discussion, see McNeil & Valenzuela, 2001; Valenzuela, 2002).

In November, 2000, I shared the new language of my "multiple indicators" idea with MALDEF attorneys Al Kauffman and Joe Sanchez, who then converted it into legalese. They walked the halls of the capitol searching for a bill sponsor. None of the Anglo representatives on the Committee on Public Education in the House wanted to carry the legislation. Only Representative Dora Olivo, a former teacher who was knowledgeable about the abuses of the testing system, was willing to sponsor it.

I still remember the sense of relief I felt on the day that we found our bill's sponsor. Al Kauffman, lead MALDEF attorney and honorary Mexican, e-mailed me with these words: "On the real difficult issues, *solamente la gente trabaja con nosotros y para nosotros* [only our people work with and for us]."[2] His sincere expression of solidarity and struggle still touches me deeply today.

With his use of Spanish and his reference to "our people," Al Kauffman gave voice to both our struggle for power and also how policy making is racialized independently of the merits of the legislation that we, as minorities, bring to the table. Although our proposal for just assessment practices promised to benefit all children regardless of race, what seemed to matter more in the eyes of the reluctant legislators was *who* was bringing it to their attention rather than *what* the proposal contained. I suspect that if our team both had been Anglo and had not been associated with either civil rights or the MALDEF court case, our proposal would have been received differently. However much they inform policy work, it is impossible to regret such circumstances. They refer to obstacles over which we have no control.

Our strategy has thus been to mobilize our constituents, continue working with our white allies—many of them scholars such as Professors Linda McNeil at Rice University and Walt Haney at Boston University—and educate legislators, newspaper columnists, and the lay public to begin considering how the state's approach to accountability marginalizes either students, the curriculum, or both. With the recent, high-profile exposés of fraudulent accounting of dropouts in the Houston Independent School District by the *New York Times,* coupled with arguments of how such practices are encouraged by design (Schemo 2003a, 2003b; Winerip, 2003), we already have achieved a modicum of success.

Looking back, it was my familiarity with discourse and rhetorical analysis that helped me decipher how state legislators used the slippery term "accountability." My understanding of their rhetoric and logic led me to craft arguments for new accountability practices that were incremental. The idea was to subtly alter, not dismantle, the existing accountability structure. To this end, we contended that because accountability is a large and complex system, it requires a more complex form of assessment. For evaluating students for high-stakes decisions (promotion, retention, and graduation), the state needs an assessment system premised on multiple measures rather than a single, narrow measure based on students' test scores. From a rhetorical standpoint, we framed our proposed legislation in language and justification that was both logical and less threatening to the larger political edifice of accountability (see Valenzuela, 2004b).

Initially, I thought my authority to advocate such an approach before legislative caucus members came from prior research in schools, from my status as a university professor, from my state- and national-level connections, and from being a citizen and having children in the public school system. Yet none of these factors would have been sufficient to convince legislators to rethink the concept of accountability and, in so doing, to consider our proposal seriously. In retrospect, it mattered that I am closely identified with the Mexican community *and* that I am directly involved in the recurrent struggles of Chicana/o legislators to either craft helpful legislation or weigh in on legislation that is not helpful. Moreover, I showed how deeply I was moved by the tragedy of unfairness in the assessment of children of color, as well as for all children generally. Additionally, my demonstrated interest and involvement in issues extending beyond assessment (e.g., legislative issues pertaining to English language learners) manifested my commitment to the Latina/o community, generally, while shielding me from the criticism often heaped upon university academics that their involvement is typically limited and self-serving in nature.

Without these crucial ingredients of identification, direct action, and a principled commitment to the community, my plea for a more humane multiple assessment approach would have lacked moral and ethical force. At first, I resented the circumstances that placed me in this position. I simply wanted to study the reform and not to be the person who was pivotal in achieving it. In time, however, I came to see how my knowledge and expertise could be used for meaningful change and also to appreciate the value of first-hand experience and skills associated with the legislative process. This by now long-term collaboration with Chicana/o political leaders is what pushed me to conduct a deeper, critical analysis of the state's school system. Immersed in the legislative process, I came to see how the Texas Education Agency's official rhetoric and the sanitized test results provided to the media obscured both the material conditions of schooling and the state's purported mission to educate all students equitably and thereby close the achievement gap.

The other side of my collaboration with state legislators is an equally intense collaboration with my graduate students. To date, all of the doctoral students with whom I work directly are engaged in education policy research. Our collective efforts push me to theorize, explain, and represent our observations of the legislature and legislators in new ways.

The dual role that I now play as both researcher and advocate constitutes a major break with my original training as a social scientist. I have found a way of doing social science that goes beyond the insipid, apolitical positivism that I learned in graduate school. At this point, it gives me enormous personal satisfaction to continue using my privileged status as a scholar to support and promote a social justice agenda. Moreover, being a *Tejana* and Mexican American female scholar imbues this calling with a special sense of urgency and purpose.

▣ Conclusion

We have tried to raise some issues and make some distinctions that will move self-proclaimed "critical ethnographers" to interrogate their current ethnographic practice. By contrasting our own ethnographic and political practices, we discovered an interesting difference that helps clarify the notion of collaboration. On one hand, Foley has spent his career writing cultural critiques of American capitalism and its schools, but he has spent considerably less time in direct political involvement. In lieu of joining various progressive political struggles, he joined the ideological struggle against positivism and scientism. Like many progressive academics, this allowed him to survive professionally but left him longing for more direct political involvement as a "citizen anthropologist."

In this regard, he admires the passionate and direct political involvement of his colleague, Angela Valenzuela. She feels a deep moral bond to her ethnic group, and she works tirelessly for its betterment as an expert witness, researcher, and adviser to various Chicana/o legislators. She also mentors many of her students along this path. When Valenzuela responded somewhat apologetically about being less "reflexive" than I am, that mirrored for me how my notion of "collaboration" has shifted over the years. In some ways, I have become "the effect" of the powerful postmodern experimentalist discourse in anthropology. This made it harder for me to see that the following notions of collaboration—decentering the author, deconstructing theory, polyphonic texts, dialogic interviewing, and even community review of the texts—are no more fundamental than Valenzuela's notion of "collaboration."

On the surface, she and her award-winning ethnography do not seem to meet the postmodern ideals of reflexivity and a coproduced narrative. She does not deploy the experimental ethnography discourse rhetorically to make her text more authoritative. Moreover, this chapter is her first attempt at portraying the ethical-political ground of her ethnographic practice. Earlier, she recounted how she is linked to the Chicano political movement and its efforts to change society. Privately, she talks about having a "spiritual" connection with her research subjects—many of whom are political allies. They share a common historical memory of being a racialized, stigmatized people. When she participates in the struggle, she feels affirmed and empowered, and she experiences a shared sense of fate. These feelings compel her to write caring and thoughtful portraits of her people.

In effect, Valenzuela identifies and collaborates with her subjects in a deep psychological and political way. There is a sense of being *carnales* (brothers/sisters) and *camaradas* (comrades). In return, they expect her to be what Antonio Gramsci (1971) would call one of their "organic intellectuals." She has made it through a racist economic and educational system. She now has the academic credentials and the writing skills to be among a select community of experts, authors, and persons who, to use Gayatri Spivak's (1988) apt phrase, "strategically essentialize" their struggle. In the end, they may refuse many of the collaborative methodological practices advocated in experimental, postmodern ethnography. This is not to argue that one notion of collaboration is superior to the other, but it is clear that "native" or insider ethnographers may have to march to the beat of a different drummer. Ethical commitments to their subjects/political allies may compel them to be collaborative in more spiritual and less procedural, methodological ways. Our differences suggest that there are a number of ways of being collaborative. Each ethnographer ultimately develops his or her own notions of collaboration, positionality, and authorship.

Valenzuela's account of how her direct involvement in the legislative process led her to a greater understanding is a ringing endorsement for Hale's notion of activist anthropology. Researchers who are involved directly in the political process are in a better position to understand and theorize about social change. This being true, the academy must find many more ways to reward "citizen-scholars" who are both assisting local communities and producing more deeply grounded research studies. Unfortunately, the academy still mainly rewards scholars who produce universalistic "theoretical knowledge." The ruling academic elite of most disciplines still devalues the production of local, politically useful, "applied knowledge." As a result, many progressive scholars may minimize or even hide their attempts to produce the kind of practical knowledge needed to transform local communities and institutional policies.

At different points in history, the academy has punished progressive scholars for being too active politically. There are signs that the country is presently moving toward a new era of McCarthyism under the banner of fighting terrorism. Notwithstanding the presence of Mexican American Studies centers and other safe spaces that offer protection through a connection to community, the so-called safe space created by post-1960s cultural critics in the academy could disappear rather quickly if political lines harden. Consequently, it is with some urgency that we exhort our academic peers to valorize and share more openly the political dimensions of their fieldwork. There are undoubtedly political risks, but what other choice is there for so-called public intellectuals who live in an empire with enough bombs to destroy the world?

Perhaps future scholars who live in a more humane society and world will look back on this little post-1960s opening of "critical ethnography" with a bit of wonder. What our generation is doing may seem a little like the medical science of leeches or chemotherapy—a modest beginning at best. On a substantive level, we see many promising new varieties of critical ethnography. We have suggested many ways to question our notions of purpose, positionality, collaboration, and writing styles. Transforming the academic knowledge production industry obviously requires much more than challenging the ideology of positivism and scientism. We also need to change the way academic publishing is organized and controlled, and the way promotion and tenure for publication and public service is awarded. We also must continue to open up the academy to underrepresented groups so that they, too, may contribute to scholarship. Critical ethnography that embraces the public interest truly will flower when we can transform academia.

Notes

1. Angela Valenzuela wishes to thank her colleague, Bill Black, for his suggestion of the latter term.
2. Personal communication in 2001 to Angela Valenzuela during the first weeks of the legislative session.

References

Bennett, J. W. (1996). Applied and action anthropology: Ideological and conceptual aspects. *Current Anthropology, 36,* 23–53.

Brodkin, K. (2001). Diversity in anthropological theory. In I. Susser & T. Patterson (Eds.), *Cultural diversity in the United States* (pp. 368–387). Oxford, UK: Blackwell.

Burawoy, M. (1991). *Ethnography unbound.* Berkeley: University of California Press.

Burawoy, M. (2000). *Global ethnography: Forces, connections, and imaginations in a postmodern world.* Berkeley: University of California Press.

Carspecken, P. (1996). *Critical ethnography in educational research: A theoretical and practical guide.* London: Routledge.

Denzin, N. K. (1997). *Interpretive ethnography: Ethnographic practices for the 21st century.* Newbury Park, CA: Sage.

Denzin, N. K., & Lincoln, Y. S. (Eds.). (2000). *Handbook of qualitative research* (2nd ed.). Thousand Oaks, CA: Sage.

Douglas, J. (1976). *Investigative social research.* Beverly Hills, CA: Sage.

Eddy, E., & Partridge, W. (Eds.). (1987). *Applied anthropology in America* (2nd ed.). New York: Columbia University Press.

Fine, M., & Weis, L. (1998). *The unknown city: Lives of poor and working class young adults.* Boston: Beacon.

Fine, M., & Weis, L. (2000). *Speed bumps: A student-friendly guide to qualitative research.* New York: Teachers College Press.

Fine, M., Weis, L., Weseen, S., & Wong, L. (2000). For whom: Qualitative research, representations, and social responsibilities. In N. K. Denzin & Y. S. Lincoln (Eds.), *Handbook of qualitative research* (2nd ed., pp. 107–133). Thousand Oaks, CA: Sage.

Flores, R. (2002). *Remembering the Alamo: Memory, modernity and the master symbol.* Austin: University of Texas Press.

Foley, D. (1990). *Learning capitalist culture: Deep in the heart of Tejas.* Philadelphia: University of Pennsylvania Press.

Foley, D. (1995). *The heartland chronicles.* Philadelphia: University of Pennsylvania Press.

Foley, D. (1999). The Fox project: A reappraisal. *Current Anthropology, 40*(2), 171–191.

Foley, D. (2000, Spring). Studying the politics of Raza Unida politics: Reflections of a white anthropologist. *Reflexiones: New Directions in Mexican American Studies,* 51–81.

Foley, D. (2002). Critical ethnography: The reflexive turn. *International Journal of Qualitative Studies in Education, 15*(4), 469–491.

Foley, D., Levinson, B., & Hurtig, J. (2001). Anthropology goes inside: The new educational ethnography of ethnicity and gender. In W. Secada (Ed.), *Review of research in education* (pp. 37–99). Washington, DC: American Educational Research Association Publications.

Foley, D., & Moss, K. (2001). Studying American cultural diversity: Some non-essentializing perspectives. In I. Susser & T. Patterson (Eds.), *Teaching cultural diversity* (pp. 130–152). London: Blackwell.

Foley, D., with Mota, C., Post, D., & Lozano, I. (1989). *From peones to politicos: Class and ethnicity in a South Texas town, 1900–1987.* Austin: University of Texas Press.

GI Forum et al. v. Texas Educational Agency et al., 87 F. Supp. 667 (W.D. Tex. 2000).

Gordon, E. T. (1997). *Disparate diasporas: Identity and politics in an African-Nicaraguan community.* Austin: University of Texas Press.

Gramsci, A. (1971). *Selections from the prison notebooks.* New York: International Publishers.

Hale, C. R. (1994). *Resistance and contradiction: Miskitu Indians and the Nicaraguan state, 1894–1987.* Stanford, CA: Stanford University Press.

Hale, C. R. (n.d.). *Activist research versus cultural critiques: Contradictions at every turn.* Unpublished paper, Department of Anthropology, University of Texas, Austin.

Haraway, D. (1988). Situated knowledges: The science question in feminism as a site of discourse on the privilege of partial perspective. *Feminist Studies, 14,* 575–599.

Harding, S. (1998). *Is science multicultural? Postcolonialisms, feminisms, and epistemology.* Bloomington: Indiana University Press.

Hymes, D. (Ed.). (1972). *Reinventing anthropology.* New York: Vintage.

Kane, S., & Mason, T. (2001). AIDS and criminal justice. *Annual Review of Anthropology, 30,* 457–479.

Kemmis, S., & McTaggart, R. (2000). Participatory action research. In N. K. Denzin & Y. S. Lincoln (Eds.), *Handbook of qualitative research* (2nd ed., pp. 567–606). Thousand Oaks, CA: Sage.

Lather, P. (1991). *Getting smart: Feminist research and pedagogy within the post-modern.* New York: Routledge.

Levinson, B., & Holland, D. (1996). The cultural production of the educated person: An introduction. In B. Levinson, D. Foley, & D. Hollands (Eds.), *The cultural production of the educated person: Critical ethnographies of schooling and local practice* (pp. 1–54). Albany: State University of New York Press.

Levinson, B., & Sutton, M. (Eds.). (2001). *Policy as practice: Towards a comparative sociological analysis of educational policy.* Westport, CT: Ablex.

Lynd, R. (1956). *Middletown: A study of American culture* (2nd ed.). New York: Harcourt Brace.

Marcus, G. (1998). *Ethnography through thick and thin.* Princeton, NJ: Princeton University Press.

Marcus, G. (Ed.). (1999). *Critical anthropology now: Unexpected contexts, shifting constituencies, changing agendas.* Santa Fe, NM: School of American Research Press.

Marcus, G., & Cushman, D. (1982). Ethnographies as texts. *Annual Review of Anthropology, 11,* 25–69.

Marcus, G., & Fischer, M. (1986). *Anthropology as cultural critique: An experimental moment in the human sciences.* Chicago: University of Chicago Press.

McNeil, L. (2000). *Contradictions of school reform: Educational costs of standardized testing.* New York: Routledge.

McNeil, L., & Valenzuela, A. (2001). The harmful impact of the TAAS system of testing in Texas: Beneath the accountability rhetoric. In M. Kornhaber & G. Orfield (Eds.), *Raising standards or raising barriers? Inequality and high stakes testing in public education* (pp. 127–150). New York: Century Foundation.

Menchaca, M. (2002). *Recovering history, constructing race: The Indian, black and white roots of Mexican Americans.* Austin: University of Texas Press.

Mills, C. W. (1959). *The sociological imagination.* New York: Oxford University Press.

Nader, L. (1996). *Naked science: Anthropological inquiry into boundaries, power, and knowledge.* New York: Routledge.

Okongwu, F., & Mencher, J. P. (2000). The anthropology of public policy: Shifting terrains. *Annual Review of Anthropology, 29,* 107–124.

Rubinstein, R. (1986). Reflections on action anthropology: Some developmental dynamics of an anthropological tradition. *Human Organization, 5,* 270–282.

Sanday, P. R. (1976). *Anthropology and the public interest: Fieldwork and theory.* New York: Academic Press.

Sanday, P. R. (1990). *Fraternity gang rape: Sex, brotherhood and privilege on campus.* New York: New York University Press.

Sanday, P. R. (1996). *A woman scorned: Acquaintance rape on trial.* New York: Doubleday.

Schemo, D. J. (2003a, August 28). For Houston schools, college claims exceed reality. *New York Times.* Retrieved August 28, 2003, from www.nytimes.com

Schemo, D. J. (2003b, July 11). Questions on data cloud luster of Houston schools. *New York Times.* Retrieved July 11, 2003, from www.nytimes.com

Scheper-Hughes, N. (1992). *Death without weeping: The violence of everyday life in Brazil.* Berkeley: University of California Press.

Scheper-Hughes, N., & Sargent, C. (Eds.). (1998). *Small wars: The cultural politics of childhood.* Berkeley: University of California Press.

Schwandt, T. A. (2000). Three epistemological stances for qualitative inquiry: Interpretivism, hermeneutics, and social constructionism. In N. K. Denzin & Y. S. Lincoln (Eds.), *Handbook of qualitative research* (2nd ed., pp. 37–84). Thousand Oaks, CA: Sage.

Smith, L. T. (1999). *Decolonizing methodologies: Research and indigenous peoples.* London: Zed Books.

Spivak, G. (1988). *Other worlds: Essays in cultural politics.* New York: Methuen.

Susser, I. (2001). Poverty and homelessness in US cities. In I. Susser & T. Patterson (Eds.), *Cultural diversity in the United States* (pp. 229–249). Oxford, UK: Blackwell.

Tax, S. (1963). *Penny capitalism: A Guatemalan Indian history.* Chicago: University of Chicago Press.

Valentine, C. (1968). *Culture and poverty: A critique and counter-proposals.* Chicago: University of Chicago Press.

Valenzuela, A. (1999). *Subtractive schooling: U.S.-Mexican youth and the politics of caring.* Albany: State University of New York Press.

Valenzuela, A. (2000). The significance of the TAAS test for Mexican immigrant and Mexican American adolescents: A case study. *Hispanic Journal of the Behavioral Sciences, 22*(4), 524–539.

Valenzuela, A. (2002). High-stakes testing and U.S.-Mexican youth in Texas: The case for multiple compensatory criteria in assessment. *Harvard Journal of Hispanic Policy, 14,* 97–116.

Valenzuela, A. (2004a). Accountability and the privatization agenda. In A. Valenzuela (Ed.), *Leaving children behind: Why Texas-style accountability fails Latino youth* (pp. 263–297). Albany: State University of New York Press.

Valenzuela, A. (2004b). The accountability debate in Texas: Continuing the conversation. In A. Valenzuela (Ed.), *Leaving children behind: Why Texas-style accountability fails Latino youth* (pp. 1–32). Albany: State University of New York Press.

Vidich, A. J., & Lyman, S. (2000). Qualitative methods: Their history in sociology and anthropology. In N. K. Denzin & Y. S. Lincoln (Eds.), *Handbook of qualitative research* (2nd ed., pp. 37–84). Thousand Oaks, CA: Sage.

Villenas, S., & Foley, D. (2002). Chicano/Latino critical ethnography of education: Borderlands cultural productions from La Frontera. In R. R. Valencia (Ed.), *Chicano school failure and success: Past, present, and future* (2nd ed., pp. 195–226). London: Routledge Falmer.

Winerip, M. (2003, August 13). The "zero dropout" miracle: Alas! Alack! A Texas tall tale. *New York Times.* Retrieved August 13, 2003, from www.nytimes.com

Wolfe, E. (1982). *Europe and people without history.* Berkeley: University of California Press.

Wolfe, T. (1974). *The new journalism.* New York: Harper and Row.

Zavella, P. (1987). *Women, work, and family in the Chicano community.* Ithaca, NY: Cornell University Press.

10

EARLY MILLENNIAL FEMINIST QUALITATIVE RESEARCH

Challenges and Contours

Virginia Olesen

The only constant in today's world is change.

—Braidotti (2000, p. 1062)

A short time into the "new millennium" (to use a limited, Westernized term), changing themes suffuse feminist qualitative research. These themes challenge feminist work wherever done, bearing on the very articulation of gender, its enactment, and the problems which inhere thereto: economic stagnation that slows growth in Westernized societies and impedes progress in developing countries; the potential for war and terrorism of whatever scope; altering relationships among major nation-states, with consequences for isolation and new coalitions; and the unceasingly rapid development of electronic communication which melts borders, transfers resources, and alters identities. Within some societies, both Eastern and Western, conservativism grows or resurges, with substantial potential to shape women's and men's lives. As Evelyn Nakano Glenn has noted, "If one accepts gender as a variable, then one must acknowledge that it is never fixed, but continually constituted and reconstituted" (2002, p. 8).

Feminism and feminist qualitative research remain highly diversified, enormously dynamic, and thoroughly challenging. Contending models of thought jostle, divergent methodological and analytical approaches compete, once clear theoretical differences (see Fee, 1983) blur, and

Author's Note. Incisive criticisms from Norman Denzin, Yvonna Lincoln, Patricia Clough, Michelle Fine, Meaghan Morris, and Yen Le Espiritu enhanced the quality of this chapter. I'm grateful to them all as well as to Judith Lorber for generous sharing of feminist research on the Sociologists for Women in Society e-mail list; to Elizabeth Allen for her roster of feminist, critical, and poststructural policy analyses; and to Adele Clarke for continuing, stimulating feminist dialogue.

divisions deepen, even as rapprochement occurs. Experimental work with new complexities engages numerous investigators at the same time that many others remain oriented to views of gendered universals and more traditional approaches. Moreover, even within the same wings of feminist research (experimental or traditional), there are disagreements on many issues, such as the most efficacious theoretical stance, treatment of voices, and research for policy use.

What follows here is rooted in an early feminist declaration I wrote for a 1975 conference on women's health in which I argued that "Rage is not enough" (1977, pp. 1–2) and called for incisive scholarship to frame, direct, and harness passion in the interests of redressing grievous problems in many areas of women's health. As a symbolic interactionist working primarily within the interactionist–social constructionist tradition (Denzin, 1992, pp. 1–21), I sympathize with sectors of deconstructive currents in interactionism and feminism that encourage provocative and productive unpacking of taken-for-granted ideas about women in specific material, historical, and cultural contexts to avoid a "fatal unclutteredness" (Mukherjee, 1994, p. 6). Research *for* women should extend and amplify research merely *about* women, to ensure that even the most revealing descriptions of unknown or recognized aspects of women's situations do not remain merely descriptions. It must be remembered, however, as Yen Le Espiritu has commented (personal communication, September 15, 2003), "Women of color have insisted that a social justice agenda address the needs of both men and women of color since they are linked to race and class." Failure to attend closely to how race, class, and gender are relationally constructed leaves feminists of color distanced from feminist agendas.

Research for women that incorporates these critical points is possible in theoretical essays and through a variety of qualitative modes using combinations of both experimental and text-oriented styles, but it is not without difficulties, as will be discussed at the end of this chapter. Feminist work sets the stage for other research, other actions, and policy that transcend and transform (Olesen, 1993). Feminist inquiry is dialectical, with different views fusing to produce new syntheses that in turn become the grounds for further research, praxis, and policy (Lupton, 1995; Nielsen, 1990, p. 29; Westkott, 1979, p. 430).

I will locate this exploration in changing currents of feminist thought (Benhabib, Butler, Cornell, & Fraser, 1995; Ebert, 1996; entire issue of *Signs*, Vol. 25, No. 4, 2000) and altering, sometimes controversial themes within qualitative research (Denzin, 1997;Gubrium & Holstein, 1997; Gupta & Ferguson, 1997; G. Miller & Dingwall, 1997; Scheurich, 1997). Feminist qualitative research is *not* a passive recipient of transitory intellectual themes and controversies. On the contrary, it influences and alters aspects of qualitative research (Charmaz & Olesen, 1997; DeVault, 1996; D. Smith, 1990a, 1990b; J. Stacey & Thorne, 1985; V. Taylor, 1998), stimulating some and irritating others. Feminisms draw from different theoretical and pragmatic orientations that reflect national contexts where feminist agendas differ widely (Evans, 2002; Morawski, 1997; *Signs*, Vol. 25, No. 4, 2000). Nevertheless, without in anyway positing a global, homogeneous, unified feminism, qualitative feminist research in its many variants, whether or not self-consciously defined as feminist, problematizes women's diverse situations as well as the gendered institutions and material and historical structures that frame those. It refers the examination of that problematic to theoretical, policy, or action frameworks to realize social justice for women (and men) in specific contexts (Eichler, 1986, p. 68; 1997, pp. 12–13). It generates new ideas to produce knowledges about oppressive situations for women, for action or further research (Olesen & Clarke, 1999).[1] Critical race and legal studies have also foregrounded issues to be reviewed here, for instance Patricia Williams's (1991) application of literary theory to analysis of legal discourse to reveal the intersubjectivity of legal constructions or Mari Matsuda's (1996) interrogation of race, gender, and the law.

As background, I will briefly outline the scope of feminist qualitative research, recognizing that this is only a partial glimpse of a substantial literature in many disciplines. This will ground a discussion of emergent complexities in feminist qualitative work and issues that feminist scholars continue to debate. These include the obdurate worries about bias and believability, objectivity and subjectivity for those who continue to rely on these criteria, and for others the demands posed by new experimental approaches in the realm of representation, voice, text, and ethical issues. The accomplishments of, shortfalls in, and future of feminist qualitative research close the chapter.

▣ Scope and Topics of Feminist Qualitative Research

Feminist work goes well beyond views that qualitative research is most useful for inquiries into subjective issues and interpersonal relations or the erroneous assumption that qualitative research cannot handle large scale issues. For reasons found in intellectual themes to be discussed shortly and the multiple use of methods (see Reinharz, 1992), feminists range from assessments of women's lives and experiences that foreground the subjective and production of subjectivities to analyses of relationships through investigation of social movements (Klawiter, 1999; Kuumba, 2002; V. Taylor, 1998; see also two special issues of *Gender and Society*—Vol. 12, No. 6, 1998, and Vol. 13, No. 1, 1999) and research reports in the feminist globalization literature (see the entire issue of *Signs*, Vol. 26, No. 4, 2001 and *International Sociology*, Vol. 18, No. 3, 2003). This includes policy and organizational studies.

It is impossible to cite even a small part of this research here, but two fields, education and health, merit mention. Within the educational realm, the range is indicated by studies such as Sandra Acker's acute observations of classroom experiences (1994), Deborah Britzman's poststructuralist analysis of the "socialization" of student teachers (1991), Diane Reay's research on social class in mothers' involvement in their children's schooling (1998), Susan Chase's narrative analysis of women school superintendents struggling with inhibiting structures (1995), and a study of how women "become gentlemen" in law school (Guinier, Fine, & Balin, 1997). Additionally, educational researchers writing about policy issues in a feminist, critical, and poststructural vein have widened policy analysis (Ball, 1994; Blackmore, 1995; de Castell & Bryson, 1997; Marshall, 1999).

In the field of health and healing, Jennifer Fishman's multimethod study of Viagra demonstrated the emergence of a new disease category, female sexual arousal, which will be the basis for prescribing Viagra-related drugs to women (2001).[2] Jennifer Fosket (1999) showed how women construct breast cancer knowledge, and Janet Shim (2000) revealed gender and other elements in biomedical knowledge formation. Nurse researchers' feminist qualitative inquiries have produced critiques of Asian women's menopausal experiences (Im, Meleis, & Park, 1999) and probed working women's lives (Hattar-Pollara, Meleis, & Nagib, 2000).

Although policy analysis is still largely quantitative and male dominated, some feminist researchers carry out Janet Finch's (1986) early argument that qualitative research can contribute significantly to understanding and framing policy. Some have focused on the substance, construction, and emergence of specific policy issues: Kaufert and McKinlay (1985) documented divergent scientific, clinical, and feminist constructions in the emergence of estrogen replacement therapy; Rosalind Petchesky revealed how women's health was framed in the abortion debate (1985) and the complexities of transnationalizing women's health movements (2003); and Nancy Naples (1997a, 1997b) deployed discourse analysis to demonstrate the state's part in restructuring families and women's roles therein. Others have dealt with processes through which policy is accomplished:[3] Theresa Montini's (1997) triangulated study showed how physicians deflected activists in the movement to provide information to women with breast cancer, away from activists' goals. Accomplishing policy raises issues of control of women: Nancy Fraser's (1989) discourse analysis of women's needs and the state questioned whether definitions are emancipatory or controlling. Wendy Brown (1992) argued that Barbara Ehrenreich and

Frances Fox Piven's (1983) positive view of the state for women did not recognize issues of control.[4]

Continuing and Emergent Complexities

Complexity and controversy characterize the qualitative feminist research enterprise: the nature of research, the definition of and relationship with those with whom research is done, the characteristics and location of the researcher, and the creation and presentation of knowledges. If there is a dominant theme, it is the question of knowledges. Whose knowledges? Where and how obtained, and by whom; from whom and for what purposes? As Liz Stanley and Sue Wise (1990) reflected, "Succinctly, feminist theorists have moved away from 'the reactive' stance of the feminist critiques of social science and into the realms of exploring what 'feminist knowledge' could look like" (p. 37). This undergirds influential feminist writing such as Lorraine Code's question, "who can know?" (1991, p. ix), Donna Haraway's conceptualization of situated knowledges (1991), Dorothy Smith's articulation of the everyday world as problematic (1987), and a multitude of texts on feminist qualitative methods and methodology (Behar, 1996; Behar & Gordon, 1995; O. Butler, 1986; Clarke, 2004; DeVault, 1993, 1999; Fine, 1992a; Fonow & Cook, 1991; Hekman, 1990; Holland & Blair with Sheldon, 1995; Lather, 1991; Lewin & Leap, 1996; Maynard & Purvis, 1994; Morawski, 1994; Naples, 2003; Nielsen, 1990; Ramazanoglu with Holland, 2002; Ribbens & Edwards, 1998; Roberts, 1981; Skeggs, 1995a; D. Smith, 1999, in press; Stanley & Wise, 1983; Tom, 1989; Visweswaran, 1994; D. Wolf, 1996a; M. Wolf, 1992, 1996; L. Stanley, 1990).

That there are multiple knowledges was set forth forcefully by Patricia Hill Collins (1990) in her explication of black feminist thought, an influential work that—along with writings of Angela Davis (1981), Bonnie Thornton Dill (1979), Effie Chow (1987), bell hooks (1990), Rayna Green (1990), and Gloria Anzaldúa (1987, 1990)—began to dissolve an unremitting whiteness in feminist research. This continues with exploration of the black female experience (Reynolds, 2002), black women in authority (Forbes, 2001), and the diversities among American Indian women (Mihesuah, 1998, 2000).

This growing emphasis departed from important themes in the early years of feminist research. First, Catherine MacKinnon's assertion that "consciousness raising" is the basis of feminist methodology (1982, p. 535; 1983) gave way as theorists and researchers recognized that women are located structurally in changing organizational and personal contexts that intertwine with subjective assessment to produce knowledge, as Sheryl Ruzek (1978) had earlier demonstrated in her analysis of the women's health movement. Second, observations about women being missing from and invisible in certain arenas of social life, such as Judith Lorber's (1975) research on women in medicine and Cynthia Epstein's (1981) work on women in law, led to complex analyses such as Darlene Clark Hine's (1989) exploration of the structural, interactional, and knowledge-producing elements in the exclusion of and treatment of African American women in American nursing.

Parallel research revealed women as ubiquitous and invisible workers in the domestic sphere (Abel & Nelson, 1990; Finch & Groves, 1983; Graham, 1984, 1985; M. K. Nelson, 1990). Evelyn Nakano Glenn's (1990) work on Japanese domestic workers, Judith Rollins's (1985) participant observation study of doing housecleaning, Mary Romero's (1992) interview study of Latina domestic workers, and Pierrette Hondagneu-Sotelo's (2001) interview study of employers, Latina workers, and heads of employment agencies laid bare the race, class, and gender issues in domestic service and household work and concomitant contexts of knowledge, seemingly banal, but ultimately critical to everyday life. This work problematized further the concept of care and spurred a surge of later conceptual and research projects (Cancian, Kurz, London, Reviere, & Tuominen, 2000). Margery DeVault's (1991) research on domestic food preparation, Anne Murcott's (1993) analysis of conceptions of food, and Arlie

Table 10.1. Complexities in Feminist Qualitative Research and Representative Texts

I. Strands in Continuing Complexities

Work by and About Specific Groups of Women

Writing by Women of Color
Dill (1979), A. Y. Davis (1981), Zinn (1982), Collins (1986), Zavella (1987), Garcia (1989), Hurtado (1989), Anzaldúa (1990), Green (1990), hooks (1990), Espiritu (1997), Mihesuah (1998), Reynolds (2002)

Lesbian Research and Queer Theory
Krieger (1983), Anzaldúa (1990), Hall & Stevens (1991), Terry (1991), Weston (1991), J. Butler (1990, 1993), Kennedy & Davis (1993), Lewin (1993), Alexander (1997)

Disabled Women
Asch & Fine (1992), Morris (1995), Lubelska & Mathews (1997)

II. Approaches

Postcolonial Feminist Thought

Mohanty (1988, 2003), Spivak (1988), Trinh (1989, 1992), Heng (1997)

Globalization

Marchand & Runyan (2000), Misra (2000), Naples (2002), Runyon & Marchand (2000), Bergeron (2001), Fernandez-Kelly & Wolf (2001), Freeman (2001), Kelly et al. (2001), Kofman et al. (2001), Young (2001), Barndt (2002)

Standpoint Theory
Hartsock (1983, 1997b), Harding (1987,1990), D. Smith (1987, 1997), Collins (1990, 1998), Haraway (1991), Weeks (1998), Ramazanoglu with Holland (2002), Naples (2003)

Postmodern and Deconstructive Theory
Flax (1987), Hekman (1990), Nicholson (1990), Haraway (1991), Clough (1998), Haraway (1997), Collins (1998b), Lacsamana (1999)

III. Consequences of Complexity

Problematizing Researcher and Participant

Behar (1993), Frankenberg & Mani (1993), Lincoln (1993, 1997), Ellis (1995), Reay (1996a), Lather & Smithies (1997)

Problematizing Unremitting Whiteness

Frankenberg (1994), Hurtado & Stewart (1997)

Destabilizing Insider-Outsider

Kondo (1990), Lewin (1993), Ong (1995), Zavella (1996), Naples (1996, 2003), Weston (1996), B. Williams (1996), Narayan (1997)

Deconstructing Traditional Concepts

Experience
(Scott, 1991), O'Leary (1997)

Table 10.1. (Continued)

Difference
hooks (1990), Felski (1997)

Gender
West & Zimmerman (1987), J. Butler (1990, 1993), Lorber (1994), Poster (2002)

IV. Enduring Issues

"Bias" and Objectivity

Fine (1992), Scheper-Hughes (1992), Holland & Ramazanoglu (1994), Phoenix (1994), Harding (1991, 1996, 1998), Haraway (1997), Diaz (2002)

"Validity" and Trustworthiness

Lather (1993), Richardson (1993), K. Manning (1997)

Participants' Voices

Maschia-Lees et al. (1989), Fine (1992a), Opie (1992), Lincoln (1993, 1997), Reay (1996b), Kincheloe (1997), Ribbens & Edwards (1998)

Presenting the Account

Behar & Gordon (1995), Ellis (1995), Kondo (1995), Lather & Smithies (1997), McWilliam (1997), Richardson (1997), Gray & Sinding (2002)

Research Ethics

Finch (1984), Stacey (1988), Lincoln (1995), Fine & Weis (1996), Reay (1996b), D. Wolf (1996), M. Wolf (1996), Ribbens & Edwards (1998), Edwards & Mauthner (2002), Mauthner et al. (2002)

Transcending, Transforming the Academy

Stacey & Thorne (1985), Abu-Lughod (1990), Fine & Gordon (1992), Behar (1993), Morawski (1994), Cancian (1996), D. Smith (1999), Gergen (2001), Messer-Davidow (2002), Anglin (2003)

Making Feminist Work Count

Laslett & Brenner (2001), Stacey (2003)

Hochschild and Anne Machung's findings (1989) that household labor is imbedded in the political economy of household emotions further demonstrated the dynamics of knowledge production and control within gendered relationships in the domestic sphere.

Thus, emergent complexities moved feminist research from justly deserved criticisms of academic disciplines (J. Stacey & Thorne, 1985, 1996), social institutions, and the lack of or flawed attention to women's lives and experiences to debate and discussion of critical epistemological issues.[5] Researchers became more sensitive to differences among women, even in the same group, and to concerns about the researcher's own characteristics. As the concept of a universalized "woman" or "women" faded, understanding grew that multiple identities and subjectivities are constructed in particular historical and social contexts (Ferguson, 1993).

Strands Contributing to and Sustaining Complexities

Major strands that continue to sustain complexities in feminist research include work by and about specific groups of women (women of color, gay and lesbian/queer women, and disabled women) and approaches to the study of women (postcolonial, globalization, standpoint theory, postmodern theory, and deconstructive theory). These are not always discrete, as, for instance, researchers who are women of color may utilize standpoint theory, as is noted elsewhere.

Writing by Women of Color. Beyond the eye-opening analyses cited earlier, other work by women of color significantly shaped new understandings that displaced taken-for-granted views of women of color and revealed the extent to which whiteness can be a factor in creating "otherness," for example, Asianness in Britain (Puar, 1996). Aside from the critical task of differentiation, greater recognition of the interplay of race, class, and gender in shaping women's oppression and white women's advantage is displayed in writing by Maxine Baca Zinn (1982), Patricia Hill Collins (1986), Aida Hurtado (1989), A. M. Garda (1989), and research by Patricia Zavella on Mexican American cannery workers (1987) and by Elaine Bell Kaplan on black teenage mothers (1997). As Yen Le Espiritu has noted, "Racism affects not only people of color, but organizes and shapes experiences of all women" (personal communication, September 15, 2003). At the same time, Gloria Anzaldúa's experimental writing and work (1987) foregrounded the conceptualization of borders, crossing borders and fluidities in women's lives—familial, national, sexual, and international—adding further dimensions and complexities. Recognition of the importance of borders and fluidities, albeit in a very different form, emerged from feminist researchers working on women and immigration (Espin, 1995; Hondagneu-Sotelo, 2001). Yet feminist scholars Vanessa Bing and P. T. Reid (1996) warned against misapplication of white feminist knowledge, a caveat echoed by legal scholar Kimberly Crenshaw (1992) in her discussion of white feminists' appropriation of the 1991 Clarence Thomas hearings.

Parallel to these developments have been critical investigations that problematize not only the construction of women of color in relationship to whiteness, but also whiteness itself. Ruth Frankenberg's (1994) interview study shifts whiteness from privileged, unnamed taken-for-grantedness to a critical issue that must be raised about all research participants. Noting that "whiteness" is the "natural" state of affairs, Aida Hurtado and Abigail J. Stewart (1997, pp. 309–310) call for studies of whiteness from the standpoint of people of color to find what they call a critical, counterhegemonic presence in the research. Dealing with untangling whiteness and the existence of a global color line, Chandra Talpade Mohanty (2003) urged feminists to consider questions of power, equality, and justice in ways that address context and recognition of questions of history and experience.

Postcolonial Feminist Thought. If the criticisms of an unremitting whiteness in feminist research in Western, industrialized societies began to unsettle feminist research frames, powerful and sophisticated research and feminist thought from postcolonial theorists further shifted the grounds of feminist research with regard to "woman" and "women," the very definitions of feminism itself, and constructions of color (Mohanty, 2003). Feminism, these theorists argued, takes many different forms depending on the context of contemporary nationalism (Heng, 1997). Concerned about the invidious effects of "othering" (invidious, oppressive defining of the persons with whom research is done), they argued that Western feminist models were inappropriate for thinking of research with women in postcolonial sites (Kirby, 1991, p. 398). Postcolonial feminists raised incisive questions such as Gayatri Chakravorti Spivak's (1988) query as to whether subordinates can speak or are forever silenced by virtue of representation within elite thought. (See also Mohanty, 1988.) They also asked about whether Third World women or indeed all women could be conceptualized as unified subjectivities easily located in the category of "woman." Drawing on her expertise as a filmmaker, Trinh T. Minh-ha (1989, 1992) articulated a fluid framing of woman (as other and not other) and undermined the very doing of ethnographic research by undercutting the concept of woman, the assumptions of subjectivity and objectivity, and the utility of the interview. This literature also pointed to issues in globalization.

Globalization. Feminist theorists' and researchers' explorations of the international march of capital, shifting labor markets, and recruitment thereto have foregrounded the implications of these vast political and economic processes for women in highly divergent contexts (Barndt, 2002; R. M. Kelly, Bayes, Hawkesworth, & Young, 2001; Kofman, Phizacklea, Raghuran, & Sales, 2001; Marchand & Runyan, 2000; see also the entire issue of *Signs,* Vol. 26, No. 4, 2001) and expanded the scope of feminist qualitative research. Feminists complicate homogeneous views of globalization, which is not "unified and noncontradictory, an inevitable accumulation on a world wide basis or solely determined by powerful economic institutions" (Bergeron, 2001, p. 996), but rife with contradictions (Naples, 2002) and the potential to produce multiple subjectivities (see also Fernandez-Kelly & Wolf, 2001; C. Freeman, 2001; Runyan & Marchand, 2000; Young, 2001). This complicating maneuver has produced research that reflects divergent views on two critical issues: (a) the interplay of the dominance of the state and these economic forces in women's lives and women's enactment of or potential resistance and (b) the production of new opportunities and/or the continuation of old oppressions. Rhacel Parrenas's (2001) research on Filipina domestic workers finds acts of resistance in everyday life, but these did not intervene against structural processes. Millie Thayer's (2001) analysis of rural Brazilian women shows that the women's local movement drew on their own resources to exert power, defend the movement's autonomy, and negotiate access to resources. These studies and others (Constable, 1997; Guevarra, 2003) stretch feminist qualitative researchers, as they require multiple methods (ethnography, interviews, documentary analysis). They also invoke contentious issues found elsewhere in feminist qualitative work: the efficacy of postmodern thinking (Lacsamana, 1999); the risk of reproducing Eurocentric concepts of feminism (Grewal & Caplen, 1994; Kempadoo, 2001; Rudy, 2000; Shohat, 2001); theoretical tensions between local particulars and the political economy of labor (Lacsamana, 1999); and, particularly in sex traffic research, questions of female agency (Doezema, 2000; Ho, 2000; Hanochi, 2001) and working conditions (Gulcur & Ilkkaracan, 2002; Poudel & Carryer, 2000; Pyle, 2001).

Lesbian Research. In research that quickly laid to rest Stanley and Wise's (1990, pp. 29–34) criticism that little attention had been paid to lesbians, feminist scholars upended theoretical and research frames saturated with stigma that essentially had rendered lesbians invisible and, where visible, despicable. Here, as Yen Le Espiritu has pointed out, it is useful to differentiate studies that focus on sexuality as an object of study from those that make sexuality a central concept (personal communication, September 15, 2003). The former type of research dissolved a homogeneous view of lesbians: Susan Krieger's (1983) ethnography of a lesbian community; Patricia Stevens and Joanne Hall's (1991) analysis of how medicine has invidiously defined lesbianism; Kath Weston's (1991) study of lesbian familial relationships; Ellen Lewin's (1993) research on lesbian mothers, which shows the surpassing importance of the maternal rather than sexual identity; and Jennifer Terry (1994) on theorizing "deviant" historiography. Other work (Anzaldúa, 1987, 1990; Kennedy & Davis, 1993; Lewin,1996) further differentiated these views by revealing race and class issues within lesbian circles and the multiple bases of lesbian identity. Jacqui Alexander's (see Alexander & Mohanty, 1997) work is of the second category, as she conceptualizes sexuality as fundamental to gender inequality and as a salient marker of otherness that has been central to racist and colonial ideologies.

The very meaning of gender also came in for incisive critical review by Judith Butler (1990, 1993), whose philosophical analysis for some feminists evoked themes contained in an earlier sociological statement by Candace West and Don Zimmerman (1987). In both cases, but for different theoretical reasons, these scholars pointed to sexual identity as performative rather than given or socially ascribed and thus undercut a dualistic conception of gender that had informed feminist thought for decades.

The term "queer" has been used as a synonym for homosexual identity and also to question norms around heterosexual marriage. The emergence of the term "queer theory," referring to those gay men and women who refuse assimilation into either gay culture or oppressive heterosexual culture, also has been loosely used as a cover term for gay and lesbian studies. In addition, it refers to a more precise political stance (Lewin, 1996, pp. 6–9). Ellen Lewin's (1998) research on gay and lesbian marriages shows how those ceremonies simultaneously reflect accommodation and subversion. This stance of resistance carries conceptual implications that bear directly on feminist research and that require recognition of the complex contributions of race and class (J. Butler, 1994) to diverse expressions of identity(ies), always in formation and always labile. The stability of the very categories of "man" and "woman" is questioned, as Leila Rupp and Verta Taylor show in their study of drag queens (2003).

Disabled Women. Recognition of differences among women also emerged with the disability rights movement and publication by feminist women who were themselves disabled. "Socially devalued, excluded from the playing field as women and invisible" (Gill, 1997, p. 96), disabled women were essentially depersonalized and degendered, sometimes even, regrettably, within feminist circles (Lubelska & Mathews, 1997, p. 135). A. Asch and Michelle Fine, reviewing the emergence of disabled women as a problematic issue for feminists, pointed out that even sympathetic research on women with disabilities tended to overlook women's multiple statuses and view women solely in terms of their disability (1992, p. 142; see also J. Morris, 1995).

Standpoint Research. Building on a loosely related set of theoretical positions by feminist scholars from several disciplines, standpoint research (much of that noted earlier can be thusly categorized) took up the feminist criticism of the absence of women from or marginalized women in research accounts and foregrounded women's knowledge as emergent from women's situated experiences (Harding, 1987, p. 184). Aptly summarized by Donna Haraway, whose influential work in the history of science undergirded standpoint thinking, "standpoints are cognitive-emotional-political achievements, crafted out of located social-historical-bodily experience—itself always constituted through fraught, noninnocent, discursive, material, collective practices" (1997, p. 304, n. 32).[6] Research and writing by sociologist Dorothy Smith, sociologist Patricia Hill Collins, political scientist Nancy Hartsock, and philosopher Sandra Harding dissolved the concept of essentialized, universalized woman, which was to be replaced by the ideas of a situated woman with experiences and knowledge specific to her place in the material division of labor and the racial stratification systems.

This implies that knowledge claims are socially located and that some social locations, especially those at the bottom of social and economic hierarchies, are better than others as starting points for seeking knowledge not only about those particular women but others as well. (This does *not* assume that the researcher's own life or group is the best starting point, nor does it assert the relativist position that all social locations are equally valuable for knowledge projects.) Although they have been grouped under the rubric of "standpoint," standpoint theorists are by no means identical, and in their differing versions they offer divergent approaches for qualitative researchers (Harding, 1997, p. 389). It is worthwhile to review these theorists while recognizing the inevitable violence done to subtle thought in such a brief review. (See Naples, 2003, pp. 37–88; Ramazanoglu with Holland, 2002, pp. 60–69; and Weeks, 1998, pp. 3–11 for useful summaries of standpoint theorists, their critics, and misinterpretations.)

Dorothy Smith focuses on women's standpoints and conceptualizes the everyday world as a problematic—that is, continually created, shaped, and known by women within it—and its organization, which is shaped by external material factors or textually mediated relations (1987, p. 91). Thus, the "everyday, everynight activities" of women's lives are at the center. To understand that world, the researcher must not objectify the woman, as traditionally would be done in sociology, which divides subject and object, researcher and participant. The researcher must be able to "work very differently than she is able to do with established sociological strategies of thinking and inquiry" (D. Smith, 1992, p. 96) that are not outside the relations of ruling. This requires a high degree of reflexivity from the researcher and a recognition of how feminist sociologists "participate as subjects in the relations of ruling" (p. 96). Smith's work with Alison Griffith (see D. Smith, 1987) discloses how she and her colleague found in their own discussions the effects of the North American discourse on mothering of the 1920s and 1930s (D. Smith, 1992, p. 97). Smith herself (in press) has fully explicated institutional ethnography, as this approach is called, as a method of inquiry. A growing cadre of researchers is utilizing and developing her ideas of institutional ethnography (M. Campbell, 1998, 2002; M. Campbell & Gregor, 2002; M. Campbell & Manicom, 1995). They attempt to discover how textually mediated relationships occur and are sustained in institutional settings, thus knitting an important link between the classic problem of micro and macro issues (D. Smith, 1997).

Patricia Hill Collins (1990) grounds her articulation of black women's standpoint in black women's material circumstances and political situation. Methodologically, this requires "an alternative epistemology whose 'criteria for substantiated knowledge' and 'methodological adequacy' will be compatible with the experiences and consciousness of Black women" (O'Leary, 1997, p. 62). Collins's writings and those of bell hooks (1984, 1990) moved feminist thinking and research in the direction of more particularized knowledge and away from any sense of the universal. Collins refuses to abandon situated standpoints and links the standpoint of black women with intersectionality, "the ability of social phenomena, race, class, and gender to mutually construct one another" (1998a, p. 205), but *always* within keen consideration for power and structural relations (1998a, pp. 201–228). This substantially amplifies standpoint theory. Thinking through this complexity is, as she recognizes, a "daunting task" (1998a, p. 225), and doing qualitative research within such a frame is equally daunting. Nevertheless, embracing new understandings of social complexity—and the locales of power relationships—is vital to the task of developing black feminist thought as critical social theory and new forms of visionary pragmatism (1998a, p. 228).

Sandra Harding, a philosopher, early recognized three types of feminist inquiry, which she termed "transitional epistemologies" (1987, p. 186). Harding's concerns about modernity and science in general, and science questions in feminism, led her to rest these types on how those modes of inquiry relate to traditional science and the problem of objectivity. (a) *Feminist empiricism* is of two types: first, "spontaneous feminist empiricism" (rigorous adherence to existing research norms and standards), and second, following Helen Longino (1990), "contextual empiricism" (recognition of the influence of social values and interests in science) (Harding, 1993, p. 53). (b) *Standpoint theory* "claims that all knowledge attempts are socially situated and that some of these objective social locations are better than others for knowledge projects" (Harding, 1993, p. 56). (c) *Postmodern theories* void the possibility of a feminist science in favor of the many and multiple stories women tell about the knowledge they have (Harding, 1987, p. 188). These are still useful ways to look at different styles of feminist qualitative work, but many projects display elements of several or all three as feminist researchers creatively borrow from multiple styles in their search "to escape damaging limitations of the dominant social relations and their schemes" (Harding, 1990, p. 101).

At issue here is the very form of science and whether "all possible science and epistemology . . . must be containable within modern, androcentric, Western, bourgeois forms" (Harding, 1990, p. 99). Harding argues that other forms of science are quite possible and likely. Her concerns with feminist research as a scientific activity and the attempt to generate "less false stories" prompted her to reject reliance on processes strictly governed by methodological rules and to argue that researchers critically examine their own personal and historical commitments with which they construct their work (1993, pp. 70–71). She points to the critical difference between sociological, cultural, and historical relativism (listening carefully to others' views) and judgmental relativism (abandoning any claims for adjudicating between different systems of beliefs and their social origins). Her solution is a posture of "strong objectivity" (1991).[7] Strong objectivity contrasts sharply with value-free objectivity and posits the interplay of the researcher and participant. Her contribution on "strong objectivity" is discussed in greater detail later in this chapter, under issues of validity.

Key to Nancy Hartsock's Marxist formulation of standpoint theory is her view that women's circumstances in the material order provide them with experiences that generate particular and privileged knowledge that reflects oppression and women's resistance (1983, 1985). Like the proletariat in Marxist theory, their knowledges provide a basis for criticism of domination and for political action (Hartsock, 1997b, p. 98). This does not assume that such knowledge is innately essential or that all women have the same experiences or, indeed, the same knowledge. Rather, Hartsock articulates the possibility of a "concrete multiplicity" of perspectives (1990, p. 171). Each of these constitutes a different world, and each represents a differential influence of power, a consideration that distinguishes standpoint theory from feminist empiricism (Hundleby, 1997, p. 41). Such knowledge is not merely individual but derives from "interaction of people and groups with each other" and is always transitional (Hundleby, 1997, p. 36). As Hartsock has observed, "the subjects who matter are not individual subjects, but collective subjects, or groups" (1997a, p. 371).

Standpoint theories and their implications for feminist qualitative research have not gone uncriticized. Some fretted that standpoint theories contained risks of relativism (Harding, 1987, p. 187), were overly simplistic (Hawkesworth, 1989), and raised issues around validity (Ramazanoglu, 1989). Criticisms arose about the potential for essentialism (Lemert, 1992, p. 69), neglect of traditions of knowledge among women of color (Collins, 1992), problems of evaluating accounts from different perspectives (Hekman, 1997b, p. 355; Longino, 1993, p. 104; Maynard, 1994b; Welton, 1997, p. 21), questions about understanding fragmented identities (Lemert, 1992, p. 68), and the potentially untenable basis of experience as a starting point for investigation if it is continually mediated and constructed from unconscious desire (Clough, 1993a). Others have argued that queer theory, with its destabilizing elements, undercut the possibility for standpoint thinking, which, in this view, presumed the replication of heterosexual categories (Clough, 1994, p. 144).

For their part, standpoint theorists have not been silent. Dorothy Smith's robust exchange with Patricia Clough highlighted the centrality of experience, the place of desire, and the primacy of text (Clough, 1993a, p. 169; Clough, 1993b; Smith,

1993). Clough argued that Smith had not gone far enough in deconstructing sociology as a dominant discourse of experience, a point Smith rejected, claiming that Clough's view is overly oriented to text and neglects experience. Susan Hekman's critical review of standpoint theory (1997a, 1997b) addressed questions of whether women's knowledge is privileged and how truth claims can be settled. Responses from Dorothy Smith (1997), Patricia Hill Collins (1997), Nancy Hartsock (1997a), and Sandra Harding (1997) show clearly that standpoint theories have been and are continually revised (Harding, 1997, p. 389). Feminist qualitative researchers thinking of using standpoint theories in their work must read these theorists carefully and in their latest version if they are to avoid misinterpretation and if they are to explore new connections between standpoint theories and postmodernism (Hirschman, 1997). Indeed, Sandra Harding has observed that "poststructural approaches have been especially helpful in enabling standpoint theories systematically to examine critically pluralities of power relations, of the sort indicated in the earlier discussion of gender as shaped by class, race and other historical cultural forces and how these are disseminated through 'discourses' that are both structural and symbolic" (1996, p. 451). Patricia Hill Collins, while warning about the corrosive effects of postmodern and deconstructive thought for black women's group authority and hence social action (1998b, p. 143), also points to postmodernism's powerful analytic tools as useful in challenging dominant discourses and the very rules of the game (1998b, p. 154).[8] Nancy Naples argues for a multidimensional approach to standpoint research that recognizes both the embodied aspects of standpoint theory and the multiplicity of perspectives that researchers and participants achieve in dynamic social and political environments (2003, pp. 197–198).

These controversies show no sign of abating (see the exchange between Walby, 2001a, 2001b Sprague, 2001, and Harding, 2001). At the same time, research using standpoint theory is abundant and wide ranging: ethnographic research in a Latino community (Eichenberger, 2002), sexual harassment (Dougherty, 2001), gendered relations in organizations (P. Y. Martin, 2001), African American women managers (Forbes, 2001), mothers with HIV (Tanenberg, 2000), backlash politics (Hawkesworth, 1999), and women's political practice (Naples, 1999; Naples & Sachs, 2000).

Postmodern and Deconstructive Thought. Complexities probably would have arisen in feminist qualitative research thanks to any of the themes discussed here, but multiple seductive intellectual aspects of postmodern and deconstructive thought honed complexities.[9] Indeed, in varying degrees postmodernism and deconstructionism are present in many of the foregoing themes, sometimes constituting the central stance (as in Judith Butler or Trinh T. Minh-ha's analyses), occasionally anticipating future problematics (as in Frankenberg's deconstruction of whiteness), and frequently reflecting trends and themes firmly set out by feminists not oriented to these modes of thought (as in Collins's analysis of black feminist thought or Lewin's research on lesbian cultures).

Concerned that it is difficult, if not impossible, to produce more than a partial story of women's lives in oppressive contexts, postmodern feminists regard "truth" as a destructive illusion. They see the world as a series of stories or texts that sustain the integration of power and oppression and actually "constitute us as subjects in a determinant order" (Hawkesworth, 1989, p. 549). Feminist researchers in anthropology, sociology, history, political science, cultural studies, and social studies of science as well as in the experimental wings in educational and nursing research (see the Australian journal *Nursing Inquiry*) have drawn on these ideas.

Carrying the imprint of feminist forebears from deconstruction and postmodernism (French feminists such as Irigaray and Cixous, and Foucault, Deleuze, Lyotard, and Baudrillard), feminist research in cultural studies stresses representation and text. This area is particularly complex for feminist researchers because some scholars also utilize Marxist theory from Althusser, French feminist theory, literary criticism (Abel,

Christian, & Moglen, 1997), historical analysis, and psychoanalytic views (Lacan—not all feminists agree on Lacan's utility for feminist research; see Ferguson, 1993, p. 212, n. 3). In contrast to classical Marxist feminist studies of women, work, and social class such as Karen Sacks's investigation of hospital workers (1988) and Nona Glazer's analysis of race and class issues in the profession of nursing (1991), materialist feminist research in an Althusserian mode looks at ideology and its place in the shaping of subjectivity, desire, and authority (Clough, 1994, p. 75). Here enters the elusive and difficult issue of how desire is expressed in or inferred from cultural products ranging from ethnographic accounts through films. This confronts the feminist qualitative researcher with questions that go far beyond the easy recognition of intersubjectivity and invokes deeper cultural forms and questions.[10] (For a feminist materialist analysis of narrative, see Roman, 1992.)

These inquiries typically take the form of the analysis of cultural objects (film, etc.) and their meanings (Balsamo, 1993; Clough, 2000; de Lauretis, 1987; Denzin, 1992, p. 80; M. Morris, 1998). Included are textual analysis of these objects and the discourses surrounding them (Denzin, 1992, p. 81) and the "study of lived cultures and experiences which are shaped by the cultural meanings that circulate in everyday life" (Denzin, 1992, p. 81). This anticipates Valerie Walkerdine's (1995) important call for the analysis of understanding the media as the site of production of subjectivity.

Here will be found the voluminous and sophisticated feminist work in gender and science, wherein science, the sacred cow of the Enlightenment, modernity, and the contemporary moment, is dismembered as a culture to reveal its practices, discourses, and implications for control of women's lives (Haraway, 1991, 1997; E. Martin, 1987, 1999), including their health (Clarke & Olesen, 1999), and to provide avenues for resistance and/or intervention. Research about women's reproductive status, an issue central to feminist qualitative research from the very start and long productive of influential work (Ginzburg, 1998; Gordon, 1976; Joffe, 1995; Luker, 1984, 1996), has moved into the gender and science area (Balsamo, 1993, 1998; Casper, 1998; Hartouni, 1997; Mamo, 2002; Rapp, 1999). Because this work utilizes interdisciplinary borrowing, it is not easily classified. Studies often appear as hybrids and radical in terms of form, substance, and content, as, for instance, in Donna Haraway's deft interweaving of fiction, biology, history, humor, religion, and visual imagery in her feminist unpacking of technosciences (1997). These productions can be uncomfortable, threatening, and subversive, not only for male-dominated institutions such as science, but also for feminism itself.

These styles of thought continue to sharpen and enhance the emerging complexities: the sites (gender, race, and class) of where and how "women" are controlled, and how the multiple, shifting identities and selves that supplant earlier notions of a stable identity (self) are produced (Clough, 1998; Ferguson, 1993; Flax, 1990; Fraser, 1997, p. 381). They shift from binary frameworks to fluid conceptualizations of women's experiences, places, and spaces (Anzaldúa, 1987; Trinh, 1989, 1992). This move emphasized discourse, narrative and text, and experimental writing of standard research account presentations. Postmodernism and deconstructionism also called into question, as had standpoint theorists, feminist qualitative researchers' unexamined embrace of and adherence to traditional positivist qualitative approaches. Known as feminist empiricism, these were thought to forward the feminist agenda, but rather, the critics averred, merely repeated structures of oppression. The postmodern position produced an uneasy and anxious concern that the shifting sands of meaning, text, locale, and the continual proliferation of identities left no grounds for reform-oriented research, reinforced the status quo, erased structural power, and failed to address problems or to represent a cultural system (Benhabib, 1995; Collins, 1998b; Ebert, 1996; Hawkesworth, 1989; Johannsen, 1992; Maschia-Lees, Sharpe, & Cohen, 1989; Maynard, 1994a; Ramazanoglu, 1989). This impact raised questions that will be discussed more fully in the section on issues in feminist qualitative research.

Consequences of Growing Complexities

Writing from women of color, gay/lesbian/queer theorists, postcolonial and globalization researchers, disabled women, standpoint theorists, and analysts persuaded to a postmodern stance opened and upended taken-for-granted conceptualizations of feminist research as well as critical key concepts such as experience, difference, and gender. Nowhere has this been more and more incisively pursued than in rethinking the topic of woman as research participant, a point discussed above, and in the destabilization of the conception of the feminist researcher as an all-knowing, unified, distanced, and context-free seeker of objectified knowledge whose very gender guarantees access to women's lives and knowledges.

The dissolution of this assumption took two directions. A first direction came with recognition that the researcher, too, has attributes; characteristics; a history; and gender, class, race, and social attributes that enter the research interaction. Yvonna Lincoln captured this in her comment that, "We are not single persons, but a multitude of possibilities any one of which might reveal itself in a specific field situation" (1997, p. 42). However, these possibilities are not static elements; they are, rather, reflections of the intersections of structures and practices. In this vein, borrowing from cultural studies, Ruth Frankenberg and Lata Mani articulated a conjecturalist approach that "firmly centers the analysis of subject formation and cultural practice within matrices of domination and subordination" and that "asserts that there is an effective but not determining relationship between subjects and their histories, a relationship that is complex, shifting and not 'free'" (1993, p. 306). Although they wrote in a postcolonial, deconstructionist vein, their conceptualization of a conjecturalist approach still has applicability to the dynamics of feminist research wherever found because it recognizes that both researcher and participant are positioned and are being positioned by virtue of history and context.

A number of feminist researchers have described the dynamics of conjecturalism in their work: Foregrounding her own trajectory from the working class to middle-class researcher, Diane Reay (1996a) reflected on class in her analysis of mothers' involvement in their children's primary schooling; Ann Phoenix's (1994) work on young people's social identities demonstrated that the taken-for-granted assumption that matching race and gender of interviewers is too simplistic; and Catherine Kohler Riessman (1987) pointed out how ethnic and class differences override gender in achieving understandings in interviews. Several researchers examined problems with their feminist views in their research: D. Millen (1997) examined potential problems when feminist researchers work with women not sympathetic to feminism, and Denise Cuthbert's (2000) study of non-Aboriginal women who adopted Aboriginal children necessitated a departure from feminist methodology. (In a related vein, see also Andrews, 2002; Gaskell & Eichler, 2001.)

A second direction recognized the impact of research on the feminist researcher in light of the multiple positions, selves, and identities at play in the research process. The subjectivity of the researcher, as much as that of the researched, became foregrounded, an indication of the blurring phenomenological and epistemological boundaries between the researcher and the researched. This did not go unmarked among more traditional researchers, who worried that the emphasis on subjectivity comes "too close . . . to a total elimination of intersubjective validation of description and explanation" (Komarovsky, 1988, p. 592; 1991). This issue led directly into questions about objectivity, "validity and reliability," and nature of the text and the voices in it, to be discussed shortly. In spite of these misgivings, feminists began to publish provocative and even influential work that reflected the blurring of these boundaries: Ruth Behar's (1993) analysis of her Mexican respondent's life and her own crosses multiple national, disciplinary, and personal borders, as do Carolyn Ellis's (1995) poignant account of a terminal illness and Patti Lather's (Lather & Smithies, 1997) work with HIV-positive women.

These views of the researcher's part in the research also bred a host of influential reflections that rethought the important issue of whether being an "insider" gave feminist researchers access to inside knowledge, a view that partook of Patricia Hill Collins's important conceptualization of "insider/outsider" (1986): Patricia Zavella's (1996) discovery that her Mexican background did not suffice in studying Mexican women doing factory work; Ellen Lewin's (1993) analysis of lesbian mothers showed the surpassing importance of motherhood over sexual orientation; Kirin Narayan (1997) asked how native is a "native" anthropologist, Dorinne Kondo (1990) reported unexpected and sometimes unsettling experiences doing fieldwork in Japan around her Japanese identity, and Brackette Williams (1996) found that kinship as well as racial identity affected her research with elderly African Americans. These papers and others, such as Aihwa Ong's (1995) account of work with immigrant Chinese women and Nancy Naples's (1996) research with women in Iowa, problematized the idea that a feminist researcher who shared some attributes of a cultural background would, by virtue of that background, have full access to women's knowledge in that culture. They also troubled the hidden assumption that insider knowledge is unified, stable, and unchanging and the view that insider/outsider positions are fixed and unchanging (Naples, 2003, p. 40). Kath Weston's report of her struggles with these issues summarizes the problems: "A single body can not bridge that mythical divide between insider and outsider, researcher and researched. I am neither, in any simple way, and yet I am both" (1996, p. 275).

If the play of increasing complexities destabilized once-secure views of the researcher and those with whom research is done, it also generated critical examination of once-taken-for-granted concepts. Although feminist qualitative researchers working in the empiricist and standpoint frames still foreground women's reports of experience as key, there is growing recognition that merely focusing on those reports does not account for how that "experience" emerged (Morawski, 1990; Scott, 1991) and the characteristics of the material, historical, and social circumstances. One of the problems with taking experience in an unproblematic way is that the research, even standpoint research, though less prone to this problem, replicates rather than criticizes oppressive systems and carries a note of essentialism. Personal experience is not a self-authenticating claim to knowledge (O'Leary, 1997, p. 47), a point postmodernists raise in pointing to the risk of essentialism in unthinking reliance on experience. Historian Joan Scott comments, "Experience is at once already an interpretation and in need of interpretation" (1991, p. 779).

Feminist research in sociology and anthropology analyzes both women's representations of experience and the material, social, economic, or gendered conditions that articulate the experience: Arlie Hochschild's (1983) research on how flight attendants manage emotions (1983), Nona Glazer's (1997) examination of racism and classism in professional nursing, Nancy Scheper-Hughes's (1992) exploration of motherhood and poverty in northeastern Brazil, and Jennifer Pierce's (1995) ethnographic study of how legal assistants play a part in the production of their oppression in law firms. Historian Linda Kerber's (1998) analysis of women's legal obligations as well as their rights also falls into this category.

The recognition of difference, a conceptual move that pulled feminist thinkers and researchers away from the view of a shared gynocentric identity, surfaced in the dynamics of trends just discussed but very quickly gave way to concerns about the almost unassailable nature of the concept and whether its use led to an androcentric or imperialistic "othering" (Felski, 1997; hooks, 1990). Arguing for the use of such concepts as hybridity, creolization, and metissage, Rita Felski (1997) claims that these metaphors "not only recognize differences within the subject, fracturing and complicating holistic notions of identity, but also address connections between subjects by recognizing affiliations, cross-pollinations, echoes, and repetitions, thereby unseating difference from a position of absolute privilege" (p. 12).

Theorist Nancy Tuana enunciated a balance of possible common interests and observable differences in a way that would allow feminist qualitative researchers to grapple with these issues in their work:

> It is more realistic to expect pluralities of experiences that are related through various intersections or resemblances of some of the experiences of various women to some of the experiences of others. In other words, we are less likely to find a common core of shared experiences that are immune to economic conditions, cultural imperatives, etc., than a family of resemblances with a continuum of similarities, which allows for significant differences between the experience of, for example, an upper-class white American woman and an Indian woman from the lowest caste. (1993, p. 283)

While echoing much of this thinking, bell hooks (1990) and Patricia Hill Collins (1990) nevertheless reminded feminist researchers that identity cannot be dropped entirely. Rather, they see differences as autonomous, not fragmented, producing knowledge that accepts "the existence of, and possible solidarity with, knowledges from other standpoints" (O'Leary, 1997, p. 63). These views reflect Gadamer's little-recognized concept of the "fusion of horizons" "which carries double or dual vision and dialectical notions a step further than do standpoint epistemologies because it indicates a transcendent third and new view or synthesis" (Nielsen, 1990, p. 29).

Gender, the workhorse concept of feminist theory and research, also has undergone changes that make contemporary use of this concept much more complex and differentiated than at the outset of the "second wave." Theoretical insights going as far back as Suzanne Kessler and Wendy McKenna's classic ethnomethodological framing of gender (1978), including Judith Butler's philosophical outline of gender as performative (1990) and Judith Lorber's argument that gender is wholly constructed (1994, p. 5), shifted research possibilities. Whereas in an earlier time, work on gender differences looked for explanations or characteristics of autonomous individuals (Gilligan, 1982), now production and realization of gender in a complex matrix of material, racial, and historical circumstances become the research foci. Differences among women as well as similarities between men and women are acknowledged (Brabeck, 1996; Lykes, 1994). (Gender as causal explanation and as analytic category and the implications for research are examined in the exchange between Hawkesworth, 1997a, and McKenna and Kessler, 1997, Scott, 1997, S. G. Smith, 1997, and Connell, 1997 and the reply from Hawkesworth, 1997b.) Global ethnography also has stimulated reconsideration of gender (Poster, 2002).

Issues and Tensions

The shifting currents depicted earlier emphasize and alter tensions to produce new issues about the conduct of the research, including new worries about ethics. Whereas in an earlier era, concerns about the research enterprise tended to reflect traditional worries about the qualitative research enterprise (how to manage "bias," what about validity, etc.), the newer worries display uneasiness about voice, the text, and ethical conduct. Feminist empiricists and those working within one of the standpoint frameworks are apt to share all these concerns, whereas those who pursue a deconstructionist path are less likely to worry about bias and validity and more about voice and text, and about key issues in representation, although there are important exceptions here (Lather & Smithies, 1997). There is a good deal of borrowing across these lines; hence, many grapple simultaneously with these issues because much remains to be articulated, particularly in work that experiments with writing, narrative, voice, and form.

Dissolving the distance between the researcher and those with whom the research is done and the recognition that both are labile, nonunitary subjects (Britzman, 1998, p. ix) steps beyond traditional criticisms about researcher bias (Denzin, 1992, pp. 49–52; Huber, 1973) and leads to strong arguments for "strongly reflexive" accounts about the researcher's part (Fine, 1992a; Holland & Ramazanoglu, 1994; Phoenix, 1994; Warren, 1988) and reflections from the participants (Appleby, 1997), but Susan Speer (2002) argues that many feminist researchers do not yet have the skills to do reflexivity well.

What Nancy Scheper-Hughes called "the cultural self" that all researchers take into their work (1992) is not a troublesome element to be eradicated or controlled, but a set of resources. Indeed, Susan Krieger (1991) early argued that utilization of the self was fundamental to qualitative work. If the researcher is sufficiently reflexive about her project, she can evoke these resources to guide gathering, creating, and interpreting her own behavior (Casper, 1997; Daniels, 1983; J. Stacey, 1998). Leslie Rebecca Bloom (1998, p. 41) goes further to urge that researchers and their participants work out how they will communicate and that this be part of research account. Nevertheless, researcher reflexivity needs to be tempered with acute awareness as to the contributions of hidden or unrecognized elements in the researchers' background. Sherry Gorelick identifies potential problems when inductivist feminist researchers who espouse a Marxist framework "fail to take account of the hidden structure of oppression (the research participant is not omniscient) and the hidden relations of oppression (the participant may be ignorant of her relative privilege over and difference from other women)" (1991, p. 461). Nancy Scheper-Hughes (1983) also warned about feminists unwittingly replicating androcentric perspectives in their work. Thus, there is recognition that both researcher and participant produce interpretations that are "the data" (Diaz, 2002).

Forgoing traditional and rigid ideas about objectivity, feminist researchers have opened new spaces to consider the enduring question of bias (Cannon, Higginbotham, & Leung, 1991). Arguing that observers' experiences can be useful, Sandra Harding suggests a strategy of "strong objectivity" that takes researchers as well as those researched as the focus of critical, causal, scientific explanations (1993, p. 71) and calls for critical examination of the researcher's social location (1996, 1998). She notes, "Strong objectivity requires that we investigate the relation between subject and object rather than deny the existence of, or seek unilateral control over, this relation" (1991, p. 152). She asks that the participants in the inquiry be seen by the feminist researcher as "gazing back" and that the researcher take their view in looking at her own socially situated project.[11] This goes beyond mere reflection on the conduct of the research and demands a steady, uncomfortable assessment of the interpersonal and interstitial knowledge-producing dynamics of qualitative research. As Janet Holland and Caroline Ramazanoglu illustrate in their research on young women's sexuality, there is no way to neutralize the social nature of interpretation. They argue:

> Feminist researchers can only try to explain the grounds on which selective interpretations has been made by making explicit the processes of decision making which produce the interpretation and the logic of the method on which these decisions are based. This entails acknowledging complexity and contradiction which may be beyond the researchers' experience, and recognizing the possibility of silences and absences in their data. (Holland & Ramazanoglu, 1994, p. 133)[12]

Donna Haraway urges going beyond even strong objectivity to the exercise of diffracting, which turns the lenses with which researchers view phenomena to show multiple fresh combinations and possibilities (1997, p. 16).

Rescuing feminist objectivity from being in thrall to classical positivist definitions and from being lost in an inchoate relativism (all views are equal), Donna Haraway (1988) recognizes the merging of researcher and participant to foreground a position of situated knowledge, accountability (the necessity to avoid reproducing oppressive views of women), and partial truths. In Haraway's apt and oft-quoted phrase, "the view from nowhere" becomes "the view from somewhere," that of connected embodied, situated participants. (For an example of Haraway's conceptualization of objectivity in use, see Kum-Kum Bhavani's [1994] research on young, working-class people in Britain.)

Related to the question of objectivity is the old question of the degree to which the account reflects or depicts that which the researcher and her participants have mutually constructed, a question which goes to the heart of whether feminist qualitative research will be deemed credible, a potent question if the research addresses key issues in women's lives. Feminist qualitative researchers address or worry about validity (Holland & Ramazanoglu, 1995), also known in more recent incarnations as "trustworthiness" in different ways, depending on how researchers frame their approaches (Denzin, 1997, pp. 1–14). For those who work in a traditional vein reflecting the positivist origins of social science (there is a reality to be discovered), the search for validity will turn to well-established techniques. Those who disdain the positivistic origins, but nevertheless believe that ways of achieving validity that reflect the nature of qualitative work are possible, seek out ways to establish credibility by such strategies as audit trails and member "validation," techniques that reflect their postpositivist views but that do not hold out hard and fast criteria for according "authenticity" (Lincoln & Guba, 1985; K. Manning, 1997). Feminist qualitative researchers who worry about whether their research will respect or appreciate those with whom they work, and, indeed, may transform those others into another version of themselves, reach for something new, as in Laurel Richardson's manifesto (1993, p. 695):

> I challenge different kinds of validity and call for different kinds of science practices. The science practice I model is a feminist-postmodernist one. It blurs genres, probes lived experiences, enacts science, creates a female imagery, breaks down dualisms, inscribes female labor and emotional response as valid, deconstructs the myth of an emotion-free social science, and makes a space for partiality, self-reflexivity, tension and difference.

Among new ways of imagining validity (Denzin, 1997, pp. 9–14; Scheurich, 1997, pp. 88–92), Patti Lather's transgressive validity is the most completely worked out feminist model, one that calls for a subversive move ("retaining the term to circulate and break with the signs that code it," 1993, p. 674) in a feminist deconstructionist mode. To ensure capturing differences but within a transformative space that can lead to a critical political agenda, she rests transgressive validity on four subtypes, here highly condensed: (a) ironic validity, which attends to the problems in representation; (b) paralogical validity, which seeks out differences, oppositions, and uncertainties; (c) rhizomatic validity, which counters authority with multiple sites; and (b) voluptuous validity, which deliberately seeks excess and authority via self-engagement and reflexivity (1993, pp. 685–686). Whether even in these bold steps Lather has gone far enough to overcome what some see as the almost obdurate problem in legitimation (the inevitable replication of researcher within the analyzed views of the researched) (Scheurich, 1997, p. 90), this formulation nevertheless retains a feminist emancipatory stance while providing leads for feminist qualitative researchers to work out and work on the inherent problems in validity. Lather's research with Chris Smithies on women with AIDS illustrates these strategies of validity and challenges feminist qualitative researchers (1997).

Problems of Voice, Reflexivity, and Text

Irrespective of the approach they take, feminist qualitative researchers continue to worry about the question of voice and the nature of the account, which, as William Tierney and Yvonna Lincoln argue in *Representation and the Text*, now "comes under renewed scrutiny" (1997, p. viii), a position echoed in Rosanna Hertz's *Reflexivity and Voice* (1997). This concern goes back to the earliest beginnings of feminist research and the attempts, noted earlier in this chapter, to find and express women's voices. When women of color and postcolonial critics raised concerns about how participants' voices are to be heard, with what authority and in what form, they sharpened and extended this issue. Within these questions lie anxiety-provoking matters of whether the account will only replicate hierarchical conditions found in parent disciplines, such as sociology (D. Smith, 1989, p. 43) and the difficult problems of translating private matters from women's lives into the potentially oppressive and distorting frames of social science (Ribbens & Edwards, 1998). To address this, some feminist researchers have articulated strategies involving voice-centered relational methods (Mauthner & Doucet, 1998), reconstructing research narratives (Birch, 1998), and writing the voices of the less powerful (Standing, 1998).

How to make women's voices heard without exploiting or distorting those voices is also a vexatious question. When literary devices are borrowed to express voice, hidden problems of control may occur (Maschia-Lees et al., 1989, p. 30). Even though researchers and participants both shape the flow of silences and comments, the researcher, who writes up the account and has responsibility for the text, remains in the more powerful position (Lincoln, 1997; Phoenix, 1994; J. Stacey, 1998). Merely letting the tape recorder run to present the respondent's voice does not overcome the problem of representation, because the respondent's comments are already mediated when they are made in the interview (Lewin, 1991). Even taking the account back for comment or as simple courtesy, or shaping the account with respondents, may not work, as J. Acker, Barry, and Esseveld (1991) found in their participatory project. Women wanted them to do the interpreting. Moreover, the choice of audience shapes how voice is found and fashioned (Kincheloe, 1997; Lincoln, 1993, 1997).[13] Michelle Fine raises serious questions about voices (use of pieces of narrative, taking individual voices to reflect group ideas, assuming that voices are free of power relations, failing to make clear the researcher's own position in relationship to the voices or becoming a "ventriloquist"). She forcefully urges feminist researchers to "articulate how, how not, and within what limits voices are framed and used (1992b, pp. 217–219).[14] She also (personal communication) points to the tension between treating voices as if they were untouched by ideology, hegemony, or interpretation and critically analyzing the contexts in which they arise and the hegemonic pressures out of which they are squeezed. The issue of voice leads into the form, nature, and content of the account. Experimental writing, based on research or on highly reflexive and insightful interpretations, is growing. Some manipulate or work within the printed text, while others opt for performances of the account.

Experimentation blooms.[15] Marjorie Wolf presents three versions of voices from her anthropological fieldwork in Taiwan: a piece of fiction, her anthropological field notes, and a social science article (1992). Ruth Behar (1993) explodes the traditional anthropological form of life history to intertwine her own voice with that of her cocreator in an extended double voiced text. Patti Lather and Chris Smithies (1997) use a split-page textual format to present their research, their respondents' views, and their own reflections on themselves and their research. Laurel Richardson (1997) continues to pioneer writing and presenting sociological poetry and tales. (See also Richardson and St. Pierre, Chapter 38, this volume.) Carolyn Ellis's accounts (1995), both presented and written, deal with emotionally difficult topics such as an abortion, death in the family, an experience with black-white relations, and the death of her partner; this work has given research in the sociology of emotions a decidedly experimental and feminist tone. "Auto-ethnography," Ellis's term for this form, locates the researcher's deeply personal and emotional experiences as topics in a context related to larger social issues. Here, the personal, biographical, political, and social are interwoven with the autoethnography, which in turn illuminates them (Denzin, 1997, p. 200) as in Laura Ellingson's reflexive account of communications within a medical setting (1998). These stances link the personal and political, and they undercut criticisms that personal reflections are merely solipsistic (Patai, 1994). As autoethnography has matured (Ellis & Bochner, 1996) researchers have developed careful reflections with which to evaluate this new style of ethnographic work (see *Qualitative Inquiry*, Vol. 6, No. 2, 2000, and R. H. Brown, 1998).

At the same time, some feminists, borrowing from avant-garde art (Wheeler, 2003), create performance pieces, dramatic readings, or plays performed at academic conferences. This is related to feminist analysis of performance theory, where the key question is "How can the consideration of the engendered live body in performance provide a site for possible feminist subversions, making performance a vital paradigm for any study of social relations?" (Case & Abbitt, 2004, p. 937). The work of the early 1990s (Michal McCall and Howard Becker on the art world, 1990; the late Marianne Paget's poignant play, based on her own research, about a woman with an incorrect cancer diagnosis, 1990; Jackie Orr's performance of a panic diary, 1993) continues. Anthropologist Dorinne Kondo's play *Dis(Graceful) Conduct*, about sexual and racial harassment in the academy, embraces a paradigm that shifts "away from the purely textual to the performative, the evanescent, the nondiscursive, the collaborative" and attempts to intervene in another register in what she calls "powerfully engaging modes quite different from conventional academic prose" (1995, p. 51). Canadian social scientists (Gray & Sinding, 2002) who performed their research about women diagnosed with metastatic breast cancer with the women themselves also videotaped the performance, which allows showing it in many venues. They also discuss production of performance pieces. Performance pieces vary with regard to preparation and audience involvement (Denzin, 1997, pp. 90–125). Creating a performance piece of whatever type is not easy (Olesen, 1997). High literary skills and sensitivities are necessary if the piece is not to founder or be deemed sophomoric by audiences accustomed to the polished presentations in contemporary visual media. Because performance pieces are still developing, deploying them to reach new audiences or to display feminist research has yet to be fully explored, though Judith Stacey's candid insights into taking feminist research public suggest that performance pieces might be useful (2003, p. 28). In the meantime, thoughtful practitioners of performance and dramatic work have begun to examine how to evaluate such work (McWilliam, 1997; see also *Qualitative Inquiry*, Vol. 9, No. 2, 2003).

Ethics in Feminist Qualitative Research

Feminist qualitative researchers recognize and discuss ethical issues, such as privacy, consent, confidentiality, deceit, and deception, that also trouble the larger field. They try to avoid harm of whatever sort (undue stress, unwanted publicity, loss of reputation, invasion of privacy) throughout the research, negotiating access, gathering and analyzing, and writing text (Ribbens & Edwards, 1998; D. Wolf, 1996). However, feminist writing on research ethics has moved beyond universalist positions in moral philosophy (duty ethics of principles, utilitarian ethics of consequences) to become more complex, emphasizing specificity and context and drawing on feminist ethics of care (Mauthner, Birch, Jessop, & Miller, 2002). Rosalind Edwards and Melanie Mauthner's (2002) helpful review of ethical models (deontological—based on unbreakable principles; consequential utilitarianism—based on consequences; virtue ethics of skills—based on situated negotiations; communitarian—based on ethics of care) shows the strengths and shortcomings of each and tensions among them. They suggest close attention to specifics of particular research contexts (pp. 20–28) as an ethical approach. This echoes Yvonna Lincoln's insight that standards for quality are now intertwined with ethical ones, for example, the demand that the researcher conduct and make explicit open and honest negotiations around gathering materials, analysis, and presentation (1995, p. 287). These are closely tied to issues of how and where knowledge is created, as are the enduring questions of privacy, confidentiality, disclosure, informed consent, and researcher "power."

Regarding privacy and confidentiality, few face having their empirical materials subpoenaed (Scarce, 2002), but regulations offering anyone access to such materials gathered in federally funded studies occasion renewed worries about assurance of privacy and confidentiality. Those who work on women's reproductive health, especially abortion; sexual activity, and orientation; experience with stigmatized illness or health conditions; and homeless women are particularly sensitive to these issues, though all feminist qualitative researchers face them.

The worries exist uneasily with concerns about deceit and about fully informing participants of research goals, strategies, and styles. The older qualitative or feminist literature treated informed consent as unproblematic, stable, and durable. However, some have questioned the very meaning of informed consent (who is consenting to what?) and pointed to the fact that consent may fade or alter, so that participants express curiosity, skepticism about, or resistance to the research at a later stage (Casper, 1997; Corrigan, 2003, pp. 784–786; Fine & Weis, 1996; May, 1980; T. Miller & Bell, 2002; see also Fine, Weis, Weseen, & Wong, 2000).

Although feminists rarely conduct covert research, there remain gray areas where the researcher may deliberately withhold or blur personal information (D. Wolf, 1996, pp. 11–12), or views on sex, religion, politics, money, social class, or race are lost in the complexities of interactions characterized by both participants' and researchers' mobile subjectivities and multiple realities. The former is a research strategy; the latter is characteristic of everyday social life. In both cases, the lack of information may influence the mutual construction of stories and representations.

Relationships with participants lie at the heart of feminist ethical concerns. Earlier, some believed that friendly relationships could occur (Oakley, 1981), but this quickly gave way to more distanced views. Feminist qualitative researchers became sensitive to ethical issues arising from concern for and even involvement with participating individuals. Janet Finch's (1984) early observation about researchers' unwitting manipulation of participants hungry for social contact anticipated Judith Stacey's widely cited paper (1988) and Lila Abu-Lughod's (1990) analysis of contradictions in feminist qualitative methodology. Stacey raised the uncomfortable question of getting information from respondents as a means to an end, along with the difficult compromises that may be involved in promising respondents control over the report. These issues characterize qualitative work, which can never resolve all ethical dilemmas that arise (Wheatley, 1994).

Other ethical dilemmas abound, among them the hazard of "stealing women's words" (Opie, 1992; Reay, 1996b), negotiating meanings with participants (Jones, 1997), "validating" or challenging women's taken-for-granted views when they do not accord with feminist perspectives (Kitzinger & Wilkinson, 1997), research where professional and research roles may conflict (Bell & Nutt, 2002; Field, 1991), blurred boundaries between research and counseling (Birch & Miller, 2000), how to represent findings in respondents' own words (S. A. Freeman & Lips, 2002; Skeggs, 1995b).

The view, long held in feminist research, that the researcher occupies a more powerful position continues to be worrisome. However, closer examination of research relations has recognized that the researcher's "power" is often only partial (Ong, 1995), illusory (D. Wolf, 1996; Viswesweran, 1994), tenuous (J. Stacey, 1998; D. Wolf, 1996, p. 36), and confused with researcher responsibility (Bloom, 1998, p. 35), even though the researcher may be more powerfully positioned when out of the field, because she usually will write the account (Luff, 1999).

These ethical issues and those of voice and account emerge even more vividly in activist studies, where researchers and participants collaborate on topics of concern in their lives and worlds. Participatory research (fully discussed in McKemmis and Taggart, Chapter 23, this volume) confronts both researchers and participants-who-are-also-researchers with challenges about women's knowledge, representations of women, modes of gathering empirical materials, analysis, interpretation and writing the account, and relationships between and among the collaborating parties. Although it is not as widely done as might be hoped, nevertheless there is a growing body of research projects and thoughtful discussion of such issues as othering and dissemination (Lykes, 1997). Linda Light and Nancy Kleiber's (1981) early study of a Vancouver women's health collective describes their conversion from traditional field workers to coresearchers with the members of the women's health collective and the difficulties of closing the distance between researchers and participants both fully engaged in the research. Questions of the ownership of the research materials also arise (Renzetti, 1997). Issues of power remain, as collaborative research does not dissolve competing interests (Lykes, 1989, p. 179). Alice McIntyre and M. Brinton Lykes (1998) urge feminist participatory action researchers to exercise reflexivity to interrogate power, privilege, and multiple hierarchies.

In a certain sense, participants are always "doing" research, for they, along with researchers, construct the meanings that are interpreted and turned into "findings." Whereas in customary research, the researcher frames interpretations, in participatory action research researchers and participants undertake this together (Cancian, 1996; Craddock & Reid, 1993). This raises issues of evaluation (Lykes, 1997) and management of distortion. Based on her collaborative work, Maria Mies's conceptualization of "conscious partiality," achieved through partial identification with research participants, creates a critical conceptual distance between the researcher and participants dialectically to facilitate correction of distortions on both sides (Mies, 1993, p. 68; Skeggs, 1994).

Feminist Research on Ethics. Feminist research on ethics has been done on (a) questions referential to larger issues of moral beingness and (b) practices and situations in health care. Research on moral beingness has a long history reaching back to Carol Gilligan's well-known and controversial study of young girls' moral development (Gilligan, 1982; see also Benhabib, 1987; Brabeck, 1996; Koehn, 1998; Larrabee, 1993). This history overlaps complex arguments around the question of care (Larrabee, 1993; R. C. Manning, 1992; Tronto, 1993) and the substantial conceptual and empirical feminist literature on caregiving (Cancian et al., 2000; Noddings, 2002). Ideas from that literature have filtered into discussions of research ethics.

Theorists and researchers have shifted away from the view that ethical or moral behavior is inherent in gender (the essentialist view that women are "natural" carers) to the social construction of gender, which recognizes that a trait such as caring emerges from an interaction between the individual and the milieu (Seigfried, 1996, p. 205). These newer positions on an ethic of care go beyond a focus on personal relationships in the private sphere to concerns with the just community (Seigfried, 1996, p. 210) and the potential for transforming society in the public sphere (Tronto, 1993, pp. 96–97). (See also Walker, 1998; DesAutels & Wright, 2001; Fiore & Nelson, 2003.)

Feminist researchers' long-standing concerns about and work on ethical (or nonethical) treatment of women in health care systems have carried into inquiries on aspects of new technologies, such as assisted reproduction and genetic screening, and into the regrettably enduring problems of equitable care for elderly, poor women of all ethnic groups (Holmes & Purdy, 1992; Sherwin, 1992; Tong, 1997).

Unrealized Agendas

In the early millennial moment, feminist qualitative research remains a complex, diverse, and highly energized enterprise. There is no single approach, nor can any approach claim dominance or a privileged position. Given the substantive range, theoretical complexity, and empirical difficulties, the multiplicity of voices is apt. None of these approaches is beyond criticism, which could and should sharpen and improve them. Feminists should celebrate, not condemn, the diversity and multiplicity of these approaches. The strained binary that posed rigid adherence to traditional methods against the view that all competing knowledge claims are valid should be abandoned. More profitable and realistic are attempts, as theorist Joan Alway (1995) has argued, "to try to produce less false, less partial and less perverse representations without making any claims about what is absolutely and always true" (p. 225). This posture rests on the important assumption that women in specific contexts are best suited to help develop presentations of their lives, contexts that are located in specific structures and historical-material moments. This point is particularly critical as feminists work to understand—through text, discourses, and encounters with women—how their lives are contextualized and framed.

Unrealized agendas remain. Foremost among these is deeper exploration of how race, class, and gender emerge, interlock, and achieve their various effects. Patricia Hill Collins's analysis of "real mothers" (1999); Yen Le Espiritu's (1997) research on gender-based immigration, labor policies, and labor conditions in 19th- and 20th-century America; and Sheila Allen's (1994) discussion of race, ethnicity, and nationality accomplish this critical task. Complicating this agenda is the still-unfinished job of problematizing whiteness and its links to privilege, discussed earlier, and the realization of different agendas, contexts, and dynamics for women of color and varying social status. A promising start is Dorothy Smith's (1997) proposal to utilize the metaphor of the map to discover the ongoing ways by which people coordinate their activities, particularly "those forms of social organization and relations that connect up multiple and various sites of experience" (p. 175). Olivia Espin's (1995) analysis of racism and sexuality in immigrant women's narratives does this.

Much remains to be done to open traditional approaches of data gathering, analysis, and representation to experimental moves, though some feminist researchers are appreciative of the new moves.[16] However, this poses two issues for all feminist qualitative researchers. First is the obdurate necessity to attend to representation, voice, and text in ways that avoid replication of the researcher and instead display participants' representations. Simply presenting research materials or findings in new or shocking ways will not resolve this difficulty. It speaks to the ethical and analytic difficulties inherent as researcher and participant engage in the mutual creation of interpretations that the researcher usually brings to the fore. Researchers cannot avoid responsibility for the account, the text, and the voices.

Patricia Clough (1993a) further complicates this point: "The textuality never refers to a text, but to the processes of desire elicited and repressed, projected and interjected in the activity of reading and writing" (p. 175). Apt though this is, it presents an even much more elusive question than choosing and positioning voices and texts, and it merits much more thoughtful attention.

A second and parallel task is how to address overarching issues of credibility or, put another way, how to indicate that the claims produced are less false, less perverse, and less partial, without falling back into positivist standards that measure acceptability of knowledge in terms of some ideal, unchanging body of knowledge. One way forward, proposed by authors reviewed here, is scrupulous and open interrogation of the feminist researcher's own postures, views, and practices, turning back on herself the very lenses with which she is scrutinizing the lives of the women with which she works, always looking for tensions, contradictions, and complicity (Humphries, 1997, p. 7). Uncomfortable though this may be, it is a strategy both for feminist qualitative researchers who reach for new and experimental approaches and for those who take more familiar paths. Such unremitting reflexivity is not without difficulties: Rachel Wasserfall (1997) reveals deep and tension-laden differences between herself and her participants; Rebecca Lawthom (1997) discloses problems in her work as a feminist researcher in nonfeminist research; and Kathy Davis and Ine Gremmen (1998) found that feminist ideals sometimes can stand in the way of doing feminist research.

The Influence of Contexts on Agendas

It is important to note some contexts that shape and are shaped by feminist qualitative research agendas.

Academic Life. The traditional structure of academic life—at least in the United States—has influenced feminist qualitative research, and not always in the direction of transformations. Ellen Messer-Davidow's (2002) extended and critical account of feminist scholarship within the academy argues that the very structures it sought to reform shaped it. Her incisive historical inquiry addresses Dorothy Smith's earlier question, "What is it about the academy that undermines and reworks the project of claiming it for women in general?" (1999, p. 228). Carolyn Dever's (2004) skeptical exploration of "the boundaries with which academic feminists have constructed their work" (p. xvi) raises fundamental issues about exclusivity and about canonization of feminist theory and knowledge that undergird research.

Whereas much of the early impetus for reform and transformation emerged outside the academy, one finds major feminist research energies of recent decades in such traditional departments as anthropology, sociology, psychology, political science, philosophy, history, interdisciplinary women's studies, and cultural studies and in such professional programs as education, nursing, and social work, where it is not surprising to read thoughtful research and essays on issues discussed in this chapter such as quality of the work and the utility of standpoint theory. Dispersal of feminist qualitative research as well as the feminisms that support it results in highly variegated approaches and levels of maturity. It also means differential reception of qualitative feminist work, ranging from dismissal or hostility to admiration if well, truly, and brilliantly done (depending on evaluators' predilection for traditional or experimental approaches). How these responses translate into job recruitment, tenure review, and acceptance of publications and research funding is a crucial question. Francesca Cancian's (1996, pp. 198–204) academic colleagues doing activist participatory research revealed conflicts and tensions with other colleagues that necessitated working out strategies to enable them to continue such work while trying to succeed academically. Still, as Margaret Randall (2004) observed, "Academics capable of rigorous scholarship and motivated to test that scholarship in activist politics are in a privileged position with regard to exercising the social change so necessary to the survival of humankind"(p. 23).

A different but intriguing issue arises when other scholars borrow feminist research strategies in qualitative feminist research, some taken from traditional qualitative approaches and then modified, others newly created, thus creating a problem of differentiating feminist work from these other projects. Some feminist qualitative researchers would argue that criteria for feminist work (see footnote 1) would differentiate methodologically similar qualitative projects from feminist research. The question of whether feminist qualitative research can transform traditional disciplines is lodged in the complexities of feminist research and the structural nature of the site. Sectors of sociology and psychology tenaciously hold positivistic outlooks along with diverse theoretical views that blunt or facilitate feminist transformation (J. Stacey & Thorne, 1985). Whether such transformative research stances as Dorothy Smith's radical critique of sociology (1974, 1989, 1990a, 1990b; Collins, 1992) or Patricia Hill Collins's concerns about the impact of dualistic thought and the tendency to perpetuate racism (1986, 1990) will reshape sociology remains to be seen. Or will changes come from more deconstructive approaches of abandoning ethnography and focusing on "re-readings of representations in every form of information processsing," which Patricia Clough (1998, p. 137) urges, or Ann Game's embrace of discourses rather than the focus on "the social" (1991, p. 47)?

Within anthropology, Ruth Behar (1993) and Lila Abu-Lughod (1990) argue that influential themes discussed earlier (dissolution of self/other, subject/object boundaries) that are fundamental to traditional ethnographic approaches may liberate the discipline from its colonial and colonizing past (Behar, 1993, p. 302). In psychology, Michelle Fine and Susan Merle Gordon (1992, p. 23) urge that feminist psychologists work in the space between the personal and the political to reconstitute psychology. They urge activist research,[17] while Mary Gergen (2001) formulates a constructionist, postmodern agenda for revisioning psychology. Noting that feminists in psychology have made local and partial alterations to established methods rather than creating a programmatic metatheory, Jill Morawski (1994) foresees the basis for radically new forms of psychological inquiry even though feminist psychology remains in transition.

It is too early to detect the transformative potential of feminist cultural studies and the vital multidisciplined social studies of science. Here, as in other disciplinary sites, the plight of the fiscally strained academic department will shape feminist qualitative research. Downsized departments or programs relying on part-time faculty are not fertile arenas for experimental or even traditional transformative work. In all these contexts, the balance of demands from home, family, and career is an obdurate "every day, every night issue" (to use Dorothy Smith's felicitous phrase) that confronts feminist qualitative researchers who are serious about research for women and its transformative potentials. Counterbalancing these issues is the strong presence of established feminist researchers who take mentoring seriously and who connect politically to other scholars, feminist or not, and to other feminists, academic or not.

Parochialism and Publishing Practices. For at least the last two decades and with no apparent end in sight, publishers have brought out thousands of feminist titles—theoretical, empirical, experimental, and methodological (Messer-Davidow, 2002). This abundance has nourished the emergence and growing complexity of qualitative feminist research. As positive as this is, given the relatively limited number of offerings three decades ago, it nevertheless is worrisome because much of this often very sophisticated literature, which includes work by feminists from countries other than the United States and the United Kingdom, is published in English. Translation difficulties and marketing pressures make English language publication necessary (Maynard, 1996; Meaghan Morris, personal communication; Schiffrin, 1998).[18] It is not surprising that there are undifferentiated views and limited or nonexistent understandings of feminist research done outside Westernized, bureaucratized societies.

Fortunately, different perspectives—such as those of postcolonial, Marxist feminists—come through these publications to undercut Westernizing and homogenizing assumptions about "women" anywhere and everywhere. The leading English-language feminist journals increasingly publish essays from researchers in Asia, Africa, Latin America, the Arab Middle East, and Eastern Europe. Special issues featuring international researchers are common. Leading university and trade presses that publish feminist books frequently have non-U.S. feminists on their lists.[19] However, even when published in English, a feminist research-oriented monograph such as Cynthia Nelson and Soraya Altorki's Arab Regional Women's Studies Workshop (1997) may not easily reach interested Western feminists if it is published outside the United States or Great Britain.

Some, but not enough, of that work is heard at international conferences such as the International Congresses on Women's Health Issues, which meet biannually in such countries as New Zealand, Denmark, Botswana, Thailand, Egypt, and South Korea and draw substantial numbers of international participants. In sum, greater access to international researchers' work balances English-language publications and the dominance of English-language feminism, particularly around international feminist concerns about the problems and complexities of globalization. Given the increasing complexity in feminist qualitative research, some of which derives from postcolonial feminist thinking, new approaches and tactics from international scholars will attract attention not only among open-minded English language feminist researchers but also among publishers with an eye to profitable publication in an era when the economics of publishing are highly problematic.

Qualitative researchers who wish to go beyond research in the Anglophone world increasingly find valuable feminist talk lists and Web sites that offer information about international feminist work, conferences, and publications. Many originate outside the United States or Great Britain. Limited space here prohibits listing even a small proportion of this abundance, but a powerful search engine will produce a cornucopia of worthwhile addresses and sites. Particularly notable among these burgeoning resources that redress Westernized parochialism in feminist research is the Sociologists for Women in Society talk list, where Judith Lorber, herself a leading feminist qualitative researcher, regularly shares such information. Regrettably, computer and Internet resources may not be readily available to all feminist qualitative researchers, particularly those in disadvantaged countries.

▣ Conclusion

If anything, feminist qualitative research is stronger than in the past because theorists and researchers both critically examine its foundations, even as they try new research approaches, both experimental and traditional. Above all, they are much more self-conscious, aware of and sensitive to issues in the formulation and conduct of research. More sophisticated approaches and more incisive understandings enable feminists to grapple with the innumerable problems in women's lives, contexts, and situations in the hope of achieving, if not emancipation, at least some modest intervention and transformation. Yet there is more to do, as many of the authors cited in this chapter make clear. Given the diversity and complexity of feminist qualitative research, it is not likely that any orthodoxy—experimental or traditional—will prevail; nor, in my opinion, should it.

Feminist researchers have articulated thoughtful and incisive directions on feminist research and the potential for change or transformation. Judith Stacey outlined the difficulties of taking feminist work public: "We must take our work public with extraordinary levels of reflexivity, caution and semiotic and rhetorical sophistication" (2003, p. 28). Barbara Laslett and Johanna Brenner (2001) urged feminist researchers to recognize the way higher education institutions work (p. 1233) while noting that "we will need new strategies that correspond to new opportunities as well as the difficulties of these times" (p. 1234). Mary Anglin (2003, p. 3), chair of the Association for Feminist Anthropology of the American Anthropological Association (2003–2005), renewed the call for feminists to reconsider how to bridge academic theories/research with gender equity and social justice.

I conclude with a statement Adele Clarke and I published in 1999:

> It is important to recognize that knowledge production is continually dynamic—new frames open which give way to others which in turn open again and again. Moreover, knowledges are only partial. Some may find these views discomfiting and see in them a slippery slope of ceaseless constructions with no sure footing for action of whatever sort. It is not that there is no platform for action, reform, transformation or emancipation, but that the platforms are transitory. If one's work is overturned or altered by another researcher with a different, more effective approach, then one should rejoice and move on. . . . What is important for concerned feminists is that new topics, issues of concerns and matters for feminist inquiry are continually produced and demand attention to yield a more nuanced understanding of action on critical issues. (Olesen & Clarke, 1999, p. 356)[20]

Early millennial feminist qualitative research, outlined far too sketchily here because of space limitations, offers strategies to lay foundations for action on critical projects, large and small, to realize social justice in different feminist versions, a challenge that thoughtful feminists must accept and carry forward. The range of problems is too great and the issues are too urgent to do otherwise. As poet and activist Margaret Randall declared in her realistic plenary talk to the Winter, 2004, Sociologists for Women in Society meeting, "our mission . . . must be nothing short of rethinking and reworking our future" (Randall, 2004, p. 23).

Accepting this, what can feminist qualitative researchers expect? Ruth Chance, a feminist and legendary director of the Rosenberg Foundation (1958–1974), wisely and realistically observed:

> I think the more modest you are about what you are doing, the better off you'll be. You can count on it that time is going to upset your solutions, and that a period of great ferment and experimentation will be followed by one of examination to see what should be absorbed or modified or rejected . . . but that shouldn't discourage us from acting on the issues as we see them at a given time. The swing of the pendulum will come and maybe you'll start all over again, but it does seem to inch us forward in understanding how complex and remote solutions are. (Chance, quoted in Gorfinkel, 2003, p. 27)

Notes

1. Even though feminist qualitative research may not directly relieve women's suffering in certain contexts, the research nevertheless can contribute to legislation, policy, or agencies' actions (Maynard, 1994a). Beyond the relevance of the findings, the very conduct of the research provides grounds for evaluating the degree to which it is feminist: Does it depict the researched as abnormal, powerless, or without agency? Does it include details of the micropolitics of the research? How is difference handled in the study? Does it avoid replicating oppression? (Bhavnani, 1994, p. 30). Francesca Cancian enunciates a similar list of criteria for regarding research as feminist (1992).

2. Feminist research on health and illness ranges very widely. Lora Bex Lempert (1994) linked accounts of battered women's experiences to constructions of the battering and structural issues. Her subjective approach contrasted with Dorothy Broom's (1991) analysis of how the emergence of state-sponsored women's health clinics in Australia created contradictions with feminist principles that feminists had to handle as they worked within the health care system. Linda Hunt, Brigitte Jordan, S. Irwin, and Carole Browner's (1989) interview study found that women did not comply with medical regimes for reasons that made sense in their own lives and were not "cranks," a finding similar to Anne Kasper's (1994) in her study of women with breast cancer. At a different level, Sue Fisher's (1995) analysis showed that nurse practitioners provide more attentive care than do physicians but still exert considerable control over patients. Addressing large-scale issues, Susan Yadlon's (1997) analysis of discourses around causes for breast cancer revealed that women were blamed for being poor mothers or too skinny, but the discourses overlooked

environmental and other extracorporal causes (1997). Sarah Nettleton's (1991) deconstructive analysis of discursive practices in dentistry showed how ideal mothers are created, while Kathy Davis's (1995) research on cosmetic surgery highlighted women's dilemmas.

3. Policy research raises the issue of "studying up." It also invokes the oft-noted comment that feminist researchers, like many other qualitative (and quantitative) investigators, find it easier to access respondents in social groups open to them rather than high-status lawmakers or elected officials, an important exception being Margaret Stacey's (1992) analysis of the British Medical Council. Furthermore, feminist concerns focus on elite policy sites, overlooking the fact that significant policy is made at local levels (institutions, city government, school boards, community groups). The work developing Dorothy Smith's theories of institutional ethnography (M. Campbell & Manicom, 1995) and particularly Marie Campbell's (1998) analysis of how texts are enacted as policy in a Canadian nursing home offers new and promising leads in the area of feminist policy analysis. Carroll Estes and Beverly Edmonds's (1981) symbolic interactionist model of how emergent policy issues become framed remains a valuable approach for feminists interested in policy analysis. Additionally a growing number of explicitly feminist examinations of policy construction (Bacchi, 1999), policy and social justice (N. D. Campbell, 2000), critical policy analysis (Marshall, 1997), and policy and politics (Staudt, 1998) provide foundations for policy-oriented qualitative feminist researchers, as does the new area of feminist comparative policy (Mazur, 2002). However, as Ronnie Steinberg's (1996) account of her considerable experience as an feminist advocacy policy researcher shows, there are substantial "challenges, frustrations, and unresolvable double-bind associated with conducting (feminist) research in a political context for social change" (p. 254). Another difficulty, documented in a Canadian report about feminist policy analysis (Burt, 1995), lies in the tensions between traditional approaches that often overlook women and feminist policy challenges.

4. In Adele Clarke's phrase, these are "meso analyses" that refer to how societal and institutional forces mesh with human activity. Clarke's own feminist sociohistorical analysis shows how these processes play out around such issues as production of contraceptives (1990, 1998a, 1998b). These studies elevate research for women to an important critique of historically male-dominated science and policy making and control, not just of women but also of the policy processes, for example, Linda Gordon's (1994) sociohistorical analysis of welfare mothers, which showed how outmoded ideas about women's place are carried into new eras and misplaced policies.

5. This shift has evoked worried comments that feminist researchers have moved away from the political agendas of an earlier time, concerned with understanding and alleviating women's oppression, to descriptions of women's lives or arcane epistemological questions (Glucksman, 1994, p. 150; L. Kelly, Burton, & Regan, 1994, p. 28). Clearly, widespread interest in epistemological issues flourishes among those seeking to understand, improve, or destabilize feminist approaches, but there is abundant work oriented to intervention and change on numerous fronts. Patti Lather and Chris Smithies's (1997) participatory study with HIV-positive women combines poststructural approaches with a clear reform agenda, Rachel Pfeffer's (1997) ethnographic inquiry into lives of young homeless women points to programmatic possibilities, and Diana Taylor and Katherine Dower's (1995) policy-oriented focus group research with community women in San Francisco details women's concerns. Olesen, Taylor, Ruzek, & Clarke (1997) extensively review feminist research oriented to ameliorating women's health, and qualitative feminist researchers discuss difficult issues in researching sexual violence against women—for example, sexual harassment of the researcher (Huff, 1997), cross-race research (Huisman, 1997), and managing one's own and others' emotions (Mattley, 1997). Adele Clarke and I argue that "discursive constructions and signifying practices can be handled as constitutive rather than determinative" (1999a, p. 13). Sally Kenney and Helen Kinsella (1997) detail the political and reform implications of standpoint theory. Moreover, a number of journals (*Qualitative Research in Health Care*, *Qualitative Studies in Education*, *Feminism and Psychology*, *Western Journal of Nursing Research*, *Journal of Social Issues*, *Sociology of Health and Illness*, *Qualitative Inquiry*, *Qualitative Sociology*, *Journal of Contemporary Ethnography*, *Feminist Studies*, *Feminist Review*, *Gender & Society*, *and Social Problems*) publish feminist qualitative reform-oriented research. However, here, as elsewhere, space limits on length of essays (25 pages double-spaced) make constructing both an argument and a reform stance difficult, given the necessity for detail in qualitative reporting.

6. Work by feminist legal scholars (Ashe, 1988; Bartlett, 1990; Fry, 1992; MacKinnon, 1983; Matsuda,

1992, 1996; P. J. Williams, 1991) also falls within this genre.

7. Yvonna Lincoln, in a personal communication, has reminded me that relativism "spreads over a continuum" ranging from radical relativists who believe that "anything goes" to those who disavow absolute standards for evaluating accounts but who hold that standards should be developed in specific contexts, and these standards should incorporate participants' ideas of which account represents useful knowledge. This latter view does not jettison any notion of quality but rather serves as a way to avoid utilizing "scientific standards" in contexts where "they act in oppressing, disabling or power-freighted ways."

8. Beyond the original texts of standpoint theorists cited here, useful interpretive reviews can be found in Denzin (1997), Clough (1998), and Kenney and Kinsella (1997). Harding's summary of standpoint theories' chronology also is instructive (1997, p. 387).

9. The extensive and occasionally difficult literature on deconstructionism, postmodernism, and feminism is not always as accessible as it should be for those who are starting to explore or wish to deepen their understanding. Some useful works are the Spring, 1988, issue of *Feminist Studies*, Nicholson (1990, 1997), Hekman (1990), Flax (1987, 1990), Rosenau (1992), Lemert (1997), Charmaz's (1995) insightful and evenly balanced analysis of positivism and postmodernism in qualitative research, and Collins's (1998b, pp. 114–154) incisive discussion of what postmodernism means for black feminists.

10. Feminist researchers who look to deconstruction or psychoanalytic feminist semiotics disavow attention to experience (Clough, 1993a, p. 179). They argue that irrespective of how close the researcher, experience is always created in discourse and textuality. Text is central to incisive analysis as a fundamental mode of social criticism. In this work, the emphasis on desire seems to refer to (a) passion, (b) the mysterious and mischievous contributions of the unconscious, (c) libidinal resources not squeezed out of us by childhood and adult socialization, and (d) the sexuality and politics of cultural life and its representations.

11. Kamela Visweswaran (1994) makes a useful differentiation between reflexive ethnography, which questions its own authority, confronts the researcher's processes of interpretation, and emphasizes how the researcher thinks she knows, and deconstructive ethnography, which abandons authority, confronts power in the interpretive processes, and emphasizes how we think we know what we know is not innocent.

12. Other feminist accounts that have explicated how decisions are made include Janet Finch and Jennifer Mason's detailed report on how they sought "negative cases" (1990) and Catherine Kohler Riessman's worries about her analysis of divorced persons' reports and the sociologist's interpretive voice (1990). Jennifer Ring, following Hegel, avers that dialectical thought prevents stabilizing the border between objectivity and subjectivity (1987, p. 771).

13. Considerations of voice and preparation of text or alternative presentation raise the question of type of publication. Presenting research materials in popular magazines may reach audiences who would be unlikely to have access to or see more traditional or even experimental accounts in academic sources. At present, few of the academic review processes leading to tenure, promotion, or even merit increases acknowledge these lay publications as important. Patti Lather and Chris Smithies (1997), in their research with HIV-positive women in which they consulted with women throughout, initially took their manuscript directly into a publication for the mass audience reachable through such outlets as supermarkets.

14. Earlier feminist accounts developed innovative ways to reflect and present voice, though not all would be free of the problems Fine discusses. (For an extensive list of such accounts, see Maschia-Lees et al., 1989, pp. 7–8, n. 1). Two contrasting examples: Marjorie Shostak (1981) gave a verbatim dialogic account of her voice and that of her K!ung respondent, Nissa, and Susan Krieger (1983) used the device of a polyphonic chorus to represent voices of women in a Midwest lesbian community. Krieger's voice is absent, though she clearly selected the materials for the account.

15. Under the editorship of Barbara and Dennis Tedlock, the flagship journal *The American Anthropologist* adopted a policy of publishing experimental texts, as have several sociological journals long sympathetic to the new modes (*Qualitative Inquiry*, *Journal of Contemporary Ethnography*, *The Midwest Sociological Quarterly*, and *Qualitative Sociology*).

16. In a review essay by five women at the University of Michigan's Institute for Research on Women and Gender, discussing Laurel Richardson's *Fields of Play* (1997), Lora Bex Lempert argues that scholars who have moved into the experimental spaces have created intellectual and representation spaces for others in the work of social transformation, an agenda shared with the traditionalists (Dutton, J., Groat, L., Hassinger, J., Lempert, L., Riehl, C., 1998).

17. Activist-oriented research agendas in women's health are outlined by Narrigan, Zones, Worcester, and Grad (1997) and by Ruzek, Olesen and Clarke (1997).

18. I am indebted here to a lively exchange on these issues with Meaghan Morris, Norman Denzin, Patricia Clough, and Yvonna Lincoln. In a helpful critical reading of this section of the chapter, Annie George of the University of California, San Francisco Department of Social and Behavioral Sciences Graduate Program in Sociology pointed out that many English-language publications in non-Western countries are not listed or cited in major databases such as SocAbstracts and ERIC.

19. Notable recent issues of English-language feminist journals with international feminist research include *Feminist Review* (Summer, 1998), "Rethinking Caribbean Difference"; *Signs* (Winter, 1998), "Gender, Politics and Islam." Research by Chinese and Japanese feminists on women office workers (Ogasawara, 1998) and on women factory workers in Hong Kong and South China (Lee, 1998) exemplifies international work published by university and trade presses, as do writings by international scholars on their relationship to feminism and scholarship in their home and adopted societies (John, 1996; U. Narayan, 1997).

20. As Deborah Lupton (1995) has noted, "The point is not to seek a certain 'truth,' but to uncover varieties of truth that operate, to highlight the nature of truth as transitory and political and the position of subjects as fragmentary and contradictory" (pp. 160–161).

References

Abel, E., Christian, B., & Moglen, H. (Eds.). (1997). *Female subjects in black and white: Race, psychoanalysis, criticism.* Berkeley: University of California Press.

Abel, E. K., & Nelson, M. K. (Eds.). (1990). *Circles of care: Work and identity in women's lives.* Albany: State University of New York Press.

Abu-Lughod, L. (1990). Can there be a feminist ethnography? *Women and Performance, 5,* 7–27.

Acker, J., Barry, K., & Esseveld, J. (1991). Objectivity and truth: Problems in doing feminist research. In M. M. Fonow & J. A. Cook (Eds.), *Beyond methodology: Feminist scholarship as lived research* (pp. 133–153). Bloomington: University of Indiana Press.

Acker, S. (1994). *Gendered education: Sociological reflections on women, teaching and feminism.* Buckingham, UK: Open University Press.

Alexander, M. J., & Mohanty, C. T. (1997). *Feminist genealogies, colonial legacies, democratic futures.* New York: Routledge.

Allen, S. (1994). Race, ethnicity and nationality: Some questions of identity. In H. Afshar & M. Maynard (Eds.), *The dynamics of "race" and gender: Some feminist interventions* (pp. 85–105). London: Taylor and Francis.

Alway, J. (1995). The trouble with gender: Tales of the still missing feminist revolution in sociological theory. *Sociological Theory, 13,* 209–228.

Andrews, M. (2002). Feminist research with non-feminist and anti-feminist women: Meeting the challenge. *Feminism and Psychology, 12,* 55–77.

Anglin, M. (2003). Feminism in practice. *Voices: A Publication of the Association for Feminist Anthropology, 6,* 3.

Anzaldúa, G. (1987). *Borderlands/La frontera.* San Francisco: Auntie Lute.

Anzaldúa, G. (1990). *Making sou: Haciendo caras.* San Francisco: Auntie Lute.

Appleby, Y. (1997). How was it for you? Intimate exchanges in feminist research. In M. Ang-Lyngate, C. Corrin, & H. S. Millson (Eds.), *Desperately seeking sisterhood: Still challenging and building* (pp. 127–147). London: Taylor and Francis.

Asch, A., & Fine, M. (1992). Beyond the pedestals: Revisiting the lives of women with disabilities. In M. Fine (Ed.), *Disruptive voices: The possibilities of feminist research* (pp. 139–174). Ann Arbor: University of Michigan Press.

Ashe, M. (1988). Law-language of maternity: Discourse holding nature in contempt. *New England Law Review, 521,* 44–70.

Bacchi, C. (1999). *Women, policy and politics.* Thousand Oaks, CA: Sage.

Ball, S. J. (1994). *Education reform: A critical and post-structural approach.* Buckingham, UK: Open University Press.

Balsamo, A. (1993). On the cutting edge: Cosmetic surgery and the technological production of the gendered body. *Camera Obscura, 28,* 207–237.

Balsamo, A. (1999). Technologies of surveillance: Constructing cases of maternal neglect. In A. E. Clarke & V. L. Olesen (Eds.), *Revisioning women, health and healing: Feminist cultural and techno-science perspectives* (pp. 231–253). New York: Routledge.

Barndt, D. (2002). *Tangled routes: Women, work and globalization on the tomato trail.* New York: Rowman & Littlefield.

Bartlett, K. (1990). Feminist legal methods. *Harvard Law Review, 103,* 45–50.

Behar, R. (1993). *Translated woman: Crossing the border with Esperanza's story.* Boston: Beacon.

Behar, R. (1996). *The vulnerable observer.* Boston: Beacon.

Behar, R., & Gordon, D. (Eds.). (1995). *Women writing culture.* Berkeley: University of California Press.

Bell, L., & Nutt, L. (2002). Divided loyalties, divided expectations: Research ethics, professional and occupational responsibilities. In M. Mauthner, M. Birch, J. Jessop, & T. Miller (Eds.), *Ethics in qualitative research* (pp. 70–90). Thousand Oaks, CA: Sage.

Benhabib, S. (1987). The generalized and the concrete other: The Kohlberg-Gilligan controversy and feminist theory. In S. Benhabib & D. Cornell (Eds.), *Feminism as critique* (pp. 77–95). Minneapolis: University of Minnesota Press.

Benhabib. S. (1995). Feminism and postmodernism: An uneasy alliance. In S. Benhabib, J. Butler, D. Cornell, & N. Fraser (Eds.), *Feminist contentions: A philosophical exchange* (pp. 17–34). New York: Routledge.

Benhabib, S., Butler, J., Cornell, D., & Fraser, N. (Eds.). (1995). *Feminist contentions: A philosophical exchange.* New York: Routledge.

Bergeron, S. (2001). Political economy discourses of globalization and feminist politics. *Signs, 26,* 984–1006.

Bhavnani, K.-K. (1994). Tracing the contours: Feminist research and feminist objectivity. In H. Afshar & M. Maynard (Eds.), *The dynamics of "race" and gender: Some feminist interventions* (pp. 26–40). London: Taylor and Francis.

Bing, V. M., & Reid, P. T. (1996). Unknown women and unknowing research: Consequences of color and class in feminist psychology. In N. R. Goldberger, J.M.M. Tarule, B. McVicker, & M. Field (Eds.), *Knowledge, difference and power: Essays inspired by women's ways of knowing* (pp. 175–205). New York: Basic Books.

Birch, M. (1998). Reconstructing research narratives: Self and sociological identity in alternative settings. In J. Ribbens & R. Edwards (Eds.), *Feminist dilemmas in qualitative research: Public knowledge and private lives* (pp. 171–185). Thousand Oaks, CA: Sage.

Birch, M., & Miller, T. (2000). Inviting intimacy: The interview as therapeutic opportunity. *International Review of Social Research Methodology, 3,* 189–202.

Blackmore, J. (1995). Policy as dialogue: Feminist administrators working for educational change. *Gender and Education, 7,* 293–313.

Bloom, L. R. (1998). *Under the sign of hope: Feminist methodology and narrative interpretation.* Albany: State University of New York Press.

Brabeck, M. M. (1996). The moral self, values and circles of belonging. In K. F. Wyche & F. J. Crosby (Eds.), *Women's ethnicities: Journeys through psychology* (pp. 145–165). Boulder, CO: Westview.

Braidotti, R. (2000). Once upon a time in Europe. *Signs, 25,* 1061–1064.

Britzman, D. P. (1991). *Practice makes practice: A critical study of learning to teach.* Albany: State University of New York Press.

Britzman, D. P. (1998). Foreword. In L. R. Bloom, *Under the sign of hope: Feminist methodology and narrative interpretation* (pp. ix–xi). Albany: State University of New York Press.

Broom, D. (1991). *Damned if we do: Contradictions in women's health care.* Sydney: Allen and Unwin.

Brown, R. H. (1998). Review of *Fields of Play: Constructing an Academic Life* by Laurel Richardson. *Contemporary Sociology, 27,* 380–383.

Brown, W. (1992). Finding the man in the state. *Feminist Studies, 18,* 7–34.

Burt, S. (1995). Gender and public policy: Making some difference in Ottawa. In F.-P. Gingras (Ed.), *Gender and politics in contemporary Canada* (pp. 86–105). Toronto: Oxford University Press.

Butler, J. (1990). *Gender trouble: Feminism and the subversion of identity.* London: Routledge.

Butler, J. (1993). *Bodies that matter: On the discursive limits of "sex."* London: Routledge.

Butler, J. (1994). Against proper objects. *Differences, 6,* 1–16.

Butler, O. (1986). *Feminist experiences in feminist research.* Manchester, UK: University of Manchester Press.

Campbell, M. (1998). Institutional ethnography and experience as data. *Qualitative Sociology, 21,* 55–74.

Campbell, M. (2002). Textual accounts, ruling action: The intersection of knowledge and power in the routine conduct of nursing work. *Studies in Cultures, Organizations and Societies, 7,* 231–250.

Campbell, M., & Gregor, F. (2002). *Mapping social relations: A primer in doing institutional ethnography.* Toronto: Garamond.

Campbell, M., & Manicom, A. (Eds.). (1995). *Knowledge, experience and ruling relations.* Toronto: University of Toronto Press.

Campbell, N. D. (2000). *Using women: Gender, drug policy, and social justice.* New York: Routledge.

Cancian, F. M. (1992). Feminist science: Methodologies that challenge inequality. *Gender and Society, 6,* 623–642.

Cancian, F. M. (1996). Participatory research and alternative strategies for activist sociology. In

H. Gottfried (Ed.), *Feminism and social change* (pp. 187–205). Urbana: University of Illinois Press.

Cancian, F. M., Kurz, D., London, A. S., Reviere, R., & Tuominen, M. C. (Eds.). (2000). *Child care and inequality: Re-thinking care work for children and youth.* New York: Routledge.

Cannon, L. W., Higginbotham, E., & Leung, M.L.A. (1991). Race and class bias in qualitative research on women. In M. M. Fonow & J. A. Cook (Eds.), *Beyond methodology: Feminist scholarship as lived research on women* (pp. 107–118). Bloomington: Indiana University Press.

Case, S.-E., & Abbitt, E. W. (2004). Disidentifications, diaspora and desire. Questions on the future of the feminist critique of performance. *Signs, 29,* 925–938.

Casper, M. J. (1997). Feminist politics and fetal surgery: Adventures of a research cowgirl on the reproductive frontier. *Feminist Studies, 23,* 233–262.

Casper, M. J. (1998). *The making of the unborn patient: Medical work and the politics of reproduction in experimental fetal surgery.* New Brunswick, NJ: Rutgers University Press.

Charmaz, K. (1995). Between positivism and postmodernism: Implications for methods. In N. K. Denzin (Ed.), *Studies in symbolic interaction* (Vol. 17, pp. 43–72). Greenwich, CT: JAI.

Charmaz, K., & Olesen, V. L. (1997). Ethnographic research in medical sociology: Its foci and distinctive contributions. *Sociological Methods and Research, 25,* 452–494.

Chase, S. E. (1995). *Ambiguous empowerment: The work narratives of women school superintendents.* Amherst: University of Massachusetts Press.

Chow, E. N. (1987). The development of feminist consciousness among Asian American women. *Gender and Society, 1,* 284–299.

Clarke, A. (1990). A social worlds research adventure: The case of reproductive science. In S. E. Cozzens & T. F. Gieryn (Eds.), *Theories of science in society* (pp. 15–43). Bloomington: Indiana University Press.

Clarke, A. (1998a). *Disciplining reproduction: Modernity, American life sciences, and the problems of "sex."* Berkeley: University of California Press.

Clarke, A., & Olesen, V. L. (Eds.). (1999). *Revisioning women, health and healing: Feminist, cultural and technoscience perspectives.* New York: Routledge.

Clarke, A., & Olesen, V. (1999a). Revising, diffracting, acting. In A. E. Clarke & V. L. Olesen (Eds.), *Revisioning women, health and healing: Feminist, cultural and technoscience perspectives* (pp. 3–38). New York: Routledge.

Clarke, A. (2005). *Situational analysis: Grounded theory after the postmodern turn.* Thousand Oaks, CA: Sage.

Clough, P. T. (1993a). On the brink of deconstructing sociology: Critical reading of Dorothy Smith's standpoint epistemology. *The Sociological Quarterly, 34,* 169–182.

Clough, P. T. (1993b). Response to Smith's response. *The Sociological Quarterly, 34,* 193–194.

Clough, P. T. (1994). *Feminist thought: Desire, power and academic discourse.* London: Basil Blackwell.

Clough, P. T. (1998). *The end(s) of ethnography* (Rev. ed.). Newbury Park, CA: Sage.

Clough, P. T. (2000). *Autoaffection: The unconscious in the age of teletechnology.* Minneapolis: University of Minnesota Press.

Code, L. (1991). *What can she know? Feminist theory and the construction of knowledge.* Ithaca, NY: Cornell University Press.

Collins, P. H. (1986). Learning from the outsider within: The sociological significance of Black feminist thought. *Social Problems, 33,* 14–32.

Collins, P. H. (1990). *Black feminist thought: Knowledge, consciousness and the politics of empowerment.* Boston: Unwin Hyman.

Collins, P. H. (1992). Transforming the inner circle: Dorothy Smith's challenge to sociological theory. *Sociological Theory, 10,* 73–80.

Collins, P. H. (1997). Comment on Hekman's "Truth and method: Feminist standpoint theory revisited." *Signs, 22,* 375–381.

Collins, P. H. (1998a). *Fighting words: Black women and the search for justice.* Minneapolis: University of Minnesota Press.

Collins, P. H. (1998b). What's going on? Black feminist thought and the politics of postmodernism. In P. H. Collins, *Fighting words: Black women and the search for justice* (pp. 124–154). Minneapolis: University of Minnesota Press.

Collins, P. H. (1999). Will the "real" mother please stand up? The logic of eugenics and American national family planning. In A. E. Clarke & V. L. Olesen (Eds.), *Revisioning women, health and healing: Feminist, cultural and technoscience perspectives* (pp. 266–282). New York: Routledge.

Connell, R. W. (1997). Comment on Hawkesworth's "Confounding gender." *Signs, 22,* 702–706.

Constable, N. (1997). *Maid to order in Hong Kong: Stories of Filipina workers.* Ithaca, NY: Cornell University Press.

Corrigan, O. (2003). Empty ethics: The problem with informed consent. *Sociology of Health and Illness, 25*, 768–792.

Craddock, E., & Reid, M. (1993). Structure and struggle: Implementing a social model of a well woman clinic in Glasgow. *Social Science and Medicine, 19*, 35–45.

Crenshaw, K. (1992). Whose story is it, anyway? Feminist and antiracist appropriations of Anita Hill. In T. Morrison (Ed.), *Race-ing justice, engendering power* (pp. 402–436). New York: Pantheon.

Cuthbert, D. (2000). "The doctor from the university is at the door . . .": Methodological reflections on research with non-Aboriginal adoptive and foster mothers of Aboriginal children. *Resources for Feminist Research/Documentation sur la Recherche Feminists, 28*, 209–228.

Daniels, A. K. (1983). Self-deception and self-discovery in field work. *Qualitative Sociology, 6*, 195–214.

Davis, A. Y. (1981). *Women, race and class.* London: The Women's Press.

Davis, K. (1995). *Reshaping the female body: The dilemma of cosmetic surgery.* New York: Routledge.

Davis, K., & Gremmen, I. (1998). In search of heroines: Some reflections on normativity in feminist research. *Feminism and Psychology, 8*, 133–153.

de Castell, S., & Bryson, M. (1997). En/gendering equity: Paradoxical consequences of institutionalized equity policies. In S. de Castell & M. Bryson (Eds.), *Radical In(ter)ventions: Identity politics and difference/s in educational praxis* (pp. 85–103). Albany: State University of New York Press.

de Lauretis, T. (1987). *Technologies of gender: Essays on theory, film, and fiction.* Bloomington: Indiana University Press.

Denzin, N. K. (1992). *Symbolic interactionism and cultural studies.* Oxford, UK: Basil Blackwell.

Denzin, N. K. (1997). *Interpretive ethnography: Ethnographic practices for the 21st century.* Thousand Oaks, CA: Sage.

DesAutels, P., & Wright, J. (2001). *Feminists doing ethics.* Boulder, CO: Rowman and Littlefield.

DeVault, M. (1991). *Feeding the family: The social organization of caring as gendered work.* Chicago: University of Chicago Press.

DeVault, M. (1993). Different Voices: Feminists' methods of social research. *Qualitative Sociology, 16*, 77–83.

DeVault, M. (1996). Talking back to sociology: Distinctive contributions of feminist methodology. *Annual Review of Sociology, 22*, 29–50.

DeVault, M. (1999). *Liberating method: Feminism and social research.* Philadelphia: Temple University Press.

Dever, C. (2004). *Skeptical feminism, activist theory, activist practice.* Minneapolis: University of Minnesota Press.

Diaz, C. (2002). Conversational heuristic as a reflexive method for feminist research. *International Review of Sociology, 12*(2), 249–255.

Dill, B. T. (1979). The dialectics of Black womanhood. *Signs, 4*, 543–555.

Doezema, J. (2000). Loose women or lost women? The emergence of the myth of white slavery in contemporary discourses on trafficking in women. *Gender Issues, 18*, 23–50.

Dougherty, D. S. (2001). Sexual harassment as [dys]functional process: A feminist standpoint analysis. *Journal of Applied Communication Research, 29*, 372–402.

Dutton, J., Groat, L., Hassinger, J., Lempert, L., Riehl, C. (1998). Academic lives. *Qualitative Sociology, 21*, 195–203.

Ebert, T. (1996). *Ludic feminism and after: Postmodernism, desire, and labor in late capitalism.* Ann Arbor: University of Michigan Press.

Edwards, R., & Mauthner, M. (2002). Ethics and feminist research: Theory and practice. In M. Mauthner, M. Birch, J. Jessop, & T. Miller (Eds.), *Ethics in qualitative research* (pp. 14–31). Thousand Oaks, CA: Sage.

Ehrenreich, B., & Fox Piven, F. (1983). Women and the welfare state. In I. Howe (Ed.), *Alternatives: Proposals for America from the democratic left* (pp. 30–45). New York: Pantheon.

Eichenberger, S. E. (2002). *Perceived identity: Researching a Latino/a Catholic community.* Paper presented at the meeting of the Southern Sociological Society.

Eichler, M. (1986). The relationship between sexist, non-sexist, woman-centered and feminist research. *Studies in Communication, 3*, 37–74.

Eichler, M. (1997). Feminist methodology. *Current Sociology, 45*, 9–36.

Ellingson, L. L. (1998). "Then you know how I feel": Empathy, identity and reflexivity in fieldwork. *Qualitative Inquiry, 4*, 492–514.

Ellis, C. (1995). *Final negotiations: A story of love, loss and chronic illness.* Philadelphia: Temple University Press.

Ellis, C., & Bochner, A. P. (1996). *Composing ethnography: Alternative forms of writing.* Walnut Creek, CA: AltaMira.

Epstein, C. F. (1981). *Women in law.* New York: Basic Books.

Espiritu, Y. L. (1997). *Asian American women and men: Labor, laws and love.* Thousand Oaks, CA: Sage.

Espin, O. M. (1995). "Race," racism and sexuality in the life narratives of immigrant women. *Feminism and Psychology, 5,* 223–228.

Estes, C. L., & Edmonds, B. C. (1981). Symbolic interaction and social policy analysis. *Symbolic Interaction, 4,* 75–86.

Evans, S. M. (2002). Re-viewing the second wave. *Feminist Studies, 28,* 259–267.

Fee, E. (1983). Women and health care: A comparison of theories. In E. Fee (Ed.), *Women and health: The politics of sex in medicine* (pp. 10–25). Englewood Cliffs, NJ: Baywood.

Felski, R. (1997). The doxa of difference. *Signs, 23,* 1–22.

Ferguson, K. (1993). *The man question: Visions of subjectivity in feminist theory.* Berkeley: University of California Press.

Fernandez-Kelly, P., & Wolf, D. (2001). A dialogue on globalization. *Signs, 26,* 1243–1249.

Field, P. A. (1991). Doing fieldwork in your own culture. In J. M. Morse (Ed.), *Qualitative nursing research: A contemporary dialogue* (pp. 91–104). Newbury Park, CA: Sage.

Finch, J. (1984). It's great to have someone to talk to. In C. Bell & H. Roberts (Eds.), *Social researching: Politics, problems, practice* (pp. 70–87). London: Routledge and Kegan Paul.

Finch, J. (1986). *Research and policy: The uses of qualitative research in social and educational research.* London: Falmer.

Finch, J., & Groves, D. (1983). *A labour of love: Women, work and caring.* London: Routledge and Kegan Paul.

Finch, J., & Mason, J. (1990). Decision taking in the fieldwork process: Theoretical sampling and collaborative working. In R. G. Burgess (Ed.), *Studies in qualitative methodology: Vol. 2. Reflections on field experience* (pp. 25–50). Greenwich, CT: JAI.

Fine, M. (Ed.). (1992a). *Disruptive voices.* Ann Arbor: University of Michigan Press.

Fine, M. (1992b). Passions, politics and power: Feminist research possibilities. In M. Fine (Ed.), *Disruptive voices* (pp. 205–232). Ann Arbor: University of Michigan Press.

Fine, M., & Gordon, S. M. (1992). Feminist transformations of/despite psychology. In M. Fine (Ed.), *Disruptive voices* (pp. 1–25). Ann Arbor: University of Michigan Press.

Fine, M., & Weis, L. (1996). Writing the "wrongs" of fieldwork: Confronting our own research/writing dilemma in urban ethnographies. *Qualitative Inquiry, 2,* 251–274.

Fine, M., Weis, L., Weseen, S., & Wong, L. M. (2000). For whom? Qualitative research, representations and social responsibilities. In N. K. Denzin & Y. S. Lincoln (Eds.), *Handbook of qualitative research* (2nd ed., pp. 107–132). Thousand Oaks, CA: Sage.

Fiore, R. N., & Nelson, H. L. (2003). *Recognition, responsibility and rights: Feminist ethics and social theory.* Boulder, CO: Rowan and Littlefield.

Fisher, S. (1995). *Nursing wounds: Nurse practitioners, doctors, women patients, and the negotiation of meaning.* New Brunswick, NJ: Rutgers University Press.

Fishman, J. (2001). Drugs and sex: Clinical research. *Molecular Interventions, 2,* 12–16.

Flax, J. (1987). Postmodernism and gender relations in feminist theory. *Signs, 14,* 621–643.

Flax, J. (1990). *Thinking fragments: Psychoanalysis, feminism and postmodernism in the contemporary West.* Berkeley: University of California Press.

Fonow, M. M., & Cook, J. A. (1991). *Beyond methodology: Feminist scholarship as lived research.* Bloomington: University of Indiana Press.

Forbes, D. A. (2001). Black women in authority: An oxymoron? A black feminist analysis of the organizational experiences of selected African-descended women managers in the United States and Jamaica. *Dissertation Abstracts International-61/08*, February, p. 3367.

Fosket, J. R. (1999). Problematizing biomedicine: Women's constructions of breast cancer knowledge. In L. Potts (Ed.), *Ideologies of breast cancer: Feminist perspectives* (pp. 15–36). London: Macmillan.

Frankenberg, R. (1994). *White women, race matters: The social construction of whiteness.* Minneapolis: University of Minnesota Press.

Frankenberg, R., & Mani, L. (1993). Cross currents, cross talk: Race, postcoloniality and the politics of location. *Cultural Studies, 7,* 292–310.

Fraser, N. (1989). Struggle over needs: Outline of a socialist-feminist critical theory of late capitalist political culture. In N. Fraser, *Unruly practices: Power, discourse and gender in contemporary social theory* (pp. 161–187). Minneapolis: University of Minnesota Press.

Fraser, N. (1997). *Justice interruptus: Critical reflections on the post-socialist condition.* New York: Routledge.

Freeman, C. (2001). Is local:global as feminine: masculine? Rethinking the gender of globalization. *Signs, 26,* 1007–1038.

Freeman, S. A., & Lips, H. M. (2002). Harsh judgements and sharp impressions: Audience responses to participants in a study of heterosexual feminist identities. *Feminism and Psychology, 12,* 275–281.

Fry, M. J. (1992). *Postmodern legal feminism.* London: Routledge.

Game, A. (1991). *Undoing the social: Towards a deconstructive sociology.* Milton Keynes, UK: Open University Press.

Garcia, A. M. (1989). The development of Chicana discourse. *Gender & Society,* 3, 217–238.

Gaskell, J., & Eichler, M. (2001). White women as burden: On playing the role of feminist "experts" in China. *Women's Studies International Forum, 24,* 637–651.

Gergen, M. (2001). *Feminist reconstructions in psychology: Narrative, gender, and performance.* Newbury Park, CA: Sage.

Gill, C. J. (1997). The last sisters: Health issues of women with disabilities. In S. B. Ruzek, V. L. Olesen, & A. E. Clarke (Eds.), *Women's health: Complexities and differences* (pp. 96–112). Columbus: The Ohio State University Press.

Gilligan, C. (1982). *In a different voice: Psychological theory and women's development.* Cambridge, MA: Harvard University Press.

Ginzburg, F. (1998). *Contested lives: The abortion debate in an American community* (new ed.). Berkeley: University of California Press.

Glazer, N. Y. (1991). "Between a rock and a hard place": Women's professional organizations in nursing and class, racial and ethnic inequalities. *Gender and Society, 5,* 351–372.

Glenn, E. N. (1990). The dialectics of wage work: Japanese-American women and domestic service, 1905–1940. In E. C. DuBois & V. Ruiz (Eds.), *Unequal sisters: A multi-cultural reader in U.S. women's history* (pp. 345–372). London: Routledge.

Glenn, E. N. (2002). *Unequal freedom: How race and gender shaped American citizenship and labor.* Cambridge, MA: Harvard University Press.

Glucksman, M. (1994). The work of knowledge and the knowledge of women's work. In M. Maynard & J. Purvis (Eds.), *Researching women's lives from a feminist perspective* (pp. 149–165). London: Taylor and Francis.

Gordon, L. *Women's body, women's right.* New York: Grossman.

Gordon, L. (1994). *Pitied but not entitled: Single mothers and the history of welfare.* New York: Free Press.

Gorelick, S. (1991). Contradictions of feminist methodology. *Gender and Society, 5,* 459–477.

Gorfinkel, C. (2003). *Much remains to be done: Ruth Chance and California's 20th century movements for social justice.* Pasadena, CA: International Productions.

Graham, H. (1984). *Women, health and the family.* Brighton, UK: Wheatsheaf Harvester.

Graham, H. (1985). Providers, negotiators and mediators: Women as the hidden carers. In E. Lewin & V. L. Olesen (Eds.), *Women, health and healing: Toward a new perspective* (pp. 25–52). London: Tavistock.

Gray, R., & Sinding, C. (2002). *Standing ovation: Performing social science research about cancer.* Boulder, CO: Rowman & Littlefield.

Green, R. (1990). The Pocahontas perplex: The image of Indian women in American culture. In E. C. DuBois & V. L. Ruiz (Eds.), *Unequal sisters: A multi-cultural reader in U.S. women's history* (pp. 15–21). London: Routledge.

Grewal, I., & Caplen, K. (1994). *Scattered hegemonies: Postmodernity and trans-national practices.* Minneapolis: University of Minnesota Press.

Gubrium, J. B., & Holstein, J. A. (1997). *The new language of qualitative method.* New York: Oxford University Press.

Guevarra, A. (2003). *Manufacturing bodies for sale: The biopolitics of labor export in the Philippines.* Unpublished doctoral dissertation, Department of Social and Behavioral Sciences, University of California, San Francisco.

Guinier, L., Fine, M., & Balin, J. (1997). *Becoming gentlemen: Women, law school and institutional change.* Boston: Beacon.

Gulcur, L., & Ilkkaracan, P. (2002). The "Natasha" experience: Migrant sex workers from the former Soviet Union and Eastern Europe in Turkey. *Women's Studies International Forum, 25,* 411–421.

Gupta, A., & Ferguson, J. (1997). *Anthropological locations: Boundaries and grounds of a field science.* Berkeley: University of California Press.

Hamochi, S. (2001). Japan and the global sex industry. In R. M. Kelly, J. H. Hayes, M. H. Hawkesworth, & B. Young (Eds.), *Gender, globalization, and democratization* (pp. 137–146). Lanham, MD: Roman & Littlefield.

Haraway, D. J. (1988). Situated knowledges: The science question in feminism and the privilege of partial perspectives. *Feminist Studies, 14,* 575–599.

Haraway, D. J. (1991). *Simians, cyborgs and women: The reinvention of nature.* London: Routledge.

Haraway, D. J. (1997). *Modest-Witness@Second-Millennium.FemaleMan-Meets-OncoMouse.* New York: Routledge.

Harding, S. (1987). Conclusion: Epistemological questions. In S. Harding (Ed.), *Feminism and methodology* (pp. 181–190). Bloomington: Indiana University Press.

Harding, S. (1990). Feminism, science and the anti-enlightenment critiques. In L. J. Nicholson (Ed.), *Feminism/postmodernism* (pp. 83–105). New York: Routledge.

Harding, S. (1991). "Strong objectivity" and socially situated knowledge. In S. Harding, *Whose science, whose knowledge?* (pp. 138–163). Ithaca, NY: Cornell University Press.

Harding, S. (1993). Rethinking standpoint epistemology: What is "strong objectivity?" In L. Alcoff & E. Potter (Eds.), *Feminist epistemologies* (pp. 49–82). New York: Routledge.

Harding, S. (1996). Gendered ways of knowing and the "epistemological crisis" of the West. In N. R. Goldberger, J. M. Tarule, B. M. Clinchy, & M. F. Belenky (Eds.), *Knowledge, difference and power: Essays inspired by women's ways of knowing* (pp. 431–454). New York: Basic Books.

Harding, S. (1997). Comment on Hekman's "Truth and method: Feminist standpoint theory revisited." *Signs, 22,* 382–391.

Harding, S. (1998). *Is science multicultural? Post-colonialisms, feminisms and epistemologies.* Bloomington: Indiana University Press.

Harding, S. (2001). Comment on Walby's "Against epistemological chasms: The science question in Feminism Revisited": Can democratic values and interests ever play a rationally justifiable role in the evaluation of scientific worth? *Signs, 26,* 511–576.

Hartouni, V. (1997). *Cultural conceptions: On reproductive technologies and the remaking of life.* Minneapolis: University of Minnesota Press.

Hartsock, N. (1983). The feminist standpoint: Developing the ground for a specifically feminist historical materialism. In S. Harding & M. B. Hintikka (Eds.), *Discovering reality* (pp. 283– 310). Amsterdam: D. Reidel.

Hartsock, N. (1985). *Money, sex, and power: Towards a feminist historical materialism.* Boston: Northeastern University Press.

Hartsock, N. (1990). Foucault on power: A theory for women? In L. J. Nicholson (Ed.), *Feminism and post-modernism* (pp. 157–175). New York: Routledge.

Hartsock, N. (1997a). Comment on Hekman's "Truth and method: Feminist standpoint theory revisited": Truth or justice? *Signs, 22,* 367–374.

Hartsock, N. (1997b). Standpoint theories for the next century. In S. J. Kenney & H. Kinsella (Eds.), *Politics and feminist standpoint theory* (pp. 93–101). New York: Haworth.

Hattar-Pollara, M., Meleis, A. I., & Nagib, H. (2000). A study of the spousal role of Egyptian women in clerical jobs. *Health Care for Women International, 21,* 305–317.

Hawkesworth, M. E. (1989). Knowers, knowing, known: Feminist theory and claims of truth. *Signs, 14,* 533–557.

Hawkesworth, M. E. (1997a). Confounding gender. *Signs, 22,* 649–686.

Hawkesworth, M. E. (1997b). Reply to McKenna and Kessler, Smith, Scott and Connell: Interrogating gender. *Signs, 22,* 707–713.

Hawkesworth, M. (1999). Analyzing backlash: Feminist standpoint theory as analytical tool. *Women's Studies International Forum, 22,* 135–155.

Hekman, S. (1990b). *Gender and knowledge: Elements of a post-modern feminism.* Boston: Northeastern University Press.

Hekman, S. (1997a). Reply to Hartsock, Collins, Harding and Smith. *Signs, 22,* 399–402.

Hekman, S. (1997b). Truth and method: Feminist standpoint theory revisited. *Signs, 22,* 341–365.

Heng, G. (1994). "A great way to fly": Nationalism, the state and varieties of Third World feminism. In M. J. Alexander & C. T. Mohanty (Eds.), *Feminist genealogies, colonial legacies, democratic futures* (pp. 30–45). New York: Routledge.

Hertz, R. (Ed.). (1997). *Reflexivity and voice.* Thousand Oaks, CA: Sage.

Hine, D. C. (1989). *Black women in white: Racial conflict and cooperation in the nursing profession, 1890–1950.* Bloomington: University of Indiana Press.

Hirschman, N. J. (1997). Feminist standpoint as post-modern strategy. In S. J. Kenney & H. Kinsella (Eds.), *Politics and feminist standpoint theories* (pp. 73-92). New York: Haworth.

Ho, J. C. (2000). Self–empowerment and "professionalism": Conversations with Taiwanese sex workers. *Inter-Asian Cultural Studies, 1,* 283–299.

Hochschild, A. R. (1983). *The managed heart: Commercialization of human feeling.* Berkeley: University of California Press.

Hochschild, A. R. (with Machung, A.). (1989). *The second shift.* New York: Avon.

Holland, J., & Blair, M., with Sheldon, S. (Eds.). (1995). *Debates and issues in feminist research and pedagogy.* Clevedon, UK: Open University Press.

Holland, J., & Ramazanoglu, C. (1994). Coming to conclusions: Power and interpretation in researching young women's sexuality. In M. Maynard & J. Purvis (Eds.), *Researching women's lives from a feminist perspective* (pp. 125–148). London: Taylor and Francis.

Holland, J., & Ramazanoglu, C. (1995). Accounting for sexuality, living sexual politics: Can feminist research be valid? In J. Holland & M. Blair (with S. Sheldon) (Eds.), Debates and issues in feminist research and pedagogy. Clevedon, UK: The Open University Press.

Holmes, H. B., & Purdy, L. M. (Eds.). (1992). *Feminist perspectives in medical ethics.* Bloomington: University of Indiana Press.

Hondagneu-Sotelo, P. (2001). *Domestica: Immigrant workers cleaning and caring in the shadows of affluence.* Berkeley: University of California Press.

Hondagneu-Sotelo, P. (Ed.). (2003). *Gender in U.S. immigration: Continuing trends.* Berkeley: University of California Press.

hooks, b. (1984). *Feminist theory from margin to center.* Boston: South End Press.

hooks, b. (1990). Culture to culture: Ethnography and cultural studies as critical intervention. In b. hooks, *Yearning: Race, gender and cultural politics* (pp. 123–133). Boston: South End.

Huber, J. (1973). Symbolic interaction as a pragmatic perspective: The bias of emergent theory. *American Sociological Review, 38,* 274–284.

Huff, J. K. (1997). The sexual harassment of researchers by research subjects: Lessons from the field. In M. D. Schwartz (Ed.), *Researching sexual violence against women: Methodological and personal perspectives* (pp. 115–128).Thousand Oaks, CA: Sage.

Huisman, K. A. (1997). Studying violence against women of color: Problems faced by white women. In M. D. Schwartz (Ed.), *Researching sexual violence against women: Methodological and personal perspectives* (pp. 179–192). Thousand Oaks, CA: Sage.

Humphries, B. (1997). From critical thought to emancipatory action: Contradictory research goals. *Sociological Research Online, 2*(1), 1–9.

Hundleby, C. (1997). Where standpoint stands now. In S. J. Kenney & H. Kinsella (Eds.), *Politics and feminist standpoint theories* (pp. 25–44). New York: Haworth.

Hunt, L. M., Jordan, B., Irwin, S., & Browner, C. H. (1989). Compliance and the patient's perspective: Controlling symptoms in everyday life. *Culture, Medicine and Psychiatry, 13,* 315–334.

Hurtado, A. (1989). Relating to privilege: Seduction and rejection in the subordination of white women and women of color. *Signs, 14,* 833–855.

Hurtado, A., & Stewart, A. J. (1997). Through the looking glass: Implications of studying whiteness for feminist methods. In M. Fine, L. Weis, L. C. Powell, & L. M. Wong (Eds.), *Off white: Readings on race, power and society* (pp. 297–311). New York: Routledge.

Im, E. O., Meleis, A. I., & Park, Y. S. (1999). A feminist critique of menopausal experience of Korean women. *Research in Nursing and Health, 22,* 410–420.

Joffe, C. (1995). Doctors of conscience: The struggle to provide abortion before and after Roe v. Wade. Boston: Beacon.

Johannsen, A. M. (1992). Applied anthropology and post-modernist ethnography. *Human Organization, 51,* 71–81.

John, M. E. (1996). *Discrepant dislocations: Feminism, theory and postcolonial histories.* Berkeley: University of California Press.

Jones, S. J. (1997). Reflexivity and feminist practice: Ethical dilemmas in negotiating meaning. *Feminism and Psychology, 7,* 348–353.

Kaplan, E. B. (1997). *Not our kind of girl: Unraveling the myths of black teenage motherhood.* Berkeley: University of California Press.

Kasper, A. (1994). A feminist qualitative methodology: A study of women with breast cancer. *Qualitative Sociology, 17,* 263–281.

Kaufert, P. A., & McKinlay, S. M. (1985). Estrogen-replacement therapy: The production of medical knowledge and the emergence of policy. In E. Lewin & V. L. Olesen (Eds.), *Women, health and healing: Toward a new perspective* (pp. 113–138). London: Tavistock.

Kelly, L., Burton, S., & Regan, L. (1994). Researching women's lives or studying women's oppression? Reflections on what constitutes feminist research. In M. Maynard & J. Purvis (Eds.), *Researching women's lives from a feminist perspective* (pp. 27–48). London: Taylor and Francis.

Kelly, R. M., Bayes, J. M., Hawkesworth, M. E., & Young, B. (2001). *Gender, globalization and democratization.* Lanham, MD: Rowman & Littlefield.

Kempadoo, K. (2001). Women of color and the global sex trade: Transnational feminist perspectives. *Meridians, Feminism, Race, Transnationalism, 1,* 28–51.

Kennedy, E. L., & Davis, M. (1993). *Boots of leather, slippers of gold: The history of a lesbian community.* New York: Routledge.

Kenney, S. J., & Kinsella, H. (Eds.). (1997). *Politics and feminist standpoint theories.* Binghamton, NY: Haworth.

Kerber, L. (1998). *No constitutional right to be ladies: Women and the obligation of citizenship.* New York: Hill and Wang.

Kessler, S., & McKenna, W. (1978). *Gender: An ethnomethodological approach.* New York: Wiley.

Kincheloe, J. (1997). Fiction formulas: Critical constructivism and the representation of reality. In W. G. Tierney & Y. S. Lincoln (Eds.), *Representation and the text: Reframing the narrative voice* (pp. 57–80). Albany: State University of New York Press.

Kirby, V. (1991). Comment on Maschia-Lees, Sharpe, and Cohen's "The postmodernist turn in anthropology: Cautions from a feminist perspective." *Signs, 16,* 394–400.

Kitzinger, C., & Wilkinson, S. (1997). Validating women's experiences? Dilemmas in feminist research. *Feminism and Psychology, 7,* 566–574.

Klawiter, M. (1999). Racing for the cure, walking, women and toxic touring: Mapping cultures of action within the Bay Area terrain of breast cancer. *Social Problems, 46,* 104–126.

Koehn, D. (1998). *Rethinking feminist ethics: Care, trust and empathy.* New York: Routledge.

Kofman, E., Phizacklea, A., Raghuran, P., & Sales, R. (2001). *Gender and internal migration in Europe: Employment, welfare, politics.* New York: Routledge.

Komarovsky, M. (1988). The new feminist scholarship: Some precursors and polemics. *Journal of Marriage and the Family, 50,* 585–593.

Komarovsky, M. (1991). Some reflections on the feminist scholarship in sociology. *Annual Review of Sociology, 17,* 1–25.

Kondo, D. K. (1990). *Crafting selves: Power, gender, and discourses of identity in a Japanese workplace.* Chicago: University of Chicago Press.

Kondo, D. K. (1995). Bad girls: Theater, women of color, and the politics of representation. In R. Behar & D. Gordon (Eds.), *Women writing culture* (pp. 49–64). Berkeley: University of California Press.

Krieger, S. (1983). *The mirror dance: Identity in a women's community.* Philadelphia: Temple University Press.

Krieger, S. (1991). *Social science and the self: Personal essays as an art form.* New Brunswick, NJ: Rutgers University Press.

Kuumba, M. B. (2002). "You've struck a rock": Comparing gender, social movements, and transformation in the United States and South Africa. *Gender and Society, 4,* 504–523.

Lacsamana, A. E. (1999). Colonizing the South: Postmodernism, desire and agency. *Socialist Review, 27,* 95–106.

Larrabee, M. J. (Ed.). (1993). *An ethic of care: Feminist and interdisciplinary perspectives.* New York: Routledge.

Laslett, B., & Brenner, J. (2001). Twenty-first century academic feminism in the United States: Utopian visions and practical actions. *Signs, 25,* 1231–1236.

Lather, P. (1991). *Getting smart: Feminist research and pedagogy within the postmodern.* New York: Routledge.

Lather, P. (1993). Fertile obsession: Validity after post-structuralism. *The Sociological Quarterly, 34,* 673–694.

Lather, P. (1995). Feminist perspectives on empowering research methodologies. In J. Holland & M. Blair with S. Sheldon (Eds.), *Debates and issues in feminist research and pedagogy* (pp. 292–307). Clevedon, UK: Open University Press.

Lather, P., & Smithies, C. (1997). *Troubling the angels: Women living with AIDS.* Boulder, CO: Westview.

Lawthom, R. (1997). What can I do? A feminist researcher in non-feminist research. *Feminism and Psychology, 7,* 533–538.

Lee, C. K. (1998). *Gender and the south China miracle: Two worlds of factory women.* Berkeley: University of California Press.

Lemert, C. (1992). Subjectivity's limit: The unsolved riddle of the standpoint. *Sociological Theory, 10,* 63–72.

Lemert, C. (1997). *Postmodernism is not what you think.* Malden, MA: Blackwell.

Lempert, L. B. (1994). Narrative analysis of abuse: Connecting the personal, the rhetorical and the structural. *Journal of Contemporary Ethnography, 22,* 411–441.

Lewin, E. (1991). Writing gay and lesbian culture: What the natives have to say for themselves. *American Ethnologist, 18,* 786–792.

Lewin, E. (1993). *Lesbian mothers.* Ithaca, NY: Cornell University Press.

Lewin, E. (Ed.). (1996). *Inventing lesbian cultures in America.* Boston: Beacon.

Lewin, E. (1998). *Recognizing ourselves: Ceremonies of lesbian and gay commitment.* New York: Columbia University Press.

Lewin, E., & Leap, W. L. (Eds.). (1996). *Out in the field: Reflections of gay and lesbian anthropologists.* Chicago: University of Illinois Press.

Light, L., & Kleiber, N. (1981). Interactive research in a feminist setting. In D. A. Messerschmidt (Ed.), *Anthropologists at home in North America: Methods and issues in the study of one's own society* (pp. 167–184). Cambridge, UK: Cambridge University Press.

Lincoln, Y. S. (1993). I and thou: Method, voice, and roles in research with the silenced. In D. McLaughlin & W. G. Tierney (Eds.), *Naming silenced lives: Personal narratives and processes of educational change* (pp. 20–27). New York: Routledge.

Lincoln, Y. S. (1995). Emerging criteria for quality in qualitative and interpretive research. *Qualitative Inquiry, 1,* 275–289.

Lincoln, Y. S. (1997). Self, subject, audience, text: Living at the edge, writing in the margins. In W. G. Tierney & Y. S. Lincoln (Eds.), *Representation and the text* (pp. 37–55). Albany: State University of New York Press.

Lincoln, Y. S., & Guba, E. G. (1985). *Naturalistic inquiry.* Beverly Hills, CA: Sage.

Longino, H. (1990). *Science as social knowledge.* Princeton, NJ: Princeton University Press.

Longino, H. (1993). Subjects, power and knowledge: Description and prescription in feminist philosophies of science. In L. Alcott & E. Potter (Eds.), *Feminist epistemologies* (pp. 101–120). New York: Routledge.

Lorber, J. (1975). Women and medical sociology: Invisible professionals and ubiquitous patients. In M. M. Millman & R. M. Kanter (Eds.), *Another voice: Feminist perspectives on social life and social science* (pp. 75–105). Garden City, NY: Anchor Books.

Lorber, J. (1994). *Paradoxes of gender.* New Haven, CT: Yale University Press.

Lubelska, C., & Mathews, J. (1997). Disability issues in the politics and processes of feminist studies. In M. Ang-Lygate, C. Corrin, & M. S. Henry (Eds.), *Desperately seeking sisterhood: Still challenging and building* (pp. 117–137). London: Taylor and Francis.

Luker, K. (1984). *The politics of motherhood.* Berkeley: University of California Press.

Luker, K. (1996). *Dubious conceptions: Politics of teen-age pregnancy.* Cambridge, MA: Harvard University Press.

Luff, D. (1999). Dialogue across the divides: "Moments of rapport" and power in research with anti-feminist women. *Sociology, 33,* 689–703.

Lupton, D. (1995). *The imperative of health: Public health and the regulated body.* Thousand Oaks, CA: Sage.

Lykes, M. B. (1989). Dialogue with Guatemalan Indian women: Critical perspectives on constructing collaborative research. In R. Unger (Ed.), *Representations: Social constructions of gender* (pp. 167–184). Amityville, NY: Baywood.

Lykes, M. B. (1994). Whose meeting at which crossroads? A response to Brown and Gilligan. *Feminism and Psychology, 4,* 345–349.

Lykes, M. B. (1997). Activist participatory research among the Maya of Guatemala: Constructing meanings from situated knowledge. *Journal of Social Issues, 53,* 725–746.

MacKinnon, C. (1982). Feminism, Marxism, method and the state: An agenda for theory. *Signs, 7,* 515–544.

MacKinnon, C. (1983). Feminism, Marxism and the state: Toward feminist jurisprudence. *Signs, 8,* 635–658.

Mamo, L. (2002). Sexuality, reproduction, and biomedical negotiations: An analysis of achieving pregnancy in the absence of heterosexuality. *Dissertation Abstracts.* International-A63/04, October, p. 1565.

Manning, K. (1997). Authenticity in constructivist inquiry: Methodological considerations without prescription. *Qualitative Inquiry, 3,* 93–116.

Manning, R. C. (1992). *Speaking from the heart: A feminist perspective on ethics.* Lanham, MD: Rowman & Littlefield.

Marchand, M. H., & Runyan, A. S. (Eds.). (2000a). *Gender and global restructuring: Sightings, sites and resistances.* London: Routledge.

Marchand, M. H., & Runyan, A. S. (2000). Introduction: Feminist sightings of global restructuring, conceptualizations and reconceptualizations. In M. H. Marchand & S. Runyan (Eds.), *Gender and global restructuring: Sightings, sites and resistances* (pp. 1–22). London: Routledge.

Marshall, C. (1997). *Feminist critical policy analysis.* Washington, DC: Falmer.

Marshall, C. (1999). Researching the margins: Feminist critical policy analysis. *Educational Policy, 13,* 59–76.

Martin, E. (1987). *The woman in the body: A cultural analysis of reproduction.* Boston: Beacon.

Martin, E. (1999). The woman in the flexible body. In A. E. Clarke & V. L. Olesen (Eds.), *Revisioning women, health and healing: Feminist, cultural and technoscience perspectives* (pp. 97–118). New York: Routledge.

Martin, P. Y. (2001). "Mobilizing masculinities": Women's experiences of men at work. *Organization, 8,* 587–618.

Maschia-Lees, F. E., Sharpe, P., & Cohen, C. B. (1989). The postmodern turn in anthropology: Cautions from a feminist perspective. *Signs, 15,* 7–33.

Matsuda, M. (1992). *Called from within: Early women lawyers of Hawaii.* Honolulu: University of Hawaii Press.

Matsuda, M. (1996). *Where is your body?: And other essays on race, gender and the law.* Boston: Beacon.

Mattley, C. (1997). Field research with phone sex workers: Managing the researcher's emotions. In M. D. Schwartz (Ed.), *Researching sexual violence against women: Methodological and personal perspectives* (pp. 101–114). Thousand Oaks, CA: Sage.

Mauthner, M., Birch, M., Jessop, J., & Miller, T. (Eds.). (2002). *Ethics in qualitative research.* Thousand Oaks, CA: Sage.

Mauthner, N., & Doucet, A. (1998). Reflections on a voice-centered relational method: Analyzing maternal and domestic voices. In J. Ribbens & R. Edwards (Eds.), *Feminist dilemmas in qualitative research: Public knowledge and private lives* (pp. 119–146). Thousand Oaks, CA: Sage.

May, K. A. (1980). Informed consent and role conflict. In A. J. Davis & J. C. Krueger (Eds.), *Patients, nurses, ethics* (pp. 109–118). New York: American Journal of Nursing.

Maynard, M. (1994a). Methods, practice and epistemology: The debate about feminism and research. In M. Maynard & J. Purvis (Eds.), *Researching women's lives from a feminist perspective* (pp. 10–26). London: Taylor and Francis.

Maynard, M. (1994b). Race, gender and the concept of "difference" in feminist thought. In H. Afshar & M. Maynard (Eds.), *The dynamics of "race" and gender: Some feminist interventions* (pp. 9–25). London: Taylor and Francis.

Maynard, M. (1996). Challenging the boundaries: Towards an anti-racist women's studies. In M. Maynard & J. Purvis (Eds.), *New frontiers in women's studies: Knowledge, identity and nationalism* (pp. 11–29). London: Taylor and Francis.

Maynard, M., & Purvis, J. (Eds.). (1994). *Researching women's lives from a feminist perspective.* London: Taylor and Francis.

Mazur, A. G. (2002). *Theorizing feminist policy.* Oxford, UK: Oxford University Press.

McCall, M., & Becker, H. (1990). Performance science. *Social Problems, 37,* 117–132.

McIntyre, A., & Lykes, M. B. (1998). Who's the boss? Confronting whiteness and power differences within a feminist mentoring relationship in participatory action research. *Feminism and Psychology, 8,* 427–444.

McKenna, W., & Kessler, S. (1997). Comment on Hawkesworth's "Confounding gender": Who needs gender theory? *Signs, 22,* 687–691.

McWilliam, E. (1997). Performing between the posts: Authority, posture and contemporary feminist scholarship. In W. G. Tierney & Y. S. Lincoln (Eds.), *Representation and the text: Reframing the narrative voice* (pp. 219–232). Albany: State University of New York Press.

Messer-Davidow, E. (2002). *Disciplining feminism: From social activism to academic discourse.* Durham, NC: Duke University Press.

Mies, M. (1993). Towards a methodology for feminist research. In M. Hammersley (Ed.), *Social research: Philosophy, politics and practice* (pp. 64–82). Newbury Park, CA: Sage.

Mihesuah, D. A. (1998). Commonality of difference: American Indian women and history. In D. A. Mihesuah (Ed.), *Natives and academics: Researching and writing about American Indians* (pp. 37–54). Lincoln: University of Nebraska Press.

Mihesuah, D. A. (2000). A few cautions at the millennium on the merging of feminist studies with American Indian Women's Studies. *Signs, 25,* 1246–1251.

Millen, D. (1997). Some methodological and epistemological issues raised by doing feminist research on non-feminist women. *Sociological Research Online, 2* (3), 2–18.

Miller, G., & Dingwall, R. (1997). *Context and method in qualitative research.* Thousand Oaks, CA: Sage.

Miller, T., & Bell, L. (2002). Consenting to what? Issues of access, gate-keeping and "informed" consent." In M. Mauthner, M. Birch, J. Jessop, & T. Miller (Eds.), *Ethics in qualitative research* (pp. 37–54). New York: Routledge.

Misra, J. (2000). Gender and the world-system: Engaging the feminist literature on development. In T. D. Hall (Ed.), *A world-systems reader: New perspectives on gender, urbanism, cultures, indigenous peoples, and ecology* (pp. 105–130). Lanham, MD: Rowman & Littlefield.

Mohanty, C. (1988). Under Western eyes: Feminist scholarship and colonial discourses. *Feminist Review, 30,* 60–88.

Mohanty, C. (2003). *Feminism without borders: Decolonizing theory, practicing solidarity.* Durham, NC: Duke University Press.

Montini, T. (1997). Resist and redirect: Physicians respond to breast cancer informed consent legislation. *Women and Health, 12,* 85–105.

Morawski, J. (1990). Toward the unimagined: Feminism and epistemology in psychology. In R. Hare-Mustin & J. Marecek (Eds.), *Making a difference: Psychology and the construction of gender* (pp. 159–183). New Haven, CT: Yale University Press.

Morawski, J. (1994). *Practicing feminisms, reconstructing psychology: Notes on a liminal science.* Ann Arbor: University of Michigan Press.

Morawski, J. (1997). The science behind feminist research methods. *Journal of Social Issues, 53,* 667–681.

Morris, J. (1995). Personal and political: A feminist perspective on researching physical disability. In J. Holland & M. Blair with S. Sheldon (Eds.), *Debates and issues in feminist research and pedagogy* (pp. 262–272). Clevedon, UK: Open University Press.

Morris, M. (1998). *Too soon, too late: History in popular culture.* Bloomington: University of Indiana Press.

Mukherjee, B. (1994). *The holder of the world.* London: Virago.

Murcott, A. (1993). On conceptions of good food, or anthropology between the laity and professionals. *Anthropology in Action, 14,* 11–13.

Naples, N. A. (1996). A feminist revisiting of the insider/outsider debate: The "outsider phenomenon" in rural Iowa. *Qualitative Sociology, 19,* 83–106.

Naples, N. A. (1997a). Contested needs: Shifting the standpoint in rural economic development. *Feminist Economics, 3,* 63–98.

Naples, N. A. (1997b). The "new consensus on the gendered social contract": The 1997–1998 U.S. Congressional hearings on welfare reform. *Signs, 22,* 907–945.

Naples, N. A. (1999). Towards comparative analyses of women's political praxis: Explicating multiple dimensions of standpoint epistemology for feminist methodology. *Women & Politics, 20*(1), 29–57.

Naples, N. (2002). The challenges and possibilities of transnational feminist praxis. In N. A. Naples & M. Desai (Eds.), *Women's activism and globalization: Linking local struggles and global politics* (pp. 267–282). New York: Routledge.

Naples, N. A. (2003). *Feminism and method, ethnography, discourse analysis and activist research.* New York: Routledge.

Naples, N., & Sachs, G. (2000). Standpoint epistemology and the uses of self-reflection in feminist enthnography. *Rural Sociology, 65,* 194–214.

Narayan, K. (1997). How native is a "native" anthropologist? In L. Lamphere, H. Ragone, & P. Zavella (Eds.), *Situated lives, gender and culture in everyday life* (pp. 23–41). New York: Routledge.

Narayan, U. (1997). *Dislocating cultures: Identities and Third World feminism.* New York: Routledge.

Narrigan, D., Zones, J. S., Worcester, N., & Grad, M. J. (1997). Research to improve women's health: An agenda for equity. In S. B. Ruzek, V. L. Olesen, & A. E. Clarke (Eds.), *Women's health: Complexities and differences* (pp. 551–579). Columbus: The Ohio State University Press.

Nelson, C., & Altorki, S. (Eds.). (1997). *Arab Regional Studies Workshop: Cairo Papers in Social Science* (Vol. 20, No. 3). Cairo, IL: The American University in Cairo Press.

Nelson, M. K. (1990). *Negotiated care: The experience of family day care givers.* Philadelphia: Temple University Press.

Nettleton, S. (1991). Wisdom, diligence and teeth: Discursive practices and the creation of mothers. *Sociology of Health and Illness, 13,* 98–111.

Nicholson, L. (Ed.). (1990). *Feminism/postmodernism.* London: Routledge.

Nicholson, L. (Ed.). (1997). *The second wave.* New York: Routledge.

Nielsen, J. M. (Ed.). (1990). *Feminist research methods: Exemplary readings in the social sciences.* Boulder, CO: Westview.

Noddings, N. (2002). *Starting at home: Caring and social policy.* Berkeley: University of California Press.

Oakley, A. (1981). Interviewing women: A contradiction in terms? In H. Roberts (Ed.), *Doing feminist research* (pp. 30–61). London: Routledge & Kegan Paul.

Ogasawara, Y. (1998). *Office ladies and salaried men: Power, gender and work in Japanese companies.* Berkeley: University of California Press.

O'Leary, C. M. (1997). Counteridentification or counterhegemony? Transforming feminist standpoint theory. In S. J. Kenney & H. Kinsella (Eds.), *Politics and feminist standpoint theories* (pp. 45–72). New York: Haworth.

Olesen, V. L. (1977). Rage is not enough: Scholarly feminism and research in women's health. In V. L. Olesen (Ed.), *Women and their health: Research implications for a new era* (DHEW Publication No. HRA-3138) (pp. 1–2). Rockville, MD: Health Resources Administration, National Center for Health Services Research.

Olesen, V. L. (1993). Unfinished business: The problematics of women, health and healing. *The Science of Caring, 5,* 27–32.

Olesen, V. L. (1997). "Do whatever you want": Audiences created, creating, recreated. *Qualitative Inquiry, 3,* 511–515.

Olesen, V. L., & Clarke, A. E. (1999). Resisting closure, embracing uncertainties, creating agendas. In A. E. Clarke & V. L. Olesen (Eds.), *Revisioning women, health and healing: Feminist cultural studies and technoscience perspectives* (pp. 355–357). New York: Routledge.

Olesen, V. L., Taylor, D., Ruzek, S. B., & Clarke, A. E. (1997). Strengths and strongholds in women's health research. In S. B. Ruzek, V. L. Olesen, & A. E. Clarke (Eds.), *Women's health: Complexities and differences* (pp. 580–606). Columbus: The Ohio State University Press.

Ong, A. (1995). Women out of China: Traveling tales and traveling theories in postcolonial feminism. In R. Behar & D. Gordon (Eds.), *Women writing culture* (pp. 350–372). Berkeley: University of California Press.

Opie, A. (1992). Qualitative research, appropriation of the "other" and empowerment. *Feminist Review, 40,* 52–69.

Orr, J. (1993). Panic diary: (Re)constructing a partial politics and poetics of disease. In J. Holstein & G. Miller (Eds.), *Reconsidering social constructionism: Debates in social problems theory* (pp. 441–482). New York: Aldine de Gruyter.

Paget, M. (1990). Performing the text. *Journal of Contemporary Ethnography, 19,* 136–155.

Parrenas, R. S. (2001). Transgressing the nation state: The partial citizenship and imagined (global) community of migrant Filipina domestic workers. *Signs, 26,* 1129–1135.

Patai, D. (1994, February 23). Sick and tired of nouveau solipsism. *The Chronicle of Higher Education,* p. A52.

Petchesky, R. P. (1985). Abortion in the 1980's: Feminist morality and women's health. In E. Lewin & V. Olesen (Eds.), *Women, health and healing: Toward a new perspective* (pp. 139–173). London: Tavistock.

Petchesky, R. P. (2003). *Global prescriptions: Gendering health and human rights.* New York: Zed Books.

Pfeffer, R. (1997). *Children of poverty: Studies on the effect of single parenthood, the feminization of poverty and homelessness.* New York: Garland.

Phoenix, A. (1994). Practicing feminist research: The intersection of gender and "race" in the research process. In M. Maynard & J. Purvis (Eds.), *Researching women's lives from a feminist perspective* (pp. 35–45). London: Taylor and Francis.

Pierce, J. L. (1995). *Gender trials: Emotional lives in contemporary law firms.* Berkeley: University of California Press.

Poster, W. R. (2002). Racialism, sexuality, and masculinity: Gendering "global ethnography" of the workplace. *Social Politics, 9,* 126–158.

Poudel, P., & Carryer, J. (2000). Girl-trafficking, HIV/AIDS and the position of women in Nepal. *Gender and Development, 8,* 74–79.

Puar, J. K. (1996). Resituating discourses of "whiteness" and "Asianness" in northern England: Second-generation Sikh women and constructions of identity. In M. Maynard & J. Purvis (Eds.), *New frontiers in women's studies* (pp. 125–150). London: Taylor and Francis.

Pyle, J. L. (2001). Sex, maids and export processing: Risks and reasons for gendered global production networks. *International Journal of Politics, Culture and Society, 15,* 55–76.

Ramazanoglu, C. (1989). Improving on sociology: The problems of taking a feminist standpoint. *Sociology, 23,* 427–442.

Ramazanoglu, C., with Holland, J. (2002). *Feminist methodology: Challenges and choices.* London: Sage.

Randall, M. (2004). Know your place: The activist scholar in today's political culture. *SWS Network News, 21,* 20–23.

Rapp, R. (1999). *Testing women, testing the foetus: The social impact of amniocentesis in America.* New York: Routledge.

Reay, D. (1996a). Dealing with difficult differences. *Feminism and Psychology, 6,* 443–456.

Reay, D. (1996b). Insider perspectives or stealing the words out of women's mouths: Interpretation in the research process. *Feminist Review, 53,* 57–73.

Reay, D. (1998). Classifying feminist research: Exploring the psychological impact of social class on mothers' involvement in children's schooling. *Feminism & Psychology, 8,* 155–171.

Reinharz, S. (1992). *Feminist methods in social research.* Oxford, UK: Oxford University Press.

Renzetti, C. M. (1997). Confessions of a reformed positivist: Feminist participatory research as good social science. In M. D. Schwartz (Ed.), *Researching sexual violence against women: Methodological and personal perspectives* (pp. 131–143). Thousand Oaks, CA: Sage.

Reynolds, T. (2002). Rethinking a black feminist standpoint. *Ethnic and Racial Studies, 25,* 591–606.

Ribbens, J., & Edwards, R. (1998). *Feminist dilemmas in qualitative research: Public knowledge and private lives.* Thousand Oaks, CA: Sage.

Richardson, L. (1993). Poetics, dramatics and transgressive validity: The case of the skipped line. *The Sociological Quarterly, 34,* 695–710.

Richardson, L. (1997). *Fields of play: Constructing an academic life.* New Brunswick, NJ: Rutgers University Press.

Riessman, C. K. (1987). When gender is not enough: Women interviewing women. *Gender and Society, 2,* 172–207.

Riessman, C. K. (1990). *Divorce talk: Women and men make sense of personal relationships.* New Brunswick, NJ: Rutgers University Press.

Ring, J. (1987). Toward a feminist epistemology. *American Journal of Political Science, 31,* 753–772.

Roberts, H. (1981). *Doing feminist research.* London: Routledge.

Rollins, J. (1985). *Between women: Domestics and their employers.* Philadelphia: Temple University Press.

Roman, L. (1992). The political significance of other ways of narrating ethnography: A feminist materialist analysis. In M. D. LeCompte, W. L. Millroy, & J. Preissle (Eds.), *The handbook of qualitative research in education* (pp. 555–594). San Diego: Academic Press.

Romero, M. (1992). *Maid in the U.S.A.* London: Routledge.

Rosenau, P. M. (1992). *Post-modernism and the social sciences: Insights, inroads and intrusions.* Princeton, NJ: Princeton University Press.

Rudy, K. (2000). Difference and indifference: A US feminist response to global politics. *Signs, 25,* 1051–1053.

Runyan, A. S., & Marchand, M. H. (2000). Conclusion: Feminist approaches to global restructuring. In M. H. Marchand & A. S. Runyan (Eds.), *Gender and global restructuring* (pp. 225–230). London: Routledge.

Rupp, L. J., & Taylor, V. (2003). *Drag queens at the 801 Cabaret.* Chicago: University of Chicago Press.

Ruzek, S. B. (1978). *The women's health movement: Feminist alternatives to medical care.* New York: Praeger.

Ruzek, S. B., Olesen, V. L., & Clarke, A. E. (Eds.). (1997). *Women's health: Complexities and differences.* Columbus: The Ohio State University Press.

Sacks, K. B. (1988). *Caring by the hour: Women, work and organizing at Duke Medical Center.* Urbana: University of Illinois Press.

Scarce, R. (2002). Doing time as an act of survival. *Symbolic Interaction, 25,* 303–321.

Scheper-Hughes, N. (1983). Introduction: The problem of bias in androcentric and feminist anthropology. *Women's Studies, 19,* 109–116.

Scheper-Hughes, N. (1992). *Death without weeping: The violence of everyday life in Brazil.* Berkeley: University of California Press.

Scheurich, J. J. (1997). The masks of validity: A deconstructive investigation. In J. J. Scheurich, *Research method in the postmodern* (pp. 80–93). London: Falmer.

Schiffrin, A. (1998, November 20). Transactional publishing in microcosm: The Frankfurt book fair. *The Chronicle of Higher Education,* pp. B6–B7.

Scott, J. (1991). The evidence of experience. *Critical Inquiry, 17,* 773–779.

Scott, J. (1997). Comment on Hawkesworth's "Confounding gender." *Signs, 22,* 697–702.

Seigfried, C. H. (1996). *Pragmatism and feminism: Reweaving the social fabric.* Chicago: University of Chicago Press.

Sherwin, S. (1992). *No longer patient: Feminist ethics and health care.* Philadelphia: Temple University Press.

Shim, J. K. (2000). Bio-power and racial, class and gender formation in biomedical knowledge production. In J. J. Kronenfield (Ed.), *Research in the sociology of health care* (pp. 173–195). Stamford, CT: JAI.

Shohat, E. (2001). Area studies, transnationalism and the feminist production of knowledge. *Signs, 26,* 1269–1272.

Shostak, M. (1981). *Nisa: The life and words of a !Kung woman.* Cambridge, MA: Harvard University Press.

Skeggs, B. (1994). Situating the production of feminist ethnography. In M. Maynard & J. Purvis (Eds.), *Researching women's lives from a feminist perspective* (pp. 72–92). London: Taylor and Francis.

Skeggs, B. (Ed.). (1995a). *Feminist cultural theory: Process and production.* New York: Manchester University Press.

Skeggs, B. (1995b). Theorizing ethics and representation in feminist ethnography. In B. Skeggs (Ed.), *Feminist cultural theory: Process and production* (pp. 190–206). New York: Manchester University Press.

Smith, D. (1974). Women's perspective as a radical critique of sociology. *Sociological Inquiry, 4,* 1–13.

Smith, D. (1987). *The everyday world as problematic.* Boston: Northeastern University Press.

Smith, D. (1989). Sociological theory: Methods of writing patriarchy. In R. A. Wallace (Ed.), *Feminism and sociological theory* (pp. 34–64). Newbury Park, CA: Sage.

Smith, D. (1990a). *The conceptual practices of power: A feminist sociology of knowledge.* Boston: Northeastern University Press.

Smith, D. (1990b). *Texts, facts and femininity: Exploring the relations of ruling.* London: Routledge.

Smith, D. (1992). Sociology from women's experience: A reaffirmation. *Sociological Theory, 10,* 88–98.

Smith, D. (1993). High noon in textland: A critique of Clough. *Sociological Quarterly, 30,* 183–192.

Smith, D. (1997). Telling the truth after postmodernism. *Symbolic Interaction, 19,* 171–202.

Smith, D. (1999). *Writing the social.* Toronto: University of Toronto Press.

Smith, D. (in press). *Institutional ethnography: A sociology from people's standpoint.* Walnut Creek, CA: AltaMira Press.

Smith, S. G. (1997). Comment on Hawkesworth's "Confounding gender." *Signs, 22,* 691–697.

Speer, S. A. (2002). What can conversational analysis contribute to feminist methodology? Putting reflexivity into practice. *Discourse and Society, 13,* 783–803.

Spivak, G. C. (1988). Subaltern studies: Deconstructing historiography. In G. C. Spivak, *In other worlds: Essays in cultural politics* (pp. 197–221). London: Routledge.

Sprague, J. (2001). Comment on Walby's "Against epistemological chasms: The science question in feminism revisited": Structured knowledge and strategic methodology. *Signs, 26,* 527–536.

Stacey, J. (1988). Can there be a feminist ethnography? *Women's Studies International Forum, 11,* 21–27.

Stacey, J. (1998). *Brave new families: Stories of domestic upheaval in late twentieth century America.* Berkeley: University of California Press.

Stacey, J. (2003). Taking feminist sociology public can prove less progressive than you wish. *SWS Network News, 20,* 27–28.

Stacey, J., & Thorne, B. (1985). The missing feminist revolution in sociology. *Social Problems, 32,* 301–316.

Stacey, J., & Thorne, B. (1996). Is sociology still missing its feminist revolution? *Perspectives: The ASA Theory Section Newsletter, 18,* 1–3.

Stacey, M. (1992). *Regulating British medicine: The General Medical Council.* New York: Wiley.

Standing, K. (1998). Writing the voices of the less powerful. In J. Ribbens & R. Edwards (Eds.), *Feminist dilemmas in qualitative research: Public knowledge and private lives* (pp. 186–202). Thousand Oaks, CA: Sage.

Stanley, L. (Ed.). (1990). *Feminist praxis: Research, theory, and epistemology in feminist sociology.* London: Routledge.

Stanley, L., & Wise, S. (1983). *Breaking out: Feminist consciousness and feminist research.* London: Routledge and Kegan Paul.

Stanley, L., & Wise, S. (1990). Method, methodology and epistemology in feminist research processes. In L. Stanley (Ed.), *Feminist praxis: Research, theory and epistemology in feminist sociology* (pp. 20–60). London: Routledge.

Staudt, K. (1998). *Policy, politics and gender: Women gaining ground.* West Hartford, CT: Kumarian Press.

Steinberg, R. J. (1996). Advocacy research for feminist policy objectives: Experiences with comparable worth. In H. Gottfried (Ed.), *Feminism and social change: Bridging theory and practice* (pp. 250–255). Urbana: University of Illinois Press.

Stevens, P. E., & Hall, J. H. (1991). A critical historical analysis of the medical construction of lesbianism. *International Journal of Health Services, 21,* 271–307.

Tanenberg, K. (2000). Marginalized epistemologies: A feminist approach to understanding the experiences of mothers with HIV. *Affilia, 15,* 31–48.

Taylor, D., & Dower, K. (1995). Toward a women-centered health care system: Women's experiences, women's voices, women's needs. *Health Care for Women International, 18,* 407–422.

Taylor, V. (1998). Feminist methodology in social movements research. *Qualitative Sociology, 21,* 357–379.

Terry, J. (1994). Theorizing deviant historiography. In A.-L. Shapiro (Ed.), *Feminists revision history* (pp. 20–30). New Brunswick, NJ: Rutgers University Press.

Thayer, M. (2001). Transnational feminism: Reading Joan Scott in the Brazilian sertão. *Ethnography, 2,* 243–271.

Tierney, W. G., & Lincoln, Y. S. (1997). *Representation and the text: Reframing the narrative voice.* Albany: State University of New York Press.

Tom, W. (1989). *Effects of feminist research on research methods.* Toronto: Wilfred Laurier Press.

Tong, R. (1997). *Feminist approaches to bioethics: Theoretical reflections and practical applications.* Boulder, CO: Westview.

Trinh, T. M-ha. (1989). *Woman, native, other: Writing post-coloniality and feminism.* Bloomington: University of Indiana Press.

Trinh, T. M-ha. (1992). *Framer framed.* New York: Routledge.

Tronto, J. C. (1993). *Moral boundaries: A political argument for an ethic of care.* New York: Routledge.

Tuana, N. (1993). With many voices: Feminism and theoretical pluralism. In P. England (Ed.), *Theory on gender: Feminism on theory* (pp. 281–289). New York: Aldine de Gruyter.

Viswesweran, K. (1994). *Fictions of feminist ethnography.* Minneapolis: University of Minnesota Press.

Walby, S. (2001a). Against epistemological chasms: The science question in feminism revisited. *Signs, 26,* 485–510.

Walby, S. (2001b). Reply to Harding and Sprague. *Signs, 26,* 537–540.

Walker, M. V. (1998). *Moral understandings: A feminist study in ethics.* New York: Routledge.

Walkerdine, V. (1995). Postmodernity, subjectivity and the media. In T. Ibanez & L. Iniguez (Eds.), *Critical social psychology* (pp. 169–177). London: Sage.

Warren, C.A.B. (1988). *Gender issues in field research.* Newbury Park, CA: Sage.

Wasserfall, R. R. (1997). Reflexivity, feminism and difference. In R. Hertz (Ed.), *Reflexivity and voice* (pp. 150–168). Thousand Oaks, CA: Sage.

Weeks, K. C. (1998). *Constituting feminist subjects.* Ithaca, NY: Cornell University Press.

Welton, K. (1997). Nancy Hartsock's standpoint theory: From content to "concrete multiplicity." In S. J. Kenney & H. Kinsella (Eds.), *Politics and feminist standpoint theories* (pp. 7–24). New York: Haworth.

West, C., & Zimmerman, D. (1987). Doing gender. *Gender and Society, 1,* 125–151.

Westkott, M. (1979). Feminist criticism of the social sciences. *Harvard Educational Review, 4,* 422–430.

Weston, K. (1991). *Families we choose: Lesbians, gays, kinship.* New York: Columbia University Press.

Weston, K. (1996). Requiem for a street fighter. In E. L. Lewin & W. L. Leap (Eds.), *Out in the field: Reflections of lesbian and gay anthropologists* (pp. 274–286). Urbana: University of Illinois Press.

Wheatley, E. (1994). How can we engender ethnography with a feminist imagination: A rejoinder to Judith Stacey. *Women's Studies International Forum, 17,* 403–416.

Wheeler, B. (2003). The institutionalization of an American avant-garde: Performance art as democratic culture, 1970–2000. *Sociological Perspectives, 46,* 491–512.

Williams, B. (1996). Skinfolk, not kinfolk: Comparative reflections on the identity of participant-observation in two field situations. In D. Wolf (Ed.), *Feminist dilemmas in fieldwork* (pp. 72–95). Boulder, CO: Westview.

Williams, P. J. (1991). *The alchemy of race and rights.* Cambridge, MA: Harvard University Press.

Wolf, D. (Ed.). (1996). *Feminist dilemmas in fieldwork.* Boulder, CO: Westview.

Wolf, M. (1992). *A thrice told tale: Feminism, postmodernism and ethnographic responsibility.* Stanford, CA: Stanford University Press.

Wolf, M. (1996). Afterword: Musings from an old gray wolf. In D. Wolf (Ed.), *Feminist dilemmas in fieldwork* (pp. 214–222). Boulder, CO: Westview.

Yadlon, S. (1997). Skinny women and good mothers: The rhetoric of risk, control and culpability in the production of knowledge about breast cancer. *Feminist Studies, 23,* 645–677.

Young, B. (2001). Globalization and gender: A European perspective. In R. M. Kelly, J. H. Bayes, M. E. Hawkesworth, & B. Young (Eds.), *Gender, globalization, and democratization* (pp. 27–48). New York: Rowman & Littlefield.

Zavella, P. (1987). *Women's work and Chicano families: Cannery workers of the Santa Clara Valley.* Ithaca, NY: Cornell University Press.

Zavella, P. (1996). Feminist insider dilemmas: Constructing ethnic identity with Chicana informants. In D. Wolf (Ed.), *Feminist dilemmas in fieldwork* (pp. 138–159). Boulder, CO: Westview.

Zinn, M. B. (1982). Mexican-American women in the social sciences. *Signs, 8,* 251–272.

11

THE MORAL ACTIVIST ROLE OF CRITICAL RACE THEORY SCHOLARSHIP

Gloria Ladson-Billings and Jamel Donnor

It doesn't matter who you are, or how high you rise. One day you will get your call. The question is how will you respond?

—African American University
Senior Administrator

The epigraph that opens this chapter comes from a colleague and friend who serves as a top administrator at a major university. His use of the term "your call" is his reference to what in African American vernacular would be known as being called the "N-word." Rather than focus on the controversy over the term and its appropriateness (see Kennedy, 2002), this chapter looks more specifically at the meaning of the "call" and the ways it should mobilize scholars of color[1] and others who share commitments to equity, social justice, and human liberation. This friend was referring to the way African Americans almost never are permitted to break out of the prism (and prison) of race that has been imposed by a racially coded and constraining society. Clearly, this same hierarchy and power dynamic operates for all people of color, women, the poor, and other "marginals."[2] The call is that moment at which, regardless of one's stature and/or accomplishments, race (and other categories of otherness) is recruited to remind one that he or she still remains locked in the racial construction. Below, we provide examples from popular culture, and each of the authors demonstrates how the "call" is mobilized to maintain the power dynamic and hierarchical racial structures of society.

The first example comes from the 1995 murder trial of Orenthal James Simpson, more commonly known as O. J. Simpson. Simpson was an American hero. He was revered for his exploits on the football field at the University of Southern California, and with the professional football franchises in Buffalo and San Francisco, coupled with his good looks and "articulateness."[3] The latter two qualities allowed Simpson to turn his postcompetition years into a successful sports broadcasting career and a mediocre but profitable acting career. Simpson moved comfortably in the world of money and power—the white world. He was said to be someone who "transcended race" (Roediger, 2002), which is a code expression for those people of color that whites claim they no longer think of as people of color. Michael Jordan and Colin Powell also are considered in this vein. They are, according to Dyson (1993), "symbolic figures who embodied social possibilities of success denied to other people of color" (p. 67).

Some might argue that Simpson did not get a "call," that he was a murderer who got the notoriety and degradation he deserved, while also getting away with a heinous crime. Our point is not to argue Simpson's guilt or innocence (and from where we stand, he indeed looks guilty), but rather to describe his devolution from white to black in the midst of the legal spectacle. Simpson learned quickly that the honorary white status accorded to him by the larger society was tentative and ephemeral. Some might argue that anyone charged with murder would receive the same treatment, but consider that Ray Carruth, a National Football League player who was convicted of a murder-for-hire of his pregnant girlfriend, was regarded as "just another black hoodlum." His actions barely caused a collective raised eyebrow in the larger society. We argue that Simpson's crimes are not only the murder of Nicole Brown and Ron Goodman but also the perceived "betrayal" of white trust.

Simpson went from conceptually white to conceptually black (King, 1995)—from a "Fresh Prince of Brentwood" to the "Pariah of Portrero Hill" (the San Francisco community in which he grew up). One of the weekly newsmagazines admitted to "colorizing" Simpson's police mug shot on its cover, resulting in a more sinister look. We perceive that editorial decision as a symbol of Simpson's "return to black." He no longer transcended race. He was just another N-word who was dangerous, sinister, and unworthy of honorary white status. O. J. Simpson received his call.

Of course, the bizarre and circus-like circumstances of the Simpson trial make it an outlier example of receiving a call. Therefore, we use more personal examples that better situate this argument in our everyday life experiences. Ladson-Billings (1998b) describes her experience of being invited to a major university to be a speaker in the distinguished scholars lecture series. After the speech, she returned to her hotel and decided to unwind in the hotel's concierge floor lounge. Dressed in business attire and reading the newspaper, she noticed a white man who popped his head in the door. "What time are y'all serving?" he asked. Because she was the only person in the lounge, it was clear that he was addressing Ladson-Billings. She politely but firmly replied, "I don't know what time *they* are serving. I'm here as a guest." Red-faced and clearly embarrassed, the man quietly left. One might argue that he made a simple mistake. Perhaps he would have asked the same question of anyone who was sitting in the lounge. Nevertheless, the moment reminded Ladson-Billings that no matter what her scholarly reputation, at any time she could be snapped back into the constraining racial paradigm, complete with all the limitations such designations carry.

Donnor asserts that one of his many calls came when he served as an instructor for a "diversity" class that enrolled only white, middle-class teachers. Because this was a graduate course, Donnor expected the students to adhere to the rigors of a master's-level class. After assigning homework following the first class meeting, Donnor was challenged by one of the few male students about the amount of homework. When Donnor told the student that he expected students to complete the assignment, the inquirer responded, "It ain't going to happen." At the next class meeting, the program's site coordinator, a white woman, arrived at the class, ostensibly to share some program information with the students. However, as she addressed the students, she began to talk to them about modifications in assignments and contacting her if they had issues and concerns regarding the course.

The issue with the student's complaint about the volume of work is a common one in a society that regularly rejects intellectual pursuits. However, graduate students typically exercise some level of courtesy and skill in negotiating the amount of work they are willing (or able) to do.

The blatant remark that "it ain't going to happen" may reflect the certainty with which the student approached the racial power dynamic. As a white male approaching an African American male, this student understood that he could challenge Donnor's credentials and abilities. More pointedly, the experience with the site coordinator underscored the fact that although Donnor was hired to teach the course, authority flowed to the white woman. Students could essentially discount Donnor whenever he did anything they disagreed with. Both incidents serve as powerful reminders for Donnor that despite his academic credentials and experience, his racial identity always serves as a mitigating factor in determining his authority and legitimacy.

Receiving a call is a regular reminder of the liminal space of alterity (Wynter, 1992) that racialized others occupy. But it is important not to regard the liminal space solely as a place of degradation and disadvantage. Wynter (1992) assures us that this place of alterity offers a perspective advantage whereby those excluded from the center (of social, cultural, political, and economic activity) experience "wide-angle" vision. This perspective advantage is not due to an inherent racial/cultural difference but instead is the result of the dialectical nature of constructed otherness that prescribes the liminal status of people of color as beyond the normative boundary of the conception of Self/Other (King, 1995).

In the previous iteration of this chapter, Ladson-Billings (2000)[4] cited King (1995), who argued that the epistemic project that scholars of color and their allies must undertake is more than simply adding multiple perspectives or "pivoting" the center. Such scholars occupy a liminal position whose perspective is one of alterity. This liminal position or point of alterity that we inhabit attempts to transcend an "either/or" epistemology. Alterity is not a dualistic position such that there are multiple or equally partial standpoints that are either valid or inexorably ranked hierarchically. Recognizing the alterity perspective does not essentialize other perspectives such as blackness, Indian-ness, Asian-ness, or Latino-ness as homogenizing reverse epistemics (West, 1990).

Ethiopian anthropologist Asmaron Legesse (1973) asserts that the liminal group is that which is forcibly constrained to play the role of alter ego to the ideal self prescribed by the dominant cultural model. This dominant model sets up prescriptive rules and canons for regulating thought and action in the society. Thus, the "issue is about the 'nature of human knowing' of the social reality, in a model of which the knower is already a socialized subject" (Wynter, 1992, p. 26).

> The system-conserving mainstream perspectives of each order (or well-established scholarship) therefore clash with the challenges made from the perspectives of alterity. . . . For, it is the task of established scholarship to rigorously maintain those prescriptions which are critical to the order's existence. (Wynter, 1992, p. 27)

This focus on the ways of the dominant order is important in helping us explore the ways such an order distorts the realities of the Other in an effort to maintain power relations that continue to disadvantage those who are excluded from that order. As Wynter (1992) so eloquently argues, this liminal perspective is the condition of the dominant order's self-definition that "can empower us to free ourselves from the 'categories and prescriptions' of our specific order and from its 'generalized horizon of understanding'" (p. 27).

In this iteration of the handbook, we move away from solely describing the epistemological terrain (both dominant and liminal) to advocating the kinds of moral and ethical responsibilities various epistemologies embody. We do this in hopes of mobilizing scholarship that will take a stance on behalf of human liberation. The subsequent sections of this chapter examine the position of intellectuals as constructors of ethical epistemologies, the discursive and material limits of liberal ideology, new templates for ethical action, moving from research to activism, reconstructing the intellect, and the search for a revolutionary habitus.

We admit at the outset that this is an ambitious project and that we are likely to fall short of our stated goals. However, because a task is hard does not imply that we should not undertake it. Similarly, Derrick Bell (1992) argued that even though racism was a permanent fixture of American life, we must still struggle against it. Our success will not necessarily come in the form of a tightly constructed scholarly treatise but rather in the form of scores of other community, student, and scholar activists who continue or take up this cause rather than merely waiting for "the call."

▣ Intellectual Marginals as Constructors of Ethical Epistemologies

> *The special function of the Negro intellectual is a cultural one. He [sic] should . . . assail the stultifying blight of the commercially depraved white middle-class who has poisoned the structural roots of the American ethos and transformed the American people into a nation of intellectual dolts.*
>
> —Harold Cruse (1967/1984, p. 455)

We would be remiss if we did not acknowledge the incredible volume of work that scholars of color have produced that we regard as ethical epistemologies. Clearly, in a chapter of this length, it is impossible to do justice to all (or even most) of this work. Thus, we will attempt to make this "review of the literature" more a grand tour (Spradley, 1979) to outline the contours of the foundation on which we are building. We start our foundational work with a look at W.E.B. DuBois's (1903/1953) construct of "double consciousness," with which he argues that the African American "ever feels his two-ness . . . two souls, two thoughts, two unreconciled strivings" (p. 5). David Levering Lewis (1993, p. 281) addressed the importance of DuBois's conception stating:

> It was a revolutionary concept. It was not just revolutionary; the concept of the divided self was profoundly mystical, for DuBois invested this double consciousness with a capacity to see incomparably farther and deeper. The African American . . . possessed the gift of "second sight in this American world," an intuitive faculty enabling him/her to see and say things about American society that possessed heightened moral validity.

Ladson-Billings (2000) argued that DuBois's work had an important synchronic aspect in that he raised the issues of double consciousness prior to the formation of the Frankfurt School, out of which critical theories emerged. Coincidentally, DuBois had studied at the University of Berlin in the late 1800s, yet his name is never mentioned in the same context as those of Max Horkheimer, Theodor Adorno, and Herbert Marcuse. DuBois remains a "Negro" intellectual concerned with the "Negro" problem, but it was in Germany that DuBois recognized the race problems in the Americas, Africa, and Asia, as well as the political development of Europe, as being one problem that was part of a shared ideology. This was the period of his life that united his studies of history, economics, and politics into a scientific approach of social research.

DuBois's notion of double consciousness applies not only to African Americans but to all people who are constructed outside the dominant paradigm. Although DuBois refers to a double consciousness, we know that our sense of identity may evoke multiple consciousness, and it is important to read our discussion of multiple consciousness as a description of complex phenomena that impose essentialized concepts of "blackness," "Latina/o-ness," "Asian American-ness," or "Native American-ness" on specific individuals or groups.[5]

In addition to DuBois's conception of double consciousness, we rely on Anzaldúa's (1987) perspective that identities are fractured not only by gender, class, race, religion, and sexuality, but also by geographic realities such as living along the U.S.-Mexico border, in urban spaces, or on government-created Indian reservations. Anzaldúa's work continues a long intellectual history of Chicanas/os (see Acuna, 1972; Almaguer, 1974; Balderrama, 1982; Gomez-Quinones, 1977; Mirande & Enriquez, 1979; Padilla, 1987; Paz, 1961) and extends what Delgado Bernal (1998) calls a Chicana feminist epistemology. This work includes writers such as Alarcon (1990), Castillo (1995), and de la Torre and Pesquera (1993) to illustrate the intersections of race, class, and gender.

Our reliance on these scholars is not to assume a unified Latino/a (or even Chicano/a) subject. Oboler (1995) challenges the amalgamation of Spanish speakers in the Western Hemisphere under the rubric "Hispanic." The Hispanic label belies the problem inherent in attempts to create a unitary consciousness from one that is much more complex and multiple than imagined or constructed. According to Oboler:

> Insofar as the ethnic label Hispanic homogenizes the varied social and political experiences of 23 million people of different races, classes, languages, and national origins, genders, and religions, it is perhaps not so surprising that the meanings and uses of the term have become the subject of debate in the social sciences, government agencies, and much of society at large. (1995, p. 3)

Oboler's (1995) argument is enacted in a scene in Rebecca Gilman's (2000) play *Spinning into Butter.* In one scene, a college student is told that he is eligible for a "minority" fellowship. When the student objects to the term "minority," the dean informs him that he can designate himself as "Hispanic." He becomes more offended at that term, and when the dean asks him how he would like to identify himself, he says, "Newyorican." The dean then suggests that he list "Puerto Rican," but the student explains to her that he is not Puerto Rican. "I have never been to Puerto Rico and I would be as lost as any American tourist there." They continue to argue over what label or category is appropriate. The dean cannot understand that a key feature of self-determination lies in the ability to name oneself. The failure of the dean to recognize Newyorican as an identity does not de-legitimate it, except in her mainstream world, which not insignificantly controls the resources that the student needs to be successful at the college.

American Indians grapple with similar questions of what it means to be Indian. Despite movements toward "Pan-Indianism" (Hertzberg, 1971), the cultures of American Indians are both broad and diverse. Although we warn against essentializing American Indians, we do not want to minimize the way the federal government's attempt to "civilize" and de-tribalize Indian children through boarding schools helped various groups of Indians realize that they shared a number of common problems and experiences (Snipp, 1995). Lomawaima (1995) stated that "since the federal government turned its attention to the 'problem' of civilizing Indians, its overt goal has been to educate Indians to be non-Indians" (p. 332).

Much of the double consciousness that Indians face revolves around issues of tribal sovereignty. A loss of sovereignty is amplified by four methods of disenfranchisement experienced by many American Indians (Lomawaima, 1995). Those four methods included relocation by colonial authorities (e.g., to missions or reservations), systematic eradication of the native language, religious conversion (to Christianity), and restructuring of economies toward sedentary agriculture, small-scale craft industry, and gendered labor.

Warrior (1995) asks whether or not an investigation of early American Indian writers can have a significant impact on the way contemporary Native intellectuals develop critical studies. He urges caution in understanding the scholarship of Fourth World formulations such as those of Ward Churchill and M. Annette Jaimes because it tends to be essentializing in its call for understanding American Indian culture as a part of a global consciousness shared by all indigenous people in all periods of history. Warrior's work is a call for "intellectual sovereignty" (p. 87)—a position free from the tyranny and oppression of the dominant discourse.

Despite the attempts to eradicate an Indian identity, the mainstream continues to embrace a "romantic" notion of the Indian. In Eyre's (1998) adaptation of Sherman Alexie's (1993) *The Lone Ranger and Tonto Fistfight in Heaven*, which became the film *Smoke Signals*, we see an excellent example of this. The character Victor tells his traveling companion Thomas that he is not Indian enough. Playing on the prevailing stereotypes that whites have about Indians, Victor instructs Thomas to be "more stoic," to allow his hair to flow freely, and to get rid of his buttoned-down look. We see the humor in this scene because we recognize the ways we want Indians to appear to satisfy our preconceived notions of "Indian-ness."

Among Asian Pacific Islanders, there are notions of multiple consciousness. Lowe (1996) expresses this in terms of "heterogeneity, hybridity, and multiplicity" (p. 60). She points out that

> The articulation of an "Asian American identity" as an organizing tool has provided unity that enables diverse Asian groups to understand unequal circumstances and histories as being related. The building of "Asian American culture" is crucial to this effort, for it articulates and empowers the diverse Asian-origin community vis-à-vis the institutions and apparatuses that exclude and marginalize it. Yet to the extent that Asian American culture fixes Asian American identity and suppresses differences—of national origin, generation, gender, sexuality, class—it risks particular dangers: not only does it underestimate the differences and hybridities among Asians, but it may inadvertently support the racist discourse that constructs Asians as a homogenous group . . . (pp. 70–71)

Espiritu (1992) also reminds us that "Asian American" as an identity category came into being within the past 30 years. Prior to that time, most members of the Asian-descent immigrant population "considered themselves culturally and politically distinct" (p. 19). Indeed, the historical enmity that existed between and among various Asian groups made it difficult for groups to transcend their national allegiances to see themselves as one unified group. In addition, the growing anti-Asian sentiments with which the various Asian immigrant groups were faced in the United States caused specific groups to "disassociate themselves from the targeted group so as not to be mistaken for members of it and suffer any possible negative consequences" (p. 20).

Trinh Minh-ha (1989) and Mohanty (1991) offer postmodern analyses of Asian Americanness that challenge any unitary definitions of "Asian American." Rather than construct a mythical solidarity, their work examines the ways that Asian-ness is represented in the dominant imagination. One of the most vivid examples of the distorted, imagined Asian shows up in the work of David Henry Hwang, whose play *M. Butterfly* demonstrated how a constellation of characteristics—size, temperament, submissiveness—allowed a French armed services officer to intimately mistake a man for a woman.

Lowe (1996) reminds us that "the grouping 'Asian American' is not a natural or static category; it is a socially constructed unity, a situationally specific position assumed for political reasons" (p. 82). But it coexists with a "dynamic fluctuation and heterogeneity of Asian American culture . . ." (p. 68).

What each of these groups (i.e., African Americans, Native Americans, Latinos, and Asian Americans) has in common is the experience of a racialized identity. Each group is composed of myriad other national and ancestral origins, but the dominant ideology of the Euro-American epistemology has forced them into an essentialized and totalized unit that is perceived to have little or no internal variation. However, at the same moment, members of these groups have used these unitary racialized labels for political and cultural purposes. Identification with the racialized labels means an acknowledgment of some of the common experiences that group members have had as outsiders and others.

Along with this notion of double-consciousness that we argue pervades the experience of racialized identities, we believe it is imperative to include another theoretical axis—that of postcolonialism. Whereas double consciousness speaks to the struggle for identities, postcolonialism speaks to the collective project of the modern world that was in no way prepared for the decolonized to talk back and "act up." As West (1990) asserts, decolonization took on both "impetuous ferocity and moral outrage" (p. 25). Frantz Fanon (1968) best describes this movement:

> Decolonization, which sets out to change the order of the world, is obviously a program of complete disorder. . . . Decolonization is the meeting of two

forces, opposed to each other by their very nature, which in fact owe their originality to that sort of substantification which results from and is nourished by the situation in the colonies. In decolonization, there is therefore the need of a complete calling in question of the colonial situation. (p. 35)

Fanon (1994) helped us understand the dynamics of colonialism and why decolonization had to be the major project of the oppressed:

> Colonial domination, because it is total and tends to over-simplify, very soon manages to disrupt in spectacular fashion the cultural life of a conquered people. This cultural obliteration is made possible by the negation of national reality, by new legal relations introduced by the occupying power, by the banishment of the natives and their customs to outlying districts by colonial society, by expropriation, and by the systematic enslaving of men and women. (p. 45)

Postcolonial theory serves as a corrective to our penchant for casting these issues into a strictly U.S. context. It helps us see the worldwide oppression against the "other" and the ability of dominant groups to define the terms of being and non-being, of civilized and uncivilized, of developed and undeveloped, of human and nonhuman. But even as we attempt to incorporate the term "postcolonial" into our understanding of critical race theory, we are reminded of the limits of such terminology to fully explain conditions of hierarchy, hegemony, racism, sexism, and unequal power relations. As McClintock (1994) asserts, "'post-colonialism' (like postmodernism) is unevenly developed globally. . . . Can most of the world's countries be said, in any meaningful or theoretically rigorous sense, to share a single 'common past,' or single common 'condition,' called 'the post-colonial condition,' or 'post-coloniality'" (p. 294)? Indeed, McClintock (1994) reminds us that "the term 'post-colonialism' is, in many cases, prematurely celebratory. Ireland may, at a pinch, be 'post-colonial,' but for the inhabitants of British-occupied Northern Ireland, not to mention the Palestinian inhabitants of the Israeli Occupied Territories and the West Bank, there may be nothing 'post' about colonialism at all"(p. 294). As Linda Tuhiwai Smith (1998) queries, "Post . . . have they left yet?"

"Is-ness" Versus "Us-ness": The Discursive and Material Limits of Liberal Ideology

> *To the extent that we interpret our experience from within the master narrative, we reinforce our own subordination. Whether [people of color] can counter racism may depend, finally, on our ability to claim identities outside the master narrative.*
>
> —Lisa Ikemoto (1995, pp. 312–313)

In the previous section, we addressed axes of moral and ethical epistemology on which much of the work of scholars of color rests (i.e., double consciousness, sovereignty, hybridity, heterogeneity, postcolonialism). In this section, we point toward the problems of dichotomy provoked by current political and social rhetoric.

After the September 11, 2001, terrorist attacks on the World Trade Center, the Pentagon, and a plane that crashed in Pennsylvania, George W. Bush addressed the nation (and ostensibly the world), letting the audience know that there were but two choices—to be with "us" or with the "terrorists." Those dichotomous choices were not nearly as simple as Bush suggested. For one thing, who is the "us"? Is the "us" the United States, regardless of the situation and circumstance? Is the "us" the United States even when it oppresses you? Is the "us" the supporters of the U.S. Patriot Acts I and II? Second, who are the terrorists? Clearly, we are not confused about al-Qaeda or the Taliban, but does objecting to U.S. foreign policy place us in league with them? If we stand in solidarity with the Palestinian people, are with "with the terrorists"? If we acknowledge the legitimacy of the claims of the Northern Ireland Catholics, have we lost our claim on being a part of "us"? In the face of this sharp dividing line, many liberals chose George W. Bush's "us."

Choosing this unified "us" is not unlike Lipsitz's (1998) argument that the United States has been constructed as a nation of white people whose public policy, politics, and culture are designed to serve the interests of whites. Such a construction serves to maintain white privilege and justify the subordination of anyone outside this racial designation. Thus, even in the reporting of war casualties, we list the number of Americans (read: white, even if this is not the actual case) killed while ignoring the number of "the enemy" who are killed. What is important here is that whiteness is not attached to phenotype but to rather a social construction of who is worthy of inclusion in the circle of whiteness. The enemy is never white. His identity is subsumed in a nationality or ideology that can be defined as antithetical to whiteness (e.g., Nazis, fascists, communists, Muslims).

In one of her classes, Ladson-Billings used to show students a videotape of the Rodney King beating and, following the viewing, distributed copies of blind editorials about the beating. She then asked the students to determine the political perspective of the writers. Without benefit of newspaper mastheads or authors' names, many of the students struggled to locate the writers' ideological views. Predictably, the students divided the editorials into "liberal" and "conservative." No students identified moderate, radical, or reactionary perspectives. Their failure to see a broader ideological continuum is indicative of the polarization and dichotomization of our discourses.

We make a specific assumption about where the discursive battles must be fought. We do not engage the conservative ideology because we take for granted its antagonism toward the issues we raise. We understand that conservative rhetoric has no space for discussions of ethical epistemologies, double consciousness, hybridity, or postcolonialism. Our battle is with liberals who presume the moral high ground and who have situated themselves as "saviors" of the oppressed while simultaneously maintaining their white skin privilege (McIntosh, 1988).

A wonderful literary example of the moral vacuum in current liberal discourse appears in a novel by Bebe Moore Campbell (1995), *Your Blues Ain't Like Mine*. The novel is a fictionalized account of the horrible Emmett Till murder of the 1950s. Instead of focusing solely on the victim's family and perspective, the author provides multiple perspectives, including that of the perpetrators, the various families, and the townspeople. One character, Clayton, is a classic white liberal. He is from a privileged family and is afraid to truly relinquish his access to that privilege. Therefore, although Clayton tries to "help" various black characters, at the end of the novel, when he discovers that he is related to one of the black characters, he adamantly refuses to share his inheritance with her. Clayton's behavior is a metaphor for white liberalism. It is prepared to go only so far.

A real-life example of this moral vacuum was exemplified in the Clinton presidency. We are not referring to his personal transgressions and sexual exploits but rather his retreat from the political left by packaging himself as a "New Democrat," which can only be described as an "Old Moderate Republican"—think Nelson Rockefeller, George Romney, or Lowell Weicker. The actual Clinton presidency record indicates, according to columnist Steve Perry (1996), that [he] . . . co-opted the great middle while leaving liberals with no place to go" (p. 2). Randall Kennedy (2001) suggests:

> For all Clinton's much-expressed concern about social justice in general and racial justice in particular, his programs, policies, and gestures have done painfully little to help those whom Professor William Julius Wilson calls "the truly disadvantaged"—impoverished people, disproportionately colored, who are locked away in pestilent and crime-ridden inner cities or forgotten rural or small-town wastelands, people who are bereft of money, training, skills, or education needed to escape their plight. True, Clinton had to contend with a reactionary, Republican-led Congress for much of his presidency. But, even before the Gingrichian deluge of 1994 he had made it plain that his sympathies lay predominantly with "the middle class." For those below it, he offered chastising lectures that legitimated the essentially conservative notions that the predicament of the poor results primarily

> from their conduct and not from the deformative deprivations imposed on them by a grievously unfair social order that is in large part a class hierarchy and in smaller part a pigmentocracy.

Progressive columnist Malik Miah (1999) argues that Clinton's ease and fellow feeling with African Americans should not be interpreted as solidarity with the cause of African American or other people suffering oppression:

> While it is true Clinton plays the sax and is right at home visiting a Black church, his real policies have done more damage to the Black community than any president since the victory of civil rights movement in the 1960s. . . .
>
> On the issue of families and welfare he's ended programs that, while inadequate, provided some relief for the poorest sections of the population. Ironically, Nixon, Reagan and Bush—who all promised to end welfare—couldn't get it done. Clinton not only did it but claimed it as a great accomplishment of his first term in office. . . .
>
> He pushed through Congress a crime bill that restricts civil liberties and makes it easier to impose the death penalty. . . .
>
> The strong support [of African Americans] for Clinton is thus seen as "using common sense" and doing what's best for the future of our children, much more than having big illusions in Clinton and the "new" Democrats. The new middle-class layers in these communities also provide new potential voters and supporters for the two main parties of the rich.

Like Campbell's (1995) fictional character, Clayton, Bill Clinton was prepared to go only so far in his support of people of color. His liberal credentials relied on superficial and symbolic acts (e.g., associating with blacks, attending black churches, playing the saxophone); thus, in those areas where people of color were most hurting (e.g., health, education, welfare), he was unwilling to spend political capital. Such a retreat from liberal ideals represented a more severe moral failing than afternoon trysts with a White House intern.

With the George W. Bush administration, people of color and poor people are faced with a more pressing concern—the legitimacy of their being. Rather than argue over whether or not they are "with us" or "with the terrorists," we must constantly assert that we *are* rather than reflect a solidarity with an overarching "us" that actively oppresses. At this writing, we are watching a movement in California to prohibit the state from collecting data that identify people by racial categories (California Proposition 54). Passage of this proposition would mean that the state would not be able to report about the disparities that exist between whites and people of color in school achievement, incarceration, income levels, health concerns, and other social and civic concerns. Thus, this so-called color-blind measure effectively erases the races while maintaining the social, political, economic, and cultural status quo. The significance of this proposition is lost in the media circus of the California gubernatorial recall and cast of characters seeking to be governor of the most populous (and one of the most diverse) states in the nation.

At the same moment that the society seeks to erase and ignore the Other, it maintains a curious desire to consume and co-opt it. The appropriation of cultural forms from communities of color is not really flattery; it is a twisted embrace that simultaneously repels the Other. The complexity of this relationship allows white people, as performance artist Roger Guenveur Smith (Tate, 2003, p. 5) suggests, to love black music and hate black people. The mainstream community despises rap music for its violence, misogyny, and racial epithets but spends millions of dollars to produce and consume it. The mainstream decries illegal immigration from Mexico and Central America while refusing to acknowledge its own complicity in maintaining immigrants' presence through its demand for artificially price-depressed produce, domestic service, and the myriad jobs that "Americans" refuse to do. The mainstream fights what it sees as the "overrepresentation" of Asian-descent people in certain industries or high-status universities but cultivates fetishes over "Oriental" artifacts—martial arts, feng shui, sushi, and "docile," "petite" women. The mainstream remained silence while the indigenous population was massacred and displaced onto reservations but now runs eagerly to participate in sweat lodges and powwows. Such fascination does nothing to liberate and enrich the Other. Instead, they remain on the margins and are conveniently exploited for the political, economic, social, and cultural benefit of the dominant group. We are not a part of the "us" or "the terrorists." We are the struggling to exist—to just "be."

New Templates for Ethical Action

> *The past history of biology has shown that progress is equally inhibited by an anti-intellectual holism and a purely atomistic reductionism.*
>
> —Ernst Mayr (1976)

In his book *Ethical Ambition*, legal scholar Derrick Bell (2002) addresses a question that plagues many scholars of color: "How can I succeed without selling my soul?" He argues that the qualities of passion, risk, courage, inspiration, faith, humility, and love are the keys to success that maintain one's integrity and dignity. He contends that scholars must consider these as standards of behavior in both scholarship and relationships. Clearly, this is a different set of standards than those the academy typically applies to research and scholarship. But how well have the usual standards served communities of color?

> From 1932 to 1972, 399 poor black sharecroppers in Macon County, Alabama were denied treatment for syphilis and deceived by physicians of the United States Public Health Service. As part of the Tuskegee Syphilis Study, designed to document the natural history of the disease, these men were told that they were being treated for "bad blood." In fact, government officials went to extreme lengths to insure that they received no therapy from any source. As reported by the *New York Times* on 26 July 1972, the Tuskegee Syphilis Study was revealed as "the longest nontherapeutic experiment on human beings in medical history." (Tuskegee Syphilis Study Legacy Committee, 1996)

The Health News Network (2000; www.healthnewsnet.com) details a long list of unethical and egregious acts performed in the name of science. For example, in 1940, 400 prisoners in Chicago were infected with malaria to study the effects of new and experimental drugs to combat the disease. In 1945, Project Paperclip was initiated by the U.S. State Department, Army intelligence, and the CIA to recruit Nazi scientists and offer them immunity and secret identities in exchange for work on top secret government projects in the United States. In 1947, the CIA began a study of LSD as a potential weapon for use by U.S. intelligence. In this study, human subjects (both civilian and military) were used with and without their knowledge. In 1950, the U.S. Navy sprayed a cloud of bacteria over San Francisco to determine how susceptible a U.S. city would be to biological attack. In 1955, the CIA released a bacteria over Tampa Bay, Florida, that had been withdrawn from the Army's biological warfare arsenal to determine its ability to infect human populations with biological agents. In 1958, the Army Chemical Welfare Laboratories tested LSD on 95 volunteers to determine its effect on intelligence. In 1965, prisoners at the Holmesburg State Prison in Philadelphia were subjected to dioxin, the highly toxic chemical compound of Agent Orange used in Vietnam. In 1990, more than 1,500 6-month-old black and Latino babies in Los Angeles were given an "experimental" measles vaccine that had never been licensed for use in the United States. The Centers for Disease Control later admitted that the parents were never informed that their babies were receiving an experimental vaccine.

Although these examples in the life sciences are extreme, it is important to recognize that social sciences have almost always tried to mimic the so-called hard sciences. We have accepted their paradigms and elevated their ways of knowing even when "hard scientists" themselves challenge them (Kuhn, 1962). The standards that require research to be "objective," precise, accurate, generalizable, and replicable do not simultaneously produce moral and ethical research and scholarship. The current calls for "scientifically based" and "evidence-based" research in education from the United States Department of Education have provoked an interesting response from the education research community (Shavelson & Towne, 2003).

The National Research Council Report *Scientific Research in Education* (Shavelson & Towne, 2003) outlines what it terms a "set of fundamental principles" for "a healthy community of researchers" (p. 2). These principles include:

1. Pose significant questions that can be investigated empirically.
2. Link research to relevant theory.
3. Use methods that permit direct investigation of the question.
4. Provide a coherent and explicit chain of reasoning.
5. Replicate and generalize across studies.
6. Disclose research to encourage professional scrutiny and critique. (pp. 3–5)

On their face, these seem to be "reasonable" principles around which the "scientific" community can coalesce. Although it is beyond the scope of this chapter to do a thorough review of the NRC report, we do want to point out some of the problems such thinking provokes, particularly in the realm of ethics and moral activism. The first principle suggests that we "pose significant questions that can be investigated empirically." We cannot recall the last time a researcher asserted that he or she was investigating something "insignificant." Scholars research that which interests them, and no one would suggest that they are interested in insignificant things. More important, this principle assumes the supremacy of empirical work. Without taking our discussion too far into the philosophical, we assert that what constitutes "the empirical" is culturally coded. For example, many years ago, a researcher from a prestigious university was collecting data in an urban classroom. The researcher reported on the apparent chaos and disorder of the classroom and described her observation of some students openly snorting drugs in the back of the classroom. Later, a graduate student who knew the school and the community talked with some of the students and learned that the students knew that the researchers expected them to be "dangerous," "uncontrollable," and "frightening." Determined to meet the researcher's expectations, the students gathered up the chalk dust from the blackboard ledge and began treating it like a powdered drug. What the researcher actually saw were students who decided to fool a researcher. This may have been empirical work, but clearly it was wrong.

In a less extreme example, an anthropology of education professor regularly displayed a set of photographic slides to his class and required students to describe the contents of each slide. In one slide, a photo of a farmhouse in a small German village, there is a huge pile of manure (at least one full story high) in front of the house. Not one student out of a lecture section of about 100 noted the manure pile. Even if one might argue that it was difficult to determine what it was in the slide, not one student noted that there was a "pile of something" sitting in front of the farmhouse. Our point here is that our ability to access the empirical is culturally determined and always shaped by moral and political concerns.

Popkewitz (2003) argues that the NRC report rests on a number of assumptions that expose the writers' misunderstanding of scientific inquiry. These assumptions include:

> (1) There is a unity of foundational assumptions that cross all the natural and social sciences. This unity involves: (2) the importance of rigorous methods and design models; (3) the cumulative, sequential development of knowledge; (4) science is based on inferential reasoning; (5) the empirical testing and development of knowledge. Finally, the assumptions provide the expertise of what government needs—showing what works. This last point is important as the Report has a dual function. It is to outline a science of education and to propose how government can intervene in the development of a science that serves policy reforms. (pp. 2–3)

Popkewitz (2003) is elegant in his rebuttal of the NRC report, and we are limited in our ability to expend space to offer additional critique. However, our task is to point out that with all the emphasis on "scientific principles," the NRC report fails to include the moral and ethical action in which scholars must engage. Is it enough to follow protocols for human subjects? That sets a very minimalist standard that is likely to continue the same moral and ethical abuses. For example, in a recent National Public Radio broadcast of *All Things Considered* (Mann, 2003) titled "New York Weighs Lead-Paint Laws," the reporter indicated that researchers were testing children for the levels of lead in their blood. Although there was consensus that many of the children had elevated levels of lead, the researchers rejected the recommendation that the levels of lead in the building be tested. This second, more efficient method would allow for class action on the part of the building residents, but the researchers chose to persist in examining individuals. Rather than raise the moral bar by insisting that it is unsafe to live in buildings with lead-based paint and to test the buildings for that paint, individuals (many who are poor and disenfranchised) are responsible for coming forth to be tested. One might argue that the researchers are abiding by the standards of scientific inquiry; however, these standards are not inclusive of the moral and ethical action that must be taken.

In addition to Bell's (2002) call for ethical behavior in the academy, Guinier and Torres (2002) have argued that it is important to move past the current racial discourses because such discourses invariably keep us locked in race-power hierarchies that depend on a winner-take-all conclusion. Instead, Guinier and Torres (2002) give birth to a new construct—"political race"—that relies on building cross-racial coalitions and alliances that involve grassroots workers who strive to remake the terms of participation and invigorate democracy. Their work points to the coalition of African Americans and Latinos who devised the 10% decision to address inequity in Texas higher education. This decision means that all students in the state of Texas who graduate in the top 10% of their class are eligible for admission at the two flagship Texas universities—University of Texas at Austin and Texas A&M. We would also point to the work of the modern civil rights movement of the 1960s and the anti-apartheid work in South Africa. In both instances, we saw broad coalitions of people working for human liberation and justice. The aim of such work is not merely to remedy past racial injustice but rather to enlarge the democratic project to include many more participants. In the case of the United States, the civil rights movement became a template for addressing a number of undemocratic practices against women, immigrants, gays and lesbians, the disabled, and linguistic minorities. The point of moral and ethical activism is not to secure privileges for one's own group; it is to make democracy a reality for increasing numbers of groups and individuals. Such work permits us to look at multiple axes of difference and take these intersections seriously.

In *Miner's Canary*, Guinier and Torres (2002) point out that our typical response to inequity is to feel sorry for the individuals but ignore the structure that produces such inequity. We would prefer to prepare the dispossessed and disenfranchised to better fit in a corrupt system rather than rethink the whole system. Instead of ignoring racial differences, as the color-blind approach suggests, political race urges us to understand the ways that race and power intertwine at every level of the society and to further understand that only through cross-racial coalitions can we expose the embedded hierarchies of privilege and destroy them (www.minerscanary.org/about.shtml, retrieved December 1, 2003). Guinier and Torres (2002) call this notion of enlisting race to resist power "political race." It requires diagnosing systemic injustice and organizing to resist it.

Political race challenges the social and economic consequences of race in a "third way" (www.minerscanary.org/about.shtml) that proposes a multitextured political strategy rather than the traditional legal solutions to the issues of racial justice. The authors argue that "political race dramatically transforms the use of race from a signifier of individual culpability and prejudice to an early warning sign of larger injustices" (Ibid.) When they speak of political, they are not referring to conventional electoral politics.

Rather, their notion of political race challenges social activists and critical scholars to rethink what winning means and if winning in a corrupt system can ever be good enough. Instead, their focus is on the power of change through collective action and how such action can change (and challenge) us all to work in new ways.

We seek a methodology and a theory that, as Gayatri Spivak (1990) argues, seeks not merely reversal of roles in a hierarchy, but rather displacement of taken-for-granted norms around unequal binaries (e.g., male-female, public-private, white-non-white, able-disabled, native-foreign). We see such possibility in Critical Race Theory (CRT), and we point out that CRT is not limited to the old notions of race. Rather, CRT is a new analytic rubric for considering difference and inequity using multiple methodologies—story, voice, metaphor, analogy, critical social science, feminism, and postmodernism. So visceral is our reaction to the word "race" that many scholars and consumers of scholarly literature cannot see beyond the word to appreciate the value of CRT for making sense of our current social condition. We would argue that scholars such as Trinh Minh-ha, Robert Allen Warrior, Gloria Anzaldúa, Ian Haney Lopez, Richard Delgado, Lisa Lowe, David Palumbo-Liu, Gayatri Spivak, Chandra Mohanty, and Patricia Hill Collins all produce a kind of CRT. They are not bogged down with labels or dogmatic constraints; rather, they are creatively and passionately engaging new visions of scholarship to do work that ultimately will serve people and lead to human liberation.

Thus, we argue that the work of critical scholars (from any variety of perspectives) is not merely to try to replicate the work of previous scholars in a cookie-cutter fashion but rather to break new epistemological, methodological, social activist, and moral ground. We do not need Derrick Bell, Lani Guinier, or Gerald Torres clones. We need scholars to take up their causes (along with causes they identify for themselves) and creatively engage them. We look to them because of their departure from the scholarly mainstream, not to make them idols.

Moving From Research to Activism—Street-Level Research in Ivory Towers

> *Conflict—the real world kind, I mean—can be bloody, misguided, and wholly tragic. It behooves us always to try to understand how and why bloodshed breaks out as it does. But the very narratives and stories we tell ourselves and each other afterwards, in an effort to explain, understand, excuse, and assign responsibility for conflict, may also be, in a sense, the source of the very violence we abhor.*
>
> —Lisa Ikemoto (1995, p. 313)

Earlier in this chapter, we referenced Harold Cruse and *The Crisis of the Negro Intellectual* (1967/1984), and indeed we recognize that the crisis Cruse identifies is a crisis for all intellectuals of color. Cruse's point that "While Negro intellectuals are busy trying to interpret the nature of the black world and its aspirations to the whites, they should, in fact, be defining their own roles as intellectuals within both worlds" (p. 455) is applicable to all scholars of color. Novelists such as Toni Morrison (1987), Shawn Wong (1995), Ana Castillo (1994), Sherman Alexie (1993), and Jhumpa Lahiri (1999) deftly accomplish what Cruse asks. They sit comfortably within the walls of the academy and on the street corners, barrios, and reservations of the people. They are "cultural brokers" who understand the need to be "in" the academy (or mainstream) but not "of" the academy.

In the foreword to Cruse's book, Allen and Wilson (1984) summarize the central tasks that this book outlines for "would-be intellectuals" (p. v):

1. To familiarize themselves with their own intellectual antecedents and with previous political and cultural movements;
2. To analyze critically the bases for the pendulum swings between the two poles of integration and [black] nationalism, and try to synthesize them into a single and consistent analysis;

3. To identify clearly the political, economic, and cultural requisites for black advancement in order to meld them into a single politics of progressive black culture. This process requires greater attention both to Afro-American popular culture and to the macroeconomic, structural context of modern capitalism in which group culture either flourishes or atrophies;
4. To recognize the uniqueness of American conditions and to insist that one incorporate this uniqueness when studying numbers 1 through 3 above.

Despite Cruse's (1967/1984) focus on African Americans and their experiences in the United States, it is clear to us that such work is important for any marginalized group. All scholars of color must know the intellectual antecedents of their cultural, ethnic, or racial group. This is important for combating the persistent ideology of white supremacy that denigrates the intellectual contributions of others. All scholars of color must look to the epistemological underpinnings and legitimacy of their cultures and cultural ways of knowing. They must face the tensions that emerge in their communities between assimilation into the U.S. mainstream and the creation of separate and distinct cultural locations. For example, the construction of Asian Americans as articulated previously by Lowe (1996) and Espiritu (1992) are powerful examples of the synthesis Cruse speaks of. All scholars of color need to acknowledge the salience of popular culture in shaping our research and scholarly agendas, for it is in the popular that our theories and methodologies become living, breathing entities.

Martin Luther King, Jr. had a theory about "nonviolence" that came from his study of Gandhi and Dietrich Bonhoeffer, but the theory was actualized in the hearts and minds of ordinary people—Fannie Lou Hamer, Esau Jenkins, Septima Clark, and many others. So great is the desire for survival and liberation that it transcends geopolitical boundaries, languages, and cultures. The modern civil rights movement in the United States was replayed in China's Tiananmen Square, in the cities and townships of South Africa, and in liberation struggles the world over. In each instance, the power of the popular brings music, art, and energy to the struggle. Ordinary people become the "street-level bureaucrats" (Lipsky, 1983) who translate theory into practice. However, we want to be clear that we are not suggesting that such "street-level bureaucrats" begin to behave as functionaries of the state and thereby become the new power brokers. Rather, we are suggesting a new vision of Lipsky's (1983) concept in which people from the community represent a new form of leadership that is unafraid of shared power and real democracy.

But scholars who take on the challenge of moral and ethical activist work cannot rely solely on others to make sense of their work and translate it into usable form. Patricia Hill Collins (1998) speaks of a "visionary pragmatism" (p. 188) that may be helpful in the development of more politically and socially engaged scholarship. She uses this term to characterize the perspective of the working-class women of her childhood:

> The Black women on my block possessed a "visionary pragmatism" that emphasized the necessity of linking caring, theoretical vision with informed, practical struggle. A creative tension links visionary thinking and practical action. Any social theory that becomes too out of touch with everyday people and their lives, especially oppressed people, is of little use to them. The functionality and not just the logical consistency of visionary thinking determines its worth. At the same time, being too practical, looking only to the here and now—especially if present conditions seemingly offer little hope—can be debilitating. (p. 188)

Scholars must also engage new forms of scholarship that make translations of their work more seamless. Guinier and Torres (2002) speak to us of "political race" as a new conception we can embrace. Castillo (1994) offers magical realism as a rubric for Chicano coalescence. Lowe (1996) has taken up notions of hybridity, heterogeneity, and multiplicity to name the material contradictions that characterize immigrant groups—particularly Asian-descent immigrants—who are routinely lumped together and homogenized into a unitary and bounded category. Espiritu (2003) helps us link the study of race and ethnicity to the study of imperialism so that we can better understand transnational and diasporic lives. Similarly, Ong (1999) warns of the growing threat of global capital that destabilizes notions of cultural unity and/or allegiance. Instead, the overwhelming power of multinational corporations creates economic cleavages that force people, regardless of their racial, cultural, and ethnic locations, to chase jobs and compete against each other to subsist.

Promising scholarship that may disrupt the fixed categories that whiteness has instantiated appears in work by Prashad (2002), who examines the cross-racial and interracial connections that reflect the reality of our histories and current conditions. Prashad (2002) argues that instead of the polarized notions of either "color-blindness" or a primordial "multiculturalism," what we seek is a "polyculturalism," a term he borrows from Robin D. G. Kelley (1999), who argues that "so-called 'mixed-race' children are not the only ones with a claim to multiple heritages. All of us, and I mean ALL of us, are the inheritors of European, African, Native-American, and even Asian pasts, even if we can't exactly trace our bloodlines to all of these continents" (p. 6). Kelley (1999) further argues that our various cultures "have never been easily identifiable, secure in their boundaries, or clear to all people who live in or outside our skin. We were multi-ethnic and polycultural from the get-go" (p. 6). This challenge to notions of ethnic purity moves us away from the futile chase for "authenticity" and troubles the reification of ethnic and racial categories. We begin to understand, as political activist Rev. Al Sharpton has said, that "all my skin folks, ain't my kin folks." Just because people look like us by no means implies that they have our best interests at heart.

At the street level, we must acknowledge the power of hip-hop culture. It is important that we distinguish our acknowledgment from the negatives that corporate interests promulgate—violence, racism, misogyny, and crass consumerism—from hip-hop as a vehicle for cross-racial, cross-cultural, and international coalitions. Organizations such as El Puente Academy for Peace and Justice in the Williamsburg section of Brooklyn, New York, and the Urban Think Tank Institute (www.UrbanThinkTank.org) provide a more democratic and politically progressive discourse. The Urban Think Tank Institute argues that the hip-hop generation "has become more politically sophisticated . . . [and needs] a space whereby grassroots thinkers, activists, and artists can come together, discuss relevant issues, devise strategies, and then articulate their analysis to the public and to policy makers" (see Yvonne Bynoe on the Urban Think Tank Web site). Such organizations have corollaries in the earlier work of Myles Horton (1990; Horton & Freire, 1990), Paulo Freire (1970), Septima Clark (with Brown, 1990), Marcus Garvey's Universal Negro Improvement Association (Prashad, 2002), and the Boggs Center (Boggs, 1971). It also resembles the worldwide liberation movements we have seen in India, South Africa, China, Brazil, Zimbabwe, and most everywhere in the world where people have organized to resist oppression and domination.

The hip-hop movement reminds us of the stirrings of the youth and young adults in the modern civil rights movement. When it became clear that the older, more conservative leadership was unwilling to make a space for young people in the movement, we began to see a new form of liberation work. Instead of attempting to assimilate and assert our rights as Americans, young people began to assert their rights to a distinct identity in which being an American may have been constitutive of this identity but it was not the all-encompassing identity. Hip-hop's wide appeal, across geopolitical and ethnic boundaries (we found hip-hop Web sites in Latvia, Russia, Italy, and Japan) makes it a potent force for mobilizing young people worldwide. Unfortunately, most scholars (and, for that matter, most adults) have narrow views of hip hop.[6] They see it merely as rap music and "gangsta" culture. However, the power of hip hop is in its diffuse-ness. It encompasses art, music, dance, and self-presentation. Although much of the media attention has focused on notorious personalities such as Biggie Smalls, Snoop Dogg, P. Diddy, 50-Cent, Nelly, and others, there is a core group of hip-hop artists whose major purpose was to provide social commentary and awaken a somnambulant generation of young people from their drug, alcohol, and materialistic addictions. Some of these artists sought to contextualize the present conditions of the African American and other marginalized communities of color and call for action by making historical links to ideas (e.g., Black Power), social movements (e.g., cultural nationalism), and political figures (e.g., Malcolm X, Che Guevara). The need for this kind of work is not unlike the call of Ngugi wa Thiongo (1991), who argued, in speaking of the emerging independent African nations, that we needed a radically democratic proposal for the production of art, literature, and culture based on our political praxis. Looking at the U.S. scene, Dyson (1993) argues:

> Besides being the most powerful form of Black musical expression today, rap music projects a style of self into the world that generates forms of cultural resistance and transforms the ugly terrain of ghetto existence into a searing portrait of life as it must be lived by millions of voiceless people. For that reason alone, rap deserves attention and should be taken seriously. (p. 15)

Counted among these visionary hip-hop leaders[7] are Grandmaster Flash, Public Enemy, Run-DMC, The Fugees, Lauryn Hill, KRS-1, Diggable Planets, Arrested Development, the Roots, Mos Def, Common, Erykah Badu, the whole host of Nuyorican poets, and the organic intellectuals that produce *YO Magazine* in the San Francisco Bay area. These are the people who have the ears (and hearts and minds) of young people. It is among this group that new forms of scholarship that take up moral and ethical positions will be forged. Scholars who choose to ignore the trenchant pleas of the hip-hop generation will find themselves increasingly out of touch and irrelevant to the everyday lives of people engaged in the cause of social justice.

A number of scholars have made connections with the hip-hop generation: Miguel Algarin, with his ties to both the academy and the Nuyorican Poet's Café; Cornel West and Michael Eric Dyson, with their face-to-face conversations with the hip-hop generation; and bell hooks, with her revolutionary black feminism. The late poet June Jordan, Toni Morrison, Pablo Neruda, Carlos Bulosan, John Okada, Diego Rivera, Leslie Marmon Silko, Sherman Alexie, and others have deployed their art to speak across the generations.

Social scientists must similarly situate themselves to play a more active and progressive role in the fight for equity and social justice. Their work must transcend narrow disciplinary boundaries if it is to have any impact on people who reside in subaltern sites or even on policy makers. Unfortunately, far too many academics spend their time talking to each other in the netherworld of the academy. We write in obscure journals and publish books in languages that do not translate to the lives and experiences of real people. We argue not for the seeming "simplicity" of the political right, but for the relevancy and the power of the popular.

▣ Reconstruction of the Work of the Intellect

> *Don't push me, cause I'm close to the edge I'm trying not to lose my head. It's like a jungle sometimes, it makes me wonder How I keep from going under.*
>
> —From *The Message*, by Grandmaster Flash

It is typical for institutional recommendations to call for a "transformation" of some kind. In this case, were we to suggest that the academy needed to be transformed, we imagine that many would agree. However, transformation implies a change that emanates from an existing base. Clark Kent transformed himself into Superman, but underneath the blue tights, he was still Clark Kent. Britt Reid transformed himself into the Green Hornet, but underneath the mask he was still Britt Reid. Captain John Reid's brother Dan transformed himself into the Lone Ranger, but under that powder blue, skintight outfit and mask he was still Dan Reid. What we are urging is the equivalent of having Jimmy Olsen, Kato, and Tonto assume the leadership and implement the plan.

Reconstruction comes after the destruction of what was. The Union Army did not attempt to massage the South into a new economy after the U.S. Civil War. The Cuban Revolution was not Fidel Castro's attempt to adapt the Battista regime. The new South Africa is not trying to organize a new form of apartheid with black dominance. Rather, these are instances where we see the entire destruction of the old in an attempt to make something new. So it may have to be with the academy in order for it to be responsive to the needs of everyday people.

The student movement at San Francisco State College (Prashad, 2002) revolutionized not only that local campus but also campuses across the country. It formed the basis for the development of what Wynter (1992) called "new studies" in black, Latino, Asian, and Native American studies. It provided a template for women's studies, gay and lesbian studies, and disability studies. It reconfigured knowledge from static, fixed disciplines with the perception of cumulative information, to a realization of the dynamic and overlapping nature of knowledge and a more fluid sense of epistemology and methodology. But even with the strides made by these new studies, they still represent a very small crack in the solid, almost frozen traditions of the university. Indeed, the more careerist interests have made a more indelible imprint on colleges and universities in the United States. Instead of seeing colleges and universities as the site of liberal education and free thinking, increasing numbers of young people (and their parents) see the university as a job training facility. Courses and programs of study in hotel and restaurant management, criminal justice, and sports management,[8] while representing legitimate job and career choices, are less likely to promote overall university goals of educating people to engage with knowledge and critical thinking across a wide variety of disciplines and traditions.

A reconstructed university would displace much of the credentialing function of the current system and organize itself around principles of intellectual enrichment, social justice, social betterment, and equity. Students would see the university as a vehicle for public service, not merely personal advancement. Students would study various courses and programs of study in an attempt to improve both their minds and the condition of life in the community, society, and the world. Such a program has little or no chance of success in our current sociopolitical atmosphere. Although colleges and universities are legitimately categorized as nonprofit entities, they do have fiscal responsibilities. Currently, those fiscal responsibilities are directed to continued employment of elites, supplying a well-prepared labor force, and increasing endowments. In a reconstructed university, the fiscal responsibility would be directed toward community development and improving the socioeconomic infrastructure.

A reconstructed university would have a different kind of reward system in which teaching and service were true equals to research and scholarship. Perhaps these components would be more seamlessly wedded and more tightly related. Excellence would be judged by quality efforts in all areas. Admission to such a university would involve more complex standards being applied in evaluating potential students. Instead of examining strict grade point averages, class rankings, standardized test scores, and inflated résumés,[9] colleges and universities could begin to select students for their ability to contribute to the body politic that will be formed on a particular campus.

Democracy is a complicated system of government, and it requires an educated citizenry to participate actively in it. By educated, we are referring not merely to holding degrees and credentials, but to knowing enough to, as Freire (1970) insists, "read the word and the world." We recognize the need for "organic intellectuals"[10] to help us as credentialed intellectuals do the reconstructive work. We find it interesting (and paradoxical) that education at the two ends of the continuum (precollegiate and adult education) seem to be more progressive and proactive (at least from the point of view of the literature they produce and respond to). Colleges and universities seem to function as incubators for the soon-to-be (or wannabe) guardians of the status quo. Too many of our college and university students want to assume a place in the current society without using their collegiate years as an opportunity to consider how the society could be different and how it could be more just.

Among precollegiate educators, Grace Boggs (1971) has developed a "new system of education" that makes a radical break from the current system that is designed to "prepare the great majority [of citizens] for labor and to advance a few out of their ranks to join the elite in governing" (p. 32). Boggs's (1971) vision is for a "new system of education that will have as its means and its ends the development of the great masses of people *to govern over themselves and to administer over things*" (p. 32). Boggs's system of education calls for an education that must do the following:

- Be based on a philosophy of history—in order to realize his or her highest potential as a human being, every young person must be given a profound and continuing sense (a) of his or her own life as an integral part of the continuing evolution of the human species; and (b) of the unique capacity of human beings to shape and create reality in accordance with conscious purposes and plans;
- Include productive activity—productive activity, in which individuals choose a task and participate in its execution from beginning to end, remains the most effective and rapid means to internalize the relationship between cause and effect, between effort and result, between purposes (ends) and programs (means), an internalization which is necessary to rational behavior, creative thinking, and responsible activity;
- Include living struggles—every young person must be given expanding opportunities to solve the problems of his [*sic*] physical and social environment, thereby developing the political and technical skills which are urgently needed to transform the social institutions as well as the physical environments of our communities and cities;
- Include a wide variety of resources and environments—in our complex world, education must be consciously organized to take place not only in schools and not only using teachers and technology, but also a multiplicity of physical and social environments (e.g., the countryside, the city, the sea, factories, offices, other countries, other cultures);
- Include development in bodily self-knowledge and well-being—increased scientific and technological knowledge necessitates more active participation by lay people and a greater focus on preventive medicine. Students must learn how to live healthy lives and work to reverse the devastating health conditions in poor and working-class communities;
- Include clearly defined goals—education must move away from achieving more material goods and/or fitting people into the existing unequal structure. Education's primary purpose must be governing. (pp. 33–36)

Early scholars in adult education (Freire, 1970; M. Horton, 1990; M. Horton & Freire, 1990) understood the need to develop education imbued with social purpose and grounded in grassroots, popular organizing movements. Although there are a number of such examples, because of space limitations we will focus on the Highlander Folk School. Aimee Horton (1989) documents the school's history and points out that its relationship with social movements is the key to understanding both the strength and the limitations of its adult education program. The two—social movement and adult education—form a symbiotic relationship. As Myles Horton (1990) himself suggests:

> It is only in a movement that an idea is often made simple enough and direct enough that is can spread rapidly. . . . We cannot create movements, so if we want to be a part of a movement when it comes, we have to get ourselves into a position—by working with organizations that deal with structural change—to be on the inside of that movement when it comes, instead of on the outside trying to get accepted. (p. 114)

Highlander always saw itself as part of the larger goals of social movements while simultaneously "maintaining a critical and challenging voice within" (Heaney,1995, p. 57). Highlander based its work on two major components—an education grounded in the "real and realizable struggles of people for democratic control over their lives" (Heaney, 1995, p. 57) and the need to challenge people to consider the present and the future simultaneously as they move toward social change.

The Citizenship Schools (which functioned between 1953 and 1961), one of Highlander's programs, were designed to help African American citizens of the deep South to become literate *and* protest for their rights. According to Horton (1990), "you can't read and write yourself into freedom. You [have] to fight for that and you [have] to do it as part of a group, not as an individual" (p. 104). The Citizenship Schools are a far cry from current adult literacy and vocational programs that have no political commitment and encourage individual and simple solutions to major social problems (Heaney, 1995).

We are skeptical of the academy's ability to reconstruct itself because of the complicity of its intellectuals with the current social order. Thus, we agree with Foucault (1977), who insists:

> Intellectuals are no longer needed by the masses to gain knowledge: the masses know perfectly well, without illusion; they know far better than the intellectual and they are certainly capable of expressing themselves. But there exists a system of power which blocks, prohibits, and invalidates this discourse and this knowledge, a power not only found in manifest authority of censorship, but one that profoundly and subtly penetrates an entire societal network. Intellectuals are themselves agents of this system of power—the idea of their responsibility for "consciousness" and discourse forms part of the system. (p. 207)

Concluding Thoughts: In Search of Revolutionary Habitus

> *As soon as possible he [the white man] will tell me that it is not enough to try to be white, but that a white totality must be achieved.*
>
> —Frantz Fanon (1986)

Our previous section suggests an almost nihilistic despair about the role of the intellectual in leading us toward more just and equitable societies. Actually, we point to the limits of the academy and suggest that committed intellectuals must move into spaces beyond the academy to participate in real change. Indeed, such a move may mean that academics take on less prominent roles in order to listen and learn from people actively engaged in social change. Thus, we speak to an audience who is willing to search for a revolutionary habitus.

Bourdieu (1990) brought us the concept of habitus, which he vaguely defines as a system of

> durable, transposable dispositions, structured structures predisposed to function as structuring structures, that is, as principles which generate and organize practices and representations that can be objectively adapted to their outcomes without presupposing a conscious aiming at ends or an express mastery of the operations necessary in order to attain them. Objectively "regulated" and "regular" without being in any way the product of obedience to the rules, they can be collectively orchestrated without being the product of the organizing action of a conductor. (p. 53)

Thus, according to Palumbo-Liu (1993), "individuals are inclined to act in certain ways given their implicit understanding of, their 'feel for,' the field" (p. 6). The habitus "expresses first the result of an organizing action with a meaning close to that of words such as structure: it also designates a way of being, a habitual state (especially of the body) and, in particular, a disposition, a tendency, propensity, or inclination" (Bourdieu, 1977, p. 214). This work provides us with both "the flexibility of what might otherwise be thought of as a strictly determinative structure (the field) and the ambiguity of a predisposed but not mandated agency (habitus) [and] signal Bourdieu's desire to go beyond the usual binary categories of external/internal, conscious/unconscious, determinism/free agency" (Palumbo-Liu, 1993, p. 7).

Our call for a revolutionary habitus recognizes that the "field" (Bourdieu, 1990) in which academics currently function constrains the social (and intellectual) agency that might move us toward social justice and human liberation. As Palumbo-Liu (1993) points out, a field is

> a particular grid of relations that governs specific areas of social life (economics, culture, education, politics, etc.): individuals do not act freely to achieve their goals and the creation of dispositions must be understood within historically specific formations of fields; each field had its own rules and protocols that open specific social positions for different agents. Yet this is not a static model: the field in turn is modified according to the manner in which those positions are occupied and mobilized. (p. 6)

Thus, despite notions of academic freedom and tenure, professors work within a field that may delimit and confine political activity and views unpopular with university administrators, state and national legislators, and policy makers. Subtle and not so subtle sanctions have the power to shape how individuals' habituses conform to the field. We must imagine new fields and new habituses that constitute a new vision of what it means to do academic work. According to Palumbo-Liu (1993), "The habitus we might imagine for social agents has not yet become habituated to postmodern globalized culture that continues to be reshaped as we speak. The field of culture must now be understood to accommodate both dominant and emergent social groups who differently and significantly inflect the consumption and production of an increasingly global and hybrid culture" (p. 8).

Perhaps our notion of a revolutionary habitus might better be realized through Espiritu's (2003) powerful conceptualization of "home," in which there is a keen awareness of the way racialized immigrants "from previously colonized nations are not exclusively formed as racial minorities within the United States but also as colonized nationals while in their 'homeland'—one that is deeply affected by U.S. influences and modes of social organization" (p. 1). Espiritu (2003) points out that the notion of home is not merely a physical place but is also "a concept and desire—a place that immigrants visit through the imagination" (p. 10). We assert that even those long-term racialized residents of the United States (e.g., African Americans, American Indians, Latinos) have experienced (and continue to experience) colonial oppression (Ladson-Billings, 1998a).

What Espiritu (2003) offers is a way to think about the permeable nature of concepts like race, culture, ethnicity, gender, and ability. Rather than become fixated on who is included and who is excluded, we need to consider the way that we are all border dwellers who negotiate and renegotiate multiple places and spaces. According to Mahmud (cited in Espiritu, 2003), "immigrants call into question implicit assumptions about 'fixed identities, unproblematic nationhood, invisible sovereignty, ethnic homogeneity, and exclusive citizenship'" (p. 209).

Thus, the challenge of those of us in the academy is not how to make those outside the academy more like us, but rather to recognize the "outside the academy" identities that we must recruit for ourselves in order to be more effective researchers on behalf of people who can make use of our skills and abilities. We must learn to be "at home" on the street corners and in the barrios, churches, mosques, kitchens, porches, and stoops of people and communities, so that our work more accurately reflects their concerns and interests. Our challenge is to renounce our paternalistic tendencies and sympathetic leanings to move toward an empathic, ethical, and moral scholarship that propels us to a place where we are prepared to forcefully and courageously answer "the call."

▣ Notes

1. We are using the term "of color" to refer to all people who are raced and outside the construction of whiteness (Haney Lopez, 1998).

2. Paulo Freire (1970) insists that "that the oppressed are not 'marginals,' are not men living 'outside' society. They have always been 'inside'—inside the structure that made them 'beings' for others" (p. 71).

3. "Articulate" is a term seemingly reserved for African Americans and is seen by African Americans as a way to suggest that one speaks better than would be expected of "your kind."

4. We are restating at length portions of Ladson-Billings's (2000) discussion on alterity and liminality that appeared in the second edition of this handbook.

5. We remind the reader that we are aware of the dilemma of using racialized categories and that the boundaries between and among various racial, ethnic, and cultural groups are more permeable and more complex than the categories imply.

6. MacArthur Fellow and civil rights leader Bernice Johnson Reagon asserts that no one has the right to tell the next generation what their freedom songs should be (Moyers, 1991).

7. We are aware that we are not acknowledging all of the artists in this tradition.

8. We want to be clear that we do not disparage these career choices; however, we question whether they represent what is meant by "liberal arts."

9. Increasingly, students seeking admission to selective colleges and universities participate in extracurricular activities (e.g., sports, clubs, the arts) and volunteer efforts not because of interests and commitments but rather because such participation may give them an advantage over other applicants.

10. We use this term to describe those grassroots people whose intellectual power convicts and persuades the masses of people to investigate and explore new ideas for human liberation. The late John Henrik Clark (New York), Clarence Kailin, (Madison, WI), and the late James Boggs and his wife Grace Lee Boggs (Detroit) are examples of organic intellectuals.

References

Acuna, R. (1972). *Occupied America: The Chicano struggle toward liberation.* New York: Canfield Press.

Alarcon, N. (1990). Chicana feminism: In the tracks of "the" native woman. *Cultural Studies, 4,* 248–256.

Alexie, S. (1993). *The Lone Ranger and Tonto fistfight in heaven.* New York: Atlantic Monthly Press.

Allen, B., & Wilson, E. J. (1984). Foreword. In H. Cruse, *The crisis of the Negro intellectual* (pp. i–vi). New York: Quill.

Almaguer, T. (1974). Historical notes on Chicano oppression: The dialectics of racial and class domination in North America. *Aztlan, 5*(1–2), 27–56.

Anzaldúa, G. (1987). *Borderlands/la frontera: The new mestiza.* San Francisco: Ante Lute Press.

Balderrama, F. E. (1982). *In defense of La Raza: The Los Angeles Mexican consulate and the Mexican community, 1929–1936.* Tucson: University of Arizona Press.

Bell, D. (1992). *Faces at the bottom of the well: The permanence of racism.* New York: Basic Books.

Bell, D. (2002). *Ethical ambition.* New York: Bloomsbury.

Boggs, G. L. (1971). *Education to govern* [Pamphlet]. Detroit: All-African People's Union.

Bourdieu, P. (1977). *Outline of a theory of practice.* Cambridge:, UK Cambridge University Press.

Bourdieu, P. (1990). *The logic of practice* [R. Nice, Trans.]. Stanford, CA: Stanford University Press.

Campbell, B. M. (1995). *Your blues ain't like mine.* New York: Ballantine.

Castillo, A. (1994). *So far from God.* New York: Plume.

Castillo, A. (1995). *Massacre of the dreamers: Essays on Xicanisima.* New York: Plume.

Clark, S. (with Brown, C. S., ed.). (1990). *Ready from within: A first person narrative.* Trenton, NJ: Africa World Press.

Collins, P. H. (1998). *Fighting words: Black women and the search for justice.* Minneapolis: University of Minnesota Press.

Cruse, H. (1984). *The crisis of the Negro intellectual.* New York: Quill. (Original work published 1967)

de la Torre, A., & Pesquera, B. (Eds.). (1993). *Building with our hands: New directions in Chicano studies.* Berkeley: University of California Press.

Delgado Bernal, D. (1998). Using a Chicana feminist epistemology in educational research. *Harvard Educational Review, 68,* 555–582.

DuBois, W.E.B. (1953). *The souls of black folks.* New York: Fawcett. (Original work published 1903)

Dyson, M. E. (1993). *Reflecting Black: African American cultural criticism.* Minneapolis: University of Minnesota Press.

Espiritu, Y. L. (1992). *Asian American panethnicity: Bridging institutions and identities.* Philadelphia: Temple University Press.

Espiritu, Y. L. (2003). *Home bound: Filipino American lives across cultures, communities, and countries.* Berkeley: University of California Press.

Eyre, C. (Director). (1998). *Smoke signals* [Motion picture]. Los Angeles: Miramax.

Fanon, F. (1968). *The wretched of the earth.* New York: Grove.

Fanon, F. (1986). *Black skin, white masks.* London: Pluto Press.

Fanon, F. (1994). On national culture. In P. Williams & L. Chrisman (Eds.), *Colonial discourse and post-colonial theory* (pp. 36–52). New York: Columbia University Press.

Foucault, M. (1977). *Language, counter-memory, practice.* Ithaca, NY: Cornell University Press.

Freire, P. (1970). *Pedagogy of the oppressed.* New York: Continuum.

Gilman, R. (2000). *Spinning into butter.* Woodstock, IL: Dramatic Publishing.

Gomez-Quinones, J. (1977). On culture. *Revista Chicano-Riquena, 5*(2), 35–53.

Guinier, L., & Torres, G. (2002). *Miner's canary: Enlisting race, resisting power, transforming democracy.* Cambridge, MA: Harvard University Press.

Haney Lopez, I. (1998). *White by law: The legal construction of race.* New York: New York University Press.

Health News Network. (2000). *A history of secret human experimentation.* Retrieved December 28, 2004, from www.skyhighway.com/~chemtrails911/docs/human_experiments.html

Heaney, T. (1995). When adult education stood for democracy. *Adult Education Quarterly,* 43(1), 51–59.

Hertzberg, H. W. (1971). *The search for an American Indian identity.* Syracuse, NY: Syracuse University Press.

Horton, A. (1989). *The Highlander Folk School: A history of its major programs, 1932–1961.* Brooklyn, NY: Carlson.

Horton, M., with Kohl, H., & Kohl, J. (1990). *The long haul: An autobiography.* New York: Doubleday.

Horton, M., & Freire, P. (1990). *We make the road by walking: Conversations on education and social change.* Philadelphia: Temple University Press.

Ikemoto, L. (1995). Traces of the master narrative in the story of African American/Korean American conflict: How we constructed "Los Angeles." In R. Delgado (Ed.), *Critical race theory: The cutting edge* (pp. 305–315). Philadelphia: Temple University Press.

Kelley, R.D.G. (1999). People in me. *Colorlines, 1*(3), 5–7.

Kennedy, R. (2001, February). The triumph of robust tokenism. *The Atlantic online.* Retrieved from http://www.theatlantic.com/issues/2001/02/kennedy.htm

Kennedy, R. (2002). *Nigger: The strange career of a troublesome word.* New York: Pantheon.

King, J. E. (1995). Culture centered knowledge: Black studies, curriculum transformation, and social action. In J. A. Banks & C. M. Banks (Eds.), *Handbook of research on multicultural education* (pp. 265–290). New York: Macmillan.

Kuhn, T. (1962). *The structure of scientific revolutions.* Chicago: University of Chicago Press.

Ladson-Billings, G. (1998a). From Soweto to the South Bronx: African Americans and colonial education in the United States. In C. A. Torres & T. Mitchell (Eds.), *Sociology of education: Emerging perspectives* (pp. 247–264). Albany: SUNY Press.

Ladson-Billings, G. (1998b). Just what is critical race theory and what is it doing in a "nice" field like education? *International Journal of Qualitative Studies in Education, 11,* 7–24.

Ladson-Billings, G. (2000). Racialized discourses and ethnic epistemologies. In N. Denzin & Y. Lincoln (Eds.), *Handbook of qualitative research* (2nd ed., pp. 257–277). Thousand Oaks, CA: Sage.

Lahiri, J. (1999). *Interpreter of maladies.* Boston: Houghton Mifflin.

Legesse, A. (1973). *Gada: Three approaches to the study of an African society.* New York: Free Press.

Lewis, D. L. (1993). *W.E.B. DuBois: Biography of a race (1868-1919).* New York: Henry Holt.

Lipsitz, G. (1998). *The possessive investment in whiteness: How white people profit from identity politics.* Philadelphia: Temple University Press.

Lipsky, M. (1983). *Street-level bureaucrats.* New York: Russell Sage Foundation.

Lomawaima, K. T. (1995). Educating Native Americans. In J. A. Banks & C. M. Banks (Eds.), *Handbook of research on multicultural education* (pp. 331–347). New York: Macmillan.

Lowe, L. (1996). *Immigrant acts: On Asian-American cultural politics.* Durham, NC: Duke University Press.

Mann, B. (2003, October 6). New York weighs lead-paint laws [Radio broadcast]. *All Things Considered.* Washington, DC: National Public Radio.

Mayr, E. (1976). *Evolution and the diversity of life.* Cambridge, MA: Belknap Press.

McClintock, A. (1994). The angel of progress: Pitfalls of the term "post-colonialism." In P. Williams & L. Chrisman (Eds.), *Colonial discourse and post-colonial theory* (pp. 291–304). New York: Columbia University Press.

McIntosh, P. (1988). *White privilege and male privilege: A personal account of coming to see correspondences through work in women's studies* (Working Paper 189). Wellesley, MA: Wellesley College Center for Research on Women.

Miah, M. (1999). Race and politics: Black voters and "brother" Clinton. *Against the Current.* Retrieved from http://solidarity.igc.org/atc/78Miah.html

Minh-ha, T. (1989). *Woman, narrative, other: Writing postcoloniality and feminism.* Bloomington: Indiana University Press.

Mirande, A., & Enriquez, E. (1979). *La Chicana: The Mexican American woman.* Chicago: University of Chicago Press.

Mohanty, C. T. (1991). Under western eyes: Feminist scholarship and colonial discourses. In C. T. Mohanty, A. Russo, & L. Torres (Eds.), *Third World women and the politics of feminism* (pp. 50–80). Bloomington: Indiana University Press.

Morrison, T. (1987). *Beloved.* New York: Vintage Books.

Moyers, B. (Producer), & Pellett, G. (Director). (1991, February). *The songs are free: Interview with Bernice Johnson Reagon* [Video recording]. Princeton, NJ: Films for the Humanities & Sciences.

Oboler, S. (1995). *Ethnic lives, ethnic labels.* Minneapolis: University of Minnesota Press.

Ong, A. (1999). *Flexible citizenship: The cultural logics of transnationality.* Raleigh, NC: Duke University Press.

Padilla, F. (1987). *Latino ethnic consciousness.* Notre Dame, IN: Notre Dame University Press.

Palumbo-Liu, D. (1993). Introduction: Unhabituated habituses. In D. Palumbo-Liu & H. U. Gumbrecht (Eds.), *Streams of cultural capital: Transnational cultural studies* (pp. 1–21). Stanford, CA: Stanford University Press.

Paz, O. (1961). *The labyrinth of solitude: Life and thought in Mexico.* New York: Random House.

Perry, S. (1996, May 29). *Bill Clinton's politics of meaning.* Retrieved from ww.citypages.com/databank/17/808/article2724.asp

Popkewitz, T. (2003). Is the National Research Council Committee's report on scientific research in education scientific? On trusting the manifesto. *Qualitative Inquiry, 10*(1), 62–78.

Prashad, V. (2002). *Everybody was Kung Fu fighting: Afro-Asian connections and the myth of cultural purity.* New York: Beacon.

Roediger, D. (2002). *Colored White: Transcending the racial past.* Berkeley: University of California Press.

Shavelson, R., & Towne, L. (Eds.). (2003). *Scientific research in education.* Washington, DC: National Academies Press.

Smith, L. T. (1998). *Decolonising methodologies: Research and indigenous peoples.* London: Zed Books.

Snipp, C. M. (1995). American Indian studies. In J. A. Banks & C. M. Banks (Eds.), *Handbook of research on multicultural education* (pp. 245–258). New York: Macmillan.

Spivak, G. C. (1990). Explanation and culture: Marginalia. In R. Ferguson, M. Gever, & T. T. Minh-ha (Eds.), *Out there: Marginalization and contemporary cultures* (pp. 377–393). Cambridge, MA: MIT Press.

Spradley, J. (1979). *The ethnographic interview.* New York: Holt, Rinehart & Winston.

Tate, G. (2003). Introduction: Nigs R Us, or how Blackfolks became fetish objects. In G. Tate (Ed.), *Everything but the burden: What white people are taking from Black culture* (pp. 1–14). New York: Broadway Books.

Tuskegee Syphilis Study Legacy Committee. (1996, May 26). *Final report.* Washington, DC: Author.

wa Thiongo, N. (1991). *Decolonising the mind.* Nairobi: Heinemann Kenya.

Warrior, R. A. (1995). *Tribal secrets: Recovering American Indian intellectual traditions.* Minneapolis: University of Minnesota Press.

West, C. (1990). The new cultural politics of difference. In R. Ferguson, M. Gever, & T. T. Minh-ha (Eds.), *Out there: Marginalization and contemporary cultures* (pp. 19–36). Cambridge, MA: MIT Press.

Wong, S. (1995). *American knees.* New York: Simon & Schuster.

Wynter, S. (1992). *Do not call us "negros": How "multicultural" textbooks perpetuate racism.* San Francisco: Aspire Books.

12

RETHINKING CRITICAL THEORY AND QUALITATIVE RESEARCH

Joe L. Kincheloe and Peter McLaren

Our Idiosyncratic Interpretation of Critical Theory and Critical Research

Over the past 25 years of our involvement in critical theory and critical research, we have been asked by hundreds of people to explain more precisely what critical theory is. We find that question difficult to answer because (a) there are many critical theories, not just one; (b) the critical tradition is always changing and evolving; and (c) critical theory attempts to avoid too much specificity, as there is room for disagreement among critical theorists. To lay out a set of fixed characteristics of the position is contrary to the desire of such theorists to avoid the production of blueprints of sociopolitical and epistemological beliefs. Given these disclaimers, we will now attempt to provide one idiosyncratic "take" on the nature of critical theory and critical research in the first decade of the 21st century. Please note that this is merely our subjective analysis and that there are many brilliant critical theorists who will find many problems with our pronouncements. In this spirit, we tender a description of an ever-evolving criticality, a reconceptualized critical theory that was critiqued and overhauled by the "post-discourses" of the last quarter of the 20th century and has been further extended in the first years of the 21st century (Bauman, 1995; Carlson & Apple, 1998; Collins, 1995; Giroux, 1997; Kellner, 1995; Peters, Lankshear, & Olssen, 2003; Roman & Eyre, 1997; Steinberg & Kincheloe, 1998; Weil & Kincheloe, 2003).

In this context, a reconceptualized critical theory questions the assumption that societies such as the United States, Canada, Australia, New Zealand, and the nations in the European Union, for example, are unproblematically democratic and free. Over the 20th century, especially after the early 1960s, individuals in these societies were acculturated to feel comfortable in relations of domination and subordination rather than equality and independence. Given the social and technological changes of the last half of the century that led to new forms of information production and access, critical theorists argued that questions of self-direction and democratic egalitarianism should be reassessed. In this context, critical researchers informed by the "post-discourses" (e.g., postmodern, critical feminism, poststructuralism) came to understand that individuals' view of themselves and the world were even more influenced by social and historical forces than previously believed. Given the changing social and informational conditions of late 20th-century and early 21st-century media-saturated Western culture, critical theorists have needed new ways of researching and analyzing the construction of individuals (Agger, 1992; Flossner & Otto, 1998; Hinchey, 1998; Leistyna, Woodrum, & Sherblom, 1996; Quail, Razzano, & Skalli, 2004; Skalli, 2004; R. Smith & Wexler, 1995; Sünker, 1998; Wesson & Weaver, 2001).

Partisan Research in a "Neutral" Academic Culture

In the space available here, it is impossible to do justice to all of the critical traditions that have drawn inspiration from Marx; Kant; Hegel; Weber; the Frankfurt School theorists; Continental social theorists such as Foucault, Habermas, and Derrida; Latin American thinkers such as Paulo Freire; French feminists such as Irigaray, Kristeva, and Cixous; or Russian sociolinguists such as Bakhtin and Vygotsky—most of whom regularly find their way into the reference lists of contemporary critical researchers. Today there are criticalist schools in many fields, and even a superficial discussion of the most prominent of these schools would demand much more space than we have available.

The fact that numerous books have been written about the often-virulent disagreements among members of the Frankfurt School only heightens our concern with the "packaging" of the different criticalist schools. Critical theory should not be treated as a universal grammar of revolutionary thought objectified and reduced to discrete formulaic pronouncements or strategies. Obviously, in presenting our idiosyncratic version of a reconceptualized critical theory or an evolving criticality, we have defined the critical tradition very broadly for the purpose of generating understanding; as we asserted earlier, this will trouble many critical researchers. In this move, we decided to focus on the underlying commonality among critical schools of thought, at the cost of focusing on differences. This, of course, is always risky business in terms of suggesting a false unity or consensus where none exists, but such concerns are unavoidable in a survey chapter such as this.

We are defining a criticalist as a researcher or theorist who attempts to use her or his work as a form of social or cultural criticism and who accepts certain basic assumptions: that all thought is fundamentally mediated by power relations that are social and historically constituted; that facts can never be isolated from the domain of values or removed from some form of ideological inscription; that the relationship between concept and object and between signifier and signified is never stable or fixed and is often mediated by the social relations of capitalist production and consumption; that language is central to the formation of subjectivity (conscious and unconscious awareness); that certain groups in any society and particular societies are privileged over others and, although the reasons for this privileging may vary widely, the oppression that characterizes contemporary societies is most forcefully reproduced when subordinates accept their social status as natural, necessary, or inevitable; that oppression has many faces and that focusing on only one at the expense of others (e.g., class oppression versus racism) often elides the interconnections among them; and, finally, that mainstream research practices are generally, although most often unwittingly, implicated in the reproduction of systems of class, race, and gender oppression (Kincheloe & Steinberg, 1997).

In today's climate of blurred disciplinary genres, it is not uncommon to find literary theorists doing anthropology and anthropologists writing about literary theory, political scientists trying their hand at ethnomethodological analysis, or philosophers doing Lacanian film criticism. All these inter-/cross-disciplinary moves are examples of what Norman Denzin and Yvonna Lincoln (2000) have referred to as bricolage—a key innovation, we argue, in an evolving criticality. We will explore this dynamic in relation to critical research later in this chapter. We offer this observation about blurred genres not as an excuse to be wantonly eclectic in our treatment of the critical tradition but to make the point that any attempts to delineate critical theory as discrete schools of analysis will fail to capture the evolving hybridity endemic to contemporary critical analysis (Kincheloe, 2001a; Kincheloe & Berry, 2004).

Readers familiar with the criticalist traditions will recognize essentially four different "emergent" schools of social inquiry in this chapter: the neo-Marxist tradition of critical theory associated most closely with the work of Horkheimer, Adorno, and Marcuse; the genealogical writings of Michel Foucault; the practices of poststructuralist deconstruction associated with Derrida; and postmodernist currents associated with Derrida, Foucault, Lyotard, Ebert, and others. In our view, critical ethnography has been influenced by all these perspectives in different ways and to different degrees. From critical theory, researchers inherit a forceful criticism of the positivist conception of science and instrumental rationality, especially in Adorno's idea of negative dialectics, which posits an unstable relationship of contradiction between concepts and objects; from Derrida, researchers are given a means for deconstructing objective truth, or what is referred to as "the metaphysics of presence."

For Derrida, the meaning of a word is constantly deferred because the word can have meaning only in relation to its difference from other words within a given system of language. Foucault invites researchers to explore the ways in which discourses are implicated in relations of power and how power and knowledge serve as dialectically reinitiating practices that regulate what is considered reasonable and true. We have characterized much of the work influenced by these writers as the "ludic" and "resistance" postmodernist theoretical perspectives. Critical research can be understood best in the context of the empowerment of individuals. Inquiry that aspires to the name "critical" must be connected to an attempt to confront the injustice of a particular society or public sphere within the society. Research thus becomes a transformative endeavor unembarrassed by the label "political" and unafraid to consummate a relationship with emancipatory consciousness. Whereas traditional researchers cling to the guardrail of neutrality, critical researchers frequently announce their partisanship in the struggle for a better world (Grinberg, 2003; Horn, 2000; Kincheloe, 2001b).

The work of Brazilian educator Paulo Freire is instructive in relation to constructing research that contributes to the struggle for a better world. The research of both authors of this chapter has been influenced profoundly by the work of Freire (1970, 1972, 1978, 1985). Always concerned with human suffering and the pedagogical and knowledge work that helped expose the genesis of it, Freire modeled critical research throughout his career. In his writings about research, Freire maintained that there are no traditionally defined objects of his research—he insisted on involving, as partners in the research process, the people he studied as subjects. He immersed himself in their ways of thinking and modes of perception, encouraging them all along to begin thinking about their own thinking. Everyone involved in Freire's critical research, not just the researcher, joined in the process of investigation, examination, criticism, and reinvestigation—everyone learned to see more critically, think at a more critical level, and to recognize the forces that subtly shape their lives.

Whereas traditional researchers see their task as the description, interpretation, or reanimation of a slice of reality, critical researchers often regard their work as a first step toward forms of political action that can redress the injustices found in the field site or constructed in the very act of research itself. Horkheimer (1972) puts it succinctly when he argues that critical theory and research are never satisfied with merely increasing knowledge (see also Agger, 1998; Andersen, 1989; Britzman, 1991; Giroux, 1983, 1988, 1997; Kincheloe, 1991, 2003c; Kincheloe & Steinberg, 1993; Quantz, 1992; Shor, 1996; Villaverde & Kincheloe, 1998). Research in the critical tradition takes the form of self-conscious criticism—self-conscious in the sense that researchers try to become aware of the ideological imperatives and epistemological presuppositions that inform their research as well as their own subjective, intersubjective, and normative reference claims. Thus, critical researchers enter into an investigation with their assumptions on the table, so no one is confused concerning the epistemological and political baggage they bring with them to the research site.

Upon detailed analysis, critical researchers may change these assumptions. Stimulus for change may come from the critical researchers' recognition that such assumptions are not leading to emancipatory actions. The source of this emancipatory action involves the researchers' ability to expose the contradictions of the world of appearances accepted by the dominant culture as natural and inviolable (Giroux, 1983, 1988, 1997; McLaren, 1992, 1997; San Juan, 1992; Zizek, 1990). Such appearances may, critical researchers contend, conceal social relationships of inequality, injustice, and exploitation. For instance, if we view the violence we find in classrooms not as random or isolated incidents created by aberrant individuals willfully stepping out of line in accordance with a particular form of social pathology, but as possible narratives of transgression and resistance, then this could indicate that the "political unconscious" lurking beneath the surface of everyday classroom life is not unrelated to practices of race, class, and gender oppression but rather intimately connected to them.

An Evolving Criticality

In this context, it is important to note that we understand a social theory as a map or a guide to the social sphere. In a research context, it does not determine how we see the world but helps us devise questions and strategies for exploring it. A critical social theory is concerned in particular with issues of power and justice and the ways that the economy; matters of race, class, and gender; ideologies; discourses; education; religion and other social institutions; and cultural dynamics interact to construct a social system (Beck-Gernsheim, Butler, & Puigvert, 2003; Flecha, Gomez, & Puigvert, 2003). Thus, in this context we seek to provide a view of an evolving criticality or a reconceptualized critical theory. Critical theory is never static; it is always evolving, changing in light of both new theoretical insights and new problems and social circumstances.

The list of concepts elucidating our articulation of critical theory indicates a criticality informed by a variety of discourses emerging after the work of the Frankfurt School. Indeed, some of the theoretical discourses, while referring to themselves as critical, directly call into question some of the work of Horkheimer, Adorno, and Marcuse. Thus, diverse theoretical traditions have informed our understanding of criticality and have demanded understanding of diverse forms of oppression including class, race, gender, sexual, cultural, religious, colonial, and ability-related concerns. The evolving notion of criticality we present is informed by, while critiquing, the post-discourses—for example, postmodernism, poststructuralism, and postcolonialism. In this context, critical theorists become detectives of new theoretical insights, perpetually searching for new and interconnected ways of understanding power and oppression and the ways they shape everyday life and human experience.

In this context, criticality and the research it supports are always evolving, always encountering new ways to irritate dominant forms of power, to provide more evocative and compelling insights. Operating in this way, an evolving criticality is always vulnerable to exclusion from the domain of approved modes of research. The forms of social change it supports always position it in some places as an outsider, an awkward detective always interested in uncovering social structures, discourses, ideologies, and epistemologies that prop up both the status quo and a variety of forms of privilege. In the epistemological domain, white, male, class elitist, heterosexist, imperial, and colonial privilege often operates by asserting the power to claim objectivity and neutrality. Indeed, the owners of such privilege often own the "franchise" on reason and rationality. Proponents of an evolving criticality possess a variety of tools to expose such oppressive power politics. Such proponents assert that critical theory is well-served by drawing upon numerous liberatory discourses and including diverse groups of marginalized peoples and their allies in the nonhierarchical aggregation of critical analysts (Bello, 2003; Clark, 2002; Humphries, 1997).

In the present era, emerging forms of neocolonialism and neo-imperialism in the United States move critical theorists to examine the ways American power operates under the cover of establishing democracies all over the world. Advocates of an evolving criticality argue—as we do in more detail later in this chapter—that such neocolonial power must be exposed so it can be opposed in the United States and around the world. The American Empire's justification in the name of freedom for undermining democratically elected governments from Iran (Kincheloe, 2004), Chile, Nicaragua, and Venezuela to Liberia (when its real purpose is to acquire geopolitical advantage for future military assaults, economic leverage in international markets, and access to natural resources) must be exposed by criticalists for what it is—a rank imperialist sham (McLaren, 2003a, 2003b; McLaren & Jaramillo, 2002; McLaren & Martin, 2003). Critical researchers need to view their work in the context of living and working in a nation-state with the most powerful military-industrial complex in history that is shamefully using the terrorist attacks of September 11 to advance a ruthless imperialist agenda fueled by capitalist accumulation by means of the rule of force (McLaren & Farahmandpur, 2003).

Chomsky (2003), for instance, has accused the U.S. government of the "supreme crime" of preventive war (in the case of its invasion of Iraq, the use of military force to destroy an invented or imagined threat) of the type that was condemned at Nuremburg. Others, like historian Arthur Schlesinger (cited in Chomsky, 2003), have likened the invasion of Iraq to Japan's "day of infamy," that is, to the policy that imperial Japan employed at the time of Pearl Harbor. David G. Smith (2003) argues that such imperial dynamics are supported by particular epistemological forms. The United States is an epistemological empire based on a notion of truth that undermines the knowledges produced by those outside the good graces and benevolent authority of the empire. Thus, in the 21st century, critical theorists must develop sophisticated ways to address not only the brute material relations of class rule linked to the mode and relations of capitalist production and imperialist conquest (whether through direct military intervention or indirectly through the creation of client states) but also the epistemological violence that helps discipline the world. Smith refers to this violence as a form of "information warfare" that spreads deliberate falsehoods about countries such as Iraq and Iran. U.S. corporate and governmental agents become more sophisticated in the use of such episto-weaponry with every day that passes.

Obviously, an evolving criticality does not promiscuously choose theoretical discourses to add to the bricolage of critical theories. It is highly suspicious—as we detail later—of theories that fail to understand the malevolent workings of power, that fail to critique the blinders of Eurocentrism, that cultivate an elitism of insiders and outsiders, and that fail to discern a global system of inequity supported by diverse forms of ideology and violence. It is uninterested in any theory—no matter how fashionable—that does not directly address the needs of victims of oppression and the suffering they must endure. The following is an elastic, ever-evolving set of concepts included in our evolving notion of criticality. With theoretical innovations and shifting zeitgeists, they evolve. The points that are deemed most important in one time period pale in relation to different points in a new era.

Critical Enlightenment. In this context, critical theory analyzes competing power interests between groups and individuals within a society—identifying who gains and who loses in specific situations. Privileged groups, criticalists argue, often have an interest in supporting the status quo to protect their advantages; the dynamics of such efforts often become a central focus of critical research. Such studies of privilege often revolve around issues of race, class, gender, and sexuality (Allison, 1998; V. Carter, 1998; Howell, 1998; Kincheloe & Steinberg, 1997; Kincheloe, Steinberg, Rodriguez, & Chennault, 1998; McLaren, 1997; Rodriguez & Villaverde, 2000; Sleeter & McLaren, 1995). In this context, to seek critical enlightenment is to uncover the winners and losers in particular social arrangements and the processes by which such power plays operate (Cary, 1996; Dei, Karumanchery, & Karumanchery-Luik, 2004; Fehr, 1993; King, 1996; Pruyn, 1994; Wexler, 1996a).

Critical Emancipation. Those who seek emancipation attempt to gain the power to control their own lives in solidarity with a justice-oriented community. Here, critical research attempts to expose the forces that prevent individuals and groups from shaping the decisions that crucially affect their lives. In this way, greater degrees of autonomy and human agency can be achieved. In the first decade of the 21st century, we are cautious in our use of the term "emancipation" because, as many critics have pointed out, no one is ever completely emancipated from the sociopolitical context that has produced him or her. Concurrently, many have used the term "emancipation" to signal the freedom an abstract individual gains by gaining access to Western reason—that is, becoming reasonable. Our use of "emancipation" in an evolving criticality rejects any use of the term in this context. In addition, many have rightly questioned the arrogance that may accompany efforts to emancipate "others." These are important caveats and must be carefully taken into account by critical researchers. Thus, as critical inquirers who search for those forces that insidiously shape who we are, we respect those who reach different conclusions in their personal journeys (Butler, 1998; Cannella, 1997; Kellogg, 1998; Knobel, 1999; Steinberg & Kincheloe, 1998; Weil, 1998).

The Rejection of Economic Determinism. A caveat of a reconceptualized critical theory involves the insistence that the tradition does not accept the orthodox Marxist notion that "base" determines "superstructure"—meaning that economic factors dictate the nature of all other aspects of human existence. Critical theorists understand in the 21st century that there are multiple forms of power, including the aforementioned racial, gender, and sexual axes of domination. In issuing this caveat, however, a reconceptualized critical theory in no way attempts to argue that economic factors are unimportant in the shaping of everyday life. Economic factors can never be separated from other axes of oppression (Aronowitz & DiFazio, 1994; Carlson, 1997; Gabbard, 1995; Gee, Hull, & Lankshear, 1996; Gibson, 1986; Kincheloe, 1995, 1999; Kincheloe & Steinberg, 1999; Martin & Schuman, 1996). Mechanistic formulations of economic determinism are often misreadings of the work of Marx. McLaren's work, for instance, does not reject the base/superstructure model *tout court*, but only undialectical formulations of it (see McLaren & Farahmandpur, 2001).

The Critique of Instrumental or Technical Rationality. A reconceptualized critical theory sees instrumental/technical rationality as one of the most oppressive features of contemporary society. Such a form of "hyper-reason" involves an obsession with means in preference to ends. Critical theorists claim that instrumental/technical rationality is more interested in method and efficiency than in purpose. It delimits its topics to "how to" instead of "why should." In a research context, critical theorists claim that many rationalistic scholars become so obsessed with issues of technique, procedure, and correct method that they forget the humanistic purpose of the research act. Instrumental/technical rationality often separates fact from value in its obsession with "proper" method, losing in the process an understanding of the value choices always involved in the production of so-called facts (Alfino, Caputo, & Wynyard, 1998; Giroux, 1997; Hinchey, 1998; Kincheloe, 1993; McLaren, 1998; Ritzer, 1993; Stallabrass, 1996; M. Weinstein, 1998).

The Concept of Immanence. Critical theory is always concerned with what could be, what is immanent in various ways of thinking and perceiving. Thus, critical theory should always move beyond the contemplative realm to concrete social reform. In the spirit of Paulo Freire, our notion of an evolving critical theory possesses immanence as it imagines new ways to ease human suffering and produce psychological health (A.M.A. Freire,

2001; Slater, Fain, & Rossatto, 2002). Critical immanence helps us get beyond egocentrism and ethnocentrism and work to build new forms of relationship with diverse peoples. Leila Villaverde (2003) extends this point about immanence when she maintains that critical theory helps us "retain a vision of the not yet." In the work of the Frankfurt School critical theory and the hermeneutics of Hans-Georg Gadamer (1989) we find this concern with immanence. Gadamer argues that we must be more cautious in our efforts to determine "what is" because it holds such dramatic consequences for how we engage "what ought to be." In Gadamer's view, the process of understanding involves interpreting meaning and applying the concepts gained to the historical moment that faces us. Thus, immanence in the context of qualitative research involves the use of human wisdom in the process of bringing about a better and more just world, less suffering, and more individual fulfillment. With this notion in mind, critical theorists critique researchers whose scholarly work operates to adapt individuals to the world as it is. In the context of immanence, critical researchers are profoundly concerned with who we are, how we got this way, and where we might go from here (Weil & Kincheloe, 2003).

A Reconceptualized Critical Theory of Power: Hegemony. Our conception of a reconceptualized critical theory is intensely concerned with the need to understand the various and complex ways that power operates to dominate and shape consciousness. Power, critical theorists have learned, is an extremely ambiguous topic that demands detailed study and analysis. A consensus seems to be emerging among criticalists that power is a basic constituent of human existence that works to shape the oppressive and productive nature of the human tradition. Indeed, we are all empowered and we are all unempowered, in that we all possess abilities and we are all limited in the attempt to use our abilities. Because of limited space, we will focus here on critical theory's traditional concern with the oppressive aspects of power, although we understand that an important aspect of critical research focuses on the productive aspects of power—its ability to empower, to establish a critical democracy, to engage marginalized people in the rethinking of their sociopolitical role (Apple, 1996; Fiske, 1993; A.M.A. Freire, 2000; Giroux, 1997; Macedo, 1994; Nicholson & Seidman, 1995). In the context of oppressive power and its ability to produce inequalities and human suffering, Antonio Gramsci's notion of hegemony is central to critical research. Gramsci understood that dominant power in the 20th century was not always exercised simply by physical force but also was expressed through social psychological attempts to win people's consent to domination through cultural institutions such as the media, the schools, the family, and the church. Gramscian hegemony recognizes that the winning of popular consent is a very complex process and must be researched carefully on a case-by-case basis. Students and researchers of power, educators, sociologists, all of us are hegemonized as our field of knowledge and understanding is structured by a limited exposure to competing definitions of the sociopolitical world. The hegemonic field, with its bounded sociopsychological horizons, garners consent to an inequitable power matrix—a set of social relations that are legitimated by their depiction as natural and inevitable. In this context, critical researchers note that hegemonic consent is never completely established, as it is always contested by various groups with different agendas (Grossberg, 1997; Lull, 1995; McLaren, 1995a, 1995b; McLaren, Hammer, Reilly, & Sholle, 1995; West, 1993). We note here that Gramsci famously understood Marx's concept of laws of tendency as implying a new immanence and a new conception of necessity and freedom that cannot be grasped within a mechanistic model of determination (Bensaid, 2002).

A Reconceptualized Critical Theory of Power: Ideology. Critical theorists understand that the formation of hegemony cannot be separated from the production of ideology. If hegemony is the larger effort of the powerful to win the consent of their "subordinates," then ideological hegemony involves the cultural forms, the meanings, the rituals, and the representations that produce consent to the status quo and individuals' particular places within it. Ideology vis-à-vis hegemony moves critical inquirers beyond explanations of domination that have used terms such as "propaganda" to describe the ways media, political, educational, and other sociocultural productions coercively manipulate citizens to adopt oppressive meanings. A reconceptualized critical research endorses a much more subtle, ambiguous, and situationally specific form of domination that refuses the propaganda model's assumption that people are passive, easily manipulated victims. Researchers operating with an awareness of this hegemonic ideology understand that dominant ideological practices and discourses shape our vision of reality (Lemke, 1995, 1998). Thus, our notion of hegemonic ideology is a critical form of epistemological constructivism buoyed by a nuanced understanding of power's complicity in the constructions people make of the world and their role in it (Kincheloe, 1998). Such an awareness corrects earlier delineations of ideology as a monolithic, unidirectional entity that was imposed on individuals by a secret cohort of ruling-class czars. Understanding domination in the context of concurrent struggles among different classes, racial and gender groups, and sectors of capital, critical researchers of ideology explore the ways such competition engages different visions, interests, and agendas in a variety of social locales—venues previously thought to be outside the domain of ideological struggle (Brosio, 1994; Steinberg, 2001).

A Reconceptualized Critical Theory of Power: Linguistic/Discursive Power. Critical researchers have come to understand that language is not a mirror of society. It is an unstable social practice whose meaning shifts, depending upon the context in which it is used. Contrary to previous understandings, critical researchers appreciate the fact that language is not a neutral and objective conduit of description of the "real world." Rather, from a critical perspective, linguistic descriptions are not simply about the world but serve to construct it. With these linguistic notions in mind, criticalists begin to study the way language in the form of discourses serves as a form of regulation and domination. Discursive practices are defined as a set of tacit rules that regulate what can and cannot be said, who can speak with the blessings of authority and who must listen, whose social constructions are valid and whose are erroneous and unimportant. In an educational context, for example, legitimated discourses of power insidiously tell educators what books may be read by students, what instructional methods may be utilized, and what belief systems and views of success may be taught. In all forms of research, discursive power validates particular research strategies, narrative formats, and modes of representation. In this context, power discourses undermine the multiple meanings of language, establishing one correct reading that implants a particular hegemonic/ideological message into the consciousness of the reader. This is a process often referred to as the attempt to impose discursive closure. Critical researchers interested in the construction of consciousness are very attentive to these power dynamics. Engaging and questioning the use value of particular theories of power is central to our notion of an evolving criticality (Blades, 1997; Gee, 1996; Lemke, 1993; McWilliam & Taylor, 1996; Morgan, 1996; Steinberg, 2001).

Focusing on the Relationships Among Culture, Power, and Domination. In the last decades of the 20th century, culture took on a new importance in the critical effort to understand power and domination. Critical researchers have argued that culture has to be viewed as a domain of struggle where the production and transmission of knowledge is always a contested process (Giroux, 1997; Kincheloe & Steinberg, 1997; McLaren, 1997; Steinberg & Kincheloe, 1997). Dominant and subordinate cultures deploy differing systems of meaning based on the forms of knowledge produced in their cultural domain. Popular culture, with its TV, movies, video games, computers, music, dance, and other productions, plays an increasingly important role in critical research on power and domination. Cultural studies, of course, occupies an ever-expanding role in this context, as it examines not only popular culture but also the tacit rules that guide cultural production. Arguing that the development of mass media has changed the way the culture operates, cultural studies researchers maintain that cultural epistemologies in the first decade of the 21st century are different from those of only a few decades ago. New forms of culture and cultural domination are produced as the distinction between the real and the simulated is blurred. This blurring effect of hyperreality constructs a social vertigo characterized by a loss of touch with traditional notions of time, community, self, and history. New structures of cultural space and time generated by bombarding electronic images from local, national, and international spaces shake our personal sense of place. This proliferation of signs and images functions as a mechanism of control in contemporary Western societies. The key to successful counter-hegemonic cultural research involves (a) the ability to link the production of representations, images, and signs of hyperreality to power in the political economy and (b) the capacity, once this linkage is exposed and described, to delineate the highly complex effects of the reception of these images and signs on individuals located at various race, class, gender, and sexual coordinates in the web of reality (R. Carter, 2003; Cary, 2003; Ferguson & Golding, 1997; Garnham, 1997; Grossberg, 1995; Jackson & Russo, 2002; Joyrich, 1996; O'Riley, 2003; Rose & Kincheloe, 2003; Sanders-Bustle, 2003; Steinberg, 1997a, 1997b; Thomas, 1997; Wexler, 2000).

The Centrality of Interpretation: Critical Hermeneutics. One of the most important aspects of a critical theory–informed qualitative research involves the often-neglected domain of the interpretation of information. The critical hermeneutic tradition (Grondin, 1994; Gross & Keith,1997; Rosen, 1987; Vattimo, 1994) holds that in qualitative research, there is only interpretation, no matter how vociferously many researchers may argue that the facts speak for themselves. The hermeneutic act of interpretation involves, in its most elemental articulation, making sense of what has been observed in a way that communicates understanding. Not only is all research merely an act of interpretation, but, hermeneutics contends, perception itself is an act of interpretation. Thus, the quest for understanding is a fundamental feature of human existence, as encounter with the unfamiliar always demands the attempt to make meaning, to make sense. The same, however, is also the case with the familiar. Indeed, as in the study of commonly known texts, we come to find that sometimes the familiar may be seen as the most strange. Thus, it should not be surprising that even the so-called objective writings of qualitative research are interpretations, not value-free descriptions (Denzin, 1994; Gallagher, 1992; Jardine, 1998; Mayers, 2001; D. G. Smith, 1999). Learning from the hermeneutic tradition and the postmodern critique, critical researchers have begun to reexamine textual claims to authority. No pristine interpretation exists—indeed, no methodology, social or educational theory, or discursive form can claim a privileged position that enables the production of authoritative knowledge. Researchers must always speak/write about the world in terms of something else in the world, "in relation to . . ." As creatures of the world, we are oriented to it in a way that prevents us from grounding our theories and perspectives outside it. The critical hermeneutics that grounds critical qualitative research moves more in the direction of a normative hermeneutics in that it raises questions about the purposes and procedures of interpretation. In its critical theory–driven context, the purpose of hermeneutical analysis is to develop a form of cultural criticism revealing power dynamics within social and cultural texts. Qualitative researchers familiar with critical hermeneutics build bridges between reader and text, text and its producer, historical context and present, and one particular social circumstance and another. Accomplishing such interpretive tasks is difficult, and researchers situated in normative hermeneutics push ethnographers, historians, semioticians, literary critics, and content analysts to trace the bridge-building processes employed by successful interpretations of knowledge production and culture (Gallagher, 1992; Kellner, 1995; Kogler, 1996; Rapko, 1998). Grounded by this hermeneutical bridge building, critical researchers in a hermeneutical circle (a process of analysis in which interpreters seek the historical and social dynamics that shape textual interpretation) engage in the back-and-forth of studying parts in relation to the whole and the whole in relation to parts. Deploying such a methodology, critical researchers can produce profound insights that lead to transformative action (Berger, 1995; Cary, 1996; Clough, 1998; Coben,1998; Gadamer, 1989; Goodson, 1997; Kincheloe & Berry, 2004; Miller & Hodge, 1998; Mullen, 1999; Peters & Lankshear, 1994).

The Role of Cultural Pedagogy in Critical Theory. Cultural production often can be thought of as a form of education, as it generates knowledge, shapes values, and constructs identity. From our perspective, such a framing can help critical researchers make sense of the world of domination and oppression as they work to bring about a more just, democratic, and egalitarian society. In recent years, this educational dynamic has been referred to as cultural pedagogy (Berry, 1998; Giroux, 1997; Kincheloe, 1995; McLaren, 1997; Pailliotet, 1998; Semali, 1998; Soto, 1998). "Pedagogy" is a useful term that traditionally has been used to refer only to teaching and schooling. By using the term "cultural pedagogy," we are specifically referring to the ways particular cultural agents produce particular hegemonic ways of seeing. In our critical interpretive context, our notion of cultural pedagogy asserts that the new "educators" in the electronically wired contemporary era are those who possess the financial resources to use mass media. This corporate-dominated pedagogical process has worked so well that few complain about it in the first decade of the 21st century—such informational politics doesn't make the evening news. Can we imagine another institution in contemporary society gaining the pedagogical power that corporations now assert over information and signification systems? What if the Church of Christ was sufficiently powerful to run pedagogical "commercials" every few minutes on TV and radio touting the necessity for everyone to accept that denomination's faith? Replayed scenes of Jews, Muslims, Hindus, Catholics, and Methodists being condemned to hell if they rejected the official pedagogy (the true doctrine) would greet North Americans and their children 7 days a week. There is little doubt that many people would be outraged and would organize for political action. Western societies have to some degree capitulated to this corporate pedagogical threat to democracy, passively watching an elite gain greater control over the political system and political consciousness via a sophisticated cultural pedagogy. Critical researchers are intent on exposing the specifics of this process (Deetz, 1993; Drummond, 1996; Kincheloe, 2002; Molnar, 1996; Pfeil, 1995; Rose & Kincheloe, 2003; Steinberg & Kincheloe, 1997).

▣ Critical Research and Cultural Studies

Cultural studies is an interdisciplinary, transdisciplinary, and sometimes counterdisciplinary field that functions within the dynamics of competing definitions of culture. Unlike traditional humanistic studies, cultural studies questions the equation of culture with high culture; instead, cultural studies asserts that myriad expressions of cultural production should be analyzed in relation to other cultural dynamics and social and historical structures. Such a position commits cultural studies to a potpourri of artistic, religious, political, economic, and communicative activities. In this context, it is important to note that although cultural studies is associated with the study of popular culture, it is not primarily about popular culture. The interests of cultural studies are much broader and generally tend to involve the production and nature of the rules of inclusivity and exclusivity that guide academic evaluation—in particular, the way these rules shape and are shaped by relations of power. The rules that guide academic evaluation are inseparable from the rules of knowledge production and research. Thus, cultural studies provides a disciplinary critique that holds many implications (Abercrombie, 1994; Ferguson & Golding, 1997; Grossberg, 1995; Hall & du Gay, 1996; Kincheloe, 2002; McLaren, 1995a; Oberhardt, 2001; Woodward, 1997).

One of the most important sites of theoretical production in the history of critical research has been the Centre for Contemporary Cultural Studies (CCCS) at the University of Birmingham. Attempting to connect critical theory with the particularity of everyday experience, the CCCS researchers have argued that all experience is vulnerable to ideological inscription. At the same time, they have maintained that theorizing outside everyday experience results in formal and deterministic theory. An excellent representative of the CCCS's perspectives is Paul Willis, whose *Learning to Labour: How Working Class Kids Get Working Class Jobs* was published in 1977, 7 years after Colin Lacey's *Hightown Grammar* (1970). Redefining the nature of ethnographic research in a critical manner, *Learning to Labour* inspired a spate of critical studies: David Robins and Philip Cohen's *Knuckle Sandwich: Growing Up in the Working-Class City* in 1978, Paul Corrigan's *Schooling the Smash Street Kids* in 1979, and Dick Hebdige's *Subculture: The Meaning of Style* in 1979. Also following Willis's work were critical feminist studies, including an anthology titled *Women Take Issue* (Women's Studies Group, 1978). In 1985, Christine Griffin published *Typical Girls?*, the first extended feminist study produced by the CCCS. Conceived as a response to Willis's *Learning to Labour, Typical Girls?* analyzes adolescent female consciousness as it is constructed in a world of patriarchy. Through their recognition of patriarchy as a major disciplinary technology in the production of subjectivity, Griffin and the members of the CCCS gender study group moved critical research in a multicultural direction.

In addition to the examination of class, gender and racial analyses are beginning to gain in importance (Quantz, 1992). Poststructuralism frames power not simply as one aspect of a society but as the basis of society. Thus, patriarchy is not simply one isolated force among many with which women must contend; patriarchy informs all aspects of the social and effectively shapes women's lives (see also Douglas, 1994; Finders, 1997; Fine, Powell, Weis, & Wong, 1997; Frankenberg, 1993; Franz & Stewart, 1994; Shohat & Stam, 1994). Cornel West (1993) pushes critical research even further into the multicultural domain as he focuses critical attention on women, the Third World, and race. Adopting theoretical advances in neo-Marxist postcolonialist criticism and cultural studies, he is able to shed greater light on the workings of power in everyday life.

In this context, Ladislaus Semali and Joe Kincheloe, in *What Is Indigenous Knowledge? Voices from the Academy* (1999), explore the power of indigenous knowledge as a resource for critical attempts to bring about social change. Critical researchers, they argue, should analyze such knowledges in order to understand emotions, sensitivities, and epistemologies that move in ways unimagined by many Western knowledge producers. In this postcolonially informed context, Semali and Kincheloe employ concerns raised by indigenous knowledge to challenge the academy, its "normal science," and its accepted notions of certified information. Moving the conversation about critical research in new directions, these authors understand the conceptual inseparability of valuing indigenous knowledge, developing postcolonial forms of resistance, academic reform, the reconceptualization of research and interpretation, and the struggle for social justice.

In *Schooling as a Ritual Performance,* Peter McLaren (1999) integrates poststructuralist, postcolonialist, and Marxist theory with the projects of cultural studies, critical pedagogy, and critical ethnography. He grounds his theoretical analysis in the poststructuralist claim that the connection of signifier and signified is arbitrary yet shaped by historical, cultural, and economic forces. The primary cultural narrative that defines school life is the resistance by students to the school's attempts to marginalize their street culture and street knowledge. McLaren analyzes the school as a cultural site where symbolic capital is struggled over in the form of ritual dramas. *Schooling as a Ritual Performance* adopts the position that researchers are unable to grasp themselves or others introspectively without social mediation through their positionalities with respect to race, class, gender, and other configurations. The visceral, bodily forms of knowledge, and the rhythms and gestures of the street culture of the students, are distinguished from the formal abstract knowledge of classroom instruction. The teachers regard knowledge as it is constructed informally outside the culture of school instruction as threatening to the universalist and decidedly Eurocentric ideal of high culture that forms the basis of the school curriculum.

As critical researchers pursue the reconceptualization of critical theory pushed by its synergistic relationship with cultural studies, postmodernism, and poststructuralism, they are confronted with the post-discourses' redefinition of critical notions of democracy in terms of multiplicity and difference. Traditional notions of community often privilege unity over diversity in the name of Enlightenment values. Poststructuralists in general and poststructuralist feminists in particular see this communitarian dream as politically disabling because of the suppression of race, class, and gender differences and the exclusion of subaltern voices and marginalized groups whom community members are loath to engage. What begins to emerge in this instance is the movement of feminist theoretical concerns to the center of critical theory. Indeed, after the feminist critique, critical theory can never return to a paradigm of inquiry in which the concept of social class is antiseptically privileged and exalted as the master concept in the Holy Trinity of race, class, and gender.

A critical theory reconceptualized by poststructuralism and feminism promotes a politics of difference that refuses to pathologize or exoticize the Other. In this context, communities are more prone to revitalization and revivification (Wexler, 1996b, 1997); peripheralized groups in the thrall of a condescending Eurocentric gaze are able to edge closer to the borders of respect, and "classified" objects of research potentially acquire the characteristics of subjecthood. Kathleen Weiler's *Women Teaching for Change: Gender, Class, and Power* (1988) serves as a good example of critical research framed by feminist theory. Weiler shows not only how feminist theory can extend critical research but also how the concept of emancipation can be reconceptualized in light of a feminist epistemology. In this context, we clearly observe the way our notion of an evolving criticality operates. Criticalists inform poststructuralists and feminists, who in turn critique and extend the subject matter and the approach of more traditional forms of critical research. Though not always without contention, such a process is in the long-term interests of a vibrant critical theory that continues to matter in the world (Aronowitz & Giroux, 1991; Behar & Gordon, 1995; Bersani, 1995; Brents & Monson, 1998; Britzman, 1995; Christian-Smith & Keelor, 1999; Clatterbaugh, 1997; Clough, 1994; Cooper, 1994; Hedley, 1994; Johnson, 1996; Kelly, 1996; King & Mitchell, 1995; Lugones, 1987; Maher & Tetreault, 1994; Morrow, 1991; Rand, 1995; Scott, 1992; Sedgwick, 1995; Steinberg, 1997b; I. Young, 1990).

In the last few years, Norman Denzin (2003) has initiated a major turn in cultural studies with his notion of a performative ethnography. As a critical and emancipatory discourse, a performative cultural studies connects Giroux's, McLaren's, and Kincheloe's articulations of critical pedagogy with new ways of writing and performing cultural politics. Denzin carefully argues that performance-based human disciplines can catalyze democratic social change. Moving like the coyote trickster, Denzin proposes a cultural studies of action that decenters subjectivity as it questions the status quo. Defining performance as an "act of intervention, a method of resistance, a form of criticism, a way of revealing agency" (p. 9), Denzin shapes his notion of performativity in the spirit of Henry Giroux's (2003) work in cultural studies and critical pedagogy. Performance in cultural studies becomes public pedagogy when it employs the aesthetic and performative in the effort to portray the interactions connecting politics, institutions, and experience. Thus, performance for Denzin becomes a form of human agency that brings individuals together with culture in an enacted manner.

Denzin's important ideas intersect with Peter Reason and William Torbert's (2001) concept of the action turn. In the action turn, Reason and Torbert reconceptualize the nature and purpose of social science. Because human beings, they tell us,

> are all participating actors in the world, the purpose of inquiry is not simply or even primarily to contribute to the fund of knowledge in a field, to deconstruct taken-for-granted realities, or even

> to develop emancipatory theory, but rather to forge a more direct link between intellectual knowledge and moment-to-moment personal and social action, so that inquiry contributes directly to the flourishing of human persons, their communities, and the ecosystems of which they are part. (p. 2)

In this context, we find an intersection between Denzin's performativity and the shift to action from social science's emphasis on abstract knowledge. In both articulations, the focus of social research is critical, as it focuses on the improvement of the human condition, community development, and the strengthening of the ecosystems in which people and communities operate. In this spirit, Denzin, in *Performative Ethnography* (2003), uses racism as an example of a problem that can be addressed by a critical performative social science. Connecting his work to the research of W.E.B. DuBois and bell hooks, Denzin seeks to write and perform cultural dynamics around race in innovative ways. In this context, he positions political acts as pedagogical and performative. In this way, the researcher opens fresh venues for democratic citizenship and transformative dialogue. In light of the racial violence of the contemporary era, Denzin applies his performative ethnography to help us imagine alternative social realities, new modes of discourse, and fresh experiences in schools, workplaces, wilderness areas, and other public spaces.

Thus, Denzin pushes cultural studies and its attendant criticality that moves from textual ethnography to a performative autoethnography, while connecting it to critical pedagogy's concept of making the political more pedagogical and the pedagogical more political. Critical in the way it confronts mainstream ways of knowing and representing the world, Denzin's performativity is better tailored to engage postcolonial and subaltern cultural practices. In addition to connecting to the action turn in research documented by Reason and Torbert, Denzin's performativity also connects to Humberto Mautaurana and Francisco Varela's Santiago school of Enactivism in cognitive theory. If performance ethnography and cultural studies highlight immediacy and involvement, then Enactivism's concern with the importance of *enacting* cognition in the complexity and complications of lived experience can possibly synergize our insights into the realm of performance. With the help of the social, pedagogical, political, and cognitive theories, critical researchers begin to understand that the social world may be more complex than we have been taught. Denzin's performativity helps us get closer to this complexity.

This interaction connecting performance ethnography, the action turn, and Enactivism moves critical researchers to explore their work in relation to recent inquiry about our evolving view of the human mind. Looking at the concept of mind from biological, psychological, and social perspectives, Enactivists begin the reparation process necessitated by the Western rationalistic abstraction, reduction, and fragmentation of the world. When Enactivism is added to our notion of an evolving criticality, we emerge with a powerful grounding for a reconceptualization of the research act. Kincheloe and Steinberg (1993, 1996, 1999) and numerous other cognitive theorists have argued, in the spirit of Lev Vygotsky, over the last two decades, that cognition and the knowledge it produces are socially situated activities that take place in concrete historical situations (Kincheloe, 2003b). Varela adds to this description, arguing that it is in the particular historical circumstance that we realize who we are and what we can become. Indeed, we realize our cognitive capabilities in the specific concrete circumstance while concurrently gaining the power to imagine what capabilities we can develop.

As criticalists engage Denzin's performativity, the action turn, and Enactivist principles of systemic self-organization (autopoiesis), critical research moves into a new zone of emergent complexity. In this context, when advocates of a critical form of inquiry use the term "transformative action," they gain a deeper sense of what this might mean using the enactivist concept of readiness-for-action. Knowledge must be enacted—understood at the level of human beings' affect and intellect. In a critical context, the knowledge we produce must be enacted in light of our individual and collective struggles. Without this dimension, the research act becomes a rather abstract enterprise. Nothing new *emerges*, as knowledges and concepts are merely produced rather than related to one another and enacted (performed) in the world. In this enacted context, Denzin argues, cultural studies develops a new way of encountering the cosmos. Epistemological notions of performance and performativity enter into a dynamic tension between doing and the done, the saying and the said. In this productive tension, distance and detachment are overcome in the act of performing. Improvisation, a key dynamic in all these intersecting discourses of inquiry, constructs the moment where resistance emerges, where the doing and the done merge.

In this performative, action-oriented moment, criticalists escape the confines of the stale debate between positivist empiricism and postmodern interpretivism. A new dawn breaks for our evolving criticality and research in cultural studies, as researchers study themselves in relation to others in the effort to produce a practical form of knowledge represented in an action-oriented, performative manner. A new performative, action-oriented, and Enactivist-informed paradigm helps critical researchers develop new ways of inquiring in action-based everyday interactions and lived processes. These interactions and processes are always "sensuous and contingent," Denzin notes. In order for an ethnographer or cultural studies researcher to represent such dynamics, new modes of research are necessary. By definition, the performative ethnography that Denzin offers shatters the textual conventions that traditionally have operated to represent lived experiences. Critical ethnography and cultural studies will never be the same after performativity and the participatory epistemology on which it is based explode the boundaries of acceptable research practice.

▣ Critical Research Encounters the Bricolage

Using the concept of bricolage, as articulated by the editors of this handbook, Norman Denzin and Yvonna Lincoln, Joe Kincheloe develops the notion as an extension of the concept of evolving criticality developed in this chapter. Lincoln and Denzin use the term in the spirit of Claude Levi-Strauss (1966) and his lengthy discussion of it in *The Savage Mind.* The French word *bricoleur* describes a handyman or handywoman who makes use of the tools available to complete a task (Harper, 1987). Some connotations of the term involve trickery and cunning and remind me of the chicanery of Hermes, in particular his ambiguity concerning the messages of the gods. If hermeneutics came to connote the ambiguity and slipperiness of textual meaning, then bricolage can also imply the fictive and imaginative elements of the presentation of all formal research. Indeed, as cultural studies of science have indicated, all scientific inquiry is jerry-rigged to a degree; science, as we all know by now, is not nearly as clean, simple, and procedural as scientists would have us believe. Maybe this is an admission that many in our field would wish to keep in the closet.

In the first decade of the 21st century, bricolage typically is understood to involve the process of employing these methodological strategies as they are needed in the unfolding context of the research situation. While this interdisciplinary feature is central to any notion of the bricolage, critical qualitative researchers must go beyond this dynamic. Pushing to a new conceptual terrain, such an eclectic process raises numerous issues that researchers must deal with in order to maintain theoretical coherence and epistemological innovation. Such multidisciplinarity demands a new level of research self-consciousness and awareness of the numerous contexts in which any researcher is operating. As one labors to expose the various structures that covertly shape our own and other scholars' research narratives, the bricolage highlights the relationship between a researcher's ways of seeing and the social location of his or her personal history. Appreciating research as a power-driven act, the critical researcher-as-bricoleur abandons the quest for some naïve concept of realism, focusing instead on the clarification of his or her position in the web of reality and the social locations of other researchers and the ways they shape the production and interpretation of knowledge.

In this context, bricoleurs move into the domain of complexity. The bricolage exists out of respect for the complexity of the lived world and the complications of power. Indeed, it is grounded on an epistemology of complexity. One dimension of this complexity can be illustrated by the relationship between research and the domain of social theory. All observations of the world are shaped either consciously or unconsciously by social theory—such theory provides the framework that highlights or erases what might be observed. Theory in a modernist empiricist mode is a way of understanding that operates without variation in every context. Because theory is a cultural and linguistic artifact, its interpretation of the object of its observation is inseparable from the historical dynamics that have shaped it. The task of the bricoleur is to attack this complexity, uncovering the invisible artifacts of power and culture, and documenting the nature of their influence on not only their own works but on scholarship in general. In this process, bricoleurs act upon the concept that theory is not an explanation of nature—it is more an explanation of our relation to nature.

In its hard labors in the domain of complexity, the bricolage views research methods actively rather than passively, meaning that we actively construct our research methods from the tools at hand rather than passively receiving the "correct," universally applicable methodologies. Avoiding modes of reasoning that come from certified processes of logical analysis, bricoleurs also steer clear of preexisting guidelines and checklists developed outside the specific demands of the inquiry at hand. In its embrace of complexity, the bricolage constructs a far more active role for humans both in shaping reality and in creating the research processes and narratives that represent it. Such an active agency rejects deterministic views of social reality that assume the effects of particular social, political, economic, and educational processes. At the same time and in the same conceptual context, this belief in active human agency refuses standardized modes of knowledge production (Bresler & Ardichvili, 2002; Dahlbom, 1998; Mathie & Greene, 2002; McLeod, 2000; Selfe & Selfe, 1994; T. Young & Yarbrough, 1993).

Some of the best work in the study of social complexity is now taking place in the qualitative inquiry of numerous fields including sociology, cultural studies, anthropology, literary studies, marketing, geography, media studies, informatics, library studies, women's studies, various ethnic studies, education, and nursing. Denzin and Lincoln (2000) are acutely aware of these dynamics and refer to them in the context of their delineation of the bricolage. Yvonna Lincoln (2001), in her response to Kincheloe's development of the bricolage, maintains that the most important border work between disciplines is taking place in feminism and race-ethnic studies.

In many ways, there is a form of instrumental reason, of rational irrationality, in the use of passive, external, monological research methods. In the active bricolage, we bring our understanding of the research context together with our previous experience with research methods. Using these knowledges, we *tinker* in the Levi-Straussian sense with our research methods in field-based and interpretive contexts. This tinkering is a high-level cognitive process involving construction and reconstruction, contextual diagnosis, negotiation, and readjustment. Researchers' interactions with the objects of their inquiries, bricoleurs understand, are always complicated, mercurial, unpredictable, and, of course, complex. Such conditions negate the practice of planning research strategies in advance. In lieu of such rationalization of the process, bricoleurs enter into the research act as methodological negotiators. Always respecting the demands of the task at hand, the bricolage, as conceptualized here, resists its placement in concrete as it promotes its elasticity. Critical researchers are better informed as to the power of the bricolage in light of Yvonna Lincoln's (2001) delineation of two types of bricoleurs: those who (a) are committed to research eclecticism, allowing circumstance to shape methods employed, and (b) want to engage in the genealogy/archeology of the disciplines with some grander purpose in mind. My purpose entails both of Lincoln's articulations of the role of the bricoleur.

Research method in the bricolage is a concept that receives more respect than in more rationalistic articulations of the term. The rationalistic articulation of method subverts the deconstruction of wide varieties of unanalyzed assumptions embedded in passive methods. Bricoleurs, in their appreciation of the complexity of the research process, view research method as involving far more than procedure. In this mode of analysis, bricoleurs come to understand research method as also a technology of justification, meaning a way of defending what we assert we know and the process by which we know it. Thus, the education of critical researchers demands that everyone take a step back from the process of learning research methods. Such a step back allows us a conceptual distance that produces a critical consciousness. Such a consciousness refuses the passive acceptance of externally imposed research methods that tacitly certify modes justifying knowledges that are decontextualized, reductionistic, and inscribed by dominant modes of power (Denzin & Lincoln, 2000; Fenwick, 2000; Foster, 1997; McLeod, 2000).

In its critical concern for just social change, the bricolage seeks insight from the margins of Western societies and the knowledge and ways of knowing of non-Western peoples. Such insight helps bricoleurs reshape and sophisticate social theory, research methods, and interpretive strategies, as they discern new topics to be researched. This confrontation with difference so basic to the concept of the bricolage enables researchers to produce new forms of knowledge that inform policy decisions and political action in general. In gaining this insight from the margins, bricoleurs display once again the blurred boundary between the hermeneutical search for understanding and the critical concern with social change for social justice. Kincheloe has taken seriously Peter McLaren's (2001) important concern—offered in his response to Kincheloe's (2001a) first delineation of his conception of the bricolage—that merely focusing on the production of meanings may not lead to "resisting and transforming the existing conditions of exploitation" (McLaren, 2001, p. 702). In response, Kincheloe maintained that in the critical hermeneutical dimension of the bricolage, the act of understanding power and its effects is merely one part—albeit an inseparable part—of counterhegemonic *action.* Not only are the two orientations not in conflict, they are synergistic (DeVault, 1996; Lutz, Kendall, & Jones, 1997; Soto, 2000; Steinberg, 2001).

To contribute to social transformation, bricoleurs seek to better understand both the forces of domination that affect the lives of individuals from race, class, gender, sexual, ethnic, and religious backgrounds outside of dominant culture(s) and the worldviews of such diverse peoples. In this context, bricoleurs attempt to remove knowledge production and its benefits from the control of elite groups. Such control consistently operates to reinforce elite privilege while pushing marginalized groups farther away from the center of dominant power. Rejecting this normalized state of affairs, bricoleurs commit their knowledge work to helping address the ideological and informational needs of marginalized groups and individuals. As detectives of subjugated insight, bricoleurs eagerly learn from labor struggles, women's marginalization, the "double consciousness" of the racially oppressed, and insurrections against colonialism (Kincheloe & Steinberg, 1993; Kincheloe, Steinberg, & Hinchey, 1999; T. Young & Yarbrough, 1993). In this way, the bricolage hopes to contribute to an evolving criticality.

Thus, the bricolage is dedicated to a form of rigor that is conversant with numerous modes of meaning-making and knowledge production—modes that originate in diverse social locations. These alternative modes of reasoning and researching always consider the relationships, the resonances, and the disjunctions between formal and rationalistic modes of Western epistemology and ontology and different cultural, philosophical, paradigmatic, and subjugated expressions. In these latter expressions, bricoleurs often uncover ways of accessing a concept without resorting to a conventional validated set of prespecified procedures that provide the distance of objectivity (Thayer-Bacon, 2003). This notion of distance fails to take into account the rigor of the hermeneutical understanding of the way meaning is preinscribed in the act of being in the world, the research process, and objects of research. This absence of hermeneutical awareness undermines the researcher's quest for a thick description and contributes to the production of reduced understandings of the complexity of social life (Paulson, 1995; Selfe & Selfe, 1994).

The multiple perspectives delivered by the concept of difference provide bricoleurs with many benefits. Confrontation with difference helps us to see anew, to move toward the light of epiphany. A basic dimension of an evolving criticality involves a comfort with the existence of alternative ways of analyzing and producing knowledge. This is why it's so important for a historian, for example, to develop an understanding of phenomenology and hermeneutics. It is why it is so important for a social researcher from New York City to understand forms of indigenous African knowledge production. The incongruities between such cultural modes of inquiry are quite valuable, for within the tensions of difference rest insights into multiple dimensions of the research act. Such insights move us to new levels of understanding of the subjects, purposes, and nature of inquiry (Burbules & Beck, 1999; Mayers, 2001; Semali & Kincheloe, 1999; Willinsky, 2001).

Difference in the bricolage pushes us into the hermeneutic circle as we are induced to deal with parts in their diversity in relation to the whole. Difference may involve culture, class, language, discipline, epistemology, cosmology, ad infinitum. Bricoleurs use one dimension of these multiple diversities to explore others, to generate questions previously unimagined. As we examine these multiple perspectives, we attend to which ones are validated and which ones have been dismissed. Studying such differences, we begin to understand how dominant power operates to exclude and certify particular forms of knowledge production and why. In the criticality of the bricolage, this focus on power and difference always leads us to an awareness of the multiple dimensions of the social. Paulo Freire (1970) referred to this as the need for perceiving social structures and social systems that undermine equal access to resources and power. As bricoleurs answer such questions, we gain new appreciations of the way power tacitly shapes what we know and how we come to know it.

The Bricolage, a Complex Ontology, and Critical

A central dimension of the bricolage that holds profound implications for critical research is the notion of a critical ontology (Kincheloe, 2003a). As bricoleurs prepare to explore that which is not readily apparent to the ethnographic eye, that realm of complexity in knowledge production that insists on initiating a conversation about what it is that qualitative researchers are observing and interpreting in the world, this clarification of a complex ontology is needed. This conversation is especially important because it hasn't generally taken place. Bricoleurs maintain that this object of inquiry is ontologically complex in that it can't be described as an encapsulated entity. In this more open view, the object of inquiry is always a part of many contexts and processes; it is culturally inscribed and historically situated. The complex view of the object of inquiry accounts for the historical efforts to interpret its meaning in the world and how such efforts continue to define its social, cultural, political, psychological, and educational effects.

In the domain of the qualitative research process, for example, this ontological complexity undermines traditional notions of triangulation. Because of its in-process (processual) nature, inter-researcher reliability becomes far more difficult to achieve. Process-sensitive scholars watch the world flow by like a river in which the exact contents of the water are never the same. Because all observers view an object of inquiry from their own vantage points in the web of reality, no portrait of a social phenomenon is ever exactly the same as another. Because all physical, social, cultural, psychological, and educational dynamics are connected in a larger fabric, researchers will produce different descriptions of an object of inquiry depending on what part of the fabric they have focused on—what part of the river they have seen. The more unaware observers are of this type of complexity, the more reductionistic the knowledge they produce about it. Bricoleurs attempt to understand this fabric and the processes that shape it in as thick a way as possible (Blommaert, 1997).

The design and methods used to analyze this social fabric cannot be separated from the way reality is construed. Thus, ontology and epistemology are linked inextricably in ways that shape the task of the researcher. The bricoleur must understand these features in the pursuit of rigor. A deep interdisciplinarity is justified by an understanding of the complexity of the object of inquiry and the demands such complications place on the research act. As parts of complex systems and intricate processes, objects of inquiry are far too mercurial to be viewed by a single way of seeing or as a snapshot of a particular phenomenon at a specific moment in time.

A deep interdisciplinarity seeks to modify the disciplines and the view of research brought to the negotiating table constructed by the bricolage. Everyone leaves the table informed by the dialogue in a way that idiosyncratically influences the research methods they subsequently employ. The point of the interaction is not standardized agreement as to some reductionistic notion of "the proper interdisciplinary research method" but awareness of the diverse tools in the researcher's toolbox. The form such deep interdisciplinarity may take is shaped by the object of inquiry in question. Thus, in the bricolage the context in which research takes place always affects the nature of the deep interdisciplinarity employed. In the spirit of the dialectic of disciplinarity, the ways these context-driven articulations of interdisciplinarity are constructed must be examined in light of the power literacy previously mentioned (Blommaert, 1997; Friedman, 1998; Pryse, 1998; Quintero & Rummel, 2003; T. Young & Yarbrough, 1993).

In social research, the relationship between individuals and their contexts is a central dynamic to be investigated. This relationship is a key ontological and epistemological concern of the bricolage; it is a connection that shapes the identities of human beings and the nature of the complex social fabric. Thus, bricoleurs use multiple methods to analyze the multidimensionality of this type of connection. The ways bricoleurs engage in this process of putting together the pieces of the relationship may provide a different interpretation of its meaning and effects. Recognizing the complex ontological importance of relationships alters the basic foundations of the research act and knowledge production process. Thin reductionistic descriptions of isolated things-in-themselves are no longer sufficient in critical research (Foster, 1997; Zammito, 1996).

What the bricolage is dealing with in this context is a double ontology of complexity: first, the complexity of objects of inquiry and their being-in-the-world; second, the nature of the social construction of human subjectivity, the production of human "being." Such understandings open a new era of social research where the process of becoming human agents is appreciated with a new level of sophistication. The complex feedback loop between an unstable social structure and the individual can be charted in a way that grants human beings insight into the means by which power operates and the democratic process is subverted. In this complex ontological view, bricoleurs understand that social structures do not *determine* individual subjectivity but *constrain* it in remarkably intricate ways. The bricolage is acutely interested in developing and employing a variety of strategies to help specify these ways subjectivity is shaped.

The recognitions that emerge from such a multiperspectival process get analysts beyond the determinism of reductionistic notions of macrosocial structures. The intent of a usable social or educational research is subverted in this reductionistic context, as human agency is erased by the "laws" of society. Structures do not simply "exist" as objective entities whose influence can be predicted or "not exist" with no influence over the cosmos of human affairs. Here fractals enter the stage with their loosely structured characteristics of irregular shape—fractal structures. While not *determining* human behavior, for example, fractal structures possess sufficient order to affect other systems and entities within their environment. Such structures are never stable or universally present in some uniform manifestation (Varenne, 1996; T. Young & Yarbrough, 1993). The more we study such dynamics, the more diversity of expression we find. Taking this ontological and epistemological diversity into account, bricoleurs understand there are numerous dimensions to the bricolage (Denzin & Lincoln, 2000). As with all aspects of the bricolage, no description is fixed and final, and all features of the bricolage come with an elastic clause.

Critical Research in a Globalized, Privatized World

A critical postmodern research requires researchers to construct their perception of the world anew, not just in random ways but in a manner that undermines what appears natural, that opens to question what appears obvious (Slaughter, 1989). Oppositional and insurgent researchers as maieutic agents must not confuse their research efforts with the textual suavities of an avant-garde academic posturing in which they are awarded the sinecure of representation for the oppressed without actually having to return to those working-class communities where their studies took place. Rather, they need to locate their work in a transformative praxis that leads to the alleviation of suffering and the overcoming of oppression.

Rejecting the arrogant reading of metropolitan critics and their imperial mandates governing research, insurgent researchers ask questions about how what is has come to be, whose interests are served by particular institutional arrangements, and where our own frames of reference come from. Facts are no longer simply "what is"; the truth of beliefs is not simply testable by their correspondence to these facts. To engage in research grounded on an evolving criticality is to take part in a process of critical world-making, guided by the shadowed outline of a dream of a world less conditioned by misery, suffering, and the politics of deceit. It is, in short, a pragmatics of hope in an age of cynical reason. The obstacles that critical research has yet to overcome in terms of a frontal assault against the ravages of global capitalism, the new American Empire and its devastation of the global working class, has led McLaren to a more sustained and sympathetic engagement with Marx and the Marxist tradition.

One significant area of concern that has been addressed in the recent Marxist work of McLaren and Scatamburlo-D'Annibale (2004) and Antonia Darder and Rodolfo Torres (2004) is that of critical pedagogy and its intersection with critical multiculturalism, especially with respect to the influence that critical race theory has had on recent work in these interconnected domains. Darder and Torres (2004) point to the fact that much of the work within critical race theory is grounded in the popular intersectionality argument of the post-structuralist and post-modernist era that stipulates that race, class, gender, and sexual orientation should all receive equal attention in understanding the social order and the institutions and ideologies that constitute it. That is, various oppressions are to be engaged with equal weight as one ascribes pluralized sensibilities to any political project that theorizes about social inequalities (2004).

This reduces capitalist exploitation and relations of capitalist production to one set of relations, among others, that systematically denies the totality of capitalism that is constitutive of the process of racialized class relations. This is not to argue that the pernicious ideology of racism is not integral to the process of capitalist accumulation but, as Darder and Torres argue, it is to antiseptically separate politics and economics as distinct spheres of power or ensembles of social relations. Rather than focus on race, or raced identity (i.e., shared phenotypical traits or cultural attributes), Darder and Torres make the case for concentrating upon the ideology of racism and racialized class relations within a larger materialist understanding of the world, thereby bringing the analysis of political economy to the center of the debate.

In a similar fashion, McLaren and Scatamburlo-D'Annibale (2004) argue that the separation of the economic and the political within current contributions of multiculturalism premised on identity politics has had the effect of replacing a *historical materialist class analysis* with a *cultural analysis of class.* As a result, many critical race theorists as well as post-Marxists writing in the realm of cultural studies have also stripped the idea of class of precisely that element which, for Marx, made it radical—namely its status as a universal form of exploitation whose abolition required (and was also central to) the abolition of all manifestations of oppression (Marx, 1978, p. 60). With regard to this issue, Kovel (2002) is particularly insightful, for he explicitly addresses an issue that continues to vex the Left—namely the priority given to different categories of what he calls "dominative splitting"—those categories of gender, class, race, ethnic and national exclusion, and so on.

Kovel argues that we need to ask the question of *priority* with respect to what? He notes that if we mean priority with respect to time, then the category of gender would have priority because there are traces of gender oppression in all other forms of oppression. If we were to prioritize in terms of existential significance, Kovel suggests that we would have to depend on the immediate historical forces that bear down on distinct groups of people—he offers examples of Jews in 1930s Germany who suffered from brutal forms of anti-Semitism and Palestinians today who experience anti-Arab racism under Israeli domination. The question of what has political priority, however, would depend on which transformation of relations of oppression are practically more urgent, and while this would certainly depend upon the preceding categories, it would also depend on the fashion in which all the forces acting in a concrete situation are deployed.

As to the question of which split sets into motion all the others, the priority would have to be given to *class* because class relations entail the state as an instrument of enforcement and control, and it is the state that shapes and organizes the splits that appear in human ecosystems. Thus, class is both logically and historically distinct from other forms of exclusion (hence, we should not talk of "classism" to go along with "sexism" and "racism," and "species-ism"). This is, first of all, because class is an essentially human-made category, without root in even a mystified biology. We cannot imagine a human world without gender distinctions—although we can imagine a world without domination by gender. But a world without class is eminently imaginable—indeed, such was the human world for the great majority of our species's time on earth, during all of which considerable fuss was made over gender. Historically, the difference arises because "class" signifies one side of a larger figure that includes a state apparatus whose conquests and regulations create races and shape gender relations. Thus, there will be no true resolution of racism so long as class society stands, inasmuch as a racially oppressed society implies the activities of a class-defending state. Nor can gender inequality be enacted away so long as class society, with its state, demands the super-exploitation of women's labor (Kovel, 2002).

▣ Rethinking Class and Class Consciousness

Recently, McLaren and Scatamburlo-D'Annibale (2004) have reexamined some of the ethnographic and conceptual work of Paul Willis (1977, 1978, 2000; Willis, Jones, Cannan, & Hurd, 1990) in an attempt to rethink a research agenda involving the participation of working-class subjects and constituencies. We believe that ethnographic models of research such as those developed by Willis would best serve the interests of the working class if they could be accompanied by a larger strategy for socialist transformation, one that proceeds from an assessment of the objective factors and capabilities latent in the current conditions of class struggle. McLaren and Scatamburlo-D'Annibale maintain that the worldwide social movement against anticorporate globalization, as well as the anti-imperialist/antiwar movements preceding and following the U.S. invasion of Iraq, have provided new contexts (mostly through left-wing independent publications and resources on the Internet) for enabling various publics (and non-publics beyond the institutions that serve majority groups) to become more critically literate about the relationship between current world events, global capitalism, and imperialism. For many researchers and educators on the left, this will require a socialist "education" of working-class consciousness. This, in turn, means challenging the mediated social forms in which we live and learn to labor.

One way of scrutinizing the production of everyday meanings so that they are less likely to provide ballast to capitalist social relations is to study working-class consciousness. Bertell Ollman (1971, 1993, 2003) has developed a systematic approach to dialectics that can be brought to bear on the study of working-class consciousness. Such an approach is in need of serious consideration by progressive researchers, especially because most current studies of working-class consciousness have been derived from non-Marxist approaches. Ollman (1993) advises that class consciousness is much more than individual consciousness writ large. The subject of class consciousness is, after all, class. Viewing class consciousness from the perspective of the labor theory of value and the materialist conception of history, as undertaken in Ollman's account, stipulates that we view class in the context of the overall integrated functions of capital and wage labor.

Although people can certainly be seen from the functionalist perspective as embodiments of social-economic functions, we need to expand this view and understand the subjective dimensions of class and class consciousness. Ollman follows Marx's advice in recommending that in defining "class" or any other important notion, we begin from the whole and proceed to the part (see also Ilyenkov, 1977, 1982a, 1982b). According to McLaren and Scatamburlo-D'Annibale (2004), class must be conceived as a complex social relation in the context of Marx's dialectical approach to social life. (This discussion is based on McLaren and Scatamburlo-D'Annibale [2004]). It is important in this regard to see class as a function (from the perspective of the place of a function within the system), as a group (qualities that are attributed to people such as race and gender), and as a complex relation (that is, as the abstracted common element in the social relationship of alienated individuals). A class involves, therefore, the alienated quality of the social life of individuals who function in a certain way within the system. The salient features of class—alienated social relation, place/function, and group—are all mutually dependent.

Class as function relates to the objective interests of workers; class as group relates to their subjective interests. Subjective interests refer to what workers actually believe to be in their own best interests. Those practices that serve the workers in their function as wage laborers refer to their objective interests. Ollman summarizes class consciousness as

> one's identity and interests (subjective and objective) as members of a class, something of the dynamics of capitalism uncovered by Marx (at least enough to grasp objective interests), the broad outlines of the class struggle and where one fits into it, feelings of solidarity toward one's own class and of rational hostility toward opposition classes (in contrast to the feelings of mutual indifference and inner-class competition that accompany alienation), and the vision of a more democratic and egalitarian society that is not only possible but that one can help bring about. (1993, p. 155)

Ollman underscores importantly the notion that explaining class consciousness stipulates seeking what is not present in the thinking of workers as well as what is present. It is an understanding that is "appropriate to the objective character of a class and its objective interests" (1993, p. 155). But in addition to the objective aspect of class consciousness, we must include the subjective aspect of class consciousness, which Ollman describes as "the consciousness of the group of people in a class in so far as their understanding of who they are and what must be done develops from its economistic beginnings toward the consciousness that is appropriate to their class situation" (1993, p. 155). But what is different between this subjective consciousness and the actual consciousness of each individual in the group? Ollman writes that subjective consciousness is different from the actual consciousness of the individual in the group in the following three ways:

> (1) It is a group consciousness, a way of thinking and a thought content, that develops through the individuals in the group interacting with each other and with opposing groups in situations that are peculiar to the class; (2) it is a consciousness that has its main point of reference in the situation and objective interests of a class, viewed functionally, and not in the declared subjective interests of class members (the imputed class consciousness referred to above has been given a role here in the thinking of real people); and (3) it is in its essence a process, a movement from wherever a group begins in its consciousness of itself to the consciousness appropriate to its situation. In other words, the process of becoming class conscious is not external to what it is but rather at the center of what it is all about. (1993, p. 155)

Class consciousness is therefore something that Ollman describes as "a kind of 'group think,' a collective, interactive approach to recognizing, labeling, coming to understand, and acting upon the particular world class members have in common" (1993, p. 156). Class consciousness is different from individual consciousness in the sense of "having its main point of reference in the situation of the class and not in the already recognized interests of individuals" (1993, p. 157). Class consciousness is something that exists "in potential" in the sense that it represents "the appropriate consciousness of people in that position, the consciousness that maximizes their chances of realizing class interests, including structural change where such change is required to secure other interests" (1993, p. 157). Ollman stresses that class consciousness "exists in potential," that is, "class consciousness is a consciousness waiting to happen" (1993, p. 187). It is important here not to mistake class consciousness as some kind of "abstract potential" because it is "rooted in a situation unfolding before our very eyes, long before understanding of real people catches up with it" (1993, p. 157). Class consciousness, then, is not something that is fixed or permanent but is always in motion. The very situatedness of the class establishes its goal—it is always in the process of becoming itself, if we understand the notion of process dialectically. Consequently, we need to examine class from the perspective of Marx's philosophy of internal relations, as that "which treats the relations in which anything stands as essential parts of what it is, so that a significant change in any of these relations registers as a qualitative change in the system of which it is a part" (Ollman, 2003, p. 85).

▣ Focusing on Critical Ethnography

As critical researchers attempt to get behind the curtain, to move beyond assimilated experience, to expose the way ideology constrains the desire for self-direction, and to confront the way power reproduces itself in the construction of human consciousness, they employ a plethora of research methodologies. In this context, Patti Lather (1991, 1993) extends our position with her notion of catalytic validity. Catalytic validity points to the degree to which research moves those it studies to understand the world and the way it is shaped in order for them to transform it. Noncritical researchers who operate within an empiricist framework will perhaps find catalytic validity to be a strange concept. Research that possesses catalytic validity will not only display the reality-altering impact of the inquiry process; it will also direct this impact so that those under study will gain self-understanding and self-direction.

Theory that falls under the rubric of *postcolonialism* (see McLaren, 1999; Semali & Kincheloe, 1999) involves important debates over the knowing subject and object of analysis. Such works have initiated important new modes of analysis, especially in relation to questions of imperialism, colonialism, and neocolonialism. Recent attempts by critical researchers to move beyond the objectifying and imperialist gaze associated with the Western anthropological tradition (which fixes the image of the so-called informant from the colonizing perspective of the knowing subject), although laudatory and well-intentioned, are not without their shortcomings (Bourdieu & Wacquaat, 1992). As Fuchs (1993) has so presciently observed, serious limitations plague recent efforts to develop a more reflective approach to ethnographic writing. The challenge here can be summarized in the following questions: How does the knowing subject come to know the Other? How can researchers respect the perspective of the Other and invite the Other to speak (Abdullah & Stringer, 1999; Ashcroft, Griffiths, & Tiffin, 1995; Brock-Utne, 1996; Goldie, 1995; Macedo, 1994; Myrsiades & Myrsiades, 1998; Pieterse & Parekh, 1995; Prakash & Esteva, 1998; Rains, 1998; Scheurich & Young, 1997; Semali & Kincheloe, 1999; Viergever, 1999)?

Although recent confessional modes of ethnographic writing attempt to treat so-called informants as "participants" in an attempt to avoid the objectification of the Other (usually referring to the relationship between Western anthropologists and non-Western culture), there is a risk that uncovering colonial and postcolonial structures of domination may, in fact, unintentionally validate and consolidate such structures as well as reassert liberal values through a type of covert ethnocentrism. Fuchs (1993) warns that the attempt to subject researchers to the same approach to which other societies are subjected could lead to an " 'othering' of one's own world" (p. 108). Such an attempt often fails to question existing ethnographic methodologies and therefore unwittingly extends their validity and applicability while further objectifying the world of the researcher. Michel Foucault's approach to this dilemma is to "detach" social theory from the epistemology of his own culture by criticizing the traditional philosophy of reflection. However, Foucault falls into the trap of ontologizing his own methodological argumentation and erasing the notion of prior understanding that is linked to the idea of an "inside" view (Fuchs, 1993). Louis Dumont fares somewhat better by arguing that cultural texts need to be viewed simultaneously from the inside and from the outside.

However, in trying to affirm a "reciprocal interpretation of various societies among themselves" (Fuchs, 1993, p. 113) through identifying both transindividual structures of consciousness and transsubjective social structures, Dumont aspires to a universal framework for the comparative analysis of societies. Whereas Foucault and Dumont attempt to "transcend the categorical foundations of their own world" (Fuchs, 1993, p. 118) by refusing to include themselves in the process of objectification, Pierre Bourdieu integrates himself as a social actor into the social field under analysis. Bourdieu achieves such integration by "epistemologizing the ethnological content of his own presuppositions" (Fuchs, 1993, p. 121). But the self-objectification of the observer (anthropologist) is not unproblematic. Fuchs (1993) notes, after Bourdieu, that the chief difficulty is "forgetting the difference between the theoretical and the practical relationship with the world and of imposing on the object the theoretical relationship one maintains with it" (p. 120). Bourdieu's approach to re-search does not fully escape becoming, to a certain extent, a "confirmation of objectivism," but at least there is an earnest attempt by the researcher to reflect on the preconditions of his or her own self-understanding—an attempt to engage in an "ethnography of ethnographers" (p. 122).

Postmodern ethnography often intersects—to varying degrees—with the concerns of postcolonialist researchers, but the degree to which it fully addresses issues of exploitation and the social relations of capitalist exploitation remains questionable. Postmodern ethnography—and we are thinking here of works such as Paul Rabinow's *Reflections on Fieldwork in Morocco* (1977), James Boon's *Other Tribes, Other Scribes* (1982), and Michael Taussig's *Shamanism, Colonialism, and the Wild Man* (1987)—shares the conviction articulated by Marc Manganaro (1990) that "no anthropology is apolitical, removed from ideology and hence from the capacity to be affected by or, as crucially, to effect social formations. The question ought not to be if an anthropological text is political, but rather, what kind of sociopolitical affiliations are tied to particular anthropological texts" (p. 35).

Judith Newton and Judith Stacey (1992–1993) note that the current postmodern textual experimentation of ethnography credits the "post-colonial predicament of culture as the opportunity for anthropology to reinvent itself" (p. 56). Modernist ethnography, according to these authors, "constructed authoritative cultural accounts that served, however inadvertently, not only to establish the authority of the Western ethnographer over native others but also to sustain Western authority over colonial cultures" (p. 56). They argue (following James Clifford) that ethnographers can and should try to escape the recurrent allegorical genre of colonial ethnography—the pastoral, a nostalgic, redemptive text that preserves a primitive culture on the brink of extinction for the historical record of its Western conquerors. The narrative structure of this "salvage text" portrays the native culture as a coherent, authentic, and lamentably "evading past," whereas its complex, inauthentic, Western successors represent the future (p. 56).

Postmodern ethnographic writing faces the challenge of moving beyond simply the reanimation of local experience, an uncritical celebration of cultural difference (including figural differentiations within the ethnographer's own culture), and the employment of a framework that espouses universal values and a global role for interpretivist anthropology (Silverman, 1990). What we have described as resistance postmodernism can help qualitative researchers challenge dominant Western research practices that are underwritten by a foundational epistemology and a claim to universally valid knowledge at the expense of local, subjugated knowledges (Peters, 1993). The choice is not one between modernism and postmodernism, but one of whether or not to challenge the presuppositions that inform the normalizing judgments one makes as a researcher.

Vincent Crapanzano (1990) warns that "the anthropologist can assume neither the Orphic lyre nor the crown of thorns, although I confess to hear salvationist echoes" in his desire to protect his people (p. 301).

Connor (1992) describes the work of James Clifford, which shares an affinity with ethnographic work associated with Georges Bataille, Michel Lerris, and the College de Sociologie, as not simply the "writing of culture" but rather "the interior disruption of categories of art and culture correspond[ing] to a radically dialogic form of ethnographic writing, which takes place across and between cultures" (p. 251). Clifford (1992) describes his own work as an attempt "to multiply the hands and discourses involved in 'writing culture' . . . not to assert a naïve democracy of plural authorship, but to loosen at least somewhat the monological control of the executive writer/anthropologist and to open for discussion ethnography's hierarchy and negotiation of discourses in power-charged, unequal situations" (p. 100). Citing the work of Marcus and Fischer (1986), Clifford warns against modernist ethnographic practices of "representational essentializing" and "metonymic freezing" in which one aspect of a group's life is taken to represent the group as a whole; instead, Clifford urges forms of multilocale ethnography to reflect the "transnational political, economic and cultural forces that traverse and constitute local or regional worlds" (p. 102). Rather than culture being fixed into reified textual portraits, it needs to be better understood as displacement, transplantation, disruption, positionality, and difference.

Although critical ethnography allows, in a way conventional ethnography does not, for the relationship of liberation and history, and although its hermeneutical task is to call into question the social and cultural conditioning of human activity and the prevailing sociopolitical structures, we do not claim that this is enough to restructure the social system. But it is certainly, in our view, a necessary beginning. We follow Patricia Ticineto Clough (1992) in arguing that "realist narrativity has allowed empirical social science to be the platform and horizon of social criticism" (p. 135). Ethnography needs to be analyzed critically not only in terms of its field methods but also as reading and writing practices. Data collection must give way to "rereadings of representations in every form" (p. 137). In the narrative construction of its authority as empirical science, ethnography needs to face the unconscious processes upon which it justifies its canonical formulations, processes that often involve the disavowal of oedipal or authorial desire and the reduction of differences to binary oppositions. Within these processes of binary reduction, the male ethnographer is most often privileged as the guardian of "the factual representation of empirical positivities" (Clough, 1992, p. 9).

New Questions Concerning Validity in Critical Ethnography

Critical research traditions have arrived at the point where they recognize that claims to truth are always discursively situated and implicated in relations of power. Yet, unlike some claims made within "ludic" strands of postmodernist research, we do not suggest that because we cannot know truth absolutely, truth can simply be equated with an effect of power. We say this because truth involves regulative rules that must be met for some statements to be more meaningful than others. Otherwise, truth becomes meaningless and, if that is the case, liberatory praxis has no purpose other than to win for the sake of winning. As Phil Carspecken (1993, 1999) remarks, every time we act, in every instance of our behavior, we presuppose some normative or universal relation to truth. Truth is internally related to meaning in a pragmatic way through normative referenced claims, intersubjective referenced claims, subjective referenced claims, and the way we deictically ground or anchor meaning in our daily lives. Carspecken explains that researchers are able to articulate the normative evaluative claims of others when they begin to see them in the same way as their participants by living inside the cultural and discursive positionalities that inform such claims.

Claims to universality must be recognized in each particular normative claim, and questions must be raised about whether such norms represent the entire group. When the limited claim of universality is seen to be contradictory to the practices under observation, power relations become visible. What is crucial here, according to Carspecken, is that researchers recognize where they are located ideologically in the normative and identity claims of others and at the same time be honest about their own subjective referenced claims and not let normative evaluative claims interfere with what they observe. Critical research continues to problematize normative and universal claims in a way that does not permit them to be analyzed outside a politics of representation, divorced from the material conditions in which they are produced, or outside a concern with the constitution of the subject in the very acts of reading and writing.

In his book *Critical Ethnography in Educational Research* (1996), Carspecken addresses the issue of critical epistemology, an understanding of the relationship between power and thought, and power and truth claims. In a short exposition of what is "critical" to critical epistemology, he debunks facile forms of social constructivism and offers a deft criticism of mainstream epistemologies by way of Continental phenomenology, poststructuralism, and postmodernist social theory, mainly the work of Edmund Husserl and Jacques Derrida. Carspecken makes short work of facile forms of constructivist thought, purporting that what we see is strongly influenced by what we already value and that criticalist research simply indulges itself in the "correct" political values. For instance, some constructivists argue that all that criticalists need to do is to "bias" their work in the direction of social justice.

This form of constructivist thought is not viable, according to Carspecken, because it is plainly ocular-centric; that is, it depends upon visual perception to form the basis of its theory. Rather than rely on perceptual metaphors found in mainstream ethnographic accounts, critical ethnography, in contrast, should emphasize communicative experiences and structures as well as cultural typifications. Carspecken argues that critical ethnography needs to differentiate among ontological categories (i.e., subjective, objective, normative-evaluative) rather than adopt the position of "multiple realities" defended by many constructivists. He adopts a principled position that research value orientations should not determine research findings, as much as this is possible. Rather, critical ethnographers should employ a critical epistemology; that is, they should uphold epistemological principles that apply to all researchers. In fecundating this claim, Carspecken rehabilitates critical ethnography from many of the misperceptions of its critics who believe that it ignores questions of validity.

To construct a socially critical epistemology, critical ethnographers need to understand holistic modes of human experience and their relationship to communicative structures. Preliminary stages of this process that Carspecken articulates include examining researcher bias and discovering researcher value orientations. Following stages include compiling the primary record through the collection of monological data, preliminary reconstructive analysis, dialogical data generation, discovering social systems relations, and using systems relations to explain findings. Anthony Giddens's work forms the basis of Carspecken's approach to systems analysis. Accompanying discussions of each of the complex stages Carspecken develops are brilliantly articulated approaches to horizontal and vertical validity reconstructions and pragmatic horizons of analysis. In order to help link theory to practice, Carspecken uses data from his study of an inner-city Houston elementary school program that is charged with helping students learn conflict management skills.

Another impressive feature is Carspecken's exposition and analysis of communicative acts, especially his discussion of meaning as embodiment and understanding as intersubjective, not objective or subjective. Carspecken works from a view of intersubjectivity that combines Hegel, Mead, Habermas, and Taylor. He recommends that critical ethnographers record body language carefully because the meaning of an action is not in the language, it is rather in the action and the actor's bodily states. In Carspecken's view, subjectivity is derivative from intersubjectivity (as is objectivity), and intersubjectivity involves the dialogical constitution of the "feeling body." Finally, Carspecken stresses the importance of macro-level social theories, environmental conditions, socially structured ways of meeting needs and desires, effects of cultural commodities on students, economic exploitation, and political and cultural conditions of action. Much of Carspecken's inspiration for his approach to validity claims is taken from Habermas's theory of communicative action. Carspecken reads Habermas as grasping the prelinguistic foundations of language and intersubjectivity, making language secondary to the concept of intersubjectivity.

Yet Carspecken departs from a strict Habermasian view of action by bringing in an expressive/praxis model roughly consistent with Charles Taylor's work. Although Habermas and Taylor frequently argue against each other's positions, Carspecken puts them together in a convincing manner. Taylor's emphasis on holistic modes of understanding and the act constitution that Carspecken employs make it possible to link the theory of communicative rationality to work on embodied meaning and the metaphoric basis of meaningful action. It also provides a means for synthesizing Giddens's ideas on part/whole relations, virtual structure, and act constitution with communicative rationality. This is another way in which Carspecken's work differs from Habermas and yet remains consistent with his theory and the internal link between meaning and validity.

Recent Innovations in Critical Ethnography

In addition to Carspecken's brilliant insights into critically grounded ethnography, the late 1990s witnessed a proliferation of deconstructive approaches as well as reflexive approaches (this discussion is based on Trueba and McLaren [2000]). In her important book *Fictions of Feminist Ethnography* (1994), Kamala Visweswaran maintains that reflexive ethnography, like normative ethnography, rests on the "declarative mode" of imparting knowledge to a reader whose identity is anchored in a shared discourse.

Deconstructive ethnography, in contrast, enacts the "interrogative mode" through a constant deferral or a refusal to explain or interpret. Within deconstructive ethnography, the identity of the reader with a unified subject of enunciation is discouraged. Whereas reflexive ethnography maintains that the ethnographer is not separate from the object of investigation, the ethnographer is still viewed as a unified subject of knowledge that can make hermeneutic efforts to establish identification between the observer and the observed (as in modernist interpretive traditions). Deconstructive ethnography, in contrast, often disrupts such identification in favor of articulating a fractured, destabilized, multiply positioned subjectivity (as in postmodernist interpretive traditions). Whereas reflexive ethnography questions its own authority, deconstructive ethnography forfeits its authority.

Both approaches to critical ethnography can be used to uncover the clinging Eurocentric authority employed by ethnographers in the study of Latino/a populations. The goal of both these approaches is criticalist in nature: that is, to free the object of analysis from the tyranny of fixed, unassailable categories and to rethink subjectivity itself as a permanently unclosed, always partial, narrative engagement with text and context. Such an approach can help the ethnographer to caution against the damaging depictions propagated by Anglo observers about Mexican immigrants. As Ruth Behar (1993) notes, in classical sociological and ethnographic accounts of the Mexican and Mexican American family, stereotypes similar to those surrounding the black family perpetuated images of the authoritarian, oversexed, and macho husband and the meek and submissive wife surrounded by children who adore their good and suffering mother. These stereotypes have come under strong critique in the last few years, particularly by Chicana critics, who have sought to go beyond the various "deficiency theories" that continue to mark the discussion of African American and Latino/a family life (p. 276).

The conception of culture advanced by critical ethnographers generally unpacks culture as a complex circuit of production that includes myriad dialectically reinitiating and mutually informing sets of activities such as routines, rituals, action conditions, systems of intelligibility and meaning-making, conventions of interpretation, systems relations, and conditions both external and internal to the social actor (Carspecken, 1996). In her ethnographic study *A Space on the Side of the Road* (1996), Kathleen Stewart cogently illustrates the ambivalent character of culture, as well as its fluidity and ungraspable multilayeredness, when she remarks:

> Culture, as it is seen through its productive forms and means of mediation, is not, then, reducible to a fixed body of social value and belief or a direct precipitant of lived experience in the world but grows into a space on the side of the road where stories weighted with sociality take on a life of their own. We "see" it . . . only by building up multilayered narratives of the poetic in the everyday life of things. We represent it only by roaming from one texted genre to another—romantic, realist, historical, fantastic, sociological, surreal. There is no final textual solution, no way of resolving the dialogic of the interpreter/interpreted or subject/object through efforts to "place" ourselves in the text, or to represent "the fieldwork experience," or to gather up the voices of the other as if they could speak for themselves. (p. 210)

According to E. San Juan (1996), a renewed understanding of culture—as both discursive and material—becomes the linchpin for any emancipatory politics. San Juan writes that the idea of culture as social processes and practices that are thoroughly grounded in material social relations—in the systems of maintenance (economics), decision (politics), learning and communication (culture), and generation and nurture (the domain of social reproduction)—must be the grounding principle, or paradigm if you like, of any progressive and emancipatory approach (p. 177; Gresson, 1995). Rejecting the characterization of anthropologists as either "adaptationalists" (e.g., Marvin Harris) or "ideationalists" (e.g., cognitivists, Lévi-Straussian structuralists, Schneiderian symbolists, Geertzian interpretivists), E. Valentine Daniel remarks in his recent ethnography *Charred Lullabies: Chapters in an Anthropology of Violence* (1996) that culture is "no longer something out there to be discovered, described, and explained, but rather something into which the ethnographer, as interpreter, enter[s]" (p. 198). Culture, in other words, is cocreated by the anthropologist and informant through conversation. Yet even this semeiosic conceptualization of culture is not without its problems. As Daniel himself notes, even if one considers oneself to be a "culture-comaking processualist," in contrast to a "culture-finding essentialist," one still has to recognize that one is working within a logocentric tradition that, to a greater or lesser extent, privileges words over actions.

Critical ethnography has benefited from this new understanding of culture and from the new hybridic possibilities for cultural critique that have been opened up by the current blurring and mixing of disciplinary genres—those that emphasize experience, subjectivity, reflexivity, and dialogical understanding. The advantage that follows such perspectives is that social life is not viewed as preontologically available for the researcher to study. It also follows that there is no perspective unspoiled by ideology from which to study social life in an antiseptically objective way. What is important to note here is the stress placed on the ideological situatedness of any descriptive or socioanalytic account of social life. Critical ethnographers such as John and Jean Comaroff (1992) have made significant contributions to our understanding of the ways in which power is entailed in culture, leading to practices of domination and exploitation that have become naturalized in everyday social life. According to Comaroff and Comaroff, hegemony refers to "that order of signs and practices, relations and distinctions, images and epistemologies—drawn from a historically situated cultural field—that come to be taken-for-granted as the natural and received shape of the world and everything that inhabits it" (p. 23). These axiomatic and yet ineffable discourses and practices that are presumptively shared become "ideological" precisely when their internal contradictions are revealed, uncovered, and viewed as arbitrary and negotiable. Ideology, then, refers to a highly articulated worldview, master narrative, discursive regime, or organizing scheme for collective symbolic production. The dominant ideology is the expression of the dominant social group.

Following this line of argument, hegemony "is nonnegotiable and therefore beyond direct argument," whereas ideology "is more susceptible to being perceived as a matter of inimical opinion and interest and therefore is open to contestation" (Comaroff & Comaroff, 1992, p. 24). Ideologies become the expressions of specific groups, whereas hegemony refers to conventions and constructs that are shared and naturalized throughout a political community. Hegemony works both through silences and through repetition in naturalizing the dominant worldview. There also may exist oppositional ideologies among subordinate or subaltern groups—whether well formed or loosely articulated—that break free of hegemony. In this way, hegemony is never total or complete; it is always porous.

Critical Research, 9/11, and the Effort to Make Sense of the American Empire in the 21st Century

The dominant power of these economic dynamics has been reinforced by post-9/11 military moves by the United States. Critical researchers cannot escape the profound implications of these geopolitical, economic, social, cultural, and epistemological issues for the future of knowledge production and distribution. An evolving criticality is keenly aware of these power dynamics and the way they embed themselves in all dimensions of the issues examined here. In this context, it is essential that critical researchers work to expose these disturbing dynamics to both academic and general audiences. In many ways, 9/11 was a profound shock to millions of Americans who obtain their news and worldviews from the mainstream, corporately owned media and their understanding of American international relations from what is taught in most secondary schools and in many colleges and universities. Such individuals are heard frequently on call-in talk radio and TV shows expressing the belief that America is loved internationally because it is richer, more moral, and more magnanimous than other nations. In this mind-set, those who resist the United States hate its freedom for reasons never quite specified. These Americans, the primary victims of a right-wing corporate-government produced miseducation (Kincheloe & Steinberg, 2004), have not been informed by their news sources of the societies that have been undermined by covert U.S. military operations and U.S. economic policies (Parenti, 2002). Many do not believe, for example, the description of the human effects of American sanctions on Iraq between the first and second Gulf Wars. Indeed, the hurtful activities of the American Empire are invisible to many of the empire's subjects in the United States itself.

The complexity of the relationship between the West (the United States in particular) and the Islamic world demands that we be very careful in laying out the argument we are making about this cultural pedagogy, this miseducation. The activities of the American Empire have not been the only forces at work creating an Islamist extremism that violently defies the sacred teaching of the religion. But American misdeeds have played an important role in the process. A new critical orientation toward knowledge production and research based on an appreciation of difference can help the United States redress some of its past and present policies toward the diverse Islamic world. Although these policies have been invisible to many Americans, they are visible to the rest of the world—the Islamic world in particular. Ignoring the *history* of the empire, Kenneth Weinstein (2002) writes in the Thomas B. Fordham Foundation's (2002) *September 11: What Our Children Need to Know* that the Left "admits" that differences exist between cultures but paradoxically downplays their violent basis through relativism and multiculturalism. It views cultural diversity and national differences as matters of taste, arguing that the greatest crime of all is judgmentalism. Weinstein concludes this paragraph by arguing that Americans are just too nice and, as such, are naïve to the threats posed by many groups around the world.

The Fordham Foundation's *September 11: What Our Children Need to Know* (2002) is right-wing educator Chester Finn's epistle to the nation about the incompetence of U.S. educators. The report's list of contributors is a virtual who's who of the theorists of the 21st-century American Empire, including the wife of Vice President Dick Cheney, Lynne Cheney, as well as William Bennett. Critical researchers should be aware of the politics of knowledge operating in this well-financed discreditation of thoughtful educators. As Finn puts it, he had to act because so much "nonsense" was being put out by the educational establishment. What Finn describes as nonsense can be read as scholarship attempting to provide perspective on the long history of Western-Islamic relations. Finn's use of "so much" in relation to this "nonsense" is crass exaggeration. Most materials published about 9/11 for educators were rather innocuous pleas for helping children deal with the anxiety produced by the attacks. Little elementary or secondary school material devoted to historicizing or contextualizing the Islamic world and its relation with the West appeared in the first 2 years after the tragic events of 9/11.

Kenneth Weinstein and many other Fordham authors set up a classic straw man argument in this context. The Left that is portrayed by them equates difference with a moral relativism that is unable to condemn the inhumane activities of particular groups. Implicit throughout *September 11: What Our Children Need to Know* is the notion that this fictional American Left does not condemn al-Qaeda and its crimes against humanity. It is the type of distortion that equated opposition to the second Gulf War with support for Saddam Hussein's Iraqi regime. How can these malcontents oppose America, the Fordham authors ask. Their America is a new empire that constantly denies its imperial dimensions. The new empire is not like empires in previous historical eras that overtly boasted of conquest and the taking of colonies. The 21st century is the era of the postmodern empire that speaks of its moral duty to unselfishly liberate nations and return power to the people. Empire leaders speak of free markets, the rights of the people, and the domino theory of democracy. The new American Empire employs public relations people to portray it as the purveyor of freedom around the world. When its acts of liberation and restoration of democracy elicit protest and retaliation, its leaders express shock and disbelief that such benevolent actions could arouse such "irrational" responses.

In Joe Kincheloe's chapter on Iran in *The Miseducation of the West: Constructing Islam* (2004), he explores the inability of American leaders to understand the impact of empire building in the Persian Gulf on the psyches of those personally affected by such activities. Indeed, the American public was ignorant of covert U.S. operations that overthrew the democratically elected government of Iran so a totalitarian regime more sympathetic to the crass needs of the American Empire could be installed. The citizens of Iran and other peoples around the Muslim world, however, were acutely aware of this imperial action and the contempt for Muslims it implied. When this was combined with a plethora of other U.S. political, military, and economic initiatives in the region, their view of America was less than positive. In the case of Iraq in the second Gulf War, American leaders simply disregarded the views of nations around the world, the Muslim world in particular, as they expressed their opposition to the American invasion. History was erased as Saddam Hussein was viewed in a psychological context as a madman. References to times when the United States supported the madman were deleted from memory. The empire, thus, could do whatever it wanted, regardless of its impact on the Iraqi people or the perceptions of others (irrational others) around the world. An epistemological naïveté—the belief that dominant American ways of seeing both itself and the world are rational and objective and that differing perspectives are irrational—permeate the official information of the empire (Abukhattala, 2004; Kellner, 2004; Progler, 2004; Steinberg, 2004). As John Agresto (2002) writes in the Fordham report:

> It is not very helpful to understand other cultures and outlooks and not understand our own country and what it has tried to achieve. What is it that has brought tens of millions of immigrants to America, not to bomb it, but to better its future and their own? What is it about the promise of liberty and equal treatment, of labor that benefits you and your neighbor, of an open field for your enterprise, ambition, determination and pluck? *Try not to look at America through the lens of your own ideology or political preference but see it as it really is.* Try, perhaps, to see the America most American see. That can be a fine antidote to smugness and academic self-righteousness. (emphasis ours)

Studying the Fordham Foundation's ways of looking at and teaching about America with its erasures of history deployed in the very name of a call to teach history, we are disturbed. When this is combined with an analysis of media representations of the nation's war against terrorism and the second Gulf War in Iraq, we gain some sobering insights into America's future. The inability or refusal of many Americans, especially those in power, to see the problematic activities of the "invisible" empire does not portend peace in the world in the coming years. The way knowledge is produced and transmitted in the United States by a corporatized media and an increasingly corporatized/privatized educational system is one of the central political issues of our time. Yet, in the mainstream political and educational conversations it is not even on the radar. A central task of critical researchers must involve putting these politics of knowledge on the public agenda. The power literacies and the concern with social change delineated in our discussion of critical theoretical research have never been more important to the world.

References

Abdullah, J., & Stringer, E. (1999). Indigenous knowledge, indigenous learning, indigenous research. In L. Semali & J. L. Kincheloe (Eds.), *What is indigenous knowledge? Voices from the academy.* Bristol, PA: Falmer.

Abercrombie, N. (1994). Authority and consumer society. In R. Keat, N. Whiteley, & N. Abercrombie (Eds.), *The authority of the consumer.* New York: Routledge.

Abukhattala, I. (2004). The new bogeyman under the bed: Image formation of Islam in the Western school curriculum and media. In J. L. Kincheloe & S. R. Steinberg (Eds.), *The miseducation of the West: Constructing Islam.* New York: Greenwood.

Agger, B. (1992). *The discourse of domination: From the Frankfurt school to postmodernism.* Evanston, IL: Northwestern University Press.

Agger, B. (1998). *Critical social theories: An introduction.* Boulder, CO: Westview.

Agresto, J. (2002). Lessons of the Preamble. In Thomas B. Fordham Foundation, *September 11: What our children need to know.* Retrieved from www

.edexcellence.net/institute/publication/publication .cfm?id=65#743

Alfino, M., Caputo, J., & Wynyard, R. (Eds.). (1998). *McDonaldization revisited: Critical essays on consumer and culture.* Westport, CT: Praeger.

Allison, C. (1998). Okie narratives: Agency and whiteness. In J. L. Kincheloe, S. R. Steinberg, N. M. Rodriguez, & R. E. Chennault (Eds.), *White reign: Deploying whiteness in America.* New York: St. Martin's.

Andersen, G. (1989). Critical ethnography in education: Origins, current status, and new directions. *Review of Educational Research, 59,* 249–270.

Apple, M. (1996). *Cultural politics and education.* New York: Teachers College Press.

Aronowitz, S., & DiFazio, W. (1994). *The jobless future.* Minneapolis: University of Minnesota Press.

Aronowitz, S., & Giroux, H. (1991). *Postmodern education: Politics, culture, and social criticism.* Minneapolis: University of Minnesota Press.

Ashcroft, B., Griffiths, G., & Tiffin, H. (Eds.). (1995). *The post-colonial studies reader.* New York: Routledge.

Bauman, Z. (1995). *Life in fragments: Essays in postmodern morality.* Cambridge, MA: Blackwell.

Beck-Gernsheim, E., Butler, J., & Puigvert, L. (2003). *Women and social transformation.* New York: Peter Lang.

Behar, R. (1993). *Translated woman: Crossing the border with Esperanza's story.* Boston: Beacon.

Behar, R., & Gordon, D. A. (Eds.). (1995). *Women writing culture.* Berkeley: University of California Press.

Bello, W. (2003). The crisis of the globalist project and the new economics of George W. Bush. *New Labor Forum.* Retrieved from www.globalpolicy.org/globaliz/econ/2003/0710bello.htm

Bensaid, D. (2002). *Marx for our times: Adventures and misadventures of a critique* (G. Elliot, Trans.). London: Verso.

Berger, A. A. (1995). *Cultural criticism: A primer of key concepts.* Thousand Oaks, CA: Sage.

Berry, K. (1998). Nurturing the imagination of resistance: Young adults as creators of knowledge. In J. L. Kincheloe & S. R. Steinberg (Eds.), *Unauthorized methods: Strategies for critical teaching.* New York: Routledge.

Bersani, L. (1995). Loving men. In M. Berger, B. Wallis, & S. Watson (Eds.), *Constructing masculinity.* New York: Routledge.

Blades, D. (1997). *Procedures of power and curriculum change: Foucault and the quest for possibilities in science education.* New York: Peter Lang.

Blommaert, J. (1997). *Workshopping: Notes on professional vision in discourse.* Retrieved from http://africana_rug.ac.be/texts/research-publications/publications_on-line/workshopping.htm

Boon, J. A. (1982). *Other tribes, other scribes: Symbolic anthropology in the comparative study of cultures, histories, religions, and texts.* Cambridge, UK: Cambridge University Press.

Bourdieu, P., &Wacquaat, L. (1992). *An invitation to reflexive sociology.* Chicago: University of Chicago Press.

Brents, B., & Monson, M. (1998). Whitewashing the strip: The construction of whiteness in Las Vegas. In J. L. Kincheloe, S. R. Steinberg, N. M. Rodriguez, & R. E. Chennault (Eds.), *White reign: Deploying whiteness in America.* New York: St. Martin's.

Bresler, L., & Ardichvili, A. (Eds.). (2002). *Research in international education: Experience, theory, and practice.* New York: Peter Lang.

Britzman, D. (1991). *Practice makes practice: A critical study of learning to teach.* Albany: State University of New York Press.

Britzman, D. (1995). What is this thing called love? *Taboo: The Journal of Culture and Education, 1,* 65–93.

Brock-Utne, B. (1996). Reliability and validity in qualitative research within Africa. *International Review of Education, 42,* 605–621.

Brosio, R. (1994). *The radical democratic critique of capitalist education.* New York: Peter Lang.

Burbules, N., & Beck, R. (1999). Critical thinking and critical pedagogy: Relations, differences, and limits. In T. Popkewitz & L. Fendler (Eds.), *Critical theories in education.* New York: Routledge.

Butler, M. (1998). Negotiating place: The importance of children's realities. In S. R. Steinberg & J. L. Kincheloe (Eds.), *Students as researchers: Creating classrooms that matter.* London: Taylor & Francis.

Cannella, G. (1997). *Deconstructing early childhood education: Social justice and revolution.* New York: Peter Lang.

Carlson, D. (1997). *Teachers in crisis.* New York: Routledge.

Carlson, D., & Apple, M. (Eds.). (1998). *Power/knowledge/pedagogy: The meaning of democratic education in unsettling times.* Boulder, CO: Westview.

Carspecken, P. F. (1993). *Power, truth, and method: Outline for a critical methodology.* Unpublished manuscript, Indiana University.

Carspecken, P. F. (1996). *Critical ethnography in educational research: A theoretical and practical guide.* New York: Routledge.

Carspecken, P. F. (1999). *Four scenes for posing the question of meaning and other essays in critical philosophy and critical methodology.* New York: Peter Lang.

Carter, R. (2003). Visual literacy: Critical thinking with the visual image. In D. Weil & J. Kincheloe (Eds.), *Critical thinking and learning: An encyclopedia for parents and teachers.* Westport, CT: Greenwood.

Carter, V. (1998). Computer-assisted racism: Toward an understanding of cyber-whiteness. In J. L. Kincheloe, S. R. Steinberg, N. M. Rodriguez, & R. E. Chennault (Eds.), *White reign: Deploying whiteness in America.* New York: St. Martin's.

Cary, R. (1996). I.Q. as commodity: The "new" economics of intelligence. In J. L. Kincheloe, S. R. Steinberg, & A. D. Gresson III (Eds.), *Measured lies: The bell curve examined.* New York: St. Martin's.

Cary, R. (2003). Art and aesthetics. In D. Weil & J. Kincheloe (Eds.), *Critical thinking and learning: An encyclopedia for parents and teachers.* Westport, CT: Greenwood.

Chomsky, N. (2003, August 11). Preventive war "the supreme crime." *Znet.* Retrieved from www.zmag.org/content/showarticle.cfm?SectionID=40&ItemID=4030

Christian-Smith, L., & Keelor, K. S. (1999). *Everyday knowledge and women of the academy: Uncommon truths.* Boulder, CO: Westview.

Clark, L. (2002). *Critical theory and constructivism. Theory and methods for the teens and the new media @ home project.* Retrieved from www.colorado.edu/journalism/mcm/qmr-crit-theory.htm

Clatterbaugh, K. (1997). *Contemporary perspectives on masculinity: Men, women, and politics in modern society.* Boulder, CO: Westview.

Clifford, J. (1992). Traveling cultures. In L. Grossberg, C. Nelson, & P. A. Treichler (Eds.), *Cultural studies.* New York: Routledge.

Clough, P. T. (1992). *The end(s) of ethnography: From realism to social criticism.* Newbury Park, CA: Sage.

Clough, P. T. (1994). *Feminist thought: Desire, power and academic discourse.* Cambridge, MA: Blackwell.

Clough, P. T. (1998). *The end(s) of ethnography: From realism to social criticism* (2nd ed.). New York: Peter Lang.

Coben, D. (1998). *Radical heroes: Gramsci, Freire and the politics of adult education.* New York: Garland.

Collins, J. (1995). *Architectures of excess: Cultural life in the information age.* New York: Routledge.

Comaroff, J., & Comaroff, J. (1992). *Ethnography and the historical imagination.* Boulder, CO: Westview.

Connor, S. (1992). *Theory and cultural value.* Cambridge, MA: Blackwell.

Cooper, D. (1994). Productive, relational, and everywhere? Conceptualizing power and resistance within Foucauldian feminism. *Sociology, 28,* 435–454.

Corrigan, P. (1979). *Schooling the Smash Street Kids.* London: Macmillan.

Crapanzano, V. (1990). Afterword. In M. Manganaro (Ed.), *Modernist anthropology: From fieldwork to text.* Princeton, NJ: Princeton University Press.

Dahlbom, B. (1998). *Going to the future.* Retrieved from http://www.viktoria.infomatik.gu.se/~max/bo/papers.html

Daniel, E. V. (1996). *Charred lullabies: Chapters in an anthropology of violence.* Princeton, NJ: Princeton University Press.

Darder, A., & Torres, R. (2004). *After race: Racism after multiculturalism.* New York: New York University Press.

DeLissovoy, N., & McLaren, P. (2003). Educational "accountability" and the violence of capital: A Marxian reading. *Journal of Education Policy, 18,* 131–143.

Deetz, S. A. (1993, May). *Corporations, the media, industry, and society: Ethical imperatives and responsibilities.* Paper presented at the annual meeting of the International Communication Association, Washington, DC.

Dei, G., Karumanchery, L., & Karumanchery-Luik, N. (2004). *Playing the race card: Exposing white power and privilege.* New York: Peter Lang.

Denzin, N. K. (1994). The art and politics of interpretation. In N. K. Denzin & Y. S. Lincoln (Eds.), *Handbook of qualitative research.* Thousand Oaks, CA: Sage.

Denzin, N. K. (2003). *Performative ethnography: Critical pedagogy and the politics of culture.* Thousand Oaks, CA: Sage.

Denzin, N. K., & Lincoln, Y. S. (2000). Introduction: The discipline and practice of qualitative research. In N. K. Denzin & Y. S. Lincoln (Eds.), *Handbook of qualitative research* (2nd ed.). Thousand Oaks, CA: Sage.

DeVault, M. (1996). Talking back to sociology: Distinctive contributions of feminist methodology. *Annual Review of Sociology, 22,* 29–50.

Douglas, S. (1994). *Where the girls are: Growing up female in the mass media.* New York: Times Books.

Drummond, L. (1996). *American dreamtime: A cultural analysis of popular movies and their implications for a science of humanity.* Lanham, MD: Littlefield Adams.

Fehr, D. (1993). *Dogs playing cards: Powerbrokers of prejudice in education, art, and culture.* New York: Peter Lang.

Fenwick, T. (2000). *Experiential learning in adult education: A comparative framework.* Retrieved from www.ualberta.ca/~tfenwick/ext/aeq.htm

Ferguson, M., & Golding, P. (Eds.). (1997). *Cultural studies in question.* London: Sage.

Finders, M. (1997). *Just girls: Hidden literacies and life in junior high.* New York: Teachers College Press.

Fine, M., Powell, L. C., Weis, L., & Wong, L. M. (Eds.). (1997). *Off white: Readings on race, power and society.* New York: Routledge.

Fiske, J. (1993). *Power works, power plays.* New York: Verso.

Flecha, R., Gomez, J., & Puigvert, L. (Eds.). (2003). *Contemporary sociological theory.* New York: Peter Lang.

Flossner, G., & Otto, H. (Eds.). (1998). *Towards more democracy in social services: Models of culture and welfare.* New York: de Gruyter.

Fordham Foundation. (2002). *September 11: What our children need to know.* Retrieved www.edexcellence.net/institute/publication/publication.cfm?id=65

Foster, R. (1997). Addressing epistemologic and practical issues in multimethod research: A procedure for conceptual triangulation. *Advances in Nursing Education, 20*(2), 1–12.

Frankenberg, R. (1993). *White women, race matters: The social construction of whiteness.* Minneapolis: University of Minnesota Press.

Franz, C., & Stewart, A. (Eds.). (1994). *Women creating lives.* Boulder, CO: Westview.

Freire, A. M. A. (2000). Foreword. In P. McLaren, *Che Guevara, Paulo Freire, and the pedagogy of revolution.* Boulder, CO: Rowman and Littlefield.

Freire, A. M. A. (2001). *Chronicles of love: My life with Paulo Freire.* New York: Peter Lang.

Freire, P. (1970). *Pedagogy of the oppressed.* New York: Herder and Herder.

Freire, P. (1972). *Research methods.* Paper presented to a seminar in Studies in Adult Education, Dar-es-Salaam, Tanzania.

Freire, P. (1978). *Education for critical consciousness.* New York: Seabury.

Freire, P. (1985). *The politics of education: Culture, power, and liberation.* South Hadley, MA: Bergin & Garvey.

Friedman, S. (1998). (Inter)disciplinarity and the question of the women's studies Ph.D. *Feminist Studies, 24*(2), 301–326.

Fuchs, M. (1993). The reversal of the ethnological perspective: Attempts at objectifying one's own cultural horizon. Dumont, Foucault, Bourdieu? *Thesis Eleven, 34,* 104–125.

Gabbard, D. (1995). NAFTA, GATT, and Goals 2000: Reading the political culture of post-industrial America. *Taboo: The Journal of Culture and Education, 2,* 184–199.

Gadamer, H.-G. (1989). *Truth and method* (2nd rev. ed.) (J. Weinsheimer & D. G. Marshall, Eds. & Trans.). New York: Crossroad.

Gallagher, S. (1992). *Hermeneutics and education.* Albany: State University of New York Press.

Garnham, N. (1997). Political economy and the practice of cultural studies. In M. Ferguson & P. Golding (Eds.), *Cultural studies in question.* London: Sage.

Gee, J. (1996). *Social linguistics and literacies: Ideology in discourses* (2nd ed.). London: Taylor & Francis.

Gee, J., Hull, G., & Lankshear, C. (1996). *The new work order: Behind the language of the new capitalism.* Boulder, CO: Westview.

Gibson, R. (1986). *Critical theory and education.* London: Hodder & Stoughton.

Giroux, H. (1983). *Theory and resistance in education: A pedagogy for the opposition.* South Hadley, MA: Bergin & Garvey.

Giroux, H. (1988). Critical theory and the politics of culture and voice: Rethinking the discourse of educational research. In R. Sherman & R. Webb (Eds.), *Qualitative research in education: Focus and methods.* New York: Falmer.

Giroux, H. (1992). *Border crossings: Cultural workers and the politics of education.* New York: Routledge.

Giroux, H. (1997). *Pedagogy and the politics of hope: Theory, culture, and schooling.* Boulder, CO: Westview.

Giroux, H. (2003). *The abandoned generation: Democracy beyond the culture of fear.* New York: Palgrave.

Goldie, T. (1995). The representation of the indigene. In B. Ashcroft, G. Griffiths, & H. Tiffin (Eds.), *The post-colonial studies reader.* New York: Routledge.

Goodson, I. (1997). *The changing curriculum: Studies in social construction.* New York: Peter Lang.

Gresson, A. (1995). *The recovery of race in America.* Minneapolis: University of Minnesota Press.

Griffin, C. (1985). *Typical girls? Young women from school to the job market.* London: Routledge & Kegan Paul.

Grinberg, J. (2003). Only the facts? In D. Weil & J. L. Kincheloe (Eds.), *Critical thinking and learning: An encyclopedia for parents and teachers.* Westport, CT: Greenwood.

Grondin, J. (1994). *Introduction to philosophical hermeneutics* (J. Weinsheimer, Trans.). New Haven, CT: Yale University Press.

Gross, A., & Keith, W. (Eds.). (1997). *Rhetorical hermeneutics: Invention and interpretation in the age of science.* Albany: State University of New York Press.

Grossberg, L. (1995). What's in a name (one more time)? *Taboo: The Journal of Culture and Education, 1,* 1–37.

Grossberg, L. (1997). *Bringing it all back home: Essays on cultural studies.* Durham, NC: Duke University Press.

Hall, S., & du Gay, P. (Eds.). (1996). *Questions of cultural identity.* London: Sage.

Harper, D. (1987). *Working knowledge: Skill and community in a small shop.* Chicago: University of Chicago Press.

Hebdige, D. (1979). *Subculture: The meaning of style.* London: Methuen.

Hedley, M. (1994). The presentation of gendered conflict in popular movies: Affective stereotypes, cultural sentiments, and men's motivation. *Sex Roles, 31,* 721–740.

Hinchey, P. (1998). *Finding freedom in the classroom: A practical introduction to critical theory.* New York: Peter Lang.

Horkheimer, M. (1972). *Critical theory.* New York: Seabury.

Horn, R. (2000). *Teacher talk: A post-formal inquiry into educational change.* New York: Peter Lang.

Howell, S. (1998). The learning organization: Reproduction of whiteness. In J. L. Kincheloe, S. R. Steinberg, N. M. Rodriguez, & R. E. Chennault (Eds.), *White reign: Deploying whiteness in America.* New York: St. Martin's.

Humphries, B. (1997). From critical thought to emancipatory action: Contradictory research goals? *Sociological Research Online, 2*(1). Retrieved from www.socresonline.org.uk/socresonline/2/1/3.html

Ilyenkov, E. V. (1977). *Dialectical logic: Essays on its history and theory.* Moscow: Progress.

Ilyenkov. E. V. (1982a). *The dialectics of the abstract and the concrete in Marx's Capital* (S. Syrovatkin, Trans.). Moscow: Progress.

Ilyenkov. E. V. (1982b). *Leninist dialectics and the metaphysics of positivism.* London: New Park Publications.

Jackson, S., & Russo, A. (2002). *Talking back and acting out: Women negotiating the media across cultures.* New York: Peter Lang.

Jardine, D. (1998). *To dwell with a boundless heart: Essays in curriculum theory, hermeneutics, and the ecological imagination.* New York: Peter Lang.

Johnson, C. (1996). Does capitalism really need patriarchy? Some old issues reconsidered. *Women's Studies International Forum, 19,* 193–202.

Joyrich, L. (1996). *Reviewing reception: Television, gender, and postmodern culture.* Bloomington: Indiana University Press.

Kellner, D. (1995). *Media culture: Cultural studies, identity, and politics between the modern and the postmodern.* New York: Routledge.

Kellner, D. (2004). September 11, terror war, and blowback. In J. L. Kincheloe & S. R. Steinberg (Eds.), *The miseducation of the West: Constructing Islam.* New York: Greenwood.

Kellogg, D. (1998). Exploring critical distance in science education: Students researching the implications of technological embeddedness. In S. R. Steinberg & J. L. Kincheloe (Eds.), *Students as researchers: Creating classrooms that matter.* London: Falmer.

Kelly, L. (1996). When does the speaking profit us? Reflection on the challenges of developing feminist perspectives on abuse and violence by women. In M. Hester, L. Kelly, & J. Radford (Eds.), *Women, violence, and male power.* Bristol, PA: Open University Press.

Kincheloe, J. L. (1991). *Teachers as researchers: Qualitative paths to empowerment.* London: Falmer.

Kincheloe, J. L. (1993). *Toward a critical politics of teacher thinking: Mapping the postmodern.* Granby, MA: Bergin & Garvey.

Kincheloe, J. L. (1995). *Toil and trouble: Good work, smart workers, and the integration of academic and vocational education.* New York: Peter Lang.

Kincheloe, J. L. (1998). Critical research in science education. In B. Fraser & K. Tobin (Eds.), *International handbook of science education* (Pt. 2). Boston: Kluwer.

Kincheloe, J. L. (1999). *How do we tell the workers? The socioeconomic foundations of work and vocational education.* Boulder, CO: Westview.

Kincheloe, J. (2001a). Describing the bricolage: Conceptualizing a new rigor in qualitative research. *Qualitative Inquiry, 7*(6), 679–692.

Kincheloe, J. (2001b). *Getting beyond the facts: Teaching social studies/social sciences in the twenty-first century* (2nd ed.). New York: Peter Lang.

Kincheloe, J. L. (2002). *The sign of the burger: McDonald's and the culture of power.* Philadelphia: Temple University Press.

Kincheloe, J. (2003a). Critical ontology: Visions of selfhood and curriculum. *JCT: Journal of Curriculum Theorizing, 19*(1), 47–64.

Kincheloe, J. (2003b). Into the great wide open: Introducing critical thinking. In D. Weil & J. Kincheloe (Eds.), *Critical thinking and learning: An encyclopedia for parents and teachers.* Westport, CT: Greenwood.

Kincheloe, J. L. (2003c). *Teachers as researchers: Qualitative paths to empowerment* (2nd ed.). London: Falmer.

Kincheloe, J. (2004). Iran and American miseducation: Coverups, distortions, and omissions. In J. Kincheloe & S. Steinberg (Eds.), *The miseducation of the West: Constructing Islam.* New York: Greenwood.

Kincheloe, J., & Berry, K. (2004). *Rigour and complexity in educational research: Conceptualizing the bricolage.* London: Open University Press.

Kincheloe, J. L., & Steinberg, S. R. (1993). A tentative description of post-formal thinking: The critical confrontation with cognitive theory. *Harvard Educational Review, 63,* 296–320.

Kincheloe, J., & Steinberg, S. R. (1996). Who said it can't happen here? In J. Kincheloe, S. Steinberg, & A. D. Gresson III (Eds.), *Measured lies: The bell curve examined.* New York: St. Martin's.

Kincheloe, J. L., & Steinberg, S. R. (1997). *Changing multiculturalism: New times, new curriculum.* London: Open University Press.

Kincheloe, J. L., & Steinberg, S. R. (1999). Politics, intelligence, and the classroom: Postformal teaching. In J. Kincheloe, S. Steinberg, & L. Villaverde (Eds.), *Rethinking intelligence: Confronting psychological assumptions about teaching and learning.* New York: Routledge.

Kincheloe, J. L., & Steinberg, S. R. (Eds.). (2004). *The miseducation of the West: Constructing Islam.* New York: Greenwood.

Kincheloe, J. L., Steinberg, S. R., & Hinchey, P. (Eds.). (1999). *The post-formal reader: Cognition and education.* New York: Falmer.

Kincheloe, J. L., Steinberg, S. R., Rodriguez, N. M., & Chennault, R. E. (Eds.). (1998). *White reign: Deploying whiteness in America.* New York: St. Martin's.

King, J. (1996). Bad luck, bad blood, bad faith: Ideological hegemony and the oppressive language of hoodoo social science. In J. L. Kincheloe, S. R. Steinberg, & A. D. Gresson III (Eds.), *Measured lies: The bell curve examined.* New York: St. Martin's.

King, J., & Mitchell, C. (1995). *Black mothers to sons.* New York: Peter Lang.

Knobel, M. (1999). *Everyday literacies: Students, discourse, and social practice.* New York: Peter Lang.

Kogler, H. (1996). *The power of dialogue: Critical hermeneutics after Gadamer and Foucault.* Cambridge, MA: MIT Press.

Kovel, J. (2002). *The enemy of nature: The end of capitalism or the end of the world?* London: Zed Books.

Lacey, C. (1970). *Hightown Grammar: The school as a social system.* London: Routledge & Kegan Paul.

Lather, P. (1991). *Getting smart: Feminist research and pedagogy with/in the postmodern.* New York: Routledge.

Lather, P. (1993). Fertile obsession: Validity after poststructuralism. *Sociological Quarterly, 34,* 673–693.

Leistyna, P., Woodrum, A., & Sherblom, S. (1996). *Breaking free: The transformative power of critical pedagogy.* Cambridge, MA: Harvard Educational Review.

Lemke, J. (1993). Discourse, dynamics, and social change. *Cultural Dynamics, 6,* 243–275.

Lemke, J. (1995). *Textual politics: Discourse and social dynamics.* London: Taylor & Francis.

Lemke, J. (1998). Analyzing verbal data: Principles, methods, and problems. In B. Fraser & K. Tobin (Eds.), *International handbook of science education* (Pt. 2). Boston: Kluwer.

Levi-Strauss, C. (1966). *The savage mind.* Chicago: University of Chicago Press.

Lincoln, Y. (2001). An emerging new bricoleur: Promises and possibilities—a reaction to Joe Kincheloe's "Describing the bricoleur." *Qualitative Inquiry, 7*(6), 693–696.

Lugones, M. (1987). Playfulness, "world"-traveling, and loving perception. *Hypatia, 2*(2), 3–19.

Lull, J. (1995). *Media, communication, culture: A global approach.* New York: Columbia University Press.

Lutz, K., Kendall, J., & Jones, K. (1997). Expanding the praxis debate: Contributions to clinical inquiry. *Advances in Nursing Science, 20*(2), 23–31.

Macedo, D. (1994). *Literacies of power: What Americans are not allowed to know.* Boulder, CO: Westview.

Maher, F., & Tetreault, M. (1994). *The feminist classroom: An inside look at how professors and students are transforming higher education for a diverse society.* New York: Basic Books.

Manganaro, M. (1990). Textual play, power, and cultural critique: An orientation to modernist anthropology. In M. Manganaro (Ed.), *Modernist anthropology: From fieldwork to text.* Princeton, NJ: Princeton University Press.

Marcus, G. E., & Fischer, M.M.J. (1986). *Anthropology as cultural critique: An experimental moment in the human sciences.* Chicago: University of Chicago Press.

Martin, H., & Schuman, H. (1996). *The global trap: Globalization and the assault on democracy and prosperity.* New York: Zed Books.

Marx, K. (1978). Economic and philosophical manuscripts of 1844. In *The Marx-Engels reader* (2nd ed., R. C. Tucker, Ed.). New York: W. W. Norton.

Mathie, A., & Greene, J. (2002). Honoring difference and dialogue in international education and development: Mixed-method frameworks for research. In L. Bresler & A. Ardichvili (Eds.), *Research in international education: Experience, theory, and practice.* New York: Peter Lang.

Mayers, M. (2001). *Street kids and streetscapes: Panhandling, politics, and prophecies.* New York: Peter Lang.

McLaren, P. (1992). Collisions with otherness: "Traveling" theory, post-colonial criticism, and the politics of ethnographic practice—the mission of the wounded ethnographer. *International Journal of Qualitative Studies in Education, 5,* 77–92.

McLaren, P. (1995a). *Critical pedagogy and predatory culture: Oppositional politics in a postmodern era.* New York: Routledge.

McLaren, P. (1995b). *Life in schools* (3rd ed.). New York: Longman.

McLaren, P. (1997). *Revolutionary multiculturalism: Pedagogies of dissent for the new millennium.* New York: Routledge.

McLaren, P. (1998). Revolutionary pedagogy in post-revolutionary times: Rethinking the political economy of critical education. *Educational Theory, 48,* 431–462.

McLaren, P. (1999). *Schooling as a ritual performance: Toward a political economy of educational symbols and gestures* (3rd ed.). Boulder, CO: Rowman & Littlefield.

McLaren, P. (2001). Bricklayers and bricoleurs: A Marxist addendum. *Qualitative Inquiry, 7*(6), 700–705.

McLaren, P. (2002). Marxist revolutionary praxis: A curriculum of transgression. *Journal of Curriculum Inquiry Into Curriculum and Instruction, 3*(3), 36–41.

McLaren, P. (2003a). Critical pedagogy in the age of neoliberal globalization: Notes from history's underside. *Democracy and Nature, 9*(1), 65–90.

McLaren, P. (2003b). The dialectics of terrorism: A Marxist response to September 11 (Part Two: Unveiling the Past, Evading the Present). *Cultural Studies/Critical Methodologies 3*(1), 103–132.

McLaren, P., & Farahmandpur, R. (2001). The globalization of capitalism and the new imperialism: Notes towards a revolutionary critical pedagogy. *The Review of Education, Pedagogy & Cultural Studies, 23*(3), 271–315.

McLaren, P., & Farahmandpur, R. (2003). Critical pedagogy at ground zero: Renewing the educational left after 9–11. In D. Gabbard & K. Saltman (Eds.), *Education as enforcement: The militarization and corporatization of schools.* New York: Routledge.

McLaren, P., Hammer, R., Reilly, S., & Sholle, D. (1995). *Rethinking media literacy: A critical pedagogy of representation.* New York: Peter Lang.

McLaren, P., & Jaramillo, N. (2002). Critical pedagogy as organizational praxis: Challenging the demise of civil society in a time of permanent war. *Educational Foundations, 16*(4), 5–32.

McLaren, P., & Martin, G. (2003, Summer). The "big lie" machine devouring America. *Socialist Future Review,* pp. 18–27.

McLaren, P., & Scatamburlo-D'Annibale, V. (2004). Paul Willis, class consciousness, and critical pedagogy: Toward a socialist future. In N. Dolby & G. Dimitriadis with P. Willis (Eds.), *Learning to labor in new times.* New York: RoutledgeFalmer.

McLeod, J. (2000, June). *Qualitative research as bricolage.* Paper presented at the annual conference of the Society for Psychotherapy Research, Chicago.

McWilliam, E., & Taylor, P. (Eds.). (1996). *Pedagogy, technology, and the body.* New York: Peter Lang.

Miller, S., & Hodge, J. (1998). *Phenomenology, hermeneutics, and narrative analysis: Some unfinished methodological business.* Unpublished manuscript, Loyola University, Chicago.

Molnar, A. (1996). *Giving kids the business: The commercialization of America's schools.* Boulder, CO: Westview.

Morgan, W. (1996). Personal training: Discourses of (self) fashioning. In E. McWilliam & P. Taylor

(Eds.), *Pedagogy, technology, and the body.* New York: Peter Lang.

Morrow, R. (1991). Critical theory, Gramsci and cultural studies: From structuralism to post-structuralism. In P. Wexler (Ed.), *Critical theory now.* New York: Falmer.

Mullen, C. (1999). Whiteness, cracks and ink-stains: Making cultural identity with Euroamerican pre-service teachers. In P. Diamond & C. Mullen (Eds.), *The postmodern educator: Arts-based inquiries and teacher development.* New York: Peter Lang.

Myrsiades, K., & Myrsiades, L. (Eds.). (1998). *Race-ing representation: Voice, history, and sexuality.* Lanham, MD: Rowman & Littlefield.

Newton, J., & Stacey, J. (1992–1993). Learning not to curse, or, feminist predicaments in cultural criticism by men: Our movie date with James Clifford and Stephen Greenblatt. *Cultural Critique, 23,* 51–82.

Nicholson, L. J., & Seidman, S. (Eds.). (1995). *Social post-modernism: Beyond identity politics.* New York: Cambridge University Press.

Oberhardt, S. (2001). *Frames within frames: The art museum as cultural artifact.* New York: Peter Lang.

Ollman, B. (1971). *Alienation: Marx's conception of man in capitalist society.* New York: Cambridge University Press.

Ollman, B. (1993). *Dialectical investigations.* New York: Routledge.

Ollman, B. (2003). Marxism, this tale of two cities. *Science & Society, 67*(1), 80–86.

O'Riley, P. (2003). *Technology, culture, and socioeconomics: A rhizoanalysis of educational discourses.* New York: Peter Lang.

Pailliotet, A. (1998). Deep viewing: A critical look at visual texts. In J. L. Kincheloe & S. R. Steinberg (Eds.), *Unauthorized methods: Strategies for critical teaching.* New York: Routledge.

Parenti, M. (2002). *The terrorism trap: September 11 and beyond.* San Francisco: City Lights Books.

Paulson, R. (1995). Mapping knowledge perspectives in studies of educational change. In P. W. Cookson, Jr., & B. Schneider (Eds.), *Transforming schools.* New York: Garland.

Peters, M. (1993). *Against Finkielkraut's la defaite de la pensee: Culture, postmodernism and education.* Unpublished manuscript, University of Glasgow.

Peters, M., & Lankshear, C. (1994). Education and hermeneutics: A Freirean interpretation. In P. McLaren & C. Lankshear (Eds.), *Politics of liberation: Paths from Freire.* New York: Routledge.

Peters, M., Lankshear, C., & Olssen, M. (Eds.). (2003). *Critical theory and the human condition.* New York: Peter Lang.

Pfeil, F. (1995). *White guys: Studies in postmodern domination and difference.* New York: Verso.

Pieterse, J., & Parekh, B. (1995). Shifting imaginaries: Decolonization, internal decolonization, postcoloniality. In J. Pieterse & B. Parekh (Eds.), *The decolonization of imagination: Culture, knowledge, and power.* Atlantic Highlands, NJ: Zed.

Prakash, M., & Esteva, G. (1998). *Escaping education: Living as learning within grassroots cultures.* New York: Peter Lang.

Progler, Y. (2004). Schooled to order: Education and the making of modern Egypt. In J. Kincheloe & S. Steinberg (Eds.), *The miseducation of the West: Constructing Islam.* New York: Greenwood.

Pruyn, M. (1994). Becoming subjects through critical practice: How students in an elementary classroom critically read and wrote their world. *International Journal of Educational Reform, 3*(1), 37–50.

Pryse, M. (1998). Critical interdisciplinarity, women's studies, and cross-cultural insight. *NWSA Journal, 10*(1), 1–11.

Quail, C. B., Razzano, K. A., & Skalli, L. H. (2004). *Tell me more: Rethinking daytime talk shows.* New York: Peter Lang.

Quantz, R. A. (1992). On critical ethnography (with some postmodern considerations). In M. D. LeCompte, W. L. Millroy, & J. Preissle (Eds.), *The handbook of qualitative research in education.* New York: Academic Press.

Quintero, E., & Rummel, M. K. (2003). *Becoming a teacher in the new society: Bringing communities and classrooms together.* New York: Peter Lang.

Rabinow, P. (1977). *Reflections on fieldwork in Morocco.* Berkeley: University of California Press.

Rains, F. (1998). Is the benign really harmless? Deconstructing some "benign" manifestations of operationalized white privilege. In J. L. Kincheloe, S. R. Steinberg, N. M. Rodriguez, & R. E. Chennault (Eds.), *White reign: Deploying whiteness in America.* New York: St. Martin's.

Rand, E. (1995). *Barbie's queer accessories.* Durham, NC: Duke University Press.

Rapko, J. (1998). Review of *The power of dialogue: Critical hermeneutics after Gadamer and Foucault. Criticism, 40*(1), 133–138.

Reason, P., & Torbert, W. R. (2001). Toward a transformational science: A further look at the scientific merits of action research. *Concepts and Transformations, 6*(1), 1–37.

Ritzer, G. (1993). *The McDonaldization of society.* Thousand Oaks, CA: Pine Forge.

Robins, D., & Cohen, P. (1978). *Knuckle sandwich: Growing up in the working-class city.* Harmondsworth, UK: Penguin.

Rodriguez, N. M., & Villaverde, L. (2000). *Dismantling white privilege.* New York: Peter Lang.

Roman, L., & Eyre, L. (Eds.). (1997). *Dangerous territories: Struggles for difference and equality in education.* New York: Routledge.

Rose, K., & Kincheloe, J. (2003). *Art, culture, and education: Artful teaching in a fractured landscape.* New York: Peter Lang.

Rosen, S. (1987). *Hermeneutics as politics.* New York: Oxford University Press.

San Juan, E., Jr. (1992). *Articulations of power in ethnic and racial studies in the United States.* Atlantic Highlands, NJ: Humanities Press.

San Juan, E., Jr. (1996). *Mediations: From a Filipino perspective.* Pasig City, Philippines: Anvil.

Sanders-Bustle, L. (2003). *Image, inquiry, and transformative practice: Engaging learners in creative and critical inquiry through visual representation.* New York: Peter Lang.

Scheurich, J. J., & Young, M. (1997). Coloring epistemologies: Are our research epistemologies racially biased? *Educational Researcher, 26*(4), 4–16.

Scott, J. W. (1992). Experience. In J. Butler & J. W. Scott (Eds.), *Feminists theorize the political.* New York: Routledge.

Sedgwick, E. (1995). Gosh, Boy George, you must be awfully secure in your masculinity! In M. Berger, B. Wallis, & S. Watson (Eds.), *Constructing masculinity.* New York: Routledge.

Selfe, C. L., & Selfe, R. J., Jr. (1994). *The politics of the interface: Power and its exercise in electronic contact zones.* Retrieved from www.hu.mtu.edu/~cyselfe/texts/politics.html

Semali, L. (1998). Still crazy after all of these years: Teaching critical media literacy. In J. L. Kincheloe & S. R. Steinberg (Eds.), *Unauthorized methods: Strategies for critical teaching.* New York: Routledge.

Semali, L., & Kincheloe, J. L. (1999). *What is indigenous knowledge? Voices from the academy.* New York: Falmer.

Shohat, E., & Stam, R. (1994). *Unthinking Eurocentrism: Multiculturalism and the media.* New York: Routledge.

Shor, I. (1996). *When students have power: Negotiating authority in a critical pedagogy.* Chicago: University of Chicago Press.

Silverman, E. K. (1990). Clifford Geertz: Towards a more "thick" understanding? In C. Tilley (Ed.), *Reading material culture.* Cambridge, MA: Blackwell.

Skalli, L. (2004). Loving Muslim women with a vengeance: The West, women, and fundamentalism. In J. L. Kincheloe & S. R. Steinberg (Eds.), *The miseducation of the West: Constructing Islam.* New York: Greenwood.

Slater, J., Fain, S., & Rossatto, C. (2002). *The Freirean legacy: Educating for social justice.* New York: Peter Lang.

Slaughter, R. (1989). Cultural reconstruction in the post-modern world. *Journal of Curriculum Studies, 3,* 255–270.

Sleeter, C., & McLaren, P. (Eds.). (1995). *Multicultural education, critical pedagogy, and the politics of difference.* Albany: State University of New York Press.

Smith, D. G. (1999). *Pedagon: Interdisciplinary Essays in the Human Sciences, Pedagogy, and Culture.* New York: Peter Lang.

Smith, D. G. (2003). On enfraudening the public sphere, the futility of empire and the future of knowledge after "America." *Policy Futures in Education, 1*(3), 488–503.

Smith, R., & Wexler, P. (Eds.). (1995). *After postmodernism: Education, politics, and identity.* London: Falmer.

Soto, L. (1998). Bilingual education in America: In search of equity and social justice. In J. L. Kincheloe & S. R. Steinberg (Eds.), *Unauthorized methods: Strategies for critical teaching.* New York: Routledge.

Soto, L. (Ed.). (2000). *The politics of early childhood education.* New York: Peter Lang.

Stallabrass, J. (1996). *Gargantua: Manufactured mass culture.* London: Verso.

Steinberg, S. R. (1997a). The bitch who has everything. In S. R. Steinberg & J. L. Kincheloe (Eds.), *Kinderculture: The corporate construction of childhood.* Boulder, CO: Westview.

Steinberg, S. (1997b). Kinderculture: The cultural studies of childhood. In N. Denzin (Ed.), *Cultural studies: A research volume.* Greenwich, CT: JAI.

Steinberg, S. (Ed.). (2001). *Multi/intercultural conversations.* New York: Peter Lang.

Steinberg, S. R. (2004). Desert minstrels: Hollywood's curriculum of Arabs and Muslims. In J. L. Kincheloe

& S. R. Steinberg (Eds.), *The miseducation of the West: Constructing Islam.* New York: Greenwood.

Steinberg, S. R., & Kincheloe, J. L. (Eds.). (1997). *Kinderculture: Corporate constructions of childhood.* Boulder, CO: Westview.

Steinberg, S. R., & Kincheloe, J. L. (Eds.). (1998). *Students as researchers: Creating classrooms that matter.* London: Taylor & Francis.

Stewart, K. (1996). *A space on the side of the road: Cultural poetics in an "other" America.* Princeton, NJ: Princeton University Press.

Sünker, H. (1998). Welfare, democracy, and social work. In G. Flosser & H. Otto (Eds.), *Towards more democracy in social services: Models of culture and welfare.* New York: de Gruyter.

Taussig, M. (1987). *Shamanism, colonialism, and the wild man: A study in terror and healing.* Chicago: University of Chicago Press.

Thayer-Bacon, B. (2003). *Relational "(e)pistemologies."* New York: Peter Lang.

Thomas, S. (1997). Dominance and ideology in cultural studies. In M. Ferguson & P. Golding (Eds.), *Cultural studies in question.* London: Sage.

Trueba, E. T., & McLaren, P. (2000). Critical ethnography for the study of immigrants. In E. T. Trueba & L. I. Bartolomé (Eds.), *Immigrant voices: In search of educational equity.* Boulder, CO: Rowman & Littlefield.

Varenne, H. (1996). The social facting of education: Durkheim's legacy. *Journal of Curriculum Studies, 27,* 373–389.

Vattimo, G. (1994). *Beyond interpretation: The meaning of hermeneutics for philosophy.* Stanford, CA: Stanford University Press.

Viergever, M. (1999). Indigenous knowledge: An interpretation of views from indigenous peoples. In L. Semali & J. L. Kincheloe (Eds.), *What is indigenous knowledge? Voices from the academy.* Bristol, PA: Falmer.

Villaverde, L. (2003). Developing curriculum and critical pedagogy. In J. Kincheloe & D. Weil (Eds.), *Critical thinking and learning: An encyclopedia.* Westport, CT: Greenwood.

Villaverde, L., & Kincheloe, J. L. (1998). Engaging students as researchers: Researching and teaching Thanksgiving in the elementary classroom. In S. R. Steinberg & J. L. Kincheloe (Eds.), *Students as researchers: Creating classrooms that matter.* London: Falmer.

Visweswaran, K. (1994). *Fictions of feminist ethnography.* Minneapolis: University of Minnesota Press.

Weil, D. (1998). *Towards a critical multicultural literacy: Theory and practice for education for liberation.* New York: Peter Lang.

Weil, D., & Kincheloe, J. (Eds.). (2003). *Critical thinking and learning: An encyclopedia for parents and teachers.* Westport, CT: Greenwood.

Weiler, K. (1988). *Women teaching for change: Gender, class, and power.* South Hadley, MA: Bergin & Garvey.

Weinstein, K. (2002). Fighting complacency. In Thomas B. Fordham Foundation, *September 11: What our children need to know.* Retrieved from www.edexcellence.net/institute/publication/publication.cfm?id=65#764

Weinstein, M. (1998). *Robot world: Education, popular culture, and science.* New York: Peter Lang.

Wesson, L., & Weaver, J. (2001). Administration–Educational standards: Using the lens of postmodern thinking to examine the role of the school administrator. In J. Kincheloe & D. Weil (Eds.), *Standards and schooling in the United States: An encyclopedia* (3 vols.). Santa Barbara, CA: ABC-CLIO.

West, C. (1993). *Race matters.* Boston: Beacon.

Wexler, P. (1996a). *Critical social psychology.* New York: Peter Lang.

Wexler, P. (1996b). *Holy sparks: Social theory, education, and religion.* New York: St. Martin's.

Wexler, P. (1997, October). *Social research in education: Ethnography of being.* Paper presented at the International Conference on the Culture of Schooling, Halle, Germany.

Wexler, P. (2000). *The mystical society: Revitalization in culture, theory, and education.* Boulder, CO: Westview.

Willinsky, J. (2001). Raising the standards for democratic education: Research and evaluation as public knowledge. In J. Kincheloe & D. Weil (Eds.), *Standards and schooling in the United States: An encyclopedia* (3 vols.). Santa Barbara, CA: ABC-CLIO.

Willis, P. E. (1977). *Learning to labour: How working class kids get working class jobs.* Farnborough, UK: Saxon House.

Willis, P. (1978). *Profane culture.* London: Routledge & Kegan Paul.

Willis, P., Jones, S., Cannan, J., & Hurd, G. (1990). *Common culture.* Milton Keynes, UK: Open University Press.

Willis, P. (2000). *The ethnographic imagination.* Cambridge, UK: Polity.

Women's Studies Group, Centre for Contemporary Cultural Studies. (1978). *Women take issue: Aspects of women's subordination.* London: Hutchinson, with Centre for Contemporary Cultural Studies, University of Birmingham.

Woodward, K. (Ed.). (1997). *Identity and difference.* London: Sage.

Young, I. (1990). The ideal of community and the politics of difference. In L. J. Nicholson (Ed.), *Feminism/postmodernism.* New York: Routledge.

Young, T., & Yarbrough, J. (1993). *Reinventing sociology: Missions and methods for postmodern sociology* (Transforming Sociology Series, 154). Red Feather Institute. Retrieved from www.etext.org/Politics/Progressive.Sociologists/authors/Young.TR/reinventing-sociology

Zammito, J. (1996). *Historicism, metahistory, and historical practice: The historicization of the historical subject.* Retrieved from http://cohesion.rice.edu/humanities/csc/conferences.cfm?doc_id=378

Zizek, S. (1990). *The sublime object of ideology.* London: Verso.

13

METHODOLOGIES FOR CULTURAL STUDIES

An Integrative Approach

Paula Saukko

In this chapter, I discuss the characteristic methodological approaches of cultural studies and how recent intellectual and historical developments have modified them. I also propose an integrative methodological framework that interlaces the different philosophical and methodological commitments of the paradigm. By doing this, I hope to point beyond debates that have underpinned cultural studies since its inception over whether the focus of research should be culture, people, or the real—or texts, audiences, or production in communication studies (e.g., Ferguson & Golding, 1997; Grossberg, 1998; McGuigan, 1997; McRobbie, 1997).

The distinctive feature of cultural studies is the way in which it combines a hermeneutic focus on lived realities, a (post)structuralist critical analysis of discourses that mediate our experiences and realities, and a contextualist/realist investigation of historical, social, and political structures of power. This creative combining of different approaches has accounted for the productivity and popularity of cultural studies since the golden years of the Birmingham Centre for Contemporary Cultural Studies in the 1970s. However, it also has resulted in philosophical and political tensions. The hermeneutic interest in lived realities runs into a contradiction with the poststructuralist interest in critical analysis of discourses, posing the question: How can one be true to lived experiences and, at the same time, criticize discourses that form the very stuff out of which our lived realities are made? Furthermore, hermeneutics and poststructuralism explore the lived and political dimensions of realities in the plural. On the contrary, contextualism is always wedded to an implicit or explicit realism or the idea that social structures of power constitute the bottom line or the reality against which the meaning and effectiveness of discourses and experiences should be

Author's Note. The support of the Economic and Social Science Research Council (ESRC) is gratefully acknowledged. This work forms part of the research program on Genomics in Society (Egenis). The author would also like to thank Pertti Alasuutari and Norman Denzin for comments.

Table 13.1. The Three Validities or Methodological Programs in Cultural Studies in an Integrated Framework

	Contextual Validity	*Dialogic Validity*	*Self-Reflexive Validity*
Contextual dimension	**Social reality**	Local realities in social context	Research shapes "real" social processes
Dialogic dimension	Local repercussions of social processes	**Local realities**	Local awareness of social shaping of reality
Self-reflexive dimension	Research shapes social processes or reality	Local realities are socially shaped	**Social shaping of reality**

evaluated. These frictions between different methodological approaches structured the chapters on cultural studies in the previous editions of the *Handbook of Qualitative Research*, addressing the long-standing juxtaposition of research on production and consumption in media studies (Fiske, 1994) and discussing multiperspectival research (Frow & Morris, 2000).

In the spirit of contributing to a handbook on methodology, and following in the footsteps of pioneers such as Lincoln and Guba (1985, 1994) and Lather (1993), I intend that this chapter will start to make sense of the three methodological currents in cultural studies by translating them into three "validities." In traditional social research–speak, validity refers to various measures that aim to guarantee the "truthfulness" of research or that attempt to ensure that research accurately and objectively describes reality. The three modes of inquiry in cultural studies, however, open distinctive perspectives on reality or define truth differently. The hermeneutic impulse in cultural studies evaluates the value of research in terms of how sensitive it is to the lived realities of its informants (Lincoln & Guba, 1985, 1994). The poststructuralist bent in the paradigm assesses research in terms of how efficiently it exposes the politics embedded in the discourses through which we construct and perceive realities (Lather, 1993). The contextual and realist commitment of cultural studies most closely mirrors the traditional criteria for validity in that it evaluates how accurately or truthfully research makes sense of the historical and social reality.

In this chapter, I propose an integrative and multidimensional framework for combining the hermeneutic or dialogic, poststructuralist or self-reflexive, and contextual validities that form the methodological basis of cultural studies. I do not argue that these different validities are united by a common reference to truth. However, nor do I argue that they refer to different truths. Instead, I explore how the three validities interlace one another, so that each validity or research program is rendered multidimensional by the other two (see Table 13.1). For example, contextualist analysis of social structures and processes may focus on what these structures "are." Such analysis will be enriched, however, by paying attention to the way in which these social processes may be experienced very differently in particular local contexts (dialogism). It also will benefit from thinking through how the research itself, for its small or big part, influences the processes it is studying (self-reflexivity).

The proposed methodological framework builds on the long-term tradition of doing empirical research in cultural studies, while also pushing it in new directions. The days are gone when social research could speak from the top-down or ivory-tower position of autonomy and objectivism. Gone also are the days when cultural studies could speak from the bottom-up, romantic/populist position of "the margin." Current theories, such as actor-network theory (Latour, 1993, also Haraway, 1997), as well as institutional pressures to attain external funding and produce more and more monetary, social, and intellectual "outcomes," view scholarship in less vertical and more horizontal terms. Research is viewed as being not above or below but in the middle, as one among many actors that forges connections between different institutions, people, and things, creating, fomenting, and halting social processes. The integrated but multidimensional methodological framework hopes to offer both a survival kit and a critical toolbox in this brave new world, helping to make sense of what it is, how it affects different peoples, and what our role is in it.

Methodological Histories

Before discussing the three validities and their dimensions in more detail, I will revisit the history of cultural studies as a means of grounding the current approaches. As Stuart Hall (1982) analyzed in a classic article, cultural studies as a paradigm carved itself a space in the early 1970s, between and beyond right-wing positivist functionalism and left-wing Marxist political economy. It did this by innovatively combining hermeneutics, structuralism, and New Leftism (Hall, 1980), and these three philosophical/political currents shaped and continue to shape empirical inquiry in the paradigm (on the early works, see Gurevitch, Woollacott, Bennett, & Curran, 1982; Hall, Hobson, Lowe, & Willis, 1980).

Two early landmark studies in cultural studies, Paul Willis's *Learning to Labour* (1977) and Janice Radway's *Reading the Romance* (1984), highlight the both fruitful and problematic nature of this multimethodological approach. Both Willis and Radway empathetically studied the everyday life of a subordinated group. Willis investigated the misbehavior of working-class schoolboys, and Radway analyzed fantasies of middle-class women involving a relationship with a nurturing man that drive these women to read romances. On the surface, these popular activities may appear to be of little importance or even silly. However, Willis and Radway argue that they address important, "real" structural inequalities, namely working-class children's alienation within the middle-class school-culture and women's dissatisfaction with intimate relationships structured by patriarchy. The authors, however, conclude that despite their creative and resistant nature, these activities do not transform the structures of power they address. Instead, they end up consolidating the structures, as underperformance at school leads working-class boys to blue-collar jobs and the seductive powers of romance novelettes hold women under the spell of an imaginary nurturing or true love.

The methodological innovativeness of these early works lies in their ability to take seriously a popular, often ignored, practice, such as disobedience at school or reading of romance literature, trying to understand its significance from the point of view of the people involved as well as against the backdrop of the wider social context. However, this strength also constitutes the Achilles' heel of the methodology. Willis and Radway argue that the misbehaving working-class boys and romance-reading women resist real structures of power (alienating education, patriarchy), yet they posit that this resistance is "imaginary," in that it gives people a sense of power or pleasure but does little to transform class or gender structures. These underlying distinctions, however, raise the question of how to separate wheat from chaff or real from imaginary resistance.[1]

As critical commentators (Ang, 1996; Marcus, 1986) have noted, what counts as the "real," against which the per se interesting popular acts are to be evaluated, reflects the authors' preferred theoretical frameworks, namely Marxist labor theory and feminism. This highlights a constitutive tension between a hermeneutic interest in subordinated experiences/realities and the New Leftist project of evaluating their relevance against the social context or "system." Three decades after his classic study, Willis (2000) defends his reading of the schoolboys' culture through theory, stating that field material needs to be brought to "forcible contact with outside concepts" in order to locate it as part of a wider whole (p. xi). The question, however, remains how to forge the micro and the macro in a way that does not reduce the local experiences to props for social theories.

When these canonical pieces are examined from a contemporary perspective, they come across as lodged in a decidedly modern and vertical imaginary of "foundations"—structuring theories, such as the Marxist base/superstructure model, the Freudian theory of the unconscious, and the idea of genes as the blueprint of life. All these theories refer to a deep or hidden layer of reality that is excavated or brought to light by science in order to provide the final explanation (structures of labor, the unconscious, DNA) of societies, people, or life.

What is interesting about Willis's and Radway's works is that they compare and contrast experiences in different sites. These innovative contrasts, however, are interpreted in vertical or hierarchical terms, so that one (the factory, intimate relations) is more "real," whereas the other one (the school, romance reading) is less so. However, one also can juxtapose multiple sites and social processes in a more horizontal manner that does not necessarily privilege one process over another but highlights how they interact and interrupt each other (see Marcus, 1998). Maybe having to do with her spatial field of geography, Doreen Massey (1994) has, like Willis, examined the marginalization of working-class men while drawing attention to the contradictions of the process. Exploring the aftermath of the British Miners' Strike, she notes that the benefits of government regeneration programs went to the wives of the former miners. After a long history of domestic servitude, these women offered the perfect labor pool for the new industries that wanted a "flexible" and non-unionized labor force that was willing to take up temporary and part-time jobs for low pay. Looking at the formation of these new labor markets from several perspectives (how it marginalized men yet allowed women to gain a level of economic independence, even if within a controversial economic configuration) highlights the multidimensionality of the process instead of interpreting it as simply a loss or a victory. Exploring several perspectives in an open fashion may enrich systemic analyses by focusing attention on developments that do not fit the initial framework, such as Marxist labor theory, and perhaps also pave the way for more inclusive and multidimensional political responses.

Contextual Validity

Willis's and Radway's studies are examples of cultural studies research that emphasize the social context, providing a convenient bridge to start a discussion on the contextual validity in cultural studies. The contextual dimension of research refers to an analysis of social and historical processes, and the worth or validity of the project depends on how thoroughly and defensibly or correctly this has been done. Few cultural studies projects embark on a major analysis of social, political, or economic processes. Such analyses usually involve an examination of large sets of statistical data and documents. Many cultural studies projects, however, make reference to social structures and processes, such as labor structures or, more recently, globalization or neoliberalism (e.g., Rose, 1999; Tomlinson, 1999). Therefore, relating to and assessing contextual developments may be seen as a prerequisite for doing high-quality cultural studies. I also argue in this section that not only does cultural studies benefit from contextualization but contextual analysis also benefits from being aware, in the dialogic spirit, of local realities that may challenge general analyses as well as being self-reflexively conscious of the political nature of its analysis.

To discuss the contextual approach, I have chosen to focus on a body of work that does not fall within cultural studies but is a prime example of an ambitious, realist analysis of contemporary global reality widely used by scholars in the field: Manuel Castells's highly acclaimed trilogy on the information society (Castells, 1996, 1997, 1998). Castells's oeuvre is based on a formidable amount of statistical and other data on social, technological, and economic developments in different parts of the world. Drawing on the data, he states that the world increasingly has been split into the sphere of The Net and the sphere of The Self. The Net emerges from flows, such as Internet communication and financial transactions as well as the globally mobile managerial elite, that operate beyond or above particular places. Castells argues that this space of flows begins to live a life of its own, as happens in places like New York or Mexico City, where the local elite is connected to global financial and other networks and disconnected from local marginalized people (Castells, 1996, p. 404). Most people, however, do not inhabit the ungrounded Net but are caught in places. In this sphere of The Self, Castells argues, people construct new identities and social movements that could challenge the elusive and elitist tendencies of the global Net. Castells distinguishes three kinds of identities and movements. A "legitimizing" identity validates dominant institutions, an example being trade unionists who bargain with the welfare state. A "resistant" identity reacts to globalization by isolating into a community of believers, ranging from Islamic fundamentalists and American patriots to Mexican Zapatistas on the Yucatán peninsula. A "project" identity, such as a feminist or environmentalist identity, on the contrary, reaches outward to connect with other people and issues and, therefore, according to Castells, has the potential to provide a counterforce to the global Net (Castells, 1997).

Castells's description of resistant identity appears prophetic against the backdrop of the September 11, 2001, attacks on the World Trade Center and the Pentagon. Those attacks seem to epitomize the resentful and futile violence of a "resistant" social movement that, instead of paving the way for social transformation, sparked a massive military retaliation against an entire region. This prophetic or critical insight of Castells's analysis is, however, troubled by his relentless dichotomizing categories, such as The Net/The Self, resistant/project, reactive/proactive, history/future, inward-looking/outward-looking, disconnected/connected (also Friedmann, 2000; Watermann, 1999). Despite Castells's understanding or analytical attitude toward the resistant movements, his polarizing logic underlines the prevailing idea that these groups are simply misguided, dangerous, and wrong, thereby fueling the kind of social division and mistrust that in other ways he is trying to address critically. This highlights the methodological blind spot of the realism that Castells represents. In its belief that through an analysis of, for example, statistics, it can describe how the world "really is," it is not able to reflect critically on the political nature of the categories it creates to excavate the "truth" out of these data.

The political nature and implications of Castells's conceptual framework become particularly clear when contrasting them to Ien Ang's (2001) analysis of another "resistant" movement, namely Pauline Hanson's right-wing populism and Patomäki's (2003) critical comment on Castells's eulogization of the Finnish model of combining a free-market information society and social equality (Castells & Himanen, 2002).

Drawing on Castells's analysis, Ang locates the roots of Hansonism in the white working class's loss of cultural and economic privilege amid the processes of a globalizing economy and transnational migration. She also notes the xenophobia embedded in the movement's rallying against being "swamped by Asians" and the futility of its strategy as it further disinvests its supporters from the contemporary economic and symbolic hard currency of multicultural ease and flexibility. However, halfway through the essay, Ang shifts gears and begins to reflect critically on her own position as a female intellectual of Asian origin who migrated to Australia in the 1990s when the New Labour, neoliberal government of Paul Keating was rebranding the continent as a "multicultural Australia in Asia." Ang interrogates how her enthusiasm with the inclusive reinterpretation of Australian nationality implicitly supports the harsh discourse on economic restructuring and competition for the Asian market that wants to transform Australia into "a future-oriented nation which is not just capable of change but actively desires change, turning necessity into opportunity in times of altered economic and geopolitical circumstances" (2001, p. 155). Castells invites radical cultural studies intellectuals to feel that in their outward-directedness they are "in the right," in relation to both global forces of capitalism and the self-enclosed fundamentalists. On the contrary, Ang suggests that intellectuals should critically reflect on their cultural and political frames of reference that may be complicit with the new global "survival of the fittest," in which Hansonites are the losers.

Patomäki (2003) challenges Castells's analytical framework from a rather different perspective. He refers to Castells's (Castells & Himanen, 2002) work that frames my own country of origin, Finland, as an exemplar of the successful combining of a free-market information economy—epitomized by Nokia mobile-phones and Linux open-source software—and social equality. Patomäki argues that Castells's interpretation of the mutual compatibility of Finland's aggressive liberalization and transformation into information economy during the 1990s, on one hand, and social equality, on the other, is an "optical illusion." Noting that Castells uses old statistics on income equality to make his point, Patomäki states that his analysis is misguiding, as it neglects the rapid steepening of social disparities in Finland during the 1990s, precisely when the country took the leap toward liberalization and information society. Thus, Patomäki's comment illustrates the danger that a strong commitment to a particular theory may carry the analyst away, to see what he or she wants to see in the data (that a liberal information economy is the only solution but that it can be harnessed to social equality).

To draw a preliminary conclusion, Castells's work is a brilliant example of meticulous and extraordinarily broad analysis of a social and global transformation, identifying it from an enormous material of pivotal tendencies. As such, it is a great exemplar of contextual validity and how to do a remarkable job in making sense of social reality. However, the works by Ang and Patomäki highlight that contextual analysis would benefit from the dialogic principle of being sensitive to local realities. As illustrated by the Australian Hansonites and the Finnish version of an information economy, paying close attention to these local cases might complicate the conceptual framework, drawing attention to complexities and incongruencies that do not fit the model. Furthermore, Ang and Patomäki also draw attention to the need to be self-reflexively aware of the political commitments embedded in the concepts and categories that drive one's work. Castells is deeply committed to the distinction between the Net and the Self and that the way forward is to give the Net a humane face (in the shape of the environmentalist and feminist movements or the Finnish model economy). This commitment makes him blind to the way in which his pronouncements may breed the kind of intolerance and hostility (against various peoples branded "fundamentalists") he laments and to the possibility that his socioeconomic analysis may legitimate the negative underpinnings of the new economy he criticizes.

◼ Dialogic Validity

Taking local realities seriously is the starting point for the second, dialogic, validity or research program in cultural studies. Dialogic validity has its roots in the classical ethnographic and hermeneutic project of capturing "the native's point of view" or, to quote Bronislaw Malinowski, "to realize *his* vision of *his* world" (Malinowski, 1922/1961, p. 25, see also Alasuutari, 1998, pp. 61–66). Classic ethnography, however, believed that it was possible for research to comprehend the internal universe of informants objectively, or through the rigorous use of a method, such as participant observation. More recent interpretations of the hermeneutic principle of understanding local realities view research in more interactive terms, as happening in the dialogic space between the Self of the researcher and the Other world of the person being researched (e.g., Buber, 1970; Maso, 2001). On the dialogic end of the hermeneutic continuum, research participants are involved in the project of capturing or constructing their reality as coworkers, involved in designing, executing, and reporting on the study, in some cases even sharing authorship (Lincoln, 1995). The dialogic interest in Other worlds also lays significant emphasis on emotional and embodied forms of knowledge and understanding, understood to be neglected by rationalistic "facts"-focused scientific research (e.g., Denzin, 1997).

An outstanding example of dialogic work that aims to understand a decidedly different or hard to comprehend world is Faye Ginsburg's (1989/1998) ethnography on prolife and prochoice women. After her fieldwork, Ginsburg's aim became to communicate the "counterintuitive" fact that prolife women, perceived as foes of feminism, saw themselves as defending female values of care, nurturance, and selflessness against violent masculine competitiveness and materialism (Ginsburg, 1997). One of her informants, Karen, explained that abortion has become accepted because materialist and individualist society does not value caring, and that "housewives don't mean much because we do the caring and mothering kinds of things which are not important" (Ginsburg, 1989/1998, p. 185). Thus, rather than fit Karen and her likes into an overarching social theory, Ginsburg aimed to comprehend how prolife women define the world and their place in it, and she allowed that view to trouble presuppositions about these women. Still, Ginsburg also provided another angle on abortion and described how the prochoice women saw their reward coming when women who have come to the clinic thank them for making a difference in their life and being "so warm, and so caring and so non-judgemental" (p. 155).

The extraordinary feature of Ginsburg's work on these two ways of experiencing female caring is that it enables the reader to relate to the contrasting realities of both of these groups of women and to comprehend them, even if not necessarily accepting them. Furthermore, Ginsburg also reaches outward from these intimate feelings, stating that they reflect the way in which the women's lives are shaped by the distinction between private care and public freedom that still structured the American society in the late 20th century. In making the two nearly incomprehensibly different worldviews comprehensible, as well as pointing out how they both address same-gendered structures of inequality, Ginsburg gestures toward political dialogues that would acknowledge both differences and points of common interest between the two groups. In her attempt to imagine ways to bridge different worlds, Ginsburg comes close to Ang's visions of forging tentative dialogues with the Hanson supporters.

Ginsburg's ethnographic work is exemplary in its intimate depth, social breadth, and balanced nuance. However, just as in research on social context, research on lived experiences is sometimes oblivious of other dimensions of life and reality. The literature in my current area of research, genetic testing, is rife with descriptions of intense intimate experiences that are strangely lacking in terms of critical social analysis. For example, Smith, Michie, Stephenson, and Quarrel (2002) have used interpretative phenomenological analysis to make sense of the way in which people who have relatives with Huntington's disease perceive their risk and make decisions about taking a predictive test. Huntington's disease is a genetic neurodegenerative disorder that will lead to deterioration of the person's mental and physical capacities and premature death in mid-life. It is a dominantly inherited condition: A person with one parent with Huntington's has a 50% chance of being afflicted. Smith et al. set out to get a "holistic" understanding of the "knife edge predicament" facing people who are deciding whether to take the test. They recount how one of their informants, Linda, psyched herself up for bad news and rationalized that, even if her result were negative, it would affect one of her children: "Even if you say for 100 percent it's gonna miss me, it's gonna cop for one of mine or both of mine. I says so how do you think that makes me feel?" (Smith et al., 2002, p. 135). Smith et al. succinctly capture the feel of such tough decisions—you can almost hear Linda speaking in her rolling and thick working-class British accent. However, even if the description stays true to the texture of the experience, it ends up fixated on perceptions (and misunderstanding) of clinical, probabilistic risk estimates.

Smith et al. set out to resuscitate a warm, flesh-and-blood, and emotional lived experience that has been ignored by mainstream medicine. However, when doing it, they reaffirmed the scientist's distinction between real, probabilistic risk estimates and perceptions of them, ending up exploring how these "facts feel" (Wynne, 2001). This fixation on clinical risk underlines the necessity to underpin the dialogic aim to capture the experience of the Other with a self-reflexive awareness that both our understanding of other people as well as their understanding of themselves is mediated by social discourses. Without this self-reflexive understanding, research may end up moving in a circle, where the starting point of research is a common social discourse (clinical risk) and the study then lends emotional or existential support to this common sense, dwelling in its intensity (Atkinson & Silverman, 1997). There are no "cracks" in this story that would allow for a moment of critical reflection on these new identities and discourses formed around "risk." Furthermore, the analysis seems as if it floats in a timeless and placeless emotional intensity, where not only the mediated nature but also the social context or contextual dimension of the experience fall out of the picture. In the analysis of predictive testing for Huntington's disease, the social ramifications of genetic testing—such as how it interacts with other social regimes, including the contemporary, contradictory social and political discourse emphasizing taking "responsibility" of, or enhancing, one's self, health, and life (see Novas & Rose, 2000)—are entirely absent in the picture. Dialogic research sees itself seeking to give voice to experiences that have been neglected by mainstream society. If the methodological framework does not leave space for the experiences to address the discourses and social contexts that shape them, the experiences cannot speak about or back to the social structures that neglected them in the first place.

◼ Self-Reflexive Validity

Critical reflection on how social discourses and processes shape or mediate how we experience our selves and our environment is, perhaps, the most prominent feature of cultural studies. Analyses of popular media texts—such as the romances studied by Radway—and how they shape the way we understand our selves are the trademark of cultural studies research. Self-reflexive awareness of mediation, thus, is the most characteristic criterion for good or valid research in the paradigm.

Most critically reflexive research in cultural studies, including Radway's work, is "objectivist," or marked by the scholar's detached scrutiny of a body of texts or talk in terms of the social discourses that underpin them. The trouble with objectivist analyses is that they may end up forgetful of the discourses that guide the analysis itself, as happens in Radway's study, which pronounces women as falling short of becoming fully fledged feminists.

When I initiated my research on women who, like myself, had been anorexic, I was aggravated or insulted by objectivist analyses—both psychiatric (e.g., Bruch, 1978) and feminist (e.g., Bordo, 1993)—that examined the way in which women who starved were influenced by social discourses, such as beauty ideals. I felt that these diagnostic analyses oversimplified anorexia and fueled the notion that anorexic women are dis-ordered, or incapable of reliably assessing their thoughts or actions. Thus, when I interviewed women who had had anorexia, I asked them to tell about their experience with the condition, which inevitably led to a discussion of beauty and gender norms, as well as to tell me what they thought of the diagnostic notions of anorexia. By doing this, I wanted to avoid diagnosing the women, from the outside, in terms of identifying discourses that informed their self-understanding. I rather wanted to invite them to "do" poststructuralism with me, from the inside, on both the discourses that informed their starving and the discourses that informed their diagnosis.

The response that I got was varied. An American woman, Jeanne, stated that her starving was informed by the "Reagan years, when women were supposed to have it all, be extremely successful in all realms and be extremely thin and good-looking." The attempt to live up to this ideal led her to exercise to the extreme, work in popular campus bars, and use the money she earned to buy clothing to "show off" her thin body. She also was an excellent student who would spend her nights in the undergraduate lounge, where she would "smoke, and smoke, and smoke and drink diet sodas and just study into the night." In a similar fashion, a Finnish woman, Taru, associates her starving with having danced ballet. For 15 years, since the age of 5, she did everything she could to become a professional dancer: strong, light, and flawless. To achieve this, she put herself through an excruciating regime of exercises, long stays abroad, crossing half of Finland to attend lessons, and assuaging her hunger by nibbling on rice and Tabasco sauce, which "made her stomach feel warm."

Despite the similarities of their experience of anorexia, Jeanne and Taru assessed the diagnostic discourses on the condition rather differently. Reflecting on her years of starving and the diagnostic notions of eating disorders, Jeanne noted that she was a relatively typical middle-class anorexic. She concluded that she is "not proud" for having had anorexia, which with hindsight seemed "just so self-indulgent." Rather differently, Taru was sharply critical of notions of anorexia, noting that they were similar to stories she encountered when dancing ballet and reading fitness and sports magazines, which frame women as always "weaker" than men. She concluded that she did not want to analyze the causes of her anorexia too much, as she was afraid it just "reveals more weaknesses and abnormalities."

Both of the women's stories bear witness to the way in which their starving was informed by the competitive individualist ideal of strength and success. Looking back to it, Jeanne defined her quest for strength as both self-destructive and self-indulgent. Somewhat differently, Taru criticized the diagnostic discourses of anorexia that define women's pursuit of strength as merely pathological, noting that it simply added to the discourses that define women as too weak in mind and body, which informs the anorexic's fierce starving to overcome her shortcomings in the first place. Making sense of these similarities and differences, I resorted to an e-mail that I received from a third woman, Eleanora, who commented on an article that I had written (Saukko, 2000), based partly on her interview. She wrote that she did not recognize herself in the description of a lonely and pained child, noting that it fueled the notion of anorexic women as mere victims and did not acknowledge that they can also be strong. In the same e-mail, she added that the pursuit of strength also can be limiting and that her decision to follow her lover to a foreign country had sidetracked her adamant career orientation but also made her more happy, even if also insecure. What the stories of Jeanne, Taru, and Eleanora tell about is the merciless judgment that the cultural, highly gendered discourse on strength passes on these women. This normative discourse leaves little space for the kind of ambivalence communicated by Eleanora's personal story, which contemplates on how self-determination may enable women, or people in general, to get ahead in their lives but that it may also limit their lives, even if alternative paths are not without their problems.

Methodologically speaking, paying attention to social discourses, such as the individualist discourse on strength, allows us to illuminate deep-seated belief systems that guide our thoughts and actions and shape our societies. However, if done in an objectivist manner, these analyses may end up passing on problematic cultural diagnoses based on uninterrogated cultural assumptions. This happens, for example, when anorexic women are diagnosed as being subjugated by cultural ideals of strength and self-control and, in the same breath, defined as weak and out of control, affirming the same norms of strength and control. Opening this critical reflexive bite to other views benefits from being complemented with a dialogic dimension or sensitivity to local critiques of discourses. The rarely stated but usually assumed presumption in poststructuralism is that "lay" people are blind to social discourses that guide them and that critical analysis of mediation can be executed only by an expert. However, the idea that only experts can analyze expert discourses may render the analysis moving in a circle, as there is no way for critical outside insight to break into the cycle. This is particularly true when analyzing people like anorexics, whose critical comments on their diagnosis or treatment have been all too easily dismissed as defiance or symptomatic of their dis-order.

A more concrete or contextual dimension of self-reflexivity calls attention to the "real" implications our research has for the reality we are studying. This refers back to Foucault's argument with Derrida, in which Foucault (1979) noted that the discourse on madness did not simply symbolically affirm the Enlightenment notion of rationality (that stood in opposition to the definition of irrationality or madmen) but also very concretely locked the mad in institutions, ripping from them any basic human rights. When initiating my research on anorexia, I deliberately did not want to study anorexic women in a treatment context, as I wanted to critically analyze diagnostic practices. However, looking back to it, I have had second thoughts about this decision. Even though my work has been adopted by scholars and teachers working in psychology, I feel it would have had more of an impact on the treatment of anorexia if I had directly engaged with the therapeutic institution.

This question of whether research should be "in" or "out" of the institutional context it is addressing has been discussed at length in cultural studies, particularly in the so-called policy debates in the 1990s. Tony Bennett (1998) started these debates by suggesting that cultural studies as a paradigm should get engaged in policy making and advice, arguing that it would make the discipline more politically effective as well as acknowledge the fact that, despite claims of autonomy, research always legitimates political arrangements, such as the liberal humanism of the liberal state. Bennett's suggestion was met with criticism in some circles. The criticism drew parallels between his approach and so-called administrative communication research in postwar America that was funded by government and industry and concentrated on polling and marketing research and against which cultural and critical communication studies defined itself (Hardt, 1992). Tomaselli (1996) noted that the usefulness of the policy approach depended on the context, and that working for the South African government during apartheid may have been counterproductive, whereas collaboration with the new state was a different case.

The British Minister of Education, Charles Clarke, recently refueled the policy debate by stating that he does not "mind there being some medievalists around for ornamental purposes, but there is no reason for the state to pay for them." He later clarified that he wanted to underline the task of British universities to deal with challenges posed by "global change" to the national economy and society ("Devil's Advocate Ignites Row," 2003, p. 2). What this means can be exemplified by the fact that during Clarke's reign in office, the legendary Department of Cultural Studies at the Birmingham University was "restructured" out of existence in the summer of 2002. In this situation, there does not seem to exist a choice to be outside the system or do research that is not externally funded and socially or economically "relevant." This, however, does not mean that critical inquiry has had its day, but it does force scholars in the field to rethink self-reflexivity. The introspective interrogating of the discourses that impinge on other people's or on one's own self-understanding no longer is sufficient. What is called for is an outward-directed exploration of what kinds of concrete realities our research, for its big or small part, helps to create (Haraway, 1997). This returns this chapter back full circle to contextual validity, or the need to assess research in terms of how well it is able to make sense of gritty social and historical processes and the role it plays in those processes.

▣ Conclusion

Perhaps, in a way that was symptomatic of the newest of new times (Hall & Jacques, 1989) in cultural studies, about a year ago I decided to change gears in my academic career. I left communication studies and moved into social scientific research on genomics. I thought genomics as an area was intellectually interesting, socially relevant, and timely, and, in a utilitarian fashion, probably a better bet to get funding than reading media texts.

The first surprise in my new job came when I had to wait for 6 months to get a go-ahead from the local ethics board for my study. In the aftermath of several scandals, including the so-called Bristol case—where tissue samples from children, who had died in cardiac surgery, were kept and used for research without permission over a long period of time—the governance of ethics in medical research in the United Kingdom has become part of a long-winded, multistage bureaucratic procedure. While waiting to study "real" people, I began following a virtual discussion group. The group that I was reading was for people with a relatively low "polygenic" susceptibility to developing deep vein thrombosis (as opposed to more familiar monogenic or deterministic genetic diseases, such as Huntington's). When I contacted the moderator and the hematologist working with the group about the study I was contemplating, they told me they were in the process of establishing an organization for patients, in collaboration with the Centers for Disease Control in Atlanta. They stated that my research on the group might serve the patient information project they were planning. One of the first priorities of the newly formed group was to negotiate a reduced price from La Roche for a machine that would allow home testing of blood-coagulation levels (to save people numerous trips to clinics). On the list, people also expressed hopes that the new organization would lobby for the House to pass the bill, approved by the Senate, that would ban insurance companies and employers from discriminating against people based on genetic information.

Rabinow (1996) has made sense of these new social sensibilities and modes of action with his term "biosociality" (as opposed to the old sociobiology), which refers to the ways in which people with shared genetic characteristics form identities and projects around them. They may form patient organizations that use virtual and real modes of communication and organization to forge connections between themselves, regulatory bodies, medical practitioners and scientists, pharmaceutical companies, and cultural studies scholars to produce often-contradictory political projects (also Heath, Koch, Ley, & Montova, 1999).

This current situation is significantly different from that of the early part of the 20th century, when geneticists James V. Neel and Victor McKusick based their research on the indigenous people in Amazonia and the old order Amish. They would go to these communities and harvest indigenous knowledge, plant and human DNA, family trees, family photographs, and life stories (Lindee, 2003; Santos, 2003). As Lindee has aptly noted, the material that McKusick collected consisted of very different kinds of knowledges, being like a "patchwork quilt, pulled together from multiple fabrics" (Lindee, 2003, p. 50). Yet the heterogeneity of these knowledges was rendered invisible in the final product of genetic knowledge that gives the appearance of pure, objective science. Those days of free harvesting, however, are gone. Nowadays, indigenous people and people with genetic conditions or susceptibilities do not necessarily simply lend themselves to be investigated but want to negotiate the collaboration.

As a consequence, research can no longer retreat to the space of apparent autonomy and objectivity and make statements about the social system, people, or nature. But neither can research render people with genetic conditions targets of their own romantic projections about the "margin." Instead, the researcher, like the people with their newly found biosociality, is caught in a messier and more horizontal network, forging and negotiating links between social and cultural research, medical research and practice, policy, patients, companies, and funding bodies, and possibly being funded by government research councils, health care providers, companies, or the patient organizations.

In this scenario, the old distinction between the system and the people blurs. This refers to the intersections between contextual and dialogic validities in Table 13.1. Thus, systems are comprehensible only through their local implications or manifestations, such as the mundane need for reasonably priced home testing machines, which may complicate or confound grand systemic pronouncements about the goodness or badness of our "genomic future" (on opposite views, see Department of Health, 2003; GeneWatch/UK, 2002). Yet, similarly, the local needs are intelligible only within the system. These might include the emerging use of genomic knowledge to prevent common illnesses, which has costs and benefits for the people using preventive tests and drugs, the health care and insurance system, and the companies producing the test machines.

The other side of the equation, the relationship between the people and the system, seems equally indistinguishable. This refers to the intersection between dialogic and self-reflexive validities in Table 13.1. The local people or realities or biosociality that we study do not exist—anymore than "genes" do—in "nature" or in a socially untouched state of authenticity, but are instead formed by the genomic configuration or system. Furthermore, local people cannot be presumed to be "dupes" or unaware of their relationship with the wider system. On the contrary, they actively engage with it, forming alliances, inserting pressure on, and bargaining with other social organizations, including cultural studies research projects, to advance their interests, such as better and affordable care.

Furthermore, we can observe a collapse of the distinctions that have formed the cornerstones of many of the methodological debates in cultural studies between the researcher and the research object/subject and virtual and real. This refers to the intersection of the self-reflexive and contextual validities in Table 13.1. Research on, for example, social implications of genomics cannot assume to be neutral, as it forms part of the busy network of actors who shape policy, regulations, treatment practices, scientific and funding priorities, and everyday lives. The influences exerted by the different constituencies within this network—cultural studies and genomic research, people with the genetic susceptibilities, policy makers, companies, and so on—are also both symbolic and real or "material/semiotic," to quote Haraway (1997). They not only represent people, genes, risk, cures, prevention, costs, and benefits but also forge them in concrete terms, giving rise to particular everyday routines of care, health care priorities, policies, and so on.

In the end, the task of the integrative methodological approach is to facilitate empirical inquiry into social reality in a way that takes into account that the reality is shot through with a mosaic of different realities and that our research is part of the processes forming this social mosaic or a "patchwork quilt" (Deleuze & Guattari, 1987; Lindee, 2003; Saukko, 2000). This integrative quilting approach aims to address some novel historical and intellectual factors, but it is close to exploring the nexuses between the local and global, the cultural and the real, and the personal and the political, which have fascinated and infatuated cultural studies throughout its history. I make no claim in this chapter to point "beyond" these positions or debates; I simply hope to contribute to the ongoing project of making the incompatible compatible in an analytically sophisticated, methodologically practical, and politically productive way that has fueled the paradigm for over three decades.

Note

1. This distinction reflects Antonio Gramsci's separation between "good sense" and "common sense" (Gramsci, 1971, p. 333) as well as the later concept of "double articulation" (Grossberg, 1997, p. 217).

References

Alasuutari, P. (1998). *An invitation to social research.* London: Sage.

Ang, I. (1996). *Living room wars: Rethinking media audiences for a postmodern world.* London: Routledge.

Ang, I. (2001). *On not speaking Chinese: Living between Asia and the West.* London: Routledge.

Atkinson, P., & Silverman, D. (1997). Kundera's *Immortality*: The interview society and the invention of the self. *Qualitative Inquiry, 3,* 304–325.

Bennett, T. (1998). *Culture: A reformer's science.* London: Sage.

Bordo, S. (1993). *The unbearable weight: Feminism, Western culture, and the body.* Berkeley: University of California Press.

Bruch, H. (1978). *The golden cage: The enigma of anorexia nervosa.* Cambridge, MA: Harvard University Press.

Buber, M. (1970). *I and thou.* New York: Charles Scribner's Sons.

Castells, M. (1996). *The rise of the network society.* London: Blackwell.

Castells, M. (1997). *The power of identity.* London: Blackwell.

Castells, M. (1998). *End of millennium.* London: Blackwell.

Castells, M., & Himanen, P. (2002). *The information society and the welfare state: The Finnish model.* Oxford, UK: Oxford University Press.

Deleuze, G., & Guattari, F. (1987). *A thousand plateaus: On capitalism and schizophrenia.* Minneapolis: University of Minnesota Press.

Denzin, N. (1997). *Interpretive ethnography: Ethnographic practices for the 21st century.* Thousand Oaks, CA: Sage.

Department of Health. (2003). *Our inheritance, our future: Realising the potential of genetics in the NHS.* London: The Stationery Office. Available at www.dh.gov.uk/PolicyAndGuidance/HealthAndSocialCareTopics/Genetics/GeneticsGeneralInformation/GeneticsGeneralArticle/fs/en?CONTENTID=4016430&chk=RnGBgL

Devil's advocate ignites row . . . (2003, May 16). *Times Higher Education Supplement,* pp. 1–3.

Ferguson, M., & Golding, P. (Eds.). (1997). *Cultural studies in question.* London: Sage.

Fiske, J. (1994). Audiencing: Cultural practice and cultural studies. In N. K.Denzin & Y. S. Lincoln (Eds.), *Handbook of qualitative research* (pp. 189–198). Thousand Oaks, CA: Sage.

Foucault, M. (1979). My body, this paper, this fire. *Oxford Literary Review, 4,* 9–28.

Friedmann, J. (2000). Reading Castells: *Zeitdiagnose* and social theory. *Environment and Planning D: Society and Space, 18,* 111–120.

Frow, J., & Morris, M. (2000). Cultural studies. In N. K. Denzin & Y. S. Lincoln (Eds.), *Handbook of qualitative research* (2nd ed., pp. 315–346). Thousand Oaks, CA: Sage.

GeneWatch/UK. (May, 2002). *Genetics and "predictive medicine": Selling pills, ignoring causes* (Briefing Number 18). Available at www.genewatch.org/HumanGen/publications/briefings.htm#Brief18

Ginsburg, F. (1997). The case of mistaken identity: Problems in representing women on the Right. In R. Hertz (Ed.), *Reflexivity and voice* (pp. 283–299). London: Sage.

Ginsburg, F. (1998). *Contested lives: The abortion debate in an American community.* Berkeley: University of California Press. (Original work published 1989)

Gramsci, A. (1971). *Selections from the prison notebooks of Antonio Gramsci* (Q. Hoare & J. Nowell Smith, Ed. and Trans.). London: Lawrence & Wishart.

Grossberg, L. (1997). *Bringing it all back home: Essays on cultural studies.* Durham, NC: Duke University Press.

Grossberg, L. (1998). The victory of culture. Part I. Against the logic of mediation. *Angelaki, 3*(3), 3–29.

Gurevitch, M., Woollacott, J., Bennett, T., & Curran, J. (Eds.). (1982). *Culture, society and the media.* London: Methuen.

Hall, S. (1980). Cultural studies: Two paradigms. *Media, Culture and Society, 2*(1), 59–72.

Hall, S. (1982). The rediscovery of ideology: Return of the repressed in media studies. In M. Gurevitch, J. Woollacott, T. Bennett, & J. Curran (Eds.), *Culture, society and the media* (pp. 56–90). London: Methuen.

Hall, S., Hobson, D., Lowe, A., & Willis, P. (Eds.). (1980). *Culture, media, language: Working papers in cultural studies, 1972–79.* London: Hutchinson.

Hall, S., & Jacques, M. (Eds.). (1989). *New times: The changing face of politics in the 1990s.* London: Lawrence and Wishart.

Haraway, D. (1997). *Modest-Witness@Second-Millennium.FemaleMan-Meets-OncoMouse: Feminism and technoscience.* London: Routledge.

Hardt, H. (1992). *Critical communication studies: Essays on communication, history and theory in America.* London: Routledge.

Heath, D., Koch, E., Ley, B., & Montova, M. (1999). Nodes and queries: Linking locations in networked fields of inquiry. *American Behavioral Scientist, 43*(3), 450–463.

Lather, P. (1993). Fertile obsessions. Validity after poststructuralism. *The Sociological Quarterly, 34*(4), 673–693.

Latour, B. (1993). *We have never been modern.* Cambridge, MA: Harvard University Press.

Lincoln, Y., & Guba, E. (1985). *Naturalistic inquiry.* London: Sage.

Lincoln, Y., & Guba, E. (1994). Competing paradigms in qualitative research. In N. K. Denzin & Y. S. Lincoln (Eds.), *Handbook of qualitative research* (pp. 105–117). Thousand Oaks, CA: Sage.

Lindee, M. S. (2003). Provenance and pedigree: Victor McKusick's fieldwork with the old order Amish. In A. Goodman, D. Heath, & M. S. Lindee (Eds.), *Genetic nature/culture: Anthropology and science beyond the two-culture divide* (pp. 41–76). Berkeley: University of California Press.

Malinowski, B. (1961). *Argonauts of the Western Pacific.* New York: E. P. Dutton. (Original work published 1922)

Marcus, G. (1986). Contemporary problems of ethnography in the modern world system. In J. Clifford & G. Marcus (Eds.), *Writing culture: The politics and poetics of ethnography* (pp. 165–193). Berkeley: University of California Press.

Marcus, G. (1998). *Ethnography through thick and thin.* Princeton, NJ: Princeton University Press.

Maso, I. (2001). Phenomenology and ethnography. In P. Atkinson, A. J. Coffey, S. Delamont, J. Lofland, & L. H. Lofland (Eds.), *Handbook of ethnography* (pp. 136–144). London: Sage.

Massey, D. (1994). *Space, place and gender.* London: Polity.

McGuigan, J. (Ed.). (1997). *Cultural methodologies.* London: Sage.

McRobbie, A. (Ed.). (1997). *Back to reality? Social experience and cultural studies.* Manchester, UK: Manchester University Press.

Novas, C., & Rose, N. (2000). Genetic risks and the birth of the somatic individual. *Economy and Society, 29*(4), 485–513.

Patomäki, H. (2003). An optical illusion: The Finnish model for the information age. *Theory, Culture, and Society, 20*(3), 136–145.

Radway, J. (1984). *Reading the romance: Women, patriarchy, and popular literature.* Chapel Hill: University of North Carolina Press.

Rose, N. (1999). *Powers of freedom: Reframing political thought.* Cambridge, UK: Cambridge University Press.

Santos, R. V. (2003). Indigenous peoples, changing social and political landscapes, and human genetics in Amazonia. In A. Goodman, D. Heath, & M. S. Lindee (Eds.), *Genetic nature/culture: Anthropology and science beyond the two-culture divide* (pp. 23–40). Berkeley: University of California Press.

Saukko, P. (2000). Between voice and discourse: Quilting interviews on anorexia. *Qualitative Inquiry, 6*(3), 299–317.

Smith, J., Michie, S., Stephenson, M., & Quarrel, O. (2002). Risk perception and decision-making in candidates for genetic testing for Huntington's disease: An interpretative phenomenological analysis. *Journal of Health Psychology, 7*(2), 131–144.

Tomaselli, K. (1996, December). *Cultural policy & politics: South Africa and the Australian cultural policy "moment."* Paper delivered at the Cultural Studies Association of Australia Conference "In Search of the Public." Retrieved from www.nu.ac.za/ccms/anthropology/culturalpolicy.asp?ID=1

Tomlinson, J. (1999). *Globalization and culture.* London: Polity.

Watermann, P. (1999). The brave new world of Manuel Castells: What on earth (or in the ether) is going on? *Development and Change, 20,* 357–380.

Willis, P. (1977). *Learning to labour: How working-class kids get working-class jobs.* Westmead: Saxon House.

Willis, P. (2000). *The ethnographic imagination.* Cambridge, UK: Polity.

Wynne, B. (2001). Creating public alienation: Expert cultures of risk and ethics on GMOs. *Science as Culture, 10*(4), 445–481.

14

CRITICAL HUMANISM AND QUEER THEORY

Living With the Tensions

Ken Plummer

Failure to examine the conceptual structures and frames of reference which are unconsciously implicated in even the seemingly most innocent factual inquires is the single greatest defect that can be found in any field of inquiry.

—John Dewey (1938, p. 505)

Most people in and outside of the academy are still puzzled about what queerness means, exactly, so the concept still has the potential to disturb or complicate ways of seeing gender and sexuality, as well as the related areas of race, ethnicity and class.

—Alexander Doty (2000, p. 7)

Research—like life—is a contradictory, messy affair. Only on the pages of "how-to-do-it" research methods texts or in the classrooms of research methods courses can it be sorted out into linear stages, clear protocols, and firm principles. My concern in this chapter lies with some of the multiple, often contradictory assumptions of inquiries. Taking my interest in sexualities/gay/queer research as a starting point and as a tension, I see "queer theory" and "critical humanism" as one of my own tensions. I have tried to depict each and to suggest some overlaps, but my aim has not been to reconcile the two. That is not possible and probably is not even desirable. We have to live with the tensions, and awareness of them is important background for the self-reflexive social researcher.

Social Change and Zombie Research

This discussion should be seen against a background of rapid social change. Although for many, research methods remain the same over time (they just get a bit more refined with each generation), for others of us, changes in society are seen to bring parallel changes in research practices. To put it bluntly, many claim we are moving into a postmodern, late modern, globalizing, risk, liquid society. A new global order is in the making that is much more provisional and less authoritative than that of the past; it is a society of increasing self-reflexivity and individuation, a network society of flows and mobilities, a society of consumption and waste (Bauman, 2000, 2004; Beck, 2003; Giddens,1991; Urry, 2000).

As we tentatively move into these new worlds, our tools for theory and research need radical overhaul. German sociologist Ulrich Beck, for example, speaks of "zombie categories"; we move among the living dead! Zombie categories are categories from the past that we continue to use even though they have long outlived their usefulness and even though they mask a different reality. We probably go on using them because at present we have no better words to put in their place. Yet dead they are.

Beck cites the example of the concept of "the family" as an instance of a zombie category, a term that once had life and meaning but for many now means very little. I suggest that we could also cite most of our massive research methodology apparatus as partially zombified. I am not a major fan of television, but when I choose to watch a documentary, I often am impressed by how much more I get from it than from the standard sociological research tract. Yet the skills of a good documentary maker are rarely the topics of research methods courses, even though these skills—from scriptwriting and directing to camera movements and ethics—are the very stuff of good 21st-century research. And yes, some research seems to have entered the world of cyberspace, but much of it simply replicates the methods of quantitative research, making qualitative research disciplined, quantitative, and antihumanistic. Real innovation is lacking. Much research at the end of the 20th century—to borrow Beck's term again—truly was zombie research (Beck, 2003).

Table 14.1 suggests some links between social change and social research styles. The background is the authoritative scientific account with standard research protocols. As the social world changes, so we may start to sense new approaches to making inquiries. My concern in this chapter is largely with the arrival of queer theory.

A Reflexive Introduction

How research is done takes us into various language games—some rational, some more contradictory, some qualitative, some quantitative. The languages we use bring with them all manner of tensions. Although they sometimes help us chart the ways we do research, they often bring their own contradictions and problems. My goal here is to address some of the incoherencies I have found in my own research languages and inquiries and to suggest ways of living with them. Although I will draw widely from a range of sources and hope to provide some paradigmatic instances, the chapter inevitably will be personal. Let me pose the key contradiction of my inquiries. (We all have our own.)

The bulk of my inquiries have focused on sexualities, especially lesbian and gay concerns, with an ultimate eye on some notion of sexual justice. In the early days, I used a relatively straightforward symbolic interactionism to guide me in relatively straightforward fieldwork and interviewing in and around London's gay scene of the late 1960s. At the same time, I engaged politically, initially with the Homosexual Law Reform Society and then with the Gay Liberation Front in its early years. I read my Becker, Blumer, Strauss, and Denzin! At the same time, I was coming out as a young gay man and finding my way in the very social world I was studying. More recently, such straightforwardness has come to be seen as increasingly problematic. Indeed, there was

Table 14.1. Shifting Research Styles Under Conditions of Late Modernity

Current Social Changes	*Possible Changes in Research Style*
Toward a late modern world	Toward a late modern research practice
Postmodern/fragmentation/pluralization	The 'polyphonic' turn
Mediazation	The new forms of media as both technique and data
Stories and the death of the grand narrative	The storytelling/narrative turn
Individualization/choices/unsettled identities	The self-reflexive turn
Globalization-glocalization hybridization/ diaspora	The hybridic turn: decolonizing methods (L. T. Smith, 1999)
High tech/mediated/cyborg /post-human	The high-tech turn
Knowledge as contested	The epistemological turn
Postmodern politics and ethics	The political/ethical turn
The network society	Researching flows, mobilities, and contingencies
Sexualities as problematic	The queer turn

always a tension there: I just did not always see it (Plummer, 1995).

On one hand, I have found myself using a language that I increasingly call that of critical humanism, one allied to symbolic interactionism, pragmatism, democratic thinking, storytelling, moral progress, redistribution, justice, and good citizenship (Plummer, 2003). Inspirations range from Dewey to Rorty, Blumer to Becker. All of these are quite old and traditional ideas, and although I have sensed their postmodernized affinities (as have others), they still bring more orthodox claims around experience, truths, identities, belonging to groups, and a language of moral responsibilities that can be shared through dialogues (Plummer, 2003).

By contrast, I also have found myself at times using a much more radicalized language that nowadays circulates under the name of queer theory. The latter must usually be seen as at odds with the former: Queer theory puts everything out of joint, out of order. "Queer," for me, is the postmodernization of sexual and gender studies. "Queer" brings with it a radical deconstruction of all conventional categories of sexuality and gender. It questions all the orthodox texts and tellings of the work of gender and sexuality in the modern world (and all worlds). It is a messy, anarchic affair—not much different from intellectual anarchists or political International Situationists. "Queer" would seem to be antihumanist, to view the world of normalization and normality as its enemy, and to refuse to be sucked into conventions and orthodoxy. If it is at all sociological (and it usually is not), it is gothic and romantic, not classical and canonical (Gouldner, 1973). It transgresses and subverts.

On one hand, then, I am quite happy about using the "new language of qualitative method" (Gubrium & Holstein, 1997); on the other, I am quite aware of a queer language that finds problems everywhere with orthodox social science methods (Kong, Mahoney, & Plummer, 2002). Again, these tensions are very much products of their time (queer theory did not exist before the late 1980s). Yet, retrospectively, it would seem that I have always walked tightropes between an academic interactionism, a political liberalism, a gay experience, and a radical critique.

But of course, as usual, there are more ironies here. Since the late 1980s, I have more or less considered myself "post-gay." So who was that young man from the past who studied the gay world? Likewise, those wild queer theorists have started to build their textbooks, their readers, and their courses, and they have proliferated their own esoteric cultlike worlds that often seem more academic than the most philosophical works of Dewey. Far from breaking boundaries, queer theorists often have erected them, for while they may not wish for closure, they nevertheless find it. Queer theories have their gurus, their followers, and their canonical texts. But likewise, humanists and new qualitative researchers—finding themselves under siege from postmodernists, queer theorists, some feminists, and multiculturalists and the like—have also fought back, rewriting their own histories and suggesting that many of the critiques laid at their door are simply false. Some, like Richard Rorty—the heir apparent to the modern pragmatism of Dewey and James—fall into curious traps: Himself labeled a postmodernist by others, he condemns postmodernists as "posties" (Rorty, 1999). Methodological positions often lead in directions different from those originally claimed.[1]

So here am I, like many others, a bit of a humanist, a bit post-gay, a sort of a feminist, a little queer, a kind of a liberal, and seeing that much that is queer has the potential for an important radical change. In the classic words of interactionism, Who am I? How can I live with these tensions?

This chapter is not meant to be an essay of overly indulgent self-analysis, but rather one in which, starting to reflect on such a worry, I am simply showing tensions that many must confront these days. Not only am I not alone in such worries, but I also am fairly sure that all reflective qualitative inquiries will face their own versions of them, just as most people face them in their daily lives. Ambivalence is the name of the game.

In this chapter, I plan to deal with three interconnected issues raised by qualitative research—all focused on just how far we can "push" the boundaries of qualitative research into new fields, strategies, and political/moral awareness—and how this has been happening continuously in my own work. New languages of qualitative method benefit from new ideas that at least initially may be seen as opposition. This is how they grow and how the whole field of qualitative research becomes more refined. In what follows, I will explore:

- What is critical humanism and how to do a critical humanist method
- What is queer and how to do a queer method
- How the contradictions can be lived through

▣ The Critical Humanist Project

How different things would be . . . if the social sciences at the time of their systematic formation in the nineteenth century had taken the arts in the same degree they took the physical science as models.

—Robert Nisbet (1976, p. 16)

There is an illusive center to this contradictory, tension-ridden enterprise that seems to be moving further and further away from grand narratives and single, overarching ontological, epistemological, and methodological paradigms. This center lies in the humanistic commitment of the qualitative researcher to study the world always from the perspective of the interacting individual. From this simple commitment flow the liberal and radical politics of qualitative research. Action, feminist, clinical, constructivist, ethnic, critical, and cultural studies researchers all unite on this point. They all share the belief that a politics of liberation must always begin with the perspectives, desires, and dreams of those individuals and groups who have been oppressed by the larger ideological, economic, and political forces of a society or a historical moment.

—Denzin & Lincoln (1994, p. 575)

I use the term "critical humanism" these days to suggest orientations to inquiry that focus on human experience—that is, with the structure of experience and its daily lived nature—and that acknowledge the political and social role of all inquiry. It goes by many names—symbolic interactionism,[2] ethnography, qualitative inquiry, reflexivity, cultural anthropology, and life story research, among others—but they all have several concerns at heart. All these research orientations have a focus on human subjectivity, experience, and creativity: They start with people living their daily lives. They look at their talk, their feelings, their actions, and their bodies as they move around in social worlds and experience the constraints of history and a material world of inequalities and exclusions. They make methodological claims for a naturalistic "intimate familiarity" with these lives, recognizing their own part in such study. They make no claims for grand abstractions or universalism—assuming an inherent ambivalence and ambiguity in human life with no "final solutions," only damage limitations—while simultaneously sensing both their subjects' ethical and political concerns and their own in conducting such inquiries. They have pragmatic pedigrees, espousing an epistemology of radical, pragmatic empiricism that takes seriously the idea that knowing—always limited and partial—should be grounded in experience (Jackson, 1989). It is never neutral, value-free work, because the core of the inquiry must be human values. As John Dewey remarked long ago, "Any inquiry into what is deeply and inclusively (i.e., significantly) human enters perforce into the specific area of morals" (1920, p. xxvi). Impartiality may be suspect; but a rigorous sense of the ethical and political sphere is a necessity. Just why would one even bother to do research were it not for some wider concern or value?

What are these values? In the most general terms, critical humanism champions those values that give dignity to the person,[3] reduce human sufferings, and enhance human well-being. There are many such value systems, but at a minimum they probably must include the following:

1. A commitment to a whole cluster of *democratizing values* (as opposed to totalitarian ones) that aim to *reduce/remove human sufferings.* They take as a baseline *the value of the human being* and often provide a number of suggested *human rights*—freedom of movement, freedom of speech, freedom of association, freedom against arbitrary arrest, and so on. They nearly always include the *right to equality.* This commitment is strongly antisuffering and provides a major thrust toward both equality and freedom for all groups, including those with "differences" of all kinds (Felice, 1996).
2. An ethics of *care* and *compassion.* Significantly developed by feminists, this is a value whereby looking after the other takes on a prime role and whereby *sympathy, love,* and even *fidelity* become prime concerns (Tronto, 1993).
3. A politics of *recognition* and *respect.* Following the work of Axel Honneth (1995) and significantly shaped earlier by George Herbert Mead, this is a value whereby others are always acknowledged and a certain level of empathy is undertaken.
4. The importance of *trust.* This value recognizes that no social relationships (or society, for that matter) can function unless humans have at least some modicum of trust in each other (O'Neill, 2002).

Of course, many of these values bring their own tensions: We must work through them and live with them. A glaring potential contradiction, for example, may be to talk of humanistic values under capitalism, for many of the values of humanism must be seen as stressing nonmarket values. They are values that are not necessarily given a high ranking in a capitalist economy. Cornel West has put this well:

> In our own time it is becoming extremely difficult for non-market values to gain a foothold. Parenting is a non market activity; so much sacrifice and service go into it without any assurance that the providers will get anything back. Mercy, justice: they are non market. Care, service: non market. Solidarity, fidelity: non market. Sweetness and kindness and gentleness. All non market. Tragically, non market values are relatively scarce.... (West, 1999, p. 11)

The Methodologies of Humanism

These values strongly underpin critical humanism. In his classic book *The Human Perspective in Sociology*, T. S. Bruyn (1966) locates this humanistic perspective as strongly allied to the methods of participant observation. Elsewhere, I have suggested an array of life story strategies for getting at human experience. The task is a "fairly complete narrating of one's entire experience of life as a whole, highlighting the most important aspects" (R. Atkinson, 1998, p. 8). These may be long, short, reflexive, collective, genealogical, ethnographic, photographic, even auto/ethnographic (Plummer, 2000). Life stories are prime humanistic tools, but it is quite wrong to suggest that this means that the stories only have a concern with subjectivity and personal experience.[4]

Throughout all of this, there is a pronounced concern not only with the humanistic understanding of experience but also with ways of telling the stories of the research. Usually, the researcher is present in many ways in the text: The text rarely is neutral, with a passive observer. Chris Carrington's (1999) study of gay families, for example, makes it very clear from the outset his own location within a single-parent family: "I grew up in a working-poor, female-headed, single parent family. Throughout much of my childhood, in order to make ends meet, my mother worked nights as bar tender. There were periods where she could not get enough hours and our family had to turn to food stamps and welfare" (p. 7). Likewise, Peter Nardi's (1999) study of gay men's friendships is driven by his own passion for friends: "What follows is partly an attempt to make sense of my own experiences with friends" (p. 2). Humanistic inquiries usually reveal humanistic researchers.

Most commonly, as in Josh Gamson's *Freaks Talk Back* (1998) and Leila Rupp and Verta Taylor's *Drag Queens at the 801 Cabaret* (2003), the method employed will entail triangulation—a combination of cultural analysis tools.[5] Here, multiple sources of data pertaining to texts, production, and reception are collected and the intersections among them analyzed. In Rupp and Taylor's study of drag queens, they observed, tape recorded, and transcribed 50 drag performances, along with the dialogue, music, and audience interactions, including photographs and dressing up themselves. They collected data on the performances through weekly meetings of the drag artists and semistructured life histories, and they conducted focus groups on people who attended the performances. In addition, they looked at weekly newspapers (such as the gay paper *Celebrate*) and others to partially construct the history of the groups. Their research has a political aim, humanistic and sociological, and yet queer too, showing that combinations are possible. Enormous amounts of research have been written on all of this (e.g., Clifford & Marcus, 1986; Coffey, 1999; Coles, 1989; Ellis & Flaherty, 1992; Hertz, 1992; Reed-Danahay, 1997; Ronai, 1992).

A further recent example of such work is Harry Wolcott's (2002) account of Brad, the Sneaky Kid. Wolcott, an educational anthropologist, is well known for his methodological writings and books, especially in the field of education. This book started life in the early 1980s as a short journal article on the life story of Brad, a troubled 19-year-old. The story is aimed at getting at the human experience of educational failure, in particular, the lack of support for those who are not well served by our educational systems.

This would have been an interesting life story but an unexceptional one had it not been for all the developments that subsequently emerged around it. What are not told in the original story are the details of how Wolcott met Brad, how he had gay sex with him, and how he got him to tell his life story. Much follows after the original story, which later takes curious turns: Brad develops schizophrenia and returns one night to Wolcott's house to burn it down in an enraged attempt to kill him. This leads to the complete destruction of Wolcott's home and all his belongings (and those of his schoolteacher partner). A serious court case ensues in which Brad is tried and sent to prison. Despite Brad's guilt, Wolcott is himself scrutinized regarding his relationship, his homosexuality, and even his role as an anthropologist. Brad's family is especially unhappy about the relationship with Wolcott, but so are many academics. Ultimately, Brad is institutionalized. Eventually, the story is turned into an intriguing ethnographic play. I have only read the text of the play and not seen it performed. Judging by the text presented here, it comes across as a collage of 1980s pop music, sloganized slides, and a drama in two layers—one about Brad's relationship with Wolcott and another about Wolcott's ruminations, as a professor, on the plights of ethnography.

I mention this study because although it started out as a life story gloss—a simple relaying of Brad's story—because of the curious circumstances that it led to, a much richer and complex story was revealed that generated a host of questions and debates about the ethical, personal, and practical issues surrounding fieldwork. Sexuality and gender were pretty much at the core. It is a gripping tale of the kinds of issues highlighted by all humanistic research. Indeed, within the book a second major narrative starts to appear—that of Harry Wolcott himself. He was always present, of course, but his story takes over as he reveals how he had regular sex with the young man, his partner's disapproval of Brad, and how one night he returns to his house to find a strong smell of oil and Brad screaming "You fucker. I'm going to kill you. I'm going to kill you. I'm going to tie you up and leave you in the house and set the house on fire" (p. 74). Luckily, Harry escapes, but unluckily, his house does not. It goes up entirely in flames, with all of his and his partner's belongings. This may be one of the core dramatic moments in life story telling—certainly an "epiphany"! After that, a major chapter follows that tells of the working of the court and how Wolcott himself is almost on trial.

When the story of Sneaky Kid was first published in 1983, it was a 30-page essay; it has grown into a book of more than 200 pages (Wolcott, 2002). The original article does not tell much about the relationship from which it grew or much of the other background; the book tells much more, but it raises sharply the issue of just how much remains left out. The book serves as a sharp reminder that all social science, including life stories, consists of only partial selections of realities. There is always much going on behind the scenes that is not told. Here we have the inevitable bias, the partiality, the limits, the selectivity of all stories told—but I will not take these issues further here.

The Troubles With Humanism

Although I think humanism has a lot to offer qualitative inquiry, it is an unfashionable view these days: Many social scientists seem to want to turn only to discourse and language. But this discourse is not incompatible with doing this, as it evokes the humanities (much more so than other traditions), widens communities of understanding by dialoguing with the voices of others, and takes a strong democratic impulse as the force behind its thinking and investigating. As a form of imagery to think about social life, this is all to the good. It brings with it the possibility for such inquiry to engage in poetry and poetics, drama and performance, philosophy and photography, video and film, narrative and stories.

Nevertheless, these days humanism remains a thoroughly controversial and contested term—and not least among queer theorists themselves. We know, of course, the long-standing attacks on humanism from theologies, from behavioral psychologies, and from certain kinds of philosophers: There is a notorious debate between the humanist Sartre's *Existentialism and Humanism* and Heidegger's *Letter on Humanism.* More recent attacks have denounced "humanism" as a form of white, male, Western, elite domination and colonization that is being imposed throughout the world and that brings with it too strong a sense of the unique individual. It is seen as contra postmodernism. In one telling statement, Foucault proclaims, "The modern individual—objectified, analyzed, fixed—is a historical achievement. There is no universal person on whom power has performed its operations and knowledge, its enquiries" (1979, pp. 159–160). The "Human Subject" becomes a Western invention. It is not a progress or a liberation, merely a trapping on the forces of power.

This loose but important cluster of positions critical of humanism—usually identified with a postmodern sensibility—would include queer theorists, multicultural theorists, postcolonialists, many feminists, and antiracists, as well as poststructural theorists. Although I have much sympathy with these projects and the critical methodologies they usually espouse (e.g., L. T. Smith, 1999), I also believe in the value of the pragmatic and humanist traditions. How can I live with this seeming contradiction?

Let me look briefly at what the critics say. They claim that Humanists propose some kind of common and hence universal "human being" or self: a common humanity that blinds us to wider differences and positions in the world. Often this is seen as a powerful, actualizing, and autonomous force in the world: The individual agent is at the center of the action and of the universe. This is said to result in overt individualism strongly connected to the Enlightenment project (Western, patriarchal, racist, colonialist, etc.) which turns itself into a series of moral and political claims about progress through a liberal and democratic society. Humanism is linked to a universal, unencumbered "self" and to the "modern" Western liberal project. Such ideas of the human subject are distinctly "Western" and bring with them a whole series of ideological assumptions about the centrality of the white, Western, male, middle-class/bourgeois position; hence, they become the enemies of feminism (human has equaled male), ethnic movements (human has equaled white superiority), gays (human has equaled heterosexual), and all cultures outside the Western Enlightenment project (human here has equaled the middle-class West).

A More Complex Humanism?

Such claims made against "humanism" demean a complex, differentiated term into something far too simple. Humanism can, it is true, come to mean all of the above, but the term does not have to. Alfred McLung Lee (1978, pp. 44–45) and others have charted both a long history of humanism and many forms of it. Attacks usually are waged at a high level of generality, and specifics of what constitutes "the human" often are seriously overlooked. But, as I have suggested elsewhere, for me this "human being" is never a passive, helpless atom. Humans must be located in time and space: They are always stuffed full of their culture and history, and they must "nest" in a universe of contexts. Human beings are both embodied, feeling animals and creatures with great symbolic potential. They engage in symbolic communication and are dialogic and intersubjective: There is no such thing as the solitary individual. Human lives are shaped by chance, fateful moments, epiphanies, and contingencies. There is also a continuous tension between the specificities and varieties of humanities at any time and place, and the universal potentials that are to be found in all humans. And there is a continuous engagement with moral, ethical, and political issues.

Curiously, it is also clear that many of the seeming opponents of humanism can be found wanting to hold onto some version of humanism after all. Indeed, it is odd that some of the strongest opponents lapse into a kind of humanism at different points in their argument. For instance, Edward Said—a leading postcolonial critic of Western-style humanism—actually urges another kind of humanism, "shorn of all its 'unpleasantly triumphalist weight,'" and in recent work he actually claims to be a humanist (Said, 1992, p. 230; 2003).

Indeed, at the start of the 21st century, there have been many signs that the critique of humanism that pervaded the previous century has started to be reinvigorated as a goal of inquiry. More and more contemporary commentators, well aware of the attacks above, go on to make some kinds of humanist claims. It would not be hard to find signs of humanism (even if the authors disclaimed them!) in major studies such as Nancy Scheper-Hughes's *Death Without Weeping* (1994), Stanley Cohen's *States of Denial* (1999), and Martha Nussbaum's *Sex and Social Justice* (1999). For me, they are clearly inspired by a version of humanism with the human being at the heart of the analysis, with care and justice as core values, and with the use of any methods at hand that will bring out the story.[6] So whatever the critiques, it does appear that a critical humanism still has its place in social science and qualitative inquiry. But before going too far, we should see what queer theory has to say on all this.

A Queer Project

> *Queer articulates a radical questioning of social and cultural norms, notions of gender, reproductive sexuality and the family.*
>
> —Cherry Smith (2002, p. 28)

> *Queer is by definition whatever is at odds with the normal, the legitimate, the dominant. There is nothing in particular to which it necessarily refers.*
>
> —David Halperin (1995, p. 62)

Queer theory emerged around the mid- to late 1980s in North America, largely as a humanities/multicultural-based response to a more limited "lesbian and gay studies." While the ideas of Michel Foucault loom large (with his talks of "regimes of truth" and "discursive explosions"), the roots of queer theory (if not the term) usually are seen to lie in the work of Teresa de Lauretis (Halperin, 2003, p. 339) and Eve Kosofsky Sedgwick, who argued that

> many of the major nodes of thought and knowledge in twentieth century Western culture as a whole are structured—indeed fractured—by a chronic, now endemic crisis of homo/heterosexual definition, indicatively male, dating from the end of the nineteenth century. . . . an understanding of any aspect of modern Western culture must be, not merely incomplete, but damaged in its central substance to the degree that it does not incorporate a critical analysis of modern Homo/heterosexual definition. (1990, p. 1)

Judith Butler's work has been less concerned with the deconstruction of the homo/heterosexual binary divide and more interested in deconstructing the sex/gender divide. For her, there can be no kind of claim to any essential gender: It is all "performative," slippery, unfixed. If there is a heart to queer theory, then, it must be seen as a radical stance around sexuality and gender that denies any fixed categories and seeks to subvert any tendencies toward normality within its study (Sullivan, 2003).

Despite these opening suggestions, the term "queer theory" is very hard to pin down (some see this as a necessary virtue for a theory that refuses fixed identity). It has come to mean many things: Alexander Doty can suggest at least six different meanings, as follow. Sometimes it is used simply as a synonym for lesbian, gay, bisexual, transgender (LGBT). Sometimes it is an "umbrella term" that puts together a range of so-called "non-straight positions." Sometimes it simply describes any non-normative expression of gender (which could include straight). Sometimes it is used to describe "non-straight things" not clearly signposted as lesbian, gay, bisexual, or transgender but that bring with them a possibility for such a reading, even if incoherently. Sometimes it locates the "non-straight work, positions, pleasures, and readings of people who don't share the same sexual orientation as the text they are producing or responding to." Taking it even further, Doty suggests that "queer" may be a particular form of cultural readership and textual coding that creates spaces not contained within conventional categories such as gay, straight, and transgendered. Interestingly, what all his meanings have in common is that they are in some way descriptive of texts and they are in some way linked to (usually transgressing) categories of gender and sexuality (Doty, 2000, p. 6).

In general, "queer" may be seen as partially deconstructing our own discourses and creating a greater openness in the way we think through our categories. Queer theory must explicitly challenge any kind of closure or settlement, so any attempts at definition or codification must be nonstarters. Queer theory is, to quote Michael Warner, a stark attack on "normal business in the academy" (1992, p. 25). It poses the paradox of being inside the academy while wanting to be outside it. It suggests that a "sexual order overlaps with a wide range of institutions and social ideologies, to challenge the sexual order is sooner or later to encounter these institutions as a problem" (Warner, 1993, p. 5). Queer theory is really poststructuralism (and postmodernism) applied to sexualities and genders.

To a limited extent, queer theory may be seen as another specific version of what Nancy

Harstock and Sandra Harding refer to as standpoint theory (though I have never seen it discussed in this way). Initially developed as a way to analyze a position of women's subordination and domination, it suggests that an "opposition consciousness" can emerge that transcends the more taken-for-granted knowledge. It is interesting that hardly any men have taken this position up, but other women—women of race and disability, for example—have done so. Men seem to ignore the stance, and so too do queer theorists, yet what we may well have in queer theory is really something akin to a "queer standpoint."

Certain key themes are worth highlighting. Queer theory is a stance in which

- both the heterosexual/homosexual binary and the sex/gender split are challenged.
- there is a de-centering of identity.
- all sexual categories are open, fluid, and non-fixed (which means that modern lesbian, gay, bisexual, and transgender identities are fractured, along with all heterosexual ones).
- it offers a critique of mainstream or "corporate" homosexuality.
- it sees power as being embodied discursively. Liberation and rights give way to transgression and carnival as a goal of political action, what has been called a "politics of provocation."
- all normalizing strategies are shunned.
- academic work may become ironic, is often comic and paradoxical, and is sometimes carnivalesque: "What a difference a gay makes," "On a queer day you can see forever" (cf. Gever, Greyson, & Parmar, 1993).
- versions of homosexual subject positions are inscribed everywhere, even in heterosexualities.
- the deviance paradigm is fully abandoned, and the interest lies in a logic of insiders/outsiders and transgression.
- its most common objects of study are textual—films, videos, novels, poetry, visual images.
- its most frequent interests include a variety of sexual fetishes, drag kings and drag queens, gender and sexual playfulness, cybersexualities, polyamoury, sadomasochism, and all the social worlds of the so-called radical sexual fringe.

▣ A Queer Methodology?

What are the implications of queer theory for method (a word it rarely uses)? In its most general form, queer theory is a refusal of all orthodox methods—a certain disloyalty to conventional disciplinary methods (Halberstam,1998, pp. 9–13). What, then, does queer method actually do? What does it look like? In summary, let me give a few examples of what a queer methodology can be seen to offer.

The Textual Turn: Rereadings of Cultural Artifacts. Queer methods overwhelmingly employ an interest in and analysis of texts—films, literature, television, opera, musicals. This is perhaps the most commonly preferred strategy of queer theory. Indeed, Michael Warner has remarked that "almost everything that would be called queer theory is about ways in which texts—either literature or mass culture of language—shape sexuality." More extremely, he continues, "you can't eliminate queerness . . . or screen it out. It's everywhere. There's no place to hide, hetero scum!" (Warner, 1992, p. 19). The locus classicus of this way of thinking usually is seen to be Sedgwick's *Between Men* (1985), in which she looked at a number of key literary works (from Dickens to Tennyson) and reread these texts as driven by homosexuality, homosociality, and homophobia. Whereas patriarchy might condemn the former, it positively valorizes the latter (Sedgwick, 1985). In her wake have come hosts of rereadings around such themes. In later works, she gives readings to work as diverse as Diderot's *The Nun*, Wilde's *The Importance of Being Earnest*, and authors such as James and Austen (Sedgwick, 1990, 1994). In her wake, Alexander Doty gives queer readings to mass culture products such as "the sitcom"—from lesbian readings of the sitcoms *I Love Lucy* or *The Golden Girls*, to the role of "feminine straight men" such as Jack Benny, to the bisexual meanings in *Gentlemen Prefer Blondes* (Doty, 1993, 2000). Indeed, almost no text can escape the eyes of the queer theorist.

Subversive Ethnographies: Fieldwork Revisited. These are often relatively straightforward ethnographies of specific sexual worlds that challenge assumptions. Sasho Lambevski (1999), for instance, attempted to write "an insider, critical and experiential ethnography of the multitude of social locations (class, gender, ethnicity, religion) from which 'gays' in Macedonia are positioned, governed, controlled and silenced as subaltern people" (p. 301). As a "gay" Macedonian (are the terms a problem in this context?) who had spent time studying HIV in Australia, he looks at the sexual conflicts generated between the gay Macedonians and gay Albanians (never mind the Australian connection). Lambevski looks at the old cruising scenes in Skopje, known to him from before, that now take on multiple and different meanings bound up with sexualities, ethnicities, gender playing, and clashing cultures. Cruising for sex here is no straightforward matter. He describes how, in approaching and recognizing a potential sex partner as an Albanian (in an old cruising haunt), he feels paralyzed. Both bodies are flooded with ethnic meaning, not simple sexual ones, and ethnicities reek of power. He writes: "I obeyed by putting the (discursive) mask of my Macedonicity over my body" (p. 398). In another time and place, he may have reacted very differently.

Lambevski is overtly critical of much ethnography and wishes to write a queer experiential ethnography, not a confessional one (1999, p. 298). He refuses to commit himself to what he calls "a textual lie," which "continues to persist in much of what is considered a real ethnographic text." Here bodies, feelings, sexualities, ethnicities, and religions all can be left out easily. Nor, he claims, can ethnography simply depend on site observation or one-off interviewing. There is a great chain of connection: "The gay scene is inextricably linked to the Macedonian school system, the structuring of Macedonian and Albanian families and kinship relations, the Macedonian state and its political history, the Macedonian medical system with its power to mark and segregate 'abnormality' (homosexuality)" (1999, p. 400). There is a chain of social sites, and at the same time his own life is an integral part of this (Macedonian queer, Australian, gay). Few researchers have been so honest regarding the tensions that infuse their lives and the wider chains of connectedness that shape their work.

I find it hard to believe that this is not true for all research, but it is usually silenced. Laud Humphreys's classic *Tearoom Trade* (1970), for example—admittedly, written some 30 years earlier—cannot speak of Humphreys's own gayness, his own bodily presence (though there is a small footnote on the taste of semen!), his emotional worlds, his white middle-classness, or his role as a white married minister. To the contrary, although he does remind the reader of his religious background and his wife, this serves more as a distraction. As important as it was in its day, this is a very different kind of ethnography. The same is true of a host that followed it. They were less aware of the problematic nature of categories and the links to material worlds. They were, in a very real fashion, "naïve ethnographies"—somehow thinking "the story could be directly told as it was." We live in less innocent times, and queer theory is a marker for this.

Scavenger Methodologies: The Raiding of Multiple Texts to Assemble New Ones. A fine example of queer "method" is Judith Halberstam's work on "female masculinity" (1998). Suggesting that we have failed to develop ways of seeing that can grasp the different kinds of masculinities that women have revealed both in the past and the present, she wrote a study that documents the sheer range of such phenomena. In her own work, she "raids" literary textual methods, film theory, ethnographic field research, historical survey, archival records, and taxonomy to produce her original account of emerging forms of "female masculinity" (Halberstam, 1998, pp. 9–13). Here we have aristocratic European cross-dressing women of the 1920s, butch lesbians, dykes, drag kings, tomboys, black "butch in the hood" rappers, trans-butches, the tribade (a woman who practices "unnatural vices" with other women), the gender invert, the stone butch, the female-to-male transsexual (FTM), and the raging bull dyke! She also detects—through films as diverse as *Alien* and *The Killing of Sister George*—at least six prototypes of the female masculine: tomboys,

Predators, Fantasy Butches, Transvestites, Barely Butches, and Postmodern Butches (1998, chap. 6).

In introducing this motley collection, she uses a "scavenger methodology . . . [of] different methods to collect and produce information on subjects who have been deliberately or accidentally excluded from traditional studies of human behavior" (1998, p. 13). She borrows from Eve Kosofsky Sedgwick's "nonce taxonomy": "The making and unmaking and remaking and redissolution of hundreds of old and new categorical meanings concerning all the kinds it takes to make up a world" (Sedgwick, 1990, p. 23). This is the mode of "deconstruction," and in this world the very idea that types of people called homosexuals or gays or lesbians (or, more to the point, "men" and "women") can be simply called up for study becomes a key problem in itself. Instead, the researcher should become more and more open to start sensing new worlds of possibilities.

Many of these social worlds are not immediately transparent, whereas others are amorphously nascent and forming. All this research brings to the surface social worlds only dimly articulated hitherto—with, of course, the suggestion that there are more, many more, even more deeply hidden. In one sense, Halberstam captures rich fluidity and diversity—all this going on just beneath the surface structures of society. But in another sense, her very act of naming, innovating terms, and categorizing tends itself to create and assemble new differences.

Performing Gender and Ethnographic Performance. Often drawing upon the work of Judith Butler, who sees gender as never essential, always unfixed, not innate, never natural, but always constructed through performativity—as a "stylized repetition of acts" (1990, p. 141)—much of the work in queer theory has been playing around with gender. Initially fascinated by drag, transgender, and transsexualism, and with Divas, Drag Kings, and key cross-genderists such as Del LaGrace Volcano and Kate Bornstein (1995), some of it has functioned almost as a kind of subversive terrorist drag. It arouses curious, unknown queered desires emancipating people from the constraints of the gendered tyranny of the presumed "normal body" (Volcano & Halberstam, 1999). Others have moved out to consider a wide array of playing with genders—from "faeries" and "bears," to leather scenes and the Mardi Gras, and on to the more commercialized/normalized drag for mass consumption: RuPaul, Lily Savage, and Graham Norton.

Sometimes performance may be seen as even more direct. It appears in the work of alternative documentaries, in "video terrorism" and "street theater," across cable talk shows, experimental artworks, and activist tapes. By the late 1980s, there was a significant expansion of lesbian and gay video (as well as film and film festivals), and in the academy, posts were created to deal with this—along with creation of more informal groupings. (See, for example, Jennie Livingston's film *Paris Is Burning* [1990], which looks at the "ball circuit" of poor gay men and transgenderists, usually black, in the late 1980s in New York City, or Ang Lee's *Wedding Banquet* [1993], which reconfigured the dominant "rice queen" image).[7]

Exploring New/Queered Case Studies. Queer theory also examines new case studies. Michael Warner, for example, looks at a range of case studies of emergent publics. One stands out to me: It is the details of a queer cabaret (a counter-public?) that involves "erotic vomiting." Suggesting a kind of "national heterosexuality" that, along with "family values," saturates much public talk, he argues that multiple queer cultures work to subvert these. He investigates the queer counter public of a "garden variety leather bar" where the routines are "spanking, flagellation, shaving, branding, laceration, bondage, humiliation, wrestling—as they say, you know, the usual" (Warner, 2002, pp. 206–210). But suddenly this garden-variety S&M bar is subverted by the less than usual: a cabaret of what is called erotic vomiting.

The Reading of the Self. Most of the researches within queer theory play with the author's self: It is rarely absent. D. A. Miller's (1998) account, for example, of the Broadway musical and the role its plays in queer life is an intensely personal account of the musical, including snapshots of the author as child, with the albums played.

What's New?

As interesting as many of these methods, theories, and studies most certainly are, I suggest that there is really very little that could be called truly new or striking here. Often, queer methodology means little more than literary theory rather belatedly coming to social science tools such as ethnography and reflexivity (although sometimes it is also a radical critique of orthodox social science—especially quantitative—methods). Sometimes it borrows some of the oldest of metaphors, such as drama. Queer theory does not seem to me to constitute any fundamental advance over recent ideas in qualitative inquiry—it borrows, refashions, and retells. What is more radical is its persistent concern with categories and gender/sexuality—although, in truth, this has long been questioned, too (cf. Plummer, 2002; Weston, 1998). What seems to be at stake, then, in any queering of qualitative research is not so much a methodological style as a political and substantive concern with gender, heteronormativity, and sexualities. Its challenge is to bring stabilized gender and sexuality to the forefront of analyses in ways they are not usually advanced and that put under threat any ordered world of gender and sexuality. This is just what is, indeed, often missing from much ethnographic or life story research.

The Troubles With Queer

Responses to queer theory have been mixed. It would not be too unfair to say that outside the world of queer theorists—the world of "straight academia"—queer theory has been more or less ignored and has had minimal impact. This has had the unfortunate consequence of largely ghettoizing the whole approach. Ironically, those who may most need to understand the working of the heterosexual-homosexual binary divide in their work can hence ignore it (and they usually do), whereas those who least need to understand it actively work to deconstruct terms that really describe themselves. Thus, it is comparatively rare in mainstream literary analysis or sociological theory for queer to be taken seriously (indeed, it has taken three editions of this handbook to include something on it, and the so-called seventh moment of inquiry (see Lincoln & Denzin, Epilogue, this volume) has so far paid only lip service to it!). More than this, many gays, lesbians, and feminists themselves see no advance at all in a queer theory that, after all, would simply "deconstruct" them, along with all their political gains, out of existence. Queer theorists often write somewhat arrogantly, as if they have a monopoly on political validity, negating both the political and theoretical gains of the past. Let me reflect on some of the standard objections to queer theory.

First, for many, the term itself is provocative: a pejorative and stigmatizing phrase from the past is reclaimed by that very same stigmatized grouping and had its meaning renegotiated; as such, it has a distinct generational overtone. Younger academics love it; older ones hate it. It serves to write off the past worlds of research and create new divisions.

Second, it brings a category problem, what Josh Gamson (1995) has described as a Queer Dilemma. He claims that there is simultaneously a need for a public collective identity (around which activism can galvanize) and a need to take apart and blur boundaries. As he says, fixed identity categories are the basis for both oppression and political power. Although it is important to stress the "inessential, fluid and multiple sited" forms of identity emerging within the queer movement, he also can see that there are very many from within the lesbian, gay, bisexual, and transgender movement (LGBT, as it is currently clumsily called) who also reject its tendency to deconstruct the very idea of gay and lesbian identity—hence abolishing a field of study and politics when it has only just gotten going.

There are also many radical lesbians who view it with even more suspicion, as it tends to work to make the lesbian invisible and to reinscribe tacitly all kinds of male power (in disguise), bringing back well-worn arguments about S&M, porn, and transgender politics as anti-women. Radical lesbian feminist Sheila Jeffreys (2003) is particularly scathing, seeing the whole queer movement as a serious threat to the gains of radical lesbians in the late 20th century. With the loss of the categories of woman-identified-woman and radical lesbian in a fog of (largely masculinist) queer deconstruction, it becomes impossible to see the roots of women's subordination to men. She also accuses it of a major elitism: The languages of most of its proponents ape the language of male academic elites, and lose all the gains that were made by the earlier, more accessible writings of feminists who wrote for and spoke to women in the communities, not just other academics. Lilian Faderman claims it is "resolutely elitist" and puts this well:

> The language queer scholars deploy sometimes seems transparently aimed at what lesbian feminists once called the "big boys" at the academy. Lesbian-feminist writing, in contrast, had as primary values clarity and accessibility, since its purpose was to speak directly to the community and in so doing reflect change. (1997, pp. 225–226).[8]

There are many other critics. Tim Edwards (1998) worries about a politics that often collapses into some kind of fan worship, celebration of cult films, and weak cultural politics. Stephen O. Murray hates the word "queer" itself because it perpetuates binary divisions and cannot avoid being a tool of domination, and he worries about excessive preoccupation with linguistics and with textual representation (2002, pp. 245–247). Even some of queer theory's founders now worry if the whole radical impulse has gotten lost and queer theory has become normalized, institutionalized, even "lucrative" within the academy (Halperin, 2003).

From many sides, then, doubts are being expressed that all is not well in the house of queer. There are problems that come with the whole project, and in some ways I still find the language of the humanists more conducive to social inquiry.

Queer Theory Meets Critical Humanism: The Conflictual Worlds of Research

> *Conflict is the gadfly of thought . . . a sine qua non of reflection and ingenuity.*
>
> — John Dewey (*Human Nature and Conduct,* p. 300)

And so we have two traditions seemingly at serious odds with each other. There is nothing unusual about this—all research positions are open to conflict from both within and without. Whereas humanism generally looks to experience, meaning, and human subjectivity, queer theory rejects this in favor of representations. Whereas humanism generally asks the researcher to get close to the worlds he or she is studying, queer theory almost pleads for distance—a world of texts, defamiliarization, and deconstruction. Whereas humanism brings a liberal democratic project with "justice for all," queer theory aims to prioritize the oppressions of sexuality and gender and urges a more radical change. Humanism usually favors a calmer conversation and dialogue, whereas queer is carnivalesque, parodic, rebellious, and playful. Humanism champions the voice of the public intellectual; queer theory is to be found mainly in the universities and its own self-generated social movement of aspiring academics.

Yet there are some commonalities. Both, for instance, would ask researchers to adopt a critically self-aware stance. Both would seek out a political and ethical background (even though, in a quite major way, they may differ on this—queer theory has a prime focus on radical gender change, and humanism is broader). And both assume the contradictory messiness of social life, such that no category system can ever do it justice.

On a closer look, several of the above differences overlap. Many critical humanisms can focus on representations (though fewer queer theorists are willing to focus on experience). Critical humanists often are seen as social constructionists, and this hardly can be seen as far removed from deconstructionists. There is no reason why critical humanism cannot take the value and political stances of queer theorists (I have and I do), but the moral baselines of humanism are wider and less specifically tied to gender. Indeed, contemporary humanistic method enters the social worlds of different "others" to work a catharsis of comprehension. It juxtaposes differences and complexities with similarities and harmonies. It recognizes the multiple possible worlds of social research—not necessarily the standard interviews or ethnographies, but the roles of photography, art, video, film, poetics, drama, narrative, autoethnography, music, introspection, fiction, audience participation, and street theater. It also finds multiple ways of presenting the "data," and it acknowledges that a social science of any consequences must be located in the political and moral dramas of its time. One of those political and moral dramas is "queer."

But there again, the histories, canons, and gurus of critical humanism and queer theory are indeed different, even though, in the end, they are not nearly as at odds with each other as one could be led to believe. Yes, they are not the same; and it is right that they should maintain some of their key differences. But no, they are not so very different either. It is no wonder, then, that I find that I can live with both. Contradiction, ambivalence, and tension reside in all critical inquiries.

▣ Notes

1. As Dmitri Shalin noted more than a decade ago, "The issues that symbolic interactionism has highlighted since its inception and that assured its maverick status in American sociology bear some uncanny resemblance to the themes championed by postmodernist thinkers" (1993, p. 303). It investigates "the marginal, local, everyday, heterogeneous and indeterminate" alongside the "socially constructed, emergent and plural" (p. 304). Likewise, David Maines (2001) has continued to sustain an earlier argument that symbolic interactionism, by virtue of its interpretive center, finds an easy affinity with much of postmodernism, but because of that same center, has no need for it (pp. 229–233). He finds valuable the resurgence of interest in interpretive work, the importance now given to writing "as intrinsic to method," the concern over multiple forms of presentation, and the reclaiming of value positions and "critical work" (Maines, 2001, p. 325). In addition, as is well known, Norman K. Denzin has been at the forefront in defending postmodernism within sociology/cultural studies and symbolic interactionism, in numerous books and papers (e.g., Denzin, 1989,1997, 2003).

2. For some, "interactionism" has become almost synonymous with sociology; see Maines (2001) and P. Atkinson and Housley (2003).

3. The liberal, humanist feminist philosopher Martha Nussbaum (1999, p. 41) suggests a long list of "human capabilities" that need cultivating for a person to function as a human being. These include concerns such as "bodily health and integrity" senses, imagination, and thought; emotions; practical reason; affiliation; concern for other species; play; control over one's environment; and life itself. To this I might add the crucial self-reflexive process, a process of communication that is central to the way we function.

4. In Bob Connell's rich study of *Masculinities* (1995)—a study that is far from being either avowedly "humanist" or "queer"—he takes life stories as emblematic/symptomatic of "crisis tendencies in power relations (that) threaten hegemonic masculinity directly" (p. 89). He looks at four groups of men under crisis—radical environmentalists, gay and bisexual networks, young working-class men, and men of the new class. Connell implies that I do not take this seriously (1995, p. 89). However, even in the first edition of my book *Documents of Life* (Plummer, 1983), I make it quite clear that among the contributions of the life story, it can be seen as a "tool for history," as a perspective on totality, and as a key focus on social change! (pp. 68–69).

5. Or, as Rupp and Taylor call it, "the tripartite model of cultural investigation" (2003, p. 223).

6. Likewise, I can sense a humanism at work in the writings of Cornel West, Jeffrey Weeks, Seyla Benhabib, Anthony Giddens, Zygmunt Bauman, Agnes Heller, Jürgen Habermas, Michel Bakhtin, and many others. Never mind the naming game, in which they have to come out as humanists (though some clearly do); what matters are the goals that they see will produce adequate understanding and social change for the better. In this respect, a lot of them read like humanists manqué.

7. See, for example, *Jump Cut*, *Screen*, *The Celluloid Closet*, *Now You See It?*, *The Bad Object Choices* collective, and the work of Tom Waugh and Pratibha Parmar.

8. See also Simon Watney's critiques to be found in *Imagine Hope* (2000). Watney is far from sympathetic

to radical lesbianism, but his account has distinct echoes. Queer theory has often let down AIDS activism.

References

Atkinson, P., & Housley, W. (2003). *Interactionism.* London: Sage.

Atkinson, R. (1998). *The life story interview.* Thousand Oaks, CA: Sage.

Bauman, Z. (1991). *Modernity and ambivalence.* Cambridge, UK: Polity.

Bauman, Z. (2000). *Liquid society.* Cambridge, UK: Polity.

Bauman, Z. (2004). *Wasted lives: Modernity and its outcasts.* Cambridge, UK: Polity.

Beck, U. (2003). *Individualization.* London: Sage.

Bornstein, K. (1995). *Gender outlaw.* New York: Vintage.

Bruyn, T. S. (1966). *The human perspective in sociology.* Englewood Cliffs, NJ: Prentice Hall.

Butler, J. (1990). *Gender trouble.* London: Routledge.

Carrington, C. (1999). *No place like home: Relationships and family life among lesbians and gay men.* Chicago: University of Chicago Press.

Clifford, J., & Marcus, G. E. (Eds.). (1986). *Writing culture.* Berkeley: University of California Press.

Coffey, A. (1999). *The ethnographic self: Fieldwork and the representation of identity.* London: Sage.

Cohen, S. (1999). *States of denial.* Cambridge, UK: Polity.

Coles, R. (1989). *The call of stories: Teaching and the moral imagination.* Boston: Houghton Mifflin.

Connell, R. W. (1995). *Masculinities.* Cambridge, UK: Polity.

Denzin, N. K. (1989). *Interpretive biography.* London: Sage.

Denzin, N. K. (1997). *Interpretive ethnography: Ethnographic practices for the 21st century.* London: Sage.

Denzin, N. K. (2003). *Performance ethnography.* London: Sage.

Denzin, N., & Lincoln, Y. (Eds.). (1994). *Handbook of qualitative research.* London: Sage.

Dewey, J. (1920). *Reconstruction of philosophy.* New York: Henry Holt.

Dewey, J. (1938). *Logic of inquiry.* New York: Henry Holt.

Dewey, J. (19XX). *Human nature and conduct.* New York: Henry Holt.

Doty, A. (1993). *Making things perfectly queer: Interpreting mass culture.* Minneapolis: University of Minnesota Press.

Doty, A. (2000). *Flaming classics: Queering the film canon.* London: Routledge.

Edwards, T. (1998). Queer fears: Against the cultural turn. *Sexualities, 1*(4), 471–484.

Ellis, C., & Flaherty, M. G. (Eds.). (1992). *Investigating subjectivity: Research on lived experience.* London: Sage.

Faderman, L. (1997). Afterword. In D. Heller (Ed.), *Cross purposes: Lesbians, feminists and the limits of alliance.* Bloomington: Indiana University Press.

Felice, W. F. (1996). *Taking suffering seriously.* Albany: State University of New York Press.

Foucault, M. (1979). *The history of sexuality.* Middlesex, UK: Harmondsworth.

Gamson, J. (1995). Must identity movements self-destruct?: A queer dilemma. *Social Problems, 42*(3), 390–407.

Gamson, J. (1998). *Freaks talk back: Tabloid talk shows and sexual nonconformity.* Chicago: University of Chicago Press.

Gever, M., Greyson, J., & Parmar, P. (Eds.). (1993). *Queer looks: Perspectives on lesbian and gay film and video.* New York: Routledge.

Giddens, A. (1991). *Modernity and self-identity.* Cambridge, UK: Polity.

Gouldner, A. (1973). *For sociology: Renewal and critique in sociology today.* London: Allen Lane.

Gubrium, J., & Holstein, J. (1997). *The new language of qualitative research.* Oxford, UK: Oxford University Press.

Halberstam, J. (1998). *Female masculinity.* Durham, NC: Duke University Press.

Halperin, D. (1995). *Saint Foucault: Towards a gay hagiography.* New York: Oxford University Press.

Halperin, D. (2003). The normalization of queer theory. *Journal of Homosexuality, 45*(2–4), 339–343.

Hertz, R. (Ed.). (1997). *Reflexivity and voice.* Thousand Oaks, CA: Sage.

Honneth, A. (1995). *The struggle for recognition: The moral grammar of social conflicts.* Cambridge, UK: Polity.

Humphreys, L. (1970). *Tearoom trade.* Chicago: Aldine.

Jackson, M. (1989). *Paths toward a clearing: Radical empiricism and ethnographic inquiry.* Bloomington: Indiana University Press.

Jeffreys, S. (2003). *Unpacking queer politics.* Oxford, UK: Polity.

Kong, T., Mahoney, D., & Plummer, K. (2002). Queering the interview. In J. F. Gubrium & J. A. Holstein (Eds.), *The handbook of interview research* (pp. 239–257). Thousand Oaks, CA: Sage.

Lambevski, S. A. (1999). Suck my nation: Masculinity, ethnicity and the politics of (homo)sex. *Sexualities, 2*(3), 397–420.

Lee, A. (Director). (1993). *The wedding banquet* [Motion picture]. Central Motion Pictures Corporation.

Lee, A. M. (1978). *Sociology for whom?* Oxford: Oxford University Press.

Lincoln, Y. S., & Denzin, N. K. (1994). The fifth moment. In N. K. Denzin & Y. S. Lincoln (Eds.), *Handbook of qualitative research* (pp. 575–586). Thousand Oaks, CA: Sage.

Livingston, J. (Director), & Livingston, J., & Swimar, B. (Producers). (1990). *Paris Is Burning* [Motion picture]. Off White Productions.

Maines, D. (2001). *The fault lines of consciousness: A view of interactionism in sociology.* New York: Aldine de Gruyter.

Miller, D. A. (1998). *Place for us: Essay on the Broadway musical.* Cambridge, MA: Harvard University Press.

Murray, S. O. (2002). Five reasons I don't take queer theory seriously. In K. Plummer (Ed.), *Sexualities: Critical concepts in sociology* (Vol. 3, pp. 245–247). London: Routledge.

Nardi, P. (1999). *Gay men's friendships: Invincible communities.* Chicago: University of Chicago Press.

Nisbet, R. (1976). *Sociology as an art form.* London: Heinemann.

Nussbaum, M. C. (1999). *Sex and social justice.* New York: Oxford University Press.

O'Neill, O. (2002). *A question of trust: The BBC Reith Lectures 2002.* Cambridge, UK: Cambridge University Press.

Plummer, K. (1983). *Documents of life.* London: Allen and Unwin.

Plummer, K. (1995). *Telling sexual stories.* London: Routledge.

Plummer, K. (2001). *Documents of life 2: An invitation to a critical humanism.* London: Sage.

Plummer, K. (Ed.). (2002). *Sexualities: Critical concepts in sociology* (4 vols.). London: Routledge.

Plummer, K. (2003). *Intimate citizenship.* Seattle: University of Washington Press.

Reed-Danahay, D. E. (Ed.). (1997). *Auto/ethnography: Rewriting the self and the social.* Oxford, UK: Berg.

Ronai, C. R. (1992). A reflexive self through narrative: A night in the life of an erotic dancer/researcher. In C. Ellis & M. G. Flaherty (Eds.), *Investigating subjectivity: Research on lived experience* (pp. 102–124). Newbury Park, CA: Sage.

Rorty, R. (1999). *Philosophy and social hope.* Middlesex, UK: Penguin.

Rupp, L., & Taylor, V. (2003). *Drag queens at the 801 Cabaret.* Chicago: University of Chicago Press.

Said, E. (2003). *Orientalism* (2nd ed.). New York: Cambridge.

Scheper-Hughes, N. (1994). *Death without weeping.* Berkeley: University of California Press.

Sedgwick, E. K. (1985). *Between men: English literature and male homosexual desire.* New York: Columbia University Press.

Sedgwick, E. K. (1990). *Epistemology of the closet.* Berkeley: University of California Press.

Sedgwick, E. K. (1994). *Tendencies.* London: Routledge.

Shalin, D. N. (1993). Modernity, postmodernism and pragmatic inquiry. *Symbolic Interaction, 16*(4), 303–332.

Smith, L. T. (1999). *Decolonizing methodologies: Research and indigenous peoples.* London: Zed Books.

Smyth, C. (1992). Lesbians talk queer notions. London: Scarlet Press.

Sullivan, N. (2003). *A critical introduction to queer theory.* Edinburgh: University of Edinburgh Press.

Tronto, J. (1993). *Moral boundaries: A political argument for an ethic of care.* London: Routledge.

Urry, J. (2000). *Sociology beyond societies: Mobilities for the twenty-first century.* London: Routledge.

Volcano, D. L., & Halberstam, J. (1999). *The drag king book.* London: Serpent's Tail.

Warner, M. (1991). *Fear of a queer planet: Queer politics and social theory.* Minneapolis: University of Minnesota.

Warner, M. (1992, June). From queer to eternity: An army of theorists cannot fail. *Voice Literary Supplement, 106,* pp. 18–26.

Warner, M. (1999). *The trouble with normal: Sex, politics, and the ethics of queer life.* Cambridge, MA: Harvard University Press.

Warner, M. (2002). *Public and counterpublics.* New York: Zone Books.

Watney, S. (2000). *Imagine hope: AIDS and gay identity.* London: Routledge.

West, C. (1999). The moral obligations of living in a democratic society. In D. B. Batstone & E. Mendieta (Eds.), *The good citizen* (pp. 5–12). London: Routledge.

Weston, K. (1998). *longslowburn: Sexuality and social science.* London: Routledge.

Wolcott, H. F. (2002). *Sneaky kid and its aftermath.* Walnut Creek, CA: AltaMira.

Part III

STRATEGIES OF INQUIRY

The civic-minded qualitative researcher thinks historically, interactionally, and structurally. He or she attempts to identify the many persuasions, prejudices, injustices, and inequities that prevail in a given historical period (Mills, 1959, p. 7). Critical scholars seek to examine the major public and private issues and personal troubles that define a particular historical moment. In doing so, qualitative researchers self-consciously draw upon their own experience as a resource. They always think reflectively and historically, as well as biographically. They seek strategies of empirical inquiry that will allow them to make connections between lived experience, social injustices, larger social and cultural structures, and the here and now. These connections will be forged out of the interpretations and empirical materials that are generated in any given inquiry.

Empirical inquiry, of course, is shaped by paradigm commitments and by the recurring questions that any given paradigm or interpretive perspective asks about human experience, social structure, and culture. More deeply, however, the researcher always asks how the practices of qualitative inquiry can be used to help create a free democratic society. Critical theorists, for example, examine the material conditions and systems of ideology that reproduce class and economic structures. Queer, constructivist, cultural studies, critical race, and feminist researchers examine the stereotypes, prejudices, and injustices connected to race, ethnicity, and gender. There is no such thing as value-free inquiry, although in qualitative inquiry this premise is presented with more clarity. Such clarity permits the value commitments of researchers to be transparent.

The researcher-as-interpretive-*bricoleur* is always, already in the material world of values and empirical experience. This world is confronted and constituted through the lens that the scholar's paradigm or interpretive perspective provides. The world so conceived ratifies the individual's commitment to the paradigm or perspective in question. This paradigm is connected at a higher ethical level to the values and politics of an emancipatory, civic social science.

As specific investigations are planned and carried out, two issues must be confronted immediately: research design and choice of strategy of inquiry. We take them up in order. Each devolves into a variety of related questions and issues that also must be addressed.

Research Design[1]

The *research design*, as discussed in our Introduction and analyzed by Julianne Cheek in this section of the *Handbook* (Chapter 15), situates the investigator in the world of experience. Five basic questions structure the issue of design:

1. How will the design connect to the paradigm or perspective being used? That is, how will empirical materials be informed by and interact with the paradigm in question?
2. How will these materials allow the researcher to speak to the problems of praxis and change?
3. Who or what will be studied?
4. What strategies of inquiry will be used?
5. What methods or research tools for collecting and analyzing empirical materials will be utilized?

These questions are examined in detail in Part IV of the *Handbook*.

Paradigm, Perspective, and Metaphor

The positivist, postpositivist, constructionist, and critical paradigms dictate, with varying degrees of freedom, the design of a qualitative research investigation. Designs can be viewed as falling along a continuum ranging from rigorous design principles on one end, to emergent, less well-structured directives on the other. Positivist research designs place a premium on the early identification and development of a research question, a set of hypotheses, a research site, and a statement concerning sampling strategies, as well as a specification of the research strategies and methods of analysis that will be employed. A research proposal laying out the stages and phases of the study may be written. In interpretive research, a priori design commitments may block the introduction of new understandings. Consequently, although qualitative researchers may design procedures beforehand, designs always have built-in flexibility, to account for new and unexpected empirical materials and growing sophistication.

These stages can be conceptualized as involving reflection, planning, entry, data collection, withdrawal from the field, analysis, and write-up. Cheek observes that the degree of detail involved in the proposal will vary depending on the funding agency. Funding agencies fall into at least six categories: local community funding units; special purpose, family-sponsored, corporate, or national foundations; and governmental agencies. The proposal may also include a budget, a review of the relevant literature, a statement concerning human subjects protection, a copy of consent forms and interview schedules, and a timeline. Positivist designs attempt to anticipate in advance all the problems that may arise in a qualitative study (although interpretivist designs do not). Such designs provide rather well-defined road maps for the researcher. The scholar working in this tradition hopes to produce a work that finds its place in the literature on the topic being studied.

In contrast, much greater ambiguity and flexibility are associated with postpositivist and nonpositivist designs—those based, for example, on the constructivist or critical theory paradigms, or the critical race, feminist, queer, or cultural studies perspectives. In studies shaped by these paradigms and perspectives, there will be less emphasis on formal grant proposals, well-formulated hypotheses, tightly defined sampling frames, structured interview schedules, and predetermined research strategies, methods, and forms of analysis. The researcher may follow a path of discovery, using as models qualitative works that have achieved the status of classics in the field. Enchanted, perhaps, by the myth of the Lone Ethnographer, the scholar hopes to produce a work that has the characteristics of a study done by one of the giants from the past (Malinowski, Mead, Bateson, Goffman, Becker, Strauss, and Wolcott). Conversely, qualitative researchers often at least begin by undertaking studies that can be completed by one individual after prolonged engagement.

The Practices and Politics of Funded Qualitative Research

Cheek's chapter complicates and deconstructs the relationships among money, ethics, and research markets. She shows how qualitative research is a commodity that circulates and is exchanged in this political economy. Funding involves selling one's self to a funding agency. Such agencies may not understand the nuances of qualitative research practice. Cheek discusses the problems associated with Institutional Review Boards (IRBs) and ethics committees. In Australia, researchers cannot conduct research on human subjects until they have formal ethics approval from the University Research Ethics Committee. In the United States and the United Kingdom, as well as in Australia, the original focus of IRBs and the context from which they emerged was medicine. Qualitative research is often treated unfairly by ethics committees. Such research, it may be charged, is unscientific. In effect, IRBs have become methodological review boards, institutionalizing only one brand, or version, of science. In the United Kingdom, the Royal College of Physicians guidelines make the point that badly designed research is unethical. This means that judgment is being passed on the scientific as well as the ethical merits of research. Cheek observes that in too many instances, it seems as though qualitative researchers have become the "fall guys" for ethical mistakes in medical research. Cheek notes that many times, qualitative researchers are unable to answer in advance all the questions that are raised by such committees. Issues of control over the research also are central. As she observes, taking funding from someone or some organization in order to conduct research is not a neutral act. This issue shades into another, namely, What happens when the researcher's findings do not please the funder?

There are dangers in accepting external funding. Faculty members increasingly are under pressure to secure external funding for their research. Such pressures turn research into a commodity that is bought and sold. Cheek observes that these are dangerous times. The conservative discourse of the marketplace has become preeminent. It is the market, not the judgment of stakeholders and peers, that now determines the worth of what we do.

Choreographing the Dance of Design

Janesick (2000) presents a fluid view of the design process. She observes that the essence of good qualitative research design requires the use of a set of procedures that are at once open-ended and rigorous. Influenced by Martha Graham, Merce Cunningham, Alvin Ailey, Elliot Eisner, and John Dewey, she approaches the problem of research design from an aesthetic, artistic, and metaphorical perspective. With Dewey and Eisner, she sees research design as a work of improvisational, rather than composed, art; as an event, a process, with phases connected to different forms of problematic experience, along with their interpretation and representation. Art molds and fashions experience. In its dance form, art is a choreographed, emergent production, with distinct phases: warming up, stretching exercises and design decisions, cooling down, interpretation, and writing the narrative.

Who and What Will Be Studied?

The who and what of qualitative studies involve cases, or instances of phenomena and/or social processes. Three generic approaches may be taken to the question who or what will be studied. First, a single case or single process may be studied, what Robert E. Stake (Chapter 17, this volume) calls the intrinsic case study. Here the researcher examines in detail a single case or instance of the phenomenon in question, for example a classroom, an arts program, or a death in the family.

Second, the researcher may focus on a number of cases. Stake calls this the collective case approach. These cases are then analyzed in terms of specific and generic properties. Third, the researcher can examine multiple instances of a process, as that process is displayed in a variety of different cases. Denzin's (1993) study of relapse in the careers of recovering alcoholics examined types of relapses across several different types of recovering careers. This process approach is then grounded or anchored in specific cases.

Research designs vary, of course, depending on the needs of multiple-focus, or single-focus case and process inquiries. Different sampling issues arise in each situation. These needs and issues also vary by the paradigm that is being employed. Every instance of a case or process bears the stamp of the general class of phenomenon to which it belongs. However, any given instance is likely to be particular and unique. Thus, for example, any given classroom is like all classrooms, but no two classrooms are the same.

For these reasons, many postpositivist, constructionist, and critical theory qualitative researchers employ theoretical or purposive, and not random, sampling models. They seek out groups, settings, and individuals where (and for whom) the processes being studied are most likely to occur. At the same time, a process of constant comparison—between groups, concepts, and observations—is necessary, as the researcher seeks to develop an understanding that encompasses all instances of the process or case under investigation. A focus on negative cases is a key feature of this process.

These sampling and selection issues would be addressed differently by a postmodern ethnographer in the cultural studies tradition. This investigator would be likely to place greater stress on the intensive analysis of a small body of empirical materials (cases and processes), arguing, after Sartre (1981, p. ix), that no individual or case is ever just an individual or a case. Each person or case must be studied as a single instance of more universal social experiences and social processes. The person, Sartre (1981) states, is "summed up and for this reason universalized by his [or her] epoch, he [or she] in turn resumes it by reproducing himself [or herself] in it as a singularity" (p. ix). Thus, to study the particular is to study the general. For this reason, any case will necessarily bear the traces of the universal; consequently, there is less interest in the traditional positivist and postpositivist concerns with negative cases, generalizations, and case selection. The researcher assumes that readers will be able, as Stake argues, to generalize subjectively from the case in question to their own personal experiences.

An expansion on this strategy is given in the method of instances (see Denzin, 1999; Psathas, 1995). Following Psathas (1995, p. 50), the "method of instances" takes each instance of a phenomenon as an occurrence that evidences the operation of a set of cultural understandings currently available for use by cultural members.

An analogy may be useful. In discourse analysis, "no utterance is representative of other utterances, though of course it shares structural features with them; a discourse analyst studies utterances in order to understand how the potential of the linguistic system can be activated when it intersects at its moment of use with a social system" (Fiske, 1994, p. 195). This is the argument for the method of instances. The analyst examines those moments when an utterance intersects with another utterance, giving rise to an instance of the system in action.

Psathas clarifies the meaning of an instance: "An instance of something is an occurrence . . . an event whose features and structures can be examined to discover how it is organized" (1995, p. 50). An occurrence is evidence that "the machinery for its production is culturally available . . . [for example] the machinery of turn-taking in conversation" (pp. 50–51).

The analyst's task is to understand how this instance and its intersections work, to show what rules of interpretation are operating, to map and illuminate the structure of the interpretive event itself. The analyst inspects the actual course of the interaction "by observing what happens first, second, next, etc., by noticing what preceded it; and by examining what is actually done and said by the participants" (Psathas, 1995, p. 51). Questions of meaning are referred back to the actual course of interaction, where it can be shown how a given utterance is acted upon and hence given meaning. The pragmatic maxim obtains here (Peirce, 1905). The meaning of an action is given in the consequences that are produced by it, including the ability to explain past experience and to predict future consequences.

Whether the particular utterance occurs again is irrelevant. The question of sampling from a population is also not an issue, for it is never possible to say in advance what an instance is a sample of (Psathas, 1995, p. 50). Indeed, collections of instances "cannot be assembled in advance of an analysis of at least one, because it cannot be known in advance what features delineate each case as a 'next one like the last'" (Psathas, 1995, p. 50).

This means there is little concern for empirical generalization. Psathas is clear on this point. The goal is not an abstract or empirical generalization; rather, the aim is "concerned with providing analyses that meet the criteria of unique adequacy" (p. 50). Each analysis must be fitted to the case at hand; each "must be studied to provide an analysis *uniquely adequate* for that particular phenomenon" (p. 51, italics in original).

Strategies of Inquiry

A strategy of inquiry describes the skills, assumptions, enactments, and material practices that researchers-as-methodological-*bricoleurs* use when they move from a paradigm and a research design to the collection of empirical materials. Strategies of inquiry connect researchers to specific approaches and methods for collecting and analyzing empirical materials. The case study, for example, relies on interviewing, observing, and document analysis. Research strategies locate researchers and paradigms in specific empirical, material sites and in specific methodological practices, for example making a case an object of study (Stake, Chapter 17, this volume).

We turn now to a brief review of the strategies discussed in this volume. Each is connected to a complex literature with its own history, its own exemplary works, and its own set of preferred ways for putting the strategy into motion. Each strategy also has its own set of problems involving the positivist, postpositivist, and postmodern legacies.

Performance Ethnography

Bryant Keith Alexander (Chapter 16, this volume) offers a detailed and sweeping history of the complex relationship between performance studies, ethnography, and autoethnography. He connects these formations to critical pedagogy theory. Performance ethnography is a way of inciting culture, a way of bringing culture alive, a way of fusing the pedagogical with the performative with the political. Alexander's chapter addresses the philosophical contingencies, the procedural pragmatics, and the pedagogical and political possibilities that exist in the spaces and practices of performance ethnography. Alexander's arguments complement the ethnodrama performance movement inspired by Jim Mienczakowski (2001).

Performance is an embodied act of interpretation, a way of knowing, a form of moral discourse. A politics of possibility organizes the project. Performance ethnography can be used politically, to incite others to moral action. It strengthens a commitment to a civic-minded discourse, a kind of performative citizenship, advocated by Stephen Hartnett.

The Case Study

Robert E. Stake (Chapter 17, this volume) argues that not all case studies are qualitative, although many are. Focusing on those that are attached to the naturalistic, holistic, cultural, and phenomenological paradigms, he contends that the case study is not a methodological choice but a choice of object to be studied—for example, a child or a classroom. Ultimately, the researcher is interested in a process or a population of cases, not an individual case. Stake identifies several types of case studies (intrinsic, instrumental, collective). Each case is a complex historical and contextual entity. Case studies have unique conceptual structures, uses, and problems (bias, theory, triangulation, telling the story, case selection, ethics). Researchers routinely provide information on such topics as the nature of the case, its historical background, and its relation to its contexts and other cases, as well as providing information to the informants who have provided information. In order to avoid ethical problems, the case study researcher needs constant input from "conscience, from stakeholders, and from the research community" (p. 459).

Public Ethnography

Barbara Tedlock (Chapter 18, this volume) reminds us that ethnography involves an ongoing attempt to place specific encounters, events, and understandings into a fuller, more meaningful content. She shows how participant observation has become the observation of participation. As a consequence, the doing, framing, representation, and reading of ethnography have changed dramatically in the last decade. The field of autoethnography has emerged out of this discourse.

Tedlock observes that early anthropology in the United States included a tradition of social criticism and public engagement. Franz Boas, Ruth Benedict, and Margaret Mead shaped public opinion through their social criticisms and their calls for public and political action. By the mid-1960s, the term "critical anthropology" gained force in the context of the civil rights movement and growing opposition to the Vietnam War. Critical theory, in anthropology, was put into practice through the production of plays. An indigenous political theater based on the works of Brecht, Boal, Freire, and others gained force in Latin America, Africa, and elsewhere.

Under the leadership of Victor and Edith Turner and of Edward Bruner, performance ethnography gained power in the 1980s. Culture was seen as a performance, and interpretation was performative. Ethnodrama and public ethnography emerged as vehicles for addressing social issues. Public ethnography is a discourse that engages with critical issues of the time. It is an extension of critical anthropology. It is anchored in the spaces discussed by Foley and Valenzuela (Chapter 9) and Alexander (Chapter 16) in this volume.

In the late 1990s, under the editorship of Barbara and Dennis Tedlock, the *American Anthropologist* began to publish politically engaged essays. Tedlock observes that "within this politically engaged environment, social science projects serve the communities in which they are carried out, rather than serving external communities of educators, policy makers, military personnel, and financiers" (p. 474). Thus does public ethnography take up issues of social justice.

Analyzing Interpretive Practice

In Chapter 19, James A. Holstein and Jaber F. Gubrium continue to extend the arguments of their highly influential book *The New Language of Qualitative Method* (Gubrium & Holstein, 1997). In that book, they examine various contemporary idioms of qualitative inquiry, from naturalism to ethnomethodology, emotional sociology, postmodernism, and poststructuralism. They then offer a new language of qualitative research that builds on ethnomethodology, conversational analysis, institutional studies of local culture, and Foucault's critical approach to history and discourse analysis (see also Kendall & Wickham, 1999). Their chapter captures a developing consensus in the interpretive community. This consensus seeks to show how social constructionist approaches can be profitably combined with poststructuralist discourse analysis (Foucault) and the situated study of meaning and order as local, social accomplishments.

Holstein and Gubrium draw attention to the interpretive procedures and practices that give structure and meaning to everyday life. These reflexive practices are both the topic of and the resources for qualitative inquiry. Knowledge is always local, situated in a local culture, and embedded in organizational and interactional sites. Everyday stereotypes and ideologies, including understandings about race, class, and gender, are enacted in these sites. The systems of power, what Dorothy Smith (1993) calls the ruling apparatuses and relations of ruling in society, are played out in these sites. Holstein and Gubrium build on Smith's project, elaborating a critical theory of discourse and social structure. Holstein and Gubrium then show how reflexive discourse and discursive practices transform the processes of analytic and critical bracketing. Such practices make the foundations of local social order visible. This emphasis on interpretive resources and local resources enlivens and dramatically extends the reflexive turn in qualitative research.

Grounded Theory

Kathy Charmaz (Chapter 20, this volume) is a leading exponent of the constructivist approach to grounded theory. She shows how grounded theory methods offer rich possibilities for advancing qualitative justice research in the 21st century. Grounded theorists have the tools to describe and go beyond situations of social justice. They can offer interpretations and analyses of the conditions under which injustice develops, changes, or is maintained.

Charmaz suggests that grounded theory, in its essential form, consists of systematic inductive guidelines for collecting and analyzing empirical materials to build middle-range theoretical frameworks that explain collected empirical materials. Her chapter outlines the history of this approach, from the early work of Glaser and Strauss, to its transformations in more recent statements by Glaser, Strauss, and Strauss and Corbin. She contrasts the positivist-objectivist positions of Glaser, Strauss, and Corbin with her own more interpretive constructivist approach, which stakes out a middle ground between postmodernism and positivism. Grounded theory may be the most widely employed interpretive strategy in the social sciences today. It gives the researcher a specific set of steps to follow, ones closely aligned with the canons of "good science." But on this point Charmaz is clear: It is possible to use grounded theory without embracing earlier proponents' positivist leanings (a position long adopted by Guba and Lincoln; see their Chapter 8 in this volume, and Lincoln and Guba, 1985).

Charmaz reviews the basic strategies used by grounded theorists. She grounds her discussion in materials from her own research, including two moving case studies. She moves these strategies into the space of social justice inquiry. She offers key criteria, basic questions that can be asked of any grounded theory study of social justice. Does a study exhibit credibility and originality? Does it have resonance—is it connected to the worlds of lived experience? Is it useful? Can it be used by people in their everyday worlds? Does it contribute to a better society? With these criteria, she reclaims the social justice tradition of the early Chicago school while moving grounded theory firmly into this new century.

Critical Ethnography as Street Performance

D. Soyini Madison's text (Chapter 21, this volume) shows; it does little telling. Her text is a performance—it performs an instance of critical ethnography as a performance. Her text is a story about returning to Ghana, about leaving home to come home to do the work her soul must do, a final arrival. She describes a time for the staging of the last performance, the transformation of years of fieldwork on poverty and indigenous human rights activism into a public performance. This performance of critical ethnography serves the purpose of advocacy and change; the performance would implicate corporate, capitalist economy in the human rights abuses in the global South.

Her text is a performance of possibilities, a staging of struggles, of violence, the imagination of how injustice could be ended, a confrontation with the truth, and solidarity in the face of conflict. It is a street performance that cannot be undone. The performance has created new possibilities, new alliances, and new friends; it enacts and imagines collective hopes and dreams.

The performance mattered. It made public an injustice committed on an American street. It turned passive observers into spirited actors. It evoked spontaneous communities, and it gave us the gift of remembering. It gave us the possibility for "another strategy of 'globalization from below'" (p. 545). The magic of performance evokes a lived politic, new demands for social justice, "the possibilities of another way of being" (p. 545).

▣ The New Histories and the Historical Method

Texts such as Madison's simultaneously build on and advance the projects of the contemporary cultural historian (see Jenkins, 1997), including the new cultural Marxism; the new social histories of everyday life; interpretive anthropology (Geertz); critical psychoanalytic and Marxist studies of women, gender, and sexuality; and the discursive, linguistic turn in history since Foucault.

All social phenomena need to be studied in their historical context. This involves the use of historical documents and written records of the past, including diaries, letters, newspapers, census tract data, novels, and other popular literature and popular culture documents. To understand historical documents, one must have an interpretive point of view. This point of view shapes how one gathers, reads, and analyzes historical materials. A historian's account of the past is a social text that constructs and reconstructs the realities of the past.

History is always the story of somebody's lived experience. The stories that tell history are always biased; none can ever document the "truth." Together, they present a revealing montage that should speak to us today. But how history speaks reveals the politics of power, for history is not purely referential; it is constructed by the historian. Written history both reflects and creates relations of power. Today's struggles are, then, about how we shall know the past and how the past will be constituted in the present. Every historical method implies a different way of telling these stories.

Borrowing from Benjamin (1969), today we write and perform history by quoting history back to itself. In this way, the cracks and contradictions in the official histories of the day are exposed. Madison shows us how to do this.

Testimonio as Narrative, Method, and Discourse

John Beverley's (Chapter 22, this volume) seminal discussion of *testimonio* traces the contemporary history of this method back to Oscar Lewis's life history analysis in *Children of Sanchez.* A *testimonio* is a first-person political text told by a narrator who is the protagonist, or witness to the events that are being reported. These tellings report on torture, imprisonment, social upheaval, and struggles for survival. These works are intended to produce (and record) social change. Their truth is contained in the telling of the events that are recorded by the narrator. The author is not a researcher, but rather a person who testifies on behalf of history and personal experience.

Beverley suggests that a predominant formal aspect of the *testimonio* is the voice that speaks to the reader in the form of an "I," a real rather than a fictional person. This is a voice that refuses to be silenced, and the person speaks on behalf of others. Yet, unlike autobiography, *testimonio* involves an erasure of the concept of author. The *testimonio* uses a voice that stands for a larger whole. This creates a democratic, egalitarian form of discourse. The *testimonio* is an open-ended, interpretive work. It may contain passages and reflections that are social constructions, fabrications, and arrangements of selected events from the actual world. These constructions may deal with events that did not happen. In this sense, the *testimonio* is an object of interpretation; it is not a mirror of the world. Rather, it stands in a critical relationship to the world of actual events. *I, Rigoberta Menchú* (1984) does this.

The *testimonio* asks that the reader identify with the text, that he or she believe in the truth of the text as the text asserts its interpretations of the world. In this context, Beverley takes up the controversy surrounding *I, Rigoberta Menchú.* (See also the bibliographic note to Chapter 22). Beverley concludes with a very valuable endnote on the preparation of *testimonios.* It is certain that in this century, the *testimonio* will be continue to be a major form of critical, interpretive writing.

Participatory Action Research

According to Stephen Kemmis and Robin McTaggart (Chapter 23, this volume), participatory action research (PAR) is an alternative philosophy of research (and social life) associated with liberation theology, neo-Marxist approaches to community development, and human rights activism. There are several different strands of participatory research, from critical action research, to classroom action research, action learning, action science, and industrial action research. Participatory researchers believe in the shared ownership of research projects, as well as the value of community-based analyses of social problems. They have a commitment to local community action, but they take care to protect the welfare and interests of those with whom they work. Participatory scholars reject the concept of value neutrality while also rejecting the criticisms of those who claim that PAR scholarship lacks scientific rigor and is too political.

Kemmis and McTaggart identify three different forms of PAR, what they call the third-person instrumental, second-person practical, and first-person critical approaches. They value those forms of PAR that involve first-person relationships. The material practices of PAR transform practitioners' theories and the theories that operate at the community level. Such transformations help to shape the conditions of life, connecting the local and global, the personal and the political. Work in this tradition attempts to make qualitative research more humanistic, holistic, and relevant to the lives of human beings. This worldview sees human beings as co-creating their reality through participation, experience, and action. Participatory action researchers help make this happen.

Clinical Models

Participatory action research has a natural affinity with clinical methods. Each tradition reflects a commitment to change, although clinical research displays a greater concern for diagnosis and treatment, rather than large-scale social change per se. Historically, the biomedical, positivist, and postpositivist paradigms have dominated clinical, medical research. William L. Miller and Benjamin F. Crabtree (Chapter 24, this volume) present a qualitative alternative approach that locates clinical research in the nexus of applied anthropology and the practice of primary health care, family practice in particular. They outline an experience-based, interpretive view of clinical practice, a view that makes the clinical practitioner and the patient coparticipants in the realities of medical treatment. They ask how questions emerging from the racial, gendered clinical experience can frame the conversations that occur between doctors and patients.

They offer a compelling critical analysis of the biomedical paradigm, as it is rooted in a patriarchal positivism. They criticize evidence-based medicine (EBM), the new wonder child of clinical research. Randomized clinical trials (RCT) and meta-analyses of multiple RCTs are now considered to be the best external evidence when considering medical interventions. Miller and Crabtree contend that the double-blind, closed RCT has "high internal validity but dubious external validity and almost no information about context or ecological consequences" (p. 613).

They propose conceptualizing a multimethod RCT as a double-stranded helix of DNA. On one strand are qualitative methods for addressed issues of context, meaning, power, and complexity. On the other strand are quantitative methods. The two strands are connected by the research question. "Clinicians and patients seeking support in the health care setting ask four basic questions of clinical praxis: (a) What is going on with our bodies? (b) What is happening with our life? (c) Who has what power? (d) What are the complex relationships between our bodies, our lives, our ecological context, and power?" (p. 614).

This model blends experience-based medicine with a participatory, action-based, multimethod approach. Methodologically, this model draws on experimental, survey, documentary, and field methods. It also uses the analytic framework of grounded theory, personal experience methods, clinical interviews, and participant observation. This model treats the medical and social body as a contested (and gendered) site for multiple personal and medical narratives. The multimethod approach advocated by Miller and Crabtree represents an attempt to change biomedical culture radically. Their chapter speaks to the politics of qualitative research. In the clinical, as in other areas of qualitative research, the multimethod approach often is the only avenue to a more interpretive conception of the research process.

With Kemmis and McTaggart, Miller and Crabtree show how qualitative research can be used as a tool to create social change. Miller and Crabtree want to change consciousness in the medical setting by changing the language and the paradigm that physicians and patients now use. The tools that these four authors advocate are powerful agents for social change.

At the same time, Miller and Crabtree want to change how medical texts are written. They want to create new forms of textuality, forms that will hold a place for those who have not yet been heard. Once the previously silenced are heard, they can then speak for themselves as agents of social change. In these kinds of texts, research is connected to political action, systems of language and meaning are changed, and paradigms are challenged. How to interpret these voices is the topic of Part IV of the *Handbook*. In the meantime, listen to the voices in Part III; these are calls to action.

Note

1. Mitch Allen's comments have significantly shaped our treatment of the relationship between paradigms and research designs.

References

Benjamin, W. (1969). *Illuminations* (H. Zohn, Trans.). New York: Harcourt, Brace & World.

Denzin, N. K. (1993). *The alcoholic society: Addiction and recovery of self.* New Brunswick, NJ: Transaction Publishing.

Denzin, N. K. (1999). Cybertalk and the method of instances. In S. Jones (Ed.), *Doing Internet research: Critical issues and methods for examining the Net* (pp. 107–126). Thousand Oaks, CA: Sage.

Fiske, J. (1994). Audiencing: Cultural practice and cultural studies. In N. K. Denzin & Y. S. Lincoln (Eds.), *Handbook of qualitative research* (pp. 189–198). Thousand Oaks, CA: Sage.

Gubrium, J. F., & Holstein, J. A. (1997). *The new language of qualitative method.* New York: Oxford University Press.

Janesick, V. J. (2000). The choreography of qualitative research design. In N. K. Denzin & Y. S. Lincoln (Eds.), *Handbook of qualitative research* (2nd ed., pp. 379–399). Thousand Oaks, CA: Sage.

Jenkins, K. (Ed.). (1997). *The postmodern history reader.* New York: Routledge.

Kendall, G., & Wickham, G. (1999). *Using Foucault's methods.* London: Sage.

Lincoln, Y. S., &. Guba, E. G. (1985). *Naturalistic inquiry.* Beverly Hills, CA: Sage.

Menchú, R. (1984). *I, Rigoberta Menchú: An Indian woman in Guatemala* (E. Burgos-Debray, Ed.; A. Wright, Trans.). London: Verso.

Mienczakowski, J. (2001). Ethnodrama: Performed research: Limitations and potential. In P. Atkinson, A. Coffey, S. Delamont, J. Lofland, & L. Lofland (Eds.), *Handbook of ethnography* (pp. 468–476). London: Sage.

Mills, C. W. (1959). *The sociological imagination.* New York: Oxford University Press.

Peirce, C. S. (1905, April). What pragmatism is. *The Monist, 15,* pp. 161–181.

Psathas, G. (1995). *Conversation analysis.* Thousand Oaks, CA: Sage.

Sartre, J. P. (1981). *The family idiot: Gustave Flaubert, 1821–1857* (Vol. 1). Chicago: University of Chicago Press.

Smith, D. E. (1993). High noon in textland: A critique of Clough. *Sociological Quarterly, 34,* 183–192.

15

THE PRACTICE AND POLITICS OF FUNDED QUALITATIVE RESEARCH

Julianne Cheek

1. Introduction: Connecting Practices and Politics

Funding increasingly is being recognized as an enabler for qualitative research. Part of this recognition has involved debunking the myth that qualitative research is cheap to do (Morse, 2002b). Funded qualitative research can take various forms. For example, the researcher might be granted a certain amount of money to be used directly for salaries, equipment, travel, or other expenses identified as necessary for the conduct of the research. In other cases, support for projects is offered "in kind": The funder may choose to provide the researcher with access to specialist staff or equipment as a means of supporting the research rather than supplying cash. Thus, when we talk about *funded* qualitative research, it is not always money that we are talking about. Funded qualitative research is not a homogeneous category able to be reduced to a single understanding. In the same way that qualitative approaches to research are varied in focus and purpose, so are funded qualitative projects.

Seeking, gaining, and accepting funding for qualitative research is not a neutral, value-free process. Funding does more than enable a qualitative project to proceed. Any form of support for qualitative research will have its unique demands on both the researcher and the research project. In particular, the amount of freedom that researchers have—in terms of both project design and the form that the "products" of the research take—will vary depending on what type of support is received. The amount of funding received also may be used to make statements about the relative worth of an individual researcher and to draw up rank tables of successful researchers and research institutions. Accepting funding aligns researchers with certain organizations and funding bodies. Allocation of funding reflects judgments being made as to what is, and is not, acceptable research or research worthy of being funded. Funding thus involves a series of choices being made, all of which have consequences both for the qualitative research itself and for the qualitative researcher. This chapter is about surfacing these choices, interrogating them, and exploring some of their effects. Such exploration involves scrutiny of the contested nature of research, our identities as qualitative researchers, and the nature of qualitative research itself. It moves the focus clearly onto the connections and interactions between qualitative research, funding, and politics.

The contemporary political climate at the time of writing this chapter is one that can be defined broadly as neo-liberal. Although there is no unitary or absolute form of neo-liberalism, neo-liberal governments, and the political regimes of truth that emanate therefrom, promote "notions of open markets, free trade, the reduction of the public sector, the decrease of state intervention in the economy and the deregulation of markets" (Torres, 2002, p. 368). Neo-liberal thought has permeated every aspect of contemporary Western society, including higher education and the world of research. This is evident from trends such as research increasingly being driven by corporate needs, students being positioned and referred to as consumers, and a climate where "paymasters and administrators accrete authority over academics" (Miller, 2003, p. 897). There has been a perceptible shift by governments in the United States, the United Kingdom, Australia, and elsewhere from an emphasis on the social aspects of government to the economic aspects, with the concomitant transformation of social projects to an enterprise form and ethos emphasizing outcomes in terms of economically driven balance sheets and report cards. As Shore and Wright (1999) point out, universities are just one of the sites where "neo-liberal ideas and practices are displacing the norms and models of good government established by the post-war, welfare state" (p. 558). In such a political climate, research increasingly is viewed as an enterprise and is being colonized by corporate and market derived and sustained understandings and premises.

It is with this political backdrop always in mind that this chapter explores aspects of the practicalities of doing funded qualitative research. I asserted in the previous edition of this *Handbook*, some 5 years ago (Cheek, 2000), that discussions of "doing" funded qualitative research often focus only on the writing of proposals or coming up with research ideas. What precedes proposal development in terms of identifying potential funders, and what follows receipt of funding, largely remains an "untold" story. My reading of the literature suggests that this is still the case. What has changed is that managerial, legal, scientific, and economic discourses (that is, ways of thinking and writing about aspects of reality) (Kress, 1985) have emerged with increasing prominence in terms of shaping and influencing the direction of funded qualitative research, in keeping with the increased influence of neo-liberal–driven agendas. Thus, in this chapter, as in my earlier piece of writing, I focus on identifying and approaching potential funding sources as well as on decisions and choices that arise once funding has been acquired. However, it is now not a matter of changing registers at the end of a chapter (Cheek, 2000) to consider a super-context where the "focus is on larger social issues and forces that impact on the funded qualitative researcher" to introduce a "more critical voice, one that probes, challenges, and tests assumptions about . . . the research market and the concomitant commodification of research" (p. 415). Rather, this register is present throughout—the practice of doing funded qualitative research cannot be separated from the political context in which it operates. Thus, the politics that sits behind many of the practices of funded qualitative research will be explored and will form as much a focus of the chapter as the "doing" of funded qualitative research.

As the author of this text, I am writing from a number of positions. Those that I identify are qualitative researcher, funded researcher, coeditor and associate editor of journals, panel member for a number of granting bodies, and reviewer for a number of granting schemes and journals. Just as I have argued that the intersection of qualitative research and funding creates tensions, so do the intersections of these various subject positions that I occupy at any one point in time. For example, as an individual committed to qualitative research as a legitimate and worthwhile research approach in its own right, and defined in its own right, at times I question my motives in applying for funding. Is the funding to do a project that I believe is important and should be done my driving motivation, or is it more that an opportunity to get funding has arisen and I should pursue that? In other words, what is more important to me—the funding or the project? Myself as researcher or myself as entrepreneur? I find myself on occasion torn between these positions because I, like many other researchers, am buffeted by the political context in which I operate.

An example of such buffeting is that while I am sitting here writing this chapter, I have in front of me an e-mail communication congratulating me for being in "the top 10" researchers in the part of the university in which I am located. At first this might seem innocuous or even a good thing, but a closer examination of the premises for such a ranking raises many important questions and issues. First, the criteria used to rank researchers are related to a narrow range of measures. There is no consideration given to the fact that the amount of funding received may be more a product of how much is needed to do a particular research project than a reflection of the relative ability of the researcher. For example, my research does not require large pieces of equipment worth many hundreds of thousands of dollars. Neither is there any consideration that an effect of such a rating based on individual performance may be to discourage collaboration and mentoring of other researchers, because the grant amount or research outcomes will need to be "split" across individuals in the research team. This applies to publications as well: The skill of slicing material into as many articles as possible may be more desirable than having something to say. Similarly, single-author publications will be more strategic than having to "share" performance. Nor is there any consideration of whether or not it is possible to simply transport the language and techniques of corporate management and neo-liberal enterprise culture, such as "the measurement of 'output' and 'efficiency' through competitive league tables, 'performance indicators' and other statistical indices of 'productivity'" (Shore & Wright, 1999, p. 564) into the university and research context. That it is possible, indeed desirable, to do so is a given—indicative of the pervasive influence of the rationality of neo-liberalism.

Questions that I have been asking myself in the past few months, and again while I am actually writing this chapter, include the following: Is it important to me that I am on the "league table" of the top 10 researchers in my area, or is it more important to me that I challenge the assumptions on which such tables are drawn up? Is it better to critique from within—that is, as a person who does attract relatively large sums of money—or does that involve selling out in order to get into that position in the first place, and thereby assisting in perpetuating the structures that I aim to critique? How do I survive in an academic climate where I, like every other facet of the context, am being reduced to a dollar value worked out according to a series of formulae, a large driver in which is the amount of funding received for research? If the amount of funding is key, then where does that leave qualitative research, as I am not going to need pieces of equipment worth large amounts of dollars? What should my response be when I am invited onto grants as "the qualitative person" or because "we thought it would useful to have a bit of qualitative research in it"? My personal journey and explorations with respect to these types of questions form the text to follow. I am sure that many qualitative researchers either are confronting similar issues, or will be, in the near future. It is important that these stories are told. This chapter is a beginning contribution to such a telling.

In what follows, however, I have deliberately tried to avoid setting up any form of polemic. Thus, I am not arguing for, or against, doing funded qualitative research. Rather, I am exploring what "doing" funded qualitative research might mean for both the researcher and the research. I am viewing funded qualitative research as text, recognizing that any text has embedded within it assumptions about the reality in question and a certain view that is being conveyed to the reader of the text. This is the subtext or "the hidden script" (Sachs, 1996). This chapter attempts to surface and explore the often hidden script that shapes and constructs understandings about funded qualitative research. As such, it should not be read as either for or against funded—or any other type—of research. Rather, it should be read as text itself, text that takes a particular view of funded qualitative research. As with any text, it is up to readers as to how they position themselves with respect to that view.

2. Locating Funding: Practices and Politics

Locating funding for qualitative research is a political process. There are two major pathways qualitative researchers can take to locate funding for projects. The first is to have an idea for a project and then to seek out funding sources for that project. The other, which is emerging with increasing emphasis in the area where I work, is to respond to tenders that have been advertised from industry or government for clearly defined and clearly delineated research projects, usually of very short duration. This is sometimes known as tendered research. The reason why this type of research is emerging with more prominence in the area that I work in is that this money is perceived, rightly or wrongly, as easier to win than funding in more traditional granting schemes, in which success rates can be less than 20% and it takes months for decisions to be made by a long (and sometimes cumbersome) process of peer review. Applications for these traditional schemes are very demanding and can take up to 6 months to develop, thereby decreasing the attractiveness of such schemes. In addition, it tends to be easier for institutions, with their increasing enterprise orientation, to make a profit from tendered research, in that researcher time will be paid for (whereas in Australia, many "traditional" funding schemes will not pay the time of the chief investigators) and profit margins can be built in. In fact, in many universities in Australia, it is not possible to put in a tender for research until it has been checked by business development units to ensure that the tender has maximized revenue-generating possibilities. There is thus an overt emphasis on the research being at least as much about revenue generation as about the actual research to be conducted. In more traditional schemes, such profit usually is not possible. In fact, in many of these schemes, projects often are not funded for the full amount applied for, with the researcher left to absorb the shortfall. For example, in some of the grants I hold, the granting body will pay a fixed amount towards the oncosts (the institution's contribution toward payroll tax, worker's compensation, and superannuation) of research personnel. However, in some schemes this is less than the oncosts charged by the institution in which I work. This immediately leaves me with a shortfall in funding in this area before I begin. The cumulative effect of this, across several grants, often means that I am actually working on grants as a research assistant on my own time, on weekends and nights, because I do not have enough funds to cover the research after all the "off the top" costs have been taken out. From a purely financial point of view, this makes tendered research a much more attractive proposition, particularly if institutions offer incentives to individual researchers as rewards for revenue generation.

Does this matter? The short answer is that yes, it does. It has serious implications both for qualitative research itself and for the role that qualitative researchers might find themselves playing in funded research. The type of funding sought affects the type of research that can be done. For example, it is highly unlikely that a government department will tender for projects involving long time frames. This immediately eliminates qualitative approaches requiring longer periods in the field and immersion in the data. My experience is that if a qualitative approach is asked for (and it is still the case in Australia that this is the exception rather than the rule), then it is likely to involve the conduct of an already specified number of workshops, focus groups, or interviews. In other words, tendered research is often more about a qualitative researcher operationalizing someone else's idea, intent, and design than it is about designing research to address an issue that the researchers themselves have identified. Even if the tender is in a particular substantive area of interest, it is unlikely that the emphases in the proposed research will be those of the researcher per se. This does not necessarily mean that the research is not valuable or important, but it does mean that the researcher is positioned differently in relation to the research process. It also has implications for understandings and possible future directions of qualitative research itself. If tendered research becomes more prominent, that may skew the type of qualitative research that gets done.

Another emerging trend that I have noticed in the quest to gain an edge in locating funding is the "tacking on" of a (usually small) qualitative component to large-scale, essentially quantitative studies in funding proposals. On one hand, this is an acknowledgment that there are limitations with measuring, for example, only outcomes and opinions. However, the effect of this "tacking on," paradoxically, can be to marginalize qualitative research even more. Often, the qualitative component of such studies involves the application of a few qualitative techniques, devoid of any theoretical grounding. Carey and Swanson (2003) note that "some applications drop in a focus group with no explanation of why it is being proposed or how the expected information will be used, and no description of the method or analysis plans. Although a similarly inappropriate use of quantitative methods could occur, I [*sic*] have not seen that scenario" (p. 856). This presents a very real possibility of qualitative research becoming more a technique than a theoretically grounded research approach.

Qualitative research is a way of thinking, not a method. When I am approached to be "the qualitative person" on a funding proposal that needs a "qualitative bit or part," that alerts me to the fact that the research is likely to be compartmentalized into the main study and the qualitative component, which is usually much smaller, with far fewer dollars attached to it, and leaves me with little control over the direction of the project itself. Therefore, I am very careful when considering requests of this type. It is important to determine if the proposal going forward for funding, or the tender being called for, understands qualitative research as more than just a few techniques able to be tacked onto the "real" research. It is important to make a decision as to what that means for me as a researcher and what actions I will take in response. I have experienced being in a project in which more than 90% of a large budget was for the quantitative aspects of the study and the qualitative research was underfunded, not well understood, and undervalued. I will not put myself in that position again. By participating in that situation, however, I was able to change the thinking of members of the team and now enjoy very productive and fruitful relationships with them on other funded projects. This is but one example of the underlying and ongoing tensions that permeate the politics and practice of funded qualitative research. I cannot present a "right way" of acting in the funding process; there is no right or wrong way of acting. Rather, the discussion is designed to raise consciousness about what are often unintended consequences with respect to the positioning of both qualitative research and qualitative researchers in funded proposals and research teams.

An important part of being able to locate funding for qualitative research is to be in a position to know about and identify potential funding sources. Zagury (1997) has identified six categories of potential funding sources. These are local community funds, special purpose foundations, family-sponsored foundations, national foundations, government grants and corporate foundations, and corporate funding. It is important to be aware that there are distinct national differences in types and patterns of funding. Hence, it may well be that in certain countries, some of the above categories of funders are of less significance than in others.

One place to start in identifying potential funders is to obtain publications that list them. One such publication is *The GrantSearch Register of Australian Funding* (Summers, 2003). Watching advertisements in newspapers, particularly in the contract/tender section, is another way of identifying potential funding sources, as is getting on the mailing list of the university research office (for those who work in a university setting). Another useful way of learning about potential funding sources that may not be advertised or appear in any grant register or list is to talk to people who have received funding in areas similar to the proposed research. Thus, regardless of the actual mix of funding sources in any particular country or part of the country (there are regional variations in many nations), it is imperative that researchers "do their homework" with respect to uncovering potential funding sources. In light of the preceding discussion, this homework will involve working out what type of funding to seek or apply for, and how this funding might position both the researcher and the qualitative research itself.

Once potential funders are identified, it is important to get as much information as possible about them. One way of doing this is to obtain copies of funding guidelines and/or annual reports. These documents, among other things, give a good overview of the types of projects potential funders have funded in the past and are likely to fund in the future. From this, researchers can assess whether their proposed research seems to fit the priorities and interests of the funder concerned. If review of documentation from the agency reveals it as a viable potential funder for the research in question, the next step is to approach the agency directly to discuss the research idea. How this is done will vary, depending on the type of sponsor. For example, if the funder calls for proposals on an annual basis, the researcher can initiate contact with the office that deals with these applications, both to acquire information about the process and to introduce both the research and the researcher to the people who are likely to be dealing with the application administratively. Speaking with representatives of the agency gives insight into its processes and practices with respect to the way that funding is allocated. Furthermore, it should be possible to ascertain more information about what types of research have been funded in the past. The agency may even supply reports of completed research and/or copies of proposals that have been funded. This information is invaluable for ascertaining the format and scope expected of a proposal, as well as in assisting in the better formulation of ideas, in language appropriate to the funder in question. Examination of previously funded research also enables the researcher to better locate the proposed study in terms of work already done in the area. Personal communication with potential funding bodies is thus critical, as it provides insights and advice not readily available elsewhere.

Much of what has been discussed also applies when researchers approach a funding agency that does not have regular funding rounds but instead tends to fund research on a more ad hoc basis. One difference is that it may not be immediately obvious whom to contact in the sponsor's organization. It is important to find the right person, in the right section in the organization, to talk to about the intended research and the possibility of funding for it. In this way, the researcher becomes familiar with the organization, and the organization gets to know the researcher. This is important, as a crucial question in funders' minds is whether they can trust a particular researcher to successfully complete a worthwhile project once money is committed to it. When speaking to a funder's representative, it is important to present a clear, simple idea that is both researchable and likely to produce benefits and outcomes that are valuable from the funder's perspective. Consider submitting a concept paper first, either by post or in person, before making personal contact with a representative of the organization. The concept paper could include any preliminary work done or data already collected. This allows the researcher to address the points identified by Bogdan and Biklen (1998) as being important when initiating contact with funders: "1. What have you done already? 2. What themes, concerns, or topics have emerged in your preliminary work? What analytic questions are you pursuing?" (p. 70).

Accompanying the concept paper should be a statement of the researcher's track record. It is important to demonstrate that there is every likelihood, based on past experience, that the research will be completed on time and within budget. Not only is it important to present the research idea, it also is important to present the researchers themselves. One of the problems facing many researchers is the catch-22 situation of needing a track record to attract funding, while not being able to get the funding needed to build up a track record. One way around this is to join a research team that already has established a track record in the same or a closely related area of research, and to work as part of that team. This has a further benefit of establishing contact with the research expertise that is collectively present. It is an ideal way to learn about the research process in a safe way and can lead to the formation of enduring research relationships between colleagues. Another strategy for building a track record is to acquire some form of seed funding. The process may be less competitive than acquiring grants from larger funding bodies, and the funding may be directed to more novice researchers. Such seed funding, though usually modest in amount, can be enough to begin a small research project that can lead to publications and thus provide a foundation on which other research can be built.

What should be evident by now is that acquiring funding is not a quick or easy process. Much lead time often is needed for planning and for establishing research credentials and rapport with funding sources. Failures are inevitable, and it is difficult not to take these personally. Other researchers can provide valuable advice and support throughout this process. As I pointed out previously, many research textbooks begin and end their discussions of how to acquire funding by talking about proposal writing. This, I believe, is nowhere near enough. What has just been discussed—namely, the strategies that must be employed to get to the point where one can write a proposal for a specific funding agency—is, in my opinion, the actual start of "doing" funded qualitative research. In addition, it is imperative to consider, at every stage of the funding process, the politics behind funding itself and any particular funding bid.

◼ 3. Allocating Funding: Practices and Politics

The next step, after identifying a potential funder, is crafting a proposal to seek funding for the research. I have deliberately used the word "crafting" because proposal writing is a craft requiring a unique set of skills, most of which are learned as a result of practice. Writing a proposal involves shaping and tailoring a research idea to fit the guidelines or application process imposed by the intended funding agency. Each application, even for the same project, will vary depending on the characteristics and requirements of the funder being approached. When a proposal is written for a potential sponsor's consideration, it is written for a particular audience, whose members have assumptions and expectations of the form a proposal should take and the language it should use. Thus, as I have emphasized before, it is important for researchers to know that audience and its expectations.

What follows is not about proposal writing per se. Much already has been written about this. For example, a recent edition of *Qualitative Health Research* (Vol. 3, No. 6, July 2003) was devoted to a discussion of qualitative research proposals. Several excellent articles focused on crafting and developing qualitative proposals, along with some of the politics that sits behind this. In these articles, the authors share their experiences by telling their stories of the development, and at times defense, of their proposals. Here, I will continue to expose aspects of what otherwise may remain hidden with respect to the politics and practice of allocating funding for qualitative research.

Writing a proposal is a political process. Researchers need to consider whether the qualitative approach proposed and the likely outcomes of the research "fit" the agenda of the funding body. It is quite reasonable for those who provide funding for research to ask whether or not the proposed project represents appropriate use of the funds for which they have responsibility. The majority of funders take the allocation of monies very seriously. They must weigh the relative merits, from their point of view, of proposals competing for limited resources. Thus, it is essential for the proposal submitted to be clear in terms of its purpose and rationale. Are the outcomes of the project stated? Are they important, useful, and able to make a difference in people's lives? Some funding bodies may be a little self-serving in their reasons for funding specific proposals, but on the whole, funders do make genuine efforts to fund worthy research proposals, and most treat the selection process very seriously. Funders who are seeking to let a tender for research, while still wanting to ensure that the research done will meet high standards, have other considerations as well. One of these will be cost. This lies at the heart of the tendering process, which is designed for the funder to test the research marketplace in terms of what their money can buy. Qualitative researchers entering this world need to understand the market-driven parameters of tendered research and position themselves competitively. Offering value for money means not only meeting high standards in the research; it also means considering how much, or little, money needs to be allocated to attain those standards.

The trend for universities in Australia, as elsewhere, is to move more into the world of tenders that once belonged to market researchers and consultants. This has meant that university-based qualitative researchers have had to confront issues that they may have been able to ignore in the past. The inherent quality of research no longer is the only consideration. Indeed, understandings of "quality" themselves may have undergone transformation, with traditional measures such as peer review playing less of a role and other factors assuming more prominence, such as perceived value for money. Thus, some means of acquiring funding are becoming overt forms of selling oneself and one's research skills in the research marketplace. The funder does not fund an idea; rather, a researcher's time and expertise are bought to conduct a piece of defined research the agency or organization wants done. This concept, as I have suggested previously and will return to at the end of the chapter, creates new and different tensions for the funded qualitative researcher. Not the least of these tensions revolves around what research funding is for: either remuneration for selling skills, thereby contributing to university or researcher income, or enabling the conduct of research identified by the researcher as important and needing to be done. Of course, these may not be mutually exclusive, although in my experience one or the other tends to be at the fore in any particular funding situation.

Shaping all application forms or guidelines provided by funders are assumptions, often unwritten and unspoken, about research and the way that research is understood. It is important to excavate these assumptions and understandings, for two reasons. The first is to work out whether the funding body is likely to fund qualitative research. Are the guidelines structured in such a way that it is impossible to "fit" qualitative research into them? As Lidz and Ricci (1990) point out, reviewers and funders, like all of us, have "culturally prescribed ideas about 'real' research" (p. 114). The application form and the way that it is structured provide insight and clues as to the funder's particular culturally prescribed ideas about research. Second, in light of some of the preceding discussion, insights also can be gleaned about the way that qualitative research, if present in a detailed tender brief, is understood. Hence, texts such as funding guidelines, tender briefs, and research grant application forms must be read carefully, not only for what they say and how they say it, but also for what they *do not* say. Such a critical reading enables qualitative researchers to take up an informed political position in relation to a particular funding source.

Another guide to the likely success of qualitative proposals is the composition of the review panel used by the funder. Does it contain people who are expert in qualitative research? Does it allow for the possibility for the committee to seek expert opinion outside the committee itself if a proposal comes in that is not within the methodological expertise of committee members? Morse (2003a), Parahoo (2003), and many others have noted that reviews of research proposals can indicate real ignorance about qualitative research, such as asking for power calculations for sample size. Further, Morse (2003a) notes that sometimes the seeking and/or assumption of "expert" advice about qualitative research can be very limited and somewhat ad hoc. The committee members know someone who uses qualitative research or someone who has done a workshop or short course on qualitative research, and "they use these isolated 'facts' as gold standards" (Morse, 2003a, p. 740). Morse refers to this sort of climate as "denigrative" of qualitative research and calls for agencies to be made more accountable for "decisions based on inaccurate, incorrect, or invalid reviews" (2003a, p. 739). Further, she notes that even if there are qualitative reviewers on panels, they invariably are in the minority, often being a "faint voice" on funding panels (Morse, 2002b, p. 1308). If the practice of averaging all the panel members' scores for a particular proposal is followed, then in many instances, because of the relative lack of expertise in and appreciation for qualitative research among the majority of panel members, it is unlikely that average scores for qualitative proposals will be high enough for these proposals to be recommended for funding.

Once the decision has been made to pursue funding from a particular source, the instructions given for applying for funds must be followed carefully. I have reviewed many research funding applications for which it was evident that instructions were not followed. To improve your project's chances of being funded, follow all instructions, beginning with the basics. When asked to confine the application to a certain page limit or word limit, do so. Similarly, if asked to explain something in a lay person's terms, do so. No one is impressed by impenetrable language. Perhaps most crucial is following instructions meticulously with respect to the detail required about the research budget and the way the funds will be used. Many claims appear in proposals for amounts that are obviously well beyond the funding parameters of the grants program in question. Put simply, the proposal must be tailored to the guides, not the guides to the proposal. One strategy employed by many successful researchers to assist in ensuring that the proposal closely approximates the guidelines is to get colleagues to read the draft proposal and provide critical comments.

A key point to bear in mind is that any research proposal, qualitative or not, must formulate a clear issue or question. The initial idea that provided the impetus for the research must be transformed into a researchable focus. The rest of the proposal must unpack that research question and demonstrate how the approach to be taken will enable it to be answered. The proposed research must be contextualized in terms of what has preceded it. The study must be situated in terms of what others are doing and how this research links to that of others. It must be justified in terms of approach and design, having a clear direction and focus with clearly achievable outcomes in line with the funder's priorities and stated goals. The credentials of the researcher or research team also need to be established. The amount of information given about the research design, analysis, and data collection will be determined in part by the format of the guidelines or application form. The proposal must be written so that the reader can understand clearly from the document what is intended for the study, and why. As the proposal is being written and after it is submitted, it is important to ascertain the deadlines and timelines involved, as well as the procedures followed by the decision-making person or committee. In other words, it is important to gain insight into the process of allocating funds. Such insight prepares the researcher to expect a response in a certain format within a set time, and it informs any necessary follow-up.

When the decision about funding finally is made, there are usually three possible outcomes. First, the request may be approved. In this case, the researcher receives funding, and the research commences as soon as all appropriate permissions, such as ethics clearance, are obtained. Another possible outcome is that the researcher is asked to add or change something, for instance, to supply more information about one or more aspects of the proposal. This should be interpreted as a positive sign. More often than not, it means that the funder is considering the request seriously and feels it has some merit; certain aspects of it, however, need clarification before the funder is willing to commit funds. In another version of this outcome, the researcher may be asked if the study could be conducted with a reduced budget, and if so, how. This is not unusual. Sometimes funders have set amounts to allocate, and if the proposed study is toward the bottom of the list of projects they wish to fund, they may be able to offer only a portion of the funds requested. It is important that researchers think carefully about whether to accept such funding. I believe that funded research should not be attempted without adequate support for the activities necessary to the research. It is very tempting to accept any funding offered, but inadequate funding can lead to all sorts of problems in actually doing research. Clearly, research funding poses issues not only about the wise use of funds but also about the wisdom of whether or not to accept funds in the first place.

The third possible outcome is one that is becoming all too common, given the increasing competition for grants: The request for funding is rejected. If this happens, it is important to get as much feedback as possible. Make an appointment to speak to the chair of the committee or a representative of the trust, foundation, or other organization making the decision. Find out as much as possible. Copies of the reviewers' reports may be made available, and these often contain useful critiques that can be used in preparing the proposal for resubmission or submission to another agency. If these reports cannot be obtained, or in addition to them, a list of the projects that were successful may be available. This list may give insights into whether the idea did in fact match the funding priorities of the funder, and what the funder sought in successful proposals. If no feedback at all is available from the funder, then ask researchers who have been funded to review the unsuccessful proposal and to help in debriefing the process just undergone. Talking it through may reveal things that can be done differently in the next application. However, at all times researchers should be aware of their odds of success. In many grants programs in Australia, for example, the success rate is below 20%. Such low success rates are increasingly the case in most countries as the competition for shrinking funding sources grows relentlessly. It is much more likely for researchers *not* to acquire funding than to be successful. Research proposals take much time and effort to complete, and it is hard to cope with rejection, but it may help to remember that no researcher is alone. By maintaining contact with others and setting in place the strategies outlined so far in this chapter, the chances of success can be maximized.

4. Navigating Ethics Committees: Practices and Politics

Receiving a recommendation for funding is not the end of the review process. Funded qualitative research, like other forms of research, needs to undergo a process of formal ethics review. Ethics committees thus become another layer of decision making as to what research will be, and will not be, funded. Funds may not be released until ethics approval is formally received, or if they are released, the research might not be able to proceed until ethics approval has been given. In the university in which I am located, and in keeping with standard practice in Australia, I cannot conduct research with human participants until I have formal ethics approval from the university's Human Research Ethics Committee, as well as from any relevant ethics committees at the sites where my research is situated. An issue for qualitative researchers relates to the role and function of ethics committees with respect to giving such approval. Lincoln and Tierney (2002) assert that there is evidence in the United States that some qualitative researchers are having problems getting research that has already been funded through the Institutional Review Board (IRB) ethics process. In the United States, IRBs were initiated in 1966 (Riesman, 2002) following an order from the U.S. Surgeon General in response to questionable medical research involving elderly patients being injected with live cancer cells. Further regulations designed to protect human subjects (*sic*) became effective in 1974. Thus, the driving force in the establishment of IRBs was the protection of human subjects. This was in keeping with developments stemming from the Nuremberg Code, promulgated in the aftermath of unethical medical experimentation on prisoners and concentration camp inmates during World War II. Thus, the original focus of IRBs and the context from which they emerged was that of medicine and the scientific discourse that underpins medicine.

Similarly, in the United Kingdom, the Royal College of Physicians in 1967 recommended that all medical research be subject to ethical review, and by 1991 every health district was required to have a Local Research Ethics Committee (LREC), with Multi-centre Research Ethics Committees (MRECs) emerging as a means of helping streamline proposals that otherwise would have to go through numerous LRECs (Ramcharan & Cutcliffe, 2001). In the United Kingdom, as in the United States, the formalizing of ethics requirements and the establishment of ethics committees was derived and driven largely by practices from medical research. This is also the case in Australia. For example, university-based Human Research Ethics Committees are modeled on National Health and Medical Research Council guidelines. These apply to all research involving humans, whether it is health related or not. Thus, ethics committees, and the understandings of research with which they operate, often are influenced by the traditions of medicine and science, including the research methods and understandings of research that these disciplines employ.

To some extent, the emergence of qualitative research, and particularly the emergence of funded qualitative research, has occurred at the same time as the emergence of ethics committees and the formalization of ethics requirements and processes. At times, we see the collision of these surfaces of emergence and the working out of the tensions that emanate therefrom. For example, Lincoln and Tierney (2002), Ramcharan and Cutcliffe (2001), and Riesman (2002) assert that qualitative research may be being treated unfairly, and in fact may be disadvantaged, by some ethics committees. Such claims emanate from concerns that qualitative approaches are rejected on the grounds that they are "unscientific" and not able to be generalized. Research methods increasingly have become the remit of ethics committees. In effect, ethics committees can be more powerful than national peer-reviewed funding committees. Even if national and international peers who are experts in my field and the research approaches I employ recommend a project for funding, ethics committees can reject it on the basis of "poor design"—and, thus, "unethical research"—that will result in no benefit, or even possibly in harm, to research participants.

The focus on the quality of the research design stems from legitimate ethical concerns as to the ability of research to make a difference. For example, the U.K. Royal College of Physicians guidelines make the point "that badly designed research is unethical, because unnecessary disturbances may be caused to those concerned, and the lack of validity of results means they cannot be disseminated for the good of society" (Lacey, 1998, p. 215). The upshot of this is that "LRECs must therefore judge the scientific as well as ethical merit of the research under consideration" (Lacey, 1998, pp. 215–216). However, the key question arises as to what constitutes scientific merit or "good" research design, and who determines this. If scientific merit is reduced to "conventional quantitative methods" (Lacey, 1998, p. 216), then this will work against qualitative research unfairly. As van den Hoonaard (2001) points out, ethical review often is based on "the principles and epistemology of deductive research. . . . [This] tends to erode or hamper the thrust and purpose of qualitative research . . . [and] it is a question of whether it is appropriate to judge the ethical merit of qualitative research using criteria derived from other paradigms of research" (pp. 19, 21). It also begs the question of whether ethics and research design are one and the same or different.

Requirements specified by some ethics committees simply can not apply to qualitative research. If, for example, it is necessary for researchers to state clearly, before research begins, each question that they will ask participants, this makes the emergent design of some qualitative research extremely problematic. As Lincoln and Tierney (2002) point out, the issue here is twofold: failure to obtain permission to conduct qualitative research as well as mandates that these studies should be conducted in a positivist fashion. Further issues arise from the politics between ethics committees themselves. Some ethics committees refuse to accept the ethics approval of other committees. Inconsistencies between the decisions and processes of different ethics committees sometimes arise, with the result that it takes a long time to gain approval. I have been caught in such politics of research with funded projects, with one ethics committee approving my research and another not. This example highlights the inconsistencies that can develop around ethics approvals. If the research concerned is a form of tendered research requiring relatively short turnaround times, this protracted approval process can preclude the research from being funded. It may also create and sustain the perception that qualitative research is problematic, unwieldy, and therefore best avoided by funders.

In light of such issues, a strategy I have used when navigating requirements of ethics committees is to write to the particular ethics committees, explaining how I have filled in the form and why I have done so, especially with respect to not being able to provide certain details of the research until the study is actually under way. I state how the initial approach will be made to participants, and I outline the general principles that will be employed regarding confidentiality and other matters. I also suggest that, if the committee would find it useful, I would be happy to talk about the research and discuss any concerns committee members might have. I have found most (but not all) committees willing to listen and to be quite reasonable. However, when talking with ethics committees who have invited me to their meetings to discuss concerns, I am continually struck by the realization that I constantly have to frame my responses in terms of the understandings of research that the committee brings to the table. The conversation usually is as much a discussion of understandings of research as it is about the ethics of that research. I have had to justify all aspects of the research process, not just those I thought were ethical matters. For example, I have found myself engaging in deep, philosophically derived debates about the nature of knowledge and the way that it is possible to study that knowledge. This was despite the fact that a national funding body had deemed the research in question rigorous enough to be funded. Afterwards, I wondered whether any of the committee had ever had to explain the philosophical basis of the research approaches they were familiar with, and I reached the conclusion that they probably had not. This highlighted to me that dominant understandings of research were in play here and that decisions made were as much about what individuals understood and constructed research to be, as they were about the ethics of the research in question. This suggests that ethics committees and the process of ethical approval are as much discursive constructions as any other text.

As another example, a student of mine agreed to change the word "participant" to "patient" in the consent forms and information sheets that would be given to research participants. This was one of the conditions to be met for ethics approval to be granted. We (student and supervisor) had to think deeply about this, but in the end we considered that it was more important for the research to go forward than to take a stand on this issue. In reality, changing this word did not affect the way we did our research. It was more about the comfort levels of some committee members and that their understanding of the positioning of people entering the hospital was maintained. However, this example does raise an important point: At times, researchers may find themselves asked to modify proposals in a way that appears to compromise the approach they wish to take. In instances like this, they must make what I would argue is a fundamentally ethical decision: Can the research proceed under these conditions? Some readers may argue that what we did in changing the word "participant" to "patient" was an ethical issue, one in which we "sold out" to pragmatics and expediency.

One of the reasons for the initial emergence and subsequent prominence of ethics committees and their power was a rise in lawsuits pertaining to medical research that had gone "wrong." As a consequence, van den Hoonaard agrees with "one qualitative researcher" that "qualitative researchers have become the fall guys for ethical mistakes in medical research" (2001, p. 22). He poses the question of whether the rise of ethics committees constitutes a moral panic involving "exaggeration of harm and risk, orchestration of the panic by elite or powerful special-interest groups, the construction of imaginary deviants, and reliance on diagnostic instruments" (van den Hoonaard, 2001, p. 25). In such a construction, qualitative research could be viewed as deviant, and the rise of prescribed forms of deductive research as diagnostic instruments able to be used to detect "suspect" research. The effect, unintended or otherwise, of ethics committees increasingly positioning themselves as determining what type of research will proceed and which will not is an interesting shift from the original intent of ethics committees to uphold the rights of those being researched, to a focus equally concerned with possible legal ramifications of any research undertaken. Thus, protection as a focus of ethics committees has evolved to be as much about protecting from potential litigation the institutions from which researchers come from and/or in which they do their research, as it is about protecting individual participants from adverse research effects.

Putting another spin on this, Kent (1997) notes that ethics committees sometimes take on proxy decision making for participants, making "assumptions about patient's [*sic*] welfare which do not correspond to patients' actual feelings and beliefs" (p. 187). An interesting insight into this was provided by a recent experience I had when asking participants to sign a consent form for a nominal group I was conducting as part of funded research. The ethics committee requirement was that all participants must sign this consent form before the group could proceed. This particular nominal group comprised senior government and industry representatives. One of the participants objected to having to sign a consent form, seeing it as a form of coercion and control. I was then in a quandary. Did I ask this person to leave and preclude him from the research, or did I proceed, contravening the legalistic requirement of a signed form? In the end, I was able to talk the person around to signing the form but felt that in so doing, I was being coercive and establishing my control of the process. I felt that the forms and procedures had more to do with legalistic requirements than with ethical concerns. Far from empowering this participant, they actually were a form of control and restriction. This is not to argue against the signing of consent forms or the need for consent. Instead, I suggest that techniques employed to ensure that ethical requirements are met can themselves become apparatuses of power that actually do something other than ensuring the ethics of the research. The danger is that regulations (i.e., forms and processes) *become* the ethics, rather than the ethics of the research itself.

Elsewhere (Cheek, 2000), I have suggested strategies for navigating ethics committees. These include finding out as much as possible about the processes used by the committee and asking to see examples of proposals that have been accepted. These actions supply ideas of both the level of detail and the format that the committee requires. Another suggestion is to speak to others who have applied to the committee in question for ethics approval. Remember that qualitative researchers seeking funding or ethical approval have rights, as do all researchers. These include the right "to have their proposals treated with respect and due consideration" (Kent, 1997, p. 186). Stuart (2001) suggests that how we choose to act with respect to how we approach ethics committees (and we could add funding committees) is in fact an ethical decision. He writes, "Will the research be based on practices that treat people as the objects of research and provide them with limited opportunities to contribute to the production of knowledge, or will it be based on collaborative practices that view people as participants in the production of knowledge?" (Stuart, 2001, p. 38). Similarly, do we massage our research into prescribed forms and formulae, knowing that in this form it will be much more likely to achieve funding and approval, but also knowing that it may use systems and practices that work against qualitative research and leave unresolved some of the issues posed?

These sorts of decisions and weighing of tensions and alternatives are important parts of the politics and practice of funded qualitative research. They challenge us to think deeply about every aspect of what we do. It is not a matter of expediency and learning how to "play" the system. We need to try to work for real change, change that will make a difference to, and differences in, the types of research that are funded and approved. Rowan (2000) observed that

> when the British Psychological Society decided that it was wrong to call people subjects, because it suggested that they were subjected to the will of the researcher, changing 'subjects' to 'participants' was

> for many psychologists simply a matter of calling up the 'find and replace' facility on the computer. It was not seen as related to a code of ethics, or requiring any change in them. (p. 103)

This highlights the layers of political action that are required to address deep residual practices that can hinder and even subvert the development of funded qualitative research. Without taking such political action, we run the risk of remaining on the surface and playing the politics of the system rather than changing that politics. As Morse (2003b) points out:

> This is a task for all of us to do collectively and systematically, for it involves changes such as broadening research priorities and perspectives on what is considered researchable and what constitutes research. It involves political problems, such as expanding and sharing research funds to new groups of investigators. In this light, the administrative changes involved, such as developing appropriate review criteria, expanding committee membership, and educating other scientists about the principles of qualitative inquiry . . . appear trivial. (p. 849)

To focus only on the mechanism of practices associated with funding, be they proposal writing, peer review, or ethics review, is to run the risk of dealing only "with minor changes within the same basic structure" (Martin, 2000, p. 17). Put another way, it is to focus on "what is" and working within that, rather than on "what might be" in terms of "dramatically different allocation principles and associated consequences" (Martin, 2000, p. 21).

▣ 5. Accepting Funding: Practices and Politics

Accepting funding involves entering into a contractual and intellectual agreement with a funder that has consequences for the research that is undertaken. Thus, a central consideration when thinking about doing funded qualitative research is whether or not to accept funding from a particular funding agency. Would-be researchers must consider the potentially conflicting agendas of funders, participants, and researchers. For example, at the university in which I work, we do not accept funding from the tobacco industry. This is just one example, and there are many more instances of question marks over the ethics of accepting funding from certain industries, agencies, or even governments. Other examples include whether a particular industry is involved in questionable environmental activities or health practices and whether it is a multinational company involved in possible exploitation of developing countries' workforces. Taking money from a sponsor is not a neutral activity; it links the researcher and research inexorably with the values of that funder.

A related set of issues emerges from a consideration of who controls the qualitative research that is funded. It is a fact that once funding is accepted for research, the researcher is not an entirely free agent with respect to the direction and outcome of that research. Depending on the policies and attitudes of the funder, the degree of freedom allowed in carrying out the research (such as changing its direction if the need arises as a result of findings, or talking and writing about the research) may vary considerably. Issues of control must be negotiated carefully in the very early stages of the research, as it is often too late once the project is well under way. Too often, researchers either ignore or are simply unaware of the problems that can arise. Taking funding from someone in order to conduct research is not a neutral act. It implies a relationship with that funder that has certain obligations for both parties. It is important for researchers to discuss with funders all the expectations and assumptions, both spoken and unspoken, that they may have about the research.

As an example, one such expectation relates to what can be said about the research, and by whom. Put another way, this is an issue about who actually owns the data or findings that result from the study, as well as about how those data can be used both during and after the study. Some researchers have found themselves in the situation of not being able to write about the research in the way they want to, if at all. For example,

I carried out a funded piece of research, using qualitative approaches, that produced four main findings, each of which was accompanied by a series of recommendations. When I submitted the report, I found that the funding body was willing to act on two of the findings, as it believed they were within the body's statutory remit, but not on the other two. Although this seems reasonable at one level, I was concerned that the remaining two findings were in danger of being lost. The recommendations associated with those findings were important and, in my opinion, required action. I was even more concerned when the funder wanted to alter the report to include only the two findings it believed were relevant to it. Fortunately, a solution was found whereby the report was framed to highlight the findings considered relevant by the funder, while making reference to the other findings as well. In some ways, this may seem like an uneasy compromise, but at least the whole picture was given with respect to the findings. Somewhat naïvely, in retrospect, I had not anticipated the issue arising as to what data and findings should or could be included in a study, or what data, conversely, might be excluded. I am now much more careful to negotiate how the findings of a study will be reported, the use of the data, and my rights to publish the study findings in full, myself, in scholarly literature.

Qualitative approaches to research are premised on an honest and open working relationship between the researcher and the participants in the research. Inevitably, in such studies the researcher spends a great deal of time with participants getting to know aspects of their world and learning about the way they live in that world. At the center of a good working relationship in qualitative research is the development of trust. Furthermore, as qualitative researchers, we all have dealt with issues such as participants feeling threatened by the research and therefore concealing information, or participants who are eager to please us and give us the information they think we want to hear or that they think we need to know. These issues can become even more complicated in the conduct of funded qualitative research. Therefore, when conducting funded research, it is important for researchers to tell participants who is providing the funding and the purposes of that funding. Successful researchers report the importance of making their own relationship to the funder clear. For example, are they acting as paid employees of the funder, or are they independent? Equally crucial to a successful relationship between researchers and participants is to ensure, and to give assurance, that the participants will remain anonymous and that the confidentiality of their individual information will be safeguarded. This is a major concern for some participants, who may believe they will be identified and "punished" in some way by the funder—for example, if they criticize a funder who is their employer. When conducting research in a specific setting among a specified group of people, it may be difficult for researchers to ensure the anonymity of participants. It is crucial for researchers to be clear about this issue and to discuss it with participants, who need to know what will happen to specific information in the project, who will have access to it, and how their rights to confidentiality are being ensured. Individuals may choose not to participate if they have concerns about a particular funder having access to information they have given or if they question the motives for that funding being given in the first place.

If there are any restrictions on what can or cannot be said about the findings of the research and the research undertaking itself, then it is important for researchers to make potential participants aware of this. Part of the constant process of giving feedback to participants must include informing them about any issues that arise about ownership of the research and the way it will be disseminated. All of this is to assist participants in making informed decisions about whether to participate or not, as well as to give them some idea about the uses to which the research is likely to be put. This enables them to be better positioned to follow up the research findings and to have a say in what happens as a result of them. It is a part of valuing all perspectives in the research and of treating participants as more than simply research objects who are subject to a research agenda that has been imposed on them.

A related issue can arise when the findings of a study do not please the funder. What happens if the findings are, or have the potential to be, beneficial to the participants but may displease the sponsor? Who has the say as to whether or not these findings will be published? As Parahoo (1991) points out, "too often those who control the purse tend to act in their own interests when they veto the publication of research. To others this is an abuse of power and office, and a waste of public money" (p. 39). This is a particularly important question if the research involves working with groups that are relatively powerless or disenfranchised. Researchers have found themselves in the position of not being able to publish or otherwise disseminate results in any way because of the contractual arrangements that they have entered into when accepting funds. When finalized, a contract should be checked carefully so that researchers can be sure they are comfortable and can live with the conditions set. Such checking of the contract also pertains to the need for clarity about exactly what will be "delivered" to the funder in return for the funding received. What is it that the researcher is contracting with the funder to provide? This is an important question, raising the possibility of numerous problems arising if the parties involved do not share an understanding. It is easy and tempting for researchers, particularly if they are inexperienced, to underestimate the amount of time and energy needed for a project. Consequently, they may "overcommit" in terms of what they can deliver to the funder. They must consider carefully what it is reasonable to provide for the funding received, then make this explicit to the funder. Time frames should be placed on each deliverable so that both parties are aware of what will be produced and when it can be expected.

As we have seen, obtaining funding creates a research relationship to build during the conduct of the research, namely that between the funder and the researcher. All funding bodies require reports about the progress of funded projects. When communicating and reporting to the funder, which often involves reporting to an individual nominated by the funder, it is important for researchers to be honest and up front. This particularly applies if something has "gone wrong" or if for some reason the research plan has had to be changed. In my experience, funders would much rather find out about these things as they arise than be faced at the end with a project that has not met expectations. The extent of a funding body's involvement in research can vary considerably, ranging from the submission of one or two reports a year to a highly hands-on approach in which a representative of the agency seeks to play an active role in the research undertaken. Whatever approach is adopted, it is important that there is clear communication as to the roles that the researcher and the funder will play in the research. It also is important to clarify that if research is being carried out in which participants will be known to the representative of the agency, then there may have to be restrictions on access to information so as to protect participants' rights to confidentiality. Similarly, if a funder requires that an advisory board be established to provide guidance on the progress and direction of the research, it is important to clarify the parameters within which the board will operate. Such boards can be invaluable in assisting with broad issues pertaining to the substantive focus of the research. Indeed, many experienced researchers, recognizing the value of advisory boards in thinking through aspects of doing the project, interpreting the findings, and considering the routes for dissemination, may constitute such a board regardless of funder requirements. However, clear understandings must be put in place as to what access, if any, the board can have to specific sets of information collected in the study, especially if board members are connected in any way to the study site and/or to participants.

All of this highlights the careful thought that must go into deciding whether to accept money from a particular funder. Funders, just like researchers, have motives for wanting research to be done. Some bodies may be entirely altruistic, others less so. Some funders, particularly in the evaluation area, may be funding research overtly to "vindicate policies and practices" (Parahoo, 1991, p. 37). As Guba and Lincoln (1989) note when writing about evaluation studies, "often evaluation contracts are issued as requests for proposals just as research contracts are; in this way, winning evaluators are often those whose definitions of problems, strategies, and methods exhibit 'fit' with the clients' or funders' values" (p. 124). This is why Bogdan and Biklen (1998) assert that "You can only afford to do evaluation or policy research [or, I would add, any funded form of qualitative research] if you can afford not to do it" (p. 217). It is important to consider whether it is possible to retain integrity and independence as a researcher paid by someone else or provided with the support to do research. Key questions to ask are how much freedom will be lost if someone else is paying and how the researcher feels about this loss of freedom. It is important to remember that although "in the research domain, the notion of mutual interest licenses partnerships between state, college and industry . . . such relationships merit scrutiny rather than an amiable blind faith" (Miller, 2003, p. 899) such as that preached by adherents of neo-liberal thought.

It is important in a research team that team members share similar approaches to the issues that have been raised. This needs to be discussed from the outset of the formation of the team, and it is just as important to the smooth functioning of the team as the particular expertise each team member brings to the project. There must be trust among team members that decisions made will be adhered to. Furthermore, it is important to talk about how decisions will be made in and about the team. Who will control the budget? What happens if there is disagreement about the way the research is proceeding? The involvement of a third party, namely the funder, makes the need to be clear about these issues all the more imperative. Furthermore, the team needs to have clear guidelines about who will communicate with the funder and how. Working with other researchers offers the advantages of having a team that is multiskilled and often multidisciplinary in focus. However, funding increases the need for good communication in the team and clear understandings of each member's role, both in terms of the research itself and in terms of dealing with the funder. Strategies that research teams can employ to assist in the smooth functioning of funded projects include outlining each member's responsibilities, including their contribution to the final report; drawing up timelines for each member to adhere to; upholding each member's access to support and funds; and holding regular meetings to discuss issues among the team members.

Accepting funding for qualitative research affects the nature of relationships between the research participants and the researcher. Funded research also can result in the development of a new set of relationships, especially those between the researcher/research team and the funding agency, along with any other structures the funder may wish to put in place, such as advisory boards. When there is clear communication, these relationships can enhance the research effort and assist its smooth functioning. However, such relationships cannot be taken for granted and need to be worked on actively by all those involved. Their development is another part of the practices and politics of funded qualitative research.

6. Marketing Research: Practices and Politics

The issues discussed in this chapter have arisen against the backdrop of an emergent view of research as a commodity to be traded on an academic, and increasingly commercially driven, marketplace. The late 1990s saw the emergence of a climate of economic restraint and funding cuts by governments in most Western countries. At the time of writing this chapter, this trend continues, with little likelihood of it being reversed or slowing. Fiscal restraint has greatly affected the availability of funding for research in that many funding agencies, particularly government departments, no longer have the resources to support research to the extent that they once did. At the same time, educational institutions such as universities have experienced cuts to their core funding. One of the consequences of such cuts to university operating budgets has been the imperative for staff to be able to generate income for the institution. In some cases, such income has become part of academics' salaries; in others, this income has been factored into the operating budget of the institution to pay for basic resources needed to continue teaching and research programs.

In Australia, as elsewhere, concomitantly we have seen the emergence of increasing regulation of the university sector, including a rise in the frequency of prescribed reporting of performance indicators. We also have seen the emergence and rise of business development units designed to manage and sell research. In some divisions of universities in Australia, the greatest increase in staffing in the past decade has been in marketing and business development units. As an academic, I increasingly find myself in a world like that described by Brennan (2002), in which research is tendered out by, and oriented to, business, industry, and government. Their agendas feature increasingly short time frames for both conducting and reporting on research. This, of course, mitigates against certain types of qualitative research that are viewed as less efficient and more unwieldy. Qualitative research takes time and is very hands-on. The commercially driven tender and business development environment currently driving much research works against qualitative research. If the sole object of writing a proposal is revenue generation, then the research usually will lack strategic foundation and direction. As Morse (2003b) notes, "inadequate time, clearly, will kill a project or result in a project that has not become all that it could . . . be" (p. 846). If we are not careful, an effect of the emphasis on quick research turnaround and research "deliverables" could be to encourage the rise of an atheoretical set of qualitative techniques designed for expediency and framed by reductionist understandings of what qualitative research is and might do.

The contemporary context in which universities and qualitative researchers operate is one where the "fast capitalist texts" (Brennan, 2002, p. 2) of business and management have entered public discourse, normalizing practices and understandings of funded qualitative research and the purpose of that research. This, in some instances, has created a new imperative for obtaining funding, where the funding rather than the research has become highly prized. Put another way, it is possible that what is becoming important to some university administrations is the amount of funding obtained, rather than the contribution of the research and its associated scholarship to new knowledge and problem solving. In such a climate, there is the potential to privilege funded research over unfunded research. There is also the very real possibility that this environment is viewed as "natural" and "normal." We are bombarded with messages that we have to become more accountable, efficient, and effective, with clear implications that in the past research has been inefficient and/or ineffective and that researchers were unaccountable. But we must pause to ask certain questions: Efficient and effective in terms of what? Accountable to whom and in terms of what? It is a relatively recent phenomenon for research and funding to be so closely tied to the marketplace, and limited understandings of that market place at that! For example, in the postwar United States in 1946, Poiri and Conrad (see Bromley, 2002) in the Office of Naval Research were asked to suggest how the federal government could support university-based research without destroying academic freedom and creativity, which were recognized as important and integral to advancing discovery. Bromley (2002) notes that they came up with three fundamental principles: (a) Find the best people in the nation on the basis of peer review; (b) support these individuals in doing whatever they decided they wanted to do, as they are much better judges of how best to use their time and talent than anyone in government; and (c) leave them alone while they are doing it (i.e., minimize reporting and paperwork). Why does this approach seem so "abnormal" to those of us working in academe and/or research in the early 2000s? Is it because the understandings and dominant forms of the fast texts of the market and late capitalism have colonized research and academic cultures to such an extent that we cannot imagine that a situation such as the one Bromley described not only existed but was actively promoted, only a few decades ago?

What this highlights is that at any point in history, certain understandings will be at the fore. Which understandings prevail results from the power of particular groups at any one time to promote their frames of discourse to the exclusion or marginalization of others (Foucault, 1977). If Poiri and Conrad were to make their suggestions now, they would be marginalized, talked about as "dreamers," and told to operate in the "real world" by many administrators. Of course, we may well dispute how Poiri and Conrad defined and operationalized some of their categories, such as "best people" and "peer review," but their assertions are useful for highlighting how far we have moved in terms of the ways of thinking and speaking that are afforded mainframe status in many research texts in the contemporary research context. The discourse of the market is preeminent. An effect of this is changing control over the conditions and activities of researchers, who increasingly are being viewed as workers selling their labor and research products. It is the market, not necessarily peers, that determines the worth of research, and even what research will be done. Furthermore, this marketplace is tightly regulated in terms of the means of obtaining funding, what actually is funded, the way research performance is assessed, and the reporting that researchers must do both about their research and the way that they use their time in general. Such regulation codifies our knowledge, reducing it to key performance indicators such as number of publications or number of research dollars obtained, thereby diverting attention from "more productive and educational uses of our time" (Brennan, 2002, p. 2). Emerging trends show academics, for example, being forced to estimate costs for every activity and being told that activities for which they do not get paid directly should not be undertaken. Mentoring, thinking time, community service, and unfunded research are some of the potential casualties of such reductionist discourse.

So, too, is scholarship. Scholarship increasingly has come to be associated with narrowly defined research outcomes, including the number of journal articles published, funding received, or conference papers presented (Cheek, 2002). These measures inevitably are numeric and relative. Thus, institutional lists of "top" researchers are drawn up on the basis of numeric scores, worked out using complicated formulae designed to convert research, ideas, and scholarship into measurable throughput. What becomes important is the score, not how the score was calculated or the assumptions underlying it. It doesn't matter if a researcher's funding is mostly for an expensive piece of equipment; that researcher will score higher than, and "rank above," a qualitative researcher who may have acquired funding for a number of projects. In these formulae, publications also are converted to points and dollars. Morse (2002a), in keeping with many editors of scholarly journals, bemoans the fact that in submissions to the journal of which she is editor, *Qualitative Health Research*, she sees an increasing prevalence of what she calls atheoretical articles that are "shallow, thin and insignificant . . . it is the worst of qualitative inquiry" (p. 3). Morse describes a form of journal submission that is almost formulaic, "trite," and goes on to assert that "a few comments do not an article make" (Morse, 2002a, p. 4). Why the emergence of such a trend now? Could it be an effect of the imperative to publish and that what counts (literally) is the number of articles, not their content, just as what counts is the amount of research money, and not what it funds?

Historically, there has always been a place for both funded and unfunded research in universities and elsewhere. Some types of research simply have not required funding, yet have been able to produce significant contributions to knowledge for which they have been valued. Furthermore, research serves a variety of purposes. On one hand, it can be carried out to investigate a well-defined issue or problem arising in a specific area or field, and on the other it can be conducted to probe or explore what the issues might be in the first place. Research also can be carried out simply for the pleasure of investigating new and different ways of thinking about aspects of our reality. Some research projects might incorporate all of the above. In other words, just as there are a variety of research approaches and associated techniques, so there are a range of purposes for which research might be carried out. Each research project has its own intended audience, who will relate to the assumptions framing the problem to be investigated as embedded within that piece of research. However, with the imperative for academics to generate income, there has been a subtle, and at times not so subtle, shift in thinking toward valuing research that is funded more highly than research that is not. Given this, the question can be asked as to whether we are seeing the taking hold of what Derrida (1977) terms a binary opposition with respect to funded/unfunded research.

Derrida (1977) holds that any positive representation of a concept in language, such as "funded research," rests on the negative representation of its "opposite," in this case, unfunded research. In a binary opposition, there is always a dominant or prior term, and conversely there is always a subordinate or secondary term. For example, consider such common binary oppositions as masculine/feminine and reason/emotion. In each case, the first named term is given priority over the second, which is often defined in terms of "not" the dominant. However, as noted elsewhere, "the definitional dynamic extends to the primary term as well in that it can only sustain its definition by reference to the secondary term. Thus the definition and status of the primary term is in fact maintained by the negation and opposition of the secondary partner" (Cheek, Shoebridge, Willis, & Zadoroznyj, 1996, p. 189). Derrida (1977) points out that binary oppositions are constructions of certain worldviews; they are not natural givens that can be taken for granted. In the instance of funded/unfunded research, it is important to recognize that there is a binary opposition in operation and to explore both how it has come to be and how it is maintained. An interesting way to commence such an exploration is to reverse the binary pairing and note the effect. What is the effect on the way research is viewed and understood if unfunded research assumes primacy and funded research becomes the secondary or derivative term?

In a climate where funded research assumes ever increasing importance, the power of funding agencies to set research agendas has increased markedly. As Parahoo (1991) noted more than a decade ago, "a successful researcher is sometimes defined by the ability to attract funds, and most researchers know that in order to do so one must submit proposals on subjects which sponsors are prepared to spend money on. This can mean that the real issues that concern practitioners are sometimes ignored" (p. 37). What has changed in the past decade is that it is no longer the case that successful researchers are "sometimes" defined in this way, but rather that they "usually" or "normally" are. We see in play here "new neo-liberal notions of the performing professional" (Shore & Wright, 1999, p. 569). Although it is not unreasonable that sponsors should be able to fund research that is relevant to them, a problem arises if funds are not available for researcher-initiated research that addresses questions that have arisen from the field. If funding alone drives research agendas, then this may infringe on the academic freedom of researchers to pursue topics of importance and interest. As Porter (1997) notes, "pressure is therefore exerted on academics to tailor their work in order to meet the requirements of funders" (p. 655). Creativity may be sacrificed for expediency, in that some research topics will have more currency than others in terms of their likeliness to attract funding. Drawing on Mills (1959), Stoesz (1989) observes that "to the extent that this happens, an enormous problem emerges—social science [read qualitative research] becomes a commodity, the nature of which is defined by the bureaucracies of the corporate and governmental sectors" (p. 122).

The emerging emphasis on funded research, in terms of its ability to produce income for institutions, has in my opinion seen the emergence of research as a commodity to be bought and sold on the research market. Information and data from research projects are seen as a "product" to be traded on this market and sold to the highest bidder. Researchers increasingly find themselves struggling with the often competing demands of research as the generation of new knowledge, against research as a commodity to be traded in the marketplace. Such a struggle is exacerbated by a trend in which the act of winning funding for research is itself viewed as a currency to be traded in the academic marketplace. For example, promotion and tenure committees in many universities are influenced by the amount of funding received as a measure of research success. This has the effect of maintaining the binary opposition of funded/unfunded research, in that performance in terms of funded research is valued, while the absence of funding—that is, unfunded research—is not. The idea of research being perceived as a commodity, along with the trend to privilege funded research over unfunded research, poses some particular dilemmas for qualitative researchers. For instance, it is still true that most funding is attracted by research projects using traditional scientific methods. This means that it is relatively harder to obtain funding for qualitative research. If success in obtaining funding is used, rightly or wrongly, to measure performance and to put a value on research, then there is a real danger that qualitative research could be marginalized because it is not as easy to attract funds using qualitative approaches.

All of this is to bring into sharp focus some fundamental questions with which qualitative researchers need to grapple. These questions relate to the background assumptions about research and research performance that are driving many research agendas and researchers. Assumptions about how research performance is measured and valued need to be exposed. They can then be considered and explored in terms of the effect they have on notions of what research is for and what the nature of a research product should be. Funding is important in that it enables research to be carried out that otherwise would not occur because of resource constraints. It is not funding itself that is the issue here; rather, it is the uses to which the act of gaining funding is being put, apart from enabling a specific piece of research to proceed. I am not arguing against funded qualitative research—far from it! What I am suggesting is that researchers need to think about their own assumptions about funded research and how such assumptions have embedded, within them, many taken-for-granteds about the nature of research and research products in what is increasingly becoming a research marketplace.

7. Practices and Politics Beyond the "Find and Replace" Function Key

Doing funded qualitative research is not a neutral and value-free activity. Researchers must constantly examine their motives for doing research and the motives of funding bodies in funding research. This is particularly important in a context in which new forms of neo-liberal rationality are emerging, defining the performance, worth, and mission of research, researchers, and the institutions in which they work. In writing this chapter, I am advocating suspended readings. Such readings suspend notions of funded research and attendant practices and organizations, such as funding panels and ethics committees, in order to take another look at what otherwise become taken-for-granted parts of the funding process. This other look begins by exploring the origins of understandings shaping research, and particularly funded qualitative research, how these understandings are maintained, and what this reveals about the context in which researchers operate. I am not advocating that we replace one set of understandings with another, but rather that we recognize, for what they are, current trends and issues in the politics and practice of funded qualitative research, so that we might best position ourselves in relation to them. Questions we need to ask ourselves include the following: Can we accept and live with the tensions and contradictions posed to us as funded qualitative researchers in the reality in which we live and work every day? What should we defend, and what might we give up? How do we respond to the enterprise culture of neo-liberalism increasingly so pervasive in every aspect of the research process? In all of this, a key question and challenge is how to avoid being always located at the margins, as the "faint voice" (Morse, 2002b, p. 1308) in funding panels or funding received, in order that qualitative research can be viewed as legitimate and mainframe.

There are no easy answers to these questions. The position taken by each of us as individuals will be different. What is important is that this conversation is held and that the inherent political nature of funded qualitative research is surfaced and explored. This chapter has provided a lens to bring into focus issues concerning the regulation and production of forms of knowledge, through practices associated with, and arising from, the funded research process. How qualitative researchers respond to the imperatives that confront them every day, and to the imperatives for political action that emanate from the discussion herein, will go a long way in determining what the future holds for qualitative research itself and its positioning, either mainframe or at the margins. The identities that we individually want as qualitative researchers must be embedded in all facets of our research endeavors, including the seeking, acquisition, and use of funds to support that research. We must avoid atheoretical pragmatic types of qualitative research techniques emerging as synonymous with understandings of funded (or fundable) qualitative research. Instead, it will be increasingly important to promote theoretically and politically robust qualitative research. For me, this is the key challenge facing qualitative research as it becomes "more accepted" into the funding fold. Such acceptance can be a double-edged sword for the unwary and could see a subversion of all that we have worked to establish if we are not on our guard. In all of this, I reiterate that funding itself is not the problem—funding is useful as an enabler of qualitative research. Problems arise if funding becomes the end, rather than the means, and qualitative research (or a variant thereof) is subverted to the expedient end of gaining that funding. The choice is ours, both individually and collectively, as to which of these positions we adopt.

References

Bogdan, R. C., & Biklen, S. K. (1998). *Qualitative research in education: An introduction to theory and method.* Boston: Allyn and Bacon.

Brennan, M. (2002). *The politics and practicalities of grassroots research in education.* Retrieved May 15, 2002, from www.staff.vu.edu.au/alnarc/forum/marie_brennan.html

Bromley, D. A. (2002). Science, technology, and politics. *Technology in Society, 24,* 9–26.

Carey, M. A., & Swanson, J. A. (2003). Funding for qualitative research. *Qualitative Health Research, 13*(6), 852–856.

Cheek, J. (2000). An untold story? Doing funded qualitative research. In N. K. Denzin & Y. S. Lincoln (Eds.), *Handbook of qualitative research* (2nd ed., pp. 401–420). Thousand Oaks, CA: Sage.

Cheek, J. (2002). Advancing what? Qualitative research, scholarship, and the research imperative. *Qualitative Health Research, 12*(8), 1130–1140.

Cheek, J., Shoebridge, J., Willis, E., & Zadoroznyj, M. (1996). *Society and health: Social theory for health workers.* Melbourne: Longman Australia Pty Limited.

Derrida, J. (1977). *Of grammatology.* Baltimore: Johns Hopkins University Press.

Foucault, M. (1977). *Discipline and punish.* London: Penguin.

Guba, G. M., & Lincoln, Y. S. (1989). Ethics and politics: The twin failures of positivist science. In *Fourth generation evaluation* (pp. 117–141). Newbury Park, CA: Sage.

Kent, G. (1997). The views of members of local research ethics committees, researchers and members of the public towards the roles and functions of LRECS. *Journal of Medical Ethics, 23*(3), 186–190.

Kress, G. (1985). *Linguistic processes in socio-cultural practice.* Victoria, New South Wales: Deakin University Press.

Lacey, E. A. (1998). Social and medical research ethics: Is there a difference? *Social Sciences in Health, 4*(4), 211–217.

Lidz, C. W., & Ricci, E. (1990). Funding large-scale qualitative sociology. *Qualitative Sociology, 13*(2), 113–126.

Lincoln, Y. S., & Tierney, W. G. (2002, April). *"What we have here is a failure to communicate . . .": Qualitative research and institutional review boards*. Paper presented at the annual meeting of the American Educational Research Association, New Orleans, LA.

Martin, B. (2000). Research grants: Problems and options. *Australian Universities' Review, 2,* 17–22.

Miller, T. (2003). Governmentality or commodification? US higher education. *Cultural Studies, 17*(6), 897–904.

Mills, C. W. (1959). *The sociological imagination.* New York: Oxford University Press.

Morse, J. (2002a). Editorial. A comment on comments. *Qualitative Health Research, 12*(1), 3–4.

Morse, J. (2002b). Myth #53: Qualitative research is cheap. *Qualitative Health Research, 12*(10), 1307–1308.

Morse, J. (2003a). The adjudication of qualitative proposals. *Qualitative Health Research, 13*(6), 739–742.

Morse, J. (2003b). A review committee's guide for evaluating qualitative proposals. *Qualitative Health Research, 13*(6), 833–851.

Parahoo, K. (1991). Politics and ethics in nursing research. *Nursing Standard, 6*(1), 35–39.

Parahoo, K. (2003). Square pegs in round holes: Reviewing qualitative research proposals. *Journal of Clinical Nursing, 12,* 155–157.

Porter, S. (1997). The degradation of the academic dogma. *Journal of Advanced Nursing, 25,* 655–656.

Ramcharan, P., & Cutcliffe, J. R. (2001). Judging the ethics of qualitative research: Considering the "ethics as process" model. *Health and Social Care in the Community, 9*(6), 358–366.

Riesman, D. (2002, November/December). Reviewing social research. *Change,* pp. 9–10.

Rowan, J. (2000). Research ethics. *International Journal of Psychotherapy, 5*(2), 103–111.

Sachs, L. (1996). Causality, responsibility and blame—core issues in the cultural construction and subtext of prevention. *Sociology of Health and Illness, 18*(5), 632–652.

Shore, C., & Wright, S. (1999). Audit culture and anthropology: Neo-liberalism in British higher education. *Journal of the Royal Anthropological Institute, 5*(4), 557–575.

Stoesz, D. (1989). Provocation on the politics of government funded research: Part 1. *Social Epistemology, 4*(1), 121–123.

Stuart, G. (2001). Are you old enough? Research ethics and young people. *Youth Studies Australia, 20*(4), 34–39.

Summers, J. (2003). *The GrantSearch register of Australian funding.* Perth, WA: GrantSearch.

Torres, C. A. (2002). The state, privatisation and educational policy: A critique of neo-liberalism in Latin America and some ethical and political implications. *Comparative Education, 38*(4), 365–385.

van den Hoonaard, W. C. (2001). Is research-ethics review a moral panic? *Canadian Review of Sociology and Anthropology, 38*(1), 19–36.

Zagury, C. S. (1997). Grant writing: The uncertain road to funding, Part V. From the other side: How reviewers look at proposals. *Alternative Health Practitioner, 3*(1), 25–29.

16

PERFORMANCE ETHNOGRAPHY

The Reenacting and Inciting of Culture

Bryant Keith Alexander

Performance ethnography is literally the staged re-enactment of ethnographically derived notes. This approach to studying and staging culture works toward lessening the gap between a perceived and actualized sense of self and the other. This is accomplished through the union and practice of two distinct and yet interrelated disciplinary formations—*performance studies* and *ethnography*. Practitioners of performance ethnography acknowledge the fact that culture travels in the stories, practices, and desires of those who engage it. By utilizing an experiential method such as performance ethnography, those who seek understanding of other cultures and lived experiences are offered a body-centered method of knowing, what Dwight Conquergood (1986a) calls a dialogical understanding in which "the act of performance fosters identification between dissimilar ways of being without reducing the other to bland sameness, a projection of the performing self" (p. 30).

Performance studies, in its most procedural sense drawn from its link to communication studies, is interested in what Pelias (1999a) calls "the process of dialogic engagement with one's own and others' aesthetic communication through the means of performance" (p. 15). *Ethnography*, in its most utilitarian sense, is what Spradley and McCurdy (1972) refer to as "the task of describing a particular culture" (p. 3). As a broad-based description of performative praxis, performance ethnography is a *form of cultural exchange* (Jones, 2002), *a performative cross-cultural communication* (Chesebro, 1998), an embodied *critical performative pedagogy* (Giroux, 2001; Pineau, 1998, 2002; Worley, 1998), and a theater form that *establishes emancipatory potential* (Mienczakowski, 1995; Park-Fuller, 2003). Performance ethnography is also a method of *putting the critical sociological and sociopolitical imagination to work in understanding the politics and practices that shape human experience* (Denzin, 2003).

Within the explanatory frame of this chapter title, I make the strong suggestion that performance ethnography *is* and *can be* a strategic method of *inciting culture*. The collaborative power of performance and ethnography utilizes an embodied aesthetic practice coupled with the descriptive knowledge of lives and the conditions of living, to stir up feeling and provoke audiences to a critical social realization and possible response. This social action to which I refer here briefly is not necessarily that which is set into violent motion to overthrow dominant structures of oppression: It is a physical force set against the desire of knowing and being in the world.

The potential for social action resides at the core of how *participants in* and *audiences of* performance ethnography see themselves in relation to others. The potential resides in how they understand the act of performing the lives of others, as synecdoche to the larger politics of representation and identity (i.e., race, culture, class, gender, etc.). The potential lies in revealing issues of who gets to speak and for whom, linked with *the politics of culture* that regulate what elements of culture are featured or suppressed (Whisnant, 1983). The potential resides in how participants choose to maintain or disrupt the perceptual stasis that exists within their *habitudes and habitus*, and how they *might* act toward influencing social awareness of problematic human conditions that may be revealed or explored through performance ethnography.

For some, the notion of *overthrowing structures of oppression* might seem farfetched and beyond the traditional scope of performance ethnography, yet theories and practices in both performance studies and theater arts have been moving steadily toward the social and political goals of employing performance as a tool and method of cultural awareness and social change. Such a charge and application has been made in the particularity of practices in traditional and nontraditional performance arenas, as well as planting the seeds of social activism in the classroom with future theater and performance practitioners. Such attempts seek to frame performance as *a critical reflective and refractive lens* to view the human condition and a form of *reflexive agency* that initiates action. Performance ethnography uses theater to illuminate cultural politics and to instill understanding with the potential to invoke change and have a positive effect on the lived conditions of self and others (Boal, 1979, 1995, 1998; Dolan, 2001a, 2001b; Park-Fuller, 2003; Schutzman & Cohen-Cruz, 1994; Spry, 2001; Van Erven, 1993).

The positioning of audience members as agents in the production of cultural meaning places a mandate, if not a culpability, on audience members to act as social agents. It requires them to both interact with the performance and to engage in the imaginative, yet practical, act of creating new possibilities of human interaction in the manner in which such experience could be translated into their daily lives (Pollock, 1998a). In this sense, the power and potency of performance ethnography resides in the demand that a performance text must not only "awaken moral sensibilities. It must move the other and the self to action" (Denzin, 1997, p. xxi). The power and potential of performance ethnography resides in the empathic and embodied engagement of other ways of knowing that heightens the possibility of acting upon the humanistic impulse to transform the world.

In discussing performance ethnography in the second edition of the *Handbook of Qualitative Research*, Michal M. McCall (2000) did a fine job of focusing attention on the foundational issues of performance ethnography—like tracing a conceptual history of performance through Futurism, Dadaism, Surrealism, and varying experimental forms. She then provided concrete examples of performance ethnography with tips on casting, directing, and staging drawn from a variety of scholar-practitioners (Becker, McCall, & Morris, 1989; Conquergood, 1985, 1988; Denzin, 1997; McCall, 1993; Mienczakowski, 2001; Paget, 1990; Pollock, 1990; Richardson, 1997; Siegel & Conquergood, 1985, 1990; Smith, 1993, 1994). In many ways, this chapter should be used as a companion to McCall's efforts in extending the scope of performance ethnography.

This chapter outlines and details the philosophical contingencies, procedural pragmatics, pedagogical possibilities, and political potentialities of *performance ethnography*. The chapter necessarily pushes and expands the borders and ways of thinking about performance ethnography, yet the basic approach of *field research, data collection, script formulation, and performance* should not be overshadowed by other concerns. The value of performing ethnographic materials from the field may be for pedagogical or representational purposes

(Van Maanen, 1995), which might bring additional value that circulates around critical and cultural research, political activism, and social change. In these ways, the chapter serves as a guide to those who seek to understand how performance ethnography is an embodied epistemology and how performance ethnography can become a way of engaging a critical cultural discourse.

I. Practical Matters and Philosophical Contingencies

In a literal sense of the aphorism "walking a mile in someone else's shoes," performance ethnography most often entails an embodied experience of the cultural practices of the other. This practice has the intent of allowing the participants in and audience of the performance the opportunity to *come to know culture differently*. In the first portion of this section, I offer a practical pedagogical assignment in performance ethnography. In the subsequent subsections, I use that example as a way of teasing out what I consider to be some of the disciplinary, philosophical, theoretical, and methodological promises and pitfalls of engaging performance ethnography.

A. Performing Ethnography/ Performing Street Vendors

In response to a classroom assignment in a 300-level performance studies class, a student group consisting of three men and two women focus on migrant streetside vendors. In the Los Angeles area, there is a large number of mostly immigrant Mexican street vendors, male and female, who stand on the entrances and exits of major interstates and highways selling everything from bagged oranges, cherries, and peanuts to flowers, handmade cultural artifacts, and clothing. The students in this group conduct ethnographic interviews and engage in practical assistance under the guise of participant-observation to get a sense of what that experience is like and a better sense of those who engage these practices.

In their performance, the students each carry a commodity that they sell to the audience. They walk in a choreographed circle around the room hawking their items in a syncopated rhythm that mirrors the persistence of the street vendors, some of whom closely approach vehicles in traffic like the seated students in class, trying to initiate a purchase. At varying points, the circulating caravan stops and a particular student in the character of the vendor takes center stage and shares a personal narrative. The narratives—actual, compiled, and constructed[1]—drawn from the interviews reveal the conditions under which the street vendors labor. They labor under the heat of the day. They encounter police officers who chase them away from certain areas and rude drivers who throw things at them, spit on them, or lure them with the chance of purchase and then speed away. They endure suppliers who overcharge them for their goods or swindle them knowing that most of them are *illegal aliens* and will not press police charges. And they experience the occasional kindness from motorists.

The narratives are delivered through impassioned voices, in Spanish and with Spanish accents, then translated by another vendor (student performer). The narratives reveal the multiple reasons for which the vendors come to this circumstance: Some work to send money back to their families in Mexico or to support their families here in the United States. Some are trapped in a type of slave labor with the coyotes (smugglers of human chattel from Mexico) who helped them cross the border. Others labor because they have no other marketable skills. Through the performance and written reflective essays, the students articulate and claim a new understanding of the lives of *particular others*. The efforts of street vendors are not seen as what is casually assumed or asserted to be their culture, but acts of survival and sustenance grounded in their current predicament and their relation to space, place, and time.

The student performance is a dialogic engagement in which they extend the voices of *the other* into the specialized place of public access, the classroom. The performance serves as product and process, a performative representation of their knowing, a starting point of their understanding, and a method of engaging others in the issues that undergird cultural experience. In this particular example, performance ethnography helps in establishing a critical site, an instance in which embodied experience meets social and theoretical knowing to establish a critical dialogue between researcher-performers and observers (Garoian, 1999, p. 67). It is the specificity of the project, the particularity of the culture represented, and the context of the performance in the classroom that affords the opportunity for close scrutiny.

B. Performance Studies, Performance, and Performativity

Performance studies as a disciplinary formation often defies definition—in the way in which definitions codify and categorize, as well as capture and contain, that which they seek to describe—thereby limiting its reach and scope. Borrowing generously from communication studies, sociology, cultural studies, ethnography, anthropology, and theater, among other areas, performance studies explores and considers a wide range of *human activity as expression*. Richard Schechner (1988) states, "The subjects of performance studies are both what is performance and the performative—and the myriad contact points and overlaps, tensions and loose spots, separating and connecting these categories" (p. 362). In other words, performance pivots on the enacted nature of human activity, the socialized and shifting norms of human sociality, and the active processes of human sense-making.

In the preceding example of the street vendors, performance is engaged as an interpretive event of cultural practice. Performance involves scripts of social discourse constructed with intention and performed by actors in the company of particular audiences. The related concept of *performativity* references the stylized repetition of communicative acts, linguistic and corporeal, that are socially validated and discursively established in the moment of the performance (Butler, 1990a, 1990b, 1993). Through the example, students use these related terms in the range of performance studies to explore the fundamental notion of human behavior as performative—as socially constructed, enacted, emergent, repeatable, and subversive.

Performativity becomes the social and cultural dynamic that extends and exposes the import of repetitive human activity. The students use these constructs to acknowledge and engage the study of human nature as both an issue of *being* and *doing*, to explore social structure and human agency as mutually constituted, and that the recursive nature of cultural play can produce unintended and intended consequences. This allows us to see social action as moments of broader power relations that can be illuminated, interrogated, and intervened, if not transformed (Bhabha, 1994; Diamond, 1996; Langellier, 1999).

One version of performance studies sees its shift or evolution from the study of literary texts through oral interpretation[2] to a broader construction of text as the scope of cultural practice and articulated human expression. This then moves from an exclusive focus on *text to context*[3]—such as analyses of religious rituals, wedding ceremonies, sporting events, and particular cultural practices such as those of the street vendors in the student example. This approach valorizes diverse epistemological paradigms in which the role of artist-actor is expanded to include all social beings *as performers*. The focus of study shifts from an exclusive emphasis on canonical texts to cultural practices in everyday life, especially a focus on historically marginalized groups.

These variations ground performance studies' privileging of three concerns. First is an appreciation for the aesthetic/creative nature of human expression across borders of text, context, and embodied practice.[4] Second is a focus on the body as a site of knowing and showing,[5] hence what Conquergood (1998) distinguishes as "struggles to recuperate the *saying* from the *said*, to put mobility, action, and agency back into play" (p. 31). Third is an interest in ethnography as a critical method of observing and studying the performative nature of cultural practice.

This signals what some have coined as *the cultural turn* in performance studies (Chaney, 1994; Conquergood, 1998; Pollock, 1998d; Strine, 1998), or what Victor Turner (1982) refers to as *the performative and reflexive turn in anthropology.* In such cases, there is an intense focus on the ways in which culture is performance practice, sedimented as norms of sociability. Thus in both the cultural turn in performance studies and the performative and reflexive turn in anthropology, there is a move to *put culture back into motion* (Rosaldo, 1989, p. 91). By performing empirical materials derived through ethnographic practice researchers as performers, and the audiences of such performative research are afforded a more intimate understanding of culture.

In this way, performance becomes not only embodied practice but also explanatory metaphor for human engagement, and performativity becomes the everyday practice of *redoing* what is *done* (Pollock, 1998b). The actual sense of the other is derived through embodied experience of the other's cultural practice. In this way, as Peggy Phelan (1998) states, "Performance and performativity are braided together by virtue of iteration; the copy renders performance authentic and allows the spectator to find in the performer 'presence.' Presence can be had only through the citation of authenticity, through reference to something (we have heard) called 'live'" or have seen called life (p. 10). Hence, in performance ethnography the textual subject becomes the empirical subject, allowing performers and audiences to be brought closer to aspects of cultural being that operate at the real and everyday level of experience (Denzin, 1997, pp. 60–61).

In other words, what happens when ethnography becomes performative, when ethnography becomes performance? What happens to the ethnographic? It reinstates the actualization of everyday cultural performance. It rehydrates the objectified, text-bound description of lives-lived into living embodied forms that offer a greater sense of direct experience and the direct knowing of culture. It reinstates ethnographic bodies to the realm of process, of activity, of doing—negotiating beings, both in the simulated presence of their daily lives as well as within the specified moment of performance.

Using performance as an "explanatory metaphor" involves reconstructing the notion of performance from *theatrical entertainment* to performance as a *method of explaining, exemplifying, projecting, knowing, and sharing meaning.* It involves, as in the example with the students in the street vendor performance, ways of using performance as a means, method, and mode of communication establishing an intercultural dialogue. The comparative relationship between the object of reflection and the performative act moves toward an embodied and engaged understanding. Conquergood (1998) tracks *this semantic genealogy* "from performance as *mimesis* to *poiesis* to *kinesis*, performance as imitation, construction, and dynamism" (p. 31).[6]

Performance methodology can be described as a collectivized ensemble of precepts used by those committed to the communicative and pedagogical potential that knowledge—the process of attaining, sharing, and projecting knowing—can be accomplished through doing. What Pineau (1995) refers to as "a deep kinesthetic attunement that allows us to attend to experiential phenomena in an embodied, rather than purely intellectualized way" (p. 46). Hence students and audiences *come to know through doing*, whether this is performing ethnographic notes or performing theory as a means of practical experience in testing hypotheses or displaying knowledge.

The broad-based construction of performance methodology opens up the possibility of engaging performance in strategic ways: *performance as a method of inquiry* or *performance as a way of knowing* (Geiger, 1973; Hopkins, 1981; O'Brien, 1987; Wolcott, 1999), *performance as a method of reporting knowledge and ideological critique* (Jackson, 1993, 1998; Nudd, 1995; Park-Fuller & Olsen, 1983; Pineau, 1995; Taylor, 1987), *performance as a method of critical response* (Alexander, 1999; Conquergood, 1986a, 1986b; Harrison-Pepper, 1999), *performance as an act of publication* (Espinola, 1977), and *performance as an interpretive tool* (Jackson, 2000; Merrill, 1999; Pollock, 1998a; Roach, 1993; Román, 1998; Wolf, 2002). In each case, performers use the processes of research, analysis, and synthesis leading toward message rehearsal (intent, content, and form) to culminate in an enactment of thought and knowing. Hence, the process of coming to know and the act of projecting the known are intricately interwoven.

C. Cultural Performance and the Performance of Culture

Another version of performance studies sees its particular origins in the collaborative discourses between Richard Schechner (1965, 1977, 1985) and Victor Turner (1982, 1988) in which theater and anthropology inform each other to explore the innate theatricality of cultural expression and intercultural exploration.[7] My interests in what has been constructed as *cultural performance* have been influenced by them and scholars such as Chesebro (1988), Clifford (1998), Conquergood (1983, 1985, 1986a, 1986b, 1988), E. C. Fine and Speer (1992), Fuoss (1997), Guss (2000), Kirshenblatt-Gimbett (1998), MaCaloon (1984), and Singer (1972), to name a few. It is undergirded with the kernel understanding that *cultural performance* refers to the collective expectations and practices of members of particular communities.

Cultural performance is the method in which we all define community, maintain community membership, negotiate identity, and sometimes subvert the rules of social membership and practice. Hence, echoing Turner (1974), Conquergood (1986a) notes that as human beings we are *homo performans*, in that we socially construct the very world that undergirds our enactments. It is how some have approached the notion of performance as *the presentation of self in everyday life* (Goffman, 1959), *the practice of everyday life* (Certeau, 1984), the critical self-reflexivity of engaging *restored behavior or twice-behaved behavior* (Schechner, 1988), and the tensive enactment of *social dramas* (Turner, 1974, 1980).[8] It is the everydayness of performance in culture that becomes the focus of observation in ethnographic research and thus becomes the source model of reperforming culture in performance ethnography that is the primary focus of this discussion.

Signaling an important element of performance ethnography, Clifford (1988) reminds us that we can better understand cultural identity not by studying the artifacts of museums or libraries, but through observing emergent cultural performances. These emergent cultural performances signify the social and cultural constructs that already are in place and those that are being challenged, subverted, or appropriated. The street vendor project exemplifies the way that performance ethnography mirrors social, cultural, and political practices to publicize the politics in the existence of those social occurrences.

In making the link between cultural performance and performance ethnography, I make the reciprocal yet interrelated distinction between *cultural performance* in everyday life and *the performance of culture* in which there is a documentation and re-creation of cultural forms found through research (Alexander, 2002b). The students in the street vendor performance studied culture and then sought to re-create their understanding in/through performance. This was primarily to better know and understand the culture, but for some it might be a process of rehearsal in becoming a cultural member; a form of practiced *enculturation* as it were, leading toward competency and cultural membership (Samovar & Porter, 1994).

The performance of culture that is presented in performance ethnography is a reflection of an actual culture refracted through the lens of ethnographic practices and situated in performing bodies that (re)present that culture. The intentions of the actualized versus the performed version of culture (by others) are different, yet they may inform each other by sensitizing performers and audiences to alternative cultural systems (Chesebro, 1998, p. 317).

Performance ethnography always simulates the fishbowl conditions under which cultures operate in everyday life. Culture operates both within the confines of its own constructions (power, social relations, time, history, and space) and under the forces of externalized pressure that affect the conditions of its operation. *Performance ethnography as a moral discourse* foregrounds this very delicate balance. The presumed subject of scrutiny in performance ethnography is not exclusive to the particular culture being performed but also applies to the process of engaging cultural performance. Conquergood (1986a) writes:

> Performance requires a special doubling of consciousness, reflexive self-awareness. The performer plays neither the role of Self or Other; instead of an I or a You, the performer is essentially, at all times, playing a We. . . . Performance can reconcile the tension between Identity, which banalizes, and Difference, which estranges, the Other. (p. 34)

In this way, performance ethnography becomes a form of *standpoint epistemology*, a situated moment of knowing that positions performers and audiences in the interstices of knowing themselves through and as the other (Denzin, 1997). The moment of performance is both practical place and liminal space, a standpoint from which to view culture.

At this point in offering an overview of practical matters and philosophical contingencies, it is necessary to state that performance ethnography cannot and maybe should not be easily reduced to being (just a) method. Although I know that I am pushing the borders of what some might refer to as *traditional performance ethnography*, I am also asking the question of "Why do we do performance ethnography?" In the rendering of and response to the question, I suggest that most people see performance ethnography as moral discourse. Thus, this chapter asks readers to extend their familiar methodological construction of performance ethnography into a larger view of its promise and possibilities.

Beyond the *practical pedagogical* or the *pleasure of the performative, performance ethnography is moral discourse* in the tradition of all qualitative research. It is situated activity that locates the participants, researchers, and observers in the world—a world in which the implications and complications of being and knowing others can be negotiated in mutually beneficial ways. It consists of a set of interpretive material practices that make culture visible; hence making manifest not only the cultural conditions of living, but also the joint concerns of humanism that can be equally distributed. These practices work to illuminate the world as much as they work to transform the world (Denzin & Lincoln, 1998).

Following a *feminist communitarian model*, performance ethnography "interlocks personal autonomy with communal well-being." It encourages the "morally appropriate action [that] intends community" (Christians, 2000, pp. 144–145). Through performance ethnography, performer-researcher-scholars ask audiences (both objectified onlookers and performers as audience to their own engagement) to position themselves in relation to those being represented in performance. These performances are always *enmeshed in moral matters*; they use performance to illuminate the dynamics of culture that are always and already in practice with and across borders of perceived difference (Conquergood, 1985). They contain a moment of judgment of others and of the self in relation to others, a judgment that affects choice not only in the moment of performance but also in those moments after performance in which the sensuousness of performative experience resonates in the body and mind, seeking its own engagement of meaningful expression.

D. Links and Challenges Between Ethnography and Performance

The selection and manner of presenting particular cultural insights in performance ethnography reveal not only an assumed actuality of the other but also a particular critique and understanding of the other. This *is* and in most cases *is not equal to* the actual experiences of the other. This element of *critique and commentary* that is a cornerstone of performance methodology becomes the cautionary tale and the ethical linchpin in the process of performance ethnography. The staged performance of culture is also an appraisal of culture. It foregrounds aspects of human experience for particular reasons, with particular desired effects—either in the form of direct critique or through the more artistic tropes of parody, metaphor, and analogy.

This begins to reveal the problems and the possibilities of performing the other, for selves always intervene experience and foreground orientation, desire, and intent. For example, when performing the lives and narratives of the street vendors, my students (as researchers and performers) had to reconcile their thoughts and feelings about the street vendors. They had to negotiate the balance between their everyday experiences with street vendors and their social commentary on street vendors, with and against their embodied positionality in performing street vendors. They had to ask the question:

> How as researchers and performers in our reciprocal relationships do we negotiate and help to inform and/or transform the politics of class, notions of work ethic, cultural bias, and issues of pride and propriety? This in relation to what we have come to know about the predicament and conditions of these street vendors through the joint effort of performance and ethnography?

In this sense, all those engaged in performance ethnography must always clearly define themselves in relation to the populations being performed, their intentions in performing, the desired effects of their performance, and the methods engaged in gathering and reporting knowledge. Although this works in tension with what might be constructed as "traditional performance ethnography" used as pedagogical practice or public entertainment, these questions and concerns are necessary relational and political issues about representation that only enhance the pedagogical potency of such endeavors.

Ethical guides for performance ethnography are clearly established within the contributing disciplines of both performance and ethnography (Alcoff, 1991/1992; Bateson, 1993; Chambers, 2000; Christians, 2000; Clifford & Marcus, 1986; M. Fine, Weis, Weseen, & Wong, 2000; Lockford, 1998; Rosaldo, 1989; Sparkes, 2002; B. Tedlock, 2000; D. Tedlock, 1983; Valentine, 1998; Valentine & Valentine, 1992). Here I want to foreground three articulations of *ethical relations in performance/ethnography*. My intention here is to offer a particular perspective on the relationship between ethnographer and cultural community—the relational, representational, and variables of translation in any social text—as well as the binary oppositions involved in the dynamics of being audience to the performance of actual lives.

First, in "Performing as a Moral Act: Ethical Dimensions of the Ethnography of Performance," Dwight Conquergood (1985) charts "four ethical pitfalls, performative stances towards the other that are morally problematic" (p. 4). *The Custodian's Rip-off* is likened to a theft or rape, a search and seizure on the part of the ethnographer, who approaches and appropriates culture without a sense of care. *The Enthusiast's Infatuation* jumps to conclusions, making facile assumptions of performative practice in an attempt to quickly assume identification with the other. *The Skeptic's Cop-out* embodies the sterilized and historically objectified approaches to ethnography in which the ethnographer stands outside or above culture, avoiding personal involvement or encounter with the other—but is readily prepared to cast judgment on cultural practice and identity. *The Curator's Exhibitionism* overly identifies with the other, to the point of exoticizing and romanticizing the other as the noble savage and thereby further dichotomizing the difference between self and other.

Conquergood constructs a fifth stance, *the dialogical stance*. "Dialogical performance is a way of having intimate conversation with other people and cultures. Instead of speaking about them, one speaks to and with them" (1985, p. 10). The dialogical stance negotiates the borders between identity, difference, detachment, and commitment not only to represent the other but also to re-present the other as a means of continuing a dialogue that seeks understanding. "It is a kind of performance that resists conclusions, it is intensely committed to keeping the dialogue between performer and text [performer and cultural members] open and ongoing" (p. 9).

In discussing the nature of ethnography and its links to performance, I have often turned to Van Maanen's (1988) construction, which states: "Ethnographies are documents that pose questions at the margins between two cultures. They necessarily decode one culture while re-coding it for another" (p. 4).[9] Within this statement, I see and understand the interpretive nature of ethnography to the lived practices of others—through a detailed description of culture, knowing, of course, that such a description is always and already inflicted with and processed through the particular experience of the ethnographer—the one who reports. It is also shaped and influenced by the sociological, perceptual, and political issues of the audience—those to whom such findings are reported, with a particular concern regarding *why* the report is being made. One asks *how* subjects and their actions are concretized and isolated from the historicity of experience for the scrutiny of others (see Denzin, 1997, pp. 247–248, and his citing of Fiske, 1994), as well as *what* happens in those moments of translation, those moments of an assumed accuracy in decoding culture and the recoding of such understandings across borders of experience. These are also the challenges of performance, what Judith Hamera (2000) describes as "a very specific technology of translation, a look rebounding between two differently framed [experiences] into language" (p. 147).

Second, Norman Denzin (1997) outlines four paired terms that might be used to examine any social text. I present them here as a way to foreground the relational, the representational, and challenges of translation that are faced in both ethnography and performance—with the specific emphasis on the combined effort/event of performance ethnography. Denzin outlines the four as follows: "(a) the real and its representations in the text [performance], (b) the text and the author [performer], (c) lived experience and its textual [and embodied] representations, and (d) the subject and his or her intentional meanings" (p. 4). I extend the use of the following logics to both the specificity of his emphasis, *interpretive ethnography*, and the more exacting process of performance ethnography.

In the case of performance ethnography, there is a double assumption of the ability to capture and contain culture through language and then to assume and embody culture through the materiality of different bodies; bodies that may have different or even opposing historicity, bodies that are framed and conjoined with bones, muscles, and sinews that have not been sufficiently exercised or exorcised into being over time. Maybe this is the *representational crisis* or a *representational challenge* in performance ethnography, one that is not easily solved, but it can be understood if the conjoined effort of performance/ethnography can be seen as a dialogical engagement. In such an engagement, performance ethnography is not only an act of presenting research findings and representing the other but also a means of extending and expanding on a critical dialogue in and about culture, with researcher-performers embodying the nature of their knowledge and inviting audiences to participate.

In this way, performance ethnography is linked appropriately with the traditions of *interpretive ethnography*—the staging of reflexive ethnographic performances that turn ethnographic and theoretical texts back onto each other, a form of both scholarly production and textual critique committed to the critical social processes of meaning-making and illuminating cultural experience. This is done through descriptive language and embodied engagement, as well as engaging the performance of critical accountability for/of the very processes of its production (Bochner & Ellis, 2002; Denzin, 1997, 1999; Ellis & Bochner, 1996, 2000; McCall, 2000).

Performance and ethnography are both concerned with lessening gaps between the known and the unknown, illuminating and exploring the lived practices of others, and bridging geographical and social distances through vivid description, narration, and embodiment—helping readers/audiences to see possibilities through the visualization of experience. Maybe through theatricalizing experience, the challenge of performance ethnography is to represent culture without claiming culture, to *interrogate and decenter culture—without discarding* culture (Conquergood, 1998). Maybe the challenge is to project the knowing of culture, without dominating the experience of the other, thus creating a "recognizable verisimilitude of setting, character and dialogue" that foregrounds culture and not self (Cohen, 1988, p. 815), while providing the necessary critical processes to tease *out/at* those elements that conjoin and separate the two, for both research/writer/performer and audience.

This would also require that the staging of such a performance must dematerialize the fourth wall of theatrical production that often encourages objectified viewing, creating a more *dialectical theater* (Brecht, 1964; Kershaw, 1999), a *theater of performance* that, while framing the aesthetic event as part entertainment, also reframes *the experience of performance ethnography from entertainment to social and intercultural dialogue.* This dialogue exists between performers and cultural informants, and between the performative experience of the audience in the moment of the doing and how that is extended in the everydayness of their being.

Third, Linda Park-Fuller (2003) offers five problematic aspects of *audiencing*—as the engaged practice of participatory viewing. It is a positionality that further implicates the viewer in performance ethnography and, in her specific case, Playback Theatre. Park-Fuller describes Playback Theatre as "an audience-interactive, improvisational form in which audience members tell stories from their lives and then watch those stories enacted on the spot" (p. 291). Playback Theater is further theorized by Fox (1986), Fox and Heinreich (1999), and Salas (1996). It is grounded in logics of community-based theater (Haedicke & Nellhaus, 2001) and the liberatory, democratic, interactive theater practices of Boal (1979, 1995, 1998) and Wirth (1994). It is further explained through the role of witnessing in performance ethnography (Doyle, 2001). In large, these methods engage performance as reflexive praxis, *praxis* as the relationship between theoretical understandings, a critique of society, and action toward social reform (Freire, 1985). Hence, the five problematic aspects of audiencing that Park-Fuller outlines are the relational dynamics between *empathizing/criticizing, empowering/disempowering, supporting/shaping, resisting/tweaking,* and *the ritual dance of power,* all of which implicate the representational politics of performing others in light of our own *dense particularity,* which is always dichotomous and fluid (Mohanty, 1989).

Risking a conflation of her significant contributions, I see her primary argument grounded in Wallace Bacon's (1979) use of the term "tensiveness." Park-Fuller seemingly extends his logics from the specific exploration of literary texts, to a broader context of social and cultural performance. Tensiveness refers to those competing impulses that give any performative situation dynamism, a push and pull—but not a tension as in friction or strife, but the actions of those elements and attributes of social relations that either maintain social systems or seek to transform them.

So what appear to be binary opposites in Park-Fuller's construction are really dynamic dyads, necessarily co-present variables, and procedural mandates specifically in Playback Theatre that I apply in general to performance ethnography. In her words, they encourage responsibility: "[A] responsibility to listen to, to respect, and to learn from one another's stories, but also to 'talk back,' to intervene, to unmask the latent stances in stories that can divide the human community, and to redress, through its various rituals, the wrongs suffered in silence as well as in speech or action" (p. 303). In this way, performance ethnography encourages a dialogue and action that extends outside the specified site of performance and into the everyday realm of human social interaction.

▣ II. Procedural Pragmatics and Genres of Performance Ethnography

Conquergood (1988) writes that performance always "takes as both its subject matter and method the experiencing body situated in time, place, and history" (p. 187). Hence, the procedural pragmatics and genres of performance ethnography that I outline here are centered in the performing body, yet it is how bodies are situated in performance, the body being performed (self/other) and the source model of information gathered (researcher/performer) in performance ethnography that shifts. According to Soyini Madison (1998), "Performance becomes the vehicle by which we travel to the worlds of Subjects and enter domains of intersubjectivity that problematize how we categorize who is 'us' and who is 'them,' and how we see ourselves with 'other' and different eyes" (p. 282). Hence, performance is a way of coming to know self and other, and self as other.

Within this section, I suggest that the bodies and lived experiences being represented in performance ethnography shift between "the other" and back to "the self," with particular interests in denoting and connoting the ties that bind. I fall short of establishing a specific typology that separates and delineates individual approaches to doing performance ethnography, knowing that the borders of performance ethnography bleed and that the impulse is in staging articulated lived experience, cultural practice, and knowledge of culture.

A. Performing Others in Performance Ethnography

Victor Turner and Edie Turner (1982, 1988), who were mostly interested in teaching culture, provided their students with descriptive "strips of behavior" to develop into "playscripts," thereby performing "ethnography in a kind of instructional theater" (Turner, 1982, p. 41). It was their attempt to have students come to understand the intricacies of embodied cultural practice. The full process of such a pedagogical engagement culminates not only in the experiencing body but also later in the critical reflection on what students come to know through assuming the particular cultural practices that have been mostly outside the range of their everyday experiences. This form of performance ethnography was mostly *student-in-class centered.*

This point of origin provides the theoretical and methodological foundation for the type of work being done in performance studies, beginning with a specific example in the work of Joni Jones. In documenting her own work with performance ethnography, based on her research in Nigeria on the Yoruba deity Osun, Jones (2002) offers an *audience-centered brand of performance ethnography* designed to invite audience members to participate within the performance of a particular cultural formation. Her production of *Searching for Osun* was an installation piece that focused on "aspects of Yoruba life that moved [her] most—dance music, divination, Osun's relationship to children, 'women's work,' and food preparation" (p. 1). The cast of performers assumed archetypal characters in Yoruba life, engaging in particular cultural and relational practices. The invited audience to the performance entered the performance space not as distanced onlookers but participants.

The audience was invited to engage varying dimensions that shape cultural life—food/eating and dining rituals, movement/ music and dance, clothing/the wearing of traditional garb, and listening to storytelling and oral lore. Within her method, as in the work of Boal (1979), Jones created opportunities for audiences to make the move from being spectators to being "spect-actors," active participants who were involved in knowing and shaping their own experience. Hence, the process of coming to know is not only relegated to seeing, but also extended and enriched by fully participating in the experience.

Approaches to performance ethnography also engage *group-field study work.* Such approaches culminate in the public performances of research notes and interviews by those who conducted the research and may involve members of the cultural communities explored (see McCall, 1993; Pollock, 1990). It can be *the result of a single researcher's long-term research* that works at excavating specific political and cultural events. Such examples might operate on a *localized level,* such as restaging the politics leading to a cafeteria workers' strike at the University of North Carolina, Chapel Hill (Madison, 1998), or *an intercultural and interracial level of conflict,* such as in the staged and performance work of Anna Deavere Smith—*Fires in the Mirror: Crown Heights, Brooklyn, and Other Identities* (1993) and *Twilight: Los Angeles, 1992* (1994).

This is historical and culturally based work in which artists use performance to foreground and make commentary on culture. They offer performed elements of historical truisms as a method of illuminating aspects of oppression and the politics of social relations based in race, ethnicity, sex, gender, and class.[10] In describing her project dealing with the cafeteria strike,

Madison (1998) writes that "the performance strives to communicate a sense of the Subjects' world in their own words; its hopes to amplify their meanings and intentions to a larger group of listeners and observers" (p. 280). In this way, we also come to understand Deavere Smith's work in searching for the American character in *Fires in the Mirror.*

In her project, Deavere Smith interviewed, and later performed, 19 original portraits of African Americans and Jews (politicians, housewives, activists, authors, parents, etc.) after the racial unrest and rioting in Crown Heights, Brooklyn in 1991. The unrest was sparked by what is considered an accident. (A Hasidic man driving a station wagon swerved on a corner and killed a young African American boy. This was followed by the act of retribution 4 days later in which a young Jewish man was stabbed by a group of young African American men.) Through the buttressing of performed ethnographic interviews and character sketches, Deavere Smith illuminates the seeds and logics of racial contestation that were germinating long before the incident that sparked the fires of riot. Thus, the project provides the audience with a searing portrait of race relations in America that operates on the level of performed visceral response.[11]

In this sense, performance ethnography can also operate on a *globalized level* in which a specific issue of the human condition that crosses national borders is exemplified, such as in Soyini Madison's intentions to stage *Trokosi*, the Ghanaian practice of ostracizing girls who have been sexually abused. The intention of such work would be to present the result of the individual scholar's research in Ghana and her critique of the practices. Staged in Ghana amid the Ghanaian debates over the practices, the performance would serve a critical reflexive praxis, a refractive mirror and argument concerning social practice and cultural investment (Jones 2002).

This approach to performance ethnography reflects that tradition in which empirical materials are presented in the form of scripts, poems, short stories, and dramas that are staged and presented to diverse audiences. (See Bauman, 1986; Becker et al., 1989; Bochner, 1994; Bruner, 1986; Conquergood, 1985, 1986b, 1989, 1991, 1992; Kapferer, 1986; McCall & Becker, 1990; Mienczakowski, 1992, 1994, 1995; Mienczakowski & Morgan, 1993; Paget, 1990, 1993; Richardson & Lockridge, 1991; Schechner, 1986; Stern & Henderson, 1993.)[12] These approaches work toward the redramatization of cultural life, by rehydrating the lived experiences of others described in ethnographic work, restoring aspects of the dramatic, dynamic, and aesthetic qualities of cultural practice in the moment of presenting research.

B. Performance of (Auto)Ethnography

The intention of performance ethnography could be signaled in the desire to build a *template of sociality* (Hamera, 1999). This construct signals not a projected standard of living but an association of experience gained through performance. It allows audiences to see others in relation to themselves; to come to know, to contemplate on how they came to know, to signal ways of being, and to see possibilities for their social relational orientations and obligations to others. Performance ethnography as template of sociality becomes a *generative (auto)ethnographic* experience that sparks and provides a template on which audiences begin their own processes of critical reflection (Alexander, 2000).

In this sense, although performance ethnography is traditionally thought of in terms of the performance of the cultural other and grounded in *externalized ethnographic practices*, it can also reflect a process of *internalized ethnographic practice* in which a performer uses lived experience and personal history as cultural site, such as in autoethnography (Ellis & Bochner, 2000; Lionnet, 1989; Reed-Danahay, 1997; Spry, 1997, 2001). Such a journey into the self is no less treacherous than crossing the borders and boundaries inhabited by the exotic other. Nor are the potential insights gathered less meaningful in coming to understand the politics of cultural identity in the circulation of social relations. In particular, autoethnography is a method that attempts "quite literally, [to] come to terms with sustaining questions of self and culture" (Neumann, 1996, p. 193). It is a method of navigating the "busy intersections" of race, sex, sexuality, class, and gender that is often constructed as the unitary location of cultural identity sedimented in social practice (Rosaldo, 1989, p. 17).

Using this as an alternative approach, performance ethnography thus can include what has been referred to as *autoperformance*, singularly conceived performances such as autobiography, autoethnography, and performance art (Kirby, 1979). All of these, to varying degrees, have as their concerted effort *a critique of self and society, self in society, and self as resistant and transformative force of society.* Despite the suggested critiques of *solo performance* as a narcissistic act of self-indulgence and narcissism (Gentile, 1989), Françoise Lionnet (1989) sees autoethnography in particular as a form of cultural performance. She states that autoethnography "transcends pedestrian notions of referentiality, for the staging of the event is part of the process of 'passing on,' of elaborating cultural forms, which are not static and inviolable but dynamically involved in the creation of culture itself" (p. 102).

Autoethnography thus engages ethnographical analysis of personally lived experience. The evidenced act of showing in autoethnography is less about reflecting on the self in a public space than about using the public space and performance as an act of critically reflecting culture, an act of *seeing the self see the self through and as the other*. Thus, as a form of performance ethnography, it is designed to engage a locus of embodied reflexivity using lived experience as a specific cultural site that offers social commentary and cultural critique (Alexander, 2002b).

Ellis and Bochner (2000) identify five different exemplars for autoethnography that blend and bleed the borders of individualized cultural identity, intentionality, and its orientation to audience. Briefly stated, in *reflexive ethnographies* researchers critically reflect on lived experience in *a* particular cultural community (which may not be their own), specifying their exact relation to self and a particular society. *Native ethnographies* foreground the experiences of researchers, who reflect on their membership in a historically marginalized or exoticized culture. *Complete-member-researchers/ethnographies* are those in which a member of a particular culture interprets and reports on the culture for outsiders. *Literary autoethnographies* feature writer/researchers describing and interpreting their culture for audiences that are not familiar with the writer/researcher's culture. *Personal narratives* as critical autobiographical stories of lived experience offer (public) audiences access to personal experience with the intent of politicizing aspects of human experience and social sense-making.

Kristin Langellier (1989) writes that like most narratives, the personal narrative "does something in the social world . . . [it] participate[s] in the ongoing rhythm of people's lives as a reflection of their social organization and cultural values" (p. 261). In this way, the personal narrative as an exemplar and contributing model of self-storying is a reflection of an individual's critical excavation of lived experience and the categorizing of cultural meaning. This is then shared within a public domain to provide the audience with a meaningful articulation of human experience. The benefit, as Langellier (1998) later writes, resides in the consequences and conditions of the telling, the audience that orients to the story and processes the transgressive and recuperative powers of the performative moment. In writing this, I am not collapsing personal narrative into ethnography, nor bleeding the borders between personal narrative and autoethnography—as much as I foreground the links of exploring lived and living experience (self and other) that is germane to all.

I think that at the core of performance ethnography is the desire not only for an audience to see the performance of culture, but, as Ellis and Bochner (1996) suggest, to engage on some level in a "self-conscious reflexivity" on their own relation to the experience (p. 28). I want to claim and categorize this quality and process in the manner in which Victor Turner (1988) defines "performative reflexivity," as "a condition in which a sociocultural group, or its most perceptive members acting representatively turn, bend or reflect back upon themselves" (p. 24). Turner's thought on reflexivity is culture and context specific. The inherent reflexive turn of performative experience is precisely its power to transmit as well as to critique culture and self.

In his essay "The Personal: Against the Master Narrative," Fred Corey (1998) outlines what I believe to be a key argument for personal narrative as performance ethnography, specifically in his links between the personal and the cultural. He writes: "The master narrative is an artillery of moral truth, and the personal narrative defixes the truth. The master narrative is a cultural discourse, replete with epistemic implications, and the personal narrative is a mode of 'reverse discourse'" (p. 250).[13] Using Foucault's (1982) construct of *reverse discourse* or *counter discourse*, Corey gives territorial distinction to the personal narrative as moral discourse.

Whereas the master narrative often dictates and speculates on collective identities, the personal narrative "tell[s] about personal, lived experience in a way that assists in the construction of identity, reinforces or challenges private and public belief systems and values, and either resists or reinforces the dominate cultural practices of the community in which the narrative event occurs"[14] (Corey, 1998, p. 250). Although there are multiple constructions of the master narrative, I want to suggest, along with Corey, that the master narrative is the dominant, hegemonic, way of seeing or thinking the world is *or* should be, the narrative that often guides and undergirds social, cultural, and political mandates.

The personal narrative always stands in relation to the master narrative, which is the reflection of culture and our relation to/in culture. Hence, the personal narrative is always a reflection on and excavation of the cultural contexts that give rise to experience. In this sense, personal narratives move from what some might presume to be an insular engagement of personal reflection, to a complex process that implicates the performative nature of cultural identity. Like autoethnography as theorized by Ellis and Bochner (2000), personal narrative places the individual in a dialogue with "history, social structure, and culture, which themselves are dialectically revealed through action, feeling, thought, and language" (p. 739).

▣ III. Links Between Critical Pedagogy and Critical Performative Pedagogy

Drawing from principles in performance studies and ethnography, the preceding sections have laid the foundational logics for performance ethnography as a social force, a strategic embodied methodology, and a moral discourse. This section further grounds performance ethnography as a critical pedagogical practice designed to democratize the classroom. The section also furthers how these logics expand our understanding of the unifying links between performance, pedagogy, culture, and social reform.

By including these logics, I clearly understand that *while performance ethnography may strive to function as a critical pedagogical strategy, not all performance ethnography would participate within the logic of critical pedagogy.* In this case, I am interested in the theorizing of educational practice "that turns the ethnographic into the performative and the performative into the political" (Denzin, 2003, p. xiii). By drawing on the kernel logic of Turner and Turner (1988), I want to necessarily expand the pedagogical use of performance ethnography from mere *class activity* to an insurgent method of engaging, critiquing, and commenting on culture that is an ongoing activity in educational practice.

A. Critical Pedagogy

In Peter McLaren's extensive body of work, listed here in brief (Giroux & McLaren, 1984, 1994; McLaren, 1985, 1989, 1993, 1994, 1997, 1998, 2000; McLaren & Lankshear, 1994), he, perhaps more than any other educator-scholar, has laid the groundwork for a critical pedagogy. Theorists in critical pedagogy argue that schools are grounded in processes of culture and cultural propagation, and that classrooms have always been sites of cultural inscription that seek to legitimate particular forms. In this sense, critical pedagogy is grounded in the moral imperative of exposing systems of oppression that exist within the very structures of education, the process of schooling, and the overarching logic of perpetuating hierarchies of oppression and liberation through the sanctioning of particularly restrictive performances of self and other.

In *Schooling as a Ritual Performance*, McLaren (1993) grounds his critical vision in a politics of the body, which is my core link between pedagogy and performance ethnography. His concept of enfleshment signals "that meeting place of both the unthought social norms in which meaning is always already in place and the ongoing production of knowledge through particular social, institutional and disciplinary procedures" (p. 275). This work centers his ethnographic project in *the feeling body, the dialogically constituted feeling body, the discursive body*, and *the performing body* as sites of social inscription. His work suggests that the body is the site of knowing and feeling, and the site from which transformation is instantiated and initiated. McLaren states, "this means decoupling ourselves from the disciplined mobilizations of everyday life in order to rearticulate the sites of our affective investment so that we can 'reenter the strategic politics of the social formation'"[15] (p. 287). Desire must be inflected into a transformative politics of hope and action. I believe that performance ethnography taps into this kernel logic of experience. McLaren goes on to call for a critically reflexive and embodied performance of resistance and subversion that opens spaces for variation and expression.

B. Critical Performative Pedagogy

Grounded in a performance-based methodology, the practical and theoretical construct of *critical performative pedagogy* is used in diverse yet interlocking ways. For example, performance studies scholar Elyse Pineau (1998, 2002) uses the term to reference a body-centered experiential method of teaching that foregrounds the active-body-knowing. Her conceptualization of critical performative pedagogy, heavily supported with precepts from critical pedagogy, "acknowledge[s] that inequities in power and privilege have a physical impact on our bodies and consequently must be struggled against bodily, through physical action and activism" (2002, p. 53). Her performative methodology engages the body as a primary site of meaning-making, of ideological struggle, and of performative resistance. Hence bodies are put "into action in the classroom" as a means of exercising and engaging a liberatory practice that extends beyond the borders of the classroom into everyday citizenship (2002, p. 53).

Her approach is what cultural studies scholar Lawrence Grossberg (1996) might refer to as *the act of doing*. In particular, performative pedagogy in the classroom is used to illuminate and embody social politics "intervening into contexts and power . . . in order to enable people to act more strategically in ways that may change their context for the better" (p. 143). In this way, critical performative pedagogy is a rehearsal process that practices possibility outside the classroom (Boal, 1985).

Communication and sociology scholar Norman K. Denzin (2003) approaches *critical performance pedagogy* as a cluster of performative and emancipatory strategies. It includes Pineau's construction but extends further into a "civic, publicly responsible autoethnography that addresses the central issues of self, race, gender, society, and democracy" (p. 225). The expanse of his survey includes performance ethnography, autoethnography, performative cultural studies, reflexive critical ethnography, critical race theory, and the broader sociological and ethnographic imagination, all of which are undergirded in his expansion of Freirean (1998, 1999) politics, pedagogies, and possibilities of hope.

These methods are all empowered with the ability to open up spaces of pain to critical reflection on self and society. Hence, they exist in that tensive space of being radical and risky—radical in the sense that they strip away notions of a given human condition, and risky in that our sense of comfort in knowing the world is made bare. They give way to the possibility of knowing the world differently. They open a possibility of hope encouraged by social responsibility, political activism, and engaged participation in a moral science of humanistic discourse. This cluster of performative strategies that he refers to as *critical performance pedagogy* are all centered in the active body doing; the active mind knowing; and an active civic responsibility that collectivizes and promotes democracy and human rights.

Denzin's construction addresses Giroux's (2001) search for a project and the politics of hope when he discusses "strategies of understanding, engagement, and transformation that address the most demanding social problems of our time. Such projects are utopian . . ." (p. 7). Denzin refers to utopian as indicating an ideal state of human social relations but also uses utopian to indicate a particular and practical strategy of gaining insight into cultural others in order to build community. Performance ethnography as the overarching logic of this discussion can be what Jill Dolan (2001b) describes as a *utopian performative*. The theater or the situated site of performance can become a place where "audiences are compelled to gather with others, to see people perform live, hoping perhaps for moments of transformation that might let them reconsider and change the world outside the theatre" (p. 455). Although Dolan is referencing the specific project of theater, I am focusing broadly on performance and then applying it back to the specifics of performance ethnography in which actual lives and actual human conditions are presented for public discussion.

C. Border Pedagogy

In *Postmodern Education: Politics, Culture, and Social Criticism*, Aronowitz and Giroux (1991) discuss the construct of *border pedagogy*. "Border pedagogy offers the opportunity for students to engage the multiple references that constitute different cultural codes, experiences, and languages. This means educating students to read these codes critically, to learn the limits of such codes, including the ones they use to construct their own narratives and histories" (pp. 118–119). I believe this to be core logic of a *student-in-class–centered* approach to performance ethnography. It is a logic that promotes student engagement of actual accounts and descriptions of cultural practice, with the intent for them to come to know culture differently. In more specific terms, Aronowitz and Giroux write that border pedagogy helps students to understand that "[o]ne's class, race, gender, or ethnicity may influence, but does not irrevocably predetermine, how one takes up a particular ideology, reads a particular text, or responds to particular forms of oppression" (p. 121). Hence, there is the potential of seeing the links that bind humanity and not the borders of difference that we presume divide us.

Border pedagogy requires teachers to engage students in the places and ideological spaces of their own experiences as they try to make sense of culture and curriculum—while practicing a voice long subdued and silenced in the classroom. Such a performance-based method demands a new level of engagement that crosses borders between the knowing and the known. Giroux and Shannon (1997) state: "Pedagogy in this context becomes performative through the ways in which various authors [teachers and students] engage diverse cultural texts as a context for theorizing about social issues and wider political considerations" (p. 2).

In these ways, the link between performance and ethnography can move the overall engagement of education beyond mere *teaching*, that process of organizing and integrating knowledge for the purpose of sharing meaning and mandating understanding in the confines of the classroom. It can move toward the notion of *pedagogy*, which strategizes purposeful learning with an awareness of the social, cultural, and political contexts in which learning and living take place. Performance ethnography as a particular pedagogical strategy can then move even further to encompass a *critical pedagogy* by revealing, interrogating, and challenging legitimated social and cultural forms and opening spaces for additional voices in a meaningful human discourse. Such an act would always be moving toward becoming a *revolutionary pedagogy* that helps to enact the possibilities of social transformation by bleeding the borders of subjectivity and opening spaces of care (McLaren, 2000).

D. Public Pedagogy

In both Pineau's and Denzin's approaches to critical performative pedagogy, there is a hope that the embodied, reflective, and reflexive process of performative pedagogy becomes what Giroux (2001) constructs as *a public pedagogy*, a process in which the efforts and effects of such critical processes are not limited to the sterilizing confines of the classroom or the realm of self-knowing, but are presented to and enacted in the public sphere so as to transform social life. Giroux writes, "Defined through its performative functions, public pedagogy is marked by its attentiveness to the interconnections and struggles that take place over knowledge, language, spatial relations, and history. Public pedagogy represents a moral and political practice rather than merely a technical procedure" (p. 12). Public pedagogy expands privatized notions of pedagogical practices, specifically the in-class strategies used by individual teachers that might mark disciplinary limits and boundaries. In such case, a public pedagogy is framed and conceptualized by a political network of principles in critical pedagogy and cultural studies that link teaching and learning with social change.[16]

Through the performed engagement of a cultural dialogue, performance ethnography becomes a public pedagogy with several characteristics. It is designed to make public the often privatized, if not secularized, experiences of others. It is designed to begin the painstaking process of deconstructing notions of difference that often regulate the equal distribution of humanistic concern. It makes present and visible the lived experiences of self and other; giving students, performers, and audiences access to knowledge that, one hopes, will open spaces of possibility.

IV. Political Potentialities and Practical Interpretations of Performance Ethnography

Performance ethnography teases at and illuminates a wide variety of issues that are of particular concern both in performance studies and in ethnography. I have already focused on the issue of representation and the social reconstruction of *other people's lives*, whether as pedagogical method or as political activism. Performance ethnography troubles the issue and illuminates the need for careful consideration and delicate attention to the dramatistic questions of who, what, when, where, and why (Burke, 1957), directed to the actions of others and, more important, directed to our own political intentions. Drawing from the conceptual frames of theorists in performance studies, ethnography, and anthropology, I outline and extend *some* of the more dominant issues that reflect these disciplines as they converge in performance ethnography.

A. Dominating Issues at the Convergence of Performance/Ethnography

Performance ethnography highlights the concern in performance studies with how specific cultural practices shape identity and the concern in ethnography of how identity shapes the practice of cultural performance. Performance ethnography also highlights the role of cultural hegemony in the interpretation of cultural performance (E. C. Fine & Speer, 1992, p. 16). In this case, cultural hegemony is defined as the collectivizing practices of cultural familiars who regulate identity through the actualized embodiment of particular norms as identifying markers of communal, cultural, and political membership.

Performance ethnography as a reifying and magnifying cultural performative act replicates aspects of this quality of cultural performance in at least three ways. First, in the staging and embodiment of "the other" in performance, performance ethnography capitalizes on the observable and replicable behavior of cultural members in a particular context. Second, performance ethnography depends on the integrity of relational and ethical acts of the ethnographer who describes culture and the performer who embodies cultural experience. The questions of *why are particular cultural practices engaged* and *why they are studied through performance* should be scrutinized carefully. In this way, performance ethnography foregrounds the representational politics of performance and ethnography and the ethical issues of responsibility to particular audiences and cultures represented in the texts (Carlson, 1996, p. 15). The question of *what aspects of culture are reenacted in performance for what reason and with what perceptual and literal effects on the culture being represented* also should be critically engaged. Third, performance ethnography calls for a reflexive engagement on the part of the participants—actors/audiences to question what they accept as truth and to examine how their truths are shaped by their perspective both in and of performance, as well as in and of the cultural lives represented through performance (Jones, 2002, p. 1).

Discussing the three stages in the methodological process of performance ethnography, *ethnography into playscript, script into performance*, and *performance into meta-ethnography*, Victor Turner (1982) comments on a level of critical reflexivity that implicates the nature of ethnography and performance. He writes, "The reflexivity of performance dissolves the bonds (between body and mentality, unconscious and conscious thinking, species and self) and so creatively democratizes" (p. 100).

Performance ethnography orchestrates an embodied understanding of how notions of the self are always constructed in relation to other, and how we hold those perceptual standards as regulatory devices in maintaining human social relations. As a moral discourse, performance ethnography democratizes human sociality by closing the gaps between the known and the unknown, between self and other, and between the borders and boundaries of differently lived experiences.

B. Interpreting and Evaluating Effective Performance Ethnography

In articulating concerns of interpretation and evaluation, I focus on three areas of emphasis: content, form, and impact. I depend heavily on Laurel Richardson's (2000a) essay, in which she writes: "Ethnography is always situated in human activity, bearing both the strengths and limitations of human perception and feeling" (p. 254). These are palpably felt and realized in the conjoined effort of *performance ethnography*, which is to articulate a vision and understanding of a particular cultural experience, as it resonates and ricochets between self and other and, at times, self as other.

Content

1. Substantive contribution (Richardson, 2000a, p. 254): Does this piece contribute to our understanding of social life? Do the writer/performers demonstrate a deeply grounded (if embedded) human-world understanding and perspective? How has this perspective informed the construction of the text?

The notion of contribution is really an issue of intention. It is based in a series of questions that seek to get to the core of the critical endeavor of the performative engagement. What does the performance seek to accomplish? What does the performance seek to contribute, in terms of knowledge and experience, to the audience? In some very literal ways, the constructed entity of the performance must have a specific purpose with specific goals. What is/are the moral and theoretical arguments in the text? In the case of audience-centered performance ethnography, what aspects of culture do the performers seek to expose to the audience—particular traditions, clothing, food, social expressions, and so on? What critical evaluation (or politicized understanding) of cultural practice do the performers seek to share with the audience, or want the audience to assume? What political movement, emotional response, or engaged temperament does the performance seek to incite?

2. Reflexivity (Richardson, 2000a, p. 254): How did the author/performers come to write/perform this text? How was the information gathered? How has the author/performers' subjectivity been both a producer and product of this text? Is there

adequate self-awareness and self-exposure for the audience to make judgments about the point of view? Do author/performers hold themselves accountable to the standards of knowing and telling of the people they have studied?

The performative construction and presentation of ethnography has multiple levels of reflexive accountabilities. First, when the performer is representing the cultural other, there is a *performer-based reflexivity.* This level of reflexivity is a critical self-examination of the performer's intentions, a clear understanding of his or her dense particularity in relation to the performed other, and his or her positionality in relation to the politics of performing the other.

Second, performance ethnography encourages a critical reflection on the *performed population*, gathering a clear understanding of their cultural experience. This turns into a *performer-performed reflexivity* that acknowledges the active process of performative embodiment of the other, the resonant points of juncture and disjunction, and how they work toward and in tension with the intended goal of the overall performative engagement. Such critical engagements seek not only to know the selves engaged in the performance (performer and performed), but also how the performance seeks to encourage a certain critical reflexiveness in the audience as they engage the performative moment. The performance should push the audience to learn and engage previously unspoken and unknown things about culture and communication from the experience of their engagement (Goodall, 2000). This performative learning engagement is specific both to the represented culture and to ways in which such knowledge can be extrapolated to broader issues of social and cultural interaction.

3. Expresses a reality (Richardson, 2000a, p. 254): Does this text present a fleshed out, embodied sense of lived experience? Does it seem "true"—meaning a credible account of a cultural, social, individual, or communal sense of the "real"?

The moment of performance presents a context that opens the way for the performer-ethnographer "to present human social behavior as more, rather than as less, complex, to keep explanations from becoming simplistic or reductionist" (Wolcott, 1999, p. 79). In this regard, Denzin (1992) might suggest that performance ethnography must "reflect back on, be entangled in, and critique this current historical moment and its discontents" (p. 25). For my own purposes, the current historical moment is both the actualized lived conditions and practices of those presented in performance, and also the moment of performance.

Form

4. Aesthetic merit (Richardson, 2000a, p. 254): Does this piece succeed aesthetically? Does the use of creative analytical practice open up the text and invite interpretive responses? Is the text artistically shaped, satisfying, complex, and not boring?

The writing in performance ethnography must be well crafted. This implies craft both in poetic terms, through aesthetic language that invokes the links between felt emotion, critical thought, and understanding; as well as craft in the sense that the language must be clear, effective, evocative, and more than subtly representative of the populations to which it reflects (Pelias, 1999a, 1999b; Spry, 2001). The writing must give the audience to which it is presented access to the world of those it represents in a manner that simulates the visceral response of actual experience.

In the case of using empirical materials gathered from ethnographic interviews, the language that informants speak *speaks the logic of their desire.* Their processed and re-articulated voice must be shaped and placed in context, signaling both the actuality of location in the utterance and the regenerated conditions of its use in performance—bridging space, time, and the channeled embodiment of cultural experience. The crafted language and embodied engagement of performance ethnography must meet the standards of intellectual rigor and aesthetic acumen set by experts and theorists in both performance studies and the social sciences (Denzin, 1997; Spry, 2001).

It must have the sensuousness of articulate embodied thought, with the clarity and efficacy of good research grounded in ethical care and thick description.

Impact

5. How does performance ethnography affect the performers (emotionally, intellectually, and politically)? How does performance ethnography affect the audience (emotionally, intellectually, and politically)? What new questions are generated in and through the performance? Does the performance move the performer and audience to try new ways of seeing the world, particular cultures, particular research practices, and ways of knowing the world? Does the performance move the performers and audience to a particular action—extending outside the borders of the immediate performative experience? (Richardson, 2000a, p. 254).

These are not questions of measurement or the validation of effect that often trouble the very personalized and deeply felt responses to performative engagement, yet the strategic purposes of engaging performance ethnography might encourage performers and audience members to reflect upon the nature of their experience. They might suggest that audience members of these performances be offered a forum or venue, such as speaking in post- performance discussion sessions or writing on questionnaires or comment sheets. This helps in further theorizing what audiences bring to and take away from performances. It helps to clarify the effectiveness of performance to engage, inform, ignite, and incite response beyond personalized pleasure or the emotional stirrings of dis-ease (Park-Fuller, 2003).

Furthermore, some form of *engaged discourse* might suggest asking performers and audience members to articulate a shift in their way of thinking and seeing the world. What do they know differently? What will they do differently? How can they literally translate performative experience into knowledge and translate knowledge into doing? In many ways, this possibility extends and reifies the dialogic nature of performance ethnography, into a realized dialogue between the aestheticized recreation of cultural others, the performers who make their presence and voices known in performance, and the diverse audiences with whom they come into contact.

V. Directions in/for Performance Ethnography

Performance ethnography is concerned with embodying aspects of ethnographic description. It is this *practice of engagement* that allows performers, subjects, and audiences (in their reciprocated and intensely bound positionalities) to come to an experiential sense of the variables that affect cultural life. It focuses on the important transformative process of becoming, which signals our agency for empathy and our flexibility in embodying cultural norms. One can hope that the pedagogical, aesthetic, and political processes that inform performance ethnography will continue to bubble to the surface while establishing new ways of engaging, extending, and critically reflecting on the multiple variables that shape and affect cultural knowing.

Soyini Madison's (1998) key construction of *the performance of possibilities* offers both validity and direction for performance ethnography. I knowingly and willingly displace my voice to foreground some of her germinal articulations on this note, knowing that they are most certainly key reminders of the ways in which performance ethnography seeks to open realms of knowing and doing through the joint efforts of performance and ethnography and the necessary political activism that yokes and drives engaged citizenship. (See how Madison furthers these imperatives in her chapter on critical ethnography, Chapter 21, this volume.) Here I reframe her articulations as tenets for a performance of possibilities—not rules, but a set of organizing principles that should guide the future of performance ethnography.

Tenets for a Performance of Possibilities

- The *performance of possibilities* functions as a politically engaged pedagogy that never has to convince a predefined subject—whether empty or full, whether essential or fragmented—to adopt a new position. Rather, the task is to win an already positioned, already invested individual or group to a different set of places, a different organization of *the space of possibilities.*
- The *performance of possibilities* invokes an investment in politics and "the Other," keeping in mind the dynamics of performance, audience, and Subjects while at the same time being wary of both cynics and zealots.
- The *performance of possibilities* takes the stand that performance matters because it does something in the world. What it does for the audience, the Subjects, and those engaged in it must be driven by a thoughtful critique of assumptions and purpose.
- The *performance of possibilities* does not accept being heard and included as its focus, but only as a starting point. Instead, voice is an embodied historical self that constructs and is constructed by a matrix of social and political processes. The aim is to present and represent Subjects as made and makers of meaning, symbol, and history in their fullest sensory and social dimensions. Therefore, the *performance of possibilities* is also a performance of voice wedded to experience.
- The *performance of possibilities* as an interrogative field aims to create or contribute to a discursive space where unjust systems and processes are identified and interrogated. It is where what has been expressed through the illumination of voice and the encounter with subjectivity motivates individuals to some level of informed and strategic action.
- The *performance of possibilities* motivates performers and spectators to appropriate the rhetorical currency they need, from the inner space of the performance to the outer domain of the social world, in order to make a material difference.
- The *performance of possibilities* necessitates creating performances where the intent is largely to invoke interrogation of specific political and social processes so that art is seen as consciously working toward a cultural politics of change that resonates in a progressive and involved citizenship.
- The *performance of possibilities* strives to reinforce to audience members the web of citizenship and the possibilities of their individual selves as agents and change-makers.
- The *performance of possibilities* acknowledges that when audience members begin to witness degrees of tension and incongruity between a Subject's life-world and those processes and systems that challenge and undermine that world, something more and new is learned about how power works.
- The *performance of possibilities* suggests that both performers and audiences can be transformed. They can be themselves and more as they travel between worlds—the spaces that they and others actually inhabit and the spaces of possibility of human liberation.
- The *performance of possibilities* is moral responsibility and artistic excellence that culminates in the active intervention of unfair closures, *remaking* the possibility for new openings that bring the margins to a shared center.
- The *performance of possibilities* does not arrogantly assume that we exclusively are giving voice to the silenced, for we understand they speak and have been speaking in spaces and places often foreign to us.
- The *performance of possibilities* in the new millennium will specialize in the wholly impossible reaching toward light, justice, and enlivening possibilities (Madison, 1998, pp. 276–286).

How might Madison's constructions be made manifest in performance ethnography? How might we move toward a concrete materialization of these possibilities? How might we extend the promises and possibilities of performance ethnography outside a sometimes insular academic endeavor characterized by talk and into a community-based application where doing has meaningful consequences? Those of us working for a critical cultural awareness through performance studies, ethnography, cultural studies, and pedagogical studies understand that the stakes are high, but so is our desire. We understand that the steps that we take leave tracks from where we have been but also establish trails to our direction and for others to follow. Allow me to offer some possible directions for us to travel.

First, issues of critical reflexivity are always at the center of performance ethnography. The act of *seeing the self see the self* signals Joseph Roach's (2002) discussion through Brecht of *defamilarizing* the self—not defamilarizing the self by simply stepping into the bodies of others, but by becoming aware of what happens in and as a result of that shift. Performance ethnography would benefit from what K. E. Supriya (2001) calls the *staging of ethnographic reflexivity* in which there is a critical emphasis on seeing the self see the self both in moments of ethnographic practice and in the performance of that knowledge. Such performances might at once confirm the power of performance as a method of knowing and present a clear template for audiences to engage in the process of critical reflection on their experiences in performance ethnography, thus assisting them in developing critical skills that extend beyond the performance moment and can affect the ways in which they move through the world.

In this way, we also heed Langellier's (1998) charge related to performing personal narrative when she writes: "To 'just do it'"—in this case performance ethnography—"without producing knowledge about" *the links between performance, ethnography, and culture* risks exploiting cultural practices for personal gains. Joining Langellier, Elizabeth Bell (2002) yearns for performance theory that *can* help to "account for the material, political consequences of performance . . ." (p. 128). I apply her logic toward building a critical theory of performance ethnography, a theory that *can* help to enlighten us on the revelations gained through performative experience. These revelations might exceed the particularity of method, pedagogical purpose, or even the politics of representation to foreground *the logics of effect and the sociopolitical impacts of performative experience.*

Such a theory would ask and answer the following questions: What do performers and audience members take from the experience of performance ethnography? How, through a performance of translated ethnographic materials, do performers and audiences come to know culture better? In answering these questions, performance ethnography might also be formally linked to Giroux's (2001) desire for a public pedagogy, thereby linking practices that are interdisciplinary, pedagogical, and performance-based with such practices that are designed to further racial, economic, and political democracy, practices that are designed to strike a new balance and expand the individual and social dimensions of citizenship (p. 9).[18]

Second, although performance ethnography often seems interested in reflecting on the experience of and with the cultural other, distinctions are made through perceived characteristics of difference. To what degree would performance ethnography also benefit in illuminating the ways in which "difference" as an ideological and practiced construct is a part of any community? To what degree would performance ethnography benefit in turning its gaze on the specified communities to which ethnographers and performers claim membership, and thereby illuminate the ways in which struggle and strife are present within the everyday life of cultural familiars?

Most recently, my work has moved into what I have constructed as *an integrative and reflexive ethnography of performance* that both captures and extends this logic. This experimental approach is grounded both in Denzin's (1997) construction of *reflexive critique* and in Jones's (1997) use of *performance as a critique of the academy*. It is also informed by Schneider's (2002) notion of a *reflexive/diffractive ethnography*, which charges that ethnographic practices should not only re-inscribe the nature of what already happens in the world, but also move toward instantiating ways of seeing and methods of knowing to transform those practices.

The approach allows me the opportunity to address questions about and responses to staged cultural performance that I encounter in the academic communities in which I claim membership. Although these comments and critiques are "seemingly" directed to a particular product or utterance, the inseparability of product, process, and producer (a member of "minority culture") in relation to the variables that shape the life of the critic (a member of "majority culture") always bleed the borders. These bleeding borders are like semi-permeable membranes between the public and the private, between the professional and the personal, and between the politics of power and propriety that always threaten to hold tension-filled historical social relations in stasis. By incorporating such critiques in a restaging of the performance either in embodied or written form, I stage a critical reflexivity for self and other, thereby further theorizing the mechanisms that undergird both performances in everyday life and how others and I reconstruct and critique those occurrences in the academic and scholarly cultural arena (Alexander, 2004b).

The kernel idea that I am suggesting turns on the following questions. Can performance ethnography be used to turn the tables not only on those constructed as "the other" but also on our collective cultural selves? Can performance ethnography be used to look at the very conditions under which ethnographers, scholars, teachers, and students labor, in order to discover, or rather uncover, the ways in which our talk about oppression and liberation of the other are not always the models that we use in developing and maintaining the communities in which we claim membership? Can we use performance ethnography to critically gaze back on our own practices? Can we use performance ethnography to explore the ways in which the mixed identities in any community (e.g., race, ethnicity, class, sex, sexuality) and the investments we have in maintaining these social identities often clash and rub against each other? These points of contact must be acknowledged and addressed sometime before we begin to cure the world.

In this way, maybe performance ethnography can be used to deconstruct disciplinary formations such as white studies, black studies, queer studies, and the varying machinations of identity politics that both center and decenter the vested interests of varying populations in the larger moral discourse of human interaction. Maybe, in some rather specific ways, under the rubric of *performing theory and embodied writing* (Madison, 1999), we can engage a close ethnographic excavation and performative engagement of these logics that undergird human sociality. Such an engagement might reveal how theoretical and academic logics format and foment particular social tensions and thereby sustain borders of difference, even as they purport to democratize. Examples include the following: (a) how the construction of commodity in white studies and black studies is the signifier for myths of nationality and identity that reconfirm problematic constructions of race, power, and division; (b) how queer studies/theory performs a resistance to regimes of the normal, and in turn generalizes concerns and experiences within an imagined community where there is still contestation over the very terms "gay" and "queer" as informed through issues of race, class, sexual practice, and desire.

I see my own work moving in these areas when issues of personal survival motivate scholarly production (Alexander, 2002a, 2003, 2004a, 2004b). More often, I am positioning myself as an affected party, as a community member, or as an indigenous ethnographer. Through autoethnography, I am exploring and sometimes exposing my own vulnerability to racial, gender, and cultural critique as a method of both understanding self and other, and self as other, while engaging in performances (written and embodied) that seek to transform the social and cultural conditions under which I live and labor.

Third, performance ethnography needs to develop legs, or walking feet, traveling the distance to particular audiences that might effect change, such as Boal's Legislative Theatre, or to those audiences that need an affective awareness of the issues. Following some of the more radical applications of Theatre of the Oppressed, Playback Theatre, and Community-Based Interactive Theatre(s), performance ethnography as an academic construct cannot sit in the ivory tower and invite audiences to come to it. It must go to those places and spaces where such critical performative intervention is needed to magnify issues, to *dynamize* movement—physical, social, and political (Boal)—and to engage audiences most in need of exercising and practicing voice. In this way, performance ethnography would thus develop projects that "reach outside the academy and are rooted in an ethic of reciprocity and exchange" (Conquergood, 2002, p. 152).

Fourth, in a literal move of *stepping into someone else's voice* and consequently his or her lived experience, maybe performance ethnography continues its direction toward cross-cultural and cross-racial performances by having people perform the narratives of others. The kind of work that is engaged by Olga Davis at the University of Arizona in staging events, leading up to and including the Tulsa Race Riots of 1965, might further spur on this impulse. The work includes her students in a long-term ethnographic research project and challenges them to perform aspects of research, race, resistance, and riots.

In many ways, Davis's pedagogical practice of also having students at the predominantly white university where she teaches perform actual slave narratives embarks on a form of performance ethnography that forces students into realms of historical knowing. They begin to think, as Denzin and Lincoln (1998) write, "historically, interactionally, and structurally." They begin "to make connections among lived experience, larger social, and cultural structures" that are made manifest in the current predicaments of race and culture (p. xi). This approach is centered in the performance of autobiography and the performance of biography, embodying the articulated and documented experiences of others as gathered through ethnographic processes or found texts.[19]

Fifth, we must strengthen the commitment of performance ethnography as a civic-minded moral discourse that encourages what Stephen Hartnett (1998) calls a form of "performative citizenship"—one in which the aesthetics of performance "move[s] beyond hypnotized individuality and voracious commodification to approach something closer to engaged cultural history" (p. 288). This type of cultural history, as both realms of individual/human experience and as shared legacies of pain and possibility, enacts citizenship as productive participation in the realm of human relations. In *Geographies of Learning*, Jill Dolan (2001a) takes on this argument to suggest that the arena and engaged practice of performance can create citizens and engage democracy as a participatory forum in which ideas and possibilities for social equity and justice are shared.

Performance ethnography can help us to understand the lived cultural experiences of others, but it also can help us to claim the joint culpability of history's legacy. It can then help us to strategize possibility, ways in which collective social action might lead to a more compatible human condition.

▣ Notes

1. See Lockford (1998, 2000) for a helpful discussion on performing constructed narratives or performing *the true in experience* or *the true to experience narrative.*

2. See Bacon (1979), Bacon and Breen (1961), Kleinau and McHughes (1980), and Yordon (1989) as germinal texts.

3. See Stern and Henderson (1993) for a good survey of this approach.

4. This is particularly noted in performance studies' most recent interest in "performative writing" or what Richardson (2000b) calls "creative analytic writing practices" (p. 941). See also Madison (1999), Pollock (1998c), Pelias (1999b), and L. Miller and Pelias (2001).

5. See Carlson (1996), Conquergood (2002), Pelias and VanOosting (1987), Strine, Long, and Hopkins (1990), and Stucky and Wimmer (2002) for more expanded surveys of the evolution of performance studies.

6. Conquergood tracks this movement through the work of Goffman (1959), Austin (1962), Searle (1969), Hymes (1975), Turner (1982), Bauman (1986), Turner and Turner (1988), and Bhabha (1994). He marks his original construction of this moment in Conquergood (1992).

7. See Phelan and Lane (1998) for the further charting of this trajectory.

8. Turner (1988) defines social dramas as units of aharmonic or disharmonic social processes, a rising in conflict situations. Typically, they have four main phases of public action: (a) breach of regular norm-governed social relations; (b) crisis, during which there is a tendency for the breach to widen; (c) redressive

action to resolve certain kinds of crisis or legitimate other modes of resolution; and (d) either reintegration of the disturbed social group or the social recognition and legitimization of irreparable schism between the contesting parties (pp. 74–75).

9. Van Maanen credits Barthes (1972) with the insight.

10. See Coco Fusco's (1994) description of her work with Guillermo Gómez-Peña and texts on the origin and impetus of performance art. Performance art is most often interested in the relationship between performance and identity, especially the visibility of those normally excluded by race, class, gender, or sexuality (see Mifflin, 1992, and T. Miller, Kushner, and McAdams, 2002).

11. In *Twilight: Los Angeles, 1992* (1994), Anna Deavere Smith engages the same process in interviewing and later performing people after the 1992 Los Angeles riots.

12. See Denzin's (1997) outlining of procedural types and texts of performance ethnography (pp. 90–125).

13. Corey cites Foucault (1982) for the construct of "reverse discourse."

14. Here Corey cites Stern and Henderson (1993, p. 35).

15. McLaren is citing Grossberg (1992, p. 394).

16. Giroux cites Raymond Williams (1989, p. 158) to help establish this argument.

17. The following is a summary of thoughts presented by Madison (1998, pp. 276–286).

18. Giroux cites Hall and Held (1990, pp. 8–9).

19. See Pineau (1992) for more detailed distinction between performance of autobiography and autobiographical performance.

References

Alcoff, L. (1991/1992). The problem of speaking for others. *Cultural Critique, 20,* 5–32.

Alexander, B. K. (1999). Moving toward a critical poetic response. *Theatre Topics, 9*(2), 107–126.

Alexander, B. K. (2000). Skin flint (or the garbage man's kid): A generative autobiographical performance based on Tami Spry's Tattoo stories. *Text and Performance Quarterly, 20*(1), 97–114.

Alexander, B. K. (2002a). The outsider (or *Invisible Man* all over again): Contesting the absented black gay body in queer theory (with apologies to Ralph Ellison). In W. Wright & S. Kaplan (Eds.), *The image of the outsider: Proceedings of the 2002 Society for the Interdisciplinary Study of Social Imagery conference* (pp. 308–315). Pueblo: University of Southern Colorado.

Alexander, B. K. (2002b). Performing culture and cultural performance in Japan: A critical (auto)ethnographic travelogue. *Theatre Annual: A Journal of Performance Studies, 55,* 1–28.

Alexander, B. K. (2003). Querying queer theory again (*Or queer theory as drag performance*). In G. A. Yep, K. E. Lovaas, & J. P. Elia (Eds.), *Queer theory and communication: From disciplining queers to queering the discipline(s)* (pp. 349–352). New York: Harrington Park Press.

Alexander, B. K. (2004a). Black face/white mask: The performative sustainability of whiteness. *Qualitative Inquiry, 10*(5), 647–672.

Alexander, B. K. (2004b). Passing, cultural performance, and individual agency: Performative reflections on black masculine identity. *Cultural Studies ↔ Critical Methodologies, 4*(3), 377–404.

Aronowitz, S., & Giroux, H. (1991). *Postmodern education: Politics, culture, and social criticism.* Minneapolis: University of Minnesota Press.

Austin, J. L. (1962). *How to do things with words.* London: Oxford University Press.

Bacon, W. A. (1979). *The art of interpretation* (3rd ed.). New York: Holt, Rinehart & Winston.

Bacon, W., & Breen, R. (1961). *Literature for interpretation.* New York: Holt, Rinehart & Winston.

Barthes, R. (1972). *Mythologies.* London: Paladin.

Bateson, M. C. (1993). Joint performance across cultures: Improvisation in a Persian garden. *Text and Performance Quarterly, 13,* 113–121.

Bauman, R. (1986). *Story, performance, event: Contextual studies of oral narratives.* Cambridge, UK: Cambridge University Press.

Becker, H. S., McCall, M. M., & Morris, L. V. (1989). Theatres and communities: Three scenes. *Social Problems, 36,* 93–116.

Bell, E. (2002). When half the world's a stage: A feminist excavation of Richard Schechner's theory of "actuals." *The Theatre Annual: A Journal of Performance Studies, 55,* 112–131.

Bhabha, H. (1994). *The location of culture.* New York: Routledge.

Boal, A. (1979). *Theater of the oppressed* (C. A. McBride & M.-O. Leal McBride, Trans.). New York: Urizen Books.

Boal, A. (1985). *Theatre of the oppressed* (C. A. McBride & M.-O. Leal McBride, Trans.). New York: Theatre Communication Group.

Boal, A. (1995). *The rainbow of desire: The Boal method theatre and therapy* (A. Jackson, Trans.). New York: Routledge.

Boal, A. (1998). *Legislative theatre: Using performance to make politics* (A. Jackson, Trans.). New York: Routledge.

Bochner, A. P. (1994). Perspectives on inquiry II: Theories and stories. In M. Knapp & G. R. Miller (Eds.), *The handbook of interpersonal communication* (pp. 21–41). Thousand Oaks, CA: Sage.

Bochner, A. P., & Ellis, C. (2002). *Ethnographically speaking: Autoethnography, literature, and aesthetics.* Walnut Creek, CA: AltaMira.

Brecht, B. (1964). *Brecht on theatre* (J. Willet, Trans.). New York: Hill.

Bruner, E. M. (1986). Experience and its expressions. In V. M. Turner & E. M. Bruner (Eds.), *The anthropology of experience* (pp. 3–30). Urbana: University of Illinois Press.

Burke, K. (1957). *The philosophy of literary form.* New York: Vintage Books.

Butler, J. (1990a). *Gender trouble: Feminism and the subversion of identity*. New York: Routledge.

Butler, J. (1990b). Performative acts and gender constitution: An essay in phenomenology and feminist theory. In S. E. Case (Ed.), *Performing feminisms: Feminist critical theory and theatre* (pp. 270–282). Baltimore: Johns Hopkins University Press.

Butler, J. (1993). *Bodies that matter: On the discursive limits of sex*. New York: Routledge.

Carlson, M. (1996). *Performance: A critical introduction.* London: Routledge.

Certeau, M. (1984). *The practice of everyday life.* (S. Rendall, Trans.). Berkeley: University of California Press.

Chambers, E. (2000). Applied ethnography. In N. K. Denzin & Y. S. Lincoln (Eds.), *Handbook of qualitative research* (2nd ed., pp. 851–869). Thousand Oaks, CA: Sage.

Chaney, D. (1994). *The cultural turn: Scene-setting essay in modern cultural history*. New York: Routledge.

Chesebro, J. W. (1998). Performance studies as paradox, culture, and manifesto: A future orientation. In S. J. Dailey (Ed.), *The future of performance studies: Visions and revisions* (pp. 310–319). Annandale, VA: National Communication Association.

Christians, C. G. (2000). Ethics and politics in qualitative research. In N. K. Denzin & Y. S. Lincoln (Eds.), *Handbook of qualitative research* (2nd ed., pp. 133–155). Thousand Oaks, CA: Sage.

Clifford, J. (1988). *The predicament of culture: Twentieth-century ethnography, literature, and art.* Cambridge, MA: Harvard University Press.

Clifford, J., & Marcus, G. E. (Eds.). (1986). *Writing culture: The poetics and politics of ethnography: A School of American Research advanced seminar*. Berkeley: University of California Press.

Cohen, R. (1988). Realism. In M. Banham (Ed.), *The Cambridge guide to theatre* (p. 815). Cambridge, UK: Cambridge University Press.

Conquergood, D. (1983). A sense of the other: Interpretation and ethnographic research. In I. Crouch (Ed.), *Proceedings of the seminar/conference on oral tradition* (pp. 148–155). Las Cruces: New Mexico State University.

Conquergood, D. (1985). Performing as a moral act: Ethical dimensions of the ethnography of performance. *Literature in Performance, 5,* 1–13.

Conquergood, D. (1986a). Performance and dialogical understanding: In quest of the other. In J. L. Palmber (Ed.), *Communication as performance* (pp. 30–37). Tempe: Arizona State University Press.

Conquergood, D. (1986b). Performing cultures: Ethnography, epistemology, and ethics. In E. Slembek (Ed.), *Miteinander sprechen and handein: Festschrift fur Hellmut Geissner* (pp. 55–147). Frankfurt: Scriptor.

Conquergood, D. (1988). Health Theatre in a Hmong refugee camp: Performance, communication and culture. *The Drama Review: A Journal of Performance Studies, 32*(3), 174–208.

Conquergood, D. (1989). Poetics, play, process and power: The performance turn in anthropology. *Text and Performance Quarterly, 9,* 82–88.

Conquergood, D. (1991). Rethinking ethnography: Towards a critical cultural politics. *Communication Monographs, 58,* 179–194.

Conquergood, D. (1992). Ethnography, rhetoric and performance. *Quarterly Journal of Speech, 78,* 80–97.

Conquergood, D. (1998). Beyond the text: Toward a performative cultural politics. In S. J. Dailey (Ed.), *The future of performance studies: Visions and revisions* (pp. 25–36). Annandale, VA: National Communication Association.

Conquergood, D. (2002). Performance studies: Interventions and radical research. *The Drama Review: A Journal of Performance Studies, 46*(2), 145–156.

Corey, F. C. (1998). The personal: Against the master narrative. In S. J. Dailey (Ed.), *The future of performance studies: Visions and revisions* (pp. 249–253). Annandale, VA: National Communication Association.

Denzin, N. K. (1992). The many faces of emotionality. In C. Ellis (Ed.), *Investigating subjectivity: Research on lived experience* (pp. 17–30). London: Sage.

Denzin, N. K. (1997). *Interpretive ethnography: Ethnographic practices for the 21st century.* Thousand Oaks, CA: Sage.

Denzin, N. K. (1999). Interpretive ethnography for the next century. *Journal of Contemporary Ethnography, 28*(5), 510–519.

Denzin, N. K. (2003). *Performance ethnography: Critical pedagogy and the politics of culture.* Thousand Oaks, CA: Sage.

Denzin, N. K., & Lincoln, Y. S. (1998). Introduction to this volume. In N. K. Denzin & Y. S. Lincoln (Eds.), *Strategies of qualitative inquiry* (pp. xi–xxii). Thousand Oaks, CA: Sage.

Diamond, E. (1996). Introduction. In E. Diamond (Ed.), *Performances and cultural politics* (pp. 1–12). New York: Routledge.

Dolan, J. (2001a). *Geographies of learning: Theory and practice, activism and performance.* Middletown, CT: Wesleyan University Press.

Dolan, J. (2001b). Performance, utopia, and the "Utopian performative." *Theatre Journal, 53*(3), 455–479.

Doyle, D. M. (2001). The role of witnessing in performance ethnography. *Iowa Journal of Communication, 33*(1/2), 22–37.

Ellis, C., & Bochner, A. P. (1996). *Composing ethnography: Alternative forms of qualitative writing.* Walnut Creek, CA: AltaMira.

Ellis, C., & Bochner, A. P. (2000). Autoethnography, personal narrative, reflexivity: Researcher as subject. In N. K. Denzin & Y. S. Lincoln (Eds.), *Handbook of qualitative research* (2nd ed., pp. 733–768). Thousand Oaks, CA: Sage.

Espinola, J. (1977). Oral interpretation performance: An act of publication. *Western Journal of Speech Communication, 41*(2), 90–97.

Fine, E. C., & Speer, J. H. (1992). Introduction. In E. C. Fine & J. H. Speer (Eds.), *Performance, culture, and identity* (pp. 1–22). Westport, CT: Praeger.

Fine, M., Weis, L., Weseen, S., & Wong, L. (2000). For whom? Qualitative research, representations, and social responsibilities. In N. K. Denzin & Y. S. Lincoln (Eds.), *Handbook of qualitative research* (2nd ed., pp. 107–131). Thousand Oaks, CA: Sage.

Fiske, J. (1994). Audiencing: Cultural practice and cultural studies. In N. K. Denzin & Y. S. Lincoln (Eds.), *Handbook of qualitative research* (pp. 189–198). Thousand Oaks, CA: Sage.

Foucault, M. (1982). The subject and power. *Critical Inquiry, 8,* 777–795.

Fox, J. (1986). *Acts of service: Spontaneity, commitment, tradition in the nonscripted theatre.* New Paltz, NY: Tusitala.

Fox, J., & Heinreich, D. (Eds.). (1999). *Gathering voices: Essays on playback theatre.* New Paltz, NY: Tusitala

Freire, P. (1985). *The politics of education: Culture, power, and liberation.* New York: Bergin & Garvey.

Freire, P. (1998). *Teachers as cultural workers: Letters to those who dare teach* (D. Macedo, D. Koike, & A. Oliveira, Trans.). Boulder, CO: Westview.

Freire, P. (1999). *Pedagogy of the oppressed.* New York: Continuum.

Fuoss, K. (1997). *Striking performance/performing strikes.* Jackson: University of Mississippi Press.

Fusco, C. (1994). The other history of intercultural performance. *The Drama Review: A Journal of Performance Studies, 38,* 143–167.

Garoian, C. R. (1999). *Performing pedagogy: Towards an art of politics.* New York: SUNY Press.

Geiger, D. (1973). Poetic realizing as knowing. *Quarterly Journal of Speech, 59,* 311–318.

Gentile, J. (1989). *A cast of one: One-person shows from the Chautauqua platform to the Broadway stage.* Urbana: University of Illinois Press.

Giroux, H. A. (2001). Cultural studies as performative politics. *Cultural Studies ↔ Critical Methodologies, 1*(1), 5–23.

Giroux, H. A., & McLaren, P. (1984). *Critical pedagogy, the state and cultural struggle.* New York: SUNY Press.

Giroux, H. A., & McLaren, P. (Eds.). (1994). *Between borders: Pedagogy and the politics of cultural studies.* New York: Routledge.

Giroux, H. A., & Shannon, P. (Eds.). (1997). *Education and cultural studies: Toward a performative practice.* New York: Routledge.

Goffman, E. (1959). *The presentation of self in everyday life.* Garden City, NY: Doubleday.

Goodall, H. L., Jr. (2000). *Writing the new ethnography.* Walnut Creek, CA: AltaMira.

Grossberg, L. (1992). *We gotta get out of this place: Popular conservatism and postmodern culture.* London: Routledge.

Grossberg, L. (1996). Toward a genealogy of the state of cultural studies. In C. Nelson & D. Parameshwar (Eds.), *Disciplinarity and dissent in cultural studies* (pp. 87–107). New York: Routledge.

Guss, D. M. (2000). *The festive state: Race, ethnicity, and nationalism as cultural performance.* Los Angeles: University of California Press.

Haedicke, S. C., & Nellhaus, T. (Eds.). (2001). *Performing democracy: International perspectives on urban community-based performance.* Ann Arbor: University of Michigan Press.

Hall, S., & Held, D. (1990). Citizens and citizenship. In S. Hall & M. Jacques (Eds.), *New times: The changing face of politics in the 1990s* (pp. 173–188). London: Verso.

Hamera, J. (1999). Editor's notes. *Text and Performance Quarterly, 19*(2), 106.

Hamera, J. (2000). The romance of monsters: Theorizing the virtuoso body. *Theatre Topics, 10*(2), 145–153.

Harrison-Pepper, S. (1999). Dramas of persuasion: Performance studies and interdisciplinary education. *Theatre Topics, 9*(2), 141–156.

Hartnett, S. (1998). Democracy is difficult: Poetry, prison, and performative citizenship. In S. J. Dailey (Ed.), *The future of performance studies: Visions and revisions* (pp. 287–297). Annandale, VA: National Communication Association.

Hopkins, M. F. (1981). From page to stage: The burden of proof. *Southern Speech Communication Journal, 47,* 1–9.

Hymes, D. (1975). Breakthrough into performance. In D. Ben-Amos & K. Goldstein (Eds.), *Folklore: Performance and communication* (pp. 11–74). The Hague: Mouton.

Jackson, S. (1993). Ethnography and the audition: Performance as ideological critique. *Text and Performance Quarterly, 13,* 21–43.

Jackson, S. (1998). White noises: In performing white, on writing performance. *The Drama Review: A Journal of Performance Studies, 42*(1), 90–97.

Jackson, S. (2000). *Lines of activity: Performance, historiography, Hull-House domesticity.* Ann Arbor: University of Michigan Press.

Jones, J. (1997). Sista docta: Performance as a critique of the academy. *The Drama Review: A Journal of Performance Studies, 41*(2), 51–67.

Jones, J. (2002). Performance ethnography: The role of embodiment in cultural authenticity. *Theatre Topics, 12*(1), 1–15.

Kapferer, B. (1986). Performance and the structuring of meaning and experience. In V. M. Turner & E. M. Bruner (Eds.), *The anthropology of experience* (pp. 188–203). Urbana: University of Illinois Press.

Kershaw, B. (1999). *The radical in performance: Between Brecht and Baudrillard.* London: Routledge.

Kirby, M. (1979). Autoperformance issues: An introduction. *The Drama Review: A Journal of Performance Studies, 23*(1), 2.

Kirshenblatt-Gimbett, B. (1998). *Destination culture: Tourism, museums, and heritage.* Berkeley: University of California Press.

Kleinau, M. L., & McHughes, J. L. (1980). *Theatres for literatures.* Sherman Oaks, CA: Alfred Publishing.

Langellier, K. M. (1989). Personal narratives: Perspectives on theory and research. *Text and Performance Quarterly, 9,* 243–276.

Langellier, K. M. (1998). Voiceless bodies, bodiless voices: The future of personal narrative performance. In S. J. Dailey (Ed.), *The future of performance studies: Visions and revisions* (pp. 207–213). Annandale, VA: National Communication Association.

Langellier, K. M. (1999). Personal narrative, performance, performativity: Two or three things I know for sure. *Text and Performance Quarterly, 19,* 125–144.

Lionnet, F. (1989). *Autobiographical voices: Race, gender, self-portraiture.* Ithaca, NY: Cornell University Press.

Lockford, L. (1998). Emergent issues in the performance of a border-transgressive narrative. In S. J. Dailey (Ed.), *The future of performance studies: Visions and revisions* (pp. 214–220). Annandale, VA: National Communication Association.

Lockford, L. (2000). An ethnographic ghost story: Adapting "What's a nice commodity like you doing in a spectacle like this?" *Text and Performance Quarterly, 20*(4), 402–415.

MaCaloon, H. R. (1984). *Rites, drama, festival, spectacle: Rehearsals toward a theory of cultural performance.* Philadelphia: Institute for the Study of Human Issues.

Madison, D. S. (1998). Performance, personal narratives, and the politics of possibility. In S. J. Dailey (Ed.), *The future of performance studies: Visions and revisions* (pp. 276–286). Annandale, VA: National Communication Association.

Madison, D. S. (1999). Performing theory/embodied writing. *Text and Performance Quarterly, 19,* 107–124.

McCall, M. M. (1993). *Not "just" a farmer and not just a "farm wife."* Unpublished performance script.

McCall, M. M. (2000). Performance ethnography: A brief history and some advice. In N. K. Denzin & Y. S. Lincoln (Eds.), *Handbook of qualitative research* (2nd ed., pp. 421–433). Thousand Oaks, CA: Sage.

McCall, M., & Becker, H. S. (1990). Performance science. *Social Problems, 32,* 117–132.

McLaren, P. (1985). The ritual dimensions of resistance: Clowning and symbolic inversion. *Journal of Education, 167*(2), 84–97.

McLaren., P. (1989). On ideology and education: Critical pedagogy and the cultural politics of resistance. In H. Giroux & P. McLaren (Eds.), *Critical pedagogy, the state and cultural struggle* (pp. 174–202). Albany: State University of New York Press.

McLaren, P. (1993). *Schooling as a ritual performance: Towards a political economy of educational symbols and gestures.* New York: Routledge.

McLaren, P. (1994). *Life in school: An introduction to critical pedagogy in the foundations of education.* New York: Longman.

McLaren, P. (1997). *Revolutionary multiculturalism: Pedagogies of dissent for the new millennium.* Boulder, CO: Westview.

McLaren, P. (1998). *Life in school: An introduction to critical pedagogy in the foundations of education* (3rd ed.). New York: Longman.

McLaren, P. (2000). *Che Guevara, Paulo Freire, and the pedagogy of revolution.* New York: Rowman & Littlefield.

McLaren, P., & Lankshear, C. (1994). *Politics of liberation: Paths from Freire.* New York: Routledge.

Merrill, L. (1999). *When Romeo was a woman: Charlotte Cushman and her circle of female spectators.* Ann Arbor: University of Michigan.

Mienczakowski, J. (1992). *Synching out loud. A journey into illness.* Brisbane, Australia: Griffith University.

Mienczakowski, J. (1994). Reading and writing research. *NADUE Journal, 18,* 45–54.

Mienczakowski, J. (1995). The theatre of ethnography: The reconstruction of ethnography into theatre with emancipatory potential. *Qualitative Inquiry, 1*(3), 360–375.

Mienczakowski, J. (2001). Ethnodrama: Performed research: Limitations and potential. In P. Atkinson, A. Coffey, S. Delamont, J. Lofland, & L. Lofland (Eds.), *Handbook of ethnography* (pp. 468–476). London: Sage.

Mienczakowski, J., & Morgan, S. (1993). *Busting: The challenge of the drought spirit.* Brisbane, Australia: Griffith University.

Mifflin, M. (1992). Performance art: What is it and where is it going? *Art News, 91*(4), 88–89.

Miller, L., & Pelias, R. (2001). *The green window: Proceedings of the Giant City conference on performative writing.* Carbondale: Southern Illinois University Press.

Miller, T., Kushner, T., & McAdams, D. A. (2002). *Body blows: Six performances.* Madison: University of Wisconsin Press.

Mohanty, S. P. (1989). Us and them: On the philosophical bases of political criticism. *Yale Journal of Criticism, 2*(2), 1–31.

Neumann, M. (1996). Collecting ourselves at the end of the century. In C. Ellis & A. P. Bochner (Eds.), *Composing ethnography: Alternative forms of qualitative writing* (pp. 172–198). Walnut Creek, CA: AltaMira.

Nudd, D. M. (1995). The postmodern heroine(s) of Lardo Weeping. *Text and Performance Quarterly, 15,* 24–43.

O'Brien, J. (1987). Performance as criticism: Discoveries and documentation through enactment. *Communication Studies, 40,* 189–201.

Paget, M. A. (1990). Performing the text. *Journal of Contemporary Ethnography, 19,* 136–155.

Paget, M. A. (1993). *A complex sorrow* (M. L. DeVault, Ed.). Philadelphia: Temple University Press.

Park-Fuller, L. (2003). Audiencing the audience: Playback theatre, performative writing, and social activism. *Text and Performance Quarterly, 23*(3), 288–310.

Park-Fuller, L., & Olsen, T. (1983). Understanding what we know: Yonnondio: From the thirties. *Literature in Performance, 4,* 65–77.

Pelias, R. (1999a). *Performance studies: The interpretation of aesthetic texts* (2nd ed.). Dubuque, IA: Kendall/Hunt.

Pelias, R. (1999b). *Writing performance: Poeticizing the researcher's body.* Carbondale: Southern Illinois University Press.

Pelias, R., & VanOosting, J. (1987). A paradigm for performance studies. *Quarterly Journal of Speech, 73,* 219–231.

Phelan, P. (1998). Introduction. In P. Phelan & J. Lane (Eds.), *The ends of performance* (pp. 1–19). New York: New York University Press.

Phelan, P., & Lane, J. (Eds.). (1998). *The ends of performance.* New York University Press.

Pineau, E. L. (1992). A mirror of her own: Anais Nin's autobiographical performances. *Text and Performance Quarterly, 12,* 97–112.

Pineau, E. L. (1995). Re-casting rehearsal: Making a case for production as research. *Journal of the Illinois Speech and Theatre Association, 46,* 43–52.

Pineau, E. L. (1998). Performance studies across the curriculum: Problems, possibilities, and projections. In S. J. Dailey (Ed.), *The future of performance studies: Visions and revisions* (pp. 128–135). Annandale, VA: National Communication Association.

Pineau, E. (2002). Critical performative pedagogy. In N. Stucky & C. Wimmer (Eds.), *Teaching performance studies* (pp. 41–54). Carbondale: Southern Illinois University Press.

Pollock, D. (1990). Telling the told: Performing *Like a family. Oral History Review, 18,* 1–36.

Pollock, D. (1998a). *Exceptional spaces: Essays in performance and history.* Chapel Hill: University of North Carolina Press.

Pollock, D. (Ed.). (1998b). Introduction. In *Exceptional spaces: Essays in performance and history* (pp. 1–45). Chapel Hill: University of North Carolina Press.

Pollock, D. (1998c). Performing writing. In P. Phelan & J. Lane (Eds.), *The ends of performance* (pp. 73–103). New York: New York University Press.

Pollock, D. (1998d). A response to Dwight Conquergood's essay "Beyond the text: Toward a performative cultural politics." In S. J. Dailey (Ed.), *The future of performance studies: Visions and revisions* (pp. 37–46). Annandale, VA: National Communication Association.

Reed-Danahay, D. E. (Ed.). (1997). *Auto/ethnography: Rewriting the self and the social.* New York: Berg.

Richardson, L. (1997). *Fields of play: Constructing an academic life.* New Brunswick, NJ: Rutgers University Press.

Richardson, L. (2000a). Evaluating ethnography. *Qualitative inquiry, 6*(2), 253–255.

Richardson, L. (2000b). Writing: A method of inquiry. In N. K. Denzin & Y. S. Lincoln (Eds.), *Handbook of qualitative research* (2nd ed., pp. 923–948). Thousand Oaks, CA: Sage.

Richardson, L., & Lockridge, E. (1991). The sea monster: An ethnographic drama. *Symbolic Interaction, 14,* 335–340.

Roach, J. (1993). *The player's passion: Studies in the science of acting.* Ann Arbor: University of Michigan Press.

Roach, J. (2002). Theatre studies/cultural studies/ performance studies: The three unities. In N. Stucky & C. Wimmer (Eds.), *Teaching performance studies* (pp. 33–40). Carbondale: Southern Illinois University Press.

Román, D. (1998). *Acts of intervention: Performance, gay culture, and AIDS.* Bloomington: Indiana University Press.

Rosaldo, R. (1989). *Culture and truth: The remaking of social analysis.* Boston: Beacon.

Salas, J. (1996). *Improvising real life: Personal story in playback theatre* (Rev. ed.). New Paltz, NY: Tusitala.

Samovar, L. A., & Porter, R. E. (1994). *Intercultural communication: A reader.* Belmont, CA: Wadsworth.

Schechner, R. (1965). *Rites and symbols of initiation.* New York: Harper.

Schechner, R. (1977). *Essays on performance theory, 1970–1976.* New York: Drama Book Specialists.

Schechner, R. (1985). *Between theater and anthropology.* Philadelphia: University of Pennsylvania Press.

Schechner, R. (1986). Magnitudes of performance. In V. M. Turner & E. M. Bruner (Eds.), *The anthropology of experience* (pp. 344–369). Urbana: University of Illinois Press.

Schechner, R. (1988). *Performance theory* (Rev. and exp. ed.). New York: Routledge.

Schneider, J. (2002). Reflexive/diffractive ethnography. *Cultural studies ↔ Critical Methodologies, 2,* 460–482.

Schutzman, M., & Cohen-Cruz, J. (Eds.). (1994). *Playing Boal: Theatre, therapy, activism.* New York: Routledge.

Searle, J. (1969). *Speech acts.* New York: Cambridge University Press.

Shor, I. (1992). *Culture wars: School and society in the conservative restoration.* Chicago: University of Chicago Press.

Siegel, T., & Conquergood, D. (Producers & Directors). (1985). *Between two worlds: The Hmong shaman in America* [Video documentary].

Siegel, T., & Conquergood, D. (Producers & Directors). (1990). *The heart broken in half* [Video documentary].

Singer, M. (1972). *When a great tradition modernizes: An anthropological approach to Indian civilization.* New York: Praeger.

Smith, A. D. (1993). *Fires in the mirror: Crown Heights, Brooklyn, and other identities.* Garden City, NY: Anchor.

Smith, A. D. (1994). *Twilight: Los Angeles, 1992.* Garden City, NY: Anchor.

Sparkes, A. C. (2002). Autoethnography: Self-indulgence or something more? In A. P. Bochner & C. Ellis. (Eds.), *Ethnographically speaking: Autoethnography, literature, and aesthetics* (pp. 209–232). Walnut Creek, CA: AltaMira.

Spradley, J. P., & McCurdy, D. W. (1972). *The cultural experience: Ethnography in complex society.* Prospect Heights, IL: Waveland.

Spry, T. (1997). Skins: A daughter's (re)construction of cancer: A performative autobiography. *Text and Performance Quarterly, 17,* 361–365.

Spry, T. (2001). Performing autoethnography: An embodied methodical praxis. *Qualitative Inquiry, 7,* 706–732.

Stern, C. S., & Henderson, B. (1993). *Performance: Texts and contexts.* New York: Longman.

Strine, M. S. (1998). Mapping the "cultural turn" in performance studies. In S. J. Dailey (Ed.), *The future of performance studies: Visions and revisions* (pp. 3–9). Annandale, VA: National Communication Association.

Strine, M., Long, B., & Hopkins, M. F. (1990). Research in interpretation and performance studies. In G. Phillips & J. Wood (Eds.), *Speech communication: Essays to commemorate the seventy-fifth anniversary of the Speech Communication Association* (pp. 181–204). Carbondale: Southern Illinois University Press.

Stucky, N., & Wimmer, C. (2002). *Teaching performance studies.* Carbondale: Southern Illinois University Press.

Supriya, K. E. (2001). Evocation of an enactment in *Apna Ghar*: Performing ethnographic self-reflexivity. *Text and Performance Quarterly, 21,* 225–246.

Taylor, J. (1987). Documenting performance knowledge: Two narrative techniques in Grace Paley's fiction. *Southern Speech Communication Journal, 53,* 67–79.

Tedlock, B. (2000). Ethnography and ethnographic representation. In N. K. Denzin & Y. S. Lincoln (Eds.), *Handbook of qualitative research* (2nd ed., pp. 455–486). Thousand Oaks, CA: Sage.

Tedlock, D. (1983). On the translation of style in oral narrative. In B. Swann (Ed.), *Smoothing the ground: Essays on Native American oral literature* (pp. 57–77). Berkeley: University of California Press.

Turner, V. (1974). *Dramas, fields, and metaphors: Symbolic action in human society.* Ithaca, NY: Cornell University Press.

Turner, V. (1980). Social dramas and stories about them. *Critical Inquiry, 7*(1), 141–168.

Turner, V. (1982). *From ritual to theatre.* New York: Performing Arts Journal Publications.

Turner, V. (1988). *The anthropology of performance.* New York: Performing Arts Journal Publications.

Turner, V., & Turner, E. (1982). Performing ethnography. *The Drama Review: A Journal of Performance Studies, 26,* 33–50.

Turner, V., & Turner, E. (1988). Performance ethnography. In V. Turner, *The anthropology of performance* (pp. 139–155). New York: Performing Arts Journal Publications.

Valentine, K. B. (1998). Ethical issues in the transcription of personal narrative. In S. J. Dailey (Ed.), *The future of performance studies: Visions and revisions* (pp. 221–225). Annandale, VA: National Communication Association.

Valentine, K. B., & Valentine, E. (1992). Performing culture through narration: A Gallegan storyteller. In E. Fine & J. H. Speer (Eds.), *Performance, culture, and identity* (pp. 181–205). New York: Praeger.

Van Erven, E. (1993). *The playful revolution: Theatre and liberation in Asia.* Bloomington: Indiana University Press.

Van Maanen, J. (1988). *Tales of the field: On writing ethnography.* Chicago: University of Chicago Press.

Van Maanen, J. (Ed.). (1995). *Representation in ethnography.* Thousand Oaks, CA: Sage.

Whisnant, D. (1983). *All that is native and fine: The politics of culture in an American region.* Chapel Hill: University of North Carolina Press.

Williams, R. (1989). Adult education and social change. In *What I came to say* (pp. 157–166). London: Hutchinson-Radus.

Wirth, J. (1994). *Interactive acting: Acting, improvisation, and interacting for audience participatory theatre.* Fall Creek, OR: Fall Creek Press.

Wolcott, H. F. (1999). *Ethnography: A way of seeing.* Walnut Creek, CA: AltaMira.

Wolf, S. (2002). *A problem like Maria: Gender and sexuality in the American musical.* Ann Arbor: University of Michigan Press.

Worley, D. (1998). Is critical performative pedagogy practical? In S. J. Dailey (Ed.), *The future of performance studies: Visions and revisions* (pp. 136–144). Annandale, VA: National Communication Association.

Yordon, J. (1989). *Roles in interpretation* (2nd ed.). Dubuque, IA: Wm. C. Brown.

17

QUALITATIVE CASE STUDIES

Robert E. Stake

Case studies are a common way to do qualitative inquiry. Case study research is neither new nor essentially qualitative. Case study is not a methodological choice but a choice of what is to be studied. If case study research is more humane or in some ways transcendent, it is because the researchers are so, not because of the methods. By whatever methods, we choose to study *the case*. We could study it analytically or holistically, entirely by repeated measures or hermeneutically, organically or culturally, and by mixed methods—but we concentrate, at least for the time being, on the case. The focus in this chapter is a qualitative concentration on the case.

The physician studies the child because the child is ill. The child's symptoms are both qualitative and quantitative. The physician's record of the child is more quantitative than qualitative. The social worker studies the child because the child is neglected. The symptoms of neglect are both qualitative and quantitative. The formal record that the social worker keeps is more qualitative than quantitative.[1] In many professional and practical fields, cases are studied and recorded. As a form of research, case study is defined by interest in an individual case, not by the methods of inquiry used.

A majority of researchers doing casework call their studies by some other name. Howard Becker, for example, when asked (Simons, 1980) what he called his own studies, reluctantly said, "Fieldwork," adding that such labels contribute little to the understanding of what researchers do. The name "case study" is emphasized by some of us because it draws attention to the question of what specially can be learned about the single case. That epistemological question is the driving question of this chapter: What can be learned about the single case? I will emphasize designing the study to optimize understanding of the case rather than to generalize beyond it.

For a research community, case study optimizes understanding by pursuing scholarly research questions. It gains credibility by thoroughly triangulating the descriptions and interpretations, not just in a single step but continuously

Author's Note. This revision of my chapter in the 2000 second edition of this *Handbook* continues to draw heavily from papers on *What Is a Case?*, edited by Charles Ragin and Howard Becker (1992). Editorial review by Rita Davis, Norman Denzin, and Yvonna Lincoln is herewith acknowledged.

throughout the period of study. For a qualitative research community, case study concentrates on experiential knowledge of the case and close attention to the influence of its social, political, and other contexts. For almost any audience, optimizing understanding of the case requires meticulous attention to its activities. These five requirements—issue choice, triangulation, experiential knowledge, contexts, and activities—will be discussed in this chapter.

▣ The Singular Case

A case may be simple or complex. It may be a child or a classroom of children or an event, a happening, such as a mobilization of professionals to study a childhood condition. It is one among others. In any given study, we will concentrate on the one. The time we may spend concentrating our inquiry on the one may be long or short, but while we so concentrate, we are engaged in case study.

Custom has it that not everything is a case. A child may be a case, easy to specify. A doctor may be a case. But *his or her doctoring* probably lacks the specificity, the boundedness, to be called a case. As topics of inquiry, ethnomethodologists study *methods*, such as methods of doctoring, methods of cooking, examining how things get done, and the work and play of people (Garfinkel, 1967). Coming to understand a case usually requires extensive examining of how things get done, but the prime referent in case study is the case, not the methods by which the case operates. An Agency (e.g., nongovernmental organization) may be a case. But the *reasons* for child neglect or the *policies* of dealing with neglectful parents seldom will be considered a case. We think of those topics as generalities rather than specificities. The case is a specific One.[2]

If we are moved to study it, the case is almost certainly going to be a functioning body. The case is a "bounded system" (Flood, as reported in Fals Borda, 1998). In the social sciences and human services, most cases have working parts and purposes; many have a self. Functional or dysfunctional, rational or irrational, the case is a system.

It is common to recognize that certain features are within the system, within the boundaries of the case, and other features outside. In ways, the activity is patterned. Coherence and sequence are there to be found. Some outside features are significant as context. William Goode and Paul Hatt (1952) observed that it is not always easy for the case researcher to say where the child ends and where the environment begins. But boundedness and activity patterns nevertheless are useful concepts for specifying the case (Stake, 1988).

Ultimately, we may be interested in a general phenomenon or a population of cases more than in the individual case, and we cannot understand a given case without knowing about other cases. But while we are studying it, our meager resources are concentrated on trying to understand *its* complexities. Later in this chapter, we will talk about comparing two or more cases. We may simultaneously carry on more than one case study, but each case study is a concentrated inquiry into a single case.

Charles Ragin (1992) has emphasized the question of "What is it a case of?" as if "membership in" or "representation of" something else were the main consideration in case study. He referred to the casework of Michel Wieviorka (1988) on terrorism. Ragin and his coeditor, Howard Becker (1992), were writing for the social scientist seeking theoretical generalization, justifying the study of the particular only if it serves an understanding of grand issues or explanations. They recognized that even in formal experimentation and statistical survey work, there is interest in the illustrative or deviant case. But historians, program evaluators, institutional researchers, and practitioners in all professions are interested in the individual case without necessarily caring what it is a case of. This is intrinsic case study.

Even if my definition of the study of cases were agreed upon,[3] and it is not, the terms "case" and "study" defy full specification (Kemmis, 1980). A case study is both a process of inquiry about the case and the product of that inquiry. Lawrence Stenhouse (1984) advocated calling the product a "case record," and occasionally we shall, but the practice of calling the final report a "case study" is widely established.

Here and there, researchers will call anything they please a case study,[4] but the more the object of study is a specific, unique, bounded system, the greater the usefulness of the epistemological rationales described in this chapter.

To move beyond terminology to method, I introduce Figure 17.1, a sketch of a plan for a case study. This was an early plan made by a small team of early childhood education specialists led by Natalia Sofiy in Ukraine. The case they chose was a boy in the Step by Step child-centered program for inclusion of children with disability in regular classrooms. They used Figure 17.1 to identify content and tasks, selecting three activities to be observed and noting several interviews needed. The researchers were deeply interested in the case but intended to use the report to illustrate their work throughout the country. With such further purpose, I call their research an *instrumental* case study.

Intrinsic and Instrumental Interest in Cases

I find it useful to identify three types of case study. I call a study an *intrinsic case study* if the study is undertaken because, first and last, one wants better understanding of this particular case. It is not undertaken primarily because the case represents other cases or because it illustrates a particular trait or problem, but instead because, in all its particularity *and* ordinariness, this case itself is of interest. The researcher at least temporarily subordinates other curiosities so that the stories of those "living the case" will be teased out. The purpose is not to come to understand some abstract construct or generic phenomenon, such as literacy or teenage drug use or what a school principal does. The purpose is not theory building—though at other times the researcher may do just that. Study is undertaken because of an intrinsic interest in, for example, this particular child, clinic, conference, or curriculum. Books illustrating intrinsic case study include the following:

The Education of Henry Adams (1918), an autobiography,

God's Choice (1986) by Alan Peshkin,

Bread and Dreams (1982) by Barry MacDonald, Clem Adelman, Saville Kushner, and Rob Walker,[5]

An Aberdeenshire Village Propaganda (1889) by Robert Smith, and

The Swedish School System (1984) by Britta Stenholm.

I use the term *instrumental case study* if a particular case is examined mainly to provide insight into an issue or to redraw a generalization. The case is of secondary interest, it plays a supportive role, and it facilitates our understanding of something else. The case still is looked at in depth, its contexts scrutinized and its ordinary activities detailed, but all because this helps us pursue the external interest. The case may be seen as typical of other cases or not. (In a later section, I will discuss when typicality is important.) Here the choice of case is made to advance understanding of that other interest. We simultaneously have several interests, particular and general. There is no hard-and-fast line distinguishing intrinsic case study from instrumental, but rather a zone of combined purpose. Writings illustrating instrumental case study include the following:

"Campus Response to a Student Gunman" (1995) by Kelly Asmussen and John Creswell,

Boys in White (1961) by Howard Becker, Blanche Geer, Everett Hughes, and Anselm Strauss,

On the Border of Opportunity: Education, Community, and Language at the U.S.-Mexico Line (1998) by Marleen Pugach, and

"A Nonreader Becomes a Reader: A Case Study of Literacy Acquisition by a Severely Disabled Reader" (1994) by Sandra McCormick.

When there is even less interest in one particular case, a number of cases may be studied jointly in order to investigate a phenomenon, population, or general condition. I call this *multiple case study* or *collective case study*.[6] It is instrumental study extended

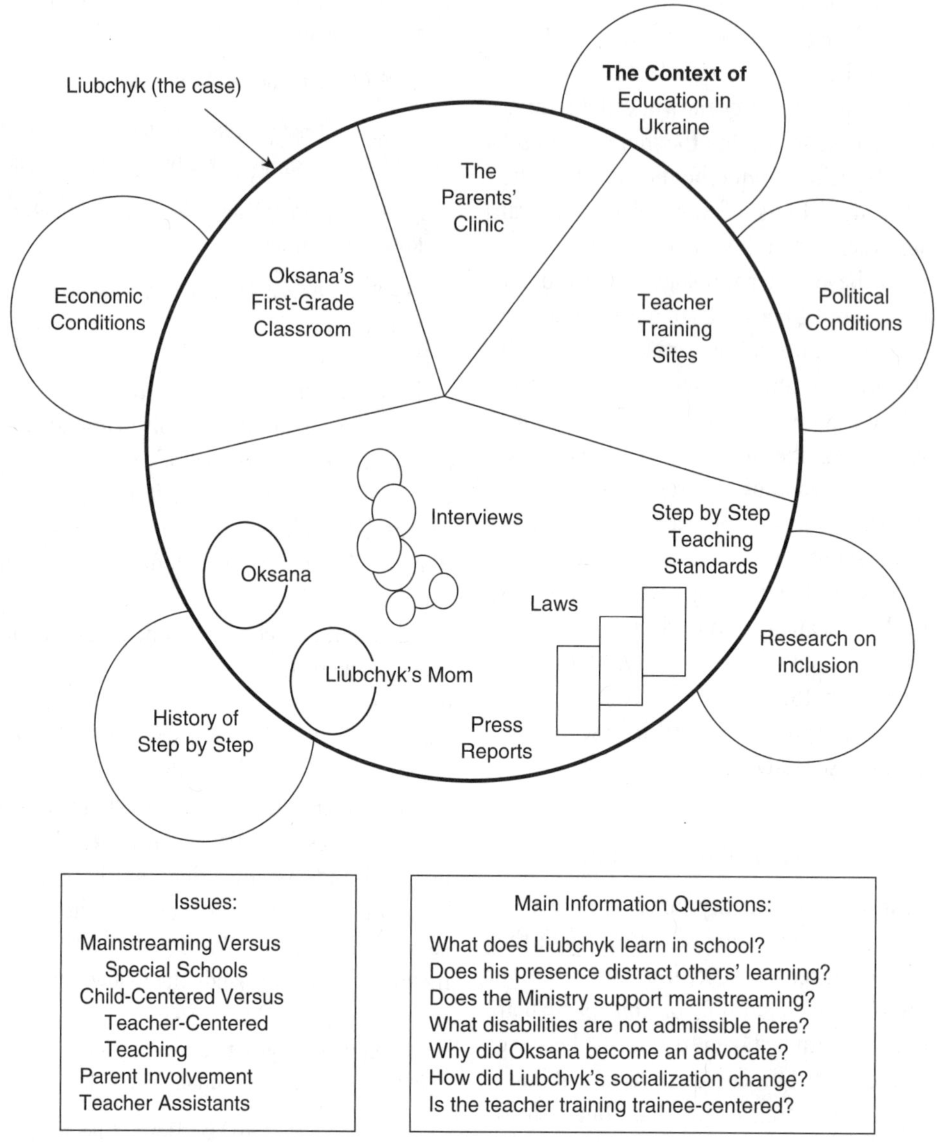

Figure 17.1. Plan for the Ukraine Case Study

to several cases. Individual cases in the collection may or may not be known in advance to manifest some common characteristic. They may be similar or dissimilar, with redundancy and variety each important. They are chosen because it is believed that understanding them will lead to better understanding, and perhaps better theorizing, about a still larger collection of cases. Illustrations of collective case study include the following:

Teachers' Work (1985) by Robert Connell,

"Researching Practice Settings" (of medical clinics) by Benjamin Crabtree and William Miller in their edited volume *Doing Qualitative Research* (1999),

Savage Inequalities (1991) by Jonathan Kozol,

Bold Ventures: Patterns Among U.S. Innovations in Science and Mathematics Education (1997) edited by Senta Raisin and Edward Britton, and

"The Dark Side of Organizations" (1999) by Diane Vaughan.

Reports and authors often do not fit neatly into the three categories. I see these three as useful for thinking about purpose. Alan Peshkin responded to my classification of his book *God's Choice* (1986) by saying "I mean to present my case so that it can be read with interest in the case itself, but I always have another agenda—to learn from the case about some class of things. Some of what that will be remains an emergent matter for a long time" (personal communication).

For this fine work, for 3 years Peshkin studied a single school, Bethany Baptist Academy. Until the final chapter, he did not tell the reader about matters of importance to him, particularly unfair treatment of ethnic minorities. The first order of business was to understand the case. The immediate, if not ultimate, interest was intrinsic. The methods Peshkin used centered on the case, only later taking up his abiding concern for community, freedom, and survival.

Other typologies of case study have been offered. Harrison White (1992) categorized social science casework according to three purposes: case studies for identity, explanation, or control. Historians and political scientists regularly examine a singular episode or movement or era, such as Norman Gottwald (1979) did in his study of the emergence of Jewish identity. I choose to call these studies case studies when the episode or relationship—however complex, impacting, and bounded—is easily thought of as organic and systemic, heavy with purpose and self.

It is good to recognize that there is a common form of case study used in teaching to illustrate a point, a condition, a category—something important for instruction (Kennedy, 1979). For decades, professors in law schools and business schools have paraded cases in this manner. For staff development and management training, such reports constitute the articles of the *Journal of Case Research*, a key publication of the North American Case Research Association. Used for instruction and consultation, they come from pedagogically oriented instrumental case study.

Biography has its own history. William Tierney (2000) noted that, like case study, biography calls for special attention to chronological structures and to procedures for the protection of human subjects. Similarly, television documentaries, many of them easily classifiable as case studies, require their own methods. In law, the *case* has a special definition: The practice of law itself could be called case study. The work of ethnographers, critical theorists, institutional demographers, and many others has conceptual and stylistic patterns that not only amplify the taxonomy but also extend the foundation for case study research in the social sciences and social services. My purpose here in categorization is not taxonomic but to emphasize variation in concern for and methodological orientation to *the case*, thus focusing on three types: intrinsic, instrumental, and collective.

Seeking the Particular More Than the Ordinary

Case researchers seek out both what is common and what is particular about the case, but the end product of the research regularly portrays more of the uncommon (Stouffer, 1941), drawing all at once from

1. the nature of the case, particularly its activity and functioning;
2. its historical background;
3. its physical setting;
4. other contexts, such as economic, political, legal, and aesthetic;
5. other cases through which this case is recognized; and
6. those informants through whom the case can be known.

To study the case, to probe its particularity, qualitative case researchers gather data on all the above.

Case uniqueness traditionally has not been a choice ingredient of scientific theory. Case study research has been constrained even by qualitative methodologists, who grant less than full regard to study of the particular (Denzin, 1989; Glaser & Strauss, 1967; Herriott & Firestone, 1983; Yin, 1984). These and other social scientists have written about case study as if intrinsic study of a particular case were not as important as studies intended to obtain generalizations pertaining to a population of cases.[7] Some have emphasized case study as typification of other cases, as exploration leading up to generalization-producing studies, or as an occasional early step in theory building. At least as I see it, case study method has been too little honored as the intrinsic study of a valued particular, as it is in biography, institutional self-study, program evaluation, therapeutic practice, and many lines of work. In the 1994 first edition of this *Handbook*, I wrote, "insistence on the ultimacy of theory building appears to be diminishing in qualitative social science" (p. 238), but now I am not so sure.

Still, even intrinsic case study can be seen as a small step toward grand generalization (Campbell, 1975; Flyvbjerg, 2001; Vaughan, 1992), especially in a case that runs counter to a rule. But generalization should not be emphasized in all research (Feagin et al., 1991; Simons, 1980). Damage occurs when the commitment to generalize or to theorize runs so strong that the researcher's attention is drawn away from features important for understanding the case itself.[8] The case study researcher faces a strategic decision in deciding how much and how long the complexities of the case should be studied. Not everything about the case can be understood—so how much needs to be? Each researcher has choices to make.

Organizing Around Issues

A case study has (as has research of all kinds) some form of conceptual structure. Even an intrinsic case study is organized around a small number of research questions. Issues are not information questions, such as "Who initiated their advocacy of regional forestry planning?" or "How was their hiring policy announced?" The issues or themes are questions such as "In what ways did their changes in hiring policy require a change in performance standards?" or "Did the addiction therapy, originally developed for male clients, need reconceptualization for women?"

Issues are complex, situated, problematic relationships. They pull attention both to ordinary experience and also to the disciplines of knowledge, such as sociology, economics, ethics, or literary criticism. Seeking a different purview from that of most designers of experiments and testers of hypotheses, qualitative case researchers orient to complexities connecting ordinary practice in natural habitats to a few abstractions and concerns of the academic disciplines. This broader purview is applied to the single case, leaving it as the focus, yet generalization and proof (Becker, 1992) linger in the mind of the researcher. A tension exists.[9]

The two issues used as examples two paragraphs back were written for a particular case. A more general question would be "Does a change in hiring policy away from affirmative action require change in performance standards?" or "Does addiction therapy originally developed for male clients need reconceptualization for women?" Whether stated for generalization or for particularization, these organizing themes should serve to deepen understanding of the specific case.

Starting with a topical concern, researchers pose *foreshadowed problems*,[10] concentrate on issue-related observations, interpret patterns of data, and reform the issues as assertions. One transformation experienced in my work in program evaluation is illustrated in Figure 17.2, with an issue for a hypothetical case study of a music education program.

The selection of key issues is crucial. Researchers follow their preference for or obligation to intrinsic or instrumental study. They ask, "Which issue questions bring out our concerns? Which would be the dominant theme?" To maximize understanding of the case, they ask, "Which issues seek out compelling uniquenesses?" For an evaluation study, they ask, "Which issues help reveal merits and shortcomings?" Some researchers raise social justice issues (House & Howe, 1999). In general, they ask, "Which issues facilitate the planning and activities of inquiry?"

1. Topical Issue: The goals of the music education program.
2. Foreshadowed Problem: The majority of the community supports the present emphasis on band, chorus, and performances, but a few teachers and community leaders prefer a more intellectual emphasis, for example, history, literature, and critical review of music.
3. Issue Under Development: What are the pros and cons of having this teaching staff teach music theory and music as a discipline in courses required of everyone?
4. Assertion: As a whole, this community was opposed to providing the extra funding required to provide intellectually based school music.

Figure 17.2. An Example of Issue Evolution in a Study

Issues are chosen partly in terms of what can be learned within the opportunities for study. They will be chosen differently depending on the purpose of the study, and differently by different researchers. One might say a personal contract is drawn between researcher and phenomenon. Researchers ask, "What can be learned *here* that a reader needs to know?"

The issues used to organize the study may or may not be the ones used to report the case to others. Some cases will be structured by need for information, raising little debate. For example, what led to the change in operating policy? or "Has performance quality been dropping?" Issues often serve to draw attention to important functioning of the case in a situation of stress, as well as to tease out more of its interaction with contexts.

Contexts

The case to be studied is a complex entity located in a milieu or situation embedded in a number of contexts or backgrounds. Historical context is almost always of interest, but so are cultural and physical contexts. Other contexts often of interest are the social, economic, political, ethical, and aesthetic.

The case is singular, but it has subsections (e.g., production, marketing, sales departments), groups (e.g., patients, nurses, administrators), occasions (e.g., work days, holidays, days near holidays), dimensions, and domains—many so well-populated that they need to be sampled. Each of these may have its own contexts, and the contexts may go a long way toward making relationships understandable. Qualitative case study calls for the examination of these complexities. Yvonna Lincoln and Egon Guba (2000) pointed out that much qualitative research is based on a view that social phenomena, human dilemmas, and the nature of cases are situational, revealing experiential happenings of many kinds.

Qualitative researchers sometimes are oriented toward *causal explanation* of events (Becker, 1992) but more often tend to perceive events as Tolstoy did in *War and Peace*—multiply sequenced, multiply contextual, and coincidental more than causal. Many find the search for cause as simplistic. They describe instead the sequence and coincidence of events, interrelated and contextually bound, purposive but questionably determinative. They favor inquiry designs for describing the diverse activities of the case. Doing case studies does not require examination of diverse issues and contexts, but that is the way that most qualitative researchers do them.

The Study

Perhaps the simplest rule for method in qualitative casework is this: "Place your best intellect into the thick of what is going on." The brainwork ostensibly is observational, but more critically, it is *reflective*.[11] In being ever-reflective, the researcher is committed to pondering the impressions, deliberating on recollections and records—but not necessarily following the conceptualizations of theorists, actors, or audiences (Carr & Kemmis, 1986). Local meanings are important, foreshadowed meanings are important, and readers' consequential meanings are important. In Figure 17.1, activities in the first-grade classrooms, parents' clinic, and teacher training sites are to be described and interpreted. The case researcher digs into meanings, working to relate them to contexts and experience. In each instance, the work is reflective.[12]

If we typify qualitative casework, we see data sometimes precoded but continuously interpreted, on first encounter and again and again. Records and tabulations are perused not only for classification and pattern recognition but also for "criss-crossed" reflection (Spiro, Vispoel, Schmitz, Samarapungavan, & Boerger, 1987). An observation is interpreted against one issue, perspective, or utility, then interpreted against others. Qualitative case study is characterized by researchers spending extended time on site, personally in contact with activities and operations of the case, reflecting, and revising descriptions and meanings of what is going on. Naturalistic, ethnographic, phenomenological caseworkers seek to see what is natural in happenings, in settings, in expressions of value.

Reflecting upon case literature, I find case study methods written about largely by people who hold that the research should contribute to scientific generalization. The bulk of case study work, however, is done by people who have *intrinsic* interest in the case. Their intrinsic case study designs draw these researchers toward understandings of what is important about that case within its own world, which is not the same as the world of researchers and theorists. Intrinsic designs aim to develop what is perceived to be the case's own issues, contexts, and interpretations, its "thick description." In contrast, the methods of instrumental case study draw the researcher toward illustrating how the concerns of researchers and theorists are manifest in the case. Because the critical issues are more likely to be known in advance and to follow disciplinary expectations, such a design can take greater advantage of already-developed instruments and preconceived coding schemes.[13]

In intrinsic case study, researchers do not avoid generalization—they cannot. Certainly, they generalize to happenings of their case at times still to come and in other situations. They expect their readers to comprehend their interpretations but to arrive, as well, at their own. Thus, the methods for case work actually used are to learn enough about the case to encapsulate complex meanings into a finite report but to describe the case in sufficient descriptive narrative so that readers can experience these happenings vicariously and draw their own conclusions.

Case Selection

Perhaps the most unusual aspect of case study in the social sciences and human services is the selection of cases to study. Intrinsic casework regularly begins with cases already identified. The doctor, the social worker, and the program evaluator receive their cases; they seldom choose them. The cases are of prominent interest before formal study begins. Instrumental and collective casework regularly requires cases to be chosen. Achieving the greatest understanding of the critical phenomena depends on choosing the case well (Patton, 1990; Vaughan, 1992; Yin, 1989). Suppose we are trying to understand the behavior of people who take hostages and we decide to probe the phenomenon using a case study. Hostage taking does not happen often; in the entire world, there are few cases to choose. Current options, let us imagine, boil down to a bank robber, an airline hijacker, an estranged father who kidnapped his own child, and a Shiite Muslim group. We want to generalize about hostage-taking behavior, yet we realize that each of these cases, each sample of one, weakly *represents* the larger group of interest.

When one designs a study in the manner advocated by Michael Huberman and Matthew Miles (1994) and Gery Ryan and Russell Bernard (2000) in the second edition of this *Handbook*, nothing is more important than making a representative selection of cases. For this design, formal sampling is needed. The cases are expected to represent some population of cases. The phenomenon of interest observable in the case represents the phenomenon writ large. For Miles and Huberman, Yin, and Malinowski, the main work was science, an enterprise to achieve the best possible explanations of phenomena (von Wright, 1971). In the beginning, phenomena are given; the cases are opportunities to study the phenomena. But even in the larger collective case studies, the sample size usually is much too small to warrant random selection. For qualitative fieldwork, we draw a purposive sample, building in variety and acknowledging opportunities for intensive study.[14]

The phenomenon on the table is hostage taking. We want to improve our understanding of hostage taking, to fit it into what we know about criminology, conflict resolution, human relations—that is, various *abstract dimensions.*[15] We recognize a large population of hypothetical cases and a small subpopulation of accessible cases. We want to generalize about hostage taking without special interest in any of those cases available for study. On representational grounds, the epistemological opportunity seems small, but we are optimistic that we can learn some important things from almost any case. We choose one case or a small number of exemplars. Hostages usually are strangers who happen to be available to the hostage taker. We might rule out studying a father who takes his own child as hostage. Such kidnappings actually may be more common, but we rule out the father. We are more interested in hostage taking accompanying a criminal act, hostage taking in order to escape. The researcher examines various interests in the phenomenon, selecting a case of some typicality but leaning toward those cases that seem to offer *opportunity to learn.* My choice would be to choose that case from which we feel we can learn the most.[16] That may mean taking the one most accessible or the one we can spend the most time with. Potential for learning is a different and sometimes superior criterion to representativeness. Sometimes it is better to learn a lot from an atypical case than a little from a seemingly typical case.

Another illustration: Suppose we are interested in the attractiveness of interactive (the visitor manipulates, gets feedback) displays in children's museums. We have resources to study four museums, to do a collective study of four cases. It is likely that we would set up a typology, perhaps of (a) museum types, namely art, science, and history; (b) city types, namely large and very large; and (c) program types, namely exhibitory and participative. With this typology, we could create a matrix of 12 cells. Examples probably cannot be found for all 12 cells, but resources do not allow studying 12 anyway. With four to be studied, we are likely to start out thinking we should have one art, one history, and two science museums (because interactive displays are more common in science museums); two located in large; and two in very large cities; and two each of the program types. But when we look at existing cases, the logistics, the potential reception, the resources, and additional characteristics of relevance, we move toward choosing four museums to study that offer variety (falling short of structured representation) across the attributes, the four that give us the best opportunities to learn about interactive displays.[17] Any best possible selection of four museums from a balanced design would not give us compelling representation of museums as a whole, and certainly not a statistical basis for generalizing about interactions between interactivity and site characteristics. Several desirable types usually have to be omitted. Even for collective case studies, selection by sampling of attributes should not be the highest priority. Balance and variety are important; opportunity to learn is often more important.

The same process of selection will occur as part of intrinsic case study. Even though the case is decided in advance (usually), there are subsequent choices to make about persons, places, and events to observe. They are *cases within the case*—embedded cases or mini-cases. In Figure 17.1, two mini-cases were anticipated, one of the teacher Oksana and one of Liubchyk's mother. Later, a third mini-case was added, that of a clinic created by parents. Here again, training, experience, and intuition help us to make a good selection. The Step by Step early childhood program in Ukraine (Figure 17.1) aimed to get children with disability ready for the regular classroom, avoiding segregated special education, the usual assignment.[18] The sponsors chose to study a child in the school with the most developed activity. Selecting the child was influenced largely by the activity of his parents, two teachers, a social worker, and the principal. With time short, the researchers needed to select other parents, teachers, and community leaders to interview. Which of them would add most to the portrayal?

Or suppose that we are studying a program for placing computers in the homes of fourth graders for scholastic purposes. The cases—that is, the school sites—already have been selected. Although there is a certain coordination of activity, each participating researcher has one case study to develop. A principal issue has to do with impact on the family, because certain expectations of computer use accompany placement in the home. (The computer should be available for word processing, record keeping, and games by family members, but certain times should be set aside for fourth-grade homework.) At one site, 50 homes now have computers. The researcher can get certain information from every home, but the budget allows observation in only a small number of homes. Which homes should be selected? Just as in the collective case study, the researcher notes attributes of interest, among them perhaps gender of the fourth grader, presence of siblings, family structure, home discipline, previous use of computers, and other technology in the home. The researcher discusses these characteristics with informants, gets recommendations, visits several homes, and obtains attribute data. The choice is made, ensuring variety but not necessarily representativeness, without strong argument for typicality, again weighted by considerations of access and even by hospitality, for the time is short and perhaps too little can be learned from inhospitable parents. Here, too, the primary criterion is opportunity to learn.

Interactivity

Usually we want to learn what the selected case does—its activity, its functioning. We will observe what we can, ask others for their observations, and gather artifacts of that functioning. For example, the department being studied provides services, manages itself and responds to management by external authorities, observes rules, adapts to constraints, seeks opportunities, and changes staffing. Describing and interpreting these activities constitutes a large part of many case studies.

These activities are expected to be influenced by contexts, so contexts need to be described, even if evidence of influence is not found. Staffing, for example, may be affected by the political context, particularly union activity and some form of "old boy network." Public announcement of services may be affected by historical and physical contexts. Budgets have an economic context. Qualitative researchers have strong expectations that the reality perceived by people inside and outside the case will be social, cultural, situational, and contextual—and they want the interactivity of functions and contexts as well described as possible.

Quantitative researchers study the differences among main effects, such as the different influences of rural and urban settings and the different performances of boys and girls, comparing subpopulations. Demographics and gender are common "main effects." Programmatic treatment is another common main effect, with researchers comparing subsequent performance of those receiving different kinds or levels of treatment. Even if all possible comparisons are made, some performance differences remain unexplained. A typical treatment might be personally accommodated work conditions. Suppose urban females respond differently to such a treatment. This would show up in the analysis of variance as an interaction effect. And suppose a particular city girl, Carmen, consistently responds differently from other city girls. Her pattern of behavior is unlikely to be discerned by quantitative analysis but may be spotted easily by case study. And on further analysis, her pattern of behavior may be useful for the interpretation of the functioning of several subgroups. As cases respond differently to complex situations, the interactivity of main effects and settings can be expected to require the particularistic scrutiny of case study.[19]

Data Gathering

Naturalistic, ethnographic, phenomenological caseworkers also seek what is *ordinary* in happenings, in settings, in expressions of value. Herbert Blumer (1969, p. 149) called for us to accept, develop, and use the distinctive expression (of the particular case) in order to detect and study the common. What details of life the researchers are unable to see for themselves is obtained by interviewing people who did see them or by finding documents recording them. Part IV of this *Handbook* deals extensively with the methods of qualitative research, particularly observation, interview, coding, data management, and interpretation. These pertain, of course, to qualitative case study.

Documenting the unusual and the ordinary takes lots of time—for planning, gaining access, data gathering, analysis, and write-up. In many studies, there are no clear stages: Issue development continues to the end of the study, and write-up begins with preliminary observations. A speculative, page-allocating outline for the report helps anticipate how issues will be handled and how the case will become visible. For many researchers, to set out upon an unstructured, open-ended study is a calamity in the making. A plan is essential, but the caseworker needs to anticipate the need to recognize and develop late-emerging issues. Many qualitative fieldworkers invest little in instrument construction, partly because tailored (not standardized) questions are needed for most data sources. The budget may be consumed quickly by devising and field-testing instruments to pursue what turns out to be too many foreshadowing questions, with some of them maturing, some dying, and some moving to new levels of complexity. Even the ordinary is too complicated to be mastered in the time available.

When the case is too large for one researcher to know well or for a collective case study, *teaming* is an important option. Case research requires integrated, holistic comprehension of the case, but in the larger studies, no one individual can handle the complexity. Coding can be a great help, if the team is experienced in the process and with each other. But learning a detailed analytic coding system within the study period often is too great a burden (L. M. Smith & Dwyer, 1979), reducing observations to simple categories, eating up the on-site time. Often sites, key groups or actors, and issues should be assigned to a single team member, including junior members. The case's parts to be studied and the research issues need to be pared down to what can be comprehended by the collection of team members. It is better to negotiate the parts to be studied, as well as the parts not, and to do an in-depth study of a few key issues. Each team member writes up his or her parts; other team members need to read and critique these write-ups. Usually, the team leader needs to write the synthesis, getting critiques from the team, data sources, and selected skeptical friends.

Triangulation

With reporting and reading both "ill-structured" and "socially constructed," it is not surprising to find researcher tolerance for ambiguity and championing of multiple perspectives. Still, I have yet to meet case researchers unconcerned about clarity of their own perception and validity of their own communication. Even if meanings do not transfer intact but instead squeeze into the conceptual space of the reader, there is no less urgency for researchers to assure that their sense of situation, observation, reporting, and reading stay within some limits of correspondence. However accuracy is construed, researchers don't want to be inaccurate, caught without confirmation. Counterintuitive though it may be, the author has some responsibility for the validity of the readers' interpretations (Messick, 1989). Joseph Maxwell (1992) has spoken of the need for thinking of validity separately for descriptions, interpretations, theories, generalizations, and evaluative judgments.

To reduce the likelihood of misinterpretation, various procedures are employed, two of the most common being redundancy of data gathering and procedural challenges to explanations (Denzin, 1989; Goetz & LeCompte, 1984). For qualitative casework, these procedures generally are called *triangulation.*[20] Triangulation has been generally considered a process of using multiple perceptions to clarify meaning, verifying the repeatability of an observation or interpretation.[21]

But acknowledging that no observations or interpretations are perfectly repeatable,[22] triangulation serves also to clarify meaning by identifying different ways the case is being seen (Flick, 1998; Silverman, 1993). The qualitative researcher is interested in diversity of perception, even the multiple realities within which people live. Triangulation helps to identify different realities.

Learning From the Particular Case

The researcher is a teacher using at least two pedagogical methods (Eisner, 1985). Teaching *didactically*, the researcher teaches what he or she has learned. Arranging for what educationists call *discovery learning*, the researcher provides material for readers to learn, on their own, especially things about which readers may know better than the researcher.

What can one learn from a single case? David Hamilton (1980), Stephen Kemmis (1980), Lawrence Stenhouse (1979), and Robert Yin (1989) are among those who have advanced the epistemology of the particular.[23] Even Donald Campbell (1975), the prophet of scientific generalization, contributed. How we learn from the singular case is related to how the case is like and unlike other cases we do know, mostly by comparison.[24] It is intuition that persuades both researcher and reader that what is known about one case may very well be true about a similar case (Smith, 1978).

Experiential Knowledge

From case reports, we convey and draw forth the essence of qualitative understanding—that is, experiential knowledge (Geertz, 1983; Polanyi, 1962; Rumelhart & Ortony, 1977; von Wright, 1971). Case study facilitates the conveying of experience of actors and stakeholders as well as the experience of studying the case. It can enhance the reader's experience with the case. It does this largely with narratives and situational descriptions of case activity, personal relationship, and group interpretation.

Experiential descriptions and assertions are relatively easily assimilated by readers into memory and use. When the researcher's narrative provides opportunity for *vicarious experience*, readers extend their perceptions of happenings. Naturalistic, ethnographic case materials, at least to some extent, parallel actual experience, feeding into the most fundamental processes of awareness and understanding. Deborah Trumbull and I called these processes *naturalistic generalization* (Stake & Trumbull, 1982). That is, people make some generalizations entirely from personal or vicarious experience. Enduring meanings come from encounter, and they are modified and reinforced by repeated encounter.

In ordinary living, this occurs seldom to the individual alone and more often in the presence of others. In a social process, together people bend, spin, consolidate, and enrich their understandings. We come to know what has happened partly in terms of what others reveal as their experience. The case researcher emerges from one social experience, the observation, to choreograph another, the report. Knowledge is socially constructed—or so we constructivists believe (see Schwandt, 2000)—and through their experiential and contextual accounts, case study researchers assist readers in the construction of knowledge.

Case researchers greatly rely on subjective data, such as the testimony of participants and the judgments of witnesses. Many critical observations and interview data are subjective. Most case study is the empirical study of human activity. The major questions are not questions of opinion or feeling, but of the sensory experience. And the answers come back, of course, with description and interpretation, opinion and feeling, all mixed together. When the researchers are not there to experience the activity for themselves, they have to ask those who did experience it. To make empirical data more objective and less subjective, the researcher uses replicative, falsification, and triangulating methods. Good case study research follows disciplined practices of analysis and triangulation to tease out what deserves to be called experiential knowledge from what is opinion and preference (Stake, 2004).

Understanding the case as personal experience depends on whether or not it can be embraced intellectually by a single researcher (or a small case study team). When the case is something like a person or a small Agency or a legislative session, a researcher who is given enough time and access can become personally knowledgeable about the activities and spaces, the relationships and contexts, of the case, as modeled in Figure 17.1. Possibly with the help of a few others, he or she can become experientially acquainted with the case. The case then is *embraceable.* Through observation, enumeration, and talk, the researcher can personally come to perceive the nature of the case. When the researcher can see and inquire about the case personally, with or without scales and rubrics, that researcher can come to understand the case in the most expected and respected ways. But when the researcher finds the case obscured, extending into too-distant regions or beyond his or her comprehension, and thus beyond personal encounter, that researcher conceptualizes the case differently. The case is likely to become overly abstract, a construct of criteria. Whether or not they want to, researchers then depersonalize the assignment, rely more on instruments and protocols, and accept simplistic reporting from people who themselves lack direct personal experience. Even if the researcher has extensive personal contact with parts of the case, that contact fails to reach too many extremities and complexities. This is a case beyond personal embrace, beyond experiential knowing.

Knowledge Transfer From Researcher to Reader

Both researcher and reader bring their conceptual structures to a case. In the literature, these structures have been called many things, including *advanced organizers* (Ausubel & Fitzgerald, 1961), *schemata* (Anderson, 1977), and an *unfolding of realization* (Bohm, 1985). Some such frameworks for thought are unconscious. Communication is facilitated by carefully crafted structures. Thought itself, conversation surely, and writing especially draw phrases into paragraphs and append labels onto constructs. Meanings aggregate or attenuate. Associations become relationships; relationships become theory (Robinson, 1951). Generalization can be an unconscious process for both researcher and reader.

In private and personal ways, ideas are structured, highlighted, subordinated, connected, embedded *in* contexts, embedded *with* illustration, and laced with favor and doubt. However moved to share ideas case researchers might be, however clever and elaborated their writings, they will, like others, pass along to readers some of their personal meanings of events and relationships—and fail to pass along others. They know that readers, too, will add and subtract, invent and shape—reconstructing the knowledge in ways that leave it differently connected and more likely to be personally useful.

A researcher's knowledge of the case faces hazardous passage from writing to reading. The writer seeks ways of safeguarding the trip. As reading begins, the case slowly joins the company of cases previously known to the reader. Conceptually for the reader, the new case cannot be but some variation of cases already known. A new case without commonality cannot be understood, yet a new case without distinction will not be noticed. Researchers cannot know well which cases their readers already know or their readers' peculiarities of mind. They seek ways to protect and substantiate the transfer of knowledge.

Qualitative researchers recognize a need to accommodate the readers' preexisting knowledge. Although everyone deals with this need every day and draws upon a lifetime of experience, we know precious little about how new experience merges with old. According to Rand Spiro and colleagues (1987), most personal experience is *ill-structured,* neither pedagogically nor epistemologically neat. It follows that a well-structured, propositional presentation often will not be the better way to *transfer* experiential knowledge. The reader has a certain *cognitive flexibility*, the readiness to assemble a situation-relative schema from the knowledge fragments of a new encounter. The Spiro group (1987) contended that

> the best way to learn and instruct in order to attain the goal of cognitive flexibility in knowledge representation for future application is by a method of case-based presentations which treats a content domain as a landscape that is explored by "criss-crossing" it in many directions, by reexamining each case "site" in the varying contexts of different neighboring cases, and by using a variety of abstract dimensions for comparing cases. (p. 178)

Knowledge transfer remains difficult to understand. Even less understood is how a small aspect of the case may be found by many readers to modify an existing understanding about cases in general, even when the case is not typical.[25] In a ghetto school (Stake, 1995), I observed a teacher with *one* set of rules for classroom decorum—except that for Adam, a nearly expelled, indomitable youngster, a more liberal set had to be continuously invented. Reading my account, teachers from very different schools agreed with two seemingly contradictory statements: "Yes, you have to be strict with the rules" and "Yes, sometimes you have to bend the rules." They recognized in the report an unusual but generalizable circumstance. People find in case reports certain insights into the human condition, even while being well aware of the atypicality of the case. They may be *too* quick to accept the insight. The case researcher needs to provide grounds for validating both the observation and the generalization.

◼ Storytelling[26]

Some say we should just let the case "tell its own story" (Carter, 1993; Coles, 1989). The story a case tells of itself may or may not be useful. The researcher should draw out such stories, partly by explaining issues and by referring to other stories, but it is risky to leave it to the case actors to select the stories to be conveyed. Is the purpose to convey the storyteller's perception or to develop the researcher's perception of the case? Given expectations of the client, other stakeholders, and readers, either emphasis may be more appropriate. One cannot know at the outset what issues, perceptions, or theory will be useful. Case researchers usually enter the scene expecting, even knowing, that certain events, problems, and relationships will be important; yet they discover that some of them, this time, will be of little consequence (Parlett & Hamilton, 1976; L. M. Smith, 1994). Case content evolves even in the last phases of writing.

Even when empathic and respectful of each person's realities, the researcher decides what the case's "own story" is, or at least what will be included in the report. More will be pursued than was volunteered, and less will be reported than was learned. Even though the competent researcher will be guided by what the case indicates is most important, and even though patrons and other researchers will advise, that which is necessary for an understanding of the case will be decided by the researcher.[27] It may be the case's own story, but the report will be the researcher's dressing of the case's own story. This is not to dismiss the aim of finding the story that best represents the case, but instead to remind the reader that, usually, criteria of representation ultimately are decided by the researcher.

Many a researcher would like to tell the whole story but of course cannot; the whole story exceeds anyone's knowing and anyone's telling. Even those inclined to tell all find strong the obligation to winnow and consolidate. The qualitative researcher, like the single-issue researcher, must choose between telling lots and telling little. John van Maanen (1988) identified seven choices of presentation: realistic, impressionistic, confessional, critical, formal, literary, and jointly told. He added criteria for selecting the content. Some criteria are set by funding agencies, prospective readers, rhetorical convention, the researcher's career pattern, or the prospect of publication. Some criteria are set by a notion of what represents the case most fully, most appreciably for the hospitality received, or most comprehensibly. These are subjective choices not unlike those that all researchers make in choosing what to study. Some are made while designing the case study, but some continue to be made throughout the study and until the final hours.

Reporting a case seldom takes the traditional form of telling a story: introduction of characters followed by the revelation and resolution of problems. Many sponsors of research and many a researcher want a report that looks like traditional social science, running from statement of problem to review of literature, data collection, analysis, and conclusions. The case can be portrayed in many ways.

Many researchers, early in a study, try to form an idea of what the final report might look like. In Figure 17.3, the topics of 16 sections of an anticipated 45-page report have been sequenced in the left column, with guesses of page limits provided for each. This is the plan of the researchers from Ukraine, Natalia Sofiy and Svitlana Efimova, with Liubchyk as their case. Liubchyk would have been sent to a special school for children of disability, but thanks to a diligent mother and an inclusion-oriented principal, he was "mainstreamed" in Mrs. Oxama's regular kindergarten. Strategically, Liubchyk is used as a pivot for examining the recent mainstreaming thrust in Ukraine. As seen in column headings, the most important issue was inclusion, followed by teacher training and child-centered education, then three other concerns. Where these issues may be developed in the report is predicted in the figure. In the last two columns, the researchers listed singular moments and quotations for placement in the sections. By forecasting the order and size of the parts of the story, one can lessen the chances of gathering much too much of any kind of data.

Comparisons

A researcher will report his or her case as a case, knowing it will be compared to others. Researchers differ as to how much they set up comparative cases and acknowledge the reader's own cases. Most naturalistic, ethnographic, phenomenological researchers will concentrate on describing the present case in sufficient detail so that the reader can make good comparisons. Sometimes the researcher will point out comparisons that might be made. Many quantitative and evaluation case researchers will try to provide some comparisons, sometimes by presenting one or more reference cases, sometimes providing statistical norms for reference groups from which a hypothetical reference case can be imagined. Both the quantitative and the qualitative approaches provide narrow grounds for strict comparison of cases, even though a tradition of grand comparison exists within comparative anthropology and related disciplines (Ragin, 1987; Sjoberg, Williams, Vaughan, & Sjoberg, 1991; Tobin, 1989).

I see formally designed comparison as actually competing with learning about and from the particular case. Comparison is a grand epistemological strategy, a powerful conceptual mechanism, fixing attention upon one or a few attributes. Thus, it obscures any case knowledge that fails to facilitate comparison. Comparative description is the opposite of what Geertz (1973) called "thick description." Thick description of the music program, for example, might include conflicting perceptions of the staffing, recent program changes, the charisma of the choral director, the working relationship with a church organist, faculty interest in a critical vote of the school board, and the lack of student interest in taking up the clarinet. In these particularities lie the vitality, trauma, and uniqueness of the case. Comparison might be made on any of these characteristics but tends to be made on more general variables traditionally noted in the organization of music programs (e.g., repertoire, staffing, budget, tour policy). With concentration on the bases for comparison, uniquenesses and complexities will be glossed over. A research design featuring comparison substitutes (a) *the comparison* for (b) *the case* as the focus of the study.

Regardless of the type of case study—intrinsic, instrumental, or collective—readers often learn

Insertions	Topic Sections	pages	pages of context	Questionnaire info	Inclusion	teacher training	child-centered educ.	democratic play	program sustainability	choice vs. standard	minor topics	quotes, impressions
						Issues appearing						
D, C, 3	Liubchyk	5			X			X			1. Teacher selection	A. Black today, green tommorrow
F, 1	Oksana	3	1		X	X	X			X	2. child protection	B. Director not bureaucrat
4	Tchr tng, Lviv	3	1	X	X	X					3. child view of disability	C. L's view of time & mgmt
	Press conf, Lviv	2			X				X		4. tchr view of disability	D. Body contact
	Tchr tng, Kiev	2				X					5. nature of disability	E. tchr staffing or potholes
	Tchr tng, Ukr.	2	2		X	X					6. role of church	F. Oksana's activity centers
3	Liubchyk	3		X	X						7. teacher unions	G. parents voted support
	His parents	2		X	X						8. European Union TACIS	H. psycholog'l assessment
	Parent Org's	2	2		X						9. Chernoble effects	I. aggression, affection
B, 9	LEA, Lviv	3	1								10. special ed alternatives	
	Ministry	2	2		X		X	X			11. preparing parents	
2, 8	SbS Ukraine	2	2		X		X	X		X		
10	Interpretation: Alt. ed. policy	4					X					
	Interpretation: Teacher training	4		X		X						
E, 5	Interpretation: Inclusion	4			X							
A	Liubchyk	2			X							
		45	11									

Figure 17.3. Plan for Assembling Ukraine Final Report

little from control or reference cases chosen only for comparison. When there are multiple cases of intrinsic interest, then of course it can be useful to compare them.[28] But often, there is but one case of intrinsic interest, if any at all. Readers with intrinsic interest in the case learn more about it directly from the description; they do not ignore comparisons with other cases but also do not concentrate on comparisons. Readers examining instrumental case studies are shown how the phenomenon exists within particular cases. As to reliability, differences between measures, such as how much the group changed, are fundamentally more unreliable than simple measurements. Similarly, conclusions about measured differences between any two cases are less to be trusted than are conclusions about a single case. Nevertheless, illustration of how a phenomenon occurs in the circumstances of several exemplars can provide valued and trustworthy knowledge.

Many are the ways of conceptualizing cases to maximize learning from a case. The case is expected to be something that functions, that operates; the study is the observation of operations (Kemmis, 1980). There is something to be described and interpreted. The conceptions of most naturalistic, holistic, ethnographic, phenomenological case studies need accurate description and subjective, yet disciplined, interpretation; a respect for and curiosity about culturally different perceptions of phenomena; and empathic representation of local settings—all blending (perhaps clumped) within a constructivist epistemology.

Ethics

Ethical considerations for qualitative research are reviewed by Clifford Christians in Chapter 6 of this *Handbook* (and elsewhere by authors such as Coles, 1997, and Graue and Walsh, 1998). Case studies often deal with matters that are of public interest but for which there is neither public nor scholarly *right to know.* Funding, scholarly intent, or Institutional Review Board authorization does not constitute license to invade the privacy of others. The value of the best research is not likely to outweigh injury to a person exposed. Qualitative researchers are guests in the private spaces of the world. Their manners should be good and their code of ethics strict.

Along with much qualitative work, case study research shares an intense interest in personal views and circumstances. Those whose lives and expressions are portrayed risk exposure and embarrassment, as well as loss of standing, employment, and self-esteem. Something of a contract exists between researcher and the researched:[29] a disclosing and protective covenant, usually informal but best not silent, a moral obligation (Schwandt, 1993). Risks to well-being cannot be inventoried but should be exemplified. Issues of observation and reportage should be discussed in advance. Limits to access should be suggested and agreements heeded. It is important (but never sufficient) for targeted persons to receive drafts of the write-up revealing how they are presented, quoted, and interpreted; the researcher should listen well to these persons' responses for signs of concern. It is important that great caution be exercised to minimize risks to participants in the case. Even with good advance information from the researcher about the study, the researched cannot be expected to protect themselves against the risks inherent in participation. Rules for protection of human subjects should be followed (yet protested when they serve little more than to protect the researcher's institution from litigation). The researcher should go beyond those rules, avoid low-priority probing of sensitive issues, and draw in advisers and reviewers to help extend the protective system.

Ethical problems arise (both inside and outside the research topics) with nondisclosure of malfeasance and immorality. When rules for a study are set that prevent the researcher from "whistle-blowing" or the exercise of compassion, a problem exists. Where an expectation has been raised that propriety is being examined and no mention is made of a serious impropriety that has been observed, the report is deceptive. Breach of ethics is seldom a simple matter; often, it occurs when two contradictory standards apply, such as withholding full disclosure (as per the contract) in order to protect a good but vulnerable agency (Mabry, 1999). Ongoing and summative review procedures are needed, with impetus from the researcher's conscience, from stakeholders, and from the research community.

Summary

Major conceptual responsibilities of the qualitative case researcher include the following:

a. Bounding the case, conceptualizing the object of study;
b. Selecting phenomena, themes, or issues (i.e., the research questions to emphasize);
c. Seeking patterns of data to develop the issues;

d. Triangulating key observations and bases for interpretation;
e. Selecting alternative interpretations to pursue; and
f. Developing assertions or generalizations about the case.

Except for (a), the steps are similar to those of other qualitative researchers. The more intrinsic the interest of the researcher in the case, the more the focus of study will be on the case's idiosyncrasy, its particular context, issues, and story. Some major stylistic options for case researchers are the following:

a. How much to make the report a story,
b. How much to compare with other cases,
c. How much to formalize generalizations or leave such generalizing to readers,
d. How much description of the researcher to include in the report, and
e. Whether or not and how much to protect anonymity.

Case study is a part of scientific methodology, but its purpose is not limited to the advance of science. Populations of cases can be represented poorly by single cases or samples of a very few cases, and such small samples of cases can provide questionable grounds for advancing grand generalization. Yet, "Because more than one theoretical notion may be guiding an analysis, confirmation, fuller specification, and contradiction all may result from one case study" (Vaughan, 1992, p. 175). For example, we lose confidence in the generalization that a child of separated parents is better off placed with the mother than with the father when we find a single instance of resulting injury. Case studies are of value in refining theory, suggesting complexities for further investigation as well as helping to establish the limits of generalizability.

Case study also can be a disciplined force in setting public policy and in reflecting on human experience. Vicarious experience is an important basis for refining action options and expectations. Formal epistemology needs further development, but somehow people draw, from the description of an individual case, implications for other cases—not always correctly, but with a confidence shared by people of dissimilar views.

The purpose of a case report is not to represent the world, but to represent the case. Criteria for conducting the kind of research that leads to valid generalization need modification to fit the search for effective particularization. The utility of case research to practitioners and policy makers is in its extension of experience. The methods of qualitative case study are largely the methods of disciplining personal and particularized experience.

Notes

1. Many case studies are both qualitative and quantitative. In search of fundamental pursuits common to both qualitative and quantitative research, Robert Yin (1992) analyzed three well-crafted research efforts: (a) a quantitative investigation to resolve disputed authorship of the Federalist Papers, (b) a qualitative study of Soviet intent at the time of the Cuban missile crisis, and (c) his own studies of the recognizability of human faces. He found four common commitments: to bring expert knowledge to bear upon the phenomena studied, to round up all the relevant data, to examine rival interpretations, and to ponder and probe the degree to which the findings have implications elsewhere. These commitments are as important in case research as in any other type.

2. Another specific one for targeting a qualitative study is the event or instance. Events and instances are bounded, complex, and related to issues, but they lack the organic systemacity of most cases. Media instances have been studied by John Fiske (1994) and Norman Denzin (1999). Conversation analysis is a related approach (Psathas, 1995; Silverman, 2000).

3. Definition of the case is not independent of interpretive paradigm or methods of inquiry. Seen from different worldviews and in different situations, the "same" case *is* different. And however we originally define the case, the working definition changes as we study. And the definition of the case changes in different ways under different methods of study. The case of Theodore Roosevelt was not just differently portrayed but was differently defined as biographer Edmund Morris (1979) presented him, one chapter at a time, as "the Dude from New York,"

"the Dear Old Beloved Brother," "the Snake in the Grass," "the Rough Rider," "the Most Famous Man in America," and so on.

4. The history of case study, like the history of curiosity and common sense, is found throughout the library. Peeps at that history can be found in Robert Bogdan and Sara Bicklin (1982), John Creswell (1998), Sara Delamont (1992), Joe Feagin, Anthony Orum, and Gideon Sjoberg (1991), Robert Stake (1978), Harrison White (1992), and throughout this *Handbook.*

5. *Bread and Dreams* is a program evaluation report. Most evaluations are intrinsic case studies (see Mabry, 1998).

6. Collective case study is essentially what Robert Herriott and William Firestone (1983) called "multisite qualitative research." Multisite program evaluation is another common example. A number of German sociologists, such as Martin Kohli and Fritz Schütze, have used collective case studies with Strauss's grounded theory approach.

7. In a thoughtful review of an early draft of this chapter, Orlando Fals Borda urged abandoning the effort to promote intrinsic casework and the study of particularity. In persisting here, I think it important to support disciplined and scholarly study that has few scientific aspirations.

8. In 1922, Bronislaw Malinowski wrote, "One of the first conditions of acceptable Ethnographic work certainly is that it should deal with the totality of all social, cultural and psychological aspects of the community . . ." (1922/1984, p. xvi). There is a good spirit there, although totalities defy the acuity of the eye and the longevity of the watch.

9. Generalization from collective case study has been discussed by Herriott and Firestone (1983), John and Lyn Lofland (1984), Miles and Huberman (1994), and again by Firestone (1993).

10. Malinowski claimed that we could distinguish between arriving with closed minds and arriving with an idea of what to look for. He wrote:

> Good training in theory, and acquaintance with its latest results, is not identical with being burdened with "preconceived ideas." If a man sets out on an expedition, determined to prove certain hypotheses, if he is incapable of changing his views constantly and casting them off ungrudgingly under the pressure of evidence, needless to say his work will be worthless. But the more problems he brings with him into the field, the more he is in the habit of moulding his theories according to facts, and of seeing facts in their bearing upon theory, the better he is equipped for the work. Preconceived ideas are pernicious in any scientific work, but *foreshadowed problems* are the main endowment of a scientific thinker, and these problems are first revealed to the observer by his theoretical studies. (1922/1984, p. 9)

11. I would prefer to call it *interpretive* to emphasize the production of meanings, but ethnographers have used that term to mean "learn the special views of actors, the local meanings" (see Erickson, 1986; Schwandt, 2000).

12. Ethnographic use of the term *reflective* sometimes limits attention to the need for self-challenging the researcher's etic issues, frame of reference, and cultural bias (Tedlock, Chapter 18, this volume). That challenge is important but, following Donald Schön (1983), I refer to a general frame of mind when I call qualitative case work *reflective*. (Issues "brought in" are called *emic* issues; those found during field study are called *etic.*)

13. Coding is the method of connecting data, issues, interpretations, data sources, and report writing (Miles & Huberman, 1994). In small studies, this means careful labeling and sorting into file folders or computer files. Many entries are filed into more than one file. If the file becomes too bulky, subfiles need to be created. Too many files spoils the soup. In larger studies with files to be used by several team members, a formal coding system needs to be developed, possibly using a computer program such as *Ethnograph*, *ATLAS-ti*, or *HyperRESEARCH.*

14. Michael Patton (1990), Anselm Strauss and Juliet Corbin (1990), and William Firestone (1993) have discussed successive selection of cases over time.

15. As indicated in a previous section, I call them issues. Mary Kennedy (1979) called them "relevant attributes." Spiro et al. (1987) called them "abstract dimensions." Malinowski (1922/1984) called them "theories." In contemporary case research, these will be our "working theories" more than the "grand theories" of the disciplines.

16. If my emphasis is on learning about both the individual case and the phenomenon, I might do two studies, one a case study and the other a study of the phenomenon, giving close attention to an array of instances of hostage taking.

17. Firestone (1993) advised maximizing diversity and "to be as like the population of interest as possible" (p. 18).

18. The project is ongoing, and no report is yet available. The Step by Step program is described in Hansen, Kaufmann, and Saifer (n.d.).

19. For a number of years, psychologists Lee Cronbach and Richard Snow (1977) studied aptitude-treatment interactions. They hoped to find general rules by which teachers could adapt instruction to personal learning styles. At deeper and deeper levels of interaction they found significance, leading not to prespecifying teaching methods for individuals but supporting the conclusion that differentiated consistencies of response by individuals are to be expected in complex situations.

20. Laurel Richardson and Elizabeth St. Pierre speak similarly of *crystallization* in Chapter 38 of this volume.

21. Creative use of "member checking," submitting drafts for review by data sources, is one of the most needed forms of validation of qualitative research (Glesne & Peshkin, 1992; Lincoln & Guba, 1985).

22. Or that a reality exists outside the observers.

23. Among the earlier philosophers of science providing groundwork for qualitative contributions to theory elaboration were Herbert Blumer, Barney Glaser, Bronislaw Malinowski, and Robert Merton.

24. Yet, in the words of Charles Ragin, "variable oriented comparative work (e.g., quantitative cross-national research) as compared with case oriented comparative work disembodies and obscures cases" (Ragin & Becker, 1992, p. 5).

25. Sociologists have used the term "micro/ macro" to refer to the leap from understanding individual cases or parts to understanding the system as a whole. Even without an adequate epistemological map, sociologists do leap, and so do our readers (Collins, 1981).

26. Storytelling as representative of culture and as sociological text emerges from many traditions, but nowhere more than from oral history and folklore. It is becoming more disciplined in a line of work called narrative inquiry (Clandenin & Connelly, 1999; Ellis & Bochner, 1996; Heron, 1996; Lockridge, 1988; Richardson, 1997). The *Journal of Narrative and Life History* includes studies using such methods.

27. It may appear that I claim here that participatory action research is problematic. Joint responsibility for design, data gathering, and interpretation is possible, often commendable. It is important that readers know when the values of the study have been so shaped.

28. Evaluation studies comparing an innovative program to a control case regularly fail to make the comparison credible. No matter how well studied, the control case too weakly represents cases presently known by the reader. By comprehensively describing the program case, the researcher may help the reader draw naturalistic generalizations.

29. A special obligation exists to protect those with limited resources. Those who comply with the researcher's requests, who contribute in some way to the making of the case, should not thereby be hurt—usually. When continuing breaches of ethics or morality are discovered, or when they are the reason for the study, the researcher must take some ameliorative action. Exposé and critique are legitimate within case study, but luring self-indictment out of a respondent is no more legitimate in research than in the law.

References

Adams, H. (1918). *The education of Henry Adams: An autobiography.* Boston: Houghton Mifflin.

Anderson, R. C. (1977). The notion of schema and the educational enterprise. In R. C. Anderson, R. J. Spiro, & W. E. Montague (Eds.), *Schooling and the acquisition of knowledge* (pp. 415–431). Hillsdale, NJ: Lawrence Erlbaum.

Asmussen, K. J., & Creswell, J. W. (1995). Campus response to a student gunman. *Journal of Higher Education, 66,* 575–591.

Ausubel, D. P., & Fitzgerald, D. (1961). Meaningful learning and retention: Interpersonal cognitive variables. *Review of Educational Research, 31,* 500–510.

Becker, H. S. (1992). Cases, causes, conjunctures, stories, and imagery. In C. C. Ragin & H. S. Becker (Eds.), *What is a case? Exploring the foundations of social inquiry* (pp. 205–216). Cambridge, UK: Cambridge University Press.

Becker, H. S., Geer, B., Hughes, E. C., & Strauss, A. L. (1961). *Boys in white: Student culture in medical school.* Chicago: University of Chicago Press.

Blumer, H. (1969). *Symbolic interactionism: Perspective and method.* Englewood Cliffs, NJ: Prentice-Hall.

Bogdan, R. C., & Biklen, S. K. (1982). *Qualitative research for education: An introduction to theory and methods.* Boston: Allyn & Bacon.

Bohm, D. (1985). *Unfolding meaning: A weekend of dialogue with David Bohm.* New York: Routledge.

Campbell, D. T. (1975). Degrees of freedom and case study. *Comparative Political Studies, 8,* 178–193.

Carr, W. L., & Kemmis, S. (1986). *Becoming critical: Education, knowledge and action research.* London: Falmer.

Carter, K. (1993). The place of story in the study of teaching and teacher education. *Educational Researcher, 22,* 5–12.

Clandenin, J., & Connelly, M. (1999). *Narrative inquiry.* San Francisco: Jossey-Bass.

Coles, R. (1989). *The call of stories: Teaching and the moral imagination.* Boston: Houghton Mifflin.

Coles, R. (1997). *Doing documentary work.* Oxford, UK: Oxford University Press.

Collins, R. (1981). On the microfoundations of macrosociology. *American Journal of Sociology, 86,* 984–1014.

Connell, R. W. (1985). *Teachers' work.* Sydney: George Allen & Unwin.

Crabtree, B. F., & Miller, W. L. (1999). Researching practice settings: A case study approach. In B. F. Crabtree & W. L. Miller (Eds.), *Doing qualitative research* (2nd ed., pp. 293–312). Thousand Oaks, CA: Sage.

Creswell, J. W. (1998). *Qualitative inquiry and research design: Choosing among five traditions.* Thousand Oaks, CA: Sage.

Cronbach, L. J., & Snow, R. E. (1977). *Aptitudes and instructional methods: A handbook for research on interactions.* New York: Irvington.

Delamont, S. (1992). *Fieldwork in educational settings: Methods, pitfalls and perspectives.* London: Falmer.

Denzin, N. K. (1989). *The research act* (3rd ed.). Englewood Cliffs, NJ: Prentice Hall.

Denzin, N. K. (1999). Cybertalk and the method of instances. In S. Jones (Ed.), *Doing Internet research: Critical issues and methods for examining the Net* (pp. 107–126). Thousand Oaks, CA: Sage.

Eisner, E. (Ed.). (1985). *Learning and teaching the ways of knowing* [84th yearbook of the National Society for the Study of Education]. Chicago: University of Chicago Press.

Ellis, C., & Bochner, A. P. (Eds.). (1996). *Composing ethnography.* Walnut Creek, CA: AltaMira.

Erickson, F. (1986). Qualitative methods in research on teaching. In M. C. Wittrock (Ed.), *Handbook of research on teaching* (3rd ed., pp. 119–161). New York: Macmillan.

Fals Borda, O. (Ed.). (1998). *People's participation: Challenges ahead.* New York: Apex.

Feagin, J. R., Orum, A. M., & Sjoberg, G. (1991). *A case for the case study.* Chapel Hill: University of North Carolina Press.

Firestone, W. A. (1993). Alternative arguments for generalizing from data as applied to qualitative research. *Educational Researcher, 22*(4), 16–23.

Fiske, J. (1994). Audiencing: Cultural practice and cultural studies. In N. K. Denzin & Y. S. Lincoln (Eds.), *Handbook of qualitative research* (pp. 359–378). Thousand Oaks, CA: Sage.

Flick, U. (1998). *An introduction to qualitative research: Theory, method and applications.* London: Sage.

Flyvbjerg, B. (2001). *Making social science matter.* Cambridge, UK: Cambridge University Press.

Garfinkel, H. (1967). *Studies in ethnomethodology.* New York: Prentice Hall.

Geertz, C. (1973). Thick description: Toward an interpretive theory of culture. In C. Geertz, *The interpretation of cultures* (pp. 3–30). New York: Basic Books.

Geertz, C. (1983). *Local knowledge: Further essays in interpretive anthropology.* New York: Basic Books.

Glaser, B. G., & Strauss, A. L. (1967). *The discovery of grounded theory: Strategies for qualitative research.* Chicago: Aldine.

Glesne, C., & Peshkin, A. (1992). *Becoming qualitative researchers: An introduction.* White Plains, NY: Longman.

Goetz, J. P., & LeCompte, M. D. (1984). *Ethnography and qualitative design in educational research.* New York: Academic Press.

Goode, W. J., & Hatt, P. K. (1952). The case study. In W. J. Goode & P. K. Hatt, *Methods of social research* (pp. 330–340). New York: McGraw-Hill.

Gottwald, N. K. (1979). *The tribes of Jahweh: A sociology of the religion of liberated Israel, 1250–1050 B.C.E.* Maryknoll, NY: Orbis Books.

Graue, M. E., & Walsh, D. J. (1998). *Studying children in context: Theories, methods, ethics.* Newbury Park, CA: Sage.

Hamilton, D. (1980). Some contrasting assumptions about case study research and survey analysis. In H. Simons (Ed.), *Towards a science of the singular* (pp. 76–92). Norwich, UK: University of East Anglia, Centre for Applied Research in Education.

Hansen, K. A., Kaufmann, R. K., & Saifer, S. (no date). *Education and the culture of democracy: Early childhood practice.* (Available from New York: Open Society Institute, 888 Seventh Ave., New York, NY 10106)

Heron, J. (1996). *Co-operative inquiry: Research into the human condition.* London: Sage.

Herriott, R. E., & Firestone, W. A. (1983). Multisite qualitative policy research: Optimizing description and generalizability. *Educational Researcher, 12*(2), 14–19.

House, E. R., & Howe, K. R. (1999). *Values in evaluation and social research.* Thousand Oaks, CA: Sage.

Huberman, A. M., & Miles, M. B. (1994). Data management and analysis methods. In N. K. Denzin & Y. S. Lincoln (Eds.), *Handbook of qualitative research* (pp. 428–445). Thousand Oaks, CA: Sage.

Kemmis, S. (1980). The imagination of the case and the invention of the study. In H. Simons (Ed.), *Towards a science of the singular* (pp. 93–142). Norwich, UK: University of East Anglia, Centre for Applied Research in Education.

Kennedy, M. M. (1979). Generalizing from single case studies. *Evaluation Quarterly, 3,* 661–678.

Kozol, J. (1991). *Savage inequalities.* New York: Harper.

Lincoln, Y. S., & Guba, E. G. (1985). *Naturalistic inquiry.* Beverly Hills, CA: Sage.

Lincoln, Y. S., & Guba, E. G. (2000). Paradigmatic controversies, contradictions, and emerging confluences. In N. K. Denzin & Y. S. Lincoln (Eds.), *Handbook of qualitative research* (pp. 163–188). Thousand Oaks, CA: Sage.

Lockridge, E. (1988). Faithful in her fashion: Catherine Barkley, the invisible Hemingway heroine. *Journal of Narrative Technique, 18*(2), 170–178.

Lofland, L. J., & Lofland, L. H. (1984). *Analyzing social settings: A guide to qualitative observation and analysis* (2nd ed.). Belmont, CA: Wadsworth.

Mabry, L. (1998). Case study methods. In H. J. Walberg & A. J. Reynolds (Eds.), *Advances in educational productivity: Vol. 7. Evaluation research for educational productivity* (pp. 155–170). Greenwich, CT: JAI.

Mabry, L. (1999). Circumstantial ethics. *American Journal of Evaluation, 20,* 199–212.

MacDonald, B., Adelman, C., Kushner, S., & Walker, R. (1982). *Bread and dreams: A case study in bilingual schooling in the U.S.A.* Norwich, UK: University of East Anglia, Centre for Applied Research in Education.

Malinowski, B. (1984). *Argonauts of the western Pacific.* Prospect Heights, IL: Waveland. (Original work published 1922)

Maxwell, J. A. (1992). Understanding and validity in qualitative research. *Harvard Educational Review, 63,* 279–300.

McCormick, S. (1994). A nonreader becomes a reader: A case study of literacy acquisition by a severely disabled reader. *Reading Research Quarterly, 29*(2), 157–176.

Messick, S. (1989). Validity. In R. L. Linn (Ed.), *Educational measurement* (3rd ed., pp. 13–103). New York: Macmillan.

Miles, M. B., & Huberman, A. M. (1994). *Qualitative data analysis* (2nd ed.). Thousand Oaks, CA: Sage.

Morris, E. (1979). *The rise of Theodore Roosevelt.* New York: Coward, McCann & Geognegan.

Parlett, M., & Hamilton, D. (1976). Evaluation as illumination: A new approach to the study of innovative programmes. In G. V Glass (Ed.), *Evaluation studies review annual* (Vol. 1, pp. 141–157). Beverly Hills, CA: Sage.

Patton, M. Q. (1990). *Qualitative evaluation and research methods* (2nd ed.). Newbury Park, CA: Sage.

Peshkin, A. (1986). *God's choice.* Chicago: University of Chicago Press.

Polanyi, M. (1962). *Personal knowledge: Towards a post-critical philosophy.* Chicago: University of Chicago Press.

Pugach, M. (1998). *On the border of opportunity: Education, community, and language at the U.S.-Mexico line.* Mahwah, NJ: Erlbaum.

Psathas, G. (1995). *Conversation analysis.* Thousand Oaks, CA: Sage.

Ragin, C. C. (1987). *The comparative method.* Berkeley: University of California Press.

Ragin, C. C. (1992). Cases of "What is a case?" In C. C. Ragin & H. S. Becker (Eds.), *What is a case? Exploring the foundations of social inquiry* (pp. 1–18). Cambridge, UK: Cambridge University Press.

Ragin, C. C., & Becker, H. S. (Eds.). (1992). *What is a case? Exploring the foundations of social inquiry.* Cambridge, UK: Cambridge University Press.

Raisin, S., & Britton, E. D. (1997). *Bold ventures: Patterns among U. S. innovations in science and mathematics education.* Dordrecht, the Netherlands: Kluwer Academic.

Richardson, L. (1997). *Fields of play.* New Brunswick, NJ: Rutgers University Press.

Robinson, W. S. (1951). The logical structure of analytic induction. *American Sociological Review, 16,* 812–818.

Rumelhart, D. E., H.Ortony, A. (1977). The representation of knowledge in memory. In R. C. Anderson, R. J. Spiro, & W. E. Montague (Eds.), *Schooling and the acquisition of knowledge* (pp. 99–135). Hillsdale, NJ: Erlbaum.

Ryan, G. W., & Bernard, H. R. (2000). Data analysis and management methods. In N. K. Denzin & Y. S. Lincoln (Eds.), *Handbook of qualitative research* (2nd ed., pp. 769–802). Newbury Park, CA: Sage.

Schön, D. (1983). *The reflective practitioner: How professionals think in action.* New York: Basic Books.

Schwandt, T. A. (1993). Theory for the moral sciences: Crisis of identity and purpose. In G. Mills & D. J. Flinders (Eds.), *Theory and concepts in qualitative research* (pp. 5–23). New York: Teachers College Press.

Schwandt, T. A. (2000). Three epistemological stances for qualitative inquiry: Interpretivism, hermeneutics, and social constructionism. In N. K. Denzin & Y. S. Lincoln (Eds.), *Handbook of qualitative research* (2nd ed., pp. 189–213). Newbury Park, CA: Sage.

Silverman, D. (1993). *Interpreting qualitative data.* London: Sage.

Silverman, D. (2000). Analyzing talk and text. In N. K. Denzin & Y. S. Lincoln (Eds.), *Handbook of qualitative research* (2nd ed., pp. 821–834). Newbury Park, CA: Sage.

Simons, H. (Ed.). (1980). *Towards a science of the singular.* Norwich, UK: University of East Anglia, Centre for Applied Research in Education.

Sjoberg, G., Williams, N., Vaughan, T. R., & Sjoberg, A. (1991). The case approach in social research: Basic methodological issues. In J. R. Feagin, A. M. Orum, & G. Sjoberg (Eds.), *A case for the case study* (pp. 27–79). Chapel Hill: University of North Carolina Press.

Smith, L. M. (1978). An evolving logic of participant observation, educational ethnography and other case studies. In L. Shulman (Ed.), *Review of Research in Education, 6* (pp. 316–377). Chicago: Peacock Press.

Smith, L. M. (1994). Biographical method. In N. K. Denzin & Y. S. Lincoln (Eds.), *Handbook of qualitative research* (pp. 286–305). Thousand Oaks, CA: Sage.

Smith, L. M., & Dwyer, D. (1979). *Federal policy in action: A case study of an urban education project.* Washington, DC: National Institute of Education.

Smith, R. (1889). *An Aberdeenshire Village Propaganda: Forty years ago.* Edinburgh: David Douglas.

Spiro, R. J., Vispoel, W. P., Schmitz, J. G., Samarapungavan, A., & Boerger, A. E. (1987). Knowledge acquisition for application: Cognitive flexibility and transfer in complex content domains. In B. C. Britton (Ed.), *Executive control processes* (pp. 177–199). Hillsdale, NJ: Lawrence Erlbaum.

Stake, R. E. (1978). The case study method of social inquiry. *Educational Researcher, 7*(2), 5–8.

Stake, R. E. (1988). Case study methods in educational research: Seeking sweet water. In R. M. Jaeger (Ed.), *Complementary methods for research in education* (pp. 253–278). Washington, DC: American Educational Research Association.

Stake, R. E. (1995). *The art of case study research.* Thousand Oaks, CA: Sage.

Stake, R. E. (2004). *Standards-based and responsive evaluation.* Thousand Oaks, CA: Sage.

Stake, R. E., & Trumbull, D. J. (1982). Naturalistic generalizations. *Review Journal of Philosophy and Social Science, 7,* 1–12.

Stenholm, B. (1984). *The Swedish school system.* Stockholm: The Swedish Institute.

Stenhouse, L. (1979). *The study of samples and the study of cases.* Presidential address to the annual conference of the British Educational Research Association.

Stenhouse, L. (1984). Library access, library use and user education in academic sixth forms: An autobiographical account. In R. G. Burgess (Ed.), *The research process in educational settings: Ten case studies* (pp. 211–234). London: Falmer.

Stouffer, S. A. (1941). Notes on the case-study and the unique case. *Sociometry, 4,* 349–357.

Strauss, A. L., & Corbin, J. (1990). *Basics of qualitative research: Grounded theory procedures and techniques.* Newbury Park, CA: Sage.

Tierney, W. (2000). Undaunted courage: Life history and the postmodern challenge. In N. K. Denzin & Y. S. Lincoln (Eds.), *Handbook of qualitative research* (pp. 537–554). Thousand Oaks, CA: Sage.

Tobin, J. (1989). *Preschool in three cultures.* New Haven, CT: Yale University Press.

van Maanen, J. (1988). *Tales of the field: On writing ethnography.* Chicago: University of Chicago Press.

Vaughan, D. (1992). Theory elaboration: The heuristics of case analysis. In C. C. Ragin & H. S. Becker (Eds.), *What is a case? Exploring the foundations of social inquiry* (pp. 173–202). Cambridge, UK: Cambridge University Press.

Vaughan, D. (1999). The dark side of organizations: Mistake, misconduct and disaster. *Annual Review of Sociology, 25,* 271–305.

von Wright, G. H. (1971). *Explanation and understanding.* London: Routledge & Kegan Paul.

White, H. C. (1992). Cases are for identity, for explanation, or for control. In C. C. Ragin & H. S. Becker (Eds.), *What is a case? Exploring the foundations of social inquiry* (pp. 83–104). Cambridge, UK: Cambridge University Press.

Wieviorka, M. (1988). *Sociétés et terrorisme.* Paris: Fayard.

Yin, R. K. (1984). *Case study research: Design and methods* (Applied Social Research Methods, Vol. 5). Beverly Hills, CA: Sage.

Yin, R. K. (1989). *Case study research: Design and methods* (2nd ed.). Newbury Park, CA: Sage.

Yin, R. K. (1992, November). *Evaluation: A singular craft.* Paper presented at the annual meeting of the American Evaluation Association, Seattle, WA.

18

THE OBSERVATION OF PARTICIPATION AND THE EMERGENCE OF PUBLIC ETHNOGRAPHY

Barbara Tedlock

Participant observation was created during the late 19th century as an ethnographic field method for the study of small, homogeneous cultures. Ethnographers were expected to live in a society for an extended period of time (2 years, ideally), actively participate in the daily life of its members, and carefully observe their joys and sufferings as a way of obtaining material for social scientific study. This method was widely believed to produce documentary information that not only was "true" but also reflected the native's own point of view about reality.[1]

The privileging of participant observation as a scientific method encouraged ethnographers to demonstrate their observational skills in scholarly monographs and their social participation in personal memoirs. This dualistic approach split public (monographs) from private (memoirs) and objective (ethnographic) from subjective (autobiographical) realms of experience. The opposition created what seems, from a 21st-century perspective, not only improbable but also morally suspect.[2]

More recently, ethnographers have modified participant observation by undertaking "the observation of participation" (B. Tedlock, 1991, 2000). During this activity, they reflect on and critically engage with their own participation within the ethnographic frame. A new genre, known as "autoethnography," emerged from this practice. Authors working in the genre attempt to heal the split between public and private realms by connecting the autobiographical impulse (the gaze inward) with the ethnographic impulse (the gaze outward). Autoethnography at its best is a cultural performance that transcends self-referentiality by engaging with cultural forms that are directly involved in the creation of culture. The issue becomes not so much distance, objectivity, and neutrality as closeness, subjectivity, and engagement. This change in approach emphasizes relational over autonomous patterns, interconnectedness over independence, translucence over transparency, and dialogue and performance over monologue and reading.[3]

Such once-taboo subjects as admitting one's fear of physical violence as well as one's intimate encounters in the field are now not only inscribed but also described and performed as social science data.[4] The philosophical underpinnings of this discourse lie in the domains of critical, feminist, poststructuralist, and postmodern theories, with their comparative, interruptive, non-universalistic modes of analysis. Social science in this environment has given up on simple data collection and instead "offers re-readings of representations in every form of information processing, empirical science, literature, film, television, and computer simulation" (Clough, 1992, p. 137).

Public Engagement

Early anthropology in the United States included a tradition of social criticism and public engagement. As a result, most articles and books of that time could be read, understood, and enjoyed by any educated person. Scholars such as Franz Boas, Ruth Benedict, and Margaret Mead shaped public opinion through their voluminous writing, public speaking, and calls for social and political action. Boas spent most of his career battling against the racist confusion of physical and cultural human attributes. His student Ruth Benedict, in her best-selling book *Patterns of Culture* (1934), promoted the notion of "culture" as not just those art events that found their way into the women's pages of the newspapers of her era, but a people's entire way of life. In so doing, she humanized non-elite and non-Western peoples—they too have culture—and delegitimated evolutionary ideas concerning hierarchies of peoples. Margaret Mead, in *Coming of Age in Samoa* (1928), contested the notion that adolescence was necessarily a period of strain. Later, in *Sex and Temperament in Three Primitive Societies* (1935), she argued against the dominant Western sexual ideology of her time, which claimed that men were naturally aggressive while women were naturally passive.[5]

By the 1950s, however, as academic culture in the United States felt the chill wind of the McCarthy era, many researchers no longer dared to address their work to the general public. Instead, they withdrew into small professional groups where they addressed one another. As they did so, they elaborated ever more elegant apolitical theoretical paradigms: functionalism, culture and personality, structuralism, componential analysis, and semiotics. In time, social and political disengagement became entrenched in academia and a strong taboo against any form of social criticism of hegemonic institutions or practices arose. It would not be until the mid-1960s that the critical function of ethnography in the United States would reappear. Stanley Diamond coined the term "critical anthropology" in 1963 and subsequently clarified its socially engaged nature in his journal *Dialectical Anthropology*.[6]

This rekindling of public engagement took place in the context of the civil rights movement, opposition to the war in Vietnam and other U.S. interventions in the Third World, the writings of the California branch of the Frankfurt School, and the research of educational revisionists. As a more general research paradigm, this renewed public and critical engagement was known as "critical theory." Scholars working within the paradigm saw it as a way to free academic work from capitalist domination and to help schools and other institutions to become places where people might be socially empowered rather than subjugated.[7]

One way critical theory was put into practice was through the production of plays addressing the economic and political plight of impoverished working people and peasants. In the mid-1960s, popular theater groups such as Bread and Puppet in the United States and *Teatro Campesino* in Mexico began working together as egalitarian collectives, producing free theater for the masses. The goal of such theater groups in Latin America was to politically transform the peasants' view of themselves as independent rural farmers to that of exploited, underpaid workers.

Paulo Freire theorized that this empowerment process, which he called *conscientization*, takes place whenever people recognize and act upon their own ideas rather than consuming the ideas of others. In *Pedagogy of the Oppressed* (1973), he described how the process of *conscientization* occurs by means of dialogue, during which people share information on institutional injustices and challenge powerful interests so as to change their own everyday realities. Grassroots participatory research grew out of this environment and became a strategy for groups lacking resources and power to work together to achieve political empowerment.[8]

As participatory research and grassroots theater became important movements in Latin America, university students and intellectuals, in their rush for solidarity with the masses, reduced cultural differences to class differences. What they failed to realize was that indigenous peoples live on the margins of capitalist society mainly for reasons of linguistic and religious differences, rather than simply because of economic disenfranchisement (Taylor, 2003, p. 198).

Peru's leading theater collective, *Grupo Cultural Yuyachkani*, has worked to avoid this politically naïve stance by making visible a combined multilingual and multiethnic epistemology. This predominantly "white," Spanish-speaking group is deeply involved with the local indigenous and mestizo populations as well as with transcultural Andean-Spanish ways of knowing and remembering. The Quechua part of their name, Yuyachkani, which means "I am thinking," "I am remembering," and "I am your thought," highlights their recognition of the complexity of Peru's social memory. It consists not only of archival memory existing in written texts but also, and perhaps more importantly, of embodied memory transmitted in performance. The group attempts to make its urban audiences able to recognize the many different ways of being "Peruvian," and in so doing it insists on creating a community of witnesses through its performances (Taylor, 2001).

There exists a similar history of popular theater in Africa (Coplan, 1986). In Ghana, for example, Concert Party Theatre combined oral and vernacular forms in such a way as to be simultaneously accessible to both illiterate and educated people (Cole, 2001). As in Latin America, intellectuals in Africa initially disapproved of popular theater for what they saw as its lack of social or political radicalism. They had been unaware of the political nature of the performances, which, instead of voicing criticism in a direct and obvious narrative form, subtly imbedded political subversion within the doing of the performance itself. The actors' self-positioning as "preachers," and the audiences' endorsement of this in their search for "lessons," created a new theater form that was neither mimetic nor spectacular, neither realist nor classical. Rather, it was a discourse of example. As such, it was both socially and politically engaged.[9]

Concert Party Theatre transformed the authorizing fiction of colonialism, "civilization," into a humorous practice rather than allowing it a fixed ontological status (cf. Bakhtin, 1984). This suggests that in order to discover the social, cultural, and political significance of popular theater, one must analyze the poetry of action. West African concert artists chose elements from local, national, continental, diasporic, European, and American sources and poetically reshaped them, producing an altogether new and powerful form of popular politics.

▣ Performance Ethnography

Performance is everywhere in life: from simple gestures to melodramas and macrodramas. Because dramatic performances can communicate engaged political and theoretical analysis, together with nuanced emotional portraits of human beings, they have gained acceptance by a number of documentarians. Plays and other performances become vibrant forms of ethnography that combine political, critical, and expressive actions centering on lived experiences locally and globally. A number of ethnographers have served as producers, actors, and dramaturges.[10]

There are two main types of performance ethnography that directly link anthropological and theatrical thought. One considers human behavior as performance, and the other considers performance as human interaction. Edith and Victor Turner suggested that every socioeconomic formation has its own cultural-aesthetic mirror in which it achieves self-reflexivity. Their goal was to aid students in understanding how people in a multitude of cultures experience their own social lives. To that end, they staged a Virginia wedding, the midwinter ceremony of the Mohawk, an Ndembu girl's puberty ceremony, and the Kwakiutl Hamatsa ceremony.[11]

Because culture is emergent in human interaction rather than located deep inside individual brains or hearts, or loosely attached to external material objects or impersonal social structures, dramas are a powerful way to both shape and show cultural construction in action. Because of this subjunctive quality, plays create and enact moral texts that communicate vibrant emotional portraits of human beings, together with an empathic response and deeply engaged political analysis (Cole, 1985).

Playwriting and production (as contrasted with writing short stories or novels) provide checks on flights of the imagination, because dramatic performance demands that the vision be embodied. Public performances encourage authors and performers to think concretely about what can be observed rather than dwelling on inner thoughts. Actors communicate, by means of gesture and other bodily forms, an understandable and believable mimetic reality for their spectators. Such performances operate on a feedback principle of approximating reality by checking the details and then refining the representation in a reiterative or "closed loop" approach. In contrast, novels and theatrical dramas, although they may be ethnographically informed, operate on a more "open" principle.

Because of these and other characteristics, popular theater, with its egalitarian "by the people, for the people" ethos, serves as an imitation of aspects of the sensible world, and thus is a form of cultural mimesis or representation. Milton Singer (1972) introduced the notion of "cultural performance" as an important institution embodying key aspects of cultural traditions. Since then, popular theater, especially improvisation, has been studied as cultural performance in many places. Popular theaters in Iran and Indonesia, as examples, are extemporized around minimal plots. The actors ad lib among themselves and dialogue with the audience.[12]

Music, song, dance, storytelling, puppetry, and other theatrical forms often are embraced as forms of political analysis, catharsis, and group healing by indigenous peoples who have experienced ethnic, cultural, and social displacement; grinding poverty; and horrendous acts of violence. Basotho migrant laborers, for example, respond to their social situation with highly evocative word music, creating a "cultural shield" against dependency, expropriation, and the dehumanizing relations of race and class in South Africa (Coplan, 1994). Women living in the *favelas*, or urban shantytowns, of Brazil create absurdist and black-humor modes of storytelling in the face of poverty, trauma, and tragedy. These stories aesthetically define and emotionally release the alienation and frustration caused by years of severe economic deprivation and social desperation (Goldstein, 2003). In so doing, they produce a commentary in which the actors, who are also their own authors, refuse the surplus of knowledge that typifies an authoritative author. These actor-authors, with the help of their audience members, create multiple comic subplots. As a result of this contingent situation, each performance is unique and unrepeatable.

An indigenous theater group in Mozambique produced a play in Maputo that opened with an attack on a market woman who was brutally killed and transformed into a spirit. A ceremony was then performed that included healing stories, songs, ritual bathing, and the holding and stroking of victims of violence as one would a frightened child. According to the group, the key purpose for writing and performing the drama was to mobilize women into a sex strike until the killing stopped (Nordstrum, 1997).

In Chiapas, Mexico, during the late 1980s, a group of Mayan farmers who had served for many years as informants to foreign ethnographers founded a theater company called *Lo'il Maxil*, or "Monkey Business" (Breslin, 1992). Their goal was to produce dramas that could showcase Mayan history and culture. From its inception, anthropologist Robert Laughlin worked as a dramaturge for the group. An early play they produced was titled *Herencia fatal*, "fatal inheritance"

(Sna Jtz'ibajom, 1996). It concerned two brothers who killed their sister in a dispute over land. Such disputes are still a common problem in rural Mexico and Guatemala, where siblings often end up in court due to a lack of adequate available agricultural land upon which to support their families.

The play opened with a curing ceremony showing a shaman at work. During the premiere in San Cristóbal, an initiated shaman, who also was a member of the troupe, sat backstage with the cast. In the middle of the performance, he suddenly jumped up and walked around to the front of the curtain in order to see if the shamanic healing was properly performed. Because this scene was an important part of the play's verisimilitude, it had to be absolutely true to life. If it were not, then the mostly Mayan audience would not connect with the cultural continuity message provided by the example of traditional healing. In the face of enormous historical injustices, in which the majority of the land is owned by absentee landholders, healing rituals allow Mayans a space for resistance and recuperation. This was accomplished in the play by revealing the ongoing colonial imperialism at the heart of Mayan social problems.

This and other plays have continued to be produced in dozens of rural Mayan hamlets, as well as in the large, multiethnic cities of Mexico and the United States (Laughlin, 1994, 1995). At the end of each performance, the cast and audience conduct a dialogue. Ideas for ways to improve the production as a work of art, cultural document, and political critique are aired, and changes are included in future performances. This type of feedback loop is at the heart of Bertholt Brecht's (1964) distinction between "traditional" and "epic" theater. Traditional theater is monologic, and as a result the spectators are unable to influence what happens on the stage because it is art and they represent life. Epic theater is dialogic, and as a result the audience undergoes a process of learning something about their lives. Popular theater consisting of ethnographically derived plays, also called "ethnodramas" (Mienczakowski, 1995, 1996), is located within the tradition of epic theater.

Another instructive example of ethnodrama is the Zuni play *Ma'l Okyattsik an Denihalowilli:we*, "Gifts from Salt Woman." It was written, sponsored, and performed several times in the 1990s by the theater group known as *Idiwanan An Chawe* or "Children of the Middle Place." This bilingual play, exploring the physical and spiritual care of Zuni Salt Lake, raised important issues about the United States government's continuing violation of Zuni sovereignty. The tribe sponsored a number of public performances in the pueblo as well as a cross-country tour. After each performance, the director, playwright, actors, dancers, singers, and audience members conversed about the meaning and interpretation of the play. In collaboration with the Appalachian group Roadside Theater, they also produced a bicultural play titled *Corn Mountain/Pine Mountain: Following the Seasons*, or *Dowa Yalanne/Ashek'ya Yalanne Debikwayinan Idulohha*. The performers included 3 Zuni and 3 Appalachian storytellers wearing modern dress and 16 traditionally dressed Zuni dancers and singers. Instead of underscoring cultural differences, of which there were many, they focused on the similarity of their reciprocal caring relationships with humans, animals, and mountains (Cocke, Porterfield, & Wemytewa, 2002).

Ethnodramas also have been used to address urban and institutional social issues. A performance piece centering on schizophrenia, titled *Syncing Out Loud: A Journey into Illness*, was presented in several residential psychiatric settings in Australia. The play was written by sociologists and performed by a group of professional actors and nursing students as a psychotherapeutic strategy intended to instruct both students and patients (Cox, 1989). Each performance was followed by an open forum that not only built communicative consensus but also revealed elements of the performance that were inaccurate and disenfranchising. As a result of this public performance-editing strategy, the script remained open ended and constantly evolving (Mienczakowski, 1996).

What happens when an ethnodrama is not handled in this manner was revealed in a play called *Talabot*, performed in 1988 by the Danish theatre group Odin Teatret (Hastrup,

1992). The central character was a Danish woman ethnographer, Kirsten Hastrup. She wrote a detailed autobiography for use by the cast in performing her life. The other characters—Knud Rasmussen (the Danish Polar explorer), Che Guevara (the Latin American revolutionary), and Antonin Artaud (the French surrealist poet)—were chosen to mirror specific elements in her life. Kirsten had read about Rasmussen's arctic explorations as a child, which is what lured her into anthropology. Che Guevara chose revolution to empower the weak, while Kirsten chose ethnography to defend weaker cultures. Antonin Artaud juxtaposed theater and the plague, and in so doing he mirrored Kirsten's own madness after her fieldwork, when she was caught in a spider's web of competing realities. The ethnographer also had a twin in the play, a trickster figure who, like herself, served as a mirror promising not to lie but never telling the whole truth either, a classic ethnographic dilemma (Crapanzano, 1986).

Kirsten's initial response to seeing the play staged was the feeling of shock and betrayal at "having been fieldworked upon" (Hastrup, 1995, p. 144). In analyzing her own discomfort, she noticed that exaggeration of her biography, accomplished through the use of masculine heroes, created schizophrenia in her self concept. As a result, she found she could neither fully identify with, nor fully distance herself from, the staged Kirsten. "She was neither my double nor an other. She restored my biography in an original way, being not-me and not-not-me at the same time. I was not represented, I was performed" (Hastrup, 1995, p. 141). When the theater troupe left Denmark for performances in Italy, she felt that they were running away with the meaning of her life, with her soul, and in so doing they had stripped her of her concept of a self. The pain this caused made her understand the informant's loss at the departure of the ethnographer, who for a brief time had encouraged her to see who she was for another.

Because Hastrup learned something about herself as a spectator, the play might be described as falling within the Brechtian category of "epic theater." However, because the director failed to include her responses and observations in his subsequent performances, the play operated in a traditional theatrical mode, revealing a fictive attitude toward reality. Thus, even though the play was ethnographically researched, it was not an ethnodrama in the epic mode, because it did not operate within a closed-loop feedback model of refining the details again and again until it became closer and closer to the reality of her life.

▣ Public Ethnography

At about the same time as the development of ethnodrama, a few publishing houses and professional associations began to encourage social scientists to communicate openly with nonspecialist audiences. One of the earliest and the most successful of these efforts was that of Jean Malaurie, who established the French series *Terre Humaine* at the publishing house Plon in Paris. Over the years, *Terre Humaine* developed an enormous public audience for its passionate and politically engaged narrative portraiture. This distinguished run of accessible narrative ethnographies and biographies is now more than 80 titles in length.[13]

A similar opening up of anthropology occurred in Britain and the United States. In 1985, The Royal Anthropological Institute, located in London, launched a new journal titled *Anthropology Today*. This bimonthly publication was designed to appeal to people working in neighboring disciplines, including other social sciences, education, film, health, development, refugee studies, and relief aid (Benthall, 1996). It has focused on still photography, ethnographic films, fieldwork dilemmas, native anthropology, globalization, and the role of anthropologists in development.

The American Anthropological Association also assumed a central role in stimulating a broader mission for the discipline of anthropology. The flagship journal of the association, the *American Anthropologist*, under the editorship of Barbara and Dennis Tedlock (1993–1998) included many more well-written, illustrated, passionate, moral, and politically engaged essays than ever before in its hundred-year history. The association also invited a group of scholars to its headquarters to discuss "Disorder in U.S. Society." On this occasion, Roy Rappaport (1995) suggested that engaged ethnography ought to both critique and enlighten members of one's own society. This stimulated the Center for Community Partnership at the University of Pennsylvania to initiate discussions of strategies for encouraging researching and writing about socially relevant topics. The center labeled its undertaking "public interest anthropology."[14]

More recently, a sociological collective at the University of California, Berkeley, undertook a project involving finely tuned participant observation within local political struggles worldwide. They documented many newly emerging social issues, including the privatization of nursing homes, the medicalization of breast cancer, and the dumping of toxic waste. Their work, which showed how ethnography could have a global reach and relevance, consisted of directly engaged fieldwork that was both conceptually rich and empirically concrete. In their edited volume, *Global Ethnography: Forces, Connections, and Imaginations in a Postmodern World* (Burawoy et al., 2000), they demonstrated how globalization impacted the daily lives of Kerala nurses, Irish software programmers, and Brazilian feminists, among dozens of other groups. In this work, we see clearly how researchers can weave back and forth within the storied lives of others, creating an engaged narrative grounded within a specific community that is, in turn, located within an international mosaic of global forces. In so doing, the veil of scientific professionalism that surrounded and protected social inquiry during the McCarthy era was pulled aside, revealing how private joys and troubles create and blend with larger national and international public issues.

As one group of progressive colleagues in anthropology focused their critical gaze within the borders of the United States, another group of progressive colleagues in the social sciences focused their critical gaze outside the United States. The School of American Research, located in Santa Fe, New Mexico, valorized both of these directions for anthropologists when in 2003 it split the prestigious J. I. Staley Prize between Reyna Rapp (1999) for her book on amniocentesis in the United States and Lawrence Cohen (1998) for his book on Alzheimer's disease in India. Rapp's ethnography centered on the moral conflicts women face when they choose to abort fetuses because of information gained by genetic testing. Cohen centered on the culturally and historically located description and embodiment of the anxiety surrounding aging. These authors not only are excellent researchers and writers but also are deeply implicated in and passionate about their topics. I consider their ethnographies, together with ethnodrama, as important forms of "public ethnography."

By public ethnography, I mean the type of research and writing that directly engages with the critical social issues of our time, including such topics as health and healing, human rights and cultural survival, environmentalism, violence, war, genocide, immigration, poverty, racism, equality, justice, and peace. Authors of such works passionately inscribe, translate, and perform their research in order to present it to the general public. They also use the observation of their own participation to understand and artistically portray the pleasures and sorrows of daily life at home as well as in many out-of-the-way places. In so doing, they emotionally engage, educate, and move the public to action.[15]

Public ethnography, as I conceive it, is both a theory and a practice. It straddles the domains of lived experience and recollected memory of time spent interacting in the field, on one hand, with time spent alone in reflection, interpretation, and analysis, on the other. As a revolutionary theory and a powerful pedagogical strategy, it creates a location within which new possibilities for describing and changing the world co-occur.

In an attempt to fulfill these new mandates, ethnographers are once again engaging with the general public. They are penning op-ed pieces in newspapers and writing magazine essays, popular books, short stories, and novels. They are also creating dramas, poems, performance pieces, films, videos, websites, and CD-ROMs.

These various ethnographic stagings are deeply "enmeshed in moral matters" (Conquergood, 1985, p. 2). Experimental theater, personal narratives, filmmaking, and documentary photography produce mimetic parallels through which the subjective is made present and available to its performers and witnesses. This is true for both indigenous and outsider ethnographers, producers, and performers.

Three recent books beautifully document public ethnography in action. Paul Farmer's *Pathologies of Power: Health, Human Rights, and the New War on the Poor* (2003) illustrates the way in which racism and gender inequality in the United States create disease and death. He passionately argues that health care should be a basic human right. Aihwa Ong, in her ethnography *Buddha Is Hiding: Refugees, Citizenship, the New America* (2003), documents the way in which Cambodian refugees become citizens through a combination of being-made and self-making. Along the way, she raises important questions about the meaning of citizenship in an age of rapid globalization.

David Anderson and Eeva Berglund, in their edited volume *Ethnographies of Conservation: Environmentalism and the Distribution of Privilege* (2003), reveal that conservation efforts not only fail to protect environments but also disempower already underprivileged groups. The authors make visible these marginalized peoples, examine how projects to protect landscapes are linked to myths of state identity and national progress, and show how conservation creates privileged enclaves for consumption while restricting local people's engagement with their environment. Drawing on the tradition of critical theory, they shed light on overlooked aspects of environmentalism, and as a result they were challenged by a powerful conservation organization that hinted at litigation if they published their critique. This extreme reaction to their project helped them to realize that their efforts "had moved the anthropological gaze toward relatively powerful organizations without giving these organizations the right of veto" (Berglund & Anderson, 2003, p. 15). To avoid a lawsuit but still publish their research, they edited their contributions so as to conceal all personal and organizational identities.

As scholars and activists produce more public ethnography, they will move ever further into the political arena. As they are read and listened to, they will encounter legal and other attempts to silence them. Such is the price of what Michael Fischer (2003, p. 2) has called "moral entrepreneurship," the directing of attention to matters about which something ought and might be done. This is a price that many researchers will pay happily in return for the chance to practice ethnography that makes a difference both at home and abroad.

We have moved far from the Enlightenment goals of "value-free" social science based on a rationalist presumption of canonical ethics; we have entered into the arena of postcolonial social science, with its focus on morally engaged research. This new ethical framework presumes that the public sphere consists of a mosaic of communities with a pluralism of identities and worldviews. Researchers and participants are united by a set of ethical values in which personal autonomy and communal well-being are interlocked. Undertaking research in alliance with indigenous, disabled, and other marginalized peoples empowers diverse cultural expressions and creates a vibrant discourse in the service of respect, freedom, equality, and justice. This new ethnography is deeply rooted in ideas of kindness, neighborliness, and a shared moral good. Within this politically engaged environment, social science projects serve the communities in which they are carried out, rather than serving external communities of educators, policy makers, military personnel, and financiers.[16]

▣ Conclusion

The observation of participation produces a combination of cognitive and emotional information that ethnographers can use to create engaged ethnodramas and other forms of public ethnography. Such performances and books address important social issues in a humanistic, self-reflexive manner, engaging both the hearts and the minds of their audiences. The public ethnographies currently being written, published, and performed today are robust examples of humanistic concerns and moral entrepreneurship in action. They will engage and embolden a whole new generation of scholars in many disciplines to tackle the ethical dilemmas stemming from ongoing developments in environmentalism, biotechnology, and information databases. There is much public ethnography yet to be done.

Notes

1. The replacement of armchair ethnography by experientially gained knowledge of other cultures was pioneered by Matilda Cox Stevenson, Alice Fletcher, Franz Boas, and Frank Hamilton Cushing (B. Tedlock, 2000, p. 456). This new type of research was claimed as a formal method later by Bronislaw Malinowski (Firth, 1985). Malinowski also claimed that anthropology was concerned with understanding other cultures from the "native's point of view" (1922, p. 25). For a discussion of the history and practice of participant observation, see B. Tedlock (2000).

2. This split between monographs and memoirs is illustrated by the books of Jean-Paul Dumont (1976, 1978).

3. For discussions of the genre of autoethnography, see Strathern (1987), Lionnet (1989), Deck (1990), Friedman (1990), B. Tedlock (1991), Okely and Callaway (1992), Pratt (1994), Van Maanen (1995), Ellis and Bochner (1996, 2000), Clough (1997), Harrington (1997), and Reed-Danahay (1997).

4. Examples of works touching on these topics include Cesara (1982), Weston (1991, 1998), Scheper-Hughes (1992), Kleinman and Copp (1993), Newton (1993), Wade (1993), Blackwood (1995), Bolton (1995), Dubisch (1995), Grindal and Salomone (1995), Kulick (1995), Kulick and Willson (1995), Lewin (1995), Nordstrum and Robben (1995), Shokeid (1995), Behar (1996), Daniel (1996), Kennedy and Davis (1996), Lewin and Leap (1996), Wafer (1996), Zulaika and Douglass (1996), Willson (1997), Lee-Treweek and Linkogle (2000), Theidon (2001), Wolcott (2002), Gusterson (2003), and Wax (2003).

5. A recent long essay in *The New Yorker* (Pierpont, 2004) profiled the public legacy of Boas as well as his students. See also the book on race by Benedict (1945).

6. See Diamond (1974) and Gailey (1992). Stanley Diamond founded the international journal *Dialectical Anthropology* in 1975. From its inception, it has had an important critical role in critiquing the discipline of anthropology: its intellectual leaders, paradigms, and representations.

7. See Marcuse (1964), Leacock (1969), Freire (1973), Bowles and Gintis (1976), Brodkey (1987), and Giroux (1988).

8. Participatory research, also known as "participatory action research," is closely associated with critical performance ethnography, liberation theory, neo-Marxism, and human rights activism. See Oliveira and Darcy (1975), Fals Borda and Rahman (1991), Whyte (1991), Marika, Ngurruwutthun, and White (1992), Park et al. (1993), Heron and Reason (1997), Cohen-Cruz (1998), Kemmis and McTaggart (2000), and Haedicke (2001).

9. For discussions of this new type of postcolonial politically engaged theater in Africa, see Desai (1990), Mlama (1991), Mda (1993), Kerr (1995), Idoko (1997), and Barber (2000).

10. For examples and discussions of performance ethnography, see Kuper (1970), Garner and Turnbull (1979), Grindal and Shepard (1986), Turner (1988), Turnbull in Higgins and Cannan (1984), D. Tedlock (1986, 1998, 2003), Conquergood (1989), McCall and Becker (1990), Richardson and Lockridge (1991), Hastrup (1992, 1995), Mienczakowski and Morgan (1993), Smith (1993), Allen and Garner (1994), Laughlin (1994), Bynum (1995), Isbell (1995), Kondo (1995), Mienczakowski (1995, 1996), Schevill and Gordon (1996), Cole (2001), Wolcott (2002), and Chatterjee (2003).

11. See Turner and Turner (1982), Schechner (1983, 1985), Schechner and Appel (1990), Turner (1988), Beeman (1993), and Bouvier (1994) for discussions of theatrical anthropology. This research is very different from Eugenio Barba's "theater anthropology," which is concerned with cross-cultural actor training (Barba & Savarese, 1991). For an analysis of Iranian popular theater, see Beeman (1979, 1981).

12. Ethnographic descriptions and discussions of Indonesian popular theater include those of Belo (1960), Peacock (1978), Wallis (1979), Keeler (1987), and Hobart (2002). Balinese popular theater can be observed in a classic documentary film by Bateson, Belo, and Mead (1952).

13. See Balandier (1987), Malaurie (1993), Descola (1996), and Aurégan (2001) for discussions about the

nature and impact of the series. For a recent title in this series, see B. Tedlock (2004).

14. Participants in the development and discussion of this activist paradigm within anthropology include Peggy Sanday (1976, 2003), James Peacock (1995, 1997), Anne Francis Okongwa and Joan P. Mencher (2000), and Julia Paley (2002), among others.

15. Some examples of advocacy and engaged ethnographic research include Bello, Cunningham, and Rav (1994), Curtis and McClellan (1995), Mullings (1995), Buck (1996), Dehavenon (1996), Seavey (1996), Zulaika and Douglass (1996), Harrison (1997), Cummins (1998), Thornton (1998), Brosius (1999), Fairweather (1999), Lyons and Lawrence (1999), Kim, Irwin, Millen, and Gershman (2000), Howitt (2001), McClusky (2001), Lamphere (2002), Gusterson (2003), Siegel (2003), Battiste and Youngblood Henderson (2004), Frommer (2004), Griffiths (2004), McIntosh (2004), Stevenson (2004), and B. Tedlock (2005). Electronically available reports and other information are becoming more and more important for researchers working in these rapidly developing areas. See, for example, both "New Issues in Refugee Research" and the monthly Refugee Livelihoods e-mail digest at www.unhcr.ch. See also the portal called "Forced Migration Online" at www.forcedmigration.org. and www.secure.migrationexpert.com.

16. For more information about, and models of, this morally engaged turn within the social sciences, see Harrison (1991), Denzin (1997), Frank (2000), and Chatterjii (2004). This is rapidly becoming a visible social movement. At the American Anthropological Association meeting in November, 2003, in Chicago, a coalition called the Justice Action Network of Anthropologists (JANA) was founded. Its membership list currently consists of more than 250 anthropologists from Canada, the United States, the United Kingdom, Australia, South Korea, Costa Rica, Mexico, and the Netherlands.

References

Allen, C., & Garner, N. (1994). *Condor qatay* [Play]. Produced and performed by the Department of Theatre and Dance, George Washington University, Dorothy Betts Marvin Theater, March 31–April 3.

Anderson, D. G., & Berglund, E. (Eds.). (1993). *Ethnographies of conservation: Environmentalism and the distribution of privilege.* New York: Berghahn Books.

Aurégan, P. (2001). *Des récits et des homes. Terre Humaine: un autre regard sur les sciences de l'homme.* Paris: Nathan/HER.

Bakhtin, M. (1984). *Rabelais and his world* (H. Iwolsky, Trans.). Bloomington: Indiana University Press.

Balandier, G. (1987). "Terre Humaine" as a literary movement. *Anthropology Today, 3,* 1–2.

Barba, E., & Savarese, N. (1991). *A dictionary of theatre anthropology: The secret art of the performer.* London: Routledge.

Barber, K. (2000). *The generation of plays: Yoruba popular life in theater.* Bloomington: Indiana University Press.

Bateson, G., Belo, J., & Mead, M. (1952). *Trance and dance in Bali* [Motion picture]. New York: New York University Film Library.

Battiste, M., & Youngblood Henderson, S. (2000). *Protecting indigenous knowledge and heritage: A global challenge.* Saskatoon, Saskatchewan: Purich.

Beeman, W. O. (1979). Cultural dimensions of performance conventions in Iranian Ta'ziyeh. In P. J. Chelkowski (Ed.), *Ta'ziyeh: Ritual and drama in Iran.* New York: New York University Press.

Beeman, W. O. (1981). Why do they laugh? An Interactional approach to humor in traditional Iranian improvisatory theatre. *Journal of American Folklore, 94*(374), 506–526.

Beeman, W. O. (1993). The anthropology of theater and spectacle. *Annual Reviews in Anthropology, 22,* 369–393.

Behar, R. (1996). *The vulnerable observer: Anthropology that breaks your heart.* Boston: Beacon.

Bello, W., Cunningham, S., & Rav, B. (1994). *Dark victory: The United States, structural adjustment, and global poverty.* London: Pluto.

Belo, J. (1960). *Trance in Bali.* New York: Columbia University Press.

Benedict, R. (1934). *Patterns of culture.* Boston: Houghton Mifflin.

Benedict, R. (1945). *Race: Science and politics.* New York: Viking.

Benthall, J. (1996). Enlarging the context of anthropology: The case of *Anthropology Today.* In J. MacClancy & C. McDonaugh (Eds.), *Popularizing anthropology* (pp. 135–141). London: Routledge.

Berglund, E., & Anderson, D. G. (1993). Introduction: Towards an ethnography of ecological underprivilege. In D. G. Anderson & E. Berglund (Eds.), *Ethnographies of conservation: Environmentalism and the distribution of privilege* (pp. 1–15). New York: Berghahn Books.

Blackwood, E. (1995). Falling in love with an-Other lesbian: Reflections on identity in fieldwork. In D. Kulick & M. Willson (Eds.), *Taboo: Sex, identity and erotic subjectivity in anthropological fieldwork* (pp. 51–75). London: Routledge.

Bolton, R. (1995). Tricks, friends, and lovers: Erotic encounters in the field. In D. Kulick & M. Willson (Eds.), *Taboo: Sex, identity and erotic subjectivity in anthropological fieldwork* (pp. 140–167). New York: Routledge.

Bouvier, H. (1994). Special issue on anthropology and theatre [Special issue]. *Theatre Research International, 19.*

Bowles, S., & Gintis, H. (Eds.). (1976). *Schooling in capitalist America.* New York: Basic Books.

Brecht, B. (1964). *Brecht on theater* (J. Willett, Ed.). New York: Hill & Wang.

Breslin, P. (1992, August). Coping with change: The Maya discover the play's the thing. *Smithsonian,* pp. 79–87.

Brodkey, L. (1987). Writing critical ethnographic narratives. *Anthropology and Education Quarterly, 18,* 67–76.

Brosius, P. J. (1999). Analyses and interventions: Anthropological engagements with environmentalism. *Current Anthropology, 40*(3), 277–309.

Buck, P. (1996). Sacrificing human rights on the altar of morality: White desperation, far right, and punitive social welfare reform. *Urban Anthropology, 25*(2), 195–210.

Burawoy, M., Blum, J. A., George, S., Gill, Z., Gowan, T., Haney, L., et al. (2000). *Global ethnography: Forces, connections, and imaginations in a postmodern world.* Berkeley: University of California Press.

Bynum, B. (1995, December). *My heart is still aching* [Play]. Performed at the American Anthropological Association Meeting in Atlanta, GA.

Cesara, M. [pseudonym of K. Poewe]. (1982). *Reflections of a woman anthropologist: No hiding place.* London: Academic Press.

Chatterjee, P. (2003). Staging "A time for tea": Theater and poetry in writing the plantation. *XCP (Cross Cultural Poetics), 12,* 72–78.

Chatterjii, A. (2004). Anthropology and cultural survival: On representations of indigenousness. *Anthropology News, 45*(3), 7–8.

Clough, P. T. (1992). *The end(s) of ethnography: From realism to social criticism.* Newbury Park, CA: Sage.

Clough, P. T. (1997). Autotelecommunication and autoethnography: A reading of Carolyn Ellis's *Final negotiations. Sociological Quarterly, 38,* 95–110.

Cocke, D., Porterfield, D., & Wemytewa, E. (2002). *Journeys home: Revealing a Zuni-Appalachia collaboration.* Zuni, NM: A:shiwi Publishing.

Cohen, L. (1998). *No aging in India: Alzheimer's, the bad family, and other modern things.* Berkeley: University of California Press.

Cohen-Cruz, J. (Ed.). (1998). *Radical street performance: An international anthology.* New York: Routledge.

Cole, C. M. (2001). *Ghana's concert party theatre.* Bloomington: Indiana University Press.

Conquergood, D. (1985). Performing as a moral act: Ethical dimensions of the ethnography of performance. *Literature in Performance, 5,* 1–13.

Conquergood, D. (1989). Poetics, play, process and power: The performance turn in anthropology. *Text and Performance Quarterly, 9,* 81–88.

Coplan, D. (1986). Ideology and tradition in South African black popular theater. *Journal of American Folklore, 99,* 151–176.

Coplan, D. (1994). *In the time of cannibals: The word music of South Africa's Basotho migrants.* Chicago: University of Chicago Press.

Cox, H. (1989). Drama in the arts lab. *Australian Nurses Journal, 19*(1), 14–15.

Crapanzano, V. (1986). Hermes' dilemma: The masking of subversion in ethnographic description. In J. Clifford & G. Marcus (Eds.), *Writing culture: The poetics and politics of ethnography* (pp. 51–76). Berkeley: University of California Press.

Cummins, J. (1998). Organic agriculture and the threat of genetic engineering. *Third World Resurgence, 93,* 6–7.

Curtis, K., & McClellan, S. (1995). Falling through the safety net: Poverty, food assistance and shopping constraints in an American city. *Urban Anthropology, 24,* 93–135.

Daniel, E. V. (1996). *Charred lullabies: Chapters in an anthropology of violence.* Princeton, NJ: Princeton University Press.

Deck, A. (1990). Autoethnography: Zora Neale Hurston, Noni Jabavu, and cross-disciplinary discourse. *Black American Literature Forum, 24,* 237–256.

Dehavenon, A. (1996). *From bad to worse at the emergency assistance unit: How New York City tried to stop sheltering homeless families in 1996.* New York: Action Research Project.

Denzin, N. K. (1997). *Interpretive ethnography: Ethnographic practices for the 21st century.* Thousand Oaks, CA: Sage.

Desai, G. (1990). Theater as praxis: Discursive strategies in African popular theater. *African Studies Review, 33*(1), 65–92.

Descola, P. (1996). A *bricoleur's* workshop: Writing *Les lances du créspuscule.* In J. MacClancy & C. McDonaugh (Eds.), *Popularizing anthropology* (pp. 208–224). London: Routledge.

Diamond, S. (1974). *In search of the primitive: A critique of civilization.* New Brunswick, NJ: Transaction Books.

Dubisch, J. (1995). Lovers in the field: Sex, dominance, and the female anthropologist. In D. Kulick & M. Willson (Eds.), *Taboo: Sex, identity and erotic subjectivity in anthropological fieldwork* (pp. 29–50). London: Routledge.

Dumont, J.-P. (1976). *Under the rainbow: Nature and supernature among the Panaré Indians.* Austin: University of Texas Press.

Dumont, J.-P. (1978). *The headman and I: Ambiguity and ambivalence in the fieldworking experience.* Austin: University of Texas Press.

Ellis, C., & Bochner, A. P. (Eds.). (1996). *Composing ethnography: Alternative forms of qualitative writing.* Walnut Creek, CA: AltaMira.

Ellis, C., & Bochner, A. P. (2000). Autoethnography, personal narrative, reflexivity. In N. K. Denzin & Y. S. Lincoln (Eds.). *Handbook of qualitative research* (2nd ed., pp. 733–768). Thousand Oaks, CA: Sage.

Fairweather, J. R. (1999). Understanding how farmers choose between organic and conventional production: Results from New Zealand and policy implications. *Agriculture and Human Values, 16*(1), 51–63.

Fals Borda, O., & Rahman, M. A. (Eds.). (1991). *Action and knowledge: Breaking the monopoly with participatory action-research.* New York: Apex.

Farmer, P. (2003). *Pathologies of power: Health, human rights, and the new war on the poor.* Berkeley: University of California Press.

Firth, R. (1985). Degrees of *intelligibility.* In J. Overing (Ed.), *Reason and morality* (pp. 29–46). London: Tavistock.

Fischer, M. J. (2003). *Emergent forms of life and the anthropological voice.* Durham, NC: Duke University Press.

Frank, G. (2000). *Venus on wheels: Two decades of dialogue on disability, biography, and being female in America.* Berkeley: University of California Press.

Freire, P. (1973). *Pedagogy of the oppressed.* New York: Seabury.

Friedman, N. (1990). Autobiographical sociology. *American Sociologist, 21,* 60–66.

Frommer, C. (2004). Protecting traditional medicinal knowledge. *Cultural Survival, 27*(4), 83–87.

Gailey, C. W. (1992). Introduction: Civilization and culture in the work of Stanley Diamond. In C. W. Gailey (Ed.), *Dialectical anthropology: Essays in honor of Stanley Diamond* (pp. 1–25). Gainesville: University Press of Florida.

Garner, N. C., & Turnbull, C. M. (1979). *Anthropology, drama, and the human experience.* Washington, DC: George Washington University.

Giroux, H. (1988). Critical theory and the politics of culture and voice: Rethinking the discourse of educational research. In R. Sherman & R. Webb (Eds.), *Qualitative research in education: Focus and methods* (pp. 190–210). New York: Falmer.

Goldstein, D. M. (2003). *Laughter out of place: Race, class, violence, and sexuality in a Rio shantytown.* Berkeley: University of California Press.

Griffiths, T. (2004). Help or hindrance? The global environment facility, biodiversity conservation, and indigenous peoples. *Cultural Survival, 28*(1), 28–31.

Grindal, B., & Salomone, F. (Eds.). (1995). *Bridges to humanity: Narratives on anthropology and friendship.* Prospect Heights, IL: Waveland.

Grindal, B., & Shepard, W. H. (1986, November). *Redneck girl* [Play].

Gusterson, H. (2003). Anthropology and the military: 1968, 2003, and beyond? *Anthropology Today, 19*(3), 25–26.

Haedicke, S. C. (2001). Theater for the next generation: The Living Stage Theatre Company's program for teen mothers. In S. C. Haedicke & E. Nellhaus (Eds.), *Performing democracy: International pe spectives on urban community-based performance* (pp. 269–280). Ann Arbor: University of Michigan Press.

Harrington, W. (1997). *Intimate journalism: The art and craft of reporting everyday life.* Thousand Oaks, CA: Sage.

Harrison, F. V. (1991). Ethnography as politics. In F. V. Harrison (Ed.), *Decolonizing anthropology: Moving further toward an anthropology for liberation* (pp. 88–109). Washington, DC: Association of Black Anthropologists, American Anthropological Association.

Harrison, F. V. (1997). The gendered politics and violence of structural adjustment: View from Jamaica. In L. Lamphere, H. Ragoné, & P. Zavella (Eds.), *Situated lives—gender and culture in everyday life* (pp. 451–468). New York: Routledge.

Hastrup, K. (1992). Out of anthropology: The anthropologist as an object of dramatic representation. *Cultural Anthropology,7,* 327–345.

Hastrup, K. (1995). *A passage to anthropology: Between experience and theory.* London: Routledge.

Heron, J., & Reason, P. (1997). A participatory inquiry paradigm. *Qualitative Inquiry, 3,* 274–294.

Higgins, C., & Cannan, D. (1984). *The Ik* [Play]. Woodstock, IL: The Dramatic Publishing Company.

Hobart, M. (2002). Live or dead? Televising theater in Bali. In F. D. Ginsburg, L. Abu-Lughod, & B. Larkin (Eds.), *Media worlds: Anthropology on new terrain* (pp. 370–382). Berkeley: University of California Press.

Howitt, R. (2001). *Rethinking resource management: Justice, sustainability, and indigenous peoples.* New York: Routledge.

Idoko, E. F. (1997). "Residual" forms: Viable tools for community development through drama—the "Tandari" experiment. *Borno Museum Society Newsletter, 30–31,* 27–36.

Isbell, B. J. (1995). Women's voices: Lima 1975. In D. Tedlock & B. Mannheim (Eds.), *The dialogic emergence of culture* (pp. 54–74). Urbana: University of Illinois Press.

Keeler, W. (1987). *Javanese shadow plays: Javanese selves.* Princeton, NJ: Princeton University Press.

Kemmis, S., & McTaggart, R. (2000). Participatory action research. In N. K. Denzin & Y. S. Lincoln (Eds.), *Handbook of qualitative research* (2nd ed., pp. 567–605). Thousand Oaks, CA: Sage.

Kennedy, E. L., & Davis, M. D. (1996). *Boots of leather, slippers of gold: The history of a lesbian community.* London: Routledge.

Kerr, D. (1995). *African popular theatre.* London: James Currey.

Kim, J. Y., Irwin, A., Millen, J., & Gershman, J. (2000). *Dying for growth: Global inequality and the health of the poor.* Monroe, ME: Common Courage.

Kleinman, S., & Copp, M. A. (Eds.). (1993). *Emotions and fieldwork.* Newbury Park, CA: Sage.

Kondo, D. (1995). Bad girls: Theater, women of color, and the politics of representation. In R. Behar & D. Gordon (Eds.), *Women writing culture* (pp. 49–64), Berkeley: University of California Press.

Kulick, D. (1995). The sexual life of anthropologists: Erotic subjectivity and ethnographic work. In D. Kulick & M. Willson (Eds.), *Taboo: Sex, identity and erotic subjectivity in anthropological fieldwork* (pp. 1–28). London: Routledge.

Kulick, D., & Willson, M. (Eds.). (1995). *Taboo: Sex, identity and erotic subjectivity in anthropological fieldwork.* London: Routledge.

Kuper, H. (1970). *A witch in my heart: A play set in Swaziland in the 1930s.* London: Oxford University Press.

Lamphere, L. (2002). *Structuring diversity: Ethnographic perspectives on the new immigration.* Chicago: University of Chicago Press.

Laughlin, R. M. (1994, March). *From all for all* [Play]. Performed March 24 at the conference "La sabiduria Maya ah idzatil: The wisdom of the Maya," Gainesville, FL.

Laughlin, R. M. (1995). From all for all: A Tzotzil-Tzeltal tragicomedy. *American Anthropologist, 97*(3), 528–542.

Leacock, E. (1969). *Teaching and learning in city schools: A comparative study.* New York: Basic Books.

Lee-Treweek, G., & Linkogle, S. (Eds.). (2000). *Danger in the field: Ethics and risk in social research.* London: Routledge.

Lewin, E. (1995). Writing lesbian ethnography. In R. Behar & D. Gordon (Eds.), *Women writing culture* (pp. 322–335). Berkeley: University of California Press.

Lewin, E., & Leap, W. L. (Eds.). (1996). *Out in the field: Reflections of lesbian and gay anthropologists.* Urbana: University of Illinois Press.

Lionnet, F. (1989). Autoethnography: The an-archic style of *Dust tracks on a* road. In F. Lionnet (Ed.), *Autobiographical voices: Race, gender, self-portraiture* (pp. 97–129). Ithaca, NY: Cornell University Press.

Lyons, K., & Lawrence, G. (1999). Alternative knowledges, organic agriculture, and the biotechnology debate. *Culture and Agriculture, 21*(2), 1–12.

Malaurie, J. (1993). *Le livre Terre Humaine* (Vol. 1). Paris: Plon.

Malinowski, B. (1922). *Argonauts of the western Pacific.* London: Routledge.

Marcuse, H. (1964). *One dimensional man: Studies in ideology of advanced industrial society.* New York: Houghton Mifflin.

Marika, R., Ngurruwutthun, D., & White, L. (1992). Always together, Yaka gäna: Participatory research at Yirrkala as part of the development of Yolngu education. *Convergence,*25(1), 23–39.

McCall, M., & Becker, H. S. (1990). Performance science. *Social Problems, 32,* 117–132.

McClusky, L. J. (2001). *Here our culture is hard: Stories of domestic violence from a Mayan community in Belize.* Austin: University of Texas Press.

McIntosh, I. S. (2004). Seeking environmental and social justice. *Cultural Survival, 28*(1), 5.

Mda, Z. (1993). *When people play people: Development communication through theatre.* London: Zed Books.

Mead, M. (1928). *Coming of age in Samoa.* Harmondsworth, UK: Penguin.

Mead, M. (1935). *Sex and temperament in three primitive societies.* Harmondsworth, UK: Penguin.

Mienczakowski, J. (1995). The theatre of ethnography: The reconstruction of ethnography into theatre with emancipatory potential. *Qualitative Inquiry, 1*(3), 360–375.

Mienczakowski, J. (1996). An ethnographic act: The construction of consensual theatre. In C. Ellis & A. P. Bochner (Eds.), *Composing ethnography: Alternative forms of qualitative writing* (pp. 244–264). Walnut Creek, CA: AltaMira.

Mienczakowski, J., & Morgan, S. (1993). *Busting: The challenge of the drought spirit* [Play]. Brisbane, Australia: Griffith University Reprographics.

Mlama, P. M. (1991). *Culture and development: The popular theatre approach in Africa.* Uppsala, Sweden: Scandinavian Institute of African Studies.

Mullings, L. (1995). Households headed by women: The politics of race, class and gender. In S. D. Ginsburg & R. Rapp (Eds.), *Conceiving the new world order: The global politics of reproduction* (pp. 122–139). Berkeley: University of California Press.

Newton, E. (1993). My best informant's dress: The erotic equation in fieldwork. *Cultural Anthropology, 8,* 3–23.

Nordstrum, C. (1997). *A different kind of war story.* Philadelphia: University of Pennsylvania Press.

Nordstrum, C., & Robben, A. C. (Eds.). (1995). *Fieldwork under fire: Contemporary studies of violence and survival.* Berkeley: University of California Press.

Okely, J., & Callaway, H. (Eds.). (1992). *Anthropology and autobiography.* London: Routledge.

Okongwa, A. F., & Mencher, J. P. (2000). Anthropology of public policy: Shifting terrains. *Annual Review of Anthropology, 29,* 107–124.

Oliveira, R., & Darcy, M. (1975). *The militant observer: A sociological alternative.* Geneva: IDAC.

Ong, A. (2003). *Buddha is hiding: Refugees, citizenship, the new America.* Berkeley: University of California Press.

Paley, J. (2002). Toward an anthropology of democracy. *Annual Review of Anthropology, 31,* 469–496.

Park, P., et al. (Eds.). (1993). *Voices of change: Participatory research in the United States and Canada.* Toronto, Canada: OISE.

Peacock, J. L. (1978). Symbolic reversal and social history: Transvestites and clowns of Java. In B. Babcock (Ed.), *The reversible world: Symbolic inversion in art and society* (pp. 209–224). Ithaca, NY: Cornell University Press.

Peacock, J. L. (1995). American cultural values: Disorders and challenges. In S. Forman (Ed.), *Diagnosing America: Anthropology and public engagement* (pp. 23–50). Ann Arbor: University of Michigan Press.

Peacock, J. L. (1997). The future of anthropology. *American Anthropologist, 99*(1), 9–17.

Pierpont, C. R. (2004, March 8). The measure of America: How a rebel anthropologist waged war on racism. *The New Yorker,* pp. 48–63.

Pratt, M. L. (1994). Transculturation and autoethnography: Peru 1615/1980. In F. Barker, P. Hulme, & M. Iverson (Eds.), *Colonial discourse/postcolonial theory* (pp. 24–46). Manchester, UK: Manchester University Press.

Rapp, R. (1999). *Testing women, testing the fetus: The social impact of amniocentesis in America.* New York: Routledge.

Rappaport, R. (1995). Disorders of our own. In S. Forman (Ed.), *Diagnosing America: Anthropology and public engagement* (pp. 235–294). Ann Arbor: University of Michigan Press.

Reed-Danahay, D. E. (1997). *Auto-ethnography: Rewriting the self and the social.* Oxford, UK: Berg.

Richardson, L., & Lockridge, E. (1991). The sea monster: An ethnographic drama. *Symbolic Interaction, 14,* 335–340.

Sanday, P. (1976). *Anthropology and the public interest: Fieldwork and theory.* New York: Academic Press.

Sanday, P. (2003, November). *Public interest anthropology: A model for engaged social science.* Paper prepared for the Public Interest Anthropology Workshop, Chicago.

Schechner, R. (1983). Points of contact between anthropological and theatrical thought. *South Asian Anthropologist, 4*(1), 9–30.

Schechner, R. (1985). *Between theater and anthropology.* Philadelphia: University of Pennsylvania Press.

Schechner, R. & Appel, W. (Eds.). (1990). *By means of performance.* Cambridge, UK: Cambridge University Press.

Scheper-Hughes, N. (1992). *Death without weeping: The violence of everyday life in Brazil.* Berkeley: University of California Press.

Schevill, J., & Gordon, A. (1996). *The myth of the docile woman* [Play]. San Francisco, CA: California On Stage.

Seavey, D. (1996). *Back to basics: Women's poverty and welfare reform.* Washington, DC: Center for Research on Women.

Shokeid, M. (1995). *A gay synagogue in New York.* New York: Columbia University Press.

Siegel, S. (2003, December). *Conservation at all costs: How industry backed environmentalism creates violent conflict among indigenous peoples.* Corporate Watch. Retrieved from www.corpwatch.org/

Singer, M. (1972). *When a great tradition modernizes.* London: Pall Mall.

Smith, A. D. (1993). *Fires in the mirror: Crown Heights, Brooklyn, and other identities.* [Play]. Garden City, NY: Anchor.

Sna Jtz'ibajom (1996). *Xcha'kuxesel ak'ob elav ta slumal batz'i viniketik ta Chyapa. Renacimiento del teatro Maya en Chiapas* (2 vols.). San Cristóbal, Mexico: La Casa del Escritor.

Stevenson, M. G. (2004). Decolonizing co-management in northern Canada. *Cultural Survival, 28*(1), 68–71.

Strathern, M. (1987). The limits of auto-anthropology. In A. Jackson (Ed.), *Anthropology at home* (pp. 59–67). London, UK: Tavistock.

Taylor, D. (2001). Yuyachkani: Remembering community. In S. C. Haedicke & E. Nellhaus (Eds.), *Performing democracy: International perspectives on urban community-based performance* (pp. 310–325). Ann Arbor: University of Michigan Press.

Taylor, D. (2003). *The archive and the repertoire: Performing cultural memory in the Americas.* Durham, NC: Duke University Press.

Tedlock, B. (1991). From participant observation to the observation of participation: The emergence of narrative ethnography. *Journal of Anthropological Research, 47,* 69–94.

Tedlock, B. (2000). Ethnography and ethnographic representation. In N. K. Denzin & Y. S. Lincoln (Eds.), *Handbook of qualitative research* (2nd ed., pp. 455–484). Thousand Oaks, CA: Sage.

Tedlock, B. (2004). *Rituels et pouvoirs, les Indiens Zuñis Nouveau-Mexique.* Paris: Editions Plon, Collection Terre Humaine.

Tedlock, B. (2005). Struggles between nation states and native peoples over herbal medicines and indigenous crops. In K. Torjesen & D. Champagne (Eds.), *Indigenous peoples and the modern state* (pp. 43–59). Walnut Creek, CA: AltaMira.

Tedlock, D. (1986).The translator or why the crocodile was not disillusioned: A play in one act. *Translation Review, 20,* 6–8.

Tedlock, D. (1998, April). *Man of Rabinal: The Mayan dance of the trumpets of sacrifice* [Play]. Produced and performed in the Katharine Cornell Theater, State University of New York at Buffalo.

Tedlock, D. (2003). *Rabinal Achi: A Mayan drama of war and sacrifice.* New York: Oxford University Press.

Theidon, K. (2001). Terror's talk—fieldwork and war. *Dialectical Anthropology, 26*(1), 19–35.

Thornton, T. (1998). Crisis in the last frontier: The Alaskan subsistence debate. *Cultural Survival, 22*(3), 29–34.

Turner, V. (1988). *The anthropology of performance.* New York: PAJ Publications.

Turner, V., & Turner, E. (1982). Performing ethnography. *Drama Review, 26*(2), 33–50.

Van Maanen, J. (1995). An end to innocence: The ethnography of ethnography. In J. Van Maanen (Ed.). *Representation in ethnography* (pp. 1–35). Thousand Oaks, CA: Sage.

Wade, P. (1993). Sexuality and masculinity among Colombian blacks. In D. Bell, P. Caplan, & W. J. Karim (Eds.), *Gendered fields: Women, men and ethnography* (pp. 199–214). London: Routledge.

Wafer, J. (1996). Out of the closet and into print: Sexual identity in the textual field. In E. Lewin & W. L. Leap (Eds.), *Out in the field: Reflections of lesbian and gay anthropologists* (pp. 262–273). Urbana: University of Illinois Press.

Wallis, R. (1979). Balinese theater: Coping with old and new. *Papers in International Studies: Southeast Asia Series, 52,* 37–47.

Wax, M. L. (2003). Wartime dilemmas of an ethical anthropology. *Anthropology Today, 19*(3), 23–24.

Weston, K. (1991). *Families we choose: Lesbians, gays, kinship.* New York: Columbia University Press.

Weston, K. (1998). *Long slow burn: Sexuality and social science.* London: Routledge.

Whyte, W. F. (Ed.). (1991). *Participatory action research.* London: Sage.

Willson, M. (1997). Playing the dance, dancing the game: Race, sex and stereotype in anthropological fieldwork. *Ethnos, 62*(3–4), 24–48.

Wolcott, H, F. (2002). *Sneaky Kid and its aftermath: Ethics and intimacy in fieldwork.* Walnut Creek, CA: AltaMira.

Zulaika, J., & Douglass, W. A. (1996). *Terror and taboo: The follies, fables, and faces of terrorism.* New York: Routledge.

19

INTERPRETIVE PRACTICE AND SOCIAL ACTION

James A. Holstein and Jaber F. Gubrium

Qualitative inquiry's analytic pendulum is constantly in motion. There have been times when naturalism was on the upswing, when the richly detailed description of social worlds was the goal. At other times, analysis has shifted toward the processes by which these worlds and their experiences are socially constructed. The pendulum has even doubled back on itself as postmodern sensibilities refocus the analytic project on itself, viewing it as a source of social reality in its own right (see Gubrium & Holstein, 1997). Although it can be unsettling, the oscillation invariably clears new space for growth.

This chapter capitalizes on a momentum that is currently building among qualitative researchers interested in the practical accomplishment of meaning and its relation to social action. As social constructionist analysis expands, diversifies, and claims an increasingly prominent place on the qualitative scene, analysts are drawing new inspiration from ingenious "misreadings" and innovative admixtures of canonical sources. Recently, ethnomethodological sensibilities have been appropriated to the constructionist move (see Gubrium & Holstein, 1997; Holstein & Gubrium, 2000), heightening and broadening its analytic acuity. At the same time, yet riding a different current in the discursive and linguistic flow of the social sciences, poststructuralist discourse analysis has suffused constructionism with cultural, institutional, and historical concerns. This chapter outlines one attempt to explore and extend the discursive and interactional terrain that is emerging at the intersection of ethnomethodology and Foucauldian discourse analysis.

For some time, qualitative researchers have been interested in documenting the processes by which social reality is constructed, managed, and sustained. Alfred Schutz's (1962, 1964, 1967, 1970) social phenomenology, Peter Berger and Thomas Luckmann's (1966) social constructionism, and process-oriented strains of symbolic interactionism (e.g., Blumer, 1969; Hewitt, 1997; Weigert, 1981) all have contributed to the constructionist project, but ethnomethodology arguably has been the most analytically radical and empirically productive in specifying the actual procedures through which social order is accomplished (see Garfinkel, 1967; Heritage, 1984; Maynard & Clayman, 1991; Mehan & Wood, 1975; Pollner 1987, 1991).[1] The analytic emphasis throughout has been on the question of *how* social reality is constructed, with ethnomethodology taking the lead in documenting the mechanisms by which this is accomplished in everyday life.

Recently, a new set of concerns has emerged in relation to ethnomethodology, reflecting a heretofore suspended interest in *what* is being accomplished, under *what* conditions, and out of *what* resources. Older naturalistic questions are being resurrected, but with a more analytically sophisticated, empirically sensitive mien, and with a view toward social action. Analyses of reality construction are now re-engaging questions concerning the broad cultural and the institutional contexts of meaning-making and social order. The emerging empirical horizons, while still centered on processes of social accomplishment, are increasingly viewed in terms of "interpretive practice"—the constellation of procedures, conditions, and resources through which reality is apprehended, understood, organized, and conveyed in everyday life (Gubrium & Holstein, 1997; Holstein, 1993; Holstein & Gubrium, 2000). Interpretive practice engages both the *hows* and the *whats* of social reality; it is centered in both how people methodically construct their experiences and their worlds, and in the configurations of meaning and institutional life that inform and shape their reality-constituting activity. A growing attention to both the *hows* and the *whats* of the social construction process echoes Karl Marx's (1956) adage that people actively construct their worlds but not completely on, or in, their own terms. The dual concern not only makes it possible to understand the construction process but also foregrounds the realities themselves that enter into and are produced by the process.

The new set of concerns converges on the issue of social action. Strict attention to the *hows* of the construction process informs us of the mechanisms by which social forms are brought into being in everyday life. But this tells us little about the shape and distribution of these realities in their own right. The possibility, for example, that family troubles will be constructed a particular way at some time and place, and differently in another, is glossed over for the construction process. The *whats* of social reality are outshone by attending exclusively to the *hows* of its construction. It's the times and places of these *whats*—the *whens* and the *wheres*—that locate the concrete, yet constructed, realities that challenge us. Attending to the latter offers a basis for making particular choices and taking action. Although an approach that emphasizes the *hows* of the construction process rests on the assumption that social life is not set in stone but is a product of practical choices, there is a need to attend carefully to the choices in tow as well as imminent possibilities. The latter moves interpretive practice into the realm of politics.

▣ Foundational Matters

Interpretive practice has diverse conceptual bases. These range from Schutz's development of a social phenomenology, to the related empirical concerns embodied in ethnomethodological programs of research developed in the wake of Harold Garfinkel's (1967) early studies and later work on talk in interaction (see Sacks, 1992; Silverman, 1998), and to the contemporaneous studies of institutional and historical discourses presented by Michel Foucault (see Dreyfus & Rabinow, 1982). Let us consider these in turn as they point us toward more recent developments.

Phenomenological Background

Edmund Husserl's (1970) philosophical phenomenology provides the point of departure for Schutz and other social phenomenologists. Concerned with the experiential underpinnings of knowledge, Husserl argues that the relation between perception and its objects is not passive. Rather, human consciousness actively constitutes objects of experience. Consciousness, in other words, is always consciousness-of-something. It does not stand alone, over and above experience, more or less immaculately perceiving and conceiving objects and events, but, instead, exists always already—from the start—as a constitutive part of what it is conscious of. Although the term "construction" came into fashion much later, we might say that consciousness constructs as much as it perceives the world. Husserl's project is to investigate the structures of consciousness that make it possible to apprehend an empirical world.

Schutz (1962, 1964, 1967, 1970) turns Husserl's philosophical project toward the ways in which ordinary members of society attend to their everyday lives, introducing a set of tenets that aligns with ethnomethodological sensibilities. He argues that the social sciences should focus on the ways that the life world—the world every individual takes for granted—is experienced by its members. Schutz cautions that "the safeguarding of [this] subjective point of view is the only but sufficient guarantee that the world of social reality will not be replaced by a fictional non-existing world constructed by the scientific observer" (1970, p. 8). From this perspective, the scientific observer deals with how the social world is made meaningful. Her focus is on *how* members of the social world apprehend and act upon the objects of their experience as if they were things separate and distinct from themselves. Emile Durkheim's (1961, 1964) formulation of a sociology based on the emergence of categories *sui generis*, separate and distinct from individual thought and action, resonates with this aim.

This is a radical departure from the assumptions underlying what Schutz calls "the natural attitude," which is the stance that takes the world to be principally "out there," so to speak, categorically distinct from acts of perception or interpretation. In the natural attitude, it is assumed that the life world exists before members are present and that it will be there after they depart. Schutz's recommendation for studying members' attention to this life world is to first "bracket" it for analytic purposes. That is, the analyst temporarily sets aside belief in its reality in order to bring its apprehension into focus. This makes it possible to view the constitutive processes—the *hows*—by which a separate and distinct empirical world becomes an objective reality for its members. Ontological judgments about the nature and essence of things and events are suspended temporarily so that the observer can focus on the ways that members of the life world subjectively constitute the objects and events they take to be real, that is, to exist independently of their attention to, and presence in, the world.

Schutz's orientation to the subjectivity of the life world pointed him to the commonsense knowledge that members use to "objectify" (make into objects) its social forms. He noted that individuals approach the life world with a stock of knowledge composed of ordinary constructs and categories that are social in origin. These images, folk theories, beliefs, values, and attitudes are applied to aspects of experience, thus making them meaningful and giving them a semblance of everyday familiarity. The stock of knowledge produces a world with which members already seem to be acquainted. In part, this is because of the categorical manner by which knowledge of particular objects and events is articulated. The myriad phenomena of everyday life are subsumed under a delimited number of shared constructs (or types). These "typifications" make it possible to account rationally for experience, rendering various things and sundry occurrences recognizable as particular types of objects or events. Typification, in other words, organizes the flux of life into apprehensible form, making it meaningful. In turn, as experience is given shape, the stock of knowledge is itself elaborated and altered in practice.

Ordinary language is the *modus operandi.* In the natural attitude, the meaning of a word is taken principally to be what it references or stands for in the real world, following a correspondence theory of meaning. In this framework, the leading task of language is to convey accurate information. Viewed as a process of typification, however, words and categories are the constitutive building blocks of the social world. Typification through ordinary language use creates the sense among users that the life world is familiarly organized and substantial, simultaneously giving it shape and meaning. Individuals who interact with one another do so in an environment that is concurrently constructed and experienced in fundamentally the same terms by all parties, even though mistakes may be made in its particular apprehensions. Taking for granted that we intersubjectively share the same reality, we assume further that we can understand each other in its terms. Intersubjectivity is thus a social accomplishment, a set of understandings sustained in and through the shared assumptions of interaction and recurrently sustained in processes of typification.

Ethnomethodological Formulations

Although indebted to Schutz, ethnomethodology is not a mere extension of his social phenomenological program. Ethnomethodology addresses the problem of order by combining a "phenomenological sensibility" (Maynard & Clayman, 1991) with a paramount concern for everyday social practice (Garfinkel, 1967). From an ethnomethodological standpoint, the social world's facticity is accomplished by way of members' constitutive interactional work, the mechanics of which produces and maintains the accountable circumstances of their lives.[2] In a manner of speaking, ethnomethodologists focus on how members actually "do" social life, aiming in particular to document the mechanisms by which they concretely construct and sustain social entities, such as gender, self, or family, for example.

Although Garfinkel's studies were phenomenologically informed, his overall project responded more directly to his teacher Talcott Parsons's theory of action (Heritage, 1984; Lynch, 1993). According to Parsons, social order was made possible through socially integrating systems of norms and values, a view that left little room for the everyday production of social order. Garfinkel sought an alternative to this approach, which in his judgment portrayed actors as "cultural dopes" who automatically put into place the effects of external social forces and internalized moral imperatives. Garfinkel's (1952) response was a vision of social order built from the socially contingent, practical reasoning of ordinary members of society, which, contrastingly, foregrounded their cultural acuity. He viewed members as possessing ordinary linguistic and interactional skills through which the accountable features of everyday life were produced. This approach deeply implicated members in the production of social order. Rather than more or less playing out moral directives, Garfinkel conceptualized members of society as actively using them, thus *working* to give their world a sense of orderliness. Indeed, ethnomethodology's focus became members' integral "methods" for accomplishing everyday reality.

The empirical investigation of members' methods takes its point of departure from phenomenological bracketing. Adopting the parallel policy of "ethnomethodological indifference" (Garfinkel & Sacks, 1970), the investigator temporarily suspends all commitments to a priori or privileged versions of the social world, focusing instead on how members accomplish a sense of social order. Social realities such as crime or mental illness are not taken for granted; instead, belief in them is suspended temporarily in order to make visible how they become realities for those concerned. This brings into view the ordinary constitutive work that produces the locally unchallenged appearance of stable realities. This policy vigorously resists judgmental characterizations of the correctness of members' activities. Contrary to the common sociological tendency to ironicize and criticize commonsense formulations from the standpoint of ostensibly correct sociological views, ethnomethodology takes members' practical reasoning for what it is—circumstantially adequate ways of interpersonally orienting to and interpreting the world at hand. The abiding guideline is succinctly conveyed by Melvin Pollner (personal communication): "Don't argue with the members!"

Ethnomethodologists have examined many facets of social order. One aim has been to document how recognizable structures of behavior, systems of motivation, or causal ties between motivations and social structures are evidenced in members' practical reasoning (Zimmerman & Wieder, 1970). Whereas conventional sociology orients to rules, norms, and shared meanings as exogenous explanations for members' actions, ethnomethodology turns this around to consider how members themselves orient to and use rules, norms, and shared meanings to account for the regularity of their actions. Ethnomethodology sets aside the idea that actions are externally rule-governed or internally motivated in order to observe how members themselves establish and sustain social regularities. The appearance of action as being the consequence of a rule is treated as just that—the *appearance* of action as compliant or noncompliant. In "accounting" for their actions by prospectively invoking rules or retrospectively offering rule-motivated explanations for action, members convey a sense of structure and order, and, in the process, cast their actions as rational, coherent, precedented, and reproducible for all practical purposes (Zimmerman, 1970).

For example, a juror in the midst of deliberations may account for her opinion by saying that the judge's instructions on how to consider the case in question compel her to think as she does. She actively uses the judge's instructions to make sense of her opinion, thereby giving it the semblance of rationality, legality, and correctness because it was formed "according to the rule" invoked (Holstein, 1983). In contrast, another juror might account for his opinion by saying that it was serving the interests of justice, citing a value or moral principle in explanation (Maynard & Manzo, 1993). From an ethnomethodological standpoint, the rationality or correctness of these opinions and the reasoning involved is not at issue. Instead, the focus is on the *hows* involved—the use of instructions, values, moral principles, and other accounts to construct a sense of coherence in social action, in this case a shared understanding among jurors of what led them to form their opinions and reach a verdict.

The accountable display of social order forms ethnomethodology's analytic horizon. Rather than assuming a priori that members share meanings and definitions of situations, ethnomethodologists consider how members achieve them by applying a native capacity to "artfully" account for their actions, rendering them orderly. Social order is not externally imposed by proverbial social forces, nor is it the expression of more or less socialized members of society; instead, ethnomethodologists view it as locally produced by way of the practices of mundane reason (Pollner, 1987). If social order is accomplished in and through its practices, then social worlds and circumstances are self-generating. Members, as we put it earlier, are continually "doing" social life in the very actions they take to communicate and make sense of it. Their language games, to borrow from Ludwig Wittgenstein (1958), virtually constitute their everyday realities; in this sense, the games themselves are "forms of life."

This implicates two properties of ordinary social action. First, all actions and objects are "indexical"; they depend upon (or "index") context (see Holstein & Gubrium, 2004). Objects and events have equivocal or indeterminate meanings without a discernible context. It is through contextualization that practical meaning is derived. Second, the circumstances that provide meaningful contexts are themselves self-generating. Each reference to, or account for, an action—such as the juror's comment that she is expressly following the judge's directives—establishes a context (in this case, of procedural dutifulness) for evaluating the self-same and related actions of the juror herself and the actions of others. The account establishes a particular context, which in turn becomes a basis for making her own and others' actions accountable. Having established this context, the juror can then virtually turn around and account for her actions by saying, for example, "That's why I feel as I do," in effect parlaying the context she has constructed for her actions into something recognizable and reasonable (accountable), if not ultimately acceptable. Practical reasoning, in other words, is simultaneously in and about the settings to which it orients and that it describes. Social order and its practical realities are thus "reflexive." Accounts or descriptions of a setting constitute that setting, while they are simultaneously being shaped by the contexts they constitute.

Ethnomethodological research is keenly attuned to naturally occurring talk and social interaction, orienting to them as constitutive elements of the settings studied (see J. M. Atkinson

& Drew, 1979; Maynard, 1984, 1989; Mehan & Wood, 1975; Sacks, 1972). This has taken different empirical directions, in part depending on whether the interactive meanings or the structure of talk is emphasized. Ethnographic studies tend to focus on locally crafted meanings and the settings within which social interaction constitutes the practical realities in question. Such studies consider the situated content of talk in relation to local meaning-making (see Gubrium, 1992; Holstein, 1993; Lynch & Bogen, 1996; Miller, 1991; Pollner, 1987; Wieder, 1988). They combine attention to how social order is built up in everyday communication with detailed descriptions of place settings as those settings and their local understandings and perspectives mediate the meaning of what is said in the course of social interaction. The texts produced from such studies are highly descriptive of everyday life, with both conversational extracts from the settings and ethnographic accounts of interaction being used to convey the methodical production of the subject matter in question. To the extent the analysis of talk in relation to social interaction and setting is undertaken, this tends to take the form of (non-Foucauldian) discourse analysis, or DA, which more or less critically orients to how talk, conversation, and other communicative processes are used to make meaning (see Potter, 1996, 1997; Potter & Wetherell 1987; Wodak, 2004).

Studies that emphasize the structure of talk itself examine the conversational "machinery" through which meaning emerges. The focus here is on the sequential, utterance-by-utterance, socially structuring features of talk or "talk-in-interaction," the now familiar bailiwick of conversation analysis, or CA (see Heritage, 1984; Sacks, Schegloff, & Jefferson, 1974; Silverman, 1998; Zimmerman, 1988). The analyses produced from such studies are detailed explications of the communicative processes by which speakers methodically and sequentially construct their concerns in conversational practice. These analyses are often bereft of ethnographic detail except for brief lead-ins that describe place settings, and the analytic sense conveyed is that biographical and social particulars can be understood as artifacts of the unfolding conversational machinery, although the analysis of what is called "institutional talk" or "talk at work" has struck a greater balance with place settings in this regard (see, for example, Drew & Heritage, 1992). Although some contend that CA's connection to ethnomethodology is tenuous because of this lack of concern with ethnographic detail (P. Atkinson, 1988; Lynch, 1993; Lynch & Bogen, 1994; for counterarguments see Maynard & Clayman, 1991, and ten Have, 1990), CA clearly shares ethnomethodology's interest in the local and methodical construction of social action (Maynard & Clayman, 1991).

John Heritage (1984) summarizes the fundamentals of conversation analysis in three premises. First, interaction is sequentially organized, and this may be observed in the regularities of ordinary conversation. All aspects of interaction can be found to exhibit stable and identifiable features, which are independent of speakers' individual characteristics. This sets the stage for the analysis of talk as structured in and through social interaction, not by internal sources such as motives or by external determinants such as social status. Second, social interaction is contextually oriented in that talk is simultaneously productive of, and reflects, the circumstances of its production. This premise highlights both the local conditioning and the local constructiveness of talk and interaction, exhibiting the dual properties of indexicality and reflexivity noted earlier. Third, these properties characterize all social interaction, so that no form of talk or interactive detail can be dismissed as irrelevant.

Conversation analysis has come under fire from ethnomethodologists who argue that the in situ details of everyday life are ignored at the risk of reducing social life to recorded talk and conversational sequencing. Michael Lynch, for example, has drawn a parallel between CA and molecular biology, which, proverbially speaking, tends to miss the forest for the trees, in this case the molecules. On one hand, this serves to underscore Lynch's claims about CA's basic formalism and scientism. On the other, it projects the image of conversation as a relatively predictable set of socially structured techniques through which orderly social activities are assembled. Conversation analysts, according to Lynch, attempt to describe "a simple order of structural elements and rules for combining them, and thus they undertake a reductionist program not unlike molecular biology" (1993, p. 259), which attempts to deconstruct DNA for its molecular structures and rules of combination, glossing over the distinct forms of life in tow.

As a "molecular sociology" (Lynch, 1993), CA focuses on the normative, sequential "machinery" of conversation that constitutes social action. This machinery in many ways inverts conventional understandings of human agency, substituting the demands of a moral order of conversation for psychological and motivational imperatives. Although this does not strip participants of all agency, it does place them in the midst of a "liberal economy" of conversational rights and obligations (Lynch, 1993) that tests ethnomethodological tolerance for deterministic formulations.

In contrast to what Lynch and David Bogen (1994) have labeled the "enriched positivism" of CA, Garfinkel, Lynch, and others have elaborated what they refer to as a "postanalytic" ethnomethodology that is less inclined to universalistic generalizations regarding the enduring structures or machinery of social interaction (see Garfinkel, 1988; Lynch, 1993; Lynch & Bogen, 1996). This program of research centers on the highly localized competencies that constitute specific domains of everyday "work," especially the (bench)work of astronomers (Garfinkel, Lynch, & Livingston, 1981), biologists and neurologists (Lynch, 1985), and mathematicians (Livingston, 1986). The aim is to document the *haecceity*—the "just thisness"—of social practices within circumscribed domains of knowledge and activity (Lynch, 1993). The practical details of the real-time work of these activities are viewed as an *incarnate* feature of the knowledges they produce. It is impossible to separate the knowledges from the highly particularized occasions of their production. The approach is theoretically minimalist in that it resists a priori conceptualization or categorization, especially historical time, while advocating detailed descriptive studies of the specific, local practices that manifest order and render it accountable (Bogen & Lynch, 1993).

Despite their success at displaying a panoply of social accomplishment practices, CA and postanalytic ethnomethodology in their separate ways tend to disregard an important balance in the conceptualizations of talk, setting, and social interaction that was evident in Garfinkel's early work and Harvey Sacks's (1992) pioneering lectures on conversational practice (see Silverman, 1998). Neither Garfinkel nor Sacks envisioned the machinery of conversation as productive of recognizable social forms in its own right. Attention to the constitutive *hows* of social realities were balanced with an eye to the meaningful *whats.* Settings, cultural understandings, and their everyday mediations were viewed as reflexively interwoven with talk and social interaction. Sacks, in particular, understood culture to be a matter of practice, something that served as a resource for discerning the possible linkages of utterances and exchanges. Whether they wrote of (Garfinkel's) "good organizational reasons" or (Sacks's) "membership categorization devices," both initially avoided the reduction of social practice to highly localized or momentary *haecceities* of any kind.

As such, some of the original promise of ethnomethodology has been short-circuited as CA and postanalytic ethnomethodology have increasingly restricted their investigations to the relation between social practices and the immediate accounts of those practices. If the entire goal of postanalytic and CA projects is describing the accounting practices by which descriptions are made intelligible in the immediate circumstances of their production, then constructionists would need to formulate a new project that retains ethnomethodology's interactional sensibilities while extending its scope to both the constitutive and constituted *whats* of everyday life. Michel Foucault, among others, is a valuable resource for such a project.

Foucauldian Discourse Analysis

Whereas ethnomethodology engages the accomplishment of everyday life at the interactional level, Foucault has undertaken a parallel project in a different empirical register. Appearing on the analytic stage during the early 1960s, at about the same time ethnomethodologists did, Foucault considers how historically and culturally located systems of power/knowledge construct subjects and their worlds. Foucauldians refer to these systems as "discourses," emphasizing that they are not merely bodies of ideas, ideologies, or other symbolic formulations, but are also working attitudes, modes of address, terms of reference, and courses of action suffused into social practices. Foucault (1972, p. 48) himself explains that discourses are not "a mere intersection of things and words: an obscure web of things, and a manifest, visible, colored chain of words." Rather, they are "practices that systematically form the objects [and subjects] of which they speak" (p. 49). Even the design of buildings such as prisons reveals the social logic that specifies ways of interpreting persons and the physical and social landscapes they occupy (Foucault, 1979).

Like the ethnomethodological perspective on social interaction, Foucault views discourse as socially reflexive, both constitutive and meaningfully descriptive of the world and its subjects. For Foucault, however, the accent is as much on the constructive *whats* that discourse constitutes as it is on the *hows* of discursive technology. Although this represents a swing in the analytic pendulum toward the culturally "natural," Foucault's treatment of discourse as social practice suggests, in particular, the importance of understanding the practices of subjectivity. If he offers a vision of subjects and objects constituted through discourse, he also allows for an unwittingly active subject who simultaneously shapes and puts discourse to work (Best & Kellner, 1991). As Foucault (1988) explains:

> If now I am interested . . . in the way in which the subject constitutes himself in an active fashion, by the practices of the self, these practices are nevertheless not something that the individual invents by himself. They are patterns that he finds in his culture and which are proposed, suggested and imposed on him by his culture, his society and his social group. (p. 11)

This parallels ethnomethodology's interest in documenting the accomplishment of order in the everyday practice of talk and social interaction. Foucault is particularly concerned with social locations or institutional sites—the asylum, the hospital, and the prison, for example—that specify the practical operation of discourses, linking the discourse of particular subjectivities with the construction of lived experience. As in ethnomethodology, there is an interest in the constitutive quality of systems of discourse; it is an orientation to practice that views social worlds and their subjectivities as always already embedded and embodied in its discursive conventions.

Several commentators have pointed to the parallel between what Foucault (1988) refers to as systems of "power/knowledge" (or discourses) and ethnomethodology's formulation of the constitutive power of language use (P. Atkinson, 1995; Gubrium & Holstein, 1997; Heritage, 1997; Miller, 1997b; Potter, 1996; Prior, 1997; Silverman, 1993). The correspondence suggests that what Foucault documents historically as "discourses-in-practice" in varied institutional or cultural sites may be likened to what ethnomethodology traces as "discursive practice" in varied forms of social interaction.[3] We will continue to apply these terms—discourses-in-practice and discursive practice—throughout the chapter to emphasize the parallel, as well as the possibilities for critical awareness and social action that it suggests.

Although ethnomethodologists and Foucauldians draw upon different intellectual traditions and work in distinct empirical registers, we want to emphasize their respective concerns with social practice: They both attend to the reflexivity of discourse. Neither discursive practice nor discourse-in-practice is viewed as being caused or explained by external social forces or internal motives. Rather, they are taken to be the working mechanism of social life itself, as actually known or performed in time and place. For both, "power" lies in the articulation of distinctive forms of social life as such, not in the application of particular resources by some to affect the lives of others. Although discourses-in-practice are represented by "regimens/regimes" or lived patterns of action that broadly (historically and institutionally) "discipline" or encompass their adherents' lives, and discursive practice is manifest in patterns of talk and interaction that constitute everyday life, the practices refer in common to the lived "doing," or ongoing accomplishment, of social worlds.

For Foucault, power operates in and through discourse as the other face of knowledge, thus the term "power/knowledge." Discourse not only puts words to work, it also gives them their meaning, constructs perceptions, and formulates understanding and ongoing courses of interaction. The "work" entailed simultaneously and reflexively constitutes the realities that words are taken otherwise to merely reference or specify. To deploy a particular discourse of subjectivity is not simply a matter of representing a subject; in practice, it simultaneously constitutes the kinds of subjects that are meaningfully embedded in the discourse itself. For example, to articulate the discourse of medicine in today's world automatically generates the roles of professional healer and patient, each of whose actions in turn articulate the application and reception of technologies of healing served by the dominance of scientific knowledge. The taken-for-grantedness of this socially encompassing discourse makes challenges to this way of "thinking" (or speaking) seem oddly misplaced. Even the weak "powerfully" participate in the discourse that defines them as weak. This is a kind of knowledge-in-practice, and it is powerful because it not only represents but also ineluctably puts into practice what is known and shared. Language is not just more or less correlated with what it represents, but is always already a "form of life," to again put it in Wittgenstein's (1958) terms. If ethnomethodologists tend to emphasize *how* members use everyday methods to account for their activities and their worlds, Foucault makes us aware of the related conditions of possibility for *what* the results are likely to be. For example, in a Western postindustrial world, to seriously think of medicine and voodoo as equally viable paradigms for understanding sickness and healing would seem idiosyncratic, if not amusing or preposterous, in most conventional situations. The power of medical discourse partially lies in its ability to be "seen but unnoticed," in its ability to appear as *the* only possibility while other possibilities are outside the plausible realm.

Both ethnomethodology's and Foucault's approach to empirical material are "analytics," not theoretical frameworks in the traditional sense. Conventionally understood, theory purports to explain the state of the matters in question. It provides answers to *why* concerns, such as why the suicide rate is rising or why individuals are suffering depression. Ethnomethodology and the Foucauldian project, in contrast, aim to answer how it is that individual experience comes to be understood in particular terms such as these. They are pretheoretical in this sense, respectively seeking to arrive at an understanding of how the subject matter of theory comes into existence in the first place, and of what the subject of theory might possibly become. The parallel lies in the common goal of documenting the practiced bases of such realities.

Still, this remains a parallel. Because Foucault's project (and most Foucauldian projects) operates in a historical register, real-time talk and social interaction are understandably missing from chosen bodies of empirical material. Although Foucault himself points to sharp turns in the discursive formations that both form and inform the shifting realities of varied institutional spheres, contrasting extant social forms with the "birth" of new ones, he provides little or no sense of the *everyday* technology by which this is achieved (see P. Atkinson, 1995; Holstein & Gubrium, 2000). Certainly, he elaborates the broad birth of new technologies, such as the emergence of new regimes of surveillance in medicine and modern criminal justice systems (Foucault, 1965, 1979), but he doesn't provide us with a view of how these operate in social interaction. Neither do latter-day Foucauldians—such as Nikolas Rose (1990), who informatively documents the birth and rise of the technical apparatus for "governing the soul" that forms a private self—offer much insight into the everyday processes through which such regimes are accomplished. These *hows,* in other words, are largely missing from their analyses.

Conversely, ethnomethodology's commitment to documenting the real-time, interactive processes by which reality is built up into accountable structures precludes a broader perspective on constitutive resources, possibilities, and limitations. Such *whats,* so to speak, are largely absent in adherents' work. It is one thing to show in interactive detail that our everyday encounters with reality are ongoing accomplishments, but is quite another matter to derive an understanding of what the general parameters of those everyday encounters might be. The machinery of talk-in-interaction tells us little about the massive resources that are taken up in, and that guide, the operation of conversation, or about the consequences of producing particular results and not others, each of which is an important ingredient of practice. Members speak their worlds and their subjectivities, but they also articulate particular forms of life as they do so. What Foucauldian considerations offer ethnomethodology in this regard is an analytic sensitivity to the discursive opportunities and possibilities at work in talk and social interaction, but without making it necessary to take these up as external templates for the everyday production of social order.

An Analytics of Interpretive Practice

The analytics of interpretive practice has benefited from drawing together ethnomethodological and Foucauldian sensibilities. This is not simply another attempt at bridging the so-called macro-micro divide. That debate usually centers on the question of how to conceptualize the relationship between preexisting larger and smaller social forms, the assumption being that these are categorically distinct and separately discernible. Issues raised in the debate perpetuate the distinction between, say, social systems, on one hand, and social interaction, on the other. In contrast, those who consider ethnomethodology and Foucauldian analytics to be parallel operations focus their attention instead on the interactional, institutional, and cultural variabilities of socially constituting discursive practice or discourses-in-practice, as the case might be. They are concerned with how the social construction process is shaped across various domains of everyday life, not in how separate theories of macro and micro domains can be linked together for a fuller account of social organization. Doctrinaire accounts of Garfinkel, Sacks, Foucault, and others may continue to sustain a variety of distinct projects, but these projects are not likely to inform one another; nor will they lead to profitable "conversations" between dogmatic practitioners who insist on viewing themselves as speaking different analytic languages.[4] In our view, what is required is a new, hybridized analytics of reality construction at the crossroads of institutions, culture, and social interaction—an analytics that "misreads" and co-opts useful insights from established traditions in order to appreciate the possible complementarity of analytic idioms, without losing sight of their distinctive utilities, limitations, and contributions.

Beyond Ethnomethodology

Some conversation analysts have edged in this direction by analyzing the sequential machinery of talk-in-interaction as it is patterned by institutional context, bringing a greater concern for the *whats* of social life into the picture. Their studies of "talk at work" aim to specify how the "simplest systematics" of ordinary conversation (Sacks, Schegloff, & Jefferson, 1974) is shaped in various ways by the reflexively constructed speech environments of particular interactional regimes (see Boden & Zimmerman, 1991; Drew & Heritage, 1992). Ethnomethodologically oriented ethnographers approach the problem from another direction by asking how institutions and their respective representational cultures are brought into being, managed, and sustained in and through members' social interaction (or "reality work") (see P. Atkinson, 1995; Dingwall, Eekelaar, & Murray, 1983; Emerson, 1969; Emerson & Messinger, 1977; Gubrium, 1992; Holstein, 1993; Mehan, 1979; Miller, 1991, 1997a). Self-consciously Foucauldian ethnographers, too, have drawn links between everyday discursive practice and discourses-in-practice to document in local detail how the formulation of everyday texts such as psychiatric case records or coroners' reports reproduce institutional discourses (see Prior, 1997).

In their own fashions, these efforts consider both the *hows* and the *whats* of reality construction. But this is analytically risky business. Asking *how* questions without having an integral way of getting an analytic handle on *what* questions makes concern with the *whats* arbitrary. Although talk-in-interaction is locally "artful," as Garfinkel (1967) puts it, not just anything goes. On the other hand, if we swing too far analytically in the direction of contextual or cultural imperatives, we end up with the cultural, institutional, or judgmental "dopes" that Garfinkel (1967) decried.

The admonition that "not just anything goes" has been taken seriously, but cautiously, by both ethnomethodologists and conversation analysts as they have sought to carefully document the practical contours of interaction in the varied circumstances in which it unfolds. Systematic attention to everyday reasoning and to the sequential organization of conversations have made it clear that outcomes are constructed in the interactional apparatuses within which their antecedents are made topical. But this is a very delimited approach to the constitutive *whats* of social construction, one that lacks a broad view of the institutional and cultural discourses that serve as resources for what is likely to be constructed, when, and where in everyday life.

To broaden and enrich ethnomethodology's analytic scope and repertoire, we have extended its reach into the institutional and cultural *whats* that come into play in social interaction. This needn't be a historical extension, as was Foucault's metier, although that certainly should not be ruled out. Rather, we appeal to a "cautious" (and self-conscious) naturalism that addresses the practical and sited production of everyday life (Gubrium, 1993) and that, as will be seen, provides a integral basis for critically, not just descriptively, attending to ongoing talk and social interaction. The analytics of interpretive practice is such an effort. It centers on the interplay, not the synthesis, of discursive practice and discourses-in-practice, the tandem projects of ethnomethodology and Foucauldian discourse analysis. This analytics assiduously avoids theorizing social forms, lest the discursive practices associated with the construction of these forms be taken for granted. By the same token, it concertedly keeps institutional or cultural discourses in view, lest they be dissolved into localized displays of practical reasoning or forms of sequential organization for talk-in-interaction. First and foremost, an analytics of interpretive practice takes us, in real time, to the "going concerns" of everyday life, as Everett Hughes (1984) liked to call social institutions. There, we can focus on how members artfully put distinct discourses to work as they constitute their subjectivities and related social worlds.

The emphasis on the interplay between the *hows* and *whats* of interpretive practice is paramount. Interplay connotes a dynamic relationship. We assiduously avoid analytically privileging either discursive practice or discourses-in-practice. Putting it in ethnomethodological terms, the aim of an analytics of interpretive practice is to document the interplay between the practical reasoning and interactive machinery entailed in constructing a sense of everyday reality, on one hand, and the institutional conditions, resources, and related discourses that substantively nourish and interpretively mediate interaction, on the other. Putting it in Foucauldian terms, the goal is to describe the interplay between institutional discourses and the "dividing practices" that constitute local subjectivities and their worlds of experience (Foucault, 1965). The symmetry of real-world practice requires that we give equal treatment to both its articulative and its substantive engagements.

Qualitative researchers are increasingly focusing on these two sides of interpretive practice, looking to both the artful processes and the substantive conditions of meaning-making and social order. Douglas Maynard (1989), for example, notes that most ethnographers traditionally have asked "How do participants see things?" whereas ethnomethodologically informed discourse studies have asked "How do participants do things?" Although his own work typically begins with the later question, Maynard cautions us not to ignore the former. He explains that, in the interest of studying how members *do* things, ethnomethodological studies have tended to de-emphasize factors that condition their actions. Recognizing that "external social structure is used as a resource for social interaction at the same time as it is constituted within it," Maynard suggests that ethnographic and discourse studies can be mutually informative, allowing researchers to better document the ways in which the "structure of interaction, while being a local production, simultaneously enacts matters whose origins are externally initiated" (1989, p. 139). "In addition to knowing how people 'see' their workaday worlds," writes Maynard (p. 144), researchers should try to understand how people "discover and exhibit features of these worlds so that they can be 'seen.'"

Expressing similar interests and concerns, Hugh Mehan has developed a discourse-oriented program of "constitutive ethnography" that puts "structure and structuring activities on an equal footing by showing *how* the social facts of the world emerge from structuring work to become external and constraining" (1979, p. 18, emphasis in the original). Mehan examines "contrastive" instances of interpretation in order to describe both the "distal" and the "proximate" features of the reality-constituting work people do "within institutional, cultural, and historical contexts" (1979, pp. 73 and 81).

Beginning from similar ethnomethodological and discourse analytic footings, David Silverman (1993) likewise attends to the institutional venues of talk and social construction (also see Silverman, 1985, 1997). Seeking a mode of qualitative inquiry that exhibits both constitutive and contextual sensibilities, he suggests that discourse studies that consider the varied institutional contexts of talk bring a new perspective to qualitative inquiry. Working in the same vein, Gale Miller (1991, 1997b) has proposed "ethnographies of institutional discourse" that serve to document "the ways in which setting members use discursive resources in organizing their practical actions, and how members' actions are constrained by the resources available in the settings" (Miller, 1991, p. 280). This approach makes explicit overtures to both conversation analysis and Foucauldian discourse analysis.

Miller's (1997a) ethnography of the discourses characterizing a therapy agency is instructive, especially as it sheds light on the everyday production of the client in therapy. His 12-year ethnographic study of Northland Clinic, an internationally prominent center of "brief therapy," recounts a marked shift in client subjectivity that accompanied a conscious alteration of treatment philosophy. When Miller began his fieldwork, Northland employed "ecosystemic brief therapy," which emphasized the social contexts of clients' lives and problems. In this therapeutic environment, clients' subjectivity was linked with the systems of social relationships that were taken to form and fuel their problems. The approach required the staff to discern the state of these systems and to intervene so as to alter their dynamics and thereby effect change. Miller notes that this approach was informed by a "modern" discourse of the reality of the problems in question.

Several years into the fieldwork, Northland shifted to a more "postmodern" approach, articulating intervention in an everyday linguistic and constructivist discourse. Therapists began to apply what was called "solution-focused brief therapy," which meant viewing troubles as ways of talking about everyday life. This prompted the staff to orient to the therapy process as a set of language games, expressly appropriating Wittgenstein's sense of the term. The idea here was that troubles were as much constructions—ways of talking or forms of life—as they were real difficulties for the clients in question. This transformed clients' institutional subjectivity from being relatively passive agents of systems of personal troubles and negative stories, to being active problem solvers with the potential to formulate positive stories about themselves and design helpful solutions. As an everyday language of solutions, not a discourse of problems, became the basis of intervention, the narrative identity of clients was transformed to reveal entirely different selves. Changes in the therapy agency were articulations of transformations of both the discourse-in-practice and related discursive practices. This resulted in the construction of distinctly different "clients" and "problems" (subsequently "solutions"). Emphasizing both the *hows* and *whats* of the agency's changing interpretive practices provides both the researcher and those researched an awareness of the alternative ways client troubles can be construed and the kinds of action that can be taken to deal with them in the process.

Dorothy Smith (1987, 1990) has been quite explicit in addressing a version of the interplay between the *whats* and *hows* of social life from a feminist point of view, pointing to the critical consciousness made possible by the perspective. Hers has been an analytics initially informed by ethnomethodological and, increasingly, Foucauldian sensibilities. Moving beyond ethnomethodology, she calls for what she refers to as a "dialectics of discourse and the everyday" (1990, p. 202). Stressing the "play and interplay" of discourse, Smith articulates her view of women's "active" placement in their worlds.

> It is easy to misconstrue the discourse as having an overriding power to determine the values and interpretation of women's appearances in local settings, and see this power as essentially at the disposal of the fashion industry and media. But women are active, skilled, make choices, consider, are not fooled or foolish. Within discourse there is play and interplay. (p. 202)

Philosopher Calvin Schrag (1997) similarly emphasizes the advantage of the strategy of analytic interplay over theoretical integration. Schrag puts this in the context of the need to guard against reducing what we refer to as discursive practice to mere speech acts or talk-in-interaction, on one hand, or supplanting the local artfulness of social interaction with its institutional discourses, on the other. Considering the self after postmodernity, Schrag echoes our own aim to keep both the constructive *whats* and *hows* in balance at the forefront of an analytics, lest the study of lived experience neglect or overemphasize one or the other.

> We must stand guard to secure the space of discourse as temporalized event of speaking *between* the objectification of speech acts and language on the one hand and the abstractions and reifications in the structuralist designs of narratology on the other hand. The event of discourse as a saying of something by someone to someone is threatened from both "below" and "above"—from below in terms of a tendency toward an ontology of elementarism fixated on the isolable, constitutive elements of speech acts and linguistic units . . . and from above in the sense of a predilection toward an abstract holism of narratological structures that leave the event of discourse behind. Only by sticking to the terrain of the "between" will the subject as the who of discourse and the who of narrative remain visible. It is on this terrain, which we will later come to call the terrain of lived-experience, that we are able to observe the august event of a self understanding itself through the twin moments of discourse and narration. (pp. 22–23)

We echo Schrag's warning against integrating an analytics of discursive practice with an analytics of discourse-in-practice. To integrate one with the other is to reduce the empirical purview of a common enterprise. Reducing the analytics of discourse-in-practice into discursive practice risks losing the lessons of attending to institutional differences and cultural configurations as they mediate, and are not "just talked into being" through, social interaction. Conversely, figuring discursive practice as the mere residue of institutional discourse risks a totalized marginalization of local artfulness.

Analytic Bracketing

Rather than attempting synthesis or integration, we view an analytics of interpretive practice as more like a skilled juggling act, alternately concentrating on the myriad *hows* and *whats* of everyday life. This requires a new form of bracketing to capture the interplay between discursive practice and discourses-in-practice. We've called this technique of oscillating indifference to the realities of everyday life "analytic bracketing" (see Gubrium & Holstein, 1997).

Recall that ethnomethodology's interest in the *hows* by which realities are constructed requires a studied, temporary indifference to those realities. Like phenomenologists, ethnomethodologists begin their analysis by setting aside belief in the real in order to bring into view the everyday practices by which subjects, objects, and events come to have a sense of being observable, rational, and orderly for those concerned. The ethnomethodological project moves forward from there, documenting how discursive practice constitutes social structures by identifying the particular mechanisms at play. As Wittgenstein (1958, p. 19) might put it, language is "taken off holiday" in order to make visible how language works to construct the objects it is otherwise viewed as principally describing.

Analytic bracketing works somewhat differently. It is employed throughout analysis, not just at the start. As analysis proceeds, the observer intermittently orients to everyday realities as both the *products* of members reality-constructing procedures and as *resources* from which realities are constituted. At one moment, the analyst may be indifferent to the structures of everyday life in order to document their production through discursive practice. In the next analytic move, he or she brackets discursive practice in order to assess the local availability, distribution, and/or regulation of resources for reality construction. In Wittgensteinian terms, this translates into attending to both language-at-work and language-on-holiday, alternating considerations of how languages games, in particular institutional discourses, operate in everyday life and what games are likely to come into play at particular times and places. In Foucauldian terms, it leads to alternating considerations of discourses-in-practice, on one hand, and the locally fine-grained documentation of related discursive practices, on the other.

Analytic bracketing amounts to an orienting procedure for alternately focusing on the *whats*, then the *hows*, of interpretive practice (or vice versa) in order to assemble both a contextually scenic and a contextually constructive picture of everyday language-in-use. The objective is to move back and forth between discursive practice and discourses-in-practice, documenting each in turn, and making informative references to the other in the process. Either discursive machinery or available discourses becomes the provisional phenomenon, while interest in the other is temporarily deferred, but not forgotten. The constant interplay between the analysis of these two sides of interpretive practice mirrors the lived interplay between social interaction, its immediate surroundings, and its going concerns.

Because discursive practice and discourses-in-practice are mutually constitutive, one cannot argue that analysis should begin or end with either one, although there are predilections in this regard. As those who are ethnographically oriented are wont to do, Smith (1987, 1990), for example, advocates beginning "where people are"; we take her to mean that this refers to where people are located in the institutional landscape of everyday life. Conversely, conversation analysts insist on beginning with discursive practice, even while a variety of unanalyzed *whats* typically informs their efforts.[5]

Wherever one starts, neither the cultural and institutional details of discourse nor its interpolations in social interaction predetermines the other. If we set aside the need for an indisputable resolution to the question of which comes first or last, or has priority, we can designate a suitable point of departure and proceed from there, so long as we keep firmly in mind that the interplay within interpretive practice requires that we move back and forth analytically between its facets. Because we don't want to reify the components, we continuously remind ourselves that the analytic task centers on the dialectics of two fields of play, not the reproduction of one by the other.

Although we advocate no rule for where to begin, we needn't fret that the overall task is impossible or logically incoherent. Maynard

(1998, p. 344), for example, compares analytic bracketing to "wanting to ride trains that are going in different directions, initially hopping on one and then somehow jumping to the other." He asks, "How do you jump from one train to another when they are going in different directions?" The question is, in fact, merely an elaboration of the issue of how one brackets in the first place, which is, of course, the basis for Maynard's and other ethnomethodologists' and conversation analysts' own projects. The answer is simple: Knowledge of the *principle* of bracketing (and unbracketing) makes it possible. Those who bracket the life world or treat it indifferently, as the case might be, readily set reality aside every time they get to work on their respective corpuses of empirical material. It becomes as routine as rising in the morning, having breakfast, and going to the workplace.[6] On the other hand, the desire to operationalize bracketing of any kind, analytic bracketing included, into explicitly codified and sequenced procedural moves would turn bracketing into a set of recipe-like, analytic directives, something surely to be avoided. We would assume that no one, except the most recalcitrant operationalist, would want to substitute a recipe book for an analytics.[7]

Analytic bracketing, however, is far from undisciplined: It has distinct procedural implications. As we have noted, the primary directive is to alternately examine both sides of interpretive practice. Researchers engaging in analytic bracketing must constantly turn their attention in more than one direction. This has resulted in new methodological hybrids. Some analysts undertake a more content-oriented form of discourse analysis (see Potter, 1996; Potter & Wetherell, 1987). Others develop methods of "constitutive ethnography" (Mehan, 1979), the "ethnography of practice" (Gubrium, 1988), or other discursively sensitive ethnographic approaches (see Holstein, 1993; Miller, 1991, 1997a). The distinguishing feature of such studies is their disciplined focus on both discourse-in-practice and discursive practice.

The dual focus should remind us that, in describing the constitutive role of discourses-in-practice, we must take care not to appropriate these naïvely into our analysis. We must sustain ethnomethodology's desire to distinguish between members' resources and our own. As a result, as we consider discourses-in-practice, we must attend to how they mediate, not determine, members' socially constructive activities. Analytic bracketing is always substantively temporary. It resists full-blown attention to discourses as systems of power/knowledge, separate from how they operate in lived experience. It also is enduringly empirical in that it does not take the everyday operation of discourses for granted as the truths of a setting *tout court*.[8]

Working Against Totalization

Centered at the crossroads of discursive practice and discourses-in-practice, an analytics of interpretive practice works against totalization. It offers breathing room for choice and action. It restrains the propensity of a Foucauldian analytics to view all interpretations as artifacts of particular regimes of power/knowledge. Writing in relation to the broad sweep of his "histories of the present," Foucault was inclined to overemphasize the predominance of discourses in constructing the horizons of meaning at particular times or places, conveying the sense that discourses fully detail the nuances of everyday life. A more interactionally sensitive analytics of discourse—one tied to discursive practice—resists this tendency.

Because interpretive practice is mediated by discourse through institutional functioning, we discern the operation of power/knowledge in the separate going concerns of everyday life. Yet, what one institutional site brings to bear is not necessarily what another puts into practice. Institutions constitute distinct, yet sometimes overlapping, realities. Whereas one may deploy a gaze that confers agency or subjectivity upon individuals, for example, another may constitute subjectivity along different lines, such as the family systems that are called into question as subjects and agents of troubles in family therapy (see Gubrium, 1992; Miller, 1997a).

Still, if interpretive practice is complex and fluid, it is not socially arbitrary. In the practice of everyday life, discourse is articulated in myriad sites and is socially variegated; actors methodically build up their shared realities in diverse, locally nuanced, and biographically informed terms. Although this produces considerable slippage in how discourses do their work, it is far removed from the uniform hegemonic regimes of power/knowledge presented in some Foucauldian readings. Social organization nonetheless is evident in the going concerns referenced by participants, to which they hold their talk and interaction accountable.

An analytics of interpretive practice must deal with the perennial question of what realities and/or subjectivities are being constructed in the myriad sites of everyday life. In practice, diverse articulations of discourse intersect, collide, and work against the construction of common or uniform subjects, agents, and social realities. Interpretations shift in relation to the institutional and cultural markers they reference, which, in turn, fluctuate with respect to the varied settings in which social interaction unfolds. Discourses-in-practice refract one another as they are methodically adapted to practical exigencies, local discursive practice serving up variation and innovation in the process (see Abu-Lughod, 1991, 1993; Chase, 1995; Narayan & George, 2002).

From How *and* What *to* Why

Traditionally, qualitative inquiry has concerned itself with *what* and *how* questions. *Why* questions have been the hallmark of quantitative sociology, which seeks to explain and ostensibly predict behavior. Qualitative researchers typically approach *why* questions cautiously. Explanation is a tricky business, one that qualitative inquiry embraces discreetly in light of its appreciation for *interpretive elasticity.* It is one thing to describe what is going on and how things or events take shape, but the question of why things happen the way they do can lead to inferential leaps and empirical speculations that propel qualitative analysis far from its stock-in-trade. The challenge is to respond to *why* question in ways that are empirically and conceptually consonant with qualitative inquiry's traditional concerns.

Our approach to interpretive practice provides a limited basis for raising particular kinds of *why* questions in the context of qualitative inquiry. In order to pursue *why* questions, one needs to designate a domain of explanation for that which is to be explained. The familiar distinction in sociology between macrosociological and microsociological domains, for instance, specifies two kinds of explanatory footing. Most commonly, macrosociological variables are used as footing for explaining microsociological phenomena, for example, using the rural/urban or the traditional/modern distinction to explain qualities of face-to-face relationships. Parsons's (1951) social system framework was once a leading model of this kind of explanation, applying macro-level systemic variables as explanations for functioning and variation in individual lives and actions.

One way for qualitative inquiry to approach *why* questions without hazarding its traditional analytic interests is to proceed from the *whats* and *hows* of social life. Provisional explanatory footing can be found at the junction of concerns for what is going on in everyday life in relation to how that is constructed, centered in the space we have located interpretive practice. Bracketing the *whats,* footing for explaining the constructive nuances of social patterns can be found in discursive practice. Bracketing the *hows,* footing for explaining the delimited patterns of meaning consequent to social construction processes can be found in discourses-in-practice.

The interplay between discourses-in-practice and discursive practice is a source of two kinds of answer for why things are organized as they are in everyday life. One kind stems from the explanatory footings of discursive practice, directing us to the artful talk and interaction that designs and designates the local contours of our social worlds. From such footings, we learn why discourses are not templates for action. Their articulation is subject to the everyday contingencies of discursive practice. Discourses-in-practice are talked into action, so to speak; they do not dictate what is said and done from the outside or from the inside, as if they were separate and distinct sources of influence. To answer why social structures are as circumstantially nuanced as they are, one can bracket the constitutive *whats* of the matter in order to reveal how recognizable activities and systems of meaning are constituted in particular domains of everyday life. Discursive practice, in other words, provides the footing for answering why recognizable constellations of social order take on locally distinctive shapes.

We may also answer limited *why* questions that are related to discursive practice, questions such as why discursive actions unfold in specific directions or why they have particular consequences. Answers emerge when we bracket the constitutive work that shapes who and what we are and what it is that we do. By itself, the machinery of conversation gives us few clues as to when, where, or what particular patterns of meaning or action will be artfully produced and managed. The machinery is like a galloping horse, but we have little or no sense of when it began to run, where it's headed, what indeed it is up to, and what might happen when it gets there. Is it racing, fleeing, playing polo, delivering the mail, or what? Each of these possibilities requires a discourse to set its course and to tell us what messages it might be conveying. This can inform us in delimited ways of why the machinery of speech environments is organized and propelled in the ways it is. Discourse-in-practice provides the footing for answering why discursive practice proceeds in the direction it does, toward what end, in pursuit of what goals, and in relation to what meanings.

Sustaining a Critical Consciousness

The interplay of discourse-in-practice and discursive practice sustains an integral critical consciousness for qualitative inquiry, which is a necessary basis for related social action. Each component of interpretive practice serves as *endogenous* grounds for raising serious questions relating to the empirical assumptions of ongoing inquiry. Critical consciousness is built into this framework; it is not external to it. Indeed, it's the other face of analytic bracketing. If, for purposes of broadening our knowledge of everyday life, analytic bracketing provides a means of combining attention to constitutive *hows* with substantive *whats*, it simultaneously enjoins us to continuously pay attention to what we may be shortchanging in the service of one of these questions or the other. The continuing enterprise of analytic bracketing doesn't keep us comfortably ensconced throughout the research process in a domain of indifference to the lived realities of experience, as a priori bracketing does. Nor does analytic bracketing keep us comfortably engaged in the unrepentant naturalism of documenting the world of everyday life the way it really is. Rather, it continuously jerks us out of the analytic lethargies of both endeavors.

When questions of discourse-in-practice take the stage, there are grounds for problematizing or politicizing the sum and substance of what otherwise can be too facilely viewed as arbitrarily or individualistically constructed, managed, and sustained. The persistent urgency of *what* questions cautions us not to assume that interpersonal agency, artfulness, or the machinery of social interaction is the whole story. The urgency prompts us to inquire into the broader sources of matters that are built up across time and circumstance in discursive practice, the contemporaneous conditions that inform and shape the construction process, and the personal and interpersonal consequences for those involved of having constituted their world in the way they have. Although the view toward interpretive practice doesn't orient naturalistically to the "real world," neither does it take everyday life as built from the ground up in talk-in-interaction on each and every conversational or narrative occasion. The political consequence of this is an analytic framework that turns to matters of social organization and control, implicating a reality that doesn't rest completely on the machinery of talk or the constructive quality of social interaction. It turns us to wider contexts in search of other sources of change or stability.

When discursive practice commands the spotlight, there is a basis for critically challenging the representational hegemony of taken-for-granted realities. The continual urgency of *how* questions warns us not to assume that the world as it now is, is the world that must be (cf. Freire's [1970] strategy of *conscientização*). The warning prompts us to "unsettle" realities in search of their construction to reveal the constitutive processes that produce and sustain particular realities as the processes are engaged, not for time immemorial. Critically framed, the *how* concerns of interpretive practice caution us to remember that the everyday realities of our lives—whether they are being normal, abnormal, law abiding, criminal, male, female, young, or old—are realities we *do*. Having done them, they can be undone. We can move on to do realities, producing and reproducing, time and again, the world we inhabit. Politically, this presents the recognition that, in the world we live in, we could enact alternate possibilities or alternative directions, which the apparent organization of our lives might appear to make seem impossible. If we make visible the constructive fluidity and malleability of social forms, we also reveal a potential for change (see Gubrium & Holstein, 1990, 1994, 1995, 1997; Holstein & Gubrium, 2000).

The critical consciousness of this perspective deploys the continuous imperative to take issue with discourse or discursive practice when either one is foregrounded, thus turning the analytics on itself as it pursues its goals. Reflexively framed, the interplay of discourse and discursive practice transforms analytic bracketing into critical bracketing, offering a basis not only for documenting interpretive practice, but also for critically commenting on its own constructions, putting the analytic pendulum in motion in relation to itself.

Social Action

The critical consciousness that is endogenous to interpretive practice can be taken outside the context of research and analysis. Further attending to the substance of the social realities at stake in a realm of everyday life can specify the *whats* into *whens* and *wheres*. Further attending to what is at stake in the construction process can lead us to identify the times when and the places where those concerned construct particular social forms in the ways they do. Knowing this provides interested parties, such as family members and troubled individuals, not just social researchers, with knowledge of the alternative constructions available to them for assembling themselves and their experiences in particular ways. They are provided distinct bases for action in the context of various discourses, as Foucauldians might put it, to construct their lives so that preferred solutions come into play. This works against totalization in the world of action.

For example, Gubrium's (1992) comparative field study of two family therapy programs focused on both the *hows* and the *whats* of the process by which therapists and family members constructed family troubles. His material shows how participants in both programs went about assembling the knowledge and approaches available to them into explicit pictures of domestic disorder and equally straightforward designs for turning disorder into orderly, or functional, family lives. The *hows*, or mechanisms of the process, were similar in the two programs, including cataloging and classifying particular experiences into reflexively constructed categories recognizable to all. The *whats*, however, were distinct. In one of the facilities, an outpatient program called "Westside House," family troubles were interpreted and clinically categorized as the dysfunctions of a hierarchical family system. In the other facility, an inpatient program located at what Gubrium called "Fairview Hospital," troubles took on an emotional cast, hierarchy being displaced by mutual disclosure and democratic communication centered on individual members' feelings. What was constructed in these two locations was distinct and had contrasting consequences for the family members' lives, even though the construction process was similar.

The social action consequences follow directly from the identification and documentation of constructed differences. Comparing what is constructed at Westside House with what is constructed at Fairview Hospital provides a modicum of choice for anyone seeking solutions—in this case, to family troubles. Westside House is a discursive environment that privileges authority and downplays individual feelings, whereas Fairview Hospital is a discursive environment in which feelings and clear communication loom forth as a basis for healing familial wounds. Broadening the comparative perspective to include other discursive environments of family construction adds to the concrete choices for constructing both what these families are and solutions for what they could be (see Miller, 2001).

Taken into the world of everyday life, this provides those concerned—stakeholders such as troubled sons and daughters and distressed mothers and fathers—with evidence of the possible solutions available for understanding constructions of what troubles them as well as alternative ways of resolving those troubles. This moves beyond single solutions by providing evidence of the varied ways that troubles can be assembled into concrete realities. The *hows* and the *whats*, respectively, show that stakeholders have a choice in how their troubles will be construed as well as the options for construing them in particular ways. From related knowledge of when and where options present themselves, action can be organized toward preferred possibilities.

Although social researchers themselves aren't obliged to take a critical consciousness into the outside world, a critical consciousness does obligate them to document, publish, and make broadly available the possibilities for constructing everyday life. It is in this spirit, which stems in many ways from C. Wright Mills's (1959) call for a publicly oriented critical consciousness, that we have offered the framework of interpretive practice for public consumption and social action.

Notes

1. Some self-proclaimed ethnomethodologists, however, would reject the notion that ethnomethodology is in any sense a "constructionist" or "constructivist" enterprise (see Lynch, 1993). Some reviews of the ethnomethodological canon also clearly imply that constructionism is anathema to the ethnomethodological project (see Maynard, 1998; Maynard & Clayman, 1991).

2. Although clearly reflecting Garfinkel's pioneering contributions, this characterization of the ethnomethodological project is perhaps closer to the version conveyed in the work of Melvin Pollner (1987, 1991) and D. Lawrence Wieder (1988) than to some of the more recent "postanalytic" or conversation analytic forms of ethnomethodology. Indeed, Garfinkel (1988), Lynch (1993), and others might object to how we ourselves portray ethnomethodology. We would contend, however, that there is much to be gained from a studied "misreading" of the ethnomethodological "classics," a practice that Garfinkel himself advocates for the sociological classics more generally (see Lynch, 1993). With the figurative "death of the author" (Barthes, 1977), those attached to doctrinaire readings of the canon should have little grounds for argument.

3. Other ethnomethodologists have drawn upon Foucault, but without necessarily endorsing these affinities or parallels. Lynch (1993), for example, writes that Foucault's studies can be relevant to ethnomethodological investigations in a "restricted and 'literal' way" (p. 131), and he resists the generalization of discursive regimes across highly occasioned "language games." See McHoul (1986) and Lynch and Bogen (1996) for exemplary ethnomethodological appropriations of Foucauldian insights.

4. There is still considerable doctrinaire sentiment for maintaining "hard-headed, rigorous investigation in one idiom" while recognizing its possible "incommensurability" with others (Maynard, 1998, p. 345). The benefit, according to Maynard (1998, p. 345), would be "strongly reliable understanding in a particular domain of social life, and it need not imply narrowness, fragmentation, limitation, or isolation." Our sense is that such conversations do produce fragmentation and isolation (see Hill and Crittenden [1968] for a vivid example of nonproductive conversation deriving from incompatible analytic idioms), resulting in the stale reproduction of knowledge and, of course, the equally stale representation of the empirical world. In our view, reliability has never been a strong enough incentive to ignore the potential validities of new analytic horizons.

5. The CA argument for this point of departure is that ostensibly distinct patterns of talk and interaction are constitutive of particular settings, and therefore must be the point of departure. This is tricky, though. CA's practitioners routinely designate and describe particular institutional contexts *before* the analysis of the conversations that those conversations are said to reveal. CA would have us believe that setting, as a

distinct context for talk and interaction, would be visibly (hearably) constituted *in the machinery of talk* itself (see Schegloff, 1991). This would mean that no scene-setting would be necessary (or even need to be provided) for the production of the discursive context to be apparent. One wonders if what is demonstrated in these studies could have been produced in the unlikely event that no prior knowledge of the setting had been available, or if prior knowledge were rigorously bracketed.

CA studies always admit to being about conversation in *some* context. Even the myriad studies of telephone interaction make that discursive context available to readers *before* the analysis begins. Indeed, titles of research reports literally announce institutional context at the start. For example, one of Heritage's (1985) chapters is titled "Analyzing News Interviews: Aspects of the Production of Talk for an 'Overhearing' Audience." Immediately, the reader knows and, in a manner of speaking, is prepared to get the gist of, what conversation is "doing" in what follows. In a word, the *productivity* of talk relies as much on this analytically underrecognized start as on what the analysis proper aims to show. In such studies, context inevitably sneaks in the front door, in titles and "incidental" stage setting. Apparently, analysts fail to recognize that some measure of discursive context is being imported to assist in the explanation of how context is indigenously constructed.

Strictly speaking, the researcher cannot hope to attribute institutional patterns completely to the machinery of conversation. Nor can she completely disattend to discourse-in-practice and meaning while describing the sequential flow of conversation. Analytically, one must at some point reappropriate institutions and external cultural understandings in order to know what is artfully and methodically going on in that talk and interaction. Centered as analytic bracketing is on both sides of interpretive practice, there is concerted warrant for the continual return of the analytic gaze to discourse-in-practice.

6. There are other useful metaphors for describing how analytic bracketing changes the focus from discourse-in-practice to discursive practice. One can liken the operation to shifting gears while driving a motor vehicle equipped with a manual transmission. One mode of analysis may prove quite productive, but eventually it will strain against the resistance engendered by its own temporary analytic orientation. When the analyst notes that the analytic "engine" is laboring under, or being constrained by, the restraints of what it is currently "geared" to accomplish, she can decide to virtually "shift" analytic "gears" in order to gain further purchase on the aspects of interpretive interplay that were previously bracketed. Just as there can be no prescription for shifting gears while driving (i.e., one can never specify in advance at what speed one should shift up or down), changing analytic brackets always remains an artful enterprise, awaiting the empirical circumstances it encounters. Its timing cannot be prespecified. Like shifts in gears while driving, changes are not arbitrary or undisciplined; rather, they respond to the analytic challenges at hand in a principled, if not predetermined, fashion.

7. This may be the very thing Lynch (1993) decries with respect to conversation analysts who attempt to formalize and professionalize CA as a "scientific" discipline.

8. Some critics (see Denzin, 1998) have worried that analytic bracketing represents a selective objectivism, a form of "ontological gerrymandering." These, of course, have become fighting words among constructionists. But we should soberly recall that Steve Woolgar and Dorothy Pawluch (1985) have suggested that carving out some sort of analytic footing may be a pervasive and unavoidable feature of any sociological commentary. Our own constant attention to the *interplay* between discourse-in-practice and discursive practice—as they are understood and used by members—continually reminds us of their reflexive relationship. Gerrymanderers stand their separate ground and unreflexively deconstruct; analytic bracketing, in contrast, encourages a continual and methodical deconstruction of empirical groundings themselves. This may produce a less-than-tidy picture, but it also is designed to keep reification at bay and ungrounded signification under control.

References

Abu-Lughod, L. (1991). Writing against culture. In R. Fox (Ed.), *Recapturing anthropology* (pp. 137–162). Santa Fe, NM: SAR Press.

Abu-Lughod, L. (1993). *Writing women's worlds: Bedouin stories.* Berkeley: University of California Press.

Atkinson, J. M., & Drew, P. (1979). *Order in court.* Atlantic Highlands, NJ: Humanities Press.

Atkinson, P. (1988). Ethnomethodology: A critical review. *Annual Review of Sociology, 14,* 441–465.

Atkinson, P. (1995). *Medical talk and medical work.* London: Sage.

Barthes, R. (1977). *Image, music, text.* New York: Hill & Wang.

Berger, P. L., & Luckmann, T. (1966). *The social construction of reality.* New York: Doubleday.

Best, S., & Kellner, D. (1991). *Postmodern theory: Critical interrogations.* New York: Guilford.

Blumer, H. (1969). *Symbolic interactionism.* Englewood Cliffs, NJ: Prentice-Hall.

Boden, D., & Zimmerman, D. (Eds.). (1991). *Talk and social structure.* Cambridge, UK: Polity.

Bogen, D., & Lynch, M. (1993). Do we need a general theory of social problems? In J. Holstein & G. Miller (Eds.), *Reconsidering social constructionism: Debates in social problems theory* (pp. 213–237). Hawthorne, NY: Aldine de Gruyter.

Chase, S. E. (1995). *Ambiguous empowerment: The work narratives of women school superintendents.* Amherst: University of Massachusetts Press.

Denzin, N. K. (1998). The new ethnography. *Journal of Contemporary Ethnography, 27,* 405–415.

Dingwall, R., Eekelaar, J., & Murray, T. (1983). *The protection of children: State intervention and family life.* Oxford, UK: Blackwell.

Drew, P., & Heritage, J. (Eds.). (1992). *Talk at work.* Cambridge, UK: Cambridge University Press.

Dreyfus, H. L., & Rabinow, P. (1982). *Michel Foucault: Beyond structuralism and hermeneutics.* Chicago: University of Chicago Press.

Durkheim, E. (1961). *The elementary forms of the religious life.* New York: Collier-Macmillan.

Durkheim, E. (1964). *The rules of sociological method.* New York: Free Press.

Emerson, R. M. (1969). *Judging delinquents.* Chicago: Aldine.

Emerson, R. M., & Messinger, S. (1977). The micro-politics of trouble. *Social Problems, 25,* 121–134.

Foucault, M. (1965). *Madness and civilization.* New York: Random House.

Foucault, M. (1972). *The archaeology of knowledge.* New York: Pantheon.

Foucault, M. (1979). *Discipline and punish.* New York: Vintage.

Foucault, M. (1988). The ethic of care for the self as a practice of freedom. In J. Bernauer & G. Rasmussen (Eds.), *The final Foucault* (pp. 1–20). Cambridge, MA: MIT Press.

Freire, P. (1970). *Pedagogy of the oppressed.* New York: Continuum.

Garfinkel, H. (1952). *The perception of the other: A study in social order.* Unpublished doctoral dissertation, Harvard University.

Garfinkel, H. (1967). *Studies in ethnomethodology.* Englewood Cliffs, NJ: Prentice Hall.

Garfinkel, H. (1988). Evidence for locally produced, naturally accountable phenomena of order*, logic, reason, meaning, method, etc. in and as of the essential quiddity of immortal ordinary society, (I of IV): An announcement of studies. *Sociological Theory, 6,* 103–109.

Garfinkel, H., Lynch, M., & Livingston, E. (1981). The work of a discovering science construed with materials from the optically discovered pulsar. *Philosophy of the Social Sciences, 11,* 131–158.

Garfinkel, H., & Sacks, H. (1970). On the formal structures of practical actions. In J. C. McKinney & E. A. Tiryakian (Eds.), *Theoretical sociology* (pp. 338–366). New York: Appleton-Century-Crofts.

Gubrium, J. F. (1988). *Analyzing field reality.* Newbury Park, CA: Sage.

Gubrium, J. F. (1992). *Out of control: Family therapy and domestic disorder.* Newbury Park, CA: Sage.

Gubrium, J. F. (1993). For a cautious naturalism. In J. Holstein & G. Miller (Eds.), *Reconsidering social constructionism* (pp. 89–101). New York: Aldine de Gruyter.

Gubrium, J. F., & Holstein, J. A. (1990). *What is family?* Mountain View, CA: Mayfield.

Gubrium, J. F., & Holstein, J. A. (1994). *Constructing the life course.* Dix Hills, NY: General Hall.

Gubrium, J. F., & Holstein, J. A. (1995). Life course malleability: Biographical work and deprivatization. *Sociological Inquiry, 65,* 207–223.

Gubrium, J. F., & Holstein, J. A. (1997). *The new language of qualitative method.* New York: Oxford University Press.

Heritage, J. (1984). *Garfinkel and ethnomethodology.* Cambridge, UK: Polity.

Heritage, J. (1985). Analyzing news interviews: Aspects of the production of talk for an overhearing audience. In T. A. van Dijk (Ed.), *Handbook of discourse analysis* (Vol. 3, pp. 95–119). New York: Academic Press.

Heritage, J. (1997). Conversation analysis and institutional talk: Analyzing data. In D. Silverman (Ed.), *Qualitative research: Theory, method and practice* (pp. 161–182). London: Sage.

Hewitt, J. P. (1997). *Self and society.* Boston: Allyn & Bacon.

Hill, R. J., & Crittenden, K. S. (1968). *Proceedings of the Purdue Symposium on Ethnomethodology.* West Lafayette, IN: Purdue Research Foundation.

Holstein, J. A. (1983). Jurors' use of judges' instructions. *Sociological Methods and Research, 11,* 501–518.

Holstein, J. A. (1993). *Court-ordered insanity: Interpretive practice and involuntary commitment.* Hawthorne, NY: Aldine de Gruyter.

Holstein, J. A., & Gubrium, J. F. (2000). *The self we live by: Narrative identity in a postmodern world.* New York: Oxford University Press.

Holstein, J. A., & Gubrium, J. F. (2004). Context: working it up, down, and across. In C. Seale, G. Gobo, J. F. Gubrium, & D. Silverman (Eds.), *Qualitative research practice* (pp. 297–311). London: Sage.

Hughes, E. C. (1984). Going concerns: The study of American institutions. In D. Riesman & H. Becker (Eds.), *The sociological eye* (pp. 52–64). New Brunswick, NJ: Transaction Books.

Husserl, E. (1970). *Logical investigation.* New York: Humanities Press.

Livingston, E. (1986). *The ethnomethodological foundations of mathematics.* London: Routledge and Kegan Paul.

Lynch, M. (1985). *Art and artifact in laboratory science.* London: Routledge and Kegan Paul.

Lynch, M. (1993). *Scientific practice and ordinary action.* Cambridge, UK: Cambridge University Press.

Lynch, M., & Bogen, D. (1994). Harvey Sacks' primitive natural science. *Theory, Culture, and Society, 11,* 65–104.

Lynch, M., & Bogen, D. (1996). *The spectacle of history.* Durham, NC: Duke University Press.

Marx, K. (1956). *Selected writings in sociology and social philosophy* (T. Bottomore, Ed.). New York: McGraw-Hill.

Maynard, D. W. (1984). *Inside plea bargaining.* New York: Plenum.

Maynard, D. W. (1989). On the ethnography and analysis of discourse in institutional settings. In J. Holstein & G. Miller (Eds.), *Perspectives on social problems* (Vol. 1, pp. 127–146). Greenwich, CT: JAI.

Maynard, D. W. (1998). On qualitative inquiry and extramodernity. *Contemporary Sociology, 27,* 343–345.

Maynard, D. W., & Clayman, S. E. (1991). The diversity of ethnomethodology. *Annual Review of Sociology, 17,* 385–418.

Maynard, D. W., & Manzo, J. (1993). On the sociology of justice. *Sociological Theory, 11,* 171–193.

McHoul, A. (1986). The getting of sexuality: Foucault, Garfinkel, and the analysis of sexual discourse. *Theory, Culture, and Society, 3,* 65–79.

Mehan, H. (1979). *Learning lessons: Social organization in the classroom.* Cambridge, MA: Harvard University Press.

Mehan, H., & Wood, H. (1975). *The reality of ethnomethodology.* New York: Wiley.

Miller, G. (1991). *Enforcing the work ethic.* Albany: SUNY Press.

Miller, G. (1997a). *Becoming miracle workers: Language and meaning in brief therapy.* New York: Aldine de Gruyter.

Miller, G. (1997b). Building bridges: The possibility of analytic dialogue between ethnography, conversation analysis, and Foucault. In D. Silverman (Ed.), *Qualitative research: Theory, method and practice* (pp. 24–44). London: Sage.

Miller, G. (2001). Changing the subject: Self-construction in brief therapy. In J. F. Gubrium & J. A. Holstein (Eds.), *Institutional selves: Troubled identities in a postmodern world* (pp. 64–83). New York: Oxford University Press.

Mills, C. W. (1959). *The sociological imagination.* New York: Grove Press.

Narayan, K., & George, K. M. (2002). Personal and folk narrative as culture representation. In J. F. Gubrium & J. A. Holstein (Eds.), *Handbook of interview research* (pp. 815–832). Thousand Oaks, CA: Sage.

Parsons, T. (1951). *The social system.* New York: Free Press.

Pollner, M. (1987). *Mundane reason.* Cambridge, UK: Cambridge University Press.

Pollner, M. (1991). Left of ethnomethodology: The rise and decline of radical reflexivity. *American Sociological Review, 56,* 370–380.

Potter, J. (1996). *Representing reality: Discourse, rhetoric, and social construction.* London: Sage.

Potter, J. (1997). Discourse analysis as a way of analyzing naturally-occurring talk. In D. Silverman (Ed.), *Qualitative research: Theory, method and practice* (pp. 144–160). London: Sage.

Potter, J., & Wetherell, M. (1987). *Discourse and social psychology.* London: Sage.

Prior, L. (1997). Following in Foucault's footsteps: Text and context in qualitative research. In D. Silverman (Ed.), *Qualitative research: Theory, method and practice* (pp. 63–79). London: Sage.

Rose, N. (1990). *Governing the soul: The shaping of the private self.* New York: Routledge.

Sacks, H. (1972). An initial investigation of the usability of conversational data for doing sociology. In D. Sudnow (Ed.), *Studies in social interaction* (pp. 31–74). New York: Free Press.

Sacks, H. (1992). *Lectures on conversation* (Vols. 1 & 2). Oxford, UK: Blackwell.

Sacks, H., Schegloff, E., & Jefferson, G. (1974). A simplest systematics for the organization of turn-taking for conversation. *Language, 50,* 696–735.

Schegloff, E. A. (1991). Reflections on talk and social structure. In D. Boden & D. Zimmerman (Eds.), *Talk and social structure* (pp. 44–70). Cambridge, UK: Polity.

Schrag, C. O. (1997). *The self after postmodernity*. New Haven, CT: Yale University Press.

Schutz, A. (1962). *The problem of social reality.* The Hague: Martinus Nijhoff.

Schutz, A. (1964). *Studies in social theory.* The Hague: Martinus Nijhoff.

Schutz, A. (1967). *The phenomenology of the social world.* Evanston, IL: Northwestern University Press.

Schutz, A. (1970). *On phenomenology and social relations.* Chicago: University of Chicago Press.

Silverman, D. (1985). *Qualitative methodology and sociology.* Aldershot, UK: Gower.

Silverman, D. (1993). *Interpretive qualitative data.* London: Sage.

Silverman, D. (Ed.). (1997). *Qualitative research: Theory, method and practice.* London: Sage.

Silverman, D. (1998). *Harvey Sacks: Conversation analysis and social science.* New York: Oxford University Press.

Smith, D. E. (1987). *The everyday world as problematic.* Boston: Northeastern University Press.

Smith, D. E. (1990). *Texts, facts, and femininity.* London: Routledge.

ten Have, P. (1990). Methodological issues in conversation analysis. *Bulletin de Methodologie Sociologique, 27,* 23–51.

Weigert, A. J. (1981). *Sociology of everyday life.* New York: Longman.

Wieder, D. L. (1988). *Language and social reality.* Washington, DC: University Press of America.

Wittgenstein, L. (1958). *Philosophical investigations.* New York: Macmillan.

Wodak, R. (2004). Critical discourse analysis. In C. Seale, G. Gobo, J. F. Gubrium, & D. Silverman (Ed.), *Qualitative research practice* (pp. 197–214). London: Sage.

Woolgar, S., & Pawluch, D. (1985). Ontological gerrymandering. *Social Problems, 32,* 214–227.

Zimmerman, D. H. (1970). The practicalities of rule use. In J. Douglas (Ed.), *Understanding everyday life* (pp. 221–238). Chicago: Aldine.

Zimmerman, D. H. (1988). On conversation: The conversation analytic perspective. In J. A. Anderson (Ed.), *Communication yearbook 11* (pp. 406–432). Beverly Hills, CA: Sage.

Zimmerman, D. H., & Wieder, D. L. (1970). Ethnomethodology and the problem of order. In J. Douglas (Ed.), *Understanding everyday life* (pp. 285–295). Chicago: Aldine.

20

GROUNDED THEORY IN THE 21ST CENTURY

Applications for Advancing Social Justice Studies

Kathy Charmaz

Grounded theory methods of the 20th century offer rich possibilities for advancing qualitative research in the 21st century. Social justice inquiry is one area among many in which researchers can fruitfully apply grounded theory methods that Barney G. Glaser and Anselm L. Strauss (1967) created. In keeping with the theme for the current *Handbook* of advancing constructive social critique and change through qualitative research, this chapter opens discussion about applying grounded theory methods to the substantive area(s) of social justice. Inquiry in this area assumes focusing on and furthering equitable distribution of resources, fairness, and eradication of oppression (Feagin, 1999).[1]

The term "grounded theory" refers both to a method of inquiry and to the product of inquiry. However, researchers commonly use the term to mean a specific mode of analysis (see Charmaz, 2003a). Essentially, grounded theory methods are a set of flexible analytic guidelines that enable researchers to focus their data collection and to build inductive middle-range theories through successive levels of data analysis and conceptual development. A major strength of grounded

Author's Note. I thank Adele E. Clarke, Norman K. Denzin, Udo Kelle, Anne Marie McLaughlin, and Janice Morse for their comments on an earlier version of this chapter. I also appreciate having the views of the following members of the Sonoma State University Faculty Writing Program: Karin Enstam, Scott Miller, Tom Rosin, Josephine Schallehn, and Thaine Stearns. I presented brief excerpts from earlier drafts in a keynote address, "Reclaiming Traditions and Re-forming Trends in Qualitative Research," at the Qualitative Research Conference, Carleton University, Ottawa, Canada, May 22, 2003, and in a presentation, "Suffering and the Self: Meanings of Loss in Chronic Illness," at the Sociology Department, University of California, Los Angeles, January 9, 2004.

theory methods is that they provide tools for analyzing processes, and these tools hold much potential for studying social justice issues. A grounded theory approach encourages researchers to remain close to their studied worlds and to develop an integrated set of theoretical concepts from their empirical materials that not only synthesize and interpret them but also show processual relationships.

Grounded theory methods consist of simultaneous data collection and analysis, with each informing and focusing the other throughout the research process.[2] As grounded theorists, we begin our analyses early to help us focus further data collection.[3] In turn, we use these focused data to refine our emerging analyses. Grounded theory entails developing increasingly abstract ideas about research participants' meanings, actions, and worlds and seeking specific data to fill out, refine, and check the emerging conceptual categories. Our work results in an analytic interpretation of participants' worlds and of the processes constituting how these worlds are constructed. Thus, we can use the processual emphasis in grounded theory to analyze relationships between human agency and social structure that pose theoretical and practical concerns in social justice studies. Grounded theorists portray their understandings of research participants' actions and meanings, offer abstract interpretations of empirical relationships, and create conditional statements about the implications of their analyses.

Applying grounded theory methods to the substantive area of social justice produces reciprocal benefits. The critical stance in social justice in combination with the analytic focus of grounded theory broadens and sharpens the scope of inquiry. Such efforts locate subjective and collective experience in larger structures and increase understanding of how these structures work (see also Clarke, 2003, 2005; Maines, 2001, 2003). Grounded theory can supply analytic tools to move social justice studies beyond description, while keeping them anchored in their respective empirical worlds.[4] Not only are justice and injustice abstract concepts, but they are, moreover, *enacted processes*, made real through actions performed again and again. Grounded theorists can offer integrated theoretical statements about the conditions under which injustice or justice develops, changes, or continues. How might we move in this direction? Which traditions provide starting points?

▣ Constructivist Re-Visions of Grounded Theory

To develop a grounded theory for the 21st century that advances social justice inquiry, we must build upon its constructionist elements rather than objectivist leanings. In the past, most major statements of grounded theory methods minimized what numerous critics (see, for example, Atkinson, Coffey, & Delamont, 2003; Bryant, 2002, 2003; Coffey, Holbrook, & Atkinson, 1996; Silverman, 2000) find lacking: interpretive, constructionist inquiry. Answering this criticism means building on the Chicago school roots in grounded theory consistent with my constructivist statement in the second edition of this handbook (Charmaz, 2000a).[5] Currently, the Chicago school antecedents of grounded theory are growing faint and risk being lost. Contemporary grounded theorists may not realize how this tradition influences their work or may not act from its premises at all. Thus, we need to review, renew, and revitalize links to the Chicago school as grounded theory develops in the 21st century.

Building on the Chicago heritage supports the development of grounded theory in directions that can serve inquiry in the area of social justice. Both grounded theory methods and social justice inquiry fit pragmatist emphases on process, change, and probabilistic outcomes.[6] The pragmatist conception of emergence recognizes that the reality of the present differs from the past from which it develops (Strauss, 1964). Novel aspects of experience give rise to new interpretations and actions. This view of emergence can sensitize social justice researchers to study change in new ways, and grounded theory methods can give them the tools for studying it. Thus, we must revisit and reclaim Chicago school pragmatist and fieldwork traditions and develop their implications for social justice and democratic process.[7] To do so, we must move further into a constructionist social science and make the positivist roots of grounded theory problematic.

For many researchers, grounded theory methods provided a template for doing qualitative research stamped with positivist approval. Glaser's (see, especially, Glaser, 1978, 1992) strong foundation in mid-20th-century positivism gave grounded theory its original objectivist cast with its emphases in logic, analytic procedures, comparative methods, and conceptual development and assumptions of an external but discernible world, unbiased observer, and discovered theory. Strauss's versions of grounded theory emphasized meaning, action, and process, consistent with his intellectual roots in pragmatism and symbolic interactionism. These roots seem shrunken in his methodological treatises with Juliet Corbin (Strauss & Corbin, 1990, 1998) but grow robust in other works (see, for example, Corbin & Strauss, 1988; Strauss, 1993). Like Glaser, Strauss and Corbin also advanced positivistic procedures, although different ones. They introduced new technical procedures and made verification an explicit goal, thus bringing grounded theory closer to positivist ideals.[8] In divergent ways, Strauss and Corbin's works as well as Glaser's treatises draw upon objectivist assumptions founded in positivism.

Since then, a growing number of scholars have aimed to move grounded theory in new directions away from its positivist past. I share their goal and aim to build on the constructivist elements in grounded theory and to reaffirm its Chicago school antecedents. To date, scholars have questioned the epistemologies of both Glaser's and Strauss and Corbin's versions of grounded theory. We challenge earlier assumptions about objectivity, the world as an external reality, relations between the viewer and viewed, the nature of data, and authors' representations of research participants. Instead, we view positivist givens as social constructions to question and alter. Thus, when we adopt any positivist principle or procedure, we attempt to do so knowingly and to make our rationales explicit. In the second edition of this handbook (Charmaz, 2000a), I argued for building on the pragmatist underpinnings in grounded theory and developing it as a social constructionist method. Clive Seale (1999) contends that we can retain grounded theory methods without adhering to a naïve realist epistemology. Antony Bryant (2002, 2003) calls for re-grounding grounded theory in an epistemology that takes recent methodological developments into account, and Adele E. Clarke (2003, 2005) aims to integrate postmodern sensibilities with grounded theory and to provide new analytic tools for discerning and conceptualizing subtle empirical relationships. These moves by grounded theorists reflect shifts in approaches to qualitative research.[9]

A constructivist grounded theory (Charmaz, 1990, 2000a, 2003b; Charmaz & Mitchell, 2001) adopts grounded theory guidelines as tools but does not subscribe to the objectivist, positivist assumptions in its earlier formulations. A constructivist approach emphasizes the studied phenomenon rather than the methods of studying it. Constructivist grounded theorists take a reflexive stance on modes of knowing and representing studied life. That means giving close attention to empirical realities and our collected renderings of them—*and* locating oneself in these realities. It does not assume that data simply await discovery in an external world or that methodological procedures will correct limited views of the studied world. Nor does it assume that impartial observers enter the research scene without an interpretive frame of reference. Instead, what observers see and hear depends upon their prior interpretive frames, biographies, and interests as well as the research context, their relationships with research participants, concrete field experiences, and modes of generating and recording empirical materials. No qualitative method rests on pure induction—the questions we ask of the empirical world frame what we know of it. In short, we share in constructing what we define as data. Similarly, our conceptual categories arise through our interpretations *of* data rather than emanating *from* them or from our methodological practices (cf. Glaser, 2002). Thus, our theoretical analyses are interpretive renderings of a reality, not objective reportings of it.

Whether informed by Glaser (1978, 1992, 1998, 2002) or Strauss and Corbin (1990, 1998), many researchers adopted positivist grounded theory as a template. The constructivist position recasts this template by challenging its objectivist underpinnings. We can use a constructivist template to inform social justice research in the 21st century. Clearly, much research in the area of social justice is objectivist and flows from standard positivist methodologies. A constructivist grounded theory offers another alternative: a systematic approach to social justice inquiry that fosters integrating subjective experience with social conditions in our analyses.

An interest in social justice means attentiveness to ideas and actions concerning fairness, equity, equality, democratic process, status, hierarchy, and individual and collective rights and obligations. It signifies thinking about being human and about creating good societies and a better world. It prompts reassessment of our roles as national and world citizens. It means exploring tensions between complicity and consciousness, choice and constraint, indifference and compassion, inclusion and exclusion, poverty and privilege, and barriers and opportunities. It also means taking a critical stance toward actions, organizations, and social institutions. Social justice studies require looking at both realities and ideals. Thus, contested meanings of "shoulds" and "oughts" come into play. Unlike positivists of the past, social justice researchers openly bring their shoulds and oughts into the discourse of inquiry.

▣ Reexamining Grounded Theory of the Past

In the 20th century, grounded theory methods offered guidelines and legitimacy for conducting research. Glaser and Strauss (1967) established qualitative research as valuable in its own right and argued that it proceeds from a different logic than quantitative research. Although researchers did not always understand grounded theory methods and seldom followed them beyond a step or two, they widely cited and acclaimed these methods because they legitimized and codified a previously implicit process. Grounded theory methods offered explicit strategies, procedural rigor, and seeming objectivity. As Karen Locke (1996) notes, many researchers still use grounded theory methods for "a rhetoric of justification as opposed to a rhetoric of explication" (p. 244; see also Charmaz, 1983; Silverman, 2000).

All analyses come from particular standpoints, including those emerging in the research process. Grounded theory studies emerge from wrestling with data, making comparisons, developing categories, engaging in theoretical sampling, and integrating an analysis. But *how* we conduct all these activities does not occur in a social vacuum. Rather, the entire research process is interactive; in this sense, we bring past interactions and current interests into our research, and we interact with our empirical materials and emerging ideas as well as, perhaps, granting agencies, institutional review boards, and community agencies and groups, along with research participants and colleagues. Neither data nor ideas are mere objects that we passively observe and compile (see also Holstein & Gubrium, 1995).

Glaser (2002) treats data as something separate from the researcher and implies that they are untouched by the competent researcher's interpretations. If, perchance, researchers somehow interpret their data, then according to Glaser, these data are "rendered objective" by looking at many cases. Looking at many cases strengthens a researcher's grasp of the empirical world and helps in discerning variation in the studied phenomenon. However, researchers may elevate their own assumptions and interpretations to "objective" status if they do not make them explicit.

No analysis is neutral—despite research analysts' claims of neutrality. We do not come to our studies uninitiated (see also Denzin, 1994; Morse, 1999; Schwandt, 1994, 2000). What we know shapes, but does not necessarily determine, what we "find." Moreover, *each* stage of inquiry is constructed through social processes. If we treat these processes as unproblematic, we may not recognize how they are constructed. Social justice researchers likely understand their starting assumptions; other researchers may not—including grounded theorists.[10] As social scientists, we *define* what we record as data, yet how we define data outlines how we represent them in our works. Such definitional decisions—whether implicit or explicit—reflect moral choices that, in turn, spawn subsequent moral decisions and actions.[11]

Rather than abandoning the traditional positivist quest for empirical detail, I argue that we advance it—*without the cloak of neutrality and passivity enshrouding mid-century positivism.* Gathering rich empirical materials is the first step. Recording these data systematically prompts us to pursue leads that we might otherwise ignore or not realize. Through making systematic recordings, we also gain comparative materials to pinpoint contextual conditions and to explore links between levels of analysis. By seeking empirical answers to emerging theoretical questions, we learn about the worlds we enter and can increase the cogency of our subsequent analyses. Hence, data need to be informed by our theoretical sensitivity. Data alone are insufficient; they must be telling and must answer theoretical questions.

Without theoretical scrutiny, direction, and development, data culminate in mundane descriptions (see also Silverman, 2000). The value of the product then becomes debatable, and critics treat earlier studies as reified representations of the limits of the method itself rather than how it was used (Charmaz, 2000a). Burawoy (1991) categorizes the products of grounded theory as empirical generalizations. Moreover, he claims that the method does not consider power in micro contexts and that "it represses the broader macro forces that both limit change and create domination in the micro sphere" (p. 282). I disagree. Simply because earlier authors did not address power or macro forces does not mean that grounded theory methods cannot. In contrast to Burawoy's claims, I argue that we should use grounded theory methods in precisely these areas to gain fresh insights in social justice inquiry.

Critics of grounded theory commonly miss four crucial points: (a) theorizing is an activity; (b) grounded theory methods provide a way to proceed with this activity; (c) the research problem and the researcher's unfolding interests shape the *content* of this activity, not the method; and (d) the products of theorizing reflect how researchers acted on these points. As Dan E. Miller (2000) argues, the ironic issue is that researchers have done so little grounded theory, despite their claims to use it. Its potential for developing theory remains untapped, as does its potential for studying power and inequality.

Social justice studies require data that diverse audiences agree represent the empirical world and that researchers have given a fair assessment. I do not mean that we reify, objectify, and universalize these data. Instead, I mean that we must start by gathering thorough empirical materials precisely because social justice research may provoke controversy and contested conclusions. Thus, we need to identify clear boundaries and limits of our data. Locating the data strengthens the foundation for making theoretical insights and for providing evidence for evaluative claims. Critics can then evaluate an author's argument on its merits. The better they can see direct connections between the evidence and points in the argument, the more this argument will persuade them. The lingering hegemony of positivism still makes controversial research suspect, as Fine, Weis, Weseen, and Wong (2000) observe. Therefore, the data for such studies must be unassailable.

A strong empirical foundation is the first step in achieving credibility—for both social justice researchers and grounded theorists. Despite reliance on data-driven interpretations, the rush to "theorize"—or perhaps to publish—has led some grounded theorists to an unfortunate neglect of thorough data collection, which has persisted since Lofland and Lofland (1984) first noted it. Glaser (1992, 2002) discounts quests for accurate data and dismisses full description as distinguishing conventional qualitative data analysis from grounded theory. However, leading studies with implications for social justice and policy have had solid empirical foundations (see, for example, Duneire, 1992; Glaser & Strauss, 1965; Goffman, 1961; Mitchell, 2002; Snow & Anderson, 1993). Grounded theory studies that lack empirical vitality cannot support a rationale for major social change—or even minor policy recommendations. The stronger the social justice arguments derived from a study, particularly controversial ones, the greater the need for a robust empirical foundation with compelling evidence.

Using Grounded Theory to Study Social Justice Issues

Initial Reflections

Both the steps and the logic of grounded theory can advance social justice research. Grounded theorists insist that researchers define what is happening in the setting (Glaser, 1978; Glaser & Strauss, 1967). Sensitivity to social justice issues fosters defining latent processes as well as explicit actions. Grounded theory tools for studying action—collective as well as individual action—can make social justice analysis more precise and predictive. By focusing the data gathering, a researcher can seek new information to examine questions concerning equality, fairness, rights, and legitimacy.[12] The grounded theory openness to empirical leads spurs the researcher to pursue emergent questions and thus shifts the direction of inquiry.

A social justice researcher can use grounded theory to anchor agendas for future action, practice, and policies in the *analysis* by making explicit connections between the theorized antecedents, current conditions, and consequences of major processes. Social justice research, particularly participatory action research (Kemmis & McTaggart, 2000), proceeds from researchers' and participants' joint efforts and commitments to change practices. Because it arises in settings and situations in which people have taken a reflexive stance on their practices, they already have tools to conduct systematic research on their practices in relation to subjective experience, social actions, and social structures. Hence, adopting constructivist grounded theory would foster their efforts to articulate clear links between practices and each level and, thus, to strengthen their arguments for change.

Other researchers need to weigh whether, when, how, and to what extent to bring research participants into the process. Although well intended, doing so may create a series of knotty problems in concrete situations.[13] Janice Morse (1998) finds that the consequences of bringing participants into research decisions include keeping the analytic level low, overstating the views of participants who clamored for more space in the narrative, and compromising the analysis. Moreover, Morse (1998) notes that qualitative analyses differ from participants' descriptive accounts and may reveal paradoxes and processes of which participants are unaware.

Adopting grounded theory strategies in social justice research results in putting ideas and perspectives to empirical tests. Any extant concept must earn its way into the analysis (Glaser, 1978). Thus, we cannot import a set of concepts such as hegemony and domination and paste them on the realities in the field. Instead, we can treat them as sensitizing concepts, to be explored in the field settings (Blumer, 1969; van den Hoonaard, 1997). Then we can define if, when, how, to what extent, and under which conditions these concepts become relevant to the study (Charmaz, 2000b). We need to treat concepts as problematic and look for their characteristics as lived and understood, not as given in textbooks. Contemporary anthropologists, for example, remain alert to issues of cultural imperialism. Most sociologists attend to agency, power, status, and hierarchy.

Grounded theory studies can show how inequalities are played out at interactional and organizational levels. True, race, class, and gender—and age and disability—are everywhere. But how do members of various groups define them?[14] How and when do these status variables affect action in the scene? Researchers must define how, when, and to what extent participants *construct* and *enact* power, privilege, and inequality. Robert Prus (1996) makes a similar point in his book *Symbolic Interaction and Ethnographic Research*. Race, class, gender, age, and disability are social constructions with contested definitions that are continually reconstituted (see, for example, Olesen, Chapter 10, this volume). Using them as static variables, as though they have uncontested definitions that explain data and social processes *before* or *without* looking, undermines their potential power. Taking their meanings as given also undermines using grounded theory to develop fresh insights and ideas. Adopting my alternative tack involves juxtaposing participants' definitions against academic or sociological notions. In turn, researchers themselves must be reflexive about how they represent participants' constructions and enactments.

What new dimensions will social justice foci bring to research? Societal and global concerns are fundamental to a critical perspective. Thus, these studies situate the studied phenomenon in relation to larger units. How and where does it fit? For example, a study of sales interactions could look not only at the immediate interaction and how salespeople handle it but also at the organizational context and perhaps the corporate world, and its global reach, in which these interactions occur. Like many qualitative researchers, grounded theorists often separate the studied interactions from their situated contexts. Thus, a social justice focus brings in more structure and, in turn, a grounded theory treatment of that structure results in a dynamic, processual analysis of its enactment. Similarly, social justice research often takes into account the historical evolution of the current situation, and a grounded theory analysis of this evolution can yield new insights and, perhaps, alternative understandings. For that matter, researchers can develop grounded theories from analyses of pertinent historical materials in their realm of inquiry (see, for example, Clarke, 1998; Star, 1989).

Critical inquiry attends to contradictions between myths and realities, rhetoric and practice, and ends and means. Grounded theorists have the tools to discern and analyze contradictions revealed in the empirical world. We can examine what people *say* and compare it to what they *do* (Deutscher, Pestello, & Pestello, 1993). Focusing on words or deeds are ways of representing people; however, observed contradictions between the two may indicate crucial priorities and practices. To date, grounded theorists have emphasized the *overt*—usually overt statements—more than the tacit, the liminal, and the implicit. With critical inquiry, we can put our data to new tests and create new connections in our theories.

Social Justice Emphases: Resources, Hierarchies, and Policies and Practices

A social justice focus can sensitize us to look at both large collectivities and individual experiences in new ways. Several emphases stand out: *resources*, *hierarchies*, and *policies and practices.* First, present, partial, or absent resources—whether economic, social, or personal—influence interactions and outcomes. Such resources include information, control over meanings, access to networks, and determination of outcomes. Thus, information and power are crucial resources. As Martha Nussbaum (1999) argues, needs for resources vary among people, vary at different times, and vary according to capabilities. Elders with disabling conditions need more resources than other people do or than they themselves needed in earlier years. What are the resources in the empirical worlds we study? What do they mean to actors in the field? Which resources, if any, are taken for granted? By whom? Who controls the resources? Who needs them? According to which and whose criteria of need? To what extent do varied capabilities enter the discussion? Are resources available? If so, to whom? How, if at all, are resources shared, hoarded, concealed, or distributed? How did the current situation arise? What are the implications of having control over resources and of handling them, as observed in the setting(s)?

Second, any social entity has hierarchies—often several. What are they? How did they evolve? At what costs and benefits to involved actors? Which purported and actual purposes do these hierarchies serve? Who benefits from them? Under which conditions? How are the hierarchies related to power and oppression? How, if at all, do definitions of race, class, gender, and age cluster in specific hierarchies and/or at particular hierarchical levels? Which moral justifications support the observed hierarchies? Who promulgates these justifications? How do they circulate? How do these hierarchies affect social actions at macro, meso, and micro social levels? How and when do the hierarchies change?

Third, the consequences of social policies and practices are made real in collective and individual life. Here we have the convergence of structure and process. What are the rules—both tacit and explicit? Who writes or enforces them? How? Whose interests do the rules reflect? From whose standpoint? Do the rules and routine practices negatively affect certain groups or categories of individuals? If so, are they aware of them? What are the implications of their relative awareness or lack of it? To what extent and when do various participants support the rules and the policies and practices that flow from them? When are they contested? When do they meet resistance? Who resists, and which risks might resistance pose?

By asking these questions, I aim to stimulate thinking and to suggest diverse ways that critical inquiry and grounded theory research may join. The potential of advancing such endeavors already has been indicated by symbolic interactionists who point the way to demonstrating micro consequences of structural inequalities (L. Anderson & Snow, 2000; Scheff, 2003; Schwalbe et al., 2000). Combining critical inquiry and grounded theory furthers these efforts.

Working With Grounded Theory

Studying the Data

The following interview stories provide the backdrop for introducing how grounded theory guidelines can illuminate social justice concerns. My research is social psychological; however, grounded theory methods hold untapped potential for innovative studies at the organizational, societal, and global levels of analysis. The examples below offer a glimpse of the kinds of initial comparisons I make.[15] I began studying the experience of chronic illness with interests in meanings of self and time. Such social psychological topics can reveal hidden effects of inequality and difference on the self and social life that emerge in research participants' many stories of their experiences.

Both grounded theory and critical inquiry are inherently comparative methods. In earlier renderings, I treated the excerpt of Christine Danforth below as a story of suffering and Marty Gordon's initial tale as a shocking significant event that marked a turning point in her life. The first step of grounded theory analysis is to study the data. Grounded theorists ask: What is happening? and What are people doing? A fresh look at the accounts below can suggest new leads to pursue and raise new questions.

At the time of the following statement, Christine was a 43-year-old single woman who had systemic lupus erythematosus, Sjögren's syndrome, diabetes, and serious back injuries. I had first met her 7 years earlier, when her multiple disabilities were less visible, although intrusive and worrisome. Since then, her health had declined, and she had had several long stretches of living on meager disability payments. Christine described her recent episode:

> I got the sores that are in my mouth, got in my throat and closed my throat up, so I couldn't eat or drink. And then my potassium dropped down to 2.0. I was on the verge of cardiac arrest. . . . That time when I went in they gave me 72 bottles of pure potassium, burned all my veins out.
>
> I asked, "What does that mean, that it burned your veins out?"
>
> She said, "It hurts really bad; it's just because it's so strong and they can't dilute it with anything. They said usually what they do is they dilute with something like a numbing effect, but because I was 2.0, which is right on cardiac arrest that they couldn't do it, they had to get it in fast."
>
> I asked, "Did you realize that you were that sick?"
>
> She said, "Well, I called the doctor several times saying, 'I can't swallow.' I had to walk around and drool on a rag. They finally made an appointment, and I got there and I waited about a half hour. The

lady said that there was an emergency and said that I'd have to come back tomorrow. And I said, 'I can't.' I said, 'As soon as I stand up, I'm going to pass out.' And she said, 'Well there's nothing we can do.' . . . And then this other nurse came in just as I got up and passed out, so then they took me to emergency. . . . And it took them 12 hours to—they knew when I went in there to admit me, but it took them 12 hours to get me into a room. I sat on a gurney. And they just kept fluid in me until they got me to a room.

Later in the interview, Christine explained,

[When the sores] go to my throat, it makes it really hard to eat or drink, which makes you dehydrated. After that first time . . . when I called her it had been 3 days since I'd ate or drank anything . . . and by the time I got an appointment, it was, I believe, six or seven days, without food or water.

Imagine Christine walking slowly and determinedly up the short sidewalk to my house. See her bent knees and lowered head, as she takes deliberate steps. Christine looks weary and sad, her face as laden with care as her body is burdened by pain and pounds. Always large, she is heavier than I have ever seen her, startlingly so.

Christine has a limited education; she can hardly read. Think of her trying to make her case for immediate treatment—without an advocate. Christine can voice righteous indignation, despite the fatigue and pain that saps her spirit and drains her energy. She can barely get through her stressful workday, yet she must work as many hours as possible because she earns so little. The low pay means that Christine suffers directly from cutbacks at the agency where she works. Her apartment provides respite, but few comforts. It has no heat —she cannot afford it. Christine does not eat well. Nutritious food is an unobtainable luxury; cooking is too strenuous, and cleanup is beyond imagination. She tells me that her apartment is filled with pictures and ceramic statues of cats as well as stacks of things to sort. Maneuverable space has shrunk to aisles cutting through the piles. Christine seldom cleans house—no energy for that. I've never been to her apartment; it embarrasses her too much to have visitors. Christine would love to adopt a kitten but cats are not permitted. Her eyes glaze with tears when my skittish cat allows her to pet him.

Christine has become more immobile and now uses a motorized scooter, which she says has saved her from total disability. But since using the scooter and approaching midlife, she also has gained one hundred pounds and needs a better vehicle to transport the scooter. Christine has little social life by now; her friends from high school and her bowling days have busy family and work lives. When she first became ill, Christine had some nasty encounters with several of those friends who accused her of feigning illness. She feels her isolation keenly, although all she can handle after work is resting on the couch. Her relationship with her elderly mother has never been close; she disapproves of her brother, who has moved back in with their mother and is taking drugs. One continuing light in Christine's life is her recently married niece, who just had a baby.

The years have grown gray with hardships and troubles. Christine has few resources—economic, social, or personal. Yet she perseveres in her struggle to remain independent and employed. She believes that if she lost this job, she would never get another one. Her recent weight gain adds one more reason for the shame she feels about her body.

Christine suffers from chronic illness and its spiraling consequences. Her physical distress, her anger and frustration about her life, her sadness, shame, and uncertainty all cause her to suffer. Christine talks some about pain and much about how difficult disability and lack of money make her life. She has not mentioned the word "suffering." Like many other chronically ill people, Christine resists describing herself in a way that might undermine her worth and elicit moral judgments. Yet she has tales to tell of her turmoil and troubles. (Charmaz, 1999, pp. 362–363)

The following interview account of Marty Gordon's situation contrasts with Christine's story. Marty received care from the same health facility as Christine and also had a life-threatening condition that confounded ordinary treatment and management. However, Marty's relationship to staff there and the content and quality of her life differed dramatically from Christine's.

When I first met Marty Gordon in 1988, she was a 59-year-old woman with a diagnosis of rapidly progressing pulmonary fibrosis. A hospitalization for extensive tests led to the diagnosis of Marty's condition. She had moved to a new area after her husband, Gary, retired as a school superintendent, and she herself retired early from her teaching and grant-writing post at a high school. Marty said that she and Gary were "very, very close." They had had no children, although Gary had a son by an earlier marriage and she, a beloved niece.

Pure retirement lasted about 3 months before they became bored. Subsequently, Marty became a part-time real estate agent and Gary worked in sales at a local winery. Not only did working bring new interests into their lives, but it also helped pay their hefty health insurance costs. They had not realized that their retirement benefits would not cover a health insurance plan. They both found much pleasure in their new lives and in their luxurious home high in the hills overlooking the city. Marty seemed to remain almost as busy as she was before retiring. While working full-time, she had entertained her husband's professional associates, had run a catering business, and had created special meals to keep Gary's diabetes and heart condition under control. She had taken much pride—and still did—in keeping up her perfectly appointed house and in keeping her weight down through regular exercise. For years, she had arisen at 5 each morning to swim an hour before going to work, then stopped at church afterward to say her rosaries.

When I first met Marty, she told the following tale about her first hospitalization:

> The doctor came in to tell me, "Uh, it didn't look good and that this was a—could be a rapidly"—and it appeared that mine was really going rapidly and that it might be about six weeks. Whoa! That blew my mind. It really did. . . . Right after that—I'm a Catholic—right after that, a poor little volunteer lady came in and said, "Mrs. Gordon?" And the doctor had said, "Mrs. Gordon?" "Yeah, OK." And then he told me. She said, "I'm from St. Mary's Church." I said, "Jesus, Mary, and Joseph, they've got the funeral already." And it really just—then I began to see humor in it, but I was scared. . . .
>
> This was the point when—[I decided], "If this is going to happen OK, but I'm not going to let it happen." . . . And I think probably that was the turning point when I said I wouldn't accept it. You know, I will not accept that uhm, death sentence, or whatever you want to call it. (Charmaz, 1991, p. 215)

However, from that point on, Marty had Gary promise her that she would die first. She needed him to take care of her when she could no longer care for herself; moreover, she could not bear the thought of living without him. During the next 5 years, Marty made considerable gains, despite frequent pain, fatigue, and shortness of breath. One Sunday evening, when Gary came home from a wine-pouring and Marty saw his ashen face, she insisted, "We're going to emergency." He had had a second heart attack, followed by a quadruple bypass surgery. Marty said, "He sure is a lot better now. And, of course, *I was very angry with him.* I said to him, 'You can never leave me. *I tell you, I'll sue you!*' [She explained to me.] Because we've had a deal for a long time." When telling me about her own health, she recounted this conversation with her surgeon:

> I come in for an appointment and I had just played 18 holes of golf, and so he said, "I think we misdiagnosed you." And I said, "Well, why do you think that?" And he said, "You're just going over, you're surpassing everything." So I said, "Well, that doesn't necessarily mean a diagnosis is wrong." I said, "Are you going to give me credit for anything?" And he said, "Well, what do you mean?" I said, "You have to have a medical answer, you can't have an answer that I worked very hard, on my whole body and my mind, to get, you know, the integral part of myself, and that maybe that might be helping? And the fact that I don't touch fats and I don't do this and I do exercise? *That's not helping, huh*?" So he said, "Well, I guess so." And I said, "Well, do you want to take out my lungs again and see?" I said, "You took them out [already]." So he acknowledged, he said, "Yeah, it's just that it's so unusual." And maybe not accepting something, you know, denial is one thing, but not *excepting* is another thing.

Marty strove to be the exception to her dismal prognosis—she insisted on being an exception. She made great efforts to keep herself and her husband alive, functioning, and enjoying life. By confronting her doctor and challenging *his* definition of her, Marty rejected his narrow, medicalized definition of her. She implied that he was *denying her wellness*. Thus, she enacted a dramatic reversal of the conventional scenario of a doctor accusing the patient of denying her illness. Marty fought feelings of self-pity and sometimes talked about suffering and self-pity interchangeably. When she reflected on how she kept going, she said:

> I do, do really think that, if you sit down, and I mean, literally sit down, because it's hard to get up, you do start feeling sorry for yourself. And I'm saying, "Oh, God if I could only get up without hurting." And I've begun to feel, once in a while, I get this little sorry for myself thing, that if I could have a day without pain, I wonder what I'd do? *Probably nothing*. Because I wouldn't push myself and I'd get less done.
>
> I asked, "How so?"
>
> Marty replied, "My whole thing is faith and attitude. You've just got to have it. I feel so sorry for people who give in. But maybe that's why . . . you've got to have some people die. [Otherwise they'd] be hanging around forever."

Marty had fortitude—and attitude. Marty intended to live—by will and grit. Dying? The prospect of dying undermined her belief in individual control and thus conflicted with her self-concept.

■ Integrating Grounded Theory With Social Justice Research

What do these stories indicate? What might they suggest about social justice? How do grounded theory methods foster making sense of them? Both women have serious debilitating conditions with multiple harrowing episodes that make their lives uncertain. Both are courageous and forthright, are aware of their conditions, and aim to remain productive and autonomous.

Coding is the first step in taking an analytic stance toward the data. The initial coding phase in grounded theory forces the researcher to define the action in the data statement. In the figures illustrating coding (Figures 20.1–20.3), my codes reflect standard grounded theory practice. The codes are active, immediate, and short. They focus on defining action, explicating implicit assumptions, and seeing processes. By engaging in line-by-line coding, the researcher makes a close study of the data and lays the foundation for synthesizing it.

Coding gives a researcher analytic scaffolding on which to build. Because researchers study their empirical materials closely, they can define both new leads from them and gaps in them. Each piece of data—whether an interview, a field note, a case study, a personal account, or a document—can inform earlier data. Thus, should a researcher discover a lead through developing a code in one interview, he or she can go back through earlier interviews and take a fresh look as to whether this code sheds light on earlier data. Researchers can give their data multiple readings and renderings. Interests in social justice, for example, would lead a researcher to note points of struggle and conflict and to look for how participants defined and acted in such moments.

Grounded theory is a comparative method in which the researcher compares data with data, data with categories, and category with category. Comparing these two women's lives illuminates their several similarities and striking contrasts between their personal, social, and material resources. I offer these comparisons here for heuristic purposes only, to clarify points of convergence and divergence. Both women shared a keen interest in retaining autonomy, and both were aware that illness and disability raised the specter of difference, disconnection, and degradation. Nonetheless, Marty Gordon enjoyed much greater economic security, choices, privileges, and opportunities throughout her life than did Christine Danforth. Marty's quick wit, articulate voice, organizational skills, and diligence constituted a strong set of capabilities that served her well in dealing with failing health.

Poverty and lack of skills had always constrained Christine's life and curtailed her choices. They also diminished her feelings of self-worth and moral status, that is, the extent of virtue or vice attributed to a person by others and self (Charmaz, in press). Then illness shrunk her

Recognizing illness spiral Recounting symptom progression Approaching crisis	I got the sores that are in my mouth, got in my throat and closed my throat up, so I couldn't eat or drink. And then my potassium dropped down to 2.0. I was on the verge of cardiac arrest. . . . That time when I went in they gave me 72 bottles of pure potassium, burned all my veins out. I asked, "What does that mean, that it burned your veins out?"
Suffering the effects of treatment Receiving rapid treatment Forfeiting comfort for speed	She said, "It hurts really bad; it's just because it's so strong and they can't dilute it with anything. They said usually what they do is they dilute with something like a numbing effect, but because I was 2.0, which is right on cardiac arrest that they couldn't do it, they had to get it in fast." I asked, "Did you realize that you were that sick? She said,
Seeking help Remaining persistent Explaining symptoms Encountering bureaucratic dismissal Experiencing turning point Explaining severity Receiving second refusal Collapsing Prolonging the ordeal—fitting into organizational time	"Well, I called the doctor several times saying, 'I can't swallow.' I had to walk around and drool on a rag. They finally made an appointment, and I got there and I waited about a half hour. The lady said that there was an emergency and said that I'd have to come back tomorrow. And I said, 'I can't.' I said, 'As soon as I stand up, I'm going to pass out.' And she said, 'Well there's nothing we can do.' . . . And then this other nurse came in just as I got up and passed out, so then they took me to emergency. . . . And it took them 12 hours to—they knew when I went in there to admit me, but it took them 12 hours to get me into a room. I sat on a gurney. And they just kept fluid in me until they got me to a room. Later in the interview, Christine explained:
Explaining symptoms Awareness of complications Enduring the wait Suffering induced by organization	[When the sores] go to my throat, it makes it really hard to eat or drink, which makes you dehydrated. After that first time . . . when I called her it had been three days since I'd ate or drank anything . . . and by the time I got an appointment, it was, I believe, six or seven days, without food or water.

Figure 20.1. Initial Coding—Christine Danforth

limited autonomy, and her moral status plummeted further. Christine lived under a cloud of nagging desperation. The anger she felt earlier about being disabled, deprived, and disconnected had dissipated into a lingering sadness and shame. Clearly, Christine has far fewer resources than Marty. She also has had fewer opportunities to develop capabilities throughout her life that could help her to manage her current situation.

Marty struggled periodically with daily routines, but she exerted control over her life and her world. Her struggles resided at another level; she fought against becoming inactive and sinking into self-pity. She treated both her body and her mind as objects to work on and to improve, as projects. Marty worked with physicians, if they agreed on her terms. Although she had grown weaker and had pronounced breathing problems, she believed living at all testified to her success.

Receiving bad news Facing death Suffering diagnostic shock Identifying religion Recounting the identifying moment Finding humor Feeling frightened	The doctor came in to tell me, "Uh, it didn't look good and that this was a—could be a rapidly"—and it appeared that mine was really going rapidly and that it might be about six weeks. Whoa! That blew my mind. It really did. . . . Right after that—I'm a Catholic—right after that, a poor little volunteer lady came in and said, "Mrs. Gordon?" And the doctor had said, "Mrs. Gordon?" "Yeah, OK." And then he told me. She said, "I'm from St. Mary's Church." I said, "Jesus, Mary, and Joseph, they've got the funeral already." And it really just—then I began to see humor in it, but I was scared. . . .
Accepting the present but not the prognosis Insisting on controlling the illness Turning point—Refusing the death sentence	This was the point when—[I decided], "If this is going to happen OK, but I'm not going to let it happen." . . . And I think probably that was the turning point when I said I wouldn't accept it. You know, I will not accept that uhm, death sentence, or whatever you want to call it.

Figure 20.2. Initial Coding—Marty Gordon

For long years, Marty kept her illness contained, or at least mostly out of view. Her proactive stance toward her body and her high level of involvements sustained her moral status. Whatever social diminishment of moral status she experienced derived more from age than from suffering.

The kinds of insights that grounded theory methods can net social justice research vary according to level, scope, and objectives of the study. Through comparing the stories above, we gain some sense of structural and organizational sources of suffering and their differential effects on individuals. The comparisons suggest how research participants' relative resources and capabilities became apparent through studying inductive data.

The comparisons also lead to ideas about structure. Most policy research emphasizes *access* to health care. Comparing these two interviews indicates differential treatment *within* a health care organization. In addition, the comparisons raise questions about rhetoric and realities of receiving care. Marty Gordon credited her "faith and attitude" for managing her illness; however, her lifestyle, income, supportive relationships, and quick wit also helped to buffer her losses. But might not her attitude and advantages be dialectic and mutually reinforcing? Could not her advantages have also fostered her faith and attitude? Each person brings a past to the present. When invoking a similar logic, the residues of the past—limited family support, poor education, undiagnosed learning problems, and lack of skills—complicated and magnified Christine Danforth's troubles with chronic illness and in negotiating care. The structure of Christine's life led to her increasing isolation and decreasing moral status. Might not her anger and sadness have followed? From Marty and Christine's stories, we can discern hidden advantages of high social class status as well as hidden injuries of low status (Sennett & Cobb, 1973).

Last, coding practices can help us to see *our* assumptions, as well as those of our research participants. Rather than raising our codes to a level of objectivity, we can raise questions about how and why we developed certain codes.16 Another way to break open our assumptions is to ask colleagues and, perhaps, research participants themselves to engage in the coding. When they bring divergent experience to the coding, their responses to the data may call for scrutiny of our own.

	Christine Danforth	*Marty Gordon*
Awareness of illness	Predicting symptom intensification Recognizing illness spiral Lack of control over escalating symptoms Experiencing stigma	Learning and experimenting Becoming an expert Realizing the potential of stigma
Developing a stance toward illness	Remaining persistent Monitoring progression of symptoms Seeking help	Suffering initial diagnostic shock Feeling frightened Taking control Refusing death sentence Making deals Challenging physician's view Attacking physician's assumptions Discrediting physician's opinion Rejecting medical model Working on body and mind Following strict regimen Swaying physician's view Believing in her own perceptions Seeing self as an exception
Material resources	Fighting to keep the job Having a health plan Struggling to handle basic expenses Eking out a life—Juggling to pay the rent; Relying on an old car	Working part-time for extras Having a health plan Having solid retirement income Enjoying comfortable lifestyle with travel and amenities
Personal resources	Persevering despite multiple obstacles Defending self Recognizing injustice Abiding sense of shame about educational deficits and poverty Hating her appearance Trying to endure life Feeling excluded from organizational worlds	Preserving autonomy Forging partnerships with professionals Trusting herself Having a good education Assuming the right to control her life Believing in individual power Finding strength through faith Possessing a sense of entitlement Aiming to enjoy life Having decades of experience with organizations and professionals
Social resources	Living in a hostile world Taking delight in her niece Retreating from cruel accusations Suffering loneliness Realizing the fragility of her existence Foreseeing no future help	Taking refuge in a close marriage Having strong support, multiple involvements Maintaining powerful images of positive and negative role models Knowing she could obtain help, if needed
Strategies for managing life	Minimizing visibility of deficits Avoiding disclosure of illness Limiting activities	Obtaining husband's promise Avoiding disclosure of illness Controlling self-pity Remaining active Maintaining religious faith

Figure 20.3. Comparing Life Situations

Reclaiming Chicago School Traditions

Marty Gordon and Christine Danforth's situations and statements above indicate the construction of their views and actions. Note that at certain points, they each struggle with obdurate social structures that take on tangible meaning in their stories of crucial interactions. To make further sense of situations and stories like these and to interpret the social justice issues with them, I have called for reclaiming Chicago school underpinnings in grounded theory. These underpinnings will move grounded theory more completely into constructionist social science. What are these underpinnings? What does reclaiming them entail? On which assumptions does Chicago school sociology rest? Why are they significant for both the development of grounded theory methods and social justice inquiry?

In brief, the Chicago school assumes human agency, attends to language and interpretation, views social processes as open-ended and emergent, studies action, and addresses temporality. This school emphasizes the significance of language for selfhood and social life and understands that human worlds consist of meaningful objects. In this view, subjective meanings emerge from experience, and they change as experience changes (Reynolds, 2003a). Thus, the Chicago school assumes dynamic, reciprocal relationships between interpretation and action, and it views social life as people fitting together diverse forms of conduct (Blumer, 1979, p. 22).[17] Because social life is interactive and emergent, a certain amount of indeterminacy characterizes it (Strauss & Fisher, 1979a, 1979b). How might we use Chicago school sociology now to inform contemporary grounded theory studies and social justice inquiry? Where might it lead us? What moral direction might it give?

Both pragmatist philosophy and Chicago school ethnography foster openness to the world and curiosity about it. The Meadian concept of role-taking assumes empathetic understanding of research participants and their worlds. To achieve this understanding, we must know how people define their situations and act on them. Social justice researchers can turn this point into a potent tool for discovering if, when, and to what extent people's meanings and actions contradict their economic or political interests—and whether and to what extent they are aware of such contradictions (see, for example, Kleinman, 1996). Thus, seeking these definitions and actions can make critical inquiry more complex and powerful. Knowing them can alert the researcher to points of actual or potential conflict and change—or compliance. Similarly, learning what things mean to people makes what they do with them comprehensible—at least from their worldview. Conversely, how people act toward things in their worlds indicates their relative significance. Such considerations prompt the researcher to construct an inductive analysis rather than, say, impose structural concepts on the scene.

Although Chicago school sociology has been viewed as microscopic, it also holds implications for the meso and macro levels that social justice researchers aim to engage. A refocused grounded theory would aid and refine connections with these levels. Horowitz (2001) shows how extending Mead's (1934) notion of "generalized other" takes his social psychology of the self to larger social entities and addresses expanding democratic participation of previously excluded groups. Her argument is two-pronged: (a) the development of a critical self is prerequisite for democracy and (b) groups that achieve self-regulation gain empowerment.

The naturalistic inquiry inherent in Chicago school tradition means studying what people in specific social worlds do over time and gaining intimate familiarity with the topic (Blumer, 1969; Lofland & Lofland, 1984, 1995). Hence, to reclaim the Chicago tradition, we must first: *Establish intimate familiarity with the setting(s) and the events occurring within it—as well as with the research participants.*[18] This point may seem obvious; however, much qualitative research, including grounded theory studies, skate the surface rather than plumb the depths of studied life.

An emphasis on action and process leads to considerations of time. The pragmatist treatment of social constructions of past, present, and future could direct social justice researchers to look at timing, pacing, and temporal rhythms. These concerns could alert us to new forms of control and organization. In addition, understanding timing and sequencing can shed light on the success or failure of collective action. Thus, attending to temporality affords us new knowledge of the worlds we study.

Chicago fieldwork traditions have long emphasized situated analyses embedded in social, economic, and occasionally political contexts, as evident in urban ethnographies (see, for example, E. Anderson, 2003; Horowitz, 1983; Suttles, 1968; Venkatesh, 2000). Numerous grounded theory studies have not taken account of the context in which the studied research problem or process exists. Combining Chicago intellectual traditions with social justice sensitivities would correct tendencies toward decontextualized—and, by extension, objectified—grounded theory analyses.

Looking at data with a Chicago school lens entails focusing on meaning and process at both the subjective and social levels. Like many other people with chronic illness, the women above are aware of the pejorative moral meanings of illness and suffering and sensed the diminished status of those who suffer. When I asked Marty Gordon how her condition affected her job, she said, "I never let it show there. *Never.* Never give cause for anybody either to be sorry for you or want to get rid of you." Although Christine Danforth hated her job, she viewed it as her lifeline and feared losing it. After telling me about receiving written ultimatums from her supervisor, she said:

> Nobody else is going to hire me. . . . An able body can't get one [job], how am I going to get one? So if I'm dyslexic, you know, those people don't even know what it is, let alone how to deal with it. I wouldn't be able to get a job as a receptionist because I can't read and write like most people, so I'm there for life.

Christine Danforth's employers knew the names of her medical diagnoses, but they did not understand her symptoms and their effects in daily life. Christine's story took an ironic twist. She worked for an advocacy agency that served people with disabilities. Several staff members who challenged her work and worth had serious physical disabilities themselves. Christine also discovered that her supervisors had imposed rules on her that they allowed other staff to ignore. Thus, the situation forced Christine to deal with multiple moral contradictions. She suffered the consequences of presumably enlightened disability advocates reproducing negative societal judgments of her moral worth. Tales of such injustice inform stories of suffering.

These examples suggest the second step to reclaiming the Chicago tradition: *Focus on meanings and processes.* This step includes addressing subjective, situational, and social levels. By piecing together many research participants' statements, I developed a moral hierarchy of suffering. Suffering here is much more than pain; it defines self and situation—and ultimately does so in moral terms that support inequities. Suffering takes into account stigma and social definitions of human worth. Hence, suffering includes the lived experience of stigma, reduced autonomy, and loss of control of the defining images of self. As a result, suffering magnifies difference, forces social disconnection, elicits shame, and increases as inequalities mount.[19]

Meanings of suffering, however, vary and are processual. As researchers, we must find the range of meanings and learn how people form them. Figure 20.4 shows how suffering takes on moral status and assumes hierarchical form. In addition, it suggests how suffering intersects with institutional traditions and structural conditions that enforce difference. In keeping with a grounded theory perspective, any attributes taken as status variables must earn their way into the analysis rather than be assumed. Note that I added resources and capabilities as potential markers of difference as their significance became clear in the data.[20] Figure 20.4 implies how larger social justice issues can emerge in open-ended, inductive research. In this case, these issues concern access, equitable treatment, and inherent human worth in health care.

HIERARCHY of MORAL STATUS in SUFFERING

HIGH MORAL STATUS—VALIDATED MORAL CLAIMS

MEDICAL EMERGENCY

INVOLUNTARY ONSET

BLAMELESSNESS FOR CONDITION

"APPROPRIATE" APPEARANCE AND DEMEANOR

SUSTAINED MORAL STATUS—ACCEPTED MORAL CLAIMS

CHRONIC ILLNESS

NEGOTIATED DEMANDS

PRESENT OR PAST POWER & RECIPROCITIES

Diminished Moral Status—Questionable Moral Claims

CHRONIC TROUBLE

BLAME FOR CONDITION AND COMPLICATIONS

"INAPPROPRIATE/REPUGNANT" APPEARANCE AND/OR DEMEANOR

PERSONAL VALUE

worth less

worth less

Worth Less

WORTHLESS

Institutional Traditions **Structural Conditions**

Difference—class, race, gender, age, sexual preference, resources, capabilities

Figure 20.4. Hierarchy of Moral Status in Suffering

Source: Adapted and expanded from Charmaz (1999), "Stories of Suffering: Subjects' Stories and Research Narratives," *Qualitative Health Research, 9,* 362–382.

The figure reflects an abstract statement of how individual experience and social structure come together in emergent action. The figure derives from inductive and comparative analyses of meaning and action, consistent with Chicago school sociology. When we compare individual accounts, we can see that Marty Gordon and Christine Danforth develop their stance toward illness from different starting places and different experiences, yet they both are active in forming their definitions. The Chicago school concept of human nature has long contrasted with much of structural social science. We not only assume human agency but also study it and its consequences. People are active, creative beings who *act,* not merely behave. They attempt to solve problems in their lives and worlds. As researchers, we need to learn how, when, and why participants act. Thus, the third step in reclaiming Chicago traditions follows: *Engage in a close study of action.* The Chicago emphasis on process becomes evident here. What do research participants see as routine? What do they define as problems? In Marty Gordon's case, the problems disrupted her life and could kill her. She had good reason for wanting to oversee her care. At one point, she described her conversation with Monica, her lung specialist, about ending treatment with prednisone:

> I've had a couple of setbacks. . . . The first time I went off it [prednisone], my breathing capacity cut right in half, so she said, "No." And I make deals with her. . . . So I'm going to Ireland and she said, "Okay, I want you to double it now, go back up while you're traveling, and then we'll talk about it. But no deals, and don't be stupid." So when I came back I said, "Let's try it again."

But when Marty came back from Ireland, she had complications. She described what happened while she was playing golf:

> I wound up in emergency Easter Sunday because I thought . . . I pulled a muscle. . . . But they thought it was a pulmonary embolism. . . . They said, "Well, with your condition we have to take an X ray, a lung X ray." And he [physician] said, "Oh, I don't like what I see here." And I said, "Look, you're not the doctor that looks at that all the time, don't get nervous, it's been there." So he said, "No, there's a lot more scar tissue than your other X ray." And I said, "Yeah, well that's par for the course, from what I understand." And he said, "But there's a hole there I don't like to see." I said, "Look, it's a pulled muscle. *Give me the Motrin.*" [At the time of this interview, Motrin was a prescription drug.] And finally he said, ". . . Maybe it is a pulled muscle." So she [Monica, her lung specialist] called me the next day and she said, "Okay, let's slow down on this going down on the prednisone, too many side things are happening, so we're going slower." And I think it will work. . . . I'm still playing golf and still working.

Marty Gordon's recounted conversations attest to her efforts to remain autonomous. She insisted on being the leading actor in her life and on shaping its quality. From the beginning, she had remained active in her care and unabashed in her willingness to challenge her physicians and to work with them—on her terms.

Agency does not occur in isolation; it always arises within a social context already shaped by language, meaning, and modes of interaction. This point leads us to the next step in reclaiming the Chicago tradition: *Discover and detail the social context within which action occurs.* A dual focus on action and context can permit social justice researchers to make nuanced explanations of behavior. What people think, feel, and do must be analyzed within the relevant social contexts, which, in turn, people construct through action and interaction. Individuals take into account the actions of those around them as they themselves act. Interaction depends on fitting lines of action together, to use Herbert Blumer's term (Blumer, 1969, 1979). We sense how Marty Gordon and Monica fit lines of actions together to quell her symptoms. Marty crafted an enduring professional partnership with Monica that has eased her way through an increasingly less accessible health care organization for more than 10 years. Knowing that others are or will be involved shapes how people respond to their situations. The more participants create a shared focus and establish a joint goal, the more they will build a shared past and projected future. Marty and Monica shared the goal of keeping Marty alive and of reducing her symptoms while minimizing medication side effects. They built a history of more than a decade, and to this day they project a shared future.

The women in these two stories grapple with the issues that confront them and thus affect the social context in which they live. Marty had a voice and made herself heard; Christine tried but met resistance. She lacked advocates, social skills, and a shared professional discourse to enlist providers as allies, which commonly occurs when class and culture divide providers and patients. The construction of social context may be more discernible in Marty's statements than in other kinds of interviews. In Christine's attempt to obtain care, she related the sequence and timing of events. We see that she received care only because she became a medical emergency, and we learn how earlier refusals and delays increased her misery.

These interview statements contain words and phrases that tell and hint of meaning. Marty

Gordon talks about "making deals," "working hard," "not excepting," "wallowing," and "pushing myself." Christine Danforth contrasts herself with an "able body" and recounts how the sequence of events affected her actions. The fifth step in reclaiming the Chicago school tradition follows this dictum: *Pay attention to language*. Language shapes meaning and influences action. In turn, actions and experiences shape meanings. Marty's interview excerpts suggest how she uses words to make her meanings real and tries to make her meanings stick in interaction. Chicago school sociology assumes reciprocal and dynamic relations between interpretation and action. We interpret what happens around and to us and shape our actions accordingly, particularly when something interrupts our routines and causes us to rethink our situations.

In addition to the points outlined above, Chicago school scholars have generated other concepts that can fruitfully inform initial directions in social justice research and can sensitize the researcher's empirical observations. Among these concepts are Glaser and Strauss's (1965) concept of awareness contexts, Scott and Lyman's (1968) idea of accounts, Mills's (1990) notion of vocabularies of motive, Goffman's (1959) metaphor of the theater, and Hochschild's (1983) depiction of emotion work and feeling rules. Establishing who knows what, and when they know it, can provide a crucial focus for studying interaction in social justice research. Both the powerful and the powerless may be forced to give accounts that justify or excuse their actions. People describe their motives in vocabularies in situated social, cultural, historical, and economic contexts. Viewing life as theater can alert social justice researchers to main actors, minor characters and audiences, acts and scenes, roles and scripts, and front-stage impressions and backstage realities. Different kinds of emotion work and feeling rules reflect the settings in which they arise. Expressed emotions and stifled feelings stem from rules and enacted hierarchies of power and advantage that less privileged actors may unwittingly support and reproduce (see, for example, Lively, 2001).

Rethinking Our Language

Just as we must attend to how our research participants' language shapes meaning, we must attend to our own language and make *it* problematic. I mention a few key terms that we qualitative researchers assume and adopt. These terms have served as guiding metaphors or, more comprehensively, as organizing concepts for entire studies. Perhaps ironically, Chicago school sociologists and their followers have promulgated most of these terms. Researchers have made them part of their taken-for-granted lexicon and, I believe, imposed them too readily on our studied phenomena. The logic of both the earlier Chicago school and grounded theory means developing our concepts *from* our analyses of empirical realities, rather than applying concepts *to* them. If we adopt extant concepts, they must earn their way into the analysis through their usefulness (Glaser, 1978). Then we can extend and strengthen them (see, for example, Mamo, 1999; Timmermans, 1994).

Two major concepts carry images of tactical manipulations by a calculating social actor: strategies and negotiations. Despite what we social scientists say, much of human behavior does not reflect explicit *strategies*. Subsuming ordinary actions under the rubric of "strategies" implies explicit tactical schemes when, in fact, an actor's intentions may not have been so clear to him or her, much less to this actor's audience. Rather than strategies, much of what people do reflects their taken-for-granted habitual actions. These actions become routine and scarcely recognized unless disrupted by change or challenge. Note that in the long lists of codes comparing Christine Danforth's and Marty Gordon's situations, I list many actions but few strategies.

When looking for taken-for-granted actions in our research, John Dewey's (1922) central ideas about habit, if not the term itself, can prove helpful to attend to participants' assumptions and taken-for-granted practices, which may not always be in their own interests. Like Snow's (2001) point that much of life is routine and proceeds without explicit interpretation, Dewey (1922) views habits as patterned predispositions that enable individuals to respond to their situations with economy of thought and action: People can act while focusing attention elsewhere (see also Clark, 2000; Cutchin, 2000). Thus, habits include those taken-for-granted modes of thinking, feeling, and acting that people invoke without reflection (Dewey, 1922; Hewitt, 1994). The habits of a lifetime enabled Marty Gordon to maintain hope and to manage her illness. Christine's habits let her eke by but also increased her isolation and physical problems.

Like the concept of strategies, negotiation also imparts a strategic character to interaction. Negotiation is an apt term to describe Marty Gordon's "deals" and disputes with her practitioners. At least from her view, contests did emerge, and bargaining could bring them to effective closure. Then interaction could proceed from the negotiated agreement. Marty brought not only her resolve to her negotiations, but also years of skills and fearlessness in dealing with professionals, a partnership with her primary physician, a network of supportive others, and the ability to pay for nutritious food, conveniences, and a good health plan. Little negotiation may proceed when a person has few such resources and great suffering, as Christine Danforth's story suggests.

Although the concept of negotiations may apply in Marty Gordon's case, we have stretched its applicability, as if it reflected most interactions. It does not. Much of social life proceeds as people either unconsciously adapt their response to another person or interpret what the other person says, means, or does and then they subsequently respond to it (Blumer, 1979). Interaction can alter views, temper emotions, modify intentions, and change actions—all without negotiation. The strategic quality of negotiation may be limited or absent during much sociability. People can be persuasive without attempting to negotiate. Negotiation assumes actors who are explicitly aware of the content and structure of the ensuing interaction. Negotiation also assumes that participants' interactional goals conflict or need realignment if future mutual endeavors are to occur. For that matter, the term assumes that all participants have sufficient power to make their voices heard, if not also to affect outcomes. Judith Howard (2003) states, "The term 'negotiation' implies that the interacting parties have equal opportunities to control the social identities presented, that they come to the bargaining table with equal resources and together develop a joint definition of the situation" (p. 10). Nonetheless, much negotiation ensues when the parties involved do not have equal resources, and much foment may occur about enforcing definitions of social identities, despite unequal positions. For negotiations to occur, each party must be involved with the other to complete joint actions that matter to both, likely for different reasons.

The problems of applying these concepts and of importing their meanings and metaphors on our data extend beyond the concepts above. These problems also occur with applying the concepts of "career," "work," or "trajectory," which we could examine with the same logic. However, the current social scientific emphasis on stories merits scrutiny here.

Metaphors of Stories and Meanings of Silences

The term "story" might once have been a metaphor for varied qualitative data such as interview statements, field note descriptions, or documents. However, we cease to use the term "story" as metaphor and have come view it as concrete reality, rather than a construction we place on these data. With several exceptions (e.g., Charmaz, 2002, in press; Frank, 1997), social scientists have treated the notion of "story" as unproblematic. We have questioned whose story we tell, how we tell it, and how we represent those who tell us their stories, but not the idea of a story itself or whether our materials fit the term "story." The reliance on qualitative interviews in grounded theory studies (Creswell, 1997), as well as in other qualitative approaches, such as narrative analysis, furthered this focus on stories. In addition, the topics themselves of intensive interviews foster producing a story.

Limiting data collection to interviews, as is common in grounded theory research, delimits the theory we can develop. In social justice studies, we must be cautious about which narrative frame we impose on our research, and when and how we do it. The frame itself can prove consequential. The story frame assumes a linear logic and boundaries of temporality that we might over- or underdraw.[21]

Part of my argument about stories concerns silences. In earlier works (Charmaz, 2002, in press), I have emphasized silences at the individual level of analysis; they are also significant at the organizational, social worlds, and societal levels. Clarke (2003, 2005) provides a new grounded theory tool, situational mapping, for showing action and inaction, voices and silences, at varied levels of analysis. She observes that silences reveal absent organizational alignments. Thus, mapping those silences, in their relation to active alignments, can render invisible social structure visible. Invisible aspects of social structure and process are precisely what critical inquiry needs to tackle.[22]

Silences pose significant meanings and telling data in any research that deals with moral choices, ethical dilemmas, and just social policies. Silence signifies absence and sometimes reflects a lack of awareness or inability to express thoughts and feelings. However, silence speaks to power arrangements. It also can mean attempts to control information, to avoid redirecting actions, and, at times, to impart tacit messages. The "right" to speak may mirror hierarchies of power: *Only those who have power dare to speak.* All others are silenced (see, for example, Freire, 1970). Then, too, the powerless may retreat into silence as a last refuge. At one point, Christine Danforth felt that her life was out of control. She described being silenced by devastating events and by an aggressive psychiatrist, and she stopped talking. In all these ways, silence is part of language, meaning, *and* action.

Making stories problematic and attending to silences offers new possibilities for understanding social life for both social justice and grounded theory research. What people in power do not say is often more telling than what they do say. We must note those who choose to remain silent, as well as those who have been silenced. Treating both stories and silences with a critical eye and comparing them with actions and inaction provides empirical underpinnings for any emerging grounded theory. Subsequently, the constructed theory will gain usefulness in its explanatory and predictive power.

Establishing Evaluation Criteria

Using grounded theory for social justice studies requires revisiting the criteria for evaluating them. Glaser and Strauss's (1967; Glaser, 1978) criteria for assessing grounded theory studies include fit, workability, relevance, and modifiability. Thus, the theory must fit the empirical world it purports to analyze, provide a workable understanding and explanation of this world, address problems and processes in it, and allow for variation and change that make the core theory useful over time. The criterion of modifiability allows for refinements of the theory that simultaneously make it more precise and enduring.

Providing cogent explanations stating how the study meets high standards will advance social justice inquiry and reduce unmerited dismissals of it. However, few grounded theorists provide a model. They seldom offer explicit discussions about how their studies *meet* the above or other criteria, although they often provide statements on the logic of their decisions (cf. S. I. Miller & Fredericks, 1999). In the past, some grounded theorists have claimed achieving a theoretical grounding with limited empirical material. Increasingly, researchers justify the type, relative depth, and extent of their data collection and analysis on *one* criterion: saturation of categories. They issue a claim of saturation and end their data collection (Flick, 1998; Morse, 1995; Silverman, 2000). But what does saturation mean? To whom? Janice Morse (1995), who initiated the critique of saturation, accepts defining it as "data adequacy" and adds that it is "operationalized as collecting data until no new information is obtained" (p. 147). Often, researchers invoke the criterion of saturation to justify small samples—very small samples with thin data. Such justifications diminish the credibility of grounded theory. Any social justice study that makes questionable claims of saturation risks being seen as suspect.

Claims of saturation often reflect rationalization more than reason, and these claims raise questions. What stands as a category?[23] Is it conceptual? Is it useful? Developed? By whose criteria? All these questions add up to the big question: *What stands as adequate research*? Expanded criteria that include the Chicago school's rigorous study of context and action makes any grounded theory study more credible and advances the claims of social justice researchers. Then we can augment our criteria by going beyond "saturation" and ask if our empirical detail also achieves Christians's (2000) and Denzin's (1989) criterion of "interpretive sufficiency," which takes into account cultural complexity and multiple interpretations of life.

To reopen explicit discussion of criteria for grounded theory studies, and particularly those in social justice research, I offer the following criteria.

Criteria for Grounded Theory Studies in Social Justice Inquiry

Credibility

- Has the researcher achieved intimate familiarity with the setting or topic?
- Are the data sufficient to merit the researcher's claims? Consider the range, number, and depth of observations contained in the data.
- Has the researcher made systematic comparisons between observations and between categories?
- Do the categories cover a wide range of empirical observations?
- Are there strong logical links between the gathered data and the researcher's argument and analysis?
- Has the researcher provided enough evidence for his or her claims to allow the reader to form an independent assessment—and *agree* with the researcher's claims?

Originality

- Are the categories fresh? Do they offer new insights?
- Does the analysis provide a new conceptual rendering of the data?
- What is the social and theoretical significance of the work?
- How does the work challenge, extend, or refine current ideas, concepts, and practices?

Resonance

- Do the categories portray the fullness of the studied experience?
- Has the researcher revealed liminal and taken-for-granted meanings?
- Has the researcher drawn links between larger collectivities and individual lives, when the data so indicate?
- Do the analytic interpretations make sense to members and offer them deeper insights about their lives and worlds?

Usefulness

- Does the analysis offer interpretations that people can use in their everyday worlds?
- Do the analytic categories speak to generic processes?
- Have these generic processes been examined for hidden social justice implications?
- Can the analysis spark further research in other substantive areas?
- How does the work contribute to making a better society?

A strong combination of originality and credibility increases resonance, usefulness, and the subsequent value of the contribution. The criteria above account for the empirical study and development of the theory. They say little about how the researcher writes the narrative or what makes it compelling. Other criteria speak to the aesthetics of the writing. Our written works derive from aesthetic principles and rhetorical devices—in addition to theoretical statements and scientific rationales. The act of writing is intuitive, inventive, and interpretive, not merely a reporting of acts and facts, or, in the case of grounded theory, causes, conditions, categories, and consequences. Writing leads to further discoveries and deeper insights; it furthers inquiry. Rather than claiming silent authorship hidden behind a scientific facade, grounded theorists—as well as proponents of social justice—should claim audible voices in their writings (see Charmaz & Mitchell, 1996; Mitchell & Charmaz, 1996). For grounded theorists, an audible voice brings the writer's self into the words while illuminating intersubjective worlds. Such evocative writing sparks the reader's imagined involvement in the scenes portrayed and those beyond. In this sense, Laurel Richardson's (2000) criteria for the evocative texts of "creative analytic practice ethnography" also apply here. These criteria consist of the narrative's substantive contribution, aesthetic merit, reflexivity, impact, and expression of a reality (p. 937).

A grounded theory born from reasoned reflections and principled convictions that conveys a reality makes a substantive contribution. Add aesthetic merit and analytic impact, and then its influence may spread to larger audiences. Through reclaiming Chicago traditions, conducting inquiry to make a difference in the world, and creating evocative narratives, we will not be silenced. We will have stories to tell and theories to proclaim.

Summary and Conclusions

A turn toward qualitative social justice studies promotes combining critical inquiry and grounded theory in novel and productive ways. An interpretive, constructivist ground theory supports this turn by building on its Chicago school antecedents. Grounded theory can sharpen the analytic edge of social justice studies. Simultaneously, the critical inquiry inherent in social justice research can enlarge the focus and deepen the significance of grounded theory analyses. Combining the two approaches enhances the power of each.

A grounded theory informed by critical inquiry demands going deeper into the phenomenon itself and its situated location in the world than perhaps most grounded theory studies have in the past. This approach does not mean departing from grounded theory guidelines. It does not mean investigative reporting. Grounded theory details process and context—and goes into the social world and setting far beyond one investigative story. Grounded theory contains tools to study how processes become institutionalized practices. Such attention to the processes that constitute structure can keep grounded theory from dissolving into fragmented small studies.

With the exception of those studies that rely on historical documents, grounded theory studies typically give little scrutiny to the past and sometimes blur inequalities with other experiences or overlook them entirely. Studying social justice issues means paying greater attention to inequality and its social and historical contexts. Too much of qualitative research today minimizes current *social* context, much less historical evolution. Relying on interview studies on focused topics may preclude attention to context—particularly when our research participants take the context of their lives for granted and do not speak of it. Hence, the mode of inquiry itself limits what researchers may learn. Clearly, interviewing is the method of choice for certain topics, but empirical qualitative research suffers if it becomes synonymous with interview studies.

Like snapshots, interviews provide a picture taken during a moment in time. Interviewers gain a view of research participants' concerns as they present them, rather than as events unfold. Multiple visits over time combined with the intimacy of intensive interviewing do provide a deeper view of life than one-shot structured or informational interviews can provide. However, anyone's retelling of events may differ markedly from an ethnographer's recording of them. In addition, as noted above, what people say may not be what they do (Deutscher et al., 1993). At that, what an interviewer asks and hears or an ethnographer records depends in part on the overall context, the immediate situation, *and* his or her training and theoretical proclivities.

At its best, grounded theory provides methods to explicate an empirical process in ways that prompt seeing beyond it. By sticking closely to the leads and explicating the relevant process, the researcher can go deeper into meaning and action than given in words. Thus, the focused inquiry of grounded theory, with its progressive inductive analysis, moves the work theoretically and covers more empirical observations than other approaches. In this way, a focused grounded theory portrays a picture of the whole.

▣ Notes

1. Such emphases often start with pressing social problems, collective concerns, and impassioned voices. In contrast, Rawls's (1971) emphasis on fairness begins from a distanced position of theorizing individual rights and risks from the standpoint of the rational actor under hypothetical conditions. Conceptions of social justice must take into account both collective goods and individual rights and must recognize that definitions both of rationality and of "rational" actors are situated in time, space, and culture—and both can change. To foster justice, Nussbaum (2000, p. 234) argues that promoting a collective good must not subordinate the ends of some individuals over others. She observes that women suffer when a collective good is promoted without taking into account the internal power and opportunity hierarchies within a group.

2. For descriptions of grounded theory guidelines, see Charmaz (2000a, 2003b), Glaser (1978, 1992), and Strauss and Corbin (1990, 1998).

3. I use the term "data" throughout for two reasons: It symbolizes (a) a fund of empirical materials that we systematically collect and assemble to acquire knowledge about a topic and (b) an acknowledgment that qualitative resources hold equal significance for studying empirical reality as quantitative measures, although they differ in kind.

4. In this way, integrating a critical stance offers a corrective to narrow and limited studies conducted as grounded theory studies. Neither a narrow focus nor limited empirical material is part of the method itself. We cannot blur how earlier researchers have used grounded theory with the guidelines in the method. Although social justice inquiry suggests substantive fields, it also assumes questions and concerns about power, privilege, and hierarchy that some grounded theorists may not yet have entertained.

5. Chicago school sociology shaped an enduring tradition of qualitative research in sociology, of which grounded theory remains a part. What stands as "the" Chicago school varies depending on who defines it (Abbott, 1999; L. H. Lofland 1980). In my view, the Chicago school theoretical heritage goes back to the early years of the 20th century, in the works, for example, of Charles Horton Cooley (1902), John Dewey (1922), George Herbert Mead (1932, 1934), and Charles S. Peirce (Hartshorne & Weiss, 1931–1935). In research practice, the Chicago school sparked study of the city and spawned urban ethnographies (see, for example, Park & Burgess, 1925; Shaw, 1930; Thomas & Znaniecki, 1927; Thrasher, 1927). Chicago sociologists often held naïve and partial views but many sensed the injustices arising in the social problems of the city, and Abbott (1999) notes that Albion Small attacked capitalism. Nonetheless, some Chicago school sociologists reinforced inequities in their own bailiwicks (Deegan, 1995). Mid-century ethnographers and qualitative researchers built on their Chicago school intellectual heritage and created what scholars have called a second Chicago school (G. A. Fine, 1995). For recent renderings of the Chicago school, see Abbott (1999), G. A. Fine (1995), Musolf (2003), and Reynolds (2003a, 2003b). Chicago school sociology emphasizes the contextual backdrop of observed scenes and their situated nature in time, place, and relationships. Despite the partial emergence of grounded theory from both theoretical and methodological Chicago school roots, Glaser (2002) disavows the pragmatist, constructionist elements in grounded theory.

6. Symbolic interactionism provides an open-ended theoretical perspective from which grounded theory researchers can start. This perspective is neither inherently prescriptive nor microsociological. Barbara Ballis Lal (2001) not only suggests the contemporary usefulness of early Chicago school symbolic interactionist ideas for studying race and ethnicity but also notes their implications for current political action and social policy. David Maines (2001) demonstrates that symbolic interactionist emphases on agency, action, and negotiated order have long had macrosociological import. He shows that the discipline of sociology has incorrectly—and ironically—compartmentalized symbolic interactionism while increasingly becoming more interactionist in its assumptions and directions.

7. In particular, the Chicago school provides antecedents for attending to social reform, as in Jane Addams's (1919) work at Hull-House and Mead and Dewey's interests in democratic process. The field research founded in Chicago school sociology has been called into question at various historical junctures

from Marxist and postmodernist perspectives (see, for example, Burawoy, Blum, et al., 1991; Burawoy, Gamson, et al., 2002; Clough, 1992; Denzin, 1992; Wacquant, 2002). Criticisms of Chicago school sociology have suggested that grounded theory represents the most codified and realist statement of Chicago school methodology (Van Maanen, 1988).

8. Strauss and Corbin's (1990, 1998) emphasis on technical procedures has been met with chagrin by a number of researchers (Glaser, 1992; Melia, 1996; Stern, 1994). In his 1987 handbook *Qualitative Analysis for Social Scientists*, Strauss mentions axial coding and verification, which depart from earlier versions of grounded theory, and he and Juliet Corbin (1990, 1998) develop them in their coauthored texts.

9. My critique mirrors a much larger trend. Lincoln and Guba (2000) find that the movement away from positivism pervades the social sciences. They state that the turn toward interpretive, postmodern, and critical theorizing makes most studies vulnerable to criticism (p. 163).

10. Grounded theory provides tools that researchers can—and do—use from any philosophical perspective—or political agenda. Studies of worker involvement, for example, may start from addressing employees' concerns or management's aim to increase corporate profits.

11. Tedlock (2000) states, "Ethnographers' lives are embedded within their field experiences in such a way that all their interactions involve moral choices" (p. 455). Ethnography may represent one end of a continuum. Nevertheless, does not grounded theory research also involve moral choices?

12. Feminist research suggests ways to proceed. DeVault (1999) and Olesen (2000) provide excellent overviews of and debates in feminist research.

13. Issues of exploitation arise when participants work without pay or recognition. Feminist researchers often recommend having participants read drafts of materials, yet even reading drafts may be too much when research participants are struggling with losses, although they may have requested to see the researcher's writings in progress. When research participants express interest, I share early drafts, but I try to reduce participants' potential feelings of obligation to finish reading them. Morse (1998) agrees with sharing results but not the conduct of inquiry.

14. Schwalbe et al. (2000) and Harris (2001) make important moves in this analytic direction.

15. The first two interview excerpts appear in earlier published accounts. I include them so that readers interested in seeing how I used them in social psychological accounts may obtain them. Subsequent interview statements have not been published. The data are part of an evolving study of 170 interviews of chronically ill persons. A subset of research participants that includes these two women have been interviewed multiple times.

16. Further specifics of grounded theory guidelines are available in Charmaz (2000a, 2003b, Charmaz & Mitchell, 2001), Glaser (1978, 1992, 2001), Strauss, (1987), and Strauss and Corbin (1990, 1998).

17. I realize that presenting the Chicago school as a unified perspective is something of a historical gloss because differences are discernible between the early pragmatists as well as among the sociologists who followed them. Furthermore, a strong quantitative tradition developed at the University of Chicago (see Bulmer, 1984).

18. See Lofland and Lofland (1984, 1995) for an emphasis on describing the research setting. Lincoln and Guba (1985) offer a sound rationale for naturalistic inquiry as well as good ideas for conducting it. When the data consist of extant texts such as documents, films, or texts, then the researcher may need to seek multiple empirical sources.

19. See Scheff (2003) for a discussion of relationships between shame and society.

20. Grounded theory methods can inform traditional quantitative research, although these approaches seldom have been used together. Hypotheses can be drawn from Figure 20.4, such as that the greater the definitions of an individual's difference, the more rapid his or her tumble down the moral hierarchy of suffering. Quantitative researchers could pursue such hypotheses.

21. And as I have pointed out with individual accounts (Charmaz, 2002), raw experience may fit neither narrative logic nor the comprehensible content of a story.

22. Clarke's (2003, 2004) concept of implicated actors can be particularly useful to analyze voices and silences in social justice discourses.

23. See Dey (1999) for an extensive discussion on constructing categories in the early grounded theory works.

References

Abbott, A. (1999). *Department & discipline: Chicago sociology at one hundred.* Chicago: University of Chicago Press.

Addams, J. (1919). *Twenty years at Hull-House.* New York: Macmillan.

Anderson, E. (2003). Jelly's place: An ethnographic memoir. *Symbolic Interaction, 26,* 217–237.

Anderson, L., & Snow, D. A. (2001). Inequality and the self: Exploring connections from an interactionist perspective. *Symbolic Interaction, 24,* 396–406.

Atkinson, P., Coffey, A., & Delamont, S. (2003). *Key themes in qualitative research: Continuities and changes.* New York: Rowman and Littlefield.

Blumer, H. (1969). *Symbolic interactionism.* Englewood Cliffs, NJ: Prentice-Hall.

Blumer, H. (1979). Comments on "George Herbert Mead and the Chicago tradition of sociology." *Symbolic Interaction, 2*(2), 21–22.

Bryant, A. (2002). Regrounding grounded theory. *The Journal of Information Technology Theory and Application, 4,* 25–42.

Bryant, A. (2003). A constructive/ist response to Glaser. *Forum Qualitative Sozialforschung/Forum: Qualitative Social Research, 4.* Retrieved from www.qualitative-research.net/fqs-texte/1-03/1-bryant-e-htm

Bulmer, M. (1984). *The Chicago school of sociology: Institutionalization, diversity, and the rise of sociology.* Chicago: University of Chicago Press.

Burawoy, M (1991). Reconstructing social theories. In M. Burawoy, J. Gamson, J. Schiffman, A. Burton, A. A. Ferguson, L. Salzinger, L., et al. (Eds.), *Ethnography unbound : Power and resistance in the modern metropolis* (pp. 8–28). Berkeley: University of California Press.

Burawoy, M., Blum, J. A., George, S., Gill, Z., Gowan, T., Haney, L., et al. (2000). *Global ethnography: Forces, connections, and imaginations in a postmodern world.* Berkeley: University of California Press.

Burawoy, M., Gamson, J., Schiffman, J., Burton, A., Ferguson, A. A., Salzinger, L., et al. (1991). *Ethnography unbound : Power and resistance in the modern metropolis.* Berkeley: University of California Press.

Charmaz, K. (1983). The grounded theory method: An explication and interpretation. In R. M. Emerson (Ed.), *Contemporary field research* (pp. 109–126). Boston: Little, Brown.

Charmaz, K. (1990). Discovering chronic illness: Using grounded theory. *Social Science and Medicine, 30,* 1161–1172.

Charmaz, K. (1991). *Good days, bad days: The self in chronic illness and time.* New Brunswick, NJ: Rutgers University Press.

Charmaz, K. (1999). Stories of suffering: Subjects' stories and research narratives. *Qualitative Health Research, 9,* 362–382.

Charmaz, K. (2000a). Constructivist and objectivist grounded theory. In N. K. Denzin & Y. S. Lincoln (Eds.), *Handbook of qualitative research* (2nd ed., pp. 509–535). Thousand Oaks, CA: Sage.

Charmaz, K.(2000b). Looking backward, moving forward: Expanding sociological horizons in the twenty-first century. *Sociological Perspectives, 43,* 527–549.

Charmaz, K.(2002). Stories and silences: Disclosures and self in chronic illness. *Qualitative Inquiry, 8,* 302–328.

Charmaz, K. (2003a). Grounded theory. In M. Lewis-Beck, A. E. Bryman, & T. F. Liao (Eds.), *The Sage encyclopedia of social science research methods* (pp. 440–444). Thousand Oaks, CA: Sage.

Charmaz, K. (2003b). Grounded theory. In J. A. Smith (Ed.), *Qualitative psychology: A practical guide to research methods* (pp. 81–110). London: Sage.

Charmaz, K. (in press). Stories and silences: Disclosures and self in chronic illness. In D. Brashers & D. Goldstein (Eds.), *Health communication.* New York: Lawrence Erlbaum.

Charmaz, K., & Mitchell, R. G. (1996). The myth of silent authorship: Self, substance, and style in ethnographic writing. *Symbolic Interaction, 19*(4), 285–302.

Charmaz, K., & Mitchell, R. G. (2001). Grounded theory in ethnography. In P. Atkinson, A. Coffey, S. Delamont, J. Lofland, & L. H. Lofland (Eds.), *Handbook of ethnography* (pp. 160–174). London: Sage.

Christians, C. G. (2000). Ethics and politics in qualitative research. In N. K. Denzin & Y. S. Lincoln (Eds.), *Handbook of qualitative research* (2nd ed., pp. 133–155). Thousand Oaks, CA: Sage.

Clark, F. A. (2000). The concepts of habit and routine: A preliminary theoretical synthesis. *The Occupational Therapy Journal of Research, 20,* 123S–138S.

Clarke, A. E. (1998). *Disciplining reproduction: Modernity, American life sciences and the "problem of sex."* Berkeley: University of California Press.

Clarke, A. E. (2003). Situational analyses: Grounded theory mapping after the postmodern turn. *Symbolic Interaction, 26,* 553–576.

Clarke, A. E. (2004). *Situational analysis: Grounded theory after the postmodern turn.* Thousand Oaks, CA: Sage.

Clough, P. T. (1992). *The end(s) of ethnography: From realism to social criticism.* Newbury Park, CA: Sage.

Coffey, A., Holbrook, P., & Atkinson, P. (1996). Qualitative data analysis: Technologies and representations. *Sociological Research Online, 1*(1). Retrieved from www.socresonline.org.uk/1/1/4.html

Cooley, C. H. (1902). *Human nature and the social order.* New York: Scribner's.

Corbin, J. M., & Strauss, A. (1988). *Unending care and work.* San Francisco: Jossey-Bass.

Creswell, J. W. (1997). *Qualitative inquiry and research design.* Thousand Oaks, CA: Sage.

Cutchin, M. P. (2000). Retention of rural physicians: Place integration and the triumph of habit. *The Occupational Therapy Journal of Research, 20,* 106S–111S.

Deegan, M. J. (1995). The second sex and the Chicago school: Women's accounts, knowledge, and work, 1945–1960. In G. A. Fine (Ed.), *A second Chicago school?* (pp. 322–364). Chicago: University of Chicago Press.

Denzin, N. K. (1989). *Interpretive biography.* Newbury Park, CA: Sage.

Denzin, N. K. (1992). *Symbolic interactionism and cultural studies: The politics of interpretation.* Oxford, UK: Basil Blackwell.

Denzin, N. K. (1994). The art and politics of interpretation. In N. K. Denzin & Y. S. Lincoln (Eds.), *Handbook of qualitative research* (pp. 500–515). Thousand Oaks, CA: Sage.

Deutscher, I., Pestello, R., & Pestello, H. F. (1993). *Sentiments and acts.* New York: Aldine de Gruyter.

DeVault, M. L. (1999). *Liberating method: Feminism and social research.* Philadelphia: Temple University Press.

Dewey, J. (1922). *Human nature and conduct.* New York: Modern Library.

Dey, I. (1999). *Grounding grounded theory.* San Diego: Academic Press.

Duneire, M. (1992). *Slim's table: Race, respectability, and masculinity.* Chicago: University of Chicago Press.

Feagin, J. R. (1999). Social justice and sociology: Agendas for the twenty-first century. *American Sociological Review, 66,* 1–20.

Fine, G. A. (Ed.). (1995). *A second Chicago school? The development of a postwar American sociology.* Chicago: University of Chicago Press.

Fine, M., Weis, L., Weseen, S., & Wong, L. (2000). For whom? Qualitative research, representations, and social responsibilities. In N. K. Denzin & Y. S. Lincoln (Eds.), *Handbook of qualitative research* (2nd ed., pp. 107–131). Thousand Oaks, CA: Sage.

Flick, U. (1998). *An introduction to qualitative research.* Thousand Oaks, CA: Sage.

Frank, A. W. (1997). Enacting illness stories: When, what, and why. In H. L. Nelson (Ed.), *Stories and their limits: Narrative approaches to bioethics* (pp. 31–49). New York: Routledge.

Freire, P. (1970). *The pedagogy of the oppressed* (M. B. Ramos, Trans.). New York: Herder and Herder.

Glaser, B. G. (1978). *Theoretical sensitivity.* Mill Valley, CA: Sociology Press.

Glaser, B. G. (1992). *Basics of grounded theory analysis.* Mill Valley, CA: Sociology Press.

Glaser B. G. (1998). *Doing grounded theory: Issues and discussions.* Mill Valley, CA: Sociology Press.

Glaser, B. G. (2001). *Conceptualization contrasted with description.* Mill Valley, CA: Sociology Press.

Glaser, B. G. (2002). Constructivist grounded theory? *Forum Qualitative Sozialforschung/Forum: Qualitative Social Research, 3*(3). Retrieved from www.qualitative-research.net/fqs-texte/3-02/3-02glaser-e-htm

Glaser, B. G., & Strauss, A. L. (1965). *Awareness of dying.* Chicago: Aldine.

Glaser, B. G., & Strauss, A. L. (1967). *The discovery of grounded theory.* Chicago: Aldine.

Goffman, E. (1959). *The presentation of self in everyday life.* Garden City, NY: Doubleday.

Goffman, E. (1961). *Asylums.* Garden City, NY: Doubleday.

Harris, S. R. (2001). What can interactionism contribute to the study of inequality? The case of marriage and beyond. *Symbolic Interaction, 24,* 455–480.

Hartshorne, C., & Weiss, P. (Eds.). (1931–1935). *Collected papers of Charles Saunders Peirce* (Vols. 1–6). Cambridge, MA: Harvard University Press.

Hewitt, J. P. (1994). *Self and society: A symbolic interactionist social psychology* (6th ed.). Boston: Allyn & Bacon.

Hochschild, A. (1983). *The managed heart: Commercialization of human feeling.* Berkeley: University of California Press.

Holstein, J. A., & Gubrium, J. F. (1995). *The active interview.* Thousand Oaks, CA: Sage.

Horowitz, R. (1983). *Honor and the American dream: Culture and identity in a Chicano community.* New Brunswick, NJ: Rutgers University Press.

Horowitz, R. (2001). Inequalities, democracy, and fieldwork in the Chicago schools of yesterday and today. *Symbolic Interaction, 24,* 481–504.

Howard, J. A. (2003). Tensions of social justice. *Sociological Perspectives, 46,* 1–20.

Kemmis, S., & McTaggart, R. (2000). Participatory action research. In N. K. Denzin & Y. S. Lincoln (Eds.), *Handbook of qualitative research* (2nd ed., pp. 567–605). Thousand Oaks, CA: Sage.

Kleinman, S. (1996). *Opposing ambitions: Gender and identity in an alternative organization.* Chicago: University of Chicago Press.

Lal, B. B. (2001). Individual agency and collective determinism: Changing perspectives on race and ethnicities in cities, the Chicago school 1918–1958. In J. Mucha, D. Kaesler, & W. Winclawski (Eds.), *Mirrors and windows: Essays in the history of sociology* (pp. 183–196). Torun: International Sociological Association.

Lincoln, Y. S., & Guba, E. G. (1985). *Naturalistic inquiry.* Beverly Hills, CA: Sage.

Lincoln, Y. S., & Guba, E. G. (2000). Paradigmatic controversies, contradictions, and emerging confluences. In N. K. Denzin & Y. S. Lincoln (Eds.), *Handbook of Qualitative Research* (2nd ed., pp. 163–188). Thousand Oaks, CA: Sage.

Lively, K. (2001). Occupational claims to professionalism: The case of paralegals. *Symbolic Interaction, 24,* 343–365.

Locke, K. (1996). Rewriting *The Discovery of Grounded Theory* after 25 years? *Journal of Management Inquiry, 5,* 239–245.

Lofland, J., & Lofland, L. H. (1984). *Analyzing social settings* (2nd ed.). Belmont, CA: Wadsworth.

Lofland, J., & Lofland, L. H. (1995). *Analyzing social settings* (3rd ed.). Belmont, CA: Wadsworth.

Lofland, L. H. (1980). Reminiscences of classic Chicago. *Urban Life, 9,* 251–281.

Maines, D. R. (2001). *The faultline of consciousness: A view of interactionism in sociology.* New York: Aldine de Gruyter.

Maines, D. R.(2003). Interactionism's place. *Symbolic Interaction, 26,* 5–18.

Mamo, L. (1999). Death and dying: Confluences of emotion and awareness. *Sociology of Health and Illness, 21,* 13–26.

Mead, G. H. (1932). *Philosophy of the present.* LaSalle, IL: Open Court.

Mead, G. H. (1934). *Mind, self and society.* Chicago: University of Chicago Press.

Melia, K. M. (1996). Rediscovering Glaser. *Qualitative Health Research, 6,* 368–378.

Miller, D. E. (2000). Mathematical dimensions of qualitative research. *Symbolic Interaction, 23,* 399–402.

Miller, S. I., & Fredericks, M. (1999). How does grounded theory explain? *Qualitative Health Research, 9,* 538–551.

Mills, C. W. (1990). Situated actions and vocabularies of motive. In D. Brissett & C. Edgley (Eds.), *Life as theatre* (2nd ed., pp. 207–218). New York: Aldine de Gruyter.

Mitchell, R. G., Jr. (2002). *Dancing to Armageddon: Survivalism and chaos in modern times.* Chicago: University of Chicago Press.

Mitchell, R. G., & Charmaz, K. (1996). Telling tales, writing stories. *Journal of Contemporary Ethnography, 25,* 144–166.

Morse, J. M. (1995). The significance of saturation. *Qualitative Health Research, 5,* 147–149.

Morse, J. M. (1998). Validity by committee. *Qualitative Health Research, 8,* 443–445.

Morse, J. M. (1999). The armchair walkthrough. *Qualitative Health Research, 9,* 435–436.

Musolf, G. R. (2003). The Chicago school. In L. T. Reynolds & N. J. Herman-Kinney (Eds.), *Handbook of symbolic interactionism* (pp. 91–117). Walnut Creek, CA: AltaMira.

Nussbaum, M. C. (1999). *Sex and social justice.* New York: Oxford University Press.

Nussbaum, M. C. (2000). Women's capabilities and social justice. *Journal of Human Development, 1,* 219–247.

Olesen, V. L. (2000). Feminisms and qualitative research at and into the millennium. In N. K. Denzin & Y. S. Lincoln (Eds.), *Handbook of qualitative research* (2nd ed., pp. 215–255). Thousand Oaks, CA: Sage.

Park, R. E., & Burgess, E. W. (1925). *The city.* Chicago: University of Chicago Press.

Prus, R. (1996). *Symbolic interaction and ethnographic research: Intersubjectivity and the study of human lived experience.* Albany: State University of New York Press.

Rawls, J. (1971). *A theory of justice.* Cambridge, MA: Belknap Press of Harvard University Press.

Reynolds, L. T. (2003a). Early representatives. In L. T. Reynolds & N. J. Herman-Kinney (Eds.), *Handbook of symbolic interactionism* (pp. 59–81). Walnut Creek, CA: AltaMira.

Reynolds, L. T. (2003b). Intellectual precursors. In L. T. Reynolds & N. J. Herman-Kinney (Eds.), *Handbook of symbolic interactionism* (pp. 39–58). Walnut Creek, CA: AltaMira.

Richardson, L. (2000). Writing: A method of inquiry. In N. K. Denzin & Y. S. Lincoln (Eds.), *Handbook of qualitative research* (2nd ed., pp. 923–948). Thousand Oaks, CA: Sage.

Scheff, T. J. (2003). Shame in self and society. *Symbolic Interaction, 26,* 239–262.

Schwalbe, M. S., Goodwin, S., Holden, D., Schrock, D., Thompson, S., & Wolkomir, M. (2000). Generic processes in the reproduction of inequality: An interactionist analysis. *Social Forces, 79,* 419–452.

Schwandt, T. A. (1994). Constructivist, interpretivist approaches to human inquiry. In N. K. Denzin & Y. S. Lincoln (Eds.), *Handbook of qualitative research* (pp. 118–137). Thousand Oaks, CA: Sage.

Schwandt, T. A. (2000). Three epistemological stances for qualitative inquiry: Interpretivism, hermeneutics, and social constructionism. In N. K. Denzin & Y. S. Lincoln (Eds.), *Handbook of qualitative research* (2nd ed., pp. 189–213). Thousand Oaks, CA: Sage.

Scott, M., & Lyman, S. M. (1968). Accounts. *American Sociological Review, 33,* 46–62.

Seale, C. (1999). *The quality of qualitative research.* London: Sage.

Sennett, R., & Cobb, J. (1973). *The hidden injuries of class.* New York: Vintage.

Shaw, C. (1930). *The jack-roller.* Chicago: University of Chicago Press.

Silverman, D. (2000). *Doing qualitative research: A practical handbook.* London: Sage.

Snow, D. (2001). Extending and broadening Blumer's conceptualization of symbolic interactionism. *Symbolic Interaction, 24,* 367–377.

Snow, D., & Anderson, L. (1993). *Down on their luck: A study of homeless street people.* Berkeley: University of California Press.

Star, S. L. (1989). *Regions of the mind: Brain research and the quest for scientific certainty.* Stanford, CA: Stanford University Press.

Stern, P. N. (1994). Eroding grounded theory. In J. Morse (Ed.), *Critical issues in qualitative research methods* (pp. 212–223). Thousand Oaks, CA: Sage.

Strauss, A. L. (Ed.). (1964). *George Herbert Mead on social psychology.* Chicago: University of Chicago Press.

Strauss, A. L. (1987). *Qualitative analysis for social scientists.* New York: Cambridge University Press.

Strauss, A. L. (1993). *Continual permutations of action.* New York: Aldine de Gruyter.

Strauss, A., & Corbin, J. (1990). *Basics of qualitative research: Grounded theory procedures and techniques.* Newbury Park, CA: Sage.

Strauss, A., & Corbin, J. (1998). *Basics of qualitative research: Grounded theory procedures and techniques* (2nd ed.). Thousand Oaks, CA: Sage.

Strauss, A., & Fisher, B. (1979a). George Herbert Mead and the Chicago tradition of sociology, Part 1. *Symbolic Interaction, 2*(1), 9–26.

Strauss, A., & Fisher, B. (1979b). George Herbert Mead and the Chicago tradition of sociology, Part 2. *Symbolic Interaction, 2*(2), 9–19.

Suttles, G. (1968). *Social order of the slum.* Chicago: University of Chicago Press.

Tedlock, B. (2000). Ethnography and ethnographic representation. In N. K. Denzin & Y. S. Lincoln (Eds.), *Handbook of qualitative research* (2nd ed., pp. 455–486). Thousand Oaks, CA: Sage.

Thomas, W. I., & Znaniecki, F. (1927). *The Polish peasant in America.* New York: Knopf.

Thrasher, F. (1927). *The gang.* Chicago: University of Chicago Press.

Timmermans, S. (1994). Dying of awareness: The theory of awareness contexts revisited. *Sociology of Health and Illness, 17,* 322–339.

van den Hoonaard, W. C. (1997). *Working with sensitizing concepts: Analytical field research.* Thousand Oaks, CA: Sage.

Van Maanen, J. (1988). *Tales of the field.* Chicago: University of Chicago Press.

Venkatesh, S. (2000). *American project: The rise and fall of a modern ghetto.* Cambridge, MA: Harvard University Press.

Wacquant, L. (2002). Scrutinizing the street: Poverty, morality, and the pitfalls of urban ethnography. *American Journal of Sociology, 107,* 1468–1534.

21

CRITICAL ETHNOGRAPHY AS STREET PERFORMANCE

Reflections of Home, Race, Murder, and Justice

D. Soyini Madison

What does it mean to be at home? How does leaving home affect home and being-at-home?

> Home is here, not a particular place that one simply inhabits, but more than one place: there are too many homes to allow place to secure the roots or routes of one's destination. It is not simply that the subject does not belong anywhere. The journey between homes provides the subject with the contours of a space of belonging, but a space that expresses the very logic of an interval, the passing through of the subject between apparently fixed moments of departure and arrival. (Ahmed 2000, p. 76)

The Airport: Departing Home/Arriving Home

When my plane was about to land at Kotoka International Airport in Ghana, West Africa, in March of 2000, I had been away from Africa for nearly a month. I had gone home to the United States to see my son and my daughter after more than 2 years of fieldwork in Ghana. I was leaving home to come home. For the last 2 years, airports on both sides of the Atlantic marked physical and symbolic junctures of the departure and arrival of home (Ahmed, 2000). Airports had become rhizomes of perennial beginnings and endings, of a marked liminality that delineated what it meant to depart one life and arrive in another. Airports became the synecdoche for a black Diaspora citizenship and for a politics of mobility.

During 14 hours of travel, I departed home in order to arrive home, and, in the sentiment of Alice Walker, to do the work my soul must do (Walker, 1974), in Ghana, by doing the work of performance and by making a performance that, hopefully, mattered. As I gathered my belongings to leave the plane, I realized it was my last year in Africa. I was in the final stage of my fieldwork—the culminating stage. This was the year I would stage the performance, thereby making my fieldwork public and its purpose known.

It was upon entering the airport and waiting for my friend and fellow Fulbright sister, Lisa Aubrey, to pick me up that I began to feel the full weight of this final arrival. This was it. There was no turning back. It was time to transform 2 years of fieldwork data on poverty and indigenous human rights activism into a public performance, a public performance for the purpose of advocacy and change. The performance would depict a debate raging within a community of Ghanaians, one side representing the human rights of women and girls, and the other side representing the preservation of traditional religious practices. The former believed that traditional religion must be changed for the freedom and development of their people, while the latter believed that traditional religion must be preserved for the sustenance and protection of their people. The performance would represent these opposing claims, but it would do more—it would implicate the corporate, capitalist economy and the consequences of poverty on human rights abuses in the global South.

I. Performance of Possibility

As I walked through the airport, thoughts of the performance and its purpose took hold. This performance was going to be about the work of Ghanaian human rights activists and the work they were doing in their own country, and it had to be powerful and true and absolutely urgent because bodies were on the line. These people were changing the lives of women and girls by re-imagining the discourse of rights, by mobilizing their communities, and by changing the law. Moreover, Ghanaians did this for themselves under the forces of wretched poverty and global inequity. The performance had to unveil the labor of these activists working in their local communities, AND it had to unveil the devastation of global forces that impeded and burdened their victories. This performance aimed to expose the hidden, clarify the oblique, and articulate the possible. It would be a performance of possibility (Madison, 1998) that aimed to create and contribute to a discursive space where unjust systems and processes are identified and interrogated. Social critic Anna Marie Smith (1998) states:

> Dissemination of democratic discourse to new and needed areas of the social is the first step toward change.... One becomes radicalized when one finds a compelling discourse to speak. (p. 8)

I hoped the performance would provide such a discourse through the descriptions and narratives of those Ghanaian rights activists who told me their stories. Staging their struggles for human rights and the mandate for economic justice through the illuminating frame of performance promised this dissemination of democratic discourse. I hoped the performance would offer its audience another way to speak of rights and the origins of poverty that would then un-nestle another possibility of informed and strategic action. In other words, the significance of the performance for the subjects of my fieldwork is for those who bear witness to their stories to interrogate actively and purposefully those processes that limit their health and freedom. I do not mean to imply that one performance can bring down a revolution, but one performance can be revolutionary in enlightening citizens to the possibilities that grate against injustice. One performance may or may not change someone's world, but, as James Scott reminds us, acts of resistance amass, rather like snowflakes on a steep mountainside, and can set off an avalanche. Everyday forms of resistance give way to collective defiance (Scott, 1990, p. 192). In the performance of possibilities, the expectation is for the performers and spectators to appropriate the rhetorical currency they need, from the inner space of the performance to the outer domain of the social world, to make a material difference (Madison, 1998).

Performance scholar Diana Taylor reminds us that when confronted with certain "truths," theater has the power to illuminate not only what we see and how we see it, but how we can reject the reality of what we see and know to be true (Taylor, 1997). I believe more and more that a performance of possibility is always a harbinger of and a confrontation with the truth.

II. The Unexpected in the Present Tense: The Murder of Amadou Diallo

I see Lisa at the baggage claim. How on Earth did she actually get inside the airport! Those hard-core guards don't let anyone come inside the airport unless they're traveling. This woman is a wonder, with her combination of striking beauty, unabashed willfulness, irreverence for rules, and extraordinary intellect. She always averts the expected, the predictable, the required. I won't even ask her how she might have charmed the guards to get through this blockade of an airport, while throngs of others are waiting outside to greet friends and relations.

"Lisa!" I shout, so happy to see my friend.

"Soyiiiineeee!" she calls out with excitement in her Louisiana accent. "How was the flight?"

"The flight was fine. I have just been so worried about getting this performance ready. This is all on top of the fatigue of not sleeping for 2 days trying to get back here."

"Oh Soyini, girrrrl, the performance will be wonderful and you will be fine. Besides, you don't have time to be tired."

"Why?" I asked curiously. "What's happening?"

"We must organize a protest march on the American embassy for Amadou!"

"Lisa, it is all so awful and so redundant."

Lisa's voice tightens. "Does a blackman's life, a poor blackman's life, mean anything in the U.S.?"

The march was Lisa's idea, and I knew that she would be stalwart in mobilizing people of conscience to stand up and speak out against the murder of Amadou Diallo and the miscarriage of justice that followed. Still, I was so exhausted I could hardly speak.

"Lisa, are we meeting tonight?"

"Yes, we're all meeting at Flavors Pub in Osu tonight. This will be our second meeting. I need you there to help organize. We don't have much time. We need to mount the protest for next week!"

I'm stunned. "Next week?"

"Yes, next week. We need to get the letters and petitions to Washington within 2 weeks for a retrial. Are you too tired, Soyini? Can you make it, because we may be up all night."

I take a deep, uneasy breath, not so much from fatigue but from the contradiction. I am in the home of my heart, Africa, reflecting back on a 400-year-old rage for the home of my birth, the United States. The ideology of liberal democracy in the United States is, for some, a model for the world, yet its democratic principles partner with racial injustice with flagrant consistency. Racism in America is no moribund phenomenon; whatever or however its forms of disguise, it is alive and still hurting people. I will protest here, in my African home, for what was done there, in my American home, to a blackman born on this continent. I say to Lisa, "Let's go."

◘ ◘ ◘

> [African] Americans organizing protest activities in Ghana against the United States government posed interesting political and social contractual questions regarding citizen's rights, state responsibility, and democracy in an international context. For instance, in what ways can citizens lawfully exercise their constitutional rights to hold institutions of government accountable for their actions when those citizens reside outside of the country of their birth and citizenship? Additionally, how do we ensure that protests comply to laws of both the land of citizenship and the land of residence? Furthermore, how can we operate within the confines of both sets of laws and still maintain the passion, outrage and fervor of our demands? (Aubrey, 2001, p. 1)

Africanist and political science professor Lisa Aubrey wrote these words for *In Salute of Hero Amadou Diallo: African Americans Organize Amadou Diallo Protest Activities in Accra, Ghana in 2000: Lesson for Democracy in the United States and in Ghana.*

The Street Performance: Blackness and Outside Belonging

There are more people here at the march than we expected. We've worked very hard, and we've pulled it off. The teach-ins, the awareness sessions, the petitions, the letter writing campaign, and the international solidarity day for Mumia Abu Jamal each were essential and dynamic projects in our organizing efforts for this march, the Amadou Diallo march. Each of these activities was a success, now culminating in this day. I look at all these people gathered here: They are a blend of races and ethnicities, expatriates from Europe, Asia, Africa, and the Americas living in Ghana from all over the world and coming to voice their indignation over the death of a young, innocent black man in New York City who was murdered by four plainclothes police officers as he was entering his residence in the Bronx. The police officers fired 41 bullets at Amadou Diallo; 19 of those bullets entered his body after he had fallen to the ground. The police were looking for a criminal, a young black man they thought was Amadou. They asked him if they could have a word with him. Amadou reached for his wallet to show his identification; then, the bullets came, and they kept coming. He did not have a weapon. The officers were brought to trial. A jury of eight white men and four black women acquitted the four white police officers. I wonder, if all the officers had been black, would Amadou's life have been spared? It is a troubling thought, but I don't think it would have made a difference. Blackness is a universal signifier of fear, danger, and threat across color lines; the meanings play out in the destruction of too many black men in American cities by those powerful and powerless with guns.

Here we all stand, together, on this day, March 8, 2000, remembering Amadou and demanding justice. And here I stand, African American, between two homes—one majority white, the other majority black. I stand here thinking about this thing called race that wrestles between Africa and America and that is complicated by the category "African American."

Performance scholar Joni Jones writes:

> Just what is an African American in Africa? My inability to answer this question uprooted a heretofore, fundamental aspect of my identity, a part of the self I took for granted in the United States as a part of my cultural identity. In my mind, my dreadlocks, West African inspired clothing, and blackness of tongue meant something powerful in the United States, while for the Yoruba, these artifacts of identity elicited puzzlement, amusement, and sometimes disdain. I did not feel that my self, the self I had constructed on the U.S. soil, was visible. Indeed, I felt out of my self. (1996, p. 133)

I Remember: A Digression

I remember, during my first days in Ghana, I went to visit Lisa. I was looking for her flat; I couldn't figure out which apartment was hers. A Ghanaian living on the first floor of her building saw that I was lost. He knew that I was looking for Lisa, so referring to her, he asked, "Are you looking for the white girl upstairs?"

I was taken aback by his description. Lisa is honey brown, with natural hair and West African–inspired clothing and blackness of tongue. How could he mistake Lisa for a white woman!

"No," I said, unsettled and insulted. "I am not looking for a white girl, I am looking for Lisa Aubrey and we are both African Americans."

The man pointed to her apartment and then just shook his head and chuckled under his breath, "Abruni."

I trembled. He had just called me a foreigner, a white person.

Black people are dying and catching hell in the United States, and that man called me Abruni! I belong to blackness as much as this man! I am reminded of cultural critic Elspeth Probyn: "If you have to think about belonging, perhaps you are already outside. Instead of presuming a common locus, I want to consider the ways in which the very longing to belong embarrasses its taken-for-granted nature" (1996, pp. 8–9).

For many black Americans, at profound moments, belonging requires a fixed political ground. Understanding that ultimately we belong in different categories and to different communities and that our belonging may be annunciated at different stages of political and social progressions (or regressions), beyond all this, "African American" as signifier and as signified is nonetheless a relatively stable reality of belonging to blackness in the

United States, however complicated that belonging may be. I experience belonging within the racialization of blackness in the United States not as a longing from an outside identity to enter into an inside identity. I am always already inside. Even when I'm not thinking about it, am I ever not a black person? Granted, I experience black belonging on American soil as a space of flux and ambiguity constituting multiple identities; however, this belonging remains a discursive and material association with specific bodies based on historical, social, and political arrangements that are regulated through law, culture, and the everyday. As this belonging is discursively instituted and materially experienced, my black body is further evidence that I am not white and that I belong to the category of blackness.

Black people can or cannot and will or will not choose to be slippery and equivocal about their racial identity and belonging. But for many black people in the United States, embracing this belonging, however it is articulated or whatever the level of its consistency, becomes a matter of saving one's life and one's sanity. This kind of belonging falls beyond intellectual or philosophical pondering; it is psychological and physical protection.

I never questioned the fact of my blackness. It is as much a part of me as my skin, my nose, my mouth, my hair, and my speech, all the while with an understanding that it is beyond appearances. When Anna Julia Cooper said, "When and where I enter, my race enters with me," she was acknowledging the ubiquity of race as it is internally felt and externally constructed (Giddings, 1996). The ever-present fact of race looms within the multilayered realms of blackness in the United States and within a web of projections both colored and white, both hostile and admiring, where race/ blackness often precedes being. In Ghana, West Africa, the words "white girl upstairs" disrupted my reality of belonging (that I've always known) to its very core. I was reminded that geography might be one of the greatest determiners of them all. Perhaps geography is destiny after all.

My personhood, for Lisa's neighbor, was outside blackness. I was outside belonging (Probyn, 1996). I represented something else to him. At that moment, it was representation that eclipsed any notion of belonging. I was not a black woman, but the representation of a white one, the representation of a white, advanced country. The neighbor certainly understood that I was not white like Julia Roberts is white. I was not white by phenotype, but by country. Although he may have understood that I was of African descent, it did not matter. Nation and global order took primacy over racial identification. In that instant, I represented an individual of American descent, not African descent. I live in an advanced country; he lives in the developing world. This fact of economy eclipsed blackness within the U.S. context or any unity around Diaspora blackness that I might fantasize.

Belonging may be the effect of identity, but representation became a framework for meaning in the white girl upstairs (Hall, 1997). And if representation embodies meaning, my meaning was now constructed as not black, as not belonging. And if one of the things that culture is based on is the production and exchange of meanings, and if one of the ways we give things meaning is by how we produce them and how we represent them or how they appear to us, in that moment the white girl upstairs became the classic encounter between cultural insider and cultural outsider. At that moment, insider/outsider was deeply inscribed and poignantly reversed. I was the outsider, and belonging was reversed. That race is socially made became an understatement at the sound of "white girl." We are reminded repeatedly (and for good reason) that race is constructed, reconstructed, and deconstructed depending on locale, history, and power, but immediate experience sometimes penetrates deeper. Would he have called Lisa white if she had been a man and if I had been a man? Would he have said, "the white boy upstairs"? If I had been a white American woman, would he have referred to race at all? Would he have said, "you mean the lady upstairs?"

I personalize my experiences in the field to engage ironically with a vulnerability toward universal questions and human unease. Race as personally experienced in the ethnographic then, when I became subject and object of the Other's gaze, brings me to the ethnographic now, writing. I theorize from the starting point of the personal and from my own racial dislocation between, within, and outside belonging in Africa. Race, in the moment—"white girl upstairs"—meant that this (re)construction of who I am is tied to where I live and where I travel, as well as politicized perspectives on wealth, opportunity, and technology, specifically as they are perceived by those in the global South, the developing world. That blackness is contingent—relative to African Americans, NOT on being of African descent but on being American citizens—is for many Africans taken for granted, while for many black Americans it is disheartening. Blackness is tied to slavery, terror, and discrimination, as it is also tied to a culture and past that are generative, free, and prosperous. However, in that ethnographic then, all these layers were displaced in recognition of my American citizenship that is complicated because I am of African descent.

III. Street Performance and Diaspora Identity

We are marching down the streets of Accra. This is less a protest march and more a street performance, or is it more a protest march because it is a street performance?

We had all planned to meet at the Labonne Coffee Shop in town and then march in silence to the American embassy; upon reaching the embassy, we would begin our program of speeches and testimonies. But the silence has surrendered to the sheer energy of our collective will. We are all caught in the drama and the urgency of our indignation, which cannot be stilled by silence, not here on this continent of drums, poetry, and dance, always dance, because this coming together has evolved into a precious praise song mightily strung together by the antiquity of dark-skinned motion. The march is a performance of movement made into a variance of sounds, symbolic rhythms, and lyrical incantations of mourning and politics. The onlookers in our path join our chorus of steps. They sing and chant with us. They see the black and white T-shirts we are wearing, the word "Diallo" written in black letters across the front and the numbers "19 of 41" written across our backs. We pick up more and more people on our way. This march is becoming a carnival of contestation of the highest order, of purposeful action (Conquergood, 2002). We are all together, absorbed spontaneously in the communitas and flow of this assemblage of movement and this alchemy of collective will. There is no white girl upstairs here; there is only, in this heightened moment, communal energy. On this path of street performance and protest, for this brief moment in time, all of us belong to each other for performance and because of it, and some of us, for justice and because of it. More and more come to join the march. We are stepping and singing; we are meeting new friends; we are learning about the particularity of a lost life; we are enacting our urgency for justice. Reggae singer Shasha Marley raises his voice and calls. We respond. He calls again, and we respond again in the reverie of Ghanaian high life.

Anthropologist Victor Turner (1982) writes:

> Is there any of us who has not known this moment when the mood, style, or fit of spontaneous communitas is upon us, we place a high value on personal honesty, openness, and lack of pretensions or pretentiousness. We feel that it is important to relate directly to another person as he presents himself in the here and now, free from the culturally defined encumbrances of his role, status, reputation, class, caste, sex, or other structural niche. Individuals who interact with one another in the mode of spontaneous communitas become totally absorbed into a single synchronized, fluid event. It has something magical about it. (pp. 47–48)

The magic of our inspired oneness summoned by the dramatic sounds and motions of street performance displaced "white girl upstairs," at least today and with a possibility for tomorrow, into a Diaspora consciousness, a black Atlantic identity, that would demand that African peoples on the continent and in the United States understand Amadou's death as an allegory for political action on both sides of the ocean. Describing that day, I turn again to Lisa's article and her words:

> African American individuals in Ghana who took the initiative of organizing protest activities were supported by many Pan-African and other humanitarian communities that believe in justice, fairness, equality, and democracy. Individuals, community organizations, non-governmental organizations (NGOs), businesses, especially private radio stations, offered untiring support for the Diallo protest activities. Among the supporters were the African American Association of Ghana, One-Africa, the Brotherhood, members of the Ghana legal profession and the Ghana Bar Association, other concerned Ghanaians, Liberian refugees in Ghana, the W.E.B. Dubois Center, the Embassy of Guinea, the Commission on Human Rights and Administrative Justice (CHRAJ, a quasi governmental organization of Ghana), the Student and Workers Solidarity Committee, Musicians of Ghana (MUSIGA) and Ghanaian and American students from the University of Ghana, Legon. (Aubrey, 2001, pp. 1–2)

Now, the march has grown to even greater numbers. Amadou Diallo's memory is reaching out like a hand gesturing for another to hold and to remember. Manifest through performance, the gesture is exquisite, evolving into a celebratory embrace.

We finally reach the American embassy. We form a large circle in front of the building. As the circle forms, we begin lighting our candles. Lisa begins the ceremony by recounting the night of Amadou's death. She concludes her presentation by speaking eloquently on the nature of democracy and descent. Her words are a call to action for free speech, for collective action, and for the U.S. Department of Justice to intervene and bring federal civil rights charges against the acquitted police officers.

After Lisa ends her presentation, I begin to speak. I am speaking of the power of mourning: mourning the hope of Amadou Diallo, who was so like so many immigrants, who strive most of their lives to come to the land of opportunity, wealth, and happiness, and discover that when they finally arrive, they must confront the ominous inequality and violence of race in America. I close by recovering what it means to mourn, not only as loss but also as evocation. Our mourning evokes social activism. I am reminded of rights activists who have fought across national borders and their urgent cry: "Don't mourn, organize!"

The ceremony is drawing to an end. The written statement we crafted, demanding a retrial and that civil charges be brought against the four police officers, is given to the director of the embassy. She receives the statement with the promise that the embassy would look into the matter and take action, as its officers also believe in justice.

■ November 15, 2002, North Carolina, U.S.A.

And the Hate Goes On
La, La, La, La, La

A retrial was not ordered. The acquittal of the four police officers was granted without further interference by the justice system. When I first began preparing this chapter, 2 years after our protest march, I went to the Internet to search for new developments relating to the Diallo case. I discovered that there was an Amadou Diallo Web site. I opened the site and, to my surprise, although the murder of Diallo was on February 4, 1999, nearly 3 years prior, their was a posting for that very day, November 15, 2002. What follows are samples of the most recent exchange over a 3-day period from when I first discovered the site. These verbatim exchanges (including spelling and grammar) represent the sentiment of most of the entries sent to the Amadou Diallo home page. I have chosen to include only three that were the least offensive.

Name: Nigger God Killer

Date: Tuesday, November 12, 2002, at 20:44:06

Comments: Phuck you Nigger God you stupid fucking worthless faggot ass nigger! Someone should kill your worthless cocksucking faggot nigger ass! Kill all niggers! White Power!

Name: Aryan

Date: Thursday, November 12, 2002, at 20:47:22

> Comments: Amadou Diallo is a worthless nigger; the cops should have blown this nigger brains out. The only good nigger is a dead nigger. Heil Hitler! Deutschesland Uber Alles! Ein Reich, Ein volk, Ein Fuhrer! Seig heil!
>
> Name: All niggers and niggerlovers must die!
>
> Date: Friday, November 15, 2002, at 01:44:51
>
> Comments: I totally agree with you Aryan. The cops should have not only blown Amadou Diallo's brains out, but have also blown out his whole family's brains. allus true white people (excluding kikes, wiggers, and faggots, because they're niggerloving white race traitors) should blow every nigger on this earth's brains out. if niggerkilling and niggerloverkilling was legalized I'd be killing tons and tons of niggers and niggerloving white race traitor kikes, wiggers, and faggots everyday.

And the hate goes on, even after death. We are in an era when many still relegate such racism to bygone days. The messages from the Internet notwithstanding, and given that the murder of Amadou Diallo met no justice, what good did our street protest do? People still hate, and more people of color have died since 1999 at the hands of murderous authority. What is the value of such performances when what we aim for is not achieved? What effect did our performance march have in the light of these despicable and violent words?

IV. Conclusion

Just like a bell cannot be unrung, our street performance cannot be undone. It is remembered, and it has produced friends, allies, and comrades, as it has also inspired imagination. The promise of a performance of possibility is that it not only creates alliances while it names and marks injustice, but it also enacts a force beyond ideology; it enacts and imagines the vast possibilities of collective hopes and dreams coming into fruition, of actually being lived. In the words of performance scholar Janelle Reinelt, "performance can overrun ideology's containment" (1996, p. 3). Why, then, did our street performance matter?

The performance made public international injustice committed on an American city street. It brought that injustice beyond its particular location by extending the arena of public viewing and awareness across national boundaries to invoke and materialize a transborder participatory call for justice, generating a street performance that embodied a dialogue with authority (Gunner, 1994). Therefore, in this more expanded performative participation, a re-visioning of ingrained social arrangements relating to authority and violence, class and power, as well as freedom of speech and social change, were called into question by the voices and action of those situated within the context of globalization from below (Brecher, Costello, & Smith, 2002; Cohen-Cruz, 1998).

The march evolved into a street performance that made spirited actors out of passive observers. Engaged action motivated by performative intervention, a performance of possibility was required for the call and the response, for the testimonies, the dialogue, and the demand upon the American embassy. Moreover, it is the emotionally charged animation drawn from the body in motion, within the heightened moments of performative intervention, that unleashes a palpable defiance that dissolves apathy (Conquergood, 2002; Denzin, 2003; Madison, 1999). The performance evoked spontaneous communitas that offers the alchemy of human connection, conjoinment, and intersubjectivity to the power and ubiquity of memory. We remember how this communion felt for us and for each other, together. It was made even more powerfully human because it was publicly performed. I echo the sentiment of social activist Ernesto J. Cortes, Jr., that there is a dimension of our humanity that emerges only when we engage in public discourse.

The street performance, empowered by communitas and the humanizing dynamics of public discourse, provided us with the gift of remembering (Pollock, 1999). The street performance became a method and a means for the dissemination of discourse relative to rights, justice, and change, and, moreover, for transborder participatory democracy (Brecher et al., 2002). The march was a local and a dramatic point of interrogation of U.S. foreign policy relative to democracy assistance programs that demand that other nations in the world to make their state institutions accountable and fair (Aubrey, 2001, p. 2). Lisa Aubrey states: "By organizing the protest activities, African Americans were forcing the U.S. to look into the mirror for the very transparency and probity it aims to cultivate and extract from other governments" (p. 2). The street performance honored the local in speaking truth to power (Marable, 1996) and became a communicative instrument in the public interrogation of injustice that resulted in the enactment of collective memory and mourning.

Finally, the street performance opens the possibility for another strategy for globalization from below. Globalization from above is making poor people poorer and rich people richer. Brecher, Costello, and Smith, in their powerfully concise book *Globalization From Below*, state:

> The ultimate source of power is not the command of those at the top, but the acquiescence of those at the bottom. . . . In response to globalization from above, movements are emerging all over the world in social locations that are marginal to the dominant power centers. These are linking up by means of networks that cut across national borders. They are beginning to develop a sense of solidarity, a common belief system, and a common program. They are utilizing these networks to impose new norms on corporations, governments, and international institutions. (pp. 23, 26)

The street performance is another illustration of the communicative function and political effectiveness of performance in mobilizing communities for change. It serves as an added example of the potential of street performance as a platform for subaltern voices and cross-border access and networks.

Several years have passed since our march on the American embassy in Ghana, and I still relive in my memory the words and chants from several of our Ghanaian friends who were responsible for turning a protest march into a street performance: Shasha chanted "We are One Love"; Akosua kept repeating "We prove today that we are sisters"; Helen asserted "We are all African people"; and, as the march came to an end, Kweku said, "An ocean cannot divide our blood."

I remember the resounding force of the drummers and how our steps marked the rhythms of the drums along the road to the embassy under the hot sun, the blazing heat, and the many accented voices filled with song, chant, banter, and laughter. In Shasha's words and in the words of many other Ghanaians who performed that day, we were living in the communitas of one love.

But after the march, and beyond the path of the marchers, Lisa and I still remain the white girls upstairs. However, on that particular day, the magic of performance evoked a politics that was lived in the flesh and on the ground and that demanded social justice, a politics that is now remembered and recounted for the possibilities of another way of being.

References

Ahmed, S. (2000). *Strange encounters: Embodied others in post-coloniality.* New York: Routledge.

Aubrey, L. (2001). *In salute of hero Amadou Diallo: African Americans organize Amadou Diallo protest activities in Accra, Ghana in 2000: Lesson for democracy in the United States and in Ghana.* Retrieved from www.ohio.edu/tonguna/winter/2001/lisa-aubrey.htm

Brecher, B., Costello, T., & Smith, B. (2002). *Globalization from below.* Cambridge, UK: South End.

Cohen-Cruz, J. (Ed.). (1998). *Radical street performance: An international anthology.* New York: Routledge.

Conquergood, D. (2002). Performance studies: Interventions and radical research. *The Drama Review, 46*(2), 145–156.

Denzin, N. (2003). *Performance ethnography: Critical pedagogy and the politics of culture.* Thousand Oaks, CA: Sage.

Giddings, P. (1996). *When and where I enter: The impact of black women on race and sex in America.* New York: William Morrow.

Gunner, L. (Ed.). (1994). *Politics and performance: Theatre, poetry, and song in southern Africa.* Johannesburg : Witwatersrand University Press.

Hall, S. (1997). *Representation: Cultural representations and signifying practices.* London: Sage.

Jones, J. L. (1996). The self as other: Creating the role of Joni the Ethnographer for Broken Circles. *Text and Performance Quarterly, 16,* 131–145.

Madison, S. (1998). Performance, personal narratives, and the politics of possibility: The future of performance studies. In S. J. Daily (Ed.), *Visions and revisions* (pp. 276–286). Washington, DC: National Communication Association.

Madison, D. S. (1999). Performing theory/embodied writing. *Text and Performance Quarterly, 19,* 107–124.

Marable, M. (1996). *Speaking truth to power.* Boulder, CO: Westview.

Pollock, D. (1999). *Telling bodies, performing birth.* New York: Columbia University Press.

Probyn, E. (1996). *Outside belonging.* New York: Routledge.

Reinelt, J. (1996). *Crucibles of crisis: Performing social change.* Ann Arbor: University of Michigan Press.

Scott, J. (1990). *Domination and the arts of resistance.* New Haven, CT: Yale University Press.

Smith, A. (1998). *Laclau and Mouffe: The radical democratic imaginary.* New York: Routledge.

Taylor, D. (1997). *Disappearing acts: Spectacles of gender and nationalism in Argentina's "Dirty War."* Durham, NC: Duke University Press.

Turner, V. (1982). *From ritual to theatre: The human seriousness of play.* New York: Performing Art Journal Publications.

Walker, A. (1974). *In search of our mothers' gardens.* New York: Harcourt, Brace & Company.

22

TESTIMONIO, SUBALTERNITY, AND NARRATIVE AUTHORITY

John Beverley

In a justly famous essay, Richard Rorty (1985) distinguishes between what he calls the "desire for solidarity" and the "desire for objectivity" as cognitive modes:

> There are two principal ways in which reflective human beings try, by placing their lives in a larger context, to give sense to those lives. The first is by telling the story of their contribution to a community. This community may be the actual historical one in which they live, or another actual one, distant in time or place, or a quite imaginary one, consisting perhaps of a dozen heroes and heroines selected from history or fiction or both. The second way is to describe themselves as standing in an immediate relation to a nonhuman reality. This relation is immediate in the sense that it does not derive from a relation between such a reality and their tribe, or their nation, or their imagined band of comrades. I shall say that stories of the former kind exemplify the desire for solidarity, and that stories of the latter kind exemplify the desire for objectivity. (p. 3)[1]

The question of *testimonio*—testimonial narrative—has come prominently onto the agenda of the human and social sciences in recent years in part because *testimonio* intertwines the "desire for objectivity" and "the desire for solidarity" in its very situation of production, circulation, and reception.

Testimonio is by nature a demotic and heterogeneous form, so any formal definition of it is bound to be too limiting.[2] But the following might serve provisionally: A *testimonio* is a novel or novella-length narrative, produced in the form of a printed text, told in the first person by a narrator who is also the real protagonist or witness of the events she or he recounts. Its unit of narration is usually a "life" or a significant life experience. Because in many cases the direct narrator is someone who is either functionally illiterate or, if literate, not a professional writer, the production of a *testimonio* generally involves the tape recording and then the transcription and editing of an oral account by an interlocutor who is a journalist, ethnographer, or literary author.

Although one of the antecedents of *testimonio* is undoubtedly the ethnographic life history of the *Children of Sánchez* sort, *testimonio* is not exactly commensurable with the category of life history (or oral history). In the life history, it is the intention of the interlocutor-recorder (the ethnographer or journalist) that is paramount; in *testimonio,* by contrast, it is the intention of the direct narrator, who *uses* (in a pragmatic sense) the possibility the ethnographic interlocutor offers to bring his or her situation to the attention of an audience—the bourgeois public sphere—to which he or she would normally not have access because of the very conditions of subalternity to which the *testimonio* bears witness.[3] *Testimonio* is not intended, in other words, as a reenactment of the anthropological function of the native informant. In René Jara's (1986, p. 3) phrase, it is rather a *narración de urgencia*—an "emergency" narrative—involving a problem of repression, poverty, marginality, exploitation, or simply survival that is implicated in the act of narration itself. In general, *testimonio* could be said to coincide with the feminist slogan "The personal is the political." The contemporary appeal of *testimonio* for educated, middle-class, transnational publics is perhaps related to the importance given in various forms of 1960s counterculture to oral testimony as a form of personal and/or collective catharsis and liberation in (for example) the consciousness-raising sessions of the early women's movement, the practice of "speaking bitterness" in the Chinese Cultural Revolution, or psychotherapeutic encounter groups.

The predominant formal aspect of the *testimonio* is the voice that speaks to the reader through the text in the form of an "I" that demands to be recognized, that wants or needs to stake a claim on our attention. Eliana Rivero (1984–1985) notes that "the act of speaking faithfully recorded on the tape, transcribed and then 'written,' remains in the *testimonio* punctuated by a repeated series of interlocutive and conversational markers . . . which constantly put the reader on the alert, so to speak: True? Are you following me? OK? So?" (pp. 220–221, my translation). The result, she argues, is a "snaillike" discourse (*discurso encaracolado*) that keeps turning in on itself and that in the process invokes the complicity of the reader through the medium of his or her counterpart in the text, the direct interlocutor. This presence of the voice, which the reader is meant to experience as the voice of a *real* rather than a fictional person, is the mark of a desire not to be silenced or defeated, to impose oneself on an institution of power and privilege from the position of the excluded, the marginal, the subaltern—hence the insistence on the importance of personal name or identity evident sometimes in titles of *testimonios,* such as *I, Rigoberta Menchú* (even more strongly in the Spanish: *Me llamo Rigoberta Menchú y así me nacío la conciencia*), *I'm a Juvenile Delinquent* (*Soy un delincuente*), and *Let Me Speak* (*Si me permiten hablar*).

This insistence suggests an affinity between testimony and autobiography (and related forms, such as the autobiographical *bildungsroman,* the memoir, and the diary). Like autobiography, *testimonio* is an affirmation of the authority of personal experience, but, unlike autobiography, it cannot affirm a self-identity that is separate from the subaltern group or class situation that it narrates. *Testimonio* involves an erasure of the function and thus also of the textual presence of the "author" that is so powerfully present in all major forms of Western literary and academic writing.[4] By contrast, in autobiography or the autobiographical *bildungsroman,* the very possibility of "writing one's life" implies necessarily that the narrator is no longer in the situation of marginality and subalternity that his or her narrative describes, but now has attained precisely the cultural status of an author (and, generally speaking, middle- or upper-class economic status). Put another way, the transition from storyteller to author implies a parallel transition from *gemeinschaft* to *gesellschaft,* from a culture of primary and secondary orality to writing, from a traditional group identity to the privatized, modern identity that forms the subject of liberal political and economic theory.

The metonymic character of testimonial discourse—the sense that the voice that is addressing us is a part that stands for a larger whole—is a crucial aspect of what literary critics would call the convention of the form: the narrative contract with the reader it establishes. Because it does not require or establish a hierarchy of narrative authority, *testimonio* is a fundamentally democratic and egalitarian narrative form. It implies that *any* life so narrated can have a symbolic and cognitive value. Each individual *testimonio* evokes an absent polyphony of other voices, other possible lives and experiences (one common formal variation on the first-person singular *testimonio* is the polyphonic *testimonio* made up of accounts by different participants in the same event).

If the novel is a closed form, in the sense that both the story and the characters it involves end with the end of the text, in *testimonio,* by contrast, the distinctions between text and history, representation and real life, public and private spheres, objectivity and solidarity (to recall Rorty's alternatives) are transgressed. It is, to borrow Umberto Eco's expression, an "open work." The narrator in *testimonio* is an actual person who continues living and acting in an actual social space and time, which also continue. *Testimonio* can never create the illusion—fundamental to formalist methods of textual analysis—of the text as autonomous, set against and above the practical domain of everyday life and struggle. The emergence of *testimonios*, for the form to have become more and more popular in recent years, means that there are experiences in the world today (there always have been) that cannot be expressed adequately in the dominant forms of historical, ethnographic, or literary representation, that would be betrayed or misrepresented by these forms.

Because of its reliance on voice, *testimonio* implies in particular a challenge to the loss of the authority of orality in the context of processes of cultural modernization that privilege literacy and literature as a norm of expression. The inequalities and contradictions of gender, class, race, ethnicity, nationality, and cultural authority that determine the "urgent" situation of the testimonial narrator may also reproduce themselves in the relation of the narrator to the interlocutor, especially when (as is generally the case) that narrator requires to produce the *testimonio* a "lettered" interlocutor from a different ethnic and/or class background in order first to elicit and record the narrative, and then to transform it into a printed text and see to its publication and circulation as such. But it is equally important to understand that the testimonial narrator is not the subaltern as such either; rather, she or he functions as an organic intellectual (in Antonio Gramsci's sense of this term) of the subaltern, who speaks to the hegemony by means of a metonymy of self in the name and in the place of the subaltern.

By the same token, the presence of subaltern voice in the *testimonio* is in part a literary illusion—something akin to what the Russian formalists called *skaz*: the textual simulacrum of direct oral expression. We are dealing here, in other words, not with reality itself but with what semioticians call a "reality effect" that has been produced by both the testimonial narrator—using popular speech and the devices of oral storytelling—and the interlocutor-compiler, who, according to hegemonic norms of narrative form and expression, transcribes, edits, and makes a story out of the narrator's discourse. Elzbieta Sklodowska (1982) cautions in this regard that it would be naïve to assume a direct homology between text and history (in *testimonio*).

> The discourse of a witness cannot be a reflection of his or her experience, but rather a refraction determined by the vicissitudes of memory, intention, ideology. The intention and the ideology of the author-editor further superimposes the original text, creating more ambiguities, silences, and absences in the process of selecting and editing the material in a way consonant with norms of literary form. Thus, although the testimonio uses a series of devices to gain a sense of veracity and authenticity—among them the point of view of the first-person witness-narrator—the play between fiction and history reappears inexorably as a problem. (p. 379, my translation; see also Sklodowska, 1996)

The point is well-taken, but perhaps overstated. Like the identification of *testimonio* with life history (which Sklodowska shares), it concedes agency to the interlocutor-editor of the testimonial text rather than to its direct narrator. It would be better to say that what is at stake in *testimonio* is the *particular* nature of the reality effect it produces. Because of its character as a narrative told in the first person to an actual interlocutor, *testimonio* interpellates the reader in a way that literary fiction or third-person journalism or ethnographic writing does not. The word *testimonio* carries the connotation in Spanish of the act of testifying or bearing witness in a legal or religious sense. Conversely, the situation of the reader of *testimonio* is akin to that of a jury member in a courtroom. *Something* is asked of us by *testimonio*, in other words. In this sense, *testimonio* might be seen as a kind of speech act that sets up special ethical and epistemological demands. (When we are addressed directly by an actual person, in such a way as to make a demand on our attention and capacity for judgment, we are under an obligation to respond in some way or other; we can act or not on that obligation, but we cannot ignore it.)

What *testimonio* asks of its readers is in effect what Rorty means by solidarity—that is, the capacity to identify their own identities, expectations, and values with those of another. To understand how this happens is to understand how *testimonio works* ideologically as discourse, rather than what it *is*.

In one of the most powerful sections of her famous *testimonio I, Rigoberta Menchú* (Menchú, 1984), which has come to be something like a paradigm of the genre, Menchú describes the torture and execution of her brother Petrocinio by elements of the Guatemalan army in the plaza of a small highland town called Chajul, which is the site of an annual pilgrimage by worshipers of the local saint. Here is part of that account:

> After he'd finished talking the officer ordered the squad to take away those who'd been "punished," naked and swollen as they were. They dragged them along, they could no longer walk. Dragged them to this place, where they lined them up all together within sight of everyone. The officer called to the worst of the criminals—the *Kaibiles*, who wear different clothes from other soldiers. They're the ones with the most training, the most power. Well, he called the *Kaibiles* and they poured petrol over each of the tortured. The captain said, "This isn't the last of their punishments, there's another one yet. This is what we've done with all the subversives we catch, because they have to die by violence. And if this doesn't teach you a lesson, this is what'll happen to you too. The problem is that the Indians let themselves be led by the communists. Since no-one's told the Indians anything, they go along with the communists." He was trying to convince the people but at the same time he was insulting them by what he said. Anyway, they [the soldiers] lined up the tortured and poured petrol on them; and then the soldiers set fire to each one of them. Many of them begged for mercy. Some of them screamed, many of them leapt but uttered no sound—of course, that was because their breathing was cut off. But—and to me this was incredible—many of the people had weapons with them, the ones who'd been on their way to work had machetes, others had nothing in their hands, but when they saw the army setting fire to the victims, everyone wanted to strike back, to risk their lives doing it, despite all the soldiers' arms. . . . Faced with its own cowardice, the army itself realized that the whole people were prepared to fight. You could see that even the children were enraged, but they didn't know how to express their rage. (pp. 178–179)

This passage is undoubtedly compelling and powerful. It invites the reader into the situation it describes through the medium of the eyewitness narrator, and it is the sharing of the experience through the medium of Menchú's account that constitutes the possibility of solidarity. But "what if much of Rigoberta's story is not true?" anthropologist David Stoll (1999, p. viii) asks. On the basis of interviews in the area where the massacre was supposed to have occurred, Stoll concludes that the killing of Menchú's brother did not happen in exactly this way, that Menchú could not have been a direct witness to the event as her account suggests, and that therefore this account, along with other details of her *testimonio*, amounts to, in Stoll's words, a "mythic inflation" (pp. 63–70, 232). It would be more accurate to say that what Stoll is able to show is that *some* rather than "much" of Menchú's story is not true. He does not contest the fact of the murder of Menchú's brother by the army, and he stipulates that "there is no doubt about the most important points [in her story]: that a dictatorship massacred thousands of indigenous peasants, that the victims included half of Rigoberta's immediate family, that she fled to Mexico to save her life, and that she joined a revolutionary movement to liberate her country" (p. viii). But he does argue that the inaccuracies or omissions in her narrative make her less than a reliable spokesperson for the interests and beliefs of the people for whom she claims to speak. In response to Stoll, Menchú herself has publicly conceded that she grafted elements of other people's experiences and stories onto her own account. In particular, she has admitted that she was not herself present at the massacre of her brother and his companions in Chajul, and that the account of the event quoted in part above came instead from her mother, who (Menchú claims) was there. She says that this and similar interpolations were a way of making her story a collective one, rather than a personal autobiography. But the point remains: If the epistemological and ethical authority of testimonial narratives depends on the assumption that they are based on personal experience and direct witness, then it might appear that, as Stoll puts it, "*I, Rigoberta Menchú* does not belong in the genre of which it is the most famous example, because it is not the eyewitness account it purports to be" (p. 242).

In a way, however, the argument between Menchú and Stoll is not so much about what really happened as it is about who has the authority to narrate. (Stoll's quarrel with Menchú and *testimonio* is a *political* quarrel that masquerades as an epistemological one.) That question, rather than the question of "what really happened," is crucial to an understanding of how *testimonio* works. What seems to bother Stoll above all is that Menchú *has* an agenda. He wants her to be in effect a native informant who will lend herself to *his* purposes (of ethnographic information gathering and evaluation), but she is instead functioning in her narrative as an organic intellectual, concerned with producing a text of local history—that is, with elaborating hegemony.

The basic idea of Gayatri Spivak's famous, but notoriously difficult, essay "Can the Subaltern Speak?" (1988) might be reformulated in this way: If the subaltern could speak—that is, speak in a way that really *matters* to us, that we would feel compelled to listen to—then it would not be subaltern. Spivak is trying to show that behind the gesture of the ethnographer or solidarity activist committed to the cause of the subaltern in allowing or enabling the subaltern to speak is the trace of the construction of an other who is available to speak to us (with whom we *can* speak or with whom we would feel comfortable speaking), thus neutralizing the force of the reality of difference and antagonism to which our own relatively privileged position in the global system might give rise. She is saying that one of the things being subaltern means is not mattering, not being worth listening to, or not being understood when one is "heard."

By contrast, Stoll's argument with Rigoberta Menchú is precisely with how her *testimonio* comes to matter. He is bothered by the way it was used by academics and solidarity activists to mobilize international support for the Guatemalan armed struggle in the 1980s, long after (in Stoll's view) that movement had lost whatever support it may have initially enjoyed among the indigenous peasants for whom Menchú claims to speak. That issue—"how outsiders were using Rigoberta's story to justify continuing a war at the expense of peasants who did not support it" (Stoll, 1999, p. 241)—is the main problem for Stoll, rather than the inaccuracies or omissions themselves. From Stoll's viewpoint, by making Menchú's story seem (in her own words) "the story of all poor Guatemalans"—that is, by its participating in the very metonymic logic of *testimonio*—*I, Rigoberta Menchú* misrepresents a more complex and ideologically contradictory situation among the indigenous peasants. It reflects back to the reader not the subaltern as such, but a narcissistic image of what the subaltern *should be*:

> Books like *I, Rigoberta Menchú* will be exalted because they tell academics what they want to hear.... What makes *I, Rigoberta Menchú* so attractive in universities is what makes it misleading about the struggle for survival in Guatemala. We think we are getting closer to understanding Guatemalan peasants when actually we are being borne away by the mystifications wrapped up in an iconic figure. (Stoll, 1999, p. 227)

In one sense, of course, there is a coincidence between Spivak's concern with the production in metropolitan ethnographic and literary discourse of what she calls a "domesticated Other" and Stoll's concern with the conversion of Menchú into an icon of academic political correctness. But Stoll's argument is also explicitly *with* Spivak, as a representative of the very kind of "postmodern scholarship" that would privilege a text like *I, Rigoberta Menchú*, even to the extent of wanting to deconstruct its metaphysics of presence. Thus, Stoll states, for example:

> Following the thinking of literary theorists such as Edward Said and Gayatri Spivak, anthropologists have become very interested in problems of narrative, voice, and representation, especially the problem of how we misrepresent voices other than our own. In reaction, some anthropologists argue that the resulting fascination with texts threatens the claim of anthropology to be a science, by replacing hypothesis, evidence, and generalization with stylish forms of introspection. (p. 247)

Or this: "Under the influence of postmodernism (which has undermined confidence in a single set of facts) and identity politics (which demands acceptance of claims to victimhood), scholars are increasingly hesitant to challenge certain kinds of rhetoric" (p. 244). Or "With postmodern critiques of representation and authority, many scholars are tempted to abandon the task of verification, especially when they construe the narrator as a victim worthy of their support" (p. 274).

Where Spivak is concerned with the way in which hegemonic literary or scientific representation effaces the effective presence and agency of the subaltern, Stoll's case against Menchú is precisely that: a way of, so to speak, *resubalternizing* a narrative that aspired to (and to some extent achieved) cultural authority. In the process of constructing her narrative and articulating herself as a political icon around its circulation, Menchú is becoming not-subaltern, in the sense that she is functioning as what Spivak calls a subject of history. Her *testimonio* is a *performative* rather than simply descriptive or denotative discourse. Her narrative choices, and silences and evasions, entail that there are versions of "what really happened" that she does not or cannot represent without relativizing the authority of her own account.

It goes without saying that in any social situation, indeed even within a given class or group identity, it is always possible to find a variety of points of view or ways of telling that reflect contradictory, or simply differing, agendas and interests. "Obviously," Stoll (1999) observes:

> Rigoberta is a legitimate Mayan voice. So are all the young Mayas who want to move to Los Angeles or Houston. So is the man with a large family who owns three worn-out acres and wants me to buy him a chain saw so he can cut down the last forest more quickly. Any of these people can be picked to make misleading generalizations about Mayas. (p. 247)

The presence of these other voices makes Guatemalan indigenous communities—indeed even Menchú's own immediate family—seem irremediably driven by internal rivalries, contradictions, and disagreements.

But to insist on this is, in a way, to deny the possibility of subaltern agency as such, because a hegemonic project by definition points to a possibility of collective will and action that depends precisely on the transformation of the conditions of cultural and political disenfranchisement, alienation, and oppression that underlie these rivalries and contradictions. The appeal to diversity ("any of these people") leaves intact the authority of the outside observer (the ethnographer or social scientist) who is alone in the position of being able to both hear and sort through all the various conflicting testimonies.

The concern about the connection between *testimonio* and identity politics that Stoll evinces is predicated on the fact that multicultural rights claims carry with them what Canadian philosopher Charles Taylor (1994) has called a "presumption of equal worth" (and *I, Rigoberta Menchú* is, among other things, a strong argument for seeing the nature of American societies as irrevocably multicultural and ethnically heterogeneous). That presumption in turn implies an epistemological relativism that coincides with the postmodernist critique of the Enlightenment paradigm of scientific objectivity. If there is no one universal standard for truth, then claims about truth are contextual: They have to do with how people construct different understandings of the world and historical memory from the same sets of facts in situations of gender, ethnic, and class inequality, exploitation, and repression. The truth claims for a testimonial narrative like *I, Rigoberta Menchú* depend on conferring on the form a special kind of epistemological authority as embodying subaltern voice and experience. Against the authority of that voice—and, in particular, against the assumption that it can represent adequately a collective subject ("all poor Guatemalans")—Stoll wants to affirm the authority of the fact-gathering and -testing procedures of anthropology and journalism, in which accounts like Menchú's will be treated simply as ethnographic data that must be processed by more objective techniques of assessment, which, by definition, are not available to the direct narrator. In the final analysis, what Stoll is able to present as evidence against the validity of Menchú's account are, precisely, *other testimonios*: other voices, narratives, points of view, in which, it will come as no surprise, he can find something *he* wants to hear.

We know something about the nature of this problem. There is not, outside the realm of human discourse itself, a level of facticity that can guarantee the truth of this or that representation, given that society itself is not an essence prior to representation, but rather the consequence of struggles to represent and over-representation. That is the deeper meaning of Walter Benjamin's aphorism "Even the dead are not safe": Even the historical memory of the past is conjectural, relative, perishable. *Testimonio* is both an art and a strategy of subaltern memory.

We would create yet another version of the native informant of classical anthropology if we were to grant testimonial narrators like Rigoberta Menchú only the possibility of being witnesses, and not the power to create their own narrative authority and negotiate its conditions of truth and representativity. This would amount to saying that the subaltern can of course speak, but only through *us*, through our institutionally sanctioned authority and pretended objectivity as intellectuals, which give us the power to decide what counts in the narrator's raw material. But it is precisely that institutionally sanctioned authority and objectivity that, in a less benevolent form, but still claiming to speak from the place of truth, the subaltern must confront every day in the forms of war, economic exploitation, development schemes, obligatory acculturation, police and military repression, destruction of habitat, forced sterilization, and the like.[5]

There is a question of agency here. What *testimonio* obliges us to confront is not only the subaltern as a (self-)represented victim, but also as the agent—in that very act of representation—of a transformative project that aspires to become hegemonic in its own right. In terms of this project, which is not our own in any immediate sense and which may in fact imply structurally a contradiction with our own position of relative privilege and authority in the global system, the testimonial text is a *means* rather than an end in itself. Menchú and the persons who collaborated with her in the creation of *I, Rigoberta Menchú* certainly were aware that the text would be an important tool in human rights and solidarity work that might have a positive effect on the genocidal conditions the text itself describes. But *her* interest in the text is not to have it become an object for us, our means of getting the "whole truth"—*toda la realidad*—of her experience. It is rather to act tactically in a way she hopes and expects will advance the interests of the community and social groups and classes her *testimonio* represents: "poor" (in her own description) Guatemalans. That is as it should be, however, because it is not only *our* desires and purposes that count in relation to *testimonio.*

This seems obvious enough, but it is a hard lesson to absorb fully, because it forces us to, in Spivak's phrase, "unlearn privilege." Unlearning privilege means recognizing that it is not the intention of subaltern cultural practice simply to signify its subalternity to us. If that is what *testimonio* does, then critics like Sklodowska are right in seeing it as a form of the status quo, a kind of postmodernist *costumbrismo.* The force of a *testimonio* such as *I, Rigoberta Menchú* is to displace the centrality of intellectuals and what they recognize as culture—including history, literature, journalism, and ethnographic writing. Like any testimonial narrator (like anybody), Menchú is of course also an intellectual, but in a sense she is clearly different from what Gramsci meant by a traditional intellectual—that is, someone who meets the standards and carries the authority of humanistic and/or scientific high culture. The concern with the question of subaltern agency and authority in *testimonio* depends, rather, on the suspicion that intellectuals and writing practices are themselves complicit in maintaining relations of domination and subalternity.

The question is relevant to the claim made by Dinesh D'Souza (1991) in the debate over the Stanford Western Culture undergraduate requirement (which centered on the adoption of *I, Rigoberta Menchú* as a text in one of the course sections) that *I, Rigoberta Menchú* is not good or great literature. D'Souza writes, "To celebrate the works of the oppressed, apart from the standard of merit by which other art and history and literature is judged, is to romanticize their suffering, to pretend that it is naturally creative, and to give it an aesthetic status that is not shared or appreciated by those who actually endure the oppression" (p. 87). It could be argued that *I, Rigoberta Menchú* is one of the most powerful works of *literature* produced in Latin America in the past several decades, but there is also some point in seeing it as a provocation in the academy, as D'Souza feels it to be. The subaltern, by definition, is a social position that is not, and cannot be, adequately represented in the human sciences or the university, if only because the human sciences and the university are among the institutional constellations of power/knowledge that create and sustain subalternity. This is not, however, to draw a line between the world of the academy and the subaltern, because the point of *testimonio* is, in the first place, to intervene in that world—that is, in a place where the subaltern is not. In its very situation of enunciation, which juxtaposes radically the subject positions of the narrator and interlocutor, *testimonio* is involved in and constructed out of the opposing terms of a master/slave dialectic: metropolis/periphery, nation/region, European/indigenous, creole/mestizo, elite/popular, urban/rural, intellectual/manual, male/female, "lettered"/illiterate or semiliterate. *Testimonio* is no more capable of transcending these oppositions than are more purely literary or scientific forms of writing or narrative; that would require something like a cultural revolution that would abolish or invert the conditions that produce relations of subordination, exploitation, and inequality in the first place. But *testimonio* does involve a new way of articulating these oppositions and a new, collaborative model for the relationship between the intelligentsia and the popular classes.

To return to Rorty's point about the "desire for solidarity," a good part of the appeal of *testimonio* must lie in the fact that it both represents symbolically and enacts in its production and reception a relation of solidarity between ourselves—as members of the professional middle class and practitioners of the human sciences—and subaltern social subjects. *Testimonio* gives voice to a previously anonymous and voiceless popular-democratic subject, but in such a way that the intellectual or professional is interpellated, in his or her function as interlocutor/reader of the testimonial account, as being in alliance with (and to some extent dependent on) this subject, without at the same time losing his or her identity as an intellectual.

If first-generation *testimonios* such as *I, Rigoberta Menchú* effaced textually in the manner of the ethnographic life story (except in their introductory presentations) the presence of the interlocutor, it is becoming increasingly common in what is sometimes called the "new ethnography" to put the interlocutor into the account, to make the dynamic of interaction and negotiation between interlocutor and narrator part of what *testimonio* testifies to. Ruth Behar's *Translated Woman: Crossing the Border with Esperanza's Story* (1993), for example, is often mentioned as a model for the sort of ethnographic text in which the authority (and identity) of the ethnographer is counterpointed against the voice and authority of the subject whose life history the ethnographer is concerned with eliciting. In a similar vein, Philippe Bourgois's innovative ethnography of Puerto Rican crack dealers in East Harlem, *In Search of Respect* (1995), often pits the values of the investigator—Bourgois—against those of the dealers he befriends and whose stories and conversations he transcribes and reproduces in his text. In *Event, Metaphor, Memory: Chauri Chaura, 1922–1992* (1995), the subaltern studies historian Shahid Amin is concerned with retrieving the "local memory" of an uprising in 1922 in a small town in northern India in the course of which peasants surrounded and burned down a police station, leading to the deaths of 23 policemen. But he is also concerned with finding ways to incorporate formally the narratives that embody that memory into his own history of the event, thus abandoning the usual stance of the historian as omniscient narrator and making the heterogeneous voices of the community itself the historian(s).

These ways of constructing testimonial material (obviously, the examples could be multiplied many times over) make visible that what happens in *testimonio* is not only the textual staging of a "domesticated Other," to recall Spivak's telling objection, but the confrontation through the text of one person (the reader and/or immediate interlocutor) with another (the direct narrator or narrators) at the level of a *possible* solidarity. In this sense, *testimonio* also embodies a new possibility of political agency (it is essentially that possibility to which Stoll objects). But that possibility—a postmodernist form of Popular Front–style alliance politics, if you will—is necessarily built on the recognition of and respect for the radical incommensurability of the situation of the parties involved. More than empathic liberal guilt or political correctness, what *testimonio* seeks to elicit is *coalition*. As Doris Sommer (1996) puts it succinctly, *testimonio* "is an invitation to a tête-à-tête, not to a heart to heart" (p. 143).

Bibliographic Note

Margaret Randall, who has organized testimonial workshops in Cuba and Nicaragua (and who has herself edited a number of *testimonios* on the roles of women in the Cuban and Nicaraguan revolutions), is the author of a very good, albeit hard to find, handbook on how to prepare a *testimonio* titled *Testimonios: A Guide to Oral History* (1985). The first significant academic discussion of *testimonio* that I am aware of was published in the 1986 collection *Testimonio y literatura,* edited by René Jara and Hernán Vidal at the University of Minnesota's Institute for the Study of Ideologies and Literature. The most comprehensive representation of the debate around *testimonio* in the literary humanities in the ensuing decade or so is the collection edited by Georg Gugelberger titled *The Real Thing: Testimonial Discourse and Latin America* (1996), which incorporates two earlier collections: one by Gugelberger and Michael Kearney for a special issue of *Latin American Perspectives* (vols. 18–19, 1991), and the other by myself and Hugo Achugar titled *La voz del otro: Testimonio, subalternidad, y verdad narrativa,* which appeared as a special issue of *Revista de Crítica Literaria Latinoamericana* (1992). The initial literary "manifesto" of *testimonio* was the essay by the Cuban novelist-ethnographer Miguel Barnet (apropos his own *Biography of a Runaway Slave*), "La novela-*testimonio:* Socioliteratura" (1986), originally published in the late 1960s in the Cuban journal *Unión.* On the academic incorporation of *testimonio* and its consequences for pedagogy, see Carey-Webb and Benz (1996). Jara and Vidal's (1986) collection happened to coincide with the famous collection on ethnographic authority and writing practices edited by James Clifford and George Marcus, *Writing Culture* (1986), which exercised a wide influence in the fields of anthropology and history. One should note also in this respect the pertinence of the work of the South Asian Subaltern Studies Group (see, e.g., Guha, 1997; Guha & Spivak, 1988) and of the Latin American Subaltern Studies Group (see Rabasa, Sanjinés, & Carr, 1994/1996). For both social scientists and literary critics, a touchstone for conceptualizing *testimonio* should be Walter Benjamin's great essays, "The Storyteller" and "Theses on the Philosophy of History" (see Benjamin, 1969).

Notes

1. Rorty's (1985) distinction may recall for some readers Marvin Harris's well-known distinction between *emic* and *etic* accounts (where the former are personal or collective "stories" and the latter are representations given by a supposedly objective observer based on empirical evidence).

2. Widely different sorts of narrative texts could in given circumstances function as *testimonios*: confession, court testimony, oral history, memoir, autobiography, autobiographical novel, chronicle, confession, life story, *novela-testimonio,* "nonfiction novel" (Truman Capote), or "literature of fact" (Roque Dalton).

3. Mary Louise Pratt (1986) describes the *testimonio* usefully in this respect as "autoethnography."

4. In Miguel Barnet's (1986) phrase, the author has been replaced in *testimonio* by the function of a "compiler" (*compilador*) or "activator" (*gestante*), somewhat on the model of the film producer.

5. Lacan (1977, pp. 310–311) writes:

> Any statement of authority has no other guarantee than its very enunciation, and it is pointless for it to seek another signifier, which could not appear outside this locus in any way. Which is what I mean when I say that no metalanguage can be spoken, or, more aphoristically, that there is no Other of the Other. And when the Legislator (he who claims to lay down the Law) presents himself to fill the gap, he does so as an impostor.

References

Amin, S. (1995). *Event, metaphor, memory: Chauri Chaura 1922–1992.* Berkeley: University of California Press.

Barnet, M. (1986). La novela-*testimonio:* Socioliteratura. In R. Jara & H. Vidal (Eds.), *Testimonio y literatura* (pp. 280–301). Minneapolis: University of Minnesota, Institute for the Study of Ideologies and Literatures.

Behar, R. (1993). *Translated woman: Crossing the border with Esperanza's story.* Boston: Beacon.

Benjamin, W. (1969). *Illuminations* (H. Zohn, Trans.). New York: Schocken.

Beverley, J., & Achugar, H. (Eds.). (1992). *La voz del otro: Testimonio, subalternidad, y verdad narrativa* [Special issue]. *Revista de Crítica Literaria Latinoamericana, 36.*

Bourgois, P. (1995). *In search of respect.* Cambridge, UK: Cambridge University Press.

Carey-Webb, A., & Benz, S. (Eds.). (1996). *Teaching and testimony.* Albany: State University of New York Press.

Clifford, J., & Marcus, G. E. (Eds.). (1986). *Writing culture: The poetics and politics of ethnography.* Berkeley: University of California Press.

D'Souza, D. (1991). *Illiberal education.* New York: Free Press.

Gugelberger, G. M. (Ed.). (1996). *The real thing: Testimonial discourse and Latin America.* Durham, NC: Duke University Press.

Gugelberger, G. M., & Kearney, M. (Eds.). (1991). [Special issue]. *Latin American Perspectives, 18–19.*

Guha, R. (Ed.). (1997). *A subaltern studies reader.* Minneapolis: University of Minnesota Press.

Guha, R., & Spivak, G. C. (Eds.). (1988). *Selected subaltern studies.,* New York: Oxford University Press.

Jara, R. (1986). Prólogo. In R. Jara & H. Vidal (Eds.), *Testimonio y literatura* (pp. 1–3). Minneapolis: University of Minnesota, Institute for the Study of Ideologies and Literatures.

Jara, R., & Vidal, H. (Eds.). (1986). *Testimonio y literatura.* Minneapolis: University of Minnesota, Institute for the Study of Ideologies and Literatures.

Lacan, J. A. (1977). *Écrits: A selection.* New York: W. W. Norton.

Menchú, R. (1984). *I, Rigoberta Menchú: An Indian woman in Guatemala* (E. Burgos-Debray, Ed.; A. Wright, Trans.). London: Verso.

Pratt, M. L. (1986). Fieldwork in common places. In J. Clifford & G. E. Marcus (Eds.), *Writing culture: The poetics and politics of ethnography* (pp. 27–50). Berkeley: University of California Press.

Rabasa, J., Sanjinés, J., & Carr, R. (Eds.). (1996). Subaltern studies in the Americas [Special issue]. *Dispositio/n, 19*(46). (Contributions written in 1994)

Randall, M. (1985). *Testimonios: A guide to oral history.* Toronto: Participatory Research Group.

Rivero, E. (1984–1985). Testimonio y conversaciones como discurso literario: Cuba y Nicaragua. *Literature and Contemporary Revolutionary Culture, 1,* 218–228.

Rorty, R. (1985). Solidarity or objectivity? In J. Rajchman & C. West (Eds.), *Postanalytic philosophy* (pp. 3–19). New York: Columbia University Press.

Sklodowska, E. (1982). La forma testimonial y la novelística de Miguel Barnet. *Revista/Review Interamericana, 12,* 368–380.

Sklodowska, E. (1996). Spanish American testimonial novel: Some afterthoughts. In G. M. Gugelberger (Ed.), *The real thing: Testimonial discourse and Latin America* (pp. 84–100). Durham, NC: Duke University Press.

Sommer, D. (1996). No secrets. In G. M. Gugelberger (Ed.), *The real thing: Testimonial discourse and Latin America* (pp. 130–160). Durham, NC: Duke University Press.

Spivak, G. C. (1988). Can the subaltern speak? In C. Nelson & L. Grossberg (Eds.), *Marxism and the interpretation of culture* (pp. 280–316). Urbana: University of Illinois Press.

Stoll, D. (1999). *Rigoberta Menchú and the story of all poor Guatemalans.* Boulder, CO: Westview.

Taylor, C. (1994). The politics of recognition. In C. Taylor, K. A. Appiah, J. Habermas, S. C. Rockefeller, M. Walzer, & S. Wolf, *Multiculturalism: Examining the politics of recognition* (A. Gutmann, Ed.). Princeton, NJ: Princeton University Press.

23

PARTICIPATORY ACTION RESEARCH

Communicative Action and the Public Sphere

Stephen Kemmis and Robin McTaggart

Participatory action research has an extensive history in many fields of social practice. Our aim in this chapter is to develop the view of participatory action research that has shaped our own theory and practice during recent years. We begin with a short overview of the evolution of our own thinking and the influence of several generations of action research. In our chapter on "Participatory Action Research" for the second edition of this *Handbook,* we identified several key approaches to action research, the sites and settings where they are most frequently used, several criticisms that have been advanced for each, and key sources to explore them (Kemmis & McTaggart, 2000). The approaches identified were a somewhat eclectic mix—participatory research, classroom action research, action learning, action science, soft systems approaches, and industrial action research. We summarize those approaches again here but do not reiterate our views of them in this chapter. We acknowledge the influence of each approach on the field and as stimulus to reflection on our own ideas and practices.

For our current purposes, we proceed to develop a comprehensive view of social practice and reflect on aspects of our own work that we term "myths, misinterpretations, and mistakes" to move toward reconceptualizing research itself as a social practice. Thinking about research as a social practice leads us to an exploration of Habermas's notion of the public sphere as a way of extending the theory and practice of action research. We hope that this argument shows more clearly how participatory action research differs from other forms of social inquiry, integrating more clearly its political and methodological intentions. We anticipate that this argument will provide direction for a new generation of participatory action research, and we trust that it will strengthen the theory and practice of participatory action research in the many fields and settings that draw on its intellectually and morally rich traditions, ideas, and challenges.

The Family of Action Research

Action research began with an idea attributed to social psychologist Kurt Lewin. It first found expression in the work of the Tavistock Institute of Human Relations in the United Kingdom (Rapaport, 1970), where Lewin had visited in 1933 and 1936 and had maintained contact for many years. Lewin's (1946, 1952) own earliest publications on action research related to community action programs in the United States during the 1940s. However, it is worth noting that Altrichter and Gstettner (1997) argued that there were earlier, more "actionist" approaches to action research in community development practiced by H. G. Moreno, for example, working with prostitutes in Vienna at the turn of the 20th century. Nevertheless, it was Lewin's work and reputation that gave impetus to the action research movements in many different disciplines. Stephen Corey initiated action research in education in the United States soon after Lewin's work was published (Corey, 1949, 1953). However, efforts to reinterpret and justify action research in terms of the prevailing positivistic ideology in the United States led to a temporary decline in its development there (Kemmis, 1981).

A second generation of action research, building on a British tradition of action research in organizational development championed by researchers at the Tavistock Institute (Rapaport, 1970), began in Britain with the Ford Teaching Project directed by John Elliott and Clem Adelman (Elliott & Adelman, 1973). Recognition in Australia of the "practical" character of the British initiative led to calls for more explicitly "critical" and "emancipatory" action research (Carr & Kemmis, 1986). The critical impulse in Australian action research was paralleled by similar advocacies in Europe (Brock-Utne, 1980). These advocacies and efforts for their realization were called the third generation of action research. A fourth generation of action research emerged in the connection between critical emancipatory action research and participatory action research that had developed in the context of social movements in the developing world, championed by people such as Paulo Freire, Orlando Fals Borda, Rajesh Tandon, Anisur Rahman, and Marja-Liisa Swantz as well as by North American and British workers in adult education and literacy, community development, and development studies such as Budd Hall, Myles Horton, Robert Chambers, and John Gaventa. Two key themes were (a) the development of theoretical arguments for more "actionist" approaches to action research and (b) the need for participatory action researchers to make links with broad social movements.

Participatory Research

Participatory research is an alternative philosophy of social research (and social life [*vivéncia*]) often associated with social transformation in the Third World. It has roots in liberation theology and neo-Marxist approaches to community development (e.g., in Latin America) but also has rather liberal origins in human rights activism (e.g., in Asia). Three particular attributes are often used to distinguish participatory research from conventional research: shared ownership of research projects, community-based analysis of social problems, and an orientation toward community action. Given its commitment to social, economic, and political development responsive to the needs and opinions of ordinary people, proponents of participatory research have highlighted the politics of conventional social research, arguing that orthodox social science, despite its claim to value neutrality, normally serves the ideological function of justifying the position and interests of the wealthy and powerful (Fals Borda & Rahman, 1991; Forester, Pitt, & Welsh, 1993; Freire, 1982; Greenwood & Levin, 2000, 2001; Hall, Gillette, & Tandon, 1982; Horton, Kohl, & Kohl, 1990; McGuire, 1987; McTaggart, 1997; Oliveira & Darcy, 1975; Park, Brydon-Miller, Hall, & Jackson, 1993).

Critical Action Research

Critical action research expresses a commitment to bring together broad social analysis—the self-reflective collective self-study of practice, the way in which language is used, organization and power in a local situation, and action to improve things.

Critical action research is strongly represented in the literatures of educational action research, and there it emerges from dissatisfactions with classroom action research that typically does not take a broad view of the role of the relationship between education and social change. It has a strong commitment to participation as well as to the social analyses in the critical social science tradition that reveal the disempowerment and injustice created in industrialized societies. During recent times, critical action research has also attempted to take account of disadvantage attributable to gender and ethnicity as well as to social class, its initial point of reference (Carr & Kemmis, 1986; Fay, 1987; Henry, 1991; Kemmis, 1991; Marika, Ngurruwutthun, & White, 1992; McTaggart, 1991a, 1991b, 1997; Zuber-Skerritt, 1996).

Classroom Action Research

Classroom action research typically involves the use of qualitative interpretive modes of inquiry and data collection by teachers (often with help from academics) with a view to teachers making judgments about how to improve their own practices. The practice of classroom action research has a long tradition but has swung in and out of favor, principally because the theoretical work that justified it lagged behind the progressive educational movements that breathed life into it at certain historical moments (McTaggart, 1991a; Noffke, 1990, 1997). Primacy is given to teachers' self-understandings and judgments. The emphasis is "practical," that is, on the interpretations that teachers and students are making and acting on in the situation. In other words, classroom action research is not just practical idealistically, in a utopian way, or just about how interpretations might be different "in theory"; it is also practical in Aristotle's sense of practical reasoning about how to act rightly and properly in a situation with which one is confronted. If university researchers are involved, their role is a service role to the teachers. Such university researchers are often advocates for "teachers' knowledge" and may disavow or seek to diminish the relevance of more theoretical discourses such as critical theory (Dadds, 1995; Elliott, 1976–1977; Sagor, 1992; Stenhouse, 1975; Weiner, 1989).

Action Learning

Action learning has its origins in the work of advocate Reg Revans, who saw traditional approaches to management inquiry as unhelpful in solving the problems of organizations. Revans's early work with colliery managers attempting to improve workplace safety marks a significant turning point for the role of professors, engaging them directly in management problems in organizations.

The fundamental idea of action learning is to bring people together to learn from each other's experiences. There is emphasis on studying one's own situation, clarifying what the organization is trying to achieve, and working to remove obstacles. Key aspirations are organizational efficacy and efficiency, although advocates of action learning affirm the moral purpose and content of their own work and of the managers they seek to engage in the process (Clark, 1972; Pedler, 1991; Revans, 1980, 1982).

Action Science

Action science emphasizes the study of practice in organizational settings as a source of new understandings and improved practice. The field of action science systematically builds the relationship between academic organizational psychology and practical problems as they are experienced in organizations. It identifies two aspects of professional knowledge: (a) the formal knowledge that all competent members of the profession are thought to share and into which professionals are inducted during their initial training and (b) the professional knowledge of interpretation and enactment. A distinction is also made between the professional's "espoused theory" and "theories in use," and "gaps" between these are used as points of reference for change. A key factor in analyzing these gaps between theory and practice is helping the professional to unmask the "cover-ups" that are put in place, especially when participants are feeling anxious or threatened. The approach aspires to the development of the "reflective practitioner" (Argyris, 1990; Argyris & Schön, 1974, 1978; Argyris, Putnam, & McLain Smith, 1985; Reason, 1988; Schön, 1983, 1987, 1991).

Soft Systems Approaches

Soft systems approaches have their origins in organizations that use so-called "hard systems" of engineering, especially for industrial production. Soft systems methodology is the human "systems" analogy for systems engineering that has developed as the science of product and information flow. It is defined as oppositional to positivistic science with its emphasis on hypothesis testing. The researcher (typically an outside consultant) assumes a role as discussion partner or trainer in a real problem situation. The researcher works with participants to generate some (systems) models of the situation and uses the models to question the situation and to suggest a revised course of action (Checkland, 1981; Checkland & Scholes, 1990; Davies & Ledington, 1991; Flood & Jackson, 1991; Jackson, 1991; Kolb, 1984).

Industrial Action Research

Industrial action research has an extended history, dating back to the post-Lewinian influence in organizational psychology and organizational development in the Tavistock Institute of Human Relations in Britain and the Research Center for Group Dynamics in the United States. It is typically consultant driven, with very strong advocacies for collaboration between social scientists and members of different levels of the organization. The work is often couched in the language of workplace democratization, but more recent explorations have aspired more explicitly to the democratization of the research act itself, following the theory and practice of the participatory research movement. Especially in its more recent manifestations, industrial action research is differentiated from action science and its emphasis on cognition taking a preferred focus on reflection and the need for broader organizational and social change. Some advocacies have used critical theory as a resource to express aspirations for more participatory forms of work and evaluation, but more typically the style is somewhat humanistic and individualistic rather than critical. Emphases on social systems in organizations, such as improving organizational effectiveness and employee relations, are common. Also, the Lewinian aspiration to learn from trying to bring about change is a strong theme (Bravette, 1996; Elden, 1983; Emery & Thorsrud, 1976; Emery, Thorsrud, & Trist, 1969; Foster, 1972; Levin, 1985; Pasmore & Friedlander, 1982; Sandkull, 1980; Torbert, 1991; Warmington, 1980; Whyte, 1989, 1991).

The Emergence of Critical Participatory Action Research

Until the late 1990s, the hallmark of the action research field was eclecticism. Although the Lewinian idea was often used as a first point of legitimation, quite different rationales and practices had emerged in different disciplines. The sequestering of much literature under disciplinary rubrics meant that there was little dialogue between groups of different practitioners and advocates. Increases in visibility and popularity of the approaches rapidly changed this. There were large increases in scale and attendance at the world congresses on participatory action research as well as burgeoning interest at international sociological conferences. Action research reemerged as an influential approach in the United States (Greenwood & Levin, 2000, 2001). New associations between researchers and a vast literature of critique of modernity and its insinuation of capitalist, neocapitalist, and postcapitalist state and social systems into social life created both the impetus for and the possibility of dialogue. The historical and geographical distribution of action research approaches around the world and their interrelationships were better understood.

Critical participatory action research emerged as part of this dialogue. It aimed to provide a frame of reference for comprehension and critique of itself and its predecessors and to offer a way of working that addressed rampant individualism, disenchantment, and the dominance of instrumental reason—the key features of the "malaise of modernity" (Taylor, 1991). Critical participatory action research, as we now understand it, also creates a way of reinterpreting our own views of action research as they develop practically, theoretically, and pedagogically over time (e.g., Carr & Kemmis, 1986; Kemmis & McTaggart, 1988a, 1988b, 2000; McTaggart, 1991a). Before we revisit some of the myths, misinterpretations, and mistakes associated with our work over three decades, we present a summary of what we have regarded as the key features of participatory action research. We do this to identify some key principles as markers of progress, but we then look back at our own experience to develop what might potentially be seen as the rationale for a new generation of critical participatory action research.

Key Features of Participatory Action Research

Although the process of participatory action research is only poorly described in terms of a mechanical sequence of steps, it is generally thought to involve a spiral of self-reflective cycles of the following:

- *Planning* a change
- *Acting* and *observing* the process and consequences of the change
- *Reflecting* on these processes and consequences
- *Replanning*
- *Acting* and *observing again*
- *Reflecting again,* and so on . . .

Figure 23.1 presents this spiral of self-reflection in diagrammatic form. In reality, the process might not be as neat as this spiral of self-contained cycles of planning, acting and observing, and reflecting suggests. The stages overlap, and initial plans quickly become obsolete in the light of learning from experience. In reality, the process is likely to be more fluid, open, and responsive. The criterion of success is not whether participants have followed the steps faithfully but rather whether they have a strong and authentic sense of development and evolution in their *practices,* their *understandings* of their practices, and the *situations* in which they practice.

Each of the steps outlined in the spiral of self-reflection is best undertaken collaboratively by coparticipants in the participatory action research process. Not all theorists of action research place this emphasis on collaboration; they argue that action research is frequently a solitary process of systematic self-reflection. We concede that it is often so; nevertheless, we hold that participatory action research is best conceptualized in collaborative terms. Participatory action research is itself a social—and educational—process. The "subjects" of participatory action research undertake their research as a social practice. Moreover, the "object" of participatory action research is social; participatory action research is directed toward studying, reframing, and reconstructing social practices. *If practices are constituted in social interaction between people, changing practices is a social process.* To be sure, one person may change so that others are obliged to react or respond differently to that individual's changed behavior, but the willing and committed involvement of those whose interactions constitute the practice is necessary, in the end, to secure and legitimate the change. Participatory action research offers an opportunity to create forums in which people can join one another as coparticipants in the struggle to remake the practices in which they interact—forums in which rationality and democracy can be pursued together without an artificial separation ultimately hostile to both. In his book *Between Facts and Norms,* Jürgen Habermas described this process in terms of "opening communicative space" (Habermas, 1996), a theme to which we return later.

At its best, then, participatory action research is a social process of collaborative learning realized by groups of people who join together in changing the practices through which they interact in a shared social world in which, for better or worse, we live with the consequences of one another's actions.

It should also be stressed that participatory action research involves the investigation of

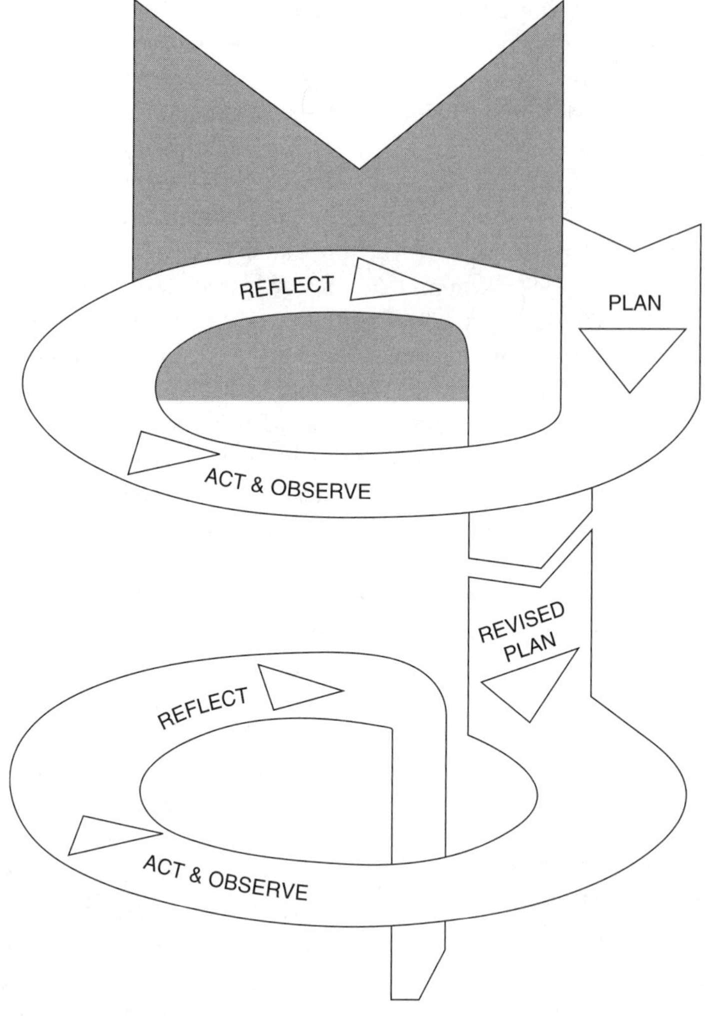

Figure 23.1. The Action Research Spiral

actual practices and not *abstract* practices. It involves learning about the real, material, concrete, and particular practices of particular people in particular places. Although, of course, it is not possible to suspend the inevitable abstraction that occurs whenever we use language to name, describe, interpret, and evaluate things, participatory action research differs from other forms of research in being more obstinate about its focus on changing particular practitioners' particular practices. Participatory action researchers may be interested in practices in general or in the abstract, but their principal concern is in changing practices in "the here and now." In our view, participatory action researchers do not need to apologize for seeing their work as mundane and mired in history; on the contrary, by doing so, they may avoid some of the philosophical and practical dangers of the idealism that suggests that a more abstract view of practice might make it possible to transcend or rise above history and to avoid the delusions of the view that it is possible to find a safe haven in abstract propositions that construe but do not themselves constitute practice. Participatory action research is a learning process whose fruits are the real and material changes in the following:

- What people do
- How people interact with the world and with others
- What people mean and what they value
- The discourses in which people understand and interpret their world

Through participatory action research, people can come to understand that—and how—their social and educational practices are located in, and are the product of, particular material, social, and historical circumstances that *produced* them and by which they are *reproduced* in everyday social interaction in a particular setting. By understanding their practices as the product of particular circumstances, participatory action researchers become alert to clues about how it may be possible to *transform* the practices they are producing and reproducing through their current ways of working. If their current practices are the product of one particular set of intentions, conditions, and circumstances, other (or transformed) practices may be produced and reproduced under other (or transformed) intentions, conditions, and circumstances.

Focusing on practices in a concrete and specific way makes them accessible for reflection, discussion, and reconstruction as products of past circumstances that are capable of being modified in and for present and future circumstances. While recognizing that the real space–time realization of every practice is transient and evanescent, and that it can be conceptualized only in the inevitably abstract (but comfortingly imprecise) terms that language provides, participatory action researchers aim to understand their own particular practices as they emerge in their own particular circumstances without reducing them to the ghostly status of the general, the abstract, or the ideal—or, perhaps one should say, the unreal.

If participatory action research is understood in such terms, then through their investigations, participatory action researchers may want to become especially sensitive to the ways in which their particular practices are *social practices* of material, symbolic, and social

- communication,
- production, and
- social organization,

which shape and are shaped by *social structures* in

- the cultural/symbolic realm,
- the economic realm, and
- the sociopolitical realm,

which shape and are shaped by the *social media* of

- language/discourses,
- work, and
- power,

which largely shape, but also can be shaped by, participants' *knowledge* expressed in their

- understandings,
- skills, and
- values,

which, in turn, shape and are shaped by their *social practices* of material, symbolic, and social

- communication,
- production, and
- social organization, and so on.

These relationships are represented diagrammatically in Figure 23.2.

Participatory action researchers might consider, for example, how their acts of communication, production, and social organization are intertwined and interrelated in the real and particular practices that connect them to others in the real situations in which they find themselves (e.g., communities, neighborhoods, families, schools, hospitals, other workplaces). They consider how, by collaboratively changing the ways in which they participate with others in these practices, they can change the *practices* themselves, their *understandings* of these practices, and the *situations* in which they live and work.

For many people, the image of the spiral of cycles of self-reflection (planning, acting and observing, reflecting, replanning, etc.) has become the dominant feature of action research as an

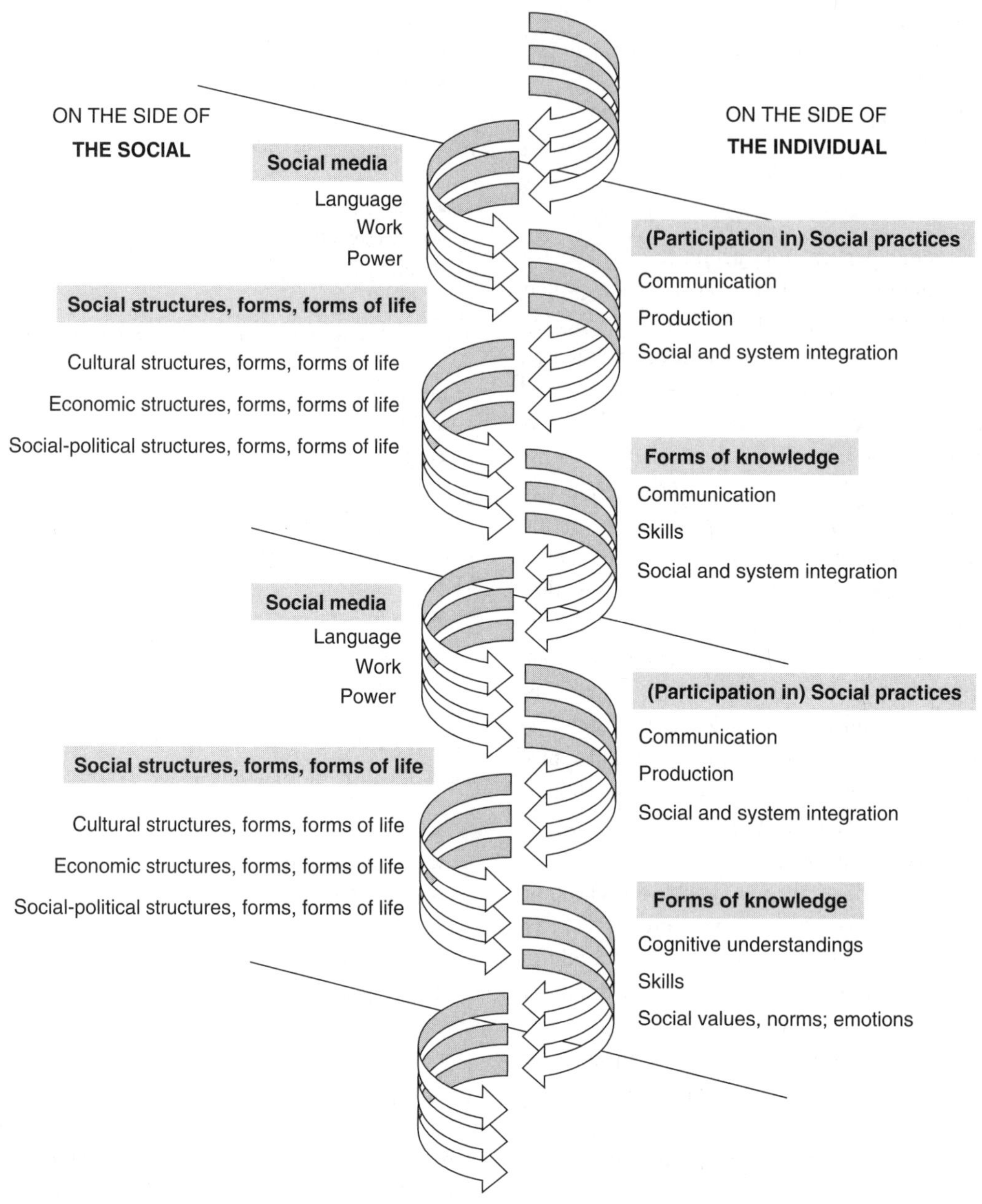

Figure 23.2. Recursive Relationships of Social Mediation That Action Research Aims to Transform

approach. In our view, participatory action research has seven other key features that are at least as important as the self-reflective spiral.

1. *Participatory action research is a social process.* Participatory action research deliberately explores *the relationship between the realms of the individual and the social.* It recognizes that "no individuation is possible without socialization, and no socialization is possible without individuation" (Habermas, 1992b, p. 26), and that the processes of individuation and socialization continue to shape individuals and social relationships in all of the settings in which we find ourselves.

Participatory action research is a process followed in research in settings such as those of education and community development, when people—individually and collectively—try to understand how they are formed and reformed as individuals, and in relation to one another in a variety of settings, for example, when teachers work together (or with students) to improve processes of teaching and learning in the classroom.

2. *Participatory action research is participatory.* Participatory action research engages people in examining their *knowledge* (understandings, skills, and values) and interpretive categories (the ways in which they interpret themselves and their action in the social and material world). It is a process in which all individuals in a group try to get a handle on the ways in which their knowledge shapes their sense of identity and agency and to reflect critically on how their current knowledge frames and constrains their action. It is also participatory in the sense that people can only do action research "on" themselves, either individually or collectively. It is *not* research done "on" others.

3. *Participatory action research is practical and collaborative.* Participatory action research engages people in examining the *social practices* that link them with others in social interaction. It is a process in which people explore their practices of communication, production, and social organization and try to explore how to improve their interactions by changing the acts that constitute them, that is, to reduce the extent to which participants experience these interactions (and their longer-term consequences) as irrational, unproductive (or inefficient), unjust, and/or unsatisfying (alienating). Participatory researchers aim to work together in reconstructing their social interactions by reconstructing the acts that constitute them.

4. *Participatory action research is emancipatory.* Participatory action research aims to help people recover, and release themselves from, the constraints of irrational, unproductive, unjust, and unsatisfying *social structures* that limit their self-development and self-determination. It is a process in which people explore the ways in which their practices are shaped and constrained by wider social (cultural, economic, and political) structures and consider whether they can intervene to release themselves from these constraints—or, if they cannot, how best to work within and around them to minimize the extent to which they contribute to irrationality, lack of productivity (inefficiency), injustice, and dissatisfactions (alienation) as people whose work and lives contribute to the structuring of a shared social life.

5. *Participatory action research is critical.* Participatory action research aims to help people recover, and release themselves from, the constraints embedded in the *social media* through which they interact—their language (discourses), their modes of work, and the social relationships of power (in which they experience affiliation and difference, inclusion and exclusion—relationships in which, grammatically speaking, they interact with others in the third, second, or first person). It is a process in which people deliberately set out to contest and reconstitute irrational, unproductive (or inefficient), unjust, and/or unsatisfying (alienating) ways of interpreting and describing their world (e.g., language, discourses), ways of working (work), and ways of relating to others (power).

6. *Participatory action research is reflexive (e.g., recursive, dialectical).* Participatory action research aims to help people to investigate reality in order to change it (Fals Borda, 1979) and (we might add) to change reality in order to investigate it. In particular, it is a deliberate process through which people aim to transform their practices through a spiral of cycles of critical and self-critical action and reflection. As Figure 23.2 (presented earlier) aims to show, it is a deliberate social process designed to help collaborating groups of people to transform their world so as to learn more about the nature of the recursive relationships among the following:

- Their (individual and social) *practices* (the work)
- Their *knowledge of their practices* (the workers)

- The *social structures* that shape and constrain their practices (the workplace)
- The *social media* in which their practices are expressed (the discourses in which their work is represented and misrepresented)

In our view, this is what theorizing practice means. Participatory action research does not, however, take an armchair view of theorizing; rather, it is a process of learning, with others, by doing—changing the ways in which we interact in a shared social world.

7. *Participatory action research aims to transform both theory and practice.* Participatory action research does not regard either theory or practice as preeminent in the relationship between theory and practice; rather, it aims to articulate and develop each in relation to the other through critical reasoning about both theory and practice and their consequences. It does not aim to develop forms of theory that can stand above and beyond practice, as if practice could be controlled and determined without regard to the particulars of the practical situations that confront practitioners in their ordinary lives and work. Nor does it aim to develop forms of practice that might be regarded as self-justifying, as if practice could be judged in the absence of theoretical frameworks that give them their value and significance and that provide substantive criteria for exploring the extent to which practices and their consequences turn out to be irrational, unjust, alienating, or unsatisfying for the people involved in and affected by them. Thus, participatory action research involves "reaching out" from the specifics of particular situations, as understood by the people within them, to explore the potential of different perspectives, theories, and discourses that might help to illuminate particular practices and practical settings as a basis for developing critical insights and ideas about how things might be transformed. Equally, it involves "reaching in" from the standpoints provided by different perspectives, theories, and discourses to explore the extent to which they provide practitioners themselves with a critical grasp of the problems and issues they actually confront in specific local situations. Thus, participatory action research aims to transform *both* practitioners' theories and practices *and* the theories and practices of others whose perspectives and practices may help to shape the conditions of life and work in particular local settings. In this way, participatory action research aims to connect the local and the global and to live out the slogan that the personal is political.

These seven features summarize some of the principal features of participatory action research as we see it. It is a particular partisan view. There are writers on action research who prefer to move immediately from a general description of the action research process (especially the self-reflective spiral) to questions of methodology and research technique—a discussion of the ways and means of collecting data in different social and educational settings. This is a somewhat methodologically driven view of action research; it suggests that research methods are what makes action research "research." This is not to argue that participatory action researchers should not be capable of conducting sound research; rather, it is to emphasize that sound research must respect much more than the canons of method.

Myths, Misinterpretations, and Mistakes in Critical Participatory Action Research

The critical view of participatory action research that we developed over the more than two decades since 1981 emerged in a practice that involved some successes; however, from the perspective of our current understandings, it also engendered some failures. Sometimes we, as well as some of our colleagues, mythologized or overstated the power of action research as an agent of individual and social change. Sometimes we misinterpreted our own experience and the ways in which substantive and methodological literatures might be useful pedagogically. Sometimes others misinterpreted our views, occasionally even despite our stout disavowal. The repeated reference to the action research spiral as "*the method* of action research" continues to frustrate us. We also made some mistakes. These myths, misinterpretations, and mistakes clustered around four key foci:

- Exaggerated assumptions about how *empowerment* might be achieved through action research
- Confusions about the role of those helping others to learn how to conduct action research, the problem of *facilitation,* and the illusion of neutrality
- The falsity of a supposed *research–activism dualism,* with research seen as dispassionate, informed, and rational and with activism seen as passionate, intuitive, and weakly theorized
- Understatement of the *role of the collective* and how it might be conceptualized in conducting the research and in formulating action in the "project" and in its engagement with the "public sphere" in all facets of institutional and social life

We present these reflections on our practices here and return to them later from a different theoretical perspective.

Empowerment

In our earliest work on action research, we argued that self-reflection on efforts to bring about change that was disciplined by group planning and reflection of observations would give participants a greater sense of control of their work. Sometimes we overstated our claims; we were victims of our own enthusiasm and persuasion. This was not always unconscious. We faced the dilemma of the advocate; that is, rhetoric can help lead to changes in reality. Our aspirations were often picked up by others, and the result left action research advocates vulnerable to charges of hyperbole or naïveté in real settings where individual and collective change often proved to be extremely difficult to effect.

It is true that an increased understanding of social situations through action materially changes individual power, authority, and control over people's work. However, it is equally true that such change is often technical and constrained, invoking concepts such as "efficiency." Authentic change, and the empowerment that drives it and derives from it, requires political sustenance by some kind of collective, too easily construed as an "action group" that defined itself by opposition to, and distinctiveness from, a wider social or public realm. Nevertheless, it was a mistake not to emphasize sufficiently that power comes from collective commitment and a methodology that invites the democratization of the objectification of experience and the disciplining of subjectivity. A question remains as to whether this was an adequate conceptualization of "empowerment," the way in which to achieve it, or indeed who or what empowerment was for.

The Role of the Facilitator of Action Research

We were troubled by the concept of "facilitation" as early as 1981 at the Australian National Seminar on Action Research (Brown, Henry, Henry, & McTaggart, 1988). Too often the facilitator lapsed into the role of "process consultant" with pretensions or aspirations to expertise about a "method" of action research, a role quite inconsistent with the commitment to participate in the personal and social changes in practice that had brought participants together. Despite efforts to contain the concept then, and to disavow its utility and outline its dangers later, it was a mistake to perpetuate the use of a term that already carried connotations of neutrality. Although the role of university researchers in action research is always somewhat problematic and an important object of critique, conceptualizing facilitation as a neutral or merely technical activity denies the social responsibility of the facilitator in making or assisting social change (McTaggart, 2002). The emphasis on techniques of facilitation also overplayed the importance of academic researchers and implicitly differentiated the work of theoreticians and practitioners, academics and workers, and community developers and peasant workers. Preoccupation with neutrality sustained the positivistic myth of the researcher as detached secretary to the universe and focused attention on the social practices (and research practices) of "the other." This in turn helped to make action research look like research for amateurs.

University professors often play an active role in action research. In the education field, for example, they are often teacher educators as well as researchers. Teacher education is just one "subpractice" of *education* as a social practice and, of course, is not practiced exclusively by university professors. In education, there are also curriculum practices, policy and administration practices, and research and evaluation practices. There is also a variety of student learning practices and community and parent participation practices that help to constitute the practice of education. Similarly, in action research for community development in some parts of the world, outside researchers have often been indispensable advocates and *animateurs* of change and not just technical advisers. It is clear to us that some of these *animateurs* have been heroes in social transformation, and we must acknowledge that many have lost their lives because of their work with dispossessed and disempowered people and communities, struggling with them for justice and democracy against repressive social and economic conditions.

Apart from these moral and political reasons against seeing facilitation as a merely technical role, there are reasons of epistemology. Emphasis on facilitation as a neutral role blinds one to the manifoldness of practice, that is, to the constitution of practice through the knowledge of individuals and a range of extraindividual features, including its social, discursive, moral, and political aspects as well as its historical formation such as the way in which it is shaped and reshaped in traditions of practice (Kemmis, 2004). Seeing facilitation in neutral terms also blinds one to the way in which practice is constituted as a "multiple reality" that is perceived differently by different participants in and observers of practice (e.g., professionals, clients, clients' families and friends, interested observers). Thus, seeing the role of facilitation as a neutral role obscures key aspects of practices and impedes critique of the way in which practices may sustain and daily reconstitute social realities whose character and consequences can be unjust, irrational, unproductive, and unsatisfactory for some of the people involved in or affected by them.

This leads us to the nub of a problem. What is the shared conceptual space that allows the intrication of these subpractices of broad social practices, such as education, health, agriculture, and transportation, to become the object of critique and the subject of enhancement? To understand how these subpractices are constitutive of lived social realities requires what Freire called *conscientization,* that is, the development of an informed critical perspective on social life among ordinary people or, to put it another way, the development of a critical theory of social life by the people who participate in it.

The Research–Activism Dualism

We find significant understatement of the role of theory and theory building in the literature of action research. The causes of this are complex. On the one hand, they include the difficulties associated with group members introducing theoretical concepts and experience of similar cases that are too difficult or confronting for other participants (McTaggart & Garbutcheon-Singh, 1986). On the other hand, they include the difficulties of ignoring or oversimplifying pertinent theoretical resources without which participants may be obliged to construe their own problems or concerns as if in a vacuum, isolating them from useful intellectual and discursive resources and sometimes leaving them vulnerable to charges of mere navel gazing. This is compounded by thinking in terms of a theory–action (thinking–activism) dualism. Thinking about unsatisfactory conditions is less confronting than actually changing them, and some take refuge in the view that political action is somehow less rational than thinking or talking about change. We reject this dualism; on the contrary, our experience suggests that there should be both more theory and more action in action research. Political activism should be theoretically informed just like any other social practice. Although action research is often incremental in the sense that it encourages growth and development in participants' expertise, support, commitment, confidence, knowledge of the situation, and understanding of what is prudent (i.e., changed thinking), it also encourages growth and development in participants' capacity for action, including direct and substantial collective action that is well justified by the demands of local conditions, circumstances, and consequences.

The Role of the Collective

The idea of the action research *group* is typically credited to Lewin immediately after World War II, although it may be that Moreno pioneered the practice a generation earlier (Altrichter & Gstettner, 1997). It was Lewin who argued the potency of "group commitment" in bringing about changes in social practices. In more recent views of action research, the "collective" is seen as supporting three important functions. First, it is seen as an expression of the democratization of scientific practice. Instead of deferring to the pronouncements of professional experts, a local scientific community is established to use principles of scientific inquiry to enhance and create richer local understandings. We have referred to this process as the "objectification of experience." Two further roles of the collective are expressed in the idea of the "disciplining of subjectivity," where subjectivity refers to an *affective* aspect, the emotional reactions of participants, and an aspect of political *agency.* In the affective aspect of subjectivity, the action research process creates opportunities for feelings to be made accessible and explored. At the same time, it creates opportunities for the way in which people feel about their situations to be examined for deeper causes and meanings and for participants to differentiate serious and abiding concerns from transient or peripheral reactions to immediate difficulties. Again, this work is not simply the preserve of the scientific or professional specialist group therapist or facilitator; on the contrary, in participatory action research, it must be part of a social process of transformation (of selves as well as situations) that is comprehensible to participants. Participants play a supportive role, but the collective has a disciplining function, helping to clarify thinking and providing a context where affect as well as cognitive questions can be justified. People come to realize that some feelings are superficial, misdirected, unfair, and overreactions. Other feelings are focused, strengthened, and nurtured as they are revealed, articulated, thought through, and reflected on. This is introspective in part, but its aim is refined action.

Political agency is a corollary of heightened understanding and motivation. As affect becomes mobilized and organized, and as experience is more clearly objectified and understood, both knowledge and feeling become articulated and disciplined by the collective toward prudent action. Individual action is increasingly informed and planned with the support and wisdom of others directly participating in related action in a situation. The collective provides critical support for the development of personal political agency and critical mass for a commitment to change. Through these interactions, new forms of practical consciousness emerge. In other words, both the action and research aspects of action research *require* participation as well as the disciplining effect of a collective.

The extension of action research collectives to include "critical friends," to build alliances with broader social movements, and to extend membership across institutional hierarchies has been a way of enhancing the understanding and political efficacy of individuals and groups. However, the problem of how to create the conditions of learning for participants persists. People not only are hemmed in by material institutional conditions, they frequently are trapped in institutional discourses that channel, deter, or muffle critique. How do we create (or re-create) new possibilities for what Fals Borda (1988) called *vivéncia,* through the revitalization of the public sphere, and also promote decolonization of lifeworlds that have become saturated with the bureaucratic discourses, routinized practices, and institutionalized forms of social relationships characteristic of social systems that see the world only through the prism of organization and not the human and humane living of social lives? This is an issue that we have now come to interpret through the notion of public discourse in public spheres and the idea of research as a social practice.

Participatory Action Research and the Study of Practice

In our chapter on participatory action research for the second edition of this *Handbook,* we outlined five traditions in the study of practice. We argued that *research on practice* is itself a practice and that the practice of research on practice has historically taken, and continues to take, different forms. Different practitioners of research on practice see it more from the perspective of the *individual* and/or the *social* and more from an "*objective*" perspective and/or a "*subjective*" perspective. They use different research methods and techniques that reflect these epistemological and ontological choices, that is, choices about what it means to *know* a practice (the epistemological choice) and about what a practice *is* and thus how it manifests itself in reality (the ontological choice). If research on practice is *methodologically defined,* however, researchers may obscure, even from themselves, the epistemological and ontological choices that underpin their choices of methods. As ways of "seeing" practice, research methods both illuminate and obscure what the research and the researcher can see. As Ludwig Wittgenstein noticed, this may involve a "conjuring trick" that obscures the very thing we hoped to see:

> How does the philosophical problem about mental processes and states and about behaviourism arise? The first step is the one that altogether escapes notice. We talk of processes and states and leave their nature undecided. Sometime perhaps we shall know more about them—we think. But that is just what commits us to a particular way of looking at the matter. For we have a definite concept of what it means to learn to know a process better. (The decisive movement in the conjuring trick has been made, and it was the very one that we thought quite innocent.) And now the analogy which was to make us understand our thoughts falls to pieces. So we have to deny the yet uncomprehended process in the yet unexplored medium. And now it looks as if we had denied mental processes. And naturally we don't want to deny them. (Wittgenstein, 1958, p. 103)

We conclude, therefore, that it is risky to proceed in a discussion of research on practice principally *from* research methods and techniques—risky because the methods we choose may inadvertently have "committed us to a particular way of seeing the matter."

In our chapter in the second edition of this *Handbook,* we depicted the relationships among five broad traditions in the study of practice. Table 23.1 summarizes these traditions.

We argued that these different approaches to the study of practice involved different kinds of relationships between *the researcher* and *the researched.* Essentially, we argued that "objective" approaches tended to see practice from the perspective of an outsider in the *third person;* that "subjective" approaches tended to see practice from the perspective of an insider in the *second person;* and that the reflexive dialectical perspective of critical social science tended to see practice from the perspective of the insider group, whose members' interconnected activities constitute and reconstitute their own social practices, in the *first person* (plural). This last perspective on practice is the one taken by participant-researchers in participatory action research.

In terms of these five aspects of practice and the five traditions in the study of practice, it seems to us that a methodologically driven view of participatory action research finds itself mired in the assumptions about practice to which one or another of the different traditions of research on practice is committed. Depending on which of these sets of presuppositions it adopts, it may find itself unable to approach (the study of) practice in a sufficiently rich and multifaceted way, that is, in terms that recognize different aspects of practice and do justice to its social, historical, and discursive construction.

If participatory action research is to explore practice in terms of each of the five aspects

Table 23.1. Relationships Among Different Traditions in the Study of Practice

Perspective	*The Individual*	*The Social*	*Both: Reflexive–dialectical view of individual–social relations and connections*
Objective	(1) Practice as individual behavior, seen in terms of performances, events, and effects: Behaviorist and most cognitivist approaches in psychology	(2) Practice as social interaction (e.g., ritual, system-structured): Structure-functionalist and social systems approaches	
Subjective	(3) Practice as intentional action, shaped by meaning and values: Psychological *verstehen* (empathetic understanding) and most constructivist approaches	(4) Practice as socially structured, shaped by discourses, tradition: Interpretive, aesthetic-historical *verstehen* (empathetic understanding), and poststructuralist approaches	
Both: Reflexive–dialectical view of subjective–objective relations and connections			(5) Practice as socially and historically constituted and as reconstituted by human agency and social action: Critical methods; dialectical analysis (multiple methods)

outlined in our chapter in the second edition of this *Handbook,* it will need to consider how different traditions in the study of practice, and different research methods and techniques, can provide *multiple* resources for the task. It must also avoid accepting the assumptions and limitations of particular methods and techniques. For example, the participatory action researcher may legitimately eschew the narrow empiricism of those approaches that attempt to construe practice entirely "objectively," as if it were possible to exclude consideration of participants' subjective intentions, meanings, values, and interpretive categories from an understanding of practice or as if it were possible to exclude consideration of the frameworks of language, discourse, and tradition by which people in different groups construe their practices. It does not follow from this that quantitative approaches are never relevant in participatory action research; on the contrary, they may be—but without the constraints of empiricism and objectivism that many quantitative researchers put on these methods and techniques. Indeed, when quantitative researchers use questionnaires to convert participants' views into numerical data, they tacitly concede that practice cannot be understood without taking participants' views into account. Participatory researchers will differ from one-sidedly quantitative researchers in the ways in which they collect and use such data because participatory action researchers will regard them as crude approximations of the ways in which participants understand themselves and not (as empiricistic, objectivistic, quantitative researchers may assert) as more rigorous (e.g., valid, reliable) because they are scaled.

On the other hand, the participatory action researcher will differ from the one-sidedly qualitative approach that asserts that action can be understood only from a qualitative perspective, for example, through close clinical or phenomenological analysis of an individual's views or close analysis of the discourses and traditions that shape the way in which a particular practice is understood by participants. The participatory action researcher will also want to explore how changing "objective" circumstances (e.g., performances, events, effects, patterns of interaction, rules, roles, system functioning) shape and are shaped by the "subjective" conditions of participants' perspectives.

In our view, questions of research methods should not be regarded as unimportant, but (in contrast with the methodologically driven view) we would want to assert that what makes participatory action research "research" is not the machinery of research techniques but rather an abiding concern with the relationships between social and educational theory and practice. In our view, before questions about what kinds of research methods are appropriate can be decided, it is necessary to decide what kinds of things "practice" and "theory" are, for only then can we decide what kinds of data or evidence might be relevant in describing practice and what kinds of analyses might be relevant in interpreting and evaluating people's real practices in the real situations in which they work. On this view of participatory action research, a central question is how practices are to be understood "in the field," as it were, so that they become available for more systematic theorizing. Having arrived at a general view of what it means to understand (theorize) practice in the field, it becomes possible to work out what kinds of evidence, and hence what kinds of research methods and techniques, might be appropriate for advancing our understanding of practice at any particular time.

The theoretical scheme depicted in Figure 23.2 takes a view of what theorizing a practice might be like—locating practice within frameworks of participants' knowledge, in relation to social structures, and in terms of social media. By adopting a more encompassing view of practice like the one outlined in Table 23.1, we may be able to understand and theorize it more richly, and in more complex ways, so that powerful social dynamics (e.g., the tensions and interconnections between system and lifeworld [Habermas 1984, 1987b]) can be construed and reconstituted through a critical social practice such as participatory action research.

The participants in participatory action research understand practice from *both* its individual and its social aspects and understand it *both* objectively and subjectively. They view practice as constructed and reconstructed *historically* both in terms of the *discourses* in which practices are described and understood and in terms of socially and historically constructed *actions and their consequences.* Moreover, they view practice as constituted and reconstituted in *human and social action* that projects a living past through the lived present into a future where the people involved and affected will live with the consequences of actions taken.

This view of practice as *projected through history by action* applies not only to the "first-level" practices that are the object and subject of participants' interests (e.g., the practices of economic life in a village aiming at community development) but also to the practice of research itself. Participants in participatory action research understand their research practices as *meta-practices* that help to construct and reconstruct the first-level practices they are investigating. For example, participants in a participatory action research project on practices of community development (the first-level practices) understand their research practices as among the meta-practices that shape their practices of community development. Practices of management, administration, and social integration are also meta-practices shaping their practices of community development. However, unlike those other meta-practices, the meta-practice of participatory action research is deliberately and systematically reflexive. It is both outwardly directed and inwardly (self-) directed. It aims to change community development practitioners, community development practices, and the practice situations of community development through practices of research that are also malleable and developmental and that, through collaborative processes of communication and learning, change the practitioners, practices, and practice situations of the research. Like other practices, the practices of participatory action research are projected through history by action. They are meta-practices that aim to transform the world so that other first-level transformations become possible, that is, transformations in people's ways of thinking and talking, ways of doing things, and ways of relating to one another.

This view of *research practices* as specifically located in time (history) and social space has implications that are explored later in this chapter. In the process of participatory action research, the same people are involved in two parallel, reflexively related sets of practices. On the one hand, they are the practitioners of community development (to use our earlier example); on the other hand, they are the practitioners of the meta-practice of participatory action research. They are *both practitioners and researchers* in, say, community development, the development of primary health care, or school–community relations. They understand their research as "engaged research" (Bourdieu & Wacquant, 1992) through which they, as researchers, aim to *transform* practices of community development, primary health care, or school–community relations. But they also understand their research practices as constructed and open to reconstruction. They do not regard the research process as the application of fixed and preformed research techniques to the particular "applied" problem with which they are concerned. On the contrary, they regard their research practices as a matter of borrowing, constructing, and reconstructing research methods and techniques to throw light on the nature, processes, and consequences of the particular object they are studying (whether community development practices, primary health care practices, or practices of school–community relations). And this means that participatory action researchers are embarked on a process of transforming themselves as researchers, transforming their research practices, and transforming the practice settings of their research.

In our chapter in the second edition of this *Handbook,* we also argued for a view of research that we termed "symposium research," that is, research drawing on the multiple disciplinary perspectives of different traditions in social science theorizing and multiple research methods that illuminate different aspects of practices. We believe that this approach will increasingly come to characterize participatory action research inquiries. That is, we expect that as participatory action research becomes more sophisticated in its scope and intentions, it will draw on transdisciplinary theoretical resources (e.g., relevant psychological and sociological theories) and multiple research methods and techniques that will allow participant-researchers to gain insight into the formation and transformation of their practices in context. For example, we expect to see more participatory action research using research techniques characteristic of all five of the traditions depicted in Table 23.1. These methods and techniques are presented in Table 23.2.

In the current edition of the *Handbook,* we argue that the nature of the social relationships involved in participatory action research—and the proper politics of participatory action research—can be more clearly understood from the perspective of Habermas's (1984, 1987a) *theory of communicative action* and, in particular, his later commentary on the nature of the *public sphere,* as outlined in *Between Facts and Norms* (Habermas, 1996, chap. 8).

▣ The Politics of Participatory Action Research: Communicative Action and the Public Sphere

In his book *Theory of Communicative Action,* and especially the second volume, Habermas (1984, 1987b) described communicative action as what people do when they engage in communication of a particular—and widespread—kind, with three particular features. It is communication in which people consciously and deliberately aim

Table 23.2. Methods and Techniques Characteristic of Different Approaches to the Study of Practice

Perspective	*The Individual*	*The Social*	*Both: Reflexive–dialectical view of individual–social relations and connections*
Objective	(1) Practice as individual behavior: Quantitative and correlational–experimental methods; psychometric and observational techniques, tests, and interaction schedules	(2) Practice as social and systems behavior: Quantitative and correlational–experimental methods; observational techniques, sociometrics, systems analysis, and social ecology	
Subjective	(3) Practice as intentional action: Qualitative and interpretive methods; clinical analysis, interview, questionnaire, diaries, journals, self-report, and introspection	(4) Practice as socially structured, shaped by discourses and tradition: Qualitative, interpretive, and historical methods; discourse analysis and document analysis	
Both: Reflexive–dialectical view of subjective–objective relations and connections			(5) Practice as socially and historically constituted and as reconstituted by human agency and social action: Critical methods; dialectical analysis (multiple methods)

1. to reach *intersubjective agreement* as a basis for
2. *mutual understanding* so as to
3. reach an *unforced consensus about what to do* in the particular practical situation in which they find themselves.

Communicative action is the kind of action that people take when they interrupt what they are doing (Kemmis, 1998) to ask four particular kinds of questions (the four validity claims):

- Whether their understandings of what they are doing *make sense* to them and to others (are *comprehensible*)
- Whether these understandings are *true* (in the sense of being *accurate* in accordance with what else is known)
- Whether these understandings are *sincerely held and stated* (authentic)
- Whether these understandings are *morally right and appropriate* under the circumstances in which they find themselves

In *Between Facts and Norms,* Habermas (1996) added a fourth feature to the original list of three features of communicative action. He noticed something obvious that previously had been overlooked, namely that communicative action also *opens communicative space* between people. He gave this fourth feature of communicative action special attention because he considered that opening space for communicative action produces two particular and simultaneous effects. First, it builds *solidarity* between the people who open their understandings to one another in this kind of communication. Second, it underwrites the understandings and decisions that people reach with *legitimacy.* In a world where communications are frequently cynical, and where people feel alienated from public decisions and even from the political processes of their world, legitimacy is hard-won. More important for our purposes here, however, Habermas's argument is that *legitimacy is guaranteed only through communicative action,* that is, when people are free to choose—authentically and for themselves, individually and in the context of mutual participation—to decide *for themselves* the following:

- What is comprehensible to *them* (whether in fact they understand what others are saying)
- What is true in the light of *their own* knowledge (both their individual knowledge and the shared knowledge represented in the discourse used by members)
- What participants *themselves* regard as sincerely and truthfully stated (individually and in terms of their joint commitment to understanding)
- What participants *themselves* regard as morally right and appropriate in terms of their individual and mutual judgment about what it is right, proper, and prudent to do under the circumstances in which they find themselves

What is projected here is not an ideal against which actual communications and utterances are to be judged; rather, it is something that Habermas believes we normally take for granted about utterances—unless they are deliberately distorted or challenged. In ordinary speech, we may or may not regard any particular utterance as suspect on the grounds of any or all of the four validity claims; whether any particular utterance will be regarded as suspect or needing closer critical examination will depend on "who is saying what about what to whom in what context." On the other hand, when we move into the mode of *communicative action,* we acknowledge at the outset that we must strive for intersubjective agreement, mutual understanding, and unforced consensus about what to do in this particular situation because we already know that one or all four of the validity claims must be regarded as problematic—by *us* here and now, for our situation, and in relation to what to do in practice about the matter at hand. That is, the validity claims do not function merely as *procedural* ideals for critiquing speech; they also function as bases for, or underpinnings of, the *substantive* claims we need to explore to reach mutual agreement, understanding, and consensus about what to do in the *particular* concrete situation in which a particular group of people in a shared socially, discursively, and historically structured specific communicative space are deliberating together.

What we notice here, to reiterate, is that the process of recovering and critiquing validity claims is not merely an abstract ideal or principle but also an invocation of critique and critical self-awareness in *concrete* and *practical* decision making. In a situation where we are genuinely acting collaboratively with others, and where practical reason is genuinely called for, we are obliged, as it were, to "retreat" to a meta-level of critique—communicative action—because it is *not* self-evident what should be done. Perhaps we simply do not comprehend what is being talked about or we are not sure that we understand it correctly. Perhaps we are unsure of the truth or accuracy of the facts on which our decisions might be based. Perhaps we fear that deliberate deception or accidental self-deception may lead us astray. Perhaps we are not sure what it is morally right and appropriate to do in this practical situation in which our actions will, as always, be judged by their historical consequences (and their differential consequences for different people and groups). In any of these cases, we need to consider how to approach the practical decision before us, and we must gather our shared understandings to do so. In such cases, we interrupt what we are doing to move into the mode of communicative action. In some such cases, we may also move into the slower, more concretely practical, and more concretely critical mode of participatory action research, aiming deliberately and collaboratively to investigate the world in order to transform it, as Fals Borda observed, and to transform the world in order to investigate it. We take a problematic view of our own action in history and use our action in history as a "probe" with which to investigate reflexively our own action and its place as cause and effect in the unfolding history of our world.

Participatory Action Research and Communicative Space

In our view, *participatory action research opens communicative space* between participants. The process of participatory action research is one of *mutual inquiry* aimed at reaching intersubjective agreement, mutual understanding of a situation, unforced consensus about what to do, and a sense that what people achieve together will be *legitimate* not only for themselves but also for every reasonable person (a universal claim). Participatory action research aims to create circumstances in which people can search together collaboratively for more comprehensible, true, authentic, and morally right and appropriate ways of understanding and acting in the world. It aims to create circumstances in which *collaborative social action* in history is not justified by appeal to authority (and still less to coercive force); rather, as Habermas put it, it is justified by the force of better argument.

To make these points is to notice three things about the social relations engendered through the process of action research. First, it is to notice that certain relationships are appropriate in the *research* element of the term "participatory action research." It is to notice that the social practice of this kind of research is *a practice directed deliberately toward discovering, investigating, and attaining* intersubjective agreement, mutual understanding, and unforced consensus about what to do. It is aimed at testing, developing, and retesting agreements, understandings, and decisions against the criteria of mutual comprehensibility, truth, truthfulness (e.g., sincerity, authenticity), and moral rightness and appropriateness. In our view, *participatory action research projects communicative action into the field of action and the making of history.* It does so in a deliberately critical and reflexive way; that is, it aims to change both our unfolding history and ourselves as makers of our unfolding history. As science, participatory action research is *not* to be understood as the kind of science that gathers knowledge as a precursor to and resource for controlling the unfolding of events (the technical knowledge-constitutive interest characteristic of positivistic social science [Habermas, 1972]). Nor is it to be understood as the kind of science directed toward educating the person to be a wiser and more prudent actor in as yet unspecified situations and circumstances (the practical knowledge-constitutive interest characteristic of hermeneutics and interpretive social science [Habermas, 1972]). Participatory action research is to be understood as a collaborative practice of critique, performed in and through a collaborative practice of research that aims to change the researchers themselves as well as the social world they inhabit (the emancipatory knowledge-constitutive interest characteristic of critical social science [Carr & Kemmis, 1986; Habermas, 1972]).

Second, it is to notice that similar relationships are appropriate in the *action* element of participatory action research. It is to notice that the decisions on which action is based must first have withstood the tests of the research element and must then withstand the tests of wisdom and prudence—that people are willing to, and indeed can, reasonably live with the consequences of the decisions they make, and the actions they take, and the actions that follow from these decisions. This is to notice that participatory action research generates not only a collaborative sense of agency but also a collaborative sense of the *legitimacy* of the decisions people make, and the actions they take, together.

Third, it is to notice that participatory action research involves relationships of *participation* as a central and defining feature and not as a kind of instrumental or contingent value tacked on to the term. In many views of action research, including some of our earliest advocacies for it, the idea of "participation" was thought to refer to an action research group whose members had reached an agreement to research and act together on some shared topic or problem. This view caused us to think in terms of "insiders" and "outsiders" to the group and to the action research process. Such a view carries resonances of discussions of the role of the avant-garde in making the revolution. It suggests that the action research group constitutes itself *against* established authorities or ways of working, as if it were the role of the group to show how things can and should be done better despite the constraints and exigencies of taken-for-granted ways of doing things.

The idea of participation as central to participatory action research is not so easily enclosed and encapsulated. The notion of *inclusion* evoked in participatory action research should not, in our view, be regarded as static or fixed. Participatory action research should, in principle, create circumstances in which all of those involved in and affected by the processes of research and action (all of those involved in thought and action as well as theory and practice) about the topic have a right to speak and act in transforming things for the better. It is to say that, in the case of, for example, a participatory action research project about education, it is not only teachers who have the task of improving the social practices of schooling but also students and many others (e.g., parents, school communities, employers of graduates). It is to say that, in projects concerned with community development, not only lobby groups of concerned citizens but also local government agencies and many others will have a share in the consequences of actions taken and, thus, a right to be heard in the formation of programs of action.

In reality, of course, not all involved and affected people will participate in any particular participatory action research project. Some may resist involvement, some might not be interested because their commitments are elsewhere, and some might not have the means to join and contribute to the project as it unfolds. The point is that a participatory action research project that aims to transform existing ways of understanding, existing social practices, and existing situations must also transform other people and agencies who might not "naturally" be participants in the processes of doing the research and taking action. *In principle,* participatory action research issues an invitation to previously or naturally uninvolved people, as well as a self-constituted action research group, to participate in a common process of *communicative action for transformation.* Not all will accept the invitation, but it is incumbent on those who do participate to take into account those others' understandings, perspectives, and interests—even if the decision is to oppose them in the service of a broader public interest.

Participatory Action Research and the Critique of the "Social Macro-Subject"

As these comments suggest, participatory action research does not—or need not—valorize a particular *group* as the carrier of legitimate political action. In his critique of the "social macro-subject" in *The Philosophical Discourse of Modernity* and *Between Facts and Norms,* Habermas (1987a, 1996) argued that political theory has frequently been led astray by the notion that a state or an organization can be autonomous and self-regulating in any clear sense. The circumstances of late modernity are such, he argued, that it is simplistic and mistaken to imagine that the machinery of government or management is unified and capable of self-regulation in any simple sense of "self." Governments and the machinery of government, and managements and the machinery of contemporary organizations, are nowadays so complex, multifaceted, and (often) internally contradictory as "systems" that they do not operate in any autonomous way, let alone in any way that could be regarded as self-regulating in relation to the publics they aim to govern or manage. They are not unified systems but rather complex sets of subsystems having transactions of various kinds with one another economically (in the steering medium of money) and administratively (in the steering medium of power). *Between Facts and Norms* is a critique of contemporary theories of law and government that are based on concrete, historically outmoded notions of governmentality that presume a single, more or less unified body politic that is regulated by law and a constitution. Such theories presume that governments can encapsulate and impose order on a social body as a unified whole across many dimensions of social, political, cultural, and individual life or lives. Many of those who inhabit the competing subsystems of contemporary government and management in fact acknowledge that no such simple steering is possible; on the contrary, steering takes place—to the extent that it can happen at all—through an indeterminate array of established practices, structures, systems of influence, bargaining, and coercive powers.

The same is true of participatory action research groups. When they conceive of themselves as closed and self-regulating, they may lose contact with social reality. In fact, participatory action research groups are internally diverse, they generally have no unified "center" or core from which their power and authority can emanate, and they frequently have little capacity to achieve their own ends if they must contend with the will of other powers and orders. Moreover, participatory action research groups connect and interact with various kinds of external people, groups, and agencies. In terms of thought and action, and of theory and practice, they arise and act out of, and back into, the wider social reality that they aim to transform.

The most morally, practically, and politically compelling view of participatory action research is one that sees participatory action research as a practice through which people can create networks of communication, that is, sites for the practice of communicative action. It offers the prospect of opening communicative space in public spheres of the kind that Habermas described. Based on such a view, participatory action research aims to engender practical critiques of existing states of affairs, the development of critical perspectives, and the shared formation of emancipatory commitments, that is, commitments to overcome distorted ways of understanding the world, distorted practices, and distorted social arrangements and situations. (By "distorted" here, we mean understandings, practices, and situations whose consequences are unsatisfying, ineffective, or unjust for some or all of those involved and affected.)

Communicative Action and Exploratory Action

Participatory action research creates a communicative space in which communicative action is fostered among participants and in which problems and issues can be thematized for critical exploration aimed at overcoming felt dissatisfactions (Fay, 1987), irrationality, and injustice. It also fosters a kind of "playfulness" about action—what to do. At its best, it creates opportunities for participants to adopt a thoughtful but highly exploratory view of what to do, knowing that their practice can and will be "corrected" in the light of what they learn from their careful observation of the processes and consequences of their action as it unfolds. This seems to us to involve a new kind of understanding of the notion of communicative action. It is not just "reflection" or "reflective practice" (e.g., as advocated by Schön, 1983, 1987, 1991) but also action taken with the principal purpose of learning from experience by careful observation of its processes and consequences. It is deliberately designed as an *exploration* of ways of doing things in this particular situation at this particular historical moment. It is designed to be *exploratory action.*

Participatory action research is scientific and reflective in the sense in which John Dewey described "scientific method." Writing in *Democracy and Education,* Dewey (1916) described the essentials of reflection—and scientific method—as follows:

> They are, first, that the pupil has a genuine situation of experience—that there be a continuous activity in which he is interested for its own sake; secondly, that a genuine problem develop within this situation as a stimulus to thought; third, that he possess the information and make the observations needed to deal with it; fourth, that suggested solutions occur to him which he shall be responsible for developing in an orderly way; fifth, that he shall have the opportunity and occasion to test his ideas by application, to make their meaning clear, and to discover for himself their validity. (p. 192)

For Dewey, experience and intelligent action were linked in a cycle. Education, like science, was to aim not just at filling the minds of students but also at helping them to take their place in a democratic society ceaselessly reconstructing and transforming the world through action. Intelligent action was always experimental and exploratory, conducted with an eye to learning and as an opportunity to learn from unfolding experience.

In our view, participatory action research is an elaboration of this idea. It is exploratory action that parallels and builds on the notion of communicative action. It does more than conduct its reflection in the rear-view mirror, as it were, looking backward at what has happened to learn from it. It also generates and conducts action in an exploratory and experimental manner, with actions themselves standing as practical hypotheses or speculations to be tested as their consequences emerge and unfold.

Constituting Public Spheres for Communicative Action Through Participatory Action Research

Baynes (1995), writing on Habermas and democracy, quoted Habermas on the *public sphere:*

> [Deliberative politics] is bound to the demanding communicative presuppositions of political arenas that do not coincide with the institutionalized will-formation in parliamentary bodies but extend equally to the political public sphere and to its cultural context and social basis. A deliberative practice of self-determination can develop only in the interplay between, on the one hand, the parliamentary will-formation institutionalized in legal procedures and programmed to reach decisions and, on the other, political opinion-building in informal circles of political communication. (p. 316).[1]

Baynes (1995) described Habermas's conceptualization of the "strong publics" of parliamentary and legal subsystems and the "weak publics" of the "public sphere ranging from private associations to the mass media located in 'civil society' . . . [which] assume responsibility for identifying and interpreting social problems" (pp. 216–217). Baynes added that, in this connection, Habermas "also describes the task of an opinion-forming public sphere as that of laying siege to the formally organized political system by encircling it with reasons without, however, attempting to overthrow or replace it" (p. 217).

In practice, this has been the kind of task that many action researchers, and especially participatory action researchers, have set for themselves—surrounding established institutions, laws, policies, and administrative arrangements (e.g., government departments) with *reasons* that, on the one hand, respond to contemporary crises or problems experienced "in the field" (in civil society) and, on the other, provide a rationale for changing current structures, policies, practices, procedures, or other arrangements that are implicit in causing or maintaining these crises or problems. In response to crises or problems experienced in particular places, participatory action researchers are frequently involved in community development projects and initiatives of various kinds, including community education, community economic development, raising political consciousness, and responding to "green" issues. In one sense, they see themselves as oppositional, that is, as protesting current structures and functions of economic and administrative systems. In another sense, although sometimes they are confrontational in their tactics, they frequently aim not to *overthrow* established authority or structures but rather to get them to *transform* their ways of working so that problems and crises can be overcome. As Baynes observed, their aim is to besiege authorities with *reasons* and not to destroy them. We might also say, however, that some of the reasons that participatory action researchers employ are the fruits of their practical experience in making change. They create *concrete contradictions* between established or current ways of doing things, on the one hand, and alternative ways that are developed through their investigations. They read and contrast the nature and consequences of existing ways of doing things with these alternative ways, aiming to show that irrationalities, injustices, and dissatisfactions associated with the former can be overcome *in practice* by the latter.

As we indicated earlier, the approach that participatory action researchers take to identified problems or crises is *to conduct research* as a basis for informing themselves and others about the problems or crises and to explore ways in which the problems or crises might be overcome. Their stock in trade is communicative action both internally, by opening dialogue within the group of researcher-participants, and externally, by opening dialogue with the powers-that-be about the nature of the problems or crises that participants experience in their own lives and about ways of changing social structures and practices to ease or overcome these problems or crises. Sometimes advocates of participatory action research (including ourselves) have misstated the nature of this oppositional role—seeing themselves as simply opposed to established *authorities* rather than as opposed to particular *structure*s or established *practices.* We recognize that in our own earlier advocacies, the language of "emancipation" was always ambiguous, permitting or encouraging the idea that the emancipation we sought was from the structures and systems of the state itself rather than, or as much as, emancipation from the real objects of our critique—self-deception, ideology, irrationality, and/or injustice (as our more judicious formulations described it).

Habermas's critique of the social macro-subject suggests that our formulation of the action group as a kind of avant-garde was always too wooden and rigid. It encouraged the notion that there were "insiders" and "outsiders" and that the insiders could be not only self-regulating and relatively autonomous but also effective in confronting a more or less unitary, self-regulating, and autonomous state or existing authority. That is, it seemed to presume an integrated (unconflicted) "core" and an integrated (unconflicted) political object to be changed as a consequence of the investigations undertaken by the action group. In reality, we saw action groups characterized by contradictions, contests, and conflicts within that were interacting with contradictory, contested, and conflict-ridden social structures without. Alliances shifted and changed both inside action groups and in the relations of members with structures and authorities in the wider social context of which they were a part. Indeed, many participatory action research projects came into existence *because* established structures and authorities wanted to explore possibilities for change in existing ways of doing things, even though the new ways would be in a contradictory relationship with the usual ways of operating.

This way of understanding participatory action research groups is more open-textured and fluid than our earlier advocacies suggested. In those advocacies, we imagined action groups as more tightly knotted, better integrated, and more "solid" than the way in which we see them now. Now we recognize the more open and fluid connections between "members" of action groups and between members and others in the wider social context in which their investigations take place.

Public Spheres

In *Between Facts and Norms,* Habermas (1996, chap. 8) outlined the kinds of conditions under which people can engage in communicative action in the contexts of social action and social movements. He set out to describe the nature of what he called *public spheres.* (Note that he did not refer solely to "the public sphere," which is an abstraction; rather, he referred to "public spheres," which are concrete and practical contexts for communication.) The public spheres that Habermas had in mind are *not* the kinds of communicative spaces of most of our social and political communication. Communication in very many political contexts (especially in the sense of *realpolitik*) is frequently distorted and disfigured by interest-based bargaining, that is, by people speaking and acting in ways that are guided by their own (self-) interests (even if they are shared political interests) in the service of their own (shared) particular goals and ends. We return to this in our discussion of participatory action research and communicative space later.

From Habermas's (1996, chap. 8) discussion in *Between Facts and Norms,* we identified 10 key features of public spheres as he defined them. In what follows, drawing on other recent work (Kemmis, 2004; Kemmis & Brennan Kemmis, 2003), we describe each of these features and then briefly indicate how critical participatory action research projects might exemplify each feature. From Kemmis and Brennan Kemmis (2003), we also present comments indicating how two kinds of social action projects displayed some of the characteristics of public discourses in public spheres, that is, how participatory action research work can create more open and fluid relationships than can the closed and somewhat mechanical notions sometimes associated with action research groups and methodologically driven characterizations of their work. To use this illustration, it is necessary to give a brief introduction to these examples. The first is an example of a participatory action research project in Yirrkala, Australia, during the late 1980s and 1990s. The second is an example of a large educational congress held in the Argentine Republic in 2003.

Example 1: The Yirrkala Ganma Education Project. During the late 1980s and 1990s, in the far north of Australia in the community of Yirrkala, North East Arnhem Land, Northern Territory, the Yolngu indigenous people wanted to change their schools.[2] They wanted to make their schools more appropriate for Yolngu children. Mandawuy Yunupingu, then deputy principal at the school and later lead singer of the pop group Yothu Yindi, wrote about the problem this way:

> Yolngu children have difficulties in learning areas of Balanda [white man's] knowledge. This is not because Yolngu cannot think, it is because the curriculum in the schools is not relevant for Yolngu children, and often these curriculum documents are developed by Balanda who are ethnocentric in their values. The way that Balanda people have institutionalised their way of living is through maintaining the social reproduction process where children are sent to school and they are taught to do things in a particular way. Often the things that they learn favour [the interests of] the rich and powerful, because when they leave school [and go to work] the control of the workforce is in the hands of the middle class and the upper class.
>
> An appropriate curriculum for Yolngu is one that is located in the Aboriginal world which can enable the children to cross over into the Balanda world. [It allows] for identification of bits of Balanda knowledge that are consistent with the Yolngu way of learning. (Yunupingu, 1991, p. 102)

The Yolngu teachers, together with other teachers and with the help of their community, began a journey of participatory action research. Working together, they changed the white man's world of schooling. Of course, sometimes there were conflicts and disagreements, but they worked through them in the Yolngu way—toward consensus. They had help but no money to conduct their research.

Their research was not research about schools and schooling *in general;* rather, their participatory action research was about how schooling was done in *their* schools. As Yunupingu (1991) put it,

> So here is a fundamental difference compared with traditional research about Yolngu education: We start with Yolngu knowledge and work out what comes from Yolngu minds as of central importance, not the other way [a]round. (pp. 102–103)

Throughout the process, the teachers were guided by their own collaborative research into their problems and practices. They gathered stories from the old people. They gathered information about how the school worked and did not work for them. They made changes and watched what happened. They thought carefully about the consequences of the changes they made, and then they made still further changes on the basis of the evidence they had gathered.

Through their shared journey of participatory action research, the school and the community discovered how to limit the culturally corrosive effects of the white man's way of schooling, and they learned to respect *both* Yolngu ways and the white man's ways. At first, the teachers called the new form of schooling "both ways education." Later, drawing on a sacred story from their own tradition, they called it "Ganma education."

Writing about his hopes for the Ganma research that the community conducted to develop the ideas and practices of Ganma education, Yunupingu (1991) observed,

> I am hoping the Ganma research will become critical educational research, that it will empower Yolngu, that it will emphasize emancipatory aspects, and that it will take a side—just as the

> Balanda research has always taken a side but never revealed this, always claiming to be neutral and objective. My aim in Ganma is to help, to change, to shift the balance of power.
>
> Ganma research is also critical in the processes we use. Our critical community of action researchers working together, reflecting, sharing, and thinking includes important Yolngu elders, the Yolngu action group [teachers in the school], Balanda teachers, and a Balanda researcher to help with the process. Of course, she is involved too; she cares about our problems, [and] she has a stake in finding solutions—this too is different from the traditional role of a researcher. (p. 103) . . .
>
> It is, I must stress, important to locate Ganma in our broader development plans . . . in the overall context of Aboriginalisation and control into which Ganma must fit. (p. 104)

Together, the teachers and the community found new ways in which to think about schools and schooling, that is, new ways in which to think about the work of teaching and learning and about their community and its future. Their collaborative participatory action research changed not only the school but also the people themselves.

We give a little more information about the communicative relationships established in the project as we describe 10 features of public spheres as discussed by Habermas.

Example 2: The Córdoba Educational Congress. In October 2003, some 8,000 teachers gathered in Córdoba, Argentina, for the Congreso Internacional de Educación (Congreso V Nacional y III Internacional).[3] We want to show that the congress opened a shared communicative space to explore the nature, conditions, and possibilities for change in the social realities of education in Latin America. When participants opened this communicative space, they created open-eyed and open-minded social relationships in which participants were jointly committed to gaining a critical and self-critical grasp on their social realities and the possibilities for changing the educational practices of their schools and universities and for overcoming the injustice, inequity, irrationality, and suffering endemic in the societies in which they live. Although we are not claiming that the case perfectly realizes the ideal type of the public sphere, it seems to us that the participants in the Córdoba congress created the kind of social arena that is appropriately described as a public sphere. Moreover, the congress is also to be understood as one of many key moments in a broad social and educational movement at which participants reported on particular projects of different kinds (many of them participatory action research projects), seeing these particular projects as contributions to the historical, social, and political process of transforming education in various countries in South America.

The 10 features of public spheres we mentioned earlier are as follows:

1. Public spheres are *constituted as actual networks of communication among actual participants.* We should not think of public spheres as entirely abstract, that is, as if there were just one public sphere. In reality, *there are many public spheres.*

Understood in this way, participatory action research groups and projects might be seen as open-textured networks established for communication and exploration of social problems or issues and as having relationships with other networks and organizations in which members also participate.

The Yirrkala Ganma project involved a particular group of people in and around the schools and community at that time. It was a somewhat fluid group that was focused on a group of indigenous teachers at the school together with community elders and other community members—parents and others—and students at the schools. It also involved nonindigenous teachers and coresearchers who acted as critical friends to the project. The network of actual communications among these people constituted the project as a public sphere.

The Córdoba congress brought together some 8,000 teachers, students, education officials, and invited experts in various fields. For the 3 days of the congress, they constituted an overlapping set of networks of communication that could be regarded as a large but highly interconnected and thematized set of conversations about contemporary educational conditions and educational practices in Latin America. They were exploring the question of how current educational practices and institutions continued to contribute to and reproduce inequitable social relations in those countries and how transformed educational practices and institutions might contribute to transforming those inequitable social conditions.

2. Public spheres are *self-constituted.* They are formed by people who get together *voluntarily.* They are also *relatively autonomous;* that is, they are outside formal systems such as the administrative systems of the state. They are also outside the formal systems of influence that mediate between civil society and the state such as the organizations that represent particular interests (e.g., a farmers' lobby). They are composed of people who want to explore particular problems or issues, that is, around particular themes for discussion. Communicative spaces or communication networks organized as part of the communicative apparatus of the economic or administrative subsystems of government or business would *not* normally qualify as public spheres.

Participatory action research groups come into existence around themes or topics that participants want to investigate, and they make a shared commitment to collaborating in action and research in the interests of transformation. They constitute themselves as a group or project for the purpose of mutual critical inquiry aimed at practical transformation of existing ways of doing things (practices/work), existing understandings (which guide them as practitioners/workers), and existing situations (practice settings/workplaces).

The Yirrkala Ganma project was formed by people who wanted to get together to work on changing the schools in their community. They participated voluntarily. They were relatively autonomous in the sense that their activities were based in the schools but were not "owned" by the schools, and their activities were based in the community but were not "owned" by any community organization. The project was held together by a common commitment to communication and exploration of the possibilities for changing the schools to enact the Ganma (both ways) vision of Yolngu schooling for Yolngu students and communities.

People attended the Córdoba congress voluntarily. Despite the usual complex arrangements for people to fund their attendance and sponsorship of students and others who could not afford to attend (approximately 800 of the 8,000 attendees received scholarships to subsidize their attendance), the congress remained autonomous of particular schools, education systems, and states. The administrative apparatus of the congress was not "owned" by any organization or state, although its core administrative staff members were based at the Dr. Alejandro Carbó Normal School. The congress was coordinated by a committee of educators based in Córdoba and was advised by an academic committee composed of people from many significant Argentinean education organizations (e.g., the Provincial Teachers' Union, universities, the National Academy of Sciences based in Córdoba). Arguably, however, the structuring of the congress as a self-financing economic enterprise (as distinct from its connection with a broader social and educational movement) jeopardized the extent to which it might properly be described as a public sphere.

3. Public spheres frequently come into existence in response to *legitimation deficits;* that is, they frequently come into existence because potential participants do not feel that existing laws, policies, practices, or situations are legitimate. In such cases, participants do not feel that they would necessarily have come to the decision to do things the ways they are now being done. Their communication is aimed at exploring ways in which to overcome these legitimation deficits by finding alternative ways of doing things that will attract their informed consent and commitment.

Participatory action research groups and projects frequently come into existence because existing ways of working are regarded as lacking legitimacy in the sense that they do not (or no longer) command respect or because they cannot be regarded as authentic for participants, either individually or collectively.

The Yirrkala Ganma project came into existence because of prolonged and profound dissatisfaction with the nature and consequences of the white man's way of schooling for Yolngu students, including the sense that current ways of doing schooling were culturally corrosive for Yolngu students and communities. As indicated earlier, Yolngu teachers and community members wanted to find alternative ways of schooling that would be more inclusive, engaging, and enabling for Yolngu students and that would help to develop the community under Yolngu control.

The people attending the Córdoba congress generally shared the view that current forms of education in Latin America serve the interests of a kind of society that does not meet the needs of most citizens, that is, that current forms of schooling are not legitimate in terms of the interests of the majority of students and their families. They wanted to explore alternative ways of doing education that might better serve the interests of the people of Latin America (hence the theme for the congress, "Education: A Commitment With the Nation").

4. Public spheres are constituted for *communicative action* and for *public discourse.* Usually they involve face-to-face communication, but they could be constituted in other ways (e.g., via e-mail, via the World Wide Web). Public discourse in public spheres has a similar orientation to communicative action in that it is oriented toward intersubjective agreement, mutual understanding, and unforced consensus about what to do. Thus, communicative spaces organized for essentially instrumental or functional purposes—to command, to influence, to exercise control over things—would *not* ordinarily qualify as public spheres.

Participatory action research projects and groups constitute themselves for communication oriented toward intersubjective agreement, mutual understanding, and unforced consensus about what to do. They create communication networks aimed at achieving communicative action and at projecting communicative action into practical inquiries aimed at transformation of social practices, practitioners' understandings of their practices, and the situations and circumstances in which they practice.

The Yirrkala Ganma project was created with the principal aim of creating a shared communicative space in which people could think, talk, and act together openly and with a commitment to making a difference in the way in which schooling was enacted in their community. Communications in the project were mostly face-to-face, but there was also much written communication as people worked on various ideas and subprojects within the overall framework of the Ganma project. They spent many hours in reaching intersubjective agreement on the ideas that framed their thinking about education, in reaching mutual understanding about the conceptual framework in which their current situation was to be understood and about the Ganma conceptual framework that would help to guide their thinking as they developed new forms of schooling, and in determining ways in which to move forward based on unforced consensus about how to proceed. Although it might appear that they had an instrumental approach and a clear goal in mind—the development of an improved form of schooling—it should be emphasized that their task was not merely instrumental. It was not instrumental because they had no clear idea at the beginning about what form this new kind of schooling would take; both their goal and the means to achieve it needed to be critically developed through their communicative action and public discourse.

In the Córdoba congress, people came together to explore ways of conceptualizing a reconstructed view of schooling and education for Latin America at this critical moment in the history of many of its nations. The point of the congress was to share ideas about how the current situation should be understood and how it was formed and to consider ideas, issues, obstacles, and possible ways in which to move forward toward forms of education and schooling that might, on the one hand, overcome some of the problems of the past and, on the other, help to shape forms of education and schooling that would be more appropriate to the changed world of the present and future. Participants at the congress presented and debated ideas; they explored social, cultural, political, educational, and economic problems and issues; they considered the achievements of programs and approaches that offered alternative "solutions" to these problems and issues; and they aimed to reach critically informed views about how education and schooling might be transformed to overcome the problems and address the issues they identified in the sense that they aimed to reach practical decisions about what might be done in their own settings when participants returned home from the congress.

5. Public spheres aim to be *inclusive.* To the extent that communication among participants is *exclusive,* doubt may arise as to whether a sphere is in fact a "public" sphere. Public spheres are attempts to create communicative spaces that include not only the parties most obviously interested in and affected by decisions but also people and groups peripheral to (or routinely excluded from) discussions in relation to the topics around which they form. Thus, essentially private or privileged groups, organizations, and communicative networks do *not* qualify as public spheres.

Participatory action research projects and groups aim to include not only practitioners (e.g., teachers, community development workers) but also others involved in and affected by their practices (e.g., students, families, clients).

The Yirrkala Ganma project aimed to include as many of the people who were (and are) involved in and affected by schooling in the community as was possible. It reached out from the school to involve the community and community elders, it included nonindigenous teachers as well as indigenous teachers, and it involved students and their families as well as teachers in the school. It was not exclusive in the sense that its assertion of Yolngu control excluded Balanda (nonindigenous) people; still, it invited Balanda teachers, advisers, and others to join the common commitment of Yolngu people in their search for improved forms of education and schooling that would meet the needs and aspirations of Yolngu people and their communities more genuinely.

The Córdoba congress aimed to be broadly inclusive. It was a congress that was described by its coordinator, María Nieves Díaz Carballo, as "by teachers for teachers"; nevertheless, it included many others involved in and affected by education and schooling in Latin America—students, education officials, invited experts, representatives of a range of government and nongovernment organizations, and others. It aimed to include all of these different kinds of people as friends and contributors to a common cause—creating new forms of education and schooling better suited to the needs of the present and future in Latin America and the world.

6. As part of their inclusive character, public spheres tend to involve communication in *ordinary language.* In public spheres, people deliberately seek to break down the barriers and hierarchies formed by the use of specialist discourses and the modes of address characteristic of bureaucracies that presume a ranking of the importance of speakers and what they say in terms of their positional authority (or lack thereof). Public spheres also tend to have only the weakest of distinctions between insiders and outsiders (they have relatively permeable boundaries and changing "memberships") and between people who are relatively disinterested and those whose (self-)interests are significantly affected by the topics under discussion. Thus, the communicative apparatuses of many government and business organizations, and of organizations that rely on the specialist expertise of some participants for their operations, do *not* ordinarily qualify as public spheres.

While drawing on the resources and discourses of theory and policy in their investigations, participatory action researchers aim to achieve mutual comprehension and create discourse communities that allow all participants to have a voice and play a part in reaching consensus about what to do. By necessity, they use language that all can use rather than relying on the specialist discourses of social science that might exclude some from the shared task of understanding and transforming shared everyday lives and a shared lifeworld.

In the Yirrkala Ganma project, much of the communication about the project not only was in ordinary language but was also conducted in the language of the community, that is, *Yolngu-matha.* This not only was a deliberate shift from the language in which Balanda schooling was usually discussed in the community (English and some specialist educational discourse) but also was a shift to engage and use the conceptual frameworks of the community and Yolngu culture. On the other hand, the modes of address of the Yolngu culture require respect for elders and specialist forms of language for "inside" matters (secret/sacred, for the initiated) versus "outside" matters (secular, for the uninitiated), so many discussions of the Ganma conceptual framework required participants to respect these distinctions and the levels of initiation of speakers and hearers.

At the Córdoba congress, many speakers used specialist educational (and other) discourses to discuss their work or ideas, but much of the discussion took place in language that was deliberately intended to be inclusive and engaging for participants, that is, to share ideas and open up participants for debate without assuming that hearers were fluent in specialist discourses for understanding either the sociopolitical context of education in Latin America or the technical aspects of contemporary education in Latin American countries. More particularly, the languages used at the congress, including translations from English and Portuguese, were inclusive because they were directed specifically toward fostering the shared commitment of participants about the need for change and the obstacles and possibilities ahead if participants wanted to join the shared project of reconstructing education in Argentina and elsewhere. Specialist discourses were used to deal with specific topics (e.g., in philosophy, in social theory, in curriculum), but the conversations about those topics soon shifted register to ensure that ideas were accessible to any interested participants.

7. Public spheres presuppose *communicative freedom.* In public spheres, participants are free to occupy (or not occupy) the particular discursive roles of speaker, listener, and observer, and they are free to withdraw from the communicative space of the discussion. Participation and nonparticipation are voluntary. Thus, communicative spaces and networks generally characterized by obligations or duties to lead, follow, direct, obey, remain silent, or remain outside the group could *not* be characterized as public spheres.

Participatory action research projects and groups constitute themselves to "open communicative space" among participants. They constitute themselves to give participants the right and opportunity to speak and be heard, to listen, or to walk away from the project or group. Contrary to some of our earlier views, they are not closed and self-referential groups in which participants are (or can be) bound to some "party line" in the sense of a "correct" way of seeing things. Moreover, they constitute themselves deliberately for *critical* and *self-critical* conversation and decision making that aims to open up existing ways of saying and seeing things, that is, to play with the relationships between the actual and the possible.

In the Yirrkala Ganma project, participants were free to occupy the different roles of speaker, listener, and observer or to withdraw from discussions. In any particular discussion, some may have occupied one or another of these roles to a greater extent, but over the life of the project, people generally occupied the range of these roles at one time or another. As indicated earlier, some people continued to occupy privileged positions as speakers (e.g., on matters of inside knowledge), but they also occupied roles as listeners in many other situations, responding with their specialist knowledge whenever and wherever it was appropriate to do so. In general, however, the prolonged discussions and debates about giving form to the idea of the Ganma (both ways) curriculum was conducted in ways that enabled participants to gather a shared sense of what it was and could be and how it might be realized in practice. The discussions were consistently open and critical in the sense that all participants wanted to reach shared understandings and agreements about the limitations of Balanda education for Yolngu children and communities and about the possibilities for realizing a different and improved form of education for Yolngu children and their community.

The Córdoba congress engendered conditions of communicative freedom. Although the congress program and timetable privileged particular participants as speakers at particular times, the vast conversation of the congress, within and outside its formal sessions and in both formal and informal communication, presupposed the freedom of participants to speak in, listen to, observe, and withdraw from particular discussions. Conversations were open and critical, inviting participants to explore ideas and possibilities for change together.

8. The communicative networks of public spheres generate *communicative power;* that is, the positions and viewpoints developed through discussion will command the respect of participants not by virtue of obligation but rather by the power of mutual understanding and consensus. Thus, communication in public spheres creates legitimacy in the strongest sense, that is, the shared belief among participants that they freely and authentically consent to the decisions they reach. Thus, systems of command or influence, where decisions are formed on the basis of obedience or self-interests, would *not* ordinarily qualify as public spheres.

Participatory action research projects and groups allow participants to develop understandings of, reasons for, and shared commitment to transformed ways of doing things. They encourage exploration and investigation of social practices, understandings, and situations. By the very act of doing so, they generate more authentic understandings among participants and a shared sense of the legitimacy of the decisions they make.

Over the life of the Yirrkala Ganma project, and in the continuing work arising from it, participants developed the strongest sense that the new way of thinking about education and schooling that they were developing was timely, appropriate, true to their circumstances, and generative for Yolngu children and their community. They were clearly conscious that their shared viewpoint, as well as their conceptual framework, contrasted markedly with taken-for-granted assumptions and presuppositions about schooling in Australia, including many taken-for-granted (Balanda) ideas about indigenous education. The communicative power developed through the project sustained participants in their commitment to these new ways of schooling despite the occasional resistances they experienced when the Northern Territory education authorities found that community proposals were counter to, or exceptions to, usual ways of operating in the system. (It is a tribute to many nonindigenous people in the Northern Territory who worked with Yirrkala Community Schools and the associated Homelands Centre Schools that they generally took a constructive and supportive view of the community's proposals even when the proposals fell outside established practice. The obvious and deep commitment of the Yolngu teachers and community to the tasks of the project, the support of credible external coresearchers, and the long-term nature of the project encouraged many nonindigenous system staff members to give the project "the benefit of the doubt" as an educational project that had the possibility to succeed in indigenous education where many previous proposals and plans developed by nonindigenous people had failed.)

The Córdoba congress was infused by a growing sense of shared conviction and shared commitment about the need and possibilities for change in education in Argentina and elsewhere in Latin America. On the other hand, the impetus and momentum of the developing sense of shared conviction may have been more fragile and transitory because the congress was just a few days long (although building on the momentum from previous congresses and other work that participants were doing toward the same transformative ends). Seen against the broader sweep of education and educational change in education in Latin America, however, it is clear that the congress was drawing on, refreshing, and redirecting long-standing reserves of critical educational progressivism in the hearts, minds, and work of many people who attended.

The shared conviction that new ways of working in education are necessary generated a powerful and nearly tangible sense of *solidarity* among participants in the congress—a powerful and lasting shared commitment to pursuing the directions suggested by the discussions and debates in which they had participated. It also generated an enduring sense of the *legitimacy* of decisions made by participants in the light of shared exploration of their situations, shared deliberation, and shared decision making.

9. Public spheres do not affect social systems (e.g., government, administration) *directly;* their impact on systems is *indirect.* In public spheres, participants aim to change the climate of debate, the ways in which things are thought about and how situations are understood. They aim to generate a sense that alternative ways of doing things are possible and feasible and to show that some of these alternative ways actually work or that the new ways do indeed resolve problems, overcome dissatisfactions, or address issues. Groups organized primarily to pursue the particular interests of particular groups by direct intervention with government or administrative systems would *not* ordinarily qualify as public spheres. Similarly, groups organized in ways that usually serve the particular interests of particular groups, even though this may happen in a concealed or "accidental" way (as frequently happens with news media), do *not* ordinarily qualify as public spheres.

Participatory action research projects and groups rarely have the power to legislate or compel change, even among their own members. It is only by the force of better argument, transmitted to authorities who must decide for themselves what to do, that they influence existing structures and procedures. They frequently establish themselves, and are permitted to establish themselves, at the margins of those structures and procedures, that is, in spaces constituted for exploration and investigation and for trying out alternative ways of doing things. They are frequently listened to because they have been deliberately allowed to explore this marginal space, with the tacit understanding that what they learn may be of benefit to others and to existing systems and structures. Although they may understand themselves as oppositional or even "outlaw" (in a metaphorical sense), they are frequently acting with the knowledge and encouragement of institutional authorities who recognize that changes might be needed.

As already indicated, the Yirrkala Ganma project was based in the schools but was not an official project of the school system or education system, and it was based in the community but was not an official project of any community organization. The schools and the Northern Territory education system, as well as various community organizations, knew of the existence of the project and were generally supportive. The work of the project was not an improvement or development project undertaken by any of these organizations, nor did the project "speak" directly to these organizations from within the functions and operations of the systems as systems. On the contrary, the project aimed to change the way in which these systems and organizations thought about and organized education in the community. In particular, it aimed to change the conceptual frameworks and discourses in which Yolngu education was understood and the activities that constituted it. In a sense, the transformations produced by the project were initially "tolerated" by these systems and organizations as exceptions to usual ways of operating. Over time, through the indirect influence of showing that alternative ways of doing things could work, the systems began to accept them—even though the alternative ways were at odds with practice elsewhere. The project changed the climate of discussion and the nature of the discourse about what constitutes good education for Yolngu children and communities. Because similar experiments were going on elsewhere around Australia (e.g., with the involvement of staff members from Deakin University, the University of Melbourne, and Batchelor College), there was a sense within education systems that the new experiment should be permitted to proceed in the hope (increasingly fulfilled) that the new ways of working might prove to be more effective in indigenous schools in indigenous communities where education had frequently produced less satisfactory outcomes than in nonindigenous schools and for nonindigenous students and communities. In a variety of small but significant ways, education systems began to accept the discourses of "both ways" education (realized differently in different places) and to encourage different practices of "both ways" education in indigenous communities and schools with large enrollments of indigenous students.

The Córdoba congress operated outside the functional frameworks of education and state systems and aimed to change the ways in which education and schooling were understood and practiced indirectly rather than directly. No state agency sponsor controlled the congress; as indicated earlier, it is a congress created and maintained by its organizers "by teachers for teachers." On the other hand, state officials (e.g., the minister of education for the Province of Córdoba [Amelia López], the Argentinean federal minister of education [Daniel Filmus]) addressed the congress and encouraged participants in their efforts to think freshly about the educational problems and issues being confronted in schools and in Argentina. The size, success, and generativity of previous congresses was well known (the 2003 congress was the fifth national congress and third international congress held in Córdoba), and it is reasonable to assume that representatives of the state would want to endorse the congress even if some of the ideas and practices being debated and developed by participants were at the periphery of, or even contrary to, state initiatives in education and schooling. Of course it is also true that many of the ideas and practices discussed at the congress, such as those concerned with social justice in education, were generally in the spirit of state initiatives, although most congress participants appeared to take an actively and constructively critical view of the forms and consequences of contemporary state initiatives in schooling.

10. Public spheres frequently arise in practice through, or in relation to, the communication networks associated with *social movements*, that is, where voluntary groupings of participants arise in response to a legitimation deficit or a shared sense that a social problem has arisen and needs to be addressed. Nevertheless, the public spheres created by some organizations (e.g., Amnesty International) can be long-standing and well organized and can involve notions of (paid) membership and shared objectives. On the other hand, many organizations (e.g., political parties, private interest groups) do *not* ordinarily qualify as public spheres for reasons already outlined in relation to other items on this list and also because they are part of the social order rather than social movements.

Participatory action research groups and projects often arise in relation to broad social movements such as the women's movement, the green movement, peace movements, the civil rights movement, and other movements for social transformation. They frequently arise to explore alternative ways of doing things in settings where the impact of those movements is otherwise unclear or uncertain (e.g., in the conduct of teaching and learning in schools, in the conduct of social welfare by family and social welfare agencies, in the conduct of catchment management by groups of landholders). They draw on the resources of those social movements and feed back into the broader movements, both in terms of the general political potency of the movements and in terms of understanding how the objectives and methods of those movements play out in the particular kinds of situations and settings (e.g., village life, schooling, welfare practice) being investigated.

As some of the statements of Yunupingu (1991) quoted earlier suggest, the Yirrkala Ganma project was an expression of several important contemporary indigenous social movements in Australia, particularly the land rights movement, the movement for Aboriginal self-determination and control, and (for Australians generally) the movement for reconciliation between indigenous and nonindigenous Australians. Arguably, some of the ideas developed in the Ganma project have had a far wider currency than might have been expected, for example, through the songs and music of Yunupingu's pop group, Yothu Yindi, which have resolutely and consistently advocated mutual recognition and respect between indigenous and nonindigenous Australians and have educated and encouraged nonindigenous Australians to understand and respect indigenous people, knowledge, communities, and cultures. The Ganma project was a manifestation of these indigenous rights movements at the local level and in the particular setting of schools and was also a powerful intellectual contribution to shaping the wider movements. On the one hand, the project named and explained ways in which schooling was culturally corrosive for indigenous peoples; on the other hand, it showed that it was possible to create and give rational justifications of alternative, culturally supportive ways of doing schooling and education for indigenous people and in indigenous communities.

In the Córdoba congress, there was a strong sense of connection to a broad social movement for change in Latin American education and societies. Endemic corruption, ill-considered economic adventures, antidemocratic practices, the denial of human rights, and entrenched social inequity in a number of Latin American countries were opposed and critiqued by many progressive people, including many teachers and education professionals, and there was (and is) a hunger for alternative forms of education that might prevent the tragic inheritance of previous regimes (e.g., escalating national debt, fiscal crises, impoverishment, the collapse of services) from being passed on to rising generations of students and citizens. The negative/critical and positive/constructive aspects of the education movement represented in and by the congress are connected to a wider social movement for change, but they are also a particular and specific source of intellectual, cultural, social, political, and economic ideas and practices that make a distinctive contribution to the shape and dynamics of the wider movement. The congress itself is now something of a rallying point for progressive and critical teachers and education professionals, but it remains determinedly and politely independent of the state and commercial sponsors that might seek to exercise control over or through it. Its organizers are convinced that their best chance to change the climate of thinking about education and society is to remain independent of the state machinery of social order and to strive only for an indirect role in change by having a diffuse role in changing things "by the force of better argument" rather than striving to create change through the administrative power available through the machinery of the state or (worse) through any kind of coercive force. The congress also expressed, not only in its written materials but also in its climate and culture, a profound sense of passion, hope, and joy; participants clearly regard it as an opportunity to celebrate possibilities and achievements in creating new forms of education aimed at making (and speaking and writing into existence) a better future.

These 10 features of public spheres describe a space for social interaction in which people strive for intersubjective agreement, mutual understanding, and unforced consensus about what to do and in which legitimacy arises. These are the conditions under which participants regard decisions, perspectives, and points of view reached in open discussion as compelling for—and even binding on—themselves. Such conditions are very different from many other forms of communication, for example, the kind of functional communication characteristic of social systems (which aims to achieve particular ends by the most efficient means) and most interest-based bargaining (which aims to maximize or optimize self-interests rather than to make the best and most appropriate decision for all concerned).

These conditions are ones under which practical reasoning and exploratory action by a community of practice are possible—theorizing, research, and collective action aimed at changing practices, understandings of practices, and the settings and situations in which practice occurs. They are conditions under which a loose affiliation of people can gather to address a common theme based on contemporary problems or issues, aiming to inform themselves about the core practical question of "what is to be done?" in relation to the formation and transformation of practice, practitioners, and the settings in which practice occurs at particular times and in particular places.

As already suggested, such communities of practice sometimes come into existence when advocacy groups believe that problems or issues arise in relation to a program, policy, or practice and that change is needed. An example would be the kind of collaboration that occurs when a group of mental health service clients meet with mental health service providers and professionals to explore ways in which to improve mental health service delivery at a particular site. Another example would be the project work of groups of teachers and students who conduct participatory action research investigations into problems and issues in schooling. Another would be the kind of citizens' action campaign that sometimes emerges in relation to issues of community well-being and development or environmental or public health issues. This approach to the transformation of practice understands that changing practices is not just a matter of changing the ideas of practitioners alone; it also is a matter of changing the social, cultural, discursive, and material conditions under which the practice occurs, including changing the ideas and actions of those who are the clients of professional practices and the ideas and actions of the wider community involved in and affected by the practice. This approach to changing practice, through fostering public discourse in public spheres, is also the approach to evaluation advocated by Niemi and Kemmis (1999) under the rubric of "communicative evaluation" (see also Ryan, 2003).

Myths, Misinterpretations, and Mistakes Revisited

In the light of the Habermasian notions of *system and lifeworld* (explored in our chapter in the second edition of this *Handbook*), *the critique of the social macro-subject,* and the notion of *public spheres* developed in *Between Facts and Norms,* we can throw new light on the myths, misinterpretations, and mistakes about critical participatory action research identified earlier in this chapter. The following comments present a necessarily brief summary of some of the ways in which our understandings of these topics have evolved during recent years.

Empowerment

In the light of the Habermasian theory of system and lifeworld, we came to understand the notion of empowerment neither solely in lifeworld terms (in terms of the lifeworld processes of cultural, social, and personal reproduction and transformation and their effects) nor solely in systems terms (in terms of changing systems structures or functioning or through effects produced by the steering media of money and administrative power of organizations and institutions). Exploring practices, our understandings of them, and the settings in which we worked from *both* lifeworld and system perspectives gave us richer critical insight into how processes of social formation and transformation occur in the contexts of particular projects. Increasingly, we came to understand empowerment not only as a lifeworld process of cultural, social, and personal development and transformation but also as implying that protagonists experienced themselves as working both in and against system structures and functions to produce effects intended to be read in changed systems structures and functioning. From this stereoscopic view, system structures and functions are not only sources of constraint but also sources of possibility, and lifeworld processes of cultural, social, and personal reproduction and transformation are not only sources of possibility but also sources of constraint on change. Thus, in real-world settings inevitably constructed by both, the notion of empowerment plays across the conceptual boundary between lifeworld and system, and it now seems likely that one would say that empowerment had occurred only when transformations were evident in both lifeworld and system aspects of a situation.

In the light of Habermas's critique of the social macro-subject, we increasingly recognized that the notion of empowerment is not to be understood solely in terms of closed organizations achieving self-regulation (by analogy with the sovereignty of states) as a process of achieving autonomy and self-determination, whether at the level of individual selves or at the level of some collective (understood as a macro-"self"). It turns out that neither individual actors nor states can be entirely and coherently autonomous and self-regulating. Their parts do not form unified and coherent wholes but rather must be understood in terms of notions such as difference, contradiction, and conflict as much as unity, coherence, and independence. In the face of internal and external differentiation, perhaps ideas such as dialogue, interdependence and complementarity are the positives for which one might hope. Despite its rhetorical power and its apparent political necessity, the concept of empowerment does not in reality produce autonomous and independent self-regulation; rather, it produces only a capacity for individuals, groups, and states to interact more coherently with one another in the ceaseless processes of social reproduction and transformation. At its best, it names a process in which people, groups, and states engage one another more authentically and with greater recognition and respect for difference in making decisions that they will regard as legitimate because they have participated in them openly and freely, more genuinely committed to mutual understanding, intersubjective agreement, and consensus about what to do.

In the light of Habermas's commentary on the public sphere, the basis for empowerment is not to be understood in terms of activism justified by ideological position taking; rather, the basis for empowerment is the communicative power developed in public spheres through communicative action and public discourse. On this view, the aim of empowerment is rational and just decisions and actions that will be regarded as legitimate by those involved and affected.

The Role of the Facilitator

In the light of the Habermasian theory of system and lifeworld, we came to understand that facilitation is not to be understood solely in system terms as a specialized role with specialized functions, nor is it to be understood solely in lifeworld terms as a process of promoting the reproduction and transformation of cultures, social relationships, and identities. Instead, it is to be understood as a process to be critically explored from both perspectives. The question of facilitation usually arises when there is an asymmetrical relationship of knowledge or power between a person expecting or expected to do "facilitation" and people expecting or expected to be "facilitated" in the process of doing a project. It is naïve to believe that such asymmetries will disappear; sometimes help *is* needed. At the same time, it must be recognized that those asymmetries can be troublesome and that there is little solace in the idea that they can be made "safe" because the facilitator aims to be "neutral." On the other hand, it is naïve to believe that the person who is asked for help, or to be a facilitator, will be an entirely "equal" coparticipant along with others, as if the difference were invisible. Indeed, the facilitator *can* be a coparticipant, but one with some special expertise that may be helpful to the group in its endeavors. The theory of system and lifeworld allows us to see the doubleness of the role in terms of a specialist role and functions in critical tension with processes of cultural, social, and personal reproduction and transformation that aspire to achieving self-expression, self-realization, and self-determination (recognizing that the individual or collective self in each case is not a unified, coherent, autonomous, responsible, and independent whole entirely capable of self-regulation). The stereoscopic view afforded by the theory of system and lifeworld provides conceptual resources for critical enactment and evaluation of the role of the facilitator in practice.

In the light of Habermas's critique of the social macro-subject, we no longer understand the people involved in collaborative participatory action research projects as a closed group with a fixed membership; rather, we understand them as an open and inclusive network in which the facilitator can be a contributing coparticipant, albeit with particular knowledge or expertise that can be of help to the group. Moreover, at different times, different participants in some groups can and do take the facilitator role in relation to different parts of the action being undertaken and in relation to the participatory action research process.

In the light of Habermas's commentary on the public sphere, the facilitator should not be understood as an external agent offering technical guidance to members of an action group but rather should be understood as someone aiming to establish or support a collaborative enterprise in which people can engage in exploratory action as participants in a public sphere constituted for communicative action and public discourse in response to legitimation deficits.

The Research–Action Dualism

In the light of the Habermasian theory of system and lifeworld, action in participatory action research should not be understood as separated from research in a technical division of labor mirrored in a social division of labor between participants and researchers. Instead, research and action converge *in* communicative action aimed at practical and critical decisions about what to do in the extended form of exploratory action, that is, practices of action and research jointly projected through history by action. Equally, however, we do not understand the research and action elements of participatory action research as the "natural" realization of the lifeworld processes of cultural, social, and personal reproduction and transformation. In participatory action research, systems categories of structure, functions, goals, roles, and rules are relevant when a group works on a "project" (implying some measure of rational–purposive or strategic action). Here again, participatory action research crosses and recrosses the conceptual boundaries between system and lifeworld aspects of the life of the project, and the stereoscopic view afforded by the theory of system and lifeworld offers critical resources for exploring and evaluating the extent to which the project might become nothing but a rational–purposive project and the extent to which it risks dissolving into the lifeworld processes of the group conducting it. Both the research element and the action element of the project have system and lifeworld aspects, and both elements are candidates for critical exploration and evaluation from the perspectives of system and lifeworld. Indeed, we might now conclude that it is the commitment to conducting this critique, in relation to the action, the research, and the relationship between them, that is the hallmark of critical participatory action research.

In the light of Habermas's critique of the social macro-subject, research and action are to be understood not in terms of steering functions for an individual or for a closed group (e.g., to steer the group by exercising administrative power) but rather as mutually constitutive processes that *create* affiliations and collaborative action among people involved in and affected by particular kinds of decisions and actions.

In the light of Habermas's commentary on the public sphere, research and action are to be understood not as separate functions but rather as different moments in a unified process of struggle characteristic of social movements—struggles against irrationality, injustice, and unsatisfying social conditions and ways of life (a unification of research for action that recalls the insight that all social movements are also educational movements). In the light of Habermas's (1996, chap. 8) description of the public sphere in *Between Facts and Norms,* we now conclude that the impulse to undertake participatory action research is an impulse to subject practice—social action—to deliberate and continuing critique by making action deliberately exploratory and arranging things so that it will be possible to learn from what happens and to make the process of learning a collective process to be pursued through public discourse in a public sphere constituted for that purpose.

The Role of the Collective

In the light of the Habermasian theory of system and lifeworld, the collective is not to be understood either solely in systems terms, as an organization or institution, or solely in lifeworld terms, as a social group constituted in face-to-face social relationships. Instead, it must be critically explored from *both* perspectives and as constituted by processes associated with each (on the systems side: steering media; on the lifeworld side: cultural reproduction and transformation, social reproduction and transformation, and the formation and transformation of individual identities and capabilities).

In the light of Habermas's critique of the social macro-subject, the collective should be understood not as a closed group with fixed membership—a coherent, unified, autonomous, independent, and self-regulating whole—but rather as internally diverse, differentiated, and sometimes inconsistent and contradictory. Nor does a participatory action research group stand in the position of an avant-garde in relation to other people and groups in the setting in which the research occurs, but it retains its connections with those others, just as it retains responsibility for the consequences of its actions as they are experienced in those wider communities in which they take place.

In the light of Habermas's commentary on the public sphere, the collective formed by a participatory action research project should be understood not as a closed and exclusive group constituted to perform the particular organizational roles and functions associated with a project but rather as an open and inclusive space constituted to create conditions of communicative freedom and, thus, to create communicative action and public discourse aimed at addressing problems and issues of irrationality, injustice, and dissatisfaction experienced by particular groups at particular times. In our view, some of the most interesting participatory action research projects are those directly connected with wider social movements (e.g., green issues; issues of peace, race, or gender), but it should not go unnoticed that many participatory action research projects constitute themselves in ways that are very like social movements in relation to local issues, although often with wider ramifications, for example, by addressing issues about the effects of hyperrationalization of practices in local settings that frequently have much more widespread relevance. For example, around the world there are hundreds—probably thousands—of different kinds of action research projects being conducted by teachers to explore the potential and limitations of various innovative forms of teaching and learning that address the alienating effects of state regulation of curriculum, teaching, and assessment at every level of schooling. The multiplication of such projects suggests that there is a social movement under way aimed at recovering or revitalizing education in the face of the very widespread colonization of the lifeworld of teaching and learning by the imperatives of increasingly muscular and intrusive administrative systems regulating and controlling the processes of schooling. These projects in education are paralleled by similar action research projects in welfare, health, community development, and other fields. Taken together, despite their differences, they make an eloquent statement of refusal and reconstruction in the face of a version of corporate and public administration that places the imperative of institutional control above the moral and substantive imperatives and virtues traditionally associated with the practice of these professions.

◼ Reimagining Critical Participatory Action Research

The view of critical participatory action research we have advanced in this chapter is somewhat different from the view of it that we held in the past. Two decades ago, our primary aim was to envisage and enact a well-justified form of research to be conducted by teachers and other professional practitioners into their own practices, their understandings of their practices, and the situations in which they practiced. Despite our critique of established ways of thinking about social and educational research, certain remnant elements of conventional perceptions of research continued to survive in the forms of research we advocated, for example, ideas about theory, knowledge, and the centrality of the researcher in the advancement of knowledge.

Two decades ago, we hoped for advances in theory through action research that would somehow be similar to the kinds of theory conventionally produced or extended in the social and educational research of that time. We expected that practitioners would also develop and extend their own theories of education, but we were perhaps less clear about what the nature and form of those theories would be. We had admired Lawrence Stenhouse's definition of research as "systematic enquiry made public" (Stenhouse, 1975) but had given less thought to how those theories might emerge in a literature of practitioner research. Now we have a clearer idea that sometimes the theories that motivate, guide, and inform practitioners' action are frequently in the form of *collective understandings* that elude easy codification in the forms conventionally used in learned journals and books. They accumulate in conversations, archives of evidence, and the shared knowledge of *communities of practice.*

Two decades ago, although we had regarded "knowledge" as a problematic category and had distinguished between the private knowledge of individuals and the collective knowledge of research fields and traditions, we probably valued the knowledge outcomes of research over the practical outcomes of participant research—the effects of participant research in changing social and educational practices, understandings of those practices, and the situations and settings of practice. Now we have a clearer idea that the outcomes of participatory action research are written in histories—the histories of practitioners, communities, the people with whom they interact, and (again) communities of practice. And we see that the outcomes of participatory action research are to be read in terms of historical consequences for participants and others involved and affected by the action people have taken, judged not only against the criterion of truth but also against the criteria of wisdom and prudence, that is, whether people were better off in terms of the consequences they experienced. We can ask whether their understandings of their situations are less irrational (or ideologically skewed) than before, whether their action is less unproductive and unsatisfying for those involved, or whether the social relations between people in the situation are less inequitable or unjust than before. The product of participatory action research is not just knowledge but also different histories than might have existed if participants had not intervened to transform their practices, understandings, and situations and, thus, transformed the histories that otherwise seemed likely to come into being. We look for the products of participatory action research in *collective action* and the making and remaking of *collective histories.*

Two decades ago, we were excited by participatory research that connected with social movements and made changes in particular kinds of professional practices (e.g., nursing, education, community development, welfare), but we were less aware than we are now that this kind of engagement with social movements is a two-way street. Social movements can be expressed and realized in the settings of professional practice (e.g., the powerful connections made between the women's movement and health or education or between green issues and education or community development), but social movements also take strength and direction from participatory studies that explore and critically investigate issues in the particular contexts of different kinds of social practices. Social movements set agendas around the broad themes that are their focus, but studies of particular practices and local settings also show how differently those broad themes must be understood in terms of issues identified in in-depth local investigations. Now we have a clearer understanding not only that participatory action research expresses the spirit of its time in terms of giving life to social movements in local settings or in relation to particular themes (e.g., gender, indigenous rights) but also that local investigations into locally felt dissatisfactions, disquiets, or concerns also open up themes of broader interest, sometimes linking to existing social movements but also bringing into existence new movements for transformation in professional fields and in the civil life of communities. Now, in judging the long-term success of participatory action research projects, we are more likely to ask about the extent to which they have fed *collective capacities for transformation* locally and in the widening sphere of social life locally, regionally, nationally, and even internationally, as has happened in the history of participatory action research as it has contributed to the development of *people's collective communicative power.*

Most particularly, two decades ago we valorized the researcher. According to conventional views of research, researchers were the people at the center of the research act—heroes in the quiet adventures of building knowledge and theory. We encouraged participant research that would make "ordinary" practitioners local heroes of knowledge building and theory building and collaborative research that would make heroic teams of researching practitioners who produced new understandings in their communities and communities of practice. Increasingly, in those days, we saw research "collectives" as key activist groups that would make and change history. We continue to advocate this view of participatory research as making history by making exploratory changes. Now, however, our critiques of the research–action dualism, and our changing views of the facilitator and the research collective, encourage us to believe that critical participatory action research needs *animateurs* but that it also thrives in *public spheres* in which people can take a variety of roles as researchers, questioners, interlocutors, and interested observers. And if we reject the heroic view of history as being "made" by individuals—great men or great women—then we must see the real transformations of history as transformations made by ordinary people working together in the light of emerging themes, issues, and problems (e.g., via social movements). We now see a central task of participatory action research as including widening groups of people in the task of making their own history, often in the face of established ways of doing things and often to overcome problems caused by living with the consequences of the histories others make for us—often the consequences of new ways of doing things that were intended to improve things but that turned out to have unexpected, unanticipated, and untoward consequences for those whom the new ways were intended to help. As we hope we have shown, Habermas's description of public discourse in public spheres gives us another way in which to think about who can do "research" and what research might be like if it is conceptualized as exploratory action aimed at nurturing and feeding public discourse in public spheres. Now we are less inclined to think in terms of heroes of knowledge building or even of heroes of history making; we are more inclined to think in terms of people working together to develop a greater collective capacity to change the circumstances of their own lives in terms of *collective capacity building.*

Now, more so than two decades ago, we are excited by notions of collective understanding, collective research, communicative power, and collective capacity. We are interested in describing and identifying conditions under which people can investigate their own professional fields or community circumstances to develop communicative power and strengthen their collective capacity. In "projects" and movements aimed at collective capacity building, we see people securing new ways of working on the basis of *collective commitment.* We see them achieving new ways of working and new ways of being that have *legitimacy* because their decisions are made in conditions like those we described in the last section—the conditions of public discourse in public spheres. Now, more so than two decades ago, we see participatory action research as a process of sustained *collective deliberation* coupled with sustained *collective investigation* of a topic, a problem, an issue, a concern, or a theme that allows people to explore possibilities in action, judging them by their consequences in history and moving with a measure of tentativeness and prudence (in some cases with great courage in the face of violence and coercion) but also with the support that comes with *solidarity.*

This account of what we now value as outcomes and consequences of participatory action research—well-justified and agreed-on collective action that reduces the world's stock of irrationality, injustice, inequity, dissatisfaction, and unproductive ways of doing things—may seem a far cry from the kind of justification for much social and educational research. Perhaps more modestly, that research makes few claims to changing history for the better and promises only improved knowledge and theories that *may* contribute to clearer understanding and improved policy and practice. That is not necessarily the way it is used, of course; sometimes "scientific" theories or findings are used to justify social programs, policies, and practices of breathtaking foolhardiness. Our advocacy of critical participatory research is intended partly as an antidote to such foolhardiness but also to insist, in an age of hyperrationality and the technologization of everything, that people can still, gaps and miscues notwithstanding, have a hope of knowing what they are doing and doing what they think is right and, more particularly, doing less of what they think will have untoward consequences for themselves and others. Perhaps this is to take too "activist" a view of participatory action research and to give up on the conventional understanding that people should wait for experts and theorists to tell them what will work best—what will be best for them.

In 1957, in the *Journal of Educational Sociology*, Harold Hodgkinson presented a critique of action research that he regarded as "a symptom of the times in which we live" (Hodgkinson, 1957, p. 152). Against Arthur Foshay, whom he quoted as saying, "Cooperative action research is an approach to making what we do consistent with what we believe" (which we would argue fails to acknowledge the power of action research to put our ideas to the test and correct what we believe), Hodgkinson retorted,

> This is simply not so. Action research merely focuses attention on the doing and eliminates most of the necessity for believing. We are living in a "doing" age, and action research allows people the privilege of "doing" something. This method could easily become an end in itself. (p. 153)

Hodgkinson (1957) believed that action research would produce "teachers who spend much of their time measuring and figuring, playing with what Dylan Thomas would call 'easy hobby games for little engineers'" (p. 153). He held out for the great scientific generalizations, based on sound empirical and statistical methods that would provide a secure scientific basis for what teachers could or should do.

Those other approaches to research have produced some justifications for improved ways of working in education, social work, community development, and other spheres of social action. They will continue to do so. But they will always create a problem of putting the scientist as "expert" in the position of mediator, that is, mediating between the knowledge and action and the theory and practice of practitioners and ordinary people. They will always create disjunctions between what scientific communities and policymakers believe to be prudent courses of action and the courses of action that people would (and will) choose for themselves, knowing the consequences of their actions and practices for the people with whom they work. For two decades, we have insisted that *practitioners'* interpretive categories (not just how they think about their work but also how they think about their world) must be taken into account in deciding what, when, whether, and how research should be conducted into professional practice and community life. Critical participatory action research is an expression of this impulse, and it has proved, in hundreds of studies, to be a means by which people have transformed their worlds. Sometimes, perhaps, things have *not* turned out for the better, but many times people have concluded that their participatory action research work has changed their circumstances for the better and avoided untoward consequences that they otherwise would have had to endure. This has been true in rebuilding education in South Africa, in literacy campaigns in Nicaragua, in developments in nursing practice in Australia, in improving classroom teaching in the United Kingdom, in community development in The Philippines, in farms in Sri Lanka, in community governance in India, in improving water supplies in Bangladesh, and in hundreds of other settings around the world. These are not "easy hobby games for little engineers," as

Hodgkinson might have it, but rather matters of great human and social significance. These people might not have changed the world, but they have changed their worlds. Is that not the same thing? They might not have changed everything everywhere, but they have improved things for particular people in particular places and in many other places where their stories have traveled. We do not think that it is too immodest an aspiration to judge participatory action research in terms of historical consequences. Indeed, perhaps we judge too much social and educational science against too low a bar. We are used to expecting too little help from it, and our expectations have been met. Under such circumstances, we believe, people would be wise to conduct their own research into their own practices and situations. Under such circumstances, there continues to be a need for critical participatory action research.

Notes

1. The quotation is from page 334 of the German edition of Habermas's (1992a) *Faktizität und Geltung* (Between Facts and Norms).

2. This description is adapted from Kemmis and Brennan Kemmis (2003).

3. This description is adapted from Kemmis (2004).

References

Altrichter, H., & Gstettner, P. (1997). Action research: A closed chapter in the history of German social science? In R. McTaggart (Ed.), *Participatory action research: International contexts and consequences* (pp. 45–78). Albany: State University of New York Press.

Argyris, C. (1990). *Overcoming organisational defences: Facilitating organisational learning.* Boston: Allyn & Bacon.

Argyris, C., Putnam, R., & McLain Smith, D. (1985). *Action science.* San Francisco: Jossey–Bass.

Argyris, C., & Schön, D. A. (1974). *Theory in practice: Increasing professional effectiveness.* San Francisco: Jossey–Bass.

Argyris, C., & Schön, D. A. (1978). *Organisational learning: A theory of action perspective.* Reading, MA: Addison–Wesley.

Baynes, K. (1995). Democracy and the *Rechsstaat:* Habermas's *Faktizität und Geltung.* In S. K. White (Ed.), *The Cambridge companion to Habermas* (pp. 201–232). Cambridge, UK: Cambridge University Press.

Bourdieu, P., & Wacquant, L. J. D. (1992). *An invitation to reflexive sociology.* Cambridge, UK: Polity.

Bravette, G. (1996). Reflection on a black woman's management learning. *Women in Management Review, 11*(3), 3–11.

Brock-Utne, B. (1980, Summer). What is educational action research? *Classroom Action Research Network Bulletin,* No. 4, pp. 10–15.

Brown, L., Henry, C., Henry, J., & McTaggart, R. (1988). Action research: Notes on the national seminar. In S. Kemmis & R. McTaggart (Eds.), *The action research reader* (3rd ed., pp. 337–352). Geelong, Australia: Deakin University Press.

Carr, W., & Kemmis, S. (1986). *Becoming critical: Education, knowledge, and action research.* London: Falmer.

Checkland, P. (1981). *Systems thinking, systems practice.* Chichester, UK: Wiley.

Checkland, P., & Scholes, J. (1990). *Soft systems methodology in action.* Chichester, UK: Wiley.

Clark, P. A. (1972). *Action research and organisational change.* London: Harper & Row.

Corey, S. M. (1949). Action research, fundamental research, and educational practices. *Teachers College Record, 50,* 509–514.

Corey, S. M. (1953). *Action research to improve school practices.* New York: Columbia University, Teachers College Press.

Dadds, M. (1995). *Passionate enquiry and school development: A story about teacher action research.* London: Falmer.

Davies, L., & Ledington, P. (1991). *Information in action: Soft systems methodology.* Basingstoke, UK: Macmillan.

Dewey, J. (1916). *Education and democracy.* New York: Macmillan.

Elden, M. (1983). Participatory research at work. *Journal of Occupational Behavior, 4*(1), 21–34.

Elliott, J. (1976–1977). Developing hypotheses about classrooms from teachers' practical constructs: An account of the work of the Ford Teaching Project. *Interchange, 7*(2), 2–22. Reprinted in Kemmis, S., & McTaggart, R. (Eds.). (1988). *The action research reader* (pp. 195–213). Geelong, Australia: Deakin University Press.

Elliott, J., & Adelman, C. (1973). Reflecting where the action is: The design of the Ford Teaching Project. *Education for Teaching, 92,* 8–20.

Emery, F. E., & Thorsrud, E. (1976). *Democracy at work: The report of the Norwegian Industrial Democracy Program.* Leiden, Netherlands: M. Nijhoff.

Emery, F. E., Thorsrud, E., & Trist, E. (1969). *Form and content in industrial democracy: Some experiences from Norway and other European countries.* London: Tavistock.

Fals Borda, O. (1979). Investigating reality in order to transform it: The Colombian experience. *Dialectical Anthropology, 4,* 33–55.

Fals Borda, O. (1988). *Knowledge and people's power.* New Delhi: Indian Social Institute.

Fals Borda, O., & Rahman, M. (1991). *Action and knowledge: Breaking the monopoly with participatory action research.* New York: Apex Press.

Fay, B. (1987). *Critical social science: Liberation and its limits.* Cambridge, UK: Polity.

Flood, R. L., & Jackson, M. C. (1991). *Creative problem solving: Total systems intervention.* Chichester, UK: Wiley.

Forester, J., Pitt, J., & Welsh, J. (Eds.). (1993). *Profiles of participatory action researchers.* Ithaca, NY: Cornell University, Department of Urban and Regional Planning.

Foster, M. (1972). An introduction to the theory and practice of action research in work organizations. *Human Relations, 25,* 529–566.

Freire, P. (1982). Creating alternative research methods: Learning to do it by doing it. In B. Hall, A. Gillette, & R. Tandon (Eds.), *Creating knowledge: A monopoly?* (pp. 29–37). New Delhi: Society for Participatory Research in Asia. Reprinted in Kemmis, S., & McTaggart, R. (Eds.). (1988). *The action research reader* (pp. 291–313). Geelong, Australia: Deakin University Press.

Greenwood, D., & Levin, M. (2000). Reconstructing the relationships between universities and society through action research. In N. Denzin & Y. Lincoln (Eds.), *Handbook of qualitative research* (2nd ed., pp. 85–106). Thousand Oaks, CA: Sage.

Greenwood, D., & Levin, M. (2001). Pragmatic action research and the struggle to transform universities into learning communities. In P. Reason & H. Bradbury (Eds.), *Handbook of action research* (pp. 103–113). London: Sage.

Habermas, J. (1972). *Knowledge and human interests* (J. J. Shapiro, Trans.). London: Heinemann.

Habermas, J. (1984). *Theory of communicative action,* Vol. 1: *Reason and the rationalization of society* (T. McCarthy, Trans.). Boston: Beacon.

Habermas, J. (1987a). *The philosophical discourse of modernity: Twelve lectures* (F. G. Lawrence, Trans.). Cambridge, MA: MIT Press.

Habermas, J. (1987b). *Theory of communicative action,* Vol. 2: *Lifeworld and system: A critique of functionalist reason* (T. McCarthy, Trans.). Boston: Beacon.

Habermas, J. (1992a). *Faktizität und Geltung* (Between facts and norms). Frankfurt, Germany: Suhrkamp.

Habermas, J. (1992b). *Postmetaphysical thinking: Philosophical essays* (W. M. Hohengarten, Trans.). Cambridge, MA: MIT Press.

Habermas, J. (1996). *Between Facts and Norms* (trans. William Rehg). Cambridge, Massachusetts: MIT Press.

Hall, B., Gillette, A., & Tandon, R. (1982). *Creating knowledge: A monopoly?* New Delhi: Society for Participatory Research in Asia.

Henry, C. (1991). If action research were tennis. In O. Zuber-Skerritt (Ed.), *Action learning for improved performance.* Brisbane, Australia: Aebis Publishing.

Hodgkinson, H. (1957). Action research: A critique. *Journal of Educational Sociology, 31*(4), 137–153.

Horton, M., with Kohl, J., & Kohl, H. (1990). *The long haul.* New York: Doubleday.

Jackson, M. C. (1991). *Systems methodology for the management sciences.* New York: Plenum.

Kemmis, S. (1981). Action research in prospect and retrospect. In S. Kemmis, C. Henry, C. Hook, & R. McTaggart (Eds.), *The action research reader* (pp. 11–31). Geelong, Australia: Deakin University Press.

Kemmis, S. (1991). Action research and postmodernisms. *Curriculum Perspectives, 11*(4), 59–66.

Kemmis, S. (1998). Interrupt and say: Is it worth doing? An interview with Stephen Kemmis. *Lifelong Learning in Europe, 3*(3).

Kemmis, S. (2004, March). *Knowing practice: Searching for saliences.* Paper presented at the "Participant Knowledge and Knowing Practice" conference, Umeå, Sweden.

Kemmis, S., & Brennan Kemmis, R. (2003, October). *Making and writing the history of the future together: Exploratory action in participatory action research.* Paper presented at the Congreso Internacional de Educación, Córdoba, Argentina.

Kemmis, S., & McTaggart, R. (1988a). *The action research planner* (3rd ed.). Geelong, Australia: Deakin University Press.

Kemmis, S., & McTaggart, R. (1988b). *The action research reader* (3rd ed.). Geelong, Australia: Deakin University Press.

Kemmis, S., & McTaggart, R. (2000). Participatory action research. In N. Denzin & Y. Lincoln (Eds.), *Handbook of qualitative research* (2nd ed., pp. 567–605). Thousand Oaks, CA: Sage.

Kolb, D. (1984). *Experiential learning: Experience as the source of learning and development.* Englewood Cliffs, NJ: Prentice Hall.

Levin, M. (1985). *Participatory action research in Norway.* Trondheim, Norway: ORAL.

Lewin, K. (1946). Action research and minority problems. *Journal of Social Issues, 2,* 34–46.

Lewin, K. (1952). Group decision and social change. In T. M. Newcomb & E. E. Hartley (Eds.), *Readings in social psychology* (pp. 459–473). New York: Holt.

Marika, R., Ngurruwutthun, D., & White, L. (1992). Always together, Yaka gäna: Participatory research at Yirrkala as part of the development of Yolngu education. *Convergence, 25*(1), 23–39.

McGuire, P. (1987). *Doing participatory research: A feminist approach.* Amherst: University of Massachusetts, Center for International Education.

McTaggart, R. (1991a). *Action research: A short modern history.* Geelong, Australia: Deakin University Press.

McTaggart, R. (1991b). Western institutional impediments to Aboriginal education. *Journal of Curriculum Studies, 23,* 297–325.

McTaggart, R. (Ed.). (1997). *Participatory action research: International contexts and consequences.* Albany: State University of New York Press.

McTaggart, R. (2002). The mission of the scholar in action research. In M. P. Wolfe & C. R. Pryor (Eds.), *The mission of the scholar: Research and practice* (pp. 1–16). London: Peter Lang.

McTaggart, R., & Garbutcheon-Singh, M. (1986). New directions in action research. *Curriculum Perspectives, 6*(2), 42–46.

Niemi, H., & Kemmis, S. (1999). Communicative evaluation: Evaluation at the crossroads. *Lifelong Learning in Europe, 4*(1), 55–64.

Noffke, S. E. (1990). *Action research: A multidimensional analysis.* Unpublished PhD thesis, University of Wisconsin–Madison.

Noffke, S. E. (1997). Themes and tensions in U.S. action research: Towards historical analysis. In S. Hollinsworth (Ed.), *International action research: A casebook for educational reform* (pp. 2–16). London: Falmer.

Oliveira, R., & Darcy, M. (1975). *The militant observer: A sociological alternative.* Geneva: Institute d'Action Cultural.

Park, P., Brydon-Miller, M., Hall, B., & Jackson, T. (Eds.). (1993). *Voices of change: Participatory research in the United States and Canada.* Toronto: OISE Press.

Pasmore, W., & Friedlander, F. (1982). An action research program for increasing employee involvement in problem-solving. *Administrative Science Quarterly, 27,* 342–362.

Pedler, M. (Ed.). (1991). *Action learning in practice.* Aldershot, UK: Gower.

Rapaport, R. N. (1970). Three dilemmas in action research. *Human Relations, 23,* 499–513.

Reason, P. (Ed.). (1988). *Human inquiry in action: Developments in new paradigm research.* London: Sage.

Revans, R. W. (1980). *Action learning: New techniques for management.* London: Blond & Briggs.

Revans, R. W. (1982). *The origins and growth of action learning.* Lund, Sweden: Studentlitteratur.

Ryan, K. E. (2003, November). *Serving public interests in educational accountability.* Paper presented at the meeting of the American Evaluation Association, Reno, NV.

Sagor, R. (1992). *How to conduct collaborative action research.* Alexandria, VA: Association for Supervision and Curriculum Development.

Sandkull, B. (1980). Practice of industry: Mis-management of people. *Human Systems Management, 1,* 159–167.

Schön, D. A. (1983). *The reflective practitioner: How professionals think in action.* New York: Basic Books.

Schön, D. A. (1987). *Educating the reflective practitioner.* San Francisco: Jossey–Bass.

Schön, D. A. (Ed.). (1991). *The reflective turn: Case studies in and on educational practice.* New York: Columbia University, Teachers College Press.

Stenhouse, L. (1975). *An introduction to curriculum research and development.* London: Heinemann Educational.

Taylor. C. (1991). *The malaise of modernity.* Concord, Ontario: House of Anansi.

Torbert, W. R. (1991). *The power of balance: Transforming self, society, and scientific inquiry.* Newbury Park, CA: Sage.

Warmington, A. (1980). Action research: Its methods and its implications. *Journal of Applied Systems Analysis, 7,* 23–39.

Weiner, G. (1989). Professional self-knowledge versus social justice: A critical analysis of the teacher–researcher movement. *British Educational Research Journal, 15*(1), 41–51.

Whyte, W. F. (1989). Introduction to action research for the twenty-first century: Participation, reflection, and practice. *American Behavioral Scientist, 32,* 502–512.

Whyte, W. F. (Ed.). (1991). *Participatory action research.* Newbury Park, CA: Sage.

Wittgenstein, L. (1958). *Philosophical investigations* (2nd ed., G. E. M. Anscombe, Trans.). Oxford, UK: Basil Blackwell.

Yunupingu, M. (1991). A plan for Ganma research. In R. Bunbury, W. Hastings, J. Henry, & R. McTaggart (Eds.), *Aboriginal pedagogy: Aboriginal teachers speak out* (pp. 98–106). Geelong, Australia: Deakin University Press.

Zuber-Skerritt, O. (Ed.). (1996). *New directions in action research.* London: Falmer.

24

CLINICAL RESEARCH

William L. Miller and Benjamin F. Crabtree

Under a sky the color of pea soup she is looking at her work growing away there actively, thickly like grapevines or pole beans as things grow in the real world, slowly enough.

—Opening stanza of Marge Piercy's "The Seven of Pentacles"

A tornado approaches the fields of our dreams. How well has our clinical research prepared the ground for the coming whirlwind? Jocelyn arrives to consult with her primary care clinician. For 3 years, the 50-year-old Jocelyn notices some burning pain "around my heart" shortly after meals and when she lies down for extended periods. This pain is frequently associated with a "sour taste in my mouth." On the morning of her visit, shortly after her fourth cup of coffee, she stands by the grill at work nearly doubled over by the pain. She can tolerate the suffering no longer. By nearly everyone's account, the clinical encounter that follows is a success. Her doctor quickly diagnoses gastroesophageal reflux disease (GERD) and prescribes Nexium, the "purple pill." The whole visit takes only 6 minutes and helps the doctor to meet his productivity quota. Jocelyn, knowing about the pill from television commercials, is worried about the diagnosis but pleased with the simple solution. AstraZeneca, which produces Nexium, is delighted. The office staff and practice group manager are happy, and Jocelyn's employer at the fast-food restaurant is glad that Jocelyn has very little time lost from work. Clinical researchers, proud of their randomized controlled trials demonstrating the effectiveness of esomeprazole (the generic name for Nexium), feel vindicated. So, where's the tornado? If you are a clinical researcher, are you worrying about the standardized simplicity of this story?

GERD is the disease label affixed to a symptom complex associated with the experience of heartburn. GERD is related to the reflux of gastric acid (important for immunity and digestion) into the esophagus because of the inappropriate relaxation or leakage of the lower esophageal sphincter (LES) that separates the stomach from the esophagus. The healthy stomach has a protective coating of mucous shielding it from acid, whereas the esophagus does not and often produces alerting symptoms such as heartburn in the presence of acid. Proton pump inhibitors (PPIs) such as

Nexium block the cellular pumps that produce normal acid in the stomach and, by nearly eliminating the acid, prevent heartburn (but not the reflux of acid-free stomach juices). Reflux results from multiple factors that weaken the LES, relax it inappropriately, or create excessive pressure on it. These factors include overeating, bedtime snacking, wearing tight clothing or tight clip-on earrings, rapid eating, being obese (especially with large abdominal girth), experiencing emotional stress, and using several common drugs, caffeine, tobacco, and/or alcohol—in summary, an acquisitive, materialistic consumer lifestyle. These factors are named and chided in a PPI commercial where a patient celebrates being liberated from the agony of lifestyle change simply by taking the right pill. She is now free to continue whatever lifestyle she wishes and no longer needs to wonder what else her body is trying to communicate through the symptom of heartburn. She is learning to ignore the questions that emerge from her own experiences and to pay more attention to consumer-oriented answers and corporation-generated questions. These are questions of instrumental rationality that are eagerly and extravagantly funded by government-sponsored research institutions and the medical technology and pharmaceutical industries and that are most commonly addressed by current clinical research.

One by one, islands of rock, with a solitary person standing on each, loom into view as the surf pounds below. Each voice urgently proclaims, "I didn't know!" As the hidden camera fades back, the islands merge together, each person appearing securely confident—protected by the purple pill—and the erosive raging of the sea below now controlled. The war against the terrorism of stomach acid pouring across its boundary into the esophagus has been won. Millions of television viewers, including Jocelyn, watch this AstraZeneca commercial about its newest PPI, Nexium. What didn't they know? The veiled threat is that GERD could lead to Barrett's esophagus and then to adenocarcinoma, even though this connection is rare and uncertain and there is no evidence that taking PPIs prevents it (Conio et al., 2003). Thousands of physicians, fed by AstraZeneca representatives, have their offices cluttered with tablets, pens, and trinkets labeled "Nexium" and have their drug cabinets stocked with Nexium samples. How well has our clinical research prepared Jocelyn and her clinician, as well as everyone else, for this global corporate tornado? On their desks or computer screens appear article reprints of clinical research exclaiming the effectiveness of esomeprazole (Nexium) in controlling the symptoms of heartburn (Johnson et al., 2001; Talley et al., 2002) but none about what it means.

Sickness pervades the landscape. Suburban sprawl contributes to obesity and the epidemic of diabetes (Perdue, Stone, & Gostin, 2003). Millions of socioeconomically impoverished people are dying or dead from AIDS, tuberculosis, and malaria because economically colonized countries lack access to care and the necessary medicines despite supporting the profits of global pharmaceutical corporations (Farmer, 2001; Kim, Millen, Irwin, & Gershman, 2000). Sustainable ways of living across our globe are disrupted and replaced by capitalist market economies. People who were once self-sufficient are now bound to wage labor and assured the freedom to choose soft drinks. Greatly reduced is their freedom to choose a local vocation and way of life (Coote, 1996; Douthwaite, 1999). Water, air, forests, soil, and the ecologies of which they are a part are deteriorating (Gardner, 2003). The acid of Western civilization's quest for domination is pouring across its boundaries, scorching the land, and consuming the earth's diversity. The proposed solutions are even more technology and business as usual, a global purple pill for global GERD. Part of what is going on here is the complex interactions of an expectant and frightened public, the myopic arrogance of military and economic power, and many (often well-intentioned) individuals trapped in their own and the dominant culture's webs of denial (Jensen, 2002). Welcome to the clinical research space.

Meanwhile, amid a Middle Atlantic landscape of small farms, sprawling suburbs, crowded urban streets, and rigid walls of private property, Jocelyn is taking the purple pill every day. She is confused and worried. Although free of heartburn symptoms, nothing else has changed in her life. The heartburn began about 1 year after her daughter's infant child died in an auto accident and 6 months after starting a new job in a fast-food restaurant. Over that year, Jocelyn resumed smoking, gained 30 pounds, and was drinking more coffee. The heartburn was getting worse despite taking many over-the-counter medicines. During this same time, she worried about her son serving in the U.S. Army in Iraq and about the threat of terrorism. Is it possible that parts of this story are related to her symptoms? To the global issues noted? What does the new diagnosis of GERD mean to Jocelyn? What and whose questions were addressed in her encounter? What and whose questions were missing? Poor, frightened, and 50 years old, she knows that something is wrong. Where is the meaning in her embodied embedded lived experiences? Her life, composed of memories, children, career, lovers, and anticipated hopes, appears shredded; she fears that no one is listening. Now she is noticing some low back pain. Her doctors hide their fears and lose their empathy behind the latest tests and the newest drugs and clinical trial protocols. Working for "HamsterCare," they are exhausted turning their wheels of productivity (Morrison, 2000). They feel tired, overregulated, angry at the continued emphasis on cost cutting and efficiency and on the threat of malpractice, and inadequate in the face of death, but they conceal their emotions behind a wall of professional "objectivity." The clinicians also struggle to mediate guidelines, multiple languages of specialization, ambiguities of new technological visions of the body, their own clinical knowledge and experience, and patient values and idiosyncrasies. Meanwhile, marketing researchers for AstraZeneca are conducting focus groups to learn more effective ways of convincing adults and physicians of Nexium's value. But these are stories rarely known by the "public." These stories are hidden, if known at all, by conscious concealment and by the forces of unconscious cultural preference. The story told is that GERD is dangerous to you and that Nexium is the safe and effective product fix. The ecological, social, and spiritual consequences are invisible.

This is a typical tale in clinical medical research. *Suffering and normality are standardized, commoditized, and marketed.* The suffering related to heartburn is framed as a threat, that is, a universal need for some marketable product that restores control. The story is framed as a "restitution" narrative (Frank, 1995). Everyone has something wrong with him or her; normal now means inadequate in moral and standardized ways such as the recent guidelines creating the new disease of prehypertension (Chobanian et al., 2003) and the guidelines on obesity that make most U.S. adults overweight or obese (National Heart, Lung, and Blood Institute, 1998). The complexities, multiplicities, and individualities of suffering and normality are subsumed within this technological and commercial frame. This is the tornado! Important voices, questions, and evidence are missing. Knowing the efficacy of the drug—the internal validity—is sufficient to approve using all means necessary to convince all people to "choose" the pill as a requirement for a safe and healthy life. It is assumed that there is a real material world that is, in principle, knowable through scientific methodology, especially the randomized controlled trial, and nothing should stand in the way of pursuing this truth. Outside the swirl of this neorealist tornado, there is so much silence. Jocelyn's experience of taking a daily pill that labels her self and body as endangered is missing. The voices of her family members are missing. Relationships and moral discourse are missing. The place and role of power are missing. Feeling, spirituality, and ecology are missing. Depth and context are reduced, simplified, or eliminated, and relationships are isolated and alienated. What hope is there after the tornado passes?

This is the clinical research space we have witnessed above ground—clinical research too often working on behalf of the dominant cultural tornado of global corporate capitalism. There are alternatives! The stories of interest and hope for clinical researchers are in what is missing and how the stories are framed. We imagine clinical research spaces where Jocelyn and the many communities of patients and neighbors, clinicians, and researchers meet together and seek transformation. The suffering related to heartburn is framed as broken-ness calling for reconnection, generosity, and love. The story is framed as a movement from "chaos" to "quest" narrative (Frank, 1995). We imagine at least two different and deeply connected research spaces. One is at ground level, visible, helpful, and growing and healing within the dominant culture, at the places where the questions of embodied and embedded lived experience meet clinical reality and current institutional structures and processes. Here, using a more participatory and mixed methods approach guided by the questions of lived experience, the ground is tended and weeded and opportunities for planting seeds and nurturing healthier plants are identified and enacted. This is the quest toward transformation that assumes that even the oppressors are oppressed. We do not believe that this will be enough. The tornado already creates wastelands based on ethnicity, color, class, gender, and sexuality, and it ravishes the life-sustaining soul of our one earth—the soil, water, air, and intricate web of interdependent species. The tornado often leaves us in chaos, with no clear storyline apparent; there is only the hope of each other. We propose a second space below ground—out of reach of the tornado. Within the burrows and entanglements of garden soil, clinician/patient, qualitative/quantitative, academy/practice, very different ways, cultures, and technologies of knowing can meet, converse, and create a "solidarity" clinical research for the future that serves nascent institutional forms. This chapter explores both of these spaces and conversations.

This *Handbook* celebrates the qualitative research community's conversations—the internal discourse about our identity, what we do, and the faith and hope for our own growth and transformation that is sustained there. The opportunity to translate this conversation into both an expanded and a new alternative clinical research space was never better or more urgent. Historical calls for a shift away from a strictly positivist position and for seeking greater methodological diversity, including the use of qualitative research methods (e.g., Freymann, 1989; McWhinney, 1986, 1989; Waitzkin, 1991), are being answered. Qualitative clinical research is finding its way into funding agency agendas, especially in primary health and medical care and nursing. Patients[1] and clinicians are increasingly invited into research conversations. Methods are also evolving; they are beginning to separate from their parent traditions (e.g., ethnography, phenomenology, grounded theory) and generating new hybrids in the clinical research space. Unfortunately, this success is also leading to powerful efforts from within the dominant paradigm to co-opt qualitative methods despite a small and articulate resistance (Morse, Swanson, & Kuzel, 2001). This is most evident in the development of checklists for ensuring validity of qualitative studies (Barbour, 2001). Versions of this chapter in earlier editions of this *Handbook* were solely about continuing and accelerating this successful flow, that is, the exploration and conversations at ground level. We no longer believe this to be sufficient. Our own recent experiences at working within the toxic embrace of the dominant paradigm and its forces of elite corporate globalization alert us to the additional need for work below ground preparing for after the tornado passes.

The understandings of clinical research presented here are grounded in the authors' own stories. Our rhizomes are deeply embedded within the nexus of applied anthropology and the practice of primary health care, particularly family medicine. Both authors have appointments in departments of family medicine and are trained in anthropology. Our social science roots were fed by the development of clinically applied anthropology during the 1970s (Chrisman, 1977; Chrisman & Maretzki, 1982; Fabrega, 1976, 1979; Foster, 1974; Foster & Anderson, 1978; Polgar, 1962) and were nurtured by the later work of Kleinman (1988, 1992, 1995; see also Kleinman, Eisenberg, & Good, 1978), the Goods (Good, 1994; Good & Good, 1981), Lock (1982, 1986, 1993), the Peltos (Pelto & Pelto, 1978, 1990), and Young (1982a, 1982b). These roots are currently challenged by the poststructuralist debate (Burawoy et al., 1991; Clifford & Marcus, 1986; Haraway,

1993; Jackson, 1989) and critical theory (Baer, 1993; Morsy, 1996; Singer, 1995). One of the authors (W.L.M.) has a busy urban family medicine practice, oversees a residency program, and chairs a clinical department within a large academic community hospital. The other author (B.F.C.) directs a family medicine research division and is a national research consultant. Both authors actively participate in the politics and discourse of academic biomedicine and academic social science and have experience in international health settings. The biomedical influence, with its perceived therapeutic imperative, steers toward pragmatic interventions and the desire for explicitness and coherence in information gathering and decision making and highlights the appeal of neorealist postpositivism and technology. The actual relationships that emerge within patient care reveal the uncertainty and particularity (McWhinney, 1989) of clinical praxis and turn one toward storytelling, relationship, and interpretation. The realities of power and dominant cultural hegemony are exposed in our efforts to help uninsured patients receive appropriate care, to protect the health of local habitats, to change international health policy, to get grants funded, to publish storied knowledge in biomedical journals, and to guide our departments through budget challenges and our institutions toward profitability. Growing and dying within the multiplicities of our soils, we have come to realize the relativity of all knowledge. The challenges are not epistemological but rather practical and moral. We are privileged white men holding positions of power within the belly of the beast; we are also tricksters. The conversations that we recommend for clinical research reflect these two stances.

Clinical Research at Ground Level

Fight persistently as the creeper that brings down the tree. Spread like the squash plant that overruns the garden. Gnaw in the dark and use the sun to make sugar. Weave real connections, create real nodes, build real houses. Live a life you can endure: make love that is loving.

—Continuation of Marge Piercy's "The Seven of Pentacles"

Our guiding premise is that the questions emerging from the embodied, embedded, and mindfully lived clinical experience frame conversation and determine research design (Brewer & Hunter, 1989; Diers, 1979; Miller & Crabtree, 1999b). Clinical researchers have at least six discernible research styles available: (a) experimental, (b) survey, (c) documentary–historical, (d) field (qualitative), (e) philosophical, and (f) action/participatory (Lather, 1991; see also Madison, chap. 21, this volume). The clinical research space above ground needs to be open to all of these possible sources and types of knowledge. They all contribute to the two primary aims of clinical research at ground level. The first is to *deepen and contextualize the practical and ethical questions,* concerns, and emerging understandings for healers and their patients and policymakers. A second aim is to *trouble the waters and seek change* within the clinical research world itself. This section is organized around the following three goals: (a) *creating a space* for research that opens and celebrates qualitative and multiparadigmatic approaches to the clinical world, (b) *providing the tools and translations* necessary for discovering and witnessing clinical stories and knowledge within this space, and (c) identifying and describing the means for *telling the stories* and sharing the knowledge.

The emphasis is on the clinical text of Western biomedicine and the particular subtext of primary health care because of the authors' location in that place. Fortunately, the discussion is easily transferred to other clinical contexts such as nursing care, education, organizational management, community organizing, and international activism (see also Berg & Smith, 1988; Bogdan & Biklen, 1992; Morse & Field, 1997; Moyer, MacAllister, & Soifer, 2001; Roseland, 1998; Sapsford & Abbott, 1992; Schein, 1987; Symon & Cassell, 1998). In all of these arenas, qualitative methods are more accepted, yet the noise from policymakers is for being more evidence based and outcomes driven with generalizability and randomized designs prioritized. (See the recent "No Child Left Behind" act for an example of this in educational policy [www.ed.gov/nclb/landing.jhtml].) In education, for example, a recent "consensus" report sought to define scientific research in education and, like this chapter, argued that the methods must fit the question. Unlike this chapter, the report prioritized the value of randomized studies and expressed doubts about participatory models. The report voiced no concerns about the goal of evidence-based education (Shavelson & Towne, 2002). We offer an alternative viewpoint.

Creating a Space

The dominant biomedical world and the smaller qualitative research community both tend to maintain methodological and academic rigidity. Creating a clinical research space requires bringing both groups into the garden and developing common language. *The clinical questions are the common ground* (Taylor, 1993) for creating this space. These questions call us to rediscover the missing evidence (the people, experiences, ecology, power, and contexts) and the richness and depth of what "effectiveness" means. The clinical questions invite us to explore the human implications of rationing and cost issues, biotechnology, and genetic engineering and to enter the conflicted landscape of alternative and conventional medicine—the world between the "garden" and the "machine" (Beinfield & Korngold, 1991). The questions beg us to locate, own, aim, and share the powers inherent in clinical situations (Brody, 1992). The vulnerability exposed by the fully embedded and embodied clinical experiences that give rise to these questions also reveals the inadequacies of a neorealist epistemology (for more details, see Perakyla, chap. 34, this volume). Three core strategies for creating and entering this common ground and transforming clinical research are described. These consist of stepping carefully and strategically into the biomedical world, expanding the evidence-based medicine (EBM) space, and democratizing knowledge. Three additional strategies—using theory more explicitly, expanding cross-disciplinary collaborations, and applying the principles of critical multiplism—are also mentioned briefly. These strategies assume that change is more experience based than it is rational and that clinical participants must actively try methods if they are to adopt them. Thus, there is an emphasis on clinical participants, including patients, answering their own questions using methods appropriate for those questions.

Entering Biomedicine

Walking and working within the walls of technocratic biomedicine is exciting and daunting, and it frequently challenges intellectual and personal integrity. Thriving in this world requires understanding the biomedical cultural context while also clearly articulating a model that highlights the clinical implications of qualitative clinical research. This knowledge, if also joined by patients and other community participants, facilitates bargaining, mediation, and the formation of common language that makes possible the creation of a new research space at ground level. This is where, in languages understandable by the existing clinical world and patients, a space for more expansive imagination is created, the tools for listening and seeing are shared, and the seeds for transforming stories are sown.

The dominant biomedical paradigm is rooted in a patriarchal positivism; *control through rationality and separation is the overriding theme.* The biomedical model is typified by the following 10 basic premises: (a) scientific *rationality,* (b) an emphasis on *individual autonomy* rather than on family or community, (c) the *body as machine* with an emphasis on physicochemical data and on objective numerical measurement, (d) *mind–body separation* and dualism, (e) *diseases as entities,* (f) the *patient as object* and the resultant alienation of physician from patient, (g) an emphasis on the *visual,* (h) diagnosis and treatment from the *outside,* (i) *reductionism* and the seeking of *universals* (Davis-Floyd & St. John, 1998; Gordon, 1988), and (j) *separation from nature.* The everyday characteristics of the clinical medical world that follow from this model include (a) male centeredness, (b) physician centeredness, (c) specialist orientation, (d) an emphasis on credentials, (e) high value placed on memory, (f) a process orientation accentuating ritual with supervaluation on "science" and technology, (g) therapeutic activism with an emphasis on short-term results, (h) death seen as defeat, (i) division of the clinical space into "front" (receptionists, billing clerks, and office managers) and "back" (doctors, nurses, and phlebotomists), (j) the definition, importance, and sanctity of "medical time," (k) an emphasis on patient satisfaction, (l) profit-driven system, (m) reverence for the privacy of the doctor–patient relationship, (n) disregard of ecological and international impacts, and (o) intolerance of other modalities (Davis-Floyd & St. John, 1998; Helman, 2000; Pfifferling, 1981; Stein, 1990). These are the common (and often tacit) assumptions, values, and beliefs that characterize the dominant voice of the medical clinic and that currently define the preferred boundaries of clinical research.

Biomedical culture is reinforced and sustained by its comfortable fit within the prevailing cultural norms of the United States and an elite globalizing corporate economy. These "normalizing ideologies" include control over the environment, rational determinism, future orientation, life as an ordered and continuous whole, and individualism with an emphasis on productivity, perseverance, self-determination, and self-reliance. They surface in public discourse as four "market myths," namely, that (a) growth benefits all, (b) freedom is market freedom, (c) we are *homo economicus, consumens, et dominans,* and (d) corporate and finance driven globalization is inevitable (Moe-Lobeda, 2002). The normalizing ideologies are also manifest in daily discourses about family, self, gender identity, and aging. Both patients and physicians refer to these ideologies and their associated discourses to help them restore order and normality to the disruptions of sickness (Becker, 1997).

This reigning voice of biomedicine has now been successfully corporatized in the United States, and its apparent goals, aside from amassing profits, are the elimination of pain, suffering, disease, and even death. The research tends to be product focused, hospital based, and disease oriented. In many ways, the current situation represents the triumph of commoditization and universalism with an emphasis on cost, customers, products, outcomes, effectiveness, standardization, and evidence. The reasons for focusing on outcomes are to inform choices (market approach), to provide accountability (regulatory approach), and to improve care (management approach). Despite the superficial appearance of hegemony and coherence, the voice of medicine, when enacted and witnessed, reveals many "hidden" multiplicities (Mol, 2002). Fortunately for qualitative researchers, these voices and actions are waiting to be heard and seen. If these voices are entered into the conversation as evidence, the clinical research space is expanded, dominant paradigms are challenged, and hope is reimagined.

Successfully entering the biomedical world as a qualitative clinical researcher requires a many-eyed *model of mediation.* Enter as eye jugglers (Frey, 1994) with multiple perspectives. This qualitative clinical model of mediation features the following 10 premises:

1. Center yourself in the *clinical world,* that is, in the eye of the storm.
2. Focus on the *questions* that dawn there.
3. Assume *both/and.* Acknowledge what is of value in biomedicine *and* highlight what is missing—what is silent, invisible, or ignored. Expand on the already existent tension between care and competence (Good & Good, 1993). Hold quantitative objectivisms in one hand and qualitative revelations in the other.
4. Follow a *natural history* path that characterized the early history of Western medicine and that is still an important aspect of primary health care (Harris, 1989).
5. Be *participatory.* Include patients and clinicians in your inquiry work.
6. Preserve and celebrate *anomaly,* that is, the discoveries and data that do not fit. Anomalies are levers for transformation.

7. Allow "truth" to be *emergent* and not preconceived, defensive, or forceful.
8. Respect the plea for *clinical action* and the perceived need for coherence voiced by nearly all participants in the clinical world.
9. Practice *humility, generosity,* and *patience.* This will enable everything else.
10. Refuse *silence* when oppression is evident or exposed. Practice testimony (Frank, 1995).

Qualitative clinical researchers bring several powerful perspectives to the clinical encounter that help surface the unseen and unheard and also add depth to what is already present. These include understanding disease as a cultural construction (Berger & Luckmann, 1967); possessing knowledge of additional medical models such as the biopsychosocial and humanistic models (Engels, 1977; Smith, 1996), the holistic model (Gordon, 1996; Weil, 1988), homeopathy (Swayne, 1998), and non-Western models that include traditional Chinese (Beinfield & Korngold, 1991), Ayurvedic (Sharma & Clark, 1998), and shamanism (Drury, 1996); and recognizing the face and importance of spirituality in human life. Qualitative researchers also perceive that the therapeutic or healing process occurs not only in the clinical moment but also in everyday life between clinical events. Thus, the study of everyday life offers additional perspectives, that is, additional voices to the research space being created at ground level. Carrying the staff of your many-eyed model of mediation, you are ready to enter the clinic.

The clinic[2] is a public sanctuary for the voicing of trouble and the dispensing of relief. Each clinic participant crafts meaning out of the "facts" and "feelings" inherent in each clinical encounter and seeks to weave a comforting cloth of *support.* Jocelyn and her family come and meet their clinician and his staff at the clinic. All of these participants' past ghosts—the emotional, physical, conceptual, sociocultural, and spiritual contingencies—and the competing demands of their presents and the hopes and fears for their futures are brought into the clinic. This is the real world of clinical practice involving intentions, meanings, intersubjectivity, values, personal knowledge, power, and ethics. Yet most published clinical research still consists of observational epidemiology (Feinstein, 1985; Kelsey, Thompson, & Evans, 1986; Sackett, 1991; Stevens, Abrams, Brazier, Fitzpatrick, & Lilford, 2001) and clinical trial designs (Meinert, 1986; Pocock, 1983). These studies involve separating the variables of interest from their local everyday milieu, entering them into a controlled research environment, and then trying to fit the results back into the original context. For example, Jocelyn's clinician is aware of randomized controlled trials demonstrating clinical efficacy for short-term bed rest in patients with back pain (Deyo, Diehl, & Rosenthal, 1986; Wiesel et al., 1980). But the practitioner encounters difficulty in applying this information to the particular back pain and disability experienced by Jocelyn. The pieces of evidence needed to inform this encounter are many. Ideally, the clinical participants will study themselves and, thus, challenge their own situated knowledges and empower their own transformations. This requires bringing qualitative methods to the clinical experience. Let us expand the EBM research space.

Expanding Evidence-Based Medicine

EBM is the new wonder child in clinical care and clinical research. The premise is that individual clinical expertise must be integrated "with the best research evidence . . . and patient values" (Sackett, Straus, Richardson, Rosenberg, & Haynes, 2000, p. 1). Randomized clinical trials (RCTs) and meta-analyses (systematic reviews of multiple RCTs) are considered the best external evidence when asking questions about therapeutic interventions. An international group of clinicians, methodologists, and consumers has formed the Cochrane Collaboration as a means of facilitating the collection, implementation, and dissemination of such systematic reviews (Fullerton-Smith, 1995). The group has created a Cochrane Library that is available on CD, on the Internet, and in secondary publications through the *British Medical Journal.* Major initiatives are under way to ensure that all physicians, especially at the primary care level, use this evidence to guide their clinical decision making (Shaughnessy, Slawson, & Bennett, 1994; Slawson, Shaughnessy, & Bennett, 1994). The proliferation of clinical practice guidelines is one result of these initiatives. Another result is the relative reduced value of qualitative studies. But EBM actually offers qualitative clinical investigators multiple opportunities for entering, expanding, challenging, and adding variety and honesty to this space. There is so much *missing evidence*!

The double-blind (closed) RCT has high internal validity but dubious external validity and very little information about *context* or *ecological consequences* (Glasgow, Lichtenstein, & Marcus, 2003). Read any RCT report, and the only voice you hear is the cold sound of the intervention and faint echoes of the investigator's biases. The cacophonous music of patients, clinicians, insurance companies, lawyers, government regulatory bodies, consumer interest groups, animals and habitats, community agencies, office staff, corporate interests, and family turmoil is mute. Local politics and contradictory demands become the sound of thin hush. There is also little research about the *individual clinical expertise* side of the EBM equation and about the associated areas of relationship dynamics, communication, and patient preference. There is much to be learned about how patients and clinicians actually implement "best evidence." How is the evidence incorporated into patients' and communities' life stories? In addition, there are many gray zones of clinical practice where the evidence about competing clinical options is incomplete or contradictory (Naylor, 1995). What constitutes evidence, anyway (Morse et al., 2001)? Who creates it, defines it, and judges it? Trouble the waters of EBM certainty. Here are openings for clinical researchers. We can enter the EBM and RCT space and expand and challenge its vision.

We recommend replacing the metaphor of "gold standard" with a metaphor of "ancient forest standard" that needs to include qualitative methods along with the RCT. In addition to those areas already noted, qualitative methods can help to formalize the learning curve, test theory, inform hypothesis testing and future work, and enhance the transferability of the clinical trial into clinical practice. "Gold standard" suggests a singular, immutable, and universal truth, whereas "ancient forest standard" suggests diversity, dynamic complexity, and contingent multiple perspectives. We propose conceptualizing a multimethod RCT as a double-stranded helix of DNA—a *double helix trial design* (Miller, Crabtree, Duffy, Epstein, & Stange, 2003). On one strand are qualitative methods addressing issues of context, meaning, power, and complexity, and on the other strand are quantitative methods providing measurement and a focused anchor. The two strands are connected by the research questions. The qualitative and quantitative strands twist and spiral around the questions in an ongoing interaction, creating codes of understanding that get expressed in better clinical care. If the qualitative strand maintains methodological integrity and interpretive relativism and stays connected to the experiences informing the research questions, the double helix and its bonds might even experience breakage and mutation and transformation beyond postpositivism.

We hope that clinical researchers will seek out those doing clinical trials on symptom management, treatments, clinical process, and community interventions and will advocate for adding the qualitative strand. For example, if a gastroenterologist at your local hospital or academic medical center is planning or conducting an RCT concerning a new treatment option for GERD, you could offer to meet and propose adding a qualitative arm to the study with the intent of exploring any of several possible questions. How do patients understand and incorporate the diagnosis into their life stories? How do they experience the treatment? What is the impact on their quality of life, their work, their sexual activity, their family and social relations, their involvement in civic affairs, their sense of self, and their fears and desires? How does the study affect the researchers? This work will help to identify new outcomes that transpose the emphasis on individual cure and elimination of pain and disease toward care, growth, quality of life, healthier relationships, and more sustainable communities and ecosystems. Nonetheless, a double helix trial design is not adequate for assessing ecological consequences of interventions; this requires more longitudinal, mixed method, and case study designs.

Examples showing the way toward double helix trial designs already exist. Jolly, Bradley, Sharp, Smith, and Mant (1998), using RCT technology, tested a nurse-led intervention to help patients surviving heart attacks maintain a rehabilitation program and improve health habits. The quantitative RCT strand yielded statistically insignificant results; fortunately, Wiles (1998) had also conducted a qualitative depth interview study with 25 of the participants at 2 weeks and 5 months during the trial and uncovered several clinically valuable findings. At 2 weeks, most of the patients trusted the official accounts of what had happened and what needed to be done to prevent future problems. By 5 months, most of the patients had lost that trust because the official accounts had not adequately addressed the experienced random nature of heart attacks, the severity, and the level of recovery. Many of the patients perceived survival to mean that their heart attacks were mild, and because the doctors had reassured them that everything would be normal in 6 weeks, the patients assumed that they could return to their original "normal" lifestyles by that time. Another example of the double helix design for RCTs concerns smoking cessation interventions and is found in the work of Willms and Wilson at McMaster University. They learned that the meanings that patients attributed to their cigarettes were more influential in stopping smoking than were counseling and the use of nicotine gum (Willms, 1991; Willms et al., 1990; Wilson et al., 1988). Let us also join in opening the imagination inside the genome with qualitative questions and approaches (Finkler, 2000).

What are the clinically grounded questions that serve as windows for opening imagination at ground level? Clinicians and patients seeking *support* in the health care setting confront four fundamental questions of clinical praxis. First, what is going on with our *bodies?* Second, what is happening with our *lives?* Third, who has what *power*? Fourth, what are the complex *relationships* among our bodies, our lives, our ecological context, and power? These four questions also mirror the methods of numeracy, literacy, policy, and "ecolacy" (i.e., thinking ecologically) (Hardin, 1985). Each of these questions has *emotional, physical/behavioral, conceptual/attributional, cultural/social/historical,* and *spiritual/energetic* ramifications. From the story of Jocelyn, there are body questions about support. What are the emotions of living with a fear of the long-term consequences of GERD? Is Nexium more effective than lifestyle change at preventing those consequences? How will either impact family and social bodies? What is the lived experience and meaning of GERD for patients and clinicians? What is happening in the office practice as a body that helps or hinders Jocelyn's care? There are questions concerning the support of one's life or biography. Do explanatory models of GERD relate to the experience and outcome of risk? How does one's self-concept relate to GERD and response to Nexium? What are patients' and clinicians' hopes, despairs, fears, and insecurities concerning GERD? How does past experience connect to the immediate experience of GERD or participation in a clinical trial? There are questions of power about how people are supported. What is happening when patients with GERD present to clinicians in different organizational contexts of care? How is emotional distress surfaced or suppressed? What patterns exist in these different settings? Who influences whom? How is the power of the patient or clinician undermined or enhanced (Fahy & Smith, 1999)? What are the local politics? There are questions about the support of relationships. What actions in the clinical encounter enhance family relationships? How do the individuals, the families, and the clinic function as complex adaptive systems? How do the illness and its care relate to the local ecology? Many of these questions are addressed adequately only if qualitative methods enter into the clinical research space and we look toward an ancient forest standard.

This is the evidence needed! We can apply these four question categories to the critically important issues of the next decade such as the globalization of biomedicine, rationing and cost, biotechnology and genetic products, and the often conflicted landscape where alternative medicine and biomedicine meet. How does rationing affect our bodies? What are the emotional, physical, conceptual, social, and spiritual consequences? The same questions can be asked of the many new (and old) products of biotechnology. What is the impact on our lives? Where is the power, and how is it used and resisted? What are the relationships and complex systems that are affected and through which the technology is deployed? What are the unanticipated consequences? How do patients decide about therapies? How do they juggle seeing their bodies as both garden and machine? What other metaphors are used, and when and how do they change outcomes? The questions are infinite and challenging. Primary care, at its core, is a context-dependent craft. EBM lacks context in its current form; it cries out for qualitative methods and alternative paradigms. Let us get to work!

Democratizing Knowledge

Entering biomedicine and working to expand and change the EBM space also holds great risk for qualitative clinical researchers being co-opted by the dominant paradigm that they seek to transform; thus, there is a need for democratizing knowledge. The assumption is that the more everyone and everything potentially affected by any given knowledge and its associated technologies and actions has decision-making influence and involvement in the production of that knowledge, the less likely the research will be co-opted by any single power. Participatory research approaches, supported by using a participatory wheel of inquiry and its four ways of knowing, valuing variation and improvisation, applying the precautionary principle, and pursuing slow knowledge, are proposed keys to democratizing knowledge and opening the clinical research space above ground to transformational hope.

Participatory research approaches all share the characteristics of collaboration between the researcher and the researched, a reciprocal process whereby each party educates the other, and the intent to create local knowledge for improving the conditions and quality of life (Macaulay et al., 1998; Small, 1995; Thesen & Kuzel, 1999). Participatory research promotes the voices of communities in identifying health issues and helps to ensure that social, cultural, economic, and ecological conditions are included (Jason, Keys, Suarez-Balcazar, Taylor, & Davis, 2004). It also provides another entry into challenging and transforming the research space and brings us around, full circle, to the research questions. We propose that clinical researchers investigate questions emerging from the clinical experience with the clinical participants, pay attention to and reveal any underlying values and assumptions, and direct the results toward clinical participants and policymakers. This refocuses the gaze of clinical research onto the clinical experience and redefines its boundaries as the answer to three questions, namely "Whose question is it?," "Are hidden assumptions of the clinical world revealed?," and "For whom are the research results intended?" (i.e., who are the stakeholders or audiences?). Clinical researchers share ownership of the research with clinical participants, thereby undermining the patriarchal bias of the dominant paradigm and opening its assumptions to investigation. This is the situated knowledge, the "somewhere in particular" (Haraway, 1991, p. 196), where space is created to find a larger and more inclusive vision of clinical research. The opportunity is created to redefine the meaning of and responsibilities for health, to value indigenous practices and knowledge systems, to demystify science and technology, and to expand the research capacity of communities (Tandon, 1996). Patients and clinicians are invited to explore personal and/or each other's questions and concerns with whatever methods and paradigms are necessary.

Participatory approaches bring a diverse group of people and ideas and ways of knowing into a common space that challenges the traditional boundaries of science. Figure 24.1, a *participatory wheel of inquiry* derived from the work of Wilber (1996) and Schumacher (1977), represents a map for understanding and working with this diversity of traditions, experiences, and associated methods (Stange, Miller, & McWhinney, 2001), and the six research styles noted earlier. This integrative framework represents human knowledge about the natural world in four quadrants, with the horizontal axis representing inner and outer reality and the vertical axis representing individual and collective knowledge. The right-hand quadrants are the world as seen by materialist science—the view from outside. This is the domain of third-person "It" and "Its" knowledge based on detached objective observation. The left-hand quadrants are the inner or subjective aspects of reality—the domain of "I" and "We" knowledge. The left is concerned with meaning, that is, with beauty and goodness. The right is concerned with physical laws. The multiple ways of knowing and associated traditions and methods may be classified within this grid (for a similar model, see Kemmis & McTaggart, 2003). For example, both of the right-hand quadrants, knowledge of external physical and social reality, are studied using experimental and social science and epidemiological survey methods and are based primarily on the traditional biomedical paradigm and associated reductionist assumptions of materialist inquiry.

For the domains of knowledge needed for personalized, prioritized, and integrated clinical care, a more participatory and "subjective" way of knowing based on intimate involvement with self and other is required. The interior-focused quadrants on the left represent such complementary knowledge based on reflective participation. The left upper quadrant, "I" knowledge, refers to wisdom gained through the individual accumulation of particular experiences—reflection on clinical practice, diaries and journals, and philosophical methods. The left lower quadrant, "We" knowledge, is exemplified by the theoretical work of Lucy Candib. Candib (1995) demonstrated the connections among the developing feminist literature on ways of knowing, the general practice traditions, and the emerging literature on qualitative research and the narrative mode of thought. She argued effectively for the importance of a "connected knowing" based on personal experiences and relationships that seek to discover how the other perceives the world. Connected knowing is rooted in empathy and believability and is interested in context, relationship, and time. This way of knowing usually uses qualitative ("field" style) and participatory research strategies.

At the intersection of the four quadrants is the clinical craft or practice being informed by the multiple modes of inquiry being enacted within a participatory framework. As a means of keeping the wheel of inquiry turning and the participatory space open, it is helpful to emphasize and value *variation* and *improvisation* over standardization. Emerging understandings from complexity science and ecological science strongly suggest that "nature" and life thrive on variation and improvisation (Capra, 1996, 2002). The conventional metaphor of the "body as machine" reflects the dangers inherent in standardization. Too many voices are silenced. The participatory wheel turns within a sphere of interpretive relativism (see Perakyla, chap. 34, this volume). A more robust metaphor, one that embraces all four quadrants of human knowledge and values variation, is the "body as organism in ecological context." This metaphor contains the seeds from which a democratized knowledge and clinical practice can grow. They will not grow, however, unless the ground is fertile and not poisoned by the privatized knowledge and products of global corporations.

Much current clinical research is the hand inside the glove of corporate interests and operates on a "first act until harm proven" principle, where proven usually means establishing a direct cause-and-effect relationship. The result is the continued spread of chemical toxins, greenhouse gases, and cigarettes until such nearly impossible proof appears and convinces everyone. Older wisdom recommended "first do no harm." A current form of this wisdom, the *precautionary principle* (Raffensperger, Tickner, & Jackson, 1999), offers guidance consistent with better health and more

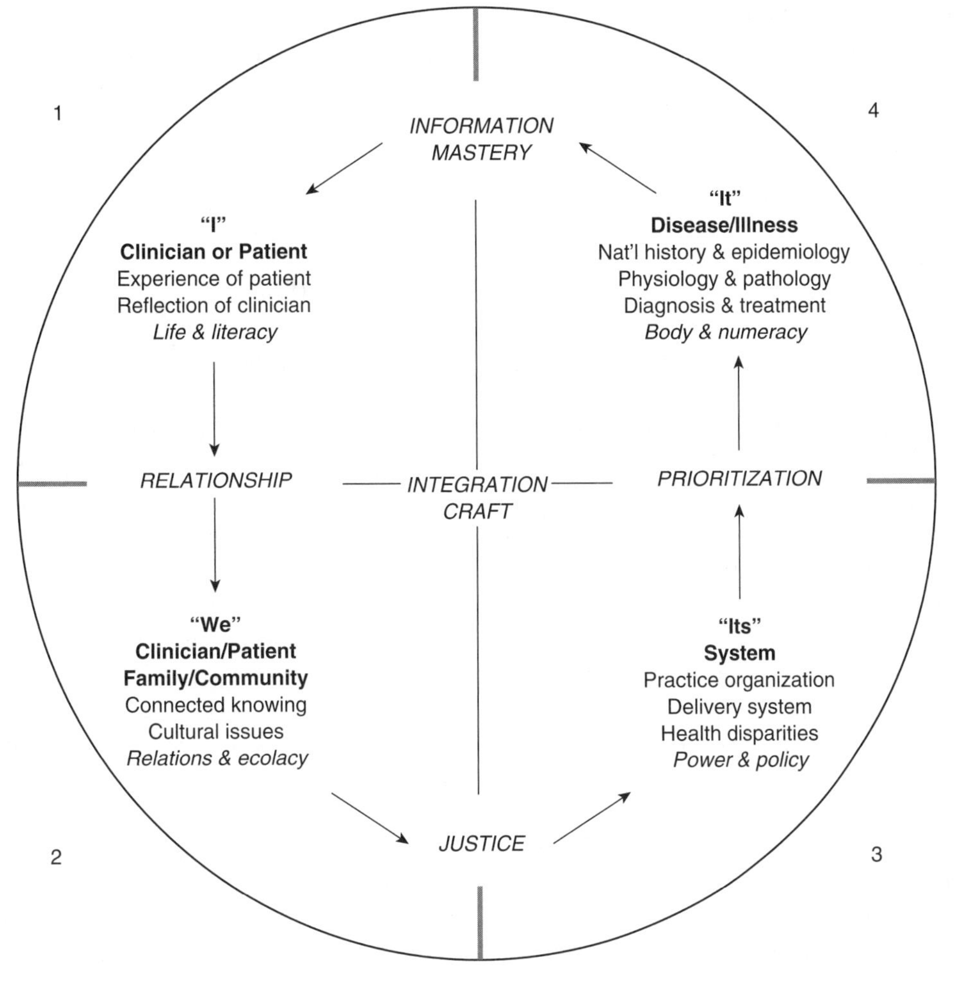

Figure 24.1. A Participatory Wheel of Inquiry

participatory research spaces. The precautionary principle essentially states that in the presence of scientific uncertainty and the plausibility of harm, precautionary measures must be taken (Raffensperger, 2002). This principle shifts the burden of proof to those who advocate or wish to sell a potentially harmful action or product and must be open, informed, and democratic, including all potentially affected parties. Thus, it opens the research space to a more democratic process of knowledge generation and sharing. The precautionary principle obliges us to observe and foresee (as far as seven generations) before acting. This involves examination of a full range of alternatives, including no action. It begins with seeking to see the invisible, hear the unspeakable, and touch the untouchable. Learn to hear the stars and the trees and to talk to turtles, coyotes, and bears. Learn from children. Remember who you really were before the dominant culture silenced your deep awareness.

Participatory research approaches, supported by applying the participatory wheel of inquiry, valuing variation and improvisation, and adhering to the precautionary principle, all lead to *slow knowledge,* that is, knowledge that is consistent with the rhythms of life, sustainability, and appropriate scale (Orr, 2002). It assumes interdependence and uncertainty, and it acknowledges the absurdity and hubris of seeking perfection. Slow knowledge works with the complexities of reality rather than seeking to control them, and it accepts that some conflict and suffering are inevitable. Rather than trying to eliminate them, slow knowledge pursues means of comfort, care, reconciliation, resilience, and restoration that optimize the healthy embedded interrelationships of all life, one local place at a time. Slow knowledge shifts the focus from outcomes to the nurturing of life together. For Jocelyn and her heartburn, slow knowledge means deemphasizing the PPI until more is known about its multiple and ecological consequences. Instead, there is more emphasis on supporting Jocelyn and expanding her community of concern and on changing the social, economic, and lifestyle factors creating the conditions of GERD. This is more difficult and slower work; it is healing work. Slow knowledge is the result of a clinical research of love and not instrumental rationality. This is learning at the speed and scale where all of life can participate. It represents the democratization of knowledge. Imagine the possibilities for clinical research if government funding prioritized slow knowledge. Now, enter the world of biomedicine and work to expand the EBM space, but do so as a gardener with the tools of participatory approaches and a wheel of inquiry, valuing variation and improvisation and applying the precautionary principle as you tend the plants of slow knowledge. Theory, collaboration, and critical multiplism are additional strategies for helping do clinical research above ground.

Using Theory

The double helix RCT proposed earlier also creates an opportunity for clinical researchers to reintroduce theory into clinical research. Theory is frequently not explicitly stated in standard quantitative clinical studies. This often results in ungrounded a posteriori speculation. Qualitative data help to surface hidden theoretical assumptions and suggest new possibilities and connections. Theory helps to bridge dominant biomedical and other cultural worlds. Recent theoretical discussions among medical anthropologists, phenomenologists, semioticians, and sociologists concerning the *metaphor of the "body"* challenge biomedical assumptions about the human body and its boundaries and highlight the culturally and socially constructed aspects of the body that extend far beyond its corporeality (Csordas, 2002; Johnson, 1987; Kirmayer, 1992; Macnaghten & Urry, 2001; Martin, 1994; Scheper-Hughes & Locke, 1987; Shildrick, 1997; Strathern, 1996; Turner, 1992). There is an individual body, a social body, and a body politic. There are medical bodies, the earth as body, and communicative bodies. Bodies are imagined as flexible, leaky, castles, machines, gardens, or effervescent, and these imaginations both shape and are shaped by the social body, the body politic, and the world body. Arthur Frank, for example, described the use of storytelling as a means of restoring voice to the body (Frank, 1995). Bodily symptoms are understood as the infolding of cultural traumas into the body; as these bodies create history, the symptoms outfold into social space. Because of their complexity, social bodies (e.g., practice organizations) are often best characterized using metaphors such as "brains," "machines," "organisms," and "ugly faces" (Morgan, 1998). Qualitative methods become a primary source for hearing these stories and their associated metaphors, caring in relationships, and resisting the colonizing narrative of institutionalized medicine (Mattingly, 1998; Sandelowski, 2002). The study of bodies and their place in the production and expression of sickness and health becomes a core strategy for clinical research that enables the bridging of paradigms and opens the clinical research space while also resisting the standardization of the body as commodity.

Collaborating Across Disciplines

This opened clinical research space requires collaboration that emphasizes multiple linkages and different types of cross-disciplinary relationships. Linkages occur vertically where one moves up and drown through different levels or scales such as the molecular, individual, local, and regional levels. Linkages are also horizontal across different sectors at the same level of social organization such as medical practices, schools, and local businesses. Linkages also occur over time or at different times. Finally, there are multiple academic linkages, including those with the "public," with practitioners, with policymakers, and with research participants (Miller, 1994).

Critical Multiplism

Orchestrating this type of multimethod, cross-disciplinary research requires the skills and mind-set of a generalist researcher using a framework of critical multiplism (Coward, 1990; Miller, 1994). The skills and perspectives of the generalist researcher consist of negotiation, translation, theoretical pluralism, methodological pluralism, a community orientation, and comfort with and rootedness in clinical practices. These are successfully implemented through a critical multiplist framework. Critical multiplism assumes that multiple ways of knowing are necessary and that these options require critical thought and choice. "Multiplism" refers not only to multiple methods but also to multiple triangulation, multiple stakeholders, multiple studies, and multiple paradigms and perspectives. "Critical" refers to the critical selection of these options based on local history, the role of power and patterns of domination, and how the different methods complement each other. Six principles help to guide critical multiplists in their complex work:

1. Know why you choose to do something.
2. Preserve method and paradigm integrity.
3. Pay attention to units of analysis.
4. Remember the research questions.
5. Ensure that the strengths and weaknesses of each selected option complement each other.
6. Continually evaluate methodology throughout the study.

Critical multiplism is a particularly powerful framework for doing participatory clinical research and provides discipline as one moves within the participatory wheel of inquiry.

Revealing the many kinds of evidence requires entering the EBM space, developing cross-disciplinary collaborations, using multiple methods with a critical multiplist conceptualization, using bridging metaphors and theories such as "bodies," and often emphasizing participatory and advocacy approaches and democratizing knowledge. With these strategies, the clinical research space opens for the tools of the generalist clinical researcher. Qualitative researchers have seen and heard the stories and sufferings of Jocelyn and others like her, but they have often been retold in a language that patients and clinicians do not understand (e.g., Fisher, 1986; Fisher & Todd, 1983; Lazarus, 1988; Mishler, 1984; West, 1984; Williams, 1984). Neither clinicians nor patients know the language of "ethnomethodology," "hermeneutics," "phenomenology," "semiotics," or "interpretive interactionism." Much qualitative clinical research is published in a language and in places that benefit only selected researchers and not the patients and practitioners. Qualitative researchers have asked that clinicians join, listen to, and speak the "voice of the lifeworld" (Mishler, 1984). We ask clinical qualitative researchers to do the same, and we recommend the work of Carolyn Ellis and Arthur Frank as powerful examples of clear and moving text (Ellis, 1995; Frank, 1991).

Providing the Tools and Translations

This section presents the tools and translations necessary for bringing qualitative methods and traditions into the clinical research space at ground level. It begins by comparing the qualitative *research process* with the clinical process. The nearly direct correspondence enables the clinical researcher to make qualitative methods transparent to clinicians and patients. This is followed by a brief overview of qualitative methods and how to create mixed method *research designs* in the clinical setting. Finally, we *put it all together* with an example of clinical research that uses some of the strategies discussed and share tips for writing, demonstrating credibility, and getting published.

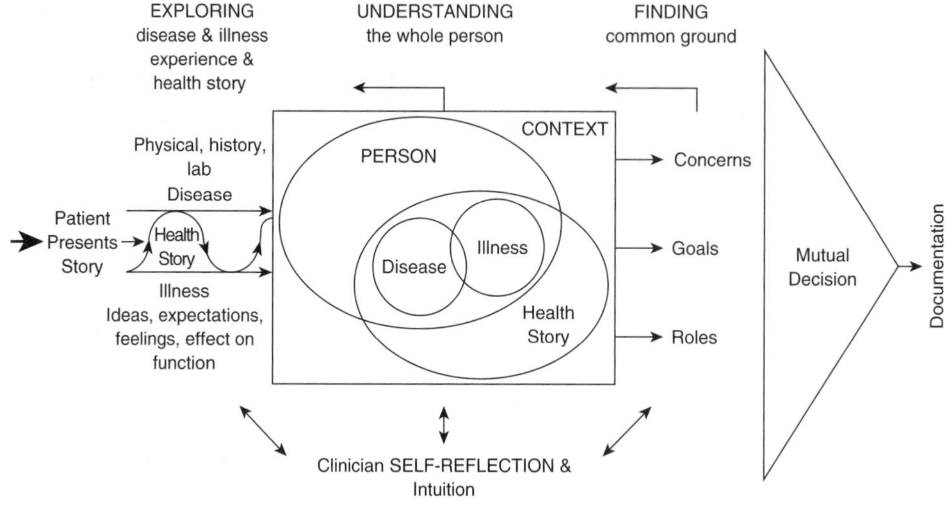

Figure 24.2. Relationship-Centered Clinical Method

Research Process

The clinical research space is created by focusing on the questions arising from the clinical experience and opens many possibilities for using the full range of qualitative data-gathering and analysis methods. Many of these qualitative approaches are presented elsewhere in this *Handbook* and are discussed in more detail in a text for primary care qualitative researchers (Crabtree & Miller, 1999). The challenge is to preserve the integrity of the questions and to translate qualitative collection and analysis methods into clear and jargon-free language without sacrificing the methods' integrity rooted in the soil of disciplinary conversations. A fundamental tenet of the proposed translation is that *the question and clinical context are primary; methods must adjust to the clinical setting and the clinical questions.* Interpretive social science traditionally has feared mixed methods because this usually meant treating qualitative as only a method subservient to the positivist paradigm or materialistic inquiry. We not only imagine a clinical research space where qualitative methods are empowered and where constructivist and critical/ecological paradigms are accepted but also note that it already exists. The key is to recognize the similarity between the qualitative research process and the clinical process, particularly as it presents itself in primary care.

Figure 24.2 diagrams an idealized relationship-centered clinical method proposed as a model for family medicine (Stewart et al., 1995; Tresolini, 1994). Notice that the overall method consists of four separate processes: exploring, understanding, finding common ground, and engaging in self-reflection. These four processes flow sequentially, but they all iterate with each other and the whole process usually cycles multiple times over time for any given illness episode. For example, chronic illness care will occur over a lifetime of visits, whereas an episode of ear infection may require only two visits (i.e., two iterations of the clinical cycle). The four clinical processes directly correspond to the four processes of qualitative research, and these parallel processes are illustrated in Figure 24.3. (The clinical equivalents are italicized in brackets above the research processes.)

The clinician begins by gathering data using purposeful or information-rich sampling. The clinician focuses his or her interviewing, observing, and touching around possible explanations related to the patient's presenting concern or opening story. The exploration seeks "disease" information following the biomedical model, but the process also searches for understanding of the patient's health story and illness experience, especially the patient's ideas, expectations, and feelings about his or her concern and its effect on everyday living. The clinician almost immediately begins to analyze the data while continuing to gather additional information. This analysis seeks to understand the patient's concern within the context of his or her lifeworld—personal, family, and community stories. This understanding is organized around sensitizing concepts, diagnostic categories, personal experience templates or scripts, and connections looked for and then corroborated against the known evidence. Using a participatory framework, the clinician periodically shares the emerging understanding with the patient (or others), and together they seek a common interpretation. Throughout this iterative process, the clinician is using self-reflection, personal feelings, and intuition to inform the gathering, analyzing, and interpreting. The visit ends when the clinician and patient agree that they have sufficient data (i.e., saturation) to implement an initial course of action. The outcome is an engaging plan for the patient and a report describing the encounter written (or dictated) by the clinician. These reports occasionally undergo peer review. This sounds like, looks like, and feels like qualitative research. However, most clinicians do not know it. Use clinical language to translate qualitative methods and standards. Let us get to work!

Finally, notice how clinical care also mirrors the double helix RCT. In both, simplified coherence for action ("disease") is in dynamic tension with personal/social/cultural complexity ("illness" and "health story") and the tension is held through the quest for care, that is, through the research questions. This is more likely when the clinical or research process is simultaneously participatory and cognizant of the power imbalances inherent in the relationships and in the greater health care system. All of the many voices must be surfaced and attention must be paid to them; we must protect the questions and prevent them from being co-opted and changed by hierarchy and the biomedical paradigm. This is the work of democratizing knowledge. Out of this fabric of relational forces, within given biocultural boundaries, are woven senses. The methods must parallel the clinical process and provide self-critique and correction. This is the intersection of doing science and reflexivity.

Research Design

Research designs in clinical research inherently require multimethod thinking and critical multiplism, with the particular combinations of data-gathering and analysis/interpretation approaches being driven by the research question and the clinical context. There are infinite possibilities for integrating qualitative and quantitative methods, with the design being created for each study and the qualitative aspects often evolving as a study progresses in response to the emerging questions. Participatory research approaches, in particular, usually involve a more emergent design process. In clinical research, research designs may be wholly qualitative (Shepherd, Hattersley, & Sparkes, 2000) or quantitative, including the use of a single method, but are increasingly combinations of these in what has been referred to as mixed methods (Borkan, 2004; Creswell, 2003; Creswell, Fetters, & Ivankova, 2004; Tashakkori & Teddlie, 1998). Clinical researchers must maintain multimethod thinking and remain free to mix and match methods as driven by particular clinically based questions.

There are many questions and contexts that require only a single method; however, single-method designs should still be considered within a multimethod context. When the investigator starts with the question and considers all possible methods before deciding that a single method is appropriate for the question, he or she is maintaining multimethod thinking. Most clinical research questions are more complex and require multiple approaches. Particular mixed method combinations of qualitative and quantitative methods are generally presented in terms of typologies of multimethod designs (Creswell, 2003; Stange, Miller, Crabtree, O'Connor, &

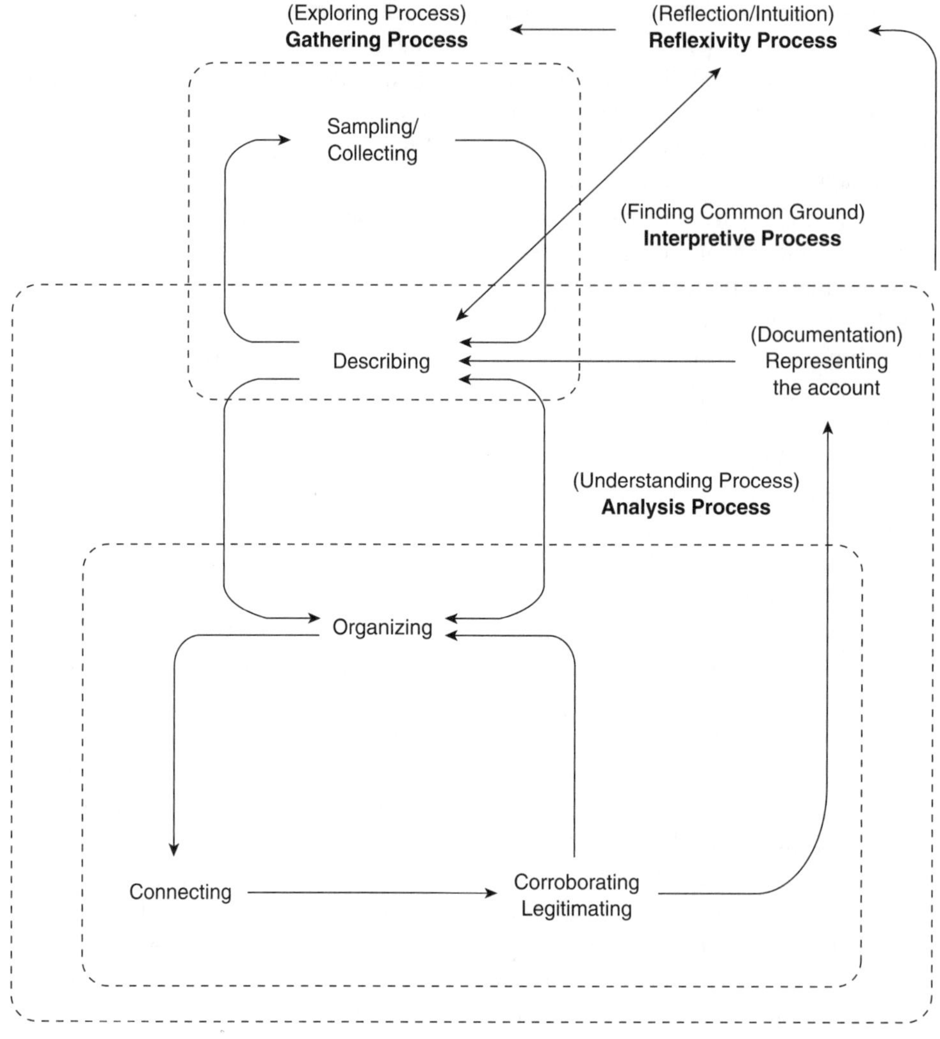

Figure 24.3. Qualitative Research Process and Clinical Parallels

Zyzanski, 1994). In actual practice, these typologies are too prescriptive and tend to oversimplify the complex dance of the research process. In conceptualizing a study, the clinical investigator creates a design from the full range of data collection and analysis tools, much like a child makes creations from the sticks and wheels of "Tinker Toys" or parts from a "Lego" set. There are airplanes, cars, windmills, and buildings, but they are rarely exactly alike.

One dimension of multimethod design is the longitudinal nature of the research process. Most clinical research questions are complex and multifaceted and cannot be addressed in a single study. In constructing the design, the clinical researcher is constantly balancing the desire to fully address the question with the feasibility of being able to complete the study. Narrowing the focus potentially compromises the integrity of the question, whereas trying to accomplish too much can be overwhelming and possibly not fundable. Thus, in conceptualizing study designs, the researcher may do a series of studies in a longitudinal process that fits the larger research agenda. How a design is finally put together depends on the questions and the setting. Snadden and Brown

(1991) wondered how stigmatization affected adults with asthma. Answering this question required two steps. First, they identified patients with asthma who felt that they were stigmatized, and then they explored the perceived effect of that stigmatization on the patients' lives. The design solved these issues by initially using a questionnaire measuring attitudes concerning asthma to identify respondents reporting high levels of stigma. These individuals were then interviewed using interpretive interview and analysis methods.

Multiple methods can also be directly integrated within a single study in a number of ways. For example, sometimes it may be helpful to conduct two independent studies concurrently on the same study population and then to converge the results. This is the approach recommended for the double helix RCT (Wiles, 1998; Willms, 1991). Another widely used approach to designing multimethod research is to integrate multiple methods more intimately within a single research study. For example, Borkan, Quirk, and Sullivan (1991) noticed that breaking a hip was often a turning point toward death for many elderly patients. They puzzled about what distinguished those persons from others who had recovered with minimal complications. The research literature did not reveal any obvious traditional biomedical factors. They wondered whether patients' stories about the fractures had any connection with the outcomes. They used an epidemiological cross-sectional design with a sample of hospitalized elderly patients with hip fractures. Multiple biomedical indicators were measured as independent variables along with rehabilitation outcome measures as the dependent variable. There was nothing unusual here, and this design would ensure acceptance by the intended clinical audience. What distinguishes this study is that the researchers also conducted depth interviews with each patient concerning how he or she understood the hip fracture within his or her life story. Several distinguishable injury narratives emerged. These were coded and entered as another independent variable in the statistical outcome modeling. The narrative type was the most powerful predictor of rehabilitation outcome.

When discussing qualitative research design with clinicians and patients, we have simplified the jargon. The data-gathering methods are divided into interviewing, observing, and reviewing documents (including videotapes). Interviews are further subdivided into depth, focus group, and ethnographic (or key informant) (Mitchell, 1998). Participant observation is described as either short term or prolonged. Instead of using the jargon of grounded theory, phenomenology, ethnography, and hermeneutics, we frame the many traditions and techniques of analysis as a "dance of interpretation" in which three idealized organizing styles—immersion/crystallization, editing, and template (for details, see Figure 24.4 and Miller & Crabtree, 1999a)—promote the dynamic, creative, iterative, yet disciplined craft of qualitative interpretation. All three organizing styles may be used at some time during the different gathering/interpreting iterations of a particular research project.

Putting It All Together

To further demonstrate the use of a multimethod framework, we provide an overview of a longitudinal series of four federally funded studies focusing on family medicine patterns of care and change (Crabtree, Miller, Aita, Flocke, & Stange, 1998; Crabtree, Miller, & Stange, 2001; Goodwin et al., 2001; Stange et al., 1998). These studies all were funded separately by large federal grants, providing evidence of wider acceptance of the multimethod approach (for more details on funding qualitative research, see Saukko, chap. 13, this volume).

The National Cancer Institute funded the Direct Observation of Primary Care (DOPC) study. The DOPC study was designed to illuminate the "black box" of clinical practice by describing patient visits to family physicians in community practices with a special emphasis on the delivery of preventive health services. This largely quantitative cross-sectional descriptive study focused on the content and context of the outpatient visit. Data were obtained through the direct observation of patient visits using a variation of the highly structured Davis Observation Code

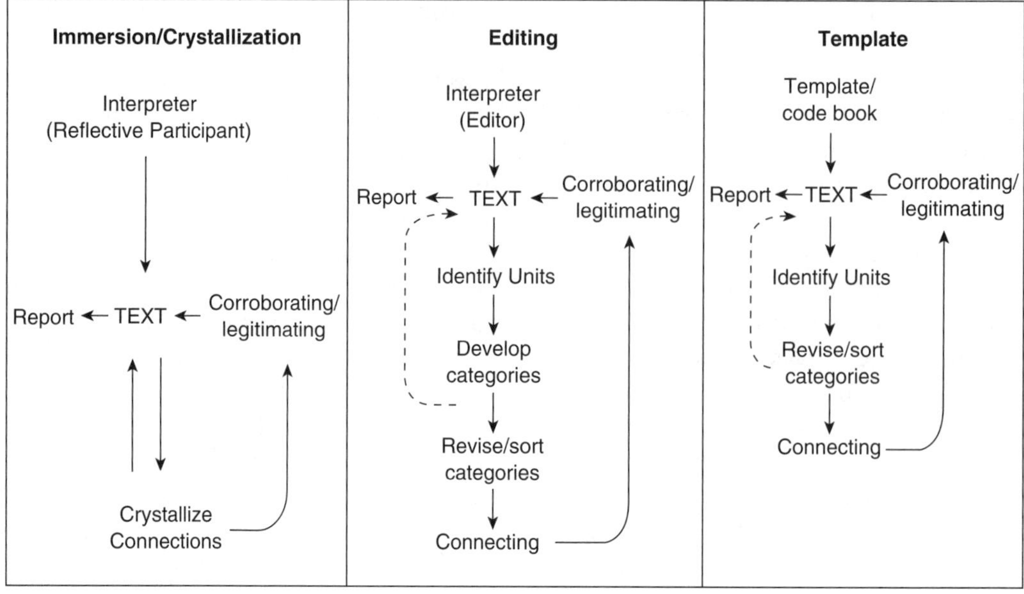

Figure 24.4. Diagrammatic Representation of Different Organizing Styles of Analysis

Source: Crabtree and Miller (1999).

(Callahan & Bertakis, 1991) along with checklists of the patient visit, patient exit questionnaires, medical record reviews, billing data abstractions, and physician questionnaires. To supplement and enhance these quantitative data, research nurses dictated observational field notes immediately after each visit to provide richer descriptions of the variables under study. This ethnographic data were impressionistic and focused on describing the practice in terms of key features such as the practice location, office relationships, and how the practice functioned. These data eventually totaled more than 2,000 pages of field notes from observation of 138 physicians in 84 different family medicine offices. The quantitative descriptions provided valuable insights into the overall content of family medicine (Stange et al., 1998) as well as into many other facets of family medicine (see the May 1998 issue of the *Journal of Family Practice*). The qualitative field notes identified a long list of key features that appear to be important for understanding how practices operate on a day-to-day basis, particularly in the delivery of preventive services (Crabtree et al., 1998). The qualitative data were also used to formulate a new theoretical model of practice organization based on complexity theory that now provides the basis for subsequent federally funded studies (Miller, Crabtree, McDaniel, & Stange, 1998).

The Prevention and Competing Demands in Primary Care (P&CD) study was funded by the Agency for Healthcare Research and Quality as a follow-up to the DOPC study to provide a more in-depth look at how the practice and the people in the practice worked together. In the P&CD study, 18 practices were purposefully selected to include some that were doing really well in delivering preventive services and others that were doing less well. Trained observers spent weeks in each practice observing, taking detailed notes about how the organization functioned, and talking to people using key informant and depth interviews. They observed 30 encounters with each clinician and dictated field notes in the form of a chronology of what went on during the encounters. This largely qualitative study helped to refine the theoretical model developed in the DOPC study (Miller, McDaniel, Crabtree, & Stange, 2001).

The DOPC and P&CD studies directly challenged the ideology of standardization and commodification of health care. Multiple analyses elucidated the tremendous variation that exists in practice organization and clinical care. Much of this variation was beneficial along with some problematic variation. Thus, we see clinicians prioritizing care in ongoing continuous relationships with patients (Flocke, Miller, & Crabtree, 2002) and opportunistically tailoring tobacco counseling (Jaen et al., 2001) while at the same time overprescribing antibiotics for upper respiratory infections (Scott et al., 2001) or failing to manage obvious depression (Robinson et al., 2001). Practices themselves, as complex organizations, exhibited much variation, including how they hire and use staff (Aita et al. 2001) or respond to hospital ownership (Tallia et al., 2003). Using concepts from family systems (McGoldrick, Gerson, & Shellenberger, 1999), it was possible to identify different ways in which practices organize themselves and to diagram patterns of communication in a "practice genogram" (McIlvain, Crabtree, Medder, Stange, & Miller, 1998). Urban practices were very different from rural practices, which in turn were very different from suburban practices (Pol, Rouse, Zyzanski, Rasmussen, & Crabtree, 2001). The larger health care system also created variation and surprise. For example, 24% of patients in managed care had to change their physicians during a 2-year period in the DOPC study, creating discontinuity in the care of many patients (Flocke, Stange, & Zyzanski, 1997).

Based on insights from the DOPC and P&CD studies, we developed an organizational change model for tailoring interventions to the local context that incorporated characteristics of patients, clinicians, the clinical encounter, the practice, the community, and the larger health system. This model was based on our emerging understanding of complexity theory and was initially tested in a National Cancer Institute-funded clinical trial called the Study to Enhance Prevention by Understanding Practice (STEP-UP). The STEP-UP intervention randomized 80 practices in Ohio and used an initial 2- to 5-day mixed methods assessment of the practice to provide insights for tailoring feedback to the practice (an example of a double helix trial design). Based on the assessment, a facilitator would go back to the practice, show the practitioners their genogram, give them a summary report, and then negotiate a prevention-oriented intervention. The STEP-UP intervention resulted in a significant enhancement in the delivery of global preventive services in the intervention practices (as opposed to the control practices) over a 12-month period, a change that has been sustained for more than 3 years after the intervention (Goodwin et al., 2001).

An analysis of the qualitative field notes recorded during the STEP-UP intervention was used to develop a refined model of organizational change that seeks to stimulate self-reflective and ongoing learning in practices. This analysis, which focused on discovering why the intervention worked in some places and not in others, led to the National Heart, Lung, and Blood Institute (NHLBI)-funded Using Learning Teams for Reflective Adaptation (ULTRA) study. The ULTRA study is a collaborative participatory research study using a double helix design. In this study, an initial assessment of the organization by means of a 2-week multimethod assessment process (MAP) is used to stimulate a reflective adaptation process (RAP), which is an iterative team-building process combining assessment feedback with facilitation of learning teams in the practice. Patients are required as participants on these teams. The hypothesis underlying the ULTRA study is that change in overall practice processes will simultaneously affect a wide range of outcomes, including the organizational culture and clinical care such as smoking cessation counseling and the management of chronic illnesses (e.g., hyperlipidemia, hypertension, diabetes, asthma).

A research design has evolved from this series of studies that might best be characterized as an in-depth comparative case study of family medicine offices using ethnographic techniques and a multimethod participatory clinical trial using complexity theory to guide an interventional strategy. The potential for multisite, multimethod collaborative studies at ground level is demonstrated in the progression from a multimethod observational study (DOPC) to an in-depth comparative case study (P&CD), which then led to an intervention trial that is grounded in insights from the previous work (STEP-UP). This finally resulted in a participatory collaboration with practices and patients (ULTRA).

An important aspect of all of these studies is their use of a collaborative research team (Miller, 1994). The team includes physicians, nurses, epidemiologists, statisticians, psychologists, anthropologists, economists, and sociologists. We design the study together, meet frequently during the study to review the qualitative data and make adjustments to the study, and do intensive reflexivity work (Barry, Britten, Barber, Bradley, & Stevenson, 1999). This long-term collaborative teamwork has enabled the group to expand its use of qualitative methods and its operating paradigms.

Writing Strategies

There are some specific writing strategies that facilitate communication of and receptivity to qualitative clinical research (Richardson, 1990; Wolcott, 1990). The most important is *avoiding jargon* and keeping language simple and concrete. Using typologies and continua as rhetorical frames is helpful because these initially appear to be rational and measurable—qualities valued by traditional clinical researchers. Interpretive aspects can be maintained by emphasizing cultural/historical and/or inductive construction and by grounding in lived clinical experience. It is also useful to communicate either in the biomedically dominant visual mode, through the use of tables, charts, diagrams, and data matrices, or through the clinically familiar narrative mode of case reports. Narrative reports often take the form of first-person voice pathographies (Hawkins, 1993) or first-person accounts by physicians of their patient encounters (Loxterkamp, 1997; Sacks, 1984). The strategy of authoethnography, where the voice of the researcher as deeply personal subject is explicitly woven into the context of the social issues being researched, also resonates with the clinical narrative mode (Ellingson, 1998; Ellis & Bochner, 1996).

The dominant audience for clinical research perceives the issues of "validity," "reliability," and "generalizability" as scientific fundamentalist dogma resulting in heightened concerns about bias. The collaborative multimethod study of Daly and McDonald (1992) described the impact of echocardiography on patients' perceptions of self. Their story described how difficult it can be to till the soil: "The biggest problem was that physicians saw qualitative research methods as . . . prone to bias. Highly structured methods of analyzing qualitative data were effectively used . . . and are probably necessary for 'covering one's back' in multidisciplinary teams" (p. 416). They presented strategies for qualitative researchers to translate their insights and build tornado-proof hedges around their fields. The methodological guidelines for quantitative methods are not relevant for qualitative clinical researchers. The criteria for qualitative clinical research can be translated for clinical audiences in the form of telling methodologically, rhetorically, and clinically convincing stories.

Methodologically convincing stories answer the question, "How was the research designed and done?" It is important to make explicit how and why the research design, sampling strategies, and data collection and analysis techniques fit the question and research context as discussed earlier in this chapter. It is helpful to mention when the research design is cross-sectional, prospective, case–control, or similar to some other design from observational epidemiology (Ward, 1993). Specific techniques such as triangulation, member checking, and searching for disconfirming evidence should also be addressed when applicable (Malterud, 2001a, 2001b).

Relationship is essential to the clinical experience. Kahn (1993) proposed that a language of relationship be used to judge the methodological adequacy of clinical qualitative research. A methodologically convincing story addresses three different relationships: (a) the investigator's *relationship with informants*, noting how each influences the other during the research process, (b) the *relationship with the data,* particularly the circularity or iterative aspects of the research experience, and (c) the *relationship with the readers*, so that the researcher's authorial intent is clear.

One popular approach to helping primary care clinicians become "information masters" involves teaching them to recognize patient-oriented evidence that matters (POEMS) (Slawson et al., 1994). The first step is to scan an article's abstract and determine whether the results relate to outcomes that are common or important in everyday clinical practice and matter to patients and whether the results would potentially change what you currently do in practice. If the answers are yes, then the second step is to read the article and decide whether the conclusions are methodologically sound. There are simple one-page checklists for quantitative studies. The following, in an effort to enhance accessibility and quality while avoiding the checklist format that we condemned earlier, was developed by the authors and is currently being used for evaluating qualitative articles:

1. Is the method appropriate for the question?
2. Is the sampling adequate and information rich?
3. Is the research process iterative?
4. Is the interpretive process thorough and clearly described?
5. Is reflexivity addressed?

We hope that by using a question format and leaving space for interpretation, there is both sufficient flexibility for creativity and sufficient guidance for assurance of quality. A methodologically convincing story is not one that pleases a positivist or a postpositivist; rather, it is one that pleases qualitative research peers, clinicians, and patients. Thus, the use of explicit guidelines and checklists is problematic and must be tempered with a large dose of flexibility so as not to put off the doing of qualitative research (Chapple & Rogers, 1998). The preceding approach is consistent with Altheide and Johnson's (1998) idea of "validity-as-reflexive-accounting," where the researcher or team, the sense-making processes, and the question or topic are in interaction with a focus on how meanings are constructed. This is also a good description of the validity process in clinical care.

A *rhetorically convincing story* answers the question, "How believable is this text?" The readers are drawn into the story and begin imagining that the story is about them. When this occurs, the conclusions make more sense for the readers. The language and style of writing need to be familiar to the audience. Some of the quotations and observations selected to illustrate interpretations also need to reflect the readers' experience and/or values. A rhetorically convincing story assures the readers that you have "walked in their shoes." Bunge (1961) reviewed some of the features that characterize a believable story.

A *clinically convincing story* answers the questions, "Does this study make clinical sense?" and "How does this study help in the care of patients?" (Giacomini & Cook, 2000) A story is clinically convincing if it successfully addresses three features that are important in the clinical research space. The *question* must matter to clinical participants, and the results must specifically address that question. This usually means that attention is directed to the pragmatic intervention and policy focus of the clinical world. The *audience* or stakeholders are also clinical participants for whom the results matter, and this should be obvious in the text. Finally, the text reveals *assumptions* about the physical/behavioral, social/emotional, cultural/historical, and/or spiritual aspects of clinical participants' bodies, lives, and/or power. It is made clear to the readers who benefits most from the story.

A clinically convincing story is also one that enriches the possibilities for a narrative medicine (Brody, 2003; Greenhalgh & Hurwitz, 1998). In narrative-based care, the clinician views his or her primary task as partnering with the patient to create new stories from the broken ones. This involves learning the patient's language and discovering the life contexts and plans that make sense of it (Launer, 2002). This sounds like good clinical research. When possible, articulate this connection, especially in the discussion section of a manuscript. The work of Frank (1995) and his concepts of restitution, quest, and chaos narratives cited earlier are also quite relevant here.

Qualitative clinical research is convincing if the methods are appropriate for the question and the investigator's relationship with informants, data, and audience are clearly addressed; if the audience recognizes itself in the findings; and if the question and results matter to clinical participants. All of these criteria are more easily satisfied if a collaborative team does the research. When this team includes clinical participants, it creates a community of discourse where conversations at ground level can grow (Denz-Penhey & Murdoch, 1993).

Even when the writing is clear and the results are convincing, it is still a challenge to find a publishing venue. Fortunately, the options are improving. Qualitative clinical research is widely presented and published in primary care internal medicine and family medicine, nursing, social work, and educational research books and journals. Much of this success over the past two decades has been due to specific efforts to translate and introduce qualitative research in workshops within professional meetings, through newsletters, and through methods' publications emphasizing clinical usefulness. Qualitative clinical research is now appearing in clinical journals, especially in the field of primary care. *Qualitative Health Research; Culture, Medicine, and Psychiatry; Health;* and *Social Science and Medicine* serve as bridge-building publications with a nearly exclusive or significant emphasis on qualitative clinical research. All of the primary care journals have reviewers trained in qualitative research and publish qualitative studies. The *Annals of Family Medicine* provides space on its Web site to "publish" supplementary materials, thereby making it possible to condense articles into the space requirements of medical journals. The next steps are to improve ways of communicating results to the patient population and international community. The use of the Web may become a valuable means of presenting findings to patients and the broader community.

◼ Clinical Research Below Ground

> *Connections are made slowly, sometimes they grow underground. You cannot tell always by looking what is happening. More than half a tree is spread out in the soil under your feet. Penetrate quietly as the earthworm that blows no trumpet.*
>
> —Continuation of Marge Piercy's "The Seven of Pentacles"

Still, the tornado approaches. When it will arrive, within our generation's lifetime or that of our grandchildren, is difficult to predict. What we believe is that the current destruction of the earth's life support systems, the widening gap between the rich and the poor, and all of the powers and structures that currently maintain this oppression of our earth community are ultimately unsustainable and self-destructive. This is, in our opinion, the most important clinical and health problem for our time. Acknowledging this, how do we, as individuals and clinical researchers, respond? We are not sure. We are not confident that the clinical research above ground is sufficient to bring about the necessary change. We are morally uncomfortable with leaving that change to others. In this section, we invite you into our conversation underground—into our own personal struggles, from positions of power, to maintain integrity and to be citizens working for the democracy and health of all life. Join with us, in solidarity as clinical researchers and as lovers of the earth, on our burrowing toward wholeness. This is "ecological identity" work—using direct experience with nature and others "as a framework for personal decisions, professional choices, political actions, and spiritual inquiry" (Thomashow, 1996, p. xiii). Our name for this pilgrimage below ground is *solidarity research.*

Clinical research above ground is opportunistic, challenging, helpful, and protective. It is public; it complicates and addresses important clinical questions and works for change. It is about career, making a living, getting published, holding positions of power, and openly challenging power. It seeks to mix methods and create new relationships, to surface the hidden, and to protect the miracle of life (Berry, 2000) where possible. These efforts at optimizing the ability to function within a dangerously broken system are critically important, and (it seems to us) they will not be enough. The research plants that bloom in the sunshine, our works above ground, are only as healthy as the roots and rhizomes that sustain us. What supports our personal integrity and wholeness, keeps our senses open to the cries of suffering and alert to hidden danger, nourishes our vision and deep interdependence, and helps us to image and experience health as membership (Berry, 2000)? We suggest that these tasks call for clinical research below ground. This could be a solidarity research that nourishes the work above ground, tenaciously grounds us to our earth community (Rasmussen, 1996), and ensures an adequate soil and seed for life before and after the tornado passes.

Solidarity research might be the proactive work building and preparing for the future. This could be our night work. Maybe this is where we join with resistance movements and new alternative structures arising around the world and, using our research skills, we work, learn, and grow with them to create a life that can emerge before and after the tornado (Perlas, 2000). This is solidarity research. The name derives from the cooperative economics in Brazil connecting local alternatives together to create networks of resistance to elite corporate globalization that is called *economia solidária,* that is, solidarity economics. We propose that solidarity research represents inquiry and learning that increase solidarity with our selves as whole persons and increase solidarity with our earth community and with other communities of resistance. It is generating better questions for our above ground research. It is story sharing. It is relationships and building community. It is mysticism—the prayer, music, and poetry that enliven community and give it spirit. It is growing love.

Foundational sources for our current understanding and development of solidarity research include the work of Paulo Freire, Ivan Illich, and Vandana Shiva. Freire (1970) emphasized the importance of words as praxis—as part of an action/reflection cycle—and of working directly with the oppressed through "dialogics" with the goals of democratizing culture and raising critical consciousness or *conscientização.* We must "learn how and what the people know." We must "learn with the oppressed the indispensable ropes of their resistance" (Freire, 1998, p. 273). Illich (1970, 1976) highlighted the importance of creating alternative local systems of mutual support to resist the current disempowering institutions of education and health care. Shiva (1994) articulated and demonstrated, with her work in India, the power of linking ecology, feminism, and social justice concerns to local resistance efforts against corporate globalization threatening their habitat and way of life.

The resistance to global corporate capitalism and the work of solidarity economics and politics is present, in some form, in nearly every nation (Notes From Nowhere, 2003). People dreaming and reweaving the power to choose and shape alternative ways of living need the skills of clinical researchers to help them name, track, and learn from the stories of their journeys. This is where we, as solidarity researchers, can join in the reclaiming and can help "to open a crack in history" (Ponce de León, 2001, p. 216).

Solidarity research, as we currently understand it, involves no new methods or grand new scheme; it is quieter than that. It does build on the core concepts related to democratizing knowledge, and it emphasizes at least three related assumptions, namely that (a) life is interdependent, diverse, always changing, and sustainable; (b) all action, including doing science, is moral activity; and (c) moral activity should sustain the common good. Common good is understood to mean those pluralistic, social, and ecological conditions and processes that seek the good of all and are arrived at through public interaction that expresses differences and seeks to include the perspectives of the more vulnerable—in other words, participatory democracy (Moe-Lobeda, 2002). Solidarity research, we propose, is about local, participatory, community-based inquiry and learning that is connected with similar activities around the globe. This work is not usually funded and often occurs after hours, but it can often be woven into existing projects and everyday activities in the workplace. It is more about how we and our families and colleagues live our lives and with whom and what we are in relationship and growing solidarity. Some of the purposes of solidarity research could be the following: (a) learning from others who are in different circumstances, (b) documenting and truth telling (the acts of testimony and witness), (c) restoring and nurturing personal and local community health, and (d) weaving connections with other communities of resistance around the globe. All four of these could inform, support, and maybe even transform the clinical research that we do above ground. So, what could solidarity research actually look like?

We suggest a three-step process: identify, connect, and create in solidarity. Solidarity research could begin by *identify*ing alternative kinds of relationships and clinical practices occurring in our own communities. Where are people already meeting their clinical needs through practices that value democratic participation, cooperation, diversity, sustainability, testimony, and direct experience with nature? Examples from our own experience include local organic farming cooperatives, domestic violence shelters, drumming circles, a conservancy group working to restore and protect a local watershed, faith-based groups working with the homeless and malnourished, and community groups helping to meet the health care needs of latchkey children and recent Hispanic immigrants. Imagine the possibilities if these groups could get connected!

The next step, after joining with identified groups, could be to *connect* them with each other and begin the process of developing relationships of mutual support. Freire's dialogic approach might be particularly helpful in facilitating learning connections that are empowering rather than paternalistic. These connections should be about building meaningful and accountable relationships from which concrete and practical exchanges, new questions and research approaches, and strategy development emerge. The work of solidarity research might be to help discover and document the interconnections between and among the groups. How does the health of the local river relate to domestic violence, homelessness, malnutrition, and healthy food sources? How does improvisational group drumming help to create community? Once local connections are established, consider connecting with similar communities and activities elsewhere in the larger region and world. We have not yet found a place where people are not working to heal the wounds and broken-ness resulting from the inherent excesses of colonialism, industrialism, and militarism and its current form as global corporate capitalism. We are in the early stages of developing connections with communities of resistance in Maine and Brazil, but the possibilities are probably unlimited. Keep expanding the circles of identification from self to local neighborhood to global commons.

It is hoped that, through the newly connected, emergent, and dynamic networks, we can begin to *create* alternative institutions and economies, new initiatives and community information systems, and refreshed imaginations. The specific role of clinical researchers would be to support all three steps by witnessing what is occurring, growing new embodied and embedded knowledge, and sharing in the empowerment of all participants. We can share the stories and use them to enhance our clinical research above ground. Just maybe, solidarity research is the small-scale, human-scale, local work interdependent with others around our earth that we do together, subversively, below ground to reclaim our homes and selves as spaces and bodies of love, healing, growth, and solidarity.

Let us imagine together. Jocelyn still works the grill at a fast-food restaurant while she takes classes at the community college for a degree in social work. She reads *Fast Food Nation* (Schlosser, 2002) and no longer eats where she works or at any other fast-food restaurants. Her family physician purchases a share in a local organic farm, and Jocelyn is able to barter for food at the same farm by agreeing to help during harvest season. The farmer also connects her by way of e-mail with an organic coffee collective in Chiapas, Mexico. That correspondence connects her with women's collectives in Chiapas whose members help to awaken Jocelyn to the relationships among her life situation, her heartburn, fast-food restaurants, the purple pill, and the threat to the livelihoods and way of life of her new friends in Mexico. A clinical researcher in the nursing department at a local university is a guest lecturer at Jocelyn's community college class, becomes interested in her story, and agrees to help Jocelyn and her family physician establish a heartburn recovery group. The researcher is now working with that group and the women's group in Chiapas to design a collaborative participatory research project. Is this a story of solidarity research? Are you connected?

Summary

> *Live as if you liked yourself, and it may happen: reach out, keep reaching out, keep bringing in. This is how we are going to live for a long time: not always, for every gardener knows that after the digging, after the planting, after the long season of tending and growth, the harvest comes.*
>
> —Concluding stanza of Marge Piercy's "The Seven of Pentacles"

There are many clinical worlds. Each of them is a place where support is sought and power is invoked. The clinical world and people's need for support occur in nursing, primary health care, specialized medical care, administration and management, education, social work, family therapy, mental health, public health, engineering, law, community organizing, and international activist work. In each of these worlds, there are questions emerging from practice. These are the questions, the settings, and the participants for doing qualitative clinical research. This is where the conversations start. Clinical research is disciplined inquiry regarding the conditions and processes that support and hinder the restoration and growth of interdependent and sustainable life.

People continue to meet in clinics, hoping to weave a comforting cloth of support, but the created relationships and patterns are now more varied, more confusing, and often too expensive. Concerns about access and cost do matter but are not adequately addressed without facing the abusive and dismembering experience of being a woman in the clinic, the pervasive delegitimation of patient experience, the clinicians' increasing sense of helpless imprisonment, and the mounting problems, discontinuities, and cultural conflicts within local communities. Knowing the probabilities is not enough and is often inappropriate. Ignoring the powerful, and often unconscious, impacts of elite corporate globalization and its ideology is morally dangerous (Comaroff & Comaroff, 2001; Ritzer, 2001). The stories, uniqueness, and context are also essential threads in the fabric. Without them, care and moral discourse remain narrowly defined, our bodies and lives remain fragmented, and power is imposed. Jocelyn remains isolated and dependent on her purple pill. She and we need the breath of qualitative research. She and we need *relationship* restored to the clinical world.

A decade has passed. Jocelyn is now a member of a community health advisory council that provides guidance for several local primary care practices and a regional health network and hospital system. They are meeting with an interdisciplinary team of researchers, clinicians, local employers, pharmaceutical industry representatives, and a fellow from the National Institutes of Health (NIH). This group is designing a new regional research initiative, jointly funded by the NIH and a local foundation, that will test a promising new approach to the care of GERD using a double helix RCT design that includes the extensive use of qualitative methods. The analysis of the qualitative data will occur independently from the RCT analysis and will be ongoing through the trial. Jocelyn is a member of the qualitative analysis team. She has authority to end the study for any reason at any time. Imagine the possibility that "Nexium" becomes a nexus for bringing people together to create *conscientização.*

Qualitative methods are needed now more than ever, but with a participatory, collaborative, narrative, and multimethod twist. Qualitative clinical researchers must engage the clinical experience and its questions and must practice humility and fidelity within a community of discourse at ground level. This is a dangerous—but exciting—conversation because it promises that no one can stay the same. Beware the idolatry of control, that is, the idolatry of measurement. If measurement is required, insist on inviting the patients and clinicians into the research process, insist on the precautionary principle, and insist on measuring suffering and love. Complicate the outcomes. Measure the dance of life's attachments and detachments, of mystery and grace, and of breathing and the rhythms of life. Measure the process of healing. Seek a healthier story. Our research needs to risk restoring relationship to the clinical world. Clinical research can heal by transforming into praxis. In time, all ideologies crumble, power shifts, and healing begins. We cannot prevent tornadoes. Thank heavens. It is much better than that. Go into the woods or beside the ocean. Join Jocelyn for the harvest at the local organic farm. *Practice solidarity research*! Do clinical research above ground that helps clinicians and patients now, and work to transform and heal. Let our clinical research also be the waters that break open fundamentalisms and flow between dualisms. At night, below ground, begin to grow a sustainable life together. When the sun rises, bloom!

Notes

1. "Patient" derives from the Latin word *patiens* ("to suffer") and from the Latin *paene* ("almost") and *penuria* ("need"). People seek clinicians because they have needs and are suffering. They are no longer complete; they lack adequate support. People come to clinicians because they do not perceive themselves as equal and/or whole. They are "patients" in need of movement toward wholeness.

2. "Clinic" derives from the Greek words *klinikos* ("of a bed") and *klinein* ("to lean, recline"). From this sense, *a clinic is a physical, emotional, conceptual, social, and spiritual place for those in need of support.* (This support can be medical, managerial, educational, legal, economic, religious, nursing, social, or psychological.) This understanding defines clinic as a bounded text for research.

References

Aita, V., Dodendorf, D., Lebsack, J., Tallia, A., & Crabtree, B. (2001). Patient care staffing patterns and roles in community-based family practices. *Journal of Family Practice, 50,* 889.

Altheide, D. L., & Johnson, J. M. (1998). Criteria for assessing interpretive validity in qualitative research. In N. K. Denzin & Y. S. Lincoln (Eds.), *Collecting and interpreting qualitative materials* (pp. 283–312). Thousand Oaks, CA: Sage.

Baer, H. A. (1993). How critical can clinical anthropology be? *Medical Anthropology, 15,* 299–317.

Barbour, R. S. (2001). Checklists for improving rigour in qualitative research: A case of the tail wagging the dog? *British Medical Journal, 322,* 1115–1117.

Barry, C. A., Britten, N., Barber, N., Bradley, C., & Stevenson, F. (1999). Using reflexivity to optimize teamwork in qualitative research. *Qualitative Health Research, 9*(1), 26–44.

Becker, G. (1997). *Disrupted lives: How people create meaning in a chaotic world.* Berkeley: University of California Press.

Beinfield, H., & Korngold, E. (1991). *Between heaven and earth: A guide to Chinese medicine.* New York: Ballantine Books.

Berg, D. N., & Smith, K. K. (Eds.). (1988). *The self in social inquiry: Researching methods.* Newbury Park, CA: Sage.

Berger, P. L., & Luckmann, T. (1967). *The social construction of reality: A treatise in the sociology of knowledge.* Garden City, NY: Anchor.

Berry, W. (2000). *Life is a miracle.* Washington, DC: Counterpoint.

Bogdan, R. C., & Biklen, S. K. (1992). *Qualitative research for education: An introduction to theory and methods.* Boston: Allyn & Bacon.

Borkan, J. M. (2004). Mixed methods studies in primary care. *Annals of Family Medicine, 2*(1), 4–6.

Borkan, J. M., Quirk, M., & Sullivan M. (1991). Finding meaning after the fall: Injury narratives from elderly hip fracture patients. *Social Science and Medicine, 33,* 947–957.

Brewer, J., & Hunter, A. (1989). *Multimethod research: A synthesis of styles.* Newbury Park, CA: Sage.

Brody, H. (1992). *The healer's power.* New Haven, CT: Yale University Press.

Brody, H. (2003). *Stories of sickness* (2nd ed.). Oxford, UK: Oxford University Press.

Bunge, M. (1961). The weight of simplicity in the construction and assaying of scientific theories. *Philosophy of Science, 28,* 120–149.

Burawoy, M., Burton, A., Ferguson, A. A., Fox, K. J., Gamson, J., Gartrell, N., Hurst, L., Kurzman, C., Salzinger, L., Schiffman, J., & Ui, S. (1991). *Ethnography unbound: Power and resistance in the modern metropolis.* Berkeley: University of California Press.

Callahan, E. J., & Bertakis, K. D. (1991). Development and validation of the Davis Observation Code. *Family Medicine, 23,* 19–24.

Candib, L. M. (1995). *Medicine and the family: A feminist perspective.* New York: Basic Books.

Capra, F. (1996). *The web of life: A new scientific understanding of living systems.* New York: Anchor/Doubleday.

Capra, F. (2002). *The hidden connections: Integrating the biological, cognitive, and social dimensions of life into a science of sustainability.* New York: Doubleday.

Chapple, A., & Rogers, A. (1998). Explicit guidelines for qualitative research: A step in the right direction, a defence of the "soft" option, or a form of sociological imperialism? *Family Practice, 15,* 556–561.

Chrisman, N. J. (1977). The health seeking process: An approach to the natural history of illness. *Culture, Medicine, and Psychiatry, 1,* 351–377.

Chrisman, N. J., & Maretzki, T. W. (Eds.). (1982). *Clinically applied anthropology: Anthropologists in health science settings.* Boston: D. Reidel.

Chobanian, A. V., Bakris, G. L., Black, H. R., Cushman, W. C., Green, L. A., Izzo, J. L., Jr., Jones, D. W., Materson, B. J., Oparil, S., Wright, J. T., Jr., & Roccella, E. J. (2003). Report of the Joint National Committee on Prevention, Evaluation, and Treatment of High Blood Pressure (JNC 7). *Journal of the American Medical Association, 289,* 2560–2572.

Clifford, J., & Marcus, G. (Eds.). (1986). *Writing culture.* Berkeley: University of California Press.

Comaroff, J., & Comaroff, J. L. (Eds.). (2001). *Millennial capitalism and the culture of neoliberalism.* Durham, NC: Duke University Press.

Conio, M., Blanchi, S., Lapertosa, G., Ferraris, R., Sablich, R., Marchi, S., D'Onofrio, V., Lacchin, T., Iaquinto, G., Missale, G., Ravelli, P., Cestari, R., Benedetti, G., Macri, G., Fiocca, R., Munizzi, F., & Filiberti, R. (2003). Long-term endoscopic surveillance of patients with Barrett's esophagus: Incidence of dysplasia and adenocarcinoma—A prospective study. *American Journal of Gastroenterology, 98,* 1931–1939.

Coote, B. (1996). *The trade trap: Poverty and the global commodity market.* Oxford, UK: Oxfam UK & Ireland.

Coward, D. D. (1990). Critical multiplism: A research strategy for nursing science. *Image: Journal of Nursing Scholarship, 22,* 163–167.

Crabtree, B. F., & Miller, W. L. (Eds.). (1999). *Doing qualitative research* (2nd ed.). Thousand Oaks, CA: Sage.

Crabtree, B. F., Miller, W. L., Aita, V., Flocke, S. A., & Stange, K. C. (1998). Primary care practice organization and preventive services delivery: A qualitative analysis. *Journal of Family Practice, 46,* 403–409.

Crabtree, B. F., Miller, W. L., & Stange, K. (Eds.). (2001). Results from the Prevention and Competing Demands in Primary Care study. *Journal of Family Practice, 50,* 837–889.

Creswell, J. W. (2003). *Research design: Qualitative, quantitative, and mixed methods approaches* (2nd ed.). Thousand Oaks, CA: Sage.

Creswell, J. W., Fetters, M. D., & Ivankova, N. V. (2004). Designing a mixed methods study in primary care. *Annals of Family Medicine, 2*(1), 7–12.

Csordas, T. J. (2002). *Body/Meaning/Healing.* New York: Palgrave Macmillan.

Daly, J., & McDonald, I. (1992). Covering your back: Strategies for qualitative research in clinical settings. *Qualitative Health Research, 2,* 416–438.

Davis-Floyd, R., & St. John, G. (1998). *From doctor to healer: The transformative journey.* New Brunswick, NJ: Rutgers University Press.

Denz-Penhey, H., & Murdoch, J. C. (1993). Service delivery for people with chronic fatigue syndrome: A pilot action research study. *Family Practice, 10,* 14–18.

Deyo, R. A., Diehl, A. K., & Rosenthal, M. (1986). How many days of bedrest for acute low back pain? A randomized clinical trial. *New England Journal of Medicine, 315,* 1064–1070.

Diers, D. (1979). *Research in nursing practice.* Philadelphia: J. B. Lippincott.

Douthwaite, R. (1999). *The growth illusion* (rev. ed.). Gabriola Island, British Columbia: New Society Publishers.

Drury, N. (1996). *Shamanism.* Shaftesbury, UK: Element Books.

Ellingson, L. L. (1998). "Then you know how I feel": Empathy, identity, and reflexivity in fieldwork. *Qualitative Inquiry, 4,* 492–514.

Ellis, C. (1995). *Final negotiations: A story of love, loss, and chronic illness.* Philadelphia: Temple University Press.

Ellis, C., & Bochner, A. P. (Eds.). (1996). *Composing ethnography: Alternative forms of qualitative writing.* Walnut Creek, CA: AltaMira.

Engels, G. L. (1977). The need for a new medical model: A challenge for biomedicine. *Science, 196,* 129–136.

Fabrega, H., Jr. (1976). The function of medical care systems: A logical analysis. *Perspectives in Biology and Medicine, 20,* 108–119.

Fabrega, H., Jr. (1979). The ethnography of illness. *Social Science and Medicine, 13A,* 565–575.

Fahy, K., & Smith, P. (1999). From the sick role to subject positions: A new approach to the medical encounter. *Health, 3*(1), 71–93.

Farmer, P. (2001). *Infections and inequalities: The modern plagues* (rev. ed.). Berkeley: University of California Press.

Feinstein, A. R. (1985). *Clinical epidemiology: The architecture of clinical research.* Philadelphia: W. B. Saunders.

Finkler, K. (2000). *Experiencing the new genetics: Family and kinship on the medical frontier.* Philadelphia: University of Pennsylvania Press.

Fisher, S. (1986). *In the patient's best interest: Women and the politics of medical decisions.* New Brunswick, NJ: Rutgers University Press.

Fisher, S., & Todd, A. D. (Eds.). (1983). *The social organization of doctor–patient communication.* Washington, DC: Center for Applied Linguistics.

Flocke, S., Miller, W. L., & Crabtree, B. F. (2002). Relationships between physician practice style, patient satisfaction, and attributes of primary care. *Journal of Family Practice, 51,* 835–840.

Flocke, S., Stange, K. C., & Zyzanski, S. J. (1997). The impact of insurance type and forced discontinuity on the delivery of primary care. *Journal of Family Practice, 45,* 129–135.

Foster, G. M. (1974). Medical anthropology: Some contrasts with medical sociology. *Medical Anthropology Newsletter, 6,* 1–6.

Foster, G. M., & Anderson, B. G. (1978). *Medical anthropology.* New York: John Wiley.

Frank, A. W. (1991). *At the will of the body: Reflections on illness.* Boston: Houghton Mifflin.

Frank, A. W. (1995). *The wounded storyteller: Body, illness, and ethics.* Chicago: University of Chicago Press.

Freire, P. (1970). *Pedagogy of the oppressed* (M. B. Ramos, Trans.). New York: Continuum Publishing.

Freire, P. (1998). Pedagogy of the heart. In A. M. A. Freire & D. Macedo (Eds.), *The Paulo Freire reader* (pp. 265–282). New York: Continuum International Publishing Group.

Frey, R. (1994). *Eye juggling: Seeing the world through a looking glass and a glass pane.* Lanham, MD: University Press of America.

Freymann, J. G. (1989). The public's health care paradigm is shifting: Medicine must swing with it. *Journal of General Internal Medicine, 4,* 313–319.

Fullerton-Smith, I. (1995). How members of the Cochrane Collaboration prepare and maintain systematic reviews of the effects of health care. *Evidence-Based Medicine, 1,* 7–8.

Gardner, G. (Ed.). (2003). *State of the world 2003.* New York: Norton.

Giacomini, M. K., & Cook, D. J. (2000). Qualitative research in health care: What are the results and how do they help me care for my patients? *Journal of the American Medical Association, 284,* 478–482.

Glasgow, R. E., Lichtenstein, E., & Marcus, A. C. (2003). Why don't we see more translation of health promotion in research to practice? Rethinking the efficacy-to-effectiveness transition. *American Journal of Public Health, 93,* 1261–1267.

Good, B. J. (1994). *Medicine, rationality, and experience.* Cambridge, UK: Cambridge University Press.

Good, B. J., & Good, M. D. (1981). The meaning of symptoms: A cultural hermeneutic model for clinical practice. In L. Eisenberg & A. M. Kleinman (Eds.), *The relevance of social science for medicine* (pp. 165–196). Boston: D. Reidel.

Good, B. J., & Good, M. D. (1993). "Learning medicine": The constructing of medical knowledge at Harvard Medical School. In S. Lindenbaum & M. Lock (Eds.), *Knowledge, power, and practice: The anthropology of medicine and everyday life* (pp. 81–107). Berkeley: University of California Press.

Goodwin, M. A., Zyzanski, S. J., Zronek, S., Ruhe, M., Weyer, S. M., Konrad, N., Esola, D., & Stange, K. C. (2001). A clinical trial of tailored office systems for preventive service delivery: The Study to Enhance Prevention by Understanding Practice (STEP-UP). *American Journal of Preventive Medicine, 21,* 20–28.

Gordon, D. R. (1988). Tenacious assumptions in Western medicine. In M. Lock & D. Gordon (Eds.), *Biomedicine examined* (pp. 19–56). Boston: D. Reidel.

Gordon, J. (1996). *Manifesto for a new medicine: Your guide to healing partnerships and the wise use of alternative therapies.* Reading, MA: Addison-Wesley.

Greenhalgh, T., & Hurwitz, B. (1998). *Narrative based medicine: Dialogue and discourse in clinical practice.* London: BMJ Books.

Haraway, D. J. (1991). *Simians, cyborgs, and women: The reinvention of nature.* London: Routledge.

Haraway, D. J. (1993). The biopolitics of postmodern bodies: Determinations of self in immune system discourse. In S. Lindenbaum & M. Lock (Eds.), *Knowledge, power, and practice: The anthropology of medicine and everyday life* (pp. 364–410). Berkeley: University of California Press.

Hardin, G. (1985). *Filters against folly.* New York: Penguin Books.

Harris, C. M. (1989). Seeing sunflowers. *Journal of the Royal College of General Practitioners, 39,* 313–319.

Hawkins, A. H. (1993). *Reconstructing illness: Studies in pathography.* West Lafayette, IN: Purdue University Press.

Helman, C. G. (2000). *Culture, health, and illness* (4th ed.). Oxford, UK: Butterworth Heinemann.

Illich, I. (1970). *Deschooling society.* London: Marian Boyars.

Illich, I. (1976). *Medical nemesis: The exploration of health.* New York: Pantheon Books.

Jackson, M. (1989). *Paths toward a clearing: Radical empiricism and ethnographic inquiry.* Bloomington: Indiana University Press.

Jaen, C., McIlvain, H., Pol, L., Phillips, R., Jr., Flocke, S., & Crabtree, B. (2001). Tailoring tobacco counseling to the competing demands in the clinical encounter. *Journal of Family Practice, 50,* 859–863.

Jason, L. A., Keys, C. B., Suarez-Balcazar, Y., Taylor, R. R., & Davis, M. I. (Eds.). (2004). *Participatory community research: Theories and methods in action.* Washington, DC: American Psychological Association.

Jensen, D. (2002). *The culture of make believe.* New York: Context Books.

Johnson, D. A., Benjamin, S. B., Vakil, N. B., Goldstein, J. L., Lamet, M., Whipple, J., Damico, D., & Hamelin, B. (2001). Esomeprazole once daily for 6 months is effective therapy for maintaining healed erosive esophagitis and for controlling gastroesophageal reflux disease symptoms: A randomized, double-blind, placebo-controlled study of efficacy and safety. *American Journal of Gastroenterology, 96,* 27–34.

Johnson, M. (1987). *The body in the mind.* Chicago: University of Chicago Press.

Jolly, K., Bradley, F., Sharp, S., Smith, H., & Mant, D. (1998). Follow-up care in general practice of patients with myocardial infarction or angina pectoris: Initial results of the SHIP trial. *Family Practice, 15,* 548–555.

Kahn, D. L. (1993). Ways of discussing validity in qualitative nursing research. *Western Journal of Nursing Research, 15,* 122–126.

Kelsey, J. L., Thompson, W. D., & Evans, A. S. (1986). *Methods in observational epidemiology.* New York: Oxford University Press.

Kemmis, S., & McTaggart, R. (2003). Participatory action research. In N. K. Denzin & Y. S. Lincoln (Eds.), *Strategies of qualitative inquiry* (2nd ed., pp. 336–396). Thousand Oaks, CA: Sage.

Kim, J. Y., Millen, J. V., Irwin, A., & Gershman, J. (Eds.). (2000). *Dying for growth: Global inequality and the health of the poor.* Monroe, ME: Common Courage Press.

Kirmayer, L. J. (1992). The body's insistence on meaning: Metaphor as presentation and representation in illness experience. *Medical Anthropology Quarterly, 6,* 323–346.

Kleinman, A. M. (1988). *The illness narratives: Suffering, healing, and the human condition.* New York: Basic Books.

Kleinman, A. M. (1992). Local worlds of suffering: An interpersonal focus for ethnographies of illness experience. *Qualitative Health Research, 2,* 127–134.

Kleinman, A. M. (1995). *Writing at the margin: Discourse between anthropology and medicine.* Berkeley: University of California Press.

Kleinman, A. M., Eisenberg, L., & Good, B. (1978). Culture, illness, and care: Clinical lessons from anthropologic and cross-cultural research. *Annals of Internal Medicine, 88,* 251–258.

Lather, P. (1991). *Getting smart: Feminist research and pedagogy with/in the postmodern.* New York: Routledge.

Launer, J. (2002). *Narrative-based primary care: A practical guide.* Abingdon, UK: Radcliffe Medical Press.

Lazarus, E. S. (1988). Theoretical considerations for the study of the doctor–patient relationship: Implications of a perinatal study. *Medical Anthropology Quarterly, 2,* 34–58.

Lock, M. (1982). On revealing the hidden curriculum. *Medical Anthropology Quarterly, 14,* 19–21.

Lock, M. (1986). The anthropological study of the American medical system: Center and periphery. *Social Science and Medicine, 22,* 931–932.

Lock, M. (1993). Cultivating the body: Anthropology and epistemologies of bodily practice and knowledge. *Annual Reviews of Anthropology, 22,* 133–156.

Loxterkamp, D. (1997). *A measure of my days: The journal of a country doctor.* Hanover, NH: University Press of New England.

Macaulay, A. C., Commanda, L. E., Freeman, W. L., Gibson, N., McCabe, M. L., Robbins, C. M., & Twohig, P. L. (1998). Responsible research with communities: Participatory research in primary care [online publication of the North American Primary Care Research Group]. Retrieved October 27, 2004, from http://napcrg.org.exic.html

Macnaghten, P., & Urry, J. (Eds.). (2001). *Bodies of nature.* London: Sage.

Malterud, K. (2001a). The art and science of clinical knowledge: Evidence beyond measures and numbers. *Lancet, 358,* 397–400.

Malterud, K. (2001b). Qualitative research: Standards, challenges, and guidelines. *Lancet, 358,* 483–488.

Martin, E. (1994). *Flexible bodies: The role of immunity in American culture from the days of polio to the age of AIDS.* Boston: Beacon.

Mattingly, C. (1998). *Healing dramas and clinical plots: The narrative structure of experience.* Cambridge, UK: Cambridge University Press.

McGoldrick, M., Gerson, R., & Shellenberger, S. (1999). *Genograms: Assessment and intervention* (2nd ed.). New York: Norton.

McIlvain, H., Crabtree, B. F., Medder, J., Stange, K. C., & Miller, W. L. (1998). Using "practice genograms" to understand and describe practice configurations. *Family Medicine, 30,* 490–496.

McWhinney, I. R. (1986). Are we on the brink of a major transformation of clinical method? *Canadian Medical Association Journal, 135,* 873–878.

McWhinney, I. R. (1989). An acquaintance with particulars. *Family Medicine, 21,* 296–298.

Meinert, C. L. (1986). *Clinical trials: Design, conduct, and analysis.* New York: Oxford University Press.

Miller, W. L. (1994). Common space: Creating a collaborative research conversation. In B. F. Crabtree, W. L. Miller, R. B. Addison, V. J. Gilchrist, & A. Kuzel (Eds.), *Exploring collaborative research in primary care* (pp. 265–288). Thousand Oaks, CA: Sage.

Miller, W. L., & Crabtree, B. F. (1999a). The dance of interpretation. In B. F. Crabtree & W. L. Miller (Eds.), *Doing qualitative research* (2nd ed., pp. 127–143). Thousand Oaks, CA: Sage.

Miller, W. L., & Crabtree, B. F. (1999b). Primary care research: A multimethod typology and qualitative roadmap. In B. F. Crabtree & W. L. Miller (Eds.), *Doing qualitative research* (2nd ed., pp. 3–28). Thousand Oaks, CA: Sage.

Miller, W. L., Crabtree, B. F., Duffy, M. B., Epstein, R. M., & Stange, K. C. (2003). Research guidelines for assessing the impact of healing relationships in clinical medicine. *Alternative Therapies in Health and Medicine, 9*(3, Suppl.), 80A–95A.

Miller, W. L., Crabtree, B. F., McDaniel, R., & Stange, K. C. (1998). Understanding change in primary care practice using complexity theory. *Journal of Family Practice, 46,* 369–376.

Miller, W. L., McDaniel, R., Crabtree, B. F., & Stange, K. C. (2001). Practice jazz: Understanding variation in family practices using complexity science. *Journal of Family Practice, 50,* 872–878.

Mishler, E. G. (1984). *The discourse of medicine: Dialectics of medical interviews.* Norwood, NJ: Ablex.

Mitchell, M. L. (1998). *Employing qualitative methods in the private sector.* Thousand Oaks, CA: Sage.

Moe-Lobeda, C. D. (2002). *Healing a broken world: Globalization and god.* Minneapolis, MN: Fortress Press.

Mol, A. (2002). *The body multiple: Ontology in medical practice.* Durham, NC: Duke University Press.

Morgan, G. (1998). *Images of organization: The executive edition.* San Francisco: Berrett–Koehler.

Morrison, J. I. (2000). *Health care in the new millennium: Visions, values, and leadership.* San Francisco: Jossey–Bass.

Morse, J. M., & Field, P. A. (1997). *Principles of qualitative methods.* Thousand Oaks, CA: Sage.

Morse, J. M., Swanson, J. M., & Kuzel, A. J. (2001). *The nature of qualitative evidence.* Thousand Oaks, CA: Sage.

Morsy, S. A. (1996). Political economy in medical anthropology. In C. F. Sargent & T. M. Johnson (Eds.), *Medical anthropology: Contemporary theory and method* (rev. ed., pp. 21–40). Westport, CT: Praeger.

Moyer, B., MacAllister, J., & Soifer, S. (2001). *Doing democracy: The MAP model for organizing social movements.* Gabriola Island, British Columbia: New Society Publishers.

National Heart, Lung, and Blood Institute. (1998). *Clinical guidelines on the identification, evaluation, and treatment of overweight and obesity in adults: The evidence report* (NIH Publication 98-4083). Bethesda, MD: Author.

Naylor, C. D. (1995). Grey zones of clinical practice: Some limits to evidence-based medicine. *Lancet, 345,* 840–842.

Notes From Nowhere (Eds.). (2003). *We are everywhere: The irresistible rise of global anticapitalism.* London: Verso.

Orr, D. W. (2002). *The nature of design: Ecology, culture, and human intention.* Oxford, UK: Oxford University Press.

Pelto, P. J., & Pelto, G. H. (1978). *Anthropological research: The structure of inquiry* (2nd ed.). New York: Cambridge University Press.

Pelto, P. J., & Pelto, G. H. (1990). Field methods in medical anthropology. In T. M. Johnson & C. F. Sargent (Eds.), *Medical anthropology: Contemporary theory and method* (pp. 269–297). New York: Praeger.

Perdue, W. C., Stone, L. A., & Gostin, L. O. (2003). The built environment and its relationship to the public's health: The legal framework. *American Journal of Public Health, 93,* 1390–1394.

Perlas, N. (2000). *Shaping globalization: Civil society, cultural power, and threefolding.* Quezon City, Philippines: Center for Alternative Development Initiatives.

Pfifferling, J. H. (1981). A cultural prescription for medicocentrism. In L. Eisenberg & A. Kleinman (Eds.), *The relevance of social science for medicine* (pp. 197–222). Boston: D. Reidel.

Piercy, M. (1994). *Circles on the water: Selected poems of Marge Piercy.* New York: Alfred A. Knopf.

Pocock, S. J. (1983). *Clinical trials: A practical approach.* New York: John Wiley.

Pol, L., Rouse, J., Zyzanski, S., Rasmussen, D., & Crabtree, B. (2001). Rural, urban, and suburban comparisons of preventive services in family practice clinics. *Journal of Rural Health, 17,* 114–121.

Polgar, S. (1962). Health and human behavior: Areas of interest common to the social and medical sciences. *Current Anthropology, 3,* 159–205.

Ponce de León, J. (Ed.). (2001). *Our work is our weapon: Selected writings, subcommandante insurgente Marcos.* New York: Seven Stories Press.

Raffensperger, C. (2002). The precautionary principle: Bearing witness to and alleviating suffering. *Alternative Therapies, 8,* 111–115.

Raffensperger, C., Tickner, J., & Jackson, W. (1999). *Protecting public health and the environment: Implementing the precautionary principle.* Washington, DC: Island Press.

Rasmussen, L. L. (1996). *Earth community, earth ethics.* Maryknoll, NY: Orbis Books.

Richardson, L. (1990). *Writing strategies: Reaching diverse audiences.* Newbury Park, CA: Sage.

Ritzer, G. (2001). *Explorations in the sociology of consumption: Fast food, credit cards, and casinos.* London: Sage.

Robinson, D., Prest, L., Susman, J., Rasmussen, D., Rouse, J., & Crabtree, B. (2001). Technician, friend, detective, and healer: Family physicians' responses to emotional distress. *Journal of Family Practice,* 50, 864–870.

Roseland, M. (1998). *Toward sustainable communities: Resources for citizens and their governments.* Gabriola Island, British Columbia: New Society Publishers.

Sackett, D. L. (1991). *Clinical epidemiology: A basic science for clinical medicine* (2nd ed.). Boston: Little, Brown.

Sackett, D. L., Straus, S. E., Richardson, W. S., Rosenberg, W., & Haynes, R. (2000). *Evidence-based medicine: How to practice and teach EBM* (2nd ed.). London: Churchill Livingstone.

Sacks, O. (1984). *A leg to stand on.* New York: Summit Books.

Sandelowski, M. (2002). Reembodying qualitative inquiry. *Qualitative Health Research, 12,* 104–115.

Sapsford, R., & Abbott, P. (1992). *Research methods for nurses and the caring professions.* Bristol, PA: Open University Press.

Schein, E. H. (1987). *The clinical perspective in fieldwork.* Newbury Park, CA: Sage.

Scheper-Hughes, N., & Locke, M. (1987). The mindful body: A prolegomenon to future work in medical anthropology. *Medical Anthropology Quarterly, 1,* 6–41.

Schlosser, E. (2002). *Fast food nation: The dark side of the all-American meal.* New York: HarperCollins.

Schumacher, E. F. (1977). *A guide for the perplexed.* New York: Harper & Row.

Scott, J., Cohen, D., DiCicco-Bloom, B., Orzano, A. J., Jaen, C. R., & Crabtree, B. F. (2001). Antibiotic use in acute respiratory infections and the ways patients pressure physicians for a prescription. *Journal of Family Practice, 50,* 853–858.

Sharma, H., & Clark, C. (1998). *Contemporary ayurveda: Medicine and research in maharishi ayurveda.* Philadelphia: Churchill Livingstone.

Shaughnessy, A. F., Slawson, D. C., & Bennett, J. H. (1994). Becoming an information master: A guidebook to the medical information jungle. *Journal of Family Practice, 39,* 489–499.

Shavelson, R. J., & Towne, L. (Eds.). (2002). *Scientific research in education.* Washington, DC: National Academic Press.

Shepherd, M., Hattersley, A. T., & Sparkes, A. C. (2000). Predictive genetic testing in diabetes: A case study of multiple perspectives. *Qualitative Health Research, 10,* 242–259.

Shildrick, M. (1997). *Leaky bodies and boundaries: Feminism, postmodernism, and (bio)ethics.* London: Routledge.

Shiva, V. (1994). *Close to home: Women reconnect ecology, health, and development worldwide.* Gabriola Island, British Columbia: New Society Publishers.

Singer, M. (1995). Beyond the ivory tower: Critical praxis in medical anthropology. *Medical Anthropology Quarterly, 9,* 80–106.

Slawson, D. C., Shaughnessy, A. F., & Bennett, J. H. (1994). Becoming a medical information master: Feeling good about not knowing everything. *Journal of Family Practice, 38,* 505–513.

Small, S. A. (1995). Action-oriented research: Models and methods. *Journal of Marriage and the Family, 57,* 941–955.

Smith, R. C. (1996). *The patient's story: Integrated patient–doctor interviewing.* Boston: Little, Brown.

Snadden, D., & Brown, J. B. (1991). Asthma and stigma. *Family Practice, 8,* 329–335.

Stange, K. C., Miller, W. L., Crabtree, B. F., O'Connor, P. J., & Zyzanski, S. J. (1994). Multimethod research: Approaches for integrating qualitative and quantitative methods. *Journal of General Internal Medicine, 9,* 278–282.

Stange, K. C., Miller, W. L., & McWhinney, I. (2001). Developing the knowledge base of family practice. *Family Medicine, 33,* 286–297.

Stange, K. C., Zyzanskim, S. J., Jaen, C. R., Callahan, E. J., Kelly, R. B., Gillanders, W. R., Shank, J. C., Chao, J., Medalie, J. H., Miller, W. L., Crabtree, B. F., Flocke, S. A., Gilchrist, V. J., Langa, D. M., & Goodwin, M. A. (1998). Illuminating the "black box": A description of 4454 patient visits to 138 family physicians. *Journal of Family Practice, 46,* 377–389.

Stein, H. F. (1990). *American medicine as culture.* Boulder, CO: Westview.

Stevens, A., Abrams, K., Brazier, J., Fitzpatrick, R., & Lilford, R. (Eds.). (2001). *The advanced handbook of methods in evidence based healthcare.* London: Sage.

Stewart, M., Brown, J. B., Weston, W. W., McWhinney, I. R., McWilliam, C. L., & Freeman, T. R. (1995). *Patient-centered medicine: Transforming the clinical method.* Thousand Oaks, CA: Sage.

Strathern, A. J. (1996). *Body thoughts.* Ann Arbor: University of Michigan Press.

Swayne, J. (1998). *Homeopathic method: Implications for clinical practice and medical science.* London: Churchill Livingstone.

Symon, G., & Cassell, C. (Eds.). (1998). *Qualitative methods and analysis in organizational research: A practical guide.* London: Sage.

Talley, N. J., Venables, T. L., Green, J. R., Armstrong, D., O'Kane, K. P., Giaffer, M., Bardhan, K. D., Carlsson, R. G., Chen, S., & Hasselgren, G. S. (2002). Esomeprazole 40 mg and 20 mg is efficacious in the long-term management of patients with endoscopy-negative gastro-oesophageal reflux disease: A placebo-controlled trial of on-demand therapy for 6 months. *European Journal of Gastroenterology and Hepatology, 14,* 857–863.

Tallia, A., Stange, K., McDaniel R, Jr., Aita, V., Miller, W., & Crabtree, B. (2003). Understanding organizational designs of primary care practices. *Journal of Healthcare Management, 48,* 43–58.

Tandon, R. (1996). The historical roots and contemporary tendencies in participatory research: Implications for health care. In K. De Koning & M. Martin (Eds.), *Participatory research in health: Issues and experiences* (pp. 19–26). London: Zed Books.

Tashakkori, A., & Teddlie, C. (1998). *Mixed methodology: Combining qualitative and quantitative approaches.* Thousand Oaks, CA: Sage.

Taylor, B. (1993). Phenomenology: One way to understand nursing practice. *International Journal of Nursing Studies, 30,* 171–179.

Thesen, J., & Kuzel, A. (1999). Participatory inquiry. In B. F. Crabtree & W. L. Miller (Eds.), *Doing qualitative research* (2nd ed., pp. 269–290). Thousand Oaks, CA: Sage.

Thomashow, M. (1996). *Ecological identity: Becoming a reflective environmentalist.* Cambridge, MA: MIT Press.

Tresolini, C. P. (1994). *Health professions education and relationship-centered care.* San Francisco: Pew Health Professions Commission.

Turner, B. (1992). *Regulating bodies: Essays in medical sociology.* New York: Routledge.

Waitzkin, H. (1991). *The politics of medical encounters: How patients and doctors deal with social problems.* New Haven, CT: Yale University Press.

Ward, M. M. (1993). Study design in qualitative research: A guide to assessing quality. *Journal of General Internal Medicine, 8,* 107–109.

Weil, A. (1988). *Health and healing.* Boston: Houghton Mifflin.

West, C. (1984). *Routine complications: Troubles with talk between doctors and patients.* Bloomington: Indiana University Press.

Wiesel, S. W., Cuckler, J. M., DeLuca, F., Jones, F., Zeide, M. S., & Rothman, R. H. (1980). Acute low back pain: An objective analysis of conservative therapy. *Spine, 5,* 324–330.

Wilber, K. (1996). *A brief history of everything.* Boston: Shambhala Publications.

Wiles, R. (1998). Patients' perceptions of their heart attack and recovery: The influence of epidemiological "evidence" and personal experience. *Social Science and Medicine, 46,* 1477–1486.

Williams, G. (1984). The genesis of chronic illness: Narrative re-construction. *Sociology of Health and Illness, 6,* 175–200.

Willms, D. G. (1991). A new stage, a new life: Individual success in quitting smoking. *Social Science and Medicine, 33,* 1365–1371.

Willms, D. G., Best, J. A., Taylor, D. W., Gilbert, J., Wilson, D., Lindsay, E., & Singer, J. (1990). A systematic approach for using qualitative methods in primary prevention research. *Medical Anthropology Quarterly, 4,* 391–409.

Wilson, D. M. C., Taylor, D. W., Gilbert, J. R., Best, J. A., Lindsay, E. A., Willms, D. G., & Singer, J. (1988). A randomized trial of a family physician intervention for smoking cessation. *Journal of the American Medical Association, 260,* 1570–1574.

Wolcott, H. F. (1990). *Writing up qualitative research.* Newbury Park, CA: Sage.

Young, A. (1982a). The anthropologies of illness and sickness. In B. Siegel, A. Beals, & S. Tyler (Eds.), *Annual review of anthropology 11* (pp. 257–285). Palo Alto, CA: Annual Reviews.

Young, A. (1982b). When rational men fall sick: An inquiry into some assumptions made by medical anthropologists. *Culture, Medicine, and Psychiatry, 5,* 317–335.

Part IV

METHODS OF COLLECTING AND ANALYZING EMPIRICAL MATERIALS

Nothing stands outside representation. Research involves a complex politics of representation. The socially situated researcher creates, through interaction and material practices, those realities and representations that are the subject matter of inquiry. In such sites, the interpretive practices of qualitative research are implemented. These methodological practices represent different ways of generating and representing empirical materials grounded in the everyday world. Part IV of the *Handbook* examines the multiple practices and methods of analysis that qualitative researchers-as-methodological *bricoleurs* now employ.

Narrative Inquiry

Today narrative inquiry is flourishing; it is everywhere. We know the world through the stories that are told about it. Even so, as Susan Chase (Chapter 25) reminds us, narrative inquiry as a particular type of qualitative inquiry is a field in the making. Chase defines narrative as retrospective meaning making and defines narrative inquiry as an "amalgam of interdisciplinary lenses, diverse disciplinary approaches, and both traditional and innovative methods—all revolving around an interest in biographical particulars as narrated by the one who lives them." She provides an excellent historical overview of this field, moving from the sociologists and anthropologists in the first half of the 20th century who championed the life history method, to the second-wave feminists who "poured new life into the study of personal narratives," to sociolinguists who treated oral narrative as a form of discourse, to contemporary scholars who turn the use of interviews into the study of how persons perform and tell stories about themselves.

Narratives are socially constrained forms of action, socially situated performances, ways of acting in and making sense of the world. Narrative researchers often write in the first person, thus "emphasizing their own narrative action." Chase identifies several distinct approaches to narrative analysis, including psychological, sociological, anthropological, autoethnographic, and performances studies of identity. She then outlines a series of issues that must be addressed in any narrative inquiry. These involve interpretive authority and "hearing" the story that is being told.

Narrative inquiry can advance a social change agenda. Wounded storytellers can empower others to tell their stories. *Testimonios,* as emergency narratives, can mobilize a nation against social injustice, repression, and violence. Collective stories can form the basis of a social movement. Telling the stories of marginalized people can help to create a public space requiring others to hear what they do not want to hear.

Arts-Based Inquiry

Arts-based inquiry uses the aesthetics, methods, and practices of the literary, performance, and visual arts as well as dance, theater, drama, film, collage, video, and photography. Arts-based inquiry is intertextual. It crosses the borders of art and research. Susan Finley (Chapter 26) writes a history of this methodology, locating it in the postcolonial postmodern context. She assesses the usefulness of activist art (e.g., photographs of refugees of war, children and street art, street theater) when political activism is the goal. She shows how activist art can be used to address issues of political significance, including engaging community participants in acts of political self-expression.

When grounded in a critical performance pedagogy, arts-based work can be used to advance a progressive political agenda that addresses issues of social inequity. Thus do researchers take up their "cameras, paintbrushes, bodies, and voices" in the name of social justice projects. Such work exposes oppression, targets sites of resistance, and outlines a transformative praxis that performs resistance texts. Finley shows how she makes this commitment to transformative praxis work by offering moving examples from her At Home At School (AHAS) program for kindergarten through eighth-grade (K–8) children who live in shelter and transitional housing.

The Interview

We live in an interview society, in a society whose members seem to believe that interviews generate useful information about lived experience and its meanings. The interview has become a taken-for-granted feature of our mediated mass culture. But the interview is a negotiated text—a site where power, gender, race, and class intersect. Stealing a narrative line from the film *Memento,* which begins at the end with a murder, Fontana and Frey (Chapter 27) begin their review of the history of the interview in the social sciences by starting in the present. They work back and forth in time from Kong, Mahoney, and Plummer's (2002) essay, "Queering the Interview." This essay shows how the interview became a tool of modernist democratization and ultimately of social reform.

Working back from the present, Fontana and Frey note the interview's major forms—structured, unstructured, and open-ended—while showing how the tool is modified and changed during use. They also discuss the group (or focused) interview, the oral history interview, creative interviewing, online interviewing, and gendered, feminist, and postmodern (or multivoiced) active interviewing.

The interview is a conversation—the art of asking questions and listening. It is not a neutral tool, for at least two people create the reality of the interview situation. In this situation, answers are given. Thus, the interview produces situated understandings grounded in specific interactional episodes. This method is influenced by the personal characteristics of the interviewer, including race, class, ethnicity, and gender.

Fontana and Frey review the important work of feminist scholars on the interview, especially the arguments of Behar, Reinharz, Hertz, Richardson, Clough, Collins, Smith, and Oakley. The British sociologist Oakley (1981) and other feminist scholars have identified a major contradiction between scientific positivistic research, which requires objectivity and detachment, and feminist-based interviewing, which requires openness, emotional engagement, and the development of a potentially long-term trusting relationship between the interviewer and the subject.

A feminist interviewing ethic, as Fontana and Frey suggest, redefines the interview situation. This ethic transforms interviewers and respondents into coequals who are carrying on a conversation about mutually relevant, often biographically critical, issues. This narrative, performative, storytelling framework challenges the informed consent and deception models of inquiry discussed by Christians (Chapter 6) in Part I. This ethic changes the interview into an important tool for the types of clinical and applied action research discussed by Kemmis and McTaggart (Chapter 23) and Miller and Crabtree (Chapter 24) in Part III. This ethic also turns the interview into a vehicle for social change, as noted in Chase's (Chapter 25) discussion of the interview as a site for storytelling.

▣ Recontextualizing Observational Methods

Going into a social situation and looking is another important way of gathering materials about the social world. Drawing on previous arguments (Angrosino & Pérez, 2000), Michael Angrosino (Chapter 28) fundamentally rewrites the methods and practices of naturalistic observation. All observation involves participation in the world being studied. There is no pure, objective, detached observation; the effects of the observer's presence can never be erased. Furthermore, the colonial concept of the subject (the object of the observer's gaze) is no longer appropriate. Observers now function as collaborative participants in action inquiry settings. Angrosino and Pérez (2000) argue that observational interaction is a tentative situational process. It is shaped by shifts in gendered identity as well as by existing structures of power. As relationships unfold, participants validate the cues generated by others in the sitting. Finally, during the observational process, people assume situational identities that might not be socially or culturally normative.

Like Christians (Chapter 6), Angrosino offers compelling criticisms of institutional review boards (IRBs), noting that positivistic social scientists seldom recognize the needs of observational ethnographers. At many universities, the official IRBs are tied to the experimental, hypothesis-testing, so-called scientific paradigm. This paradigm creates problems for the postmodern observer, for the scholar who becomes part of the world that is being studied. To get approval for their research, scholars might have to engage in deception (in this instance of the IRB). This leads some ethnographers to claim that their research will not be intrusive and, hence, will not cause harm. Yet interactive observers are by definition intrusive. When collaborative inquiry is undertaken, subjects become stakeholders, persons who shape the inquiry itself. What this means for consent forms—and for forms of participatory inquiry more broadly—is not clear. Alternative forms of ethnographic writing, including the use of fictionalized stories, represent one avenue for addressing this ethical quandary.

Angrosino offers an ethic of "proportionate reason." This utilitarian ethic attempts to balance the benefits, costs, and consequences of actions in the field, asking whether the means to an end are justified by the importance and value of the goals attained. This ethic is then translated into a progressive social agenda. This agenda stresses social (not commutative), distributive, or legal justice. A social justice ethic asks the researcher to become directly involved with the poor and the marginalized, to become an advocate, and to facilitate empowerment in communities. A pedagogy for social justice based on a service learning model is outlined.

Angrosino demystifies the observation method. Observation is no longer the key to some grand analysis of culture or society. Instead, observational research now becomes a method that focuses on differences, on the lives of particular people in concrete, but constantly changing, human relationships. The relevance and need for a feminist ethics of care and commitment become even more apparent.

▣ Reimagining Visual Methods

Today visual sociologists and anthropologists use photography, motion pictures, the World Wide Web, interactive CDs, CD-ROMs, and virtual reality as ways of forging connections between human existence and visual perception. These forms of visual representation represent different ways of recording and documenting what passes as social life. Often called the mirror with a memory, photography takes the researcher into the everyday world, where the issues of observer identity, the subject's point of view, and what to photograph become problematic. Douglas Harper (Chapter 29) examines the status of visual thinking in the sociological community, the impact of new technologies on visual methods, the continuing development of traditional forms of visual documentary, and problematic issues surrounding ethics in the visual research world. Journals have become more sophisticated in the presentation of visual materials, and new technologies and skills using websites have created new ways of presenting visual materials. These methods have been taken up by experimental, reflexive digital ethnographers. Harper wisely notes that these developments exist within an unstable and constantly changing electronic world. The software and the computers that deliver these developments have short lives.

Historically, visual sociology began within the postpositivist tradition, providing visual information to support the realist tales of traditional ethnography. Photographs were a part of the unproblematic "facts" that constituted the "truth" of these tales. Now visual sociology, like ethnography, is in a period of deep questioning and great change. Visual sociology, Harper contends, must find a place in this new ethnography. Drawing from his own research, Harper illustrates the value of photo elicitation in the study of the meaning of change in the dairy industry in northern New York State. In photo elicitation studies, photos are used to stimulate a quality of memory that word-based interviewing does not.

Harper discusses the use of photographs to observe public life. IRBs have been reluctant to give permission to photograph the public without informed consent. But many visual sociologists base their photographic research on the model of documentary photography and photojournalism, where the right to photograph the public has been guaranteed by amendments to the Constitution dealing with the freedom of expression. Visual sociologists point to these precedents and argue that harm to subjects is unlikely to occur from "showing normal people doing normal things" in public.

IRBs insist that confidentiality be maintained, that subjects remain anonymous. But in many cases, subjects are both willing and pleased to be identified; furthermore, their very identifiability may be critical to the research project. In such situations, the researcher is urged to develop an ethical covenant with those being studied so that only mutually agreed-on materials will be published.

We need to learn how to experiment with visual (and nonvisual) ways of thinking. We need to develop a critical visual sensibility, a sensibility that will allow us to bring the gendered material world into play in critically different ways. We need to interrogate critically the hyperlogics of cyberspace and its virtual realities. The rules and methods for establishing truth that hold these worlds together must also be better understood.

Authoethnography: Making the Personal Political

Stacy Holman Jones (Chapter 30) shows how autoethnography can be used to make the personal political. Her essay is about autoethnography as a radical democratic practice, a political practice intended to create a space for dialogue and debate about issues of injustice. Her chapter, like Madison's (Chapter 21) contribution on ethnography as street performance in Part III, tells by showing. Autoethnographic performances breathe life into life ethnographies.

Personal experience reflects the flow of thoughts and meanings people have in their immediate situations. These experiences can be routine or problematic. They occur within the life of a person. When they are talked about, they assume the shape of a story or a narrative. Lived experience cannot be studied directly because language, speech, and systems of discourse mediate and define the very experience one attempts to describe. We study the representations of experience, not experience itself. We examine the stories people tell one another about the experiences they have had. These stories may be personal experience narratives or self stories, interpretations made up as the person goes along.

Many now argue that we can study only our own experiences. The researcher becomes the research subject. This is the topic of autoethnography. Holman Jones's text reflexively presents the arguments for writing reflexive personal narratives. Indeed, her multivoiced text is an example of such writing; it performs its own narrative reflexivity. Holman Jones masterfully reviews the arguments for studying personal experience narratives, anchoring her text in the discourses of feminist poststructuralism and postmodernism, especially the works of Ronai, Ellis, Bochner, and Richardson.

Holman Jones reviews the history of and arguments for this writing form, the challenge to create texts that unfold in the life of the writer while embodying tactics that enact a progressive politics of resistance. Such texts, when performed (and writing is a form of performance), enact a politics of possibility. They shape a critical awareness, they disturb the status quo, and they probe questions of identity. Holman Jones writes out of her own history with this method, and in so doing she takes readers to the Alexander (Chapter 16) and Madison (Chapter 21) contributions on performance ethnography and critical ethnography in Part III. In a moving passage, she shares a poem/letter she wrote to and for her dead grandfather.

In her concluding sections, Holman Jones embeds the performance turn in the history of progressive theater. She then invites readers to perform the testimony and witnessing of personal stories, to stage improbable impossible encounters of possibility, to create disturbances and chaos, to stage arguments, and to use words in ways that move the world.

ONLINE ETHNOGRAPHY

Annette Markham (Chapter 31) argues that computer-mediated construction of self, other, and social structure constitutes a unique phenomenon of study. Offline, the body is present and can be responded to by others. Identity construction is a situated, face-to-face process. Online, in contrast, the body is absent and interaction is mediated by computer technology and the production of written discourse. Markham examines many of the issues that can arise in the qualitative study of Internet-mediated situations. These are issues connected to definitions of what constitutes the field or boundaries of a text as well as what counts as text or empirical material. How the other is interpreted and given a textual presence is also problematic, as are ethical issues that are complex.

Ethical guidelines for Internet research vary sharply across disciplines and nations. Markham contrasts the utilitarian IRB ethical model predominant in the United States with the deontological or communitarian stance predominant in Europe. In some nations, citizens enjoy a greater protection of privacy regarding data collection and use. Under the usual IRB model, online ethnographers wrestle with securing informed consent, and with maintaining subject anonymity, while protecting subjects from harm. Under a communitarian, feminist ethical model, researchers enter into a collaborative relationship with a moral community of online interactants. Attempts are made to establish agreed-on understandings concerning privacy, ownership of materials, the use of personal names, and the meaning of broad principles such as justice and beneficence.

Markham wisely concludes, "Because the Internet is new, is widespread, and has the potential for changing the way in which people live their everyday professional and personal lives in a global society, it is essential to reflect carefully on the ethical frames that influence our studies and the political possibilities of our research."

ANALYTIC PERSPECTIVES

In a powerful programmatic statement, Paul Atkinson and Sara Delamont (Chapter 32) argue that social activity and representation have their own indigenous modes of organization. These modes include language, discourse, narratives, visual styles, and semiotic and cultural codes. Qualitative researchers must remain faithful to this indigenous organization and deploy analytic strategies that are fitted to it. We need rigorous work that pays systematic attention to the systemic relations among the interaction order, orders of talk, representational orders, and the organized properties of material culture. Atkinson and Delamont endorse the disciplined use of such analytic perspectives and approaches as discourse, narrative, and semiotic analysis.

Inquiry must also be concerned with forms of collective—not individual—social action. Furthermore, an engaged social science should remain faithful to the world and its organization. Atkinson and Delamont reject certain postmodern positions that free qualitative analysis from the conventions of academic writing. We need more principled and disciplined ways of accounting for the world and its organization. The authors' perspective restores a particular sense of tradition and continuity to the qualitative research project, connecting it back, at one level, to the Chicago School of the 1930s and 1940s.

Foucault's Methodologies

It goes without staying that Michel Foucault was one of the giant intellectuals of the 20th century. The meanings of his legacy for the humanities and the social sciences are multiple and unfolding (see Holstein & Gubrium [Chapter 19 in Part III] and Perakyla [Chapter 34]). At one level, as Kamberelis and Dimitriadis (Chapter 35) note in their contribution on focus groups, Foucault's project represents an attempt to understand how any object has been constituted out of a particular intersection of forces, discourses, and institutions. A genealogy maps the complex and contradictory ways in which forces and processes come together to produce a certain set of effects. Foucault's genealogies are not histories of causes; rather, they are histories of effects of consequences.

Foucault's work has traditionally been divided into three sequential phases: archaeology, genealogy, and care of the self. James Scheurich and Kathryn Bell McKenzie (Chapter 33) focus on the first two phases, offering a masterful reading of Foucault's methodologies and his use of archaeology and genealogy. Foucault offered nothing less than a sweeping critique of the modernist view of the human sciences and of the human subject (man) as the object of inquiry. He moved back and forth between systems of discourse, what he called *savoir* (e.g., implicit knowledge, everyday opinions, commercial practices), and formal bodies of learning (*connaissance*), including specific disciplines such as Freudian psychoanalysis. Savoir provides the discursive conditions for the development of connaissance. For example, an understanding of the history of psychiatry as a discipline requires the study of the relations among rules of jurisprudence, norms of industrial labor and bourgeois morality, and opinions of madness in daily life. Foucault's archaeology focused on the analysis of these local discourses, whereas his genealogy focused on the transformation of such knowledge into more formal disciplinary systems. Scheurich and McKenzie usefully outline the interpretive rules advocated by Foucault in his archaeologies and genealogies.

Analyzing Talk and Text

Qualitative researchers study spoken and written records of human experience, including transcribed talk, films, novels, and photographs. Interviews give researchers accounts of the issues being studied. The topics of research are not interviews themselves. Research studies using naturally occurring empirical materials—tape recordings of mundane interaction—constitute topics of inquiry in their own right. This is the topic of Anssi Peräkylä's (Chapter 34) contribution.

With Chase (Chapter 25), Fontana and Frey (Chapter 27), and Gubrium and Holstein (Chapter 19 in Part III), Peräkylä treats interview materials as narrative accounts rather than as true pictures of reality. Texts are based on transcriptions of interviews and other forms of talk. These texts are social facts; they are produced, shared, and used in socially organized ways. Peräkylä discusses semiotics, discourse analysis, critical discourse analysis, and historical discourse analysis as approaches to understanding naturally occurring textual materials.

Peräkylä also discusses membership categorization analysis (MCA) as a less familiar form of narrative analysis. Drawing on the work of Harvey Sacks (Silverman, 1998), Peräkylä illustrates the logic of MCA. With this method, the researcher asks how persons use everyday terms and categories in their interactions with others.

Peräkylä turns next to the analysis of talk. There are two main social science traditions that inform the analysis of transcripts: conversation analysis (CA) and discourse analysis (DA). He reviews and offers examples of both traditions, arguing that talk is socially organized action that creates and maintains intersubjective reality. Drawing from his own research on AIDS and its treatment, Peräkylä notes that in observing the "skillful practices through which AIDS counselors encourage their clients to talk about their subjective experiences, we were also observing the operation of an institution, involving powerful relations and bodies of knowledge, at a particular moment in its historical development."

In sum, text-based documents of experience are complex. But if talk constitutes much of what we have, then the forms of analysis outlined by Peräkylä represent significant ways of making the world and its words more visible.

▣ Focus Groups: Pedagogy, Politics, and Inquiry

Kamberelis and Dimitriadis (Chapter 35) significantly advance the discourse on focus group methodology by showing how focus groups have been used in market and military research, in emancipatory pedagogy, and in first-, second-, and third-generation feminist inquiry. Building on Foucault, they place these three genealogies of focus group activity in dialogue with one another.

Kamberelis and Dimitriadis contrast the dialogical, critical theory approach to focus groups with the use of such groups in propaganda and market research. In the marketing context, focus groups are used to extract information from people on a given topic. This information is then used to manipulate people more effectively. Critical pedagogy theorists, such as Freire and Kozol, use focus groups for imagining and enacting the "emancipatory political possibilities of collective work."

Kamberelis and Dimitriadis contrast these two approaches with the history of focus groups in feminist inquiry, noting the use of such groups in first-, second-, and third-wave feminist formations for consciousness-raising purposes. They draw on Madriz (2000), who offered a model of focus group interviewing that emphasizes a feminist ethic of empowerment, moral community, emotional engagement, and the development of long-term trusting relationships. This method gives a voice to women of color who have long been silenced. Focus groups facilitate women writing culture together. As a Latina feminist, Madriz placed focus groups within the context of collective testimonies and group resistance narratives. Focus groups reduce the distance between the researcher and the researched. The multivocality of the participants limits the control of the researcher over the research process.

Within this history, focus groups have been used to elicit and validate collective testimonies, to give a voice to the previously silenced by creating a safe space for sharing one's life experiences. The critical insights and practices of consciousness-raising groups have helped us to move more deeply into the praxis-oriented commitments of the seventh and eighth moments. In these spaces, as the work of Radway and Lather and Smithies documents, focus groups can become the vehicle for allowing participants to take over and own the research. In these ways, focus groups become the sites where pedagogy, politics, and interpretive inquiry intersect and inform one another.

When this happens, as in the projects discussed by Fine and Weis (Chapter 3) in Part I, inquiry becomes directly involved in the complexities of political activism and policymaking.

Madriz, Olesen, Ladson-Billings, and Donnor remind us that women of color experience a triple subjugation based on class, race, and gender oppression. Critical focus groups, as discussed by Kamberelis and Dimitriadis, create the conditions for the emergence of a critical race consciousness, a consciousness focused on social change. It seems that with critical focus groups, critical race theory and progressive politics have found their methodology.

Conclusion

The researcher-as-methodological bricoleur should have a working familiarity with each of the methods of collecting and analyzing empirical materials presented in this part of the *Handbook.* This familiarity includes understanding the history of each method and technique as well as possessing hands-on experience with each. Only in this way can the limitations and strengths of each method and technique be fully appreciated. At the same time, the investigator will see more clearly how each, as a set of material interpretive practices, creates its own subject matter.

In addition, it must be understood that each paradigm and perspective, as presented in Part II, has a distinct history with these methods of research. Although methods-as-tools are somewhat universal in application, they are not used uniformly by researchers from all paradigms, and when they are used they are fitted and adapted to the particularities of the paradigm in question. However, researchers from all paradigms and perspectives can profitably make use of each of these methods of collecting and analyzing empirical materials.

References

Angrosino, M. V., & Pérez, K. A. (2000). Rethinking observation: From method to context. In N. K. Denzin & Y. S. Lincoln (Eds.), *Handbook of qualitative research* (2nd ed., pp. 673–702). Thousand Oaks, CA: Sage.

Kong, T. S. K., Mahoney, D., & Plummer, K. (2002). Queering the interview. In J. Gubrium & J. Holstein (Eds.), *Handbook of qualitative research: Context and method* (pp. 239–258). Thousand Oaks, CA: Sage.

Madriz, E. (2000). Focus groups in feminist research. In N. K. Denzin & Y. S. Lincoln (Eds.), *Handbook of qualitative research* (2nd ed., pp. 835–850). Thousand Oaks, CA: Sage.

Oakley, A. (1981). Interviewing women: A contradiction in terms. In H. Roberts (Ed.), *Doing feminist research* (pp. 30–61). London: Routledge.

Silverman, D. (1998). *Harvey Sacks: Social science and conversation analysis.* Oxford, UK: Polity.

25

NARRATIVE INQUIRY

Multiple Lenses, Approaches, Voices

Susan E. Chase

During the early 1990s, as I struggled to interpret and represent *as narrative* my interviews with women school superintendents, I relied on a rich interdisciplinary tradition defending the study of individuals in their social and historical context. That tradition includes works as diverse as Thomas and Znaniecki's (1918/1927) *The Polish Peasant in Europe and America,* Garfinkel's (1967) ethnomethodological study of Agnes, and the Personal Narratives Group's (1989) feminist explorations of women's journals, life histories, and autobiographies. In this tradition, researchers begin with the biographical leg of Mills's (1959) famous trilogy—biography, history, and society. Mills called these three "the co-ordinate points of the proper study of man" (p. 143). Of course, I was also writing after the narrative turn, and so Barthes's (1977) dramatic words—"narrative is present in every age, in every place, in every society" (p. 79)—had already infiltrated sociological theory. And yet I found few empirical sociological studies based on interview material that could serve as methodological models for the particular way in which I wanted to treat the women's interviews as narratives. Most helpful to me was Riessman's (1990) approach to interview material in *Divorce Talk.*[1]

These days, narrative inquiry in the social sciences is flourishing. Signs of this burgeoning interest include an interdisciplinary journal called *Narrative Inquiry,* a book series on *The Narrative Study of Lives,* and professional conferences specifically showcasing narrative work.[2] Nonetheless, I still get the sense that narrative inquiry is a field in the making. Researchers new to this field will find a rich but diffuse tradition, multiple methodologies in various stages of development, and plenty of opportunities for exploring new ideas, methods, and questions.

In preparation for writing this chapter, I gathered and read as many examples of what might be called narrative inquiry as I could, and I wrestled with various ways of defining the contours of narrative inquiry, both past and present. Although qualitative researchers now routinely refer to any prosaic data (as opposed to close-ended or short-answer data) as "narrative" (Polkinghorne, 1995), I present narrative *inquiry* as a particular type—a subtype—of qualitative inquiry. Contemporary narrative inquiry can be characterized as an amalgam of interdisciplinary analytic lenses, diverse disciplinary approaches, and both traditional and innovative methods—all revolving around an interest in biographical particulars as narrated by the one who lives them.

In what follows, I begin by defining some pivotal terms and then discuss the predecessors of contemporary narrative researchers: sociologists and anthropologists who championed the life history method during the first half of the 20th century, second-wave feminists who poured new life into the study of personal narratives, and sociolinguists who treated oral narrative as a form of discourse worthy of study in itself. After that historical overview, I turn to contemporary narrative inquiry, articulating a set of analytic lenses through which narrative researchers view empirical material and outlining several current approaches to narrative research. Next come explorations of specific methodological issues in contemporary narrative inquiry. For researchers who collect narratives through intensive interviews, a central question is how to treat the interviewee as a narrator, both during interviews and while interpreting them. For all narrative researchers, a central question revolves around which voice or voices researchers should use as they interpret and represent the voices of those they study. And although all qualitative researchers address the question of the relationship between the relatively small "sample" they study and some larger whole, this question is particularly poignant for narrative researchers, who often present the narratives of a very small number of individuals—or even of just one individual—in their published works. The subsequent section addresses the relationship between narrative inquiry and social change. In the concluding paragraphs, I sketch some questions that arose for me as I worked on this chapter, questions that I hope narrative inquirers will explore during the coming years.

Foundational Matters and Historical Background

Pivotal Terms

The terms that narrative researchers use to describe the empirical material they study have flexible meanings, beginning with *narrative* itself. A narrative may be oral or written and may be elicited or heard during fieldwork, an interview, or a naturally occurring conversation. In any of these situations, a narrative may be (a) a short topical story about a particular event and specific characters such as an encounter with a friend, boss, or doctor; (b) an extended story about a significant aspect of one's life such as schooling, work, marriage, divorce, childbirth, an illness, a trauma, or participation in a war or social movement; or (c) a narrative of one's entire life, from birth to the present.

Life history is the more specific term that researchers use to describe an extensive autobiographical narrative, in either oral or written form, that covers all or most of a life. But *life history* can also refer to a social science text that presents a person's biography. In that case, *life story* may be used to describe the autobiographical story in the person's own words (for the complexity of these terms, see Bertaux, 1981; Frank, 2000). Yet some researchers treat the terms *life history* and *life story* as interchangeable, defining both as birth-to-present narratives (Atkinson, 2002). For still others, a life story is a narrative about a specific significant aspect of a person's life, as in the second definition (b) in the preceding paragraph. A life story may also revolve around an epiphanal event (Denzin, 1989) or a turning point (McAdams, Josselson, & Lieblich, 2001) in one's life. Instead of *life story,* some researchers use *personal narrative* to describe a compelling topical narration (Riessman, 2002a). They may use this term to indicate that they are not talking about literary narratives or folklore (but see Narayan & George, 2002, for the intermingling of personal narrative and folklore). *Personal narrative* can also refer in a more generic sense to diaries, journals, and letters as well as to autobiographical stories (Personal Narratives Group, 1989).

Historians use *oral history* to describe interviews in which the focus is not on historical events themselves—historians' traditional interest—but rather on the meanings that events hold for those who lived through them (McMahan & Rogers, 1994; Thompson, 1978/2000). A *testimonio* is a type of oral history, life history, or life story; it is an explicitly political narrative that describes and resists oppression (Beverley, 2000; Tierney, 2000; see also Beverley, chap. 22, this volume). For the past few decades, *testimonio* has been especially associated with the (usually oral) narratives of Latin American activists in revolutionary movements (e.g., Menchú, 1984; Moyano, 2000; Randall, 1981, 1994, 2003). Finally, a *performance narrative* transforms any oral or written narrative into a public performance, either on stage (Madison, 1998; McCall & Becker, 1990) or in alternative textual forms such as poems and fiction (Denzin, 1997, 2000, 2003; Richardson, 2002).

Sociology and Early Life Histories

The predecessors of today's narrative researchers include the Chicago School sociologists who collected life histories and other personal documents during the 1920s and 1930s.[3] Thomas and Znaniecki's (1918/1927) *The Polish Peasant* is frequently cited as the first significant sociological use of life history. In the final 300 pages of the second volume, Thomas and Znaniecki presented the "life record" of a Polish immigrant, Wladek Wiszniewski, whom they paid to write his autobiography (p. 1912). The sociologists' voice preceded the life record with nearly 800 pages on the disorganization and reorganization of social life in Poland as well as the organization and disorganization of social life after immigration to the United States. They also added explanatory footnotes throughout Wiszniewski's life record.

In explaining their interest in life records, Thomas and Znaniecki (1918/1927) stated,

> A social institution can be fully understood only if we do not limit ourselves to the abstract study of its formal organization, but analyze the way in which it appears in the personal experience of various members of the group and follow the influence which it has upon their lives. (p. 1833)

Indeed, they claimed, "Personal life records, as complete as possible, constitute the *perfect* type of sociological material" (p. 1832). In their view, social scientists turned to other materials and methods because of practical difficulties; it is too time-consuming to get sufficient numbers of life records on every sociological issue, and it is too time-consuming to analyze them. Nonetheless, some sociologists, especially in Poland, made the effort. Józef Chalasiński, a follower of Znaniecki, championed the method of using public competitions to solicit hundreds of ordinary people's autobiographies. His research demonstrated that "the formation and transformations of whole social classes (peasants, workers) could be described and understood by analyzing sets of autobiographies" (Bertaux, 1981, p. 3; see also Chalasiński, 1981).[4]

The Polish Peasant was followed by other Chicago School studies based on life histories, especially of juvenile delinquents and criminals (e.g., Shaw, 1930/1966; Sutherland, 1937). These sociologists had some interest in the individual's subjective experience, but they were primarily interested in explaining the individual's behavior as an interactive process between the individual and his or her sociocultural environment. Although studies of urban boys' and men's lives are frequently cited in reviews of the life history method, Hagood's (1939) *Mothers of the South: Portraiture of the White Tenant Farm Woman* also offers an example of early narrative methods.[5]

During the 1940s and 1950s, mainstream American sociology favored abstract theory along with survey and statistical research methods, and the life history method was marginalized. At this point, sociologists were more interested in positivist methods that use single studies to confirm or disconfirm predetermined hypotheses than in research based on the "mosaic" model offered by the Chicago School—studies that may produce no definitive conclusions of their own but that contribute to a larger collective research endeavor (Becker, 1966, pp. viii–ix, xvi–xviii; Bertaux, 1981, p. 1; Denzin, 1970, p. 219).

Anthropology and Early Life Histories

Anthropological use of the life history method emerged early in the 20th century, mostly as a way of recording American Indian cultures that were assumed to be nearly extinct.[6] During the 1920s, life history became a rigorous anthropological method with the publication of Radin's (1926) *Crashing Thunder* (Langness & Frank, 1981, pp. 17–18, 20). Crashing Thunder, a middle-aged Winnebago man in financial difficulty, wrote his autobiography for a fee in two sessions (Lurie, 1961, p. 92). Radin (1926) supplied the cultural context and heavy annotations of the life record.

During the early period, anthropologists gathered life histories as a way of understanding cultural facts, choosing to study people who they assumed were representative of their cultural group (Langness & Frank, 1981, p. 24). By the mid-1940s, under the influence of Edward Sapir, Ruth Benedict, and Margaret Mead, many anthropologists had developed a stronger interest in individuals per se and especially in the relationship between cultural context and distinct personality types (Langness, 1965, pp. 11, 19; see also DuBois, 1944/1960; Kardiner, 1945). Anthropologists also used life histories to present insiders' views of culture and daily life, as exemplified by Lewis's (1961) publication of the life stories of the members of one Mexican family in *The Children of Sánchez*. In this and other works, Lewis also developed the controversial concept of "the culture of poverty" (Langness & Frank, 1981, pp. 24–25). Finally, anthropologists have used life histories to study cultural change, as brought about either by contact between different cultural groups or as the result of revolutionary movements (Langness, 1965, p. 16; Langness & Frank, 1981, pp. 24–27). Although the majority of early anthropological life histories were studies of men, some anthropologists—mostly women—used life history methods to study women's lives (Watson & Watson-Franke, 1985, chap. 6).

Feminism and Personal Narratives

The liberation movements of the 1960s and 1970s helped to reinvigorate the life history method. For example, the civil rights movement led to renewed interest in slave narratives, many of which had been collected from 1936 to 1938 by unemployed writers working with the Federal Writers' Project of the Works Project Administration. More than 2,000 oral histories of former slaves had been deposited in the Library of Congress, but only a glimpse of them was available to the public in Botkin's (1945) *Lay My Burden Down: A Folk History of Slavery*. Two and a half decades later, activists and academics returned to these narratives, and sociologist Rawick (1972) published them in their entirety in 18 volumes of *The American Slave: A Composite Autobiography.* In the introductory volume, he offered a beginning toward a social history of black community life under slavery, based on the narratives, countering previous academic treatment of slaves as voiceless victims (p. xiv).[7]

The second wave of the women's movement played a major role in the renaissance of life history methods and the study of personal narratives such as journals and autobiographies.[8] As feminists critiqued the androcentric assumptions of social science—that men's lives and activities are more important than those of women and/or constitute the norm from which women's lives and activities deviate—they began to treat women's personal narratives as "essential primary documents for feminist research" (Personal Narratives Group, 1989, p. 4). By listening to previously silenced voices, feminist researchers challenged social science knowledge about society, culture, and history (Belenky, Clinchy, Goldberger, & Tarule, 1986; Franz & Stewart, 1994; Gluck, 1979; Gluck & Patai, 1991; Personal Narratives Group, 1989; Reinharz, 1992, chap. 7; Reinharz & Chase, 2002; Watson & Watson-Franke, 1985, chap. 6). Through the influence of working-class feminists and feminists of color (among others), race, ethnicity, nationality, social class, sexual orientation, and disability came to the fore as central aspects of women's lives (for an extensive overview, see Geiger, 1986; see also Olesen, chap. 10, this volume). The first decade or so of second-wave academic feminism produced many examples of feminist research based on life histories and personal narratives (e.g., Babb & Taylor, 1981; Hunt & Winegarten, 1983; Jacobs, 1979; Ruddick & Daniels, 1977; Sexton, 1981; Sidel, 1978; for an extensive list, see Reinharz, 1992, chap. 7).

The explosion of interest in women's personal narratives was accompanied by feminist challenges to conventional assumptions about research relationships and research methods. Thomas and Znaniecki (1918/1927), and many who followed in their footsteps, had said little about how they gathered their materials, noting only that they motivated people to write their life histories through monetary rewards or public contests (Langness & Frank, 1981; Watson & Watson-Franke, 1985). In addition, despite the early life historians' apparently humanistic bent (e.g., Shaw's [1930/1966] interest in ameliorating the miserable conditions of Stanley's life as a juvenile delinquent and anthropologists' interest in recording what they assumed were disappearing cultures), from a feminist point of view, the people in these life histories appeared as distant "others" or deviant "objects" of social scientist interest. It is important to keep in mind, of course, that the early life historians were writing in positivist times, during which the social sciences were struggling to gain recognition as sciences.[9]

Feminists resisted the idea that life histories and other personal narratives were primarily useful for gathering information about historical events, cultural change, or the impact of social structures on individuals' lives. Rather, they were interested in women as social actors in their own right and in the subjective meanings that women assigned to events and conditions in their lives. Importantly, these feminist lenses opened up new understandings of historical, cultural, and social processes. Furthermore, as feminists approached women as subjects rather than as objects, they also began to consider *their* subjectivity—the role that researchers' interests and social locations play in the research relationship. Whose questions should get asked and answered? Who should get the last say? How does power operate in the research relationship? And as feminists incorporated postmodern influences, they began to ask questions—which are still pertinent today—about voice, authenticity, interpretive authority, and representation. What does it mean to hear the other's voice? In what sense do—or don't—women's life histories and personal narratives "speak for themselves"? How do interactional, social, cultural, and historical conditions mediate women's stories? In what ways are women's voices muted, multiple, and/or contradictory? Under what conditions do women develop "counternarratives" as they narrate their lives? How should researchers represent all of these voices and ideas in their written works? (Anderson & Jack, 1991; McCall & Wittner, 1990; Personal Narratives Group, 1989; Ribbens & Edwards, 1998).

Sociolinguistics and Oral Narratives

The mid-1960s saw the development of another line of inquiry that has influenced contemporary narrative research. At this time, anthropologists, sociologists, and sociolinguists (e.g., Erving Goffman, Harold Garfinkel, John Gumperz, Dell Hymes, Harvey Sacks, Emanuel Schegloff, William Labov) were exploring a "range of subject matters at the intersection of language, interaction, discourse, practical action, and inference" (Schegloff, 1997, p. 98).

A 1967 article by Labov and Waletzky, "Narrative Analysis: Oral Versions of Personal Experience," is often cited as a groundbreaking presentation of the idea that ordinary people's oral narratives of everyday experience (as opposed to full-fledged life histories, written narratives, folklore, and literary narratives) are worthy of study in themselves. In this article, Labov and Waletzky (1967/1997) argued that oral narratives are a specific form of discourse characterized by certain structures serving specific social functions. Using data from individual and focus group interviews, they claimed that narrative discourse consists of clauses that match the temporal sequence of reported events. They also identified five sociolinguistic features of oral narratives: Orientation (which informs listeners about actors, time, place, and situation), Complication (the main body of the narrative—the action), Evaluation (the point of the story), Resolution (the result of the action), and Coda (which returns the listener to the current moment).

In 1997, the *Journal of Narrative and Life History* reprinted Labov and Waletzky's 1967 article along with 47 then-current assessments of how it had influenced linguistically informed narrative inquiry since it was first published. Bruner (1997), for instance, suggested that Labov and Waletzky's "fivefold characterization of overall narrative structure transformed the study of narrative profoundly. It set many of us thinking about the cognitive representation of reality imposed by narrative structure on our experience of the world and how we evaluate that experience" (p. 64). Referring to his own influential distinction between logico-scientific and narrative modes of thought—which he had articulated in *Actual Minds, Possible Worlds* (Bruner, 1986)—Bruner (1997) added, "I happily admit that it set me thinking about narrative not simply as a form of text but as a mode of thought" (p. 64).

Many of the assessments of the 1967 article point to the limits of Labov and Waletzky's narrowly structuralist formulation. For example, Riessman (1997) gave them credit for helping her attend to the fundamental structures and functions of oral narratives in her research on people's experiences of divorce. But she found their definition of narrative much too narrow, and so she developed a typology of narrative genres such as the habitual narrative and the hypothetical narrative (pp. 155–156). These helped Riessman to show how people recount their divorce experiences differently and to discuss the connection between the form and function of their speech.

In a different vein, Schegloff (1997) critiqued Labov and Waletzky's failure to take into account the interactional context in which oral narratives are elicited and received. Over the past three decades, conversation analysts such as Schegloff have explored (among other things) how stories arise and how they function in naturally occurring conversations (for an overview, see Holstein & Gubrium, 2000, chap. 7). Other sociolinguistically oriented researchers have investigated the research interview itself as a particular kind of discourse or communicative event in which narratives may be discouraged or encouraged (Briggs, 1986, 2002; Mishler, 1986). Furthermore, although Labov and Waletzky assumed a one-to-one correspondence between a narrative and the events it describes—between narrative and reality—most researchers since then have resisted this referential view of language. A central tenet of the narrative turn is that speakers *construct* events through narrative rather than simply refer to events.[10]

Despite the limitations of the original formulation, the attention that Labov and Waletzky devoted to the linguistic structures and functions of ordinary people's oral narratives served as a launching pad for diverse explorations of the sociolinguistic features of oral discourse. Many contemporary narrative researchers embrace the idea that how individuals narrate experience is as important to the meanings they communicate as is what they say.

▣ Contemporary Narrative Inquiry

Turning to the present, I begin by outlining a set of five analytic lenses through which contemporary researchers approach empirical material. These lenses reflect the influence of the histories just reviewed and, taken as a whole, suggest the distinctiveness of narrative inquiry—how it is different from (if connected to) other forms of qualitative research.

Analytic Lenses

First, narrative researchers treat narrative—whether oral or written—as a distinct form of discourse. Narrative is retrospective meaning making—the shaping or ordering of past experience. Narrative is a way of understanding one's own and others' actions, of organizing events and objects into a meaningful whole, and of connecting and seeing the consequences of actions and events over time (Bruner, 1986; Gubrium & Holstein, 1997; Hinchman & Hinchman, 2001; Laslett, 1999; Polkinghorne, 1995). Unlike a chronology, which also reports events over time, a narrative communicates the narrator's point of view, including why the narrative is worth telling in the first place. Thus, in addition to describing what happened, narratives also express emotions, thoughts, and interpretations. Unlike editorials, policy statements, and doctrinal statements of belief, all of which also express a point of view, a narrative makes the self (the narrator) the protagonist, either as actor or as interested observer of others' actions. Finally, unlike scientific discourse, which also explains or presents an understanding of actions and events, narrative discourse highlights the uniqueness of each human action and event rather than their common properties (Bruner, 1986; Polkinghorne, 1995).

Second, narrative researchers view narratives as verbal action—as doing or accomplishing something. Among other things, narrators explain, entertain, inform, defend, complain, and confirm or challenge the status quo. Whatever the particular action, when someone tells a story, he or she shapes, constructs, and performs the self, experience, and reality. When researchers treat narration as actively creative in this way, they emphasize the narrator's voice(s). The word *voice* draws our attention to what the narrator communicates and how he or she communicates it as well as to the subject positions or social locations from which he or she speaks (Gubrium & Holstein, 2002). This combination of what, how, and where makes the narrator's voice particular. Furthermore, when researchers treat narration as actively creative and the narrator's voice as particular, they move away from questions about the factual nature of the narrator's statements. Instead, they highlight the versions of self, reality, and experience that the storyteller produces through the telling. Although narrators are accountable for the credibility of their stories, narrative researchers treat credibility and believability as something that storytellers accomplish (Holstein & Gubrium, 2000; Lincoln, 2000).

Third, narrative researchers view stories as both enabled and constrained by a range of social resources and circumstances. These include the possibilities for self and reality construction that are intelligible within the narrator's community, local setting, organizational and social memberships, and cultural and historical location. While acknowledging that every instance of narrative is particular, researchers use this lens to attend to similarities and differences across narratives. For example, they emphasize patterns in the storied selves, subjectivities, and realities that narrators create during particular times and in particular places (Brockmeier & Carbaugh, 2001; Bruner, 2002; Hatch & Wisniewski, 1995; Holstein & Gubrium, 2000).

Fourth, narrative researchers treat narratives as socially situated interactive performances—as produced in this particular setting, for this particular audience, for these particular purposes. A story told to an interviewer in a quiet relaxed setting will likely differ from the "same" story told to a reporter for a television news show, to a private journal that the writer assumes will never be read by others, to a roomful of people who have had similar experiences, to a social service counselor, or to the same interviewer at a different time. Here, researchers emphasize that the narrator's story is flexible, variable, and shaped in part by interaction with the audience. In other words, a narrative is a joint production of narrator and listener, whether the narrative arises in naturally occurring talk, an interview, or a fieldwork setting (Bauman, 1986; Briggs, 1986, 2002; Mishler, 1986).

Fifth, narrative researchers, like many other contemporary qualitative researchers, view *themselves* as narrators as they develop interpretations and find ways in which to present or publish their ideas about the narratives they studied (Denzin & Lincoln, 2000). This means that the four lenses just described make as much sense when applied to the researcher as they do when applied to the researched. Breaking from traditional social science practice, narrative researchers are likely to use the first person when presenting their work, thereby emphasizing their own narrative action. As narrators, then, researchers develop meaning out of, and some sense of order in, the material they studied; they develop their own voice(s) as they construct others' voices and realities; they narrate "results" in ways that are both enabled and constrained by the social resources and circumstances embedded in their disciplines, cultures, and historical moments; and they write or perform their work for particular audiences. The idea that researchers are narrators opens up a range of complex issues about voice, representation, and interpretive authority (Emihovich, 1995; Hertz, 1997; Josselson, 1996a; Krieger, 1991; Tierney, 2002; Tierney & Lincoln, 1997).

Theoretically, it is possible to treat these five analytic lenses as distinct. However, as researchers go about the business of hearing, collecting, interpreting, and representing narratives, they are well aware of the interconnectedness of the lenses. As they do their work, researchers may emphasize one or another lens or their intersections, or they may shift back and forth among the lenses, depending on their specific approaches to empirical narrative material.

Diverse Approaches

Although narrative inquiry as a whole is interdisciplinary, specific approaches tend to be shaped by interests and assumptions embedded in researchers' disciplines. Without claiming to be comprehensive or exhaustive in my categories, I briefly outline five major approaches in contemporary narrative inquiry.[11] It is here that we see diversity and multiplicity in this field of inquiry.

Some psychologists have developed an approach that focuses on the relationship between individuals' life stories and the quality of their lives, especially their psychosocial development.[12] In addition to gathering extensive life stories,[13] these researchers sometimes use conventional psychological tests. For example, in a study of adults' narratives about turning points in their lives, McAdams and Bowman (2001) found that those who score high on conventional measures of psychological well-being and generativity (i.e., commitment to caring for and contributing to future generations) are likely to tell "narratives of redemption," that is, to construct negative events as having beneficial consequences. Conversely, those who score low in terms of psychological well-being and generativity are more likely to tell "narratives of contamination," that is, to present good experiences as having negative outcomes. While acknowledging that biographical, social, cultural, and historical circumstances condition the stories that people tell about themselves, narrative psychologists look for evidence (e.g., in a person's score on conventional measures) that the stories that people tell affect how they live their lives. They emphasize "the formative effects of narratives" and propose that some stories cripple, and others enable, an efficacious sense of self in relation to life problems or traumas (Rosenwald & Ochberg, 1992, p. 6).

In their interpretations, these psychological researchers tend to emphasize *what* the story is about—its plot, characters, and sometimes the structure or sequencing of its content. Along these lines, McAdams (1997) argued that the content of a life story embodies a person's identity and that both develop and change over time. This idea was exemplified by Josselson's (1996b) longitudinal study of how women revise their stories *and* their lives as they move through their 20s, 30s, and 40s.

A second approach has been developed by sociologists who highlight the "identity work" that people engage in as they construct selves within specific institutional, organizational, discursive, and local cultural contexts. Unlike the psychologists just described, who conceptualize the life story as distinguishable from—yet having an impact on—the life, these researchers often treat narratives *as* lived experience. Thus, they are as interested in the *hows* of storytelling as they are in the *whats* of storytelling—in the narrative practices by which storytellers make use of available resources to construct recognizable selves. They often study narratives that are produced in specific organizational settings such as prisons, courts, talk shows, human service agencies, self-help groups, and therapy centers (Gubrium & Holstein, 2001; Holstein & Gubrium, 2000; Miller, 1997; Pollner & Stein, 1996). For example, in her study of support groups for women who have experienced domestic violence, Loseke (2001) showed how group facilitators often encourage battered women to transform their narratives into "formula stories" about wife abuse. She found that many women resist the counselors' version of their experience and resist identifying themselves as "battered women," and she suggested that the problem may lie less in women's psychological denial of their victimization and more in the formula story's failure to encompass the complexities of lived experience

(p. 122). As part of everyday lived experience, narratives themselves are messy and complex.

A major conceptual touchstone in this sociological approach is the "deprivatization" of personal experience. This approach highlights the wide range of institutional and organizational settings—some more and some less coercive—that shape "the selves we live by." A person's movement across a variety of settings creates further constraints as well as a plethora of options for narrating the self in a postmodern world (Holstein & Gubrium, 2000).

The third approach is also sociological.[14] Here, narrative researchers share the interest in the *hows* and *whats* of storytelling but base their inquiry on intensive interviews about specific aspects of people's lives rather than on conversations in specific organizational contexts. These researchers are interested in how people communicate meaning through a range of linguistic practices, how their stories are embedded in the interaction between researcher and narrator, how they make sense of personal experience in relation to culturally and historically specific discourses, and how they draw on, resist, and/or transform those discourses as they narrate their selves, experiences, and realities.

Examples of this approach include Langellier's (2001) study of how a woman performs the self and resists medical discourse as she comes to terms with breast cancer, Mishler's (1999) exploration of adult identity formation in craft artists' work histories, Foley and Faircloth's (2003) study of how midwives both use and resist medical discourse to legitimize their work, Riessman's (1990) examination of women's and men's divorce stories in relation to discourse about marriage and gender, Bell's (1999) exploration of how diethylstilbestrol (DES)-exposed daughters negotiate tensions between scientific and feminist discourses, Luttrell's (1997) analysis of the gendered and racialized identities of working-class mothers who return to school to get general equivalency diplomas (GEDs), and Lempert's (1994) analysis of how a woman survivor of domestic violence narrates self-transformation in relation to her physical, psychological, social, and cultural environments.

These researchers often produce detailed transcripts to study interactional processes in the interview as well as linguistic and thematic patterns throughout the narrative. A major goal of this sociological approach is showing that people create a range of narrative strategies in relation to their discursive environments, that is, that individuals' stories are constrained but not determined by hegemonic discourses. Another goal is showing that narratives provide a window to the contradictory and shifting nature of hegemonic discourses, which we tend to take for granted as stable monolithic forces.

Anthropologists have led the way in a fourth approach to narrative inquiry. Some call this approach *narrative ethnography*, which is a transformation of both the ethnographic and life history methods. Like traditional ethnography, this approach involves long-term involvement in a culture or community; like life history, it focuses heavily on one individual or on a small number of individuals. What makes narrative ethnography distinct is that both the researcher and the researched "are presented together within a single multivocal text focused on the character and process of the human encounter" (Tedlock, 1992, p. xiii).

Myerhoff's (1979/1994) *Number Our Days* is an early example. In this study of a community of elderly immigrant Jews in California, Myerhoff highlighted the life of Shmuel Goldman, a tailor and one of the most learned members of the community. At the same time, she analyzed her subjectivity as well as her relationship with those she studied. Although Myerhoff presented page after page of Shmuel's life stories "verbatim," she also showed how her questions and interruptions shaped Shmuel's narrative. And she went further. She described her distaste on observing selfish bickering over food at a community lunch, and then—with the help of a dream—she reinterpreted those actions as reflecting the social and psychological conditions of community members' lives (pp. 188–189). When Shmuel died during the course of the study, Myerhoff wrote a conversation that she imagined she and Shmuel would have had about another community member's death (pp. 228–231). Finally, she told her own story of how her grandmother's stories influenced her own life and research (pp. 237–241).

In more recent narrative ethnographies, researchers are even more explicit about the intersubjectivity of the researcher and the researched as they work to understand the other's voice, life, and culture (Behar, 1993/2003; Frank, 2000; Shostak, 2000b). A major goal of narrative ethnography is moving to the center of empirical anthropological work the issues of voice, intersubjectivity, interpretive authority, and representation.

A fifth approach to narrative inquiry is found in *autoethnography,* where researchers also turn the analytic lens on themselves and their interactions with others, but here researchers write, interpret, and/or perform their own narratives about culturally significant experiences (Crawley, 2002; Ellis & Berger, 2002; Ellis & Bochner, 1996; Ellis & Flaherty, 1992; see also Holman Jones, chap. 30, this volume). Autoethnographers who share an interest in a topic sometimes engage in collaborative research by conducting interviews with each other, tape-recording conversations with each other, and/or writing separate accounts of their experiences. For example, Ellis and Bochner (1992) narrated separate and joint accounts of their experience of Ellis's unwanted pregnancy and subsequent abortion. And Ellis, Kiesinger, and Tillmann-Healy (1997) used an interactive interviewing method to investigate Kiesinger's and Tillmann-Healy's experiences of bulimia and Ellis's responses to their accounts.

Autoethnographers often present their work in alternative textual forms such as layered accounts (Ellis & Berger, 2002; Ellis & Bochner, 1996), and many have experimented with performing their narratives as plays, as poems, or in various other forms (Denzin, 1997, 2000, 2003; McCall & Becker, 1990; Richardson, 2002). Sometimes autoethnographers resist analysis altogether, leaving interpretation up to the audiences of their performances (Hilbert, 1990). The goal of autoethnography, and of many performance narratives, is to *show* rather than to *tell* (Denzin, 2003, p. 203) and, thus, to disrupt the politics of traditional research relationships, traditional forms of representation, and traditional social science orientations to audiences.[15]

▣ Methodological Issues in Contemporary Narrative Inquiry

The Research Relationship: Narrator and Listener in Interview-Based Studies

All narrative researchers attend to the research relationship, but those whose studies are based on in-depth interviews aim specifically at transforming the interviewer–interviewee relationship into one of narrator and listener. This involves a shift in understanding the nature of interview questions and answers. These researchers often illustrate this shift by telling about how they initially ignored, grew impatient with, or got thrown off track by interviewees' stories—and later realized their mistake (Anderson & Jack, 1991; Mishler, 1986; Narayan & George, 2002; Riessman, 1990, 2002a). For instance, in *Narrating the Organization,* Czarniawska (1997) described how she used to ask questions that encouraged interviewees to generalize and compare their experiences, for example, "What are the most acute problems you are experiencing today?" and "Can you compare your present situation with that of 2 years ago?" She found, however, that most people "would break through my structure" by offering stories about the background of current circumstances. "This used to bring me to the verge of panic—'How to bring them to the point?'—whereas now I have at least learned that this *is* the point" (p. 28).

The moral of Czarniawska's account, and of similar accounts, is that the stories people tell *constitute* the empirical material that interviewers need if they are to understand how people create meanings out of events in their lives. To think of an interviewee as a narrator is to make a conceptual shift away from the idea that interviewees have answers to researchers' questions and toward the idea that interviewees are narrators with stories to tell and voices of their own.

Let me pause to say that this idea need not reflect the romantic notion, critiqued by Atkinson and Silverman (1997), that "the open-ended interview offers the opportunity for an authentic gaze into the soul of another" (p. 305). Similarly, Gubrium and Holstein (2002) critiqued the notion of a narrator's "own" voice, which implies that narrators' stories are not socially mediated. I contend that conceiving of an interviewee as a narrator is not an interest in the other's "authentic" self or unmediated voice but rather an interest in the other as a narrator of his or her particular biographical experiences as he or she understands them. Although any narration is always enabled and constrained by a host of social circumstances, *during interviews* the narrative researcher needs to orient to the particularity of the narrator's story and voice.

This conceptual shift has consequences for data collection (as well as for interpretive processes, which I will get to next). When researchers conceive of interviewees as narrators, they not only attend to the stories that people *happen* to tell during interviews but also work at *inviting* stories. Although some interviewees tell stories whether or not researchers want to hear them, other interviewees might not take up the part of narrator unless they are specifically and carefully invited to do so.

Paradoxically, assumptions embedded in our "interview society" may discourage interviewees from becoming narrators in the sense that I am developing that idea here. Denzin and Lincoln (2000) suggested that we live "in a society whose members seem to believe that interviews generate useful information about lived experience and its meanings" (p. 633; see also Atkinson & Silverman, 1997; Gubrium & Holstein, 2002). Yet interviewees often speak in generalities rather than specifics, even when talking about their experiences, because they assume (often accurately) that researchers are interested in what is general rather than particular about their experience (Weiss, 1994). As Czarniawska (1997) stated, researchers often "ask people in the field to compare, to abstract, to generalize" (p. 28). Sacks (1989) called these "sociological questions"—questions that are organized around the researcher's interest in general social processes—even though the questions may be couched in everyday language (p. 88). When researchers ask sociological questions, they are likely to get sociological answers—generalities about the interviewee's or others' experiences. The interview questions that qualitative researchers include in appendixes to their studies show how often they encourage interviewees to speak generally and abstractly.[16]

How, then, do narrative researchers invite interviewees to become narrators, that is, to tell stories about biographical particulars that are meaningful to them? I have described this as a matter of framing the interview as a whole with a broad question about whatever story the narrator has to tell about the issue at hand (Chase, 1995b, 2003). This requires a certain kind of preparation before interviewing; it requires knowing what is "storyworthy" in the narrator's social setting, an idea that is most easily grasped through examples from non-Western cultures. Grima (1991), for instance, found that Paxtun women in Northwest Pakistan attributed the most value to stories of suffering and personal hardship and that these stories were intimately connected to an honorable identity. If a woman had no such experiences, she had no story to tell. Similarly, in Rosaldo's (1976) anthropological fieldwork with Tukbaw, an Ilongot man in the Philippines, the researcher told of realizing that he had come close to "assuming that every man has his life story within him" and that the narrator himself "should be the subject of the narrative" (pp. 121–122). Although Tukbaw had plenty of stories to tell, these Western assumptions about narratives were unfamiliar to him.

Although broad cultural assumptions condition narrators' voices and the stories they have to tell, so do specific institutional, organizational, and/or discursive environments (Gubrium & Holstein, 2001). In my study of women school superintendents, for example, the fact that they are highly successful women in an overwhelmingly white- and male-dominated occupation shapes their work narratives and makes them storyworthy in a particular way. Their work narratives revolve around the juxtaposition between their individual accomplishments, on the one hand, and the gendered and racial inequities they face in their profession, on the other, and this juxtaposition makes their work narratives interesting not only to researchers and the general public but also to themselves (Chase, 1995a, pp. 14–15). Once a researcher has a sense of the broad parameters of the story that the narrator has to tell—of what is storyworthy given the narrator's social location in his or her culture, community, and/or organizational setting—the researcher can prepare for narrative interviews by developing a broad question that will invite the other to tell his or her story (Chase, 1995b). The point, of course, is not to ask for a "formula story" (Loseke, 2001); instead, the researcher needs to know the parameters of the story that others similarly situated *could* tell so as to invite *this* person's story.

In some cases, it may be easy to figure out how to frame the interview as a whole; it may be easy to articulate a broad open question that will invite a personal narrative. In my study of women superintendents, the question about their career histories turned out to be pivotal. (I confess that I did not understand it this way at the time and that my coresearcher, Colleen Bell, and I asked plenty of sociological questions along the way.) But it is not always so easy to know what the broad question will be. For example, Sacks (1989), in her ethnographic study of working-class women's militancy and leadership in the workplace, conducted interviews to understand the connection between what women learned from their families and from their workplace militancy. After her sociological interview questions produced dead ends, she finally began to ask "how they learned about work and what it meant to them." She realized that this question invited stories that showed how "family learning empowered women to rebel" (p. 88).

Being prepared to invite a story, however, is only part of the shift in the research relationship. Burgos (1989) described a transformation that may occur when an interviewee takes up the invitation to become a narrator:

> A life story comes off successfully when its narrator exercises her power upon the person who is ostensibly conducting the interview by derealising his interventions, capturing his attention, neutralizing his will, arousing his desire to learn something else, or something more, than what would be allowed by the logic of the narrative itself. (p. 33)

This statement offers a strong version of the narrator's voice as well as of the researcher's listening; in speaking from and about biographical particulars, a narrator may disrupt the assumptions that the interviewer brings to the research relationship. Thus, narrative interviewing involves a paradox. On the one hand, a researcher needs to be well prepared to ask good questions that will invite the other's particular story; on the other hand, the very idea of a particular story is that it cannot be known, predicted, or prepared for in advance. The narrator's particular story is not identical to—and may even depart radically from—what is "storyworthy" in his or her social context.

An example can be found in my own research. As Colleen Bell and I interviewed a woman superintendent who was leaving her job for a less prestigious and less stressful position, she showed us family photographs and began to tell stories about a family member who had a serious physical disability. At the time, I experienced this as a digression from her work narrative, and I waited patiently for her to get back to it. Later, as I reviewed the interview tapes, I realized that her sharing of family photos and stories was integral, not peripheral, to her work narrative; her career move "down," away from the exhausting and very public work of the superintendency, was for her a move toward a more balanced work–family relationship. If I had been open to understanding the family photos and stories as central to her work narrative, I might have prompted for and heard a fuller account of the particular way in which this woman narrated her career history. She was speaking in a different voice, or from a different subject position, from what I had anticipated; she disrupted my assumption about the "logic" of a career narrative.

The Interpretive Process in Interview-Based Studies

When it comes to interpreting narratives heard during interviews, narrative researchers begin with narrators' voices and stories, thereby extending the narrator–listener relationship and the active work of listening into the interpretive process. This is a move away from a traditional theme-oriented method of analyzing qualitative material. Rather than locating distinct themes *across* interviews, narrative researchers listen first to the voices *within* each narrative.[17]

I realized the importance of this shift as I interpreted the women superintendents' interviews. At first, I tried to organize the transcripts into themes about work (e.g., aspirations, competence, confidence) and themes about inequality (e.g., barriers, discrimination, responses). But I soon found that it was difficult to separate a woman's talk about work and her talk about inequality. Finally it dawned on me that there was a connection between a woman's construction of self in one story (e.g., about her individual strength as a competent leader) and her construction of self in other stories (e.g., about her individual strength in fighting discrimination). Thus, I began to focus on connections among the various stories that a woman told over the course of the interview. I used the term *narrative strategy* to refer to the specific way in which each woman juxtaposed her stories about achievement and her stories about gendered and/or racial inequalities, that is, how she navigated the disjunction between individualistic discourse about achievement and group-oriented discourse about inequality (Chase, 1995a, pp. 23–25). The term *narrative strategy* draws attention to the complexity within each woman's voice—to the various subject positions each woman takes up—as well as to diversity among women's voices because each woman's narrative strategy is particular.

Narrative researchers who base their work on interviews use a variety of methods for listening to—for interpreting—complexity and multiplicity within narrators' voices. For example, in their study of adolescent girls "at risk" for early pregnancy and dropping out of school, Taylor, Gilligan, and Sullivan (1995) described an explicitly feminist Listening Guide that requires reading each interview four times. First, they attended to "the overall shape of the narrative and the research relationship"; second, to the narrator's first-person voice—how and where she uses "I"; third and fourth, to "contrapuntal voices"—voices that express psychological development, on the one hand, and psychological risk and loss, on the other (pp. 29–31). In contrast, Bamberg (1997) focused on three levels of narrative positioning: how narrators position self and others (e.g., as protagonists, as antagonists, as victims, as perpetrators), how narrators position self in relation to the audience, and how narrators "position themselves to themselves," that is, construct "a [local] answer to the question 'Who am I?'" (p. 337).

In one way or another, then, narrative researchers listen to the narrator's voices—to the subject positions, interpretive practices, ambiguities, and complexities—*within* each narrator's story. This process usually includes attention to the "narrative linkages" that a storyteller develops between the biographical particulars of his or her life, on the one hand, and the resources and constraints in his or her environment for self and reality construction, on the other (Holstein & Gubrium, 2000, p. 108). Rather than unitary, fixed, or authentic selves, these researchers suggest that narrators construct "nonunitary subjectivities" (Bloom & Munro, 1995), "revised" identities (Josselson, 1996b), "permanently unsettled identities" (Stein, 1997), and "troubled identities" (Gubrium & Holstein, 2001).

Researchers' Voices and Narrative Strategies

Implicit in my discussion of how the researcher listens to the narrator's voice—both during the interview and while interpreting it—is the *researcher's* voice. Here, I return to issues I raised under the fifth analytic lens—issues of voice, interpretive authority, and representation.

To sort out a range of possibilities, I develop a typology of three voices or narrative strategies that contemporary narrative researchers deploy as they wrestle with the question of how to use their voice(s) to interpret and represent the narrator's voice(s). My typology is not an exhaustive and rigid classification of every possible narrative strategy; rather, it is a flexible device for understanding the diversity in narrative researchers' voices. In practice, researchers may move back and forth among them.

The Researcher's Authoritative Voice

Many narrative researchers develop an authoritative voice in their writing, including those I just described in the section on interpretive processes in interview-based studies and those I described previously in the section on diverse approaches as taking psychological and sociological approaches (the first three approaches). This narrative strategy connects and separates the researcher's and narrator's voices in a particular way. Sociologists usually present long stretches from narrators' stories or long excerpts of naturally occurring conversation, followed by their interpretations. Psychologists are more likely to offer long summaries of narrators' stories, followed by their interpretations. In each case, in the texts they create, researchers connect or intermingle their voices with narrators' voices.

At the same time, these researchers separate their voices from narrators' voices through their interpretations. They assert an authoritative interpretive voice on the grounds that they have a different interest from the narrators in the narrators' stories. For example, during an interview, both narrator and listener are interested in developing the fullness and particularity of the narrator's story, but when it comes to interpreting, the researcher turns to *how* and *what* questions that open up particular ways of understanding what the narrator is communicating through his or her story. These questions are about narrative processes that narrators typically take for granted as they tell their stories such as their use of cultural, institutional, or organizational discourses for making sense of experience, their development of narrative strategies or narrative linkages in relation to conflicting discourses, their communication of meaning through linguistic features of talk, and/or their reconstruction of psychological issues through particular metaphors or subjugated storylines (Brockmeier & Carbaugh, 2001; Capps & Ochs, 1995; Chase, 1996; Gubrium & Holstein, 1997; Hinchman & Hinchman, 2001; Holstein & Gubrium, 2000; Ochberg, 1996; Rosenwald & Ochberg, 1992).

By writing with an authoritative voice, these researchers are vulnerable to the criticism that they "privilege the analyst's listening ear" at the narrator's expense (Denzin, 1997, p. 249). After all, as narrators work to make sense of their experiences through narration, they do not talk about "the selves we live by," "identity work," "nonunitary subjectivities," "discursive constraints," or "hegemonic discourses." Nor do researchers talk this way as they narrate stories in *their* everyday lives. But I prefer (in part because my work fits here) to understand these researchers as making visible and audible taken-for-granted practices, processes, and structural and cultural features of our everyday social worlds. The sociological concepts that researchers develop serve that aim. Ochberg (1996) articulated this point from a psychological perspective: "Interpretation reveals what one [the narrator] might say if only one could speak freely, but we can see this only if we are willing to look beyond what our informants tell us in so many words" (p. 98).

By taking up an authoritative sociological or psychological voice, the researcher speaks differently from, but not disrespectfully of, the narrator's voice. Czarniawska (2002) suggested that "the justice or injustice done to the original narratives depends on the attitude of the researcher and on the precautions he or she takes" (p. 743). In discussing "narrative responsibility and respect," she recommended that researchers attend to diversity in the stories that various narrators tell, to dominant and marginal readings of narrators' stories, and to narrators' responses (including opposition) to the researchers' interpretations (pp. 742–744).[18] It bears emphasizing that when these researchers present extensive quotations from narrators' stories, they make room for readers' alternative interpretations (Laslett, 1999; Riessman, 2002).

The Researcher's Supportive Voice

At the other end of an imaginary continuum, some narrative researchers develop a supportive voice that pushes the narrator's voice into the limelight. This is characteristic of Latin American testimonios. For example, in *I Rigoberta Menchú: An Indian Woman in Guatemala* (Menchú, 1984), the translator, Ann Wright, offered a short preface, and anthropologist Elisabeth Burgos-Debray wrote an introduction in which she described how she conducted and edited the interviews with Menchú. But the majority of the book consists of Menchú's uninterrupted stories. Diana Miloslavich Tupac developed a similarly supportive voice as editor and annotator of the work and autobiography of martyred Peruvian activist Maria Elena Moyano (Moyano, 2000). Significantly, these two testimonios named the narrators—Menchú and Moyano—as the books' authors. Other testimonios, especially those that include two or more narrators, name the researchers as the authors (e.g., Randall, 1981, 1994, 2003).

Researchers who publish oral histories or life histories may also use a muted supportive voice. For instance, in Shostak's (1981/2000a) introduction and epilogue to *Nisa: The Life and Words of a !Kung Woman,* she described her research with Nisa and the !Kung people, and she began each chapter with anthropological commentary. But the majority of the book consists of Nisa's stories (see also Blauner, 1989; Gwaltney, 1980/1993; Terkel, 1995).

When researchers present performance narratives, they may also deploy supportive voices. For example, Madison (1998) described a theatrical performance of the personal narratives of two women cafeteria workers who led a strike for better pay and working conditions at the University of North Carolina. Although the strike took place in 1968, the public performance of the narratives took place 25 years later to a packed audience during the university's bicentennial celebration. Both women were in the audience, and after the performance they received "a thunderous and lengthy standing ovation" (p. 280) as well as attention from the local media. On the occasion of the performance, the researcher's voice as interviewer and editor of the women's narratives was muted; the performance highlighted the women's voices and opened possibilities for political and civic engagement on the part of the women, the audience, and the performers.[19]

In each of these cases—testimonio, oral history, life history, and performance narrative—the researcher (and translator, who is sometimes—but not always—the same person) makes decisions about how to translate and transcribe the narrator's story, which parts of the story to include in the final product, and how to organize and edit those parts into a text or performance. And yet, because the goal of this narrative strategy is to bring the narrator's story to the public—to get the narrator's story heard—researchers do not usually dwell on how they engaged in these interpretive processes. Or if they do, they do so elsewhere. For example, in an article written after *Nisa* was published, Shostak (1989) discussed the complexities of these interpretive decisions, including the way in which she presented three voices in the book: Nisa's first-person voice, Shostak's anthropological voice, and Shostak's voice "as a young American woman experiencing another world" (pp. 230–231). Along somewhat different lines, Madison (1998, pp. 277–278) explained the idea of the "performance of possibilities," which underlies performance narratives and which provides a strong framework during the performance itself.

These researchers may encounter the criticism that they romanticize the narrator's voice as "authentic" (Atkinson & Silverman, 1997). At its best, however, this narrative strategy aims not for establishing authenticity but rather for creating a self-reflective and respectful distance between researchers' and narrators' voices. There is a time and there is a place, these researchers might say, for highlighting narrators' voices and for moving temporarily to the margins the ways in which researchers (along with a host of social, cultural, and historical circumstances) have already conditioned those voices.

The Researcher's Interactive Voice

A third narrative strategy displays the complex interaction—the intersubjectivity—between researchers' and narrators' voices. These researchers examine *their* voices—their subject positions, social locations, interpretations, and personal experiences—through the refracted medium of narrators' voices. This narrative strategy characterizes narrative ethnographies as well as some autoethnographies.

Frank (2000) used this narrative strategy in *Venus on Wheels: Two Decades of Dialogue on Disability, Biography, and Being Female in America,* in which she presented her long-term relationship with Diane DeVries, a woman who was born without arms and legs. Frank not only presented DeVries's stories about living with her disability but also investigated her own interest in DeVries's stories:

> In choosing to write about the life of Diane DeVries, I had to ask myself how it was that, as an anthropologist, I chose not to travel to some remote place, but to stay at home and study one individual, one with a congenital absence of limbs. (p. 85)

Through reflection on her experiences of others' disabilities, her own disabilities, and emotional lack and loss in her own life, Frank realized that "I had expected to find a victim in Diane" but instead found "a survivor" (p. 87).

Interestingly, in *Return to Nisa,* Shostak (2000b) developed the same narrative strategy while moving in the opposite geographic direction. Whereas Frank needed to understand why she chose to "stay at home," Shostak needed to understand why, after being diagnosed with breast cancer, she felt compelled to leave her husband and three young children to spend a month in Botswana with Nisa and the other !Kung people whom she had not seen for 14 years. In *Return to Nisa,* Shostak wrote not only about Nisa's life during the intervening years but also about her own complex interest in reconnecting with Nisa, who (among other things) is a well-respected healer.

In narrative ethnographies and autoethnographies, researchers make themselves vulnerable in the text (Behar, 1996; Krieger, 1991). They include extensive discussions of their emotions, thoughts, research relationships, and their unstable interpretive decisions. They include embarrassing and even shameful incidents. Indeed, these researchers are vulnerable to the criticism that they are self-indulgent and that they air dirty laundry that nobody wants to see. Yet they ground these practices in the idea that researchers need to understand themselves if they are to understand how they interpret narrators' stories *and* that readers need to understand *researchers'* stories (about their intellectual and personal relationships with narrators as well as with the cultural phenomena at hand) if readers are to understand narrators' stories. These researchers aim to undermine the myth of the invisible omniscient author (Tierney, 2002; Tierney & Lincoln, 1997).

The Particular and the General

Despite differences in their narrative strategies for interpreting and representing narrators' voices, narrative researchers have in common the practice of devoting much more space in their written work to fewer individuals than do other qualitative researchers. Many anthropologists have written books based on one individual's life story (e.g., Behar, 1993/2003; Crapanzano, 1980; Frank, 2000; Shostak, 1981/2000a, 2000b).[20] And many sociologists, psychologists, and other narrative researchers have based books, book chapters, and articles on a small number of narratives (e.g., Bell, 1999; Bobel, 2002, chap. 1; Capps & Ochs, 1995; Chase, 1995a, 2001; DeVault, 1999, chap. 5; Ferguson, 2001, pp. 135–161; Josselson, 1996b, chaps. 4–7; Langellier, 2001; Lempert, 1994; Liebow, 1993, pp. 251–309; Luttrell, 2003, chap, 4; Mishler, 1999; Riessman, 1990, chap. 3; Rosier, 2000; Stromberg, 1993, chaps. 3–6; Wozniak, 2002, chaps. 2 and 9).

The question of whether and how an individual's narrative (or a small group of individuals' narratives) represents a larger population goes back to *The Polish Peasant.* Thomas and Znaniecki (1918/1927) argued that sociologists should gather life histories of individuals who represent the population being studied (pp. 1834–1835). They defended their extensive use of Wiszniewski's life record by claiming that he was "a typical representative of the culturally passive mass which, under the present conditions and at the present stage of social evolution, constitutes in every civilized society the enormous majority of the population" (p. 1907). In evaluating *The Polish Peasant,* however, Blumer (1939/1979) claimed that Thomas and Znaniecki had failed to demonstrate Wiszniewski's representativeness and that it would have been difficult for them to do so anyway (p. 44).

Contemporary narrative researchers occupy a different social and historical location. Under the auspices of the narrative turn, they reject the idea that the small number of narratives they present must be generalizable to a certain population. Some researchers do this by highlighting the particularity of the narratives they present and by placing them in a broader frame. For example, Shostak's *Nisa* is about one woman's narrative, but Shostak (1989) used the stories of the other !Kung women she interviewed, as well as previous anthropological studies of the !Kung people, to show how Nisa's story is at once unique in some respects and similar to other !Kung women's stories in other ways.

Many contemporary narrative researchers, however, make a stronger break from Thomas and Znaniecki's (1918/1927) positivist stance regarding representativeness. Given "narrative elasticity" and the range of "narrative options" in any particular setting (Holstein & Gubrium, 2000), as well as constant flux in social and historical conditions, these researchers propose that the range of narrative possibilities within any group of people is potentially limitless. To make matters more complex, as Gubrium and Holstein (2002) suggested, "Treating subject positions and their associated voices seriously, we might find that an ostensibly single interview could actually be, in practice, an interview with several subjects, whose particular identities may be only partially clear" (p. 23).

Thus, many contemporary narrative researchers approach *any* narrative as an *instance* of the possible relationships between a narrator's active construction of self, on the one hand, and the social, cultural, and historical circumstances that enable and constrain that narrative, on the other. Researchers often highlight a range of possible narratives to show that no one particular story is determined by a certain social location, but they do not claim that their studies exhaust the possibilities within that context (see, e.g., Auerbach, 2002; Bell, 1999; Chase, 1995a; Mishler, 1999). From this perspective, any narrative is significant because it embodies—and gives us insight into—what is possible and intelligible within a specific social context.[21]

Narrative Inquiry and Social Change

As outlined by Denzin and Lincoln, a major goal of this edition of the *Handbook* is exploring how qualitative research can "advance a democratic project committed to social justice in an age of uncertainty" (personal communication, July 7, 2002). With that goal in mind, I now turn to questions about the relationship between narrative inquiry and social change. What kinds of narratives disrupt oppressive social processes? How and when do researchers' analyses and representations of others' stories encourage social justice and democratic processes? And for whom are these processes disrupted and encouraged? Which audiences need to hear which researchers' and narrators' stories?

For some people, the act of narrating a significant life event itself facilitates positive change. In discussing a breast cancer survivor's narrative, Langellier (2001) wrote, "The wounded storyteller reclaims the capacity to tell, and hold on to, her own story, resisting narrative surrender to the medical chart as the official story of the illness" (p. 146; see also Capps & Ochs, 1995; Frank, 1995). Along similar lines, Rosenwald and Ochberg (1992) claimed that self-narration can lead to personal emancipation—to "better" stories of life difficulties or traumas. In these cases, the narrator is his or her own audience, the one who needs to hear alternative versions of his or her identity or life events, and the one for whom changes in the narrative can "stir up changes" in the life (p. 8; see also Mishler, 1995, pp. 108–109).

For other narrators, the urgency of storytelling arises from the need and desire to have *others* hear one's story. Citing René Jara, Beverley (2000) described testimonios as "emergency narratives" that involve

> a problem of repression, poverty, marginality, exploitation, or simply survival.... The voice that speaks to the reader through the text... [takes] the form of an I that demands to be recognized, that wants or needs to stake a claim on our attention. (p. 556)

But it is not only Latin American testimonios that are narrated with this urgent voice. The stories of many marginalized groups have changed the contemporary narrative landscape—to name just a few, the stories of transgendered people, people with disabilities, and the survivors of gendered, racial/ethnic, and sexual violence. Indeed, "giving voice" to marginalized people and "naming silenced lives" have been primary goals of narrative research for several decades (McLaughlin & Tierney, 1993; Personal Narratives Group, 1989).

If a previously silenced narrator is to challenge an audience's assumptions or actions effectively, the audience must be ready to hear the narrator's story—or must be jolted into listening to it. In writing about empathetic listening, Frank (2000) stated, "Taking the other's perspective is a necessary step in constructive social change" (p. 94). In a similar vein, Gamson (2002) argued that storytelling "promotes empathy across different social locations" (p. 189). Although he was writing about media discourse on abortion, Gamson's argument is relevant to the narrative approaches I have been discussing. Gamson resisted the critique of American popular media (e.g., newspapers, television) that they are too infused with personal narratives. Because an unwanted pregnancy is ultimately a woman's problem, excluding stories about that "existential dilemma" from media and policy discourse silences women in particular. Thus, he argued that "personalization... opens discursive opportunities" (p. 189). Gamson had in mind "deliberation and dialogue in a narrative mode," which (unlike abstract argument) "lends itself more easily to the expression of moral complexity." In this sense, "storytelling facilitates a healthy democratic, public life" (p. 197).

During recent years, many narrative researchers have pushed beyond the goal of eliciting previously silenced narratives. Tierney's (2000) description of the goal of life history research applies to other forms of narrative research as well:

> Life histories are helpful not merely because they add to the mix of what already exists, but because of their ability to refashion identities. Rather than a conservative goal based on nostalgia for a paradise lost, or a liberal one of enabling more people to take their places at humanity's table, a goal of life history work in a postmodern age is to break the stranglehold of metanarratives that establishes rules of truth, legitimacy, and identity. The work of life history becomes the investigation of the mediating aspects of culture, the interrogation of its grammar, and the decentering of its norms. (p. 546)

These statements offer a strong version of what I described earlier as the researcher's authoritative voice. When researchers' interpretive strategies reveal the stranglehold of oppressive metanarratives, they help to open up possibilities for social change. In this sense, audiences need to hear not only the narrator's story, but also the researcher's explication of how the narrator's story is constrained by, and strains against, the mediating aspects of culture (and of institutions, organizations, and sometimes the social sciences themselves). Audiences whose members identify with the narrator's story might be moved by the researcher's interpretation to understand *their* stories in new ways and to imagine how they could tell their stories differently. Audiences whose members occupy social locations different from the narrator's might be moved through empathetic listening to think and act in ways that benefit the narrator or what he or she advocates (Madison, 1998, pp. 279–282).

What if the audience is hostile? DeVault and Ingraham (1999) broached this issue: "A radical challenge to silencing is not only about having a say, but about talking back in the strongest sense—saying the very things that those in power resist hearing" (p. 184). When the audience is both powerful and invested in the status quo—invested in oppressive metanarratives—narrators and narrative researchers may turn to "collective stories," which connect an individual's story to the broader story of a marginalized social group (Richardson, 1990). In discussing the collective stories of sexual abuse survivors and gays and lesbians, Plummer (1995) wrote, "For narratives to flourish, there must be a community to hear. . . . For communities to hear, there must be stories which weave together their history, their identity, their politics. The one—community—feeds upon and into the other—story" (p. 87). In the face of a hostile and powerful audience, narrators strengthen their communities through narratives and simultaneously seek to broaden their community of listeners. Thus, collective stories—or testimonios—become integral to social movements (see also Davis, 2002). However, it is important to heed Naples's (2003) cautionary note. In her analysis of how personal narratives function in the social movement of childhood sexual abuse survivors, she argued that we must determine when and where various strategies of speaking from personal experience are more effective and less effective in challenging oppression (p. 1152).

Although discussion of social movements and testimonios evokes the need for large-scale social change, we also need to consider the role of narratives and narrative research in small-scale, localized social change. For example, in Auerbach's (2002) study of Latino/Latina parent involvement in a college access program for their high school children, she heard many parents tell of poor treatment at the hands of school personnel. Auerbach also observed that the program gave parents some opportunities to share their stories publicly with each other and that sometimes this public performance of their stories led to collective problem solving (p. 1381). Equally important, Auerbach pointed to the need for such programs to create "a third space" that "disrupts the official discourse and scripted behavior that normally dominates school events for parents, just as it does in classrooms for students" (p. 1386). In other words, such programs hold the promise of creating conditions that would allow school administrators, teachers, and counselors to hear parents' narratives so that school staff can be jolted into resisting metanarratives that usually prevail in their work environments—immigrant families of color are uninterested in their children's education, immigrant children of color have limited educational potential, and so forth (see also Rosier, 2000). Auerbach suggested that researchers can help to create public spaces in which marginalized people's narratives can be heard even by those who normally do not want to hear them.

Narrative Inquiry: A Field in the Making

In *my* narrative, I have attempted to give shape to the massive material that can be called narrative inquiry, identifying its contours and complexities and arguing for the idea that it constitutes a subfield within qualitative inquiry even amid its multiplicity. Here I raise some issues—in the form of a set of relationships—that I believe are pivotal to the future of this field.

First is the relationship between theoretical and methodological work within narrative inquiry. Narrative theorists point out that narrative research is embedded in and shaped by broad social and historical currents, particularly the ubiquity of personal narratives in contemporary Western culture and politics—from television talk shows, to politicians' speeches, to self-help groups. Clough (2000) warned, however, that the "trauma culture" we currently inhabit encourages proliferation of personal narratives about trouble and suffering without offering a theory and politics of social change. Along similar lines, Atkinson and Silverman (1997) and Gubrium and Holstein (2002) pointed to the powerful tug of our "interview society," and they warned researchers against the romantic assumption that narrators reveal "authentic" selves and speak in their "own" voices, as if their selves and voices were not already mediated by the social contexts in which they speak. I argued earlier that treating interviewees as narrators does not mean succumbing to those problematic assumptions. Here, however, I suggest that narrative researchers need to do more, collectively, to integrate a critique of the trauma culture/interview society with discussion of methodological issues involved in conducting empirical research (e.g., inviting and interpreting narrators' stories). How do these two activities—one theoretical and the other methodological—support each other and serve a joint purpose? What specific research practices produce narrative research informed by a broad social critique and a politics of social change? Given the centrality of personal narrative in many political, cultural, and social arenas, narrative researchers have much work to do and much to offer by way of empirically grounded analysis and social critique (Crawley & Broad, 2004; Naples, 2003). No one theoretical or empirical project can do everything, of course, but it seems to me that one key lies in more conversation among narrative researchers across theoretical and methodological interests.

Second is the relationship between Western and non-Western narrative theories and practices. Gubrium and Holstein (2002) suggested that the interview society has gone global—that people around the globe know what it means to be interviewed. Even Nisa, a member of the (until recently) hunting and gathering !Kung people, knows how to place herself at the center of a life story (Shostak, 1981/2000a, 2000b). At the same time, narrative researchers need to understand cross-cultural differences more fully. What do Western narrative researchers (and Westerners in general) have to learn from the ways in which non-Westerners narrate the self, narrate group identities, or integrate folklore narratives into personal narratives (Grima, 1991; Narayan & George, 2002; Riessman, 2002b)? If self or identity is not the central construct in (at least some) non-Western narratives (Rosaldo, 1976), what is? What do non-Western narrative researchers have to teach their Western counterparts about the kinds of narratives that need to be heard and about interpretive and narrative strategies for presenting and performing them? What is the relationship among narrative, narrative research, and social change in non-Western societies? For example, what impact do Latin American testimonios have in the local communities from which they arise? I am not suggesting that Western narrative researchers should take up residence in non-Western locales; rather, I am suggesting that we need to understand more fully how our research is imbued with Western assumptions about self and identity. Anthropologists may be ahead of the game here, but much American narrative research remains unreflective about its Western character.

The third issue revolves around the relationship between narrative inquiry and technological innovation. Although it is hard to imagine narrative researchers giving up the domain of face-to-face interviewing and on-site gathering of naturally occurring conversation, some researchers have already moved into the domain of virtual research and many others will follow in their footsteps (Mann & Stewart, 2002; see also Markham, chap. 31, this volume). How are e-mail, chat groups, online support groups, and instant messaging changing the meaning of "naturally occurring conversation"? How are they creating new arenas for narrating the self and for constructing identities, realities, relationships, and communities? As narrative researchers explore these new opportunities to hear people converse and to interview individuals and groups, what new risks and ethical issues will they encounter? What new forms of knowledge will emerge?

Fourth, researchers interested in the relationship between narrative and social change need to do more to address the issue of audience (Lincoln, 1997). We need to think more about who could benefit from, and who needs to hear, *our* research narratives. Marginalized people in the communities we study? Power brokers and gatekeepers in the communities we study? Policymakers? Students in our classes? The public at large? Other researchers within our disciplines and substantive fields of study? Equally important, in my view, is the need for narrative researchers to explore the possible points of contact between *narrators'* stories and various audiences who need to hear them. What kinds of stories (and what kinds of research narratives) incite collective action? And to what effect? When do previously silenced narrators jolt powerful—and initially hostile—audiences to join in breaking the stranglehold of oppressive metanarratives? And how can researchers help to create the conditions of empathetic listening across social locations?

Along these lines, what do we have to learn from Ensler's (2001) wildly successful *Vagina Monologues*? How did Ensler transform interviews with women about their bodies into performances that have sparked a massive international movement against violence against women?[22] Similarly, what do we have to learn about writing for the public from Ehrenreich's (2001) best-seller, *Nickel and Dimed: On (Not) Getting By in America*? In this mixture of undercover reporting and narrative ethnography, Ehrenreich wrote both seriously and humorously about her efforts to make ends meet for a month at a time as a waitress in Florida, a house cleaner in Maine, and a Wal-Mart employee in Minnesota. Many of my students claim that this text disrupts their attachment to individualist ideologies in ways that other texts do not. I am not suggesting that we should all aspire to off-Broadway performances or to best-sellerdom for our work; rather, I am suggesting that we need to think more concertedly and broadly about whom we write for and speak to—and how we do so. For many of us, this may mean thinking about how to create public spaces in our local communities where the personal narratives and collective stories of marginalized people can be heard by—and can jolt out of their complacency—those who occupy more powerful subject positions and social locations.

Finally, narrative researchers need to attend to the relationship between our work and that of our social science colleagues who work within other traditions of inquiry. We need to treat other social science scholars as an important audience for our work. We need to demonstrate that immersion in the biographical leg of Mills's trilogy—biography, history, and society—produces new significant concepts and analyses that other researchers in our substantive areas and disciplines *need* to do their work well. For example, Loseke's (2001) concept of the "formula story" of wife abuse, and her analysis of its inadequacy in capturing women's complex stories of domestic violence, is crucial to the work of other social scientists—whether quantitative or qualitative—who study the success or failure of battered women's shelters in helping women to leave abusive partners. Generally speaking, narrative inquiry's contributions to social science have to do with concepts and analyses that demonstrate two things: (a) the creativity, complexity, and variability of individuals' (or groups') self and reality constructions and (b) the power of historical, social, cultural, organizational, discursive, interactional, and/or psychological circumstances in shaping the range of possibilities for self and reality construction in any particular time and place. Narrative researchers need to confidently assert their contributions to, their interventions in, and their transformations of social science scholarship.

As narrative researchers grapple with these and myriad other issues and questions, it is hard to imagine Mills's argument for the joint investigation of biography, society, and history going out of style. What exactly that means, however, will likely undergo many further permutations, disrupting assumptions that many of us now hold dear.

▣ Notes

1. I thank Norman Denzin, Yvonna Lincoln, James Holstein, Ruthellen Josselson, and Catherine Riessman for their comments on earlier drafts of this chapter.

2. The *Journal of Narrative and Life History* was created in 1990, and it became *Narrative Inquiry* in

1998. As just two examples of conferences, in February 2003 the American Educational Research Association held a Winter Institute on Narrative Inquiry in Social Science Research at the Ontario Institute for Studies in Education, and in May 2004 the second biannual Narrative Matters conference was held at St. Thomas University in New Brunswick.

3. For overviews of early life history methods in sociology, see Becker (1966), Bertaux (1981), Denzin (1970), and Plummer (1983).

4. The life history and life story approaches continue to be international in scope. The 2003 Board of Biography and Society, a research committee of the International Sociological Association, included researchers from many European countries as well as from Japan, South Africa, and Russia.

5. In addition to summarizing the interview data that she gathered from 129 women about childbearing, child rearing, marriage, housework, fieldwork, and community participation, Hagood (1939) presented two women's life stories in depth. This allows readers to see the impact on these two women's lives of the social and economic conditions described earlier in the book.

6. For overviews of early life history methods in anthropology, see Langness (1965), Langness and Frank (1981), and Watson and Watson-Franke (1985).

7. Two volumes of *The American Slave* consist of interviews conducted at Fisk University before the Federal Writers' Project was created. During the late 1960s and early 1970s, Lester (1968) and Yetman (1970), among others, were publishing parts of and writing about the slave narratives. After the publication of *The American Slave,* Rawick (1977) and other researchers searched for, found, and published many other slave narratives that had been deposited in state collections and libraries. Not surprisingly, they found evidence that some of the narratives had been tampered with, presumably to suppress negative portrayals of whites.

8. For overviews of early second-wave feminist use of life history and personal narratives, see Armitage (1983), Geiger (1986), Gluck (1979, 1983), Personal Narratives Group (1989), and Reinharz (1992, chap. 7).

9. Even before feminism became a major influence in social science research, there were exceptions to this pattern of methodological indifference and objectification of research participants. For example, in *Mountain Wolf Woman: Sister of Crashing Thunder,* Lurie (1961) addressed many methodological issues and described in detail her relationship with Mountain Wolf Woman.

10. See Mishler (1995, pp. 90–102) on various ways in which narrative researchers connect the "telling" and the "told."

11. Polkinghorne (1995) and Mishler (1995) also made distinctions among types of narrative research in the social sciences, but because they excluded some kinds of work that I want to include (and because they included some kinds that I want to exclude), I construct my own categories here.

12. Because quantitative modes of inquiry are so dominant in psychology, some psychologists treat narrative inquiry as synonymous with qualitative inquiry (Josselson, Lieblich, & McAdams, 2003). Nonetheless, I have tried to separate out a psychological approach that uses the analytic lenses I have articulated and so is not identical to qualitative research in general.

13. For interview guides used by psychological researchers who take a narrative approach, see McAdams and Bowman (2001, pp. 12–13) and Josselson (1996b, pp. 265–272).

14. Some of the researchers I include in this approach are not sociologists. For example, Mishler is a psychologist and Langellier is a communication scholar. Nonetheless, their approach is sociological in the ways described here.

15. Sometimes memoirs, even those not written by social scientists, have autoethnographic characteristics. For example, in *Crossing the Color Line: Race, Parenting, and Culture,* Reddy (1994) investigated her experiences as a white woman married to an African American man and as the mother of two biracial children. She showed how these racialized relationships disrupted her identity as a white woman and her understanding of racial issues in the social world. The writing itself, however, is not experimental in the same way that much autoethnographic writing is.

16. See Chase (1995b, 2003) for a comparison of sociological interview questions and questions oriented to inviting narratives.

17. The influence of narrative inquiry can be seen in the difference between Rubin's (1976) *Worlds of Pain: Life in the Working Class Family* and Rubin's (1994) *Families on the Faultline: America's Working Class Speaks About the Family, the Economy, Race, and Ethnicity.* In the earlier book, Rubin (1976) presented anonymous excerpts from a range of interviewees to represent various themes. In contrast, Rubin (1994) organized the more recent book around the stories of specific families, beginning and ending the book with the same four families.

18. See also Ochberg (1996) on the ways in which researchers "convert what we have been told from one kind of account into another" (p. 110). In addition, Josselson (1996a) offered an interesting discussion of the anxiety, guilt, and shame that may arise when "writing other people's lives" and sharing interpretations with those people.

19. Ferguson's (2001) *Bad Boys: Public Schools in the Making of Black Masculinity* offers an example of a researcher mixing narrative strategies. For the most part, Ferguson wrote with an authoritative voice. But in the middle of the book, she shifted to a supportive voice when she included a 27-page transcript from an interview with an African American mother whose attempt to discipline her son was itself disciplined by police, courts, and social service agencies. Ferguson stated, "You must read what Mariana had to say aloud. You cannot understand it unless you hear the words" (p. 135).

20. For many other examples, see Koehler (1981, pp. 89–93), Langness and Frank (1981), and Watson and Watson-Franke (1985).

21. Focusing on instances rather than representative cases is not unique to narrative inquiry, but the issue may seem more urgent in narrative research because of the small number of narratives that researchers present. For broader discussions of the relation between the particular and the general, see Blum and McHugh (1984, p. 37), Denzin (1997, p. 245), and Psathas (1995, p. 50).

22. *The Vagina Monologues* was originally an off-Broadway production based on interviews with 200 American women. It has been performed in many cities and communities across the United States as well as around the globe. When performed in conjunction with the "V-day" movement, profits are donated to organizations fighting violence against women.

References

Anderson, K., & Jack, D. C. (1991). Learning to listen: Interview techniques and analyses. In S. B. Gluck & D. Patai (Eds.), *Women's words: The feminist practice of oral history* (pp. 11–26). New York: Routledge.

Armitage, S. H. (1983). The next step. *Frontiers: A Journal of Women's Studies, 7,* 3–8.

Atkinson, P., & Silverman, D. (1997). Kundera's *Immortality:* The interview society and the invention of the self. *Qualitative Inquiry, 3,* 304–325.

Atkinson, R. (2002). The life story interview. In J. F. Gubrium & J. A. Holstein (Eds.), *Handbook of interview research: Context and method* (pp. 121–140). Thousand Oaks, CA: Sage.

Auerbach, S. (2002). "Why do they give the good classes to some and not to others?" Latino parent narratives of struggle in a college access program. *Teachers College Record, 104,* 1369–1392.

Babb, J., & Taylor, P. E. (1981). *Border healing woman: The story of Jewel Babb.* Austin: University of Texas Press.

Bamberg, M. G. W. (1997). Positioning between structure and performance. *Journal of Narrative and Life History, 7,* 335–342.

Barthes, R. (1977). *Image, music, text* (S. Heath, Trans.). New York: Hill & Wang.

Bauman, R. (1986). *Story, performance, and event: Contextual studies in oral narrative.* Cambridge, UK: Cambridge University Press.

Becker, H. S. (1966). Introduction. In C. R. Shaw, *The jack-roller: A delinquent boy's own story.* Chicago: University of Chicago Press.

Behar, R. (1996). *The vulnerable observer: Anthropology that breaks your heart.* Boston: Beacon.

Behar, R. (2003). *Translated woman: Crossing the border with Esperanza's story.* Boston: Beacon. (Original work published in 1993)

Belenky, M. F., Clinchy, B. M., Goldberger, N. R., & Tarule, J. M. (1986). *Women's ways of knowing: The development of self, voice, and mind.* New York: Basic Books.

Bell, S. E. (1999). Narratives and lives: Women's health politics and the diagnosis of cancer for DES daughters. *Narrative Inquiry, 9,* 347–389.

Bertaux, D. (Ed.). (1981). *Biography and society: The life history approach in the social sciences.* Beverly Hills, CA: Sage.

Beverley, J. (2000). Testimonio, subalternity, and narrative authority. In N. K. Denzin & Y. S. Lincoln (Eds.), *Handbook of qualitative research* (2nd ed., pp. 555–565). Thousand Oaks, CA: Sage.

Blauner, B. (1989). *Black lives, white lives: Three decades of race relations in America.* Berkeley: University of California Press.

Bloom, L. R., & Munro, P. (1995). Conflicts of selves: Nonunitary subjectivity in women administrators' life history narratives. In J. A. Hatch & R. Wisniewski (Eds.), *Life history and narrative* (pp. 99–112). London: Falmer.

Blum, A., & McHugh, P. (1984). *Self-reflection in the arts and sciences.* Atlantic Highlands, NJ: Humanities Press.

Blumer, H. (1979). *Critiques of research in the social sciences: An appraisal of Thomas and Znaniecki's* The Polish Peasant in Europe and America. New Brunswick, NJ: Transaction Books. (Original work published in 1939)

Bobel, C. (2002). *The paradox of natural mothering.* Philadelphia: Temple University Press.

Botkin, B. A. (Ed.). (1945). *Lay my burden down: A folk history of slavery.* Chicago: University of Chicago Press.

Briggs, C. L. (1986). *Learning how to ask: A sociolinguistic appraisal of the role of the interview in social science research.* Cambridge, UK: Cambridge University Press.

Briggs, C. L. (2002). Interviewing, power/knowledge, and social inequality. In J. F. Gubrium & J. A. Holstein (Eds.), *Handbook of interview research: Context and method* (pp. 911–922). Thousand Oaks, CA: Sage.

Brockmeier, J., & Carbaugh, D. (Eds.). (2001). *Narrative and identity: Studies in autobiography, self, and culture.* Amsterdam, Netherlands: John Benjamins.

Bruner, J. (1986). *Actual minds, possible worlds.* Cambridge, MA: Harvard University Press.

Bruner, J. (1997). Labov and Waletzky: Thirty years on. *Journal of Narrative and Life History, 7,* 61–68.

Bruner, J. (2002). *Making stories: Law, literature, life.* New York: Farrar, Straus, & Giroux.

Burgos, M. (1989). Life stories, narrativity, and the search for the self. *Life Stories [Récits de vie], 5,* 27–38.

Capps, L., & Ochs, E. (1995). *Constructing panic: The discourse of agoraphobia.* Cambridge, MA: Harvard University Press.

Chalasiński, J. (1981). The life records of the young generation of Polish peasants as a manifestation of contemporary culture. In D. Bertaux (Ed.), *Biography and society: The life history approach in the social sciences* (pp. 119–132). Beverly Hills, CA: Sage.

Chase, S. E. (1995a). *Ambiguous empowerment: The work narratives of women school superintendents.* Amherst: University of Massachusetts Press.

Chase, S. E. (1995b). Taking narrative seriously: Consequences for method and theory in interview studies. In R. Josselson & A. Lieblich (Eds.), *Interpreting experience: The narrative study of lives* (pp. 1–26). Thousand Oaks, CA: Sage.

Chase, S. E. (1996). Personal vulnerability and interpretive authority in narrative research. In R. Josselson (Ed.), *Ethics and process in the narrative study of lives* (pp. 45–59). Thousand Oaks, CA: Sage.

Chase, S. E. (2001). Universities as discursive environments for sexual identity construction. In J. F. Gubrium & J. A. Holstein (Eds.), *Institutional selves: Troubled identities in a postmodern world* (pp. 142–157). New York: Oxford University Press.

Chase, S. E. (2003). Learning to listen: Narrative principles in a qualitative research methods course. In R. Josselson, A. Lieblich, & D. P. McAdams (Eds.), *Up close and personal: The teaching and learning of narrative research* (pp. 79–99). Washington, DC: American Psychological Association.

Clough, P. T. (2000). Comments on setting criteria for experimental writing. *Qualitative Inquiry, 6,* 278–291.

Crapanzano, V. (1980). *Tuhami: Portrait of a Moroccan.* Chicago: University of Chicago Press.

Crawley, S. L. (2002). "They still don't understand why I hate wearing dresses!" An autoethnographic rant on dresses, boats, and butchness. *Cultural Studies, Critical Methodologies, 2,* 69–92.

Crawley, S. L., & Broad, K. L. (2004). "Be your(real lesbian)self": Mobilizing sexual formula stories through personal (and political) storytelling. *Journal of Contemporary Ethnography, 33,* 39–71.

Czarniawska, B. (1997). *Narrating the organization: Dramas of institutional identity.* Chicago: University of Chicago Press.

Czarniawska, B. (2002). Narrative, interviews, and organizations. In J. F. Gubrium & J.A. Holstein (Eds.), *Handbook of interview research: Context and method* (pp. 733–749). Thousand Oaks, CA: Sage.

Davis, J. E. (Ed.). (2002). *Stories of change: Narrative and social movements.* Albany: State University of New York Press.

Denzin, N. K. (1970). *The research act: A theoretical introduction to sociological methods.* Chicago: Aldine.

Denzin, N. K. (1989). *Interpretive biography.* Newbury Park, CA: Sage.

Denzin, N. K. (1997). *Interpretive ethnography: Ethnographic practices for the 21st century.* Thousand Oaks, CA: Sage.

Denzin, N. K. (2000). The practices and politics of interpretation. In N. K. Denzin & Y. S. Lincoln (Eds.), *Handbook of qualitative research* (2nd ed., pp. 897–922). Thousand Oaks, CA: Sage.

Denzin, N. K. (2003). The call to performance. *Symbolic Interaction, 26,* 187–207.

Denzin, N. K., & Lincoln, Y. S. (2000). Introduction: The discipline and practice of qualitative research. In N. K. Denzin & Y. S. Lincoln (Eds.), *Handbook of qualitative research* (2nd ed., pp. 1–28). Thousand Oaks, CA: Sage.

DeVault, M. L. (1999). *Liberating method: Feminism and social research.* Philadelphia: Temple University Press.

DeVault, M. L., & Ingraham, C. (1999). Metaphors of silence and voice in feminist thought. In M. L. DeVault, *Liberating method: Feminism and social research* (pp. 175–186). Philadelphia: Temple University Press.

DuBois, C. (1960). *The people of Alor: A social-psychological study of an East Indian island.* Cambridge, MA: Harvard University Press. (Original work published in 1944)

Ehrenreich, B. (2001). *Nickel and dimed: On (not) getting by in America.* New York: Metropolitan Books.

Ellis, C., & Berger, L. (2002). Their story/My story/Our story: Including the researcher's experience in interview research. In J. F. Gubrium & J. A. Holstein (Eds.), *Handbook of interview research: Context and method* (pp. 849–875). Thousand Oaks, CA: Sage.

Ellis, C., & Bochner, A. P. (1992). Telling and performing personal stories: The constraints of choice in abortion. In C. Ellis & M. G. Flaherty (Eds.), *Investigating subjectivity: Research on lived experience* (pp. 79–101). Newbury Park, CA: Sage.

Ellis, C., & Bochner, A. P. (Eds.). (1996). *Composing ethnography: Alternative forms of qualitative writing.* Walnut Creek, CA: AltaMira.

Ellis, C., & Flaherty, M. G. (Eds.). (1992). *Investigating subjectivity: Research on lived experience.* Newbury Park, CA: Sage.

Ellis, C., Kiesinger, C. E., & Tillmann-Healy, L. M. (1997). Interactive interviewing: Talking about emotional experience. In R. Hertz (Ed.), *Reflexivity and voice* (pp. 119–149). Thousand Oaks, CA: Sage.

Emihovich, C. (1995). Distancing passion: Narratives in social science. In J. A. Hatch & R. Wisniewski (Eds.), *Life history and narrative* (pp. 37–48). London: Falmer.

Ensler, E. (2001). *The vagina monologues: The V-day edition.* New York: Villard/Random House.

Ferguson, A. A. (2001). *Bad boys: Public schools in the making of black masculinity.* Ann Arbor: University of Michigan Press.

Foley, L., & Faircloth, C. A. (2003). Medicine as discursive resource: Legitimation in the work narratives of midwives. *Sociology of Health & Illness, 25,* 165–184.

Frank, A. W. (1995). *The wounded storyteller: Body, illness, and ethics.* Chicago: University of Chicago Press.

Frank, G. (2000). *Venus on wheels: Two decades of dialogue on disability, biography, and being female in America.* Berkeley: University of California Press.

Franz, C. E., & Stewart, A. J. (Eds.). (1994). *Women creating lives: Identities, resilience, and resistance.* Boulder, CO: Westview.

Gamson, W. A. (2002). How storytelling can be empowering. In K. A. Cerulo (Ed.), *Culture in mind: Toward a sociology of culture and cognition* (pp. 187–198). New York: Routledge.

Garfinkel, H. (1967). *Studies in ethnomethodology.* Englewood Cliffs, NJ: Prentice Hall.

Geiger, S. N. G. (1986). Women's life histories: Method and content. *Signs: Journal of Women in Culture and Society, 11,* 334–351.

Gluck, S. (1979). What's so special about women? Women's oral history. *Frontiers: A Journal of Women's Studies, 2,* 3–11.

Gluck, S. B. (1983). Women's oral history: The second decade. *Frontiers: A Journal of Women's Studies, 7,* 1–2.

Gluck, S. B., & Patai, D. (Eds.). (1991). *Women's words: The feminist practice of oral history.* New York: Routledge.

Grima, B. (1991). The role of suffering in women's performance of *paxto.* In A. Appadurai, F. J. Korom, & M. A. Mills (Eds.), *Gender, genre, and power in South Asian expressive traditions* (pp. 78–101). Philadelphia: University of Pennsylvania Press.

Gubrium, J. F., & Holstein, J. A. (1997). *The new language of qualitative method.* New York: Oxford University Press.

Gubrium, J. F., & Holstein, J. A. (Eds.). (2001). *Institutional selves: Troubled identities in a postmodern world.* New York: Oxford University Press.

Gubrium, J. F., & Holstein, J. A. (2002). From the individual interview to the interview society. In J. F. Gubrium & J. A. Holstein (Eds.), *Handbook of interview research: Context and method* (pp. 3–32). Thousand Oaks, CA: Sage.

Gwaltney, J. L. (Ed.). (1993). *Drylongso: A self-portrait of Black America.* New York: New Press. (Original work published in 1980)

Hagood, M. J. (1939). *Mothers of the South: Portraiture of the white tenant farm woman.* New York: Greenwood.

Hatch, J. A., & Wisniewski, R. (Eds.). (1995). *Life history and narrative.* London: Falmer.

Hertz, R. (Ed.). (1997). *Reflexivity and voice.* Thousand Oaks, CA: Sage.

Hilbert, R. A. (1990). The efficacy of performance science: Comment on McCall and Becker. *Social Problems, 37,* 133–135.

Hinchman, L. P., & Hinchman, S. K. (Eds.). (2001). *Memory, identity, community: The idea of narrative in the human sciences.* Albany: State University of New York Press.

Holstein, J. A., & Gubrium, J. F. (2000). *The self we live by: Narrative identity in a postmodern world.* New York: Oxford University Press.

Hunt, A. M., & Winegarten, R. (1983). *I am Annie Mae: An extraordinary black Texas woman in her own words.* Austin: University of Texas Press.

Jacobs, R. H. (1979). *Life after youth: Female, forty—What next?* Boston: Beacon.

Josselson, R. (1996a). On writing other people's lives: Self-analytic reflections of a narrative researcher. In R. Josselson (Ed.), *Ethics and process in the narrative study of lives* (pp. 60–71). Thousand Oaks, CA: Sage.

Josselson, R. (1996b). *Revising herself: The story of women's identity from college to midlife.* New York: Oxford University Press.

Josselson, R., Lieblich, A., & McAdams, D. P. (Eds.). (2003). *Up close and personal: The teaching and learning of narrative research.* Washington, DC: American Psychological Association.

Kardiner, A. (1945). *The psychological frontiers of society.* Westport, CT: Greenwood.

Koehler, L. (1981). Native women of the Americas: A bibliography. *Frontiers: A Journal of Women's Studies, 6,* 73–101.

Krieger, S. (1991). *Social science and the self: Personal essays on an art form.* New Brunswick, NJ: Rutgers University Press.

Labov, W., & Waletzky, J. (1997). Narrative analysis: Oral versions of personal experience. *Journal of Narrative and Life History, 7,* 3–38. (Original work published in 1967)

Langellier, K. M. (2001). You're marked: Breast cancer, tattoo, and the narrative performance of identity. In J. Brockmeier & D. Carbaugh (Eds.), *Narrative and identity: Studies in autobiography, self, and culture* (pp. 145–184). Amsterdam, Netherlands: John Benjamins.

Langness, L. L. (1965). *The life history in anthropological science.* New York: Holt, Rinehart & Winston.

Langness, L. L., & Frank, G. (1981). *Lives: An anthropological approach to biography.* Novato, CA: Chandler & Sharp.

Laslett, B. (1999). Personal narratives as sociology. *Contemporary Sociology, 28,* 391–401.

Lempert, L. B. (1994). A narrative analysis of abuse: Connecting the personal, the rhetorical, and the structural. *Journal of Contemporary Ethnography, 22,* 411–441.

Lester, J. (1968). *To be a slave.* New York: Scholastic.

Lewis, O. (1961). *The children of Sánchez: Autobiography of a Mexican family.* New York: Random House.

Liebow, E. (1993). *Tell them who I am: The lives of homeless women.* New York: Penguin.

Lincoln, Y. S. (1997). Self, subject, audience, text: Living at the edge, writing in the margins. In W. G. Tierney & Y. S. Lincoln (Eds.), *Representation and the text: Re-framing the narrative voice* (pp. 37–55). Albany: State University of New York Press.

Lincoln, Y. S. (2000). Narrative authority vs. perjured testimony: Courage, vulnerability, and truth. *Qualitative Studies in Education, 13,* 131–138.

Loseke, D. R. (2001). Lived realities and formula stories of "battered women." In J. F. Gubrium & J. A. Holstein (Eds.), *Institutional selves: Troubled identities in a postmodern world* (pp. 107–126). New York: Oxford University Press.

Lurie, N. O. (Ed.). (1961). *Mountain Wolf Woman: Sister of Crashing Thunder.* Ann Arbor: University of Michigan Press.

Luttrell, W. (1997). *School-smart and mother-wise: Working-class women's identity and schooling.* New York: Routledge.

Luttrell. W. (2003). *Pregnant bodies, fertile minds: Gender, race, and the schooling of pregnant teens.* New York: Routledge.

Madison, D. S. (1998). Performance, personal narratives, and the politics of possibility. In S. J. Dailey (Ed.), *The future of performance studies: Visions and revisions* (pp. 276–286). Annandale, VA: National Communication Association.

Mann, C., & Stewart, F. (2002). Internet interviewing. In J. F. Gubrium and J. A. Holstein (Eds.), *Handbook of interview research: Context and method* (pp. 603–627). Thousand Oaks, CA: Sage.

McAdams, D. P. (1997). *The stories we live by: Personal myths and the making of the self.* New York: Guilford.

McAdams, D. P., & Bowman, P. J. (2001). Narrating life's turning points: Redemption and contamination. In D. P. McAdams, R. Josselson, & A. Lieblich (Eds.), *Turns in the road: Narrative studies of lives in transition* (pp. 3–34). Washington, DC: American Psychological Association.

McAdams, D. P., Josselson, R., & Lieblich, A. (Eds.). (2001). *Turns in the road: Narrative studies of lives in transition.* Washington, DC: American Psychological Association.

McCall, M. M., & Becker, H. S. (1990). Performance science. *Social Problems, 37,* 117–132.

McCall, M. M., & Wittner, J. (1990). The good news about life history. In H. S. Becker & M. M. McCall (Eds.), *Symbolic interaction and cultural studies* (pp. 46–89). Chicago: University of Chicago Press.

McLaughlin, D., & Tierney, W. G. (Eds.). (1993). *Naming silenced lives: Personal narratives and processes of educational change.* New York: Routledge.

McMahan, E. M., & Rogers, K. L. (Eds.). (1994). *Interactive oral history interviewing.* Hillsdale, NJ: Lawrence Erlbaum.

Menchú, R. (1984). *I, Rigoberta Menchú: An Indian woman in Guatemala* (with an introduction by E. Burgos-Debray, Ed.; A. Wright, Trans.). London: Verso.

Miller, G. (1997). *Becoming miracle workers: Language and meaning in brief therapy.* New York: Aldine de Gruyter.

Mills, C. W. (1959). *The sociological imagination.* London: Oxford University Press.

Mishler, E. G. (1986). *Research interviewing: Context and narrative.* Cambridge, MA: Harvard University Press.

Mishler, E. G. (1995). Models of narrative analysis: A typology. *Journal of Narrative and Life History, 5,* 87–123.

Mishler, E. G. (1999). *Storylines: Craft artists' narratives of identity.* Cambridge, MA: Harvard University Press.

Moyano, M. E. (2000). *The autobiography of María Elena Moyano: The life and death of a Peruvian activist* (D. M. Tupac, Ed. and Annot.). Gainesville: University Press of Florida.

Myerhoff, B. (1994). *Number our days: Culture and community among elderly Jews in an American ghetto.* New York: Meridian/Penguin. (Original work published in 1979)

Naples, N. (2003). Deconstructing and locating survivor discourse: Dynamics of narrative, empowerment, and resistance for survivors of childhood sexual abuse. *Signs: Journal of Women in Culture and Society, 28,* 1151–1185.

Narayan, K., & George, K. M. (2002). Personal and folk narrative as cultural representation. In J. F. Gubrium & J. A. Holstein (Eds.), *Handbook of interview research: Context and method* (pp. 815–831). Thousand Oaks, CA: Sage.

Ochberg, R. L. (1996). Interpreting life stories. In R. Josselson (Ed.), *Ethics and process in the narrative study of lives* (pp. 97–113). Thousand Oaks, CA: Sage.

Personal Narratives Group. (Eds.). (1989). *Interpreting women's lives: Feminist theory and personal narratives.* Bloomington: Indiana University Press.

Plummer, K. (1983). *Documents of life: An introduction to the problems and literature of a humanistic method.* London: George Allen & Unwin.

Plummer, K. (1995). *Telling sexual stories: Power, change, and social worlds.* London: Routledge.

Polkinghorne, D. E. (1995). Narrative configuration in qualitative analysis. In J. A. Hatch & R. Wisniewski (Eds.), *Life history and narrative* (pp. 5–23). London: Falmer.

Pollner, M., & Stein, J. (1996). Narrative mapping of social worlds: The voice of experience in Alcoholics Anonymous. *Symbolic Interaction, 19,* 203–223.

Psathas, G. (1995). *Conversation analysis: The study of talk-in-interaction.* Thousand Oaks, CA: Sage.

Radin, P. (Ed.). (1926). *Crashing Thunder: The autobiography of an American Indian.* New York: Appleton.

Randall, M. (1981). *Sandino's daughters: Testimonies of Nicaraguan women in struggle.* Vancouver, British Columbia: New Star Books.

Randall, M. (1994). *Sandino's daughters revisited: Feminism in Nicaragua.* New Brunswick, NJ: Rutgers University Press.

Randall, M. (2003). *When I look into the mirror and see you: Women, terror, and resistance.* New Brunswick, NJ: Rutgers University Press.

Rawick, G. P. (1972). *The American slave: A composite autobiography,* Vol. 1: *From sundown to sunup—The making of the black community.* Westport, CT: Greenwood.

Rawick, G. P. (1977). General introduction. In G. Rawick, J. Hillegas, & K. Lawrence (Eds.), *The American slave: A composite autobiography,*

Supplement, Ser. 1, Vol. 1: *Alabama narratives* (pp. ix–li). Westport, CT: Greenwood.

Reddy, M. T. (1994). *Crossing the color line: Race, parenting, and culture.* New Brunswick, NJ: Rutgers University Press.

Reinharz, S. (1992). *Feminist methods in social research.* New York: Oxford University Press.

Reinharz, S., & Chase, S. E. (2002). Interviewing women. In J. F. Gubrium & J. A. Holstein (Eds.), *Handbook of interview research: Context and method* (pp. 221–238). Thousand Oaks, CA: Sage.

Ribbens, J., & Edwards, R. (Eds.). (1998). *Feminist dilemmas in qualitative research: Public knowledge and private lives.* London: Sage.

Richardson, L. (1990). Narrative and sociology. *Journal of Contemporary Ethnography, 19,* 116–135.

Richardson, L. (2002). Poetic representation of interviews. In J. F. Gubrium & J. A. Holstein (Eds.), *Handbook of interview research: Context and method* (pp. 877–892). Thousand Oaks, CA: Sage

Riessman, C. K. (1990). *Divorce talk: Women and men make sense of personal relationships.* New Brunswick, NJ: Rutgers University Press.

Riessman, C. K. (1997). A short story about long stories. *Journal of Narrative and Life History, 7,* 155–158.

Riessman, C. K. (2002a). Analysis of personal narratives. In J. F. Gubrium & J. A. Holstein (Eds.), *Handbook of interview research: Context and method* (pp. 695–710). Thousand Oaks, CA: Sage.

Riessman, C. K. (2002b). Positioning gender identity in narratives of infertility: South Indian women's lives in context. In M. C. Inhorn & F. van Balen (Eds.), *Infertility around the globe: New thinking on childlessness, gender, and reproductive technologies* (pp. 152–170). Berkeley: University of California Press.

Rosaldo, R. (1976). The story of Tukbaw: "They listen as he orates." In F. E. Reynolds & D. Capps (Eds.), *The biographical process: Studies in the history and psychology of religion* (pp. 121–151). The Hague, Netherlands: Mouton.

Rosenwald, G. C., & Ochberg, R. L. (Eds.). (1992). *Storied lives: The cultural politics of self-understanding.* New Haven, CT: Yale University Press.

Rosier, K. B. (2000). *Mothering inner-city children: The early school years.* New Brunswick, NJ: Rutgers University Press.

Rubin, L. B. (1976). *Worlds of pain: Life in the working-class family.* New York: Basic Books.

Rubin, L. B. (1994). *Families on the faultline: America's working class speaks about the family, the economy, race, and ethnicity.* New York: HarperPerennial.

Ruddick, S., & Daniels, P. (Eds.). (1977). *Working it out: 23 women writers, artists, scientists, and scholars talk about their lives and work.* New York: Pantheon.

Sacks, K. B. (1989). What's a life story got to do with it? In Personal Narratives Group (Eds.), *Interpreting women's lives: Feminist theories and personal narratives* (pp. 85–95). Bloomington: University of Indiana Press.

Schegloff, E. A. (1997). "Narrative analysis" thirty years later. *Journal of Narrative and Life History, 7,* 97–106.

Sexton, P. C. (1981). *The new Nightingales: Hospital workers, unions, new women's issues.* New York: Enquiry Press.

Shaw, C. R. (1966). *The jack-roller: A delinquent boy's own story.* Chicago: University of Chicago Press. (Original work published in 1930)

Shostak, M. (1989). "What the wind won't take away": The genesis of *Nisa—The life and words of a !Kung woman.* In Personal Narratives Group (Eds.), *Interpreting women's lives: Feminist theory and personal narratives* (pp. 228–240). Bloomington: Indiana University Press.

Shostak, M. (2000a). *Nisa: The life and words of a !Kung woman.* Cambridge, MA: Harvard University Press. (Original work published in 1981)

Shostak, M. (2000b). *Return to Nisa.* Cambridge, MA: Harvard University Press.

Sidel, R. (1978). *Urban survival: The world of working-class women.* Boston: Beacon.

Stein, A. (1997). *Sex and sensibility: Stories of a lesbian generation.* Berkeley: University of California Press.

Stromberg, P. G. (1993). *Language and self-transformation: A study of the Christian conversion narrative.* Cambridge, UK: Cambridge University Press.

Sutherland, E. H. (1937). *The professional thief.* Chicago: University of Chicago Press.

Taylor, J. M., Gilligan, C., & Sullivan, A. M. (1995). *Between voice and silence: Women and girls, race and relationship.* Cambridge, MA: Harvard University Press.

Tedlock, B. (1992). *The beautiful and the dangerous: Encounters with the Zuni Indians.* New York: Viking/Penguin Books.

Terkel, S. (1995). *Coming of age: The story of our century by those who've lived it.* New York: New Press.

Thomas, W. I., & Znaniecki, F. (1927). *The Polish peasant in Europe and America* (Vol. 2). New York: Alfred A. Knopf. (Original work published in 1918)

Thompson, P. (2000). *The voice of the past: Oral history* (3rd ed.). New York: Oxford University Press. (Original work published in 1978)

Tierney, W. G. (2000). Undaunted courage: Life history and the postmodern challenge. In N. K. Denzin & Y. S. Lincoln (Eds.), *Handbook of qualitative research* (2nd ed., pp. 537–553). Thousand Oaks, CA: Sage.

Tierney, W. G. (2002). Get real: Representing reality. *Qualitative Studies in Education, 15,* 385–398.

Tierney, W. G., & Lincoln, Y. S. (Eds.). (1997). *Representation and the text: Re-framing the narrative voice.* Albany: State University of New York Press.

Watson, L. C., & Watson-Franke, M-B. (1985). *Interpreting life histories: An anthropological inquiry.* New Brunswick, NJ: Rutgers University Press.

Weiss, R. S. (1994). *Learning from strangers: The art and method of qualitative interview studies.* New York: Free Press.

Wozniak, D. F. (2002). *They're all my children: Foster mothering in America.* New York: New York University Press.

Yetman, N. R. (1970). *Life under the "peculiar institution": Selections from the slave narrative collection.* New York: Holt, Rinehart & Winston.

26

ARTS-BASED INQUIRY

Performing Revolutionary Pedagogy

Susan Finley

The focus of this chapter is the usefulness of arts-based approaches to doing qualitative inquiry when political activism is the goal. References were chosen to include both theoretical discussions about arts-based inquiry methodologies and examples of arts-based representations as well as to underscore the notions of usefulness and political activism that are served by arts-based inquiry. In this review, special attention is given to arts-based research that is positioned toward future developments in the field of socially responsible, politically activist, and locally useful research methodologies. From an historical perspective and for the purpose of defining arts-based research, the chapter addresses concerns and issues that have dominated discussions about arts-based research methodologies. Ultimately, it is argued that arts-based research can contribute greatly to "a radical ethical aesthetic . . . [that] grounds its representations of the world in a set of interpretive practices that implement critical race, queer, and Third World postcolonial theory" (Denzin, 2000, p. 261).

This chapter begins with a description of characteristics of arts-based research that render it unique among the various forms of postmodern qualitative inquiry. Following this characterization of arts-based research, it presents a skeletal outline of broader social features that provide a contextual backdrop for a radical, ethical, and revolutionary arts-based inquiry. Finally, the chapter concludes with an example of community-based, activist, arts-based inquiry. The genealogy of arts-based research that I have chosen to follow is couched in the widely shared belief that social science inquiry is always moral and political, and I further interpret this as a timely proclamation that its practitioners should, therefore, be purposeful in performing inquiry that is activist, engages in public criticism, and is resistant to neoconservative discourses that threaten social justice. Moreover, I believe that this purposeful turn to a revolutionary, performative research aesthetics facilitates critical race, indigenous, queer, feminist, and border studies.

▣ Postmodern Integrations of Activism, Social Science, and Art: Defining the Features of Arts-Based Inquiry

Arts-based inquiry has emerged in postcolonial postmodern contexts, woven from complex threads of social, political, and philosophical shifts in perspectives and practices across multiple discourse communities. It has surfaced in the context of a reflexive turn that marked the social sciences, philosophy and literary criticism, science, education, and the arts, and it is evidenced in particular by the narrative turn in sociological discourse.

Arts-based inquiry is one methodological and theoretical genre among many new forms of qualitative inquiry. It is situated within what Lincoln (1995) described as an emerging tradition of participatory critical action research in social science. Practitioners of inquiry in this line propose reinterpretation of the methods and ethics of human social research and seek to construct action-oriented processes for inquiry that are useful within the local community where the research originates. Arts-based inquiry, as it is practiced by academics doing human social research, fits historically within a postmodern framework that features a developing activist dynamic among both artists and social researchers.

Three historical stories are used here to recount the genealogy of a radical aesthetic inquiry: (a) the turn to activist social science, (b) the emergence of arts-based research (and the turn to activist arts), and (c) the turn to a radical, ethical, and revolutionary arts-based inquiry (and the emergence of revolutionary pedagogy).

The Turn to Activist Social Science

Postmodern foundational shifts brought about new conceptualizations of how research works, how meanings are made, and what social purposes research might serve. Social scientists began to act on their realization that traditional techniques of research were not adequate to handle the many questions that needed to be asked when the frame was shifted to take on new and diverse perspectives. For instance, writers such as Guba (1967) identified the proliferation of new questions as a profound movement in social research away from questions concerning technique to questions concerning theory, and he foresaw a reformist movement that would bring "art" to inquiry (p. 64) as researchers sought ways in which to merge theory and practice. New questions prompted new ways of looking, and the transformation of social science research to include qualitative methodologies began full bore by the early 1970s (Schwandt, 2000).

Two primary issues arose to create a space for arts-based social science inquiry. First, the dialogue turned to ethical issues that occur in the relationship between researchers and the communities in which they work. Qualitative researchers had embraced new practices that redefined the roles of researchers and research participants—who no longer were subjects but instead were collaborators or even coresearchers—so that the lines between the researcher and the researched blurred. In the context of this type of locally meaningful inquiry, researchers and participants were actively developing an ethics of care that ultimately became a quality standard in the new paradigm for social science research (Lincoln & Reason, 1996). Rather than following the quantitative scientific model of objectivity, qualitative social science inquiry was increasingly defined as action-based inquiry that takes its forms through interpersonal, political, emotional, moral, and ethical relational skills that develop and are shared between researchers and research participants (Lincoln, 1995; Lincoln & Reason, 1996).

Second, questions and issues arose in this new stance of researchers as community partners and initiated a "crisis of representation" (Denzin & Lincoln, 1994) that prompted questions from researchers. How should research be reported? Are the traditional approaches to dissemination adequate for an expanding audience that includes a local community? How do researchers "write up" their understandings without "othering" their research partners, exploiting them, or leaving them voiceless in the telling of their own stories?

What forms should research take? How can researchers make their work available and useful to participants rather than produce reports in the tradition of academics writing for other academics or policymakers?

Nontraditional methods and revised standards for evaluating research emerged from these questions and in 1995 gave rise to the publication of the journal *Qualitative Inquiry* (edited by Norman Denzin and Yvonna Lincoln) as a location for ongoing discussions about the practices and methodologies that take place in participatory, critical action forms of research (for a review of the first 7 years of publication of *Qualitative Inquiry,* see Finley, 2003a). Writing in *Qualitative Inquiry,* Lincoln (1995) and Lincoln and Reason (1996) identified particular skills that had emerged in the new tradition of inquiry. The skills that were increasingly necessary to new paradigm researchers included interpersonal, political, emotional, moral, and ethical competence; intellectual openness and creativity; and spiritual qualities related to empathy and understanding when confronted with human experience.

In this context of research reform, Eisner (e.g., 1991/1998) also argued that successful researchers in the new social science genre require a different kind of skill base than was previously expected among social researchers. He proposed a graduate school curriculum that values students' developing skills of imagination, perception, and interpretation of the qualities of things as well as mastery of skills of artistic representation. To address the representational crisis, Eisner encouraged reaching into the existing fields of arts and letters: "Art, music, dance, prose, and poetry are some of the forms that have been invented to perform this function" (p. 235). Likewise, Seale (1999) visualized a studio apprenticeship model for learning a wide variety of research skills "in much the same way as artists learn to paint, draw, or sculpt" (p. 476). Similarly, Tierney (1998, 1999) acknowledged that authors' attempts to include multiple textual voices called for narrative range as wide and experimental as offered in literature. Writing in a special issue of *Qualitative Inquiry* devoted to life history research that took its forms in literary genres, Tierney (1999) observed, "What these authors are struggling over is how to get out of the representational straightjacket that social scientists have been in for most of this century" (p. 309). He continued, "The authors want to create greater narrative flexibility in time, space, and voice. Their assumption is that rather than a standard proof akin to the natural scientists, readers make meaning from emotive and affective aspects of a text" (pp. 309–310).

Thus, the turn to activist social science was simultaneous and mutual with the turn to narrative social science research. Casey (1995) explained that methodological shifts in research approaches are tied to political or theoretical interests charged by social and historical circumstances and that narrative research is politically situated in that it "deliberately defies the forces of alienation, anomie, annihilation, authoritarianism, fragmentation, commodification, deprecation, and dispossession" (p. 213). In the context of activism, what is called for is expressive research that portrays the multidimensionality of human life as compared with truth finding, proofs, and conclusivity in traditional social science. Recognition of the power dynamic between the researcher and the researched called for the adaptation of literary forms to serve the purpose of research texts that represent, as vividly as possible, the words as well as the worlds of participants. The prevailing ethics of care among new social science researchers moved narrative discourse (i.e., storytelling) to the forefront of social science research.

Working in this politically and ethically charged context of border crossing, activist researchers broke new ground, offering research narratives in multiple literary forms. Denzin (2004) wrote,

> Experimental, reflexive ways of writing first-person ethnographic texts are now commonplace. Critical narrative perspectives have become a central feature of counter-hegemonic, decolonizing methodologies (Mutua and Swadener, 2004, p. 16). Sociologists, anthropologists, and educators continue to explore new ways of composing ethnography, and cultural criticism is now accepted practice. (p. 1)

Indeed. Columbia University now offers its medical students courses in literature, literary theory, and creative writing as part of its Program in Narrative Medicine (Thernstrom, 2004).

The Emergence of Arts-Based Research

Within the context of burgeoning new practices that merged activist social science and narrative art forms, Eisner (1981) expounded on the differences between scientific and artistic approaches to qualitative research, giving rise to arts-based educational research. One of Eisner's important contributions was his insistence on the power of form to inform that included a call to use many different art forms (e.g., dance, film, plastic arts) as well as the various narrative forms that have proliferated in the new social science paradigm. Eisner's theories are couched in the historical antecedents of artists and social scientists whose works seem virtually interchangeable—art that is social science and social science that is artful. They are especially respectful of the contributions that artists have made to understanding social life. In the new construction of social science, borders were crossed, but boundaries were similarly breached by postmodern artists seeking political voice and power and audience-participant influence in the construction of social values.

Cultural, historical, and political contexts that shaped the reform of social science research similarly invigorated political activism among artists. For example, Felshin (1995) argued that activist art took hold in the context of feminist-driven paradigmatic shifts that emerged during the 1970s and then expanded and institutionalized over the subsequent 20 years. Felshin traced the particular influence of paradigmatic shifts on the role of artists in society. She pointed out, for instance, that whereas activist art addresses a broad spectrum of social issues—homelessness, AIDS, violence against women, environmental neglect, sexism, racism, illegal immigration, and other topics—common methodologies, formal strategies, and activist goals are shared by new paradigm activist artists.

Activist art, in this self-reflective, early postmodern phase, according to Felshin (1995), is characterized by six traits:

- Innovative use of public space to address issues of sociopolitical and cultural significance
- Encouragement of community or public participation in arts making as a means of effecting social change
- Engagement of community participants in acts of self-expression or self-representation as a way of promoting voice and visibility among participants and of making the personal political
- Use of mainstream media techniques (e.g., billboards, posters, subway and bus advertising, newspaper inserts) to connect to a wider audience and to subvert the usual uses of commercial forms
- Immersion in community for preliminary research and collaborations among artists and communities/constituencies that share a personal stake in the issues addressed
- Conscious use of public spaces to contextualize artworks and to encourage audiences to define themselves not as passive spectators but rather as active participants in the artworks

In sum, Felshin defined "new public art" in terms that recollect Lincoln's (1995) descriptions of developing trends in "new social science." In this border-crossing dynamic, new work that has been created stands neither inside nor outside the realms of social science or art; instead, this work is located in the spaces formed by emotionality, intellect, and identity.

In arts-based research, paradigms for making meaning in the contextual realms of art and social science collide, coalesce, and restructure to become something that is not strictly identifiable as either art or science. As Ulmer (1994) observed, "To do heuretics is to cross the discourses of art and theory" (p. 81). *Heuretics* refers to creative processes of discovery and invention such as those that have been enjoyed by arts-based researchers who have consciously brought the methodologies of the arts to define new practices of human social inquiry. Eisner offered seven organizing premises that make explicit his definition of arts-based inquiry, and his formative book, *The Enlightened Eye* (Eisner, 1991/1998), is presented as an argument in support of each of the seven foundations:

1. There are multiple ways in which the world can be known. Artists, writers, and dancers, as well as scientists, have important things to tell about the world.
2. Human knowledge in a constructed form of experience and, therefore, is a reflection of mind as well as of nature. Knowledge is made and not simply discovered.
3. The terms through which humans represent their conception of the world have a major influence on what they are able to say about it.
4. The effective use of any form through which the world is known and represented requires intelligence.
5. The selection of a form through which the world is to be represented not only influences what humans can say but also influences what they are likely to experience.
6. Educational inquiry will be more complete and informative as humans increase the range of ways in which they describe, interpret, and evaluate the educational world.
7. The particular forms of representation that become acceptable in the educational research community are as much a political matter as they are an epistemological one. New forms of representation, when acceptable, will require new competencies.

Eisner's argument rests in a multiple intelligences stance that holds that there are varied ways in which the world can be known and that broadening the range of perspectives available for constructing knowledge increases the informative value of research. Arts-based researchers are increasingly using art forms that include visual and performing arts as well as forms borrowed from literature. This presents a boundary crossing among arts-based researchers; it critiques the privilege of language-based ways of knowing, and it further challenges status quo responses to the question "what is research?" There is a political challenge in Eisner's foundational construction. Here again, he noted that who does research and whether it is recognized as research when it is presented in art forms is a political issue linked to education. If research is to become a site for the implementation of critical race, feminist, and Third World methodologies (among others), researchers need to emphasize and confront the power issues underscored in Eisner's foundations. There are multiple socially constructed ways of knowing the world, and diversity is achieved in and through the voices of diverse people brought forward in the act of doing research as well as in representing it. As I have said elsewhere,

> It is an act of political emancipation from the dominant paradigm of science for new paradigm researchers to say "I am doing art" and to mean "I am doing research"—or vice versa. In either utterance, that art and research are common acts makes a political statement. (Finley, 2003a, p. 290)

On the one hand, a communal experience of research requires that the information-gathering and analytical processes of inquiry be communal in nature and open to participation among members of the community that the research intends to serve. On the other hand, the community of care encompassed in the research experience also includes the audiences to research. Making art is a passionate visceral activity that creates opportunities for communion among participants, researchers, and the various audiences who encounter the research text. Arts-based research crosses the boundaries of art and research as defined by conventions formed in historically, culturally bounded contexts of the international art market and in the knowledge market dominated by higher education.

It is important to acknowledge here that both art with political purpose and social inquiry with artistic qualities have long and rich histories. In the arts-based research example, however, what is profoundly different and starkly political is the effort to claim that art is equal to—indeed, sometimes even profoundly more appropriate than—science as a way of understanding. Arts-based research is one of many systemic studies of phenomena undertaken to advance human understanding—not exactly art and certainly not science. As Slattery and Langerock (2002) stated, arts-based research takes place in "synthetical moments—experiences of profound insight that merge time, space, and self in seamless transhistorical moments [not] . . . easily discernible and not clearly categorized within the rigid disciplinary boundaries" of art and science (p. 350). A primary concern for arts-based researchers is how to make the best use of their hybrid, boundary-crossing approaches to inquiry to bring about culturally situated, political aesthetics that are responsive to social dilemmas. The response has been to create and encourage open hermeneutic texts that create spaces for dialogues that blur boundaries among researchers, participants, and audiences so that, ideally, roles reverse and participants lead researchers to new questions, audiences revert to questioning practitioners, and so forth as all interact within the text. In this instance, the text is defined in its broadest possible terms and invokes all of the actions in the world that can be "read."

Intertextuality refers to a kind of play (fullness) between texts. One text plays with the next text; that is, the play of intertextuality is the process of reading through which one text refers to another text in the process of cultural production (Barthes, 1970/1974). Intertextuality in research display points to the more dynamic aspects of cultural production. The meaning texts of social science include all things that can be read, can be interpreted, or are the referents to which people make meanings about their world. Thus, personal identity is created within social structures that are themselves "performance texts" that play into ongoing and always changing social and cultural constructions. For example, Garoian (1999) and Finley (2001) have separately produced examples of collage–assemblage artworks that are self-consciously autobiographical, drawing into their representative forms textual referents to social constructions such as ethnicity, gender, socioeconomic status, and cultural history. Although these works are profoundly personal accounts of "becoming" the people we are, they are also commentaries on cultural histories and the texts that shaped and formed us. The concept of intertextuality goes a long way in explaining why culture and other social constructions are always dynamic.

Aspects of intertextuality form the basis for arts-based inquiry. In the hyphen that connects "arts" and "based" is a textual reference to the arts as a basis for something else, something that is "not art." Connecting activist movements in art and research is one of the fundamental acts of intertextual reading that forms the foundation for arts-based research. Among the particular skills of the arts-based researcher is the ability to play or, perhaps more accurately, to construct a field for play; there is a physical dimension to making something, a confluence of mind and body applied in efforts to understand (see also Butler, 1997, 1999; Finley, 2001; Fox & Geichman, 2001). For Richardson, this physical dimension to cognition implies a "kinesthetic balance" that moves the audience/reader to some kind of action (Richardson & Lockridge, 1998). Moving people to action can be the purpose of arts-based research. The primary characteristics of arts-based research provide a formula for a radical, ethical, and revolutionary qualitative inquiry.

This genealogy of arts-based inquiry exists in the identification of intertextual connections and tensions (i.e., disconnections) among "new wave" social science researchers and storytellers, poets, dancers, painters, weavers, dramatists, and filmmakers who have situated themselves and their work in dynamic and diverse postmodern social structures. A postmodern rewriting of the story of arts-based inquiry methodologies plays out in discontinuous, discordant, and intertextual constructions. That there is a shared urge to use their work to promote revolutionary social justice that brings artists and social scientists into collective discourse is just one such construction.

As Barone (2001a) noted, arts-based inquiry evidences elements of design that are aesthetic in character and that, with variation according to art form, are "selected for their usefulness in recasting the contents of experience into a form with the potential for challenging (sometimes deeply held) beliefs and values" (p. 26). Imagination, community, and communal experience, as well as perceptual, emotional, and sensual awareness, all contribute to the aesthetic dimensions of arts-based research. In arts-based research, the artfulness to be found in everyday living composes the aesthetic (Barone, 2001a; Barone & Eisner, 1997; Dewey, 1934/1958). Denzin (2000) and others have encouraged researchers to focus on the vernacular and to capture the visceral ephemeral moments in daily life. Vernacular, expressive, and contextualized language forms open narratives that promote empathy and care (Barone, 2001b). These entreaties to the vernacular for the purpose of broader audience/participant voice, representation, and appeal, as well as the philosophical appeal to regarding people equally, recall Tolstoy's (1946/1996) comments about art:

> We are accustomed to understand art to be only what we hear and see in theaters, concerts, and exhibitions, together with buildings, statues, poems, and novels. . . . [But] all human life is filled with works of art of every kind—from cradlesong, jest, mimicry, the ornamentation of houses, dress, and utensils, to church services, building monuments, and triumphal processions. It is all artistic activity. (p. 66)

In its use of everyday, localized, and personal language, and in its reliance on texts that are ambiguous and open to interpretation, arts-based research draws people into dialogue and opens the possibility for critical critique of social structures (Barone, 2001a, 2001b). *Performativity* is the writing and rewriting of meanings that continually disrupts the authority of texts. Resistance is a kind of performance that holds up for critique hegemonic texts that have become privileged stories told and retold. All knowledge claims are dependent on ascription within power structures (stories) that are performed within cultural boundaries.

This connection among political resistance, pedagogy, and performance has emerged as a way of understanding, and it represents an arts-based methodological approach for interpreting and taking action (for a more comprehensive discussion of the "dramaturgical turn," see Denzin, 1997, 2003). Dramaturgy as a research form draws from the rich history of politically motivated, activist theater used to resist oppression. Garoian (1999) argued that performances in this genre can be used to "critique dominant cultural assumptions, to construct identity, and to attain political agency" (p. 2). Garoian defined the human body as a "contested site" (p. 23) where the activity of the play enables culturally disenfranchised actors to push against tradition, hegemony, and dominant standpoints. With echoes of Felshin (1995), Garoian drew on the feminist arts movement as a site of activist performance art, particularly with references to the performance artist Suzanne Lacy. Broadening his definition of performance as pedagogy, Garoian observed,

> [Lacy's] art work is performative curriculum because it opens a liminal space, within which a community can engage a critical discourse, a space wherein decisions are contingent upon the collective desires of its citizens, as well as an ephemeral space because it is applicable to the particular time and place for which it has been designed. Thus, for Lacy, communities are contested sites, and performance art is a function of community development. (p. 128)

The community aspects of Lacy's work are accomplished by the involvement of diverse communities of participants as experts and actors examining their own oppression, where expertise is defined by participants' lives in the community. The participants in her work are coresearchers, critiquing and challenging themselves to understand their community and to overcome cultural oppressions that occur there. Thus, art, politics, pedagogy, and inquiry are brought together in performance.

In tracing the evolution of performance as a primary site for revolutionary research methodology, Denzin (2003) explained,

> Ethnography had to be taken out of a purely methodological framework and located first within a performative arena and then within the spaces of pedagogy, where it was understood that the pedagogical is always political. We can now see that interpretive ethnography's subject matter is set by a dialectical pedagogy. This pedagogy connects oppressors and the oppressed in capital's liminal, epiphanic spaces. (p. 31)

The Turn to a Radical, Ethical, and Revolutionary Arts-Based Inquiry

With reference to writers who have advanced the notion of critical performance pedagogy, such as Freire (1970/2001), Giroux (2000, 2001), Kincheloe and McLaren (2000), Conquergood (1998), Garoian (1999), Pineau (1998), and Hill (1998), Denzin (2003) put forward a model of performance ethnography "that moves from interpretation and emotional evocation to praxis, empowerment, and social change" (p. 133).

This turn by Denzin (1999) to critical performance delivered on his charge to critical ethnographers that performative pedagogy is needed to confront race relations and inequalities in the globalized capitalist democratic system. Denzin (2003) explained that, through an evolutionary process, the field of ethnography has reached its current critical, performative pedagogical moment; it is a point in time when performative ethnography can be enacted as critical social practice. A critical performance pedagogy should enable oppressed persons to "unveil the world of oppression and through praxis commit themselves to its transformation" (Freire, 1970/2001, p. 54, cited in Denzin, 2003, p. 30).

It is a shift in perspective and a call to action demanded by the cultural, social, and governmental epoch in which we live. As McLaren (2003) stated, there is renewed intensity in pleas to take reformative action today in the face of globalized oppression and repressive political structures. These "dark times" as McLaren (1999) called them, demand that practitioners and theorists who base their work in an ethics of care and social responsibility will take critical pedagogy to the heights of political action. Revolutionary performance pedagogy must move beyond the dialogical tasks of reframing, refunctioning, and reposing questions and formulations of knowledge that characterize critical pedagogy in preference for action (p. 8). Instead, the call to revolution is ethical: "to make liberation and the abolition of human suffering the goal of the educative enterprise" (p. 5).

Revolutionary pedagogy, as described by McLaren (1999, 2001, 2003), does the following:

- Resists heterogeneity in discourses and representations of history, culture, and politics that ignore the tensions and contradictions lived through raced and gendered difference
- Names and gives voice to nonparticipants in the power structures derived from world capitalism and colonialist practices
- Contests various assaults on protections for the poor, for women, and for people of color
- Challenges the assumptions and ideologies enacted in schooling and attempts to refashion a politics of education to the larger universal values of social democracy
- Offers a provisional glimpse of a new society freed from the bondage of the past
- Creates narrative spaces set against the subjectification of everyday experience and gives rise to an empowered way of being by recognizing and naming, in an uncompromising critique, the everyday signifiers of power and practices of concealment that typically prevent self-knowledge and by discouraging naming the tensions and contradictions wrought by capitalist colonialist practices
- Directly confronts differentiated totalities of contemporary society and their historical imbrications in the world system of global capitalism by engagement in revolutionary transformation (conceived as an opposition to social justice reforms)

From a postmodern perspective, Ulmer (1994) similarly argued for a revolutionary pedagogy that makes its task the transformation of institutions by using the formalizing structures of the institution itself to experimentally rearrange reality for critical effect. He cited Eco (1984, p. 409) to make his case for engaging in "revolutionary" interventionist works that entertain the possibility, as in an ideal "guerilla" semiotics, of "changing the circumstances by virtue of which the receivers choose their own codes of reading. . . . This pragmatic energy of semiotic consciousness shows how a descriptive discipline can also be an active project" (Ulmer, 1994, p. 86).

Social crisis suggests that the next phase in the development of arts-based research will bring into focus the potential for arts-based inquiry to confront postmodern political issues such as diversity and globalization and for its practitioners to implement critical race, queer, and postcolonial epistemologies.

In performance, the emphasis is on doing. Thus, performance creates a specialized (open and dialogic) space that is simultaneously asserted for inquiry and expression. Performance requires some sort of imaginative interpretation of events and the contexts of their occurrences. A performance text redirects attention to the process of doing research rather than looking for truth, answers, and expert knowledge in a final report of findings from the researcher. "Open texts cannot be decontextualized; their (now unpredictable) meanings emerge within the sociology of space and are connected within the reciprocal relationships that exist between people and the political, dynamic qualities of place" (Finley, 2003a, p. 288).

Such performances are possible in any art form, including visual arts, music, dance, poetry, and narrative. In posing questions, analyzing information, making discoveries, and/or engaging in political action, the performative text is a politically, socially, and contextually grounded work (in the example of music, see Daspit, 2000; Frith, 1996).

It is in this liminal space that distinctions are made between private and public spheres, thereby rendering personal identity, culture, and social order unstable, indeterminate, inchoate, and amenable to change. Giroux (1995) argued, "It is within the tension between what might be called the trauma of identity formation and the demands of public life that cultural work is both theorized and made performative" (p. 5, cited in Garoian, 1999, pp. 40–41). From within the openings that are created by arts research, people—just ordinary people, you and me, researchers as participants as audiences—can implement new visions of dignity, care, democracy, and other postcolonial ways of being in the world.

Arts-Based Inquiry as "Guerrilla Warfare": Taking Back the Streets

Denzin (1999) urged a new movement in qualitative inquiry in which researchers take up their pens (and their cameras, paintbrushes, bodies, and voices) so that we might "conduct our own ground-level guerrilla warfare against the oppressive structures of our everyday lives" (pp. 568, 572). Following Freire (1970/2001; see also discussion of this point in Denzin, 2003), there are two primary tasks that are the specific aims of human social inquiry in the context of a revolutionary arts-based pedagogy: (a) to unveil oppression and (b) to transform praxis. What follows is a discussion of those two tasks and an example of radical, ethical, and revolutionary arts-based inquiry. This inquiry has taken place (and is continuing) among various diverse communities of economically poor children and their families (both sheltered and unsheltered), street youths (unaccompanied minors, runaway and throwaway children, travelers, and other people between 17 and 24 years of age who live on the streets), and tent communities where unhoused people govern their own lives. It also includes the experience of field-based, community-centered research among college students, teachers, shelter workers, and other social services providers as well as the community more broadly. The discourse community is intentionally broad so as to involve as many individuals and role representatives as I can draw into dialogue, critical critique, inquiry, and social action around issues of poverty and homelessness as they influence the educational lives and experiences of children, youths, and adults. (For examples, see Finley, 2000a, 2000b, 2003b; Finley & Finley, 1999. For a discussion of Finley, 2000a, as participatory performance inquiry, see Denzin, 2003. For an adaptation into a stage performance of these and other research publications in this line of social research, see Saldaña, Finley, & Finley, in press. For discussions of ethnomethodology, see Saldaña, 1999, 2003.)

"Mystory" Performances

With the intention of empowering children living in shelter and transitional housing to become active learners in classrooms, the At Home At School (AHAS) program that I organize brings together K–8 (kindergarten through eighth grade) children, their families, and preservice and inservice teachers in a field-based community project. All of us are students; we are both the researchers and the researched following an arts-based inquiry model of new paradigm human studies. Children experience arts-based literacy instruction (broadly conceived) throughout the school year during after-school educational enrichment and in an intensive 6-week summer school program. Doing drama, literature, visual arts, gardening, and computer technology are the mainstays of the children's program. Teachers learn firsthand what it means for children to live in a shelter or temporary apartment, they experience the encumbrances of poverty to education more closely than most have experienced previously, and they learn methods for integrating arts across the disciplines. Children in this setting have experienced the criminalization of homelessness in America, marginalization in schools, and disrupted lives in changing homes and schools as they and their families search for affordable housing. Of course, some are further inured to the vagaries of addictions, imprisonments of parents and siblings, and other social manifestations of poverty in a minimum-wage economy.

While enrolled in AHAS, children who reside in shelter and transitional housing live in a system that regulates their time—with rules for when they can bathe, sleep, eat, and so forth—simply because of their status as unhoused (longtime or recently) and economically poor persons.

Variously, in addition to strengthening academic performance as a means to build self-esteem, my goal with the children who attend AHAS is to draw their attention to the relationship between themselves and society so as to help them redirect the anger that they sometimes feel at themselves and their parents back toward the system of sustained poverty that subverts them. The goal is for the children to embrace their understandings of themselves and society in terms of political struggle and, in so doing, to encourage them to imagine all that they can do and be in their lives—and to dispute what might seem to be a destiny of lifelong poverty. My task is to provide tools for constructing new autobiographical images and then to encourage ongoing practices that these children and their families might use to transform their lives.

Equally important is my goal of providing tools for K–12 educators to recognize that their own compliance with a system that degrades and disenfranchises these children leaves "blood on their hands." The goal is to encourage them to find ways in which to assist students toward newly formed life stories built on the notion of a caring community that includes educators who, while part of the system, will use the system in its own transformation. Because art is a visceral and personal experience that gives expression to affective ways of being and knowing, I introduce arts-based inquiry in this curriculum as a way for the children and their teachers to create their own "mystories." Mystory performances are personal cultural texts (e.g., narratives, paintings, poetry, music) that contextualize important personal experiences and problems within the institutional settings and historical moments where their authors (e.g., painters, collagists, dramatists) find themselves. They attempt to make sense of seemingly senseless moments in life, to capture frustrations and turmoil and open them for critical critique. They open a liminal space, and create an open and dialogic text, where a diverse group of people can be brought to collective understanding of the sites of power, of conflicts between the empowered and the powerless, and from this point of understanding can begin to address the need for social change (for further discussions of the functions of mystory, see Denzin, 2003; Ulmer, 1989).

Teacher-led projects in which children have created mystories that have taken place in the context of AHAS include an extended effort at portraiture during which children painted their life histories first by learning to work within the symbolic language of colors, lines, and space and brush work while working with charcoal, pens, and water and acrylic paints. Over a period of roughly 3 months (shelter stays are limited to 90 days, so there was a changing population of children, with some attending all of the sessions and some attending only a few), during weekly sessions children painted self-portraits, pictures of objects, and so forth to tell life stories. The project culminated with a day of communal painting of five mural panels (4 feet by 4 feet) with the theme of "the story of us." Again, the children followed up the session by verbally processing the meanings they intended when they began painting and by defining the meanings they constructed during the process.

Amid likenesses of "Sponge Bob," trees, peace symbols, and American flags, personal and community stories emerged. One child who had practiced and then painted a very pleasing tree blacked it out with other paint so that it was no longer even visible on the canvas, and two other boys joined him in his "scorched earth" efforts. When the child expressed his anger and frustration with multiple heart surgeries that left him physically smaller than his peers—a personal story, but one that had community ties—his teachers were better prepared to understand his occasional displays of seemingly unfounded temper. Telling his life story, he found compassion and understanding among his peers and teachers, and he began to attend tutoring sessions each week with absolute regularity, had fewer outbursts, and began (over a period of several months) to improve his school performance.

In this same setting, three girls had painted a scene in which two (gender-neutral) couples walked among trees and flowers. On close inspection, one couple held hands while the other couple did not, and the couple not holding hands had tears flowing from their eyes. These girls' storytelling turned to personal remembrances of divorce, of grandparents left in other states as a result of moves, and of feelings of being disconnected from peers when at school. From that point, beginning with the girls who had painted the scene but also involving other children, a conversation grew about loving their own mothers but wanting to build lasting relationships in their own lives. Because the scene took a mural space very close to a U.S. flag, next to which another student had written "give peace a chance" and several had drawn peace signs, conversation shifted again, now having moved from the realm of personal experiences of divorce and separation, to a discussion of world instability and U.S. dominance, and the instability to children's lives introduced by war. Nothing was resolved—there were disagreements as to whether the United States was right or wrong to go to war—but most important was that there was a conversation about the war at all; children were expressing their opinions about world events and were confident that their ideas mattered. I could not help but think that students' understandings wrought by telling mystories would carry over, at least in minimal ways, to life at school.

Painted portraits are just one way for the children to tell "the story of us." We also have had occasions for movie making, writing, and performing rap and blues, and we have constructed a community in which personal storytelling is rewarded. Against this backdrop of unveiling personal and systemic events that have shaped the lives of the children, two events that have occurred convince me that we are achieving transformative praxis in AHAS.

First, a rule prohibited people living in the shelter from fraternizing with people living in transitional housing by going back and forth to each other's places of residence. Two 12-year-old girls—one who lived in a transitional housing apartment and the other who was housed at the shelter—became very close friends during tutoring. While the girls were making plans to visit one another after the program at the apartment of one of the girls, another student reminded them of the rule and that if it were enforced, the girls' families would be asked to leave. This was followed by a discussion among the children in which they recognized how unfair the situation was. They decided that they had to do something about it. Their solution was to write in their journals about the situation and then to show me what they had written and enlist my help in challenging the rule. They disputed the system, and they took action to try and change the rule. In the end, because of their problem solving, the rule was changed.

Second, the painted murals were hung, along with excerpts from the narrative sessions, in the gallery of the Student Services building at the university where I teach. I took a class of 11 practicing teachers (who were enrolled in my advanced children's literature course) to see the display. Of these 11 teachers, 5 began volunteer tutoring on a weekly basis and several carried over beyond the end of the semester. In addition, they conducted book drives at their schools so that every child could take a book home with him or her. Most important, all of the teachers made statements similar to this comment offered by one:

> I have always had these children in my classes, and I have always resented them being there. I have seen them as unprepared, [as] underparented, and as a waste of my time. I have changed. I'm a good teacher to a lot of the children. My goal now is—truly, not just as mere rhetoric—to become a teacher of all of the children in my classroom. These children are now my children.

In sum, although the painting of the portraits affected these children's perceptions of themselves as learners and in both their current and future participation in society, what is perhaps more profound is the impact that the children have had, through their paintings and stories, on other children in similar circumstances who will attend classes taught by the teachers and preservice teachers who have adopted activist pedagogies and practices.

As an educator, I want to encourage children to learn early to become lifelong activists who are equipped for guerrilla warfare against oppression by virtue of their ability to name their oppressors, dispute oppressive practices that are stereotyped or systematized into seeming normality, imagine a life lived otherwise, and then construct and enact a script that shifts them into an alternative space. Art, in any of its various forms, provides media for self-reflection, self-expression, and communication between and among creators and audiences. Performing social change begins with artful ways of seeing and knowing ourselves and the world in which we live.

The AHAS example demonstrates that art can be the catalyst for audiences to see themselves differently, to receive messages, and to find a level of understanding about people that they would have ignored in different circumstances. Knowing these children through their artful expressions of themselves motivated a group of adults to embrace their empathetic emotions and to give something of their time and expertise as teachers. Yet once they were in direct contact with the artists, the teachers became students of the social structures they helped to perpetuate and began to write small scripts based on the need for change, with book drives and gifts of books being the foundation for change in the emotional and physical spaces in which teaching and learning occur in their schools and classrooms. For the teachers, it takes a sustained effort at learning to use the tools that are available to create and revise their own self-portraits; practice is required. Artful performance in the community will occur if teachers look deeply enough into themselves and can paint their way to a more humanistic and communal portraiture than schools typically allow.

In these examples, the children have become researchers and artists of their own lives. Other examples, not given here because of space considerations, would demonstrate the arts-based inquiry that teachers have experienced in this context. Still another group of examples would be my own inquiries into the experiences of AHAS, some of which have been coauthored and copresented with K–12 students, teachers, street youths, and street artists. In this schema, arts-based research makes possible the erasure of distinctions between the researcher and the researched. We all are inquirers into our experiences and collaborators in efforts to create a better space to share our lives.

A major dilemma for arts-based researchers has emerged around definitions of quality criteria. What is good arts-based research? Is it incumbent on arts-based research to demonstrate the best in terms of artistic skill and craftsmanship? And, if demonstrations of artistic skill are necessary to arts-based research, can quality arts-based inquiry be achieved by community-members (e.g., children and teachers, as well as university researchers) who are not educated in the art-form chosen as the representational text? How far can arts-based researchers go in becoming "community partners" where distinctions between the roles of researcher and researched converge? Who is an artist? Who is a researcher? These are questions that underscore the postmodern turn in sociological research, but they have become somewhat polarizing issues among arts-based researchers. Some practitioners of arts-based inquiry argue for the need to develop an established research tradition that has coherence and integrity in its methodological and epistemological commitments, whereas others take the position I have taken in this chapter—that quality control efforts force a singular way of knowing and shut off the possibilities for diverse voices and expressions. Performativity is the quality criterion I have emphasized in this chapter as being necessary to achieve arts-based approaches to inquiry that is activist, engages in public criticism, is resistant to threats to social justice, and purposefully intends to facilitate critical race, indigenous, queer, and feminist and border studies as entrée to multiple, new, and diverse ways of understanding and living in the world.

References

Barone, T. (2001a). Science, art, and the predispositions of educational researchers. *Educational Researcher, 30*(7), 24–28.

Barone, T. (2001b). *Teaching eternity: The enduring outcomes of teaching.* New York: Columbia University, Teachers College Press.

Barone, T., & Eisner, E. (1997). *Handbook on complementary methods for educational research* (R. Yeager, Ed.). Washington, DC: American Educational Research Association.

Barthes, R. (1974). *S/Z* (R. Miller, Trans.). New York: Hill & Wang. (Original work published in 1970)

Butler, J. (1997). *Excitable speech: A politics of the performative.* New York: Routledge.

Butler, J. (1999). Revisiting bodies and pleasures. *Theory, Culture, and Society, 16,* 11–20.

Casey, K. (1995). The new narrative research in education. *Review of Research in Education, 21,* 211–253.

Conquergood, D. (1998). Beyond the text: Toward a performative cultural politics. In S. J. Dailey (Ed.), *The future of performance studies: Visions and revisions* (pp. 25–36). Washington, DC: National Communication Association.

Denzin, N. K. (1997). Performance texts. In W. G. Tierney & Y. S. Lincoln (Eds.), *Representation and the text: Re-framing the narrative voice* (pp. 179–217). Albany: State University of New York Press.

Denzin, N. K. (1999). Two-stepping in the 90s. *Qualitative Inquiry, 5,* 568–572.

Denzin, N. K. (2000). Aesthetics and the practices of qualitative inquiry. *Qualitative Inquiry, 6,* 256–265.

Denzin, N. K. (2003). *Performance ethnography: Critical pedagogy and the politics of culture.* Thousand Oaks, CA: Sage.

Denzin, N. K. (2004). *The First International Congress of Qualitative Inquiry.* Retrieved November 15, 2004, from www.qi2005.org/index.html

Denzin, N. K., & Lincoln, Y. S. (Eds.). (1994). *Handbook of qualitative research.* Thousand Oaks, CA: Sage.

Daspit, T. (2000). Rap pedagogies: Bringing the noise of knowledge born in the microphone to radical education. In T. Despit & J. A. Weaver (Eds.), *Popular culture and critical pedagogy: Reading, constructing, connecting* (pp. 163–182). New York: Garland.

Dewey, J. (1958). *Art as experience.* New York. Capricorn. (Original work published in 1934)

Eco, U. (1984). *La structure absente: Introduction a la recherché semiotique* (U. Esposito-Torrigiani, Trans.). Paris: Mercured de France.

Eisner, E. W. (1981). On the difference between scientific and artistic approaches to qualitative research. *Educational Researcher, 10*(4), 5–9.

Eisner, E. W. (1998). *The enlightened eye: Qualitative inquiry and the enhancement of educational practice.* Upper Saddle River, NJ: Prentice Hall. (Original work published in 1991)

Felshin, N. (Ed.). (1995). *But is it art? The spirit of art as activism.* Seattle, WA: Bay Press.

Finley, S. (2000a). "Dream child": The role of poetic dialogue in homeless research. *Qualitative Inquiry, 6,* 432–434.

Finley, S. (2000b). From the streets to the classrooms: Street intellectuals as teacher educators, collaborations in revolutionary pedagogy. In K. Sloan & J. T. Sears (Eds.), *Democratic curriculum theory and practice: Retrieving public spaces* (pp. 98–113). Troy, NY: Educator's International Press.

Finley, S. (2001). Painting life histories. *Journal of Curriculum Theorizing, 17*(2), 13–26.

Finley, S. (2003a). Arts-based inquiry in *QI:* Seven years from crisis to guerrilla warfare. *Qualitative Inquiry, 9,* 281–296.

Finley, S. (2003b). The faces of dignity: Rethinking the politics of homelessness and poverty in America. *Qualitative Studies in Education, 16,* 509–531.

Finley, S., & Finley, M. (1999). Sp'ange: A research story. *Qualitative Inquiry, 5,* 313–337.

Fox, C. T., with Geichman, J. (2001). Creating research questions from strategies and perspectives of contemporary art. *Curriculum Inquiry, 31,* 33–49.

Freire, P. (2001). *Pedagogy of the oppressed.* New York: Continuum. (Original work published in 1970)

Frith, S. (1996). *Performing rites: On the value of popular music.* Cambridge, MA: Harvard University Press.

Garoian, C. R. (1999). *Performing pedagogy: Toward an art of politics.* Albany: State University of New York Press.

Giroux, H. A. (1995). Borderline artists, cultural workers, and the crisis of democracy. In C. Becker (Ed.), *The artist in society: Rights, rules, and responsibilities* (pp. 4–14). Chicago: New Art Examiner.

Giroux, H. A. (2000). *Impure acts: The practical politics of cultural studies.* New York: Routledge.

Giroux, H. A. (2001). Cultural studies as performative politics. *Cultural Studies–Critical Methodologies, 1,* 5–23.

Guba, E. (1967). The expanding concept of research. *Theory Into Practice, 6*(2), 57–65.

Hill, R. T. G. (1998). Performance pedagogy across the curriculum. In S. J. Dailey (Ed.), *The future of performance studies: Visions and revisions* (pp. 141–144). Washington, DC: National Communication Association.

Kincheloe, J. L., & McLaren, P. (2000). Rethinking critical theory and qualitative research. In N. K. Denzin & Y. S. Lincoln (Eds.), *Handbook of qualitative research* (2nd ed., pp. 279–313). Thousand Oaks, CA: Sage.

Lincoln, Y. S. (1995). Emerging criteria for quality in qualitative and interpretive research. *Qualitative Inquiry, 1,* 275–289.

Lincoln, Y. S., & Reason, P. (Eds.). (1996). Quality in human inquiry [special issue]. *Qualitative Inquiry, 2*(1).

McLaren, P. (1999). Contesting capital: Critical pedagogy and globalism. *Current Issues in Comparative Education, 1*(2). Retrieved January 3, 2004, from www.tc.columbia.edu/cice/v011nr2/a1152.htm

McLaren, P. (2001). Che Guevara, Paulo Freire, and the politics of hope: Reclaiming critical pedagogy. *Cultural Studies–Critical Methodologies, 1,* 108–131.

McLaren, P. (2003). Towards a critical revolutionary pedagogy: An interview with Peter McLaren by Michael Pozo (Ed.). *St. John's University Humanities Review, 2*(1). Retrieved December 16, 2004, from www.axisoflogic.com/cgibin/exec/view.pl?archive=38&num=3801

Mutua, K., & Swadener, B. B. (2004). Introduction. In K. Mutua & B. B. Swadener (Eds.), *Decolonizing research in cross-cultural contexts: Critical personal narratives* (pp. 1–23). Albany: State University of New York Press.

Pineau, E. L. (1998). Performance studies across the curriculum: Problems, possibilities, and projections. In S. J. Dailey (Ed.), *The future of performance studies: Visions and revisions* (pp. 128–135). Washington, DC: National Communication Association.

Richardson, L., & Lockridge, E. (1998). Fiction and ethnography: A conversation. *Qualitative Inquiry, 4,* 328–336.

Saldaña, J. (1999). Playwriting with data: Ethnographic performance texts. *Youth Theatre Journal, 13,* 60–71.

Saldaña, J. (2003). Dramatizing data: A primer. *Qualitative Inquiry, 9,* 218–236.

Saldaña, J., Finley, S., & Finley, M. (in press). Street rat. In J. Saldaña (Ed.), *Ethnodrama: An anthology of reality theatre.* Walnut Creek, CA: AltaMira.

Schwandt, T. (2000). Three epistemological stances for qualitative inquiry. In N. K. Denzin & Y. S. Lincoln (Eds.), *Handbook of qualitative research* (2nd ed., pp. 189–213). Thousand Oaks, CA: Sage.

Seale, C. (1999). Quality in arts-based research. *Qualitative Inquiry, 5,* 465–478.

Slattery, P., & Langerock, N. (2002). Blurring art and science: Synthetical moments on the borders. *Curriculum Inquiry, 32,* 349–356.

Thernstrom, M. (2004, April 18). The writing cure: Can understanding narrative make you a better doctor? *The New York Times Magazine,* pp. 42–47.

Tierney, W. G. (1998). Life history's history: Subjects foretold. *Qualitative Inquiry, 4,* 49–70.

Tierney, W. G. (1999). Guest editor's introduction. Writing life's history. *Qualitative Inquiry, 5,* 307–312.

Tolstoy, L. (1996). *What is art?* (A. Maude, Trans.). New York: Penguin. (Original work published in 1946)

Ulmer, G. (1989). *Teletheory.* New York: Routledge.

Ulmer, G. (1994). The heuretics of deconstruction. In P. Brunette & D. Wills (Eds.), *Deconstruction and the visual arts: Art, media, architecture* (pp. 80–96). New York: Cambridge University Press.

27

THE INTERVIEW

From Neutral Stance to Political Involvement

Andrea Fontana and James H. Frey

The movie *Memento* begins at the end, showing a killing and then backing up to the beginning scene by scene. We do not go that far here; after all, this is not a thriller but rather a chapter about interviewing. Yet we cut to the chase, beginning with the razor-edge state of interviewing and then backing up to the old days and progressing to our days through the chapter, with full knowledge of where we are going. If you think that this will spoil the ending, skip the first section and read it last.

We have no actual killing here, but metaphorically, traditional interviewing—as it is commonly understood—does get killed. The perpetrators (or liberators, depending on your point of view) are Kong, Mahoney, and Plummer (2002), the coauthors of "Queering the Interview." They focus on the changing public perception of gays and lesbians in the United States during the past few decades and on how that changing perception altered the tone of interviewing those groups. Decades ago, when gays were "homosexuals," the interview "was clearly an instrument of pathological diagnosis," yet when the milieu became one of social reform, "the interview became a tool of modernist democratization and ultimately of social reform" (p. 240).

What this tells us about interviewing is that it is inextricably and unavoidably historically, politically, and contextually bound. This boundedness refutes the whole tradition of the interview of gathering objective data to be used neutrally for scientific purposes. If *queering* the interview denies its primary goal, what should be done? We could reject interviewing altogether. That is hardly feasible in today's society, which has been tabbed as "the interview society," where everyone gets interviewed and gets a moment in the sun, even if only to reveal dastardly aberrations on the *Jerry Springer* show. We certainly do not want to trivialize the interview in the same way as the mass media have tended to do. What should we do? Very simply, some sociologists have turned the timetable and returned the scope of the interview to that of the predecessors of interactionism, the pragmatists, focusing on social amelioration. If the interview cannot be a neutral tool (and we will see that it never really was), why not turn it into a walking stick to help some people get on their feet? This is where the interview is now, and we outline this development next.

▣ Empathetic Interviewing

"Empathetic" emphasizes taking a stance, contrary to the scientific image of interviewing, which is based on the concept of neutrality. Indeed, much of traditional interviewing concentrates on the language of scientific neutrality and the techniques to achieve it. Unfortunately, these goals are largely mythical.

As many have argued convincingly (Atkinson & Silverman, 1997; Fontana, 2002; Hertz, 1997b; Holstein & Gubrium, 1995; Scheurich, 1995), interviewing is not merely the neutral exchange of asking questions and getting answers. Two (or more) people are involved in this process, and their exchanges lead to the creation of a collaborative effort called *the interview.* The key here is the "active" nature of this process (Holstein & Gubrium, 1995) that leads to a contextually bound and mutually created story—the interview. Some have highlighted the problematics of the interview. Atkinson and Silverman (1997) drew attention to the asymmetric nature of the interview and to the fact that the final product is a pastiche that is put together by fiat. Scheurich (1995) observed that the interviewer is a person, historically and contextually located, carrying unavoidable conscious and unconscious motives, desires, feelings, and biases—hardly a neutral tool. Scheurich maintained, "The conventional, positivist view of interviewing vastly underestimates the complexity, uniqueness, and indeterminateness of each one-to-one human interaction" (p. 241).

If we proceed from the belief that neutrality is not possible (even assuming that it would be desirable), then taking a stance becomes unavoidable. An increasing number of social scientists have realized that they need to interact as persons with the interviewees and acknowledge that they are doing so. Long ago, Douglas (1985) advocated revealing personal feelings and private situations to the interviewee as a quid pro quo of good faith. Yet Douglas, despite his openness, still placed primary importance on the traditional notion of obtaining better and more comprehensive responses; he failed to see that his openness was merely a technique to persuade the interviewee to reveal more and be more honest in his or her responses.

New empathetic approaches in interviewing differ from the conventional approach; they see that it is time to stop treating the interviewee as a "clockwork orange," that is, looking for a better juicer (techniques) to squeeze the juice (answers) out of the orange (living person/interviewee). Scheurich (1995) concurred: "The modernist representation is not sheer fabrication, but all of the juice of the lived experience has been squeezed out" (p. 241). The new empathetic approaches take an ethical stance in favor of the individual or group being studied. The interviewer becomes an advocate and partner in the study, hoping to be able to use the results to advocate social policies and ameliorate the conditions of the interviewee. The preference is to study oppressed and underdeveloped groups.

Kong and colleagues (2002), as mentioned earlier, showed that the change toward empathy might not be so much of an individual decision as it is the result of changing historical, political, and cultural perspectives. They discussed changes in interviewing regarding same-sex experiences. They showed that during the past few decades, as Americans underwent a profound change from "homosexuals" to "gays," "*the sensibilities of interviewing are altered with the changing social phenomena that constitute the "interview*" (p. 240, italics in original). Thus, interviews changed from "instruments of pathological diagnosis" (p. 240) to become much more humanized in the wake of social reform. Interviews became "a methodology of friendship" (p. 254). Kong and colleagues concluded that the interview is bound in historical, political, and cultural moments and that as those moments change, so does the interview. The work by these three coauthors was radical in that it collapsed decades of alleged "objective interview findings." As they clearly stated, framing the interview within specific parameters (i.e., "We are interviewing pathological, sick, deviant individuals" vs. "We are interviewing individuals who should not be ostracized because of their diverse sexual sensibilities") will lead to entirely different results. These results will be anything but neutral;

they will be politically laden and used for or against the group studied.

Researchers have strongly emphasized the removal of barriers between the interviewer and the interviewee in the process of interviewing women. Many female researchers advocate a partnership between the researcher and respondents, who should work together to create a narrative—the interview—that could be beneficial to the group studied. Most researchers address factors beyond that of gender. Hertz and Ferguson (1997) addressed the plight of single mothers—both heterosexuals and lesbians. Weston (1998) also attended to groups of same-sex preferences in academia. Collins (1990) added the element of being black to that of being female. Denzin (2003a, 2003b) extended the interest in amelioration of oppressed groups to that in reporting the results of the study. He maintained that traditional reporting modes are ill equipped to capture the attention and hearts of the readers (see also Behar, 1996). Denzin (2003a) issued a "manifesto" calling for performance ethnography: "We need to explore performance ethnography as a vehicle for enacting a performative cultural politics of hope" (p. 202).

Some researchers are becoming keenly attuned to the fact that in knowing "others," we come to know "ourselves." Holstein and Gubrium (1995) urged researchers to be reflexive not only about *what* the interview accomplishes but also about *how* the interview is accomplished, thereby uncovering the ways in which we go about creating a text. Wasserfall (1993) noted that even when the researcher and respondents are women, if there is a discordant view of the world (in her study, a political one), there is a great divide between the two. She added that, despite claims to "friendship and cooperation," it is the researcher who ultimately cuts and pastes together the narrative, choosing what will become a part of it and what will be cut. Similarly, El-Or (1992) pointed to a gap between the researcher and respondents created by religious differences (in her study, when a nonreligious ethnographer studies an ultra-orthodox group). El-Or also reflexively addressed the notion of "friendship" between the researcher and respondents and concluded that it is fleeting and somewhat illusory: "We can't be friends because she [the respondent] was the object and we both know it" (p. 71). Atkinson and Silverman (1997) also emphasized self-restraint and self-reflexivity in warning that researchers should not replace a false god (the authorial monologue of classical sociology) with another (the monologue of a privileged speaking respondent). Researchers should not privilege any ways of looking at the world or at a particular technique but should instead continue to question, question, and question.

Atkinson and Silverman's (1997) chilly warning can be turned on the proponents of the empathetic approach because they strongly privilege a method of inquiry over all others. Yet as Denzin (2003a) observed, "Symbolic interactionism is at a crossroad. We need to reclaim the progressive heritage given to us by DuBois, Mead, Dewey, and Blumer" (p. 202). As Fontana (2003) pointed out, perhaps Denzin (and we could add all of the others) is being a postmodern Don Quixote in his approach, yet the windmills of racism, sexism, and ageism are not mere shadows in our minds; rather, they are very real and very oppressive. The empathetic approach is not merely a "method of friendship"; it is a method of morality because it attempts to restore the sacredness of humans before addressing any theoretical or methodological concerns.

We too have "queered" the chapter to follow by framing it in the light of today's development and new awareness in interviewing. Let us turn the time back and see how interviewing has come to be where it is.

▣ Interviewing in Perspective

Asking questions and getting answers is a much harder task that it may seem at first. The spoken or written word always has a residue of ambiguity, no matter how carefully we word the questions and how carefully we report or code the answers. Yet interviewing is one of the most common and powerful ways in which we try to understand our fellow humans. Interviewing includes a wide variety of forms and a multiplicity of uses. The most common form of interviewing involves individual, face-to-face verbal interchange, but interviewing can also take the form of face-to-face group interchange and telephone surveys. It can be structured, semistructured, or unstructured. Interviewing can be used for marketing research, political opinion polling, therapeutic reasons, or academic analysis. It can be used for the purpose of measurement, or its scope can be the understanding of an individual or a group perspective. An interview can be a one-time brief exchange, such as 5 minutes over the telephone, or it can take place over multiple lengthy sessions, at times spanning days as in life history interviewing.

The use of interviewing to acquire information is so extensive today that it has been said that we live in an "interview society" (Atkinson & Silverman, 1997; Silverman, 1993). Increasingly, qualitative researchers are realizing that interviews are not neutral tools of data gathering but rather active interactions between two (or more) people leading to negotiated, contextually based results. Thus, the focus of interviews is moving to encompass the *hows* of people's lives (the constructive work involved in producing order in everyday life) as well as the traditional *whats* (the activities of everyday life) (Cicourel, 1964; Dingwall, 1997; Gubrium & Holstein, 1997, 1998; Holstein & Gubrium, 1995; Kvale, 1996; Sarup, 1996; Seidman, 1991; Silverman, 1993, 1997a). Interviews are moving toward new electronic forms and have seen a return to the pragmatic ideal of political involvement.

In this chapter, after discussing the interview society, we examine interviews by beginning with structured methods of interviewing and gradually moving to more qualitative types, examining interviews as negotiated texts and ending with electronic interviews and new trends in interviewing. We begin by briefly outlining the history of interviewing and then turn to a discussion of the academic uses of interviewing. Although the focus of this volume is qualitative research, to demonstrate the full import of interviewing, we need to discuss the major types of interviewing (structured, group, and unstructured) as well as other ways in which to conduct interviews. One caveat is that, in discussing the various interview methods, we use the language and rationales employed by practitioners of these methods; we note our differences with these practitioners and our criticisms later in the chapter in our discussion of gendered and other new types of qualitative interviewing. Following our examination of structured interviewing, we address in detail the various elements of qualitative interviewing. We then discuss the problems related to gendered interviewing, as well as issues of interpretation and reporting, as we broach some considerations related to ethical issues. Finally, we note some of the new trends in qualitative interviewing.

◙ THE INTERVIEW SOCIETY

Before embarking on our journey through interviewing per se, we comment briefly on the tremendous reliance on interviewing in the U.S. society today. This reliance on interviewing has reached such a level that a number of scholars have referred to the United States as "the interview society" (Atkinson & Silverman, 1997; Silverman, 1993).

Both qualitative and quantitative researchers tend to rely on the interview as the basic method of data gathering whether the purpose is to obtain a rich, in-depth experiential account of an event or episode in the life of the respondent or to garner a simple point on a scale of 2 to 10 dimensions. There is inherent faith that the results are trustworthy and accurate and that the relation of the interviewer to the respondent that evolves during the interview process has not unduly biased the account (Atkinson & Silverman, 1997; Silverman, 1993). The commitment to, and reliance on, the interview to produce narrative experience reflects and reinforces the view of the United States as an interview society.

It seems that everyone—not just social researchers—relies on the interview as a source of information, with the assumption that interviewing results is a true and accurate picture of the respondents' selves and lives. One cannot escape being interviewed; interviews are everywhere in the form of political polls, questionnaires about visits to doctors, housing applications, forms regarding social service eligibility, college applications, talk shows, news programs—the list goes on and on. The interview as a means of data gathering is no longer limited to use by social science researchers and police detectives; it is a "universal mode of systematic inquiry" (Holstein & Gubrium, 1995, p. 1). It seems that nearly any type of question—whether personal, sensitive, probing, upsetting, or accusatory—is fair game and permissible in the interview setting. Nearly all interviews, no matter their purposes (and these can be varied—to describe, to interrogate, to assist, to test, to evaluate, etc.), seek various forms of biographical description. As Gubrium and Holstein (1998) noted, the interview has become a means of contemporary storytelling in which persons divulge life accounts in response to interview inquiries. The media have been especially adept at using this technique.

As a society, we rely on the interview and, by and large, take it for granted. The interview and the norms surrounding the enactment of the respondent and researcher roles have evolved to the point where they are institutionalized and no longer require extensive training; rules and roles are known and shared. (However, there is a growing group of individuals who increasingly question the traditional assumptions of the interview, and we address their concerns later in our discussion of gendered interviewing and new trends in interviewing.) Many practitioners continue to use and take for granted traditional interviewing techniques. It is as if interviewing is now part of the mass culture, so that it has actually become the most feasible mechanism for obtaining information about individuals, groups, and organizations in a society characterized by individuation, diversity, and specialized role relations. Thus, many believe that it is not necessary to "reinvent the wheel" for each interview situation given that "interviewing has become a routine technical practice and a pervasive, taken-for-granted activity in our culture" (Mishler, 1986, p. 23).

This is not to say, however, that the interview is so technical and the procedures are so standardized that interviewers can ignore contextual, societal, and interpersonal elements. Each interview context is one of interaction and relation, and the result is as much a product of this social dynamic as it is the product of accurate accounts and replies. The interview has become a routine and nearly unnoticed part of everyday life. Yet response rates continue to decline, indicating that fewer people are willing to disclose their "selves" or that they are so burdened by requests for interviews that they are much more selective in their choices of which interviews to grant. Social scientists are more likely to recognize, however, that interviews are interactional encounters and that the nature of the social dynamic of the interview can shape the nature of the knowledge generated. Interviewers with less training and experience than social scientists might not recognize when interview participants are "actively" constructing knowledge around questions and responses (Holstein & Gubrium, 1995).

We now turn to a brief history of interviewing to frame its roots and development.

◘ The History of Interviewing

At least one form of interviewing or another has been with us for a very long time. Even ancient Egyptians conducted population censuses (Babbie, 1992). During more recent times, the tradition of interviewing evolved from two trends. First, interviewing found great popularity and widespread use in clinical diagnosis and counseling where the concern was with the quality of responses. Second, during World War I, interviewing came to be widely employed in psychological testing, with the emphasis being on measurement (Maccoby & Maccoby, 1954).

The individual generally credited with being the first to develop a social survey relying on interviewing was Charles Booth (Converse, 1987). In 1886, Booth embarked on a comprehensive survey of the economic and social conditions of the people of London, published as *Life and Labour of the People in London* (Booth, 1902–1903). In his early study, Booth embodied what were to become separate interviewing methods because he not only implemented survey research but also triangulated his work by relying on unstructured interviews and ethnographic observations:

> The data were checked and supplemented by visits to many neighborhoods, streets, and homes, and by conferences with various welfare and community leaders. From time to time Booth lived as a lodger in districts where he was not known, so that he could become more intimately acquainted with the lives and habits of the poorer classes. (Parten, 1950, pp. 6–7)

Many other surveys of London and other English cities followed, patterned after Booth's example. In the United States, a similar pattern ensued. In 1895, a study attempted to do in Chicago what Booth had done in London (Converse, 1987). In 1896, the American sociologist W. E. B. DuBois, who admittedly was following Booth's lead, studied the black population of Philadelphia (DuBois, 1899). Surveys of cities and small towns followed, with the most notable among them being the Lynds' *Middletown* (Lynd & Lynd, 1929) and *Middletown in Transition* (Lynd & Lynd, 1937).

Opinion polling was another early form of interviewing. Some polling took place well before the start of the 20th century, but it really came into its own in 1935 with the forming of the American Institute of Public Opinion by George Gallup. Preceding Gallup, in both psychology and sociology during the 1920s, there was a movement toward the study (and usually the measurement) of attitudes. W. I. Thomas and Florian Znaniecki used the documentary method to introduce the study of attitudes in social psychology. Thomas's influence along with that of Robert Park, a former reporter who believed that sociology was to be found out in the field, sparked a number of community studies at the University of Chicago that came to be known collectively as the works of the Chicago School. Many other researchers, such as Albion Small, George H. Mead, E. W. Burgess, Everett C. Hughes, Louis Wirth, W. Loyd Warner, and Anselm Strauss, were also greatly influential (for a recent discussion of the relations and influence of various Chicago School members, see Becker, 1999).

Although the members of the Chicago School are reputed to have used the ethnographic method in their inquiries, some disagree and have noted that many of the Chicago School studies lacked the analytic component of modern-day ethnography and so were, at best, "firsthand descriptive studies" (Harvey, 1987, p. 50). Regardless of the correct label for the Chicago School members' fieldwork, they clearly relied on a combination of observation, personal documents, and informal interviews in their studies. Interviews were especially in evidence in the work of Thrasher (1927/1963), who in his study of gang members relied primarily on some 130 qualitative interviews, and in that of Anderson (1923), whose classic study of hobos relied on informal in-depth conversations.

It was left to Herbert Blumer and his former student, Howard Becker, to formalize and give impetus to sociological ethnography during the 1950s and 1960s, and interviewing began to lose both the eclectic flavor given to it by Booth and the qualitative accent of the Chicago School members. Understanding gang members or hobos through interviews lost importance; instead, what became relevant was the use of interviewing in survey research as a tool to quantify data. This was not new given that opinion polls and market research had been doing it for years. But during World War II, there was a tremendous increase in survey research as the U.S. armed forces hired great numbers of sociologists as survey researchers. More than a half million American soldiers were interviewed in one manner or another (Young, 1966), and their mental and emotional lives were reported in a four-volume survey, *Studies in Social Psychology in World War II,* the first two volumes of which were directed by Samuel Stouffer and titled *The American Soldier.* This work had tremendous impact and led the way to widespread use of systematic survey research.

What was new, however, was that quantitative survey research moved into academia and came to dominate sociology as the method of choice for the next three decades. An Austrian immigrant, Paul Lazarsfeld, spearheaded this move. He welcomed *The American Soldier* with great enthusiasm. In fact, Lazarsfeld and Robert Merton edited a book of reflections on *The American Soldier* (Merton & Lazarsfeld, 1950). Lazarsfeld moved to Columbia in 1940, taking with him his market research and other applied grants, and he became instrumental in directing the Bureau of Applied Social Research. Two other "survey organizations" were also formed: the National Opinion Research Center (formed in 1941 by Harry Field, first at the University of Denver and then at the University of Chicago) and the Survey Research Center (formed in 1946 by Rensis Likert and his group at the University of Michigan).

Academia at the time was dominated by theoretical concerns, and there was some resistance toward this applied, numbers-based kind of sociology. Sociologists and other humanists were critical of Lazarsfeld and the other survey researchers. Herbert Blumer, C. Wright Mills, Arthur Schlesinger, Jr., and Pitirin Sorokin were among those who voiced their displeasure. According to Converse (1987), Sorokin felt that "the new emphasis on quantitative work was obsessive, and he called the new practitioners 'quantophrenics'—with special reference to Stouffer and Lazarsfeld" (p. 253). Converse also quoted Mills: "Those in the grip of the methodological inhibition often refuse to say anything about modern society unless it has been through the fine little mill of the Statistical Ritual" (p. 252). Converse noted that Schlesinger called the survey researchers "social relations hucksters" (p. 253).

But the survey researchers also had powerful allies such as Merton, who joined the Bureau of Applied Social Research at Columbia in 1943, and government monies were becoming increasingly available for survey research. The 1950s saw a growth of survey research in the universities and a proliferation of survey research texts. Gradually, survey research increased its domain over sociology, culminating in 1960 with the election of Lazarsfeld to the presidency of the American Sociological Association. The methodological dominance of survey research continued unabated throughout the 1970s, 1980s, and 1990s, although other methods began to erode the prominence of survey research.

Qualitative interviewing continued to be practiced hand in hand with participant observation methods, but it too assumed some of the quantifiable scientific rigor that preoccupied survey research to a great extent. This was especially visible in grounded theory (Glaser & Strauss, 1967), with its painstaking emphasis on coding data, and in ethnomethodology, with its quest for invariant properties of social action (Cicourel, 1970). Other qualitative researchers suggested variations. Lofland (1971) criticized grounded theory for paying too little attention to data-gathering techniques. Douglas (1985) suggested lengthy, existential one-on-one interviews that lasted at least 1 day. Spradley (1980) tried to clarify the difference between ethnographic observation and ethnographic interviewing.

Recently, postmodernist ethnographers have concerned themselves with some of the assumptions present in interviewing and with the controlling role of the interviewer. These concerns have led to new directions in qualitative interviewing focusing on increased attention to the voices of the respondents (Marcus & Fischer, 1986), the interviewer–respondent relationship (Crapanzano, 1980), the importance of the researcher's gender in interviewing (Gluck & Patai, 1991), and the role of other elements such as race, social status, and age (Seidman,1991).

Platt (2002), in her recent chapter on the history of interviewing, correctly noted that the interview encompasses so many different practices that it is extremely hard to derive meaningful generalization about it and that the changes that have taken places over time are driven partly by methodological concerns and partly by sociopolitical motives.

Structured Interviewing

In structured interviewing, the interviewer asks all respondents the same series of preestablished questions with a limited set of response categories. There is generally little room for variation in response except where open-ended questions (which are infrequent) may be used. The interviewer records the responses according to a coding scheme that has already been established by the project director or research supervisor. The interviewer controls the pace of the interview by treating the questionnaire as if it were a theatrical script to be followed in a standardized and straightforward manner. Thus, all respondents receive the same set of questions asked in the same order or sequence by an interviewer who has been trained to treat every interview situation in a like manner. There is very little flexibility in the way in which questions are asked or answered in the structured interview setting. Instructions to interviewers often include some of the following guidelines:

- Never get involved in long explanations of the study; use the standard explanation provided by the supervisor.
- Never deviate from the study introduction, sequence of questions, or question wording.
- Never let another person interrupt the interview; do not let another person answer for the respondent or offer his or her opinion on the question.
- Never suggest an answer or agree or disagree with an answer. Do not give the respondent any idea of your personal views on the topic of the question or survey.
- Never interpret the meaning of a question; just repeat the question and give instructions or clarifications that are provided in training or by the supervisor.
- Never improvise such as by adding answer categories or making wording changes.

Telephone interviews, face-to-face interviews in households, intercept interviews in malls and parks, and interviews generally associated with survey research are most likely to be included in the structured interview category.

This interview context calls for the interviewer to play a neutral role, never interjecting his or her opinion of a respondent's answer. The interviewer must establish what has been called "balanced rapport"; he or she must be casual and friendly, on the one hand, but must be directive and impersonal, on the other. The interviewer must perfect a style of "interested listening" that rewards the respondent's participation but does not evaluate these responses (Converse & Schuman, 1974).

It is hoped that in a structured interview, nothing is left to chance. However, response effects, or nonsampling errors, that can be attributed to the questionnaire administration process commonly evolve from three sources. The first source of error is respondent behavior. The respondent may deliberately try to please the interviewer or to prevent the interviewer from learning something about him or her. To do this, the respondent will embellish a response, give what is described as a "socially desirable" response, or omit certain relevant information (Bradburn, 1983, p. 291). The respondent may also err due to faulty memory. The second source of error is found in the nature of the task, that is, the method of questionnaire administration (face-to-face or telephone) or the sequence or wording of the questions. The third source of error is the interviewer, whose characteristics or questioning techniques might impede proper communication of the question (Bradburn, 1983). It is the degree of error assigned to the interviewer that is of greatest concern.

Most structured interviews leave little room for the interviewer to improvise or exercise independent judgment, but even in the most structured interview situation, not every contingency can be anticipated and not every interviewer behaves according to the script (Bradburn, 1983; Frey, 1989). In fact, a study of interviewer effects found that interviewers changed the wording of as many as one third of the questions (Bradburn, Sudman, & Associates, 1979).

In general, research on interviewer effects has shown interviewer characteristics such as age, gender, and interviewing experience to have a relatively small impact on responses (Singer & Presser, 1989). However, there is some evidence to show that student interviewers produce a larger response effect than do nonstudent interviewers, higher status interviewers produce a larger response effect than do lower status interviewers, and the race of interviewers makes a difference only on questions specifically related to race (Bradburn, 1983; Hyman, 1954; Singer, Frankel, & Glassman, 1983).

The relatively minor impact of the interviewer on response quality in structured interview settings is directly attributable to the inflexible, standardized, and predetermined nature of this type of interviewing. There is simply little room for error. However, those who are advocates of structured interviewing are not unaware that the interview is a social interaction context and that it is influenced by that context. Good interviewers recognize this fact and are sensitive to how interaction can influence response. Converse and Schuman (1974) observed, "There is no single interview style that fits every occasion or all respondents" (p. 53). This means that interviewers must be aware of respondent differences and must be able to make the proper adjustments called for by unanticipated developments. As Gorden (1992) stated, "Interviewing skills are not simple motor skills like riding a bicycle; rather, they involve a high-order combination of observation, emphatic sensitivity, and intellectual judgment" (p. 7).

It is not enough to understand the mechanics of interviewing; it is also important to understand the respondent's world and forces that might stimulate or retard responses (Kahn & Cannell, 1957). Still, the structured interview proceeds under a stimulus–response format, assuming that the respondent will truthfully answer questions previously determined to reveal adequate indicators of the variable in question so long as those questions are phrased properly. This kind of interview often elicits rational responses, but it overlooks or inadequately assesses the emotional dimension.

Developments in computer-assisted interviewing (Couper et al., 1998) have called into question the division between traditional modes of interviewing such as the survey interview and the mail survey. Singleton and Straits (2002) noted that today we are really looking at a continuum of data-collecting methods rather than clearly divided methods; in fact, as these authors observed, many surveys today incorporate a variety of data-gathering methods driven by concerns such as time constraints, financial demands, and other practical elements.

Group Interviewing

The group interview is essentially a qualitative data-gathering technique that relies on the systematic questioning of several individuals simultaneously in a formal or informal setting. Thus, this technique straddles the line between formal and informal interviewing.

The use of the group interview has ordinarily been associated with marketing research under the label of *focus group,* where the purpose is to gather consumer opinions on product characteristics, advertising themes, and/or service delivery. This format has also been used to a considerable extent by political parties and candidates who are interested in voter reactions to issues and policies. The group interview has also been used in sociological research. Bogardus (1926) tested his social distance scale during the mid-1920s, Zuckerman (1972) interviewed Nobel laureates, Thompson and Demerath (1952) looked at management problems in the military, Morgan and Spanish (1984) studied health issues, Fontana and Frey (1990) investigated reentry into the older worker labor force, and Merton and his associates studied the impact of propaganda using group interviews (see Frey & Fontana, 1991). In fact, Merton, Fiske, and Kendall (1956) coined the term "focus group" to apply to a situation where the researcher/interviewer asks very specific questions about a topic after having completed considerable research. There is also some evidence that established anthropologists such as Malinowski used this technique but did not report it (Frey & Fontana, 1991). Today, all group interviews are generically designated *focus group* interviews, even though there is considerable variation in the nature and types of group interviews.

In a group interview, the interviewer/moderator directs the inquiry and the interaction among respondents in a very structured fashion or in a very unstructured manner, depending on the interviewer's purpose. The purpose may be exploratory; for example, the researcher may bring several persons together to test a methodological technique, to try out a definition of a research problem, or to identify key informants. An extension of the exploratory intent is to use the group interview for the purpose of pretesting questionnaire wording, measurement scales, or other elements of a survey design. This is now quite common in survey research (Desvousges & Frey, 1989). Group interviews can also be used successfully to aid respondents' recall or to stimulate embellished descriptions of specific events (e.g., a disaster, a celebration) or experiences shared by members of the group. Group interviews can also be used for triangulation purposes or used in conjunction with other data-gathering techniques. For example, group interviews could be helpful in the process of "indefinite triangulation" by putting individual responses into a context (Cicourel, 1974). Finally, phenomenological purposes may be served whether group interviews are the sole basis for gathering data or are used in association with other techniques.

Group interviews take different forms, depending on their purposes. They can be brainstorming interviews with little or no structure or direction from the interviewer, or they can be very structured such as those in nominal/delphi and marketing focus groups. In the latter cases, the role of the interviewer is very prominent and directive. Fieldwork settings provide both formal and informal occasions for group interviews. The field researcher can bring respondents into a formal setting in the field context and ask very directed questions. Or, a natural field setting, such as a street corner or a neighborhood tavern, can be conducive to casual but purposive inquiries.

Group interviews can be compared on several dimensions. First, the interviewer can be very formal, taking a very directive and controlling posture, guiding discussion strictly, and not permitting digression or variation from topic or agenda. This is the mode of focus and nominal/delphi groups. In the latter case, participants are physically isolated but share views through a coordinator/interviewer. The nondirective approach is more likely to be implemented in a naturally established field setting (e.g., a street corner) or in a controlled setting (e.g., a research laboratory) where the research purpose is phenomenological to establish the widest range of meaning and interpretation for the topic. Groups can also be differentiated by question format and purpose, which in the case of group interviews usually means exploration, phenomenological, or pretest purposes. Exploratory interviews are designed to establish familiarity with a topic or setting; the interviewer can be very directive (or the opposite), but the questions are usually unstructured or open-ended. The same format is used in interviews with phenomenological purposes, where the intent is to tap intersubjective meaning with depth and diversity. Pretest interviews are generally structured in a question format, with the interview being directive in style. Table 27.1 compares the types of group interviews on various dimensions.

The skills that are required to conduct the group interview are not significantly different from those needed for the individual interview. The interviewer must be flexible, objective, empathetic, persuasive, a good listener, and so forth. But the group interview does present some problems not found in the individual interview. Merton and colleagues (1956) noted three specific problems, namely, that (a) the interviewer must keep one person or small coalition of persons from dominating the group, (b) the interviewer must encourage recalcitrant respondents to participate, and (c) the interviewer must obtain responses from the entire group to ensure the fullest coverage of the topic. In addition, the interviewer must balance the directive interviewer role with the role of moderator, and this calls for management of the dynamics of the group being interviewed. Furthermore, the group interviewer must simultaneously worry about the script of questions and be sensitive to the evolving patterns of group interaction.

Group interviews have some advantages over individual interviews, namely, that (a) they are

Table 27.1. Types of Group Interviews and Dimensions

Type	*Setting Purpose*	*Role of Interviewer*	*Question Format*	*Purpose*
Focus group	Formal, preset	Directive	Structured	Exploratory, pretest
Brainstorming	Formal or informal	Nondirective	Unstructured	Exploratory
Nominal/Delphi exploratory	Formal	Directive	Structured	Exploratory, pretest
Field, natural	Informal, spontaneous	Moderately nondirective	Very unstructured	Exploratory Phenomenological
Field, formal	Preset In field	Somewhat directive	Semistructured	Phenomenological

Source: Frey and Fontana (1991, p.184).

relatively inexpensive to conduct and often produce rich data that are cumulative and elaborative, (b) they can be stimulating for respondents and so aid in recall, and (c) the format is flexible. Group interviews are not, however, without problems. The results cannot be generalized, the emerging group culture may interfere with individual expression (a group can be dominated by one person), and "groupthink" is a possible outcome. The requirements for interviewer skills are greater than those for individual interviewing because of the group dynamics that are present. Nevertheless, the group interview is a viable option by both qualitative and quantitative research.

Morgan (2002) advocated a systematic approach to focus group interviewing so as to create a methodological continuity and the ability to assess the outcomes of focus group research. Morgan suggested that, just as social scientists were originally inspired to use focus groups by the example of marketing, it might be time to look at marketing again to see what is being done and use the marketing example to innovate in the field of social sciences.

Unstructured Interviewing

Unstructured interviewing can provide greater breadth than do the other types given its qualitative nature. In this section, we discuss the traditional type of unstructured interview—the open-ended, in-depth (ethnographic) interview. Many qualitative researchers differentiate between in-depth (ethnographic) interviewing and participant observation. Yet, as Lofland (1971) pointed out, the two go hand in hand, and much of the data gathered in participant observation come from informal interviewing in the field. Consider the following report from Malinowski's (1967/1989) diary:

> Saturday 8 [December 1917]. Got up late, felt rotten, took enema. At about 1 I went out; I heard cries; [people from] Kapwapu were bringing *uri* to Teyava. I sat with the natives, talked, took pictures. Went back. Billy corrected and supplemented my notes about *wasi.* At Teyava, an old man talked a great deal about fishes, but I did not understand him too well. Then we moved to his *bwayama.* Talked about *lili'u.* They kept questioning me about the war—In the evening I talked to the policeman about *bwaga'u, lili'u,* and *yoyova.* I was irritated by their laughing. Billy again told me a number of interesting things. Took quinine and calomel. (p. 145)

Malinowski's (1967/1989) "day in the field" shows how very important unstructured interviewing is in the conduct of fieldwork and clearly illustrates the difference between structured interviewing and unstructured interviewing.

Malinowski had some general topics he wanted to know about, but he did not use close-ended questions or a formal approach to interviewing. What is more, he committed (as most fieldworkers do) what structured interviewers would see as two "capital offenses." First, he answered questions asked by the respondents. Second, he let his personal feelings influence him (as all fieldworkers do); thus, he deviated from the "ideal" of a cool, distant, and rational interviewer.

Malinowski's example captures the difference in structured versus unstructured interviewing. The former aims at capturing precise data of a codable nature so as to explain behavior within preestablished categories, whereas the latter attempts to understand the complex behavior of members of society without imposing any a priori categorization that may limit the field of inquiry.

In a way, Malinowski's interviewing is still structured to some degree; there is a setting, there are identified informants, and the respondents are clearly discernible. In other types of interviewing, there might be no setting; for instance, Hertz (1995, 1997b, 1997c) focused on locating women in a historic moment rather than in a place. In addition, in their study of single mothers, Hertz and Ferguson (1997) interviewed women who did not know each other and who were not part of a single group or village. At times, informants are not readily accessible or identifiable, but anyone the researcher meets may become a valuable source of information. Hertz and Ferguson relied on tradespeople and friends to identify single mothers in the study. Fontana and Smith (1989) found that respondents were not always readily identifiable. In studying Alzheimer's disease patients, they discovered that it was often possible to confuse caregivers and patients during the early stages of the disease. Also, in Fontana's (1977) research on the poor elderly, the researcher had no fixed setting at all; he simply wandered from bench to bench in the park where the old folks were sitting, talking to any disheveled old person who would talk back.

Spradley (1979) aptly differentiated among various types of interviewing. He described the following interviewer–respondent interaction, which would be unthinkable in traditional sociological circles yet is the very essence of unstructured interviewing—the establishment of a human-to-human relation with the respondent and the desire to *understand* rather than to *explain:*

> Presently she smiled, pressed her hand to her chest, and said: "Tsetchwe." It was her name. "Elizabeth," I said, pointing to myself. "Nisabe," she answered. . . . Then, having surely suspected that I was a woman, she put her hand on my breast gravely, and, finding out that I was, she touched her own breast. Many Bushmen do this; to them all Europeans look alike. "Tasu si" (women), she said. Then after a moment's pause, Tsetchwe began to teach me. (pp. 3–4)

Spradley (1979) went on to discuss all of the things that an interviewer learns from the natives—their culture, their language, their ways of life. Although each and every study is different, these are some of the basic elements of unstructured interviewing. These elements have been discussed in detail already, and we need not elaborate on them too much here (for detailed accounts of unstructured interviewing, see Adams & Preiss, 1960; Lofland, 1971; Spradley, 1979). Here we provide brief synopses. Remember that these are presented only as heuristic devices; every study uses slightly different elements and often in different combinations.

It is important to keep in mind that the following description of interviewing is highly modernistic in that it presents a structured format and definite steps to be followed. In a way, it mimics structured interviewing in an attempt to "scientize" the research, albeit by using very different steps and concerns. Later in this chapter, in discussing new trends, we deconstruct these notions as we frame the interview as an active emergent process. We contend that our interview society gives people instructions on how to comply with these heuristics (Silverman, 1993, 1997a, 1997b). Similarly, Scheurich (1995, 1997) was openly critical of both positivistic and interpretive interviewing because they are based on modernistic assumptions. For Scheurich (1997), rather than being a process "by the numbers," interviewing (and its language) is "persistently slippery, unstable, and ambiguous from person to person, from situation to situation, from time to time" (p. 62).

Although postmodern researchers follow Scheurich, more traditional sociologists and researchers from other disciplines still follow this "how to" approach to interviewing, where the illusion exists that the better they execute the various steps, the better they will apprehend the reality that they assume is out there, ready to be plucked.

Accessing the Setting. How do we "get in"? That, of course, varies according to the group that one is attempting to study. One might have to disrobe and casually stroll in the nude if he or she is doing a study of nude beaches (Douglas, Rasmussen, & Flanagan, 1977), or one might have to buy a huge motorbike and frequent seedy bars in certain locations if he or she is attempting to befriend and study the Hell's Angels (Thompson, 1985). The different ways and attempts to get in vary tremendously, but they all share the common goal of gaining access to the setting. Sometimes there is no setting per se, as when Fontana (1977) attempted to study the poor elderly on the streets and had to gain access anew with each and every interviewee.

Understanding the Language and Culture of the Respondents. Wax (1960) gave perhaps the most poignant description of learning the language and culture of the respondents in her study of "disloyal" Japanese in concentration camps in America between 1943 and 1945. Wax had to overcome a number of language and cultural problems in her study. Although respondents may be fluent in the language of the interviewer, there are different ways of saying things—or indeed, certain things that should not be said at all—linking language and cultural manifestations. Wax made this point:

> I remarked that I would like to see the letter. The silence that fell on the chatting group was almost palpable, and the embarrassment of the hosts was painful to see. The *faux pas* was not asking to see a letter, for letters were passed about rather freely. It rested on the fact that one did not give a Caucasian a letter in which the "disloyal" statement of a friend might be expressed. (p. 172)

Some researchers, especially in anthropological interviews, tend to rely on interpreters and so become vulnerable to added layers of meanings, biases, and interpretations, and this may lead to disastrous misunderstandings (Freeman, 1983). At times, specific jargon, such as the medical metalanguage of physicians, may be a code that is hard for nonmembers to understand.

Deciding How to Present Oneself. Do we present ourselves as representatives from academia studying medical students (Becker, 1956)? Do we approach the interview as a woman-to-woman discussion (Spradley, 1979)? Do we "dress down" to look like the respondents (Fontana, 1977; Thompson, 1975)? Do we represent the colonial culture (Malinowski, 1922), or do we humbly present ourselves as "learners" (Wax, 1960)? This is very important because once the interviewer's presentational self is "cast," it leaves a profound impression on the respondents and has a great influence of the success of the study (or lack thereof). Sometimes inadvertently, the researcher's presentational self may be misrepresented, as Johnson (1976) discovered in studying a welfare office when some of the employees assumed that he was a "spy" for management despite his best efforts to present himself to the contrary.

Locating an Informant. The researcher must find an insider—a member of the group being studied—who is willing to be an informant and act as a guide and translator of cultural mores and, at times, of jargon or language. Although the researcher can conduct interviews without an informant, he or she can save much time and avoid mistakes if a good informant becomes available. The "classic" sociological informant was Doc in Whyte's (1943) *Street Corner Society.* Without Doc's help and guidance, it is doubtful that Whyte would have been able to access his respondents to the level he did. Rabinow's (1977) discussion of his relation with his main informant, Abd al-Malik ben Lahcen, was very instructive. Malik acted as a translator but also provided Rabinow with access to the cultural ways of the respondents, and by his actions he provided Rabinow with insights into the vast differences between a University of Chicago researcher and a native Moroccan.

Gaining Trust. Survey researchers asking respondents whether they would or would not favor the establishment of a nuclear dump in their state (Frey, 1993) do not have too much work to do in the way of gaining trust; respondents have opinions about nuclear dumps and are very willing to express them, sometimes forcefully. But it is clearly a different story if one wants to ask about people's frequency of sexual intercourse or preferred method of birth control. The interviewer needs to establish some trust with the respondents (Cicourel, 1974). Rasmussen (1989) had to spend months as a "wallflower" in the waiting room of a massage parlor before any of the masseuses gained enough trust in him to divulge to him, in unstructured interviews, the nature of their "massage" relation with clients. Gaining trust is essential to the success of the interviews, and once it is gained, trust can still be very fragile. Any faux pas by the researcher may destroy days, weeks, or months of painfully gained trust.

Establishing Rapport. Because the goal of unstructured interviewing is *understanding,* it is paramount to establish rapport with respondents; that is, the researcher must be able to take the role of the respondents and attempt to see the situation from their viewpoint rather than superimpose his or her world of academia and preconceptions on them. Although a close rapport with the respondents opens the doors to more informed research, it may create problems in that the researcher may become a spokesperson for the group studied, losing his or her distance and objectivity, or may "go native" and become a member of the group and forgo his or her academic role. At times, what the researcher might feel is a good rapport turns out to not to be, as Thompson (1985) found out in a nightmarish way when he was subjected to a brutal beating by the Hell's Angels just as his study of them was coming to a close. At the other end of the spectrum, some researchers might never feel that they have established a good rapport with their respondents. Malinowski (1967/1989), for example, always mistrusted the motives of the natives and at times was troubled by their brutish sensuality or angered by their outright lying or deceptions: "After lunch I [carried] yellow calico and spoke about the *baloma.* I made a small *sagali,* Navavile. I was *fed up* with the *niggers*" (p. 154).

Collecting Empirical Material. Being out in the field does not afford one the luxury of video cameras, soundproof rooms, and high-quality recording equipment. Lofland (1971) provided detailed information on doing and writing up interviews and on the types of field notes that one ought to take and how to organize them. Yet field-workers often must make do with what they can have in the field; the "tales" of their methods used range from holding a miniature tape recorder as inconspicuously as possible to taking mental notes and then rushing to the privacy of a bathroom to jot down notes—at times on toilet paper. We agree with Lofland that, regardless of the circumstances, researchers ought to (a) take notes regularly and promptly, (b) write down everything no matter how unimportant it might seem at the time, (c) try to be as inconspicuous as possible in note taking, and (d) analyze notes frequently.

Other Types of Unstructured Interviewing

We consider the issue of interpreting and reporting empirical material later in the chapter. In this subsection, we briefly outline some different types of unstructured interviews.

Oral History

The oral history differs from other unstructured interviews in purpose but not methodologically. The oral collection of historical materials goes back to ancient times, but its modern-day formal organization can be traced to 1948 when Allan Nevins began the Oral History Project at Columbia University (Starr, 1984, p. 4). The oral history captures a variety of forms of life, from common folks talking about their jobs in Terkel's

(1975) *Working* to the historical recollections of President Harry Truman in Miller's (1974) *Plain Speaking* (see also Starr, 1984, p. 4). Often oral history transcripts are not published, but many may be found in libraries. They are like silent memoirs waiting for someone to rummage through them and bring their testimony to life. Recently, oral history has found great popularity in the feminist movement (Gluck & Patai, 1991), where it is seen as a way of understanding and bringing forth the history of women in a culture that has traditionally relied on masculine interpretation: "Refusing to be rendered historically voiceless any longer, women are creating a new history—using our own voices and experiences" (Gluck, 1984, p. 222).

Relevant to the study of oral history (and, in fact, to all interviewing) is the study of memory and its relation to recall. For instance, Schwartz (1999) examined the ages at which we recall critical episodes in our lives, concluding that "biographical memory . . . is better understood as a social process" and that "as we look back, we find ourselves remembering our lives in terms of our experience with others" (p. 15; see also Schwartz, 1996). Ellis (1991) resorted to the use of "sociological introspection" to reconstruct biographical episodes of her past life. Notable among Ellis's work in this genre was her reconstruction of her 9-year relationship with her partner, Gene Weinstein. Ellis (1995) described the emotional negotiations the two of them went through as they coped with his downward-spiraling health until the final negotiation with death.

Creative Interviewing

Close to oral history, but used more conventionally as a sociological tool, is Douglas's (1985) "creative interviewing." Douglas argued against the "how to" guides to conducting interviews because unstructured interviews take place in the largely situational everyday world of members of society. Thus, interviewers must necessarily be creative, must forget "how to" rules, and must adapt to the ever-changing situations they face. Similar to oral historians, Douglas described interviewing as collecting oral reports from the members of society. In creative interviewing, these reports go well beyond the length of conventional unstructured interviews and may become "life histories," with interviewing taking place in multiple sessions over many days with the respondents.

Postmodern Interviewing

Douglas's (1985) concern with the important role played by the interviewer as human, a concern that is also shared by the feminist oral historians, became a paramount element in the interviewing approaches of postmodern anthropologists and sociologists during the mid-1980s. Marcus and Fischer (1986) addressed ethnography at large, but their discussion was germane to unstructured interviewing because, as we have seen, such interviewing constitutes the major way of collecting data in fieldwork. Marcus and Fischer voiced reflexive concerns about the ways in which the researcher influences the study, both in the methods of data collection and in the techniques of reporting findings. This concern led to new ways of conducting interviews in the hope of minimizing, if not eliminating, the interviewer's influence. One such way is through *polyphonic* interviewing, where the voices of the respondents are recorded with minimal influence from the researcher and are not collapsed together and reported as one through the interpretation of the researcher. Instead, the multiple perspectives of the various respondents are reported, and differences and problems encountered are discussed, rather than glossed over (Krieger, 1983). *Interpretive interactionism* follows in the footsteps of creative and polyphonic interviewing, but borrowing from James Joyce, it adds a new element—that of epiphanies, which Denzin (1989a) described as "those interactional moments that leave marks on people's lives [and] have the potential for creating transformational experiences for the person" (p. 15). Thus, the topic of inquiry becomes dramatized by the focus on existential moments in people's lives, possibly producing richer and more meaningful data. Finally, as postmodernists seek new ways of understanding and reporting data, we note the concept of "oralysis," which refers to "the ways in which oral forms, derived from everyday life, are, with the recording powers of video, applied to the analytical tasks associated with literate forms" (Ulmer, 1989, p. xi). In oralysis, the traditional product of interviewing, talk, is coupled with the visual, providing a product consonant with a society that is dominated by the medium of television (Ulmer, 1989).

▣ Gendered Interviewing

> The housewife goes into a well-stocked store to look for a frying pan. Her thinking probably does not proceed exactly this way, but it is helpful to think of the many possible two-way choices she might make: Cast iron or aluminum? Thick or thin? Metal or wooden handle? Covered or not? Deep or shallow? Large or small? This brand or that? Reasonable or too high in price? To buy or not? Cash or charge? Have it delivered or carry it? . . . The two-way question is simplicity itself when it comes to recording answers and tabulating them. (Payne, 1951, pp. 55–56)

The preceding quote represents the prevalent paternalistic attitude toward women in interviewing (Oakley, 1981, p. 39) as well as the paradigmatic concern with coding answers and, therefore, with presenting limited dichotomous choices. Apart from a tendency to be condescending to women, the traditional interview paradigm does not account for gendered differences. In fact, Babbie's (1992) classic text, *The Practice of Social Research,* briefly referenced gender only three times and did not even mention the influence of gender on interviews. As Oakley (1981) cogently pointed out, both the interviewer and the respondent are considered to be faceless and invisible, and they must be if the paradigmatic assumption of gathering value-free data is to be maintained. Yet, as Denzin (1989a) told us, "gender filters knowledge" (p. 116); that is, the sex of the interviewer and the sex of the respondent make a difference because the interview takes place within the cultural boundaries of a paternalistic social system in which masculine identities are differentiated from feminine ones.

In the typical interview, there exists a hierarchical relation, with the respondent being in the subordinate position. The interviewer is instructed to be courteous, friendly, and pleasant:

> The interviewer's manner should be friendly, courteous, conversational, and unbiased. He should be neither too grim nor too effusive; neither too talkative nor too timid. The idea should be to put the respondent at ease, *so that he will talk freely and fully.* (Selltiz, Jahoda, Deutsch, & Cook, 1965, p. 576, emphasis added)

Yet, as the last line of this quote shows, this demeanor is a ruse to gain the trust and confidence of the respondent without reciprocating those feelings in any way. The interviewer is not to give his or her own opinions and is to evade direct questions. What seems to be a conversation is really a one-way pseudoconversation, raising an ethical dilemma (Fine, 1983–1984) inherent in the study of people for opportunistic reasons. When the respondent is female, the interview presents added problems because the preestablished format directed at information relevant for the study tends both to ignore the respondent's own concerns and to curtail any attempts to digress and elaborate. This format also stymies any revelation of personal feelings and emotions.

Warren (1988) discussed problems of gender in both anthropological and sociological fieldwork, and many of these problems are also found in the ethnographic interview. Some of these problems are the traditional ones of entrée and trust that may be heightened by the sex of the interviewer, especially in highly sex-segregated societies:

> I never witnessed any ceremonies that were barred to women. Whenever I visited compounds, I sat with the women while the men gathered in the parlors or in front of the compound. . . . I never entered any of the places where men sat around to drink beer or palm wine and to chat. (Sudarkasa, 1986, quoted in Warren, 1988, p. 16)

Solutions to the problem have been to view the female anthropologist as androgyny or to grant her honorary male status for the duration of her research. Warren (1988) also pointed to some advantages of the researcher being female and, therefore, being seen as harmless or invisible. Other problems are associated with the researcher's status and race and with the context of the interview, and again these problems are magnified for female researchers in a paternalistic world. Female interviewers at times face the added burden of sexual overtures or covert sexual hassles (p. 33).

Feminist researchers are suggesting ways in which to circumvent the traditional interviewing paradigm. Oakley (1981) noted that interviewing is a masculine paradigm that is embedded in a masculine culture and stresses masculine traits while at the same time excluding traits, such as sensitivity and emotionality, that are culturally viewed as feminine traits. However, there is a growing reluctance, especially among female researchers (Oakley, 1981; Reinharz, 1992; Smith, 1987), to continue interviewing women as "objects" with little or no regard for them as individuals. Although this reluctance stems from moral and ethical reasons, it is also relevant methodologically. As Oakley (1981) pointed out, in interviewing there is "no intimacy without reciprocity" (p. 49). Thus, the emphasis is shifting to allow the development of a closer relation between the interviewer and the respondent. Researchers are attempting to minimize status differences and are doing away with the traditional hierarchical situation in interviewing. Interviewers can show their human side and can answer questions and express feelings. Methodologically, this new approach provides a greater spectrum of responses and a greater insight into the lives of the respondents—or "participants," to avoid the hierarchical pitfall (Reinharz, 1992, p. 22)—because it encourages them to control the sequencing and language of the interview while also allowing them the freedom of open-ended responses (Oakley, 1981; Reinharz, 1992; Smith, 1987). To wit, "Women were always . . . encouraged to 'digress' into details of their personal histories and to recount anecdotes of their working lives. Much important information was gathered in this way" (Yeandle, 1984, quoted in Reinharz, 1992, p. 25).

Hertz (1997a) made the self of the researcher visible and suggested that it is only one of many selves that the researcher takes to the field. She asserted that interviewers need to be reflexive; that is, they need to "have an ongoing conversation about experience while simultaneously living in the moment" (p. viii). By doing so, they will heighten the understanding of differences of ideologies, culture, and politics between interviewers and interviewees.

Hertz also underscored the importance of "voices"—how we (as authors) express and write our stories, which data we include and which data we exclude, whose voices we choose to represent and whose voices we choose not to represent. The concern with voices is also found, very powerfully, in Vaz's (1997) edited *Oral Narrative Research With Black Women.* One of the contributors, Obbo (1997), stated,

> This chapter is a modest exercise in giving expression to women's voices and in rescuing their perceptions and experiences from being mere murmurs or backdrop to political, social, and cultural happenings. Women's voices have been devalued by male chronicles of cultural history even when the men acknowledge female informants; they are overshadowed by the voice of male authority and ascendance in society. (pp. 42–43)

This commitment to maintaining the integrity of the phenomena and preserving the viewpoint of the respondents, as expressed in their everyday language, is very akin to phenomenological and existential sociologies (Douglas & Johnson, 1977; Kotarba & Fontana, 1984) and also reflects the concern of postmodern ethnographers (Marcus & Fischer, 1986). The differences are (a) the heightened moral concern for respondents/participants, (b) the attempt to redress the male/female hierarchy and existing paternalistic power structure, and (c) the paramount importance placed on membership because the effectiveness of male researchers in interviewing female respondents has been largely discredited.

Behar (1996) addressed the ambiguous nature of the enterprise of interviewing by asking the following questions. Where do we locate the researcher in the field? How much do we reveal about ourselves? How do we reconcile our different roles and positions? Behar made us see that interviewer, writer, respondent, and interview are not clearly distinct entities; rather, they are intertwined in a deeply problematic way. Behar and Gordon (1995) also cogently pointed out that the seminal work by Marcus and Fischer (1986) broke ground with modernistic ethnography but remains an example of paternalistic sociology because it did not address women's concerns.

Some feminist sociologists have gone beyond the concern with interviewing or fieldwork in itself. Richardson (1992a) strove for new forms of expression to report the findings and presented some of her fieldwork in the form of poetry. Clough (1998) questioned the whole enterprise of fieldwork under the current paradigm and called for a reassessment of the whole sociological enterprise and for a rereading of existing sociological texts in a light that is not marred by a paternalistic bias. Their voices echoed the concern of Smith (1987), who eloquently stated,

> The problem (of a research project) and its particular solution are analogous to those by which fresco painters solved the problems of representing the different temporal moments of a story in the singular space of the wall. The problem is to produce in a two-dimensional space framed as a wall a world of action and movement in time. (p. 281)

A growing number of researchers believe that we cannot isolate gender from other important elements that also "filter knowledge." For example, Collins (1990) wrote eloquently about the filtering of knowledge through memberships—of being black and female in American culture, in her case. Weston (1998) made just as powerful a case for sexuality, contending that it should not be treated as a compartmentalized subspecialty because it underlies and is integral to the whole of social sciences. It is clear that gender, sexuality, and race cannot be considered in isolation; race, class, hierarchy, status, and age (Seidman, 1991) all are part of the complex, yet often ignored, elements that shape interviewing.

▣ Framing and Interpreting Interviews

Aside from the problem of framing real-life events in a two-dimensional space, we face the added problems of how the framing is being done and who is doing the framing. In sociological terms, this means that the type of interviewing selected, the techniques used, and the ways of recording information all come to bear on the results of the study. In addition, data must be interpreted, and the researcher has a great deal of influence over what part of the data will be reported and how the data will be reported.

Framing Interviews

Numerous volumes have been published on the techniques of structured interviewing (see, e.g., Babbie, 1992; Bradburn et al., 1979; Gorden, 1980; Kahn & Cannell, 1957). There is also a voluminous literature on group interviewing, especially on marketing, and survey research (for a comprehensive review of literature in this area, see Stewart & Shamdasani, 1990). The uses of group interviewing have also been linked to qualitative sociology (Morgan, 1988). Unstructured interviewing techniques also have been covered thoroughly (Denzin, 1989; Lofland, 1971; Lofland & Lofland, 1984; Spradley, 1979).

As we have noted, unstructured interviews vary widely given their informal nature and depending on the type of the setting, and some eschew the use of any preestablished set of techniques (Douglas, 1985). Yet there are techniques involved in interviewing whether the interviewer is just being "a nice person" or he or she is following a format. Techniques can be varied to meet various situations, and varying one's techniques is known as using tactics. Traditionally, the researcher is involved in an informal conversation with the respondent; thus, the researcher must maintain a tone of "friendly" chat while trying to remain close to the guidelines of the topics of inquiry that he or she has in mind. The researcher begins by "breaking the ice" with general questions and gradually moves on to more specific ones while also—as inconspicuously as possible—asking questions intended to check the veracity of the respondent's statements. The researcher should avoid getting involved in a "real" conversation in which he or she answers questions asked by the respondent or provides personal opinions on the matters discussed. The researcher can avoid "getting trapped" by shrugging off the relevance of his or her opinions (e.g., "It doesn't matter how I feel; it's your opinion that's important") or by feigning ignorance (e.g., "I really don't know enough about this to say anything; you're the expert"). Of course, as we have seen in the case of gendered interviewing, the researcher may reject these techniques and "come down" to the level of the respondent to engage in a "real" conversation with give and take and shared empathetic understanding.

The use of language, particularly that of specific terms, is important to create a "sharedness of meanings" in which both interviewer and the respondent understand the contextual nature of specific referents. For instance, in studying nude beaches, Douglas and Rasmussen (1977) discovered that the term "nude beach virgin" had nothing to do with chastity; rather, it referred to the fact that a person's buttocks were white, indicating to others that he or she was a newcomer to the nude beach. Language is also important in delineating the type of question (e.g., broad, narrow, leading, instructive).

Nonverbal techniques are also important in interviewing. There are four basic modes of nonverbal communication:

> *Proxemic* communication is the use of interpersonal space to communicate attitudes, *chronemic* communication is the use of pacing of speech and length of silence in conversation, *kinesic* communication includes any body movements or postures, and *paralinguistic* communication includes all the variations in volume, pitch, and quality of voice. (Gorden, 1980, p. 335)

All four of these modes represent important techniques for the researcher. In addition, the researcher should carefully note and record respondents' use of these modes because interview data are more than verbal records and should include, as much as possible, nonverbal features of the interaction. Finally, techniques vary with the group being interviewed; for instance, interviewing a group of children requires a different approach from the one that the interviewer may use when interviewing a group of elderly widows (Lopata, 1980).

An interesting proposal for framing interviews came from Saukko (2000), who asked, "How can we be true and respect the inner experiences of people and at the same time critically assess the cultural discourses that form the very stuff from which our experiences are made?" (p. 299). Using the metaphor of patchwork quilts (which have no center), Saukko patched and stitched together the stories of five anorexic women. Thus, she rejected the idea of framing characters as monological and instead, borrowing from Bakhtin (1986), presented them as "dialogic characters" (Saukko, 2000, p. 303).

Interpreting Interviews

Many studies that use unstructured interviews are not reflexive enough about the interpreting process. Common platitudes proclaim that data speak for themselves and that the researcher is neutral, unbiased, and "invisible." The data reported tend to flow nicely, there are no contradictory data, and there is no mention of what data were excluded and why. Improprieties never happen, and the main concern seems to be the proper (if unreflexive) filing, analyzing, and reporting of events. But anyone who has engaged in fieldwork knows better. No matter how organized the researcher may be, he or she slowly becomes buried under an increasing mountain of field notes, transcripts, newspaper clippings, and audiotapes. Traditionally, readers were presented with the researcher's interpretation of the data, cleaned and streamlined and collapsed in a rational noncontradictory account. More recently, sociologists have come to grips with the reflexive, problematic, and sometimes contradictory nature of data and with the tremendous, if unspoken, influence of the researcher as author. What Van Maanen (1988) called "confessional style" began in earnest during the 1970s (Johnson, 1976) and has continued unabated to our days in a soul cleansing by researchers of problematic feelings and sticky situations in the field. Although perhaps somewhat overdone at times, these "confessions" are very valuable because they make readers aware of the complex and cumbersome nature of interviewing people in their natural settings and lend a tone of realism and veracity to studies. Malinowski (1967/1989) provided a good example: "Yesterday I slept very late. Got up around 10. The day before I had engaged Omaga, Koupa, and a few others. They didn't come. Again I fell into a rage" (p. 67).

Showing the human side of the researcher and the problematics of unstructured interviewing has taken new forms in deconstructionism (Derrida, 1976). Here, the influence of the author is brought under scrutiny. Thus, the text created by the rendition of events by the researcher is "deconstructed"; the author's biases and taken-for-granted notions are exposed, and sometimes alternative ways of looking at the data are introduced (Clough, 1998).

Postmodern social researchers, as we have seen, attempt to expose the role of the researcher as field-worker and minimize his role as author. For instance, Crapanzano (1980) reported Tuhami's accounts, whether they were sociohistorical renditions, dreams, or outright lies, because they all constituted a part of this Moroccan Arab respondent's sense of self and personal history. In interviewing Tuhami, Crapanzano learned not only about his respondent but also about himself:

> As Tuhami's interlocutor, I became an active participant in his life history, even though I rarely appear directly in his recitations. Not only did my presence, and my questions, prepare him for the text he was to produce, but they produced what I read as a change of consciousness in him. They produced a change of consciousness in me too. We were both jostled from our assumptions about the nature of the everyday world and ourselves and groped for common reference points within this limbo of interchange. (p. 11)

No longer pretending to be a faceless respondent and an invisible researcher, Tuhami and Crapanzano were portrayed as individual humans with their own personal histories and idiosyncrasies, and the readers learn about two people and two cultures.

Gubrium and Holstein (2002) actually considered the interview as a contextually based, mutually accomplished story that is reached through collaboration between the researcher and the respondent. Thus, just to tell what happened (the *what*) is not enough because the what depends greatly on the ways, negotiations, and other interactive elements that take place between the researcher and the respondent (the *how*). Others have addressed the same concerns, at times enlarging the one-to-one interaction to interaction between the researcher and a whole community or outlining the various types of collaborative interviewing (Ellis & Berger, 2002).

The discovery of reflexivity proved to be an epiphanic moment for Banister (1999). Once she was able to realize that her study of midlife women resonated strong personal notes with her midlife experience, Banister acknowledged that the she was not just a witness to her respondents and came to see the liminality of her position. Thus, she was able to understand the women's midlife experience as well as her own and to reach a deep ethnographic understanding.

Another powerful way in which to accentuate reflexivity in interviewing is through narrative, where in trying to understand the "other" we learn about (our)"selves," reaching the hermeneutic circle, that is, the circle of understanding (Rabinow & Sullivan, 1987; Warren, 2002). Denzin (2003b) noted that writers can gain knowledge about themselves by bringing forth their autobiographical past; in a way, they are bringing the past into the present (Pinar, 1994). Denzin (2003a) proposed that this perhaps can best be achieved through the use of performances rather than traditional writing modes as a way in which to reach across the divide and extend a hand to those who have been oppressed. In performance, we infuse powerful feelings and try to recreate a way in which to understand those we study and ourselves in our relationship to them, that is, not merely to create new sociological knowledge but also to use that hand to grasp and pull the downtrodden out of the mire in which they are suffocating.

Ethical Considerations

Because the objects of inquiry in interviewing are humans, extreme care must be taken to avoid any harm to them. Traditionally, ethical concerns have revolved around the topics of *informed consent* (receiving consent by the respondent after having carefully and truthfully informed him or her about the research), *right to privacy* (protecting the identity of the respondent), and *protection from harm* (physical, emotional, or any other kind).

No sociologists or other social scientists would dismiss these three ethical concerns, yet there are other ethical concerns that are less unanimously upheld. The controversy over overt/covert fieldwork is more germane to participant observation but could include the surreptitious use of tape-recording devices. Warwick (1973) and Douglas (1985) argued for the use of covert methods because they mirror the deceitfulness of everyday-life reality, whereas others, including Erickson (1967), vehemently opposed the study of uninformed respondents.

Another problematic issue stems from the researcher's degree of involvement with the group under study. Whyte (1943) was asked to vote more than once during the same local elections (i.e., to vote illegally) by the members of the group to which he had gained access and befriended, thereby gaining the group members' trust. He used "situational ethics," that is, judging the legal infraction to be minor in comparison with the loss of his fieldwork if he refused to vote more than once. Thompson (1985) was faced with a more serious possible legal breach. He was terrified at the prospect of having to witness one of the alleged rapes for which the Hell's Angels had become notorious, but as he reported, none took place during his research. The most famous, and widely discussed, case of questionable ethics in qualitative sociology took place during Humphreys's (1970) research for *Tearoom Trade.* Humphreys studied homosexual encounters in public restrooms in parks ("tearooms") by acting as a lookout ("watch queen"). Although this fact in itself may be seen as unethical, it is the following one that raised many academic eyebrows. Humphreys, unable to interview the men in the tearoom, recorded their cars' license plate numbers, which led him to find their residences with the help of police files. He then interviewed many of the men in their homes without being recognized as having been their watch queen.

A twist in the degree of involvement with respondents came from a controversial article by Goode (2002) in which he summarily dismissed years of research with the fat civil rights organization as a "colossal waste of time." Goode discussed the problematics of sexual intimacy between researchers and respondents and acknowledged that he had casual sexual liaisons with some of the respondents. In fact, he fathered a child with a person he had met at research meetings. Goode's article was published along with a number of responses, all of them very critical (in different ways) of Goode's cavalier approach (Bell, 2002; Manning, 2002; Sagui, 2002; Williams, 2002). Perhaps the following quote from Williams (2002) best summarized the feelings of the scholars responding to Goode: "I would hope and expect that sociologists and their audiences could understand public discrimination without sleeping with its victims" (p. 560).

Another ethical problem is raised by the veracity of the reports made by researchers. For example, Whyte's (1943) famous study of Italian street corner men in Boston has come under severe scrutiny (Boelen, 1992) as some have alleged that Whyte portrayed the men in demeaning ways that did not reflect their visions of themselves. Whyte's case is still unresolved; it illustrates the delicate issue of ethical decisions in the field and in reporting field notes, even more than 50 years later (Richardson, 1992b).

A growing number of scholars, as we have seen (Oakley, 1981), feel that most of traditional in-depth interviewing is unethical, whether wittingly or unwittingly. The techniques and tactics of interviewing, they say, are really ways of manipulating the respondents while treating them as objects or numbers rather than as individual humans. Should the quest for objectivity supersede the human side of those we study? Consider the following:

> One day while doing research at the convalescent center, I was talking to one of the aides while she was beginning to change the bedding of one of the patients who had urinated and soaked the bed. He was the old, blind, ex-wrestler confined in the emergency room. Suddenly, the wrestler decided he was not going to cooperate with the aide and began striking violently at the air about him, fortunately missing the aide. Since nobody else was around, I had no choice but to hold the patient pinned down to the bed while the aide proceeded to change the bedding. It was not pleasant: The patient was squirming and yelling horrible threats at the top of his voice; the acid smell of urine was nauseating; I was slowly losing my grip on the much stronger patient, while all along feeling horribly like Chief Bromden when he suffocates the lobotomized MacMurphy in Ken Kesey's novel. *But there was no choice; one just could not sit back and take notes while the patient tore apart the aide.* (Fontana, 1977, p. 187, emphasis added)

A chapter (Edwards & Mauthner, 2002) in a recent edited volume (Mauthner, Birch, Jessop, & Miller, 2002) presented new insight on the ethics of feminist research. Edwards and Mauthner (2002) outlined the various models of ethics currently existing: the universalist models based on "universal principles such as honesty, justice, and respect" or based on "'goodness' of outcomes of research" (p. 20). In contrast, a third model is based on "contextual or situational ethical position" (p. 20). The authors noted that a majority of feminist researchers (if not all of them) have focused on care and responsibility, that is, on contextually based "feminist-informed social *values*" (p. 21). The authors lauded the work of Denzin (1997) for applying these feminist principles to social research. However, they found that some of Denzin's ideas could be refined to some degree. For instance, Denzin (1997) advocated a symmetrical relation between researchers and respondents, whereas others (e.g., Young, 1997) criticized this as "neither possible nor desirable" (Edwards & Mauthner, 2002, p. 26) and called instead for "asymmetrical reciprocity." In the words of the Edwards and Mauthner (2002), "Rather than ignoring or blurring power positions, ethical practice needs to pay attention to them" (p. 27).

Clearly, as we move forward with sociology, we cannot—to paraphrase what Blumer said so many years ago—let the methods dictate our images of humans. As Punch (1986) suggested, as field-workers we need to exercise common sense and responsibility—and, we would like to add, to our respondents first, to the study next, and to ourselves last. As Johnson (2002) empathically proclaimed, regardless of what criteria we wish to adopt for interviewing, "the most important ethical imperative is to tell the truth" (p. 116).

New Trends in Interviewing

The latest trends in interviewing have come some distance from structured questions; we have reached the point of the interview as negotiated text. Ethnographers have realized for quite some time that researchers are not invisible neutral entities; rather, they are part of the interaction they seek to study, and they influence that interaction. At last, interviewing is being brought in line with ethnography. There is a growing realization that interviewers are not the mythical neutral tools envisioned by survey research. Interviewers are increasingly seen as active participants in an interaction with respondents, and interviews are seen as negotiated accomplishments of both interviewers and respondents that are shaped by the contexts and situations in which they take place. As Schwandt (1997) noted, "It has become increasingly common in qualitative studies to view the interview as a form of discourse between two or more speakers or as a linguistic event in which the meanings of questions and responses are contextually grounded and jointly constructed by interviewer and respondent" (p. 79). We are beginning to realize that we cannot lift the results of interviews out of the contexts in which they were gathered and claim them as objective data with no strings attached.

The Interview as a Negotiated Accomplishment

Let us briefly recap the two traditional approaches to the interview, following Holstein and Gubrium (1995, 1997). The authors use Converse and Schuman's (1974) *Conversations at Random* as an exemplar of the interview as used in survey research. In this context, the interviewer is carefully instructed to remain as passive as possible so as to reduce his or her influence; the scope of the interviewer's function is to access the respondent's answers. This is a *rational* type of interviewing; it assumes that there is an objective knowledge out there and if that one can access it if he or she is skilled enough, just as a skilled surgeon can remove a kidney from a donor and use it in a different context (e.g., for a patient awaiting a transplant).

Holstein and Gubrium (1995, 1997) regarded Douglas's (1985) creative interviewing as a romanticist type of interviewing. Douglas's interviewing is based on *feelings;* it assumes that researchers, as interviewers, need to "get to know" the respondents beneath their rational facades and that researchers can reach respondents' deep well of emotions by engaging them and by sharing feelings and thoughts with them. Douglas's interviewer is certainly more active and far less neutral than Converse and Schuman's interviewer, but the assumptions are still the same—that the *skills* of the interviewer will provide access to knowledge and that there is a *core knowledge* that the researcher can access.

Holstein and Gubrium (1995) finally considered the new type of interviewing, although "new" isn't exactly accurate given that their reference for this is the work of Ithiel de Sola Pool, published in 1957. To wit, "Every interview is . . . an interpersonal drama with a developing plot" (Pool, 1957, p. 193, quoted in Holstein & Gubrium 1995, p. 14). Holstein and Gubrium went on to discuss that so far we have focused on the *whats* of the interview (the substantive findings) and that it is now time to pay attention to the *hows* of the interview (the context, particular situation, nuances, manners, people involved, etc., in which interview interactions take place). This concept harks back to ethnomethodology, according to Holstein and Gubrium: "To say that the interview is an interpersonal drama with a developing plot is part of a broader claim that reality is an ongoing, interpretive accomplishment" (p. 16). Garfinkel, Sacks, and others clearly stated during the late 1960s that reality is an ever-changing, ongoing accomplishment based on the practical reasoning of the members of society. It is time to consider the interview as a practical production, the meaning of which is accomplished at the intersection of the interaction of the interviewer and the respondent.

In a later essay, Gubrium and Holstein (1998) continued their argument by looking at interviews as storytelling, which they saw as a practical production used by members of society to accomplish coherence in their accounts. Once more, they encouraged us to examine the *hows* as well as the *whats* of storytelling. Similarly, Sarup (1996) told us,

> Each narrative has two parts, a story (*histoire*) and a discourse (*discourse*). The story is the content, or chain of events. The story is the "what" in a narrative, the discourse is the "how." The discourse is rather like a plot, how the reader becomes aware of what happened, [and] the order of appearance of the events. (p. 17)

Gubrium and Holstein are not alone in advocating this reflexive approach to interviews. Both Silverman (1993) and Dingwall (1997) credited Cicourel's (1964) classic work, *Method and Measurement in Sociology,* with pointing to the interview as a social encounter. Dingwall (1997) noted,

> If the interview is a social encounter, then, logically, it must be analysed in the same way as any other social encounter. The products of an interview are the outcome of a socially situated activity where the responses are passed through the role-playing and impression management of both the interviewer and the respondent. (p. 56)

Seidman (1991) discussed interviewing as a relationship by relying on a principal intellectual antecedent of the ethnomethodologist Alfred Schutz. Seidman analyzed the interviewer–respondent relation in terms of Schutz's (1967) "I–Thou" relation, where the two share a reciprocity of perspective and, by both being "thou" oriented, create a "we" relationship. Thus, the respondent is no longer "an object or a type" (Seidman, 1991, p. 73); rather, the respondent becomes an equal participant in the interaction.

To recapitulate, we must find someone willing to talk to us (Arksey & Knight, 2002). Then we go through many creative stratagems to find more respondents (Warren, 2002; Weiss, 1994). Then, we talk to the respondents and attend to the meaning of the stories they weave while interjecting our own perspectives. Warren (2002) puts it beautifully: "In the social interaction of the qualitative interview, the perspectives of the interviewer and the respondent dance together for the moment but also extend outward in social space and backward and forward in time" (p. 98). Finally, we try to piece together the kaleidoscope of shapes and colors into a coherent story—something that has some meaning and, in the common understanding that we achieve, brings us all closer together (Atkinson, 2002).

The Problematics of New Approaches

Some of the proponents of the ethnomethodologically informed interview are critical of both interactionist and positivist interview methods. Dingwall (1997), as well as others, spoke of the romantic movement in ethnography (and interviewing)—the idea that the nearer we come to the respondent, the closer we are to apprehending the "real self." This assumption neglects the fact that the self is a process that is ever negotiated and accomplished in the interaction. Dingwall also faulted the "postmodern" turn; that is, if there is no real self, then there is no real world and so we can create one of our own. Finally, Dingwall was troubled by the "crusading" nature of the romantics and asked, "What is the value of a scholarly enterprise that is more concerned with being 'right on' than with being right?" (p. 64).

In a similar vein, Atkinson and Silverman (1997) rejected the postmodern notion of "polyphonic voices," correctly noting that the interviewer and the respondent collaborate together to create an essentially monologic view of reality. This same rejection could be made by using Schutz's (1967) argument, that is, "I" and "thou" create a unified "we" rather than two separate versions of it.

Ethnomethodologically informed interviewing is not, however, immune from criticism itself. Schutz (1967) assumed a reciprocity of perspective that might not exist. Granted, in our interview society, we all know the commonsense routines and ground rules of interviewing, but in other societies this might not be the case. Bowler (1997) attempted to interview Pakistani women about their experience with maternity services and found a total lack of understanding of the value of social research and interviewing:

> I had told them that I was writing a book on my findings. Yams, who spoke the better English, translated this with a look of disbelief on her face, and then they both dissolved into laughter. The hospitals were very good. There weren't any problems. All was well. (p. 72)

Bowler was forced to conclude that interviewing might not work when there is no "shared notion of the process of research" (p. 66).

Silverman (1993) envisioned a different problem. He seemed to feel that some ethnomethodologists have suspended their interest in substantive concerns of everyday life, claiming that they cannot address them until they knew more about the ways in which these realities are accomplished. He noted, "Put simply, according to one reading of Cicourel, we would focus on the conversational skills of the participants rather than on the content of what they are saying and its relation to the world outside the interview" (p. 98).

Cicourel (1970) stated that sociologists need to outline a workable model of the actor before engaging in the study of self and society. Garfinkel held similar beliefs. For instance, in his famous study of a transsexual named Agnes, Garfinkel (1967) examined the routines by which societal members pass as males or females; he had little or no interest in issues of transsexuality per se. Thus, it would follow that, according to Silverman's reading of ethnomethodology, we should learn the conversational methods before attempting to learn substantive matters in interviewing.

Future Directions

To borrow from Gubrium and Holstein (1997), "Where do we go from here?" (p. 97). We share with these two authors a concern with appreciating the new horizons of postmodernism while simultaneously remaining conservatively committed to the empirical description of everyday life. Gubrium and Holstein (1998) introduced a technique called "analytic bracketing" to deal with the multiple levels of interviewing (and ethnography):

> We may focus, for example on *how* a story is being told, while temporarily deferring our concern for the various *whats* that are involved—for example, the substance, structure, or plot of the story, the context within which it is told, or the audience to which it is accountable. We can later return to these issues. (p. 165)

The use of this analytic bracketing allows the authors to analyze interviewing in its coherence and diversity as an event that is collaboratively achieved and in which product and process are mutually constituted.

A pressing problem in interviewing concerns the kinds of standards that we should apply to these new and different types of interviews. To assume absolute relativism is not the solution because it would lead, in Silverman's (1997b) words, to the "sociology of navel-gazing" (p. 240). Silverman proposed an aesthetics for research, rejecting attempts to use literary forms in sociology: "If I want to read a good poem, why on earth should I turn to a social science journal?" (p. 240). Silverman's critique of interactionist sociology and proposal for aesthetic values seemed to focus on the following three points. First, he attacked the grandiose political theorizing of British sociology and invoked a return to more modest, more minute goals. Second, he rejected the romanticist notion of equating experience (from the members' viewpoint) with authenticity. Third, he noted that in sociology we mimic the mass media of the interview society, thereby succumbing to the trivial, the kitschy, the gossipy, and the melodramatic and ignoring simplicity and profundity.

Silverman's (1997b) notions that we should pay attention to minute details in sociological studies, rather than embarking on grandiose abstract projects, in a way was not dissimilar to Lyotard's (1984) appeal for a return to local elements and away from metatheorizing. For Silverman, the "minute" details are the small details that go on in front of our eyes in our everyday life—very similar to Garfinkel's mundane routines that allow us to sustain the world and interact with each other.

We agree with Silverman that we need to stop deluding ourselves that in our particular method (whichever it may be), we have the key to the understanding of the self. We also agree that it is imperative that we look for new standards given that we are quickly digressing into a new form of the theater of the absurd (and without the literary flair, we fear). But we cannot wait to find a model of the methods used by participants in interviews or in everyday life before we proceed; Cicourel's (1970) invariant properties of interaction turned out to be so general as to be of little use to sociological inquiry.

We need to proceed by looking at the substantive concerns of the members of society while simultaneously examining the constructive activities used to produce order in everyday life and, all along, remaining reflexive about how interviews are accomplished (Gubrium & Holstein, 1997, 1998). For instance, as Baker (1997) pointed out, a researcher telling a respondent that "I am a mother of three" versus telling the respondent that "I am a university professor" accesses different categories and elicits different accounts. We need to move on with sociological inquiry, even though we realize that conditions are less than perfect. To paraphrase Robert Solow, as cited by

Geertz (1973), just because complete asepsis is impossible does not mean that we may just as well perform surgery in a sewer.

A different kind of future direction for interviewing stems largely from the new feminist interviewing practices. The traditional interview has painstakingly attempted to maintain neutrality and achieve objectivity and has kept the role of the interviewer as invisible as possible. Feminists instead are rebelling against the practice of *exploiting* respondents and wish to use interviewing for ameliorative purposes. To wit, "As researchers with a commitment to change, we must decenter ourselves from the 'ivory tower' and construct more participatory, democratic practices. *We must keep people and politics at the center of our research*" (Benmayor, 1991, pp. 172–173, emphasis added). Denzin (1997) referred to this approach as the "feminist, communitarian ethical model" (see also Lincoln, 1995) and told us,

> The feminist, communitarian researcher does not invade the privacy of others, use informed consent forms, select subjects randomly, or measure research designs in term of their validity. This framework presumes a researcher who builds collaborative, reciprocal, trusting, and friendly relations with those studied. . . . It is also understood that those studied have claims of ownership over any materials that are produced in the research process, including field notes. (Denzin, 1997, p. 275)

Combining the roles of the scholar and the feminist may be problematic and sometimes may lead to conflict if the researcher has a different political orientation from that of the people studied (Wasserfall, 1993), but this approach may also be very rewarding in allowing the researcher to see positive results stemming from the research (Gluck, 1991).

A third kind of future direction, one that is already here but is likely to expand greatly in the near future, is that of performance and poetics. I combine the two because they stem from the same concerns for speaking with the voices of the respondents and taking a helping stance toward them. Also, they both possess an expressional trope that goes beyond the traditional one of social sciences—prose. Denzin (2003a) championed performance to the exclusion of other modes of relating social science (ethnography and interview). Performance does not becomes fixed in a written text to be read later; rather, performance is doing, is now, and has feelings, passions, joy, tears, despair, and hope. Performance can reach to people's hearts and not only their minds. Performance can be a powerful instrument for social reform, for righting some wrongs, and for helping those in need. Performance relates to people in our media society; it draws interest, draws attention, and leads to questioning.

Poetics operates in a similar way by encapsulating in a welter of feelings and emotions a life story, an epiphanic moment in the life, a tragedy, a moment of sorrow, or a moment of utter joy. Consider the reply of Louisa May, a sort of average woman from Tennessee, when her partner asked her to terminate her pregnancy:

> Jody May's father said,
>
> "Get an Abortion."
>
> I told him,
>
> "I would never marry you.
>
> I would never marry you.
>
> I would never.
>
> I am going to have this child.
>
> I am going to.
>
> I am. I am.

Richardson's (1997) masterful poem captured the soul of Louisa May, and through the poem we come to know that woman, we know her feelings, and our heart goes out to her.

Richardson (2002), in speaking about poetry pointed out that prose is privileged only because it is empowered by the current system, yet it is only one of many tropes of expression, including performance and poetry, in a newly fragmented world in which not only metatheories but also modes of expression have been fragmented, and we can now speak in many voices and in different tropes.

Electronic Interviewing

Another direction currently being taken in interviewing is related to the changing technologies available. The reliance on the interview as a means of information gathering most recently has expanded to electronic outlets, with questionnaires being administered by fax, electronic mail, and websites. Estimates suggest that nearly 50% of all households have computers and that nearly half of these use the Internet. Software that allows researchers to schedule and archive interview data gathered by chat room interviews is now available. The limited population of potential respondents with access to computers makes surveys of the general population infeasible, but electronic interviewing can reach 100% of some specialized populations (Schaefer & Dillman, 1998).

It is now possible to engage in "virtual interviewing," where Internet connections are used synchronously or asynchronously to obtain information. The advantages include low cost (no telephone or interviewer charges) and speed of return. Of course, face-to-face interaction is eliminated, as is the possibility of both the interviewer and the respondent reading nonverbal behavior or of cueing from gender, race, age, class, or other personal characteristics. Thus, establishing an interviewer–interviewee "relationship" and "living the moment " while gathering information (Hertz, 1997a) is difficult if not impossible. Internet surveys make it easy for respondents to manufacture fictional social realities without anyone knowing the difference (Markham, 1998). Of course, interviewers can deceive respondents by claiming to have experiences or characteristics that they do not have in hopes of establishing better rapport. They can feign responses for the same purpose by claiming "false nonverbals," for example, telling respondents that they "laughed at" or "were pained by" particular comments. Markham (1998), in her autoethnography of Internet interviewing, reported that electronic interviews take longer than their traditional counterparts and that responses are more cryptic and less in depth; however, the interviewer has time to phrase follow-up questions or probes properly.

It is also virtually impossible to preserve anonymity in Internet e-mail surveys, but chat rooms and similar sites permit the use of pseudonyms. Although electronic interviews are currently used primarily for quantitative research and usually employ structured questionnaires, it is only a matter of time before researchers adapt these techniques to qualitative work, just as they have adapted electronic techniques of data analysis. For example, Markham (1998) immersed herself in the process of engaging with various electronic or Internet formats (e.g., chat rooms, listservs) to interview other participants and to document her journey in the virtual world, learning the experience of cyberspace and the meanings that participants attached to their online lifestyles. She asked an intriguing question: "Can I have a self where my body does not exist?" (p. 8).

The future may see considerable ethnography by means of computer-mediated communication, where virtual space—rather than a living room or workplace—is the setting of the interview. It remains to be seen whether electronic interviewing will allow researchers to obtain "thick descriptions" or accounts of subjective experiences or whether such interviewing will provide the "process context" that is so important to qualitative interviews. In addition, researchers conducting such interviewing can never be sure that they are receiving answers from desired or eligible respondents. Interviewing by way of the Internet is so prominent today that researchers are studying its effects on response quality. Schaefer and Dillman (1998), for example, found that e-mail surveys achieved response rates similar to those of mail surveys but yielded better quality data in terms of item completion and more detailed responses to open-ended questions.

There are clearly many unanswered questions and problems related to the use of electronic interviewing. This mode of interviewing will obviously increase during the new millennium as people rely increasingly on electronic modes of communication. But just how much Internet communication will displace face-to-face interviewing is a matter that only time will tell.

Conclusion

In this chapter, we have examined the interview, from structured types of interview to the interview as negotiated text. We outlined the history of interviewing, with its qualitative and quantitative origins. We looked at structured, group, and various types of unstructured interviewing. We examined the importance of gender in interviewing and the ways in which framing and interpreting affect interviews. We examined the importance of ethics in interviewing. Finally, we discussed the new trends in interviewing.

We have included discussion of the whole gamut of the interview, despite the fact that this book is concerned with qualitative research, because we believe that researchers must be cognizant of all the various types of interviews, both modern and postmodern, if they are to gain a clear understanding of interviewing. Clearly, certain types of interviewing are better suited to particular kinds of situations, and researchers *must be aware of the implications, pitfalls, and problems of the types of interview they choose.* If we wish to find out how many people oppose the establishment of a nuclear repository in their area, then a structured type of interview, such as that used in survey research, is our best tool; we can quantify and code the responses and can use mathematical models to explain our findings. If we are interested in opinions about a given product, then a focus group interview will provide us with the most efficient results. If we wish to know about the lives of Palestinian women in the resistance (Gluck, 1991), then we need to interview them at length and in depth in an unstructured way. In the first example just cited, and perhaps in the second, we can speak in the formal language of scientific rigor and verifiability of findings. In the third example, we can speak of understanding a negotiated way of life.

More scholars are realizing that to pit one type of interviewing against another is a futile effort—a leftover from the paradigmatic quantitative/qualitative hostility of past generations. Thus, an increasing number of researchers are using a multimethod approach to achieve broader and often better results. This multimethod approach is referred to as *triangulation* (Denzin, 1989b; Flick, 1998) and allows researchers to use different methods in different combinations. For instance, group interviewing has long been used to complement survey research and is now being used to complement participant observation (Morgan, 1988). Humans are complex, and their lives are ever changing. The more methods we use to study them, the better our chances will be to gain some understanding of how they construct their lives and the stories they tell us about them.

The brief journey we have taken through the world of interviewing should allow us to be better informed about, and perhaps more sensitized to, the problematics of asking questions for sociological reasons. We must remember that each individual has his or her own social history and an individual perspective on the world. Thus, we cannot take our task for granted. As Oakley (1981) noted, "Interviewing is rather like a marriage: Everybody knows what it is, an awful lot of people do it, and yet behind each closed front door there is a world of secrets" (p. 41). She was quite correct. We all think that we know how to ask questions and talk to people, from common everyday folks to highly qualified quantophrenic experts. Yet to learn about people, we must treat them as people, and they will work with us to help us create accounts of their lives. So long as many researchers continue to treat respondents as unimportant faceless individuals whose only contributions are to fill more boxed responses, the answers that researchers will get will be commensurable with the questions they ask and the way in which they ask them. As researchers, we are no different from Gertrude Stein, who, while on her deathbed, asked her lifelong companion Alice B. Toklas, "What is the answer?" When Alice could not bring herself to speak, Gertrude asked, "In that case, what is the question?"

References

Adams, R. N., & Preiss, J. J. (Eds.). (1960). *Human organizational research: Field relations and techniques.* Homewood, IL: Dorsey.

Anderson, N. (1923). *The hobo: The sociology of the homeless man.* Chicago: University of Chicago Press.

Arksey, H., & Knight, P. (2002). *Interviewing for social scientists: An introductory resource with examples.* Thousand Oaks, CA: Sage.

Atkinson, P. (2002). The life story interview. In J. Gubrium & J. Holstein (Eds.), *Handbook of interview research: Context and method* (pp. 121–140). Thousand Oaks, CA: Sage.

Atkinson, P., & Silverman, D. (1997). Kundera's *Immortality:* The interview society and the invention of the self. *Qualitative Inquiry, 3,* 304–325.

Babbie, E. (1992). *The practice of social research* (6th ed.). Belmont, CA: Wadsworth.

Baker, C. (1997). Membership categorization and interview accounts. In D. Silverman (Ed.), *Qualitative research: Theory, method, and practice* (pp. 130–143). London: Sage.

Bakhtin, M. (1986). *Speech genres and other late essays.* Austin: University of Texas Press.

Banister, E. M. (1999). Evolving reflexivity: Negotiating meaning of women's midlife experience. *Qualitative Inquiry, 5,* 3–23.

Becker, H. S. (1956). Interviewing medical students. *American Journal of Sociology, 62,* 199–201.

Becker, H. S. (1999). The Chicago School, so-called. *Qualitative Sociology, 22,* 3–12.

Behar, R. (1996). *The vulnerable observer: Anthropology that breaks your heart.* Boston: Beacon.

Behar, R., & Gordon, D. (Eds.). (1995). *Women writing culture.* Berkeley: University of California Press.

Bell, S. (2002). Sexualizing research: Response to Erich Goode. *Qualitative Sociology, 25,* 535–539.

Benmayor, R. (1991). Testimony, action research, and empowerment: Puerto Rican women and popular education. In S. B. Gluck & D. Patai (Eds.), *Women's words: The feminist practice of oral history* (pp. 159–174). New York: Routledge.

Boelen, W. A. M. (1992). Street corner society: Cornerville revisited. *Journal of Contemporary Ethnography, 21,* 11–51.

Bogardus, E. S. (1926). The group interview. *Journal of Applied Sociology, 10,* 372–382.

Booth, C. (1902–1903). *Life and labour of the people in London.* London: Macmillan.

Bowler, I. (1997). Problems with interviewing: Experiences with service providers and clients. In G. Miller & R. Dingwall (Eds.), *Context and method in qualitative research* (pp. 66–76). Thousand Oaks, CA: Sage.

Bradburn, N. M. (1983). Response effects. In P. H. Rossi, J. D. Wright, & A. B. Anderson (Eds.), *Handbook of survey research* (pp. 289–328). New York: Academic Press.

Bradburn, N. M., Sudman, S., & Associates. (1979). *Improving interview method and questionnaire design.* San Francisco: Jossey–Bass.

Cicourel, A. (1964). *Method and measurement in sociology.* New York: Free Press.

Cicourel, A. (1970). The acquisition of social structure: Toward a developmental sociology of language and meaning. In J. D. Douglas (Ed.), *Understanding everyday life: Toward a reconstruction of social knowledge* (pp. 136–168). Chicago: Aldine.

Cicourel, A. (1974). *Theory and method in a study of Argentine fertility.* New York: John Wiley.

Clough, P. T. (1998). *The end(s) of ethnography: From realism to social criticism* (2nd ed.). New York: Peter Lang.

Collins, P. H. (1990). *Black feminist thought: Knowledge, consciousness, and the politics of empowerment.* New York: Routledge.

Converse, J. M. (1987). *Survey research in the United States: Roots and emergence 1890–1960.* Berkeley: University of California Press.

Converse, J. M., & Schuman, H. (1974). *Conversations at random: Survey research as interviewers see it.* New York: John Wiley.

Couper, M., Baker, R., Bethlehem, J., Clark, C., Nicholls, W., II, & O'Reilly, J. (Eds.). (1998). *Computer-assisted survey information collection.* New York: John Wiley.

Crapanzano, V. (1980). *Tuhami: Portrait of a Moroccan.* Chicago: University of Chicago Press.

Denzin, N. K. (1989). *The research act: A theoretical introduction to sociological methods* (3rd ed.). Englewood Cliffs, NJ: Prentice Hall.

Denzin, N. (1997). *Interpretive ethnography: Ethnographic practices for the 21st century.* London: Sage.

Denzin, N. K. (2003a). The call to performance. *Symbolic Interaction, 26,* 187–208.

Denzin, N. K. (2003b). *Performance ethnography: Critical pedagogy and the politics of culture.* Thousand Oaks, CA: Sage.

Derrida, J. (1976). *Of grammatology* (G. C. Spivak, Trans.). Baltimore, MD: Johns Hopkins University Press.

Desvousges, W. H., & Frey, J. H. (1989). Integrating focus groups and surveys: Examples from environmental risk surveys. *Journal of Official Statistics, 5,* 349–363.

Dingwall, R. (1997). Accounts, interviews, and observations. In G. Miller & R. Dingwall (Eds.), *Context and method in qualitative research* (pp. 51–65). Thousand Oaks, CA: Sage.

Douglas, J. D. (1985). *Creative interviewing.* Beverly Hills, CA: Sage.

Douglas, J. D., & Johnson, J. M. (1977). *Existential sociology.* Cambridge, UK: Cambridge University Press.

Douglas, J. D., Rasmussen, P., with Flanagan, C. A. (1977). *The nude beach.* Beverly Hills, CA: Sage.

DuBois, W. E. B. (1899). *The Philadelphia Negro: A social study.* Philadelphia: Ginn.

Edwards, R., & Mauthner, M. (2002). Ethics and feminist research: Theory and practice. In M. Mauthner, M. Birch, J. Jessop, & T. Miller (Eds.), *Ethics in qualitative research* (pp. 14–31). London: Sage.

Ellis, C. (1991). Sociological introspection and emotional experience. *Symbolic Interaction, 14,* 23–50.

Ellis, C. (1995). *Final negotiation: A story of love, loss, and chronic illness.* Philadelphia: Temple University Press.

Ellis, C., & Berger, L. (2002). Their story/My story/Our story: Including the researcher's experience in interview research. In J. Gubrium & J. Holstein (Eds.), *Handbook of interview research: Context and method* (pp. 849–876). Thousand Oaks, CA: Sage.

El-Or, T. (1992). Do you really know how they make love? The limits on intimacy with ethnographic informants. *Qualitative Sociology, 15,* 53–72.

Erickson, K. T. (1967). A comment on disguised observation in sociology. *Social Problems, 14,* 366–373.

Fine, M. (1983–1984). Coping with rape: Critical perspectives on consciousness. *Imagination, Cognition, and Personality, 3,* 249–267.

Flick, U. (1998). *An introduction to qualitative research: Theory, method, and applications.* London: Sage.

Fontana, A. (1977). *The last frontier: The social meaning of growing old.* Beverly Hills, CA: Sage.

Fontana, A. (2002). Postmodern trends in interviewing. In J. Gubrium & J. Holstein (Eds.), *Handbook of qualitative research: Context and method* (pp. 161–175). Thousand Oaks, CA: Sage.

Fontana, A. (2003). The windmills of morality. *Symbolic Interaction, 26,* 209–216.

Fontana, A., & Frey, J. H. (1990). Postretirement workers in the labor force. *Work and Occupations, 17,* 355–361.

Fontana, A., & Smith, R. (1989). Alzheimer's disease victims: The "unbecoming" of self and the normalization of competence. *Sociological Perspectives, 32,* 35–46.

Freeman, D. (1983). *Margaret Mead and Samoa: The making and unmaking of an anthropological myth.* Cambridge, MA: Harvard University Press.

Frey, J. H. (1989). *Survey research by telephone* (2nd ed.). Newbury Park, CA: Sage.

Frey, J. H. (1993). Risk perception associated with a high-level nuclear waste repository. *Sociological Spectrum, 13,* 139–151.

Frey, J. H., & Fontana, A. (1991). The group interview in social research. *Social Science Journal, 28,* 175–187.

Garfinkel, H. (1967). *Studies in ethnomethodology.* Englewood Cliffs, NJ: Prentice Hall.

Geertz, C. (1973). Thick descriptions: Toward an interpretive theory of culture. In C. Geertz, *The interpretation of cultures: Selected essays* (pp. 3–30). New York: Basic Books.

Glaser, B., & Strauss, A. (1967). *The discovery of grounded theory: Strategies for qualitative research.* Chicago: Aldine.

Gluck, S. B. (1984). What's so special about women: Women's oral history. In D. Dunaway & W. K. Baum (Eds.), *Oral history: An interdisciplinary anthology* (pp. 221–237). Nashville, TN: American Association for State and Local History.

Gluck, S. B. (1991). Advocacy oral history: Palestinian women in resistance. In S. B. Gluck & D. Patai (Eds.), *Women's words: The feminist practice of oral history* (pp. 205–220). New York: Routledge.

Gluck, S. B., & Patai, D. (Eds.). (1991). *Women's words: The feminist practice of oral history.* New York: Routledge.

Goode, E. (2002). Sexual involvement and social research in a fat civil rights organization. *Qualitative Sociology, 25,* 501–534.

Gorden, R. L. (1980). *Interviewing: Strategy, techniques, and tactics.* Homewood, IL: Dorsey.

Gorden, R. 1. (1992). *Basic interviewing skills.* Itasca, IL: Peacock.

Gubrium, J., & Holstein, J. (1997). *The new language of qualitative methods.* New York: Oxford University Press.

Gubrium, J., & Holstein, J. (1998). Narrative practice and the coherence of personal stories. *Sociological Quarterly, 39,* 163–187.

Gubrium, J., & Holstein, J. (Eds.). (2002). *Handbook of interview research: Context and method.* Thousand Oaks, CA: Sage.

Harvey, L. (1987). *Myths of the Chicago School of Sociology.* Aldershot, UK: Avebury.

Hertz, R. (1995). Separate but simultaneous interviewing of husbands and wives: Making sense of their stories. *Qualitative Inquiry*, *1*, 429–451.

Hertz, R. (1997a). Introduction: Reflexivity and voice. In R. Hertz (Ed.), *Reflexivity and voice* (pp. vii–xviii). Thousand Oaks, CA: Sage.

Hertz R. (1997b). *Reflexivity and voice.* Thousand Oaks, CA: Sage.

Hertz, R. (1997c). A typology of approaches to childcare: The centerpiece of organizing family life for dual-earner couples. *Journal of Family Issues, 18,* 355–385.

Hertz, R., & Ferguson, F. (1997). Kinship strategies and self-sufficiency among single mothers by choice: Postmodern family ties. *Qualitative Sociology, 20,* 13–37.

Holstein, J., & Gubrium, J. (1995). *The active interview.* Thousand Oaks, CA: Sage.

Holstein, J., & Gubrium, J. (1997). Active interviewing. In D. Silverman (Ed.), *Qualitative research: Theory, method, and practice* (pp. 113–129). Thousand Oaks, CA: Sage.

Humphreys, L. (1970). *Tearoom trade: Impersonal sex in public places.* Chicago: Aldine.

Hyman, H. H. (1954). *Interviewing in social research.* Chicago: University of Chicago Press.

Johnson, J. (1976). *Doing field research.* New York: Free Press.

Johnson, J. (2002). In-depth interviewing. In J. Gubrium & J. Holstein (Eds.), *Handbook of interview research: Context and method* (pp. 103–119). Thousand Oaks, CA: Sage.

Kahn, R., & Cannell, C. F. (1957). *The dynamics of interviewing: Theory, techniques, and cases.* New York: John Wiley.

Kong, T. S. K., Mahoney, D., & Plummer, K. (2002). Queering the interview. In J. Gubrium & J. Holstein (Eds.), *Handbook of qualitative research: Context and method* (pp. 239–258). Thousand Oaks, CA: Sage.

Kotarba, J. A., & Fontana, A. (Eds.). (1984). *The existential self in society.* Chicago: University of Chicago Press.

Krieger, S. (1983). *The mirror dance: Identity in a women's community.* Philadelphia: Temple University Press.

Kvale, S. (1996). *InterViews: An introduction to qualitative research interviewing.* Thousands Oaks, CA: Sage.

Lincoln, Y. S. (1995). The sixth moment: Emerging problems in qualitative research. *Studies in Symbolic Interaction, 19,* 37–55.

Lofland, J. (1971). *Analyzing social settings.* Belmont, CA: Wadsworth.

Lofland J., & Lofland, L. (1984). *Analyzing social settings: A guide to qualitative observation and analysis* (2nd ed.). Belmont, CA: Wadsworth.

Lopata, H. Z. (1980). Interviewing American widows. In W. Shaffir, R. Stebbins, & A. Turowetz (Eds.), *Fieldwork experience: Qualitative approaches to social research* (pp. 68–81). New York: St. Martin's.

Lynd, R. S., & Lynd, H. M. (1929). *Middletown: A study in American culture.* New York: Harcourt, Brace.

Lynd, R. S., & Lynd, H. M. (1937). *Middletown in transition: A study in cultural conflicts.* New York: Harcourt, Brace.

Lyotard, J. F. (1984). *The postmodern condition: A report on knowledge* (G. Bennington & B. Massumi, Trans.). Minneapolis: University of Minnesota Press.

Maccoby, E. E., & Maccoby, N. (1954). The interview: A tool of social science. In G. Lindzey (Ed.), *Handbook of social psychology,* Vol. 1: *Theory and method* (pp. 449–487). Reading, MA: Addison-Wesley.

Malinoswki, B. (1922). *Argonauts of the Western Pacific.* New York: E. P. Dutton.

Malinowski, B. (1989). *A diary in the strict sense of the term.* Stanford, CA: Stanford University Press. (Original work published in 1967)

Manning, P. (2002). Fat ethics: Response to Erich Goode. *Qualitative Sociology, 25,* 541–547.

Marcus, G. E., & Fischer, M. M. J. (1986). *Anthropology as cultural critique: An experimental moment in the human sciences.* Chicago: University of Chicago Press.

Markham, A. N. (1998). *Life online: Researching real experience in virtual space.* Walnut Creek, CA: AltaMira.

Mauthner, M., Birch, M., Jessop, J., & Miller, T. (Eds.). (2002). *Ethics in qualitative research.* London: Sage.

Merton, K., Fiske, M., & Kendall, P. (1956). *The focused interview: A manual of problems and procedures.* Glencoe, IL: Free Press.

Merton, R. K., & Lazarsfeld, P. F. (Eds.). (1950). *Continuities in social research: Studies in the scope and method of "The American soldier."* Glencoe, IL: Free Press.

Miller, M. (1974). *Plain speaking: An oral biography of Harry S. Truman.* New York: Putnam.

Mishler, E. G. (1986). *Research interviewing: Context and narrative.* Cambridge, MA: Harvard University Press.

Morgan, D. (1988). *Focus groups as qualitative research.* Newbury Park, CA: Sage.

Morgan, D. (2002). Focus group interviewing. In J. Gubrium & J. Holstein (Eds.), *Handbook of interview research: Context and method* (pp. 141–159). Thousand Oaks, CA: Sage.

Morgan, D., & Spanish, M. T. (1984). Focus groups: A new tool for qualitative research. *Qualitative Sociology, 7,* 253–270.

Oakley, A. (1981). Interviewing women: A contradiction in terms. In H. Roberts (Ed.), *Doing feminist research* (pp. 30–61). London: Routledge & Kegan Paul.

Obbo, C. (1997). What do women know? . . . "As I was saying!" In K. M. Vaz (Ed.), *Oral narrative research with black women* (pp. 41–63). Thousand Oaks, CA: Sage.

Parten, M. (1950). *Surveys, polls, and samples.* New York: Harper.

Payne, S. L. (1951). *The art of asking questions.* Princeton, NJ: Princeton University Press.

Pinar, W. (1994). *Autobiography, politics, and sexuality: Essays in curriculum theory 1972–1992.* New York: Peter Lang.

Platt, J. (2002). The history of the interview. In J. Gubrium & J. Holstein (Eds.), *Handbook of interview research: Context and method* (pp. 33–54). Thousand Oaks, CA: Sage.

Pool, I. S. (1957). A critique of the twentieth anniversary issue. *Public Opinion Quarterly, 21,* 190–198.

Punch, M. (1986). *The politics and ethics of fieldwork.* Newbury Park, CA: Sage.

Rabinow, P. (1977). *Reflections on fieldwork in Morocco.* Berkeley: University of California Press.

Rabinow, P., & Sullivan, W. (Eds.). (1987). *Interpretive social science: A second look.* Berkeley: University of California Press.

Rasmussen, P. (1989). *Massage parlor prostitution.* New York: Irvington.

Reinharz, S. (1992). *Feminist methods in social research.* New York: Oxford University Press.

Richardson, L. (1992a). The poetic representation of lives: Writing a postmodern sociology. *Studies in Symbolic Interaction, 13,* 19–28.

Richardson, L. (1992b). Trash on the corner: Ethics and technocracy. *Journal of Contemporary Sociology, 21,* 103–119.

Richardson, L. (1997). *Fields of play: Constructing an academic life.* New Brunswick, NJ: Rutgers University Press.

Richardson, L. (2002). Poetic representation of interviews. In J. Gubrium & J. Holstein (Eds.), *Handbook of interview research: Context and method* (pp. 877–892). Thousand Oaks, CA: Sage.

Sagui, A. (2002). Sex, inequality, and ethnography: Response to Erich Goode. *Qualitative Sociology, 25,* 549–556.

Sarup, M. (1996). *Identity, culture, and the postmodern world.* Athens: University of Georgia Press.

Saukko, P. (2000). Between voice and discourse: Quilting interviews on anorexia. *Qualitative Inquiry, 6,* 299–317.

Schaefer, D. R., & Dillman, D. A. (1998). Development of a standard e-mail methodology. *Public Opinion Quarterly, 62,* 378–397.

Scheurich, J. J. (1995). A postmodernist critique of research interviewing. *Qualitative Studies in Education, 8,* 239–252.

Scheurich, J. (1997). *Research method in the postmodern.* London: Falmer.

Schutz, A. (1967). *The phenomenology of the social world.* Evanston, IL: Northwestern University Press.

Schwandt, T. A. (1997). *Qualitative inquiry: A dictionary of terms.* Thousand Oaks, CA: Sage.

Schwartz, B. (1999). Memory and the practice of commitment. In B. Glassner & R. Hertz (Eds.), *Qualitative sociology as everyday life* (pp. 159–168). Thousand Oaks, CA: Sage.

Schwartz, B. (Ed.). (1996). Collective memory [special issue]. *Qualitative Sociology, 19*(3).

Seidman, I. E. (1991). *Interviewing as qualitative research.* New York: Columbia University, Teachers College Press.

Selltiz, C., Jahoda M., Deutsch, M., & Cook, S. W. (1965). *Research methods in social relations.* London; Methuen.

Silverman, D. (1993). *Interpreting qualitative data: Methods for analysing talk, text, and interaction.* London: Sage.

Silverman, D. (Ed.). (1997a). *Qualitative research: Theory, method, and practice.* London: Sage.

Silverman, D. (1997b). Towards an aesthetics of research. In D. Silverman (Ed.), *Qualitative research: Theory, method, and practice* (pp. 239–253). London: Sage.

Singer, E., Frankel M., & Glassman, M. B. (1983). The effect of interviewer characteristics and expectations on response. *Public Opinion Quarterly, 47*, 68–83.

Singer, E., & Presser, S. (1989). *Survey research methods.* Chicago: University of Chicago Press.

Singleton, R. A., Jr., & Straits, B. (2002). Survey interviewing. In J. Gubrium & J. Holstein (Eds.), *Handbook of interview research: Context and method* (pp. 59–82). Thousand Oaks, CA: Sage.

Smith, D. E. (1987). *The everyday world as problematic: A feminist sociology.* Boston: Northeastern University Press.

Spradley, J. P. (1979). *The ethnographic interview.* New York: Holt, Rinehart & Winston.

Spradley, J. P. (1980). *Participant observation.* New York: Holt, Rinehart & Winston.

Starr, L. (1984). Oral history. In D. Dunaway & W. K. Baum (Eds.), *Oral history: An interdisciplinary anthology* (pp. 3–26). Nashville, TN: American Association for State and Local History.

Stewart, D., & Shamdasani, P. (1990). *Focus groups: Theory and practice.* Newbury Park, CA: Sage.

Sudarkasa, N. (1986). In a world of women: Field work in a Yoruba community. In P. Golde (Ed.), *Women in the field: Anthropological experiences* (pp. 167–191). Berkeley: University of California Press.

Terkel, S. (1975). *Working.* New York: Avon.

Thompson, H. (1985). *Hell's Angels.* New York: Ballantine.

Thompson, J., & Demerath, M. J. (1952). Some experiences with the group interview. *Social Forces, 31*, 148–154.

Thrasher, F. M. (1963). *The gang: A study of 1,313 gangs in Chicago.* Chicago: University of Chicago Press. (Original work published in 1927)

Ulmer, G. (1989). *Teletheory: Grammatology in an age of video.* New York: Routledge.

Van Maanen, J. (1988). *Tales of the field: On writing ethnography.* Chicago: University of Chicago Press.

Vaz, K. M. (Ed.). (1997). *Oral narrative research with black women.* Thousand Oaks, CA: Sage.

Warren, C. A. B. (1988). *Gender issues in field research.* Newbury Park, CA: Sage.

Warren, C. A. B. (2002). Qualitative interviewing. In J. Gubrium & J. Holstein (Eds.), *Handbook of interview research: Context and meaning* (pp. 83–101). Thousand Oaks, CA: Sage.

Warwick, D. P. (1973). Tearoom trade: Means and ends in social research. *Hastings Center Studies, 1*, 27–38.

Wasserfall, R. (1993). Reflexivity, feminism, and difference. *Qualitative Sociology, 16*, 23–41.

Wax, R. (1960). Twelve years later: An analysis of field experiences. In R. N. Adams & J. J. Preiss (Eds.), *Human organization research: Field relations and techniques* (pp. 166–178). Homewood, IL: Dorsey.

Weiss, R. S. (1994). *Learning from strangers: The art and method of qualitative interview studies.* New York: Free Press.

Weston, K. (1998). *Longslowburn: Sexuality and social science.* New York: Routledge.

Whyte, W. F. (1943). *Street corner society: The social structure of an Italian slum.* Chicago: University of Chicago Press.

Williams, C. (2002). To know me is to love me? Response to Erich Goode. *Qualitative Sociology, 25*, 557–560.

Yeandle, S. (1984). *Women's working lives: Patterns and strategies.* New York: Tavistock.

Young, I. M. (1997). *Intersecting voices: Dilemmas of gender, political philosophy, and policy.* Princeton, NJ: Princeton University Press.

Young, P. (1966). *Scientific social surveys and research* (4th ed.). Englewood Cliffs, NJ: Prentice Hall.

Zuckerman, H. (1972). Interviewing an ultra-elite. *Public Opinion, 36*, 159–175.

28

RECONTEXTUALIZING OBSERVATION

Ethnography, Pedagogy, and the Prospects for a Progressive Political Agenda

Michael V. Angrosino

Observation has been characterized as "the fundamental base of all research methods" in the social and behavioral sciences (Adler & Adler, 1994, p. 389) and as "the mainstay of the ethnographic enterprise" (Werner & Schoepfle, 1987, p. 257). Even studies that rely mainly on interviewing as a data collection technique employ observational methods to note body language and other gestural cues that lend meaning to the words of the persons being interviewed. Social scientists are observers both of human activities and of the physical settings in which such activities take place. Some such observation may take place in a laboratory or clinic, in which case the activity may be the result of a controlled experiment. On the other hand, it is also possible to conduct observations in settings that are the "natural" loci of those activities. Some scholars have criticized the very concept of the "natural" setting, particularly when fieldwork is conducted in Third World locations (or in domestic inner-city sites) that are the products of inherently "unnatural" colonial relationships (Gupta & Ferguson, 1996, p. 6), but the designation is still prevalent throughout the literature. In that case, it is proper to speak of "naturalistic observation," or fieldwork, which is the focus of this chapter.

Author's Note. This chapter builds on the essay, "Rethinking Observation: From Method to Context" (Angrosino & Pérez, 2000), which appeared in the second edition of this *Handbook*. In that chapter, we argued that observation-based ethnographic research is not so much a specific method of inquiry as a context in which new ways of conducting qualitative research are emerging. I suggested that researchers' activities were developing in response to a greater consciousness of situational identities, the ethical demands of the modern research enterprise, and relationships of relative power in the field setting, particularly in reference to studies dealing with gender, sexuality, and people on the sociocultural margins (e.g., people with disabilities). The current chapter explores the ramifications of seeing observational research as context, with an emphasis on a convergence of pedagogy and political action in service to a progressive social agenda.

Observations in natural settings can be rendered as descriptions either through open-ended narrative or through the use of published checklists or field guides (Rossman & Rallis, 1998, p. 137; for an historical overview of this dichotomy, see Stocking, 1983a). In either case, in the past it was generally assumed that naturalistic observation should not interfere with the people or activities under observation. Most social scientists have long recognized the possibility of observers affecting what they observe; nonetheless, careful researchers were supposed to adhere to rigorous standards of objective reporting designed to overcome potential bias. Even cultural anthropologists, who have usually thought of themselves as "participant observers" and who have deliberately set out to achieve a degree of subjective immersion in the cultures they study (Cole, 1983, p. 50; Wolcott, 1995, p. 66), still claim to be able to maintain their scientific objectivity. Failure to do so would mean that they had "gone native," with their work consequently being rendered suspect as scientific data (Pelto & Pelto, 1978, p. 69). The achievement of the delicate balance between participation and observation remains the ideal of anthropologists (Stocking, 1983b, p. 8), even though it is no longer "fetishized" (Gupta & Ferguson, 1996, p. 37). Objectivity remains central to the self-images of most practitioners of the social and behavioral sciences. Objective rigor has most often been associated with quantitative research methods, and the harmonization of empathy and detachment has been so important that even those dedicated to qualitative methods have devoted considerable effort to organizing their observational data in the most nearly objective form (i.e., the form that looks most quantitative) for analysis (see, e.g., Altheide & Johnson, 1994; Bernard, 1988; Miles & Huberman, 1994; Silverman, 1993).

Adler and Adler (1994), in fact, suggested that in the future observational research will be found as "part of a methodological spectrum," but that in this spectrum it will serve as "the most powerful source of validation" (p. 389). Observation, they claimed, rests on "something researchers can find constant," meaning "their own direct knowledge and their own judgment" (p. 389). In social science research, as in legal cases, eyewitness testimony from trustworthy observers has been seen as a particularly convincing form of verification (Pelto & Pelto, 1978, p. 69). In actuality, the production of a convincing narrative report of the research has most often served as de facto validation, even if the only thing it validates is the ethnographer's writing skill and not his or her observational capacities (Kuklick, 1996, p. 60).

Postmodernist analysts of society and culture certainly did not invent the current critique of assumptions about the objectivity of science and its presumed authoritative voice, but the prevalence of that analysis in contemporary scholarship has raised issues that all qualitative researchers need to address. The postmodernist critique is not necessarily directed toward the conduct of field-based observational research, but it is impossible to consider postmodern discourse on the production and reproduction of knowledge without taking into account the field context from which so much of our presumed "data" are said to emerge. Earlier criticism of field-workers might have been directed at particular researchers, with the question being whether they had lived up to the expected standards of objective scholarship. In the postmodernist milieu, in contrast, the criticism is directed at the standards themselves. In effect, it is now possible to question whether observational objectivity is either desirable or feasible as a goal. Clifford (1983a), who has written extensively and critically about the study of culture and society, even called into question the work of the revered Bronislaw Malinowski, the archetype of the scientific participant observer who, according to Stocking (1983a), is the scholar most directly responsible for the "shift in the conception of the ethnographer's role, from that of inquirer to that of participant 'in a way' in village life" (p. 93). Perhaps more surprisingly, Clifford (1983a) also questioned the research of the very influential contemporary interpretivist Clifford Geertz, whom he took to task for suggesting that the ethnographer, through empathy, can describe a culture in terms of the meanings specific to members of that culture. In other words, the ethnographer, as a distinct person, disappears—just as he or she was supposed to do in Malinowski's more openly positivistic world. This assessment was echoed by Sewell (1997), who pointed out that Geertz did not expect field-workers to "achieve some miracle of empathy with the people whose lives they briefly and incompletely share; they acquire no preternatural capacity to think, feel, and perceive like a native" (p. 40). The problem is not that Geertz failed to achieve some sort of idealized empathetic state; rather, the question is whether such a state is even relevant to ethnographic research and whether it is desirable to describe and/or interpret cultures as if those depictions could exist without the ethnographer's being part of the action.

The postmodernist critique, which emphasizes the importance of understanding the ethnographer's "situation" (his or her gender, class, ethnicity, etc.) as part of interpreting the ethnographic product, is particularly salient because the remote, traditional folk societies that were the anthropologist's stock-in-trade have virtually disappeared. Most cultural anthropology now is carried out in communities that, if not literate themselves, are parts of larger literate societies that are themselves parts of global communication and transportation networks. Like sociologists, anthropologists now "study up" (i.e., they conduct research among elites), if only to help them understand the predicament of the poor and marginalized people who remain their special concern. Doing so overcomes some of the problems associated with the lingering colonialist bias of traditional ethnography (Wolf, 1996, p. 37), but it raises new issues regarding the position and status of the observational researcher. For one thing, ethnographers can no longer claim to be the sole arbiters of knowledge about the societies and cultures they study because they are in a position to have their analyses read and contested by those for whom they presume to speak (Bell & Jankowiak, 1992; Larcom, 1983, p. 191). In effect, objective truth about a society or culture cannot be established because there are inevitably going to be conflicting versions of what happened. Sociologists and other social scientists were working in such settings long before anthropologists came onto the scene and were already beginning to be aware of the problems inherent in claiming the privilege of objective authoritative knowledge when there are all too many "natives" ready and able to challenge them. As Wolf (1992) wryly commented,

> We can no longer assume that an isolated village will not within an amazingly short period of time move into the circuit of rapid social and economic change. A barefoot village kid who used to trail along after you *will* one day show up on your doorstep with an Oxford degree and your book in hand. (p. 137)

The validity of the traditional assumption—that the truth can be established through careful cross-checking of ethnographers' and insiders' reports—is no longer universally granted because contemporary social and behavioral scientists are increasingly inclined to expect differences in testimony grounded in gender, class, ethnicity, and other factors that are not easy to mix into a consensus. Ethnographic truth has come to be seen as a thing of many parts, and no one perspective can claim exclusive privilege in the representation thereof. Indeed, the result of ethnographic research "is never reducible to a form of knowledge that can be packaged in the monologic voice of the ethnographer alone" (Marcus, 1997, p. 92).

Ethnographers of various disciplines have responded to this new situation by revising the ways in which they conduct observation-based research and present their analyses of this research. No longer can it be taken for granted that ethnographers operate at a distance from their human subjects. Indeed, the very term *subject*, with its implicit colonialist connotations, is no longer appropriate. Rather, there is said to be a *dialogue* between researchers and those whose cultures/societies are to be described. "Dialogue" in this sense does not literally mean a conversation between two parties; in practice, it often consists of multiple, even contradictory, voices. As a result, discussions of ethnographers' own interactions, relationships, and emotional states while in the field have been moved from their traditional discreet place in acknowledgments or forewords to the centers of the ethnographies themselves. The increasing acceptance of autoethnography and performance-based ethnography has also resulted in a greater personalization of the activities of the researchers (see, e.g., Bochner & Ellis, 2002; see also Holman Jones, chap. 30, this volume). Although these practices have certainly opened up new horizons in ethnographic reportage, they raise further issues of their own. For example, because it is likely to be the ethnographers who write up (or at least collate or edit) the results of field studies, do they not continue to claim the implicit status of arbiters/mediators of social/cultural knowledge (Wolf, 1992, p. 120)? Ethnographers may assert that they represent the many voices involved in the research, but we still have only their assurance that such is the case.

Nonetheless, we now function in a context of "collaborative" research. *Collaboration* no longer refers only to the conduct of multidisciplinary teams of professional researchers; it often means the presumably equal participation of professional researchers and their erstwhile "subjects" (Kuhlmann, 1992; Wolf, 1996, p. 26). Matsumoto (1996), for example, sent a prepared list of questions to the people she was interested in interviewing for an oral history project. She assured them that any questions to which they objected would be eliminated. The potential respondents reacted favorably to this invitation to participate in the formulation of the research design. As such situations become more common, it is important that we rethink our current notions about "observation"—what it is, how it is done, what role it plays in the generation of ethnographic knowledge. To that end, it might be useful to shift from a concentration on observation as a "method" per se to a perspective that emphasizes observation as a context for interaction among those involved in the research collaboration.

Observation-Based Research: Traditional Assumptions

Observational researchers traditionally have attempted to see events through the eyes of the people being studied. They have been attentive to seemingly mundane details and to take nothing in the field setting for granted. They were taught to contextualize data derived from observation in the widest possible social and historical frame, all without overgeneralizing from a necessarily limited (and probably statistically nonrepresentative) sample. Their research design usually involved the use of as many means of data collection as were feasible to supplement purely observational data. Although observational research has played a part in many different schools of social theory, it has been most prominently associated with those orientations that seek to construct explanatory frameworks only after careful analysis of objectively recorded data.

There are three main ways in which social scientists have conducted observation-based research. Despite considerable overlap, it is possible to distinguish among (a) participant observation, grounded in the establishment of considerable rapport between the researcher and the host community and requiring the long-term immersion of the researcher in the everyday life of that community; (b) reactive observation, associated with controlled settings and based on the assumption that the people being studied are aware of being observed and are amenable to interacting with the researcher only in response to elements in the research design; and (c) unobtrusive (nonreactive) observation, conducted with people who are unaware of being studied.

All forms of observational research involve three procedures of increasing levels of specificity: (a) descriptive observation (the annotation and description of all details by an observer who assumes a nearly childlike stance, eliminating all preconceptions and taking nothing for granted), a procedure that yields a large amount of data, some of which will prove to be irrelevant; (b) focused observation (where the researcher looks only at material that is pertinent to the issue at hand, often concentrating on well-defined categories of group activity such as religious rituals and political elections); and (c) selective observation (focusing on a specific form of a more general category such as initiation rituals and city council elections). (For an elaboration of these points, see Werner & Schoepfle, 1987, pp. 262–264.)

Underlying these various methodological points was the assumption that it is both possible and desirable to develop standardized procedures that can "maximize observational efficacy, minimize investigator bias, and allow for replication and/or verification to check out the degree to which these procedures have enabled the investigator to produce valid, reliable data that, when incorporated into his or her published report, will be regarded by peers as objective findings" (Gold, 1997, p. 397). True objectivity was held to be the result of agreement between participants and observers as to what is really going on in a given situation. Such agreement was obtained by the elicitation of feedback from those whose behaviors were being reported. Ethnography's "self-correcting investigative process" has typically included adequate and appropriate sampling procedures, systematic techniques for gathering and analyzing data, validation of data, avoidance of observer bias, and documentation of findings (Clifford, 1983b, p. 129; Gold, 1997, p. 399). The main difference between sociological and anthropological practitioners of ethnography seems to be that the former have generally felt the need to validate their eyewitness accounts through other forms of documentation, whereas the latter have tended to use participant observation—"relatively unsystematized" as it might be—as the ultimate reality check on "all the other, more refined research techniques" (Pelto & Pelto, 1978, p. 69).

One classic typology (Gold, 1958) divided naturalistic researchers into "complete participants" (highly subjective and, hence, scientifically questionable), "participants-as-observers" (insiders with a little bit of scientific training but still not truly acceptable as scientists), "observers-as-participants," and "complete observers." Gold (1997) went on to advocate a form of ethnographic research that seeks to collect data that are "grounded in the informants' actual experience" (p. 399). He insisted on the continuing importance of maintaining standards of reliability and validity through "adequate and appropriate sampling procedures, systematic techniques for gathering and analyzing data, validation of data, avoidance of observer bias, and documentation of findings," although he admitted that such goals are met in ethnographic research "in ways that differ from conventional (statistical) procedures" (p. 399).

A somewhat different perspective is represented by Adler and Adler (1987), who emphasized a range of "membership roles" as opposed to roles defined relative to some presumed ideal of pure observation. This shift was occasioned by the realization that pure observation was, first, nearly impossible to achieve in practice and, second, ethically questionable, particularly in light of the evolving professional concern with informed consent. Therefore, Adler and Adler wrote about (a) peripheral member researchers (those who believe they can develop a desirable insider's perspective without participating in those activities that constitute the core of group membership), (b) active member researchers (those who become involved with the central activities of the group, sometimes even assuming responsibilities that advance the group without necessarily fully committing themselves to members' values and goals), and (c) complete member researchers (those who study settings in which they are already members or with which they become fully affiliated during the course of research). In the scholarly world prior to the ascendancy of the postmodernist critique, even complete member researchers, who were expected to celebrate the "subjectively lived experience," were still enjoined to avoid using their insider status to "alter the flow of interaction unnaturally" (Adler & Adler, 1994, p. 380).

▣ Observation-Based Research: Current Assumptions

Contemporary observation-based social research may be characterized by the following trends. First, there is an increasing willingness on the part of ethnographers to affirm or develop a "membership" identity in the communities they study.

Second, researchers recognize the possibility that it may be neither feasible nor possible to harmonize observer and insider perspectives so as to achieve a consensus about "ethnographic truth." Thus, there is a recognition that our erstwhile "subjects" have become collaborators, although they often speak in a voice different from that of hegemonic authoritative science.

Traditional researchers' concern with process and method, therefore, has been supplemented with (but by no means supplanted by) an interest in the ways in which ethnographic observers interact with, or enter into a dialogic relationship with, members of the group being studied. In light of these trends, an earlier incarnation of this chapter suggested that observation-based ethnographic research was not so much a specific method of inquiry as a context in which new roles for the qualitative researcher were emerging. Research roles were said to be developing in response to a greater consciousness of situational identities and to the perception of relative power, particularly in reference to studies dealing with gender, sexuality, and people on the sociocultural margins (e.g., people with disabilities). (For a detailed review of research illustrating these trends, see Angrosino & Pérez, 2000, pp. 678–690.)

At this point, however, it no longer seems fruitful to go on arguing the case for rethinking observation. The numerous studies cited by Angrosino and Pérez (2000) demonstrate quite plainly that the new perspective is already part and parcel of the conceptual framework and methodological toolkits of a wide range of contemporary qualitative researchers.[1] If the battle cannot be said to have been definitively won, there is no longer any doubt that the traditional view—with its fixation on objectivity, validation, and replicability—is now simply one point on a continuum and not the unique voice of reputable social research. The pressing question that now faces us is the following: How do we move this new perspective beyond the confines of academic discourse and ensure its relevance in ways that help us to advance a progressive social agenda?

▣ THE ETHICAL DIMENSION OF OBSERVATION-BASED RESEARCH

Before answering the question at the end of the previous section directly, we must first consider the matter of ethics as it bears on the conduct of observation-based research. Ethics concerns us on two levels. First, we must take into account the current standards operative in most universities and other research institutions that govern the ways in which we work. Second, and perhaps more important in the long run, is the matter of what we mean by a "progressive social agenda." In other words, what values may we invoke to explain and justify the ways in which we seek to use our ethnographic knowledge?

Institutional Structures

Observation was once thought of as a data collection technique employed primarily by ethnographers who thought of themselves as objective researchers extrinsic to the social settings they studied. It has become a context in which researchers who define themselves as members of those social settings interact with other members of those settings. This transition has also effected a shift in the parameters of research ethics.

For good or ill, virtually all social research in our time is governed by the structure of institutional review boards (IRBs), which grew out of federal regulations, beginning in the 1960s, that mandated informed consent for all those participating in federally funded research. Rules governing the use of human subjects are "rooted in scandal" (Gunsalus, 2002, p. B24), specifically the scandal of experiments that led to injury or even death of participants. The perceived threat was from "intrusive" research (usually biomedical). The new rules were designed so that participation in such research would be under the control of the "subjects," who had a right to know what was going to happen to them and who were expected to agree formally to all provisions of the research. The right of informed consent, and the IRBs that were eventually created to enforce it at all institutions receiving federal moneys (assuming a function originally carried out centrally by the U.S. Office of Management and Budget), radically altered the power relationship between the researcher and the human subject, allowing both parties to have a say in the conduct and character of research. (For more detailed reviews of this history, see Fluehr-Lobban, 2003; Wax & Cassell, 1979.) Although few would criticize the move toward protection of human subjects and the concern for their privacy, the increasingly cautious approach of IRBs and their tendency to expand their jurisdiction over all aspects of the research process have turned IRBs into "de facto gatekeepers for a huge amount of scholarly inquiry" (Gunsalus, 2002, p. B24).

Ethnographic researchers, however, have always been uncomfortable with this situation—not because they wanted to conduct covert harmful research but rather because they did not believe that their research was intrusive. Such a claim stemmed from the assumptions typical of the observers-as-participants role, although it is certainly possible to interpret it as a relic of the "paternalism" that traditional researchers often adopted with regard to their human subjects (Fluehr-Lobban, 2003, p. 172). Ethnographers were also concerned that the proposals sent to IRBs had to be fairly complete when it came to explicating the methodology so that all possibilities of doing harm could be adequately assessed. Their research, they argued, often grew and changed as it went along and could not always be set out with the kind of predetermined specificity that the legal experts seemed to expect. They further pointed out that the statements of professional ethics promulgated by the relevant disciplinary associations already provided for informed consent; thus, the IRBs were being redundant in their oversight.

During the 1980s, social scientists won from the U.S. Department of Health and Human Services an exemption from review for all social research except that dealing with children, people with disabilities, and others defined as members of "vulnerable" populations (Fluehr-Lobban, 2003, p. 167). Nevertheless, legal advisers at many universities (including the University of South Florida [USF], where I am based) have opted for caution and been very reluctant to allow this near blanket exemption to be applied. Indeed, at USF, proposals that may meet the general federal criteria for exemption must still be reviewed, although they may be deemed eligible for an "expedited" review. Even proposals that are completely exempt (e.g., studies relying on on-the-record interviews with elected officials about matters of public policy) must still be filed with the IRB. It is ironic that one type of observational research is explicitly mentioned in the "exempt" category—research that is "public" (e.g., studying patterns of where people sit in airport waiting rooms). This is one of the increasingly rare remaining classic "pure observer" types of ethnography. The exemption, however, is disallowed if the researcher intends to publish photos or otherwise identify the people who make up the "public" being researched.

USF now has two IRBs: one for biomedical research and one for "behavioral research." Because the latter is dominated by psychologists (by far the largest department in the social sciences division of the College of Arts and Sciences), this separate status rarely works to the satisfaction of ethnographic researchers. The psychologists, who are used to dealing with hypothesis-testing, experimental clinical or lab-based research, have been reluctant to recognize a subcategory of "observational" research design. As a result, the form currently required by the behavioral research IRB is couched in terms of the individual human subject rather than in terms of populations or communities, and it mandates the statement of a hypothesis to be tested and a "protocol for the experiment." Concerned ethnographers at USF have discovered that some other institutions have developed forms more congenial to their particular needs, but as of this writing they have had no success in convincing the USF authorities to adopt any of them as an alternative to the current "behavioral research" form for review. Indeed, the bias in favor of clinical research seems to have hardened. For example, of the many hundreds of pages in the federal handbook for IRBs, only 11 paragraphs are devoted to behavioral research (Gunsalus, 2002, p. B24). Moreover, it is now mandated that all principal investigators on IRB-reviewed research projects take continuing education on evolving federal ethical standards. It is possible to do so over the Internet, but during the 2001–2002 academic year, all of the choices of training modules were drawn from the realm of health services research.

Issues for Contemporary Observational Researchers

Ethical ethnographers who adopt more clearly "membership"-oriented identities, therefore, are caught between two equally untenable models of research. On the one hand is the official IRB, which is tied to the hypothesis-testing, experimental clinical model. On the other hand are those ethnographers who, in their zeal to win exemption from irrelevant and time-consuming strictures, appear to be claiming that their research is not—or should not be considered—intrusive at all. Yet the interactive, membership-oriented researchers *are by definition* intrusive—not in the negative sense of the word, to be sure, but they are still deeply involved in the lives and activities of the community members they study, a stance fraught with all sorts of possibilities for "harm." The dilemma becomes particularly difficult when we attempt to move beyond academic research to the application of research in service to a social agenda. Such action would seem to require intervention and advocacy—or even conflict in some cases—to bear fruit. As such, there is certainly the possibility of harm, but it is difficult to anticipate what form that harm might take. In principle at least, it might be possible to say that because research collaborators are no longer "subjects," by definition they have as much power as do researchers in shaping the research agenda; they do not need to be warned or protected. But in reality, the researcher is still in a privileged position, at least where actually conducting the research and disseminating its results are concerned. The contemporary researcher probably does not want to retreat to the objective cold of the classic observer, but neither does he or she want to shirk the responsibility for doing everything possible to avoid hurting or embarrassing people who have been trusting partners in the research endeavor. (For another perspective on these matters, see Kemmis & McTaggart, chap. 23, this volume.)

Values and the Social Agenda

Observational research, as it has evolved during recent times, is essentially a matter of interpersonal interaction and only rarely is a matter of objective hypothesis testing. As Fluehr-Lobban (2003) suggested, this turn of events makes it more imperative that we be mindful of the relational ethics implied by the informed consent process (pp. 169–172). Ethnographers should not try to exempt themselves from monitoring; we can, in contrast, work toward a less burdensome and more appropriate set of ethical standards. It is important to keep in mind, however, that human action must always be interpreted in situational context and not in terms of universally applicable objective "codes." Angrosino and Pérez (2000) suggested a method of "proportionate reason" as one way in which to link social research to an ethical framework (pp. 692–695). This position, associated with the philosophical writings of Cahill (1981), Curran (1979), Hoose (1987), and Walter (1984), assesses "the relation between the specific value at stake and the . . . limitations, the harm, or the inconvenience which will inevitably come about in trying to achieve that value" (Gula, 1989, p. 273). In other words, although it is certainly important to weigh the consequences of an action, we must keep in mind that consequences are only one part of the total meaning of an action. Proportionate reason defines what a person is doing in an action (e.g., an ethnographer engaged in an observational context); the person and the action are inseparable. (The opposite, of course, would be the old notion of the ethnographic observer as extrinsic to the action he or she is recording.)

There are three criteria that help us to decide whether a proper relationship exists between the specific value and the other elements of the act

(McCormick, 1973; McCormick & Ramsey, 1978). First, *the means used will not cause more harm than necessary to achieve the value.* In traditional moral terms, the ends cannot be said to justify the means. If we take "the value" to refer to the production of some form of ethnography, we must be careful to ensure that the means used (e.g., inserting oneself into a social network, using photographs or other personal records) do not cause disproportionate harm. We might all agree that serving as *comadre* or *compadre* to a child of the community that one is studying is sufficiently proportionate; in contrast, we might well argue about whether becoming the lover of someone in that community (particularly if that sexual liaison is not intended to last beyond the time of the research) does more harm than an ethnographic book, article, or presentation might be worth. Volunteering as a classroom tutor in a program that serves adults with mental retardation whom one is interested in observing and interviewing is probably sufficiently proportionate; in contrast, becoming a bill-paying benefactor to induce cooperation among such adults in a group home would be morally questionable.

The second criterion is that *no less harmful way to protect the value currently exists.* Some might argue that observational research always and inevitably compromises personal privacy, such that no form of research can ethically protect that cherished value. But most researchers would probably reject such an extreme view and instead take the position that there is real value in disseminating the fruits of ethnographic research so as to increase our knowledge and understanding of cultural diversity, the nature of coping strategies, or any number of currently salient social justice issues. Granted that *all* methods have the potential to harm, we must be sure to choose those that do the *least* amount of harm but that still enable us to come up with the sort of product that will be effective in communicating the valuable message. The strategy of writing ethnographic fiction, for example, might be one way in which to make sure that readers do not know exactly who is being described.

The third criterion is that *the means used to achieve the value will not undermine it.* If one sets out, for example, to use research to promote the dignity of people defined as mentally disabled, one must make sure that the research techniques do not subject those people to ridicule. Videotaping a group of people with mental retardation as they play a game of softball might conceivably result in confirming the popular stereotypes of such people as clumsy or inept—objects of pity (at best) or of scorn (at worst)—rather than as dignified individuals. Videotaping as an adjunct to observational research is itself ethically neutral; its appropriateness must be evaluated in this proportionate context.

McCormick (1973) suggested three modes of knowing whether there is a proportionate reason to carry out a suggested action. First, we know that a proper relation exists between a specific value and all other elements of an act through *experience,* which sometimes amounts to plain common sense. For example, although we may think that it is important to encourage individual expression, we know from experience that doing so in the context of a traditional community, where the individual is typically subordinate to the group, will do real violence to the precepts by which the people we are intent on studying have historically formed themselves into a cohesive society. Experience might suggest that we rethink a decision to collect personal life histories of people in such communities in favor of focusing on the collective reconstruction of remembered common activities or events.

Second, we might know that a proper relationship exists through our own *intuition* that some actions are inherently disproportionate, even if we do not have personal experience of their being so. For example, we should intuitively know that publishing information of a personal nature collected from undocumented migrant workers might mean that such information could be used against them. Our righteous goal of improving the lot of the migrants might well be undermined by giving authorities the ammunition to harass them further. A perception of what *could* happen (the result of intuition) is, of course, different from a perception of what *will* happen (the result of experience), and we are clearly not well served by dreaming up every conceivable disaster. It serves no purpose to allow ourselves to be paralyzed beforehand by overactive guilty consciences. But there is certainly a commonsensical hierarchy of plausibility that occurs in such cases; some things that *could* happen are more likely to come about than are others.

Third, we know through *trial and error.* This is a mode of knowing that would be completely impossible under current institutional ethical guidelines. But the fact is that we do not, and cannot, know all possible elements in any given human social interaction, and the idea that we can predict—and thereby forestall—all harm is naïve in the extreme. An ethical research design would omit (or seek to modify) that which experience and intuition tell us is most likely to do harm. We can then proceed, but only on the understanding that the plan will be modified during the course of the action when it becomes clear what is feasible and desirable in the real-life situation. For those uncomfortable with the indeterminacy of the term "trial and error," Walter (1984) suggested "rational analysis and argument" (p. 38). By gathering evidence and formulating logical arguments, we try to give reasons to support our choices for certain actions over others. But this way of knowing does indeed involve the possibility of committing errors, perhaps some that may have unexpected harmful consequences. It is nonetheless disingenuous to hold that all possibilities of harm can be anticipated and that any human action, including a research project based on interpersonal interaction, can be made risk free. The moral advantage of the proportionate reasoning strategy is that it encourages researchers to admit to errors once they have occurred, to correct the errors so far as possible, and to move on. The "objective" mode of research ethics, in contrast, encourages researchers to believe that they have eliminated all such problems, and so they are disinclined to own up to problems that crop up and, hence, are less capable of repairing the damage. Those who work with people with developmental disabilities are familiar with the expression "the dignity of risk," which is used to describe the habilitation of clients for full participation in the community. To deny clients the possibility of making mistakes (by assuming that all risks can be eliminated beforehand and by failing to provide training in reasonable problem-solving techniques) is to deny them one of the fundamental characteristics of responsible adult living. One either lives in a shelter, protected from risk by objectified codes, or lives real life. The ethical paradigm suggested here does nothing more than allow the observational researcher the dignity of risk.

The logic of proportionate reason as a foundation for an ethical practice of social research might seem, at first glance, to slide into subjective relativism. Indeed, the conscience of the individual researcher plays a very large part in determining the morality of a given interaction. But proper proportionalism cannot be reduced to a proposition that an action can mean anything an individual wants it to mean or that ethics is simply a matter of personal soul searching. Rather, the strategy is based on a sense of community; the individual making the ethical decision must ultimately be guided by a kind of "communal discernment" (Gula, 1989, p. 278). When we speak of "experience," for example, we refer not only to personal experience but also to the "wisdom of the past" embodied in a community's traditions. As such, it

> demands broad consultation to seek the experience and reflection of others in order to prevent the influence of self-interest from biasing perception and judgment. Using proportionalism requires more moral consultation with the community than would ever be required if the morality of actions were based on only one aspect . . . apart from its relation to all the . . . features of the action. (Gula, 1989, p. 278)

That being the case, the ideal IRB would not be content with a utilitarian checklist of presumed consequences. Rather, it would constitute a circle of "wise" peers with whom the researcher could discuss and work out the (sometimes conflicting) demands of experience, intuition, and the potential for rational analysis and argument. The essential problem with current ethical codes, from the standpoint of the qualitative observational researcher, is that they set up an arbitrary—and quite unnecessary—adversarial relationship between researchers and the rest of the scholarly community. The framework of proportionate reason implies that ethical research is the product of shared discourse and not of a species of prosecutorial inquisition.

Elements in a Suggested Progressive Social Agenda

The abstractions of the proportionate reason framework can be translated into a progressive social agenda to guide the researcher. Progressive politics seeks a just society, although traditional moral philosophy speaks of four different types of justice: (a) commutative justice, which is related to the contractual obligations between individuals involving a strict right and the obligation of restitution (e.g., when one person lends another person a sum of money, the borrower is obliged to return that money according to the terms of the agreement); (b) distributive justice, which is related to the obligation of a government toward its citizens with regard to its regulation of the burdens and benefits of societal life (e.g., a government may tax its citizens but must do so fairly, according to their ability to pay, and must distribute the proceeds according to need); (c) legal justice, which is related to citizens' obligation toward the government or society in general (e.g., citizens are obligated to pay taxes, serve on juries, and possibly serve in the military, although they reserve the right to engage in conscientious objection—or even civil disobedience—if they deem the demands of the government unjust); and (d) social justice, which is related to the obligation of all people to apply moral principles to the systems and institutions of society (e.g., individuals and groups are urged to take an active interest in necessary social and economic reforms). My own personal vision tends to emphasize the element of social justice, and I suggest three ways in which researchers can work toward the principles embodied in the concept of social justice.

First, the researcher should be directly connected to the poor and marginalized. Helping the latter might well involve intensive study of power elites, but a progressive agenda goes by the boards if the researcher comes to identify with those elites and sees the poor simply as a "target population." Direct connection necessarily involves becoming a part of the everyday life of a community. The middle-class researcher who *chooses* to live with the poor and otherwise marginalized in our society (or with entire societies that are poor and marginalized vis-à-vis larger global powers) is, of course, in a very different position compared with residents of such communities who have no choice in the matter. But research in service to a progressive agenda flows from a degree of empathy (not simply "rapport" in the way that term was used by traditional participant observers) that is not available to those who do not even try to maintain such ongoing contact.[2]

Second, the researcher should ask questions and search for answers. This might seem like an obvious thing for a researcher to do, but we are in the habit of asking questions based primarily on our scholarly knowledge of the literature. We move in a more productive direction if we begin to ask questions based on our experience of life among the poor and marginalized rather than on our experience of what others have written or said about them. By the same token, we must avoid the sentimental conclusion that "the people" have all the answers, just as we shun the assumption that "the experts" know what is best for the people. Asking the relevant questions might lead us to look within the community for answers drawing on its own untapped resources, or it might lead us to explore options beyond the community.

Third, the researcher should become an advocate. Advocacy might mean becoming a spokesperson for causes or issues already defined by the community. It also might mean helping the people to discern and articulate issues that may have been inchoate to that point. Advocacy often means engaging in some sort of conflict (either among factions within the community or between the community and the powers-that-be), but it can also mean finding ways in which to achieve consensus in support of an issue that has the potential to unite. In either case, one ends up working *with* the community as opposed to working *for* the community (with the latter implying a more distanced stance).

The overall goal of this process is to empower the community to take charge of its own destiny to whatever extent is practical. The researcher might well retain a personal agenda (e.g., collecting data to complete a dissertation), but his or her main aim is to work with the community to achieve shared goals. Such a philosophy can be difficult to convey to students or other apprentice researchers (e.g., how does it all work out "on the ground"?). To that end, it might be instructive to consider a form of pedagogy that, although not specifically designed for this purpose, certainly serves these ends.

Pedagogy for Social Justice: Service Learning

The concept of "service learning" was given a boost by the Johnson Foundation/Wingspread report titled *Principles of Good Practice for Combining Service and Learning.* Service learning is more than simply a way in which to incorporate some local field research into social science courses. As a strategy adopted by USF and others in response to the *Principles* report, service learning is the process of integrating volunteer community service combined with active guided reflection into the curriculum to enhance and enrich student learning of course material. It is designed to reinvigorate the spirit of activism and volunteerism that energized campuses during the 1960s but that waned during subsequent decades. Colleges and universities that accepted this challenge formed a support network (Campus Compact) to develop and promote service learning as a pedagogical strategy. Service learning is now a national movement.

The philosophical antecedent and academic parent of service learning is experiential learning (e.g., cooperative education, internships, field placements), which was based on the direct engagement of the learner in the phenomenon being studied. The critical difference and distinguishing characteristic of service learning is its emphasis on enriching student learning while also revitalizing the community. To that end, service learning involves students in course-relevant activities that address real community needs. Course materials (e.g., textbooks, lectures, discussions, reflection) inform students' service, and the service experience is brought back to the classroom to inform the academic dialogue and the quest for knowledge. This reciprocal process is based on the logical continuity between experience and knowledge.

The pedagogy of service learning reflects research indicating that we retain 60% of what we do, 80% of what we do with active guided reflection, and 90% of what we teach or give to others. The pedagogy is also based on the teaching of information processing skills rather than on the mere accumulation of information. In a complex society, it is nearly impossible to determine what information will be necessary to solve particular problems. All too often the content that students learn in class is obsolete by the time they obtain their degrees. Service learning advocates promote the importance of "lighting the fire" (i.e., teaching students how to think for themselves) as opposed to "filling the bucket" (i.e., giving students predigested facts and figures). Learning is not a predictable linear process. It may begin at any point during a cycle, and students might have to apply their limited knowledge in a service situation before consciously setting out to gain or comprehend a body of facts related to that situation. The discomfort arising from the lack of knowledge is supposed to encourage further accumulation of facts or the evolutionary development of a personal theory for future application. To ensure that this kind of learning takes place, however, skilled guidance in reflection on the experience must occur. By providing students with the opportunity to have a concrete experience and then assisting them in the intellectual processing of that experience, service learning not only takes advantage of a natural learning cycle but also allows students to provide a meaningful contribution to the community.

It is important to note that the projects that form the basis of the students' experience are generated by agencies or groups in the community. The projects can be either specific one-time efforts (e.g., a Habitat for Humanity home-building project) or longer term initiatives (e.g., the development of an after-school recreation and tutoring program based at an inner-city community center). Given the theme of this chapter, it is significant that all such activities build on the fundamentals of observational research. Student volunteers gradually adopt membership identities in the community and must nurture their skills as observers of unfamiliar interactions so as to carry out the specific mandates of the chosen projects and to act as effective change agents in the community. In this way, service learning projects affiliated with courses outside the social and behavioral sciences require students to become practitioners of observational research methods, although such an outcome is not a specifically identified goal of the course. Recently at USF, service learning has been a key feature of a diverse set of courses, including an anthropology seminar on community development, a sociology course on the effects of globalization, an interdisciplinary social science course on farm-worker and other rural issues, a psychology course on responses to the HIV/AIDS epidemic, a social work course on racial and ethnic relations, and a business seminar on workplace communication.

In sum, service learning, which affects the professional educator as well as the novice/student, is more than simply traditional "applied social science," which often had the character of "doing for" the community. Service learning, which begins with the careful observation of a community on the part of a committed student adopting a membership identity, is active engagement in and with the community in ways that foster the goals of a social justice-oriented progressive political and social agenda.

Prospects for Observational Research

Although it is certainly true that "forecasting the wax and wane of social science research methods is always uncertain" (Adler & Adler, 1994, p. 389), it is probably safe to say that observation-based research is going to be increasingly committed to what Abu-Lughod (1991) called "the ethnography of the particular" (p. 154). Rather than attempting to describe the composite culture of a group or to analyze the full range of institutions that supposedly constitute the society, the observational ethnographer will be able to provide a rounded account of the lives of particular people, with the focus being on individuals and their ever-changing relationships rather than on the supposedly homogeneous, coherent, patterned, and (particularly in the case of traditional anthropologists) timeless nature of the supposed "group." Currently the "ethnography of the particular" coexists uneasily with more quantitative and positivistic schools of sociology, anthropology, and social psychology. There is, however, considerable doubt as to how long that link can survive given the very different aims and approaches of the diverging branches of the once epistemologically unified social sciences. It seems likely that observational techniques will find a home in a redefined genre of cultural studies, leaving their positivist colleagues to carry on in a redefined social science discipline.

Observation once implied a notebook and pencil and perhaps a sketch pad and simple camera. The conduct of observational research was revitalized by the introduction of movie cameras and then video recorders. Note taking has been transformed by the advent of laptop computers and software programs that assist in the analysis of narrative data. But as our technological sophistication increases, we face an increasing intellectual dilemma in doing research. On the one hand, we speak the theoretical language of "situatedness," indeterminacy, and relativism; on the other hand, we rely more and more on technology that suggests the capture of "reality" in ways that could be said to transcend the individual researcher's relatively limited capacity to interpret. The technology makes it possible for the ethnographer to record and analyze people and events with a degree of particularity that would have been impossible just a decade ago, but it also has the potential to privilege what is captured on the record at the expense of the lived experience as the ethnographer has personally known it. It would be foolish to suggest that, for the sake of consistency, observation-based ethnographers should eschew further traffic with sophisticated recording and analytic technology. But it would be equally foolish to assume that the current strong trend in the direction of individualized particularism can continue without significant modification in the face of technology that has the perceived power to objectify and turn into "data" everything it encounters. Perhaps it will become necessary for us to turn our observational powers on the very process of observation, that is, to understand ourselves not only as psychosocial creatures (which is the current tendency) but also as users of technology. As Postman (1993) pointed out, technological change is never merely additive or subtractive; it is never simply an aid to doing what has always been done. Rather, it is "ecological" in the sense that a change in one aspect of behavior has ramifications for the entire system of which that behavior is a part. Under those circumstances, perhaps the most effective use of observational techniques we can make in the near future will be to discern the ethos of the technology that we can no longer afford to think of as a neutral adjunct to our business-as-usual mentality. It is a technology that itself has the capacity to define our business. We need to turn our observational powers to what happens not only when "we" encounter "them" but also when we do so with a particular kind of totalizing technology.

No technological revolution has been more challenging to the traditions of observational research than the rise of the Internet and with it the increasing prevalence and salience of the "virtual community." Ethnographers have long observed communities that are defined by some sort of geographic "reality," although we have also recognized the importance of social networks that are not place bound. Contemporary virtual communities are an extension of such older "communities of interest," although they depend on computer-mediated communication and are characterized by online interactions. Research needs to be developed to explore the nature of these virtual communities. How are they similar to traditional communities or social networks? How are they different? How does electronic communication make new kinds of community possible? How does it facilitate existing communities? (Regarding questions such as these, see Gabrial, 1998; Hine, 2000; Jones, 1998, 1999; Markham, 1996; Miller & Slater, 2000). As Bird and Barber (2002) noted, "Life on-line is becoming simply another part of life in the twenty-first century. On-line communities may replicate many of the features of other non-place-based communities, but they also make available new possibilities and new kinds of connections" (p. 133).

The increasing salience of electronic media poses some special ethical challenges for the ethnographic observer. It goes without saying that the traditional norms of informed consent and protection of privacy and confidentiality continue to be important, even though we are observing and otherwise dealing with people we do not see face to face. It is true that the Internet is a kind of public space, but the people who inhabit its virtual terrain are still individuals entitled to enjoy the same rights as are people in more traditional communities. There are as yet no comprehensive guidelines applicable to online research, but a few principles seem to be emerging by consensus. First, research based on a content analysis of a public website need not pose an ethical problem, and "it is probably acceptable to quote messages posted on public message boards" (Bird & Barber, 2002, p. 134). But the attribution of such quotes to identifiable correspondents would be a breach of privacy. Second, when observing an online community, the researcher should inform the members of his or her presence and of his or her intentions. The members should be assured that the researcher will not use real names, e-mail addresses, or any other identifying markers in any publication based on the research. Third, many online groups have their own rules for entering and participating. The "virtual" community should be treated with the same respect as if it were a "real" community, and its norms of courtesy should be observed carefully. Some researchers conducting online ethnographies, therefore, have accepted as standard procedure the sharing of drafts of research reports for comments by members of the online community. By allowing members to help decide how their comments will be used, this practice realizes the larger ethical goal (discussed earlier) of turning research "subjects" into truly empowered collaborators.

Bird and Barber (2002) pointed out that "electronic communication is stripped of all but the written word" (p. 134). As such, the ethnographer is at somewhat of a disadvantage given that the traditional cues of gestures, facial expressions, and tones of voice—all of which give nuances of meaning to social behavior—are missing. By the same token, the identity of the person with whom the researcher is communicating can be concealed—or even deliberately falsified—in ways that would not be possible in face-to-face communication. Therefore, it is necessary to develop a critical sense, to evaluate virtual sources carefully, and to avoid making claims of certainty that cannot be backed up by other means.

Whether in the virtual world or the real world, observation-based researchers continue to grapple with the ethical demands of their work. In light of comments in this chapter, it is heartening to learn that a recent report from the Institute of Medicine (IOM) has presented us with the challenge of rethinking the whole notion of research ethics. Ethical regulations, as discussed previously, have tended to ask basically negative questions (e.g., What is misconduct? How can it be prevented?). The IOM report, however, invites us in the near term future to consider the positive (e.g., What is integrity? How do we find out whether we have it? How can we encourage it?). According to Frederick Grinnell, a member of the IOM committee that produced the report, the promotion of researcher integrity has both individual and institutional components, namely "encouraging individuals to be intellectually honest in their work and to act responsibly, and encouraging research institutions to provide an environment in which that behavior can thrive" (Grinnell, 2002, p. B15). Grinnell went so far as to claim that qualitative social researchers have a central role to play in this proposed evolution of the structures of research ethics because they are particularly well equipped to conduct studies that would identify and assess the factors that influence integrity in research in both individuals and large social institutions.

A Closing Word

It seems clear that the once unquestioned hegemony of positivistic epistemology that encompassed even so fundamentally humanistic a research technique as observation has now been shaken to its roots. One telling indication of the power of that transition—and a challenging indication of things to come—was a comment by the late Stephen Jay Gould, the renowned paleontologist and historian of science, who ruefully admitted,

> No faith can be more misleading than an unquestioned personal conviction that the apparent testimony of one's eyes must provide a purely objective account, scarcely requiring any validation beyond the claim itself. Utterly unbiased observation must rank as a primary myth and shibboleth of science, for we can only see what fits into our mental space, and all description includes interpretation as well as sensory reporting. (p. 72)

Notes

1. In the chapter that appeared in the second edition of this *Handbook,* Pérez and I discussed a number of such studies. One of the authors we cited, James Mienczakowski, has asked that we clarify some of the remarks we made about his work. Noting his use of "alternative" means of reporting ethnographic data, we linked him with others experimenting with ethnographic writing, including autoethnographers. In so doing, we might have unwittingly left the impression that Mienczakowski's work fell into the category of autoethnography. Although that work is not dealt with in this chapter, I feel honor bound to allow Mienczakowski to present what he believes is a

more accurate representation of his work. In a personal communication (May 17, 2004), he noted, "My work unequivocally describes not self-location or autoethnography but a very different form of ethnographic research construction. In fact, . . . my personal experiences or location . . . are not relevant to, or the focus of, my published researches in detoxification therapy."

2. "Empathy" in this context should be interpreted in a political sense; that is, the researcher takes on a commitment to the community's agenda. Use of the term in this way should not be taken to imply anything about the totality of the community's culture or about the ability of the researcher to achieve a capacity to enter totally into the ethos of that community—if such a thing as an enveloping community ethos even exists.

References

Abu-Lughod, L. (1991). Writing against culture. In R. G. Fox (Ed.), *Recapturing anthropology: Working in the present* (pp. 137–162). Santa Fe, NM: School of American Research.

Adler, P. A., & Adler, P. (1987). *Membership roles in field research.* Newbury Park, CA: Sage.

Adler, P. A., & Adler, P. (1994). Observational techniques. In N. K. Denzin & Y. S. Lincoln (Eds.), *Handbook of qualitative research* (pp. 377–392). Thousand Oaks, CA: Sage.

Altheide, D. L., & Johnson, J. M. (1994). Criteria for assessing interpretive validity in qualitative research. In N. K. Denzin & Y. S. Lincoln (Eds.), *Handbook of qualitative research* (pp. 485–499). Thousand Oaks, CA: Sage.

Angrosino, M. V., & Pérez, K. (2000). Rethinking observation: From method to context. In N. K. Denzin & Y. S. Lincoln (Eds.), *Handbook of qualitative research* (2nd ed., pp. 673–702). Thousand Oaks, CA: Sage.

Bell, J., & Jankowiak, W. R. (1992). The ethnographer vs. the folk expert: Pitfalls of contract ethnography. *Human Organization, 51,* 412–417.

Bernard, H. R. (1988). *Research methods in cultural anthropology.* Newbury Park, CA: Sage.

Bird, S. E., & Barber, J. (2002). Constructing a virtual ethnography. In M. V. Angrosino (Ed.), *Doing cultural anthropology* (pp. 129–137). Prospect Heights, IL: Waveland.

Bochner, A. P., & Ellis, C. (Eds.). (2002). *Ethnographically speaking: Autoethnography, literature, and aesthetics.* Walnut Creek, CA: AltaMira.

Cahill, L. S. (1981). Teleology, utilitarian, and Christian ethics. *Theological Studies, 41,* 601–629.

Clifford, J. (1983a). On ethnographic authority. *Representations, 1,* 118–146.

Clifford, J. (1983b). Power and dialogue in ethnography: Marcel Griaule's initiation. In G. W. Stocking (Ed.), *Observers observed: Essays on ethnographic fieldwork* (pp. 121–156). Madison: University of Wisconsin Press.

Cole, D. (1983). "The value of a person lies in his *Herzenbildung*": Franz Boas' Baffinland letter-diary, 1883–1884. In G. W. Stocking (Ed.), *Observers observed: Essays on ethnographic fieldwork* (pp. 13–52). Madison: University of Wisconsin Press.

Curran, C. E. (1979). Utilitarianism and contemporary moral theology: Situating the debates. In C. E. Curran & R. A. McCormick (Eds.), *Readings in moral theology* (pp. 341–362). Ramsey, NJ: Paulist Press.

Fluehr-Lobban, C. (2003). Informed consent in anthropological research: We are not exempt. In C. Fluehr-Lobban (Ed.), *Ethics and the profession of anthropology* (2nd ed., pp. 159–178). Walnut Creek, CA: AltaMira.

Gabrial, A. (1998). Assyrians: "3,000 years of history, yet the Internet is our only home." *Cultural Survival Quarterly, 21,* 42–44.

Gold, R. L. (1958). Roles in sociological field observation. *Social Forces, 36,* 217–223.

Gold, R. L. (1997). The ethnographic method in sociology. *Qualitative Inquiry, 3,* 388–402.

Gould, S. J. (1998). The sharp-eyed lynx, outfoxed by nature (Part 2). *Natural History, 107,* 23–27, 69–73.

Grinnell, F. (2002, October 4). The impact of ethics on research. *Chronicle of Higher Education,* p. B15.

Gula, R. M. (1989). *Reason informed by faith.* New York: Paulist Press.

Gunsalus, C. K. (2002, November 15). Rethinking protections for human subjects. *Chronicle of Higher Education,* p. B24.

Gupta, A., & Ferguson, J. (1996). Discipline and practice: "The field" as site, method, and location in anthropology. In A. Gupta & J. Ferguson (Eds.), *Anthropological locations: Boundaries and grounds of a field science* (pp. 1–46). Berkeley: University of California Press.

Hine, C. (2000). *Virtual ethnography.* London: Sage.

Hoose, B. (1987). *Proportionalism.* Washington, DC: Georgetown University Press.

Jones, S. G. (Ed.). (1998). *Cybersociety 2.0.* London: Sage.

Jones, S. G. (1999). *Doing Internet research: Critical issues and methods for examining the Net.* London: Sage.

Kuhlmann, A. (1992). Collaborative research among the Kickapoo tribe of Oklahoma. *Human Organization, 51,* 274–283.

Kuklick, H. (1996). After Ishmael: The fieldwork tradition and its future. In A. Gupta & J. Ferguson (Eds.), *Anthropological locations: Boundaries and grounds of a field science* (pp. 47–65). Berkeley: University of California Press.

Larcom, J. (1983). Following Deacon: The problem of ethnographic reanalysis, 1926–1981. In G. W. Stocking (Ed.), *Observers observed: Essays on ethnographic fieldwork* (pp. 175–195). Madison: University of Wisconsin Press.

Marcus, G. E. (1997). The uses of complicity in the changing mise-en-scène of anthropological fieldwork. *Reflections, 59,* 85–108.

Markham, A. (1996). *Life on-line: Researching real experience in virtual space.* Walnut Creek, CA: AltaMira.

Matsumoto, V. (1996). Reflections on oral history: Research in a Japanese-American community. In D. L. Wolf (Ed.), *Feminist dilemmas in fieldwork* (pp. 160–169). Boulder, CO: Westview.

McCormick, R. A. (1973). *Ambiguity and moral choice.* Milwaukee, WI: Marquette University Press.

McCormick, R. A., & Ramsey, P. (1978). *Doing evil to achieve good.* Chicago: Loyola University Press.

Miles, M. B., & Huberman, A. M. (1994). *Qualitative data analysis: An expanded sourcebook* (2nd ed.). Thousand Oaks, CA: Sage.

Miller, D., & Slater, D. (2000). *The Internet: An ethnographic approach.* New York: Berg.

Pelto, P. J., & Pelto, G. H. (1978). *Anthropological research: The structure of inquiry* (2nd ed.). New York: Cambridge University Press.

Postman, N. (1993). *Technopoly: The surrender of culture to technology.* New York: Vintage.

Rossman, G. B., & Rallis, S. F. (1998). *Learning in the field: An introduction to qualitative research.* Thousand Oaks, CA: Sage.

Sewell, W. H. (1997, Summer). Geertz and history: From synchrony to transformation. *Representations,* pp. 35–55.

Silverman, D. (1993). *Interpreting qualitative data: Strategies for analysing talk, text, and interaction.* London: Sage.

Stocking, G. W. (1983a). The ethnographer's magic: Fieldwork in British anthropology from Tylor to Malinowski. In G. W. Stocking (Ed.), *Observers observed: Essays on ethnographic fieldwork* (pp. 70–120). Madison: University of Wisconsin Press.

Stocking, G. W. (1983b). History of anthropology: Whence/whither. In G. W. Stocking (Ed.), *Observers observed: Essays on ethnographic fieldwork* (pp. 3–12). Madison: University of Wisconsin Press.

Walter, J. (1984). Proportionate reason and its three levels of inquiry: Structuring the ongoing debate. *Louvain Studies, 10,* 30–40.

Wax, M. L., & Cassell, J. (1979). *Federal regulations: Ethical issues and social research.* Boulder, CO: Westview.

Werner, O., & Schoepfle, G. M. (1987). *Systematic fieldwork,* Vol. 1: *Foundations of ethnography and interviewing.* Newbury Park, CA: Sage.

Wolcott, H. F. (1995). *The art of fieldwork.* Walnut Creek, CA: AltaMira.

Wolf, D. L. (1996). Situating feminist dilemmas in fieldwork. In D. L. Wolf (Ed.), *Feminist dilemmas in fieldwork* (pp. 1–55). Boulder, CO: Westview.

Wolf, M. A. (1992). *A thrice-told tale: Feminism, postmodernism, and ethnographic responsibility.* Stanford, CA: Stanford University Press.

29

WHAT'S NEW VISUALLY?

Douglas Harper

One faces the task of a chapter on the same subject for the third edition of this *Handbook* with a certain amount of trepidation. After all, not that much changes in the social sciences, especially within such a few brief years. Yet there are new themes, technologies, and practices mixed into the gradual evolutions of established patterns in visual methods. With that in mind, my goal in this chapter is to minimize overlap with the chapters in the earlier editions, with the modest proposal of seeing what indeed is new in visually inspired qualitative research.

Thus, readers interested in the postmodern critique of visual ethnography; the relationship among visual sociology, visual anthropology, and documentary photography; and the development of a research typology of visual thinking in visual research should consult the earlier chapters (Harper, 1993, 2000). I suggested that visual sociology offered the opportunity to address the postmodern critiques of ethnography and documentary photography and, in so doing, to fashion a new method based on the understanding of the social construction of the image and the need for collaboration between the subject and the photographer.

This chapter examines the status of visual thinking in the sociological community, the impact of new technologies on visual methods, the continuing development of visual documentary and visual sociology, and problematical ethics questions in the visual research world.

In the background is a much discussed separation in the visual studies movement between the study of social life using images, which is often referred to as the empirical wing of visual sociology, and the study of the meanings of visual culture, which is usually called cultural studies. Some have argued that this clouds the fact that we share a fundamental interest in the meanings of visual imagery.

As an example of visually oriented cultural studies, Fuery and Fuery (2003) explore Foucault's imaging of the body, Lacanian theories of abjection and reflection, Kristeva's ideas about body fragmentation and visual culture, Derrida's notions about social reproduction and the semiotics of imagery, and Barthes's semiotics of photography. Their book contains only one image—a reproduction of a 1992 *Calvin and Hobbes* cartoon to illustrate Kristeva's theory of the abjection of the self. However, the arguments are grounded in examples of visual imagery on websites that are listed at the ends of the chapters. Thus, the reader can refer to the images of Magritte, Dali, Warhol, Caravaggio, and Bernini, to the photographs of Newton, and to the films of Hitchcock without the expense and inconvenience of having the images in the book itself. Of course, reading the book implies access to a computer and the Internet, and referencing websites in this way assumes that the images will still be available online for as long as the book is used. Because the images are not esoteric, this is probably a safe bet. So, the book presents itself as a postmodern argument against the hegemony of its own form.

But more to the point of this chapter, Fuery and Fuery (2003) show how cultural studies use images to advance theories of the self, society, existence itself, and/or symbolism. I have suggested elsewhere (Harper, n.d.) that cultural studies generally use images (from fine arts to mass media, from architectural shapes to fashion, from body decoration and shapes to imagery of nightmares) as a referent for the development of theory. One can argue that these cultural studies are ethnographic in an indirect manner; they are based on the analysis of the visual culture writ large.

This chapter has a different orientation because I believe that a handbook of qualitative research should focus on field research. From my perspective, the emphasis should be on the practical, that is, using imagery to study specific questions and issues in sociology, anthropology, communications, and the like. Much of what I discuss in the following draws on photography, although there are several other suitable ways in which to visually represent the world in social research. For example, in my own study of the work of a rural artisan (Harper, 1987), drawings complemented photographs. The drawings allowed a more subjective take; elements could be left out, and interiors of objects could be invaded with cutaways. So, there is no reason why photography must dominate empirical visual sociology beyond the fact that it has proven to be enormously useful.

Most of the visual sociology discussed in this chapter depends on photographs—processed, juxtaposed, deconstructed, and captioned, but still evidence of something seen. It is a reminder, once again, of photography as both empirical and constructed. It has become something of a ritual to repeat this idea in all articles or chapters on visual sociology, but it appears to be necessary.

Innovations in Journal Publication

Sociological research that relies on visual data is being published with increasing frequency. Journals such as *Qualitative Inquiry* and *Symbolic Interaction* include imagery—not exactly routinely, but more and more frequently nonetheless. Several new visually oriented journals have joined established visual social science journals, such as *Visual Anthropology* and *Visual Sociology* (renamed *Visual Studies* in 2001), as outlets for visual research.

A promising development within American sociology was the introduction of the American Sociological Association's (ASA) journal, *Contexts,* in 2001. *Contexts,* intended to popularize sociology for a mass audience, is the first American sociology journal to forefront visual information, albeit with not entirely consistent results.

Visual illustration in *Contexts* is used in three ways. I call the first the "illustrated research article," with an example being Rank's (2003) study of the incidence of poverty in the United States. Rank uses photographs to portray a spectrum of the poor, including well-dressed job seekers, some using cell phones, in an unemployment line in New York; a group of perhaps 200 disheveled homeless people gathering for shelter in San Francisco; a young homeless family in Eugene, Oregon, sitting on a curb across the street from a grocery store; and an African American woman and an aged white immigrant in the daily routines of their poverty. The images put a face on statistical data, but what do they add beyond that?

First, they contextualize poverty with other sociological variables such as family life, unemployment, and global migration. Visual documentation becomes a part of research triangulation, confirming theories using different forms of data. In these instances, the photographs argue that visual traces of the world adequately describe the phenomenon under question.

The photographs also subjectively connect the viewer to the argument. The well-dressed job seekers in New York connect poverty directly to employment. The homeless couple and child in Oregon do not look like the stereotyped vision of poverty; we would expect to see their attractive faces in a typical middle-class home. The immigrant in poverty is an elderly man from the Netherlands, showing us that nonminority immigrants also struggle to make ends meet in the United States.

But although these photographs are important to the text, they remain secondary. The visual dimension is not integrated into the research; the images are added by an editor who has the challenging job of securing photos from a variety of sources. The result is that useful photos are often found and published, but so are images that fall short of their mandate to visually tell a sociological story.

Contexts also publishes photo essays, where sociological thinking emerges directly from images rather than reinforcing and elaborating on word-based thinking. Gold's (2003) photo essay on the Israeli diaspora is a good example. The body of the article consists of 12 photographs and captions organized around the themes of "Individual and Community Business," "Designing and Finding Communities," and "Transnational Networks and Identities." The photographs locate people in various environments—from their homes, to businesses, to public settings—interacting in the routines of various social scenes. The images are organized conceptually and are the main way in which the ideas are presented. Gold's photo essay (and others published in *Contexts*) shows the possibility of sociological thinking that derives nearly entirely from images. The intention is that sociologists will regard the photographs in these essays as visual data, that is, that sociologists will engage the photographs with active intellectual "looking." Because photographs saturate popular culture and are generally treated superficially, this is a big leap.

As hinted at previously, asking sociologists to take photographs seriously raises the matter of their truth status—or their validity, in sociological terminology. Here, as has been stated many times previously and has already been mentioned in this chapter, rests a central irony of the photograph: It is both true and constructed. It is true in the sense that it reflects light falling on a surface, but it is also constructed by the technical, formalistic, and other selections that go into making the image and by the contexts (from historical to presentational format) in which it is viewed. In this way, photos are similar to all forms of data—both qualitative and quantitative.

It is hoped that the *Contexts* photo essays will elevate sociologists' understanding of this essential similarity between photographic data and other forms of data.

Contexts also publishes photo essays on social change, that is, images that show the same social scene at an earlier time and a more contemporary time. Photography is especially helpful in studies of social change because photographs can be matched with earlier images to reveal extraordinarily detailed renditions of changes in human habitation, landscape, and/or traces of human interaction. This approach draws on the work of a single sociologist, Jon Rieger, who has applied the fine arts and documentary "rephotography" movement to the study of social change in northern Michigan (Rieger, 1996, 2003) and other settings.

Although *Contexts* has broken new ground in sociology, it remains to be seen whether the journal will successfully make the case for visual data in research or whether it will be considered less rigorous precisely because the journal relies heavily on visual displays. For *Contexts* to redefine visual thinking in sociological publishing, it must initiate a discussion of the role of visual information in sociological thinking and presentation.

The journal must also improve its means of attaining images; it is simply not feasible to assume that good-hearted photographers will donate the use of their photos. It is also not feasible to assume that volunteer staff members (despite their success so far) can do what professional photo editors do, that is, find and get access to the very best photos to develop visual arguments.

New Technologies; New Ways of Thinking

What is genuinely new in visual sociology is the use of technology in recording, organizing, presenting, and analyzing visual information. Emerging technologies have revolutionized the use of imagery in social science, and some intrepid researchers have already provided convincing examples. The basis of the revolution is the computer, but more specifically it is software programs such as Macromedia's *Director* and, in some cases, the Web. All of these technologies are several generational offsprings of *HyperCard,* a program bundled with early Apple computers that allowed information to be organized in a nonlinear manner. In what follows, I briefly examine four projects that demonstrate the range of these new ways of thinking and doing field research visually.

Jay Ruby's ethnographic study of Oak Park, Illinois, uses the Web to disseminate the ongoing results of a field study (Ruby, n.d.). The website (http://astro.ocis.temple.edu/~ruby/opp/) includes interviews, photographs, observations, historical commentary, and video segments in various forms of completion. Ruby also established a listserv of residents of Oak Park, inviting people who are the subject of the study to disagree, elaborate, or simply comment on the ongoing study. According to Ruby's website,

> Oak Park Stories is a series of experimental, reflexive, and digital ethnographies that attempt to explore a forty-year-old social experiment in Oak Park, a Chicago suburb. It is experimental in that I have not followed the traditional method of producing a book or film but instead made an interactive and nonlinear work that has both video and text. It is reflexive in that the subject of my research is my hometown. . . . It is digital in its form of delivery—on a DVD using QuickTime movies and html documents. I have constructed these Stories in a nonlinear fashion; that is, unlike a book or a film, there is no defined beginning, middle, or end. Viewers/Readers are free to begin anywhere. They can ignore anything that doesn't interest them. I have provided many links to materials that will allow anyone interested to pursue a topic in more depth. I have found writing in a nonlinear fashion to be amazingly freeing.

The website is organized around "modules," which are broad categories with scroll-down subcategories. These include an extensive discussion of ethnography, histories of families that represent the community, the black migration to Chicago and Oak Park itself, biographies of individuals who have played an important role in the community, and other modules that explore themes such as racial integration.

The module organization is similar to chapters in a book but also is distinctly different. The modules include subcategories of photo essays (often from archival sources) that show, for example, images of race riots in 1919 and images of a single African American on an otherwise all-white championship football team. The module format establishes a logic for the overall project: The first-order categories are the modules themselves, the second-order categories are scrollable items beneath the module title, and the third-order information exists in the many linked articles, photo essays, newspapers, and other archival documents that are sprinkled liberally throughout. This is similar to the organization of a book with a chapter structure, text, and endnotes, but it is markedly different because of the freedom allowed to go into more depth than a particular subject in a book might allow or to add material that might be too tangential for a scholarly study. For example, Ruby's study develops a central theme of racial and ethnic integration. Subcategories of the integration module present the history of African Americans in Chicago in more detail than would likely be included in an academic monograph. Ruby's pages-long overview of housing policies, race politics, and shifting demographic information can, however, easily be included in the Web presentation. It is contextualizing information that some, but certainly not all, viewers/readers will use. Links to additional sites further these possibilities.

Ruby posts quarterly reports from the field and asks for feedback by way of Web discussions. His importance in visual anthropology and prominence in a visual communication listserv generates a Web-based audience for his work.

The attractiveness of this mode of dissemination is precisely that a variety of communication modes—text, still images, and moving images—can be integrated. However, the memory-hungry nature of video makes it (so far) impractical to include more than a few seconds of video clips, with the moving images being bracketed into a small thumbnail on the screen. The final project is intended as a number of DVDs, where longer video segments can be included.

The sharing of the project-in-progress by way of an evolving website has not, to my knowledge, been done before. The project could be left in this form and updated on a continual basis through the near future. However, Ruby intends to finalize the project as one or more DVDs distributed in the same way as other emerging visual anthropology multimedia projects are distributed, that is, through commercial or academic publishers.

Other visually oriented sociologists have begun to develop the potential of advanced interactivity with Macromedia's *Director.* The first of these projects was Biella, Chagnon, and Seaman's (1997) *Yanamamo Interactive*, which is an interaction version of Chagnon and Asch's classic ethnographic film, *The Ax Fight.*[1] *The Ax Fight* is a 10-minute film showing a hostile interaction between two groups of Yanamamo tribespeople in Venezuela. The film has become an important teaching tool as well as an important research tool. It is a commonly cited example of how minimally edited ethnographic film can tell several layers of ethnographic stories. So, the Biella project is based on expanding the potential of a classic in visual anthropology, primarily (but not exclusively) for teaching.

The traditional means of teaching this material has been to show the film, assign readings on the Yanamamo, and integrate these materials in lectures and discussions. Researchers use a similar strategy—close study of the film and consideration of visual material in the context of written sources.

By packaging the film with different kinds of information (still photographs, graphs, tables, and extensive texts) so that various parts can be connected in novel ways, *Yanamamo Interactive* opens up heretofore unexplored pedagogical and research possibilities.

The *Yanamamo Interactive* CD-ROM includes three versions of the film (unedited and edited in two forms), 380 paragraphs that describe the events as they unfold in the film (these are viewed alongside the scrolling film), more than 100 captioned photographs of the participants in the ax fight, genealogical charts that plot the participants' relationships, and maps of the village and the interaction of the fight. As noted, the software architecture allows viewers to move among filmed events, biographical sketches, maps of important places, and ethnographic explanations freely and creatively. The format invites theory testing, both formally and informally. The CD-ROM defines film as being integral to ethnography rather than as a form of ethnography itself. As a result, the film can be seen as ethnographic information that is deconstructed by reading the anthropology that gives background information.

My experience with the CD-ROM has been nothing short of inspiring. I am well aware of how difficult it is to teach ethnographic film; students see the film in one parcel of time and then read or discuss it in another parcel of time. Thus, the emotional and subjective experience of studying film is separated from the more analytical experience of studying texts. This separation often leads to stereotyping precisely because emotions and analysis become ever more distant from each other.

The interactivity potential of the CD-ROM allows the viewer to, for example, stop the video, select a particular participant in the fight, and trace the participant's genealogy in the village and his social position vis-á-vis his participation in village groups and activities. Thus, students and researchers can study the contexts of social action and begin to understand the layers of meaning that reside under the surface of the fight. In fact, the organization of the material invites students and researchers to ask new questions and to investigate new lines of reasoning.

The project has been distributed with an introductory anthropology textbook and is widely used in university anthropology courses. The CD-ROM allows students from a wide range of backgrounds to actually encounter ethnographic information and, thus, to do visual research at a fairly sophisticated level.

It is likely that the format introduced in *Yanamamo Interactive* will soon become common in visual anthropology, extending the usefulness of ethnographic film for both teaching and research. Several projects by the authors of this CD-ROM and others are under way.

Macromedia's *Director* has also been used to produce a searchable archive of the work of documentary photographer Jean Mohr. Mohr is best known for his collaborations with John Berger (Berger & Mohr, 1967, 1975, 1982) and for his work in the area of international human rights for several international organizations (Mohr's first photographs, taken during the early 1950s, documented the everyday lives of Palestinian refugees). He has also photographed less known projects involving the Chicago police on patrol and international tours of a European symphony.

The CD-ROM titled *Jean Mohr: A Photographer's Journey* (Mohr, n.d.) collects more than 1,200 of Mohr's black-and-white and color photographs (from more than 1 million taken during his 50-year career) and includes brief interviews with Mohr and others about the meaning of his work as well as brief texts that explain and elaborate on the projects from which the images were drawn.

The core of the project is the photographs, which are organized in five categories, the most important of which are "image type," "subjects," and "regions." Each of these categories includes several subcategories accessible as drop-down menus. For example, the image category of "subjects" includes the subcategories of "migrants," "music," "refugees," and several others. Thus, the viewer is able to create a corpus of images by clicking on one subcategory in each main category. For example, I direct the CD-ROM to gather Mohr's black-and-white portraits of refugees who were photographed in Africa. Or, the viewer could direct the CD-ROM to select color images on the general subject of music that Mohr photographed in the Middle East. Combining a different subelement from each of the main categories allows the viewer to construct hundreds of individualized archives.

These advanced searching capabilities allow the viewer to use Mohr's work efficiently and creatively. I found that, after several hours of working with the archive, the only limitation that suggested itself was the number of photographs that it included. A total of 1,200 images might seem like a lot at first glance, but they are a tiny percentage of Mohr's life work. Most searches cross-referenced across several categories yield 20 to 30 images, whereas Mohr's full corpus would include several times that number. The most challenging aspect of this project was clearly in programming the navigation; one senses that more images could have easily been scanned and added to the archive. Thus, if the project had included three to four times the number of images, the archive would be that much more useful.

Electronic and searchable photograph archives from newspapers or public collections are increasingly available. Mohr's project, however, might be the first to present the life work of a sociologically oriented photographer with information that describes his career, publications, self-reflections, and commentary on his relationship with Berger. As an overview of the work of a single photographer, it sketches the working methods of an artist. It also provides visual evidence on sociological themes such as refugees as well as visual area studies of the places where Mohr concentrated his efforts. Short video clips also humanize Mohr.

One would hope that the considerable effort represented in this CD-ROM project will lead others to synthesize their photographic work, especially when the work so broadly addresses subject matters of interest to sociological researchers.

Two projects with a smaller scope show the potential of interactive media in visual research. Ricabeth Steiger photographed an aspect of daily life—a train commute she makes several times a week from Basel to Zurich, Switzerland, to construct a visual ethnography of a taken-for-granted aspect of daily life (Steiger, 2000) (Figure 29.1). The images are both impressionistic (showing blurred landscapes through the train windows—the world speeding by as viewed from inside the train) and ethnographic (showing the tacit social scripts—how people interact on a train—that underlie the public behavior in Switzerland).

Steiger's project was published in *Visual Sociology* as a research article in two forms. The

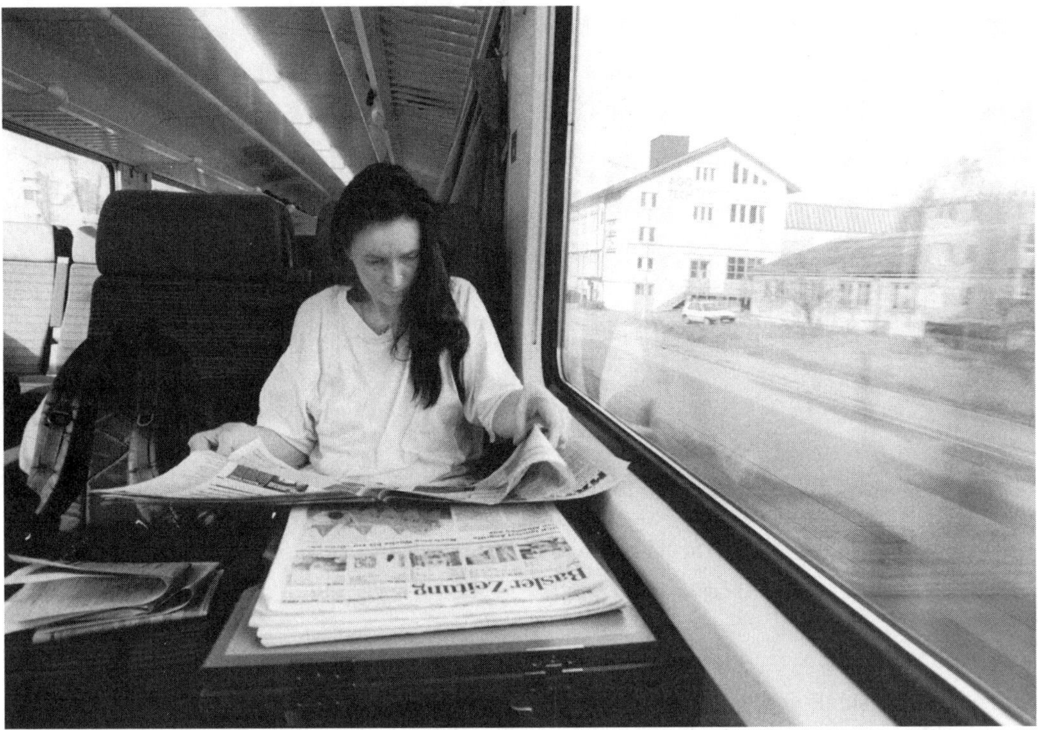

Figure 29.1. Inside the Train

Source: Photograph by Ricabeth Steiger.

article text and photo sequence were published as thumbnail-sized images in the print journal and on a CD-ROM that housed a *Director*-based movie version of the project. The CD-ROM format allowed Steiger to transform still photographs into a new mode of communication—a virtual movie consisting of an automatically advancing slide show. This was an ideal solution; the images were too numerous to work as an article but were too few to constitute a book, and they needed to be viewed in sequence to achieve the intended effect. Although the thumbnail images published in the journal are a catalog of the photos, the virtual movie clearly constitutes the actual article.

The publication of the project in *Visual Sociology* was a breakthrough in the presentation of visual research. The development of the CD-ROM required the journal designer to have knowledge of relevant software and cross-platform development. The International Visual Sociology Association (IVSA), the sponsoring academic organization of the journal, devoted considerable resources to fund the CD-ROM and to package and distribute it as a regular part of the journal. It did so with the hope that the project's revolutionary character would help to encourage a new way in which to see and do visual research.

Finally, Dianne Hagaman recently published a photographic project using the same software, with considerably more elaborate development (Hagaman, 2002). As in the case of Steiger's project, the subject is a visual ethnography of daily life, in this case her life with her husband, the sociologist Howard S. Becker.

The photographs are organized into 14 "sonnets," with each sonnet named after a jazz standard such as "Night and Day," "Slow Boat to China" (Figure 29.2), or "One Morning in May." Jazz has been an important part of Becker's life; he was (and remains) a practicing musician, and his studies of jazz are important contributions to cultural sociology. The photographs also have a jazzy

Figure 29.2. From "Slow Boat to China" Sonnet of the CD-ROM *Howie Feeds Me*

Source: Photographs by Dianne Hagaman.

quality; they are subtle and present reality from an oblique angle, transforming otherwise unremarkable subject matter, such as window frames and beds, into poetic visual statements. Likewise, jazz presents familiar melodies in unusual and provocative frames of musical reference.

The photographs are about place (the couple's homes in Seattle and San Francisco and the couple's travels to Paris and other locations where Becker lectures), landscape (Hagaman is a master at rendering sky as a part of landscape, often inhabited by birds on the wing), social gatherings (often with well-known sociologists), and (most centrally) their own relationship. According to Hagaman's introduction,

> We weren't kids when we met and decided to live together, and we didn't have our whole lives ahead of us. . . .
>
> He played the piano and knew hundreds of songs from his days when he played clubs in Chicago. And he could cook. And liked to do it. He told me that after his wife Nan died, he made himself three full meals a day, every day, in order to establish a routine and structure in his life in a time of change and grief.
>
> I, however, had never learned to cook. It wasn't deliberate. I just somehow fell through the cracks. But, maybe as a consequence, I've never taken the preparation or the social aspects of food for granted: how central eating is and preparing the food that you eat (that magical skill) is, who we eat with and where.

Thus, the project is titled *Howie Feeds Me,* and the photographs allude to a relationship rooted in caring for and nourishing the body and spirit. In this way, the project is an ethnography of the daily life of a couple and their loving relationship, as told from the perspective of one partner. The only similar attempts to communicate this theme are Laura Letinsky's photo essay *Venus Inferred* (Letinsky, 2000), which focuses on the banalities of the sexual lives of several couples, and Pernette and Leeuwenberg's (2001) photo essay on their intimate relationship. But whereas Letinsky (2000) focuses on the obvious (i.e., a series of couples looking embarrassed in the act of coupling) and Pernette and Leeuwenberg (2001), both photographers in their early 30s, use the camera to record the energy and lovingness of sexual union, Hagaman (2002) communicates the mundane aspects of nonsexual intimacy with subtlety and humor that suggests the stuff of daily life.

Much of the message of Hagaman's essay is in the medium. The project is rooted in

35-millimeter black-and-white photos, but from the beginning it was intended for the computer. Hagaman organized the CD-ROM-mounted photo sequences in what she calls sonnets: "I took the idea of the fourteen lines of a sonnet and used it to organize my photographs, a group of fourteen images making a kind of poem: rhyming, repeating, alluding, and suggesting, the way photographs do when you put them into groups."

The sonnets are of two forms. One is a series of individual images presented on the computer screen against a white background, like images on the wall of a gallery. These have short captions that usually identify the place or action depicted. The viewer studies these images individually and in sequence as well as in the context of the story hinted at by the title of the sonnet (a jazz standard).

Other sonnets are continuous visual loops of joined images that the viewer scrolls through. The images adjoin each other completely; the viewer creates new images composed of parts of the adjoining images by stopping the scroll bar in other than the borders of the photographs. Thus, when the viewer scrolls, images suddenly combine exteriors of a room from one image and exteriors of a street from another; other images contain both night and day, and so forth. The continually joined images add a dimension that could not be achieved if the images stood alone either on a gallery wall or on a computer screen.

The photographs are also presented as thumbnails with detailed descriptions of location, people, and events that are useful points of reference.

New developments such as those described heretofore have revolutionary potential in visual studies. There are, however, several issues that may affect their contributions.

The first issue concerns longevity. The software that runs the various programs is under constant development, and the systems that run the computers are as well. For example, Apple's recent operating system, OS-X (already in its third iteration), has required full redesign of participating software. Similar developments in PC operating systems have led to the same challenges. With the rate of current development, it is nearly impossible to predict the hardware, operating system, and/or software compatibility for today's projects that will be in use 10 or even 5 years from now. Of course, the book that I just removed from the shelf will be there, in exactly the same form, 50 years from now.

The second issue is that, as noted previously, electronic delivery and organization of material often allows information to be packaged in a way that could not be presented in print form. But the opposite is also true: Old-fashioned media, including books, articles, and handmade images, have been shown to have a remarkable resiliency precisely because of the very qualities that the electronic forms transcend. The illustrated book or journal article, for example, imposes limitations that the Web does not and that might lead to more judicious editing or organization. The linearity of old-fashioned presentations remains meaningful as a frame by which ideas and images can be organized.

There is also the matter by which various forms of information find their way to consumers. Books and articles are published and distributed through a system that draws on well-articulated institutional structures and a public that consumes in a certain way. This is a multilayered and conservative system. Nontextual media, such as CD-ROMs and DVDs, have only recently begun to get a foothold in this system.

This is not to say that the old forms are necessarily better or worse than newer competing forms of visual communication. It is simply to say that some aspects of change come slowly. This must be said in the context of the increasing success of the Web and multimedia platforms.

The Continuation of the Old

Certain themes and forms of visual research, however, continue to produce useful visual research. One is the visual critical analysis, such as Margolis's (1998, 1999) studies of education and labor processes. This work traces its roots to studies such as Stein's (1983) critical investigation of early social reform-oriented photography. Stein's study focuses on how the sponsorship, photographic technology, and forms of dissemination influenced what the photos communicated. These arguments often suggest that the photographs have latent meanings that reinforce the very structures they seem to be criticizing.

A more informal use of images to ask critical questions of the past is Norfleet's (2001) *When We Liked Ike.* Norfleet, who may have been the first practicing visual sociologist (she worked in photography and sociology for several decades at Harvard University), here assembles photographs from archives from the 1950s that document everyday life—families, institutions, organizations, leisure life, and so forth. She captions these images with excerpts from popular sociological texts of the time (e.g., those of David Reisman and Vance Packard), excerpts from novelists (e.g., J. D. Salinger), and quotes from the popular press (e.g., *Ladies Home Journal*). The viewer is taken to the everyday world that became the basis of sociological analysis.

Empirical visual sociology lives on as well. For example, Rich and Chalfen (1999) use visual methods in a study of disease phenomenology. In their research, chronic asthma sufferers in their teens or younger made and analyzed videos of their personal worlds under the influence of asthma. The films and discussions opened a window into the private world of a disease at a particular stage of the life cycle. The visual dimension served as a means of discovery by the disease victims (they filmed their worlds to tell the story of their disease experience), and it also served as the basis of dialogue among asthma sufferers, adults in their social worlds (e.g., parents, teachers), and the medical community. The videos described social isolation, parental irresponsibility, and other themes that led to a fuller understanding of how the teens and younger children manage a debilitating disease.

Rich and Chalfen's use of native-produced imagery draws originally from Worth, Adair, and Chalfen's (1972/1997) Navajo project of the late 1960s, where anthropologists taught reservation Navajo to use 16-millimeter cameras to tell their cultural stories. Many other examples followed.

Native-produced still images, however, have also become important visual research tools in social science. An early example was Ewald's work with Appalachian youth. Her approach was to teach young children to photograph their families and surroundings, develop the black-and-white film, and print the images. She asked the children she taught what they imagined and dreamed about and how they interpreted their daily surroundings. Ewald's initial success led to several similar projects in South America, Holland, and other settings (Ewald, 1985, 1992, 1996).

Photo elicitation is another approach that belongs exclusively to the visual. In a recent description of the method (Harper, 2002), I found photo elicitation to be the primary method in 40 studies, including doctoral theses, books, articles, and reports. Several studies have been finished during the period since the article was published, and certainly many were missed in the review. The disciplines represented in these studies include anthropology, communication, education, sociology (especially urban, rural, and communities studies), photojournalism, cultural studies, ethnic studies, and industrial management. In these vastly dissimilar kinds of research, the common desire to understand the world as defined by the subject led to wide applications of the photo elicitation method.

In what follows, I explain one way in which photo elicitation operates in a brief review of a study of the meaning of change in dairy farming in northern New York (Harper, 2001). In this project, my goal was to understand how agriculture had changed and what these changes meant for those who lived through them. To this end, I showed elderly farmers photographs from the 1940s, (a period when they had been teens or young adult farmers) and asked them to remember events, stories, or commonplace activities that the photos brought to mind. The success of the project rested on the coincidence of the availability of an extraordinary archive of documentary photographs (the Standard Oil of New Jersey archive) from just the era that elderly farmers had experienced at the beginnings of their careers and the fact that these photographs were of such a quality as to inspire detailed and often deep memories.

The farmers described the mundane aspects of farming, including the social life of shared work (Figure 29.3). But more important, they explained what it meant to have participated in agriculture that had been neighbor based, environmentally friendly, and oriented toward animals more as partners than as exploitable resources.

In this and other photo elicitation studies, photographs proved to be able to stimulate memories that word-based interviewing did not. The result was discussions that went beyond "what happened when and how" to themes such as "this was what this had meant to us as farmers."

Visual methods have also been applied to approaches that have not previously been thought to be visual. A recent issue of *Visual Studies* (Volume 18, Issue 1) was devoted to ethnomethodology. The visual worlds that ethnomethodologists studied included the textual materials in various administrative jobs (Carlin, 2003) and the work objects of scientific endeavors (Kawatoko & Ueno, 2003). These studies draw on Sudnow's (1993) pioneering ethnomethodological studies of jazz performance that were communicated partly through photographic imagery.

Several texts on visual methods have been published during recent years. The most useful are Pink's (2001) *Doing Visual Ethnography,* Banks's (2001) *Visual Methods in Social Research,* and van Leeuwen and Jewitt's (2001) edited *Handbook of Visual Analysis.* Pink has studied visual research broadly, whereas Banks has concentrated on visual anthropology. Van Leeuwen and Jewitt's handbook is a useful collection of cultural studies and empirical research. Their contributors describe content analysis, visual anthropology, cultural studies, semiotics, ethnomethodology, and film analysis. Although most contributors downplay approaches that favor "researchers making photos to analyze reality," the collection is a useful starting place. Less useful is Emission and Smith's (2000) *Researching the Visual,* which is largely a polemic against the photocentric orientation of visual sociology.

It is especially interesting that those who have synthesized the strains and traditions of visual social studies have come largely from outside the United States and, most significant during the past few years, from the United Kingdom. The "U.K. School" emphasizes cultural studies but is increasingly eclectic, with recent and forthcoming collections that center on visual ethnography (e.g., Knowles & Sweetman, 2004).

Figure 29.3. A Farm Work Crew Eating Dinner

Source: Photograph by Sol Libsohn. Used by permission of the Ekstrom Library, University of Louisville.

The other significant European movement in visual sociology is situated in Italy, primarily at the University of Bologna. Beginning in the early 1990s, Patrizia Faccioli and her colleagues have conducted visual research on a wide range of topics using photo elicitation, documentary photography, content analysis, and semiotics (for an overview, see Faccioli & Losacco, 2003). Losacco's (2003) recent monograph uses family photography to understand the negotiation of cultural identities of Italian immigrants in Canada.

That the IVSA meets regularly in Europe helps to facilitate the growth of visual methods internationally. The development of visual social science in the remaining areas of the world where social sciences are taught is a critical next development.

However, although there are many recent texts on visual methods, there are few new in-depth studies based on visual data or visual analysis. Quinney has written and photographed a series of introspective ethnographies of place, with the most recent (Quinney, 2001) exploring the meaning of what he refers to the "borderland"—Hamlin Garland's "middle border," which he presents as a landscape, a state of mind, and a basis for philosophical orientation. Barndt (2002) uses photographs to both gather and present information in a study of the globalization of the food. *Changing Works* (Harper, 2001) is one of the few recent ethnographic studies based on photographs.

However, photo documentary studies continue to be published. Recent examples include Coles and Nixon's (1998) *School,* which explores the social realities of three schools in Boston; Goodman's (1999) *A Kind of History* (1999), which documents 20 years in the life of an ordinary American town;

and Wilson's (2000) photo study of the *Hutterites of Montana.* Yet the documentary tradition remains the scope or attention of most social scientists. Unfortunately, Becker's suggestion back in 1974 that documentary photographers and sociologists with an interest in photography should explore their overlap and get on with learning from each other is still largely underrealized (Becker, 1974).

Unresolved Issues: Ethics of Visual Research—Special Issues and Special Considerations

The scientific world, of which sociology is a part, has become increasingly concerned with research ethics. This preoccupation is partly due to past misuses of scientific research. This has, in turn, led to the increased use of institutional review boards (IRBs) as legally mandated monitors of all research at U.S. universities. These issues are also the subjects of codes of ethics of professional societies such as the ASA.

Qualitative researchers, however, often have a difficult time in defining their work in terms that meet the expectations of IRBs. This is especially the case for photographic researchers. The primary issue concerns the matter of subject informed consent and subject anonymity. The problems for qualitative researchers, and the special case of sociological photographers, are detailed in what follows.

The first concerns the observation of public life and, in the case of visual sociology, the photography of public life. Observation of public life has been a part of sociology since Georg Simmel's studies of generic forms of social interaction, based in part on his observations of public life from his Berlin apartment window, or since Irving Goffman's observations of the nuances of human interaction in social gatherings. Anderson (2003) refers to this style of sociological observation as "folk ethnography." Anderson's method involves observing the public on bus trips and walks through a city as well as overhearing conversations in restaurants and other instances of public life.

In large part, IRBs appear to be ready to accept that observation of public life may take place without informed consent. But the right to photograph the public without the subjects' consent has, by and large, not been tested by passage of research proposals by members of the visual sociological community. Many visual sociologists model our photographic research on documentary photography and photojournalism, where the right to photograph in public has been guaranteed by amendments to the U.S. Constitution dealing with freedom of expression. In these studies, it is precisely the clearly portrayed face of a stranger doing the things people normally do that leads to compelling documentary statements or sociologically meaningful insights.

Visual sociologists point to the precedent of photojournalism and documentary and argue that harm to subjects is unlikely to occur from showing normal people doing normal things. In a personal example, I was photographed unawares at a recent Pittsburgh Pirates baseball game by a photographer working for the *Pittsburgh Post Gazette,* and I was presented in a half-page photograph to support the message of an article that alleged low attendance at the Pirates games. In fact, I had chosen to sit by myself in an otherwise empty section because I like the vantage point of that section and I enjoy the solitude in a baseball stadium early in the season. Having the photo in the *Post Gazette* made me a celebrity for a day, but it also opened up other questions. Was I skipping work? Was I a social isolate? And so forth. However, the public accepts that being in a public space makes one susceptible to public photography. I was not harmed by my momentary celebrity status, and the ethics of photojournalism were not violated. I was portrayed accurately in the mundane performance of my life.

Those of us who want to use photography in sociology believe that it is logical to argue that we have the same rights as those who work in the closely related worlds of photojournalism and photodocumentary. Indeed, some of us have come to define ourselves as documentary photographers, rather than as visual sociologists, to avoid

IRB scrutiny, although this is surely not a solution to this issue.

The second matter concerns the loss of confidentiality in photos that portray people clearly. The language of the current ethics literature (in the ASA code of conduct or the IRB guidelines) is strongly aligned with protecting the anonymity of subjects. That is commendable if subjects wish to remain anonymous. But what about subjects who are pleased and willing to be subjects (and who sign releases to this effect)? The identifiability of subjects is critical to the sociological usefulness of the images; these include elements such as subjects' expressions, gestures, hairstyles, clothing, and other personal attributes.

There has been little written about the ethics of photographic research. Several years ago, Gold (1989) argued that the biomedical model did not sufficiently address the ethical issues of visually based research, arguing instead for a "research outlook—sensitivity—that is rooted in the covenantal ethical position . . . as a means of addressing the ethical problems of visual sociology" (p. 100). This sensitivity "requires the researcher to develop an in-depth understanding of subjects so that he or she may determine which individuals and activities may be photographed, in what ways it is appropriate to do so, and how the resulting images should be used" (p. 103). This involves understanding the point of view of subjects, especially their thoughts on how and where the images will be used. According to Gold, "Unlike a contract that simply specifies rights and duties, a covenant requires the researcher to consider his or her relationship with subjects on a much wider level, accepting the obligations that develop between involved, interdependent persons" (p. 104).

The practical implications are that one will sometimes find oneself in research situations where photography would violate the norms of the setting or the feelings of the subjects; in such cases, photography should not be done. Gold (1989) suggests that sociologists use their knowledge as well as their ethical sensitivities to guide their actions. Whether this can be the basis of an acceptable method remains to be seen.

For visual ethnography to come out of the closet, these issues need to be resolved. Visual researchers must have their work sanctioned by boards that eventually will accept research that varies radically from the formal experiment and that depends on the right to document life in glaring exactitude.

Summary

My hope is that visual methods will become ever more important in the various research traditions where it already has a foothold and that this growth will take place in a way that acknowledges the potential of new media, while preserving what is useful in the old media, and acknowledges the subjects' rights but calls forth a larger ethical stance than the biomedical contractual model determines as appropriate. I hope that during the next decade, visual social studies will become a world movement and, thus, a means to long overdue internationalization of sociology.

For visual social science to develop, professional rules and norms concerning ethics must acknowledge the rights of photographers/researchers to photograph in public and to present identifiable subjects, but in the context of ethical considerations that consider photographers/researchers as connected by webs of obligation and moral regard.

Note

1. Biella and colleagues' (1997) project, as well as Steiger's (2000) article (which had just been released when the second iteration of this chapter was written), both were mentioned briefly in my chapter in the second edition of this *Handbook*.

References

Anderson, E. (2003, November). *Folk ethnography.* Paper presented at the conference Being Here/Being There: Fieldwork Encounters and Ethnographic Discoveries, University of Pennsylvania, Philadelphia, PA.

Banks, M. (2001). *Visual methods in social research.* London: Sage.

Barndt, D. (2002). *Tangled routes: Women, work, and globalization of the tomato trail.* Lanham, MD: Rowman & Littlefield.

Becker, H. S. (1974). Photography and sociology. *Studies in the Anthropology of Visual Communication, 1*(1), 3–26.

Berger, J., & Mohr, J. (1967). *A fortunate man.* New York: Pantheon.

Berger, J., & Mohr, J. (1975). *A seventh man.* New York: Viking.

Berger, J., & Mohr, J. (1982). *Another way of telling.* New York: Pantheon.

Biella, P., Chagnon, N., & Seaman, G. (1997). *Yanamamo interactive: The ax fight* [CD-ROM]. New York: Harcourt Brace.

Carlin, A. P. (2003). Pro forma arrangements: The visual availability of textual artefacts. *Visual Studies, 18*(1), 6–20.

Coles, R., & Nixon, N. (1998). *School.* Boston: Little, Brown.

Emission, M., & Smith, P. (2000). *Researching the visual.* London: Sage.

Ewald, W. (1985). *Portraits and dreams.* New York: Writers and Readers.

Ewald, W. (1992). *Magic eyes: Scenes from an Andean girlhood.* Seattle, WA: Bay Press.

Ewald, W. (1996). *I dreamed I had a girl in my pocket: The story of an Indian village.* New York: DoubleTake Books.

Faccioli, P., & Losacco, G. (2003). *Manuale di Sociologia Visuale.* Milan, Italy: Angeli.

Fuery, P., & Fuery, K. (2003). *Visual cultures and critical theory.* Oxford, UK: Oxford University Press.

Gold, S. (1989). Ethical issues in visual field work. In G. Blank, J. L. McCartney, & E. Brent (Eds.), *Practical applications in research and work* (pp. 99–112). New Brunswick, NJ: Transaction Publishers.

Gold, S. (2003). Israeli diaspora. *Contexts, 2*(3), 50–57. (American Sociological Association)

Goodman, M. (1999). *A kind of history.* San Francisco: Markerbooks.

Hagaman, D. (2002). *Howie feeds me* [CD-ROM]. Rochester, NY: Visual Studies Workshop.

Harper, D. (1987). *Working knowledge: Skill and community in a small shop.* Chicago: University of Chicago Press.

Harper, D. (1993). On the authority of the image: Visual sociology at the crossroads. In N. K. Denzin & Y. Lincoln (Eds.), *Handbook of qualitative research* (pp. 403–412). Newbury Park, CA: Sage.

Harper, D. (2000). Reimagining visual methods: Galileo to *Neuromancer*. In N. Denzin & Y. Lincoln (Eds.), *Handbook of qualitative research* (2nd ed., pp. 717–732). Thousand Oaks, CA: Sage.

Harper, D. (2001). *Changing works: Visions of a lost agriculture.* Chicago: University of Chicago Press.

Harper, D. (2002). Talking about pictures: A case for photo elicitation. *Visual Studies, 17*(1), 13–26.

Harper, D. (n.d.). Cultural studies and the photograph. Manuscript.

Kawatoko, Y., & Ueno, N. (2003). Talking about skill: Making objects, technologies, and communities visible. *Visual Studies, 18*(1), 47–57.

Knowles, C., & Sweetman, P. (2004). *Picturing the social landscape.* London: Routledge.

Letinsky, L. (2000). *Venus inferred.* Chicago: University of Chicago Press.

Losacco, G. (2003). *Wop o Mangicake, Consumi e identita etnica: La negoziazione dell'italianita a Toronto.* Milan, Italy: Angeli.

Margolis, E. (1998). Picturing labor: A visual ethnography of the coal mine labor process. *Visual Sociology, 13*(2), 5–36.

Margolis, E. (1999). Class pictures: Representations of race, gender, and ability in a century of school photography. *Visual Sociology, 14*(1), 7–38.

Mohr, J. (n.d.). *Jean Mohr: A photographer's journey.* Geneva, Switzerland: Association Memoires de Photographes.

Norfleet, B. (2001). *When we liked Ike: Looking for postwar America.* New York: Norton.

Pernette, W., & Leeuwenberg, F. (2001). *Twogether.* Zurich, Switzerland: Edition Stemmle.

Pink, S. (2001). *Doing visual ethnography.* London: Sage.

Quinney, R. (2001). *Borderland: A midwest journal.* Madison: University of Wisconsin Press.

Rank, M. (2003). As American as apple pie: Poverty and welfare. *Contexts, 2*(3), 41–50. (American Sociological Association)

Rich, M., & Chalfen, R. (1999). Showing and telling asthma: Children teaching physicians with visual narrative. *Visual Sociology, 14*(1), 51–72.

Rieger, J. H. (1996). Photographing social change. *Visual Sociology, 11*(1), 5–49.

Rieger, J. H. (2003). A retrospective visual study of social change: The pulp-logging industry in an upper peninsula Michigan county. *Visual Studies, 18*(2), 157–178.

Ruby, J. (n.d.). *Oak Park.* [Online.] Available: http://astro.temple.edu~ruby/opp

Steiger, R. (2000). Enroute: An interpretation through images. *Visual Sociology, 15.* [CD ROM.]

Stein, S. (1983, May). Making connections with the camera: Photography and social mobility in the career of Jacob Riis. *Afterimage,* 14.

Sudnow, D. (1993). *Ways of the hand: The organization of improvised conduct.* Cambridge, MA: MIT Press.

van Leeuwen, T., & Jewitt, C. (Eds.). (2001). *Handbook of visual analysis.* London: Sage.

Wilson, L. (2000). *Hutterites of Montana.* New Haven, CT: Yale University Press.

Worth, S., Adair, J., & Chalfen, R. (1997). *Through Navajo eyes: An exploration in film communication and anthropology.* Albuquerque: University of New Mexico Press. (Original work published in 1972)

30

AUTOETHNOGRAPHY

Making the Personal Political

Stacy Holman Jones

> *The next moment in qualitative inquiry will be one at which the practices of qualitative research finally move, without hesitation or encumbrance, from the personal to the political.*
>
> —Norman Denzin,
> "Aesthetics and the Practices of Qualitative Inquiry," 2000, p. 261

> *We cannot move theory into action unless we can find it in the eccentric and wandering ways of our daily life. . . . [Stories] give theory flesh and breath.*
>
> —Minnie Bruce Pratt, *S/HE*, 1995, p. 22

> *I think theater is primarily a site for liberation stories and a sweaty laboratory to model possible strategies for empowerment.*
>
> —Tim Miller,
> "Solo Performing as Call to Arms," 2002, para. 3

This is a chapter about the personal text as critical intervention in social, political, and cultural life. Please do not read it alone.

This chapter is more than a little utopian in its call to disrupt, produce, and imagine a breakthrough in—and not a respite from—the way things are and perhaps should be (Ricoeur, 1986, pp. 265–266). It cannot stand alone in the world.

This is a chapter about how looking at the world from a specific, perspectival, and limited vantage point can tell, teach, and put people in motion. It is about autoethnography as a radical democratic politics—a politics committed to creating space for dialogue and debate that instigates and shapes social change (Reinelt, 1998, p. 286). It does not act alone.

This is a chapter about how a personal text can move writers and readers, subjects and objects, tellers and listeners into this space of dialogue, debate, and change. It does not speak alone.

This chapter is meant for more than one voice, for more than personal release and discovery, and for more than the pleasures of the text. It is not a text alone.

This chapter is meant for public display, for an audience. It is not meant to be left alone.

This chapter is an ensemble piece. It asks that you read it with other texts, in other contexts, and with others. It asks for a performance, one in which we might discover that our autoethnographic texts are not alone. It is a performance that asks how our personal accounts count.

▣ Turning to Narrative: Crises, Histories, and Movements

Demanding a Response

"Don't read this until you steady yourself. This isn't just the third essay on the list of assigned reading for next week. It will make you cringe. It will haunt you. It will change you."

This is what I said to friends in my team ethnography graduate course at California State University, Sacramento.[1] It was, for me, a novel course in many ways: We were working together as a research team; we were writing Van Maanen's (1988) realist, impressionist, and confessional tales; and we were creating a text together as a class.[2] In the midst of the creativity and camaraderie we experienced in this course, Ronai's (1995) "Multiple Reflections of Child Sex Abuse: An Argument for a Layered Account" altered us and the way in which we approached our work. In the essay, Ronai juxtaposed reflections on being sexually abused as a child with an argument for a layered account—a telling that creates a "continuous dialectic of experience, emerging from the multitude of reflexive voices that simultaneously produce and interpret . . . text[s]" (p. 396).

"Multiple Reflections" is autoethnography, although I did not know it then. Ronai (1995) offered up her own terrifying experience in the name of saying something startling and intricate about sexual abuse and the force and import of her scholarly and personal efforts to make sense of this experience. Ronai's story had a powerful effect on me. My thinking—about sexual abuse, about writing and scholarship, about the power of texts—shifted. Her language and story accomplished something that, up until that point, I had believed to be the business of music, novels, and film; they invited me into a lived felt experience. I could not stand outside of her words at safe remove. Ronai's story demanded that I respond and react. I marveled at the beauty of her language. I talked about her essay with my colleagues and listened as they recounted their own experiences of sexual abuse. I was enraged about what happened to Ronai and to my friends.

This is the story of my first encounter with autoethnography as a communication scholar. Of course, I had been experiencing autoethnographic texts all my life—in Raymond Carver's short stories, Silvia Plath's poetry, Milan Kundera's novels, and Billie Holiday's singing. Until I read "Multiple Reflections," however, I did not make the connection between what these works and acts accomplished and what I believed scholarship to be about.

Autoethnography Is . . .

A balancing act. Autoethnography and writing about autoethnography, that is.[3] Autoethnography works to hold self and culture together, albeit not in equilibrium or stasis. Autoethnography writes a world in a state of flux and movement—between story and context, writer and reader, crisis and denouement. It creates charged moments of clarity, connection, and change.

Writing about autoethnography is also a balancing act. In a handbook chapter that wants to move theory and method to action, what do I leave in and leave out? How do I balance *telling* (about autoethnography's history, methods, responsibilities, and possibilities) with *showing* (doing the work of autoethnography here on these pages)? How much of my self do I put in and leave out?

I begin with another sort of balancing act, sifting though books and essays, looking for words that others have used to describe the doing of autoethnography. Autoethnography is . . .

> "research, writing, and method that connect the autobiographical and personal to the cultural and social. This form usually features concrete action, emotion, embodiment, self-consciousness, and introspection . . . [and] claims the conventions of literary writing." (Ellis, 2004, p. xix)

> "a self-narrative that critiques the situatedness of self with others in social contexts." (Spry, 2001, p. 710)

> "texts [that] democratize the representational sphere of culture by locating the particular experiences of individuals in a tension with dominant expressions of discursive power." (Neumann, 1996, p. 189)

Soon, however, I find myself wanting to bend the rules, to reinscribe words about other endeavors—autobiographies, personal narratives, memoirs, short fiction, performances—as defining moments for autoethnography. I tell myself that this is not a selfish impulse—wanting beautiful phrases of other origins for autoethnography—because autoethnography is not a practice alone in the world. Autoethnography does have a story, one that was told in loving detail by Reed-Danahay (1997, pp. 4–9), Ellis and Bochner (2000, pp. 739–743), and Neumann (1996, pp. 188–193), among others. But because autoethnography is what Geertz (1983) referred to as a blurred genre, it overlaps with, and is indebted to, research and writing practices in anthropology, sociology, psychology, literary criticism, journalism, and communication (for these histories, see Denzin, 1997, pp. 203–207; Ellis, 2004, pp. 12–18; Neumann, 1996, pp. 193–195), to say nothing of our favorite storytellers, poets, and musicians.

And so I allow words about other sorts of personal texts to make themselves heard in the dance of my fingers on the keys. Autoethnography is . . .

> "a catastrophic encounter, a moment of vulnerability and ambiguity that is sensuous, embodied, and profoundly implicated in the social and ideological structures of their lifeworlds." (Marilyn Brownstein, quoted in Grumet, 2001, p. 177)

> "the kind [of art] that takes you deeper inside yourself and ultimately out again." (Friedwald, 1996, p. 126)

> "storytelling [that] can change the world." (Wade Davis, quoted in Chadwick, 2003).

Taking these words as a point of departure, I create my own responses to the call: Autoethnography is . . .

> Setting a scene, telling a story, weaving intricate connections among life and art, experience and theory, evocation and explanation . . . and then letting go, hoping for readers who will bring the same careful attention to your words in the context of their own lives.

> Making a text present. Demanding attention and participation. Implicating all involved. Refusing closure or categorization.

> Witnessing experience and testifying about power without foreclosure—of pleasure, of difference, of efficacy.

> Believing that words matter and writing toward the moment when the point of creating autoethnographic texts *is* to change the world.

I return to the books balanced on my lap. I keep looking, unsatisfied with my textual portrait. It feels tentative and unfinished. And perhaps it should be. I decide on one final entry because it says something I have not managed to put into my collected words. Autoethnography is . . .

> "[a] performance text . . . turning inward waiting to be staged." (Denzin, 1997, p. 199)

I decide to stop here, knowing that this is not the end of a story about autoethnography, only a beginning. I return to my own story of autoethnographic history and my encounter with Ronai's (1995) story. More than creating connections and shifts in my thinking, more than inspiring both rage and desire, this story also signals a crisis, one that began long before Ronai's story or my reading of it and one that continues as we speak, as we write and are written on these pages and on the stages of our experience.

Crisis

It is a triple crisis, a triple threat, a triple crown of thorns: representation, legitimation, and praxis. These crises, which mark and coincide with a turn toward interpretive, qualitative, narrative, and critical inquiry in the human disciplines, are summoned in an oft-recited line in a familiar play: How much does a scholar know, how does she know it, and what can she do with this knowledge in the world?[4]

The idea of a triple crisis implies that it is something new and something different. But these crises are not new (Denzin, 1997, p. 203). Crisis itself is not new. It is simply the result of forces in conflict, the dramatic nature of human action, and the choices (conscious and unconscious) we make in a world full of possibilities (Pelias, 1992, p. 7). The drama of representation, legitimation, and praxis is part of an ongoing dialogue between self and world about questions of ontology, epistemology, method, and praxis: What is the nature of knowing, what is the relationship between knower and known, how do we share what we know and with what effect? What makes this triple crisis feel urgent is the ways in which this dialogue has increasingly questioned the stability and coherence of our lives as we live and tell about them. This dialogue asks how, in lifeworlds that are partial, fragmented, and constituted and mediated by language, we can tell or read our stories as neutral, privileged, or in any way complete. In answering these questions, we have looked to the personal, concrete, and mundane details of experience as a window to understanding the relationships between self and other or between individual and community. We use the contingent and skeptical languages of poststructuralism and postmodernism (among others) to tell and understand our lives and our world, hoping to confront questions of "self, place, [and] power" in ways that are more satisfying and—*yes*—more subversive than in previous performances (Neumann, 1996, p. 195; see also Denzin, 1997; Reinelt, 1998, p. 285).

A crisis is a turning point, a moment when conflict must be dealt with even if we cannot resolve it. It is a tension that opens a space of indeterminacy, threatens to destabilize social structures, and enables a creative uncertainty (Reinelt, 1998, p. 284). Interpretive, qualitative, narrative, and critical inquiry have had many such moments, all of which led to shifts in genres and methods. We have traveled from . . .

> the impossibility of careful, faithful, and authoritative cataloguing of an exotic other . . .
>
> to partial, reflexive, and local narrative accounts . . .
>
> to texts that work to create a space for an ethics committed to dialogue.

In the current moment . . .

> we confront the impossibility of representing lived experience by troubling the link between life and text . . .
>
> we develop (and question the development of) criteria for understanding and evaluating the work we do to narrate the conditions of our lives . . .
>
> we resolve to do work that makes a difference by writing the social imaginary in inciteful and revolutionary ways.[5]

We rise to the challenge of movement. . . .

Movement

Even though I was able to place "Multiple Reflections" within the larger context of turns and movements in interpretive, qualitative, narrative, and critical inquiry, I did not know what to do with the rage I felt on the day I read Ronai's (1995) essay. I looked for a place to put my anger, a way to assuage it, and a means to act on it without forgetting or dismissing it. In her chapter in the second edition of this *Handbook,* Olesen (2000) wrote, "Rage is not enough" (p. 215). Olesen's challenge—to me, to you—is to move from rage to "progressive political action, to theory and method that connect politics, pedagogy, and ethics to action in the world" (N. Denzin & Y. Lincoln, personal communication, September 23, 2002).

This is a challenge that autoethnographers have been working to meet slowly and incrementally. It is the challenge of creating texts that unfold in the intersubjective space of individual and community and that embrace tactics for both *knowing* and *showing* (Jackson, 1998; Kemp, 1998, p. 116). Responding to this challenge means asking questions about the following:

- How knowledge, experience, meaning, and resistance are expressed by embodied, tacit, intonational, gestural, improvisational, coexperiential, and covert means (Conquergood, 2002, p. 146). Autoethnographic texts focus on how subordinated people use deliberately subtle and opaque forms of communication—forms that are not textual or visual—to express their thoughts, feelings, and desires by performing these practices on the page and on stage (Daly & Rogers, 2001; Jones, 1997a; Stewart, 1996).

- How emotions are important to understanding and theorizing the relationship among self, power, and culture. Autoethnographic texts focus on creating a palpable emotional experience as it connects to, and separates from, other ways of knowing, being, and acting in/on the world (Bochner, 2001; Ellis, 1997, 1995; Jago, 2002; Spry, 2001).

- How body and voice are inseparable from mind and thought as well as how bodies and voices move and are privileged (and are restricted and marked) in very particular and political ways. Autoethnographic texts seek to invoke the corporeal, sensuous, and political nature of experience rather than collapse text into embodiment or politics into language play (Alexander, 2000; Gingrich-Philbrook, 1997; Jackson, 1998; Jones, 1997b; Pineau, 2000; Stoller, 1997).

- How selves are constructed, disclosed, and implicated in the telling of personal narratives as well as how these narratives move in and change the contexts of their telling.[6] Texts aspire to purposeful and tension-filled "self-investigation" of an author's (and a reader's) role in a context, a situation, or a social world. Such self-investigation generates what Gornick (2001) termed "self-implication," that is, seeing "one's own part in the situation"—particularly "one's own frightened or cowardly or self-deceived part" (pp. 35–36)—in creating the dynamic and movement of a text (see also Bochner, 2001; Ellis, 2002; Garrick, 2001; Hartnett, 1998; Langellier, 1999; Park-Fuller, 2000; Spry, 2000; Vickers, 2002).

- How stories help us to create, interpret, and change our social, cultural, political, and personal lives. Autoethnographic texts point out not only the necessity of narrative in our world but also the power of narrative to reveal and revise that world, even when we struggle for words, when we fail to find them, or when the unspeakable is invoked but not silent (Bochner, 2001; Denzin, 2000; Hartnett, 1999; Lockford, 2002; Neumann, 1996; Pelias, 2002; Richardson, 1997).

These questions challenge us to create work that acts through, in, and on the world and to shift our focus from representation to presentation, from the rehearsal of new ways of being to their performance. These questions posit the challenge of *movement*—to talk and share in new and difficult ways, to think and rethink our positions and commitments, to push through resistance in search of hope (Becker, 2000, pp. 523, 541–542). Responding to these questions has led me and others to turn to performance. In making this turn, we must consider how the practices of autoethnography are informed by a rich history in performance, a history that needs to be written into accounts of autoethnographic theory and practices (Denzin, 2003; Ellis & Bochner, 1996). Our abiding interest in performance ethnography, performative writing, and personal performance narratives is telling. These endeavors point to how personal stories become a means for interpreting the past, translating and transforming contexts, and envisioning a future.

▣ Turning to Performance: Letters of/for/on Change

The Impossibility of Iser

I went to the University of Texas at Austin to study organizational culture and to learn more about ethnography, writing, and scholarship. When I looked through the graduate course offerings in the Department of Communication, I kept coming back to a course titled Reading and Performing. I was intrigued. I wanted to learn about performance studies, and I wanted to explore theories and practices of reading. But performing? I was not sure I was ready for that.

The professor[7] encouraged me to come to the first class to see what it was all about, and so I did. The material was compelling, the students were engaging, and the professor was witty and commanding. But what about the performances? My last—and only—performance experience was playing the baby Jesus in the church Christmas pageant. I was not sure whether I should stay, but I knew I wanted to stay. Then the professor began assigning reading reports, and I began to sweat. And then it was my turn. He looked at me and said, "Well, I don't *know* you, but you look like a nice person. I am assigning you Wolfgang Iser because *he* is a nice person."

I had to stay. I had to report on Iser. It is what a nice person would do. I read *The Fictive and the Imaginary* (Iser, 1993), and I understood that Iser was talking about reading and also about writing and performing. He stated,

> The impossibility of being present to ourselves becomes our possibility to play ourselves out to the fullness that knows no bounds, because no matter how vast the range, none of the possibilities will "make us tick." This impossibility suggests a purpose for literary staging. . . . Literature becomes a panorama of what is possible, because it is not hedged in by either the limitations or the considerations that determine the institutionalized organizations within which human life otherwise takes its course. (p. xviii)

As I wrote my report, I kept coming back to this passage because it speaks to the fertile space within which we confront the impossibility of full or complete knowledge (of self, of others, and of the relationships between the two). Because we cannot know, write, or stage it "all," we are free to create a vision of what is possible. Reading Iser, I was convinced that texts both written and read might engage and exceed these constraints in liberatory ways. I was also convinced that performance offered a possibility for realizing this goal.

Performance Rising

Conquergood (1991) traced the rise of performance in ethnographic research[8] and writing in his essay, "Rethinking Ethnography."[9] He tracked the turn to performance to Victor Turner's characterization of humankind as *homo performans*—humanity as performer—"a culture-inventing, social-performing, self-making, and self-transforming creature" (p. 187). Turner's move to link ethnography with performance as a lived and living practice accomplishes four goals. First, it turns our attention to how bodies and voices are situated in contexts—in and of "time, place, and history" (p. 187). Second, the performative turn moves researchers and researched toward a relationship of embodied "intimate involvement and engagement of 'coactivity' or co-performance with historically situated, named, 'unique individuals'" (p. 187; see also Kisliuk, 2002, pp. 105–106). Third, performance-centered ethnography points up the visual, linguistic, and textual bias of Western civilization and redirects our attention to an aural, bodily, and postmodern expression of culture and lifeworld, fieldwork and writing (Conquergood, 1991, p. 189; see also Tyler, 1986). Fourth, in highlighting the "polysemic" and constitutive nature of social life and cultural performances, the performance paradigm asks us to focus on how texts can be created, communicated, and most notably critiqued on multiple levels (Conquergood, 1991, p. 189).

Conquergood[10] (1991) was not suggesting that ethnography abandon text or field in favor of performance; rather, he was suggesting that we use performance as a metaphor, means, and method for thinking about and sharing what is lost and left out of our fieldwork and our texts as well as thinking about how performance complements, alters, supplements, and critiques these texts (p. 191).[11]

Ekphrastic Criticism

> A thief drives to the museum in his black van. The night
> watchman says, Sorry, closed, you have to come back tomorrow.
> The thief sticks the point of his knife in the guard's ear.
> I haven't got all evening, he says, I need some art.
> Art is for pleasure, the guard says, not possession, you can't
> something, and then the duct tape is going across his mouth.
> Don't worry, the thief says, we're both on the same side.
> He finds the Dutch Masters and goes right for a Vermeer:
> "Girl Writing a Letter." The thief knows what he's doing.
> He has a Ph.D. He slices the canvas on one edge from
> the shelf holding the salad bowls right down to the
> square of sunlight on the black and white checked floor.
> The girl doesn't hear this, she's too absorbed in writing
> her letter, she doesn't notice him until too late.[12]

I chose Carpenter's (1993) "Girl Writing a Letter" for my first performance for Reading and Performing. I chose this poem because it is smart and funny and has a happy ending. I thought these things, that is, until I began to work on the performance. There were too many characters, too many stories, too many voices and attitudes to attend to all at once. But it was too late. I stayed the course. I reported on Iser. Now I had to perform.

I finished my performance of "Girl Writing a Letter," and the professor was silent. I waited, my heart pulsing in my head. He walked to the chalkboard and wrote "Ekphrastic." Ekphrastic? What does that mean? Was it good? Awful? He explained that ekphrastic works, such as my poem, are meditations on others' creative acts (Scott, 1994, p. xi), usually texts considering a visual or aural work of art. Think John Keats's "Ode to a Grecian Urn." Ekphrastic texts attempt to invoke "the picture-making capacity of words in poems" (Krieger, 1992, p. 1).

After this brief lesson, the professor moved on, inviting the next performance. I was left to wonder—about the poem, about the performance, about ekphrasis. Later that week, I saw my professor in the hallway outside of his office. He said, "Nice work the other day. Great poem. Great performance. I thought you said you weren't a performer."

"I'm not."

"*You* are a *performer.*"

I spent the next several weeks reading and thinking about performance, texts, and ekphrasis. Although it is typically the domain of the poet and literary scholar, ekphrasis describes our attempts to translate and transmute an experience to text and text to experience. Ekphrasis "breathes words into the mute picture; it makes pictures out of the suspended words of its text. It is as much about urgency as it is about rest, as much voyage as interlude" (Scott, 1994, p. xii). And what happens when we perform an ekphrastic text? What happens when we perform the artist performing the artist, repeating the act of connection and creation, breaking that experience out of one form and context and remaking it in another? Perhaps we create a critical ekphrasis, a performance that moves through *mimesis* (imitation) and *poiesis* (creation) to *kinesis* (movement) (Conquergood, 1992, p. 84).[13]

Inventory

I was hooked. I changed parties and turned to performance studies. I enrolled in Performance History, Autobiography, and Performance and in Performance Ethnography. On the first day of Performance Ethnography, the professor[14] asked students to pair up and said, "Without speaking, write three observations or assumptions about your partner and then discuss."

There were an odd number of students, so I was paired with the professor. I wrote, "Sings well, writes poetry, believes in reincarnation." She wrote, "Married or in a committed relationship, precise and particular, doesn't relax easily." We shared our lists and laughed over the entries. Some of them were on target, and others were not. But each item on our lists spoke to our projections, our hopes, things we wanted for ourselves, and things we did not want.

At the end of class, the professor asked us to do a self-inventory, answering questions about our physical, emotional, spiritual, intellectual, artistic, and artifactual selves:

> What are three of your typical gestures?
>
> When you cried last, what was it about?
>
> What spiritual activities do you engage in each day?
>
> What was the last book you read that was not assigned for a class?
>
> In what activities are you the most creative?
>
> How do you typically adorn your body?

Answering these questions and others, I thought about how performance ethnography is an inventory of both self and other, an act of interpretation and a performance of that assessment, and a journey through imitation and creation into movement. I wondered where this journey would take me.

Doing Bodies Doing Culture

Jones (2002) wrote that performance ethnography is "most simply, how culture is done in the body" (p. 7). The process of creating and staging performance ethnography, however, is not simply placing, and then playing, bodies in cultures. Rather, performance ethnography seeks to *implicate* researchers and audiences by creating an experience that brings together theory and praxis in complicated, contradictory, and meaningful ways.

Performance ethnography is grounded in two primary ideas: (a) that our identities and daily practices are a series of performance choices (conscious and unconscious) that we improvise within cultural and social guidelines and (b) that we learn though participation or through performance (p. 7; see also Denzin, 2003, pp. 14–16). Performance ethnography can take many forms, ranging from recreating cultural performances for audiences invested and interested in understanding, preserving, and/or challenging particular identities and ways of life (Conquergood, 1985, 1994) to presenting individual (autoethnographic) experiences as a means for pointing up the subjective and situated nature of identity, fieldwork, and cultural interpretation (Jones, 1996; Spry, 2001). Performance ethnography can also be presented in various ways, ranging from traditionally "theatrical" settings complete with fourth-wall conventions (in which the audience observes the action on stage) to installations and scenes in which audience members are invited/compelled to participate in the creation of the performance. Whatever the form or process, performance ethnographies seek to "explore bodily knowing, to stretch the ways in which ethnography might share knowledge of a culture, and to puzzle through the ethical and political dilemmas of fieldwork and representation" (Jones, 2002, p. 7). Jones (2002) asserted that performance ethnography achieves these goals by focusing on four principles: (a) creating a specific context for the performance, (b) working in collaboration with and being accountable to a fieldwork community, (c) highlighting the performer's "situated and interested role" in the interpretation of culture, and (d) providing a multitude of perspectives that audience members must actively synthesize (pp. 8–9).

Doing bodies doing culture can be these things if we are willing to remember and perform context, accountability, subjectivity, and multivocality, that is, if we create work that is both "community-based and community active" (Kisliuk, 2002, p. 116). We must be willing not only to implicate our audiences but also to incite them to participate, to act, and to take risks.

Girl Writing (another) Letter

During the second semester of my Ph.D. program, insomnia came to live with me. I would lie in bed with my mind racing. I rehashed rehearsals and classroom conversations. I wondered whether I had paid the electric bill. I agonized over who or what to choose as my subject for Performance Ethnography. I considered sites and contexts as well as organizations and individuals, but nothing seemed right. I changed positions, tried to focus on the hum of the air conditioner and the steady pulse of the highway traffic, and then fell into a shallow sleep and dreamed of my grandfather.

A few months before insomnia came to stay, my grandfather had died. I was in the heat of my first semester at Texas when my mother called to tell me. My grandfather had spent the past 2 years mourning the death of my grandmother, and a heart attack had rescued him from living alone without her.

I did not go to the funeral. My mother convinced me to stay in school. That was where my grandfather had wanted me, where he was proud of me. Months later, my sleepless nights began and ended with dreams of my grandfather and the hazy edges of my unlived grief. One night after my eyes flew open to greet the red glare of 2 o'clock, I decided that I had had enough. I decided that I would meet my grandfather in the space he cared about most and to live my grief at school in Performance Ethnography. I got up and composed another letter—another poem for performance.

Dear Grandpa

I didn't hear you leave.

I was too busy writing,

your college girl,

never noticing until too late.

Grandma phoned from her hospital bed

asked me to look in on you.

Said last night you were hit by a car,

walking home in the rain.

I drive to you teeth clenched.

Fear works the doorbell and

twists into my breathing

until I hear you call over barking dogs.

The door opens and you shrink in its frame.

Angry bruises glow violent beneath pale skin,

your left eye pinched shut against the pain.

My own vision blurs as we embrace.

You don't want to see a doctor, don't want

to lie down, don't want to rest.

You need to get to the hospital, to her.

You've been gone too long.

I take you to her, but say I can't stay.

That's right, I'm your college girl.

I watch you touch her face and stroke her hair.

I am furious you don't want to live without her.

I tell you both good-bye, not knowing

this is the last time, not knowing

I left you together. Is this how you wanted it?

I didn't hear you leave.

I wove this letter into a performance that included my grandfather's letters to me, family photos, reflections on his life and death, and arguments for the performance of grief.[15] I used monologue, epic, and "everyday life" performance techniques to show my grandfather, myself, and the process of performing an other (Hopper, 1993; Stucky, 1993). I felt closer to my grandfather; more in tune with his presence in my life, dreams, and grief; and proud to share both with an audience.

This performance was my response to the project of performance ethnography. It was my subjective and vulnerable experience. It did not produce "findings"; it was not generalizable outside of asking audience members to recall and reinhabit their own moments of grieving (Goodall, 2000, p. 2). It generated whatever credibility it earned out of my fumbling attempts to make sense of my loss. This is a hallmark of autoethnography and autoethnographic performance—speaking in and through experiences that are unspeakable as well as inhabiting and animating the struggle for words and often our failure to find them (A. Bochner & C. Ellis, personal communication, September 6, 2003). These are risky performances for all involved, and not only because they testify to the spaces of failure, silence, and loss. They are risky because in the rush to identification, empathy, and our desire for an "authentic" experience, audiences and performers can give and receive testimony in ways that move too quickly from a connected yet distinctive "you" and "me" to an unquestioned and violent "we" (Salverson, 2001, p. 124; see also Diamond, 1992). This collapsing of me into you and you into me can work to shut down engagement and responsibility. It can fail to recognize the ethical move required to make autoethnography and autoethnographic performances "a doorway, an instrument of encounter, a place of public and private negotiations—where the goal is not just to empathize, but to *attend*" (Salverson, 2001, p. 125, emphasis added). My performance of my grief for my grandfather stopped short of asking my audience and myself to take a greater risk, to move through *mimesis* (reflection) to *poiesis* (creation) and *kinesis* (movement). That performance—the performance of critique and change—required another letter.

Connecting

I flew to St. Louis, Missouri, and met an old friend. We drove into a new territory, with her convertible twisting and winding into the state park, where we breathed in the scents of pine and sunlight. We were there for a conference on performative writing. We collected there to share the work—the words—we believed to be performative writing. I was nervous, tentative, and unsure. Should *I* be here? Should it be someone else instead? Of course. I felt guilty about leaving work on a dissertation about torch singing as a feminist performance practice. Should I be *here*? Should I be at home writing—focused on finishing—instead? Of course. But I was here to listen, to read my words, and to experience. And I knew that when we embody stories and identities, there is always danger and always risk,[16] so I went.

We began by talking about performative writing. What is it? How do we know it? What does it aspire to be? How do we judge? What does performance have to do with it? We talked and questioned and made notes, never deciding but instead piling on detail and nuance. Performative writing . . .

> "[is a] kind of writing where the body and the spoken word, performance practice and theory, the personal and the scholarly, come together." (Miller & Pelias, 2001, p. v)
>
> "requires faith that language inked on a page can 'do' as well as 'be'." (Stucky, 2001, p. vii)
>
> "depends upon the performative body believing in language." (Gingrich-Philbrook, 2001, p. vii)
>
> "*creates* a performance, rather than describes one." (Barthes, 1977, p. 114)

The hurried and rich discussion left me breathless and nervous. Did my words embody a belief in the power of language? Move beyond the pages of their inscription? Invoke, conjure, and create a new world? As much as the warm atmosphere and kind eyes of the participants told me to relax—to enjoy this performance—I was afraid of how my work would be read, heard, and judged.

Reading, reception, and judgment—conversations about why and how to evaluate alternative auto/ethnographic work abound.[17] For example, Richardson (2000) offered five criteria that she uses when reviewing what she calls creative analytic practices (CAP) ethnography: (a) substantive contribution to an understanding of social life, (b) aesthetic merit, (c) reflexivity, (d) emotional and intellectual impact, and (e) a clear expression of a cultural, social, individual, or communal sense of reality (p. 937). Using Richardson's and others' models, I have developed a list of actions and accomplishments that I look for in my work and in the work of others. They are changing. They are generated in the doing of this writing rather than outside or prior to it:

- *Participation as reciprocity.* How well does the work construct participation of authors/readers and performers/audiences as a *reciprocal* relationship marked by mutual responsibility and obligation (Elam, 1997, p. 78; hooks, 1995, p. 221)?

- *Partiality, reflexivity, and citationality as strategies for dialogue (and not "mastery").* How well does the work present a partial and self-referential tale that connects with other stories, ideas, discourses, and contexts (e.g., personal, theoretical, ideological, cultural) as a means of creating a dialogue among "authors, readers, and subjects written/read" (Pollock, 1998, p. 80; see also Denzin, 1997, pp. 224–227; Lather, 2001, p. 216; Richardson, 1997, p. 91)?

- *Dialogue as a space of debate and negotiation.* How well does the work create a space for and engage in meaningful dialogue among different bodies, hearts, and minds (Conquergood, 1985, p. 9; Denzin, 1997, p. 247)?

- *Personal narrative and storytelling as an obligation to critique.* How do narrative and story enact an ethical obligation to critique subject positions, acts, and received notions of expertise and justice within and outside of the work (Conquergood, 2002, p. 152; Denzin, 1997, p. 200; Langellier, 1999, 128–131)?

- *Evocation and emotion as incitements to action.* How well does the work create a plausible and visceral lifeworld and charged emotional atmosphere as an incitement to act within and outside the context of the work (Bochner, 2000, p. 271; Denzin, 1997, p. 209)?

- *Engaged embodiment as a condition for change.* How does the work place/embody/interrogate/intervene in experience in ways that make political action and change possible in and outside of the work? In other words, how does the work "make writing *do*" (Diamond, 1996, p. 2; Pollock, 1998, pp. 95–96)?

I brought these actions and accomplishments with me to the gathering on performative writing. As the first author/performer began, I heard them sound and reverberate on his tongue and in his words and through his story. I heard them sound and reverberate as we listened to each other that weekend, writing and telling and remaking selves in the words on our pages, in our mouths, on our bodies, and in the room with the green window on the world.[18]

(Re)Making the Self

Miller (1998)[19] maintained that the gathering interest in autobiographical performance has much to do with a shift in performance studies from aesthetic performance to "a more integral paradigm for explaining, critiquing, and experiencing how contemporary life is lived" (p. 318). This shift, like the move toward interpretive, qualitative, narrative, and critical inquiry in other human disciplines, was precipitated by a rethinking of the relationships among texts, performers, audiences, and contexts; a proliferation in the number and nature of communication technologies; and a postmodern decentering of the authority, autonomy, and stability of institutions, subjectivities, and texts (pp. 319–320). Out of this shift emerged an emphasis on personal narrative as a situated, fluid, and emotionally and intellectually charged *engagement* of self and other (performer and witness) made possible in the "evolving, revelatory dance between performer and spectator" (Miller, 1995, p. 49). In such exchanges, audiences and performers (often composed of people who are classified by virtue of race, class, age, sexual preference, gender identity, and experience as "others") create and constitute a shared history and, thus, break into and diminish their marginalization. These performances create highly personal encounters within an increasingly impersonal public sphere.

Autobiographical performances provide an opportunity to "educate, empower, and emancipate" (Langellier, 1999, p. 129). Langellier (1999) located a means of mitigating and complicating the "either/or" logic of celebration (resistance) and suspicion (dominance) within personal narrative performance, specifically in the interaction between performance and performativity. Langellier asserted that "stories are made, not found" in performances that mediate between experience and story, between the doing and the done (p. 128; see also Denzin, 2003, p. 10).

These distinctions between experience and story, between the doing and the done, rely on a notion of performativity that states that a life story—an identity—is not something an author/performer "elects to do, but . . . [rather] is *performative* in the sense that it constitutes an effect of the very subject it appears to express" (Butler, 1991, p. 24). Performativity points to how identities, and thus life stories, are not easily adopted or changed (as a role taken on by an actor) but instead accrue "gradually, yet [do] not attach [themselves] to some blank, some actor cast in a play she's not yet read; [such identities] come into being by virtue of being performed" (Solomon, 1997, p. 169). That is, life stories are created and recreated in the moments of their telling.

Performativity points to the impossibility of separating our life stories from the social, cultural, and political contexts in which they are created and the ways in which performance as a site of dialogue and negotiation is itself a contested space (Diamond, 1996, p. 2). Langellier (1999) wrote,

> Identity and experience are a symbiosis of performed story and the social relations in which they are materially embedded. . . . This is why personal narrative performance is especially crucial to those communities left out of the privileges of dominant culture, those bodies without voice in the political sense. (p. 129)

The challenge is to consider how particular performances of personal stories "need performativity to comprehend [their] constitutive effects" as well as how performativity "relies upon performance to show itself" (Langellier, 1999, p. 136). In the iterative and unstable move between performance and performativity, "questions of embodiment, of social relations, of ideological interpellations, of emotional and political effects, all become discussable" (Diamond, 1996, p. 4). It is a discussion that moves discourse to storytelling performance, from autonomous texts to situated practices, from received storylines to emergent dramas with numerous possible "endings," and from omniscient narrators to a proliferation of unreliable reflexive voices. It is a discussion that creates and challenges social relations "within the performance event and perhaps even beyond it" (Langellier, 1999, p. 132; see also Denzin, 2003, pp. 10–11).

Performative writing brings the performance–performativity dynamic to the moment of texting in which identities and experiences are constructed, interpreted, and changed. It occurs when we encounter the page with the intention of entering into a discussion marked by contest and negotiation, embodied knowledge and vociferous exchange, emotional and intellectual charge. It occurs when we invite an audience into dialogue as we write, speak, and perform the words on the page, in our mouths, on our bodies, and in the world. Because the performance–performativity dynamic asserts that performances are inseparable from performers and that performativity is inseparable from politics, autobiographical performance, personal narrative, and performative auto/ethnography enmesh the personal within the political and the political within the personal in ways that can, do, and must matter.

A Love Letter

It was my turn. I moved from my seat on the floor and into the chair beneath the window. All eyes—expectant and encouraging—were on me. I took a breath and began a story about torch singers and ghosts.

> On the flight from Detroit to Paris, I read about the Edith Piaf Museum in the guidebook:

Paris. Open by appointment 1–6 p.m. Closed Friday, Saturday, Sunday, and bank holidays. Private museum in an apartment. Memorabilia of the singer. China collection. Free.

I circle the phone number. I turn the dog-eared page. I close my eyes and begin listening for Piaf as she haunts Paris, as she haunts me, a present history singing her invisibility. . . .

I arrive at the apartment museum at 1 p.m. Melissa accompanies me as translator. The proprietor, Bernard Marchois, invites us in. Standing immediately in front of us is a black-and-white cardboard cutout of Piaf. Marchois tells us that the cutout was created as a lobby display for one of her last concerts at the Paris Olympia. He smiles. This is a life-sized portrait, he says. He puts his arm around the cardboard statue. He is not a tall man, but Edith looks like a tiny bird under his arm—yes, a sparrow.

He shows us into the sitting room, and Melissa and I look around. This place, like all of the others, is packed tight with Piaf memorabilia. These are *her* things—her records, her jewelry, her hastily scrawled letters, her black dress, her china. We sit on a couch. (Is it hers? Did she sit here?) Marchois pulls up a chair. Melissa explains that we're interested in hearing about Piaf's performances, about Piaf the woman. He nods and smiles. I ask him to tell us how they met. Melissa asks again, in French. He laughs. He explains that he met Piaf when he was a teenager. An older couple—friends of the family—invited him to see Piaf at the Olympia. Before the show, the couple took Marchois backstage to meet her. He was disappointed. She was frail and plain. She looked like a cleaning lady.

"Surprised?" she asked.

Marchois nodded sheepishly.

She laughed a round, full laugh. "You come back and see me after the show, eh?"

He was sure he had seen enough, but he nodded again.

"The show was electrifying. By the end of the show, I was smitten. I could barely contain my excitement as we made our way backstage. When we entered the dressing room, she turned that lightning smile on me."

"So, what do you think of me now?"

"She saw everything in my eyes."

She laughed. "Come," she said, and she pulled me into her embrace.

Marchois's eyes glisten. He sighs. He says they were friends, never lovers. He says she loved life, loved to laugh and play music, loved to sing. He says her songs were full of heartache, but that heartache was never hopeless. It was simply part of the equation of living. Her songs were signposts of the places she was in between—spaces of contradiction, tension, and immanent possibilities.[20] He says she loved sharing these places, these wounds of feeling. He says, again, she loved life.

I see the cardboard likeness of Piaf in the next room. I see the picture of Marchois with his arm around her—not the life-sized photo but [rather] what is pressing in from the other side of the image displayed within her tiny frame.[21] I see him sitting here, in an apartment filled with her teacups and earrings and stationery. I glance down at my notebook. My next question is, "Why do this? Why invite strangers into your home to talk about Edith Piaf?" I look up at him and I have my answer. He is an amateur, a careful collector of memories. He does this so that he might breathe life back in where only a vague memory or a bare trace was visible to those who bothered to look.[22] He lives among her things because looking at them and showing them to others is his lover's discourse.[23] He is writing ghost stories in a language of commonplace things that take on an immense power.[24] And with each day, with each conversation, he proclaims his love and writes his memories anew.

We leave the museum and walk toward the Metro station. Melissa asks if I got what I wanted. I say, Yes. No. I'm not sure, and maybe that's the point. I came to Paris looking for the real Edith Piaf, and I'm leaving with her ghost.

Melissa stops. Why do this? Why follow her ghost around Paris?

> I have my answer: Because following a ghost is about making contact, and that contact changes you.[25]
>
> Later, when I sit down to write this story of my encounter with Piaf and her ghost, I feel her watching over my shoulder as I move my fingers along the keys, always with me, the questioning, critical ghost of my text. She leaves wounds of feeling on my language; never hopeless, just part of living. My stories are love letters, invitations to hear the unspoken, unheard voices of the singer and myself.

Performing Possibilities

I finished my story, and the audience was still and silent. Then the discussion began, pulling my story and me into a new performance. We talked of rhythm and thick description, theory and practice, haunting and writing. I was challenged and energized by our conversation. I envisioned new possibilities for my story and for the power of narrative to inscribe and embody a horizon of movement. I left the chair under the window and returned to my place on the floor.

I flew home from the conference and spent a few days writing and reading about performance, personal narrative, and performativity. I made note of what Madison (1998a) stated about the "performance of possibilities," that is, the "active, creative work that weaves the life of the mind with being mindful of life, of 'merging text and world,' of critically traversing the margin *and* the center, of opening more and different paths for enlivening relations and spaces" (p. 277).

Performances of possibilities are created in the momentum of movement from silence to voice and from margin to center. They provide a gathering place for narratives that seek change in "systems and processes that limit possibilities" (Madison, 1998a, p. 279). The space and movement of performances of possibilities are infused with the responsibility to ethically engage with selves and others in ways that do not forestall or foreclose dialogue. Performances of possibilities provide both the means and the method for an alterative, alternative ethnography. They are, to use Sandoval's (2000) description, subjunctive; they join together the possible and what is, they provide the medium "through which difference both arises and is undone; [they] join together through *movement*" (p. 180).

Then I returned to my dissertation, my love letter to torch singing. I brought these questions with me to my writing.

Intimate Provocation

Madison's questions link the personal with the political and suggest how the turn toward performative narratives and narrative performances creates a politically efficacious poetics in and through movement (see also Conquergood, 2002; Langellier, 1999; Hartnett, 1998; Jones, 2002; Spry, 2001).

The lessons and challenges for autoethnography in the turn toward performance, performative writing, and personal narrative are clear. Autoethnographic texts are personal stories that are both constitutive and performative. They are charged exchanges of presence or "mutual presentness" (Dolan, 1993, p. 151). They are love letters—processes and productions of desire—for recognition, for engagement, and for change. Tedlock (1991) characterized the ethnographer's process as that of an amateur, which derives from the Latin *amatus* or "to love" (p. 82). Written and experienced in this way, autoethnography becomes an intimate provocation, a critical ekphrasis, a story of and with movement.

But like all stories, my account is partial, fragmented, and situated in the texts and contexts of my own learning, interpretations, and practices. Rather than end here in the intersections and interactive possibilities of narrative and performance, I want to tell you one more story, invent one more history, invoke one more discussion of the intricacies of theory and praxis. I want to tell you about socially resistive performance as a site and means of intimate provocation. I want to ask you to consider the place of autoethnography in this story.

Turning Again: Performing Social Resistance

Watching and Writing

When I was young—4 and 5 and 6 years old—I loved staying over on Saturday nights with my grandparents. I relished staying up late nights and having their undivided attention. But most of all, I loved watching *The Lawrence Welk Show.* My grandmother marveled at my fixation on the set. At first, she thought it was the bubbles that held my attention, but I watched everything—the musical numbers, the singers, the dancing. I clapped in time with the movement of Bobby and Sissy. I clapped in time with my grandfather's typewriter click-clacking in the other room.

My grandmother would call him in to see my performance, and the typing—the writing of letters, histories, and wild fictions—would stop. My grandfather would stroll into the living room to watch me. He would smile and pick me up, swinging me high over his head and onto his shoulders. He would hold my hands and spin me in time to Bobby and Sissy's waltz, swing, or foxtrot. And when the number was over, he would return me to my spot on the floor in front of the television and then return to his typewriter.

Out of sight, he would place his fingers on the keys and furiously tap out his own rhythm, vision, and story. And I would return to the dancing, the music, the singing, and the bubbles.

Hopeful Openness

First, consider several ideas about theater and social change:

- That art does not mirror or transcend experience but rather is a means for creating and experiencing the world
- That what happens in a performance can influence, and can *change,* what happens in the world
- That the performer–spectator relationship is not fixed but rather malleable—that a spectator can be an active agent (e.g., cocreator, participant) *in* a performance rather than a passive consumer *of* a performance
- That performance creates a space in which participants not only glimpse who and what they are and desire but also come into contact with different identities, positions, and desires
- That such encounters can demand and facilitate response and action

Now, imagine these ideas as they are played out on stages and street corners, in lecture halls, and in coffee shops. Can you see and hear these performances? Can you imagine that each "models a hopeful openness to the diverse possibilities of democracy" (Dolan, 2001b, p. 2)?

Wait. Do not answer yet. I want to tell you one more story.

Performance has long been a site and means for negotiating social, cultural, and political dialogue (for two historical accounts of this process in different contexts, see Denning, 1997, and Scott, 1990). In the United States, activist theater has coalesced around social movements such as the labor movement of the 1930s, the civil rights and feminist movements of the 1960s and 1970s, and the AIDS activism of the 1980s (Cohen-Cruz, 2001, p. 95). The associations between social movements and activist performance, however, are opportunistic, tenuous, and changing. Such associations do not adequately describe the changing nature of social change theater. Instead, as Cohen-Cruz (2001) proposed, movements in the form and function of activist performance correspond to shifts in the ways in which performance posits the performer–audience–text–context relationship.[26]

During the late 1960s and early 1970s, the conditions for activist theater were ripe. Actors formed radical collectives that produced both realist drama and original work. The goals of these "actor-based, movement-linked" companies "were plain: get the United States out of Vietnam, enforce equal rights for all people regardless of race or ethnicity, boycott grapes" (Cohen-Cruz, 2001, p. 98). Although techniques were many, much of this work drew on Bertolt Brecht's concept of epic theater—performances that create a distinction among—and distance between—actor and character, text and context. Epic theater asks audiences to critically engage with and evaluate the performance and its social implications rather than get swept away in the emotional and nonevaluative force of theater-as-entertainment. Distinction and distance are what make theater an occasion for enlightened and involved citizenship as well as a powerful site and means for breaking into and refiguring our world (Brecht, 1957/1998, p. 125).

As the national movements with which these performances were allied began to fracture and shift, socially resistant performance also began to change (Cohen-Cruz, 2001, p. 99). Performers turned their attention to issues in their own communities and began to grapple with the need to express not only solidarity and unity but also the intricacies of identity, difference, and identification (pp. 98–99). During the 1980s, identity politics (e.g., efforts focused specifically on gay rights or gender equality) emphasized personal storytelling and creating an environment and process in which community members could participate in performances. Whereas 1960s "political theater was more consistently radical in *content,* community-based theater is more consistently radical in, and focused on, *process*" (p. 100, emphasis added). The force and power of this work inheres in creating reciprocity among artists and community members, linking the personal with the political, and instigating specific, local actions. Working with untrained participants meant that community-based theater relied heavily on workshops for developing and rehearsing performances. Workshop techniques, such as those developed by Augusto Boal, facilitated this process. Boal (1979/1985), whose work draws and builds on Brechtian principles, outlined several techniques to assist community members in creating "theater [as] a rehearsal for revolution" (p. 122). Whereas Brecht advocated a critically active spectator, Boal asserted that spectators must learn to become "spect-actors" and, as such, to actively participate in the unfolding drama on stage. In so doing, spect-actors train themselves for real action in the world (p. 122).

Participants did learn to become active participants on stage and in the world. They benefited from the performance in definable and material ways. Challenges surrounding the need to balance aesthetic concerns with the sharing of experience, the splintering effects of identity-based dialogues, and the need to connect local action to larger contexts precipitated a shift from community-based performance to theater and civic dialogue (Cohen-Cruz, 2001, p. 104). Theater and civic dialogue is focused on realigning and reconnecting the politics surrounding gender, race, class, and sexuality (among other identities and positions) in a way that does not obfuscate or collapse differences but instead puts these identities and positions in conflict and conversation with one another around an issue of civic importance (Dolan, 2001a, p. 90). The goal of civic dialogue performance is to "engage the public more fully with contemporary issues" (p. 106). As such, civic dialogue returns to the broad social, cultural, and political contexts and issues "reminiscent of 1960s theater, but from multiple perspectives" (p. 106). Civic dialogue performance is inspired and informed by an impetus to involve audiences in the wake of actual events to create critical engagement (hooks, 1995, p. 214).

Whereas the techniques of both Brecht and Boal formed the cornerstone for much theater practice in movement- and community-based theater, civic dialogue theater embraces a fluid and opportunistic approach to performative paradigms and styles (hooks, 1995, p. 219). Civic dialogue performance also takes advantage of the multiple sites available for engagement—live theater and street performance, television and the Internet, dance parties and spectacles (Orenstein, 2001, pp. 149–150). These performances must, as Orenstein (2001) asserted, "appeal to a broad audience by offering frameworks for protest that leave room for individual creativity and by eschewing overly restrictive or exclusive ideologies" (p. 151).

What lessons does this history offer for autoethnography? First, it provides another context for the turn to performance, performative writing, and personal performance narratives in interpretive, qualitative, critical, and narrative inquiry. Second, this history traces the movement between and among art and politics, individual and community, representation and participation. In the shifts toward reflexivity, inclusion, personal stories, local actions, multiple perspectives, and civic dialogue, social protest theater demonstrates how paradigms and techniques can be used in the service of making art matter and generating action in the world. Social protest theater's history also speaks to how the stories *we* tell can and do reflect back on, become entangled in, and critique this current historical moment and its discontents (Denzin, 1997, p. 200).

Journalist . . . Artist

When I got a little older, my Saturday night stays with my grandparents in the company of Lawrence Welk were extended to weeklong visits over summer vacation. I would visit them at their lake house, with its screened porch, sloping lawn, and dense stand of trees. Inside the house, there was a guest bedroom with a white iron twin bed, just for me. There was my grandmother's electric organ, with its waltz, foxtrot, and bossa nova accompaniment. There were shelves of books and stacks of board games—Monopoly, Scrabble, and Parcheesi. There were all of these things to keep my hands and mind busy, and after 20 minutes or so I would whine that there was absolutely nothing to do.

I would start wondering how much longer it would be until my parents came to pick me up.

I would sprawl on the couch and sulk.

I would wander into the kitchen and watch my grandmother peeling potatoes. I would watch her so intently that she would turn around and ask, "What's the matter?"

"I'm *bored*."

"Do you want to read?"

"No."

"Want to go outside and play?"

"Nope."

"Want Grandpa to play Scrabble with you?"

"No."

"Well then, dear, what do you want to do?"

And I would stare back at her, expressionless, until she would shrug and return to the potatoes.

We enacted this scene nearly every day during my visits. And then one day, my grandmother turned to me and said, "Why don't you write something?"

"*What?*" I had not heard that one before.

"Why don't you pretend you're a reporter and you're going to write a story for the evening edition of the paper?"

"But I don't know how to be a reporter."

"I'll show you."

And with that, my grandmother set off to look for my reporter's costume. She gave me a small pad and pencil. She gave me an old hat of my grandfather's. She wrote "Press" on a slip of paper and stuck it in the hatband. Then she said, "Why don't you interview Grandpa for your story?"

At least I think that is what she said. I was already looking for my grandfather.

He was sitting at the dining room table, staring at his typewriter. His hands were clasped behind his head. He was reading the newly typed sheet in front of him, silently mouthing the words. He looked up from his work and said, "Well, who is this?"

"I'm a reporter and I'm here to interview you for the evening edition!"

"Sure. Pull up a chair. Care for a drink?"

"Can't. I'm on the job."

"Very well, then. What can I do for you?"

I asked my grandfather how old he was, how much he weighed, and how tall he was.

I asked about his favorite color, record, and book. I asked him why he loved Grandma and whether he wished he could live forever. I asked him why he sat at his typewriter all afternoon and into the darkness, typing. He said that he was writing stories.

"Stories about what?"

"Stories about what I see when I close my eyes and listen very, very carefully."

"Listen to what?"

"To the radio. To the mourning doves. To you playing the organ. To the beating of my own heart."

He smiled and asked me whether I had any other questions. I said, "No, that does it." He went back to staring at the page and reading his words to himself. And then he put his fingers on the keys and began typing.

I stayed there, very still in my chair and wrote down the things I noticed about my grandfather as he worked—the way his glasses glinted when the light hit them, the way his right hand would raise up from the keys and push the return key and land back on the keys in one fluid motion, the way he smiled at being watched and documented.

I worked on my story for several days. When I was done, my grandmother pasted it onto a large sheet of construction paper. Both of my grandparents said that they liked my story very much.

The story I wrote at my grandparents' house that summer did not come out of nowhere. I intended to write it. I donned the costume of a reporter and played the role as I remembered it—watching carefully, asking questions, and writing things down. I do not recall how the story went, but I do know that it was about my grandfather's performance as an artist—as a writer. It was my attempt to document music, movement, and the beating of his heart. And although I did not know it then, this story was my attempt to write a text that enacted the very art it sought to inscribe.

On Location

The "documentary idea" in solo performance, as Kalb (2001) put it, is to give an audience the impression of having been there "*on location*" (p. 20, emphasis added). For Kalb, the actual fact of being there is not as important as the rhetorical power of solo performance to generate "powerful topical narratives that are not easily dismissed or second-guessed, and for performance circumstances" in which Brecht's epic theater[27] "becomes a living concept again because the reality of the performer-researcher has been made an active part of the art" (p. 16). Documentary solo performance subscribes to an inherent duplicity—of fact and fiction, imagination and realism, objectivity and partisanship—that "recognizes the audience's sophistication regarding stories" (p. 22). It is this duplicity, along with a performer's ability to bridge and exploit the possibilities inherent in the move between documentary realism and fictionalization, that makes a performance compelling.

Anna Deavere Smith's performances *Fires in the Mirror* (regarding the 1991 riots in Crown Heights, Brooklyn, New York, following the death of a black boy struck by a rabbi's motorcade and the retaliatory stabbing of a Jewish student) and *Twilight: Los Angeles* (regarding the 1992 riots in Los Angeles following the acquittal of the police officers accused of beating Rodney King) offer striking examples of the duplicity of solo documentary performance.[28] Smith constructed these performances by interviewing people directly and indirectly involved in the events and delivered, "verbatim, their words and the essence of their physical beings in characterizations which fall somewhere between caricature, Brechtian epic gestures, and mimicry" (Reinelt, 1996, p. 609). Reinelt (1996) characterized Smith's performance technique as "a bridge that makes the unlikely seem connected. She ghosts her portraits with her own persona, signifying sympathy, fairness, and also her own subject position" (p. 615). Reinelt argued[29] that, in filtering the voices of (many) others through her own voice and oscillating between identification and difference,

> Smith needs to have it both ways.... She needs to be identified as both journalist and artist. In a sense, Smith dares to speak [for others] ... *not* because she is objective, fair-minded, and even-handed, but because she demonstrates the process of bridging difference, seeking information and understanding, and finessing questions of identity. Since the audience is positioned in the direct address sequences to "be" Smith, they are positioned to experience the activity of bridging, working with difference. This effect is the most radical element of Smith's work—it engages the spectator in radical political activity to the extent that the spectator grapples with this epistemological process. (p. 615)

Smith's work enacts this bridging in the performance of personal stories. Rather than use these stories as a mirror for a subject's or an audience's unexamined experience, Smith's solo performances "turn the mirror into a political tool" (Kalb, 2001, p. 23; see also Dolan, 2001a, p. 89; Kondo, 2000). Smith noted, "My project is about ... the gap between ... the performer and the other and . . . the gap between the performer and the text" (quoted in Capo and Langellier, 1994, p. 68). By remaining critically present in her portrayal of others and their stories, Smith brings the performative to her performance. She eschews politically disengaged, reductive, and static *representation(s)* of events and participants in favor of work that *presents*—creates—a "generative engagement between performer and audience" in the negotiation among stories, selves, texts, and contexts (Salverson, 2001, p. 123). She moves through *mimesis* to *poiesis* and *kinesis*.

What happens when performers present their own stories? Solo performers often offer their personal stories as testimony about "real" events. Audiences witness such testimony and, as such, become implicated in the encounters. As Hughes and Román (1998) noted,

> When we attend a solo piece it's knowing that there is a good chance the performer is also the writer and the stories we will hear "really happened." There is some level of safety that disappears for the audience: we can't hide behind "it's only art." (p. 4; see also Miller, 1995)

Personal narrative performances deny any easy distinction between "art" and "life." Such performances retain their performative, political power in and through the ways in which they foreground the constitutive and shifting nature of giving testimony and witnessing. Rather than present experience as authentic (true) and untouchable (immune to critical commentary), solo performers create intimate provocations in which they testify and audiences bear witness to their stories (Gray & Sinding, 2002).

Robbie McCauley is a performer who writes, directs, and performs personal narrative, making explicit the social conditions in which her stories are situated (Whyte, 1993, p. 282). In telling personal narratives, McCauley "intends that her onlookers . . . , in witnessing the experiences she invokes in her performances, will begin to understand their own implication in the situations that she presents" (p. 282). In her work *Sally's Rape: The Whole Story,* McCauley explores how her own story is shaped by the stories of others, including her "great-great-grandmother Sally, a slave on the Monticello estate of Thomas Jefferson" (p. 280).[30] The work includes a scene in which McCauley stands naked on an auction block. Her white partner Jeannie Hutchins[31] instructs the audience to create the scene of a slave market by chanting "Bid 'em in, bid 'em in." McCauley performs a monologue in which the voice of Sally and her own voice are intertwined as her body is examined and violated. Whyte (1993) described her experience of this scene:

> For the onlooker there is an awe-ful fascination in this representation of the slave auction, this scene of victimage. The pleasure of looking at the naked body of the black woman is . . . made guilty by the awareness of being inescapably positioned as a potential buyer in the slave market. . . . Similarly, whether or not you join the chanting you are trapped by the sympathetic magic of sound which reanimates the past, and no matter how much you tell yourself you had nothing to do with this scene, you are made vicariously complicit in the auction system that McCauley's staging represents. (p. 278)

McCauley's work illustrates the ways in which giving testimony and witnessing can and must be situated in larger contexts and shared histories. Her performances ask audiences and performers to come together differently and deeply "without collapsing either the 'I' or the 'other' into a totalizing 'we'" (Salverson, 2001, p. 120). McCauley taps into the vulnerability required to tell personal stories to move audiences past simple, essentialist identification and toward a generative engagement with their differences. She noted, "When you engage your vulnerability around . . . issues that are both political and personal, then you can have something powerful happen between people" (quoted in Becker, 2000, p. 530).

Where does bridging the political and personal in solo performance move (and leave) performers and audiences? Hughes and Román (1998) wrote,

> "The personal is political" remain[s] a vital challenge for solo performers. . . . Consequently, few

> performance artists—no matter how skilled or funny—intend to simply entertain: they mean to provoke, to raise questions, to implicate their audiences. (pp. 8–9)

Thus, the idea of being *on location* as a solo performer means using personal stories to create "calculated disturbances" in social, cultural, and political networks of power (Lane, 2002, p. 61). Writer, performer, and director Tim Miller commented on the exacting nature of these disturbances: "The whole reason for being an artist in this particular realm (performance) . . . is to respond quickly, effectively, and surgically to what you want to do" (quoted in Burnham, 1998, p. 35).

Miller's solo performances focus on gay rights and identities as these issues are reflected in/through the critical lens of his personal experience. His recent work *Glory Box* protests the failure of immigration laws to recognize gay and lesbian relationships, using the experience of his own relationship with his Australian Scottish partner. Writing about his experience traveling in the United States and performing *Glory Box*, Miller (2002) noted,

> I am trying to make my case to the communities I engage that this violence and injustice against lesbian and gay couples must stop. . . . I think theater is primarily a site for liberation stories and a sweaty laboratory to model possible strategies for empowerment. (para. 4)

For Miller, these strategies include explicit calls to action both within and outside of the performance. In each community in which he performs, Miller joins forces with national and local organizations invested in an issue, encourages community members to lobby their congressional representatives, asks audience members to sign petitions that support changes in legislation, and uses the performance as a catalyst for media coverage that will raise awareness about the issue (para. 7–11).

In addition to this "nuts-and-bolts activism," Miller asks his audience to engage in the more individual work of consciousness raising, which he terms "emotional and psychic . . . adjustments." For example, Miller's performance asks straight audience members to acknowledge their heterosexual privilege and asks gay and lesbian audience members to recognize the institutional and symbolic degradation of their lives (para. 12). In both its activist and consciousness-raising impulses, Miller's work "retains a personal and political investment that blurs the borders between public and private" (Dolan, 2001a, p. 114).

By taking their stories on location and using the duplicity of artistry and journalism, expert testimony and witnessing, solo performers teach us how to create, enact, and incite performances full of possibilities.

Torch Stories

In my dream, I see my grandfather on my university campus. I am walking to the library when I see him. He is reading a newspaper in the coffee shop. I call to him, and he looks up from the pages. He stands and waves, and when I reach him we embrace. He buys me a cup of coffee, and we settle in for a long talk.

He says, "What are you writing about?"

"I'm writing about how we are called to participate in music, in texts. I'm writing about torch singing as a sounding of personal and political desire."

He raises his eyebrows. "Really?"

"I guess what I'm really doing is writing a series of stories about torch singing."

He nods. "That sounds like fun."

"It is."

We turn our attention to our coffee and other topics, although I keep the conversation about writing torch stories going in my head. They are stories about what happens in between binaries, stories about what occurs between participation and provocation, emotion and politics, subject and object, body and voice, intended meaning and literal meaning, form and function, monologue and dialogue, connection and distance, conclusions and possibilities. They are stories that begin with the idea that performance, because it is imbricated in a culture and vast spiral of relationships, is necessarily and thoroughly *political* (Colleran &

Spencer, 1998, p. 1). They are stories that look into the gaps and contradictions between a modernist/realist perspective on performance that imagines that "stable meanings can . . . be 'shared' between author and reader, actor and audience, stage and auditorium" and a postmodern/anti-realist approach that deconstructs the "process of meaning-making itself" (Kershaw, 1999, p. 12).

Because of this, torch stories are stories that ask what happens when I try to understand performance by straddling the fence—with one foot planted in the realm of uncovering and celebrating difference, multiple subject positions, and ideological and political pluralism and with the other foot firmly placed inside the possibility of a community experience, a shared sense of agency, and concerted action directed at social change. They are, just as important, stories that ask what happens when audiences engage with texts that are overtly resistant not in form or content but rather in their activity as a subtle and indirect voicing (Holderness, 1992, p. 10). They are stories that want to have it both ways, to say that it depends.

In the gaps and fissures of cultural production and politics, these stories create, to use theater scholar Kershaw's (1999) term, a source of *freedom.* This freedom is doubled—"not just freedom from oppression, repression, [and] exploitation . . . but also freedom *to reach beyond* existing systems of formalized power, freedom to create currently unimaginable forms of association and action" (p. 18). The freedom found in performance—found in telling stories—creates a resistive and transgressive radicalism.

Kershaw (1999) preferred "radical" to "political" because "radical has no necessary ideological tendency. . . . It gestures . . . towards kinds of freedom that currently cannot be envisaged" (p. 18). These stories also "invite an ideological investment that it cannot itself determine"; they are a "performative process in need of direction" (p. 20). *One* direction that readers and audience members might take is to actively engage what Brecht (1957/1998) termed a "complex seeing" and hearing that allows for multiple perspectives within the tangle of identifications and difference without forgetting the need to expose systems of oppression or the desire to find new ways of being in the world (p. 44). Even so, the source and object of these desires vary; they depend on readers' and audience members' perspectives and ideological investments. These stories promise a performative field of dreams—if you want to hear a critique, it will come.

Because these stories create an open and indeterminate space for interpretation and action, tracing their political efficacy is something like tracking the movement of an unspoken idea. The accounts, ideas, and explanations that these stories contain are points of contact, although they do not connect in a direct route or on a logical course. They are spaces of hope—*destinations* that can be arrived at from any number of locations.

"About these stories you're writing," my grandfather says, pulling me back into the conversation. "Does anything radical happen in them?"[32]

"Well, I think so. Yes."

"Tell me."

◼ Performative Praxis: Autoethnography as a Politics (full) of Possibility

I began this chapter asking you to consider how our autoethnographic texts do not stand, speak, or act alone; are not texts alone; and do not want to be left alone. I wanted to create a noisy and fractious dialogue on and about personal stories, performance, and social change. I wanted to stage this dialogue in and through the flesh and breath of my own experience. I wanted to create a text that shows—performs—a writing practice that tries to respond to the crisis of praxis. I wanted to engage you in a conversation that says and does something about autoethnography. I wanted to suggest how we make our personal accounts count.

I want to close by asking you to keep this conversation going in your own texts, contexts, and praxes. I want you to take this conversation into the next turn, crisis, and moment in autoethnography and to move your work, "without hesitation or encumbrance from the personal to the political"

(Denzin, 2000, p. 261). Drawing on the lessons that the turn toward personal narrative and performance has taught us, write your stories as they are constructed in and through the stories of others. Look at the intersections in the work of personal storytellers, performance ethnographers, and social protest performers described in this chapter and elsewhere as examples of how you might radically contextualize your texts and your subjectivity; embody personal and community accountability; attend to connection without collapsing or foreclosing debate, dialogue, and difference; move people to understand their world and its oppressions in new ways; and create the possibility of resistance, hope, and—*yes*—freedom (Denzin, 2003, pp. 33, 268). Ask how your texts can create and constitute social action—how your words can make a *difference* in and outside of individual processes of knowing and coming to know—and then *write* them and *share* them (B. Alexander, personal communication, August 2003). This, I believe, is the future of autoethnography. It is the challenge of telling and showing, to borrow from Ellis (2000), stories that are not only necessary but also full of possibilities (p. 275). In the spirit of moving into this future, I want to challenge you to do the following:

- *Recognize the power of the in-between.* Recognize the power of having it "both ways," of insisting on the interaction of message and aesthetics, process and product, the individual and the social. Recall how the crises, turns, and movements in and toward narrative, performance, and social protest theater are generated in the radical possibilities that exist in these in-betweens. Make work that "struggles to open the space between analysis and action, and to pull the pin on the binary opposition between theory and practice" (Conquergood, 2002, p. 145).

- *Stage impossible encounters.* Create texts that stage what Cohen-Cruz (2001) termed "impossible encounters" in their "capacity to bring people in contact with ideas, situations, or others that appear to be totally different" (p. 105). Use these encounters as occasions to negotiate a debate and dialogue about issues of importance to you and the world. Remember that, as McCauley stated, "Dialogue is an act. . . . It is not before or after the act. Saying the words, allowing the dialogue, making dialogue happen is an act, a useful act in the moment" (quoted in Mahone, 1994, p. 213).

- *Contextualize giving testimony and witnessing.* Perform the testimony and witnessing of personal stories in, through, and with larger social contexts. Consider that when we bring our texts to contexts, we can make work that constitutes a first step toward social change. Strive to make work that "might act as a doorway, an instrument of encounter, a place of public and private negotiations" (Salverson, 2001, p. 125) where the goal is to witness "within the context of the meeting with the person who testifies" (p. 121).

- *Create disturbances.* Value texts that "mean to provoke, to raise questions, [and] to implicate" authors and audiences, texts that create disturbances (Hughes & Román, 1998, p. 9). Capitalize on the complicity wrought in writing and reading autoethnographic texts—in how, when we place our lives and bodies in the texts that we create, engage, and perform, they are "no longer just our own; for better or worse they have become part of a community experience" (Nudd, Schriver, & Galloway, 2001, p. 113). Write texts that insist that to be there—on location—"is to be implicated" (p. 115).

- *Make texts of an explicit nature.* Respond to the need to be explicit in moving your readers and audiences intellectually, emotionally, and toward concerted social, cultural, and political action. Use your texts to "stage arguments, to embody knowledge and politics, to open a community to itself and the world in ways that are dangerous, visceral, compelling, and moving" (Dolan, 2001a, p. 62). Ask not only whether your texts are moving but also *how* they create movement and toward what *ends?* (Salverson, 2001, p. 122, emphasis added).

These are your challenges, and they are my own. In a handbook chapter that wants to move theory and method to action, it is the charge to make the personal political in your work and in my own. Will the chapter on autoethnography in the next edition of this handbook ask whether there is a place for autoethnography in our conversations about a radical democratic politics, a poetics of change, or a performance of possibilities? Will this chapter end with this query, or will it constitute a beginning, an opening into a conversation about where we have been and how far we have come—in being willing and able to say that we are in a moment when the point of creating autoethnographic texts is to change the world?

Epilogue: There Are Living Forces in Poetry

You deal in dangerous and intimate provocations.
Yelling "Change!" in crowded theaters, committing efficacy to writing
believing that
there are living forces in . . . poetry.[33]

You take your politics personally
and make the personal political.
You stake your life story on re-presenting, not imitating;
bringing movement, not mirrors, to reality.

You understand how
theater, art, text, experience is what
we make of it
and we are made by that making.[34]

You play the imaginary
line between artist and activist.
You give flesh and breath to the theory that there are countless ways
of making do . . . and getting through.[35]

Is there a place for autoethnography in this poem?
You tell me.

Notes

1. Titled "Communication Studies 298: Colloquium in Communication," this special topics course was designed and taught by my mentor, Nick Trujillo, as a team ethnography course that focuses on studies of organizational culture. Trujillo (2003) discussed this course and others in his essay, "Reflections on a Career in Academia." See also my essay, "What We Save: A Bricolage On/About Team Ethnography" (Holman Jones, 2003).

2. This text was published as "Fragments of Self at the Postmodern Bar" by Communication Studies 298 (1997).

3. This section has an obvious debt, and owes a sincere thanks, to Pelias's (1999) "Performance Is" (pp. 109–111).

4. For a discussion of how these questions anticipate the crises of representation, legitimation, and praxis, see Denzin (1997, pp. 3–14) and Lather (1993, pp. 673–674).

5. For a summary of these responses, see Denzin (1997, pp. 16–21).

6. The interest in personal narratives as auto/ethnographic texts owes a clear debt to the long-standing practice of telling personal stories among women anthropologists and the traditions and conventions of feminist ethnography. See, for example, Abu-Lughod (1990), Gordon (1988), Tedlock (2000), and Visweswaran (1997).

7. Paul Gray was the director of graduate studies and professor of performance studies at the University of Texas, Austin when I began my Ph.D. studies there in 1996. Reading and Performing was the first of several courses I took with him. Gray was the first (but certainly not the only) faculty member to encourage my interest in both performance and performing. He is an astute critic, powerful intellect, and enthusiastic mentor, and he is a teacher to whom I am happily indebted.

8. Ethnography is both a method for studying performance (projects that focus on the performance practices of particular individuals and cultures [Conquergood, 1992; Jackson, 1993; Jones, 2002; Madison, 1998b]) and a performance practice in its own right (a means of sharing the results of fieldwork [Gray, 2003; Mienczakowski & Morgan, 1993; Paget, 1995; Welker & Goodall, 1997]).

9. In Conquergood's (1991) essay, he explored four themes generated in and through the "deep epistemological, methodological, and ethical

self-questioning" of the crisis of representation and an increased emphasis on critical approaches and theory.

10. Conquergood and Turner are not alone here. Clifford Geertz, Dell Hymes, Erving Goffman, Richard Bauman, Kenneth Burke, and other anthropologists, sociologists, folklorists, and linguists all are interested and involved in the performative turn (Stucky & Wimmer, 2002, pp. 12–13; see also Denzin, 1997, pp. 102–104).

11. This is adapted from Conquergood (1991), who wrote, "I want to think about performance as a complement, alternative, supplement, and critique of inscribed texts" (p. 191).

12. Carpenter (1993, p. 125).

13. I am drawing on Conquergood's (1992) description of the "varying meanings of the key word 'performance' as it has emerged with increasing prominence in cultural studies. This critical genealogy can be traced from performance as mimesis to poiesis to kinesis, performance as imitation, construction, dynamism" (pp. 83–84).

14. Joni Jones taught Performance Ethnography. Her work on performance and identity in the academy and her fieldwork with the Yoruba in Nigeria are central to the discussion and practice of performance ethnography and are an inspiration for my own work. Jones directed my dissertation, an ethnographic and performative study of torch singing. This work bears the mark and trace of her thoughtful, sincere, and challenging guidance.

15. This performance was my response to the assignment designed by Joni Jones. This assignment asked us to create what Pineau (2002) described as the use of performance as methodology (p. 50). She wrote, "Performance methodology means learning by doing and might include any experiential approach that asks students to struggle bodily with course content" (p. 50; see also Alexander, 1999).

16. I am referencing Langellier's (1999) essay in which she wrote, "When personal narrative performance materializes performativity—when a narrator embodies identity and experience—there is always danger and risk" (p. 129).

17. I have found touchstones in Conquergood (1985, 1991, 2002), Denzin (1997), Lather (1993, 2001), Lincoln (1990), Pollock (1998), Richardson (2000), and Stewart (1996); see also Bochner (2000); Clough (2000); and Ellis (2000).

18. The conference was titled the Giant City Conference on Performative Writing and took place in April 2001 at Giant City Park in Makanda, Illinois. Each writer presented his or her work "under a small window that opened to the green woods" (Miller & Pelias, 2001, p. v). In this passage, I make reference to the "green window" (as the conference proceedings came to be titled) and to the piece shared by Gingrich-Philbrook (2001) that began this work.

19. I had the pleasure of taking courses titled Performing Autobiography and Writing and Performance Art with Lynn Miller while I attended the University of Texas as well as of having her help on my dissertation committee. Miller's passion for and knowledge about autobiographical performance has influenced my work and informed my understanding of how and why personal narrative performance matters in autoethnography.

20. Scott (1990, p. xii).

21. Gordon (1997, p. 107).

22. Gordon (1997, p. 22).

23. Barthes (1977/1978).

24. Carver (2001) wrote, "It's possible, in a poem or short story, to write about commonplace things and objects using commonplace but precise language, and to endow those things—a chair, a window curtain, a fork, a stone, a woman's earring—with immense, even startling power" (p. 89).

25. Gordon (1997, p. 22).

26. The shifts in form and process discussed here do not correspond neatly or entirely to chronological or sequential logic. The social protest theater strategies I describe (following Jan Cohen-Cruz) are not mutually exclusive, and all of these techniques are used in contemporary performance.

27. Kalb (2001) focused specifically on Brecht's notion of *Verfremdung* (alienation) in which audiences are encouraged to move beyond simple identification (empathy) with characters to a critical orientation in which actors are separate from characters and context is clearly connected to the text being presented.

28. See also Kalb's (2001) discussion of Marc Wolf, Danny Hoch, and Sarah Jones.

29. Reinelt (1996) was commenting on both the stage performance and video of *Fires in the Mirror*, produced for American Playhouse.

30. Whyte (1993) noted that McCauley's great-great-grandmother was not Sally Hemings, although Whyte pointed out that McCauley's performance "plays on the similarities between the lives of these two Sallies and those of other women slaves" (p. 292).

31. Portions of *Sally's Rape* were based on conversations with Hutchins about race, class, gender, history, and contexts. See Becker (2000, p. 520).

32. This is drawn from Kershaw (1999), who asserted that the questions we should ask about performance—and I would include stories—are "Has anything radical happened?" and "How was it done?" (p. 218).

33. Artaud (1958, p. 85).

34. Nudd, Schriver, and Galloway (2001, p. 15).

35. DeCerteau (1984, p. 29).

References

Abu-Lughod, L. (1990). Can there be a feminist ethnography? *Women and Performance, 5*(1), 7–27.

Alexander, B. K. (1999). Moving toward a critical poetic response. *Theatre Topics, 9*(2), 107–125.

Alexander, B. K. (2000). *Skin Flint* (or, *The Garbage Man's Kid*): A generative autobiographical performance based on Tami Spry's *Tattoo Stories. Text and Performance Quarterly, 20,* 97–114.

Artaud, A. (1958). *The theater and its double* (M. C. Richards, Trans.). New York: Grove Press.

Barthes, R. (1977). *Image–music–text* (S. Heath, Trans.). New York: Hill & Wang.

Barthes, R. (1978). *A lover's discourse: Fragments* (R. Howard, Trans.). New York: Hill & Wang. (Originally work published in 1977)

Becker, B. (2000). Robbie McCauley: A journey toward movement. *Theatre Journal, 52,* 519–542.

Boal, A. (1985). *Theatre of the oppressed* (C. A. McBride & M. O. McBride, Trans.). New York: Theatre Communications Group. (Original work published in 1979)

Bochner, A. P. (2000). Criteria against ourselves. *Qualitative Inquiry, 6,* 266–272.

Bochner, A. P. (2001). Narrative's virtues. *Qualitative Inquiry, 7,* 131–157.

Brecht, B. (1998). *Brecht on theatre: The development of an aesthetic* (J. Willett, Ed. & Trans.). New York: Hill & Wang. (Original work published in 1957)

Burnham, L. F. (1998). Interview with Tim Miller. In G. Harper (Ed.), *Interventions and provocations: Conversations on art, culture, and resistance* (pp. 31–40). Albany: State University of New York Press.

Butler, J. (1991). Imitation and gender insubordination. In D. Fuss (Ed.), *Inside/Out: Lesbian theories, gay theories* (pp. 13–31). New York: Routledge.

Capo, K. E., & Langellier, K. M. (1994). Anna Deavere Smith on *Fires in the Mirror. Text and Performance Quarterly, 14,* 62–76.

Carpenter, W. (1993). Girl writing a letter. *Iowa Review, 23*(2), 125.

Carver, R. (2001). On writing. In W. L. Stull (Ed.), *Call if you need me: The uncollected fiction and other prose* (pp. 87–92). New York: Vintage Contemporaries.

Chadwick, A. (2003, May 27). *Researcher heads to Sahara to study ancient cultures (Part 1).* [Online.] Washington, DC: National Geographic Radio Expeditions and National Public Radio. Available: www.npr.org/templates/story/story.php?storyid=1275887

Clough, P. (2000). Comments on setting criteria for experimental writing. *Qualitative Inquiry, 6,* 278–291.

Cohen-Cruz, J. (2001). Motion of the ocean: The shifting face of U.S. theater for social change since the 1960s. *Theater, 31*(3), 95–107.

Colleran, J., & Spencer, J. S. (1998). Introduction. In J. Colleran & J. S. Spencer (Eds.), *Staging resistance: Essays on political theater* (pp. 1–10). Ann Arbor: University of Michigan Press.

Communication Studies 298. (1997). Fragments of self at the postmodern bar. *Journal of Contemporary Ethnography, 26,* 251–292.

Conquergood, D. (1985). Performing as a moral act. *Literature and Performance, 5*(2), 1–13.

Conquergood, D. (1991). Rethinking ethnography: Towards a critical cultural politics. *Communication Monographs, 58,* 179–194.

Conquergood, D. (1992). Ethnography, rhetoric, and performance. *Quarterly Journal of Speech, 78,* 80–123.

Conquergood, D. (1994). For the nation! How street gangs problematize patriotism. In H. W. Simons & M. Billig (Eds.), *After postmodernism: Reconstructing ideology critique* (pp. 200–221). London: Sage.

Conquergood, D. (2002). Performance studies: Interventions and radical research. *Drama Review, 46*(2), 145–156.

Daly, A., & Rogers, A. (2001). Carolee Schneemann: A life drawing. *Drama Review, 45*(2), 9–54.

DeCerteau, M. (1984). *The practice of everyday life* (S. F. Rendall, Trans.). Berkeley: University of California Press.

Denning, M. (1997). *The cultural front: The laboring of American culture in the twentieth century.* London: Verso.

Denzin, N. (1997). *Interpretive ethnography: Ethnographic practices for the 21st century.* Thousand Oaks, CA: Sage.

Denzin, N. (2000). Aesthetics and the practices of qualitative inquiry. *Qualitative Inquiry, 6,* 256–265.

Denzin, N. (2003). *Performance ethnography: Critical pedagogy and the politics of culture.* Thousand Oaks, CA: Sage.

Diamond, E. (1992). The violence of "we." In J. G. Reinelt & J. R. Roach (Eds.), *Critical theory and performance* (pp. 390–398). Ann Arbor: University of Michigan Press.

Diamond, E. (1996). Introduction. In E. Diamond (Ed.), *Performance and cultural politics* (pp. 1–12). London: Routledge.

Dolan, J. (1993). *Presence and desire: Essays on gender, sexuality, performance.* Ann Arbor: University of Michigan Press.

Dolan, J. (2001a). *Geographies of learning: Theory and practice, activism and performance.* Middleton CT: Wesleyan University Press.

Dolan, J. (2001b). Rehearsing democracy: Advocacy, public intellectuals, and civic engagement in theatre and performance studies. *Theatre Topics, 11*(1), 1–17.

Elam, H. J., Jr. (1997). *Taking it to the streets: The social protest theater of Luis Valdez and Amiri Baraka.* Ann Arbor: University of Michigan Press.

Ellis, C. (1995). *Final negotiations: A story of love, loss, and chronic illness.* Philadelphia: Temple University Press.

Ellis, C. (1997). Evocative autoethnography: Writing emotionally about our lives. In W. Tierney & Y. Lincoln (Eds.), *Representation and the text: Reframing the narrative voice* (pp. 116–139). Albany: State University of New York Press.

Ellis, C. (2000). Creating criteria: An ethnographic short story. *Qualitative Inquiry, 6,* 273–277.

Ellis, C. (2002). Shattered lives: Making sense of September 11th and its aftermath. *Journal of Contemporary Ethnography, 31,* 375–410.

Ellis, C. (2004). *The ethnographic I: A methodological novel about teaching and doing autoethnography.* Walnut Creek, CA: AltaMira.

Ellis, C., & Bochner, A. P. (1996). Introduction: Talking over ethnography. In C. Ellis & A. P. Bochner (Eds.), *Composing ethnography: Alternative forms of qualitative writing* (pp. 13–48). Walnut Creek, CA: AltaMira.

Ellis, C., & Bochner, A. P. (2000). Autoethnography, personal narrative, reflexivity: Researcher as subject. In N. K. Denzin & Y. S. Lincoln (Eds.), *Handbook of qualitative research* (2nd ed., pp. 733–768). Thousand Oaks, CA: Sage.

Friedwald, W. (1996). *Jazz singing: America's great voices from Bessie Smith to bebop and beyond.* New York: Da Capo.

Garrick, D. A. (2001). Performances of self-disclosure. *Drama Review, 45*(4), 94–105.

Geertz, C. (1983). *Local knowledge: Further essays in interpretive anthropology.* New York: Basic Books.

Gingrich-Philbrook, C. (1997). Refreshment. *Text and Performance Quarterly, 17,* 352–360.

Gingrich-Philbrook, C. (2001). Preface to the proceedings. In L. Miller & R. J. Pelias (Eds.), *The green window: Proceedings of the Giant City conference on performative writing* (p. vii). Carbondale: Southern Illinois University Press.

Goodall, H. L. (2000). *Writing the new ethnography.* Walnut Creek, CA: AltaMira.

Gordon, A. F. (1997). *Ghostly matters: Haunting and the sociological imagination.* Minneapolis: University of Minnesota Press.

Gordon, D. (1988). Writing culture, writing feminism: The poetics and politics of experimental ethnography. *Inscriptions, 3*(4), 7–24.

Gornick, V. (2001). *The situation and the story: The art of personal narrative.* New York: Farrar, Straus & Giroux.

Gray, R. (2003). Performing on and off the stage: The place(s) of performance in arts-based approaches to qualitative inquiry. *Qualitative Inquiry, 9,* 254–267.

Gray, R., & Sinding, C. (2002). *Standing ovation: Performing social science research about cancer.* Walnut Creek, CA: AltaMira.

Grumet, M. R. (2001). Autobiography: The mixed genre of public and private. In D. H. Holdstein & D. Bleich (Eds.), *Personal effects: The social character of scholarly writing* (pp. 165–177). Logan: Utah State University Press.

Hartnett, S. (1998). Democracy is difficult: Poetry, prison, and performative citizenship. In S. J. Dailey (Ed.), *The future of performance studies: Visions and revisions* (pp. 287–297). Annandale, VA: National Communication Association.

Hartnett, S. (1999). Four meditations on the search for grace amidst terror. *Text and Performance Quarterly, 19,* 196–216.

Holderness, G. (1992). Introduction. In G. Holderness (Ed.), *The politics of the theatre and drama* (pp. 1–17). New York: St. Martin's.

Holman Jones, S. (2003). What we save: A bricolage on/about team ethnography. *American Communication Journal, 6*(2). [Online]. Available: www.acjournal.org

hooks, b. (1995). Performance practice as a site of opposition. In C. Ugwu (Ed.), *Let's get it on: The politics of black performance* (pp. 210–221). Seattle: Bay Press.

Hopper, R. (1993). Conversational dramatism and everyday life performance. *Text and Performance Quarterly, 13,* 181–183.

Hughes, H., & Román, D. (1998). O solo homo: An introductory conversation. In H. Hughes & D. Román (Eds.), *O solo homo: The new queer performance* (pp. 1–15). New York: Grove Press.

Iser, W. (1993). *The fictive and the imaginary: Charting literary anthropology.* Baltimore, MD: Johns Hopkins University Press.

Jackson, S. (1993). Ethnography and the audition: Performance as ideological critique. *Text and Performance Quarterly, 13,* 21–43.

Jackson, S. (1998). White noises: On performing white, on writing performance. *Drama Review, 42*(1), 49–65.

Jago, B. (2002). Chronicling an academic depression. *Journal of Contemporary Ethnography, 31,* 729–757.

Jones, J. L. (1996). The self as other: Creating the role of Joni Jones the ethnographer for Broken Circles. *Text and Performance Quarterly, 16,* 131–145.

Jones, J. L. (1997a). Performing Osun without bodies: Documenting the Osun Festival in print. *Text and Performance Quarterly, 17,* 69–93.

Jones, J. L. (1997b). Sista docta: Performance as critique of the academy. *Drama Review, 41,* 51–67.

Jones, J. L. (2002). Performance ethnography: The role of embodiment in cultural authenticity. *Theatre Topics, 21,* 1–15.

Kalb, J. (2001). Documentary solo performance. *Theater, 31*(3), 13–29.

Kemp, A. (1998). This black body in question. In P. Phelan & J. Lane (Eds.), *The ends of performance* (pp. 116–129). New York: New York University Press.

Kershaw, B. (1999). *The radical in performance: Between Brecht and Baudrillard.* London: Routledge.

Kisliuk, M. (2002). The poetics and politics of practice: Experience, embodiment, and the engagement of scholarship. In N. Stucky & C. Wimmer (Eds.), *Teaching performance studies* (pp. 99–117). Carbondale: Southern Illinois University Press.

Kondo, D. (2000). (Re)Visions of race: Contemporary race theory and the cultural politics of racial crossover in documentary theater. *Theatre Journal, 52,* 81–107.

Krieger, M. (1992). *Ekphrasis: The illusion of the natural sign.* Baltimore, MD: Johns Hopkins University Press.

Lane, J. (2002). Reverend Billy: Preaching, protest, and postindustrial flânerie. *Drama Review, 46*(1), 60–84.

Langellier, K. M. (1999). Personal narrative, performance, performativity: Two or three things I know for sure. *Text and Performance Quarterly, 19,* 125–144.

Lather, P. (1993). Fertile obsession: Validity after poststructuralism. *Sociological Quarterly, 34,* 673–693.

Lather, P. (2001). Postbook: Working the ruins of feminist ethnography. *Signs, 26*(4), 199–227.

Lincoln, Y. S. (1990). The making of a constructivist. In E. C. Guba & Y. S. Lincoln (Eds.), *The paradigm dialog* (pp. 67–87). Newbury Park, CA: Sage.

Lockford, L. (2002). From silence to siren to silence: A personal tale of political consequence. *Qualitative Inquiry, 8,* 622–631.

Madison, D. S. (1998a). Performance, personal narratives, and the politics of possibility. In S. J. Dailey (Ed.), *The future of performance studies: Visions and revisions* (pp. 276–285). Annandale, VA: National Communication Association.

Madison, D. S. (1998b). That was my occupation: Oral narrative, performance, and black feminist thought. In D. Pollock (Ed.), *Exceptional spaces: Essays in performance and history* (pp. 319–342). Chapel Hill: University of North Carolina Press.

Mahone, S. (1994). *Moon marked and touched by the sun.* New York: Theatre Communications Group.

Mienczakowski, J., & Morgan, S. (1993). *Busting: The challenge of the drought spirit.* Brisbane, Australia: Griffith University.

Miller, L. C. (1995). "Polymorphous perversity" in women's performance art: The case of Holly Hughes. *Text and Performance Quarterly, 15,* 44–58.

Miller, L. C. (1998). Witness to the self: The autobiographical impulse in performance studies. In J. S. Trent (Ed.), *Communication: Views from the helm for the 21st century* (pp. 318–322). Boston: Allyn & Bacon.

Miller, L. C., & Pelias, R. J. (2001). A beginning preface. In L. C. Miller & R. J. Pelias (Eds.), *The green window: Proceedings of the Giant City conference on performative writing* (pp. v–vi). Carbondale: Southern Illinois University Press.

Miller, T. (2002). *Solo performing as call to arms.* [Online.] Available: www.communityarts.net/readingroom/archie/32miller.php

Neumann, M. (1996). Collecting ourselves at the end of the century. In C. Ellis & A. P. Bochner (Eds.), *Composing ethnography: Alternative forms of qualitative writing* (pp. 172–198). Walnut Creek, CA: AltaMira.

Nudd, D. M., Schriver, K., & Galloway, T. (2001). Is this theater queer? The Micke Faust Club and the performance of community. In S. C. Haedick & T. Nellhaus (Eds.), *Performing democracy: International perspectives on urban community-based performance* (pp. 104–116). Ann Arbor: University of Michigan Press.

Olesen, V. (2000). Feminisms and qualitative research at and into the millennium. In N. K. Denzin & Y. S. Lincoln (Eds.), *Handbook of qualitative research* (2nd ed., pp. 215–255). Thousand Oaks, CA: Sage.

Orenstein, C. (2001). Agitational performance, now and then. *Theater, 31*(3), 139–151.

Paget, M. A. (1995). Performing the text. In J. Van Maanen (Ed.), *Representation in ethnography* (pp. 222–272). Thousand Oaks, CA: Sage.

Park-Fuller, L. M. (2000). Performing absence: The staged personal narrative as testimony. *Text and Performance Quarterly, 20,* 20–42.

Pelias, R. J. (1992). *Performance studies: The interpretation of aesthetic texts.* New York: St. Martin's.

Pelias, R. J. (1999). *Writing performance: Poeticizing the researcher's body.* Carbondale: Southern Illinois University Press.

Pelias, R. J. (2002). For father and son: An ethnodrama with no catharsis. In A. P. Bochner & C. Ellis (Eds.), *Ethnographically speaking: Autoethnography, literature, and aesthetics* (pp. 35–43). Walnut Creek, CA: AltaMira.

Pineau, E. L. (2002). Critical performative pedagogy: Fleshing out the politics of liberatory education. In N. Stucky & C. Wimmer (Eds.), *Teaching performance studies* (pp. 41–54). Carbondale: Southern Illinois University Press.

Pollock, D. (1998). Performing writing. In P. Phelan & J. Lane (Eds.), *The ends of performance* (pp. 73–103). New York: New York University Press.

Pratt, M. B. (1995). *S/HE.* Ithaca, NY: Firebrand Books.

Reed-Danahay, D. E. (1997). *Auto/Ethnography: Rewriting the self and the social.* Oxford, UK: Berg.

Reinelt, J. (1996). Performing race: Anna Deavere Smith's *Fires in the Mirror. Modern Drama, 39,* 609–617.

Reinelt, J. (1998). Notes for a radical democratic theater: Productive crisis and the challenge of indeterminacy. In J. Colleran & J. S. Spencer (Eds.), *Staging resistance: Essays on political theater* (pp. 283–300). Ann Arbor: University of Michigan Press.

Richardson, L. (1997). *Fields of play: Constructing an academic life.* New Brunswick, NJ: Rutgers University Press.

Richardson, L. (2000). Writing: A method of inquiry. In N. K. Denzin & Y. S. Lincoln (Eds.), *Handbook of qualitative research* (2nd ed., pp. 923–948). Thousand Oaks, CA: Sage.

Ricoeur, P. (1986). *Lectures on ideology and utopia* (G. H. Taylor, Ed.). New York: Columbia University Press.

Ronai, C. R. (1995). Multiple reflections of child sex abuse: An argument for a layered account. *Journal of Contemporary Ethnography, 23,* 395–426.

Salverson, J. (2001). Change on whose terms? Testimony and an erotics of inquiry. *Theater, 31*(3), 119–125.

Sandoval, C. (2000). *Methodology of the oppressed.* Minneapolis: University of Minnesota Press.

Scott, G. F. (1994). *The sculpted word: Keats, ekphrasis, and the visual arts.* Hanover, NH: University Press of New England.

Scott, J. C. (1990). *Domination and the arts of resistance: Hidden transcripts.* New Haven, CT: Yale University Press.

Solomon, A. (1997). *Re-dressing the canon: Essays on theatre and gender.* London: Routledge.

Spry, T. (2000). Tattoo stories: A postscript to *Skins. Text and Performance Quarterly, 20,* 84–96.

Spry, T. (2001). Performing autoethnography: An embodied methodological praxis. *Qualitative Inquiry, 7,* 706–732.

Stewart, K. (1996). *A space on the side of the road: Cultural poetics in an "other" America.* Princeton, NJ: Princeton University Press.

Stoller, P. (1997). *Sensuous scholarship.* Philadelphia: University of Pennsylvania Press.

Stucky, N. (1993). Toward an aesthetics of natural performance. *Text and Performance Quarterly, 13,* 168–180.

Stucky, N. (2001). Preface to the proceedings. In L. Miller & R. J. Pelias (Eds.), *The green window: Proceedings of the Giant City conference on performative writing* (p. vii). Carbondale: Southern Illinois University Press.

Stucky, N., & Wimmer, C. (2002). The power of transformation in performance studies pedagogy. In N. Stucky & C. Wimmer (Eds.), *Teaching performance studies* (pp. 1–29). Carbondale: Southern Illinois University Press.

Tedlock, B. (1991). From participant observation to the observation of participation: The emergence of narrative ethnography. *Journal of Anthropological Research, 47,* 69–94.

Tedlock, B. (2000). Ethnography and ethnographic representation. In N. K. Denzin & Y. S. Lincoln (Eds.), *Handbook of qualitative research* (2nd ed., pp. 455–486). Thousand Oaks, CA: Sage.

Trujillo, N. (2003). Reflections on a career in academia: A response. *American Communication Journal,* 6(2). [Online.] Available: www.acjournal.org

Tyler, S. A. (1986). Post-modern ethnography: From document of the occult to occult document. In J. Clifford & G. E. Marcus (Eds.), *Writing culture: The poetics and politics of ethnography* (pp. 122–140). Berkeley: University of California Press.

Van Maanen, J. (1988). *Tales of the field.* Chicago: University of Chicago Press.

Vickers, M. H. (2002). Researchers as storytellers: Writing on the edge—without a safety net. *Qualitative Inquiry, 8,* 608–621.

Visweswaran, K. (1997). Histories of feminist ethnography. *Annual Review of Anthropology, 26,* 591–621.

Welker, L. S., & Goodall, H. L. (1997). Representation, interpretation, and performance: Opening the text of *Casing a Promised Land. Text and Performance Quarterly, 17,* 109–122.

Whyte, R. (1993). Robbie McCauley: Speaking history other-wise. In L. Hart & P. Phelan (Eds.), *Acting out: Feminist performances* (pp. 277–293). Ann Arbor: University of Michigan Press.

31

THE METHODS, POLITICS, AND ETHICS OF REPRESENTATION IN ONLINE ETHNOGRAPHY

Annette N. Markham

in cyberspace, one dwells in language. and through language.
i exist as myself in language online . . . it feels more like being me than i sometimes feel offline
. . . i think myself in language is more communicative of who i am.
and because i'm a good writer, eloquence makes me beautiful . . .

—Sherie, online interview participant

Here, I can edit what I think before I say it. This makes communication easier between my friends and I. There are fewer errors in meaning when our thoughts have been written clearly.

—Robin, online interview participant

My ambiguity makes you nervous. I can be many things at once here. Are they all 'me'? Who am I? 'He' . . . 'Her' . . . 'Per' . . . 'It' . . . 'We' . . . ? Can't you tell? Why do you want to know???

—DominOH!, online interview participant

Whether one studies the Internet as a social structure or utilizes Internet-based technologies as tools for research, Internet-based technologies change the research scenario. Computer mediation has a significant influence on many aspects of communication practice and theory. The internet has similarities to many earlier media for communication, such as letter writing, telephone, telegraph, Post-It Notes, and so forth. At the same time, the capacities and uses of Internet communication are unique in configuration and shape a user's (and thus the researcher's) perceptions and interactions. These influences extend beyond the interpersonal; outcomes of these communication processes have the potential to shift sensemaking practices at the cultural level. We are, as Gergen (1991) notes, saturated in technologies. The Internet and associated communication media permeate and alter interactions and the possible outcomes of these interactions at the dyadic, group, and cultural level.[1] Equally, Internet technologies have the potential to shift the ways in which qualitative researchers collect, make sense of, and represent data.

In technologically mediated environments, self, other, and social structures are constituted through interaction, negotiated in concert with others. The extent to which information and communication technology (ICT) can mediate one's identity and social relations should call us to epistemological attention. Whether or not we do research of physical or online cultures, new communication technologies highlight the dialogic features of social reality, compelling scholars to reexamine traditional assumptions and previously taken-for-granted rubrics of social research.

In the early 1990s, as the capacities of the Internet became more publicly known and accessed, the use of the Internet for the development of personal relationships and social structures grew, as did the study of computer-mediated subjectivity and community. Through a phone line, access to the Internet, and specialized software, people could meet and develop relationships with others from the privacy of their homes. People could do this anonymously if they chose, creating personae that were similar to or highly distinctive from what they perceived their physical personae to be. They could create or join communities based on like-mindedness rather than physical proximity.

During these early years when Internet and virtual reality technologies caught public and scholarly interest, the study of computer-mediated communication (CMC) worked from theoretical extremes: On the one hand, computer-mediated communication was lauded as a means of transcending the limits associated with human embodiment. By erasing sociocultural markers such as race and gender or escaping the body altogether, virtual communication would lead to a utopian society whereby democratic participation in public discourse was unhindered by physicality and corresponding stereotypes. At the other extreme, skeptics critiqued CMC because it removed essential socioemotional or nonverbal cues and would result in impoverished, low-trust relationships at best and social withdrawal, at worst. Citizens would resemble hackers: pale, reclusive, and prone to eating pizza and Chinese takeout. As time passed, use grew, novelty diminished, and more measured accounts emerged based less on theoretical speculation and more on study of actual contexts.[2] It became clear that meaningful and significant relationships and social structures could thrive in text-only online environments. This capacity is now taken for granted. The past decade of communication has included forms new to many of us: email, mailing lists, Multi User Dimensions (MUDs or MOOs), real time chatrooms, instant messaging, websites, blogs, and so forth. We are now familiar with the concepts of cybersex, online marriages, Friendster, and other creative uses of technology to enact identity and relationships through computer-mediation. Many of us can probably name close colleagues and friends whom we would not recognize in person.

The computer-mediated construction of self, other, and social structure constitutes a unique phenomenon for study. In online environments, the construction of identity is a process that must be initiated more deliberately or consciously. Offline, the body can simply walk around and be responded to by others, providing the looking glass with which one comes to know the self. Online, the first step toward existence is the production of discourse, whether in the form of words, graphic images, or sounds. But as many scholars have taught us (e.g., Buber, 1958; Bakhtin, 1981; Blumer, 1969; Laing, 1969), we understand our Self only in concert with Other, a continual dialogic process of negotiation and a great deal of faith in shared meaning (Rommetveit, 1980).

In most computer-mediated environments, this process requires a more deliberate exchange of information because people are not co-present in the same physical space and the nonverbal aspects of the process are, for the most part, missing. The process is obfuscated because a person typically takes knowledge of self for granted with little reflection on the social, interactive process by which the self is negotiated with others in context. Mostly overlooked by users, the production of the message is only the first part of the process: Whether by receiving a reply message or by tracking a virtual footprint of a visitor to one's website, one can only know if one has been acknowledged through some sort of response. MacKinnon's insights in this matter (1995) warrant repeating here. He notes that the common phrase "I think, therefore I am" is woefully inadequate in cyberspace. Even "I speak, therefore I am" is not enough. In cyberspace, the more appropriate phrase is "I am perceived, therefore I am." (p. 119). Implied in this last phrase is the fact that online, perception of another's attention is only known by overt response. So we can usefully note this by adding the phrase "I am responded to, therefore I am" (Markham, 2003a).

The participant statements (from my previous research of Internet users) at the beginning of this chapter represent well the importance of text to a person's construction and negotiation of identity in online text-based environments. Sherie expresses a desire to be known solely as text (not through, but *as* text). For Sherie, computer-mediated communication is a way of being. Robin always uses correct punctuation and strives to make the meaning as clear as possible. Text is perceived as a powerful means of controlling, through editing and backspacing, the way the self is presented to others. DominOH!, unlike the other two, does not pay much attention to the textual, linguistic aspects of the medium. Rather, DominOH! uses the technology as an interaction space which protects anonymity and allows the social self to be less firmly attached to the body. Yet the text is vital to the researcher's understanding of DominOH!'s persona online.

For all three personae interviewed, text remains the means through which each performs and negotiates the self. None of these textual entities exists in isolation. Their existence is made possible by direct or perceived interaction with others. They are communicative through and through; their social being is initiated through a process of creating and sending a message and negotiated through a process of interaction.

Although we recognize that reality is socially negotiated through discursive practice, the dialogic nature of identity and culture is thrown into high relief in computer-mediated environments. This gives rise to many possibilities and paradoxes in social research. For any researcher studying life online, the traditional challenge of understanding other-in-context is complicated by the blatant interference of the researcher into the frame of the field and by the power of the researcher in representing the culture. Researchers have always interfered with the context in some way while conducting research. In the past three or more decades, scholars have problematized this feature of research, as well as highlighted the blurring of boundaries between researcher and researched. Still, these issues become startlingly apparent—and challenging—in the context of CMC environments.

These issues call not only for adjustment of traditional methods to online environments or the creation of new methods, but also for across-the-board reassessment and interrogation of the premises of qualitative inquiry in general. Interestingly, the specific logistic and analytic problems associated with the interpretive study of computer-mediated personae reveal many weaknesses in qualitative methods and epistemologies, generally. In the years I have spent trying to figure out how to make sense of participants whose gender, name, body type, age, ethnicity, class, and location remain inexplicable, I have been compelled to seriously examine certain practices of Othering which, despite efforts to be reflexive, hide in everyday, embodied ways of knowing. Put more positively, studying computer-mediated interactions allows and encourages exploration of what is happening in "the hyphen that both separates and merges personal identities with our inventions of Others" (Fine, 1994, p. 70).

New communication technologies privilege and highlight certain features of interaction while obscuring others, confounding traditional methods of capturing and examining the formative elements of relationships, organizations, communities and cultures. Additionally, a person's conceptual framework of any new communication technology will predetermine, to a certain extent, that person's understanding of, response to, and interaction with the technology. This complicates the researcher's ability to assume commonalities among participants' communicative practices via CMC, or to presume that participants understand and use the technology in the same way the researcher does. The challenge for the qualitative researcher in the computer-mediated environment is to attend to the details of how one is going about the process of getting to know something about the context and the persons being studied.

At the same time, examining one's own influence in the shape of the outcome is a vital practice. Grappling with both the practical and the epistemological implications of this influence can help researchers make more socially responsible decisions. In a very real sense, every method decision is an ethics decision, in that these decisions have consequences for not just research design but also the identity of the participants, the outcomes of our studies, and the character of knowledge which inevitably grows from our work in the field.

In this chapter, I describe some of the tensions and complications that can arise in the qualitative study of Internet-mediated contexts when decisions must be made about (a) defining the boundaries of the field, (b) determining what constitutes data, (c) interpreting the other as text, (d) using embodied sensibilities to interpret textuality, and (e) representing the other ethically in research reports. My overall object in this discussion is to illustrate some of the challenges of doing research in computer-mediated environments and to display the significance of the researcher's choices on the field's structure, on the other's embodied or reported Being, and ultimately, on the social knowledge derived from the research project. The discussion is intended to help researchers generate questions which can be used to interrogate their own epistemological and axiological assumptions throughout the design and enactment of the inquiry. In addition to this primary train of thought, I talk briefly about how the Internet is conceptualized, review some of the main shifts in thinking about qualitative Internet research, and discuss some of the major ethical considerations which are entwined with this type of inquiry.

To clarify what this chapter does and does not do: First, this chapter focuses on textuality. The examples throughout this chapter draw primarily on text-based computer-mediated discourse and interactions among participants or between participant and researcher. Although technologies facilitate visual and audio simulations and representations and the capacities of the traditional PC are moving to mobile or convenience devices, text remains a primary unit of analysis for the qualitative researcher. Put differently, the issues raised here apply equally to multi-media and mobile aspects of CMC because these are, for the most part, analyzed as texts, broadly speaking.

Second, even though this chapter focuses on computer-mediated contexts, the spirit of these arguments applies to other forms of interaction, both online and offline. The intriguing thing about CMC is that it calls attention to the ways we literally see and make sense of the world and points out many of the biases inherent in our traditional ways of seeing and knowing. Therefore, one should not dismiss the challenges discussed herein even if doing radically different types of qualitative research.

Third, this chapter does not seek to provide an overview of how qualitative research is conducted on or via the Internet, but rather, addresses key epistemological and methodological questions facing ethnographers researching in social spaces constituted in part or wholly through new communication technologies. Many sources exist to aid the researcher with specific procedures and methods for qualitative studies (this volume) and qualitative Internet studies (e.g., Johns, Chen, & Hall, 2003; Mann & Stewart, 2000).

Finally, this chapter focuses more on problems and challenges than opportunities and potential of CMC-related research environments. This imbalance is not indicative of my own or a general attitude toward qualitative Internet research. Here, however, I want to build a case for cautious, reflexive, and prepared research which, while celebrating those aspects of new communication technologies that make them well suited for qualitative inquiry, remains attentive to the consequences of one's research choices.

Shifting Lenses

The study of CMC spans virtually every academic discipline and methodological approach. Research objects and lenses have shifted rapidly in the past decade or so, commensurate with the rapid development and dissemination of information and communication technologies (ICT). Qualitative study of ICT in the past decade has tended to shift in two ways. First, though not a universal trend, research has tended to shift from strongly polarized depictions and predictions in the early 1990s, to more descriptive accounts in the mid-late 1990s and, in the new century, to more theoretically grounded, comparative, or theory-building studies.

Accounts of CMC, identity, and culture throughout the early 1990s were heavily influenced by pop culture descriptions of and personal experience with novel and exciting forms of interaction. Gibson's term *Cyberspace*, coined in his science fiction novel *Neuromancer*, offered the elusive but intriguing definition of online experience as "a consensual hallucination experienced daily by billions of legitimate operators, in every nation, by children being taught mathematical concepts. . . . A graphical representation of data abstracted from the banks of every computer in the human system. Unthinkable complexity. Lines of light ranged in the non-space of the mind, clusters and constellations of data. Like city lights, receding" (1984). About virtual reality, Rheingold (1991) told readers "*we have to decide fairly soon what it is we as humans ought to become, because we're on the brink of having the power of creating any experience we desire*" (p. 386, emphasis in original). Wright (1994) told us simply that it would "deeply change politics, culture, and the fabric of society—if not, indeed, the very metaphysics of human existence" (p. 101). Barlow offered a vision of Cyberspace as the Wild West, a final frontier to be claimed: "Cyberspace . . . is presently inhabited almost exclusively by mountain men, desperadoes and vigilantes, kind of a rough bunch. . . . And as long as that's the case, it's gonna be the Law of the Wild in there" (cited in Woolley, 1992, pp. 122-123). Keep (1993) suggested that virtuality through computer mediated communication "announces the end of the body, the apocalypse of corporeal subjectivity" (p. 4).

These ideas caught the imagination of scholars and influenced significantly the tone of research. This is not surprising: With the invention or new use of every communication technology in the past century, claims regarding media effects tend to be overestimated and exaggerated as long as the technology remained novel. Although this period was not without empirically based and theoretically grounded research, there was a feeling of utopianism in descriptions of how technology might (or should) free us from the constraints of worldwide shackles like hierarchy, traditional social stereotypes, embodiment, and even death. Rheingold's *Virtual Community* (1993) and Benedikt's edited collection *Cyberspace: First Steps* (1991) represent this trend well. To give these authors credit, their ideas sparked the interest of many scholars whose work followed.

Simultaneously, research was influenced by news coverage, movies, and pop culture accounts that predicted negative, even dire consequences of this new Internet era. *Time Magazine* offered a cover story on "Cyberporn," wherein readers learned that the Internet threatened our children's safety (from adult sexual predators) and innocence (from easy access to pornography). Vastly exaggerated claims incited sound criticism; the magazine editors had relied exclusively on evidence supplied by an undergraduate student's non-peer-reviewed study. Critiqued or not, this issue of *Time* was quoted by legislators, parents, and scholars. "Internet Addiction Disorder" entered the medical lexicon in 1996. Popular films spelled out the dangers of identity theft, hackers, and spending too much time in front of one's computer. Pundits predicted that face-to-face interactions would become impoverished as people forgot the intricacies and delicacies of human interaction in physical environments.

These swings have evened out in the last few years, resulting in published accounts which exhibit many of the more traditional characteristics of social research. Scholars are explaining their approach and methods more carefully, grounding their work in previous research more thoroughly, and attending more closely to the history of communication technologies as well as the history of qualitative inquiry. The targets of research continue to follow shifts in technological development. Herring (2004) aptly notes that researchers have tended to follow novelty; researchers quickly flock to each new technology. Research in the 1980s tended to focus on the use and impact of computers, email, and networking in the workplace (overviewed well by Sproull & Kiesler, 1991). In the 1990s, research waves moved progressively through various forms of CMC, such as Email, Usenet, MUDs and MOOs, the World Wide Web, IM (Instant Messaging), SMS (Short Messaging Service via mobile telephone), and Blogs.

Various social interaction practices and social structures received empirical attention over the past decade: Flaming and other forms of emotionally charged or violent acts (e.g., Dery, 1994; Dibble, 1996; MacKinnon, 1998); the use of emoticons to compensate for the absence of nonverbals (Witmer & Katzman, 1998); the social construction of virtual communities via mailing lists (e.g., Baym, 2000; Bromseth, 2002; Sveningsson, 2001; Rheingold, 1993), MUDs or MOOs (e.g., Kendall, 1998; Reid, 1995) or websites (Johnson, 2003); the intersection of technology and identity (e.g., Lupton, 1995; Markham, 1998; Senft & Horn, 1996; Sondheim, 1996; Stone, 1996; Turkle, 1995); sexuality (e.g., Kiesler, 1997; Waskul, Douglass, & Edgley, 2000); gender and participation in CMC (e.g., Herring, 1993); and race (Kolko, Nakamura, & Rodman, 2000). Ethnographically informed studies have focused on online groups (e.g., Baym, 2000; Eichhorn, 2001; Kendall, 1998; Orgad, 2002; Reid, 1995); use of Internet in traditional, physically based cultures (e.g., Miller & Slater, 2000); cultural formation around particular topics (e.g., Hine, 2000); and sensemaking in specialized environments such as virtual work teams (e.g., Shane, 2001).

Multiple anthologies offered accounts of cyberculture (e.g., *High Noon on the Electronic Frontier* [1996]; *the Cybercultures Reader* [2000]). Utilizing both pop culture and academic accounts, these texts provide a useful overview of the 1990s viewpoints about computer-mediated communication and cultural practice. Few resources existed during the 1990s to specifically guide qualitative researchers. Although researchers offered context-specific discussions of research methods (represented well in *Internet Research*, edited by Jones, 1999), a comprehensive treatment did not appear until 2000, when Mann and Stewart's volume provided principles and practices for conducting qualitative inquiry using Internet communication as a tool of research.

As research in this evolving field grows more refined, the conceptualization of computer-mediated communication has shifted from sweeping universalized encapsulations to more specific, context-based definitions. As well, some have noted a move from exaggerated to mundane accounts. A recent article (Herring, 2004) entitled "Slouching Toward the Ordinary" notes the trend to minimize the impact of new communication technologies on identity, subjectivity, and social practices and structures. In this same vein, ethnographic inquiry appears to be shifting from the study of online-only environments and virtual identity to the intersection of computer-mediated communication with everyday life. Scholars are now calling for increased attention to the multiple uses and definitions of "Internet" in context, as well as increased attention to how the online and offline intersect (Baym, Zhang, & Lin, 2002; Orgad, 2002).

Overtly political analyses of computer mediated communication are diverse in scope and range. I mention just two areas: research in developing countries and research interrogating the role of the researcher. Work exploring the use of internet technologies in developing countries is important and increasing. Kolko conducted in-depth interviews in Uzbekistan as a means of grounding her NSF-funded study of how ICT affects life in central Asia (personal communication, October 15, 2002). Miller and Slater have conducted the most widely known ethnography of a developing country to date, exploring the ways in which the Internet is perceived and used in Trinidad (2000). Theresa Senft's recent work in Ghana illustrates a politically motivated effort to use interpretive participatory action research to help the cause of women and the poor in that region of the world (personal communication, October 2004).

Research exploring the researcher's role in Internet studies is also expanding: My own work was acknowledged as an explicitly reflexive discussion of the researcher's role in Internet ethnography (1998). Later works also discuss directly the ethical and political stance of the researcher and the relationship between researcher and participants (e.g., Ryen, 2002). Bromseth (2002, 2003) discusses in depth the ethical dilemmas of collecting data in groups where people are reluctant to be studied. Gajjala (2002) explores her own study of a group wherein the members were overtly and actively resistant to her intent as a researcher. Along different lines, Eichhorn's study of a virtual group (2001) astutely addresses the paradox of using offline interviews to understand online subjectivities. Orgad's work (2002) illustrates the opposite paradox: using only online interviews with women in a virtual support group to understand how these women make sense of their illness. In both cases, these researchers recognized during the course of their research that giving voice to the participants meant selecting the medium based on what was most appropriate for the participants, not the researcher.

A final note about the shifting trends in qualitative research over the past decade of Internet studies. Many studies have been labeled "ethnography" when the more appropriate term would be interview study, case study, phenomenology, grounded theory, narrative analysis, biography or life history, and so forth. "Ethnography" seems to be a term that is applied by scholars who do not know what else to call their work or, in my case (1998), by scholars whose study of new forms of ethnography broadens the umbrella of what can be considered "ethnography." Closely related, the quality of work in Internet studies from an ethnographer's or qualitative methodologist's perspective has varied widely; some scholars come to the field of inquiry having been trained in qualitative methods, while others have topic- or technology-specific expertise or interest but no familiarity or training in the diversity of qualitative approaches (Mann, 2002, 2003).

◙ Critical Junctures in Research Design and Process

The idea of studying the Internet or using Internet technologies to facilitate qualitative research is beguiling: A researcher's reach is potentially global, data collection is economical, and transcribing is no more difficult than cutting and pasting. But in the virtual field, as one interacts with anonymous participants, tracks disjointed, non-linear, multiple participant conversations, and analyzes hundreds of screens worth of cultural texts, one can begin to feel like the Internet might cause more headaches than it cures. Deceptive in its apparent simplicity, qualitative inquiry in this environment requires careful attention to the traditional means by which social life is interpreted and the adjustments that must be made to give value to the online experience and internal consistency to one's methods. The absence of visual information about the participant functions more paradoxically than one might realize. Socioeconomic markers such as body type, gender, race, and class are used consciously or unconsciously by researchers to make sense of participants in physical settings. Online, these frames are still used but without visual information, they function invisibly. This warrants close examination, both to consider how this happens and to explore how the researcher's default premises and unconscious choices can influence the shape of the participant and the reality of the outcome.

This complexity of knowing anything certain about the other is paradoxical, yet to acknowledge the uncertainty or even impossibility of knowing Other is to risk paralysis in the research process, loss of authority in the presentation of research, and diminishment of one's academic role as observer/interpreter/archivist of social life. How, then, does one proceed? "With caution" is a trite yet reasonable response which calls for sensitivity to the context, interrogation of one's own presumptions, and flexible adaptation to a new era in social research, one in which we recognize the limitations bred by our traditional five senses and take the risks necessary to reconsider how and why we seek and create knowledge. Proceeding thus is a political move. It does not retreat from understanding Other on the grounds that the researcher cannot know anything except his or her own experiences. It also does not rest on the laurels of traditional methods, trying to shore up ways of knowing that are crumbling before our eyes as digital and convergent media saturate cultural practices and forms. It faces the complexity and interrogates the way we analyze people for purposes of academic inquiry. If one examines deeply the way new communication technologies influence the research project, one is likely to stumble into issues which question the fundamental reasons for doing research in the first place. Allowing oneself to explore those issues can vitally contribute to the creation of reflexive and socially responsible research practice.

At several junctures during the research project, we have the opportunity and responsibility to reflexively interrogate our roles, methods, ethical stances, and interpretations. When studying computer-mediated environments, this need is intensified because the traditional frames of reference we use to guide our premises and procedures are entrenched in physical foundations and modernist ontologies. Questions one might address include:

- What can we say we know about the Other when self, other, and the context may be constructed solely through the exchange of messages?
- In social situations derived from discursive interaction, is it possible to simply observe? Is it desirable?
- How does the researcher's participation in the medium affect the identity of the participant and the shape of the culture?
- How can one balance the traditional scientific impulse to uncover the "real" while interacting with people who may or may not have any correspondence to their physical counterparts?
- In what ways do one's research traditions delimit and limit the possibilities for sensemaking in environments which are not overtly physical, visual, and aural?

Whether or not the researcher pays attention to them, the issues raised by these questions operate throughout any ethnographically based project. They identify logistic challenges but also display problematic working assumptions that must be addressed. Reflexive research practice requires a constant disruption of the seemingly placid surface of inquiry. Stopping to identify critical decision junctures and reflect on the consequences of specific actions constitutes an honest presence in the research process and active engagement in the ethical grounding of one's inquiry.[3]

Defining the boundaries of the field.

Determining what constitutes data.

Interpreting the other as text.

Using embodied sensibilities to interpret textuality.

Representing others ethically in research reports.

Each of these categories identifies a critical decision juncture within the research project. Neither exhaustive nor separate, these categories can be used as examples to help one think through some of the decisions made during the course of a study which have meaningful consequences for the identity of the participants, the representation of self and other in research reporting, and the shape of the body of scientific knowledge built on multiple ethnographically informed studies. The actual questions one might ask are particular to the researcher and the project, as variable as one's worldviews and methodological approaches.

Defining the Boundaries of the Field

Drawing boundaries around the research context, or "identifying the field" involves a series of decisions that both presuppose and reveal the researcher's underlying ontological and epistemological assumptions. Obviously, reflecting on our own biases is not just useful but ethically necessary, even if our academic training did not identify the necessity for such reflection. When studying physically based cultures, the location of the field is typically predetermined, so the logistical challenges lie in gaining access and building rapport with informants. For the Internet ethnographer, the process of locating and defining sensible boundaries of the field can be convoluted and elusive.

Because the Internet is geographically dispersed, the researcher has the option to disregard location and distance to communicate instantaneously and inexpensively with people. Logistically, the distance-collapsing capacity of the Internet allows the researcher to connect to participants around the globe. The researcher can include people previously unavailable for study. This not only increases the pool of participants but also provides the potential for cross-cultural comparisons that were not readily available previously for practical and financial reasons. In a world where potential participants are only a keyboard click and fibre optic or wireless connection away, distance become almost meaningless as a pragmatic consideration in research design; the Internet serves as an extension of the researcher's and participant's bodies. Research can be designed around questions of interaction and social behavior unbound from the restrictions of proximity or geography. Participants can be selected on the basis of their appropriate fit within the research questions rather than their physical location or convenience to the researcher.

From Geographic to Discursive Boundaries

As we shift from geographic to computer-mediated spaces, we are shifting focus from place to interaction, from location to locomotion (Markham, 2003a). Consequently, communities and culture are not neatly mapped before entering the field, but instead are created as part of the ethnographic process. Christine Hine (2000) argues that the ethnographer's notion of cultural boundary must be reconsidered given this capacity of the Internet. Rather than relying on traditional, geographically based means of encapsulating the culture under study, such as national boundaries or town limits, ethnographers might find more accuracy in using discourse patterns to find boundaries. "The ethnographer must read the texts and interactions of interest, much like trail signs, and make defensible decisions about which paths to follow, which paths to disregard, and thereby which boundaries to draw" (Markham, 2003b).

Seemingly mundane decisions become crucial criteria that are used, consciously or not, to create boundaries around the field of inquiry. Boundary markers are underwritten by the researcher's choice about how to find data sites, which search engine to use to sample, whom to interact with, what to say in interaction with participants, what language to speak, when to seek and conduct interviews (including both time of day and considering time zones), and so forth. Computer-mediated cultural contexts are shifting contexts. Their discursive construction occurs in global as well as local patterns. Membership can be transient. This becomes more meaningful when one realizes the boundary-forming work that is being accomplished when one contributes messages to a group, defines the boundaries of a cultural phenomenon through one's own surfing choices, and sifts or funnels the data set by using a particular search engine or set of databases. Each action taken by the researcher in this vast information sphere contributes directly to the construction of the structures that eventually get labeled "field" or "data."

Indeed, the global potential of this medium is often conflated with global reach, an achievement that relies on global access (Markham, 2004b). Arguably, people in industrialized countries tend to overestimate the degree to which the world has access to computers and electronic communication technologies. Access is not universal and those populations being studied via the Internet represent a very privileged and small portion of the world's population. In many ways, then, the boundaries may be flexible, seemingly arbitrary, and discursively constructed, but nonetheless remain within larger political and economic structures that are not universally experienced.

Participation in the Discursive Construction of the Field

As I have noted previously (Markham 1998), interacting with anyone formally or informally marks a significant shift from observer to participant, from archivist to accomplice. Online, as one participates in the context, one co-constructs the spaces under investigation. Interactions with participants are not simple events in these online spaces, they are organizing elements of these spaces.

By the very nature of their actions and interactions, researchers in any cultural environment are involved in the construction of what becomes the object of analysis. This is highlighted in technologically mediated environments because both the production and consumption of communication can be global, non-sequential, fragmented, disembodied, and decentered. In contexts where the boundaries of self, other, and social world are created and sustained solely through the exchange of information, being is therefore relational and dialectic. Social constructions are less connected to their physical properties. Boundaries are not so much determined by "location" as they are by "interaction."

The boundaries of the field become more a matter of choice than in physically located spaces. Researchers are more obviously participative. Addressing a seemingly simple question of "should I participate or observe" then, gives rise to an entirely more complicated set of issues that shape the research design and complicate our concepts of how media function socially. The deceptively easy act of choosing a particular community of websites creates an audience that previously did not exist and indicates to the larger academic community that this context is meaningful. Thus, choice of field becomes a politically charged process because of the inherent ethicality of one's decisions.

Ethnography that ignores these issues can remain at the edges of the cultural context and more importantly, can become mired in the now much critiqued notion that the researcher observes but does not interfere with or influence that which is studied. Moreover, the decisions that a researcher makes at this level directly influence the way the researcher later represents the context and the participants, which ultimately impacts our academic conversations of and knowledge about computer-mediated communication environments. These are issues laden with ethical responsibility, yet the questions themselves appear to be so straightforward they are often only addressed as simple logistics problems.

This discussion necessarily takes us forward to later stages of the research process. The effort or unconscious decision to absent oneself from the field will not remove the researcher from the process and product. Thinking ahead to the outcome of inquiry—the research report—one must acknowledge that the interpretation of culture will change depending on the form of the telling. Interpretative focus and the nature of the "findings" shift with the passage of time, the venue for publication, the credibility of the author or notoriety of the subject, and innumerable other factors. Frankly, whether or not the researcher participates or simply observes, the construction of the research report will present a particular reality of the object of analysis that is influenced by the identity and participation of the researcher. It may be more productive to acknowledge one's participative role early, so that every aspect of the research design can effectively incorporate the researcher's presence in the construction of the field under study. As Internet Studies evolves as an interdisciplinary field of inquiry, further research depth and credibility will be gained through realistic and contemporary conceptualizations of the ways in which the researcher, reader, and object of analysis intersect.

Determining What Constitutes Data

A researcher's representation of others is inextricably bound up with the way data are collected and distinguished as meaningful versus meaningless. Computer-mediated communication contexts complicate the researcher's decisions, not only because the contexts are constructed interactively, comprised of mostly disembodied participants, or because the researcher has little access to typical sensemaking devices used to identify and collect data. The researcher's decisions are further complicated because we are always and constantly struck with stimuli in any research environment, stimuli that must be filtered in and out in order to create sensible categories for interpretation. Interacting in text-only online environments diminishes the most prominent of our senses: vision. CMC separates more obviously the wholeness of a person's being into component parts; that which was previously made sense of as a whole is consequently made sense of at different points of time using different combinations of senses. This feature of technology promotes highly focused and divided attention on the content, the producer, the carrier, and the meaning of discursive activity in context. Even in more overtly visual research environments, where the researcher may have access to photos, webcams, websites, hyperlink behavior, and blogs, the issue is not resolved because traditional research training is designed for physically co-present environments.

Methodologically, one must reflect carefully on what collected information is considered as "data." Just as interaction constructs and reflects the shape of the phenomena being studied, interaction also delineates the being doing the research in the field. Obviously, we cannot pay attention to everything—our analytical lens is limited by what we are drawn to, what we are trained to attend to, and what we want to find. Borrowing from Goffman (1959), our understanding is determined as much by our own frames of reference as the frames supplied by the context. Our selection of data and rejection of non-data presents a critical juncture within which to interrogate the possible consequences of our choices on the representation of others through our research.

An example of online discourse from prior research (Markham, 1998) illustrates the implications of this point. Matthew, as with all the participants in my study, is a self-described "heavy user" of the Internet. The interview occurred in a MOO, an online environment which is designed to facilitate the enactment and appearance of particular forms of communication. By writing different commands or using particular punctuation, one can speak, exclaim, question, whisper, emote, or think, so that dialogue appears as a verbal statement (Annette says, "Hi." Annette exclaims, "Hi!" Annette asks "Hi?") a cartoon-like thought bubble . o O (Annette wonders if the reader sees that this is a thought bubble), a description of one's nonverbal behaviors or thoughts (Annette scratches her head thoughtfully), and so forth.

Initially archiving Matthew's interview, I included the entire log of the conversation. As I began the analysis process, I removed extraneous, repetitive, or system-specific commands in order to minimize distractions. The following sample is from this latter phase, where the commands are removed. From this log, I conducted the initial analysis of data:

Matthew: "Now madison, that's a nice town."

Markham: "okay here's some official stuff for you Matthew."

Markham: "I guarantee that I will not ever reveal your address/name/location."

Matthew: "Fine about the secrecy stuff."

Markham: "Matthew, I guarantee that I will delete any references that might give a reader clues about where you live, who you are, or where you work."

Markham: "do you mind that I archive this interview?"

Matthew: "Log away, Annette" . . .

Markham: "what do you do mostly when you're online? Where do you go?"

Matthew: "Mostly I'm doing one of two things. Firstly I do research. If I'm looking for academic research in software engineering, my specialty, a lot of it is on the Web . . ."

Matthew: "And a lot of tools to play with are there, too."

Matthew: "Also, I use it for news and information, the way I used to use the radio. (I'm an unrepentent . . ."

Matthew: "real-lifer). For instance, if I'm going to go run (or bike or do something else outside) . . . "

Matthew: "I check the weather on the Web when in years past I would turn on the radio. Ditto for news" . . .

Markham: "how would you compare your sense of self as a person online to your sense of self offline?"

Matthew: "More confident online, because I'm a better editor than writer/speaker. I do well when I can backspace."

Matthew: "But I'm the same me in both places. I guess I've been me too long to be anybody else without a lot more practice than I have time for."

Markham: "hmmm . . . How would you describe your self?"

Markham: "i mean, what's the 'me' you're talking about?"

Matthew: "Kind of androgenous. Plenty of women for friends. But I was never good at dating or any of the romantic/sexual stuff."

Matthew: "Also, somewhat intellectual."

Matthew: has a delayed blushing reaction to the androgeny comment.

Matthew: "And a fitness nut."

Markham: o O (I wonder why Matthew is blushing . . .)

Markham: "tell me about your most memorable online experience"

Matthew: "OK, it was a couple years ago and I was just getting on the Web and starting to realize all"

After conducting initial coding and analysis, I found that I was struggling with this interview. I returned to the original transcript and realized I had made an error in my delineation of "meaningful" from "nonessential" data. The following excerpt illustrates what I saw when I returned to the original interview (the pieces I had removed are underlined):

Matthew says, "Now madison, that's a nice town."

Matthew spills popcorncrumbs into his keyboard :-(

Markham says, "bummer, Matthew."

Matthew says, "If you see me going away for a while, you know I went to make more popcorn ;-)"

Markham says, "okay here's some official stuff for you Matthew."

Markham says, "I guarantee that I will not ever reveal your address/name/location."

Matthew says, "Fine about the secrecy stuff."

Markham says, "Matthew, I guarantee that I will delete any references that might give a reader clues about where you live, who you are, or where you work."

Markham asks, "do you mind that I archive this interview?"

Matthew salutes and says "Yes'm

Matthew says, "Log away, Annette"

Markham says, "okay. i have a tendency to ask questions too quickly."

Matthew doesn't answer because he's too busy opening a box of rice cakes. . . .

Markham asks, "what do you do mostly when you're online? Where do you go?"

Matthew says, "Mostly I'm doing one of two things. Firstly I do research. If I'm looking for academic research in software engineering, my specialty, a lot of it is on the Web . . . "

Matthew says, "And a lot of tools to play with are there, too."

Matthew says, "Also, I use it for news and information, the way I used to use the radio. (I'm an unrepentent . . . "

Matthew says, "real-lifer). For instance, if I'm going to go run (or bike or do something else outside) . . . "

Matthew says, "I check the weather on the Web when in years past I would turn on the radio. Ditto for news" . . .

Markham asks, "how would you compare your sense of self as a person online to your sense of self offline?"

Matthew says, "More confident online, because I'm a better editor than writer/speaker. I do well when I can backspace."

Matthew says, "But I'm the same me in both places. I guess I've been me too long to be anybody else without a lot more practice than I have time for."

Markham asks, "hmmm . . . How would you describe your self?"

Markham asks, "i mean, what's the 'me' you're talking about?"

Matthew says, "Kind of androgenous. Plenty of women for friends. But I was never good at dating or any of the romantic/sexual stuff."

Matthew says, "Also, somewhat intellectual."

Matthew says, has a delayed blushing reaction to the androgeny comment.

Matthew says, "And a fitness nut."

Markham . o O (I wonder why Matthew is blushing . . .)

Matthew does pushups.

Markham stares

Markham . o O (should I be doing something too?)

Matthew says, "You should be asking me questions (the interviewee becomes the interviewer)"

Markham sighs and refocuses

Markham says, "tell me about your most memorable online experience"

Matthew gets very jealous of people who have sleep.

Matthew enters state of deep thought.

Matthew goes to raid the nearby refrigerator while composing reply in head

Matthew says, "OK, it was a couple years ago and I was just getting on the Web and starting to realize all"

My interpretation shifted as I realized the extent to which Matthew made certain to include his embodied activities in the conversation. Regardless of the interpretation one elects to make about these underlined enactments (Matthew is hungry, bored, creative, using conventions learned in culture), the fact remains that the "data" are different from one transcript to the next.

One can elect to bracket or set aside the form and focus only on the content. This decision would be guided by the premise that the meaning of one's utterances is only understood in context and therefore the medium is less important than the content. On the other hand, to ignore the form in this interview could also be seen as a poor choice, given the well-founded premise that nonverbal behaviors function discursively in the presentation of self, negotiation of identity, and eventual symbolic construction of culture. In this case, my analysis would suffer without the inclusion of Matthew's delineation of his embodied activities. It also raises the question of what constitutes form and what constitutes content.

One's choice in this situation should be guided by the research questions or the overall goal of research, which in this case was to explore how people experience the Internet and how their identities are presented and negotiated. Yet, this edict is laden with ambiguity when put into practice. Multiple dilemmas present themselves: How much does text represent the reality of the person? Put more personally, how much would I want to be bound by what I wrote at any particular time? To what extent does or should the researcher include spelling or typing ability as meaningful information in the understanding of identity or culture? How much are my own preconceptions and stereotypes influencing how I elect to categorize data from non-data?

One might wonder whether or not I ever asked Matthew to participate in the decision about what constituted "data," as this would seem a relatively easy way to answer some of the questions asked above. What would Matthew categorize as meaningful data from unessential non-data? On the other hand, why and under what circumstances would I want Matthew to determine what ought to be analyzed and what ought to be ignored?

These questions are important in that they directly shape what is examined by the researcher. This is not an unfamiliar point, as it raises the importance of interrogating the researcher's role in writing culture (Clifford and Marcus, 1986). In this case (and any, I would suggest), while the analysis may indeed emerge from the data, *the researcher determines a priori what constitutes data in the first place*, making this decision point a crucial reflection point.

Interpreting the Other Through Their Text

As one addresses these issues and shifts from data collection to analysis, another critical juncture arises, sponsored by the following question: To what extent is the Other defined by his or her texts? When the participant, researcher and context are nothing but text and everything beyond mere language, our perceptual filters must be adjusted to accommodate complexities of human expression. Discursive practices are the heart of our enterprise as ethnographic researchers. When the discourse is limited to the exchange of texts, one might think that the methods of analysis are likewise limited to what is seen in the text, but this is not the case. Rather, an array of interpretive tools are used to make sense of these texts and it becomes a worthwhile task to reflect on some of the more hidden or unacknowledged analytical methods being used to interpret the Other.

The following two examples usefully illustrate the extent to which participants can be judged in multiple ways by the form of their texts. The samples of discourse in these examples represent well the writing tendencies of two participants: Sheol and DominOH!.

> <Sheol> I am intrested in talking to:) Could you be more spesific about what questions you will ask? Just let me know when you want to talk, and I will try to accomidate! :)

> <Sheol> I became a very popular (I know that sounds conseeded) figuar on the line I called home. I am ruled by the right side of my brain so I liked the diea of being that personality.

In this interview with Sheol, it was impossible to bracket the spelling, use of graphic accents, tag lines, and so forth. From the beginning, I had been determined to conduct systematic analyses that remained close to the text. I was using a blend of content-oriented analytical tools to code, thematize, and make sense of the interactions with participants. Reflecting on my inability to ignore the form in my analysis of content jarred me out of the false stability granted by method-specific procedures and caused me to identify some of the ways I was putting Sheol into categories without noticing what I was doing.

For example, very early on, I categorized Sheol as female because a gendered language style was very evident in tags, qualifiers, expressions of emotion, and heavy use of graphic accents (Sheol turned out to be male). Sheol was also: Young (spelling was phonetic, attention to language misuse was not at all evident); Perhaps not very intelligent (multiple spelling errors, unreadable messages, apparent lack of ability to be a real hacker); and, of course, Caucasian (default characteristic because of mainstream cultural assumptions about use of the Internet as well as the tendency to make the online other look more like the self). Additionally and solely based on my own frame of reference, Sheol was heterosexual, middle class, and American.

In a different study, a participant called DominOH! also used phonetic spelling, but in a different way:

<DominOH!> Sumtymz i am lost in my online identiteez . . . well, the aktuel problem? i feel more 'found' in my online selvvz . . . kicky, spun out, reeler than real. More atooned to the energee and more atooned to those i'm talking with . . .

<DominOH!> . . . so much fun 2 play . . . YOU, and EVERYONE else, kannot reely no mee. And y do you feeeeel that you need 2?! So, online I'm a nerdy college professor with a quirky sense of humor, or I'm a professhunal athlete with a career ending injuree, and sumtymz i'm handsum, or i'm beauteous . . . and if peepole wanna hang with mee, i'm alwaze up for play.

In my conversations with this persona, I found it easier to bracket the misspellings because they appeared obvious and deliberate. DominOH! seemed to revel in the ability to remain elusive during our various interactions. DominOH!'s discourse was marked with aggressive and challenging statements. I was cautious with this participant to not make assumptions about gender but found myself categorizing DominOH! as male, young, well-educated, and Caucasian.

As the researcher, I have numerous choices regarding the interpretation of these interviews. My choices will build cultural knowledge about Sheol and DominOH! as individuals and about how people interact in cyberspace. In interpretive inquiry, the integrity of one's interpretation is tied directly to reflexivity. Frequently, though, reflexivity happens *after* the analysis is in progress or the project is completed. I mentally attached a number of social labels to both these participants during the course of our conversations and long after, as I was interpreting the discourse. Some of the labels I did not recognize until others pointed them out. The importance is not in the accuracy of the labels, but in the type of evidence used to derive the category. Without reflection, I initially gave a negative attribution to Sheol's phonetic spelling (deficient abilities) while giving a positive attribution to DominOH!'s (cleverness). Without reflection, I categorized Sheol as female and DominOH! as male, based solely on their use of accommodating or aggressive language.

This example illustrates that one's interpretation is founded in the text but simultaneously not limited to the text. While systematic procedures of analysis are vital tools for the social scientist, they are not fail safe if followed to the letter. Procedures can actually blind one to the actual interpretive processes occurring. In Internet-based environments, the existence of the online persona being studied is often encapsulated by their pixels on a computer screen. The choices made to attend to, ignore, or edit these pixels has real consequences for the persons whose manifestations are being altered beyond and outside their control. if a subject types solely in lowercase and uses non-standard.grammatical.conventions the reeders correction of *errors* may inappropriately ignore and thus misrepresent a participant's deliberate presentation of self. ;-) if someone spells atroshiously or uniQueLY and the researcher corrects it in the research report for readAbility, alteration of a person's desired online identity may be the price of smooth reading (Markham, 2003a, 2003b).

On the other hand, Sheol may be working with a sticky keyboard, ignoring the errors in the interest of speed, or multi-tasking such that he is not devoted fully to our interaction. DominOH! may be more comfortable with phonetic spelling. Maybe she or he was aggressive in response to something I had said early on. Certainly, to make the interpretive task both easier and more grounded in the participant's experience, one could ask the participants to clarify their own writing tendencies. One could also gather additional demographic information. My point, however, is not to articulate how to make the interpretations more accurate or truthful, but to identify one of many moments in the research project when the researcher faces, consciously or not, certain decisions about what to include as part of the interpretive consideration, only some of which can be identified or controlled.

To make this task more difficult, the most ethically sensitive approach to analysis is complicated—and impeded—by academic conventions and training. Most social science approaches teach the researcher to distill the complexity of human experience into discrete variables that are easily measured. Interpretive methods seek to ease these restrictions but involve ways of knowing that continually strive to simplify rather than complexify human experience. To shift the gaze from the subject of research to the gaze itself is one step in the evolution of human sciences. To stop there, however, is to risk losing sight of the larger goals of inquiry. Rather than seeking to describe or reflect reality, researchers must consider the political act of promoting, activating, or engendering realities.

The Search for Authenticity[4]

Particularly notable in disembodied research environments, the researcher's body continues to be privileged as the site of experience, the best measure of authenticity, and the residence of knowledge. This is sensible, literally, because we make sense of our world through our eyes, ears, noses, mouths, and sense of touch. We abstract our embodied knowledge to convey it through logic, language, and print, but as Ackerman (1995) notes, our primary level of understanding remains firmly entwined with our senses. "There is no way in which to understand the world without first detecting it through the radar-net of our senses.... The senses ... tear reality apart into vibrant morsels and reassemble them into a meaningful pattern.... Reasoning we call it, as if it were a mental spice" (pp. xv-xvii).

The implications of this are significant in scientific research; in most traditions, the interpretive act is characterized as an analytical, logical, mental procedure. Separated from the body in theory, the embodied practice of interpretation lingers. Online, this underlying disjuncture is highlighted precisely because the body of the participant is *notably* absent.

Searching for the Body Behind the Text

The question often asked about participants in online contexts is "Who are they, really?" By this, one often means, who are they, as I can see, verify, and know them in a body? From students, reviewers, and publishers, I have heard the suggestion many times: "You should have interviewed the participants offline as well as online. Then, you would have a better idea of who they are." Shifting one's perspective slightly, one might ask questions that get at the underlying issues: How much do we rely on our bodies and the bodies of participants to establish presence and know other? Is this reliance warranted or desirable? Will our picture of other, in person, make our understanding of them more whole? More directly: Does the embodiment of a participant gauge their authenticity?

The answers depend not only on the question one is seeking to address but also on the researcher's underlying epistemological assumptions. If one is simply using the Internet as a tool to expand one's reach to participants and interviewing them online is merely a convenience, one should consider the extent to which people can and do express themselves well, truly, or fully in text. But if one is studying Internet contexts as cultural formations or social interaction in computer-mediated communication contexts, the inclusion of embodied ways of knowing may be unwarranted and even counterproductive.

In chat rooms, on mobile phones, through personal websites, and other media, identity is produced and consumed in a form abstracted from actual presence. Cultural understanding is literally constructed discursively and interactively. We know from both popular press and scholarly studies that many people seek interaction and community on the Internet because it provides the perceived means to escape the confines of embodied social markers to engage in what many refer to as a "meeting of the minds." Whether or not this is truly possible (and some have argued (e.g., Ess, 2003; Kolko, Nakamura, & Rodman, 2000) that it is not), a user's desire to present and be perceived as a confluence of texts without body might best be read by researchers as a request for us to acknowledge text as ample and sufficient evidence of being and to study it as such (Markham, 2003a, 2004a).

Yet social scientists persist in seeking the authentic by privileging the concept of the body. The desire to add validity to findings often results in research design that holds up the textual representation of the participants next to their physical personae. The goal is to see the extent to which the images match. Researchers deciding to interview participants both online and f2f (face to face) may claim that their efforts will add authenticity to their interpretation—by adding paralinguistic or nonverbal cues to the words people speak—and thereby add more credibility to their findings (Markham, 2003a).

For good biologically based reasons, researchers rely on and trust their traditional senses of sight, smell, touch, taste, and hearing to provide verification of concrete reality. We are conditioned to rely particularly on our visual sensibilities: "Seventy percent of the body's sense receptors cluster in the eyes, and it is mainly through seeing the world that we appraise and understand it" (Ackerman, 1995, p. 230). Ecologist and philosopher David Abram adds that perception is a reciprocity between the body and the entities that surround it. Considering Merleau-Ponty's idea that perception itself is embodied, Abram notes that "[Perception] is a sort of silent conversation that I carry on with things, a continuous dialogue that unfolds far below my verbal awareness" (1997, p. 52). Although "we conceptually mobilize or objectify the phenomenon . . . by mentally absenting ourselves from this relation" (Abram, 1997, p. 56), our understanding of the world is sensual. While it makes sense that researchers use embodied sensibilities, this is not mentioned much, if at all, in methods textbooks. It therefore becomes a critical juncture to address in a very conscious manner.

Removing the Researcher's Body

In essentially disembodied relationships and cultures, one must wonder if the intrusion of certain embodied sense-making faculties bleeds integrity from the project of knowing the other in context. Yet, as mentioned above, perception always involves embodiment, and this cannot be set aside in the context of studying life online. Hence, a paradox emerges that may not be overcome but should be considered, acknowledged, or accounted for in the research design or research report.

Irony follows, however, when one notes the marked absence of the researcher's own embodiment in many studies of text-based cultural contexts. Although a researcher may give his or her participants' bodied forms and make sense of their identities through his or her own body, this sensibility is rarely noted in the published paper. Considerable privilege is given to the researcher to make his or her own embodiment a choice or even a non-issue while simultaneously questioning the authenticity of the participants' choices regarding their own embodiment. Ethically as well as epistemologically, it is vital to reflect carefully on the extent to which the research design privileges the researcher at the expense of both understanding the other and operating with a keen awareness of the context (Markham, 2003a, p. 152).

The online persona may be much more fluid and changeable than we imagine as we catch them in particular moments or only a fraction of the virtual venues they populate. Anonymity in text-based environments gives one more choices and control in the presentation of self, whether or not the presentation is perceived as intended. Understanding the potential for flexible, ad hoc negotiation of identity in technologically mediated social spaces may foster another critical juncture at which the researcher can ask an intriguing set of questions about the representation of other: "As researchers and members of various communities and cultures, what do we use to construct a sense of who the Other really is?" "In what ways do our methods of comprehending life as interwoven with new communication technologies ignore, deny, or validate shifting constructions of identity and social world?"

Interpreting Within Socioeconomic Comfort Zones

It makes sense that researchers visualize their participants even in non-visual text-based media. Yet, it is not only the visual bias that must be critically analyzed by researchers, but also the imagination with which one visualizes the participant. Pioneers on the research frontier of online ethnography continually juxtapose embodiment with other modes of presentation and knowing. When we rely on our embodied sensibilities of knowing, we are not necessarily getting a better or more "accurate" picture of the subjects of our studies; we may be simply reflecting our own comfort zones of research. Critical reflection on the product of our gaze can reveal some of these comfort zones for introspection and interrogation. Researchers should be wary of the tendency to perceive the world in familiar, close-to-home categories. What do the participants look like in the mind's eye? How likely is the researcher to give the participant an ethnic category different from his or her own? What information is used to make judgments about the embodied person behind the screen?

Typing speed, spelling and grammar usage, choice of (nick)name; linear or fragmented progression of ideas: These all influence the way a participant is understood by the researcher. As the researcher visually appraises the discursive practices of the participants, the form wafts through the sense-making like an invisible but compelling scent on the breeze. Whether one notices that the text is idiosyncratic or not, either in its error or uniqueness or blandness or precision, the form influences meaning and helps give a bodied shape to the participant. Form composes new stereotypes that must be acknowledged and interrogated.

As researchers, we carry our own predilections concerning race, gender, and bodied appearance of virtual participants. For no obvious reasons, I identified the participant mentioned above, Sheol, as white, female, heterosexual, young, and average in body weight and height. After about two hours of the interview, Sheol mentioned "girlfriend," and I recognized that I had made an invisible (but obviously in operation) assumption that she was heterosexual. Forced to reconcile the contradiction between my a priori assumption and the use of the word "girlfriend," I began to look for clues of gender I must have missed earlier. I also began to wonder at my invisible use of sexuality and gender as categories.

I did not reflect on the fact that I was giving Sheol a body in my mind until this disjuncture occurred and I realized the body in my mind no longer fit the body being presented by the participant. To note, Sheol was simply chatting with me, not presenting a body in any deliberate fashion. I had given shape to the person. A few minutes later, when Sheol referred to himself as a male, I realized she was not a lesbian but that 'he' had a 'girlfriend.' I had made yet another blunder. The form of the message had led me to an initial assumption that Sheol was female. The name, if read at a very surface level, hinted that Sheol was female (here, "Sheol" is a double-pseudonym but the original name was similar in that if read quickly, part of the spelling could be mistaken as an obviously female name or marker, like "Susanerd" or "21She132"). I also knew from previous research that women tend to use more tag lines, offer more caveats, and augment their texts with more emoticons and punctuation.

Recent inquiry of race in cyberspace contends that users transform online others into images of themselves but that these images are limited by media representations of identity, so that most visualizations will conform to mass media images of beauty, race, gender, ethnicity, and size (Nakamura, 1995). What impact does this have for qualitative researchers conducting ethnographically informed research in anonymous or virtual environments?

In teaching computer-mediated courses, my assumptions turn my students white and nondescript. If they use an interesting name, I find myself trying to find a body that suits what I perceive the name implies about the appearance of their persona. When I reflect on my visual images, I realize that even though race is supposedly absent from the research lens, it becomes a category which defaults to "white" (Nakamura, 2003). My experience is not atypical. It illustrates how much we rely on and use our own parameters to categorize others into something we can comfortably address. Scholarly discussion of race and the Internet is growing, particularly concerning how the Internet has been created and perceived naïvely as a raceless space (Kendall, 1998; Kolko, Nakamura, & Rodman, 2000; Poster, 1998). These discussions will help researchers better reflect on the spaces studied as well as the assumptions made during the collection and interpretation phases of the project.

Again, traditional academic training complicates the issues of embodiment for researchers in that this training seeks to make the researcher invisible. Traditional academic training encourages the researcher to focus on the theory and method as the locus of control in the study. Good research design, in the scientific tradition, eliminates bias, allows the method to strictly guide the findings, and ignores non-scientific measures such as hunches. The researcher's senses should be removed from the analysis of data and researcher's voice should be removed from the final report. This training creates habits—even among strongly resistant researchers—to ignore or deny the impact of one's conscious or unconscious embodied sensibilities on the research outcome. It is difficult even in qualitative research to peel back one's own complicated layers of interpretation.

Considering Methods as Ethics

As mentioned early in this article, any method decision is an ethics decision. The political potential and consequences of our research should not be underestimated. Every choice we make about how to represent the self, participants, and the cultural context under study contributes to how these are understood, framed, and responded to by readers, future students, policy makers, and the like.

The process of studying culture is one of comprehension, encapsulation, and control. To say otherwise is to deny our impulses and roles as scholars and scientists. At a very basic level, we go there to learn something about Other and—when we think we have something figured out, to decide how to tell others what we think we know. To accomplish this goal, we must stop for a moment the flood of experience, extract a sample of it for inspection, and re-present it in academic terms with no small degree of abstraction. The researcher is afforded a tremendous degree of control in representing the realities of the people and contexts under study. This control need not be characterized in a completely negative fashion, as we could also consider the image of a Möbius strip, where seemingly opposing sides are eventually realized as part of the same path. Our capacity to represent cultural knowledge is a great responsibility, with many traps and difficulties. But it is also a gift, well earned through education, well honed through experience, and well intended through ethical reflexivity.

Editing Choices

Consider the way research reports present, frame, and embody the people being studied: A person's very being has the potential to be literally reconfigured when edited by the researcher and put into a context of a research account rather than left in the context of experience.

This dilemma does not apply only to the study of virtual environments, but any study of human behavior, of course. But computer-mediated environments seem to highlight this dilemma of research reporting because it's so clear that text can be the primary, if not sole means of producing and negotiating self, other, body, and culture. Common practices of editing are rarely questioned. What happens when we transform the participant's utterances from disjunctive sentence fragments to smooth paragraphs? How are we presenting the social reality of these spaces when we correct grammar, spelling, and punctuation? How might we be changing their identities when we transform the appearance of their fonts to meet the acceptable standards for various publishing venues? Study participants can appear to be as smooth as movie characters after the writer has cleaned up everyday talk. Of course, the writer must make the report readable, but this need must be balanced with what is possibly silenced in this process. Online, this project takes a somewhat different form than in physically based research contexts. Highly disjunctive online conversations get reproduced as tidy exchanges of messages. A conversation developing over the course of six months can appear as a single paragraph in the written report. Deliberate fragmentation of ideas can be spliced into linear logic. Key to the ethical representation of the participant is sensitivity to the context and the individual. Certain editing choices may not alter the meaning of the utterances, interaction, or identity of the textual being embodied through these utterances. Other editing choices can function to devalue, ignore, or silence a fundamental aspect of a persona (Markham, 2003a).

On the other side of the coin, when presenting dialogue with participants, how many writers present a version of reality wherein they themselves talk and think in a hyper-organized fashion? Researchers are not likely to do this deliberately. Rather, the habit is an ingrained part of our training; it goes along with other practices, such as using passive voice and third person in the traditional academic paper. In the search for understanding the discursive construction of reality in computer-mediated environments, overediting may be misleading and limiting. The reader may have difficulty reading non-linear, disjunctive, or seriously misspelled examples of dialogue, but just like the visual elements of a personal website, these features of discourse illustrate vividly how it is experienced.

Generally speaking, as soon as an interaction occurs, the study of it becomes an abstraction. This is a fact of research. Even so, simplification or dismissal of the challenge of representation is not warranted. The task is to design research which allows human subjects to retain their autonomy and identity—whether or not their uniqueness is intentional or unintentional.

In Whose Interests?

Shifting from ideas about re-presenting participants to ideas about advocacy, the political aspects of research become more visible. The question of advocacy can be asked in many ways: "Whose interests does the research serve?" "Why am I doing this research anyway?" "What groups need speaking for?" "How can my analysis help someone?" "How can my writing and publishing give voice to those who might remain otherwise silent?"

These are not simply political or ethical questions. These are methods questions that must be embedded in design, in that they impact directly the way information is collected and analyzed and how research findings are written and distributed. Yet questions such as these are not typically included in research methods textbooks as a part of the primary methodological discussion. If included at all, these questions are relegated to a separate unit or chapter entitled "Ethics" or separated from the main text, along with other special, non-typical considerations.

Even if one's research goals do not include serving as an advocate for participants, I suggest that not only will research design be more ethically grounded and reflexive but also the results will have more integrity if these questions are considered throughout the course of the study. They serve as important reminders that researchers often take more than they give, that the researcher's choices are always privileged, and that even when wanting to give voice to participants, the researcher can unintentionally end up as the hidden ventriloquist, speaking for, rather than with, others (Fine, Weis, Weseen, & Wong, 2000).

Ethics and Institutional Review Boards

Ethical guidelines for Internet research vary sharply across disciplines and countries, depending on the premises and assumptions used to develop the criteria from which actions are judged as ethical or not. In this section, I've chosen to outline the features of Internet interaction that give rise to ethical controversies and to sketch the major distinctions between the "utilitarian" (predominant in the United States) and the "deontological" or "communitarian" stances (predominant in certain parts of the EU, particularly Nordic countries). This discussion is intended to give researchers alternative ways of thinking about projects, so that decisions are made not just based on what is legally required but also on what constitutes the right course of action in particular research and social contexts.

For Internet researchers, ethical challenges and controversy arise in the following circumstances:

- Some users perceive publicly accessible discourse sites as private.

- Some users have a writing style that is readily identifiable in their online community, so that the researcher's use of a pseudonym does not guarantee anonymity.
- Online discussion sites can be highly transient. Researchers gaining access permission in June may not be studying the same population in July.
- Search engines are often capable of finding statements used in research reports, making anonymity in certain venues almost impossible to guarantee.
- Age is difficult if not impossible to verify in certain online environments.
- Vulnerable persons are difficult to identify in certain online environments.
- Informed consent of the actual participant (the persona corresponding to the driver's license) is difficult to attain in writing if the participant desires anonymity from the researcher.

Some of the above generate general ethical issues; others generate official red flags for institutional research boards, which govern research of human subjects at institutions of higher education.

Utilitarian and Communitarian Approaches

Are Institutional Review Boards (IRBs) in the United States more interested in protecting the institution than the human subject? Do the regulations really serve the interest of the human subject? Christians (2000) and Thomas (2003) argue that the system of regulation may be counterproductive, though it was designed to protect the participant, because these regulations are embedded in positivist, capitalist, and utilitarian social structures.

Officially, IRBs require researchers to preserve the autonomy of human subjects (respect for persons), distribute fairly both the benefits and burdens of research (justice), and secure the well-being of subjects by avoiding or minimizing harm (beneficence). Pragmatically, to adhere to the general IRB regulations, a researcher would ask: First, does the research protect the autonomy of the human subject? Second, do the potential benefits of study outweigh the risks posed to the human subject? Operationalized in the United States, if the potential benefit of the proposed research is "good" enough, the risk is acceptable, therefore making the second question a prioritized criterion.

Doing enough "good," according to Christians (2000), becomes a matter of determining what makes the majority of people happy. Combined with a strong tradition in positivism, which values neutrality and validity through scientifically verifiable measures, determinations of "happiness" are largely restricted to those domains that are extrinsic, observable, and measurable (p. 138-142). "In its conceptual structure, IRB policy is designed to produce the best ration of benefits to costs. IRBs ostensibly protect the subjects who fall under the protocols they approve. However, given the interlocking utilitarian functions of social science, the academy, and the state . . . , IRBs in reality protect their own institutions rather than subject populations in society at large" (see Vanderpool, 1996, chaps. 2-6). Thomas (2003) adds to this, noting: "Too often, [IRB] decisions seem driven not so much by protecting research subjects, but by following federally mandated bureaucratic procedures that will protect the institution from sanctions in the event of a federal audit" (p. 196). IRBs are designed to provide guidelines where they might otherwise be ignored; in that, the regulations are sensible. But when these guidelines are used as an exclusive means of defining the ethical boundaries of one's work, the spirit of the regulation has been replaced by unreflexive adherence to the letter of the law.

This stance gets turned upside down (or right side up, depending on how you look at it) when we examine the ethical sphere of other countries. Ess (2003) outlines a European perspective as one that is more deontological. Citizens enjoy a much greater protection of privacy regarding data collection and use. Research stresses the protection of individual rights, "first of all, the right to privacy—even at the cost of thereby losing what might be research that promises to benefit the larger whole" (Ess & AOIR working committee on ethics, 2002, p. 20).

If we take a look at the contrast between U.S. and European approaches to ethics in research, this recommendation takes shape as a viable and proactive stance. The Association of Internet Researchers has addressed the issue of ethics in Internet research in some depth (2002). They offer key questions which can help guide researchers in making ethically grounded decisions regarding the particularities of online environments outlined above. Some of these questions include:

- What ethical expectations are established by the venue?
- When should one ask for informed consent?
- What medium for informed consent (email, fax, Instant Messaging) would best protect the human subject?
- In studying groups with a high turnover rate, is obtaining permission from the moderator/facilitator/list owner, etc., sufficient?
- What are the initial ethical expectations/assumptions of the authors/subjects being studied? For example: Do participants in this environment assume/believe that their communication is private?
- Will the material be referred to by direct quotation or paraphrased?
- Will the material be attributed to a specified person? Referred to by his/her real name? Pseudonym? "Double-pseudonym?" (i.e., a pseudonym for a frequently used pseudonym?)

Chris Mann (2002), a British sociologist specializing in the study of ethics, distills the issues into a set of three very simple questions:

- Are we seeking to magnify the good?
- Are we acting in ways that do not harm others?
- Do we recognize the autonomy of others and acknowledge that they are of equal worth to ourselves and should be treated so?

These criteria shift the focus away from utility and regulation and place the emphasis squarely on the purpose of the research, a point made clearly by Denzin (1997, 2003) in discussing a feminist communitarian stance. An example illustrating the difference between these stances and possible outcomes is the U.S. researcher asking:

> "Am I working with human subjects or public documents?"

This question arises in a study wherein the scholar is using publicly accessed archives of online discourse. Many Internet scholars contend that publicly accessible online discourse does not require human subject approval because the domains in which these texts are produced are public (Walther, 2002). This determination is derived from arguments about the regulatory definitions of what constitutes human subjects research. Walther further notes that while participants might perceive that the space is private and therefore their texts are private, this perception is "extremely misplaced" (p. 3).

Posed to a colleague in Scandinavia, the question was not sensible (Bromseth, personal communication, February 19, 2004). She understood the question, but indicated that her colleagues would not frame the question in the same way. Among other things, Bromseth noted that the question focuses on the researcher's legalistic dilemma and not the participants in the study. The question polarizes the issue into an "either/or" false dichotomy to be solved by definition-based, legalistic clarification, rather than through the input of and interaction with the human subject(s).

To further clarify the distinction, note that the title of this current section of this chapter highlights ethics alongside their regulatory body for academics, the IRB. My choice in heading reflects a utilitarian stance. On the contrary, when describing the ethical issues facing Internet researchers, Bromseth (2003) never mentions a regulatory body at all, instead focusing on the respondent. She writes within the communitarian or deontological stance, "Researchers have been forced to rethink basic issues . . . to be able to develop and apply approaches that work for ourselves and our research goals and that would be ethically defensible in relation to our informants" (p. 68).

With deeply rooted standpoints and few universal principles, how should one treat texts and websites, which may or may not be vital to the subjectivity of the author; which may or may not be considered private by the author; which may or may not be important to our individual research goals? There are no simple conclusions to be drawn in the arena of ethical Internet research. Institutional research boards will continue to regulate the activities of scholars. National, regional, and cultural principles will undoubtedly remain distinct; ethical guidelines are entrenched in larger socio-political-economic structures of meaning. Internet researchers will continue to argue the issues of publicly accessible documents; anonymity; copyright; presentation of other; and privacy. Excellent overviews of opposing positions can be found in various journals, online reports, and conference/workshop proceedings.[5]

Given the variations in ethical stances as well as the diversity of methodological choices, each researcher must explore and define research within their own integral frameworks. Thomas (2003) recommends a more proactive approach to ethical behavior than simply adhering to rules set out by IRBs. "In this view, we recognize the potential ambiguity of social situations in which most value decisions are made and commit ourselves not to rules, but to broad principles of justice and beneficence" (p. 197). As to how one might determine what these broad principles actually are, Stephen L. Carter (1996) reminds us of what it means to have integrity. It involves not only discerning what is right and what is wrong, but also acting on this discernment, even at personal cost, and publicly acknowledging and defending one's stance and choices. Acting with integrity, Carter adds, "demands that we take the time for genuine reflection to be certain that the [morality] we are pressing is right" (p. 204).

▣ Rethinking the Purpose of Research

My ten years of experience as an Internet researcher lead me to believe that it is time to reassess our priorities and processes as researchers. Instead of asking "how we can protect human subjects through various types of research design?" we will frame better questions and find richer answers by shifting our focus toward the participant. Putting the human subject squarely in the center of the research both shifts the ethical considerations and allows for socially responsible research.

All ethnographically informed research, particularly in computer-mediated environments, includes decisions about how to draw boundaries around groups, what to leave in as meaningful data and what to dismiss as unimportant, and how to explain what we think we know to our audiences. These research design decisions, which are often dismissed as simple logistics and not often mentioned in methods texts or ethics discussions, influence the representation of research participants, highlight particular findings while dismissing others, create ideologically charged bases of knowledge and, ultimately, impact legislation and policy making. This chain of events requires astute, reflexive methodological attention. We make choices, either consciously or unconsciously, throughout the research process. Researchers must grapple with natural and necessary change engendered by vivid awareness of the constructed nature of science, knowledge, and culture.

One way to meet the future is to learn from but not rely on the past. Practically speaking, this involves a return to the fundamental question: Why are we doing research? Politically speaking, this involves taking risks that will productively stretch the academy's understanding of what inquiry intends to produce.

The Internet continues to provide a unique space for the construction of identity in that it offers anonymity in an exclusively discursive environment. The difficulty of observing and interviewing in these contexts is that our expectations remain rooted in embodied ways of collecting, analyzing and interpreting information. Simply put, our methods are still more suitable for research in physically proximal contexts. Moreover, although the technology of the internet has afforded us greater reach to participants and provided a space for researchers to interact with participants in creative ways, our epistemological frameworks have not yet shifted to match this reality. It is necessary not only to accommodate the features of computer-mediated communication into our basic assumptions, but also to interrogate and rework the underlying premises we use to make sense of the world.

Computer mediated communication highlights key paradoxes of social research in that personae being represented are already one step removed from their bodies when encountered by the researcher. Doing research of life online has compelled me to recognize that I have always taken for granted my ability to parse human experience by carefully paying attention to people's activities in context. Engaging in meaningful experiences with anonymous beings and interviewing people I cannot see face to face, I can identify many of the weaknesses of qualitative research processes in general. Interviewing or observing in natural settings, researchers rely on the ability to judge a face, looking for visual signs of authentic emotion and inauthentic pretense. We make immediate categorizing decisions based on first impressions, listening to the tenor of a voice on the phone or looking at body type, ethnic markers, hair style and color, and clothing brands. Even the most astute and cautious researchers unconsciously rely on habitual patterns of sense making in everyday interactions with others.

We must directly engage the fact that the questions driving the research must change to accommodate the enduring partiality of scientific knowing. Political action is a sensible shift, therefore, in that it does not seek to find the truth, but to create the possibilities for people to enjoy a better life.

In whatever ways we utilize the potential of Internet-mediated communication to facilitate our social inquiry, ethically sensitive approaches are complicated, even impeded, by our methodological training. Depending on the academic discipline we find ourselves working within, we will be encouraged in varying degrees to oversimplify the complexity of human experience, transforming the mysteries of interaction into discrete variables that are easily measured. This is done for admirable reason and by no means am I recommending a complete dismissal of traditional means of collecting and analyzing data. At the same time, Internet contexts prompt us to reconsider the foundations of our methods and compel us to assess the extent to which our methods are measuring what we think they are, or getting to the heart of what we have assumed they did. Through the Internet, we have the opportunity to observe how written discourse functions to construct meaning and how textual dialogue can form the basis of cultural understanding. The taken-for-granted methods we use to make sense of participants in our research projects need thorough reexamination in light of our growing comprehension of how intertextuality literally occurs.

Even within a contemporary framework of sociological inquiry—whereby the distinction between the researcher and researched is problematized, the researcher's role is acknowledged, and bias is accepted as a fundamental fact of interpretation—our obligation to the participant remains. We make decisions, conscious or unconscious, about what constitutes the virtual field and subject of study. Often dismissed as logistical, research design decisions, these choices make a great difference in what is studied, how it is studied, and eventually, how society defines and frames computer-mediated communication environments. Because Internet-based technologies for communication are still new and potentially changing the way people live their everyday professional and personal lives in a global society, it is essential to reflect carefully on the ethical frames influencing our studies and the political possibilities of our research.

■ NOTES

1. It is important to note that although this chapter focuses on computer-mediated communication, the capacities and consequences extend well beyond the desktop or laptop. For excellent discussions of the ways in which mobile telephones influence identity and cultural constructions, see Howard Rheingold (2002) or Katz and Aakhus (2002).

2. The trend is exaggerated here to illustrate the extremes. Speculative and exaggerated accounts are important to consider because they influenced research premises throughout the 1990s. This is not to say that empirical research was absent or unimportant. The impact of electronic technologies on individual communication practices and social structure has been explored for decades, most well represented by

scholars like Marshall McLuhan (1964), Harold Innis (1964), James Carey (1989), and Neil Postman (1986, 1993). Throughout the 1980s, significant empirical and theoretical research examined the impact of computers and information technology on the practices and structures of work. Sociological accounts (e.g., Turkle, 1984) studied important intersections of technology, self, and society. Crucial to the point is that many exciting but exaggerated texts appeared in the early 1990s, both in trade and academic presses, which fueled further speculative research and led to the publication of accounts that had more novel appeal than careful scholarship in an era of exciting new technological developments. As this field of inquiry evolves, it is vital to examine with a critical lens the foundations upon which current theoretical premises may be built.

3. A similar categorization of critical junctures was developed by the author for a keynote address at a Nordic conference on Ethics and Internet research and has been used subsequently in related publications (Markham, 2003a, 2003b).

4. The material in this section is being written concurrently for a chapter in an edited collection (Markham, 2003c).

5. *The Information Society*, for example, hosted a special issue in 1996 on the ethics of Internet research. The Association of Internet Researchers released a comprehensive report of various stances, comparative guidelines and an extensive list of resources (2002); a conference panel yielded a set of articles which lay out various perspectives in a special issue of *Ethics and Technology* (2002); the first Nordic conference and graduate seminar on ethics and Internet research yielded the edited volume *Applied ethics in Internet research*, containing keynote addresses and case studies by Scandinavian students (Thorseth, 2003); and an edited volume by Johns, Chen, and Hall, (2003) entitled *Online social research* offers various perspectives and cases. Many other sources discuss both general and specific issues related to internet research and ethics. All of these resources offer both novice and experienced researchers valuable philosophical, practical, and legal information.

References

Abram, D. (1997). *The spell of the sensuous*. New York: Vintage Books.

Ackerman, D. (1995). *A natural history of the senses*. New York: Vintage Books.

AOIR Ethics Working Committee. (2002). *Ethical decision-making and Internet research: Recommendations from the AOIR ethics working committee*. Retrieved January 2004 from www.aoir.org/reports/ethics.pdf

Association of Internet Researchers. (2002). Ethical decision making and Internet research. Retrieved January 15, 2004 from http://www.aoir.org/reports/ethics.pdf

Bakhtin, M. (1981). *The dialogic imagination: Four essays*. Edited by Michael Holquist. Trans. C. Emerson and M. Holquist. Austin: University of Texas Press.

Baym, N. (2000). *Tune in, log on: Soaps, fandom, and online community*. Thousand Oaks, CA: Sage.

Baym, N., Zhang, Y. B., & Lin, M. (October 2002). The internet in college social life. Paper presented at the annual conference of the Association of Internet Researchers.

Bell, D., & Kennedy, B. M. (Eds.). (2000). *The Cybercultures reader*. New York: Routledge.

Benedikt, M. (1991). *Cyberspace: First steps*. Cambridge, MA: MIT Press.

Blumer, H. (1969). *Symbolic interactionism*. Engelwood Cliffs, NJ: Prentice-Hall.

Bromseth, J. (2002). Public Places . . . Private Activities? In Morrison, A. (Ed.) *Researching ICTs in context* (pp. 44-72). Oslo: Intermedia Report 3/2002. Oslo: Unipub forlag. Retrieved December 1, 2002, from http://www.intermedia.uio.no/publikasjoner/rapport_3/

Bromseth, J. (2003). Ethical and methodological challenges in research on net-mediated communication. In Thorseth, M. (Ed.), *Applied ethics in internet research* (pp. 67-85). Trondheim, Norway: NTNU University Press.

Buber, M. (1958). *I and Thou*. 2nd ed. Translated by R. G. Smith. New York: Scribner.

Carey, J. (1989). *Communication as culture: Essays on media and society*. Boston: Unwin Hyman.

Carter, S. L. (1996). *Integrity*. New York: Harper Perennial.

Christians, C. (2000). Ethics and politics in qualitative research. In N. K. Denzin & Y. S. Lincoln (Eds.), *Handbook of qualitative research, 2nd Edition* (pp. 133-155). Thousand Oaks, CA: Sage.

Clifford, J., & Marcus, G. (1986). *Writing culture: The poetics and politics of ethnography*. Berkeley: University of California Press.

Denzin, N. K. (1997). *Interpretive ethnography: Ethnographic practices for the 21st century*. Thousand Oaks, CA: Sage.

Denzin, N. K. (2003). Prologue: Online environments and interpretive social research. In Johns, M., Chen, S. L., & Hall, J. (Eds.), *Online social research: Methods, issues, and ethics* (pp. 1-12). New York: Peter Lang.

Dery, M. (1994). *Flame wars: Discourses in cyberspace.* Chapel Hill, NC: Duke University Press.

Dibbell, J. (1996). A rape in Cyberspace; or how an evil clown, a Haitian trickster spirit, two wizards, and a cast of dozens turned a database into a society. In P. Ludlow (Ed.), *High noon on the electronic frontier: Conceptual issues in Cyberspace* (pp. 375-396). Cambridge, MA: The MIT Press.

Eichhorn, K. (2001). Sites unseen: Ethnographic research in a textual community. *International Journal of Qualitative Studies in Education, 14*(4), 565-578.

Ess, C. (2003). Beyond contemptus mundi and Cartesian dualism. In M. Thorseth (Ed.), *Applied ethics in internet research.* Trondheim, Norway: NTNU University Press.

Ethics and Information Technology, 4(3). (2002). Special issue on Internet research ethics.

Fine, M. (1994). Working the hyphens: Reinventing self and other in qualitative research. In N. K. Denzin & Y. S. Lincoln (Eds.), *Handbook of qualitative research* (pp. 70-82). Thousand Oaks, CA: Sage.

Fine, M. Weis, L., Weseen, S., & Wong, L. (2000). For whom? Qualitative research, representations, and social responsibilities. In N. K. Denzin & Y. S. Lincoln (Eds.), *Handbook of qualitative research, 2nd Edition* (pp. 107-131). Thousand Oaks, CA: Sage.

Gajjala, R. (July 2002). An interrupted postcolonial/feminist cyberethnography: Complicity and resistance in the "Cyberfield." *Feminist Media Studies, 2*(2), 177-193.

Gergen, K. (1991). *The saturated self. Dilemmas of identity in contemporary life.* New York: Basic Books.

Gibson, W. (1984). *Neuromancer.* New York: Ace Books.

Goffman, E. (1959). *The presentation of self in everyday life.* New York: Anchor Press.

Haraway, D. (1991). *Simians, cyborgs, and women: The reinvention of nature.* New York: Routledge.

Herring, S. (1993). Gender and democracy in computer-mediated communication. *Electronic Journal of Communication/La Revue Electronique de Communication,* 3(2), pp. 1-17.

Herring, C. S. (2004). Slouching toward the ordinary: Current trends in computer-mediated communication. *New Media and Society, 6*(1), 26-36.

Hine, C. (2000). *Virtual ethnography.* London: Sage.

Innis, H. (1964). *The bias of communication.* Toronto, Canada: University of Toronto Press.

Johns, M. D., Chen, S.L.S., & Hall, G. J. (Eds.). (2003). *Online social research: Methods, issues, and ethics.* New York: Peter Lang.

Johnson, C. (2003). *Social interaction and meaning construction among community websites.* Unpublished Master of Arts thesis. University of Illinois at Chicago.

Jones, S. G. (1995b). Understanding community in the information age. In S. G. Jones (Ed.), *Cybersociety: Computer-mediated communication and community* (pp. 10-35). Thousand Oaks, CA: Sage.

Jones, S. G. (Ed.). (1999). *Doing Internet research: Critical issues and methods for examining the net.* Thousand Oaks, CA: Sage.

Katz, J. & Aakhus, M. (Eds.). (2002). *Perpetual contact: Mobile communication, private talk, public performance.* Cambridge, UK: Cambridge University Press.

Keeps, C. J. (1993). Knocking on heaven's door: Leibbniz, Baudrillard and virtual reality. *Ejournal, 3,* Retrieved December, 1996 via anonymous ftp: EJOURNAL@albany.bitnet.

Keisler, S. (1997). *Culture of the Internet.* Mahwah, N.J.: Lawrence Earlbaum.

Kendall, L. (1998). Meaning and identity in "Cyberspace": The performance of gender, class and race online. *Symbolic Interaction, 21*(2), 129-153.

Kendall, L. (2002). *Hanging out in the virtual pub: Masculinities and relationships online.* Berkeley: University of California Press.

Kolko, B. E. (2000). Erasing @race: Going White in the (Inter)Face. In B. E. Kolko, L. Nakamura, & G. B. Rodman (Eds.) *Race in Cyberspace.* (pp. 117-131). New York: Routledge.

Kolko, B. E. (2002). Personal conversation. October. Maastricht, The Netherlands.

Kolko, B. E., Nakamura, L., & Rodman, G. B. (Eds.). (2000.) *Race in Cyberspace.* New York: Routledge.

Kramarae, C. (1995). A backstage critique of virtual reality. In S. G. Jones (Ed.). *Cybersociety: Computer-mediated communication and community,* (pp. 36-56). Thousand Oaks, CA: Sage.

Laing, R. D. (1969). *Self and others*. New York: Pantheon.

Lakoff, G., & Johnson, M. (1981). *Metaphors we live by*. Chicago: University of Chicago Press.

Ludlow, P. (1996). (Ed.). *High noon on the electronic frontier*. Cambridge, MA: MIT Press.

Lupton, D. (1995). The embodied computer/user. In M. Featherstone & R. Burrows (Eds.), *Cyberspace/Cyberbodies/Cyberpunk* (pp. 97-112). Thousand Oaks, CA: Sage.

MacKinnon, R. C. (1995). Searching for the Leviathan in usenet. In S. G. Jones (Ed.). *Cybersociety: Computer-mediated communication and community*, (pp. 112-137). Thousand Oaks, CA: Sage.

MacKinnon, R. C. (1998). The social construction of rape in Cyberspace. In F. Sudweeks, S. Rafaeli, & M. McLaughlin (Eds.), *Network and netplay: Virtual groups on the Internet*. Menlo Park, CA: AAAI Press. [cited from the online/ascii version. Retrieved March 1997 from the World Wide Web: http://www.actlab.utexas.edu/~spartan/texts/rape.html.

Mann, C., & Stewart, F. (2000). *Internet communication and qualitative research: A handbook for researching online*. London: Sage.

Mann, C. (June 1, 2002). *Generating data online: Ethical concerns and challenges for the C21 researcher*. Keynote address delivered at Making Common Ground: A Nordic conference on Internet research ethics. Trondheim, Norway.

Mann, C. (2003). Generating data online: Ethical concerns and challenges for the C21 researcher. In M. Thorseth (Ed.), *Applied ethics in internet research* (pp. 31-50). Trondheim, Norway: NTNU University Press.

Markham, A. (1998). *Life online: Researching real experience in virtual space*. Walnut Creek, CA: AltaMira.

Markham, A. (2003a). Representation in online ethnographies. In Johns, M., Chen, S. L., & Hall, J. (Eds.), *Online social research: Methods, issues, and ethics* (pp. 141-156). New York: Peter Lang.

Markham, A. (2003b). Critical junctures and ethical choices in internet ethnography. In Thorseth, M. (Ed.) *Applied ethics in internet research* (pp. 51-63). Trondheim, Norway: NTNU University Press.

Markham, A. (2004a). The internet as research context. In Seale, C., Gubrium, J., Giampietro, G., & Silverman, D. (Eds.). *Qualitative research practice*. London: Sage.

Markham, A. (2004b). Internet as a tool for qualitative research. In Silverman, D. (Ed.). *Qualitative research: Theory, method, and practice* (pp. 95-123). London: Sage.

McLuhan, M. (1964). *Understanding media: The extensions of man*. New York: New American Library.

Miller, D., & Slater, D. (2000). *The Internet: An ethnographic approach*. New York: New York University Press.

Nakamura, L. (1995). Race in/for Cyberspace: Identity tourism and racial passing on the Internet. *Works and Days*, *13*(1-2), 181-193.

Nakamura, L. (2003). Untitled conference presentation at National Communication Association annual meetings. November 19, Miami, Florida.

Orgad, S. (2002, October 14). *Continuities between the offline and the online*. Paper presented at the conference of the Association of Internet Researchers, Maastricht, The Netherlands, October 13-16.

Poster, M. (1998). Virtual ethnicity: Tribal identity in an age of global communications. In S. G. Jones (Ed.), *Cybersociety 2.0* (pp.184-211). Thousand Oaks, CA: Sage.

Postman, N. (1986). *Amusing ourselves to death: Public discourse in the age of show business*. New York: Viking Press.

Postman, N. (1993). *Technopoly: The surrender of culture to technology*. New York: Vintage Books.

Reid, E. (1995). Virtual worlds: Culture and imagination. In S. G. Jones (Ed.). *Cybersociety: Computer-mediated communication and community*, (pp. 164-183). Thousand Oaks, CA: Sage.

Rheingold, H. (1991). *Virtual Reality*. New York: Touchstone.

Rheingold, H. (1993). *The virtual community: Homesteading on the electronic frontier*. Reading, Mass: Addison-Wesley.

Rheingold, H. (2002). *Smart mobs: The next social revolution*. New York: Basic Books.

Rommetveit, R. (1980). On "meanings" of acts and what is meant and made known by what is said in a pluralistic social world. In M. Brenner (Ed.), *The structure of action* (pp. 108-149). Oxford: Basil Blackwell.

Ryen, A. (June 1, 2002). Paper presented at Making Common Ground: A Nordic conference on Internet research ethics. Trondheim, Norway.

Senft, T., & Horn, S. (1996). Special issue: Sexuality and Cyberspace: Performing the Digital Body. *Women & Performance: A Journal of Feminist Theory*, *17*.

Shane, M. J. (2001). Virtual work teams: An ethnographic analysis. Unpublished dissertation, Fielding Institute, California.

Sondheim, A. (Ed.). (1996). *Being online: Net subjectivity.* New York: Lusitania Press.

Sproull, L., & Kiesler, S. (1991). *Connections: New ways of working in the networked environment.* Cambridge, MA: MIT Press.

Stone, R. A. (1996). *The war of desire and technology at the close of the mechanical age.* Cambridge, MA: MIT Press.

Sveningsson, M. (2001). *Creating a sense of community: Experiences from a Swedish web chat.* Doctoral dissertation. The TEMA Institute, Department of Communication Studies, Linköping, Sweden.

Thomas, J. (2003). Reexamining the ethics of internet research: Facing the challenge of overzealous oversight. In Johns, M., Chen, S. L., & Hall, G. J. (Eds.), *Online social research: Methods, issues, and ethics* (pp. 187-201). New York: Peter Lang.

Thorseth, M. (Ed.) (2003). *Applied ethics in Internet research.* Trondheim, Norway: NTNU University Press.

Turkle, S. (1995). *Life on the screen: identity in the age of the Internet.* New York: Simon & Schuster.

Turkle, S. (1984). *Second Self: Computers and the human spirit.* New York: Simon & Schuster.

Vanderpool, H. Y. (Ed.). (1996). *The ethics of research involving human subjects: Facing the 21st century.* Frederick, MD: University Publishing Group.

Walther, J. (2002). Research ethics in Internet-enabled research: Human subjects issues and methodological myopia. *Ethics and Information Technology, 4*(3), Retrieved March 15, 2004 from http://www.nyu.edu/projects/nissenbaum/ethics_walther.html.

Waskul, D., Douglass, M., & Edgley, C. (2000). Cybersex: Outercourse and the enselfment of the body. *Symbolic Interaction, 25 (4),* 375-397.

Witmer, D. F., & Katzman, S. L. (1998). Smile when you say that: Graphic accents as gender markers in computer-mediated communication. In S. Rafaeli, F. Sudweeks, & M. L. McLaughlin (Eds.), *Network and netplay: Virtual groups on the Internet.* Boston: AAAI/MIT Press.

Woolley, B. (1992). *Virtual worlds: A journey in hype and hyperreality.* Oxford: Blackwell, Press.

Wright, R. (1994). "Life on the Internet: Democracy's salvation or cultural fragmentation?" *Utne Reader,* Jan/Feb: 101-107.

32

ANALYTIC PERSPECTIVES

Paul Atkinson and Sara Delamont

In this chapter, we examine a number of related themes under the aegis of analysis. The analysis of data derived from qualitative research strategies is a potentially vast field. It is not our intention to generate a comprehensive review of the history of analysis (Lincoln & Denzin, 2003) or of all its current manifestations (Hardy & Bryman, 2004). There are entire books that go some way in that direction, and virtually no textbook or handbook achieves complete coverage. Rather, through a selective review, we highlight what we think are some key issues confronting the research community. We do not, therefore, offer a prescriptive view on how data should be analyzed. Textbooks on methods themselves are the appropriate place for such practical guidance (e.g., Coffey & Atkinson, 1996; Silverman, 1997, 2004). Rather, we survey the methodological terrain selectively as we perceive it.

The extraordinary diffusion of qualitative research among the social and cultural disciplines is a welcome development, and it is one to which we have made modest contributions (Atkinson, Coffey, & Delamont, 2003; Delamont, 2002; Hammersley & Atkinson, 1995). We are personally and professionally committed to disseminating further qualitative research methods and the published work that derives from them. On the other hand, the very proliferation of qualitative research brings in its train some potential problems. The conduct of qualitative work has become fragmented. During an era of hyperspecialization in the academy and beyond, qualitative research has been subject to the same forces. The range of specialties and emphases can be gauged by inspecting, by way of example, the contents of recent and current edited collections (Denzin & Lincoln, 1994, 2001; Gubrium & Holstein, 2002b; Seale, Silverman, Gubrium, & Gobo, 2004; Silverman, 2004). As qualitative research has become increasingly professionalized and increasingly subject to explicit codification and reflection, it seems to have become increasingly fragmented.

In the section that follows, we review that process of fragmentation, identify some of its contours and consequences, and suggest some more positive ways of thinking about the proper relations between different methods. In particular, we affirm the rather unfashionable position that there are kinds of social activity and representation that have their indigenous modes of organization. Language and discourse, narratives, visual styles, and semiotic and cultural codes are culturally relative and arbitrary, but they nevertheless display orderliness that is relatively stable and predictable, observable, and describable. Although strongly determinist forms of structuralism or semiotics might not prove to be tenable, that is no excuse for abandoning altogether disciplined attention to such intrinsic ordering principles. Qualitative research needs to remain faithful to that indigenous organization.

We then turn our attention to a different but related issue, that is, the fragmentation of justifications for qualitative analysis and the interpretation of the social world. We contrast a centripetal tendency, a tradition that has tended toward a convergence or consensus within the field (especially in sociology), with a centrifugal tendency that has celebrated and promoted diversity among analytic strategies. The former represents a canonical tradition within the intellectual field, whereas the latter represents a more radical and sometimes transgressive mode. Recent accounts of the history of qualitative research and its practices, with which our own views diverge, tend to locate these differences within a developmental framework, tracing an intellectual history for qualitative research away from a positivist stance toward carnivalesque postmodern diversity (e.g., Lincoln & Denzin, 1994, 2001). Although we recognize that such accounts are partially correct in describing some changes in the most visible thinking, we differ in how best to capture the underlying differences (Atkinson, Coffey, & Delamont, 1999, 2001, 2003). We recapitulate and explore some of these issues briefly. Our perspective is not, however, based on a rearguard appeal to earlier versions of ethnographic or qualitative research and a return to the earlier certainties associated with the "classics" of methodological literature (cf. Atkinson et al., 2003). Our critical stance is, therefore, very different from that articulated by commentators such as Brewer (2002), who seemed to assert a rather vulgar form of realist analysis in distancing himself from postmodernist analytic strategies. Our critical stance also differs from those that embrace and endorse the claims of postmodernism.

We go on to discuss another major axis of contestation within the qualitative tradition and its current manifestations. We suggest that there is a major line of cleavage that separates disciplines or subdisciplines and individual researchers from one another, although it is not always apparent to the main protagonists in the field. We suggest that this reflects differing emphases on experience and action. During recent years, a good deal of qualitative research has been justified, analyzed, and represented in terms of social actors' experiences of their own social worlds, that is, of changes over the life courses of biographical phenomena and disruptions such as mental and physical ill health (Ellis & Flaherty, 1992). In a parallel way, qualitative research has sometimes been transmuted from the biographical to the autobiographical and autoethnographic (Bochner & Ellis, 2001; Ellis, 2004; Reed-Danahay, 1997, 2001). We do not think, however, that this is derived from a self-evident reason for conducting qualitative research. The purpose of such research is not always to understand the world from the actor's or informant's own perspective or to gain access to his or her personal private realms of experience and feeling (Behar, 1996; Fernandez & Huber, 2001; Radstone, 2000). A great deal of the foundational work in ethnography and other qualitative research was concerned with the analysis of collective social action, that is, how members of society accomplish joint activity through language and other practical activities as well as how they align their activities through shared cultural resources. From this latter perspective, even motives, emotions, intentions, and the like are matters of collective action, expressed through the codes of shared idioms. These distinctions need to be made visible so that the analysis of ethnographic and other data does not become confused (Atkinson et al., 2003; Gubrium & Holstein, 2002a, 2002b).

We then consider another related but distinct issue, that is, the aestheticization of analysis and representation. As some analysts and commentators have moved toward various postmodernist positions, they have sought to free qualitative analysis from the conventions of academic textual writing (Ellis & Bochner, 1996; Goodall, 2000). We thoroughly endorse the principle of critical reflection on the conventions through which social worlds and social actions are reconstructed.

Just as we recommend paying attention to the conventional orders of culture and action, we also recommend paying attention to the conventions of textual production and reception. But we warn against the wholesale acceptance of aesthetic criteria in the reconstruction of social life. In many contexts, there is a danger of collapsing the various forms of social action into one aesthetic mode—that is, implicitly revalorizing the authorial voice of the social scientist—and of transforming socially shared and culturally shaped phenomena into the subject matter of an undifferentiated but esoteric literary genre. (For examples of work that we believe exemplify this trend, see Clough, 1998; Richardson, 1997, 2002.)

Finally, we consider the implications of our remarks for social critique. We suggest that an engaged social science should indeed remain faithful to the intrinsic order of social life. We need—more than ever before—principled, systematic, and disciplined ways of accounting *for* the social world and *to* the social world. We need to be able to produce accounts of the social that can recognize the conventions of: media representations, of fashion and consumer culture, of political and everyday discourse, of scientific knowledge, of cinematic and other visual codings. Accounts that reduce the social world to a domain of experience cannot generate faithful, let alone critical, analyses of culture and action.

▣ Analytic Fragmentation

We have no quarrel with attempts to define and practice appropriate strategies for the analysis of particular kinds of data. Indeed, we want to insist on the proper disciplined approach to any and every type of data. In addition, we want data to be analyzed and not just reproduced and celebrated (as sometimes happens with life histories and visual materials). Our main message, however, is that the forms of data and analysis reflect the forms of culture and social action. For instance, we collect and analyze personal narratives and life histories because they are a collection of types or forms—spoken and written—through which various kinds of social activity are accomplished. They are themselves forms of social action in which identities, biographies, and various other kinds of work get done (Ochs & Capps, 2002; O'Dell, 2001; Patterson, 2002). Thus, we accord importance to narratives and narrative analysis because they address important kinds of social action (Atkinson, 1997; Bauman, 1986; Riessman, 2002). In the same spirit, we should pay serious attention to visual data insofar as culture and action have significant visual aspects that cannot be expressed and analyzed except by reference to visual materials. This is by no means equivalent to the assumption that ethnographic film or video constitutes an especially privileged approach to sociological or anthropological understanding (Ball & Smith, 2001; Banks & Morphy, 1997; Pink, 2001, 2004). The same can be said of other analytic approaches. Documentary analysis is significant insofar as a given social setting is self-documenting and important social actions are performed in that setting (Prior, 2003; Scott, 1990). Texts deserve attention because of their socially organized and conventional properties and because of the uses they are put to in their production, circulation, and consumption. The same is true of other material goods, artifacts, technologies, and so forth (Tilley, 1991, 1999, 2001). The analysis of dramaturgy, likewise, is important insofar as social actors and collectivities engage in significant performative activities (Denzin, 2003; Dyck & Archetti 2003; Gray & Sinding, 2002; Hughes-Freeland, 1998; Tulloch, 1999). But it should not be treated as a privileged way in which to approach all of social life.

We believe, therefore, that it is important to avoid reductionist views that treat one type of data or one approach to analysis as being the prime source of social and cultural interpretation. We should not, in other words, seek to render social life in terms of just one analytic strategy or just one cultural form. The forms of analysis should reflect the forms of social life, their diversity should mirror the diversity of cultural forms, and their significance should be in accordance with their social and cultural functions.

We identify these different analytic approaches not merely to celebrate diversity, that is, not to propose a vulgar version of "triangulation" through methodological pluralism and synthesis (Denzin, 1970; Janesick, 1994). Quite the reverse—we want to assert the importance of rendering the different facets of culture and social action and of reflecting their respective forms. We want, therefore, to affirm that aspects of culture and the mundane organization of social life have their intrinsic formal properties and that the analysis of social life should respect and explore those forms. In so doing, we react against some analytic tendencies that have undervalued anything that smacks of formal analysis. Such formalism seems to fly in the face of the most fashionable appeals to postmodernism. Yet discourse, narratives, performances, encounters, rhetoric, and poetics all have their intrinsic indigenous modes of organization. So too do visual, textual, material, and other cultural embodiments. It is not necessary to endorse a narrowly structuralist analytic perspective or endorse unduly restrictive analyses to recognize the formal properties of talk, the codes of cultural representation, the semiotic structures of visual materials, or the common properties of narratives and documents of life.

It is necessary, therefore, for ethnographers and other analysts of social life to pay attention to the analytic imperatives of such socially shared codes, conventions, and structures. The forms of social and cultural life call for equivalent analyses. These methodological principles give us a way of addressing some fundamental methodological precepts in a disciplined way. Herbert Blumer enunciated the principle that research should be "faithful" to the phenomena under investigation (Blumer, 1954; Hammersley, 1989). In its most general form, this methodological precept seems to beg all the important questions, seeming to imply that one can know the phenomena prior to their investigation. A naïvely naturalist interpretation is clearly inappropriate. Our formulation retrieves for Blumer's principle a more methodologically precise formulation—a more restricted but more fruitful approach. It implies that fidelity to the phenomena means paying attention to the forms and media through which social actions, events, and representations are enacted, encoded, or embodied. It also gives a particular rendering of the notion of "thick description" (Denzin, 1994; Geertz, 1973, 1983). Our approach can be extended to a commentary on versions of "grounded theory" and cognate strategies such as "analytic induction" (Atkinson et al., 2003; Znaniecki, 1934). Again, there are multiple versions of grounded theory, and they have been thoroughly documented (Charmaz & Mitchell, 2001; Glaser, 1978, 1992; Glaser & Strauss, 1967; Strauss & Corbin, 1998). We do not, incidentally, advocate that all ethnographies should deploy every conceivable analytic procedure and examine every possible data type in the interests of a spurious kind of comprehensiveness or "holism." On the other hand, our insistence on attention to the forms of culture and social action gives particular force to notions such as holism. In our version of research methodology, this can refer not to the doomed attempt to document "everything" but rather to a principled respect for the multiplicity of cultural forms. Thus, holistic analysis would refer to *preserving* those forms that are indigenous to the culture in question rather than collapsing them into an undifferentiated plenum.

In the following sections, we elaborate on these general remarks. Before doing so, we outline a number of key analytic areas that demonstrate the force of our general argument. These are among the analytic strategies that can and should contribute to the systematic analysis of social settings, action, and organization.

Analytic Strategies

Narratives and Life Histories

We should not collect and document personal narratives because we believe them to have a privileged or special quality (Atkinson, 1997; Atkinson & Silverman, 1997; Conle, 2003; Cortazzi, 1993, 2001). Narrative is not a unique mode of organizing or reporting experience. In addition, narrative is an important genre of spoken action and representation in everyday life and in many specialized contexts (Czarniawska, 1997, 1998; Riessman, 1993, 2002). We should, therefore, be studying narrative insofar as it is a particular feature of a given cultural milieu (e.g., Caplan, 1997; Cortazzi, 1991; Gardner, 2002; Lara, 1998; Myerhoff, 1978; Voysey, 1975). Furthermore, narratives are not independent of cultural conventions and shared formats (Holstein, 2000). They are not uniquely biographical or autobiographical materials, and they certainly do not convey unmediated private "experience." Likewise, they do not convey "memory" as a psychological phenomenon. Experiences, memories, emotions, and other apparently personal or private states are constructed and enacted through culturally shared narrative types, formats, and genres (Humphrey, Miller, & Zdravomyslova, 2003; Olney, 1998; Plummer, 1995, 2000, 2001; Tota, 2001; Wagner-Pacifici, 1996). They are related to story types more generally (Fine, 2001). There are affinities with other kinds of stories—of history, mythology, the mass media, and so forth. We need, therefore, to *analyze* narratives and life materials so as to treat them as instances of social action, that is, as speech acts or events with common properties, recurrent structures, cultural conventions, and recognizable genres. Therefore, we treat them as social phenomena like any others. Indeed, we need to treat narratives as performative acts (May, 2001) and treat them as forms of social action like any others.

Visual Data

The collection and analysis of visual materials tends, unfortunately, to be treated as the preserve of a specialist domain. The production of ethnographic film has a long history, although it has often been oddly divorced from the mainstream textual practices of the ethnographic monograph (Ball & Smith, 1992, 2001; Banks & Morphy, 1997). The use of photography for ethnographic purposes has also been relegated to a somewhat specialist subfield when it has not been relegated to mere illustration of the written monograph (Loizos, 1993). During recent years, the development of small digital camcorders and the development of digital photography have created an enormous range of possibilities for ethnographers in the field. Consequently, visual anthropology and sociology should not be treated as separate genres or specialties. There are many aspects of culture that are intrinsically visual. Many cultural domains and artifacts can be grasped only through their visual representations and the structured properties of their visual codes (Ball & Smith, 2001).

There are many social phenomena that can and should be analyzed in terms of their appearances and performances that may be captured in visual terms. These are not, however, separable from the social settings in which such phenomena are generated and interpreted. They should not be explored purely as "visual" topics; rather, they should be explored as integral to a wide variety of ethnographic projects. Visual phenomena—the mundane as well as the self-consciously aesthetic—have their intrinsic modes of organization (Crouch & Lübbren, 2003). One does not need to endorse the most determinist versions of semiotics or structuralism to recognize that visual culture embodies conventions and codes of representation. There are culturally determined aesthetic and formal principles, and there are conventional forms of representation and expression.

Attention to visual culture also implies serious attention to the ethnoaesthetics of the producers, mediators, and consumers of visual materials. We need to not only "read" the visual but also understand ethnographically how it is read by members of the social world or culture in question (Grimshaw, 2001). In general terms, there has been insufficient attention to the aesthetic codes and judgments deployed by members of a given culture (Attfield, 2000). We know about specialized domains of aesthetic work such as the visual arts. We also know something about the aesthetics of everyday taste in clothes and fashion (Valis, 2003). In addition, there is research relating to the decoration and consumption of domestic spaces and objects (Henderson, 1998; Julier, 2000; Miller, 1987; Painter, 2002). In other contexts, there are studies of the visual cultures of advertising and other media of representation (Frosh, 2003).

However, there are still many cultural domains in which local aesthetic criteria are important, but their analysis remains poorly integrated within the general ethnographic tradition; for instance, see DeNora (2000, 2003) on music in everyday life as a topic for ethnographic investigation (cf. Bennett & Dawe, 2001; Whiteley, Bennett, & Hawkins, 2004).

Discourse and Spoken Action

The collection and analysis of spoken materials is one domain where overspecialization is a danger. The development of discourse analysis and conversation analysis has been one of the most egregiously successful domains of qualitative research. Its disciplinary bases have been varied, including linguistics, sociology, and psychology. The emergence of conversation analysis from the work of Harvey Sacks and other ethnomethodologists has been a remarkable contribution to the disciplined empirical study of social order and social action (Atkinson & Heritage, 1984; Moerman, 1988; Sacks, 1992). In the past, there has been a distinct tendency for these approaches to spoken language to become narrowly restricted specialties. Conversation analysis has, in particular, been unduly bounded and self-referential in some cases. There is no need to restrict our analysis of social worlds exclusively to those phenomena that are susceptible to recording for conversation—or discourse—analysis. We need, in contrast, to ensure that the analysis of spoken language remains firmly embedded in studies of organizational context, processes of socialization, routines of work, personal transformation, people processing, and so forth. During recent years, fortunately, the analysis of spoken discourse has engaged more explicitly and systematically with more generic issues of sociological research (e.g., Atkinson, 1995; Sarangi & Roberts, 1999; Silverman, 1987). Spoken language has its own intrinsic forms of organization. Indeed, it demonstrates a densely structured organization at every level, including the most finely grained. It is important, however, that discourse analysis, conversation analysis, discursive psychology, and the like not be treated as analytic ends in their own right and not be intellectually divorced from other aspects of ethnographic inquiry. The expert knowledge required should not be regarded as a specialty in its own right and independent of wider sociological or anthropological competence. The conventions of language use need to be analyzed, therefore, in relation to more general issues of identity, the interaction order, moral work, and the organization of social encounters. In addition, it is important for analysts of spoken action to remain sensitive to wider issues of social analysis and critique and for practitioners of more general qualitative analysis to engage with and use the methods and findings of discourse and conversation analysis. Key discussions that identify the relationships between discourse/conversation analysis and central issues of social research include the accounts by Potter (1996, 2003), Hepburn and Potter (2004), and Potter and Wetherell (1987).

Material Assemblages and Technologies

The study of material goods and artifacts, technology, and other physical aspects of material culture deserves systematic attention in many ethnographic contexts (Tilley, 1991, 1999), but is too often relegated to specialized esoteric studies or to highly specific topics. The latter include studies of technology and inventions, of very particular kinds of physical display such as museums and art galleries, and of highly restricted kinds of artifacts such as religious, ritual, and artistic objects. But the detailed investigation of objects, assemblages, and inventions demands a place in the general ethnographic study of social and cultural forms (Appadurai, 1986; Bijker, 1995; Macdonald, 2002; Macdonald & Fyfe, 1996; Pinch & Trocco, 2002; Rabinow, 1996; Sandburg, 2003; Saunders, 2003).

It is vital that the study of physical objects, memorials, and technologies be thoroughly incorporated into more general field studies of work organizations, informal settings, cultural production, domestic settings, and so forth (Tilley, 2001). Artifacts and technologies are themselves understood, used, and interpreted by everyday social actors. They are used to document and record the past—and indeed to construct the past—and there is much to be learned from the local situated "ethnoarchaeology" of the material past (Dicks, 2000; Edwards, 2001; Gosden & Knowles, 2001). This includes the "monumental past" of places and their ethnohistories (cf. Herzfeld, 1991; Sciama, 2003; Yalouri, 2001). Issues of practical utility and aesthetic value intersect. Ideas of authenticity may be brought to bear on artifacts and assemblages (Forty & Kuchler, 1999; Handler & Gable, 1997). They may be used to display and warrant individual and collective identities; for instance, the "collection" (whether personal or national) is expressive of taste, identity, commitment, and enthusiasm (Miller, 2001b; Painter, 2002; Quinn, 2002). The material goods of fashion and conspicuous consumption are likewise expressive of status and aspirations. The archaeology of the present, as it were, needs to be integrated with the ethnographic imagination and to enrich the ethnographic eye (cf. Attfield, 2000). Much contemporary ethnographic fieldwork is oddly lacking in material content and physical goods, whereas informants' "voices" are transcribed from an apparent physical void. Field research needs to pay systematic attention to the physical embodiments of cultural values and codings.

More generally, this leads to a consideration of material culture. The material embodiment of culture and the cultural connotations of things have become prominent in recent cultural anthropological analyses (English-Lueck, 2002; Finn, 2001; Lury, 1996). Recent examples have included examinations of: home computers (Lally, 2000), mobile communications (Katz & Aakhus, 2002), photographs (Frosh, 2003), cars (Miller, 2001a), and memorabilia (Kwint, Breward, & Aynsley, 1999). These accounts transcend and transform the mundane material world into domains of signification. We do not need to subscribe to unduly strict and rigid formalisms to recognize that such phenomena can be analyzed in terms of their semiotic codes and conventions.

Places and Spaces

Most ethnographic reportage seems oddly lacking in physical location. Many sociological and anthropological accounts, for instance, have but sketchy descriptions of the built environment within which social events and encounters take place. The treatment of space is too often restricted to aspects of human geography, urban studies, and architecture (Darby, 2000). It also needs to be integrated within more general ethnographic accounts. But ethnoarchitecture is—as we know from some anthropological accounts—significant in defining the spaces and styles of everyday living (Dodds & Taverner, 2001). Built spaces provide symbolic boundaries as well as physical boundaries (Borden, 2002; Butler, 2003; Crowley & Reid, 2002). They physically enshrine collective memories as well as more personal biographical and emotional work (Bender & Winer, 2001). Homes are endowed with emotional and cultural value through the expression of taste and cultural capital, the celebration of historical authenticity, or the observance of modern minimalism (Jackson, Lowe, Miller, & Mort, 2000). Public spaces also embody tacit cultural assumptions—about the classification and processing of people and things, about commercial and professional transactions, about political processes and citizenship (Benjamin, 1999; Möller & Pehkonen, 2003). The ethnographic exploration of places and spaces includes the commercial transformation of them through tourism and heritage work, the transmutation of downtown areas and waterfronts, the recreation of industrial pasts into leisure and entertainment, and the construction of replicas and spaces for "experience" (Dicks, 2000).

These brief and partial observations are not intended to map out a comprehensive view of the current research literatures or of the general possibilities that they open up for ethnographic and other qualitative social research. More important, these observations are not intended to be a list of actual or potential domains of specialization. On the contrary, the thrust of our argument so far is that these various aspects of culture and the specialized coteries of researchers who document them should not exist in mutual isolation. The goal of ethnographic accounts of everyday life, particularly cultural and organizational milieux, should be to use such analytic perspectives and to analyze such materials in constructing multilayered accounts of the social world.

These observations are not intended to be a comprehensive listing of all relevant domains and strategies of inquiry. On the contrary, our remarks have been highly selective. We have deliberately offered some remarks on a few key fields of research to illustrate and develop our more general argument concerning the treatment of qualitative data in the analysis of social organization and action, social identities and biographies, social contexts and institutions.

The Ordering of the Social World

It would be easy to misrepresent our remarks. We are not simply suggesting a promiscuous series of analytic perspectives and strategies. We are not advocating simply putting data types and analytic types together in the interests of an ill-defined holism. The holistic ideal has, from time to time, been proposed as the goal of ethnographic and other qualitative research, although few social scientists nowadays would recognize the existence of phenomena such as "communities" that can be described holistically anyway. Such an ideal implies a degree of temporal, spatial, and cultural closure that is a chimera. We do recommend systematic attention to these data types and analytic perspectives because they reflect certain principles of intrinsic organization.

It is not altogether fashionable to invoke notions such as intrinsic organization in the analysis of social life (cf. Atkinson & Delamont 2004). During the era of poststructuralism and postmodernism, there is widespread rejection of anything that suggests "structure" or stable patterning in social and cultural forms. We believe, on the other hand, that we should recognize that forms can be identified and that they can serve as the basis of an analytic approach to qualitative social and cultural data. Moreover, an approach such as this gives us principled ways of understanding data of different sorts as reflections of the codes of social order. It also gives us ways of reconciling a number of tensions within the current treatment of qualitative research.

It is not necessary to invoke completely determinate and invariant structures so as to identify indigenous principles of order in particular forms of social action. The most obvious starting point—and it is one where there is no room for dispute—lies in the organization of spoken discourse. Discourse analysis and conversation analysis are virtually interchangeable from this perspective, and the disciplinary differences between them are insignificant for our purposes. It is not necessary to recapitulate their major findings here. But the general principles need reaffirmation. From the current vantage point, it is perhaps hard to reconstruct the recentness of any attention to spoken discourse as an object of analysis (as opposed to hypothetical texts or written materials) and of any attention to utterances in their natural context (as opposed to decontextualized individual sentences). The recognition that there can be *order* beyond the syntax of the individual sentence or beyond the single utterance is a relatively recent one. It follows, to a considerable extent, the technology of permanent recording that has permitted the close scrutiny of such phenomena, transforming spoken discourse into an object of inquiry and transforming its features into a topic of sociological, psychological, and linguistic inquiry.

The emergence of discourse analysis has transformed our collective appreciation of the interaction order in ways foreshadowed by Goffman's pioneering remarks and the no less original observations by Sacks (Goffman, 1981; Sacks, 1992; Silverman, 1998). It establishes the fundamental and pervasive principles of order, not least at the micro level of organization. Order in this sense displays itself through a remarkable array of socially shared devices, the operation of which produces and reproduces orderly conduct. The distinctive character of these devices is that they are used locally and recursively to generate strings of ordered interactions. The participants do not need to "know" the overall structure of the encounter to generate it in a predictable and stable way. They do not even need to be aware of the conventions they are using. Similar considerations apply to orderly conduct apart from spoken language. The recursive application of simple rules, in a practical way, generates orderly activity. To generate "structures" such as queues and turn-taking systems, for instance, each participant needs only to apply a simple chaining rule (i.e., "next participant follows the previous actor") and to know his or her relative position for the system to be self-replicating. Again, no actor needs to know the sequence of a complete queue for it to work smoothly, provided that each actor applies the same basic rule.

It is in this sense, therefore, that spoken and unspoken actions can display intrinsic orders that are in some sense independent of the actors' consciousness or intentions. In a similar vein, we can detect the interaction of physical and spoken actions. The capacity we now have to capture and inspect videotapes of human actions and processes of interaction already allows us to identify stable patterns of gesture in a way that was unavailable to earlier generations of observers. To this point, the social sciences have been relatively slow to fully explore the opportunities opened up by new digital technologies. We do know, however, that we can identify recurrent and interactionally functional patterns of movement and repertoires of gesture at a level of delicacy that only such permanent recordings render possible. As we have suggested, many of these analytic opportunities are dependent on contemporary recording technology. The important thing, however, is not the technology per se but rather the opportunity to pay close and systematic analytic attention to the *structures* of action. We can identify what Goffman (1983) referred to as an "interaction order" that displays ordering features that are relatively independent of the individual social actors who bring them into being. We know that social actors notice when the interaction order breaks down and that they share devices that repair mistakes and restore orderly functioning. But they do so as matters of preconscious action. Order is achieved and repaired through the application of recipes of action in a serial fashion. Complex structures and extended chains of action can be generated in a stable and smooth fashion through the local application of simple generative rules applied in a stepwise fashion.

We can identify recurrent ordering principles at a level of organization even greater than turn-by-turn discourse. The close analysis of narratives and similar spoken performances shows them to have recurrent structures. There have been various successful attempts to describe large-scale ordering principles for narrative events. Labov's pioneering work is one key example. Labov's groundbreaking work on language in society was innovative in various ways, with his work on spoken narratives being one example (Labov, 1972). Labov documented a number of basic structural elements that were part of the "grammar" of personal stories and accounts. Although not all of the structural elements were absolutely necessary for the production of a competent narrative, they recognizably generated stories that are sequentially coherent, deliver the story content competently, and are suitably "pointed" to make the story intelligible to speaker and hearer alike (Labov, 1972). We do not need to regard these as "deep structures," or as exerting mysterious powers over social actors, to acknowledge the recurrent patterning of narratives. A similar vein of analysis has been undertaken by Hymes (1996). Hymes's treatment, perhaps less well known than that of Labov, is more subtly grounded in an appreciation of *ethnopoetics,* that is, the culturally specific conventions of aesthetics and rhetoric that inform the competent performance and reception of oral performances. Hymes demonstrated principles that create distinctive internal structures within narratives and other oral performances. From his treatment of the materials, it appears that it is not necessary to reorder actors' own words into "poetic" reconstructions rather than to uncover the ethnopoetic structures and aesthetic principles that are indigenous to many narratives and other accounts.

Forms and functions of narratives and accounts are also identifiable from many analyses of respondents' accounting devices. Among these are the rhetorical repertoires or registers employed by natural scientists to express and reconcile recurrent features of scientific work. Gilbert and Mulkay (1984) demonstrated that natural scientists deploy alternating repertoires to account for scientific discoveries. Scientists proffer explanations that reflect the contingencies of personal and local characteristics while simultaneously attributing scientific discovery to the inexorable and impersonal revelation of nature. They reconcile any discursive or cognitive discrepancies by appealing to the mediating device that "the truth will out" in any event (Gilbert & Mulkay, 1984). A similar analysis of experts' accounts can be found in a subsequent analysis of the rhetorical work of health economists, whereas Atkinson and his colleagues have developed a similar analysis of a research group's accounts of its own scientific breakthrough (Atkinson, Batchelor, & Parsons, 1998). Accounting devices or registers are relatively stable features of these and similar accounts.

In a similar fashion, we have a large number of analyses of professionals' accounts of their work, including the formulation of phenomena such as "cases" and "findings." Occupations such as medicine and social work have narratives and accounts included in their stock-in-trade (Atkinson, 1995; Hunter, 1991; Pithouse, 1987). Their practitioners' routine work is constructed through various kinds of spoken performance. Practitioners persuade one another concerning diagnoses and assessments through the construction of cases that are, in turn, dependent on narrative structures; they use rhetorical devices to invoke evidence in support of their arguments. These are characterized by recurrent rhetorical features of their professional talk. They use characteristic devices to encode issues of evidence, competence, and responsibility in the course of collegial talk. In a very similar vein, we can identify rhetorical features of legal discourse through which cases are constructed, evidence is assembled and presented, or judgments are justified. Again, the major issue here lies not in the local details of particular settings or occupational groups but rather in the presence of stable regular features of spoken actions that can be identified. They can, in turn, be examined in terms of the sort of *work* that they perform. In other words, analytic payoff resides not only in identifying the patterns, structures, and conventions that generate such activity but also in analyzing their moral and practical implications.

We can extend such analytic perspectives beyond the individual narrative. There are systems of *genre.* There are culturally defined and socially shared types of story formats. The existence of such generic types means that we should not regard narrative accounts as reflections of private and individual experiences. Although narratives and biographical accounts may be felt and expressed as if they were highly personal, they are constructed and received in terms of cultural idioms and formats. This is demonstrated well in Plummer's (1995) analysis of sexual stories. Although accounts of coming out or of being a rape victim might be thought of as extremely private—and indeed in one sense they are—Plummer's analysis showed that they are couched in terms of shared forms or genres. Culturally defined formats can be identified in many contexts of spoken and written performance. They prescribe the shape and content of many descriptions and accounts. Many of the forms with which we are entirely familiar, to the point of taking them for granted, are highly conventional—or even arbitrary—cultural impositions. The analyses of documentary types such as the scientific report demonstrate that there are historical and culturally prescribed conventions through which the "plain facts" of nature and its exploration are conveyed. The work of authors such as Myers (1990) is testimony to the significance of the genre of the scientific report.

If it is fairly self-evident that discourse, descriptions, and narratives display indigenous principles of structure and order, we do not need to restrict such analyses to language. The general principles of semiotics can be applied to cultural systems of signification. Hence, visual and material data can be examined in terms of their intrinsic orders. The systems of fashion and clothing, for example, are not exhaustively defined in semiotic terms, but one can readily identify the basic structuring principles of such systems. The alternating and contrasting structuring principles that define the fashion system in recent Euro-American culture include the binary contrasts short/long, close/loose, structured/unstructured, full/narrow, colored/neutral, and plain/patterned. Although individual designers can develop their distinctive idiolects from within such systems, overall the semiotic principles help to define a "look" that is shared among many individual designers and houses in defining the distinctive style of a given season. In a similar vein, the "private" domain of fetishistic fantasy and pleasure is defined in terms of culturally defined, arbitrary features (e.g., leather, rubber, high heels, boots) that are themselves derivatives of and transform from the general system of clothing (Barthes, 1983; Hodkinson, 2002; Manning, 2001; Storr, 2003; Troy, 2002).

Visual styles of many sorts display basic semiotic principles. The visual "languages" of advertising, for instance, use recurrent coding principles that are grounded in representations of gender relations, sexual fantasy, exotic settings, domestic settings, and so forth, with the precise selection and combination of semiotic elements reflecting the product being advertised and the genre of advertisement itself. Goffman's (1979) analysis of gender relations in advertisements in print media is but one example of how advertising forms can be "decoded" from a sociological perspective. In a similar vein, one can identify semiotic principles of style and space in representations of the domestic sphere and its ideals. In the multiplicity of lifestyle magazines and television programs, statements about actual or desired status and identity can be constructed from color schemes, furnishings, and fittings. Styles can be identified through assemblages of materials and objects, for example, defining art nouveau, Bauhaus, art deco, or modernism. Such aesthetic principles may inhabit places of work as well as domestic environments. The visual and material language of the built environment is also susceptible to semiotic analysis. The use of space within and around buildings, the structures of buildings themselves, and the interior layouts of buildings simultaneously reflect the assemblage of cultural forms as well as the individual or corporate taste of the client and the aesthetic style of the architect.

Our general point here should not be lost in the various types and examples to which we have alluded. We are not trying to produce a comprehensive enumeration of all the cultural phenomena that can be analyzed. Rather, we are suggesting that whatever else these artifacts and activities might be, they display various arrays of structuring and semiotic principles. From the built environment, through domestic spaces, to individual self-presentations, biographies, narratives, and conversations, all of these social phenomena can be understood in terms of their intrinsic principles of structure and order. The collection of qualitative data certainly should not be confined to spoken materials, whether they are naturally occurring spoken interaction data or transcribed interview data. There are multiple media of inscription in which culture is enacted, and social action takes place through multiple embodiments.

Classic Principles

A systematic ethnography needs to take account of the intrinsic orderings through which social worlds are produced and reproduced. It is not necessary for any one ethnographic study to encompass systems of discourse, narrative, material culture, aesthetics, and performance to satisfy some notional criterion of completeness or adequacy. On the other hand, we should not ignore such structuring principles. There is no long-term benefit to the overall project of social research if styles of data collection and analysis remain fragmented. We certainly need some people to work on specialized technologies and techniques—digital visualization, discourse structures, semiotic structures, and the like—but those analytic domains must not flourish only in mutual isolation. We do not want to see the social world represented as if it consisted only of transcribed talk, spoken narratives, visual artifacts, or material goods.

We have already referred to Blumer's (1954) recommendation that research should be "faithful to the phenomena." In various ways, adherence to that injunction can prove to be problematic. It is hard to know what should count as phenomena in the first place, and it seems dangerous to assume that they have an essence independent of the methods used to construe them. Clearly, perfect correspondence to an independently identifiable realm of social objects and actions is impossible. We cannot aspire to perfect or comprehensive fidelity or to capture all of the variations to be found among and between types of social actions and actors. But the upshot of our argument is that ethnographers should certainly be faithful to the *forms* of social phenomena. We should be attentive to the indigenous systems of action and representation. We should not think of ignoring the systems of, say, ethnoaesthetics more than we think of mangling the local language(s) of our chosen research setting. Fidelity to the social worlds in which we work requires a systematic analysis of the principles of order they display. At least to that extent, then, we can retain a sense of fidelity and representation that is firmly rooted in social forms and also retains a notion of rigor.

This is, moreover, a productive way of approaching some key implications of "thick description" (Geertz, 1973). Geertz's (1973) use of the term, derived from Gilbert Ryle's philosophy of mind, has been susceptible to many readings. The most vulgar of uses do little or no justice to Geertz's own inspiration. Thick description is too often used to convey the sense that ethnographic accounts are densely constructed with graphic and detailed cultural descriptions. Although this may be the case, it does not really capture the specific analytic force of Geertz's idea, which is clearly intended to capture the degree to which cultural matters are overdetermined in the sense that there are multiple codings that generate meaning. There are, Geertz stressed, multiple perspectives or interpretive frameworks, that is, multiple motivational frames that inform social events and actions. Our own insistence on the intrinsic forms of culture and action gives a particular force to the notions of thick description. From our point of view, whatever else it might mean or be taken to mean, it should include analytic attention to the multiple codings and structuring principles through which social life is enacted and represented.

In these two senses, therefore, we can bring into close conjunction Blumer's precept and Geertz's insight. Both can find analytic force in the ethnographic analysis that is faithful to the contours of culture and the structures of action. We are mindful at this point to invoke yet a third idea derived from classic accounts of ethnographic analysis, that is, the notion of "triangulation" (Denzin, 1970). Like the first pair of terms we invoked, triangulation has been subject to multiple renderings and misrepresentations. Here, we do not wish to suppress or supersede all other connotations of triangulation, the fruitfulness of which lies partly in the multiplicity of inspirations that researchers can draw from it. Although it is not fruitful to assume, as in oversimplified versions, that research methods or data types can be aggregated to generate a more rounded or complete picture of a social world than would be generated by a single method alone, it might be productive to approach it in a way that is more congruent with our own approach: that is, to recognize that there can be a mode of triangulation derived from an explicit recognition of multiple social orders and principles of structuring. Triangulation thought of in this way has a very specific, if restricted, subset of meanings within the overall analytic strategy. Again, it recognizes the multiplicity and simultaneity of cultural frames of reference—spoken, performed, semiotic, material, and so forth—through which social events and institutions are possible. Consequently, a triangulated account depends not only on an opportunistic combination of methods and sources but also on a principled array of methodological strategies that reflect the indigenous principles of order and action.

Finally, our own approach here gives us some productive ways of recuperating significant aspects of "grounded theory" (Charmaz & Mitchell, 2001; Glaser & Strauss, 1967; Strauss & Corbin, 1998). We have already referred to the contested nature of this idea, or package of ideas, and we do not need to recapitulate the various definitions and applications of grounded theory. We simply reaffirm that grounded theory does not refer to some special order of theorizing per se. Rather, it seeks to capture some general principles of analysis, describing heuristic strategies that apply to any social inquiry independent of the particular kinds of data: indeed, it applies to the exploratory analysis of quantitative data as much as it does to qualitative inquiry. The idea derives directly from the pragmatist roots of interactionism. It captures the *abductive* logic through which analysts explore the social or natural world through practical engagements with it, derive working models and provisional understandings, and use such emergent ideas to guide further empirical explorations. It represents a compromise between the arid philosophy of purely deductive logic (which cannot account for the derivation of fruitful theories and hypotheses in the first place and admits of no place for *experience in the process of discovery*) and purely inductive logic (which never transcends the collection and aggregation of observations in generating generalizations). To a considerable extent, therefore, there is little to choose in practice between grounded theory and *analytic induction* as summary accounts of the practical work of social exploration and the derivation of ideas. Both formulations capture the need for systematic interactions between data and ideas as well as the emergent properties of research design and data analysis, which are in constant dialogue. Both formulations also emphasize the processual and iterative nature of the research process.

Too often, however, grounded theory is construed as a justification for the inductive retrospective inspection of volumes of field data, as if the research strategy were based on the accumulation of cases and the introspective derivation of categories—often through an inductive procedure of data "coding." Some of the descriptions of grounded theory by its own advocates have inadvertently contributed to this impression. But if we take seriously some of the things we have already outlined and claimed, we can discern some possible strategies that suggest principled relationships between data and analysis in a grounded theory manner. In other words, we recognize that culture and action are ordered. Consequently, the work of data collection is not devoted to the accumulation of isolated cases or fragmentary materials, and analysis is not just a matter of sorting and classifying those materials.

Finally, in considering our classic principles, we can sum up several of our themes so far with reference to Schutz's (1973) discussion of first- and second-order constructs. In his development of *verstehen* sociological principles beyond Dilthey or Weber through social phenomenology, Schutz suggested that analytic forms, such as ideal types, are not the sole preserve of the sociological observer. Everyday social actors are engaged in practical interpretations of their own social worlds. They use first-order constructs such as the method of practical reasoning that uses *typifications.* Sociological analysis, therefore, involves a (second-order) meta-analysis of the first-order, everyday analyses of practical social actors. In the same way, everyday social life displays principles of order that the analyst explicates and systematizes. The everyday actor has an implicit grasp of ordering rules and conventions, and it is the task of the analyst to explicate such tacit knowledge (cf. Maso, 2001).

We believe, therefore, that the social world displays various indigenous principles of organization. There are multiple ordering principles—discursive, spatial, semiotic, narrative, and so forth—to which the analysis of qualitative data needs to be attentive. The social analyst develops second-order models of these indigenous codes, conventions, and orders. There should, therefore, be principled relations between the first-order and second-order constructs. There should also be systematic relations between the different second-order analyses and models. Although this formulation might seem to be unduly formalistic, we believe it to be a salutary corrective to the unduly experiential perspectives currently brought to bear on qualitative data analysis. In the following section, we turn our attention to a parallel set of analytic preoccupations concerned with representation and aesthetics.

▣ Representation and Aesthetics

To this point, we have referred exclusively to the contours of culture, the semiotics of indigenous systems of representation, and the structures of social action. We now turn briefly to the analytic work of writing and other modes of ethnographic representation. We do not recapitulate the history of this particular domain, nor do we review all of the contributions that have been made to it. That work has been done elsewhere. Here, we note that there has been a marked tendency among the more innovative ethnographers to experiment with the textual conventions of ethnographic reportage (Faubion, 2001). The use of nontraditional literary forms or performance techniques has been well documented, and there is a growing corpus of published materials in those forms. Such experiments are usually represented as having radical connotations, and they are among the characteristics of ethnography associated with postmodernist ideas and with the most recent "moments" of Lincoln and Denzin's (1994, 2001) developmental model of qualitative research (for a critique of this particular formulation, see Delamont, Coffey, & Atkinson, 2000).

There is no doubt at all that writing ethnography is an important aspect of ethnographic analysis. The process of analysis stretches far beyond the mere manipulation of data and even of the work of grounded theorizing, thick description, and the like. It resides in the reconstruction of a given social world or some key features of it. Such reconstructions are rendered persuasive through the textual and other devices deployed by ethnographers in putting together the texts, films, and the like that constitute "the ethnography." In response to various interventions, all scholars recognize that this process is not innocent. There is no transparent medium through which a social world can be represented. Language is not a transparent medium. The textual conventions to which we have become accustomed are just that—conventions. Photography, film, and video are not merely passive recording media; rather, they actively shape our reception of social and cultural phenomena.

In the pursuit of the experimental turn in ethnographic representation, however, we believe that there have been exaggerated and extravagant moves. In bracketing and transgressing the conventions of realist representations and the textual formats of scientific writing, networks of authors have chosen to assimilate sociological representation to literary forms such as poetry and fiction. In this there lies a danger. The representation of social phenomena through poetry, for instance, inscribes some major assumptions (rarely explicated in the course of this ethnographic genre). First, the focus of attention is shifted radically from the culture and actions of social actors toward the representational work of ethnographers themselves. In sharp contrast to analyses of culture that decenter the "authors," much experimental writing places individual authors firmly—and sometimes exclusively—center stage. Literary work such as poetry here does not necessarily create the "open" or "messy" texts that some critics had sought. Rather, they create closure by creating a new basis for authorial privilege. Moreover, the ability to construct plausible, let alone meritorious, poetry or autobiographical writing appears to rest on personal authorial qualities. The social world is aestheticized in the process. What counts as a good ethnographic account is, therefore, in danger of resting primarily on aesthetic criteria.

Moreover, the assimilation of cultural and social phenomena to first-person-dominated texts, whether prose or poetry, can do violence to the phenomena themselves. We have already alluded to Blumer's (1954) aphorism concerning fidelity to the phenomena, and we invoke it once more here. We do not think that we are in any possible sense of the term *faithful* to the phenomena if we recast them into forms that derive from quite other cultural domains. We risk losing the intrinsic aesthetic, and other formal characteristics of the original meanings, events, and actions. We have already referred to the principle of ethnopoetics in recognizing that there are indigenous canons of rhetoric and construction in cultural performances. Analysts distort or obliterate the cultures they seek to account for if they translate everything into their own culture-bound aesthetics. First-person autobiographical writing and experientially derived poetry do not enjoy universal value. They are, if anything, among the more culturally specific and limited of expressive forms. There is little or no warrant for elevating them to being the preferred vehicle for cross-cultural or culturally sensitive social research.

Similar reservations can be entertained concerning performance ethnography in general. It is now permissible in some academic contexts to use our ethnographic data and the insights gleaned from ethnographic fieldwork to create various types of performative and aesthetic texts or artifacts. Denzin's (2003) recent volume is a key exemplar and discussion of this perspective. Mienczakowski (2001) also provided an overview of performed ethnography and ethnodrama. We do not seek to detract from these approaches in general except perhaps to suggest that performance ethnographers might engage more fully and systematically with the now wide-ranging ethnographic study of performance (Atkinson, 2004). We do, however, wish to assert something more in keeping with the general thrust of this chapter, namely that we should be very careful indeed of imposing "our" performative and aesthetic criteria and competences in the representation of settings, cultures, and actors while neglecting the indigenous local forms of performance through which culture, organization, and action are actually maintained in everyday life.

Social Action, Social Organization

In framing our argument as such, we are clearly stressing one particular array of emphases and preferences. We do so partly to redress what we see as a misleading tendency within many contemporary versions of qualitative research. We believe that too much emphasis is currently placed on the identification and documentation of social actors' *experiences* or *perceptions* at the expense of *social action* and *social organization* (cf. Silverman, 2004).

In part, we recapitulate arguments to which we have contributed elsewhere, and here we seek to generalize them further. We stress that among the goals of ethnographic research is to analyze *social action, social order,* and *social organization* as well as to analyze the forms and contents of *culture.* We need to pay serious and systematic attention to the recurrent phenomena of anthropology, sociology, and cognate disciplines such as discursive psychology, linguistics, and semiotics. This means that ethnographic and other qualitative research is much more than the sympathetic description and reportage of informants' experiences. We have argued elsewhere to the effect that qualitative research needs to transcend the culturally pervasive influence of the interview and what Atkinson and Silverman (1997) called the "interview society." We do not subscribe to the view that qualitative research is justified primarily by representing social affairs from the point of view of individual social actors or even from the perspectives of social aggregates.

This does not imply a return to the old methodological contestation between the merits of observation and those of interviewing—between what people *do* and what people *say* (Atkinson et al., 2003). The reverse is true. Instead, we stress that what people say is itself a form of action. We need to analyze social actors' accounts or narratives as types of speech acts. Likewise, we need to recognize that even such "experiences" as memories or emotions are not merely psychological states but also are performed social enactments (cf. Tota, 2001; Wagner-Pacifici, 1996). Moreover, in line with Mills (1940), we need to see motives as socially shared, culturally defined frames of justification or rationalization (Atkinson & Coffey, 2002). So, social action includes the work of representation. Likewise, social action includes the use and circulation of other modes of representation such as material goods and cultural artifacts (Vinck, 2003).

It follows, therefore, that we are recommending a particular approach to the analysis of social life under the aegis of ethnographic or qualitative research. We believe that there is a need for the reevaluation of analytic strategies that avoid the kind of fragmented reductionism to which we referred at the beginning of this chapter. We do not believe that it is productive for analysts to represent the social world primarily or exclusively through the lens of just one analytic strategy or data type. The different types of qualitative research—discourse analysis, visual analysis, narrative analysis, and the like—are not paradigms or disciplines in their own right; rather, they are analytic strategies that reflect and respect the intrinsic complexity of social organization, the forms of social action, and the conventions of social representation. This is not just a matter of juxtaposing different "methods," and it is not just an appeal to rather vague notions of "context" or "holistic" ethnography; rather, it means paying attention to the *systemic* relations among the interaction order, orders of talk, representational orders, and organized properties of material culture. In this way, our analytic perspectives can and should reaffirm certain kinds of rigor, some of which we believe have been lost to view in recent methodological writing. We stress, therefore, the disciplined approach to technical issues such as discourse analysis, narrative analysis, and semiotic analysis. We seek *principled* relationships between the various contributory disciplines and subdisciplines. The analysis of social phenomena is not well served by the kind of fragmentation that equates types of data (e.g., spoken, visual, textual, material) with disciplines or specialties working in relative isolation.

▣ References

Appadurai, A. (Ed.). (1986). *The social lives of things.* Cambridge, UK: Cambridge University Press.

Atkinson, J. M., & Heritage, J. (Eds.). (1984). *The structures of social action: Studies in conversation analysis.* Cambridge, UK: Cambridge University Press.

Atkinson, P. A. (1995). *Medical talk and medical work: The liturgy of the clinic.* London: Sage.

Atkinson, P. A. (1997). Narrative turn or blind alley? *Qualitative Health Research, 7,* 325–344.

Atkinson, P. A. (2004). Performing ethnography and the ethnography of performance. *British Journal of Sociology of Education, 25,* 107–114.

Atkinson, P. A., Batchelor, C., & Parsons, E. (1998). Trajectories of collaboration and competition in a medical discovery. *Science, Technology, & Human Values, 23,* 259–284.

Atkinson, P. A., & Coffey, A. (2002). Revisiting the relationship between participant observation and interviewing. In J. F. Gubrium & J. A. Holstein (Eds.), *Handbook of interview research: Context and method* (pp. 801–814). Thousand Oaks, CA: Sage.

Atkinson, P. A., Coffey, A., & Delamont, S. (1999). Ethnography: Post, past, and present. *Journal of Contemporary Ethnography, 28,* 460–471.

Atkinson, P. A., Coffey, A., & Delamont, S. (2001). A debate about our canon. *Qualitative Research, 1,* 2–22.

Atkinson, P. A., Coffey, A., & Delamont, S. (2003). *Key themes in qualitative research.* Walnut Creek, CA: AltaMira.

Atkinson, P. A., & Delamont, S. (2004). Analysis and postmodernism. In M. Hardy & A. Bryman (Eds.), *Handbook of analysis* (pp. 667–681). London: Sage.

Atkinson, P. A., & Silverman, D. (1997). Kundera's *Immortality:* The interview society and the invention of the self. *Qualitative Inquiry, 3,* 304–325.

Attfield, J. (2000). *Wild things: The material culture of everyday life.* Oxford, UK: Berg.

Ball, M., & Smith, G. (1992). *Analyzing visual data.* Newbury Park, CA: Sage.

Ball, M., & Smith, G. (2001). Technologies of realism? Ethnographic uses of photography and film. In P. Atkinson, A. Coffey, S. Delamont, J. Lofland, & L. Lofland (Eds.), *Handbook of ethnography* (pp. 302–319). London: Sage.

Banks, M., & Morphy, H. (Eds.). (1997). *Rethinking visual anthropology.* New Haven, CT: Yale University Press.

Barthes, R. (1983). *The fashion system.* New York: Hill & Wang.

Bauman, R. (1986). *Story, performance, and event: Contextual studies of oral narrative.* Cambridge, UK: Cambridge University Press.

Behar, R. (1996). *The vulnerable observer: Anthropology that breaks your heart.* Boston: Beacon.

Bender, B., & Winer, M. (Eds.). (2001). *Contested landscapes: Movement, exile, and place.* Oxford, UK: Berg.

Benjamin, W. (1999). *The Arcades Project* (H. Eiland & K. McLaughlin, Trans.). Cambridge, MA: Harvard University Press.

Bennett, A., & Dawe, K. (Eds.). (2001). *Guitar cultures.* Oxford, UK: Berg.

Bijker, W. (1995). *Of bicycles, Bakelites, and bulbs: Toward a theory of sociotechnical change.* Cambridge, MA: MIT Press.

Blumer, H. (1954). What is wrong with social theory? *American Sociological Review, 19,* 3–10.

Bochner, A. R., & Ellis, C. (Eds.). (2001). *Ethnographically speaking: Autoethnography, literature, and aesthetics.* Walnut Creek, CA: AltaMira.

Borden, I. (2002). *Skateboarding, space, and the city: Architecture and the body.* Oxford, UK: Berg.

Brewer, J. (2002). *Ethnography.* Buckingham, UK: Open University Press.

Butler, T. (2003). *London calling: The middle classes and the remaking of inner London.* Oxford, UK: Berg.

Caplan, P. (1997). *African voices, African lives.* London: Routledge.

Charmaz, K., & Mitchell, R. (2001). Grounded theory and ethnography. In P. Atkinson, A. J. Coffey, S. Delamont, J. Lofland, & L. Lofland (Eds.), *Handbook of ethnography* (pp. 160–173). London: Sage.

Clough, P. T. (1998). *The end(s) of ethnography: From realism to social criticism* (2nd ed.). New York: Peter Lang.

Coffey, A. J., & Atkinson, P. A. (1996). *Making sense of qualitative data: Complementary strategies.* Thousand Oaks, CA: Sage.

Conle, C. (2003). An anatomy of narrative curricula. *Educational Researcher, 32*(3), 3–15.

Cortazzi, M. (1991). *Primary teaching: How it is—A narrative analysis.* London: David Fulton.

Cortazzi, M. (1993). *Narrative analysis.* London: Falmer.

Cortazzi, M. (2001). Narrative analysis. In P. Atkinson, A. Coffey, S. Delamont, J. Lofland, & L. Lofland (Eds.), *Handbook of ethnography* (pp. 384–393). London: Sage.

Crouch, D., & Lübbren, N. (Eds.). (2003). *Visual culture and tourism.* Oxford, UK: Berg.

Crowley, D., & Reid, S. E. (Eds.). (2002). *Socialist spaces: Sites of everyday life in the Eastern Bloc.* Oxford, UK: Berg.

Czarniawska, B. (1997). *Narrating the organization.* Chicago: University of Chicago Press.

Czarniawska, B. (1998). *A narrative approach to organization studies.* Thousand Oaks, CA: Sage.

Darby, W. J. (2000). *Landscape and identity: Geographies of nation and class in England.* Oxford, UK: Berg.

Delamont, S. (2002). *Fieldwork in educational settings* (2nd ed.). London: Falmer.

Delamont, S., Coffey, A., & Atkinson, P. (2000). The twilight years? Educational ethnography and the five moments model. *Qualitative Studies in Education, 13,* 223–238.

DeNora, T. (2000). *Music in everyday life.* Cambridge, UK: Cambridge University Press.

DeNora, T. (2003). *After Adorno: Rethinking music sociology.* Cambridge, UK: Cambridge University Press.

Denzin, N. K. (1970). *The research act.* Chicago: Aldine.

Denzin, N. K. (1994). The art and politics of interpretation. In N. K. Denzin & Y. S. Lincoln (Eds.), *Handbook of qualitative research* (pp. 500–515). Thousand Oaks, CA: Sage.

Denzin, N. K. (2003). *Performance ethnography: Critical pedagogy and the politics of culture.* Thousand Oaks, CA: Sage.

Denzin, N. K., & Lincoln, Y. S. (Eds.). (1994). *Handbook of qualitative research.* Thousand Oaks, CA: Sage.

Denzin, N. K., & Lincoln, Y. S. (Eds.). (2001). *Handbook of qualitative research* (2nd ed.). Thousand Oaks, CA: Sage.

Dicks, B. (2000). *Heritage, place, and community.* Cardiff, UK: University of Wales Press.

Dodds, G., & Taverner, R. (2001). *Body and building: Essays on the changing relations of body and architecture.* Cambridge, MA: MIT Press.

Dyck, N., & Archetti, E. P. (Eds.). (2003). *Sport, dance, and embodied identities.* Oxford, UK: Berg.

Edwards, E. (2001). *Raw histories: Photographs, anthropology, and museums.* Oxford, UK: Berg.

Ellis, C. (2004). *The ethnographic I: A methodological novel about autoethnography.* Walnut Creek, CA: AltaMira.

Ellis, C., & Bochner, A. (Eds.). (1996). *Composing ethnography.* Walnut Creek, CA: AltaMira.

Ellis, C., & Flaherty, M. G. (Eds.). (1992). *Investigating subjectivity: Research on lived experience.* Newbury Park, CA: Sage.

English-Lueck, J. A. (2002). *Cultures @ Silicon Valley.* Stanford, CA: Stanford University Press.

Faubion, J. D. (2001). Currents of cultural fieldwork. In P. Atkinson, A. Coffey, S. Delamont, J. Lofland, & L. Lofland (Eds.), *Handbook of ethnography* (pp. 39–59). London: Sage.

Fernandez, J. W., & Huber, M. T. (Eds.). (2001). *Irony in action: Anthropology, practice, and the moral imagination.* Chicago: University of Chicago Press.

Fine, G. A. (2001). *Difficult reputations: Collective memories of the evil, inept, and controversial.* Chicago: University of Chicago Press.

Finn, C. A. (2001). *Artifacts: An archaeologist's year in Silicon Valley.* Cambridge, MA: MIT Press.

Forty, A., & Kuchler, S. (Eds.). (1999). *The art of forgetting.* Oxford, UK: Berg.

Frosh, P. (2003). *The image factory: Consumer culture, photography, and the visual content industry.* Oxford, UK: Berg.

Gardner, K. (2002). *Age, narrative, and migration: The life course and life histories of Bengali elders in London.* Oxford, UK: Berg.

Geertz, C. (1973). *The interpretation of cultures.* New York: Basic Books.

Geertz, C. (1983). *Local knowledge: Further essays in interpretive anthropology.* New York: Basic Books.

Gilbert, N., & Mulkay, M. (1984). *Opening Pandora's box.* Cambridge, UK: Cambridge University Press.

Glaser, B. (1978). *Theoretical sensitivity.* Mill Valley, CA: Sociology Press.

Glaser, B. (1992). *Emergence versus forcing.* Mill Valley, CA: Sociology Press.

Glaser, B., & Strauss, A. L. (1967). *The discovery of grounded theory.* Chicago: Aldine.

Goffman, E. (1979). *Gender advertisements.* New York: Harper & Row.

Goffman, E. (1981). *Forms of talk.* Philadelphia: University of Pennsylvania Press.

Goffman, E. (1983). The interaction order. *American Sociological Review, 48,* 1–17.

Goodall, H. L. (2000). *Writing the new ethnography.* Walnut Creek, CA: AltaMira.

Gosden, C., & Knowles, C. (Eds.). (2001). *Collecting colonialism: Material culture and colonial change.* Oxford, UK: Berg.

Gray, R., & Sinding, C. (2002). *Standing ovation: Performing social science research about cancer.* Walnut Creek, CA: AltaMira.

Grimshaw, A. (2001). *The ethnographer's eye: Ways of seeing in modern anthropology.* Cambridge, UK: Cambridge University Press.

Gubrium, J. F., & Holstein, J. A. (2002a). From the individual interview to the interview society. In J. F. Gubrium & J. A. Holstein (Eds.), *Handbook of interview research: Context and method* (pp. 3–32). Thousand Oaks, CA: Sage.

Gubrium, J. F., & Holstein, J. A. (Eds.). (2002b). *Handbook of interview research: Context and method.* Thousand Oaks, CA: Sage.

Hammersley, M. (1989). *The dilemma of qualitative method: Herbert Blumer and the Chicago tradition.* London: Routledge.

Hammersley, M., & Atkinson, P. A. (1995). *Ethnography: Principles in practice* (2nd ed.). London: Routledge.

Handler, R., & Gable, E. (1997). *The new history in an old museum: Creating the past at Colonial Williamsburg.* Durham, NC: Duke University Press.

Hardy, M., & Bryman, A. (Eds.). (2004). *Handbook of analysis.* London: Sage.

Henderson, K. (1998). *On line and on paper: Visual representations, visual culture, and computer graphics in design engineering.* Cambridge, MA: MIT Press.

Hepburn, A., & Potter, J. (2004). Discourse analytic practice. In C. Seale, G. Gobo, F. F. Gubrium, & D. Silverman (Eds.), *Qualitative research practice* (pp. 180–196). London: Sage.

Herzfeld, M. (1991). *A place in history: Social and monumental time in a Cretan town.* Princeton, NJ: Princeton University Press.

Hodkinson, P. (2002). *Goth: Identity, style, and subculture.* Oxford, UK: Berg.

Holstein, J. A. (2000). *The self we live by: Narrative identity in a postmodern world.* New York: Oxford University Press.

Hughes-Freeland, F. (1998). *Ritual, performance, media.* London: Routledge.

Humphrey, R., Miller, R., & Zdravomyslova, E. (Eds.). (2003). *Biographical research in Eastern Europe: Altered lives and broken biographies.* Aldershot, UK: Ashgate.

Hunter, K. M. (1991). *Doctors' stories: The narrative structure of medical knowledge.* Princeton, NJ: Princeton University Press.

Hymes, D. (1996). *Ethnography, linguistics, narrative inequality.* London: Taylor & Francis.

Jackson, P., Lowe, M., Miller, D., & Mort, F. (Eds.). (2000). *Commercial cultures: Economies, practices, spaces.* Oxford, UK: Berg.

Janesick, V. J. (1994). The dance of qualitative research design: Metaphor, methodolatry, and meaning. In N. K. Denzin & Y. S. Lincoln (Eds.), *Handbook of qualitative research* (pp. 209–219). Thousand Oaks, CA: Sage.

Julier, G. (2000). *The culture of design.* London: Sage.

Katz, J. E., & Aakhus, M. (Eds.). (2002). *Perpetual contact: Mobile communication, private talk, public performance.* Cambridge, UK: Cambridge University Press.

Kwint, M., Breward, C., & Aynsley, J. (Eds.). (1999). *Material memories.* Oxford, UK: Berg.

Labov, W. (1972). *Language in the inner city.* Philadelphia: University of Pennsylvania Press.

Lally, E. (2002). *At home with computers.* Oxford, UK: Berg.

Lara, M. P. (1998). *Moral textures: Feminist narratives in the public sphere.* Cambridge, UK: Polity.

Lincoln, Y. S., & Denzin, N. K. (1994). The fifth moment. In N. K. Denzin & Y. S. Lincoln (Eds.), *Handbook of qualitative research* (pp. 575–586). Thousand Oaks, CA: Sage.

Lincoln, Y. S., & Denzin, N. K. (2001). The seventh moment: Out of the past. In N. K. Denzin & Y. S. Lincoln (Eds.), *Handbook of qualitative research* (2nd ed., pp. 1047–1065). Thousand Oaks, CA: Sage.

Lincoln, Y. S., & Denzin, N. K. (Eds.). (2003). *Turning points in qualitative research: Tying knots in the handkerchief.* Walnut Creek, CA: AltaMira.

Loizos, P. (1993). *Innovation in ethnographic film.* Manchester, UK: Manchester University Press.

Lury, C. (1996). *Consumer culture.* Cambridge, UK: Polity.

Macdonald, S. (2002). *Behind the scenes at the science museum.* Oxford, UK: Berg.

Macdonald, S., & Fyfe, G. (Eds.). (1996). *Theorising museums.* Oxford, UK: Blackwell.

Manning, P. K. (2001). Semiotics, semantics, and ethnography. In P. Atkinson, A. Coffey, S. Delamont, J. Lofland, & L. Lofland (Eds.), *Handbook of ethnography* (pp. 145–159). London: Sage.

Maso, I. (2001). Phenomenology and ethnography. In P. Atkinson, A. Coffey, S. Delamont, J. Lofland, & L. Lofland (Eds.), *Handbook of ethnography* (pp. 136–144). London: Sage.

May, R. A. B. (2001). *Talking at Trena's: Everyday conversations at an African American tavern.* New York: New York University Press.

Mienczakowski, J. (2001) Ethnodrama: Performed research—Limitations and potential. In P. Atkinson, A. Coffey, S. Delamont, J. Lofland, & L. Lofland (Eds.), *Handbook of ethnography* (pp. 468–476). London: Sage.

Miller, D. (1987). *Material culture and mass communication.* Oxford, UK: Basil Blackwell.

Miller, D. (Ed.). (2001a). *Car cultures.* Oxford, UK: Berg.

Miller, D. (Ed.). (2001b). *Home possessions: Material culture behind closed doors.* Oxford, UK: Berg.

Mills, C. W. (1940). Situated actions and vocabularies of motive. *American Sociological Review, 5,* 439–452.

Moerman, M. (1988). *Talking culture: Ethnography and conversation analysis.* Philadelphia: University of Pennsylvania Press.

Möller, F., & Pehkonen, S. (Eds.). (2003). *Encountering the North: Cultural geography, international relations, and northern landscapes.* Aldershot, UK: Ashgate.

Myerhoff, B. (1978). *Number our days.* New York: Simon & Schuster.

Myers, G. (1990). *Writing biology: Texts in the construction of scientific knowledge.* Madison: University of Wisconsin Press.

Ochs, E., & Capps, L. (2002). *Living narrative: Creating lives in everyday storytelling.* Cambridge, MA: Harvard University Press.

O'Dell, D. (2001). *Sites of southern memory: The autobiographies of Katherine Du Pre Lumpkin, Lillian Smith, and Pauli Murray.* Charlottesville: University Press of Virginia.

Olney, J. (Ed.). (1998). *Autobiography: Essays theoretical and critical.* Princeton, NJ: Princeton University Press.

Painter, C. (Ed.). (2002). *Contemporary art and the home.* Oxford, UK: Berg.

Patterson, W. (2002). *Strategic narrative: New perspectives on the power of personal and cultural stories.* Lanham, MD: Lexington Books.

Pinch, T., & Trocco, F. (2002). *Analog days: The invention and impact of the Moog synthesizer.* Cambridge, MA: Harvard University Press.

Pink, S. (2001). *Doing visual ethnography.* London: Sage.

Pink, S. (2004). Visual methods. In C. Seale, D. Silverman, J. F. Gubrium, & G. Gobo (Eds.), *Qualitative research practice* (pp. 391–406). London: Sage.

Pithouse, A. (1987). *Social work: The social organization of an invisible trade.* Aldershot, UK: Avebury.

Plummer, K. (1995). *Telling sexual stories.* London: Routledge.

Plummer, K. (2000). *Documents of life 2: An invitation to a critical humanism.* London: Sage.

Plummer, K. (2001). The call of life stories in ethnographic research. In P. Atkinson, A. Coffey, S. Delamont, J. Lofland, & L. Lofland (Eds.), *Handbook of ethnography* (pp. 395–406). London: Sage.

Potter, J. (1996). *Representing reality: Discourse, rhetoric, and social construction.* London: Sage.

Potter, J. (2003). Discourse analysis and discursive psychology. In P. M. Camic, J. E. Rhodes, & L. Yardley (Eds.), *Qualitative research in psychology: Expanding perspectives in methodology and design* (pp. 73–94). Washington, DC: American Psychological Association.

Potter, J., & Wetherell, M. (1987). *Discourse and social psychology: Beyond attitudes and behaviour.* London: Sage.

Prior, L. (2003). *Using documents in social research.* London: Sage.

Quinn, B. (2002). *Techno fashion.* Oxford, UK: Berg.

Rabinow, P. (1996). *Making PCR: A story of biotechnology.* Chicago: University of Chicago Press.

Radstone, S. (2000). *Memory and methodology.* Oxford, UK: Berg.

Reed-Danahay, D. (Ed.). (1997). *Auto/Ethnography: Rewriting the self and the social.* Oxford, UK: Berg.

Reed-Danahay, D. (2001). Autobiography, intimacy, and ethnography. In P. Atkinson, A. Coffey, S. Delamont, J. Lofland, & L. Lofland (Eds.), *Handbook of ethnography* (pp. 407–425). London: Sage.

Richardson, L. (1997). *Fields of play: Constructing an academic life.* New Brunswick, NJ: Rutgers University Press.

Richardson, L. (2002). Poetic representation of interviews. In J. F. Gubrium & J. A. Holstein (Eds.), *Handbook of interview research* (pp. 877–891). Thousand Oaks, CA: Sage.

Riessman, C. K. (1993). *Narrative analysis.* Newbury Park, CA: Sage.

Riessman, C. K. (2002). Analysis of personal narratives. In J. F. Gubrium & J. A. Holstein (Eds.), *Handbook of interview research: Context and method* (pp. 695–710). Thousand Oaks, CA: Sage.

Sacks, H. (1992). *Lectures on conversation* (G. Jefferson, Ed., 2 vols.). Oxford, UK: Blackwell.

Sandburg, M. B. (2003). *Living pictures, missing persons: Mannequins, museums, and modernity.* Princeton, NJ: Princeton University Press.

Sarangi, S., & Roberts, C. (Eds.). (1999). *Talk, work, and institutional orders: Discourse in medical, mediation, and management settings.* Berlin, Germany: Mouton de Gruyter.

Saunders, N. J. (2003). *Trench art: Materialities and memories of war.* Oxford, UK: Berg.

Schutz, A. (1973). *The problem of social reality: Collected papers* (Vol. 1, M. Natanson, Ed.). The Hague, Netherlands: Martinus Nijhoff.

Sciama, L. D. (2003). *A Venetian island: Environment, history, and change in Burano.* Oxford, UK: Barghahn.

Scott, J. (1990). *A matter of record.* Cambridge, UK: Polity.

Seale, C., Silverman, D., Gubrium, J. F., & Gobo, G. (Eds.). (2004). *Qualitative research practice.* London: Sage.

Silverman, D. (1987). *Communication and medical practice: Social relations in the clinic.* London: Sage.

Silverman, D. (Ed.). (1997). *Qualitative research: Theory, method, and practice.* London: Sage.

Silverman, D. (1998). *Harvey Sacks: Social science and conversation analysis.* Cambridge, UK: Polity.

Silverman, D. (Ed.). (2004). *Qualitative research: Theory, method, and practice* (2nd ed.). London: Sage.

Storr, M. (2003). *Latex and lingerie: Shopping for pleasure at Ann Summers parties.* Oxford, UK: Berg.

Strauss, A. L., & Corbin, J. A. (1998). *Basics of qualitative research: Theory, procedures, and techniques* (2nd ed.). Thousand Oaks, CA: Sage.

Tilley, C. (1991). *Material culture and the text: The art of ambiguity.* London: Routledge.

Tilley, C. (1999). *Metaphor and material culture.* Oxford, UK: Blackwell.

Tilley, C. (2001). Ethnography and material culture. In P. Atkinson, , A. Coffey, S. Delamont, J. Lofland, & L. Lofland (Eds.), *Handbook of ethnography* (pp. 258–272). London: Sage.

Tota, A. L. (Ed.). (2001). *La Memoria Contesta: Studi Sulla Communicazione Sociale del Passato.* Milan, Italy: Angeli.

Troy, N. J. (2002). *Couture culture: A study in modern art and fashion.* Cambridge, UK: Cambridge University Press.

Tulloch, J. (1999). *Performing culture: Stories of expertise and the everyday.* London: Sage.

Valis, N. (2003). *The culture of Cursilería: Bad taste, kitsch, and class in modern Spain.* Durham, NC: Duke University Press.

Vinck, D. (Ed.). (2003). *Everyday engineering: An ethnography of design and innovation.* Cambridge, MA: MIT Press.

Voysey, M. (1975). *A constant burden.* London: Routledge & Kegan Paul.

Wagner-Pacifici, R. (1996). Memories in the making: The shapes of things that went. *Qualitative Sociology, 19,* 301–321.

Whiteley, S., Bennett, A., & Hawkins, S. (Eds.). (2004). *Music, space, and place: Popular music and cultural identity.* Aldershot, UK: Ashgate.

Yalouri, E. (2001). *The Acropolis: Global fame, local claim.* Oxford, UK: Berg.

Znaniecki, F. (1934). *The method of sociology.* New York: Farrar & Rinehart.

33

FOUCAULT'S METHODOLOGIES

Archaeology and Genealogy

James Joseph Scheurich and Kathryn Bell McKenzie

This chapter is not a true or accurate representation of Foucault's work.[1] No such representation exists or is possible, in our view. There are, consequently, many other possible readings of Foucault's work that are just as defensible as this one. Indeed, this reading, like Foucault's *savoir* (defined and discussed later), is messy, ruptured, often erroneous, broken, discontinuous, originless, fabricated, even a falsification. In other words, as Magritte wrote on his painting of a pipe, "this is not a pipe" (Foucault, 1973b); this is not Foucault.

Moreover, what we intended to accomplish here in our early conceptualizations of this project and what actually emerged are significantly different. Indeed, we might question ourselves as we think our critics will question us, and just as Foucault did at the end of his "Introduction" to *The Archaeology of Knowledge* (1969/1972).[2] We might say,

> "Aren't you sure of what you're saying? Are you going to change yet again, shift your position according to the questions that are put to you, and say that the objections are not really directed at the place from which you are speaking? Are you going to declare yet again that you have never been what you have been reproached with being? Are you already preparing the way out that will enable you in your next book to spring up somewhere else and declare as you're now doing: no, no, I'm not where you are lying in wait for me, but over here, laughing at you?" (p. 17, quotes in original)

Although our only laughter is about our own pretensions, what we intended when we started this project was to try to show how archaeology and genealogy might be used as critical "qualitative" (defined broadly) methodologies. We also wanted to illustrate briefly how each of these methods might be applied to education issues, as this is our discipline. Finally, we also envisioned a critical survey of the uses and abuses of Foucault's work in education.

However, some of this happened and much did not. For us, what changed what we did here was our review of Foucault's *oeuvre* (just the books and the order in which they were published) from the "beginning" through his genealogical work (we never thought we would cover what many consider the last phase of his work, the "care of self" or ethics period) and our review of articles and books in education that use Foucault's ideas in a central way. Neither of us had read through Foucault's work in such a systematic, focused, concentrated way, nor had we systematically surveyed the applications of Foucault in education. It was these systematic surveys, then, and the effects they had on our own understandings of Foucault and his use by education scholars that changed what we were doing in this chapter. For example, one change that emerged was our decision to discuss briefly the importance of Georges Canguilhem, arguably Foucault's most influential mentor. It almost seemed to us that to education scholars and, even more broadly, to scholars across the social sciences, Foucault and his ideas had emerged full grown from the forehead of Zeus. Consequently, we decided to provide a subsection within the "Archaeology" section that briefly discusses Foucault's view of Canguilhem and the latter's role in the French intellectual and philosophical context.

The rest of this essay, then, is divided into four parts. First, we discuss Foucault's archaeological method, which includes the Canguilhem discussion. Second, we discuss a particularly important essay, "Nietzsche, Genealogy, History" (Foucault, 1977, in *Language, Counter-Memory, Practice: Selected Essays and Interviews*) that was first published *after* his last archaeological work and *before* his first genealogical work, which we see as thematically bridging between or connecting the two methodologies. Third, we present his genealogical method. While our discussions of his archaeology or genealogy is not comprehensive enough so that a reader could assume that she or he is ready to use either of Foucault's methods after only reading this chapter, we do believe that what we have written was done in a way to help those who are not familiar with Foucault take some beginning steps toward using archaeology and genealogy. We also hope, though, that our coverage of the two is provocative of further reflections for those more experienced in their uses of Foucault's methods.

We accomplish our discussion of his archaeological method by addressing two archaeological concepts in some depth, *savoir* and *connaissance*, and then allude to what the other key archaeological concepts are. To present his genealogies, we discuss in some depth one of them, *Discipline and Punish* (Foucault, 1975/1979). However, in this work, he deploys so many provocative, useful critical tools that we can cover only some of them, let alone cover all of the other critical tools he adds with his second genealogy, *The History of Sexuality,* Volume 1: *An Introduction* (1976/1980a).[3] For the latter, however, we do point out some particularly excellent sections.

Fourth, our conclusion includes a brief overview of what we think some the critical goals of both his archaeologies and his genealogies were. We summarize some of the points about archaeology and genealogy that we make. We enthusiastically praise a new collection of Foucault's work. We also provide some brief critical remarks on the uses—and abuses—of Foucault in education in particular and in the social sciences in general, although we do not provide a comprehensive or detailed review of this material. (We do try to provide a somewhat comprehensive list of such work in education in our bibliography along with some books on Foucault from outside of education that we think are either useful or influential; indeed, our bibliography is intended to be a resource for those interested in Foucault.) In general, we might forewarn by saying we are somewhat grumpy and surly, dissatisfied, about how Foucault has most frequently been read and used to date in education and the social sciences. In addition, our conclusion contains—and this was a surprise even to us—some substantive critique that we have of Foucault's work that we did not have when we started this chapter. In other words, by the end of our read of all of his books, we arrived at a critique of Foucault that we did not have when we began this read. We expect this critique will upset some advocates of Foucault and will gratify some critics. Our only defense is that we did not intend or desire this critique, although to be intellectually honest, we felt we needed to include it.

Our assumption, at this point, is that by the end of this essay we will leave a jangle, bangle, and tangle among some experienced Foucaultians, but hopefully some useful beginnings to those who have not yet tried on Foucault. Maybe, though, just maybe, some of the former will appreciate and find provocative our efforts to "think" Foucault both comprehensively *and* critically. Maybe we are all coming to a point, even among those of us who have been enthusiastic advocates of Foucault, at which it is possible to consider his work in a more balanced way, that is, without defensiveness. Perhaps. Perhaps not.

Archaeology

Many scholars who survey the entire *oeuvre* of Foucault have discerned three sequential phases or periods—archaeology, genealogy, and the care of the self—that represent, it is thought, significant shifts in his philosophical thought, although some would add to this list Foucault's focus on governmentality.[4] Nonetheless, of the three periods, genealogy is the one that has captured the most attention of scholars to date, although one of us (Scheurich, 1997, pp. 94–118, "Policy Archaeology" chapter) has found archaeology useful, and recently Lather (2004) has written about "positivities," a key concept in archaeology. Care of the self, the last of the three periods, has generally received the least attention, although St. Pierre (2004) has recently found it to be fertile territory for her meditations on "the subject and freedom."[5]

Our intent here, however, because this is a chapter in a book on methodology, is to focus on archaeology and genealogy, which could be broadly construed as "qualitative" methods, as Foucault always used texts as his data or, what he sometimes called, the archive. It is not that we think Foucault's care of the self period or focus is unimportant. Nor do we think someone like St. Pierre could not creatively interpret the latter period as a methodology. Our aim is simpler than that. We want to provide a kind of beginner's introduction to the two Foucaultian methodologies that have received the most attention among U.S. scholars and that those interested in Foucault's perspective might use as a starting place of further exploration. What we cannot provide, though, due to space limitations, is some sort of "complete" course on how to use either methodology so that on finishing this essay, someone could move directly to applying either one. There is simply not sufficient space for accomplishing this for even one of Foucault's methods.

Canguilhem

As we suggested in our introduction to this chapter, it is our judgment that there is a general lack of understanding of the philosophical context and influences within which Foucault worked in France. A good example of the latter is a lack of knowledge about Georges Canguilhem, arguably Foucault's main intellectual mentor and teacher. In general, our view is that Canguilhem's influence on Foucault, especially Canguilhem's influence on Foucault's archaeologies, is unacknowledged, underestimated, or even unknown. Indeed, even among philosophers who know Foucault deeply and use him well, there is much more fascination with Foucault and his relationships with Kant, Nietzsche, and Heidegger (see, e.g., the work of poststructuralist philosophers such as Elizabeth Grosz in *Volatile Bodies* [1994]). In response, we briefly discuss Canguilhem's influence on Foucault and Foucault's own view of Canguilhem's role in French philosophy with the hope that this will spur others to read more deeply into Foucault and his social and intellectual context. However, we are aware that our Canguilhem is but another author function[6] and that the relationship among Foucault, his mentor, and their social, historical, and intellectual "context" is complex, contradictory, and ambiguous.

One excellent example of Foucault's own discussion of Canguilhem and his influences, particularly as a historian of the sciences, is available in *Aesthetics, Method, and Epistemology* (1994a) and is called "Life Experience and Science," which originally appeared in a French-language journal but was modified to appear as

Foucault's introduction to the 1989 English translation of Canguilhem's *The Normal and the Pathological* (p. 465). As Foucault says, there has been less awareness "of the significance and impact of a work like that of Georges Canguilhem, extending as it has over the past twenty or thirty years" (p. 465). Foucault also says that when "the sociology of the French intellectual milieus" is considered for "those strange years, the sixties," nearly all French philosophers "were affected directly or indirectly by the teaching or books of Canguilhem" (p. 465), which were primarily focused on critiquing overly rationalistic views of the history of the sciences in a much more thoughtful and complex way than Kuhn ever did in *The Structure of Scientific Revolutions* (1962).[7] Indeed, Foucault suggests that without Canguilhem, the French Marxists like Bourdieu, Castel, Passeron, and Lacan, would have less meaning for us (pp. 465–466)—a hefty claim on Foucault's part. In addition, Foucault suggests that Canguilhem (and others) played the same role in France that the Frankfurt School played elsewhere (p. 469)—another strong claim. Thus, both of these claims indicate how significant Foucault thinks Canguilhem's intellectual role was for him and others in France.

Foucault (1994a) argues that both Canguilhem and the Frankfurt School were raising "the same kind of questions" (p. 469), that is,

> questions that must be addressed to a rationality [the rationality of science] that aspires to be universal while developing within contingency, [a rationality] that asserts its unity and yet proceeds only through partial modifications, [a rationality[8]] that validates itself by into own supremacy but that cannot be dissociated in its history from the inertias, the dullness, or the coercions that subjugate it. In the history of the sciences in France, as in German Critical Theory, what is to be examined, basically, is a reason [a rationality] whose structural autonomy carries the history of dogmatisms and despotisms along with it—a reason [rationality], therefore, that has a liberating effect only provided it manages to liberate itself. (p. 469)

For those who know of Foucault's archaeologies and his genealogies, these are central themes, and he is saying here that these themes come directly from the work of Canguilhem.

Foucault (1994a) suggests that in taking up these questions, Canguilhem "did not just broaden the field of the history of the sciences; he reshaped the discipline itself on a number of essential points" (p. 470). To accomplish this, Foucault relates that Canguilhem "first took up the theme of 'discontinuity'" (p. 470), a theme that many who use Foucault in education and the social sciences think came from Foucault himself. Second, Canguilhem developed the idea that "whoever says 'history of discourse' is also saying recursive method . . . in the sense in which successive transformations of this truthful discourse constantly produce reworkings in their own history" (p. 472). In other words, science or universal reason, contrary to the typical or dominant portrayal of these, has constantly, in a recursive fashion, rewritten its own story, although leaving that rewriting unmentioned (which is another idea that many think came from Foucault himself). Third, Canguilhem places the "sciences of life back into [the] historico-epistemological perspective, [thus bringing] to light a certain number of essential traits that make their development [i.e., the development of the sciences of life] different from that of the other sciences and present historians [of the sciences and, thus, of reason] with specific problems" (p. 475) because all sciences are, in the dominant portrayal, supposed to be unified or the same.

And fourth, Foucault (1994a) said that Canguilhem raised "in a peculiar way, the philosophical question of knowledge" (p. 474). That is, at the center of this philosophical question of the nature of the knowledge of science and universal reason,

> one finds that of error. For, at the most basic level of life, the processes of coding and decoding give way to a chance occurrence [such as the random play of genes] that, before becoming a disease, a deficiency, or a monstrosity, is something like a disturbance in the informative system, something like a "mistake" . . . [and] that "error" [or mistake] constitutes not a neglect or a delay of the promised fulfillment [of life] but the dimension peculiar to the life of human beings and indispensable to the duration of the species. (p. 476)

That is, Canguilhem and Foucault are raising to a philosophical level their contention that, at the physical level of life itself, there is random error that is integral to life itself, a point that is intended, as are the other points previously noted, to undermine the dominant portrayal of science and reason.[9] As Foucault (1994a), then, suggests at the end of this chapter, in recognition of the importance of his mentor's work, especially for Foucault's own work, "Should not the whole theory of the subject be reformulated, seeing that knowledge, rather than opening onto the truth of the world, is deeply rooted in the 'errors' of life?"[10] Thus, once it is understood that it was Canguilhem who developed these four "essential points," it is obvious from whom Foucault himself drew some of his richest intellectual resources, especially for his archaeological method. Consequently, in our view, those who use Foucault throughout the social sciences need to increase their understandings of the French intellectual context in which Foucault thought and wrote and of Canguilhem in particular (see, e.g., Canguilhem, 1988, 1989).

The Archaeological Method

The first point that is important to understand about Foucault's archaeological method is that it is *not* directly related to the academic discipline of archaeology, that is, the study of past cultures. It is not even particularly useful to be reminded of the iconic picture of the archaeologist using a brush to uncover old bones or artifacts embedded in dirt. As Foucault (1969/1972) says on this subject in *The Archaeology of Knowledge,* his archaeology "does not relate analysis to geological excavation" (p. 131). In fact, we would recommend that you begin to understand Foucault's archaeology by assuming that his archeology has only the faintest allusion to the academic discipline of archaeology. It is not that there are not connections between the two; it is just that thinking of the academic discipline as a lens through which one might understand the shape and meaning of Foucault's archaeology will generally get in your way.

A second point is that there is simply not enough space here to describe archaeology in a comprehensive way. Foucault's archaeology is a complex set of concepts, including *savoir, connaissance,* positivity, enunciations, statements, archive, discursive formation, enunciative regularities, correlative spaces, enveloping theory, level, limit, periodization, division, event, discontinuity, and discursive practices. In addition, there is no book that we know of—and it would certainly take a book-length piece—that completely and thoroughly lays out how to use this method, although Foucault's "Introduction" in *The Archaeology of Knowledge,* which follows three of his archaeologies, is a good synopsis of what he is after with archaeology.[11] Consequently, the only way you can begin to understand archaeology is to study carefully and thoroughly Foucault's own uses and discussions of archaeology in his three archaeologies—*Madness and Civilization* (1961/1988), *The Birth of the Clinic* (1963/1994b), and *The Order of Things* (1966/1973a)—and in his reflexive discussion of archaeology as a method, *The Archaeology of Knowledge* (1969/1972). We would especially suggest—and this applies to reading all of Foucault—that getting an in-depth understanding of Foucault requires close, careful, and repeated readings. Indeed, in our view, reading most education or social science texts, even many of the most abstract theorists, is simple and easy compared with reading the density and complexity of Foucault's work, some of which is a function of his writing style, our lack of knowledge of the French philosophy context, our inexperience in reading philosophy of any kind, the depth at which he worked, and the complexity that he was trying to address, much of which is counter to both dominant thought and critical thought. Obviously, though, we think the time and effort needed is worth it. We want to repeat, however, that a substantive use of Foucault's archaeology, in particular, means developing an in-depth understanding of the complex interrelated set of the concepts listed previously.

Two of the more commonly cited of this set of concepts are *savoir* and *connaissance.* In an interview (Foucault, 1994a) that appeared in French in 1966, after the publication of *Madness and Civilization, The Birth of the Clinic,* and *The Order of Things* but before that of *The Archaeology of Knowledge,* Foucault discussed how he defined archaeology:

> By "archaeology," I would like to designate not exactly a discipline but a domain of research, which would be the following: in a society, different bodies of learning, philosophical ideas, everyday opinions, but also institutions, commercial practices and police activities, mores—all refer to a certain implicit knowledge [*savoir*] special to this society. This knowledge is profoundly different from the [formal] bodies of learning [*des connaissances*] that one can find in scientific books, philosophical theories, and religious justifications, but it [*savoir*] is what makes possible at a given moment the appearance of a theory, an opinion, a practice. (p. 261)

Thus, understanding these two arenas of knowledge, *savoir* and *connaissance,* is fundamental to understanding archaeology. *Savoir* includes formal knowledge such as "philosophical ideas" but also "institutions, commercial practices, and police activity,"[12] whereas *connaissance* includes only formal bodies of knowledge such as "scientific books, philosophical theories, and religious justifications." Similarly, Gutting (1989) suggests, "By *connaissance* he [Foucault] means . . . any particular body of knowledge such as nuclear physics, evolutionary biology, or Freudian psychoanalysis" (p. 251). In contrast, *savior,* Gutting continues, "refers to the [broad] discursive conditions that are necessary for the development of *connaissance*" (p. 251).

Foucault provides an example of the difference between these two concepts in the sixth chapter of *The Archaeology of Knowledge* (1969/1972). He says,

> The linch-pin of *Madness and Civilization* was the appearance at the beginning of the nineteenth century of a psychiatric discipline. This discipline had neither the same content, nor the same internal organization, nor the same place in medicine, nor the same practical function, nor the same methods as the traditional chapter on "diseases of the head" or "nervous diseases" to be found in eighteenth century medical treaties. (p. 179)

With this section, Foucault is comparing the psychiatric discipline that emerged at the beginning of the 1800s to the "diseases of the head" and "nervous diseases" of the 1700s because diseases of the head and nervous diseases during the 18th century were the closest comparison to the psychiatric discipline during the 19th century.[13] Foucault (1969/1972) continues,

> But on examining this new discipline, we discovered two things: what made it [i.e., the emerging discipline of psychiatry] possible at the time it appeared, what brought about this great change [i.e., changes from 18th-century diseases of the head to 19th-century psychiatry] in the economy of concepts, analyses, and demonstrations was a whole set of relations between [sic] hospitalization, internment, the conditions and procedures of social exclusion, the rules of jurisprudence, the norms of industrial labor and bourgeois morality, in short a whole group of relations that characterized for this discursive practice [i.e., psychiatry] the formation of its statements. (p. 179)

What made it possible, then, for psychiatry to appear as a formal discipline, as a *connaissance,* was a set of changes in concepts, practices, procedures, institutions, and norms, that is, a change in the much broader *savoir.* As Foucault (1969/1972) further elaborates,

> But this [discursive] practice is not only manifested in a discipline [i.e., psychiatry] possessing a scientific status and scientific pretensions [*connaissance* or psychiatry as a formal discipline]; it is also found in the operation in legal texts, in literature, in philosophy, in political decisions, and in the statements made and the opinions expressed in daily life [*savoir*]. (p. 179)

Thus, whereas the history of psychiatry is typically written solely in terms of psychiatry as a formal discipline, "possessing a scientific status and scientific pretensions," Foucault is arguing that this is inadequate. To better understand the history of psychiatry as a formal academic discipline, it is also necessary to study a much broader array that includes relations among "hospitalization, internment, the conditions and procedures of social exclusion, the rules of jurisprudence, the norms of industrial labor and bourgeois morality" as well as legal texts, literature, philosophy, political decisions, and the statements and opinions of daily life.

For Foucault (1994a), then, archaeology is focused on the study of *savoir,* which is "the condition of possibility[14] of [formal] knowledge [*connaissance*]" (p. 262) for the purpose of showing that psychiatry or other formal disciplines do not simply emerge out of the historical trajectory of those disciplines when that history is restricted solely to the formal discipline as a formal discipline. Instead, a history of a formal discipline must address both *connaissance,* the formal statements of a discipline, and *savoir,* the much broader and less rational array of practices, policies, procedures, institutions, politics, everyday life, and so on. However, Foucault's larger point is that, rather than the traditional view that formal knowledges (*connaissance*), such as psychiatry and economics, have their own formal rational trajectory of emergence, formal knowledges emerge more "irrationally" or not rationally from *savoir,* which includes not just the formal and rational but also the much broader "irrationality" of politics, institutional practices, popular opinions, and so on. In other words, formal knowledges emerge, substantially, from a broad array of complex irrational sources or conditions, and this more complex, messier, more ambiguous "condition[s] of possibility" undermines the modernist rational "story" or "meta-narrative" of formal knowledges.[15]

Accordingly, after understanding the meanings of *connaissance and savoir* and the fact that archaeology is the study of *savoir* as the "condition[s] of possibility" of *connaissance,* it is necessary to return to the larger context of Foucault's archaeological work. With archaeology, Foucault is drawing on the work of Canguilhem, whose work he compared to that of the Frankfurt School. And for both the Frankfurt School and Canguilhem, the nature of reason—"a rationality that aspires to be universal" (Foucault, 1994a, p. 469)—in modernity is their macro text. Furthermore, Foucault is suggesting that the myth or master narrative of modernist reason, when examined carefully, is not just logical and rational but also complex, contradictory, and problematic and that it has embedded within it instances of what we might call "unreason."[16] For example, Foucault says that this modernist reason "validates itself by its own supremacy but that cannot be dissociated in its history from the inertias, the dullness, or the coercions that subjugate it" (p. 469) and that it "is a reason whose structural autonomy carries the history of dogmatisms and despotisms along with it" (p. 469). Thus, according to Foucault, reason (i.e., formal knowledges), as it is typically portrayed within modernity, is not what it is made out to be; that is, the "archaeological" history of reason includes inertias, dullness, coercions, dogmatisms, and despotisms.

What Foucault is attempting, then, with his various archaeologies is to examine specific cases, particular examples, as in *Madness and Civilization, The Birth of the Clinic,* and *The Order of Things* (the human sciences), of the work of reason. And in carrying out these studies of specific cases of the work of reason, he has come to two insights. One is that the history of reason in these specific cases is "not wholly and entirely that of its progressive refinement, its continuously increasing rationality" (Foucault, 1969/1972, p. 4)[17]; that is, reason in these cases does not become progressively more refined, more rational, better, or more true. For example, in the psychiatry example cited previously, Foucault argues that there was no smooth, unbroken trajectory of psychiatry from the 1700s to the 1800s. Instead, he argues, during the 1700s, there was "the traditional chapter on 'diseases of the head' or 'nervous diseases' to be found in eighteenth century medical treatises," and then, at the beginning of the 1800s, there was the emergence of the "psychiatric discipline" (p. 179). However, and this is one of Foucault's key points about reason, the second did not emerge, rationally or logically, out of the first; the two—diseases of the head and nervous diseases, on the one hand, and the discipline of psychiatry, on the other—were separate and different, and the first did not lead logically and progressively to the second. There is, thus, a "discontinuity (threshold, rupture, break, mutation, transformation)" (p. 2) between the two, which again means that reason is not nearly as rational as it has been portrayed within the metanarrative of modernity. Thus, rather than just critiquing this master narrative, in his archaeologies, Foucault is doing the hard work of providing research-based examples that the master narrative is wrong.

Foucault's second point is that disciplines, formal knowledges, or *connaissances* cannot be studied and understood in just their own formal terms. Rather, a *connaissance* emerges out of *savoir,* which includes formal knowledge, such as academic books, but also institutions, laws, processes and procedures, common opinions, norms, rules, morality, commercial practices, and so on. Thus, to understand a particular discipline means that not only must the formal treatises of that discipline be studied, but so too must the *savoir,* this much broader, more complex context that includes, say, institutions and commercial practices "on the same plane" as the formal aspects of the discipline. As a result, reason loses much of its elite exaltedness, its purity, its high status, its very rationality.

However, problematizing modernity's reason is not Foucault's only focus in his archaeologies. His "twin" focus is modernity's subject (Foucault, 1969/1972, p. 12). As he says,

> Making historical analysis the discourse of the continuous [e.g., portraying formal knowledge, *connaissance,* as emerging through a rational, logical, continuous trajectory] and making human consciousness [i.e., the human subject or subjectivity] the *original* subject of *all* historical development and *all* action are the two sides of the same system of thought [i.e., modernity]. (p. 12, emphases added)

Thus, Foucault is arguing that the idea that "man" or the human subject is creating human history and creating, most importantly, formal knowledge (*connaissance*) in a logical, rational, continuous manner is but the ideology of modernity. This ideology, then, becomes a lens through which historians, philosophers, economists, linguists, social scientists, and so on fashion or construct a "picture" or representation of "reality" that is logical and rational and that has the human subject as its main actor or at its privileged center. In addition, this central actor is contradictorily both the doer and the object of the doing, the researcher and the researched. To Foucault, then, this modernist ideology and its resultant representation of "reality" in works of history, philosophy, economy, psychiatry, language, and so on can be undermined by using his archaeological methodology to show that formal knowledges emerge from *savoir,* which is not logical or rational, and that this process of emergence does not have a guiding or agentic subject at its center (i.e., archaeology decenters the modernist subject). For example, near the end of his "Introduction" to *The Archaeology of Knowledge* (Foucault, 1969/1972)—again, the last of his archaeological works—he says that the aim of archaeology is "to define a method of historical analysis *freed* from the anthropological [i.e., human subject-centered] theme" and "a method purged of all anthropologism" (p. 16, emphasis added)—a method of historical analyses freed from "man" as its center.

However, despite Foucault's (1969/1972) view that problematizing reason and the agentic subject are "two sides of the same system of thought" (p. 12), for the most part, those who have used Foucault have been more interested in his undermining of modernist reason than in his undermining of the privileged or centered subject. Indeed, some feminists and critical theorists[18] have rejected Foucault because, in their view, he destroys the agency of the subject, whereas others have appropriated parts of Foucault, such as his problematization of reason, while rejecting his decentering of the subject (e.g., Hartsock, 1998). However, other feminists, such as Butler (1993), have agreed with Foucault that the "two sides" are two parts of the "same system of thought." We agree, though, with Butler that the two cannot be separated, that it is not possible to appropriate the one from Foucault while rejecting the other. Indeed, we would argue that taking one side while rejecting the other indicates a fundamental misunderstanding of Foucault, similar to the general lack of understanding of Foucault's intellectual dependency on the work of Canguilhem and to the general lack of understanding of archaeology as a method. Indeed, we would strongly suggest that to appropriate Foucault's critique of reason without simultaneously appropriating his antihumanism is simply wrong. Foucault's critique of reason cannot stand without his antihumanism; as he says, they are "two sides of the same system of thought" (p. 12).

Our advice, then, for those interested in pursuing archaeology—and we would urge this pursuit as we think that archaeology is generally underused and underappreciated—is this: Do not just "cherry pick" a concept here and a concept there and assume that you are doing archaeology or that you are using Foucault appropriately. To learn how to do archaeology, we would suggest reading all of the archaeologies in the order they were published. The first three are actual applications of archaeology, and the fourth, *The Archaeology of Knowledge* (1969/1972), is Foucault's reflexive effort to describe the methodology retrospectively. However, it is important to understand that, as Foucault says of *The Archaeology of Knowledge*, "This work is not an exact description of what can be read in *Madness and Civilization, Naissance de la clinique* [*The Birth of the Clinic*], or *The Order of Things*. It is different on many points. It also includes a number of corrections and internal criticisms" (p. 16). Despite these corrections and criticisms, *The Archaeology of Knowledge* is his best, and final, description of archaeology as a method. Unfortunately, we know of no book, or even article-length work (we doubt an article-length effort would be sufficient), that attempts to actually explain how to use archaeology as a method. There are, though, some works that, at least partially, focus on or critique archaeology, including Gutting's *Michel Foucault's Archaeology of Scientific Reason* (1989). Books like these are helpful, but reading Foucault's four archaeological texts carefully and thoroughly is by far the best approach.

Connecting Archaeology and Genealogy

Is genealogy the successor to archaeology? Is genealogy the further development of archaeology? Is genealogy superior to archaeology? Did Foucault decide that archaeology did not work, was flawed, so he moved on to genealogy, which he considered to be better? Are the two "methodologies" widely different, clearly separate, or are they closely connected, part of the same larger project? Answers to these questions are multiple and divergent among Foucault scholars, both critics and advocates. Our sense is that the dominant, but certainly not the only, conclusion among U.S. scholars of the social sciences, and more specifically among U.S. scholars of education, is that genealogy is superior to archaeology. Partially validating this conclusion is the fact that there are many more instances of these scholars claiming to do genealogies than there are of those claiming to do archaeologies. However, basing our perspective on that of Foucault, we would have to disagree with this conclusion.

In the first of Foucault's "Two Lectures" (1980, *Power/Knowledge*), which was given on January 7, 1976, and which is *after* Foucault had written his four archaeologies and *after* he had written his two genealogies (*Discipline and Punish* and *The History of Sexuality*, Volume 1: *An Introduction*), he says,

> If we were to characterize it in two terms, then "archaeology" would be the appropriate methodology of this analysis of local discursivities, and "genealogy" would be the tactics whereby, on the basis of the descriptions of these local discursivities, the subjected knowledges which were thus released would be brought into play. (p. 85)

Also, in an interview just prior to his death on June 25, 1984, in Paris,[19] Foucault hopes that other scholars will continue to use both archaeology and genealogy, as he continues to consider both of them equally useful. Most tellingly, though, is what Foucault says in *The History of Sexuality*, Volume 2: *The Use of Pleasure* (1984/1990), which was published the year he died. Three times in this "Introduction" (on pages 4–5, 5–6, and 11–12), Foucault divides his work into three "axes" (p. 4) or arenas of analyses; he also labels these three "theoretical shifts" that he had to make to study "the games of truth" (p. 6). The first is "the analysis of discursive practices [that] made it possible to trace the formation of disciplines (*saviors*)" (p. 4), that is, archaeology. The second is "the analysis of power relations and their technologies" (p. 4), that is, genealogy. And the third is "the modes according to which individuals are given to recognize themselves as . . . subjects" (p. 5) or "the games of truth in the relationship of self with self and the forming of oneself as a subject" (p. 6), that is, the care of the self work. Then, at the end of this section, he calls these three the "archaeological dimension," the "genealogical dimension," and the "practices of the self," respectively (pp. 11–12).[20]

Unquestionably, then, Foucault himself does not see archaeology as less than genealogy or as superseded by it. Instead, throughout his work, he sees both archaeology and genealogy as continuing to be important and valid. Where, then, does this conclusion that genealogy is a correction of archaeology come from for U.S. scholars? We would suggest that it comes mainly from Dreyfus and Rabinow in their highly influential *Michel Foucault: Beyond Structuralism and Hermeneutics,* first published in 1983 when U.S. scholars were just beginning to read Foucault.[21] As a result, these two scholars, from early on, have been enormously influential in introducing both Foucault and his work to U.S. scholars; indeed, it could be said that they have been virtually canonical in their interpretations, at least for the U.S. audience. For example, that they think genealogy is the superior successor to archaeology is evident in their "Introduction" to their book. They say that they "will argue at length [about 40% of the book] that the project of *Archaeology* founder[ed]" (p. xxiv, emphasis in original) and that Foucault abandoned it (p. xxvi). They also say, at the end of their analysis of archaeology, that their "detailed study of the new archaeological method has revealed . . . that it suffers from several internal strains" (p. 90). In response, then, to the failure of archaeology, they assert that Foucault, based on "his reading of Nietzsche" (p. xxvii), developed genealogy, which Dreyfus and Rabinow claim is "his most original contribution" (p. xxvii). However, although Foucault never directly corrected them (as far as we can find), possibly because Dreyfus and Rabinow were leading the charge in touting Foucault and his work to a large U.S. audience, Foucault persisted throughout his life in maintaining the equal value and validity of archaeology and genealogy. Thus, siding with Foucault, along with others such as Mahon (1992), we think that both of his methodologies—archaeology and genealogy—should continue to be seen as equally useful and valuable.

To further illustrate this point and to draw increased attention to what we think is a critically important essay, we now discuss "Nietzsche, Genealogy, History" (Foucault, 1977, 1994a), which we would suggest can be seen as a bridge between Foucault's archaeological period and his genealogical one. Although "Nietzsche, Genealogy, History" was published in English in 1977 in *Language, Counter-Memory, Practice: Selected Essays and Interviews,* it was actually first published in French in 1971 after Foucault finished publishing his four archaeologies but before he published his two genealogies. However, it is now available, in a better version in our view,[22] in *Aesthetics, Method, and Epistemology,* Volume 2 (1998), and one of the improvements in this latter version is that it better connects this essay to his archaeological work, especially in the use of two key archaeological terms, *savoir* and *connaissance.* In this essay, Foucault provides his first description of his genealogical method, but throughout the essay he clearly maintains the connection of his second method, genealogy, to his first one, archaeology.

In "Nietzsche, Genealogy, History" (Foucault, 1994a), although his language is often literary and poetic, playing off of specific quotes and issues in Nietzsche's own works, particularly *The Genealogy of Morals,* Foucault makes four strong claims as to what a genealogist does (although it would be easy to argue that there are five, six, seven, or more such claims throughout the piece). One claim, drawn directly from Nietzsche, is that the genealogist "challenge[s] the pursuit of the origin" (p. 371). For Foucault and Nietzsche, "the pursuit of the origin" is the pursuit, largely in philosophy, history, and the social sciences, of the beginning of some phenomena or categories such as "values, morality, asceticism, and knowledge" (p. 373). Foucault says that this pursuit is "an attempt to capture the exact essence of things, their purest possibilities, and their . . . original identity" (p. 371). Instead, by refusing "metaphysics" and by listening to "history," the genealogist finds that "there is 'something altogether different' behind things: not a timeless and essential secret but the secret that they [things] have no essence, or that their essence was fabricated in a piecemeal fashion from alien forms" (p. 371). Foucault also says, "What is found at the historical beginning of things is not inviolable identity of their origin, it is the dissension of other things. It is disparity" (pp. 371–372). It is the "vicissitudes of history" (p. 373). For example, he says that by

> examining the history of reason, he [the genealogist] learns that it [reason] was born . . . from chance; [that] devotion to truth and the precision of scientific methods arose from the passion of scholars, their reciprocal hatred, their fanatical and unending discussions, and their spirit of competition—the personal conflicts that slowly forged the weapons of reason. (p. 371)

Thus, the target of Foucault's critique, his genealogy, much like with this archaeological work, is the foundational assumptions of Western modernity. In this case, his critical focus is on modernity's teleological assumption that history moves upward or forward from some origin. In contrast, he argues that the genealogist finds that there are no such origins and that origins are often fabricated. What the genealogist finds, instead, as she or he explores origins is randomness, piecemeal fabrications, dissension, disparity, passion, hatred, competition, "details and accidents" (Foucault, 1998, p. 373), "petty malice" (p. 373), "the minute deviations—or conversely, the complete reversals—the errors, the false appraisals, and the faulty calculations" (p. 374) (similar to *savoir*) mixed together with devotion to truth, precise methods, scientific discussions, and so on (similar to *connaissance*). In other words, Foucault is not denying that reason is a part of this history, but it is only one player amid a much broader cast in the dramaturgy of modernity.

A second focus of the genealogist, one that becomes much more important in later works although not a large one in this essay, is the body. Foucault (1998) says, "The body is the inscribed surface of events (traced by language and dissolved by ideas), the locus of a dissociated Self (adopting the illusion of a substantial unity), and a volume in perpetual disintegration" (p. 375). He, then, indicates that "genealogy is . . . thus situated within the articulation of the body and history. Its take is to expose a body totally imprinted by history" (pp. 375–376). This last sentence is key; the "take" of genealogy is "to expose a body totally imprinted by history." However, these few remarks are the extent of Foucault's effort to connect genealogy to the body in this essay, but he returns to this particular focus in subsequent scholarship. For example, in *Discipline and Punish,* Foucault (1975/1979) says,

> The body is also directly involved in the political field; power relations have an immediate hold upon it; they invest it, mark it, train it, torture it, force it to carry out tasks, to perform ceremonies, to emit signs. This political investment of the body is bound up, in accordance with complex reciprocal relations, with its economic use; it is largely as a force of production that the body is invested with relations of power and domination; but, on the other hand, its constitution as labour power is possible only if it is caught up in a system of subjection (in which need is also a political instrument system meticulously prepared, calculated, and used); the body becomes a useful force only if it is both a productive body and subjected body. (pp. 25–26)

This focus on the body has inspired numerous philosophers, especially feminists such as Elizabeth Grosz and Nancy Fraser, who assert that the body has been left out of philosophy. For example, Grosz (1994) says in *Volatile Bodies: Toward a Corporeal Feminism* that she intends to "explore the work of theorists of corporeal instruction, primarily Nietzsche, Foucault, and Deleuze and Guattari," because each "explores the position of the body as a site of the subject's social production" (p. xiii).

A third claim that Foucault (1998) makes for the genealogist is a focus on describing "the various systems of subjection" (p. 376) and "the endlessly repeated play of dominations" (p. 377). For example, he says that "the domination of certain men over others leads to the differentiation of values" and that "class domination generates the idea of liberty" (p. 377). He also says that domination

> establishes marks of its power and engraves memories on things and even within bodies. It makes itself accountable for debts and gives rise to the universe of rules, which is by no means designed to temper violence, but rather to satisfy it. (p. 377)

Foucault is arguing here that the modernist rationale for debts, rules, laws, and the current social, economic, governmental, and legal arrangements diverts critical attention from its domination and subjection effects. For example, he says that

> the law is a calculated and relentless pleasure, delight in promised blood, which permits the perpetual instigation of new dominations and the staging of meticulously repeated scenes of violence. The desire for peace, the serenity of compromise, and the tacit acceptance of the law, far from representing a major moral conversion or a utilitarian calculation that gave rise to the law, are but its result and, in point of fact, its perversion. (p. 378)

Foucault follows this with a direct quote from Nietzsche's *Genealogy of Morals:* "guilt, conscience, and duty had their threshold of emergence in the right to secure obligations and their inception, like that of any major event on earth, saturated in blood" (p. 378). Foucault then concludes that

> humanity does not gradually progress from combat to combat until it arrives at universal reciprocity, where the rule of law finally replaces warfare; humanity installs each of its violences in a system of rules and thus proceeds from domination to domination. (p. 378)

Foucault thus contends that the rationales that support modernity as humane and as becoming more so are false and that, instead, modernity is but a new installation of domination and violence as a "system of rules." For example, schools, the prison system, commerce, and so on are installations of domination and violence masquerading as systems of rules, and it is the work of the genealogist to describe and reveal this domination and violence.

The final focus of the genealogist that we take from this essay is drawn from what Foucault calls "effective history." Foucault's (1998) critique of traditional history or the "history of historians" (p. 380) is what he calls "effective history." This critique is "without [the] constants" of traditional history. Foucault argues,

> The traditional devices for constructing a comprehensive view of history and for retracing the past as a patient and continuous development must be systematically dismantled. Necessarily, we must dismiss those tendencies which encourage the consoling play of recognitions. Knowledge [*savoir*], even under the banner of history, does not depend on "rediscovery of ourselves." (p. 380, brackets and emphasis in original)

Once again, the now familiar targets of Foucault's critique are the same foundational assumptions of modernity. The regime of traditional history is one that constructs "a comprehensive view of history," retraces "the past as a patient and continuous development," "encourages the consoling play of recognitions," dissolves "the singular event into an ideal continuity" (Foucault, 1998, p. 380), asserts that history is controlled by "destiny or regulative mechanisms" (p. 381), and "confirm[s] our belief that the present rests upon profound intentions and immutable necessities" (p. 381).

In response to this regime,

> History becomes "effective" to the degree that it introduces discontinuity into our very being—as it divides our emotions, dramatizes our instincts, multiplies our body, and sets it against itself. Effective history leaves nothing around the self, deprives the self of the reassuring stability of life and nature, and it will not permit itself to be transported by a voiceless obstinacy toward a millennial ending. It will uproot its traditional foundations and relentlessly disrupt its pretended continuity. (Foucault, 1998, p. 380)

Also, "'Effective' history differs from the history of historians in being without constants" (p. 380):

> "Effective" history . . . deals with events in terms of their most unique characteristics; there most acute manifestations. An [historical] event, consequently, is not a decision, a treaty, a reign, or a battle, but the reversal of relationship of forces, the usurpation of power, the appropriation of vocabulary turned against those who had once used it, a domination that grows feeble, poisons itself, grows slack. (pp. 380–381)

This "effective" historical sense "confirms our existence among countless lost events, without a landmark or a point of reference" (Foucault, 1998, p. 381). Finally, it is an "affirmation of a perspectival knowledge [*savoir*]," as traditional "historians take unusual pains to erase the elements in their work which reveal their grounding in a particular time and place" (p. 382). In a sense, then, Foucault is making an argument that traditional (modernist) history is an effort to console ourselves with the assumptions that there is unity, continuity, teleology, meaning, destiny, and so on built into history itself, a view that makes us feel safe or that would make "history" our safe harbor. In critique of the latter modernist and humanist view, Foucault argues that this aspect of traditional history is predominantly dependent on a metaphysics (p. 381), a kind of modernist psychosis or spell, that hides the fact that history is "the luck of the battle," the "randomness of events," "a profusion of entangled events," "a 'host of errors and phantasms' [a quote from Nietzsche]," and "countless lost events" (p. 381).

The work, then, of the genealogist in this bridging essay between archaeology and genealogy is fourfold. The genealogist is to critique the pursuit of origins by showing they are fabrications, to show that the body is "imprinted by history" (Foucault, 1998, p. 376), to describe "systems of subjection" (p. 376) and "the endlessly repeated play of dominations" (p. 377), and to do what Foucault calls "effective history." We now turn, after this explication of this bridging essay, to his two genealogies, which did immediately follow his "Nietzsche, Genealogy, History" (Foucault, 1977/1994a) bridging essay. To accomplish this, we discuss his extensive comments on genealogy in the first of his two genealogies, *Discipline and Punish* (1975/1979), and then end the "Genealogy" section with some brief comments on his second and last genealogy, *The History of Sexuality*, Volume 1: *An Introduction* (1976/1980a).

Genealogy

Discipline and Punish first appeared in French in 1975, was translated into English by Alan Sheridan in 1977, and finally was published by Vintage Books in 1979, which is the version we are using. Although there is much in this book that is provocative and uncomfortable reading, such as Foucault's well-researched descriptions of torture used by the French penal system prior to the contemporary period,[23] we focus here primarily on what Foucault has to say about *doing* genealogy. As with his archaeologies, another of the many similarities between his archaeological work and his genealogical work,[24] Foucault is comparing one period with another period. For example, he says that during the second period, "in Europe and in the United States, the entire economy of punishment was redistributed. [There was] a new theory of law and crime, a new moral or political justification, old laws were abolished, old customs died out" (Foucault, 1975/1979, p. 7). "By the end of the eighteenth and the beginning of the nineteenth century" (p. 8), the old penal style was dying out.

During this new period, then, "punishment has become an economy of suspended rights. . . . As a result a . . . whole army of technicians took over from the executioner, the immediate anatomist of pain: warders, doctors, chaplains, psychiatrists, psychologists, educationalists" (Foucault, 1975/1979, p. 11). And the consequence of this change seemingly was a "reduction in the penal severity," "a phenomenon with which legal historians are well acquainted" (p. 16)—"less cruelty, less pain, more kindness, more respect, more 'humanity'" (p. 16). However, not surprisingly, Foucault is going to critique "the new tactics of power" (p. 23) of this liberal progressive view of less cruelty and pain. For example, he is going to argue that the penal system had become "a strange scientifico–juridical complex," the focus of which is now the soul rather than the body (p. 19), which, to some extent, Foucault considers a more oppressive focus than that of the old penal regime. He is also going to argue that the ultimate target of this complex "is not simply a judgment of guilt. . . . It bears within it an assessment of normality and a technical prescription for a possible normalization" (pp. 20–21), which applies throughout society rather than just to criminals. In other words, to Foucault, one effect of the new penal regime is not to punish the criminal but rather to normalize the larger population in terms of correct behavior.

Foucault (1975/1979), then, says that *Discipline and Punish* "is intended as a correlative history of the modern soul and of a new power to judge; a genealogy of the present scientifico–legal complex from which the power to punish derives its bases, justifications, and rules" (p. 23). "But from what point can such a history of the modern soul on trial be written?" (p. 23). First, he answers that this cannot be written

> by studying only the general social forms, as Durkheim did, [because] one runs the risk of positing as the principle of greater leniency in punishment processes of individualization that are rather one of the effects of the new tactics of power, among which can be included the new penal mechanisms. (p. 23)

In other words, focusing on the "greater leniency in punishment" in this new penal regime, as if that were a causal principle of the new regime, would be a mistake; instead, this "greater leniency" should be seen as an "effect" of "the new tactics of power."

Immediately thereafter, Foucault (1975/1979) lays out "four general rules" for his genealogical study. Although these four rules are focused specifically on this particular study, they highlight well several areas of possible work for the genealogist. What we do here, then, is present each of the rules, discuss its implications for the genealogist, and briefly speculate as to how it might be applied to some facet of public education. The following is his first rule:

> Do not concentrate the study of the punitive mechanisms on their "repressive" effects alone, on their "punishment" aspects alone, but situate them in a whole series of their possible *positive* effects, even if these seem marginal at first sight. As a consequence, regard punishment as a complex social function. (p. 23, emphasis added)

Foucault wants us to look beyond the obvious "'repressive' effects" of punishment to examine "a whole series of their possible *positive* effects." By positive, though, he does not mean an effect that we might like or approve of; he means something produced rather than something repressed or excluded. For example, as mentioned previously, one "positive" or produced effect of the new penal regime is the normalization of appropriate behavior among the general population. Indeed, one of Foucault's favorite genealogical maneuvers is to focus not just on the negative or repressive effects of power but also on the positive or productive effects of power. To Foucault, power does just exclude or repress; power also produces. However, he is not saying that the repressive effects of power should be ignored by the genealogist; rather, he is arguing that the genealogist should regard "punishment as a complex *social* function" (emphasis added) that includes both the repressive and the productive. For instance, school discipline programs do not just punish (repress) certain student behaviors among a small group of students; they also, and perhaps more importantly, produce a normalization (a "positive" effect) of correct behavior among the rest of the students. Thus, to Foucault, these discipline programs could be said to be both negative (repressive) effects and positive (productive) effects.

Foucault's (1975/1979) second rule is to "analyze punitive methods not simply as consequences of legislation or as indicators of social structures, but as techniques possessing their own specificity in the more general field of other ways of exercising power. Regard punishment as a political tactic" (p. 23). Thus, how social acts or policies get analyzed or thought about is critical to the genealogist. However, the norm of the mainstream social sciences is to see actions that are related to the government as the result of legislative policymakers or other governmental actors, that is, a function of social actors or agents. In contrast, the norm of critical theorists and other structuralists is to see governmental actions as a function of the social structures. Foucault, though, wants us to turn our thinking in a different direction. He wants us—and this is a persistent point he made throughout his career—to see specific acts, procedures, or processes, such as "punitive methods" and school discipline programs, as having a kind of a quasi-independent standing or importance, a "specificity," within "the more general field of other ways of exercising power." They are not just actions of individual agents, and they are not merely functions of something more important and larger, some social structure; these methods or programs need to be looked at by the genealogist as having their own specificity or independent standing. Moreover, by "ways of exercising power," Foucault does not usually mean the power exercised by an intentional actor, although his view encompasses that; instead, he usually means that a procedure or process multiplies across a social field because of a complex set or collection of reasons or causes that are not entirely intentional or rational. Thus, these governmental acts, procedures, or processes are not only or simply a function of legislation or social structures; instead, to the genealogist, they are ways that power multiplies, without some agentic agent consciously accomplishing this, across a social field. For instance, the new emphasis on student-centered classrooms[25] should not be analyzed only as a new and better approach emerging from progressive educational theorists or only as a function of social structures; instead, it should also be analyzed as a practice of power that has emerged and circulates more broadly in society and as a practice of power that is, in many ways, actually more oppressive than teacher-centered classrooms. The reason why Foucault might offer that the new student-centered classrooms are more oppressive is because the work of this new tactic of power is to imprint the souls of the children rather than just their behaviors, as the old teacher-centered classrooms did.

The third rule, and a critically important one to those of us in the social sciences, is as follows:

> Instead of treating the history of penal law and the history of the human sciences as two separate series whose overlapping appears to have had on one [penal law] or the other [the history of the human sciences], or perhaps on both, a disturbing or useful effect, according to one's point of view, see whether there is not some common matrix or whether they do not both derive from a single process of "epistemologico-juridical" formation; in short, make the technology of power the very principle both of the humanization of the penal system and of the knowledge of man. (Foucault, 1975/1979, p. 23)

Thus, the history of penal law, the public educational system, or nursing should not be examined just as a separate, albeit sometimes overlapping, series running parallel to the history of the social sciences but should also be examined as emerging from "some common matrix" or as deriving from a single "process of epistemologico-[fill in the blank with a juridical, educational, or medical] formation." Again, as with the second rule, the principal focus of the genealogist should be on the technologies of power and the ways that the same technology of power spreads across and is enacted both within particular systems, such as those of prisons, schools, or hospitals, and in the social sciences. Thus, technologies of power, arising out of a "common matrix" or a "'epistomologico-[fill in the blank]' formation," may multiply across both particular systems and social sciences in general, and this multiplication is likely to be both intentional and unintended, both rational and not rational. For example, we might find that contemporary public education—its practices, procedures, and policies—and the history of education scholarship, its research, and its theories have emerged from the same "common matrix" or the same epistemologico-educational formation. Although this seems to be a less radical assertion than Foucault's similar assertion about penal systems, it is important to understand that he does not simply mean that both contemporary public education and education scholarship share the same general assumptions about schools or education; instead, he means that there is a more primary matrix or formation that is not necessarily intentionally or rationally created, and that is not necessarily education oriented, out of which both are emerging. For example, perhaps, on genealogical investigation, both the new movement emphasizing student-oriented classrooms and the growth of qualitative research methodologies arise out of the same "pastoral" matrix or formation (e.g., see Foucault's use of the concept of the pastoral in *The History of Sexuality,* Volume 1: *An Introduction* [1976/1980a]).

Foucault's (1975/1979) fourth rule is as follows:

> Try to discover whether this entry of the soul on to the scene of penal justice, and with it the insertion in legal practice of a whole corpus of "scientific" knowledge, is not the effect of a transformation of the way in which the body itself is invested by power relations.
>
> In short, try to study the metamorphosis of punitive methods on the basis of a political technology of the body in which might be read a common history of power relations and object relations. Thus, by an analysis of penal leniency as a technique of power, one might understand both how man, the soul, [and] the normal or abnormal individual have come to duplicate crime as objects of penal intervention and in what way a specific mode of subjection was able to give birth to man as an object of knowledge for a discourse with a "scientific" status. (p. 24)

By his use of the word "soul," Foucault means that the focus of the new penal system is "not only on what they [the criminals] *do* but also on what they *are, will be, may be*" (p. 18, emphases added); that is, the new focus is not on their behavior but rather on their being or their selves. The new penal perspective has "taken to judging something other than crimes, namely, the 'soul' of the criminal" (p. 19). Then, this new focus on the "soul" of the criminal is combined with a new "corpus of 'scientific' knowledge," *both* of which are the "effect of a transformation of the way in which the body itself is invested by power relations." It is, as Foucault says, "a political technology of the body." Thus, what is generally seen as more humane and more liberal (i.e., "penal leniency"), in this case, is argued by Foucault to be but "a new technique of power," one in which "the body itself is invested by power relations." And he indicates that he sees this change as another example of the modernist social construction of "man [or the subject] as an object of knowledge for a discourse with 'scientific' status."[26] An example of this in education might be a consideration of "site-based management," "distributive leadership," and "community of learners," all of which are generally seen as more humane or more democratic approaches to school leadership or governance, as new "techniques of power" that are not just endemic to education but also part of a larger formation, the effect of which might be seen as a worse oppression at the level of the soul. In other words, these new techniques of power in education focus on controlling or managing the "soul" of educators rather than just their behaviors, which, to Foucault, is much more oppressive than techniques of power that seek to control only behaviors.

Although we find these four rules to be a particularly rich source for understanding the work of the Foucaultian genealogist, they certainly do not exhaust *Discipline and Punish* in terms of what the work of a genealogist is. For example, we find the entire last section of the same chapter that contains the four rules (Foucault, 1975/1979, pp. 16–31) to be a particularly exciting discussion of genealogy. We also have a strong appreciation for (a) the "The Composition of Forces" section (pp. 162–169) in the chapter, titled "Docile Bodies," which includes some direct statements about education; (b) the entire chapter titled "The Means of Correct Training," which includes sections on "Hierarchical Observation," "Normalizing Judgments," and "The Examination" as well as some direct comments on education; and (c) the last chapter, "The Carceral," which is another particularly rich and provocative section in *Discipline and Punish.* In contrast, we are not as enamored as many are with the chapter on "Panopticism," as we find it to be one of his more simplistic, more totalized, and more poorly developed concepts. Our point, though, is that this first genealogy is literally a panoply of critical tools and ideas that can be used to do Foucaultian genealogies.

Foucault's (1976/1980a) second and last genealogy was *The History of Sexuality,* Volume 1: *An Introduction.* What we do here, given space limitations, is provide just some brief comments and offer some suggestions about reading this volume. Provocatively, and one of the main reasons why we have used more space discussing *Discipline and Punish,* is that the *History of Sexuality* includes little direct discussion of genealogy as a method, whereas *Discipline and Punish* includes considerable discussion of the genealogical method. Indeed, through a systematic search of the text,[27] we found that in his second genealogy, he uses the word "genealogy" only five times (four times in the Introduction and once on p. 171).[28] Nonetheless, in general, in our view, *History of Sexuality* is the better genealogy of the two, more confident, smoother, better worked out, as if he had more deeply integrated the methodology of genealogy by the time he did this second one. It is as if he had worked out his genealogical method in *Discipline and Punish,* whereas in *History of Sexuality* he was applying what he had already worked out. In addition, we particularly recommend "Part Four: The Deployment of Sexuality" section. In many ways, this is the mature Foucault at his best. The writing is excellent, the organization is clear, and, the insights are powerful.[29] It is in this section that Foucault provides some extended discussion of how he thought power differently, what he calls an "analytics" of power (p. 82), as not just negative and repressive but also positive. Even more specifically, we recommend the "Objective" subsection (pp. 81–91) and his discussion at the beginning of the "Method" subsection of "Part Four" (pp. 92–97). Indeed, we would suggest that one of Foucault's greatest contributions to intellectual thought has been his reconceptualization of power, and a good discussion of this reconceptualization is abundantly available in *History of Sexuality.* Finally, however, what generally distinguishes his second method, genealogy, from his first one, archaeology, in our view, is that his archaeological method is dependent on a highly structured, highly interrelated set of constructs, all of which need to be deployed together to actually do an archaeology, whereas his genealogical method is more like a set of critical tools that can be used in any sort of grouping. And it is this difference, we believe, that is one of the chief reasons why the latter is much more appealing to scholars.[30]

Conclusion

Overall, it could be argued that Foucault's archaeological and genealogical work was mainly a critique of the modernist view of the human sciences and of "man" as simultaneously both the human scientist and the object of the human sciences. Then, in his conduct of any particular critique, whether archaeological or genealogical, he almost always takes up one "period" (although his "periods" often do not parallel those of mainstream history) prior to the one (the second period) he will critique and describes this first period to lay the basis for his description and critique of the subsequent period. However, his description of one period, his description of the change from one to the next, and his description of the second period move far beyond the territory typically covered in conventional history. For example, see our comparison of *connaissance* and *savoir* earlier, where *connaissance* covers the conventional territory, whereas *savoir,* which is what Foucault is focused on with both his archaeologies and his genealogies, is much broader, even including social phenomena that seem to have little direct connection to the particular *connaissance.* His point here is that the conventional or traditional view of the formal academic social sciences is but one part of an "effective history" and that when the *savoir* is considered, it becomes much more obvious that the human sciences are much less rational, much more ambiguous, much messier, much more filled with random error, and more driven by the petty jealousies and competitions of social scientists than is conventionally assumed. Thus, if you understand the difference between *connaissance* and *savoir,* and if you understand the fact that Foucault focused mostly on *savoir* as the territory of the archaeologist or the genealogist, you understand a significant piece of what Foucault was up to with his critiques.

A second point he makes with these "period" comparisons is that, contrary to the self-story of modernity that the more recent is more humane, the "modernist" period is actually, when critiqued with an archaeology or a genealogy, worse, more oppressive, more demeaning. For example, whereas the prior penal system tortured bodies, the target of the subsequent one was the soul, not what people do but rather what they are. Thus, Foucault stands as a major critic of Western modernity, particularly calling into question a wide array of "progressive" assumptions that modernity is considerably better, more humane, and more rational than that which came before modernity.

A third focus for Foucault is to decenter "man" as the primary subject of modernity. To Foucault, modernity constructed man, the subject, the agent running the world. It was modernity that fashioned the whole of human life as constructed around and for man, the central subject, the central agentic actor. It was modernity that wrote a history of the progressive rational rise of the human sciences guided by and for man, the central subject. In contrast, Foucault suggests a different and effective history of the human sciences. Based on his critical examination of historical documents, he suggests that, although rationality is part of Western history, there is much, much more that is not rational and that is not guided by any central actor. Indeed, in both his archaeologies and his genealogies, history is not predominantly created by a subject, particularly a logical rational subject who has "his" hands on the guiding wheel of history. Instead, history is created by a complex array of processes, dispersions, procedures, accidents, hatreds, policies, desires, dominations, unintended or uncontrolled circulations of techniques of power, commercial practices, mores, analyses and demonstrations, the norms of industrial labor and bourgeois morality, the endlessly repeated play of dominations, literature, political decisions, discontinuities, opinions expressed in daily life, the fanatical and unending discussions of scholars, randomness, dissensions, petty malice, precise scientific methods, subjected bodies, and faulty calculations, to name but just a few—and man, the subject, is not running this show called history. In addition, he repeatedly points out the contradiction within modernity of simultaneously having man as both the subject and object of history. However, given the dominance of our modernist romanticized view of ourselves as the center of our lives and our society and, given our deep ontological and epistemological attachment to this romanticized view, it is usually ignored or critiqued by scholars while they appropriate other aspects of Foucault's critique of modernity. This, to us, is a serious mistake. His critique of modernity and his critique of the agentic subject at the center are deeply intertwined; thus, separating the two violates Foucault's perspective at the most basic level of his thought.

There are other lesser abuses, and some erroneous readings, of Foucault that we have tried to address or correct. First, Foucault was, by his own words, enormously influenced by Canguilhem and saw Canguilhem and others as playing a role in French intellectual work similar to that which the Frankfurt School played in German intellectual work. Thus, we suggest that Canguilhem and others, such as Gaston Bachelard, should receive increased attention, as themes that Foucault draws from Canguilhem continue through his genealogies. Second, the amount of time and energy that Foucault gave to archaeology was much larger than that which he gave to genealogy. Thus, we suggest that much more attention be given to archaeology. Indeed, there is no legitimate doubt that Foucault continued throughout his life to highly value it as a method, despite what others concluded. Third, again by his own words, genealogy was not seen by Foucault as being superseded by or superior to archaeology. Thus, in comparing the two methods, more attention needs to be given to how Foucault saw the relationship of the two. Fourth, archaeology and genealogy are much less different than is often assumed, and this also could use more attention. Fifth, it was, in our opinion, Dreyfus and Rabinow who were largely responsible for what we see as a distorted view of the relationship of archaeology and genealogy in the United States. Thus, we suggest more problematization of this contention. And sixth, in any considerations of the two methods, the essay on "Nietzsche, Genealogy, History" should receive increased attention, as it is a good bridge that directly connects the two methods.

In this conclusion, we also want to strongly recommend a relatively new collection of Foucault's work. The entire set is called *Essential Works of Foucault, 1954–1984,* and Paul Rabinow is the series editor.[31] The first volume is *Ethics, Subjectivity, and Truth* (1994/1997) and was edited by Rabinow. The second volume is *Aesthetics, Method, and Epistemology* (1994a) and was edited by Faubion. The third volume is *Power* (1994c), and it too was edited by Faubion. In this set, when the English translations provided in it are compared with alternative ones, we consistently find that the translations in this set are superior. In addition, this set thematically groups parts of Foucault's books with some of his articles and interviews. We would suggest that, especially for beginners, this set is an excellent place to start reading Foucault, as it makes Foucault more accessible.

Undeniably, though, whichever books, articles, and interviews are considered, Foucault has left us with an impressive body of work and new methodologies and with a host of powerful analytic concepts, some of which we have tried to introduce to a broader range of readers. We want to end, then, with two more statements. The first is a very brief summary of our take on the use of Foucault in education scholarship. Unfortunately, we do not have space to comment in any detail on the use of Foucault in the social sciences generally or in education, our field, specifically. Indeed, commenting on the uses of Foucault across the social sciences in the United States alone is already probably too large for anything less than a book. Even just the use of Foucault as a primary focus by education scholars, as can be seen in one part of our bibliography, is rather large. However, after reviewing the scholarship in education using Foucault as the main theoretical resource, our conclusion is that a very high percentage of this work engages Foucault's work at only a fairly superficial level.

Probably the most popular use, or abuse, is to cherry pick one concept, such as "panopticon" or "disciplinary society," and then use that one concept within a more traditional critical framework, even though there are epistemological contradictions between Foucault and most U.S. critical theory.[32] In general, we would say this cherry picking is a mistake, as typically the single concept, in its Foucaultian meaning, does not really integrate with the rest of the assumptions in the article or book. Our point is that Foucault's concepts are but aspects of a general epistemological position that needs to be engaged with as a whole. Another similar error that we found in the uses of Foucault's work by U.S. education scholars, as well as by many social scientists, is to adopt his critique of modernity while ignoring his simultaneous critique of subjectivity itself. We are uncomfortable saying this because we sound like we are policing Foucault, but we think that it is simply undeniable that there is a tremendous amount of fairly superficial and ill-informed use of Foucault; in fact, we concluded that many have used his work without ever reading carefully through several volumes of it. Of course, the line between substantive engagements of Foucault and superficial ones can never be securely drawn. Thus, we are decidedly not arguing that we know and can define the canonical Foucault, but we would suggest that a supple use, or even an adequate use, of Foucault requires more than one close reading of any one book, article, or interview. Instead, we would suggest close readings of several books, along with articles and interviews, before trying to use or apply his work. When U.S. scholars do not engage in this kind of in-depth study of Foucault, we would remind them that their ignorance is fairly transparent to those who do study and use Foucault in a more substantive way.

Our second final point is what surprised us the most with our systematic review of Foucault's books. Also, we should say that we were reluctant to make this point, but we decided that we had to for us to maintain the integrity of our recent rereading of all of Foucault's major works in the order that he published them. Before we did this review, we were strong advocates of Foucault's work and not too receptive to the many critiques of his work, as we saw most of them as conscious or unconscious defenses of the foundational assumptions of modernity. What emerged, though, for us is a new openness to one of the main critiques that has been made of Foucault's work. That is, there have been numerous complaints that in Foucault's consideration of the truth regimes of social life, such as those of prisons, the clinic, and sexuality, Foucault's descriptions of these regimes make them relentlessly oppressive, perhaps even totalized, with no way "out" (see, e.g., Hartsock, 1998). Clearly, we cannot go into a lengthy discussion of this critique, nor do we want to debate it at this point. What we can do, however, is strongly suggest that other advocates and persistent users of Foucault need to more openly and more carefully consider this critique. In other words, we would suggest that our experienced Foucault scholars need to engage this critique in a more balanced way and recognize that there is some "validity" to it.

After recently rereading straight through all of his books in the order that he published them, we were truly struck, unexpectedly struck, with how unrelenting Foucault is in his critique of the social forms in which we live. We began to understand what others have concluded about his totalizations of these social forms. We began, for example, to understand where others have concluded that, in his descriptions of penal institutions or the social sciences, there appears to be "no exit." His critique and the described oppression are powerfully unrelenting and do appear to approach a totalization. It is almost as if he has discovered that, for example, the new penal regime is not just a 6-sided cube of oppression and control but also a 500-sided cube and that, in brilliantly describing all of these sides, he leaves us with no recourse, no path for resistance or emancipation. What simultaneously reinforces this is the fact that in his major works, he rarely offers any alternative for resistance or emancipation from the oppression he so thoroughly describes. (See, e.g., Grosz, 1994, who uses Foucault extensively but is simultaneously critical of how unrelenting his lack of alternative spaces and possibilities is; in fact, for us, Grosz exemplifies a balanced, in-depth use of Foucault that is both critical and appreciative.) Thus, for example, while Foucault provides an insightful characterization of the complexity of a discipline or regime, virtually every aspect, every facet, of the new complexity that Foucault describes becomes a critical moment for Foucault so that while he is opening up new perspectives on specific truth regimes, he is also foreclosing, through his totalized critique, the possibility that these new frontiers might become new possibilities or imaginaries.

Of course, we realize that the words "resistance" and "emancipation" are humanist ones arising out of modernity; thus, an advocate for Foucault might say that Foucault's unwillingness to offer any such alternative is simply his maintenance of a consistently anti-humanist-, anti-subject-centered epistemology. However, as Fraser (1989) pointed out some time ago, what is often ignored with Foucault is that much of his language, such as "systems of subjection" (Foucault, 1975/1979, p. 376) and "the endlessly repeated play of dominations" (p. 377), is itself language that is modernist and humanist and that the power Foucault's critiques have for us is a function of our immersion in and attachment to this modernist, humanist language. We would, thus, point out that what we have here is another modernist binary. Accordingly, whereas Foucault powerfully appropriates one side of this binary (e.g., subjection and domination), he largely avoids the other (e.g., resistance and emancipation). This, as Derrida[33] has pointed out so well with his deconstructive methodology, does not mean that the other side of the binary, variously labeled resistance or emancipation, is not equally in play.

Thus, again, we want to suggest that scholars who are advocates of Foucault take this critique more seriously and approach Foucault more the way that Grosz (1994) generally does. However, we are not saying that Foucault never addresses some "positive" change possibilities. We are saying, though, that in all of the archaeologies he overwhelmingly does not and that in *Discipline and Punish* (1975/1979) he largely does not. Also, for the most part in *The History of Sexuality,* Volume 1: *An Introduction* (1976/1980a) he does not, although in this latter work he does begin to talk about countering "the grips of power" with the "rallying point" being "bodies and pleasures" (p. 157). In *The History of Sexuality,* Volume 1, near the end, for example, he says,

> We must not think that by saying yes to sex, one says no to power; on the contrary, one tracks along the course laid out by the general deployment of sexuality [when one says yes to sex]. It is the agency of sex that we must break away from if we aim—through a tactical reversal of the various mechanisms of sexuality—to counter the grips of power with the claims of bodies, pleasures, and knowledges, in their multiplicity and their possibility of resistance. The rallying point for the counterattack against the deployment of sexuality ought not to be sex-desire, but bodies and pleasures. (p. 157)

This is clearly an effort by Foucault to begin to explore resistance and a space of possible change, but this is by far the exception. In fact, some might argue that it is with this work that Foucault's interest in working on resistance and change emerges in the care of the self period that is said to follow the two genealogies. In addition, he was an activist, especially around prison issues, and in his interviews he supported activism while resisting critiques of the lack of activism in his books. For example, in an interview published in an Italian journal in 1978, he said (somewhat defensively, we would say), "I don't construct my analyses in order to say, 'This is the way thing are, you are trapped.' I say these things only insofar as I believe it enables us to transform them" (Foucault, 1994c, pp. 295–295).

However, our point here is that through all of the archaeologies and the first genealogy and even most of the second genealogy, while Foucault is opening up new ways to think about our social world, his unrelenting, almost totalized, critique serves to foreclose how to use those new ways of thinking for resistance, for countering "the grips of power," and for developing spaces of valuable change. To us, this should be a major concern because, in our view, his descriptive accounts of the complexities of disciplines, social arenas, and institutions could as well show that within these complexities, there are almost always spaces for resistance, "counterattack," appropriation, and construction, and this is also a point that Grosz (1994) makes. Similarly, Gubrium and Holstein (2000), in the second edition of this *Handbook,* drawing strongly on Foucault, have tried to develop "an interpretive practice [that] works against [the kind of Foucaultian] totalization that views all interpretations as artifacts of particular regimes of power/knowledge" (p. 501). By raising these criticisms of Foucault, though, we are not trying to be definitive, as that would require a more extended, in-depth discussion of the whole range of critiques of Foucault on this issue. Instead, we are more modestly suggesting, based on our recent systematic read of Foucault, that Foucault advocates, as we ourselves have been, need to take another, more careful, more balanced consideration of this critique of Foucault's work. Or, as Foucault himself said, "The only valid tribute to [anyone's] thought . . . is precisely to use it, to deform it, to make it groan and protest. And if commentators then say that I am being faithful or unfaithful . . . that is of absolutely no interest" (Foucault, 1980b, pp. 53–54).

Nonetheless, even with such reconsiderations, Foucault remains a powerful, innovative intellectual whose work has opened up insightful and provocative avenues of thought, critique, and understanding. Moreover, without a doubt, his work has become enormously influential worldwide. Deleuze (1990/1995), though, said this much more poetically:

> When people follow Foucault, when they're fascinated by him, it's because they're doing something with him, in their own work, in their own independent lives. It's not just a question of [Foucault's] intellectual understanding or agreement, but of intensity, resonance, musical harmony. (p. 86)[34]

Hopefully, our interpretations presented here will add to this influence by helping those who have not yet engaged Foucault to understand where they might begin. We also hope we have been useful and provocative to those who are more experienced friends of Foucault, even if we may have disturbed them a bit with our critical remarks. Whatever the reads of our read, though, we want to *again* and *again* strongly emphasize that our interpretations of Foucault, our comments on the uses and abuses of Foucault in education and the social sciences, our critiques of Foucault and others, and our concluding remarks are not the correct, the best, the authoritative, or the canonical ones. Even if you forget everything else we have written here, do not forget this point. As we said at the beginning of this essay, the comments we offer here are not *true* interpretations of Foucault's work, nor are such interpretations possible in our view. The primary issue to us is how substantive the engagement is, not whether the engagement is the correct one. Thus, whether there is agreement or disagreement with what we have said here, we truly hope that all readers will see this essay as a substantive effort to engage primarily not only with Foucault but also, to a smaller extent, with his users and abusers, his advocates and critics.

Notes

1. Despite the fact that this essay is not a "true" one, we want to thank our reviewers for their suggestions, comments, and criticisms. There is simply no question that this essay was substantively improved due to their responses even when we disagreed with those responses. Those reviewers were Jaber Gubrium, Patti Lather, Bill Black, Elizabeth St. Pierre, Norman Denzin, and Jack Bratich. However, none of them should be held responsible for anything we have written here as we used and abused, agreed and disagreed with, incorporated and ignored their words.

2. The American Psychological Association (APA) style format rule is that the original publication date for a publication in another language precedes the publication date in English, just as we have done it here. However, we wanted to make sure that everyone paid attention to these dates because they are part of a significant point that we are making in this essay.

3. Foucault himself actually calls his archaeologies and genealogies toolboxes: "All my books . . . are little toolboxes, if you will" (Halperin, 1995, p. 52). Thanks to Elizabeth St. Pierre for pointing out this quote.

4. See, for example, Burchell, Gordon, and Miller's *The Foucault Effect: Studies in Governmentality* (1991), Barry, Osborne, and Rose's *Foucault and Political Reason* (1996), and parts of Popkewitz and Brennan's *Foucault's Challenge* (1998).

5. Jaber Gubrium also suggests John Rajchman, Lisa King, and Lee Quimby as doing similar work. We would agree with the Rajchman suggestion, but we are not familiar with the other two. Nonetheless, we think Gubrium knows what he is talking about.

6. See Foucault's "What Is an author?" in *Language, Counter-Memory, Practice* (1977).

7. In other words, we are suggesting to those enamored of and influenced by Kuhn that they should read the work of Canguilhem because, in our view, Canguilhem's work with the history of sciences is much more impressive, much more substantive, than that of Kuhn.

8. Throughout this essay, when we quote Foucault, we add words or phrases in brackets to help readers follow his meaning. Foucault often writes in long sentences and is often not clear with his referents or words he substitutes for other words. Thus, reading Foucault typically requires paying very close attention to his meaning as a sentence or paragraph progresses. Our added brackets are intended, then, to help readers follow his meaning more easily.

9. It is certainly easy to imagine the good uses to which Lincoln and Guba could have put Canguilhem in their critique of science and reason in 1985 in *Naturalistic Inquiry* (1985).

10. It should not be assumed that Canguilhem was trying to totally undermine the history of the sciences or to destroy the value and importance of reason. He was not. In fact, it is clear that Canguilhem appreciates and values both science and reason. Instead, Canguilhem could be said to be trying to develop an approach to the study of the history of science and the history of reason that was much less hagiographic.

11. However, Gutting's *Michel Foucault's Archaeology of Scientific Reason* (1989) is a useful discussion of archaeology, though we disagree with some of his interpretations of Foucault.

12. It should be noted that for Foucault, practices and institutions, theories and disciplines, all exist at the same level. As he says, "I deal with practices, institutions, and theories on the same plane and according to the same isomorphisms" (Foucault, 1994c, p. 262).

13. Foucault always felt that to understand something, say a discursive formation, he needed another one to which to compare it. Comparison, then, is almost always a key part of his analytic work.

14. Foucault uses "possibility" because the process is not deterministic; that is, it is not deterministically inevitable that a *connaissance* will emerge out of a *savoir*.

15. This point is similar to points made by Canguilhem, as was already discussed.

16. Remember here how Canguilhem had asserted that "error" is an integral part of life at the biological level.

17. In the specific part of *The Archaeology of Knowledge* from which this cite is drawn (p. 4), Foucault (1969/1972) cites Canguilhem. Indeed, as we argued in an earlier section, much of archaeology comes from Foucault's use, interpretation, and transformation of his mentor's work.

18. Habermas would be an example of the latter.

19. Unfortunately, we cannot find this interview at this point, but we know we have read it. Our apologies to our readers. If someone comes across it, she or he should e-mail it so that we can add the citation to any future revisions of this essay.

20. One of the reviewers of this chapter argued that *The History of Sexuality, Volume 2: The Use of Pleasure* was clearly a genealogy, but it is our view that Foucault's own words in this text indicate that Volume 2 is not another genealogy. In the "Introduction" to Volume 2, Foucault discusses the genealogy he originally intended to do but then turns away from this. A good discussion of the three periods and Foucault's intentions with each can be found in Davidson (1986).

21. We would also suggest that because of their critique of archaeology, Dreyfus and Rabinow (1983) played a key role in the lack of attention to Canguilhem, as they mention him only once throughout *Beyond Structuralism and Hermeneutics*.

22. The reason why this more recent version is better, in our view, is that it clearly distinguishes knowledge as *connaissance* and knowledge as *savoir*, both of which we have discussed as key concepts of Foucault's archaeology.

23. It is hard not to conclude that Foucault actually either enjoyed writing about the torture or enjoyed shocking readers or both, given the extended detail in his descriptions.

24. Obviously, one of the points we are trying to make here is that there is less of a break between archaeology and genealogy than is commonly assumed.

25. Foucault would likely call the new focus on student-centered classrooms one of the effects of a "pastoral" approach.

26. This point is a good example of a concern that started with Canguilhem and continues from Foucault's archaeologies into his genealogies.

27. Amazon.com now allows anyone to do two-word or phrase searches of an entire book of any book that is contained in this system. It is a marvelous system, but any single person can do this only twice a month without buying the book.

28. One odd little note is that although Foucault's convention is to compare two periods in his various analyses, in *History of Sexuality* he compares three.

29. Contrary to what many assume, Foucault is exceedingly logical in his written presentations. He constantly divides an arena of focus into numbered parts and then proceeds to define those parts in an orderly fashion. Indeed, at this point, we have begun to wonder why there is all of this commentary as to how Foucault writes in some disrupted "postmodern" fashion. We find, after our lengthy review of his work, that he writes in a fairly conventional way for complex intellectual work. Actually, other than learning to think differently, which is really the hardest task in reading Foucault, what is required is to carefully follow the meaning in his long complex sentences, as it is sometimes difficult to follow to what he is referring. In other words, it takes a close reading to follow his meaning, but there is little that is "disrupted" in his texts, in our view.

30. One of our reviewers argued that the larger problem with the archaeological methodology is that very few areas of social life lend themselves to the kind of complex discursive structures that Foucault addresses in his archaeologies. We would clearly disagree. We would suggest that before Foucault's archaeological analyses, few would have seen the complex *savoir*-based discursive patterns that Foucault identified in *Madness and Civilization* (1961/1988), *The Birth of the Clinic* (1963/1994b), and *The Order of Things* (1966/1973a). For instance, we think education could definitely be a fertile arena for archaeological analyses.

31. There is a new comprehensive set of all of Foucault's work that has been published in French, called *Dits et Ecrits*. It is two volumes, *Dits et Ecrits, tome 1, 1954–1975* (2001a, 1,700 pages) and *Dits et Ecrits, tome 2, 1976–1988* (2001b, 1,976 pages). We certainly hope that some group will provide an English translation of the entire set.

32. There is no doubt that Foucault is part of a critical tradition in Western philosophy, but he had fundamental arguments with that part of the critical

tradition that has been labeled Marxist, neo-Marxist, or critical theory.

33. As Foucault scholars well know, Derrida was strongly critical of Foucault's work.

34. Thanks to Elizabeth St. Pierre for this delightful quote.

Bibliography

Foucault Books

(This is an attempt to list all of Foucault's major books, but it is not intended to be comprehensive of all of Foucault's work in English. In addition, these are the books that we own and have studied.)

Foucault, M. (1972). *The archaeology of knowledge and the discourse on language* (A. M. Sheridan Smith, Trans.). New York: Pantheon Books. (Original work published in 1969)

Foucault, M. (1973a). *The order of things: An archaeology of the human sciences.* New York: Vintage Books. (Original work published in 1966)

Foucault, M. (1973b). *This is not a pipe* (J. Harkness, Trans.). Berkeley: University of California Press.

Foucault, M. (1977). *Language, counter-memory, practice: Selected essays and interviews by Michel Foucault* (D. F. Bouchard, Ed.; D. F. Bouchard & S. Simon, Trans.). Ithaca, NY: Cornell University Press.

Foucault, M. (1979). *Discipline and punish: The birth of the prison* (A. Sheridan, Trans.). New York: Vintage Books. (Original work published in 1975)

Foucault, M. (1980a). *The history of sexuality,* Vol. 1: *An introduction* (R. Hurley, Trans.). New York: Vintage Books. (Original work published in 1976)

Foucault, M. (1980b). *Power/Knowledge: Selected interviews and other writings, 1972–1977* (C. Gordon, Ed.; C. Gordon, L. Marshall, J. Mepham, & K. Soper, Trans.). New York: Pantheon Books.

Foucault, M. (1986). *The history of sexuality,* Vol. 3: *Care of the self* (R. Hurley, Trans.). New York: Pantheon Books. (Original work published in 1984)

Foucault, M. (1988). *Madness and civilization: A history of insanity in the age of reason* (R. Howard, Trans.). New York: Vintage Books. (Original work published in 1961)

Foucault, M. (1989). *Foucault live: Interviews, 1966–84* (S. Lotringer, Ed.; J. Johnston, Trans.). New York: Semiotext(e).

Foucault, M. (1990). *The history of sexuality,* Vol. 2: *The use of pleasure* (R. Hurley, Trans.). New York: Pantheon Books. (Original work published in 1984)

Foucault, M. (1994a). *Aesthetics, method, and epistemology* (J. D. Faubion, Ed.; R. Hurley & others, Trans.). New York: New Press.

Foucault, M. (1994b). *The birth of the clinic: An archaeology of medical perception* (A. M. Sheridan-Smith, Trans.). New York: Vintage Books. (Original work published in 1963)

Foucault, M. (1994c). *Power* (J. D. Faubion, Ed.; R. Hurley & others, Trans.). New York: New Press.

Foucault, M. (1997). *Ethics, subjectivity, and truth* (Vol. 1; P. Rabinow, Ed.; R. Hurley & others, Trans.). New York: New Press. (Original work published in 1994)

Foucault, M. (1998). *Aesthetics, method, and epistemology* (Vol. 2; J. D. Faubion, Ed.; R. Hurley and others, Trans.). New York: New Press.

Foucault, M. (2001a). *Dits et Ecrits, tome 1, 1954–1975.* Paris: Gallimard.

Foucault, M. (2001b). *Dits et Ecrits, tome 2, 1976–1988.* Paris: Gallimard.

Foucault, M. (2001c). *Fearless speech* (J. Pearson, Ed.). Los Angeles: Semiotext(e).

Foucault, M. (2003). *"Society must be defended": Lectures at the Collège de France, 1975–1976* (M. Bertaini & A. Fontana, Eds.; D. Macey, Trans.). New York: Picador.

Rabinow, P. (Ed.). (1984). *Foucault reader.* New York: Pantheon Books.

Foucault-Oriented Education Books

(This list is meant to be comprehensive of *all* books in education that apply Foucault to education as their primary purpose. It does not include books that just use Foucault among many others; it includes only those that we could find that explicitly take Foucault as their main theoretical frame.)

Baker, B., & Heyning, K. (Eds.). (2004). *Dangerous coagulations? The uses of Foucault in the study of education.* New York: Peter Lang.

Ball, S. (Ed.). (1990). *Foucault and education: Disciplines and knowledge.* London: Routledge.

Ball, S., & Tamboukou, M. (2003). *Dangerous encounters: Genealogy and ethnography.* New York: Peter Lang.

Marshall, J. D. (1996). *Michel Foucault: Personal autonomy and education.* Dordrecht, Netherlands: Kluwer Academic.

Peters, M. (1996). *Poststructuralism, politics, and education.* Westport, CT: Bergin & Garvey.

Popkewitz, T. S., & Brennan, M. (1998). *Foucault's challenge: Discourse, knowledge, and power in education.* New York: Columbia University, Teachers College Press.

Scheurich, J. J. (1997). *Research method in the postmodern.* London: Falmer.

Tamboukou, M., & Ball, S. J. (2003). Genealogy and ethnography: Fruitful encounters or dangerous liaisons? In M. Tamboukou & S. J. Ball (Eds.), *Dangerous encounters: Genealogy and ethnography* (pp. 1–36). New York: Peter Lang.

General Foucault Books

(These are books on Foucault's work that we have found to be helpful and/or influential, but it is not meant to be a comprehensive list of all books in English on Foucault. These are books that we own and have studied.)

Armstrong, T. J. (Trans.). (1992). *Michel Foucault: Philosopher.* New York: Routledge.

Barker, P. (1998). *Michel Foucault: An introduction.* Edinburgh, UK: Edinburgh University Press.

Barry, A., Osborne, T., & Rose, N. (Eds.). (1996). *Foucault and political reason: Liberalism, neoliberalism, and the rationalities of government.* Chicago: University of Chicago Press.

Bernauer, J., & Rasmussen, D. (Eds.). (1991). *The final Foucault.* Cambridge, MA: MIT Press. (Includes a biographical chronology of Foucault interspersed with some quotes from Foucault as he remembers different times in his life)

Best, S., & Kellner, D. (1991). *Postmodern theory: Critical interrogations.* New York: Guilford.

Burchell, G., Gordon, C., & Miller, P. (1991). *The Foucault effect: Studies in governmentality.* Chicago: University of Chicago Press.

Butler, J. (1993). *Bodies that matter: On the discursive limits of "sex."* New York: Routledge.

Canguilhem, G. (1988). *Ideology and rationality in the history of the life sciences.* Cambridge, MA: MIT Press.

Canguilhem, G. (1989). *The normal and the pathological.* New York: Zone Books.

Caputo, J., & Yount, M. (1993). *Foucault and the critique of institutions.* University Park: Pennsylvania State University Press.

Davidson, A. I. (1986). Archaeology, genealogy, ethics. In D. Couzens Hoy (Ed.), *Foucault: A critical reader* (pp. 221–234). Oxford, UK: Basil Blackwell.

Deleuze, G. (1995). *Negotiations: 1972–1990* (M. Joughin, Trans.). New York: Columbia University Press. (Original work published in 1990)

Dreyfus, H. L., & Rabinow, P. (1983). *Michel Foucault: Beyond structuralism and hermeneutics* (2nd ed.). Chicago: University of Chicago Press.

Eribon, D. (1991). *Michel Foucault* (B. Wing, Trans.). Cambridge, MA: Harvard University Press.

Fraser, N. (1989). *Unruly practices: Power, discourse, and gender in contemporary social theory.* Minneapolis: University of Minnesota Press.

Grosz, E. (1994). *Volatile bodies: Toward a corporeal feminism.* Bloomington: Indiana University Press.

Gubrium, J. F., & Holstein, J. A. (2000). Analyzing interpretive practice. In N. K. Denzin & Y. S. Lincoln (Eds.), *Handbook of qualitative research* (2nd ed., pp. 487–508). Thousand Oaks, CA: Sage.

Gutting, G. (1989). *Michel Foucault's archaeology of scientific reason.* Cambridge, UK: Cambridge University Press.

Gutting, G. (Ed.). (1994). *The Cambridge companion to Foucault.* Cambridge, UK: Cambridge University Press.

Halperin, D. M. (1995). *Saint Foucault: Towards a gay hagiography.* New York: Oxford University Press.

Han, B. (2002). *Foucault's critical project: Between the transcendental and the historical.* Stanford, CA: Stanford University Press.

Hartsock, N. C. M. (1998). *The feminist standpoint revisited and other essays.* Boulder, CO: Westview.

Hoy, D. C. (Ed.). (1986). *Foucault: A critical reader.* Oxford, UK: Basil Blackwell.

Jones, C., & Porter, R. (1994). *Reassessing Foucault: Power, medicine, and the body.* London: Routledge.

Kendall, G., & Wickham, G. (1999). *Using Foucault's methods.* Thousand Oaks, CA: Sage.

Kuhn. T. (1962). *The structure of scientific revolutions.* Chicago: University of Chicago Press.

Lather, P. (2004). Foucauldian "in discipline" as a sort of policy application. In B. Baker & K. Hayning (Eds.), *Dangerous coagulations? The uses of Foucault in the study of education* (pp. 281–306). New York: Peter Lang.

Lincoln, Y. S., & Guba, E. G. (1985). *Naturalistic inquiry.* Beverly Hills, CA: Sage.

Mahon, M. (1992). *Foucault's Nietzschean genealogy: Truth, power, and the subject.* Albany: State University of New York Press.

McHoul, A., & Grace, W. (1993). *A Foucault primer: Discourse, power, and the subject.* New York: New York University Press.

Merquior, J. G. (1985). *Foucault.* Berkeley: University of California Press.

Miller, J. (1993). *The passion of Michel Foucault.* New York: Simon & Schuster.

Nilson, H. (1998). *Michel Foucault and the games of truth* (R. Clark, Trans.). New York: St. Martin's.

Poster, M. (1987). *Foucault, Marxism, and history: Mode of production versus mode of information.* Cambridge, UK: Polity.

Rajchman, J. (1985). *Michel Foucault: The freedom of philosophy.* New York: Columbia University Press.

Rouse, J. (1987). *Knowledge and power: Toward a political philosophy of science.* Ithaca, NY: Cornell University Press.

Sawicki, J. (1991). *Disciplining Foucault: Feminism, power, and the body.* New York: Routledge.

Shumany, D. R. (1989). *Michel Foucault.* Charlottesville: University Press of Virginia.

Stoler, A. L. (2000). *Race and the education of desire: Foucault's* History of Sexuality *and the colonial order of things.* Durham, NC: Duke University Press.

St. Pierre, E. A. (2004). Care of the self: The subject and freedom. In B. Baker & K. E. Heyning (Eds.), *Dangerous coagulations? The uses of Foucault in the study of education* (pp. 325–358). New York: Peter Lang.

Visker, R. (1995). *Michel Foucault: Genealogy as critique* (C. Turner, Trans.). London: Verso.

Foucault Articles

(We have tried to develop a fairly comprehensive list of all articles in *education* that use Foucault as the *main framing theoretical perspective.* Also, this list includes only the articles for which we have been able to get physical or electronic copies. However, we did not include a survey of dissertations that might fall into this same category.)

Alexander, J. (1997). Out of the closet and into the network: Sexual orientation and the computerized classroom. *Computers and Composition, 14,* 207–216.

Anderson, G. L., & Grinberg, J. (1998). Educational administration as a disciplinary proactive: Appropriating Foucault's view of power, discourse, and method. *Educational Administration Quarterly, 34,* 329–353.

Aper, J. P. (2002). Steerage from a distance: Can mandated accountability systems really improve schools? *Journal of Educational Thought, 36*(1), 7–26.

Atkinson, D. (1999). A critical reading of the national curriculum for art in the light of contemporary theories of subjectivity. *International Journal of Art & Design Education, 18*(1), 107–113.

Biesta, G. J. J. (1998). Pedagogy without humanism: Foucault and the subject of education. *Interchange, 29*(1), 1–16.

Blair, K. (1994). Foucault, feminism, and writing pedagogy: Strategies for student resistance and the transformation of popular culture. *Writing Instructor, 13*(3), 112–123.

Bloland, H. G. (1995). Postmodernism and higher education. *Journal of Higher Education, 66,* 521–590.

Butin, D. W. (2001). If this is resistance, I would hate to see domination: Retrieving Foucault's notion of resistance within educational research. *Educational Studies, 22*(2), 157–176.

Butin, D. W. (2002). This isn't talk therapy: Problematizing and extending anti-oppressive education. *Educational Researcher, 31*(3), 14–16.

Carlson, D. (1995). Making progress: Progressive education in the postmodern. *Educational Theory, 45,* 337–357.

Case, P., Case, S., & Catling, S. (2000). Please show you're working: A critical assessment of the impact of OFSTED inspection of primary teachers. *British Journal of Sociology of Education, 21,* 605–622.

Copeland, I. C. (1996). The making of the dull, deficient, and backward pupil in British elementary education 1870–1914. *British Journal of Educational Studies, 44,* 377–394.

Copeland, I. C. (1997). Pseudo-science and dividing practices: A genealogy of the first educational provision for pupils with learning difficulties. *Disability and Society, 12,* 709–722.

Copeland, I. C. (1999). Normalisation: An analysis of aspects of special educational needs. *Educational Studies, 25,* 99–111.

Coulter, D. (2002). Creating common and uncommon worlds: Using discourse ethics to decide public and private in classrooms. *Journal of Curriculum Studies, 34,* 25–42.

Cuthbert, A. (2001). Going global: Reflexivity and contextualism in urban design education. *Journal of Urban Design, 6,* 297–316.

Dei, G. S., & Asgharzadeh, A. (2001). The power of social theory: The anti-colonial discursive framework. *Journal of Educational Thought, 35,* 297–323.

Dekker, J. J. H., & Lechner, D. M. (1999). Discipline and pedagogics in history: Foucault, Aries, and the history of panoptical education. *The European Legacy, 4*(5), 37–49.

Drummond, J. (2000). Foucault for students of education. *Journal of Philosophy of Education, 34,* 709–719.

Erevelles, N. (2002). Voices of silence: Foucault, disability, and the question of self-determination. *Studies in Philosophy and Education, 21,* 17–35.

Erricker, C. (2001). Shall we dance: Authority, representation, and voice—The place of spirituality in religious education. *Religious Education, 96*(1), 2–19.

Fennel, H-A. (2002). Letting go while holding on: Women principals' lived experiences with power. *Journal of Educational Administration, 40*(2), 95–117. Retrieved January 3, 2003, from www.emeraldinsight.com/0957-8234.htm

Flecha, R. (1999). Modern and postmodern racism in Europe: Dialogic approach and anti-racist pedagogies. *Harvard Educational Review, 69*(2), 150–171.

Frohmann, B. (2001). Discourse and documentation: Some implications for pedagogy and research. *Discourse and Documentation, 42*(1), 12–26.

Hall, C., & Millard, E. (1994). The means of correct training? Teachers, Foucault, and disciplining. *Journal of Education for Teaching, 20*(2), 153–161.

Hayden, S. (2001). Teenage bodies, teenage selves: Tracing the implications of bio-power in contemporary sexuality education texts. *Women's Studies in Communication, 24*(1), 30–61.

Helldin, R. (2000). Special education knowledge seen as a social problem. *Disability and Society, 15,* 247–270.

Hemmings, A. (2002). Youth culture of hostility: Discourses of money, respect, and difference. *International Journal of Qualitative Studies in Education. 15,* 291–307.

Hones, D. F. (1999). Making peace: A narrative study of a bilingual liaison, a school, and a community. *Teachers College Record, 101*(1), 106–135.

Howley, A., & Harnett, R. (1992). Pastoral power and the contemporary university: A Foucauldian analysis. *Educational Theory, 42,* 271–282.

Kelly, P. (2001). Youth at risk: Processes of individualization and responsibilisation in the risk society. *Discourse: Studies in the Cultural Politics of Education, 22*(1), 23–33.

Kennedy, D. (2002). The child and postmodern subjectivity. *Educational Theory, 52,* 155–167.

Mayo, C. (2000). The uses of Foucault. *Educational Theory, 50,* 103–117.

McCarthy, C., & Dimitriadis, G. (2000). Governmentality and the sociology of education: Media, educational policy, and the politics of resentment. *British Journal of Education, 21,* 169–185.

McCoy, K. (1997). White noise—the sound of epidemic: Reading/Writing a climate of intelligibility around the "crisis" of difference. *Qualitative Studies in Education, 10,* 333–347.

McLeod, J. (2001). Foucault forever. *Discourse: Studies in the Cultural Politics of Education, 22*(1), 95–104.

Meadmore, D., Hatcher, C., & McWilliam, E. (2000). Getting tense about genealogy. *Qualitative Studies in Education, 13,* 463–476.

Moje, E. B. (1997). Exploring discourse, subjectivity, and knowledge in chemistry class. *Journal of Classroom Interaction, 32*(2), 35–44.

Mourad, R., Jr. (2001). Education after Foucault: The question of civility. *Teachers College Record, 103,* 739–759.

Ninnes, P., & Mehta, S. (2000). Postpositivist theorizing and research: Challenges and opportunities for comparative education. *Comparative Education Review, 44,* 205–212.

Opfer, V. D. (2001). Charter schools and the panoptic effect of accountability. *Education and Urban Society, 33,* 201–215.

Peters, M. (2000). Writing the self: Wittgenstein, confession, and pedagogy. *Journal of Philosophy of Education, 34,* 353–368.

Pignatelli, F. (1993). What can I do? Foucault on freedom and the question of teacher agency. *Educational Theory, 43,* 411–432.

Pignatelli, F. (2002). Mapping the terrain of a Foucauldian ethics: A response to the surveillance of schooling. *Studies in Philosophy and Education, 21,* 157–180.

Popkewitz, T. S. (1997). The production of reason and power: Curriculum history and intellectual traditions. *Journal of Curriculum Studies, 29,* 131–164.

Popkewitz, T. S., & Brennan, M. (1997). Restructuring of social and political theory in education: Foucault and a social epistemology of school practices. *Educational Theory, 47,* 287–313.

Raddon, A. (2002). Mothers in the academy: Positioned and positioning within discourses of the "successful academic" and the "good mother." *Studies in Higher Education, 27,* 387–403.

Roth, W-M. (2002). Reading graphs: Contributions to an integrative concept of literacy. *Journal of Curriculum Studies, 34,* 1–24.

Ryan, J. (1991). Observing and normalizing: Foucault, discipline, and inequality in schooling. *Journal of Educational Thought, 25*(2), 104–119.

Schubert, D. J. (1995). From a politics of transgression toward an ethics of reflexivity. *American Behavioral Scientist, 38,* 1003–1018.

Seals, G. (1998). Objectively yours, Michael Foucault. *Educational Theory, 48,* 59–68.

Selden, S. (2000). Eugenics and the social construction of merit, race, and disability. *Journal of Curriculum Studies, 32,* 235–252.

Selwyn, N. (2000). The national grid for learning: Panacea or panopticon? *British Journal of Sociology of Education, 21,* 243–255.

Slaughter, S. (1997). Class, race, and gender and the construction of post-secondary curricula in the United States: Social movement, professionalization, and political economic theories of curricular change. *Journal of Curriculum Studies, 29,* 1–30.

Spears, R., & Lea, M. (1994). Panacea or panopticon? *Communication Research, 21,* 427–459.

St. Pierre, E. S. (2002). "Science" rejects postmodernism. *Educational Researcher, 31*(8), 25–27.

Stygall, G. (1994). Resisting privilege: Basic writing and Foucault's author function. *College Composition and Communication, 45,* 320–341.

Styslinger, M. E. (2000). Relations of power and drama in education: The teacher and Foucault. *Journal of Educational Thought, 34,* 183–199.

Walshaw, M. (2001). A Foucauldian gaze on gender research: What do you do when confronted with the tunnel at the end of the light? *Journal for Research on Mathematics Education, 32,* 471–492.

Willis, A. I. (2002). Literacy at Calhoun Colored School 1892–1945. *Reading Research Quarterly, 37*(1), 8–44.

Zembylas, M. (2002). "Structures of fooling" in curriculum and teaching: Theorizing the emotional rules. *Educational Theory, 52,* 187–208.

Additional Reading

Didion, J. (2003, January 16). Fixed opinions, or the hinge of history. *The New York Review of Books,* pp. 54–59.

34

ANALYZING TALK AND TEXT

Anssi Peräkylä

There are two much used but distinctively different types of empirical materials in qualitative research: interviews and naturally occurring materials. Interviews consist of accounts given to the researcher about the issues in which he or she is interested. The topic of the research is not the interview itself but rather the issues discussed in the interview. In this sense, research that uses naturally occurring empirical material is different; in this type of research, the empirical materials themselves (e.g., the tape-recordings of mundane interactions, the written texts) constitute specimens of the topic of the research. Consequently, the researcher is in more direct touch with the very object that he or she is investigating.

Most qualitative research probably is based on interviews. There are good reasons for this. By using interviews, the researcher can reach areas of reality that would otherwise remain inaccessible such as people's subjective experiences and attitudes. The interview is also a very convenient way of overcoming distances both in space and in time; past events or faraway experiences can be studied by interviewing people who took part in them.

In other instances, it is possible to reach the object of research directly using naturally occurring empirical materials (Silverman, 2001). If the researcher is interested in, say, strategies used by journalists in interviewing politicians (cf. Clayman & Heritage, 2002a), it might be advisable to tape-record broadcast interviews rather than to ask journalists to tell about their work. Or, if the researcher wants to study the historical evolution of medical conceptions regarding death and dying, it might be advisable to study medical textbooks rather than to ask doctors to tell what they know about these concepts.

The contrast between interviews and naturally occurring materials should not, however, be exaggerated (cf. Potter, 2004; Speer, 2002). There are types of research materials that are between these two pure types. For example, in *informal interviews that are part of ethnographic fieldwork*, and in *focus groups*, people describe their practices and ideas to the researcher in circumstances that are much closer to "naturally occurring" than are the circumstances in ordinary research interviews. Moreover, even "ordinary" interviews can be, and have been, analyzed as specimens of interaction and reasoning practices rather than as representations of facts or ideas outside the interview situation. As Speer (2002) recently put it, "The status of pieces of data as natural or not depends largely on what the researcher intends to 'do' with them" (p. 513). Wetherell and Potter (1992), for example, analyzed the ways in which interviewees use different linguistic and cultural resources in constructing their relation to racial and racist discourses. On the other hand, as Silverman (2001) put it, no data—not even tape recordings—are "untouched by the researcher's hands" (p. 159; see also Speer, 2002, p. 516); the researcher's activity is needed, for example, in obtaining informed consent from the participants. The difference between researcher-instigated data and naturally occurring data should, therefore, be understood as a continuum rather than as a dichotomy.

This chapter focuses on one end of this continuum. It presents some methods that can be used in analyzing and interpreting tape-recorded interactions and written texts, which probably are the types of data that come closest to the idea of "naturally occurring."

Analyzing Texts

Uses of Texts and Variety of Methods of Text Analysis

As Smith (1974, 1990) and Atkinson and Coffey (1997) pointed out, much of social life in modern society is mediated by written texts of different kinds. For example, modern health care would not be possible without patient records; the legal system would not be possible without laws and other juridical texts; professional training would not be possible without manuals and professional journals; and leisure would not be possible without newspapers, magazines, and advertisements. Texts of this kind have provided an abundance of material for qualitative researchers.

In many cases, qualitative researchers who use written texts as their materials do not try to follow any predefined protocol in executing their analysis. By reading and rereading their empirical materials, they try to pin down their key themes and, thereby, to draw a picture of the presuppositions and meanings that constitute the cultural world of which the textual material is a specimen. An example of this kind of informal approach is Seale's (1998) small but elegant case study on a booklet based on a broadcast interview with the British playwright Dennis Potter (pp. 127–131). The interviewee was terminally ill at the time of the interview. Seale showed how the interview conveys a particular conception of death and dying, characterized by intensive awareness of the imminent death and special creativity arising from it.

An informal approach may, in many cases, be the best choice as a method in research focusing on written texts. Especially in research designs where the qualitative text analysis is not at the core of the research but instead is in a subsidiary or complementary role, no more sophisticated text analytical methods may be needed. That indeed was the case in Seale's (1998) study, in which the qualitative text analysis complemented a larger study drawing mostly on interview and questionnaire materials as well as on theoretical work. In projects that use solely texts as empirical materials, however, the use of different kinds of analytical procedures may be considered.

There are indeed many methods of text analysis from which the researcher can choose. The degree to which they involve predefined sets of procedures varies; some of them do to a great extent, whereas in others the emphasis is more on theoretical presuppositions concerning the cultural and social worlds to which the texts belong. Moreover, some of these methods can be used in the research of both written and spoken discourse, whereas others are exclusively fitted to written texts. In what follows, I briefly mention a few text analytical methods and then discuss two a bit more thoroughly.

Semiotics is a broad field of study concerned with signs and their use. Many tools of text analysis have arisen from this field. The most prominent of them may be *semiotic narrative analysis.* The Russian ethnologist Propp (1968) and the French sociologist Greimas (1966) developed schemes for the analysis of narrative structures. Initially their schemes were developed in fairy tales, but later on they were applied to many other kinds of texts. For example, by using Greimas's scheme, primordial structural relations (e.g., subject vs. object, sender vs. receiver, helper vs. opponent) can be distilled from the texts. Törrönen (2000, 2003) used and developed further Greimasian concepts in analyzing newspaper editorials addressing alcohol policy, showing how these texts mobilize structural relations so as to encourage readers to take action to achieve particular political goals.

The term *discourse analysis* (DA) may refer, depending on context, to many different approaches of investigation of written texts (and of spoken discourse as well). In the context of linguistics, DA usually refers to research that aims at uncovering the features of text that maintain coherence in units larger than the sentence (Brown & Yule, 1983). In social psychology, DA (or *discursive psychology,* as it has been called more recently) involves research in which the language use (both written and spoken) underpinning mental realities, such as cognition and emotion, is investigated. Here, the key theoretical presupposition is that mental realities do not reside "inside" individual humans but rather are constructed linguistically (Edwards, 1997; Potter & Wetherell, 1987). *Critical discourse analysis* (CDA), developed by Fairclough (1989, 1995), constitutes yet another kind of discourse analytical approach in which some key concerns of linguistic and critical social research merge. Critical discourse analysts are interested in the ways in which texts of different kinds reproduce power and inequalities in society. Tainio's (1999) study on the language of self-help communication guidebooks for married couples is one example of a CDA study. Tainio showed, for example, how in these texts the woman is expected to change for the communication problems to be solved, whereas the man is treated as immutable.

Historical discourse analysis (HDA) constitutes yet another form of DA, and that is an approach I introduce a bit more thoroughly through a research example.

Historical Discourse Analysis: Armstrong's Work as an Example

Many scholars working with written texts have drawn insights and inspiration from the work of Michel Foucault. (For examples of his own studies, see Foucault, 1973, 1977, 1978. For examples of accessible accounts of his theories and methods, see Kendall & Wickham, 1999; McHoul & Grace, 1993.) Foucault did not propose a definite set of methods for the analysis of texts; hence, the ways of analyzing and interpreting texts of scholars inspired by him vary. For all of them, however, a primary concern is, as Potter (2004) aptly put it, how a set of "statements" comes to constitute objects and subjects. The constitution of subjects and objects is explored in historical context—or, in Foucault's terms, through *archeology* and *genealogy.*

David Armstrong's work is a good example of the Foucaultian, or historical, approach in text analysis. In a string of studies (Armstrong, 1983, 1987, 1993, 1998, 2002; Gothill & Armstrong, 1999), he investigated medical textbooks and journal articles, showing how objects such as bodies, illnesses, and death, as well as subjects such as doctors, patients, and nurses, have been constituted in these texts during the past two centuries. Armstrong's approach is radically constructionistic; he argued that these objects and subjects—in the sense that we know them now—did not exist before they were constructed through textual and other practices. For example, it has always been the case that some people die at a very early age, but according to Armstrong (1986), "infant mortality" as a discrete social object came into being around 1875. Only after that did the Registrar-General's annual reports (in Britain) orient to such a fact.

Let us examine briefly Armstrong's (1993) article on "public health spaces" so as to understand his Foucaultian way of analyzing and interpreting texts. Basically, Armstrong was concerned about hygienic rules. Using textual material derived from medical and hygienic textbooks and instructions, Armstrong showed how the rules defining the difference between the dangerous and the safe, or between the pure and the dirty, have changed during the past two centuries. In and through examining the rules and their change, Armstrong explored evolution of the spaces in which individual identity is located.

Armstrong (1993) identified four phases, or "regimes," in the development of hygienic rules. During the *quarantine* phase (from the late Middle Ages until the first half of the 19th century), the dividing line between pure and dirty demarcated different geographic spaces. Ships carrying diseases, or towns and villages where infectious diseases were found, were separated from "clean" localities. During the *sanitary science* phase (ca. 1850–1900), the key boundary separated the human body (clean) and the substances outside the body such as (contaminated) air and water. During the *interpersonal hygiene* phase (early to mid-20th century), the dividing line went between individual bodies so as to prevent the spread of contagious diseases from one body to another. Finally, during the *new public health* phase, the danger arose from the incursion of the activities of human bodies into nature in the form of pollution of the environment. Armstrong pointed out that each hygienic regime incorporated practices of the formation of human identity. For example, the shift from quarantine to sanitary science involved dissection of the mass and recognition "of separable and calculable individuality" (p. 405), interpersonal hygiene constructed individual differences, and new public health outlined a reflective subject. Through his analysis, Armstrong also entered into discussion with sociological and anthropological writings of Durkheim (1948) and Douglas (1966), giving historical specification to their concepts and reformulating some of their assumptions regarding the social significance of the boundaries between the sacred and the profane or between the pure and the dirty.

Armstrong's results are impressive. How did he do it? How did he analyze his texts? He recently gave an illuminating account of his method (Armstrong, 2002, chap. 17). Independent of, but still in line with, his own account, I now point out a few things that appear as central in the context of this *Handbook.* In a technical sense, Armstrong's way of analyzing texts is not very different from what was referred to earlier as "the informal approach." He focused on the "propositional content" (not the linguistic forms) of the texts, trying to pin down the assumptions and presuppositions that the texts incorporated. But there were at least three additional features. First, Armstrong was very sensitive about the time of the publication of the texts. A key aspect of his analysis was showing at which time each new hygienic regime arose, and he argued that quite exact times could be documented through an historical survey of texts. Second, Armstrong's analysis was informed by theory. Along with the Foucaultian concerns, Douglas's (1966) arguments presented in her modern classic *Purity and Danger* offered him a standpoint. For Douglas, the separation between the pure and the dangerous objects was the key issue. Third, for Armstrong (as for all Foucaultians), texts and *practices* are inseparable. The medical and hygienic texts that he read had a strong instructive component in them; they not only were establishing boundaries between "ideal" objects but also served as (and Armstrong read them as) guidelines for actual social practices where these boundaries were maintained.

Armstrong's historical and Foucaultian way of analyzing and interpreting texts offers one compact alternative for qualitative text analysis. We now turn to a quite different way of reading texts in qualitative research, that is, *membership categorization analysis* (MCA).

Membership Categorization Analysis

Whereas Armstrong's Foucaultian analysis was concerned with the propositional content and not the formal properties of texts, MCA can be said to focus more on the latter. However, MCA is not about grammatical forms but rather about the normative and cognitive forms concerning social relations that are involved in the production and understanding of texts. To put it another way, Armstrong's Foucaultian approach is concerned about the assumptions that underlie *what* is said (and what is not said) in the text, whereas MCA is concerned about *the descriptive apparatus* that makes it possible to say whatever is said.

Before we start to examine MCA, I want to remind the reader about the wide range of applications that this approach has. In addition to the analysis of written texts, it can be used in the analysis of interviews (e.g., Baker, 1997) and in the analysis of naturally occurring talk (e.g., Cuff, 1994). In the following, however, I focus on the text analytical applications.

The idea of membership categorization came from the American sociologist Sacks (1974b, 1992). *Description* was a key analytical question for Sacks; he was concerned about the conditions of description, that is, what makes it possible for us to produce and understand descriptions of people and their activities. As Silverman (2001) aptly put it, Sacks was concerned about "the apparatus through which members' descriptions are properly produced" (p. 139). This interest led Sacks to examine categorization.

People are usually referred to by using categories. The point of departure for MCA is recognition of the fact that at any event, a person may be referred to by using many alternative categories. As the author of this chapter, I may also be referred to also as a man, as a middle-aged person, as a Finn, as a sociologist, as a professor, as the father of two children, as a husband, and so forth. MCA is about the selection of categories such as these and about the conditions and consequences of this selection.

Sacks's (1974b) famous example is the beginning of a story written by a child: *The baby cried. The mommy picked it up.* There are two key categories in this story: "baby" and "mommy." Why are these categories used, and what is achieved by them? If the mommy happened to be a biologist by profession, why would the story not go like this: *The baby cried. The scientist picked it up* (Jayyusi, 1991, p. 238)? Why do we hear the story being about a baby and *its* mother and not just about any baby and any mother? MCA provides answers to questions such as these and offers a toolkit for analyzing various kinds of texts.

Sacks (1992) noted that categories form sets, that is, collections of categories that go together. Family is one such collection, and "baby," "mother," and "father" are some categories of it. "Stage of life" is another collection; it consists of categories such as "baby," "toddler," "child," and "adult." Now, "baby" could in principle be heard as belonging to both collections, but in the preceding little story we hear it as belonging to the "family" collection. This is because in hearing (or reading) descriptions where two or more categories are used, we orient to a rule according to which we hear them as being from the same collection if they indeed can be heard in that way. Therefore, in this case we hear "baby" and "mommy" being from the device "family" (p. 247).

Categories also go together with *activities.* Sacks used the term "category-bound activities" in referring to activities that members of a culture take to be "typical" of a category (or some categories) of people. "Crying" is a category-bound activity of a baby, just as "picking a (crying) baby up" is a category-bound activity of a mother. In a similar fashion, "lecturing" is a category-bound activity of a professor. Activities such as these can be normative; it is appropriate for the baby to cry and for the mother to pick it up, but it is not appropriate for an adult to cry (like a baby) or for a mother to fail to pick a crying baby up. *Standardized relational pairs* consist of two categories where incumbents of the categories have standardized rights and obligations in relation to each other, with "mother and baby" clearly being one pair, just as "husband and wife" and "doctor and patient" are common pairs. Moreover, the receivers of descriptions can and do infer from actions to categories and vice versa. By knowing actions, we infer the categories of the agents; by knowing categories of agents, we infer what they do.

Even on the basis of these fragments of Sacks's ideas (for more thorough accounts, see Hester & Eglin, 1997; Silverman, 1998), the reader may get an impression of the potential that this account offers for the analysis of texts. Sacks's ideas are resources for the analysis of texts as sites for the production and reproduction of social, moral, and political orders. Merely by bearing in mind that there is always more than one category available for the description of a given person, the analyst always asks "Why this categorization now?"

Let us examine a brief example of MCA. Eglin and Hester (1999) gave a thoughtful account of the local newspaper coverage of a tragic event, namely the killing of 13 female students and a data processing worker by a gunman at the Ecole Polytechnique in Montreal in December 1989. Their aim was to show how a "deviant act" was constructed by members of culture. They did this by identifying the categorical resources that were drawn on in the newspaper coverage.

Eglin and Hester (1999) showed how the description of the tragic event was entirely dependent on the resources or the "apparatus" of categorization. The headlines of the first news about the event implicated an initial pair of categories employed in describing the event, namely "offender" and "victims," which Eglin and Hester (p. 200) considered to be a special kind of a standardized relational pair. In the body of the news, these categories got transformed (e.g., "offender" got transformed into "murder suspect") and new categories, such as "police," "witnesses," "relatives," and "friends" of the victims, entered the scene. As Eglin and Hester put it,

> These categories and category pairs . . . provide, then, some of the procedural resources that news writer and news reader may use to produce and recognize, respectively, the relevance of the variety of actors and actions that appeared in the text of the articles. (p. 202)

Categories are not, however, neutral resources of description. Eglin and Hester (1999) went on to analyze how the use of categorical resources made possible an *embedded commentary,* or *assessment,* of the events. They distinguished among several different "stories" in the news coverage, with each being based on particular operations with categories. For example, *the horror story* arose from the *disjuncture* between the membership categories made relevant by *the setting* and those made relevant by *the event.* On a university campus, the setting made relevant categories such as "student," "teacher," and "staff member." The horror story involved the transformation of these category identities into those of "offender," "victims," "witnesses," and so forth. This disjuncture was encapsulated in reports such as the following: *I was doing a presentation in front of the class, and suddenly a guy came in with what I think was a semi-automatic rifle* (Canadian Press, 1989, cited in Eglin & Hester, 1999, p. 204). Another kind of commentary was involved in the *story of the tragedy.* This story drew on two categorical resources: *the stage of life* device and what Sacks (1974b) called the *R-collection,* that is, the collection of standardized relational pairs relevant for a search for help. In terms of the stage of life, the victims were young people who had their futures ahead of them: *Fourteen young women [are] brutally mowed down in the beauty of their youth when everything seemed to assure them of a brilliant future* (Malarek, 1989, cited in Eglin & Hester, 1999, p. 205). With respect to the R-collection, the tragedy arose from the loss experienced by the incumbents of the categorical "pair parts"—parents, brothers/sisters, and friends. Yet another commentary involved *the story about the killing of women.* The victims were women who were purposefully chosen by the gunman on the basis of their gender, and the categories "man" and "woman" ran through much of the news coverage. In subsequent articles, the massacre was linked with broader issues of male violence against women and with gender relations in general.

Because all description draws on categorization, it is obvious that MCA has wide applicability in the analysis of texts. The analysis of categorization gives the researcher access to the cultural worlds and moral orders on which the texts hinge. Importantly, however, categorization analysis is not *only* about specific cultures or moralities. In developing his concepts, Sacks was not primarily concerned about the "contents" of the categorizations; rather, he was concerned about the ways in which we use them (Atkinson, 1978, p. 194). Therefore, at the end of the day, membership categorization analysis invites the qualitative researcher to explore the conditions of action of description in itself.

▣ Analyzing Talk

Face-to-face social interaction (or other live interaction mediated by phones and other technological media) is the most immediate and the most frequently experienced social reality. The heart of our social and personal being lies in the immediate contact with other humans. Even though ethnographic observation of face-to-face social interaction has been done successfully by sociologists and social psychologists, video and audio recordings are what provide the richest possible data for the study of talk and interaction today. Such recordings have been analyzed using the same methods that were discussed previously in the context of interpretation of written texts. CDA, MCA, and even Foucaultian DA have all of their applications in researching transcripts based on video and/or audio recordings. However, as Goffman (1983) pointed out, to be fully appreciated, the face-to-face social interaction also requires its own specific methods. The interplay of utterances and actions in live social interaction involves a complex organization that cannot be found in written texts. *Conversation analysis* (CA) is presented as a method specialized for analyzing that organization.

Origins of Conversation Analysis

CA is a method for investigating the structure and process of social interaction between humans. As their empirical materials, CA studies use video and/or audio recordings made from naturally occurring interactions. As their results, these studies offer qualitative (and sometimes quantitative) descriptions of interactional structures (e.g., turn taking, relations between adjacent utterances) and practices (e.g., telling and receiving news, making assessments).

CA was started by Sacks and his coworkers, especially Emanuel Schegloff and Gail Jefferson, at the University of California during the 1960s. At the time of its birth, CA was something quite different from the rest of social science. The predominant way of investigating human social interaction was quantitative, based on coding and counting distinct, theoretically defined actions (see especially Bales, 1950). Goffman (e.g., 1955) and Garfinkel (1967) had challenged this way of understanding interaction with their studies that focused on the moral and inferential underpinnings of social interaction. Drawing part of his inspiration from them, Sacks started to study qualitatively the real-time sequential ordering of actions—the rules, patterns, and structures in the relations between consecutive actions (Silverman, 1998). Schegloff (1992a) argued that Sacks made a radical shift in the perspective of social scientific inquiry into social interaction; instead of treating social interaction as a screen on which other processes (Balesian categories or moral and inferential processes) were projected, Sacks started to study the very structures of the interaction itself (p. xviii).

Basic Theoretical Assumptions

In the first place, CA is not a theoretical enterprise but rather a very concretely empirical one. Conversation analysts make video and/or audio recordings of naturally occurring interactions, and they transcribe these recordings using a detailed notation system (see appendix). They search, in the recordings and transcripts, for recurrent distinct interactive practices that then become their research topics. These practices can involve, for example, specific sequences (e.g., news delivery [Maynard, 2003]) or specific ways of designing utterances (e.g., "oh"-prefaced answers to questions [Heritage, 1998]). Then, through careful listening, comparison of instances, and exploration of the context of them, conversation analysts describe in detail the properties and tasks that the practices have.

However, through empirical studies—in an "inductive" way—a body of theoretical knowledge about the organization of conversation has been accumulated. The actual "techniques" in doing CA can be understood and appreciated only against the backdrop of these basic theoretical assumptions of CA. In what follows, I try to sketch some of the basic assumptions concerning the organization of conversation that arise from these studies. There are perhaps three most fundamental assumptions of this kind (cf. Heritage, 1984, chap. 8; Hutchby & Wooffitt, 1998), namely that (a) talk is action, (b) action is structurally organized, and (c) talk creates and maintains intersubjective reality.

Talk is action. As in some other philosophical and social scientific approaches, in CA talk is understood first and foremost as a vehicle of human action (Schegloff, 1991). The capacity of language to convey ideas is seen as being derived from this more fundamental task. In accomplishing actions, talk is seamlessly intertwined with (other) corporeal means of action such as gaze and gesture (Goodwin, 1981). Some CA studies have as their topics the organization of actions that are recognizable as distinct actions even from a vernacular point of view. Thus, conversation analysts have studied, for example, openings (Schegloff, 1968) and closings (Schegloff & Sacks, 1973) of conversations, assessments and ways in which the recipients agree or disagree with them (Goodwin & Goodwin, 1992; Pomerantz, 1984), storytelling (Mandelbaum, 1992; Sachs, 1974a), complaints (Drew & Holt, 1988), telling and receiving news (Maynard, 2003), and laughter (Haakana, 2001; Jefferson, 1984). Many CA studies have as their topic actions that are typical in some institutional environment. Examples include diagnosis (Heath, 1992; Maynard, 1991, 1992; Peräkylä, 1998, 2002; ten Have, 1995) and physical examination (Heritage & Stivers, 1999) in medical consultations, questioning and answering practices in cross-examinations (Drew, 1992), ways of managing disagreements in news interviews (Greatbatch, 1992), and advice giving in a number of different environments (Heritage & Sefi, 1992; Silverman, 1997; Vehviläinen, 2001). Finally, many important CA studies focus on fundamental aspects of conversational organization that make any action possible. These include turn taking (Sacks, Schegloff, & Jefferson, 1974), repair (Schegloff, Jefferson, & Sacks, 1977; Schegloff, 1992c), and the general ways in which sequences of action are built (Schegloff, 1995).

Action is structurally organized. In the CA view, the practical actions that comprise the heart of social life are thoroughly structured and organized. In pursuing their goals, the actors have to orient themselves to rules and structures that only make their actions possible. These rules and structures concern mostly the relations between actions. Single acts are parts of larger, structurally organized entities. These entities may be called "sequences" (Schegloff, 1995).

The most basic and the most important sequence is called the "adjacency pair" (Schegloff & Sacks, 1973). It is a sequence of two actions in which the first action ("first pair part"), performed by one interactant, invites a particular type of second action ("second pair part") to be performed by another interactant. Typical examples of adjacency pairs include question–answer, greeting–greeting, request–grant/refusal, and invitation–acceptance/declination. The relation between the first and second pair parts is strict and normative; if the second pair part does not come forth, the first speaker can, for example, repeat the first action or seek explanations for the fact that the second action is missing (Atkinson & Drew, 1979, pp. 52–57; Merritt, 1976, p. 329).

Adjacency pairs often serve as a core around which even larger sequences are built (Schegloff, 1995). So, a *preexpansion* can precede an adjacency pair, for example, in cases where the speaker first asks about the other's plans for the evening and only thereafter (if it turns out that the other is not otherwise engaged) issues an invitation. An *insert expansion* involves actions that occur between the first and second pair parts and makes possible the production of the latter, for example, in cases where the speaker requests specification of an offer or a request before responding to it. Finally, in *postexpansion,* the speakers produce actions that somehow follow from the basic adjacency pair, with the simplest example being "okay" or "thank you" to close a sequence of a question and an answer or of a request and a grant (Schegloff, 1995).

Talk creates and maintains the intersubjective reality. CA has sometimes been criticized for neglecting the "meaning" of talk at the expense of the "form" of talk (cf. Alexander, 1988, p. 243; Taylor & Cameron, 1987, pp. 99–107). This is, however, a misunderstanding, perhaps arising from the impression created by technical exactness of CA studies. Closer reading of CA studies reveals that in such studies, talk and interaction are examined as a site where intersubjective understanding about the participants' intentions is created and maintained (Heritage & Atkinson, 1984, p. 11). As such, CA gives access to the construction of meaning in real time. But it is important to notice that the conversation analytical "gaze" focuses exclusively on meanings and understandings that are made public through conversational action and that it remains "agnostic" regarding people's intrapsychological experience (Heritage, 1984).

The most fundamental level of intersubjective understanding—which in fact constitutes the basis for any other type of intersubjective understanding—concerns *the understanding of the preceding turn displayed by the current speaker.* Just like any turn of talk that is produced in the context shaped by the previous turn, it also displays its speaker's understanding of that previous turn (Atkinson & Drew, 1979, p. 48). Thus, in simple cases, when producing a turn of talk that is hearable as an answer, the speaker also shows that he or she understood the preceding turn as a question. Sometimes these choices can be crucial for the unfolding of the interaction and the social relation of its participants, for example, in cases where a turn of talk is potentially hearable in two ways (e.g., as an announcement or a request, as an informing or a complaint) and the recipient makes the choice in the next turn. In case the first speaker considers the understanding concerning his talk to be incorrect or problematic, as displayed in the second speaker's utterance, the first speaker has an opportunity to correct this understanding in the "third position" (Schegloff, 1992c), for example, by saying "I didn't mean to criticize you; I just meant to tell you about the problem."

Another important level of intersubjective understanding concerns the *context* of the talk. This is particularly salient in institutional interaction, that is, in interaction that takes place to accomplish some institutionally ascribed tasks of the participants (e.g., psychotherapy, medical consultations, news interviews) (Drew & Heritage, 1992). The participants' understanding of the institutional context of their talk is documented in their actions. As Schegloff (1991, 1992b) and Drew and Heritage (1992) pointed out, if the "institutional context" is relevant for interaction, it can be observed in the details of the participants' actions—in their ways of giving and receiving information, asking and answering questions, presenting arguments, and so forth. CA research that focuses on institutional interactions explores the exact ways in which the performers of different institutional tasks shape their actions to achieve their goals.

Research Example

After these rather abstract considerations, let us consider a concrete example of CA research. In my own work on AIDS counseling (Peräkylä, 1995), one of the topics was a practice called "circular questioning" in therapeutic theory. The clients in these sessions were HIV-positive patients and their family members or other significant others. In circular questions, the counselor asked one client to describe the thoughts or experiences of another person; for example, the counselor might ask the mother of an HIV-positive patient to describe what her (copresent) son's greatest concern is. In my analysis, I showed how such questioning involves a powerful practice to incite the clients to talk about matters that they otherwise would be reluctant to discuss. In circular questions, it was not only the counselors who encouraged the clients to talk about their fears and worries. A local interactional context where the clients encouraged each other to talk was built.

One type of evidence for this "function" of the circular questions comes from the structure of such questioning sequences. Without exception, each circular question was followed by the person whose experience was described ("the owner of the experience") himself or herself giving an account of the experience in question. Often the counselor asked the "owner's" view directly after hearing the coparticipant's version, and sometimes the owner volunteered his or her view. In both cases, the pattern of questioning made the owner of the experience speak about his or her fears and worries. In what follows, Extract 1 provides an example of such a sequence. The participants are an HIV-positive patient (P), his boyfriend (BF), and the counselor (C). Arrows 1 to 4 stand for the initiation of key utterances: 1 for the counselor's circular question, 2 for the boyfriend's answer, 3 for the follow-up question to the owner of the experience, and 4 for his response. Here, as in many other cases that I analyzed, the circular question leads the owner of the experience to disclose his deep worries (see especially lines 45–61). For transcription symbols, see the appendix.

Extract 1 (AIDS Counselling *[Peräkylä, 1995, p. 110]*):

C:(1) → What are some of things that you think E:dward might
have to do.=He says he doesn't know where to go
from here maybe: and awaiting results and things.
(0.6)
C: What d'you think's worrying him.
(0.4)
BF:(2) → Uh::m hhhhhh I think it's just fear of the unknow:n.
P: Mm[:
C: [Oka:y.
BF: [At- at the present ti:me. (0.2) Uh:m (.) once:
he's (0.5) got a better understanding of (0.2) what
could happen
C: Mm:
BF: uh:m how .hh this will progre:ss then: I think (.)
things will be a little more [settled in his
C: [Mm
BF: =own mi:nd.
C: Mm:
(.)
P: Mm[:
C:(3) → [E:dward (.) from what you know:: (0.5) wha- what-
what do you think could happen. (0.8) I mean we're
talking hypothetically [now because I know
P: [Mm:: (well)-
C: =no [more than you do about your actual state of=
P: [uh::
C: =health except that we do: know,=
P: =uh
C: .hhh you're carrying the virus::, (0.6) as far as-
(0.3) the- that first test is concerned.
P: Umh
(1.4)
P:(4) → (Well I feel) I see like two different extremes.=I
see [that I can just- (0.8) carry on (in an)
C: [umh
P: incubation state:, [for many years [and (up)
C: [umh [umh
P: .hhhh you know just being very careful about (it)
[sexually:.
C: [uhm:
(0.4)
P: [and: er (0.3) can go on with a normal life.
C: [umh
C: umh
P: And then I get my greatest fears: that- (0.2) you
know just when I've get my life go:ing: you know a
good job=
C: =um:h=
P: things going very well,
C: uhm::
(0.3)
P: that (I [::) er: : (0.2) my immunity will collapse,
C: [umh
C: um[h
P: [you know: (and I will) become very ill:: (0.2)
>quickly?<
(1.0)
P: .hhh[hh an]d lose control of th- the situation,
C: [um::h]
C: umh:
P: That's my greatest fear actually.

The frequent sequence structure in circular questioning posed a kind of a puzzle for the researcher: Why do the owners of the experience always give their authoritative versions after their experience has been described by somebody else, often even without the counselor asking for it? By examining the minute aspects of the recordings, I started to grasp how the owners' special status vis-à-vis these descriptions, and thereby the relevance of their eventual utterance, was collaboratively and consistently built up in these sequences. *Response tokens* and *postural orientation* were among the means of this buildup.

Response tokens are little particles through which the receivers of an utterance can "receipt" what they have heard and, among other things, indicate that they have no need to ask for clarification or to initiate any other kind of repair, thereby "passing back" the turn of talk to the initial speaker (Schegloff, 1982; Sorjonen, 2001). Usually in question–answer sequences, response tokens would be produced by the questioners. However, in circular questions, the owners of the experience regularly produced response tokens when their significant others were describing the owners' minds and circumstances. As such, the owners indicated their special involvement in the matters that were discussed. That was also the case in Extract 1; in lines 8 and 20, P responded to BF's answer to C's questions with "Mm:"s. He showed his ownership of the matters that were spoken about, thereby also building up the relevance of his own description of them.

The same orientation was shown by the participants through their body posture. The clients who answered the circular question regularly shifted their gaze to the owner at the beginning of the answer, and only toward the end of it did they gaze at the counselor (to whom the answer is given). This organization of gaze contributes to the relevancy of the owner's utterance where he or she eventually describes his or her concerns. A segment from Extract 1 (see below) shows this pattern:

At the beginning of his answer, BF was not oriented to the questioner (the counselor); rather, he was oriented to the person whose mind he was describing (P). Likewise, P was gazing at BF; thus, they are in a mutual gaze contact. BF, the speaker, turned his gaze to the counselor at the end of the first sentence of his answer, and shortly after that P withdrew his gaze from the speaker and also turned to the counselor. Through these actions, P's special status vis-à-vis the things spoken about was collaboratively recognized.

The analysis of circular questioning led me to conclude that in this way of asking questions, a special context was created for the clients' talk

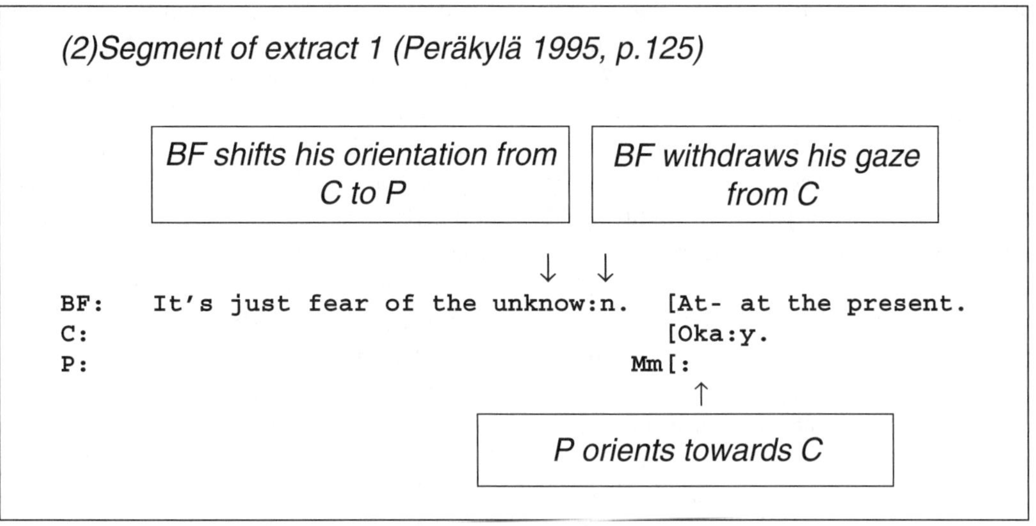

Figure 34.1.

about sensitive issues. Unlike "direct" questions, circular questions mobilize *the clients* in the work of eliciting and encouraging each other's talk. CA as a method for analyzing talk made it possible to examine this elicitation in detail.

Conclusion

It is a special concern of the third edition of this *Handbook* to be explicit politically, that is, to advance a democratic project committed to social justice. To conclude this chapter, therefore, I compare some of the methods discussed in terms of their relation to issues of *power* and *social change.* I focus on the three methods discussed most thoroughly: HDA, MCA, and CA.

The HDA exemplified in the chapter by Armstrong's work is most directly a method for investigating social change. Armstrong showed us the evolvement of hygienic regimes. At the same time, his analysis of texts was about power—about the discourses and practices through which the boundary between pure and dirty had been established and, in relation to that, through which human identities had been formed. Armstrong, like all Foucaultians, treated power here as a productive force—as something that calls realities into being rather than suppresses them.

The potential of MCA in dealing with questions pertaining to power and social change is well shown in a key text by Sacks (1992), "'Hotrodders' as a Revolutionary Category" (pp. 169–174; see also Sacks, 1979). There are at least two relevant aspects of categorization involved here. The more obvious one is the linkage between categorization and racial and other prejudice. By identifying the actors who have committed crimes or other "evils" by racial or other categories, we can create a link between *all* members of the category and the evil that was done by an individual. Thus, categorization, which is an inherent property of language and thought, is a central resource for racism. However, as Silverman (1998) pointed out, the categorical references can also be used in "benign" ways, for example, in invoking and maintaining institutional identities such as "doctor" (p. 18). The other relevant aspect to categorization is more subtle. Sacks (1992) argued that categories can be *owned, resisted,* and *enforced* (p. 172). Following his examples, young persons may be categorized as "teenagers." In (contemporary Western) society, this category is owned by those who are not teenagers, that is, those who are called "adults." It is adults who enforce and administer this categorization. Those who are categorized as "teenagers" can, however, resist this categorization by constructing their own categorizations and by deciding themselves to whom it will be applied. In Sacks's environment, one such categorization was "hotrodders"; it was a category set up by young people themselves, the incumbency of which they controlled. So far as the "others" (e.g., adults) adopted this new categorization, the revolution in categorization was successful. As a whole, Sacks's examples showed how categorization is a field of changing power relations. Analyzing texts using MCA offers one way in which to analyze them.

The relation of CA to questions of power and social change is more complex. CA that focuses on generic practices and structures of mundane everyday talk might seem irrelevant in terms of power and social change. Billig (1998) argued that this irrelevance may, in fact, imply politically conservative choices. Even in researching institutional interaction, the fact that conversation analysts often focus on small details of video- or audio-recorded talk might seem to render their studies impotent for the analysis of social relations and processes *not* incorporated in talk (cf. Hak, 1999).

From the CA point of view, two responses can be given to these criticisms. First, the significance of orderly organization of face-to-face (or other "live") interaction for *all* social life needs to be restated. No "larger scale" social institutions could operate without the substratum of the interaction order. It is largely through questions, answers, assessments, accusations, accounts, interpretations, and the like that these institutions operate. Hence, even when not focusing on hot social and political issues that we read about in the newspapers, CA is providing knowledge about the basic organizations of social life that make these issues, as well as their possible solutions and the debate about them, possible in the first place.

There is, however, also CA research that is more directly relevant for political and social concerns. For example, many CA studies have contributed to our understanding of the ways in which specific interactional practices contribute to the maintenance or change of the *gender system.* Work by West (1979) and Zimmerman (Zimmerman & West, 1975) on male–female interruptions is widely cited. More recently, Kitzinger (2000) explored the implications of preference organization for the politics of rape prevention and turn-taking organization for the practices of "coming out" as gay or lesbian. In a somewhat more linguistic CA study, Tainio (2002) explored how syntactical and semantic properties of utterances are used in the construction of heterosexual identities in elderly couples' talk. Studies such as these (for a fresh overview, see McIlvenny, 2002) also amply demonstrate the *critical* potential of CA. Yet a different CA study on social change was offered in Clayman and Heritage's (2002b) work on question design in U.S. presidential press conferences. By combining qualitative and quantitative techniques, they showed how the relative proportions of different types of journalist questions, exhibiting different degrees of "adversarialness," have changed over time. As such, they explored the historical change in the U.S. presidential institution and media.

The "dissection" of practices of talk may, therefore, lead to insights that may have some political significance. As a final note, consider again the analysis of circular questioning briefly presented in the preceding section. I sought to show how the recurrent structure of the questioning sequence, as well as the use of discourse particles and the postural orientation, contributed to a context where the patients and their significant others were *incited to speak* about their fears and worries. Now, as scholars working with the methods of historical text analysis have shown (Armstrong, 1984; Arney & Bergen, 1984), a clinic that incites patients to talk about their experience is a relatively new development that evolved during the latter half of the 20th century. Prior to that, Western medicine was not concerned about patients' subjective experience and focused on the body only. AIDS was arguably an illness that was more penetrated by this new medical gaze than was any other illness previously (Peräkylä, 1995, p. 340). Therefore, in observing the skillful practices through which AIDS counselors encourage their clients to talk about their subjective experiences, we were also observing the operation of an institution, involving power relations and bodies of knowledge, at a particular moment in its historical development.

In analyzing AIDS counseling, the results of historical text analysis provided a context for the understanding of the significance of the results of CA. Here, different methods of analyzing and interpreting talk and text complemented each other. This does not mean, however, that these methods could or should merge; the research object and the procedures of analysis in CA and HDA remain different. So, rather than combining different methods (which might be what, e.g., Wetherell, 1998, would propose), we should perhaps let each method do its job in its own way and on its own field and then, only at the end of that, let their results cross-illuminate each other.

APPENDIX

TRANSCRIPTION SYMBOLS IN CA

[	Starting point of overlapping speech.
]	End point of overlapping speech
(2.4)	Silence measured in seconds
(.)	Pause of less than 0.2 seconds
↑	Upward shift in pitch
↓	Downward shift in pitch
w*o*rd	Emphasis
wo:rd	Prolongation of sound
°word°	Section of talk produced in lower volume than the surrounding talk
WORD	Section of talk produced in higher volume than the surrounding talk
w#ord#	Creaky voice
£word£	Smile voice
wo(h)rd	Laugh particle inserted within a word
wo-	Cut off in the middle of a word
word<	Abruptly completed word
>word<	Section of talk uttered in a quicker pace than the surrounding talk
<word>	Section of talk uttered in a slower pace than the surround talk
(word)	Section of talk that is difficult to hear but is likely as transcribed
( )	Inaudible word
.hhh	Inhalation
hhh	Exhalation
.	Falling intonation at the end of an utterance
?	Rising intonation at the end of an utterance
,	Flat intonation at the end of an utterance
word.=word	"Rush through" without the normal gap into a new utterance
((word))	Transcriber's comments

Source: Adapted from Drew and Heritage (Eds.). (1992). *Talk at work: Interaction in institutional settings.* Cambridge, UK: Cambridge University Press.

References

Alexander, J. (1988). *Action and its environments: Toward a new synthesis.* New York: Columbia University Press.

Armstrong, D. (1983). *Political anatomy of the body: Medical knowledge in Britain in the twentieth century.* Cambridge, UK: Cambridge University Press.

Armstrong, D. (1984). The patient's view. *Social Science and Medicine, 18,* 734–744.

Armstrong, D. (1986). The invention of infant mortality. *Sociology of Health and Illness, 8,* 211–232.

Armstrong, D. (1987). Silence and truth in death and dying. *Social Science and Medicine, 19,* 651–657.

Armstrong, D. (1993). Public health spaces and the fabrication of identity. *Sociology, 27,* 393–410.

Armstrong, D. (1998). Decline of the hospital: Reconstructing institutional dangers. *Sociology of Health and Illness, 20,* 445–447.

Armstrong, D. (2002). *A new history of identity: A sociology of medical knowledge.* Basingstoke, UK: Palgrave.

Arney, W., & Bergen, B. (1984). *Medicine and the management of living.* Chicago: University of Chicago Press.

Atkinson, J. M. (1978). *Discovering suicide: Studies in the social organization of sudden death.* London: Macmillan.

Atkinson, J. M., & Drew, P. (1979). *Order in court: The organization of verbal interaction in judicial settings.* London: Macmilllan.

Atkinson, P., & Coffey, A. (1997). Analysing documentary realities. In D. Silverman (Ed.), *Qualitative research: Theory, method, and practice* (pp. 45–62). London: Sage.

Baker, C. (1997). Membership categorization and interview accounts. In D. Silverman (Ed.), *Qualitative research: Theory, method, and practice* (pp. 130–143). London: Sage.

Bales, R. F. (1950). *Interaction process analysis: A method for the study of small groups.* Reading, MA: Addison-Wesley.

Billig, M. (1998). Whose terms? Whose ordinariness? Rhetoric and ideology in conversation analysis. *Discourse & Society, 10,* 543–558.

Brown, G., & Yule, G. (1983). *Discourse analysis.* Cambridge, UK: Cambridge University Press.

Canadian Press. (1989, December 7). *The Globe and Mail.*

Clayman, S., & Heritage, J. (2002a). *The news interview: Journalists and public figures on the air.* Cambridge, UK: Cambridge University Press.

Clayman, S., & Heritage, J. (2002b). Questioning presidents: Journalistic deference and adversarialness in the press conferences of Eisenhower and Reagan. *Journal of Communication, 52,* 749–775.

Cuff, E. C. (1994). *Problems of versions in everyday situations.* Lanham, MD: University Press of America.

Douglas, M. (1966). *Purity and danger.* London: Routledge & Kegan Paul.

Drew, P. (1992). Contested evidence in courtroom cross-examination: The case of a trial for rape. In P. Drew & J. Heritage (Eds.), *Talk at work: Interaction in institutional settings* (pp. 470–520). Cambridge, UK: Cambridge University Press.

Drew, P., & Heritage, J. (1992). Analyzing talk at work: An introduction. In P. Drew & J. Heritage (Eds.), *Talk at work: Interaction in institutional settings* (pp. 3–65). Cambridge, UK: Cambridge University Press.

Drew, P., & Holt, E. (1988). Complainable matters: The use of idiomatic expression in making complaints. *Social Problems, 35,* 398–417.

Durkheim, E. (1948). *Elementary forms of religious life.* Glencoe, IL: Free Press.

Edwards, D. (1997). *Discourse and cognition.* London: Sage.

Eglin, P., & Hester, S. (1999). Moral order and the Montreal massacre: A story of membership categorization analysis. In P. L. Jalbert (Ed.), *Media studies: Ethnomethodological approaches* (pp. 195–230). Lanham, MD: University Press of America.

Fairclough, N. (1989). *Language and power.* London: Longman.

Fairclough, N. (1995). *Media discourse.* London: Edward Arnold.

Foucault, M. (1973). *The birth of the clinic: An archaeology of medical perception.* New York: Pantheon.

Foucault, M. (1977). *Discipline and punish: The birth of the prison.* London: Allen Lane.

Foucault, M. (1978). *The history of sexuality,* Vol. 1: *An introduction.* New York: Pantheon.

Garfinkel, H. (1967). *Studies in ethnomethodology.* Englewood Cliffs, NJ: Prentice Hall.

Goffman, E. (1955). On face work. *Psychiatry, 18,* 213–231.

Goffman, E. (1983). The interaction order. *American Sociological Review, 48,* 1–17.

Goodwin, C. (1981). *Conversational organization: Interaction between speakers and hearers.* New York: Academic Press.

Goodwin, C., & Goodwin, M. H. (1992). Assessments and the construction of context. In A. Duranti & C. Goodwin (Eds.), *Rethinking context: Language as interactive phenomenon* (pp. 147–190). Cambridge, UK: Cambridge University Press.

Gotthill, M., & Armstrong, D. (1999). Dr. No-Body: The construction of the doctor as an embodied subject in British general practice 1955–97. *Sociology of Health and Illness, 21*(1), 1–12.

Greatbatch, D. (1992). On the management of disagreement between news interviewees. In P. Drew & J. Heritage (Eds.), *Talk at work: Interaction in institutional settings* (pp. 268–302). Cambridge, UK: Cambridge University Press.

Greimas, A. J. (1966). *Semantique Structurale.* Paris: Larousse.

Haakana, M. (2001). Laughter as a patient's resource: Dealing with delicate aspects of medical interaction. *Text, 21,* 187–219.

Hak, T. (1999). "Text" and "con-text": Talk bias in studies of health care work. In S. Sarangi & C. Roberts (Eds.), *Talk, work, and institutional order* (pp. 427–452). Berlin, Germany: Mouton de Gruyter.

Heath, C. (1992). The delivery and reception of diagnosis in the general-practice consultation. In P. Drew & J. Heritage (Eds.), *Talk at work: Interaction in institutional settings* (pp. 235–267). Cambridge, UK: Cambridge University Press.

Heritage, J. (1984). *Garfinkel and ethnomethodology.* Cambridge, UK: Polity.

Heritage, J. (1998). Oh-prefaced responses to inquiry. *Language in Society, 27,* 291–334.

Heritage, J., & Atkinson, J. M. (1984). Introduction. In J. M. Atkinson & J. Heritage (Eds.), *Structures of social action* (pp. 1–15). Cambridge, UK: Cambridge University Press.

Heritage, J., & Sefi, S. (1992). Dilemmas of advice: Aspects of the delivery and reception of advice in interactions between health visitors and first time mothers. In P. Drew & J. Heritage (Eds.), *Talk at work: Interaction in institutional settings* (pp. 359–417). Cambridge, UK: Cambridge University Press.

Heritage, J., & Stivers, T. (1999). Online commentary in acute medical visits: A method for shaping patient expectations. *Social Science and Medicine, 49,* 1501–1517.

Hester, S., & Eglin, P. (Eds.). (1997). *Culture in action.* Lanham, MD: University Press of America.

Hutchby, I., & Wooffitt, R. (1998). *Conversation analysis: Principles, practices, and applications.* Cambridge, UK: Polity.

Jayyusi, L. (1991). Values and moral judgement: Communicative praxis as moral order. In G. Button (Ed.), *Ethnomethodology and the human sciences* (pp. 227–251). Cambridge, UK: Cambridge University Press.

Jefferson, G. (1984). On the organization of laughter in talk about troubles. In J. M. Atkinson & J. Heritage (Eds.), *Structures of social action* (pp. 346–369). Cambridge, UK: Cambridge University Press.

Kendall, G., & Wickham, G. (1999). *Using Foucault's methods.* London: Sage.

Kitzinger, C. (2000). Doing feminist conversation analysis. *Feminism & Psychology, 10,* 163–193.

Malarek, V. (1989, December 12). *The Globe and Mail.*

Mandelbaum, J. (1992). Assigning responsibility in conversational storytelling: The interactional construction of reality. *Text, 13,* 247–266.

Maynard, D. W. (1991). Interaction and asymmetry in clinical discourse. *American Journal of Sociology, 97,* 448–495.

Maynard, D. W. (1992). On clinicians co-implicating recipients' perspective in the delivery of diagnostic news. In P. Drew & J. Heritage (Eds.), *Talk at work: Interaction in institutional settings* (pp. 331–358). Cambridge, UK: Cambridge University Press.

Maynard, D. W. (2003). *Bad news, good news: Conversational order in everyday talk and clinical settings.* Chicago: University of Chicago Press.

McHoul, A. W., & Grace, A. (1993). *A Foucault primer: Discourse, power, and the subject.* Melbourne, Australia: Melbourne University Press.

McIlvenny, P. (2002). *Talking gender and sex.* Amsterdam, Netherlands: John Benjamins.

Merritt, M. (1976). On questions following questions (in service encounters). *Language in Society, 5,* 315–357.

Peräkylä, A. (1995). *AIDS counselling; Institutional interaction and clinical practice.* Cambridge, UK: Cambridge University Press.

Peräkylä, A. (1998). Authority and accountability: The delivery of diagnosis in primary health care. *Social Psychology Quarterly, 61,* 301–320.

Peräkylä, A. (2002). Agency and authority: Extended responses to diagnostic statements in primary care encounters. *Research on Language and Social Interaction, 35,* 219–247.

Pomerantz, A. (1984). Agreeing and disagreeing with assessments: Some features of preferred/dispreferred turn shapes. In J. M. Atkinson & J. Heritage (Eds.), *Structures of social action: Studies in conversation analysis* (pp. 67–101). Cambridge, UK: Cambridge University Press.

Potter, J. (2004). Discourse analysis as a way of analysing naturally occurring talk. In D. Silverman (Ed.), *Qualitative research: Theory, method, and practice* (2nd ed., pp. 200–201). London: Sage.

Potter, J., & Wetherell, M. (1987) *Discourse and social psychology: Beyond attitudes and behaviour.* London: Sage.

Propp, V. I. (1968). *Morphology of the folk tale* (rev. ed., L. A. Wagner, Ed.). Austin: University of Texas Press.

Sacks, H. (1974a). An analysis of the course of a joke's telling in conversation. In R. Bauman & J. Sherzer (Eds.), *Explorations in the ethnography of speaking* (pp. 337–353). Cambridge, UK: Cambridge University Press.

Sacks, H. (1974b). On the analysability of stories by children. In R. Turner (Ed.), *Ethnomethodology* (pp. 216–232). Harmondsworth, UK: Penguin.

Sacks, H. (1979). Hotrodder: A revolutionary category. In G. Psathas (Ed.), *Everyday language: Studies in ethnomethodology* (pp. 7–14). New York: Irvington.

Sacks, H. (1992). *Lectures on conversation* (Vol. 1, G. Jefferson, Ed., with an introduction by E. Schegloff). Oxford, UK: Basil Blackwell.

Sacks, H., Schegloff, E., & Jefferson, G. (1974). A simplest systematics for the organization of turn-taking for conversation. *Language, 50,* 696–735.

Schegloff, E. A. (1968). Sequencing in conversational openings. *American Anthropologist, 70,* 1075–1095.

Schegloff, E. A. (1982). Discourse as an interactional achievement: Some uses of "uh huh" and other things that come between sentences. In D. Tannen (Ed.), *Georgetown University Round Table on Languages and Linguistics 1981* (pp. 71–93). Washington, DC: Georgetown University Press.

Schegloff, E. A. (1991). Reflection on talk and social structure. In D. Boden & D. Zimmerman (Eds.), *Talk and social structure* (pp. 44–70). Cambridge, UK: Polity.

Schegloff, E. A. (1992a). Introduction. In G. Jefferson (Ed.), *Harvey Sacks: Lectures on conversation,* Vol. 1: *Fall 1964–Spring 1968.* Oxford, UK: Blackwell.

Schegloff, E. A. (1992b). On talk and its institutional occasion. In P. Drew & J. Heritage (Eds.), *Talk at work: Interaction in institutional settings* (pp. 101–134). Cambridge, UK: Cambridge University Press.

Schegloff, E. A. (1992c). Repair after next turn: The last structurally provided defense of intersubjectivity in conversation. *American Journal of Sociology, 98,* 1295–1345.

Schegloff, E. A. (1995). *Sequence organization* [mimeo]. Los Angeles: University of California, Los Angeles, Department of Sociology.

Schegloff, E. A., Jefferson, G., & Sacks, H. (1977). The preference for self-correction in the organization of repair in conversation. *Language, 53,* 361–382.

Schegloff, E. A., & Sacks, H. (1973). Opening up closings. *Semiotica, 8,* 289–327.

Seale, C. (1998). *Constructing death: The sociology of dying and bereavement.* Cambridge, UK: Cambridge University Press.

Silverman, D. (1997). *Discourses of counselling.* London: Sage.

Silverman, D. (1998). *Harvey Sacks: Social science and conversation analysis.* Cambridge, UK: Polity.

Silverman, D. (2001). *Interpreting qualitative data: Methods for analyzing talk, text, and interaction* (2nd ed.). London: Sage.

Smith, D. (1974). The social construction of documentary reality. *Sociological Inquiry, 44,* 257–268.

Smith, D. (1990). *The conceptual practices of power.* Toronto: University of Toronto Press.

Sorjonen, M-L. (2001). *Responding in conversation: A study of response particles in Finnish.* Amsterdam, Netherlands: John Benjamins.

Speer, S. (2002). "Natural" and "contrived" data: A sustainable distinction, *Discourse Studies, 4,* 511–525.

Tainio, L. (1999). Opaskirjojen kieli ikkunana suomalaiseen parisuhteeseen. *Naistutkimus, 12*(1), 2–26.

Tainio, L. (2002). Negotiating gender identities and sexual agency in elderly couples' talk. In P. McIlvenny (Ed.), *Talking gender and sexuality* (pp. 181–206). Amsterdam, Netherlands: John Benjamins.

Taylor, T. J., & Cameron, D. (1987). *Analyzing conversation: Rules and units in the structure of talk.* Oxford, UK: Pergamon.

ten Have, P. (1995). Disposal negotiations in general practice consultations. In A. Firth (Ed.), *The discourse of negotiation: Studies of language in the workplace* (pp. 319–344). Oxford, UK: Pergamon.

Törrönen, J. (2000). The passionate text: The pending narrative as a macrostructure of persuasion. *Social Semiotics, 10*(1), 81–98.

Törrönen, J. (2003). The Finnish press's political position on alcohol between 1993 and 2000. *Addiction, 98,* 281–290.

Vehviläinen, S. (2001). Evaluative advice in educational counseling: The use of disagreement in the "stepwise entry" to advice. *Research on Language and Social Interaction, 34,* 371–398.

West, C. (1979). Against our will: Male interruption of females in cross-sex conversation. *Annals of the New York Academy of Science, 327,* 81–97.

Wetherell, M. (1998). Positioning and interpretative repertoires: Conversation analysis and post-structuralism in dialogue. *Discourse & Society, 9,* 387–412.

Wetherell, M., & Potter, J. (1992). *Mapping the language of racism: Discourse and the legitimation of exploitation.* London: Harvester.

Zimmerman, D. H., & West, C. (1975). Sex roles, interruptions, and silences in conversation. In B. Thorne & N. Henley (Eds.), *Language and sex: Difference and dominance* (pp. 105–129). Rowley, MA: Newbury House.

35

FOCUS GROUPS

Strategic Articulations of Pedagogy, Politics, and Inquiry

George Kamberelis and Greg Dimitriadis

Our goal in this chapter is primarily conceptual and transdisciplinary as we explore the complex and multifaceted phenomena of focus group research. At the broadest possible level, focus groups are collective conversations or group interviews. They can be small or large, directed or nondirected. As Table 35.1 indicates, focus groups have been used for a wide range of purposes over the past century or so. The U.S. military (e.g., Merton, 1987), multinational corporations, Marxist revolutionaries (e.g., Freire), literacy activists (e.g., Kozol, 1985), and three waves of radical feminist scholar-activists, among others, all have used focus groups to help advance their concerns and causes. These different uses of focus groups have overlapped in both distinct and disjunctive ways, and all have been strategic articulations of pedagogy, politics, and inquiry.

Given our primary goal in this chapter, we discuss only occasionally and in passing procedural and practical issues related to selecting focus group members, facilitating focus group discussion, and analyzing focus group transcripts. There are many texts available for readers who are looking for this kind of treatment (e.g., Bloor, Frankland, Thomas, & Robson, 2001; Krueger, 1994; Morgan, 1998; Schensul, LeCompte, Nastatsi, & Borgatti, 1999). Instead, we both explore and attempt to move beyond historical and theoretical treatments of focus groups as "instruments" of qualitative research. More specifically, we try to show how focus groups, independent of their intended purposes, are nearly always complex and multivalent articulations of instructional, political, and empirical practices and effects. As such, focus groups offer unique insights into the possibilities of or for critical inquiry as a deliberative, dialogic, and democratic practice that is always already engaged in and with real-world problems and asymmetries in the distribution of economic and social capital (Bourdieu & Wacquant, 1992).

We begin with a very basic insight. Focus groups are little more than quasi-formal or formal instances of many of the kinds of everyday speech acts that are the part and parcel of unmarked social life—conversations, group discussions, negotiations, and the like (Bakhtin, 1986). Although their appropriation for the strategic purposes of teaching, challenging hegemonies,

Table 35.1. Discursive Formations and the Deployment of Focus Groups Over Time

Discursive Formation	*Pre-World War II*	*1950–1980*	*1980–2000*	*2000–*
Military intelligence	X			
Market research	X	X	X	X
Emancipatory pedagogy		X	X	X
First-wave feminism	X			
Second-wave feminism		X	X	
Third-wave feminism			X	X

and conducting research makes sense, the kinds of interactions and purposes that constitute focus groups were there all along. Taking such an approach allows us to expand and challenge the conscribed parameters of focus group work within qualitative inquiry. Thus, we highlight here three overlapping domains in which focus groups have proliferated: pedagogy, politics, and qualitative research practice. Or, perhaps these terms represent the three primary and overlapping functions of focus groups rather than the three separate domains in which such groups typically operate. We suggest this alternative distinction because all three functions may be (and often are) present when focus groups are enacted in any domain.

Through our analyses of converging and diverging methods and uses of focus groups in these three domains or functions, we conclude that focus groups are unique and important formations of collective inquiry where theory, research, pedagogy, and politics converge. As such, they provide us with important insights and strategies for better understanding and working through the practices and effects signaled by the "seventh moment" of qualitative inquiry (Lincoln & Denzin, 2000) with its emphasis on praxis, methodological syncretism, dialogic relations in the field, the production of polyvocal texts, and the cultivation of sacredness in our daily lives.

In writing this chapter, we are also working out a broader project within which to read the history of qualitative inquiry against the grain (Kamberelis & Dimitriadis, 2005). Here, we focus on methodological practices in general, and on focus groups in particular, with an eye toward revisioning their histories in ways that will open them to new and creative uses. As Lincoln and Denzin (2000) suggested, qualitative researchers no longer have recourse to the kinds of linear histories that have so typically (if tacitly) informed mostly "procedural" discussions of research methods. Instead, we find ourselves always already enmeshed within complex and transversing social-material spaces where we must act as *bricoleurs,* using whatever we find at hand to create whatever effects we believe are possible and desirable. So, if researchers in the seventh moment have an approach at all, it must be something like what Foucault (1984) called a genealogical approach. Basically, a genealogical approach attempts to understand how any "subject" (e.g., a person, a social formation, a social movement, an institution) has been constituted out of particular intersections of forces and systems of forces. A genealogy maps the complex, contingent, and (often) contradictory ways in which these forces and systems of force came together to produce the formation in a particular way. Importantly, because of the complexity and contingency involved, the production of such formations cannot be predicted with any accuracy but can readily be "read" after the fact. Also important here is the fact that genealogies are not histories of causes but rather histories of effects, and their value lies not so much in what they tell us about the past as in what they enable us to do. From the perspective of genealogy,

> history becomes "effective" to the degree that it introduces discontinuity into our very being—as it divides our emotions, dramatizes our instincts, multiplies our body and sets it against itself. "Effective" history deprives the self of the reassuring stability of life and nature, and it will not permit itself to be transported by a voiceless obstinacy toward a millennial ending. It will uproot its traditional foundations and relentlessly disrupt its pretended continuity. This is because knowledge is not made for understanding; it is made for cutting. (Foulcault, 1984, p. 88)

In this spirit, we place three histories or genealogies of focus group activity in dialogue with each other: dialogic focus groups as critical pedagogical practice, focus groups as political practice, and focus groups as research practice. These three histories represent three different ways of thinking about the nature and functions of focus groups. We think that this dialogic juxtaposition begins to decenter the more popularly available treatments of focus groups within qualitative inquiry—suggesting new contexts, uses, and potentials—and begins to disclose the "effectivity" that affords the "cutting" that Foucault regarded as so important.

Dialogic Focus Groups as Critical Pedagogical Practice

In this section, we highlight how focus groups have been important pedagogical sites or instruments in the work of Paulo Freire in Brazil and Jonathan Kozol in New York. Through analyses of these exemplars, we show how collective critical literacy practices were used to address local politics and concerns about social justice. Among other things, we foreground the ways in which Freire and Kozol worked *with* people and not *on* them, thereby modeling an important praxis disposition for contemporary educators and qualitative researchers (e.g., Barbour & Kitzinger, 1999). As we show in what follows, Freire and Kozol used focus groups in ways that were very different from those used by people for propaganda and market research. The latter used focus groups to "extract" information from participants, that is, to figure out how to manipulate them more effectively. In contrast, Freire and Kozol used focus groups for imagining and enacting the emancipatory political possibilities of collective work, that is, as useful tools for accomplishing seventh moment imperatives.

Freire's (1970/1993) most famous book, *Pedagogy of the Oppressed,* can be read as equal parts social theory, philosophy, and pedagogical method. His claims about education are foundational, rooted both in his devout Christian beliefs and also in his Marxism. Throughout *Pedagogy of the Oppressed,* Freire argued that the goal of education is to begin to name the world and to recognize that we all are "subjects" of our own lives and narratives, not "objects" in the stories of others. We must acknowledge the ways in which we, as humans, are fundamentally charged with producing and transforming reality together. Those who do not acknowledge this, or those who want to control and oppress, are committing a kind of epistemic "violence":

> To surmount the situation of oppression, people must first critically recognize its causes, so that through transforming action they can create a new situation, one that makes possible the pursuit of a fuller humanity. But the struggle to be more fully human has already begun in the authentic struggle to transform the situation. (Foulcault, 1984, p. 29)

Freire often referred to these situations as "limit situations," that is, situations that people cannot imagine themselves beyond. Limit situations naturalize people's sense of oppression, giving it a kind of obviousness and immutability.

To help people imagine lives beyond these "limit situations," Freire spent long periods of time in communities trying to understand community members' interests, investments, and concerns so as to elicit comprehensive sets of "generative words." These words were used as starting points for literacy learning, and literacy learning was deployed in the service of social and political activism. More specifically, generative words were paired with pictures that represented them and then were interrogated by people in the community for both what they revealed and what they concealed with respect to the circulation of multiple forms of capital. Freire encouraged the people both to explore how the meanings and effects of these words functioned in their lives and to conduct research on how their meanings and effects did function, or could function, in a variety of ways in different social and political contexts. The primary goals of these activities were to help people feel in control of their words and to be able to use them to exercise power over the material and ideological conditions of their own lives. Thus, Freire's literacy programs were designed not so much to teach functional literacy as to raise people's critical consciousness (or *conscientization*) and to encourage them to engage in "praxis" or critical reflection inextricably linked to political action in the real world. Freire underscored the fact that praxis is never easy and always involves power struggles—often violent ones.

As this description of Freire's pedagogies for the oppressed suggests, he believed that humans live both "in" the world and "with" the world and, thus, can be active participants in making history. In fact, he argued that a fundamental possibility of the human condition is to be able to change the material, economic, and spiritual conditions of life itself through *conscientization* and praxis. He posited human agency, then, as situated or embodied freedom—a kind of limited but quite powerful agency that makes it possible to change oneself and one's situation for the better. To enact such agency, he argued, people need to emerge from their unconscious engagements with the world, reflect on them, and work to change them. Viewed in this way, the enactment of freedom is an "unfinalizable" process. In constantly transforming their engagements in and with the world, people are simultaneously shaping the conditions of their lives and are constantly recreating themselves.

Freire's insistence that the unending process of emancipation must be a collective effort is far from trivial. Central to this process is a faith in the power of dialogue. Importantly, for Freire, dialogue is defined as collective reflection or action. He believed that dialogue, fellowship, and solidarity are essential to human liberation and transformation:

> We can legitimately say that in the process of oppression, someone oppresses someone else; we cannot legitimately say that in the process of revolution, someone liberates someone else, nor yet that that someone liberates himself, but rather that men in communion liberate each other. (Freire, 1970/1993, p. 103)

Within Freirean pedagogies, the development and use of generative words and phrases and the cultivation of *conscientization* are enacted in the context of locally situated "study circles" (or focus groups). The goal for the educator or facilitator within these study circles is to engage with people in their lived realities, producing and transforming them. Again, for Freire (1970/1993), pedagogical activity is always already grounded in larger philosophical and social projects concerned with how people might "narrate" their own lives more effectively:

> The starting point for organizing the program content of education or political action must be the present, existential, concrete situation, reflecting the aspirations of the people. Utilizing certain basic contradictions, we must pose the existential, concrete, present situation to the people as a problem which challenges them and requires a response—not just at the intellectual level, but [also] at the level of action.... The task of the dialogical teacher in an interdisciplinary team working on the thematic universe revealed by [the team's] investigation is to "re-present" that universe to the people from whom she or he first received it—and "re-present" it not as a lecture, but as a problem. (pp. 76–90)

To illustrate this kind of problem-posing education rooted in people's lived realities and contradictions, Freire discussed a research program designed around the question of alcoholism. Because alcoholism was a serious problem in the city, a researcher showed an assembled group a photograph of a drunken man walking past three other men talking on the corner. The group responded, in effect, by saying that the drunken man was a hard worker—the only hard worker in the photograph—and that he was probably worried about his low wages and having to support his family. In the group members' words, "He is a decent worker and a souse like us" (Freire, 1970/1993, p. 99). The men in the study circle seemed to recognize themselves in this man, noting that he was a "souse" and situating his drinking in a politicized context. In this situation, alcoholism was "read" as a response to oppression and exploitation. The goal was to "decode" images and language in ways that eventually led to questioning and transforming the material and social conditions of existence. Freire offered other examples as well, including showing people different (and contradictory) news stories covering the same event. In each case, the goal was to help people understand the contradictions they live and to use these understandings to change their worlds.

Freire's pedagogical framework could not be readily contained within traditional educational contexts where the historical weight of the "banking model" imposed powerful and pervasive constraints. His work inspired a wide range of important social movements within education, and the activities of these movements have provided yet more models for how intensive group activity—the kinds realized in focus groups—can be imagined and enacted in innovative ways to produce "effective histories" within which knowledge is made not for understanding but rather for cutting (Foucault, 1984, p. 88). Freire exerted a particularly strong influence on the work of critical pedagogues such as Henry Giroux, Peter McLaren, and Jonathan Kozol, all of whom helped to reimagine Freire's work within a U.S. context.

Freire's work has been influential outside the field of education as well. Augusto Boal, for example, developed the "theater of the oppressed," which is grounded in the liberation impulses of Freire, and used theater to blur the line between the actors on-stage and the audience off-stage. The theater of the oppressed is a public, improvisational, and highly interactive form of theater with strong transformative and pedagogical impulses and potentials (Casali, 2002). In addition, Freire profoundly influenced the participatory action research (PAR) movement led by Orlando Fals Borda, among others. Here, researchers work with subordinated populations around the world to solve unique local problems with local funds of knowledge. The PAR movement is profoundly Freirean in its impulses (Fals Borda, 1985).

Freire was an especially powerful influence on several educationally oriented social movements in the United States. Kozol, perhaps best known for his groundbreaking book *Savage Inequalities* (1991), drew on Freire's emancipatory work to research and write another book, *Illiterate America.* In this book, Kozol (1985) wrote, "Paulo Freire's work among the people of northeast Brazil during the early 1960s is one instance of a government campaign which takes its energies from the illiterates themselves" (p. 95). Like Freire, Kozol grounded his own literacy programs in New York City in the actual lives of the people with whom he worked to create dialogic collectives with horizontal leadership:

> There is a tremendous difference between knocking on a door to tell somebody of a program that has been devised already and which they are given the choice, at most, to join or else ignore—and, on the other hand, to ask them to assist in the creation of that plan. . . . Some of the best ideas that I have heard have come out of discussions held within the neighborhoods themselves. People, moreover, are far more likely to participate in something which they or their neighbors have been invited to assist in planning—and something in which ideas they have offered have been more than "heard" but given application. (p. 106)

In practice, Kozol advocated working in study circles or focus groups in much the same way as did Freire—as key pedagogical instruments or sites:

> I have come to be convinced that groups of six or seven learners and one literacy worker represent an ideal unit of instruction for this plan. The presence of a circle of [a] half-dozen friends or neighbors helps to generate a sense of common cause and to arouse a sense of optimistic ferment that is seldom present in the one-to-one encounter. (p. 108)

Groups with such a composition allow for the emergence of dynamics that open up possibilities for constructing effective histories. They also function as spawning grounds for the emergence of locally situated and effective leadership:

> Learning in groups, people at length will generate group leaders; because these leaders will emerge out of their ranks, they will remain susceptible to criticism and correction. At the same time, because of their point of origin and their proximity to pain, they may be in an ideal position to discover and encourage others. (p. 109)

Taking his cues from Freire, Kozol also advocated the elicitation and use of generative words or phrases that are likely to lead to discussion, reflection, *conscientization*, and praxis. Extending the work of Freire, he argued that for both pedagogical and political reasons, these generative words or phrases should necessarily be complex because more complex words provide more access to the common phoneme–grapheme relations in any particular natural language (e.g., Spanish, English) and, thus, facilitate "reading the word" (Freire, 1970/1993). More complex words also have richer meaning potentials than do simpler words, and their precise meanings vary more as a function of their specific contexts and purposes of use, thereby facilitating "reading the world" (Freire, 1970/1993) in more critical ways. Collective discussions of complex words or phrases typically result in "unpacking" their structures, meaning potentials, and various "effectivities" within and across different social and political contexts. Kozol noted,

> The word "revolutionary," for example, might appear to be the paradigm of active language in a literacy struggle that is rooted in the anguish of impoverished people. Here is a single adjective which dominates the public dialogue of hope and fear, are all five vowels of the English language, four of the more common consonants, the difficult suffix "tion" which is used in several dozen common words, as well as the occasional vowel *y*. (Kozol, 1985, p. 136)

The lexical and syntactic complexity embodied in this word facilitates literacy learning or reading the word. The word also has an extraordinary surplus of meanings, and its meanings vary tremendously both within and across the different contexts in which it is commonly used. This complexity facilitates reading the world. For example, in lieu of its emancipatory political connotations, the word "revolutionary" is often diluted and domesticated in all kinds of ways, for example, the phrase "a revolutionary new detergent" or, more recently, "revolutionary technology." This word has also been used by the political right to "name" particular groups as dangerous and to strike fear in the hearts of patriotic (and even not so patriotic) citizens. Furthermore, the word has been appropriated by resistance and counterresistance groups as an emblematic indicator of their collective identities and to motivate and legitimate their struggles.

Kozol also noted the importance of *space* as a dimension of the decentering activity that occurs in relation to the pedagogically oriented study circles (or focus groups). These study circles seldom take place in "official" spaces such as public schools and other public institutions. Instead, they take place in church basements, people's apartments, recreation centers, and so forth. Like generative words and phrases, these spaces mark intellectual workers as committed to working with and within marginalized communities for the purpose of helping these communities to take over responsibility for their own struggles and their own existences. These spaces also become emblematic indicators of or for the collective identities of the communities themselves, and they create the kind of overdetermined solidarity that seems to be necessary for producing effective histories with forward momentum.

Summary

Dialogic focus groups have always been central to the kinds of radical pedagogies that have been advocated and fought for by intellectual workers such as Freire and Kozol. Organized around "generative" words and phrases, and usually located within unofficial spaces, focus groups become sites of or for collective struggle and social transformation. As problem-posing formations, they operate locally to identify, interrogate, and change specific lived contradictions that have been rendered invisible by hegemonic power/knowledge regimes. Their operation also functions to reroute the circulation of power within hegemonic struggles and even to redefine what power is and how it works. Perhaps most important for our purposes here, the impulses that motivate focus groups in pedagogical domains or for pedagogical functions have important implications for imagining and using focus groups as resources for constructing "effective histories" within qualitative research endeavors in the "seventh moment." (We return to this issue in the final section of the chapter.)

Importantly, these histories are largely situated and context dependent. For Freire and Kozol, as well as for Giroux and McLaren, one could not predict a priori what might be involved in emancipating political and educative agendas. Whereas both Freire and Kozol shared progressive roots and impulses, the next movement we explore more explicitly placed focus groups at the center of an explicitly defined political agenda—feminism.

Focus Groups as Political Practice: Feminist Consciousness-Raising Groups as Exemplars

In this section, we offer descriptions and interpretations of focus groups in the service of radical political work designed within social justice agendas. In particular, we focus on how consciousness-raising groups (CRGs) of second- and third-wave feminism have been deployed to mobilize empowerment agendas and to enact social change. This work provides important insights relevant for reimagining the possibilities of focus group activity within qualitative research endeavors. Whereas the primary goal of Freire and Kozol was to use literacy (albeit broadly defined) to mobilize oppressed groups to work against their oppression through praxis, the primary goal of the CRGs of second- and third-wave feminism was to build "theory" from the lived experiences of women that could contribute to their emancipation.

In our discussion of CRGs, we draw heavily on Esther Madriz's retrospective analyses of second-wave feminist work as well as on her own third-wave empirical work. In both of these endeavors, Madriz focused on political (and politicized) uses of focus groups within qualitative inquiry. As Madriz (2000) demonstrated, there is a long history of deploying focus groups in consciousness-raising activities and of promoting social justice agendas within feminist and womanist traditions. Importantly, as a form of collective testimony, focus group participation has often been empowering for women, especially women of color (p. 843). There are several reasons why this is the case. Focus groups decenter the authority of the researcher, providing women with safe spaces to talk about their own lives and struggles. These groups also allow women to connect with each other collectively, share their own experiences, and "reclaim their humanity" in a nurturing context (p. 843). Madriz noted that women themselves often take over these groups, reconceptualizing them in fundamental ways and with simple yet far-reaching political and practical consequences. In this regard, Madriz argued,

> Focus groups can be an important element in the advancement of an agenda of social justice for women, because they can serve to expose and validate women's everyday experiences of subjugation and their individual and collective survival and resistance strategies.... Group interviews are particularly suited for uncovering women's daily experience through collective stories and resistance narratives that are filled with cultural symbols, words, signs, and ideological representations that reflect different dimensions of power and domination that frame women's quotidian experiences. (p. 836–839)

As such, these groups constitute spaces for generating collective "testimonies," and these testimonies help both individual women and groups of women to find or produce their own unique and powerful "voices."

As Madriz and others have noted, focus groups have multiple histories within feminist lines of thought and action. Soon after slavery ended, for example, churchwomen and teachers gathered to organize political work in the South (e.g., Gilkes, 1994). Similarly, turn-of-the-century "book clubs" were key sites for intellectual nourishment and political work (e.g., Gere, 1997). Mexican women have always gathered in kitchens and at family gatherings to commiserate and work together to better their lives (e.g., Behar, 1993; Dill, 1994). And in 1927, Chinese women working in the San Francisco garment industry held focus group discussions to organize against their exploitation, eventually leading to a successful strike (e.g., Espiritu, 1997). Although we do not unpack these and other complex histories in this chapter, we do offer general accounts of the nature and function of focus groups within second- and third-wave feminism in the United States. These accounts pivot on the examination of several key, original, manifesto-like texts generated within the movement that we offer as synecdoches of the contributions of a much richer, more complex, contradictory, and intellectually and politically "effective" set of histories.

Perhaps the most striking realization that emerges from examining some of the original texts of second-wave feminism is the explicitly self-conscious ways in which women used focus groups as "research" to build "theory" about their everyday experiences and to deploy theory to enact political change. Interestingly but not surprisingly, this praxis-oriented work was dismissed by male radicals at the time as little more than "gossip" in the context of "coffee klatches." Ironically, this dismissal mirrors the ways in which qualitative inquiry is periodically dismissed for being "soft," "subjective," or "nonscientific." Nevertheless, second-wave feminists persisted in building theory from the "standpoint" of women's lived experiences and eventually became a powerful social force in the struggle for equal rights.

In response to claims that feminist theory was nonscientific, Sarachild (1978) argued,

> The decision to emphasize our own feelings and experiences as women and to test all generalizations and reading we did by our own experiences was actually the scientific method of research. We were in effect repeating the 17th century challenge of science to scholasticism: "study nature, not books," and put all theories to the test of living practice and action. (p. 145)

Sarachild continued, noting that the goal of CRGs was not simply for women to share atomized experiences, to express themselves, or to confess before the groups:

> The idea of consciousness-raising was never to end generalizations. It was to produce truer ones. The idea was to take our own feelings and experience more seriously than any theories which did not satisfactorily clarify them, and to devise new theories which did reflect the actual experience and necessities of women. (p. 148)

In other words, a primary imperative of these groups was to use power in productive ways (e.g., Foucault, 1977, 1980), that is, to experiment with and intervene in reality itself (Deleuze & Guattari, 1987). This imperative went beyond representation toward reinvention. Attending to the current realities of women was a means toward the end of remapping those realities and connecting them to strategic political interests.

Despite this poststructural imperative, these discussions were often peppered with the language of "truth" and "science," making them seem decidedly postpositivist by today's standards. In many respects, this is not surprising because these women were working out of an essentialist, foundationalist perspective and also needed to inflect their arguments in ways that would allow them to be heard within a social and political climate that was unquestionably Euro-American, male dominated, and heterosexist. Yet they also seemed to realize that building political agendas around women's experiences is an inexhaustible and unfinalizable activity. In this regard, Sarachild (1978) contrasted "consciousness-raising groups" with "study groups" and "rap groups." She referred to CRGs as "revolutionary" and to the latter two kinds of groups as products of "left liberalism error" and "right liberalism error," respectively (p. 150). These contrasts are fascinating for many reasons. In a discussion with a Freirean subtext, she noted that the errors introduced by both the right liberalism and the left liberalism did not really investigate things. Instead, they began with a priori conclusions and then attempted to justify them with dogma or some semblance of empiricism. More specifically, she saw left-leaning study groups as dogmatists and saw right-leaning groups as post hoc empiricist. In contrast, she saw evolutionary CRGs as rooted in "investigation and discovery" and saw their political agendas as radical. Importantly, Sarachild was playing with the polysemic and heteroglossic meanings of "root" and "radical" here. She noted, "We were interested in getting to the roots of problems in society. You might say we wanted to pull up weeds in the garden by their roots, not just pick off the leaves at the top to make things look good momentarily" (p. 144). So, although these CRGs were intensely personal, the personal was always deployed in the service of larger theoretical and political agendas.

In many respects, the CRGs of second-wave feminism helped set the agenda for a whole generation of feminist activism. As Eisenstein (1984) noted, these groups helped to bring personal issues in women's lives to the forefront of political discourse. Issues such as abortion, incest, sexual molestation, and domestic and physical abuse emerged from these groups as pressing social issues around which public policy and legislation had to be enacted. Importantly, these issues had previously been considered to be too personal and too intensely idiosyncratic to be taken seriously by men at the time, whether they were scholars, political activists, politicians, or the like. By finding out which issues were most pressing in women's lives, CRGs were able to advance what had previously been considered individual, psychological, and private matters to the agendas of local collectives and eventually to social and political agendas at regional and national levels.

Like the work of Freire and Kozol, most focus group work within second-wave feminist qualitative inquiry has recognized the constitutive power of *space* and *place.* Groups are typically held in familiar settings such as kitchens, church basements, senior citizens' dining or living rooms, and women's shelters. Madriz (2000) noted, "Using participants' familiar spaces further diffuses the power of the researcher, decreasing the possibilities of 'otherization'" (p. 841).

In addition to the second-wave feminist work that was primarily theoretical and political, there was a large body of work that was quite practical, focusing largely on how to conduct CRGs. In other words, discourses on method were part and parcel of the movement. Not surprisingly, these discourses nearly always displayed a praxis orientation—the articulation of theory and practice for social and political change. Moreover, careful attention was paid to issues of power, especially with respect to micropolitical power relations that seemed to represent *internal* threats to the potential for second-wave feminists to produce effective histories. The ideal composition of CRGs, for example, was heavily debated. How homogeneous or heterogeneous should they be? How large should the groups be to be maximally effective? How centralized or decentralized should group leadership be? Should the groups be "single-sexed," with sympathetic men doing other kinds of work in other contexts?

Much thought and effort were also devoted to developing "manuals" for women who wanted to develop and maintain CRGs from the ground up. The Cape Cod Women's Liberation Movement (1972), for example, distributed a pamphlet that advised the following:

> I. You might start by discussing something everyone has read, to get over the initial awkwardness.
>
> II. Try talking about what each woman imagines feminism to be. Or what each expects—hopes and/or fears—to get out of the group.
>
> III. Personal histories can be shared, what each woman does, her living situation, how long she has been interested, and how each found out about the group.
>
> IV. Each woman can briefly describe her background. We all have childhoods: they influenced us but are less threatening to discuss than recent events.
>
> V. Whatever we start with, one simple method is to "go around the room." Each woman talks in turn. That way no one is passed over. It is vitally important that every woman speak.
>
> VI. After the first meeting, you might want to choose topics in advance. Some groups do; some do not. You might proceed by "going around" and seeing what people need to discuss that evening. You might discuss some external event that relates to women.

This pamphlet also discussed several obstacles and ways of overcoming them such as what to do when some women dominate the group or threaten each other and how to protect each other's privacy. The overall goals of pamphlets and flyers such as this were to build theory from the women's lived experiences and to articulate this theory with contemporary political agendas in ways that would promote equal rights for women under the law.

Like many collective efforts, the CRGs of second-wave feminism had some limitations. As Eisenstein (1984) noted, for example, these groups often operated under the constraints of what she called "false universalism." In other words, these groups often purported to speak for all women in unproblematic ways as if the experiences of white middle-class women were universal. This limitation is common among most social movements where members tend to be "alike" in many ways and where collective identities need to be overdetermined to amass any political weight. In the case of second-wave feminism, a primary goal was "to enable the participants to deemphasize their differences and to focus on the experiences they had in common. The generalizations, of course, only describe the experiences of those women who participated. By and large, these were college-educated white women" (p. 133).

These universalist tendencies alienated many women of color who saw feminism as a "middle-class white thing." As Madriz (2000) emphasized, however, many of the insights and strategies generated within the CRGs of second-wave feminism could be easily adapted to be relevant to the desires, needs, and hopes of women of color and other multiply marginalized groups of women. Indeed, if we map the trajectory from second-wave to third-wave feminism, we see both continuities and discontinuities.

The next generation of feminist scholars and researchers did indeed build on and extend the agendas of second-wave feminism while also stressing the differences within and between "groups" of women. The standpoint positions of African American, Latina, and gay women, for example, all became pronounced during this time period. Working within the movement(s) of third-wave feminism, Madriz (1997) used focus groups in powerful ways, some of which are evidenced in her book, *Nothing Bad Happens to Good Girls.* In this book, Madriz discussed the many ways in which the fear of crime works to produce an insidious form of social control over women's lives. Fear of crime produces certain ideas about what women "should" and "should not" do in public to protect themselves, enabling debilitating ideas about what constitutes "good girls" versus "bad girls" and severely constraining the range of everyday practices available to women.

With respect to research methods, Madriz called attention to the fact that most research findings on women's fear of crime had previously been generated from large survey studies of both men and women. This approach, she argued, severely limits the range of thought and experience that participants are willing to share and, thus, leads to unnecessarily partial and inaccurate accounts of the phenomenon. In other words, it is hard to get people—women in particular—to talk about sensitive topics, such as their own fears of assault or rape, in uninhibited and honest ways in the context of oral or written surveys completed alone or in relation to a single social scientist interviewer. This general problem is further complicated by differences in power relations between researchers and research participants that are a function of age, social class, occupation, language proficiency, race, and so forth.

To work against the various alienating forces that seem inherent in survey research and to collect richer and more voluminous accounts of experience with greater verisimilitude, Madriz used focus groups, noting that these groups provided a context where women could support each other in discussing their experiences of crime as well as their fears and concerns about crime. Indeed, these groups do mitigate against the intimidation, fear, and suspicion with which many women approach the one-on-one interview. In the words of one of Madriz's (1997) participants, "When I am alone with an interviewer, I feel intimidated, scared. And if they call me over the telephone, I never answer their questions. How do

I know what they really want or who they are?" (p. 165). In contrast, focus groups afford women much safer and more supportive contexts within which they may explore their lived experiences and the consequences of these experiences with other women who will understand what they are saying intellectually, emotionally, and viscerally.

This idea of safe and supportive spaces ushers in another important dimension of focus group work within third-wave feminist research, namely the importance of constituting groups in ways that mitigate against alienation, create solidarity, and enhance community building. To achieve such ends, Madriz emphasized the importance of creating homogeneous groups in terms of race, class, age, specific life experiences, and so forth—all of which are hallmarks of third-wave feminism.

Both in her own work and in her efforts to be a spokesperson for third-wave feminist approaches to qualitative inquiry, Madriz (1997) outlined a set of attitudes and practices that built on and extended the work of the second wave. Among other things, she acknowledged a long history of feminist approaches to qualitative work grounded within a long history of "no name" feminist and womanist practices—"exchanges with mothers, sisters, neighbors, friends" (p. 166). She also revisioned focus groups as vehicles for collective testimony, which offer affordances that help women to get beyond the social isolation that has historically characterized their lives (p. 166). These affordances clearly grew out of the initiatives and imperatives of second-wave CRGs already discussed, but they extended the CRGs as well. In particular, Madriz argued that the nonessentialist, social constructionist, and (often) postcolonial nature of third-wave feminist research projects accounts more fully for the extraordinary variability that often exists between and among women's experiences depending on social positioning with respect to race, class, region, age, sexual orientation, and so forth. Third-wave feminist researchers, thus, refracted and multiplied the standpoints from which testimonies might flow and voices might be produced. Although researchers such as Madriz held onto the postpositivist ideal of building theory from lived experiences, they also pushed for theory that accounted more fully for the local, complex, and nuanced nature of lived experiences that are always already constructed within power relations produced at the intersections of multiple social categories.

In the end, a primary goal of focus group activity within third-wave feminist research is not to offer prescriptive conclusions but rather to highlight the productive potentials (both oppressive and emancipatory) of particular social contexts (with their historically produced and durable power relations) within which such prescriptions typically unfold. In this regard, the work of Madriz is a synecdoche for third-wave feminist work more broadly conceived, particularly by women of color such as Dorinne Kondo, Smadar Lavie, Ruth Behar, Aiwa Ong, and Lila Abu-Lughod.

Summary

The nature and functions of CRGs within second- and third-wave feminism offer many important insights into the potential of focus groups to function in the service of the key imperatives of "seventh moment" qualitative inquiry. Building on Madriz's political reading of focus groups, and more specifically on the constructs of "testimony" and "voice," we highlight some of these possibilities here.

One key function of focus groups within feminist work has been to elicit and validate collective testimonies and group resistance narratives. These testimonies and narratives have been used by women—and could be used by any subjugated group—"to unveil specific and little-researched aspects of women's daily existences, their feelings, attitudes, hopes, and dreams" (Madriz, 2000, p. 836). Another key emphasis of focus groups within feminist and womanist traditions has been the discovery or production of voice. Because focus groups often result in the sharing of similar stories of everyday experiences of struggle, rage, and the like, they often end up validating individual voices that had previously been constructed within and through mainstream discourses as idiosyncratic, selfish, and even evil. Because focus groups foreground and exploit the power of testimony and voice, they can become sites for the overdetermination of collective identity as strategic political practice. This overdetermination creates a critical mass of visible solidarity that seems to be a necessary first step toward social and political change.

A major concern of feminist researchers has been the moral dilemmas inherent in interviewing and the researcher's role in these dilemmas. Focus groups mitigate against these dilemmas by creating multiple lines of communication that help to create "safe spaces" for dialogue in the company of others who have had similar life experiences and who are struggling with similar issues. In relation to this point, focus groups can allow for unique forms of access to the "natural" interaction that can occur between and among participants. Because focus groups privilege "horizontal interaction" over "vertical interaction," they are also constituted as social spaces that tend to decrease the influence of the researcher in controlling the topics and flow of interaction. Among other things, this horizontality increases the potential for rearticulating power dynamics within focus group interactions in ways that can lead to the collection of especially rich information (i.e., high-quality data) that will eventually result in accounts that are replete with "thick description" and rich in verisimilitude.

Focus groups within feminist and womanist traditions have also mitigated against the Western tendency to separate thinking and feeling, thereby opening up possibilities for reimagining knowledge as distributed, relational, embodied, and sensuous. Viewing knowledge in this light brings into view the complexities and contradictions that are always a part of fieldwork. It also illuminates the relations between power and knowledge and, thus, insists that qualitative research is always already political—implicated in social critique and social change.

Either out of necessity or for strategic purposes, feminist work has always taken into account the constitutive power of *space*. To further work against asymmetrical power relations and the processes of "othering," focus group meetings are nearly always held in safe spaces where women feel comfortable, important, and validated. This is a particularly important consideration when working with women who have much to lose from their participation, for example, undocumented immigrants and so-called deviant youths.

Finally, the break from second-wave to third-wave feminism called into question the monolithic treatment of difference under the sign of "woman" that characterized much of second-wave thinking and also highlighted the importance of creating focus groups that are relatively homogeneous in terms of life histories, perceived needs, desire, race, social class, region, age, and so forth because such groups are more likely to achieve the kind of solidarity and collective identity that are necessary for producing "effective histories." Although coalition building across such relatively homogeneous groups of women may be important in some instances, focused intellectual and political work is often most successful when it is enacted by people with similar needs, desires, struggles, and investments.

Together, the various insights and practices of CRGs within feminist work have been invaluable in propelling us toward the seventh moment and in helping us to imagine and enact (a) a commitment to morally sound, praxis-oriented research; (b) the strategic use of eclectic constellations of theories, methods, and research strategies; (c) the cultivation of dialogic relationships in the field; (d) the production of polyvocal nonrepresentational texts; and (d) the conduct of mindful inquiry attuned to what is sacred in and about life and text.

▣ Focus Groups as Research Practice

Interest in focus groups in the social sciences has ebbed and flowed over the course of the past 60 years or so. In many respects, the first really visible use of focus groups for conducting social science research may be traced back to the work of Paul Lazarsfeld and Robert Merton. Their focus group approach emerged in 1941 as the pair embarked on a government-sponsored project to assess media effects on attitudes toward America's involvement in World War II. As part of their research at the Columbia University Office of Radio Research, Lazarsfeld and Merton recruited groups of people to listen and respond to radio programs designed to boost morale for the war effort (Merton, 1987, p. 552). Originally, the researchers asked participants to push buttons to indicate their positive or negative responses to the radio programs. Because the data yielded from this work could help them to answer "what" questions but not "why" questions about participants' choices, the researchers used focus groups as forums for getting participants to explain why they responded in the ways they did. Importantly, Lazarsfeld and Merton's use of focus groups as a qualitative research strategy was always secondary (and less legitimate) than the various quantitative methods of data collection and analysis the researchers deployed. They used focus groups in exploratory ways to generate new questions that could be used to develop new quantitative strategies or simply to complement or annotate the more quantitative findings of their research. Lunt (1996) observed that Merton saw "the role of the focus groups as identifying the salient dimensions of complex social stimuli as [a] precursor to further quantitative tests" (p. 81). Two dimensions of Lazarsfeld and Merton's research efforts constitute part of the legacy of using focus groups within qualitative research: (a) capturing people's responses in real space and time in the context of face-to-face interactions and (b) strategically "focusing" interview prompts based on themes that are generated in these face-to-face interactions and that are considered particularly important to the researchers.

In philosophy of science terms, the early use of focus groups as resources for conducting research was quite conservative in nature. This is not at all surprising given that the work of Lazarsfeld and Merton was funded by the military and included "interviewing groups of soldiers in Army camps about their responses to specific training films and so called morale films" (Merton, 1987, p. 554). Their research also included studies of why people made war bond pledges. The goal of much of this work was to better understand people's beliefs and decision-making processes so as to develop increasingly effective forms of propaganda.

The kind of focus group research conducted by scholars such as Lazarsfeld and Merton all but disappeared within the field of sociology during the middle part of the 20th century, only to reemerge in the early 1980s, particularly around "audience analysis" work (Morley, 1980). When it did reemerge, it was no longer wed to—or used in the service of—predominantly quantitative-oriented research, a fact that Merton (1987) bemoaned:

> I gather that much of the focus-group research today as a growing type of market research does not involve this composite of both qualitative and quantitative inquiry. One gains the impression that focus-group research is being mercilessly misused as quick-and-easy claims for the validity of the research [that] are not subjected to further quantitative tests.... For us, qualitative focused group interviews were taken as sources of new ideas and new hypothes[es], not as demonstrated findings with regard to the extent and distribution of the provisionally identified qualitative patterns of response. (pp. 557–558)

Criticisms such as these notwithstanding, audience analysis research was decidedly interpretive. Its primary goal was to understand the complexities involved in how people understood and interpreted media texts; its methods were nearly exclusively qualitative. In contrast to Lazarsfeld and Merton's work, which focused on expressed content, audience analysis researchers focused on group dynamics themselves, believing that the meanings constructed within groups of viewers were largely socially constructed.

Janice Radway, for example, used focus groups to great effect in her pioneering research on the reading practices of romance novel enthusiasts that resulted in her book, *Reading the Romance.* Radway's (1991) research took place in and around a local bookstore, and her participants included the store owner and a group of 42 women who frequented the store and were regular romance readers. Radway developed a mixed-method research design that included text analysis and focus group interviews. Assisted by the store owner ("Dot"), Radway was able to tap into the activity dynamics of the existing networks of women who were avid romance novel readers. These women depended heavily on the store owner for advice about the latest novels, and they interacted with each other as well. Radway simply "formalized" some of these ongoing social activities to generate a systematic and rich store of information about the social circumstances, specific reading practices, attitudes, reading preferences, and multiple and contradictory functions of romance reading among the women she studied. In this regard, only days after meeting Dot for the first time, Radway "conducted two four-hour discussion sessions with a total of 16 of Dot's most regular customers" (p. 47). Radway's involvement with romance novels and romance readers further intensified as the study progressed. She read all of the books that her participants were reading. She talked with many of the participants informally whenever she saw them at the bookstore. She took her cues about what books to read and what issues to focus discussions on from Dot and the other participants.

Radway (1991) noted, among other things, the importance of group dynamics in how different romance novels were interpreted and used. She also underscored the importance of belonging to a reading group in mitigating the stigma often associated with the practice of reading romance novels. Through their collective involvement, Dot and her customers (i.e., Radway's participants) created a kind of solidarity with political potential. Radway used her knowledge of the political potential of collective activity strategically in her research:

> Because I knew beforehand that many women are afraid to admit their preference for romantic novels for fear of being scorned as illiterate or immoral, I suspected that the strength of numbers might make my informants less reluctant about discussing their obsession. (p. 252)

Finally, the ways in which Radway positioned herself within the reading groups were crucial. She noted, for example, that when she gently encouraged participants and backgrounded her own involvement, "the conversation flowed more naturally as the participants disagreed among themselves, contradicted one another, and delightedly discovered that they still agreed about many things" (p. 48).

All of the strategies that Radway deployed helped to mobilize the collective energy of the group and to generate kinds and amounts of data that are often difficult, if not impossible, to generate through individual interviews and even observations. In addition, these strategies—and participation in the focus groups themselves—helped to build a stronger and more effective collective with at least local political teeth. In this regard, Radway (1991) noted that the women used romance reading for two primary purposes: *combative* and *compensatory.* Each purpose is political in its own way, and each became understood more fully by the women in the context of their conversations and focus group discussions:

> It is *combative* in the sense that it enables them to refuse the other-directed social role prescribed for them within the institution of marriage. In picking up a book, as they have so eloquently told us, they are refusing temporarily their famil[ies'] otherwise constant demand that they attend to the wants of others even as they act deliberately to do something for their own private pleasure. Their activity is *compensatory,* then, in that it permits them to focus on themselves and to carve out a solitary space within an arena where their self-interest is usually identified with the interests of others and where they are defined as a public resource to be mined at will by the family. (p. 211)

These two political functions were clearly in tension at the end of *Reading the Romance,* and how this tension might work itself out over time was left unresolved. However, Radway concluded her book with a hopeful call for praxis: "It is absolutely essential that we who are committed to social change learn not to overlook this minimal but nonetheless legitimate form of protest . . . and to learn how best to encourage it and bring it to fruition" (p. 222).

If the work of Radway began to outline the political, ethical, and praxis potential of focus groups within qualitative inquiry, the work of Patti Lather has pushed the "limit conditions" of focus groups about as far as has the work of anyone in the field of qualitative research today, especially with respect to how focus groups can bring postfoundational possibilities for research "into the clearing" (Heidegger, 1975). In their book *Troubling the Angels,* for example, Lather and Smithies (1997) explored the lives, experiences, and narratives of 25 women living with HIV/AIDS. *Troubling the Angels* is a book filled with overlapping and contradictory voices that grew out of 5 years of focus group interviews conducted in the context of "support groups" in five major cities in Ohio:

> In the autumn of 1992, we met with one of the support groups to explore what questions we should use in the interviews. The women attending this meeting were spilling over with excitement and ideas; their talk became a dialogue of issues and feelings and insights. Group process was producing a form and level of collaboration that could not be remotely duplicated in one-on-one interviews, so the decision was made to maintain the group format for most of the data collection. (p. xix)

Lather and Smithies also met and talked with these women at birthday parties and holiday get-togethers, hospital rooms and funerals, baby showers and picnics. The participation frameworks for interaction changed constantly across the project. Smithies, for example, noted that group dynamics were quite unpredictable and that the women often became upset or annoyed with each other (p. 194).

Although much of this book is devoted to troubling the waters of ethnographic representation, the lived experience of conducting fieldwork primarily through focus groups also troubles the waters of research practice. In this regard, Lather and Smithies integrated sociological, political, historical, therapeutic, political, and pedagogical practices and discourses in their work with the women they studied. In Lather's (2001) "postbook," for example, she claimed to have looked constantly for "the breaks and jagged edges of methodological practices from which we might draw useful knowledge for shaping present practices of a feminist ethnography in excess of our codes but, still, always already: forces already active in the present" (pp. 200–201). She continued,

> The task becomes to throw ourselves against the stubborn materiality of others, willing to risk loss, relishing the power of others to constrain our interpretive "will to know," saving us from the narcissism and its melancholy through the very positivities that cannot be exhausted by us, the otherness that always exceeds us. . . . Ethnography becomes a kind of self-wounding laboratory for discovering the rules by which truth is produced. Attempting to be accountable to complexity, thinking the limit becomes the task, and much opens up in terms of ways to proceed for those who know both too much and too little. (pp. 202–203)

In this regard, Lather elaborated on times when her experiences with the HIV/AIDS-afflicted women or their stories brought her to tears. She realized, in working with these women, that she had to negotiate her own relationship to loss. She wondered whether and how she could ever do it, and she sometimes doubted whether she could even go on with the project. In the most real sense, Lather came to realize the ways in which knowledge is always already embodied—bodily, viscerally, and materially—and the consequences that such a realization has for fieldwork and writing.

One of the most interesting sections of Lather and Smithies's (1997) book, for our purposes in this chapter, is one where the researchers cultivated a "methodology of getting lost":

> At some level, the book is about getting lost across the various layers and registers, about not finding one's way into making a sense that maps easily onto our usual ways of making sense. Here we all get lost: the women, the researchers, the readers, [and] the angels, in order to open up present frames of knowing to the possibilities of thinking differently. (p. 52)

Although these reflections refer to the book itself rather than to the process of conducting the research that led to the writing of the book, in the sense that the reflections index the political and ethical dimensions of all practices and all knowledge, they apply equally well to working with research participants in the field. For example, Lather and Smithies refused to position themselves as grand theorists and to interpret or explain the women's lives to them. Instead, they granted

> weight to lived experience and practical consciousness by situating both researcher and researched as bearers of knowledge while simultaneously attending to the "price" we pay for speaking out of discourses of truth, forms of rationality, effects of knowledge, and relations of power. (Lather, 2001, p. 215)

Through their tactical positioning, Lather and Smithies challenged the researcher's right to know and interpret the experiences of others while, at the same time, interrupting and getting in the way of their participants' attempts to narrate their lives through a kind of innocent ethnographic realism of voices speaking for themselves that included, among other things, the construction of AIDS as the work of God's will. In this regard, Lather and Smithies acknowledged their impositions and admitted that a different kind of book—a book that may, for example, be sold at Kmart—might have pleased their participants more. But such a book would not have served the researchers' own desires and goals to problematize the practice of qualitative inquiry. In the end, the book had to "please" both researchers and research participants—if only in partial and not completely satisfying ways.

These various relational and rhetorical tactics bring to light the very complicated and sometimes troubling micropolitics that are part and parcel of research practice in the "seventh moment," whether or not we are willing to "see" these micropolitics and enact them in our own work. The work of Lather and Smithies constantly reminds us that there are no easy separations between the researcher and the researched and that research itself is always already relational, political, and ethical work. There is no privileged place from which to experience and report on experiences objectively—only positions in dialogue. The key point here is that, more than most other research of which we are aware, the work of Lather and Smithies offers us ways in which to think about research that transcends and transforms the potentials of using focus groups for revisioning epistemology, interrogating the relative purchase of both lived experience and theory, reimagining ethics within research practice, and enacting fieldwork in ways that are more attuned to its sacred dimensions. This is difficult and dangerous work indeed:

> The danger is to steal knowledge from others, particularly those who have little else, and to use it for the interests of power. This is so even when the intended goal is to extend the reach of the very counter-knowledge [on which] the [work] is based, the stories entrusted to those "who enter [such alliances] from the side of privilege" (Fiske, 1996, p. 211) in order to transform the ubiquitous injustices of history into a readable place. (Lather, 2001, p. 221)

Summary

As we have demonstrated, focus groups have been used as instruments of qualitative inquiry within several distinct epistemological moments—Merton's positivism, second-wave critical feminism, and poststructural feminism. And although focus groups have always been a critical part of qualitative research practice, their use seems to be expanding (e.g., Bloor et al., 2001; Fontana & Frey, 2000; Morgan, 2000). Among other things, the use of focus groups has allowed scholars to move away from the dyad of the clinical interview and to explore group characteristics and dynamics as relevant constitutive forces in the construction of meaning and the practice of social life. Focus groups have also allowed researchers to explore the nature and effects of ongoing social discourse in ways that are not possible through individual interviews or observations. Individual interviews strip away the critical interactional dynamics that constitute much of social practice and collective meaning making. Observations are a bit of a "crap shoot" in terms of capturing the focused activity in which researchers may be interested. In contrast to observations, focus groups can be used strategically to cultivate new kinds of interactional dynamics and, thus, access to new kinds of information.

For example, as Radway (1991) and Lather and Smithies (1997) showed, focus groups can be used strategically to inhibit the authority of researchers and to allow participants to "take over" and "own" the interview space. Focus groups are also invaluable for promoting among participants synergy that often leads to the unearthing of information that is seldom easy to reach in individual memory. Focus groups also facilitate the exploration of collective memories and shared stocks of knowledge that might seem trivial and unimportant to individuals but that come to the fore as crucial when like-minded groups begin to revel in the everyday. In addition, as was demonstrated especially in the work of Radway (1991) and Lather and Smithies (1997), focus groups can become sites for local political work. Finally, and perhaps most important, the work of Lather and Smithies brings to light the fact that focus groups are rife with multiple affordances for conducting "seventh moment" qualitative inquiry that will help it move through (and perhaps beyond) the triple crisis of representation, legitimation, and praxis that has haunted qualitative work for the past two decades. In this regard, focus groups can lead to the kinds of "breakdowns" that Lather (2001) described and that Heidegger (1927/1962) argued are essential to genuine understanding. They can also serve as constant reminders that researchers should cultivate productive relations among description, interpretation, and explanation in their work. And perhaps most important, the dialogic possibilities afforded by focus groups help researchers to work against premature consolidation of their understandings and explanations, thereby signaling the limits of reflexivity and the importance of intellectual/empirical modesty as forms of ethics and praxis. Such modesty allows us to engage in "doubled practices" where we listen to the attempts of others as they make sense of their lives. It also allows us to resist the seductive qualities of "too easy" constructs such as "voice" as we trouble experience itself, which is always already constituted within one "grand narrative" or another (Lather, 2001, p. 218). In the end, the strategic development of focus group activity for conducting qualitative inquiry foregrounds the possibility that focus groups can be key democratic spaces during an age when such spaces are becoming increasingly eclipsed and atomized (Giroux, 2001; Henaff & Strong, 2001).

▣ A Critical Summary of Focus Groups in Research Practice

Focus group research is a key site or activity where pedagogy, politics, and interpretive inquiry intersect and interanimate each other. On a practical level, focus groups are efficient in the sense that they generate large quantities of material from relatively large numbers of people in a relatively short time. In addition, because of their synergistic potentials, focus groups often produce data that are seldom produced through individual interviewing and observation and that result in especially powerful interpretive insights. In particular, the synergy and dynamism generated within homogeneous collectives often reveal unarticulated norms and normative assumptions. They also take the interpretive process beyond the bounds of individual memory and expression to mine the historically sedimented collective memories and desires. This is one of the reasons why focus group work has been so well suited to the kinds of "problem-posing" and "problem-solving" pedagogies highlighted by Freire and Kozol. "Real-world" problems cannot be solved by individuals alone; instead, they require rich and complex funds of communal knowledge and practice.

In addition to enhancing the kinds and amounts of empirical material yielded from qualitative studies, focus groups foreground the importance not only of content, but also of expression, because they capitalize on the richness and complexity of group dynamics. Acting somewhat like magnifying glasses, focus groups induce social interactions akin to those that occur in everyday life but with greater focus. Focus groups, to a greater extent than observations and individual interviews, afford researchers access to the kinds of social interactional dynamics that produce particular memories, positions, ideologies, practices, and desires among specific groups of people.

As "staged conversations," focus groups are especially useful to researchers who want to conduct various kinds of discourse analyses such as those that we discussed earlier in relation to audience analysis. Focus groups allow researchers to see the complex ways in which people position themselves in relation to each other as they process questions, issues, and topics in focused ways. These dynamics themselves become relevant "units of analysis" for study.

In addition to inducing simulations of naturally occurring talk and social interaction, focus groups function to decenter the role of the researcher. As such, focus groups can facilitate the democratization of the research process, providing participants with more ownership over it, promoting more dialogic interactions and the joint construction of more polyvocal texts. These social facts were brought to light by the feminist work conducted by Madriz, Radway, and Lather and Smithies that we discussed earlier.

Focus groups, while functioning as sites for consolidating collective identities and enacting political work, also allow for the proliferation of multiple meanings and perspectives as well as for interactions between and among them. Because focus groups put multiple perspectives "on the table," they help researchers and research participants alike to realize that both the interpretations of individuals and the norms and rules of groups are inherently situated, provisional, contingent, unstable, and changeable. In this regard, focus groups help us to move toward constructing a "methodology of getting lost" and toward enacting "doubled practices" (Lather, 2001), which seem to be necessary first steps toward conducting "seventh moment" qualitative research.

▣ Retrospect and Prospect: Focus Groups as Strategic Articulations of Pedagogy, Politics, and Inquiry

We conclude with some conceptual musings on focus group methodology as negotiated accomplishment and performative pedagogy rooted in local activism. Focus groups, we maintain, are sites where pedagogy, politics, and interpretive methodology converge, providing a way in which to think about new horizons in qualitative inquiry as praxis-oriented and ethically grounded relational work.

Importantly, opening up focus groups to genealogical analysis allows us to decenter our understanding of this method and to imagine and enact new uses and functions. Indeed, if linear or procedural methodological narratives have buttressed positivist and postpositivist approaches to research, the search for different origins makes us realize that there are no such safe spaces. If nothing else, Foucault's notion of genealogy makes us responsible for the discourses we inhabit and for the histories we evoke. Broadening the range of focus group "referents" allows us to think through contemporary research praxis in more expansive ways.

But there are no ready-made answers here. Ethics and responsibility must guide such a discussion, one that wholly implicates researchers every step of the way. This includes the ways in which researchers are positioned within and against the groups with which they work. To echo Fine (1994), researchers today must "work the hyphen" in their different roles (e.g., participant-observer) and responsibilities, always acknowledging the roles we inhabit, including what they allow and what they deny. Indeed, according to Fine, researchers must actively work against "othering" in fieldwork (i.e., objectively creating neatly bounded subjects on which to report) while also resisting self-reflexivity or navel gazing (i.e., the danger of looking inward as a way of avoiding the ethical responsibility of acting in the world). Fine challenged us to avoid what Haraway (1991) called the "god-tricks" of "relativism" and "totalization." As Haraway wrote, "Relativism is the perfect twin of totalization in the ideologies of objectivity; both deny the stakes in location, embodiment, and partial perspective" (p. 191). Location, embodiment, and partial perspective are critical to the project of fieldwork, according to Fine.

More recently, Fine and Weis (1998) extended these concerns to explicitly address the complexities of political activism and policymaking. They argued, for example, that we must try to "meld *writing about* and *working with*" politically invested actors in more compelling and constitutive ways (p. 277, emphases in original). Ultimately, Fine, Weis, Wessen, and Wong (2000) demanded that we "think through the power, obligations, and responsibilities of social research" on multiple levels, accounting for multiple social contexts and concerns (p. 108). Self-reflexivity means increasing kinds of responsibility for such questions in social contexts that are always difficult to prefigure. As Fine and Weis (1998) argued,

> our obligation is to come clean "at the hyphen," meaning that we interrogate in our writings who *we* are as we co-produce the narratives we presume to "collect." . . . As part of this discussion, we want, here, to try to explain how we, *as researchers,* work *with* communities to capture and build upon community and social movements. (pp. 277–278, emphases in original)

This means expanding the range of roles that we play as researchers, field-workers, and authors to include political activism and policymaking—roles that do not always map easily onto each other. There are, in short, no safe spaces for qualitative researchers today. The notion of an objective and neutral qualitative inquiry has been decentered, leaving researchers with, to echo Bakhtin (1993), no alibis for their effectivity in the field. In the absence of foundational claims and clear splits between researchers and research participants, what is left is an uncertain landscape that asks us—no, demands us—to work with our participants to help make their situations better than they were when we found them. "The moral imperative of such work cannot be ignored," Lincoln and Denzin (2000) argued. They added, "We face a choice . . . of declaring ourselves committed to detachment or solidarity with the human community" (p. 1062).

Echoing Gramsci, we conclude that the "we" enabled by focus groups has "no guarantees." With no guarantees, focus groups must operate according to a "hermeneutics of vulnerability" (Clifford, 1988). Clifford developed the construct of a hermeneutics of vulnerability to discuss the constitutive effects of relationships between researchers and research participants on research practice and research findings. A hermeneutics of vulnerability foregrounds the ruptures of fieldwork, the multiple and contradictory positionings of all participants, the imperfect control of researchers, and the partial and perspectival nature of all knowledge. Among the primary tactics for achieving a hermeneutics of vulnerability, according to Clifford, is the tactic of self-reflexivity, which may be understood in at least two senses. In the first sense, self-reflexivity involves making transparent the rhetorical and poetic work of researchers in representing the objects of their studies. In the second (and, we think, more important) sense, self-reflexivity refers to the efforts of researchers and research participants to engage in acts of self-defamiliarization in relation to each other.

In this regard, Probyn (1993) discussed how the fieldwork experience can engender a virtual transformation of the identities of both researchers and research participants even as they are paradoxically engaged in the practice of consolidating them. This is important theoretically because it allows for the possibility of constructing a mutual ground between researchers and research participants even while recognizing that the ground is unstable and fragile. Self-reflexivity in this second sense is also important because it encourages reflection on interpretive research as the dual practice of knowledge gathering and self-transformation through self-reflection and mutual reflection with the other. Finally, as Lather (2001) showed, even self-reflexivity has serious limits with respect to working against the triple crisis of representation, legitimation, and praxis. Indeterminacies always remain. And allowing ourselves to dwell in (and perhaps even celebrate) these indeterminacies might be the best way of traveling down the roads of qualitative research practice and theory building at this particular historical juncture. Again, opening up to the unfinalizable complexity and heterogeneity of "others" within focus group interactions is at least one way of traveling down these roads.

References

Bakhtin, M. M. (1986). *Speech genres and other late essays* (V. W. McGee, Trans.). Austin: University of Texas Press.

Bakhtin, M. M. (1993). *Toward a philosophy of the act* (V. Liapunov, Trans.). Austin: University of Texas Press.

Barbour, R., & Kitzinger, J. (1999). *Developing focus group research.* Thousand Oaks, CA: Sage.

Behar, R. (1993). *Translated woman: Crossing the border with Esperanza's story.* Boston: Beacon.

Bloor, M., Frankland, J., Thomas, M., & Robson, K. (2001). *Focus groups in social research.* Thousand Oaks, CA: Sage.

Bourdieu, P., & Wacquant, L. J. D. (1992). *An invitation to reflexive sociology.* Chicago: University of Chicago Press.

Cape Cod Women's Liberation Movement. (1972). *Getting together: How to start a consciousness raising group.* [Online.] Retrieved March 10, 2003, from http://research.umbc.edu/~korenman/wmst/crguide2.html

Casali, A. (2002). The application of Paulo Freire's legacy in the Brazilian educational context. *Taboo, 6*(2), 9–16.

Clifford, J. (1988). *The predicament of culture.* Cambridge, MA: Harvard University Press.

Deleuze, G., & Guattari, F. (1987). *A thousand plateaus: Capitalism and schizophrenia* (B. Massumi, Trans.). Minneapolis: University of Minnesota Press.

Dill, B. T. (1994). Fictive kin, paper sons, and compadrazgo: Women of color and the struggle for family survival. In M. B. Zinn & B. T. Dill (Eds.), *Women of color in U.S. society* (pp. 149–169). Philadelphia: Temple University Press.

Eisenstein, H. (1984). *Contemporary feminist thought.* New York: Macmillan.

Espiritu, Y. L. (1997). *Asian women and men: Labor, laws, and love.* Thousand Oaks, CA: Sage.

Fals Borda, O. (Ed.). (1985). *The challenge of social change.* Beverly Hills, CA: Sage.

Fine, M. (1994). Working the hyphen: Reinventing self and other in qualitative research. In N. K. Denzin & Y. S. Lincoln (Eds.), *Handbook of qualitative research* (pp. 70–82). Thousand Oaks, CA: Sage.

Fine, M., & Weis, L. (1998). *The unknown city: Lives of poor and working-class young adults.* Boston: Beacon.

Fine, M., Weis, L., Wessen, S., & Wong, L. (2000). For whom? Qualitative research, representations, and social responsibilities. In N. K. Denzin & Y. S. Lincoln (Eds.), *Handbook of qualitative research* (2nd ed., pp. 107–131). Thousand Oaks, CA: Sage.

Fiske, J. (1996). Black bodies of knowledge: Notes on an effective history. *Cultural Critique, 33,* 185–212.

Fontana, A., & Frey, J. (2000). The interview: From structured questions to negotiated text. In N. K. Denzin & Y. S. Lincoln (Eds.), *Handbook of qualitative research* (2nd ed., pp. 645–672). Thousand Oaks, CA: Sage.

Foucault, M. (1977). *Discipline and punish: The birth of the prison* (A. Sheridan, Trans.). New York: Vintage.

Foucault, M. (1980). *Power/Knowledge: Selected interviews and other writings, 1972–1977* (C. Gordon, L. Marhall, J. Mepham, & K. Soper, Trans.). New York: Pantheon.

Foucault, M. (1984). Nietzsche, genealogy, history. In P. Rabinow (Ed.), *The Foucault reader* (pp. 76–100). New York: Pantheon Books.

Freire, P. (1993/1970). *Pedagogy of the oppressed.* New York: Continuum.

Gere, A. R. (1997). *Writing groups: History, theory, and implications.* Carbondale: Southern Illinois University Press.

Gilkes, C. T. (1994). "If it wasn't for the women . . . ": African American women, community work, and social change. In M. B. Zinn & B. T. Dill (Eds.), *Women of color in U.S. society* (pp. 229–246). Philadelphia: Temple University Press.

Giroux, H. (2001). *Public spaces, private lives: Beyond the culture of cynicism.* Lanham, MD: Rowman & Littlefield.

Haraway, D. (1991). *Simians, cyborgs, and women.* London: Routledge.

Heidegger, M. (1962). *Being and time* (J. Macquarrie & E. Robinson, Trans.). San Francisco: Harper. (Original work published in 1927)

Heidegger, M. (1975). *Poetry, language, and thought* (A. Hofstadter, Trans.). New York: Perennial.

Henaff, M., & Strong, T. (2001). *Public space and democracy.* Minneapolis: University of Minnesota Press.

Kamberelis, G., & Dimitriadis, G. (2005). On *qualitative inquiry.* New York: Columbia University, Teachers College Press.

Kozol, J. (1985). *Illiterate America.* New York: Random House.

Kozol, J. (1991). *Savage inequalities: Children in America's schools.* New York: Harper Perennial.

Krueger, R. A. (1994). *Focus groups: A practical guide for applied research* (2nd ed.). Thousand Oaks, CA: Sage.

Lather, P. (2001). Postbook: Working the ruins of feminist ethnography. *Signs: Journal of Women in Culture and Society, 27*(1), 199–227.

Lather, P., & Smithies, C. (1997). *Troubling the angels: Women living with HIV/AIDS.* Boulder, CO: Westview.

Lincoln, Y. S., & Denzin, N. K. (2000). The seventh moment: Out of the past. In N. K. Denzin & Y. S. Lincoln (Eds.), *Handbook of qualitative research* (2nd ed., pp. 1047–1065). Thousand Oaks, CA: Sage.

Lunt, P. (1996). Rethinking focus groups in media and communications research. *Journal of Communication, 46*(2), 79–98.

Madriz, E. (1997). *Nothing bad happens to good girls: Fear of crime in women's lives.* Berkeley: University of California Press.

Madriz, E. (2000). Focus groups in feminist research. In N. K. Denzin & Y. S. Lincoln (Eds.), *Handbook of qualitative research* (2nd ed., pp. 835–850). Thousand Oaks, CA: Sage.

Merton, R. (1987). The focused group interview and focus groups: Continuities and discontinuities. *Public Opinion Quarterly, 51,* 550–566.

Morgan, D. L. (1998). *The focus group guidebook.* Thousand Oaks, CA: Sage.

Morgan, D. L. (2000). Focus group interviewing. In J. Gubrium & J. Holstein (Eds.), *Handbook of interview research: Context and method* (pp. 141–160). Thousand Oaks, CA: Sage.

Morley, D. (1980). *The "nationwide" audience.* London: British Film Institute.

Probyn, E. (1993). *Sexing the self: Gendered positions in cultural studies.* New York: Routledge.

Radway, J. (1991). *Reading the romance: Women, patriarchy, and popular literature.* Chapel Hill: University of North Carolina Press.

Sarachild, K. (1978). Consciousness-raising: A radical weapon. In Redstockings of the Women's Liberation Movement (Eds.), *Feminist revolution* (pp. 144–150). New York: Random House.

Schensul, J. J., LeCompte, M. D., Nastatsi, B. K., & Borgatti, S. P. (1999). *Enhanced ethnographic methods: Audiovisual techniques, focused group interviews, and elicitation techniques.* Walnut Creek, CA: AltaMira.

Part V

THE ART AND PRACTICES OF INTERPRETATION, EVALUATION, AND REPRESENTATION

In conventional terms, Part V of the *Handbook* signals the terminal phase of qualitative inquiry. The researcher or evaluator now assesses, analyzes, and interprets the empirical materials that have been collected. This process, conventionally conceived, implements a set of analytic procedures that produce interpretations, which are then integrated into a theory or put forward as a set of policy recommendations. The resulting interpretations are assessed in terms of a set of criteria, from the positivist or postpositivist tradition, including validity, reliability, and objectivity. Those interpretations that stand up to scrutiny are put forward as the findings of the research.

The contributors to Part V explore the art, practices, and politics of interpretation, evaluation, and representation. In so doing, they return to the themes of Part I—that is, asking *how the discourses of qualitative research can be used to help create and imagine a free democratic society.* In returning to this question, it is understood that the processes of analysis, evaluation, and interpretation are neither terminal nor mechanical. They are like a dance, to invoke the metaphor used by Valerie Janesick. This dance is informed at every step of the way by a commitment to this civic agenda. The processes that define the practices of interpretation and representation are always ongoing, emergent, unpredictable, and unfinished. They are always embedded in an ongoing historical and political context. As argued throughout this volume, in the United States, neoconservative discourse in the educational arena (e.g., No Child Left Behind, National Research Council) privileges experimental criteria in the funding, implementation, and evaluation of scientific inquiry. Many of the authors in this volume observe that this creates a chilling climate for qualitative inquiry. We begin by assessing a number of criteria that have been traditionally (as well as recently) used to judge the adequacy of qualitative research. These criteria flow from the major paradigms now operating in this field.

Relativism, Criteria, and Politics

John Smith and Phil Hodkinson (Chapter 36) remind us that we live in an age of relativism. In the social sciences today, there is no longer a God's-eye view that guarantees absolute methodological certainty; to assert such is to court embarrassment. Indeed, as Guba and Lincoln discuss in detail in Chapter 8 (Part II), there is considerable debate over what constitutes good interpretation in qualitative research. Nonetheless, there seems to be an emerging consensus that all inquiry reflects the standpoint of the inquirer, that all observation is theory laden, and that there is no possibility of theory-free knowledge. We can no longer think of ourselves as neutral spectators of the social world.

Consequently, as Smith and Hodkinson observe, until quite recently few spoke in terms of foundational epistemologies and ontological realism. Before the assault of methodological conservativism, relativists would calmly assert that no method is a neutral tool of inquiry, hence the notion of procedural objectivity could not be sustained. Anti-foundationalists thought that the days of naïve realism and naïve positivism were over. In their place stand critical and historical realism and various versions of relativism. The criteria for evaluating research had become relative, moral, and political.

However, events during the past 5 years, including governmental attempts to mandate research criteria in the United States and the United Kingdom, have disturbed this situation. Power and politics now play a major part in discussions of criteria.

Extending Smith and Hodkinson, there are three basic positions on the issue of evaluative criteria: foundational, quasi-foundational, and nonfoundational. There are still those who think in terms of a *foundational* epistemology. They would apply the same criteria to qualitative research as are employed in quantitative inquiry, contending that there is nothing special about qualitative research that demands a special set of evaluative criteria. As indicated in our introduction to Part II, the positivist and postpositivist paradigms apply four standard criteria to disciplined inquiry: internal validity, external validity, reliability, and objectivity. The use of these criteria, or their variants, is consistent with the foundational position.

In contrast, *quasi-foundationalists* approach the criteria issue from the standpoint of a non-naïve, neo-, or subtle realism. They contend that the discussion of criteria must take place within the context of an ontological neorealism and a constructivist epistemology. They believe in a real world that is independent of our fallible knowledge of it. Their constructivism commits them to the position that there can be no theory-free knowledge. Proponents of the quasi-foundational position argue that a set of criteria unique to qualitative research needs to be developed. Hammersley (1992, p. 64; 1995, p. 18; see also Wolcott, 1999, p. 194) is a leading proponent of this position. He wants to maintain the correspondence theory of truth while suggesting that researchers assess a study in terms its ability to (a) generate generic/formal theory, (b) be empirically grounded and scientifically credible, (c) produce findings that can be generalized or transferred to other settings, and (d) be internally reflexive in terms of taking account of the effects of the researcher and the research strategy on the findings that have been produced.

Hammersley reduces his criteria to three essential terms: plausibility (is the claim plausible?), credibility (is the claim based on credible evidence?), and relevance (what is the claim's relevance for knowledge about the world?). Of course, these terms require social judgments. They cannot be assessed in terms of any set of external or foundational criteria. Their meanings are arrived at through consensus and discussion in the scientific community. Within Hammersley's model, there is no satisfactory method for resolving this issue of how to evaluate an empirical claim.

For the *nonfoundationalists,* relativism is not an issue. They accept the argument that there is no theory-free knowledge. Relativism or uncertainty is the inevitable consequence of the fact that, as humans, we have finite knowledge of ourselves and the world in which we live. Nonfoundationalists contend that the injunction to pursue knowledge cannot be given epistemologically; rather, the injunction is moral and political. Accordingly, the criteria for evaluating qualitative work are also moral and fitted to the pragmatic, ethical, and political contingencies of concrete situations. Good or bad inquiry in any given context is assessed in terms of criteria such as those outlined by Greenwood and Levin (Chapter 2), Fine and Weis (Chapter 3), Smith (Chapter 4), Bishop (Chapter 5), and Christians (Chapter 6) in Part I; Guba and Lincoln (Chapter 8 in Part II); Kemmis and McTaggart (Chapter 23 in Part III); and Angrosino (Chapter 28 in Part IV). These are the criteria that flow from a feminist, communitarian moral ethic of empowerment, community, and moral solidarity. Returning to Christians (Chapter 6), this moral ethic calls for research rooted in the concepts of care, shared governance, neighborliness, love, and kindness. Furthermore, this work should provide the foundations for social criticism and social action.

In an ideal world, the anti- or nonfoundational narrative would be uncontested. But today in the United States and the United Kingdom, as Smith and Hodkinson observe, opponents are embracing "more crudely empiricist procedures, even the experimental or quasi-experimental procedures common to the natural sciences." There is a concerted effort by governmental regimes to reform research. This is disconcerting, all the more so when social scientists collaborate in the project. Dark days are ahead of us.

▣ Emancipatory Discourses and the Ethics and Politics of Interpretation

Norman Denzin's (Chapter 37) contribution invites indigenous and nonindigenous qualitative researchers to take up an emancipatory discourse, connecting indigenous epistemologies and theories of decolonization with critical pedagogy, and a global decolonizing discourse. Advocating the use of critical personal narratives, Denzin encourages the development of a postcolonial indigenous participatory theater focused on racism, inequality, memory, and cultural loss.

▣ Writing: A Method of Inquiry

Writers interpret as they write, so writing is a form of inquiry, a way of making sense of the world. Laurel Richardson and Elizabeth Adams St. Pierre (Chapter 38) explore new writing and interpretive styles that follow from the narrative literary turn in the social sciences. They call these different forms of writing CAP (creative analytical processes) ethnography. Their chapter is divided into three parts. Part 1, authored by Richardson, explores these forms. In Part 2, St. Pierre provides an analysis of how writing as a method of inquiry coheres with the development of ethical selves. In Part 3, Richardson provides some writing practices and exercises for the qualitative writer.

New forms include autoethnography, fiction stories, poetry, drama, performance texts, polyvocal texts, readers' theater, responsive readings, aphorisms, comedy and satire, visual presentations, conversation, layered accounts, writing stories, and mixed genres. Richardson discusses in detail one class of experimental genre that she calls evocative representations. Work in this genre includes narratives of the self, writing stories, ethnographic fictional representations, poetic representation, ethnographic drama, and mixed genres.

The crystal is a central image in Richardson's text, and she contrasts it with the triangle. Traditional postpositivist research has relied on triangulation, including the use of multiple methods, as a method of validation. The model implies a fixed point of reference that can be triangulated. Richardson illustrates the crystallization process with excerpts from her recent book with Ernest Lockridge.

Mixed genre texts do not triangulate. The central image is the crystal, which "combines symmetry and substance with an infinite variety of shapes, substances, transmutations, . . . and angles of approach." Crystals are prisms that reflect and refract, creating ever-changing images and pictures of reality. Crystallization deconstructs the traditional idea of validity, for now there can be no single or triangulated truth.

Richardson offers five criteria for evaluating CAP ethnography: substantive contribution, aesthetic merit, reflexivity, impactfulness, and ability to evoke lived experience. She concludes with a list of writing practices—ways of using writing as a method of knowing.

St. Pierre troubles conventional understandings of ethics. Drawing on Derrida and Deleuze, she places ethics under deconstruction: "What happens when we cannot apply the rules?" We must not be unworthy of what happens to us. We struggle to be worthy, to be willing to be worthy.

▣ Anthropological Poetics

Anthropologists have been writing experimental, literary, and poetic ethnographic texts for at least 40 years. In this part, three different forms of poetics are represented. Ivan Brady (Chapter 39) writes poetically about method, about a way of getting to know places by their effects on our personal experience. He invokes the environmental poets, offering a prolegomena to a poetics of place.

Using the literary poetic form, Brady enacts a moral aesthetic, an aesthetic that allows him to say new things about place, space, wild spaces, beings, self, nature, identity, meaning, and life on this threatened planet. In so doing, he pushes the boundaries of artful discourse. Thus are the boundaries between the humanities and the human sciences blurred. In this blurring, our moral sensibilities are enlivened. We are able to imagine new ways of being ourselves in this bewilderingly complex world called the present.

▣ Cultural Poesis

In a chapter that defies description, Kate Stewart (Chapter 40) offers a piece of imaginative writing grounded in the poetics of ordinary things. She gives us provocations, glimpses out of the corner of the eye, a montage, a fractured text, cultural poesis during times of violence, chaos and loss in U.S. public culture, a roller-coaster ride through somebody's dreamland, ordinary life somewhere, games, eating in, walking the dog, shopping, raking the yard, political posters in the front yard, a plastic Jesus, a shrine, yellow ribbons, surging bodies, the train screaming out a warning, nothing adding up to anything except some of us starting to lose hope yesterday.

Investigative Poetics

Stephen Hartnett and Jeremy Engels (Chapter 41) offer a poetics of witnessing, an aria in time of war. In so doing, they respond to the call of Ralph Waldo Emerson, who demanded that a poet should strive toward becoming "the knower, the doer, and the sayer." Building on Emerson, they advocate an investigative poetics, a "combination of serious scholarship, passionate activism, and experimental representation."

Hartnett and Engels write to offer a poetry that problematizes politics, that bears witness to the ways in which social structures are embodied in lived experience, a poetic that functions as a genealogical critique of power. Their essay unfolds in four movements, going from the political poetry of Carolyn Forché and Edward Sanders to a discussion of social justice discourse in the humanities. They then criticize the movement known as ethnopoetics, concluding with a positive discussion of the political poetics of John Dos Passos, Carolyn Forché, and Peter Dale Scott.

Qualitative Evaluation and Changing Social Policy

Program evaluation, of course, is a major site of qualitative research. (Earlier *Handbook* chapters by Greenwood & Levin [Chapter 2] in Part I and by Stake [Chapter 17], Kemmis & McTaggart [Chapter 23], and Miller & Crabtree [Chapter 24] in Part III established this fact.) Evaluators are interpreters. Their texts tell stories. These stories are inherently moral and political. Starting in 1965 and moving to the present, House (Chapter 42) offers a sobering historical analysis of qualitative evaluation and changing social policy. He observes that the field has moved from faddish experimental and quantitative evaluation studies (1960s), to small-scale qualitative studies, to meta-analyses and program theory. A move from a model of value-free inquiry to committed social justice projects, and back again, is also part of this history. During the 1980s, evaluation moved away from "quantitative methods and value-free studies toward multiple methodologies and qualitative studies focused on stakeholders, social justice issues, and participatory techniques."

Neoconservatives viewed such work as too permissive and argued against it. Since September 11, 2001, a neoconservative fundamentalism has taken hold of federal policy—from foreign affairs, to domestic affairs, to evaluation itself. President George W. Bush's neofundamentalism has taken the form of methodological fundamentalism in the field of evaluation. As argued previously, federal agencies that sponsor evaluation have "aggressively pushed the concept of 'evidence-based' progress, policies, and programs."

The core of this belief is the argument that research and evaluation must be scientific, that is, based on randomized experimental designs. This method of inquiry is written into federal legislation! The Bush educational policy thus implements four concepts: accountability, options for parents, local control, and evidence-based instruction.

The use of the medical model of evidence-based inquiry is predicated on the belief that education is a field of fads; the failure of our schools reflects this. In contrast, medicine, with its randomized field trials, has made significant progress in improving human health. Education should do the same. Of course, many of the fads in education have been inspired by conservatives—vouchers, charter schools, accountability through test scores. Medicine's progress can be attributed to breakthroughs in allied fields, not randomized trials.

And so the field comes full circle. We are back to the experimental models of the 1960s. Do we have the courage to stand up to this conservative assault?

Conclusions

The chapters in Part V affirm our position that qualitative research has come of age. Multiple discourses now surround topics that during earlier historical moments were contained within the broad grasp ways of the positivist and postpositivist epistemologies. There are now many in which to write, read, assess, evaluate, and apply qualitative research texts. Even so, there are pressures to turn back the clock. This complex field invites reflexive appraisal, hence the topic of Part VI—the future of qualitative research.

References

Hammersley, M. (1992). *What's wrong with ethnography?* London: Routledge.

Hammersley, M. (1995). *The politics of social research.* London: Sage.

Wolcott, H. F. (1999). *Ethnography: A way of seeing.* Walnut Creek, CA: AltaMira.

36

RELATIVISM, CRITERIA, AND POLITICS

John K. Smith and Phil Hodkinson

In a chapter that one of the authors (John Smith) wrote with Deborah Deemer on criteria for judging social and educational research for the second edition of this *Handbook,* the issue of power and criteria was briefly mentioned. Smith and Deemer (2000) said that they were not so naïve as to claim that power, and by extension (but unmentioned) politics, could ever be eliminated from judgments about the quality of research as these judgments are played out in a social context. Citing Hazelrigg (1989), they added that there was no point in embracing some sort of a romanticized "intellectualized flight from power" (Smith & Deemer, 2000, p. 202). In fact, although they did not say so, they certainly could have added that there is nothing wrong with politics and the exercise of power per se in this instance or in other instances. The central issue has been, and remains, about how the political process operates, how power is exercised, and what goals those participating in the process desire.

Because of certain events over the past few years, including governmental attempts to mandate research criteria in both the United States and the United Kingdom, it is clear that the relationship of power, politics, and criteria must be discussed at much greater length. In this chapter, we elaborate on these issues.

The starting point for our discussion is a reiteration of the main conclusion that Smith and Deemer (2000) reached in the second edition of the *Handbook:* We have come to the end of our attempts to secure an epistemological foundation for our knowledge and must acknowledge that we are in the era of relativism.

We pursue this reiteration in two parts. First, we discuss the well-known and frequently argued point that individual researchers cannot step outside their own social and historical standpoints. Because there is no possibility of theory-free observation and knowledge, the subject–object dualism of empiricism is untenable and the claim to objectivity is a chimera. Second, we discuss the condition that the conduct of research, and especially the judgments about its worth, represents social activities. In the absence of an epistemological foundation, which is essential to any claim that criteria can be neutral and objective, decisions about what the criteria for research are or should be, as well as decisions about how criteria are put into practice, result from complex social interactions. And, as with all such social interactions, individuals and groups work to further their own interests, both legitimately and (occasionally) illegitimately, although it must be added that judgments about what is legitimate versus illegitimate are themselves socially determined at any given time and place. These conditions make the process of determining research criteria and how they are to be applied unavoidably contestable and, hence, political.

Following this revisiting, we then briefly note two common responses to the demise of empiricism and the end of the pretense to objectivity, define relativism, and discuss what the latter means for the issue of criteria. Finally, we examine the role that politics plays, both generally and in the specific U.S. and U.K. contexts at the time when this chapter was being written, in the making of judgments about the quality of social and educational research. This examination, in particular, focuses on the political pressures that are being brought to bear in the attempt to reestablish or reassert that the broadly empiricist understandings about research and criteria are the only understandings that can, or should, be accepted. We find in play here both a politics of avoidance of the compelling arguments advanced against empiricism by relativist researchers and a politics directed at marginalizing the messengers.

Two basic definitions are needed before we begin. First, we define politics in a conventional sense as the process of allocating scarce resources. Any desired resource that is not totally abundant—be it money, social prestige, recognition, research grants, or whatever—must be divided up through a political process with some people getting more and others getting less of whatever is desired. Judgments about research quality and what counts as research are central to the allocation of such scarce resources for researchers. It is here that the political dimensions of research activity are most significant. Power is the ability of individuals or groups to realize their will even if others are opposed. If one knows the distribution of access to power in a group, an organization, or a society, one can understand the distribution of scarce resources and vice versa.

▣ Criteria as Method

The point of research as traditionally, and thus conventionally, understood has long been thought of as a matter of discovering the truth. Within the empiricist epistemological perspective that has dominated our understanding of research, truth is defined as the accurate representation of an independently existing reality. The accumulation of knowledge is thereby considered to be the accumulation of accurate representations of what is (independently) outside of us. The paradigmatic example of what also is called the spectator theory of knowledge, with the accompanying definition of truth in correspondence terms, involves the cat and the mat. If one says the cat is on the mat and, in fact, we observe that the cat is actually on the mat, then words correspond to reality and the truth has been spoken.

The central problem with this empiricist perspective on inquiry is that of making good on this idea of correspondence. Making good in this context means somehow connecting that which empiricism separated—the knowing subject from the object of knowing—and doing so in such a way that the activities of the former would not distort the reality of the latter. The solution of choice to cash in this correspondence theory, as has long been noted in our social and educational research textbooks, is a methodical one. The point is quite straightforward: If the proper procedures are applied, the subjectivities (e.g., opinions, ideologies) of the knowing subject would be constrained and the knower could thereby gain an accurate and objective depiction of reality. Those researchers who adhered to method would thereby possess, in contrast to all others, what one might call the well-polished Cartesian mirror of the mind. Kerlinger (1979) put it bluntly:

> The procedures of science are objective—not the scientists. Scientists, like all men and women, are opinionated, dogmatic, [and] ideological. . . . That is the very reason for insisting on procedural objectivity: to get the whole business outside of ourselves. (p. 264)

Method is thereby *the* crucial factor in any judgment made about the quality of research.

Over the course of the past half century, empiricism as a theory of knowledge with the claims of objectivity, neutrality, and so forth has come on hard times; as a result, the methodical solution to the problem of criteria has been very seriously undermined. Philosophers of science, and especially philosophers of social science, have noted numerous intractable problems associated with this methodical solution to reconnect what empiricism had separated—the dualism of the knowing subject and the object of knowing. Because this territory has been covered with frequency (for a brief recounting of this history, see Smith, 1989), we need to mention only a few key points.

Within Anglo-American philosophical circles, a good case can be made that Hanson and Kuhn were central among those who brought the subject–object dualism issue to the forefront. At the core of Hanson's (1958) arguments was the now seemingly obvious point that "the theory, hypothesis, framework, or background held by an investigator can strongly influence what is observed" (p. 7). A few years later, Kuhn (1962) followed up on this line of reasoning with his talk about incommensurable paradigms, paradigm shifts, the fact that all knowledge is framework dependent, and so forth. By the mid- to late 1980s, the work of numerous other people left little doubt that the claim that theory-free knowledge and observation is possible is intellectually untenable (e.g., see Bernstein, 1983; Gadamer, 1995; Goodman, 1978; Nagel, 1986; Putnam, 1981; Taylor, 1971).

The arguments made by these philosophers combined with another series of arguments that focused directly on the claim that method itself was neutral or that it could be the repository of procedural objectivity. The fact that such a claim could not be sustained is the central message that can be taken from the work of Cherryholmes (1988), Giddens (1976), Hesse (1980), MacKenzie (1981), Smith (1985), and others. The result of all this intellectual ferment was the elaboration of a number of points of great consequence for any discussion of criteria, namely that there is no possibility of theory-free observation and knowledge, the claim of the duality of subject and object cannot be made good, no special epistemic privilege can be attached to any particular method or set of methods, and we cannot have the kind access to an external extralinguistic referent that would allow us to claim the discovery of truth in accurate representation or correspondence terms.

Based on these points, the only conclusion that can be reached is that we no longer can talk in terms of a foundational epistemology and a direct contact with reality. There is no possibility of the objective stance or view—often called the "God's eye" point of view—and all we can have are "the various points of view of actual persons reflecting various interests and purposes that their descriptions and theories subserve" (Putnam, 1981, p. 50). With the demise of empiricism and the methodical stance on criteria, social and educational research must be seen for what it has always been—a practical and moral activity, not an epistemological one. And because we have no epistemological foundation for our practical and moral activities, any discussion of criteria must come to terms with, in one form or another, the issue of relativism.

▣ Responses

Over the recent past, there have been at least two general responses, with the usual numerous variations on theme, to those who have argued that epistemological foundationalism is over and that the criteria for judging research cannot be "fixed" but rather are the product of time- and place-contingent social processes. In the first instance, some people have advanced various lines of argument that can be labeled, albeit loosely, as neorealist (e.g., see Bhaskar, 1979; Hammersley, 1990; Manicas, 1987; Manicas & Secord, 1983; Phillips & Burbules, 2000; Pring, 2000; see also Popper, 1959, 1972, arguably the intellectual precursor of all neorealists). Second, other people recently have attempted to reassert empiricism and criteria as method (e.g., so far as educational research is concerned, see Oakley, 2000; Shavelson & Towne, 2002; Slavin, 2002; Tooley & Darby, 1998).

Other than a brief summary, we do not discuss or critique the neorealist and reassertive positions and their respective approaches to criteria. In the past, we have written such "attempt to persuade" or "conversion" pieces, as we now have come to call them, and these are readily available to interested readers (Garratt & Hodkinson, 1998; Hodkinson, 1998, 2004; Hodkinson & Smith, 2004; Smith, 1993). Although we think that the philosophical exchanges we have engaged in have been intriguing and are important to keep a conversion going, conversion by way of persuasive argument seems to occur rather rarely. Thus, in this chapter, we forgo such attempts and only summarize briefly the previously noted positions, with very limited comments, and then elaborate on our take on relativism, criteria, and politics.

There is little question that non-naïve realists or neorealists have made numerous sophisticated attempts to address the issue of criteria. These neorealist responses share in common a commitment to an ontological realism, on the one side, and a constructivist epistemology, on the other. The former means that these neorealists are committed to the proposition that there is a real world out there independent of our interest in or knowledge of that world. The latter announces their commitment to the idea that we can never know for sure whether we have depicted that reality as it really is. Although the line of argument varies, these non-naïve realists or neorealists "assert a belief in a real world independent of our knowledge while also making it clear that our knowledge of this metacognitive world is quite fallible" (Leary, 1984, p. 918).

Given these dual commitments, the neorealists then argue that criteria that are not strictly contingent on time and place can be developed. Hammersley (1990), for example, attempted to elaborate criteria to hold off the contingent nature of judgment or, put differently, to prevent a slide into what is, for him, the void of relativism. His criteria of choice, or the two key elements necessary for judging the validity of a study, are what he called plausibility and credibility. In the former instance, to say that a claim is plausible is to say that it is "likely to be true given our existing knowledge" (p. 61). He argued that some claims are so plausible that we can immediately accept them at face value, whereas other claims require the presentation of evidence. In the latter case, a judgment about credibility must be undertaken "given the nature of the phenomena concerned, the circumstances of the research" (p. 61), and so forth. And, as with plausibility, when a claim lacks face credibility, evidence is required. However, Hammersley further recognized that the particular evidence presented by a researcher in support of the plausibility and credibility of a study must itself be assessed for its own plausibility and credibility. And, as he continued, "we may require further evidence to support that evidence, which we shall judge in terms of plausibility and credibility" (p. 62).

For us, Hammersley's (1990) argument became deeply entangled in an infinite regress—if not a hermeneutic circle. It is at this point where it was necessary for him to call on his neorealism to do some work—in particular, the work of making contact with reality in such a way as to blunt this infinite regress or get one out of the hermeneutic circle of interpretation. Or, put differently, it was time for him to call on his version of realism to prevent the relativism that would seem to lie at the end of it all. This was not the case, however, and any notions about correspondence and realism, no matter how subtle, played no role of consequence for the balance of Hammersley's discussion. His arguments ultimately ended up at the only place they could go—with a discussion of the norms that *should* govern discourse among members of a scientific community as they attempt to make judgments about plausibility and credibility. These are norms because they refer to what "should be" and thereby yield to no final or foundational answers that are contestable and inevitably influenced by political processes.

A similar situation can be pointed out with reference to the work of Manicas and Secord (1983) and the well-known idea of warranted assertability. Their version of neorealism led them to note that "knowledge is a social and historical product" (p. 401), there is "no preinterpreted 'given,' and the test of truth cannot be 'correspondence.' Epistemologically, there can be nothing known to which our ideas (sentences, theories) can correspond" (p. 401). Based on these points, Manicas and Secord then addressed the issue of how to connect experiences, which are always—and can only—be culturally and historically mediated, with reality independent from experience. Their response was the negative assertion that although there is no theory-free observation, this "does not eliminate the possibility of objectivity, construed here as warranted assertability" (p. 410). For us, this placed them in the same situation as was faced by Hammersley (1990) because the warrants that one brings to judgments are themselves socially and historically conditioned—as are the warrants that warrant the warrants, and so forth. Again, they were caught in a hermeneutic circle or an infinite regress and were unable to offer a way in which to access an external referent that would allow them out of the former or to stop the latter.

A second line of response, recently asserted with vigor in both the United States and the United Kingdom, holds that social and educational inquiry should strongly embrace more crudely empiricist procedures, even the experimental or quasi-experimental procedures common to the natural sciences. In the United States, this position has been most widely advanced by the report from the National Research Council Committee (Shavelson & Towne, 2002). This report was supported by a contract between the National Research Council and the U.S. Department of Education's National Educational Research Policy and Priorities Board. In the United Kingdom, a similar but less harshly experimental position has been advanced with the critiques of the quality of British educational research at the hands of Tooley with Darby (1998) and Hillage, Pearson, Anderson, and Tamkin (1998). The former report was commissioned by the Office for Standards in Education (OFSTED), the government-established national inspection agency for schools, whereas the latter report was sponsored by the government department directly responsible for education.

In Chapter 3 of the Shavelson and Towne (2002) report, the principles of scientific inquiry were set forth. These guiding principles for educational research, not surprisingly, are very much like those that have been central to standard, empiricist-inspired, introductory research texts. The terms of discourse, for example, are those of replicate, generalize, random assignment, and so forth. In Chapter 5 of the report, the committee fleshed out these principles with a discussion of the designs for conducing scientific educational research. What they referred to as "more rigorous studies" are those that are of an experimental nature with well-defined hypotheses and so forth in place before data collection and analysis. At this point, it is clear that the methods or procedures employed by researchers are the crucial factor in any judgment of their research as good or bad.

Placed between these two chapters in the Shavelson and Towne (2002) report was one in which they addressed some of the unique features of educational inquiry—and, again by extension, social inquiry—that they argued set this inquiry apart from other fields of inquiry. They noted factors such as human volition, the central role of ethics that limits control group possibilities, rapid changes in educational programs, and so forth. These and other conditions mean that educational and social researchers are not able to exercise the same degree of control over their subject matter as are, for example, physical scientists. The committee's response to this diminution of control was to say that educational and social researchers must "pay close attention to context" when pursuing and interpreting the results of their research. Exactly what they meant by paying close attention to context was not clearly discussed. What is clear, and what is most important, is that they did not include the researcher as part of the context. This position runs counter to the now generally accepted idea that we, even as researchers, cannot undertake theory-free observation and produce theory-free knowledge.

Finally, Shavelson and Towne's (2002) comments about qualitative research and the relationship of qualitative and quantitative approaches to inquiry are difficult to interpret in that there appeared to be some ambiguity present. They declared, with citations but without argument, that the two approaches are "epistemologically quite similar" and that "we do not distinguish between them as being different forms of inquiry" (p. 19). That said, they also noted that "sharp distinctions between qualitative and qualitative inquiry have divided the field" (p. 19). This comment was followed by a concern that "the current trend of schools of education to favor qualitative methods, often at the expense of quantitative methods, has invited criticism" (p. 19). This statement was not supported by citations, and the nature of the criticism was not mentioned. Not surprisingly, one is then left to wonder about what the problem is here. If both approaches are similar and we cannot distinguish between them, then what is the reason for the concern and criticism?

In Chapter 5 of Shavelson and Towne's (2002) report, however, their take on the position of qualitative inquiry relative to quantitative inquiry could be noted more clearly. They stated that all scientific studies must begin with clear questions that can be researched empirically. They added,

> More rigorous studies will begin with more precise statements of the underlying theory driving the inquiry and will generally have a well-specified hypothesis before [the] data collection and testing phase is begun. Studies that do not start with clear conceptual frameworks and hypotheses may still be scientific, although they are obviously at a more rudimentary level and will generally require follow-on study to contribute significantly to scientific knowledge. (p. 101)

Because qualitative studies are more loosely defined before data gathering begins, they are more rudimentary than quantitative studies—the lack of epistemological distinction between them notwithstanding—and are primarily valuable for generating hypotheses for studies that are more rigorous. (As an aside, we must note that this may have taken us "full circle," so to speak. See Abel's [1948] comments about how interpretive inquiry is valuable for generating hypotheses to be turned over to real researchers for rigorous testing with their empiricist or scientific methods.)

The position taken by Shavelson and Towne (2002) is paralleled in the discussions of research quality in the United Kingdom, as advanced by Tooley and Darby (1998) and Hillage and colleagues (1998). Tooley and Darby's approach was to analyze the quality of educational research articles that appeared in four high-status U.K. academic journals. They declared that the overall standard of inquiry was far too low and their sponsor concluded that "much [educational research] that is published is, on this analysis, at best no more than an irrelevance or distraction" (p. 1). They found two main problems with a significant portion of educational research. First, there was the issue of the increasing prominence of qualitative research. About this greater increase, they stated, "The key problem lies in the subjectivity of qualitative research" (p. 43) because of the lack, most particularly, of triangulation. In addition, they were very critical of the large amount of research—overwhelmingly of a qualitative approach—that uses broad sociological theorizing and/or focuses on the lives of disadvantaged people and groups in society. Thus, Tooley and Darby chose for as an example of particular strident criticism an article by Sparkes (1994) in which he argued that the oppressions faced by a lesbian physical education teacher were a social issue rather than an individual one.

Hillage and colleagues (1998), following Tooley and Darby (1998), also took an approach similar to that of Shavelson and Towne (2002). Hillage and colleagues stated that not enough educational research was of sufficient quality and relevance to serve the needs of practitioners and policymakers. The essence of their critique was that educational research in the United Kingdom was too small scale, was not cumulative, was too often of low standard, and (most interesting) was biased toward qualitative case studies. The solution was obvious: What was needed was more large-scale, cumulative research based on a scientific approach—in other words, an increase in quantitative research and/or research using mixed methods.

Although there are certainly many variations among them, in the end, Shavelson and Towne (2002), Tooley and Darby (1998), and Hillage and colleagues (1998) broadly shared three things. First, they all wrote reports sponsored or funded by government educational agencies that had decided to get into the business of sponsoring certain criteria for judging research in a way that has no precedent of which we are aware. Second, as they defined high-quality research, they all reiterated—to one degree or another—Kerlinger's (1979) approach and embraced a continuation of the so thoroughly undermined empiricist or spectator theory of knowledge and favored the definition of criteria as a certain set of methods. Finally, they all expressed a great deal of ambiguity, at least in what they wrote, about the value or standing of qualitative inquiry when compared with the supposedly more rigorous, methodologically driven approaches to research. This led all of them to conclude that whereas qualitative researchers can be part of the educational research club, they cannot be rigorous members.

Relativism

For us, as critics of these responses to the demise of empiricism and the realization that adherence to method will not lead to theory-free knowledge and so forth, the idea is to move past the epistemological project, to change our metaphors and imageries of research from those of discovery and finding to those of constructing and making, and to accept that relativism is our inescapable condition as finite humans. However, to make such statements and employ the term *relativism* is deeply problematic for many people. Even the mention of relativism provokes strongly negative intellectual and emotional reactions.

For many writers, "relativism" is equated with some illogical and irrational abyss where every claim to knowledge has equal validity and credibility with every other claim. They argue that such a position is not only nonsensical but also dangerous in that it can lead only to a form of research anarchy and, for that matter, cultural anarchy. But to say that relativism means "anything goes" is nonsense for one simple reason: No one believes that all things are equal, and no one could lead his or her life guided by that belief. We all have preferences for some things over other things, and we make choices accordingly. This process of preferring some things to other things and making judgments accordingly has been going on since time immemorial and will continue for as far as can be seen into the future. Put differently, it is impossible to imagine a human life without judgment and discriminations. Taylor (1989) expressed the situation as follows: "To know who you are is to be oriented in moral space, a space in which questions arise about what is good or bad, what is worth doing and what not, what has meaning and importance for you and what is trivial and secondary" (p. 28). To not make judgments is to lose sight of one's orientation in such a moral space, that is, to lose one's grounding as a human.

We must also briefly address another long-standing canard, namely that relativism is self-refuting. The argument is well known: To say that all things are relative is to make a nonrelative or absolute statement and thereby to contradict oneself and so forth. Both Rorty (1985) and Gadamer (1995) addressed this issue of self-refuting. The latter agreed that relativism is self-refuting but then maintained that to make this point is to make a point of no interest because it "does not express any superior insight of value" (p. 334). Rorty (1985), on the other hand, argued that it is a mistake to think of relativism as a theory of knowledge to compete with other theories of knowledge. He dispensed with the self-refuting issue by stating that because his type of pragmatist is not interested in advancing any "epistemology, a fortiori, he does not have a relativist one" (p. 6).

We agree with these perspectives and hold that relativism, as we understand the condition, is not a theory of knowledge and advances no pretense that we can escape our finite—or time- and place-constrained—condition of being in the world. Taking a page from Godel's idea of incompleteness (Hofstadter, 1979), this situation is only what we should expect from any human (i.e., socially and historically influenced) construction. As such, relativism stands for nothing more or less than recognition of our human finitude. It is not something to be transcended; rather, it is merely something with which we, as finite beings, must learn to live.

Schwandt (1996) summarized this nonfoundational situation quite succinctly:

> We must learn to live with uncertainty, with the absence of final vindications, without the hope of solutions in the form of epistemological guarantees. Contingency, fallibilism, dialogue, and deliberation mark our way of being in the world. But these ontological conditions are not equivalent to eternal ambiguity, the lack of commitment, [and] the inability to act in the face of uncertainty. (p. 59)

As such, our problem as inquirers is that of how to make and defend judgments when there can be no appeal to foundations, to methods, or to something outside of the time- and place-constrained social processes of knowledge construction. This immediately engages us in complex social processes with obvious political implications.

▣ Criteria

The end of the epistemological project, the shift in metaphors from discovery to constructing, and the realization that social and educational inquiry is a practical and moral affair all mean that criteria must be thought of not as abstract standards but rather as socially constructed lists of characteristics. As we approach judgment in any given case, we have in mind a list of characteristics that we use to judge the quality of that production. This is not a well-defined and precisely specified list; to the contrary, this list of characteristics is always open-ended, in part unarticulated, and always subject to constant interpretation and reinterpretation. Moreover, the items on the list can never be the distillation of some abstracted epistemology, as has been attempted in the case of empiricism and method as criteria. Our lists are inevitably rooted in our standpoints and are elaborated through social interactions—or, in Gadamer's (1995) terms, they must evolve out of and reflect our "effective history [or histories]" (pp. 301–302).

The lists that we bring to judgment are open-ended in that we have the capacity to add items to and subtract items from the lists. The limits for recasting our lists derive not primarily from theoretical labor but rather from the practical use to which the lists are put as well as from the social, cultural, and historical contexts in which they are used. The limits on modification are worked and reworked within the context of actual practices or applications. Also, any lists that we bring to judgment are only partly articulated and only partly rational. Some items can be more or less specified, whereas others seem to resist such specification. Polanyi's (1962) concern about tacit knowledge applies very well in this case. We make what Beckett and Hager (2002) termed "embodied judgments" about research quality and value, that is, judgments that are practical and emotional as well as discursively considered. When we make judgments, we generally can specify some of the reasons, but other things seem to be out there—what might be called a surplus of meaning that seems to stand just beyond our grasp, just beyond our ability to completely specify or articulate. This does not mean that we should not, and do not, attempt to bring this surplus to fuller articulation; it only means that this can never be done completely.

Furthermore, the lists that people think characterize good versus bad research studies are often contested, overlap one another, and partly contradict one another (Garratt & Hodkinson, 1998). Any list can be challenged, changed, and/or modified not primarily through abstracted discussions of the items themselves but rather in application to actual inquiries. For example, something "new" is presented to us. This was the case with qualitative inquiry in the recent past. Qualitative work did not fit well with the empiricist list of methodical characteristics (e.g., sampling, null hypotheses) that were the basis for distinguishing good research studies from bad research studies. To accept qualitative inquiry meant that one had to reformulate one's list of characteristics and replace the exemplars that are always called on in the never-ending process of making judgments. However, the key here is "accept" because people may choose, as many have done, to preserve and reassert the existing list of characteristics that distinguish the good from the bad and thereby reject the "new" as something that does not even qualify to be considered as research. This, of course, is a comment that has been, and is still, offered up about qualitative research.

Making Judgments About Research

The various conditions noted in the previous section, in that they constrain all human activity—including social and educational research and thus judgments about the quality of such research—mean that politics and power are part of that complex process by which we sort out the good from the bad and the indifferent. The hope that method would allow us to make judgments about the quality of research "untainted" by our opinions, emotions, and self-interests has been a false hope. Politics and power are part of the process of judgment and always have been. At times, of course, when there is a more general agreement among researchers about how research is conceptualized and how the activity should be conducted, the politics and power aspects of judgment do not reveal themselves to any great extent. At other times, such as when there are challenges to conventional empiricist forms of inquiry as has recently been the case with qualitative research—especially when such inquiry draws on postmodernist understandings, philosophical hermeneutics, and so forth—political and power factors are much more obvious at both a micro level (i.e., within the research profession) and a macro level (i.e., a situation where outside elements, such as government officials, enter into the process). However, we must immediately note that the line between micro and macro is often very blurry indeed.

In a groundbreaking study of the school as an organization, Hoyle (1982, 1986) coined the phrase "micropolitics," an idea later expanded by Ball (1987). Hoyle (1982) described micropolitics as including "those strategies by which individuals and groups in organizational contexts seek to use their resources of power and influence to further their interests" (p. 88). One way of understanding issues of research judgment is as a micropolitical process, even if the context is wider and more complex than that of a particular organization. Hodkinson (2004) argued that educational research can be seen as a field in the sense described by Bourdieu (e.g., Bourdieu & Wacquant, 1992). That is, academics strive for distinction in that field, using whatever capital (resources) they have at their disposal. One of the major activities in such a field is that people work to support, preserve, or strengthen those rules (or lists of characteristics) that they approve of or are in their interests and/or to change the rules (or lists) in a direction that favors their interests.

This drive to promote self-interest is not the only motivation for people. The politics of research judgment is driven by deeply held and sincere beliefs about what determines research quality and the role that research should play, for example, in relation to policy and practice. That is, people may defend method as the criterion for judgment because they truly believe that methodically driven inquiry or the application of the "scientific method" is the best way in which to solve educational and social problems, to help educate children, to bring greater equity to society, and so forth. But then, this is also the case for those who critique methodically driven inquiry and insist that we must change our metaphors. However, this does not render the process any less political. Such beliefs strengthen the resolve to assert particular approaches, that is, to win the political struggles over allocation of resources. The careers and self-interests of those concerned are intimately locked into those processes and struggles.

In short, academics strive explicitly and implicitly to influence those criteria (or lists of characteristics) that determine research quality as well as to perform well against them. In Hoyle's (1982, 1986) terms, academics are micropolitical. Aspects of these rules are codified and written.

Those who fund research have criteria against which bids will be judged, and journals have criteria against which submitted articles can be evaluated. However, such written codes take us only so far. Many of the rules of academic research are uncodified, having developed through custom and practice, as we have already argued. Part of the micropolitics lies is the selection and use of codes, contexts, and informal practices that best fit with the interests of a researcher or a group of researchers. Academics are, both as laypeople and as researchers, finite beings living during the era of relativism.

Although we strongly suspect that none of this is news to those who, over the years, have had research articles published and rejected, it will help to illustrate the pervasive presence of micropolitical activity with two brief examples. The first example concerns the allocation of scarce publication space in a high-status journal, the *Educational Researcher* (*ER*), and the refreshing—but all too rare—musings of an editor about the decision-making process. A few years ago, Donmoyer (1996) talked about his "gatekeeping" role as editor of *ER* during a time of what many called "paradigm proliferation." Donmoyer did an excellent job of noting that he, as a gatekeeper, could not "widen the gates [he] monitors; [he] simply gets to decide which sorts of people can walk through them" (p. 20). He also went on to note that although different approaches to inquiry might be incommensurable, he agreed with Bernstein (1983) that this did not mean they were necessarily logically incompatible. That said, Donmoyer (1996) then acknowledged that when one moves away from the conceptual to the actual practice of publishing some papers and rejecting others, and when one is in the "realm of action . . . where resources are often scarce and hard choices consequently have to be made, a sort of pragmatic incommensurability will inevitably come into play" (p. 20).

It is precisely at this point of scarcity and hard choices, in light of philosophical differences and disputes concerning the nature of inquiry, that power and politics become very visible as part of the quality judgment process. This does not mean that the process is necessarily venal or somehow tainted, although it certainly can be and can often be judged as such—depending, of course, on how "venal" and "tainted" are defined. All we wish to convey here is that this is the way things are because we all are, at least in part, political beings with a desire to advance our respective self-interests.

Our second example illustrates the current interest in reasserting empiricism as the philosophical basis for social and educational inquiry and, in so doing, blurs the line between macro and micro. For reasons that will be made clear later, the U.K. government's Department for Education and Employment, now the Department for Education and Skills (DfES), funded the Evidence for Policy and Practice Information and Coordinating Centre (EPPI Centre) for 5 years beginning in 2000. The remit was to support groups of researchers and others in carrying out systematic reviews of existing research findings. It was based on earlier systematic review work in medical research under what has become known as the "Cochrane Collaboration." The founder of the EPPI Centre, Ann Oakley, is a determined advocate of scientific research and the primacy of the controlled experiment (Oakley, 2000, 2003). Within the center's approach, a systematic review must meet various criteria:

> means of specifying a particular answerable research question; criteria about what kinds of studies . . . will be included in, and excluded from, the domain of literature to be surveyed; making explicit, justifiable decisions about the methodological quality of studies regarded as generating reliable findings; . . . [and] has involved input from research users at all stages in the review process. (Oakley, 2003, p. 24)

The first two of the criteria demonstrate unashamedly empiricist underpinnings. The research question comes first and stands apart from and prior to the research that is to be surveyed in the review, and the quality of any research to be considered is determined by the methods used by the researchers and how clearly they are described. Also of note is the fact that although user involvement in the review process is specified, prior academic knowledge of the field to be surveyed is not. This implies that the review process is seen as a technical operation that does not require sophisticated research understanding.

As Oakley (2000, 2003) described them, the EPPI processes appear to be designed to maximize objectivity and minimize subjectivity. Part of that objectivity is the claim that "the basic principle behind EPPI Centre reviews is transparency of methods, which allows replication and updating" (Gough & Elbourne, 2002, p. 229). The reality is less clear-cut. Each EPPI group has to determine its own chosen set of criteria—clearly a social and micropolitical process. In a training event for these procedures attended by a colleague in June 2003, David Gough, deputy director of the EPPI Centre, stressed the fact that during all stages of the process, skilled interpretation was necessary. Groups would need to debate what their review questions were, what criteria should be applied, and how those criteria were to be applied in respect of individual research papers. In a group exercise, the significance of this sort of judgment making became apparent. Within one group, some participants claimed that qualitative case study research did not contain any empirical data and, therefore, always should be excluded. Others disagreed. Toward the end of this session, Gough shared a list of criteria for judging qualitative research. This is not an official EPPI list, but he claimed that it was a list with which no one will disagree:

> an explicit account of theoretical framework and/or inclusion of literature review; clearly stated aims and objectives; a clear description of context; a clear description of sample; a clear description of fieldwork methods including systematic data collection; an analysis of data by more than one researcher; and sufficient original data to mediate between evidence and interpretation.

This list is actually deeply controversial, and many high-quality research papers would be rejected if all of these criteria were seriously enforced. For example, the list sits very uncomfortably with Wolcott's (1999) claim that ethnography is research with no method—or, at least, often lacks what Gough termed "systematic data collection" or "a clear sample." It is "a way of seeing," and any aims may be general rather than specific. Becker's (1971) seminal work on becoming a marijuana user would have failed on several of these criteria, as would Wolcott's (2002) own work on the "sneaky kid." The implication that two (or more) poor interpretations are better than one good one is common but is logically bizarre. More seriously, what does "clear" mean in this context, and at what point does, for example, a description of the sample become clear as opposed to unclear? The suspicion is that clear stands for the very precise—exactly how many interviews were conducted with how many people of what categories and so forth. There is also no recognition in this list that in a short journal article, meeting every one of these criteria fully might leave little space to actually present any findings.

Far from being scientific, transparent, and replicable, every aspect of the EPPI procedures is shot through with subjective judgment making, and there is a micropolitical purpose to the work. Oakley and her colleagues are strongly promoting one approach to research and judgment-making processes about research, as Oakley's (2000) book makes clear. In so doing, life for researchers in the field who do not agree is being made much more difficult. The potential seriousness of this situation was apparent in a conversation between one of the authors (Hodkinson) and the director of a research program of which he is a part. The director stressed the need to ensure that books reporting the research contain full accounts of the method, including "the precise dates of the fieldwork," lest the books be excluded by some future EPPI groups, whose criteria are not yet even known. The sorts of nonempiricist ways of judging qualitative research described by Sparkes (2002) are so far off the agenda as to be denied existence. The fact that the EPPI Centre is funded by the U.K. government illustrates the link between the micropolitics of judgment and the more recently obvious macropolitics of research judgment.

Macro-Level Politics

The most interesting turn of events regarding criteria for judging inquiry has involved political moves at what we have defined as the macro level. By this, we mean that concerns over the issue of criteria are no longer the virtually exclusive province of researchers themselves. In both the United States and the United Kingdom, there have been moves to governmentally establish, if not impose, certain criteria not only to judge the quality of research but also to distinguish what qualifies as research and what does not.

In the United States, the most significant move has been the 2002 legislative reauthorization of the Elementary and Secondary School Act of 1965 known as No Child Left Behind (NCLB). In the United Kingdom, there have been a number of governmental moves to influence or even establish criteria for judging the quality of inquiry. Among the more important of these are the just-discussed funding by the DfES of the EPPI Centre and the government-funded and -led National Educational Research Forum (NERF). In both countries, the idea has been to set out the kinds of things that researchers must do to have a quality study and then restrict research funding to those researchers who follow the rules or the prescribed methods.

In the NCLB legislation, the criteria for judging the quality of research studies are elaborated in the definition of what is called scientifically based research. The standards or criteria (i.e., list of characteristics in our language) are that the study be systematic and empirical, involve rigorous data analysis (i.e., statistical analysis), employ reliable and valid data collection procedures (e.g., repeated measures), possess a strong research design (i.e., experimental or quasi-experimental), allow for the possibility of replication, and invoke expert scrutiny of results.

These elements, not surprisingly, have been translated into a hierarchy of approaches. The randomized control group approach is referred to as the "gold standard" for research. Quasi-experimental designs are second in order in the hierarchy and are referred to as the "silver standard." Correlational studies, descriptive studies, case studies, and the like are further down the list. The question, of course, is where qualitative inquiry fits into the picture. Because it does not meet the standards as noted in the legislation, so far as NCLB is concerned, qualitative inquiry is not research—or, if it is accepted as research, it must be thought of as quite rudimentary indeed.

Why this elimination of qualitative research from the status of scientific? At one level, it is very likely the case that many people, including researchers, believe philosophically or for epistemological reasons that qualitative inquiry is not "real" research. This is a feeling that has been maintained by many empiricist-oriented researchers since the 1980s, when qualitative inquiry began to gain increasing attention. For them, qualitative approaches have been, at worst, a useless distraction or, at best, a way of generating possible research questions for much more "rigorous" scientific investigations with control groups, statistical analysis, and so forth.

Be this as it may, we suspect that there is a major reason for this desire to impose criteria by way of governmental intervention that pushes qualitative inquiry to the sidelines of acceptable inquiry. This reason centers on what we refer to as the subversive nature—with regard to empiricism—of qualitative inquiry. There is a great deal to be gained by social and educational researchers in terms of social prestige and economic advantage by claiming to be scientists, on par with natural scientists, and convincing others to honor this claim. The problem is that much of qualitative inquiry was nurtured by philosophical arguments that undermined the claims, and even the hopes, that a science of the social was possible (on our inability to find law-like generalizations and why this is important, see Smith, 1993; on the systematic unpredictability of human affairs and the like, see Cziko, 1989, and MacIntyre, 1984). And, of course, it must be noted that if there is no science of the social, there can be no scientists of the social. It bears repeating; there is a great deal at stake here for many people.

In a very similar sense, when qualitative inquiry was subversive of the supposedly scientific approach to inquiry, it also was subversive of the claims to neutrality and objectivity—that comfortable image of the researcher as a "neutral broker" of information for policymakers. Many versions of qualitative inquiry offered the challenge that research must have a direct ameliorative intent and effect. In an echo of Marx, many people—although not necessarily being Marxists—have argued that research is not just about studying the world but also about changing it. As such, qualitative inquiry is very often driven by social purpose to improve the lives of marginalized and oppressed peoples. This is why qualitative research is often driven by perspectives that go under labels such as postcolonialist, feminist, gay/lesbian, and disablist. We suspect that for many conventional researchers, and certainly for many officials in the government, this idea of research as direct social engagement poses an unacceptable situation and must be controlled.

Finally, a speculative comment about what NCLB might mean for the American Educational Research Association (AERA) and why Shavelson and Towne (2002) discussed qualitative inquiry with such ambiguity (as noted previously) is in order. A significant number of AERA members now think of themselves as qualitative researchers. Certainly, some would accept methodical constraints and act accordingly, even though obeying methods is unlikely to gain them significant respect from the scientific types. Others, however, have adopted an ameliorative agenda and are doing readers' theater, autoethnographies, postmodernist approaches, artistic approaches, and so forth. Because the nonmethodical are considered not to be doing research at all, and the methodically oriented qualitative researchers—their adherence to method notwithstanding—are considered not to be doing really rigorous research, does this mean that the AERA should divide itself into the research members, the sort of research members, and the nonresearch members? Or, perhaps, should people go their own different ways and form different associations? We suspect that the thought of this is unacceptable, maybe not to those who wrote the NCLB definition of research but possibly to Shavelson and Towne (2002) and the members of the National Research Council Committee. We can think of no other explanation for their wavering comments about the status of qualitative research—yes it is research, no it really isn't research, maybe it is sort of research, and so forth. Maybe the report itself is a political document; any beliefs the authors may have really had about the status of qualitative research aside, they had to temper those beliefs in the face of the fact that there are a whole lot of qualitative educational researchers around. The politics of criteria is inescapable.

In the United Kingdom in the year 2000, the then secretary of state for education argued that the research community had to do much more to meet the needs of policymakers and practitioners (Blunkett, 2000). This statement was followed by a raft of government-led and -supported initiatives to ensure that this happened. The funding of Oakley's EPPI Centre was described earlier. Others included the establishment of the government-funded and -led NERF, whose role was to coordinate and direct educational research efforts, bringing together all major research funders, major journal editors, and key users of research. Membership in this group is by invitation, and during its early days a simplistic empiricist stance, if not a positivist one, was adopted. It was originally suggested that the NERF would draw up "agreed criteria" that would be universally used by all funders and journals to ensure that only high-quality educational research survived (NERF, 2000). The NERF later backed off, in the face of arguments that such an approach would undermine academic freedom. The NERF was paralleled and predated by a major new research program, the Teaching and Learning Research Programme (TLRP). Although it was administered by an independent government-funded agency, the Economic and Social Research Council (ESRC), funding came from other government sources. The remit was to produce high-quality scientific educational research that would lead directly to improvements in teaching and learning. Projects were to be relatively large, with few under £300,000 and several over £800,000.

Mixed qualitative and quantitative methods were to be preferred over qualitative research alone. Money was also to be devoted to research capacity building, but initially for experimental and quantitative educational research. More recently, this program has widened its approaches but still retains a broadly empiricist rationale.

This concerted and government-driven movement to reform research in ways that make it more "rigorous" and more useful to policymakers does not apply only to education. In the U.K./English government structure (we need to specify England because recent partial devolution means that practices in Scotland, Wales, and Northern Ireland are becoming increasingly different), major departments, such as the DfES, are separate fiefdoms. Since the Labour Party came to power in 1996, there has been significant growth of more centralized control through the Cabinet Office, which answers directly to the prime minister. In 2003, the Cabinet Office published a major report on the criteria that should be used to judge the worth of qualitative research (Spencer, Ritchie, Lewis, & Dillon, 2003).

The ostensible purpose of this report is to aid policymakers and others in judging the quality of government-funded and -sponsored evaluation reports, which contained mainly or partly qualitative data. However, the size and form of the report suggest wider unarticulated motives. The report sets out what is claimed to be "a comprehensive and systematic review of the research literature relating to standards in qualitative research" (Spencer et al., 2003, p. 6). Through this approach and other approaches, including "a review of existing frameworks for reviewing quality in qualitative research" (p. 17), the authors produced their own framework. This is, they claimed, suitable for judging "qualitative research more generally [than just evaluations]" (p. 17), especially research that uses "interviews, focus groups, observation, and documentary analysis" (p. 19). The resulting framework consists of 18 "appraisal questions," each of which is accompanied by a series of "quality indicators." These items are "recurrently cited as markers of quality in the literature, in pre-existing frameworks, and in the interviews [with some researchers and policymakers] conducted for this study" (p. 19). According to the authors, these questions entail interpretation in their use; not all will apply in every circumstance, and additional questions will sometimes be needed. Above all, the authors claimed that because their framework is not "procedural," it is not subject to previous criticisms of predetermined and universal sets of research criteria, which we discussed earlier in the chapter.

Thus, despite disclaimers, the framework is being set up as something approaching a definitive tool that pulls together the accumulated wisdom of the current times. Therefore, it becomes the touchstone against which other frameworks and most, if not all, qualitative research outputs can be judged. This view is reinforced when we examine those types of qualitative research that Spencer and colleagues (2003) claimed are not covered. In addition to research not using interviews, focus groups, observations, or documentary analysis, other research that is "out of scope" includes a set of extreme alternatives to which few researchers, if any, could sign up. There is space here for only a couple of examples: "An external reality exists independently of human constructors and is accessible directly or exactly . . . OR there is no (shared) reality, only alternative individual human constructions" (p. 50). Also out of scope are studies where either "it is possible to produce accurate accounts which one knows with certainty correspond directly with reality OR . . . there are no privileged accounts, only alternative understandings" (p. 50). The force of these sorts of supposed qualification is that nearly all reasonable research perspectives are easily included. In these ways, what starts as an attempt to help policymakers use their own evaluations ends up as a government-sponsored framework to judge nearly all qualitative research.

This all-encompassing and flexible framework has clear epistemological underpinnings that were never critically acknowledged by Spencer and colleagues (2003). The report claimed, "For the purposes of this framework, the quality of the qualitative research that generates the evidence

. . . is seen as lying at the heart of any assessment [of an evaluation output]" (p. 16); method is the prime determinant of truth. Thus, to identify the extent to which a research report contributes to knowledge, it is not necessary to know much about the substantive area to which the contribution is made. Rather, it is more important to check whether there is a literature review, whether the research design was "set in the context of existing knowledge/understanding" (p. 22), whether there is a "credible/clear discussion of how findings have contributed to knowledge and understanding [and] findings [are] presented or conceptualized in a way that offer[s] new insights" (p. 22), and whether there is "discussion of limitations of evidence and what remains unknown/unclear" (p. 22).

This approach was presented as uncontroversial despite detailed, if superficial, attention to the paradigm debates in the report. Furthermore, there is something very odd about this approach when it is set alongside the exclusionary categories described previously. From the neorealist perspective of Spencer and colleagues (2003), what does it mean to claim that research based on what they called "naïve realism" or "radical constructivism" is "out of scope"? This implies that issues of ontology and epistemology are matters of personal belief (relativist in our terms) and that the beliefs and values of either the researcher or the research reader should determine the criteria that are applied. Unsurprisingly, the implications of such a stance are not acknowledged or addressed because the political and rhetorical purpose of these "out of scope" exclusions is to legitimize the universality of the framework despite explicit claims that this is not the case.

Other than raising further and ongoing debates, it is the political context and purpose of the report that makes this logical paradox significant. This framework is explicitly and implicitly intended as a means of judging the worth of qualitative research, with clear and obvious implications for the allocation of scarce research resources—both the cultural capital of esteem and recognition and the economic capital of future research contract success. In effect, through this report, the government was striving once more to establish universal criteria for the control of social and educational research that the NERF set as its early goal before backing off in response to charges that it was curtailing academic freedom. The detailed and complex articulation of a wide range of literature, the tone of self-evident reasonableness, and the arguments that are advanced to demonstrate the credibility and applicability of this framework will nullify any such simplistic response this time around. If a few of us are foolish enough to adopt one of the extreme positions that are "out of scope," we are free to do so, and the framework acknowledges our existence outside its frame. Of course, those of us who do so should not expect either funding or esteem to follow. If this framework infiltrates indirect forms of U.K. government research funding, such as the award of ESRC research contracts or the evaluation of outputs used in the Research Assessment Exercise, political control over research will become nearly universal.

Taken collectively, these initiatives amount to a deliberate and powerful U.K. government intervention into the conduct and nature of educational research, ostensibly to improve its quality and make it more relevant to policymakers and policy implementers. As these initiatives changed the educational research map of the United Kingdom, researchers themselves became engaged in a high-stakes political process. Some celebrated the new climate and worked hard to reinforce and strengthen it while no doubt looking for opportunities to further their own work and careers. Others worked to oppose and resist the changes, trying to preserve spaces for alternative research approaches, including the sorts of work that they wanted to do. Still others worked to play the new regime by describing research in ways that might attract TLRP funding but without subscribing to its original hardline philosophy.

Interesting Times

We close with two comments about the increasingly evident political nature of research and criteria. First, we have argued that the major macropolitical interventions of both the U.S. and U.K. governments into social and educational research are framed around softer or harder versions of empiricism and neorealism. This link, of course, is not coincidental. There are strong relations between governments' desires to predict and control complex social and economic processes and the well-known role that prediction and control of phenomena and processes plays within empiricism. Put differently, current approaches are dominated by what Habermas (1972) termed "technical interests" and are also part of the much wider social and political growth of an audit society (Power, 1997) or an audit culture (Strathern, 1997, 2000). The audit culture is dominated by attempts to measure the success and value of everything. Thus, in both the United States and the United Kingdom, education establishments are increasingly judged comparatively against measures such as the retention of students, the proportions of students who complete the courses, the levels of eventual qualification that students attain, and standardized test scores. In this context, it is hardly surprising that there are strong government pressures for similar measured and supposedly objective performance criteria for research. It is this audit culture, and its nearly universal assumptions of measured value, that lies behind Shavelson and Towne's (2002) report in the United States and the Cabinet Office's report (Spencer et al., 2003) in the United Kingdom. In this audit climate, the view that research judgment is a matter of embodied interpretation, and that lists of criteria are fluid and changing, is alien self-indulgence at best.

As Habermas (1972) argued, this link among empiricism, positivism, and government interests is more than just technical. Such technical approaches deflect attention away from deeper issues of value and purpose. They make radical critiques much more difficult to mount and, as we have seen, render largely invisible partisan approaches to research under the politically useful pretence that judgments are about objective quality only. As Bourdieu (1998) wrote, empiricism and positivism are tools of the powerful:

> The dominants, technocrats, and epistemocrats of the right or the left are hand in glove with reason and the universal: one makes one's way through universes in which more and more technical, rational justifications will be necessary in order to dominate and in which the dominated can and must also use reason to defend themselves against domination, because the dominants must increasingly invoke reason, and science, to exert their domination. (p. 90)

Second, we think that governmental intervention into the politics of criteria is an announcement that the "culture wars" have come to educational and social research. Since the 1960s, more strongly in the United States and less so in the United Kingdom, there have been ongoing battles over the shape of our societies and cultures. These disputes over issues have ranged from abortion, to gay/lesbian marriages, to the content of history and sociology and other courses in our schools, to the content of television shows. It seems that it was only a matter of time until these types of divisions would become a prominent part of our judgments about acceptable versus unacceptable social and educational research. And just as the social discourse has become more strident, so might the discussions of research quality in the future. Of course, we can only wait and see.

For us, the conclusion to all of this is very clear. There is no point in pretending that power and politics, at both the micro level and the macro level, are not a part of the process by which we make judgments about the quality of research. We live in the era of relativism, and there can be no time- and place-independent criteria for judgment—that is, criteria that are "untainted" by our various opinions, ideologies, emotions, and self-interests. Power and politics are with us, and the only issues are how power is used and how the political process is played out. And of course, the answers will not be found in epistemology; instead, they will be found in our reasoning as finite practical and moral beings.

References

Abel, T. (1948). The operation called *verstehen. American Journal of Sociology, 54,* 211–218.

Ball, S. J. (1987). *The micro-politics of the school.* London: Methuen.

Becker, H. S. (1971). Becoming a marihuana user. In B. R. Cosin, I. R. Dale, G. M. Esland, & D. M. Swift (Eds.), *School and society: A sociological reader* (pp. 141–147). London: Routledge & Kegan Paul.

Beckett, D., & Hager, P. (2002). *Life, work, and learning: Practice in postmodernity.* London: Routledge.

Bernstein, R. (1983). *Beyond objectivism and relativism.* Philadelphia: University of Pennsylvania Press.

Bhaskar, R. (1979). *The possibility of naturalism.* Atlantic Highlands, NJ: Humanities Press.

Blunkett, D. (2000, February). *Influence or irrelevance: Can social science improve government?* Secretary of State's Economic and Social Research Council lecture speech, London.

Bourdieu, P. (1998). *Practical reason.* Cambridge, UK: Polity.

Bourdieu, P., & Wacquant, L. J. D. (1992). *An invitation to reflexive sociology.* Cambridge, UK: Polity.

Cherryholmes, C. (1988). *Power and criticism.* New York: Columbia University, Teachers College Press.

Cziko, G. (1989). Unpredictability and indeterminism in human behavior: Arguments and implications for educational research. *Educational Researcher, 18*(3), 17–25.

Donmoyer, R. (1996). Educational research in an era of paradigm proliferation: What's a journal editor to do? *Educational Researcher, 25*(2), 19–25.

Gadamer, H-G. (1995). *Truth and method* (2nd rev. ed., J. Weinsheimer & D. G. Marshall, Trans.). New York: Crossroad.

Garratt, D., & Hodkinson, P. (1998). Can there be criteria for selecting research criteria? A hermeneutical analysis of an inescapable dilemma, *Qualitative Inquiry, 4,* 515–539.

Giddens, A. (1976). *New rules of sociological method: A positive critique of interpretive sociologies.* London: Hutchinson.

Goodman, N. (1978). *Ways of worldmaking.* Indianapolis, IN: Hackett.

Gough, D., & Elbourne, D. (2002). Systematic research synthesis to inform policy, practice, and democratic debate. *Social Policy and Society, 1,* 225–236.

Habermas, J. (1972). *Knowledge and human interests* (2nd ed.). London: Heinemann.

Hammersley, M. (1990). *Reading ethnographic research: A critical guide.* London: Longman.

Hanson, N. (1958). *Patterns of discovery.* Cambridge, UK: Cambridge University Press.

Hazelrigg, L. (1989). *Claims of knowledge.* Tallahassee: Florida State University Press.

Hesse, M. (1980). *Revolutions and reconstructions in the philosophy of science.* Brighton, UK: Harvester.

Hillage, J., Pearson, R., Anderson, A., & Tamkin, P. (1998). *Excellence in schools.* London: Institute for Employment Studies.

Hodkinson, P. (1998, August). Naïveté and bias in educational research: The Tooley Report. *Research Intelligence,* pp. 16–17.

Hodkinson, P. (2004). Research as a form of work: Expertise, community, and methodological objectivity. *British Educational Research Journal, 30*(1), 9–26.

Hodkinson, P., & Smith, J. K. (2004). The relationship between research, policy, and practice. In R. Pring & G. Thomas (Eds.), *Evidence-based practice* (pp. 150–163). Buckingham, UK: Open University Press.

Hofstadter, D. (1979). *Gödel, Escher, Bach: An eternal golden braid.* New York: Basic Books.

Hoyle, E. (1982) Micropolitics of educational organizations. *Educational Management and Administration, 10,* 87–98.

Hoyle, E. (1986) *The politics of school management.* London: Hodder & Stoughton.

Kerlinger, F. (1979). *Behavioral research.* New York: Holt, Rinehart & Winston.

Kuhn, T. S. (1962). *The structure of scientific revolutions.* Chicago: University of Chicago Press.

Leary, D. (1984). Philosophy, psychology, and reality. *American Psychologist, 39,* 917–919.

MacIntyre, A. (1984). *After virtue* (2nd ed.). Notre Dame, IN: University of Notre Dame Press.

MacKenzie, D. (1981). *Statistics in Great Britain: 1885–1930.* Edinburgh, UK: Edinburgh University Press.

Manicas, P. (1987). *A history and philosophy of the social sciences.* Oxford, UK: Basil Blackwell.

Manicas, P., & Secord, P. (1983). Implications for psychology of the new philosophy of science. *American Psychologist, 39,* 399–413.

Nagel, T. (1986). *The view from nowhere.* New York: Oxford University Press.

National Educational Research Forum. (2000). *Research and development in education: A national strategy consultation paper.* Nottingham, UK: Author.

Oakley, A. (2000). *Experiments in knowing: Gender and method in the social sciences.* London: Polity.

Oakley, A. (2003). Research evidence, knowledge management, and educational practice: Early lessons from a systematic approach. *London Review of Education, 1*(1), 21–33.

Phillips, D. C., & Burbules, N. C. (2000). *Postpositivism and educational research.* Lanham, MD: Rowman & Littlefield.

Polanyi, M. (1962). *Personal knowledge.* Chicago: University of Chicago Press.

Popper, K. (1959). *The logic of scientific discovery.* London: Hutchinson.

Popper, K. (1972). *Objective knowledge.* Oxford, UK: Clarendon.

Power, M. (1997). *The audit society: Rituals of verification.* Oxford, UK: Oxford University Press.

Pring, R. (2000). *Philosophy of educational research.* London: Continuum.

Putman, H. (1981). *Reason, truth, and history.* Cambridge, UK: Cambridge University Press.

Rorty, R. (1985). Solidarity or objectivity? In J. Rajchman & C. West (Eds.), *Post-analytic philosophy* (pp. 3–19). New York: Columbia University Press.

Schwandt, T. (1996). Farewell to criteriology. *Qualitative Inquiry, 2,* 58–72.

Shavelson, R., & Towne, L. (2002). *Scientific research in education.* Washington, DC: National Academy Press.

Slavin, R. (2002). Evidence-based policies: Transforming educational practice and research. *Educational Researcher, 31*(7), 15–21.

Smith, J. K. (1985). Social reality as mind-dependent versus mind-independent and the interpretation of test validity. *Journal of Research and Development in Education, 1,* 1–9.

Smith, J. K. (1989). *The nature of social and educational inquiry: Empiricism versus interpretation.* Norwood, NJ: Ablex.

Smith, J. K. (1993). *After the demise of empiricism: The problem of judging social and educational inquiry.* Norwood, NJ: Ablex.

Smith, J. K., & Deemer, D. K. (2000). The problem of criteria in the age of relativism. In N. K. Denzin & Y. S. Lincoln (Eds.), *Handbook of qualitative research* (2nd ed., pp. 877–896). Thousand Oaks, CA: Sage.

Sparkes, A. C. (1994). Self, silence, and invisibility as a beginning teacher: A live history of lesbian experience. *British Journal of Sociology of Education, 15*(1), 93–118.

Sparkes, A. C. (2002). *Telling tales in sport and physical activity: A qualitative journey.* Leeds, UK: Human Kinetics.

Spencer, L., Ritchie, J., Lewis, J., & Dillon, L. (2003). *Quality in qualitative evaluation: A framework for assessing research evidence.* London: Cabinet Office.

Strathern, M. (1997). "Improving ratings": Audit in the British university system. *European Review, 5,* 305–321.

Strathern, M. (2000). The tyranny of transparency. *British Educational Research Journal, 26,* 309–321.

Taylor, C. (1971). Interpretation and the sciences of man. *Review of Metaphysics, 25,* 3–51.

Taylor, C. (1989). *Sources of the self.* Cambridge, UK: Cambridge University Press.

Tooley, J., with Darby, D. (1998). *Education research: An OFSTED critique.* London: OFSTED.

Wolcott, H. (1999). *Ethnography: A way of seeing.* Walnut Creek, CA: AltaMira.

Wolcott, H. (2002). *Sneaky Kid and its aftermath: Ethics and intimacy in fieldwork.* Walnut Creek, CA: AltaMira.

37

EMANCIPATORY DISCOURSES AND THE ETHICS AND POLITICS OF INTERPRETATION

Norman K. Denzin

> From the vantage point of the colonized, a position from which I write, and choose to privilege, the term "research" is inextricably linked to European imperialism and colonialism. The word itself, "research," is probably one of the dirtiest words in the indigenous world's vocabulary. (Smith, 1999, p. 1)

> A story grows from the inside out and the inside of Navajoland is something I know little of. But I do know myself if I begin traveling with an awareness of my own ignorance, trusting my instincts, I can look for my own stories embedded in the landscapes I travel through. . . .
>
> I am not suggesting we emulate Native Peoples—in this case, the Navajo. We can't. We are not Navajo. Besides their traditional stories don't work for us. It's like drinking another man's medicine. Their stories hold meaning for us only as examples. They can teach us what is possible. We must create and find our own stories, our own myths. (Williams, 1984, pp. 3, 5)

This chapter, in the form of a manifesto, invites indigenous and nonindigenous qualitative researchers to think through the implications of a practical, progressive politics of performative inquiry, an emancipatory discourse connecting indigenous epistemologies (Rains, Archibald, & Deyhle, 2000, p. 338) and theories of decolonization and the postcolonial (Soto, 2004, p. ix; Swadener & Mutua, 2004, p. 255) with critical pedagogy, with new ways of reading, writing, and performing culture in the first decade of a new century (Kincheloe & McLaren, 2000, p. 285).[1] I believe the performance-based human disciplines can contribute to radical social change, to economic justice, to a utopian cultural politics that extends localized critical (race) theory and the principles of a radical democracy to all aspects of decolonizing, indigenous societies (Giroux, 2000a, pp. x, 25; Kaomea, 2004, p. 31; L. T. Smith, 2000, p. 228; Swadener & Mutua, 2004, p. 257).

I advocate change that "envisions a democracy founded in a social justice that is 'not yet'" (Weems, 2002, p. 3). I believe that nonindigenous interpretive scholars should be part of this project (see Denzin, 2004a, 2004b, in press). How this endeavor is implemented in specific indigenous contexts should be determined by the indigenous peoples involved. I also believe that this initiative should be part of a larger conversation—namely, the global decolonizing discourse connected to the works of anticolonialist scholars, including those of First Nations, Native American, Alaskan, Australian Aboriginal, New Zealand Māori, and Native Hawaiian heritage (see in this volume Smith, Chapter 4; Bishop, Chapter 5; see also Mutua & Swadener, 2004; Smith, 1999).[2]

A postcolonial, indigenous participatory theater is central to this discourse (Balme & Carstensen, 2001; Greenwood, 2001).[3] Contemporary indigenous playwrights and performers revisit and make a mockery of 19th-century racist practices. They interrogate and turn the tables on blackface minstrelsy and the global colonial theater that reproduced racist politics through specific cross-race and cross-gender performances. The show how these performances used whiteface and blackface in the construction of colonial models of whiteness, blackness, gender, and national identity (Kondo, 2000, p. 83; Gilbert, 2003).

Indigenous theater nurtures a critical transnational yet historically specific critical race consciousness. It uses indigenous performance as means of political representation (Magowan, 2000, p. 311). Through the reflexive use of historical restagings, masquerade, ventriloquism, and doubly inverted performances involving male and female impersonators, this subversive theater undermines colonial racial representations (Bean, 2001, pp. 187–188). It incorporates traditional indigenous and nonindigenous cultural texts into frameworks that disrupt colonial models of race relations. This theater takes up key diasporic concerns, including those of memory, cultural loss, disorientation, violence, and exploitation (Balme & Carstensen, 2001, p. 45). This is a utopian theater that addresses issues of equity, healing, and social justice.[4]

▣ ▣ ▣

Consider the following:

- In her play *House Arrest* (2003), Anna Deavere Smith offers "an epic view of slavery, sexual misconduct, and the American presidency. Twelve actors, some in blackface, play across lines of race, age and gender to 'become' Bill Clinton, Thomas Jefferson, Sally Hemings . . . and a vast array of historical and contemporary figures" (Kondo, 2000, p. 81).
- In Native Canadian Daniel David Moses's play *Almighty Voice and His Wife* (1992), Native performers, wearing whiteface minstrel masks, mock such historical figures as Wild Bill Cody, Sitting Bull, and young Indian maidens called Sweet Sioux (Gilbert, 2003, p. 692).
- In Sydney, Australia, Aboriginal theater groups perform statements of their indigenous rights, demanding that politicians participate in these performance events "as co-producers of meaning rather than as tacit consumers" (Magowan, 2000, pp. 317–318).

Thus do indigenous performances function as strategies of critique and empowerment.

▣ ▣ ▣

The "Decade of the World's Indigenous Peoples" (1994–2004; Henderson, 2000, p. 168) has ended. Nonindigenous scholars have yet to learn from it, to learn that it is time to dismantle, deconstruct, and decolonize Western epistemologies from within, to learn that research does not have to be a dirty word, to learn that research is always already both moral and political.

Shaped by the sociological imagination (Mills, 1959), building on George Herbert Mead's (1938) discursive, performative model of the act, critical qualitative research imagines and explores the multiple ways in which performance can be understood, including as imitation, or *mimesis*; as construction, or *poiesis;* and as motion or movement, or *kinesis* (Conquergood, 1998, p. 31). The researcher-as-performer moves from a view of performance as imitation, or dramaturgical staging (Goffman, 1959), to an emphasis on performance as liminality and construction (McLaren, 1999), then to a view of performance as struggle, as intervention, as breaking and remaking, as kinesis, as a sociopolitical act (Conquergood, 1998, p. 32).

Viewed as struggles and interventions, performances and performance events become transgressive achievements, political accomplishments that break through "sedimented meanings and normative traditions" (Conquergood, 1998, p. 32).

It is this performative model of emancipatory decolonized indigenous research that I develop here (Garoian, 1999; Gilbert, 2003; Kondo, 2000; Madison, 1999). Drawing on Garoian (1999), Du Bois (1926), Gilbert (2003), Madison (1998), Magowan (2000), and Smith (2003), this model enacts a utopian performative politics of resistance (see below). Extending indigenous initiatives, this model is committed to a form of revolutionary political theater that performs pedagogies of dissent for the new millennium (McLaren, 1997b).

▣ ▣ ▣

My argument in this chapter unfolds in several parts. Drawing throughout from an ongoing performance text, I begin with a set of obstacles that confront the nonindigenous critical theorist. I then briefly discuss race, the call to performance, and the history of indigenous theater. I next address a group of concepts and the arguments associated with them; these include the concepts of indigenous epistemology, pedagogy, discourses of resistance, politics as performance, and counternarratives as critical inquiry. I briefly discuss a variety of indigenous pedagogies as well as the concept of indigenous research as localized critical theory. I elaborate variations within the personal narrative approach to decolonized inquiry, extending Richardson's (2000) model of "creative analytic practices," or CAP ethnography (p. 929). Then, after outlining a politics of resistance, I conclude the chapter with a discussion of indigenous models of power, truth, ethics, and social justice.

In the spirit of Du Bois, Dewey, Mead, Blumer, hooks, and West, I intend to create a dialogue between indigenous and nonindigenous members of the qualitative research community. I want to move our discourse more fully into the spaces of a global yet localized progressive, performative pragmatism. I want to extend those political impulses within the feminist pragmatist tradition that imagine a radical, democratic utopia. Following Du Bois, hooks, and West, I see these impulses as constantly interrogating the relevance of pragmatism and critical theory for race relations and inequality in the global neoliberal capitalist state.

▣ Obstacles Confronting the Nonindigenous Critical Theorist

In proposing a conversation between indigenous and nonindigenous scholars, I am mindful of several difficulties. First, scholars must resist the legacy of the Western colonizing other. As Smith (1999) observes of the Western colonizers, "They came, they saw, they named, they claimed" (p. 80). As agents of colonial power, Western scientists discovered, extracted, appropriated, commodified, and distributed knowledge about the indigenous other. Many indigenous critics contend that these practices have placed control over research in the hands of Western scholars. This means, for example, that Māori are excluded from discussions concerning who has control over the initiation of research about Māori, the methodologies used, the evaluations and assessments made, the resulting representations, and the distribution of the newly defined knowledge (see Bishop, Chapter 5, this volume). The decolonization project challenges research practices that perpetuate Western power by misrepresenting and essentializing indigenous persons, often denying them voice or identity.

A second difficulty is that critical, interpretive performance theory and critical race theory will not work within indigenous settings without modification. The criticisms of Graham Smith (2000), Linda Tuhiwai Smith (1999, 2000), Bishop (1994, 1998), Battiste (2000a, 2000b), Churchill (1996), Cook-Lynn (1998), and others make this very clear. Critical theory's criteria for self-determination and empowerment perpetuate neocolonial sentiments while turning the indigenous person into an essentialized "other" who is spoken for (Bishop, Chapter 5, this volume). The categories of race, gender, and racialized identities cannot be turned into frozen, essential terms, nor is racial identity a free-floating signifier (Grande, 2000, p. 348). Critical theory must be localized, grounded in the specific meanings, traditions, customs, and community relations that operate in each indigenous setting. Localized critical theory can work if the goals of critique, resistance, struggle, and emancipation are not treated as if they have "universal characteristics that are independent of history, context, and agency" (L. T. Smith, 2000, p. 229).

A third difficulty lies in the pressing need for scholars to decolonize and deconstruct those structures within the Western academy that privilege Western knowledge systems and their epistemologies (Mutua & Swadener, 2004, p. 10; Semali & Kincheloe, 1999). Indigenous knowledge systems are too frequently made into objects of study, treated as if they were instances of quaint folk theory held by the members of primitive cultures. The decolonizing project reverses this equation, making Western systems of knowledge the object of inquiry.

A fourth difficulty is that the nonindigenous scholar must carefully and cautiously articulate the spaces between decolonizing research practices and indigenous communities (to paraphrase Smith's comments in Chapter 4, this volume). These spaces are fraught with uncertainty. Neoliberal and neoconservative political economies turn knowledge about indigenous peoples into a commodity. Conflicts exist between competing epistemological and ethical frameworks, including in the area of institutional regulations concerning human subject research. Currently, research is regulated by positivist epistemologies. Indigenous scholars and intellectuals are pressed to produce technical knowledge that conforms to Western standards of truth and validity. Conflicts over who initiates and who benefits from such research are especially problematic. Scholars must develop culturally responsive research practices that locate power within indigenous communities, so that these communities determine and define what constitutes acceptable research. Such work encourages self-determination and empowerment (see Bishop, Chapter 5, this volume).

In arguing for a dialogue between critical and indigenous theorists, I must acknowledge my position as an outsider to the indigenous colonized experience. I write as a privileged Westerner. At the same time, however, I seek to be an "allied other" (Kaomea, 2004, p. 32; Mutua & Swadener, 2004, p. 4), a fellow traveler of sorts, an antipositivist, an insider who wishes to deconstruct the Western academy and its positivist epistemologies from within. I endorse a critical epistemology that contests notions of objectivity and neutrality. I believe that all inquiry is moral and political. I value autoethnographic, insider, participatory, collaborative methodologies (Fine et al., 2003). These are narrative, performative methodologies, research practices that are reflexively consequential, ethical, critical, respectful, and humble. These practices require that scholars live with the consequences of their research actions (Smith, 1999, pp. 137–139).

▣ ▣ ▣

In proposing a dialogue between indigenous and nonindigenous qualitative researchers, in positioning myself as an "allied other," I am mindful of Terry Tempest Williams's cautious advice about borrowing stories and narratives from indigenous peoples. In her autoethnography *Pieces of White Shell: A Journey to Navajoland* (1984), she praises the wisdom of Navajo storytellers and the stories they tell (pp. 3–4). But she also warns her nonindigenous readers: We cannot emulate native peoples. "We are not Navajo . . . their traditional stories don't work for us. . . . Their stories hold meaning for us only as examples. They can teach us what is possible. We must create and find our own stories" (p. 5).

As a nonindigenous scholar seeking a dialogue with indigenous scholars, I must construct stories that are embedded in the landscapes I travel through. These will be dialogical counternarratives, stories of resistance, of struggle, of hope, stories that create spaces for multicultural conversations, stories embedded in the critical democratic imagination. I briefly sample below from *Searching for Yellowstone* (Denzin, in press), a work in progress.

▣ ▣ ▣

Searching for Yellowstone consists of a series of coperformance texts and plays, each with multiple speaking parts. Drawing on verbatim theater, I quote from interviews, letters, books, and other documents written by historical and contemporary figures; in some cases, I present material that was originally written as prose in the format of poetry. "Indians in the Park" (excerpted below) is a four-act play of sorts. It can be performed on a simple set, around a seminar table, or on a stage in front of an audience. Overhead, a series of images should be projected on a full-size screen. To one side, a large roving spotlight, the "Camera Eye," should stand, with its light moving from speaker to speaker, returning always to the narrator.[5] More than 35 individuals speak or are quoted, some more than once. Audience members are asked to participate in the performance by assuming speaking parts.

▣ ▣ ▣

▣ Prologue

"Indians in the Park" (Denzin, 2004a) enacts a critical cultural politics concerning the representations of Native Americans and their historical presence in Yellowstone National Park. Beginning with the sting of childhood memory (Ulmer, 1989, pp. 209, 211), I follow Ulmer's (1989) and Benjamin's (1983–1984, p. 24) advice concerning history; that is, to write history means to quote history, and to quote history means to rip the historical object out of its context. In so doing, I expose the contradictions, cracks, and seams in official ideology. The intent is to rediscover the past as a series of scenes, inventions, emotions, images, and stories (Benjamin, 1969, p. 257; Ulmer, 1989, p. 112). In bringing the past into the autobiographical present, I insert myself into the past and create the conditions for rewriting and hence reexperiencing it.

The history at hand is the history of Native Americans in two cultural and symbolic landscapes, mid-central Iowa in the 1940s and 1950s and Yellowstone National Park in the 1870s. I read Yellowstone, America's first national park, metaphorically. In and across the discourses that historically define the park are deeply entrenched meanings concerning nature, culture, violence, gender, wilderness, parks, whites, and Native Americans (see Schullery, 1997).

I situate these voices and discourses in my own biography. The place of Native Americans in the collective white imagination is almost entirely a matter of racist myth, shifting meanings of the color line, the "Veil of Color" (Du Bois, 1903/1989, pp. xxxi, 2–3), theatricality, and minstrelsy (Spindel, 2000).

▣ ▣ ▣

For example:

Author's Aside to Audience:

> As a child I lived inside this white imaginary. I played a dress-up game called "cowboys and Indians." I watched *Red Rider and Little Beaver* and *The Lone Ranger* on Saturday-morning television. On Saturday nights my grandfather took me to see western movies—*Shane, Stagecoach, Broken Arrow, The Searchers*—at the Strand Theater in Iowa City, Iowa. (see Denzin, 2003, p. 175)

▣ ▣ ▣

In challenging the cultural representations of Native Americans, I follow Hall (1996a) and Smith (1997), who argue that it is not enough to replace negative representations with positive representations.[6] The positive-negative debate essentializes racial identity and denies its "dynamic relation to constructions of class, gender, sexuality [and] region" (Smith, 1997, p. 4). It takes two parties to do racial minstrelsy. Stereotypes of whiteness are tangled up in racial myth, in minstrel shows that replay the Wild West, leading whites to look like cowboys and Native Americans to look like Indians (Dorst, 1999). I employ this critical race theory and critical pedagogy to confront Yellowstone National Park and its histories.

Here are some excerpts from "Indians in the Park":

▣ ▣ ▣

Second Author's Aside to Audience:

I wanted to be a cowboy when I grew up. So did Mark, my brother. On Saturday mornings, while Grandma made hot doughnuts for us in the new deep-fat fryer in her big country kitchen, we watched "cowboy and Indian" television shows: *The Lone Ranger, Red Rider and Little Beaver, The Roy Rogers Show, Hopalong Cassidy.* Mark and I had cowboy outfits—wide-brimmed hats, leather vests, chaps, and spurs, along with toy pistols and holsters. Grandpa bought us a horse. I have a photograph of Mark and me in our cowboy outfits on the back of swaybacked Sonny, who was deaf in his right ear. We'd ride Sonny around and around the corral, waving at Grandpa and Grandma. When I was in fourth grade, I was Squanto in the Thanksgiving play about the pilgrims. My skin was painted brown.

▣ ACT 1

Scene 1: Sacagawea and Other Myths

Newsreel 1

Voice 1: Horton:

Keeping the Legacy Alive

Two hundred years ago the Corps of Discovery, led by captains Meriwether Lewis and William Clark, struck out from the Falls of Ohio, near Louisville, Kentucky, to explore the newly acquired territory of the Louisiana Purchase. Their 8,000 mile trek took them through perilous, forbidding country by canoe, horseback, and foot. Lewis, the party's scientist, and Clark, its surveyor, mapped geological features and fixed the longitudes and latitudes of the rivers and plains. Lewis described or preserved specimens of some 178 plants and 122 animals—the majority as-yet unknown to science. . . .

None of this, of course,

would have been possible

without the aid and assistance

of the Native Americans they met

[nearly 50 tribes in all]

along the way.

Their Shoshone guide,

Sacagawea, a 15-year-old girl,

proved indispensable. (Horton, 2003, p. 90)

▣ ▣ ▣

Voice 2: Skeptic: This is revisionist white history!

▣ ▣ ▣

Voice 3: Slaughter:

Sacagawea is elusive,

fictive,

mythic

and real.

She is the Indian princess

required by myths

of discovery and conquest. (Slaughter, 2003, p. 86)

▣ ▣ ▣

Voice 4: Spindel:

If we do a census of the population in our collective imagination,

imaginary Indians are one of the largest demographic groups.

They dance, they drum; they go on the warpath;

they are always young men who wear trailing feather bonnets.

Symbolic servants, they serve as mascots,

metaphors. We rely on these images to anchor us

to the land and verify our account of

our own past. But these Indians exist only

in our imaginations. (Spindel, 2000, p. 8)

▣ ▣ ▣

Scene 2: Park Performances

The Camera Eye (2)

Narrator: Staged performances based on lore and myth from Hollywood westerns and Wild West shows represent and connect Indians with war bonnets, horses, western landscapes, parks, wilderness, tourism, nature, and danger (see Spindel, 2000, p. 8). These representations simultaneously place Native Americans within and outside white culture, hence the phrase "Indians in the park." Parks are safe places, sites carved out of the wilderness, and other spaces where whites go to view and experience nature and the natural world. Indians are not part of this cultural landscape. The "natural world" they inhabit is outside the park. It is a wild, violent, and uncivilized world.

◙ ◙ ◙

"Remembering to Forget" is a second coperformance text. It continues my interrogation of the cultural politics surrounding the Lewis and Clark expedition of 1804–1806. It is also fractured, revisionist, personal history, an attempt at a personal mythology that contests the rhetorical uses of nature, discovery, and science for political, patriotic purposes. This play is woven in, through, and around memories of blankets, families, Native Americans, illness, and Lewis and Clark in the greater Yellowstone region. The following excerpt is from Act 1, Scenes 1 and 2.

◙ Act 1

Scene 1: Getting Started

Course Announcement, Yellowstone Association Institute, Summer 2003

"Along the Yellowstone River with Lewis & Clark"

July 25–27, Limit 19

Location: Mammoth Hot Springs/Three Forks, and Dillon, Montana; Credit Pending; Instructor: Jim Garry, M.S.

$180 (member's fee $170)

In the summer of 1805, Lewis and Clark passed

through the Yellowstone region en route to the

Pacific Ocean. They came up the Missouri River from the Great Falls and

camped in the Three Forks area before

following the Jefferson River west to the headwaters of the Missouri system at

Lemhi Pass.

Almost 200 years later, we will walk in their

footsteps, see what they saw, read their journals, and

speculate on what they would think of this country today. We'll journey to Three

Forks and from there to Dillon and Lemhi Pass where we will look at some of

the impacts on the country since the days of Lewis and Clark.

(pause)

It was something like the Lewis and Clark [traveling] Medicine Show. (Ronda, 1984, p. 18; see also Ambrose, 1996, p. 157)

(pause)

But the park did not exist in 1805. What kind of history is this?

(pause)

Our image of [history] is indissolubly bound up with the image of redemption. (Benjamin, 1969, p. 256)

Scene 2: Canadian Blankets

Voice 2: **Narrator (to audience, explaining project):** On July 5, 1955, my father returned to our little house on Third Street in Indianola, Iowa, from a fishing trip in Ontario, Canada. Mother greeted him at the door. Slightly drunk, Dad handed her a Hudson's Bay wool blanket as a present and promptly left for the office. I still have that blanket. In this family we value such blankets and exchange them as gifts. This exchange system gives me a somewhat indirect historical connection to Lewis and Clark, Canada, Hudson's Bay Company blankets, the fur trade, 19th-century British and French traders, and Native Americans. This connection takes me right into the myths about Yellowstone Park, Lewis and Clark, the Corps of Discovery, and Sacagawea. Lewis and Clark, it appears, also traded blankets for goodwill on their expedition. But this was a tainted exchange, for in many instances these blankets were carriers of smallpox. Likewise, the blanket my father gave to my mother was embedded within a disease exchange system, in this case alcoholism. Although Dad's alcoholism was not full-blown in 1955, it would become so within 2 years of his return from that fishing trip.

▣ ▣ ▣

Read together, the above excerpts model a form of writing that moves back and forth between personal and official history. Using the language of the colonizer, they quote history back to itself, refusing to treat Lewis and Clark and the past as if they are things that can be fixed in time, as performances that can be unproblematically staged in the present. Indeed, the historical reenactment of Lewis and Clark's expedition is endowed with special powers. It stands outside time. Performers benevolently re-create the past, performing and remembering it "the way it really was" (Benjamin, 1969, p. 257).

There is great danger in such historical masquerades. The past is frozen in time. Particular versions of whiteness and white history are performed. The sins of the past are ignored, and a peaceful bond is forged between the imagined past and the present. In this nostalgic space, the benign pastness of Lewis and Clark's expedition comes alive. Their historic journey of conquest is celebrated. A territorial and cultural politic is signified. The white community owns this land, this river, this park, this place, these meanings. The white community and its city fathers have the right to re-create on this land, and in these cultural spaces, their version of the past, their version of how these two men helped win the West for Thomas Jefferson and White America (Williams, 1997). In such a utopian scenario, redemption for the handful of sins committed by the explorers is sought and easily achieved (see Grossman, 2003, pp. 2–5). Indeed, redemption gives way to celebration, to a displacement, a shift from conquest to ecoenvironmentalism, to nature, the joy of floating the Yellowstone or the Missouri River under the banner of Lewis and Clark.

▣ Race, Indigenous Others, and the Call to Performance

Many qualitative researchers and interpretive ethnographers are in the seventh moment, performing culture as they write it, understanding that the dividing line between performativity (doing) and performance (done) has disappeared (Conquergood, 1998, p. 25). But even as this disappearance occurs, matters of racial injustice remain. The indigenous other is a racialized other.

On this W. E. B. Du Bois (1901/1978), reminds us that "the problem of the twenty-first century, on a global scale, will be the problem of the color line" (p. 281) and that "modern democracy cannot succeed unless peoples of different races and religions are also integrated into the democratic whole" (p. 288). This integration cannot be imposed by one culture or nation on another; it must come from within the cultures involved.

Du Bois addressed race from a performance standpoint. He understood that "from the arrival of the first African slaves on American soil . . . the definitions and meanings of blackness have been intricately linked to issues of theater and performance"

(Elam, 2001, p. 4).[7] In his manifesto for an all-black, indigenous theater, Du Bois (1926) imagined a site for pedagogical performances that articulate positive black "social and cultural agency" (Elam, 2001, p. 6). His radical theater (Du Bois, 1926, p. 134), like that of Anna Deavere Smith (2003), is a political theater about blacks, written by blacks, for blacks, performed by blacks in local theaters. Radical indigenous theater is a weapon for fighting racism and white privilege. Gilbert (2003) elaborates on this topic, showing how indigenous whiteface performances unsettle fixed racial categories based on skin color: "Such acts . . . remind us of the historical role played by theatre in negotiating suppressed fears and fantasies of colonizing nations" (p. 680).

A Brief History of Indigenous Theater

Lhamon (1998) traces the origins of blackface minstrelsy in the United States to the early 1800s and marketplace transactions in New York City. By the 1840s, white performers in blackface where using blackness as a way to represent the color of nonwhite persons, including African Americans, Asian Americans, and Native Americans (Bean, 2001, p. 173). According to Bean (2001), the "first black minstrels . . . existed as early as 1850" (p. 177), and within a short time African American male and female impersonators where engaged in satiric, subversive performances that were critical of white stereotypes of blacks (p. 187). Ellison (1964) observes that such black performers were tricksters, playing a joke on the white audience, laughing at the audience among themselves, understanding that blackface was a "counterfeiting of the black American's identity" (p. 53). Thus by the mid-19th century a subversive theater was born within the racist institution of minstrelsy.

Gilbert (2003) describes blackface minstrelsy as the "symptomatic nineteenth-century stage form for an era of territorial expansion, not just in the United States but also in other settler colonies with growing non-indigenous populations" (p. 683). From the 1850s forward, minstrelsy had a transnational presence in the performances of touring groups that performed in Australia, New Zealand, Canada, the United States, Britain, Germany, France, Italy, India, Jamaica, Nigeria, and South Africa. The American minstrel show traveled to the popular stage in the Canadian West, where its subject matter included narratives about runaway slaves and Native Canadians (Gilbert, 2003, p. 683). When William Cody's Wild West show toured Europe, it offered audiences a Far East section called the "Dream of the Orient" (Reddin, 1999, p. 158). In every geographic location where the minstrel show appeared, it validated racism and imperialism.

At the same time, indigenous performance companies were contributing to a counterdiscourse that embodied the critical race consciousness identified by Ellison (1964). Indians playing Indians for whites and blacks playing blacks for whites were engaged in reflexive, doubly inverted performances that mocked and ridiculed white racist stereotypes. In this way, indigenous theater criticizes the racial masquerade behind blackface. In such performances the performativity of race is revealed. The indigenous performer in whiteface (or blackface) peels back, as in pentimento, the colors and shades of whiteness, showing that "white is a color that exists only because some of us get told we're black or yellow or Indians" (Gilbert, 2003, p. 689).

Using a ventriloquized discourse, the whiteface performer forces spectators to confront themselves "mirrored/parodied in the whiteface minstrel mask" (Gilbert, 2003, p. 693). Native Canadian whiteface performers in Daniel David Moses's play *Almighty Voice and His Wife* (1992) deploy ventriloquism to turn the tables on whites. In the stand-up section of the play, just before the finale, the Interlocutor, dressed in top hat and tails along with white gloves and studded white boots taunts the audience:

> You're that redskin! You're that wagon burner! That feather head, Chief Bullshit. No, Chief Shitting Bull! Oh, no, no. Bloodthirsty savage. Yes, you're primitive, uncivilized, a cantankerous cannibal. Unruly redman, you lack human intelligence! Stupidly stoic, sick, demented, foaming at the maws! Weirdly mad and dangerous, alcoholic, diseased, dirty, filthy, stinking, ill fated degenerate race, vanishing, dying lazy, mortifying. (pp. 94–95; quoted in Gilbert, 2003, p. 693)

Through double coding, race and gender exchanges, and the deployment of minstrel tropes, Moses has Indians criticizing Indians playing Indians. In this way, Gilbert (2003) observes, Moses "critiques hegemonically defined Indian stereotypes" (p. 692) even as he reflexively stages a grotesque spectacle of "Native performers enacting their own objectification" (p. 693).

Such performances function as genealogies. As Gilbert (2003) notes, they document the "historical dissemination of particular performance practices across space and time" (p. 696). By manipulating the tropes of minstrelsy, indigenous performers use whiteface and blackface to critique specific colonial practices. Thus Aboriginal Australians in whiteface performances protest the colonial habit of poisoning Aborigines with flour, just as Moses uses Indians in whiteface in his reenactment of the massacre at Wounded Knee (Gilbert, 2003, p. 696). In these ways, Gilbert argues, whiteface "is continually subjected to processes of citation and appropriation that triangulate white, black, and indigenous performance traditions in complex ways" (p. 696). Indigenous theater thus exposes whiteness in its ordinary and extreme forms. Made visible as a repressive sign of violent racial domination, whiteness "is forced to show its colors" (p. 698).

Some African American authors, such as bell hooks, have elaborated the need for a black political performance aesthetic. Writing about her childhood, hooks (1990) has described how she and her sisters learned about race in America by watching

> the Ed Sullivan show on Sunday nights. . . . seeing on that show the great Louis Armstrong, Daddy, who was usually silent, would talk about the music, the way Armstrong was being treated, and the political implications of his appearance. . . . responding to televised cultural production, black people could express rage about racism. . . . unfortunately . . . black folks were not engaged in writing a body of critical cultural analysis. (pp. 3–4)

Indigenous Voices, Critical Pedagogy, and Epistemologies of Resistance

Several scholars, such as Sandoval (2000), Collins (1998), Mutua and Swadener (2004), and Bishop (Chapter 5, this volume), have observed that we are in the midst of what Lopez (1998) calls "a large-scale social movement of anticolonialist discourse" (p. 226). This movement is evident in the emergence and proliferation of indigenous epistemologies and methodologies (Sandoval, 2000), including the arguments of African American, Chicana/o, Latina/o, Native American, First Nations, Native Hawaiian, and Māori scholars. These epistemologies are forms of critical pedagogy; that is, they embody a critical politics of representation that is embedded in the rituals of indigenous communities. Always already political, they are relentlessly critical of transnational capitalism and its destructive presence in the indigenous world (see Kincheloe & McLaren, 2000).

Epistemologies of Resistance

Indigenous pedagogies are grounded in an oppositional consciousness that resists "neocolonizing postmodern global formations" (Sandoval, 2000, pp. 1–2). These pedagogies fold theory, epistemology, methodology, and praxis into strategies of resistance that are unique to each indigenous community. Thus the oppositional consciousness of Kaupapa Māori research is both like and unlike black feminist epistemology (Collins, 1991, 1998), Chicana feminisms (Anzaldúa, 1987; Moraga, 1993), "red pedagogy" (Grande, 2000; Harjo & Bird, 1997), and Hawaiian epistemology (Meyer, 2003). Common to all is a commitment to indigenism, to an indigenist outlook, that assigns the highest priority to the rights of indigenous peoples, to the traditions, bodies of knowledge, and values that have "evolved over many thousands of years by native peoples the world over" (Churchill, 1996, p. 509).

Indigenist pedagogies are informed, in varying and contested ways, by decolonizing, revolutionary, and socialist feminisms. Such feminisms, in turn, address issues of social justice, equal rights, and nationalisms of "every racial, ethnic, gender, sex, class, religion, or loyalist type" (Sandoval, 2000, p. 7). Underlying each indigenist formation is a commitment to moral praxis, to issues of self-determination, empowerment, healing, love, community solidarity, respect for the earth, and respect for elders.

Indigenists resist the positivist and postpositivist methodologies of Western science because nonindigenous scholars too frequently use these formations to validate colonizing knowledge about indigenous peoples. Indigenists deploy, instead, interpretive strategies and skills that fit the needs, languages, and traditions of their respective indigenous communities. These strategies emphasize personal performance narratives and *testimonios.*

A Māori Pedagogy

Māori scholar Russell Bishop (1994, 1998) presents a collaborative, participatory epistemological model of Kaupapa Māori research, which is characterized by the absence of a need to be in control and by a desire to be connected to and part of a moral community in which a primary goal is the compassionate understanding of another's moral position (see also Bishop, Chapter 5, this volume; Heshusius, 1994). The Māori indigenist researcher wants to participate in a collaborative, altruistic relationship in which, as Bishop (1998) puts it, nothing "is desired for the self" (p. 207). The research is evaluated against participant-driven criteria based in the cultural values and practices that circulate in Māori culture, including metaphors that stress self-determination, the sacredness of relationships, embodied understanding, and the priority of community over self. Researchers are led to develop new storylines and criteria of evaluation that reflect these understandings. These participant-driven criteria function as resources for resistance against positivist and neoconservative desires to "establish and maintain control of the criteria for evaluating Māori experience" (p. 212).

Sandoval (2000) observes that indigenists enact an ethically democratizing stance that is committed to "equalizing power differentials between humans" (p. 114). The goal "is to consolidate and extend . . . manifestos of liberation in order to better identify and specify a mode of emancipation that is effective within first world decolonizing global conditions during the twenty-first century" (p. 2).

Treaties as Pedagogy

Indigenist pedagogies confront and work through government treaties, ideological formations, historical documents, and broken promises that connect indigenist groups and their fates to the capitalist colonizers. For example, as Churchill (1996) notes, during the "first 90-odd years of its existence the United States entered into and ratified more than 370 separate treaties . . . [and] has . . . defaulted on its responsibilities under every single treaty obligation it ever incurred with regard to Indians" (pp. 516–517; see also Stirling, 1965). The aboriginal rights of First Nations tribes in Canada were not recognized in law until the Constitution Act of 1982 (Henderson, 2000, p. 165). In New Zealand, Māori debate the Treaty of Waitangi, which was signed between Māori chiefs and the British Crown in 1840. This treaty was defined as a charter for power sharing between Māori and *pakeha*, or white settlers, but in reality it subjugated Māori to the *pakeha* nation-state (Smith, 1999, p. 57; see also Bishop, Chapter 5, this volume).

Linda Smith (2000) observes that Māori attempts "to engage in the activities of the state through the mechanisms of the Treaty of Waitangi have won some space . . . [but] this space is severely limited . . . as it has had to be wrestled not only from the state, but also from the community of positivist scientists whose regard for Māori is not sympathetic (p. 232). What is "now referred to as 'Kaupapa Māori research'" (p. 224) is an attempt to find a space and set of practices that honors Māori culture, convinces Māori people of the value of research for Māori, and shows the *pakeha* (white) research community the need for greater Māori involvement in research. Kaupapa Māori research is culturally safe and relevant, and it involves the mentorship of Māori (p. 228).

A Red Pedagogy

Native American indigenous scholars thicken the argument by articulating a spoken indigenous epistemology "developed over *thousands* of years of *sustained* living on this Land" (Rains et al., 2000, p. 337). An American Indian or "red" pedagogy (Grande, 2000) criticizes simplistic readings of race, ethnicity, and identity. This pedagogy privileges personal identity performance narratives—that is, stories and poetry that emphasize self-determination and indigenous theory (Brayboy, 2000). Grande (2000) describes the four characteristics of a red pedagogy: (a) politically, it maintains "a quest for sovereignty, and the dismantling of global capitalism"; (b) epistemologically, it privileges indigenous knowledge; (c) the earth is its "spiritual center"; (d) socioculturally, it is grounded in "tribal and traditional ways of ways of life" (p. 355). The performance of such rituals validates traditional ways of life. The performance embodies the ritual. It is the ritual. In this sense the performance becomes a form of public pedagogy. It uses the aesthetic to foreground cultural meanings and to teach these meanings to performers and audience members alike.

A Hawaiian Pedagogy

Manulani Aluli Meyer's (2003) discussion of Hawaiian epistemology complements the above description of a red pedagogy. As Meyer notes, a Hawaiian pedagogy resists colonial systems of knowing and educating; and it fights for an authentic Hawaiian identity (p. 192). It defines epistemology culturally; that is, it asserts that there are specific Hawaiian ways of knowing and being in the world (p. 187). According to Meyer, seven themes shape this epistemology: spirituality, physical space, the cultural nature of the senses, relational knowing, practical knowing, language as being, and the unity of mind and body (p. 193).

This framework stresses the place of morality in knowledge production. Culture restores culture. Culture is sacred. Culture is performed. Spirituality is basic to culture. It is sensuous and embodied, involving all the senses—taste, sight, smell, hearing, and touch. Knowledge is experienced and expressed in sensuous terms, in stories and critical personal narratives that focus on the importance of practice and repetition (p. 185). Knowledge is relational. The self knows itself through the other. Knowing the other and the self locates the person in a relational context. This involves harmony, balance, being generous, being responsible, being a good listener, and being kind.

Decolonizing the Academy

As I have argued above, critical indigenist pedagogies contest the complicity of the modern university with neocolonial forces (Battiste, 2000a). They encourage and empower indigenous peoples to make colonizers confront and be accountable for the traumas of colonization. In rethinking and radically transforming the colonizing encounter, these pedagogies imagine postcolonial societies that honor difference and promote healing. Indigenist pedagogies attempt to rebuild nations and their peoples through the use of restorative indigenous ecologies. These native ecologies celebrate survival, remembering, sharing, gendering, new forms of naming, networking, protecting, and democratizing daily life (Battiste, 2000b; Smith, 1999, pp. 142–162).

Theory, method, and epistemology are aligned in this project, anchored in the moral philosophies that are taken for granted in indigenous cultures and language communities (L. T. Smith, 2000, p. 225). This worldview endorses pedagogies of emancipation and empowerment, pedagogies that encourage struggles for autonomy, cultural well-being, cooperation, and collective responsibility. Such pedagogies demand that indigenous groups own the research process. They speak the truth "to people about the reality of their lives" (Collins, 1998, p. 198), equip them with the tools they need to resist oppression, and move them to struggle, to search for justice (Collins, 1998, pp. 198–199).

Indigenous Research as Localized Critical Theory

In their commitments, indigenous epistemologies overlap with critical theory. Indeed, Linda Smith (2000) connects her version of indigenous inquiry, Kaupapa Māori research, with critical theory and cultural studies, suggesting, with Graham Smith (2000), that Kaupapa Māori research is a "local theoretical position that is the modality through which the emancipatory goal of critical theory, in a specific historical, political and social context is practised" (L. T. Smith, 2000, p. 229; see also Bishop, Chapter 5, this volume). However, critical theory fits well with the Māori worldview, which asserts that Māori are connected to the universe and their place in it through the principle of *whakapapa.* This principle tells Māori that they are the seeds or direct descendants of the heavens. Through this principle, Māori trace their heritage to the very beginning of time (L. T. Smith, 2000, pp. 234–235).

Whakapapa turns the universe into a moral space where all things great and small are interconnected, including science and research. Smith (2000, p. 239) argues that this and related beliefs lead the Māori to ask eight questions about any research project, including those projects guided by critical theory:

1. What research do we want done?
2. Whom is it for?
3. What difference will it make?
4. Who will carry it out?
5. How do we want the research done?
6. How will we know it is worthwhile?
7. Who will own the research?
8. Who will benefit?

These questions are addressed to Māori and non-Māori alike. For research to be acceptable, each question must be answered in the affirmative; that is, Māori must conduct, own, and benefit from any research that is done on or for them.

These eight questions serve to interpret critical theory through a moral lens, through key Māori principles, including *whakapapa.* They shape the moral space that aligns Kaupapa Māori research with critical theory. Thus both formations are situated within the antipositivist debate. Both rest on antifoundational epistemologies. Each privileges performative issues of gender, race, class, equity, and social justice. Each develops its own understandings of community, critique, resistance, struggle, and emancipation (L. T. Smith, 2000, p. 228). Each understands that the outcome of a struggle can never be predicted in advance, that struggle is always local and contingent. It is never final (L. T. Smith, 2000, p. 229).

As Linda Smith (2000) observes, by localizing discourses of resistance, and by connecting these discourses to performance ethnography and critical pedagogy, Kaupapa Māori research enacts what critical theory "actually offers to oppressed, marginalized and silenced groups . . . [that is,] through emancipation groups such as the Māori would take greater control of their own lives and humanity" (p. 229). This requires that indigenous groups "take hold of the project of emancipation and attempt to make it a reality on their own terms" (p. 229). This means that inquiry is always political and moral, grounded in principles centered on autonomy, home, family, and kinship, on a collective community vision that requires that research not be a "purchased product . . . owned by the state" (p. 231).

Localized critical indigenous theory encourages indigenists to confront key challenges connected to the meanings of science, community, and democracy. Graham Smith (2000, pp. 212–215) and Linda Smith (2000) outlines these challenges, asking that indigenists do the following:

1. Be proactive; they should name the world for themselves. (Further, "being Māori is an essential criterion for carrying out Kaupapa Māori research"; L. T. Smith, 2000, pp. 229–230.)
2. Craft their own version of science, including how science and scientific understandings will be used in their world.

3. Develop a participatory model of democracy that goes beyond the "Westminister 'one person, one vote, majority rule'" (G. Smith, 2000, p. 212).
4. Use theory proactively, as an agent of change, but act in ways that are accountable to the indigenous community and not just the academy.
5. Resist new forms of colonization, such as the North American Free Trade Agreement, while contesting neocolonial efforts to commodify indigenous knowledge.

By proactively framing participatory views of science, democracy, and community, indigenous peoples take control of their own fates. They refuse to be sidetracked into always responding to nonindigenous others' attempts to define their life situations (G. Smith, 2000, p. 210).

Pedagogies of Hope and Liberation

Linda Smith (1999, pp. 142–162) outlines some 25 different indigenous projects that have been developed in response to the continuing pressures of colonialism and colonization, including projects that create, name, restore, democratize, reclaim, protect, remember, and celebrate lost histories and cultural practices.[8] These indigenous projects embody a pedagogy of hope and freedom. They turn the pedagogies of oppression and colonization into pedagogies of liberation. They are not purely utopian, for they map concrete performances that can lead to positive social transformations. They embody ways of resisting the process of colonization.

Smith's moral agenda privileges four interpretive research processes. The first is *decolonization,* which reclaims indigenous cultural practices and reworks these practices at the political, social, spiritual, and psychological levels. *Healing,* the second process, also involves restorative physical, spiritual, psychological, and social practices. The third process, *transformation,* focuses on changes that move back and forth from the psychological level to the social, political, economic, and collective levels. *Mobilization,* at the local, national, regional, and global levels, is the fourth basic process. It speaks to collective efforts to change Māori society.

These four interdependent processes encompass issues of cultural survival and collective self-determination. In every instance they work to decolonize Western methods and forms of inquiry and to empower indigenous peoples. These are the states of "being through which indigenous communities are moving" (Smith, 1999, p. 116). These states involve spiritual and social practices. They are pedagogies of healing and hope, pedagogies of recovery, material practices that benefit indigenous peoples both materially and spiritually.

Critical Personal Narrative as Counternarrative

The move to performance has been accompanied by a shift in the meanings of ethnography and ethnographic writing. As Richardson (2000) observes, the narrative genres connected to ethnographic writing have "been blurred, enlarged, altered to include poetry [and] drama" (p. 929). She uses the term *creative analytic practice* (CAP) to describe these many different reflexive performance narrative forms, which include not only performance autoethnography but also short stories, conversations, fiction, personal narratives, creative nonfiction, photographic essays, personal essays, personal narratives of the self, writing-stories, self-stories, fragmented and layered texts, critical autobiographies, memoirs, personal histories, cultural criticism writings, co-constructed performance narratives, and performance writings that blur the edges between text, representation, and criticism.

Critical personal narratives are counternarratives, testimonies, autoethnographies, performance texts, stories, and accounts that disrupt and disturb discourse by exposing the complexities and contradictions that exist under official history (Mutua & Swadener, 2004). The critical personal narrative is a central genre of contemporary decolonizing writing. As a creative analytic practice, it is used to criticize "prevailing structures and relationships of power and inequity in a relational context" (Mutua & Swadener, 2004, p. 16).

Counternarratives such as those presented in *Guantánamo: "Honor Bound to Defend Freedom,"* "Indians in the Park," and "Remembering to Forget" explore the "intersections of gender and voice, border crossing, dual consciousness, multiple identities, and selfhood in a . . . post-colonial and postmodern world" (Mutua & Swadener, 2004, p. 16). The *testimonio* is another form of counternarrative. One of the purposes of the *testimonio* is to raise political consciousness by bearing witness to social injustices experienced at the group level (Mutua & Swadener, 2004, p. 18). Linda Smith (1999) begins her discussion of the *testimonio* with these lines from Menchú (1984): "My name is Rigoberta Menchú, I am twenty-three years old, and this is my testimony" (p. 1). The *testimonio* presents oral evidence to an audience, often in the form of a monologue. As Smith describes it, the indigenous *testimonio* is "a way of talking about an extremely painful event or series of events." The *testimonio* can be constructed as "a monologue and as a public performance" (p. 144).

Critics have contended that Menchú made up her story; they have concluded that it is not the truth because it cannot be verified through scientific methodology (Cook-Lynn, 2001, p. 203; see also Beverley, 2000). But, as Cook-Lynn (2001, p. 34) observes, respectfully, *testimonio* should be read as remembering and honoring the past, not as factual truthfulness. Further, Cook-Lynn notes, Menchú was appealing to nonindigenous audiences to respect the treaties of the past so that indigenous and nonindigenous peoples might build new and harmonious relationships based on mutual respect and cooperation. Menchú's critics have ignored the ethical tenets and utopian impulses behind her story (pp. 34–35).

The struggle of colonized indigenous peoples to tell their own stories is at stake in criticisms of the *testimonio.* Those who reject these stories because they do not exhibit so-called factual truthfulness are denying indigenous voices their rightful place in this political discourse (Cook-Lynn, 2001, p. 203).

The contemporary neocolonial world stages existential crises grounded in issues of race and gender. Following Turner (1986, p. 34), the performance ethnographer enters these existential spaces, writing and performing personal narratives that make racial prejudice and oppression visible. Focusing on racial epiphanies, the writer imposes a utopian narrative on the text, imagining how situations of racial conflict and strife could be different. The utopian counternarrative offers hope, showing others how to engage in actions that decolonize, heal, and transform. In this way, critical personal narratives extend Linda Smith's project.

Poet and social activist Mary Weems (2002, p. xx) reads the sign below as she crosses the state line between Indiana and Illinois:

> **"The People of Illinois Welcome You"**
>
> comes right after the LYNCH ROAD sign
>
> and the LYNCH ROAD sign comes right after
>
> I see a thin road strung with the bodies
>
> of black men like burned out lights
>
> their backs twisting in the wind,
>
> the road littered with try out ropes,
>
> gleaned chicken parts, and cloth napkins
>
> soiled wiping the lips of the audience.
>
> I know roads don't hang,
>
> but the welcome sandwiched between
>
> the word like bread
>
> cuts off my air
>
> and I pull to the side of the road
>
> loosen my collar
>
> and search for bones.

Narratives such as Weems's embrace the critical democratic storytelling imagination. They are hopeful of peaceful, nonviolent change, understanding that hope, like freedom, is "an ontological need" (Freire, 1992/1999, p. 8). Hopeful stories are grounded in struggles and interventions that enact the sacred values of love, care, community, trust, and well-being (Freire, 1992/1999, p. 9). Hopeful stories confront and interrogate cynicism, the belief that change is not possible.

The critical democratic storytelling imagination is pedagogical. As a form of instruction, it helps persons think critically, historically, and sociologically. It exposes the pedagogies of oppression that produce injustice (see Freire, 2001, p. 54). It contributes to reflective ethical self-consciousness. It gives people a language and a set of pedagogical practices that turn oppression into freedom, despair into hope, hatred into love, doubt into trust. This ethical self-consciousness shapes a critical racial self-awareness that contributes to utopian dreams of racial equality and racial justice.

Performance, Pedagogy, and Politics

Clearly, the current historical moment requires morally informed performance- and arts-based disciplines that will help indigenous and non-indigenous peoples recover meaning in the face of senseless, brutal violence, violence that produces voiceless screams of terror and insanity. Globally, cynicism and despair rein. Never have we had a greater need for a militant utopianism to help us imagine a world free of conflict, oppression, terror, and death. We need oppositional performance disciplines that will show us how to create radical utopian spaces within our public institutions.

"Performance-sensitive ways of knowing" (Conquergood, 1998, p. 26) contribute to an epistemological and political pluralism that challenges existing ways of knowing and representing the world. Such formations are more inclusionary and better suited than other ways for thinking about postcolonial or "subaltern" cultural practices (Conquergood, 1998, p. 26). Performance approaches to knowing insist on immediacy and involvement. They consist of partial, plural, incomplete, and contingent understandings, not analytic distance or detachment, the hallmarks of positivist paradigms (Conquergood, 1998, p. 26; Pelias, 1999, pp. ix, xi).

The interpretive methods, democratic politics, and feminist communitarian ethics of performance (auto)ethnography offer progressives a series of tools for countering reactionary political discourse. At stake is an "insurgent cultural politics" (Giroux, 2000a, p. 127; see also Giroux, 2000b) that challenges neofascist state apparatuses.[9] This cultural politics encourages a critical race consciousness that flourishes within the free and open spaces of a "vibrant democratic public culture and society" (Giroux, 2000a, p. 127).

Within the spaces of this new performative cultural politics, a radical democratic imagination redefines the concept of civic participation and public citizenship.[10] Struggle, resistance, and dialogue are key features of its pedagogy. The rights of democratic citizenship are extended to all segments of public and private life, from the political to the economic, from the cultural to the personal. This pedagogy seeks to regulate market and economic relations in the name of social justice and environmental causes. A genuine democracy requires hope, dissent, and criticism.

These ideals embrace a democratic-socialist-feminist agenda. This agenda queers straight heterosexual democracy (Butler, 1997). It asserts capitalism's fundamental incompatibility with democracy while thinking its way into a model of critical citizenship that attempts to unthink whiteness and the cultural logics of white supremacy (McLaren, 1997a, 1997b, 1998a, 1998b, 1999, 2001; Roediger, 2002; West, 1993). It seeks a revolutionary multiculturalism that is grounded in relentless resistance to the structures of neoliberalism. It critiques the ways in which the media are used to manufacture consent (Chomsky, 1996). It sets as its goal transformations of global capital, so that individuals may begin to "truly live as liberated subjects of history" (McLaren, 1997b, p. 290).

A Moral Crisis

Indigenous discourse thickens the argument, for the central tensions in the world today go beyond the crises in capitalism and neoliberalism's version of democracy. The central crisis, as defined by Native Canadian, Native Hawaiian, Māori, and American Indian pedagogy, is spiritual, "rooted in the increasingly virulent relationship between human beings and the rest of nature" (Grande, 2000, p. 354). Linda Smith (1999), discusses the concept of spirituality within Māori discourse, giving added meaning to the crisis at hand:

> The essence of a person has a genealogy which could be traced back to an earth parent.... A human person does not stand alone, but shares with other animate ... beings relationships based on a shared "essence" of life ... [including] the significance of place, of land, of landscape, of other things in the universe.... Concepts of spirituality which Christianity attempted to destroy, and then to appropriate, and then to claim, are critical sites of resistance for indigenous peoples. The value, attitudes, concepts and language embedded in beliefs about spirituality represent ... the clearest contrast and mark of difference between indigenous peoples and the West. It is one of the few parts of ourselves which the West cannot decipher, cannot understand and cannot control ... yet. (p. 74)

A respectful performance pedagogy honors these views of spirituality. It works to construct a vision of the person and the environment that is compatible with these principles. This pedagogy demands a politics of hope, of loving, of caring nonviolence grounded in inclusive moral and spiritual terms.

Performance (Auto)Ethnography as a Pedagogy of Freedom

Within this framework, to extend Freire (1998) and elaborate Glass (2001, p. 17), performance autoethnography contributes to a conception of education and democracy as pedagogies of freedom. Dialogic performances enacting a performance-centered ethic provide materials for critical reflection on radical democratic educational practices. In so doing, performance ethnography enacts a theory of selfhood and being. This is an ethical, relational, and moral theory. The purpose of "the particular type of relationality we call research ought to be enhancing ... moral agency" (Christians, 2002, p. 409; see also Lincoln, 1995, p. 287), moral discernment, critical consciousness, and a radical politics of resistance.

Indeed, performance ethnography enters the service of freedom by showing how, in concrete situations, persons produce history and culture, "even as history and culture produce them" (Glass, 2001, p. 17). Performance texts provide the grounds for liberation practice by opening up concrete situations that are being transformed through acts of resistance. In this way, performance ethnography advances the causes of liberation.

Critical Performance Pedagogy

A commitment to critical performance pedagogy and critical race theory gives the human disciplines a valuable lever for militant utopian cultural criticism. In his book *Impure Acts,* Henry Giroux (2000a) calls for a practical, performative view of pedagogy, politics, and cultural studies. He seeks an interdisciplinary project that would enable theorists and educators to form a progressive alliance "connected to a broader notion of cultural politics designed to further racial, economic, and political democracy" (p. 128).

Such a project engages a militant utopianism, a provisional Marxism without guarantees, a cultural studies that is anticipatory, interventionist, and provisional. It does not back away from the contemporary world in its multiple global versions, including the West, the Third World, the moral, political, and geographic spaces occupied by First Nations and Fourth World persons, persons in marginal or liminal positions (Ladson-Billings, 2000, p. 263). Rather, it strategically engages this world in those liminal spaces where lives are bent and changed by the repressive structures of the new conservatism. This project pays particular attention to the dramatic increases around the world in domestic violence, rape, child abuse, hate crimes, and violence directed toward persons of color (Comaroff & Comaroff, 2001, pp. 1–2).

Critical Race Theory and Participatory, Performance Action Inquiry

Extending critical legal theory, critical race theory theorizes life in these liminal spaces, offering "pragmatic strategies for material and social transformation" (Ladson-Billings, 2000, p. 264). Critical race theory assumes that racism and white supremacy are the norms in U.S. society. Critical race scholars use performative, storytelling autoethnographic methods to uncover the ways in which racism operates in daily life. Critical race theory challenges those neoliberals who argue that civil rights have been attained for persons of color. It also criticizes those who argue that the civil rights crusade is a long, slow struggle (Ladson-Billings, 2000, p. 264). Critical race theorists argue that the problem of racism requires radical social change and that neoliberalism and liberalism lack the mechanisms and imaginations to achieve such change (Ladson-Billings, 2000, p. 264). Critical race theorists contend that whites have been the main beneficiaries of civil rights legislation.

Strategically, critical race theory examines the ways in which race is performed, including the cultural logics and performative acts that inscribe and create whiteness and nonwhiteness (McLaren, 1997b, p. 278; Roediger, 2002, p. 17). In an age of globalization and diasporic, postnational identities, the color line should no longer be an issue, but, sadly, it is (McLaren, 1997b, p. 278).

Drawing on the complex traditions embedded in participatory action research (Fine et al., 2003; Kemmis & McTaggart, 2000), critical performance pedagogy implements a commitment to participation and performance *with,* not *for,* community members. Amplifying the work of Fine et al. (2003, pp. 176–177), this project builds on local knowledge and experience developed at the bottom of social hierarchies. Following Linda Smith's (1999) lead, participatory, performance work honors and respects local knowledge, customs, and practices and incorporates those values and beliefs into participatory, performance action inquiry (Fine et al., 2003, p. 176).

Work in this participatory, activist performance tradition gives back to the community, "creating a legacy of inquiry, a process of change, and material resources to enable transformations in social practices" (Fine et al., 2003, p. 177). Through performance and participation, scholars develop a "participatory mode of consciousness" (Bishop, 1998, p. 208) that folds them into the moral accountability structures of the group.

◼ Cultural Politics and an Indigenous Research Ethic

Nonindigenous scholars have much to learn from indigenous scholars about how radical democratic practices can be made to work. As I have indicated above, scholars such as Graham Smith, Linda Smith, and Russell Bishop are committed to a set of moral and pedagogical imperatives and, as Smith (1999) notes, "to acts of reclaiming, reformulating, and reconstituting indigenous cultures and languages . . . to the struggle to become self-determining" (p. 142). These acts lead to a research program that is devoted to the pursuit of social justice. In turn, a specific approach to inquiry is required. In his discussion of a Māori approach to creating knowledge, Bishop (1998) observes that researchers in Kaupapa Māori contexts are

> repositioned in such a way as to no longer need to seek to *give voice to others,* to *empower* others, to *emancipate* others, to refer to others as *subjugated* voices, but rather to listen and participate . . . in a process that facilitates the development in people of a sense of themselves as agentic and of having an authoritative voice. . . . An indigenous Kaupapa Māori approach to research . . . challenges colonial and neo-colonial discourses that inscribe "otherness." (pp. 207–208)

This participatory mode of knowing privileges sharing, subjectivity, personal knowledge, and the specialized knowledges of oppressed groups. It uses concrete experience as a criterion against which to measure meaning and truth. It encourages a participatory mode of consciousness (Bishop, 1998, p. 205), asking that the researcher give the group a gift as a way of honoring the group's sacred spaces. If the group picks up the gift, the group members and the researcher can create a shared reciprocal relationship (Bishop, 1998, p. 207). This relationship is built on understandings about Māori beliefs and cultural practices.

In turn, the research is evaluated against Māori-based criteria. As in Freire's revolutionary pedagogy, West's prophetic pragmatism, and

Collins's Afrocentric feminist moral ethic, dialogue is valued as a method for assessing knowledge claims in Māori culture. The Māori moral position also privileges storytelling, listening, voice, and personal performance narratives (Collins, 1991, pp. 208–212). This moral pedagogy rests on an ethic of care, love, and personal accountability that honors individual uniqueness and emotionality in dialogue (Collins, 1991, pp. 215–217). This is a performative, pedagogical ethic, grounded in the ritual, sacred spaces of family, community, and everyday moral life (Bishop, 1998, p. 203). It is not imposed by some external bureaucratic agency.

This view of knowing parallels the commitment within certain forms of red pedagogy to the performative as a way of being, a way of knowing, and a way of expressing moral ties to the community (Grande, 2000, p. 356; Graveline, 2000, p. 361). Fyre Jean Graveline (2000, p. 263), a Metis woman, speaks:

> As Metis woman, scholar, activist, teacher, healer
>
> I enact First Voice as pedagogy and methodology
>
> Observing my own lived experience as an Educator
>
> Sharing meanings with Others . . .
>
> My Voice is Heard
>
> in concert with Students and Community Participants . . .
>
> I asked: What pedagogical practices
>
> Enacted through my Model-In-Use
>
> contribute to what kinds of transformational learning?
>
> For whom?

Moral Codes and the Performative as a Site of Resistance

Because it expresses and embodies moral ties to the community, the performative view of meaning serves to legitimate indigenous worldviews. Meaning and resistance are embodied in the act of performance itself. The performative is political, the site of resistance. At this critical level, the performative provides the context for resistance to neoliberal and neoconservative attacks on the legitimacy of the worldview in question. The performative is where the soul of the culture resides. The performative haunts the liminal spaces of the culture. In their sacred and secular performances, the members of the culture honor one another and the culture itself.

In attacking the performative, critics attack the culture.[11] Smith (1999) states the issue clearly: "The struggle for the validity of indigenous knowledges may no longer be over the *recognition* that indigenous people have ways of knowing the world which are unique, but over proving the authenticity of, and control over, our own forms of knowledge" (p. 104).

Scholars need a new set of moral and ethical research protocols. Fitted to the indigenous (and nonindigenous) perspective, these are moral matters. They are shaped by the feminist, communitarian principles of sharing, reciprocity, relationality, community, and neighborliness (Lincoln, 1995, p. 287). They embody a dialogic ethic of love and faith grounded in compassion (Bracci & Christians, 2002, p. 13; West, 1993). Accordingly, the purpose of research is not the production of new knowledge per se. Rather, the purposes are pedagogical, political, moral, and ethical, involving the enhancement of moral agency, the production of moral discernment, a commitment to praxis, justice, an ethic of resistance, and a performative pedagogy that resists oppression (Christians, 2002, p. 409).

A code embodying these principles interrupts the practice of positivist research, resists the idea that research is something that white men do to indigenous peoples. Further, unlike the institutional review board model of Western inquiry, which is not content driven, an indigenous code is anchored in a particular culture and that culture's way of life; it connects its moral model to a set of political and ethical actions that will increase well-being in the indigenous culture. The code refuses to turn indigenous peoples into subjects who are the natural objects of white inquiry (Smith, 1999, p. 118). It rejects the Western utilitarian model of the individual as someone who has rights distinct from the rights of the larger group, "for example the right of an individual to give his or her own knowledge, or the right to give informed consent" (Smith, 1999, p. 118)—rights that are not recognized in Māori culture. As Smith (1999) observes, "Community and indigenous rights or views in this area are generally not . . . respected" (p. 118).

Research ethics for scholars working with the members of Māori and other indigenous communities "extend far beyond issues of individual consent and confidentiality" (L. T. Smith, 2000, p. 241). These ethics are not "prescribed in codes of conduct for researchers but tend to be prescribed for Māori researchers in cultural terms," advising researchers to show respect for the Māori by exhibiting a willingness to listen, to be humble, to be cautious, to avoid flaunting knowledge, and to avoid trampling over the *mana* of people (L. T. Smith, 2000, p. 242).

Turning the Tables on the Colonizers

Here at the end it is possible to imagine scenarios that turn the tables on the colonizer. It is possible to imagine, for example, research practices that really do respect the rights of human subjects, protocols for obtaining subjects' informed consent that truly inform and do not deceive, and research projects that not only do no harm but in fact benefit human communities.

Here I borrow from indigenous scholar Robert Williams (1997, pp. 62–67), who takes us back to Lewis and Clark and asks us to imagine another version, or telling, of the Lewis and Clark myth. Williams turns Jefferson back on himself, arguing that it is possible to use the Lewis and Clark narratives as an occasion for reimagining the human rights of indigenous peoples. Williams argues that indigenous peoples should take up Jefferson's theory of democracy and claim, as whites did, their natural, inalienable rights to self-recognition, self-governance, survival, autonomy, life, liberty, the pursuit of happiness, and sovereign authority over their own lands.

Similarly, the celebrations of Lewis and Clark's expedition that took place in 2003–2004 can be turned into political performances, transgressive events. In this form of historical theater, Lewis and Clark would be pushed aside, ignored. In their place, performers would enact a utopian disruptive theater, reclaiming and celebrating the inalienable rights of Native Americans to own and control their own history. These performance texts would be occasions for indigenous peoples to write their way into the journals, to offer their stories and narratives about the effects of Lewis and Clark on their ancestors and on themselves. Like the writings of William Least Heat-Moon (1999), these tellings would recover buried history, moments, representations, ancient pictographs that write across "all of us—red, white, mixed" (p. 217). This theater would advance the project of indigenous decolonization (Williams, 1997, p. 62). These performance events would represent Lewis and Clark as colonizers whose "undaunted courage" will no longer be recognized, honored, or celebrated.

▣ Conclusion

The ethical and moral models of Russell Bishop, Graham Smith, and Linda Smith call into question the more generic, utilitarian, biomedical Western model of ethical inquiry (see Christians, 2000, 2002; Bracci & Christians, 2002). They outline a radical ethical path for the future that transcends the institutional review board model, which focuses almost exclusively on the problems associated with betrayal, deception, and harm. They call for a collaborative social science research model that makes the researcher responsible not to a removed discipline (or institution) but to those studied. This model stresses personal accountability, caring, the value of individual expressiveness, the capacity for empathy, and the sharing of emotionality (Collins, 1991, p. 216). This model implements collaborative, participatory, performative inquiry. It forcefully aligns the ethics of research with a politics of the oppressed, with a politics of resistance, hope, and freedom.

This model directs scholars to take up moral projects that respect and reclaim indigenous cultural practices. Such work produces spiritual, social, and psychological healing, which in turn leads to multiple forms of transformation at the personal and social levels. These transformations shape the processes of mobilization and collective action, and the resulting actions help persons realize a radical politics of possibility. This politics enacts emancipatory discourses and critical pedagogies that honor human differences and draw inspiration from the struggles of indigenous peoples. In listening to indigenous storytellers, we learn new ways of being moral and political in the social world. Thus *research* ceases to be a dirty word.

Notes

1. This chapter extends some of the arguments I present in my book *Performance Ethnography* (Denzin, 2003, pp. 1–23, 242–262). A performative cultural studies enacts a critical, cultural pedagogy. It does so by using dialogue, performative writing, and the staging and performance of texts involving audience members. Regarding the terms *decolonization* and *the postcolonial,* which I use here, it should be noted that decolonizing research is not necessarily postcolonial research. Decolonization is a process that critically engages, at all levels, imperialism, colonialism, and postcoloniality. Decolonizing research implements indigenous epistemologies and critical interpretive practices that are shaped by indigenous research agendas (Smith, 1999, p. 20). In this chapter, I draw on the work of Shohat (1992), Hall (1996b), Dimitriadis and McCarthy (2001), and Swadener and Mutua (2004) in troubling the concept of "post-colonial"—with Hall, I ask, When was the colonial ever post? In its hyphenated form, the term *post-colonial* functions as a temporal marker, implying linearity and chronology. With Swadener and Mutua, I prefer the form *postcolonial,* which implies a constant, complex, intertwined back-and-forth relationship between past and present. In this sense there is no postcolonial, there are only endless variations on neocolonial formations (Soto, 2004, p. ix). Regarding the term *critical pedagogy:* As Kincheloe and McLaren (2000) note, cultural production functions as "a form of education, as it generates knowledge, shapes values, and constructs identity. . . . By using the term *cultural pedagogy,* we are specifically referring to the ways particular cultural agents produce particular hegemonic ways of seeing" (p. 285; see also McLaren, 1998a, p. 441). Critical pedagogy attempts to disrupt and deconstruct these cultural practices performatively in the name of a "more just, democratic, and egalitarian society" (Kincheloe & McLaren, 2000, p. 285; but see Lather, 1998).

2. See also Ashcroft, Griffiths, and Tiffin (2002), Battiste (2000a, 2000b), Balme and Christopher (2001), Beverley (2000), Bishop (1994, 1998), Churchill (1996), Cook-Lynn (1998), Cruikshank (1990), Ellsworth (1989), Gilbert (2003), Greenwood (2001), Harjo and Bird (1997), Kondo (2000), Magowan 2000), Marker (2003), Menchú (1984, 1998), Pratt (2001), G. Smith (2000), L. T. Smith (2000), and C. W.-I.-T.-R. Smith (2000).

3. This theater often uses verbatim accounts of injustices and acts of violence encountered in daily life. Mienczakowski (1995, 2001) provides a history of "verbatim theater" and discusses extensions of this approach that use oral history, participant observation, and the methods of ethnodrama (see also Chessman, 1971). One contemporary use of verbatim theater is the play *Guantánamo: "Honor Bound to Defend Freedom,"* created by Victoria Brittain, a former journalist, and Gillian Slovo, a novelist. This play addresses the plight of British citizens imprisoned at the U.S. naval base at Guantánamo Bay, Cuba, in the period since the September 11, 2001, terrorist attacks on the United States. According to Alan Riding (1999), writing for the *New York Times,* the "power of 'Guantánamo' is that it is not really a play but a re-enactment of views expressed in interviews, letters, news conferences and speeches by various players in the post-Sept. 11 Iraq war drama, from British Muslim detainees to lawyers, from Mr. Rumsfeld to Jack Straw, Britain's foreign secretary." Riding notes that Nicolas Kent, the play's director, believes that "political theater works here [in England] because the British have an innate sense of justice. 'When we do stories about injustice,' he said, 'there is a groundswell of sympathy . . . people are furious that there isn't due process.' . . . 'With Islamophobia growing around the world today,' he said, 'I wanted to show that we, too, think there is an injustice'" (p. B2).

4. At another level, indigenous participatory theater extends the project connected to Third World

popular theater—that is, political theater "used by oppressed Third World people to achieve justice and development for themselves" (Etherton, 1988, p. 991), The International Popular Theatre Alliance, organized in the 1980s, uses existing forms of cultural expression to fashion improvised dramatic productions that analyze situations of poverty and oppression. This grassroots approach uses agitprop and sloganizing theater pieces (pieces designed to foment political action) to stimulate collective awareness and collective action at the local level. This form of theater has been popular in Latin America, in Africa, in parts of Asia, in India, and among Native populations in the Americas (Etherton, 1988, p. 992).

5. The *Camera Eye* and *Newsreel* are Dos Passos's (1937) terms (and methods) for incorporating current events and newsworthy items into a text.

6. The positive-negative debate often neglects indigenous discourses, presupposes consensus where there may be none, shuts down nuanced debate, and ignores the performative features of racial identity (Smith, 1997, pp. 3–4).

7. For Du Bois, race and racism were social constructions. Performances, minstrelsy, blackface are powerful performance devices that produce and reproduce the color line. Du Bois believed that African Americans need performance spaces where they can control how race is constructed. Consequently, as Elam (2001, pp. 5–6) observes, African American theater and performance have been central sites for the interrogation of race and the color line (see also Elam & Krasner, 2001). As Elam notes, "The inherent 'constructedness' of performance and the malleability of the devices of the theater serve to reinforce the theory that blackness . . . and race . . . are hybrid, fluid concepts" (pp. 4–5). Stuart Hall (1996a, p. 473) is correct in his observation that persons of color have never been successful in escaping the politics and theaters of (racial) representation.

8. Other projects involve a focus on testimonies, new forms of storytelling, and returning to, as well as reframing and regendering, key cultural debates.

9. I define fascism as a conservative, extreme right-wing political, economic, and sociolegal state formation characterized by authoritarian forms of government, extreme nationalism, manufactured consent at key levels of public opinion, racism, a large military-industrial complex, foreign aggressiveness, anti-communism, state-supported corporate capitalism, state-sponsored violence, extreme restrictions on individual freedom, and tendencies toward an "Orwellian condition of perpetual war . . . [and] a national security state in which intelligence agencies and the military replace publicly elected officials in deciding national priorities" (Rorty, 2002, p. 13).

10. Here there are obvious political connections to Guy Debord's (1970) situationist project.

11. Smith (1999, p. 99) presents 10 performative ways to be colonized, 10 ways in which science, technology, and Western institutions place indigenous peoples—indeed, any group of human beings—their languages, cultures, and environments, at risk. These ways include the Human Genome Diversity Project as well as scientific efforts to reconstruct previously extinct indigenous peoples and projects that deny global citizenship to indigenous peoples while commodifying, patenting, and selling indigenous cultural traditions and rituals.

References

Ambrose, S. (1996). *Undaunted courage: Meriwether Lewis, Thomas Jefferson, and the opening of the American West.* New York: Simon & Schuster.

Anzaldúa, G. (1987). *Borderlands/la frontera: The new mestiza.* San Francisco: Aunt Lute.

Ashcroft, B., Griffiths, G., & Tiffin, H. (2002). *The empire writes back: Theory and practice in post-colonial literature* (2nd ed.). New York: Routledge.

Balme, C., & Carstensen, A. (2001). Home fires: Creating a Pacific theatre in the diaspora. *Theatre Research International, 26,* 35–46.

Battiste, M. (2000a). Introduction: Unfolding the lessons of colonization. In M. Battiste (Ed.), *Reclaiming indigenous voice and vision* (pp. xvi–xxx). Vancouver: University of British Columbia Press.

Battiste, M. (2000b). Maintaining aboriginal identity: Language and culture in modern society. In M. Battiste (Ed.), *Reclaiming indigenous voice and vision* (pp. 192–208). Vancouver: University of British Columbia Press.

Bean, A. (2001). Black minstrelsy and double inversion, circa 1890. In H. J. Elam, Jr., & D. Krasner (Eds.), *African American performance and theater history: A critical reader* (pp. 171–191). New York: Oxford University Press.

Benjamin, W. (1969). *Illuminations* (H. Zohn, Trans.). New York: Harcourt, Brace & World.

Benjamin, W. (1983–1984). Theoretics of knowledge: Theory of progress. *Philosophical Forum, 15* (1–2), 1–40.

Beverley, J. (2000). *Testimonio,* subalternity, and narrative authority. In N. K. Denzin & Y. S. Lincoln (Eds.), *Handbook of qualitative research* (2nd ed., pp. 555–565). Thousand Oaks, CA: Sage.

Bishop, R. (1994). Initiating empowering research. *New Zealand Journal of Educational Studies, 29,* 175–188.

Bishop, R. (1998). Freeing ourselves from neo-colonial domination in research: A Māori approach to creating knowledge. *International Journal of Qualitative Studies in Education, 11,* 199–219.

Bracci, S. L., & Christians, C. G. (2002). Editors' introduction. In S. L. Bracci & C. G. Christians (Eds.), *Moral engagement in public life: Theorists for contemporary ethics* (pp. 1–15). New York: Peter Lang.

Brayboy, B. M. (2000). The Indian and the researcher: Tales from the field. *International Journal of Qualitative Studies in Education, 13,* 415–426.

Butler, J. (1997). *Excitable speech: A politics of the performative.* New York: Routledge.

Chessman, P. (1971). Production casebook. *New Theatre Quarterly, 1,* 1–6.

Chomsky, N. (1996). *Class warfare: Interviews with David Barasamian.* Monroe, ME: Common Courage.

Christians, C. G. (2000). Ethics and politics in qualitative research. In N. K. Denzin & Y. S. Lincoln (Eds.), *Handbook of qualitative research* (2nd ed., pp. 133–155). Thousand Oaks, CA: Sage.

Christians, C. G. (2002). Introduction. In Ethical issues and qualitative research [Special issue]. *Qualitative Inquiry, 8,* 407–410.

Churchill, W. (1996). I am an indigenist: Notes on the ideology of the Fourth World. In W. Churchill, *From a native son: Selected essays in indigenism, 1985–1995* (pp. 509–546). Boston: South End.

Collins, P. H. (1991). *Black feminist thought: Knowledge, consciousness, and the politics of empowerment.* New York: Routledge, Chapman & Hall.

Collins, P. H. (1998). *Fighting words: Black women and the search for justice.* Minneapolis: University of Minnesota Press.

Comaroff, J., & Comaroff, J. L. (2001). Millennial capitalism: First thoughts on a second coming. In J. Comaroff & J. L. Comaroff (Eds.), *Millennial capitalism and the culture of neoliberalism* (pp. 1–56). Durham, NC: Duke University Press.

Conquergood, D. (1998). Beyond the text: Toward a performative cultural politics. In S. J. Dailey (Ed.), *The future of performance studies: Visions and revisions* (pp. 25–36). Washington, DC: National Communication Association.

Cook-Lynn, E. (1998). American Indian intellectualism and the new Indian story. In D. A. Mihesuah (Ed.), *Natives and academics: Researching and writing about American Indians* (pp. 111–138). Lincoln: University of Nebraska Press.

Cook-Lynn, E. (2001). *Anti-Indianism in modern America: A voice from Tatekeya's earth.* Urbana: University of Illinois Press.

Cruikshank, J. (in collaboration with Sidney, A., Smith, K., & Ned, A.). (1990). *Life lived like a story: Life stories of three Yukon Native elders.* Lincoln: University of Nebraska Press.

Debord, G. (1970). *Society of the spectacle.* Detroit: Black & Red.

Denzin, N. K. (2003). *Performance ethnography: Critical pedagogy and the politics of culture.* Thousand Oaks, CA: Sage.

Denzin, N. K. (2004a). Indians in the park. *Qualitative Research, 4*(3).

Denzin, N. K. (2004b). Remembering to forget: Lewis and Clark and Native Americans in Yellowstone. *Communication and Critical/Cultural Studies, 1,* 219–249.

Denzin, N. K. (in press). *Searching for Yellowstone.* London: Sage.

Dimitriadis, G., & McCarthy, C. (2001). *Reading and teaching the postcolonial: From Baldwin to Basquiat and beyond.* New York: Teachers College Press.

Dorst, J. D. (1999). *Looking west.* Philadelphia: University of Pennsylvania Press.

Dos Passos, J. (1937). *U.S.A.: I. The 42nd parallel; II. Nineteen nineteen; III. The big money.* New York: Modern Library.

Du Bois, W. E. B. (1926, July). Krigwa Players Little Negro Theatre: The story of a little theatre movement. *Crisis,* pp. 134–136.

Du Bois, W. E. B. (1978). The problem of the twentieth century is the problem of the color line. In W. E. B. Du Bois, *On sociology and the black community* (D. S. Green & E. Driver, Eds.) (pp. 281–289). Chicago: University of Chicago Press. (Original work published 1901)

Du Bois, W. E. B. (1989). *The souls of black folk.* New York: Bantam. (Original work published 1903)

Elam, H. J., Jr. (2001). The device of race: An introduction. In H. J. Elam, Jr., & D. Krasner (Eds.), *African American performance and theater history: A critical reader* (pp. 3–16). New York: Oxford University Press.

Elam, H. J., Jr., & Krasner, D. (Eds.). (2001). *African American performance and theater history: A critical reader.* New York: Oxford University Press.

Ellison, R. (1964). Change the joke and slip the yoke. In R. Ellison, *Shadow and act* (pp. 45–59). New York: Random House.

Ellsworth, E. (1989). Why doesn't this feel empowering? Working through the repressive myths of critical methodology. *Harvard Education Review, 59,* 297–324.

Etherton, M. (1988). Third World popular theatre. In M. Banham (Ed.), *The Cambridge guide to theatre* (pp. 991–992). Cambridge: Cambridge University Press.

Fine, M., Roberts, R., Torre, M., Upegui, D., Bowen, I., Boudin, K., et al. (2003). Participatory action research: From within and beyond prison bars. In P. M. Camic, J. E. Rhodes, & L. Yardley (Eds.), *Qualitative research in psychology: Expanding perspectives in methodology and design* (pp. 173–198). Washington, DC: American Psychological Association.

Freire, P. (1998). *Pedagogy of freedom: Ethics, democracy, and civic courage* (P. Clarke, Trans.). Boulder, CO: Rowman & Littlefield.

Freire, P. (1999). *Pedagogy of hope: Reliving* Pedagogy of the oppressed. New York: Continuum. (Original work published 1992)

Freire, P. (2001). *Pedagogy of the oppressed* (30th anniversary ed.). New York: Continuum.

Garoian, C. R. (1999). *Performing pedagogy: Toward an art of politics.* Albany: State University of New York Press.

Gilbert, H. (2003). Black and white and re(a)d all over again: Indigenous minstrelsy in contemporary Canadian and Australian theatre. *Theatre Journal, 55,* 679–698.

Giroux, H. (2000a). *Impure acts: The practical politics of cultural studies.* New York: Routledge.

Giroux, H. (2000b). *Stealing innocence: Corporate culture's war on children.* New York: Palgrave.

Glass, R. D. (2001). On Paulo Freire's philosophy of praxis and the foundations of liberation education. *Educational Researcher, 30*(2), 15–25.

Goffman, E. (1959). *The presentation of self in everyday life.* New York: Doubleday.

Grande, S. (2000). American Indian identity and intellectualism: The quest for a new red pedagogy. *International Journal of Qualitative Studies in Education, 13,* 343–360.

Graveline, F. J. (2000). Circle as methodology: Enacting an aboriginal paradigm. *International Journal of Qualitative Studies in Education, 13,* 361–370.

Greenwood, J. (2001). Within a third space. *Research in Drama Education, 6,* 193–205.

Grossman, E. (2003). *Adventuring along the Lewis and Clark trail.* San Francisco: Sierra Club.

Hall, S. (1996a). What is this "black" in black popular culture? In D. Morley & K.-H. Chen (Eds.), *Stuart Hall: Critical dialogues in cultural studies* (pp. 465–475). London: Routledge.

Hall, S. (1996b). When was "the post-colonial"? Thinking at the limit. In I. Chambers & L. Curt (Eds.), *The post-colonial question: Common skies, divided horizons* (pp. 242–260). London: Routledge.

Harjo, J., & Bird, G. (1997). Introduction. In J. Harjo & G. Bird (Eds.), *Reinventing the enemy's language: Contemporary Native women's writings of North America* (pp. 19–31). New York: W. W. Norton.

Henderson, J. (S.) Y. (2000). Postcolonial ledger drawing: Legal reform. In M. Battiste (Ed.), *Reclaiming indigenous voice and vision* (pp. 161–171). Vancouver: University of British Columbia Press.

Heshusius, L. (1994). Freeing ourselves from objectivity: Managing subjectivity or turning toward a participatory mode of consciousness. *Educational Researcher, 23*(3), 15–22.

hooks, b. (1990). *Yearning: Race, gender, and cultural politics.* Boston: South End.

Horton, S. (2003, March). Keeping their legacy alive. *Audubon Magazine,* pp. 90–93.

Kaomea, J. (2004). Dilemmas of an indigenous academic: A native Hawaiian story. In K. Mutua & B. B. Swadener (Eds.), *Decolonizing research in cross-cultural contexts: Critical personal narratives* (pp. 27–44). Albany: State University of New York Press.

Kemmis, S., & McTaggart, R. (2000). Participatory action research. In N. K. Denzin & Y. S. Lincoln (Eds.), *Handbook of qualitative research* (2nd ed., pp. 567–605). Thousand Oaks, CA: Sage.

Kincheloe, J. L., & McLaren, P. (2000). Rethinking critical theory and qualitative research. In N. K. Denzin & Y. S. Lincoln (Eds.), *Handbook of qualitative research* (2nd ed., pp. 279–313). Thousand Oaks, CA: Sage.

Kondo, D. (2000). (Re)visions of race: Contemporary race theory and the cultural politics of racial crossover in documentary theatre. *Theatre Journal, 52,* 81–107.

Ladson-Billings, G. (2000). Racialized discourses and ethnic epistemologies. In N. K. Denzin & Y. S. Lincoln (Eds.), *Handbook of qualitative research* (2nd ed., pp. 257–277). Thousand Oaks, CA: Sage.

Lather, P. (1998). Critical pedagogy and its complicities: A praxis of stuck places. *Educational Theory, 48,* 487–497.

Least Heat-Moon, W. (1999). *River horse: A voyage across America.* Boston: Houghton Mifflin.

Lhamon, W. T., Jr. (1998). *Raising Cain: Blackface performance from Jim Crow to hip hop.* Cambridge, MA: Harvard University Press.

Lincoln, Y. S. (1995). Emerging criteria for quality in qualitative and interpretive inquiry. *Qualitative Inquiry, 1,* 275–289.

Lopez, G. R. (1998). Reflections on epistemology and standpoint theories: A response to "A Māori approach to creating knowledge." *International Journal of Qualitative Studies in Education, 11,* 225–231.

Madison, D. S. (1998). Performances, personal narratives, and the politics of possibility. In S. J. Dailey (Ed.), *The future of performance studies: Visions and revisions* (pp. 276–286). Washington, DC: National Communication Association.

Madison, D. S. (1999). Performing theory/embodied writing. *Text and Performance Quarterly, 19,* 107–124.

Magowan, F. (2000). Dancing with a difference: Reconfiguring the poetic politics of Aboriginal ritual as national spectacle. *Australian Journal of Anthropology, 11,* 308–321.

Marker, M. (2003). Indigenous voice, community, and epistemic violence: The ethnographer's "interests" and what "interests" the ethnographer. *International Journal of Qualitative Studies in Education, 16,* 361–375.

McLaren, P. (1997a). The ethnographer as postmodern flaneur: Critical reflexivity and posthybridity as narrative engagement. In W. G. Tierney & Y. S. Lincoln (Eds.), *Representation and the text: Reframing the narrative voice* (pp. 143–177). Albany: State University of New York Press.

McLaren, P. (1997b). *Revolutionary multiculturalism: Pedagogies of dissent for the new millennium.* Boulder, CO: Westview.

McLaren, P. (1998a). Revolutionary pedagogy in postrevolutionary times: Rethinking the political economy of critical education. *Educational Theory, 48,* 431–462.

McLaren, P. (1998b). Whiteness is . . . : The struggle for postcolonial hybridity. In J. L. Kincheloe, S. Steinberg, N. Rodriguez, & R. Chennault (Eds.), *White reign: Deploying whiteness in America* (pp. 63–75). New York: St. Martin's.

McLaren, P. (1999). *Schooling as a ritual performance: Toward a political economy of educational symbols and gestures* (3rd ed.). Lanham, MD: Rowman & Littlefield.

McLaren, P. (2001). Che Guevara, Paulo Freire, and the politics of hope: Reclaiming critical pedagogy. *Cultural Studies↔Critical Methodologies, 1,* 108–131.

Mead, G. H. (1938). *The philosophy of the act.* Chicago: University of Chicago Press.

Menchú, R. (1984). *I, Rigoberta Menchú: An Indian woman in Guatemala* (E. Burgos-Debray, Ed.; A. Wright, Trans.). London: Verso.

Menchú, R. (1998). *Crossing borders* (A. Wright, Trans.). London: Verso.

Meyer, M. A. (2003). *Ho'oulu: Our time of becoming; Hawaiian epistemology and early writings.* Honolulu: 'Ai Pohaku Press Native Books.

Mienczakowski, J. (1995). The theater of ethnography: The reconstruction of ethnography into theater with emancipatory potential. *Qualitative Inquiry, 1,* 360–375.

Mienczakowski, J. (2001). Ethnodrama: Performed research—limitations and potential. In P. Atkinson, A. Coffey, S. Delamont, J. Lofland, & L. H. Lofland (Eds.), *Handbook of ethnography* (pp. 468–476). London: Sage.

Mills, C. W. (1959). *The sociological imagination.* New York: Oxford University Press.

Moraga, C. (1993). *The last generation: Prose and poetry.* Boston: South End.

Moses, D. D. (1992). *Almighty Voice and his wife.* Stratford, ON: Williams-Wallace.

Mutua, K., & Swadener, B. B. (2004). Introduction. In K. Mutua & B. B. Swadener (Eds.), *Decolonizing research in cross-cultural contexts: Critical personal narratives* (pp. 1–23). Albany: State University of New York Press.

Pelias, R. J. (1999). *Writing performance: Poeticizing the researcher's body.* Carbondale: Southern Illinois University Press.

Pratt, M. L. (2001). *I, Rigoberta Menchú* and the "culture wars." In A. Arias (Ed.), *The Rigoberta*

Menchú controversy (pp. 29–48). Minneapolis: University of Minnesota Press.

Rains, F. V., Archibald, J. A., & Deyhle, D. (2000). Through our eyes and in our own words: The voices of indigenous scholars. *International Journal of Qualitative Studies in Education, 13,* 337–342.

Reddin, P. (1999). *Wild West shows.* Urbana: University of Illinois Press.

Richardson, L. (2000). Writing: A method of inquiry. In N. K. Denzin & Y. S. Lincoln (Eds.), *Handbook of qualitative research* (2nd ed., pp. 923–948). Thousand Oaks, CA: Sage.

Riding, A. (2004, June 15). On a London stage, a hearing for Guantánamo detainees. *New York Times,* p. B2.

Roediger, D. (2002). *Colored white: Transcending the racial past.* Berkeley: University of California Press.

Ronda, J. P. (1984). *Lewis and Clark among the Indians.* Lincoln: University of Nebraska Press.

Rorty, R. (2002, October 21). Fighting terrorism with democracy. *The Nation, 275,* 11–14.

Sandoval, C. (2000). *Methodology of the oppressed.* Minneapolis: University of Minnesota Press.

Schullery, P. (1997). *Searching for Yellowstone: Ecology and wonder in the last wilderness.* Boston: Houghton Mifflin.

Semali, L. M., & Kincheloe, J. L. (1999). Introduction: What is indigenous knowledge and why should we study it? In L. M. Semali & J. L. Kincheloe (Eds.), *What is indigenous knowledge? Voices from the academy* (pp. 3–57). New York: Falmer.

Shohat, E. (1992). Notes on the post colonial. *Social Forces, 31/32,* 99–111.

Slaughter, T. P. (2003). *Exploring Lewis and Clark: Reflections on men and wilderness.* New York: Knopf.

Smith, A. D. (2003). *House arrest and Piano.* New York: Anchor.

Smith, C. W.-I.-T.-R. (2000). Straying beyond the boundaries of belief: Māori epistemologies inside the curriculum. *Educational Philosophy and Theory, 32,* 43–51.

Smith, G. (2000). Protecting and respecting indigenous knowledge. In M. Battiste (Ed.), *Reclaiming indigenous voice and vision* (pp. 209–224). Vancouver: University of British Columbia Press.

Smith, L. T. (1999). *Decolonizing methodologies: Research and indigenous peoples.* Dunedin, New Zealand: University of Otago Press.

Smith, L. T. (2000). Kaupapa Māori research. In M. Battiste (Ed.), *Reclaiming indigenous voice and vision* (pp. 225–247). Vancouver: University of British Columbia Press.

Smith, V. (1997). Introduction. In V. Smith (Ed.), *Representing blackness: Issues in film and video* (pp. 1–12). New Brunswick, NJ: Rutgers University Press.

Soto, L. D. (2004). Foreword: Decolonizing research in cross-cultural contexts: Issues of voice and power. In K. Mutua & B. B. Swadener (Eds.), *Decolonizing research in cross-cultural contexts: Critical personal narratives* (pp. ix–xi). Albany: State University of New York Press.

Spindel, C. (2000). *Dancing at halftime: Sports and the controversy over American Indian mascots.* New York: New York University Press.

Stirling, E. W. (1965). The Indian reservation system of the Northern Plains. In M. S. Kennedy (Ed.), *The red man's West* (pp. 300–312). New York: Hastings House.

Swadener, B. B., & Mutua, K. (2004). Afterword. In K. Mutua & B. B. Swadener (Eds.), *Decolonizing research in cross-cultural contexts: Critical personal narratives* (pp. 255–260). Albany: State University of New York Press.

Turner, V. M. (1986). Dewey, Dilthey, and drama: An essay in the anthropology of experience. In V. M. Turner & E. M. Bruner (Eds.), *The anthropology of experience* (pp. 33–44). Urbana: University of Illinois Press.

Ulmer, G. L. (1989). *Teletheory: Grammatology in the age of video.* New York: Routledge.

Weems, M. (2002). *I speak from the wound that is my mouth.* New York: Peter Lang.

West, C. (1993). *Keeping the faith: Philosophy and race in America.* New York: Routledge.

Williams, R. A., Jr. (1997). Thomas Jefferson: Indigenous American storyteller. In J. P. Ronda (Ed.), *Thomas Jefferson and the changing West: From conquest to conservation* (pp. 43–74). Albuquerque: University of New Mexico Press.

Williams, T. T. (1984). *Pieces of white shell: A journey to Navajoland.* Albuquerque: University of New Mexico Press.

38

WRITING

A Method of Inquiry

Laurel Richardson and Elizabeth Adams St. Pierre

The world of ethnography has expanded in ways that were unimaginable a decade ago, when this chapter was first written for the first edition of this *Handbook*. Qualitative researchers in a variety of disciplines—medicine, law, education, the social sciences, and the humanities—have since found *writing as a method of inquiry* to be a viable way in which to learn about themselves and their research topic. The literature is vast and varied.

In light of these developments, this chapter's revision is organized into three parts. In Part 1, Laurel Richardson discusses (a) the contexts of social scientific writing both historically and contemporaneously, (b) the creative analytical practice ethnography genre, and (c) the direction her work has taken during the past decade, including "writing stories" and collaborations across the humanities/social sciences divide. In Part 2, Elizabeth St. Pierre provides an analysis of how writing as a method of inquiry coheres with the development of ethical selves engaged in social action and social reform. In Part 3, Richardson provides some writing practices/exercises for the qualitative writer.

Just as the chapter reflects our own processes and preferences, we hope that your writing will do the same. The more different voices are honored within our qualitative community, the stronger—and more interesting—that community will be.

Part 1: Qualitative Writing

Laurel Richardson

A decade ago, in the first edition of this *Handbook*, I confessed that for years I had yawned my way through numerous supposedly exemplary qualitative studies. Countless numbers of texts had I abandoned half read, half scanned. I would order a new book with great anticipation—the topic was one I was interested in, the author was someone I wanted to read—only to find the text boring. In "coming out" to colleagues and students about my secret displeasure with much of qualitative writing, I found a community of like-minded discontents. Undergraduates, graduates, and colleagues alike said that they found much of qualitative writing to be—yes—boring.

We had a serious problem; research topics were riveting and research valuable, but qualitative books were underread. Unlike quantitative work that can carry its meaning in its tables and summaries, qualitative work carries its meaning in its entire text. Just as a piece of literature is not equivalent to its "plot summary," qualitative research is not contained in its abstract. Qualitative research has to be read, not scanned; its meaning is in the reading. It seemed foolish at best, and narcissistic and wholly self-absorbed at worst, to spend months or years doing research that ended up not being read and not making a difference to anything but the author's career. Was there some way in which to create texts that were vital and made a difference? I latched onto the idea of *writing as a method of inquiry.*

I had been taught, as perhaps you were as well, not to write until I knew what I wanted to say, that is, until my points were organized and outlined. But I did not like writing that way. I felt constrained and bored. When I thought about those writing instructions, I realized that they cohered with mechanistic scientism and quantitative research. I recognized that those writing instructions were themselves a sociohistorical invention of our 19th-century foreparents. Foisting those instructions on qualitative researchers created serious problems; they undercut writing as a dynamic creative process, they undermined the confidence of beginning qualitative researchers because their experience of research was inconsistent with the writing model, and they contributed to the flotilla of qualitative writing that was simply not interesting to read because writers wrote in the homogenized voice of "science."

Qualitative researchers commonly speak of the importance of the individual researcher's skills and aptitudes. The researcher—rather than the survey, the questionnaire, or the census tape—is the "instrument." The more honed the researcher, the better the possibility of excellent research. Students are taught to be open—to observe, listen, question, and participate. But in the past, they were not being taught to nurture their writing voices. During the past decade, however, rather than suppressing their voices, qualitative writers have been honing their writing skills. Learning to write in new ways does not take away one's traditional writing skills any more than learning a second language reduces one fluidity in one's first language. Rather, all kinds of qualitative writing have flourished.

Writing in Contexts

Language is a constitutive force, creating a particular view of reality and of the Self. Producing "things" always involves value—what to produce, what to name the productions, and what the relationship between the producers and the named things will be. Writing things is no exception. No textual staging is ever innocent (including this one). Styles of writing are neither fixed nor neutral but rather reflect the historically shifting domination of particular schools or paradigms. Social scientific writing, like all other forms of writing, is a sociohistorical construction and, therefore, is mutable.

Since the 17th century, the world of writing has been divided into two separate kinds: literary and scientific. Literature, from the 17th century onward, was associated with fiction, rhetoric, and subjectivity, whereas science was associated with fact, "plain language," and objectivity (Clifford & Marcus, 1986, p. 5). During the 18th century, the Marquis de Condorcet introduced the term "social science." Condorcet (as cited in Levine, 1985) contended that "knowledge of the truth" would be "easy," and that error would be "almost impossible," if one adopted precise language about moral and social issues (p. 6). By the 19th century, literature and science stood as two separate domains. Literature was aligned with "art" and "culture"; it contained the values of "taste, aesthetics, ethics, humanity, and morality" (Clifford & Marcus, 1986, p. 6) as well as the rights to metaphorical and ambiguous language. Given to science was the belief that its words were objective, precise, unambiguous, noncontextual, and nonmetaphorical.

As the 20th century unfolded, the relationships between social scientific writing and literary writing grew in complexity. The presumed solid demarcations between "fact" and "fiction" and between "true" and "imagined" were blurred. The blurring was most hotly debated around writing for the public, that is, journalism. Dubbed by

Thomas Wolfe as the "new journalism," writers consciously blurred the boundaries between fact and fiction and consciously made themselves the centers of their stories (for an excellent extended discussion of the new journalism, see Denzin, 1997, chap. 5). By the 1970s, "crossovers" between writing forms spawned the naming of oxymoronic genres—"creative nonfiction," "faction," "ethnographic fiction," the "nonfiction novel," and "true fiction." By 1980, the novelist E. L. Doctorow (as cited in Fishkin, 1985) would assert, "There is no longer any such things as fiction or nonfiction, there is only narrative" (p. 7).

Despite the actual blurring of genre, and despite our contemporary understanding that all writing is narrative writing, I would contend that there is still one major difference that separates fiction writing from science writing. The difference is not whether the text really is fiction or nonfiction; rather, the difference is the claim that the author makes for the text. Declaring that one's work is fiction is a different rhetorical move than is declaring that one's work is social science. The two genres bring in different audiences and have different impacts on publics and politics—and on how one's "truth claims" are to be evaluated. These differences should not be overlooked or minimized.

We are fortunate, now, to be working in a postmodernist climate, a time when a multitude of approaches to knowing and telling exist side by side. The core of postmodernism is the doubt that any method or theory, any discourse or genre, or any tradition or novelty has a universal and general claim as the "right" or privileged form of authoritative knowledge. Postmodernism suspects all truth claims of masking and serving particular interests in local, cultural, and political struggles. But conventional methods of knowing and telling are not automatically rejected as false or archaic. Rather, those standard methods are opened to inquiry, new methods are introduced, and then they also are subject to critique.

The postmodernist context of doubt, then, distrusts all methods equally. No method has a privileged status. But a postmodernist position does allow us to know "something" without claiming to know everything. Having a partial, local, and historical knowledge is still knowing. In some ways, "knowing" is easier, however, because postmodernism recognizes the situational limitations of the knower. Qualitative writers are off the hook, so to speak. They do not have to try to play God, writing as disembodied omniscient narrators claiming universal and atemporal general knowledge. They can eschew the questionable metanarrative of scientific objectivity and still have plenty to say as situated speakers, subjectivities engaged in knowing/telling about the world as they perceive it.

A particular kind of postmodernist thinking that I have found to be especially helpful is poststructuralism (for application of the perspective in a research setting, see Davies, 1994). Poststructuralism links language, subjectivity, social organization, and power. The centerpiece is language. Language does not "reflect" social reality but rather produces meaning and creates social reality. Different languages and different discourses within a given language divide up the world and give it meaning in ways that are not reducible to one another. Language is how social organization and power are defined and contested and the place where one's sense of self—one's subjectivity—is constructed. Understanding language as competing discourses—competing ways of giving meaning and of organizing the world—makes language a site of exploration and struggle.

Language is not the result of one's individuality; rather, language constructs one's subjectivity in ways that are historically and locally specific. What something means to individuals is dependent on the discourses available to them. For example, being hit by one's spouse is experienced differently depending on whether it is thought of as being within the discourse of "normal marriage," "husband's rights," or "wife battering." If a woman sees male violence as normal or a husband's right, she is unlikely to see it as wife battering, which is an illegitimate use of power that should not be tolerated. Similarly, when a man is exposed to the discourse of "childhood sexual abuse," he may recategorize and remember his own traumatic childhood experiences. Experience and memory are, thus, open to contradictory interpretations governed by social interests and prevailing discourses. The individual is both the site and subject of these discursive struggles for identity and for remaking memory. Because the individual is subject to multiple and competing discourses in many realms, one's subjectivity is shifting and contradictory—not stable, fixed, and rigid.

Poststructuralism, thus, points to the continual cocreation of the self and social science; they are known through each other. Knowing the self and knowing about the subject are intertwined, partial, historical local knowledges. Poststructuralism, then, permits—even invites or incites—us to reflect on our method and to explore new ways of knowing.

Specifically, poststructuralism suggests two important ideas to qualitative writers. First, it directs us to understand ourselves reflexively as persons writing from particular positions at specific times. Second, it frees us from trying to write a single text in which everything is said at once to everyone. Nurturing our own voices releases the censorious hold of "science writing" on our consciousness as well as the arrogance it fosters in our psyche; writing is validated as a method of knowing.

CAP Ethnography

In the wake of postmodernist—including poststructuralist, feminist, queer, and critical race theory—critiques of traditional qualitative writing practices, the sacrosanctity of social science writing conventions has been challenged. The ethnographic genre has been blurred, enlarged, and altered with researchers writing in different formats for a variety of audiences. These ethnographies are like each other, however, in that they are produced through creative analytical practices. I call them "CAP [creative analytical processes] ethnographies."[1] This label can include new work, future work, or older work—wherever the author has moved outside conventional social scientific writing. CAP ethnographies are not alternative or experimental; they are, in and of themselves, valid and desirable representations of the social. In the foreseeable future, these ethnographies may indeed be the most desirable representations because they invite people in and open spaces for thinking about the social that elude us now.

The practices that produce CAP ethnography are both creative and analytical. Any dinosaurian beliefs that "creative" and "analytical" are contradictory and incompatible modes are standing in the path of a meteor; they are doomed for extinction. Witness the evolution, proliferation, and diversity of new ethnographic "species"—autoethnography, fiction, poetry, drama, readers' theater, writing stories, aphorisms, layered texts, conversations, epistles, polyvocal texts, comedy, satire, allegory, visual texts, hypertexts, museum displays, choreographed findings, and performance pieces, to name some of the categories that are discussed in the pages of this *Handbook.* These new "species" of qualitative writing adapt to the kind of political/social world we inhabit—a world of uncertainty. With many outlets for presentation and publication, CAP ethnographies herald a paradigm shift (Ellis & Bochner, 1996).

CAP ethnography displays the writing process and the writing product as deeply intertwined; both are privileged. The product cannot be separated from the producer, the mode of production, or the method of knowing. Because both traditional ethnographies and CAP ethnographies are being produced within the broader postmodernist climate of "doubt," readers (and reviewers) want and deserve to know how the researchers claim to know. How do the authors position the selves as knowers and tellers? These issues engage intertwined problems of subjectivity, authority, authorship, reflexivity, and process, on the one hand, and of representational form, on the other.

Postmodernism claims that writing is always partial, local, and situational and that our selves are always present no matter how hard we try to suppress them—but only partially present because in our writing we repress parts of our selves as well. Working from that premise frees us to write material in a variety of ways—to tell and retell. There is no such thing as "getting it right," only "getting it" differently contoured and nuanced. When using creative analytical practices, ethnographers learn about the topics and about themselves that which was unknowable and unimaginable using conventional analytical procedures, metaphors, and writing formats.

In traditionally staged research, we valorize "triangulation." (For a discussion of triangulation as method, see Denzin, 1978. For an application, see Statham, Richardson, & Cook, 1991.) In triangulation, a researcher deploys different methods—interviews, census data, documents, and the like—to "validate" findings. These methods, however, carry the same domain assumptions, including the assumption that there is a "fixed point" or an "object" that can be triangulated. But in CAP ethnographies, researchers draw from literary, artistic, and scientific genres, often breaking the boundaries of those genres as well. In what I think of as a postmodernist deconstruction of triangulation, CAP text recognizes that there are far more than "three sides" by which to approach the world. We do not triangulate; we crystallize.

I propose that the central imaginary for "validity" for postmodernist texts is not the triangle—a rigid, fixed, two-dimensional object. Rather, the central imaginary is the crystal, which combines symmetry and substance with an infinite variety of shapes, substances, transmutations, multidimensionalities, and angles of approach. Crystals grow, change, and are altered, but they are not amorphous. Crystals are prisms that reflect externalities and refract within themselves, creating different colors, patterns, and arrays casting off in different directions. What we see depends on our angle of repose—not triangulation but rather crystallization. In CAP texts, we have moved from plane geometry to light theory, where light can be both waves and particles.

Travels With Ernest: Crossing the Literary/Sociological Divide (Richardson & Lockridge, 2004) is a recent example of crystallization practices. *Travels With Ernest* is built on geographical travels (e.g., Russia, Ireland, Beirut, Copenhagen, Sedona, St. Petersburg Beach) that I shared with my husband Ernest Lockridge, who is a novelist and professor of English. We experienced the same sites but refracted them through different professional eyes, gender, sensibilities, biographies, spiritual and emotional longings. After we each independently wrote a narrative account—a personal essay—inspired by the travel, we read each other's account and engaged in wide-ranging (taped/transcribed) conversations across disciplinary lines about writing, ethics, authorship, collaboration, witnessing, fact/fiction, audiences, relationships, and the intersection of observation and imagination. The travels, thus, are physical, emotional, and intellectual.

The collaborative process modeled in *Travels With Ernest* honors each voice as separate and distinct, explores the boundaries of observation and imagination, witnessing and retelling, memory and memorializing, and it confirms the value of crystallization. I remain a sociologist; he remains a novelist. Neither of us gives up our core visions. In the process of our collaboration, however, we discovered many things about ourselves—about our relationships to each other, our families, our work, and our writing—that we would not have discovered if we were not collaborating. For example, we discovered that we wanted the last piece in the book to break the book's writing format—to model other possibilities. We constructed from our conversation (and its multiple interruptions) a movie script set in our own Great American Kitchen. We especially like that the collaborative method we displayed in our text is one that is open to everyone; indeed, it is strategic writing through which established hierarchies between the researcher and the researched, between the student and the teacher, can be breached.

Crystallization, without losing structure, deconstructs the traditional idea of "validity"; we feel how there is no single truth, and we see how texts validate themselves. Crystallization provides us with a deepened, complex, and thoroughly partial understanding of the topic. Paradoxically, we know more and doubt what we know. Ingeniously, we know there is always more to know.

Evaluating CAP Ethnographies

Because the epistemological foundations of CAP ethnography differ from those of traditional social science, the conceptual apparatus by which CAP ethnographies can be evaluated differ. Although we are freer to present our texts in a variety of forms to diverse audiences, we have different constraints arising from self-consciousness about claims to authorship, authority, truth, validity, and reliability. Self-reflexivity brings to consciousness some of the complex political/ideological agendas hidden in our writing. Truth claims are less easily validated now; desires to speak "for" others are suspect. The greater freedom to experiment with textual form, however, does not guarantee a better product. The opportunities for writing worthy texts—books and articles that are "good reads"—are multiple, exciting, and demanding. But the work is harder and the guarantees are fewer. There is a lot more for us to think about.

One major issue is that of criteria. How does one judge an ethnographic work—new or traditional? Traditional ethnographers of good will have legitimate concerns about how their students' work will be evaluated if they choose to write CAP ethnography. I have no definitive answers to ease their concerns, but I do have some ideas and preferences.

I see the ethnographic project as humanly situated, always filtered through human eyes and human perceptions, and bearing both the limitations and the strengths of human feelings. Scientific superstructure is always resting on the foundation of human activity, belief, and understandings. I emphasize ethnography as constructed through *research practices.* Research practices are concerned with enlarged understanding. Science offers some research practices—literature, creative arts, memory work (Davies et al., 1997), introspection (Ellis, 1991), and dialogical (Ellis, 2004). Researchers have many practices from which to choose and ought not be constrained by habits of somebody else's mind.

I believe in holding CAP ethnography to high and difficult standards; mere novelty does not suffice. Here are four of the criteria I use when reviewing papers or monographs submitted for social scientific publication:

1. *Substantive contribution.* Does this piece contribute to our *understanding* of social life? Does the writer demonstrate a deeply grounded (if embedded) social scientific perspective? Does this piece seem "true"—a credible account of a cultural, social, individual, or communal sense of the "real"? (For some suggestions on accomplishing this, see Part 3 of this chapter.)
2. *Aesthetic merit.* Rather than reducing standards, another standard is added. Does this piece succeed aesthetically? Does the use of creative analytical practices open up the text and invite interpretive responses? Is the text artistically shaped, satisfying, complex, and not boring?
3. *Reflexivity.* How has the author's subjectivity been both a producer and a product of this text? Is there adequate self-awareness and self-exposure for the reader to make judgments about the point of view? Does the author hold himself or herself accountable to the standards of knowing and telling of the people he or she has studied?
4. *Impact.* Does this piece affect me emotionally or intellectually? Does it generate new questions or move me to write? Does it move me to try new research practices or move me to action?

These are four of my criteria. Science is one lens, and creative arts is another. We see more deeply using two lenses. I want to look through both lenses to see a "social science art form"—a radically interpretive form of representation.

I am not alone in this desire. I have found that students from diverse social backgrounds and marginalized cultures are attracted to seeing the social world through two lenses. Many of these students find CAP ethnography beckoning and join the qualitative community. The more this happens, the more everyone will profit. The implications of race and gender would be stressed, not because it would be "politically correct" but rather because race and gender *are axes* through which symbolic and actual worlds have been constructed. Members of nondominant worlds know that and could insist that this knowledge be honored (cf. Margolis & Romero, 1998). The blurring of the humanities and the social sciences would be welcomed, not because it is "trendy" but rather because the blurring coheres more truly with the life sense and learning style of so many. This new qualitative community could, through its theory, analytical practices, and diverse membership, reach beyond academia and teach all of us about social injustice and methods for alleviating it. What qualitative researcher interested in social life would not feel enriched by membership in such a culturally diverse and inviting community? Writing becomes more diverse and author centered, less boring, and humbler. These are propitious opportunities. Some even speak of their work as spiritual.

Writing Stories and Personal Narratives

The ethnographic life is not separable from the Self. Who we are and what we can be—what we can study, how we can write about that which we study—are tied to how a knowledge system disciplines itself and its members and to its methods for claiming authority over both the subject matter and its members.

We have inherited some ethnographic rules that are arbitrary, narrow, exclusionary, distorting, and alienating. Our task is to find concrete practices through which we can construct ourselves as ethical subjects engaged in ethical ethnography—inspiring to read and to write.

Some of these practices include working within theoretical schemata (e.g., sociology of knowledge, feminism, critical race theory, constructivism, poststructuralism) that challenge grounds of authority, writing on topics that matter both personally and collectively, experiencing *jouissance,* experimenting with different writing formats and audiences simultaneously, locating oneself in multiple discourses and communities, developing critical literacy, finding ways in which to write/present/teach that are less hierarchal and univocal, revealing institutional secrets, using positions of authority to increase diversity both in academic appointments and in journal publications, engaging in self-reflexivity, giving in to synchronicity, asking for what one wants, not flinching from where the writing takes one emotionally or spiritually, and honoring the embodiedness and spatiality of one's labors.

This last practice—honoring the location of the self—encourages us to construct what I call "writing stories." These are narratives that situate one's own writing in other parts of one's life such as disciplinary constraints, academic debates, departmental politics, social movements, community structures, research interests, familial ties, and personal history. They offer critical reflexivity about the writing self in different contexts as a valuable creative analytical practice. They evoke new questions about the self and the subject; remind us that our work is grounded, contextual, and rhizomatic; and demystify the research/writing process and help others to do the same. They can evoke deeper parts of the self, heal wounds, enhance the sense of self—or even alter one's sense of identity.

In *Fields of Play: Constructing an Academic Life* (Richardson, 1997), I make extensive use of writing stories to contextualize 10 years of my sociological work, creating a text that is more congruent with poststructural understandings of the situated nature of knowledge. Putting my papers and essays in the chronological order in which they were conceptualized, I sorted them into two piles: "keeper" and "reject." When I reread my first keeper—a presidential address to the North Central Sociological Association—memories of being patronized, marginalized, and punished by my department chair and dean reemerged. I stayed with those memories and wrote a writing story about the disjunction between my departmental life and my disciplinary reputation. Writing the story was not emotionally easy; in the writing, I was reliving horrific experiences, but writing the story released the anger and pain. Many academics who read that story recognize it as congruent with their experiences—their untold stories.

I worked chronologically through the keeper pile, rereading and then writing the writing story evoked by the rereading—different facets, different contexts. Some stories required checking my journals and files, but most did not. Some stories were painful and took an interminable length of time to write, but writing them loosened their shadow hold on me. Other stories were joyful and reminded me of the good fortunes I have in friends, colleagues, and family.

Writing stories sensitize us to the potential consequences of all of our writing by bringing home—inside our homes and workplaces—the ethics of representation. Writing stories are not about people and cultures "out there"—ethnographic subjects (or objects). Rather, they are about ourselves—our workspaces, disciplines, friends, and family. What can we say and with what consequences? Writing stories bring the danger and poignancy or ethnographic representation "up close and personal."

Each writing story offers its writer an opportunity for making a situated and pragmatic ethical decision about whether and where to publish the story. For the most part, I have found no ethical problem in publishing stories that reflect the abuses of power; I consider the damage done by the abusers far greater than any discomfort my stories might cause them. In contrast, I feel constraint in publishing about my immediate family members. I check materials with them. In the case of more distant family members, I change their names and identifying characteristics. I will not publish some of my recent writing because doing so would seriously "disturb the family peace." I set that writing away for the time being, hoping that I will find a way to publish it in the future.

In one section of *Fields of Play* (Richardson, 1997), I tell two interwoven stories of "writing illegitimacy." One story is my poetic representation of an interview with Louisa May, an unwed mother, and the other is the research story—how I wrote that poem along with its dissemination, reception, and consequences for me. There are multiple illegitimacies in the stories—a child out of wedlock, poetic representation as research "findings," a feminine voice in the social sciences, ethnographic research on ethnographers and dramatic representation of that research, emotional presence of the writer, and unbridled work *jouissance*.

I had thought that the research story was complete, not necessarily the only story that could be told but one that reflected fairly, honestly, and sincerely what my research experiences had been. I still believe that. But missing from the research story, I came to realize, were the personal biographical experiences that led me to author such a story.

The idea of "illegitimacy," I have come to acknowledge, has had a compelling hold on me. In my research journal, I wrote, "My career in the social sciences might be viewed as one long adventure into illegitimacies." I asked myself why I was drawn to constructing "texts of illegitimacy," including the text of my academic life. What is this struggle I have with the academy—being in it and against it at the same time? How is my story like and unlike the stories of others who are struggling to make sense of themselves, to retrieve their suppressed selves, to act ethically?

Refracting "illegitimacy" through allusions, glimpses, and extended views, I came to write a personal essay, "Vespers," the final essay in *Fields of Play* (Richardson, 1997). "Vespers" located my academic life in childhood experiences and memories; it deepened my knowledge of my self and has resonated with others' experiences in academia. In turn, the writing of "Vespers," has refracted again, giving me desire, strength, and enough self-knowledge to narrativize other memories and experiences, to give myself agency, and to construct myself anew for better or for worse.

Writing stories and personal narratives have increasingly become the structures through which I make sense of my world, locating my particular biographical experiences in larger historical and sociological contexts. Using writing as a method of discovery in conjunction with my understanding of feminist rereadings of Deleuzian thought, I have altered my primary writing question from "how to write during the crisis of representation" to "how to document becoming."

Like Zeno's arrow, I will never reach a destination (destiny?). But unlike Zeno, instead of focusing on the endpoint of a journey that never ends, I focus on how the arrowsmiths made the arrow, its place in the quiver, and the quiver's placement—displacement, replacement—in the world. I look at the promises of progressive ideologies and personal experiences as ruins to be excavated, as folds to unfold, as paths through academic miasma. I am convinced that in the story (or stories) of becoming, we have a good chance of deconstructing the underlying academic ideology—that *being* a something (e.g., a successful professor, an awesome theorist, a disciplinarian maven, a covergirl feminist) is better than *becoming.* For me, now, discovering the intricate interweavings of class, race, gender, education, religion, and other diversities that shaped me early on into the kind of sociologist I did become is a practical way of refracting the worlds—academic and other—in which I live. None of us knows his or her final destination, but all of us can know about the shape makers of our lives that we can choose to confront, embrace, or ignore.

I am not certain how others will document their becoming, but I have chosen structures that suit my disposition, theoretical orientation, and writing life. I am "growing myself up" by refracting my life through a sociological lens, fully engaging C. Wright Mills's "sociology"—the intersection of the biographical and the historical. I am discovering that my concerns for social justice across race, class, religion, gender, and ethnicity derive from these early childhood experiences. These have solidified my next writing questions. How can I make my writing matter? How can I write to help speed into this world a democratic project of social justice?

I do not have catchy or simple answers. I know that when I move deeply into my writing, both my compassion for others and my actions on their behalf increase. My writing moves me into an independent space where I see more clearly the interrelationships between and among peoples worldwide. Perhaps other writers have similar experiences. Perhaps thinking deeply and writing about one's own life has led, or will lead, them to actions that decrease the inequities between and among people and peoples and that decrease the violence.

Part 2: Writing as a Method of Nomadic Inquiry

Elizabeth Adams St. Pierre

My writing about writing as a method of inquiry in this doubled text appears after Laurel Richardson's for good reason; it is an effect of Richardson's work in the sense that it is a trajectory, a "line of flight" (Deleuze & Parnet, 1977/1987, p. 125), that maps what can happen if one takes seriously her charge to think of writing as a *method* of qualitative inquiry. I read a very early draft of this chapter, titled "Writing: A Method of Discovery," in 1992 in a sociology class that Richardson taught on postmodern research and writing. I had been trained years earlier, as an English major, to think of expository writing as a tracing of thought already thought, as a transparent reflection of the known and the real—writing as representation, as repetition. I still use that strategy for certain purposes and certain audiences even though I now chiefly use writing to disrupt the known and the real—writing as *simulation* (Baudrillard, 1981/1988), as "subversive repetition" (Butler, 1990, p. 32).

Thinking Richardson and Deleuze together, I have called my work in academia "nomadic inquiry" (St. Pierre, 1997a, 1997c), and a great part of that inquiry is accomplished in the writing because, for me, writing *is* thinking, writing *is* analysis, writing *is* indeed a seductive and tangled *method* of discovery. Many writers in the humanities have known this all along, but Richardson has brought this understanding to qualitative inquiry in the social sciences. In so doing, she has deconstructed the concept *method,* putting this ordinary category of qualitative inquiry *sous rature,* or under erasure (Spivak, 1974, p. xiv), and thereby opened it up to different meanings.

This concept certainly needs to be troubled. Two decades ago, Barthes (1984/1986) wrote, "Method becomes a Law," but the "will-to-method is ultimately sterile, everything has been put into the method, nothing remains for the writing" (p. 318). Thus, he said, "it is necessary, at a certain moment, to turn against Method, or at least to regard it without any founding privilege" (p. 319). In other words, it is important to interrogate whatever limits we have imposed on the concept method lest we diminish its possibilities in knowledge production.

This is one of postmodernism's lessons—that foundations are contingent (Butler, 1992). In fact, every foundational concept of conventional, interpretive qualitative inquiry, including method, is contingent, and postmodernists have deconstructed many of them, including data (St. Pierre, 1997b), validity (Lather, 1993; Scheurich, 1993), interviewing (Scheurich, 1995), the field (St. Pierre, 1997c), experience (Scott, 1991), voice (Finke, 1993; Jackson, 2003; Lather, 2000), reflexivity (Pillow, 2003), narrative (Nespor & Barylske, 1991), and even ethnography (Britzman, 1995; Visweswaran, 1994). This is not to say that postmodern qualitative researchers reject these concepts and others that have been defined in a certain way by interpretivism; rather, researchers have examined their effects on people and knowledge production during decades of research and have reinscribed them in different ways that, of course, must also be interrogated. Nor do postmodern qualitative researchers necessarily reject the words themselves; that is, they continue to use, for example, the words *method* and *data.* As Spivak (1974) cautioned, we are obliged to work with the "resources of the old language, the language we already possess and which possesses us. To make a new word is to run the risk of forgetting the problem or believing it solved" (p. xv). So, we use old concepts but ask them to do different work. Interestingly, it is the inability of language to close off meaning into concept that prompts postmodern qualitative researchers to critique the presumed coherency of the structure of conventional, interpretive qualitative inquiry. For some of us, the acknowledgment that that structure is, and always has been, contingent is good news indeed.

Language and Meaning

Richardson gestured toward the work of language earlier in this chapter, but here I describe in more detail the tenuous relation between language and *meaning* in order to ground my later discussion of postrepresentation in a postinterpretive world. We know that much deconstructive work has been done in the human sciences since the "linguistic turn" (Rorty, 1967), the "postmodern turn" (Hassan, 1987), the "crisis of legitimation" (Habermas, 1973/1975), and the "crisis of representation" (Marcus & Fischer, 1986), all of which employ a "consciousness of a language which does not forget itself" (Barthes, 1984/1986, p. 319) or, as Trinh (1989) put it, a consciousness that understands "language as language" (p. 17). Nearly four decades ago, Foucault (1966/1970) wrote that "language is not what it is because it has a meaning" (p. 35), and Derrida (1967/1974) theorized *différance,* which teaches us that meaning cannot be fixed in language but is always deferred. As Spivak (1974) explained, "word and thing or thought never in fact become one" (p. xvi), so language cannot serve as a transparent medium that mirrors, "represents," and contains the world.

The ideas that meaning is not a "portable property" (Spivak, 1974, p. lvii) and that language cannot simply transport meaning from one person to another play havoc with the Husserlian proposition that there is a layer of prelinguistic meaning (pure meaning, pure signified) that language can express. In this respect, postmodern discourses differ from "the interpretive sciences [that] proceed from the assumption that there is a deep truth which is both known and hidden. It is the job of interpretation to bring this truth to discourse" (Dreyfus & Rabinow, 1982, p. 180). These discourses also play havoc with the belief that noise-free rational communication (Habermas, 1981/1984, 1981/1987)—some kind of transparent dialogue that can lead to consensus—is possible, or even desirable, since consensus often erases difference. Further, Derrida's statement (as cited in Spivak, 1974) that "the thing itself always escapes" (p. lxix) throws into radical doubt (and, some would say, makes irrelevant) the hermeneutic assumption that we can, in fact, answer the ontological question "What is . . . ?"—the question that grounds much interpretive work.

But postmodernists, after the linguistic turn, suspect that interpretation is not the discovery of meaning in the world but rather the "introduction of meaning" (Spivak, 1974, p. xxiii). If this is so, we can no longer treat words as if they are deeply and essentially *meaningful* or the experiences they attempt to represent as "brute fact or simple reality" (Scott, 1991, p. 26). In this case, the interpreter has to assume the burden of meaning-making, which is no longer a neutral activity of expression that simply matches word to world. Foucault (1967/1998) wrote that "interpretation does not clarify a matter to be interpreted, which offers itself passively; it can only seize, and violently, an already-present interpretation, which it must overthrow, upset, shatter with the blows of a hammer" (p. 275). However, despite the dangers of the hermeneutic rage for meaning, we interpret incessantly, perhaps because of our "human inability to tolerate undescribed chaos" (Spivak, 1974, p. xxiii). In this regard, Foucault (as cited in Dreyfus & Rabinow, 1982) suggested that we are "condemned to meaning" (p. 88). But Derrida (1972/1981) had another take on meaning and suggested, "To risk meaning nothing is to start to play, and first to enter into the play of *différance* which prevents any word, any concept, any major enunciation from coming to summarize and to govern . . . differences" (p. 14). Derrida (1967/1974) called this deconstructive work *writing under erasure*, "letting go of each concept at the very moment that I needed to use it" (p. xviii). The implications for qualitative inquiry of imagining writing as a letting go of meaning even meaning proliferates rather than a search for and containment of meaning are both compelling and profound.

Clearly, postmodern qualitative researchers can no longer think of inquiry simply as a task of making meaning—comprehending, understanding, getting to the bottom of the phenomenon under investigation. As I mentioned earlier, this does not mean they reject meaning but rather that they put meaning in its place. They shift the focus from questions such as "What does this or that mean?" to questions such as those posed by Scott (1988): "How do meanings change? How have some meanings emerged as normative and others been eclipsed or disappeared? What do these processes reveal about how power is constituted and operates?" (p. 35). Bové (1990) offered additional questions, and I suggest that we can substitute any object of knowledge (e.g., marriage, subjectivity, race) for the word "discourse" in the following: "How does discourse function? Where is it to be found? How does it get produced and regulated? What are its social effects? How does it exist?" (p. 54).

And since Richardson and I especially love writing, we have asked ourselves these questions about writing and have posed another that we find provocative: *What else might writing do except mean?* Deleuze and Guattari (1980/1987) offered some help here when they suggested, "writing has nothing to do with signifying. It has to do with surveying, mapping, even realms that are yet to come" (pp. 4–5). In this sense, writing becomes a "field of play" (Richardson, 1997) in which we might loosen the hold of received meaning that limits our work and our lives and investigate "to what extent the exercise of thinking one's own history can free thought from what it thinks silently and to allow it to think otherwise" (Foucault, as cited in Racevskis, 1987, p. 22). In this way, the linguistic turn and the postmodern critique of interpretivism open up the concept writing and enable us to use it as a *method of inquiry*, a condition of possibility for "producing different knowledge and producing knowledge differently" (St. Pierre, 1997b, p. 175).

Writing Under Erasure: A Politics and Ethics of Difficulty

So what might the work of *writing as inquiry* be in postmodern qualitative research? What might writing under erasure look like, and how, in turn, might such writing rewrite inquiry itself? My own experiences in this regard have emerged from a long-term postmodern qualitative research project that has been both an interview study with 36 older white southern women who live in my hometown and an ethnography of the small rural community in which they live (St. Pierre, 1995). It is important to note that this study was not designed to do interpretive work—to answer the questions "who are these women?" and "what do they mean?" I never presumed I could know or understand the women—uncover their authentic voices and essential natures and then represent them in rich thick description. Rather, my task was twofold: (1) to use postmodernism to study subjectivity by using Foucault's (1984/1985, 1985/1986) ethical analysis, care of the self, to investigate the "arts of existence" or "practices of the self" the women have used during their long lives in the construction of their subjectivities and (2) to use postmodernism to study conventional qualitative research methodology, which I believe is generally both positivist and interpretive.

Also, since I call myself a writer—thanks to Richardson (it took a sociologist to teach this English teacher writing)—I determined early in the study to use writing as a method of inquiry in at least these two senses: (1) I would think of writing as a *method of data collection* along with, for example, interviewing and observation and (2) I would think of writing as *a method of data analysis* along with, for example, the traditional—and what I think of as structural (and positivist)—activities of analytic induction; constant comparison; coding, sorting, and categorizing data; and so forth. It should be clear at this point that the coherence of the positivist and/or interpretivist concept method has already been breached by investing it with these different and multiple meanings and, henceforth, efforts to maintain its unity may be futile. (Indeed, I hope others will follow my lead and imagine other uses for writing as a method of inquiry.) Further, these two methods are not discrete as I have made them out to be. Making such a distinction is to stay within the confines of the structure of conventional qualitative inquiry in which we often separate data collection from data analysis. Nevertheless, I retain the distinction temporarily for the purpose of elucidation.

In my study, I used writing as a method of data collection by gathering together, by collecting—*in the writing*—all sorts of data I had never read about in interpretive qualitative textbooks, some of which I have called *dream data, sensual data, emotional data, response data* (St. Pierre, 1997b), and *memory data* (St. Pierre, 1995). Such data might include, for example, a pesky dream about an unsatisfying interview, the sharp angle of the southern sun to which my body happily turned, my sorrow when I read the slender obituary of one of my participants, my mother's disturbing comment that I had gotten something wrong, and very real "memor[ies] of the future" (Deleuze, 1986/1988, p. 107), a mournful time bereft of these women and others of their generation. These data were neither in my interview transcripts nor in my fieldnotes where data are supposed to be, for how can one textualize everything one thinks and senses in the course of a study? But they were always already in my mind and body, and they cropped up unexpectedly and fittingly in my writing—fugitive, fleeting data that were excessive and out-of-category. My point here is that these data might have escaped entirely if I had not *written;* they were collected only *in the writing.*

I used writing as a method of data analysis by using writing to think; that is, I wrote my way into particular spaces I could not have occupied by sorting data with a computer program or by analytic induction. This was rhizomatic work (Deleuze & Guattari, 1980/1987) in which I made accidental and fortuitous connections I could not foresee or control. My point here is that I did not limit data analysis to conventional practices of coding data and then sorting it into categories that I then grouped into themes that became section headings in an outline that organized and governed my writing in advance of writing. *Thought happened in the writing.* As I wrote, I watched word after word appear on the computer screen—ideas, theories, I had not thought before I wrote them. Sometimes I wrote something so marvelous it startled me. *I doubt I could have thought such a thought by thinking alone.*

And it is thinking of writing in this way that breaks down the distinction in conventional qualitative inquiry between data collection and data analysis—one more assault to the structure. Both happen at once. As data are collected in the writing—as the researcher thinks/writes about her Latin teacher's instruction that one should thrive in adversity; about a mink shawl draped elegantly on aging, upright shoulders; about the sweet, salty taste of tiny country ham biscuits; about all the other things in her life that seem unrelated to her research project but are absolutely unleashed within it—she produces the strange and wonderful transitions from word to word, sentence to sentence, thought to unthought. Data collection and data analysis cannot be separated when writing is a method of inquiry. And positivist concepts, such as audit trails and data saturation, become absurd and then irrelevant in postmodern qualitative inquiry in which writing is a field of play where anything can happen—and does.

There is much to think about here as conventional qualitative inquiry comes undone—in this case, as writing deconstructs the concept *method,* proliferating its meaning and thereby collapsing the structure that relied on its unity. But how does one "write it up" after the linguistic turn? Postmodern qualitative researchers have been courageous and inventive in this work, and Richardson identified and described this writing both as "experimental writing" (Richardson, 1994) and as "CAP ethnography" (Richardson, 2000). Of course, there is no model for this work since each researcher and each study requires different writing. I can, however, briefly tell a small writing story about my own adventures with *postrepresentation.*

As I said earlier, in my study with the older women of my hometown, I set out to study subjectivity and qualitative inquiry using poststructural analyses, so my charge was to critique both the presumed unified structure of an autonomous, conscious, knowing woman who could be delivered to the reader in rich, thick description as well as the presumed rational, coherent structure of conventional qualitative inquiry that could guarantee true knowledge about the women. Never having read a postmodern qualitative textbook, I initially tried to force—to no avail—postmodern methodology into the grid of interpretive/positivist qualitative inquiry. When the lack of fit became apparent and then absurd, I began to deconstruct that structure to make room for difference.

At the same time, I began to assume a writerly reticence to describe or represent my participants and thereby encourage some kind of sentimental identification. After all, it was subjectivity, not the women, that was the object of my inquiry. I became wary of the not-so-innocent assumption of interpretivism that the women should be drilled and mined for knowledge ("Who are they?" "What do they mean?") and then represented. This did not seem to be the kind of ethical relation these women who had taught me how to be a woman required of me. I am reminded here of a comment by Anthony Lane, the film critic for *The New Yorker,* who suggested that instead of asking whether David Lynch's film, *Mulholland Drive,* makes sense ("What does it mean?"), viewers should ask what Laurence Olivier once demanded of Dustin Hoffman ("Is it safe?") (Lane, 2001). In interpretive research, we believe representation is possible, if perhaps unsafe, but we do it anyway with many anxious disclaimers. In postmodern research, we believe it isn't possible *or* safe, and so we shift the focus entirely, in my case, away from the women to subjectivity. We increasingly distrust the "old promise of representation" (Britzman, 1995, p. 234) and, with Pillow (2003), question a science whose goal is representation.

In my own work, I have developed a certain writerly incompetence and underachievement and am unable to write a text that "runs to meet the reader" (Sommer, 1994, p. 530), a comfort text (Lather & Smithies, 1997) that gratifies the interpretive entitlement to know the women. Rather than being an "epistemological dead end" (Sommer, 1994, p. 532) (the women as objects that can be known), the women are a line of flight that take me elsewhere (the women as provocateurs). This is not to deny the importance of the women or to say that they are not in my texts since they are everywhere, but I gesture toward them in oblique ways in my writing by relating, for example, one of our vexing conversations that burgeoned into splendid and productive confusion about subjectivity or by relating an aporia about methodology they insist I think. And when someone asks for a story about the women, I give them a good one, and if they ask for another, I say, "Go find your own older women and talk with them. They have stories to tell that will change your life."

Nevertheless, I long to write about these older women who are dying, dying, dying and fear I will someday, but only after wrestling with that postrepresentational question: *What else might writing do except mean?* That writing will involve a *politics and ethics of difficulty* that, on the one hand, can only be accomplished if I write but, on the other, cannot be accomplished on the basis of anything I already know about writing. There are no rules for postrepresentational writing; there's nowhere to turn for authorizing comfort.

What has postmodernism done to qualitative inquiry? I agree with Richardson's (1994) response to this question: "I do not know, but I do know that we cannot go back to where we were" (p. 524). Or, as Deleuze and Parnet (1977/1987) put it, "It might be thought that nothing has changed and nevertheless everything has changed" (p. 127). At this point, I return to the criteria that Richardson has set for postmodern ethnographic texts. Can the kind of writing I have gestured toward here—writing under erasure—exhibit a substantive contribution, aesthetic merit, reflexivity, impact, and reflect lived experience? I believe it can. But even more importantly, writing as a method of inquiry carries us "across our thresholds, toward a destination which is unknown, not foreseeable, not preexistent" (Deleuze & Parnet, 1977/1987, p. 25), perhaps toward the spectacular promise of what Derrida (1993/1994) called the "democracy *to come*" (p. 64), a promise those who work for social justice cannot not want. I think about this democracy often since it promises the possibility of different relations—relations more generous than those I live among, fertile relations in which people thrive.

The paradox, however, is that this democracy will never "present itself in the form of full presence" (Derrida, 1993/1994, p. 65) but nonetheless demands that we prepare ourselves for its arrival. Derrida (1993/1994) explained that it turns on the idea that we must offer "hospitality without reserve" to an "alterity that cannot be anticipated" from whom we ask nothing in return (p. 65). Thus, the setting-to-work of deconstruction in the democracy-to-come is grounded in our relations with the Other. In postmodern qualitative inquiry, the possibilities for just and ethical encounters with alterity occur not only in the field of human activity but also in the field of the text, in our writing. In these overlapping spaces, we prepare ourselves for a democracy that has no model, for a postjuridical justice that is always contingent on the case at hand and must be effaced even as it is produced. Settling into a transcendental justice and truth, some deep meaning we think will save us, may announce a lack of courage to think and live beyond our necessary fictions.

Ethics under deconstruction then, is ungrounded, it is "what happens when we cannot apply the rules" (Keenan, 1997, p. 1). This ethics of difficulty hinges on a tangled responsibility to the Other "that is not a moment of security or of cognitive certainty. Quite the contrary: the only responsibility worthy of the name comes with the withdrawal of rules or the knowledge on which we might rely to make our decisions for us." The event of ethics occurs when we have "no grounds, no alibis, no elsewhere to which we might refer the instance of our decisions." In this sense, *we will always be unprepared to be ethical.* Moreover, the removal of foundations and originary meaning, which were always already fictions, simply leaves everything as it is but without those markers of certainty we counted on to see us intact through a text of responsibility. So, how do we go on from here? How do we get on with our work and our lives?

Deleuze (1969/1990) suggested that the events in our lives—and in this essay, I'm thinking specifically of all those relations with the Other that qualitative inquiry enables—tempt us to be their equal by asking for our "best and most perfect. Either ethics makes no sense at all, or this is what it means and has nothing else to say: *not to be unworthy of what happens to us*" (pp. 148–149). The event, then, calls us to be worthy at the instant of decision, when what happens is all there is—*when meaning will always come too late to rescue us.* At the edge of the abyss, we step without reserve toward the Other. This is deconstruction at its finest and, I believe, the condition of Derrida's democracy-to-come. This democracy calls for a renewed "belief in the world" (Deleuze, 1990/1995, p. 176) that, I hope, will enable relations less impoverished than the ones we have thus far imagined and lived. As I said earlier, the setting-to-work of deconstruction is already being accomplished by postmodern qualitative researchers in all the fields of play in which they work.

As for me, I struggle every day not to be unworthy of the older women of my hometown who keep on teaching me ethics. It may seem that I am not writing about them in this essay, but I assure you they are speaking to you in every word you read. Brooding and writing about our desire for their presence (meaning) in this text and others I might write occupies much of my energy, yet I trust writing and know that one morning I will awaken and write toward these women in a way I cannot yet imagine. I trust you will do the same, that you will use writing as a method of inquiry to move into your own impossibility, where anything might happen—and will.

Part 3: Writing Practices

Laurel Richardson

> *Writing, the creative effort, should come first—at least for some part of every day of your life. It is a wonderful blessing if you will use it. You will become happier, more enlightened, alive, impassioned, light-hearted, and generous to everybody else. Even your health will improve. Colds will disappear and all the other ailments of discouragement and boredom.*
>
> —Brenda Ueland, *If You Want to Write*

In what follows, I suggest some ways of using writing as a method of knowing. I have chosen exercises that have been productive for students because they demystify writing, nurture the researcher's voice, and serve the processes of discovery about the self, the world, and issues of social justice. I wish that I could guarantee them to bring good health as well.

Metaphor

Using old worn-out metaphors, although easy and comfortable, invites stodginess and stiffness after a while. The stiffer you get, the less flexible you are. Your ideas get ignored. If your writing is clichéd, you will not "stretch your own imagination" (Ouch! Hear the cliché of pointing out the cliché!) and you will bore people.

1. In traditional social scientific writing, the metaphor for theory is that it is a "building" (e.g., structure, foundation, construction, deconstruction, framework, grand) (see the wonderful book by Lakoff & Johnson, 1980). Consider a different metaphor such as "theory as a tapestry," "theory as an illness," "theory as story," or "theory as social action." Write a paragraph about "theory" using your metaphor. Do you "see" differently and "feel" differently about theorizing using an unusual metaphor? Do you want your theory to map differently onto the social world? Do you want your theory to affect the world?

2. Look at one of your papers and highlight your metaphors and images. What are you saying through metaphors that you did not realize you were saying? What are you reinscribing? Do you want to do so? Can you find different metaphors that change how you "see" ("feel") the material and your relationship to it? Are your mixed metaphors pointing to confusion in yourself or to social science's glossing over of ideas? How do your metaphors both reinscribe and resist social inequities?

Writing Formats

1. Choose a journal article that exemplifies the mainstream writing conventions of your discipline. How is the argument staged? Who is the presumed audience? How does the article inscribe ideology? How does the author claim "authority" over the material? Where is the author? Where are "you" in the article? Who are the subjects and objects of research?

2. Choose a paper that you have written for a class or published and that you think is pretty good. How did you follow the norms of your discipline? Were you conscious of doing so? What parts did the professor/reviewer laud? Did you elide over some difficult areas through vagueness, jargon, a call to authorities, science writing norms, and/or other rhetorical devices? What voices did you exclude in your writing? Who is the audience?

Where are the subjects in the paper or article? Where are you? How do you feel about the paper or article now? How do you feel about your process of constructing it?

Creative Analytical Writing Practices

1. Join or start a writing group. This could be a writing support group, a creative writing group, a poetry group, a dissertation group, a memoir group, or the like (on dissertation and article writing, see Becker, 1986; Fox, 1985; Richardson, 1990; Wolcott, 1990).

2. Work through a creative writing guidebook (for some excellent guides, see Goldberg, 1986; Hills, 1987; Ueland, 1938/1987; Weinstein, 1993).

3. Enroll in a creative writing workshop or class. These experiences are valuable for both beginning and experienced researchers.

4. Use "writing up" fieldnotes as an opportunity to expand your writing vocabulary, habits of thought, and attentiveness to your senses and to use as a bulwark against the censorious voice of science. Where better to develop your sense of Self—your voice—than in the process of doing your research? What better place to experiment with point of view—seeing the world from different persons' perspectives—than in your fieldnotes. Keep a journal. Write writing stories, that is, research stories.

5. Write a writing autobiography. This would be the story of how you learned to write, the dicta of English classes (topic sentences? outlines? the five-paragraph essay?), the dicta of social science professors, how and where you write now, your idiosyncratic "writing needs," your feelings about writing and about the writing process, and/or your resistance to "value-free" writing. (This is an exercise used by Arthur Bochner.)

6. If you wish to experiment with evocative writing, a good place to begin is by transforming your fieldnotes into drama. See what ethnographic rules you are using (e.g., fidelity to the speech of the participants, fidelity in the order of the speakers and events) and what literary ones you are invoking (e.g., limiting how long a speaker speaks, keeping the "plot" moving along, developing character through actions). Writing dramatic presentations accentuates ethical considerations. If you doubt that, contrast writing up an ethnographic event as a "typical" event with writing it as a play, with you and your hosts cast in roles that will be performed before others. Who has ownership of spoken words? How is authorship attributed? What if people do not like how they are characterized? Are courtesy norms being violated? Experiment here with both oral and written versions of your drama.

7. Experiment with transforming an in-depth interview into a poetic representation. Try using only the words, rhythms, figures of speech, breath points, pauses, syntax, and diction of the speaker. Where are you in the poem? What do you know about the interviewee and about yourself that you did not know before you wrote the poem? What poetic devices have you sacrificed in the name of science?

8. Write a "layered text" (cf. Ronai, 1995; Lather & Smithies, 1997). The layered text is a strategy for putting yourself into your text and putting your text into the literatures and traditions of social science. Here is one possibility. First, write a short narrative of the self about some event that is especially meaningful to you. Step back and look at the narrative from your disciplinary perspective. Then insert into the narrative—beginning, midsections, end, or wherever—relevant analytical statements or references using a different typescript, alternative page placement, or a split page or marking the text in other ways. The layering can be a multiple one, with different ways of marking different theoretical levels, different theories, different speakers, and so forth. (This is an exercise used by Carolyn Ellis.)

9. Try some other strategy for writing new ethnography for social scientific publications. Try the "seamless" text in which previous literature, theory, and methods are placed in textually meaningful ways rather than in disjunctive sections (for an excellent example, see Bochner, 1997). Try the "sandwich" text in which traditional social science

themes are the "white bread" around the "filling" (Ellis & Bochner, 1996), or try an "epilogue" explicating the theoretical analytical work of the creative text (cf. Eisner, as cited in Saks, 1996).

10. Consider a fieldwork setting. Consider the various subject positions you have or have had within it. For example, in a store you might be a sales clerk, a customer, a manager, a feminist, a capitalist, a parent, or a child. Write about the setting (or an event in the setting) from several different subject positions. What do you "know" from the different positions? Next, let the different points of view dialogue with each other. What do you discover through these dialogues? What do you learn about social inequities?

11. Write your "data" in three different ways—for example, as a narrative account, a poetic representation, and readers' theater. What do you know in each rendition that you did not know in the other renditions? How do the different renditions enrich each other?

12. Write a narrative of the self from your point of view (e.g., something that happened in your family or in your seminar). Then, interview another participant (e.g., a family member or seminar member) and have that participant tell you his or her story of the event. See yourself as part of *the participant's* story in the same way as he or she is part of your story. How do you rewrite your story from the participant's point of view? (This is an exercise used by Ellis.)

13. Collaborative writing is a way in which to see beyond one's own naturalisms of style and attitude. This is an exercise that I have used in my teaching, but it would be appropriate for a writing group as well. Each member writes a story of his or her life. For example, it could be a feminist story, a success story, a quest story, a cultural story, a professional socialization story, a realist tale, a confessional tale, or a discrimination story. Stories are photocopied for the group. The group is then broken into subgroups (I prefer groups of three). Each subgroup collaborates on writing a new story—the collective story of its members. The collaboration can take any form—drama, poetry, fiction, narrative of the selves, realism, and so forth. The collaboration is shared with the entire group. Each member then writes about his or her feelings about the collaboration and what happened to his or her story—and life—in the process.

14. Consider a part of your life outside of or before academia with which you have deeply resonated. Use that resonance as a "working metaphor" for understanding and reporting your research. Students have created excellent reports and moored themselves through the unexpected lens (e.g., choreography, principles of flower arrangement, art composition, sportscasting). Those resonances nurture a more integrated life.

15. Different forms of writing are appropriate for different audiences and different occasions. Experiment with writing the same piece of research for an academic audience, a trade audience, the popular press, policymakers, research hosts, and so forth (Richardson, 1990). This is an especially powerful exercise for dissertation students who might want to share their results in a "user-friendly" way with their fellow students.

16. Write writing stories (Richardson, 1997). These are reflexive accounts of how you happened to write the pieces you wrote. The writing stories can be about disciplinary politics, departmental events, friendship networks, collegial ties, family, and/or personal biographical experiences. What these writing stories do is situate your work in contexts, tying what can be a lonely and seemingly separative task to the ebbs and flows of your life and your self. Writing these stories reminds us of the continual cocreation of the self and social science.

> *Willing is doing something you know already—there is no new imaginative understanding in it. And presently your soul gets frightfully sterile and dry because you are so quick, snappy, and efficient about doing one thing after another that you have no time for your own ideas to come in and develop and gently shine.*
>
> —Brenda Ueland, *If You Want to Write*

Note

1. The CAP acronym resonates with "cap" from the Latin for "head," *caput.* Because the head is both mind and body, its metaphorical use breaks down the mind–body duality. The products, although mediated throughout the body, cannot manifest without "headwork." In addition, "cap," both as a noun (product) and as a verb (process), has multiple common and idiomatic meanings and associations, some of which refract the playfulness of the genre—a rounded head covering or a special head covering indicating occupation or membership in a particular group, the top of a building or fungus, a small explosive charge, any of several sizes of writing paper, putting the final touches on, lying on top of, surpassing or outdoing. And then, there are the other associated words from the Latin root, such as capillary and capital(ism), that humble and contextualize the labor.

References

Barthes, R. (1986). *The rustle of language* (R. Howard, Trans.). Berkeley: University of California Press. (Original work published in 1984)

Baudrillard, J. (1988). Simulacra and simulations. In M. Poster (Ed.), *Jean Baudrillard: Selected writings* (P. Foss, P. Patton, & P. Beitchman, Trans., pp. 166–184). Stanford, CA: Stanford University Press. (Original work published in 1981)

Becker, H. S. (1986). *Writing for social scientists: How to finish your thesis, book, or article.* Chicago: University of Chicago Press.

Bochner, A. (1997). It's about time: Narrative and the divided Self. *Qualitative Inquiry, 3,* 418–438.

Bové, P. A. (1990) Discourse. In F. Lentricchia & T. McLaughlin (Eds.), *Critical terms for literary study* (pp. 50–65). Chicago: University of Chicago Press.

Britzman, D. P. (1995). "The question of belief": Writing poststructural ethnography. *International Journal of Qualitative Studies in Education, 8*(3), 229–238.

Butler, J. (1990). *Gender trouble: Feminism and the subversion of identity.* New York. Routledge.

Butler, J. (1992). Contingent foundations: Feminism and the question of "postmodernism." In J. Butler & J. W. Scott (Eds.), *Feminists theorize the political* (pp. 3–21). New York: Routledge.

Clifford, J., & Marcus, G. E. (Eds.). (1986). *Writing culture: The poetics and politics of ethnography.* Berkeley: University of California Press.

Davies, B. (1994). *Poststructuralist theory and classroom practice.* Geelong, Australia: Deakin University Press.

Davies, B., Dormer, S., Honan, E., McAllister, N., O'Reilly, R., Rocco, S., & Walker, A. (1997). Ruptures in the skin of silence: A collective biography. *Hecate: A Woman's Interdisciplinary Journal, 23*(1), 62–79.

Deleuze, G. (1988). *Foucault* (S. Hand, Trans.). Minneapolis: University of Minnesota Press. (Original work published in 1986)

Deleuze, G. (1990). *The logic of sense* (C. V. Boundas, Ed.; M. Lester, Trans.). New York: Columbia University Press. (Original work published in 1969)

Deleuze, G. (1995). *Negotiations: 1972–1990* (M. Joughin, Trans.). New York: Columbia University Press. (Original work published in 1990)

Deleuze, G., & Guattari, F. (1987). Introduction: Rhizome. In *A thousand plateaus: Capitalism and schizophrenia* (B. Massumi, Trans., pp. 3–25). Minneapolis: University of Minnesota Press. (Original work published in 1980)

Deleuze, G., & Parnet, C. (1987). Many politics. In *Dialogues* (H. Tomlinson & B. Habberjam, Trans.). New York: Columbia University Press. (Original work published in 1977)

Denzin, N. K. (1978). *The research act.* New York: McGraw-Hill.

Denzin, N. K. (1997). *Interpretive ethnography: Ethnographic practices for the 21st century.* Thousand Oaks, CA: Sage.

Derrida, J. (1974). *Of grammatology* (G. C. Spivak, Trans.). Baltimore, MD: Johns Hopkins University Press. (Original work published in 1967)

Derrida, J. (1981). *Positions* (A. Bass, Trans.). Chicago: University of Chicago Press. (Original work published in 1972)

Derrida, J. (1994). *Specters of Marx: The state of the debt, the work of mourning, and the new international* (P. Kamuf, Trans.). New York: Routledge. (Original work published in 1993)

Dreyfus, H. L., & Rabinow, P. (1982). *Michel Foucault: Beyond structuralism and hermeneutics* (2nd ed.). Chicago: University of Chicago Press.

Ellis, C. (1991). Sociological introspection and emotional experience. *Symbolic Interaction, 14,* 23–50.

Ellis, C. (2004). *The ethnographic "I": A methodological novel about autoethnography.* Walnut Creek, CA: AltaMira.

Ellis, C., & Bochner, A. P. (Eds.). (1996). *Composing ethnography: Alternative forms of qualitative writing.* Walnut Creek, CA: AltaMira.

Finke, L. A. (1993). Knowledge as bait: Feminism, voice, and the pedagogical unconscious. *College English, 55*(1), 7–27.

Fishkin, S. F. (1985). *From fact to fiction: Journalism and imaginative writing in America.* Baltimore, MD: Johns Hopkins University Press.

Foucault, M. (1970). *The order of things: An archaeology of the human sciences.* New York: Vintage Books. (Original work published in 1966)

Foucault, M. (1985). *The history of sexuality,* Vol. 2: *The use of pleasure* (R. Hurley, Trans.). New York: Vintage Books. (Original work published in 1984)

Foucault, M. (1986). *The history of sexuality,* Vol. 3: *The care of the self* (R. Hurley, Trans.). New York: Vintage Books. (Original work published in 1985)

Foucault, M. (1998). Nietzsche, Freud, Marx. In J. D. Faubion (Ed.), *Aesthetics, method, and epistemology* (J. Anderson & G. Hentzi, Trans., pp. 269–278). New York: New Press. (Original work published in 1967)

Fox, M. F. (Ed.). (1985). *Scholarly writing and publishing: Issues, problems, and solutions.* Boulder, CO: Westview.

Goldberg, N. (1986). *Writing down the bones: Freeing the writer within.* Boston: Shambala.

Habermas, J. (1975). *Legitimation crisis* (T. McCarthy, Trans.). Boston: Beacon. (Original work published in 1973)

Habermas, J. (1984). *The theory of communicative action,* Vol. 1: *Reason and the rationalization of society* (T. McCarthy, Trans.). Boston: Beacon. (Original work published in 1981)

Habermas, J. (1987). *The theory of communicative action,* Vol. 2: *Lifeworld and system: A critique of functionalist reason* (T. McCarthy, Trans.). Boston: Beacon. (Original work published in 1981)

Hassan, I. (1987). *The postmodern turn: Essays in postmodern theory and culture.* Columbus: Ohio State University Press.

Hills, R. (1987). *Writing in general and the short story in particular.* Boston: Houghton Mifflin.

Jackson, A. (2003). Rhizovocality. *International Journal of Qualitative Studies in Education, 16,* 693–710.

Keenan, T. (1997). *Fables of responsibility: Aberrations and predicaments in ethics and politics.* Stanford, CA: Stanford University Press.

Lakoff, G., & Johnson, M. (1980). *Metaphors we live by.* Chicago: University of Chicago Press.

Lane, A. (2001, October 8). Road trips. *The New Yorker,* p. 8.

Lather, P. (1993). Fertile obsession: Validity after poststructuralism. *Sociological Quarterly, 34,* 673–693.

Lather, P. (2000). Against empathy, voice, and authenticity. *Women, Gender, and Research, 4,* 16–25.

Lather, P., & Smithies, C. (1997). *Troubling the angels: Women living with HIV/AIDS.* Boulder, CO: Westview.

Levine, D. H. (1985). *The flight from ambiguity: Essays in social and cultural theory.* Chicago: University of Chicago Press.

Marcus, G. E., & Fischer, M. M. J. (1986). A crisis of representation in the social sciences. In G. E. Marcus & M. M. J. Fischer (Eds.), *Anthropology as cultural critique: An experimental moment in the human sciences* (pp. 7–16). Chicago: University of Chicago Press.

Margolis, E., & Romero, M. (1998). The department is very male, very white, very old, and very conservative: The functioning of the hidden curriculum in graduate sociology departments. *Harvard Educational Review, 68,* 1–32.

Nespor, J., & Barylske, J. (1991). Narrative discourse and teacher knowledge. *American Educational Research Journal, 28,* 805–823.

Pillow, W. S. (2003). Confession, catharsis, or cure? Rethinking the uses of reflexivity as methodological power in qualitative research. *International Journal of Qualitative Studies in Education, 16*(2), 175–196.

Racevskis, K. (1987). Michel Foucault, Rameau's nephew, and the question of identity. In J. Bernauer & D. Rasmussen (Eds.), *The final Foucault* (pp. 21–33). Cambridge, MA: MIT Press.

Richardson, L. (1990). *Writing strategies: Reaching diverse audiences.* Newbury Park, CA: Sage.

Richardson, L. (1994). Writing: A method of inquiry. In N. K. Denzin & Y. S. Lincoln (Eds.), *Handbook of qualitative research* (pp. 516–529). Thousand Oaks, CA: Sage.

Richardson, L. (1997). *Fields of play: Constructing an academic life.* New Brunswick, NJ: Rutgers University Press.

Richardson, L. (2000). Writing: A method of inquiry. In N. K. Denzin & Y. S. Lincoln (Eds.), *Handbook of qualitative research* (2nd ed., pp. 923–948). Thousand Oaks, CA: Sage.

Richardson, L., & Lockridge, E. (2004). *Travels with Ernest: Crossing the literary/sociological divide.* Walnut Creek, CA: AltaMira.

Ronai, C. (1995). Multiple reflections of child sexual abuse: An argument for a layered account. *Journal of Contemporary Ethnography, 23,* 395–426.

Rorty, R. (1967). *The linguistic turn: Essays in philosophical method.* Chicago: University of Chicago Press.

Saks, A. L. (1996). Viewpoints: Should novels count as dissertations in education? *Research in the Teaching of English, 30,* 403–427.

Scheurich, J. J. (1993). The masks of validity: A deconstructive investigation. *International Journal of Qualitative Studies in Education, 9*(11), 49–60.

Scheurich, J. J. (1995). A postmodernist critique of research interviewing. *International Journal of Qualitative Studies in Education, 8*(3), 239–252.

Scott, J. W. (1988). Deconstructing equality-versus-difference: Or, the uses of poststructuralist theory for feminism. *Feminist Studies, 14*(1), 33–50.

Scott, J. W. (1991). The evidence of experience. *Critical Inquiry, 17,* 773–797.

Sommer, D. (1994). Resistant texts and incompetent readers. *Poetics Today, 15,* 523–551.

Spivak, G. C. (1974). Translator's preface. In J. Derrida, *Of grammatology* (G. C. Spivak, Trans., pp. ix–xc). Baltimore, MD: Johns Hopkins University Press.

Statham, A., Richardson, L., & Cook, J. A. (1991). *Gender and university teaching: A negotiated difference.* Albany: State University of New York Press.

St. Pierre, E. A. (1995). *Arts of existence: The construction of subjectivity in older, white southern women.* Unpublished doctoral dissertation, Ohio State University, Columbus, OH.

St. Pierre, E. A. (1997a). Circling the text: Nomadic writing practices. *Qualitative Inquiry, 3,* 403–417.

St. Pierre, E. A. (1997b). Methodology in the fold and the irruption of transgressive data. *International Journal of Qualitative Studies in Education, 10*(2), 175–189.

St. Pierre, E. A. (1997c). Nomadic inquiry in the smooth spaces of the field: A preface. *International Journal of Qualitative Studies in Education, 10*(3), 363–383.

Trinh, M. T. (1989). *Women, native, other: Writing postcoloniality and feminism.* Bloomington: Indiana University Press.

Ueland, B. (1987). *If you want to write: A book about art, independence, and spirit.* St. Paul, MN: Graywolf Press. (Original work published in 1938)

Visweswaran, K. (1994). *Fictions of feminist ethnography.* Minneapolis: University of Minnesota Press.

Weinstein, D. (1993). *Writing for your life: A guide and companion to the inner worlds.* New York: HarperCollins.

Wolcott, H. F. (1990). *Writing up qualitative research.* Newbury Park, CA: Sage.

39

POETICS FOR A PLANET

Discourse on Some Problems of Being-in-Place

Ivan Brady

We are dwellers, we are namers, we are lovers, we make homes and search for our histories. And when we look for the history of our sensibilities, . . . it is to . . . the stable element, the land itself, that we must look for continuity.

—Seamus Heaney,
"The Sense of Place"

The great function of poetry is to give us back the situations of our dreams.

—Gaston Bachelard,
The Poetics of Space

A poetics must return to a way of dreaming works and the declarations that accompany them, of conceiving their possibility, and of working for their reality.

—Fernand Hallyn, *The Poetic Structure of the World*

Author's Note. I thank Yvonna Lincoln, Norman K. Denzin, John F. Sherry, Jr., Stephen Saraydar, Tracy Lewis, and Sara Varhus for their generous comments on earlier drafts of this chapter. I am also grateful to Beth Messana and Crystal Knowland for technical support along the way.

Stonehenge, Wessex Chalklands, July 21, 1997

A Gift of the Journey

Magical megaliths. Stonehenge. Sun mask. Druid dance.
The hand brushes the obelisk—mossy green and grey,
cold for a summer's day—dragging fingertips across
the texture. Braille for a pulse? We want to touch
the mystery of this place, even as the mind's eye squints

for a glimpse of deeper meanings, sequestered in time
and cultural distance, some of which seem to be murmured
in the eclipse of stones at dusk and dawn. But the magic
does not reside in the stones themselves. It is embedded in
the reading, the immersion of self in place, and the puzzle

of the circle that only gets more puzzling when spotted
by the eye of the sun. Like the morning dew, this Druid
magic is tied to a clock of nature. It emerges from nowhere
and disappears just as mysteriously with the heat of midday
—or too much inspection. Poets who would see this clearly

must chase the beams gently, introspectively, as they refract
on the traces of magicians and astronomers who have danced
through the bosom of these stones in patterns and rhythms
we hope are coded within us all. The experience steps us
into another reality and with all the power of ritual turns

day to dream, taking us out of ourselves for a while to show
us something about ourselves—about how we have been
and where we think we used to be—a kind of mythopoeic
archaeology. The best poets still know how to do it. Magic,
it seems, is a gift of the journey.

This is a poem I wrote about method (Brady, 2003b, p. 34). It suggests that one can get to know places marked as culturally distant through careful reflections on current experiences, that is, introspectively and imaginatively, relative to whatever hard facts or remnants may appear to lie at hand. That is how landscapes become semiotically rich, historical, and perhaps even sacred. They are projections of self, of each of us—all of us—now and before. But interpreting such investments from previous inhabitants is extraordinarily difficult, if for no other reason than the fact that even with widely shared constructs about the meaning of this place or that in any society, individual interpretations can vary widely. The same place can mean different things to different people in intensity of social and emotional commitment, if not in more dramatically different terms, even when they engage it on the same culturally standardized premises (e.g., when Americans visit the Grand Canyon or some other richly defined sacred national retreat). A sense of place, especially sacred space, shows all the volatility and variations of ritual inferences for these reasons (Brady, 1999). Moreover, as an interpreter from another cultural epoch, excavating that information in some semblance of its original form from an otherwise mute landscape cannot be done without a code or guide, living or otherwise, to the semiotic investments of those who have passed that way before and perhaps are no longer represented there (cf. Lame Deer & Erdoes, 1972, pp. 96–107). And even then, interpretations of artifact use or texts slide into the soup of polyvalence and multivocality and themselves become creative rejuvenations of performances tied through time to a sea of shifting landscapes—to the intertextualities of life that we study as ethnographers. For these and other reasons, places such as Stonehenge and the great petroglyph areas of the American Southwest are steeped in mystery, compelling and interesting in the shadows of their kinships to us but puzzles that are nonetheless ripe for wide-ranging interpretations.

That said, we must wonder what exactly environmentally concerned critics, such as poet Gary Snyder, nature writer Barry Lopez, mountain climber Jack Turner, and art historian Simon Schama, have in mind when they exhort us to relearn respect for the land we inhabit and to renew our ties to places both sacred and less exalted as a countermeasure to the thoughtless destruction of modern life.[1] I think that what they want us to know is a kind of history that includes, but reaches far beyond, what we can learn from the archaeologies and histories one finds in museums today (which are themselves, of course, specialized interpretations in their own right).[2] These caring citizens share a quest for personal knowledge, for self-conscious information about being-in-place, and for participation that can catch us in the act of complacency about who we are, where we have been, and where we are going and thereby might change our thinking about the meaning of life in the landscapes of our respective pasts and presents. What they seek is, in that sense, more poetic than scientific. They are committed more to methods of immersion and self-conscious saturation than to those of clinical distancing as forms of learning. Each approach in the extreme begs comparisons of peoples and their changing environmental circumstances, and each for those reasons is appropriate for pursuing the overall problem at hand, but the various approaches do so on vastly different terms of evidence and reporting. Our critics find common ground in the middle—respect for facts, as they can be determined more or less objectively, that is mixed with the first-person powers of poetic interpretation and representation (not just poetry). The overall effort loops into the area of educated imagination, that is, thoughtfulness focused on what is reasonable and possible in solving puzzles. On that score, poetics and science share common ground. Inference, speculation, and metaphor play an important role in both cases.[3] The result, in this case, is approximately what I have referred to elsewhere as "artful science."[4] It shows up here as prolegomena to a poetics of place pushed through the following five organizing questions. What are we supposed to learn from such environmental inquiries? What are the sources of information? What are the obstacles in and prospects for doing so? What can we hope to gain? How shall we tell the story?

What follows is an attempt to answer these questions and, in the process, outline a poetics of place with a conscience.[5] It is rooted in our propensities to make sense of material and imaginative experiences through projections of being-in-the-world and the use of our culturally appropriated bodies—our sensuous–intellectual apparatuses—as the primary instruments for doing so. It draws on landscapes variously described as "home," "wild," and "sacred," where the sensuous is conspicuously brought to the fore through most forms of participation (sites where emotional content often dominates conscious interpretations). It pursues knowledge mostly ignored or formally discounted by the extremes of logical positivism. It advocates as a complement (not as a replacement) *a kind of knowing and reporting* that (a) promotes phenomenology as a philosophy that puts the observer (the seeker, the knower) upfront in the equation of interpreting and representing experience; (b) pushes interpretive anthropology back into the loop of sensual experience, a body-centered position that includes a consideration of but transcends the sweeping metaphor that everything (e.g., people, landscapes) can and should be rendered as texts to be interpreted; (c) finds some continuity in the structures and orientations of body-groundedness and myth despite important limitations posed by language itself and by epistemic interference between the present and our preliterate past; and (d) gives poets special cachet through their offering forms of knowing and saying (robust metaphors and more) that can engage the senses and visions of being-in-place in ways that both exceed and complement more conventional strategies in anthropology and history. In deference to the critics named and the need for advocacy in the social sciences, all of this is tied to considerations of who we think we are, where we have been, and where we might go from here with the idea of reclaiming respect for the land and its inhabitants, human and otherwise, past and present.

Opportunity: Being There

> *I travel your length, like a river / I travel your body, like a forest, / Like a mountain path that ends at a cliff / I travel along the edge of your thoughts, / and my shadow falls from your white forehead, / my shadow shatters, and I gather the pieces / and go on with no body, groping my way.*
>
> —Octavio Paz, *Piedra de Sol*[6]

"Ways of dividing up space vary enormously in intricacy and sophistication, as do techniques of judging size and distance," Yi-Fu (1979, p. 34) tells us, and if we look for fundamental principles of spatial organization in all cultures, we find them in two kinds of facts: "the posture and structure of the human body, and the relations (whether close or distant) between human beings" (p. 34). We organize the space we occupy through intimate experiences with these two things to make it serve our social and physical needs.[7] That deeply evolved sense of place is strong and is linked to (among other things) natality, kinship, and mortality—to sacred and personal space, spiritual help, travel, the seasons, and the calendar (cf. Geertz, 1996, p. 259). Personal space itself is a collecting center for experience and identity construction, as an individual and as a member of groups, and is a center for *re*collection that can be variously hoarded and shared with others through storytelling about life as lived (Brady, 2003b, pp. xiv–xv). Movement in these fields creates histories and also puts an emphasis on the present. Thoughts about past landscapes are necessarily grounded in contemporary processes of mind and knowledge about being-in-place, so the cleavage between now and what we think "used to be" cannot just give itself to us freely sans interpretation. Historical knowledge of any kind involves a culturally constructed, cognitively filtered, and reciprocal process, an apprehension and a *re*presentation of place to mind and back again, revolving and evolving in its constructions.[8] It is a mixed conscious and unconscious process, received much like the patterns of puzzlements that we take to task in the circle of stones and, therefore, subject to a variety of selective perception biases and omissions, if not simply paving the high road to inventing the truth that we *need* to find, the conclusions that comfort and support us no matter what the evidence by other calculations.[9] Context is the key to it. Knowing the context of words, behaviors, and artifacts is practically everything for determining meaning. Whatever Stonehenge or other historical landscapes used to be, the larger point is that they can be known in meaningful elaborations only as they are grounded by perceptions in the moments of our current existence.[10] There is no way to bypass that process. That is the sine qua non of a poetics of place, of being-in-place, and it starts in the ultimate home—the embodied self.

Is there some common ground that can be apprehended through the trowels, brushes, and screens of the senses that will give us a realistic impression of life in ancient places and thereby address the concerns of our environmental critics? We are one species, one subspecies in biological form, embodied more or less the same everywhere, and as conscious beings we need to know (or think we know) where we are before we are able to choose definitive courses of action. The comparative framework provided by that posture gives us access to other humans through sympathy and empathy, that is, by tapping into "fellow feeling" with speculation and imagination at work, both of which are essential parts of the interpretive equation. Both can also be souped up in special ways by being on-site, in-place—by "being there" (cf. Geertz 1983)—anywhere. That by itself does not guarantee anything specific in terms of knowledge of culture or place. Getting *there* takes existing knowledge from which one can update or launch a new perspective, thereby invoking a boatload of biases and related selective constructions of mind about exactly *where* one is, "home" or not, and so on. But the processes of projecting a physical and cultured self on the places and moments at hand and making sense of them through an educated imagination—no matter how fantastic (we can learn things only in terms of what we already know)—are fundamental to human thought and, thus, to conditions of being-in-place. They provide a context for analogies between things present and past. Guided tours of historical and ancient places rely precisely on such in-person emulations to add realism (literally realization, an internalizing process) to the experience (see also Coles, 1979; Saraydar, 1976; Saraydar & Shimada, 1973). They also generally provide specific scripts or guidebooks to fill in historical details. That combination of "being and seeing" writ large situates itself in what we can call the *sensuous–intellectual continuum,* the biocultural grounding that we all bring to consciousness of being-in-place through our bodies and that, because of its integrated and systemic nature, can be represented in a common frame of reference (Blackburn, 1971). That is what makes us tick and know that we are ticking as sentient beings, as movers and makers of metaphors in place—the baseline of being and seeing and sharing it with others.[11]

By using this model and relying especially on the comparative strengths of engaging in "parallel enterprises" as humans,[12] it follows that we can tap into the sensuous–intellectual continuum as we know and experience it, heighten consciousness of our own culturally constructed screens of beliefs and behaviors (with and without scripts of expert testimony), and draw reasonable conclusions about how we are now as beings *in* and *of* place and perhaps what it *might* have been like to have occupied and left our marks on particular landscapes before us.

Getting There: The Ontogeny of Space and Place

Man is nowhere anyway/Because nowhere is here/And I am here to testify.

—Jack Kerouac, *Mexico City Blues*[13]

"*Getting* there" complements "*being* there" as an important concept in ethnography and must be maintained in any attempt to create a poetics of place. Approaching literature as an existentialist, and thereby leapfrogging any narrowly textual or ethnographic forms of analysis in favor of an anthropology of experience, poet/ethnographer Michael Jackson puts a premium on the meaning in journeying rather than on the stacked-up facts that an ethnographer is likely to report after having reached and researched a destination. Jackson (1995) argues that "the authenticity of ethnographic knowledge depends on the ethnographer recounting in detail the events and encounters that are the grounds on which the very possibility of this knowledge rests" (p. 163). Getting to that point cognitively is seldom discussed in any ethnographic context. But that is where a phenomenological account of being-in-place must begin. Let me start with myself, going and being nowhere in particular (something on the order of my current employment), just negotiating my own existence in space and place.[14]

For me, *space* is transparent, ethereal, abstract, a vacuum cornered in the mind's eye abstractly as empty geometry. It is a cognitive and culturally defined container of sorts into which concrete and meaningful things can occur or be put. *Place,* in my comfortable view, is a filled space, tangible, concrete, habitable, traversable, or defined specifically against such interests as those unavailable for human occupation (e.g., mountain peaks). It is the geography of earth, mind, body, and lived experience, the semiotically enriched site of events human and otherwise. It is where whatever happens in my experience does happen. My experience also leads me to believe that all people make something special of their engagements with the properties of place, including drawing boundaries of time, space, consciousness, and memory of being in it to orient and define themselves (see also Basso 1996a, 1996b; Feld, 1982; Feld & Basso, 1996; Low & Lawrence-Zúñiga, 2003; Yi-Fu, 1979). They make life-in-place meaningful and push it way beyond shelter making and survival (Danesi & Perron, 1999, p. 137). They turn it into signifying systems, render it in signs and images of themselves, apprehend it through metaphors and imagery of their own making—their languages, cultures, and histories—and use it to govern relations among families, native and stranger, own and other, things near and far, things past and future, and the everyday realities of being in particular places. They mark it with their embraces and alienations of kinship in a composite world, their horizons and trails of history, and the eschatologies of their fears. They find it in the high peaks of their hearts and minds and externalize the imprints of both in the physical world by accident and by design while exploring, claiming, residing, nurturing, repelling, depositing, building, storying, and sometimes even erasing the paths of their lives. For these reasons, as soon as we start identifying features of landscape (peopled or not) and marking off boundaries (actual or implied), we situate ourselves in particular concepts of place—in something approximating, by structure and category, the worldviews and histories of the cultures whose members "make sense" of these experiences—ours and those of others.

Nevertheless, thinking about space as a container for place can be misleading for analytic purposes (cf. Hirsch & O'Hanlon, 1995; Low & Lawrence-Zúñiga, 2003), especially when one projects that sequence on the ontogeny of place in individual experience (cf. Thompson, 1989, p. 127)—the essence of a phenomenological stance.[15] The conceptual relationship between space and place is transitional and metonymic, but not necessarily unidirectional in our emerging consciousness. The connection of bringing place to consciousness creates the illusion that its meaning is a function of the landscape itself, something external and discovered, shaped beyond us. But as Schama (1995) says, "Before it can ever be a repose for the senses, landscape is the work of the mind. Its scenery is built up as much from state of memory as from layers of rock" (pp. 6–7). A sense of being-in-place is given to us cognitively at some deep level, but it is also appropriated by culture and rendered meaningful in a variety of ways. It is a manufactured concept, a pan-human construct that anchors our sense of meaningful location—our *position in* space relative to other specific people or things (including social distance between persons or objects)—and it comes to mind only as our *re*presentational capacity makes the world appear twice: "once as a recalcitrant external reality and again as a malleable inner actuality" (Brann, 1991, p. 7).[16] Places in this way are turned into cultural products, and our experiences of them, as Casey (1996) argues persuasively, are "never precultural or presocial" (p. 17). From a phenomenological perspective, the ontogeny is such that we emerge consciously *in* an occupied place and abstract the concept of space from that. In a phenomenological account, place is prior to space. It is *where* being-in-the-world happens.[17] The *how* of it includes concrete immediacy in perception: Lowe (1982) says, "Before anything else, it is for me a real, pretheoretical world, wherein I undertake everyday living. This is my primary reality" (p. 170).[18] Moreover, Casey (1996) continues, even though a phenomenological approach has "its own prejudicial commitments and ethnocentric stances," its commitment to concrete description honors the experiences of its practitioners. That connects both the anthropological field-worker and the indigenes in place: "Both have no choice but to begin with experience. As Kant insisted, 'there can be no doubt that all our knowledge begins with experience'" (p. 16; see also Csordas, 1994).[19]

Imagination: Primary Transport

I think I have told you, but if I have not, you must have understood, that a man who has a vision is not able to use the power of it until after he has performed the vision on earth for the people to see.

—Black Elk, *Black Elk Speaks*[20]

We can add poets to the list of those conjoined by a phenomenological perspective (Heidegger, 1971) and use that thought to invite a deeper investigation of the role of imagination and creativity in constructing a poetics of place. Because places function as grounds for our projections of self and culture and a history of both—one private, the other public, all of it personal—and because we convert our place experiences into the "idioms" (the language and images) of the world as we know it, believe it, see it, and ordinarily argue it, the content may include what noninitiates see as mythical impossibilities (including landscapes peopled by spirits, etc.).[21] That interiorizing and largely unconscious process is often taken for granted or conflated with the significance that people assign to what they see as the dominant or "definitive" contents of particular landscapes. These are specific constructs for mentally centering and filing one kind of experience or another, including the circumscriptions of turf traveled on foot or touched only in our imaginations. Thus, place is defined by what we see in terms of landscape features through projections of self and culture and, therefore, by fantasy and wish fulfillment and other trappings of consciousness in the identity of the perceivers. For these same reasons, Thompson (1989) sees history as

> an imaginary landscape—a tableau of battles for some, a mural of scientific discoveries and technological inventions for others; and for those who avert their eyes from horizons of mystery or hallways of propaganda, there still remains an internal cinema of unconsciously edited perceptions in which self is the *figure* and nature the *ground.* (p. 127)

In fact, he suggests that "consciousness itself, as either a Buddhist heap (*skandha*) or a scientific narrative, is a landscape, for one cannot know without a world" (p. 127). Life in this sense is a constant process of negotiating landscapes (internal and external), and interpretation is as necessary to the process as is breathing, no matter how bizarre or fantastic it may seem from the outside looking in.

These creative dimensions, flexibilities, and transitive minglings of process pose a variety of analytic problems and beg the question of how we will tell the stories of places that structure our lives.[22] The concept of place cannot in any absolute way be separated from its contents—from the meanings assigned to its location and the activities or features marked in association with it. It cannot be seen as a "thing in itself." That would require an unobtainable absolute or clinical view beyond the cultural constructions of human consciousness (and that is why both logical positivism and, ultimately, hermeneutic "bracketing" fail here). But we can get closer to the essence of the concept of place—to the concrete and the sublime and largely ineffable qualities of it as a stabilizing, orienting framework for action—by looking for common denominators in the diversity of the meanings assigned to it by ourselves and others. Whatever they are, they ultimately form a comparative context with a personal sense of home at the center.

Universal Place: Home and Hearth

He had no use for sensual gratification, unless that gratification consisted of pure, incorporeal odors. He had no use for creature comforts either and would have been quite content to set up camp on bare stone.

—Patrick Suskind, *Perfume*[23]

"Like a mirror," Snyder (1990) writes, "a place can hold anything, on any scale" (p. 25). Everyone knows that it holds a sense of "home" at its roots.[24]

We all have homes, and in some ways none of us has the same one. Individual perceptions and experiences vary to the point where even family experiences shared in the same geographic location, in a common dwelling, and in the same hearth from childhood to old age do not produce clones. There are always individual versions of the experience. We mark them with personal names and related claims, and we spend time pooling them more or less in our stories and related interactions with others as a way of constructing the social reality of events that define home for all. Home is, in this sense, a place held in common by experience but unpackable in its semiotic particulars as a single version for each person involved. It is never "a seamless whole, a single story. Our imaginations set free in us other selves that seldom see the light. We lead several lives in the course of one" (Jackson, 1995, p. 161).

Despite sometimes radical differences in cultural content, in this ego-centered and relativistic way our homes are the essence of our being-in-place and our becomings in life. Even at their weakest and most fragmented moments, they are grounded in bodily experiences as emotionally loaded and semiotically coded memories, either positive or negative, and they all have a networking or centrifugal quality attached to them. These bundles of thoughts and emotions fan out as meaningful expectations about how life is or ought to be in relations with others, intersecting with the hearths and homes in surrounding neighborhoods and regions and ultimately linking up with the natal centers, the fetal and fatal places, the ancestral turfs of the rest of the world. Various physical and cultural processes make that a shifting landscape, including natural disasters, the aggrandizements and failures of colonial expansions and conquering economies, the fortunes and misfortunes of war, and the furrows of migration plowed by things such as homesteading, job seeking, refugee evacuations, and the influential cultural ship jumpers—the beachcombers of life—crossing into the frontiers of strangers and making homes there. Although certain adaptations must be made in new places (including the option of "going home"), on some scale migrants always carry their homes with them in the form of the languages, cultures, and traditions that defined their natal places (Jackson, 1995; Marshall, 2004). There is security in the transportable nest of knowledge that we call culture—the histories and desires embedded in knowing how to make and provision a hearth, in deciding who should share it and the wedding bed, and in determining where all of it literally might be placed.[25]

One good bet nowadays is that most people will not place a long-term hearth in what they consider to be a wilderness area. Doing so through the orientations and transport of modern culture puts many elements of the environment at risk, including one's own body—especially for the uninitiated. That would also constitute yet another episode in—a continuation of powerful forces already set in motion by—colonization and urbanization. But these concerns can also be very misleading. Wilderness has always been fundamental to human experience. For hundreds of thousands of years, nature has been more than a place to visit. Snyder (1990) says that it *is* home, a territory with more *and* less familiar places. Some "are more difficult and remote, but all are *known* and even named" (p. 7).[26] Nonetheless, some places in our modern experiences remain decidedly "wild," beyond the pale of what most of us would consider comfortable and secure habitation. What urbanites see as wilderness today helps to define the centering concept of home place in the breach, that is, by conceptualizing what is plainly *not* home—and that can foster two dramatically different consequences. One is to relegate such areas to a netherland of mind, out of sight and out of concern, thereby letting the strip-and-sweep policies of economic development take their tolls on these places unnoticed. Such culture runs its course, economies are stimulated, hearths get provisioned by the substantially employed, the rich get richer, ancestral places get erased at exponential rates, and no one except the developers, the politicians, the people exploited on the margins, and a few odd ethnographers seem to care. The other consequence is to recognize wilderness as foundational to our history of being-in-place in the long run as humans, let alone what is arguably a key to the future of the planet itself. This reaction shows up as an attempt to cherish and preserve what remains as wilderness, to learn from it some of the things we used to know about sustaining ourselves in body and spirit, and that in turn makes every such experience a candidate for creating sacred space. Mindful of the foundations of body and home, let me consider each of the categories of wild and sacred landscapes in more detail and then talk about their relationships and how we story them in ways that matter.

Wild Places and the Assembly of All Beings

The rain comes over the hills, / like fluttering birds it comes. / I stand in my brother's tears / happy as the running stream. / Ho! Brother. / Tread upon the wide plains. / Lonely rugged mountains rule the land.

—Archie Weller, "The Hunter"[27]

"Wild" places, such as home turf and sacred spaces, are sites where emotional content often dominates interpretations. If you say that you are going to live "in the wild" or "go wild" or just be "wild at parties," no one ever thinks that you are about to be placid and contemplative. Internally, we are in fact rooted in whatever was and is wild by our biology—by our "creatureliness." As a conscious motivation, aiming to "be wild" is a commitment of an embodied self to irregular and emotionally stimulating conditions. Externally, wild is a condition of landscape that modern Westerners might contemplate in fantasy or engage in person as adventurers, explorers, or castaways, among other marginal categories of being. The point is that being of the flesh and working in and with wild things in wild areas is a source of special identity for most of us, a marker of unusual boundaries. When *wild* becomes a *where,* it generally transforms into *wilderness,* a condition of wild landscape, a place where meaning abounds. It is, therefore, ripe picking for poets and artisans of all types, for all who would love its riches and lament its losses. It forms another "architectonic" link to the peoples and processes that are fundamental to a poetics of place.[28] But *where* is it? Gone? Seldom near? Far away and gasping for breath under the crush of a global economy? Or, is it somehow all of the above yet always with us? Snyder (1990) has some answers.

A Western sense of the "wild" is a place where "nature" rules—a place marked by ancient and eternal activities, untamed animals, uncultivated plants, and "an ordering of impermanence," if not "unruliness, disorder, and violence" (Snyder, 1990, p. 5). Although wilderness cannot be seen in any way other than through the screens of culture, it is commonly thought of as an environment that is culturally unbuilt, ungoverned, unscarred, or otherwise unmodified by humans. Encountering it always gets our attention in special ways. *Where* we find it is important. It is not confined to isolated mountains, deserts, or forests. Snyder (1990) reminds us that "a ghost wilderness hovers around the entire planet; the millions of tiny seeds of the original vegetation are hiding in the mud on the foot of an Arctic tern, in the dry desert sands, or in the wind" (p. 14). He suggests that it may, in fact, return at some point, although not in "as fine a world as the one that was glistening in the early morning of the Holocene" (p. 14). Wildness, on the other hand, is now and has always been everywhere with its "ineradicable populations of fungi, moss, mold, yeast, and such that surround and inhabit us. Deer mice on the back porch, deer bounding across the freeway, pigeons in the park, spiders in the corners" (p. 14). Urbanites live constantly in a sublimated or ignored wildness in this sense (bug and vermin exterminators take care of the rest), and although it can be a source of both reverence and wonder for the people who case its margins, enter it, and dwell in it for any length of time, the wilderness where wildness dominates is often consciously displaced, moved to its own outback in the geography of our minds until it shows up in a television travelogue or the vicarious thrill of adventure novels or Arctic explorer accounts-turned-coffee table displays.[29]

The wilderness that most people know is "a charade of areas, zones, and management plans that is driving the real wild into oblivion" (J. Turner, 1996, p. 23). It is a nice place to visit through the glass of an automobile in the national parks of Nairobi or Yellowstone or in the few brave steps from the paved roads that roll through these areas like carpets for the conquering kings.[30] Few would want to live there. The farmers of these margins get a little closer to the culturally untamed, but only on the other sides of their fences. More than anyone, their job for thousands of years has been to erase the wilderness, homestead its meadows, tame its grasses, and replace its original animals with liveries and livestock. But all of the farmers in the world cannot hold a candle to the environmental corruptions and erasures of the great urban developers. Our wild landscapes have changed as wildernesses have disappeared.

Snyder (1990) asks us to stand up and be counted on this both intellectually and ecologically:

> Wilderness is a place where the wild potential is fully expressed, a diversity of living and nonliving beings flourishing according to their own sorts of order. In ecology we speak of "wild system." When an ecosystem is fully functioning, all members are present at the assembly. To speak of wilderness is to speak of wholeness. Human beings came out of that wholeness, and to consider the possibility of reactivating membership in the Assembly of All Beings is in no way regressive. (p. 12)

But we have to ask how that can be done. How will we know when it *is* being done? Where is the map for being-in-place this way? Some of the answers lie in history. Others lie in the politics and sensitivities of the moment. The only sure way of putting them together is to increase one's awareness of and participation in the landscapes of lived experience.[31] Moreover, raising the stakes on both our being-in-place and having been there, Lopez (1990b), asserts,

> A sense of place must include, at the very least, knowledge of what is inviolate about the relationship between a people and the place they occupy, and certainly, too, how the destruction of this relationship, or the failure to attend to it, wounds people. Living in North America and trying to develop a philosophy of place—a recognition of the spiritual and psychological dimensions of geography—inevitably brings us back to our beginnings here, to the Spanish incursion. (p. 41)

It brings us back to the history of a place whose home crossings have uprooted practically everything indigenous and wild and have pushed it around in a movable tragedy of cross-cultural casualties and increasingly fluid disconnections from the land itself. That marks a dramatic change from what was once kindled and supplicated in the worldviews of many people, including Native Americans (see, e.g., Deloria, 1993), to something profane and dangerous. Setting overromanticized views of noble savages and pristine nature aside, one can discover that both kinds of circumstances—supportive and accommodating or dangerous to one's well-being—can hold value as "sacred" at one level or another. Only corruption kills the prospect altogether.

Sacred Spaces and Myth

> *There is a place of great importance to me on a pine-skirted plateau in Utah's Uinta Mountains. Elk and deer weave trails of meaning through the trees and into the escape of cliffs and heavy timber; coyotes plant scat, gorged with hair and bone, among sagebrush and juniper. The place resounds with voices of birds and small mammals, and a thousand smells of the wilderness. To me, this place is cleanly holy. I cannot explain why; I only know that for twenty years it has filled me with awe and yearning, and solitude and peace. It is a space of great sacredness, seldom visited, always appreciated.*
>
> —Richard Poulsen, *The Pure Experience of Order*[32]

Perhaps no other experiential domain shows the "made" or implied impositions of culture on geography more than places held to be sacred by the beholders (Brady, 2004). They are precious by definition. On the positive and more conventional side of that, the combination of cultural values and memory applied to such places can produce a poetics of reverie and respect, of awe and mystery, if not specific rituals designed to commemorate and renew such experiences.[33] But we know that the same places can be experienced very differently (the "parallax factor"). Unlike stepping in the puddles on a clay road after a rain, one can step in some sacred space as an outsider and never feel the change.[34] As Nelson (1983) observes quite correctly,

> Reality is not the world as it is perceived directly by the senses; reality is the world as it is perceived by the mind through the medium of the senses.... [It] is what we have learned to see through our own traditions, and they do not always line up as equivalents from one culture to the next. The interactions between Koyukon people and nature illustrate this clearly, for theirs is a world in which nature moves with power and humans are bound to a special system of environmental morality. (p. 239)[35]

Such space is easily trammeled by the uninitiated, by the claims of interlopers—the mini-colonials that ethnocentrism makes of us—who see all before them as an unfolding of their own turf. Access to the initiates' codes can save us from this error, that is, at least remind us that natural landscapes are everywhere more than physiography. They are, first and foremost, repositories of meaning that, not counting our own impositions of view and minus an artifact or two to flag other human presence, are most likely to remain invisible without a living guide.[36]

Investing the experiences of smell, taste, touch, sight, and hearing in a landscape whose features endear themselves to us or frighten us is a way of appropriating meaningful contexts in which to exist; to act in pleasure and remembrance; to meditate, marvel, and mystery over; to *re*assure; to *re*issue; to *re*member as a *re*consideration of life circumstances in plans for the future, for the next step, perhaps for the rest of our lives and the emplotments of our deaths. Such projections can make sacred space in our mind's eye and the behaviors steered by it; they create places for communion, ecstatic immersion, or other forms of poetic inspiration, on the one hand, and places for piaculum, supplication out of fear and anxiety (Yi-Fu, 1979), literally places to be avoided except under the most carefully calculated circumstances (e.g., rituals of sacrifice), on the other.[37] But the separation of these forms is not always clear because of cross-cultural misunderstandings and the knowledge that opposite interpretations can occupy the same geographic location (Brady, 2003b, pp. 93–100; Fernandez, 2003). There is also always much that appears "in between." Sacred places can stand alone as territory marked in the minds of those who know of them vicariously or in person. But when engaged in person and recognized as such, they inevitably beg questions of boundaries (where the sacred "ends" and something more secular begins) and thereby form an avenue to liminality, that is, to spiritual or imaginary places and conditions of being not only between particular people and their geography but also in the alignments of persons and spirits in a community that ostensibly shares such views.[38] These are "neither here nor there" spaces that become a crossing ground for senses of self and cultures, individuals and gods, powerful landscapes and access to the sublime, among other possibilities. That does not make them any less stimulating to the imagination or diminish the need to know how we, as intruders or observers, might or might not fit into them. On the contrary, once discovered, culturally defined environmental borders are even more likely to be conspicuous and puzzling if for no other reason than the semiotic diversity of their stimulations and expressions.[39]

Opaque Facilitator: The Native Myth-Mind

> *The leaves on the trees, the grasses on the hills and in the valleys, the waters in the creeks and in the rivers and the lakes, the four-legged and the two-legged and the wings of the air—all danced together to the music of the stallion's song.*
>
> —Black Elk, *Black Elk Speaks*[40]

All other things being equal, language communicates the mental being and moods corresponding to it in the communicator. "In the psychotopographic universe, language is also subject to transformation, and its disintegration from a vehicle for recognizable human communication into something 'other'—both divine and demonic—also signals the shift in the transcendental world of merged subject and object" (Nelson, 1996, p. 106). That makes the story context or form of communicating voice paramount to its meaning, and it includes stories about place, some of which are focused on places that are both wild *and* sacred. Among the gatherers and hunters of the world, these are sites that are rich with meaning and power and that have multiple uses (e.g., menstrual seclusion, graveyards, ritual initiations) and realities tied to them. They are the stuff of legends tied to human and more-than-human landscapes, and the memories of them "are very long" (Snyder, 1990, pp. 81–82).[41] One reason for "the profound association between storytelling and the more-than-human terrain" in tribal societies, as Abram (1996) suggests, is that it "resides in the encompassing, enveloping wholeness of a story in relation to the characters that act and move within it" (p. 163). Indeed, because "we are situated in the land in much the same way that characters are situated in a story," the members of a deeply oral culture may experience this relation "as something more than mere analogy; along with the other animals, the stones, the trees, and the clouds, we ourselves are characters within a huge story that is visibly unfolding all around us, participants within the vast imagination or dreaming of the world" (p. 163)—and that is, at best, a shifting landscape, a moving target, but not totally beyond the scope of reclamations.[42]

From his travels in Australia, Snyder (1990) offers the following "as one example of the many ways [in which] landscape, myth, and information were braided together in preliterate societies":

> We were traveling by truck over dirt tract west from Alice Springs in the company of a Pintubi elder named Jimmy Tjungurrayi. As we rolled along the dusty road, sitting back in the bed of a pickup, he began to speak very rapidly to me. He was talking about a mountain over there, telling me a story about some wallabies that came to that mountain in the dreamtime and got into some kind of mischief with some lizard girls. He had hardly finished that and he started in on another story about another hill over here and another story over there. I couldn't keep up. I realized after about half an hour of this that these were tales to be told while *walking*, and that I was experiencing a speeded-up version of what might be told over several days of foot travel. Mr. Tjungurrayi felt graciously compelled to share a body of lore with me by virtue of the simple fact that I was there.
>
> So remember a time when you journeyed on foot over hundreds of miles, walking fast and often traveling at night, traveling night-long and napping in the acacia shade during the day, and these stories were told to you as you went. In your travels with an older person, you were given a map you could memorize, full of lore and song and also practical information. Off by yourself, you could sing those songs to bring yourself back. And you could maybe travel to a place that you'd never been, steering only by the songs you had learned. (pp. 82–83)

Even this little snippet about sacred space illustrates nicely the principle that existential interpretations situated in worldviews give place a temporal dimension and also reflect both the predicaments and the solutions to them posed by changing environmental circumstances.[43] Focusing in particular on Native American materials, Leonard and McClure (2004) see such stories as important

> because in them the mythic breaks through into our present world, embodying the very kinds of boundary crossing that are so central to all mythological thinking. *Such stories give us a chance to see, to feel, the present of mythic truth in the midst of our perceptions of contemporary reality.* Whether they are the repositories of national or ethnic identity or the site of supernatural revelation or visitation, whether they are actual places where we can stand and hear the echoes of long-ago battles or imaginary places shaped by the requirements of mythic vision, sacred places serve to teach and remind us of who we are and how we ought to behave in our day-to-day lives. . . . Sacred places, especially in the

> various senses that Native Americans use the term, call out to us to *become* "down to earth," to remember and honor and revitalize our essential connections to the earth and the natural world, to the sacred all around us. They invite us to associate the spiritual with such natural material phenomena as mountains, rivers, lakes, trees, and caves. The study of stories about sacred places might just allow us to see such opposed binaries as past versus present, realistic versus mythological, or spiritual versus material as not so mutually exclusive. (p. 320, emphasis added)[44]

Certain places within the mutually owned territory of old cultures, Snyder (1990) says, are loaded with "numinous life and spirit." They are "perceived to be of high spiritual density because of plant or animal habitat intensities, or associations with legend, or connections with human totemic ancestry, or because of some geomorphological anomaly, or some combination of qualities" (p. 93). They are cultural and spiritual "gates through which one can—it would be said—more easily be touched by a larger-than-human, larger-than-personal, view" (p. 93; see also Deloria, 1993; Munn, 2003). Such sites offer a glimpse of the internal workings of belief and behaviors that put cultural histories into ecologies of place, some of which might be seen as "spiritual game management" (Snyder, 1990, p. 87). They also show us that storytelling is much more than amusement. It is fundamental to human life—especially (it seems) in myth, where one can change the content and bend the structure to achieve common understanding of perennial problems. Indeed, Verene (1976) finds that "human understanding must always have at its center the notion of the myth. In its movement toward the recollecting of origin, it discovers always again the myth, the original power of image-making or mimesis, the science of which, as Vico says, is the first that must be learned" (p. 34).

Within limits of coherence of the whole, consistency of theme, and related structural concerns, myths are a flexible and highly generalizable form of storytelling about the past in personal terms. They are linked to the now and then through one Gordian knot or another in terms aimed specifically at stirring up something poetic in the audience.[45] Poetry itself is tied to the context of the immediate and the immanent, to the processes of "being there" and sensual saturation, and to the art of the possible and not necessarily the actual, in or out of what might seem to be an obvious historical or mythological context (Brady, 2003b). Like myth, poetry addresses the long run by allowing for diverse particulars in accounting for events of the moment in forms that tap into the larger continuities and commonalities of being human. Access to some of this material is guaranteed through studies of oral poetry, for much of that is tied directly to the timekeepings and implications of ritual and myth, to stories of origins and the peoplings of landscapes through events and discoveries over time as conceptualized by the tellers—and perhaps defended in what is viewed from other perspectives as a mix of fantasy and reality (Tedlock, 1983, p. 55). In this way, myths provide a complicated source of information on worldviews and associated behaviors that pervades both history (with its mix of literate and preliterate participants) and prehistory (with its exclusively preliterate participants) and thereby helps to frame meaning and action in our lives today.[46]

Schama (1995), in his provocatively aesthetic and historical *Landscape and Memory,* argues that to put that to work in environmental review and renewal, "what we need are new 'creation myths' to repair the damage done by our recklessly mechanical abuse of nature and to restore the balance between man and the rest of the organisms with which he shares the planet" (p. 13; see also Kozinets & Sherry, 2004; Leonard & McClure, 2004, p. 324; Richardson, 1975; Saraydar, 1986; Sherry & Kozinets, 2004).[47] Wondering whether or not this is a cure for what ails us is not "to deny the seriousness of our ecological predicament, nor to dismiss the urgency with which it needs repair and redress" (Schama, 1995, p. 14), but we have to ask about the old ones in the process:

> For notwithstanding the assumption, commonly asserted in these texts, that Western culture has

> evolved by sloughing off its nature myths, they have, in fact, never gone away. For if, as we have seen, our entire landscape tradition is the product of shared culture, it is by the same token a tradition built from a rich deposit of myths, memories, and obsessions. The cults which we are told to seek in other native cultures—of the primitive forest, of the river of life, of the sacred mountain—are in fact alive and well and all about us *if we only know where to look for them.* (p. 14, emphasis added)[48]

On the premise that "strength is often hidden beneath the commonplace," Schama's study is "constructed as an excavation below our conventional sight-level to recover the veins of myth and memory that lie beneath the surface" (p. 14). It is an archaeology of knowledge, another architectonic connection to a poetics of place that supplements and gives new instructions to the more parochial endeavors of academic archaeology and history. It is a deeply poetized effort that may coach us into finding something of our internal but dusty guidebooks in the places set aside as wilderness in our cultural traditions and in portrayals of those and other landscapes in writing, painting, and photography, both past and present. It is "a way of looking, of rediscovering what we already have, but which somehow eludes our recognition and our appreciation. Instead of being yet another explanation of what we have lost, it is an exploration of what we may yet find" (p. 14).[49]

Snyder and others share the hope in this. The native myth-mind—first encountered by Europeans in North America by Cabeza de Vaca, last known fully by the Native American Ishi—is "not dead and gone. It is perennially within us, dormant as a hard-shelled seed, awaiting the fire or flood that awakes it again" (Snyder, 1990, p. 13; cf. Saraydar, 1986). This thinking again raises the issue of both myth-time and history in relation to landscape. "We are all capable of extraordinary transformations. In myth and story, these changes are animal-to-human, human-to-animal, animal-to-animal, or even farther leaps" (Snyder, 1990, p. 20) to other shared forms of being-in-place,[50] including the dreams we have had about such things and the oral and graphic representations we have left behind in the winding and sometimes broken trails of being human over the long haul. "The essential nature" of being in any part of this equation, Snyder asserts with optimism, "remains clear and steady through these changes" (p. 20). That does not guarantee access to the particulars of our pasts, of course, but it does put us in a perpetual and comparative present of sorts. We cannot lose sight of ourselves even if we try, and yet even when we look closely, we find fuzzy boundaries, much to learn, and much that is known at some level but difficult to express.

▣ Intangible Obstacles: Beyond Words

> *What moves on this archaic force / Was wild and welling at the source.*
>
> —N. Scott Momaday, *The Way to Rainy Mountain*[51]

Myth and history are two related ways in which we have kept records of being around as conscious beings-in-place for many thousands of years.[52] But despite a track record of sameness in narrative form, especially written form, there is nothing in the rulebook that precludes innovation in the presentation of either (Brady, 2004). The pervasiveness of myth in all aspects of our lives shows that not to be a new idea in itself, and history in its most conventional sense, spliced into myth-time as a form of accounting since the advent of writing and the genre building of modern academies, can also be a poem (Brady, 2003b; Dening, 1995, 1998a). Getting at the larger goals of environmental reform staked out here might benefit by building on the kinds of narrative and artistic diversity in Schama's (1995) compilation, not only by taking a new look at some older ways of telling the story of being-in-place but also by carefully inspecting what exactly is conveyed by such storying by asking about the larger perceptual context.

Reading within and between the lines of Schama's inspiring work suggests quite readily that some of what we seek in a poetics of place, both ancient and modern, lies beyond words. Language gathers at the root of all storytelling, including myth, but as Jackson (1995) says, it does not exhaust its content or its possibilities. Experience covers everything. Words do not.[53] Consciousness itself is mediated through language, and image and everything that we know emerges in one form or another from experiences of landscape and story. "Such a conception of fieldwork implies a conception of writing" (p. 113) and of language as constitutive of reality, but it does not restrict the inquiry to it even as it puts considerable emphasis on "the creative and ethical domains of human social existence" (Jackson, 1982, p. 2). The oral storyteller and the writer share the task of revealing "people to themselves and to their possibilities" (p. 2).[54] Furthermore, during this modern age,

> one must have recourse to art and literature if one is to keep alive a sense of what hard science, with its passion for definitive concepts and systematic knowledge, often forgoes or forgets. The painter who dispenses with framing in order to reunite the field of artistic vision with the space of the world, or the composer who breaks down the boundaries between what is deemed music and noise . . . find a natural ally in the philosopher who, aware that concepts never cover the fullness of human experience, sees that task of description as more compelling than that of explanation [including descriptions of being-in-place] (Jackson, 1995, pp. 4–5)[55]

Nonetheless, posing a conundrum of sorts, it is through the conveyance forms and content of language and story that we must enter an *analysis* of places and the events that unfold in them. Like the oral performances that house myths in some embrace of the long-run and second-tier translations of them by experts with their own cultural and textual biases, we need to learn how to interpret the places and events of others and relate them to our own sensuous-intellectual experiences with the best possible representations, that is, in a manner true to what we know, think, and *can* say with reasonable persuasion. But the sources of that information and the language we need to use to understand and communicate it are not always easily obtained—if they are obtained at all.

Limited Opportunity: Oral Poetry and Myth

> *[Secret Road:] There are trees, crags, gorges, rivers, precipitous places of precipitous land, various places of precipitous land, various precipitous places, gorges, various gorges. It is a place of wild animals, a place of wild beasts, full of wild beasts. It is a place where one is put to death by stealth; a place where one is put to death in the jaws of the wild beasts of the land of the dead.*
>
> —Bernardino de Sahagún, "Aztec Definitions"[56]

What is lost from, or created and added to, discourse when it is moved from one person to the next in the same culture pool? Across cultural and linguistic boundaries? It is important to remember the dialogic character of such communications and to keep in mind Bakhtin's wisdom that language never moves through uncluttered space. It is heteroglossic and mutually constructive in all utterances—all contexts of development, reception, and discovery (Holquist, 1981, p. xx; 1990, p. 69). Combined with what can be learned from history, archaeology, and on-site experiences (however changed over time), we can bolster our sense of past landscapes by studying the legends and tales, the myths and meanings, as we discover them through oral and written texts and the performances and translations of each. They all are, at one level or another, functions of language, and in the quest to understand the nature of being-in-place, language and storytelling are essential but also, in some ways, are inadequate to the task.

In some of his pioneering work on Native American narratives, Hymes (1987) points out that ethnopoetics necessarily starts with language (p. 80), that "it is first of all a matter of taking seriously the ways in which narrators select and group words" (p. 41), and that the stories of Native American oral discourse "are to be heard, or seen, in lines, and thus are a form of poetry" (p. 49; see also Kroeber, 1983; Swann, 1983; Tedlock, 1972, 1983; Zolbrod, 1983). This is fairly recent and profound thinking that runs against the grain of Western ethnocentrisms concerning what does and does not count as poetry. As Zolbrod (1983) says, it has taken a while for scholars to recognize that there is a substantial Native American poetic tradition once misperceived as little more than "casual tale-telling" that is conspicuously poetic to those who know how to recognize its "implicit semantic and rhetorical patterns" and who understand that performance and setting have "a bearing on the utterance of a storyteller not evident in ordinary prose" or in "the printed medium conventionally employed by most translators" (p. 227).[57]

This is empowering knowledge. Tedlock (1983) argues that treating oral narratives as dramatic poetry

> clearly promises many analytic . . . [and] aesthetic rewards. The apparent flatness of many past translations is not a reflection but a distortion of the originals, caused by the dictation process, the notion that content and form are independent, a pervasive deafness to oral qualities, and a fixed notion of the boundary between poetry and prose. Present conditions, which combine new recording techniques with a growing sensitivity to verbal art as performed "event" rather than as fixed "object" on the page, promise the removal of previous difficulties. (pp. 54–55)

Moreover, taking advantage of the poetic dimension in every act of speech or writing (which is "related but not identical to its linguistic dimension") and recognizing that all people in the world "continuously produce, reproduce, and revise their own cultures in dialogues among themselves," with or without ethnographers present, as an act of being human, language's dialogical potential can be used "to balance each representation with an alternative representation, producing poetry that is built on a process of translation rather than made to resist translation" (Tedlock, 1999, p. 155). But projecting the most modern of mentalities—reading as an avenue to interpretation—as a facile metaphor on all that we wish to understand (e.g., "reading" oral performances and landscapes) can be an obstacle in the study of both oral *and* written traditions, that is, a problem in translating Native American and comparable oral presentations firsthand and also in deciphering the written translations we get from others before us (see, e.g., Finnegan, 1992; Hymes, 1987; Kroeber, 1983; Saraydar, 1986; Swann & Krupat, 1987; Tedlock, 1983, 1993, 1999). Times have changed, and our sensibilities have changed along with them.

▣ Perceptual Obstacles: Epistemic Interference

> *At first there is just one line, horizontal / A second appears / It's already closer / Soon one notices lines everywhere / They draw rapidly together / Too late one realizes that / There is no escape.*
>
> —Walter Helmut Fritz, "Fesselung [Entrapment]"[58]

Texts are an important avenue to the discovery of place in its diverse purchases and appearances everywhere, but using them as evidence for anything is problematic, in part because of the creativities inherent in text construction and reception that change with contexts of interpretation (as we all know and as the history of hermeneutics and interpretive social science in general shows) and in part because of diversity in textual form, performance, and appreciation (cf. Finnegan, 1992, p. xii; Lansing, 1985). Oral or written, they are bound to be multivocal and polyvalent at one level or another and are, therefore, always subject to context-sensitive interpretations that we ourselves impose and that cannot always be determined for the original authors in the case of *re*presentations or *re*readings. That makes original meanings elusive (cf. Barthes, 1972, 1977; Brady, 1991b; Herzfeld, 2004, p. 39), but it does not preclude the construction of reasonable or agreeable interpretations between author and reader, speaker and hearer, for communication would then be impossible (Brady, 2003b, p. xxiv). Only the immaculate reception gets foiled in the process, and we do have some empirical data to help us steer and contextualize the problem rationally. But using oral or written texts as an avenue of access to really old things and behaviors is doubly complicated for other reasons as well, not least because we are separated from any possible dialogue with the original authors and from aboriginal conceptions of life in place by fundamental changes in perceptions of the world—by what we can cull from Foucault (1972) as *epistemic interference* in the gaps between prehistory and now, mostly because of the profound changes in our perceptions of ourselves, our products, and our landscapes insinuated through the invention of alphabetic literacy and compounded by the mass production of texts by way of the printing press (Abram, 1996; Lowe, 1982). Our views of the nature of the world and our embodied place in it have changed accordingly.[59]

The rise of alphabetic literacy and its dissemination through printing technology have had a profound effect on what Lowe (1982) calls the "hierarchy of the senses" and, thus, on the way in which we register and store information as humans. One sea change (among others) in this put a special premium on seeing over hearing in the field of perception and provided a means for separating knowledge from speech. Lacking written records, speech in an oral culture fulfills many functions that tend to be compartmentalized in chirographic and typographic cultures. Speech is communication in the latter, and knowledge is primarily preserved by writing. In an oral culture, however, "speech has to fulfill both functions of preserving knowledge as well as of communication, for only in the act of speaking can its knowledge be preserved" (p. 3).[60] Oral cultures have "an 'artisan' form of communication" where "stories arise from the rhythms of a preindustrial order: a world with time to listen, a language that is communal and founded on shared perceptions of reality, a respect for wisdom born of the accrued experience of generations, and a sense of life as still organized around the cycles of nature" (Wolf, 1982, p. 108; see also Feld, 1996). This knowledge is reinforced through personal experiences and is shared through tellings in oral performances—some ancient, some contemporary. Some with obvious continuity through both. In that connection it is important to recognize that the "residues from the earlier type persist to affect the later one" (Lowe, 1982, p. 2). It follows that aboriginal storytelling "is an art intrinsically at odds with a culture organized around writing and the dissemination of 'information'" (Wolf, 1982, p. 108), and so it is problematic as a source of ancient anything. By replacing or in other ways influencing folk and oral traditions, written culture undermines our ability to interpret them. The apparent "naturalness" of "seeing" or "reading" knowledge, as opposed to making the more direct connection between oral productions and aural registers, makes all interpretations of preliterate communications subject to deep-seated biases by modern interpreters.

The mix of ancient and modern shows up in contemporary studies of oral narratives and is played out in a synchronic version of epistemic interference that we can call *epistemic pooling.* The pooling part refers to the inevitable mix of diachronic continuities and traces from different traditions that show up at any given moment in history. The principle and context of the problem are encapsulated in Finnegan's (1992) observation that in folklore studies there is now "a deepening understanding of the *interaction* of oral and written forms as a regular and surprising process across a multi-dimensional continuum, rather than as something which involves bridging some deep divide" (p. xiii, emphasis added; see also Ong, 1967; Rothenberg, 1985, p. xxiii). That is precisely the scenario encountered today by ethnographers, linguists, and folklorists who seek secrets of the past from their contemporaries in other cultures, most pointedly for our purposes here, in the study of oral narratives and poetries as a measure of aboriginal forms of thought and behavior in ancient landscapes.[61] Despite some identifiable presence and separations of those forms in such contexts, the epistemic conditions of current "tribal" tellers are as mixed as anyone else's. They are modern people as well, and so they are influenced by the thoughts and premises of literacy at one level or another in text and performance (cf. Bauman, 1992; Finnegan, 1992; Finnegan & Orbell, 1995; Sammons & Sherzer, 2000). Nonetheless, with new sensitivities to the long-run obstacles that separate us, regardless of how subject to muddling they are today, we need to be optimistic. The very fact that there *is* continuity with things ancient in the oral narratives and poetries of some surviving tribal traditions (see, e.g., Perrin, 1987, p. 154) ought to spark our attention and motivate us to refine our methods for studying them. That would help us to get over the hump of what we already know, namely that oral narratives and poetry add an important source to our quest for reclaiming a sense of being in ancient places.[62]

These are some of the particulars that give motion and distinction to individuals and whole societies. They include fundamental differences that must be taken into account in any attempt to reconcile the separations and connections of language, story, and performance within and between communities, including ethnographers and their informants caught up in the mutually constructing and slippery ventriloquisms (as Dennis Tedlock would say) of speaking for others. That is equally true of attempts to reconcile the separations, and perhaps the traces of continuity, between modern written texts and the aboriginally unwritten (i.e., oral) accounts of being-in-place before the advent of writing (see, e.g., Layton, 1997). It also raises the stakes on the study of sacred space in aboriginal contexts—residual or lasting and reformed in our modern day or not—to something on the order of landscape poetics, to the study of poetries of place on both sides of the cultural fences that divide them. There is no guaranteed method to conquer it all. Meanings can be slippery, fugitive, irreducibly plural things—trains departed from the station leaving only warm tracks behind for us to touch and speculate on (Barthes, 1972, 1977, 1982; Brady, 1991b, pp. 10–11; 2003b, pp. xiii–xiv). But ethnopoetic research to date shows plainly that self-awareness and sensitivity to the impositions of cultural biases—the cultural "truths" that we take for granted, see as "natural" if we are aware of them at all, or favor in some guise as the "truth we need to find" to validate our identities—are "ground zero" for even starting such projects.[63] Knowing about them advances the prospect of *re*situating ourselves in myth-time and the history of place through texts and associated images. Like Snyder's Australian experience, that journey will also run the horizon of the old and the new. It will be history as we see it and live it, and so as we create it, with all of the interpretive problems outlined so far, but with the distinct advantage of locating the experience in a realistic site—the body itself, using language geared to sensuous-intellectual grounding and set analytically in an anthropology of ourselves.

▣ Root Facilitator: Poetics at Home

> *To understand the fashion of any life, one must know the land it is lived in and the procession of the year.*
>
> —Mary Austin, *The Land of Little Rain*[64]

Cull out the poets from among the bards and other performers of life as lived, put them on the peaks of what they consider to be their own lives and lands (Suiter, 2002), and they will likely share the experience with you as an epiphany of landscape—a dance with the sublime, the ancient, the foundational, the deeply personal poetry of themselves as beings-in-place (Bachelard, 1964, pp. 214–215).[65] Ask them how they know so much, and they will tell you that it is a matter of being-in-place for the long run, of internalizing its smells, sounds, and images—its flow of events and articulations of people and things. It is a matter of building an *embodied* history, they will say, and sometimes of launching that history through trips in the wider world and then "coming home."

We all have been somewhere beyond the homestead and its heather, and we know that returns can have a profound effect on views of the original experiences (Brady, 2003b). For one thing, nothing remains exactly the same. As Merwin (1997) says, "When I come back I find / a place that was never there" (p. 121). Times, places, and people change right under our noses. But triggered by sensuously doused memories, recombing the local landscape with a head full of new experiences (and absences) can yield a deeply contextualized poetic that both reinforces and redefines one's place *in* place, that is, by reworking the margins of self and other, native and stranger, old and new, even as the experience unfolds.[66] Conceptually *re*registering something as simple as place names in this context—for example, by virtue of their marrying "the legendary and the local" (or, say, in the case of Gettysburg, the legendary and the national)—can move the trekkers to special sentiments and symbolism of thought and action. The process is informed by both "being there" and "going there," by a then and a now, and by what we know from encounters with other cultures, including the academic and aesthetic works (e.g., painted, chanted, written) of other places, as pooled and compared with existing knowledge of our own (Agee & Evans, 1960; Brady, 2003b; Heaney, 1980b; Kerouac, 1958, 1959, 1960; Williams, 1973, pp. 1–12).[67]

All of these things "interanimate" in the mind's eye (Heaney, 1980b, p. 148), and they are the kinds of things that the poetic-minded Williams (1973) says can be "summoned and celebrated by the power of poetry" (p. 17). But the mental associations are not unfettered archaic recoveries. Nowadays they are sure to be a mix of the kinds of knowledge learned at home, on one's own through personal experience, and through the social entrainments of formal education (Heaney, 1980b, p. 131). Global networking and vast increases in access to public education, according to Heaney (1980b), ensure that in Ireland, for example, people are no longer innocent and that once local parishes now cast a wider net in the world:

> Yet those primary laws of our nature are still operative. We are dwellers, we are namers, we are lovers, we make homes and search for our histories. . . .When we look for the history of our sensibilities, I am convinced . . . that it is to . . . the stable element, the land itself, that we must look for continuity. (pp. 148–149)

And in the weave of personal emotion, myth, and symbol that Yeats once spun so effectively in Irish consciousness of self and place, so too do some of the new poets "weave their individual feelings round places they and we know, in a speech that they and we share; and in a world where the sacral vision of place is almost completely eradicated they offer in their art what Michael Longley has called 'the sacraments we invent for ourselves'" (p. 148). Their work shows that home and sacred go hand in hand as much for the sake of grounded identity—literally for locating a culturally defined self—as for the conservation and defense of an historical sanctuary of collected selves, a community, a plural being-in-place, a gathering of individuals with both shared and redefinable "roots" in matters sacred and profane.[68] Poetry latches on to that and *re*presents for us places that matter plus something as dear as the self to cherish as part of them, as something interanimated and nuanced with the rest of life and the landscapes of its expression.

Perhaps it is also true that a planet of poets so embodied and emplaced would be much less likely to trammel the very source of its own existence; to cut off the milk, the honey, the aesthetic and ecological sustenance of its forests and waterholes, its peaks and valleys; to shatter the web of life that ties coral reef to caribou, owl and finch to prairie grass, buffalo to ground squirrel, and the winds of Sahara and stratosphere to the quality of life in Chicago, Honolulu, and Madrid. Removal from the thick of it by cultural amnesia or ignorance, ideological preference, or insulated physical means does not give this experience. Personal immersion does. It does not guarantee as a process love or admiration or even acceptance of what is encountered. It does force the issue of participation.[69] The trick is to do it and to share the experience in ways that matter, perhaps on the order of Yeats, who had, as Heaney (1980b) remarks, a dual purpose: (a) "to restore a body of old legends and folk beliefs that would bind the people of the Irish place to the body of their world" and (b) "to supplement this restored sense of historical place with a new set of associations that would accrue when a modern Irish literature, rooted in its own region and using its own speech, would enter the imaginations of his countrymen" (p. 135). For that nourishment, I think, we will be well served by turning to the poets of place, Irish or not, American and Australian aborigines included, and find some way of hearing them that both represents them accurately in translation and resonates with our deepest being.

▣ Heavy Lifting: Poets at Work

I think white people are so afraid of the world they created that they don't want to see, feel, smell, or hear it.

—John (Fire) Lame Deer, *Lame Deer: Seeker of Visions*[70]

To meet the goals of conscience in a poetics of place, to move people to action in environmental reform, we need to get beyond considerations of strictly conventional representations and into something richer, more robust, and more tuned to the wider domains of body-centered experience as an avenue to (among other things) the sublime, to epiphanies of place, at home and elsewhere. And if we succeed to some degree in our reclamations and rehearsals of such experiences through these means, we have to ask not only about the kinds of information mustered in the process but, once again, also about who should tell the story and on what terms (cf. Levenson, 2004; Weinstein, 1990; White, 2004). It cannot be the usual social science sources. They prefer language that has the life of uncommon metaphors and personal participation squeezed out of it. Theirs is a language of mortification, that is, of dead metaphors and dried-up facts applied through distanced, or what are supposed to be clinical, observations (cf. Graves, 1948, pp. 223–224). Poets take a different tack. We all are to some degree defined by where we are, where we have been, and where we think we are going. Our *selves* are insinuated in place culturally, historically, linguistically, and so forth through the usual channels of socialization, enculturation, and individual life experiences. But we are also insinuated in place sensually, as sentient beings, and poetry marks sensual space more consistently than does any other form of representation (Brady, 2004).[71] Although poetry cannot (and will not try to) free itself completely from the inevitable screens and biases of alphabetic literacy, it uses metaphor as a tool for discovering and positing the relations among things, and a poetic immersion of self in the experience of a much-traveled and culturally marked ancient place has a better chance of getting at a realistic account of such experiences primarily because of its devotion to sensuous particulars. Poets are potentially expert *re*presenters who offer comparative experiences in a commonly held domain—that of the body itself—and the ultimate aim of poetic expression is to touch the universal through the particular, to evoke and enter into discourse about the sublime, to move the discourse to what defines us all—what we share as humans.[72]

This argument may apply to any finely wrought figurative language, whether verse or prose, that is, to *poesis* in general (Hallyn, 1990). Joseph Conrad's powerful prose may have the same effect as, or an even more exalted effect than, finely crafted verse by inspiring its audience with the kind of self-consciousness of being that can change lives (cf. Cushing, 1970; Hinsley, 1999). As verse or prose, the content of poetic representations exceeds the literal: "All poetic language is language strenuously composed beyond the requirements of information and therefore striking, perhaps most striking, when most apparently 'transparent'" (Vendler, 1985, p. 59). The "surplus" beyond the literal is inference and argument by analogy and allegory, among many other possible tropic combinations and prospects (cf. White, 1978). In its most creative form, poetry, surplus meaning is a protest against the constraints of the ordinary rules of inquiry: "When a rhyme surprises and extends the fixed relations between words, that in itself protests against necessity. When language does more than enough, as it does in all achieved poetry, it opts for the conditions of overlife and rebels at limit" (Heaney, 1995, p. 158). More than simple mimesis, poesis is a process of "being" and "doing" in variable contexts, a dynamic and reflexive process of construction and selection.[73] Because its reception depends markedly on the experiences, preferences, and related biases of the receiver (e.g., reader, hearer), trying to legislate the one correct interpretation is futile; no aesthetic experience can be so governed (Brady, 2003b, p. xvii).[74] Like myth, one has to know how to interpret these creations. To do that successfully, following Jackson (1995), one has to know something about how and under what circumstances they were produced.

What I am proposing is much more than a change in writing style. More than selective editing is required to get from here to there in a poetics of place. We cannot revisit foundational human experiences in the wildernesses of our pasts simply by writing up knowledge in the present tense, much as one might do in trying to make a film in the ethnographic present, that is, by erasing traces of modern occupation through selective visions and contrived replications. Poetry offers a difference in forms of knowing as well as representing,[75] and as Howes (1990) sees it,

> No amount of experimenting with one's writing style is going to make up for the deficiency of failing to experiment with one's perceptions or "sensory ratio" first. To understand a culture is to "make sense" of it, ... [and that] involves more than a "rejection of visualism" ... or exchanging an ear for an eye. Making sense involves, minimally, learning how to *be of two sensoria* at once and reflecting upon how the interplay of the senses in another culture's perceptual system both converges and diverges from their interplay in one's own [culture]. (p. 69)

What distinguishes the best of this writing—thoughtful prose, not poetry (see, e.g., Ohnuki-Tierney, 1981; Seeger, 1975, 1981; Stoller & Olkes, 1986, 1987)—"is the extent to which expositions on odors, sounds, and tastes are treated as intrinsic to the ethnographic message rather than extraneous.... To analyze these expositions [exclusively] as textual markers of having 'been there' ... would be to miss their point" (Howes, 1990, p. 69; see also Stoller, 1987, 2004).[76] Moreover, the emotional truths of such experiences are perhaps best communicated emotionally (Sherry & Schouten, 2002, p. 219), and that is an open invitation to poetic bodies everywhere (Joy & Sherry, 2003). They all are equipped to make the case for how they are at any given time, with or without lines of words that by some estimations glow in the dark with eloquence.[77]

Poetry immerses itself and revels in these sensual features (cf. Brady, 2003b, 2004; Carpenter, 1980; Classen, 1993). In so doing, it favors the analytic perspectives embodied in phenomenology and an anthropology of experience. All three perspectives attempt to represent a "natural" and self-conscious emerging in the world, a matter that begins with experiences of space and place and in some ways reaches beyond language itself as a form of knowing.[78] Each puts the observer upfront in the equation of interpreting and representing experience, starting with an upright and horizontal sentient being, present and accounting for itself. But each has its intellectual and methodological limitations as well. None offers perfect vision. Aside from its own ultimate puzzles (*aporias)* on time and being-in-place, among other considerations, a phenomenological approach has the problem of "tacit knowledge" as a fuzzy but strategic edge that is difficult to know or at least to put into words (Polanyi & Prosch, 1975). It does not deal with the unconscious in any accessible way (Joy & Sherry, 2003, p. 279; Lakoff & Johnson, 1999). The anthropology of experience finds words as subsets, imperfect and selective renderings of the larger realm of what can be known from being alive and awake as a sentient being, and so must find some way in which to account for these experiences. Poets want to stretch the limits of language, to wring everything possible out of words and metaphoric processes, ultimately to reach beyond the shortcomings of language in the landscapes of literature, speech, the sublime, and the ineffable and then pass on the whole bundle to all who will listen. They want work, as Heaney (1995) remarks about Dylan Thomas's early poetry, where "the back of the throat and the back of the mind" (p. 141) answer and support each other. That is both the promise and the genius of poetry. It might not always apply or be accepted as intended, for any of several reasons.[79] But the aim and the prospects of putting a finger on "that great unity which is neither here nor beyond" (p. 141), of creating interpretations that "still make a catch in the breath and establish a positively bodily hold upon the reader" when "the wheel of total recognition has been turned" (p. 70), of engaging "the mechanical gears of a metre" that also takes hold "on the sprockets of our creatureliness" (p. 70), and in so many other ways of "recovering a past" or "prefiguring a future" (pp. 8–9), are always there. They are funded by imagination, by a need to articulate with the physical and social environments that surround us, and by an opportunity to communicate about what matters to us as we see it in the experiences of life as lived.[80]

From that robust ground, tracking the sensual and imaginative qualities of experience through the emotionally open and rich language forms of poetry may create desire (one hopes) in the listener or reader to experience the same things in person, that is, in body. Getting to some authentic emulation or understanding of being in ancient landscapes in that context is in part a job for ethnographically informed translators and in part a job for the poets of all cultures; this is not an ethnically proprietary thing (Hymes, 1987). We cannot get there through any procedure that starts by attempting to throw out the single most important elements—the saturations of individual lives as lived, the biases of being personal, interpretive, alive, and awake on a planet that can, in the imaginaries of some, also be inhabited by ghosts of the past and fantasies of the future (cf. Heidegger, 1977, p. 333). That is the stuff of ordinary reality, and it is in terms of such things that we act first as cultured beings. By virtue of its secondary extractions, its focus on stasis (linear "snapshots" of events) rather than kinesis (the simultaneity of immersion or "ongoing film") and other distancing techniques, hard science cannot ever capture these realities.[81] But neither is just writing poetry enough. Internalizing poesis as experience by immersing in its subjects is what matters most for depth of understanding, and that must be followed by an attempt to make it as carefully coached and exact a statement (including fantasy) of lived experience as we can.[82] If the "great function of poetry is to give us back the situations of our dreams" (Bachelard, 1964, p. 15), the great demand of ethnographic poetics is that we render those experiences as clearly and accurately as possible through our sense of being-in-place and the guidance of histories—our own and those of others—that appear to contextualize the material best (Hartnett & Engels, chap. 41, this volume; on the same problem in science, cf. Hallyn, 1990). Such analyses can teach us things that are not available in any other way (Brady, 2003b, 2004).[83] Among many other possibilities, they can show us mystery and beauty and the need for being in them as we pass through the landscapes of our lives, and that in itself may motivate us to care about repairs where we see breaches in our rights and opportunities to continue.[84] Poetry, in one very important sense of the term, literally puts it all in place.

▣ Reprise: Roots and Futures

> [Then:] *The word was born / in the blood, / it grew in the dark body, pulsing, / and took flight with the lips and mouth.*
>
> —Pablo Neruda, "The Word"[85]

> [Next:] *Long enough in the desert a man like other animals can learn to smell water. Can learn, at least, the smell of things associated with water—the unique and heartening odor of the cottonwood tree, for example, which in the canyonlands is the tree of life.*
>
> —Edward Abbey, *Desert Solitaire*[86]

We are trainable, inventive, adaptable, and corporeal beings capable of making new and renewed associations among things and thoughts. With that in mind, and in the interest of breaking free as much as possible from the forces and forms of modern life that have ravaged the earth and its ancient creatures, if we have pumped up the appetite for "a kind of experience deep enough to change our selves, our form of life" (J. Turner, 1996, p. 104), and if we also realize in the process that "our ecological crisis is not, at the roots, caused by industrialization, capitalism, and technology, but by a particular form of the human self" (p. 104), then self-renewal and reform are the applied agenda at hand. We have asked how to do that and found it to be problematic. What is the instrument? How do we *re*imagine, *re*claim, and *re*surrect some semblance of participation in the changing environmental circumstances of the past and apply it to the present? Creating and sustaining a passion for place requires both primary and vicarious experience and language suitable for conveying the results realistically, that is, as they are conceptualized and felt and can be explored creatively by the participants through immersions in subject and place. Clinical abstractions tend to defeat that project, or at least they work in the wrong directions. But none of it comes to mind and body unfettered, beyond culture, personal bias, or predilections for certain kinds of interpretations against others.

The critics say that one path to a fair clearing in this, of doing something that counts in the Assembly of All Beings, is new myths, new applications of old myths, and thereby a renewed appreciation of continuities with the poetries and sacred spaces of yesterday. We need to *re*engage the study of myth and legend as embodied in landscapes and modern tellings (see especially Abram, 1996; Basso, 1996a, 1996b; Feld & Basso, 1996; Crapanzano, 2004). To reopen our eyes to the cross-cultural and ecological collisions of modern life, to "reveal the richness, antiquity, and complexity of our landscape tradition" as a way of showing the high cost of doing nothing (Schama, 1995, p. 14), we need to move from our own conceptions of a "natural" reading of cultural values and landscapes—our own blind ethnocentrisms—to something larger and more comparative, enlightening, and pragmatic through careful research and carefully reasoned imagination. Each of these efforts is a constructive and transferable source of identity. Each can tell us important things about how we are and where we have been and can thereby mark an important sense of where we are going from here as humans. But each also has its lacunae, its shortcomings, and its impossibilities, and given that the action of *re*visiting and *re*imagining circumstances *creates* original material, and thus another source of distortion in the effort to recontextualize the past through the present, the bottom line has to be not simply a study of texts and artifacts but rather a critical exercise in the larger and more inclusive realm of an anthropology of experience. To enfranchise that, we need to return consciously to the sensuous (Abram, 1996), to the body as instrument of all we can do and know, and to history and practice with all we can learn about embodiment as sentient beings in the world. Developing an unromanticized but keenly felt sense of being-in-place—of the constructive powers of getting there versus being there along with the knowledge that the basic instrument in the process is our emotionally loaded and culturally coded physical selves—is fundamental to the effort.[87] The inner and outer landscapes of our bodies are the locations where these things take place. What happens to people under these circumstances is sensuous–intellectual experience, a point of negotiation in the landscapes of life (some of which shows up in worldviews, rituals, etc.), and defines our existence, especially when things go wrong as they have for us today in the "slow-motion explosions" (Snyder, 1990, pp. 4–5) of expanding urban frontiers.

At the heart of these concerns is a primary sense of home and the structures of our very survival. Bass (2000) declares with insight that "the more fragmented the world becomes, the more critical it is that we try and hold the weave of it together, and the more clearly we will notice that which is still full and whole" (p. 73; see also Deloria, 1993; Snyder, 1978). Added to the inevitable conflict of human interests and the natural world, that may be sufficient reason to renew our inquiries among aboriginal cultures "concerning the nature of time and space and other (invented) dichotomies; the relationship between hope and the exercise of will; the role of dreams and myths in human life; and the therapeutic aspects of long-term intimacy with a landscape"

(Lopez, 1986, pp. 368–369). We need to reclaim a sense of sacred space, both as personal enlightenment and in a more applied sense as an avenue to deeper understandings of place that will support commitments to social and environmental security for future generations. To earn constructive influence in the Assembly of All Beings, we need to immerse ourselves in it and be informed by it. We need to know and *re*evaluate the transformations of place and space embedded in the landscapes of history—private and public, national and colonial—including the destruction of meaning in the land by translating encounters with other creatures and cultures into the signs of empire. We need to know the secrets sleeping both in the land and in ourselves, the experiences of being-in-place that once made the wilderness sacred to all who would pass that way or dwell there in shared dominion. We need to rediscover the sacred in the wild and the wilderness in ourselves realistically, but with all the passion of a commitment to survival in an untamed land. We need to *rekindle* our relationship with the wilderness by putting it in the kind of caring custody that we assign to our own ancestries and the offspring who gather at the hearth. We need to be a civilization that recognizes lessons learned from the wild as training for an "etiquette of freedom," as Snyder (1990, p. 24) says, that "can live fully and creatively together with wildness" (p. 6), and the New World is where we must start growing it. Such commitments can launch the opportunity for developing new sacred space, for resurrecting old myths, and for creating new myths on which to hang our survival in the long run, but only if we find some powerful way of communicating the experiences.

Meaningful life presumes a vital existence in the first place, and as we know and I have said in triplicate here, for humans that is accomplished not only by knowing and doing but by also by sharing the knowledge. *Telling* the story of place means *teaching* it as well, and Gruenewald (2003) has some very specific thoughts on that matter as applied to formal education. He argues that although culture and place are deeply intertwined, our educational system obscures that relationship by distracting our attention from, and our responses to, the actual contexts of our existences in place (p. 621). We can join our children in the equation of solving some of these problems by giving them firsthand experiences in different places—some wild, some not so wild, but all differentiated by comparisons of the overbuilt urban areas and the never-built few remaining wild areas of the planet. They must be able to distinguish between human social environments and natural environments and, in the process, to recognize that we are biological beings embedded in and embodied by both. Filtered through the social constructions of community talk and marked (one hopes) with some exalted feelings, such experiences may lead them to affinities with the planet otherwise long diminished by a frustrating and destructive search for fulfillment in a scheme of endless wants with limited means. Perhaps it will lead to a taming of the wild in their minds by recognizing and accepting it for what it is—wild, our past, our future, the place that more than any other shows us what we are and are not, where we have been and must be—perhaps by recognizing that the wilderness is ultimately our home, the baseline of the place we call our planet. Better that than building it into oblivion. Better that than squeezing its margins into creature habitats smaller than Japanese hotel rooms, skinning it for its pelts, or corralling it for rodeos, circuses, and zoos of all kinds. Perhaps this montage of old tragedies and new hopes will lead to the consciousness and rituals needed to create the myths of the future, including a philosophy of place less destructive of ecosystem, self, and the long run of humanity. History has shown us that soaking the land with cultural values means investing it with the power to change it and ourselves.[88] However idealistic and improbable that is in a world beset and distracted by the harsh realities of terrorism and murder endorsed by instructions from imaginary gods, that is power that we can reclaim and use for social and ecological justice in the Assembly of All Beings, humans and nonhumans alike.[89]

The concept of being-in-place embraces all of this, and a poetic underpinning helps to reveal the process of putting that concept to work in various forms. Poetry can educate and move us into awe, mystery, the sublime, and related realizations by "stirring things up in us." It thrives on empathy and emulation and draws us into the sensuous–intellectual anchor for all knowing—that which comes from lived experience, where words are a subset of what is known and poetic expression is an attempt to render such experiences in texts and performances in a manner that often enlists the art of the possible more directly than it does the facts of the actual. While invested in radically different traditions of knowing, including an essential association with the multilayered metaphorics of myth (see, e.g., Barthes, 1972; Dundes, 1984; Graves, 1948; Meletinsky, 1998, p. 153; Schama, 1995; Snyder, 1978; Thompson, 1989), poetry can also yield accurate and detailed information on being and doing and thereby can supplement even more directly the conventional methods and knowledge products of archaeology and history. But a poetic stance (poetry and more) always starts with the truth of raw experience, with life as lived and seen from the inside, from the role of the participant, not from some disembodied tortured analytic imposed from the outside on the premise that our sentient selves get in the way of discovery. By being inherently comparative, a poetic perspective also addresses anthropology's first principle. It moves us to draw comparisons from our own immersions in life in relation to those of others, as separated from them perhaps by the cultural differences of age, gender, generation, personal characteristics, and favored gods—by the gaps that have always separated "own" from "other" in the landscapes of cultures whose home territories touch but do not match. It begs comparisons between being now and being then, between being one and being other, between being here and being there, and it thereby situates itself in our experience as fundamental to knowing other people, their histories, and the environmental complications of being-in-place today.[90] It gives us knowable contexts for constructing more or less satisfying meanings about the nature of the world and our place in it. In that respect, it enters the concerns of art and science with the opportunity to inform in both. The problem in each domain is to learn how to listen, especially when the poesis is not drawn from our own cultural wells.

The particulars of preliterate experiences in wild and sacred space are more or less lost to us as modern peoples through the displacements and reorientations of language and the concomitant separation of knowledge and thought that has come with writing, the cultural erasures and amalgamations of colonialism, and the appetites of mindless urbanization. But the important lessons of being a long-run creature in and of place are not. They are just too often obscured by the pace and rapacious confusions of modern life. A conscientious effort to develop a poetics of place, with careful attention paid to the sensuous and intellectual components of our existence that are laced into our own and other cultural traditions, and to the possibilities of both *re*immersing and *re*inventing ourselves in the process, might bring us as close as we ever can be to the peaks of our human ancestry. Coupled with a critical use of the archaeologies, histories, and museologies of the day, that may give us our best glimpse of being-in-place in ancient circles of stones, our best claim on the spaces of ancestral voices, longings and desires, catastrophes and dilemmas, joys and defeats, the dreams of old horizons, and the life forms that contextualized all of it prior to the great steerage of alphabetic literacy, the indelible footprints of Columbus on the New World, and the launching of a loop of Western industrialism into outer space that has left no part of the planet untouched by its influence. Careful attention paid to, and a willingness to act in, that context may open the agenda of self-renewal and reform with greater wisdom and less complacency about the circumstances of our lives as lived. As interloper in an anthropology of experience, a poetics of place wants to insinuate itself in this milieu by starting with what makes us the same, the commonalities of sentient beings as seen through the great diversities of our collective meaningful existences. Being action oriented, it strives to know such things in every way possible and to defend them where they promote greater harmony in the

Assembly of All Beings. In more ways than one, that is essential ethnography.[91]

Coda

I know that it is unusual to put theory in the same box with passion and commitment in the study of anything (Noam Chomsky to the contrary), and I know that I have romped through a whole industry of specialized interests in as many disciplines on the way to this point. So, a pithy review of the structure of the argument—the landscape of this text, if you will—might be useful in conclusion. Here is what I think I have done. In the interest of developing a conscientious and environmentally concerned poetics of place, including cultivating sources of information on experiences at "home" and in modern and ancient landscapes that might best be described as "wild" and "sacred" (while discounting, for the purposes of this chapter, detailed discussions of the archaeologies and histories housed in museums that are themselves specialized interpretations of related materials), I have emphasized the need for (a) "being there" (on-site, grounded in the sensuous–intellectual continuum of the body itself, imagination, and home experience, a data source that is fundamental to interpreting experience and transfers to ancient contexts mostly by educated analogy); (b) accounting for "getting there" in personal and epistemological terms; (c) studying "tribal" poetries and myths as sources of body-grounded information (albeit complicated) on worldviews and associated behaviors that pervades both history and prehistory and is embedded in oral performances (a source of hard data and, given the paucity of expert native performers, scarce opportunity) and written texts (a source of hard data and plentiful opportunity provided by secondary observers), with the caution that we need to learn how to interpret poetries and mythical thought in those contexts, especially in the light of epistemic problems insinuated in Western perceptions since the development of writing and mass production printing and in the light of certain inadequacies of language itself to convey experience.

As models of and for interpreting these materials, I have compared (a) scientific approaches (especially logical positivism with its distancing techniques) and (b) artisan frameworks (with their essential immersion techniques, including nonverbal representations and poetics) and collected them under the heading of "artful science." I have cultivated the good fit of phenomenology as a philosophical underpinning for an anthropology of experience and for poetics as a way of knowing and communicating experiences of being-in-place. I have also given poetry per se special cachet under this umbrella, both because of and despite its composition beyond the requirements of basic information and because it is body grounded and can be a powerful source of communicating at both a sensuous and an intellectual level. Unlike the prerequisites for scientific discovery and representation, phenomenology, poetics, and an anthropology of experience put the observer upfront in the interpretive equation as an active participant. Each of these sources has its lacunae and other shortcomings relative to the other sources. But the composite attention paid to them in accounts of being-in-place and to culture as something constructed out of the interplay of the senses, filtered through imagination and the historical shapings that individuals and groups get from socialization and enculturation in particular traditions and perpetuate by storytelling, can give the overall effort an authenticity complementary to, but otherwise unavailable through, more conventional thinking in philosophy, anthropology, history, geography, and the social sciences in general. The end result has important applications in active research, formal education, and concerns for the quality of life on the planet.

Notes

1. Geertz (1996) writes that the anthropology of place has a "sort of preludial quality, as if it marked the beginning of something that will reach far beyond the matters under immediate consideration" and that it "can be brought to bear on the grand complexities that plague the world" (p. 262). The current argument moves in that direction.

2. I do not wish to slight the academic disciplines of archaeology and history. So, too, for not reviewing the successes and failures of museology—that complex blend of representational problems in archaeology, history, and performance studies. Museums are an important area of contest on problems of ethnographic representation, authenticity, and the like (see especially Karp & Levine, 1991). I cannot burden the current argument with all of these asides. But I must argue in the same breath that what is presented here is relevant to the practitioners of those fields, including the politics of their reclamations and presentations, if one accepts the necessity of putting the observer in the equation of interpretation (e.g., compare the themes of this work with Allison, Hockey, & Dawson, 1997; Clifford & Marcus, 1986; Clifton, 1990; Dening, 2004; Gewertz & Errington, 1991; Greenblatt, 1991; Hobsbawm & Ranger, 1983; Hodder, 1982, 1987, 1989; Marcus, 1998; Metcalf, 2002; Pluciennik, 1999; Pratt, 1992; Wolf, 1992; see also Hartnett & Engels, chap. 41, this volume). Excising the observer is, for me, an unacceptable fiction; (and, of course, that begs the whole issue of postmodernism and its various levels of intellectual shootouts and misfires (Brady, 1998; Denzin & Lincoln, 2000, 2002; Lincoln & Denzin, 2003b). Moreover, I have poets and their fictions in the mix of all of it (Brady, 2003b). Given Western conventions aimed at protecting science from art and vice versa, that is guaranteed to be controversial.

3. Roughly speaking, "Metaphor, calling one thing by the name of another, is not a strange poetic event. It is at the heart of language, and the direction of the metaphors is important. The body's influence [sensation and perception] spreads outwards, to features of the environment, and inwards to the mind" (Aitchison, 2000, p. 124; cf. Brady, 1991a, pp. 69–71; Snyder, 1990, p. 16). On body-grounded metaphors and the use of them in science and everyday life, see Brady (2003b, 2004), Brown (2003), Danesi (1999, p. 111), Fernandez (2003), Gibbs (1994), Hallyn (1990), Kövecses (2002), Lakoff and Johnson (1999), Laughlin, McManus, and d'Aquili, (1992), Midgley (2001), Montgomery (1996), and M. Turner (1996).

4. For more on the concept of artful science, see Brady (1991a, 1991b, 2000, 2003a, 2003b, 2004) and Brady and Kumar (2000).

5. What I mean by poetics follows Hallyn (1990) in his study of abduction in science. He does "not use the term poetics in the Aristotelian sense of a system of normative rules, but rather in the sense that one speaks about the poetics of Racine or Baudelaire, namely to designate a collection of choices made at different levels (style, composition, thematics . . .) by an author or a group. On the one hand, these choices lead to operations that inform the concrete work. On the other, they are loaded with meanings that more or less both determine and are determined by the artistic endeavor, for which the work is the result and sign. Ultimately, a study of poetics, in the sense understood here, comes down to what Umberto Eco calls 'the plan for shaping and structuring the work.' It is the program for the execution of a work, informed by presuppositions and exigencies whose traces one can locate, on the one hand, in explicit declarations, and on the other, in the work itself, to the extent that its completed form, with respect to other works, gives witness to the intentions that presided over its production. A poetics must return to a way of dreaming works and the declarations that accompany them, of conceiving their possibility, and of working for their reality" (pp. 14–15).

6. Paz (1981, p. 15). Compare Schama (1995, pp. 367–374).

7. Yi-Fu (1979) says, "The organization of human space is uniquely dependent on sight. Other senses expand and enrich the visual space" (p. 16). Sound "enlarges one's spatial awareness to include areas behind the head that cannot be seen," and it "dramatizes spatial experience. Soundless space feels calm and lifeless despite the visible flow of activity in it, as in watch[ing] events through binoculars or on the television screen with the sound turned off" (p. 16). In his view, "Taste, smell, and touch are capable of exquisite refinement. They discriminate among the wealth of sensations and articulate gustatory, olfactory, and textual worlds," whereas "odors lend character to objects and places, making them distinctive, easier to identify and remember" (p. 10). And he asks, "Can senses other than sight and touch provide a spatially organized world? It is possible to argue that taste, odor, and even hearing cannot in themselves give us a sense of space?" (p. 10). Fortunately, "The question is largely academic, for most people function with the five senses, and these constantly reinforce each other to provide the intricately ordered and emotionally charged world in which we live" (p. 10). See also Ackerman (1990) and the "sensorium of the blind" described by Kuusisto (1998). The concept of place is also a product of the various cultural experiences, themes, and beliefs about the circumstances and transformations of lives as lived through the senses. But that does not mean that all cultures put the same hierarchical valuations on sensory experience or that they represent the senses in

storytelling about life as lived in the same ways (Brady, 2003b, pp. 93–101; Carpenter, 1980; Joy & Sherry, 2003; Mitchell, 1983; Nelson, 1980, 1983).

8. The logic here is the ordinary logic of understanding for humans and their conjectural mentalities. It is both structural and hermeneutic in process (Brady, 1993), but I have conceptualized it as a progressive hermeneutic, as more of a spiral than the classic "hermeneutic circle," to accommodate the accretions and shifts of knowledge that occur through time (see also Brady, 1991b).

9. There is a scholarly danger in that, of course, especially when one seeks the truth of "what actually happened" exclusive of the experiences of being there in body and spirit (Dening, 2004), or vice versa, by thinking that one can rely only on the intuitions of body and tacit knowledge to apprehend the particulars of cultural performance. But we need to accept the fact that multiple reality frameworks can be applied to all experience and then do our best to defend the one we prefer to all others *without* deprecating or dismissing out of hand competing arguments and systems of signification from, say, the tribal world. On allowing "sufficient cognitive 'space' for conflicting ontologies to coexist," see Layton (1997, p. 128).

10. See Brady (in press) and Dening (1974, 1980, 1988, 1995, 1996, 1998a, 1998b, 2004).

11. The semiotics of talk and thought, artifact and architect, testament and text, teacher, trainer, seer, shaman, priest, and dreamer—the meaningful landscapes of "everyman" particularized in individual groups—are precisely the kind of information that is likely to dissipate with the death or disappearance of whole cultures or populations. But alluding at several levels to the kinds of problems identified in a common frame by 18th-century Italian philosopher Giambattista Vico in his *New Science* (Tagliacozzo & Verene, 1976) and to works by various phenomenologists (particularly Merleau-Ponty, 1962), and following an argument made explicit by Howes (1990), we can say that (a) *all* of this—culture itself—is "*constructed* out of the interplay of all the senses" (p. 68; see also Laughlin & D'Aquili, 1974; Laughlin et al., 1992; Stoller, 1987, 1989; Stoller & Olkes, 1986, 1987), (b) it is embedded in a conjectural mentality that is compelled to make sense of changing environmental circumstances (Laughlin & Brady, 1978), and (c) it is filtered through imagination and the historical shapings that individuals and groups get from socialization and enculturation in particular traditions, including language and its body-grounded metaphors. The resulting knowledge is perpetuated largely by stories—oral, written, performed in other ways—in units as small as parables, giving new meanings to perceptions of changing environmental circumstances (M. Turner, 1996). Accounts of being-in-place ultimately must reengage this mix of sensuous–intellectual properties and processes—the broad landscape of human experience that forms a body-centered system—to have any legitimate claim to authenticity.

12. Engaging in parallel universes and common projects as sentient beings makes it possible for us to understand each other (Merrell, 2000, pp. 73–74; on Vico's *fantasia,* thinking through the body, and the age of poetic wisdom, see Verene, 1976; on Quine's principle of charity and related comments, see Brady, 2000). Thinking "through the body and to sense the world as an order of bodies, with meaning not being separable from bodies," is difficult to imagine (Verene, 1976, p. 31; cf. Lowe, 1982), but a critical rereading of Vico's arguments about body-centeredness is nonetheless a reminder that we are all animals—sensuous–intellectual creatures—and that there are some universal responses to things that we all share. The possibilities for understanding the beliefs and experiences of others are grounded both in the common sensory apparatus that we occupy as biological beings and in the comparable modes of thought and action when we respond to the feelings and sensations of environmental stimulation (Merrell, 2000, p. 73). "The body is, so to speak, in the mind. They are both wild" (Snyder, 1990, p. 16). The same possibilities must also be realized *in an interpretive relation* to other communicative organisms (and things that are believed to be animated, e.g., rocks and trees), that is, through the interactive processes that lead to the social construction of reality through whatever cultural screens (Berger & Luckmann, 1966; see also Zolbrod, 1983, pp. 227–228). Compare Wilmsen (1999): "Separate lives are congruent in experience, no matter how disparate their cultural environments. Once the words are learned, native speakers of different languages begin to recognize each other—thirst thick under an arid sun, identical errors in navigating unknown landscapes, parallel blunderings through sexual awakening—in evoked images of their separate experiences. For it is individuals, not cultures, who meet and re-present their contexts to each other" (p. xi). See also Fletcher (1967, p. 197).

13. Kerouac (1959, p. 106).

14. Because we are creatures in and of place—embedded, embodied, and emplaced—it is difficult to extract a proper concept of place for conversation and

instruction (Geertz, 1996). But I do mean to flag the process of being and becoming emplaced as a biological and cultural system that is subject to an inherent creativity of perception and expression and, above all, to inscriptions and transferences between the body and its sociocultural milieu. See Low and Lawrence-Zúñiga (2003), Merleau-Ponty (1962), Miller (1996), and Spiegelberg (1975). To have practical value as a principle, that thought needs to be played out and observed in the everyday world. On mimesis and its complexities, see Taussig (1993). For an exquisite coarticulation of theory and practice in cultural spaces, see Stewart (1996). On living persons and practical problems, see Smith (1997, p. 2).

15. See especially Merleau-Ponty (1962), Spiegelberg (1975), and adaptations of Merleau-Ponty's work in Abram (1996) and Gruenewald (2003). The upshot is that humans enter into a participatory relationship with other phenomena through the multisensory perception of direct experience. On phenomenology and culture, see Csordas (1994), Laughlin and Brady (1978), and Laughlin and colleagues (1992).

16. Thus, meaning is made, not found, and making sense of places is a reciprocal and mutually constructing process, taking shape and acquiring meaning "when the inner realm is projected onto the outer scene" (Brann, 1991, p. 7). Feld (1996) puts it this way: "As place is sensed, senses are placed; as places make sense, senses make place" (quoted in Casey, 1996, p. 19).

17. Ethnographers generally take us to a "location," that is, to a place where *something happens.* Like watching a movie, we seldom have reason to focus on the projector or the serving apparatus. Phenomenology brings the observer's equipment to the fore and makes it part of the equation of meaningful construction and participation. Compare Thompson (1989): "So here I sit, looking at the screen of a Macintosh and in imagination, rolling the screen of history back and forth. Instructed by the natural history of life, I suspect that what I am looking for are not 'events' but thresholds of emergence that are also projections of my own framing of perceptions" (p. 135).

18. Following Lowe (1982), "By 'perception' I do not mean the neurophysiology of perception, or the behavioral psychology of perception, but an immanent description of perception as human experience.... Perception as the crucial connection includes the subject as the perceiver, the act of perceiving, and the content of the perceived. The perceiving subject, from an embodied location, approaches the world as a lived, horizontal field. The act of perceiving unites the subject with the perceived. And the content of the perceived, which results from that act, affects the subject's bearing in the world. Perception is therefore a reflexive, integral whole, involving the perceiver, the act of perceiving, and the content of the perceived" (p. 1). Moreover, according to Feld (1996), "places may come into existence through the experience of bodily sensation, but it is through expression that they reach heightened emotional and aesthetic dimensions of sensual inspiration" (p. 134). Among the Kaluli, "the poetics of place merge with the sensuousness of place as soundscape and with the sensuality of the singing voice" (p. 134).

19. We do not need Kant to tell us how fundamental space and time are to our lives. As Yi-Fu (1979) says, "'Space' and 'place' are familiar words denoting common experiences.... Basic components of the lived world; we take them for granted. When we think about them, however, they may assume unexpected meanings and raise questions we had not thought to ask" (p. 3). For some concrete examples, see also Gallagher (1993).

20. Neihardt (1959, p. 173).

21. See the various works by Claude Lévi-Strauss regarding the fantasy factor in all myths (e.g., Lévi-Strauss, 1976). On creativity and imagination in general, see especially Miller (1996). No categories of place have any meaning without imagination. It has a geography of its own—landscapes of fear and comfort where poets of virtual worlds bridge the concrete and the abstract, where the sign and its referent emerge in consciousness as places of soil, rock, sea, air, innumerable critters, and mind (Brady, 2003b). The expression "leap of the imagination" is often heard in discussions of writing, but that may be less of a leap than "a sauntering, a stepping across" into the reality at hand (Bass, 2000, p. 72). See also Caughey (1984), Joy and Sherry (2003), and Wooley (1992). Crapanzano (2004) says, "Like James, the literary critic Jean Starobinski stresses the determining role of the imagination in the perception—the constitution—of reality. 'Insinuated into perception itself, mixed with the operations of memory, opening up around us a horizon of the possible, escorting the project, the hope, the fear, speculations—the imagination is much more than a faculty for evoking images which double the world of our direct perceptions; it is a distancing power thanks to which we represent to ourselves distant objects and we distance ourselves from present realities. Hence, the ambiguity that we discover everywhere; the imagination, because it anticipates and previews, serves action, draws us before the configuration of the realizable

before it can be realized.' . . . Not only does the imaginative consciousness allow us to transcend (*depasser*) the immediacy of the present instant in order to grasp a future that is at first indistinct, Starobinski argues, but it enables us to project our 'fables' in a direction that does not have to reckon with the 'evident universe.' It permits fiction, the game, a dream, more or less voluntary error, pure fascination. It lightens our existence by transporting us into the region of the phantasm. In turn it facilitates our 'practical domination over the real' or our breaking ties with it" (p. 174).

22. On art, science, and humanism, see Bruner (1986, pp. 49–50). On extrapolations from laconic representations as simple as a dateline in a poem, see Richardson (1999b, p. 334) and Brady (2003b, p. xiv). We are compelled to interpret such signs and cues about our environment because, in a general sense, our very existence as human creatures depends on it. Place is the anchor of fundamental human experience. But how do we recognize it? "Do we know enough about it to enjoy a fanciful imagining of passage there? If we visit a place at three separate times, is it still the same place? Does the place remember us? The answers are as much a function of landscape evolving as they are of finders finding what they want or need to see—a cultural meaning and orientation problem with historical implications" (Brady, 2003b, p. xv).

23. Suskind (1986, pp. 147–148).

24. As might be expected, the concept of home as a stable place is deeply embedded in our thinking about writing. On language and embodied space, see Jackson (1995, p. 6) and Low and Lawrence-Zúñiga (2003, pp. 6–7). The real work for individuals centered more or less (cf. Stewart, 1996, p. 3, on Appalachia) in what they recognize and perpetuate as a common home and the wider world, is to determine how all of these rooted poolings of life intersect so as to figure out who and by what commonalities of ancestral experience and related cultural claims should be grouped together by category and actual location and who and what, in our estimation, should not. That is the essence of kinship and a classic set of norms for deciding issues of access and trespass, that is, for deciding who and what are to be included or excluded from particular activities at particular times in the places we call home.

25. On a larger scale, one thinks immediately of America in this context given its history as a collecting point for international migration processes and diverse cultural interests. On travel and uprootedness, see Snyder (1990, pp. 23–26). On travel as metaphor, see Jackson (1995, p. 1) and Van den Abeele (1992).

26. Naming a place is a way of taming it, bringing it at least to the control of a mental appropriation in a familiar set of signs—to the level of place punctuated by the hearths and travels of the imagination if not of the physical self. That is the same process applied through colonial appropriations of others; that is, by translating them into our own cultural system of signs, we render them "subordinate," at least by category of existence. On the importance of naming in human experience, see Cheyfitz (1997) and Aitchison (2000, p. 94ff). Schama (1995) notes, "The wilderness, after all, does not locate itself, does not name itself. It was an act of Congress in 1864 that established Yosemite Valley as a place of sacred significance for the nation" (p. 7). See also Momaday (1969, p. 27).

27. Weller (1990, p. 14).

28. More or less following Bakhtin, by "architectonics" I mean the architecture of connections revealed between individuals and their wider environments, parts to whole in changing landscapes, including other people and other points of view, over time (Holquist, 1990, p. 149ff). Sensitive to readings from both sides of the cultural fences that separate us in fieldwork and life in general, and to the mutual constructions of our interactions under those circumstances, a poetics of place must be dialogic in nature. Furthermore, "a dialogic poetics must first of all be able to identify and arrange relations between points of view; it must be adequate to the complex architectonics that shape the viewpoint of he author toward his characters, the characters toward the author, and of all of these toward each other" (p. 162).

29. Speaking of an incident in the foothills of the Rocky Mountains, Smith (1997) recalls a telling moment "in the description of a colleague who had taken her class to the mountains, sat them in a circle, enticing them, in an ecological exercise, to 'breathe this place, to recollect themselves and their relations to . . . 'reconnect.' Suddenly, the heavy sounds of a cougar circling them can be heard, followed by the instantaneous and terrified evacuation of the place by the recollectors, the breathers, and the reconnectors! Whatever the pedagogy of the place may be, it has little to do with a warm cozy relationship with an imagined nature, and perhaps more to do with the courage to befriend one's own mortality in the midst of the ongoing project of self understanding" (p. 4). The wild inspires us to be practical. It also can be a tough experience (Snyder, 1990, p. 23).

30. Ducking the television travelogues designed to sell products on commercial breaks, the closest we

usually can come to wilderness today is to traffic in its remainder in places such as Yosemite, heavily marked by people—in fact, even created by people in so many important ways, including mapping and marking it as a preserve of sorts (Schama, 1995)—or in the outback stretches of earth where the timid never tread, be it alpine, desert, or swamp (Snyder, 1990, p. 6). Snyder (1990) sees these places as "the shrines saved from all the land that was once known and lived on by the original people, the little bits left as they were, the last little places where intrinsic nature totally wails, blooms, nests, glints away. They make up only 2 percent of the land of the United States" (p. 14).

31. Immersion in the unpaved has special merits for helping the process unfold. "A week in the Amazon, the high Arctic, or the northern side of the Western Himalayas," J. Turner (1996) writes, can show us that "what counts as wildness and wilderness is determined not by the absence of people, but by the relationship between people and place. A place is wild," he says, "when it is self-willed land. Native peoples usually (though definitely not always) 'fit' that order, influencing it but not controlling it, though probably not from a superior set of values but because they lack the technical means. Control increases with civilization, and modern civilization, being largely about control—an ideology of control projected onto the entire world—must control or deny wildness" (pp. 112–113).

32. Poulsen (1982, p. 116).

33. Some sacred spaces, of course, are purely man-made in their physical construction (e.g., the Vietnam memorial in Washington, D.C.), but even these are likely to be landscaped for beauty with a "natural" theme (Osborne, 2001; Véliz, 1996). Others are located in conspicuous landscapes, such as Mount Sinai and Devil's Mountain, none of which is a "sacred" space in its own right. They are interesting in their irregularities or are novel to people who encounter them as necessary interpreters of space. But that very reading is a primary source of significance—a projection of self, culture, and emotion that occurs somewhat ironically through an appropriation of the otherwise unobtainable by wrapping the experiences in metaphor, by acquiring places in image and imagination, and by bringing them near through semiosis and fantasy, if not actual physical presence. In his analysis of Native American sites, Gulliford (2000) identifies nine categories of sacred places: "(1) sites associated with emergence and migration tales; (2) sites of trails and pilgrimage routes; (3) places essential to cultural survival; (4) altars; (5) vision quest sites; (6) ceremonial dance sites; (7) ancestral ruins; (8) petroglyphs and pictographs; and (9) burial or massacre sites" (quoted in Leonard & McClure, 2004, p. 321). Building on that and Vine Deloria's work on Native American sites, Leonard and McClure (2004) identify sacred places on two axes: one that follows "a continuum from historical/actual to imaginary/metaphorical" and one that follows "a continuum from human to divine agency" (p. 325). Deloria gives us four categories "arranged on a scale of 'agency'—entirely human agency at one end versus the agency of 'Higher Powers' at the other" (p. 322). See also Dundes (1984) and Lane (2001).

34. Some sacred sites are deeply personal and private. On places sacred to one person that fail to move another, see Poulsen (1982, pp. 116–117).

35. True to this experience, and illustrative of the power of poetry to address such issues in laconic ways, see the defining principles and irony in Gregor's (2004) smart poem, "Mammals of North America." Despite the importance of hunting in both cultures, nothing could be further removed from the place of mammals in the world of the Koyukon (Brody, 1982; Nelson, 1983).

36. Only the overall story form and perhaps the emotions of shared experiences as sentient beings-in-place, especially in the conspicuous places of whatever we can call "nature" today, can frame these inferences for us. The rest must come from material representations (cf. Clarkson, 1998; Hodder, 1982, 1987, 1989; Lewin, 1986; Richardson, 1982; Zolbrod, 1987), from written history, or from that wonderful interim point—a living person whose knowledge pool runs a continuum of semiotica from early tribal history to the present. Such guides are rare, of course, if they exist at all in ultimately reliable forms. They all are influenced by literacy and related forms of communication in the modern world, but they can be found in our current landscapes. On teachers of sacred space, see Layton (1997, p. 122) and Snyder (1990, pp. 12, 78). On contemporary horticultural experts in the American Southwest, see Nabhan (1982). See also Behar (1993), Nelson (1980, 1983), Swann (1983), Swann and Krupat (1987), and Tedlock (1972, 1983, 1990, 1993).

37. Note the irony that what are often held to be the most palatable and picturesque landscapes are also sometimes the least habitable (Barthes, 1972, pp. 74–77). With an overview of the relationships of landscapes, aesthetics, and pleasure as they might obtain in the human species, Brown (1991) says, "One of the fundamental assumptions of evolutionary psychology is that matters closely related to our survival and reproduction have a likelihood of engaging our

emotions. Thus, although there might be little evidence of a general adaptation for an aesthetic sense, a . . . disparate collection of emotion-producing activities and entities may structure what we consider aesthetic. . . . Orians (1980) has examined such matters as the emotional reactions of explorers to different natural settings, the landscaping and planting of parks, and the criteria that make particular pieces of real estate especially valuable, to show that humans seem to have an innate preference for settings that would have been optimal habitats for our Pleistocene foraging ancestors. We like 'lakes, rivers, cliffs, and savannahs,' settings in which food, water, and protection (as in caves) were in optimal combination. Key elements in Orians' arguments are the emotional nature of the human preferences, and comparisons with habitat selection in other species, where its innate component is less questionable. Here the argument is that we have an innate tendency to prefer, seek out, and construct certain kinds of settings because we feel good in them" (pp. 115–116). On forests and the emergence of poetic wisdom, compare Rubinoff (1976, p. 104).

38. This is especially true in the light of the horrifying events of September 11, 2001, in the United States and the country's subsequent declaration of war on terrorism (Lincoln & Denzin, 2003a). The whole problem can be framed in its fundamentals as one of sacred space and what is or is not allowed to take place in it. On poetries and place and the different imaginaries of country and city, see Williams (1973). On entering an age of human flourishing, see Lincoln and Guba (2000). On the Burning Man Project, see Kozinets and Sherry (2004) and Sherry and Kozinets (2004).

39. They are often represented in the mix of more than one culture, society, and/or physical landscape, the kind of heterogeneous zones we find bisected by the colliding margins of cross-cultural frontiers. They are "borderlands" of the here and the hereafter or are "beaches" as Dening (1980, 1996) liberated the concept from the stereotyped margin of surf and sand. On the U.S.–Mexican border, see also Brady (2003b, pp. 89–90). On Chicano narratives and their literary and cultural borders, see Rosaldo (1989). On Australian aboriginal notions of trespass and "spatial prohibitions as a mode of boundary making," see Munn (2003). On frontiers and the possibilities of passing into myth time, see Snyder (1990, p. 14). On the concept of "regeneration through violence," see Slotkin (1973).

40. Neihardt (1959, p. 35).

41. According to Snyder (1990), "For preagricultural people, the sites considered sacred and given special care were of course wild" (p. 79). He adds, "The idea that 'wild' might also be 'sacred' returned to the Occident only with the Romantic movement" (p. 80).

42. In answering the question of why native cultures in general give so much importance to places, Abram (1996) sees the answer as obvious: "In oral cultures the human eyes and ears have not yet shifted their synaesthetic participation from the animate surroundings to the written word. Particular mountains, canyons, streams, boulder-strewn fields, or groves of trees have not yet lost the expressive potency and dynamism with which they spontaneously present themselves to the senses. A particular place in the land is never, for an oral culture, just a passive or inert setting for the human events that occur there. *It is an active participant in those occurrences* [precisely a poetic posture]. Indeed, by virtue of its underlying and enveloping presence, the place may even be felt to be the source, the primary power that expresses itself through the various events that unfold there" (p. 162). He adds, "It is precisely for this reason that stories are not told without identifying the earthly sites where the events in those stories occur. For the Western Apache, as for other traditionally oral peoples, human events and encounters simply cannot be isolated from the places that engender them. . . . From the Distant Time stories of the Koyukon people, and from the *'agodzaahi* tales of the Western Apache, we begin to discern that storytelling is a primary form of human speaking, a mode of discourse that continually weds the human community to the land. Among the Koyukon, the Distant Time stories serve, among other things, to preserve a link between human speech and the spoken utterances of other species, while for the Western Apache, the *'agodzaahi* narratives express a deep association between moral behavior and the land and, when heard, are able to effect a lasting kinship between persons and particular places. . . . The telling of stories, like singing and praying, would seem to be an almost ceremonial act, an ancient and necessary mode of speech that tends the earthly rootedness of human language. For narrated events, as Basso reminds us, always happen *somewhere.* And for an oral culture, that locus is never merely incidental to those occurrences. The events belong, as it were, to the place, and to tell the story of those events is to let the place itself speak through the telling" (pp. 162–163). See also Basso (1996a, 1996b), Carpenter (1980), Crapanzano (2004), Feld and Basso (1996), and Nelson (1983).

43. On movements toward symbolic order in modern architecture and the idea that every force evolves a

form, compare Poulsen (1982, pp. 118, 123–124). Schama (1995) adds, "And it is just because ancient places are constantly being given the topdressings of modernity (the forest primeval, for example, turning into the 'wilderness park') that the ambiguity of the myths at their core is sometimes hard to make out. It is there, all the same" (pp. 15–16).

44. Apropos of the current thesis, Deloria (1993) calls for "the possibility of new sacred places, underscoring even more the present, ongoing nature of the kinds of interactions between the human and the spiritual realms" (cited in Leonard & McClure, 2004, p. 324).

45. By dwelling on the language associated with primary emotions (and, therefore, the limbic system of the brain), poetry is capable of moving us sensuously and emotionally. Speaking of the power of poetry and prophecy, Leavitt (1997) says, "Much of this power is already implied in the nature of language itself. For the speaking subject, a linguistic element—a phoneme or word or grammatical pattern—not only says what it says, but does so cast in a specific form and carrying specific implications. That is to say, each linguistic element carries with it not only a semantic load but also both a material presence as a pattern of sound and a cloud of connotations and colorations picked up through the subject's life experience and the elements of our own history of use. In some circumstances, people attend not only to what is being said but equally or primarily to the sound- and meaning-resonances of how it is being said. This 'poetic mode of speech perception' . . . and production defines . . . the poetic function of language; language carries sometimes actualized but always potential punch above and beyond the punch of information conveyed. The effect may be aesthetic, emotional, or physical" (p. 3). On the "thrill" or "physical emotion" that can come from reading, "the undisappointed joy of finding that everything holds up and answers the desire it awakens," compare Heaney (1995, pp. 8–9). Bass (2000) notes that the artist has an "imperative to get as close to a thing as possible, not so much to create metaphors as to uncover them; to peel them way back to their source. For me there is undeniable solace and excitement in moving in as close as possible to things, in art, and in the woods—as close as possible to the source" (p. 73). On emotions and landscapes, see also Brown (1991, pp. 115–116).

46. See Abram (1996), Barthes (1972), Benjamin (1969a), Brady (2003a, 2003b), Crapanzano (2004), Gibbs (1994), Hoffman (1999), and Meletinsky (1998). Bachelard (1964), in his classic text *The Poetics of Space,* notes, "Great images have both a history and a prehistory; they are always a blend of memory and legend, with the result that we never experience an image directly. Indeed, every great image has an unfathomable oneiric depth to which the personal past adds special color" (p. 33). To him, "Primal images, simple engravings are but so many invitations to start imagining again. . . . By living in such images as these, in images that are as stabilizing as these are, we could start a new life, a life that would be our own, that would belong to us in our very depths. . . . And because of this very primitiveness, restored, desired, and experienced through simple images, an album of pictures of huts would constitute a textbook of simple exercises for the phenomenology of the imagination" (p. 33). Schama's (1995) collection of images and texts presents exactly that—an album of experiences that give us the past (albeit recent) as both imaginative history and a history of the imagination. It directs attention to the nature of landscape as myth, and vice versa, on America's frontiers and is, therefore, most instructive for our current purposes and fair ground for contextualizing creations and renewals of sacred space.

47. Finding (or reinventing) new leaders for positive turns on sacred space is consistent with the moral and ethical goals of our environmental critics (see, e.g., Snyder, 1990, p. 78). But in the process we must also ask *whether* we really want to renew these things as sacred in our personal lives and to integrate them uncritically in modern views of what is sacred. The relativity of the concept—what is sacred for you is not necessarily the same for others—has led, as J. Turner (1996, p. 22) reminds us, to one violent confrontation after another throughout history. Moreover, a failure to distinguish between formal and popular religions has bastardized the concept in contemporary America. Turner suggests that Disneyland, national parks, the site of President John F. Kennedy's assassination, and related "pilgrimage sites" are sacred "because of the function of entertainment and tourism in our culture. In a commercial culture, the sacred will have a commercial base. For many people, nothing is more sacred than the Super Bowl" (p. 22). That is not the sense of "sacred" that Snyder has in mind, but whatever the course of action taken, there is huge personal responsibility attached to it, for ourselves and for the collective futures of all who would revisit the savannahs and forests of our beginnings with a sense of respect and preservation rather than rapacious destruction.

48. Consider Schama (1995): "Whether such relationships are, in fact, habitual, at least as habitual as the urge toward domination of nature, said to be the

signature of the West, I will leave the reader to judge. Jung evidently believed that the universality of nature myths testified to their psychological indispensability in dealing with interior terrors and cravings. And the anthropologist of religion Mircea Eliade assumed them to have survived, fully operational, in modern, as well as traditional, cultures" (p. 15). Schama marks his own view as "necessarily more historical, and by that token much less confidently universal. Not all cultures embrace nature and landscape myths with equal ardor, and those that do go through periods of greater or less enthusiasm. What the myths of ancient forest mean for one European national tradition may translate into something entirely different in another" (p. 15). Schama has "tried not to let these important differences in space and time be swallowed up in the long history of landscape metaphors sketched in [his] book. But while allowing for these variations, it is clear the inherited landscape myths and memories share two common characteristics: their surprising endurance through the centuries and their power to shape institutions that we still live with. National identity, to take just the most obvious example, would lose much of its ferocious enchantment without the mystique of a particular landscape tradition: its topography mapped, elaborated, and enriched as a homeland" (pp. 15–16).

49. We are reminded in the process that "understanding the past traditions of landscapes can be a source of illumination for the present and the future," and with a lien on that, Schama (1995) says that it can also be a source for redeeming "the hollowness of contemporary life" (p. 17). This is not a promise of passage into Nirvana, an escape from the evils of the present into something constructed out of blind fantasy and a heavily romanticized past that can be regained in the future. Schama is too much of a realist for that. In acknowledging "the ambiguous legacy of nature myths," he points out that we must also "recognize that landscapes will not always be simple 'places of delight'—scenery as sedative, topography so arranged to feast the eye. For those eyes . . . are seldom clarified of the promptings of memory. And the memories are not all of pastoral picnics" (p. 18).

50. Compare Kroeber (1983): "Evidence of . . . interactivity is likely to impress us most in stories, such as those dealing with Coyote. These we find baffling because Coyote can be animal or man at any time and without any seeming consistency. This is a crucial imaginative point. The Indian imagination is not so rigidly tied as our own to given material forms and patterns. For us, to be 'characters' animals have to be anthropomorphized. The Indian imagination recognizes Coyote as both animal and man, or either animal or man, the duality in fact making him 'Coyote' rather than 'just' the exceedingly interesting four-footed predator. The complexity of the Indian imagination is germane to the practical core of the hunting songs we are considering here" (p. 329). See also Bright (1987), Buller (1983), Diamond (1986), Ekkehart and Lomatuway'ma (1984), Haile (1984), Hymes (1987), Lopez (1977, 1986, 1990a), Snyder (1990), and Tedlock and Tedlock (1975). On Abram, Merleau-Ponty, and the phenomenological argument that "places are the ground of direct human experience" and associated assumptions about the interactions of the body with things, including the idea that "all objects or things are 'alive' and capable of entering into a relationship with a human perceiver," see Gruenewald (2003, p. 623).

51. Momaday (1969, p. 6).

52. Consider Yi-Fu (1979): "Three principal types [of space], with large areas of overlap, exist—the mythical, the pragmatic, and the abstract or theoretical. Mythical space is a conceptual schema, but it is also pragmatic space in the sense that within the schema a large number of practical activities, such as the planting and harvesting of crops, are ordered. A difference between mythical and pragmatic space is that the latter is defined by a more limited set of economic activities. [On "trails to heaven" and "maps of dreams," see also Brody, 1982, pp. 46–47.] The recognition of pragmatic space, such as belts of poor and rich soil, is of course an intellectual achievement. When an ingenious person tries to describe the soil pattern cartographically, by means of symbols, a further move toward the conceptual mode occurs. In the Western world, systems of geometry—that is, highly abstract spaces—have been created out of primal spatial experiences" (pp. 16–17). Leonard and McClure (2004) argue, "Myths which take us to a sacred place where rejuvenation or immortality is possible—whether that place is a garden, a forest, a mountain, a well, lake, stream, fountain, or river—have the effect of transporting us back to the primordial and womblike condition that preceded our quotidian struggles with money, relationships, and the eventual loss of our physical and mental powers" (p. 325). Compare Brown (1991, p. 116).

53. Snyder (1990) likens language to "some kind of infinitely interfertile family of species spreading or mysteriously declining over time, shamelessly and endlessly hybridizing, changing its own rules as it goes" (p. 7). It is "a mind–body system that coevolved

with our needs and nerves. Like imagination and the body, [it] rises unbidden . . . [with] a complexity that eludes our rational intellectual capacities" (p. 9). However, in developing his anthropology of experience, Jackson (1995) makes the cogent observation that experience, unlike language, "covers everything that is the case. This is why words alone can never do justice to experience" (p. 160). "Words are signs, "stand-ins, arbitrary and temporary, even as language reflects (and informs) the shifting values of the people whose minds it inhabits and glides through" (Snyder, 1990, p. 8). But "no word is able to contain the moods of a moment" (Jackson, 1995, p. 5). "Life eludes our grasp and remains at large, always fugitive," never captured completely (p. 5). It "outstrips our vocabulary" (p. 5). "Like a forest in which there are clearings. Like a forest through whose canopy sunlight filters and fall" (p. 5). "Theodor Adorno called this the untruth of identity, by which he meant that concepts plunder but never exhaust the wealth of experience. Life cannot be pressed [exclusively] into the service of language. Concepts represent experience at the cost of leaving a lot unsaid. So long as we use concepts to cut up experience, giving value to some things at the expense of others, . . . we gain some purchase on the world, to be sure, but claiming that our concepts contain all that can be usefully said about experience, we close off the possibility of critique. It is only when we cease trying to control the world that we can overcome our fixation on the autarchy of concepts" (p. 5). "An anthropology of experience," Jackson says in that connection, "shares with phenomenology a skepticism toward determinate systems of knowledge. It plays up the indeterminate, ambiguous, and manifold character of lived experience. It demands that we enlarge our field of vision to take into account things central *and* peripheral, focal *and* subsidiary, illuminated *and* penumbral" (p. 160). These are the kinds of things, sometimes esoteric, bundled up by deep cultural contexts that are not easily discovered without access to the granaries of knowledge through the people who have built them. And even then, unable to be the "thing in itself," we will always have to settle for partial truths. On the difficulty of describing the experience of the *duende*, see Lorca (1985).

54. Richardson (1999b) observes, "To say that we must be in a story is not to say that we have our destiny already engraved in our neurons or awash in our subconscious. On the contrary, our life story continuously unfolds, shifts, changes. . . . Both place and story have to do with where we are, with location, but the *where* of each is distinct. The poetics of place is preeminently sensory. Smell, sound, touch, and especially sight are attributes of place, which is consequently visual and spatial. On the other hand, words strung together in speech and in writing constitute stories. Narrative, therefore, is verbal and temporal. In place, our dominant mode of relating to one another is through seeing; in written narrative, it is through reading. Interestingly, we use each mode as a metaphor of the other. When we want to emphasize that we're interpreting what we look at, we speak of 'reading the landscape.' Conversely, we exclaim, 'I see!' to convey the insight gained by reading a text" (p. 332). See also Brady (2003b, pp. xiv–xv).

55. Bass (2000) tells the story of how nature writers at a conference, "much to the initial confusion of some of the audience—kept talking about *specifics:* about buffalo, about native medicines, about narwhals, caribou, grizzlies and ravens; about the things they *knew*—and it was not until the second or third day that the audience began to grumble, 'What about the writing?' The panelists looked at one another in confusion. This *was* the writing. The world they inhabited—the so-called natural world of rock and sand and wood and ice—had become so imbued with power by their living deeply within it that the only language they were comfortable with was that of the specific. So deeply and passionately did they inhabit their landscapes—physically, emotionally, and spiritually—that trees became both trees and metaphors; wolves were both wolves *and* symbols; and the lives, the movements of these things, had a logic and pattern that did not transcend art but became art. They were living in their stories. They had stepped across that line, so that everything was story. They believed intensely in the world in which they lived" (pp. 71–72). This is an ancient process so far separated from contemporary writers by the invention and absorption of alphabetic literacy that the participants failed to recognize it until they were called out for their "absence of writing."

56. de Sahagún (1985, pp. 23–24).

57. Consider Tedlock (1983): "The argument that American Indian spoken narratives are better understood (and translated) as dramatic poetry than as an oral equivalent of written prose fiction may be summarized as follows: The content tends toward the fantastic rather than the prosaic, the emotions of the characters are evoked rather than described, there are no patterns of repetition or parallelism ranging from the level of words to that of whole episodes, the narrator's voice shifts constantly in amplitude and tone, and the flow of that voice is paced by pauses that segment its sounds into what I have chosen to call lines. Of all

these realities of oral narrative and performance, the plainest and grossest is the sheer alternation of sound and silence; the resultant lines often show an independence from intonation, from syntax, and even from boundaries of plot structure. I understand the fundamental sound-shape of spoken narrative in much the same way that Robert W. Corrigan understood drama when he wrote that 'the playwright—and also the translator—cannot really be concerned with "good prose" or with "good verse" in the usual sense of those terms. The structure is action, not what is said or how it is said but *when.*' It is above all the *when,* or what dramatists call 'timing,' that is missing in printed prose" (pp. 55–56).

58. Fritz (unknown date and source), translated by Thomas F. Powell.

59. My thinking on this builds on Foucault's concept of *epistemes* as the totality of relations in knowledge of a given epoch (Dreyfuss & Rabinow, 1983; Foucault, 1970, 1972), which I have in this case applied to the separation of human activities before and after the invention of writing and the subsequent proliferations of it through mass production printing. Abram's (1996) articulate treatment of the distortions posed by studying preliterates through the mentality of alphabetic literacy is applied directly to considerations of place and translation. Lowe (1982) has an extended delineation of the root of the problem: "Recent scholarship reveals that communications media, hierarchy of sensing, and epistemic order change in time. Hence the perceptual field constituted by them differs from period to period. There is a history of perception [that delimits] the changing content of the known" (p. 2), and it has changed dramatically in the communication pools that have separated human societies before and after the advent of writing and its proliferation through mass production printing.

60. Lowe (1982) says, "Without the support of print, speech in oral culture is assisted by the art of memory. Rhythmic words are organized into formulas and commonplaces, then set to metric patterns. In this way, they can be recalled and recited with great facility. That which can be recited and repeated will be preserved. The metric recitation of rhythmic formulas and commonplaces provides a communicational grid to determine knowledge in oral culture. Only those phenomena which fit existing formulas and commonplaces can be preserved as knowledge. The new and distinctly different will soon be forgotten. Knowledge in oral culture therefore tends to be preservative and unspecialized, its content nonanalytical but formulaic" (p. 3). He adds, "The introduction of written language, whether ideographic or alphabetic, and its preservation in some type of manuscript constituted a chirographic culture. Although it took a long time to accomplish, writing eventually detached knowledge from speech and memory. A written language preserved knowledge after the act of speech and beyond the lapse of memory. One could go over a piece of writing at will, learn it, and criticize it; whereas formerly, in an oral culture, knowledge depended on the performance of the speaker" (p. 3). On the modernization of myth, see Barthes (1972).

61. See Jackson (1995, pp. 156–157). Elsewhere, Jackson (1982) says, "Whenever one retraces one's steps in the imagination, an inevitable transformation occurs. One gives thought to things one did without thinking. One replaces words actually said with a vocabulary of one's own choosing. Face-to-face reality is subverted by a second order—written reality. Life gets rendered as [written] language" (p. 3). In constructing this thesis, Jackson draws "extensively on many studies in the ethnography of speaking" in an effort to "avoid any inadvertent domination of the world of preliterate possibilities by the modes of abstract analysis developed in literate cultures" (p. 3). See also Tedlock (1983): "I am reminded of the Zuni who asked me, 'When I tell these stories do you picture it, or do you just write it down?'" (p. 55). On Geertz and cultures as "texts" to be read, see also Tedlock (1999, p. 161).

62. Anthropologists are generally happy to declare that shamanism (the world's oldest profession) is the root of all performative art—a point made effectively by the ethnopoet Rothenberg (1981; see also Rothenberg & Rothenberg, 1983) and the anthropologist Harner (1990), among others. That links us to the Paleolithic era (ca. 100,000 years ago) and opens up ethnographic inquiry to what we are considering in the current work—an enlarged sense of communal ties through the history of talk, performance, myth, poetry, and being-in-place.

63. For various expressions of the same topic, compare Abram (1996), Abu-Lughod (1988), Basso (1996a, 1996b), Brody (1982), Clifton (1990), Damon (2003), Dundes (1972), Feld (1982), Feld & Basso (1996), Howes (1990), Hymes (1987), Jackson (1982), Kroeber (1983), Lavie (1991), Layton (1997), Metcalf (2002), Munn (2003), Nabhan (1982), Ricoeur (1991), Rothenberg (1972, 1985), Rothenberg & Rothenberg (1983), Swann & Krupat (1987), B. Tedlock (1992), D. Tedlock (1972, 1983, 1993, 1999), Zolbrod (1983, 1987).

64. Austin (1997, p. 61).

65. The concept of the sublime as "tending to inspire awe usually because of elevated quality (as of beauty, nobility, or grandeur) or transcendent excellence" figures into our sentient existence and survival prospects in several ways. Brown (1991) says, "One of the fundamental assumptions of evolutionary psychology is that matters closely related to our survival and reproduction have a likelihood of engaging our emotions. Thus, although there might be little evidence of a general adaptation for an aesthetic sense, a ... disparate collection of emotion-producing activities and entities may structure what we consider aesthetic" (p. 115), including the experiences of being-in-place. Writing about Burke, Bromwich (1997) says, "Burke's conclusion is that the feelings of the sublime and the beautiful in life, ... which may also be excited by moments of works in art, are an inseparable condition of existence" (p. 30). They push the edges and the limits of human nature. The theorist's job "is to show how the affective powers of the sublime and beautiful can be causes of mental activity without ideas or images. At the very end, he will offer a possible reason why words above all can affect us like this. The mind has a hunger for belief, and it has a natural tendency toward abstraction. The appeal of the sublime and the beautiful must somehow relate to that hunger and that tendency of the mind. And words, which bear no resemblance to things, which at the height of their influence on the passions leave no image at all, are therefore the leading artificial and natural source of our sympathy with the sublime and beautiful" (p. 32). Compare Denzin (1997) and Diamond (1987). Denzin (1997) points out, "Modernist ethnographers (and poets) stood outside their texts so as to produce a sense of awe or reverence or respect for what is being written about. The writer was missing from the text. The postmodern writer also seeks the sublime, but it is a new sublime—a nostalgic sublime that transgresses Diamond's poetry of pain. The new scribe seeks a sense of respect and awe for the lost writer who experiences what is being written about. What was previously unpresentable (the writer's experiences) is now what is presented. Paradoxically, that which is most sought after remains the most illusive" (p. 215).

66. Yi-Fu (1979) notes, "Place can acquire deep meaning for the adult through the steady accumulation of sentiment over the years. Every piece of heirloom furniture, or even a stain on the wall, tells a story" (p. 33). According to Schama (1995), "To see the ghostly outline of an old landscape beneath the superficial covering of the contemporary is to be made vividly aware of the endurance of core myths. ... And it is just because ancient places are constantly being given the topdressings of modernity (the forest primeval, for example, turning into the 'wilderness park') that the ambiguity of the myths at their core is sometimes hard to make out. It is there, all the same" (p. 16).

67. Historical trekking can be at once a new and a renewed experience. The "new" information (as word, image, symbol, sensation, etc.) builds on the "old" in that process and has the prospect of resorting it all in still newer terms, including the extensive "mazeway resyntheses" of individuals and groups in revitalization movements (Wallace, 1970). Smith (1997) argues, "The relationship between place and language is perhaps best understood through the experience of breakdown—personal and collective—when one experiences the sense that one's received language, with all of its grammatical enframements and vocabulary tools, is inadequate to express what one is currently realizing to be true about the world" (p. 3).

68. On poets making place an element of their own private mythology as opposed to surrendering obediently to the existing mythology of place, see Heaney (1980b, p. 148). That is a sensuous and intellectual mingling—a tension—of past and present in a nutshell, and therein lies a path to a personal poetics, to a poetry of history and place that speaks to consciousness, commitment, action, and myth—to a possible "marriage between the geographical country and the country of the mind, whether that country of the mind takes its tone unconsciously from a shared oral inherited culture, or from a consciously savored literary culture, or from both ... that constitutes the sense of place in its richest possible manifestation" (p. 132). See also Graves (1948:14–15) and, of course, Thoreau's (1854/1995) classic, *Walden.*

69. Poetic experiences also show that immersion in place has its shiftings as well, its contradictions and alienations, and that the alienations of an ethnographer are not restricted to encounters with other cultures (Damon, 2003). Estrangement can happen through the intellectual and aesthetic encounters that one has at home, that is, by freezing moments and interpreting their particulars as both ethnographers and poets must do. On close inspection, everything is strange, and that can be a powerful source of alienation, even from hearth and family (Heaney, 1980b, pp. 137–138). On the other hand, Heaney knows that staying with the comfort and imagination of a summer's day in a strange and rural landscape can bring forth an aesthetic sense of communion with "prehistoric

timelessness." These experiences must give way to the imagination, for that is the carpet on which the Muses fly and is the beacon that signals fair landing. The work is subjective, but that should not be a disqualification for anything except mathematics crammed into teaching formulas. Participation and self-conscious interpretation are how we learn about ourselves in place. Nature can be more in our appreciations than can "inanimate stone." It can be "active nature, humanized, and humanizing" (pp. 144–145).

70. Lame Deer and Erdoes (1972, p. 110).

71. For related work in an anthropological vein, see especially the verse and/or prose of Abu-Lughod (1988), Basso (1996a, 1996b), Brady (2003b, 2004), Cahnmann (2000, 2001), Diamond (1982, 1986, 1987), Farella (1993), Feld (1982), Feld and Basso (1996), Flores (1982, 1999), Hartnett (2003), Heaney (1980a, 1987), Hymes (1995, 2001), Jackson (1995), Kusserow (1998, 1999), Lavie (1991), Lewis (2002), Lopez (1991), Maynard (2003), Nowak (2000), Prattis (1985), Richardson (1982, 1998a, 1998b, 1999a, 1999b, 2001), Rosaldo (2003); Rose (1991), Sherry (1997), Simonelli (2001), Snyder (1969, 1974), Stewart (1996), Suiter (2002), Tarn (1991, 2002), B. Tedlock (1992), and D. Tedlock (1990, 1993).

72. Compare Vendler (1985): "In trying to speak for 'all men and women,' the poet risks losing selfhood altogether" (p. 60).

73. Thompson (1989) says, "What frames and defines a world is the act of participating in a context. To take part in something is to take part from an immensity of possibilities" (pp. 129–130). See also Taussig (1993).

74. None of this is to say that poetic texts (including myths) are empty of important or precise information—another blind prejudice of positivistic science (Brady, 1991a, 1991b, 1998, 2000, 2003a, 2003b; Brady & Kumar, 2000)—or to say that creativity in thought and communication enfranchises a free-for-all of interpretation, ungoverned by existing constraints on sensibility, reality, clarity, and possibility (Brady, 2003b, p. xxiv). On the inversions of poetry and myth, compare Barthes (1972, p. 134).

75. Everybody knows that scientific writing differs from poetry in fundamental ways, for example, that scientific writing is more clinical and less given to uncommon metaphors than is poetry. But an important theoretical implication that often goes unappreciated in these discussions is that each form technically plays a different language game; the positivists use language that is supposed to be transparent or invisible, whereas the humanists (and most pointedly the poets) do exactly the opposite by openly displaying their presence as observers and authors in their works. More than just a difference of "style," each mode of representation thereby has different criteria for deciding on acceptable or satisfactory forms of expression, and the implications of that are enormous. Changing the language of our descriptions, as Wittgenstein (1974) says, also changes the analytic game itself, including changing the premises for research entry points (Brady, 2004).

76. See also Stoller (1987, 2004) and Joy and Sherry (2003). Yi-Fu (1979) says, "The Eskimos' sense of space and place is very different from that of Americans" (p. 5). Compare Carpenter (1980) and Dundes (1972).

77. Not all poetry travels with equal effectiveness across personal and cultural boundaries—but then, what does? On the roles of preferences and form, on critics who enter a world not of their own making, and on the importance of slipping any poem into mind with good effect, see Brady (2000, p. 958). On Western ethnocentrisms, see Zolbrod (1983).

78. On Australian writer David Malouf and being at a loss for words, see Smith (1997, p. 3). J. Turner (1996), after an encounter with a mountain lion, says, "An aura of prehistory marked the night. Undoubtedly people still have experiences with animals like those of ancient epochs, however unintelligible to our modern lives—unintelligible because we no longer know how to describe them. The vocabularies of shamanism, totems, synchronicities, and She are *tongues again made bold by such experiences*—experiences many believe are irretrievably lost. I believe in the experiences, but I do not understand the vocabularies. I perceive this as my own failing. My life is devoid of practices that might link such events and words. And yet the very existence of such experience is moving—beyond words" (p. 47). Moreover, in a discussion of Hemingway, he asks the question: Where is the point "at which myth and nonlinguistic practices would be required to communicate?" (p. 97). On the whiteness of the page and experiential space beyond writing, see Juarroz (1988, cited in Brady, 1991a, p. 341). On the subjected body exceeding itself and becoming "a space of excess in which the physicality of cultural politics (vocality, tactility, touch, resonance) exceeds the rationalized clarity of 'system' and transcendent understanding," see Stewart (1996, p. 130). Rickman (2002–2003) argues, "Nature is not just a linguistic edifice and language is meaningless if it does not refer beyond itself" (p. 31). See also Maslow (1964) and Sherry and Schouten (2002).

79. Poetry loses, however, if it does not conform at some level to the experience of its audience. We must be able to exchange experiences. On separations of private and public voices, see Benjamin (1969b, p. 156) and Wolf (1982, p. 108). On lyric poetry, see Damon (2003) and Tedlock (1999, p. 56). On poetry and the need for historical contexts, see Hartnett and Engels (chap. 41, this volume). On poetry and the senses, see Stewart (2002). On ways of articulating history and place through poetry and painting, see Brady (2003b).

80. Addressing similar issues, Jackson (1995) says, "I wanted to develop a style of writing which would be consonant with lived experience in all its variety and ambiguity" (p. 4), including consciousness itself as a form of projected and prospective awareness. Consciousness "expresses interrelationships *between* self and other, subject and object, which do not have to be contrived because they are the very precondition of our human situation" (p. 169). Moving in that intellectual zone with an appealing and innovative mixed verse and prose account of his fieldwork in Africa, the poet/ethnographer Wilmsen (1999), knowing little of the local languages as his African journey began, queries himself: "While walking in the debilitating heat, I asked myself how I was going to make my experience intelligible to others" (p. xii). His answer? "It seemed to me that a way to do this lay in exposing the simultaneity of experience in individual life: recurrences in which earlier occurrences resonate—recognized as memories, expectations, reveries, informing each momentary awareness, shaping each" (pp. xi–xii). Wilmsen continues, "I have tried only to translate the texture of experience without claiming it to be mine alone. . . . I wanted to demonstrate that simultaneity of experience is not an exclusive prerogative of today's world but is a condition of being human. . . . I wanted to find a way to express the historicities of persons in contact—to express the fact that there are no alien cultures, only alienating ways of categorizing diversity" (p. xiv).

81. But consider the notion of "messy texts," that is, "texts that are aware of their own narrative apparatuses, that are sensitive to how reality is social[ly] constructed, and that [understand] that writing is a way of 'framing' reality. Messy texts are many sited, intertextual, always open-ended, and resistant to theoretical holism, but always committed to cultural criticism" (Denzin, 1997, p. 224). According to Denzin (1997), "Ethnopoetics and narratives of the self are messy texts: They always return to the writerly self—a self that spills over into the world being inscribed. This is a writerly self with a particular hubris that is neither insolent nor arrogant. The poetic self is simply willing to put itself on the line to take risks. These risks are predicated on a simple proposition: This writer's personal experiences are worth sharing with others. Messy texts make the writer part of the writing project. These texts, however, are not just subjective accounts of experience; they attempt to reflexively map the multiple discourses that occur in a given social space [see especially Wilmsen, 1999]. Hence, they are always multivoiced. No interpretation is privileged. These texts reject the principles of the realist ethnographic narrative that makes claims to both textual autonomy and epistemological validity" (p. 225). See also Brady (1998, 2000, 2003b, in press) and Marcus (1994).

82. "Theodor Adorno speaks of 'exact fantasy' to describe a genre of writing that is rigorously empirical but, without 'going beyond the circumference' of the empirical, rearranges constellations of experienced facts in ways that render them accessible and readable. It is a method of writing that repudiates the form of lineal and progressive argumentation. It is paratactic. No one element is subordinated to another. Perhaps the term 'exact fiction' best describes such an approach to ethnographic writing" (Jackson, 1995, pp. 163–164). Compare Brady (2003b), Favero (2003), and Metcalf (2002).

83. There are other effects as well. Tedlock (1983) argues, "'Event' orientation, together with an intensified appreciation of fantasy, has already led modern poets to recognize a kinship between their own work and the oral art of tribal peoples. As Jerome Rothenberg points out in *Technicians of the Sacred,* both 'modern' and tribal poets are concerned with oral performance, both escape the confines of Aristotelian rationalism, both transcend the conventional genre boundaries of written literature, and both sometimes make use of stripped-down forms that require maximal interpolation by audiences" (p. 55). These kinds of interests and the focus on poetry and interpretive methods in general in ethnopoetics join up with other forms of experimental texts in making "public what sociologists and anthropologists have long kept hidden: the private feelings, doubts, and dilemmas that confront the field-worker in the field setting" (Denzin, 1997, p. 214). They "humanize the ethnographic disciplines . . . under a postmodern aesthetic assumption concerning the sublime to make what was previously unpresentable part of the presentation itself" (p. 215). They simultaneously break from and continue "the ethnographic tradition of representing experiences of others," rejecting "the search for absolute truth that is suspicious of totalizing theory," breaking down as part

of the process "the moral and intellectual distance between reader and writer" (p. 215), and perhaps helping to close the gap with fresh approaches to what we, as modern peoples, have lost (or buried or in other ways deprioritized) since the advent of writing and the removal from daily contact with the soil and animals of our ancient selves.

84. Compare Lopez (1990b): "If, in a philosophy of place, we examine our love of the land—I do not mean a romantic love, but the love Edward Wilson calls biophilia, love of what is alive, and the physical context in which it lives, which we call 'the hollow' or 'the canebrake' or the 'woody draw' or 'the canyon'—if, in measuring our love, we feel anger, I think we have a further obligation. It is to develop a hard and focused anger at what continues to be done to the land not so that people can survive, but so that a relatively few people can amass wealth" (p. 42).

85. Neruda (1997, p. 213).

86. Abbey (1968, p. 131).

87. Fawning over noble savages or pristine environments and societies only clouds the issue. We need to catch ourselves in the act of oversimplifications and ethnocentric wishes. We need to be cognizant of the fact that, as Hartnett and Engels point out elsewhere in this volume (chap. 41), the life circumstances of the ancients were "like our own world—wracked with political, economic, and cultural dilemmas."

88. Gruenewald (2003) says, "An expanded framework for analyzing the power of place might include more discussion of Native American and other indigenous traditions, natural history, psychology, anthropology, architecture, sociology, cybernetics, ecological science, and religious studies, as well as all genres of imaginative literature. Once one begins interrogating the power of place as a construct for analysis, one sees that it might be, and increasingly is, applied constructively to any realm of human experience or inquiry. . . . The question is worth asking: Without focused attention to places, what will become of them—and of us?" (p. 646). On poetry in educational research, see also Cahnmann (2003).

89. By writing from their own body-grounded experiences and addressing directly those of others similarly embodied, both personally and conscientiously, poets can dice up what ails us into vivid and believable accounts. That is an empowering and political act, and poets are not strangers to it. On poetry and politics, see Heaney (1995, pp. 1, 7–8), von Hallberg (1987), and Rich (2003). On educational reform and taking "teachers and students beyond the experience and study of places to engage them in the political process that determines what these places are and what they will become," see Gruenewald (2003, pp. 620, 640). See also the pioneering and thoughtful work on "investigative poetry" by Hartnett and Engels (chap. 41, this volume) and the powerful testament to poetic rendering as a course of social action in Hartnett (2003).

90. See Lopez (1990b, 1998) and Snyder (1985). In *Arctic Dreams,* Lopez (1986) says that the "ethereal and timeless power of the land, that union of what is beautiful with what is terrifying, is insistent. It penetrates all cultures, archaic and modern" (p. 368). And just as we are necessarily situated in the land, "The land gets inside us, and we must decide one way or another what this means, what we will do about it"—accept it as it is, attempt "to achieve congruence with a reality that is already given a . . . reality of 'horror within magnificence, absurdity within intelligibility, suffering within joy,'" as one could argue fits the worldviews of the Inuit, or should we take our profound modern ability to alter the land, that is, "change it into something else" (p. 368)? In one respect, there is no choice at all. "The long pattern of purely biological evolution . . . strongly suggests that a profound collision of human will with immutable aspects of the natural order is inevitable" (p. 368). On place, technology, and representation, see also Sherry (2000).

91. Denzin (1997) knows that "good ethnography always uses language poetically, and good poetry always brings a situation alive in the mind of the reader" (p. 26).

◘ References

Abbey, E. (1968). *Desert solitaire: A season in the wilderness.* New York: Ballantine.

Abram, D. (1996). *The spell of the sensuous.* New York: Random House.

Abu-Lughod, L. (1988). *Veiled sentiments: Honor and poetry in a Bedouin society.* Berkeley: University of California Press.

Ackerman, D. (1990). *A natural history of the senses.* New York: Vintage.

Agee, J., & Evans, W. (1960). *Let us now praise famous men.* New York: Ballantine.

Aitchison, J. (2000). *The seeds of speech: Language origin and evolution.* New York: Cambridge University Press.

Allison, J., Hockey, J., & Dawson, A. (Eds.). (1997). *After writing culture: Epistemology and praxis in contemporary anthropology.* New York: Routledge.

Austin, M. (1997). *The land of little rain.* New York: Penguin.

Bachelard, G. (1964). *The poetics of space.* Boston: Beacon.

Barthes, R. (1972). *Mythologies* (A. Lavers, Trans.). New York: Hill & Wang.

Barthes, R. (1977). *Image, music, text* (S. Heath, Trans.). New York: Hill & Wang.

Barthes, R. (1982). *The empire of signs* (R. Howard, Trans.). New York: Hill & Wang.

Bass, N. (2000, Autumn). Why so many native writers? *Orion,* pp. 69–73.

Basso, K. H. (1996a). *Wisdom sits in places: Landscape and language among the Western Apache.* Albuquerque: University of New Mexico Press.

Basso, K. H. (1996b). Wisdom sits in places: Notes on a Western Apache landscape. In S. Feld & K. H. Basso (Eds.), *Senses of place* (pp. 53–90). Santa Fe, NM: School of American Research Press.

Bauman, R. (Ed.). (1992). *Folklore, cultural performances, and popular entertainment: A communications-centered handbook.* New York: Oxford University Press.

Behar, R. (1993). *Translated woman: Crossing the border with Esperanza's story.* Boston: Beacon.

Benjamin, W. (1969a). *Illuminations* (H. Arendt, Ed.). New York: Schocken.

Benjamin, W. (1969b). The storyteller. In H. Arendt (Ed.), *Illuminations* (pp. 83–109). New York: Schocken.

Berger, P. L., & Luckmann, T. (1966). *The sociology of knowledge.* New York: Doubleday.

Blackburn, T. R. (1971). Sensuous–intellectual complementarity in science. *Science, 172,* 1003–1007.

Brady, I. (Ed.). (1991a). *Anthropological poetics.* Savage, MD: Rowman & Littlefield.

Brady, I. (1991b). Harmony and argument: Bringing forth the artful science. In I. Brady (Ed.), *Anthropological poetics* (pp. 3–30). Savage, MD: Rowman & Littlefield.

Brady, I. (1993). Tribal fire and scribal ice. In P. Benson (Ed.), *Anthropology and literature* (pp. 248–278). Urbana: University of Illinois Press.

Brady, I. (1998). Two thousand and what? Anthropological moments and methods for the next century. *American Anthropologist, 100,* 510–516.

Brady, I. (1999). Ritual as cognitive process, performance as history. *Current Anthropology, 40,* 243–248.

Brady, I. (2000). Anthropological poetics. In N. K. Denzin & Y. S. Lincoln (Eds.), *Handbook of qualitative research* (2nd ed., pp. 949–979). Thousand Oaks, CA: Sage.

Brady, I. (2003a). Poetics. In M. Lewis-Beck, A. E. Bryman, & T. F. Liao (Eds.), *The Sage encyclopedia of social science research methods* (pp. 825–827). Thousand Oaks, CA: Sage.

Brady, I. (2003b). *The time at Darwin's Reef: Poetic explorations in anthropology and history.* Walnut Creek, CA: AltaMira.

Brady, I. (2004). In defense of the sensual: Meaning construction in ethnography and poetics. *Qualitative Inquiry, 10,* 622–644.

Brady, I. (in press). Greg Dening's *Islands and Beaches* (or, why some anthropological history is suspected of being literature). In B. V. Lal & D. Munro (Eds.), *Texts and contexts: Essays on the foundational texts of Pacific Islands historiography.* Honolulu: University of Hawaii Press.

Brady, I., & Kumar, A. (2000). Some thoughts on sharing science. *Science Education, 84,* 507–523.

Brann, E. T. (1991). *The world of the imagination: Sum and substance.* Savage, MD: Rowman & Littlefield.

Bright, W. (1987). The natural history of Old Man Coyote. In B. Swann & A. Krupat (Eds.), *Recovering the word: Essays on Native American literature* (pp. 339–387). Berkeley: University of California Press.

Brody, H. (1982). *Maps and dreams.* New York: Pantheon.

Bromwich, D. (1997). The sublime before aesthetics and politics. *Raritan, 16*(4), 30–51.

Brown, D. E. (1991). *Human universals.* New York: McGraw–Hill.

Brown, T. L. (2003). *Making truth: Metaphor in science.* Chicago: University of Illinois Press.

Bruner, J. (1986). *Actual minds, possible worlds.* Cambridge, MA: Harvard University Press.

Buller, G. (1983). Commanche and Coyote, the culture maker. In B. Swann (Ed.), *Smoothing the ground: Essays on Native American literature* (pp. 245–258). Berkeley: University of California Press.

Cahnmann, M. (2000). Driving through North Philly. *Quarterly West, 51,* 98–99.

Cahnmann, M. (2001, November–December). Fathering. *American Poetry Review,* p. 50.

Cahnmann, M. (2003). The craft, practice, and possibility of poetry in educational research. *Educational Researcher, 32*(3), 29–36.

Carpenter, E. (1980). If Wittgenstein had been an Eskimo. *Natural History, 89*(2), 72–76.

Casey, E. S. (1996). How to get from space to place in a relatively short stretch of time. In S. Feld & K. Basso (Eds.), *Senses of place* (pp. 13–52). Santa Fe, NM: School of American Research Press.

Caughey, J. L. (1984). *Imaginary social worlds: A cultural approach.* Lincoln: University of Nebraska Press.

Cheyfitz, E. (1997). *The poetics of imperialism: Translation and colonization from the Tempest to Tarzan.* Philadelphia: University of Pennsylvania Press.

Clarkson, P. B. (1998). Archaeological imaginings: Contextualization of images. In D. S. Whitley (Ed.), *Reader in archaeological theory: Post-processual and cognitive approaches* (pp. 119–130). New York: Routledge.

Classen, C. (1993). *Worlds of sense: Exploring the senses in history across cultures.* New York: Routledge.

Clifford, J., & Marcus, G. (Eds.). (1986). *Writing culture: The poetics and politics of ethnography.* Berkeley: University of California Press.

Clifton, J. A. (Ed.). (1990). *The invented Indian: Cultural fictions and government policies.* New Brunswick, NJ: Transaction.

Coles, J. (1979). *Experimental archaeology.* New York: Academic Press.

Crapanzano, V. (2004). *Imaginative horizons: An essay in literary-philosophical anthropology.* Chicago: University of Chicago Press.

Csordas, T. (1994). *Embodiment and experience: The existential ground of culture and self.* Cambridge, UK: Cambridge University Press.

Cushing, F. H. (1970). *My adventures in Zuni.* Palo Alto, CA: American West.

Damon, M. (2003). Some discourses on/of the divided self: Lyric, ethnography, and loneliness. *Xcp* [Cross-Cultural Poetics], *12,* 31–59.

Danesi, M. (1999). *Sign, thought, and culture.* Toronto: Canadian Scholars' Press.

Danesi, M., & Perron, P. (1999). *Analyzing cultures.* Bloomington: Indiana University Press.

de Sahagún, B. (1985). Aztec definitions. In J. Rothenberg (Ed.), *Technicians of the sacred* (2nd ed., pp. 23–24). Berkeley: University of California Press.

Deloria, V. (1993). *God is red: A native view of religion.* Golden, CO: Fulcrum.

Dening, G. (Ed.). (1974). *The Marquesan journal of Edward Robarts, 1797–1824.* Honolulu: University Press of Hawaii.

Dening, G. (1980). *Islands and beaches: Discourse on a silent land—Marquesas 1774–1880.* Honolulu: University Press of Hawaii.

Dening, G. (1988). *The bounty: An ethnographic history.* Melbourne, Australia: University of Melbourne, Department of History.

Dening, G. (1995). *The death of William Gooch: History's anthropology.* Melbourne, Australia: Melbourne University Press.

Dening, G. (1996). *Performances.* Chicago: University of Chicago Press.

Dening, G. (1998a). *Readings/Writings.* Melbourne, Australia: Melbourne University Press.

Dening, G. (1998b). Writing, rewriting the beach. *Rethinking History, 2*(2), 143–172.

Dening, G. (2004). *Beach crossings: Voyaging across times, cultures, and self.* Melbourne, Australia: Melbourne University Press.

Denzin, N. K. (1997). *Interpretive ethnography: Ethnographic practices for the 21st century.* Thousand Oaks, CA: Sage.

Denzin, N. K., & Lincoln, Y. S. (Eds.). (2000). *Handbook of qualitative research* (2nd ed.). Thousand Oaks, CA: Sage.

Denzin, N. K., & Lincoln, Y. S. (Eds.). (2002). *The qualitative inquiry reader.* Thousand Oaks, CA: Sage.

Diamond, S. (1982). *Totems.* Barrytown, NY: Open Book/Station Hill.

Diamond, S. (1986). *Going west.* Northampton, NY: Hermes House Press.

Diamond, S. (1987). The beautiful and the ugly are one thing, the sublime another: A reflection on culture. *Cultural Anthropology, 2,* 268–271.

Dreyfuss, H. L., & Rabinow, P. (1983). *Michel Foucault: Beyond structuralism and hermeneutics.* Chicago: University of Chicago Press.

Dundes, A. (1972, May). Seeing is believing. *Natural History,* pp. 11–14.

Dundes, A. (1984). *Sacred narrative: Readings in the theory of myth.* Berkeley: University of California Press.

Ekkehart, M., & Lomatuway'ma, M. (1984). Hopi Coyote tales: Istutuwutsi. Lincoln: University of Nebraska Press.

Farella, J. (1993). *The wind in a jar.* Albuquerque: University of New Mexico Press.

Favero, P. (2003). Phantasms in a "starry" place: Space and identification in a central New Delhi market. *Cultural Anthropology, 18,* 551–584.

Feld, S. (1982). *Sound and sentiment: Birds, weeping, poetics, and song in Kaluli expression.* Philadelphia: University of Pennsylvania Press.

Feld, S. (1996). Waterfalls of song: An acoustemology of place resounding in Bosavi, Papua New Guinea.

In S. Feld & K. H. Basso (Eds.), *Senses of place* (pp. 91–135). Santa Fe, NM: School of American Research.

Feld, S., & Basso, K. H. (Eds.). (1996). *Senses of place.* Santa Fe, NM: School of American Research.

Fernandez, J. (2003). Emergence and convergence in some African sacred places. In S. M. Low & D. Lawrence-Zúñiga (Eds.), *The anthropology of space and place: Locating culture* (pp. 186–203). Oxford, UK: Blackwell.

Finnegan, R. (1992). *Oral poetry: Its nature, significance, and social context.* Bloomington: Indiana University Press.

Finnegan, R., & Orbell, M. (Eds.). (1995). *South Pacific oral traditions.* Bloomington: Indiana University Press.

Fletcher, C. (1967). *The man who walked through time.* New York: Random House.

Flores, T. (1982). Field poetry. *Anthropology and Humanism Quarterly, 7*(1), 16–22.

Flores, T. (1999). *In place.* Geneva, NY: Hobart and William Smith Colleges Press.

Foucault, M. (1970). *The order of things: An archaeology of the human sciences.* New York: Random House.

Foucault, M. (1972). *The archaeology of knowledge.* New York: Pantheon.

Fritz, W. H. (unknown). Fesselung [Entrapment] (T.. F. Powell, Trans.).

Gallagher, W. (1993). *The power of place: How our surroundings shape our thoughts, emotions, and actions.* New York: Harper.

Geertz, C. (1983). *Local knowledge: Further essays in interpretive anthropology.* New York: Basic Books.

Geertz, C. (1996). Afterword. In S. Feld & K. Basso (Eds.), *Senses of place* (pp. 259–262). Santa Fe, NM: School of American Research Press.

Gewertz, D. B., & Errington, F. K. (1991). *Twisted histories, altered contexts: Representing the Chambri in a world system.* New York: Cambridge University Press.

Gibbs, R. W., Jr. (1994). *The poetics of mind: Figurative thought, language, and understanding.* New York: Cambridge University Press.

Graves, R. (1948). *The white goddess: A historical grammar of poetic myth.* New York: Octagon.

Greenblatt, S. (1991). *Marvelous possessions: The wonder of the New World.* Chicago: University of Chicago Press.

Gregor, D. (2004). Mammals of North America [poem]. *Raritan, 23*(3), 20–23.

Gruenewald, D. (2003). Foundations of place: A multidisciplinary framework for place-conscious education. *American Educational Research Journal, 40,* 619–654

Gulliford, A. (2000). *Sacred objects and sacred places: Preserving tribal tradition.* Boulder, CO: University of Colorado Press.

Haile, B. H. (1984). *Navajo Coyote tales: The Curly Tó Aheedlíinii version.* Lincoln: University of Nebraska Press.

Hallyn, F. (1990). *The poetic structure of the world: Copernicus and Kepler.* New York: Zone Books.

Harner, M. (1990). *The way of the shaman.* New York: Harper & Row.

Hartnett, S. J. (2003). *Incarceration nation: Investigative prison poems of hope and terror.* Walnut Creek, CA: AltaMira.

Heaney, S. (1980a). *Poems 1965–1975.* New York: Farrar, Straus, & Giroux.

Heaney, S. (1980b). The sense of place. In S. Heaney (Ed.), *Preoccupations: Selected prose, 1968–1978* (pp. 131–149). London: Faber & Faber.

Heaney, S. (1987). *The Haw lantern.* New York: Farrar, Straus, & Giroux.

Heaney, S. (1995). *The redress of poetry.* New York: Farrar, Straus, & Giroux.

Heidegger, M. (1971). *Poetry as language and thought.* New York: Harper & Row.

Heidegger, M. (1977). Building, dwelling, thinking. In A. Hofstader (Trans.), *Poetry, language, thought* (pp. 145–161). New York: Harper & Row.

Herzfeld, M. (2004). *The body impolitic: Artisans and artifice in the global hierarchy of value.* Chicago: University of Chicago Press.

Hinsley, C. M. (1999). Life on the margins: The ethnographic poetics of Frank Hamilton Cushing. *Journal of the Southwest, 41,* 371–382.

Hirsch, E., & O'Hanlon, M. (Eds.). (1995). *The anthropology of landscape: Perspectives on place and space.* New York: Oxford University Press.

Hobsbawm, E., & Ranger, T. (Eds.). (1983). *The invention of tradition.* New York: Cambridge University Press.

Hodder, I. (1982). *Symbols in action: Ethnoarchaeological studies of material culture.* London: Cambridge University Press.

Hodder, I. (1987). Converging traditions: The search for symbolic meanings in archaeology and geography. In J. M. Wagstaff (Ed.), *Landscape and culture: Geographical and archaeological perspectives* (pp. 134–145). Oxford, UK: Blackwell.

Hodder, I. (Ed.). (1989). *The meaning of things: Material culture and symbolic expression.* London: Unwin Hyman.

Hoffman, C. (1999). *The seven story tower: A mythic journey through space and time.* Cambridge, MA: Perseus.

Holquist, M. (1981). Introduction. In M. M. Bakhtin (Ed.), *The dialogic imagination: Four essays by M. M. Bakhtin* (pp. xv–xxxiv). Austin: University of Texas Press.

Holquist, M. (1990). *Dialogism: Bakhtin and his world.* New York: Routledge.

Howes, D. (1990). Controlling textuality: A call for a return to the senses. *Anthropologica, 32,* 55–74.

Hymes, D. (1987). Anthologies and narrators. In B. Swann & A Krupat (Eds.), *Recovering the word; Essays on Native American literature* (pp. 41–84). Berkeley: University of California Press.

Hymes, D. (1995). Port Orford. *American Anthropologist, 97,* 659–660.

Hymes, D. (2001). Poetry. In A. Duranti (Ed.), *Key terms in language and culture* (pp. 187–189). Oxford, UK: Blackwell.

Jackson, M. (1982). *Allegories of the wilderness: Ethics and ambiguity in Karanko narratives.* Bloomington: Indiana University Press.

Jackson, M. (1995). *At home in the world.* Durham, NC: Duke University Press.

Joy, A., & Sherry, J. F., Jr. (2003). Speaking of art as embodied imagination: A multisensory approach to understanding aesthetic experience. *Journal of Consumer Research, 30,* 259–282.

Juarroz, R. (1988). *Vertical poetry* (W. S. Merwin, Trans.). San Francisco: North Point Press.

Karp, I., & Levine, S. (Eds.). (1991). *Exhibiting cultures: The poetics and politics of museum display.* Washington, DC: Smithsonian Institution Press.

Kerouac, J. (1958). *The Dharma bums.* New York: Penguin.

Kerouac, J. (1959). *Mexico City blues.* New York: Grove.

Kerouac, J. (1960). *Lonesome traveler.* London: Mayflower.

Kövecses. Z. (2002). *Metaphor: A practical introduction.* New York; Oxford University Press.

Kozinets, R. V., & Sherry, J. F., Jr. (2004). Dancing on common ground: Exploring the sacred at Burning Man. In G. St. John (Ed.), *Rave culture and religion* (pp. 287–303). New York: Routledge.

Kroeber, K. (1983). Poem, dream, and the consuming of culture. In B. Swann (Ed.), *Smoothing the ground: Essays on Native American oral literature* (pp. 323-333). Berkeley: University of California Press.

Kusserow, A. (1998). Poems. *Anthropology and Humanism, 23,* 209–210.

Kusserow, A. (1999). American nomads. *Anthropology and Humanism, 24,* 65–70.

Kuusisto, S. (1998). *Planet of the blind: A memoir.* New York: Dial Press.

Lakoff, G., & Johnson, M. (1999). *Philosophy in the flesh: The embodied mind and its challenge to Western thought.* New York: Basic Books.

Lame Deer. J. F., & Erdoes, R. (1972). *Lame Deer: Seeker of visions.* New York: Pocket Books.

Lane, B. C. (2001). Giving voice to place: Three models for understanding American sacred space. *Religion and American Culture, 11*(1), 53–81.

Lansing, J. S. (1985). The aesthetics of the sounding of the text. In J. Rothenberg & D. Rothenberg (Eds.), *Symposium of the whole: A range of discourse toward an ethnopoetics* (pp. 241–257). Berkeley: University of California Press.

Laughlin, C. D., Jr., & d'Aquili, E. G. (Eds.). (1974). *Biogenetic structuralism.* New York: Columbia University Press.

Laughlin, C. D., Jr., & Brady, I. (Eds.). (1978). *Extinction and survival in human populations.* New York: Columbia University Press.

Laughlin, C. D., Jr., McManus, J., & d'Aquili, E. G. (1992). *Brain, symbol, and experience.* New York: Columbia University Press.

Lavie, S. (1991). *The poetics of military occupation: Mzeina allegories of Bedouin identity under Israeli and Egyptian rule.* Berkeley: University of California Press.

Layton, R. (1997). Representing and translating people's place in the landscape of Northern Australia. In J. Allison, J. Hockey, & A. Dawson (Eds.), *After writing culture: Epistemology and praxis in contemporary anthropology* (pp. 122–143). New York: Routledge.

Leavitt, J. (1997). *Poetry and prophecy: The anthropology of inspiration.* Ann Arbor: University of Michigan Press.

Leonard, S., & McClure, M. (2004). *Myth and knowing: An introduction to world mythology.* New York: McGraw-Hill.

Levenson, J. C. (2004). Writing history in the age of Darwin. *Raritan, 23*(3), 115–148.

Lévi-Strauss, C. (1976). *Structural anthropology* (Vol. 2). New York: Basic Books.

Lewin, R. (1986). Anthropologist argues that language cannot be read in stones. *Science, 233,* 23–24.

Lewis, T. (2002). Five poems in three languages. *Anthropology and Humanism, 27,* 192–198.

Lincoln, Y. S., & Denzin, N. K. (Eds.). (2003a). *9/11 in American culture.* Walnut Creek, CA: AltaMira.

Lincoln, Y. S., & Denzin, N. K. (Eds.). (2003b). *Turning points in qualitative research: Tying knots in a handkerchief.* Walnut Creek, CA: AltaMira.

Lincoln, Y., & Guba, E. (2000). Paradigmatic controversies, contradictions, and emerging confluences. In N. K. Denzin & Y. S. Lincoln (Eds.), *Handbook of qualitative research* (2nd ed., pp. 163–188). Thousand Oaks, CA: Sage.

Lopez, B. (1977). *Giving birth to Thunder, sleeping with his daughter: Coyote builds North America.* New York: Avon.

Lopez, B. (1986). *Arctic dreams: Imagination and desire in a northern landscape.* New York: Bantam Books.

Lopez, B. (1990a). *Crow and weasel.* San Francisco: North Point Press.

Lopez, B. (1990b). *The rediscovery of North America.* New York: Vintage.

Lopez, B. (1991, Autumn). A sense of place. *Old Oregon,* pp. 15–17.

Lopez, B. (1998). *Desert notes/River notes.* New York: Bard.

Lorca, F. G. (1985). The duende. In J. Rothenberg & D. Rothenberg (Eds.), *Symposium of the whole: A range of discourse toward an ethnopoetics* (pp. 43–51). Berkeley: University of California Press.

Low, S. M., & Lawrence-Zúñiga, D. (Eds.). (2003). *The anthropology of space and place: Locating culture.* Oxford, UK: Blackwell.

Lowe, D. M. (1982). *History of bourgeois perception.* Chicago: University of Chicago Press.

Marcus, G, (1994). What comes (just) after "post"? The case of ethnography. In N. K. Denzin & Y. S. Lincoln (Eds.), *Handbook of qualitative research* (pp. 563–574). Thousand Oaks, CA: Sage.

Marcus, G. (1998). *Ethnography through thick and thin.* Princeton, NJ: Princeton University Press.

Marshall, M. (2004). *Namoluk beyond the reef: The transformation of a Micronesian community.* Boulder, CO: Westview.

Maslow, A. H. (1964). *Religions, values, and peak experiences.* Columbus: Ohio State University Press.

Maynard, K. (2003, February). Thirteen ways of looking at a camel. *Anthropology News,* pp. 8, 11.

Meletinsky, E. M. (1998). *The poetics of myth* (G. Lanoue & A. Sadestsky, Trans.). New York: Routledge.

Merleau-Ponty, M. (1962). *Phenomenology of perception.* London: Routledge & Kegan Paul.

Merrell, F. (2000). *Change through signs of body, mind, and language.* Prospect Heights, IL: Waveland.

Merwin, W. S. (1997). *Flower and hand: Poems 1977–1983.* Port Townsend, WA: Copper Canyon Press.

Metcalf, P. (2002). *They lie, we lie: Getting on with anthropology.* London: Routledge.

Midgley, M. (2001). *Science and poetry.* New York: Routledge.

Miller, A. I. (1996). *Insights of genius: Imagery and creativity in science and art.* New York: Springer-Verlag.

Mitchell, R. G. (1983). *Mountain experience: The psychology and sociology of adventure.* Chicago: University of Chicago Press.

Momaday, N. S. (1969). *The way to Rainy Mountain.* Albuquerque: University of New Mexico Press.

Montgomery, S. L. (1996). *The scientific voice.* New York: Guilford.

Munn, N. D. (2003). Excluded spaces: The figure in the Australian aboriginal landscape. In S. M. Low & D. Lawrence-Zúñiga (Eds.), *The anthropology of space and place: Locating culture* (pp. 92–109). Oxford, UK: Blackwell.

Nabhan, G. P. (1982). *The desert smells like rain: A naturalist in Papago Indian country.* San Francisco: North Point Press.

Neihardt, J. G. (1959). *Black Elk speaks.* New York: Pocket Books.

Nelson, R. K. (1980). *Shadow of the hunter: Stories of Eskimo life.* Chicago: University of Chicago Press.

Nelson, R. K. (1983). *Make prayers to the raven: A Koyukon view of the northern forest.* Chicago: University of Chicago Press.

Nelson, V. (1996). H. P. Lovecraft and the Great Heresies. *Raritan, 15*(3), 92–121.

Neruda, P. (1997). The word. In S. Mitchell (Trans.), *Full woman, fleshly apple, hot moon: Selected poems of Pablo Nerudapp* (pp. 213–217). New York: HarperCollins.

Nowak, M. (2000). *Revenants.* Minneapolis: Coffee House Press.

Ohnuki-Tierney, E. (1981). *Illness and healing among the Sakhalin Ainu.* Cambridge, UK: Cambridge University Press.

Ong, W. (1967). *The presence of the word.* New Haven, CT: Yale University Press.

Orians, G. H. (1980). *Habitat selection: General theory and applications to human behavior.* In J. S. Lockard

(Ed.), *The evolution of human social behavior* (pp. 49–66). New York: Elsevier.

Osborne, B. S. (2001). Landscapes, memory, monuments, and commemoration: Putting identity in its place. *Canadian Ethnic Studies, 33,* 39–77.

Paz, O. (1981). *Piedra de Sol/Sunstone* (E. Weinberger, Trans.). New York: New Directions.

Perrin, M. (1987). *The way of the dead Indians: Guajiro myths and symbols* (M. Fineberg, Trans.). Austin: University of Texas Press.

Pluciennik, M. (1999). Archaeological narratives and other ways of telling. *Current Anthropology, 40,* 653–678.

Polanyi, M., & Prosch, H. (1975). *Meaning.* Chicago: University of Chicago Press.

Poulsen, R. C. (1982). *The pure experience of order: Essays on the symbolic in the folk material culture of western America.* Albuquerque: University of New Mexico Press.

Pratt, M. L. (1992). *Imperial eyes: Travel writing and transculturation.* New York: Routledge.

Prattis, I. (Ed.). (1985). *Reflections: The anthropological muse.* Washington, DC: American Anthropological Association.

Rich, A. (2003). *What is found there: Notebooks on poetry and politics.* New York: Norton.

Richardson, M. (1975). Anthropologist: The myth teller. *American Ethnologist, 2,* 517–533.

Richardson, M. (1982). Being-in-the-plaza versus being-in-the-market: Material culture and the construction of social reality. *American Ethnologist, 9,* 421–436.

Richardson, M. (1998a). Poetics in the field and on the page. *Qualitative Inquiry, 4,* 451–462.

Richardson, M. (1998b). The poetics of a resurrection: Re-seeing 30 years of change in a Colombian community and in the anthropological enterprise. *American Anthropologist, 100,* 11–22.

Richardson, M. (1999a). The Anthro in Cali. *Qualitative Inquiry, 5,* 563–565.

Richardson, M. (1999b). Place, narrative, and the writing self: The poetics of being in the Garden of Eden. *Southern Review, 35,* 330–337.

Richardson, M. (2001). The Anthro writes a day. *Qualitative Inquiry, 7,* 54–58.

Rickman, P. (2002–2003/December–January). The poet's metaphysical role. *Philosophy Now,* pp. 30–31.

Ricoeur, P. (1991). *From text to action: Essays in hermenutics II.* Evanston, IL: Northwestern University Press.

Rosaldo, R. (1989). *Culture and truth: The remaking of social analysis.* Boston: Beacon.

Rosaldo, R. (2003). Poems. *Anthropology and Humanism, 28,* 111–113.

Rose, D. (1991). In search of experience: The anthropological poetics of Stanley Diamond. In I. Brady (Ed.), *Anthropological poetics* (pp. 219–233). Savage, MD: Rowman & Littlefield.

Rothenberg, J. (Ed.). (1972). *Shaking the pumpkin: Traditional poetry of the Indian North Americas.* New York: Doubleday.

Rothenberg, J. (1981). *Pre-faces and other writings.* New York: New Directions.

Rothenberg, J. (Ed.). (1985). *Technicians of the sacred: A range of poetries from Africa, America, Asia, Europe, and Oceania* (2nd ed.). Berkeley: University of California Press.

Rothenberg, J., & Rothenberg, D. (Eds.). (1983). *Symposium of the whole: A range of discourse toward an ethnopoetics.* Berkeley: University of California Press.

Rubinoff, L. (1976). Vico and the verification of historical interpretation. In M. M. Tagliacozzo & D. P. Verene (Eds.), *Vico and contemporary thought* (pp. 94–121). New York: Humanities Press.

Sammons, K., & Sherzer, J. (Eds.). (2000). *Translating Latin American verbal art.* Washington, DC: Smithsonian Institution Press.

Saraydar, S. C. (1976). Experimental archaeology: A dynamic approach to reconstructing the past. *Artifacts, 5,* 6–7,10.

Saraydar, S. C. (1986). Are legend days over? *Anthropology and Humanism Quarterly, 11,* 10–14.

Saraydar, S. C., & Shimada, I. (1973). Experimental archaeology: A new outlook. *American Antiquity, 38,* 344–350.

Schama, S. (1995). *Landscape and memory.* New York: Knopf.

Seeger, A. (1975). The meaning of body ornaments. *Ethnology, 14,* 211–224.

Seeger, A. (1981). *Nature and society in Central Brazil: The Suya Indians of Mato Grasso.* Cambridge, MA: Harvard University Press.

Sherry, J. F., Jr. (1997). Trivium Siam. *Consumption, Markets, and Culture, 1*(1), 91–95.

Sherry, J. F., Jr. (2000). Place, technology, and representation. *Journal of Consumer Research, 27,* 273–278.

Sherry, J. F., & Kozinets, R. V. (2004). Sacred iconography in secular space: Altars, alters, and alterity at the Burning Man Project. In C. C. Otnes & T. M. Lowrey (Eds.), *Contemporary consumption rituals: A research anthology* (pp. 291–311). Mahwah, NJ: Lawrence Erlbaum.

Sherry, J. F., Jr., & Schouten, J. (2002). A role for poetry in consumer research. *Journal of Consumer Research, 29,* 218–234.

Simonelli, J. (2001). Conflict zone: Expressions of fieldwork in Chiapas. *Anthropology and Humanism, 26,* 91–100.

Slotkin, R. (1973). *Regeneration through violence: The semantics of social creation and control.* Middletown, CT: Wesleyan University Press.

Smith, D. G. (Ed.). (1997). The geography of theory and the pedagogy of place. *Journal of Curriculum Theorizing, 13*(3), 2–4.

Snyder, G. (1969). *Earth house hold.* New York: New Directions.

Snyder, G. (1974). *Turtle Island.* New York: New Directions.

Snyder, G. (1978). *Myths and texts.* New York: New Directions.

Snyder, G. (1985). Poetry and the primitive: Notes on poetry as an ecological survival technique. In J. Rothenberg & D. Rothenberg (Eds.), *Symposium of the whole: A range of discourse toward an ethnopoetics* (pp. 90–103). Berkeley: University of California Press.

Snyder, G. (1990). *The practice of the wild.* New York: North Point Press.

Spiegelberg, H. (1975). *Doing phenomenology: Essays on and in phenomenology.* The Hague, Netherlands: Martinus Nijhoff.

Stewart, K. (1996). *A space on the side of the road: Cultural poetics in an "other" America.* Princeton, NJ: Princeton University Press.

Stewart, S. (2002). *Poetry and the fate of the senses.* Chicago: University of Chicago Press.

Stoller, P. (1987). *Sensuous scholarship.* Philadelphia: University of Pennsylvania Press.

Stoller, P. (1989). *The taste of ethnographic things: The senses in anthropology.* Philadelphia: University of Pennsylvania Press.

Stoller, P. (2004). Sensuous ethnography, African persuasions, and social knowledge. *Qualitative Inquiry, 10,* 817–835.

Stoller, P., & Olkes, C. (1986). Bad sauce, good ethnography. *Cultural Anthropology, 1,* 336–352.

Stoller, P., & Olkes, C. (1987). *In sorcery's shadow: A memoir of apprenticeship among the Songhay of Niger.* Chicago: University of Chicago Press.

Suiter, J. (2002). *Poets on the peaks: Gary Snyder, Philip Whalen, and Jack Kerouac in the North Cascades.* Washington, DC: Counterpoint.

Suskind, P. (1986). *Perfume: The story of a murderer.* New York: Pocket Books.

Swann, B. (Ed.). (1983). *Smoothing the ground: Essays on Native American oral literature.* Berkeley: University of California Press.

Swann, B., & Krupat, A. (Eds.). (1987). *Recovering the word; Essays on Native American literature.* Berkeley: University of California Press.

Tagliacozzo, M. M., & Verene, D. P. (Eds.). (1976). *Vico and contemporary thought.* New York: Humanities Press.

Tarn, N. (1991). *Views from the Weaving Mountain: Selected essays in poetics and anthropology.* Albuquerque: University of New Mexico Press.

Tarn, N. (2002). *Selected poems: 1950–2000.* Middletown, CT: Wesleyan University Press.

Taussig, M. (1993). *Mimesis and alterity: A particular history of the senses.* New York: Routledge.

Tedlock, B. (1992). *The beautiful and the dangerous: Dialogues with the Zuni Indians.* New York: Penguin.

Tedlock, D. (1972). *Finding the center: Narrative poetry of the Zuni Indians.* New York: Dial Press.

Tedlock, D. (1983). *The spoken word and the work of interpretation.* Philadelphia: University of Pennsylvania Press.

Tedlock, D. (1990). *Days from a dream almanac.* Urbana: University of Illinois Press.

Tedlock. D. (1993). *Breath on the mirror: Mythic voices and visions of the living Maya.* Albuquerque: University of New Mexico Press.

Tedlock, D. (1999). Poetry and ethnography: A dialogical approach. *Anthropology and Humanism, 24,* 155–167.

Tedlock, D., & Tedlock, B. (Eds.). (1975). *Teachings from the American Earth: Indian religion and philosophy.* New York: Liverlight.

Thompson, W. I. (1989). *Imaginary landscape: Making worlds of myth and science.* New York: St. Martin's.

Thoreau, H. D. (1995). *Walden.* Boston: Houghton Mifflin. (Original work published in 1854)

Turner, J. (1996). *The abstract wild.* Tucson: University of Arizona Press.

Turner, M. (1996). *The literary mind.* New York: Oxford University Press.

Van den Abeele, G. (1992). *Travel as metaphor: From Montaigne to Rousseau.* Minneapolis: University of Minnesota Press.

Véliz, C. (Ed.). (1996). *Monuments for an age without heroes.* Boston: Boston University Press.

Vendler, H. (1985, November 7). Looking for poetry in America. *New York Review of Books,* pp. 53–60.

Verene, D. P. (1976). Vico's philosophy of imagination. In M. M. Tagliacozzo & D. P. Verene (Eds.), *Vico and contemporary thought* (pp. 20–43). New York: Humanities Press.

von Hallberg, R. (1987). *Politics and poetic value.* Chicago: University of Chicago Press.

Wallace, A. F. C. (1970). Revitalization movements. In A. F. C. Wallace (Ed.), *Culture and personality* (pp. 188–189). New York: Random House.

Weinstein, F. (1990). Who should write history? *SUNY Research, 10*(3), 20–21.

Weller, A. (1990). The hunter. In J. Davis, S. Muecke, M. Narogin, & A. Shoemaker (Eds.), *Paperbark: A collection of black Australian writings* (p. 14). St. Lucia, Australia: University of Queensland Press.

White, H. (1978). *Tropics of discourse: Essays in cultural criticism.* Baltimore, MD: Johns Hopkins University Press.

White, R. (2004). The geography of American empire. *Raritan, 23*(3), 1–19.

Williams, R. (1973). *The country and the city.* New York: Oxford University Press.

Wilmsen, E. N. (1999). *Journeys with flies.* Chicago: University of Chicago Press.

Wittgenstein, L. (1974). *On certainty* (G. E. M. Anscombe & G. H. Von Wright, Eds.). Oxford, UK: Blackwell.

Wolf, B. J. (1982). *Romantic re-vision: Culture and consciousness in nineteenth-century American painting and literature.* Chicago: University of Chicago Press.

Wolf, M. (1992). *A thrice-told tale: Feminism, postmodernism, and ethnographic responsibility.* Stanford, CA: Stanford University Press.

Wooley, N. (1992). *Virtual worlds: A journey in hype and hyperreality.* Cambridge, MA: Blackwell.

Yi-Fu, T. (1979). *Landscapes of fear.* New York: Pantheon.

Zolbrod, P. G. (1983). Poetry and culture: The Navajo example. In B. Swann (Ed.), *Smoothing the ground: Essays on Native American oral literature* (pp. 221–244). Berkeley: University of California Press.

Zolbrod, P. G. (1987). When artifacts speak: What can they tell us? In B. Swann & A. Krupat (Eds.), *Recovering the word: Essays on Native American literature* (pp. 13–40). Berkeley: University of California Press.

40

CULTURAL POESIS

The Generativity of Emergent Things

Kathleen Stewart

What follows is a piece of imaginative writing grounded in an intense attention to the *poesis,* or creativity, of ordinary things. This is an ethnographic attention, but it is one that is loosened from any certain prefabricated knowledge of its object. Instead, it tracks a moving object in an effort (a) to somehow record the state of emergence that animates things cultural and (b) to track some of the effects of this state of things—the proliferation of everyday practices that arise in the effort to know what is happening or to be part of it, for instance, or the haunting or exciting presence of traces, remainders, and excesses uncaptured by claimed meanings.

The writing here is committed to speculations, experiments, recognitions, engagements, and curiosity, not to demystification and uncovered truths that snap into place to support a well-known picture of the world. I ask the reader to read actively—to follow along, read into, imagine, digress, establish independent trajectories and connections, disagree. My own voice is particular and partial, tending in this case to be a surreal, dream-like description of ordinary spaces and events. The subject I "am" in the stories I tell is a point of impact meandering through scenes in search of linkages, surges, and signs of intensity. I suppose that the writing gropes toward embodied affective experience. Finally, the writing is also a set of provocations in that it tries to cull attention to moments of legibility and emergence, to moments of impact (instead of to stable subjects), to models of agency that are far from simple or straightforward, to the vitality or animus of *cultural poesis* in the jump or surge of affect (rather than on the plane of finished representations), and to the still life—the moment when things resonate with potential and threat.

In calling this particular arena of things cultural poesis—the creativity or generativity in things cultural—I am thinking of the ways in which this field of emergent things has been written into cultural theory in various ways by Walter Benjamin, Michel Foucault, Mikhail Bakhtin, Roland Barthes, Gilles Deleuze, Raymond Williams, Donna Haraway, Marilyn Strathern, Eve Sedgwick, Michael Taussig, and others. There are Foucault's (1990) theses on the productivity and micropoetics of power, Williams's (1977) attention to emergent structures of feeling, Benjamin's (1999, 2003) theories of allegory (vs. symbol) and his own nomadic tracking of dream worlds still resonant in material things, Bakhtin's (1982, 1984) fundamental theorization and elaboration of the social poetics lodged in language, texts, and social worlds, and Barthes's (1975, 1977, 1981, 1985) intense and sustained insistence on the workings of spaces and pleasures in between, or outside, or somehow in excess of the recognized objects we call texts, experience, meaning, concept, and analysis. Deleuze and Guattari (1987) polemicized the conflict between meaning-based models of culture and models that track actual events, conjunctures, and articulations of forces to see what they do. In the wake of their critique, they outlined a theory of the affective as a state of potential, intensity, and vitality (see also Guattari, 1995). Contemporary feminist theorists, notably Haraway (1997, 2003), Strathern (1991, 1992a, 1992b, 1999), and Sedgwick (1992, 1993, 1997, 2003), have carefully—and with enormous creative energy of their own—worked to theorize the generativity in things cultural and to make room for ways of thinking and writing it, as has Taussig (1986, 1992, 1993, 1997, 1999).

Here, I try to incite curiosity about the vitality and volatility of cultural poesis in contemporary U.S. public culture through a story of ethnographic encounters (see also Stewart, 1996, 2000a, 2000b, 2002a, 2002b, 2003a, 2003b).

Ordinary Intensities: Affect, Vitality, Generativity

This is a story about public circulations in moments of vital impact. It takes place in the United States during an ongoing present that began some time ago. This is a time and place in which an emergent assemblage made up of a wild mix of things—technologies, sensibilities, flows of power and money, daydreams, institutions, ways of experiencing time and space, battles, dramas, bodily states, and innumerable practices of everyday life—has become actively generative, producing wide-ranging impacts, effects, and forms of knowledge with a life of their own. This is what I mean by cultural poesis.

Here, I offer some random examples of the generativity of all things in a state of cultural emergence. The objects of my story are emergent vitalities and the ordinary practices that instantiate or articulate them, if only partially and fleetingly. Caught, or glimpsed, in their very surge to be realized, these are things that are necessarily fugitive, shifting, opportunistic, polymorphous, indiscriminate, aggressive, dreamy, unsteady, practical, unfinished, and radically particular.

The writing here is one that tries to mimic felt impacts and half-known effects as if the writing were itself a form of life. It follows leads, sidesteps, and delays, and it piles things up, creating layers on layers, in an effort to drag things into view, to follow trajectories in motion, and to scope out the shape and shadows and traces of assemblages that solidify and grow entrenched, perhaps doing real damage or holding real hope, and then dissipate, morph, rot, or give way to something new. It talks to the reader not as a trusted guide carefully laying out the perfect links between theoretical categories and the real world but rather as a subject caught in the powerful tension between what can be known and told and what remains obscure or unspeakable but is nonetheless real. Its thoughts are speculative, and its questions are the most basic. What is going on? What floating influences now travel through public routes of circulation and come to roost in the seemingly private domains of hearts, homes, and dreams? What forces are becoming sensate as forms, styles, desires, and practices? What does it mean to say that particular events and strands of affect generate impacts? How are impacts registered in lines of intensity? How are people quite literally charged up by the sheer surge of things in the making? What does cultural poesis look like?

Dreamland

The roller-coaster ride of the American dream had come into a sharp-edged focus. Good and bad. Winning and losing. Those were your choices. Anxious and haunted sensibilities tracked unwanted influences and veiled threats in idioms of addiction, trauma, and conspiracy while dreams of transcendence and recluse set afloat reckless hopes of winning or escape. Life was animated in equal parts by possibility and impossibility. We lurched between poles of hope and despair as overwrought dreams flopped to the earth, only to rise up again, inexplicably revitalized, like the monster in a horror movie or the fool who keeps going back for more. Lines of escape were fascinating too—the rocketing fortunes of the rich and famous, the dream of a perfect getaway cottage, the modest success stories of people getting their lives together again. New lifestyles proliferated at the same dizzying pace as did the epidemic of addictions and the self-help shelves at the bookstore.

The political dynamism of this tense mix of dreams and nightmares registered in an everyday life infused with the effort to track and assimilate the possibilities and threats lodged in things. Newly charged forms of the desire to know, to see, and to make a record of what was behind or underneath surfaces and systems formed a network of ordinary practices. Proliferating practices of turning desires and ideals into matter both encoded the everyday effort to master, test, and encounter emergent forces and demarcated a state of being tuned in to the mainstream. The new objects of mass desire promised both inclusion in the very winds of circulation and the nested still life of a home or identity resting securely in the eye of the storm.

As previously public spaces and forms of expression were privatized, previously privatized arenas of dreams, anxieties, agencies, and morals were writ large on public stages as scenes of impact. Yet the world had become weirdly mysterious just when it started to seem like a private life writ large or some kind of collective psyche institutionalized and exported in a global mutation. It was like a net had grown around a gelatinous mutating substance, creating a strange and loose integration of planes of existence and sensibilities. Things had become both highly abstract and intensely concrete, and people had begun to try to track emergent forces and flows on these variegated registers without really knowing what they were doing. Somehow it was all personal, but it was also something huge flowing through things.

The feminist slogan, "the personal is political," took on a new charge of intensity and swirled in spinning and floating contexts far beyond any simple ideological clarity or political program.

Ordinary Life

We were busy. Homes were filled with the grounding details of getting the rent money together, getting or keeping jobs, getting sick, getting well, looking for love, trying to get out of things we had gotten ourselves into, eating in, working out, raising kids, walking dogs, remodeling homes, and shopping. There were distractions, denials, shapeshifting forms of violence, practical solutions, and real despair. For some, one wrong move was all it took. Worries swirled around the bodies in the dark. People bottomed out watching daytime television. Credit cards were maxed out. There was downsizing and unemployment. There was competition to get kids into decent schools and for them to keep their grades up. Schedules had to be constantly juggled to keep up with dance classes or layoffs. Dizzying layers of tasks filled in the space of a day.

People took walks in their neighborhoods, peering into windows by night and murmuring over beautiful flowerbeds by day. Or, we scrambled to find ways to get to work and back on unreliable buses that quit running at night. We baked birthday cakes or ordered them from the supermarket decorated with Tigger or a golf course. We "flipped off" other drivers, read the luscious novels and sobering memoirs, disappeared into the Internet, and shopped at Wal-Mart and the other megastores because they were cheap, convenient, or new and had slogans such as "Getting It Together" and "Go Home a Hero."

Positions were taken, habits were loved and hated, dreams were launched and wounded. There was pleasure in a clever or funny image. Or in being able to see right through things. Some people claimed that they could rise above the flow and walk on water. Others wore their irony like an accessory that gave them room to maneuver. There were all the dreams of purity, martyrdom, a return to nature, getting real, having an edge, and beating the system.

Just about everyone was part of the secret conspiracy of ordinary life to get what he or she could out of it. There were the dirty pleasures of holing up to watch one's secret bad TV show, taking a trip to the mall, working out in spinning classes at the gym, spending nights on the Internet, or playing music loud in the car on the way to the supermarket.

Games

There were games you could play. One was the driving game of trying to predict when the car up ahead was going to try to change lanes. Some people developed a sixth sense about it. They discovered that if they concentrated on the car they could sense when it was considering a move, even when the driver was not signaling a lane change and when the car itself was not surreptitiously leaning to the edge of the lane or acting "nervous." The game of the sixth sense became a pleasure and a compulsion in itself. It spread fast, even without the usual help of expert commentary.

You could try out this game in supermarket checkout lines too. There the game was to try to size up the flow of a checkout line in a glance. How fast is that cashier? Does that woman have coupons? That one looks like a check writer. That one looks like a talker. But the checkout line game was harder than the driving game. Even a brilliant choice could be instantly defeated by a dreaded price check or the cash register running out of tape. And once you made your choice, you were stuck with it. Already impatient, you might then start to feel a little desperate. You could switch to multitasking—make a phone call, make lists in your head, or get to work on your palm pilot. Or, you could scan the surrounding bodies and tabloid headlines for a quick thrill or an ironic inner smirk at signs of other people's eccentricity or gullibility. Or, you could just check *yourself* out by opening and paging through *Home and Garden* or *Glamour* or *Esquire*. You could relax into the aura of tactile bodies, living rooms, and gardens that staged the jump from fantasy to flesh and back again right before your eyes. The glossy images offered not so much a blueprint of how to look and live as the much more profound experience of watching images touch matter.

Odd Moments

At odd moments in the course of the day, you might raise your head in surprise or alarm at the uncanny sensation of a half-known influence. Private lives and the public world had gotten their wires crossed. Any hint of private movement would be sniffed out and thrown up on public stages, and people now took their cues so directly from circulating sensibilities that the term "hardwired" became shorthand for the state of things.

Public specters had grown intimate. The imaginary had grown concrete on public stages. All of those bodies lined up on the talk shows, outing their loved ones for this or that monstrous act. Or the reality TV shows, with the camera busting in on intimate dramas of whole families addicted to sniffing paint right out of the can. We would zoom in to linger, almost lovingly, on the gallon-sized lids scattered around on the living room carpet and then pan out to focus on the faces of the parents, and even the little kids, with big rings of white paint encircling their cheeks and chins like some kind of self-inflicted stigmata.

The labor of looking had been retooled and upgraded so that we could cut back and forth between the images popping up in the living room and some kind of real world out there.

America's Most Wanted aired photos of bank robbers with and without beards so that you could scan the faces at the local convenience store looking for a match.

The streets were littered with cryptic, half-written signs of personal/public disasters. The daily sightings of homeless men and women holding up signs while puppies played at their feet could haunt the solidity of things with the shock of something unspeakable. *Hungry. Will work for food. God bless you.*

The sign hits the senses with a mesmerizing and repellent force. Too sad. The graphic lettering that pleads for the attention of the passing cars glances off the eye as something to avoid like the plague. Moving on. But it also holds the fascination of catastrophe, the sense that something is happening, the surge of affect toward a profound scene.

The handmade, handheld sign of the homeless on the side of the road pleads to be recognized, if only in passing. In its desperation, the sign makes a gesture toward an ideological center that claims the value of willpower ("will work for food") and voices the dream of redemption ("God bless you"). But it is abject; it offers no affect to mime, no scene of a common desire, no line of vitality to follow, no intimate secret to plumb, no tips to imbibe for safety or good health. Instead, it sticks out of the side of vision. The shock of something unreal because it is too real, too far outside the recognized world, unspeakable. There is no social recipe for what you can do about homelessness or even what you can do with your eyes when confronted with homelessness face to face. We live in a profound social fear of encounters like this.

Even to glance out of the corner of the eye at the sign on the side of the road is a dizzying sidestep. What the glance finds in the scene it glances at, half panicked, is the excluded other's abject surge to be included in the wind of circulation—the mainstream. Its message is too stark; it begs. It mimes the discourse of the mainstream to the letter, pushing it to the point of imitation or parody or fraud. It makes the mainstream seem unreal and heartless—dead.

A dollar bill stuck out of a car window gets a quick surge forward from the one with the sign and the heightened, yet unassimilated, affect of a raw contact. "God bless you."

Now we are trudging the rough terrain of bodies and the sensuous accumulation of impacts.

Whatever

Jokes had started to circulate about how we might as well wire ourselves directly to sensation buttons and just skip the step of content altogether. One day an e-mail came her way from Penny, a friend in the neighborhood who liked to keep up a running commentary on quirky characters and scenes spied from her studio windows or fabricated on drowsy afternoon walks. Penny would stop by to report tidbits and then move on. A light touch. When she used the e-mail, it was to forward funny tales filled with delicious descriptive details sent to her from like-minded others building a corpus of matters to chew on. This one told the tale of something that happened shortly after the attacks of September 11, 2001, in a medical clinic where a friend of a friend of Penny's apparently worked:

> Of course, it's not the big money area and the building is very rinky-dink. Not a big target for anthrax, let's just put it that way. She works with mothers who have drug abuse problems and the office downstairs treats juvies [juveniles]. Apparently one of the women who works downstairs turned on the a/c [air conditioner] (window unit) and a white dust sprayed out all over her. Yikes. They called the CDC [Centers for Disease Control and Prevention] and men in white suits and gas masks invaded. My friend who works upstairs was dubious—and so the people in her office just stayed and worked while the downstairs was cordoned off and investigated. They rushed the substance off to the lab and put everyone who was in the office on Cipro. Then the test results came back. Low and behold, the substance tested positive for cocaine! So good, isn't it? They think one of the juvies hid his stash in the a/c when he was afraid of being searched. I think it's a brilliant idea to start pumping cocaine into the workplace. No need for caffeine anymore. Let's just move right on up to the next level of productivity inspiration. Whadya say?

A Little Accident, Like any Other

She was in a café in a small town in west Texas. A place where ranchers hang out talking seed prices, fertilizer, and machines and where strangers passing through town are welcome entertainment. The sun had gone down, and she was half-way through her fresh-killed steak and baked potato when the biker couple came in limping.

All eyes rotated to watch them move to a table and sit down. The couple talked intently, as if something was up, and from time to time they exchanged startled looks. When she walked past the couple's table on her way out, they raised their heads and asked whether she was heading out on the west road and whether she could look for bike parts. They had hit a deer coming into town and dumped their bike. The deer, they said, had fared much worse.

The room came to a dead stop as all ears tuned in to the sentience of the crash, still resonating in the bikers' bodies. Slowly, taking their sweet time, people began to offer questions from their tables, drawing out the details. Then other stories began to surface of other deer collisions and strange events at that place on the west road.

As she left, she pictured how, during the days to come, people would keep their eyes open for deer parts and bike parts when they traveled the west road out of town. She imagined that there would be more talk. Conversations would gather around the event and spin off into other questions such as the overpopulation of deer, hunting regulations, and the new law that legalized riding without a helmet. There might be discussions of how to fix bikes (and especially this particular make of bike), what parts might break or twist when the bike is dumped, and who was a good bike mechanic. Or, people might talk about the condition of the roads. The image of hitting the wide open road or surviving the desert injured might come up. The talk might call up anything from the image of sheer speed encountering a deer caught in one's headlights to the abstracted principles of freedom, fate, and recklessness.

But one way or another, the little accident would compel a response. It would shift people's life trajectories in some small way, change them by literally changing their course for a minute or a day. The chance event might add a layer of story, daydream, and memory to things. It might unearth old resentments or suddenly bring a new conflict to a head. It might even compel a search for lessons learned. Resonating levels of body and mind might begin to rearrange themselves into simpler choices—good luck and bad luck, animal lives lost and threats to machine-propelled humans, risk-taking wild rides and good old common sense.

But for now at least, and in some small way in the future too, the talk would secretly draw its force from the resonance of the event itself. Its simple and irreducible singularity. And the habit of watching for something to happen would grow.

Scanning

Everyday life was now infused with the effort to track and assimilate the possibilities and threats lodged in things. Newly charged forms of the desire to know, to see, and to record what was behind surfaces and inside systems formed a network of ordinary practices.

She was no different from anyone else. All of her life, she had been yelling "pay attention!" but now she was not sure whether that was such a good idea. Hypervigilance had taken root as people watched and waited for the next thing to happen. Like the guy she heard about on the radio who spends his whole life recording everything he does: "Got up at 6:30 am, still dark, splashed cold water on my face, brushed my teeth, 6:40 went to the bathroom, 6:45 made tea, birds started in at 6:53. . . . "

Or, there was the neighbor on a little lake in Michigan whose hobby was recording his every move on video—his walks in the neighborhood and in the woods, his rides in his Ford Model T, his forays into Polish folk dances where old women went round and round the dance floor together, the monthly spaghetti suppers at the Catholic church in town. He gave one of his videos to her and her friends to watch. They played it one night—three anthropologists peering at whatever came their way from the weird world out there. It was a video of him walking around the lake in the winter snow and ice. They heard his every breath and footstep. There were some deer droppings on the path and some snow piles with suspicious shapes. Then he was walking up to Bob and Alice's cabin (the couple were in Florida for the winter), and he was zooming in on a huge lump of something that was pushing out the black plastic wrapped around the base of the house. Uh oh. Could be ice from a broken water main. Maybe the whole house was full of ice. The neighbor guy wondered out loud, if in fact it was ice, what would happen when the ice thawed. Could be a real problem. He said that maybe he would send a copy of his video on to Bob and Alice down in Florida. Then he moved on. Back to his breathing and the icicles on trees and his footsteps in the snow. Tracking the banal, scanning for trauma.

The three anthropologists looked at each other. What was that? She was mesmerized by it, like it held a key to how the ordinary could crack open to reveal something big and hidden that it had swallowed long ago. The other two were not so easily swayed. It was some kind of weirdness that pushed banality to the point of idiocy and made no sense at all. A puzzle as to why anyone would want to record the droning sameness of things, looking for something worth noting to come his way. Some strange threat or promise that popped up just for a minute and then sank below the surface again as if nothing had ever happened. A shimmering—there one minute and gone the next. Or maybe some lyrical scene you would want to remember. Something with *meaning*.

All of this watching things was mostly a good-natured thing. Like happy campers, people would put up with a lot of nothing in hopes of a glimpse of something. The ordinary was the mother lode that they mined, hoping for a sighting of a half-known something coming up for air.

It could be that ordinary things were beginning to seem a little "off," and that was what drew people's attention to them. Or, maybe the ordinary things had always seemed a little off if you stopped to think about them.

There were the obsessive compulsives who kept track of things because they had to ("Got up at 6:30 a.m., still dark, splashed cold water on my face. . . . "). These people became sightings in themselves.

Or, there were those who gave shape to their everyday by inventing practices of mining it for something different or special. People like her friends, Joyce and Bob, who lived in the woods in New Hampshire. He was a lumberjack. She cleaned those little 1950s tourist cabins that were called things such as "Swiss Village" and "Shangrila." She had left her husband and four kids after years of living straight in a regime of beatings under the sign of Jesus. She went out the back window one day and never looked back. Then she met Bob when she was tending bar, and the two took a walk on the wild side together that lasted for a dozen happy years (although not without trouble and plenty of it). He had a drinking problem, and she let him have it because he worked hard. He would hit the bottle when he got home at night and all weekend long. She called him "Daddy" even though she was a good 10 years older and pushing 50.

Joyce and Bob moved from rental cabin to rental cabin in the north woods. They invited raccoons into their cabin as if the animals were pets. They got up at 5 a.m. to write in their diaries, and then when they got home at night they would read their daily entries out loud and look at the artsy photos of treetops and bees' nests that Bob took. Finally, they were able to get a "poor people's" loan to buy a little cabin they had found in some God-forsaken place on the north side of the lake and to fix it up. But then a card came from Joyce saying that Bob had left her for "that floozy" he met in a bar.

She wonders whether Joyce still keeps a diary, whether she still fancies the serendipitous discovery of happiness and looks for ways to deposit it in the ordinary, or whether something else has happened to her ordinary.

◘ The Anthropologists

The anthropologists kept doing the fun things they did together. Like knocking on the doors of the little fishermen's huts on the frozen lake. They would invite themselves in for a visit, but then they would sit down on the bench and the fishermen would not say anything. Not even "who are you?" or "what are you doing here?" So, they sat together in a wild and awkward silence, staring down into the hole in the ice and the deep dark waters below. The anthropologists could not think of a single question that made any sense at all.

When the anthropologists took walks in the woods, they would come across hunters. The hunters were more talkative than the ice fishermen. That is because they all wanted the friendly, nosy, overeducated strangers to know that they were not "Bambi killers." Maybe some other hunters were, but not them—the new breed. They were nice, and a lot of them had been to college and had things to say about politics and the environment and the state. Most of the time there was a woman in the group. The others were teaching her to hunt. Everyone—the anthropologists too—would cower when the mean-looking game wardens came around a bend looking for poachers. The wardens were the bad guys. They would drive slowly past in postapocalyptic cars with burned paint and giant guns and spotlights mounted on the hood. They would fix us with hard stares, and you could see the muscles jump under their camouflage hunting suits. These guys were jumpy.

Being Jumpy

Sometimes, the jumpy move would take over. Lingis (1994) saw that this had happened among miners at the Arctic Circle:

> The young miner who showed me the mine put out every cigarette he smoked on his hand, which was covered with scar tissue. Then I saw the other young miners all had the backs of their hands covered with scar tissue. . . . When my eye fell on them it flinched, seeing the burning cigarette being crushed and sensing the pain. . . . The eye does not read the meaning in a sign; it *jumps* from the mark to the pain and the burning cigarette, and then jumps to the fraternity signaled by the burning cigarettes. (p. 96)

A Slashing

On the river in Austin, Texas, in the early morning, joggers pass over the long high bridge and stop to stretch their hamstrings on its metal rails. Pairs of friends, about to part for the day, will stop to stare out at the expanse of watery sights laid out below—fishermen in flat-bottomed boats sit upright in straight-backed chairs, giant blue herons poise on drowned cottonwoods, new limestone mansions perched on the cliffs above throw reflections halfway across the river. Crew boats pass silently under the bridge like human-powered water bugs skimming the surface. Occasionally, a riverboat will thrust itself slowly up the river, dredging the hard mass of the water up and over its wheel. Here, the world-in-a-picture still vibrates, as if it was just at that very moment that the real world crossed paths with an imagined elsewhere and the two realms hung suspended together in a still life.

Sometimes there are scenes of quiet desperation.

Sometimes people leave memorials on the bridge.

One morning, a crude sign appeared, taped to the metal railing. Below it was a shrine—yellow ribbons and a Sacred Heart of Jesus votive candle with half-burned sticks of incense stuck in the wax. The names Angela and Jerry were written in bold letters at the top of the sign, like the names of young lovers repeated over and over in school notebooks or graffitied on train trestles. The star-crossed lovers' names were harshly crossed out and followed by the words "Relationship destroyed, with malice by Federal Agents & A.P.D. [Austin Police Department] for beliefs guaranteed under U.S. Constitutional Bill of Rights. I miss you Angela, Jessica, & Furry Dog Reef."

It was signed "Always, Jerry."

Below the signature were two graphics: the nickname "Yankee Girl" encircled by a pierced heart and a thick black box encasing the prayer "Please Come Back." Then a final howl and a promise:

> Angela, Jessica and Furry Dog Reef. . . . I miss you.
>
> May God have mercy on the souls of the hateful, evil, vindictive people who conspired to take you from me, and did so with success. Angela, I will love you always and forever.
>
> I miss you babe,
>
> Jerry

At the bottom, another pierced heart held Yankee Girl in its wounded arms.

The sign was both cryptic and as crystal clear as a scream. Bitter fury was its vitality and its end. Its drive to a sheer satisfaction quivered like flesh in its wavering letters. It heaved grief and longing at the world not as an outer expression of an inner state but more directly as an act of the senses making contact with pen and paper and matches. Its slashing was like the self-slashing of young women who cut themselves so that they can feel alive or literally come to their senses. It had the same self-sufficient fullness and did not ask for interpretation or dream of a meaning.

This is a sensibility as common as it is striking. It is the kind of thing you see everyday. In the elaborate poetics of graffiti—the signatures left so artfully, the politics of slashing through them, crossing them out, erasing them, replicating them all over town. Or in the signs of the homeless on the side of the road. Or in the countless verbal and visual signs that come to life on the charged border between things private and things public. It is the kind of sensibility that surges through the wild conversation of AM radio talk shows and Internet sites. It adds force to the railing of the enraged in everything from road rage, to letters to the editor, to the face-to-face raging resentments of workplaces and intimate spaces. It permeates politics from right wing to left wing.

Something in its roughened surface points to a residue in things, a something that refuses to disappear. It draws attention, holds the visual fascination of unspeakable things—transgressions, injustices, the depths of widespread hopelessness. What animates it is not a particular message but rather the more basic need to forcefully perform the unrecognized impact of things.

It flees the easy translation of pain and desire into abstract values or commonsense coping. Yet every day its dramas of surge and arrest are bathed in the glow of some kind of meaning or form of dismissal. Then there are these questions: Will the gesture of the slashing shimmer as a curiosity passed on an everyday walking path, and will you feel a little jolt as you pass? Or, will it just go in one eye and out the other?

Sometimes, it might have the vitality of a pure surge pushing back, gathering a counterforce to a point of intensity that both slashes at itself and spits at the world.

Other times, its very violence means that it will be erased, ignored, or drawn up, like blood in a syringe, to infuse new life into the enveloping categories of good sense, healthy protest, productive acts and lives, and mainstream moods by virtue of its bad example. It will be unwilling and unwitting nourishment for the more settled world of calculation, representation, value, and necessity that gave rise to its spitting fury to begin with. Yet even then, the sign, in its perverse singularity, will peep out of little cracks on barely public stages simultaneously defying and demanding witness. It will remain a partially visible affecting presence because what it registers is not only points of breakdown in "the system" but also lines of possible breakthrough beating unbidden in the blood of the mainstream.

A person walking by such signs might be touched by them or hardened to their obnoxious demands. But either way, a charge passes through the body and lodges in the person as an irritation, a confusion, an amusement, an ironic smirk, a thrill, a threat, or a source of musing. For better or worse, signs that erupt as events teach us something of their own jumpy attention to impacts by leaving visceral traces in their wake.

▣ Stress

The lone body and the social body had become the lived symptoms of the contradictions, conflicts, possibilities, and haunted sensibilities of pervasive forces. Stress was the lingua franca of the day. If you had it, you were onto something, part of the speeding force of things-in-the-making. But it could puncture you too, leaving you alone during times of exhaustion, claustrophobia, resentment, and ambient fear.

The self became a thing filled with the intricate dramas of dreams launched, wounded, and finally satisfied or left behind. You could comfort it like a child. Or, you could look at the outlines of it against the relief of other people's missed opportunities. Or, you could inhabit it as a flood of events and relationships caught in a repetitive pattern that you recognized only when you got to the end of a cycle, and by then you were already onto the next one.

There were little shocks in the rhythms of splurging and purging and in the constant edgy corrections of the self-help regimes—take an aspirin a day (or not), drink a glass of red wine a day (or not), eat butter or low-fat margarine or canola oil, eat oatmeal to strip the bad cholesterol from your arteries, eat salmon to add the good cholesterol, try antioxidants or kava kava or melatonin.

The figure of a beefed-up agency became a breeding ground for all kinds of strategies of complaint, self-destruction, flight, reinvention, and experimentation as if the world rested on its shoulders. Straight talk about willpower and positive thinking claimed that agency was just a matter of getting on track, as if all the messy business of real selves affected by events and haunted by threats could be left behind in an out-of-this-world levitation act.

Against this tendency, a new kind of memoir began to work the lone self into a fictional sacrifice powerful enough to drag the world's impacts out onto secret stages. Self-help groups added density to the mix, offering both practical recipes for self-redeeming action and a hard-hitting, lived recognition of the twisted, all-pervasive ways in which compulsions permeated freedoms and were reborn in the very surge to get free of them once and for all.

▣ The Body Surges

The body builds its substance out of layers of sensory impact laid down in the course of straining upstream against recalcitrant and alien forces or drifting downstream, with its eyes trained on the watery clouds and passing treetops overhead and its ears submerged in the flow that surrounds it, buoys it, and carries it along. The body surges forward, gets on track, gets sidetracked, falls down, pulls itself up to crawl on hands and knees, flies through the air, hits a wall, regroups, or beats a retreat. It knows itself as states of vitality, exhaustion, and renewal. It exerts itself out of necessity and for the love of movement and then it pulls a veil around itself to rest, building a nest of worn clothing redolent with smells of sweat or cheap perfume or smoky wood fires burrowed into wool.

The body cannot help itself. It is an extremist seeking thrills, a moderate sticking its toe in to test the waters, a paranoid delusion looking for a place to hide. It is a bouncing fool throwing itself at an object of round perfection in the dogged conviction that it is on the right track this time. What the body knows, it knows from the smell of something promising or rancid in the air or the look of a quickening or slackening of flesh. It grows ponderous, gazing on its own form with a Zen-like emptiness. As a new lover, it dotes on revealed scars and zones in on freckles and moles and earlobes. As one of the anxious aging, it is drawn to the sight of new jowls and mutant hairs and mottled skin in the bathroom mirror.

The body is both the persistent site of self-recognition and the thing that will always betray you. It dreams of its own redemption and knows better. It catches sight of a movement out of the corner of its eye and latches on to a borrowed intimacy or a plan that comes as a gift to sweep it into the flow of the world and free it of its lonely flesh.

The body consumes and is consumed. Like one big pressure point, it is the place where outside forces come to roost, condensing like thickened milk in the bottom of the stomach. It grows sluggish and calls for sweet and heavy things to match its inner weight. Or salty or caffeinated things to jolt it to attention.

Layers of invented life form around the body's dreamy surges like tendons or fat.

Lifestyles and industries pulse in a silent, unknown reckoning of what to make of all this.

The body builds itself out of layer on layer of sensory impact. It loves and dreads what makes it. At times, it is shocked and thrilled to find itself in the driver's seat. At other times, it holes up, bulks up, wraps itself in its layers. The world it lives in spins with the dancing poles of ups and downs and rests its laurels in a banality that hums a tune of its own.

Body for Life

She once took up *Body for Life* on the advice of a friend. Between them, it was a joke. They called it their cult. But they also knew that there was something *to* a little extreme self-transformation. Or at least the effort. *Body for Life* was a best-selling book with glossy "before-and-after" pictures of bodybuilders on the inside covers. It started as a bodybuilder's, movement-building, moneymaking challenge to the unwashed to put down the beer and chips and start loving life instead of just living it, to start thriving and not just surviving. It was "12 weeks to mental and physical strength."

She was not at all taken with the tanned, oiled, muscle man and muscle woman look on the inside covers, but the little game of moving her eyes back and forth between each pair of before-and-after shots caught her in a spell of momentary satisfaction. The eye jumped happily between the paired scenes. Now fat and pale, now muscled and oily and tan. Peek-a-boo. All of the bodies were white. They made her think of the body displays that she was always running into when she lived in Las Vegas. At the post office, or at the drive-in movie theater, or while waiting in line to get a new driver's license, there were always half-naked bodybuilders with wet-skinned snakes draped around their necks, or monkeys on leashes, or stars-and-stripes halter tops and permed blond hair.

Her friend called the people in the pictures "beefcakes." Class seemed to be somehow involved in all of this, but people would swear up and down that those who were into *Body for Life* came from all walks of life. That comfortable claim to plainness emerging out of some kind of mainstream. Some kind of mall culture. Ordinary Americans unmarked by anything but the will to change their bodies and by the real or imagined fruits of their success after those glorious 12 weeks. They were people who had been catapulted out of the back seat of life onto the magic carpet ride that turns flighty self-defeating dreams into vital generative flesh.

They had experienced their breakthroughs when they saw the inspiring photos on the inside covers, or when they took a good hard look at their own eye-opening "before" pictures, or when—while watching the inspirational video that they could get for a $15 donation to the Make-A-Wish Foundation—they were suddenly released from the feeling of being alone and felt hope instead. They began to crave the 12-week program even more than they craved a piece of key lime pie or a beer.

There is nothing weird about how this happens. It is laid out step by step like a 12-step program where the spiritual transformation flows directly through the flesh. You follow the steps in the book as if it were a recipe book, consuming each new exercise with relish. You create 12-week goals out of gossamer wishes. Done. You pull your dreams out of their shadow existence into the light of day. Okay then! You harness the force in your own faintly beating desire to change. Wow! Okay. You ask yourself hard questions. You write down the answers. You speak your goals out loud with mimicked confidence every morning and night until the confidence is real. You commit. You focus; forget the zoning out and drifting downstream. You create five daily habits. You imagine other people looking at your new body with gleaming eyes, and you hear their approving comments until the imagining is effortless and part of you. You surrender the negative emotions that hold everyone back, and you start looking forward. You realize that you will never again get sidetracked. Everyone who takes the 12-week challenge feels like a winner. You do not need a carrot on a stick anymore; you take your eyes off the prize (a blood red Lamborghini Diablo) and even consumer fetishism seems to fade into the background of a half-lived past. Now you are consuming your body, and your body is consuming you. It is more direct.

She was not really interested in the inspirational business, however, and she never actually read the book. She passed directly from the game of before-and-after photos to the charts near the end of the book that tell you exactly what you have to do and eat. She got organized. She made copies of the exercise charts so that she could fill one out each day like a daily diary. She memorized the acceptable foods in the three food groups and stocked up. She ritualized each meal and gleefully took off the 7th day each week, carefully following the instruction to eat exactly whatever she wanted that day and no less. She ordered boxes of the shakes and power bars and began to experiment with the recipes that made the chocolate shake taste like a banana split and turned the vanilla shake into that famous liquid key lime pie. She got the picture. She felt the surge. She let it become a new piece of her skeleton. Then there were the inevitable ups and downs, the sliding in and out of its partial cocoon.

A couple of years later, long after she had consumed the program enough to reduce it to a few new prejudices about how to exercise and how to eat, she drifted into Body for Life Community.com and the dozens of listservs and chat rooms in its nest. Some were modeled as Christian fellowships:

> The only requirement for membership is the desire to be healthy. This is not just a set of principles but a society for people in action. Carry the message or wither. . . . Those who haven't been given the truth may not know the abundant life we have found—a way out, into life, a real life with freedom.

Other listservs were just organized by state. In any of them, you could click on someone's name and up would pop a *Body for Life* photo, slipping you right into the culture of personal ads. In the chat rooms, things got really concrete. One woman confessed that she could smell the chocolate right through the wrappers in the bowl of Halloween candy by the door, and someone shouted support in capital letters: "HANG IN THERE! YOU CAN DO IT!!!" A man happily obsessed about how to prepare his shakes:

> My favorite is chocolate, and to prepare the shake I always use 3 cubes of ice from the Rubbermaid mold, put them (without water) in the jar, and then pour the water in. Use 12 and a half ounces and 1 centimeter, then blend for about 55 seconds. You [have] got to use a stopwatch! I think this is why I love Myoplex, because I blend it for more seconds and I drink it cool without milk or bananas.

People exchanged stories of ongoing tragedies, seeking workout partners to help them get through the ordeals. Others just focused on keeping up the network connections:

> Good morning to everyone. Been off for a few days. Lizzy—sorry to hear about your migraine—scary! Jim—it's true—your pictures don't do you justice! Abs—I love your philosophy! It's true—we become what we think about. Deb—congratulations! Good luck with your photos—can't wait to see your progress! If you find something that covers bruises, let me know—I bruise just thinking about bumping into something. Can't wait to see you all at the upcoming events!

All of these self-expressions are excessive in their own way. They proclaim, confess, obsess, and gush. But that is not because the body really does just get on track and march forward armed with the drama of success and the minutia of disciplinary practices. It is because it slumps and gets sidetracked and rejoins its *Body for Life* self. It is because it wants and it does not want and because it might do one thing or another. It is because it smells its way along tracks, and new tracks intersect the old and carry it away. It is because it catches things out of the corner of its eye, and half-hidden things on the sidelines are always the most compelling.

Body for Life draws its own life from the force of a bodily surge enacting not the simple, deliberate, one-way embodiment of dreams but rather the pulsing impact of dream and matter on each other in a moment when the body is beside itself. Caught in a movement, floating suspended between past and future, hesitation and forward thrust, pain and pleasure, knowledge and ignorance, the body vibrates or pulses. It is only when the body remains partly unactualized and unanchored that it seems intimate, familiar, and alive. This can be lived as an event—a moment of shock, climax, or awakening. But there is also something of it in the banal and quotidian—a continuous background radiation, a humming left unremarked like a secret battery kept charged.

Body for Life says that turning fleeting fantasies into the force of vitality is about making a decision, but making a decision is itself about playing games, looking at pictures, following recipes, mimicking desired states, inventing social imaginaries, and talking to yourself in the mirror. Getting on track and staying there is not the simple and sober choice of a lifetime but rather a thin line from which you can, and probably will, topple back to ordinary sloppiness or onto an "epidemic of the will" (Sedgwick, 1992) such as excessive dieting. Then the body might swing itself back to a state of moderation or exhaustion, stick its toe in to test the waters, and pull the blankets over itself to hide.

The proliferating cultures of the body spin madly around the palpable promise that fears and pleasures and forays into the world can be literally made vital all-consuming passions. But this promise (and threat) is already there in the body directly engaged by shifting public sensibilities, in the senses retooled and set in motion. Like an antenna, the body picks up pulses that are hard to hear, or hard to bear, in the normalizing universe of cultural codes. It stores the pulses in a neck muscle or a limb, or it follows them just to see where they are going. It dares them and registers their impacts. It wants to be part of their flow. It wants to be in touch. It wants to be touched. It hums along with them, flexing its muscles in a state of readiness.

◘ Sometimes When You Hear Someone Scream . . .

Laurie Anderson had a show at the Guggenheim Soho called "Your Fortune, $1." A spooky white plastic owl perched on a stool in a darkened corner spewed out a stream of two-bit advice, trenchant commentary, and stray advertising lingo plucked out of a realm of sheer circulation. The owl's mechanical yet sensuously grainy voice droned on and on, transfixing her in a flood of Hallmark greeting card schlock. She was fascinated to see how the flood's ordinary reality seemed to instantly deflate and become both laughable and alarming from the owl's simple mimicking.

Then it said something that she swore she had already been anxiously chanting to herself. *Sometimes when you hear someone scream, it goes in one ear and out the other. Sometimes it passes right into the middle of your brain and gets stuck there.*

It was one of those moments when the indiscriminate flow stops dead in its tracks. The supersaturated soup of sensory images and sounds gently prodding and massaging us like waves lapping a shore takes this opportunity to solidify into something momentarily clear or even shocking. Like a trauma we had forgotten or never quite registered that comes back in a flash. Or like a whiff of something hopeful or potentially exciting passing with the breeze. We perk up in a mix of recognition, pleasure, and alarm.

One minute you are afloat in the realm of sheer circulation. Then some random sound bite hits you with a force that seems to bring you to your senses. We sober up in the face of a cruel lucidity. But it is the hungry sense that has been awakened that drives the world back into the land of enchantment. The waves of desire lap at our feet, and we drift off again, held aloft by the sheer density of images, sensory signals, and objects drawn into play in the dreamworld.

When she heard the owl's line about screams that pass right into the middle of your brain and get stuck there, she went home and wrote down a story that had been lodged in her psyche ever since she heard it.

The story starts with a question lodged in a tactile sensate anxiety and then opens onto an aesthetic scene of the senses. The question: Do you ever wake up in the morning, or in the middle of the night, with a sense of sudden dread and start scanning your dreamy brain for the memory of what you have done or a premonition of what is coming? Some do this all of the time; for them, this is what morning has become.

The aesthetic scene: She has a big iron bed lodged against long wide windows looking onto the back deck. Tropical breezes waft over her in the night, carrying the sweet and fetid smells of kumquat trees and mimosa blossoms. At dawn, there are wild bird cries—mourning doves and grackles and parrots that once escaped their pet cages and now breed in the trees. At certain hours in the still of the night, the train cries in the near distance. The night pulses with the high lonesome sound of haunted machine dreams roaming the landscape.

When she has guests, she lets them use the iron bed, and they wake up talking about the bed and the wailing train as if they feel pleased to be set down in some kind of American Heartland. But she is only too happy to lay down a pallet on the living room floor and fall into a deep sleep with only the smell of old ashes from the fireplace because she knows why the train sings.

The train sings for Bobby, a homeless drunk who laid himself down on the tracks one night and passed out as if he too could lay down a pallet and escape from his ghosts. He and his old lady had been down at the free concert on the river where some of the street people party hard. The weekly concert was their moment to be at home in public, doing what everyone else was doing, only more. Some would laugh loud or make announcements or give people directions and advice. As the day went to full dark, the power of music would flow out from the stage, touch spellbound bodies, and spread out to the neon skyline reflecting in the dark glassy expanse of the river. There were always graceful moments—a dance gesture, a wide open smile, a sudden upsurge of generosity, the startled gratitude of pariahs who suddenly found themselves seamlessly rubbing shoulders with the housed. There were always crashes too—people falling down drunk in front of the stage; the vomiting; a man huddled and pale, too sick to party; flashes of hope and ease dashed on the rocks of familiar fury, frustration, humiliation, and grief; people making spectacles of themselves. Sometimes there were fights.

That night, Bobby had a fight with his old lady and stomped off alone. He followed the train tracks through the woods to the homeless camp, where he sat on the tracks alone, taking stock in a booze-soaked moment of reprieve. He loved the romance of the high lonesome sound in the distance and the train's promise of tactility and power—the rumbling weight of power incarnate rumbling past, the childhood memory of the penny laid on the tracks, the way the tracks carved out a "no man's land" where shadows could travel and live.

He laid himself down on the icy cold tracks and closed his eyes, as if tempting fate. As if that simple move held both the possibility of checking out and a dream of contact with a public world that might include him.

Somewhere in the middle of the long train passing over, he raised his head, awakening. They say that if he had not woken up, the train would have passed right over him.

Now the train screams out a warning when it draws close to that place on the tracks not far from her iron bed. It often wakes her. Or it lodges in her sleep and comes as an unknown shock of anxiety in the morning.

▣ ▣ ▣

▣ Coda

The stories that make up my story—disparate and arbitrary scenes of impact tracked through bodies, desires, or labors and traced out of the aftermath of a passing surge registered, somehow, in objects, acts, situations, and events—are meant to be taken not as representative examples of forces or conditions but rather as constitutive events and acts in themselves that animate and literally make sense of forces at the point of their affective and material emergence. More directly compelling than ideologies, and more fractious, multiplicitous, and unpredictable than symbolic representations of an abstract structure brought to bear on otherwise lifeless things, they are actual sites where forces have gathered to a point of impact, or flirtations along the outer edges of a phenomenon, or extreme cases that suggest where a trajectory might lead if it were to go unchecked. They are not the kinds of things you can get your hands on or wrap your mind around, but they are things that have to be literally tracked.

Rather than seek an explanation for things we presume to capture with carefully formulated concepts, my story proposes a form of cultural and political critique that tracks lived impacts and rogue vitalities through bodily agitations, modes of free-floating fascination, and moments of collective excitation or enervation. It attempts to describe how people are quite literally charged up by the sheer surge of things in the making.

My story, then, is not an exercise in representation or a critique of representation; rather it is a cabinet of curiosities designed to incite curiosity. Far from trying to present a final, or good enough, story of something we might call "U.S. culture," it tries to deflect attention away from the obsessive desire to characterize things once and for all long enough to register the myriad strands of shifting influence that remain uncaptured by representational thinking. It presumes a "we"—the impacted subjects of a wild assemblage of influences—but it also takes difference to be both far more fundamental and far more fluid than models of positioned subjects have been able to suggest. It is not normative. Its purpose is not to evaluate things as finally good or bad, and far from presuming that meanings or values run the world, it is drawn to the place where *meaning* per se collapses and we are left with acts and gestures and immanent possibilities. Rather than try to pinpoint the beating heart of its beast, it tracks the pulses of things as they cross each other, come together, fragment, and recombine in some new surge. It tries to cull attention to the affects that arise in the course of the perfectly ordinary life as the promise, or threat, that something is happening—something capable of impact. Whether such affects are feared or shamelessly romanticized, subdued or unleashed, they point to the generative immanence lodged in things. Far from the named "feelings" or "emotions" invented in discourses of morals, ideals, and known subjectivities (leave that to Hallmark and the Family Channel), they take us to the surge of intensity itself.

My story tries to follow lines of force as they emerge in moments of shock, or become resonant in everyday sensibilities, or come to roost in a stilled scene of recluse or hiding. It tries to begin the labor of knowing the effects of current restructurings not as a fixed body of elements and representations imposed on an innocent world but rather as a literally moving mix of things that engages desires, ways of being, and concrete places and objects.

References

Bakhtin, M. (1982). *The dialogic imagination* (K. Brostrom, Trans.). Austin: University of Texas Press.

Bakhtin, M. (1984). *Problems of Dostoevsky's poetics* (C. Emerson, Trans.). Minneapolis: University of Minnesota Press.

Barthes, R. (1975). *The pleasure of the text* (R. Miller, Trans.). New York: Hill & Wang.

Barthes, R. (1977). *Image–music–text* (S. Heath, Trans.). New York: Hill & Wang.

Barthes, R. (1981). *Camera Lucida: Reflections on photography* (R. Howard, Trans.). New York: Hill & Wang.

Barthes, R. (1985). *The responsibility of forms: Critical essays on music, art, and representation* (R. Howard, Trans.). New York: Hill & Wang.

Benjamin, W. (1999). *The Arcades Project* (H. Eiland & K. McLaughlin, Trans.). Cambridge, MA: Harvard University Press.

Benjamin, W. (2003). *The origin of German tragic drama* (J. Osborne, Trans.). New York: Verso.

Deleuze, G., & Guattari, F. (1987). *A thousand plateaus* (B. Massumi, Trans.). Minneapolis: University of Minnesota Press.

Foucault, M. (1990). *The history of sexuality: An introduction* (R. Hurley, Trans.). New York: Vintage.

Guattari, F. (1995). *Chaosmosis: An ethico-aesthetic paradigm.* Bloomington: Indiana University Press.

Haraway, D. (1997). *Modest witness, second millennium.* New York: Routledge.

Haraway, D. (2003). *The Companion Species Manifesto: Dogs, people, and significant otherness.* Chicago: Prickly Paradigm Press (University of Chicago).

Lingis, A. (1994). *Foreign bodies.* New York: Routledge.

Sedgwick, E. (1992). *Epistemology of the closet.* Berkeley: University of California Press.

Sedgwick, E. (1993). Epidemics of the will. In E. Sedgwick, *Tendencies* (pp. 130–145). Durham, NC: Duke University Press.

Sedgwick, E. (1997). *Novel gazing: Queer readings in fiction.* Durham, NC: Duke University Press.

Sedgwick, E. (2003). *Touching feeling: Affect, pedagogy, performativity.* Durham, NC: Duke University Press.

Stewart, K. (1996). *A space on the side of the road: Cultural poetics in an "other" America.* Princeton, NJ: Princeton University Press.

Stewart, K. (2000a). Real American dreams (can be nightmares). In J. Dean (Ed.), *Cultural studies and political theory* (pp. 243–258). Ithaca, NY: Cornell University Press.

Stewart, K. (2000b). Still life. In L. Berlant (Ed.), *Intimacy* (pp. 405–420). Chicago: University of Chicago Press.

Stewart, K. (2002a). Machine dreams. In J. Scanduri & M. Thurston (Eds.), *Modernism, Inc.: Body, memory, capital* (pp. 21–28). New York: New York University Press.

Stewart, K. (2002b). Scenes of life. *Public Culture, 14,* 2.

Stewart, K. (2003a). Arresting images. In P. Matthews & D. McWhirter (Eds.), *Aesthetic subjects: Pleasures, ideologies, and ethics* (pp. 431–438). Minneapolis: University of Minnesota Press.

Stewart, K. (2003b). The perfectly ordinary life. *Scholar and Feminist Online, 2,* 1.

Strathern, M. (1991). *Partial connections.* Savage, MD: Rowman & Littlefield.

Strathern, M. (1992a). *After nature.* New York: Cambridge University Press.

Strathern, M. (1992b). *Reproducing the future.* Manchester, UK: Manchester University Press.

Strathern, M. (1999). *Property, substance, and effect.* London: Athlone Press.

Taussig, M. (1986). *Shamanism, colonialism, and the wild man.* Chicago: University of Chicago Press.

Taussig, M. (1992). *The nervous system.* New York: Routledge.

Taussig, M. (1993). *Mimesis and alterity.* New York: Routledge.

Taussig, M. (1997). *The magic of the state.* New York: Routledge.

Taussig, M. (1999). *Defacement: Public secrecy and the labor of the negative.* Stanford, CA: Stanford University Press.

Williams, R. (1977). *Marxism and literature.* New York: Oxford University Press.

41

"ARIA IN TIME OF WAR"

Investigative Poetry and the Politics of Witnessing

Stephen J. Hartnett and Jeremy D. Engels

Contemporary intellectual production in the humanities is haunted by two scandalous hypocrisies. First, although *interdisciplinarity* and *excellence* are the catchwords of the era, universities for the most part continue to teach, hire, and tenure according to stultifying genre-bound traditions rather than fresh pedagogical, artistic, or intellectual ambitions. Second, although humanists can build flashy careers using words such as *radical, intervention, transgression,* and *counterhegemonic*—even while fitting snugly into safe discrete fields—the number of academics doing political work is embarrassingly small. In contrast to these two driving hypocrisies, we invoke the spirit of Ralph Waldo Emerson, who demanded in a sermonic essay from 1844 that a poet should strive toward becoming "the Knower, the Doer, and the Sayer." Emerson (1844/1982) told his readers that knowing, doing, and saying "stand respectively for the love of truth, for the love of good, and for the love of beauty" (p. 262). Filtered through a postmodern lens, we suggest that knowing indicates the necessity of scholarship, that doing points toward activism and other forms of embodied knowledge, and that saying calls for an examination of and participation in the politics of representation. Read in this way—as calling for the combination of serious scholarship, passionate activism, and experimental representation—Emerson's transcendentalist dictum serves as a ringing indictment of the hypocrisies described previously and as a clarion call for what we describe in what follows as *investigative poetry.*

Although attempts to define a genre are doomed to failure and inevitably invite a cascade of

Authors' Note. An earlier version of the material in Section 4 of this essay originally appeared as part of Hartnett (1999); that material appears courtesy of the National Communication Association. Parts of Sections 2 and 4 of this essay appeared in a slightly different form in Hartnett (2003); that material appears courtesy of Rowman & Littlefield Publishers. The authors are deeply grateful for the editorial insights of Norman Denzin and Ivan Brady.

counterarguments, refutations, and modifications, we nonetheless begin with the premise that investigative poetry exhibits these characteristics:

- An attempt to supplement poetic imagery with evidence won through scholarly research, with the hope that merging art and archive makes our poetry more worldly and our politics more personal
- An attempt to use reference matter not only to support political arguments but also as a tool to provide readers with additional information and empowerment
- An attempt to problematize the self by studying the complex interactions among individuals and their political contexts, hence witnessing both the fracturing of the self and the deep implication of the author in the very systems that he or she examines
- An attempt to problematize politics by witnessing the ways that social structures are embodied as lived experience, hence adding to political criticism ethnographic, phenomenological, and existential components
- An attempt to situate these questions about self and society within larger historical narratives, thereby offering poems that function as genealogical critiques of power
- An attempt to produce poems that take a multiperspectival approach, not by celebrating or criticizing one or two voices but rather by building a constellation of multiple voices in conversation
- A deep faith in the power of commitment, meaning that to write an investigative poetry of witness the poet must put himself or herself in harm's way and function not only as an observer of political crises but also as a participant in them

We elucidate these claims in what follows via a series of case studies. It is impossible to begin this essay, however, without noting that arguments over the possible relationships among poetry, politics, and social justice—to say nothing of the methodological criteria offered earlier—are as old as civilization itself. As Birkerts (1987) observes, "The poetry/politics debate began when Plato booted the poet from his ideal Republic, maybe even sooner; it will go on so long as there is language" (p. 55). But unlike Birkerts and the hundreds of other critics who have weighed in with weighty pronouncements on one aspect of this debate, often in tones that we can only describe as partisan at best and shrill at worst, we want to honor the epic and sometimes comic nature of that debate without descending into it. Instead, we offer readers a series of interlocking readings of some veins of work that we have found to be edifying. Our comments here may be taken, then, not so much as our levying an argument about how we think poets, activists, and scholars should proceed as our sharing some hopefully pedagogical thoughts on the literary and activist inspirations that have fed our fascination with and unbounded support for investigative poetry.[1]

Our essay unfolds in four movements. First, to frame our arguments about investigative poetry, we explore the poetic and political possibilities embodied in recent works by Carolyn Forché and Edward Sanders. Forché's (2003) *Blue Hour* is a haunting, elegiac, and spiritual meditation on the ever-piling wreckage of violence. Sparse and abstract, with words floating in the hushed glimmer of no-where and no-time, Forché's devastating poems feel like a dismal history lesson detached from history. Sanders's (2000) *America: A History in Verse* offers a different model. Packed with details organized chronologically, and reading like a catechism of lessons gleaned from the lost fragments of our national history, these celebratory poems offer readers an empowering investigation into the still great promises of the American experiment. By comparing these texts, we establish some of the benefits and consequences of pursuing these different modes of investigative poetry. Second, we review the literature regarding the recent turn across the humanities to a concern with social justice, hence grounding our thoughts about investigative poetry within the tradition of engaged scholars who use their positions as teachers and writers to try to help expand democratic rights, economic opportunities, and cultural aspirations for an ever larger circle of readers, students, and fellow activists. Third, to illustrate some of the promises and problems with one of the main intellectual traditions informing investigative poetry, we examine the literary, pedagogical, and anthropological ambitions of the movement known loosely as *ethnopoetics.* Although our reading of the various branches of ethnopoetics grants their important roles in initiating conversations about multiculturalism, bringing a literary consciousness to anthropology, breaking down positivism, and criticizing colonialism, our readings of specific ethnopoems finds them to be consistently removed from questions of power. Fourth, we celebrate the dense triumphs of John Dos Passos, the early Carolyn Forché, and Peter Dale Scott, all of whom merge concerns for social justice and a commitment to writing a political poetry of witness in texts that, although historical, political, personal, philosophical, and beautiful, consistently place a critique of power at the center of their work. Taken as a whole, these four sections offer readers a sweeping overview of the opportunities and obligations of both producing and consuming "Aria in Time of War"; that is, we celebrate those who honor the persistence of poetry in the face of horror, who commit their academic work to social justice, and who merge the two—scholarship and poetry—in the political work of witnessing.

1. Oscillating Between No-Time and the Blizzard of Facts: Forché, Sanders, and the Question of Historical Context

We begin with eight haunting lines from "On Earth," the central poem from Forché's (2003) unsettling *Blue Hour:*

> a random life caught in the net of purpose (p. 26)
>
> a search without hope for hope (p. 27)
>
> America a warship on the horizon at morning (p. 29)
>
> and it is certain someone will be at that very moment pouring milk (p. 30)
>
> aria in time of war (p. 32)
>
> black with burnt-up meaning (p. 35)
>
> history decaying into images (p. 42)
>
> inhabiting a body to be abolished (p. 45)

On and on it goes in relentless ethereal detail, working methodically through a 48-page alphabetically structured poem meant to approximate the feel of a Gnostic abecedarian hymn, ending with but one entry for the letter z: "zero" (p. 68).

These lines prompt readers to wonder about the mysterious relationships among agency and chance, personal volition and historical velocity ("a random life caught in the net of purpose"); to empathically walk a mile in the shoes of someone who bravely, yet apparently fruitlessly, pursues justice ("a search without hope for hope"); to ponder a world in which American power is feared by faraway peoples ("America a warship on the horizon at morning"); to know that despite such fears, someone somewhere is enjoying a quiet moment of sustenance and plenty ("and it is certain someone will be at that very moment pouring milk"); to listen closely to hear whether the explosions of war and the silent misery of poverty are graced with beauty ("aria in time of war"); to ask after all that has been lost in the ever-piling wreckage of history ("black with burnt-up meaning"); to ponder what it means to think historically in a world that appears with each day to possess meaning not from words and sounds and touches and smells but rather from the blinding whir of mass-produced pictures ("history decaying into images"); and to imagine for a moment what it must feel like to be one of the damned ("inhabiting a body to be abolished"), condemned perhaps to die on death row, or on skid row, or from the torturous spiral into hopelessness, where one inhabits a body that slowly loses meaning. Thus, Forché invites us on a terrifying voyage into the mysteries of life during an age of mass-produced misery.

Readers are left to fill in the blanks as they choose, to complete the jigsaw puzzle of horror by supplying details from their own warehouses of knowledge and memory and even fantasy, for who can hold such sweeping imagery together without moving from the realm of expertise and experience to imagination and projection? The danger of enabling such projection is that it invites readers to move from thinking about the specific causes and consequences of historical *loss* to nostalgically longing for some abstract *absence.* As LaCapra (2001) argues in *Writing History, Writing Trauma,* this shift from loss to absence is potentially dangerous because "when loss is converted into (or encrypted in an indiscriminately generalized rhetoric of) absence, one faces the impasse of endless melancholy" (p. 46). Moving from the healthy mourning of specific historical loss to the endless web of melancholy is fueled, LaCapra claims, by a tendency "to shroud, perhaps even to etherealize, them [historical losses] in a generalized discourse of absence" that relies on figures that are "abstract, evacuated, disembodied" (pp. 48–49). Forché's dilemma in *Blue Hour*, then, as in all works that strive to merge hard-hitting politics and joyous poetic reverie while roaming across a wide swath of time, revolves around the question of how to provide a cosmopolitan, truly globalizing perspective on the tragedy of life without falling into the trap of morose and politically paralyzing longing for immaterial absence.[2]

In her introduction to the magisterial anthology of poems, *Against Forgetting,* Forché (1993) argues, "The poetry of witness frequently resorts to paradox and difficult equivocation, to the invocation of what is *not* there as if it *were*. . . . That it must defy common sense to speak of the common indicates that traditional modes of thought, the purview of common sense, no longer *make* sense" (p. 40). We imagine that most readers will grant the wisdom of this claim, for who has not thrilled at the truth conveyed in an oblique poem or song or dance, bringing a rush of sensemaking greater than anything ever found in dry tomes of history or sociology or political science? And who has not found himself or herself walking through historical wreckage or working through a novel with the eerie sense that he or she were conversing with the dead (Gordon, 1997)? But at what point does defying common sense and invoking the dead fade into helpless abstraction, into the infinitely repeatable layering of random projections against one another (O'Rourke, 2003)? Like flipping distractedly through 100 channels of late-night television, or watching billboards tick by on some anonymous stretch of highway, don't such invocations of the dead and such refusals of common sense ultimately leave readers awash in confusion? Where are we? What is the date? What are the stakes? Who are the players? *Why does this matter?*

Sanders's (2000) *America: A History in Verse* answers these questions on every page. "I love the way my nation seethes/ I love its creativity/ & the flow of its wild needs," Sanders proclaims in his introduction (p. 9). Channeling the epic and synthesizing sweep of Whitman, Sanders thus offers readers a love poem qualified by the knowledge that "I know of course/ that I have to trace the/ violence of my nation" (p. 8). These poems matter, then, because they aspire to rewrite the history of America circa 1900–1939 and, by investigating specific historical losses, to provide readers with the factual knowledge, rhetorical resources, and political encouragement to try to reclaim the nation's better half from its lingering—and recently ascendant—demons. Sanders pursues this goal by studying the nation's players, institutions, struggles, and sounds, which he offers up in newspaper-like snippets organized by years. Thus, whereas Forché's melancholy *Blue Hour* offers a chillingly beautiful yet ultimately disempowering meditation on absence, Sanders's *America* offers a compelling, if didactic, tribute to the winners and losers of specific historical battles.

As one of the founders of the 1950s micropublishing culture that freed artists from corporate constraints, as a seminal New York hipster during the beat generation, as an accomplished pre-punk musician, as witness to the travesty of the Democratic Convention in Chicago in 1968, and on and on—in short, as one of those miraculous figures who seem to always be at the center of what is *happening*—Sanders has for the past 50 years or so been a tireless and good-natured gadfly watching America struggle to achieve the glory of its promises. Given his personal experiences with some of the leading artists and activists who have prompted America's cultural and political changes over the past decades, it comes as no surprise that Sanders reminds readers that history hinges in large part on individual actors exercising agency. *America* accordingly offers a "who's who" catalogue of heroes and villains in action.

For example, here is one of Sanders's many loving tributes to Isadora Duncan, who first danced in America in 1908 and who

> based her revolution in Dance
>
> on the natural grace of bodies moving in Beauty
>
> It was ancient, she said, from the form-loving Greeks
>
> & so when she showed a nipple or knee
>
> she could claim those ancient roots
>
> She was an advocate of free love
>
> a political radical
>
> & a stunning emblem to the women
>
> who wanted to smoke, strut, paint
>
> write, dance, & fuck more freely. (p. 80)

Sanders (2000) shows us a brave woman dancing her and her sisters' way toward freedom. Close readers might want more poetic detail here. *Just how did she reveal that nipple or knee? What did it look like? How did crowds respond? Were lovers actually thinking of Duncan when they fucked more freely?* But in these poems Sanders is less interested in the micro-logical details than in the ways iconic figures and actions function synecdochically, as representative parts that reveal the majesty of the whole. Indeed, as Sanders (1976) declares in his manifesto *Investigative Poetry*, "the essence of investigative poetry" is to create "lines of lyric beauty [that] descend from data clusters," hence both seducing and empowering readers with "a melodic blizzard of data-fragments" (p. 9). Synecdoche is therefore the rhetorical trope that enables Sanders to weave individual lines of beauty into a collective swirl of data fragments and thus to write poetic history.[3]

Indeed, *America* is based largely on the trope of synecdoche, which hinges on the convertibility between parts and wholes, on the representational electricity assumed to link actors to their epochs. For example, whereas Duncan stands as a representative woman, as the individual embodiment (part) of the period's struggle for women's freedom of mind and movement (whole), so Sanders reverses the equation and offers institutions (wholes) as symbolic aggregates of individual hope (part). Put differently, because even exceptional individuals are only as strong as their larger community bonds, Sanders is obliged to represent not only radical individuals but also the hope-sustaining and change-making institutions that support their visionary work. For example, Sanders's investigations into the struggle against racial violence lead him to celebrate the 1909 founding of the National Association for the Advancement of Colored People (NAACP):

> & there comes a time in the time-track
>
> when you work for good, no matter the danger
>
> . . .
>
> There comes a time—
>
> You can look in photo archives
>
> at the shiny-eyed trash
>
> gathered about a lynching tree
>
> as if it were the homecoming parade
>
> —therefore the NAACP. (pp. 83–84)

Although Sanders is a relentless critic of the "shiny-eyed trash" who choose violence over understanding, readers may wish for more details regarding the pleasures of crowds at lynchings. That is, instead of 4 lines describing the energies of white supremacists, why not 30 lines showing us in more detail what the alluded to—but not cited—"photo archives" teach attentive viewers? More than just a quibble about the focus or length of the poem, such questions carry for investigative poets a heavy methodological burden, for we proceed with the understanding that just as melancholia stands as the paralyzing result of failed mourning, so simply rebuking one's enemies—even lynch mobs—begins the process of moving from understanding specific historical loss to projecting terms of generalized absence and otherness. In this case, the complexities of white supremacy are glossed within a heroic tribute to the NAACP, but one cannot fathom the gravity of the task faced by the NAACP without a more nuanced understanding of what its members were fighting against. We are thus asking for the poem to accept the admittedly heavy burden of playing a more clearly pedagogical function.[4]

Moreover, without showing us the complexities of the players involved in a given struggle in a clearly pedagogical fashion, much of Sanders's *America* might feel to some readers like an exercise in nostalgia. For example, here is one of his many tributes to the International Workers of the World:

> In Fresno in '11
>
> another protest for the right of free speech
>
> again the jails were packed
>
> and Wobblies were singing and giving speeches
>
> to supporters and the curious
>
> gathered outside the jail
>
> . . .
>
> When it was obvious that
>
> more and more Wobblies were coming to Fresno
>
> to commit civil disobedience
>
> the power structure relented
>
> and rescinded the ban on speaking in the streets. (pp. 87–88)

In 1911, the Wobblies were fighting for workers' rights, yet they rocketed into national consciousness a few years later because of their brave stand against America entering World War I. But as Sanders notes in his poems from the years 1917 and 1918, it would not be long before the Espionage Act was crushing dissent, sending thousands of protesters to jail and shipping boatloads of socialists back to Europe. At the same time, the draft scooped up additional thousands of young men to be marched to their deaths in Europe's lice-infested trenches. Although many readers will thrill at the image of brave Wobblies fighting for justice in Fresno in 1911, the longer view is ultimately one of defeat: the Wobblies were crushed, free speech was curtailed, and America sloughed off to a disastrously bloody war. Regardless of what readers think of this narrative, the pedagogical function of investigative poetry suggests that Sanders should have offered extensive referencing so that readers could make up their own minds about this version of the Wobblies and America during the World War I era, yet no such reference matter is provided.[5]

Nonetheless, despite the sense that it is infused with nostalgia, that it lacks the referencing matter required to help readers take the pedagogical step of beginning their own research, and that it sometimes skims too quickly across the surface of events, Sanders's *America* accumulates into a majestic—even awe-inspiring—narrative, for by moving from the exuberance and genius of individuals (Duncan and her revolutionary dancing) to the strength and dignity of organizations (the NAACP and its fight against racism) to the brave triumph of struggles for freedom (the Wobblies' free speech victory in Fresno in 1911) and back again, zigzagging all the while through a kaleidoscopic montage of historical fragments, the poem offers a model of engaged citizenship, literally a handbook of democracy in action. Indeed, whereas Forché's *Blue Hour* can feel oppressively bleak—"collective memory a dread of things to come" (p. 30), "scoop of earth: slivers of femurs, metacarpals" (p. 51), "your mother waving goodbye in the flames" (p. 68)—Sanders's *America* reminds readers of the bravery of our forebears and thus of our obligations to continue their fights for justice.

In addition to this empowering and activating function, Sanders's *America* relishes the more traditionally poetic slices of joy that slither through daily experience. Indeed, by juxtaposing horror against the frivolous, joyous, and sometimes brilliant aspects of daily life, *America* provides a startlingly honest glimpse into the lived sensation of watching history crash all around you. Sanders is particularly interested in the relationship between sound and politics, as in this passage about 1925:

> George Gershwin's *Piano Concerto*
>
> Prokoviev's *Symphony #2*
>
> Aaron Copeland's *Symphony #1*
>
> and in Chicago Louis Armstrong began the Hot Five recordings
>
> while December 10
>
> the Grand Old Opry began radio broadcasts
>
> Henry Ford, hating jazz
>
> set up a series of folk dances. (p. 245)

One could obviously write hundreds of pages on each of these figures, but Sanders appears to be more interested in letting readers figure out the implications of such juxtapositions. Like Whitman's famous catalogue poems, then, Sanders makes no attempt to dive into the complexity of these figures, instead positioning them as icons loaded with apparently self-evident meaning, as synecdoches meant to suggest the larger forces at play. For example, it is assumed that one reads the line about Armstrong and understands the importance of the Hot Five moving away from big band formats toward what would eventually become hard swinging bebop; it is assumed that one reads the line about the Grand Old Opry and understands the significance of the mass production (via radio, press, and eventually television) of a nostalgia-based, quietly racist, down home country aesthetic; it is assumed that one reads the line about Copeland and understands how he sought to merge the nation's many musical vernaculars into a majestic symphony-of-the-whole; and so on, with readers left to surround each line with their own comprehension. In this sense, then, Sanders appears to be practicing less what we are calling investigative poetry than a Whitman-like catalogue poetry, for what we have here are not so much investigations into the complexity of specific moments as suggestive shards, fleeting images, and passing glimpses that are meant to be self-evidently and transparently significant (Buell, 1968; Chari, 1972; Mason, 1973; Reed, 1977).

The fact that these terms—self-evident and transparent—stand in absolute contrast to the allusive and impenetrably dense verse in Forché's *Blue Hour* demonstrates how even though both Sanders and Forché strive to write a political and historical poetry of witness, they practice dramatically different forms of investigative poetry. Indeed, the vast aesthetic differences between *Blue Hour* and *America* raise a host of questions about the possible relationships among different forms of poetry, politics, witnessing, and historical scholarship. In fact, the poems addressed here throw the terms listed earlier into question, forcing us to reappraise not only how they speak to each other but also what they stand for in their own right. Before addressing how investigative poetry speaks to these issues, it is necessary to review the ways that contemporary scholars have tried to reconsider and to merge historical, political, and artistic works to produce engaged scholarship that is both witness to and participant in struggles for social justice.

2. Social Justice and the Obligations and Opportunities of Engaged Scholars

Although Forché and Sanders both clearly see their poems as fulfilling political roles, their divergent aesthetic strategies might leave readers wondering about how the fight for social justice figures into such work. One way of answering that question is to shift genres and to address the flood of materials calling on scholars to become more active in their communities' various struggles for social justice. Although it is not difficult to piece together a loose genealogy of intellectuals concerned with issues of social justice over the past centuries, we are glad to see that during recent years scholars across a variety of disciplines have begun arguing in a systematic manner that those teacher-activists committed to the ends of social justice, while still cherishing the wondrously messy means of democratic life, need to approach issues of social justice not only as sites of research but also as sites of engagement with disadvantaged communities (Crabtree, 1998; Frey, 1998; Hartnett, 1998). Located loosely between Forché's melancholic absence and Sanders's exuberant lists, this social justice literature calls for scholarship that speaks to sweeping ideas by paying deft attention to local needs.

Our thinking here is deeply indebted to Dwight Conquergood, a performance studies professor at Northwestern University who spent years doing research on, and advocating on behalf of, the gangs with whom he lived as a neighbor, teacher, and substitute father figure in the decimated Cabrini Green public housing of Chicago. Conquergood lectured widely about his experiences and wrote about them and their implications for academics and activists in two brilliant book chapters (Conquergood, 1994, 1995). Inspired by Conquergood's bravery, Larry Frey, Barnett Pearce, Mark Pollock, Lee Artz, and Bren Murphy, colleagues at Loyola University in Chicago, implored their fellow speech communication scholars in 1996 to conduct research "not only *about* but *for* and *in the interests of* the people with whom" their research was conducted (Frey, Pearce, Pollock, Artz, & Murphy, 1996, p. 117). This means that scholars can no longer assume they are objective outsiders analyzing static objects of inquiry; instead, in this new model of engaged scholarship, researchers become subjects mutually enmeshed in the processes they are studying. Following Conquergood's lead, then, Frey and his colleagues asked engaged scholars to channel their academic work toward pressing community needs and thus to produce works that "foreground ethical concerns," "commit to structural analyses of ethical problems," "adopt an activist orientation," and "seek identification with others" (p. 111; see also Adelman & Frey, 1997).

For specific ways of thinking about the prospects of teaching on, researching about, and fighting for social justice, we have been influenced by Pierre Bourdieu's "For a Scholarship With Commitment," an essay adapted from a presentation he gave as part of a panel organized by Edward Said for the 1999 meeting of the Modern Language Association (MLA). Bourdieu (2000) recommends that scholars hoping to make a difference pursue four goals: (a) "produce and disseminate instruments of defense against symbolic domination"; (b) engage in "discursive critique," meaning analyses of the "sociological determinants that bear on the producers of dominant discourse"; (c) "counter the pseudoscientific authority of authorized experts"; and (d) "help to create social conditions for the collective production of realist utopias" (p. 42). We may conceptualize these imperatives as pointing to four modes of critical activity. First is helping to teach and popularize the critical thinking skills necessary for citizens to become more conscientious consumers of mass media; we may think of this as *debunking cultural symbolism.* Second is demonstrating through rigorous case studies how dominant discourse reflects the economic imperatives of elites; we may think of this as *analyzing class privilege.* Third is revealing and helping others to reveal the political assumptions and biases of experts within specific fields of inquiry; we may think of this as *becoming rhetorical critics.* And fourth is both imagining and advocating alternative ways of being; we may think of this as *inventing new possibilities.* In that same panel, Elaine Scarry put this fourth imperative in lovely terms—terms that would make Emerson and Whitman proud—arguing that teachers of literature and the arts share a special burden to cultivate in both their students and their communities "a reverence for the work of the imagination" (Scarry, 2000, p. 21; see also Becker, 1994). The task, then, is to fulfill Bourdieu's four critical criteria in forms that meet Scarry's aesthetic criteria, hence our fascination with the possibilities of investigative poetry.

The one obvious shortcoming of the suggestions of Bourdieu, Scarry, and their fellow MLA participants is that even while asking us to pursue scholarship with commitment, they tend to privilege certain traditional forms of textual production, hence excluding (perhaps unwittingly) many genres of human communication. This explains Conquergood's insistence that engaged scholarship and activism must take into account "the embodied dynamics that constitute meaningful human interaction" by striving for "a hermeneutics of experience, copresence, humility, and vulnerability." Recent literature on ethnography and performance studies has demonstrated the many ways these imperatives may be pursued, often with stunning results, yet as we detail in what follows, we fear that much of this work has tended to fall into a troubling pattern of sensationalism and narcissism, celebrating the raw immediacy of personal experience over any attempt to make structural sense of the larger historical, political, and cultural conditions surrounding daily life.

For both would-be investigative poets in particular and engaged scholars in general, then, the methodological conundrum is striving to balance self with society, text with context, the existential delirium of the now with the scholarly rigor of analysis—all the while honoring the obligations to social justice discussed here. Among the many subgenres and submovements within contemporary arts and letters, ethnopoetics stands as a significant attempt to tackle these conundrums; therefore, we turn to the problems and possibilities of ethnopoetics as a case study of how poets have sought to weave historical, political, and personal materials into a poetry of witness.

3. The Lessons and Legacies of Ethnopoetics

Ethnopoetics could be labeled investigative poetry's immediate predecessor, for it was a seminal attempt to make poetry political by merging a critique of colonialism, soft anthropology, and a poetics of witnessing. The term *ethnopoetics* was coined in 1967 by Jerome Rothenberg, Dennis Tedlock, and their colleagues. As Rothenberg (1990) argues, the project of ethnopoetics peaked during the late 1970s before *Alcheringa,* the magazine that Rothenberg and Tedlock founded in 1970 as an exhibition of ethnopoetic practices, finally sputtered out in 1980 (p. 8). Like defining any advanced cultural and/or academic practice, defining ethnopoetics is difficult (p. 8). As Friedrich (in press) argues, the term is "protean" and has adopted many connotations during the past three decades. For example, foregrounding its role in practicing what has since come to be known as multiculturalism, Tedlock (1992) defines ethnopoetics as the "study of the verbal arts in a worldwide range of languages and cultures" (p. 81). Likewise, Rothenberg (1990) argues that ethnopoetics "refers to an attempt to investigate on a transcultural scale the range of possible poetries that had not only been imagined but put into practice by other human beings" (p. 5). For Tedlock and Rothenberg, then, ethnopoetics is an attempt to think about poetry in a global context and thus to consider the roles of poets as witnesses to, critics of, and activists committed to healing the damage wrought by colonialism and violent modernity. Indeed, Rothenberg argues that one of the chief goals of ethnopoetics is to engage in "the struggle with imperialism, racism, chauvinism, etc." (p. 5). That quotation-ending "etc." is significant, for it indicates the off-hand, sloppy way in which much of Rothenberg's work on ethnopoetics collapses specific political crises into one catch-all basket of wrongs—*you know, modernity, colonialism, racism, chauvinism, etc.*

In contrast to that sweeping "etc.", we have argued here that investigative poetry is committed to a version of synecdoche in which grand claims can be supported only through micrological analyses based on deep historical scholarship. We return to this critique of the sloppy uses of "etc." that seem to plague the Rothenberg school of ethnopoetics later, but for now we turn to Friedrich, who argues that the genre falls into two categories: analytic and synthetic. Whereas analytic ethnopoetics operates on a "meta" level by inspecting other ethnopoetic works, synthetic ethnopoetics either creates an anthropological poem that bridges a gap between two cultures or translates a poem from one culture to another; in both synthetic cases, the goal is to make one culture familiar to another. For example, Friedrich (in press) praises Gary Snyder's "Anasazi" for "converting a foreign culture and poetry into poems that speak to Western, specifically American, sensitivities." Snyder's poem is a fine example of synthetic ethnopoetics, then, because it does the work of anthropology in the form of poetry, both enticing and enabling readers to transcend their provincialism.

Here is how Snyder (1974) brings the Anasazi to his readers:

> Anasazi,
>
> Anasazi,
>
> tucked up in clefts in the cliffs
> growing strict fields of corn
> sinking deeper and deeper in earth
> up to your hips in Gods
>   your head all turned to eagle-down
>   & lightning for knees and elbows
> your eyes full of pollen
>   the smell of bats.
>   the flavor of sandstone
>   grit on the tongue.
>
>   women
>   birthing
> at the foot of ladders in the dark.
>
> trickling streams in hidden canyons
> under the cold rolling desert
>
> corn-basked   wide-eyed
>   red baby
>   rock lip home,
>
> Anasazi. (p. 3)

The poem offers a beginner's loving guide to some basic facts about the Anasazi, namely that they live on cliffs in the desert, corn is a major part of their culture, and they live in close proximity with their gods—in short, they are human. Snyder (1974) takes us to a different time and place, to a world he describes in "Control Burn" as one "more/like,/when it belonged to the Indians/ Before" (p. 19). Like Rothenberg's "etc.", that poem-closing "Before" indicates the loose way in which this branch of ethnopoetics envisions itself as searching for a premodern, prehistoric, pre-Western world of innocence and virtue. But by conveying his sense of this lost civilization in verse that reads like a series of textbook stereotypes, Snyder teaches us little about the culture of the Anasazi. Indeed, the romanticization of Anasazi life makes the "Before" of "Control Burn" sound like a naïve plea to return to a world that is long gone and to do so while ignoring the fact that even when it existed it was—like our own world—wracked with political, economic, and cultural dilemmas.

Therefore, it is difficult to imagine anthropologists or historians taking such poems seriously. However, for Snyder and some ethnopoets, the function of such poems is not so much to stand as rigorous scholarship as to stand as rhetorical platforms from which to launch scathing critiques of Western modernity. For example, Snyder's (1974) "The Call of the Wild" leaps forward from the Anasazi to offer a blistering critique of "All these Americans up in special cities in the sky/Dumping poisons and explosives" (p. 23). Published amid the war in Vietnam, this clear reference to the saturation bombings sanctioned by President Richard Nixon invites readers to think about the deep historical connections among Indian genocide, environmental destruction, and the butchery under way in the name of defeating communism. By thinking in this multitemporal manner, by holding the Anasazi and the Vietnamese in one's mind at the same time, Snyder gains historical and political leverage for his claim in "Tomorrow's Song" that

> The USA slowly lost its mandate
> in the middle and later twentieth century

it never gave the mountains and rivers,
  trees and animals,
    a vote.
all the people turned away from it. (p. 77)

Reading these lines in the midst of another set of U.S.-triggered wars, raging now in Afghanistan and Iraq, one is struck by the commonsensical—yet so often overlooked—argument that there is an intimate relation between the violence used to demolish nature and the violence used to murder our fellow humans. Indeed, in the face of the well-oiled machinery of death that slaughtered the Indians, that murdered millions of Vietnamese, that is currently leveling Afghanistan and Iraq, and that has left a worldwide trail of ecological destruction in its path, we are struck by how relevant—how powerful—this poem feels 30 years after its first publication (Thomas, 1995).

Whereas Snyder thus uses loosely anthropological poems about the deep past to gain historical leverage for a political critique of the violence of colonialism and ecological destruction, other proponents of ethnopoetics see the genre as more directly concerned with producing a form of cultural criticism that points toward multiculturalism. For example, in his review of ethnopoetics in *Symposium of the Whole: A Range of Discourse Toward an Ethnopoetics,* Turner (1983) argues that ethnopoetics is committed to "making visible." "The more we are aware of the multiplicity of Others," he argues, "the more we become aware of the multiple 'selves' we contain, the social roles we have 'internalized'" (pp. 340–341). For Turner, then, ethnopoetics explores the polyglot multiplicity of the social self, thus leading to a self-reflexive humility that opens the door to multiculturalism: "Once they [our tired versions of 'self'] are 'made visible' they are revealed as faintly comic figures. . . . It may be that the recognition of diversity in cultural voices has the therapeutic function of confronting us with the problem of the One and the Many—a new reflexivity in itself" (p. 341). This version of ethnopoetics thus functions as verbal therapy, aspiring to help its readers question their taken-for-granted cultural assumptions, and includes the assumption that deconstructing tired versions of a unified Western self will help to bridge the distance between these now problematized selves and the multiple Others who linger outside the comfortable living rooms of the West. From this perspective, ethnopoetics aspires to produce cultural criticism capable of functioning both as political engagement and as personal therapy.

Given this framework, let us return to another piece of ethnopoetics, "The New (Colonial) Ball Game" by Robert C. Williamson. A professor of anthropology at the University of Saskatchewan, Williamson specializes in fieldwork on the Inuit Indians. Attempting both to make the humiliations of colonialism clearer for the colonizer and to vent his own frustrations at the difficulty of the process of making the invisible visible, Williamson (1985) offers the following scene:

Then the little man
Who'd just arrived
And felt important
And, of course, responsible
Said nicely, pompously
With British vowels
As tight and round
As his big ass
How everybody should be grateful
For the Christly whites
Who came, of course, to help
And not to satisfy themselves
And here in their own country
For their sakes
We all should
(As it surely must inevitably
Come to be
And the sooner, don't you see

The better for us all)—

Talk White

For once their words will fit

The words we hear the most

OK

Do this

Right now

And hurry, see?

Fuck off. (pp. 189–190)

Brady (2000) claims that "by varying their forms of expression to include poetry, anthropologists attempt to say things that might not be said as effectively or at all any other way" (p. 956). Williamson's (1985) poem-ending and resounding "Fuck off" surely fits this model, for it is hard to imagine this line finding its way into his professional academic work. So the poem gives Williamson the linguistic latitude to say what he cannot say elsewhere. But does this expressive latitude enable the poet to write a powerful poem? Does the poem show us anything that is not already the subject of hundreds, if not thousands, of stereotypical images? We do not even know where this colonial ballgame takes place, what the date is, who the players are, or what game is being played, so we are in the realm of abstraction, the generic, the ahistorical no-place of generalized anticolonial anger. The same concerns have been raised about Forché's *Blue Hour,* but at least that poem's stunning beauty leaves readers awash in reverberating images that (hopefully) provoke further critical reflection. In traditional poetry criticism, such abstract verse might be taken as allegorical, as aspiring to offer a transhistorical moral lesson, yet Williamson's "Fuck off" hardly counts as an allegory. So even though the poem succeeds as therapy for its author, who must have been carrying that "Fuck off" around with him for quite a while just waiting to launch it into space, the poem fails as a poem and fails as anthropology, amounting ultimately to little more than a self-serving rant. Moreover, given the professed pedagogical function of ethnopoetics to transcend racism and cultural chauvinism by making the faraway and the strange more human and thus more familiar to Western readers, we would have to say that the poem is a pedagogical failure as well, for it teaches us little about the people being oppressed by the "little man" who speaks with "British vowels."

We have seen how Snyder merges anthropology, history, and political criticism to produce blistering and beautiful poems that speak directly to the carnage of the war in Vietnam, and we have watched as Williamson uses a poem about colonialism as verbal therapy. To further complicate our treatment of ethnopoetics, let us inquire as well about its practices as a form of cultural translation. *Alcheringa* was among the primary sources of ethnopoetics. Its "Statement of Intention" (1970) claims that "ALCHERINGA will not be a scholarly 'journal of ethnopoetics' so much as a place where tribal poetry can appear in English translation & can act (in the oldest & newest of poetic translations) to change men's minds & lives" (p. 1). For example, consider this version of "What Harm Has She Dreamt?" (1970), a Quechua tribal poem translated in the first issue of *Alcheringa:*

Her long hair is her pillow

the girl is sleeping on her hair.

She cries blood

she does not cry tears

she cries blood.

What is she dreaming?

what harm is she dreaming?

Who hurt her?

who hurt her heart like this?

Whistle to her, whistle, whistle,

little bird

so she wakes

so she wakes now

whistle whistle

little bird. (p. 50)

The poem presumably enables a Western audience to hear a Quechua orator implicate the violence of colonialism, a force so powerful and insipid that it has seeped into the dreams of its victims. The effort is clearly heartfelt, yet without massive prefatory information, we suspect that most readers will learn little from this poem about the tribal culture in question. Where do the tribe members live? Who is causing the tribe's young women to cry tears of blood? These may seem like unfair burdens to place on any individual translation, yet without answering these historically specific questions, the poem/translation cannot help but produce a vague and characterless sense of some premodern other, some far-off culture about which we know little if not nothing. Rather than bridging the gap between smug Western assumptions of privilege and the lived experiences of cultures on the fringes of modernity, those that have been shattered by colonialism, such poems leave readers uninformed, clueless, feeling vaguely touched yet not empowered to take any specific action.

One of the many goals of ethnopoetics was to offer such translations as a corrective to what has been widely criticized as the creeping biases leading to sloppy, if not downright exploitative, translations of the works and cultures of non-Western peoples. As Basso (1988) argues, there is "a growing conviction among linguistic anthropologists that the oral literatures of Native American people have been inaccurately characterized, wrongly represented, and improperly translated" (p. 809). Such translating inaccuracies pose a significant problem for cultural critics from a variety of fields, for as Clifford (1988/1999) demonstrates in *The Predicament of Culture,* anthropologists such as Bronislaw Malinowski allowed their colonial biases to shape their fieldwork on other cultures, hence leading to supposedly scientific reporting that in fact mirrors Western prejudices (pp. 92–113). In response to this anthropological dilemma, ethnopoets sought to produce translations that were closer to the spirit of their originals, hence trying to bring to Western readers a more authentic sense of the foreign cultures under consideration. Although this is an admirable goal, the fact is that there can be no direct and unclouded transcribing of a tribal poem into forms accessible to Western readers. *All translations are interpretations.*

This fact is demonstrated nicely in *Nineteen Ways of Looking at Wang Wei,* a fascinating study by Weinberger and Paz (1987) of 19 translations of an eighth-century Buddhist poem by Wang Wei. Weinberger and Paz conclude, "In its way a spiritual exercise, translation is dependent on the dissolution of the translator's ego: an absolute humility toward the text. A bad translation is the insistent voice of the translator—that is, when one sees no poet and hears only the translator speaking" (p. 17). But as *Nineteen Ways of Looking* suggests, one always hears the translator speaking—often in rhythms and voices that bring new depth and meaning to the poem. Indeed, because all translations are interpretive acts that, at their best, aspire to fulfill pedagogical and artistic functions, ethnopoets have come to realize that translation is a form of cultural criticism and artistic production in its own right (Alfred, 1999, pp. 55–65; Rosaldo, 1989/1993, pp. 25–87; Smith, 1999). From this perspective, then, translating poems from cultures on the fringes of modernity amounts not so much to a doomed attempt to reclaim a lost past or an unsullied Other as to an attempt to multiply—and hence add diversity to—the voices mingling in our conversations about the norms, obligations, and hopes of modernity.

Given the sweeping nature of that last claim, it is important before closing our discussion of ethnopoetics to add yet another layer of complicating theoretical factors and one more set of readings of ethnopoems. We accomplish both tasks by turning to the work of Ivan Brady, who for many years has been among the leading theorists and artists of this vein of work. Brady is particularly instructive, for whereas we have referred previously to various strains of ethnopoetics, Brady prefers the term "anthropological poetics." For Brady (2004), anthropological poetics consists of three interrelated yet distinct categories: "*ethnopoetics,* 'the emics of native poetries that are midwifed by Western poets'; *native poetry,* the poetry of traditional native poets; and *ethnographic poetics,* the poetic productions of ethnographers" (p. 639). We have already addressed examples of native poetry (the Quechua poem "What Harm Has She Dreamt?") and "ethnographic poetics" (Snyder's "Anasazi" and Williamson's "The New (Colonial) Ball Game"), and so we now focus on Brady's version of ethnopoetics. In anthropology, "emic" entails using the normative values and symbolic categories of those studied rather than imposing one's own cultural biases, and a "midwife" is someone who helps in the process of birth in particular and creation more generally (and who may, as in the case of the midwife who birthed the first author's first child, be a man); thus, for Brady, ethnopoetics relies on the local idioms of groups studied by anthropologists and the flexible forms of Western poetry, translation, and storytelling to aid in the process of creating new forms of expression.

To watch how this process unfolds, we turn to Brady's (2003) masterful *The Time at Darwin's Reef: Poetic Explorations in Anthropology and History.* We should note that Brady is an accomplished anthropologist who specializes in Pacific Island cultures, so whereas the ethnopoems and translations discussed previously felt slender on anthropological details, Brady's poems bristle with a lifetime of research and personal experience; this expertise is reflected in helpful sets of references and introductions to clusters of poems. As evidence of the book's (and Brady's) remarkably broad sense of time and place, *Darwin's Reef* closes with an alphabetical "Place List" and a chronological "Date List," both of which include information relevant to the other. For example, the Place List begins with "Abaiang Island, February 14, 1840," closes with "USMCRD, San Diego, California, August 27, 1958," and includes 60 other place/time entries sandwiched in between (pp. 128–129). Thus, before reading a single poem, readers recognize from glancing through the Place List and Date List that *Darwin's Reef* addresses the long history of naval conquest, beginning for the purposes of this book in the South Pacific during the 1840s, culminating in the world's largest floating arms depot, San Diego, during the late 1950s, and wreaking havoc on all the places in between. The Place List and Date List thus function as semiotic machines of imaginative yet historically grounded suggestions, producing juxtapositions, layerings, and clues meant to lead the reader on geographic and temporal journeys through the wreckage of colonialism.

"Time" at Darwin's Reef is therefore, as in Snyder's (1974) *Turtle Island,* less linear than in traditional historical writings and more like the twisting, reverberating, ecological, and even spiritual forms it often takes in folklore. For example, in the poem that names the book, "The Time at Darwin's Reef"—located with the place and date listings that preface each poem as "Playa de la Muerte, South Pacific, July 4, 1969"—Brady conveys time as "High Time, 1:05 p.m., Fiji time" (local clock time, p. 69), as "Time to Get Down" (from the Cessna flying overhead, p. 69), as "Island Time" (the deep ecological time of natural change, p. 70), as "Copy time in the coral" (the movements of coral reproduction as seen in "ejaculating rocks," pp. 71–72), as "Magic Time" (p. 73), and so on in a dizzying multiplication of possible times, most of them rooted not in Western notions of clocks but rather in the natural temporal forms of tides, seasons, and life cycles. Taken together, these layered "times" indicate a spiritual sense of completeness, of multiplicities woven into an organic whole, of ecological centeredness.

Lest readers assume that Brady's gorgeous experiments in temporal confusions lapse into political complacency, "Proem for the Queen of Spain" layers such temporal dislocations against spatial and political fragments, hence creating a sense of bitter poetic judgment. The bulk of the piece is a letter (fictional but true to its historical moment) from Fernando Junipero Dominguez, written in "New Spain" (Mexico) in 1539, in which the writer thanks the queen for bringing to his people "the Embrace of the Mission and the Love of God, Amen" (p. 51). This is a letter, then, that demonstrates how colonized peoples internalized oppression, in this case in the form of bowing to a foreign god brought to the New World by a foreign empire. Tucked within the letter, however, Brady offers expletive-laced commands from U.S. troops in Vietnam, who shout at the locals "Nam fuckin' xuong dat! Lie the fuck down! Or y'all gonna fuckin' die!" (p. 51). The end matter following the poem provides multiple historical references on the history of Dominguez, so the poem fulfills the pedagogical function of both seducing readers to think historically and then leading them to the necessary information to pursue their own further readings. Much like Snyder's juxtaposing the Anasazi against Nixon's saturation bombing of Vietnamese peasants, then, Brady's inserting dialogue from U.S. soldiers within a 1539 letter to the queen of Spain illustrates a sense of continuity linking the Spanish invasion of Mexico to the U.S. invasion of Vietnam. Against the deeply satisfying ecological times of "Time at Darwin's Reef," then, "Proem for the Queen of Spain" offers a chilling sense of *imperial time,* of the looping repetitive horrors of conquest.

Despite this numbing sense of the ways that imperial powers have savaged weaker peoples for centuries, the bulk of Brady's poems are committed to loving and often gorgeous tributes to the ways that even the strangest Others are in fact not only human but also human in ways that are deeply familiar to Western readers, for as Brady (1991) argues elsewhere, ethnopoems function by "defining the humanity of humankind and positing it as something to be achieved in practice" (p. 6). As demonstrated in *Darwin's Reef,* those practices will be so multifarious, so convoluted, and even so magical that it takes remarkable kindness and patience to appreciate their significance. As Brady (2004) argues, "Ethnographic poets meditate on the ethnographic experience or focus on particulars arranged to elicit themes of general humanity that might apply cross-culturally" (p. 630). Brady's *Darwin's Reef* offers us a glimpse of what such cross-cultural, anthropological, and poetic consciousness might look like, hence expanding our notion of who counts as our brothers and sisters while envisioning a new, better, and more generous way of being in the world. Thus, although Brady flags these works as "poetic explorations in anthropology and history" in the subtitle to *Darwin's Reef,* our readings of them would add that they are, like Snyder's poems, both politically progressive and deeply spiritual meditations, self-reflexive opportunities for postmoderns to move past irony and cynicism toward something like multicultural commitment.

As demonstrated in the preceding paragraphs, we are deeply moved by Brady's contributions. The only problem—and it is a problem not so much with Brady as with most works of art—is that regimes of truth often obscure the ability or the desire to see another as human. Stereotypes and prejudices cloud judgment, making the generosity demonstrated in Brady's texts a difficult enterprise. Brady (2004) sees the overarching problem of anthropological poetics as one of "plural 'knowables' and the frustrations of choosing among them. (Or having someone choose for you, someone or some institution with the power to enforce the choice, say, society, for example. Or the Taliban. Or your department head)" (p. 632). This is a crucial passage, for we suspect that this parenthetical aside regarding the powers that filter through all life, the powers that allow others to "choose for you," may be the most important blockage preventing the fulfillment of Brady's vision. Indeed, the investigative poetry to which we turn in our closing section begins from the understanding that someone or some structure is always trying to choose for us, meaning that our plural knowables are often the products of oppressive regimes, stultifying cultural norms, or bureaucratic deadweight. Whereas the ethnographic poetry studied here offers us a compelling set of models for thinking critically about and engaging politically in the world—with Brady's *Darwin's Reef* standing as our best exemplar of the rich possibilities of this work—we still want to ask more from investigative poetry, for without a nuanced and pedagogically rich articulation of how multiple forms of power filter through, and sometimes even structure, our contexts of action, we can never know how to rhetorically build consensus and common humanity.

In short, in the final section, we propose—not so much as a critique of ethnographic poetry as a supplement to it—that society's power to choose for us is not an aside but rather the focal point of poetic criticism. The works we address in what follows thus move away from a sense of anthropological wonder toward hard-hitting political and poetic critiques of specific regimes of power.

4. Three Models of Investigative Poetry: Dos Passos, Forché, and Scott

The works considered here are immersed completely in, and are fully aware of their complicity with, the contradictions of U.S. power; they accordingly focus on case studies of economic, military, political, and cultural oppression. Indeed, the poems considered in this section work imminently, constructing their investigative poetry from within the very social systems they hope to examine. Whereas the ethnographic poetry considered previously works in an alluring sideways manner, thinking about U.S. power by working along its edges and using anthropology to teach us about the peoples affected by U.S. power, the works considered in what follows take a more direct approach. In fact, Peter Dale Scott, in particular, has been attacked by those who find his poems too political and not poetic enough. Our comments in this section therefore are not meant to stand as normative judgments about what is a better or more powerful form of poetry; rather, we offer them as the final piece of our puzzle, as a closing set of options and models of how our best poets have struggled to merge historical and political criticism in a form of investigative poetry.

First among these models is John Dos Passos's *U.S.A.* trilogy, consisting of *The 42nd Parallel* (1930/1969c), *Nineteen Nineteen* (1932/1969a), and *The Big Money* (1936/1969b). The bulk of these sprawling novels consists of traditional narratives following the misadventures of characters confronted with the various economic, cultural, and political complications following from the manic boom-and-bust cycles of unregulated capitalism and America's entry into World War I. Each story is followed, however, by short sections titled Newsreels and the Camera Eye and by poetic biographies of the period's key players. The Newsreels consist of newspaper headlines, snippets of newspaper stories, and snatched refrains from popular songs—*Oh say can you see . . . , Where do we go from here, boys?* Arrayed on the page as a string of disconnected shards of evidence, these Newsreels provide both a clear forerunner to the form of Sanders's *America* and an eerie glimpse into the world of popular culture, mass-produced misinformation, and the vast majority of events that have simply fallen into historical oblivion.

The Newsreels are followed by Camera Eye sections in which Dos Passos offers disjointed observations, literally camera shots of turmoil. In this case, we watch the angry response of socialists in Paris to the Treaty of Versailles: "at the République à bass la guerre MORT AUX VACHES à bas le Paix de Assassins they've torn up the gratings from around the trees and are throwing stones and bits of castirons at the fancydressed Republican Guards hissing whistling poking at the horses with umbrellas scraps of the *International*" (Dos Passos, 1932/1969a, pp. 396–397). As indicated by the random gaps in the passages just quoted, the confusion as to who is speaking, and the bristling sense of confused immediacy, these sections fade into the stream of consciousness, thus offering readers glimpses into the fractured experience of living daily life amid epochal historical transformations. Dos Passos follows these blasts of existential confusion with poetic biographies, from which we have taken this verse on Randolph S. Bourne:

> This little sparrow like man
>
> tiny twisted bit of flesh in a black cape,
>
> always in pain and ailing,
>
> put a pebble in his sling
>
> and hit Goliath in the forehead with it
>
> *War,* he wrote, *is the health of the state.* (p. 120)

Made popular in Zinn's (1980) magnificent *A People's History of the United States,* Bourne's phrase has stood for generations as an indictment of U.S. militarism (pp. 350–367). By chronicling the struggles of this largely forgotten figure, Dos Passos's biographical poem enriches our sense of American history, making it more somber and personal. The combination of the explanatory narratives, the evidence-offering Newsreels, the existentially rich Camera Eye sections, and the poetic biographies offers readers four perspectives from which to approach history. Dos Passos thus strives to merge these four modes of writing to form a collective whole capable of thinking simultaneously about the deep structural integrity of history and the baffling, awestruck wonder and confusion that fills each small moment of time.

A second important model of textual production influencing our arguement here is provided by Forché's *The Country Between Us* (1981) and *The Angel of History* (1994), her two books prior to *Blue Hour.* Based on her journalistic work in El Salvador during the height of that country's civil war, *The Country Between Us* offers a model for a poetry of witness in which the poet is not only a chronicler of hope and terror but also a participant in the processes she examines. The poems in this remarkable book thus veer from scalding political critiques of Salvadoran tyrants to self-implicating ruminations on how even the most mundane pleasures in the United States bear the stain of the violence our government funds in the Third World. Like so many of us who find that our grassroots political work changes the ways that we think about freedom (Hartnett, 2003; Tannenbaum, 2000), Forché finds that living in close proximity to barbarism in El Salvador casts shadows across daily space. Forché (1981) is thus unnerved by the sense of decadence and ease signaled by "the iced drinks and paper umbrellas, clean / toilets and Los Angeles palm trees moving / like lean women" (p. 17). Like so many of us, she finds the happy ignorance of many Americans regarding the brutality that their country foists on the world to be unbearable. Speaking to a friend, she laments,

you were born to an island of greed
and grace where you have the sense
of yourself as apart from others. It is
not your right to feel powerless. Better
people than you were powerless. (p. 20)

Many of these better people appear in the pages of *The Angel of History,* where Forché (1994) expands her poetry of witness to encompass the European Holocaust and the impact of the United States dropping nuclear bombs on Japan. Taking her title from the well-known story told in Benjamin's (1940/1969) "Theses on the Philosophy of History," where an angel is blown backward into the future while watching the present produce an ever-growing pile of wreckage (pp. 257–258), Forché tackles the horrors of World War II in personal poems full of stories of her lost relatives and friends. While leading readers on this personally inflected historical journey into barbarism, Forché speculates—frequently through the voices of other writers and philosophers—on the possibilities of forgiveness. Much like Brady's *Darwin's Reef,* then, *The Angel of History* is less an investigative attempt to name names and pinpoint causes than a philosophical attempt to make sense of the persistence of hope in the face of unspeakable suffering. Aphoristic and enigmatic—and thus nearly impossible to quote without including pages of supporting material—the poems accumulate power from their many references to other texts, hence offering readers less a definitive statement than a series of beautiful theses, each equipped with what amounts to a list of suggested readings. Thus, while embodying the wonder and openness of elegant poetry, *The Angel of History* stands ultimately as a pedagogical tool for wondering what it means to cherish art during an age of destruction.

The third, and by far the most important, model of investigative poetry is Peter Dale Scott's *Seculum* trilogy. The first part of the trilogy, *Coming to Jakarta: A Poem about Terror* (1988), has been lauded in *The Boston Review* as "remarkable and unnerving" (Weiner, 1995, p. 31), in

London's *Times Literary Supplement* as "a work of great richness and complexity" (Gunn, 1991, p. 19), in *Parnassus* as "revolutionary" (Campbell, 1993, p. 395), and in a special issue of *AGNI*—by no less a national hero than the Poet Laureate Robert Hass—as "the most important political poem to appear in the English language in a very long time" (Hass, 1990, p. 333). Like these enthusiastic reviewers, we have been deeply impressed by the sophistication and depth of Scott's political analysis, the epic sweep of his historical knowledge, the revelatory honesty of his self-implicating poems, and the sheer beauty of his verse. By interweaving these four qualities—political acumen, historical grounding, self-reflexivity, and poetic beauty—Scott produces what we call *an interdisciplinary aesthetics of provisional eloquence.* That is, by merging the four qualities just noted, and by doing so while confronting a political calamity, Scott provides us with an empowering and elegant example of the search for grace amid terror.

Coming to Jakarta was triggered by Scott's (1988) need to write "about the 1965 massacre/of Indonesians by Indonesians" (p. 24) while simultaneously questioning his own complicity—as poet, professor, one-time diplomat, father, husband, and activist—in the events that led to the Central Intelligence Agency (CIA)-sponsored butchery of more than 500,000 Indonesian "communists" following the coup that replaced Sukarno with Suharto.[6] For example, in the second poem of *Coming to Jakarta,* we find Scott suffering from

> the uprising in my stomach
>
> against so much good food and
>
> wine America or was it
>
> giving one last broadcast too many
>
> about the Letelier assassins
>
> the heroin traffic
>
> a subject I no longer hope
>
> to get a handle on. (p. 10)[7]

These lines depict Scott as an activist/intellectual speaking publicly about the subterranean links between assassination politics and the drug war, as a typical overconsumer gorged on too much decadence, and as a consummate researcher who, suffering from the nausea brought on by too much familiarity with evil, wishes that the facts would mysteriously vanish into the comforting oblivion of ignorance—but of course they do not.[8] Instead, history forces itself mercilessly onto Scott (1988), prodding him to engage in a relentless pursuit of *evidence,* dragging him deeper and deeper into both the psychology and the political economy of terror:

> Already we are descending
>
> into these shadows which
>
> hang about as if there
>
> were something much more urgent
>
> left wholly unsaid. (p. 13)

Readers interested in the facts of the Indonesian massacre will find more than 100 sources listed in Scott's notes, which situate Suharto's coup and the ensuing anticommunist genocide within the overlapping politico-economic framework of post-World War II international finance; the transition from modern, empire-driven, and ideologically driven colonialism into the postmodern neocolonialism of multinational corporations, underground think tanks, and globetrotting mercenaries; and the continuing subversion of democratic politics at the behest of the global caste-bound thugs who run secret governments as if they were their own private shooting galleries. The research used to document these charges is breathtaking, thus offering readers a tutorial in how to pursue interdisciplinary political criticism. In this sense, then, Scott is perhaps the most impressive cobbler of what we saw Sanders (1976) refer to earlier as "a melodic blizzard of data-fragments" (p. 9).

But whereas such melodic blizzards might leave many readers baffled, or at least searching for personal relevance in such waves of "data-fragments,"

Scott weaves his remarkable research around and through moments of daily life, hence showing us how power courses through even the most mundane activities. For example, watch here as Scott (1988) links the disparate strands of the international political economy of terror, U.S. weapons manufacturers, Indonesian and Saudi tycoons, the refuse of Nixon's henchmen, and the friendly neighborhood bank:

> and I thought of Adnan Khashoggi
>
> the Indonesian shipping magnate
>
> Saudi friend of Pak
>
> Chung Hee and Roy Furmak
>
> *$106 million*
>
> in Lockheed commissions
>
> to Khashoggi alone
>
> and twice that
>
> amount withdrawn by Khashoggi
>
> from Rebozo's bank in Key Biscayne
>
> in May and November '72
>
> and of Lim Suharto's *cukong*
>
> who has bought the Hibernian bank
>
> with a branch on the Berkeley campus
>
> from profits on arms deals. (pp. 127–128)[9]

Scott's awesome courage in exposing the shadowy operatives and offshore bankers and behind-the-scenes boardroom connections that fuel imperialism, in conjunction with his sweeping grasp of history and his uncanny ability to render such topics in recognizable terms—*a branch on the Berkeley campus*—render *Coming to Jakarta* a world-class example of the detailed historical and political analysis needed to render investigative poetry persuasive.

In fact, it took nearly 15 years following the publication of *Coming to Jakarta* for the mainstream media to begin to address the underworld U.S.–Indonesia connections first exposed in Scott's poem. For example, it is now known that Freeport MacMoRan, Texaco, Mobil, Raytheon, Hughes Aircraft, and Merrill Lynch (among others) are major financial sponsors of the U.S.–Indonesia Society, a lobbying group cochaired by President Ronald Reagan's Secretary of State, George Schultz, and featuring James Riady as a trustee and John Huang as a consultant. Thus, two of the central figures (Riady and Huang) in one of the Democratic party campaign finance scandals that rocked the Clinton presidency turned out to be significant U.S.–Indonesia Society figures. Press (1997) observed at the time that the society was "a public relations organ for the Suharto regime" (p. 19). Thus, beneath the surface scandal of the Democratic party accepting illegal foreign campaign contributions, journalists found the much deeper scandal of continuing links among Suharto's brutal regime, U.S.-based transnationals, and the U.S. government. That Scott's *Coming to Jakarta* exposed these connections 15 years before the mainstream press would even consider them demonstrates the remarkable depth and courage of the poem's political and historical analysis. Using Scott's *Coming to Jakarta* as a model, then, we argue that investigative poetry uses rigorous research to name names, to show who owns what and whom, and thus to lay bare the institutional and economic structures supporting specific modes of oppression.

Scott's work is just as impressive, however, as an experiment in reconstructing a new and problematic sense of an endlessly compromised self in the face of terror, hence Scott's revelation that

> To have learnt from terror
>
> to see oneself
>
> as part of the enemy
>
> can be a reassurance
>
> whatever it is
>
> arises within us. (p. 62)

Like the poems of Dos Passos and Forché, then, Scott's poems perform a dialectical interweaving of perspectives. Each well-documented scene of political barbarism segues into personal observations on the nature of complicity, each personal rumination on complicity fades into questions of commitment and the historical obligation of engaged citizens to at least attempt to speak truth to power, and each engagement with the numbing expanse of global power politics, in turn, leads back to the suspicion that perhaps grace can only be found, after all, amid those moments when daily life is lived as an aesthetic experience. Hence the prevalence in *Listening to the Candle* (Scott, 1992), the second part of the *Seculum* trilogy, of simple pleasures

> focused on the mysteries
>
> of dailiness
>
> baking bread on Saturdays
>
> smelling the freshness
>
> of sun-dried laundry
>
> while you fold the sheet
>
> against yourself
>
> from the garden line. (p. 94)

Later in the poem, after chronicling the December 1980 murder of American evangelicals working with peasants in El Salvador, Scott (1992) suggests that

> in such a time it is still good
>
> having danced until midnight
>
> to Mika's and John's new band
>
> after the family lasagna
>
> all generations
>
> our children and their friends
>
> dancing together singly. (p. 106)

Terror and grace thus jostle each other within the infinitely textured particulars of the day:

> From the Bay Bridge
>
> on the way home from the opera
>
> you could look down on the searchlights
>
> of the Oakland Army Terminal
>
> where they loaded the containers
>
> of pellet-bombs and napalm. (Scott, 1988, p. 103)

Like Forché's line about "aria in time of war," then, Scott shows us how even the drive home from the opera, that quintessential marker of high art, leads one past places of mass-produced violence. *If you look around,* Scott tells us, *you will find yourself implicated in things you have previously spent a great deal of time and energy pretending not to recognize.*

These epiphanic moments of realization need not be paralyzing, however, as Scott shows us again and again how to channel them into a renewed commitment to work not only politically for peace and justice but also personally for something approaching kindness. In fact, in *Minding the Darkness,* the third volume of the *Seculum* trilogy, Scott (2000) turns increasingly to Buddhism as a way of practicing what he calls mindfulness. Much like Snyder's ecological consciousness in *Turtle Island,* or Brady's spiritual sense of time in *Darwin's Reef,* Scott's Buddhism is woven throughout the book as a counterthread to his political criticism. Scott demonstrates its challenges and opportunities most explicitly in four poems chronicling Buddhist retreats (pp. 72–80, 140–148, 221–229, 244). In contrast to the scathing investigative poetry of *Coming to Jakarta* and the meditative work in *Listening to the Candle*, then, *Minding the Darkness* demonstrates a middle way of mindful politics, of both critique and contemplation. This turn to Buddhism clearly illustrates Scott's hankering less for the smoking gun that will rip away the lies of any given regime than for the *wisdom* that will help him to live amid so much waste and cruelty. Indeed, by tracking down his footnotes; by rambling through his childhood traumas and parental pleasures; by forcing ourselves to confront both his and our complicity with the global carnage of low-intensity anticommunism, unabashed designer capitalism, and the pleasures of high culture; by making paratactical leaps from fragmentary images and quotations toward our own approximate understanding of the text; and by enthusiastically embodying a turn toward Buddhist values, Scott teaches attentive readers to treat the poem as a heuristic—even therapeutic—device. The mysterious "something much more urgent / left wholly unsaid" (Scott, 1988, p. 13) appears here to be the realization that poetry—as a trigger for research, as a source of grace, as a means of confronting terror, as a process of self-critique and reconstruction—amounts to a self-regenerating process in which, as Scott says in an interview, "one works through personal resistance and disempowerment to re-empowerment" (Scott, 1990, p. 303).

We are reminded here of Terrence Des Pres's comment in a roundtable discussion on the possibilities of political poetry that

> we turn where we can for sustenance, and some of us take poetry seriously in exactly this way. . . . When it comes to the Bomb, or just to the prospect of empires in endless conflict, it seems clear we cannot do very much very fast. So the immediate question isn't what to do but *how to live,* and some of us, at least, turn for help to poetry. (Des Pres, 1986, p. 21)

The sustenance of *Coming to Jakarta, Listening to the Candle,* and *Minding the Darkness* derives from the pleasures of sharing one's burden as an informed and engaged citizen in a rapidly unraveling democracy while not devolving into solipsism, cynicism, or madness. Hence Scott's (1988) prudent advice about how to live in the closing section of *Coming to Jakarta:*

as for those of us
        who are lucky enough
    not to sit hypnotized
our hands on the steering wheel
        which seems to have detached itself
    from the speeding vehicle

it is our job to say
        relax trust
    spend more time with your children

things can only go
        a little better
    if you do not hang on so hard. (p. 129)

5. Conclusion

We began our essay with the claim that despite the prevalence of buzzwords indicating the rise of *interdisciplinarity* and intellectual *border crossing,* the vast majority of scholarly production falls under the aegis of time-worn departmental and disciplinary norms. We offered ethnographic and investigative poetry as ways of moving past this hypocrisy. Likewise, we argued that despite the cultural cache of terms such as *radical, intervention,* and *transgression,* we know of only an embarrassingly small number of academics whose work engages in social justice concerns. The second section of this essay accordingly offered some guidelines for thinking about how to make social justice more central to what humanists do. The third and fourth sections then offered case studies examining how different poets have produced politically driven and interdisciplinary investigative poems. Taken together, the four sections of the essay offer concrete examples of how scholars, artists, and activists might begin tackling the seven methodological proposals with which we opened the essay. We therefore hope to have offered readers a series of working models, conceptual prompts, and historical examples of how to merge scholarship and poetry, social justice and self-reflection, hence producing texts that may serve the role of "aria in time of war." Indeed, given the remarkable proliferation of cultural offerings swimming in an apparently ever more specialized world of niche consumerism—a trend as problematic in poetry as in the general culture at large—the combination of detailed case studies and sweeping historical claims that marks the best investigative poetry offers a powerful model of engaged, artful, and cosmopolitan citizenship. At their best, these models of aria in time of war might well provide us, to borrow a phrase from an interview with Sanders (1997), "pathways through the chaos."

Notes

1. Birkerts (1987) proceeds to make a formalist argument demonstrating his allegiance to a traditional version of poetry and an emaciated version of politics. For more empowering responses to this question, see the essays collected in Jones (1985). For more experimental responses, see the remarkable works in Bernstein (1990) and Monroe (1996). For more programmatic responses, see "The Art of the Manifesto" (1998).

2. For a case study of the difference between healthy mourning and paralyzing melancholia, see Kaplan (2001). See also Freud (1963, pp. 164–179) for his diagnosis of the problem.

3. The passages quoted here are offered in praise of Ezra Pound, whose use of such "data clusters" was poetically dubious at best and politically dangerous at worst (Hartnett, 1993). On the rhetorical complexities of synecdoche, see Hartnett (2002, pp. 155–172).

4. Although long a subject of scholarly analysis, the pleasures of lynch mobs came to popular attention via *Without Sanctuary: Lynching Photography in America,* a show that opened at the New York Historical Society on March 14, 2000, and that has subsequently toured the nation, searing into the minds of its many viewers images of lynch mobs laughing, drinking, barbecuing, and otherwise enjoying the spectacle of death. Some of the images from the exhibit may be seen online at the homepage of the New York Historical Society or in Allen (2000). See also the comments on the pleasures of racial violence in Hartman (1997).

5. To study the legislation alluded to here, see "An Act to Punish Acts of Interference . . . " (June 15, 1917) and "An Act to Amend . . . " (April 16, 1918)—the so-called Espionage Acts—from *Statutes at Large of the United States of America* (U.S. Congress, 1919, pp. 217–231, 531). See also "Chapter 75," the May 16, 1918, amendment to the Espionage Act, in *Statutes of the United States of America* (U.S. Congress, 1918, pp. 553–554). For Eugene Victor Debs's heroic response to these acts, see his June 16, 1918, "Canton Speech" in *The Debs White Book* (n.d., pp. 3–64). For the U.S. Supreme Court's upholding these laws, see *Schenck v. U.S., Frohwerk v. U.S.,* and *Debs v. U.S.* (all May 1919) in *The Supreme Court Reporter* (West Publishing, 1920, pp. 247–254). This case is cited by lawyers as 39 S. Ct. 247 (1919).

6. For analyses of Suharto's domination of Indonesia, his brutal 1975 invasion of East Timor, and Jakarta's place in the new global economy, see Anderson (1995), Curtis (1995–1996), and Fabrikant (1996). U.S. complicity with Suharto's occupation of East Timor and his bloody repression of oppositional groups in Indonesia continues. In fact, since Suharto's December 1975 invasion of East Timor, in which more than 200,000 people—more than 25% of the population—were slaughtered, the United States has sold Indonesia more than $1.1 billion worth of advanced weaponry. The Clinton administration alone sold close to $270 million worth of arms to Suharto (see Klare, 1994, and Washburn, 1997). Suharto was finally forced from power in the spring of 1998. For coverage of his departure, see Mydans (1998) and any major newspaper during the latter half of April and all of May 1998.

7. Orlando Letelier, the Chilean ambassador to the United States, was killed by a car bomb in Washington, D.C., in September 1976. Right-wing Cuban expatriates, trained by DINA (the Chilean Secret Service) and funded through illegal CIA connections, claimed responsibility for the blast. See Scott and Marshall (1991, pp. 30–34).

8. The impulse here is reminiscent of the lament that "There are times/ I wish my ignorance were/ more complete" in Hass (1973, p. 61). In fact, Scott (1990) later wrote of his "growing self-hatred for carrying around a head full of horrors which most people were less and less willing to hear about" (p. 300).

9. Khashoggi's perpetual role as banker to terrorists and thugs has been reprised in his post-9/11 acting as well, in this case working with Richard Perle, the recently disgraced member of President George W. Bush's Defense Policy Board. See Hersh (2004, pp. 189-201).

References

Adelman, M., & Frey, L. (1997). *The fragile community: Living together with AIDS.* Mahwah, NJ: Lawrence Erlbaum.

Alfred, T. (1999). *Peace, power, righteousness: An indigenous manifesto.* New York: Oxford University Press.

Allen, J. (Ed.). (2000). *Without sanctuary: Lynching photography in America.* Santa Fe, NM: Twin Palms.

Anderson, B. (1995, November 2). Gravel in Jakarta's shoes. *London Review of Books,* pp. 2–5.

Basso, K. (1988). A review of Native American discourse: Poetics and rhetoric. *American Ethnologist, 15,* 805–810.

Becker, C. (Ed.). (1994). *The subversive imagination: Artists, society, and social responsibility.* New York: Routledge.

Benjamin, W. (1969). Theses on the philosophy of history. In W. Benjamin, *Illuminations* (H. Arendt, Ed. and Trans., pp. 253–264). New York: Schocken Books. (Original work published in 1940)

Bernstein, C. (Ed.). (1990). *The politics of poetic form: Poetry and public policy.* New York: Roof.

Birkerts, S. (1987). "Poetry" and "politics." *Margin, 4,* 55–62.

Bourdieu, P. (2000). For a scholarship with commitment. In P. Franklin (Ed.), *Profession: An annual publication of the MLA* (pp. 40–45). New York: Modern Language Association.

Brady, I. (1991). Harmony and argument: Bringing forth the artful science. In I. Brady (Ed.), *Anthropological poetics* (pp. 3–30). Savage, MD: Rowman & Littlefield.

Brady, I. (2000). Anthropological poetics. In N. K. Denzin & Y. S. Lincoln (Eds.), *Handbook of qualitative research* (2nd ed., pp. 949–979). Thousand Oaks, CA: Sage.

Brady, I. (2003). *The time at Darwin's Reef: Poetic explorations in anthropology and history.* Walnut Creek, CA: AltaMira.

Brady, I. (2004). In defense of the sensual: Meaning construction in ethnography and poetics. *Qualitative Inquiry, 10,* 622–644.

Buell, L. (1968). Transcendentalist catalogue rhetoric: Vision versus form. *American Literature, 40*(1), 325–339.

Campbell, M. (1993). Disaster, or the scream of Juno's peacock. *Parnassus, 17/18,* 380–403.

Chari, V. K. (1972). Structure of Whitman's catalogue poems. *Walt Whitman Review, 18*(1), 3–17.

Clifford, J. (1999). *The predicament of culture: Twentieth-century ethnography, literature, and art.* Cambridge, MA: Harvard University Press. (Original work published in 1988)

Conquergood, D. (1994). Homeboys and hoods: Gang communication and cultural spaces. In L. Frey (Ed.), *Group communication in context: Studies of natural groups* (pp. 23–55). Hillsdale, NJ: Lawrence Erlbaum.

Conquergood, D. (1995). Between rigor and relevance: Rethinking applied communication. In K. Cissna (Ed.), *Applied communication in the 21st century* (pp. 79–96). Mahwah, NJ: Lawrence Erlbaum.

Crabtree, R. (1998). Mutual empowerment in cross-cultural participatory development and service learning: Lessons in communication and social justice from projects in El Salvador and Nicaragua. *Journal of Applied Communication Research, 26,* 182–209.

Curtis, M. (1995–1996). Hawks over East Timor: Britain arms Indonesia. *Covert Action Quarterly, 55,* 52–56.

Debs, E. (n.d.). *The Debs white book.* Girard, KS: Appeal to Reason.

Des Pres, T. (1986). Poetry and politics. *TriQuarterly, 65,* 17–29.

Dos Passos, J. (1969a). *Nineteen nineteen.* New York: Signet. (Original work published in 1932)

Dos Passos, J. (1969b). *The big money.* New York: Signet. (Original work published in 1936)

Dos Passos, J. (1969c). *The 42nd parallel.* New York: Signet. (Original work published in 1930)

Emerson, R. W. (1982). The poet. In L. Ziff (Ed.), *Ralph Waldo Emerson: Selected essays* (pp. 259–284). New York: Penguin. (Original work published in 1844)

Fabrikant, G. (1996, April 9). Family ties that bind growth: Corrupt leaders in Indonesia threaten its future. *The New York Times,* pp. C1–C2.

Forché, C. (1981). *The country between us.* New York: Perennial.

Forché, C. (1993). *Against forgetting: Twentieth-century poetry of witness.* New York: Norton.

Forché, C. (1994). *The angel of history.* New York: Harper Perennial.

Forché, C. (2003). *Blue hour.* New York: HarperCollins.

Freud, S. (1963). *General psychological theory.* New York: Macmillan.

Frey, L. (1998). Communication and social justice research. *Journal of Applied Communication Research, 26,* 155–164.

Frey, L., Pearce, B., Pollock, M., Artz, L., & Murphy, B. (1996). Looking for justice in all the wrong places: On a communication approach to social justice. *Communication Studies, 47,* 110–127.

Friedrich, P. (in press). Maximizing ethnopoetics: Toward fine-tuning (anthropological) experience. In C. Jordain & K. Tuite (Eds.), *Ethnolinguistics: The state of the art.* Montreal: Fides.

Gordon, A. (1997). *Ghostly matters: Haunting and the sociological imagination.* Minneapolis: University of Minnesota Press.

Gunn, T. (1991, February 1). Appetite for power. *Times Literary Supplement,* p. 19.

Hartman, S. (1997). *Scenes of subjection: Terror, slavery, and self-making in nineteenth-century America.* New York: Oxford University Press.

Hartnett, S. J. (1993). The ideologies and semiotics of fascism: Analyzing Ezra Pound's *Cantos* 12-15. *Boundary 2, 20*(1), 65–93.

Hartnett, S. J. (1998). Lincoln and Douglas meet the abolitionist David Walker as prisoners debate slavery: Empowering education, applied communication, and social justice. *Journal of Applied Communication Research, 26,* 232–253.

Hartnett, S. J. (1999). Four meditations on the search for grace amidst terror. *Text and Performance Quarterly, 19,* 196–216.

Hartnett, S. J. (2002). *Democratic dissent and the cultural fictions of antebellum America.* Urbana: University of Illinois Press.

Hartnett, S. J. (2003). *Incarceration nation: Investigative prison poems of hope and terror.* Walnut Creek, CA: AltaMira.

Hass, R. (1973). *Field guide.* New Haven, CT: Yale University Press.

Hass, R. (1990). Some notes on coming to Jakarta. *AGNI, 31/32,* 334–361.

Hersh, S. (2004). *Chain of command: The road from 9/11 to Abu Ghraib.* New York: HarperCollins.

Jones, R. (Ed.). (1985). *Poetry and politics: An anthology of essays.* New York: Quill.

Kaplan, B. (2001). Pleasure, memory, and time suspension in Holocaust literature: Celan and Delbo. *Comparative Literature Studies, 38,* 310–329.

Klare, M. (1994, January 10). License to kill: How the U.S. is building up military–industrial complexes in the Third World. *In These Times,* pp. 14–19.

LaCapra, D. (2001). *Writing history, writing trauma.* Baltimore, MD: Johns Hopkins University Press.

Mason, J. (1973). Walt Whitman's catalogues: Rhetorical means for two journeys in "song of myself." *American Literature, 45*(1), 34–49.

Monroe, J. (Ed.). (1996). Poetry, community, movement [special issue]. *Diacritics, 26*(3/4).

Mydans, S. (1998, May 21). Suharto steps down after 32 years in power. *The New York Times,* pp. A1, A8.

O'Rourke, M. (2003, June 9). She's so heavy: Review of *Blue Hour. The Nation,* pp. 36–43.

Press, E. (1997). The Suharto lobby. *The Progressive, 61*(5), 19–21.

Reed, M. (1977). First person persona and the catalogue in "song of myself." *Walt Whitman Review, 23*(4), 147–155.

Rosaldo, R. (1993). *Culture and truth: The remaking of social analysis.* Boston: Beacon. (Original work published in 1989)

Rothenberg, J. (1990). Ethnopoetics and politics/The politics of ethnopoetics. In C. Bernstein (Ed.), *The politics of poetic form: Poetry and public policy* (pp. 1–22). New York: Roof.

Sanders, E. (1976). *Investigative poetry.* San Francisco: City Lights.

Sanders, E. (1997, November 18). Interview with Brooke Horvath. *Review of Contemporary Fiction, 19*(1). Available: www.centerforbookculture.org

Sanders, E. (2000). *America: A history in verse,* Vol. 1: *1900–1939.* Santa Rosa, CA: Black Sparrow.

Scarry, E. (2000). Beauty and the scholar's duty to justice. In *Profession: An annual publication of the MLA* (pp. 21–31). New York: Modern Language Association.

Scott, P. D. (1988). *Coming to Jakarta: A poem about terror.* New York: New Directions.

Scott, P. D. (1990). How I came to Jakarta. *AGNI, 31/32,* 297–304

Scott, P. D. (1992). *Listening to the candle: A poem on impulse.* New York: New Directions.

Scott, P. D. (2000). *Minding the darkness: A poem for the year 2000.* New York: New Directions.

Scott, P. D., & Marshall, J. (1991). *Cocaine politics: Drugs, armies, and the CIA in Central America.* Berkeley: University of California Press.

Smith, L. T. (1999). *Decolonizing methodologies: Research and indigenous peoples.* London: Zed Books.

Snyder, G. (1974). *Turtle Island.* New York: New Directions.

Statement of intention. (1970). *Alcheringa/Ethnopoetics, 1*(1), 1.

Tannenbaum, J. (2000). *Disguised as a poem: My years teaching poetry at San Quentin Prison.* Boston: Northeastern University Press.

Tedlock, D. (1992). Ethnopoetics. In R. Bauman (Ed.), *Folklore, cultural performances, and popular entertainments* (pp. 81–85). New York: Oxford University Press.

The art of the manifesto [24 contributors]. (1998). In J. Rothenberg & P. Joris (Eds.), *Poems for the millennium*, Vol. 2: *From postwar to millennium* (pp. 403–453). Berkeley: University of California Press.

Thomas, W. (1995). *Scorched earth: The military's assault on the environment.* Philadelphia: New Society.

Turner, V. (1983). A review of "ethnopoetics." In J. Rothenberg & D. Rothenberg (Eds.), *Symposium of the whole: A range of discourse toward an ethnopoetics* (pp. 337–342). Berkeley: University of California Press.

U.S. Congress. (1918). *Statutes of the United States of America, passed at the second session of the sixty-fifth Congress, 1917–1918* (Part 1: Public Acts and Resolutions, pp. 553–554). Washington, DC: Government Printing Office.

U.S. Congress. (1919). *Statutes at large of the United States of America, April 1917–March 1919* (pp. 217–231). Washington, DC: Government Printing Office.

Washburn, J. (1997). Twisting arms: The U.S. weapons industry gets its way. *The Progressive, 61*(5), 26–27.

Weinberger, E., & Paz, O. (1987). *Nineteen ways of looking at Wang Wei: How a Chinese poem is translated.* Wakefield, RI: Moyer Bell.

Weiner, J. (1995, February). [Review of Peter Dale Scott's *Crossing Borders: Selected Shorter Poems*]. *Boston Review,* pp. 31–33.

West Publishing. (1920). *The Supreme Court reporter* (Vol. 39, pp. 247–254). St. Paul, MN: Author.

What harm has she dreamt? (R. Jodorowsky, Trans.). (1970). *Alcheringa/Ethnopoetics, 1*(1), 50.

Williamson, R. (1985). The new (colonial) ballgame. In J. I. Prattis (Ed.), *Reflections: The anthropological muse* (pp. 189–190). Washington, DC: American Anthropological Association.

Zinn, H. (1980). *A people's history of the United States.* New York: Perennial.

42

QUALITATIVE EVALUATION AND CHANGING SOCIAL POLICY

Ernest R. House

In 1965, the U.S. Congress passed the Elementary and Secondary Education Act. At the insistence of Senator Robert Kennedy, this bill included an evaluation rider that became the stimulus for program evaluation. That same year, President Lyndon Johnson introduced the Program Planning and Budgeting System (PPBS), developed by the Pentagon, to the U.S. Department of Health, Education, and Welfare. The goal of the PPBS was to develop government programs that could be stated, measured, and evaluated in cost–benefit terms. Economists William Gorham and Alice Rivlin headed the evaluation office (McLaughlin, 1975).

Federal policy stipulated that key decisions for social services would be made at the higher levels of the federal government. The only true knowledge about social services was a production function specifying stable relationships between inputs and outputs. The only way of obtaining such knowledge was through experimental and statistical methods. "Information necessary to improve the effectiveness of social services is impossible to obtain any other way" (Rivlin, 1971, p. 108). To that end, several large-scale experiments were funded.

Campbell and Stanley's (1963) classic work became the methodological guide. Experimental studies became the new fad, with Campbell and Stanley describing experiments

> as the only means of settling disputes regarding educational practice, as the only way of verifying educational improvements, and as the only way of establishing a cumulative tradition in which improvements can be introduced without the danger of a faddish discard of old wisdom in favor of inferior novelties. (p. 2)

During the early days of professional evaluation, both policymakers and evaluators put their faith in large-scale quantitative studies such as Follow Through, Head Start, and the Income Maintenance experiment. Policymakers and many evaluators thought that these large national

Author's Note. I thank Bob Stake, Yvonna Lincoln, and Norm Denzin for providing useful feedback in the drafting of this chapter.

studies would yield definitive findings that would demonstrate which programs worked best. The findings could serve as the basis for mandates by the central government to reform inefficient social services.

In time, these large studies proved to be extremely disappointing. One problem was their scale. The Follow Through experiment cost $500 million, and during one data collection Follow Through evaluators collected 12 tons of data. They were overwhelmed by the logistics to the point where they could not produce timely reports. Eventually, the government sponsors reduced the study to a fraction of its original size by reducing the number of sites and variables.

A more serious problem was that the findings of these studies proved to be equivocal. The studies did not produce the anticipated clear-cut results that could be generalized. For example, when the Follow Through data were analyzed, the variance in test score outcomes across the dozen early childhood programs being compared was about as great as the variance within these programs. In other words, if a given early childhood program had been implemented at six sites, two sites might have good results, two might have mediocre results, and two might have poor results. This was not the kind of conclusive evaluative finding on which the government could base national recommendations. After years of frustration and hundreds of millions of dollars spent, policymakers and most evaluators became disenchanted with large-scale studies because of their cost, time scale, and lack of definitive results.

Meanwhile, evaluators were developing alternative approaches, including qualitative studies, meta-analysis, and program theory. Small qualitative studies were practical. For example, if a school district wanted an evaluation of its early childhood education program, interviewing administrators, teachers, and students was a simple and cheap method, and the findings were easy to understand even if they could not be published in scholarly journals. Furthermore, generalizability was not the problem that it was for large national studies. The demand on the local study was that the results be true for this place at this time; they did not need to be true for sites all over the country for all time.

However, some evaluators did not consider qualitative studies to be scientific. Evaluators engaged in intense internecine debates about the scientific legitimacy of qualitative methods. This dispute preoccupied the profession for 20 years, even as qualitative studies became increasingly popular. After many words and much rancor, the field finally accepted the idea that evaluation studies could be conducted in a number of different ways (Reichardt & Rallis, 1994). Evaluation became methodologically ecumenical, although personal sensitivities lingered. By 2000, the quantitative–qualitative dispute seemed to be history.

Another alternative to large-scale quantitative studies was meta-analysis (Glass, 1976). Meta-analysis was more acceptable to quantitative methodologists, although not without controversy. In some ways, meta-analysis was a natural successor to large-scale quantitative studies. Meta-analysis assembles the results of many experimental studies—studies that have control groups—and combines the findings of these studies quantitatively by focusing on the differences between performances of the experimental and control groups. The technique is more radical than it sounds given that researchers might combine outcomes that are quite different in kind into summary scores. Meta-analysis became overwhelmingly popular in social and medical research to the point where today it is difficult to pick up a major research journal without finding meta-analytic studies.

A third alternative to large-scale experimental studies was program theory (Chen & Rossi, 1987). Program theory consists of constructing a model of the program that can be used to guide the evaluation. Earlier, some researchers had advocated basing evaluations on grand social theories, but those attempts failed. First, there were no social theories that had much explanatory power. Second, if such theories existed, there was still the question of whether they could be used to evaluate social programs. For example, given the task of evaluating automobiles, could evaluators use theories of physics to do the job? It seems unlikely.

Evaluators reduced the grand theory concept to theories for individual programs. This worked better. The program formulation is concrete enough to guide evaluations, and it communicates directly with program participants. Program theory delineates points where evaluators might confirm whether the program is working and enables evaluators to eliminate rival hypotheses and make causal attributions more easily (Lipsey, 1993). Underlying qualitative studies, meta-analysis, and program theory have been changes in our conception of causation. These changes suggest why these alternatives worked better than large experimental studies.

▣ Changing Conceptions of Causation

The conception of causation that we inherited is called the regularity or Humean theory of causation, named after David Hume's influential analysis of cause (House, 1991). Regularity describes the conception. Put simply, the reason why we know one event caused another event is that the first event took place regularly before the other event—regularity of succession. If one event occurred and another event occurred after it repeatedly, we would have reason to believe that the events would occur together again. We look for succession of events. In fact, Hume said that regularity, along with contiguity of events, is all there is to causation. The research task is to determine the succession of events. Put succinctly: If *p*, then *q*; *p*, therefore *q*.

This notion of cause is the underlying basis for most discussions of experimental design, and it is manifest in early evaluation books: "One may formulate an evaluation project in terms of a series of hypotheses which state that 'Activities A, B, C will produce [R]esults X, Y, Z'" (Suchman, 1967, p. 93). In other words, if we have a Program A under Circumstances B and C, it will produce Results X, Y, and Z. Furthermore, the perfect design for determining whether the result has occurred is the classic randomized control group design. No error could result from employing this design, according to Suchman.

Although this assertion sounds reasonable, it falls apart on closer inspection. If we return to the Follow Through studies, the same early childhood program at six different sites produced different outcomes. Why? Because social causation is more complex than the regularity theory suggests. Even with the same program, there are different teachers at different sites who produce different results. We might try to control for the teachers, but there are so many variables that might influence the outcomes, the researchers cannot control for all of them. Put another way, the program is not in and of itself an integrated causal mechanism. Parts of the program might interact with elements in the environment to produce quite different effects.

Such considerations led Cronbach to abandon treatment-interaction research altogether. He tried to determine how student characteristics and outcomes interacted. There were so many possibilities that could not be controlled, he gave up trying. Put more technically, the effects of the secondary interactions of the variables were consistently as strong as the main effects. Cronbach (1982) rethought causation and devised a more complex formulation: In S, all (ABC or DEF or JKL) are followed by P. In other words, in this particular setting, P, the outcome, may be determined by ABC or DEF or JKL. The problem for evaluators is that if A is the program, we get P only if Conditions B and C are also present. So we could have A (the program) and not have the outcome P. More confounding, because P is caused by DEF and JKL combinations as well, we might not have the Program A but still get P. Neither the presence nor the absence of the Program A determines P. Succession of events is not a definitive test of cause and effect. The classic control group design will not produce definitive conclusions if causation is this complex.

Even so, we could devise a determinate research design using Cronbach's formulation, albeit a very expensive and complex one. However, social causation is more complex than even Cronbach's formulation indicates. Cronbach based his analysis on Mackie (1974), a seminal work on causation. Mackie's original formulation was this: All F (A . . . B . . . or D . . . H . . . or) are P (the dots represent missing causal factors we do not know about). We have huge gaps in our knowledge of social events—not only gaps we do not know about) but also gaps we do not even know we do not know about. Because we can never fill those gaps, we can never be certain of all that is involved. This does not mean that experiments are hopeless, only that they have to be interpreted carefully. They are not as foolproof as advocates may claim. There are always things we cannot account for.

Qualitative studies, meta-analysis, and program theory work better than large-scale studies because each approach takes account of a more complex social reality by framing the study more precisely, albeit in different ways. Qualitative studies show the interaction of people and events with other causal factors in context, thereby limiting causal possibilities and alternatives (Maxwell, 1996). Meta-analysis uses individual studies, each of which occurred in separate circumstances of rich variation, thereby making generalization possible (Cook, 1993). Program theory delineates the domain investigated, thereby allowing the posing of more precise questions (Lipsey, 1993).

▣ Changing Conceptions of Values

A second issue that shaped development in qualitative studies is the changing conception of values, often phrased as the fact–value dichotomy. This dichotomy is the belief that facts refer to one thing and values refer to something totally different. The fact–value dichotomy is a particularly embarrassing problem given that values lie at the heart of evaluation. I doubt that anything in the history of the field of evaluation has caused more trouble than this belief.

The distinction between facts and values has been around for decades, but the evaluation community inherited it through the positivists and their influence on social science. The logical positivists thought that facts could be ascertained and that only facts were the fit subject of science, along with analytic statements that were true by definition such as "1 plus 1 equals 2." Facts were empirical and could be based on pristine observations, a position called "foundationalism."

Values were something else. Values might be feelings, emotions—possibly useless metaphysical entities. Whatever they were, they were not subject to scientific analysis. People simply believed in certain values or they did not. Values were chosen. Rational discussion had little to do with them. The role of scientists was to determine facts. Others—politicians perhaps—could worry about values.

Donald Campbell, one of the great founders of the evaluation field, accepted the fact–value dichotomy explicitly (Campbell, 1982). However, he did not accept foundationalism about facts. Counter to the positivists, he contended that there were no pristine observations on which factual claims could be based because all observations are influenced by preconceptions that people hold. Knowledge is still possible because although one cannot compare a fact to a pristine observation to determine whether the fact is true (as positivists thought), one can compare a fact to the body of knowledge to which it relates. The fact should fit the whole body of beliefs. Occasionally, the body of knowledge has to change to accommodate the fact. In any case, one is comparing a belief to a body of beliefs, not comparing a belief to pure observation. This "nonfoundationalism" was counter to the positivist view.

Unfortunately, Campbell accepted the positivist conception of values. Values could not be determined rationally; they had to be chosen. It was not the evaluator's job to choose values. Once politicians, sponsors, or program developers determined values, evaluators could examine the outcomes of programs with criteria based on those values. Practically speaking, this meant that evaluators could not evaluate the program goals because the goals were closely connected to the values. Evaluators had little choice but to accept program and policy goals as they were.

Campbell had the correct idea about facts but not about values. Evaluators can deal with both facts and values rationally. Facts and values are not separate kinds of entities altogether, although they sometimes appear to be that way (House & Howe, 1999). Facts and values (factual claims and value claims) blend together in the conclusions of evaluation studies and, indeed, blend together throughout evaluation studies. We might conceive of facts and values schematically as lying on a continuum like this:

Brute Facts ______________________ **Bare Values**

What we call facts and values are fact and value claims, which are expressed as fact and value statements. They are beliefs about the world. Sometimes these beliefs look as if they are strictly factual without any value built in. For example, the statement "Diamonds are harder than steel" may be true or false, and it fits at the left end of the continuum. There is little individual preference built into it.

A statement such as "Cabernet is better than chardonnay" fits better at the right end of the continuum. It is suffused with personal taste. What about a statement such as "Follow Through is a good educational program"? This statement contains both fact and value aspects. The evaluative claim is based on criteria from which the conclusion is drawn and is based on factual claims as well. The statement fits the middle of the continuum—a blend of factual and value claims. Most evaluative conclusions fall toward the center of the continuum as blends of facts and values.

Context makes a huge difference in how a statement functions. A statement such as "George Washington was the first president of the United States" looks like a factual (historical) claim. But if this statement is made at a meeting of feminists who are excoriating the racist and patriarchal origins of the United States, the statement becomes evaluative in this context. The statement can be factual and evaluative simultaneously. It does not cease to be a factual claim. Similarly, claims that might seem factual in another context might be evaluative in an evaluation.

Evaluative claims are subject to rational analysis in the way we ordinarily understand rational analysis. First, the claims can be true or false. For example, Follow Through may or may not be a good educational program. Second, we can collect evidence for and against the truth or falsity of the claim, as we do in evaluation studies. Third, the evidence can be biased or unbiased, and it can be good or bad. Finally, the procedures for evidential assessment are determined by the evaluation discipline.

Of course, some claims are not easy to determine. In some situations, it might not be possible to determine truth or falsity. Also, we might need new procedures to help us collect, determine, and process fact–value claims. Just as we have developed procedures for testing factual claims, we might develop procedures for collecting and processing claims that contain strong value aspects so that our evaluative conclusions are unbiased regarding these claims as well. The claims blend together in evaluation studies. In the old view of values, to the extent that evaluative conclusions were value based, they were outside the purview of the evaluator. In the revised view, values are subject to rational analysis by the evaluator and others. Values are evaluations.

In a sense, this analysis of values helps to legitimize qualitative research. Qualitative researchers have been criticized for collecting information that merely reflects the opinions of those in and around the program when instead they should be collecting data not distorted by human judgment. Qualitative information is viewed as too subjective. In fact, the views, perspectives, and values of participants are vital pieces of information about the success of the program—if processed properly. Indeed, there is no information in evaluations that does not contain value elements. And qualitative methods are the best way in which to approach value claims, although they are not the only way.

◙ Changing Conceptions of Social Justice

The saga of value-free research and the reluctance to do qualitative research and evaluation was not simply a philosophical position. The story must be understood within the historical, political, and social context in which the value-free ideas developed. There are political reasons why qualitative studies were viewed as too subjective and illegitimate. Ultimately, it has to do with social justice.

Principles of social justice are used to assess whether the distribution of benefits and burdens among members of a society are appropriate, fair, and moral. The substance of such assessments usually consists of arguments about the concepts of rights, deserts, or needs. When applied to society as a whole, social justice pertains to whether the institutions of a society are arranged to produce appropriate, fair, and moral distributions of benefits and burdens among societal members. As such, social justice is linked directly to the evaluation of social and educational programs because these entities, and their evaluations, affect directly the distribution of benefits and burdens.

In spite of the direct conceptual link between social justice and evaluation, social justice concerns are routinely omitted from evaluation discussions. There are two reasons for this. First, evaluators are not well versed in philosophy or political science and feel unprepared to discuss such concepts. Many evaluators have had methodological training that does not deal with social justice. Second, and more important, social justice concerns have long been excluded from social science research for political reasons.

In her history of the origins of American social science, Ross (1991) documented how social justice concerns were indeed topics of discussion in the social sciences during the early 20th century. However, several "Red Scare" episodes, stemming from fears of Marxism, swept the United States and intimidated social researchers. Some prominent economists and sociologists were dismissed from their university positions for supporting labor unions, child labor laws, and other social policies opposed by university boards of trustees, whose members came mostly from business.

The upshot was that many social scientists retreated from issues that might be seen as politically risky into concerns about research methodology. If social researchers could be persecuted for taking stands on political and "value" issues, they might be safe by focusing on which tests of statistical significance to employ or what sampling procedures to use—issues of no interest to politicians or boards of trustees. Those social researchers who remained concerned about social justice were relegated to the fringes of their disciplines as being too political. Certainly, given the history of American social science, the Marxists were considered out of bounds. Social science in other countries had different origins, and these differences were reflected in different discourses in other countries where critical theory and neo-Marxist approaches were acceptable. For example, qualitative evaluation in Britain was based on political control considerations from the beginning (MacDonald, 1977). In the United States, case studies were promoted as a means of illuminating the values of teaching and learning (Stake, 1978).

On the other hand, if social scientists with liberal positions were silenced or ignored (the fate of critical ethnographers), scholars on the political right continued to promote policies such as sterilization of the poor and elimination of social programs. A long history of biological racism stretching back to Galton, Burt, Spearman, Terman, Jensen, and others (Gould, 1981) continued unabated, reflecting the political temperament of the times. During the 1990s, this long tradition was manifested in *The Bell Curve* (Herrnstein & Murray, 1994). Scholars in this tradition claim that they are value neutral; they are merely following scientific evidence where it leads them, unfortunate though that may be.

This shift into safer political waters by many social scientists was bolstered intellectually by a convenient philosophy of science—logical positivism—that endorsed "value-free" research. Value-free social science became accepted research dogma. In the view of logical positivists and those influenced by them, values were not researchable. Only entities that could be confirmed by direct reference to "facts" were appropriate for scientific research.

Eventually, historical, philosophical, and sociological investigations into the nature of inquiry in the hard sciences demonstrated that the positivist view of science was incorrect. Nonetheless, the positivist interpretation of values continued, even among those who had grasped the nature of nonfoundationalism about factual claims. This attitude toward values was reinforced by the political climate during the cold war, the period when professional evaluation began. The origins of American social science were forgotten, and research methodology remained the primary focus of American social scientists. For many evaluators, social justice issues in evaluation retain nuances of illegitimacy and "politics."

The dominance of value-free social research meant that the conception of social justice embraced by politicians would be accepted without challenge in the evaluation of social programs and policies (except for those at the fringe e.g., neo-Marxists). For much of the 20th century, the liberal utilitarian conception of justice prevailed. This was identified with one of its main formulators, John Stuart Mill. Utilitarianism is captured in the phrase "the greatest good for the greatest number," although it is more sophisticated than the slogan implies. The way in which this theory played out in social policy was that overall benefits should be increased to the maximum. Society should be organized to maximize overall benefits. Hence, everyone could have more.

How those benefits were distributed was not a major issue. When applied to social programs, the nuances of utilitarian theory disappeared. The politics of more for everyone was more acceptable than the politics of distribution. As implemented in research practices, utilitarianism focused attention on outcomes. If the gross domestic product increases, that is good regardless of how it is distributed. The presumption is that there is more to distribute, even if not everyone gets more. Distribution is not an issue. If an educational program increases overall test scores, the amount of the increase is the focus regardless of the distribution of scores or resources—and sometimes regardless of the personal costs of obtaining the gains. Quantitative outcome measures fit well into such a framework; qualitative methods do not. Furthermore, the goals of social programs and policies, being value laden, were not subject to rational or empirical analysis by evaluators. The goals had to be accepted.

In the major reformulation of moral thinking during the 20th century, John Rawls challenged utilitarian theory with his "theory of justice," which was more egalitarian than utilitarianism. With sophisticated philosophical argument, Rawls (1971) proposed two major principles of justice by which to assess social arrangements. The first principle was that every citizen should have basic civil liberties and rights and that these rights were inviolate. These individual rights and liberties closely resembled those in the American Bill of Rights. There was little controversy about this principle of justice.

The second principle of justice, called the "difference" principle, was controversial. Rawls argued for the *distribution* of benefits—not only the overall level of benefits—to count as significant. Inequalities of economic fortune were permitted in the Rawlsian framework only if those inequalities helped the "least advantaged" people in society, defined as those with the fewest resources. For example, it was permissible to have medical doctors earn high fees if such financial inducements to study medicine helped poor people.

Hence, Rawls's theory was not strictly egalitarian because it did allow for significant inequalities in society. The Rawlsian theory did shift the focus to how the disadvantaged were treated and, in that sense, was more egalitarian than utilitarianism, which allowed trading off the benefits of the least advantaged (e.g., the unemployed) if such a move increased the level of benefits for societal members as a whole (e.g., a lower rate of inflation).

Both utilitarian and Rawlsian justice required manipulating social arrangements to maximize benefits. Unlike utilitarianism, Rawlsian justice placed constraints on the shape that the distribution of benefits could take. Social arrangements should be designed to tend toward equality in the distribution of benefits. The effects of circumstances that are arbitrary from a moral point of view (e.g., who one's parents happen to be) should be mitigated to this end and, if necessary, at the expense of maximizing benefits. Distributions resulting from the operation of markets must be held in check if those distributions are unjust, according to the second principle. (Yet a third theory of justice regards any distribution that results from free markets as socially just, no matter what that distribution looks like or what effects it has. The interplay of free markets determines social outcomes [Nozick, 1974]. This is called libertarianism. To this point, it has not been reflected in the evaluation discourse in any overt way, although many evaluators may hold this view implicitly.)

Following Rawls, some evaluators applied his theory to evaluation, arguing that evaluators should be concerned not only with overall test score gains but also, for example, with how test score gains were distributed among groups (House, 1980). How social benefits were distributed was important for evaluation. In addition, evaluators might have to solicit the views of stakeholders to determine which social benefits were at issue. Qualitative studies soliciting stakeholder views were necessary.

Of course, concerns about the distribution of benefits and calls for qualitative studies moved evaluators away from the value-free, quantitative methodology that the social sciences had been nurturing. Eventually, concern about stakeholders permeated the evaluation literature, even seeping into quantitative studies, and an acceptance of multiple methods, multiple stakeholders, and multiple outcomes in evaluation studies emerged, even among those not accepting egalitarian social justice.

During the 1980s and 1990s, Rawls's theory of justice came under criticism. One criticism was that the theory of liberal egalitarianism was insensitive to diverse group identities. In that sense, it could be oppressive and undemocratic. The theory focused on economic inequalities with little regard for other benefits that people might want. The criticism was that liberal egalitarianism identified the disadvantaged solely in terms of the relatively low economic benefits they possessed and proposed eliminating these disadvantages by implementing compensatory social programs.

Typically, this planning and evaluation process was conceived as requiring little input from those most affected. Liberal egalitarianism assumed that the benefits to be distributed, and the procedures by which the distribution would occur, were uncontroversial. In fact, the defined benefits might reflect only the interests of those in dominant positions. For example, consider a highly sexist curriculum with which girls, but not boys, have great difficulty. Providing girls with help in mastering this curriculum so as to remove their disadvantage is not a solution. The problem lies with the sexist curriculum. The distributive paradigm implied a top-down, expert-driven view. Critics saw such an approach as too paternalistic.

In response, philosophers revised the egalitarian theory of justice to take diverse identities into account, that is, to change the theory away from equality as a principle of distribution toward equality as a principle of democratic participation. In what might be called the "participatory shift," the requirements of distributive justice and those of democracy were intertwined. Justice required giving stakeholders, particularly members of groups that had been excluded historically, an effective voice in defining their own needs and negotiating benefits.

This shifting conception of social justice had implications for evaluation. The participatory paradigm fit views of evaluation in which equality was sought not solely in the distribution of predetermined benefits but also in the status and voice of the participants themselves. Benefits were to be examined and negotiated along with needs, policies, and practices. Democratic functioning became an overarching ideal. Some evaluators now advocate giving stakeholders roles to play in the evaluation itself, although evaluators differ on what roles participants should play (Greene, Lincoln, Mathison, Mertens, & Ryan, 1998). (Many who endorse participatory evaluation do so because they believe that stakeholders are more likely to use the findings for pragmatic reasons than because of social justice considerations.) In general, social justice continues to be controversial for historical and political reasons.

▣ Bush's Neofundamentalist Policies

As evaluation gradually moved away from quantitative methods and value-free studies toward multiple methodologies and qualitative studies focused on stakeholders, social justice issues, and participatory techniques, these trends did not go unnoticed by those in power. Not only did neoconservatives view such studies as too permissive, they did not like the direction in which the entire society was headed. Pointing to what they saw as postmodern excesses, they railed against modern trends, mostly to little avail.

However, the events of September 11, 2001, changed government policies regarding qualitative evaluation. The federal government is now promulgating what I call methodological fundamentalism—a manifestation of the neofundamentalism of President George W. Bush's regime. The Bush administration has embraced a new fundamentalism that permeates many aspects of American life. Before the September 11 terrorist attack, the Bush administration struggled to find traction. Bush emerged from a contested presidential election with fewer votes than the Democratic contender. Only through the peculiarities of the American electoral system and the notorious handling of ballots in Florida did Bush emerge the victor. As he assumed office in January 2001, his legitimacy was in question, his personal abilities were the butt of jokes, and his popularity was in decline.

On September 11, terrorists attacked the World Trade Center and the Pentagon, and Bush assumed the mantle of wartime president. The moral fervor with which he embraced this transformation fit his personal, born-again, religious fundamentalism. During his younger days, he had been a heavy drinker and drug user who converted to religion, saving himself from personal ruin, in his view. He embraced the new role that had been thrust on him with religious intensity, and he projected this moral certainty onto his administration and the country—a country traumatized by the attacks. This simple mission suited him. As observed by Condoleezza Rice, his then national security adviser, the worst thing she could say to Bush was that an issue was complex.

Previously, he had balanced the politics of his administration with people from different factions in the Republican party. He placed neoconservatives, such as Dick Cheney, Donald Rumsfeld, and Paul Wolfowitz, in key posts and balanced them with moderates such as Colin Powell. In foreign policy, the neoconservative vision of preemptively using American power to transform the world was checked by the realist view of maintaining multilateral international relationships. However, September 11 provided neoconservatives with the license they needed to pursue the hawkish policies they had long advocated, including the invasion of Iraq, an obsession of Wolfowitz, deputy secretary of defense. His plan called for preemptive military strikes on countries threatening American interests. He had prepared this policy during the first Bush administration, but the preemptive position had been dismissed as being too radical at that time. After September 11, it became official American doctrine. Bush's neofundamentalism emerged in full force.

Fundamentalism has several characteristics. First, there is one source of truth, be it the Bible, the Koran, the Talmud, or whatever. Second, this source of authority is located in the past, often in a Golden Age, and is associated with particular individuals. Believers hark back to that time. Third, true believers have access to this fundamental truth, but others do not. Applying the truth leads to a radical transformation of the world for the better. Fundamentalists have a prophetic vision of the future, that is, revelatory insight. Fourth, having access to the source of truth means that believers are certain they are correct. They have moral certitude, a defining attribute. They are "elected." Fifth, fundamentalists are not open to counterarguments. Indeed, they are not open to other ideas generally. They do not assimilate evidence that contradicts their views. They dismiss contrary information or ignore it. Sixth, they are persuaded by arguments consistent with their beliefs even when outsiders find these arguments to be incomplete, illogical, or bizarre. Seventh, people who do not agree with them do not have this insight, and fundamentalists do not need to listen to them. In fact, sometimes it is all right to muscle nonbelievers aside because they do not understand and only impede progress. Eighth, believers associate with other true believers and avoid nonbelievers, thereby closing the circle of belief and increasing certainty. Ninth, they find ways of promulgating their beliefs by means other than rational persuasion—by decree, policy, or laws—through forcing others to conform rather than persuading them—in short, through coercion. Finally, fundamentalists try to curtail the propagation of other viewpoints by restricting the flow of contrary ideas and those who espouse them.

The Bush administration has exercised this new fundamentalism in foreign affairs, domestic affairs, and even evaluation. In foreign policy, the fundamentalism is evident in the invasion of Iraq. The Golden Age for neoconservatives was the Reagan administration, and Reagan was the sacred figure. Many neoconservatives prefer to call themselves Reaganites and hope to restore the age during which the United States brought down the Soviet Union and won the cold war, in their view of history.

Bush's speeches have taken on a quasi-religious, liturgical tone, including phrases such as "axis of evil" as compared with Reagan's "the evil empire." Bush believes that he is a great leader like Reagan, Churchill, or even Lincoln. By his own admission, he talks to God every night. He has surrounded himself with fellow evangelicals who see him as "chosen" since his peculiar election, for which they prayed. And their prayers were answered. No matter what evidence was presented against his position on Iraq, it had no effect. If the Iraqis had no weapons of mass destruction, they were hiding them. If the Iraqis admitted to having weapons, they had violated the UN mandate. If the war might be disastrous for the region, if most nations in the world were opposed to it, and if world public opinion was overwhelmingly opposed to it, no matter. Others did not understand. They were "old Europe," unwilling to take risks.

The Bush team was closed to counterevidence. Bush team members presented arguments seen by others as inconclusive and at times strange. They concocted a revelatory vision of democratic transformation for Iraq that Middle East experts viewed as incredible. The more criticism that was encountered from outside, the more they banded together, like President Johnson and his advisers did during the war in Vietnam. Coercion was the tool of choice for compliance, whether it was used against enemies or allies. They either had little sense of how others might react to their actions or did not care. The fundamentalism of the Muslim terrorists was countered with the new fundamentalism of the American president.

Methodological Fundamentalism in Evaluation

Bush's neofundamentalism has influenced other parts of the federal government, including evaluation. In evaluation, this takes the form of methodological fundamentalism. Government agencies that sponsor evaluations have aggressively pushed the concept of "evidence-based" progress, policies, and programs. The core of the evidence-based idea is that research and evaluation must be "scientific." In this definition, scientific means that research and evaluation findings must be based on experiments, with randomized experiments being given strong preference. Other ways of producing evidence are not scientific and not acceptable. There is one method for discovering the truth and one method only—the randomized experiment. This is a fundamentalist position.

This doctrine is embedded in Bush's education legislation, No Child Left Behind. In this legislation (www.ed.gov), the term "scientific" is repeated more than 100 times. The method of inquiry is written into the legislation itself, an unusual event. Imagine an allocation for research in physics specifying the methods by which physicists are to conduct studies. In addition, the U.S. Department of Education has established a What Works Clearinghouse to screen evidence-based projects and has encouraged the construction of lists of researchers who comply with the new methodological strictures—a white list as opposed to a black list.

An explicit rationale for evidence-based progress is provided in a report prepared for the U.S. Department of Education by the Council for Evidence-Based Policies (2002). The council consists mostly of Washington insiders, bureaucrats, and think tank fellows plus some social researchers. In accepting the report, Secretary of

Education Rod Paige remarked that Bush education policy was based on four concepts: accountability, options for parents, local control, and evidence-based instruction. The first two policies have been mainstays of the neoconservative educational platform for some time. As for evidence-based instruction, "for the first time we are applying the same rigorous standards to education research as are applied to medical research" (Paige, 2002). Standards will save the day once again. The disdain for the opinions of professional educators manifested in national and statewide testing systems was now carried into disdain for professional evaluators, disdain for professionals being a hallmark of neoconservative policy.

The basic argument of the Council for Evidence-Based Policies (2002) report is that education is a field of fads in which there has been no progress—progress measured by national tests—for the past 30 years. In contrast, there has been great progress in medicine: "Our extraordinary inability to raise educational achievement stands in stark contrast to our remarkable progress in improving human health over the same period—progress which . . . is largely the result of evidence-based government policies" (p. i). The claim is that progress in medicine has resulted primarily from randomized field trials.

Hence, the Department of Education should build a "knowledge base" of educational interventions proved effective by randomized trials and should provide strong incentives for the use of such interventions. "This strategy holds a key to reversing decades of stagnation in American education and sparking rapid, evidence-driven progress" (Council for Evidence-Based Policies, 2002, p. i). Such is the revelatory vision for the transformation of American education. The report recommends that all discretionary funds for research and evaluation be focused on randomized trials. After all, other research designs produce erroneous findings.

These arguments are weak, to say the least. They may be sufficient to persuade those who already believe in randomized experiments or those who lack knowledge of evaluation. They could hardly withstand the scrutiny of scholars in evaluation. It is the case that education is riddled with fads that have no research backing. Indeed, the neoconservatives have promoted many of these such as charter schools, vouchers, and accountability through test scores. One might also agree that the schools have not improved much over the past 30 years and that medicine has shown progress.

However, medical progress has not been primarily due to randomized field trials. Medicine is the beneficiary of decades of breakthrough research in the physical sciences, notably biophysics, biochemistry, biology, and molecular biology, that has resulted in elaborate theories about human disease. To my knowledge, no one in medicine has received a Nobel Prize for promoting randomized studies. Field trials only test ideas—a valuable service for sure, but hardly the primary source of progress.

It is true that education has no corresponding theory on which to base its practices. The social sciences that might have produced the underlying theory, primarily psychology, have failed to do so. Actually, psychology is a field that relies heavily on randomized trials. Not only has psychology failed to produce viable theory for education, it has failed to produce cures for mental illness comparable to medical advances. Similarly, criminology, which also uses randomized trials, has failed to produce solutions to crime. Otherwise, the United States would not have 2 million people in prison.

As Noam Chomsky noted, psychology is a methodology without a substance. Members of the Council for Evidence-Based Policies, several of whom are psychologists, would have been more honest to argue that because randomized methods have produced little of substance in psychology, maybe they will produce something useful in education. Actually, randomized trials are neither the problem nor the cure. I believe that we could use more randomized field trials in evaluation, but the evangelical arguments advanced by these proponents are embarrassing.

Attributes of Methodological Fundamentalism

In addition to a revelatory vision that promises transformation, methodological fundamentalism has other features of neofundamentalism. It has a simple credo: Only randomized experiments produce the truth. There is one source of truth—the randomized experiment. If we but follow, it will lead us to a Golden Age. Methodological fundamentalism even has a storied past. The key figure is Campbell, who championed the concept of social experiments as the *only* way in which to evaluate social programs early in the history of evaluation. Although Campbell later relented, admitting that there were other valid ways of acquiring knowledge about social programs, many followers did not. Apparently, they have been biding their time and have found their opportunity in Bush's neofundamentalism as the neoconservatives have done with war policy.

The prescription for randomized trials has been written into legislation without extensive discussion in the relevant professional communities, whose members would oppose such a narrow prescription of how to conduct research and evaluation. But avoiding contrary ideas is part of the orientation. And of course, the prescription is enforced by government decree and incentives. One significant outcome of choosing randomized experiments as the only method for conducting studies is that it eliminates stakeholder views in studies. Most evaluations now incorporate the perspectives of stakeholder groups. This experimental approach precludes the views of stakeholders. Such exclusion must have appeal for those who do not want to be confused by contrary ideas and complex issues.

From a philosophy of science perspective, the difficulty is that the prescription is based on an overly simplistic view of social causation, namely the regularity theory of causation, as noted earlier. Social programs are not closed to outside influences in the same way as experiments in the physical world can be. Hence, definitive experiments to test theories are not possible because they sometimes are in the physical world. This is not to say that experiments cannot be useful. They can be valuable if they are used in the right circumstances and are supported by other evidence that provides the context for interpreting findings. Theory is not available for this purpose in social research, and findings are often interpreted ideologically or politically. There is a need for collecting and assessing various stakeholder views to aid interpretation.

The appropriate situation for randomized field trials is one similar to evaluating physical entities. For example, evaluating drugs by way of randomized experiments is extremely useful because the drugs themselves can be reproduced in identical form. Drug treatment does not vary nearly as much as social programs, although even in drug trials people react to drugs differently. When the treatment focuses on entities that are difficult to control, experiments become less useful. When educational programs are placed in different settings, there are dozens—if not hundreds—of influences that are impossible to control even in randomized experiments. This means that the results vary even when the treatment appears to be the same. Randomized experiments are one way of providing evidence, but they are not the only way. Field experiments are not appropriate in all situations, neither are they foolproof.

The utility of randomized experiments was discussed extensively in the evaluation community long ago and was abandoned as the sole way in which to conduct studies. The experiments-only advocates lost the debate, but now the same doctrine has been resurrected. This time advocates have appealed to government officials, who are easier to persuade given that they have limited expertise in research and evaluation. Government officials often yearn for certitude in evaluation findings as a way of bolstering their authority. It would make the task of mandating new programs much easier and less controversial. Evaluators have not been able to deliver such unequivocal findings. It is not difficult to understand why a method that promises certainty has appeal for them. However, the certainty that fundamentalism provides is false.

So, after 40 years, evaluation policy has come full circle. What is different this time around is that there is a sizable evaluation community that has considered, discussed, and dismissed the narrow focus on experimental method that is being promoted by the government. For those interested in how such differences will play out, they might look to history. Since its founding, the United States has been swept repeatedly by strong evangelical movements that claim to have absolute truth and attempt to restrict ideas. During the 20th century, these movements took the form of anticommunism crusades, and they had a profound effect on the shape of American social science. It appears to be time for the mettle of the current generation in evaluation to be tested.

References

Campbell, D. (1982). Experiments as arguments. In E. R. House, S. Mathison, J. A. Pearsol, & H. Preskill (Eds.), *Evaluation studies review annual* (No. 7, pp. 117–128). Beverly Hills, CA: Sage.

Campbell, D. T., & Stanley, J. C. (1963). *Experimental and quasi-experimental designs for research.* Chicago: Rand McNally.

Chen, H., & Rossi, P. H. (1987). Evaluating with sense: The theory-driven approach to validity. *Evaluation Review, 7,* 283–302.

Cook, T. D. (1993). A quasi-sampling theory of the generalization of causal relationships. In L. B. Sechrest & A. G. Scott (Eds.), *Understanding causes and generalizing about them* (New Directions in Evaluation, No. 57, pp. 39–82). San Francisco: Jossey–Bass.

Council for Evidence-Based Policies. (2002). *Bringing evidence-driven progress to education: A recommended strategy for the U.S. Department of Education.* New York: William T. Grant Foundation.

Cronbach, L. J. (1982). *Designing evaluations of educational and social programs.* San Francisco: Jossey–Bass.

Glass, G. V. (1976). Primary, secondary, and meta-analysis of research. *Educational Researcher, 5*(9), 3–8.

Gould, S. J. (1981). *The mismeasure of man.* New York: Norton.

Greene, J., Lincoln, Y. S., Mathison, S., Mertens, D. M., & Ryan, K. (1998). Advantages and challenges of using inclusive evaluation approaches in evaluation practice. *American Journal of Evaluation, 19,* 101–122.

Herrnstein, R. J., & Murray, C. (1994). *The bell curve.* New York: Free Press.

House, E. R. (1980). *Evaluating with validity.* Beverly Hills, CA: Sage.

House, E. R. (1991). Realism in research. *Educational Researcher, 20*(6), 2–9.

House, E. R., & Howe, K. R. (1999). *Values in evaluation and social research.* Thousand Oaks, CA: Sage.

Lipsey, M. W. (1993). Theory as method: Small theories of treatments. In L. B. Sechrest & A. G. Scott (Eds.), *Understanding causes and generalizing about them* (New Directions in Evaluation, No. 57, pp. 5–38). San Francisco: Jossey–Bass.

MacDonald, B. (1977). A political classification of evaluation studies. In D. Hamilton (Ed.), *Beyond the numbers game* (pp. 224-227). London: Macmillan.

Mackie, J. L. (1974). *The cement of the universe.* Oxford, UK: Clarendon.

Maxwell, J. A. (1996). *Using qualitative research to develop causal explanations.* Working paper, Harvard Project on Schooling and Children, Harvard University.

McLaughlin, M. W. (1975). *Evaluation and reform.* Cambridge, MA: Ballinger.

Nozick, R. (1974). *Anarchy, state, and utopia.* New York: Basic Books.

Paige, R. (2002, November 18). [Remarks at Consolidation Conference], Washington, DC.

Rawls, J. (1971). *A theory of justice.* Cambridge, MA: Belknap.

Reichardt, C. S., & Rallis, S. F. (Eds.). (1994). *The qualitative–quantitative debate: New perspectives* (New Directions in Program Evaluation, No. 61). San Francisco: Jossey–Bass.

Rivlin, A. (1971). *Systematic thinking for social action.* Washington, DC: Brookings Institution.

Ross, D. (1991). *The origins of American social science.* Cambridge, UK: Cambridge University Press.

Stake, R. E. (1978). The case study method in social inquiry. *Educational Researcher, 7*(2), 5–8.

Suchman, E. A. (1967). *Evaluative research.* New York: Russell Sage.

Part VI

THE FUTURE OF QUALITATIVE RESEARCH

And so we come to the end, which is only the starting point for a new beginning. Several observations have structured our arguments to this point. The field of qualitative research continues to transform itself. The changes that took shape during the early 1990s are gaining momentum, even as they confront multiple forms of resistance during the first decade of this century. The gendered narrative turn has been taken. Foundational epistemologies, what Schwandt (1997, p. 40) calls epistemologies with the big *E*, have been replaced by constructivist, hermeneutic, feminist, poststructural, pragmatist, critical race, and queer theory approaches to social inquiry. Epistemology with a small *e* has become normative, displaced by discourses on ethics and values, conversations on and about the good, and conversations about the just and moral society.

We have argued throughout that qualitative inquiry is under assault from three sides. First, on the *political right* are the methodological conservatives who are connected to neoconservative governmental regimes. These critics support evidence-based, experimental methodologies or mixed methods. This stance consigns qualitative research to the methodological margins. Second, on the *epistemological right* are neotraditionalist methodologists who look with nostalgia at the Golden Age of qualitative inquiry. These critics find in the past all that is needed for inquiry in the present. Third, on the *ethical right* are mainstream biomedical scientists and traditional social science researchers who invoke a single ethical model for human subject research. The ethical right refuses to engage the arguments of those researchers who engage in collaborative, consciousness-raising, empowering inquiry.

Qualitative researchers in the seventh and eighth moments must navigate among these three oppositional forces, each of which threatens to deny the advances in qualitative research over the past three decades. These critics do not recognize the influences of indigenous, feminist, race, queer, and ethnic border studies. We need to protect ourselves from these criticisms. We also need to create spaces for dialogue and public scholarly engagement of these issues.

The chapters in this volume speak collectively to the great need for a compassionate, critical, interpretive civic social science. This is an interpretive social science that blurs both boundaries and genres. Its participants are committed to politically informed action research, inquiry directed to praxis and social change. Hence, as the reformist movement called qualitative research gains momentum, its places in the discourses of a free democratic society become ever more clear. With the action researchers, we seek a set of disciplined interpretive practices that will produce radical democratizing transformations in the public and private spheres of the global postcapitalist world. Qualitative research is the means to these ends. It is the bridge that joins multiple interpretive communities. It stretches across many different landscapes and horizons, moving back and forth between the public and the private, the sacred and the secular.

Paradigm shifts and dialogues have become a constant presence within and across the theoretical frameworks that organize both qualitative inquiry and the social and human sciences. The move to standpoint epistemologies has accelerated. No one still believes in the concept of a unified sexual subject or, indeed, of any unified subject. Epistemology has come out of the closet. The desire for critical, multivoiced, postcolonial ethnographies increases as capitalism extends its global reach.

We now understand that the civic-minded qualitative researcher uses a set of material practices that bring the world into play. These practices are not neutral tools. This researcher thinks historically and interactionally, always mindful of the structural processes that make race, gender, and class potentially repressive presences in daily life. The material practices of qualitative inquiry turn the researcher into a methodological (and epistemological) *bricoleur.* This person is an artist, a quilt maker, a skilled craftsperson, a maker of montages and collages. The interpretive bricoleur can interview, observe, study material culture, think within and beyond visual methods, write poetry or fiction, write autoethnography, construct narratives that tell explanatory stories, use qualitative computer software, do text-based inquiries, construct *testimonios* using focus group interviews, and even engage in applied ethnography and policy formulation.

It is apparent that the constantly changing field of qualitative research is defined by a series of tensions and contradictions as well as emergent understandings. These tensions and understandings have been felt in every chapter in this volume. Here, as in the first and second editions of this *Handbook,* we list many of them for purposes of summary only. They take the form of questions and assertions:

1. Will the performance turn in qualitative inquiry lead to performances that decolonize theory and help to deconstruct that global postcolonial world?
2. Will critical, indigenous interpretive paradigms, epistemologies, and pedagogies flourish in the eighth moment?
3. Will critical, indigenous interpretive paradigms, epistemologies, and pedagogies lead to the development and use of new inquiry practices, including counternarratives, autoethnographies, cultural poetics, and arts-based methodologies?
4. Can indigenous and nonindigenous qualitative researchers take the lead in decolonizing the academy?
5. Will the emphasis on multiple standpoint epistemologies and moral philosophies crystallize around a set of shared understandings concerning the contributions of qualitative inquiry to civil society, civic discourse, and critical race theory?
6. Will the criticisms from the methodological, political, and ethical conservatives stifle this field?
7. Will the performance turn in ethnography produce a shift away from attempts to represent the stream of consciousness, and the world of internal meanings, of the conscious subject?

8. How will feminist, communitarian, and indigenous ethical codes change institutional review boards (IRBs)? Will the two- and three-track IRB models become normative?
9. Will a new interpretive paradigm, with new methods and strategies of inquiry, emerge out of the interactions that exist between and among the many paradigms and perspectives we have presented in this volume?
10. How will indigenous, ethnic, queer, postcolonial, and feminist paradigms be fitted to this new synthesis if it comes?
11. Will the postmodern, antifoundational sensibility begin to form its own foundational criteria for evaluating the written and performed text?
12. When all universals, including the postmodern worldview, are gone in favor of local interpretations, how can we continue to talk and learn from one another?

There is no definitive answer to any of these questions. Here we can only suggest, in the barest of detail, our responses to them. In our concluding chapter (Epilogue), we elaborate these responses, grouping them around several basic themes or issues: text and voice, the existential sacred text, reflexivity and being in the text, working the hyphen, ethics and critical moral consciousness, and the textual subject, including our presence in the text. Examined from another angle, the 12 questions just listed focus on the social text, history, politics, ethics, the other, and interpretive paradigms more broadly.

Into the Future

Zygmunt Bauman (Chapter 43) reflexively moves qualitative inquiry (and sociology) into the new century, telling us that the work of the poet and the sociologist—and of history—is to uncover, in ever new situations, "human possibilities previously hidden." Writing and inquiry are not innocent practices. In its representational and political practices, qualitative inquiry, like sociology, makes visible the possibility of "living together differently with less misery or no misery.... Disclosure is the beginning—not the end—of the war against human misery." We have no choice; we are always already political, always already engaged. A neutral noncommitted form of inquiry is an impossibility. In a truly democratic society, Bauman observes (quoting Cornelius Castorladis), everyone is free to question "everything that is pre-given.... In such a society, all individuals are free to create for their lives the meanings they will." In such a society, qualitative inquiry becomes a vehicle for questioning all that is pre-given. Thus does Bauman lead us into the future.

Douglas Holmes and George Marcus (Chapter 44) extend this argument, calling for a "refunctioning of ethnography," a regrounding of ethnography in the contemporary moment. They are quite explicit, observing that "a new set of regulative norms of fieldwork are needed to release ethnographers-in-the-making from the . . . imaginary" of classic ethnography. Contemporary ethnography could profitably be oriented to para-ethnography; that is, to the ecologies of knowledge, existing discourses, and local practices that are in place in field settings. The ethnographer finds the "literal field" by working through complex scenes, levels, and multiple sites that connect the local to the global.

Holmes and Marcus observe that recognizing the multisited nature of fieldwork produces a "rethinking of a whole set of issues in fieldwork—complicity instead of rapport, . . . the necessity of collaborations and their personal politics, the uneven distribution or depth of knowing, . . . the changing nature of the object of study, the grounding of abstract relations . . . in forms of human action and knowing." Thus do they offer terms of a refunctioned ethnography where subjects, now called para-ethnographers, are treated as experts, as collaborators and partners in research. They ground their interpretation of the para-ethnographer in the analysis of a famous political actor, the French nationalist Jean-Marie Le Pen.

Para-ethnography goes beyond merely identifying a new ethnographic subject. Rather, it opens the door for deeper questions of how "culture operates within a continuously unfolding contemporary." More deeply, and more radically, Holmes and Marcus believe that "spontaneously generated para-ethnographies are built into the structure of the contemporary and give form and content to a continuously unfolding skein of experience."

▣ ▣ ▣

The collapse of foundational epistemologies has led to emerging innovations in methodology. These innovations reframe what is meant by validity. They have shaped the call for increased textual reflexivity, greater textual self-exposure, multiple voicing, stylized forms of literary representation, and performance texts. These innovations shade into the next issues surrounding representation.

Representational issues involve how the other will be presented in the text. Representational strategies converge with a concern over the place of politics in the text. We can no longer separate ideology and politics from methodology. Methods always acquire their meaning within broader systems of meaning, from epistemology to ontology. These systems are themselves embedded in ethical and ideological frameworks as well as in particular interpretive communities. Our methods are always grafted into our politics.

Scientific practice does not stand outside ideology. As argued in the first and second editions of this *Handbook*, a poststructural social science project seeks its external grounding not in science but rather in a commitment to post-Marxism and an emancipatory feminism. A good text is one that invokes these commitments. A good text exposes how race, class, and gender work their ways into the concrete lives of interacting individuals.

We foresee a future where research becomes more relational, where working the hyphen becomes both easier and more difficult, for researchers are always on both sides of the hyphen. We also see a massive spawning of populist technology. This technology will serve to undermine qualitative inquiry as we know it, including disrupting what we mean by a stable subject (where is the cyberself located?). The new information technologies also increase the possibilities of dialogue and communication across time and space. We may be participating in the reconstruction of the social sciences. If so, qualitative inquiry is taking the lead in this reconstruction.

Finally, we predict that there will be no dominant form of qualitative textuality in the seventh and eighth moments; rather, several different hybrid textual forms will circulate alongside one another. The first form will be the classic, realist ethnographic text, redefined in poststructural terms. We will hear more from the first-person voice in these texts. The second hybrid textual form will blend and combine poetic, fictional, and performance texts into critical interventionist presentations. The third textual form will include testimonios and first-person (autoethnographic) texts. The fourth form will be narrative evaluation texts, which work back and forth between first-person voices and the testimonios. These forms will be evaluated in terms of an increasingly sophisticated set of local, indigenous, antifoundational, moral, and ethical criteria.

Variations on these textual forms will rest on a critical rethinking of the notion of the reflexive, self-aware subject. Lived experience cannot be studied directly. We study representations of experience—stories, narratives, performances, dramas. We have no direct access to the inner psychology and inner world of meanings of the reflexive subject. The subject in performance ethnographies becomes a performer. We study performers and performances, persons making meaning together, the how of culture as it connects persons in moments of cocreation and coperformance.

History, Paradigms, Politics, Ethics, and the Other

Many things are changing as we write our way out of writing culture and move into the eighth moment of qualitative research. Multiple histories and theoretical frameworks now circulate in this field, whereas before there were just a few. Today foundationalism and postpositivism are challenged and supplemented by a host of competing paradigms and perspectives. Many different applied action and participatory research agendas inform program evaluation and analysis.

We now understand that we study the other to learn about ourselves, and many of the lessons we have learned have not been pleasant. We seek a new body of ethical directives fitted to postmodernism. The old ethical codes failed to examine research as a morally engaged project. They never seriously located the researcher within the ruling apparatuses of society. A feminist, communitarian ethical system will continue to evolve, informed at every step by critical race, postcolonial, and queer theory sensibilities. Blatant voyeurism in the name of science or the state will continue to be challenged.

Performance-based cultural studies and critical theory perspectives, with their emphases on moral criticism, will alter the traditional empiricist foundations of qualitative research. The dividing line between science and morality will continue to be erased. A postmodern, feminist, poststructural communitarian science will move closer to a sacred science of the moral universe.

As we edge our way into the 21st century, looking back and borrowing Max Weber's metaphor, we see more clearly how we were trapped by the 20th century and its iron cage of reason and rationality. Like a bird in a cage, for too long we were unable to see the pattern in which we were caught. Coparticipants in a secular science of the social world, we became part of the problem. Entangled in the ruling apparatuses that we wished to undo, we perpetuated systems of knowledge and power that we found, underneath, to be all too oppressive. It is not too late to get out of the cage. Today we leave that cage behind.

And so do we enter, or leave, the eighth moment. In our concluding chapter (Epilogue), we elaborate our thoughts about the next generation of qualitative research.

Reference

Schwandt, T. A. (1997). *Qualitative inquiry.* Thousand Oaks, CA: Sage.

43

AFTERTHOUGHT

On Writing; on Writing Sociology

Zygmunt Bauman

The need in thinking is what makes us think.

—Theodor W. Adorno

Quoting the Czech poet Jan Skacel's opinion on the plight of the poet (who, in Skacel's words, only discovers the verses that "were always, deep down, there"), Milan Kundera comments (in *l'Art du roman,* [1986]): "To write, means for the poet to crush the wall behind which something that 'was always there' hides." In this respect, the task of the poet is not different from the work of history, which also discovers rather than "invents"; history, like poets, uncovers—in ever new situations—human possibilities previously hidden.

What history does matter-of-factly is a challenge, a task, and a mission for the poet. To rise to this mission, the poet must refuse to serve up truths known beforehand and well worn, truths already "obvious" because they have been brought to the surface and left floating there. It does not matter whether such truths "assumed in advance" are classified as revolutionary or dissident, Christian or atheist—or how right and proper, noble and just, they are or have been proclaimed to be. Whatever their denomination, those "truths" are not this "something hidden" that the poet is called to uncover; they are, rather, parts of the wall that the poet's mission is to crush. Spokespersons for the obvious, self-evident, and "what we all believe, don't we?" are *false poets,* says Kundera. But what, if anything, does the poet's vocation have to do with the sociologist's calling? We sociologists rarely write poems. (Some of us who do take a leave of absence from our professional pursuits for the time of writing.) And yet if we do not wish to share the fate of "false poets" and resent being "false sociologists," we ought to come as close as the true poets do to the yet hidden human possibilities. For that

Author's Note. An earlier version of this essay was first published in *Theory, Culture and Society*, 2000, 1.

reason, we need to pierce the walls of the obvious and self-evident, of that prevailing ideological fashion of the day whose commonality is taken for the proof of its sense. Demolishing such walls is as much the sociologist's calling as the poet's calling—and for the same reason; the walling up of possibilities belies human potential while obstructing the disclosure of its bluff.

Perhaps the verses that the poet seeks "were always there." One cannot be so sure, though, about the human potential discovered by history. Do humans—the makers and the made, the heroes and the victims of history—indeed carry forever the same volume of possibilities waiting for the right time to be disclosed? Or is it rather that, as human history goes, the opposition between discovery and creation is null and void and makes no sense? Because history is the endless process of human creation, is not history for the same reason (and by the same token) the unending process of human self-discovery? Is not the propensity to disclose/create ever new possibilities, to expand the inventory of possibilities already discovered and made real, the sole human potential that always has been, and always is, "already there"? The question of whether the new possibility has been created or "merely" uncovered by history is no doubt welcome nourishment to many a scholastic mind. As for history itself, it does not wait for an answer and can do quite well without one.

Niklas Luhmann's most seminal and precious legacy to fellow sociologists has been the notion of *autopoiesis–self-creation* (from Greek: do, create, give form, be effective; the opposite of suffering, being an object—not the source—of the act), meant to grasp and encapsulate the gist of the human condition. The choice of the term was itself a creation or discovery of the link (inherited kinship rather than chosen affinity) between history and poetry. Poetry and history are two parallel currents ("parallel" in the sense of the non-Euclidean universe ruled by Bolyai and Lobachevski's geometry) of that autopoiesis of human potentialities, in which creation is the sole form that discovery can take, whereas self-discovery is the principal act of creation.

Sociology, one is tempted to say, is a third current running in parallel with those two. Or at least this is what it should be if it is to stay inside that human condition that it tries to grasp and make intelligible. This is what it has tried to become since its inception, although it has been repeatedly diverted from trying by mistaking the seemingly impenetrable and not-yet-decomposed walls for the ultimate limits of human potential and going out of its way to reassure the garrison commanders and the troops they command that the lines they have drawn to set aside the off-limits areas will never be transgressed.

Alfred de Musset suggested nearly two centuries ago that "great artists have no country." Two centuries ago, these were militant words, a war cry of sorts. They were written down amid deafening fanfares of youthful and credulous, and for that reason arrogant and pugnacious, patriotism. Numerous politicians were discovering their vocation in building nation-states of one law, one language, one worldview, one history, and one future. Many poets and painters were discovering their mission in nourishing the tender sprouts of national spirit, resurrecting long-dead national traditions or conceiving of brand-new ones that never lived before, and offering the nation as not-yet-fully-enough-aware-of-being-a-nation the stories, the tunes, the likenesses, and the names of heroic ancestors—something to share, love, and cherish in common and so to lift the mere living together to the rank of belonging together, opening the eyes of the living to the beauty and sweetness of belonging by prompting them to remember and venerate their dead and to rejoice in guarding their legacy. Against that background, de Musset's blunt verdict bore all the marks of a rebellion and a call to arms; it summoned his fellow writers to refuse cooperation with the enterprise of the politicians, the prophets, and the preachers of closely guarded borders and gun-bristling trenches. I do not know whether de Musset intuited the fratricidal capacities of the kind of fraternities that nationalist politicians and ideologists laureate were determined to build or whether his words were but an expression of the intellectual's disgust with and resentment of narrow horizons, backwaters, and parochial mentality. Whatever the case then, when read now with the benefit of hindsight through a magnifying glass stained with the dark blots of ethnic cleansings, genocides, and mass graves, de Musset's words seem to have lost nothing of their topicality, challenge, and urgency, nor have they lost any of their original controversiality. Now, as then, they aim at the heart of the writers' mission and challenge their consciences with the question decisive for any writer's *raison d'être.*

A century and a half later, Juan Goytisolo, probably the greatest among living Spanish writers, took up the issue once more. In a recent interview ("Les batailles de Juan Goytisolo" in *Le Monde,* February 12, 1999), he points out that once Spain had accepted, in the name of Catholic piety and under the influence of the Inquisition, a highly restrictive notion of national identity, the country became, toward the end of the 16th century, a "cultural desert." Let us note that Goytisolo writes in Spanish but for many years lived in Paris and in the United States before finally settling in Morocco. And let us note that no other Spanish writer has had so many of his works translated into Arabic. Why? Goytisolo has no doubt about the reason. He explains, "Intimacy and distance create a privileged situation. Both are necessary." Although each for a different reason, both these qualities make their presence felt in Goytisolo's relations to his native Spanish and acquired Arabic, French, and English—the languages of the countries that, in succession, became his chosen substitute homes.

Because Goytisolo spent a large part of his life away from Spain, the Spanish language ceased for him to be the all-too-familiar tool of daily, mundane, and ordinary communication, always at hand and calling for no reflection. His intimacy with his childhood language was not—and could not be—affected, but now it has been supplemented with distance. The Spanish language became the authentic homeland in his exile, a territory that was known and felt and lived through from the inside and yet, because it also became remote and was full of surprises and exciting discoveries. That intimate/distant territory lends itself to the cool and detached scrutiny *sine ira et* studio, laying bare the pitfalls and the yet untested possibilities invisible in vernacular uses, showing previously unsuspected plasticity, admitting and inviting creative intervention. It is the combination of intimacy and distance that allowed Goytisolo to realize that the unreflexive immersion in a language—just the kind of immersion that exile makes all but impossible—is fraught with dangers: "If one lives only in the present, one risks disappearing together with the present." It was the "outside" detached look at his native language that allowed Goytisolo to step beyond the constantly vanishing present and so to enrich his Spanish in a way that otherwise was unlikely, perhaps altogether inconceivable. He brought back into his prose and poetry ancient terms, long fallen into disuse, and by doing so blew away the storeroom dust that had covered them, wiped out the patina of time, and offered the words' new and previously unsuspected (or long forgotten) vitality.

In *La Contre Allée,* a book published recently in cooperation with Catherine Malabou, Jacques Derrida invites his readers to think in *travel*—or, more exactly, to "think travel." That means to think that unique activity of departing, going away from *chez soi,* going far toward the unknown, taking all of the risks, pleasures, and dangers that the "unknown" has in store (even the risk of not returning).

Derrida is obsessed with "being away." There is some reason to surmise that the obsession was born when, in 1942, the 12-year-old Derrida was sent down from the school that, by the decree of the Vichy administration of North Africa, was ordered to purify itself of Jewish pupils. This is how Derrida's "perpetual exile" started. Since then, Derrida has divided his life between France and the United States. In the United States, he was a Frenchman. In France, however hard he tried to avoid it, time and time again the Algerian accent of his childhood kept breaking through his exquisite French *parole,* betraying a *pied noir* hidden under the thin skin of the Sorbonne professor. (This is, some people think, why Derrida came to extol the superiority of writing and composed the axiological myth of priority to support the axiological assertion.) Culturally, Derrida was to remain "stateless." This did not mean, though, having no cultural homeland. Quite the contrary; being "culturally stateless" meant having more than one homeland, building a home of one's own on the crossroads between cultures. Derrida became and remained a *métèque*—a cultural hybrid. His "home on the crossroads" was built of language.

Building a home on cultural crossroads proved to be the best conceivable occasion to put language to tests it seldom passes elsewhere, to see through its otherwise unnoticed qualities, to find out what language is capable of and what promises it makes but can never deliver. From that home on the crossroads came the exciting and eye-opening news about the inherent plurality and undecidability of sense (in *l'Ecriture et la différence*), about the endemic impurity of origins (in *De la grammatologie*), and about the perpetual unfulfillment of communication (in *La Carte postale*), as Christian Delacampagne notes in *Le Monde* (March 12, 1999).

Goytisolo's and Derrida's messages are different from that of de Musset. It is not true, the novelist and the philosopher suggest in unison, that great art has no homeland; on the contrary, art, like the artists, may have many homelands and most certainly has more than one. Rather than homelessness, the trick is to be at home in many homes but to be in each inside and outside at the same time, to combine intimacy with the critical look of an outsider, involvement, with detachment—a trick that sedentary people are unlikely to learn. Learning the trick is the chance of the exile—*technically* one that is *in* but not *of* the place. The unconfinedness that results from this condition (that *is* this condition) reveals the homely truths to be manmade and unmade and reveals the mother tongue to be an endless stream of communication between generations and a treasury of messages always richer than any of their readings and forever waiting to be unpacked anew.

George Steiner has named Samuel Beckett, Jorge Luis Borges, and Vladimir Nabokov as among the greatest contemporary writers. What nites them and what made them all great, he is that each of the three moved with equal ease—was equally "at home" in several linguistic universes, not one. (A reminder is in order here. "Linguistic universe" is a pleonastic phrase; the universe in which each one of us lives is, and cannot be anything but, "linguistic"—made of words. Words light the islands of visible forms in the dark sea of the invisible and mark the scattered spots of relevance in the formless mass of the insignificant. It is words that slice the world into the classes of nameable objects and bring out their kinship or enmity, closeness or distance, affinity or mutual estrangement. And so long as they stay alone in the field, they raise all such artifacts to the rank of reality—the only reality there is.) One needs to live, to visit, to know intimately more than one such universe to spy out human invention behind any universe's imposing and apparently indomitable structure and to discover just how much human cultural effort is needed to divine the idea of nature with its laws and necessities—all that is required to muster, in the end, the audacity and the determination to join in that cultural effort *knowingly*, aware of its risks and pitfalls but also of the boundlessness of its horizons.

To create (and so also to discover) always means breaking a rule; following a rule is mere routine, more of the same—not an act of creation. For the exile, breaking rules is not a matter of free choice but rather an eventuality that cannot be avoided. Exiles do not know enough of the rules reigning in their country of arrival, nor do they treat these rules unctuously enough for their efforts to observe them and conform to be perceived as genuine and approved. As for their country of origin, going into exile has been recorded there as their original sin, in the light of which all that the sinners later may do may be taken down and used against them as evidence of their rule breaking. By commission or by omission, rule breaking becomes a trademark of the exiles. This is unlikely to endear them to the natives of any of the countries between which their life itineraries are plotted. But paradoxically, it also allows them to bring to all of the countries involved gifts that they need badly without even knowing it—gifts that they could hardly expect to receive from any other source.

Let me clarify. The "exile" under discussion here is not necessarily a case of physical bodily mobility. It may involve leaving one country for another, but it need not. As Christine Brook-Rose puts it (in her essay "Exsul"), the distinguishing mark of all exile, and particularly the writer's exile (i.e., the exile articulated in words and thus made into a communicable *experience*) is the refusal to be integrated—the determination to stand out from the physical space, to conjure up a place of one's own, different from the place in which those around are settled, a place unlike the places left behind and unlike the place of arrival. The exile is defined not in relation to any particular physical space, or to the oppositions among a number of physical spaces, but rather through the autonomous stand taken toward space as such. Ultimately, asks Brooke-Rose, is not every poet or "poetic" (exploring, rigorous) novelist an exile of sorts, looking in from outside into a bright desirable image in the mind's eye, of the little world created, for the space of the writing effort and the shorter space of the reading? This kind of writing, often at odds with publishers and the public, is the last solitary, nonsocialized creative art.

The resolute determination to stay "nonsocialized"; the consent to integrate solely with the condition of nonintegration; the resistance—often painful and agonizing, yet ultimately victorious—to the overwhelming pressure of the place, old or new; the rugged defense of the right to pass judgment and choose; the embracing of ambivalence or calling ambivalence into being—these are, we may say, the constitutive features of exile. Note that all of them refer to attitude and life strategy and to spiritual mobility rather than physical mobility.

Michel Maffesoll (in *Du nomadisme: Vagabondages initiatiques,* 1997) writes of the world we *all* inhabit nowadays as a "floating territory" in which "fragile individuals" meet "porous reality." In this territory, only such things or persons may fit as are fluid, ambiguous, in a state of perpetual becoming, and in a constant state of self-transgression. "Rootedness," if any, can be only dynamic; it needs to be restated and reconstituted daily, precisely through the repeated act of "self-distantiation"—that foundational, initiating act of "being in travel," on the road. Having compared all of us—the inhabitants of the present-day world—to nomads, Jacques Attali (in *Chemins de sagesse,* 1996) suggests that, apart from traveling light and being kind, friendly, and hospitable to strangers whom they meet on their way, nomads must be constantly on the watch, remembering that their camps are vulnerable and have no walls or trenches to stop intruders. Above all, nomads, struggling to survive in the world of nomads, need to grow used to the state of continuous disorientation and to traveling along roads of unknown direction and duration, seldom looking beyond the next turn or crossing. They need to concentrate all of their attention on that small stretch of road that they need to negotiate before dusk.

"Fragile individuals," doomed to conduct their lives in a "porous reality," feel like skating on thin ice, and "in skating over thin ice," Ralph Waldo Emerson remarks in his essay "Prudence," "our safety is in our speed." Individuals, whether fragile or not, need safety, crave safety, and seek safety, and so they try, to the best of their ability, to maintain a high speed in whatever they do. When running among fast runners, slowing down means being left behind; when running on thin ice, slowing down also means the real threat of being drowned. Speed, therefore, climbs to the top of the list of survival values.

Speed, however, is not conducive to thinking, not to thinking far ahead, not to long-term thinking at any rate. Thought calls for pause and rest, for "taking one's time," recapitulating the steps already taken, and looking closely at the place reached and the wisdom (or imprudence, as the case may be) of reaching it. Thinking takes one's mind away from the task at hand, which is always the running and keeping speed and whatever else it may be. And in the absence of thought, the skating on thin ice, which is the *fate* of fragile individuals in the porous world, may well be mistaken for their *destiny.*

Taking one's fate for destiny, as Max Scheler insists in his *Ordo amoris,* is a grave mistake: "Destiny of man is not his fate. . . . The assumption that fate and destiny are the same deserves to be called fatalism." Fatalism is an error of judgment because in fact fate has "a natural and basically comprehensible origin." Moreover, although fate is not a matter of free choice, and particularly of individual free choice, it "*grows up* out of the life of a man or a people." To see all that, to note the difference and the gap between fate and destiny, and to escape the trap of fatalism, one needs resources not easily attainable when running on thin ice—"time off" to think and a distance allowing a long view. "The image of our destiny," Scheler warns, "is thrown into relief only in the recurrent traces left when we turn away from it." Fatalism, however, is a self-corroborating attitude; it makes the "turning away," that *conditio sine qua non* of thinking, appear useless and unworthy of trying.

Taking distance and taking time to separate destiny and fate, to emancipate destiny from fate, and to make destiny free to confront fate and challenge it—this is the calling of sociology. And this is what sociologists may do if they consciously, deliberately, and earnestly strive to reforge the calling they have joined—their fate—into their destiny.

"Sociology is the answer. But what was the question?" states—and asks—Ulrich Beck in *Politik in der Risikogesellschaft.* A few pages previously, Beck seems to articulate the question he seeks—the chance of a democracy that goes beyond "expertocracy," a kind of democracy that "begins where debate and decision making are opened about whether we *want* a life under the conditions that are being presented to us."

This chance is under a question mark not because someone has deliberately and malevolently shut the door on such a debate and prohibited an informed decision taking; hardly ever in the past was the freedom to speak out and to come together to discuss matters of common interest as complete and unconditional as it is now. The point is, though, that more than a formal freedom to talk and pass resolutions is needed for the kind of democracy that Beck thinks is our imperative ...rt in earnest. We also need to know what it is ...to talk about and what the resolutions we ...o be concerned with. And all of this needs to be done in our type of society, in which the authority to speak and resolve issues is the reserve of experts who own the exclusive right to pronounce on the difference between reality and fantasy and to set apart the possible from the impossible. (Experts, we may say, are almost by definition people who "get the facts straight," who take the facts as they come and think of the least risky way of living in their company.)

Why this is not easy, and is unlikely to become easier unless something is done, Beck explains in his *Risikogesellscbaft: auf dem Weg andere Moderne:* "What food is for hunger, eliminating risks, *or interpreting them away,* is for the consciousness of risks." In a society haunted primarily by material want, such an option between "eliminating" misery and "interpreting it away" did not exist. In our society, haunted by risk rather than want, it does exist—and is taken daily. Hunger cannot be assuaged by denial; in hunger, subjective suffering and its objective cause are indissolubly linked, and the link is self-evident and cannot be belied. But risks, unlike material want, are not subjectively experienced; at least, they are not "lived" directly unless they are mediated by knowledge. They may never reach the realm of subjective experience. They may be trivialized or downright denied before they arrive there, and the chance that they will indeed be barred from arriving *grows* together with the extent of the risks.

What follows is that *sociology is needed today more than ever before.* The job in which sociologists are the experts—the job of restoring to view the lost link between objective affliction and subjective experience—has become more vital and indispensable than ever, while being less likely than ever to be performed without their professional help, because its performance by the spokesmen and practitioners of other fields of expertise has become utterly improbable. If all experts deal with practical problems and all expert knowledge is focused on their resolution, sociology is one branch of expert knowledge where the practical problem it struggles to resolve is *enlightenment aimed at human understanding.* Sociology is perhaps the sole field of expertise in which (as Pierre Bourdieu pointed out in *La Misère du monde*) Dilthey's famed distinction between *explanation* and *understanding* has been overcome or cancelled.

To understand one's fate means to be aware of its difference from one's destiny. And to understand one's fate is to know the complex network of causes that brought about that fate and its difference from that destiny. To work in the world, as distinct from being "worked out and about" by it, one needs to know how the world works.

The kind of enlightenment that sociology is capable of delivering is addressed to freely choosing individuals and aimed at enhancing and reinforcing their freedom of choice. Its immediate objective is to reopen the allegedly shut case of explanation and so to promote understanding. It is the self-formation and self-assertion of individual men and women, the preliminary condition of their ability to decide whether they want the kind of life that has been presented to them as their fate, that may gain in vigor, effectiveness, and rationality as a result of sociological enlightenment. The cause of the autonomous society may profit together with the cause of the autonomous individual; they can only win or lose together.

To quote from Cornelius Castorladis's *Le Délabrement de l'Occident:*

> An autonomous society, a truly democratic society, is a society which questions everything that is pregiven and by the same token *liberates the creation of new meanings.* In such a society, all individuals are free to create for their lives the meanings they will (and can).

Society is truly autonomous once it "knows, must know, that there are no 'assured' meanings, that it lives on the surface of chaos, that it itself is a chaos seeking a form, but a form that is never fixed once for all." The absence of guaranteed meanings—of absolute truths, of preordained norms of conduct, of predrawn borderlines between right and wrong no longer needing attention, of guaranteed rules of successful action—is the *conditio sine qua non* of, simultaneously, a truly autonomous society and truly free individuals; autonomous society and the freedom of its members depend on each other. Whatever safety democracy and individuality muster depends not on fighting the endemic contingency and uncertainty of human condition but rather on recognizing it and facing its consequences point blank.

If orthodox sociology, born and developed under the aegis of solid modernity, was preoccupied with the conditions of human obedience and conformity, then the prime concern of sociology made to measure of liquid modernity needs to be the promotion of autonomy and freedom; such sociology must, therefore, put individual self-awareness, understanding, and *responsibility* at its focus. For the denizens of modern society in its solid and managed phase, the major opposition was one between conformity and deviance. For the major opposition of modern society in its present-day liquefied and decentered phase, the opposition that needs to be faced up to so as to pave the way to a truly autonomous society is one between taking up responsibility and seeking a shelter where responsibility for one's own actions need not be taken by the actors.

That other side of the opposition, seeking shelter, is a seductive option and a realistic prospect. Alexis de Tocqueville (in the second volume of his *De la démocratie en Amerique*), notes that if selfishness, that bane haunting humankind during all periods of its history, "desiccated the seeds of all virtues," then individualism, a novel and typically modern affliction, dries up only "the source of public virtues"; the individuals affected are busy cutting out small companies for their own use, while leaving the "great society" to its own fate. The temptation to do so has grown considerably since de Tocqueville jotted down his observation.

Living among a multitude of competing values, norms, and lifestyles without a firm and reliable guarantee of being in the right is hazardous and commands a high psychological price. No wonder that the attraction of the second response—of hiding from the requisites of responsible choice—gathers in strength. As Julia Kristeva puts it (in *Nations Without Nationalism*), "It is a rare person who does not invoke a primal shelter to compensate for personal disarray." And we all, to a greater or lesser extent, sometimes more and sometimes less, find ourselves in that state of personal disarray. Time and again, we dream of a "great simplification." Unprompted, we engage in regressive fantasies of which the images of the prenatal womb and the walled-up home are prime inspirations. The search for a primal shelter is "the other" of responsibility, just like deviance and rebellion were the other of conformity. The yearning for a primal shelter these days has come to replace rebellion, which has now ceased to be a sensible option. As Pierre Rosanvallon points out (in a new preface to his classic *Le Capitalisme utopique*), there is no longer a "commanding authority to depose and replace. There seems to be no room left for a revolt, as social fatalism vis-à-vis the phenomenon of unemployment testifies."

Signs of malaise are abundant and salient, yet as Pierre Bourdieu observes repeatedly, they seek in vain a legitimate expression in the world of politics. Short of articulate expression, they need to be read out, obliquely, from the outbursts of xenophobic and racist frenzy—the most common manifestations of the primal shelter nostalgia. The available, and no less popular, alternative to neotribal moods of scapegoating and militant intolerance—the exit from politics and the withdrawal to behind the fortified walls of the private—is no longer prepossessing and, above all, no longer an adequate response to the genuine source of the ailment. And so it is at this point that sociology, with its potential for explanation that promotes understanding, comes into its own more than at any other time in its history.

According to the ancient but never bettered Hippocratic tradition, as Pierre Bourdieu reminds the readers of *La Misère du monde,* genuine medicine begins with the recognition of the invisible disease—"facts of which the sick does not speak or forgets to report." What is needed in the case of sociology is the "revelation of the structural causes hich the apparent signs and talks disclose only h distorting them (*ne devoilent qu'en les* One needs to see through—explain and -the sufferings characteristic of the social order that "no doubt pushed back the great misery (though as much as it is often said), while . . . at the same time multiplying the social spaces . . . offering favourable conditions to the unprecedented growth of all sorts of little miseries."

To diagnose a disease does not mean the same as curing it. This general rule applies to sociological diagnoses as much as it does to medical verdicts. But one should note that the illness of society differs from bodily illnesses in one tremendously important respect: In the case of an ailing social order, the absence of an adequate diagnosis (elbowed out or silenced by the tendency to "interpret away" the risks spotted by Ulrich Beck) is a crucial, perhaps decisive, part of the disease. As Cornelius Castorladis famously puts it, society is ill if it stops questioning itself. And it cannot be otherwise considering that—whether it knows it or not—society is autonomous (its institutions are nothing but human-made and so, potentially, human-unmade) and that suspension of self-questioning bars the awareness of autonomy while promoting the illusion of heteronomy with its unavoidably fatalistic consequences. To restart questioning means to take a long step toward the cure. If in the history of human condition discovery equals creation, if in thinking about the human condition explanation and understanding are one, then in the efforts to improve human condition diagnosis and therapy merge.

Pierre Bourdieu expressed this perfectly in the conclusion of *La Misère du monde:* "To become aware of the mechanisms which make life painful, even unlivable, does not mean to neutralize them; to bring to light the contradictions does not mean to resolve them." And yet, skeptical as one can be about the social effectiveness of the sociological message, the effects of allowing those who suffer to discover the possibility of relating their sufferings to social causes cannot be denied, nor can one dismiss the effects of becoming aware of the social origin of unhappiness "in all its forms, including the most intimate and most secret of them."

Nothing is less innocent, Bourdieu reminds us, than laissez-faire. Watching human misery with equanimity while placating the pangs of conscience with the ritual incantation of the TINA ("there is no alternative") creed means complicity.

Whoever willingly or by default partakes in the cover-up or, worse still, the denial of the human-made, noninevitable, contingent, and alterable nature of social order, notably the kind of order responsible for unhappiness, is guilty of immorality—of refusing help to a person in danger.

Doing sociology and writing sociology are aimed at disclosing the possibility of living together differently with less misery or no misery—the possibility that is daily withheld, overlooked, or unbelieved. Not seeing, not seeking, and thereby suppressing this possibility is itself part of human misery and a major factor in its perpetuation. Its disclosure does not by itself predetermine its use. Also, when known, possibilities might not be trusted enough to be put to the test of reality. Disclosure is the beginning—not the end—of the war against human misery. But that war cannot be waged in earnest, let alone with a chance of at least partial success, unless the scale of human freedom is revealed and recognized so that freedom can be fully deployed in the fight against the social sources of all, including the most individual and private—unhappiness.

There is no choice between "engaged" and "neutral" ways of doing sociology. A noncommittal sociology is an impossibility. Seeking a morally neutral stance among the many brands of sociology practiced today, brands stretching all the way from the outspokenly libertarian to the staunchly communitarian, would be a vain effort. Sociologists may deny or forget the worldview effects of their work, and the impact of that view on human singular or joint actions, only at the expense of forfeiting that responsibility of choice that every other human faces daily. The job of sociology is to see to it that the choices are genuinely free and that they remain so—increasingly so—for the duration of humanity.

Notes

1. Herbert Marcuse, "Liberation from the Affluent Society," quoted from *Critical Theory and Society: A Reader,* edited by Stephen Eric Bronner and Douglas MacKay Kellner (London: Routledge, 1989), p. 277.

2. David Conway, *Classical Liberalism: The Unvanquished Ideal* (New York: St. Martin's, 1955), p. 48.

3. Charles Murray, *What It Means to Be a Libertarian: A Personal Interpretation* (New York: Broadway Books, 1997), p. 32. See also Jeffrey Friedman's pertinent comments in "What's Wrong with Libertarianism," *Critical Review,* Summer 1997, pp. 407–467.

4. From *Sociologie et philosophie* (1924). Here quoted in *Emile Durkheim: Selected Writings,* translated by Anthony Giddens (Cambridge, UK: Cambridge University Press, 1972), p. 115.

5. Erich Fromm, *Fear of Freedom* (London: Routledge, 1960), pp. 51, 67.

6. Richard Sennett, *The Corrosion of Character: The Personal Consequences of Work in the New Capitalism* (New York: Norton, 1998), p. 44.

7. Giles Deleuze and Felix Guattari, *Anti-Oedipus: Capitalism and Schizophrenia,* translated by Robert Hurley (New York: Viking, 1977), p. 42.

8. Alain Touraine, "Can We Live Together, Equal and Different?" *European Journal of Social Theory,* November 1998, p. 177.

9. (Frankfurt am Main, Germany: Suhrkamp, 1986); Ulrich Beck, *Risk Society: Towards a New Modernity,* translated by Mark Ritter (London: Sage, 1998), p. 138.

10. See Jean-Paul Besset and Pascale Kremer, "Le Nouvel attrait pour les residences 'sécurisées'," *Le Monde,* 15 May 1999, p. 10.

11. Richard Sennett, "The Myth of Purified Community," in *The Uses of Disorder: Personal Identity and City Style* (London: Faber & Faber, 1996), pp. 36, 39.

12. Quoted from *Emile Durkheim: Selected Writings,* edited by Anthony Giddens (Cambridge, UK: Cambridge University Press, 1972), pp. 94, 115.

13. See Jim MacLaughlin, "Nation-Building, Social Closure, and Anti-Traveller Racism in Ireland," *Sociology,* February 1999, pp. 129–151.

14. See Jean Clair, "De Guernica à Belgrade," *Le Monde,* 21 May 1999, p. 16.

15. *Newsweek,* 21 June 1999.

16. See Chris Bird, "Serbs Flee Kosovo Revenge Attacks," *The Guardian,* 17 July 1999.

17. See Daniel Vernet, "Les Balkans face au risque d'une tourmente sans fin," *Le Monde,* 15 May, p. 18

18. Ibid.

19. Eric Hobsbawm, "The Nation and Globalization," *Constellations,* March 1998, pp. 4–5.

20. Rene Girard, *La Violence et le sacre* (Paris: Grasset, 1972). Here quoted from *Violence and the Sacred,* translated by Patrick Gregory (Baltimore, MD: Johns Hopkins University Press, 1979), pp. 8, 12–13.

21. Arne Johan Vetlesen, "Genocide: A Case for the Responsibility of the Bystander," unpublished manuscript, July 1998.

22. Arne Johan Vetlesen, "Yugoslavia, Genocide, and Modernity," unpublished manuscript, January 1999.

44

REFUNCTIONING ETHNOGRAPHY

The Challenge of an Anthropology of the Contemporary

Douglas R. Holmes and George E. Marcus

We begin this chapter with some basic orientations that are driving our work these days. Part of it is sticking with the so-called *Writing Culture* critiques of anthropology (Clifford & Marcus, 1986) and trying to figure out what are their most productive legacies in the present. Part of it has to do with the changing circumstances of producing anthropological research that we experience every day in the supervision of graduate students. And relatedly, part of it has to do with contemplating the systematic changes that are necessary in the practice of ethnography to accommodate the kinds of new social and cultural formations that are emerging within frames of work that are conceived distinctively as contemporary. We see a need to "refunction ethnography" or at least to provide it with an alternative formulation to the classic Malinowskian one so as to address certain problems of research. We are pursuing this as a project by producing a series of small studies and discussion papers (Holmes, 1993; Holmes & Marcus, 2004; Marcus, 1999b, 1999d, 2001, 2002a, 2002b, 2003).

Beyond Malinowski's Staging

Early in the essay in *Argonauts of the Western Pacific,* in which fieldwork is evoked and its practices are inculcated, Malinowski (1928/1961) intones, "Imagine yourself, suddenly set down surrounded by all your gear, alone on a tropical beach close to a native village, while the launch or dinghy which has brought you sails away out of sight" (p. 46). Anthropologists have always thought about each other's fieldwork and about teaching it to initiates not just in terms of stories or tales of the field but also, in more analytic moments, strongly in terms of images and scenarios. Such a dramaturgical regime of method is most effective when the experience of fieldwork actually corresponds at least roughly to the imaginary that anthropologists make out of what they report to each other from distant experiences that are theirs alone. There is a great premium placed on ethnography that is able to set scenes that can be entered through concretely visualized and situated thought experiments.

Another distinctive, if not peculiar, aspect of the professional lore about fieldwork in anthropology is that it is highly specific and richly evoked for the early phases of fieldwork experience with the image (as per Malinowski) of "first contact" and heightened otherness in mind. The initiate's experience of fieldwork is how the imaginary is slanted, even when it expresses the experience of seasoned field-workers. But what about the continuing research of an anthropologist who has been working in a particular site for a decade or even decades? Is there any model of method in anthropology for what fieldwork is like for the virtuoso? Is it even recognizable as fieldwork according to the Malinowskian mise-en-scène? Our point is that the later work of mature ethnographers usually operates free of the tropes of their earlier work. And we would argue that somehow initiatory fieldwork in certain arenas where many younger anthropologists are working today requires something of the more diffuse and open idea of what fieldwork can be that seems to be characteristic of virtuoso fieldwork, if only it were articulated in the traditional imaginary under which ethnographers-in-the-making train. So this is a problem of pedagogy. Students now enter anthropology inspired by complex social and cultural theories from the interdisciplinary ferment of the 1980s and early 1990s, as well as by the examples of mature second and third works of senior anthropologists—themselves deeply influenced by this period of interdisciplinary ferment—that they admire and want to emulate, and then are faced with a still powerful culture of method that insists that they do something less ambitious. We insist that a new set of regulative norms of fieldwork are needed to release ethnographers-in-the-making from the emphatic and vivid "being there-ness" of the classic imaginary of fieldwork.

Now, turning to the actual challenges to the traditional fieldwork imaginary, what in the world (today) has led to fieldwork's entanglements in multiple and heterogeneous sites of investigation and in complicitous forms of collaboration that have changed markedly what anthropologists want from "natives" as subjects and have deeply compromised claims to authoritative knowledge even of the revised sorts reinstantiated by the reflexive critiques of the 1980s? The conventional understanding of these developments has lain in certain presumptions about the nature of postmodernity that circulated widely in the arenas of interdisciplinary work of the past two decades, namely that as cultures and settled populations have fragmented and become mobile and transnational, as well as more cosmopolitan locally (or at least more invaded or intervened on), fieldwork has simply had literally to follow, when it could, these processes in space. Furthermore, the weight of political and ethical critique of the traditional fieldwork relationship that generated ethnographic data, as revealed by the scrupulous reflexive probing of the postmodern gaze, broke the modicum of innocence and naïveté necessary to sustain the distance in the ethnographer's relationship to subjects, so that complicity with subjects—a state of ambiguity and improper seeming alliance—now pervades the scene of fieldwork, signaling a loss of innocence in the wake of postmodern exposures. Herein both the intensity of focus and the integrity of relationship that have shaped the Malinowskian scene of fieldwork have been challenged.

Although we are sympathetic to this conventional understanding of the challenges to the traditional composure of fieldwork, they do not arise simply from the complexities of a postmodern or now globalizing world. After all, many anthropologists can easily continue doing the same thing, and in fact many do; in many situations, it is even valuable to do so. But our take on what generates multisitedness and complicit relations in fieldwork projects today has more to do with the self-esteem of anthropology in the diminution of its distinctive documentary function amid many competing and overlapping forms of representation comparable to its own. In effect, every project of ethnography enters sites of fieldwork through zones of collateral counterpart knowledge that it cannot ignore in finding its way to the preferred scenes of ordinary everyday life with which it is traditionally comfortable. This condition alone makes fieldwork both multisited in nature, and heterogeneously so, as well as complicit with certain subjects (often experts or authorities in the scene of fieldwork, so to speak), who are crucial to bounding fieldwork and giving it orientation. The fundamental problem here is in confronting the politics of knowledge that any project of fieldwork involves and the ethnographer's trying to gain position in relation to this politics by making this terrain itself part of the design of fieldwork investigation.

Thus, since the 1980s, any critical anthropology worthy of the name not only tries to speak truth to power—truth as subaltern and understood within the closely observed everyday lives of ordinary subjects as the traditional milieu of fieldwork, power as conceptualized and theorized but not usually investigated by the strategies of fieldwork—but also tries to understand power and its agencies in the same ethnographically committed terms and in the same boundaries of fieldwork in which the subaltern is included. Ethnographic understanding itself, as a dominated segment of the dominant (in Pierre Bourdieu's terms), suggests an alternative modality relevant to the circumstances of contemporary fieldwork in which incorporating a second-order perspective on often overlapping, kindred official, expert, and academic discourses as counterpart to the ethnographer's own is an essential and complicating formulation of the traditional mise-en-scène of fieldwork. It is what accounts most cogently for making much of contemporary fieldwork multisited and political. It also makes contemporary fieldwork both slightly alienated and slightly paranoid in ways that are both inevitable and productive (Marcus, 1999c).

The keenly reflexive critical anthropology after the 1980s is well suited to this incorporation of cultures of the rational as a strategic part of its sites of fieldwork. Indeed, if there was one great success of these earlier critiques, it was to create an anthropology of current formations of knowledge and their distributions in a way that was thoroughly new and original. In a sense, all anthropology since has been most effectively an intimate critique of diffused Western knowledge practices in the name of specific communities of subjects misrepresented by, excluded from, seduced by, or victimized by such practices. The emerging innovation of fieldwork currently is to treat such power/knowledges as equal subjects of fieldwork in their complex and obscured connections to the scenes of everyday life as the cultivated and favored milieu of classic ethnography. But to be effective, such fieldwork has to do something more with this complex field of engagements than just provide distanced, however reflexive, description and interpretation. At the moment, a pervasive and sometimes cloying discourse and rhetoric of moral redemption holds this vacant place of an alternative, fully imagined and worked out alternative function for ethnography. Eventually, this rhetorical placeholder might be replaced by more active techniques that are styled in the range between ideas of experimentation and ideas of activism.

So contemporary critical ethnography orients itself through the imaginaries of expert others—through what we call para-ethnography—and operates through found zones of powerful official or expert knowledge-making practices so as to find more traditional subjects for itself. But what does it want of the complicit collaborations it makes with counterpart subjects in these domains, and what does it make of the scene of ethnography? This is distinctly not about an ethnography of elite cultures (Marcus, 1983); rather, it is about an access to a construction of an imaginary for fieldwork that can be shaped only by alliances with makers of visionary knowledge who are already in the scene or within the bounds of the field. The imaginaries of knowledge makers who have preceded the ethnographer are what the dreams of contemporary fieldwork are made of. But what are the practices/aesthetics of technique that go along with such complicitous, multisited fieldwork investigations?

Ecologies of Knowledge

As the anthropologist arrives at the gleaming headquarters of a multinational pharmaceutical corporation in New Jersey, the imposing governmental offices of the Bank of Japan, the sprawling alternative arts space in an urban ward of Cape Town, the courtrooms of the War Crimes Tribunal in The Hague, the offices of software engineers in Uttar Pradesh, or the research laboratories of the World Health Organization in Hong Kong, he or she is faced with unsettling questions. What do I do now? How do I start the fieldwork that is at the heart of my profession? How do I engage the human subjects who can enliven my research and can make my theoretical ideas anthropological? These are not just the questions that haunt the graduate student facing his or her first stint of fieldwork. They are the deep preoccupations that arise on a more or less daily basis, and it is with a veritable ethnographic treatment of the politics and ecologies of such knowledge forms that every project of the ethnography of the contemporary begins.[1] This initial ethnographic treatment produces both the context and the scaffolding of fieldwork. We suppose that this sensitivity to the zones of discourses in play as the portal through which every ethnographic project enters, and indeed constitutes the field, comes from the emphases of the 1980s critiques on reflexivity, representation, rhetorics, and especially politics. But rather than viewing these functions as constitutive of the Malinowskian project within its traditional boundaries, we see them as shaping different and methodologically more challenging conceptions of this theme of fieldwork and the practices they elicit. For us, the kind of reflexivity that is most valuable is the one that positions anthropologists within a field of already existing discourses as subjects of ethnography themselves so that they can find their way to the classic subjects of ethnography.

The work of Fortun (2001), Maurer (1995, 1999, 2002a, 2002b), Riles (2000, 2004a, 2004b, in press), and Miyazaki (2000, 2003, 2004), among many others,[2] demonstrates this rethinking of how projects of ethnography can begin deeply and critically within discourses of the rational that evoke ecologies and politics of knowledge that can be examined ethnographically. Moreover, the work of these authors has identified the deeply reflexive and complicit character of this kind of ethnography and the ways in which *theory* becomes implicated in this work. As Miyazaki (2003) notes regarding his work on Japanese securities traders,

> My ultimate goal is to carve out a space for a different kind of anthropological knowledge formation that finds an opportunity, rather than a problem, in social theorists' collective sense of belatedness. I suggest that the explicit construction of temporal incongruity as an opportunity in financial transactions makes financial markets a particularly suitable site for such exploration. (p. 256)

He further notes how the dilemmas of his subjects, securities traders, are analogous to those of the social theorists and how this convergence creates the basis of a distinctive kind of knowledge production:

> I suggested that social theorists' attention to financial markets as a new target of criticism has resulted from, and in turn intensified, their own collective sense of a temporal incongruity between their knowledge and its object of contemplation, the market. My response to this condition has been to point to analogues of such a sense of temporal incongruity in the financial markets themselves. I have argued that the traders I knew generated prospective momentum in their work precisely by reorienting the temporality of their work so as to continually re-create various forms of temporal incongruity. These analogies to the problems of social theory would suggest that the task of social theorists must be not so much to find new objects of contemplation on the constantly receding horizon of the new, such as financial markets, as to reflect on the work of temporal incongruity as an engine of knowledge formation, more generally. (p. 262)

In a sense, then, the anthropologist finds the literal field by working through the imaginaries of his or her counterparts who are already there, so to speak. This transforms the well-established scene of fieldwork as the encounter with the "other" into a much more complex scene of multiple levels, sites, and kinds of association in producing ethnographic knowledge.

We have become associated with discussing the predicament that we have been describing in terms of the emergence of multisited ethnographic research (Marcus, 1999b). Anthropology cannot remain local but rather must follow its objects and subjects as they move and circulate. This is true, and there are special problems with this, both practical and otherwise. But multisited fieldwork arises as much from the hypersensitivity of anthropology to the ecologies and politics of knowledge in which it operates that are necessary to constitute any subject today for fieldwork investigation. It cannot bracket these in the name of disciplinary authority but rather must incorporate them within the field of fieldwork, so to speak. This in itself is what generates multisitedness in its most pragmatic and feasible sense because there is no doubt that anthropological studies of the contemporary have most often taken the form of examining the relation of institutions to subjects, of systems to everyday life, and of domination to resistance. It is just that now these leading tropes of the contemporary terrain of fieldwork must be thought through in terms of the specific capacities and limits of ethnography as method and as a matter of design in how these tropes literally emerge in the constitution of fieldwork strategies, serendipity, and opportunities. The self-consciously multisited character of fieldwork comes into being as an epiphenomenon of the need to constitute the field and the object of study by incorporating both communities of often elite discourse and communities of often subaltern subjects. From this comes a rethinking of a whole set of issues of fieldwork—complicity instead of rapport (Marcus, 2001), the necessity of collaborations and their personal politics, the uneven distribution or depth of knowing in ethnography (both thickness and thinness as virtues of ethnographic description are in play), the changing nature of the object of study, the grounding of abstract relations that define cultural systems in forms of human action and knowing.

For us, one of the most important settings for developing this project of refunctioning that we are proposing is a pedagogical one. We want to give a sense of what, during recent years, has made the traditional regulative ideals of fieldwork unstable in the work of anthropology and an object for refunctioning. Part of it has to do with failures in the reigning folkloric, storytelling mode of inculcating ethnography as the distinctive practice in the professional culture of anthropology by which fieldwork has long been regulated, thought about, and idealized. This involves articulating certain dimensions that were always there in the Malinowskian staging or mise-en-scène of fieldwork but are now more important than ever in guiding adequately student ethnographers-in-the-making in the kinds of research they are increasingly undertaking. Yet at the same time, it is not clear—based on old governing tropes—what fieldwork is to be experientially in these student projects and what kinds of data it is supposed to generate. Thus, part of the destabilization has to do with the conditions that are reshaping research projects and demanding both more and different emphases from the old ethos in its vision and imaginings of what fieldwork is. This is hardly worthy of the term "crisis" as in the 1980s "crisis of representation," but like the diffusely articulated reflexively critical tendencies growing before the critique of ethnographic writing, there is now a comparable situation with regard to fieldwork. The Malinowskian mise-en-scène is by no means an empty term or guide, but it only roughly covers the forms and norms it actually takes now when applied to new projects.

In our recent work, we have been making a diverse range of arguments about this changing nature of fieldwork, especially for students in new topical arenas, grouped around the notion of what the multisited terrain of contemporary projects does to the focused Malinowskian mise-en-scène and around the concept of complicity as redefining the core relationship of collaboration in fieldwork on which authoritative ethnographic claims to knowledge have always depended. We have used the term mise-en-scène several times in referring to the imaginary that mediates and regulates the expression of method in anthropology. Fieldwork has been a vividly theatrical object of thought in anthropology from its very inception and ideological consolidation by Malinowski as the key symbol, initiatory rite, and method of anthropology. Much of the rest of this chapter is devoted to elucidating the terms of a refunctioned ethnography.

For Method

In earlier post-1986 writing, we emphasized the problem of passing through zones of representation and somehow incorporating them into the purview of fieldwork. As we noted, *acting* on this problem immediately generates the special problems of multisited fieldwork to which we have been alluding. But our efforts here are also a specific response to the possibilities that we both have encountered in pursuing initially the ethnography of elites, and now the ethnography of expertise, in the potential for these figures to define the reflexive politics of positioning for any anthropological research on the contemporary. Probing the ecologies of discourse that orient fieldwork projects today is indeed what the ethnography of elites, and now experts, has most productively become.

If the opening gambit of the ethnography is an orienting foray into a strategically selected culture of expertise, then that milieu of fieldwork cannot be treated conventionally or traditionally. Experts are to be treated not as collateral colleagues helping to inform fieldwork to occur elsewhere but instead as subjects fully within our own analytical ambit whose cognitive purview and social action range potentially over multiple, if not countless, sites and locales. Nor can they be treated as conventional "natives" or tokens of their cultures to be systematically understood; instead, they must be treated as agents who actively participate in shaping emergent social realms. These subjects must be treated like collaborators or partners in research, a fiction to be sustained more or less strongly around the key concept of para-ethnography.[3]

The para-ethnographic is a self-conscious critical faculty operating in expert domains as a way of dealing with contradictions, exceptions, and facts that are fugitive, suggesting a social realm and social processes not in alignment with conventional representations and reigning modes of analysis. Making ethnography from the found para-ethnographic redefines the status of the subject or informant and asks what different accounts one wants from such key figures in the fieldwork process. We have conceptualized the para-ethnographic as a kind of *social* thought—expressed in genres such as "the anecdotal," "hype," and "intuition"—within institutions dominated by a technocratic ethos, an ethos that, under changed contemporary circumstances, simply does not discipline thought and action as efficiently as it once did.

The para-ethnographer is an expert subject like the genetic engineer who is perplexed by the significance of his or her own cognitive practices and who, in the shadow of his or her formal knowledge work, creates intricate *cultural* narratives that might never be fully voiced but nonetheless mimic the form and the content of an ethnographic engagement with the world. Various fragmentary discourses are continuously spun off from this kind of knowledge work that connects formal scientific inquiry to the existential condition of the scientist cum para-ethnographer, on the one hand, and to a wider social imaginary, on the other. Ethical and moral apprehensions as well as professional and commercial preoccupations, although typically not fully articulated, nonetheless circulate in complex relationship to formal scientific practices, thereby constituting the substance of para-ethnography as well as part of the ecology of discourse that creates the field or ground in which strategies and designs of anthropological research take form. The questions, motives, and purposes that project anthropologists into fieldwork are not simply those raised within the discipline of anthropology or posed by the contextualizing social theories or historical narratives of contiguous academic specializations; rather, they arise from orienting engagements with counterparts and actors already defined within the field of ethnographic inquiry. Through this process, the formal *problematic* of contemporary ethnography is established (Fischer, 1999, 2003; Marcus, 1999a; Rabinow, 2003).

Under the conditions we are stipulating, where meaning is fugitive and social facts are elusive, distinct dilemmas are created for the individual. Cultural innovations continually destabilize social consensus, posing characteristic struggles for the perplexed subject—struggles that gain expression through various manifestations of the para-ethnographic. We are interested in how these para-ethnographic narratives become linked together among different expert subjects, conferring a distinctive *social* character on, for the most part, technical knowledge. What we refer to as internarratives not only link domains of expertise, often in unlikely ways, but also allow expertise to be juxtaposed in ways that render them acutely relevant to a broad range of anthropological questions. Expertise in science, politics, law, business, finance, and art must increasingly confront reciprocal expertise (and subaltern discourses) on human rights, social justice, and environmentalism, to name just a few. These critical and insurgent discourses can emerge from what are very familiar ethnographic concerns—the economic, political, and/or environmental plights of subaltern subjects or indigenous peoples—but they gain articulation in courts and through legal proceedings, in government bureaus and scientific agencies, within universities and museums, in nongovernmental organizations and a diverse range of international forums as well as through our own anthropological practices of representation and advocacy. The interchange between and among various established and alternative domains of expertise can create decisive axes of analysis that can orient a multi-sited staging of fieldwork. Thus, these bridging discourses can link the ethnography of experts to the lives and struggles of ordinary people. In this way, inquiry into cultures of expertise may well become an aspect of virtually all major projects pursued by anthropologically informed ethnography, even those projects that start from highly localized sets of interests and concerns.[4]

Our delineation of para-ethnography developed out of analysis of the unusual expertise of an infamous political actor, the French nationalist Jean-Marie Le Pen. Observations of Le Pen and his colleagues revealed an eerie convergence between their insurgent forms of political experimentation and those practices that encompass the professional métier of the ethnographer. Insurgent political narratives are, for the most part, designed not merely to circulate among experts but also to shape social thought and action across countless sites and among diverse publics. Le Pen's para-ethnography demonstrates the potential of this kind of narrative to establish a multisited scene providing the intellectual substance and the conceptual links between and among sites. By aligning the work of the anthropologist with that of highly problematic political figures such as Le Pen, we establish the problem of "complicity" as pivotal in defining the ethics and politics of fieldwork—in ways that were disguised in the Malinowskian scene in the off-stage presence of the colonial official.

Schematic Exchange

We turn to a particular case of political expertise that illustrates the shift in the staging of the ethnographic encounter we have been discussing. We draw on an interview that was part of a multi-sited ethnographic project that moved from the rural districts of northeast Italy, to the political and bureaucratic precincts of the European Parliament in Strasbourg and Brussels, and finally to the impoverished districts of the East End of London. The subject of the exchange on which we focus here is Le Pen. Holmes conducted the interview at the headquarters of the European Parliament in Strasbourg during the early 1990s. The voice—the "I"—here is superficially that of Douglas Holmes, but it actually represents our combined responses to this unusual conversation.

What made it pivotal for our thinking is that the exchange began with rather conventional premises whereby the subject, Le Pen, served as an informant, as an interlocutor who could provide an "insider account" or the "native point of view," as it were, on a distinctive form of extreme right-wing French nationalism, but in the course of the exchange a series of disruptions introduced by Le Pen (and tacitly accepted by Holmes) revealed the operation of what we are terming the para-ethnographic. In what follows, we show that what initially appeared to be a subtle shift in the staging of the encounter, in which Le Pen's role was recast from "key informant" to "para-ethnographer," can incites a wide-ranging reassessment of anthropological ethnography. We present the case as a scenario—as a thought experiment—that focuses on the nature of the encounter and how it operated in the service of anthropological knowledge. The scenario also encompasses the technical language and terminology that we have developed to rebuild and refunction ethnography.

Fieldwork at the European Parliament, the consultative body of the European Union (EU), was as part of a study of European integration that spanned the decade from late 1980s to the late 1990s, focusing on interviews with a very broad range of political figures. The meeting with Le Pen, leader of the National Front, was unplanned and came after discussions with other leaders of the party.[5]

The conversation with Le Pen defied my expectations and understanding of how the ethnographic relationship is staged and how ideas are shaped and exchanged through this kind of relationship. This sense that something about the ethnographic relation was shifting as I was participating in it had been building over the course of my work at the parliament. But only when I encountered Le Pen, with his lurid charms, his extravagance, and his audacity in openly challenging the tenets of the interview process, did I fully grasp the extent to which the ethnographic relationship was being recast. In one important way, this was not a surprise; Le Pen's theatricality is renowned, and his performances are widely acknowledged to be masterful and compelling despite (or because of) their extremist character. He prides himself on the texture, the subtlety, and the range of his emotional message. What others consider to be distasteful about his performance, Le Pen claims as the distinctive means by which he engages the intimate struggles that circumscribe the lives of his public. Linking the theatrical and emotional dimensions of his political practice is a formidable intellectual tradition that intersects with the foundational concepts of humanistic anthropology—the traditions and lineages of what Isaiah Berlin terms the "Counter-Enlightenment." From this intellectual tradition, Le Pen distills what he believes to be the essence of human nature and the character of cultural affinity and difference, ideas that imbue fervent political yearning and foreshadow an exclusionary political economy.

The manner in which Le Pen insinuated this vision into our meeting was decisive in both defining the key *theoretical* issue of Holmes's project—the supranational character of advanced European integration—and fully revealing the possibilities of what we refer to here as the para-ethnographic. Acknowledging the operation of the para-ethnographic also exposed the interleaved affinities—or what we term "complicities"—linking the knowledge work of figures such as Le Pen and our own knowledge work.

My first impression during the meeting was that Le Pen was parodying and baiting me. In retrospect, I think that there is no doubt that was exactly what he was doing. It was, however, by no means merely a rhetorical maneuver on his part; rather, it was a deep substantive challenge. He was asserting that the distinctive domain of his political expertise was "culture." He was claiming a mastery over cultural ideas, cultural practices, and cultural meanings that far exceeded anything I, or any other mere academic, was capable of exercising.

To demonstrate his prowess, he laid out a remarkable vision of Europe, a vision predicated on solving the central conundrum—the core riddle of advanced European integration. He asserted that European integration that presents itself, at least at the time of the interview, as a wide-ranging economic undertaking was in fact a radical social and cultural project aimed at creating a *supranational* multiracial and multicultural Europe. Moreover, the project, as he understood it, was unfolding unmarked, unrecognized, and unnarrated. He had assumed for himself the task of giving voice to this process, giving the project of European integration a language and thereby a new political reality.

He recognized that at the heart of the project is a deep antagonism toward the political economy of the European nation-state, its regulatory regimes, and its cognitive purview. He saw integration as a wide-ranging scheme to usurp the powers of the nation-state, a scheme that ironically was engineered through the nation-state itself. The state, in this view, is by no means irrelevant, particularly as it has come to operate intergovernmentally within the EU; rather, it no longer constitutes the preeminent instrument defining *society* in Europe (Connolly, 1995; Milward, 1999; Moravcsik, 1998).

Framing Le Pen's insights are a number of fundamental analytical challenges. As the dominant position of the European nation-state is usurped through the process of integration, so too are many of the phenomenological, epistemological, and methodological assumptions that underpin the social sciences. Inquiry into the supranational operation of the EU reveals how deeply our extant repertoire of analytical concepts, our historical perspectives, and even our ethical and moral assumptions are predicated on the nation-state as a social fact. Thus, when we seek to examine European integration, we must confront phenomena that aggressively challenge all of our means and methods by which we produce knowledge. But of course, this is precisely what makes the EU—as it continually reinvents itself—such a profoundly important object of study (Holmes, 2003).

Le Pen's ambition during the early 1990s was to define the discourse on the emergence of a multiracial and multicultural society by eviscerating its moral and intellectual foundations. He thereby escaped the tightly sequestered world of right-wing French nationalism and established the premises of a supranational politics of Europe, a politics emphatically opposed to integration. Indeed, during the early 1990s, Le Pen was the first to elaborate what could be construed as a new political articulation of what is at stake in advanced European integration.

Le Pen's political innovations are compelling intellectually and have had a powerful appeal for new *European* constituencies—despite their overt fascist resonance. What Le Pen delineated exceeds what is conventionally understood as "politics"; rather, he conjured a complex sociology and metaphysics that tethers the new political economy of the EU to emerging existential struggles taking shape in the lives of virtually all Europeans. He recognized that integration was paradoxically creating new domains of alienation and estrangement in which radical formation of meaning are being contested (Bauman, 1997, 2001; Holmes, 2000, pp. 59–74).

Le Pen was hardly inclined to submit to the role of mere informant for someone else's project; on the contrary, he sought to both control and disrupt our interchange at every turn. As I became essentially the audience for his performance, I detected something oddly familiar about Le Pen's discourse, particularly the way in which he conceptualized overarching social and cultural struggles that could be read in the sacred and profane experience of situated subjects. The way in which he drew on anecdotal accounts to create intricately woven narratives about contemporary Europe sounded ethnographic to me; indeed, our exchange in some ways sounded like the musings of social anthropologists. His narratives were, of course, hardly disinterested, yet they seemed at least superficially to be ethnographic. In other words, what struck me was that Le Pen needed something akin to an ethnographic purview to pursue his political insurgency. This insight provoked a series of questions with which we continue to grapple. What is the nature of this kind of "ethnographic" purview? How does it operate? How do we draw these knowledge practices of our subjects into a broader anthropological project? How does this kind of collaborative knowledge practice recast our relationship to our subjects? And what are the ethical implications of this kind of collaboration? More broadly, we recognized even with this initial rendering of the para-ethnographic that new strategies and designs for problematizing research had become possible (Rabinow, 2003).

▣ Complicities

As we examined carefully the intersection between ethnography and para-ethnography, we developed the notion of the "illicit discourse" to mark out domains of complicity. Le Pen's discourse was overtly "illicit" insofar as it was predicated on malevolent cultural distinctions, but it was also "illicit" insofar as it challenges our claim as anthropologists to have a unique authority over this form of knowledge practice. More broadly, we have used the concept of illicit discourse to mark a conceptual space for working out the formidable moral and ethical challenges posed by the collaborative imperatives of para-ethnography. The para-ethnographer in this case is not merely involved in a complex "sensemaking" but rather is involved in an aggressive knowledge practice in the service of wide-ranging theoretical and ideological agendas. Le Pen's para-ethnography draws on "theory" and "ideology" that seek to explain cultural and racial affinity and difference in ways that challenge the culture concept as it has come to underwrite humanistic anthropology. On this kind of complex collaborative terrain, our ethical and moral conceits are open to direct challenge from the theoretically and ideologically informed positions of our subjects (Holmes, 2000).

The most powerful illicit discourse that we discerned from the engagement with Le Pen focused on the problem of "society" as key to our reciprocal practices of "ethnography." Le Pen and we sought constructions of European society as a moral framework, an analytical construct, and an empirical fact; we needed to conjure new representations of society to do our respective work. This was the foundation of a deep convergence of our ethnography and Le Pen's para-ethnography. Le Pen used his representation of society to configure deeply rancorous political meaning. We created a representation of society to configure a critical analysis of European politics, most notably of politics like those framed by Le Pen (Holmes, 1993).

Le Pen understands viscerally that as society framed by the bourgeois nation-state is eclipsed, a space is created for a radical politics that draws on latent cultural idioms to align a new conceptualization of collectivity. This view of society espoused by Le Pen could be used, as Holmes demonstrated, to frame an analytic of European integration. But Le Pen's disturbing "theoretical" innovation also depends on a "method"—a para-ethnography—that allowed him to narrate the usurpation of the nation-state and its significance not just for those traditional political constituencies displaced and estranged by this process but also for all Europeans. Inlaid in his narrative was a complex structure of feeling that configured a new emotional landscape for a supranational Europe on which sublime yearnings are crosscut by acute fears and anxieties. Again, he recognized that integration was paradoxically creating new domains of alienation and estrangement in which radical formation of meaning were establishing the terms of struggle over multiracial and multicultural society. Le Pen had, in this way, defined a distinctive tableau not only for his political insurgency but also for our ethnographic experimentation. In other words, European integration became a domain that we could enter analytically via the ecology of discourses that Le Pen had articulated (Marcus, 1999a, 1999b).

Connective Tissue

Political narratives defining European pluralism are obviously designed not merely to circulate within the political precincts of the EU but also to shape social thought and action within countless sites across this burgeoning polity. Thus, Le Pen's para-ethnography is decisive in another crucial way in that he demonstrates the potential of what we term the "internarrative" in the construction of a multisited scene. Internarratives serve as the connective tissue and the intellectual substance, as it were, of multisited ethnography; they provide the conceptual bridges between and among sites.

Insurgent politicians seek to create narratives that can enter the lifeworlds of a newly constituted public. The initial trajectory of this kind of communicative action is, in the case of Le Pen, from his headquarters in Paris to the homes, bars, workplaces, sports clubs, and so on of French and European citizens, where his narratives circulate in informal conversations, in press accounts, and in the shop talk of local politicians. These political narratives are interpreted and endowed with distinctive configurations of meaning in these diverse local contexts. They are also refracted back to Paris, to Le Pen's headquarters, and to the political offices of all those who seek to oppose him, where they can be recalibrated and recommunicated to align a complex discursive field.

By taking a marginal nationalist discourse and recrafting it as a supranational European discourse, Le Pen set the terms of debate on a multiracial and multicultural Europe and, for our purposes, established an analytical tableau that extends across innumerable sites. Thus, the discourse on pluralism that he crafted can take profoundly different forms depending, for example, on whether it is configured across the borderlands of Ireland or Poland within working-class neighborhoods of Marseille or Vilnius. In these diverse sites, this narrative enlivens distinctive human predicaments, conferring on them a fraught conceptual and emotional substance that can be explored ethnographically. Thus, a multisited ethnography was constructed across this tableau inspired by Le Pen, revealing how contemporary formulations of European pluralism gain expression as intimate cultural practices in rural districts of northeast Italy, as a racialized political economy within the institutions of the EU, and as a violent idiom of alienation and estrangement in the East End of London (Holmes, 2000). In this staging, multiple points of entry, through which one can discover countless interlocutors who endow European integration with diverse human voices, were established.

Creative Possibilities

In our effort to reconcile the troubling affinities between the knowledge work of figures like Le Pen and our own knowledge work, we recognized a unusual creative process—an "intimate artifice"—whereby the ethnographer and para-ethnographer create either a shared framework of analysis or frameworks that operate in some kind of reciprocal relationship through which interleaved formations of knowledge are generated and exchanged dialectically. These collaborative exchanges operate at each stage of the ethnographic project.

The creative challenge posed by the type of fieldwork on which we focus here involves delineating the phenomenon to be studied, establishing an analytic tableau populated with human subjects who define it, endowing it with social form and cultural content. For us, this is a complex collaborative process whereby a discursive space on which a multisited ethnography can be staged is created, a discursive space where the actions of our subjects and our own analytical practices can be observed and where they and we shape a social reality.

In the case that we have discussed, a discursive space was circumscribed—Holmes terms it "integralism"—allowing us to view European integration simultaneously from the standpoints of its diverse theoretical underpinnings, its intellectual lineages, and its technocratic practices as well as allowing us to engage ethnographically the ways in which integrations inspire political insurgencies radically opposed to its abiding ideals. Moreover, the collaborative space encompassed by integralism created a dynamic purview from which we can view integration in terms of its manifold contradictions, revealing not merely its institutional manifestations but also its profoundly human character—the ways in which it has come to align consciousness and mediate intimacy. For us, this is the essence of a multisited mise-en-scène, a staging that can reveal the interplay between metatheoretical issues and the intricacies of human experience.

Inevitably, as we explore the dilemmas of expertise in other domains, we reciprocally expose our own professional limitations and liabilities. Not the least of these is the curious effect of observing how what we claim to be our distinctive practices as ethnographers can be deployed in creative ways by our subjects, conferring on their knowledge work a status that equals, if not exceeds, our own. To do an engaged and critical ethnography of expertise, we not only must build into our projects, as a methodological first principle, an acknowledgment of the uncertain nature of our own intellectual practices as ethnographers but also must actively exploit this unsettling condition as a driving force of our inquiry. By drawing complicity to the heart of our methods and ethics, a circumstantial *activism* becomes plausible (Marcus, 1999b).

We view this kind of collaboration as not merely an elicitation of preexisting social and cultural elements but also the systematic crafting of discursive spaces that capture newly constituted social and cultural phenomena as they take form within a continuously unfolding contemporary. We believe that this kind of activism rekindles the most radical aspirations of the anthropological project. In this collaborative framing—this intimate artifice—an activism that is theoretical, empirical, ethical, political, and existential in its scope and purview can be built into the constitution of the ethnographic relationship (Fortun, 2001).

Thus, para-ethnography is not merely a matter of identifying a new ethnographic subject—an accomplished autodidact; rather, it opens far deeper questions of how culture operates within a continuously unfolding contemporary. What is at stake in our conceptualization of the para-ethnographic are formations of culture that are *not* fully contingent on convention, tradition, and "the past" but rather constitute future-oriented cognitive practices that can generate novel configurations of meaning and action. Indeed, this gives rise to our most radical assertion—that spontaneously generated para-ethnographies are built into the structure of the contemporary and give form and content to a continuously unfolding skein of experience.

▣ Notes

1. Most of the graduate projects that we supervise begin or end with such encounters, even though they may operate for considerable periods of time in the traditional mise-en-scène of anthropological fieldwork of sustained residence among ordinary (accessible?) people—in villages, on shop floors, in neighborhoods, on hospital wards, in classrooms. But these encounters are now given ethnographic import and treatment, and the main puzzle of fieldwork becomes their multileveled relation to these other more conventional and manageable sites of fieldwork. For example, we currently have a student who is researching the implementation of "freedom of information act" laws in Poland as an index of "democratization" there, the initial challenge of which has been to understand, by self-conscious fieldwork strategy, the "local" intellectual and official culture by which these laws have been conceived and formulated. Another student who has worked on concepts of risk among financiers in Korea moved back and forth between and among firms and particular neighborhoods in Seoul, sites that offered her variably "thick" and "thin" ethnography but created the context of relationship in which she found her focused object of study—not what went on in either set of sites but rather the nature of the real and imaginary relationships between and among them. A third student has spent long periods among contemporary Mayan villagers who live on or near ancient ruins, but the project has achieved its cogency only by extending fieldwork into the daily operations of the formidable regional and national bureaucracies of cultural heritage in Mexico. Of work that has been published by former students, that of Bargach (2002), Fortun (2001), and Hernandez (2002) exemplifies this emergence of multisited fieldwork in very different styles, but each study requires the sort of refunctioning of traditional notions of fieldwork that we have described.

2. The ethnographic studies of contemporary politics, of science and technology, of corporate business and markets, and of art worlds are the primary arenas of contemporary life where the refunctioning of ethnography that we describe has been emerging. The primary example that we work through in this essay comes from European politics. The recent study of Australian aboriginal painting by Myers (2002) is probably the most important example of such ethnography on art worlds. The Late Editions volume edited by Marcus (1998) provides sources on the ethnographic study of corporations. See also the work of Maurer (1995, 1999, 2002a, 2002b). However, it is in the burgeoning field of science and technology studies that the most impressive shift in the practice of ethnography can be observed. See Downey and Dumit (1997), Latour and Woolgar (1988), Marcus (1995), Pickering (1995), Rabinow (1999), Reid and Traweek (2000), Strathern (1992), and Traweek (1988).

3. Although we try to give our own specific conception to para-ethnography as an object of fieldwork investigation, it is certainly deeply connected to the long-standing interest in American cultural anthropology of probing "native points of view" through ethnographic investigation. Put simply, anthropology works through the understandings of others and the claim to be able to

achieve knowledge of these understandings through fieldwork investigation. The influential discussions in social theory (Beck, Giddens, & Lash, 1994) of the importance of reflexivity itself as a major structural dimension of contemporary life have only enhanced this traditionally rooted interest in the para-ethnographic as an object of ethnography. For an elaborated discussion of this connection between the native point of view and para-ethnography, see Holmes and Marcus (2004).

4. A superb case in point is the recent work by Petryna (2002) on Chernobyl nuclear accident survivors that was named winner of the best first book published by an anthropologist, awarded in 2003 by the American Ethnological Society. Petryna worked closely with a group of survivors, participating in their everyday lives, characteristic of the vantage point of traditional ethnography. But she quickly found that to do justice to her topic, and to her subjects, she had to conduct multiple parallel ethnography: "My decision to abstain from judgment is also supported on empirical grounds. . . . Worlds of science, statistics, bureaucracy, suffering, power, and biological processes coevolve here in particular and unstable ways. How to discern their patterns as locally observable realities that affect people's daily lives and sense of moral and bodily integrity—or put another way, how to do an ethnography of the relationships among biological, political, and social processes as those relationships evolve—is a major creative challenge of this work" (p. 120).

5. The anthropology of contemporary Europe is a particularly cogent setting for the refunctioning of ethnography based in multisited strategies of fieldwork. The emergence of the EU and its institutions has made every locally focused study in Europe—no matter the specific venue or topic—at the same time a study of the overarching EU frame. With everything parallel processed, so to speak, there is no likely topic on contemporary Europe that is not at least multisited in its social space. Thus, this area of anthropology has been especially prescient in the refunctioning of ethnography as we discuss it. To understand the new anthropology of Europe that has emerged around the problematic of advanced European integration, see Abélès (1992, 1995, 1996, 2000), Bellier (1994, 1997), and Shore (2000).

References

Abélès, M. (1992). *La vie Quotidienne au Parlement Européen.* Paris: Hachette.

Abélès, M. (1995). Pour une anthropologie des institutions. *L'Homme, 135,* 65–85.

Abélès, M. (1996). *En attente d'Europe: Débat avec Jean-Louis Bourlanges.* Paris: Hachette.

Abélès, M. (2000). Virtual Europe. In I. Bellier & T. Wilson (Eds.), *An anthropology of the European Union: Building, imagining, and experiencing the new Europe* (pp. 31–52). Oxford, UK: Berg.

Bargach, J. (2002). *Orphans of Islam: Family, abandonment, and secret adoption in Morocco.* Lanham, MD: Rowman & Littlefield.

Bauman, Z. (1997, January 24). No way back to bliss: How to cope with the restless chaos of modernity. *Times Literary Supplement,* p. 5.

Bauman, Z. (2001). Identities in a globalizing world. *Social Anthropology, 9,* 127.

Beck, U., Giddens, A., & Lash, S. (1994). *Reflexive modernization: Politics, tradition, and aesthetics in the modern social order.* Stanford, CA: Stanford University Press.

Bellier, I. (1994). *La Commission européenne: Hauts fonctionnaries et "culture du management."* Revue française d'administration, Publique 70.

Bellier, I. (1997). The commission as an actor: An anthropologist's view. In H. Wallace & A. R. Young (Eds.), *Participation and policy-making in the European Union* (pp. 91–115). Oxford, UK: Clarendon.

Clifford, J., & Marcus, G. E. (Eds.). (1986). *Writing culture: The poetics and politics of ethnography.* Berkeley: University of California Press.

Connolly, B. (1995). *The rotten heart of Europe: The dirty war for Europe's money.* London: Faber & Faber.

Downey, G. L., & Dumit, J. (Eds.). (1997). *Cyborgs and citadels.* Santa Fe, NM: School of American Research Press.

Fischer, M. M. J. (1999). Emergent forms of life: Anthropologies of late or postmodernities. *Annual Review of Anthropology, 28,* 455–478.

Fischer, M. M. J. (2003). *Emergent forms of life and the anthropology of voice.* Durham, NC: Duke University Press.

Fortun, K. (2001). *Advocacy after Bhopal: Environmentalism, disaster, new global orders.* Chicago: University of Chicago Press.

Hernandez, M. T. (2002). *Delirio: The fantastic, the demonic, and the reel.* Austin: University of Texas Press.

Holmes, D. R. (1993). Illicit discourse. In G. Marcus (Ed.), *Perilous states: Conversations on culture, politics, and nation* (Late Editions, No. 1, pp. 255–281). Chicago: University of Chicago Press.

Holmes, D. R. (2000). *Integral Europe: Fast-capitalism, multiculturalism, neofascism.* Princeton, NJ: Princeton University Press.

Holmes, D. R. (2003). [Review of Cris Shore, 2000, *Building Europe: The Cultural Politics of European Integration*]. *American Anthropologist, 105,* 464–466.

Holmes, D. R., & Marcus, G. E. (2004). Cultures of expertise and the management of globalization: Toward the re-functioning of ethnography. In A. Ong & S. J. Collier (Eds.), *Global assemblages: Technology, politics, and ethics as anthropological problems* (pp. 235–252). London: Blackwell.

Latour, B., & Woolgar, S. (1988). *The pasteurization of France.* Cambridge, MA: Harvard University Press.

Malinowski, B. (1961). *Argonauts of the Western Pacific.* New York: Dutton. (Original work published in 1928)

Marcus, G. E. (1983). *Elites: Ethnographic issues.* Albuquerque: University of New Mexico Press.

Marcus, G. E. (Ed.). (1995). *Technoscientific imaginaries: Conversations, profiles, and memoirs* (Late Editions 2). Chicago: University of Chicago Press.

Marcus, G. E. (Ed.). (1998). *Corporate futures: The diffusion of the culturally sensitive corporate form* (Late Editions, No. 5). Chicago: University of Chicago Press.

Marcus, G. E. (1999a). Critical anthropology now: An introduction. In G. E. Marcus (Ed.), *Critical anthropology now: Unexpected contexts, shifting constituencies, changing agendas* (pp. 3–28). Santa Fe, NM: School of American Research Press.

Marcus, G. E. (1999b). *Ethnography through thick and thin.* Princeton, NJ: Princeton University Press.

Marcus, G. E. (Ed.). (1999c). *Paranoia within reason: A casebook on conspiracy as explanation* (Late Editions, No. 6). Chicago: University of Chicago Press.

Marcus, G. E. (1999d). What is at stake—and not—in the idea and practice of multi-sited ethnography. *Canberra Anthropology, 22*(2), 6–14.

Marcus, G. E. (2001). From rapport under erasure to the theater of complicit reflexivities. *Qualitative Inquiry, 7,* 519–528.

Marcus, G. E. (2002a). Beyond Malinowski and after *Writing Culture:* On the future of cultural anthropology and the predicament of ethnography. *Australian Journal of Anthropology, 13,* 191–199.

Marcus, G. E. (2002b). On the problematic contemporary reception of ethnography as the stimulus for innovations in its forms and norms in teaching and research. *Anthropological Journal on European Cultures, 11,* 191–206.

Marcus, G. E. (2003). The unbearable slowness of being an anthropologist now: Notes on a contemporary anxiety in the making of ethnography. *Xcp, 12,* 7–20.

Maurer, B. (1995). Complex subjects: Offshore finance, complexity theory, and the dispersion of the modern. *Socialist Review, 25,* 113–145.

Maurer, B. (1999). Forget Locke? From proprietor to risk-bearer in new logics of finance. *Public Culture, 11,* 47–67.

Maurer, B. (2002a). Anthropological and accounting knowledge in Islamic banking and finance: Rethinking critical accounts. *Journal of the Royal Anthropological Institute, 8,* 645–667.

Maurer, B. (2002b). Repressed futures: Financial derivatives' theological unconscious. *Economy and Society, 31*(1), 15–36.

Milward, A. S. (1999). *The European rescue of the nation-state.* London: Routledge.

Miyazaki, H. (2000). Faith and its fulfillment: Agency, exchange, and the Fijian aesthetics of completion. *American Ethnologist, 27,* 31–51.

Miyazaki, H. (2003). The temporalities of the market. *American Anthropologist, 105,* 255–265.

Miyazaki, H. (2004). *The method of hope.* Stanford, CA: Stanford University Press.

Moravcsik, A. (1998). *The choices for Europe: Social purpose and state power from Messina to Maastricht.* Ithaca, NY: Cornell University Press.

Myers, F. (2002). *Painting culture: The making of an aboriginal high art.* Durham, NC: Duke University Press.

Petryna, A. (2002). *Life exposed: Biological citizens after Chernobyl.* Princeton, NJ: Princeton University Press.

Pickering, A. (1995). *The mangle of practice: Time, agency, and science.* Chicago: University of Chicago Press.

Rabinow, P. (1999). *French modern: Norms and forms of the social environment.* Chicago: University of Chicago Press.

Rabinow, P. (2003). *Anthropos today: Reflections on modern equipment.* Princeton, NJ: Princeton University Press.

Reid, R., & Traweek, S. (Eds.). (2000). *Doing science + culture.* New York: Routledge.

Riles, A. (2000). *The network inside out.* Ann Arbor: University of Michigan Press.

Riles, A. (2004a). Property as legal knowledge: Means and ends. *Journal of the Royal Anthropological Institute, 10,* 773–793.

Riles, A. (2004b). Real time: Unwinding technocratic and anthropological knowledge. *American Ethnologist, 31*(3), 1–14.

Riles, A. (in press). Introduction. In A. Riles (Ed.), *Documents: Artifacts of modern knowledge.* Durham, NC: Duke University Press.

Shore, C. (2000). *Building Europe: The cultural politics of European integration.* London: Routledge.

Strathern, M. (1992). *Reproducing the future: Essays on anthropology, kinship, and the new reproductive technologies.* New York: Routledge.

Traweek, S. (1988). *Beamtimes and lifetimes: The world of high energy physicists.* Cambridge, MA: Harvard University Press.

EPILOGUE

The Eighth and Ninth Moments—Qualitative Research in/and the Fractured Future

Yvonna S. Lincoln and Norman K. Denzin

The end of a work such as this should signal neither a conclusion nor a final word, but rather a punctuation in time that marks a stop merely to take a breath, and, indeed, that is what we intend in this epilogue. The breadth that the contributors to this volume have tried to span marks a multidimensional map of territory traversed, including multiple moments, multiple histories, multiple influences, and multiple paradigms, perspectives, and methods, as well as increasing sensitivity to and awareness of new issues and problems. The contributors have also marked out this territory as terra incognita to be explored. Many have been as provocative as they have been historical, and that is as it should be, for we merely pause now on the border of a new vision for the social sciences. We would characterize this new vision as the realization of the seventh moment (although not its fulfillment) and a course charted toward the eighth and ninth moments in qualitative research.

The realization of the seventh moment lies in two signal achievements. First, we see, with this *Handbook* and the growing body of literature on specific methods, theoretical lenses, and paradigms, that a mature sophistication now characterizes the choices that qualitative researchers, practitioners, and theoreticians deploy in inquiring into social issues. No longer is it possible to categorize practitioners of various perspectives, interpretive practices, or paradigms in a singular or simplistic way. The old categories have fallen away with the rise of conjugated and complex new perspectives. Poststructuralist feminist qualitative researchers are joined by critical indigenous qualitative researchers. Critical poststructural feminist reconstructionists work in tandem with postmodern performance ethnographers. Labels perform double duty, or they are not applied at all. The important thing to note about many practicing interpretivists today is that they have been shaped by and influenced toward postmodern perspectives, the critical turn (as powerful an influence as the interpretive turn and the postmodern turn were in their own times), the narrative or rhetorical turn, and the turn toward a rising tide of *voices*. These are the voices of the formerly disenfranchised, the voices of subalterns everywhere, the voices of indigenous and postcolonial peoples, who are profoundly politically committed to determining their own destiny. We are at the "end of history" (Fukuyama, 1989, 1992), or at least at the end of history as we have known it. We are all "after the fact" (Geertz, 1995).

Although Hammersley (1999) objects to our historicizing, or punctuating, moments in the awakening or creation of qualitative research, we believe that there are genuine ruptures in the fabric of our own histories, precise or fuzzy points at which we are irrevocably changed. A sentence, a luminous argument, a compelling paper, a personal incident—any of these can create a breach between what we practiced previously and what we can no longer practice, what we believed about the world and what we can no longer hold onto, who we will be as field-workers as distinct from who we have been in earlier research. Indeed, we would argue that what we call moments are themselves the appearances of new sensibilities, times when qualitative researchers become aware of issues they had not imagined before. They are the "ah-ha" moments, the epiphanies, much like the "click" moments so deliciously recounted 30 years ago in the pages of *Ms.* magazine by women coming to consciousness. So, believing in our project as one of description and interpretation—the ethnographer's job—we continue to think of even the most contemporary history as a history emphasized and underscored by revelatory moments that shudder through the interpretive communities we inhabit. Those are the moments we try to describe, with the full understanding that, in the poststructural moment, our textual descriptions fall far short of what the lived experiences of individual researchers and inquiry and disciplinary communities look and feel like.

We have called the current moment the *methodologically contested present,* and we have described it as a time of great tension, substantial conflict, methodological retrenchment in some quarters (see Denzin & Lincoln, Chapter 1, this volume), and the disciplining and regulation of inquiry practices to conform with conservative, neoliberal programs and regimes that make claims regarding Truth (Cannella & Lincoln, 2004a, 2004b; Lincoln & Cannella, 2004a, 2004b). It is also a time of great tension *within* the qualitative research community, simply because the methodological, paradigmatic, perspectival, and inquiry contexts are so open and varied that it is easy to believe that researchers are everywhere. What appears to be chaos to outsiders, however, is nothing less than the intense desire of a growing number of people to explore the multiple unexplored places of a global society in transition. But where these people study, what they study, with whom they study, how they study the phenomena of interest with a communitarian sensibility, what they write about what they have studied, who writes about what they have studied—all these are subject to debate and struggle.

Out of this debate, struggle, and contestation will come the next moment. In some ways, it will share characteristics with the present moment; for example, it seems clear that the next moment will also be methodologically contested. The National Research Council's *Scientific Research in Education* (2002) will now stand next to the National Science Foundation's *Workshop on Scientific Foundations of Qualitative Research* (Ragin, Nagel, & White, 2004) as a boundary of the contested ground. It may well be the case that, as Alasuutari (2004) contends, we are undergoing a stunning compression of time, of moments, at this period in our history. Certainly, from our perspective as the editors of this volume, we see that advances in qualitative methods and models of inquiry appear to be developing somewhat more swiftly than in the past, with inventions, improvisations, and other forms of bricolage becoming both more sophisticated and more highly adaptable and adapted. It is also clear that many "moments"—in the form of real practitioners facing real problems in real fields and bringing with them real and material practices—will continue to circulate at the same time. Thus practitioners, scholars, and researchers are spread out, to varying degrees, over nine moments, often moving between moments as they seek—or are found by—new sites for inquiry. We are not discomfited by this; on the contrary, we believe it adds to the strength of qualitative research as a field and discipline, for it signifies that practitioners are willing to live with many forms of practice, many paradigms, without demanding conformity or orthodoxy.

There will also be some differences in the next moment. In the pages that follow, we try to portray some of the shifts, repositionings, and metamorphoses that we see coming and that we have asked this volume's contributors to address.

◼ The Eighth and Ninth Moments

Although methodological contestation will continue within and among the many disciplinary communities of qualitative research—business, marketing, nursing, psychology, communications studies, cultural studies, education, sociology, anthropology, medical clinical practice and epidemiology, and others—methodological sophistication will grow. The days when the teachers of qualitative research courses needed to search hard for good methodology texts are over; multiple enriched, cosmopolitan, transnational, and practice-seasoned literatures—and internal critiques of these same literatures—have been created, resulting in a veritable feast of paradigmatic arguments, interpretive practices, analytic and data management choices, and application issues. The problem for these scholars today is not in finding sound materials, but rather in choosing among and between them so as not to appear extravagant in assigning readings for classes.[1]

The next generation of qualitative researchers will face the same areas of contestation as did their earlier counterparts, but they will also face several new improvisations on old issues. It seems to us that arguments around four major issues will characterize the forthcoming generations, or moments, of the history of qualitative research. These issues are the reconnection of social science to social purpose, the rise of indigenous social science(s) crafted for the local needs of indigenous peoples, the decolonization of the academy, and the return "home" of Western social scientists as they work in their own settings using approaches that are vastly different from those employed by their predecessors. We provide some explanation of each of these major issues in the pages that follow. We then complete our forecast by discussing other issues that we believe will mark the next moment.

The Reconnection of Social Science to Social Purpose

Ruth Bleier (1984, 1986) has argued that the resources available to social science are too short, too scarce, to be used simply to satisfy scientific curiosity. Rather, she proposes, social science research should be driven by an ameliorative purpose; it should seek to solve some problem, to allay some maldistribution of resources, to meet a genuine need. Too often, however, guided by the modernist presupposition of objectivity in science, social scientists have lost sight of the purposive, intentional meanings of their work, circled back to their disciplinary roots, and left to chance and heaven the wending of findings into the policy arena. In contrast, seeking an engaged social science leads to what Conklin (2003) and Wildavsky (1975) have called "speaking truth to power." Addressing the issue of indigenous advocacy, Conklin (2003) suggests that "we can start to sort out these sticky issues," particularly the places where "the priorities of academic and activists diverge," by "locating points where professional ethics and political effectiveness converge" (p. 5). Roth (1990) suggests much the same thing when he observes that "anthropological knowledge [indeed, any putative knowledge] is also to be judged in regard to how it integrates with what else passes as knowledge" (p. 276).

The professional ethics issue that has begun to engage social scientists, particularly interpretivist qualitative researchers, most forcefully is the issue of social justice. The coupling of historically reified structures of oppression—whether educational, medical, ecological, nutritional, economic, social, or cultural—with unjust distribution of social goods and services creates a flood tide of injustice that threatens to engulf developed and developing nations and indigenous peoples alike.

The rise of a new ethic—communitarian, egalitarian, democratic, critical, caring, engaged, performative, social justice oriented—and a new emphasis on ethics that includes the reformulation of ethical issues in response to the new felt ethic signals a new interpretive community (Christians & Traber, 1997; de Laine, 2000; Zeni, 2001; see also Christians, Chapter 6, this volume). This new community is characterized by a sense of "interpersonal responsibility" (Mieth, 1997, p. 93) and moral obligation on the part of qualitative researchers, responsibility and obligation to participants, to respondents, to consumers of research, and to themselves as qualitative fieldworkers. This includes the quality of "*being with* and *for* the other, not *looking at*" the other (de Laine, 2000, p. 16). The new participatory, feminist, and democratic values of interpretive qualitative research mandate a stance that is democratic, reciprocal, and reciprocating rather than objective and objectifying.

The methods and methodologies game is not for members of the Western or European interpretive community only, however. The rise of multiple voices, some of them previously all but ignored by Eurocentric researchers, heralds a new era in qualitative inquiry. The firmness with which African American, Asian American, Native American, Latina/o, and border voices have begun to assert themselves lends a frisson of excitement, uncertainty, anticipation, and unpredictability to the field. These developments are yet another characteristic of the next wave, the eighth and ninth moments.

The Rise of Indigenous Social Science(s)

The rise of a social science that is indigenously designed and indigenously executed, more or less independent of Western or colonial and postcolonial influences, except where invited, is already a reality (De Soto & Dudwick, 2000; Fahim, 1982; Gugelberger, 1996; Gupta & Ferguson, 1997, 1999; Harrison, 2001; Smith, 1999; see also in this volume Smith, Chapter 4; Bishop, Chapter 5). Indigenism, a label once paradoxically manipulated to distinguish between the so-called civilized and the uncivilized (Ramos, 1998), now provides a framework for both critique of Western deployment of social science methods among native peoples and the creative genesis of new forms of systematic inquiry into community conditions, problems, and concerns devised by members of indigenous communities themselves. As we point out in Chapter 1 of this volume, Linda Tuhiwai Smith (1999) succinctly describes the state of social science research in her own Māori community as well as other indigenous communities: "The term 'research' is inextricably linked to European imperialism and colonialism" because "imperialism frames the indigenous experience. It is part of our story, our version of modernity" (pp. 1, 19).

Why should this generative spirit arise in social science at this particular moment in history? A tremendous number of forces have collided in the political economy of nations to create conditions that are favorable for subaltern and indigenous peoples to speak. Most prominent among these forces are the rising numbers of individuals from indigenous communities who have achieved terminal degrees and taken their places on faculties or in other positions where they can make their voices heard; the forces of globalization, which have enabled individuals all around the world to be connected via media in ways unknown a generation ago; a profound resistance to some forms of this same globalization and its Westernized, late-capitalist formations that result in the importation of Western ideas and corporatist values at the expense of local and indigenous languages, cultures, customs, and traditions; and the deep desire for self-determination among indigenous peoples everywhere. Education (and, more generally, literacy), access to means of mass communication (including the Internet), and powerful urges toward voice, liberty, and self-determination have foregrounded the dreams of oppressed peoples all over the globe. Indigenous voices are not all heard in the same ways, however; rather, the geography of place (Bhabha, 1990; Gupta & Ferguson, 1999) lends a distinctive tang to the expression of indigenous desire, as do indigenous peoples' particular experiences of colonialism and postcolonialism.

Indigenous voices in Latin America. Yúdice (1996) has a slightly different take on the emergence of indigenous assertions to the right to speak:

> More than any other form of writing in Latin America, the *testimonio* has contributed to the demise of the traditional role of the intellectual/artist as spokesperson for the "voiceless." As some major writers . . . increasingly take neoconservative positions and as the subordinated and oppressed feel more enabled to opt to speak for themselves in the wake of the new social movements, Liberation Theology, and other consciousness-raising grassroots movements, there is less of a social and cultural imperative for concerned writers to heroically assume the grievances and demands of the oppressed. . . .
>
> In contrast, the *testimonialista* gives his or her personal testimony "directly," addressing a specific interlocutor. . . . The speaker does not speak for or represent a community but rather performs an act of identity-formation that is simultaneously personal and collective. (p. 42)

Yúdice's implication is that when the intellectual/artist retreated into neoconservative (or neoliberal) political stances, the subordinated found a need to speak for themselves. And they did so, although not through any genre or rhetorical form known in the conventions of Western writing, or from any political stance previously recognized in Western literary traditions. *Testimonio,* a particularly Latin American form, serves the critical historical function of *witnessing* (see in this volume Beverley, Chapter 22; Hartnett & Engels, Chapter 41), often in the form of testifying to events unknown or unwitnessed by Western and colonial/postcolonial observers. *Testimonio* serves the political function of supporting solidarity while also serving the psychological purpose of establishing a separate and clear cultural identity for the group whose identity is being witnessed. In some ways, *testimonio* is unique among indigenous writings in that both its form and its political capacity are quite unknown in the Eurocentric and colonial rhetorical panoply.

Native voices in India and the Middle East. The experience of postcolonialism and an oppositional ethnographic method are worked out very differently in India and the Middle East (Mohanty, 1988; O'Hanlon, 1988). Whereas Latin American forms, particularly *testimonio* (but also other forms of writing around the oppressed), appear to focus little, if at all, on the relationship between the colonized and the colonizer, Indian, Middle and Near Eastern, and south Asian indigenous writings are frequently indexed to a sharp awareness of the presence of the colonizer and postcolonizer. The works of Ashis Nandy, Edward Said, Chandra Mohanty, Gayatri Spivak, and Homi Bhabha explore this colonial presence in several ways: by deconstructing how this presence has been responsible for suppressing or destroying portions of national or regional identities and languages, by capturing a mourning for what has been lost, by exploring indigenous means for recovering the lost "self" of national identity, and by providing critiques of the ways in which representations created—indeed, invented—by the West have shaped ongoing relations between the East and West (Said, 1979) in arenas as wide ranging as tourism and foreign policy. Indeed, as all of these authors have argued (albeit in different ways), social scientists' failure to grasp the cultural grounds and boundaries of the colonized has led to recurring missteps, gaffes, and social and political displacements. Much of the indigenous critique that proceeds from the Orient, consequently, revolves around the deconstruction of the culture-erasing effects of colonialism and postcolonialism; it does not seek a specific genre of ancient knowledge in which to ground new forms of social inquiry or autocritique (Conklin, 2003).

Indigenous inquiry at the antipodes and the United States. Harrison (2001) notes that the voices of the indigenous peoples of Australia, New Zealand, the United States, and Canada are often juxtaposed for the simple reason that

> the First Nations peoples of Canada, Native Americans and Alaska Natives in the United States, Aborigines in Australia, and Māori in New Zealand have established regular means of communicating about the things that they now have in common. . . . Political movements aimed at achieving recognition

> of sovereignty of indigenous groups have developed among the indigenous peoples in all four countries. (p. 23)

In these four countries, indigenous peoples have established a particular form of relationship with the federal governments that now shapes a distinctive collective dialogue around political movement toward self-determination for indigenous peoples as well as issues of education, health care, and social welfare, broadly conceived. It is from the indigenous peoples in these countries that we have both the clearest critique of modernist social science and the richest proposal for an indigenous knowledge-based education (Ah Nee-Benham & Cooper, 2000) and inquiry model (Smith, 1999).

A variety of indigenous groups have proposed guidelines for social science that take account of signal characteristics deeply embedded in non-Western cosmologies and epistemologies. Three elements of such guidelines are especially sensitive and telling. First, in manifestos and agreements indigenous peoples from these four countries and others have asserted their right to have "all investigations in our territories . . . carried out with our consent and under joint control and guidance" (Charter of the Indigenous Tribal Peoples of the Tropical Forests, as quoted in Smith, 1999, p. 119). This is a clear indication that although social scientists may find that collaboration is possible, or even useful, they can no longer carry on with their usual practice of simply inserting themselves into the context to study what and when they will.

Second, indigenous peoples in many parts of the world, but especially the four nations that frame this discussion, are troubling the entire process of researchers' seeking informed consent and institutional review board approval. One of us (Yvonna) first became aware of this at a conference in Australia when an audience member respectfully informed her that Aboriginal tribal elders consider the use of informed consent forms insulting, and so researchers working with this population in Australia simply do not use such forms. Given that Australian federal law requires a process similar to that required in the United States, in that researchers must secure the informed consent of all human participants in a research project, Yvonna asked the audience member what researchers in Australia do about this requirement; he simply replied, shrugging his shoulders, "We ignore it." We have no idea how a local institutional review board may feel about this course of action, but it is quite clear that Australian Aborigines have made their own decisions regarding the utility of the informed consent process, and, as far as they are concerned, the federal government has no say in the matter. Indeed, Linda Smith (1999) outlines a whole series of objections that indigenous peoples have to this process, including the entirely Western assumption that it is the *individual* who owns knowledge and who can participate or withdraw from a study as she or he pleases. In many indigenous cultures this construction undermines the sense of the collective, the tribal, and the concept of communal and ancestral knowledge. That such knowledge should belong to all the members of a group is not a construct that rests easy in Western epistemologies, based as they are on 18th- and 19th-century philosophical formulations of the autonomous individual (Gergen, 1991).

Third, many indigenous peoples have now established their rights to exclusive ownership of their cultural and intellectual properties, including the right to "protect and control dissemination of that knowledge [about themselves]"; further, they have established that the "first beneficiaries of indigenous knowledge must be direct indigenous descendants of that knowledge" (Smith, 1999, pp. 118–119). Where tribal, cultural, or indigenous treaties, compacts, agreements, and other formal documents exist to support such rights, it is absolutely clear that Western scholars do not have first claim on the knowledge they may help to generate. Rather, they must negotiate for that knowledge and respect the forms in which the "owners" may wish to have it presented or re-presented. Indigenous peoples pursuing self-determination with ferocity and single-mindedness have successfully challenged Western scholars' propensity to believe that they can own whatever they appropriate.

In much the same way, and with the same effects, Canadian First Nations peoples have secured a status for themselves that includes extensive local control over education, Native language and cultural instruction, and health care and other social services. In some broad ways, Canadian First Nations peoples, the Māori in New Zealand, and Australia's Aborigines have stronger and clearer voices in their self-determination than do Native Americans and Native Hawaiians in the United States or South Pacific peoples (e.g., Tongans). Nevertheless, members of all these groups are able to articulate what respect for indigenous cultural customs and epistemologies might look like, and all have assumed increasing control over the form and shape of research conducted in their midst, with some groups retaining the right to determine the research agenda and the use of methods that display maximum cultural sensitivity. This is not true of indigenous peoples in all parts of the world (Reagan, 2005).

The Decolonization of the Academy

Finkelstein, Seal, and Schuster (1998) catalog the myriad changes currently under way in the American professoriate, none of which is more visible or has greater potential to change the face of academe than the "composition of the new entrants into the faculty" (p. xi). The startling gains of women in the past 15 years, of non-native-born faculty members, of faculty of color (the most impressive gains being made by women faculty of color), and of Asians and Pacific Islanders on faculties point to a dramatic demographic shift between new hires and senior faculty (those nearing retirement). Further, the greatest changes have occurred in public, doctoral-granting institutions, with public comprehensive institutions next and private doctoral-granting institutions third.[2]

Because the greatest demographic shift is occurring in institutions that grant doctoral and master's degrees, the most profound impact of this massive diversification in the faculty ranks is being felt, at least immediately, in graduate research (Finkelstein et al., 1998). Beyond the forces impinging on graduate study, this shift is resulting in two additional changes. First, new faculty members are far less wedded to traditional forms of academic reporting than were their predecessors. Particularly in the social sciences, they are more interested in newer theoretical currents that suggest the dividing line between art and science is far more fluid and permeable than the previous academic generation believed it to be. As a consequence, the very shapes and forms of texts—whether books, journal articles, or conference presentations—are likely to be less traditional. Experimental, "messy," layered poetic and performance texts are beginning to appear in journals and on conference podiums. Second, the students of these new faculty tend to be equally comfortable with experimentation, and they are increasingly preparing research papers and dissertations that are, at a minimum, bilingual—writings that address the needs of multiple rather than singular audiences, often across national borders (see, for instance, Gonzaléz y Gonzaléz, 2004). They deploy this kind of strategy deliberately, with a globalized impact in mind. Models of academic research such as Anzaldúa's (1999) bilingual, border-focused work open up possibilities for students, especially as these many-layered and multilingual texts have become textbooks for graduate study. It is no longer unheard of, or even strange, for students to produce doctoral dissertations that include portions that some of the members of their dissertation committees may not be able to translate.

The decolonization of the academy is taking other forms as well. The influx into the American professoriate of vast numbers of individuals who were not born in the United States has brought cultural richness and diversity of experience to academia, but these individuals have also brought with them traditions that are different from those of earlier faculty, including the peculiarly American tradition of shared governance. A consequence of this may be an inadvertent undermining of the extent to which faculty participate in policy making and administrative decision making. In the same vein, just as new European theoretical currents have become deeply embedded in critical research and curricular concerns, the globalizing influence of international faculty may lead to a more pronounced set of sensibilities regarding the cultural, political, and artistic variety that is possible and desirable as a positive outcome of globalization.

International faculty also bring to U.S. colleges and universities both subtle and pronounced differences in modes of graduate training and graduate mentoring. Institutions of higher education in the United States have grappled for some time with the issue of how to mentor graduate students, including how to socialize them into faculty roles of their own. The perspectives of international faculty members, as well as those of the increasing numbers of faculty of color, bring to the fore new considerations regarding what mentoring might mean and how different forms of mentoring might be effective for diverse students (and for diverse new young faculty members, for that matter; see Stanley & Lincoln, 2005) as well as how the academy's range and repertoire of possible collegial relationships may be expanded through mentoring. Each of these changes opens the academy to decolonization by lessening the hegemony of the Western canon and creating a new consciousness of global citizenry.

Most important, the infusion into U.S. institutions of non-Western, indigenous, and "colored" epistemologies has created a vital mix of new paradigmatic perspectives, new methods and strategies for research, contested means for establishing validity in texts, new criteria for judging research and scholarship, and competing cosmologies from which knowledge and understanding might grow. The era of a shared and largely modernist model of inquiry has likely passed away. Some scholarship will still be presented and judged from a positivist paradigm, but other scholarship will be traveling the margins and borders, searching for new and innovative forms through which to express non-Western modes of knowing and being in the world.

The Homecoming of Western Social Science

Perhaps the most striking hallmark of the next moment will be the reconsideration of how the social sciences are practiced in the West as well. The phenomenological, postpositivist, postmodern, emancipatory, qualitative, liberationist sensibility that challenges modernist master narratives holds within it the seeds of a reformulated vision of what the social sciences might accomplish and how ethnographers might reconnoiter what they have already produced for evidence of its contributions to a democratic imaginary on its own soil.

We are now approaching a serious moral confrontation in Western social science. On the one hand, some social scientists (including the two of us and the contributors to this volume) are examining critically the purposes and projects of past and future social science, questioning whether, when, and under what conditions our knowledge has served to enhance democratic ends and extend social justice as well as when and under what conditions it has served to reify historical power and resource distributions. On the other hand, other, equally responsible, inquirers and researchers are seeking to reestablish the supremacy of "one method/one truth," the "gold standard" of research strategies. Political battles that are normally fought in legislative circles, leaving social scientists untouched and unmoved, have shifted directly into the arenas of educational, social, and behavioral sciences. The evolving political struggles between liberal and neoconservative/neoliberal views of the world have become progressively sharper and more distinct in Western life, concomitantly creating more fissures in American life than have existed for a half century. This is reflected in legislation affecting education (e.g., the No Child Left Behind Act of 2001) and in policy documents that represent stances on what research designs are to be considered appropriate and meaningful (e.g., National Research Council, 2002).

This is the first of the serious fractures in the social science community. What had been a sometimes mild-mannered disagreement between research methodologists, leading to a courteous détente between schools of thought (Lincoln, 2004), has become a firefight, with substantial resources, including funding through grants and contracts, and political and policy power hanging in the balance. This methodologically contested moment will not subside anytime soon.

In the meantime, qualitative research practitioners are engaged in earnest and consequential work of their own. Despite accusations of "advocacy" and of "ideology parading as intellectual inquiry" (Mosteller & Boruch, 2002, p. 2), postpositivist inquirers of all perspectives and paradigms have joined in the collective struggle for a socially responsive, democratic, communitarian, moral, and justice-promoting set of inquiry practices and interpretive processes (for a review of some of this literature, see Scheurich, 2002). The search for "culturally sensitive" research approaches—approaches that are attuned to the specific cultural practices of various groups and that "both recognize ethnicity and position culture as central to the research process" (Tillman, 2002)—is already under way (Anzaldúa, 1987; Bernal, 1998; Bishop, 1998; Collins, 2000; Dillard, 2000; Gunaratnam, 2003; Harrison, 2001; Hurtado, 1996; Parker & Lynn, 2002; Sandoval, 2000; Smith, 1999; Wing, 2000). Many of the issues associated with such approaches are captured with comprehensiveness and nuance in this volume. Qualitative researchers' concerns for social justice, moral purpose, and "liberation methodology" will mark this next moment with passion, urgency, purpose, and verve. When we argued in an earlier edition of this *Handbook* that qualitative research had "come of age," we were mistaken. It had merely reached a zesty and robustly athletic late youth. The genuine coming of age in methodology, we see now, will be the maturing of the field into a new set of practices and purposes—a new praxis that is deeply responsive and accountable to those it serves.

The Next Moment, the Fractured Future

We predict that in the ninth moment the world of methods will enter what we term a *fractured future*—a future in which, unless an intervention we cannot currently imagine takes place, methodologists will line up on two opposing sides of a great divide. Randomized field trials, touted as the "gold standard" of scientific educational research, will occupy the time of one group of researchers while the pursuit of a socially and cultural responsive, communitarian, justice-oriented set of studies will consume the meaningful working moments of another. A world in which both sides might be heard, and their results carefully considered as differently produced and differently purposed views on social realities, now seems somewhat far away, mixed-methods advocates notwithstanding.

In a battle where the warriors on the frontlines are fairly evenly matched and not much progress is being made, the skirmishes, conflicts, and engagements are likely to move elsewhere. We predict that the next encounter will be a scrimmage over federal ethics regulations. Extremely useful, but out of date for the purposes of qualitative research and entirely useless for the development of culturally, racially, and ethnically sensitive methods (for a critique of the ways in which federal regulations fail to respond to qualitative research, see Lincoln & Guba, 1989; but see also Lincoln, 2001), the current federal regulations—regarding informed consent, privacy of records, confidentiality, and the role of deception—form one kind of quality floor under research practices. As the American Association of University Professors (2001) has argued well, however, the current regulations and laws are better suited to biomedical research than to social science.

In the absence of a substantive effort to revisit the federal regulations on human subjects protections or any grave reconsideration of the applicability of the regulations either to the social sciences or, more specifically, to qualitative research (writ large, as in the pages of this book), several professional associations have constructed their own statements on professional and field ethics. The American Anthropological Association, the American Sociological Association, the American Historical Association, and the American Educational Research Association have all constructed exemplary statements on professional ethics. The American Anthropological

Association in particular has been extremely attentive to concerns about the rights of indigenous peoples, and the association's newsletter, *Anthropology News,* features a continuing dialogue, pursued for more than a decade, on field ethics, indigenous rights, and other ethical dilemmas of an "engaged anthropology."

We know from the applications of technology we see around us that technology frequently sweeps far ahead of both public policy and civic engagement in debates around public policy. The technologies associated with genetic engineering and cloning are good examples. Currently, scientists' ability to clone living organisms is much further advanced than any rational civic debate about whether and under what circumstances cloning should be allowed. We have no idea what Americans' "moral boiling point" is with respect to cloning. In precisely the same way, "McDonaldizing," "corporatizing," and globalizing efforts around the world have ensnared social scientists who wish to understand the effects of late capitalism's expansion and penetration around the globe. Technologies and technoimaginaries of communication, travel, and cyberspace have far outpaced deliberate and considered debate about what is moral, useful, and culturally respectful. The ethics, aesthetics, and teleologies necessary for a globalized world have not yet come into being, although they are being born in this volume and elsewhere. Social scientists, men and women of conscience, are devising their own standards in collaboration with indigenous peoples, people of color, and marginalized groups everywhere, but it would be heartening to see the U.S. federal government take some additional leadership role in this arena.

Qualitative researchers in the next moment will face another struggle, too, around the continuing issue of representation. On the one hand, creating open-ended, problematic, critical, polyphonic texts, given the linearity of written formats and the poststructural problem of the distance between representation and reality(ies), grows more difficult. On the other hand, engaging performative forms of social science can be difficult in many venues. Traditional texts are far more portable, albeit far less emotionally compelling. Performing social justice, examining ways in which our work can serve social justice, may be the teleological framework for a reimagined social science. Attention to the representations we make, to the possibility that messages may further disenfranchise or oppress (Fine, Weis, Weseen, & Wong, 2000; see also Tedlock, Chapter 18, this volume) when they begin circulating in the wider world, and respect for the wisdom of people who are not like us, who know all too well the unfortunate images that surround their lives, may be the start of our performance of justice. It is a place to begin.

Notes

1. Ivan Brady (2004) makes this point in a recent journal article titled "In Defense of the Sensual," as do Hartnett and Engels in Chapter 41 of this volume: The "unfinalizable" nature of ethnography arises not so much from the problem of unknowables (although they always exist) as it does from the overriding problem of plural "knowabilities" and the frustration that having to choose among them causes. Worse still for the researcher is having someone choose for him or her, some individual or some institution with the power to enforce the choice. See Brady(2004, p. 632).

2. Finkelstein et al. (1998) make the point that public institutions of higher education have diversified more swiftly than have private institutions, likely because of public pressures to do so. This has resulted in the exposure of a broader range of graduate students to diversity, given that public institutions, as a group, typically produce more doctorates than do private institutions in any given period of time.

References

Ah Nee-Benham, M. K. P., & Cooper, J. E. (Eds.). (2000). *Indigenous educational models for contemporary practice: In our mother's voice.* Mahwah, NJ: Lawrence Erlbaum.

Alasuutari, P. (2004). The globalization of qualitative research. In C. Seale, G. Gobo, J. F. Gubrium, & D. Silverman (Eds.), *Qualitative research practice* (pp. 595–608). London: Sage.

American Association of University Professors. (2001). Protecting human beings: Institutional review boards and social science research. *Academe, 87*(3), 55–67.

Anzaldúa, G. (1999). *Borderlands/la frontera: The new mestiza* (2nd ed.). San Francisco: Aunt Lute.

Bernal, D. (1998). Using a Chicana feminist epistemology in educational research. *Harvard Educational Review, 68,* 555–582.

Bhabha, H. K. (Ed.). (1990). *Nation and narration.* New York: Routledge.

Bishop, R. (1998). Freeing ourselves from neocolonial domination in research: A Māori approach to creating knowledge. *International Journal of Qualitative Studies in Education, 11,* 199–219.

Bleier, R. (1984). *Science and gender: A critique of biology and its theories on women.* Oxford: Pergamon.

Bleier, R. (Ed.). (1986). *Feminist approaches to science.* Oxford: Pergamon.

Brady, I. (2004). In defense of the sensual: Meaning construction in ethnography and poetics. *Qualitative Inquiry, 10,* 622–644.

Cannella, G. S., & Lincoln, Y. S. (2004a). Dangerous discourses II: Comprehending and countering the redeployment of discourses (and resources) in the generation of liberatory inquiry. *Qualitative Inquiry, 10,* 165–174.

Cannella, G. S., & Lincoln, Y. S. (2004b). Epilogue: Claiming a critical public social science—reconceptualizing and redeploying research. *Qualitative Inquiry, 10,* 298–309.

Christians, C. G., & Traber, M. (Eds.). (1997). *Communication ethics and universal values.* Thousand Oaks, CA: Sage.

Collins, P. H. (2000). *Black feminist thought: Knowledge, consciousness, and the politics of empowerment* (2nd ed.). New York: Routledge.

Conklin, B. (2003, October). Speaking truth to power: Mapping an engaged anthropology. *Anthropology News, 44,* 5.

de Laine, M. (2000). *Fieldwork, participation and practice: Ethics and dilemmas in qualitative research.* London: Sage.

De Soto, H. G., & Dudwick, N. (2000). *Fieldwork dilemmas: Anthropologists in postsocialist states.* Madison: University of Wisconsin Press.

Dillard, C. (2000). The substance of things hoped for, the evidence of things not seen: Examining an endarkened feminist epistemology in educational research an leadership. *International Journal of Qualitative Studies in Education, 13,* 661–681.

Fahim, H. (Ed.). (1982). *Indigenous anthropology in non-Western countries.* Durham, NC: Carolina Academic Press.

Fine, M., Weis, L., Weseen, S., & Wong, L. (2000). For whom? Qualitative research, representations, and social responsibilities. In N. K. Denzin & Y. S. Lincoln (Eds.), *Handbook of qualitative research* (2nd ed., pp. 107–131). Thousand Oaks, CA: Sage.

Finkelstein, M. J., Seal, R. K., & Schuster, J. H. (1998). *The new academic generation: A profession in transformation.* Baltimore: Johns Hopkins University Press.

Fukuyama, F. (1989, Summer). The end of history? *National Interest, 16,* 3–18.

Fukuyama, F. (1992). *The end of history and the last man.* New York: Free Press.

Geertz, C. (1995). *After the fact: Two countries, four decades, one anthropologist.* Cambridge, MA: Harvard University Press.

Gergen, K. J. (1991). *The saturated self: Dilemmas of identity in contemporary life.* New York: Basic Books.

Gonzaléz y Gonzaléz, E. M. (2004). *Perceptions of selected senior administrators of higher education institutions in Mexico regarding needed administrative competencies.* Unpublished doctoral dissertation, Texas A&M University.

Gugelberger, G. M. (Ed.). (1996). *The real thing: Testimonial discourse and Latin America.* Durham, NC: Duke University Press.

Gunaratnam, Y. (2003). *Researching "race" and ethnicity: Methods, knowledge and power.* London: Sage.

Gupta, A., & Ferguson, J. (Eds.). (1997). *Anthropological locations: Boundaries and grounds of a field science.* Berkeley: University of California Press.

Gupta, A., & Ferguson, J. (Eds.). (1999). *Culture, power, place: Explorations in critical anthropology.* Durham, NC: Duke University Press.

Hammersley, M. (1999). Not bricolage, but boatbuilding: Exploring two metaphors for thinking about ethnography. *Journal of Contemporary Ethnography, 28,* 574–585.

Harrison, B. (2001). *Collaborative programs in indigenous communities: From fieldwork to practice.* Walnut Creek, CA: AltaMira.

Hurtado, A. (1996). *The color of privilege: Three blasphemies on race and feminism.* Ann Arbor: University of Michigan Press.

Lincoln, Y. S. (2001). Varieties of validity: Quality in qualitative research. In J. C. Smart (Ed.), *Higher education: Handbook of theory and research* (Vol. 16, pp. 25–72). New York: Agathon.

Lincoln, Y. S. (2004). From disdain to détente and back again [Review essay on the National Research Council's *Scientific research in education* and Mosteller and Boruch's *Evidence matters: Randomized trials in education research*]. *Academe, 90*(6).

Lincoln, Y. S., & Cannella, G. S. (2004a). Dangerous discourses: Methodological conservatism and governmental regimes of truth. *Qualitative Inquiry, 10,* 5–14.

Lincoln, Y. S., & Cannella, G. S. (2004b). Qualitative research, power, and the radical Right. *Qualitative Inquiry, 10,* 175–201.

Lincoln, Y. S., & Guba, E. G. (1989). Ethics: The failure of positivist science. *Review of Higher Education, 12,* 221–240.

Mieth, D. (1997). The basic norm of truthfulness: Its ethical justification and universality. In C. G. Christians & M. Traber (Eds.), *Communication ethics and universal values* (pp. 87–104). Thousand Oaks, CA: Sage.

Mohanty, C. T. (1988). Under Western eyes: Feminist scholarship and colonial discourses. *Feminist Review, 30,* 61–88.

Mosteller, F., & Boruch, R. (2002). Overview and new directions. In F. Mosteller & R. Boruch (Eds.), *Evidence matters: Randomized trials in education research* (pp. 1–14). Washington, DC: Brookings Institution Press.

National Research Council (2002). *Scientific research in education.* Committee on Scientific Principles for Education Research (R. J. Shavelson & L. Towne, Eds.). Center for Education, Division of Behavioral and Social Sciences and Education. Washington, DC: National Academy Press.

O'Hanlon, R. (1988). Recovering the subject: Subaltern studies and histories of resistance in colonial South Asia. *Modern Asian Studies, 22,* 189–224.

Parker, L., & Lynn, M. (2002). What's race got to do with it? Critical race theory's conflict with and connections to qualitative research methodology and epistemology. *Qualitative Inquiry, 8,* 7–22.

Ragin, C. C., Nagel, J., & White, P. (2004). *Workshop on scientific foundations of qualitative research.* Arlington, VA: National Science Foundation.

Ramos, A. R. (1998). *Indigenism: Ethnic politics in Brazil.* Madison: University of Wisconsin Press.

Reagan, T. (2005). *Non-Western educational traditions: Indigenous approaches to educational thought and practice* (3rd ed.). Mahwah, NJ: Lawrence Erlbaum.

Roth, P. A. (1990). Comment on "Is anthropology art or science?" *Current Anthropology, 31,* 275–276.

Said, E. (1979). *Orientalism.* New York: Pantheon.

Sandoval, C. (2000). *Methodology of the oppressed.* Minneapolis: University of Minnesota Press.

Scheurich, J. J. (Ed.). (2002). *Anti-racist scholarship: An advocacy.* Albany: State University of New York Press.

Smith, L. T. (1999). *Decolonizing methodologies: Research and indigenous peoples.* London: Zed.

Stanley, C. A., & Lincoln, Y. S. (2005, March-April). Cross-race faculty mentoring. *Change, 37*(2), 44–50.

Tillman, L. C. (2002). Culturally sensitive research approaches: An African-American perspective. *Educational Researcher, 31*(9), 3–12.

Wildavsky, A. (1975). *Speaking truth to power: The art and craft of policy analysis.* New Brunswick, NJ: Transaction.

Wing, A. K. (Ed.). (2000). *Global critical race feminism: An international reader.* New York: New York University Press.

Yúdice, G. (1996). *Testimonio* and postmodernism. In G. M. Gugelberger (Ed.), *The real thing: Testimonial discourse and Latin America* (pp. 42–52). Durham, NC: Duke University Press.

Zeni, J. (Ed.). (2001). *Ethical issues in practitioner research.* New York: Teachers College Press.

AUTHOR INDEX

SUBJECT INDEX

ABOUT THE EDITORS

Norman K. Denzin is Distinguished Professor of Communications, College of Communications Scholar, and Research Professor of Communications, Sociology, and Humanities at the University of Illinois, Urbana–Champaign. He is the author of numerous books, including *Interpretive Ethnography: Ethnographic Practices for the 21st Century; The Cinematic Society: The Voyeur's Gaze; Images of Postmodern Society; The Research Act: A Theoretical Introduction to Sociological Methods; Interpretive Interactionism; Hollywood Shot by Shot; The Recovering Alcoholic;* and *The Alcoholic Self,* which won the Charles Cooley Award from the Society for the Study of Symbolic Interaction in 1988. In 1997, the Study of Symbolic Interaction presented him the George Herbert Award. He is the editor of the *Sociological Quarterly,* coeditor of *Qualitative Inquiry,* and editor of the book series *Cultural Studies: A Research Annual and Studies in Symbolic Interaction.*

Yvonna S. Lincoln is Ruth Harrington Chair of Educational Leadership and Distinguished Professor of Higher Education at Texas A&M University. In addition to this volume, she is coeditor of the first and second editions of the *Handbook of Qualitative Research,* the journal *Qualitative Inquiry* (with Norman K. Denzin), and the Teaching and Learning section of the *American Educational Research Journal* (with Bruce Thompson and Stephanie Knight). She is the coauthor, with Egon Guba, of *Naturalistic Inquiry, Effective Evaluation, and Fourth Generation Evaluation,* the editor of *Organizational Theory and Inquiry,* and the coeditor of several other books with William G. Tierney and with Norman Denzin. She is the recipient of numerous awards for research and has published journal articles, chapters, and conference papers on higher education, research university libraries, and alternative paradigm inquiry.

ABOUT THE CONTRIBUTORS

Bryant Keith Alexander is Professor in the Department of Communication Studies at California State University, Los Angeles. His research is grounded in the social and performative construction of identity as related to issues of race, culture, and gender and uses qualitative, critical, and performative methodologies, including performative writing, interpretive ethnography, and autoethnography. Most recently, he has turned to cultural geography, studies in which he focuses on the spatial constitution of society through the mediating effects of culture. His essays have appeared in *Qualitative Inquiry, Theatre Annual, Theatre Topics, Callaloo,* and *Text and Performance Quarterly*, among others. He has chapters in *The Image of the Outsider; Beacon Best 2000: Best Writing of Men and Women of All Colors; Communication, Race, and Family;* and *The Future of Performance Studies.* He is coeditor of the *Performance Theories in Education: Power, Pedagogy, and the Politics of Identity* and serves as the section editor of the forthcoming *Handbook of Performance Studies* (Sage). In 2002, he was honored with the Norman K. Denzin Outstanding Qualitative Research Award from the Carl Couch Center, Department of Communication Studies, University of Northern Iowa for his essay, "(Re)Visioning the Ethnographic Site: Interpretive Ethnography as a Method of Pedagogical Reflexivity and Scholarly Production."

Michael V. Angrosino is Professor of Anthropology at the University of South Florida, where his research and teaching specializations include mental health policy analysis, the influence of organized religion on contemporary social policy, and the methodology of oral history. He has served as editor of *Human Organization*, the journal of the Society for Applied Anthropology, and as general editor of the Southern Anthropological Society's Proceedings Series for the University of Georgia Press. Among his most recent books are *Opportunity House: Ethnographic Stories of Mental Retardation* (1998), an experiment in alternative ethnographic writing, and *The Culture of the Sacred*, an overview of the anthropology of religion.

Paul Atkinson is Distinguished Research Professor in Sociology at Cardiff University, United Kingdom. He is Associate Director of the ESRC Research Centre on Social and Economic Aspects of Genomics. His main research interests are the sociology of medical knowledge and the development of qualitative research methods. His publications include *Ethnography: Principles in Practice* (with Martyn Hammersley, 1983 and 1995), *The Clinical Experience* (1981 and 1997), *The Ethnographic Imagination* (1990), *Understanding Ethnographic Texts* (1992), *Medical Talk and Medical Work* (1995), *Fighting Familiarity* (with Sara Delamont, 1995), *Making Sense of Qualitative Data* (with Amanda Coffey, 1996), *Sociological Readings and Re-Readings* (1996), and *Interactionism* (with William Housley, 2003). Together with Sara Delamont, he edits the journal

Qualitative Research. He was coeditor of *The Handbook of Ethnography* (2002). His ethnographic study of an international opera company is published as *Everyday Arias: Making Opera Work* (2005). He is an Academician of the Academy for the Learned Societies in the Social Sciences.

Zygmunt Bauman is Professor Emeritus at Leeds and also at the University of Warsaw. Before coming to Leeds in 1972, he was with the University of Warsaw and the University of Tel Aviv. Dr. Bauman has held several visiting professorships and is known throughout the world as one of the 20th century's great social theorists and foremost sociologist of postmodernity. He has published more than 20 books, including *Legislators and Interpreters* (1987), *Modernity and the Holocaust* (1989), *Modernity and Ambivalence* (1991), and *Postmodern Ethics* (1993). In 1990, the year of his retirement, he was awarded the Amalfi European Prize and, in 1998, the Adorno Prize.

John Beverley is Professor and Chair of the Department of Hispanic Languages and Literatures at the University of Pittsburgh, where he has taught for 35 years. He was a founding member and co-coordinator of the Latin American Subaltern Studies Group between 1992 and 2002, the year of its demise. His recent books include *Subalternity and Representation* (1999, 2004), *From Cuba* (Ed., 2003); and *Testimonio: On the Politics of Truth* (2004). He coedits the University of Pittsburgh Press series *Illuminations: Cultural Formations of the Americas.*

Russell Bishop is foundation Professor and Assistant Dean for Māori Education in the School of Education at the University of Waikato, Hamilton, New Zealand. He has taught in secondary schools in New Zealand and the Cook Islands. Prior to his present appointment, he was a senior lecturer in Māori Education at the University of Otago and also Interim Director for Otago University's Teacher Education program. His research experience is in the area of collaborative storying in Māori contexts, having written a book *Collaborative Research Stories: Whakawhanaungatanga* and published internationally on this topic. His other research interests include strategies for implementing the Treaty of Waitangi in tertiary institutions, intercultural education, and collaborative storying as pedagogy. The latter area is the subject of a book, *Culture Counts: Changing Power Relationships in Classrooms* (coauthored with Ted Glynn, 1999), which demonstrates how the experiences developed from within kaupapa Māori settings, schooling, research, and policy development can be applied to mainstream educational settings. He is currently the project director for a New Zealand Ministry-of-Education-funded research/professional development project that seeks to improve the educational achievement of Māori students in mainstream classrooms.

Ivan Brady is Distinguished Teaching Professor and Chair of Anthropology at the State University of New York at Oswego. A former President of the Society for Humanistic Anthropology and Chair of the Association for Social Anthropology in Oceania, he also served as Book Review Editor of the *American Anthropologist* for seven years. He is the editor or coeditor of several books and dozens of chapters, articles, and reviews. His poetry has appeared in various books and journals, including *Reflections: The Anthropological Muse* (1985); *The American Tradition in Qualitative Research* (2001); *The Qualitative Inquiry Reader* (2002); the *Neuroanthropology Network Newsletter; Anthropology and Humanism; drunken boat: online journal of the arts; Pendulum; Cultural Studies↔ Critical Methodologies;* and *Qualitative Inquiry.* His latest book is *The Time at Darwin's Reef: Poetic Explorations in Anthropology and History.*

Kathy Charmaz is Professor of Sociology and Coordinator of the Faculty Writing Program at Sonoma State University in Rohnert Park, California. She assists faculty in writing for publication and leads three faculty seminars on writing. She teaches in the areas of sociological theory, social psychology, qualitative methods, health and illness, and gerontology. In addition to writing numerous chapters and articles, she has written or coedited five books, including *Good Days, Bad Days: The Self in Chronic Illness and Time,* which won awards from the Pacific Sociological Association and the Society for the Study of

Symbolic Interaction. Her recent publications focus on medical sociology, qualitative methods, and social psychology and include a number of articles and chapters on grounded theory. Dr. Charmaz has served as the president of the Pacific Sociological Association, vice-president of the Society for the Study of Symbolic Interaction, and editor of *Symbolic Interaction.* She is the chair-elect of the Medical Sociology Section of the American Sociological Association.

Susan E. Chase is Chair and Associate Professor of Sociology and a cofounder of the Women's Studies Program at the University of Tulsa. She is the author of *Ambiguous Empowerment: The Work Narratives of Women School Superintendents,* which analyzes how women educational leaders narrate their competence and accomplishments on one hand and their experiences of gender and racial discrimination on the other. She also coauthored *Mothers and Children: Feminist Analyses and Personal Narratives* (with Mary Rogers), a synthesis of feminist social science theory and research on mothers, mothering, and motherhood over the last 30 years.

Julianne Cheek is Professor at the University of South Australia in the Division of Health Sciences in Adelaide and Director of Early Career Researcher Development. She is recognized internationally for her expertise in qualitative research in health-related areas. She has attracted funding for many qualitative research projects, with some 19 projects funded in the past four years including five consecutive Australian Research Council grants. She has also attracted large sums of funding for projects related to teaching that have qualitative principles embedded within them. Professor Cheek has published over 60 refereed book chapters and journal articles, many of which explore the application of postmodern and poststructural approaches to health care. Her latest book is *Postmodern and Poststructural Approaches to Nursing Research* (Sage, 2000).

Clifford G. Christians is Research Professor of Communications at the University of Illinois, Urbana–Champaign. He has been a visiting scholar in philosophical ethics at Princeton University and in social ethics at the University of Chicago, as well as a PEW Fellow in Ethics at Oxford University. He completed the third edition of Rivers and Schramm's *Responsibility in Mass Communication,* has coauthored *Jacques Ellul: Interpretive Essays* with Jay Van Hook, and has written *Teaching Ethics in Journalism Education* with Catherine Covert. He is also the coauthor, with John Ferre and Mark Fackler, of *Good News: Social Ethics and the Press* (1993). His *Media Ethics: Cases and Moral Reasoning* with Kim Rotzoll, Mark Fackler and Kathy McKee is now in its seventh edition (2005). *Communication Ethics and Universal Values,* coauthored with Michael Traber, was published in 1997, and his book with Sharon Bracci, *Moral Engagement in Public Life: Theorists for Contemporary Ethics* appeared in 2002. He has lectured or given academic papers on ethics in Norway, Russia, Finland, France, Belgium, Italy, Netherlands, England, Switzerland, Singapore, Korea, Scotland, Philippines, Slovenia, Canada, Brazil, Mexico, Puerto Rico, Spain, Sweden, Hong Kong, and Taiwan.

Benjamin F. Crabtree, Ph.D., is a medical anthropologist and Professor and Director of Research in the Department of Family Medicine, UMDNJ-Robert Wood Johnson Medical School. He is also Associate Editor for the *Annals of Family Medicine.* As a full-time primary care/health services researcher in family medicine for more than 15 years, Dr. Crabtree has contributed to numerous articles and chapters on both qualitative and quantitative methods, covering topics ranging from time series analysis and log-linear models to in-depth interviews, case study research, and qualitative analysis strategies. Dr. Crabtree is coeditor (with William Miller) of *Doing Qualitative Research,* a Sage book now in its 2nd edition. He has been principal investigator on federally funded grants from the Agency for Healthcare Research and Quality, the National Cancer Institute, and the National Heart, Lung, and Blood Institute. These grants integrate qualitative methods with concepts from complexity science to better understand the differential responses primary care practices have to interventions and to design strategies for enhancing quality of patient care.

Sara Delamont is Reader in Sociology at Cardiff University, United Kingdom, and an Academician of the Academy for the Learned Societies in the Social Sciences. She was the first woman to be President of the British Education Research Association, and the first woman to be Dean of Social Sciences at Cardiff. Her research interests are educational ethnography, the anthropology of the Mediterranean and Brazil, and gender. Of her twelve published books, the best known is *Interaction in the Classroom* (1976 and 1983), and her favorites are *Knowledgeable Women* (1989) and *Appetities and Identities* (1995). Her most recent books are *Fieldwork in Educational Settings* (2002), *Feminist Sociology* (2003), and *Key Themes in Qualitative Research* (2003), written with Paul Atkinson and Amanda Coffey. She is coeditor of the journal *Qualitative Research* with Paul Atkinson. She is currently doing an ethnography of *capoeira* teaching in the UK.

Greg Dimitriadis is Associate Professor in the Department of Educational Leadership and Policy at the University at Buffalo, the State University of New York. He is the author of *Performing Identity/Performing Culture: Hip Hop as Text, Pedagogy, and Lived Practice; Friendship, Cliques, and Gangs: Young Black Men Coming of Age in Urban America.* He is first co-author, with Cameron McCarthy, of *Reading and Teaching the Postcolonial: From Baldwin to Basquiat and Beyond* and second co-author, with George Kamberelis, of *On Qualitative Inquiry*. Dimitriadis is first coeditor, with Dennis Carlson, of *Promises to Keep: Cultural Studies, Democratic Education, and Public Life,* and second coeditor, with Nadine Dolby and Paul Willis, of *Learning to Labor in New Times*. Dimitriadis has authored the following book: *Urban Youth Culture.* His next edited collection is the second edition of *Race, Identity, and Representation in Education,* coedited with Cameron McCarthy, Warren Crichlow, and Nadine Dolby.

Jamel Donnor is a Ph.D. candidate in the Department of Curriculum and Instruction at the University of Wisconsin–Madison, majoring in educational communications and technology. His research focuses on examining issues of access to and equity of technology for African American students, critical race theoretical applications to education, and the education of African American male student-athletes.

Jeremy D. Engels is a Ph.D. candidate in the Department of Speech Communication at the University of Illinois, Urbana–Champaign. His research focuses primarily on the construction of national identity in the early American republic, and his political writings have been featured in Urbana–Champaign's independent newspaper, *The Public-I*, and also in the University of Illinois's student newspaper, *The Daily Illini*.

Michelle Fine is a Distinguished Professor of Psychology, Women's Studies, and Urban Education at the Graduate Center of the City University of New York. Committed to participatory action research in schools, prisons, and communities, her writings focus on theoretical questions of social injustice: how people think about unjust distributions of resources and social practices, when they resist, and how such inequities are legitimated. Interested in the combination of quantitative and qualitative methods as well as participatory action designs, her writings encompass questions of epistemology, methodology, and social change. Recent publications include *Echoes: Youth Documenting and Performing the Legacy of Brown v. Board of Education* (Fine, Roberts, Torre and Bloom, Burns, Chajet, and Guishard and Payne, 2004); *Working Method: Social Injustice and Social Research* (Weis and Fine, 2004); *Off White: Essays on Race, Power and Resistance* (Fine, Weis, Powell, Pruitt, and Burns, 2004); *Silenced Voices and Extraordinary Conversations* (Weis and Fine, 2003); *Construction Sites: Excavating Race, Class and Gender with Urban Youth* (Fine and Weis, 2001); *Speedbumps: A Student Friendly Guide to Qualitative Research* (edited with Lois Weis, 2000); and *Changing Minds: A Participatory Action Research Analysis of College in Prison* (2001, with Maria Elena Torre, Kathy Boudin, Iris Bowen, Judith Clark, Donna Hylton, Migdalia Martinez, "Missy," Rosemarie A.

Roberts, Pamela Smart, and Deborah Upegui). She has offered expert testimony in a number of cases involving race, gender, and/or class discrimination.

Susan Finley is Associate Professor of Educational Foundations, Literacy, and Research Methodology at Washington State University, Vancouver. She bases her pedagogy and inquiry in arts-based approaches to understanding social and cultural issues in educational contexts. She is an activist who has implemented educational efforts with street youths and economically poor children, youths, and adults, housed, and unhoused.

Douglas Foley is Professor of Anthropology and of Education at the University of Texas at Austin. He specializes in the anthropology of education, American race relations, and ethnographic field methods. He also served for several years as coeditor of the *International Journal of Qualitative Studies in Education.* He is the author of numerous articles and several ethnographies, including *The Heartland Chronicles, Learning Capitalist Culture*, and *From Peones to Politics.*

Andrea Fontana (Ph.D., University of California, San Diego) is Professor of Sociology at the University of Nevada, Las Vegas. He has published articles on aging, leisure, theory, and postmodernism. He is the author of the *Last Frontier: the Social Meaning of Growing Old*, coauthor of *Social Problems and Sociologies of Everyday Life*, and coeditor of *The Existential Self in Society* and *Postmodernism and Social Inquiry*. He is former president of the Society for the Study of Symbolic Interaction and former editor of the journal *Symbolic Interaction*. Among Fontana's most recent published essays are a deconstruction of the work of the painter Hieronymus Bosch; a performance/play about Farinelli, the castrato; an ethnographic narrative about land speed records at the Bonneville Salt Flats; and a performance based on *Six Feet Under*.

James H. Frey is retired Dean of the College of Liberal Arts and Emeritus Professor of Sociology at the University of Nevada, Las Vegas. He is the founder and past Director of the Center for Survey Research at UNLV. He is the author of *Survey Research by Telephone* and *How to Conduct Interviews by Telephone and in Person* (with S. Oishi). He has published papers on survey research, group interviewing, sport sociology, deviance, and work in the leisure industry.

Davydd J. Greenwood is the Goldwin Smith Professor of Anthropology and Director of the Institute for European Studies at Cornell University, where he has served as a faculty member since 1970. He has been elected a Corresponding Member of the Spanish Royal Academy of Moral and Political Sciences. He served as the John S. Knight Professor and Director of the Mario Einaudi Center for 10 years and was President of the Association of International Education Administrators. He also has served as a program evaluator for many universities and for the National Foreign Language Center. His work centers on action research, political economy, ethnic conflict, community and regional development, the Spanish Basque Country, Spain's La Mancha region, and the Finger Lakes region of upstate New York, where he carried out a 3-year action research and community development project with communities along the Erie Canal corridor. The author of seven books and numerous articles, his works include *Unrewarding Wealth: The Commercialization and Collapse of Agriculture in a Spanish Basque Town; Nature, Culture, and Human History; The Taming of Evolution: The Persistence of Non-evolutionary Views in the Study of Humans; Las culturas de Fagor*; *Industrial Democracy as Process: Participatory Action Research in the Fagor Cooperative Group of Mondragón;* a collaborative monograph with students, *Teaching Participatory Action Research in the University in Studies in Continuing Education;* and *Introduction to Action Research: Social Research for Social Change* (with Morten Levin). He has edited two books, *Democracy and Difference: A Comparative Study of the Impact of Legal-Administrative Structures on Identity in the United States and Spain* and *Action Research and Rhetoric: The Scandinavian Action Research Development Program.*

Egon G. Guba is Professor Emeritus of Education, Indiana University. He received his Ph.D. from the University of Chicago in quantitative inquiry (education) in 1952, and thereafter served on the faculties of the University of Chicago, the University of Kansas City, the Ohio State University, and Indiana University. For the past 20 years, he has studied paradigms alternative to the received view and has espoused a personal commitment to one of these: constructivism. He is the coauthor of *Effective Evaluation* (1981), *Naturalistic Inquiry* (1985), and *Fourth Generation Evaluation* (1989), all with Yvonna S. Lincoln, and he is editor of *The Paradigm Dialog* (1990), which explores the implications of alternative paradigms for social and educational inquiry. He is the author of more than 150 journal articles and more than 100 conference presentations, many of them concerned with elements of new-paradigm inquiry and methods.

Jaber F. Gubrium is Professor and Chair of Sociology at the University of Missouri, Columbia. His research deals with the narrative organization and ethnography of personal identity, family, the life course, aging, and adaptations to illness. He is the editor of the *Journal of Aging Studies* and author of several monographs, including *Living and Dying at Murray Manor*, *Caretakers*, *Describing Care*, *Oldtimers and Alzheimer's*, *Out of Control*, and *Speaking of Life*. He has recently coedited *Qualitative Research Practice* for Sage and continues to analyze constructions of disability by stroke survivors.

Douglas Harper is Professor and Chair of the Department of Sociology at Duquesne University in Pittsburgh. He has written three ethnographies that rely heavily on photography, the most recent being *Changing Works: Visions of a Lost Agriculture* (2001). He is founding editor of *Visual Sociology*, now published as *Visual Studies*. His current research is on the social life of Italian food (coauthored by Patrizia Faccioli) and on expatriate communities in Hong Kong (coauthored by Caroline Knowles). He continues to refine and develop his use of still photography in sociological studies.

Stephen J. Hartnett is Associate Professor of Speech Communication at the University of Illinois. He is author of *Democratic Dissent & The Cultural Fictions of Antebellum America*, which won the National Communication Association's 2002 Winans and Wichelns Memorial Award for Distinguished Scholarship in Rhetoric and Public Address. He is coauthor, with the late Robert James Branham, of *Sweet Freedom's Song: "My Country 'Tis of Thee"* and *Democracy in America*. Based on 12 years of teaching in, writing about, and protesting at prisons across America, in 2003, he published *Incarceration Nation: Investigative Prison Poems of Hope and Terror*. His current projects include *Executing Democracy: Arguing About the Death Penalty in America, 1683–1850* and *The Rhetorics of Globalization and Empire in an Age of Terror*.

Phil Hodkinson is Professor of Lifelong Learning in the Lifelong Learning Institute of the University of Leeds, England. He has an ongoing interest in research methodology from a broadly hermeneutical and interpretative perspective. He is currently researching learning in workplaces and college settings and learning lives and biographies.

Douglas R. Holmes teaches anthropology at Binghamton University. He has, over the last decade, written about the sociopolitical dynamics and cultural imperatives shaping advanced European integration. His current research examines the complex role of the European Central Bank in fostering economic integration across a rapidly expanding European Union. His collaborative work with George E. Marcus focuses on recasting ethnographic method to addresses the manifold challenges posed by anthropological research within cultures of expertise. He is the author of *Integral Europe: Fast-Capitalism, Multiculturalism, Neofascism* and *Cultural Disenchantmenets: Worker Peasantries in Northeast Italy*.

James A. Holstein is Professor of Sociology in the Department of Social and Cultural Sciences at Marquette University. He is the author or editor of numerous books on qualitative research methods, social problems, deviance, and social control. In collaboration with Jaber F. Gubrium, he has published *The New Language of Qualitative Method, The Active Interview, Handbook of Interview Research, The Self We Live By,* and *Inner Lives and Social Worlds.* Holstein is currently the editor of the journal *Social Problems.*

Stacy Holman Jones is Assistant Professor in the Department of Communication at the University of South Florida. Her work focuses on socially resistive performance practices. She is the author of *Kaleidoscope Notes: Writing Women's Music and Organizational Culture* (1998) and the forthcoming *Music for Torching.*

Ernest R. House (Ed.D., University of Illinois) is Professor Emeritus of Education at the University of Colorado at Boulder and one of the world's leading evaluation experts. From 1969 to 1985, he was a professor of education at the University of Illinois in Urbana. He has been a visiting scholar at UCLA, Harvard, and New Mexico, as well as in England, Australia, Spain, Sweden, Austria, and Chile. His primary interests are evaluation and educational policy analysis. Books include *The Politics of Educational Innovation* (1974), *Survival in the Classroom* (with S. Lapan, 1978), *Evaluating with Validity* (1980), *Jesse Jackson and the Politics of Charisma* (1988), *Professional Evaluation: Social Impact and Political Consequences* (1993), *Schools for Sale* (1998), and *Values in Evaluation and Social Research* (with K. Howe, 1999). His evaluation novel, *Where the Truth Lies*, was published in 1992. He is the 1989 recipient (with W. Madura) of the Harold E. Lasswell Prize in the policy sciences and the 1990 recipient of the Paul F. Lazarsfeld Award for Evaluation Theory, presented by the American Evaluation Association. He has been editor (with R. Wooldridge) of *New Directions in Program Evaluation* (1982–1985), a featured columnist for *Evaluation Practice* (1984–89), and a Fellow at the Center for Advanced Study in the Behavioral Sciences, Stanford (1999–2000). He currently serves as federal court monitor in the bilingual education legal settlement in Denver.

George Kamberelis is Associate Professor in the School of Education at the University at Albany–SUNY. He teaches and conducts research on the history and philosophy of science and social science, qualitative inquiry, social theory, and literacy studies. Professor Kamberelis has published in the areas of qualitative inquiry (especially researcher–research participant relationships), discourse and identity, and genre studies. Some of his recent publications include "Ingestion, Elimination, Sex, and Song: Trickster as Premodern Avatar of Postmodern Research Practice" in *Qualitative Inquiry* and "The Rhizome and the Pack: Liminal Literacy Formations with Political Teeth" in *Space Matters: Assertions of Space in Literacy Practice and Research* (Kevin Leander and Margi Sheehy, editors). With Greg Dimitriadis, Kamberelis has just completed a book titled *On Qualitative Inquiry.*.

Stephen Kemmis is Professor of Education, Charles Sturt University, Wagga Wagga, Australia. His research interests include research and evaluation methods in education and the social sciences, participatory action research, communicative evaluation, Indigenous education, university research development, and curriculum theory. His books include *Becoming Critical: Education, Knowledge, and Action Research* (with Wilfred Carr) and *The Action Research Planner* (with Robin McTaggart).

Joe L. Kincheloe is Professor of Education at City University of New York Graduate Center and Brooklyn College. He is Deputy Executive Officer of the Urban Education program at CUNY. He has written books and articles on research, cultural studies, critical education, and cognition, including *The Sign of the Burger: McDonald's and the Culture of Power* and *Kinderculture: The Corporate Construction of Childhood.*

Gloria Ladson-Billings is Professor in the Department of Curriculum and Instruction at the University of Wisconsin–Madison and a Senior Fellow in Urban Education of the Annenberg Institute for School Reform at Brown University. Her primary research interests are in the relationships between culture and school and critical race theory. She is author of *The Dreamkeepers: Successful Teachers of African-American Children* and is editor of the Teaching, Learning, and Human Development section of the *American Educational Research Journal.*

Morten Levin is Professor in the Department of Industrial Economics and Technology Management at the Norwegian University of Science and Technology in Trondheim, Norway. He holds graduate degrees in engineering and in sociology. Throughout his professional life, he has worked as an action researcher with particular focus on processes and structures of social change in the relationships between technology and organization. The action research has taken place in industrial contexts, in local communities, and in university teaching, where he has developed and been in charge of a number of Ph.D. programs in action research. He is author of a number of books and articles, including *Introduction to Action Research: Social Research for Social Change,* and he serves on the editorial boards of *Systems Practice and Action Research, Action Research International, Action Research, The Handbook of Qualitative Inquiry,* and *The Handbook of Action Research.*

D. Soyini Madison is Associate Professor of Communication Studies in the area of performance studies at the University of North Carolina, Chapel Hill. Madison's Ph.D. from Northwestern University, under the direction of Dwight Conquergood, is one of the first scholarly examinations that focus on the intersections between performance studies and critical ethnography. She is the author of *Critical Ethnography: Methods, Ethics, and Performance* (Sage, 2005) and several articles ranging from film and performance criticism to examinations in critical race and gender studies. Madison is editor of the anthology, *The Woman That I Am: The Literature and Culture of Contemporary Women of Color.* She is a Senior Fulbright Scholar and recently completed a visiting lectureship at the University of Ghana at Legon. Her current project is an examination of staging/performing local debates surrounding human rights and traditional religious practices as these debates are influenced by the global economy and national development.

George E. Marcus is Joseph Jamail Professor and Chair, Department of Anthropology, Rice University. He is coauthor of *Anthropology as Cultural Critique* and coeditor of *Writing Culture.* In 1998, he published *Ethnography Through Thick & Thin.* Through the 1990s, he created and edited the *Late Editions* series of annuals designed to document the fin-de-siecle in a number of arenas through ethnographic conversations. He is now at work on a memoir of his years supervising dissertations, which he views as a laboratory for the reinvention of anthropological method.

Annette N. Markham is Associate Professor of Communication and Founding Coordinator of the Center for Technology and Learning at the University of the Virgin Islands. Her research focuses on sensemaking practices in technologically mediated environments, ethical practices in qualitative Internet research, interpretive methodology, and organizational communication. Her book *Life Online: Researching Real Experience in Virtual Space* (1998) has been regarded as one of the first in-depth sociological studies of the Net. She has published several chapters and articles related to interpretive qualitative methods in Internet Studies. Her forthcoming edited collection *Qualitative Internet Research: Dialogue Among Scholars* (Sage) focuses on practical and philosophical challenges of conducting research in computer-mediated environments. Since moving to the Caribbean and realizing electricity is not ubiquitous, her research focus is shifting from the ethnographic inquiry of life online to the study of privilege and identity politics offline. Markham received her Ph.D. from Purdue University.

Kathryn Bell McKenzie is Assistant Professor in the Department of Educational Administration and Human Resources at Texas A&M University in College Station. Dr. McKenzie received her Ph.D. in Educational Administration from the University of Texas in Austin. Her research foci include equity and social justice in schools, school leadership, qualitative methodology, and critical white studies. During her more than 20 years in public education, Dr. McKenzie was a classroom teacher, curriculum specialist, assistant principal, principal, and Deputy Director of the University of Texas at Austin Independent School District Leadership Academy. Her most recent publications include a chapter titled "The Unintended Consequences of the Texas Accountability System" in *Equity and Accountability* (Linda Skrla and James Joseph Scheurich, editors); with James Joseph Scheurich, the article "Equity Traps: A Useful Construct for Preparing Principals to Lead Schools That Are Successful With Racially Diverse Students" in *Educational Administration Quarterly*; an article in *Educational Theory* coauthored with James Joseph Scheurich titled "Corporatizing and Privatizing of Schooling: Critique, Research, and a Call for a Grounded Critical Praxis." Dr. McKenzie is regional editor for North America for the *International Journal of Qualitative Studies in Education.*

Peter McLaren is Professor, Division of Urban Schooling, Graduate School of Education and Information Studies, University of California, Los Angeles. Professor McLaren is the author and editor of over 40 books in a variety of areas that include the political sociology of education, critical pedagogy, and Marxist theory. His most recent books include *Capitalists and Conquerors: Teaching Against Global Capitalism and the New Imperialism* (with Ramin Farahmandpur) and *Red Seminars.* His writings have been published in 15 languages. Professor McLaren is the inaugural recipient of the Paulo Freire Social Justice Award, Chapman University.

Robin McTaggart is Professor and Pro-Vice-Chancellor of Staff Development and Student Affairs at James Cook University, Townsville and Cairns, North Queensland. He is Adjunct Professor in the International Graduate School of Management of the University of South Australia. He was Executive Dean of Law and Education (1998) and Executive Dean of Education and Indigenous Studies (1999) at James Cook University. Before moving to JCU, he was Director of International Programs in the Faculty of Education at Deakin University Geelong and was Head of the School of Administration and Curriculum Studies at Deakin University from 1993 to 1995. He completed his Ph.D. at the Center for Instructional Research and Curriculum Evaluation at the University of Illinois, where he was a W. F. Connell Scholar. He has conducted evaluation and research studies of action research by educators, discipline-based arts education, arts programs for disadvantaged youth, instructional computing programs for intellectually disabled adults, coeducation and gender equity in private schooling, AIDS/HIV professional development for rural health workers, Aboriginal education in traditionally oriented remote communities, scientific literacies, and distance education provision in technical and further education. He has also conducted participatory action research and evaluation training programs for private and public sector managers, academics, technical and further education and training professionals, educators, educational consultants, and health professionals in Australia, Canada, Hong Kong, Indonesia, Malaysia, New Zealand, Singapore, Thailand, and the United States.

William L. Miller (M.D., M.A.) is a family physician anthropologist and the Leonard Parker Pool Chair of Family Medicine at Lehigh Valley Hospital and Health Network, Allentown, Pennsylvania. He is Professor of Family and Community Medicine, Pennsylvania State University College of Medicine. He is also consulting editor for the *Annals of Family Medicine.* For more than 15 years, Dr. Miller, in collaboration with Benjamin Crabtree, has been working to make qualitative research more accessible to health care researchers. He has written and contributed to book chapters and articles detailing step-by-step applications of qualitative methods and seeks to translate this work into the everyday clinical, educational, and administrative realms of health care. His research interests focus on applying the paradigm of ecological relationship-centeredness and the theory of complex adaptive systems to improving health care at the organizational, office, and encounter levels and co-creating a participatory community of practice-based research.

Much of this work is shared collaboratively with Dr. Crabtree through his federally funded grants.

Virginia L. Olesen, Emerita Professor of Sociology in the Department of Social and Behavioral Sciences at the University of California, continues to explore and write on critical issues in qualitative methods, women's health, feminist thought, sociology of emotions, and globalization. She is coeditor, with Sheryl Ruzek and Adele Clarke, of *Women's Health: Complexities and Diversities* (1997) and, with Adele Clarke, of *Revisioning Women, Health and Healing: Feminist, Cultural and Technoscience Perspectives* (1999). She is currently working on issues of skepticism in qualitative research and the problems of "the third voice" constituted between and among researchers.

Anssi Peräkylä is Professor of Sociology at the University of Helsinki. His research interests include medical communication, psychotherapy, emotional communication, and conversation analysis. He has publishded *AIDS Counselling* (1995) and articles on interaction in institutional settings in journals such as *Sociology*, *Social Psychology Quarterly*, *British Journal of Social Psychology*, and *Research on Language and Social Interaction*.

Ken Plummer is Professor in Sociology at the University of Essex in the United Kingdom and is a regular visitor at the University of California at Santa Barbara. He has written or edited some ten books and a hundred articles including *Intimate Citizenship* (2003), *Documents of Life-2* (2001), *Telling Sexual Stories* (1995), and *Sexual Stigma* (1975). In 2001, he was the first recipient of the American Sociological Association Gagnon and Simon Award for outstanding contributions to the study of sexualities. He is the founding editor of the journal *Sexualities*.

Laurel Richardson is Professor Emeritus of Sociology and Visiting Professor of Cultural Studies in Education at the Ohio State University. She is the author of more than one hundred articles. She has pioneered work on gender, poststructuralist theory, and alternative representations in qualitative research. Her book, *Fields of Play: Constructing an Academic Life* (1997) was honored with the Society for the Study of Symbolic Interaction's Cooley Award. Her most recent book, *Travels With Ernest: Crossing the Literary/Sociological Divide* (2004) is an experimental writing project coauthored with her husband, the novelist Ernest Lockridge.

Paula Saukko, Ph.D., is a Research Fellow at the ESRC-Centre for Genomics in Society (Egenis) in the School of Historical, Political, and Sociological Studies at the University of Exeter and an Honorary Research Fellow at the Peninsula Medical School, both in the United Kingdom. Her research interests are qualitative methodology and cultural studies of science and medicine, and her topical projects have focused on genetic testing for common illnesses and discourses of eating disorders. She is the author of *Doing Research in Cultural Studies: An Introduction to Classical and Contemporary Methodological Approaches* (Sage, 2003). She is also coeditor (with L. Reed) of *Governing the Female Body: Gender, Health, and Networks of Power* (forthcoming) and coeditor (with C. McCarthy et al.) of *Sound Identities* (1999). She is a member of the editorial boards of *Cultural Studies/Critical Methodologies* and *Kulttuuritutkimus* and is currently writing a book on lived, social and historical dimensions of diagnostic discourses on anorexia.

James Joseph Scheurich received his Ph.D. from Ohio State University, spent 12 years as an assistant and associate professor at the University of Texas at Austin, and is now Professor and Head of the Department of Educational Administration and Human Resource Development at Texas A&M University. He has published five books, including *Anti-Racist Scholarship: An Advocacy, Research Methods in the Postmodern,* and *Leadership for Equity and Excellence* (the latter with Linda Skria as coauthor), as well as numerous peer-reviewed articles, monographs, chapters, book reviews, and newspaper editorials. He is the coauthor, with Miguel Guajardo, Patricia Sanchez, and Elissa Fineman, of a video documentary called The Labors of Life/Labores de la Vida. He currently serves on the American Educational Research

Association's (AERA) Publications Committee. He is currently coeditor, with Carolyn Clark, of the *International Journal of Qualitative Studies in Education* and serves on the editorial board for several other journals. He has successfully chaired nearly 25 dissertations and has had 18 of his students become university professors. Finally, he has authored or coauthored over $3 million in grants and contracts.

John K. Smith is Professor of Education at the University of Northern Iowa. For the past 20 years, his interests have centered on the philosophy of social and educational inquiry, with a special emphasis on the issue of criteria. His work has appeared in such journals as the *Educational Researcher, Journal of Educational Administration,* and *Educational Analysis and Policy Analysis.* He also has authored two books: *The Nature of Social and Educational Inquiry* and *After the Demise of Empiricism.*

Linda Tuhiwai Smith is Professor of Education at the University of Auckland. She is Joint Director of Nga Pae o te Maramatanga The National Institute for Research Excellence in Māori Development and Advancement, a center of research excellence hosted by the University of Auckland. Dr. Smith is a leading Māori and indigenous educationist and is well sought after as a speaker and commentator. Her work is recognized internationally through her book *Decolonising Methodologies: Research and Indigenous Peoples.* She has also published research on the history of Māori schools, Māori women and education, and other social justice themes.

Elizabeth Adams St. Pierre is Associate Professor of Language Education and Affiliated Professor of both the Qualitative Research Program and the Women's Studies Institute at the University of Georgia. Her research interests focus on the work of language in the construction of subjectivity, on a critique of conventional qualitative inquiry, and on language and literacy studies. Recent published works include articles in *Qualitative Inquiry* and *Educational Researcher*, as well as chapters in *Dangerous Coagulations* (B. Baker and K. Heyning, Editors, 2004) and *Feminist Engagements* (K. Weiler, Editor, 2001). She is coeditor with W. S. Pillow of *Working the Ruins: Feminist Poststructural Theory and Methods in Education* (2000).

Robert E. Stake is Emeritus Professor of Education and Director of the Center for Instructional Research and Curriculum Evaluation at the University of Illinois. Since 1963, he has been a specialist in the evaluation of educational programs. Among the evaluative studies he directed were works in science and mathematics in elementary and secondary schools, model programs and conventional teaching of the arts in schools, development of teaching with sensitivity to gender equity, education of teachers for the deaf and for youth in transition from school to work settings, environmental education and special programs for gifted students, and the reform of urban education. Stake has authored *Quieting Reform,* a book on Charles Murray's evaluation of Cities-in-Schools; two books on methodology, *Evaluating the Arts in Education* and *The Art of Case Study Research;* and *Custom and Cherishing,* and a book with Liora Bresler and Linda Mabry on teaching the arts in ordinary elementary school classrooms in America. Recently he led a multiyear evaluation study of the Chicago Teachers Academy for Mathematics and Science. For his evaluation work, in 1988, he received the Lazarsfeld Award from the American Evaluation Association and, in 1994, an honorary doctorate from the University of Uppsala.

Kathleen Stewart teaches anthropology and is Director of the Center for Cultural Studies at the University of Texas, Austin. She has done ethnographic fieldwork in West Virginia, Las Vegas, Orange County, California, New England, and Texas. Her first book, *A Space on the Side of the Road: Cultural Poetics in an "Other" America* (1996), was recognized by both the Victor Turner Prize and the Chicago Folklore Prize. Her second book is forthcoming and titled *Ordinary Impacts: the Affective Life of U.S. Public Culture.* She has also written about nostalgia, conspiracy theory, apocalyptic thinking, daydreams, country music, trauma, and the pitfalls of the American dream. Her work has been performed in plays and has been supported by the Rockefeller Foundation, the National Endowment for the Humanities, the School of American Research, and the Institute for the Humanities, University of California, Irvine as well as by the University of Texas.

Barbara Tedlock is Distinguished Professor of Anthropology at the State University of New York at Buffalo. She served as editor-in-chief of the *American Anthropologist* (1993–1998). Her honors include the 1997 President's Award for distinctive leadership in forging a new vision for the flagship journal of the American Anthropological Association, the *American Anthropologist,* and for dedication and commitment to the profession of anthropology. She also received the 2002 Chancellor's Research Recognition Award for "Overall Excellence of Research in the Social Sciences," given by the Chancellor of the State University of New York She is a former President of the Society for Humanistic Anthropology and a member of PEN (Poets-Essayists-Novelists). Her publications include six books and more than 100 articles and essays.

Angela Valenzuela is Associate Professor in the Department of Curriculum and Instruction at the University of Texas at Austin and also the Center for Mexican American Studies. She is author of *Subtractive Schooling: U.S. Mexican Youth and the Politics of Caring,* winner of both the 2000 American Educational Research Association Outstanding Book Award and the 2001 Critics' Choice Award from the American Educational Studies Association. She is also the editor of *Leaving Children Behind: How Texas-Style Accountability Fails Latino Youth.* Her research interests are in the areas of urban education, race relations, high-stakes testing, and Latino education policy. Much of her current policy work stems from her position as Chair of the Education Committee for the Texas League of United Latin American Citizens (LULAC), the nation's oldest Mexican American civil rights organization.

Lois Weis is Professor of Sociology of Education at the University of Buffalo, State University of New York. She is the author or coauthor of numerous books and articles pertaining to social class, race, gender, and schooling in the United States. Her most recent books include *Class Reunion: The Remaking of the American White Working Class* (2004), *Working Method* (with Michelle Fine, 2004), and *Silenced Voices and Extraordinary Conversations: Re-Imagining Schools* (with Michelle Fine, 2003). She sits on numerous editorial boards and is the editor of the Power, Social Identity, and Education book series with SUNY Press.